CONTENTS

TRADE & TRAVEL *HANDBOOKS*

"A travel guide business that looks set to sweep the world."

The Independent

"*The* ***India Handbook*** *(formerly the South Asian Handbook) has reminded me of how much I do not know about the sub-continent!*"

Mark Tully, BBC India correspondent

"*More info - less blah.*"

Readers's letter, Germany

"*By far the best, most comprehensive guides: in a class of their own. Unreservedly recommended - a Handbook will pay for itself many times over.*"

Journey Latin America

"*On Bible thin paper with distinctive covers. The miraculous result is that they are, at the same time, sturdy, exhaustive and light-weight.*"

Fort Lauderdale Sun Sentinel

"*Mines of information and free of pretentiousness: make other guidebooks read like Butlins brochures.*"

Bookshop review

"*Accurate and reliable down to the minutest detail. Amazingly so.*"

Reader's letter, Canada

"*By far the most informative guide to Burma published in recent years. Miraculously, the information appears to be up-to-date, rare for books in this genre.*"

Far Eastern Economic Review

PREFACE

After the political crises of the last two years India shows all the signs of making quiet economic progress and almost unnoticed change throughout 1994. Although some political problems, notably Kashmir, remain unresolved, with an inevitable impact on the opportunities for travelling, the great majority of India and Sri Lanka remain among the safest and yet most stimulating places to visit anywhere in the world.

This year the *Handbook* itself has undergone some radical changes, for while it retains many of the characteristics which led many people to write so encouragingly to us, its rapid growth has forced a major revision.

The major change in the 1995 *Handbook* is that it focuses on India, while retaining important sections on Sri Lanka, Bhutan and the Maldives. This change has allowed a significant expansion of the India section, making it by far the most comprehensive guide to India available in any language. Its cover has been augmented at every level: more places of interest are described in detail, and more sites discussed in each place.

As usual, this year's annual revision has involved a complete review of accommodation and travel arrangements. There is more - and more detailed - information on trains and buses than ever before. We have also tried to make the material even more accessible. A particular feature has been the introduction of new route maps, showing distances between all the places named on the major routes shown. This will make it much easier to plan travel by bus or train, not just down well beaten paths but branching out on your own.

To make this planning even easier this revision of the *Handbook* also introduces new categories of Budget hotels, giving details of accommodation for many places not mentioned in any other guide. Furthermore many of the maps have been thoroughly amended, and some new maps have been added. The revisions have been based on extensive field research in every part of India and its region.

We have already benefited from the letters and suggestions of many people using the *South Asian Handbook* over the last three years. Even with full annual revision, however, many things change. We would be very pleased to hear from you if you have any comments, suggestions or information to include for next year's edition.

Robert Bradnock
The Editor

THE EDITOR

Robert Bradnock

Born in India in 1943, Robert Bradnock went to India overland in 1966 as a research student at Cambridge, and lived in South India for a year, travelling throughout Tamil Nadu, Kerala, Karnataka and Andhra Pradesh. The return trip allowed him his first visit to several states of northern India, including Haryana, Punjab and Jammu and Kashmir. That journey was the first of many research visits living and working throughout the sub-continent. Since joining the School of Oriental and African Studies in 1968 as a lecturer in Geography with special reference to South Asia, he has carried out and supervised research in all of the major countries of the region, including Sri Lanka and the Maldives.

An international authority on India and its neighbours, Robert Bradnock has broadcast frequently on TV and radio about South Asian current affairs for the BBC and many other networks across the world. He lectures extensively on South Asia in Britain and Europe, and he is currently Editor of the Royal Geographical Society's *Geographical Journal*.

ACKNOWLEDGEMENTS

Original text for the first edition of the South Asian Handbook was written by: India introduction, East India, South India, Sri Lanka and the Maldives - Robert Bradnock; North and West India, Sikkim and Bhutan - William Whittaker.

A very large number of people have helped with the preparation of this edition of the India Handbook. We are also indebted to Dr. David Snashall for his authoritative piece on health for travellers in South Asia.

The Editor travelled through Delhi, UP, Haryana, Punjab, Karnataka and Goa in 1993 and 1994. A number of other researchers have reported on extended research visits. We are particularly grateful to Rupert Linton who spent six months in Kerala, Karnataka and Tamil Nadu and made a major contribution to updating information on South India. We are also indebted to Craig Voller (eastern UP and Bihar), and James Dawson (western UP and Rajasthan); Marlies Beschorner (throughout India, including Kashmir); Sarah Chamberlain and Alex Watson (Assam, West Bengal, Orissa, Maharashtra and Goa); Alison Henley (Karnataka, Pondicherry and Tamil Nadu); and Mark Povey and Katia Camps-Campins (UP and Nepal border crossings).

Toni Laroque provided helpful updating of the Maldives; Jaideep Mukherji gave advice on trekking and trekking destinations in India. Françoise Pommaret totally revised the Bhutan section.

Many people offered us and our researchers hospitality and practical help in many ways during our travels in South Asia in 1993 and 1994. We wish to thank: Gita Agarwal, Nirula's Hotel, New Delhi; Manager, Komala Hotel, Alappuzha; Mr. S. Palit, Madikere, Coorg; Mr. Sahu, Kovalam; Prof. and Mrs. C.P. Singh, New Delhi; Dheer Singh of Sariska; Mr. and Mrs. G.B. Singh, New Delhi; Sanjai Singh of Bissau, Jaipur; Mr Bhola Thapa, Kathmandu; Amrita Verma, New Delhi; Mr. Venugopal, Kovalam; Major S.K. Yadav, New Delhi; Ashwani Bamba, Dharamshala and Rajiv Trehan, Span Tours, Shimla.

We acknowledge the co-operation of several tourist offices and their directors, including Nabendu Bhattacharjee, ITDC; Roma Dewan Bhoosan, M.P. State Tourism, New Delhi; Nalini Netto, Kerala Tourism, Thiruvananthapuram; Sri Prithviraj Patil, Maharashtra Tourism, Bombay, P.J. Varghese, Tourist Desk, Cochin, Kerala; KTDC Tourist Officer, Kovalam and Mr Vinod Kalia, Tourism Officer, Chandigarh.

We would also like to acknowledge contributions from others over the last year and thank them for the interest they have taken. From the U.K.: Robert Archway, Farnham, Surrey; Catherine L. Bennett, London; Rachel Craig, Ballinger, Bucks; Richard Graves, Weston Super Mare; Henry Greenfield, Little Kingshill, Bucks; Jane A Harries, Newport, Dyfed; Richard Heaton, London; Richard and Diana Hollingworth, Newcastle; Barnaby Jones, Birmingham; Sonia McKay, London; Michael Lewis, Wakefield, Yorks; Paul Newton, Oxford; Matthew Price, St. Albans, Herts; J. Rao, Cambridge; J.F. Roebuck, Ormskirk, Lancashire; T.F.S. Scott, Lewes, E. Sussex; Edward Tenison, Little Chalfont, Bucks; Arabella Tresilian, Marshfield, Wilts; Jane Trobridge, Birmingham; David Winter, London; Alex Watson, London; Tom Woodhatch, London.

From elsewhere: Orlando Claudio Angelino, Rome, Italy; Manager, Annapurna Guest House, Bhuj, India;

Linda Bartolomei, Melbourne, Australia; Mr. and Mrs. Mark Boekstein, Cape Town, South Africa; Samantha Clayton, Varanasi; Axel Ebert, Essen, Germany; Udita Jhunjhunwala, Bombay; Ad van Elzakker and Marion van der Plas, Nieuwegein, Holland; Benjamine Gasselin, Toulon, France; Jack Hart, Palmerston North, New Zealand; Purnananda Jee, Cuttack, India; Manager, Ramanathan Mansion Lodge, Chidambaram, India; Ad van Schaik, Utrecht, The Netherlands; Angelika Schatzmann, Wien, Austria; Thomas Schweiger, Vienna, Austria; V. K. Shrivastava, Gorakhpur, India; Kanwal Singh, New Delhi, India; Terin S Smith, Marina Del Rey,California; Jeevan Thiagarajah, Colombo, Sri Lanka; Michael Trost, Gross Birer Rhein, Germany; Guido Villa, Milan, Italy.

Catherine and Nicola Lewis, James Bradnock and Michael Lewis all gave extensive help with proof reading and we are very grateful for the hard work of Debbie Wylde, Jo Burdall and Lorraine Horler at Trade & Travel in Bath.

Copyright citations

We are grateful to the following publishers or authors for permission to quote their work:

The Archaeological Survey of India *Arunachalam*, Prof B.B. Lal, Debala Mitra, H. Sarkar of the Archaeological Survey of India; **Bharatiya Vidya Bhavan** *Ramayana*, C. Rajagopalachari; **Cambridge University Press** *The Rise of Civilisation in India and Pakistan*, 1982, Bridget and Raymond Allchin; **George Allen & Unwin** *A Hindu View of Life*, S. Radhakrishnan, 1927; **MacMillan Ltd** *Pakistan under Bhutto, 1971-1977* (2nd ed.), Javed Burki; Koch, Dr Ebba *Shah Jahan and Orpheus*, *Pietre Dure Decoration* and *The Programme of Shah Jahan's Thrones in the Red Fort of Dehli* (Graz: Akademische Druck und Verlaganstalt, 1988); **Methuen** *India and Pakistan* (3rd ed), 1967, O.H.K. Spate & A.T.A. Learmonth; *An Introduction to South Asia*, 1983, B.H. Farmer; S. Cary Welch from *India: Art and Culture 1300-1900*. Copyright c 1986 by the Metropolitan Museum of Art. Reprinted with Permission. **Munshiram Manoharlal Publishers Pvt Ltd** *Encyclopaedia of Indian Architecture* (2 vols), 1990, A. Ghosh; **National Institute of Historical and Cultural Research, Islamabad** *Uchchh: a history and architecture 1980*, Dr. Ahmad Nabi Khan; **Oxford University Press** *A cultural history of India* (1975), A.L. Basham (Ed.) and J.F. Jordans, Chapter XVIII, and *The Heart of India* by L.D. Barnett (Murray 1913), pp 111-12, *Peasant State and Society in Medieval South India*, 1980, Burton Stein, *Siva: the erotic ascetic*, W.D. O'Flaherty (1973); **Penguin** *Hindu myths and legends*, 1975, W.D. O'Flaherty, *A History of India*, Vol 2, Romila Thapar. **Princeton University Press** *Tamil Temple Myths: sacrifice and divine marriage in South Indian Saivite tradition*, 1982, David Shulman; **Sidgwick and Jackson** *The Wonder that was India*, Vol 1 A.L. Basham, Vol 2 S. Rizvi; **Taraporevala Sons and Co Pvt Ltd.** *Indian Architecture* (2 vols) 6th ed, 1965, Percy Brown; **Viking/Penguin** *The Encyclopaedia to the Monuments of India* 1989, Vol 1 G.Michell, Vol 2 P. Davies, *Mughal India* by G.H.R. Tillotson; **Yale** *The tradition of Indian architecture*, 1989, by G.H.R. Tillotson.

HOW TO USE THIS HANDBOOK

The *India Handbook* is a unique source of information for independent travellers to India, Bhutan, Sri Lanka and the Maldives. The text is thoroughly revised every year: a new edition is published annually on 1 September, based on extensive personal travel, information from official tourist authorities, notes from correspondents and visitors and the wide range of statistical and other material.

Editorial logic

The *Handbook* starts with practical advice on travel and health, and an introduction to the land and people of the region as a whole. Thereafter it is organised on a national and regional basis. India is divided into major regions, the other countries are treated as single units.

- The capital city or regional centre is the first place covered. Routes which radiate from the regional centre, and the places of interest that lie along them, are then described in clockwise order, starting with routes running north. The routes link the most interesting places and are not necessarily the shortest.

- Rail, road and air are all widely used means of travel in South Asia. It is often assumed that if you are travelling in India rail is 'the only way to do it'. Rail certainly still offers a unique experience, and is often an excellent way of travelling long distances.

- This *Handbook* is unique in providing the essential information every train traveller needs to plan ahead and to make life easier in the booking office: the number, name and departure times of the best trains **from** more than 250 towns **to** over 1000 destinations, and the time of the journey. For ease of use these details are printed for each town after the description of their places of interest and local information.

- Because so many places of interest do not lie directly on the rail network the main route structure is designed to follow major roads.

- Buses now reach virtually every part of the sub-continent, offering a cheap, if often uncomfortable means of visiting places off the rail network.

- It is now possible to hire cars with drivers in many places, often at cheaper rates than self-drive car hire in Europe, though self-drive itself is still difficult and in many areas not advised. A car shared by 3 or 4 can be good value and save time.

- Increasing numbers of people are travelling by bike and motorbike, both of which can be very attractive alternatives.

- Road travel is often the only choice for reaching many of the places of outstanding interest in which South Asia is so rich.

- **All the road and rail networks and the centres of interest referred to in the text are shown on the state maps.**

- Many routes are now illustrated on special route maps. These show the distance in kilometres between all places

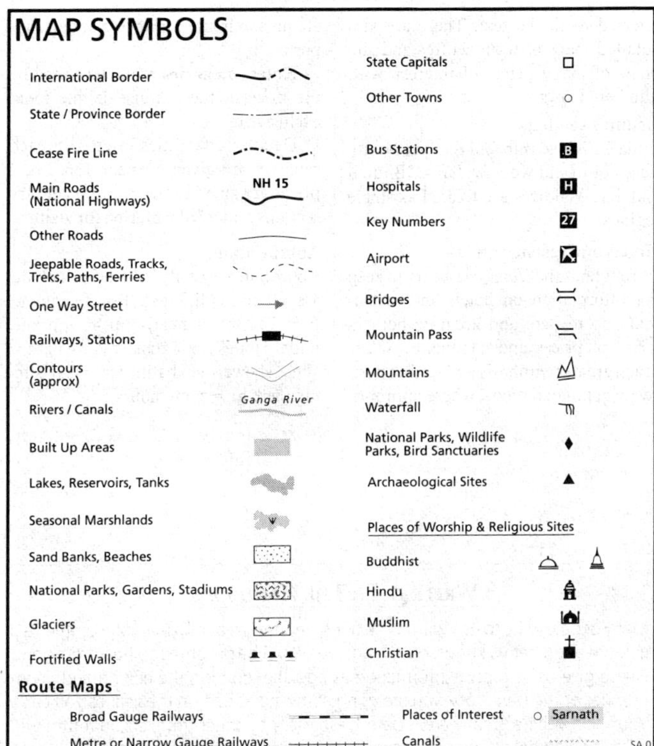

mentioned in the text. Places of special interest are highlighted. Broad gauge and metre gauge railway lines are also shown.

- Social indicators and basic stations are printed for all states, taken from the latest official publications. Population figures are from the 1991 Census or later official estimates where available.

Cross referencing, indexing and glossaries

There is a complete place index at the end of the book. Entries are extensively cross-referenced. For ease of use the 'see page' entry has been highlighted in heavier type. On the page referred to, you will find the entry again emphasised in heavier type. In addition, there are 3 glossaries listing General terms, Architectural terms and Names.

Maps

Good maps and reliable street plans are often very hard to find in South Asia. This *Handbook* has drawn on extensive field visits and a wide range of authoritative sources to compile a series of over 300 original maps, all drawn with the most up to date information available. The Bartholomew maps show the main physical features of South Asia, the major surface transport networks and a wide range of towns and cities. Each of the major regions is introduced by a detailed map, showing all the places of interest referred to in the text. There are also detailed maps of town centres and site plans of many places of interest, with numbered keys.

Country sections

India is divided into four regions, North, East, South and West. Sri Lanka, Bhutan and The Maldives are treated as single regions.

Hotels and restaurants

Throughout the *Handbook* we try to keep the information on hotels and restaurants up to date and accurate both in terms of prices and comments. While much greater emphasis is placed on positive recommendations, where appropriate unfavourable comments are also reported.

Hotel categories are determined by the price of the average double room exclusive of local taxes.

Details of facilities offered in each category are given on page 136. Local prices are given in the relevant country sections under **Information for visitors**.

Abbreviations

Abbreviations used in the book include: a/c = air-conditioned; T = telephone; F = Fax; nr = near; opp = opposite; under Hotels rm = room/rooms, bath = WC, shower or bath; rec = recommended, hr = hour/hours.

Writing To The Handbook

Many people write to us – with corrections, new information, or simply comments. If you want to let us know something, we would be delighted to hear from you. Please give us as precise information as possible, quoting the edition and page number of the *Handbook* you are using and send as early in the year as you can. Your help will be greatly appreciated, especially by other travellers. In return we will send you details about our special guidebook offer.

For hotels or restaurants, send us:

- its name
- phone and fax number
- number of rooms, whether a/c or aircooled, attached (clean?) bathroom
- location – how far from the station or bus stand, for example, or distance (walking time) from a prominent landmark
- if it's not already on one of our maps, can you place it
- your comments – either good or bad – as to why it is distinctive
- address
- tariff cards

For places of interest:

- location
- entry charge
- access – by whatever means of transport is most appropriate, e.g. time of main buses or trains to and from the site
- facilities – nearby drinks stalls, restaurants
- any problems, e.g. steep climb, monkeys, unofficial guides
- opening hours
- site guides

HEALTH INFORMATION

CONTENTS

The following information has been compiled for us by Dr. David Snashall, Senior Lecturer in Occupational Health, United Medical Schools of Guy's and St Thomas' Hospitals and Chief Medical Adviser, Foreign and Commonwealth Office, London.

The traveller to India is inevitably exposed to health risks not encountered in North America or Western Europe. Despite the fact that most of the area lies geographically within the Tropics, the climate is far from tropical in, for example, the Himalayas and so tropical diseases are often not a major problem for visitors. Because much of the area is economically underdeveloped, infectious diseases still predominate in a way in which they used to predominate in the West some decades ago. There is an obvious difference in health risks between the business traveller who tends to stay in international class hotels in large cities, and the back-packer trekking through the rural areas. There are no hard and fast rules to follow; you will often have to make your own judgements on the healthiness or otherwise of your surroundings.

There are many well qualified doctors in the area, a large proportion of whom speak English but the quality and range of medical care diminishes very rapidly as you move away from big cities. In some of the countries such as India, there are systems and traditions of medicine wholly different from the Western model and you may be confronted with unusual modes of treatment such as herbal medicine and acupuncture. At least you can be sure that local Practitioners have a lot of experience with the particular diseases of their region. If you are in a City, it may be worthwhile calling on your Embassy to provide a list of recommended Doctors.

If you are a long way away from medical help, a certain amount of self medication may be necessary and you will find many of the drugs available have familiar names. However, always check the date stamping and buy from reputable pharmacies because the shelf life of some items, especially vaccines and antibiotics, is markedly reduced in hot conditions. Unfortunately, many locally produced drugs are not subjected to quality control procedures and so can be unreliable. There have, in addition, been cases of substitution of inert materials for active drugs.

With the following precautions and advice, you should keep as healthy as usual. Make local enquiries about health risks if you are apprehensive and take the general advice of European and North American families who have lived or are living in the Area.

Before you go

Take out Medical Insurance. You should have a dental check up, obtain a spare glasses prescription and, if you suffer from a longstanding condition such as diabetes, high blood pressure, heart/lung disease or a nervous disorder, arrange for a check up with your doctor who can at the same time provide you with a letter explaining details of your disability. Check the current practice for malaria prophylaxis (prevention) for the countries you intend to visit.

Inoculations

See above.

Infectious Hepatitis (jaundice)

This is common throughout India. It seems to be frequently caught by travellers. The main symptoms are stomach pains, lack of appetite, nausea, lassitude and yellowness of the eyes and skin. Medically speaking, there are 2 types: the less serious but more common is hepatitis A for which the best protection is careful preparation of food, the avoidance of contaminated drinking water and scrupulous attention to toilet hygiene. Human normal immuno-globulin (gamma globulin) confers considerable protection against the disease and is particularly useful in epidemics. It should be obtained from a reputable source and is certainly recommended for travellers who intend to live rough. The injection should be given as close as possible to your departure and, as the dose depends on the likely time you are to spend in potentially infected areas, the manufacturer's instructions should be followed.

The other, more serious, version is hepatitis B, which is acquired as a sexually transmitted disease, from a blood transfusion or an injection with an unclean needle or possibly by insect bites. The symptoms are the same as hepatitis A but the incubation period is much longer.

You may have had jaundice before or you may have had hepatitis of either type before without becoming jaundiced, in which case it is possible that you could be immune to either hepatitis A or B. This immunity can be tested for before you travel. If you are not immune to hepatitis B already, a vaccine is available (3 shots over 6 months) and if you are not immune to hepatitis A already, then you should consider having gamma globulin.

AIDS

In India AIDS is increasing in its prevalence as in most countries but with a pattern closer to that of developing societies. Thus, it is not wholly confined to the well known high risk sections of the population i.e., homosexual men, intravenous drug abusers, prostitutes and the children of infected mothers. Heterosexual transmission is probably now the dominant mode and so the main risk to travellers is from casual sex. The same precautions should be taken as when encountering any sexually transmitted disease. In some of the countries, almost the whole of the female prostitute population is HIV positive and in other parts, intravenous drug abuse is common. The AIDS virus (HIV) can be passed via unsterile needles which have been previously used to inject a HIV positive patient but the risk of this is very small indeed. It would, however, be sensible to check that needles have been properly sterilised or disposable needles used. The chance of picking up hepatitis B in this way is much more of a danger. Be wary of carrying disposable needles yourself; Customs officials may find them suspicious. The risk of receiving a blood transfusion with blood infected with the HIV virus is greater than from dirty needles because of the amount of fluid exchanged. Supplies of blood for transfusion are now largely screened for HIV in all reputable hospitals, so the risk must be very small indeed. Catching the AIDS virus does not necessarily produce an illness in itself; the only way to be sure if you feel you have been put at risk is to have a blood test for HIV antibodies on your return to a place where there are reliable laboratory facilities. The test does not become positive for many weeks.

Common problems

Altitude

Acute mountain sickness can strike from about 3000m upwards. It is more likely to affect those who ascend rapidly (e.g. by plane) and those who over-exert themselves. Teenagers seem to be particularly prone. Past experience is not always a good guide: the Author, having spent years in Peru travelling constantly between sea level and very high altitude never suffered the slightest symptoms, then was severely affected climbing Kilimanjaro in Tanzania.

On reaching heights above 3000m, heart pounding and shortness of breath, especially on exertion are almost universal and a normal response to the lack of oxygen in the air. Acute mountain sickness takes a few hours or days to come on and presents with headache, lassitude, dizziness, loss of appetite, nausea and vomiting. Insomnia is common and often associated with a suffocating feeling when lying down in bed. Keen observers may note that their breathing tends to wax and wane at night and their face tends to be puffy in the mornings – this is all part of the syndrome. If the symptoms are mild, the treatment is rest, painkillers (preferably not Aspirin based) for the headache and anti-sickness pills for vomiting. Oxygen may help at very high altitudes but is unlikely to be available.

The best way of preventing acute mountain sickness is a relatively slow ascent and, when trekking through the Himalayas to high altitude, some time spent in the foothills getting fit and adapting to moderate altitude is beneficial. On arrival at places over 3000m, a few hours rest in a chair and the avoidance of alcohol, cigarettes and heavy food will go a long way towards preventing acute mountain sickness. Should the symptoms be severe and prolonged, it is best to descend to a lower altitude and to re-ascend slowly or in stages. The symptoms disappear very quickly with even a few 100m of descent. If a slow staged attempt is impossible because of shortage of time, then the drug Acetazolamide (Diamox) can be used as a preventative and continued during the ascent. There is good evidence of the value of this drug in the prevention of acute mountain sickness but some people do experience funny side effects. The usual dose is 500 mgs of the slow release preparation each night, starting the night before ascending above 3000m.

Other problems experienced at high altitude are sunburn, excessively dry air causing skin cracking, sore eyes (it may be wise to leave your contact lenses out) and stuffy noses. It is unwise to ascend to high altitude if you are pregnant, especially in the first 3 months, or if you have any history of heart, lung or blood disease, including sickle cell.

There is a further, albeit rare, hazard due to rapid ascent to high altitude – a kind of complicated mountain sickness presenting as acute pulmonary oedema or acute cerebral oedema. Both conditions are more common the higher you go. Pulmonary oedema comes on quite rapidly with breathlessness, noisy breathing, cough, blueness of the lips and frothing at the mouth. Cerebral oedema usually presents with confusion, going on to unconsciousness. Anybody developing these serious conditions must be brought down to low altitude as soon as possible and taken to hospital.

Rapid descent from high places will aggrevate sinus and middle ear infections and make bad teeth ache. The same problems are sometimes experienced during descent at the end of an aeroplane flight. Do not ascend to high altitude in the 24 hrs following scuba-diving. Remember that the Himalayas and other Indian mountain ranges are very high, very cold, very remote and potentially very dangerous. Do not travel in them alone, when you are ill or if you are poorly equipped. As telephone communication can be non-existent, mountain rescue is extremely difficult and medical services may not be up to much.

Despite these various hazards (mostly preventable) of high altitude travel, many people find the environment healthier and more invigorating than at sea level.

Heat and cold

Full acclimatisation to high temperatures takes about 2 weeks and during this period, it is normal to feel relatively apathetic, especially if the relative humidity is high. Drink plenty of water (up to 15 litres a day are required when working physically hard in the tropics), use salt on your food and avoid extreme exertion. Tepid showers are more cooling than hot or cold ones. Large hats do not cool you down but prevent sunburn. Remember that, especially in the mountains, there can be a large and sudden drop in temperature between sun and shade and between night and day, so dress accordingly. Loose fitting cotton clothes are still the best for hot weather. Warm jackets and woollens are essential after dark at high altitude.

Insects

These can be a great nuisance. Some of course are carriers of serious diseases such as malaria, dengue fever or filariasis and various worm infections. The best way of keeping mosquitoes away at night is to sleep off the ground with a mosquito net and to burn mosquito coils containing Pyrethrum. Aerosol sprays or a "flit" gun may be effective as are insecticidal tablets which are heated on a mat which is plugged into the wall socket (if taking your own, check the voltage of the area you are visiting so that you can take an appliance that will work. Similarly, check that your electrical adaptor is suitable for the repellent plug.)

Or you can use personal insect repellent of which the best contain a high concentration of Diethyltoluamide. Liquid is best for arms and face (take care around eyes and make sure you do not dissolve the plastic of your spectacles). Aerosol spray on clothes and ankles deter mites and ticks. Liquid DET suspended in water can be used to impregnate cotton clothes and mosquito nets. If you are bitten, itching may be relieved by cool baths and anti-histamine tablets (care with alcohol or driving), corticosteroid creams (great care – never use if any hint of sepsis) or by judicious scratching. Calamine lotion and cream have limited effectiveness and anti-histamine creams have a tendency to cause skin allergies and are, therefore, not generally recommended. Bites which become infected (commonly in the tropics) should be treated with a local antiseptic or antibiotic cream such as Cetrimide as should infected scratches. Skin infestations with body lice, crabs and scabies are unfortunately easy to pick up. Use Gamma benzene hexachloride for lice and Benzyl benzoate for scabies. Crotamiton cream alleviates itching and also kills a number of skin parasites. Malathion lotion 5% is good for lice but avoid the highly toxic full strength Malathion used as an agricultural insecticide.

Intestinal upsets

Practically nobody escapes this one, so be prepared for it. Some of these countries lead the world in their prevalence of diarrhoea. Most of the time, intestinal upsets are due to the insanitary preparation of food. Do not eat uncooked fish or vegetables or meat (especially pork), fruit with the skin on (always peel your fruit yourself) or food that is exposed to flies (especially salads). Tap water may be unsafe, especially in the monsoon and the same goes for stream water or well water. Filtered or bottled water is usually available and safe. If your hotel has a central hot water supply, this is safe to drink after cooling. Ice for drinks should be made from boiled water but rarely is, so stand your glass on the ice cubes, instead of putting them in the drink. Dirty water should first be strained through a filter bag (available from camping shops) and then boiled or treated. Bringing the water to a rolling boil at sea level is sufficient but at high altitude you have to boil the water for longer to ensure that all the microbes are killed. Various sterilising methods can be used and there are proprietary preparations containing chlorine or iodine compounds. Pasteurised or heat treated milk is now widely available, as is ice cream and yogurt produced by the same methods. Unpasteurised milk products, including cheese, are sources of tuberculosis, brucellosis, listeria and food poisoning germs. You can render fresh milk safe by heating it to 62°C for 30 minutes, followed by rapid cooling or by boiling it. Matured or processed cheeses are safer than fresh varieties.

Diarrhoea is usually the result of food poisoning, occasionally from contaminated water. There are various causes – viruses, bacteria, protozoa (like amoeba), salmonella and cholera organisms. It may take one of several forms, coming on suddenly, or rather slowly. It may be accompanied by vomiting or by severe abdominal pain and the passage of blood or mucus when it is called dysentery. How do you know which type you have and how do you treat them? All kinds of diarrhoea, whether or not accompanied by vomiting respond favourably to the replacement of water and salts taken as frequent small sips of some kind of rehydration solution. There are proprietary preparations, consisting of sachets of powder which you dissolve in water, or you can make your own by adding half a teaspoonful of salt (3.5 grams) and 4 tablespoonfuls of sugar (40 grams) to a litre of boiled water.

- If you can time the onset of diarrhoea to the minute, then it is probably viral or bacterial and/or the onset of dysentery. The treatment, in addition to rehydration, is Ciprofloxacin 500 mgs every 12 hrs. The drug is now widely available.
- If the diarrhoea has come on slowly or intermittently, then it is more likely to be protozoal, i.e. caused by amoeba or giardia and antibiotics will have no effect. These cases are best treated by a doctor as should any diarrhoea continuing for more than 3 days. If there are severe stomach cramps, the following drugs may help: Loperamide (Imodium, Arret) and Diphenoxylate with Atropine (Lomotil).

Thus, the lynch pins of treatment for diarrhoea are rest, fluid and salt replacement, antibiotics such as Ciprofloxacin for the bacterial types and special diagnostic tests and medical treatment for amoeba and giardia infections. Salmonella infections and cholera can be devastating diseases and it would be wise to get to a hospital as soon as possible if these were suspected. Fasting, peculiar diets and the consumption of large quantities of yogurt have not been found useful in calming travellers' diarrhoea or in rehabilitating inflamed bowels. Oral rehydration has, especially in children, been a life-saving technique and as there is some evidence that alcohol and milk might prolong diarrhoea, they should probably be avoided during and immediately after an attack. There are ways of preventing travellers' diarrhoea for short periods of time when visiting these countries by taking antibiotics but these are ineffective against viruses and, to some extent, against protozoa, so this technique should not be used, other than in exceptional circumstances. Some preventives such as Entero-vioform can have serious side effects if taken for long periods.

Malaria

Malaria is prevalent in India. It remains a serious disease and you are advised to protect yourself against mosquito bites as above and to take prophylactic (preventive) drugs. Start taking the tablets a few days before exposure and continue to take them 6 weeks after leaving the malarial zone. Remember to give the drugs to babies and children and pregnant women also. The subject of malaria prevention is becoming more complex as the malaria parasite becomes immune to some of the older drugs. In particular, there has been an increase in the proportion of cases of falciparum malaria which is particularly dangerous. Some of the preventive drugs can cause side effects, especially if taken for long periods of time, so before you travel you must check with a reputable agency the likelihood and type of malaria in the countries which you intend to visit and take their advice on prophylaxis and be prepared to receive conflicting advice. Because of the rapidly changing situation in the area I have not included the names and dosage of the drugs. You can catch malaria even when taking prophylactic drugs, although it is unlikely. If you do develop symptoms (high fever, shivering, severe headache, sometimes diarrhoea) seek medical advice immediately. The risk of the disease is obviously greater the further you move from the cities into rural areas with primitive facilities and standing water.

Snake bite

If you are unlucky enough to be bitten by a venomous snake, spider, scorpion, centipede or sea creature try (within limits) to catch the animal for identification. The reactions to be expected are fright, swelling, pain and bruising around the bite, soreness of the regional lymph glands, nausea, vomiting and fever. If, in addition, any of the following symptoms supervene get the victim to a doctor without delay: numbness, tingling of the face, muscular spasm, convulsions, shortness of breath or haemorrhage. Commercial snake bite or scorpion sting kits may be available but are only useful for the specific type of snake or scorpion for which they are designed. The serum has to be given intravenously, so is not much good unless you have had some practice in making injections into veins. If the bite is on a limb, immobilise the limb and apply a tight bandage between the bite and the body, releasing it for 90 seconds every 15 minutes. Reassurance of the bitten person is very important because death from snake bite is, in fact, very rare. Do not slash the bite area and try to suck out the poison because this sort of heroism does more harm than good. Hospitals usually hold stocks of snake bite serum. Best precaution: do not walk in snake territory with bare feet, sandals or shorts.

If swimming in an area where there are poisonous fish such as stone or scorpion fish (also called by a variety of local names) or sea urchins on rocky coasts, tread carefully or wear plimsolls. The sting of such fish is intensely painful and this can be helped by immersing the stung part in water as hot as you can bear for as long as it remains painful. This is not always very practical and you must take care not to scald yourself, but it does work. Avoid spiders and scorpions by keeping your bed away from the wall, look under lavatory seats and inside your shoes in the morning. In the rare event of being bitten, consult a doctor.

Sunburn and heat stroke

The burning power of the tropical sun is phenomenal, especially at high altitude. Always wear a wide brimmed hat and use some form of sun cream or lotion on untanned skin. Normal temperate zone suntan lotions (protection factor up to 7) are not much good. You need to use the types designed specifically for the tropics or for mountaineers or skiers with a protection factor between 7 and 15. Glare from the sun can cause conjunctivitis so wear sunglasses, especially on tropical beaches.

There are several varieties of 'heat stroke'. The most common cause is severe dehydration. Avoid dehydration by drinking lots of non-alcoholic fluid.

Other afflictions

Remember that **rabies** is endemic in India so do not go near any wild animal or an unknown dog. If you are bitten by a domestic animal, try to have it captured for observation and see a doctor at once. Treatment with human diploid vaccine is now extremely effective and worth seeking out if the likelihood of having contracted rabies is high. A course of anti-rabies vaccine might be a good idea before you go.

Dengue fever is present in India. It is a virus disease, transmitted by mosquito bites, presenting with severe headache and body pains. Complicated types of dengue known as haemorrhagic fevers occur throughout Asia but usually in persons who have caught the disease a second time. Thus, although it is a very serious type, it is rarely caught by visitors. There is no treatment, you must just avoid mosquito bites.

Athlete's foot and other fungal infections are best treated by sunshine and a proprietary preparation such as Tolnaftate.

Influenza and **respiratory diseases** is common, perhaps made worse by polluted cities and rapid temperature and climatic changes.

Intestinal worms are common and the more serious ones, such as hook worm can be contracted by walking barefoot on infested earth or beaches.

Leishmaniasis – this can be a serious disease taking several forms and transmitted by sand flies. These should be avoided in the same way as mosquitoes.

Prickly heat A very common itchy rash is avoided by frequent washing and by wearing loose clothing. It is helped by the use of talcum powder to allow the skin to dry thoroughly after washing.

When you return home

Remember to take your anti-malaria tablets for 6 weeks. If you have had attacks of diarrhoea, it is worth having a stool specimen tested in case you have picked up amoebic dysentery. If you have been living rough, a blood test may be worthwhile to detect worms and other parasites.

Further information

The following organisations give information regarding well trained English speaking Physicians throughout the world: International Association for Medical Assistance to Travellers, 745 5th Avenue, New York, 10022; Intermedic 777, Third Avenue, New York, 10017.

Information regarding country by country malaria risk can be obtained from the World Health Organisation (WHO) or the Ross Institute, The London School of Hygiene and Tropical Medicine, Kepple Street, London WClE 7HT, which publishes a strongly recommended book entitled: *The Preservation of Personal Health in Warm Climates.*

The organisation MASTA (Medical Advisory Service for Travellers Abroad) also based at the London School of Hygiene and Tropical Medicine, Telephone 071 631-4408 – Telex 895 3474) will provide country by country information on up to date health risks.

Further information-on medical problems overseas can be obtained from the new edition of *Travellers' Health: How to Stay Healthy Abroad*, edited by Richard Dawood (Oxford University Press,1992). We strongly recommend this revised and updated edition, especially to the intrepid travellers who go to the more out-of-the-way places.

INDIA AND ITS REGION

Contents

Introduction

The heart of India beats in the densely populated plains of the Ganga, settled and cultivated for millennia, and the home of great civilizations which shape the lives of 900 million people today. To the south lies the Peninsula, politically always more fragmented than the Plains and agriculturally less fertile, but with mineral resources which have supplied empires from the Indus Valley Civilization over 4000 years ago to the rapidly developing Indian economy of the present. Beyond lies one of India's great natural frontiers, the Indian Ocean, stretching from the Arabian Sea in the west to the Bay of Bengal in the east, and offering nothing but scattered island chains between Kanykumari and Antarctica.

To the north of the plains stand the Himalaya, which Sir Thomas Holditch, the nineteenth Surveyor General of India described as 'the finest natural combination of boundary and barrier that exists in the world. It stands alone. For the greater part of its length only the Himalayan eagle can trace it. It lies amidst the eternal silence of vast snowfield and icebound peaks. Could you stand alone on one of the outer ranges in Kashmir, or in Garhwal, or at Darjeeling, and watch on some clear day the white outline of the distant snowy range, you would then realise that never was there such a God-given boundary set to such a vast impressive and stupendous frontier.'

Yet each of these three major physical regions – the Himalaya, the Ganga plains and the Peninsula – have their own great diversity. In the eastern foothills of the Himalaya, for example, are some of the wettest, jungle clad regions in the world, while in their western ranges are the high altitude deserts of Ladakh. Similarly the Ganga plains stretch from the fertile and wet delta of Bengal to the deserts of northern Rajasthan. Even the Peninsula ranges from the tropical humid climate of the west coast to the dry plateaus inland.

India's most holy river, the Ganga, runs across the vital heartland of the country and through the mythology of Hinduism. Joined by other holy rivers along its route, such as the Yamuna (Jumna), its waters are a vital source of irrigation. Its path is dotted with towns and settlements of great sanctity, and it is a vital economic asset as well as the focus of devotion for hundreds of millions. To the south the great rivers of the Peninsula – the Narmada, Krishna, Tungabhadra and Kaveri to name only the largest – also have a spiritual significance to match their current role as providers of water and power. Most rise within 50 km of the Arabian Sea and flow east to the Bay of Bengal, the Narmada and the Tapi being the exceptions, flowing west beneath the great scarp of the Vindhyan mountains.

LAND AND LIFE

CONTENTS

MAPS

Basics

OFFICIAL NAME: The Republic of India

NATIONAL FLAG: A horizontal tricolour with equal bands of saffron, white and green from top to bottom. At the centre is an Asoka wheel in navy blue.

NATIONAL ANTHEM: *Jana Gana Mana*

KEY STATISTICS: *Population*: 900mn 1994; *Annual increase*: 18mn; *Area*: 3,287,000 sq km; *Literacy*: 52% (Male 64%, Female 39%); *Birth rate per '000*: Urban 27, Rural 34; *Death rate per '000*: Urban 7, Rural 12; *Infant mortality rate*: Urban 62, Rural 105; *Religion*: Hindu 730mn, Muslim 104mn, Christian 23mn, Sikh 19mn, Buddhist 7mn, Jain 4mn, Scheduled castes 134mn; Scheduled tribes 66mn.

Geology and landscape

India falls into 3 major geological regions. The N is enclosed by the great arc of the Himalaya. Along their southern flank lie the alluvial plains of the Ganga (Ganges), and to the S again is the Peninsula. Geologically, Sri Lanka is a continuation of the Indian Peninsula, separated by the 30 km wide shallows known as Adam's Bridge. In contrast, the island chains of the Laccadives and Minicoy off the W coast of India, and the Maldives to the SW, are coral atolls, formed on 3 submarine ridges formed the Arabian Sea.

The origins of India's landscapes

Only 100 million years ago the Indian Peninsula was still attached to the great land mass of what geologists call 'Pangaea', of which S Africa, Antarctica and India were a part. It included some of the world's oldest rocks, such as crystalline granites and gneisses which today make up a large part of India S of the Ganga Plains. In sharp contrast, the Ganga Plains themselves and the Himalaya to their N resulted from the dramatic collision of the Indian Plate as it has pushed N under the Asian landmass of modern Tibet during the last 100 million years.

As recently as 50 million years ago the land mass S of the line Jaisalmer – Delhi – Calcutta lay in the S hemisphere. Many of the rocks which form the Indian Peninsula were formed alongside their then neighbours in S Africa, S America, Australia and Antarctica. Thus the *Archaean* rocks of the Peninsula are some of the oldest in the world. They are generally crystalline, contorted and faulted. The oldest series are the *Charnockites*, named after the founder of Calcutta and enthusiastic amateur geologist, Job Charnock, see p 605. Along with the *Khondalite* rocks, these are over 3,100 million years old. Some of the most striking examples are found in the Nilgiri and Palani Hills in Tamil Nadu. Other major areas of gneissic rocks are found in the E Ghats, in Rajasthan and the Aravalli-Delhi belt, and in Bihar and Orissa. The Charnockites themselves extend into the highlands of Sri Lanka.

The first ranges of the Himalaya to begin the mountain building process were probably the Karakoram, in modern Pakistan, about 100 million years ago. The central core of the Himalayan ranges did not begin to rise until about 35 million years ago, followed by further

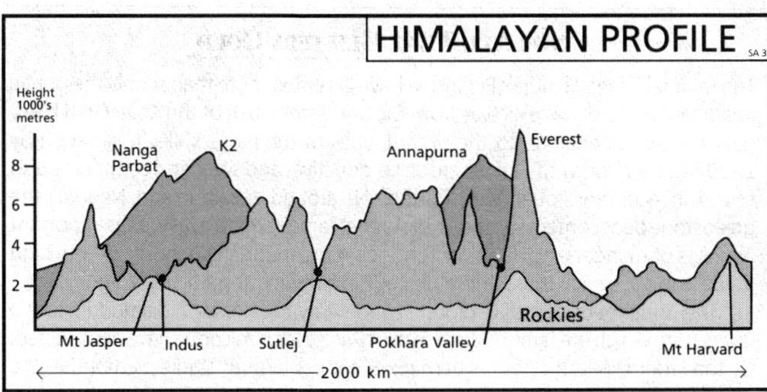

major movements between 25 and 5 million years ago. The latest mountain building period, responsible for the Shiwaliks, began less than 5 million years ago and is still continuing. The rocks of the central core of the Himalaya were formed under the intense pressure and heat of the mountain building process. Before that the present Himalayan region and what is now the Tibetan plateau had lain under the sea.

As the Himalaya began their dramatic uplift the newly formed rivers eroded massive quantities of rock, stone and silt. The finer material was washed down onto the plains fronting the newly forming mountain ranges, which were themselves sinking as the mountains to the N were rising. The trough which formed as a result of this process was steadily filled, creating the Indo-Gangetic plains. Today the alluvium reaches depths of over 5,000m in places, being deepest between Delhi and Orissa. The boundary between the plains and the Himalayan ranges is a zone of continuing violent earth movement, with earthquakes common from the W borderlands of Pakistan, through Nepal to Assam.

The Himalaya

Dominating the entire N borders of S Asia, the Himalaya stretch 2500 km from NW to SE and between 150 and 400 km from N to S. They provide a dramatic barrier between S Asia and China. The Himalayan Mountains proper, stretching from the Pamirs in Pakistan to the easternmost bend of the Brahmaputra in Assam, can be divided into 3 broad zones.

On the S flank are the Shiwaliks, or Outer Ranges. To their immediate N run the parallel Middle Ranges of Panjal and Dhauladhar, and to the N again is the third zone, the Inner Himalaya, which has the highest peaks, many of them in Nepal.

The scale of the Himalaya is unparalleled anywhere in the world. Of

Silt And Mud

The Indo-Gangetic plains are still being extended and modified. The S part of Bangladesh and of W Bengal only emerged from the sea during the last 5,000 years. The Ganga and the Indus have each been estimated to carry over 1 million tonnes of silt every year – considerably more than the Mississippi. The silts have made it possible for intensive rice cultivation to be practised continuously for hundreds of years, though they cause problems for modern irrigation development. Dams in the Himalayan region are being rapidly filled by silt, over 33 million tonnes being deposited behind the Bhakra Dam on the Sutlej River alone.

Nor All That Glisters Gold

The mineral riches of India's Peninsula have captured more than simply the poetic imagination. Gold made its way from the greenstone belt of the Kolar Gold Field, near modern Bangalore, to the distant cities of the Indus Valley Civilization by 2300 BC. Even today the mines are still productive, and silver and copper are also found in economic quantities. Further N, around Jabalpur and Nagpur, the greenstone beds contain some of India's most famous marble, as well as important deposits of manganese. However, it is their more mundane deposits of very high grade iron ore which make these geological formations particularly significant.

The upper beds of India's oldest sedimentary rocks have 2 diamond bearing layers from which the famous diamonds of Panna and Golconda have been mined. Of the latter the Koh-i-noor is perhaps the most famous single diamond in the world. Beds of sandstones, limestones and shales often 4000m thick cover over 100,000 sq km from W Bihar to the gneissic rocks of the Aravallis and Mount Abu. They form particularly dramatic ridges in the Vindhyan mountains just N of the Narmada River, where they are strikingly visible in the sharp-fronted scarp overlooking the Son.

Red sandstones have made an enormous contribution to Indian architecture as the source of the red sandstone of which the Mughals made such extensive use in their city building.

Coal, least glamorous but none the less prized of minerals for industrial development, is also found most extensively in the Peninsula. The deposits were laid down in 3 main belts: a tract along the Damodar Valley in W Bengal; an extensive outcrop along the upper reaches of the Mahanadi River in Madhya Pradesh; and a series of troughs along the upper Godavari River from Nagpur to the river's delta.

the 94 mountains in Asia above 7,300 m, all but 2 are in the Himalaya (including the Karakoram). Nowhere else in the world are there mountains as high. Although the ranges themselves are recently formed, they include rocks from all the major geological periods.

The Ganga Plains

Rising within 200 km of each other, the Ganga and its tributaries have created one of the world's most densely populated alluvial plains. They stretch apparently endlessly and unchangingly from E to W. Yet there are extremely important differences in soil and local relief which have a great effect on agriculture. Generations of farmers have practised agriculture with enormous subtlety and sensitivity to their environment. The plains have some of the largest reserves of underground water in the world which have made possible extensive well irrigation, especially in NW India, contributing to the rapid agricultural changes which have taken place.

The Peninsula

As the Indian Peninsula moved away from the African coastline just over 60 million years ago a mass of volcanic lava welled up through cracks in the earth's surface, and covered some 500,000 sq km of N Karnataka, Maharashtra, N into Gujurat and Madhya Pradesh. The deepest lava –over 3000m–was near the fissures themselves, just inland of Bombay. They thin rapidly E.

As the Indian plate moved NE away from Africa, the fault line was marked by a N-S ridge of mountains, known today as the Western Ghats, set back from the sea by a coastal plain which varies from 10 to over 80 km wide. In the S, the Nilgiris and

Palanis are over 2,500m high.

From the crest line of the Western Ghats, the Peninsula slopes generally eastwards, interrupted on its E edge by the much more broken groups of hills sometimes referred to as the Eastern Ghats. The E flowing rivers have created flat alluvial deltas which have been the basis of successive peninsular kingdoms and empires from the Pallavas, Pandiyans and Cholas in the far S to the Kalingans in Orissa.

Sri Lanka

Except for the limestone outcrops of the Jaffna Peninsula and the NW coast, the whole of Sri Lanka is composed of the same pre-Cambrian rocks characteristic of S India. They have been raised in 3 tiers from sea level, each separated from the next by a dramatic scarp front. These steep scarps have themselves been deeply eroded. The alternation of steep slopes and deep cut valleys contributes to Sri Lanka's often stunningly beautiful scenery, but in the past it often made it very difficult to get in to many parts of the central highlands.

Climate

India is divided almost exactly by the Tropic of Cancer, stretching from the near-Equatorial Kanyakumari to the Mediterranean latitudes of Kashmir – roughly the same span as from the Amazon to San Francisco or from Lagos to Madrid. Not surprisingly, climate varies considerably. High altitudes modify local climates, often dramatically.

The monsoon

An Arabic word meaning 'season', the term monsoon refers to the wind reversal which replaces the dry northeasterlies, characteristic of winter and spring, with the very warm and wet southwesterlies of the summer.

Many myths surround the onset of the monsoon. You will often be told that 'the monsoon starts on...' or 'it never rains before....' and then be given a firm date. In fact the arrival of the monsoon is as variable as is the amount of rain which it brings. What makes the Indian monsoon quite exceptional is not its regularity but the depth of moist air which passes over the sub-continent. Over India, for example, the moist airflow is over 6,000m thick. This compares with a moist airmass in Japan's summer monsoon of only 2,000m. This airmass is highly unstable, and gives rise to India's characteristic thunderstorms which mark out the wet season.

Winter

In winter high pressure builds up over C Asia. Most of India is protected from the cold NE monsoon winds that result by the massive bulk of the Himalaya, and daytime temperatures rise sharply in the sun.

Further E frost becomes less common, but right across the Ganga plains night temperatures fall to below 5°C in Jan and Feb. As you move further S so the winter temperatures increase. Madras, for example, has average minimum temperatures of 20°C.

Winter westerlies often result in the Punjab, Haryana and western Uttar Pradesh receiving Mediterranean depressions which bring vitally important winter rains. Although much of N India often has beautiful weather from Nov through to Mar, there are sometimes periods when it is cool and overcast. Elsewhere, however, the winter is a dry season through nearly all of India.

The low winter night temperatures across N India, coupled with high atmospheric pressure and increasing pollution in the larger cities such as Delhi and Calcutta, contribute to the growing problem of morning fog in Dec-Jan. Occasionally this may last all day and be so unpleasant that the sight of people wearing smog masks is no longer a rarity. It can also have a severely disrupting effect on air travel, as Delhi is the hub of N India's internal air network, as well as of its main international connections.

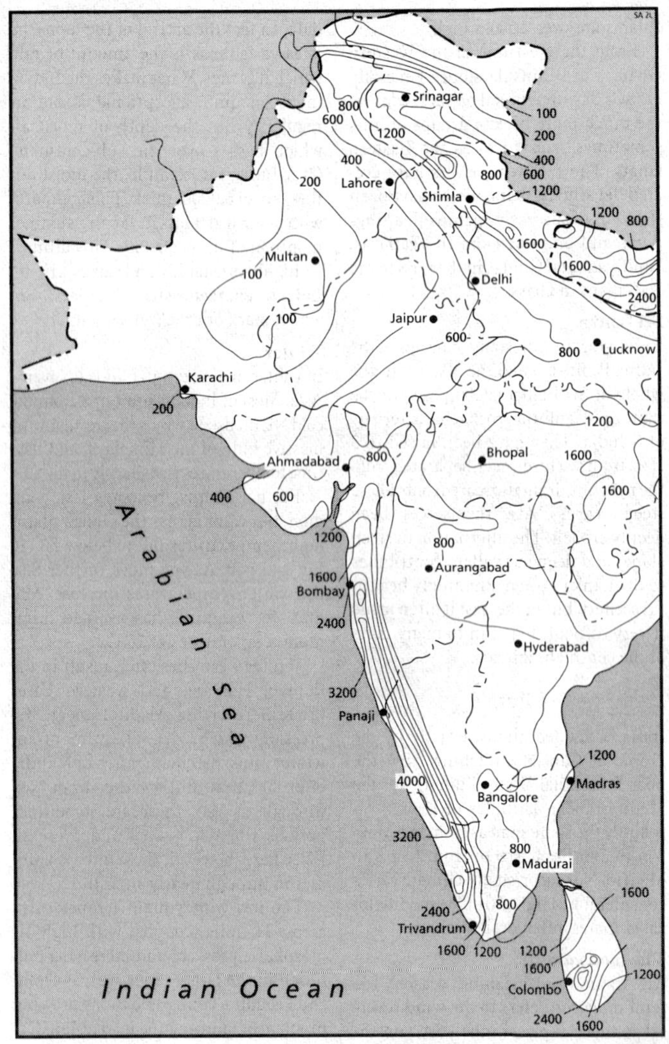

Summer

From Apr onwards much of India becomes almost unbearably hot. In the 6 weeks or so before the SW monsoon sets in, heat builds up over the land mass of both India and continental Asia to the N. Temperatures are generally over 40°C, and temperatures of over 50°C are not unknown. It is a time of year to get up to the hills.

At the end of May the upper air westerly jet stream, which controls the atmos-

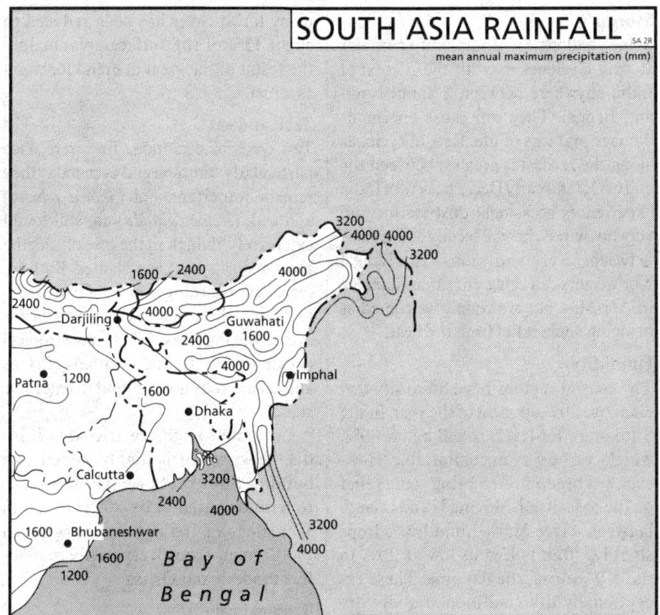

Maps: Publisher's note
The Government of India states that "The external boundaries of India are neither correct or authenticated." The maps in the *Handbook* are not intended to have any political significance.

pheric system over the Indo-Gangetic plains through the winter, suddenly breaks down. It re-forms to the N of Tibet, thus allowing very moist southwesterlies to sweep across S India and the Bay of Bengal. They then double back northwestwards, bringing rain across the Indo-Gangetic Plains to NW India.

The wet season

From a visitor's point of view the monsoon season can be even worse, for it brings an enveloping dampness which makes cooling down impossible. It also makes it very difficult to keep things dry – particularly important for photographic equipment and films. Depending on the region the rainy season lasts from between 3 and 5 months before the northeasterlies reassert themselves.

Many parts of the W coast receive over 2,500 mm of rain a year, and the Shillong plateau has received as much as 26m in one year! If you are travelling in the wetter parts of India during the monsoon you need to be prepared for extended periods of torrential rain. This often disrupts travel arrangements. However, many parts of India receive a total of under 1,000 mm a year, and although much of this comes in the monsoon season it is mainly in the form of heavy isolated showers. Rainfall generally decreases towards the NW, Rajasthan and N Gujarat merging imperceptibly into genuine desert. Tamil Nadu in the SE has an exceptional rainfall pattern. It receives most of its rain in the period of the retreating monsoon, Oct-Dec.

Storms

Some regions of India suffer major storms. Cyclones may hit the E coast of India anywhere between S Tamil Nadu and Bengal. They can cause enormous damage and loss of life. Risk of cyclones along the E coast is greatest between the end of Oct and early Dec. The NW of India experiences occasional dust storms and very hot winds, known locally as *'the Loo'*, between Apr and Jun. In Bengal Nor'westers can cause enormous damage in Apr-May, but are widely welcomed as bringing some relief from the heat.

Humidity

The coastal regions have humidity levels above 70% for most of the year. In the S it is rare for levels to fall below 80%, which can be very uncomfortable. However, sea breezes often bring some relief on the coast itself. Moving N and inland, between Dec-May humidity drops sharply, often falling as low as 20% in the NW during the daytime. These exceptionally dry conditions rapidly dry out the skin – most people travelling across the N between Mar-May find that they need plenty of skin cream.

Warning In the monsoon travelling by road, especially off the National Highways, can be hazardous. Many river causeways become unpassable and occasionally bridges are washed away. Railway timetables can also be unpredictably disrupted and some lines close for the monsoon season.

Vegetation, land and wildlife

Vegetation

India's tropical location and its position astride the wet monsoonal winds ensured that the original vegetation cover of most parts of India was tropical deciduous forest. Areas with more than 1700 mm of rainfall had tropical semi-evergreen to moist tropical deciduous, while much of the remainder had dry tropical deciduous woodland. However, today forest cover has been reduced to about 13% of the surface area, mainly the result of the great demand for wood as a fuel.

Teak and sal

Two types of deciduous tree were once particularly common and even today they remain important. Sal (*Shorea robusta*) and teak (*Tectona grandis*) are still found extensively, though in the case of teak the great majority has been planted. Both are resistant to burning, which helped to protect them where man used fire as a means of clearing the forest. While most tropical deciduous forest is highly varied both teak and sal are commonly found in extensive stands.

Sal is now largely restricted to E India. Teak, which is highly valued as a building timber because of its resistance to termites, used to be concentrated in W regions of India, but is now much more widely spread, especially in Madhya Pradesh and Orissa.

Tropical rainforest

In wetter areas, particularly along the Western Ghats, you can still find *tropical evergreen forest*, but even these forests are now extensively managed. Across the drier areas of the peninsula heavy grazing has reduced the forest cover to little more than thorn scrub.

In W Rajasthan drought-tolerant shrubs become common. In these agriculturally marginal lands, small changes in climate can be very significant. Much of Rajasthan is now known to have been significantly wetter as little as 8,000 years ago, when the pastoral settlements of the NW were beginning to develop into settled agricultural communities.

Mountain forests

At between 1000m and 2000m in the E hill ranges of India, and in Bhutan, for example, wet hill forest include evergreen oaks and chestnuts. Further W in the foothills of the Himalaya are belts of subtropical pine at roughly the same altitudes. Deodars (*Cedrus deodarus*) form large stands, and moist temperate forest, with pines, cedars, firs and spruce, is dominant, giving many of the valleys a beautifully fresh, Alpine feel.

Rhododendrons
Between 3000m and 4000m alpine forest predominates. The famous belts of rhododendron are often mixed with other forest types. Birch, juniper and pine are widespread, and poplars are found from Kashmir in the W to Bhutan in the E.

Grasslands
There are some areas of savanna grassland, resulting directly from man's action. There are several varieties of coarse grassland along the S edge of the Terai. Alpine grasses are important for grazing above altitudes of 2000 m. A totally distinctive grassland is the bamboo region of the E Himalaya. Bamboo (*Dendo calamus*), widespread throughout India, is now widely used in the NE for the paper making industry.

Soils

The fertile alluvial soils of the Indo-Gangetic plains and the deltas of the E coast of India often deteriorate rapidly if green manure and fertiliser are not applied. Others are at risk of becoming encrusted with salts if irrigated without proper drainage. Yet the heartland of N India is dependent on them.

The largest broad category of soils in peninsular India are the red soils. Light, sandy and often gravelly, usually easily worked, they are poor in plant nutrients and dry out very quickly. There are limited areas of genuine tropical laterites, as in Orissa and Kerala for example.

The most important exception to these broad regional soil types are the

Green Gold – India's Rare Forest Resources

The forests are far more than just "natural vegetation". They have always been a resource, but today some of their species give products of great economic value. Commercial pressures are also taking their toll. Indian rosewood, much favoured for its use in high quality furniture making, is now restricted to very limited areas in S India. The fragrant sandalwood, still a favourite medium for carving small images of Hindu deities, is so valuable that its exploitation is totally controlled by the government. In 1994 police in Tamil Nadu and Karnataka were continuing to fight organised smuggling rings, and vast sums of money are said to be at stake in the illegal trade in sandalwood.

One of the most striking features of the peninsular landscape is the wide variety of palm tree. Coconut palms (*Cocos nucifera*) dominate the entire W coast of India and are also common in S and E India. The large green fruit of the tender coconut, which looks so different from the small hairy brown inner nut which is seen in markets and on coconut shies in Europe, is widely available on street corners in towns and villages. It gives one of the most refreshing – and healthy – drinks available.

The palmyra palm (*Borassus flabellifer*), is more common in SE and E India. When cut off, its palm fronds pour profuse quantities of sap. This is widely collected and then boiled to produce sugar. Alternatively, if left to ferment for a few hours, the juice makes the highly alcoholic local drink, arrack or toddy. Not surprisingly, perhaps, this makes it a very popular tree with some, though disliked as the source of the demon drink by many rural women. Prohibition campaigns have been successful political platforms among women in S India, but the juice of the palmyra palm has also provided an economic way of life for whole castes of S Indian "toddy tappers".

Elephants - A Future In The Wild?

Elephants are both the most striking of the mammals and the most economically important, for there are many areas where they are put to work. The Indian elephant (*Elephas maximas*), smaller than the African, is the world's second largest land mammal. Unlike the African elephant, the male rarely reaches a height of over 3m; it also has smaller ears. Other distinguishing features include the rounded shape of the back and the smooth trunk with a single "finger" at the end. Also the female is often tuskless or bears small ones called *tushes*, and even the male is sometimes tuskless (makhnas). Much of the elephants' natural habitat has been destroyed, but there are approximately 6,500 elephants living in the wild in northern W Bengal, Assam and Bhutan. There are a further 200 in the Chittagong Hill Tracts of Bangladesh, 2,000 in C India and 6,000 in the 3 S Indian States of Kerala, Tamil Nadu and Karnataka, as well as further herds in Sri Lanka. There are plans for a new elephant reserve on the borders of Bhutan and India.

black cotton soils of the Deccan plateau. On the 500,000 sq km of the so-called Deccan Trap the volcanic lavas have given rise to heavy black soils, often referred to as cotton soils, as they have proved extremely well suited to cotton growing, though they are often too heavy to irrigate successfully.

Wildlife

India's has over 2,000 species of birds, more than 500 species of mammals and several hundred species of reptiles and amphibians. Most of India's species were adapted to forest conditions, and thus are particularly at risk from the destruction of their natural habitat. South Asia has 4 times as many species of bird, for example, as does Europe, but they too are threatened, along with the more widely publicised animals such as tigers and lions.

Tigers were reduced to the verge of extinction by the early 1970s, but now they are reported to be increasing steadily in several of the game reserves. The same is true of other, less well known species. Their natural habitat has been destroyed both by people and by domesticated animals. India alone has some 250 million cattle and 50 million sheep and goats.

National parks All the S Asian countries are taking steps to preserve their wildlife heritage. The larger countries have created national parks. Even the tiny state of Bhutan has declared approximately one fifth of its total area to be a natural reserve. In India, 25,000 sq km were set aside in 1973 for Project Tiger, just part of a much wider programme covering 250 reserves in total. There are big reserves in Sri Lanka, and the Maldives is taking a strict line on exploitation of its precious species of coral. Collin's *Handguide to Birds of the Indian Sub-Continent*, *The Book of Indian Birds* and *The Book of Indian Animals* published by the Bombay Natural History Society are recommended.

Mammals

India has over 400 species of mammal, ranging from elephants and rhinos to muntjac deer and civet cats. Elephants are not yet an endangered species, but other large S Asian mammals are very much under threat. The sub-continent's second largest mammal, the One-horned rhinoceros, was once found right across the Indo-Gangetic plains. Now there are only 1,500 left.

The numbers of the cat family have also been drastically reduced. Tiger numbers fell to around 2,000 in India, with a further 600-700 scattered among the sub-Himalayan regions and Bangladesh. The Bengal Tiger has a warm tan coat and narrow, almost black stripes.

Just Let Them Be Monkeys

In any city of India both the Rhesus macaque and the Common langur, the 2 commonest species, are widely evident. They have many related species, some of which are now extremely rare. In the extreme S of India, for example, there are about 800 Lion-tailed macaque monkeys left in the rain forests of Kerala, while the Assamese macaque, the Pig-tailed macaque of the Naga Hills and the Bonnet macaque all live in the N regions of India. The Common langur, which is found in most Indian forests, also has several variants: the Nilgiri langur, the Capped langur of Assam and the Chittagong Hill Tracts, and the Golden Langur of Bhutan. Sri Lanka has its own varieties of macaque and langur monkeys, such as the Ceylon Grey Langur and the Bear monkey.

Prof. Meredith F. Small of Cornell University has written to point out that macaque monkeys, common thoughout Asia, are often seriously mistreated. He writes that 'it is inappropriate, unkind and misguided to purchase monkeys or to feed them.' He goes on to write that in the course of years of research on macaques he has been appalled ' to see tourists tease the monkeys, slap them and feed them candy and cigarettes, and scream when monkeys jumped on them.' He also points out that it is common for monkeys to be chained up at hotels and restaurants.' He urges travellers 'just let them be monkeys, and enjoy them as they are.'

The male, often 1m high at the shoulder and 3m long, can weigh over 200 kg. It is more powerful than a lion, and nocturnal, catching its prey at the end of a jungle trail or by a water hole. It only turns into a man-eater, when it is injured or sick. Cheetahs are already extinct, and the only lion species, the Gir, was down to fewer than 200 until a successful breeding programme in the Gir sanctuary in Gujarat brought some recovery in their numbers.

India has 3 varieties of leopard. Snow leopards are found in the high Himalaya of Bhutan. The arboreal Clouded leopard is still found in N Assam and Bhutan, while India's most famous leopard, the Black panther is still found virtually throughout its original territory.

Desert and jungle cats are found in NW India, as are the Caracal, which hunt birds as their prey. Lynx live up to altitudes of 3,000m in the ranges of Gilgit and Ladakh, and the Himalaya remain a vitally important region for other species of wildlife such as Brown, Black and Sloth bears. Black bears are fairly common up to heights of 3,700m, and Sloth bears, which live on fruit, insects and wild bees, are still found in Nepal, and in 2 reserves in India.

Wild cattle Both in the Himalayan region and in game reserves in the Peninsula there is a wide range of wild species of cattle, sheep and goats. One of the most impressive is the huge Gaur, or jungle bison, which is found in the S Indian game reserves of Madumalai and Bandipur, and in parts of Nepal. Wild buffalo live in the forests of Assam and C India, and in addition to the domesticated varieties there are wild yaks in Ladakh. There are 4 Indian species of wild sheep and 5 species of wild goat. The Nilgiri tahrs, found as their name implies in the S hills of India up to altitudes of 1,800m, are also found at much higher altitudes in the Himalaya.

Deer used to roam across the whole region. Some herds can still be seen even in densely populated areas, such as Haus Khas on the outskirts of New Delhi. Reserves have made it possible for the large Barasingha, or swamp deer, to survive in W Nepal, Assam and Madhya Pradesh. The smaller Muntjac, or Barking deer, are

Birds Of Prey

Pakistan and N India are the home of some of the world's finest birds of prey. **Eagles** and **falcons** used to be very common. Although there are still over 20 species their survival is seriously threatened by systematic hunting. In contrast there are several common species of vulture and of kite which remain highly visible in many parts of S Asia. Equally, fishing birds such as egrets are a common sight along stretches of water or in irrigated fields.

But while all of the states of India have splendid examples of the largest birds of prey, they also have an enormous variety of small and colourful birds. Parakeets, woodpeckers and kingfishers abound, while various songbirds such as the Indian shama and the famous Indian mynah bird complement the range. The latter is not to be confused with its much more common but untuneful relative, seen very widely throughout India. The wealth and colour of India's bird life is symbolised most effectively perhaps in the dramatic plumage of India's national bird, the peacock.

found extensively on the lower wooded slopes of the Himalaya, and in forests of S India. Musk deer live in the birch woods and higher forests of the Himalaya.

Carnivores Rudyard Kipling made the mongoose famous in his story of Rikki-Tikki-Tavi, the mongoose that killed a giant cobra. Various species of mongoose (Herpestinae) are found across both the Indian mainland and in Sri Lanka. The 3 commonest species are small: the Grey mongoose, the small Indian mongoose and the Desert mongoose. There are also 3 larger but rare species. They are valued (and sometimes tamed) for their ability to fight effectively even the most deadly of snakes such as the cobra, although one of the mongoose species in Assam and Nepal has made freshwater crab the chief element of its diet. Snake charmers who gather round the tourist centres of India will often offer the visitor the spectacle of a mongoose fighting a cobra – all carefully controlled so that neither gets hurt.

Omnivores There is an enormous range of small mammals, some of which are omnivorous. Civet cats are widespread from Sri Lanka northwards, for example. In the Himalaya and in S India otters are found, and in the Sundarbans of W Bengal have been trained to catch fish. There are over 24 species of weasels, ferrets and badgers.

Insectivores such as shrews, hedgehogs and moles are common, and if you visit any caves you will come across bats. In many parts of the region the Flying fox is common, and rodents and squirrels are ubiquitous. The small striped Indian squirrel is one of the commonest sights right across India, treating humans with scant regard and scurrying in and out of buildings as well as trees and bushes.

Dolphins and porpoises Mammalian life is not restricted to the land. In the rivers of the Ganga-Brahmaputra delta are dolphins and porpoises, also found in the Indus. Gangetic dolphins often move far inland as they tolerate fresh as well as salt water.

Reptiles

Visitors to India very rarely see snakes, although they remain very common in the countryside. There are over 200 different species or subspecies of snakes alone, many of which are non-poisonous.

Cobras and kraits are the most feared species. The King cobras, which live in the tropical rainforests and may reach lengths of over 5m, are by far the largest poisonous snakes, though both the Rock python and the Reticulated python, which have recorded lengths of over 7m and weights of over 115 kg, are even bigger.

Kraits are less than 0.5m long, but they move exceptionally fast and have one of the most deadly venoms. Vipers, such as the Himalayan Pit Viper and the Bamboo viper, and several species of sea snake are poisonous. By and large, fresh water snakes, some of which look impressive if you come across them while bathing in hill rivers, are generally not poisonous.

Crocodiles and turtles The Blunt Nosed or Marsh crocodile (the Magar) is still found in the Terai of Nepal, but the Gharial has only just survived as a result of government efforts to protect it. The big Estuarine crocodile in still found from the Ganga in Bangladesh to the Mahanadi in Orissa. All 5 species of Monitor lizard, found in both deserts and forests, are endangered. However India retains important breeding beaches for a number of species of turtle. In Orissa there are about 300,000 Olive Ridley turtles breeding; others live in the Sundarbans of Bengal, and Hawksbill turtles breed in S Tamil Nadu.

Birds

Most of India's 2000 species originated in the tropical oriental region, although some undoubtedly have African origins. There are also large numbers of migratory birds such as ducks, cranes, swallows and fly-catchers which come annually from C Asia over the Himalaya.

The peoples of India

India, with nearly 900 million people in 1994, is the second most populated country in the world after China. That population size reflects the long history of human occupation and the fact that an astonishingly high proportion of India's land is relatively fertile. This is illustrated by the fact that 60% of India's surface area is cultivated today, compared with about 10% in China and 20% in the United States.

Although the birth rate has fallen steadily over the last 40 years, death rates have fallen just as fast, so the rate of population increase has continued to be above 2% – or 18 million – a year. Today nearly 30% of the population lives in towns, and cities have grown dramatically. In 1971, 109 million people lived in towns and cities. The figure grew to about 235 million in 1994, equal to the total population of the United States. The largest cities were Bombay (13 million), Calcutta (11 million), Delhi (8.5 million), Madras (5.5 million), Hyderabad (4.5 million) and Bangalore (4 million).

Indo-Aryans and Dravidians – Distinct Races?

An ancient Tamil myth has long held the Tamils to be the original race in India, and Indo-Aryans have similarly cherished a belief in their racial distinctiveness. Recent genetic research suggests that *homo sapiens* originated in Africa less than 300,000 years ago. Southern and northern Indian types developed distinct genetic characteristics less than 40,000 years ago as they moved out of their central Asian homeland, first into West Asia and then into India, disproving all ideas of racial purity. Early Mediterranean groups form the main component of the Dravidian speakers of the 4 S Indian states and N Sri Lanka. Later Mediterranean types also seem to have come from the NW and down the Indus Valley, but more important were the Indo-Aryans, who migrated from the steppes of Central Asia from around 2000 BC. There are recognisable differences in physical type across the subcontinent. People in the S tend to have darker complexions, a lighter build and to be shorter than those in the N. In the NE many people have Mongoloid features. Numerically tiny groups of Australoid peoples such as the Sentinelese on the Andaman Islands, form exceptions.

HISTORY AND POLITICS

CONTENTS

MAPS

Settlement and early history

The first village communities in South Asia grew up on the arid western fringes of the Indus Plains 10,000 years ago. Over the following generations successive waves of settlers – sometimes bringing goods for trade, sometimes armies to conquer territory, and sometimes nothing more than domesticated animals and families in search of land to cultivate and peace to live – moved across the Indus and into India. They left an indelible mark on the landscape and culture of all the countries of modern South Asia.

The first settlers

Recent research suggests ever earlier dates for the first settlements. A site at Mehrgarh, where the Indus Plains meet the dry Baluchistan Hills, has revealed evidence of agricultural settlement as early as 8500 BC. By 3500 BC agriculture had spread throughout the Indus Plains, and in the thousand years following it there were independent settled villages well to the E of the Indus. Between 3000 BC and 2500 BC many new settlements sprang up in the heartland of what became the Indus Valley civilization, but

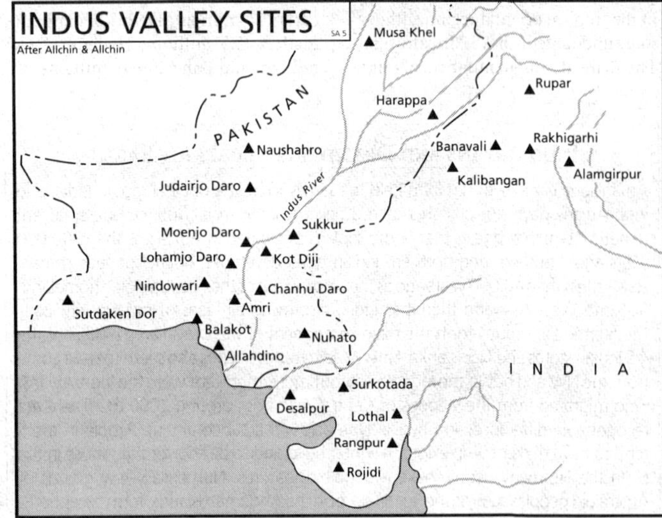

KEY DATES: INDUS VALLEY CIVILIZATION

BC	Northern S Asia	Peninsular India	External events	BC
900,000 500,000	Earliest hominids in W. Asia. Lower Palaeolithic sites from NW to the Peninsula; Pre-Soan and Soan stone industries in NW	Earliest Palaeolithic sites – Narmada Valley; Karnataka; Tamil Nadu and Andhra	First occupation of N China. First Homo sapiens in E Asia. First human settlement in Americas (Brazil)	450,000 120,000 30,000
10,000	Beginning of Mesolithic period	Continuous occupation of caves and riverside sites	Earliest known pottery – Kukui, Japan. Ice Age retreats – Hunter gatherers in Europe	10,500 8,300
8000	First wheat and barley grown in Indus plains	Mesolithic	First domesticated wheat, barley in fertile crescent; first burials in N America	8000
7500	Pottery at Mehrgarh; development of villages	Increase in range of cereals in Rajasthan	Agriculture begins in New Guinea	7000
6500	Humped Indian cattle domesticated	Cultivation extends S	Britain separated from Continental Europe by rising sea level	6500
6000	Farming widespread on margins of Indus plains		High altitude grain in Peru; potato cultivation; pigs and dogs domesticated in China	6300
5000	Origins of Indus valley civilisation, settled agriculture and trade with Middle East		Wet rice cultivation in China; rising sea level separates New Guinea and Tasmania from mainland Australia	5000
4000	Agriculture continues to develop		Guyana: first pottery in Americas	4000
3500	Potter's wheel in use. Long distance trade. Indus sees expansion of agricultural settlements		Sumeria, Mesopotamia: first urban civilisation	3500
3000	Incipient urbanisation in the Indus plains	First Neolithic settlements in S Deccan (Karnataka). Ash mounds, cattle herding	First Egyptian state; Egyptian hieroglyphics; walled citadels in Mediterranean Europe	3100
2500	Indus valley civilisation cities of Moenjo Daro, Harappa and many others	Chalcolithic ('copper' age) in Rajasthan; Neolithic continues in S	Great Pyramid of Khufu China: walled settlements; European Bronze Age begins; hybridisation of maize in S. America	2530 2500
2000	Occupation of Moenjo Daro ends	Chalcolithic in Malwa Plateau, Maharashtra Utnur and Piklihal – Neolithic ends in S: in Karnataka and Andhra – rock paintings	Earliest ceramics in Peruvian Andes. Collapse of Old Kingdom in Egypt. Stonehenge in Britain. Minoan Crete	2300 2150 2000
1750	Indus valley civilisation ends	Hill-top sites in S. India	Joseph sold into Egypt – Genesis	1750

development also took place in many other parts of S Asia.

Despite the almost continuous flow of people from outside, most cultural, religious and political developments in South Asia over that period owed more to local development than to external control. The earliest evidence from the magnificent remains of Moenjo Daro, going back to before 2500 BC, shows that South Asia had extensive contacts with other regions, notably with Mesopotamia. At its height the Indus Valley civilization covered as great an area as Egypt or Mesopotamia. However, the culture that developed was distinctively S Asian. The language, which is still untranslated, may well have been an early form of the Dravidian languages which today are found largely in S India. The only written forms of the Indus Valley language are found on seals in the form of short inscriptions. Aside from linguistic evidence, a clue to the possibility of Dravidian origins, however, may be the presence of the Dravidian Brahui language in the region today. 250,000 Brahui speaking people live on the Pakistan-Afghan border. The Indus Valley civilization spread S along the W seaboard and E to the Ganga.

India from 2000 BC to the Mauryas

In about 2000 BC Moenjo Daro became deserted, and within the next 250 years the entire Indus Valley civilization disintegrated. The causes remain uncertain: the violent arrival of new waves of Aryan immigrants, increasing desertification of the already semi-arid landscape, a shift in the course of the Indus, and internal political decay have each been suggested as instrumental in its downfall. Whatever the causes, some features of Indus Valley culture were carried on by succeeding generations.

From 1500 BC the N region of South Asia entered what has been called the Vedic period. Aryan settlers from the NW moved further and further E towards the Ganga valley. Grouped into tribes, conflict was common. Even at this stage it is possible to see the development of classes of rulers – *rajas* – and priests – *brahmins*. In one battle of this period a confederacy of tribes known as the Bharatas defeated another grouping of 10 tribes. They gave their name to the region to the E of the Indus which is the official name for India today – Bharat.

The centre of population and of culture shifted E from the banks of the Indus to the land between the rivers Yamuna and Ganga. This region, known as the doab (pronounced *doe-ahb*, literally 'two waters'), became the heart of emerging Aryan culture, which, from 1500 BC onwards, laid the literary and religious foundations of what ultimately became Hinduism.

The Vedas

The first fruit of this development was the Rig Veda, the first of 4 Vedas, composed, collected and passed on orally by Brahmin priests from 1300 BC to about 1000 BC. In the later Vedic period, from about 1000 BC to 600 BC, the Sama, Yajur and Artha Vedas show that the Indo-Aryans developed a clear sense of the *doab* as 'their' territory. Modern Delhi lies just to the S of this region, central both to the development of history and myth in South Asia. Later texts extended the core region from the Himalaya in the N to the Vindhyans in the S, and to the Bay of Bengal in the E. Beyond this core region lay the land of mixed peoples and then of barbarians, beyond the pale of Aryan society.

The Mahabharata

Details of the great battle recounted in the Mahabharata are unclear. Tradition puts its date at precisely 3102 BC, the start of the present era. Evidence suggests however that it was fought around 800 BC, about 100 km N of modern

Delhi. Delhi itself is on the site of Indraprastha, clearly identifiable from the Mahabharata, along with Kurukshetra, the site of the battle.

From the 6th to the 3rd centuries BC the region from the foothills of the Himalaya across the Ganga plains to the edge of the Peninsula was governed under a variety of kingdoms or Mahajanapadhas – 'great states'. Trade gave rise to the birth of towns in the Ganga plains themselves, many of which have remained occupied to the present. Varanasi (Benaras) is perhaps the most famous example, but a trade route was established that ran from Taxila (20 km from modern Islamabad in Pakistan) to Rajagriha 1500 km away in what is now Bihar. It was into these kingdoms of the Himalayan foothills and N plains that

KEY DATES: 1750 BC TO THE MAURYAS

BC	Northern S Asia	Peninsular India	External events	BC
1750 1500	Successors to Indus valley. Aryans invade in successive waves. Cemetery H at Harappa. Development of Indo-Aryan language	Copper age begins, but neolithic continues; cattle raising, gram and millet cultivation. Hill terracing for cultivation. Cattle, goats and sheep	Anatolia: Hittite empire New Kingdom in Egypt First metal working in Peru. First inscriptions in China; Linear B script in Greece	1650 1570 1500 1400
1400	Indo-Aryan settlement spreads E and S onto Ganga – Yamuna doab	Horses introduced into S. Cave paintings, burials	Tutankhamun buried in Valley of Kings	1337
1200	Composition of Rig Veda begins?	Iron age sites at Hallur, Karnataka	Middle America: first urban civilisation in Olmec; collapse of Hittite empire	1200
1000	Earliest Painted Grey Ware in Upper Ganga Valley; Brahmanas begin to be written, see page 300.	Iron Age becomes more widespread across Peninsula	Australia: large stone-built villages; David King of Israel Kingdom of Kush in Africa,,	
800	Mahabharata war – origin of Bhagavad Gita; Aryan invaders reach Bengal. Rise of city states in Ganga plains, based on rice cultivation		First settlement at Rome. Celtic iron age begins in N & E of Alps	850 800
		Megalithic grave sites	Greek city states	750
700	Upanishads begin to be written; concept of transmigration of souls develops; Pannini's Sanskrit grammar		Iliad composed	700
600 599 563	Northern Black Pottery Ware Mahavir born – founder of Jainism Gautama Buddha born		First Latin script; first Greek coins. First iron production in China; Zoroastrianism becomes official religion in Persia	600 550
500	Upanishads finished; Taxila and Charsadda become important towns and trade centres	Aryans colonise Sri Lanka. Irrigation practised in Sri Lanka	Wet rice cultivation introduced to Japan	500

KEY DATES: MAURYAS TO THE GUPTAS

BC	Northern S Asia	Peninsular India	External events	BC
326 321	Alexander at Indus. Chandragupta establishes Mauryan Dynasty	Megalithic cultures	Crossbow invented in China	350
300 297	Bindusara extends Mauryan power as far as Mysore	First Ajanta caves; Sarnath stupa in original form	Mayan writing and ceremonial centres established	300
272- 232 250	Asoka's empire. Death of Asoka. Brahmi script	Chola, Pandiya, Chera kingdoms: earliest Tamil inscriptions	Ptolemy. First towns in SE Asia. Rome captures Spain	285 250 206
185	Shunga dynasty, centred on Ujjain	Megalithic cultures in hills of S	Romans destroy Greek states	146
100	Kharavela King of Kalingans in Orissa. Final composition of Ramayana	S Indian trade with Indonesia and Rome. Roman pottery and coins in S. India	Indian religions spread to SE Asia. Introduction of Julian calendar	100 46
AD 100 50	Vaishnavism spreads in N and NW	Satavahanas control much of Peninsula. Discovery of monsoon winds. Irrigation in Sri Lanka. Thomas brings Christianity to S India. Tamil Sangam poems	Rome population of 1 million; pyramid of the sun at City of Teotihuacan, Mexico	**AD** 50
78 120?	Kushan rulers in NW followed by Scythians. Taxila a major centre; strong links with Roman empire. Kanishka accedes to throne (date strongly disputed); capital at Peshawar	Arikamedu – trade with Rome	Buddhism reaches China Paper introduced in China; first metal work in SE Asia	68 100
125 200	Lawbook of Manu Gandharan art Hinayana/Mahayana Buddhist split	Mahayana Buddhism spreads. Nagarjunakomda major centre in Andhra Pradesh. First cities on Deccan plateau	Hadrian's wall in Britain	125
300 319	Chandra Gupta founds Gupta dynasty: Classical age of Indian art and sculpture; Samdra Gupta (335), Chandra Gupta II (376), Kumara Gupta (415)	Rise of Pallavas	Classic period of Mayan civilization; wet rice agriculture through Japan. Edict of Milan – Christianity tolerated in Roman Empire. Constantinople founded	300 313 330
454	Skanda Gupta, the last imperial Gupta, takes power. Dies 467		End of Roman Empire Teotihuacan, Mexico, pop.200,000	476 500
540 578	Gupta rule ends	Bhakti movement Chalukya dynasty, Badami cave temple; Last Ajanta paintings	Saint Sophia, Constantinople. Buddhism arrives in Japan	532 550

both Mahavir, founder of Jainism, and the Buddha, were born.

The Mauryas to the Guptas

Alexander the Great

Small communities of Greek origin settled in the Punjab and NW Frontier following Alexander's invasion of 326 BC. Although his stay was brief, the Hellenistic influence in NW India gave rise to a distinct style of Greco-Indian art termed Gandhara which persisted until the 5th century AD and influenced the later Guptas.

Within a year of the retreat of Alexander the Great from the Indus, Chandragupta Maurya established the first indigenous empire to exercise control over much of the sub continent. Under his successors that control was extended to all but the extreme S of peninsular India.

The centre of political power had shifted steadily E into wetter, more densely forested but also more fertile regions. The Mauryans had their base in the region known as Magadh (now Bihar), and their capital at Pataliputra, near modern Patna. Their power was based on massive military force and a highly efficient, centralised administration. Chandragupta's army may have had as many as 9,000 elephants, 30,000 cavalry and 600,000 infantry. Bindusara, his successor, extended the empire S as far as Mysore.

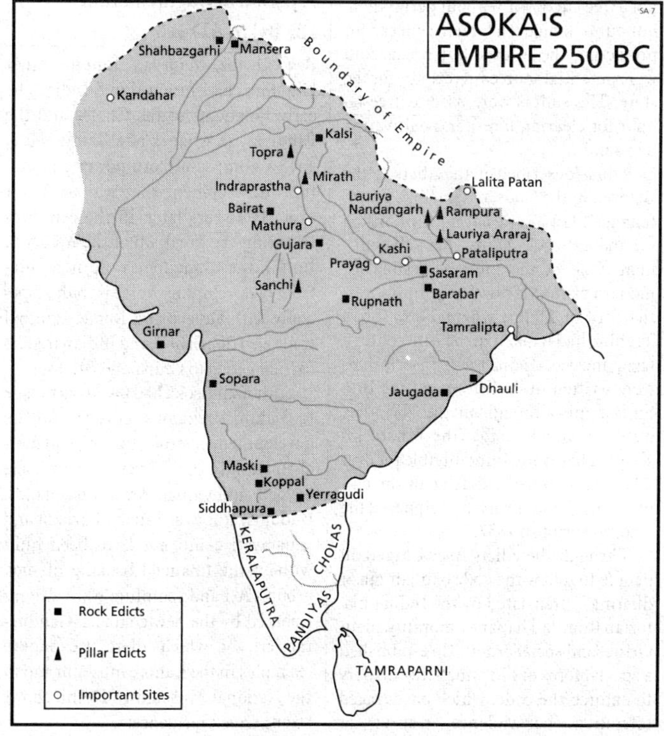

Asoka

The greatest of the Mauryan emperors, took power in 272 BC. He inherited a full blown empire, but extended it further by defeating the Kalingans in modern Orissa, before turning his back on war and preaching the virtues of Buddhist pacifism (see page 738). Asoka's empire stretched from Afghanistan to Assam, and from the Himalaya to Mysore. He inherited a structure of government set out by Chandragupta's Prime Minister, Kautilya, in a book on the principles of government, the Arthashastra. The state maintained itself by raising revenue from taxation – on everything, from agriculture, to gambling and prostitution. He decreed that 'no waste land should be occupied and not a tree cut down' without permission, not out of a modern 'green' concern for protecting the forests, but because all were potential sources of revenue for the state. The sudras were used as free labour for clearing forest and cultivating new land.

Asoka (described on the edicts as 'the Beloved of the Gods, of Gracious Countenance') left a series of inscriptions on pillars and rocks across the sub-continent. One of the most accessible for modern visitors is now in the Indraprastha fort in Delhi, where Feroz Shah Tughluq had it taken in the 14th century. Over most of India these inscriptions were written in Prakrit, using the Brahmi script, although in the NW they were in Greek using the Kharoshti script. They were unintelligible for over 2000 years after the decline of the empire until James Prinsep deciphered the Brahmi script in 1837.

Through the edicts Asoka urged all people to follow the code of dhamma or dharma – translated by the Indian historian Romila Thapar as 'morality, piety, virtue, and social order'. He established a special force of dhamma officers to try to enforce the code, which encouraged toleration, non-violence, respect for priests and those in authority and for human dignity. In addition to exercising a liberal domestic policy, Asoka had good relations with his neighbours, notably King Tissa in Sri Lanka, and with the Cholas, Pandiyas, Keralaputras and Satiyaputras in the extreme S.

However, Romila Thapar suggests that the failure to develop any sense of national consciousness, coupled with the massive demands of a highly paid bureaucracy and army, proved beyond the abilities of Asoka's successors to sustain. Within 50 years of Asoka's death in 232 BC the Mauryan Empire had disintegrated, and with it the whole structure and spirit of its government.

A period of fragmentation: 185 BC to AD 300

Beyond the Mauryan Empire other kingdoms had survived in S India. The early kingdoms of the Cholas and the Pandiyas, in what is now Tamil Nadu, gave a glimpse of both power and cultural development that was to flower over 1000 years later. In the centuries following the break up of the Mauryan Empire these kingdoms were in the forefront of developing overseas trade, especially with Greece and Rome. Internal trade also flourished, and Indian traders carried goods to China and SE Asia.

Although Asoka had given patronage to Buddhist religious orders it was the development of strong trading and merchant guilds that extended patronage beyond individual royal households. Buddhist stupas at Sanchi, Barhaut and Amaravati could not have been built without the financial backing of such groups. Art and sculpture were also influenced by the new contacts. Gandharan art, of which there are superb examples in the Lahore museum and in the National Museum in Delhi, shows strong Greek influence.

The Classical Period – the Gupta Empire AD 319-467

Although the political power of Chandra Gupta and his successors never approached that of his unrelated namesake nearly 650 years before him, the Gupta Empire which was established with his coronation in AD 319 produced developments in every field of Indian culture. Their influence has been felt profoundly across S Asia to the present.

Geographically the Guptas originated in the same Magadhan region that had given rise to the Mauryan Empire. Extending their power by strategic marriage alliances, Chandra Gupta's empire of Magadh was extended by his son, Samudra Gupta, who took power in AD 335, across N India. He also marched as far S as Kanchipuram in modern Tamil Nadu, but the heartland of the Gupta Empire remained the plains of the Ganga.

Eventually the Gupta Empire crumbled in the face of repeated attacks from the NW, this time by the Huns. By the end of the 6th century Punjab and Kashmir had been prised from Gupta control, and the last great Hindu Empire to embrace the whole of N India and part of the Peninsula was at an end.

Regional kingdoms and cultures

The collapse of Gupta power in the N opened the way for successive smaller kingdoms to assert themselves. In doing so the main outlines of the modern regional geography of South Asia began to take clear shape. After the comparatively brief reign of **Harsha** in the mid 7th century, which recaptured something both of the territory and the glory of the Guptas, the Gangetic plains were constantly fought over by rival groups, none of whom were able to establish unchallenged authority.

Regional kingdoms developed, often around comparatively small natural regions. Thus in Orissa, the delta of the Mahanadi and Brahmani rivers was the focus of several small kingdoms which only united, along with tracts of central Orissa, in the 10th and 11th centuries. This fusion of power culminated in the 12th century, when Kalinga was united with central and N Orissa. Today's Jagannath festival in Puri, an attempt to provide a focus of cultural integration through the worship of Vishnu, dates back to this period.

The central Peninsula

This was under the control of the Rashtrakutas. To their S the Pandiyas, Cholas and Pallavas controlled the Dravidian lands of what is now Kerala, Tamil Nadu and coastal Andhra Pradesh. The Pallavas, responsible for building the temples at Mamallapuram, just S of modern Madras, had come to power in the 7th century. They warded off attacks both from the Rashtrakutas to their N and from the Pandiyans, who controlled the S deltas of the Vaigai and Tamraparni Rivers, with Madurai as their capital.

In the 8th century Kerala began to develop its own regional identity with the rise of the Kulashekharas in the Periyar Valley. Caste was a dominating feature of the kingdom's social organisation, but with the distinctive twist that the Nayars, the most aristocratic of castes, developed a matrilineal system of descent.

However, it was the Cholas who came to dominate the S from the 8th century. Overthrowing the Pallavas, they controlled most of Tamil Nadu, S Karnataka and S Andhra Pradesh from 850 AD to 1278 AD. They often held the Kerala kings under their control. Under their kings Rajaraja I (984-1014) and Rajendra (1014-1044) the Cholas also controlled N Sri Lanka, sent naval expeditions to SE Asia, and successful military campaigns N to the Ganga plains. They lavished endowments on temples, and also extended the gifts of land to Brahmins instituted by the Pallavas and Pandiyans. Many thousands of Brahmin priests were brought S to serve in major temples such as those in Chidambaram, and Rajendra wished to be remembered above all as the king who brought water from the holy Ganga all the way to his kingdom.

The Rajputs

The political instability and rivalry that resulted from the ending of Gupta power in the N opened the way for new waves of immigrants from the NW, and for new groups and clans to seize power. Among these were the Rajputs (meaning '*sons of kings*'). Claiming to be descended from a mythical figure who rose out of a sacrificial pit near Mount Abu, the Rajput clans probably originated from outside India, either the Huns or from C Asian tribes who accompanied the Huns on their forceful migration into India.

KEY DATES: REGIONAL KINGDOMS AND CULTURES

AD	Northern S Asia	Peninsular India	External events	AD
600	Period of small Indian states.	Chalukyan dynasty in W and C Deccan		
629	Hiuen Tsang travels round		Death of Mohammad.	632
630	India	Pallavas in Tamil Nadu: Narasimhavarman	Buddhism reaches Tibet	645
670		Mamallapuram shore temples		
712	Arabs arrive in Sind	Nandivarman II in Tamil Nadu. Pandiyas in Madurai. Pala dynasty in Bengal and E	Muslim invasions of Spain	711
750	Rajputs become powerful force in NW	India. Rashtrakutas dominate C		
775		Peninsula		
		Kailasanath Temple, Ellora	Charlemagne crowned	
		Cholas overthrow Pallavas in		800
		Tamil Nadu.	Settlement of New	
850		Tamil philosopher Shankaracharya	Zealand.	850
			Cyrillic script developed	
				863
		Rajaraja I		
950	Khajuraho temples			
984	started.		Sung dynasty in China.	979
1001	Mahmud of Ghazni raids Indus plains.		Easter Island stone carvings	1000
	Rajput dynasties grow.	Rajendra Chola. Chola kings – navies sent to		
1014	Sufism in N India.	SE Asia: Chola bronzes.		
1050	Rajput dynasties in NW Senas in Bengal	Kalinga becomes united kingdom in E Peninsula. Polonnaruwa becomes capital of Sri Lanka in place of Anuradhapura	Norman conquest of England	1066
1100			First European universities	1100
			Angkor Wat, Cambodia;	
1192	Rajputs defeated at Battle of Tarain by Mu'izzu'd Din		paper making spreads	1137
			from Muslim world	1150
1198	First mosque built in Delhi; Qutb Minar, Delhi.	Konarak Sun Temple, Orissa	Rise of Hausa city states in West Africa	1200
1206	Delhi Sultanate established: Khalji Sultans		Mongols begin conquest of Asia under Gengis Khan	1206

From the 7th century AD Rajputs were always a force to be reckoned with in the NW. Independent Rajput dynasties became vital centres of power, albeit at a comparatively local level. The temples at Khajuraho in C India, one of contemporary India's most remarkable sites, were built during the Rajput dynasty of the Chandelas (916-1203). However, the Rajputs never succeeded in forging a united front strong enough to establish either effective central government control internally or protection from external attack.

The spread of Islamic power

The Delhi Sultanate

From about 1000 AD the external attacks which inflicted most damage on Rajput wealth and power came increasingly from the Arabs and Turks. Mahmud of Ghazni raided the Punjab virtually every year between 1000 and 1026, attracted both by the agricultural surpluses and the wealth of India's temples. By launching annual raids during the harvest season Mahmud financed his struggles in C Asia and his attacks on the profitable trade conducted along the Silk Road between China and the Mediterranean. The enormous wealth in cash, golden images and jewellery of N India's temples drew him back every year, and his greed for gold, used to re-monetise the economy of the remarkable Ghaznavid Sultanate of Afghanistan, was insatiable. He sacked the

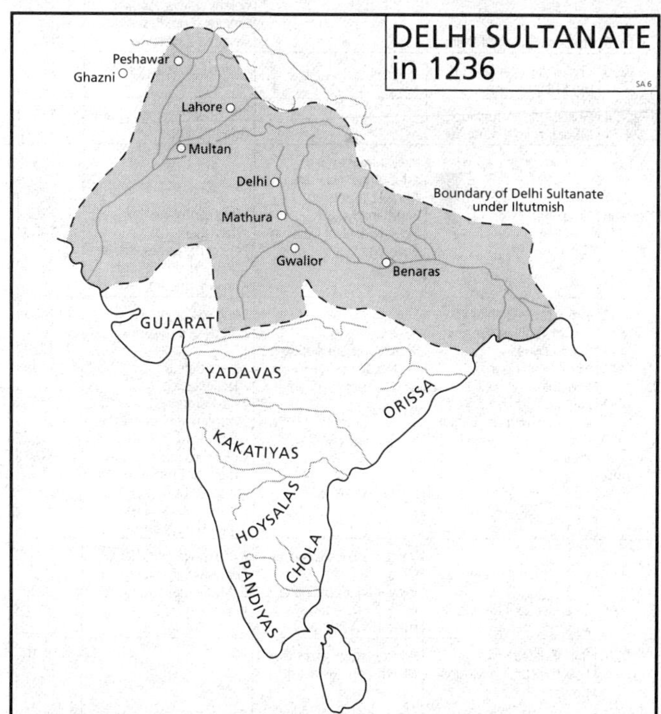

wealthy centres of Mathura (UP) in 1017, Thanesar (Haryana) in 1011, Somnath (Gujarat) in 1024 and Kanuaj (UP). He died in 1030, to the Hindus just another *mlechchha* ('impure' or sullied one), as had been the Huns and the Sakas before him, soon to be forgotten. Such raids were never taken seriously as a long term threat by kings further E, and as the Rajputs continually feuded among themselves the NW plains became an attractive prey.

Muslim political power was heralded by the raids of Mu'izzu'd Din and his defeat of massive Rajput forces at the Second Battle of Tarain in 1192. Mu'izzu'd Din left his deputy, Qutb ud Din Aibak, to hold the territorial gains from his base at Indraprastha. Mu'izzu'd Din made further successful raids in the 1190s, inflicting crushing defeats on Hindu opponents from Gwalior to Benaras. The foundations were then laid for the first extended period of such power, which came under the Delhi sultans.

Qutb ud din Aibak took Lahore in 1206, although it was his lieutenant

KEY DATES: THE DELHI SULTANATE

AD	Northern S Asia	Peninsular India	External events	AD
1206	Turkish 'slave dynasty'	Pandiyas rise	Srivijaya Kingdom at its height in Java; Angkor empire at greatest	1170
1229	Iltutmish Sultan of Delhi		First Thai kingdom	1220
1290	Khaljis in Delhi; Jalal ud Din Khalji		Marco Polo reaches China	1275
1320-24	Ghiyas ud Din Tughluq		Black death spreads from Asia to Europe	1348
1324-51	Mohammad bin Tughluq			
1336		Vijayanagar empire established, Harihara I		
1347		Ala'ud Din sets up Bahmani dynasty, independent of Delhi, in Gulbarga		
1351-88	Firuz Shah		Ming dynasty in China established.	1368
			Peking the largest city in the world; collapse of Khmer kingdom	1400
1398	Timur sacks Delhi.		Ming sea going expeditions to Africa	1405
1412	End of Tughlaq dynasty.			
1414	Sayyid Dynasty.	Bidar/Bahmani kingdom in Deccan		1428
1440	Mystic Kabir born in Benaras.		Aztecs defeat Atzcapatzalco.	1438
1451	Afghan Lodi dynasty established under Bahlul.		Incas centralise power. Byzantine Empire falls to Ottomans.	1453
1469	Guru Nanak born in Punjab		Columbus reaches the Americas; Spanish begin conquest of N. African coast; Arabs and Jews expelled from Spain	1492
1482		Fall of Bahmanis		
		Vasco da Gama reaches India	Inca Empire at its height.	1498
1500		Vijayanagar dominates S. India; Krishnadevraya rules 1509-30	Spanish claim Brazil; Safavid empire founded in Persia	1500
1506	Sikander Lodi founds Agra			
1526	Babur defeats Ibrahim Lodi to establish Mughal power	Albuquerque seizes Goa; Nizamshahis establish independent Ahmadnagar sultanate		1510

Iltutmish who really established control from Delhi in 1211. Qutb ud din Aibak consolidated Muslim dominion by an even-handed policy of conciliation and patronage. In Delhi he converted the old Hindu stronghold of Qila Rai Pithora into his Muslim capital and began several magnificent building projects, including the Quwwat ul Islam mosque and the Qutb Minar, a victory tower. Iltutmish was a Turkish slave – a *Mamluk* – and the Sultanate continued to look W for its leadership and inspiration. However, the possibility of continuing control from outside India was destroyed by the crushing raids of Genghis Khan through C Asia, and from 1222 Iltutmish ruled from Delhi completely independently of outside authority. He annexed Sind in 1228 and all the territory E to Bengal by 1230.

A succession of dynasties followed, drawing on refugees from Genghis Khan's raids and from still further to the W to strengthen the leadership. In 1290 the first dynasty was succeeded by the Khaljis, which in turn gave way to the Tughluqs in 1320. Muhammad bin Tughluq (r1324-51), was described by the Moorish traveller Ibn Batuta as 'a man who above all others is fond of making presents and shedding blood'. Returning from a victorious campaign to his capital Tughluqabad in Delhi, he had erected a splendid pavilion, secretly designed by his engineer to collapse fatally upon the sultan at the first tread of his elephant, see page 179. Despite its periodic brutality, this period marked a turning point in Muslim government in India, as Turkish mamluks gave way to government by Indian Muslims and their Hindu allies. The Delhi sultans were open to local influences and employed Hindus in their administration. In the mid 14th century their capital, Delhi, was one of the leading cities of the contemporary world. In 1398 their control came to an abrupt end with the arrival of the Mongol Timur.

Timur's limp caused him to be called Timur-i-leng (Timur the Lame, known to the W as Tamburlaine). This self-styled 'Scourge of God' was illiterate, a devout Muslim, an outstanding chess player and a patron of the arts. Five years before his arrival in India he had taken Baghdad and 3 years before that he had ravaged Russia, devastating land and pillaging villages. India had not been in such danger from Mongols since Genghis Khan had arrived on the same stretch of the Indus 200 years before.

Timur cut a bloody swathe through to Delhi. When a reconnaissance party led by Timur himself was attacked and beaten off by Indian troops, 50,000 prisoners in his camp failed to conceal their excitement that his campaign might fail. Within the space of an hour all were butchered. Timur did not stay long in India. With captured elephants, rhinos, booty which needed 20,000 pack animals for its transport, craftsmen and slaves, he returned home. He had been in the country for less than 6 months but left behind a carnage, unprecedented in India's long history. He is believed to have been responsible for 5 million deaths. Famine followed the destruction caused by his troops and plague resulted from the corpses left behind.

After Timur, it took nearly 50 years for the Delhi kingdom to become more than a local headquarters. Even then the revival was slow and fitful. The last Tughluqs, were succeeded by an undistinguished line of Sayyids, who began as Timur's deputies, who were essentially Afghan soldier/administrators, but later called themselves sultans, and 3 Lodi kings (1451-1526). They moved their capital to Agra. Nominally they controlled an area from Punjab to Bihar but they were, in fact, in the hands of a group of factious nobles.

The Deccan kingdoms

The forces of the Delhi Sultanate were in disarray, while all over N India Hin-

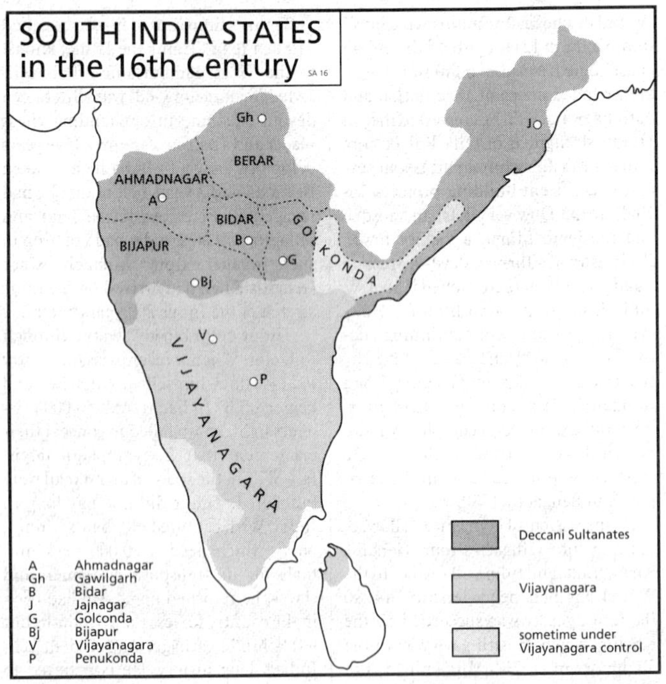

dus had lost power. Many were forced into the Himalaya, where they formed 'Pahari' (Hill) kingdoms, for example in Garhwal, Chamba and Kangra. Only in Rajasthan had they held out, but here they were deeply divided by clan rivalry. In the Deccan they had given way to the Muslim Bahmanis, whilst in the S the hold of the Vijayanagar empire was more precarious than it seemed.

The Delhi Sultanate never achieved the dominating power of earlier empires or of its successor, the Mughal Empire. It exercised political control through crushing military raids and the exaction of tribute from defeated kings, but there was no real attempt to impose central administration. Power depended on maintaining vital lines of communication and trade routes, and keeping fortified strongholds, and making regional alliances. In the Peninsula to the S, the Deccan, regional powers contested for survival, power and expansion. Most of these were Muslim ruled – the Bahmanis being the forerunner of a succession of Muslim dynasties, sometimes competing with each other, sometimes collaborating against a joint external enemy.

The Vijayanagar Empire

Across W and S India today are the remains of the only major medieval Hindu empire to resist effectively the Muslim advance. The ruins at Hampi demonstrate the power of a Hindu coalition that rose to power in the S Deccan in the first half of the 14th century, only to be defeated by its Muslim neighbours in 1565, see page 1044.

For over 200 years Vijayanagar (*'city of victory'*) kings fought to establish supremacy. It was an Empire that, in the words of one Indian historian, made it 'the nearest approach to a war state ever made by a Hindu kingdom'. At times its power reached from Orissa in the NE to Sri Lanka. In 1390 King Harihara II claimed to have planted a victory pillar in Sri Lanka. Much of modern Tamil Nadu and Andhra Pradesh were added to the core region of Karnataka in the area under Vijayanagar control.

The Mughal Empire

Within 150 years of taking power in Delhi the Delhi sultans had lost control of both Bengal and Kashmir. These came under the rule of independent Muslim sultans until nearly the end of the 16th century, when the Mughals brought them firmly back under central authority.

In N India it is the impact of the Mughal rule that is most strikingly evident today. The descendants of conquerors, with the blood of both Tamerlane (Timur) and Gengis Khan in their veins, they came to dominate Indian politics from Babur's victory near Delhi in 1526 to Aurangzeb's death in 1707. Their legacy was not only some of the most magnificent architecture in the world, but a profound impact on the culture, society and future politics of S Asia.

Babur (*the tiger*)

Founder of the Mughal dynasty, Babur was born in Russian Turkestan in 1482. He established the Mughal Empire by leading his cavalry and artillery forces to a stupendous victory over the combined armies of Ibrahim Lodi, last ruler of the Delhi Sultanate, and the Hindu Raja of Gwalior, at Panipat, 80 km N of Delhi, in 1526. When he died 4 years later, the Empire was still far from secured, but he had not only laid the foundations of political and military power but also begun to establish courtly traditions of poetry, literature and art which became the hallmark of subsequent Mughal rulers.

First impressions Babur, used to the delights of Persian gardens and the cool of the Afghan hills, was not impressed initially by what he saw of India. In his autobiography he wrote: 'Hindustan is a country that has few pleasures to recommend it. The people are not handsome. They have no idea of the charms of friendly society, of frankly mixing together, or of familiar intercourse. They have no genius, no comprehension of mind, no politeness of manner, no kindness or fellow-feeling, no ingenuity or mechanical invention in planning or executing their handicraft works, no skill or knowledge in design or architecture; they have no horses, no good flesh, no grapes or musk melons, no good fruits, no ice or cold water, no good food or bread in their bazaars, no baths or colleges, no candles, no torches, not a candlestick.'

Humayun

Babur's depressing catalogue was the view of a disenchanted outsider. Within 2 generations the Mughals had become

Babur's Hunt

The American art historian Stuart Cary Welsh quotes Babur's vivid description of a hunting incident: "A hunting circle was formed on the plain of Kattawaz where deer and wild-ass are always plentiful and always fat. Masses went into the ring; masses were killed. During the hunt I galloped after a wild-ass, on getting near shot one arrow, shot another, but did not bring it down, it only running more slowly for the two wounds. Spurring forward and getting into position quite close to it, I chopped at the nape of its neck behind the ears, and cut through the windpipe; it stopped, turned over and died. My sword cut well! The wild-ass was surprisingly fat. Its rib may have been a little under one yard in length."

fully at home in their Indian environment, and brought some radical changes. Babur had a charismatic appeal to his followers. He ruled by keeping the loyalty of his military chiefs, giving them control of large areas of territory, see page 783.

However, their strength posed a problem for Humayun, his successor. Almost immediately after Babur's death

KEY DATES: THE MUGHAL EMPIRE

AD	Northern S Asia	Peninsular India	External events	AD
1526	**Babur** founds Mughal empire in Delhi	Dutch, French, Portuguese and Danish traders	Ottomans capture Syria, Egypt and Arabia Spaniards overthrow Aztecs in Mexico. Potato introduced to Europe from S America	1516 1519 1525
1538	Sher Shah forces **Humayun** into exile			
1542 1555	**Humayun** re-conquers Delhi, **St. Francis Xavier** reaches Goa			
1556	**Akbar** Emperor			
1565		Vijayanagar defeated	Wm Shakespeare born	1564
		First printing press in India	Dutch E India Co set up	1566 1602
1603 1605 1608	Guru Granth Sahib compiled. **Jahangir** Emperor. East India Co base at Surat		Tokugawa Shogunate in Japan. First permanent English settlement in America. Telescope invented in Holland	1603 1607 1609
1628	**Shah Jahan** Emperor		Masjid-i-Shah Mosque in Isfahan. First Europeans land in Australia	1616 1629
1632-53 1639 1658	Taj Mahal built **Aurangzeb** Emperor	Fort St. George, Madras, founded by E India Co	Manchus found Ch'ing dynasty. Tasman 'discovers' New Zealand. The Fire of London	1644 1645 1666
1677 1690 1699 1703 1707 1724 1739	Calcutta founded. Guru Gobind Singh forms Sikh Khalsa Death of Aurangzeb; Mughal rulers continue to rule from Delhi until 1858 Nawabs of Avadh. The Persian Nadir Shah captures Delhi and massacres thousands	**Shivaji** and Marathas Regional powers dominate through 18th century: Nawabs of Bengal (1703); Nawabs of Arcot (1707); Maratha Peshwas (1714); Nizams of Hyderabad (1724)	Chinese occupy Outer Mongolia. Foundation of St. Petersburg, capital of Russian Empire	1697 1703
1757	Battle of Plassey; British power extended from E India	E India Co strengthens trade and political power through 18th century		

Humayun was forced to retreat from Delhi by 2 of his brothers and one of his father's lieutenants, Sher Shah Suri, who had administered Babur's Bengal territory. Humayun fled through Sind with his pregnant wife and a few servants before being given refuge by Shah Tahmasp, the Safavid ruler of Iran. His son Akbar, who was to become the greatest of the Mughal emperors, was born at Umarkot in Sindh, modern Pakistan, during this period of exile on 23 Nov 1542.

Humayun found the artistic skills of the Iranian court stunningly beautiful, and he surrounded himself with his own group of Iranian artists and scholars. In 1545 he was given Iranian help to recapture Kandahar and Kabul from his brother, Kamran. Initially he forgave his brother repeated acts of treachery, but ultimately was forced by his nobles to have him blinded – reminiscent of the fate of Shakespeare's King Lear, written some 50 years later. Planning his move back into India proper, Humayun urged his group of artists to join him, and between 1548 and his return to power in Delhi in 1555 he was surrounded by this highly influential entourage, see page 173.

Akbar

One year after his final return to Delhi, Humayun died from the effects of a fall on the stairs of his library in the Purana Qila. Akbar was therefore only 13 when he took the throne in 1556. The next 44

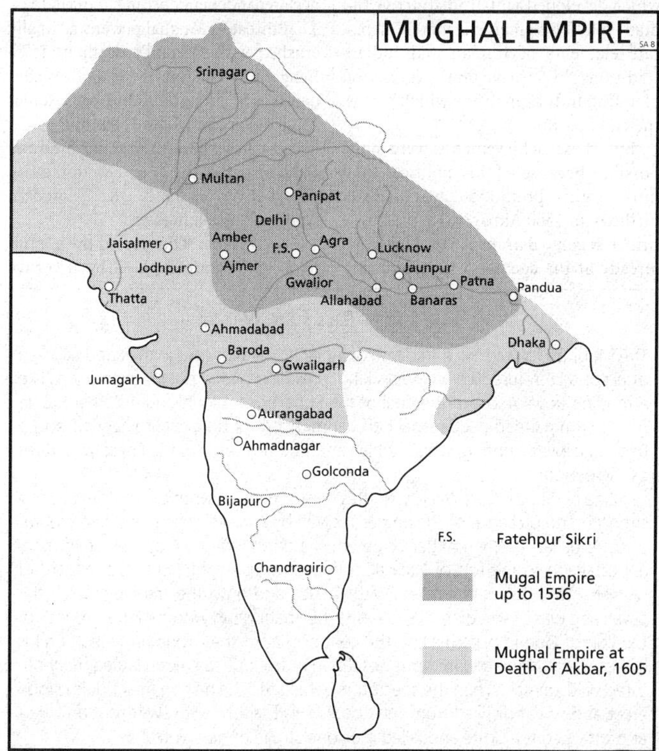

years were one of the most remarkable periods of S Asian history, paralleled by the Elizabethan period in England, where Queen Elizabeth 1st ruled from 1558 to 1603. Although Akbar inherited the throne, it was he who really created the empire. He also gave it many of its distinguishing features.

Through his marriage to a Hindu princess he ensured that Hindus were given honoured positions in government, as well as respect for their religious beliefs and practices. He sustained a passionate interest in art and literature, matched by a determination to create monuments to his empire's political power, and he laid the foundations for an artistic and architectural tradition which developed a totally distinctive Indian style. This emerged from the separate elements of Iranian and Indian traditions by a constant process of blending and originality of which he was the chief patron.

But these achievements were only possible because of his political and military gifts. From 1556 until his 18th birthday in 1560 Akbar was served by a prince regent, Bairam Khan. However, already at the age of 15 he conquered Ajmer and large areas of C India. Chittor and Ranthambor (now famous for its National Park) fell to him in 1567-68, bringing most of what is now Rajasthan under his control.

This opened the door S to Gujarat, which he took in 1573 in an astonishing military feat. He marched the 1000 km from his new capital city, Fatehpur Sikri, to Ahmadabad, with 3,000 horsemen in 9 days. On the 11th day after his departure he defeated the massed armies of Gujarat, and 32 days later was back in Fatehpur Sikri. He celebrated his victory by building the massive Buland Darvaza (gate) in his new capital city.

Afghans continued to cause his empire difficulties, including Daud Karrani, who declared independence in E India in 1574. That threat to Mughal power was finally crushed with Karrani's death in 1576. Bengal was far from the last of his conquests. He brought Kabul back under Mughal control in the 1580s and established a presence from Kashmir, Sind and Baluchistan in the N and W to the Godavari River on the N edge of modern Andhra Pradesh in the S.

It was Akbar who created the administrative structure employed by successive

THE FIRST ART FESTIVALS?

The Mughals followed in a tradition of Indian Muslim princes in their appreciation of art and literature. For an Indian king, presiding over a poetry festival was like attending Royal Ascot or the final of the Superbowl. Like his grandfather Babur, Akbar commanded deep respect and admiration for his extraordinary gifts. Like Babur, he loved hunting, scenes which are shown in some of the finest miniatures of the period.

Again, Stuart Cary Welch quotes a stunning description of the physical strength and presence of the Emperor given by Akbar's close friend and biographer, Abul Fazl. "When Akbar's crescent standards cast their rays on the territory appertaining to the fort of Narwar, a tiger such as might terrify the leopard of heaven came out of the forest with 5 cubs and onto the track by which the cavalcade was proceeding. His majesty, the Shahinshah who had the strength of the lion of God in his arms and the coat of mail of the Divine protection on his breast, went alone and without hesitation in front of that lion-clawed, fiery-natured wild animal. When the spectators beheld this the hair on their bodies stood erect and sweat distilled from their pores. His Majesty, with swift foot and alert arm attacked the brute and killed it by one stroke of his sword."

Mughal emperors to sustain their power. Revenue was raised using detailed surveying methods. Rents were fixed according to the quality of the soil in a move which was carried through into British revenue raising systems. The basis of the system had already been fixed by Sher Shah. Akbar modified it, introducing a new standard measure of length and calculating the assessment of tax due on the basis of a 10 year average of production. Each year the oldest record was dropped out of the calculation, while the average produce for the current year was added. The government's share of the produce was fixed at one quarter.

Akbar deliberately widened his power base by incorporating Rajput princes into the administrative structure and giving them extensive rights in the revenue from land. He abolished the hated tax on non-Muslims (jizya)—ultimately re-instated by his strictly orthodox great grandson Aurangzeb—ceased levying taxes on Hindus who went on pilgrimage and ended the practice of forcible conversion to Islam.

Akbar was a patron not just of art but of an extraordinary range of literature. His library contained books on 'biography, theology, comparative religion, science, mathematics, history, astrology, medicine, zoology, and anthropology'. Almost hyper-active throughout his life, he required very little sleep, using moments of rest to commission books and works of art.

The influence of his father Humayun's Iranian artists is still clearly evident in the earlier of these works, but the works were not just those of unidentified 'schools' of artists, but of brilliant individuals such as **Basawan** and **Miskin**, unparalleled in their ability to capture animal life. Examples of their work can be seen not just in India, but at major museums in Europe and the United States.

Artistic treasures abound from Akbar's court – paintings, jewellery, weapons – often bringing together material and skills from across the known world. Emeralds were particularly popular, with the religious significance which attaches to the colour green in mystic Islam adding to their attraction. Some came from as far afield as Colombia. Akbar's intellectual interests were extraordinarily catholic. He met the Portuguese Jesuits in 1572, and welcomed them to his court in Fatehpur Sikri, along with Buddhists, Hindus and Zoroastrians, every year between 1575 and 1582.

Akbar's eclecticism had a purpose, for Akbar was trying to build a focus of loyalty beyond that of caste, social group, region or religion. Like Roman emperors before him, he deliberately cultivated a new religion in which the emperor himself attained divinity, hoping thereby to give the Empire a legitimacy which would last. While his religion disappeared with his death, the legitimacy of the Mughals survived another 200 years, long after their real power had almost disappeared.

Despite their artistic achievements, Mughal politics could also be cruel and violent. Akbar himself ordered that the beautiful **Anarkali**, a member of his harem, should be buried alive when he suspected that she was having an affair with his son Jahangir.

Jahangir

Akbar died of a stomach illness in 1605. He was succeeded by his son, Prince Salim, who inherited the throne as Emperor Jahangir (*'world seizer'*). He added little to the territory of the empire, consolidating the Mughals' hold on the Himalayan foothills and parts of C India but restricting his innovative energies to pushing back frontiers of art rather than of land. He commissioned works of art and literature, many of which directly recorded life in the Mughal court. Hunting scenes were not just romanticised accounts of rural life, but conveyed the real dangers of hunting lions or tigers; implements, furniture, tools and weapons were made with lavish care and often exquisite design.

From early youth Jahangir had shown an artistic temperament, but he also became addicted to alcohol and then to opium. The drinking cups and vessels such as the opium cup now in the Bharat Kala Bhavan in Benaras Hindu University were in regular use.

In his autobiography, Jahangir described his addiction: 'I had not drunk until I was 18, except in the time of my infancy 2 or 3 times my mother and wet nurses gave it by way of infantile remedy, mixed with water and rose water to take away a cough...years later a gunner said that if I would take a glass of wine it would drive away the feeling of being tired and heavy. It was the time of my youth, and as I felt disposed towards it ordered an intoxicating draught.... After that I took to drinking wine, and increased from day to day until wine made from grapes ceased to intoxicate me, and I took to drinking arrack (local spirits). By degrees my potions rose to 20 cups of doubly distilled spirits, 14 during the daytime and the remainder at night.'

Although Jahangir cut back on his perilously high level of alcohol intake on the advice of his doctors, he subsequently became addicted to opium. Yet his greatest pleasures came from the works of art that his outstandingly gifted artists continued to produce for him. Paintings, carpets, daggers, jewels – all embellished the court.

Nur Jahan

Jahangir's favourite wife, Nur Jahan, brought her own artistic gifts to the Mughal court. Born the daughter of an Iranian nobleman, she had been brought to the Mughal court along with her family as a child, and moved to Bengal as the wife of Sher Afgan, see page 312. She made rapid progress after her first husband's accidental death in 1607, which caused her to move from Bengal to be a lady in waiting for one of Akbar's widows.

Early in 1611, she was playing with her ladies-in-waiting at being a shopkeeper in the bazar. There she met Jahangir. Mutually enraptured, they were married in May. Jahangir gave her the title Nur Mahal (Light of the Palace), soon increased to Nur Jahan (Light of the World). Aged 34, she was strikingly beautiful, and had an astonishing reputation for physical skill and intellectual wit. She was a crack shot with a gun, highly artistic, determined yet philanthropic. Throughout her life Jahangir was captivated by her, so much so that he flouted Muslim convention by minting coins bearing her image.

By 1622 Nur Jahan effectively controlled the empire. She commissioned and supervised the building in Agra of one of the Mughal world's most beautiful buildings, the I'timad ud-Daula (meaning 'Pillar of government'), as a tomb for her father and mother. Her father, Ghiyas Beg, an Iranian nobleman, had risen to become one of Jahangir's most trusted advisers, and Nur Jahan was determined to ensure that their memory was adequately honoured. She was less successful in her wish to deny the succession after Jahangir's death at the age of 58 to Prince Khurram. Acceding to the throne in 1628, he took the title of Shah Jahan (*Ruler of the World*), and in the following 30 years his reign represented the height of Mughal power.

Shah Jahan

The Mughal Empire was under attack in the Deccan and the NW when Shah Jahan became Emperor. He tried to re-establish and extend Mughal authority in both regions by a combination of military campaigns and skilled diplomacy. He was much more successful in pushing S than he was in consolidating the Mughal hold in Afghanistan, and most of the Deccan was brought firmly under Mughal control.

But he too commissioned art, literature, and above all architectural monuments, on an unparalleled scale. The Taj Mahal may be the most famous of these, but a succession of brilliant achievements can be attributed to his reign. From miniature paintings and manuscripts, which had been central features of Mughal artistic development from Babur onwards, to massive fortifications such as the Red Fort in Delhi, Shah Jahan added to the already great body of outstanding Mughal art, see page 314.

Buildings such as the fort and mosque complexes in Delhi, Agra and Lahore were magnificent, not only in scale but in their detail. Wonderful examples of the superbly executed carved marble screens (known as *jalis*), perforated both for decoration and to allow cooling breezes to penetrate the buildings, illustrate the attention paid to minute details by Mughal artists and craftsmen.

Akbar's craftsmen had already carved outstandingly beautiful jalis for the tomb of Salim Chistin in Fatehpur Sikri, but Shah Jahan developed the form further. Undoubtedly the finest tribute to these skills is forced in the Taj Mahal, the tribute to his beloved wife Mumtaz Mahal, who died giving birth to her 14th child in 1631.

Aurangzeb

The need to expand the area under Mughal control was felt even more strongly by Aurangzeb (*'The jewel in the throne'*) than by his predecessors, see page 1168. He had shown his intellectual gifts in his grandfather's court when held hostage to guarantee Shah Jahan's good behaviour, learning Arabic, Persian, Turkish and Hindi. When he seized power at the age of 40, he needed all his political and military skills to hold on to an unwieldy empire that was in permanent danger of collapse from its own size.

If the empire was to survive, Aurangzeb realised that the resources of the territory he inherited from his father were not enough, and thus through a

A Monument To Grief?

The grief that Mumtaz' death caused may have been the chief motivating force behind Shah Jahan's determination to build a monument not just to his love for her but also to the supremacy of Mughal refinement and power. However, that power had to be paid for, and the costs were escalating. Shah Jahan himself had inherited an almost bankrupt state from his father. Expenditure on the army had outstripped the revenue collected tribute from kings and from the chiefs given the rights and responsibility over territories often larger than European countries. Financial deficits forced Shah Jahan onto the offensive in order to guarantee greater and more reliable revenue.

Despite major reforms which helped to reduce the costs of his standing army, maintaining the force necessary to control the huge territories owing allegiance to the emperor continued to stretch his resources to the full. By 1648, when he moved his capital to Delhi, the empire was already in financial difficulties, and in 1657 the rumour that Shah Jahan was terminally ill immediately caused a series of battles for the succession between his 4 sons.

Aurangzeb, the second son and sixth child of Shah Jahan and Mumtaz Mahal – tough, intriguing and sometimes cruel, but also a highly intelligent strategist – emerged the winner, to find that Shah Jahan had recovered. Rather than run the risk of being deposed, Aurangzeb kept his father imprisoned in Agra Fort, where he had been taken ill, from June 1658 until his death in February 1666.

series of campaigns he pushed S, while maintaining his hold on the E and N. Initially he maintained his alliances with the Rajputs in the W, which had been a crucial element in Mughal strategy. In 1678 he claimed absolute rights over Jodhpur and went to war with the Rajput clans. However, for the remaining 39 years of his reign he was forced to struggle continuously to sustain his power.

The East India Company and the Rise of British power

Early European contacts

The British were unique among the foreign rulers of India in coming by sea rather than through the NW, and in coming first for trade rather than for military conquest. The ports that they established – Madras, Bombay and Calcutta – became completely new centres of political, economic and social activity. Before them Indian empires had controlled their territories from the land. The British dictated the emerging shape of the economy by controlling sea-borne trade. From the middle of the 19th century railways transformed the economic and political structure of S Asia, and it was those 3 centres of British political control, along with the late addition of Delhi, which became the foci of economic development and political change.

The East India Company in Madras and Bengal

In its first 90 years of contact with S Asia after the Company set up its first trading post at **Masulipatnam**, on the E coast of India, it had depended almost entirely on trade for its profits. However, in 1701, only 11 years after a British settlement was first established at Calcutta, the Company was given rights to land revenue in Bengal.

The Company was accepted, and sometimes welcomed, partly because it offered to bolster the inadequate revenues of the Mughals by exchanging silver bullion for the cloth it bought. However, in the S the Company moved further and faster towards consolidating its political base. Wars between S India's regional factions gave the East India Company's servants the opportunity to extend their influence by making alliances, and offering support to some of these factions in their struggles, which were complicated by the extension to Indian soil of the European contest for power between the French and the British.

Robert Clive

The British established effective control over both Bengal and SE India in the middle of the 17th century. Robert Clive, in alliance with a collection of disaffected Hindu landowners and Muslim soldiers, defeated the new Nawab of Bengal, the 20 year old Siraj-ud-Daula, in June 1757. The battlefield was at Plassey, about 100 km N of Calcutta, though the battle itself was little more than a skirmish, see page 646. Eight years later Clive took over the management of the revenues of the whole of Bengal. By 1788 Calcutta, which 100 years earlier had been nothing more than a collection of small villages, had become the chief city of E India, with a population of a quarter of a million.

Hastings and Cornwallis

In 1773 Calcutta had already been put in charge of Bombay and Madras. The essential features of British control were mapped out in the next quarter of a century through the work of Warren Hastings, Governor-General from 1774 until 1785, and Lord Cornwallis who took over in 1786 and remained in charge until 1793. Cornwallis was responsible for putting Europeans in charge of all the higher levels of revenue collection and administration, and for introducing government by the rule of law, making even government officers subject to the courts.

The decline of Muslim power

The extension of East India Company power in the Mughal periphery of India's S and E took place against a background of weakening Mughal power at the centre in Delhi and on the Peninsula. Some of the Muslim kingdoms of the Deccan refused to pay the tribute to the Mughal Empire that had been forced on them after defeats in 1656. This refusal, and their alliance with the rising power of Sivaji and his Marathas, had led Aurangzeb to attack the Shi'i-ruled states of Bijapur (1686) and Golconda (1687), in an attempt to re-impose Mughal supremacy.

Sivaji

Sivaji was the son of a Hindu who had served as a small-scale chief in the Muslim ruled state of Bijapur. The weakness of Bijapur encouraged Sivaji to extend his father's area of control, and he led a rebellion. The Bijapur general Afzal Khan, sent to put it down, agreed to meet Sivaji in private to reach a settlement. In an act which is still remembered by both Muslims and Marathas, Sivaji embraced him with steel claws attached to his fingers and tore him apart. It was the start of a campaign which took Maratha power as far S as Madurai and to the doors of Delhi and Calcutta, see page 1155.

Sivaji had taken the fratricidal struggle for the succession which brought Aurangzeb to power as the signal and the opportunity for launching a series of attacks against the Mughals. This in turn brought a riposte from Aurangzeb, once his hold on the centre was secure. However, despite the apparent expansion of his power the seeds of decay were already germinating. Although Sivaji himself died in 1680 Aurangzeb never fully came to terms with the rising power of the Marathas, though he did end their ambitions to form an empire of their own.

Nor was Aurangzeb able to create any wide sense of identity with the Mughals as a legitimate popular power. Instead, under the influence of Sunni Muslim theologians, he retreated into insistence on Islamic purity. He imposed Islamic law, the *sharia*, promoted only Muslims to positions of power and authority, tried to replace Hindu administrators and revenue collectors with Muslims, and re-imposed the *jizya* tax on all non-Muslims. By the time of his death in 1707 the empire no longer had either the broadness of spirit or the physical means to survive.

Bahadur Shah

The decline was postponed briefly by the 5 year reign of Aurangzeb's son. Sixty-three when he acceded to the throne, Bahadur Shah restored some of its faded fortunes. He made agreements with the Marathas and the Rajputs and defeated the Sikhs in Punjab, before taking the last Sikh guru into his service.

The decay of the Mughal Empire has been likened to 'a magnificent flower slowly wilting and occasionally dropping a petal, its brilliance fading, its stalk bending ever lower'. Nine emperors succeeded Aurangzeb between his death and the exile of the last Mughal ruler in 1858. It was no accident that it was in that year that the British ended the rule of its East India Company and decreed India to be its Indian empire.

Successive Mughal rulers saw their political control diminish and their territory shrink. Nasir ud Din Muhammad Shah, known as Rangila (*'the pleasure loving'*), who reigned between 1719 and 1748, presided over a continued flowering of art and music, but a disintegration of political power. Hyderabad, Bengal and Oudh (the region to the E of Delhi) became effectively independent states; the Marathas dominated large tracts of C India, the Jats captured Agra, the Sikhs controlled Punjab.

Muhammad Shah remained in his capital of Delhi, resigning himself to enjoying what Carey Welch has called 'the conventional triad of joys: the wine was excellent, as were the women, and for him the song was especially rewarding.' The idyll was rudely shattered by the invasion of **Nadir Shah** in 1739, an Iranian marauder who slaughtered thousands in Delhi and carried off priceless Mughal treasures, including the Peacock Throne, see page 185.

The Maratha confederacy

Nadir Shah's invasion was a flash in the pan. Of far greater substance was the development through the 18th century of the power of the **Maratha confederacy**. They were unique in India in uniting different castes and classes in a nationalist fervour for the region of Maharashtra. As Spear has pointed out, when the Mughals ceded the C district of Malwa the Marathas were able to pour through the gap created between the Nizam of Hyderabad's territories in the S and the area remaining under Mughal control in the N. They rapidly occupied Orissa in the E and raided Bengal.

By 1750 they had reached the gates of Delhi. When Delhi collapsed to Afghan invaders in 1756-57 the Mughal minister called on the Marathas for help. Yet again Panipat proved to be a decisive battlefield, the Marathas being heavily defeated by the Afghan forces on 13 Jan 1761. However Ahmad Shah was forced to retreat to Afghanistan by his own rebellious troops, demanding 2 years arrears of pay, leaving a power vacuum.

The Maratha confederacy dissolved into 5 independent powers, with whom the incoming British were able to deal separately. The door to the N was open.

The East India Company's push for power

Alliances

In the century and a half that followed the death of Aurangzeb the **British East India Company** extended its economic and political influence into the heart of India. As the Mughal Empire lost its power India fell into many smaller states. The Company undertook to protect the rulers of several of these states from external attack by stationing British troops in their territory. In exchange for this service the rulers paid subsidies to the Company. As the British historian Christopher Bayly has pointed out, the cure was usually worse than the disease, and the cost of the payments to the Company crippled the local ruler. The British extended their territory through the 18th century as successive regional powers were annexed and brought under direct Company rule.

Progress to direct British control was uneven and often opposed. The Sikhs in Punjab, the Marathas in the W, and the Mysore sultans in the S, fiercely contested British advances. **Haidar Ali** and **Tipu Sultan**, who had built a wealthy kingdom in the Mysore region, resisted attempts to incorporate them. Tipu was finally killed in 1799 at the battle of Srirangapatnam, an island fort in the Kaveri River just N of Mysore, where Arthur Wellesley, later the Duke of Wellington, began to make his military reputation.

The Marathas were not defeated until the war of 1816-18, a defeat which had to wait until Napoleon was defeated in Europe and the British could turn their wholehearted attention once again to the Indian scene. Even then the defeat owed as much to internal faction fighting as to the power of the British-led army. Only the NW of the sub-continent remained beyond British control until well into the 19th century. The Punjab and the NW frontier were the remotest regions from the ports through which the British had extended their power. In 1799 **Ranjit Singh** set up a Sikh state in Punjab which survived until the late 1830s.

In 1818 India's economy was in ruins and its political structures destroyed. Irrigation works and road systems had fallen into decay, and gangs terrorised the countryside. **Thugs** and **dacoits** controlled much of the open countryside in central India and often robbed and murdered even on the outskirts of towns. The peace and stability of the Mughal period had long since passed. Between 1818 and 1857 there was a succession of local and uncoordinated revolts in different parts of India. Some were bought off, some put down by military force.

A period of reforms

While existing political systems were collapsing, the first half of the 19th century was also a period of radical social change in ther territories governed by the East India Company. Lord William Bentinck became Governor-General at a time when England was entering a period of major reform. In 1828 he banned the burning of widows on the funeral pyres of their husbands (**sati**), and then moved to suppress **thuggee** (the ritual murder and robbery carried out in C India in the name of the goddess Kali). But his most far reaching change was to introduce education in English.

The resolution of 7 Mar 1835 stated that 'the great objects of the British government ought to be the promotion of European literature and science'. It went on to promise that funds 'should henceforth be employed in imparting to the native population the knowledge of English literature and science through the medium of the English language'. Out of this concern were born new educational institutions such as the Calcutta Medical College. From the late 1830s massive new engineering projects began to be taken up; first canals, then railways.

The innovations stimulated change, and change contributed to the growing unease with the British presence, particularly under the Governor-Generalship of the Marquess of Dalhousie (1848-56). The development of the telegraph, railways and new roads, 3 universities, and the extension of massive new canal irrigation projects in N India seemed to threaten traditional society, a risk increased by the annexation of Indian states to bring them under direct British rule. The most important of these was Oudh.

The Mutiny

Out of the growing discontent and widespread economic difficulties, came the mutiny of 1857. In May and June the atmosphere in the Bengal army, which had a large component of Brahmins, reached an explosive peak. At that moment the army issued new Lee Enfield rifles to its troops, whose cartridges were smeared with a mixture of cow and pig fat, taken as a direct affront to both Muslim and Hindu feeling. On 10 May 1857 troops in Meerut, under 70 km NE of Delhi, mutinied. They reached Delhi the next day, where Bahadur Shah, the last Mughal Emperor, took sides with the mutineers. Troops in Lucknow joined the rebellion and Gwalior was captured on 20 June. For 3 months Lucknow and other cities in the N were under siege. Appalling scenes of butchery and reprisals marked the struggle, only put down by troops from outside.

The period of Empire

The 1857 rebellion marked the end not only of the Mughal Empire but also of the East India Company, for the British Government in London took overall control in 1858. Yet within 30 years a movement for self-government had begun, and there were the first signs of a demand among the new western educated elite that political rights be awarded to match the sense of Indian national identity.

The Indian National Congress

The movement for independence went through a series of steps. The creation of the Indian National Congress in 1885 was the first all-India political institution, and was to become the key vehicle of demands for independence. However, the educated Muslim elite of what is now Uttar Pradesh saw a threat to Muslim rights, power and identity in the emergence of democratic institutions which gave Hindus, with their built in natural majority, significant advantages. Sir Sayyid Ahmad Khan, who had founded a Muslim University at Aligarh in 1877, advised Muslims against joining the Congress, seeing it as a vehicle for Hindu, and especially Bengali, nationalism.

The Muslim League

The educated Muslim community of N India remained deeply suspicious of the Congress, making up less than 8% of those attending its conferences between 1900-1920. Muslims from UP created the All-India Muslim League in 1906. However, the demands of the Muslim League were not always opposed to those of the Congress. In 1916 it concluded the Lucknow Pact with the Congress, in which the Congress won Muslim support for self-government, in exchange for the recognition that there would be separate constituencies for Muslims. The nature of the future Independent India was still far from clear, however. The British conceded the principle of self-government in 1918, but however radical the reforms would have seemed 5 years earlier they already fell far short of heightened Indian expectations.

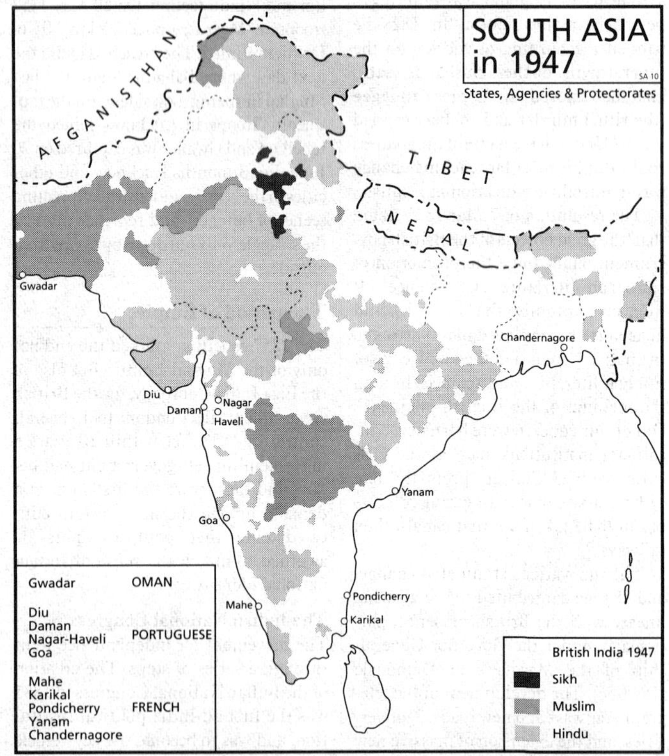

Mahatma Gandhi

Into a tense atmosphere Mohandas Karamchand Gandhi returned to India in 1915 after 20 years practising as a lawyer in S Africa. On his return the Bengali Nobel Laureate poet, Rabindranath Tagore, had dubbed him 'Mahatma' – Great Soul. The name became his. He arrived as the government of India was being given new powers by the British parliament to try political cases without a jury and to give provincial governments the right to imprison politicians without trial. In opposition to this legislation Gandhi proposed to call a *hartal*, when all activity would cease for a day, a form of protest still in widespread use. Such protests took place across India.

The protests were often accompanied by riots. On 13 Apr 1919 a huge gathering took place in the enclosed space of Jallianwala Bagh in Amritsar, see page 482. It had been prohibited by the government, and General Dyer ordered troops to fire on the people without warning, killing 379 and injuring at least a further 1,200. It marked the turning point in relations with Britain and the rise of Gandhi to the key position of leadership in the struggle for complete independence.

The thrust for Independence

In 1930 the Congress declared that 26 Jan would be Independence day – still celebrated as Republic Day in India today. The Leader of the Muslim League, Mohammad Iqbal, took the opportunity of his address to the League in the same year to suggest the formation of a Muslim state within an Indian Federation. Also in 1930 a Muslim student in Cambridge, Chaudhuri Rahmat Ali, coined a name for the new Muslim state – Pakistan. The letters were to stand P for Punjab, A for Afghania, K for Kashmir, S for Sind with the suffix *stan*, Persian for country. The idea still had little real shape however, and waited on developments of the late 1930s and 1940s to bear fruit.

By the end of the Second World War the positions of the Muslim League, now under the leadership of Mohammad Ali Jinnah, and the Congress led by Jawaharlal Nehru, were irreconcilable. While major questions of the definition of separate territories for a Muslim and non-Muslim state remained to be answered, it was clear to General Wavell, the British Viceroy through the last years of the War, that there was no alternative but to accept that independence would have to be given on the basis of separate states.

Independence and Partition

One of the main difficulties for the Muslims was that they made up only a fifth of the total population. Although there were regions both in the NW and the E where they formed the majority, Muslims were also scattered throughout India. It was therefore impossible to define a simple territorial division which would provide a state to match Jinnah's claim of a '*two-nation theory*'. On 20 February 1947, the British Labour Government announced its decision to replace Lord Wavell as Viceroy with Lord Mountbatten, who was to oversee the transfer of power to new independent governments. It set a deadline of June 1948 for British withdrawal. The announcement of a firm date made the Indian politicians even less willing to compromise, and the resulting division satisfied no-one.

When independence arrived – on 14 Aug for Pakistan and 15 Aug for India, because Indian astrologers deemed the 15th to be the most auspicious moment – many questions remained unanswered. Several key Princely States had still not decided firmly to which country they would accede. Kashmir was the most important of these, with results that have lasted to the present day.

Modern India

Politics

When India became Independent on 15 Aug 1947 it faced 3 immediate crises. Partition left it with a bitter struggle between Hindus, Muslims and Sikhs which threatened to tear the new country into pieces at birth. 13 million people migrated between the 2 new countries, and perhaps 1 million were killed in the slaughter that accompanied the migration. Almost immediately it was plunged into an inconclusive 15 month war with Pakistan over Kashmir. Finally it had the task of developing a constitution which would allow the often conflicting interest groups which made up Indian society to cement their allegiance to the new State.

In the 45 years since independence, striking political achievements have been made. With the 2 year exception of 1975-77, when Mrs Gandhi imposed a state of emergency in which all political activity was banned, India has sustained a democratic system in the face of tremendous pressures. The General Elections of May-Jun 1991, tragically interrupted by the assassination of Rajiv Gandhi, were the country's tenth.

The constitution

Establishing itself as a sovereign democratic republic, the Indian parliament accepted Nehru's advocacy of a secular constitution. The President is formally vested with all executive powers, always understood to be exercised under the authority of the Prime Minister. That assumption has been challenged from time to time, but never seriously put to the test, although the President has been able to use very limited discretionary power.

Effective power under the constitution lies with the Prime Minister and Cabinet, following the British model. In practice there have been long periods when the role of the Cabinet has been much reduced compared to that of the

Mahatma Gandhi

Gandhi was asked by a journalist when he was on a visit to Europe what he thought of Western civilisation. He paused and then replied: "It would be very nice, wouldn't it." The answer illustrated just one facet of his extraordinarily complex character. A westernised, English educated lawyer, who had lived outside India from his youth to middle age, he preached the general acceptance of some of the doctrines he had grown to respect in his childhood, which stemmed from deep Indian traditions – notably *ahimsa*, or non-violence. From 1921 he gave up his Western style of dress and adopted the hand spun dhoti worn by poor Indian villagers, giving rise to Churchill's jibe that he was a 'naked fakir' (holy man). Yet if he was a thorn in the British flesh, he was also fiercely critical of many aspects of traditional Hindu society. He preached against the iniquities of the caste system which still dominated life for the overwhelming majority of Hindus. Through the 1920s much of his work was based on writing for the weekly newspaper *Young India*, which became The Harijan in 1932. The change in name symbolised his commitment to improving the status of the outcastes, Harijan (*person of God*) being coined to replace the term outcaste. Often despised by the British in India he succeeded in gaining the reluctant respect and ultimately outright admiration of many. His death at the hands of an extreme Hindu chauvinist in January 1948 was a final testimony to the ambiguity of his achievements: successful in contributing so much to achieving India's Independence, yet failing to resolve some of the bitter communal legacies which he gave his life to overcome.

Prime Minister's secretariat. In principle parliament chooses the Prime Minister. The Parliament has a lower house (the *Lok Sabha*, or 'house of the people') and an upper house (the *Rajya Sabha* – Council of States). The former is made up of directly elected representatives from the 543 parliamentary constituencies (plus 2 nominated members from the Anglo-Indian community), the latter of a mixture of members elected by an electoral college and of nominated members. Constitutional amendments require a two-thirds majority in both houses.

India's federal constitution devolves certain powers to elected state assemblies. Each state has a Governor who acts as its official head. Many states also have 2 chambers, the upper generally called the Rajya Sabha and the lower (often called the Vidhan Sabha) being of directly elected representatives. In practice many of the state assemblies have had a totally different political complexion from that of the Lok Sabha. Regional parties have played a far more prominent role, though in many states central government has effectively dictated both the leadership and policy of state assemblies.

States and Union Territories Union territories are administered by the President "acting to such an extent as he thinks fit". In practice Union territories have varying forms of self-government. Pondicherry has a legislative Assembly and Council of Ministers. The 69th Amendment to the Constitution 1991 provided for a legislative assembly and council of Ministers for Delhi, elections for which were held in December 1993. The Assemblies of Union Territories have more restricted powers of legislation than full states. Some Union Territories – Dadra and Nagar Haveli, Daman and Diu, all of which separated from Goa in 1987 when Goa achieved full statehood – Andaman and Nicobar Islands, and Lakshadweep, have elected bodies known as Pradesh Councils. These councils have the right to discuss and make recommendations on matters relating to their territories. An example of this power is the freedom of the former Portuguese colonies to sell alcohol in contrast to their neighbouring prohibitionist state of Gujarat.

Secularism One of the key features of India's constitution is its secular principle. This is not based on the absence of religious belief, but on the commitment to guarantee freedom of religious belief and practice to all groups in Indian society. The commitment to a secular constitution is under increasing challenge, especially from the Hindu nationalism of the Bharatiya Janata Party, the BJP, which played a prominent part in the campaign to replace the Babri mosque in Ayodhya with a temple dedicated to Rama. The destruction of the mosque in December 1992 created deep unease across India, only slowly receding with the setbacks to the BJP in the 1993 state assembly elections.

The judiciary India's Supreme Court has similar but somewhat weaker powers to those of the United States. The judiciary has remained effectively independent of the government except under the Emergency between 1975-77.

The civil service India continued to use the small but highly professional administrative service inherited from the British period. Re-named the Indian Administrative Service (IAS), it continues to exercise remarkable influence across the country. The administration of many aspects of central and regional government is in the hands of this elite body, who continue to act largely by the constitutional rules which bind them as servants of the state. Many Indians accept the continuing efficiency and high calibre of the top ranking officers in the administration while believing that the bureaucratic system as a whole has been overtaken by widespread corruption.

The police India's police service is divided into a series of groups, numbering nearly 1 million. While the top ranks of the Indian Police Service are comparable to the IAS, lower levels are extremely poorly trained and very low paid. In addition to the domestic police force there are special groups: the Border Security Force, Central Reserve Police and others. They may be armed with modern weapons, and are called in for special duties.

The armed forces Unlike its immediate neighbours India has never had military rule. It has over 1.25 million men in the army – one of the largest armed forces in the world. Although they have remained out of politics the armed services have been used increasingly frequently to put down civil unrest.

The Congress Party Indian national politics has been dominated by the Congress Party. Its strength in the Lok Sabha has often overstated the volume of its support in the country, however, and state governments have frequently been formed by parties – and interests – only weakly represented at the centre.

The Congress won overall majorities in 7 of the 9 general elections held before the 1991 election. However, in no election did the Congress obtain more than 50% of the popular vote, yet it has won huge majorities on the basis of the lack of a united opposition. It has been defeated only when the opposition has agreed to field only one candidate against the Congress candidate, in 1977 and in 1989. In the latter election it still gained the largest number of seats, though not enough to form a government on its own, and it was unable to find allies.

The Congress had built its broad based support partly by championing the causes of the backward castes and the minorities. Rajiv Gandhi began to place an emphasis on a new image of modernisation and change. He pushed hard for economic reform, but lost the support of key members of his Cabinet. In Nov 1989 the Congress was defeated for only the second time in its history, deeply wounded by charges of corruption at the highest levels. It regained power in mid-1991 in the wake of Rajiv Gandhi's death.

The Non-Congress Parties Political ac-

THE NEHRU FAMILY DYNASTY

Within the Congress Party the Nehru family played the pivotal role from 1947 until Rajiv Gandhi's assassination in 1991. From 1950 until his death in 1964 Jawaharlal Nehru was the Party's undisputed leader. His daughter Indira Gandhi took up the leadership after the unexpected death of his immediate successor, Lal Bahadur Shastri. She set about radically transforming it into a vehicle of her own power, centralising the structure of the party and of the government. Her hope to install her younger son Sanjay as successor were destroyed by his death in a flying accident. Rajiv, her elder son, reluctantly agreed to take his place in political life, but was still far from securely established as a political figure when, in 1984, Mrs Gandhi was assassinated at the hands of her Sikh bodyguard. After a brief political honeymoon which followed his sweeping parliamentary victory in December 1984, Rajiv himself lost power. He never regained it, himself being assassinated during the 1992 election campaign. Some members of the Congress Party leadership tried to persuade Rajiv Gandhi's widow Sonia to accept the leadership after his assassination, but she refused, and although Rajiv's son and daughter are predicted by some to be possible successors, for the time being at least the dynasty is at an end.

PRIME MINISTERS AND PRESIDENTS SINCE 1947

Date	Prime Minister	President
1947-64	Jawaharlal Nehru	
1948-50		C. Rajagopalachari
1950-62		Rajendra Prasad
1962-67		S. Radhakrishnan
1964-66	Lal Bahadur Shastri	
1966-77	Indira Gandhi	
1967-69		Zakir Hussain
1969-74		V.V. Giri
1974-77		Fakhruddin Ali Ahmed
1977-79	Morarji Desai	
1977-82		Neelam Sanjiva Reddy
1979-80	Charan Singh	
1980-84	Indira Gandhi	
1982-87		Giani Zail Singh
1984-89	Rajiv Gandhi,	
1987-1992		R. Venkataraman
1989-90	V.P.Singh	
1990-91	S. Chandrasekhar	
1991-	P.V. Narasimha Rao	

tivity outside the Congress can seem bewilderingly complex. There are no genuinely national parties. The only alternative governments to the Congress have been formed by coalitions of regional and ideologically based parties. Parties of the left – Communist and Socialist – have never broken out of their narrow regional bases. The Communist Party of India split into 2 factions in 1964, with the Communist Party of India Marxist (CPM) ultimately taking power in W Bengal and Kerala. In the 1960s the Swatantra Party (a liberal party) made some ground nationally, opposing the economic centralisation and state control supported by the Congress. In the N a peasants' party, the Lok Dal also made some headway under the leadership of a powerful Jat leader, Charan Singh.

At the right of the political spectrum, the Jan Sangh has been seen as a party of right wing Hindu nationalism with a concentrated but significant base in parts of the N, especially among higher castes and merchant communities. The most organised political force outside the Congress, the Jan Sangh merged with the Janata Party for the elections of 1977. After the collapse of that government it reformed itself as the Bharatiya Janata Party (BJP). In 1990-91 it developed a powerful campaign focusing on reviving Hindu identity against the minorities. The elections of 1991 showed it to be the most powerful single challenger to the Congress.

The power of the BJP remained confined largely to N India. Elsewhere a succession of regional parties dominated politics in several key states. The most important were Tamil Nadu and Andhra Pradesh in the S. In Tamil Nadu power has alternated since 1967 between the Dravida Munnetra Kazhagam (the DMK) and a faction which split from it, the All India Anna DMK, named after one of the earliest leaders of the Dravidian political movement, C. N. Annadurai ('Anna'). In Andhra Pradesh, The Telugu Desam offered a similar regional alternative to Congress rule.

Recent developments The minority Congress government elected in June 1991, after Rajiv Gandhi's assassination, seemed set to face colossal problems, and many gave it little chance of survival. In the event the new Prime Minister, Narasimha Rao, and his Finance Minister Manmohan Singh, embarked on a radical programme of economic liberalisation and reform. At the same time India's foreign policy underwent rapid change, the search for new and more positive relationships with both China and the United States being major departures from policies of the previous 20 years. Until late 1992 it seemed that Narasimha Rao had transformed his government into an effective majority. His popularity was seriously dented in 1993, following the destruction of the Babri Mosque in Ayodhya, but his own fortunes improved with those of the Congress as a result of the December 1993 State Assembly elections. Although these were far from an outright triumph for the Congress, they were deeply disappointing for the BJP, and gave the Congress government a breathing space. Internationally, however, uncertainty remained in relations with Pakistan, especially over Kashmir, where in 1994 Indian troops were still tied down in the Vale trying to contain violent opposition to the government's rule. Assam also remained troubled. In the Punjab, in contrast, the situation was steadily returning to normal after a decade of bitter violence.

Economy

Agriculture and fishing

Although agriculture now accounts for less than 30% of India's GDP it remains the most important single economic activity. More than half India's people depend directly on agriculture, and the success of the annual harvest has a crucial effect on the remainder of the economy.

Indian agriculture is enormously varied, reflecting the widely different conditions of climate, soil and relief. Cereal farming dominates most areas. Wheat, grown as a winter crop, is most important in W Uttar Pradesh through Haryana to Punjab. Total wheat production in 1994 rose above 50 million tonnes, double the figure 20 years earlier. Rice, the most important single foodgrain, is concentrated in the wetter regions of the E and S. Output rose from 40 million tonnes to over 60 million tonnes between 1971 and 1994.

Other cereal crops – sorghum and the millets – predominate in C India and unirrigated parts of the N. In addition to its cereals, and a range of pulses, India produces important crops of tea, cotton and sugar cane. All have seen significant growth, tea and cotton manufactures making important contributors to export earnings.

Between independence and the late 1960s most of the increase in India's agricultural output came from extending the cultivated area. Over 57% of the total area is now cultivated. In the last 20 years increasingly intensive use of land through greater irrigation and use of fertiliser, pesticides and high yielding varieties of seeds (hyvs) has allowed growth to continue. The area under irrigation has risen to over 35% in 1994, while fertiliser use has increased 25 times since 1961. Indian agriculture is dominated by small holdings. Only 20% of the land is farmed in units of more than 10 ha, compared with 31% 20 years ago, while nearly 60% of farms are less than 1 ha.

Resources and industry

India has extensive resources of iron ore, coal, bauxite and some other minerals. Reserves of coal at likely rates of use are estimated at well over 100 years (at least 30 bn tonnes, plus 6 bn tonnes of coking coal). Medium and high grade iron ore reserves (5 bn tonnes) will last over 200 years at present extraction rates. Although iron ore is found widely across peninsular India, coal is largely restricted to the West Bengal, Bihar, and Orissa. India's coal output reached over 200 million tonnes in 1992, and iron ore 52 million tonnes, much of which was exported to Japan.

The search for oil intensified after the oil price rises of the 1970s and late 1980s. Development of the Bombay High, off the coast of Gujarat, have contributed to the total output of over 30 million tonnes. Oil, coal and gas provide the energy for just over half India's 70 millin kw electric generation capacity, 18 million kw being hydro and 1.3 million mw nuclear.

Power generation By 1994 India's power production had grown to over 260 bn kwh, but demand has risen so fast that many states continue to have power blackouts or 'loadshedding'. Firewood is estimated to provide nearly 30% of the total energy requirement, agricultural waste 9% and cow dung, a universal fuel in some poorer areas, 7%.

India's Five Year Plans

In the early 1950s India embarked on a programme of planned industrial development. Borrowing planning concepts from the Soviet Union, the government tried to stimulate development through massive investment in the public sector, imposing a system of tight controls on foreign ownership of capital in India, and playing a highly interventionist role in all aspects of economic policy. The private sector was allowed to continue to operate in agriculture, and in a wide range of 'non-essential' industrial sectors.

Although significant achievements were made in the first 2 Five Year Plans (1951-56, 1956-61), the Third Five Year Plan failed catastrophically. Agriculture was particularly hard hit by 3 poor monsoons. After a period of dependence on foreign aid at the end of the 1960s, the economy started moving forward again. The 'Green Revolution', a package of practices designed to increase farm output, enabled Indian agriculture to increase production faster than demand, and through the 1980s it was producing surplus foodgrains, enabling it to build up reserves.

Industrial development continued to lag behind expectations, however. Although India returned to the programme of Five Year Plans (in 1991 it began its Eighth Plan), central control has been progressively loosened. Indira Gandhi began to move towards liberalising imports and foreign investment. Rajiv Gandhi pursued this policy much more strongly in the first 2 years of his government, although many vested interests saw their protected status at risk and the programme slowed to a halt. The Government of Narasimha Rao inherited a foreign exchange and inflation crisis in July 1991, and in its first 2 years in office renewed the effort to encourage foreign investment and liberalisation of controls, including making the Rupee fully convertible in March 1993. Defence spending has been cut from 3.8% to 3.2% of GNP. In 1994 the economy was moving back into growth with only modest inflation, foreign exchange reserves had increased and the first signs of a major increase in foreign investment were visible in the surge on the Bombay stock market.

Achievements and problems

India today has a far more diversified industrial base than seemed imaginable at independence. It produces goods from aeroplanes and rockets to watches and computers, from industrial and transport machinery to textiles and consumer goods. The influence of India's manufacturing industry reaches every village. Yet despite the successes, many in India claim that the weaknesses remain profound. Perhaps half of the population continues to live in absolute poverty, and despite surplus grain production many still lack an adequate diet.

While India's industrial economy is producing a range of modern products, most are uncompetitive on world markets. Furthermore, critics within India increasingly argue that goods are made in factories that often fail to observe basic safety and health rules, and that emit enormous pollution into the environment. On top of that, the industrial expansion barely seems to have touched the problems of unemployment. Employment in India's organised industry has risen from 12 million in 1961 to over 25 million in 1994, yet during the same period the number of registered unemployed rose from 1.6 million to 34 million.

RELIGION

CONTENTS

MAPS

It is impossible to write briefly about religion in India without greatly oversimplifying. Over 80% of Indians are Hindu, but there are significant minorities. Muslims number about 100 million, and there are over 20 million Christians, 18 million Sikhs, 6 million Buddhists and a number of other religious groups. See page 180. One of the most persistent features of Indian religious and social life is the caste system. This has undergone substantial changes since independence, especially in towns and cities, but most people in India are still clearly identified as a member of a particular caste group. The Government has introduced measures to help the backward, or 'scheduled' castes, though in recent years this has produced a major political backlash.

Hinduism

It has always been easier to define Hinduism by what it is not than by what it is. Indeed, the name Hinduism was given by foreigners to the peoples of the sub-continent who did not profess the other major faiths, such as Muslims or Christians. The beliefs and practices of modern Hinduism began to take shape in the centuries on either side of the birth of Christ. But while some aspects of modern Hinduism can be traced back more than 2000 years before that, other features are recent. Hinduism has undergone major changes both in belief and practice. Such changes came from outside as well as from within. As early as the 6th century BC the Buddhists and Jains had tried to reform the religion of Vedism (or Brahmanism) which had been dominant in some parts of S Asia for 500 years. Great philosophers such as Shankaracharya (7th and early 8th centuries AD) and Ramanuja (12th century AD) transformed major aspects of previous Hindu thought.

Modern Hinduism

A number of ideas run like a thread through intellectual and popular Hinduism. According to the great Indian philosopher and former President of India, S. Radhakrishnan, religion for the Hindu 'is not an idea but a power, not an intellectual proposition but a life conviction. Religion is consciousness of ultimate reality, not a theory about God.'

Some Hindu scholars and philosophers talk of Hinduism as one religious and cultural tradition, in which the enormous variety of belief and practice can ultimately be interpreted as interwoven in a common view of the world. Yet there is no Hindu organisation, like a church, with the authority to define belief or establish official practice. There are spiritual leaders and philosophers who are widely revered, and there is an enormous range of literature that is treated as sacred.

That reverence does not necessarily carry with it belief in the doctrines enshrined in the text. Thus the Vedas are still regarded as sacred by most Hindus, but virtually no modern Hindu either shares the beliefs of the Vedic writers or their practices, such as sacrifice, which died out 1500 years ago. Not all Hindu groups believe in a single supreme God. In view of these characteristics, many authorities argue that it is misleading to think of Hinduism as a religion at all.

Be that as it may, the evidence of the living importance of Hinduism is visible across India. Hindu philosophy and practice has also touched many of those who belong to other religious traditions, particularly in terms of social institutions such as caste.

Darshana

One of Hinduism's recurring themes is 'vision', 'sight' or 'view' – **darshana**. Applied to the different philosophical systems themselves, such as *yoga* or *vedanta*, 'darshana' is also used to describe the sight of the deity that worshippers hope to gain when they visit a temple or shrine. Equally it may apply to the religious insight gained through meditation or prayer.

The four human goals

Many Hindus also accept that there are 4 major human goals; material prosperity (*artha*), the satisfaction of desires (*kama*), and performing the duties laid down according to your position in life (*dharma*). Beyond those is the goal of achieving liberation from the endless cycle of rebirths into which everyone is locked (*moksha*). It is to the search for liberation that the major schools of Indian philosophy have devoted most attention. Together with dharma, it is basic to Hindu thought.

Dharma

The Mahabharata lists 10 embodiments of dharma: good name, truth, self-control, cleanness of mind and body, simplicity, endurance, resoluteness of character, giving and sharing, austerities and continence. In Dharmic thinking these are inseparable from 5 patterns of behaviour: non-violence, an attitude of equality, peace and tranquillity, lack of aggression and cruelty, and absence of envy. Dharma represents the order inherent in human life. It is essentially secular rather than religious, for it doesn't depend on any revelation or command of God.

The Four Stages Of Life

It is widely believed that an ideal life has 4 stages: that of the student, the householder, the forest dweller and the wandering dependent or beggar (sannyasi). These stages represent the phases through which an individual learns of life's goals and of the means of achieving them, in which he "carries out his duties and raises sons", and then retires to meditate alone; and then finally when he gives up all possessions and depends on the gifts of others. It is an ideal pattern which some still try to follow.

One of the most striking sights is that of the saffron clad sadhu, or wandering beggar, seeking gifts of food and money to support himself in the final stage of his life. There may have been sadhus even before the Aryans arrived. Today, most of these wanderers, who have cast off all the moral requirements of their surrounding cultures, are devotees of popular Hindu beliefs. Most give up material possessions, carrying only a strip of cloth, a staff (*danda*), a crutch to support the chin during meditation (*achal*), prayer beads, a fan to ward off evil spirits, a water pot, a drinking vessel, which may be a human skull, and a begging bowl. You may well see one, almost naked, covered only in ashes, on a city street.

The age in which we live is seen by Hindu philosophers as a dark age, the *kaliyuga*. The most important behaviour enjoined on Hindus for this period was that of fulfilling the obligations of the householder. However, each of the stages is still recognised as a valid pattern for individuals.

KARMA - AN EYE TO THE FUTURE

According to karma, every person, animal or god has a being or self which has existed without beginning. Every action, except those that are done without any consideration of the results, leaves an indelible mark on that self. This is carried forward into the next life, and the overall character of the imprint on each person's 'self' determines 3 features of the next life. It controls the nature of his next birth (animal, human or god) and the kind of family he will be born into if human. It determines the length of the next life. Finally, it controls the good or bad experiences that the self will experience. However, it does not imply a fatalistic belief that the nature of action in this life is unimportant. Rather, it suggests that the path followed by the individual in the present life is vital to the nature of its next life, and ultimately to the chance of gaining release from this world.

Karma

The idea of *karma* 'the effect of former actions' – is central to achieving liberation. As C Rajagopalachari, a leading Tamil philosopher, put it: 'Every act has its appointed effect, whether the act be thought, word or deed. If water is exposed to the sun, it cannot avoid being dried up. The effect automatically follows. It is the same with everything. The cause holds the effect, so to say, in its womb. If we reflect deeply and objectively, the entire world will be found to obey unalterable laws. That is the doctrine of karma.'

Rebirth

The belief in the transmigration of souls (samsara) in a never-ending cycle of re birth has been Hinduism's most distinctive and important contribution to Indian culture. The earliest reference to the belief is found in one of the Upanishads, around the 7th century BC, at about the same time as the doctrine of karma made its first appearance. By the late Upanishads it was universally accepted, and in Buddhism and Jainism there is never any questioning of the belief.

Ahimsa

A.L. Basham pointed out that belief in transmigration must have encouraged a further distinctive doctrine, that of non-violence or non-injury – ahimsa. Buddhism and Jainism campaigned particularly vigorously against the existing practice of animal sacrifice. The belief in rebirth meant that all living things and creatures of the spirit – people, devils, gods, animals, even worms – possessed the same essential soul. One inscription which has been found in several places threatens that anyone who interferes with the rights of Brahmins to land given to them by the king will 'suffer re birth for eighty thousand years as a worm in dung'. Belief in the cycle of rebirth was essential to give such a threat any weight!

It is common now to talk of 6 major schools of Hindu philosophy. The best known are yoga and vedanta.

Yoga

Yoga is concerned with systems of meditation that can lead ultimately to release from the cycle of rebirth. It can be traced back as a system of thought to at least the 3rd century AD. It is just one part of the wider system known as Vedanta, literally the final parts of the Vedantic literature, the Upanishads. The basic texts also include the Brahmasutra of Badrayana, written about the 1st century AD, and the most important of all, the Bhagavad-gita, which is a part of the epic the Mahabharata.

Vedanta

There are many interpretations of these basic texts. Three major schools of vedanta are particularly important:

The Duty Of Tolerance

One of the reasons why the Hindu faith is often confusing to the outsider is that as a whole it has many elements which appear mutually self-contradictory but which are reconciled by Hindus as different facets of the ultimate truth. S. Radhakrishnan suggests that for a Hindu "tolerance is a duty, not a mere concession. In pursuance of this duty Hinduism has accepted within its fold almost all varieties of belief and doctrine and accepted them as authentic expressions of the spiritual endeavour." Such a tolerance is particularly evident in the attitude of Hindus to the nature of God and of divinity. C. Rajagopalachari writes that there is a distinction that marks Hinduism sharply from the other monotheistic faiths such as Christianity or Islam. This is that "the philosophy of Hinduism has taught and trained the Hindu devotee to see and worship the Supreme Being in all the idols that are worshipped, with a clarity of understanding and an intensity of vision that would surprise the people of other faiths. The Divine Mind governing the Universe, be it as Mother or Father, has infinite aspects, and the devotee approaches him or her, or both, in any of the many aspects as he may be led to do according to the mood and the psychological need of the hour."

Advaita Vedanta According to this school there is no division between the cosmic force or principle, Brahman, and the individual self, *atman* (which is also sometimes referred to as soul). The fact that we appear to see different and separate individuals is simply a result of ignorance. This is termed *maya*, sometimes translated as illusion, but Vedanta philosophy does not suggest that the world in which we live is an illusion. Rather it argues that it is only our limited understanding which prevents us seeing the full and real unity of self and Brahman.

Shankaracharya, who lived in the 7th century AD, and is the best known Advaitin Hindu philosopher, argued that there was no individual self or soul separate from the creative force of the universe, or Brahman, and that it was impossible to achieve liberation, or moksha, through any kind of action, including meditation and devotional worship. He saw these as signs of remaining on a lower level, and of being unprepared for true liberation.

Vishishtadvaita Shankaracharya's beliefs were repudiated by the school of Vedanta associated with the 12th century philosopher, Ramanuja. He transformed the idea of God from an impersonal force to a personal God. His school of philosophy, known as Vishishtadvaita, views both the self and the world as real but only as part of the whole. In contrast to Shankaracharya's view, devotion is of central importance to achieving liberation, and service to the Lord becomes the highest goal of life.

Dvaita Vedanta The 14th century philosopher Madhva believed that Brahman, the self and the world are completely distinct. Worship of God is a key means of achieving liberation.

Worship

The abstractions of philosophy do not mean much for the millions of Hindus living across S Asia today, nor have they in the past. S. Radhakrishnan puts a common Hindu view very briefly: 'It does not matter what conception of God we adopt so long as we keep up a perpetual search after truth.'

The sacred in nature Some Hindus believe in one all powerful God who created all the lesser gods and the universe. The Hindu gods include many whose origins lie in the Vedic deities of the early Aryans.

Pilgrimage

Most Hindus regard it as particularly beneficial to worship at places where God has been revealed. They will go great distances on pilgrimage, not just to the most famous sites such as those like Varanasi, on the banks of the Ganga, but to temples, hill tops and rivers across India.

Holy sites Certain rivers and towns are particularly sacred. Thus there are 7 holy rivers – the Ganga, Yamuna, Indus and mythical Sarasvati in the N, and the Narmada, Godavari and Kaveri in the Peninsula. There are also 7 holy places – Haridwar, Mathura, Ayodhya, and Varanasi, again in the N, Ujjain, Dwarka and Kanchipuram to the S. In addition to these 7 holy places there are 4 holy abodes: Badrinath, Puri and Ramesvaram, with Dwarka in modern Gujarat having the unique distinction of being both a holy abode and a holy place.

These were often associated with the forces of nature, and Hindus have revered many natural objects. Mountain tops, trees, rocks and above all rivers, are regarded as sites of special religious significance. They all have their own guardian spirits. You can see the signs of the continuing lively belief in these gods and demons wherever you travel in India. In S India, for example, trees are often painted with vertical red and white stripes and will have a small shrine at their base. Hill tops will frequently have a shrine of some kind at the highest point, dedicated to a particularly powerful god.

Those gods have constantly undergone changes. Rudra (the Roarer), the great Vedic god of destruction, became Siva, one of the 2 most worshipped deities of Hinduism. Other gods disappeared. All the time the creative spirit of Hindus gave new names to forces to be worshipped, because, as Basham says, 'the universe for the simple Hindu, despite its vastness, is not cold and impersonal, and though it is subject to rigid laws, these laws find room for the soul of man. The world is the expression of ultimate divinity; it is eternally informed by God, who can be met face to face in all things.'

Puja

For most Hindus today worship (often referred to as 'performing puja') is an integral part of their faith. The great majority of Hindu homes will have a shrine to one of the gods of the Hindu pantheon. Individuals and families will often visit shrines or temples, and on special occasions will travel long distances to particularly holy places such as Benaras or Puri. Such sites may have temples dedicated to a major deity but will always have numerous other shrines in the vicinity dedicated to other favourite gods.

Acts of devotion are often aimed at the granting of favours and the meeting of urgent needs for this life – good health, finding a suitable wife or husband, the birth of a son, prosperity and good fortune. In this respect the popular devotion of simple pilgrims of all faiths in S Asia is remarkably similar when they visit shrines, whether Hindu, Buddhist or Jain temples, the tombs of Muslim saints or even churches such as Bom Jesus in Goa, where St Francis Xavier lies entombed.

Performing puja involves making an offering to God, and darshana – having a view of the deity. Although there are devotional movements among Hindus in which singing and praying is practised in groups, Hindu worship is generally an act performed by individuals. Thus Hindu temples may be little more than a shrine in the middle of the street, housing an image of the deity which will be tended by a priest and visited at special times when a darshan of the resident God can be obtained. When it has been consecrated, the image, if exactly made, becomes the channel for the godhead to work.

Festivals
Every temple has its special festivals. Some, like the Jagannath temple in Puri, have festivals that draw Hindus from all over India. Others are village and family events. At festival times you can see villagers walking in small groups, brightly dressed and often high spirited, sometimes as far as 80 to 100 km. For the celebration of the Kumbh Mela at Allahabad in 1989 13 million worshippers gathered to bathe where 2 of India's most holy rivers, the Ganga and Yamuna, are believed to be joined by the third, invisible, stream, the Saraswati.

Images
The image of the deity may be in one of many forms. Temples may be dedicated to Vishnu or Siva, for example, or to any one of their other representations. Parvati, the wife of Siva, and Lakshmi, the wife of Vishnu, are the focus of many temple shrines. The image of the deity becomes the object of worship and the centre of the temple's rituals. These often follow through the cycle of day and night, as well as yearly lifecycles. The priests may wake the deity from sleep, bathe, clothe and feed it. Worshippers will be invited to share in this process by bringing offerings of clothes and food. Gifts of money will usually be made, and in some temples there is a charge levied for taking up positions in front of the deity in order to obtain a darshan at the appropriate times.

Hindu sects

Three Gods are widely seen as all-powerful: Brahma, Vishnu and Siva. Their functions and character are not readily separated. While Brahma is regarded as the ultimate source of creation, Siva also has a creative role alongside his function as destroyer. Vishnu in contrast is seen as the preserver or protector of the universe. There are very few images and sculptures of Brahma, Vishnu and Siva are far more widely represented and have come to be seen as the most powerful and important. Their followers are referred to as Vaishnavite and Shaivites respectively, and numerically they form the two largest sects in India.

Brahma
Popularly Brahma is interpreted as the creator in a trinity alongside Vishnu as preserver and Siva as destroyer. In the literal sense the name Brahma is the masculine and personalised form of the neuter word Brahman.

In the early Vedic writing *Brahman* represented the universal and impersonal principle which governed the Universe. Gradually as Vedic philosophy moved towards a monotheistic interpretation of the universe and its origins this impersonal power was increasingly personalised. In the Upanishads Brahman was seen as a universal and elemental creative spirit. Brahma, described in early myths as having been born from a golden egg and then to have created the Earth, assumed the identity of the earlier Vedic deity Prajapati and became identified as the creator.

Some of the early Brahma myths were later taken over by the Vishnu cult. For example in one story Brahma was believed to have rescued the earth from a flood by taking the form of a fish or a tortoise, and in another he became a boar, raising the Earth above the flood waters on his tusk. All these images were later associated with Vishnu.

By the 4th and 5th centuries AD, the height of the classical period of Hinduism, Brahma was seen as one of the trinity of Gods – *Trimurti* – in which Vishnu, Siva and Brahma represented 3 forms of the unmanifested supreme being. It is from Brahma that Hindu cosmology takes its structure. The basic cycle through which the whole cosmos passes is decribed as one day in the life of Brahma – the *kalpa*. It equals 4320 mn years, with an equally long night. One year of Brahma's life – a cosmic year – lasts 360 days and nights. The universe is expected to last for 100 years of Brahma's life, who is currently believed to be 51 years old.

By the 6th century AD Brahma worship had effectively ceased – before the great period of temple building, which accounts for the fact that there are remarkably few temples dedicated to Brahma, the most famous one being at Pushkar in Rajasthan. None the less images of Brahma are found in most temples. Characteristically he is shown with 4 faces, a fifth having been destroyed by Siva's third eye. In his 4 arms he holds a variety of objects, usually including a copy of the Vedas, a sceptre and a water jug or a bow. He is accompanied by the goose, symbolising knowledge.

Sarasvati

The 'active power' of Brahma, popularly seen as his consort, Sarasvati has survived into the modern Hindu world as a far more important figure than Brahma himself. In popular worship Sarasvati represents the goddess of education and learning. She represents thee ch and the word itself, which began to be deified as part of the process of the writing of the Vedas, which ascribed magical power to words themselves. The development of her identity represented the re-birth of the concept of a mother goddess, which had been strong in the Indus Valley Civilization over 1000 years before, and which may have been continued in popular ideas through the worship of female spirits. It is possible that her origins are associated with the now dry River Sarasvati in Rajasthan, but unlike Brahma she plays an important part in modern Hindu worship. Normally shown as white coloured and riding on a swan, she usually carries a book, and is often shown playing a vina. She may have many arms and heads, representing her role as patron of all the sciences and arts. She has an honoured place in schools, colleges and universities.

Vishnu

Vishnu is seen as the God with the human face. From the 2nd century a new and passionate devotional worship of Vishnu's incarnation as Krishna developed in the S. By 1000 AD Vaishnavism had spread across S India, and it became closely associated with the devotional form of Hinduism preached by Ramanuja. Re birth and reincarnation were already long-established by the time Ramanuja's followers spread the worship of Vishnu and his 10 successive incarnations in animal and human form. For Vaishnavites, God took these different forms in order to save the world from impending disaster. In the table, A.L. Basham has summarised the 10 incarnations.

Rama and Krishna By far the most influential incarnations of Vishnu are those in which he was believed to take recognisable human form, especially as

Vishnu, preserver of the Universe

Krishna, eighth and most popular incarnation of Vishnu

Vishnu's Ten Incarnations

Name	Form	Story
1. *Matsya*	Fish	The earth was covered in a flood. Vishnu took the form of a fish to rescue Manu (the first man), his family and the Vedas. The story is similar to that of Noah's ark.
2. *Kurma*	Tortoise	Vishnu became a tortoise to rescue all the treasures that were lost in the flood. These included the divine nectar (ambrosia or Amrita) with which the gods preserved their youth. The gods put a mountain (*Mount Kailasa*) on the tortoise's back, and when he reached the bottom of the ocean they twisted the divine snake round the mountain. They then churned the ocean with the mountain by pulling the snake. The ambrosia rose to the top of the churning waters along with other treasures, and the Goddess *Lakshmi*, Vishnu's consort.
3. *Varaha*	Boar	Vishnu appeared again to raise the earth from the ocean's floor where it had been thrown by a demon, Hiranyaksa. The story probably developed from a non-Aryan cult of a sacred pig, incorporated into the Vishnu myth. The boar incarnation was an important focus of worship in the 4th century AD.
4. *Narasimha*	Half man half lion	The demon *Hiranyakasipu* had persuaded Brahma to guarantee that he could not be killed either by day or night, by god, man or beast. He then terrorised everybody. When the gods pleaded for help, Vishnu burst out from a pillar in the demon's palace at sunset, when it was neither day nor night, in the form of a half man and half lion and killed Hiranyakasipu.
5. *Vamana*	A dwarf	Bali, another demon, achieved enormous supernatural power by following a course of asceticism. To protect the world Vishnu appeared before him in the form of a dwarf and asked him a favour. Bali agreed, and Vishnu asked for as much land as he could cover in three strides. Once granted, Vishnu became a giant, covering the earth in three strides. He left only hell to the demon.
6. *Parasurama*	Rama with the axe	Vishnu took human form as the son of a brahman, Jamadagni. *Parasurama*, killed the wicked king for robbing his father. The king's sons then killed Jamadagni, and in revenge Parasurama destroyed all male *kshatriyas*, twenty one times in succession.
7. *Rama*	The Prince of Ayodhya	In this form he came to the world to rescue it from the dark demon, *Ravana*. His story, told in the *Ramayana*, is seen by his devotees as one of long suffering and patience, shown particularly by his faithful wife Sita. This epic also saw the creation of Hanuman, the monkey-faced god who is the model of a strong and faithful servant, and who remains one of the most widely worshipped minor deities across India.
8. *Krishna*	The charioteer for Arjuna. Many forms	The stories of his incarnations, childhood and youth, in the words of A.L. Basham 'meet almost every human need. As the divine child he satisfies the warm maternal drives of Indian womanhood. As the divine lover, he provides romantic wish-fulfilment in a society still tightly controlled by ancient norms of behaviour which give little scope for freedom of expression in sexual relations. As charioteer of the hero Arjuna on the battlefield of Kurukshetra, he is the helper of all those who turn to him, even saving them from evil rebirths, if he has sufficient faith in the Lord.'
9. *The Buddha*		Probably incorporated into the Hindu pantheon in order to discredit the Buddhists, the dominant religious group in some parts of India until the 6th century AD. One of the earliest Hindu interpretations however suggests that Vishnu took incarnation as Buddha in order to show compassion for animals and to end sacrifice.

Rama (twice) and Krishna. As the Prince of Ayodhya, history and myth blend, for Rama was probably a chief who lived in the 8th or 7th century BC – perhaps 300 years after King David ruled in Israel and the start of the Iron Age in central Europe, or at about the same time as the Greeks began to develop city states.

In the earliest stories about Rama he was not regarded as divine. Although he is now seen as an earlier incarnation of Vishnu than Krishna, he was added to the pantheon very late, probably after the Muslim invasions of the 12th century AD. The story has become part of the cultures of SE Asia.

Rama (or Ram – pronounced with a long a, as in arm) is a powerful figure in contemporary India. His supposed birthplace at Ayodhya has become the focus of fierce disputes between Hindus and Muslims. Some Hindus identified Ram's birthplace as a site occupied by a mosque. One of India's leading historians, Romila Thapar, argues that there is no historical evidence for this view, but it has taken widespread hold. A massive demonstration was allowed to proceed by local authorities and the BJP – led state government, and the mosque was destroyed on 6 Dec 1992. The Government of India is planning to re-build it along with a temple to Rama on the same site.

Krishna is worshipped extremely widely as perhaps the most human of the gods. His advice on the battlefield of the Mahabharata is one of the major sources of guidance for the rules of daily living for many Hindus today.

Hanuman
The faithful monkey assistant of Rama in his search for Sita, Hanuman is worshipped across India. The Ramayana tells how he went at the head of his monkey army in search of the abducted Sita across India and finally into the demon Ravana's forest home of Lanka. He used his powers to jump the sea channel separating India from Sri Lanka and managed after a series of heroic and magical feats to find and rescue his master's wife. Whatever form he is shown in he remains almost instantly recognisable. Often painted red, there has been a recent increase in the number of Hanuman shrines in parts of northern India as part of the political campaign by the BJP to make capital out of the Ramayana story. These are readily distinguished from traditional local shrines by their strategic siting at road junctions and by their obviously modern construction and brightly painted decoration.

Siva
Siva is interpreted as both creator and destroyer, the power through whom the universe evolves. He lives on Mount Kailasa with his wife Parvati and two sons, the elephant-headed Ganesh and the 6-headed Kartikkeya, known in S India as Subrahmanyam. Siva is always accompanied by his 'vehicle', the bull (*nandi*). They form a model of sorts for family life.

Siva is often seen as rather more remote than Vishnu, but he is also widely portrayed in sculpture and art, most famously as the dancing Natarajan of S Indian bronzes, the Lord of the Cosmic

Siva as Nataraj,
Lord of the Dance

The Story Of Linga Worship

"Once in the past, when all the universe had become a single ocean, Brahma, Vishnu and Rudra arose from the water. Their arrival was unwitnessed, and even wise men do not know it. The earth, which had been the domain of former beings, had been destroyed for a piercing wind had arisen and dried up the 7 oceans. A single sun appeared, rising in the E, and then a second in the S, just like the first, drying up all the water with its rays and burning all that moved and was still. Then in the W a third sun arose, and in the N there arose a fourth, burning all that moved or was still; later on 8 more arose, and there were 12.

Rudra, the Fire of Doomsday, arose from the subterranean hell and filled all the regions out of the sky. The exalted one, as he is known everywhere, burnt all of the underworld above and sideways, without exception, and then he went to his own dwelling-place which he had made before. Then clouds arose and rained in all directions, flooding the whole earth and all the regions of the sky with waters; afterwards they plunged into the single ocean which the universe had become. There was no earth, nor any regions of the sky, no space, no heaven; everything was like a giant cask filled to the brim.

Then the 3 eternal gods arose from the midst of the water – Brahma, Vishnu and Rudra, whose arrivals are unwitnessed. The 2 – Ka and Vishnu – bowed and said to Sarva, who blazed with sharp energy and embraced the sakti of Rudra, 'You are the lord of everything, our lord. Perform creation as you wish.' 'I will perform it' he said to them, and then he plunged into the waters and remained immersed for 1,000 celestial years. Then they said to one another, 'What will we do without him? How will creation take place?' Hari said to the creator. 'Do as I tell you Grandfather: let no more time elapse, but make an effort to create progeny. For you are capable of creating various creatures in the worlds; I will give you your own sakti, so that you will be the creator.' Thus encouraged by the words that Vishnu had spoken to him, he thought about creating, and then he created everything conducive to happiness – gods, demons, Gandharvs, Yaksas, serpents, Raksasas. When that creation had been performed, Sambhu emerged from the water, desirous of creating and thinking about it in his mind. But when he saw the whole universe stretching above and below with the gods, demons, Gandharvs, Yaksas, serpents, Raksasas and men, the great god's heart was filled with anger, and he thought, 'What shall I do? Since creation has been performed by Brahma, I will therefore destroy, cutting off my own seed.' When he said this, he released from his mouth a flame which burnt everything.

When Brahma saw that everything was on fire, he bowed to the great lord with devotion and praised the lord...Sankara was pleased by Brahma's praise and told him,'I am Sankara. I will always accomplish everything that is to be done for anyone who seeks refuge with me, devotedly. I am pleased with you; tell me what you desire in your heart.' When Brahma heard this he said,'I created an extensive range of progeny; let that be as it was, O Lord, if you are pleased with me. 'When Rudra heard this he said to Ka,'That energy which I gathered in excess in order to destroy your creation – tell me, what shall I do with it for you?' Brahma thought carefully for the sake of the world, and then he said to Sankara, 'Cause your own energy to enter the sun, since you are lord over the sun; for you are the creator, protector and destroyer. Let us live together with all the immortals in the energy of the sun, and we will receive with devotion the sacred image of the 3 times (past, present and future) that was given by mankind. Then great god, at the end of the aeon you will take the form of the sun and burn this universe, moving and still, at that moment.'

He agreed to this and laughed, for he was secretly amused, and he said to Brahma, 'There is no good use for this linga except for the creation of progeny.' And as he said this he broke it off and threw it upon the surface of the earth. The linga broke through the earth and went to the very sky. Vishnu sought the end of it below, and Brahma flew upwards, but they did not find the end of it, for all their vital effort. Then a voice arose out of the sky as the 2 of them sat there, and it said.'If the linga of the god with braided hair is worshipped, it will certainly grant all desires that are longed for in the heart.' When Brahma and Vishnu heard this, they and all the divinities worshipped the linga with devotion, with their hearts set upon Rudra."

Ardhanarishvara, the male/female form of Siva

Parvati, daughter of Parvata (Himalaya) and wife of Siva

Dance. He is also shown as an ascetic, sitting among the mountain peaks around Mount Kailasa, accompanied by his wife Parvati and meditating on the nature of the universe.

More widely than either of these forms, Siva is also represented in Shaivite temples throughout India by the lingam, or phallic symbol, a symbol of energy, fertility and potency. This has become the most important form of the cult of Siva. Professor Wendy O'Flaherty suggests that the worship of the linga of Siva can be traced back to the pre-Vedic societies of the Indus Valley civilisation (c.2000 BC), but that it first appears in Hindu iconography in the 2nd century BC.

From that time a wide variety of myths appeared to explain the origin of linga worship. The myths surrounding the 12 jyoti linga (linga of light) found at centres like Ujjain go back to the 2nd century BC, and were clearly developed in order to explain and justify linga worship. O'Flaherty has translated this story of competition between the gods, in which Siva (in the form of Rudra) terrorises the other gods into worshipping him with a devotion to the linga.

Ganesh, bringer of prosperity

Durga, Mother-goddess, destroyer of demons

Her translation of the Puranic myth is summarised below. Note that the gods appear in several forms; Siva as Rudra, Sambha and Sankara, Vishnu as Hari, Brahma as Ka.

Ganesh

Ganesh is one of Hinduism's most popular gods. He is seen as the great clearer of obstacles. Shown at gateways and on door lintels with his elephant head and pot belly, his image is revered across India. Meetings, functions and special family gatherings will often start with prayers to Ganesh, and any new venture, from the opening of a building or inaugurating a company to the commissioning by Air India of a Jumbo Jet (seen in India as a highly auspicious name), will often not be deemed complete without a Ganesh puja.

Shakti, The Mother Goddess

One of the best known cults is that of Shakti, a female divinity often worshipped in the form of Durga. The worship of female goddesses developed into the widely practised form of devotional worship called Tantrism. Goddesses such as Kali became the focus of worship which often involved practices that flew in the face of wider Hindu moral and legal codes. Animal and even human sacrifices and ritual sexual intercourse were part of Tantric belief and practice, the evidence for which may still be seen in the art and sculpture of some major temples. Tantric practice affected both Hinduism and Buddhism from the 8th century AD, its influence is shown vividly in the sculptures of Khajuraho and Konarak and in the distinctive Hindu and Buddhist practices of the Kathmandu Valley in Nepal.

Kali, the bloodthirsty consort of Siva

Hindu society

Dharma is seen as the most important of the objectives of individual and social life. But what were the obligations imposed by dharma? Hindu law givers, such as those who compiled the code of Manu (AD 100-300), laid down rules of family conduct and social obligations related to the institutions of caste and jati which were beginning to take shape at the same time.

Caste

Although the word caste was given by the Portuguese in the 15th century AD, the main feature of the system emerged at the end of the Vedic period. Two terms – varna and jati – are used in India itself, and have come to be used interchangeably and confusingly with the word caste.

Varna, which literally means colour, had a fourfold division. By 600 BC this had become a standard means of classifying the population. The fair-skinned Aryans distinguished themselves from the darker skinned earlier inhabitants. The priestly varna, the Brahmins, were seen as coming from the mouth of Brahma; the Kshatriyas (or Rajputs as they are commonly called in NW India) were warriors, coming from Brahma's arms; the Vaishyas, a trading community, came from Brahma's thighs, and the Sudras, classified as agriculturalists, from his feet. Relegated beyond the pale of civilised Hindu society were the untouchables or outcastes, who were left with the jobs which were regarded as impure, usually associated with dealing with the dead (human or animal) or with excrement.

Jati Many Brahmins and Rajputs are conscious of their status, but the great majority of Indians do not put themselves into one of the 4 varna categories, but into a jati group.

There are thousands of different jatis across the country. None of the groups regard themselves as equal in status to any other, but all are part of local or regional hierarchies. These are not organised in any institutional sense, and traditionally there was no formal record of caste status. While individuals found it impossible to change caste or to move up the social scale, groups would sometimes try to gain recognition as higher caste by adopting practices of the Brahmins such as becoming vegetarians. Many used to be identified with particular activities, and occupations used to be hereditary. Caste membership is decided simply by birth. Although you can be evicted from your caste by your fellow members, usually for disobedience to caste rules such as over marriage, you can't join another caste, and technically you become an outcaste.

Right up until independence in 1947 such punishment was a drastic penalty for disobeying one's dharmic duty. In many areas all avenues into normal life could be blocked, families would disregard outcaste members, and it could even be impossible for the outcaste to continue to work within the locality.

The Harijans Gandhi spearheaded his campaign for independence from British colonial rule with a powerful campaign to abolish the disabilities imposed by the

The Sacred Thread

The highest 3 varnas were classified as "twice born", and could wear the sacred thread symbolising their status. The age at which the initiation ceremony (upanayana) for the upper caste child was carried out, varied according to class – 8 for a Brahmin, 11 for a kshatriya and 12 for a Vaishya.

The boy, dressed like an ascetic and holding a staff in his hand, would have the sacred thread (yajnopavita) placed over his right shoulder and under his left arm. A cord of 3 threads, each of 9 twisted strands, it was made of cotton for Brahmans, hemp for kshatriyas or wool for Vaishyas. It was – and is – regarded as a great sin to remove it.

The Brahmin who officiated would whisper a verse from the Rig Veda in the boy's ear, the *Gayatri mantra*. Addressed to the old solar god Savitr, the holiest of holy passages, the Gayatri can only be spoken by the 3 higher classes. A.L. Basham translated it as: "Let us think on the lovely splendour of the god Savitr, that he may inspire our minds."

caste system. Coining the term *Harijan* (meaning 'person of God'), which he gave to all former outcastes, Gandhi demanded that discrimination on the grounds of caste be outlawed. Lists – or 'schedules' – of backward castes were drawn up during the early part of this century in order to provide positive help to such groups. Today many former outcastes refer to themselves as 'dalits' – the 'oppressed'.

Affirmative action Since 1947 the Indian government has extended its positive discrimination (a form of affirmative action) to scheduled castes and scheduled tribes, particularly through reserving up to 30% of jobs in government-run institutions and in further education leading to professional qualifications for these groups, and members of the scheduled castes are now found in important positions throughout the economy. Furthermore, most of the obvious forms of social discrimination, particularly rules which prohibit eating or drinking with members of lower castes, or from plates and cups that have been touched by them, have disappeared. Yet caste remains an extremely important aspect of India's social structures.

Marriage, which is still generally arranged, continues to be dictated almost entirely by caste rules. Even in cities, where traditional means of arranging marriages have often broken down, and where many people resort to advertising for marriage partners in the columns of the Sunday newspapers, caste is frequently stated as a requirement. Marriage is generally seen as an alliance between 2 families. Great efforts are made to match caste, social status and economic position, although the rules which govern eligibility vary from region to region. In some groups marriage between even first cousins is common, while among others marriage between any branch of the same clan is strictly prohibited.

Caste also remains an explosive political issue. Attempts to improve the social and economic position of harijans and what are termed 'other backward castes' (OBCs) continues to cause sometimes violent conflict.

Hindu reform movements

Hinduism today is more self-conscious a religious and political force than it was even at independence in 1947. Reform movements of modern Hinduism can be traced back at least to the early years of the 19th century. These movements were unique in Hinduism's history in putting the importance of political ideas on the same level as strictly religious thinking, and in interrelating them.

In the 19th century English education and European literature and modern scientific thought, alongside the religious ideas of Christian missionaries, all became powerful influences on the newly emerging western educated Hindu opinion. That opinion was challenged to re-examine inherited Hindu beliefs and practice.

Some reform movements have had regional importance. Two of these originated, like the Brahmo Samaj, in Bengal. The **Ramakrishna Mission**, named after a temple priest in the **Kali** temple in S Calcutta, **Ramakrishna** (1834-1886), who achieved all-India fame as a mystic, preaching the basic doctrine that 'all religions are true.' He believed that the best religion for any individual was that into which he or she was born. One of his followers, **Vivekenanda**, became the founder of the Ramakrishna Mission, which has been an important vehicle of social and religious reform, notably in Bengal. See page 618.

Aurobindo Ghose (1872-1950) links the great reformers from the 19th century with the post-independence period. Educated in English – and for 14 years in England itself – he developed the idea of India as 'the Mother', a concept linked with the pre-Hindu idea of Sakti, or the

From Liberal Reform To A New Fundamentalism

The first major reform movement was launched by the Bengali Brahmin, Ram Mohan Roy (1772-1833). A close study of Christian teaching, as well as of Arabic, Persian and Classical Sanskrit texts, led him to challenge traditional Hindu practices such as untouchability, widow burning, female infanticide and child marriage, without leading him to accept Christian doctrine. He founded the Brahmo Samaj, the Society of God, in 1828, 'to teach and to practise the worship of the one God'. Services were modelled closely on those of the Unitarian Church, but he never broke with orthodox Hinduism.

The Brahmo Samaj became very influential, particularly in Bengal, even though it divided, and its numbers remained tiny. In N India reform was carried out under the leadership of what one writer has called "the Luther of modern Hinduism", Dayananda Saraswati (1824-83). Rejecting idolatry and many of the social evils associated with mid-19th century Hinduism, Dayananda Saraswati established the Arya Samaj (the Aryan Society). In the early 19th century the Arya Samaj launched a major attack on the caste system, through recruiting low caste Hindus and investing them with high caste status. At the same time they encouraged a movement for the re-conversion of Christians and Muslims (the *suddhi* movement). By 1931 the Arya Samaj claimed about one million members. With a strongly Hindu nationalist political line, its programme underlay the rise in post-Independence India of the Jana Sangh Party and the present day BJP.

Mother Goddess. For him 'nationalism was religion'. After imprisonment in 1908 he retired to Pondicherry, where his ashram became a focus of an Indian and international movement. See page 854.

Islam

Islam is a highly visible presence in India today. Even after partition in 1947 over 40 million Muslims remained in India, and today there are just over 100 million.

Islam is the most recent of imported religions. Islamic contact with India was first established by the navies of the Arab Muhammad bin Qasim. These conquerors of Sindh made very few converts, although they did have to develop a legal recognition for the status of non-Muslims in a Muslim ruled state. From the creation of the Delhi Sultanate in 1206, by Turkish rather than Arab power, Islam became a permanent living religion in India.

The victory of the Turkish ruler of Ghazni over the Rajputs in AD 1192 established a 500 year period of Muslim power in India. By AD 1200 the Turkish sultans had annexed Bihar in the E, in the process wiping out the last traces of Buddhism with the massacre of a Buddhist monastic order, sacked Benaras and captured Gwalior to the S. Within 30 years Bengal had been added to the Turkish empire, and by AD 1311 a new Turkish dynasty, the Khaljis, had extended the power of the Delhi Sultanate to the doors of Madurai in the extreme S.

The contact between the courts of the new rulers and the indigenous Hindu populations produced innovative developments in art and architecture, language and literature. Hindus and Hindu culture were profoundly affected by the spread and exercise of Muslim political power, but Islam too underwent major modifications in response to the new social and religious context in which the Muslim rulers found themselves.

The early Muslim rulers looked to the

Islamic Patronage

During many periods of Muslim government, Muslim and Hindu lived and worked side by side. The intermingling of people of the different faiths is still evident in the cities of many parts of India. The spread of Islam across India was achieved less by forcible conversion than by the patronage offered by the new rulers to Muslim saints and teachers. These were particularly influential in achieving mass conversions among the lower castes of Hindus. As Welch has suggested, in the courts there was also the subtle influence of the demonstration effect on Hindus who saw the advantages in terms of jobs and power of being a Muslim.

Islam underwent important modifications as it became entrenched in India. From the outset the Muslim invaders had to come to terms with the Hindu majority population. If they had treated them as idolators they would have been forced, under Qur'anic law, to give them the choice of conversion or death. The political impossibility of governing as a tiny minority on those terms encouraged them to give Indian subjects the status of 'protected peoples'.

Turkish ruling class and to the Arab caliphs for their legitimacy, and to the Turkish elite for their cultural authority. From the middle of the 13th century, when the Mongols crushed the Arab caliphate, the Delhi sultans were left on their own to exercise Islamic authority in India. From then onwards the main external influences were from Persia. Small numbers of migrants, mainly the skilled and the educated, continued to flow into the Indian courts. Periodically their numbers were augmented by refugees from Mongol repression in the regions to India's NW as the Delhi Sultanate provided a refuge for craftsmen and artists from the territories the Mongols had conquered from Lahore westwards.

Muslim populations

Muslims only became a majority of the S Asian population in 2 areas, the plains of the Indus and W Punjab, and in parts of Bengal. Elsewhere across N India they formed important minorities, notably in the towns of the central heartland such as Lucknow. The concentration at the E and W ends of the Ganga valley reflected the policies pursued by successive Muslim rulers of colonising forested and previously uncultivated land. In the central plains there was already a densely populated, Hindu region, where little attempt was made to achieve converts.

The Mughals wanted to expand their territory and their economic base. To pursue this they made enormous grants of land to those who had served the empire, and particularly in Bengal, new land was brought into cultivation. At the same time, shrines were established to Sufi saints who attracted peasant farmers. The mosques built in E Bengal were the centres of devotional worship where saints were venerated. By the 18th century many Muslims had joined the **Sunni** sect of Islam. The characteristics of Islamic practice in both these regions continues to reflect this background.

In some areas Muslim society shared many of the characteristic features of the Hindu society from which the majority of them came. Many of the Muslim migrants from Iran or Turkey, the elite ashraf communities, continued to identify with the Islamic elites from which they traced their descent. They held high military and civil posts in imperial service. In sharp contrast, many of the non-ashraf Muslim communities in the towns and cities were organised in social groups very much like the jatis of their neighbouring Hindu communities. While the elites followed Islamic prac-

Islam In South India

Not all Muslim contact was by land through the passes of Afghanistan or Baluchistan. In the Deccan of S India, where the power of the Delhi-based empires was always much weaker than in the N plains, a succession of Muslim-ruled states maintained strong contact with Arab communities through trade.

From the 15th century to the 18th century much of S India was ruled under independent Muslim kings. Hyderabad, for example, developed a distinctive cultural and artistic life, drawing on a mixed population of Indian Muslims and Hindus,Turks, Persians, Arabs and Africans, see page 1071. Until the Mughals conquered the Deccan kingdoms in 1687, Hyderabad was one of the great centres of Arab learning outside the Middle East, a link maintained through trade across the Arabian Sea with Egypt, Yemen and Iraq.

tices close to those based on the Qur'an as interpreted by scholars, the poorer, lessliteratecommunitiesfolloweddevotional and pietistic forms of Islam. The distinction is still very clear today, and the importance of veneration of the saints can be seen at tombs and shrines across Pakistan, India and Bangladesh.

Muslim beliefs

The beliefs of Islam (which means 'submission to God') could apparently scarcely be more different from those of Hinduism. Islam has a fundamental creed; 'There is no God but God; and Mohammad is the Prophet of God' (*La Illaha illa 'llah Mohammad Rasulu 'llah.*) One book, the Qur'an, is the supreme authority on Islamic teaching and faith. Islam preaches the belief in bodily resurrection after death, and in the reality of heaven and hell.

The idea of heaven as paradise is pre-Islamic. Alexander the Great is believed to have brought the word into Greek from Persia, where he used it to describe the walled Persian gardens that were found even 3 centuries before the birth of Christ. For Muslims, Paradise is believed to be filled with sensuous delights and pleasures, while hell is a place of eternal terror and torture, which is the certain fate of all who deny the unity of God.

Islam has no priesthood. The authority of Imams derives from social custom, and from their authority to interpret the scriptures, rather than from a defined status within the Islamic community. Islam also prohibits any distinction on the basis of race or colour, and there is a strong antipathy to the representation of the human figure. It is often thought, inaccurately, that this ban stems from the Qur'an itself. In fact it probably has its origins in the belief of Mohammad that images were likely to be turned into idols.

Muslim Sects

During the first century of its existence Islam split in 2 sects which were divided on political and religious grounds, the Shi'is and Sunni's. The religious basis for the division lay in the interpretation of verses in the Qur'an and of traditional sayings of Mohammad, the Hadis. Both sects venerate the Qur'an but have different *Hadis.* They also have different views as to Mohammad's successor.

The Sunnis – always the majority in South Asia – believe that Mohammad did not appoint a successor, and that Abu Bak'r, Omar and Othman were the first 3 caliphs (or viceregents) after Mohammad's death. Ali, whom the Sunni's count as the fourth caliph, is regarded as the first legitimate caliph by the Shi'is, who consider Abu Bak'r and Omar to be usurpers. While the Sunni's

The Four Islamic Obligations

There are 4 obligatory requirements imposed on Muslims. Daily prayers are prescribed at daybreak, noon, afternoon, sunset and nightfall. Muslims must give alms to the poor. They must observe a strict fast during the month of ***Ramadan.*** They must not eat or drink between sunrise and sunset. Lastly, they should attempt the pilgrimage to the Ka'aba in Mecca, known as the Hajj. Those who have done so are entitled to the prefix Hajji before their name.

Islamic rules differ from Hindu practice in several other aspects of daily life. Muslims are strictly forbidden to drink alcohol (though some suggest that this prohibition is restricted to the use of fermented grape juice, that is wine, it is commonly accepted to apply to all alcohol). Eating pork, or any meat from an animal not killed by draining its blood while alive, is also prohibited. Meat prepared in the appropriate way is called Halal. Finally usury (charging interest on loans) and games of chance are forbidden.

believe in the principle of election of caliphs, Shi'is believe that although Muhammad is the last prophet there is a continuing need for intermediaries between God and man. Such intermediaries are termed Imams, and they base both their law and religious practice on the teaching of the Imams.

The 2 major divisions are marked by further sub-divisions. The Sunni Muslims in India have followers of the Hanafi, Shafei, Maliki and Hanbali groups, named after their leaders. Numerically one of the smallest groups in South Asia is that of the Ismailis, who regard their leader, the Aga Khan, as their spiritual head.

From the Mughal emperors, who enjoyed an unparalleled degree of political power, down to the poorest peasant farmers of Bengal, Muslims in India have found different ways of adjusting to their Hindu environment. Some have reacted by accepting or even incorporating features of Hindu belief and practice in their own. Akbar, the most eclectic of Mughal emperors, went as far as banning activities like cow slaughter which were offensive to Hindus and celebrating Hindu festivals in court.

The Mughal prince Dara Shikoh, who died in 1659, even argued that the study of Hindu scriptures was necessary to obtain a complete understanding of the Qur'an. The 16th century Bengali poet Sayyed Sultan wrote an epic in which the main Hindu gods were shown as prophets who preceded Adam, Noah, Abraham, Moses, Jesus and Mohammad, and the idea of prophet was matched to the Hindu concept of *avatar*, or incarnation.

In contrast, the later Mughal Emperor, Aurangzeb, pursued a far more hostile approach to Hindus and Hinduism, trying to point up the distinctiveness of Islam and denying the validity of Hindu religious beliefs. That attitude generally became stronger in the 20th century, related to the growing sense of the Muslim's minority position within South Asia, and the fear of being subjected to Hindu rule. It was a fear that led to the creation of the separate Muslim majority state of Pakistan in 1947 and which still permeates political as well as religious attitudes across South Asia.

The Muslim year

The first day of the **Muslim calendar** is 16 Jul 622 AD. This was the date of the Prophet's migration from Mecca to Medina, the Hijra, from which the date's name is taken (AH = Anno Hijrae).

The Muslim year is divided into 12 lunar months, alternating between 29

Calculating The Hijra Year

Murray's Handbook for travellers in India gave a wonderfully precise method of calculating the current date in the Christian year from the AH date: "To correlate the Hijra year with the Christian year, express the former in years and decimals of a year, multiply by .970225, add 621.54, and the total will correspond exactly with the Christian year."

and 30 days. The first month of the year is *Moharram,* followed by *Safar, Rabi-ul-Awwal, Rabi-ul-Sani, Jumada-ul-Awwal, Jumada-ul-Sani, Rajab, Shaban, Ramadan, Shawwal, Ziquad* and *Zilhaj*.

Significant dates 1st day of *Moharram* – New Year's Day; 9th and 10th of *Moharram* – Anniversary of the killing of the Prophet's grandson Hussain, commemorated by Shi'i Muslims; 12th of *Rabi-ul-Awwal* – Birthday of the Prophet (Milad-ul-Nabi); 1st of *Ramadan* – Start of the fasting month; 21st of *Ramadan* – Night of prayer (Shab-e-Qadr); 1st of *Shawwal: Eid-ul-Fitr* – Three day festival to mark the end of Ramadan; 10th of *Zilhaj: Eid-ul-Ajha* – Two day festival commemorating the sacrifice of Ismail; the main time of pilgrimage to Mecca (the Haj).

Ramadan

From the point of view of the tourist it is very important to note that many aspects of life are significantly altered during Ramadan. Muslims do not eat between sunrise and sunset, and food and drink are not publicly available in Muslim states. For the next 10 years Ramadan falls in the winter. The date for 1995 is approximately Feb 2nd – Mar 1st. The exact date is determined by the appearance of the new moon.

Buddhism

India was the home of **Buddhism**, but today it is practised only on the margins of the sub-continent, from Leh, Ladakh, Nepal and Bhutan in the N to Sri Lanka in the S, where it is the religion of the majority Sinhalese community. Although there are approximately 5 million Buddhists in India, most are very recent converts, the last adherents of the early schools of Buddhism having been killed or converted by the Muslim invaders of the 13th century.

India has sites of great significance for Buddhists around the world. Some say that the Buddha himself spoke of the 4 places his followers should visit. Lumbini, the Buddha's birthplace, is in the Nepali foothills, near the present border with India. Bodh Gaya, where he attained what Buddhists term his 'supreme enlightenment', is about 80 km S of the modern Indian city of Patna; the deer park at Sarnath, where he preached his first sermon and set in motion the Wheel of the Law, is just outside Varanasi; and Kushinagara, where he died at the age of 80, is 50 km E of Gorakhpur. In addition there are remarkable monuments, sculptures and works of art, from Gandhara in modern Pakistan to Sanchi and Ajanta in central India, where it is still possible to see the vivid evidence of the flowering of Buddhist culture in South Asia. In Sri Lanka, Bhutan and Nepal the traditions remain alive.

The Buddha's life

Siddharta Gautama, who came to be given the title of the Buddha – the Enlightened One – was born a prince into the warrior caste in about 563 BC. He was married at the age of 16 and his wife had a son. When he reached the age of 29 he left home and wandered as a beggar and ascetic. After about 6 years he spent some time in Bodh Gaya. Sitting under the Bo tree, meditating, he

The Buddha's Four Noble Truths

The Buddha preached Four Noble Truths: that life is painful; that suffering is caused by ignorance and desire; that beyond the suffering of life there is a state which cannot be described but which he termed nirvana ; and that nirvana can be reached by following an eightfold path.

The concept of nirvana is often understood in the W in an entirely negative sense – that of "non-being". The word has the rough meaning of "blow out" or "extinguish", meaning to blow out the fires of greed, lust and desire. In a more positive sense it has been described by one Buddhist scholar as "the state of absolute illumination, supreme bliss, infinite love and compassion, unshakeable serenity, and unrestricted spiritual freedom." The essential elements of the eightfold path are the perfection of wisdom, morality and meditation.

The Buddha in Dharmacaka-mudra; calling the earth to witness

was tempted by the demon Mara, with all the desires of the world. Resisting these temptations, he received enlightenment.

These scenes are common motifs of Buddhist art. The next landmark was the preaching of his first sermon on 'The Foundation of Righteousness' in the deer park near Benaras. By the time he died the Buddha had established a small band of monks and nuns known as the Sangha, and had followers across N India. His body was cremated, and the ashes, regarded as precious relics, were divided up among the peoples to whom he had preached. Some have been discovered as far W as Peshawar, in the NW frontier of Pakistan, and at Piprawa, close to his birthplace.

After the Buddha's Death

From the Buddha's death – or parinirvana – to the destruction of Nalanda (the last Buddhist stronghold in India) in 1197 AD, Buddhism in India went through 3 phases. These are often referred to as Hinayana, Mahayana and Vajrayana, though they were not mutually exclusive, being followed simultaneously in different regions.

Hinayana

The Hinayana or Little Way, insists on a monastic way of life as the only path to achieving nirvana, see box p 86. Divided into many schools, the only surviving Hinayana tradition is the Theravada Buddhism, which was taken to Sri Lanka by the Emperor Asoka's son Mahinda, where it became the state religion under King Dutthagamini in the 1st century AD.

Mahayana

In contrast to the Hinayana schools, the followers of the Mahayana school (the Great Way) believed in the possibility of salvation for all. They practised a far

The Buddhist Resurgence

The 1951 Census of India recorded only 181,000 Buddhists. However, in October 1956 ***Dr. B.R. Ambedkar***, a Hindu leader of the outcaste community and writer of the Indian Constitution, embraced Buddhism, and was joined by 200,000 other outcastes. The movement has continued, particularly in W India, and there are now approximately 7 million Buddhists. However, India's Buddhist significance is now mainly as the home for the extraordinarily beautiful artistic and architectural remnants of what was for several centuries the region's dominant religion.

more devotional form of meditation, and new figures came to play a prominent part in their beliefs and their worship – the Bodhisattvas, saints who were predestined to reach the state of enlightenment through thousands of rebirths. They aspired to Buddhahood, however, not for their own sake but for the sake of all living things. The Buddha is believed to have passed through numerous existences in preparation for his final mission. One of the most notable Mahayana philosophers was the 2nd or 3rd century saint, Nagarjuna. Mahayana Buddhism became dominant over most of S Asia, and its influence is evidenced in Buddhist art from Gandhara in N Pakistan to Ajanta in central India and Sigirya in Sri Lanka.

Vajrayana

The Diamond Way resembles magic and yoga in some of its beliefs. The ideal of Vajrayana Buddhists is to be 'so fully in harmony with the cosmos as to be able to manipulate the cosmic forces within and outside himself'. It had developed in the N of India by the 7th century AD, matching the parallel growth of Hindu Tantrism.

Buddhist beliefs

Buddhism is based on the Buddha's own preaching. However, when he died none of those teachings had been written down. He developed his beliefs in reaction to the Brahmanism of his time, rejecting several of the doctrines of Vedic religion which were widely held in his lifetime; the Vedic gods, scriptures and priesthood, and all social distinctions based on caste. However, he did accept the belief in the cyclical nature of life, and that the nature of an individual's existence is determined by a natural process of reward and punishment for deeds in previous lives – the Hindu doctrine of karma, see page 69. In the Buddha's view, though, there is no eternal soul.

Following the Buddha's death a succession of councils was called to try and reach agreement on doctrine. The first 3 were held within 140 years of the Buddha's death, the fourth being held at Pataliputra (modern Patna) during the reign of the Emperor Asoka (272-232 BC), who had recently been converted to Buddhism. Under his reign Buddhism spread throughout S Asia and opened the routes through NW India for Buddhism to travel into China, where it had become a force by the 1st century AD.

Buddhism's decline

The decline of Buddhism in India probably stemmed as much from the growing similarity in the practice of Hinduism and Buddhism as from direct attacks. **Mahayana Buddhism**, with its reverence for Bodhisattvas and its devotional character, was more and more difficult to distinguish from the revivalist Hinduism characteristic of several parts of N India from the 7th to the 12th centuries AD. The Muslim conquest dealt the final death blow, being accompanied by the large scale slaughter of monks and the destruction of monasteries. Without

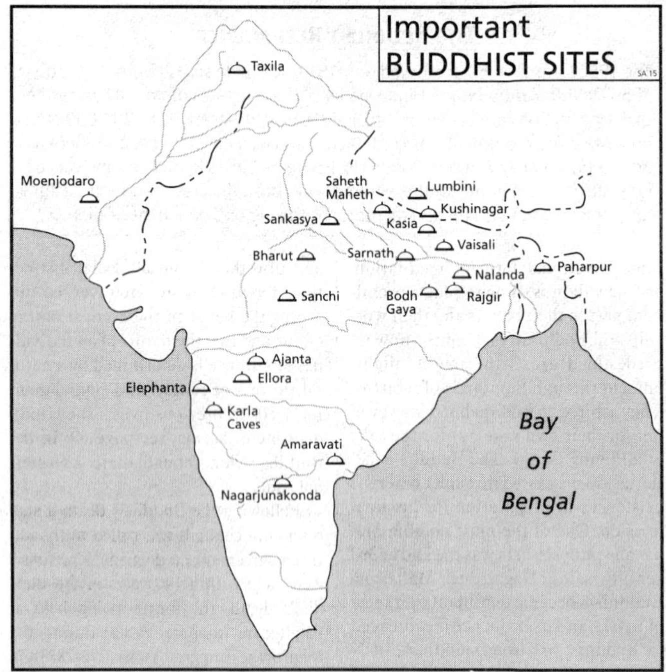

their institutional support Buddhism faded away.

Jainism

Like Buddhism, Jainism started as a reform movement of the Brahmanic religious beliefs of the 6th century BC. Its founder was a widely revered saint and ascetic, Vardhamma, who became known as Mahavir – 'great hero'. Mahavir was born in the same border region of India and Nepal as the Buddha, just 50 km to the N of modern Patna, probably in 599 BC. Thus he was about 35 years older than the Buddha. His family, also royal, were followers of an ascetic saint, Parvanatha, who according to Jain tradition had lived 200 years previously.

Unlike Buddhism, Jainism never spread beyond India, but it has survived continuously into modern India, claiming 4 million adherents. In part this may be because Jain beliefs have much in common with puritanical forms of Hinduism, and are greatly respected and admired. Some Jain ideas, such as vegetarianism and reverence for all life, are widely recognised by Hindus as highly commendable, even by those who don't share other Jain beliefs. The value Jains place on non-violence has contributed to their importance in business and commerce, as they regard nearly all occupations except banking and commerce as violent.

From the time of the Emperor Chandragupta Maurya in the 3rd century BC, Jains have enjoyed official patronage in various parts of India at different times, though Jainism became strongest in the W and parts of the S. Remarkable Jain temples can be found from Jaisalmer in

Deepavali

Mahavir's life story is embellished with legends, but there is no doubt that he left his royal home for a life of the strict ascetic. He is believed to have received enlightenment after 12 years of rigorous hardship, penance and meditation. Afterwards he travelled and preached for 30 years, stopping only in the rainy season. He died aged 72 in 527 BC. His death was commemorated by a special lamp festival in the region of Bihar, which Jains claim is the basis of the now-common Hindu festival of lights, Deepavali.

W Rajasthan to Orissa in the E, and as far S as southern Karnataka. The 18m high free standing statue of Gommateshvara at Sravana Belgola near Mysore (built about 983 AD) is just one outstanding example of the contribution of Jain art to India's heritage.

Jain beliefs

Jains (from the word Jina, literally meaning 'descendants of conquerors') believe that there are 2 fundamental principles, the living (*jiva*) and the non-living (*ajiva*). The essence of Jain belief is that all life is sacred, and that every living entity, even the smallest insect, has within it an indestructible and immortal soul. Jains developed the view of ahimsa – often translated as 'non-violence', but better perhaps as 'non-harming'. Ahimsa was the basis for the entire scheme of Jain values and ethics, and alternative codes of practice were defined for householders and for ascetics.

The five vows may be taken both by monks and by lay people: Not to harm any living beings (Jains must practise strict vegetarianism—and even some vegetables, such as potatoes and onions, are believed to have microscopic souls). To speak the truth; Not to steal; To give up sexual relations and practice complete chastity; To give up all possessions—for the Digambara sect that includes clothes.

Celibacy is necessary to combat physical desire. Jains also regard the manner of dying as extremely important. Although suicide is deeply opposed, vows of fasting to death voluntarily may be regarded as earning merit in the proper context. Mahavir himself is believed to have died of self-starvation, near Rajgir in modern Bihar.

In principle the objectives for both lay and ascetic Jains is the same, and many lay Jains pass through the stage of being a householder, and then accept the stricter practices of the monks. The essence of all the rules is to avoid intentional injury, which is the worst of all sins. Like Hindus, the Jains believe in karma, by which the evil effects of earlier deeds leave an indelible impurity on the soul. This impurity will remain through endless rebirths unless burned off by extreme penances.

Jain sects

Jains have 2 main sects, whose origins can be traced back to the 4th century BC. The more numerous Svetambaras – the 'white clad' – concentrated more in E and W India, separated from the Digambaras – or 'sky-clad'– who often go naked. The Digambaras may well have been forced to move S by drought and famine in the N region of the Deccan, and they are now concentrated in the S of India.

Unlike Buddhists, Jains accept the idea of God, but not as a creator of the universe. They see him in the lives of the 24 Tirthankaras (prophets, or literally 'makers of fords' – a reference to their role in building crossing points for the spiritual journey over the river of life), or leaders of Jainism, whose lives are

The Jain Spiritual Journey

The 2 Jain sects differ chiefly on the nature of proper ascetic practices. The **Svetambara** monks wear white robes, and carry a staff, some wooden pots, and a woollen mop for sweeping the path in front of them, wool being the softest material available and the least likely to hurt any living thing swept away. The highest level of **Digambara** monks will go completely naked, although the lower levels will wear a covering over their genitalia. They carry a waterpot made of a gourd, and peacock feathers to sweep the ground before they sit down.

Jains believe that the spiritual journey of the soul is divided into 14 stages, moving from bondage and ignorance to the final destruction of all karma and the complete fulfilment of the soul. The object throughout is to prevent the addition of new karma to the soul, which comes mainly through passion and attachment to the world. Bearing the pains of the world cheerfully contributes to the destruction of karma.

recounted in the Kalpsutra – the 3rd century BC book of ritual for the Svetambaras. Mahavir is regarded as the last of these great spiritual leaders. Much Jain art details stories from these accounts, and the Tirthankaras play a similar role for Jains as the Bodhisattvas do for Mahayana Buddhists.

Jainism's austere injunctions against harming any form of life probably prevented it from achieving lasting popularity, but in its prime it spread over most of India. Jains often became traders, an occupation regarded as the least physically harmful. In the orthodox Hindu hierarchy trade was a lower occupation than that of the priest or warriors, activities performed by the Brahmins and Kshatriyas, and later many of the Rajput states and capitals had influential Jain merchants who were allowed to construct temples – see Gwalior, Osian, Jaisalmer, Mount Abu, Ranakpur and Kumbhalgarh.

Sikhism

The Sikhs (derived from the Sanskrit word for 'disciples') are perhaps one of India's most recognisable groups. Beards and turbans give them a very distinctive presence, and although they represent less than 2% of the population they are both politically and economically significant. There are Sikhs living in all the major cities of India and playing an important role in all India's major institutions.

Sikh beliefs

From Hinduism came an acceptance of the ideas of samsara – the cycle of rebirths – and karma, see page 69. However, Sikhism is unequivocal in its belief in the oneness of God, rejecting idolatry and any worship of objects or images. Possibly reflecting the influence of Islamic beliefs, Guru Nanak also fiercely opposed discrimination on the grounds of caste.

Some of Guru Nanak's teachings are close to the ideas of the Benaras mystic **Kabir**, who, in common with the Muslim mystic sufis, believed in mystical union with God. Guru Nanak believed that God is One, formless, eternal and beyond description. However, he also saw God as present everywhere, visible to anyone who cared to look, and essentially full of grace and compassion.

Kabir's belief in the nature of God was matched by his view that man was deliberately blind and unwilling to recognise God's nature. He transformed the Hindu concept of maya into meaning the unreality of the values commonly held by the world. Guru Nanak held that salvation depended on accept-

SIKHISM'S GURUS

Guru	Teachings & practice	Developments & events	External** powers
1. **Nanak** 1469-1539	Born just W of Lahore, grew up in what is now the Pakistani town of Sultanpur. The life stories (**janam-sakhis**) of Guru Nanak, written between 50 and 80 years after his death, recorded wide travels, including Bengal in the E and Mecca in the W, studying different faiths before returning to Panjab. One of the many stories about his travels tells of how he was rebuked on his visit to Mecca for sleeping with his feet pointing towards the Qa'aba, an act Muslims would consider sacrilegious. Apologising profusely, he is said to have replied 'If you can show me in which direction I may lie so that my feet do not point towards God I will do so.'	Devotional and mystic tradition established by Guru Nanak, similar to that of Kabir. Guru Nanak had contact with Muslim families, and while he was still young organised community hymn singing when both Hindus and Muslims were welcomed. Along with a Muslim servant in the home in which he was working he also organised a common kitchen where Hindus of all castes and Muslims could eat together, thereby deliberately breaking one of the strictest of caste rules.	Delhi sultanates
2. **Angad** 1504-1538	Developments took place in Sikh worship, moving from purely individual acts of inner devotion to the introduction of special ceremonies and festivals.	,	
3. **Amar Das** 1509-1574	Introduction of worship in Gurudwaras. Continued development of the Sikh community.	Portuguese make first contacts with India.	Mughal Empire
4. **Ram Das** 1534-1581	Built first lake temple in Amritsar; the first hereditary guru.Widening of congregational worship.	Akbar. Tolerance for religious experiment.	
5. **Arjan Dev** 1563-1606	Collected the hymns and sayings of the first 3 Gurus, as well as of other Sikh saints and mystics. He brought these together with many of his father's and his own in a single volume in 1603-4 which became known as the **Adi Granth** (the 'original scripture'). Started the Golden Temple at Amritsar.	The **Adi Granth** comprises nearly 6,000 hymns composed by the first 5 gurus, 974 attributed to Guru Nanak himself. Written in the **Gurumukhi** script, which was developed from Panjabi by the second Guru, this later became known as the Guru Granth Sahib.	Akbar and Jahangir. Arjan Singh executed by Jahangir at Lahore.
6. **Har Gobind** 1595-1645	Jat caste becomes dominant influence. Sikhs began to take up arms, largely to protect themselves against Mughal attacks. Hargobind decided to withdraw to the Siwalik Hills.	McLeod, the British historian of the Sikhs, believes that the Sikh's martial traditions stemmed from the fact that the next 4 Gurus all spent much of their time as Gurus outside Punjab in the Siwalik Hills, where they developed such martial traditions as honouring the sword.	Mughal Emperors Jahangir and Shah Jahan.
7. **Har Rai** 1630-1661			Shah Jahan

SIKHISM'S GURUS

Guru	Teachings & practice	Developments & events	External** powers
8. **Har Krishna** 1656-1664		Died at Delhi.	Aurangzeb
9. **Tegh Bahadur** 1622-1675		Executed by Aurangzeb.	Aurangzeb
10. **Gobind Singh** 1666-1708	Reformed Sikh government. It is widely believed among Sikhs that **Guru Gobind Singh** introduced the features now universally associated with Sikhism. On April 15th 1699, he started the new brotherhood called the Khalsa (meaning 'the pure', from the Persian word *khales*). An inner core of the faithful, accepted by baptism (amrit). The 'five k's' date from this period: kesh (uncut hair), kangha (comb), kirpan (dagger or short sword), kara (steel bangle) and kachh ('boxer' shorts). The most important is the uncut hair, adopted before the other four. The comb is sometimes designated specifically as wooden. The dagger and the shorts reflect military influence, while the bangle may be a form of charm like the thread Hindu girls may tie on their brothers' arms, see page 239. Assassinated at Nanded in Maharashtra.	The **Khalsa** was open to both men and women, who on admission were to replace their caste names with the names **Singh** (lion) and **Kaur** ('lioness' or 'princess') respectively (the reason why the great majority of Sikh men have the surname Singh, though there are many other non-Sikhs who are also called Singh). In addition to the compulsory 'five k's', the new code prohibited smoking, eating halal meat, and sexual intercourse with Muslim women. These date from the 18th century, when the Sikhs were often in conflict with the Muslims. Other strict prohibitions include: idolatry, caste discrimination, hypocrisy, and pilgrimage to Hindu sacred places. The khalsa also explicitly forbade the seclusion of women, one of the common practices of Islam. It was only under the warrior king Ranjit Singh (1799-1838) that the idea of the Guru's presence in meetings of the Sikh community (the Panth) gave way to the now universally held belief in the total authority of the Guru Granth – the recorded words of the Guru in the scripture.	Aurangzeb

ing the nature of God. If man recognised the true harmony of the divine order (hukam) and brought himself into line with that harmony he would be saved. However, Guru Nanak rejected the prevailing Hindu belief that such harmony could be achieved by ascetic practices. In their place he emphasised 3 actions; meditating on and repeating God's name (nam), giving or charity (dan) and bathing (isnan).

Sikh worship

The meditative worship he commended is a part of the life of every devout Sikh today. Many Sikh homes will have a room set aside which houses a copy of the **Guru Granth**, and members of the house will start each day with private meditation and a recitation of the meditative verses of Guru Nanak himself, the **Japji**. However, from the time of the 3rd Guru, Sikhs have also worshipped as congregations in temples known as

Distribution Of The Sikhs

Before the partition of India and Pakistan in 1947 the Sikh community was spread evenly across the Punjab, but the region was divided in 2 by the international boundary created between India and Pakistan. Partition was preceded by savage Muslim-Sikh riots, and although some of their most sacred places were in Pakistan, Sikhs opted to become part of India, where the secular constitution seemed to offer better guarantees of long term security.

Over 2.5 million Sikhs left Pakistan for India. However, their loss of rich agricultural land, and the reduced opportunities in military and other services, led to a sense of resentment and demands for fuller political autonomy within India. Although in 1965 they won the demand for a Panjabi speaking state, Punjab has remained a centre of political unrest. Today over 90% of the 15 million Sikhs in India live in the Punjab, Haryana and Delhi. There are also significant emigrant communities abroad.

Gurudwara ("gateway to the Guru"). The Golden Temple in Amritsar, built by Guru Arjun Dev at the end of the 16th century, is the holiest site of Sikhism.

The present institutions of Sikhism owe their origins to reform movements of the 19th century. Under the Sikh Gurudwaras Act of 1925 all temples were restored to the management of a Central Gurudwara Management Committee, thereby removing them from the administrative control of the Hindus under which many had come. This body has acted as the religion's controlling body ever since.

Christianity

There are about 23 million Christians in India, and Christianity ranks third in terms of religious affiliation after Hinduism and Islam. More numerous in the south than the north, there are Christian congregations in all the major towns of India.

The great majority of the Protestant Christians in India are now members of the Church of S India, formed from the major Protestant denominations in 1947, or the Church of N India, which followed suit in 1970. Together they account for approximately half the total number of Christians. Roman Catholics make up the majority of the other 50%. Many of the church congregations, both in towns and villages, are active centres of Christian worship, the great majority using the local regional language rather than English, which is typical of some of the larger city-based churches.

Origins

Some of the churches owe their origin either to the modern missionary movement of the late 18th century onwards, or to the colonial presence of the European powers. However, Christians probably arrived in India during the 1st century after the birth of Christ. There is evidence that one of Christ's Apostles, Thomas, reached India in 52 AD, only 20 years after Christ was crucified. He settled in Malabar and then expanded his missionary work to China. It is widely believed that he was martyred in Tamil Nadu on his return to India in 72 AD, and is buried in Mylapore, in the suburbs of modern Madras. St Thomas' Mount, a small rocky hill just N of Madras airport, takes its name from him. Today there is still a church of Thomas Christians in Kerala.

The Syrian church

Kerala was linked directly with the Middle East, when Syrian Christians embarked on a major missionary movement in the 6th century AD. The

The Spread Of Christianity

The spread of Roman Catholicism was uneven, but was much stronger in the south. Jesuits concentrated their missionary efforts on work among the high caste Hindus, the most striking example of which was that of Robert de Nobili, who followed a Brahmin way of life in Madurai for many years.

Both the Roman Catholic and subsequently the Protestant denominations struggled to come to terms with the caste system. By the late 18th century the Roman Catholic church had moved substantially to abolishing discrimination on grounds of caste, a pattern which the main Protestant communities tried to follow. The American Mission in Madurai, for example, instituted "agap meals", or "love feasts", to which Christians of all castes were invited to eat meals together cooked by members of low castes.

Thomas Christians have forms of worship that show very strong influence of the Syrian church, and they still retain a Syriac order of service. They remained a close knit community, coming to terms with the prevailing caste system by maintaining strict social rules very similar to those of the surrounding upper caste Hindus. They lived in an area restricted to what is now Kerala, where trade with the Middle East, which some centuries later was to bring Muslims to the same region, remained active.

Roman Catholicism

The third major development took place with the arrival of the Portuguese. The Jesuit St Francis Xavier landed in Goa in 1542, and in 1557 Goa was made an Archbishopric, see page 1213. Goa today bears rich testimony to the Portuguese influence on community life and on church building. They set up the first printing press in India in 1566 and began to print books in Tamil and other Dravidian languages by the end of the 16th century.

Northern missions

The nature and the influence of Christian missionary activity in N India were different. There are far fewer Christians in N India than in the S, but Protestant missions in Bengal from the end of the 18th century had a profound influence on cultural and religious development. On November 9th 1793 the Baptist missionary William Carey reached the Hugli River. Although he went to India to preach, he had wide-ranging interests, notably in languages and education, and the work of 19th century missions rapidly widened to cover educational and medical work as well.

Converts were made most readily among the backward castes and in the tribal areas. The Christian populations of the tribal hill areas of Nagaland and Assam stem from such late 19th century and 20th century movements. But the influence of Christian missions in education and medical work was greater than as a proselytising force. Education in Christian schools stimulated reformist movements in Hinduism itself, and mission hospitals supplemented government run hospitals, particularly in remote rural areas. Some of these Christian-run hospitals, such as that at Vellore, continue to provide high class medical care alongside Government run medical services.

Christian beliefs

Christian theology had its roots in Judaism, with its belief in one God, the eternal Creator of the universe. Judaism saw the Jewish people as the vehicle for God's salvation, the 'chosen people of God', and pointed to a time when God would send his Saviour, or Messiah. Jesus, whom Christians believe was 'the

Christ' or Messiah, was born in the village of Bethlehem, some 20 km S of Jerusalem. Very little is known of his early life except that he was brought up in a devout Jewish family. At the age of 29 or 30 he gathered a small group of followers and began to preach in the region between the Dead Sea and the Sea of Galilee. Two years later he was crucified in Jerusalem by the authorities on the charge of blasphemy – that he claimed to be the son of God.

Christians believe that all people live in a state of sin, in the sense that they are separated from God and fail to do his will. They believe that God is personal, 'like a father'. As God's son, Jesus accepted the cost of that separation and sinfulness himself through his death on the cross. Christians believe that Jesus was raised from the dead on the third day after he was crucified, and that he appeared to his closest followers. They believe that his spirit continues to live today, and that he makes it possible for people to come back to God.

The New Testament of the Bible, which, alongside the Old Testament, is the text to which Christians refer as the ultimate scriptural authority, consists of 4 'Gospels' (meaning 'good news'), and a series of letters by several early Christians referring to the nature of the Christian life.

Denominations

Between the 2nd and the 4th centuries AD there were numerous debates about the interpretation of Christian doctrine, sometimes resulting in the formation of specific groups focussing on particular interpretations of faith. One such group was that of the Nestorian Christians, who played a major part in the theology of the Syrian Church in Kerala. They regarded the Syrian patriarch of the E their spiritual head, and followed the Nestorian tradition that there were 2 distinct natures in Christ, the divine and human. The Roman Catholic church believes that Christ declared that his disciple Peter should be the first spiritual head of the Church, and that his successors should lead the Church on earth. Modern Catholic churches still recognise the spiritual authority of the Pope and cardinals.

The reformation which took place in Europe from the 16th century onwards resulted in the creation of the Protestant churches, which became dominant in several European countries. They reasserted the authority of the Bible over that of the church. A number of new denominations were created. This process of division left a profound mark on the nature of the Christian church as it spread into S Asia. The re-unification of the church which has taken significant steps since 1947 has progressed faster in S Asia than in most other parts of the world. Most main Protestant denominations in India are now part either of the *church of S India* or the *church of N India*, and relations with both the Roman Catholic and Protestant churches are much closer than at any time in the past.

Zoroastrianism

The first Zoroastrians arrived on the W coast of India in 936 AD, forced out from their native Iran by persecution of the invading Islamic Arabs. Until 1477 they lost all contact with Iran, and then for nearly 300 years maintained contact with Persian Zoroastrians through a continuous exchange of letters. They became known by their now much more familiar name, the Parsis (or Persians).

Although they are a tiny minority (approximately 100,000), even in the cities where they are concentrated, they have been a prominent economic and social influence, especially in W India. Parsis adopted westernised customs and dress, and took to the new economic opportunities that came with colonial industrialisation. Families in W India such as the Tatas continue to be among

India's leading industrialists, just part of a community that in recent generations has spread to Europe and N America.

Origins

Zoroastrians trace their beliefs to the prophet Zarathustra, who lived in NE Iran around 7th or 6th century BC. His place and even date of birth are uncertain, but he almost certainly enjoyed the patronage of the father of Darius the Great. The passage of Alexander the Great through Iran severely weakened support for Zoroastrianism, but between the 6th century BC and the 7th century AD it was the major religion of peoples living from N India to central Turkey. The spread of Islam reduced the number of Zoroastrians dramatically and forced those who did not retreat to the desert to emigrate altogether.

Parsi beliefs

The early development of Zoroastrianism marked a movement towards belief in a single God. **Ahura Mazda**, the Good Religion of God, was shown in rejecting evil and in purifying thought word and action. Fire plays a central and symbolic part in Zoroastrian worship, representing the presence of God. There are 8 Atash Bahram – major fire temples– in India; 4 are in Bombay, 2 in Surat and one each in Navsari and Udwada. There are many more minor temples, where the rituals are far less complex – perhaps 40 in Bombay alone.

Earth, fire and air are all regarded as sacred, while death is the result of evil. Dead matter pollutes all it touches. Where there is a suitable space therefore dead bodies are simply placed in the open to be consumed by vultures, as at the towers of silence in Bombay. However, burial and cremation are also common.

CULTURE

Contents

Art and architecture

Over the 4,000 years since the Indus Valley civilization flourished art and architecture have developed with a remarkable continuity through successive regional and religious influences and styles.

The Buddhist art and architecture of the 3rd century BC left few remains, but the stylistic influence on early Hindu architecture was profound. From the 6th century AD the first Hindu religious buildings to have survived into the modern period were constructed in S and E India, alongside a continuing development of the Buddhist tradition elsewhere. Although Hindu buildings across India had many features in common, regional styles began to develop. Coming into India as vanquishing hordes, the early Muslims destroyed much that was in their path. Temples that had been encrusted with jewels were left bare. Mosques were built out of the stones of destroyed temples, often with bizarre results, as in the Qutb complex in Delhi. To the E, the Muslims finally completed the decline of Buddhism in India by destroying the last remaining Buddhist monasteries, notably the great monastery at Nalanda.

Introducing concepts of religious building from a faith completely different from that of the Hinduism into which it was transplanted, the new Islamic rulers also brought alien cultural concepts – notably from Persia. Yet the greatest flowering of Islamic architecture India ever saw, under the Mughals, was not simply a transplant from another country or region. It grew out of India's own traditions as a new and distinctive architecture, yet with recognisable links to the culture which surrounded it. That continuity reflected many forces, not least the use made by the great Mughal emperors of local skilled craftsmen and builders at every stage of their work. Constantly in contact not just with Hindu religious buildings, but with the secular buildings of the Rajputs to their S and W, the Mughal emperors took up themes present in the Hindu traditions of their time, and bent them to a new and developing purpose.

Painting, sculpture, inlay work, all blended skills from a variety of sources, and craftsmen – even occasionally from Europe. These were sometimes employed to embellish the great works. What emerged was another stepping stone in a tradition of Indian architecture, which, far from breaking the threads of Hindu tradition actually wove them into new forms. The Taj Mahal was the ultimate product of this extraordinary process.

Yet great contrasts do exist. Regional styles developed their own special features, and the main thrust of Hindu and Muslim religious buildings remains fundamentally different.

Hindu temple building

The principles of religious building were laid down in the *Sastras*, sets of rules compiled by priests. Every aspect of Hindu, Jain and Buddhist religious building is identified with conceptions of the structure of the universe. This applies as much to the process of building – the timing of which must be undertaken at astrologically propitious times – as to the formal layout of the buildings. The cardinal directions of N,S,E, and W are the basic fix on which buildings are planned. The E-W axis is nearly always a fundamental building axis. George Michell, suggests that in addition to the cardinal directions, number is also critical to the design of the religious building. The key to the ultimate scale of the building is derived from the measurements of the sanctuary at its heart.

Indian temples were nearly always built to a clear and universal design, which had built into it philosophical understandings of the universe. This cosmology, of an infinite number of universes, isolated from each other in space, proceeds by imagining various possibilities as to its nature. Its centre is seen as dominated by *Mt Meru* which keeps earth and heaven apart. The concept of *separation* is crucial to Hindu thought and social practise. Continents, rivers, and oceans occupy concentric rings around the mountain, while the stars encircle the mountain in another plane. Humans live on the continent of Jambudvipa, characterised by the rose apple tree (*jambu*).

The Sastras show plans of this continent, organised in concentric rings and entered at the cardinal points. This type of diagram was known as a mandala. Such a geometric scheme could then be subdivided into almost limitless small compartments, each of which could be designated as having special properties or be devoted to a particular deity. The centre of the mandala would be the seat of the major god. Mandalas provided the ground rules for the building of stupas and temples across India, and provided the key to the symbolic meaning attached to every aspect of religious buildings.

Temple design

Hindu temples developed characteristic plans and elevations. The focal point of the temple lay in its sanctuary, the home of the presiding deity, known as the womb-chamber (*garbhagriha*). A series of doorways, in large temples leading through a succession of buildings, allowed the worshipper to move towards the final encounter with the deity himself and to obtain *darshan* – a sight of the god. Both Buddhist and Hindu worship encourages the worshipper to walk clockwise around the shrine, performing *pradakshina*.

The elevations are designed to be symbolic representations of the home of the gods. Mountain peaks such as Kailasa are common names for the most prominent of the towers. In N and E Indian temples the tallest of these towers rises above the *garbagriha* itself, symbolising the meeting of earth and heaven in the person of the enshrined deity. In later S Indian temples the gateways to the temple come to overpower the central tower. In both, the basic structure is usually richly embellished with sculpture. When first built this would usually have been plastered and painted, and often covered in gems. In contrast to the extraordinary profusion of colour and life on the outside, the interior is dark and cramped. Here is the true centre of power.

Temple development

Buddhist and Hindu architecture probably began with wooden building, for the rock carving and cave excavated temples show clear evidence of copying styles which must have been developed first in wooden buildings. The 3rd-2nd century BC caves of the Buddhists were followed in the 7th and 8th centuries AD by free standing but rock-cut temples such as those at Mamallapuram, see page 849. They were subsequently replaced by temples built entirely out of assembled material, usually stone. By the 13th century AD most of India's most remarkable Hindu temples had been built, from the Chola temples of

HINDU AND URDU LANGUAGE

Hindi and Urdu developed as a common language in the Delhi region out of the fusion of the local language with the import of many words of Persian origin, brought by the Muslim rulers and their camp followers. During the 19th century Hindustani, as it was known by the British, divided along religious lines. Hindi moved towards its Sanskrit Hindu roots. It used the Devanagari script, now common across the N states of India from Haryana to Bihar. Urdu, on the other hand, with its script derived from Persian and Arabic, was taken up particularly by the Muslim community. It consciously incorporated Persian words, and thus while the common spoken languages of Hindi and Urdu were – and are – quite easily understood by speakers of the other language, the higher literary forms of both languages became quite distinct.

the S to the Khajuraho temples of the N Peninsula. Only the flowering of Vijayanagar architecture in S India produced continuing development, culminating in the Meenakshi Temple in Madurai, see page 915.

Muslim religious architecture

Although the Muslims adapted many Hindu features, they also brought totally new forms. Their most outstanding contribution, dominating the architecture of many N Indian cities, are the mosques and tomb complexes (*dargah*). The use of brickwork was widespread, and they brought with them from Persia the principle of constructing the true arch. Muslim architects succeeded in producing a variety of domed structures, often incorporating distinctively Hindu features such as the surmounting finial. By the end of the great period of Muslim building in 1707, the Muslims had added magnificent forts and palaces to their religious structures. Both were testaments to imperial splendour, a statement of power as well as of aesthetic taste.

European buildings

Nearly 2 centuries of architectural stagnation and decline followed the demise of Mughal power. The Portuguese built a series of churches in Goa that owed nothing to local traditions and everything to baroque developments in Europe. Despite their apparently decaying exteriors many of these remain extraordinary buildings. Not until the end of the Victorian period, when British imperial ambitions were at their height, did the British colonial impact begin to be felt. Fierce arguments divided British architects as to the merits of indigenous design. The ultimate plan for New Delhi was carried out by men who had little time for Hindu architecture and believed themselves to be on a civilizing mission, see page 162. Others at the end of the 19th century wanted to recapture and enhance a tradition for which they had great respect. They have left a series of buildings, both in formerly British ruled territory and in the Princely States, which illustrate this concern through the development of what became known as the Indo-Saracenic style.

In the immediate aftermath of the colonial period, Independent India set about trying to establish a break from the immediately imperial past, but was uncertain how to achieve it. In the event foreign architects were commissioned for major developments, such as Le Corbusier's design for Chandigarh and Louis Kahn's buildings in Dhaka and Ahmadabad. The latter, a centre for training and experiment, contains a number of new buildings such as those of the Indian architect Charles Correa.

Language

The graffiti written on the walls of any Indian city bear witness to the number of major languages spoken across the country, many with their own distinct scripts. In all the capital cities of South Asia an Indo-Aryan language – the easternmost group of the Indo-European family – is predominant; Hindi in Delhi, Urdu and Panjabi in Islamabad, Bengali in Dhaka, Sinhalese in Colombo and Nepali in Kathmandu. Even Divehi in the Maldives is an Indo-European language.

Sir William Jones, the great 19th century scholar, discovered the close links between German, Greek and Sanskrit. He showed that all these languages must have originated in the common heartland of Central Asia, being carried W, S and E by the nomadic tribes who shaped so much of the subsequent history of both Europe and Asia.

Sanskrit

It is believed that as the pastoralists from Central Asia moved into South Asia from 2000 BC onwards, the Indo-Aryan languages they spoke were gradually modified. **Sanskrit** developed from this process, emerging as the dominant classical language of India by the 6th century BC, when it was classified in the grammar of **Panini**. It remained the language of the educated until about AD 1000, though it had ceased to be in common use several centuries earlier. The Muslims brought Persian into South Asia as the language of the rulers. Like Sanskrit before it, and English from the 18th century onwards, Persian became the language of the numerically tiny but politically powerful elite across South Asia.

Hindi and Urdu

All the modern languages of N India, Pakistan, Bangladesh and Nepal owe

Some of the major scripts of South Asia

Script	*Language*	*Where used*
ستیہ میو جیتے	Urdu	Pakistan & North India
ਸਤਯਮੇਵ ਜਯਤੇ	Panjabi/Gurumukhi	North West India
सत्यमेव जयते	Devanagari	North India
সত্যমেব জয়তে	Bengali	East India & Bangladesh
ସତ୍ୟମେବ ଜୟତେ	Oriya	East India
સત્યમેવ જયતે	Gujarati	West India
సత్యమేవ జయతే	Telugu	South East India
ಸತ್ಯಮೇವ ಜಯತೇ	Kannada	South West India
சத்தியமேவ ஜயதே	Tamil	South/East India
സത്യമേവ ജയതേ	Malayalam	South West India
සත්‍යමේව ජයති	Sinhala	Sri Lanka

Roughly translated, these words mean 'truth alone triumphs'. The Government of India prints an everyday example of the scripts on its bank notes.

their origins to the blending of the earlier Indo-Aryan languages, with the later additions coming from Muslim influence. The most striking example of that influence is that of the 2 most important languages of India and Pakistan, Hindi and Urdu respectively. Most of the other modern N Indian languages were not written until the 16th century or after.

Bengali

While Hindi developed into the language of the heartland of Hindu culture, stretching from Punjab in the W to Bihar in the E, and from the foothills of the Himalaya in the N to the marchlands of Central India to the S, the Indo-Aryan languages of the early invaders developed into quite different languages on the margins of that NW core region. At the E end of the Ganga plains Hindi gives way to Bengali (known officially in Bangladesh today as Bangla), the language today of over 115 million people in Bangladesh, as well as more than 50 million in India. It is close to both Assamese to the N and Oriya to the S.

Gujarati and Marathi

Travelling S and SW of the main Hindi and Urdu belt of India and Pakistan you meet a series of quite different Indo-Aryan languages. Sindhi in Pakistan, and Panjabi in both Pakistan and India (on the Indian side of the border written in the Gurumukhi script), and further S in India, Gujarati and Marathi, all have common features with Urdu or Hindi, but are major languages in their own right. There are also 2 'outliers' of Indo-Aryan languages in the form of Sinhala in Sri Lanka and Divehi in the Maldives. Both owe their origins to the southwards movement of Buddhist missionaries. They took with them the language of Pali, which originated in the 4th century BC. This is still used in the Buddhist scriptures and was a major influence on the development of Sinhala, which developed its own character, separated by nearly 1500 km from its Indo-Aryan heartland.

The Dravidian languages

The invading Indo-Aryan speakers who came into South Asia over 3,500 years ago encountered people who spoke languages belonging to the other major language family of South Asia today, Dravidian. Four of South Asia's major living languages belong to this family group – Tamil, Telugu, Kannada and Malayalam, spoken in Tamil Nadu (and northern Sri Lanka), Andhra Pradesh, Karnataka and Kerala respectively.

Each has its own script. All the Dravidian languages were influenced by the prevalence of Sanskrit as the language of the ruling and educated elite. There have been recent attempts to rid **Tamil** of its Sanskrit elements, and to recapture the supposed purity of a literature that stretches back to the early centuries BC. Kannada and Telugu were clearly established by AD 1000, while Malayalam, which started as a dialect of Tamil, did not develop its fully distinct form until the 13th century. Today the 4 main Dravidian languages are spoken by over 180 million people.

Scripts

It is impossible to spend even a short time in India or the other countries of South Asia without coming across several of the different scripts that are used. The earliest ancestor of scripts in use today was **Brahmi**, in which Asoka's famous inscriptions were written in the 3rd century BC. Written from left to right, a separate symbol represented each different sound.

Devanagari

For about a thousand years the major script of N India has been the Nagari or Devanagari, which means literally 'the script of the city of the gods'. Hindi, Nepali and Marathi join Sanskrit in their use of Devanagari. The Muslim rulers developed a right to left script

THE MAHABHARATA

Dhrtarastra captured the throne of the Kurus. Being blind, however, he was not eligible to rule. His younger brother Pandu became king, but having been cursed, was forced to become a hermit in the Himalaya with his 2 wives, and Dhrtarastra reclaimed the throne. Pandu's 5 sons, Yudhisthira, Bhima, Arjuna, Nakula and Sahadeva (the Pandavas) were brought up after his death with Dhrtarastra's own children in the capital of Hastinapur.

Duryodhana, Dhrtarastra's eldest son, and the other brothers, resented the Pandavas, and planned to prevent them assuming the throne. The 5 Pandava brothers foiled several assassination attempts before deciding to flee, travelling through neighbouring countries as mercenaries. Arjuna, one of the sons, won the Princess Draupadi to be his bride in a *svayamvara*, a contest in which Draupadi's father challenged those contesting for his daughter to string a steel bow, then shoot an arrow through a slit in a revolving target. Arjuna was the only successful contestant. However, Draupadi wanted to avoid jealousy among the brothers, and agreed to become their joint wife.

At court the Pandavas met Krishna, chief of the Yadavas, who was to become their main ally. They returned to Hastinapur when Dhrtarastra recalled them, sharing out his kingdom between them and his own sons. The Pandavas then built a new capital at Indraprastha (now in modern Delhi), **see page 163**.

Dhrtarastra's sons were deeply unhappy with the arrangement. Yudhisthira, the eldest of the Pandava sons, accepted an invitation from Duryodhana to a great gambling match, not realising that the result was fixed. He lost his whole kingdom, his brothers and their joint wife, but Duryodhana accepted a compromise in which the Pandavas and Draupadi would be banished for 13 years, after which he would give them back their kingdom.

At the end of the period, Duryodhana went back on his promise, so the brothers got ready to fight. They gathered an enormous army, while the Kauravas (Duryodhana and his brothers) also made preparations, and the armies met on the plain of Kurukshetra. Greeks, Bactrians and Chinese were all reputed to back one side or the other.

The battle lasted 18 days, after which the only chiefs left alive were the 5 brothers and Krishna. Yudhisthira was crowned king, ruling peacefully for many years. Eventually he enthroned Arjuna's grandson Pariksit, as king, walking into voluntary exile with Draupadi and his brothers to the summit of Mount Meru, where they entered the city of the Gods.

The Mahabharata introduced the new God, Krishna, to the Vedic pantheon. Krishna's role in the battle was to serve as one of the charioteers of Arjuna. On the battlefield, Arjuna hesitated, for he could not reconcile himself to slaughtering his own family. He asked Krishna's advice, which was given in what came to be known as the Bhagavad Gita. Krishna advised him that he should obey his dharmic duty and fight, which he was finally persuaded to do with the result outlined above. The story tells how Krishna himself was accidentally killed some 36 years later by a hunter's arrow which hit his only vulnerable spot – his left heel.

Ravana, demon king of Lanka

based on Persian and Arabic.

Dravidian scripts

The Dravidian languages were written originally on leaves of the palmyra palm. Cutting the letters on the hard palm leaf made particular demands which had their impact on the forms of the letters adopted. The letters became rounded because they were carved with a stylus. This was held stationary while the leaf was turned. The southern scripts were carried overseas, contributing to the form of the non-Dravidian languages of Thai, Burmese and Cambodian.

Numerals

Many of the Indian alphabets have their own notation for numerals. This is not without irony, for what in the western world are called 'Arabic' numerals are in fact of Indian origin. In some parts of South Asia local numerical symbols are still in use, but by and large you will find that the Arabic number symbols familiar in Europe and the West are common.

The role of English

English now plays an important role across India. It is widely spoken in towns and cities, and even in quite remote villages it is usually not difficult to find someone who speaks at least a little English. Other European languages are almost completely unknown. English has undergone some important modifications during nearly 4 centuries of use in South Asia. The accent in which it is spoken is often affected strongly by the mother tongue of the speaker, and there have been changes in common grammar which sometimes make it sound unusual. Many of these changes are not mere quirks but have become standard Indian English usage, as valid as any other varieties of English used around the world. Oxford University Press in India have published a grammar of Indian English if you want to read more about common English use in South Asia.

Literature

Sanskrit was the first all-India language. Its literature has had a fundamental influence on the religious, social and political life of the entire region. Its early

THE STORY OF RAMA

Under Brahmin influence, ***Rama*** was transformed from the human prince of the early versions into the divine figure of the final story. Rama, the 'jewel of the solar kings', became deified as an incarnation of Vishnu. The story tells how Rama was banished from his father's kingdom. In a journey that took him as far as Sri Lanka, accompanied by his wife Sita and helper and friend Hanuman (the monkey-faced God depicted in many Indian temples, shrines and posters), Rama finally fought the king **Ravana**, again changed in late versions into a demon. Rama's rescue of Sita was interpreted as the Aryan triumph over the barbarians. The epic is widely seen as S Asia's first literary poem, and like the Mahabharata is known and recited in all Hindu communities.

literature was memorised and recited, and it is still impossible to date with any accuracy the earliest Sanskrit hymns. They are in the Rig Veda, which probably did not reach its final form until about the 6th century BC, but the earliest parts of which may go back as far as 1300 BC – approximately the period of the fall of Mycenean Greece in Europe.

The Vedas

The Rig Veda is a collection of 1028 hymns, not all directly religious. Its main function was to provide orders of worship for priests responsible for the sacrifices which were central to the religion of the Indo-Aryans. Two further texts that began to be created towards the end of the period in which the Rig Veda was being written down, the Yajurveda and the Samaveda, served the same purpose. A fourth, the Atharvaveda, is largely a collection of magic spells.

The Brahmanas

Central to the Vedic literature was a belief in the importance of sacrifice. At some time after 1000 BC a second category of Vedic literature, the Brahmanas, began to take shape. Story telling developed as a means to interpret the significance of sacrifice. The most famous and the most important of these were the Upanishads, probably written at some time between the 7th and 5th centuries BC. The origin, composition and ultimately writing of the Sanskrit classics was thus taking place at approximately the same time as the epics of Homer were taking shape, being recited and ultimately written down on the W coast of what is now Turkey.

The Mahabharata

The Brahmanas gave their name to the religion emerging between the 8th and 6th centuries BC, Brahmanism, the still distant ancestor of Hinduism. Two texts from about this period remain the best known and most widely revered epic compositions in South Asia, the Mahabharata and the Ramayana, known and loved by Hindus in every town and village in India.

Dating the Mahabharata

The details of the great battle recounted in the Mahabharata are unclear. Tradition puts its date at precisely 3102 BC, the start of the present era, and also suggests that the author of the poem was a sage named Vyasa. Evidence suggests however that the battle was fought around 800 BC, at Kurukshetra, see page 493. It was another 400 years before priests began to write the stories down, a process which was not complete until 400 AD. The Mahabharata was probably an attempt by the warrior class, the Kshatriyas, to merge their brand of popular religion with the ideas of Brahmanism. It was an uneasy process that took hundreds of years to complete. The original version of the Mahabharata was probably about 3,000 stanzas long, but it now contains over 100,000 – 8 times as long as Homer's Iliad and the Odyssey put together.

Good and evil

The battle was seen as a war of the forces of good and evil, the **Pandavas** being interpreted as gods and the **Kauravas** as devils. The arguments were elaborated and expanded until about the 4th century AD by which time, as Shackle says 'Brahmanism had absorbed and set its own mark on the religious ideas of the epic, and Hinduism had come into being'. A comparatively late addition to the Mahabharata, the Bhagavad-Gita is the most widely read and revered text among Hindus in South Asia today.

The Ramayana

Valmiki, is thought of in India as the author of the second great Indian epic, the Ramayana, though no more is known of his identity than is known of Homer's. Like the Mahabharata, it underwent several stages of development before it reached its final version of 48,000 lines.

Sanskrit literature

Sanskrit was always the language of the court and the élite. Other languages replaced it in common speech by the 3rd century BC, but it remained in restricted use for over 1000 years after that period, essentially as a medium for writing. The remarkable Sanskrit grammar of Panini (see page 752) helped to establish grammar as one of the 6 disciplines essential to pronouncing and understanding the texts of the Vedas properly, and to conducting Vedic rituals. The other 5 were phonetics, etymology, meter, ritual practice and astronomy. Sanskrit literature continued to be written long after it had ceased to be a language of spoken communication. Thus perhaps the greatest Sanskrit poet, Kalidasa, wrote in the 5th century AD, and the tradition of writing in Sanskrit in the courts continued until the Muslims replaced it with Persian.

Literally 'stories of ancient times', the Puranas are about the 3 major deities, Brahma, Vishnu and Siva. Although some of the stories may relate back to real events that occurred as early as 1500 BC, they were not compiled until the Gupta period in the 5th century AD. Margaret and James Stutley record the belief that 'during the destruction of the world at the end of the age, Hayagriva is said to have saved the Puranas. A summary of the original work is now preserved in Heaven!'

The stories are often the only source of information about the period immediately following the early Vedas. The Stutleys go on to say that each Purana was intended to deal with 5 themes: 'the creation of the world (sarga); its destruction and re-creation (pratisarga); the genealogy of gods and patriarchs (vamsa); the reigns and periods of the Manus (manvantaras); and the history of the solar and lunar dynasties'.

The Muslim influence

Persian

In the first 3 decades of the 10th century AD, just before the Norman conquest of England, the Turk Mahmud of Ghazni carried Muslim power across the plains of the Punjab into India. For considerable periods until the 18th century, Persian became the language of the courts. Classical Persian literature was the dominant influence, with Iran as its country of origin and Shiraz its main cultural centre, but India developed its own Persian-based style. Two writers stood out at the end of the 13th century AD, when Muslim rulers had established a sultanate in Delhi, the Indian-born poet Amir Khusrau, who lived from 1253 to 1325, and the mystic poet Amir Hasan, who died about AD 1328.

Turki

Muslim power was both confirmed and extended by the Mughals, the most notable of whom as a sponsor of literature was Akbar (1556-1605), himself illiterate. Babur left one of the most remarkable political autobiographies of any generation, the Babur-nama (History of Babur), written in Turki and translated into Persian. His son Akbar commissioned a biography, the Akbar-nama, which reflected his interest in all the world's religions. His son Jahangir left his memoirs, the Tuzuk-i Jahangiri, in Persian. They have been described as intimate and spontaneous, and an insatiable interest in things, events and people. Iranians continued to be drawn into the Indian courts of Delhi and the region of the Deccan around Hyderabad, and poetry flourished.

The colonial period

Persian was already in decline during the reign of the last great Muslim Emperor, **Aurangzeb**, and as the British extended their political power so the role of English grew. There is now a very wide Indian literature accessible in English, which has thus become the latest of the languages to be used across the whole of S Asia.

In the 19th century English became a vehicle for developing nationalist ideals. However, notably in the work of Rabindranath Tagore, it became a medium for religious and philosophical prose and for a developing poetry. Tagore himself won the Nobel Prize for Literature in 1913 for his translation into English of his own work, Gitanjali. Leading S Asian philosophers and thinkers of the 20th century have written major works in English, including not only M.K. Gandhi and Jawaharlal Nehru, the 2 leading figures in India's independence movement, but S. Radhakrishnan, Aurobindo Ghose and Sarojini Naidu, who all added to the depth of Indian literature in English.

Some suggestions for reading are listed in the Introduction and Hints (see page 152). However, several South Asian regional languages have their own long traditions of both religious and secular literature which are discussed in the relevant regional sections of this Handbook.

Science

The science of early India

Although it is still impossible to evaluate the scientific knowledge of the Indus Valley civilisation, mathematics and geometry were already developed. The extremely precise weights, cut out of grey chert, are in the exact ratios 1:2:8/3:4:8:16:32:64:160:200:320:640. It was a system unique to the Indus Valley. There is then a gap of nearly 1500 years before written evidence as to development of scientific thought becomes available. By about 500 BC texts illustrated the calculation of the calendar, although the system itself almost certainly goes back to the 8th or 9th century BC. The year was divided into 27 **nakshatras**, or fortnights, years being calculated on a mixture of lunar and solar counting.

Views of the universe

Early Indian views of the universe were based on the square and the cube. The earth was seen as a square, one corner pointing S, rising like a pyramid in a series of square terraces with its peak, the mythical Mount Meru. The sun moved round the top of Mount Meru in a square orbit, and the square orbits of the planets were at successive planes above the orbit of the sun. These were seen therefore as forming a second pyramid of planetary movement. Mount Meru was central to all early Indian schools of thought, Hindu, Buddhist and Jain.

However, about 200 BC the Jains transformed the view of the universe based on squares by replacing the idea of square orbits with that of the circle. The earth was shown as a circular disc, with Mount Meru rising from its centre and the Pole Star directly above it. The mathematics that was derived from the interpretations of the universe was put to use in the rules developed for building altars.

Conceptions of the universe and the mathematical and geometrical ideas that accompanied them were comparatively advanced in S Asia by the time of the Mauryan Empire. So also was technology. The only copy of Kautiliya's treatise on government (which was only discovered in 1909) dates from about 100 BC. It describes the weapons technology of catapults, incendiary missiles, and the use of elephants, but it is also evident that gunpowder was unknown. Large scale irrigation works were developed, though the earliest examples of large tanks may be those of the Sri Lankan King Panduwasa at Anuradhapura, built in 504 BC.

Chandra Gupta II

Chandra Gupta II reigned for 39 years

from AD 376, and was a great patron of the arts. Political power was much less centralised than under the Mauryans, and as Thapar points out, collection of land revenue was deputed to officers, who were entitled to keep a share of the revenue, rather than to highly paid bureaucrats. Trade – with SE Asia, Arabia and China – all added to royal wealth.

That wealth was distributed to the arts on a previously unheard of scale. Some went to religious foundations, such as the Buddhist monastery at Ajanta, which produced some of its finest murals during the Gupta period. But Hindu institutions also benefitted, and some of the most important features of modern Hinduism date from this time. The sacrifices of Vedic worship were given up in favour of personal devotional worship, known as bhakti. Tantrism, both in its Buddhist and Hindu forms, with its emphasis on the female life force and worship of the Mother Goddess, developed. The focus of worship was increasingly towards a personalised and monotheistic deity, represented in the form of either Siva or Vishnu. The myths of Vishnu's incarnations also arose at this period.

The Brahmins, in the key position to shape and mediate change, re-focused earlier literature to give shape to the emerging religious philosophy. In their hands the Mahabharata and the Ramayana were transformed from secular epics to religious stories. At an individual level the excellence of sculpture both reflected and contributed to an increase in image worship and the growing role of temples as centres of devotion.

Romila Thapar has recounted the remarkable developments in science made during the Gupta period. Metallurgy made dramatic progress, evidenced in the extraordinarily pure iron pillar which can be seen in the Qutb Minar complex in Delhi. In mathematics, Indians were using the concept of zero and decimal points. Furthermore in AD 499, just after the demise of the Gupta Empire, the astronomer Aryabhata 'calculated Pi as 3.1416 and the length of the solar year as 365.358 days. He also postulated that the earth was a sphere rotating on its own axis and revolving around the sun, and that the shadow of the earth falling on the moon caused eclipses'.

Science in South India

The development of science in S Asia was not restricted to the Gupta court. In S India, Tamil kings developed extensive contact with Roman and Greek thinkers during the first 4 centuries of the Christian era. Babylonian methods used for astronomy in Greece remained current in Tamil Nadu until very recent times. The basic texts of astronomy which influenced Indian development were completed by AD 400, when the **Surya Siddhanta** was completed.

This was also an age of great literature. **Kalidasa**, one of the 'nine gems' of Chandragupta II's court, and one of South Asia's greatest poets, contributed to the development of Sanskrit as the language of learning and the arts. Vatsyana's Kamasutra not only explores the diversity of physical love but sheds light on social customs. In architecture the Nagara and Dravida styles were first developed. The Brahmins also produced theses on philosophy and on the structure of society, but these had the negative effect of contributing to the extreme rigidity of the caste system which became apparent from this period onwards.

Music and dance

Music

Indian music can trace its origins to the metrical hymns and chants of the Vedas, in which the production of sound according to strict rules was understood to be vital to the continuing order of the

Universe. Over more than 3,000 years of development, through a range of regional schools, India's musical tradition has been handed on almost entirely by ear. The chants of the **Rig Veda** developed into songs in the **Sama Veda** and music found expression in every sphere of life, closely reflecting the cycle of seasons and the rhythm of work.

Over the centuries the original 3 notes, which were sung strictly in descending order, were extended to 5 and then 7 and developed to allow freedom to move up and down the scale. The scale increased to 12 with the addition of flats and sharps and finally to 22 with the further subdivision of semitones. Books of musical rules go back at least as far as the 3rd century AD. Classical music was totally intertwined with dance and drama, an interweaving reflected in the term *sangita*.

At some point after the Muslim influence made itself felt in the N, North and South Indian styles diverged, to become Karnatak music in the S and Hindustani music in the N. However, they still share important common features: *svara* (pitch), *raga* (the melodic structure), and *tala* or *talam* (metre).

Hindustani music probably originated in the Delhi Sultanate during the 13th century, when the most widely known of N Indian musical instruments, the *sitar*, was believed to have been invented. Amir Khusrau is also believed to have invented the small drums, the *tabla*. Hindustani music is held to have reached its peak under *Tansen*, a court musician of Akbar. The other important northern instruments are the stringed sarod, the reed instrument shahnai and the wooden flute. Most Hindustani compositions have devotional texts, though they encompass a great emotional and thematic range. A common classical form of vocal performance is the *dhrupad*, a 4-part composition.

The essential structure of a melody is known as a raga which usually has 5 to 7 notes, and can have as many as 9 (or even 12 in mixed ragas). The music is improvised by the performer within certain governing rules and although theoretically thousands of ragas are possible, because of the need to be aesthetically pleasing only a few hundred exist of which around a hundred are commonly performed. Ragas have become associated with particular moods and specific times of the day. Music festivals often include all night sessions to allow performers a wider choice of repertoire.

Karnatak music

Contemporary S Indian music is traced back to Tyagaraja (1759-1847), Svami Shastri (1763-1827) and Dikshitar (1775-1835), 3 musicians who lived and worked in Thanjavur. They are still referred to as 'the Trinity'. Their music placed more emphasis on extended compositions than Hindustani music. Perhaps the best known S Indian instrument is the stringed *vina*, the flute being commonly used for accompaniment along with the violin (played rather differently to the European original), an oboe-like instrument called the *nagasvaram* and the drums, *tavil*.

Music festivals

Many cities hold annual festivals, particularly during winter months. Some important ones include: **Jan** Sangeet Natak Akademi's Festival, New Delhi; Tyagaraja Festival, Tiruvayyaru, nr Thanjavur. **Feb** ITC Sangeet Sammelan, New Delhi. **Mar** Shankar Lal Festival, New Delhi. **Aug** Vishnu Digambar Festival, New Delhi. **Sep** Bhatkhande Festival, Lucknow. **Oct** Shanmukhananda, Bombay. **Nov** Sur-Singar Festival, Bombay. **Dec** Tansen Festival, Gwalior; Music Academy Festival, Madras; Music and Dance Festival, Madras.

Dance

India is rich with folk dance traditions. The rules for classical dance were laid down in the Natya shastra in the 2nd century BC. It is still one of the bases for modern dance forms, although there are many regional variations. The most common sources for Indian dance are the epics, but there are 3 essential aspects of the dance itself, Nritta (pure dance), Nrittya (emotional expression) and natya (drama). Like the music with which it is so closely intertwined, dance has expressed religious belief and deep emotion. The religious influence in dance was exemplified by the tradition of temple dancers, *devadasis*, girls and women who were dedicated to the deity in major temples to perform before them. In S and E India there were thousands of *devadasis* associated with temple worship, though the practice fell into widespread disrepute and was banned in independent India.

Handicrafts

The richness of India's traditional handicrafts is known across the world. The traditions are alive in the living traditions handed on through families that have practised them for generations. The variety and the often outstandingly high quality of the work is still astonishing. Each region has its own specialities. Details are given in the regional sections of the Handbook.

SOME INTERESTING ROUTES

The opportunities for independent travellers are now so wide that it may be difficult to know where to begin. Delhi, Bombay and Madras are all easy starting or finishing points for a tour. Several airlines make it possible to enter India from one of these cities and leave from another, so you are not bound to a circular route. A number of options for tours lasting between 10 days and 3 weeks are published by the Indian Tourist Development Corporation. Below we list a few outline suggestions. The suggested length of the tour allows for some sectors being flown. Allow a little more as the minimum time if you are planning to travel entirely by road and rail. However, if you use overnight trains for longer journeys you can cover almost as much ground in the same time as flying. Some of the tours can easily be shortened by cutting out some centres.

1. The Himalayan foothills

Delhi – Corbett – Shimla – Kulu – Manali – Leh – Delhi 18 days. Delhi gives access to some of the most beautiful sights in the Himalayan foothills, and up to the high plateaus of Leh and Ladakh. This route goes to the Corbett National Park, India's first and possibly most magnificent reserve. It then goes W via Shimla, the British summer capital and summer hill resort to Manali and Kulu, then up to the high altitude Tibetan-Buddhist area of Leh. Even if Kashmir is closed to visitors access is still possible.

2. Delhi and Rajasthan to Bombay

Delhi – Agra – Jaipur – Bikaner – Jaisalmer – Jodhpur – Udaipur – Mt. Abu – Ahmadabad – Bombay. If you fly on some sectors this tour can be done in 18 days. The most interesting sites of Mughal and Rajput India, the Jain and Hindu shrines at Mt. Abu and the distinctive Gujarat architectural style of Ahmadabad, culminating in the colonial hub of Bombay.

3. Delhi, East India and Khajuraho

Delhi – Gangtok – Darjiling – Calcutta – Bhubaneswar – Konarak – Puri – Varanasi – Khajuraho – Agra – Delhi. 21 days. Some flights desirable. Considerably longe. by land. A chance to see some of India's most sacred Hindu sites such as Puri and Varanasi, and some of the most magnificent temples at Konarak and Khajuraho. The tour would start by visiting the foothills of the Himalayas in Sikkim, with its distinctive Buddhist influences, and Darjiling, famous for its tea estates and magnificent views of Kanchengdzonga, then passes S through Calcutta, early capital of the British in India, to Orissa. It concludes with the return to Delhi, stopping at Agra to see the finest Mughal buildings, including the Taj Mahal.

4. Central India tour

Delhi – Agra – Gwalior – Jhansi – Orchcha – Bhopal – Sanchi – Indore – Mandu – Bombay – Belgaum – Badami – Hampi – Goa – Bombay. 21 days. This tour starts in the centre of Muslim influence, and goes S through some of the great Rajput cities and forts (Gwalior, Jhansi and Orchcha) to Bhopal. Around Bhopal are some of the finest prehistoric rock paintings in the world, and early Buddhist remains. Continuing through Bombay you can visit Badami, with its 6th century *Chalukya* temples, and Hampi, capital of the medieval Hindu Vijayanagar Empire. Return via the former Portuguese colony of Goa, with its churches and beaches, to Bombay.

5. **From North to South**

Delhi – Agra – Jaipur – Ajanta – Ellora – Bombay – Goa – Cochin – Madurai – Madras. 18 days if flying some sectors. Starting with the Mughal and Rajput N, the tour goes on to the magnificent Buddhist and Hindu cave temples of Ajanta and Ellora, passes through Bombay to Goa, and then samples the completely different world of the S. The great temple city of Madurai gives an excellent view of the temple life and architecture of the Tamil cultural heartland, returning to the colonial city of Madras.

6. **Tamil Nadu and Southern Karnataka**

Bombay – Cochin – Periyar – Madurai – Trichy – Thanjavur – Madras – Bangalore – Belur – Halebid – Bangalore – Bombay. 18 days. A quite brief southern tour, with so much to see that it can easily be extended. From Bombay down the W coast to Cochin, a fascinating meeting point of cultures – Hindu, Christian, Jew and Muslim, Indian, European and even a touch of Chinese – then S to one of India's game reserves at Periyar, high in the Western Ghats. From Periyar down to the Tamil plains, visiting Madurai, Trichy and Thanjavur, centres of successive Tamil kingdoms, and on to Madras and Bangalore. There are several fascinating excursions possible if you have time to extend the tour. The route then goes on to Mysore, Belur and Halebid, with remarkable Hindu and Jain monuments, returning to Bangalore and then Bombay.

7. **A South Indian circuit**

Bombay – Ajanta and Ellora – Hyderabad – Madras – Trichy – Madurai – Bangalore – Mysore – Belur – Halebid – Goa – Bombay. 14 days. In 2 weeks it is possible to see some of S. India's most stunning sites, including the Hindu and Buddhist caves of Ajanta and Ellora, the city of Hyderabad, former capital of the Muslim Nizam, reputedly one of the wealthiest men in the world, and the centres of Tamil culture. The tour returns through southern Karnataka via Bangalore, Mysore and the religious sites of Belur and Halebid.

8. **Bombay to Delhi**

Across central India Bombay – Aurangabad – Udaipur – Jaipur – Agra – Khajuraho – Varanasi – Delhi. 14 days. Across the heart of central India, in 14 days it is possible to see some of the best examples of Buddhist, Hindu and Muslim art and architecture. Travelling by road or rail, you also see a range of India's varied scenery and agriculture, going first across the Deccan plateau, with its rich black lava soils, then over the northern edge of the Peninsula to the centre of the Ganga plains at Varanasi, possibly India's holiest site.

9. **Special wildlife tour**

Bombay – Sasan Gir – Bombay – Bangalore – Mysore – Ranganathittoo – Bandipur – Mudumalai – Cochin – Periyar – Bombay; Bombay – Bhopal – Jabalpur – Kanha – Nagpur – Calcutta – Kaziranga – Delhi – Corbett – Bharatpur – Sariska – Delhi. 30 days. The suggested tour falls into 2 halves, the 1st being mainly the S, with a brief excursion to the lion sanctuary at Sasan Gir in Gujarat, the 2nd the centre and N. If you have time to do the whole tour you have the chance to see nearly the full range of Indian wildlife habitats. Much of the route has to be covered by land.

SPECIAL INTEREST HOLIDAYS AND TREKKING

Opportunities are now being developed to visit India with a specific interest or sport in mind.

Buddhist sites

The country is attracting Buddhists, particularly from Japan to undertake a circuit although Bihar state where several places of special interest are sited lacks good roads and hotels at present.

When he entered the state of Parinirvana, the Buddha named 4 places that a devout believer should visit – *Lumbini* grove in Nepal, his birthplace, *Bodhgaya* the place of Enlightenment, the Deer Park in *Sarnath* where he pronounced the Wheel of Law and *Kushinagar* where he entered the state of Parinirvana. There are 4 other sacred places of pilgrimage where the Buddha performed miracles – Sravasti, Sankasya, Rajagriha and Vaisali. The pilgrimage or *Dhammayatra* of old, undertaken by Emperor Asoka in the 3rd century BC, has been extended today to include great centres of Buddhist art and sculpture – Sanchi, Bharaut, Amaravati, Nagarjunakonda, Ajanta and Ellora, Karla and Bhaja.

Wildlife tours

These are offered by travel agents to the better known of India's 54 National Parks and over 370 sanctuaries. Most popular are Ranthambhor, Corbett, Bharatpur, Sariska, Kanha, Bandhavgarh, Kaziranga, Thekkadi (Periyar), Mudumalai, Nagarhole and Sasan Gir. It is quite possible to organise your own itinerary. See section on **Some interesting routes** above.

Golf

India has a number of beautiful and challenging courses. Mountain courses, as at Gulmarg in Kashmir or Udhagamandalam (Ooty) in Tamil Nadu, offer beautiful scenery, but there are long established clubs in all the major cities.

Adventure holidays

New opportunities in adventure sports are being offered and it is quite possible to combine a conventional sight-seeing tour with one or more of these. Trekking still remains the great favourite, discussed at some length below. Apart from the options listed here, it is possible to join a mountaineering expedition or try skiing, hang gliding, rock climbing or even motor rallying.

River running/white-water rafting

These are often combined with a trekking holiday giving the traveller a chance to experience the challenges of rapids provided by the snow-fed rivers mainly in North India flowing through Kashmir, Himachal and Uttar Pradesh and Sikkim in the East. The popular waters range from grades II-III for amateurs (Zanskar, Indus) to the greater challenges of grades IV-VI for the experienced (eg Chenab, Lidder, Sutlej, Rangit, Tons). The options ranging from a half-day trip to one lasting several days again allows a chance to see scenery, places and people off-the-beaten track. The rivers can sometimes be dangerous except when low in Aug and Sep.

The sport, which is fairly new in India, is organised and managed by professional teams who have trained abroad.

Water-sports

Water-sports (wind surfing, yachting, scuba diving etc) are being promoted particularly successfully in the Maldives

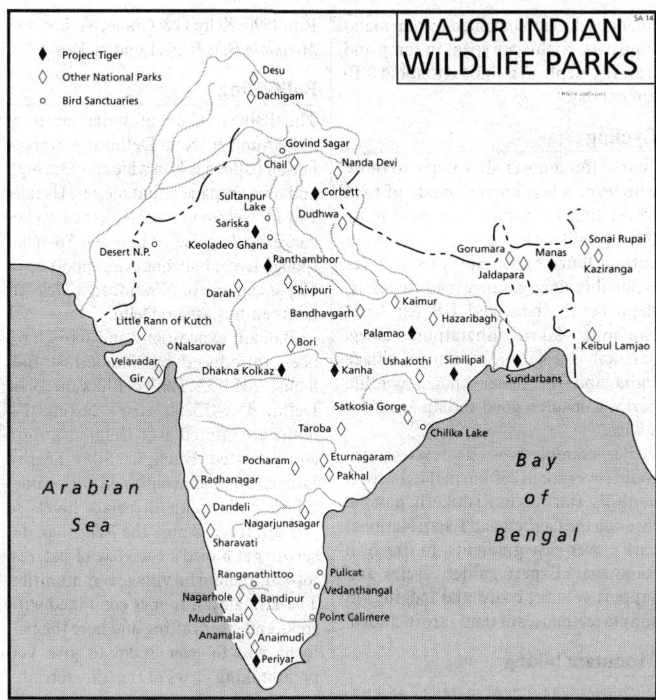

and Sri Lanka, and and now on a small scale in India, in the Andaman and Nicobar Islands and the Lakshadweeps. Ask for details at the Tourist Office.

Camel safaris

In the 16th century, traders in camel caravans crossed the mountains to the N along well trodden paths, laden with precious jewels and spices. Today's camel safaris attempt to recreate something of that spirit of adventure. The Thar desert with its vast stretches of sand, dotted with dunes and its own specially adapted shrubs and wildlife is ideal territory; the guides are expert navigators and the villages and villagers on the way, add colour to an unforgettable experience if you are prepared to sit out the somewhat uncomfortable ride (see box in Rajasthan page 475).

Horse safaris

These are gaining in popularity and are offered in Rajasthan. Conditions are similar to camel safaris with grooms (and often the horse owner) accompanying. The best months are Nov-Mar when it is cooler in the day (and often cold at night). The trails chosen usually enable you to visit small villages, old forts and temples, and take you through a variety of terrain and vegetation including scrub covered arid plains to forested hills. The charges can be a lot higher than for a camel safari but the night stays are often in comfortable palaces, forts or *havelis*.

Elephant safaris

Specialist companies offer tours of the forests in UP or Kerala on *howdahs* elephant back, supplemented by other land transport. Nights are spent in camp and travel by elephant is limited to about 8-10 km per day.

Cycling

Tours offer a novel alternative to those who want a less hurried mode of road travel than a car or bus; it offers a more flexible and at the same time, healthier option! Touring on locally hired bicycles is possible along country roads in Rajasthan, South India and UP (eg Agra, Fatehpur Sikri, Bharatpur, Deeg, Sariska) – ideal if you want to see village India and the lesser known wildlife parks. Consult a good Indian agent for advice.

For example a 6-8 day cycling trip could cover about 250 km in the Garhwal foothills, starting in Rishikesh, passing through the Corbett and Rajaji National Parks, over easy gradients, to finish in Ramnagar. Expert guides, cycles and support vehicle, board and lodging (in simple resthouses or tents) are included.

Mountain biking

With over 5000 km of metalled and unmetalled mountain road ranging in altitude from 400-5000m, a vast number of biking opportunities exist. From short day-trips in the foothills to extended tours over the highest road passes in the world there are tours to suit any biker. The Leh-Manali road, Himachal, Garhwal and Sikkim provide particularly attractive destinations with vehicle and camping support always easily arranged through local trekking agents.

Good quality mountain bikes are not available for purchase or hire so it is advisable (and sometimes obligatory) to take one over – quite easy if you dismantle it and pack it in its original shipping carton. Also be sure to take essential spares though roadside blacksmiths can fix some problems.

Suggested reading: Ballantyne, Richard: *Richard's New Bicycle Book*, London, Pan, 1990. Kelly, C & Crane, N: *Richard's Mountain Bike Book*, London, Pan, 1993.

Ballooning

The Balloon Club of India meets at Safdarjung in New Delhi; the average hot-air balloon is 15m wide and 23m high and uses propane or butane gas. Usually 2 to 3 travel up in a strengthened wicker basket and cruise at between 70-160m though larger balloons can support up to 10 passengers. In November, a *Mela* attracts enthusiasts to Delhi.

Balloon expeditions and tours have been introduced by Wanderlust Balloons, M51-52 Palika Bhawan, New Delhi, T 6875200. Trips lasting 1-4 hours are offered over Delhi city, Agra and deserted Fatehpur Sikri nearby. Longer tours are combined with camel safaris with nights in palace hotels so you can travel across the Rajasthan desert to get a bird's eye view of palaces, forts and colourful village communities. The Himalayan tour is combined with treks and river rafting and here the balloons rise to over 300m to give you breathtaking views of the hilly terrain.

Trekking

The Himalaya offer unlimited opportunities to view not only the natural beauty of mountains and the unique flora and fauna that are preserved there but also the diverse groups of people who inhabit the ranges and valleys, many of whom have retained unique cultural identities because of their isolation.

Trekking is becoming increasingly popular since many of these Himalayan regions of India and Bhutan are magnificent trekking country while the hills in Sri Lanka and other parts of India offer attractive opportunities for hikers. Details of treks appear under Uttar Pradesh, Himachal Pradesh, Kashmir, Ladakh, Darjiling and Sikkim and Bhutan.

NB: In the Himalaya some trails fall

within the 'Inner Line' for which permits are required.

Organising a trek

The success of a trek depends on your physical fitness, your equipment and advance planning and how much you enjoy venturing into areas with a culture very different to your own. Various options are open when considering organising the trek.

- **Independent trekking**

This is usually not easy since you will be in unfamiliar territory where you may not be able to communicate with the local people. There are some outstandingly beautiful treks, though they are often not through the "wilderness" sometimes conjured up.

WARNING: **Trekking alone** is not recommended as you may fall and break a limb, be severely incapacitated and not have help at hand.

The backpacking camping approach Hundreds of people arrive each year with a pack and some personal equipment, buy some food and set off trekking, carrying their own gear and choosing their own campsites or places to stay.

NB: Supplies of fuel wood are scarce and flat ground suitable for camping rare. It is not always easy to find isolated and 'private' campsites.

Trekking without a tent Comparatively cheap, this demands less equipment and uses the local inns, *Rest Houses* and *Log Huts* but facilities are basic. Probably most suited to those who have trekked before.

You carry clothes and bedding, as with youth hostelling, and for food and shelter you rely on inns or homes along the trekking route where for a few rupees a night you get a space on the floor, a wooden pallet or a camp bed, or in the more luxurious inns, a room and shower. The food is simple, usually vegetable curry, rice and *dal* which although repetitive, is healthy and can be tasty. This approach brings you into more contact with the local population, the limiting factor being the routes where accommodation is available.

NB: Treks described in this handbook are only for guidance. Independent trekkers should get a specialist publication with detailed route descriptions and a good map.

- **The locally organised trek with a *sardar* and/or porters**

Porters can usually be hired through an agent in the town or village at the start of a trek. They will help carry your baggage, someatimes cook for you, and communicate with the local people. A good porter will know the area and can often tell you about local customs and point out interesting details en route.

Although some porters speak a little English (or another foreign language) you may have communication problems and misunderstandings. Remember you may be expected to provide your porter's warm clothing and protective wear including shoes, gloves and goggles on high altitude treks.

WARNING: Porters hired in the bazar may be cheaper than agency porters but may be unreliable.

Hiring a *sardar* and crew is more expensive but well worthwhile since he will speak some English, act as a guide, take

LOW IMPACT TRAVEL

Travellers can put new strains on the environment and on local communities. Litter and the use of scarce resources such as firewood, are problems associated with some trekking areas. Over recent years the illegal removal of antiquities has also been a major problem. More detailed comments are made in the appropriate country and regional sections of this *Handbook*.

care of engaging porters and cooks, arrange for provisions and sort out all logistical problems. A *sardar* will cost more and although he may be prepared to carry a load, his principal function will be as a guide and overseer for the porters.

NB: Make sure your *sardar* or porter is experienced in the area you will be travelling in and can show good references which are his own and not borrowed. An older, experienced man is often more reliable.

● Using a trekking agent

Planning your own trek Trekking agents based in Delhi or at hill stations (eg Shimla, Manali, Dharamshala, Leh, Darjiling, Gangtok) will organise treks for a fee and provide a sardar, porters, cooks, food and equipment but it requires effort and careful thought on your part. This method is recommended for a group, preferably with some experience, that wants to follow a specific itinerary.

NB: You have to follow a pre-arranged itinerary in some areas, as required by the government, and also as porters expect to arrive at certain points on schedule.

You can make arrangements from abroad in advance, often a protracted business if Fax facilities are not available as the postal service can be slow. Alternatively, wait until you get to India but allow at least a week to make arrangements.

Reputable agencies offer an excellent service and will probably insist that you take a sardar with you as leader who will act in your interest and on your instructions. He is usually highly skilled and will make every reasonable effort to accommodate you.

The fully organised and escorted trek A company or individual with local knowledge and expertise organises a trip and sells it. Some or all camp equipment, food, cooking, planning the stages, decision-making based on progress and weather conditions, liaison with porters, shopkeepers etc are all taken care of. When operating abroad, the agency may take care of all travel arrangements, ticketing, visas and permits.

NB: Make sure that both you and the trekking company understand exactly who is to provide what equipment.

This has the advantage of being a good, safe introduction to the country. You will be able to travel with limited knowledge of the region and its culture and get to places more easily which as an individual you might not reach, without the expense of completely kitting yourself out. You should read and follow any advice in the preparatory material you are sent, as your enjoyment greatly depends on it. This applies particularly to recommendations concerning physical fitness.

An escorted trek involves going with a group; you will camp together but not necessarily all walk together. If you are willing to trade some of your independence for careful, efficient organisation and make the effort to ensure the group works well together, the experience can be very rewarding. Ideally there should be no more than 20 trekkers (preferably around 12). Check the itinerary (is it too demanding, or not adventurous enough?), whether the leader is qualified and is familiar with the route, and what exactly is provided by way of equipment, before booking.

With an organised group, companies have reputations to maintain and try to comply with western concepts of hygiene.

● Security

Thefts and muggings are very rare but on the increase. Guard your money at the point of departure. Keep your valuables with you at all times, make sure the tent 'doors' are closed when you are going for meals, and lock your room door in lodges. Be particularly careful with rucksacks carried atop buses on long journeys – always keep a watch on them when other passengers are loading/ unloading their belongings. Be particularly careful of pickpockets at the start of a trek. Thieves sometimes hang around groups of trekkers knowing that many will be carrying all their money for the trek in cash.

● **Local Agents**

Tourist Offices and government approved Trekking Agents in Delhi and the hill stations will organise fairly inexpensive treks (on some routes, it is compulsory to trek in this way). Tour operators and travel agents are listed in each town. Several travel agents in Delhi organse treks. The following are recommended: *Abercrombie & Kent*; *Cox and Kings*, Connaught Circus, T 3321028; *Ibex*, G-66 E of Kailash, T 632641, F 6846403; *Mercury Himalayan Explorations*, Jeevan Tara Bldg, Parliament St, T 312008, F 351413; *Peak Adventure Tours*, B 29A Kailash Colony, T 6432894, F 6440866; *Sita*, F-12 Connaught Pl, T 3313103; *Travel Corp of India* (TCI), N-49 Connaught Circus, T 3327468, F 3316705; *Wanderlust*, M 51-52 Palika Bhawan, opp Hyatt Regency, T 6875200, T 6885188.

The following Govt organisations can advise and also organise treks: *Himalayan Mountaineering Institutes* in hill stations in UP and Himachal and Darjiling, West Bengal; *Garhwal Mandal Vikas Nigam*, Mountaineering Div, Tourist Bungalow, Muni-ki-Reti, Rishikesh, T 373; *Parbat Tours*, Kumaon Mandal Vikas Nigam, TRC, Tallital, Nainital; *Indian Institute of Ski and Mountaineering*, Gulmarg, Kashmir, T 246; *Gujarat Mountaineering Institute*, Mount Abu, Rajasthan.

● **Foreign operators**

These, having contacts with agents in India, offer relatively expensive trips to include mess tents, dining tables, chairs, food, porters, cooks, *sardar* (guide), toilet tent.

Australia: *Adventure World*, 73 Walker St, North Sydney, PO Box 480, T 956 7766, F 956 7707 and 3rd Flr, 43 Little Collins St, Melbourne, Victoria 3000, T 670 0125, F 670 0505 and 2nd Flr, 8 Victoria Ave, Perth 6000, T 221 2300, F 221 2337; *Abercrombie & Kent*, 90 Bridport St, PO Box 22, Albert Park, 3206, T 69 9766, F 699 9308; *Travel Corp of India*, 7 Bridge St, Balmain 2041, Sydney, NSW, T 555 1079, F 555 1279. Canada: *Trek Holidays*, 8412-109 St, Edmonton, Alberta, T6G 13Z, T 439 9118; *Canadian Himalayan Expeditions*, 2 Toronto St, Suite 302, Toronto, Ontario, M5C 2B6, T 360 4300. Denmark: *Everest Travels*, Vesterbrogade 11 A, 2 van. DK-1620, Copenhagen V, T 212160, F 212125. France: *Nouvelle Frontières*, 87 Blvd de Grenelle, 75015 Paris, T 730568; *Peuple du Mode*, 10 rue de Montmorency, 75003, Paris, T 725036; *Terre d'Aventure*, 16 rue Saint Victor, 75005 Paris, T 299450, T 299631; *Voyageurs en Inde*, 45 rue St-Anne, 75001 Paris, T 61 77 08, F 61 45 86. Germany: *DAV Summit Club*, München 81545, Am Per Lacher Forst 186, T 6510720, 61507272; *Ikarus Tours*, Königstein, Fasanerweg 1, T 29020, F 22952; *Mercury Himalayan Explorations*,

6 Kurhessenstrasse, 6000 Frankfurt/Main 50, T 512620, F 521849. Holland: *Ganesh Reizen*, Lijsterstraat 27, 3514 TA Utrecht, T 719239, F 721265; *Himalaya Trekking*, Xonstant Erzeystraat 49, 3523 VT Utrecht, T 871420, F 888517. Ireland: *Club Travel Service*, 30 Lower Abbey St, Dublin 1, T 729922, F 729079. Japan: *Mercury Himalayan Explorations*, 204 Villa Hirose, 2-30-2 Yoyogi Shibuya-Ku-Tokyo, T 375 7908, F 375 7916. New Zealand: *Himalayan Travellers*, PO Box 2618, Wellington, T 863325, F 5206629. Sweden: *Himalayaresor*, Box 17, 123 21 Farsta, Stockholm, T 6055760, F 6049470. Switzerland: *Nouvelle Frontières*, Chantepoulet 10, 1201 Genève, T 7320303, F 7380193.

UK: *Capricorn Adventure*, Pen-y-Crueddyn, Apple Farm, Gladsydden, nr Llandudno, Gwynedd, North Wales, LL31 9JL, T 549733; *Exodus Expeditions*, 9 Wier Rd, London, SW12 0LT, T 081 675 5550, F 673 0779; *Explore Worldwide*, 1 Frederick St, Aldershot, Hamps, GU11 1LQ, T 319448, F 343170; *Guerba Expeditions*, 101 Eden Vale Rd, Westbury, Wiltshire, BA13 3QX, T 826611, F 826689; *High Places*, The Globeworks, Penstone Rd, Sheffield S6 3AE, T 757500, F 768190; *Himalayan Connections*, 4 Melville Pl, Edinburgh EH3 7PR, T 226 4651, F 557 5911; *Himalayan Kingdom*, 20 THe Mall, Clifton, Bristol, BS8 4DR, T 237163, F 744993; *Karakoram Experience*, 32 Lake Rd, Keswick, Cumbria CA12 5DQ, T 73966, F 74693; *Ramblers Holidays*, PO Box 43, Welwyn Garden City, Herts, AL5 6PQ, T 331133, F 333276; *Rockford Travel*, 83 Mortimer St, London, W1H 71B, T 071 436 2401, T 636 5554; *Sherpa Expedition*, 131A Heston Rd, Houslow, Middx TW5 0RD, T 081 577 2717; *Voyage Jules Verne*, 21 Dorset Sq, London NW1 6QG, T 486 8080, F 723 8629; *West Himalayan Holidays*, 54 High St East, Uppingham, Leices, LE15 9PZ, T 821330, F 821072; *World Expeditions*, 8 College RIse, Maidenhead, Berks, SL6 6BP, T 741074, F 74312.

USA: *Himalaya Trekking*, 1900 8th St, Berkeley, Ca 94710, T 540 8031, F 644 1777; *Himalure*, 10901 Rathburn, Northridge, Ca 91326, T 366 3700, F 366 1888; *Journeys*, 4011 Jackson Rd, Ann Arbor, MI 48103, T 665 4407; *Lute Jerstad Adventures*, Box 19537, Portland, OR 97280, T 244 6075; *Mercury Himalayan Explorations*, 2nd Flr, 300 E 42nd St, NY, T 661 0380, F 983 5692; *Mountain Travel*, Box 912, Westport, CT 06881, T 226 8531; *One World Expeditions*, PO Box 10538, Aspen, Colorado 81612, T 497 8368, F 925 6704; *Overseas Adventure Travel*, 349 Broadway, Cambridge, MA 02139, T 876 0533; *Sita World Travel*, 8127 San Fernando Rd, Sun Valley Ca 91352, and 9001 Airport Blvd No 202, Houston TX 77061, T 626 0134; *Tiger Tops International*, 2627 Lombard St, San Fransisco, CA 94123, T 346 3402; *Wilderness Travel*, 801 Allston Way, Berkeley, Ca 94710, T 548 0420, F 548 0347.

Trekking Seasons

These vary with the area you plan to visit and the elevation. Autumn is best in most parts of the Himalaya though March to May can be pleasant. The monsoons (mid-Jul to end-Aug) can obviously be very wet (start on your trek early in the morning as the monsoon approaches), but ocalised thunderstorms can occur at any time, particularly in the spring and summer. The Kulu valley is unsuitable for trekking during the monsoons but areas beyond the central Himalayan range eg Ladakh, Zanskar, Lahul and Spiti are largely unaffected. Be prepared for extremes in temperatures in all seasons so come prepared with light clothing as well and enough waterproof protection. Winters can be exceptionally cold; high passes can be closed and you need more equipment.

NB: Winter treks on all but a few low altitude ones (up to 3200m) are only recommended for the experienced trekker accompanied by a knowledgeable local guide.

West Himalaya UP: an all season trekking destination beacause of its variety of climate and terrain. It is perhaps best in May-Jun when days are cool and clear. Even with the onset of the monsoons when mist covers the mountains you may get breaks of 3 or 4 days in the rain. Clouds can lift to give you some good mountain views. Equipment may feel a little damp. The mountains are best for flowers in Jul-Aug. Aug to end-Oct are again good for trekking.

Himachal: trekking is possible May-Oct when all passes are open; in Jul-Sep high altitude flowers are in bloom including summer rhododendrons.

Kashmir: trekking is ideal between Apr-Nov. In Ladakh (the area open to trekkers), the motorable road from Manali to Leh is open from mid-Jun to Oct though flights to Leh from Delhi operate all year round. Most treks cross passes above 4500m and are passable from early July to Sep. Currently risky because of the political situation.

East Himalaya Darjiling area: Apr-May has a chance of occasional shower but the rhododendrons and magnolias are in full bloom; Oct-Nov are usually dry with excellent visibility. Early Dec is possible but very cold.

Sikkim: mid-Feb to late May and again Oct-early Dec are possible; Apr-May, Oct-Nov are best.

Bhutan: Mar-May, Sep-Nov are best.

NB: Trekking routes are described within each of the above regions.

Away from the Himalaya: some hill stations offer opportunities for short treks which are best undertaken outside the rainy season, preferably in Mar-May and Sep-Nov.

Satpura (MP) Pachmarhi: to Mahadeo and Dhupgarh peaks.

Aravallis (Rajasthan) Mount Abu: to Shikhar, Achalgarh and Gaumukh.

Western Ghats Madikere: Tala Cauvery, Igutappa, Tadiandamole, Virajpet, Ponnampet, Srimangala, Nagarhole.

Nilgiris Around Udhagamandalam: Coonoor, Pollachi, Topslip, Monamboli, Valparai, Grass Hills, Vaguvarai, Chanduvarai, Kilavarai, Kodaikkanal

WARNING: When trekking in the monsoon, beware of **leeches**. They sway on the ground waiting for a passer by and get in boots when you are walking. When they are gorged with blood they drop off. Don't try pulling one off as the head will be left behind and cause infection. Put some salt (or hold a lighted cigarette to it) which will make it quickly fall off. It helps to spray socks and bootlaces with an insect repellent before starting off in the morning. No leeches in Kashmir, Ladakh, Lahl and Himachal as these areas are too cool for them.

Practical information

The Sierra Club motto is worth remembering: 'Leave only footprints, take only photographs'. **Please burn or bury litter** including toilet paper. Carry a pocket lighter if you prefer to burn. Do not use firewood or encourage its use.

Hints on social behaviour When trekking, do not give money, cigarettes, sweets or other items indiscriminately, but do give to pilgrims and holy men who live on alms. Do not swim or bathe nude in rivers or hot springs.

Accommodation The popular treks have reasonable hotels or *Rest Houses* with private rooms (occasionally with attached showers) and catering. On less popular routes there are camp sites and simple huts with dormitories as well as rooms in village homes.

NB: Bed bugs are common and kitchen hygiene may be poor.

The daily routine Local porters and guides usually eat little breakfast whilst not working, preferring a large meal around 1000. On trek, however, the locally recruited staff will have a large rice meal whilst you have breakfast and then a second meal later in the day after reaching camp. On an organised trek you will probably be woken at around 0600, have a full breakfast comprising cereals or cornflakes, toast or chapathis, jam, eggs etc, start walking at around 0800, stopping for a packed picnic lunch around midday before walking another 2-3 hr reaching camp about 1500. Tea with biscuits is usually served as soon as the staff have got the kitchen running followed by a hot dinner served about 0700 and then hot drinks. Most people are usually asleep by 2100.

Footpaths Away from roads, the footpath is the principal line of communication between villages. Tracks tend to be very good, well graded and in good condition but without many flat stretches. In remoter areas away from all habitation, tracks may be indistinct and a local guide is recommended.

Health

● Acclimatisation and mountain sickness

You will probably experience Mountain Sickness in its mildest form if you go over 3000m (very occasionally at lower altitudes).

2500m It may occur when a too rapid ascent above about 2500m is attempted (or after a flight from low altitude). The body tries to adapt to the reduced concentration of oxygen in the atmosphere at higher altitudes. Mild symptoms are a slight shortness of breath, a mild headache, and increased urine output. If the trekker remains at the altitude where these symptoms first appeared, they usually gradually disappear as the body becomes acclimatised. These mild symptoms are nothing to worry about. Most people are affected, regardless of age, sex or physical fitness. Drinking large quantities of fluids always helps to counter some of these effects.

Some may suffer from acute or chronic altitude sickness. It is difficult to predict who may fail to acclimatise or become affected by high altitude often after a period of 2-3 days. The only solution is descent. Acute altitude sickness is quite rare if basic and sensible precautions are taken.

The maxim 'walking high, sleeping low' is worth remembering. You can go quite high and manage for short periods and all will be well if you camp much lower. The *Himalayan Rescue Association* has a good pamphlet on Mountain Sickness (try the Alpine Club or the British Mountaineering Association). Diamox and portable oxygen can help. The portable hyper-baric chamber bag, invented in 1989, which can replciate lower altitude pressure has saved many lives.

It is sensible to seek advice from experienced high altitude trekkers and climbers if you are going to high altitudes for the first time.

WARNING: A continued rapid ascent beyond the body's ability to adjust may ultimately induce a total breakdown in the acclimatisation process. This condition is potentially fatal. It can be prevented by understanding the causes and taking the necessary precautions. Do not climb more than 600m per day when above 2000m.

NB: It is essential to read **Altitude** under **Common problems** in **Health Information** section above on page 14.

● **Other health hints**

Take extra care to avoid sun burn and snow blindness. Take great care of your feet and have a dental check. Dehydration in cold dry air is a constant threat at altitude due to excessive exhaling and perspiring. Thirst is not a reliable indicator of your body's needs; drink as much as possible, preferably 3-4 litres per day.

Consult your doctor beforehand if you suffer from even a minor chronic problem. The heart is particularly vulnerable; anyone suffering from heart disease may be restricted to remaining below 3000m. Inexperienced trekkers may do well to attempt a hike/trek near home beforehand to check fitness and also get into shape.

Women Carry extra tampons or sanitary napkins as these are not easily available. High altitude can affect the menstrual cycle and cause irregular periods. It is advisable not to take oral contraceptives if spending any time above 4000m (13,000 ft). Because of potential blood clotting problems associated with the pill, it is best to discontinue taking it several weeks before going to altitude.

Trekking permits

Trekking is permitted in all areas other than those described as Restricted or Protected and within the "Inner Line" so that you may not go close to the international boundary in many places. Often, destinations falling within these "sensitive" zones which have recently been openened for trekking, require treks to be organised by an recognized Indian Travel Agent for groups (min 4, individual tourists not permitted) travelling on a specified route, accompanied by a representative/liason officer. Sometimes there are restrictions on the maximum number of days, season and type of transport used. Special exemptions apply in places: the 'Inner Line' runs parallel and 40 km inside the international boundary; Kaza (Himachal Pradesh), however, is now open to group trekkers though overnight stay is not allowed at Puh, Khabo, Sumdo, Dankar Gompa and Tabo. Other areas now open to tourists include Kalini Khal (Garhwal), Milam Glacier (Kumaon), Khardung La, Tso Morari and Pangong (Ladakh; the Manali-Leh road, already popular is being upgraded), Tsangu Lake, Lachung and Yumthang Sikkim) and Kameng Valley (Arunachal Pradesh).

Issuing authorities When applying for a Visa at an Indian Mission abroad, it is necessary to mention the States you intend to travel in; a trekking permit may considerably delay your application at this stage. On arrival in India, Govt approved trekking agencies can obtain permits relatively easily within 3/4 days usually.

Areas where individual trekking is permitted you do not need a permit. For restricted areas, permits are issued at the Foreigners' Regional Registration Offices in Delhi, Bombay, Calcutta and Madras (and sometimes at a local FRRO), from Immigration officers at points of entry and sometimes at the District Magistrates. The local Tourist Office will advise.

There are also entrance fees for the various National Parks and conservation areas

WARNING: Always carry your passport. There are regular trekking permit inspection points along most trails. Without one you can be turned back or, if in a restricted area, be deported.

Mountaineering courses

Information on mountaineering from *Indian Mountaineering Federation*, Benito Juarez Marg, New Delhi, T 671211. *The Mountaineering Institute and Allied Sports Complex* (T 42), 1.5 km out of Manali, organises courses in mountaineering, skiing, watersports, high altitude trekking and mountain-rescue courses. *Garhwal Mandal Vikas Nigam* (GMVN), Muni-ki-Reti, T 372, organises trekking, mountaineering and allied sports activities from Rishikesh. *Himalayan Mountaineering Institute*, Nehru Hill, Darjiling conducts the following courses (Mar-Dec): 28-day Basic and 32-day Advanced Mountaineering (incl acclimatisation, trekking up to 4500m, field training) and a 20-day Adventure courses (incl trekking, canoeing, rock climbing, available to foreigners); apply direct. *The Nehru Institute of Mountaineering*, Uttarkashi offers mountaineering courses (ask travel agents). *Indian Institute of Ski and Mountaineering*, Gulmarg, T 246.

Equipment and clothing

If you have good equipment, it is worth taking it. You are strongly advised to bring your own boots and these should be comfortable, especially in hot weather, and well worn in, blisters can ruin a trek. Mountaineering & trekking equipment can sometimes be hired from various hill stations. Ask the *Institutes of Mountaineering* and *Tourist Offices* there. Other sources are clubs, eg *Nainital Mountaineering Club*.

Clothes Waterproof jacket with hood and over-trousers (Gore-tex and similar makes that are windproof, waterproof and 'breather' are particularly good); warm sweater; woollen shirt or fibre-pile jacket. Good lightweight walking boots (light yet durable boots have replaced old-style heavy ones, insoles help); spare laces, Good running shoes (for resting the feet; also suitable for many low-level treks, except in snow and off the trails); polypropylene undersocks, heavy walking socks.

Track suit or lightweight wool trousers; Gore-tex overtrousers; walking shorts (villagers may be offended by women in brief shorts) ; skirt; cotton T shirts; gloves; cotton underwear; warm underwear (vests, longjohns, gloves, balaclavas in Polypropylene (or similar) light, warm with 'wicking' properties are best); woollen hat; sun hat; sunglasses (UV blocking), swimming costume. Also take an umbrella, a sleeping bag (plus liner), ground cloth, about 10m length of cord, a compass and binoculars and a day pack.

It is worth carrying fabrics that can be easily washed in cold water streams. It would be considered a kind gesture to offer clothes you can part with, to your porter.

Carry salt and insecticide spray against leeches during the rainy season. See also the **Checklist** at the end of this section.

Kit for independent trekkers A tent (in certain areas); kerosene stove and strong fuel container (suitable for high altitudes, kerosene is usually easy to find); water containers; nesting cooking pots (at least 2); enamel mug and spoon. Bags for provisions; local foods (grains, lentils, some fruit, vegetables and nuts, milk for boiling, eggs, oil) will be available along the trail. Sizeable towns and those popular with trekkers will stock milk powder, packet soups, packet noodles, chocolate bars and usually a limited variety of tinned foods. Carry freeze dried foods.

Maps and books

● Maps

For map distributors outside South Asia see page 155. In India: Survey of India has started producing trekking maps, Scale 1:250,000; a few only are available covering the Himachal and UP areas. Nest & Wings booklets (see **Books** below) offer suggestions of routes and include map/maps. See also **Maps** above on page 154.

● Books

The following is a short selection, several of which are available in India. Nest & Wings, Post Box 4531, New Delhi 110016, T 6442245 are updating their series of 'Trekking', 'Holiday & Trekking' and 'Trekking Map' titles (Rs 40-140) which cover most of the trekking destinations in the Indian Himalaya; trekking itineraries are listed in brief but some booklets give additional insight into the history and culture of the area. However, places en route are sometimes difficult to locate as the order is confused and an index is often missing.

Also useful are Himalayan Club's *Himalayan Journal* (annual) from PO Box 1905, Bombay 400001 and Indian Mountaineering Foundation's *Indian Mountaineer* (6-monthly) from Benito Juarez Rd, North Delhi 110021.

Ali, S. *Indian hill birds*, OUP.

Atkinson, E.T. *Religion in the Himalayas*, Delhi, Cosmos, 1974.

Chabloz, P. & Cremieu, N. *Hiking in Zanskar and Ladakh*, Geneva, Olizane, 1986.

Iozawa, T. *Trekking in the Himalayas*, Delhi, Allied Publishers, 1980.

Keay, J. *Where men and mountains meet*, London, Murray, 1977.

Khosla, G.D. *Himalayan circuit*, OUP, 1989.

Noble, C. *Over the high passes*, Collins, 1988.

Polunin, O. & Stanton, A. *Flowers of the Himalaya*, OUP, 1984.

Pommaret, F. & Imaeda, Y. *Bhutan*.

Randhawa, M.S. *Travels in the western Himalayas*, Delhi, Thomson, 1974.

Rizvi, J. *Ladakh*, OUP, 1983.

Singh, M. *Himalayan art*, Macmillan, 1968.

Swift, H. *Trekking in Pakistan and India*, London, Hodder & Stoughton, 1990.

Thukral, G. & E. *Garhwal Himalaya*, North Delhi, Frank Brothers, 1987.

Weare, G. *Trekking in the Indian Himalaya*, South Yarra (Australia), Lonely Planet, 1986.

See also **Further reading**, page 152.

HIMALAYAN ENVIRONMENT TRUST CODE OF PRACTICE

Campsite Leave it cleaner than you found it.

Deforestation Make no open fires and discourage others making one for you. Limit use of water heated by firewood (use of dead wood is permitted – available in Sikkim but scarce elsewhere). Choose accommodation where kerosene or fuel efficient wood stoves are used.

Litter Remove it. Burn or bury paper and carry away non-degradable litter. If you find other people's litter, remove their's too! Pack food in biodegradable containers. Carry away all batteries/ cells.

Water Keep local water clean. Do not use detergents and pollutants in streams and springs. Where there are no toilets be sure you are at least 30 m away from water source and bury or cover waste. Do not allow cooks or porters to throw rubbish in nearby streams and rivers.

Plants Do not take cuttings, seeds and roots – it is illegal in all parts of the Himalayas.

Giving to children, encourages begging. **Donations** to a project, health centre or school is more constructive.

Respect **local traditions and cultures**.

Respect **privacy** and ask permission before taking photographs.

Respect **holy places**. Never touch or remove religious objects. Remove shoes before entering temples.

Respect local **etiquette**. Dress modestly particularly when visiting temples and shrines and while walking through villages; loose, lightweight clothes are preferable to shorts, skimpy tops an tight-fitting outfits. Avoid holding hands and kissing in public.

Photography

The wealth of photographic opportunity justifies good equipment. The following are recommended:

A single reflex camera with interchangeable lenses: wide angle (28-35mm), telephoto (70-200), macro lense (for good close-ups).

Ultra violet and a polarising filter for high altitudes.

Plenty of film (a roll a day!) and extra batteries (they are affected by very low temperatures). Good quality print and transparency film can now be reliably bought from the more reputable photostores in Bombay, Delhi and sometimes even in places like Darjiling. **NB** Make sure it is well within the 'Sell by' date and the film has not been tampered with.

Waterproof covering for all equipment.

Refer to advice on photography on page 134.

Equipment suppliers

A selection: *YHA Adventure* shops including 174 Kensington High St, London W8 7RG, T 071 938 1911; *Blacks Camping and Leisure* shops incl 42-53 Rathbone Pl, London W1P 1AN, T 071 636 6645; *Nomad*, 3-4 Wellington Terrace, Turnpike Lane, London N8 0PX, T 081 889 7014; *Cotswold Camping* (shops in Betwys-y-Coed, Cirencester, London, Manchester, Reading, South Cerney and mail order from 42 Uxbridge Rd, London W12 8ND, T 081 743 2976); *Army Surplus* shops.

By Mail Order: *Field & Trek*, 3 Wates Way, Brentwood, Essex, CM15 9TB, T 0277 233122; *International Supplies Ltd*, Alpha Close, Garth Rd, Morden, Surrey, SM4 4LX, T 081 337 0161; *MASTA*, Keppel St, London WC1E 7HT, T 071 631 4408.

For mosquito nets: *Clothtec*, 92 Par Green, Par, Cornwall, PL24 2AG, T 0726 813602; *Oasis*, 1 High St, Stoke Ferry, Norfolk PE33 9SF, T 0366 501122.

INFORMATION FOR VISITORS

Contents

Before you go

Entry requirements

● Visas and permits

The Government of India has changed the rules regarding visas frequently over the last 3 years. They may change again, so it is essential to check details and costs. In mid 1994 the following visa rules applied:

Tourist visa 1 month validity. Entry must be within 1 month from date of issue, and it allows a stay of 1 month from the date of arrival. Fee £3.

Tourist visa up to 6 months validity. **NB** This is only valid for 6 months from the date of issue, not from the date of entry. Multiple entry. No extensions are allowed. Fee £16.

Business visa up to 1 year validity from the date of issue. Fee £32.

Business visa up to 2 year validity from the date of issue. Fee £63.

Visa up to 5 years validity (Indian origin only; proof must be shown). Fee £63.

Student visa up to 1 year validity from the date of issue. Fee £32. (Applications must be accompanied by letter of acceptance from Indian educational institution. Allow up to 3 months for approval.)

Applications must normally be accompanied by 3 passport photos. Some High Commissions, Embassies and Consulates will issue visas by post. Applications must be made on the prescribed form and the passport must be valid to cover the period of visit. Transit visas are issued to those passing through India en route to another country. Nationals of Bhutan and Nepal do not require a Visa – they only require a suitable means of identification. Arrangements for visa application and collection vary from office to office, and should be confirmed by phone with the relevant office. Tourists from countries which do not have Indian representatives may apply to resident British representatives, or enquire at the Air India Office.

Visa extensions

Applications should be made to the Foreigners' Regional Registration Offices at New Delhi, Bombay, Calcutta or Madras, or an office of the Superintendent of Police in the District Headquarters.

Restricted and protected areas

Parts of the country require special permits – **Arunachal Pradesh**, **Manipur**, **Mizoram**, **Nagaland** and **Sikkim**. For Sikkim, 7 day permits are issued to individuals wishing to visit Gangtok, Rumtak and Phodong, and organised groups trekking in Dzongri may enter for 15 days if sponsored by a recognised Indian travel agency. Applications to Under Secretary, Ministry of Home Affairs, Foreigners Division, Lok Nayak Bhavan, Khan Market, New Delhi 110003 at least 4 weeks in advance. Foreign visitors may apply to visit Imphal town in Manipur if they travel to and from Imphal by air.

Special permission is needed for **Assam**, **Meghalaya** and **Tripura**.

Andaman and Nicobar Islands Individuals may visit Port Blair, Jolly Buoy and Cinque Islands for up to 15 days, permission for which is available on arrival at Port Blair. Organised groups may also visit Snob, Red Skin, Grub and Boat Islands.

Lakshadweep Islands Individuals may visit Bangaram and Suheli Islands after obtaining a permit from the Lakshadweep Administration, Wellington Island, Harbour Rd, Cochin 3.

Registration No foreigners need to register within the 180 day period of their visa.

Income tax clearance All foreign visitors who stay in India for more than 180 days are required to get an income tax clearance exemption certificate from the Foreign Section of the Income Tax Dept in Delhi, Bombay, Calcutta or Madras.

Work permits All foreigners require work permits. Apply to the Indian representative in your country of origin.

Liquor permits Periodically some Indian states have tried to enforce prohibition. Permits are obtainable for foreigners.

● Vaccinations

Small-pox vaccination is no longer required. Neither is cholera vaccination, despite the fact that the disease is endemic in Bangladesh and can occur in India. Yellow fever vaccination is not required either, although you may be asked for a certificate if you have been in a country affected by yellow fever immediately before travelling to India. The following vaccinations are recommended:

Typhoid (monovalent): 1 dose followed by a booster in 1 month's time. Immunity from this course lasts 2-3 years. An oral preparation is currently being marketed in some countries.

Polio-myelitis: This is a live vaccine generally given orally and a full course consists of 3 doses with a booster in tropical regions every 3-5 years.

Tetanus: 1 dose should be given with a booster at 6 weeks and another at 6 months and 10 yearly boosters thereafter are recommended. Children should, in addition, be properly protected against diphtheria, whooping cough, mumps and measles. Teenage girls, if they have not had the disease, should be given rubella (German measles) vaccination. Consult your doctor for advice on BCG innoculation against tuberculosis; the disease is still common in the region.

Meningococcal Meningitis and Japanese B Encephalitis (JBE): Immunisation (effective in 10 days) gives protection for around 3 years. There is an extremely small risk, though it varies seasonally and from region to region. Consult a Travel Clinic such as British Airways or Thomas Cook, or MASTA (see below for details).

Hepatitis A: The new vaccine gives protection for 1 year after 2 injections (10 days to be effective) and 10 years if a 3rd is taken between 6-12 months. Alternatively, 1 gamma globulin injection to cover up to 6 months' travel is effective immediately. Regular travellers should have a blood test first to check whether they are already immune.

Rabies: Pre-exposure vaccination gives anyone bitten by a suspect animal time to get treatment (so particularly helpful to those visiting remote areas) and also prepares the body to produce antibodies quickly; cost of vaccine can be shared by 3 receiving vaccination together.

Malaria: Prophylactic tablets are strongly advised for visitors to affected countries but since a particular course of treatment is recommended to a specific part of the world (which can change in time) seek up-to-date advice from the Malaria Reference Laboratory, T 0891 600 350 (recorded message, premium rate) or the Liverpool School of Tropical Medicine, T 051 708 9393. In the USA, try Centre for Disease Control, Atlanta, T 404 332 4555.

● Representation overseas

In South Asia **Bangladesh**, House 120, Road 2, Dhanmondi RA, Dhaka-2, T 507670, Tx 642336. Consulates: Chittagong T 210291, Rajshahi T 3641; **Bhutan**, India House Estate, Thimpu, T 2162, Tx 211; **Maldives**, Mafabbu Aage 37, Orchid Magu, Male 20-02, T 323015, Tx 66044; **Nepal**, Lainchour, PO Box No 292, Kathmandu, T 410900, Tx 2449; **Pakistan**, 482-, Sector G-6/4, Islamabad, T 826718, Tx 5849. Consulate: Karachi T 522275; **Sri Lanka**, 36-38 Galle Road, Colombo 3, T 21605, Tx 21132. Consulate: Kandy T 22430.

Elsewhere **Australia**, 3-5 Moonah Place, Yarralumla, Canberra, T 733999, Tx AA-62362. Consulates: Sydney T 927055, Melbourne T 3503351; **Austria**, Kärntner Ring 2, A-1015 Vienna, T 50 58 666-669, F 50 59 219, Tx: 113 721; **Belgium**, 217-Chaussée de Vleurgat, 1050 Brussels, T 640 93 73, F 648 9638. Consulates: Ghent T 091/263423, Antwerp T (03) 234 1122; **Canada**, 10 Springfield Rd., Ottawa, Ontario K1M 1C9, T (613) 744-3751, Tx 053-4172. Consulates: Toronto T (416) 960-0751, Vancouver T (926-6080; **Denmark**, Vangehusvej 15, 2100 Copenhagen, T (01) 18288, Tx 15964; **Finland**, Satamakatu 2 A8, 00160 Helsinki-16, T 60 89 27, Tx 125202; **France**, 15 Rue Alfred Dehodencq, Paris, T 4520-3930, Tx 610621; **Germany**, Adenauerallee, 262/264, 5300 Bonn-1, T 54050, Tx 8869301. Consulates: Berlin T 881-7068, Frankfurt T 069-271040, Hamburg T 338036, Munich T 089-92562067, Stuttgart T 0711-297078; **Ireland**, 6 Lesson Park, Dublin 6, T 0001-970843, Tx 30670; **Italy**, Via XX Settembre 5, – 00187 Rome, T 464642, Tx 611274. Consulates: Milan T 02 869 0314, Genoa T 54891; **Japan**, 2-11, Kudan Minami 2-Chome, Chiyoda-ku, Tokyo 102, T (03) 262-2391, F (03) 234-4866, Tx 2324886. Consulate: Kobe T 078-241 8116; **Korea**, 37-3, Hannam-dong, Yongsan-Ku, Seoul, T 798-4257, F 796-9534, Tx 24641; **Malaysia**, 20th Floor Wisma Selangor Dredging, West Block, 142-C, Jalan Apang, 50450 Kuala Lumpur, T 03-261 7000, Tx 30317.

Netherlands (Consul), Buitenrustweg 2, The Hague (2517KD), T 070-46 97 71, Tx 33543; **New Zealand**, 10th floor, Princess Tower, 180 Molesworth Street, (PO Box 4045) Wellington, T 736 390/1, Tx NZ 31676; **Norway**, 30 Niels Jules Gate, 0272 Oslo-2, T 443194, Tx 78510; **Singapore**, India House, 31 Grange Road, Singapore 0923, T 7376777, Tx 25526; **Spain**, Avenida Pio XII 30-32, 28016 Madrid, T 457-02-09, Tx 22605. Consulate: Barcelona T 93/2120422; **Sweden**, Adolf Fredriks Kyrkogata 12, Box 1340, 11183 Stockholm, T 08-10 70 08, Tx 11598, F 08-24 85 05; **Switzerland**, 17 Weltpoststrasse 17, 3015 Berne, T 031-44 01 9, Tx 911829 INDE CH, F 26 26 87; **Thailand**, 46, Soi 23 (Prasarn Mitr) Sukhumvit 23, Bangkok 10110, T 2580300-6, Tx 82793; **UK**, India House, Aldwych, London WC2B 4NA, T 071-836 8484, Tx 267166, F 836 4331. Consulate: Birmingham, 82-86 New St, B2 4BA, T 643 0829; **USA**, 2107 Massachusetts Ave, Washington DC 20008, T (202) 939-7000, Tx 64333, F (202) 939-7027. Consulates: New Orleans T (504) 582 8105, New York T (212) 879-7800, San Francisco T (415) 668-0662, Chicago T (312) 781680, Cleveland T 216/696.

● Indian Tourist Offices

Indian Tourism Ministry of Tourism, Transport Bhavan, Parliament Street, T (11) 384111, Tx 312827, New Delhi 110001 India.

Overseas Australia, Level 5, 65 Elizabeth St, Sydney, NSW 2000, T (02) 232-1600, F (02) 223-3003; **Canada**, 60 Bloor Street, West Suite No 1003, Toronto, Ontario, T 416-962 3787, F 416-962 6279; **France**, 8 Boulevard de la Madeleine, 75009 Paris, T 42-65-83-86; **Germany**, 77 (III) Kaiserstrasse, D-6000 Frankfurt 1, T 235423, F 069-234724; **Italy**, Via Albricci 9, Milan 20122, T 804952; **Japan**, Pearl Building, 9-18 Chome Ginza, Chuo Ku, Tokyo 104, T (03) 571-5062; **The Netherlands**, Rokin 9-15, 1012 Amsterdam, T 020-208891; **UK**, 7 Cork Street, T 071-437 3677/8, F 071-494 1048, London W1X 2AB, UK; **USA**, 30 Rockefeller Plaza, Room 15, North Mezzazine, T (212) 586 4901/2/3, F (212) 582 3274, New York, NY 10020, USA.

When to go

● Best time to visit

In most of India by far the most pleasant time to visit is from the end of the monsoon in November to the beginning of April. However, there are important exceptions. The hill statioins in the Himalaya and the Nilgiris are beautiful in the hot weather months of April to early June, and the western Himalaya, including the Vale of Kashmir, can be excellent through to September. The *Handbook* gives temperatures and rainfall details for all regions and many cities, indicating the best times to visit.

Health

● Staying healthy

Travellers to India are often worried about becoming ill. However, providing you take basic precautions, you should be able to stay healthly. The main points are to eat and drink sensibly. You should not drink tap water which has not been sterilised.

● Medical services

Health and facilities are good in the main cities and details of doctors, chemists and hospitals are given town by town.

● Further health information

See **Vaccinations**, page 126 and read the main health section on page 13.

Money

● Currency

Indian currency is the Rupee. New notes are

printed in denominations of Rs 500, 100, 50, 20, 10, 5, 2, though some Rs 1 notes are still in circulation. The Rupee is divided into 100 Paise. Coins are minted in denominations of Rs 2, 1, 50, 25, 20, 10 and 5 Paise. It can be useful to keep a supply of small denomination notes.

● Credit cards

Major credit cards are increasingly acceptable in the major centres, though in smaller cities and towns it is still rare to be able to pay by credit card. Payment by credit card can sometimes be more expensive than payment by cash. However shopping by credit card for items such as handicrafts, clothing, and carpets from larger dealers does not mean that you have to accept the first price asked. Bargaining is still expected and essential. American Express cardholders can use their cards to obtain either cash or travellers' cheques in the major cities. They have offices in Coimbatore, Hyderabad, Pune, Ahmadabad, Baroda, Goa, Trivandrum and Guwahati. Diners, Master Card and Visa are widely used.

● Money changing

NB **Retain your encashment certificate**.

This gives proof of exchange through an authorised dealer. Some banks, including at Delhi airport, can be reluctant to give encashment certificates. Insist on it. It allows you to change Indian Rupees back to your own currency (you are not allowed to take any Rupees out of India). At airports do this before going through passport control – no exchange facilities 'airside'. It also enables you to use Rupees to pay hotel and other bills for which payment in foreign exchange is compulsory.

If you want cash on arrival it is best to get it at the airport bank. Many international flights arrive during night hours, and it is generally far easier and less time consuming to change money at the airport than at banks in the city. Banks often give a substantially better rate of exchange than hotels. Large hotels change money 24 hr a day.

Black market The decision to make the Rupee fully convertible has virtually ended the black market. Premiums are very small.

WARNING: Changing money through unauthorised dealers is illegal and may be risky.

● Travellers' cheques (TCs)

Most TCs are accepted without difficulty, but some organisations, like Indian Airlines, only accept TCs from the biggest companies. If you are travelling widely and off the beaten track it can be useful to have TCs from different companies, eg American Express and Thomas Cook. They nearly always have to be exchanged in banks or hotels, and can only very rarely be used directly for payment. Identification documents, usually a passport, need to be shown. Except in hotels, encashing TCs nearly always takes up to half an hour or longer, so it is worth taking larger denomination TCs and changing enough money to last for some days. Hotels will normally only cash TCs for resident guests, but the rate is often poorer than in banks. Most banks will accept sterling and other major currency TCs. Dollars are accepted nearly everywhere.

WARNING: If you use sterling always make certain that you have been given Rupees at the sterling rate and not the dollar rate.

NOTE: If you are travelling to remote areas it can be worth buying Indian Rupee TCs from a major bank. These are more widely accepted than foreign exchange TCs.

● Cost of living

Indian costs of living remain well below those in the industrialised world. Most food, accommodation, and public transport, especially rail and bus, are exceptionally cheap. Even the most expensive hotels and restaurants in the major cities are much less expensive than their counterparts in Europe, Japan or the United States. There is a widening range of moderately priced but clean hotels and restaurants outside the big cities, making it possible to get a great deal for your money.

What to take

Travellers tend to take more than they need though requirements vary with the destination and the type of travel that is to be undertaken. Laundry services are generally cheap and speedy. A travelpack, a hybrid backpack/suitcase, rather than a rigid suitcase, covers most eventualities and survives bus boot, roof rack and plane/ship hold travel with ease. Serious trekkers will need a framed backpack.

Light cotton clothes are useful almost anywhere in India at any time of year. It is a good idea to have some very lightweight long sleeve cottons and trousers for evenings, preferably light in colour, as they also give some protection against mosquitoes. Between Dec-Feb it can be cool at night even on the plains in North and East India, and at altitudes above 1500m right across India some woollens are essential.

Dress is rarely formal. In the large cities short-sleeved shirts and ties are often worn for business. For travelling loose clothes are most comfortable. Comfortable shoes with socks as feet may swell in hot weather. Modest dress for women including a sunhat and headscarf. It is worth shopping locally for cotton items which are very good value.

● **Checklist**:

Air cushions for hard seating
Bumbag
Contact lens cleaning equipment – not readily available in South Asia
Earplugs
Eye mask
Insect repellent and/or mosquito net, electric mosquito mats, coils
Neck pillow
International driving licence
Photocopies of essential documents
Short wave radio
Socks: take a thick pair for visiting temples and mosques
Spare passport photographs
Sun hat
Sun protection cream – factor 10 plus
Sunglasses
Swiss Army knife
Tissues/toilet paper
Torch and spare batteries
Umbrella (excellent protection from sun and unfriendly dogs)
Wipes (*Damp Ones* or equivalent)
Zip-lock bags

Those intending to stay in budget accommodation might also include:

Cotton sheet sleeping bag
Money belt
Padlock (for hotel room and pack)
Plastic sheet to protect against bed bugs on mattresses
Soap
Student card
Towel
Toilet paper
Universal bath plug

● **Health kit**:

Antiacid tablets
Anti-diarrhoea tablets
Anti-malaria tablets
Anti-infective ointment
Condoms
Contraceptives
Dusting powder for feet
First aid kit and disposable needles
Flea powder
Sachets of rehydration salts
Tampons
Travel sickness pills
Water sterilizing tablets

Getting there

Air

Most international flights arrive at Delhi, but there are also international airports at Bombay, Madras, Calcutta, Trivandrum, Tiruchirappalli and Goa. Some carriers permit "open-jaw" travel (arriving in, and departing from, different cities in India).

● **To Delhi**

From Europe The most direct flights are from London, Paris, Frankfurt, Rome, Geneva or Zurich. There are connections from all other European capitals. From **London**: approx time, London to Delhi or Bombay (non-stop): 9 hrs. British Airways and Air India have daily flights and Thai International 3 flights a week. Some East European, Central Asian and Middle Eastern airlines offer sharply discounted rates, but prices for all flights are highly seasonal. Christmas and July are the highest price periods into India.

From **Amsterdam**: KLM flies 3 times to Delhi. Gulf Air Summer schedule incl direct flights from Amsterdam to Delhi via Frankfurt, Bahrain and Muscat. From **Frankfurt**: Lufthansa 5 flights a week, Air India 6 and PIA 4. Lufthansa subsidiary Condor operate Charters during season, incl hotels, transfers, sightseeing. Min stay 7 days. From **Moscow**: Air India flies 3 times a week and Aeroflot 4 times. From **Paris**: Air France has 4 flights a week and Air India 5. From **Rome**: with Alitalia and Air India, both twice a week. Swissair flights leave **Zurich** 3 times a week and there are 2 from **Geneva** with Air India.

From the USA and Canada Approx Time from **New York**: 17 hrs. Air India flies 4 times a week from New York and twice a week from **Toronto**.

From Australasia You can fly to Delhi from **Sydney** via Singapore with Singapore Airlines. KLM once a week or Air India twice from **Singapore**.

From the Far East Air India flights from **Tokyo** 3 times a week, Alitalia twice and Japan Airlines once. From **Singapore**: (approx 5 hrs), Singapore Airlines has 3 flights a week, Aeroflot and Air India 2 and Turkish Airlines one. KLM flies twice a week from **Jakarta** and there are 2 flights a week each from **Kuala Lumpur** with Malaysian Airlines and Air India. **Hong Kong** has Air India flights twice a week, British Airways 5 times, Air France twice and Alitalia once. You can fly from **Bangkok** (approx 4 hr) with Thai International 5 times a week, Air India 4 times, Air France twice and Japan Airlines once.

From the Middle East Gulf Air has 5 flights a week from **Bahrain**.

NB: If you are in **transit in Delhi**, do not go through Green Channel since you are not allowed back in until 4 hr before departure. There are no facilities for refreshments immediately outside. Airport Manager's office has a Freephone to airlines' offices. Airport dormitories (Rs 55) are clean, with lockers, showers and fans. Transit passsengers connecting within 2 hr may now check in at the "transfer desk".

● **To Bombay**

From Europe There is a very wide choice of flights. **Paris** with Air India 4 times and Air France 3 times a week. **Amsterdam** with Biman Bangladesh Airlines weekly and KLM 3 times a week. **London Heathrow** with British Airways 5 times a week, Singapore Airlines twice and Air India daily. **Frankfurt** (with connections from San Francisco) with PIA 3 times a week, Lufthansa 5 times, Air India 6 times. **Rome** with Alitalia and Air India both twice a week. **Geneva** with Air India twice a week and **Zurich** with Swissair, 4 flights a week.

From USA and Canada From **New York** (JFK): daily flights with Air India and 3 with PIA. PIA also has 6 flights a week from LA via JFK and 3 from **San Francisco** via Frankfurt. Air India has twice weekly flights from **Toronto**.

From Australasia Qantas flies 5 days a week (from **Sydney, Melbourne, Perth, Brisbane** and **Cairns**) via Singapore in partnership with Singapore Airlines and Air India.

From the Far East Many flights on all main routes. From **Tokyo**: Air India flies 4 times a week. From **Singapore**: Singapore Airlines has 3 flights a week, Air India 6 and Turkish Airlines one. There are weekly flights from **Jakarta** with Swissair and from **Kuala Lumpur** with Air India and CSA. From **Hong Kong**: Cathay Pacific flies 4 times a week, Air India, Air France and British Airways twice, and Swissair 3 times. From **Bangkok**: Air India and Cathay Pacific have 4 flights a week, and Air France 3.

From the Middle East Gulf Air has daily flights from **Bahrain**, Air India 2 a week and Kuwait Airways 3.

● **To Calcutta**

From Europe There are connections via Bombay, Amman, Delhi, Frankfurt and Dhaka and Amsterdam. There is a weekly Aeroflot flight from **Moscow**.

From USA and Canada Passengers should travel via Europe.

From Australasia and the Far East Thai International flies via Bangkok to Calcutta on several routes: **Sydney** twice a week, **Jakarta, Kuala Lumpur** and **Hong Kong** 3 times. Also from **Hong Kong**: Cathay Pacific has 6 flights a week via Bangkok. From **Bangkok**: there are direct flights with Indian Airlines and Alisarda 3 times a week and Air India once. **Singapore** has a twice weekly connection with Singapore Airlines and there is a weekly Air India flight from **Tokyo**.

From the Middle East there is a weekly flight from **Bahrain** via Dhaka with Biman Bangladesh Airlines.

● To Madras

From Europe Various flights are available. From **Paris** with Air India once a week. **London Heathrow** has a weekly direct flight with Air India and 2 a week with British Airways with connections from **Oslo, Helsinki, San Francisco** and **New York** (JFK).

From USA and Canada Travel via Europe.

From Australasia Travel via Singapore or Bangkok or with Malaysian Airlines have a twice weekly connection from **Sydney** via Kuala Lumpur.

From the Far East Fights from **Singapore** with Air India 6 times a week and with Singapore Airlines 3 times. From Kuala Lumpur: flights with Air India twice a week, Malaysian Airlines 6 times and British Airways twice. Malaysian Airlines have flights which connect with their Kuala Lumpur-Madras route from **Jakarta** twice a week and from **Bangkok** 5 times.

NB: Airline schedules change frequently, so it is essential to check with a travel agent before making travel arrangements.

● Discounts

It is possible to obtain significant discounts, especially outside European holiday times, most notably from London, even on non-stop flights. Shop around and book early. It is also possible to get discounts from Australasia, South-East Asia and Japan. Mid-July to mid-August is the peak season and most expensive. Some Middle Eastern, Central European and Central Asian airlines offer highly discounted fares.

● Group tickets

Groups of 10 or more can obtain tickets to visit the member countries of the South Asian Association of Regional Co-operation (SAARC). Therefore if you plan to visit 2 or more South Asian countries in 3 weeks or less you may obtain discounts of 30% on your full-fare international tickets. Information is available through the National Tourist offices.

● Stop-overs and round the world tickets

You can arrange several stop-overs in South Asia on round the world and other longer distance tickets. RTW tickets allow you to fly in to Delhi and out from another international airport such as Bombay, Madras, Calcutta or Kathmandu. Different travel agents organise different deals. Trailfinders of London, one of the world's biggest agencies, has a range of discounted deals. Contact at 194 Kensington High St, London W8 7RG, T 071 938 3939. Competitive rates are quoted by Campus Travel and STA in many towns.

● Airline security

International airlines vary in their arrangements and requirements for security, in particular the carrying of equipment like radios, tape-recorders, lap top computers and batteries. It is advisable to ring the airline in advance to confirm what their current regulations are. **Note that internal airlines often have different rules from the international carriers.** You are strongly advised not to pack valuables in your luggage (reports of vandalised cases and theft, particularly on Air India) and avoid having to repack at the airport.

Indian Airlines fly to Pakistan, Nepal, Bangladesh, Sri Lanka and the Maldives. Flights operated by **PIA, Royal Nepal Airlines, Druk Air**, Bangladesh **Biman** and **Air Lanka** link India with Pakistan, Nepal, Bhutan, Bangladesh and Sri Lanka and the Maldives respectively.

It is also possible to get good air travel arrangements for some internal flights using international carriers. Air India flights to Delhi or Bombay can be extended to include Madras, Goa and Calcutta for example for considerably less than the tickets bought individually on Indian Airlines. Such arrangements must be made in advance.

International air tickets can be bought in India. At the time of writing payment must be made in foreign exchange, but this rule may be relaxed. Check to see if you are eligible for a discount, which are available on some routes.

Train

● From Pakistan

The only train crossing is from Lahore to Amritsar via the Wagha border post. Timing is subject to political relations between India and Pakistan. A daily service normally operates leaving Lahore at 0900, arriving in Amritsar by 1600.

Road

● Land border crossings

Between India and its neighbours are subject to the political relationships between them. Several border crossings between India and Nepal and India and Bangladesh are open periodically, but permission to cross cannot be guaranteed. Those listed below are the main crossings which are normally open throughout the year to tourists.

● From Pakistan

The Wagha border is the only crossing open. Minibuses and taxis go from central Lahore (railway station) to the border. You walk across through Pakistani and Indian immigration and customs. Porters are always available to carry luggage. Taxis and minibuses are available on the Indian side to go to Amritsar.

● From Nepal

Three crossings are in common use. In London enquire from the Nepal Embassy on T 071 229 1594/229 6231, F 229 9861.

Sonauli-Bhairawa This is the shortest and fastest route from New Delhi and Varanasi. The best route by train to/from New Delhi is via Gorakhpur. See page 273.

To/from Varanasi, it is possible to travel via Bhairawa 6 km inside the Nepal border, and Nautanwa or Sonauli on the Indian border, $3\frac{1}{2}$ hrs from Varanasi. See page 296.

The border crossing at **Pharenda** is shorter than the route via Sonauli, but the road may be closed.

Raxaul-Birganj This crossing is used by travellers between Patna, Bihar (with its Buddhist and Jain sites) and Nepal. Several buses run daily between Patna and Raxaul, (5-7 hrs). However, timings are difficult and the buses are crowded and uncomfortable. Night buses from Patna reach the border in early morning; morning buses from Patna connect with the night bus to Kathmandu. Either way you have to have at least 1 night bus journey unless you stay at Birganj or Raxaul which is not recommended. The bus journey between Kathmandu or Pokhara and the border takes about 11-12 hrs. Even Express buses are slow and packed. 'Tourist' Minibuses are the only moderately comfortable option. For details see **Patna**, page 770.

Kakarbhitta, a border town lacks suitable accommodation. This crossing is convenient for those travelling between Kathmandu and Darjiling/Siliguri. For details see under **Darjiling**, page 660.

● From Bangladesh

Bangaon-Benapol The most commonly used crossing, and most reliably open, is the Bangaon-Benapol border between Calcutta and Jessore (37 km beyond the border). The road follows the broad gauge railway line which originally went from Calcutta to Jessore. Buses and minibuses are available from Bangaon railway station to the border. On the Bangladesh side rickshaws are available for the 1 km distance to Benapol. Buses also run from Calcutta.

WARNING: Regulations about the land crossing are subject to change. It is essential to enquire in Calcutta or Dhaka before making the land crossing. Arrive at the border before 1500, as crossing often takes time. In mid-1994 crosings between NE India and Bangladesh were closed to tourists and the crossing from Siliguri to Bangladesh only open periodically. In London enquire from Bangladesh High Commission, T 071 584 0081, F 225 2130.

● From Bhutan

The road from Bagdogra (the nearest Indian airport) enters Bhutan at Phuntsholing, the border town. It is a 3-4 hr drive from Bagdogra airport; from Darjiling or Gangtok, it can take 7 hr to the border and another 6 hr to Thimphu (or Paro).

Sea

No regular passenger liners operate to India. Round the world cruise ships do stop at some South Asian ports like Bombay, Marmagao, Cochin, Madras, and Colombo. The main shipping lines operating such cruises are American President Lines, British India, Cunard, Holland Line of America, McKinnon & McKenzie, Salen Linblad Cruising, Costa Cruises, Hapag Lloyd, the Royal Cruise Line, Mitsui O.S.K. Line, Royal Viking Line, Black Sea Shipping Co. and Far Eastern Shipping Co.

● From Sri Lanka and Maldives

It is very unusual for foreign tourists to arrive by sea but shipping agents in Colombo, Sri Lanka or Male, Maldives may allow passengers on their cargo boats to Tuticorin in Tamil Nadu.

Customs

● Duty free allowance
Tourists are allowed to bring in all personal effects "which may reasonably be required" without charge. The official customs allowance includes 200 cigarettes or 50 cigars, 0.95 litres of alcohol, a camera with 5 rolls of film, a pair of binoculars. Valuable personal effects or professional equipment must be registered on a Tourist Baggage Re-Export Form (TBRE), including jewellery, special camera equipment and lenses, lap top computers, sound and video recorders. These forms require the serial numbers of such equipment. It saves considerable frustration if you know the numbers in advance and are ready to show the serial numbers on the equipment. In addition to the forms, details of imported equipment may be entered into your passport. **It is essential to keep these forms** for showing to the customs when leaving India, otherwise considerable delays are very likely at the time of departure.

● Duty free shopping
Delhi and Bombay airports have new and competitive duty free shops.

● Currency regulations
There are no restrictions on the amount of foreign currency or travellers' cheques a tourist may bring into India. If you are carrying more than US$ 10,000 or its equivalent in cash or travellers' cheques in 1994 you had to fill in a currency declaration form. This could change with a relaxation in the currency regulations.

● Prohibited items
The import of dangerous drugs, live plants, gold coins, gold and silver bullion and silver coins not in current use are either banned or subject to strict regulation. It is illegal to import firearms into India without special permission. Enquire at Consular offices abroad for details.

● Export restrictions
Export of gold jewellery purchased in India is allowed up to a value of Rs 2000 and other jewellery (including settings with precious stones) up to a value of Rs 10,000.

WARNING: Export of antiquities and art objects over 100 years old is restricted. Skins of all animals, snakes and articles made from them are banned. You may, however, take out an article made of a reasonable quantity of peacock feathers.

When you arrive

● Arrival and departure
Arrival The formalities on arrival in India have been increasingly streamlined during the last 5 years and the physical facilities at the major international airports greatly improved. However, arrival can still be a slow and confusing process. Disembarkation cards, with an attached customs declaration, are handed out to passengers during the inward flight. The immigration form should be handed in at the immigration counter on arrival. The customs slip will be returned, for handing over to the customs on leaving the baggage collection hall. Transit passengers, see note under 'To Delhi' above.

NB: Pre-paid taxis to the city are available at all major airports. Some airports have up to 3 categories of pre-paid service, "limousine", "luxury" and ordinary. The first 2 are usually much more prominent than the ordinary taxi service, so you may have to insist if you want to use the standard service.

WARNING: Do not take advice from unofficial "Tourist Offices" at airports.

Departure Tax Rs 300 is payable for all international departures in mid-1994. This must be paid in Rupees: it is worth setting the amount aside for when you leave.

● Begging
The number of beggars on the streets of the larger cities of India, some of whom may be badly physically handicapped, can be very distressing. It is best to give any donations to an organisation rather than to individuals. A coin to one child or a destitute woman on the street will make you the focus of demanding attention from a vast number before long. There are also networks of beggar rings that operate in various cities which are run on a business scale. Some people find it appropriate to give food to beggars rather than money.

Young children sometimes offer to do 'jobs' such as call a taxi, carry shopping, clean your shoes (apart from shoe-shine boys), or pose for a photo. You may want to give a small coin in exchange.

● Conduct
Courtesy and appearance Cleanliness and modesty are appreciated even in informal situations. Nudity is not permitted on beaches in India, and although there are some places where this ban is ignored, it causes widespread

offence. Displays of intimacy are not considered suitable in public and will probably draw unwanted attention. Unaccompanied women may find problems of harrassment, though this is rare.

Great warmth and hospitality will be experienced by most travellers, but with it comes an open curiosity about personal matters. You should not be surprised by total strangers on a train, for example, asking details of your job, income and family circumstances. Outside Westernised circles, Indian women are shy and may appear to be ignored, although they perform a vital social and economic role in many areas.

Religious sites Visitors to **Hindu** temples should observe customary courtesy especially in clothing. Shoes must always be removed outside (and leather items in Jain temples), take thick socks for protection when walking on sun-baked stone floors. Non-Hindus are sometimes not permitted into the inner sanctum of Hindu temples and occasionally even into the temple itself. Look for signs or ask. Donations if desired should not be handed to priests or monks since they may be forbidden to touch money but should be left in a bowl or plate provided. It is also not customary to shake hands with a priest or monk.

Special rules apply to visiting **Buddhist** shrines. Walk on the left of shrines and stupas. Also walk on the left hand side inside monasteries. Buddhist monasteries are open to all. You may even visit the resident lama (priest). If you wish to make a contribution, put money in the donation box. It will be used for the upkeep of the temple or monastery.

In **Sikh** gurudwaras, everyone should cover their heads (even if it is with a handkerchief). **Muslim** mosques may be closed to non-Muslims shortly before prayers. In mosques women should be covered from head to ankle.

Social behaviour Use your right hand for giving, taking, eating or shaking hands as the left is considered to be unclean. Women do not shake hands with men as this form of contact is not traditionally acceptable between acquaintances. Do not photograph women without permission.

The greeting when meeting or parting used universally among the Hindus across India is the palms joined together as in prayer, sometimes accompanied with the word *Namaste* (N and W) *Namoshkar* (E) and *Vanakkam* (Tamil Nadu), translated as 'I salute all divine qualities in you.' "Thank you" is often expressed by a smile and occasionally with the somewhat formal *Dhannyabad* or *Shukriya* (N and W), *Dhonnyobad* (E) and *nandri* (S).

● Electricity

220-240 volts AC. Some top hotels have transformers to enable visitors to use their appliances. There may be pronounced variations in the voltage, and power cuts are common. Socket sizes vary so you are advised to take a universal adaptor (available at airports).

● Hours of business

Banks 1000-1400, Mon-Fri; 1000-1230, Sat. Top hotels sometimes have 24 hr service.

Post Offices 1000-1700, Mon-Fri; Sat mornings.

Government offices 0930-1700, Mon-Fri; 0930-1300, Sat (some open on alternate Sat only).

Shops 0930-1800, Mon-Sat. Bazars keep longer hours.

NB: There are regional variations.

● Official time

GMT + $5\frac{1}{2}$ hr. Conception of "time" is different in South Asia, being rather vague. Unpunctuality can therefore be frustrating so patience is needed.

● Photography

It is advisable to take rolls of films and batteries although they are available at major tourist centres. There are strict restrictions on photography of airports, military installations, bridges, tribal areas and 'sensitive border areas' and it is often necessary to obtain permits at sites on payment of a fee in addition to the entrance charge. Bhutan is especially strict – no 16 mm film is allowed and tourist permits are needed to enter and visit temples etc. Many monuments now charge a camera fee, with higher fees for video use. Charges range from approximately Re 1 to Rs 10 for still cameras, and may be as high as Rs 500 for video cameras. A much higher charge may be levied at wildlife sanctuaries. Special permits are needed from the Archaeological Survey of India for photographing monuments with the use of tripods and artificial lights. Photo **films**: only buy from a reputable shop. Hawkers and roadside stalls may pass off used film as new.

● Police

Even after taking all reasonable precautions

people do have valuables stolen. This can cause great inconvenience. You can minimise this by keeping a record of vital documents, including your passport number and travellers' cheque numbers in a completely separate place from the documents themselves. If you have items stolen, they should be reported to the police as soon as possible. Larger hotels will be able to assist in contacting and dealing with the police.

WARNING: Dealings with the police can be very difficult and in the worst regions even dangerous. The paper work involved in reporting losses can be time consuming and irritating, and your own documentation (e.g. passport and visas) may be demanded. In some states the police themselves sometimes demand bribes, though tourists should not assume, however, that if procedures move slowly they are automatically being expected to offer a bribe. If you have to go to a police station if possible take someone with you. If you face really serious problems, for example in connection with driving accidents, you should contact your consular offices as quickly as possible.

● Safety

Confidence tricksters These are particularly common where people are on the move, notably around railway stations. A common plea is some sudden and desperate calamity. Sometimes a letter will be produced in English to back up the claim. The demands are likely to increase sharply if sympathy is shown. Forewarned may be fore-armed. It is also essential to take care that credit cards are not run off more than once when making a purchase. Gems offered for sale on the street or by some traders are often fake.

Personal security In general the threats to personal security for travellers in India are remarkably small. In most areas it is possible to travel either individually or in groups without any risk of personal violence. However, care is necessary in some places, and basic common sense needs to be used with respect to looking after valuables.

Some parts of India are subject to political violence. In Punjab, Kashmir and Assam, politically motivated violence occurred in the early 1990s. Punjab was quiet again by 1993 and life had returned largely to normal. Access to Kashmir was possible though potentially dangerous, and parts of the Indian NE were still closed. North and North-East Sri Lanka have been suffering civil war for over a decade, though the rest of the island was largely open to visitors.

NB: It is often better to seek advice on security from your own consulate than from travel agencies or national tourist organisations.

Some areas in India have long been noted for banditry. In the great majority of areas visited by tourists, however, violent crime and personal attacks are extremely rare. Goa is becoming an exception to this rule, where incidents of petty theft and violence directed specifically at tourists have been on the increase, and the police have also been involved in extorting money from tourists. Specific dangers are discussed in the relevant sections.

Theft is not uncommon. It is essential to take good care of personal valuables both when you are carrying them, and when you have to leave them in hotels or other places. **You cannot regard hotel rooms as automatically safe.** It is wise to use hotel safes for valuable items, though even they cannot guarantee security. It is best to keep travellers' cheques and passports with you at all times. Money belts **worn under clothing** are one of the safest options. It can be difficult to protect your valuables if travelling alone by train. 1st class a/c and 1st class compartments are self-contained and normally completely secure, although nothing of value should be left close to open train windows. Two tier a/c compartments in India, which have much to recommend them, are larger, allowing more movement of passengers. Attendants are always present in each carriage, and personal security is not at risk, but it is necessary to keep close care of personal possessions.

WARNING: Travelling bags and cases should be made of tough material, if possible not easily cut, and external pockets (both on bags and on clothing) should never be used for carrying either money or important documents. Strong locks for travelling cases are invaluable. Extra security can be obtained from surrounding conventional cases with a leather strap. Pickpockets and other thieves do operate in the big cities. Crowded areas are particularly high risk, and it is impossible to travel far on railways without being in crowded areas from time to time. Keep valuables as close to the body as possible. Women may prefer to make use of compartments which are reserved for women.

● **Shopping**

Bazars (the local markets), are often a great experience, but you must be prepared to bargain. It pays to first look around. Street hawkers often pass off fake marble, ivory, silver, semi-precious stones, coral etc as real. Taxi drivers and couriers sometimes insist on recommending certain shops where they expect a commission and prices are likely to be inflated. Export of certain items such as antiquities, ivory, furs and skins is controlled or banned, so it is essential to get a certificate of legitimate sale and permission for export. You can get excellent examples of the handicrafts of different states from the government handicrafts emporia in the major cities. These are listed under the shopping sections. The official emporiums are generally the safest bet for guaranteed quality at reasonable prices. There is no bargaining. In private shops and markets bargaining is normally essential and you can get excellent material at bargain prices.

Some shops offer to pack and post your purchases. Many small private shops cannot be trusted. Unless you have a specific recommendation from a person you know well, only make such arrangements in Government emporia.

NB See departure regulations above for items that are prohibited for export.

WARNING We have had several letters from women travellers complaining of being molested while being measured for clothing in tailors shops, especially in northern India. If possible be accompanied by a friend when having a fitting.

● **Tipping**

In the largest hotels a tip of Rs 5 per piece of luggage carried would be appropriate. In restaurants 5% or rounding off the bill with small change is completely acceptable. Indians do not tip taxi drivers. Tour companies sometimes make recommendations for 'suitable tips' for coach drivers and guides. Some of the figures may seem modest by non-Indian standards but are very inflated if compared with normal Indian earnings. Some group companies recommend a tip of Rs 50 per day for drivers and guides. This can safely be regarded as generous, though some will try to persuade you otherwise.

The more expensive hotels and restaurants frequently add a service charge to the bill. Otherwise 10% is the usual amount to leave in expensive hotels, less elsewhere. Taxi drivers do not expect to be tipped but a small extra amount over the fare is welcomed and particularly if a large amount of luggage is being carried. Porters at airports and railway stations often have a fixed rate displayed but will usually press for more. Ask fellow passengers what the fair rate is – they will nearly always advise.

When shopping outside Government emporia and the biggest hotels, expect to bargain hard.

● **Weights and measures**

India now uses the metric system for weights and measures. It has come into universal use in the cities. In remote rural areas local measures are sometimes used. The more common are listed in the glossary at the end of the Handbook, where a conversion table is also provided.

Where to stay

● **Hotels**

There is a very wide range of accommodation. You can stay safely and very cheaply by western standards right across India. In all the major cities there are also high quality hotels, offering a full range of personal and business facilities, though some find their food bland and uninspired. In small centres even the best hotels are far more variable. In the peak season (Oct to Apr for most of India) bookings can be extremely heavy. It is therefore desirable to reserve bookings well in advance if you are making your own arrangements, or to arrive reasonably early in the day. If you travel out from the major centres it will often be necessary to accept much more modest accommodation.

In Rajasthan, old maharajas' palaces have been privately converted into comfortable, unusual hotels. Hotels in beach resorts and hill-stations, because of their location and special appeal, often deviate from the description of the different categories given below. The Indian Tourism Development Corporation (ITDC) with the 'Ashok' chain, and State Tourism Development Corporations, also run a number of hotels throughout the country, often located in places of special interest. These are usually reasonably priced, though restaurant service is often slow and menus may be limited in the modest ones.

Budget hotels A special feature of the *India Handbook 1995* is the budget category of hotels. Many hotels in the **F** category have rooms for Rs 50 and under and sometimes have dormitory beds for Rs 20 or less. These are always very basic, but can be clean and excellent value. Dormitories may sometimes be quite small, having as few as 4 to 6 beds. Some more expensive hotels have rooms in this price range, so if you are looking for good really cheap accommodation, start here!

Prices for luxury hotels are sometimes comparable with the West. Hotels which charge more than Rs 1200 a night per single room have to levy up to 35% extra in taxes. Many try to evade this law by advertising double rooms which cost up to Rs2400 as if they were 2 singles. This is just one of the irritations of some middle and upper range hotels. Another is that many also have different rates for Indians and non-Indian guests, foreigners having to pay the "dollar rate". This may be as much

HOTEL CLASSIFICATIONS

The first 6 categories used in this Handbook are based on prices of the best double rooms, as at mid-1994. They are **not** star ratings, and individual facilities vary considerably. Normally the following facilities will be found as standard in the given classes.

In late 1994 most **AL** and some **A** category hotels charged all foreigners, except those working in India, a 'dollar price'. This is between 30% and 100% more than the 'rupee price'. This policy may change in the next 12 months.

AL Rs 3000+ – International class luxury hotels, usually found only in the regional capitals and the largest cities. All facilities for business and leisure travellers to the highest international standard.

A Rs 2000-3000 – International class. Central a/c, rooms with attached baths, telephone and TV with video channel, a business centre, multicuisine restaurants, bar, and all the usual facilities including 24 hr room service, shopping arcade, exchange, laundry, travel counter, swimming pool and often other sports such as tennis and squash. Accept credit cards. They often have hairdresser, beauty parlour and a health club.

B Rs 1200-2000 – Most of the facilities of **A** but perhaps not business centre, swimming pool and sports and lacking the feeling of luxury.

C Rs 600-1200 – Often the best hotels available in medium and small towns, but not always the best value. The entrance and reception areas is usually more 'grand' than **D** and **E** price hotels, but the quality of the rooms is often no better despite the higher price. However, they often serve excellent value meals. Usually central a/c, comfortable, with restaurant, exchange facilities, travel agent, shops and swimming pool.

D Rs 250-600 – Many hotels in this category will have a range of rooms, some at the bottom of the price range and a few at the top, sometimes a/c rooms with bath attached. Most have TV as standard. Restaurant and rm service normally available. Most medium to large towns will have at least 1 hotel in this category.

Budget hotels – **NB** Many hotels which charge up to Rs 250 per night for a double room also have much cheaper accommodation.

E Rs 100-250 – Simple rm with fan (occasionally a/c), shower or bucket 'bath'. May have shared toilet facilities. Limited rm service may include meals brought in when no restaurant available. At the lower end of this scale, some may not provide sheets, pillow cases and towels.

F Below Rs 100 – Very basic, usually with shared toilet facilities (often "squat"), but sometimes very good value, especially in South India. May be in noisy or remote locations. Very variable cleanliness and hygiene. These often have rooms for under Rs 50 and dormitory beds for under Rs 20.

as 50% more than the Rupee rate charged to Indians.

There are some excellent value hotels in the cheaper categories, though quality and cleanliness vary much more. The price for each category is a guide to what you would pay for the best standard double room, remembering that taxes vary widely from state to state and can sometimes add considerably to the basic price: see **Surcharges** below.

Prices away from large cities tend to be lower for the comparable standard of hotel and you will notice that, particularly in South India, you will often find a comfortable hotel in the **D** category and certainly clean, adequate rooms in the **E**. **C** grade hotels are often overpriced in terms of room quality, but some have excellent value meals. Restaurants in modest (**D**, **E**, **F**) hotels in certain parts of the country, especially in the S and W, may only offer vegetarian food.

Off-season rates Large reductions are made by hotels in all categories during the offseason in many resort centres. Always ask if any is available.

WARNING: Many visitors complain of **incorrect hotel bills**, even in the most expensive hotels. The problem particularly afflicts visitors who are part of groups, when last minute extras sometimes appear mysteriously on some guests' bills. **Check the evening before departure, and keep all receipts. It is essential to check carefully again when paying your bill**.

Surcharges Sales Tax and Luxury Tax are applicable, though they vary from state to state. The government has been changing tax and foreign exchange rules which could affect hotel rates.

Short term stays For people travelling off the beaten track there are several cheap options for short stay or temporary accommodation. Railway stations often have 'Retiring Rooms' or 'Rest Rooms'. These may be hired for periods of between 1 and 24 hrs by anyone holding a train ticket. They are cheap, usually provide a bed and a fan, and some have a couple of a/c rooms, but they are often very heavily booked. They can be extremely convenient for short stops if travelling extensively by train.

In many areas outside the biggest cities there are government guest houses, ranging from ***dak bungalows*** to ***circuit houses***. The latter are now reserved almost exclusively for travelling government officers, but dak and travellers' bungalows are sometimes available for overnight stays. Usually extremely basic, for example rarely having a cook or kitchen facilities, they can be attractive places to stay. Travelling officials always take precedence, even over booked guests.

Indian style hotels New-style hotels for Indian businessmen are springing up fast in or on the outskirts of many small and medium sized towns. They will often have individual air-conditioning, showers rather than baths and 'squat' toilets. They are more variable in quality than hotels run by the major hotel chains, but it is increasingly possible to find excellent value accommodation even in remote areas.

WARNING: You have to be prepared for difficulties which are uncommon in Europe, America or Australasia. In some states power cuts are common, or tap water may be restricted to certain times of day. The largest hotels have their own generators but it is advisable to have a good torch.

Unmarried people sharing hotel rooms usually causes no difficulties. **NB** Some cheaper hotels in India attracting tourists do not allow Indian guests (to avoid "unwanted harrassment").

Air-conditioning Only the larger hotels have central a/c. Elsewhere a/c rooms are cooled by individual units and occasionally large "air-coolers". These can be noisy and unreliable. When they fail to operate tell the management as it is often possible to get a rapid repair, or to transfer to a room where the unit is working. Fans are provided in all but the cheapest of hotels.

Toilet facilities Apart from the **AL** and **A** categories, 'baths' do not necessarily refer to bathrooms with Western bathtubs. Other hotels may provide a bathroom with a toilet, basin and a shower. In the lower priced hotels and outside large towns, a bucket and tap may replace the shower, and an Indian 'squat' toilet instead of a Western WC. During the cold weather and in hill stations, hot water will be available at certain times during the day, sometimes in buckets. Even medium sized hotels which are clean and pleasant do not always provide towels, soap and toilet paper.

Water supply In some regions water supply is rationed periodically. Water from the taps should never be regarded as safe to drink. The biggest hotels will supply boiled water. Bottled mineral water is now widely available (check seal when buying) although not all bottled water is mineral water. Some is simply purified water from an urban supply. It is safe unless the seal is broken. See page 16, under **Health**. Always take plenty with you when travelling.

Noise In cities is difficult to avoid, so if you are in a non-a/c room, be prepared for it. People wake up early in India, and temple and bazar loudspeakers often play very loud music!

Insects The odd mosquito may penetrate even the best hotels. In cheap hotels you need to be prepared for a wider range of insect life, including flies, cockroaches, spiders, ants, and harmless house lizards. Poisonous insects, including scorpions, are extremely rare in towns. Hotel managements are nearly always prepared with insecticide sprays, and will come and spray rooms if asked. It is worth taking your own repellent creams if you are travelling to places off the main hotel routes. Remember to shut windows and doors after dusk. Electrical devices, used with insecticide pellets, are now widely available. Many small hotels in mosquito-prone areas have mosquito nets. Dusk and early evening are the worst times for mosquitoes. Trousers and long-sleeved shirts are advisable, especially out of doors.

● Camping

Some states, notably Maharashtra, are beginning to provide new camping facilities. Regional tourist offices have details of new developments. For information on YMCA camping facilities contact: **YMCA**, The National General Secretary, National Council of YMCAs of India, PB No 14, Massey Hall, Jai Singh Rd, New Delhi 1.

● Youth hostels

The Dept of Tourism runs 16 hostels, each with about 40 beds, usually organised into dormitory accommodation.

In some parts of India travellers may also stay in religious hostels (*dharamshalas*) of various kinds, often for up to 3 days, sometimes free of charge or in exchange for voluntary offerings. Usually only vegetarian food is permitted; smoking and alcohol are not.

Food and drink

● Food

Most visitors are surprised – and often delighted – at the enormous variety of delicious food, some bearing little relation to the various 'curries' available outside India. You find just as much variety in dishes and presentation crossing India as you would on an equivalent journey across Europe. Furthermore, on top of the variety of main meals is a remarkable range of delicious savoury snacks (for example, *chaat* in North India) and sweets.

Given the limited basic ingredients, the diversity is surprising. Rice is the almost universal basis of meals in the South and East, while wheat is more common in the North. But accompanying these essential grains is a huge variety of dishes, many of them spiced, but not always with the kind of hot spices usually associated with Indian food abroad. Chilli was only introduced to India by the Portuguese, adding just one more ingredient to the already richly flavoured and spiced diet. Spices are essential to giving each region its distinctive combination of flavours. The cooking medium is generally oil. Clarified butter – *ghee* – is now both too expensive and too rich in fat to be as lavishly used as it once was, but mustard oil in the North and East, sesame in the South and East, and coconut oil in the West, are widely used substitutes.

If there is a typical meal it is the '*thali*'. Served on a banana leaf or metal tray, several preparations, placed in small bowls, surround the central serving of wholewheat puris and rice. In a private home you might well find that the dishes were placed in large bowls on the table and you would serve yourself to fill the small dishes which would surround your plate. Fish, mutton or chicken are popular non-vegetarian dishes. Vegetable dishes depend on seasonal availability, but there would always be *dal* (lentils) and usually some kind of yoghurt. In the North this is often served as a marinade for a salad vegetable such as cucumber. In the South it is usually served plain. It is widely regarded as offering a bland cooling dish to accompany highly spiced food, and as an excellent aid to digestion. Surrounding the thali would be placed a variety of sweet and hot pickles – mango and lime are two of the most popular, but there are many others. These can be exceptionally hot, and are designed to be taken in minute quantities alongside the main dishes.

Vegetarians are particularly well provided for in India, as some groups, notably most Brahmins, are strictly vegetarian. South Indian Brahmin food is wholly distinctive, tamarind and coconut being typical ingredients, while clear peppery soups such as *rasam* add a unique touch. Boiled rice provides the basis of the main meal in South India, with several vegetable dishes (not cooked with hot spices), *sambhar*, another soup-like preparation but much thicker than rasam, and coconut chutney and pickles as side dishes.

The South is also particularly known for 3 of its snacks – *dosai*, *idli* and *vadai*. Their popularity has swept the country. The dosai is a pancake made of a mixture of fermented rice and lentil flour, and may be served with a savoury filling (*masala dosai*) or without (*ravai* or *plain dosai*). Idlis are steamed rice cakes, a bland breakfast food given flavour by its spiced accompaniment, while vadai are deep fried.

North Indian cooking is often called *Mughlai*, hinting at the Muslim influence on North Indian diet over the last 6 centuries. Cream and ghee are favourite cooking mediums, and spices, herbs, nuts and fruit are all added ingredients to dishes which usually have meat as the main focus of the meal. Several different kinds of kebab, meat balls (*kofta*) and minced meat preparations (*keema*) are served alongside *biriyani* (fried rice, saffron, vegetables and marinated lamb) and *pulao*, similar to biriyani but usually served as a vegetarian dish. *Tandoori* dishes, marinated meat cooked in a special earthen oven, come from the far North-west, but are widely popular.

East India has long specialised in fish. River fish from the Ganga and freshwater fish from ponds and streams are favourite, *hilsa* and *bekti* being the best known. *Bekti* is often served as fried fish, while hilsa tends to be the centrepiece of a curried stew, though the smoked *hilsa* is a real delicacy – if exceptionally bony. However, if the Indian regions achieve national fame for a particular contribution to the nation's diet, Bengal's is that of its sweets. *Sandesh* and *rasgollah* are made from curds (though most people would never guess), steeped in syrup. In place of plain yoghurt, which is not part of the Bengali diet, there is the exceptional *mishti doi*, a sweet yoghurt.

West India also has its distinctive cuisine. Maharashtrian vegetarian cooking, which uses both wheat and rice, specialises in sprouted lentils, relatively lightly spiced, but with a number of sweet and sour dishes. The Parsis of Bombay and the West coast have introduced *dhansak*, chicken or lamb cooked with lentils. To India's seemingly never ending array of sweets the West has contributed *gulab jamun* and *barfi*, and *jelabis*, *laddus* and *halvas*.

One of the best known features of Indian diets right across the country is *paan*, with which all main meals would be expected to end. The *paan* leaf is the vehicle for a succession of pastes and spices, the making of which is regarded as an art. Areca nuts, cardomom, cloves, lime for the digestion, tobacco and a number of other ingredients will go into the bright green leaf, to be carefully folded and then chewed, seemingly endlessly.

It is still very exceptional for Indians to drink alcohol with a meal, water being on hand but not usually drunk until the end of the meal.

In the big cities there are many good restaurants, offering excellent value, outside the hotels. Popular local restaurants are often obvious from the number of people eating in them – follow their example! However, it is necessary to be careful in eating food prepared outside the best hotels or private homes. Raw food such as salads and unpeeled fruit should be avoided. If you are unused to spicy food have a simple plain meal regularly to give your system time to adjust.

Some foods that are common in Europe are both less readily available and of much lower quality in India. Cheese and chocolates are two. Bringing small quantities of such foods can help. They can also be very acceptable as small presents for Indian hosts, but you need to be certain of being able to keep them cool.

Fruit India has many delicious tropical and semi tropical fruits. Some are highly seasonal – mangos in the hot season, for example, while others are available throughout the year, such as bananas.

● Drink

Alcoholic drinks are generally either imported and extremely expensive, or local and of poor quality. This applies particularly to wines and spirits, though Indian whisky and rum are now widely accepted. Some local brands of beer are also increasingly popular. International and safe local brands of soft bottled drinks are very widely available. However, do check that the bottle top is original, as in some areas old bottles are re-filled with coloured water. Branded mineral water and cartons of fruit juice are now widely available at reasonable prices. Do not add ice cubes to drink as the water from which the ice is made is very unlikely to be pure. Tea and coffee are almost universally available and are generally safe.

Some states have dry days or varying degrees of Prohibition. Details are available from the Indian Mission/Tourist Office abroad. When applying for your visa you can ask for an All India Liquor Permit which will enable you to buy a certain specified quantity of alcoholic drinks in a specified time provided the State laws allow the use of the Liquor Permit. You can also get the Permit from any Govt of India Tourist Office in Bombay, Calcutta, Delhi or Madras on arrival.

Getting around

● Sensitive areas in India

Some regions are politically sensitive and require special permits to visit them. Border regions, tribal areas and some of the Himalayan zones are subject to restrictions and special permits may be needed to visit them. See page 125, **Restricted and protected areas**.

● Air

In addition to **Indian Airlines** (the nationalised carrier) there is now a growing number of private airlines, mostly regional (eg Damania, East-West, Jet Airways, Modiluft, Sahara) Indian Airlines has a fleet of Airbuses, Boeing 737s and Avro HS 748s. It is essential to book as early as possible, especially in the peak season. All the major airline offices are connected to the central reservation system. However, the more you can get done before you leave home, the better, as buying tickets can be time consuming and frustrating. Indian Airlines has restructured schedules and attempted to ensure same-day returns and acceptable night arrivals (no later than 2230). However, it has a poor record of time-keeping. Some of the new airlines are highly recommended. The service and time-keeping of Modi Luft and East-West Airlines were reputedly better than Indian Airlines in 1994.

Air ticket pricing Foreigners buying air tickets in India must use foreign exchange and pay the 'Dollar rate', whether on Indian Airlines or any of the new private airlines. Major credit cards, travellers' cheques and cash (with encashment certificate) are accepted. Most airlines have been charging the same prices, but in early 1994 there were the first signs of a price war.

Special fares Indian Airlines offers special fares for tourists which can be bought abroad. Trailfinders (in London) will confirm reservations if main ticket is with Air India or BA. If

flying with other airlines, confirmation can take weeks. At the time of going to press they include:

Discover India Unlimited travel within India on Indian Airlines for 21 days. US$ 400.

India Wonderfares Unlimited travel in ONE Indian region (N,S,E or W) for 7 days. US$ 200.

South India excursion 30% discount on US dollar fare on selected sectors in S. India.

Youth fare 25% of US$ fare for tourists between ages of 12 and 30.

Delays Be prepared for delays. For long journeys flying saves time – but often not as much as you may hope! Unfortunately the worst time for air travel, especially in northern India, is also climatically the best time of year to visit. The problems stem from the fact that Indian Airlines' northern routes all originate in New Delhi. From early Dec through to Feb, smog has become an increasingly common morning hazard at Delhi airport, sometimes delaying departures of all flights by several hours. These delays then affect the whole northern system for the rest of that day. Travelling by air can be a very frustrating experience, and for short distances on some routes is not necessarily quicker than train.

Passengers with international tickets flying with most major airlines may book Jet Airways internal flights from any part of the world.

Air travel tips

- If you do not have a confirmed booking it pays to arrive early at the airport and to be persistent in enquiring about your position in the queue.
- Indian Airlines sometimes do not permit batteries in luggage checked in but allow them in hand luggage or on your person. You need to collect small tags from the check-in desk to mark every piece taken into the cabin. However, rules change, so check.
- If your flight is delayed Indian Airlines may issue a ticket for refreshments if you ask for it.
- There is a free telephone service at major airports to contact any hotel of your choice.

● Train

There are special high-speed Tourist Trains like the ***Rajdhani Express*** (Delhi-Calcutta, Delhi-Bombay), ***Shatabdi Express*** (Delhi to Agra, Gwalior, Jhansi and Bhopal, and a number of other major routes) or the convenient ***Taj Express*** to Agra and ***Pink City Express*** to Jaipur. For a special experience of travelling in 'royal style' the ***New Palace on Wheels*** gives visitors an opportunity to see some of the 'royal' cities in Rajasthan during the winter months. See under **Rajasthan** for details, page 397.

There are special quotas for tourists on many trains. Thus, when tickets are not available over the general sales counter, it may still be possible to travel on a tourist quota ticket. Payment must be in foreign exchange or in Rupees, as long as you have your currency exchange certificate. (This requirement may not be necessary when the Rupee has been made fully convertible.) Although these schemes are designed to help tourists they do have disadvantages. In some booking offices, notably Calcutta, the booking process itself is much slower in the tourist section than in the open booking hall. If you are buying tickets for a single journey, it may be advisable to check first whether places are available under the general quota.

There are the following classes of travel: *A/c 1st Cl* (Bed rolls provided); *A/c Sleeper* also known as *2-Tier A/c Sleeper* which are clean and comfortable (bed-rolls can be ordered); *A/c Chair Car* (reclining for long inter-city journeys and tickets include meals); ***1st Cl non-a/c*** (cheaper than 2nd Cl a/c) can be hot and dusty during the warm weather; ***2nd Cl (non-a/c) 2-tier and 3-tier*** provide exceptionally cheap travel.

Very cheap by Western standards, the a/c 2-tier sleeper and chair-car trains are very comfortable. They all have toilets (not always very clean); if there is a choice of Western or Indian style it is nearly always better to use the Indian style as they are better maintained. Meals and drinks are available on long distance trains. It is usually necessary to book train tickets in advance. Indian Railways offer discounts and special passes for foreign tourists. These can offer excellent value.

Indrail Passes Tourists (foreigners and Indians resident abroad) may buy passes which allow travel across the network, without route restrictions, and without incurring reservation fees, sleeper charges and supplementary fees. Reservations however must be made, which can be done well in advance when purchasing your Pass. They may be obtained for periods ranging from 7 to 90 days from the tourist sections of railway booking offices at the fol-

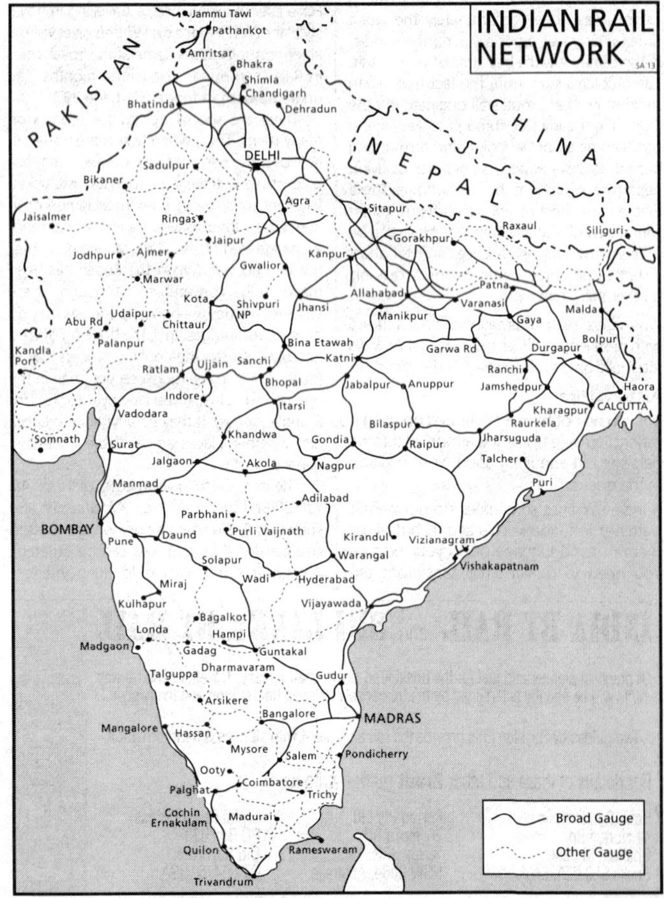

Indian Railways: Fare Structure

Distance kms	1	2	3	4	5	6	7	8
50	159	125	70	49	58	30	14	9
100	255	167	107	66	58	30	24	14
200	385	244	172	105	58	30	46	24
500	816	459	360	214	120	58	96	46
1000	1334	737	588	326	197	84	157	67
2000	2243	1180	981	530	277	127	221	101
3000	3122	1528	1362	719	343	168	274	134
4000	3998	1877	146	909	410	209	328	167
5000	4876	2221	2128	1099	478	250	382	200

Columns represent:

1 A/c 1st class
2 A/c sleeper (2-tier)
3 1st class
4 A/c chair-car
5 Sleeper (Mail/Express)
6 Sleeper (ordinary)
7 2nd class (Mail/Express)
8 2nd class (Ordinary)

lowing stations: Ahmadabad, Agra Cantt, Amritsar, Aurangabad, Bangalore City, Bombay, Calcutta, Chandigarh, Gorakhpur, Hyderabad, Jaipur, Madras, New Delhi, Rameswaram, Secunderabad, Trivandrum, Vasco da Gama, Vadodara and Varanasi. In mid-1994 payment still had to be in foreign currency, or Rupees against a currency exchange certificate. A Blue ticket allows 1st Cl a/c travel, a Green, A/c Sleeper, 1st Cl and A/c Chair Car travel and the Yellow card only 2nd Cl travel. Special 1 day passes are also available for single journeys, but only if bought abroad.

Indrail passes can also conveniently be bought abroad. The **UK** agent is ***SD Enterprises Ltd***, 103, Wembley Park Drive, Wembley, Middx HA9 8HG, England, T 081-903 3411, F 081 903 0392. They make all necessary reservations, and offer excellent advice.

Other international agents are: **Australia**: ***Adventure World***, 8th Floor, 37 York St, Sydney NSW 2000; ***Penthouse Travel***, 5th Level, 72 Pitt St, Sydney NSW 2000. **Canada**: ***Hari World Travels Inc***, Royal York Hotel, 106 Front St West, Arcade Level, Toronto, Ontario M5J 1E3. **Denmark**: ***Danish State Railways***, DSW Travel Agency Division, Reventlowsgade – 10, DK 1651 Kobenhaven V. **Finland**: ***Intia-Keskus Ltd***, Yrjonkatu 8-10, 00120 Helsinki, Finland. **France**: ***Le Monde de L'Inde et de L'Asie***, 15 Rue Des Ecoles, Paris 75005. **Germany**: ***Asra-Orient***, Kaiserstrasse 50, D-6000 Frankfurt/M.I. **Malaysia**: ***City East West Travels Sdn***, BhD, No 28-A, Loreng Bunus, 6, Jalan Masjid India, Kuala Lumpur. **Hong Kong**: ***Thomas Cook Travel Services (HK) Ltd***, 6/F D'Aguilar Place, 1-13 D'Aguilar Street, Central, Hong Kong. **Japan**: ***Japan Travel Bureau Inc***, Overseas Travel Division, 1-6-4 Marunouchi, Chiyoda-ku, Tokyo-100. **Thailand**: ***S.S. Travel Service***, 10/12-13 Convent Road, S.S. Building, Bangkok. **USA**: ***Hari World Travels Inc***, 30 Rockefeller Plaza, Shop No 21, Mezzanine North, New York 10112.

Indrail Pass rates

Period	A/c 2 tier US$
1 day	35
7 days	135
15 days	165
21 days	200
30 days	250
60 days	360
90 days	440

A/c First Class costs approximately double the above rate, and non A/c Second Class approximately half. Children aged 5 to 12 travel at half the adult price shown. Senior citizens of 65 and above may obtain 25% discount on journeys over 500 kms on proof of age.

Rail fares for individual journeys are based on distance covered and reflect both the class travelled in and the type of train. Higher rates apply on the Shatabdi and Rajdhani trains.

Shatabdi Express fares Prices for A/c Chair car on the Shatabdi trains range from Rs 95 from Kalka to Chandigarh to Rs 465 from New Delhi to Bhopal. A/c 1st Class is double that price.

Rajdhani Express fares Prices for A/c Chair car on selected routes: From New Delhi-to Howrah Rs 550; Kanpur Rs 345; Allahabad Rs

Riding The Rails

The travel writer Christopher Portway has written that 'there is a common popular conception about Indian trains: they all consist of dilapidated wagons overflowing – onto running boards and roof – with semi-naked Indian bodies. This may have held an element of truth a decade or more ago; indeed, I have experienced some horrendous journeys in my time – but today's long-distance expresses are a very different breed.'

He goes on to suggest that 'For observing this vast country, to travel the length and breadth of it, Indian Railways offer by far the best means of so doing. No longer is riding her trains a hardship and the experience will teach you much about India and yourself.

As the Indian Trains at a Glance timetable (obtainable at main stations) and Cook's Overseas Timetable will confirm, the 70,000 km 3 gauge rail system runs 7000 passenger trains a day carrying 11 million passengers between 7000 stations through the gigantic ferment of India.'

Indian Railways has the world's 2nd largest network. Computerised booking has brought some major changes to rail travel in India since 1988. In theory it is now very straightforward to get your own rail tickets from any sales window in any of the major cities. However, 'purchasing a ticket can still remain something of a hassle since Indian stations are a frenzy of humanity, full of theatrical confusion and a microcosm of India.'

To make a reservation a form has to be completed, and 'in due course, one's name, probably misspelt, appears on a reservation chart at the station or platform of departure and/or on the side of your designated coach. Should the train be fully booked your name will be entered on a waiting list likewise displayed.'

430; Bombay Rs 640; Bhopal Rs 745; Secunderabad Rs 580. A/c 2 tier costs twice this rate and A/c 1st Class 4 times the rate.

Some key distances Examples of the distances between major points on the rail network are: **New Delhi** to: Shimla 364 km, Varanasi 788 km, Calcutta 1441 km, Bombay 1542 km, Madras 2194 km; Cochin 2833 km. **Calcutta** to: Bombay 1980 km, Madras1663 km. **Bombay** to: Porbander 959 km, Madras 1279 km.

Rail travel tips

- Trains can still be the cheapest and most comfortable means of travelling long distances, despite increases in 1st and 2nd Cl a/c fares in 1993. Overnight trains save hotel expenses, and travelling by train allows you to use station retiring rooms, a very useful facility from time to time.

- A/c 1st Cl is cheaper than flying, and is recommended for long journeys if you would like to arrive fresh at your destination. A/c 2 tier Sleeper and A/c Chair Car provide an excellent alternative (these are very popular so book well in advance if you have an itinerary planned). Remember that a/c compartments can get very cold, so have a thick jumper easily accessible. 2nd Cl non a/c is very cheap, but can be very uncomfortable and toilet facilities can be unpleasant. A/c is not available on all routes.

- A Blue or Green Indrail Pass is worthwhile if you plan to make more than 1 journey and wish to travel in a/c comfort. Although there is little financial saving buying a Green Pass, preferential bookings and freedom from restrictions make for easier travel. Buying a day pass before you leave home allows you to make a reservation from outside India, which can be useful if you want to travel by train soon after arriving. Yellow Passes give few advantages.

- Regional timetables are available cheaply from station bookstalls which also list principal long distance trains.

- Always allow time for booking and for making connections. Delays are common on all means of transport.

• If you do not have a reservation for a particular train, you may get one with your Indrail Pass by arriving about 3 hr early or asking if the Superintendent on duty can help. Ask for separate Tourist Quota counter and Ladies counter at main stations. Fill up reservation forms while queuing.

• Booking offices can be very confusing places. INDRAIL passes always have to be validated and a specific reservation issued. This can be done in the railway booking offices in the major cities. Non-INDRAIL PASS tickets can be bought over the counter. It is always best to book as far in advance as possible. However, a large number of spaces are technically reserved as 'quotas' for various groups of travellers, such as civil servants, military personnel etc. In addition many stations have their own quota for particular trains, so that a train may be 'fully booked' when there are still some tickets available from the quota of other stations. These quotas are only released to the public on the day of departure, and therefore passengers are wait-listed. You need to know the train **name** and **number**, its time of departure and destination. These have to be entered on the booking form. If you cannot get a confirmed booking, or if you have any problems at a railway station, ask to see the Station Superintendent or the Chief Reservations Supervisor.

• Women's ticket queues are available at most railway booking offices outside the main centres.

• A woman travelling alone overnight can ask to be put in a compartment with other women.

• Keep valuables close to you, securely locked, and away from windows. For security, carry a good lock to attach your luggage to the chains sometimes provided on trains. Note that zipped luggage is particularly vulnerable.

• Avoid touts offering tickets or money changing.

• If you are travelling extensively, allow free time to recover.

• Always carry plenty of liquid. Bottled water and/or juice and soft drinks in cartons are the safest options. Tea and coffee are also widely available. Although you can order meals in 1st class and 2nd class a/c, and on many 2nd class non A/c Express trains, a supply of fruit and biscuits can be useful.

• Take a good supply of toilet paper.

• It is often worth asking for upper berths, which offer some protection against theft, and can be used in the day time when the lower seats may all be occupied by sitting passengers.

Road

Bus Very few villages are now more than 2 or 3 km from a bus stop. Buses fall into 3 categories. Special tourist **'luxury' coaches** can be hired, either for day trips or for longer journeys. They may be a/c. It is increasingly common for groups to use hired buses for at least some sections of the tour, but apart from the very best they are often not very comfortable for really long journeys.

Express buses are run both by private companies and state enterprises, on long distance routes. These are often called 'video coaches', and frequently run overnight. The video coach can be an appalling experience, unless you appreciate very loud film music blasting through the night. Ear plugs may ease the pain. However, buses are often the quickest way of covering medium to long distances.

Local buses These are often very crowded and quite slow, but on many routes they can be a friendly and easy way of getting about, especially for quite short distances. Even where signboards are not in English someone will usually give you directions.

Mini buses Many larger towns have minibus services which pick up and drop passengers on request. Often very crowded, and with restricted headroom, they are the fastest way of getting about many of the larger towns.

Bus travel tips

• Avoid the back half of the bus if possible, as the ride is often very bumpy.

• Note that many towns have different bus stations for different destinations. These are detailed in the town sections.

• It is possible to reserve tickets on many long distance bus journeys. Booking on major routes in several states is now computerised, and it is worth booking in advance where possible.

Car Tourists may import their own vehicles into India with a Carnet de Passage (Triptyques) issued by any recognised automobile association or club affiliated to the Alliance Internationale de Tourisme in Geneva. Cars may be imported free of duty for up to 6 months. The vehicle must be re-exported at the end of 6 months **even where the Carnet has a validity of one year**. In India it is also advisable to obtain an International Certificate for Motor Vehicles (ICMW) and an International Driving Permit (IDP). An IDP should be obtained from the tourist's own licensing authority. IDPs obtained through an automobile association must be endorsed by the regional licensing authority in which the tourist arrives in India.

Vehicles drive on the left – in theory. India has a very extensive road network, and roads offer the only way of reaching many sites of great interest. Routes around the major cities are usually crowded with lorry traffic, and the main roads are often poor and slow in comparison with those in Europe or the United States. There are no motorways, and many main roads are single track. District roads are often quiet, and although they are not fast they can be an excellent way of seeing the country and village life. On main roads across India petrol stations are reasonably frequent, but there are areas which are poorly served, and in remote areas service stations often only have diesel pumps. Some will still carry small reserves of petrol. Always carry a spare can.

- Diesel is widely available and normally much cheaper than petrol. Petrol is rarely above 92 octane.

- Drivers must have third party insurance. This may have to be with an Indian insurer, or with a foreign insurer which has a national guarantor.

Self-drive car hire This is still in its infancy. Indian roads are often in poor condition, driving conditions are extremely slow and drivers usually have only a limited amount of English. Furthermore, the most widely used hire car, the Hindustan Ambassador is not the most reliable of cars. Comfort is perhaps a matter of taste, and Ambassador cars still have their devotees, but many find it extremely uncomfortable for long journeys. It also seems designed to break down frequently, perhaps to provide work for the thousands of mechanics across India who can get it back on the road again – for a time. For a similar price, Maruti cars and vans are much more reliable.

Car hire with driver The cost of a non-a/c Ambassador for long journeys will be between Rs 3 and Rs 4 per km with a minimum coverage of 250 km per day. The driver charge will be between Rs 60 and Rs 100 per day, bringing the total to approximately $30 a day. Cars can be hired through the ITDC or through private companies, but some ITDC cars are worse than those available privately. International companies such as **Hertz**, **Europcar** and **Budget** have begun operating in the major cities. Their rates are generally higher than those of local firms. The price of the top of the range imported cars is approximately 3 times that of the Ambassador.

NB: Drivers may stay in the car overnight, though hotels often provide special facilities for drivers. They are responsible for all their expenses (including petrol). A tip of up to Rs 30 per day is perfectly acceptable. It is also necessary to pay some inter-state taxes. Occasionally drivers are forced to pay small bribes to police to be allowed to continue their journey.

Cars can be hired for the day for between Rs 400 and Rs 600 for 8 hrs and 80 kms, an extra Rs 3 to Rs 4 being charged for each extra km. The total cost of a 10-day journey of 2500 km would be about US$300 from a local firm, and up to 50% more from an international company. Many companies are happy to arrange to pick you up almost anywhere in India and to drive you where you want to go if you hire a car and driver, the only additional cost being the extra time for the car and driver to get to and from their base in addition to your own travel. Longer tours do provide a chance to travel off the beaten track, and give unrivalled opportunities for seeing something of India's great variety of villages and small towns. Drivers may also be very helpful company.

Car travel tips

- If you drive yourself it is essential to take great care. Pedestrians, cattle and a wide range of other animals roam at will. This can be particularly dangerous when driving after dark especially as even other vehicles often carry no lights. Accidents often produce large and angry crowds very quickly. It is best to leave the scene of the accident and report it to the police as quickly as possible thereafter.

- Ensure that you have adequate food and drink, and a basic tool set in the car.

- The Automobile Association offers a range of services to members. **Delhi**: AA of Upper India, Lilaram Building, 14F Connaught Place, New Delhi; **Bombay**: Western India AA, Lalji Narainji Memorial Building, 76, Vir Nariman

Rd, Bombay; **Calcutta**: AA of Eastern India, 13 Promothesh Barua Sarani, Calcutta; **Madras**: AA of Southern India, 187 Anna Salai, Madras.

Taxis Yellow-top taxis in cities and large towns are metered, although tariffs change frequently. These changes are shown on a fare chart which should be read in conjunction with the meter reading. Increased night time rates apply in some cities, and a surcharge may be levied for luggage. In some cities taxis refuse to use the meter. Official advice is to call the police. This also may not work, but it is worth trying. Other taxis and auto-rickshaws do not always have a meter so a fare should be negotiated before starting the journey. You always need to negotiate with drivers of cycle rickshaws and *tongas**.

Taxi tips

- Always try to insist on the taxi meter being 'flagged' in your presence. Do not assume that the price asked by an unmetered vehicle driver is the fair rate, so try to bargain down to a reasonable fare by first asking at the hotel desk for a guide price, if you have not already made a similar journey before.

- At stations and airports it is often possible to share taxis to a central point. It is worth looking for fellow passengers who may be travelling in your direction.

Hitch Hiking is almost unheard of in India, partly because public transport is so cheap. If you try you are likely to spend a very long time on the roadside. Trucks do sometimes give lifts, especially in emergencies, but they rarely average more than 40 kph.

Motor Cycling is increasingly common across South Asia. It is easy to buy new Indian-made or assembled motorcycles in India and imported ones elsewhere if you pay direct with foreign exchange. Among the Indian models are the 350 cc Enfield Bullet and several 100 cc models, including Suzuki and Hondas, made in collaboration with Indian firms. Buying second hand in Rupees takes more time but is quite possible. Repairs are usually easy to arrange and quite cheap. Carry appropriate tools with you.

Cycling It is easy to hire bikes in most small towns. Indian bikes are heavy and without gears, but they can be an excellent means of exploring comparatively short distances outside towns. It is also quite possible to tour more extensively. Imported bikes have the advantage of lighter weight and gears, but the disadvantage of greater difficulty of maintenance and repair, and the much greater risk of being stolen or damaged. One recent correspondent wrote that it was comfortably possible to cover 80 to 110 km per day, and that it was a wonderful way of seeing the quiet by-ways of South Asia. Many would agree (see also cycling and mountain biking, page 113).

Travelling with children Children of all ages are widely welcomed, being greeted with a warmth in their own right which is often then extended to those accompanying them. In the big hotels there is no difficulty with obtaining safe baby foods, though disposable nappies are not readily available in many areas. Packets and jars may be carried if the child is used to them before starting the journey. It doesn't harm a child to eat an unvaried and limited diet of familiar food for a few weeks if the local dishes are not acceptable, but it may be an idea to give vitamin and mineral supplements. To help young children to take anti-malarial tablets, one suggestion is to crush them between spoons and mix with a teaspoon of dessert chocolate (for cake-making) bought in a tube.

Extra care must be taken to protect children from the heat by creams, hats, umbrellas etc and by avoiding being out in the hottest part of the day. Cool showers or baths help if children get too hot. Dehydration may be counteracted with plenty of drinking water – bottled, boiled (furiously for 5 minutes) or purified with tablets. Preparations such as "Dioralyte" may be given if the child suffers from diarrhoea. Moisturiser, zinc and castor oil (for sore bottoms due to change of diet) are worth taking. Mosquito nets or electric insect repellents at night may be provided in hotel rooms which are not a/c, but insect repellent creams are a must. It is best to visit South Asia in the cooler months, especially when travelling with young children. The biggest hotels provide babysitting facilities.

Communications

● Language

Hindi is India's official language. The use of English is also enshrined in the Constitution for a wide range of official purposes, notably communication between Hindi and non-Hindi speaking states. In addition to Hindi there are several hundred other Indian languages, though the 10 most important account for over 90% of the total population. After Hindi (spoken by 350 million people) Bengali (65 million), Marathi (63 million), Urdu (45 million), Gujarati (42 million), Oriya (29 million) and Punjabi (22 million) are the most widely spoken Indo-Aryan languages, while among the Dravidian languages Telugu (68 million), Tamil (57 million), Kannada (33 million) and Malayalam (31 million) are the most widely used. Most of these languages have their own scripts. There are over 700 minor languages and dialects.

● Postal services

In recent years the post has frequently become unreliable, and delays are common. It is advisable to use a post office where it is possible to hand over mail for franking across the counter, or a hotel post box. Post between Europe and South Asia can easily take 2 weeks, and from the United States 4 weeks. Valuable items should only be sent by Registered Mail. Government Emporia or shops in the larger hotels will send purchases home if the items are difficult to carry. Airmail service to Europe, Africa and Australia takes at least a week and a little longer for the Americas.

NB: Sending parcels can take 2 hr. Check that post office offers the service and holds necessary customs declaration forms (2/3 copies needed). Write "No commercial value" if returning used clothes, books etc. Air Mail is expensive; Sea Mail slow but reasonable (10 kg, Rs 800). Take your parcel in an open cardboard box so items can be inspected. "Packers" outside Post office will do all necessary cloth covering, sealing etc for Rs 20-50; you address the parcel, obtain stamps from a separate counter; stick stamps and one customs form to the parcel with glue available (the other form/s must be partially sewn on). Post at the Parcels Counter and obtain Registration slip. It is theoretically possible to insure the parcel but may prove difficult.

WARNING: Many people complain that private shops offering a postal service actually send cheap substitutes. It is usually too late to complain when the buyer finds out, so it is essential to take advice if making such arrangements.

Poste restante facilities are widely available in even quite small towns at the GPO where mail is held for 1 month. Ask for mail to be addressed to you with your surname in capitals and underlined. When asking for mail at Poste Restante check under surname as well as Christian name. DHL and similar courier services are available in the larger towns.

● Telephone services

International Direct Dialling is now widely available in privately run call boxes, usually labelled on yellow boards with the letters "PCO-STD-ISN". You dial the call yourself, and the time and cost are displayed on a computer screen. They are by far the best places from which to telephone abroad. Telephone calls from hotels are usually much more expensive. Check price before calling. Fax services are also becoming widely available.

International codes for India (010 or 00) 91. STD codes for towns are printed after the town name.

Entertainment

● Newspapers

India has a large English language press. The best known are The Hindu, The Hindustan Times, The Independent, The Indian Express, The Times of India, and The Statesman. The Economic Times is possibly the best for independent reporting and world coverage. The Telegraph (published in Calcutta) has good foreign coverage. The Indian Express has stood out as being consistently critical of the Congress Party and Government. They all have extensive analysis of contemporary Indian and some international issues. There is a wide range of weekly and fortnightly magazines. Some of the most widely read are The Illustrated Weekly (generally an entertainment weekly, with some political and social content), Sunday, India Today and Frontline, all of which are current affairs journals on the model of Time or Newsweek. In all the major cities it is possible to buy international newspapers, often stocked by bookshops in the top hotels, and occasionally by booksellers elsewhere. There is a flourishing local press.

● Television and radio

India's national radio and television network, Doordarshan, broadcasts in national and regional languages. Many Indians have now switched off DD, as it is known, to watch satellite TV, including the BBC World Service TV, CNN and other some international channels are currently relayed through the Star Network. BBC World Service radio has a large Indian audience in both English and regional languages.

Holidays and festivals

There are numerous religious festivals and special celebrations throughout the country which may vary from state to state – only a few count as full public holidays: **26 Jan** Republic Day; **15 August** Independence Day; **2 October** Mahatma Gandhi's Birthday; **25 December** Christmas Day.

Religious and folk festivals fall on different dates each year, depending on the lunar calendar, so check with the Tourist Office. Certain festivals are associated with a particular state or town, others are celebrated throughout the country. Some major national and regional festivals are listed below, while others appear under the particular state or town.

● Festivals and the Indian calendar

Since 1957 the official Indian national calendar has been based on the *Saka* era. The new year starts on 22 March, and has exactly the same length as the Gregorian calendar. The first month is *Chaitra*.

India has an extraordinary wealth of festivals. Only a few are genuinely national, and many are specific to a very narrow locality or even a particular temple. Furthermore many are determined by the lunar/solar calendar and are therefore variable from year to year. The following list is of major festivals:

Jan 1 *New Year's Day* is accepted officially when following the Gregorian calendar but there are regional variations which fall on different dates which in some places coincides with spring/harvest time. *Losar* in Ladakh, *Naba Barsha* in Bengal, *Goru* in Assam, *Ugadi* in Andhra, *Vishu* in Kerala and *Jamshed Navroj* for the Parsi community.

Desert Festival – Jaisalmer, Rajasthan. *International Kite Festival* – Ahmadabad, Gujarat. *Elephant March* – Kerala. *Ganga Sagar Mela* – West Bengal. **26** *Republic Day Parade* – New Delhi.

Feb *Vasant Panchami* The Spring (Vasant) festival when people where bright yellow clothes to mark the advent of the season with singing, dancing and feasting. In Bengal it is also Saraswati Puja when the goddess of learning is worshipped in schools, colleges, homes and community marquees. Students pray for her blessing and good luck at exams, and place books at her feet.

Ramadan, the Muslim fasting month (in 1995-Feb). During the month food and drink are only taken between sunset and sunrise. *Id ul Fitr*, the 3-day festival which marks its end, is celebrated by Muslims across India. The precise timing is determined by the sighting of the new moon (in 1995 Mar).

Surajkund Crafts Mela – Surajkund, Haryana. *Nagaur Camel Fair* – Nagaur, Rajasthan. *International Yoga Festival* – Rishikesh, UP. *Elephanta Festival* – Elephanta, Rajasthan. *Konark Festival* – Konark, Orissa.

Feb-Mar *Sivaratri* marks the night when Siva danced his celestial dance of destruction (*Tandava*) celebrated with feasting and fairs at Siva temples, but preceded by a night of devotional readings and hymn singing. Orthodox Saivites fast during the day and offer prayers every 3 hrs; devotees who remain awake through the night believe they will win the Puranic promise of prosperity and salvation.

Holi, the festival of colours, marks the climax of spring. The previous night bonfires are lit in parts of North India symbolising the end of winter (and conquering of evil). People have fun throwing coloured powder and water at each other and in the evening some gamble with friends. If you don't mind getting covered in colours, you can risk going out but celebrations can sometimes get rowdy. For days afterwards, many people's clothes carry the telltale marks of splashed colour. Some link the festival to worship of Kama the god of pleasure; some worship Krishna who defeated the demon Putana.

Mar *Ellora Festival of Classical Dance and Music* – Ellora Caves, Maharashtra. *Khajuraho Dance Festival* – Khajuraho, MP. *Holi*. *Gangaur* – Jaipur, Rajasthan.

Apr *Mahavir Jayanti*. *Baisakhi* – North India. *Carnival* – Goa.

Apr/May *Sikkim Flower Festival* – Gangtok, Sikkim. *Bihu* – Assam. *International Spice Festival* – Cochin, Kerala.

May *Buddha Jayanti* The first full moon night in May marks the birth of the Buddha. Celebrations are held in several parts of the country. *Pooram* – Kerala.

Id-ul-Zuha/Bakr-Id Muslims commemorate Ibrahim's sacrifice of his son according to God's commandment. An animal (goat) is sacrificed and special meat and vermicelli dishes are prepared.

Jun/Jul *Rath Yatra* – Puri, Orissa. *Hemis Festival* – Leh, Ladakh. *Teej* – Jaipur, Rajasthan. *International Mango Festival* – Saharanpur, UP.

Jul/Aug *Raksha Bandhan* (literally 'protection

bond') symbolising the bond between brother and sister, celebrated mainly in North India at full-moon. A sister says special prayers for her brother and ties coloured (silk) threads around his wrist to remind him of the special bond. He in turn gives a gift and promises to protect and care for her. Sometimes *rakshas* are exchanged as a mark of friendship. *Narial Purnima* on the same full-moon, Hindus particularly in coastal areas of West and South India, make offerings of *narial* (coconuts) to the Vedic god Varuna (Lord of the waters) by throwing them into the sea.

Aug 15 *Independence Day* A national secular holiday. In some large cities it is marked by special events, and in Delhi there is an impressive flag hoisting ceremony at the Red Fort.

Muharram Muslims commemorate the martyrdom of Hussein the Prophet Muhammad's grandson. Decorated *tazias* (replicas of the martyr's tomb) are carried in procession by devout wailing followers who beat their chests to express their grief. Hyderabad and Lucknow are famous for their grand *tazias*. Shias fast for the 10 days.

Ganesh Chaturthi. *Rakhi*. *Tarnetar Mela* – Gujarat.

Aug/Sep *Janamashtami* The birth of Krishna is celebrated at midnight at Krishna temples. Special festivities are held in Mathura his birth place and nearby at Vrindavan where Rasalilas (dance dramas are performed through the night.

Sep/Oct *Dasara* In North India, celebrations for the 9 nights, are marked with *Ramlila*. During this period various episodes of the Ramayana story (See section on **Hinduism**, page 74) are enacted and recited, with particular reference to the battle between the forces of good and evil. It celebrates *Rama's* victory over the Demon king *Ravana* of Lanka with the help of loyal Hanuman (Monkey). Huge effigies of *Ravana* made of bamboo and paper, are burnt on the 10th day (*Vijaya dasami*) of *Dasara* in public open spaces.

Onam – Kerala.

Navaratri (9 nights) The goddess *Parvati* (*Durga*) is worshipped for 9 nights. An oil lamp is kept alight by household 'temples' for the 9 days and nights. Durga puja is of special significance in Bengal.

Oct 2 *Gandhi Jayanti* Mahatma Gandhi's birthday is remembered with prayer meetings and devotional singing.

Oct/Nov *Diwali/Deepavali* (a row of lamps/ the festival of lights). Some Hindus celebrate Krishna's victory over the demon Narakasura, some Rama's return after his 14 years' exile in the forest when citizens lit his way with earthen oil lamps. See also page 88. It falls on the dark *chaturdasi* (14th) night, (the one preceding the new moon) when rows of lamps or candles are lit in remembrance, and *rangolis* are ainted on the floor as a sign of welcome. Fireworks have become an integral part of the celebration which are often set off days before Diwali. Equally, Lakshmi, the Goddess of Wealth (as well as Ganesh) is worshipped by merchants and the business community (especially in West India) who open the new year's account on the day. Most people wear new clothes; some play games of chance.

Pushkar Fair – Ajmer, Rajasthan.

Nov 2 *Guru Nanak Jayanti* commemorates the birth of Guru Nanak. *Akhand Pat* (unbroken reading of the holy book) takes place and the book itself (*Granth*) is taken out in procession.

Sonepur Fair – Sonepur, Bihar

Dec 25 *Christmas Day* Indian Christians celebrate the birth of Christ in much the same way as in the west; many churches hold services/mass at midnight. There is an air festivity in city markets which are specially decorated and illuminated.

Shekhavati Festival – Shekhavati, Rajasthan. *Hampi-Vijaynagar Festival* – Karnataka.

FURTHER READING

The literature on South Asia is as huge and varied as the subcontinent itself. Below are a few suggestions:

● Travel

Cameron, J. *An Indian summer*, London, 1974. Beautifully written and perceptive view.

Ellis, R. *India by Rail*. The 1992 edition brings this rail enthusiast's guide up to date.

Mohd Farook *The Fascinating Maldives*, Male, Novelty Printers, 1985.

Finlay, H. et al. *India: a travel survival kit*, Latest ed 1993. The most popular guide to India in the 1980s. Despite its trienniel increase in bulk, remarkably thin coverage of many areas, encouraging modern Lonely Planet pilgrims to follow the same well-beaten paths. The latest edition introduces some nice little colour photos, but Insight Guides have nothing to fear.

Frater, A. *Chasing the monsoon*, London, Viking, 1990. (India) An attractive and prize winning account of the human impact of the monsoon's sweep across India.

Godden R. & J. *Two under the Indian Sun.* A beautifully painted account of the two sisters' childhood in Bengal.

Hatt, J. *The tropical traveller: the essential guide to travel in hot countries*, 3rd ed 1992. Excellent, wide ranging and clearly written common sense, based on extensive experience and research.

Insight Guides Beautifully illustrated guides to each of the major countries of South Asia. Recent editions carry much improved brief text. *India. Nepal. Pakistan. Sri Lanka.*

Murphy, D. A number of entertaining books on travels in the region: *Full tilt: Dunkirk to Delhi by bike; A winter in Baltistan; and On a shoestring to Coorg.*

Naipaul, V.S. *A million mutinies now*, London, 1990. The latest – revisionist – of the author's insights into India (India).

A Handbook for travellers in India, Pakistan, Nepal, Bangladesh and Sri Lanka, John Murray, 1982 (22nd edition). Still a remarkable guide, based entirely on rail routes and rich in British historical material.

Swift H. *Trekking in Pakistan and India*, London, Hodder & Stoughton, 1990. Detailed practical guide, based on first hand experience.

● Novels and short stories

Desai A. *The village by the sea*, Penguin.

Farrell, J.G. *The siege of Krishnapur.*

Forster, E.M. *A Passage to India*, London.

Fraser, G.M. *Flashman*, London, Pan, (Pakistan); *Flashman in the Great Game*, London, Pan, 1976 (The 1857 Mutiny).

Godden R. *Kingfishers catch fire*, 1955.

Holmstrom, L. Has recently collected a series of short stories by Indian women, translated into English. *The Inner Courtyard*, Rupa, 1992.

Narayan, R.K. Has written many gentle and humourous novels and short stories of South India. *The Man-eater of Malgudi* and *Under the Banyan tree and other stories* are two examples, London, Penguin, 1985, (India).

Rushdie, S. *Midnight's children*, London, 1981. A novel of India since Independence, while his later *Shame* focuses on Pakistan. At the same time funny and bitterly sharp critiques of contemporary South Asian life.

Scott, P. *The Raj Quartet*, London, Panther, 1973; *Staying on*, London, Longmans, 1985. Outstandingly perceptive novels of the end of the Raj.

● Popular history

Allen, C. & Dwivedi, S. *Lives of the Indian Princes*, London, Century Publications, 1984. Colourful view of an often romanticised past.

Chauduri, N.C. 4 books give vivid, witty and often sharply critical accounts of India across the 20th century. *The autobiography of an unknown Indian*, MacMIllan, London, and *Thy Hand, Great Anarch!*, London, Chatto & Windus, 1987. *The continent of Circe* and *Hinduism: A religion to live by*, New Delhi, B.I. Publications, 1979.

Gascoigne, B. *The Great Moghuls*, London, Cape, 1987.

Hopkirk, P. *The Great Game: on secret service in High Asia*, John Murray, 1990.

Keay, J. *When men and mountains meet*, 1973; *The Gilgit game*, John Murray, 1979.

Mason, P. *Men who ruled India* and *The Guardians*, London, Cape, 1985.

Nehru, J. *The discovery of India*, New Delhi, ICCR, 1976.

Russell, R. *Khurshidul Islam Ghalib: Life and letters*, London, Allen & Unwin, 1969.

Spear, P. & Thapar, R. *A history of India*, 2 vols, London, Penguin, 1978.

Wolpert, S. *A new history of India*, Oxford University Press, 1990.

● Mountaineering

Bonnington, C. *Annapurna South face*, London, Cassell, 1971; *Everest the hard way*, London, Hodder & Stoughton, 1979.

Hillary, E. *High adventure*, New York, Dutton, 1955.

Tilman, H.M. *Two mountains and a river*, Cambridge University P., 1948. (Pakistan).

They are all classic accounts of Himalayan mountaineering.

● People and places

Anderson, M.M. *Festivals of Nepal*, London, Allen & Unwin, 1971.

Furer-Haimendorf, C von. A world authority on tribal people of South Asia, *The Sherpas of Nepal*, Berkeley, Univ of California, 1964 and *The Naked Nagas* are two sensitively written anthropologies.

Heyerdahl, T. *The Maldive mystery*, London,

Allen & Unwin, 1986.

Maloney, C. *Peoples of South Asia*, New York, Holt, Rheinhart & Winston, 1974. A wide ranging and authoritative review, perhaps over-emphasising the Dravidian connection.

Messerli, B. & Ives J.D. *Himalayan crisis: reconciling development and conservation*, London, Routledge & K Paul, 1989. Excellent review of the debate over environmental change in the Himalaya.

S. Mutthiah *Madras discovered*, 1987, East West Press Pvt Ltd.

Johnson B.L.C. has written books on the geography of each of the larger South Asian countries which contain much helpful factual material. *India: resources and development*; *Pakistan*; *Bangladesh*; and *Sri Lanka* (written with M. Le M. Scrivenor) are all published by Heinemann and Barnes and Noble.

Stainton, J.D.A. *Forests of Nepal*, London, Murray, 1972.

● Architecture

Brown, P. *Indian Architecture*, 2 vols, Bombay, Taraporevala, 1976. A classic, dated but still an invaluable reference.

Mitra, D. *Buddhist monuments*, Calcutta, Sahitya Samsad, 1971.

Morris, J. & Winchester S. *Stones of Empire*, Oxford, OUP, 1983.

Mumtaz, K.K. *Architecture in Pakistan*, Singapore, Concept Media, 1985.

Tillotson G.H.R. *The Rajput Palaces*, Yale, 1987; *Mughal architecture*, London, Viking, 1990; *The tradition of Indian architecture*, Yale 1989. Superbly clear writing on development of Indian architecture under Rajputs, Mughals and the British.

● Political commentaries

Tully, M. *No full stops in India*, Viking, 1991. An often superbly observed but controversially interpreted view of contemporary India.

● Academic and reference books

Allchin, B. & R. *The Rise of civilisation in India and Pakistan*, Cambridge, CUP, 1982. The most authoritative survey of the origins of Indian civilisations.

Basham, A.L. (ed.) *A Cultural history of India*, Oxford, OUP, 1975. A collection of excellent academic essays, which wear their learning lightly.

Basham, A.L. *The Wonder that was India*, London, Sidgwick & Jackson, 1985. Still one of the most comprehensive and readable accounts of the development of India's culture.

Bock, K.R. *A Guide to the common reef fish of West Indian Oceans*, London, Macmillan, 1987.

Farmer, B.H. *An introduction to South Asia* (2nd ed 1993), Methuen. Perhaps the best and most balanced short introduction to modern South Asia.

Fleming, R.L. & others *Birds of Nepal*, Kathmandu, Avalok, 1979. Excellent reference.

Gandhi, M.K. *An Autobiography*, London, 1982.

Ghosh, A. *An Encyclopaedia of Indian archaeology*, E.J. Brill, 1990. Superb but expensive 2 volume reference work.

O'Flaherty, W. *Hindu Myths*, London, Penguin, 1974. A sourcebook translated from the Sanskrit.

Rajagopalachari, C. *The Mahabharata*, Bombay, Bharatiya Vidya Bhavan, 1979; *Ramayana*, Bombay, Bharatiya Vidya Bhavan, 1978.

Robinson F. (ed.) *Cambridge Encyclopedia of India, Pakistan*, 1989, ed, Cambridge. Excellent and readable introduction to many aspects of South Asian society.

Shackle, C. *South Asian languages*, London, SOAS, 1985.

Snellgrove, D.L. *Buddhist Himalaya*, Oxford, Bruno Cassirer, 1957.

Stutley M.J. *Dictionary of Hinduism*.

Maps

The Bartholomew 1:4m map sheet of India is the most authoritative, detailed and easy to use map available. It can be bought worldwide, or from John Bartholomew & Son Ltd, 12 Duncan Street, Edinburgh EH9 1TA, Scotland. Nelles' regional maps of South Asia at the scale of 1:1.5m, published by Nelles Verlag BmbH, D 8000 München 45, Germany offer generally clear route maps,though they are not always reliable. State maps and town plans are published by the TT Company, PO Box 21, 328 GST Rd, Chromepet, Madras 600044. These are constantly being updated and improved and are the best available. For the larger cities they provide the most compact yet clear map sheets (generally 50 mm x 75 mm format).

The US Army Series (AMS) U502 at the scale

of 1:250,000 are available from selected booksellers in the United States and Europe. Showing contours at 250 or 500 feet, the series was completed before 1960, so some features, notably roads, are out of date. However, they provide good topographic information. Sources of maps outside India: ***Stanford International Map Centre***, 12-14 Long Acre, London WC2E 9LP; ***Zumsteins Landkartenhaus***, Leibkerrstrasse 5, 8 München 22, Germany; ***Geo Buch Verlag***, Rosenthal 6, D-6000 München 2, Germany; ***GeoCenter GmbH***, Honigwiessenstrasse 25, Postfach 800830, D-7000 Stuttgart 80, Germany; ***Libreria Alpina***, Via C. Coroned-Berti, 4 40137 Bologna, Zona 370-5, Italy; ***Library of Congress***, 101 Independence Ave, Washington, DC 20540, USA; ***Michael Chessler Books***, PO Box 2436, Evergreen, CO 80439, USA T 800 654 8502, 303 670 0093; NOAA Distribution Branch (N/CG33), National Ocean Service, Riverdale MD 20737.

The Survey of India publishes large scale 1:10,000 town plans of approximately 70 cities. These detailed plans are the only surveyed town maps in India, though some are 20 years old. The Survey also has topographic maps at the scale of 1:25,000 and 1:50,000 in addition to its 1:250,000 scale coverage, some of which are as recent as the late 1980s. However, maps are regarded as highly sensitive and it is only possible to obtain the above maps from main agents of the Survey of India. It is illegal to sell large scale maps of any area within 80 km of the coast or an international border. The export of large scale maps from India is prohibited. For anyone interested in the geography of India, trying to buy good maps is a depressing experience.

NORTH INDIA

Contents

Route Maps

Introduction

North India is the largest region in India. From the high peaks of the Himalaya it embraces the great flat plains of the Ganga valley and the upland plateaus of the northern Peninsula. This enormously diverse landscape is home to an equally wide range of peoples, from those of Mongolian and Tibetan stock in Leh and Ladakh to the tribal peoples in Madhya Pradesh. Delhi, centrally located in the region and well connected with all parts of the country, has the style and facilities of a modern and sophisticated capital.

Environment

The states of North India

North India has 2 Union territories – Delhi and Chandigarh – and 7 states, covering 1,452,602 sq km, 44% of India's land area. UP alone has 140 million people, 16% of the nation's total, and population density is equally high in Haryana and Punjab. These 3 states, along with Delhi and Chandigarh, form a heavily populated belt stretching from the NW to SE. This corresponds to the distribution of fertile alluvial soils on the Gangetic plain, along the Yamuna and the Punjab river system.

The mountain regions of Jammu & Kashmir, Himachal Pradesh and the hill region of UP are sparsely populated, but the cultivated area is relatively limited because of the mountainous terrain and its altitude. In terms of the land available for agriculture the densities are as high as those on the plains. Rajasthan (34 mn) has extensive deserts and semi-arid regions while Madhya Pradesh (52 mn) still has extensive forests.

Land

The Himalaya

The mountain region is magnificent with many striking contrasts. The Himalaya (Abode of Snow) stretches from Kashmir to Nepal. To the N is Tibet. Over 1000 km long, it varies in width from 160 km in Garhwal and Kumaon to 400 km in Kashmir and Ladakh. In places the mountains tower to almost 8000m.

To the S of the Himalaya are the **Shiwaliks**, a range of foothills, sometimes separated from the **Lesser Himalaya** by valleys (duns). In Kashmir the **Pir Panjal** range rises to nearly 5000m, forming the S wall to the **Vale of Kashmir**. Lower ranges, such as the **Zanskar** and **Ladakh** ranges, reach 6000m. These 2 are often referred to as the **Trans-Himalaya**, as the area is transitional between the Himalaya proper and the Tibetan plateau. Because the High Himalaya intercept the rain bearing monsoon, the Ladakh region receives only 100 mm of rain per year, making agriculture difficult. This dry region extends into Lahul and Spiti in Himachal Pradesh.

The mountains to the S of the Great Himalayan axis receive enough rain to allow 2 crops a year to be grown up to an altitude of approximately 3000m. The N presents a bleak contrast, alpine desert with a stark, stony beauty and deep gorges. The Indus River runs through Ladakh before entering Baltistan in Pakistan. Within Kashmir there is immense diversity. Ladakh is strongly Buddhist, its asceticism seemingly at home in this austere environment. The Vale of Kashmir in contrast is well-wooded, lush, and moist, with a number of large lakes, and predominantly Muslim. To its S is Jammu, where the Hindu majority have more affinities with the Punjab than the regions to the N.

Himachal Pradesh

This is also a beautiful mountain region. Valleys include the **Kulu Valley**, the Kangra and Chamba. Garhwal and Kumaon in the UP Himalaya can claim to be the home of the gods. The sacred **Ganga** and almost equally sacred **Yamuna** have their sources at Gangotri and Yamunotri. **Nanda Devi** (7816m) is the highest and one of the most beautiful and mysterious mountains in the entire range. Garhwal and Kumaon are Himalayan trekking's best kept secret – see page 253.

Punjab and the Gangetic Plain

When Indians speak of 'the North', they are usually referring to a broad belt of land from UP to Punjab, containing a very large proportion of the country's population. Its flat alluvium has created an ideal farming environment suited to large scale irrigation (see page 23).

Across the unrelentingly flat plain flows the **Ganga**, the physical as well as spiritual life force of northern India. At **Haridwar**, the gateway to the hills, it is nearly 300m above sea level. When it crosses the UP border with Bihar, it has fallen only 220m over more than 1000 km. The Ganga and Yamuna join at Allahabad (Prayag).

Central Plateau and Uplands

Running diagonally across Rajasthan from Mount Abu (1300m) to the Delhi Ridge are the Aravalli Hills. To the S is a region of hill and plateaus, up to 1150m high, while to the N is the Thar Desert. Delhi is strategically sited at the narrowest point between the Aravallis and the Himalaya. In Madhya Pradesh the Malwa plateau belongs to outliers of the Western Ghats. The old erosion front in the N of the state is strikingly beautiful, presenting bare cliffs and densely forested ravines which have long formed an important barrier to movement from the plains.

Thar Desert

The Great Indian or Thar desert lies N of the Aravallis and the Luni river. There are shifting sand dunes W of Jaisalmer but as you move E the desert becomes gently undulating and stony. Jodhpur dominates the central part.

Climate

There are wide variations in climate. Winter, spring, summer, monsoon and autumn are experienced by all regions except Ladakh and the Lahul/Spiti region, which lie beyond the Great Himalayan Axis and therefore do not receive the monsoon.

Temperature

Generally Dec and Jan are cool with maximum daily temperatures on the plains reaching 20°C and the minimum around 7°C, increasing as you move S. After dark it can get quite cold. Winter showers occur sporadically and mist or morning fog is relatively common. In the hills there is snow down to around 2000m. In Nainital the daily minimum in Jan is 2°C, and the maximum 10°C. In Leh it can reach as low as -35°C in summer rising to over 30°C. Sunstroke and frostbite are equally possible in Ladakh, where unsettled weather can originate from the Tibetan plateau bringing cold wind and snow or rain.

In the hills Feb and Mar are very pleasant months. Snow lies above 3500m and Ladakh is still snow bound, though daytime temperatures are pleasantly warm. To the S it is gradually hotting up. Bhopal can reach 34°C. Delhi is a few degrees cooler. Because of low rainfall the landscape is often dusty looking and humidity levels are low.

The hot weather lasts from Apr to mid-Jun. Delhi and Agra become very hot in May with daytime temperatures consistently over 40°C whilst at night they fall to around 27°C.The low humidity makes it bearable, but air conditioning becomes a necessity.

During the monsoon maximum daytime temperatures fall to around 35°C on the plains and 21°C in the hills. Humidity is high, the atmosphere enervating and clothes always seem damp.

When the monsoon finishes the weather pattern settles down. From Oct to Dec the skies clear, it is pleasantly warm and the countryside looks delightful. As winter approaches, night time temperatures fall and the mornings can be quite cool. It is an excellent time to travel.

Rain and snow fall

Most of the region receives its precipitation largely in the Jun to Oct monsoon. The onset of the rainy season is traditionally celebrated in rural areas because of its importance to crop growth. All areas except Ladakh and Lahul/Spiti receive 75% of their annual rainfall over this 5 month period. Flooding is common over much of the Gangetic Plain and communications can be disrupted. This is a difficult and unpleasant time for travelling, even though some places such as Mandu in Madhya Pradesh look their best. Kashmir is one of the few places that receives comparatively little rain over this period, and its relatively high altitude make it the perfect time to visit when political conditions permit.

History

North India lay at the heart of the development of Indian civilisation and political power from the growth of the Indus Valley civilisation until the arrival of the British. Thus much of the early history of the sub-continent is at the same time the history of northern India, and has been discussed in the Introduction to South Asia. See pages 34-66.

Modern North India

Politics

North India was at the centre of major political unrest in 1992-93 as the gathering Hindu political movement's campaign to build a temple on the supposed birthplace of Rama at Ayodhya culminated in the destruction of the 16th century Babri mosque. The Bharatiya Janata Party (BJP), the political party which had made this issue its major campaigning platform for over five years, had already made striking gains in earlier elections in several northern states, forming the government in Rajasthan, Madhya Pradesh, Uttar Pradesh and Himachal Pradesh. The 1991 Lok Sabha election saw the BJP make significant advances in many parts of the region. The gains were most pronounced in UP, where it won 50 of the 82 seats contested to the Janata Dal's 22 and the Congress Party's 5. The destruction of the mosque on December 6th 1992 led to riots in several major cities across India and at least 2000 deaths in police shootings, overwhelmingly of Muslims.

Elsewhere in the north political developments brought mixed results for the central government of Narasimha Rao. For the first time in 10 years the political violence in the Punjab showed signs of receding. Elections to the state assembly in summer 1992 produced only a minute turnout, reflecting at least in part the ability of terrorist separatists to keep even villagers away from polling booths. By spring 1993, however, local elections saw a dramatic shift in mood, with large scale voter turnout and a growing sense of optimism that a semblance of political normality was returning to what is still India's most prosperous agricultural state. In Kashmir, however, the situation remained bleak. Claimed by both India and Pakistan, and with a strong movement demanding independence from both, Kashmir continues to suffer great unrest and to be under tight military clampdown. Although some visitors entered the state in 1992-93, the situation remained tense and unpredictable.

Economy

Agriculture

Punjab is by far the most productive area with four-fifths of the cultivated area irrigated and impressive yields. Large parts of western UP and Haryana are not far behind and farmers have increased their yields more than 5 times since Independence. Wheat and rice are grown as commercial crops. In the hill region of UP, Himachal Pradesh, and extensive areas of Rajasthan and MP, farmers produce for their own consumption, sometimes having to import grain from the plains.

Up to an altitude of about 3000m, there are 2 cropping seasons. The *rabi* season runs from Oct to Mar/Apr. The *kharif* is the monsoon growing season, in which as much arable land as possible is sown. Wheat is the major rabi crop throughout the region and on poorer soils such as those in Ladakh is replaced with barley. The northern region produces the bulk of the nation's wheat and all its surplus. This is in contrast to E and S India which are rice growing regions. Rice is the most important kharif crop, thriving in the wetter conditions. Sugar cane is important along the Indo-Gangetic belt, cotton in southern Rajasthan and Madhya Pradesh, and market gardening around the urban centres such as Delhi.

In the alpine regions and semi arid areas of Rajasthan, where there is often only one cropping season, goats and sheep are popular for their wool production and, to a lesser extent, for their meat, which is acceptable to Muslims and less orthodox Hindus. Cattle are kept as draught animals and for milk production.

Forests

Pressure of population has caused a drastic reduction in the region's forests. Good reserves exist in the less accessible areas in the hills and over E Madhya Pradesh. Wood is a vital cooking fuel, and as the population increases the remaining forest resources are in jeopardy. In the towns kerosene and electricity are the main sources of energy for cooking for middle class households, but the poor burn cow dung, leaves, charcoal and wood.

Manufacturing

Various types of industry are distributed across the plains. Kanpur was one of the first textile factory cities in India and is a major processing centre for agricultural products, chemicals and leather. It is also a centre of the aircraft industry. Textiles are important in Rajasthan and Madhya Pradesh, which are well endowed with minerals ranging from diamonds from Panna to high grade iron and tin ore. There are steel plants at Bhilai, heavy electrical enterprises at Bhopal and an aluminium plant at Korba. Heavy industry includes the construction of railway rolling stock in Rajasthan along with zinc and copper smelting. Punjab on the other hand has practically no mineral resources, producing consumer goods such as bicycles. Haryana is the largest producer of automobile spare parts in India. Light industrial zones have been established in Central and southern Rajasthan around Kota, Jaipur, Udaipur and Bhilwara.

NB: Forced child labour and bonded labour are common in north India, especially in the carpet industry. The South Asian Coalition on Child Servitude (SACCS), a non Governmental organization set up to eradicate child labour in all the countries of South Asia, estimates that there are 300,000 children working in the Indian carpet industry alone, with a further 500,000 in Pakistan and 200,000 in Nepal. Many of these are either forcibly abducted or sold by parents to factory owners. Some 60 factory owners have now united in the Carpet Manufacturers' Association without Child Labour, and there is growing pressure to insist on an international rug mark certifying that carpets have not been made using child labour.

Other industry Kashmir has long been reliant on its high quality handicrafts such as carpets, papier mâché goods and shawls. In terms of its contribution to the regional economy tourism is relatively insignificant. However, in the popular areas such as Delhi, Agra, Rajasthan, and Kashmir, Ladakh and the hill stations, tourism has generated employment and income.

Communications

These are generally good throughout the region. The plains have an extensive road and rail network though the quality of roads is often poor and they are increasingly heavily used. Roads have been built into remote hill areas of the N for strategic reasons. This has increased their reliance on the more productive regions rather than aided local economic development.

NEW DELHI

CONTENTS

MAPS

New Delhi is the capital of India and a Union Territory and is the fastest growing large city in India, rapidly catching up the colonial cities of Bombay and Calcutta in size, and long since eclipsing them in political importance. In some areas it remains a spacious, garden city, tree-lined and with beautiful parks, but it can also be crowded and raucous with nightmarish traffic. Turbaned Sikhs, colourfully dressed Rajasthani and Gujarati women working as manual labourers on building sites, Muslim shopkeepers along Chandni Chowk in Old Delhi, Tibetans and Ladakhis in the street stalls along Janpath, and Kashmiris in the handicraft emporia around Connaught Place, all add to the cosmopolitan feel of the city.

BASICS *Area*: 434 sq km. *Altitude*: 216m. *STD Code*: 022. *Main languages*: Hindi, Urdu, Punjabi and English. *Distance of Connaught Circus*: to airport 23 km (Indira Gandhi International), 15 km (Palam Domestic).

CLIMATE The monsoon lasts from mid-Jun to mid-Sep. May and June are very hot and dry. Dec and Jan can be colder than most people realise, particularly at night, so woollens are recommended.

SOCIAL INDICATORS *Population*: 9.1mn (Scheduled castes 18%). *Literacy*: M 84% F 68%. *Birth rate*: *Rural* 33:1000, *Urban* 27:1000. *Death rate*: *Rural* 8:1000, *Urban* 7:1000. *Registered graduate job seekers*: 64,000. *Religion*: *Hindu* 84%, *Muslim* 8%, *Sikh* 6%, *Christian* 1%.

Arrival

From Indira Gandhi International Airport you drive along the broad tree-lined streets of New Delhi, in marked contrast to Old Delhi where your senses are bombarded by noise, bustle, smells and apparent chaos. Outside the railway stations taxi drivers, rickshaw wallahs and hotel touts jostle for attention. Often street names appear in 4 scripts – Devanagari, Gurmukhi, Urdu and English. East and west, old and new, traditional and modern, simple and sophisticated, are all juxtaposed. Un-

CLIMATE: NEW DELHI

	Jan	Feb	Mar	Apr	May	Jun	Jul	Aug	Sep	Oct	Nov	Dec	Av/Tot
Max (°C)	21	24	30	36	41	40	35	34	34	35	29	23	32
Min (°C)	7	10	15	21	27	29	27	26	25	19	12	8	19
Rain (mm)	25	22	17	7	8	65	211	173	150	31	1	5	715

representative of much of the rest of India, Delhi and its inhabitants nevertheless suggest great confidence and vitality.

The site

Sited on the W bank of the Yamuna River at the narrowest point between the Aravalli hills to the SW and the Himalaya, Delhi has commanded the route from the vital NW frontier into the rich agricultural hinterland of the Ganga plains. From Tughluqabad in S Delhi you can get an excellent view of Delhi's strategic position.

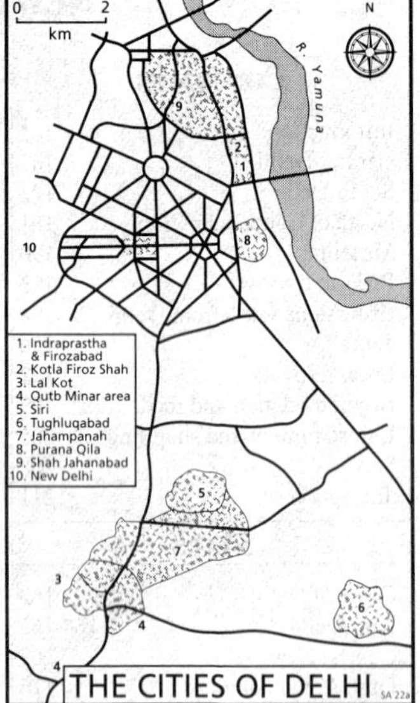

THE CITIES OF DELHI

The Cities of Delhi

Delhi today is essentially 3 cities, spreading over the remains of nearly a dozen earlier centres which once occupied this vital strategic site.

Old Delhi or Shah Jahanabad, was built by the Mughal Emperor Shah Jahan in the first half of the 17th century. Focusing on the great imperial buildings of the Red Fort and the Jama Masjid, this old city is a dense network of narrow alleys and tightly packed markets and houses, Muslims, Sikhs and Hindus living side by side, but separated in their own defined quarters.

The new cities Immediately to the S is the British-built capital of New Delhi, a self conscious attempt to match the imperial grandeur of the Mughal capital. It retains the monumental buildings and street layout of its imperial builders, but it has already been engulfed by the sprawl of the modern city. Spreading in all directions from the twin centres of Old and New Delhi, post-Independence Delhi has accelerated its suburban expansion with government built and privately-owned flats and houses.

But there is also a 3rd city, often scarcely seen. Unlike Bombay and Calcutta, notorious for the desperate housing problems of the poor, Delhi has confined much of its worst housing to the areas distant from the main centres. Yet squatter settlements provide the only shelter for at least ⅓ of Delhi's 9 million people, and their growth continues remorselessly.

New Delhi: the origins

New Delhi's present position as capital was only confirmed on 12 December 1911, when the King Emperor George V announced at the Delhi Durbar that the capital of India was to move from Calcutta to Delhi. It was to be an emphatic statement of the magnificence and permanence of British rule in India. The planning of New Delhi began as soon as the 1911 Durbar was over under the leadership of Edwin Lutyens. The new city was inaugurated on 9 Feb 1931.

Lutyens and Baker For an architect, the project was a dream. The new city was to cover 26 sq km and include the boldest expressions anywhere in the world of British imperial ambitions. Lutyens decided that he would design the palatial

Viceroy's House and his friend **Herbert Baker** would design the nearby Government Secretariat and Imperial Legislative Assembly. Between them they would style the symbolically important approach to these magnificent structures.

The King Emperor favoured something in form and flavour similar to the Mughal masterpieces but fretted over the horrendous expense that this would incur. A petition signed by eminent public figures such as Bernard Shaw and

The Cities Of Delhi

City	Date	Site	Remains
1 **Indraprastha**	9th century BC- 4th century AD	In Purana Qila, Nr Pragati Maidan	Recent archaeological finds at Shergarh support the view that this was the site of Delhi's earliest city. Nothing remains
2 **Lal Kot**	850 AD. Built by the Rajput Tomar kings	Qutb Minar complex	Recent archaeological finds: nothing is standing
3 **Lal Kot** enlarged	1180 AD Built by the Rajput king Prithviraj	Qutb Minar complex	Some walls of the fort
4 **Qutb Minar** area	1193 AD	Qutb Minar	Mosques, Qutb Minar, walls
5 **Siri**	1304 AD Built by Ala-ud-din Khalji, major trading centre through 14th century	Nr Hauz Khas	Walls remain
6 **Tughluqabad**	1321-25. Built by Ghiyas ud Din Tughluq	8 km E of Qutb	Walls and some ruined buildings
7 **Jahanpanah**	Mid-14th century. Built by Md. Tughluq	Between Siri and Qutb Minar	A few remnants of defensive walls
8 **Firozabad**	Built 1354 by Firoz Tughluq, capital until Sikander Lodi chose Agra	7 km NE of Siri – Feroze Shah Kotla	Only the Asoka pillar rising from the ruins remains
9 **Purana Qila** (Old Fort)	Built in 1534 by Humayun, the 2nd Mughal Emperor	ESE of India Gate	High gates, walls, mosque, and a great baoli (well)
10 **Shergarh**	Mid 16th century. Built by Sher Shah during Humayun's enforced exile	Around the Purana Quila	Kabuli and Lal Darwaza gates and the Sher Mandal
11 **Shah Jahanabad**	Mid-17th century. Built by Shah Jahan as his capital when he moved from Agra	The existing Old Delhi	The Red Fort, Jama Masjid, main streets of Old Delhi (eg Chandni Chowk), long sections of walls and several city gates
12 **New Delhi**	1920s. King George V announced the move of the capital from Calcutta to Delhi in 1911. Main buildings completed 20 years later	Centred on Connaught Circus and Rajpath	All the main British buildings

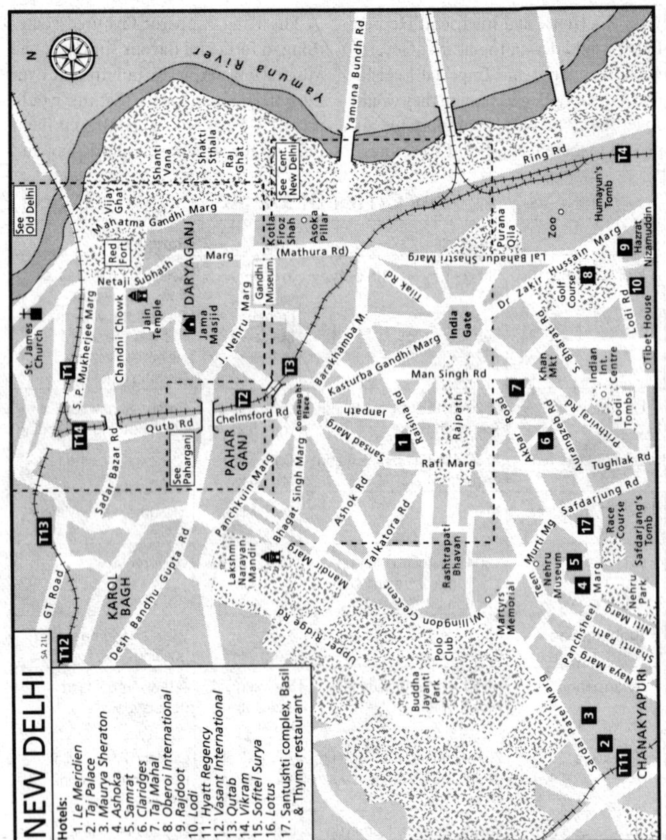

A New Law To Beef About?

In April 1994 the Delhi Assembly passed new legislation making it a criminal offence subject to up to five years in prison to possess any meat product of bulls or cows. Muslim-run abbattoirs were finding new severe restrictions on their normal trade, nominally to reduce the volume of animal waste dumped in the Yamuna every day. This has been estimated as sufficient to fill an Olympic swimming pool with blood and offal. For millions of goats, whose meat is often classified as the ubiquitous 'mutton', the decision may spell a brief reprieve, but it remains to be seen how effective the ban will be, and how long the consequent dramatic rise in meat prices will last.

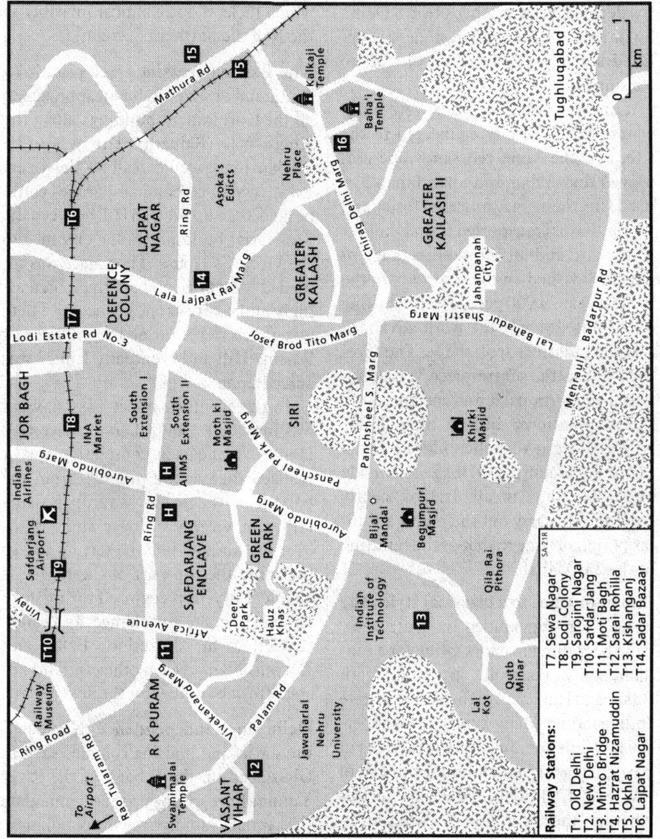

Thomas Hardy advocated an Indian style and an Indian master builder. Herbert Baker had made known his own views even before his appointment when he wrote "first and foremost it is the spirit of British sovereignty which must be imprisoned in its stone and bronze". Lord Hardinge, the Viceroy suggested 'Western architecture with an Oriental motif'. As Tillotson has shown, Lutyens was appalled by the political pressure to adopt any Indian styles. For one thing, he despised Indian architecture. "Even before he had seen any examples of it," writes Tillotson, "he pronounced Mughal architecture to be 'piffle', and seeing it did not disturb that conviction." Yet in the end, the compromise was what Lutyens was forced to settle for.

The choice of site The city would accommodate 70,000 people and have boundless possibilities for future expansion. A foundation stone was hastily cut and laid by King George V at the Durbar, but when Lutyens and his team arrived and toured the site on elephant back they decided that it was unsuitable. The Viceroy decided on an another site in S Delhi. So in 1913 the foundation stone was uplifted and moved on a bullock cart to Raisina Hill.

Land was levelled, roads were built, water and electricity connected to the site, and the same red sandstone employed that Akbar and Shah Jahan had used in their magnificent forts and tombs. It was transported from Dholpur to the site and an impressive range of marble lavished on the interiors. In the busiest year 29,000 people were working on the site. Slowly the work advanced and the buildings took shape. The Viceroy's house, the centre-piece, was of imperial proportions; it was one km round the foundations, bigger than Louis XIV's palace at Versailles, had a colossal dome surmounting a long colonnade and 340 rooms in all. It took nearly 2 decades to carry out the plans, a similar period of time to that of the building of the Taj Mahal.

Indian touches to a classical style The project was surrounded by controversy from beginning to end. Opting for a fundamentally classical structure, both Baker and Lutyens sought to incorporate Indian motifs. Many were entirely superficial. While some claim that Luytens in particular achieved a unique synthesis of the two traditions, Tillotson queries whether "the sprinkling of a few simplified and classicised Indian details (especially *Chhattris*) over a classical palace" could be called a synthesis. The chief exception was the dome of the Viceroy's house itself, which made strong allusions to the Buddhist stupa at Sanchi while marrying it to an essentially classical form, see page 361. A striking irony in the overall design came as a result of the late necessity of building a council chamber for the representative assembly which was created by political reforms in 1919. This now houses the Lok Sabha, but its centrality to the current Indian constitution is belied by Baker's design which tucks it away almost invisibly to the N of the northern Secretariat.

The Raisina crossing (See page 169.) The grand design was for an approach to all the Government buildings along the King's Way (Rajpath). This was to be 2.4 km long, would lead to the Great Palace where ceremonial parades could be held, then up Raisina Hill between the Secretariat buildings to the entrance to the Viceroy's House. The palace was intended to be in view at all times, increasingly impressive as one got nearer. There was much debate over the gradient of Raisina Hill and eventually 1 in 22 was agreed upon.

In the event the effect was not what was intended. Only when the Viceroy's House was nearing completion was it realised that as you progress from the bottom of the Kings Way up Raisina Hill, the Viceroy's House sinks down over the horizon like the setting sun so that only the top part of the palace is visible. Lutyens recognised the mistake too late to make any change, and called this effect his 'Bakerloo'. Baker and Lutyens blamed each other and did not speak to one another for the next 5 years.

Delhi since Independence New satellite towns and housing colonies such as Ghaziabad on the E bank of the River Yamuna have sprung up to accommodate the capital's rapidly growing population. Government Ministries and Departments have spread across S Delhi but it is also one of the world's greenest cities, with many trees and attractive parks. However, beyond the range of New Delhi's broad avenues is another city. At least ⅓ of the city's population continue to live in 'jhuggies' (squatter huts). In the 1970s Sanjay Gandhi, Mrs. Gandhi's younger son, pushed through a programme of bulldozing squatter settlements from the more public places, but some argue that the housing problem has simply been pushed a little further from sight.

One attempt to meet the most basic problems of shelter has been the provision of night shelters for homeless workers. By 1994 they catered for over 125,000 people every night for a nominal charge. The largest is near Old Delhi Railway Station. Each centre has fans and air coolers; cleaners go through daily, and 100,000 blankets are washed every day.

Current political developments

Delhi has its own Assembly, though its political powers as the government of a Union Territory of under 10 million voters are very limited. Right wing Hindu parties have always been a force in Delhi politics, and in the December 1993 elections the BJP swept Delhi's electoral board. They will continue to press that Delhi be given the full status of a state. The Chief Minister, Madan Lal Khurana, appears to have won significant Sikh support in the elections by promising to pursue the prosecution of those responsible for the anti-Sikh riots following Mrs. Gandhi's assassination in 1984. That promise may be difficult to deliver, but there has already been one surprising result of the BJP's takeover in the city – a dramatic clamp down on meat supplies.

Places of interest

The sites of interest are grouped in 3 main areas. **Shah Jahanabad** is about 7 km to the N of Connaught Circus. 10 km to the S is the Qutb Minar complex, with the old fortress city of Tughluqabad 8 km to its E. In the centre is the British built capital of New Delhi, with its government buildings and wide avenues. You can visit each separately, or link routes together into a day-tour to include the most interesting sites. This description starts near the centre of the modern political and administrative centre of Indian government. The 2nd section describes sites in the S and the 3rd, the city of Shah Jahanabad.

Central Delhi

India Gate

A tour of New Delhi will usually start with a visit to India Gate. This war memorial is situated at the E end of Rajpath. Designed by Lutyens, it commemorates more than 70,000 Indian soldiers who died in World War I. 13,516 names of British and Indian soldiers killed on the NW Frontier and in the Afghan War of 1919 are engraved on the arch and foundations. Under the arch is the Amar Jawan Jyoti, commemorating Indian armed forces' losses in the Indo-Pakistan War of 1971. The arch (43m high) stands on a base of Bharatpur stone and rises in stages. Below the cornice are Imperial Suns and on both sides of the arch is inscribed INDIA flanked by the dates MCMXIV (1914 left) and MCMXIX (1919). Facing the arch is an open cupola which once contained a statue of King George V. Similar to the Hindu *chhattri* signifying regality, it is decorated with nautilus shells symbolising British Maritime power.

To the NW of India Gate are 2 impressive buildings, **Hyderabad House** and **Baroda House**, built as residences for the Nizam of Hyderabad and the Gaekwar of Baroda. Now used as offices, both were carefully placed to indicate the paramountcy of the British Raj over the Princely States. The *Nizam*, reputed to be the richest man in the world, ruled over an area equal to that of France. The *Gaekwar* belonged to the top level of Indian Princes and both, along with the Maharajas of Mysore, Jammu and Kashmir and Gwalior were entitled to receive 21 gun salutes.

Rajpath leads W from India Gate towards Janpath. To the N are the **National Archives**. Formerly the Imperial Record Office, and designed by Lutyens, this was intended to be a part of a much more ambitious complex of public buildings. To the S is the **Na-**

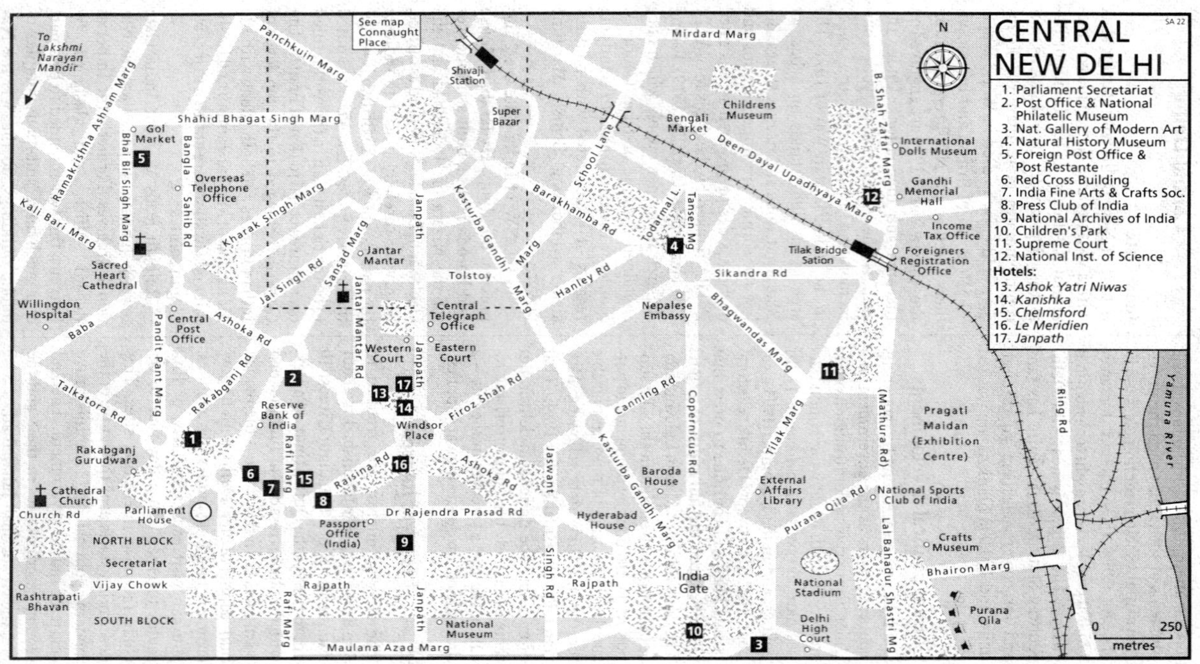
CENTRAL NEW DELHI
SA 22
1. Parliament Secretariat
2. Post Office & National Philatelic Museum
3. Nat. Gallery of Modern Art
4. Natural History Museum
5. Foreign Post Office & Post Restante
6. Red Cross Building
7. India Fine Arts & Crafts Soc.
8. Press Club of India
9. National Archives of India
10. Children's Park
11. Supreme Court
12. National Inst. of Science
Hotels:
13. Ashok Yatri Niwas
14. Kanishka
15. Chelmsford
16. Le Meridien
17. Janpath
N
To Lakshmi Narayan Mandir
See map Connaught Place
Panchkuin Marg
Shivaji Station
Mirdard Marg
Childrens Museum
Super Bazar
Shahid Bhagat Singh Marg
Gol Market
Bengali Market
Ramakrishna Ashram Marg
Bhai Bir Singh Marg
Bangla Sahib Rd
Overseas Telephone Office
School Lane
Deen Dayal Upadhyaya Marg
B. Shah Zafar Marg
International Dolls Museum
Gandhi Memorial Hall
Kali Bari Marg
Kharak Singh Marg
Janpath
Kasturba Gandhi Marg
Barakhamba Rd
Todarmal L.
Tansen Mg
Income Tax Office
Sacred Heart Cathedral
Sansad Marg
Jantar Mantar
Tolstoy
Tilak Bridge Sation
Foreigners Registration Office
Jai Singh Rd
Hanley Rd
Sikandra Rd
Willingdon Hospital
Central Post Office
Jantar Mantar Rd
Central Telegraph Office
Nepalese Embassy
Baba
Ashoka Rd
Western Court
Eastern Court
Bhagwandas Marg
Pandit Pant Marg
Rakabganj Rd
Talkatora Rd
Reserve Bank of India
Windsor Place
Firoz Shah Rd
Canning Rd
Copernicus Rd
(Mathura Rd)
Pragati Maidan (Exhibition Centre)
Ring Rd
Yamuna River
Tilak Marg
Rakabganj Gurudwara
Rafi Marg
Raisina Rd
Jaswant Singh Rd
Baroda House
External Affairs Library
National Sports Club of India
Cathedral Church
Church Rd
Parliament House
Dr Rajendra Prasad Rd
Hyderabad House
Purana Qila Rd
Passport Office (India)
NORTH BLOCK
Secretariat
Crafts Museum
Bhairon Marg
Vijay Chowk
Rajpath
India Gate
National Stadium
Lal Bahadur Shastri Mg
Rashtrapati Bhavan
SOUTH BLOCK
National Museum
Delhi High Court
Purana Qila
Maulana Azad Marg
0 250 metres

tional **Museum** (see under Museums). The foundation stone was laid by Jawarharlal Nehru in 1955 and the building completed in 1960. Rajpath continues to the foot of Raisina Hill, now called Vijay Chowk.

The Secretariats

These stand on both sides of Raisina Hill. **North Block** houses the Home and Finance Ministries, **South Block** the Ministry of Foreign Affairs. These long classical buildings, topped by Baroque domes, designed by Baker, are similar to his Government Buildings of Pretoria, and were derived from Wren's Royal Naval College at Greenwich. The towers were originally designed to be twice the height of the buildings, and to act as beacons guarding the way to the inner sanctum. Their height was reduced, and with it their impact. The domes are decorated with lotus motifs and elephants, while the N and S gateways are Mughal in design. On the N Secretariat is the imperialistic inscription 'Liberty will not descend to a people: a people must raise themselves to liberty. It is a blessing which must be earned before it can be enjoyed'.

In the Great Court between the Secretariats are the 4 **Dominion Columns**, donated by the governments of Australia, Canada, New Zealand and South Africa – ironically, as it turned out. The resemblance to Baker's domes to his work in Pretoria is also striking and ironic! Each is crowned by a bronze ship sailing east, symbolising the maritime and mercantile supremacy of the British Empire. In the centre of the court is the Jaipur column of red sandstone and topped with a white egg, bronze lotus and 6-pointed glass star of India (4-pointed, 2 centre-front and rear. As it evolved the star of India became a 5 pointed star, as today.). Across the entrance to the **Great Court** is a 205m wrought iron screen.

At Secretariat and Rashtrapati Bhavan gates mounted and unmounted troops parade in full uniform. Sat 1030, worth attending.

Rashtrapati Bhavan

The Viceroy's House, now called Rashtrapati Bhavan, is the official residence of the President of India. Designed by Lutyens, it combines western and eastern styles and has been described by Philip Davies as a masterpiece of symmetry, discipline, silhouette and harmony. Inside is the Durbar Hall, 23m in diameter with coloured marble from all parts of India. To the W of the Viceroy's House the garden extends the principles of hierarchy and order.

To the S is Flagstaff House, formerly the residence of the Commander-in-Chief. Renamed **Teen Murti Bhawan** it now houses the Nehru Memorial Museum (see below). Designed by Robert Tor Russell, in 1948 it became the Prime Minister's residence. The **Martyr's Memorial**, at the junction of Sardar Patel Marg and Willingdon Crescent, is a magnificent 26m long, 3m high bronze sculpture by D. P. Roy Chowdhury. The 11 statues of national heroes are headed by Mahatma Gandhi.

Parliament House

NE of the Viceroy's House is the Council House, now Sansad Bhavan. Baker designed this and Lutyens suggested that it be circular (173m diameter). Originally, it was intended to have a dome but this plan was dropped. Inside is the library and chambers for the Council of State, Chamber of Princes and Legislative Assembly – the Lok Sabha.

Just opposite the Council House is the **Rakabganj Gurudwara** in Pandit Pant Marg. This 20th century white marble shrine in a style that is a subtle integration of the late Mughal and Rajasthani styles marks the spot where the headless body of Guru Tej Bahadur, the 9th Sikh Guru (see page 92) was cremated in 1657. W of the Council House is the **Cathedral Church of the Re-**

demption (1927-35) by Henry Medd whose design (after Palladio's II Redentore in Venice) won an architectural competition. The altar was donated by York Minster to mark its thirteenth centenary. To the N is Medd's Italianate Roman Catholic **Church of the Sacred Heart** (1930-4), the winning design in another competition.

Connaught Place

Connaught Place and its outer ring, **Connaught Circus**, comprise 2-storeyed arcaded buildings, ranged radially. Designed by Robert Tor Russell, they have become the main commercial centre of Delhi. Architecturally, they are very distinctive, very un-Indian and the complete antithesis to Shah Jahan's Chandni Chowk. To the S in Janpath (the People's Way) the E and W Courts were hostels for the members of the newly convened Legislative Assembly. With their long colonnaded verandahs, these are Tuscan in character.

The Birla Temple

To the W of Connaught Circus is the **Lakshmi Narayan Mandir** in Mandir Marg. Financed by the prominent industrialist Raja Baldeo Birla in 1938, this is one of the most popular Hindu shrines in the city and one of Delhi's few striking examples of Hindu architecture. Dedicated to Lakshmi, the goddess of well-being, it is commonly referred to as Birla Mandir. The design is in the Orissan style with tall curved towers (*sikhara*) capped by large *amalakas*. The exterior is faced with red and ochre stone and white marble. Built around a central courtyard, the main shrine has images of Narayan and his consort Lakshmi while 2 separate cells have icons of Siva (the Destroyer) and his consort Durga (the 10-armed destroyer of demons). The temple is flanked by a *dharamshala* (rest house) and a Buddhist *vihara* (monastery).

E from the Birla temple, down Kali Bari Marg to Baba Kharag Singh Marg (Irwin Rd), is the **Hanuman Mandir**. This small temple appears to have been built in 1724 by Maharaja Jai Singh of Jaipur at about the same time that the Jantar Mantar was constructed. Of no great architectural interest, in the last 10 years the temple has become increasingly popular with devotees. The **Mangal haat** (Tuesday Fair) is a popular market for local people.

Jai Singh's observatory

Just to the E of the Hanuman Mandir in Sansad Marg (Parliament St) is the **Jantar Mantar** (observatory). The Mughal Emperor Muhammad Shah (r1719-1748) entrusted the renowned astronomer Maharaja Jai Singh of Jaipur with the task of revising the calendar and correcting the astronomical tables used by contemporary priests – see page 403. Daily astral observations were made for years before construction began and plastered brick structures were favoured for the site instead of brass instruments. It was built in 1725 and is slightly smaller than that at Jaipur. A small Bhairav temple E of the instruments appears to have been built at the same time. Guide books available.

The Road to Raj Ghat

There are several interesting and important sites immediately to the E and NE of Connaught Circus. Travel NE from Connaught Circus under the Minto Bridge to the open space of the Ramlila grounds, part of which still serves as a camp site. Along their N side run the shops of Asaf Ali Road, which conceal what used to be the wall of Shah Jahanabad. To the left is the old Ajmeri Gate. To the right the road runs past the old Delhi Gate (where the main road N into the city turns sharp left into the often chaotically noisy, fume-ridden Daryaganj) to the Yamuna.

The Memorial Ghats

Beyond Delhi Gate lie the banks of the Yamuna, marked by a series of memorials to India's leaders. The river itself, now a km away is invisible from the road, protected by a low rise and banks of trees. The most prominent memorial, immediately opposite the end of Jawaharlal Nehru Rd is that of Mahatma Gandhi at **Raj Ghat**. To its N is **Shanti Vana** ('forest of peace'), landscaped gardens where Prime Minister Jawaharlal Nehru was cremated in 1964, and subsequently his grandson Sanjay Gandhi in 1980, daughter Indira Gandhi in 1984 and elder grandson, Rajiv, in 1991. To the N again is **Vijay Ghat** ('Victory bank') where Prime Minister Lal Bahadur Shastri was cremated in 1965.

Kotla Firoz Shah

Moving S down the Mathura Rd (now Lal Bahadur Shastri Marg) is a succession of sites illustrating Delhi at its most modern and its most ancient. Immediately to the S of Raj Ghat is the Yamuna Velodrome and the Indraprastha Stadium, one of India's biggest sports stadiums. Between that and the Mathura Rd is Kotla Firoz Shah, the citadel of Firozabad, built by Firoz Shah Tughluq (r1351-1388) in 1351. Little remains as the ruins of Firozabad were extensively used for the later cities of Sher Shah (Shergarh) and Shah Jahan (Shah Jahanabad). At its height it stretched from Hauz Khas in the S to N of the Delhi ridge, and E to the Yamuna river.

From Bahadurshah Zafar Marg you enter the central enclosure, the largest of the 3 originals (covered for the most part by modern buildings). The most striking feature is the tapering 14m high monolithic polished sandstone Asoka pillar (3rd century BC). Firoz Shah was deeply interested in antiquities and had it brought from Topra (Haryana), 100 km away, wrapped in silk and muslin, on a 42-wheeled carriage drawn apparently by 200 men at each wheel. The Brahmi inscription carries the Emperor Asoka's message of goodwill to his subjects – see page 40. Nearby is a a circular *baoli* (well) and a ruined mosque. In its original state it is said to have accommodated over 10,000 worshippers and was where the Mongol Timur prayed during his sacking of Delhi in 1398. Apparently, he was so impressed by it that the Samarkand mosque was modelled on it. If popular legends are to be believed, S Asia is riddled with secret underground tunnels. It is said that 3 secret passages lead from the Kush-ki-Firoz (Palace of Firoz) to the river, his hunting lodge on the Ridge and to Jahanpanah near the Qutb Minar. To the S of Kotla Firoz Shah is the Pragati Maidan, a permanent exhibition centre for trade fairs and other public exhibitions. Immediately to its S, is the Purana Qila.

Purana Qila (Old Fort)

Entrance by W gate. Guide books and postcards available. A small museum near the Humayun Darwaza houses finds from the excavations. Open 0800-1830. Clean toilets.

The venue of Delhi's annual flower show, the Purana Qila is now an attractive and quiet park. However, in the 16th century it witnessed the crucial struggle between the Mughal Emperor Humayun and his formidable Afghan rival Sher Shah Suri. The massive gateways and walls were probably built by Humayun, who laid the first brick of his new capital Dinpanah in 1534. The few surviving buildings within this roughly octagonal fort were the work of Sher Shah, who defeated Humayun in 1540, razed Dinpanah to the ground and started to build his own capital Shergarh on the same site. Humayun regained his throne in 1555 and destroyed Shergarh, but he died a year later.

The massive double-storeyed **Bara Darwaza** (Great Gate) is the main entrance to the fort. The 2 bay-deep cells on the inside of the enclosure were used after the Partition of India in 1947 to provide shelter for refugees from Pakistan. The S gate, the **Humayun Darwaza**, bears an ink inscription mentioning Sher Shah and the date 950 AH (1543-4), while the N gate is known as the **Talaqi Darwaza** (Forbidden Gate). The **Qila-i-Kuhna Masjid** (mosque of the Old fort) was built by Sher Shah and is considered one of the finest examples of Indo-Afghan architecture. The arches, tessellations and rich ornamentation in black and white marble against red sandstone became very popular during the Mughal period. Though the Fort is in ruins, the mosque is in good condition.

Sher Mandal, a small octagonal tower S of the mosque was probably built by Sher Shah as a pleasure pavilion from which to view the river. Humayun later used it as a library, spending hours poring over his cherished collection of miniatures and manuscripts. It is said that when he heard the *muezzin's* call to prayer he hurried down the steps of the building and slipped. The fall proved fatal. Trenches dug south of Sher Mandal in 1955 revealed pieces of Grey Ware, also discovered at other sites and associated with the *Mahabharata* (c1100 BC), reinforcing the tradition that this was also the site of the legendary Indraprasth.

Outside the Purana Qila and across Mathura Rd is **Khairul Manzil Masjid** ("Most Auspicious of houses" Mosque), built in 1561 by Maham Anga, a wet-nurse to Akbar, who is said to have held considerable influence over him. Alongside this is Sher Shah Darwaza, the S gate to Shergarh.

South Delhi

The southern part of the city can conveniently be seen separately from those described above, though you can continue on the route as follows. The spacious layout of New Delhi has been preserved despite the building on empty sites and the sub-division of previously large gardens. Still close to the centre, there are several attractive high class residential areas, such as Jor Bagh near the Lodi Gardens, while beyond the Ring Road sprawling estates of flats and larger apartments and huge shopping and commercial centres such as Nehru Place, have pushed the limits of Delhi to Tughluqabad and the Qutb Minar.

The Lodi Gardens

A further km to the S of the Purana Qila, the Mathura Rd is joined on the right by Lodi Rd, leading to the Lodi Gardens and the **Lodi Tombs**. The gardens now are beautiful parks. Set in the heart of one of the best residential districts of Delhi, they are much used by anyone from joggers to those out for a gentle stroll. The mellow stone tombs of the 15th and 16th century Lodi rulers are situated in the gardens. In the middle of the garden facing the E entrance from Max Mueller Rd is **Bara Gumbad** (Big Dome), a mosque built in 1494. The raised courtyard, ascended by steps from the N is provided with an imposing gateway and *mehman khana* (guest rooms). The platform in the centre appears to have had a tank for ritual ablutions.

The Sheesh (Shish) **Gumbad** (Glass Dome, late 15th century) is built on a raised incline a few metres N of the Bara Gumbad and was once decorated with glazed blue tiles, painted floral designs and Koranic inscriptions. The façade gives the impression of a 2-storeyed building, typical of Lodi architecture. **Mohammad Shah's Tomb** (1450) is that of the 3rd Sayyid ruler. It has sloping buttresses, an octagonal plan, projecting eaves and lotus patterns on the ceiling. **Sikander Lodi's tomb**, built by his son in 1517 is also an octagonal structure decorated with Hindu motifs. A structural innovation is the double dome which was later refined under the Mughals. **Athpula** (Bridge of 8 Piers) is nearby, used for entering the garden from the NE, and is believed to have been built in the 16th century by Nawab Bahadur, a nobleman at Akbar's court.

Safdarjang's Tomb

At the E end of Lodi Road is Safdarjang's Tomb which has the advantage of not being full of tourists. Open sunrise to sunset. Nominal entry fee. This tomb was built by Nawab Shuja-ud-Daulah for his father Mirza Mukhim Abdul Khan, entitled Safdarjang, who was Governor of Oudh during the reign of Muhammad Shah (1719-1748), and Wazir of his successor Ahmad Shah (1748-1754). Safdarjang died in 1754. With its high enclosure walls, *char bagh* layout of gardens, fountain and central domed mausoleum, it follows the tradition of Humayun's tomb but despite its attractiveness and the elements reminiscent of the Taj Mahal, it shows a weakening of form typical of a late architectural style. Typically, the real tomb is just below ground level. Flanking the mausoleum are pavilions used by Shuja-ud-Daulah and his family as their Delhi residence. Immediately to its S is the battlefield where Timur and his Mongol horde crushed Mahmud Shah Tughluq on 12 December 1398.

Hazrat Nizamuddin

At the W end of the Lodi Road is Hazrat Nizamuddin Dargah. Nizamuddin *basti* (village), now tucked away behind the residential suburb of Nizamuddin West, off Mathura Rd, grew up around the tomb and shrine of Sheikh Nizamuddin Aulia (1236-1325), the 4th Chishti saint. The original tomb no longer exists and the present structure was built in 1526 and subsequently extensively renovated. Legend states that the then emperor Ghiyas'ud-din Tughluq tried to prevent workmen from building the shrine as his own city Tughluqabad was then being constructed. The craftsmen worked at night and when the emperor forbade the sale of oil, they used water from the sacred baoli (well) near the N gate, to fuel the lamps.

W of the central shrine is the **Jama-at-khana Mosque** (1325). Its decorated arches are typical of the Khalji design also seen at the Ala'i Darwaza at the Qutb Minar. S of the main tomb and behind finely crafted screens is the grave of princess Jahanara, Shah Jahan's eldest and favourite daughter. She shared the emperor's last years when he was imprisoned at Agra fort – see page 309. The grave, open to the sky, is in accordance with the epitaph written by her "Let naught cover my grave save the green grass, for grass suffices as the covering of the lowly".

Pilgrims congregate at the shrine twice a year for the *Urs* (fair) held to mark the anniversaries of Hazrat Nizamuddin Aulia and his disciple **Amir Khusrau**, whose tomb is nearby. An evening visit (around 1900) is rewarding as *qawwalis* are sung after *namaaz* (prayer).

Humayun's Tomb

It is a popular place because it is the most interesting and best preserved tomb in Delhi and is therefore included in organised sightseeing tours. Proximity to railway stations means peace is destroyed by constant train noise. Open daily, sunrise to sunset. Nominal entry fee, Fri free. **NB:** Video cameras Rs 25. Transport: located in Nizamuddin, ¼ hr by taxi from Connaught Circus. Allow ¾ hr there. Soft drinks, guide books and postcards sold at the entrance.

In most other countries Humayun's tomb would be considered a great monument. Eclipsed later by the Taj Mahal and the Jama Masjid, it is the best example in Delhi of the early Mughal style of tomb and is well worth a visit, preferably before visiting the Taj Mahal in Agra. Humayun, the 2nd Mughal Emperor, was forced into exile in Persia after being heavily defeated by the Afghan Sher Shah in 1540. He returned to India in 1545, finally re-capturing Delhi in 1555. For the remaining year of his life the emperor spent much of his time in the octagonal Sher Mandal at Sher Shah's fort (now Purana Qila), poring over his cherished collection of miniatures and manuscripts (see page172).

Humayun's tomb was built by his senior widow and mother of his son Akbar, Hamida Begum. A Persian from Khurasan, after her pilgrimage to Mecca she was known as Haji Begum. She supervised the entire construction of the tomb (1564-1573), camping on the site. Her design was before its time, though it was copied soon afterwards in the much smaller tomb of Atkah Khan.

The plan The first substantial example of Mughal architecture in India, it has an octagonal plan, lofty arches, pillared kiosks and the double dome of Central Asia origin, which appears here for the first time in India. Outside Gujarat, Hindu temples make no use of the dome, but the Indian Muslim dome had until now been of a flatter shape, much like a half grapefruit as opposed to the tall Persian dome rising on a more slender neck. Here also is the first standard example in India of the garden tomb concept: the *char bagh* (garden divided into quadrants), water channels and fountains. This form culminated in the gardens of the Taj Mahal. However, the tomb also shows a number of distinctively Hindu motifs. Tillotson has pointed out that in Humayun's tomb, Hindu *Chhattris* (small domed kiosks), complete with temple columns and *chajjas* (broad eaves), surround the central dome. The bulbous finial on top of the dome and the star motif in the spandrels of the main arches are also Hindu, the latter being a solar symbol.

The approach From the car park you enter the Bu Halima garden before reaching the admission kiosk. The tomb enclosure has 2 high double-storeyed gateways: the entrance to the W and the other to the S. A *baradari* occupies the centre of the E wall, and a bath chamber that of the N wall. Several Moghul princes, princesses and Haji Begum herself lie buried here. During the 1857 Mutiny Bahadur Shah II, the last Moghul Emperor of Delhi, took shelter here with his 3 sons. Over 80, he was seen as a figurehead by Muslims opposing the British. When captured he was transported to Rangoon for the remaining 4 years of his life.

The platform on which the tomb stands measures 47.5m square. The corners of the octagonal tomb are similarly large. The dome (38m high) does not have the swell of the Taj Mahal and the decoration of the whole edifice is much simpler. It is of red sandstone with some white marble to highlight the lines of the building. There is some attractive inlay work, and some *jalis* in the balcony fence, and on some of the recessed keel arch windows.

The interior is austere and consists of 3 storeys of arches rising up to the dome. The Emperor's tomb is of white marble and quite plain without any inscription. The overall impression is that of a much bulkier, more squat building than the Taj Mahal or Safdarjang's tomb. The cavernous space under the main tombs is an ideal home for great colonies of bats.

Minor sites south of the tomb 3 km S of Humayun's tomb, 500m to the W of the Mathura road is an **Asokan Rock Edict**, at Okhla. Discovered in 1966, this is one of Asoka's (272-232BC) minor Rock Edicts. It confirms that ancient Delhi was an important town on a trunk route connecting commercial centres with provincial capitals. The 18th century **Kalkaji temple** is close by and is dedicated to the goddess Kali (see Calcutta) who, having killed all the demons who terrorised the neighbourhood, installed herself on the hill nearby to be worshipped.

From here it is possible either to continue on an outer circuit of Delhi by going S to Tughluqabad (see page 179) or travelling W on a shorter inner circuit of the southern city. The **Begumpuri Masjid** (a 14th century mosque built by Khan-i-Jahan) lies just off Aurobindo Marg, S of its junction with Panscheel Marg. The 94m by 88m courtyard of this imposing rubble-built mosque is enclosed by arched cloisters and contains a prayer hall to the West.

About 1 km to the N is **Bijai Mandal** (Victory Palace), an unusual octagonal building with sloping sides and a doorway at each cardinal point. It is not clear whether it was the bastion of Muhammad-bin Tughluq's Jahanpanah or a tower to review his troops from. It is said that an **underground passage** links it with Tughluqabad (S) and Kotla Firoz Shah (N). 1 km to the SE is the **Khirki Masjid** (the Mosque of Windows), built in 1380 by the *Wazir* of Firoz Shah Tughluq. It is a covered mosque with 4 open courts. The upper storey wall is broken with *khirkis* (windows), hence its name.

Hauz Khas

Immediately to the N again, and entered off either Aurobindo Marg on the E side or Africa Ave on the W side, is Hauz Khas. Ala-ud-din Khalji (r1296-1313) created a large tank here for the use of the inhabitants of Siri, the 2nd capital city of Delhi founded by him. 50 years later Firoz Shah Tughluq cleaned up the silted tank and raised several buildings on its E and S banks which are known as Hauz Khas or Royal Tank.

Firoz Shah's austere tomb is found here. The multi storeyed wings, on the N and W of Firoz Shah's tomb, were built by him in 1354 as a *madrasa* (college). The octagonal and square *Chhattris* were built as tombs, possibly to the teachers at the college. Nearby is the **Idgah mosque** built in 1405.

Hauz Khas is now widely used as a park for early morning recreation – walking, running and yoga exercises. Classical music concerts, dance performances and a son et lumière show are held in the evenings when monuments are illuminated by thousands of earthen lamps and torches; 1 hr cultural show, daily, 1845, Rs 100 (check with Delhi Tourism). Huaz Khas won the PATA 1993 Heritage Award. Restaurants and shops have opened.

The courts of the Delhi Lawn Tennis Association, where Indian Davis Cup matches are played when held in Delhi, are just to the N of the gardens on Africa Ave. To the NE of Hauz Khas between Aurobindo Marg and the Ring Rd in South Extension is the **Moth ki Masjid**. Sikander Lodi (r1488-1517) is said to have picked up a grain of lentil *(moth)* from a mosque and given it to his Prime Minister *(Wazir)* Miyan Bhuwa. The grain was sown and it multiplied until enough had been earned to build this mosque. Possibly the finest example of Lodi architecture, the design shows innovation in the decoration of its *mihrab* and arches, special treatment of the central arch and the construction of domes over the prayer hall. In these it anticipates several features of later Mughal architecture.

The Qutb Minar Complex

ACCESS Open sunrise to sunset. Small entry fee.

History

Muhammad Ghuri conquered NW India at the very end of the 12th century. The conquest of the Gangetic plain down to Benares was undertaken by Muhammad's Turki slave and chief general, Qutb-ud-din-Aibak, whilst another general took Bihar and Bengal. In the process, temples were reduced to rubble, the remaining Buddhist centres were dealt their death blow and their monks slaughtered. When Muhammad was assassinated in 1206, his gains passed to the loyal Qutb-ud-din-Aibak. Thus the first sultans or Muslim kings of Delhi became known as the Slave Dynasty (1026-1290).

For the next 3 centuries the Slave Dynasty and the succeeding Khalji (1290-1320), Tughluq (1320-1414), Sayyid (1414-45) and Lodi (1451-1526)

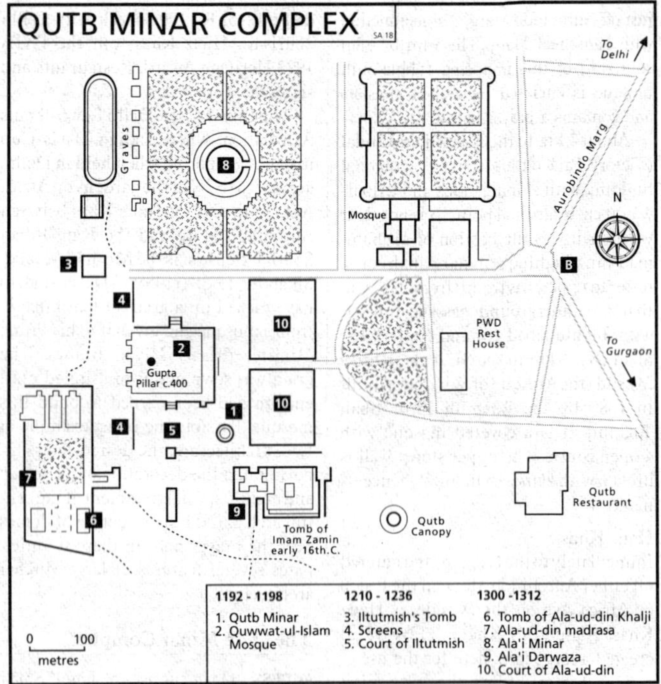

dynasties provided Delhi with fluctuating authority. The legacy of their ambitions survives in the tombs, forts, palaces that litter Delhi Ridge and the surrounding plain.

Qutb-ud-din-Aibak died after only 4 years in power, but he left his mark with the **Qutb Minar** and his **citadel**. The Qutb Minar, built to proclaim the victory of Islam over the infidel (unbeliever), dominates the countryside for miles around. Visit the Minar first.

Qutb Minar (1)

The construction In 1199 work began on what was intended to be the most glorious tower of victory in the world and was to be the prototype of all minars (towers) in India. (Occasionally local guides will say that the tower was originally a Rajput building; this is totally untrue). Qutb-ud-din-Aibak had probably seen and been influenced by the brick victory pillars in Ghazni in Afghanistan, but this one was to also serve as the minaret attached to the Might of Islam Mosque. From here the muezzin could call the faithful to prayer, though without the aid of modern speakers he would have had great difficulty in making himself heard. Later every mosque would incorporate its minaret.

As a mighty reminder of the importance of the ruler as Allah's representative on earth, the **Qutb Minar** (literally 'axis minaret') stood at the centre of the community and the world revolved around it. A pivot of Faith, Justice and Righteousness, its name also carried the message of Qutb-ud-din's ('Axis of the Faith') own achievements. The inscriptions carved in kufi script tell that 'the tower was erected to cast the shadow of God over both East and West'. For Qutb-ud-din-Aibak it marked the eastern limit of the empire of the One God. Its western counterpart is the **Giralda tower** built by Yusuf in Seville.

The decoration The Qutb Minar is 73m high and consists of 5 storeys. The diameter of the base is 14.4m and 2.7m at the top. Qutb-ud-din built the first 3 and his son-in-law Iltutmish embellished these and added a 4th. This is indicated in some of the Persian and Nagari (N Indian) inscriptions which also record that it was twice damaged by lightning in 1326 and 1368. While repairing the damage caused by the 2nd, Firoz Shah Tughluq added a 5th storey and used marble to face the red and buff sandstone. This was the first time contrasting colours were made a deliberate decorative feature. The later Mughals used this effect to its fullest. Firuz's 5th storey was topped by a graceful cupola but this fell down during an earthquake in 1803. A new one was added by a Major Robert Smith in 1829 but was so out of keeping that it was removed in 1848 and now stands in the gardens.

The original storeys are heavily indented with different styles of fluting, alternately round and angular on the bottom, round on the 2nd and angular on the 3rd. The beautifully carved honeycomb detail beneath the balconies are reminiscent of the Alhambra Palace in Spain. The calligraphy bands are verses from the Koran and praises to its patron builder. The staircase inside the tower to the balconies has been closed following an accident in 1979 when a party of schoolgirls panicked when the lights failed. Some were crushed to death in the resultant scramble to reach the exit.

Quwwat-ul-Islam Mosque (2)(The Might of Islam Mosque)

This, the earliest surviving mosque in India is to the NW of the Qutb Minar. It was begun in 1192, immediately after Qutb-ud-din's conquest of Delhi, and completed in 1198, using the remains of no fewer than 27 local Hindu and Jain temples.

The architectural style contained elements that Muslims brought from Arabia, including buildings made of mud and brick and decorated with glazed tiles, *squinches* (arches set diagonally across the corners of a square chamber to facilitate the raising of a dome and to effect a transition from a square to a round structure), the pointed arch and the true dome. Finally, Muslim buildings came alive through ornamental calligraphy and geometric patterning. This was in marked contrast to indigenous Indian styles of architecture. Hindu, Buddhist and Jain buildings relied on the post-and-beam system in which spaces were traversed by corbelling, ie shaping flat-laid stones to create an arch. The arched screen that runs along the W end of the courtyard beautifully illustrates the fact that it was Hindu methods that still prevailed at this stage, for the 16m high arch uses Indian corbelling, the corners being smoothed off to form the curved line.

The screen (4) The idea of a screen may have been borrowed from the sanctuary in the courtyard of the Prophet's mosque at Medina in Arabia. Whatever the influence, Qutb-ud-din's screen formed the façade of the mosque and, facing in the direction of Mecca, became the focal point. The sandstone screen is carved in the Indo-Islamic style, lotuses mingling with Koranic calligraphy. The later screenwork and other extensions (1230) are fundamentally Islamic in style, the flowers and leaves having been replaced by more arabesque patterns.

Indian builders mainly used stone, which from the 4th century AD had been intricately carved with representations of the gods. In their first buildings in India the Muslim architects designed the buildings and local Indian craftsmen built them and decorated them with typical motifs such as the vase and foliage, tasselled ropes, bells, cows and leaves.

Iltutmish's extension

The mosque was enlarged twice. In 1230 Qutb-ud-din's son-in-law and successor **Shamsuddin Iltutmish** doubled its size by extending the colonnades and prayer hall – 'Iltutmish's extension'. This accommodated a larger congregation, and in the more stable conditions of Iltutmish's reign Islam was obviously gaining ground. The arches of the extension are nearer to the true arch and are similar to the Gothic arch that appeared in Europe at this time. The decoration is Islamic.

Almost 100 years after Iltutmish's death, the mosque was enlarged again, by **Ala-ud-din Khalji**. The conductor of tireless and bloody military campaigns, Ala-ud-din proclaimed himself "God's representative on earth". His architectural ambitions, however, were not fully realised, because on his death in 1316 only part of the N and E extensions were completed.

Ala'i Minar and the Ala'i Darwaza

To the N of the Qutb complex is the **Ala'i Minar (8)**, intended to surpass the tower of the Qutb, but not completed beyond the first storey. It stands at just over 26m. He did complete the S gateway to the building, the **Ala'i Darwaza (9)**. Inscriptions on its surface testify that it was built in 1311 (the Muslim year 710 AH). Ala-ud-din benefited from events in Central Asia. Since the beginning of the 13th century Mongol hordes had been sweeping down from Central Asia and fanning out E and W, destroying the civilisation of the Seljuk Turks in W Asia, and refugee artists, architects, craftsmen and poets fled East. Employed by Ala-ud-din they brought to India features and techniques that had developed in Byzantine Turkey, some of which can be seen in the Ala'i Darwaza.

The gate-house is a large sandstone cuboid, 17m square and 18m high, into which are set small cusped arches with carved *jali* screens. The lavish ornamentation of geometric and floral designs in red sandstone and white marble produced a dramatic effect when viewed against the surrounding buildings.

The inner chamber, 11m square, has a doorway in each side and, for the first time in India, true arches. Above each of these doorways is an Arabic inscription with its creators name and one of his self-assumed titles – 'The Second Alexander'. The N doorway, which is the main entrance, is the most elaborately carved. The dome, raised on squinched arches is flat and shallow, and topped with a button finial. Of the effects employed, the arches with their 'lotus-bud' fringes are Seljuk, as is the dome and rounded finial and the general treatment of the façade. These now became trademarks of the **Khalji style**, remain-

The Gupta Pillar

In the courtyard of the Quwwat-ul-Islam Mosque (2) is the **iron pillar**. This dates from the 4th century AD and bears a Sanskrit inscription in the Gupta style of the period, telling that it was erected as a flagstaff in honour of Vishnu and in memory of the Gupta King Chandragupta II (375-413). Originally the pillar was topped by an image of Garuda, Vishnu's charge or vehicle and it probably stood facing a Vishnu temple. The purity of its wrought iron (98%) is extraordinary, and it has survived 1600 years virtually without blemish. A local tradition regards the pillar as having magical qualities. Anyone who can encircle it with their hands behind their back will have good fortune. Plenty seem to manage it.

ing virtually unchanged until their further development in Humayun's tomb.

Iltutmish's Tomb (3)
Built in 1235 this lies in the NW of the compound midway along the W wall of the mosque. It is the first surviving tomb of a Muslim ruler in India. 2 other tombs also stand within the perimeter of the extended Might of Islam Mosque.

The idea of a tomb was quite alien to Hindus, who had been practising cremation since around 400 BC. Blending Hindu and Muslim styles, the outside is relatively plain, with 3 arched and decorated doorways. The interior carries reminders of the nomadic origins of the first Muslim rulers. Like a Central Asian *yurt* (tent) in its decoration, it combines the familiar Indian motifs of the wheel, bell, chain and lotus with the equally familiar geometric arabesque patterning. The W wall is inset with 3 *mihrabs* that indicate the direction of Mecca in any Muslim shrine.

The tomb originally supported a dome resting on *squinches* which you can still see. The dome collapsed, as can be seen from the slabs of stone lying around, suggesting that the technique was as yet unrefined. Since these squinches are corbelled, it may be assumed that the dome was corbelled too, on the principles of the corbelled domes in contemporary Gujarat and Rajput temples. The blocks of masonry were fixed together using the Indian technology of iron dowels. In later Indo-Islamic buildings lime plaster was used for bonding.

To the SW of this uncompleted mosque, an L-shaped ruin marks the site of **Ala-ud-din Khalji's tomb** (6) within the confines of a *madrasa* (7). This is the first time in India that a tomb and madrasa are found together, another custom inherited from the Seljuks.

Immediately to the E of the Ala'i Darwaza stands the **Tomb of Imam Zamin**, a sufi 'saint' from Turkestan who arrived in India at the beginning of the 16th century. It is an octagonal structure with a plastered sandstone dome and has *jali* screens, a characteristic of the Lodi style of decoration.

Tughluqabad and the Baha'i temple

ACCESS Less than 8 km E of the Qutb Minar. Despite its desolate and ruined appearance, Tughluqabad retains a sense of the power and energy of the newly arrived Muslims in India. Open sunrise-1700. Entry free. Allow 45-60 min.

Ghiyas'ud-Din Tughluq (r1321-1325), after ascending the throne of Delhi, selected this site for his capital, see page 45. For strategic reasons he built a massive fort around his capital city which stands high on a rocky outcrop of the Delhi Ridge. The fort is roughly octagonal in plan with a circumference of 6.5 km. Its 10-15m high rubble walls are provided with bastions and gates and are pierced with loopholes and are crowned with a line of battlements of solid stone. At present the fort has 13 gates and there are 3 inner gates to the citadel. The vast size, strength and obvious solidity of the whole give it an air of massive grandeur. From the walls you get a magnificent impression of the strategic advantages of the site.

It is worth visiting Tughluqabad to see the style of fort construction and to compare it with the later Red Fort in Old Delhi. You can see how the various functions of the capital were combined in the garrison, palace and city. It was not until Babur (r1526-1530) that dynamite was used in warfare, so this is a very defensible site.

The plan
Tughluqabad was divided into 3 parts. To the E of the main entrance is the rectangular citadel. A wider area immediately to the W and bounded by walls contained the palaces. Beyond this to the N lay the city. Now marked by the ruins

of houses, the streets were laid out in a grid fashion. Inside the citadel enclosure is a tower known as Vijay Mandal and the remains of several halls including a long underground passage. The fort also contained 7 tanks. To the S of the fort was a vast reservoir created by erecting bunds between the hills.

A causeway connects the fort with the tomb of Ghiyas'ud-Din Tughluq while a wide embankment near its SE corner gave access to the fortresses of **Adilabad** about 1 km away, built a little later by Ghiyas'ud-Din's son Muhammad. The tomb is very well preserved, and has red sandstone walls with a pronounced slope (the first Muslim building in India to have sloping walls) crowned with a white marble dome. This dome, like that of the Ala-i-darwaza at the Qutb, is crowned by a cogwheel-like finial called *amalaka*, a feature of Hindu architecture. Also Hindu is the trabeate arch at the tomb's fortress wall entrance. According to Percy Brown this distinctive slope reflects the fact that Ghiyas'ud-Din modelled the design on a mausoleum he was building over 300 km away at Multan (now in Pakistan). Lack of building stone in the Indus plains meant that they had to be built of brick, subsequently covered in plaster. Inside are 3 cenotaphs belonging to Ghiyas'ud-Din, his wife and son Muhammad.

Ghiyas'ud-Din Tughluq quickly found that military victories were no guarantee of lengthy rule. When he returned home after a victorious campaign the welcoming pavilion erected by his son and successor, **Muhammad-bin Tughluq**, was deliberately collapsed over him. Tughluqabad was abandoned shortly afterwards and was thus only inhabited for 5 years.

Baha'i Temple in Bahapur

To the N of Tughluqabad on the way back into Delhi is the Baha'i Temple. Open 1 Apr-30 Sep 0900-1900, 1 Oct-31 Mar 0930-1730. Closed Mon. Audio visual shows in English at 1100, 1200, 1400 and 1530. Shoes must be left at the entrance. The volunteer staff are very friendly and helpful. There is a library on the left of the main entrance.

The structure Architecturally it is a remarkably striking building. Constructed in 1980-1, the latest of 7 Baha'i temples in different parts of the world, it is built out of white marble and in the characteristic Baha'i temple shape of a lotus flower. In appearance it is reminiscent of the Sydney Opera House. The temple is 34m from floor to apex, 70m in diameter and with a seating capacity for 1300 worshippers. 45 lotus petals form the walls in the form of the opening lotus flower. Internally it creates a feeling of light and space. It is a simple design, brilliantly executed and very elegant in form. All Baha'i temples are 9 sided, symbolising 'comprehensiveness, oneness and unity'. The Delhi temple is surrounded by 9 pools, not only making an attractive feature but helping to keep the building cool.

Baha'i Houses of Worship everywhere are 'dedicated to the worship of God, for peoples of all races, religions or castes. Within their portals only the Holy Scriptures of the Baha'i Faith and earlier revelations are read or recited, according to arranged programmes'. Visitors are welcome to such services, and at other times the temple is open for silent meditation and prayer in the very peaceful atmosphere.

The Baha'i faith was founded by a Persian, **Baha'u'llah** (meaning 'glory of God': 1817-1892). It preaches that "all revelations are from the same divine source, brought to mankind progressively in different ages, through manifestations of the supreme creator, for the sole purpose of the spiritual and social upliftment of the entire human race, for carrying forward an ever-advancing civilisation. Baha'i's believe that Baha'u'llah is the manifestation of God for this age. His teachings were directed towards the unification of the human race, the establishment of a permanent universal peace, the formation of a world commonwealth of nations. "The earth is but one country, and mankind its citizens". Baha'i's claim 1.8 million adherents, though it is not clear what such adherence means.

North of Connaught Circus

Shah Jahanabad (Old Delhi)

Today, Shah Jahan (r1628-1658) is chiefly remembered for the astonishing achievement of the Taj Mahal. However, the Red Fort and the Jama Masjid in Delhi, both part of Shah Jahan's city, are also remarkable examples of the mature Mughal style that developed under his patronage. Both are well worth visiting, though the Red Fort in Delhi could be sacrificed for the Red Fort in Agra if time is at a premium. *Old Delhi: 10 Easy Walks* by Gaynor Barton and Lauraine Malone published by Rupa and Co, is an excellent short guide.

The city Shah Jahan decided to move back from Agra to Delhi in 1638. Within 10 years the huge city of Shah Jahanabad, now known as Old Delhi, was built. Much of the building material was taken from the ruins of Firozabad and Shergarh. The city was laid out in blocks with wide roads, residential quarters, bazars and mosques. Its principal street was

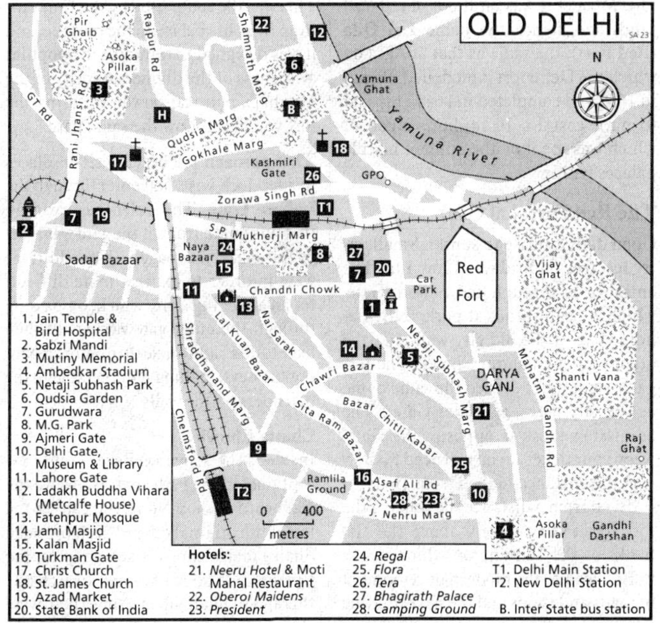

Chandni Chowk which had a tree-lined canal flowing down its centre and which quickly became renowned throughout Asia. Today, Chandni Chowk retains some of its former magic, though now it is a bustling jumble of shops, of labyrinthine alleys running off a main thoroughfare with craftsmen's workshops, hotels, mosques and temples. Here goldsmiths, silversmiths, ivory workers, silk traders and embroiderers can all be found.

The city of Shajahanabad was protected by rubble-built walls, some of which still survive. These walls were pierced by 14 main gates. The most important of these still in existence are **Ajmeri Gate**, **Turkman Gate** (often referred to by auto-rickshaw *wallas* as 'Truckman Gate'!), **Kashmiri Gate** and **Delhi Gate**. Between this new city and the River Yamuna Shah Jahan built a fort. Most of it was built out of red (*lal*) sandstone, hence the name **Lal Qila** (Red Fort), the same as that at Agra on which the Delhi fort is modelled. Begun in 1639 and completed in 1648, it is said to have cost Rs 10 million, much of which was spent on the opulent marble palaces within.

The Red Fort (Lal Qila)

Open daily sunrise to sunset. Small entry fee, free on Fridays. Allow 1 hr. The entrance is through the Lahore Gate, which is nearest the car park. (**NB:** Lahore Gate of the old city wall is at the other end of Chandni Chowk. The fort gates sometimes carried the same name as the city gates, eg Delhi Gate.) The admission kiosk is opposite the Gate. Keep your ticket as you will need to show it at the entrance to the Drum House.

Even from a distance the walls of the fort towered massively above the flat banks of the Yamuna on which it was built. Despite the modern development of roads and shops and the never ending traffic, that dominating impression is still immensely powerful. The Fort is built as an octagon measuring 900m by 550m. It was surrounded by a 9m deep moat, now empty, fed by the Yamuna river. The river itself has now shifted more than 1 km to the E and is invisible beyond its high bank and the trees along it. In front of the fort is a massive *Maidan* (open space) which has been used for political rallies ever since the time of the Independence Movement. From the Lahore Gate overlooking the Maidan, the Prime Minister addresses enormous crowds on 15 August, Independence Day.

What is not obvious today is the symbolism of the plan of Shah Jahan's new city. If you look back from the gateway you can still make out the axis which Chandni Chowk represents between the seat of religious authority enshrined in the Jama Masjid to the W and the centre of political authority represented by the Diwan-i-Am in the heart of the Fort. This was the route used by the Emperor to go from his palace to the mosque, and it was designed to reinforce the popular awareness of the divine authority of the Mughal's political power. Entering the fort you now follow the same path.

The approach It is best to visit the places inside, clock-wise. You enter through the **Lahore Gate.** The defensive barbican that juts out in front of the gate was built by Aurangzeb, see page 53. The additions were in order to make it more difficult for an attacking army which, on passing through the outer gateway, would then have to do a right angle turn before reaching the next, making it vulnerable to the defenders on the walls.

Chatta Chowk

Inside is the 'Covered Bazar', quite exceptional in the 17th century. Above the signboard of shop No 19 you can see the top of the original cusped arch of one of Shah Jahan's shops. Each shop on the lower arcade must have had an arch like this and in Shah Jahan's time there were shops on both upper and lower levels. Today the upper levels are the dwellings of Indian Army families and the shops

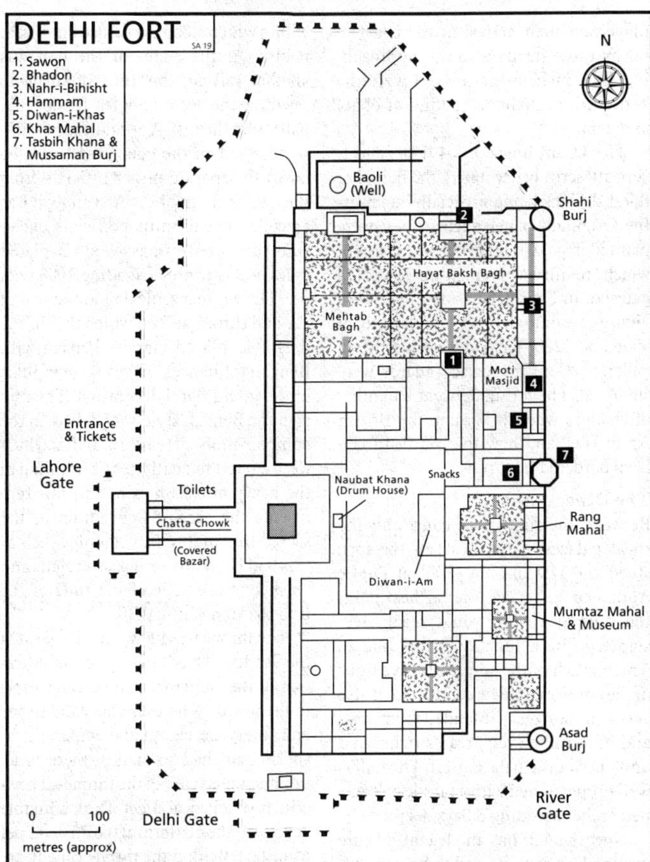

specialise in souvenirs. Originally they catered to the luxury trade of the Imperial household and carried stocks of silks, brocades, velvets, gold and silver ware, jewellery and gems. There were coffee shops too for nobles and courtiers. Walk through the left-hand archway and you will see a small building on your right near the Art Corner shop. These are the only visitor's toilets in the Red Fort, but are particularly unpleasant.

The Naubat khana

Also called Nakkar Khana (music gallery), it is immediately beyond the bazar. This marked the entrance to the inner apartments of the fort. Here everyone except the princes of the royal family had to dismount and leave their horses or elephants (*hathi*), hence its other name of **Hathi Pol** (Elephant Gate). But as well as a gate-house, the Drum House was a music gallery. Five times a day ceremonial music was played to the glory of the Emperor. Also, various princes are believed to have had their own special signature tunes which were played on their arrival at the court to notify those inside who was approaching. The instruments played were the kettle drum, shahnais (a kind of oboe) and cymbals.

The **Drum house** has 4 floors and is very attractively decorated, the herbal or floral designs being especially noteworthy. Originally panels such as these were painted in gold or other colours, traces of which are still visible on the interior of the gateway. In Shah Jahan's day, the Drum House gave onto an inner courtyard 165m wide and 128m long, around which ran galleries. Here the palace guards were stationed. The fort underwent a number of changes when it became the British Army H.Q. and now the courtyard is a lawn bordered by shrubs.

The Diwan-i-Am

Between the first inner court and the royal palaces at the heart of the fort, stood the Diwan-i-am (Hall of Public Audience). This was the farthest point the normal visitor would reach. Designed to be a functional building in which much of the administrative work of the empire could be conducted, it also acts as a showpiece intended to impress and hint at the even greater riches and opulence of the palace itself. The hall is well proportioned with a façade of 9 cusped arches standing 3 bays deep.

Now the hall has an elegant if spare beauty. However, it used to be very different. In Shah Jahan's time the sandstone was hidden behind a very thin layer of white plaster, *chunam*, polished to shine like white marble. This was then decorated with floral motifs in many colours, especially gilt. There used to be silk carpets and heavy curtains hung from the outside of the building – you can see the canopy rings above the pillars. These could be raised and lowered by a system of ropes.

The throne surround At the back of the hall is a platform for the emperor's throne. Around this was a gold railing, within which stood the princes and great nobles. At the edges of the hall was another railing, this time of silver, to separate the lesser nobles (inside the hall) from the rest. A 3rd railing of sandstone stood in the courtyard (now the lawn) to separate minor officials from the general public. A canopy was erected above the minor officials' enclosure, supported by massive silver-plated poles and capable of shading 1000 people. The white marble dais at the rear of the hall throne and on which the throne itself was placed marries Persian with Bengali influences. The Persian input is in the inlaid floral decoration. The roof is in the Bengali style – modelled on the bamboo roofs of eastern India which were curved to facilitate the draining of the heavy monsoon rains and this represents the archaic convention of the sacred tree umbrella. Canopies such as this had been protecting sovereigns and teachers since at least the time of the Buddha (6th century BC).

The throne was known as 'The Seat of the Shadow of God', giving a clear indication of the emperor's self-perceived role in the world. Wherever you stand in the hall (everyone except the emperor's favourite son had to stand), there is an uninterrupted view of the throne – a powerful psychological effect. The low marble bench was the platform of the *Wazir* (Chief Minister). Behind the throne canopy are 12 marble inlaid panels. Figurative workmanship is very unusual in Islamic buildings, and this one panel is the only example in the Red Fort.

Shah Jahan's day Shah Jahan used to spend about 2 hours a day in the **Diwan-i-Am**. According to Bernier, the French traveller, the subjects waited patiently, their eyes downcast and their hands crossed. The emperor would enter to a fanfare and mounted the throne by a flight of moveable steps. The business conducted was a mixture of official and domestic administration. There would

A Gift From Florence?

The contact with Italy Ebba Koch suggests that in all there are 318 ***Florentine pietra dura*** plaques in the niche behind the throne, showing flowers, birds, and lions as well as the central figure of Orpheus, playing to the beasts. In between these Italian panels are Mughal pietra dura works with flowery arabesques in the lower area, and birds, fashioned like those in the Italian plaques, in the lunette-shaped sections of the wall. Ebba Koch argues that the techniques employed by the Mughal artisans are exactly the same as the Italian ones, so there must have been a direct connection.

This is not to say that there was no independent development of Mughal inlay craftsmanship. Such a view has been described by Tillotson as the result of wishful thinking by Europeans, eager to claim a stake in the superb work. In fact the Mughals had an equally fine tradition of stone carving and of inlay work on which to draw as had the Florentine princes, as can be seen from the work in the **Jami Masjid** in Ahmadabad, built in 1414, see page 1241. The development in technique under Shah Jahan parallelled that in Italy, but the view that this resulted from the presence of European lapidaries in the Mughal court needs careful scrutiny.

As Ebba Koch concludes, the similar tastes and interests of the Mughal patrons and artists (scientific naturalism and involvement in precious stones and their courtly uses), led to similar artistic expressions even if some of the lessons came from European teachers. She argues that the Mughals were quick to realise the potential of the European form for their own needs, and in the end similar solutions might have been produced by an artistic development that had become quite independent from its initial impetus.

be reports from the provinces, tax and revenue matters and official appointments. On the personal side, Shah Jahan would listen to accounts of illness, dream interpretations and anecdotes from his ministers and nobles. Many animals would be paraded across the courtyard for inspection. Wednesday was the day of judgment. Sentences were often brutal but swift and sometimes the punishment of dismemberment, beating or death was carried out on the spot. The hangmen were close at hand with axes and whips to mete out rough justice. On Fri, the Muslim holy day, there would be no business.

The inner palace buildings

The **Diwan-i-am** has seen many dramatic events – the destructive whirlwind of the Persian Nadir Shah in 1739 and of Ahmad Shah the Afghan in 1756, and the trial of the last 'King of Delhi' – *Baoli* Bahadur Shah II in 1858. Behind the Hall of Public Audience is the private enclosure of the fort in which Shah Jahan set 6 small palaces (5 survive). These are along the E wall of the fort overlooking the river Yamuna. Also within this compound are the harem, the Life-Bestowing Garden and the Nahr-i-Bihisht (Stream of Paradise). Leave the throne canopy area by the steps to your left, follow the path and carry on until you reach the white marble garden pavilion (see Map).

Life-Bestowing Gardens (*Hayat Baksh Bagh*)

Like all Islamic formal gardens these were designed to imitate the heavenly gardens of paradise. Though the present layout is new, the original was landscaped according to the Persian *char bagh* with pavilions, fountains and water courses dividing the garden into various but regular beds. The 2 pavilions named **Sawan** (1) and **Bhadon** (2) reveal something of the character of the garden.

Sawan is the 1st month of the rainy season (Jul) and Bhadon the 2nd (Aug). The garden used to be so alive with water as to create the effect of the monsoon and contemporary accounts tell us that in the pavilions, some of which were especially erected for the Hindu festival of *Teej* which marks the arrival of the monsoon, the royal ladies would sit in silver swings and watch the rains.

Water flowed from the back wall of the pavilion through a slit above the marble shelf and over the niches in the wall. Gold and silver pots of flowers were placed in these alcoves during the day whilst at night candles were lit to create a glistening and colourful effect. The water then flowed from along a channel to a square pool in the centre of the garden. The pool area is now filled with grass and there is a sandstone pavilion built in the 19th century in the centre of it. During Shah Jahan's reign apparently there was also a pavilion hidden by the jets of water from the 281 fountains surrounding it. To the W is **Mehtab Bagh** which has a *Baoli* (step well) to its NW.

The Shahi Burj

From here you can walk to the next pavilion which is opposite and then to the Shahi Burj tower at the right hand side. It was from the pavilion next to the tower that the canal known as the **Nahr-i-Bihisht** (3, Stream of Paradise) began its journey along the Royal Terrace. The octagonal Royal Tower is closed to the public as it was seriously damaged in 1857 and is still unsafe. It has 3 storeys. The lower one contained a tank from which water was raised to flow into the garden. The view from the wall by the tower shows that there is some distance to the River Yamuna. In Shah Jahan's time it lapped the walls and in 1784 a Prince, concerned that he might be about to lose his life, jumped from the Royal Tower into the river, swam across it and fled to Lucknow. Shah Jahan used the tower as his most private working place and only his sons and 3 or 4 senior ministers were allowed with him. Looking along the length of the Royal Terrace you can see the Stream of Paradise flowing S to the next building along the walls. These are the Royal Baths.

Moti Masjid

To the right are the 3 marble domes of the 'Pearl Mosque'. Please remove shoes at the entance. Built in 1662 by Aurangzeb for his personal use, it is a small building and, except for the cupolas, completely hidden behind a wall of red sandstone, now painted white. It is of polished marble and like a pearl it is small, white and with some exquisite decoration. Aurangzeb's style is more ornate than Shah Jahan's. All the surfaces are highly decorated in a fashion similar to rococo, which was developed at the same time in Europe. The prayer hall is on a raised platform which is unusual in a mosque and the hall is inlaid with the outlines of individual prayer mats (*musallas*) in black marble. Interestingly the interior and exterior walls are not aligned with each other. The outer walls are aligned to the cardinal points, for this was the layout of all the buildings in the fort (see Map). But, in order for the Mosque to be correctly facing Mecca the inner walls were positioned so that in fact they are out of true with the rest of the buildings.

The Royal Baths

Move back towards the wall to the first of a line of buildings. The **Hammam** (4) has 3 apartments separated by corridors with canals to carry water to each room. The 2 rooms flanking the entrance had hot and cold baths and were for the royal children. The room furthest away from the door has 3 fountain basins which emitted rose water. It is reputed that 4 tonnes of wood were required to heat the water.

The Diwan-i-Khas (5)

Beyond is the single-storeyed 'Hall of Private Audience', the hub of the court,

Peacock Throne

In the centre of the Diwan-i-Khas (5) is a marble pedestal on which stood the Peacock Throne (2m x 1.3m) which Shah Jahan commissioned on his accession in 1627 and took 7 years to execute. The throne which was originally in Agra, was designed with 2 peacocks standing behind with a parrot carved out of a single emerald, between them . It was inlaid with a vast number of precious stones – sapphires, rubies, emeralds, pearls and diamonds; even the 6 solid gold feet were inlaid with rubies, emeralds and diamonds. Over the top was a gem encrusted gold canopy edged with pearls, supported by 12 pillars.

The throne was carried off by Nadir Shah, a Turk who after conquering Persia, sacked Delhi in 1739. Soon after his occupation of Delhi a riot broke out in which 900 of his soldiers were killed. Nadir Shah himself rode through the streets of Delhi to assess the situation when some residents were rash enough to throw stones at him. Enraged, Nadir Shah ordered the entire population of Delhi to be massacred, resulting in 30,000 dead. In the evening the 'Great' Mughal (Mohammad Shah) begged for mercy, and such was Nadir Shah's control over his troops that he was able immediately to halt the carnage. The invaders packed up to go, taking with them as much as they could extort from all the nobles and rich citizens. The Mughal Emperor was forced to hand over the keys of the treasury, jewels, and the Peacock Throne (which he later replaced with a poor imitation).

The rich haul enabled Nadir Shah to suspend taxes in Persia for the next 3 years. The throne was later broken up by Nadir Shah's assassins in 1747; some of the jewels are believed to have been incorporated into the late Shah of Iran's throne.

topped by 4 Hindu-style *Chhattris* and built completely of white marble. The *dado* (lower part of the wall) on the interior was richly decorated with inlaid precious and semi-precious stones. The ceiling was silver but was removed by the Marathas in 1760 – see page 55. Outside, the hall used to have a marble pavement and an arcaded court. Both have gone.

The office of state It was in the Diwan-i-Khas that all the important affairs of state and policies were decided. It was the Mughal 'Oval Office' or 10 Downing Street. Here the emperor would also inspect paintings and miniatures or review select animals and birds such as cheetahs and hawks that would be presented in the forecourt. Shah Jahan spent 2 hours (1000-1200) in the Diwan-i-Khas before retiring for a meal, siesta and prayers. In the evening he would return to the Hall for more work before going to the harem. He usually retired to bed at around 2200 and liked to be read to, his particular favourite being the *Babur-i-nama*, the autobiography of his great-great-grandfather. Such was the splendour of the hall that in the eyes of many there was little reason to doubt the words of the 14th century poet **Amir Khusrau** inscribed above the corner arches of the N and S walls: "Agar Firdaus bar rue Zamin-ast/ Hamin ast o Hamin ast o Hamin ast". (If there be a paradise on earth, it is here, it is here, it is here.)

The Royal Palaces
Next to the Diwan-i-Khas is the **Khas Mahal** (6, Private Palace). This consists of 3 rooms. To the N, nearest the Diwan-i-Khas, is the **Tasbih Khana** (7, Chamber for the Telling of Rosaries). Here the Emperor would worship privately with his rosary of 99 beads, one for each of the mystical names of Allah. After the death of his beloved wife Mumtaz, for whom the Taj Mahal was constructed, Shah

Jahan became quite devout. In the centre is the **Khwabgah** (*'Palace of Dreams'*) which gives on to the octagonal tower. Here Shah Jahan would be seen each morning. A balcony was added to the tower in 1809 and here George V and Queen Mary appeared in the Durbar of 1911. The levée was held before them on the open space between the Fort and the Yamuna, caused by its receding (see above). The Durbar celebrated their coronation and coincided with the announcement of the decision to move the capital from Calcutta to Delhi.

To the S is a long hall with painted walls and ceiling, the **Tosh Khana** (*Robe Room*). At the N end is a beautiful marble screen. This is carved with the scales of justice – above the filigree grille. If you are standing with your back to the Diwan-i-Khas you will see a host of circulating suns but if your back is to the next building, ie The Rang Mahal, you will see moons surrounding the scales. The sun was widely used to symbolise royalty, eg Louis XIV of France (*Le Roi Soleil*). It is most appropriate for the suns to be there as that particular side faced the throne of the 'Sun' himself, Shah Jahan. All these rooms were sumptuously decorated with fine silk carpets, rich silk brocade curtains and lavishly decorated walls. Beneath the Khas Mahal is the **Khirzi Gate**. This is neglected now, but was an important and convenient private entrance for the Emperor and his most senior nobles. After 1857 the British used the Khas Mahal as an officer's mess and sadly it was defaced.

The Palace of Colours Next again to the S is the **Rang Mahal** (*Palace of Colours*), the residence of the chief *sultana*. It was also the place where the emperor ate most of his meals. To protect the rich carpets, calico-covered leather sheets were spread out. It was divided into 6 apartments. Privacy and coolness was ensured by the use of marble *jali* screens. Like the other palaces it was beautifully decorated with a silver ceiling ornamented with golden flowers to reflect the water in the channel running through the building. The N and S apartments were both known as **Sheesh Mahal** (Palace of Mirrors) since into the ceiling were set hundreds of small mirrors. In the evening when candles were lit a starlit effect would be produced. This type of decoration was a favourite in Rajasthan before the Mughals arrived (see page 412 – Amber Fort).

Through the palace ran the Life-bestowing Stream and at its centre is a lotus shaped marble basin which had an ivory fountain. As might be expected in such a cloistered and cossetted environment, the ladies sometimes got bored. In the 18th century the Empress of Jahandar Shah sat gazing out at the river and remarked that she had never seen a boat sink. Shortly afterwards a boat was deliberately capsized so that she could be entertained by the sight of people bobbing up and down in the water crying for help. In the summer the ladies went underground. Access is not permitted but the rooms would have been cool because they were cellars and had water running above them.

Museum The southernmost of the palaces is the **Mumtaz Mahal** (*Palace of Jewels*) which was also used by the harem. The lower half of its walls are of marble and it contains 6 apartments. After the Mutiny of 1857 it was used as a guardroom and since 1912 it has been a **museum** with exhibits of textiles, weapons, carpets, jade and metalwork as well as works depicting life in the court. It should not be missed. Open daily except Fri, 0900-1700.

Between the Mumtaz Mahal and Rang Mahal was a small palace known as **Choti Baithak** (Little Sitting Room) but this has disappeared. The other parts of the Red Fort are inaccessible. You leave the same way as you entered.

Diagambar Jain Mandir The impressive red sandstone façade of the temple standing at the E end of Chandni Chowk, faces this Red Fort. Built in 1656, it contains an image of Adinath. The bird hospital within this compound, releases the birds on recovery (instead of returning them to their owners); many remain within the temple precincts.

Jama Masjid (The Friday Mosque)

1 km to the W of the Red Fort is the magnificent Jama Masjid, the largest mosque in India and the last great architectural work of Shah Jahan, intended to dwarf all mosques that had gone before it. It also has the distinction of being one of the few mosques, either in India or elsewhere, that was designed to produce a pleasing external effect.

With the Fort it dominates Old Delhi. Both symbolise the mighty aspirations of their maker and demonstrate the gulf that existed between monarch and subject. Each Friday the emperor and his male retinue would travel the short distance from the fort to attend the midday prayers, the foremost service of the Muslim week.

The Jama Masjid is much simpler in its ornamentation than Shah Jahan's secular buildings, a judicious blend of red sandstone and white marble. Marble and sandstone are interspersed in the domes, minarets and cusped arches. All these features are intended to emphasise the architectural merits of the building rather than to merely act as decoration.

The gateways The Mosque has 3 huge gateways, the largest being on the E. This was reserved for the royal family, who gathered in a private gallery in its upper storey. Today, the faithful enter through the E gate on Fri and on the occasion of the 2 annual **Id** festivals to mark the end of Ramadan, **Id-ul-Fitr**, and **Id-ul-Adha**, which commemorates Abraham's (Ibrahim) sacrificial offering of his son Ishmael (Ismail). Islamic traditions varies from the Jewish and Christian tradition that Abraham offered to sacrifice Isaac, Ishmael's brother. The general public enter by the N gate.

The purpose of gateways is symbolic as well as practical for they separate the sacred and secular worlds (see also The Taj Mahal). So, the threshold is a place of great importance where one steps to a higher plane. Shoes must be removed. Visitors should cover their heads.

The courtyard The 900m square *sahn* acts as an extended prayer hall which can accommodate over 20,000 worshippers. The mosque itself comprises a façade which includes the main arch *(iwan)*, 5 smaller arches on each side and 2 flanking minarets. Behind sit 3 bulbous domes, a large central one flanked by 2 smaller ones, all perfectly proportioned and placed in relation to one another. The effect of the *iwan* is to draw the worshippers attention into the building.

Hauz In the centre of the courtyard is a tank. Water plays an important role in Islam just as it does in Hinduism. It is used as a means of initiation. The ablution tank is placed between the inner and outer parts of a building to remind the worshipper that it is through the ritual of baptism that one first enters the community of believers.

Dikka In front of the ablution tank stands a raised platform about 3m high. Muslim communities grew so rapidly that by the 8th century it became necessary in many places to introduce a second prayer leader (*muballigh*). This was his platform, and his role was to copy the postures and chants of the *imam* who was inside the building and thus relay them to a much larger congregation. With the introduction of the loudspeaker and amplification, the dikka and the muballigh became redundant.

The Kawthar Inscription Set up in 1766, the inscription commemorates the place where a worshipper had a vision of the Prophet standing by the celestial tank in paradise. It is here that the Prophet will stand on Judgment Day. In most Islamic buildings, the inscriptions are passages from the Koran or Sayings of the Prophet. Shah Jahan, however, preferred to have sayings extolling the virtues of the builder and architect as well. The 10 detailed panels on the façade indicate the date of construction (1650-1656), the cost (10 lakhs – one million rupees), the history of the building, the architect (Ustad Khalil) and the builder (Nur Allah Ahmed, probably the son of the man who did most of the work on the Taj Mahal).

North of the Red Fort

The centre of gravity of the city has shifted steadily S since 1947. The old civil lines area to the N of Kashmiri Gate and the Red Fort, is now often bypassed. However, there are several sites of interest.

Going N past the Old Delhi Post Office, just before Kashmiri Gate (now bypassed by the main road), is **St James Church**, completed in 1836. It was built by Colonel James Skinner, who had a great military reputation in the Punjab. See page 824.

Kashmiri Gate was built by the British, along with other bastions in Shah Jahan's original city walls, in 1835. It was blown up in the Mutiny of 1857. Immediately to the N of the gate today is the main inter-state bus terminal. On the opposite side of the road are the **Qudsia Gardens**, named after the wife of the Mughal Emperor Muhammad Shah, who laid out the gardens in 1748.

The *Oberoi Maiden's Hotel* is 1 km further N, in the heart of the Civil Lines, and just to the N again a mound on which Tamerlane camped when he attacked Delhi. The Civil Lines were the centre of British Administration until New Delhi was completed.

Running N to S is the **Delhi Ridge**. At the S end of the Ridge is the President's Estate in New Delhi. However, it was on the N end that the major monuments of British India, before New Delhi itself was thought of, were built. To reach the crest of the ridge, still covered in low scrub, go down Raj Niwas Rd, just S of the *Oberoi Maidens Hotel*. At the end of Raj Niwas Marg turn left and then right into Hindu Rao Marg, named after Hindu Rao, whose house (now a hospital on the W facing the Ridge) played a vital role in the British troops defence after the Mutiny. The road makes the short but quite steep climb up the Ridge. Turning left at the top of the ridge, an Asokan pillar is just off to the left. Further down the road is the Gothic **Mutiny Memorial**. There are excellent views over the old city. To the SW is **Sabzi Mandi**, the old city's vegetable market, to the SE the Jama Masjid. Running N from the Mutiny Memorial, the Ridge Road (now Rani Jhansi Marg) goes to the University.

Museums

The National Museum

Janpath, T 3019538. 1000-1700, closed Mon. Entry free. This is one of the best museums in the country. It gives an excellent overview of the cultural development of S Asia. The collection was formed from the nucleus of the Exhibition of Indian Art, London (1947) which brought together selected works from state museums and private collections. Now merged with the Asian Antiquities Museum it displays a rich collection of the artistic treasure of Central Asia and India. The museum provides a comprehensive review of ethnological objects from prehistoric archaeological finds to the late Medieval period. Research is facilitated by a library. Films are screened every day (1430). Replicas of exhibits on display and books on Indian culture and art are on sale at the entrance.

Ground Floor Prehistoric. Included are seals, figurines, toy animals and jewellery from the Harappan civilization (2400-1500 BC). Maurya Period.

Terracottas and stone heads from the Sunga period (3rd century BC) include the *chaturmukha lingam*, a 4-faced phallic symbol connected with the worship of Siva (1st century BC). Gandhara School, a series of stucco heads showing the Graeco Roman influence. Gupta terracottas c400 AD include 2 life size images of the river goddesses Ganga and Yamuna and the 4-armed bust of Vishnu from a temple near Lal Kot. S Indian sculpture from Pallava and early Chola temples and relief panels from Mysore are presented. 10th century AD sculptures. Bronzes from the Buddhist monastery at Nalanda.

1st Floor Illustrated manuscripts includes the *Babur-i-nama* in the emperor's own handwriting and an autographed copy of Jahangir's memoirs. Miniature paintings includes the 16th century Jain School, the 18th century Rajasthani School and the Pahari (Hill) Schools of Garhwal, Basoli and Kangra. Aurel Stein Collection consists of antiquities recovered by him during his explorations of Central Asia and the western borders of China at the turn of the century.

2nd Floor Pre-Columbian and Mayan artefacts. Anthropological Section devoted to Indian tribal artifacts and folk arts. Sharan Rani Bakkiwal Gallery of Musical Instruments displays over 300 instruments collected by the famous *sarod* player Sharad Rani and donated to the museum in 1980.

Airforce Museum
Palam Marg, T 393461. 1000-1330, Closed Mon. Guns, bullets, uniforms and photographs record the history of the Indian Air Force. Excellent aircraft which include a Westland 'Wapiti'.

Crafts Museum
Pragati Maidan, Bhairon Rd, T 3317641. 1000-1700, Sun and Public Holidays 1000-2000. Contains over 20,000 pieces of traditional Indian crafts from all parts of the country. A rich collection of 18th-20th century objects including terracottas, bronzes, enamel work, wood painting and carving, brocades and jewellery. Library.

Dolls Museum
Nehru House, Bahadur Shah Zafar Marg. 1000-1800, Closed Mon. Entry Re 1 Adults, Re 0.25 Children. Started in 1954 by the well known journalist Shankar. Over 6000 dolls. The BC Roy Children's Library has a wide selection of books and a play corner for those below reading age. Membership restricted to under 16s. Films for members on 2nd Saturdays.

Field Museum
Purana Qila, Mathura Rd. 1000-1700, Closed Mon. Archaeological finds of excavations at this site, below which lies the legendary city of Indraprastha, see page 163. Coins from the early Sunga period (200-100 BC), red earthenware from the Kushan period (100 BC-300 AD), seals and figurines from the Gupta period (200-600 AD) and stone sculptures (700-800 AD). Later artefacts include Rajput coins (900-1200 AD), glazed ware and coins from the Sultanate period (1206-1526).

Gandhi Darshan
Raj Ghat. 1000-1700, Closed Mon. Five pavilions bring together in sculpture, photographs and paintings the life of Gandhi, the history of the *Satyagraha* movement, the philosophy of non-violence and the Constructive Programme formulated by Gandhi. A children's section recreates the history of the freedom movement.

Gandhi Smarak Sangrahalaya
Raj Ghat. 0930-1730, Closed Th. Displays some of Gandhi's personal belongings: walking stick, spinning wheel, sandals, watch and spectacles. Small library and collection of tape recordings of speeches. Films on the *Sarvodaya* movement and allied subjects are screened on Sundays: 1600 Hindi, 1700 English.

National Gallery of Modern Art

Jaipur House, nr India Gate, T 382835. 1000-1700, Closed Mon. Housed in the former Delhi residence of the Maharaja of Jaipur. Excellent collection of Indian modern art. Some of the best exhibits are on the ground floor which is devoted to post-1930 works. Visitors who would like to view the collections chronologically are advised to begin their tour on the first floor. Some of the collections displayed: Amrita Shergil (Grd Fl), contains over 100 examples of her work, including one self portrait. Her style was a synthesis of the flat treatment of Indian painting with a realistic tone. Rabindranath Tagore (Grd Fl). An invaluable collection by the poet who for a brief but intense spell in the 1930s expressed himself through painting as well as poetry. The Bombay School (or Company School) (1st Fl). This includes Western painters who documented their visits to India. Foremost among them is the British painter Thomas Daniell. With a style that seems to anticipate the camera, the realism characteristic of this school is reflected in Indian painting of the early 19th century represented by the schools of Avadh, Patna, Sikkim and Thanjavur. The Bengal School (the late 19th century Revivalist Movement). Artists such as Abanindranath Tagore and Nandalal Bose have their works exhibited here. Western influence was discarded in response to the nationalist movement. Inspiration derived from Indian folk art is evident in the works of Jamini Roy and those of Y.D. Shukla. The Japanese influence can be seen in the use of wash techniques and a miniature style. Some of the works would benefit from better labelling. Postcards, booklets and prints are available at the reception.

Natural History Museum

FICCI Bldg, Barakhamba Rd. 1000-1700, Closed Mon. A small but well assembled introduction to India's natural heritage. A Discovery Room offers children the opportunity to handle specimens and take part in creative activities such as animal modelling. Daily film-show (1130-1530), regular lectures and exhibitions organised in conjunction with other natural history organisations.

Nehru Memorial Museum and Library

Teen Murti Bhavan, T 3016734. Museum 1000-1700, Closed Mon. Library 0900-1900, Closed Sun. The official residence of India's first Prime Minister, Jawaharlal Nehru, was converted after his death (1964) into a national memorial consisting of a museum and research library. The reception, study and bedroom have been preserved as they were. Note his extensive reading and wide interests. A Jyoti Jawahar, kept burning day and night in the garden, is a symbol of the eternal values he inspired, and a granite rock is carved with extracts from his historic speech at midnight 14-15 August 1947. Library resources include unpublished records, private correspondence and micro-film facilities. Films are screened in the auditorium and a *son et lumière* is held after sunset. Very informative and vivid history of the Independence Movement.

Philatelic Museum

Dak Tar Bhavan, Parliament St. 1030-1230, 1430-1630, Closed Mon. Entry passes are available from the basement of the Parliament St Head Post Office. Extensive stamp collection including the first stamp issued in India by the Sindh Dak (1854) and stamps issued before Independence by the ruler of the Princely States. A record is maintained of contemporary stamps issued by the Government. Library.

Pragati Maidan

Mathura Rd. 0930-1730, Sun and Public Holidays 0930-2000. A sprawling exhibition ground containing a restaurant, children's park, shopping centre and cinema theatres where Indian and foreign films are screened daily. The 5 permanent exhibitions include The Nehru

Pavilion displaying a small but comprehensive exhibition on Jawaharlal Nehru. The Son of India Pavilion features the life of Sanjay Gandhi and the Atomic Energy and Defence Pavilions demonstrate through models, photographs and statistics the country's technological and industrial achievements. The 7 acre Village Complex recreates a village scene with about 10 kinds of rural dwellings. Musical instruments, deities, folk arts and crafts and items of everyday use are displayed inside.

Rabindra Bhavan
Copernicus Marg. Housing the national academies of literature (Sahitya Akademi), fine arts and sculpture (Lalit Kala Akademi) and the performing arts (Sangeet Natak Akademi) in separate wings. Founded in 1954 at the inspiration of Maulana Abul Kalam Azad. All have libraries and display galleries which also have postcards and reproductions on sale.

Rail Transport Museum
Chanakyapuri, T 601816. 0930-1730, Closed Mon. Entry R 1 Adults, R 0.50 Children. Opened in 1977, the museum preserves a memorable account of 125 years of the history of Indian Railways. The collection includes 26 vintage locomotives, 17 carriages and saloons including the 4-wheeled saloon used by the Prince of Wales (Edward VII) in 1876 and the Maharaja of Mysore's saloon made of seasoned teak and laced with gold and ivory. The open display recreates a yard and facilitates the movement of stock. Guide books on sale.

Red Fort Museum
Mumtaz Mahal, Lal Qila, T 267961. 1000-1700, Closed Mon. On display are the swords, hookahs, chess sets, armoury, carpets etc of the Mughal emperors from Babur to Bahadurshah Zafar. Miniatures depict life at the court, maps and monuments of Delhi and portraits.

Tibet House
Institutional Area, Lodi Rd, T 611515. 1000-1300, 1400-1700, Closed Sun. Tibetan Art.

Libraries

Central Secretariat Library, Shastri Bhavan. 0900-1800, Closed Sun. Suitable for the social sciences with a strong political science and economics section.

Delhi Public Library, SP Mukherjee Marg. 1400-1945, Closed Sun. The biggest public library in Delhi with branches at Karol Bagh, Patel Nagar and Shahdara.

National Archives, Janpath. 0900-1630, Closed Sun. The archives contain 75,000 bound volumes and 4 million unbound documents.

Parliament House Library, Sansad Bhavan. 1000-1700, Closed Sun and the Second Sat. in the month. Was once the meeting hall of the Chamber of Princes. Panelled in dark wood, the walls are lined with the insignia of the former princely states of India. The library is especially good for political science and modern history.

Parks & zoos

Delhi has many very well kept parks, ideal places to relax. They are also good places for casual birdwatching. Delhi's Birdwatching Society has listed over 350 species of birds seen in the city. Peacocks, weaver-birds, spotted owlets, kingfishers and the koel are relatively common. The arrival of the pied-crested cuckoo heralds the monsoon. Visit Sultanpur and Bharatpur if you are a serious birdwatcher. Parks open 0600-2000.

NB: Although Delhi is safe by the standards of many cities, after dark visitors should be careful as muggings and theft are not unknown.

Buddha Jayanti Park
Sardar Patel Marg, opp Assam House. Commemorates the 2500th anniversary

of Gautama Buddha's attainment of nirvana. A sapling of the original bodhi tree taken to Sri Lanka by Emperor Asoka's daughter in the 3rd century BC is planted here. Rockeries, streams, bridges and the sloping terrain create an atmosphere of peace and tranquillity.

Central Fountain Park
Connaught Pl. A well used park in the heart of the city.

Children's Park
India Gate. A small children's recreation complex.

District Park, Hauz Khas
Deer in the Chinkara complex near to Hauz Khas. Heavily used for early morning yoga exercises, jogging and walking.

Lodi Gardens
Lodi Estate. Officially named Lady Willingdon Park, a very popular and pleasant park set around the 14th and 15th century Lodi and Sayyid tombs.

Mughal Gardens
Rashtrapati Bhavan Estate. A carefully tended Mughal style garden laid out in the classic *char bagh* style. Open to the public one month a year in Feb-Mar when the flowers are in full bloom. For an entry permit at other times contact the India Tourist Office.

National Rose Garden
Safdarjang's Tomb. Worth a visit during the winter months. For bird-watchers, the ornamental pool behind the tomb is likely to have white-fronted and common kingfishers.

Nehru Park
Chanakyapuri. An 85 acre landscaped garden. Sayings of the late Jawaharlal Nehru are inscribed on the rocks. Swimming pool and snack bar at the S end.

Qudsia Bagh
Near Kashmiri Gate. Laid out in 1748 by Qudsia Begum, a slave who became the favourite mistress of the Mughal Emperor Mohammad Shah and mother of his successor. From here the British opened fire on Kashmiri Gate during the Mutiny of 1857. The imposing gateway with pavilions at each end overlooks the river. Peacocks are common.

Roshanara Gardens
Gulabi Bagh. Laid out in 1640 by Princess Roshanara, Shah Jahan's younger daughter, shortly after the completion of Shah Jahanabad. In recent years the garden has been landscaped in Japanese style.

Talkatora Gardens
Talkatora Stadium. Small Japanese garden with mini lake and fountains.

Yamuna Waterfront
Near Inter-State Bus Terminal. River bank developed with Mughal style gardens.

Zoological Gardens
Purana Qila. 0900-1700 Winter, 0800-1800 Summer. Entry Re 0.50. The enclosures house over 1000 animals, reptiles and birds. The most popular attractions are the white tiger from Rewa and the elephant who plays the harmonica! Well laid out. Worth a visit.

Excursions south from Delhi

ROUTES The route along NH 2 from **Delhi** to **Agra** via **Mathura** is described under Uttar Pradesh section. You can take a day trip SW of Delhi into Haryana following the Jaipur road.

Surajkund (Sun pool)

11 km from the Qutb Minar, on the Badarpur-Mehrauli road is a perennial lake surrounded by rock-cut steps. This was built by the Rajput king Surajpal Tomar, and according to tradition this is where the Rajputs first settled before Anangpal Tomar built Lal Kot in Delhi in the 11th century AD. At the head of the reservoir, to the E, are the ruins of what is believed to have been a sun temple (the Rajput dynasties often associated themselves with the Sun or

Moon). A little S is **Siddha Kund**, a pool of fresh water trickling from a rock crevice. This is said to have healing properties. About 2 km west is the **Anangpur dam,** made by depositing local quartzite rocks across the mouth of a narrow ravine. The whole area has become something of a picnic spot for Delhi-ites. The Haryana Tourism *Resort* provides facilities for comfortable 1-day or weekend trips out of Delhi. **Accommodation C** *Raj Hans*, T 6830766, a/c rm, restaurant, bar; *Annexe*, T 8275357. **D** *Tourist Huts*, T 8276099, set in landscaped lawns, deer park, 9-hole golf, boating, facilities open to non-residents.

Local festival

The annual *Craft Mela*, held in Feb in the village complex, draws crafts people from all over India – potters, weavers, metal and stone workers, painters, printers, wood carvers, embroiderers and many more. In addition, folk singers, dancers, magicians and acrobats perform for the crowds. It is a unique opportunity to see the traditional handicrafts being produced, buy direct from the craftsmen, and to sample village food in a rural atmosphere, served on banana leaves and in clay pots. Special bus services from Delhi, Faridabad and Gurgaon during Mela.

ROUTES Surajkund is something of a diversion because you reach it by driving S on NH2 then turning right halfway to Faridabad. This road will bring you back to NH8 at **Gurgaon** (37 km from Delhi; *Pop* 89,000; *STD Code* 01272). **Accommodation D** *Shama* (Haryana Tourism), T 20683, restaurant, bar.

Sultanpur Jheel

46 km from Delhi, just beyond Gurgaon, this is a small bird sanctuary. A *jheel* is a shallow expansive lake. Reeds and other waterside plants grow round the rim and there are some small mud-spits in the water. Best time, Nov-Feb, when there are northern migratory birds. The large and handsome *Sarus*, the only indigenous Indian crane, breed in the reed beds. The migratory demoiselle, the smallest member of the crane family, comes to the lakeside in huge flights late in the winter evenings. The greylag and bar-headed geese and most of the migratory duck species visit the *jheel* including the ruddy shelduck, mallard, teal, gadwall. Coots are common as are white (rosy) pelicans, flamingos and a variety of waders. Of the indigenous birds visiting Sultanpur, the grey pelican, cormorant, painted stork, grey heron and pond heron, egret, are all to be seen plus a few white ibis and the blacknecked stork. Further information from the Project Officer, Haryana Tourism, Chanderlok Bldg, Delhi.

- **Accommodation D** *Rosy Pelican Complex* (Haryana Tourism), Sultanpur Bird Sanctuary, restaurant, a/c rm, camper huts, camping site, birdwatching, facilities open to visitors.

- **Transport Road Bus**: take a blue Haryana bus to Gurgaon from Delhi (dep every 10 min from Dhaula Khan). At Gurgaon take a Chandu bus (3/4 daily) and get off at Sultanpur.

Rewari

83 km from Delhi, was founded in 1000 AD by Raja Rawat and reputedly named after his daughter. There are the ruins of a still older town east of the 'modern' walls. The Rajas of Rewari were partially independent, even under the Mughals, coined their own currency called 'Gokal Sikka' and built the mud fort of Gokalgarh near the town. Rewari fell first to the Marathas and then to the Jat Rajas of Bharatpur. In 1805 it came under direct British rule. It has been a prosperous centre for the manufacture of iron and brass vessels. To the southwest of the town is an attractive tank with ghats built by Tej Singh and also Jain temples. **Accommodation** Haryana Tourism's **D** *Sandpiper Motel*, T 5224, restaurant, bar.

Jahazgarh

20 km N of Rewari, is a corruption of

Georgegarh (George's fort). It was supposedly built by George Thomas, a military adventurer in the late 18th century. With the erosion of central authority in the 18th century, local resources were denied the centre and used by local chiefs for local wars of supremacy. By the end of the century in the Punjab any adventurer who could gather some followers might seize a fort and terrorise the countryside. George Thomas was one of these. In 1801 the Marathas ousted him. Abandoning his conquests, he retired to safety in Berhampur in British territory.

Tours

Guided sightseeing tours can be arranged through approved travel agents and tour operators (see Tour companies & travel agents section). There are many small establishments clustered together in commercial areas, eg opposite New Delhi Rly Station. Although they offer seemingly unusual itineraries their standards cannot be guaranteed and their rates are not significantly lower. India Tourism Development Corporation (ITDC) and Delhi Tourism both run city sightseeing tours. Concessional fares are available for Old Delhi and New Delhi tours combined on the same day, but this can be very tiring. A/c services are particularly recommended during the summer months. The tour price includes transport, entry fees to monuments and museums and guide services. All tend to be whistle stop tours. **NB:** As transport costs tend to be high, a group of 3 or 4 people should consider hiring a car and doing the tour at their own pace. Approved tourist guides may be engaged through the India Tourist Office and travel agents for local and outstation sightseeing. Rates: Delhi only, Half day Rs 60 approx, Full day Rs 100 approx.

Delhi Tourism Tours

Departure point: Bombay Life Bldg, N-Block, Connaught Pl. **New Delhi Tour** (0900-1400): Jantar Mantar, Qutb Minar, Lakshmi Narayan temple, Safdarjang's Tomb, Diplomatic Enclave, India Gate. **Old Delhi Tour** (1415-1715): Jama Masjid, Red Fort (Lal Qila), Shanitvana, Raj Ghat, Kotla Firoz Shah. **Evening Tour** (1800-2200): Lakshmi Narayan Temple (evening prayer), India Gate, Purana Qila (floodlit monument), *son et lumière* (Red Fort), Jama Masjid (dinner at a Mughlai and tandoori restaurant included in the tour price). **Museum Tour**, Sunday only, check time: Air Force, Rail and Transport, and National Museums, Indira Gandhi Memorial, Nehru Planetarium, Museum of Natural History and Dolls Museum.

ITDC Tours

Departure point: L-Block Connaught Pl. **New Delhi Tour** (0900-1400): Jantar Mantar, Lakshmi Narayan temple, India Gate, Nehru Pavilion, Pragati Mai-

dia Gate, Nehru Pavilion, Pragati Maidan (closed Mon), Humayun's tomb, Qutb Minar. **Old Delhi Tour** (1400-1700): Kotla Firoz Shah, Raj Ghat, Shantivana, Jama Masjid and Red Fort. Good value, entry fees included.

Local festivals

Consult the weekly *Delhi Diary* (available at hotels and many shops and offices around town) for exact dates. The following list gives an approximate indication of the dates.

Jan: *Lohri* (13th), the climax of winter is celebrated with bonfires and singing. *Republic Day* Parade (26th), Rajpath. A spectacular fly past and military march past, with colourful pageants and tableaux from every state, dances and music. Tickets through travel agents and most hotels. Cost approx. Rs 100. You can see the full dress preview free, usually 2 days before. (See under Secretariats) Week long celebrations during which government buildings are illuminated. *Beating the Retreat* (29th), Vijay Chowk, a stirring display by the armed forces bands marks the end of the Republic Day Celebrations. *Martyr's Day* (30th) marks Mahatma Gandhi's death anniversary; devotional *bhajans* and Guard of Honour at Raj Ghat. *Delhi Rose Show* (moveable), Safdarjang Tomb. *Shankarlal Sangeet Sammelan* (moveable), N Indian music festival.

Feb: *Basant Panchami* (2nd) celebrates the first day of spring. The Mughal Gardens are opened to the public for a month. *Delhi Flower Show*, Purana Qila. *Horse Show*, Lal Qila. *Thyagaraja Festival* Homage, S Indian music and dance, Vaikunthnath temple, opp J Nehru University.

Mar: *Basant Ritu Sammelan*, N Indian music festival.

Apr: *Amir Khusrau's* Birth Anniversary, a fair in Nizamuddin celebrates this with prayers and *qawwali* singing at his tomb. *National Drama Festival*, Rabindra Bhavan.

May: *Buddha Jayanti*. The first full moon night in May marks the birth of the Buddha and prayer meetings are held at Ladakh Buddha Vihara, Ring Rd and Buddha Vihara, Mandir Marg.

Aug: *Janmashtami* observed as the birth anniversary of the Hindu god Krishna. Special *puja*, Lakshmi Narayan Mandir. *Independence Day* (15th) Impressive flag hoisting ceremony at the Red Fort. *Vishnu Digambar Sammelan*, N Indian music and dance festival.

Sept: *Phoolwalon ki Sair* (30th), Festival of Flower Vendors, dating back to Mughal times symbolises communal harmony.

Oct: *Gandhi Jayanti* (2nd), Mahatma Gandhi's birthday; devotional singing at Raj Ghat. *Dasara* celebrations for 10 nights; over 200 Ramlila performance ana story (see Introduction on Hinduism, page 74). The *Ramlila Ballet* at Delhi Gate is performed for a month and is the most spectacular. The effigy of the demon king Ravana is burnt on the 9th night of Dasara on every large public open space and is noisy and flamboyant, signifying the triumph of good over evil. Special *dasara* discounts at State Government Emporia and Khadi Gram Udyog Bhavan, Connaught Place. *National Drama Festival*, Shri Ram Centre. *Diwali*, the festival of lights; lighting of earthen lamps, candles and firework displays. Diwali greetings are exchanged. Innumerable Diwali melas (fairs). National Drama Festival, Rabindra Bhavan.

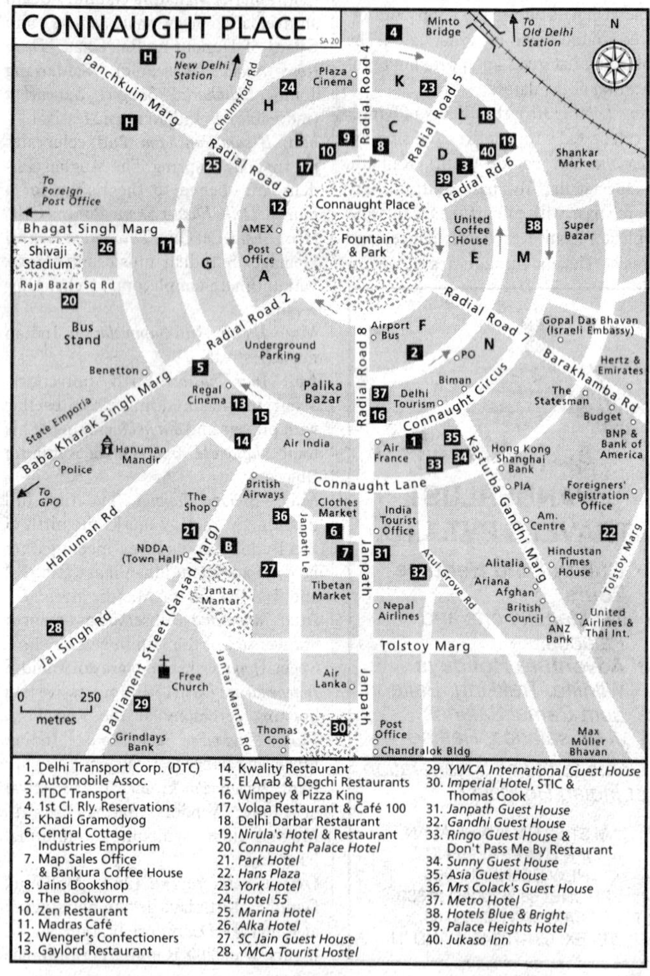

Nov: *Children's Day* (14th), Jawaharlal Nehru's birthday; *Bal Mela* (Children's Fair), India Gate; special programmes at the Dolls Museum, Bal Bhavan and Teen Murti Bhavan.

Dec: *Chrysanthemum Show*, YMCA. *Christmas* (25th). Special Christmas Eve entertainments at all major hotels and restaurants; midnight mass and services at all churches. *Ayyappa Temple Festival*, Ayyappa Swami temple, Ramakrishnapuram; S Indian music. *New Year's Eve* (31st) Widely celebrated in all hotels and restaurants offering special food and entertainment with prices ranging from expensive to exorbitant.

Local information

Accommodation & food

● Accommodation

10% Luxury Tax, 10% Service Charge, 20% Expenditure Tax on hotels with room rates over Rs 1200 per night. See page 138 for hotel classification and advice on billing. Payment in these hotels must be made in foreign exchange (cash, travellers cheque, credit card, or on production of Foreign Exchange Encashment Certificate). Hotels in this category also often insist that foreigners pay a 'dollar rate', which may be up to 50% more than the 'Rupee rate' which is charged to Indians. Children under 12 years are generally free if sharing a room with parents. Extra beds are available for a 3rd person sharing a room. Most down to **D** have a/c rm with bath. Some hotels offer large discounts out of season (Apr-Sep).

Price guide
AL Rs 3,000+ **A** Rs 2,000-3,000
B Rs 1,200-2,000 **C** Rs 600-1,200
D Rs 250-600 **E** Rs 100-250 **F** Up to Rs 100.

NB: The symbols shown represent the distance from the international airport (✈), New Delhi railway station (®) and the city centre (©).

AL *Ashok* , 50-B Chanakyapuri, T 600121, F 6873216. 571 large rm, ✈ 15 km, ® 9 km, ITDC's flagship hotel, garden bar and sunny coffee shop, quiet but not central; **AL** *Holiday Inn Crown Plaza*, Barakhamba Ave, Connaught Pl, T 3320101, F 3325335, 500 rm, ✈ 20 km, ® 2 km, © 0.5 km, 25-storey hotel, described as resembling a 'Russian prison', unattractive lobby, poor report, for its class, in 1994; **AL** *Hyatt Regency*, Bhikaiji Cama Pl, Ring Rd, T 6881234, F 6886833, 535 rm, ✈ 12 km, © 8 km, good pool plus disco, geared to the business traveller; **AL** *Le Meridien*, Windsor Pl, Janpath, T 3710101, F 3714545, 358 rm, ✈ 23 km, ® 2 km, © 0.5 km, just S of Connaught Pl, visually striking, dramatic atrium, good views, elevated pool, rooftop restaurant; **AL** *The Oberoi*, Dr Zakir Hussain Marg, T 363030, F 360484, 288 rm, ✈ 20 km, ® 9 km, © 8 km, one of the 'Leading Hotels of the World' with Raj overtones, known for its quiet efficiency and dignity, overlooks Golf Course with fine views; **AL** *Taj Mahal*, 1 Mansingh Rd, T 3016162, F 3017299, 300 rm, ✈ 18 km, ® 5 km, © 5 km, known as Taj Man Singh to distinguish it from the Taj Palace, an excellent, lavishly finished and very well run hotel with good views over the city, especially from higher floors; **AL** *Taj Palace Inter-Continental*, 2 Sardar Patel Marg, Diplomatic Enclave, T 3010404, F 3011252, 504 rm, ✈ 12 km, ® 9 km, © 10 km, location good for airport but away from centre, purpose-built for conventions, tour groups and business travellers; **AL** *Maurya Sheraton Hotel and Towers*, Sardar Patel Marg, Diplomatic Enc, T 3010101, F 3010908, 500 rm, ✈ 12 km, ® 8 km, © 10 km, excellent decor and service, Executive Club for business travellers, splendid pool (solar heated), tennis, disco, *Dum Phukt* particularly renowned restaurant for *handi* cuisine.

The following **A** category hotels have the Govt 5 Star classification but are not in the same class as the **AL** category hotels. **A** *Centaur*, Gurgaon Rd, nr International Airport, T 5452223, 376 rm, ✈ 2 km, ® 16 km, © 16 km, floodlit tennis court and putting green, service unreliable – but free transport to airport and centre; **A** *Claridges*, 12 Aurangzeb Rd, T 3010211, F 3010625, 167 rm, ✈ 20 km, ® 6 km, © 4 km, colonial atmosphere, elegant reception, attractive restaurants and good food, rec; **A** *Imperial*, Janpath, T 3325332, F 3314542, 175 rm, ✈ 20 km, ® 2 km, modernised but retaining Colonial feel, especially in bedrooms, well tended gardens, in the heart of town, good pool, Thomas Cook, STIC offices, increasingly has the feel of a tourist package hotel, service reluctant, book in advance; ITDC **A** *Kanishka*, 19 Ashoka Rd, T 3324422, 317 rm, ✈ 20 km, ® 2.5 km, © 0.5 km, excellent views from upper floors and rooftop restaurant but otherwise rather characterless, service can be slow.

A *Oberoi Maidens*, 7 Sham Nath Marg, T 2525464, F 2929800, 53 rm, ✈ 30 km, ® 10 km (Old Delhi) 2 km, many large rm (especially suites) with verandahs; some rm are enclosed and windowless, attractive colonial style hotel (one of the oldest) in quiet area of Old Delhi set in spacious gardens, reasonably priced with more personal attention than in larger hotels, lacks arcade shops but has a disco and tennis; **A** *Park*, 15 Parliament St, T 352447, F 352025, 234 rm, ✈ 20 km, ® 2 km, central, small pool, very central with views over Jantar Mantar, friendly service, exclusive Bengali cuisine, modern and comfortable rooms but walls too thin!; **A** *Qutab*, off Sri Aurobindo Marg, T 660060, 64 rm, ✈ 15 km, ® 15 km, © 15 km, pool, tennis, bowling alley, also 30 small apartments with kitchenette but no rm service; ITDC **A** *Samrat*, Chanakyapuri, T 603030, 268 rm, ✈ 15 km, ® 9 km, modern but already looking run down; **A** *Siddharth*, 3 Rajendra Pl, T 5712501, F 5729581, 100 rm, ✈ 15 km, ® 4 km, © 4 km; **A** *Sofitel Surya*, New Friends Colony, T 6835070, 230 rm, ✈ 18 km, ® 12 km, © 10 km, isolated, but courtesy coach to airports and centre, good views; **A** *Vasant Continental*, Vasant Vihar, T 678800, F 6873842, 110 rm, ✈ 10 km, ® 13 km, © 10 km, convenient for airports; smaller hotel with a more Indian atmosphere, courtesy coach, large pool and gardens; **A** *Taj Ambassador*, Sujan Singh Park, T 690391, 69 rm, ✈ 12 km, ® 6 km, © 5 km, no pool but disco and garden, excellent restaurant: *Dasaprakash* (S Indian), reserve ahead.

B *Connaught Palace*, 37 Shaheed Bhagat Singh Marg, T 344225, F 310757, good location, 80 rm, flexible checkout, no pool, adequate but uninspired. Hotel car-hire service restricts you to their choice hotels for out-of-city trips (US$190 for 5-day 'triangle'); **B** *Hans Plaza*, 15 Barakhamba Rd, T 3316868, F 3314830, 70 rm, ✈ 20 km, ® 2 km, © 1 km, excellent location, no pool, business centre, health club, superb views, clean and quiet, on 16th-20th Fl, excellent value if you like heights!; **B** *Diplomat*, 9 Sardar Patel Marg, T 3010204, F 3018605, 25 rm, ✈ 10 km, ® 10 km, © 10 km, no pool, quietly located in Diplomatic area; **B** *Janpath*, Janpath, T 3320070, 213 rm, ✈ 20 km, ® 2 km, © 0.5 km, no pool, good location but poor rm (awaiting refurbishment) and indifferent service; **B** *Marina*, G-59 Connaught Circus, T 3324658, 93 rm, ✈ 20 km, ® 1 km, central, the oldest hotel in New Delhi, refurbished in 1982, some rm cramped, attractive public rm, one recent report of poor service, but quite good value.

All **C** hotels have central a/c and TV. **C** *Nirula's*, L-Block, Connaught Circus, T 3322419, F 332 4669, 29 rm, ✈ 22 km, ® 1 km, very central, so often full; friendly reception, *Potpourri* restaurant, fast, clean and very popular – excellent light meals & snacks, own ice cream parlour – a focus for Delhi social life!; New, less expensive sister hotel C-135 Sector2, NOIDA, T 8926512, with occasional free transfer to town centre, similar *Potpourri* and bar, pleasant atmosphere, friendly, 16 km out-of-town location a disadvantage; **C** *Jukaso Inn*, 50 Sunder Nagar, T 690308, 50 clean rm, ✈ 21 km, ® 9 km, © 8 km, restaurant, garden, pleasant, in quiet location, friendly staff, also at L-1 Connaught Circus, T 3329694, 40 rm, ✈ 20 km, ® 1 km, central, restaurant, travel, exchange, a bit run-down; **C** *Rajdoot*, Mathura Rd, T 699583, 55 rm, ✈ 16 km, ® 7 km (close to Hazrat Nizammuddin Rly), © 6 km, pool, 'nightclub'; **C** *Alka*, G, 16/90 Connaught Circus, T 344328, 23 rm, ✈ 20 km, ® 1.5 km, central, rm, small but modern, clean & comfortable, good Indian restaurant, very good value; friendly, efficient staff, book ahead; **C** ***Asian International***, Janpath Le, T 3321636, 33 rm, ✈ 20 km, ® 3 km, © 1 km, a/c, restaurant, coffee shop, exchange, entrance off-putting, but clean rm, good service, rec as good value; **C** ***Broadway***, 4/15A Asaf Ali Rd, T 273821, 32 clean rm, ✈ 15 km, ® 2 km, © 2 km, good restaurant, bar, 24 hr coffee shop, exchange, refurbished.

C ***India International Centre***, Lodi Estate, T 619431, good restaurants, often full; **C** ***Lodhi***, Lala Lajpat Rai Marg, T 362422, 207 rm, ✈ 22 km, ® 8 km (1 km Nizamuddin Rly), © 7 km, restaurant *Woodlands*, highly rec S Indian food, bar, shops, pool; **C** ***Lotus Inn***, C-5 Kalkaji, opp Nehru Place Shopping Complex, T 6477049, 20 rm, some a/c with bath, in business style hotel with Secretarial/Fax services; **C** ***President***, 4/23B Asaf Ali Rd, T 3277836, 20 rm, some comfortable, ✈ 17 km, ® 3 km, © 2 km, restaurant *Tandoor*, good quality tandoori food, indian music, coffee shop, bar, travel; ITDC **C** ***Ranjit***, Maharaja Ranjit Singh Rd, T 3311256, 186 rm, about half a/c, ✈ 26 km, ® 2 km, © 3 km, good restaurant (veg), exchange, coffee shop, bar, pool, well located for Old Delhi sights but rm needs renovation; **C** ***Sartaj***, A-3 Green Park Main, T 667759, 45 simple rm, ✈ 10 km, ® 11 km, © 10 km, restaurant, bar, travel; **C** ***Vikram***, Ring Rd, Lajpatnagar, T 6436451, 72 rm, ✈ 12 km, ® 13 km, © 12 km, restaurant, bar, travel, exchange, pool, lacks attention; **C** ***York***, K-Block, Connaught Circus, T 3323769, 28 simply furnished rm on upper Fl, ✈ 20 km, ® 1 km, central, good restaurant, pool, good value.

Most **D** hotels now have TV in at least some rm. **D** ***La Sagrita Tourist Home***, 14 Sunder Nagar, T 4698572, F4636956, 25 rm with phone, close to Supreme Court, Pragati Maidan, © 4 km, central a/c, some rm noisy, good restaurant, travel, lawns, very helpful staff, strict hygiene and good service, quiet location and excellent value for money for Delhi; **D** ***Sobti***, 2397 Hardian Singh Rd, Karolbagh, T 5729035, 27 rm, ✈ 21 km, ® 4 km, © 5 km, restaurant, garden; **D** ***YMCA Tourist Hostel***, Jai Singh Rd, T 311915, 123 rm, ® 3 km, © 1 km, open to both sexes, a/c rm with bath (B block, non a/c and shared bath), small membership charge, max stay 15 days, restaurant (reasonably priced), pool, exchange, travel, shop, gardens, tennis, good value, can reserve ahead; **D** ***YWCA International Guest House***, Sansad Marg (nr Jantar Mantar), T 311561, 24 a/c rm, © 1 km, open to both sexes, restaurant (poor value, mainly Western food), convenient location; ITDC **D** ***Ashok Yatri Niwas***, 19 Ashok Rd, T 3324511, 547 rm, ® 3 km, © 1 km, 547 rm, good self-service restaurant, bar, exchange, PO, good views from higher floors, but rm up to floor 14 not very clean, poorly lit, lifts inadequate, service at main desk can be very slow, and sometimes demand full payment in advance; grumpy management, expensive for poor facilities, not rec. However, *Coconut Grove* (S Indian restaurant), pleasant atmosphere, good value.

D ***Maharani Guest House***, 3 Sunder Nagar, T 693128, © 4 km, quiet location. Indian meals, roof terrace, good value; **D** ***Woodstock Motel***, 11 Golf Links, T 619571, 16 a/c rm, © 4 km, restaurant, guest house rec for friendly attention, quiet location and pleasant garden; **D** ***Yatri Paying Guest House***, corner of Panch Kuin Rd and Mandir Marg, T 525463, large clean, well kept rm, some a/c, quiet location, garden, reserve ahead; **D** ***Fifty Five***, H-55 Connaught Pl, T 3321244, F 3320769, 15 small a/c rm, central, central a/c, 24-hr rm service (no restaurant), travel, terrace, cramped and dim, but rec for good service, Visa only; **D** ***Central Court***, N Block Connaught Circus, T 3315013, 36 a/c rm, ® 1 km, central, restaurant, coffee shop, exchange and refrigerator; **D** ***Flora***, Dayanand Rd, Daryaganj, T 3273634, 24 a/c rm, ® 3 km, © 2 km, restaurant, 63 small but clean rm upstairs, ® 2 km (4 km Old Delhi Rly), © 3 km, 29 a/c rm, restaurant; **D** ***Host Inn***, F-33 Connaught Pl, T 3310704, 10 a/c rm, ® 1 km, central, central a/c, TV, run-down and seedy; **D** ***Manor***, 77 Friends Colony, T 632171, 24 a/c rm, ® 10 km, © 8 km, restaurant, travel, pool, tennis; **D** ***Metro***, N-49 Connaught Circus, T 3313856, 10 rm, half a/c, ® 2 km, central, check rm first; **D** ***Rajdeep***, 34 Bank St, Karol Bagh, T 5717354, central a/c, restaurant, travel; **D** ***Regal***, S. P. Mukherjee Marg, T 2526197, 37 rm, some a/c, ® 6 km (2 km Old Delhi Rly), © 6 km; ***Sodhi Lodge***, E-2 East of Kailash, T 6432381, 9 a/c rm, ® 10 km, © 8 km, restaurant; **D** ***Tourist Delux***, Ram Nagar, T 770985, comfortable rm, nr New Delhi Rly, © 1 km; the neighbouring **D** ***Tourist***, Ram Nagar, T 510334, 65 rm, some a/c, restaurant (veg), travel, set back from road; **D** ***Tourist Holiday Home***, 7 Link Rd, Jangpura, T 618797, 16 rm, some a/c, ® 6 km, © 6 km.

● **Budget hotels**

E *S Indian*, Ajmal Khan Rd, Karol Bagh, T 5717126, 25 rm, some a/c, ® 2 km, © 2 km, restaurant, travel; **E** *Satkar*, Green Park, T 664572, 9 rm, ® 12 km, © 10 km, some a/c rm, restaurant (veg).

Very cheap accommodation: is concentrated around Janpath, Paharganj and Chandni Chowk. Well patronised but basic and usually cramped, they are good places for meeting other budget travellers. Govt of India Tourist Office on Janpath has information, as does the Student Travel Information Centre at *Imperial Hotel*, Janpath.

In the Connaught Pl area: **E** *Bright*, M-85 Connaught Pl, T 3320444, 18 rm, ® 2 km, central, exchange, noisy at night, downstairs disco, poorly maintained; **E** *Palace Heights*, D-Block Connaught Circus, 3rd Fl, T 3321369, 18 simple rm, some with bath, ® 2 km, central, breakfast and drinks only; **E** *Janpath Guest House*, nr Tourist Office, 82 Janpath, T 3321935, reasonable but small rm, some a/c (more expensive but better), most with bath; solar powered hot water – only when the sun shines!; **E** *Royal Guest House*, 44 Janpath, nr Nepal Airlines, some rm with bath, clean; **E** *RC Mehta*, 3rd Fl, 52 Janpath; **E** *Jain's Guest House*, 7 Pratap Singh Bldg, Janpath Le, rm without bath, quiet, clean; **E** *Mrs Colacks Guest House*, Janpath Le, T 3328758, small simple rm.

On and around Kasturba Gandhi Marg: **E** *Asia Guest House*, 14 Scindia House, Kasturba Gandhi Marg, above Air France office, T 3313393, rm with hot showers, some a/c, spartan but clean, good service, very good value, friendly, helpful management, rec by many; **E** *Ringo Guest House*, 17 Scindia House, T 3310605, small, simple rm and crowded dorm (beds 15cm apart!), when full, cheap beds on rooftop, no hot showers, smelly toilets and dirty rm reported in 1994, lockers, meals 0700-2300, courtyard for tea, popular with backpackers; **E** *Gandhi Guest House*, 80 Tolstoy Marg, 9 rm, cheap dorm, hot water in winter, tatty, grim, but less crowded than Ringo; **E** *Sunny Guest House*, 152 Scindia House, T 3312909, basic rm and dorm, excellent breakfasts.

Paharganj area: (along Main Bazar, nr New Delhi Rly station and N of it, about 20 min walk from Connaught Circus): there are several fairly cheap, noisy, basic hotels, mostly with shared bath. Outside there are plenty of eating houses. It is best to inspect before deciding. **Note**: It can get very muddy here, especially during and after the monsoons. **E** *Ajanta*, 36 Arakashan Rd, Ram Nagar, T 7520925, F 7532223, central, 300m from New Delhi Rly, 58 rm, some dearer a/c rm, with bath and TV, restaurant (indifferent service), coffee shop, travel, terrace, overlooks park, Indian businessmen's hotel, reports of poor service in 1994, not good value; **E** *Anoop*, 1566 Main Bazar, T 735219, rm with bath, some with air-cooler, very clean though basic, rooftop restaurant shared with *Hare Krishna Hotel*, convenient area for international phone calls, rec;R **E** *Apsara Tourist Lodge*, 8126 Arakashan Rd, Ramnagar, T 527121, basic rm, clean linen, visitor in 1994 found a mouse!; **E** *The Nest*, Corner House, 11 Qutb Rd, T526614, 18 rm, ® 1 km, © 1 km, some a/c rm, exchange, rm service; **E** *Satyam*, fairly clean rm; **E** *Shiela*, Pawha House, 9 Qutb Rd, T 525603, 44 rm, ® 1 km, © 1 km, some a/c rm, travel; **E** *Chanakya*, Rajguru Rd, pleasant; **E** *Vivek*, 1550 Main Bazar, T 521948, some reasonable rm with bath, few with hot water, restaurant; **E** *Vishal*, few doors down, some rm with bath, restaurants (not rec), additional problem of pestering 'trinket' salesmen; **E** *Rail Yatri Nivas*, behind New Delhi Rly Station (3 min walk from Ajmeri Gate in 8-storey bldg), 36 rm with shower, 172 dorm beds, restaurant, reserve in advance through ITB (see Transport by rail below) or direct to New Delhi Rly Station, Gate 2 or T 3315445, quoting ticket no and send money order for accommodation and 'key deposit', max stay 3 nights, check-out 1000 when you may be lucky at weekends and find a vacancy if you arrive without pre-booking.

Some are even cheaper but most suffer from noise, particularly noticeable at night, when your sleep can be disturbed. **F** *Airlines*, Qutb Rd; **E** *Ajay*, 5084a Main Bazar, T 7777617, very clean rm, popular, easy to meet others, good value, opp, under same management; **E** *Hare Rama*, is similar with additional dorm beds, basic rooftop restaurant (24-hr); **F** *Little Star*, between Main Bazar and Desh Bandhu Gupta Rd; **F** *Mohak Palace*, Multani Dhanda, clean, friendly, safe to leave luggage; **F** *Natraj*, Chuna Mandi, T 522699, reasonably clean rm; **F** *Navrang*, friendly and cheap;. **F** *Venus*, 1566 Main Bazar; **F** *White House Tourist Lodge*, 8177 Main Bazar; **F** *Tourist Lodge*,

In Old Delhi: **E** *Tera* and Restaurants, 2802 Bara Bazar, Kashmiri Gate, T 239660, 42 rm, some

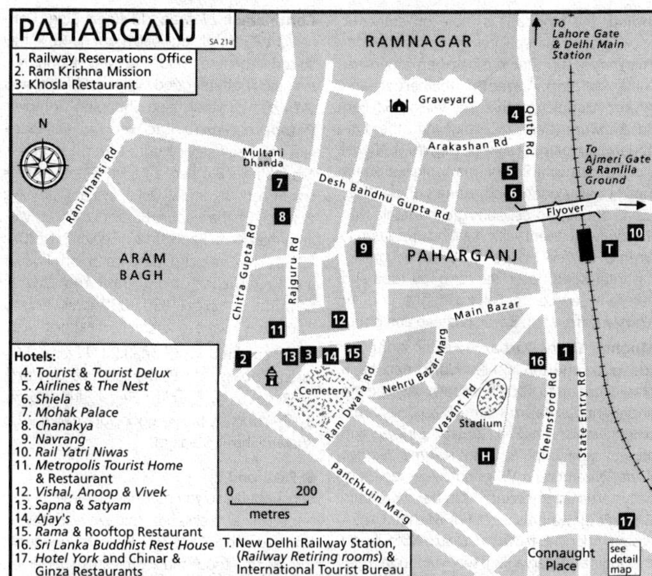

a/c, ® 4 km (0.5 km Old Delhi Rly), © 4 km, restaurant, coffee shop, TV; **E** *Bhagirath Palace*, opp Red Fort, Chandni Chowk, T 236223, 18 rm, ® 5 km (1 km Old Delhi Rly), © 5 km, some a/c rm, bar, TV; **E** *Neeru*, 10 Netaji Subhash Marg, Daryaganj, T 278522, 24 rm, ® 2 km, © 2 km, some a/c rm, restaurant.

Paying guest accommodation: a number of Delhi families welcome tourists as paying guests. Consult Govt of India Tourist Office, 88 Janpath for full details.

Airport Retiring Rooms, T 391351, simple rm at Rs 200 (D) and Rs 100 (S), contact Airport Manager, room allocation on 'first come, first served' basis for confirmed ticket holders only; *Rly Retiring Rooms*, at Old and New Delhi Rly Stations, for 12 and 24 hr. Dorm beds (10 rm, 6 a/c are usually pre-booked), only for train ticket-holders, basic, noisy, but convenient. For **E** *Rail Yatri Nivas*, see above.

● Youth Hostels

E *Vishwa Yuvak Kendra* (International Youth Centre), Circular Rd, Chanakyapuri, T 3013631, ✈ 12 km, © 8 km, 36 rm, some with bath and dorm, open to all ages, cafeteria, on 620 bus route to Connaught Pl, reservations: The Manager; **F** *Youth Hostel*, 5 Naya Marg, Chanakyapuri, T 3016285, basic dorm, breakfast, preference to International YHA members, popular and rec.

● Camping

F *New Delhi Tourist Camp*, Nehru Marg, opp JP Narayan Hospital, T 3272898, clean rm in huts plus cheaper dorm beds in tents, hot water, restaurant, exchange, travel, gardens, nr New Delhi Rly and centre, EATS bus to airports (Rs 25/35); **F** *Tourist Camp*, Qudsia Gardens, opp Inter-State Bus Terminal, T 2523121, camping and huts, food available.

● Places to eat

The larger hotels have some very good restaurants – for cuisine, decor and ambience. Buffets (breakfast, lunch or dinner) cost Rs 80-350. Alternatively you can have an excellent Indian vegetarian *thali* at the smaller *Taj* and some C grade hotels (Rs 75-120) or a quick evening meal (Rs 100 for 2) at *Bar-e-Kabab* (*Ashoka*). Restaurants outside hotels can be excellent; they open around 1930. Eating out is very popular in Delhi and Indian families sometimes eat very late; without a reservation, you are advised to arrive early. **NB:** Alcohol is not served in restaurants outside hotels. Some restaurants close on Sun.

Indian: the emphasis is more on authentic cooking for Indian palates than on elegant or imaginative surroundings. ***Amber***, expensive, lightly spiced; ***Angeethi*** (barbecue) and ***Ankur*** (Mughlai), both in The Village, Siri Fort Rd; ***Bankura*** (Central Cottage Industries Emporium), Janpath for snacks; ***Degchi***, 13 Regal Bldg, Connaught Pl, unremarkable surroundings but very good food; ***Kaka's***, Plaza Bldg, *Handi* dishes and delicious green masala fish; ***Regency***, excellent valuc, seating upstairs, rec; ***United Coffee House***, E-15 Connaught Pl, has interesting decor, rec for good food and excellent service. In Paharganj the popular ***Khosla Café***, Main Bazar, is cheap and good.

Mughlai: ***Delhi Darbar***, 49 Connaught Circus, good mutton dishes; ***Flora***, opp Jama Masjid (option to sit on floor cushions) and the unpretentious ***Karim's***, Jama Masjid, serve excellent *kalmi* chicken kebab, *biryani* and breads, very popular. Also ***Karim's Nemat Kada***, Nizamuddin W, good value, rec especially after sightseeing; ***Khyber***, Kashmiri Gate, Peshawari dishes; ***Mini Mahal***, C-25A Vasant Vihar; ***Moti Mahal***, *Delux*, NDSE II, and the original at Daryaganj, serve tandoori food, pleasanter tented section outside, closed Tues, branch at M-13 Gt Kailash I; ***Mughlai***, M-17 Connaught Pl, also serves good Indian sweets; *Dhaba* style open-air ***Chic-Fish***, Malviya Nagar and ***Aalis***, Panchsheel Enclave are rec, the latter for '*kathis*' (spicy meat kebabs rolled in *paratha* bread); ***Peshawari***, 3707 Subhash Marg, Daryaganj, tiny with tiled walls, serves delicious chicken, closed Tue.

S Indian: In hotels *Ambassador* and *Lodhi*. Outside, ***Andhra Bhavan***, nr India Gate, ***Sagar***, Defence Colony, and ***S Indian Boarding House***, opp Shankar Market are rec. ***Ranjit*** does good veg *thalis*.

Chinese & Japanese: *Zen*, Connaught Pl, stylish, impersonal but popular, generous portions for Chinese (try Shanghai Chicken), more expensive options – Japanese and seafood rec; ***Berco's***, L-Block Connaught Pl, generous helpings; ***Ginza***, K-Block Connaught Pl; ***Don't Pass Me By***, next to *Ringos*, 17 Scindia House, huge portions, tasty, happy staff, 'incredibly cheap'; ***Daitchi***, E-19A NDSE II; ***Dynasty***, M-17 Connaught Pl. Away from the centre: ***Fujiya***, 12/48 Malcha Marg, has Japanese dishes too; ***Golden Dragon***, C-2 Vasant Vihar, attractive decor, popular with diplomats; ***Hong Kong***, M-31 Greater Kailash I; ***Chopsticks***, The (Asiad) Village, Siri Fort Rd; ***Akasaka*** and ***Faley's***, Defence Colony Market.

Continental: ***El Arab***, 13 Regal Bldg, Connaught Pl, slightly dull decor but good, lightly spiced Lebanese food; non-veg, highly rec, evening buffets good value; ***Fisherman's Wharf***, A-1 Moolchand Shopping Complex; ***Potpourri***, *Nirula's Hotel*, very popular, excellent value self-service buffet from lunchtime. *Nirula's* have 8 other fast food restaurants/ice cream parlours across Delhi, incl at *Chanakya Cinema*, Chanakyapuri; Basant Lok Mkt, Vasant Vihar; Karol Bagh; C135, Sector 2, NOIDA; 13/30 Ajmal Khan Rd, Defence Colony Flyover and New Friends Colony. ***Basil and Thyme***, Santushti Complex (1030-1830) is rec. Also try Hauz Khas Village for a variety of eating places.

Multi-cuisine: in Connaught Pl are: Mirrored ***Embassy***, 11-D; the subdued ***Gaylord***, 14 Regal Bldg; ***Kwality***, Regal Bldg; ***Volga***, B-19; ***Yorks***, K-Block, good for snacks. Also ***Shivaji***, Shivaji Stadium.

● Fast food

Very popular, so you may have to wait a while (especially at weekends); hippy-wear may be frowned upon. ***Café 100***, B Block Connaught Circus, fast food and ice creams specialties; ***American Pie***, Asiad Village (1100-2400); ***Wimpy's***, N-5, bright, shiny, burger bar (no *beef* but excellent lamb burgers and free iced water!), popular with backpackers;P ***Sona Rupa***, 46 Janpath, rec for veg snacks (1030-2400). When shopping in the State Emporia, walk across to Mohan Singh Pl Bldg on Baba Kharak Singh Marg for excellent coffee and snacks on top floor. In Connaught Pl: ***Nizam's Kathi Kebabs***, H-5 Plaza; ***Nirula's***, L-Block, for good breakfasts, snacks, pastries and ice creams in a cluster of shops; other outlets listed under Continental; ***Tej's***, N-Block; ***The Treat*** for good snacks and ***Kaveri*** for good veg at Palika Parking Complex, busy at lunch times, deserted at night; ***The Regency Midtown***, B-29, has relaxed atmosphere; Popular ***Pantry***, M-15; ***Kalpana***, Tolstoy Le, behind Air India, rec for breakfasts. Look out for '*Colonelz Kebabz*' outlets – good fast food, at Defence Colony Mkt, RK Puram and elsewhere.

● Tea lounges

The old fashioned 'tea on the lawns' still served at the *Imperial* and in the *Claridges'* courtyard – sit inside for a/c if you prefer. Some others offer tea, coffee and cold drinks with light snacks. Unique tea-tasting at ***Aapki Pasand***, 15 Netaji Subhash Marg, before you buy.

● 24-Hour coffee shops

Usually pleasantly situated by a hotel garden or poolside, often offering substantial snacks and fast service. Rec: ***Cafe Promenade*** (*Hyatt Regency*), with palms and 'waterfall', pleasant for breakfast; ***Machan*** (*Taj Mahal*), a 'jungle lookout'; ***Isfahan*** (*Taj Palace*) with Persian decor; ***Samovar*** (*Ashok*) for good breakfasts and salads; ***Verandah*** (*Imperial*) along a very pleasant garden setting.

● Confectioners

Outside hotels: ***Chocolate Wheel***, 55 Jorbagh. Connaught Pl has: ***Nirula's Pastry Shop***, L-Block; ***Wengers***, A-Block. Major markets now have excellent confectioners and patisseries.

● Bars

1st and 7th day of each month and national holidays are 'dry' when liquor stores and hotel bars are closed but you can get a drink through room service. Normally hotel restaurants, bars and clubs serve alcohol. Restaurants outside hotels often do not, exceptions incl *Delhi Durbar*, Connaught Pl. All the top hotels have bars.

Entertainment & shopping

The weekly *Delhi Diary*, free from hotels and many other outlets round the city gives information on what is on.

● Clubs

Chelmsford Club, Raisina Rd. ***Delhi Gymkhana Club***, Safdarjang Rd, membership mostly for government and defence personnel, long waiting list, squash, tennis, swimming, bar and restaurant. ***Roshanara Club***, Roshanara Rd, cricket club and ground, used in the film 'Gandhi'.

● Cultural Centres

Alliance Française de Delhi, M-5 NDSE Part II, T 6440128. French classes. Library of French literature. Theatre activities and active film club. 1000-1700, closed Sun. ***American Centre*** (US Information Service), 24 Kasturba Gandhi Marg, T 3316841. Large library (20,000 books). American fine arts and performing arts are energetically promoted. 0930-1800, closed Sun. ***British Council***, 17 Kasturba Gandhi Marg, T 3711401. Extensive library with an excellent reference section for the sciences. Special facilities include large print and audio visual sections and a postal loan service. Membership. 0900-1800, closed Sun. ***French Cultural Centre***, 2 Aurangzeb Rd, T 3014682. ***Italian Cultural Centre***, 38 Ring Rd, T 623441. ***Japan Cultural Centre***, 32 Feroze Shah Rd, T 329803. Language classes, films, exhibitions and lectures. 0900-1300 and Tues-Fri 1400-1700, closed Sun. ***Max Mueller Bhawan***, 3 Kasturba Gandhi Marg, T 3329506. Houses the Goethe Institute of German. Language classes, cultural programmes, lectures, discussions, seminars and films. Good library for sociology and art. 0900-1400, 1500-1800, closed Sun. ***House of Soviet Culture***, 24 Feroze Shah Rd, T 386629. Regular exhibitions and films promoting both Indian and Soviet culture. 1000-1700, Closed Sun. ***Triveni Theatre Complex***, Tansen Marg, between Bengali market and India Gate. A centre for the performing and visual arts, the Triveni has theatres (excellent English and Hindi plays, and classical Indian dance), four different galleries (modern sculpture, paintings, cartoons etc.) and an excellent open air cafe.

● Discotheques

Oasis, *Hyatt Regency*. ***Ghungroo***, *Maurya Sheraton* (residents only). ***No. 1***, *Taj Mahal*. ***CJ's***, *Le Meridien*, selective entry, cover charge. All popular (2200 until early hr).

● Son et Lumière

Red Fort: 1800-1900 (Hindi), 1930-2030 (English). Entry Rs 5 and Rs 10. Tickets available at the Red Fort. Enquiries T 600121 ext. 2156 and 274580 (after 1700). (Be sure to take mosquito cream). **Teen Murti House**: 'A Tryst with Destiny': 1800-1900 (Hindi), 1915-2015 (English). Entry Rs 2 and Rs 5. Tickets available at Teen Murti House. Enquiries T 3015026. Both *son et lumière* shows do not usually operate over the monsoon period. Check in *Delhi Diary*. **Hauz Khas**: 1 hr cultural show in illuminated ruins, daily, 1845, Rs 100.

● Sports

Boating: paddle and row boats are available for hire at Purana Qila lake, Mathura Rd. 0600-1800.

Bowling: the ***Qutab Hotel*** has a 4 lane semi-automatic bowling alley, T 62537.

Flying: ***Delhi Flying and Gliding Clubs***, Safdarjang Airport, T 618271. Temporary membership available. 1300-1800. Gliding season Mar-Jun and Sept-Nov.

Golf: ***Delhi Golf Club***, Dr Zakir Hussein Marg, T 699236. Country's busiest. A sanctuary attracting over 300 species of birds. Temporary membership available with clubs for hire. 6,972 yard, par 72, 18-hole course and 9-hole beginners' course. Open all year. Another at Suraj Kund (see under excursions).

Polo: ***Delhi Polo Club***, President's Estate, Rashtrapati Bhawan, T 375604). Temporary membership available. Apply to The Secretary, c/o The President's Body Guard.

Riding: ***Delhi Riding Club***, Safdarjang Rd, T 3011891. Open to all. Information from the Club Secretary and to book the day before. Rides 0630-0930 and 1400-1900. ***Children's Riding Club***, T 3012265.

Skating: rink at Pragati Maidan.

Swimming: many hotels empty their pools over the winter (Dec-Feb). *Samrat Hotel*, allows outsiders to use the pool and health club. By far the cheapest of the hotel pools. The *Maurya Sheraton's* is solar heated and open all year round. When open, the *Taj Mahal*, *Oberoi* and *Imperial* pools are very good. The *Maurya*, *Ashok*, *Claridges* and *Imperial* allow non-residents to use their pools at daily charges of Rs 100-250. ***NMDC Pools***, at Nehru Park near *Hotel Ashok* and Block Sarojini Nagar.

Tennis: ***Delhi Lawn Tennis Association***, Africa Ave, T 653955. Asian Games Village.

● Shopping

Shops generally open from 1000-1930 (Winter 1000-1900). Food stores, chemists stay open later. Most shopping areas close on Sun including Connaught Circus, Khan Market, Jor Bagh, Sundernagar, Chandni Chowk, Sadar Bazar. However, Defence Colony, Janpura, Karol Bagh, Nizamuddin and S Extension are closed on Mon, and Green Park, Haus Khaz and Sarojini Nagar Markets are closed on Tues. Banks tend to follow the same pattern.

● Books

Many booksellers will pack and post books abroad but have to assess the cost at a Post Office and so requires a return visit. ***Oxford Book and Stationery***, Scindia House, Connaught Circus, (nr Janpath) and ***Bookworm***, B-29 Connaught Pl, have a wide selection, including fiction. ***Jain's Bookshop*** in C block, Connaught Pl, is the Govt book agency. ***E D Galgotia*** at 17B and ***New Book Depot*** at 18 B Connaught Pl are highly rec. ***The Central News Agency***, P 23/90 Connaught Circus, has a range of foreign newspapers and journals as well as newspapers from all over India. All around Connaught Pl there are street booksellers selling a wide range of foreign authors' works at a fraction of the original price. Janpath has a line of small bookshops, including the Karachi Stationery Mart, some offering bargains.

Hotel booksellers often carry a good selection of imported books about India, though some charge inflated prices. Among those who have specialist academic and art books focusing on India are ***Jainson's***, *Janpath Hotel*; ***The Book House***, *Hotel Kanishka*; ***Krishan Book Shop***, Claridge's; and ***Khazana***, the *Taj Mahal* and *Taj Palace hotels*. In the old city ***Moti Lal Benarsi Das***, Nai Sarak, Chandni Chowk, has books on Indology. In Khan Market, ***The Bookshop***, has a wide choice (also at Jor Bagh Market), as do ***Bahri & Sons***. ***Prabhu Service*** at Gurgaon village beyond the airport is a good second-hand bookshop.

● Clothing

Tailoring is not as cheap as it used to be and styles tend to be somewhat dated. Nearly all big hotels have a fabric/tailor's shop. Allow about 24-hr for stitching. Some may allow fabric purchased elsewhere but your bargaining power over tailoring cost will be reduced. Readymade clothes (Western style) can be found in the small shops along Janpath nr the Tibetan Market, and between Parliament St and Janpath, and also at the underground Palika Bazar (Junc of Janpath and Connaught Circus).

Top quality clothes in the latest western styles and fashionable fabrics are virtually unobtainable – it seems that India exports all this, but a modest selection together with table linen and printed bed spreads can be found at ***The Shop***, in the parade of shops nr Regal Cinema on Connaught Pl and at ***Fab India***, 14 N Greater Kailash. ***Archana*** in Gt Kailash I has several boutiques. Indian style clothing is readily available from the ***Khadi shop***, nr the Regal building, and more regional styles of dress at the state on Baba Kharak Singh Marg. Sari shops abound. The shopping centres at Chandni Chowk, catering to Indian taste, and Sunder Nagar which is more western-oriented are also worth visiting. ***Benetton*** in the *Ashoka Hotel* has western style clothes at excellent prices.

Some designer wear in European styles are available from ***Hauz Khas village*** – a series of authentic, old village houses converted into designer shops selling a whole range of handicrafts, ceramics, antiques and furniture in addition to luxury wear. You will also find art galleries and restaurants. Many shops are expensive, but 3 good value shops are: ***Dastkar***, an excellent, cooperative outlet; the tucked away ***Andaz***; and ***Khaas*** for clothing and linen.

● **Food**

Delicatessen: products like cold meats, cheeses, yoghurts can be bought at ***Steakhouse***, Jorbagh Market and ***Modern Bazar***, Vasant Vihar market.

Fresh fruit and vegetables: at *INA Market*, *Bengali Market* and *Khan Market* among others.

Groceries: try shops along Janpath or ***Super Bazar*** on the outer circle of Connaught Circus.

Indian sweets: some of the best, freshest (hence safest) are at ***Bhim Sen's***, Bengali Market (end of Tansen Marg not far from Connaught Pl).

Snacks: pre-packaged *namkeen* (savoury snack) is widely available.

Tea: excellent Indian Teas ***Cottage Industries Emporium***, ***Modern Bazar*** and from ***Tea City*** outlets which are widely advertised. Also at the charming shop in the small ***Kaka Nagar Market*** on Zakir Hussain Marg, opp the Golf Course (well worth a visit). *The Taj Mahal Hotel* has an excellent bakery. Some of the best sweets in Delhi are available from ***Nathus***, in the Bengali market. Also excellent snacks, South Indian food and fresh juice, all very cheap.

● **Handicrafts**

Carpet: shops in most hotels and a number round Connaught Pl, not necessarily fixed-price. If you are visiting Agra, check out the prices there first. Remember to bargain.

Earthenware: unglazed earthenware *khumba matkas* (water pots) are sold round New Delhi Rly Station (workshops behind the main road).

Emporium: *Central Cottage Industries Emporium*, Janpath, is Govt run and has fixed prices. The range and quality of goods is generally excellent. Hassle-free shopping under one roof. They will also pack and post your purchases overseas. Exchange counter, gift wrapping and tickets for cultural shows. Coffee shop next door. Other Govt are ***Khadi Gramodyog Bhawan***, for inexpensive homespun cotton kurta (loose shirts), pyjamas and cotton/silk waistcoats, linen (off-white). Also Jaipuri paintings. ***Handicrafts and Handloom Export Corp***, Lok Kalyan Bhawan, 11A Rouse Ave Le. ***Kashmir Govt Arts Emporium***, 5 Prithviraj Rd. Each state has its own emporium and all these are conveniently located on Baba Kharak Singh Marg which runs off Connaught Pl. Among them Bengal, Delhi (silk). Bihar (excellent Madhubani paintings, gems), Gujarat (good quilts, bedspreads), Kashmir (papier mâché, carpets), Maharashtra (bedspreads), Assam (blankets, silk), Rajasthan, Tripura (wood sculptures, cane work), Orissa (stoneware, wood sculpture), UP, Andhra Pradesh (dolls), Kerala (sandalwood), MP. Small stalls along Janpath can be fun to explore but bargain hard. The fashionable ***Santushti Complex*** opp *Hotel Samrat* has attractive a/c 'Units' in a garden setting. Shops sell good quality crafts, linen, saris, ceramics among others. ***Anokhi*** has a good selection.

Ivory: craftsmen carving ivory can be seen at ***Ivory Mart*** in Chawri Bazar behind the Jama Masjid. Finished works on sale (certificates are necessary for exporting purchases).

Jewellery: traditional silver and goldsmiths in Dariba Kalan, off Chandni Chowk.

Leather: ***Khan Market and S Extension*** are good for leather goods and shoes, as are the shops at the *Taj Mahal*, *Taj Palace* and *Maurya Sheraton hotels*. ***Bharat Leather Shop***, opp *Nirula's* on Connaught Pl and the ***Central Cottage Industries Emporium***, Janpath have good selections whilst ***Bata*** and ***Baluja***, both on Connaught Pl have good readymade shoes (not in very large sizes). ***Bata*** also has a selection of leather bags and cases.

Marble: if you want to see marble inlay, Agra is the place though much of it is soapstone, not marble.

Markets: the ***Tibetan Market*** of streetside shops and stalls along Janpath has plenty of trinkets, curios. Nearly all the items have been made recently and are rapidly aged to look old or authentic. The ***Sunder Nagar Market*** has become one of the largest markets in Asia for fine quality Indian handicrafts. It also specializes in antiques and jewellery (precious and semi-precious). Well worth visiting.

● **Maps**

The Survey of India Map Sales Office above the *Bankura* café next to the Central Cottage Industries Emporium on Janpath has a selection of guide maps of different Indian cities and states. Typical Indian Govt office. See page 154. 1000-1700.

● **Photography**

Delhi Photo Company, 78 Janpath, rec for reprints. ***Fotofare***, N-54 Connaught Pl. ***Goyal Colour Photo Labs***, C-24 Connaught Pl. ***Imperial Photo Stores***, opp State Bank of India, Chandni Chowk. ***Kodak***, A-22 Janpath.

Quick Colour Lab, Kanishka Shopping Plaza. *Simla Studio*, 4 Regal Bldg, Connaught Pl and many others.

Services

● Airline offices

Domestic: **Indian Airlines**, Reservation, 18 Barakhamba Rd, T 3313732. Airport 3295433. Enquiries, T 3014433. Safdarjang. T 4520556. Office on Safdarjang Rd (by Tomb). Very efficient. Open Sun. To avoid delays be there at 0830. **Citilink**, Hotel Janpath. T 3319146, Reservations T 5452238, F 5452330. **Damania**, whose operations concentrate on W India, T 673440. **East-West**, T 3755167, 3755166. **Jagsons**, 12 E Vandana Bldg, 11 Tolstoy Marg, T 3721593, F 3324693. **Modiluft**, T 643051. The only one to offer 1st Cl. **Palam Airport** (Domestic), T 391361, Ext 2268. Chartered: **Archana Airways**, T 6820559, Airport T 3295519, F 3295768. Reservations, T 6841690.

International: **Aeroflot**, BMC House, N-1 Connaught Pl, T 3312843. **Air Canada**, 105 Indraprakash Bldg, Barakhamba Rd, T 3325876. **Air France**, 6 Scindia House, Janpath, T 3310407. Airport, T 394308. **Air India**, Jeevan Bharati Bldg, 124 Connaught Circus, T 3311225. Airport, T 5452050. **Alitalia**, 19 Kasturba Gandhi Marg, T 3311019. Airport, T 393140. **Ariana Afghan Airlines**, 19 Kasturba Gandhi Marg, T 3311432. **Bangladesh Biman**, City Office, T 3312197. **British Airways**, DLF Bldg, Parliament St, T 3327428. Airport, T 5452077. **Cathay Pacific**, Tolstoy House, Tolstoy Marg, T 3325789. **Delta**, 36 Janpath, T 3322359. **Druk Air**, Malbro Travels, 403 Nirmal Towers, 26 Barakhamba Rd, T 3322859. **Gulf Air**, Marina Arcade, G-12 Connaught Circus, T 3324293. Airport, T 5952065. **Japan Airlines**, Chandralok Bldg, Janpath, T 3327104. Airport, T 5452082. **KLM**, Prakash Deep, Tolstoy Marg, T 3315841. Airport, T 392192, Ext 2219. **Lufthansa**, 56 Janpath, T 3323310. Airport, T 5452063. **Malaysian Airlines**, G-55 Connaught Circus, T 3326302. **PIA**, 26 Kasturba Gandhi Marg, T 3313161. Airport, T 5452093. **Philippine Airlines**, City Office, T 3325888. **Qantas**, Mohandev, 13 Tolstoy Marg, T 3321434. **Royal Nepal Airlines**, 44 Janpath, T 3320817. Airport, T 393876. **Sabena**, Himalaya House, Kasturba Gandhi Marg, T 3312701. **Saudi Arabian Airlines**, Hansalaya, 15 Barakhamba Rd, T 3310466. Airport, T 391357. **SAS**, City Office, T 3327668. **Singapore Airlines**, G-11 Connaught Circus, T 3320145. Airport, 394200. **Swissair**, 56 Janpath, T 3325511. **Thai Airways**, Ambadeep Bldg, 14 Kasturba Gandhi Marg, T 3327667. Airport, T 5482526. **TWA**, City Office, T 3327418. **United Airlines**, City Office, T 3715079.

● Banks & money changers

Open Mon-Fri 1000-1400, Sat 1000-1200. **NB**: Localities in Delhi, including banks, close in rotation on different days of the week. See under 'Shopping' for closing days. Cash against Visa can take up to 1 hr. It is usually quicker to change foreign cash and travellers cheques at hotel exchange counters, though the exchange rate may be slightly poorer.

Foreign Banks: **American Express**, A-Block Connaught Pl. One of the best places to change money. **Bank of America**, 15 Barakhamba Rd. **Bank of Tokyo**, Jeevan Vihar, Sansad Marg. **Banque Nationale de Paris**, 2nd Fl, Suryakiran Bldg, Kasturba Gandhi Marg. **Citibank**, Jeevan Vihar Bldg, Parliament St. **Grindlays**, Sansad Marg. **Mercantile**, 28 Kasturba Gandhi Marg.

Indian Banks dealing in foreign exchange: **Open 24 hr**: **Central Bank of India**, *Ashok Hotel*. **State Bank of India**, Palam Airport.

Normal hours: **Bank of Baroda**, 16 Parliament St. **Bank of India**, Bahadur Shah Zafar Marg. **Canara Bank**, 7 Tolstoy Marg. **Federal Bank Ltd.**, M-73 Connaught Circus. **Indian Overseas Bank**, Rachna Bldg, Rajendra Pl. **New Bank of India**, 1 Tolstoy Marg. **Punjab National Bank**, 28 Kasturba Gandhi Marg. **Punjab National Bank**, 5 Sansad Marg. **State Bank of India**, SBI Bldg, Sansad Marg. **The Chartered Bank**, 17 Sansad Marg.

● Chambers of Commerce

International Trade Fairs are held in Delhi from time to time. The **Trade Fair Authority of India**, Pragati Maidan, T 3318374 have details. *Confederation of Indian Industries*, 23, 26 Institutional Area, Lodi Rd, T 4629994. *Federation of Indian Chambers of Commerce and Industry*, Federation House, Tansen Marg, T 3319251. *Punjab Haryana and Delhi Chambers of Commerce and Industry*, T 665425. *Indo-American Chamber of Commerce*, T 669021. *Indo-Italian Chamber of Commerce*, T 665425 all at PHD House, 4-2 Siri Institutional Area. *Indo-German Chamber of Commerce*, 86 FG Himalaya House, Kasturba Gandhi Marg, T 3314151. *Indo-French Chamber of*

Commerce and *Indo-Polish Chamber of Commerce*, Philips Bldg, 9A Connaught Pl, T 3327421. *World Bank*, 55 Lodi Estate, T 619496.

● High Commissions & Embassies

Afghanistan, Shantipath, Chanakyapuri, T 606625; **Algeria**, 15 Anand Lok, T 6445216; **Argentina**, B8/9 Vasant Vihar, T 671345; **Australia,** 1/50G Shantipath, Chanakyapuri, T 601336; **Austria,** EP 13 Chandra Gupta Marg, Chanakyapuri, T 601112; **Bangladesh,** 56 MG Rd, Lajpat Nagar III, T 6934668; **Belgium**, 50 Chanakyapuri, T 607957; **Bhutan**, Chandra Gupta Marg, Chanakyapuri, T 604076; **Canada**, 7-8 Shantipath, T 608161; **China**, 50-D Shantipath, Chanakyapuri, T 600238; **CIS**, Shantipath, T 605875; **Denmark,** 2 Golf Links, T 616273; **Finland**, Nyaya Marg, T 605409; **France,** 2/50E Shantipath, T 604004; **Germany,** 6/50G Shantipath, T 604861; **Greece**, 16 Sunder Nagar, T 617800; **Indonesia,** 50-A Chanakyapuri, T 602352; **Ireland**, 13 Jor Bagh, T 617435; **Italy**, 50E Chandragupta Marg, Chanakyapuri, T 618311; **Israel**, Gopal Das Bhavan, 28 Barakhamba Rd.

Japan, 4/50G Chanakyapuri, T 604071; **Korea** (Republic) 9 Chandragupta Marg, T 601601; **Laos,** 20 Jor Bagh, T 615865; **Malaysia**, 50 M Satya Marg, T 601291; **Mauritius,** 5 Kautilya Marg, T 3011112; **Myanmar**, 3/50-F Nyaya Marg, Chanakyapuri, T 600251/2; **Nepal**, Barakhamba Rd, T 3329969; **Netherlands**, 6/50 Shantipath, Chanakyapuri, T 609571; **New Zealand**, 25 Golf Links, T 697296; **Norway,** Shantipath, T 605982; **Pakistan,** 2/50 G Shantipath, Chanakyapuri, T 600601; **Poland**, 50 M Shantipath, Chanakyapuri, T 608596; **Portugal**, A-24 West End Colony, T 674596; **Russia**, Shantipath T 606026; **Singapore,** E 6 Chandragupta Marg, T 608149; **Somalia,** 12-A Golf Links, T 619559.

Spain, 12 Prithviraj Rd, T 3015892; **Sri Lanka,** 27 Kautilya Marg, T 3010201; **Sweden,** Nyaya Marg, T 604961; **Switzerland,** Nyaya Marg, T 604225/6; **Thailand**, 56 Nyaya Marg, T 607807; **UK,** Shantipath, Chanakyapuri T 601371; **USA,** Shantipath, T 600651. **NB:** Thai & Chinese Visa applications 0900-1200. Collect next day. Easy.

● Hospitals & medical services

Chemists: (24 hr) *All India Institute of Medical Sciences*, Sri Aurobindo Marg. *Hindu Rao Hospital*, Sabzi Mandi. *Super Bazar*, Connaught Circus, T 3310166. *Dr Ram Manohar Lohia Hospital*, Willingdon Crescent.

Hospitals: High Commissions, Embassies, Consulates have lists of rec doctors and dentists. Most hotels (Category C upwards) have doctors on call. Several hospitals and nursing homes have doctors approved by IAMAT (International Association for Medical Assistance to Travellers), listed in a Directory. Casualty and emergency wards in both private and government hospitals are open 24 hr. *All India Institute of Medical Sciences*, Sri Aurobindo Marg, T 661123. *Dr Ram Manohar Lohia Hospital*, Willingdon Crescent, T 345525. *Freemasons Poly Clinic*, Tolstoy Marg, T 3327935. *Hindu Rao Hospital*, Sabzi Mandi, T 2522362. *Holy Family Hospital*, Okhla, T 631626. *Lok Nayak Jai Prakash Narain Hospital*. J. Nehru Marg, T 3316271. *Safdarjang General Hospital*, Sri Aurobindo Marg, T 665060. *Sucheta Kripalani Hospital*, Panchkuin Rd, T 344037. The chemist attached to the Marina Hotel, Connaught Circus, sells Paludrine tablets – difficult to obtain in India.

● Post & telecommunications

Fax services: available at 15 Telegraph offices; they will also receive messages. 0800-2000. Inland Rs 30, neighbouring countries Rs 90, others Rs 110-25. Central Telegraph Office, Eastern Court, Janpath, 24 hr. Also Nehru Pl, Palam airport. Overseas Communication Service (Telex, Telephone), Bangla Sahib Rd, 24 hr.

Post offices: there are post offices throughout the city. Stamps can often be obtained from the Bell Captain in the larger hotels. Head Post Office, Parliament St, 1000-1830 Mon-Sat. Eastern Court PO, Janpath, 1000-2300 Mon-Sat. Connaught Pl PO, A-Block, 1000-1700 Mon-Sat (parcel packing service outside). GPO, Ashoka Pl, 1000-1700 Mon-Fri, 1000-1300 Sat. GPO, Kashmiri Gate, 1000-1900 Mon-Fri, 1000-1230 Sat. Safdarjung Sorting Office open 24 hr. Speedpost available to 39 countries from 22 centres.

Poste restante: Foreign Post Office (c/o The Postmaster), Bhai Bir Singh Marg, New Delhi 110001. Make sure senders specify New Delhi and the Pin Code (Post Code or Zip). Collect from 1st Fl, 0900-1700, until 1300 Sat; c/o American Express, Hamilton House, A-Block, Connaught Pl, New Delhi 11001. If you are staying at a hotel and intend returning, mail can also be directed there. When asking for mail, it pays to be quite persistent. Some hotels are not as well organised in their mail storage as you would expect. **Note**: The Tourist Office, 88 Janpath, offers a Poste restante Service but it is not recommended. Letters are not secure, anyone can browse through without checks and the staff seem to take no interest in the letter rack.

Courier services: numerous offices incl *Apollo Exp*, N-44, Connaught Circus, T 3313216, *Blue Dart*, Chandni Chowk, T 2526113, *OCS Overseas Couriers*, 43 Nehru Pl, T 6449196, *Overnite Exp*, T732411.

International telephone calls: see page 150. **NB:** Calls from hotels usually attract a heavy surcharge, even when it is a 'collect call'. Areas with modest hotels have good STD-ISD booths, eg Paharganj.

● Places of Worship

Only some are listed: **Hindu**: *Lakshmi Narayan Temple*, Mandir Marg. *Swami Malai Temple*, RK Puram. *Devi Katyayani Mandir*, Chattarpur. **Muslim**: *Jama Masjid*, opp Red Fort. *Sonchri Mosque*, Chandni Chowk. **Christian**: *Cathedral Church of The Redemption*, Church Rd. *Free Church*, Parliament St. **Sikh**: *Gurudwara Bangla Sahib*, Ashoka Rd.

● Tour companies & travel agents

Agents can be found in all the major hotels and clustered in several different centres of Delhi. The most important are Connaught Circus (especially F to H blocks), Paharganj, Rajendra Pl and Nehru Pl. Most belong to national and international associations foremost among which are the International Air Transport Association (IATA), the Pacific Area Travel Association (PATA) and the Travel Agents' Association of India (TAAI). Complaints can be addressed to the association if the agency's service is not satisfactory. Many of these agencies will send their representative to your hotel to discuss your plans. The following is a short list of some of the best (see also list under Trekking).

American Express, A-Block, Connaught Pl, T 3327617; *Ashok Tours and Travels*, Kanishka Shopping Plaza, 19 Ashok Rd, T 3324422; *Balmer and Lawrie*, 32-33 Nehru Pl, T 6419222; *Cox and Kings*, Connaught Circus, T 3321028; *Everett*, C-11 Connaught Pl, T 3321117; **Hans Travel**, *Vishal Hotel*, Main Bazar, Pahar Ganj, T 527629; *Indtravels*, *Hotel Imperial*, Janpath, T 3322887; *Kashmir Himalayan Expeditions*, 17 Indian Oil Bhawan, Janpath, T 3302663, F 3327749; *Mackinnon*, 16 Parliament St, T 3323741; *Maruti*, 3171, Sangtrashan, Paharganj, BD Gupta Rd, T 7515978; *Mercury*, Jeevan Tara Bldg, Parliament St, T 312008. *Peak Adventure Tours*, B 29A, Kailash Colony, T 6432894, F 644866, respresents major UK operators; *Royal Expeditions*, S-43, Greater Kailash I, T 6461921, F 6450210, offers a unique experience in N India; *Sita*, F-12 Connaught Pl, T 3313103; *STIC*, *Hotel Imperial*, Janpath, T 3327582; *Sunshine*, Hotel Metro, M-13 Connaught Circus, T 3323122; *Swagatam*, 55 Ram Nagar, T 772177; *Thomas Cook*, Hotel Imperial, Janpath, T 3328468; *Trade Wings*, 60 Janpath, T 351637; *Travel Corp of India* (TCI), N-49 Connaught Circus, T 3327468, F 3316705; *Travel House*, 102 AVG Bhavan, M-3 Connaught Pl, T 3329609.

Warning Beware of travel agents' touts at New Delhi Rly Station, offering 'adventure tours' and other services. These are often overpriced and poor.

● Tourist Offices

Information Offices: **Govt of India Tourist Office**, 88 Janpath, T 3320008. Helpful assistance. Issues permits for visits to Rashtrapati Bhavan and gardens. 0900-1800. Closed Sun. Also at Indira Gandhi International Airport, T 39117. **Delhi Tourism Dev Corp** (Delhi Tourism), N-Block Connaught Pl, T 3313637. Counters at: 18, DDA Office Complex, Moolchand, T 618374; Indira Gandhi International Airport, T 392297; New Delhi Rly Station, T 350574; Inter-State Bus Terminal (ISBT), T 2512181; Delhi Rly Station, T 2511083. **ITDC**, L-Block Connaught Pl, T 3320331. Not very helpful. Counters at ITDC Hotels (Ashok Group): *Ashok*, T 600121 Ext 2155. *Ashok Yatri Niwas*, T 3324511 Ext 15. *Janpath*, T 3320070 Ext 814. *Kanishka*, T 3324422 Ext 2336. *Lodi*, T 362422 Ext 207. *Ranjit*, T 3311256 Ext 630. Indira Gandhi International Airport; (Domestic), T 392825; (International) T 394410.

State Tourist Offices: each state has a tourist office in Delhi. Some have useful information available and, often, tourist maps. Most are open 1000-1800, Mon-Fri.

A number are on Kharak Singh Marg: **Assam**, B-1,T 345897; **Bihar**, A-5, T 311087; **Gujarat**, A-6, T 343173; **Karnataka**, T 343862; **Maharashtra**, T 343281; **Manipur**, T 343497; **Orissa**, T 344580; **Tamil Nadu**, T 343913. Several others in the **Chandralok Bldg, 36 Janpath Rd** opp *Hotel*

Imperial: **Haryana**, T 3324911; **Himachal Pradesh**, T 3324764; **Rajasthan**, T 3322332; **Uttar Pradesh**, T 3322251; **West Bengal**, T 343775.

A few others are in the Kaniksha Shopping Plaza, 19 Ashok Rd: **Jammu and Kashmir**, T 3325373; **Madhya Pradesh**, T 3015545; **Punjab**, T 385431. Some are particularly helpful incl Orissa, Karnataka, Assam.

Others are: **Andaman and Nicobar Islands**, F-105, Curzon Rd Hostel, Kasturba Gandhi Marg, T 387015. **Andhra Pradesh**, 1 Ashok Rd, T 389182; **Kerala**, 3 Jantar Mantar Rd, T 353424; **Nagaland**, 4 Rao Tula Ram Marg, T 679177; **Sikkim**, Chanakyapuri, T 3014981; and **Tripura**, Kautliya Marg, T 3014607.

● Useful addresses

Emergency Numbers: Ambulance (24 hr) T 102. Police T 100. Traffic police are identified by their blue and white uniforms and white helmets. Women officers wear green saris and white blouses. The Central Reserve Police Force (CRPF) in khaki uniforms and berets are mainly concerned with assisting in traffic operations, patrolling and riot control. All police stations register complaints. This can be a very lengthy process. **Foreigners' Registration Office**: 1st Fl, Hans Bhawan, Tilak Bridge.

Local transport

● Bus

The city bus service run by the Delhi Transport Corp connects all important points in the city. There are over 300 routes. Information is available at DTC assistance booths and at all major bus stops. Don't be afraid to ask conductors or fellow passengers. Indians are usually very helpful if they understand what you are saying. Buses are often hopelessly overcrowded so only use at off-peak.

Directional Route Classification: 1st digit of bus route number (1-9) determines the direction in which it travels and also indicates the terminal depot: **1** Azadpur (NW); **2** Kashmiri Gate (NE); **3** ITO (Income Tax Office) and Indraprastha (Central); **4** Lajpat Nagar (SE); **5** All-India Medical School (S); **6** Sarojini Nagar (SW); **7,8,9** Dhaula Khan, Raja Garden and Punjabi Bagh respectively (W). **Night services**: a skeletal service 2300-0130. This can also take extremely roundabout routes, double backing on themselves frequently. Tickets are Rs 1, 2 and 3. DTC Head Office, T 3315085. Local enquiries T 3319847. ISBT Office T 2518836.

Private buses and mini buses: also operate on DTC routes. Tickets are Rs 1 and 2. To avoid overcrowded buses choose 'Green Line', Rs 4, or 'white line', Rs 6, which are comfortable and run on all key routes at regular intervals. For transport to and from airport, see 'By air', under Long Distance connections below.

WARNING If travelling on a crowded bus, beware of pickpockets. The row of seats along the kerb side of the bus is for women, who are entitled to ask any male to vacate it. So-called 'Eve teasing' (bottom pinching) can be a problem.

● Taxis

Yellow-top taxis: are easily available. Most large hotels have stands outside and the doorman will call one for you. Also numerous taxi stands around town or hail one on the road. The meter should read Rs 5 when it is 'flagged down'. Meters often have not been changed after the last price rise, so a surcharge may apply; ask to see the conversion card. Add 25% night charge (2300-0500) plus 50p for each piece of heavy luggage (over 20 kg). These extras apply to scooter-rickshaws as well. For complaints, T 3319334.

● Car hire

Private taxis/cars: full day local running (non a/c) is Rs 450, half day Rs 220. **Adarsh Tourist Transport Service**, 38 Yashwant Pl. **Auto Rental Service**, YMCA Hostel, Jai Singh Rd. **Delhi Transport Service**, Arambagh, Panchkuin Rd. **Hindustan Tourist Taxis**, 36 Janpath. **Goel**, 16 Sunder Nagar Market, T 618755. **Karachi Taxi Service**, 36 Janpath, T 3323830. **All India Road Tourist Taxis**, *Hotel Imperial*. **Venus Travels**, 16-1708, Arya Samaj Rd, Karol Bagh. **Western Court Tourist Taxis**, 36 Janpath. **American Express Taxis**, 36 Janpath. **Ex-Soldiers Tourist Taxis**, opp 16 Dr Rajendra Prasad Marg. **Hertz**, T 3318695, **Europcar**, Travel House, M3 Connaught Circus. T 6862248 and **Budget**, G3, Arunachal, Barakhamba Rd, T 3715657, G5, Vaikunth, 82 Nehru Pl, T 6452634. Central Reservations: T 671671, F 3712990. They charge higher prices but provide very dependable service: about 80 km/8 hr, Rs 650-950. Self drive 24 hr/150 km Rs 1000. Weekly rentals chauffeur Rs 150/day.

● Cycle-rickshaws

Also **Tongas** (Horse drawn traps) are available in the Old city. They are not allowed into Connaught Pl. Rates negotiable. Be prepared to haggle over the price, remembering that it should be cheaper than motorised transport.

● **Motorcycle-rickshaws**

Matador Taxis (4 seater plus). For point-to-point travel only at fixed charges, eg between railway stations and a residential area. **Matador Motorbike taxi** (Harley Davidson), nr Palika Bazar, fixed routes, fixed rates.

● **Scooter-rickshaws**

Widely available at about half the cost of taxis (Rs 4 for the first km). Normal capacity for foreigners is 2 persons. Extra passengers may be taken; agree the raised fare in advance. Surcharges as for taxis.

● **Cycle hire**

Shops are near Minto Bridge, off Connaught Pl, on Mohan Singh Pl near Rivoli cinema and in Paharganj. Rentals costs about Rs 5/hr to Rs 20/day plus a refundable deposit.

● **Suburban trains**

The Delhi suburban railway is neither very popular nor convenient. A ring route operates 3 times a day – 0755, 1625, 1725, starting from Hazrat Nizamuddin station.

● **Travel tips**

Check that scooter and taxi meters are cleared and try and insist on the meter being used. If you wish to travel a short distance, e.g from Janpath to the New Delhi Rly Station, often *rickshaw wallahs* may ask Rs 30 or more, 4 or 5 times the proper rate. Similarly, if you are staying away from the centre, it may be difficult to get a scooter or taxi late at night. If this is the case, go to a hotel and get the doorman to call you one. For this service, a small tip should be given. Carry plenty of coins and small notes. As a last resort you can threaten drivers with police action if they prove to be particularly difficult. Whilst you do not want the trouble that this entails, drivers can lose their permits if they attempt to cheat. However, it is common that with fare revisions, the meter is not always changed. Drivers must carry a card with the revised fares, so if a driver asks for more than is on the meter, ask to see the card to check. Most will oblige. Official night rates for taxis apply after 2200.

Long distance connections

● **Air**

Indian Airlines connects Delhi with the following Indian cities. **Agra**, ½ hr; **Ahmadabad**, 1¼ hr; **Allahabad**; **Amritsar**, 50 min; **Aurangabad**, 4¼ hr, 3 stops; **Bagdogra** for Darjiling, 2 hr; **Bangalore**, 2½ hr; **Bhopal**, 2 hr: 1 stop; **Bhubaneswar**, 4 hr, 2 stops; **Bombay**, 1¾ hr, first 0615, last 2020; **Calcutta**, 2 hr; **Chandigarh**, 1 hr; **Kochi**, 4 hr, 1 stop; **Dabolim** (Goa), 2½ hr; **Gorakhpur**, Guwahati, 3¼ hr, 1 stop; **Gwalior**, Hyderabad, 2 hr; **Imphal**; **Indore**, 2¾ hr, 2 stops; **Jabalpur**, 2¼hr; **Jaipur**, ½ hr; **Jammu**; **Jodhpur**, 1¾ hr, 1 stop; **Kanpur**; **Khajuraho**, 1¾ hr, 1 stop; **Leh**, 2 hr, 1 stop; **Lucknow**, 1 hr; **Madras**, 2½ hr, 1 stop; **Nagpur**, Patna, 1½ hr; **Pune**, 2 hr; **Raipur**; **Ranchi**; **Srinagar**, 1¼ hr; **Thiruvananthapuram**, 5 hr, 2 stops; **Udaipur**, 2¾ hr, 2 stops; **Vadodara**; **Varanasi**, 1¼ hr. **Indian Airlines** international services also connect Delhi to Dhaka, Kabul, Kathmandu, Lahore and Karachi. **Air India** offers discounts on its domestic flights taking off at night to Bombay, Calcutta and Madras.

Private operators: **Jagson Airlines** have a service to Kulu, Shimla and Dehra Dun; **Citilink Airways** to **Calcutta**, **Bombay** and **Ludhiana** 6 weekly flights (BAC 1-11) and daily to **Kula** and **Chandigarh**. **Trans Bharat Aviation (TBA)** started 6 flights a week to **Kulu**, with free transport to Manali. **Modiluft** flies daily to **Bangalore**, 2¾ hr, on to **Kochi**, 4 hr, on Tu,Th,Sa; **Bombay**, 2 hr, twice; **Calcutta**, 2hr; **Goa**, 2½ hr, M,W,F,Su; **Jammu**, except Su, 1¾ hr; **Madras**, 2¾ hr.

Transport to and from the airport: **Taxi**: from the airport into the city. **NB:** The International and Domestic terminals have **pre-paid taxi counters** which ensure that you pay the right amount (specify luggage), see page 133. Keep your receipt to show the driver at the end of the journey. Further payment is not required, nor is a tip. If you do not take a pre-paid taxi, the driver will usually demand an inflated fare. From the International terminal: during the day Rs 120 is reasonable for the town-centre (Connaught Pl area); at night, Rs 200. Rates are lower from the Domestic terminal; about Rs 90 at night. Europcar charges more. Free shuttle between the 2 terminals every ½ hr.

Bus: run by Ex-Servicemen's Airlink Transport Service (**EATS**) from the 2 terminals go via some hotels, and central budget areas to F-Block Connaught Pl. It leaves from IA office in Connaught Pl at regular intervals from 0430-2300 and connects with most flights. Rs 15-20 per person. There is a booth just outside the arrival terminals at the International and Domestic airports. This is a safe, economical option, particularly for the first-time visitor on a budget.

● Train

New Delhi Rly Station (ND) is the focus of the broad gauge network and connects Delhi with all major destinations in India. International Tourist Bureau (ITB), 1st Fl, Main Bldg. Computerised Reservations in separate building 200m away. **Old Delhi Rly Station (OD)** is on the metre gauge network of the Western Railways and connects Delhi with Jaipur, Ajmer, Jodhpur, Bikaner, Udaipur and Ahmadabad and many more. Some of the principal services to major destinations are: **Agra**: *Shatabdi Exp* 2002, daily, ND 0615, 2 hr (Rs 400, 1st Cl a/c incl meal); *Taj Exp* 2180, daily, ND, 0705, 2¾ hr. **Amritsar**: *Dadar-Amritsar Exp* 1057, daily, 0805, 10½ hr; *New Delhi-Amritsar Exp* 2459, daily, 1420, 7¼ hr; *Flying Mail*, 4647, daily, 1215, 8¾ hr; *Shane Punjab Exp* 2497, daily, 0645, 7 hr. **Bangalore**: *Rajdhani Exp* Sat, 36 hr. **Bikaner**: *Bikaner Exp* 4789, daily, OD, 0830, 11¾ hr; *Bikaner Mail*, 4791, daily, OD, 2100, 11½ hr. **Bhopal**: *Shatabdi Exp* 2002, daily, ND, 0615, 7¾ hr. **Bombay** (Central): *Rajdhani Exp* 2952, daily except Tu, ND, 1605, 16½ hr; *Paschim Exp* 2926, daily, ND, 1700, 22 hr; *Frontier Mail*, 2904, daily, ND, 0825, 22½ hr; *Jammu Tawi-Bombay Exp* 2972, Tu,W,Fr,Sa, ND 2145, 20½ hr; *Bombay Exp* 9020, daily, ND, 2210, 30¼ hr.

Calcutta: *Rajdhani Exp* 2302, daily except Su, ND, 1715, M-W, F,Sa, 17½ hr; *Haora Exp* 3012, daily, OD, 2210, 32 hr; *AC Exp* 2382, Tu,Th,Sa, ND, 1600, 26 hr. **Chandigarh** Dep ND, *Himalayan Queen* 4095, daily, 0600, 4¼ hr. *Shatabdi Exp* 2005, Daily, 1625, 3½ hr. From OD: *Haora-Kalka Mail* 2311, daily, 2245, 15 hr. **Gwalior**: *Shatabdi Exp* 2002, daily, N. Del 0615, 3¼ hr. **Haridwar**: *Bombay-Dehra Dun Exp* 9019, daily, 0735, 7 hr; *Mussoorie Exp* 4041, daily, 2225, 7 hr. **Jabalpur**: *Mahakoshal Exp* 1450, daily, 1620, 18¼ hr. **Jaipur**: *Pink City Exp* 2901, daily, OD 0600, 5 hr. **Jammu**: (for Kashmir): *Jhelum Exp* 4677, daily, ND, 2140, 13½ hr. **Jhansi**: *Shatabdi Exp* 2002, daily, 4½ hr; *Jhelum Exp* 4678, daily, 1050, 7½ hr; *Karnataka Exp* 2628, daily, 2320, 5½ hr; *Tamil Nadu Exp* 2622, daily, 5½ hr; *AP Exp* 2724, daily, 1430, 5½ hr. **Jodhpur**: Jodhpur Mail, 4893, daily, dep OD, 2030, 14¼ hr; *Mandore Exp* 2461, daily, OD, 1810, 11½ hr.

Kanpur: *Shatabdi Exp* 2004, Mon-Fri, ND, 0620, 5 hr; *Prayag Raj Exp* 2418, daily, 2200, 6¾ hr; *Vaishali Exp* 2554, daily, 1930, 6½ hr. **Lucknow**: *Neelachal Exp* 8476, Tu,Th,Su, ND, 0540, 8 hr; *Lucknow Mail* 4230, daily, ND 2130, 9¾ hr; *Gomti Exp* 2420, daily except Tu, ND, 1440, 8¼ hr. **Madras**: *Rajdhani* M, 0650, 30 hr; *GT Exp* 2304, M,W,F,Su, ND 1840 (36¼ hr); *Tamil Nadu Exp* 2622, daily, ND, 2230, 33¼ hr; *6068/6032 Exp* M,W,F,Su, ND (Originates OD, 1435) 1500, 45½ hr. **Mathura**: *Taj Exp* 2180, daily, 0705, 2 hr.

Shimla: Dep OD: *Haora-Kalka Mail* 2311 (change at Kalka to 253 Mail), daily, 1955, 16½ hr. ND *Himalayan Queen* 4095 (change at Kalka to 251), daily, 0521, 5¼ hr. **Udaipur**: *Chetak Exp* 9615, daily, OD, 1300, 20¼ hr. **Varanasi**: *A/c Exp* 2382, Tu,Th,Sa, ND, 1600, 13¼ hr; *Neelachal Exp* 8476, Tu,Th,Su, ND, 0540, 13¼ hr; *Ganga-Yamuna Exp* 3284 on Tu,W,F,Su, 3214 on M,Th,Sa, OD, 2145, 17 hr; *Saryu Yamuna Exp* 2450, M,Th,Sa, ND, 2105, 15¼ hr.

● Road

Delhi is well connected by road with major cities: by NH2 to Agra (200 km), Ajmer (399 km), by NH1 to Amritsar (446 km), Bhopal (741 km), Chandigarh (249 km), Gwalior (319 km), by NH8 to Jaipur (261 km), Jammu (586 km), Jodhpur (604 km), Kanpur (490 km), Kota (505 km), by NH24 to Lucknow (569 km), Pathankot (478 km), Simla (368 km), Srinagar (876 km), Udaipur (635 km) and Varanasi (765 km). All road journeys in India are slow. Main roads out of Delhi are very heavily congested. The best time to leave Delhi is very early morning.

Bus: Delhi is linked to most major centres in N India. Services are provided by Delhi Transport Corp (DTC) and the State Road Transport Corporations (SRTCs) of neighbouring states. Most inter-state buses leave from the Inter-State Bus Terminal (ISBT) Kashmiri Gate which has a restaurant, left luggage, bank and telephones. Allow about 30 mins for buying a ticket and finding the right bus. Enquiries: **ISBT** Enquiries, T 2519083. **Haryana Roadways**, ISBT, T 2521262. **Himachal Pradesh** RTC, ISBT, T 2516725. **Jammu and Kashmir** RTC, *Hotel Kanishka*, T 3324422 Ext. 2243. **Punjab Roadways**, ISBT, T 2517842. **Rajasthan** SRTC, ISBT, T 2514417. Deluxe services, Bikaner House, Pandara Rd, T 383469. **U P** Roadways, Ajmeri Darwaza (Gate), T 2518709.

Among others: Agra, 239 km, 5 hr (quicker by rail); Almora, 399 km, 5 hr; Bharatpur, 186 km, 5 hr; Bikaner, 500 km, 11 hr; Dehra Dun, 259 km, 6 hr (via Roorkee); Jaipur, 275 km, 5 hr; Shimla, 344 km, 9-10 hr; Kathmandu, 3 days.

UTTAR PRADESH

CONTENTS

MAPS

Uttar Pradesh ('Northern Province') is India's most populous state with about a 7th of the nation's population. India's fourth largest state (294,413 sq km), the region of today's UP has been the heart of much of India's contemporary religious and cultural life.

UP contains the source of the sacred river Ganga – "Ganga Ma" or Mother Ganga – regarded by Hindus as the physical and spiritual life source of the country. To bathe in it is to wash away guilt. To drink the water is meritorious. To be cremated on its banks at Varanasi, India's holiest city, holds the promise of removing all the stains of one's karma and finding release from the endless cycle of re-births. Along it are a number of towns of religious significance; where it leaves the hills at Rishikesh and Haridwar, one of the scenes of the great Kumbh Mela festival; Allahabad, at its confluence with its principal tributary the Yamuna and with the mystical Saraswati river flowing from heaven, is another. Mathura, S of Delhi and on the banks of the Yamuna river, is regarded as the birthplace of Lord Krishna. Haridwar, Mathura and Varanasi are 3 of Hinduism's 7 holy cities, and each year vast numbers of pilgrims travel through the state. The region has also shaped both **Buddhism** and **Islam**. The Buddha was born on the borders of eastern UP and Bihar, while UP became the heartland of various Muslim dynasties, especially the Mughals. The Muslim influence lives on in the State's 20 million Muslims. UP has some beautiful hill stations such as Mussoorie and Nainital. Although it contains some of the poorest parts of India, the W of the state has shared in the dynamic growth of the entire Delhi region.

SOCIAL INDICATORS *Population*: 148 mn (Urban 18%, Scheduled Castes 21%, Scheduled Tribes 0.2%). *Literacy*: M 39% F 14%. *Birth rate*: *Rural* 39:1000, *Urban* 29:1000. *Death rate*: *Rural* 14:1000, *Urban* 8:1000. *Infant mortality*: *Rural* 156:1000, *Urban* 99:1000. *Religion*: *Hindu* 83%, *Muslim* 16%, *Christian* 0.2%, *Sikh* 0.1%.

Environment

Land

Area: 294,000 sq km. UP shares one third of its N boundary with Tibet and two-thirds with Nepal. In the mountains it adjoins Himachal Pradesh in the NW whilst on the plains its neighbours are: Haryana and Delhi (W), Rajasthan (SW), Madhya Pradesh (S) and Bihar (E). About 75% of UP comprises plain, the rest being the Shiwalik hills and the Himalaya in the N and the Vindhya Hills and central plateau in the S.

There are 4 physical regions. In the N are the **Himalaya**, see page 23. **Nanda Devi** (7816m) and other peaks such as **Kamet**, **Trisul**, **Badrinath**, **Dunagiri** and **Shivling**, are all permanently snow-capped and over 6400m. This part of the Himalaya more than any other can justly claim to be the throne room of the Gods. The **Ganga** also has its source here. Soils tend to be easily drained but thin, stony, and poor.

To the S the **Shiwaliks** form a low range of hills running parallel with the Himalaya. To their S is the Bhabar and Terai. Formed of coarse gravels, many mountain streams disappear below the quite steep slopes of the Bhabar during the dry season. On the plains side of this is the Terai, a belt of jungle approximately 65 km wide, originally running from the Ganga gorge at Haridwar to Bihar. Here the streams that vanish in the Bhabar, resurface.

The Gangetic Plain occupies the largest part of the state. The elevation of the plain gradually decreases from 365m in the NW at Haridwar to 80m in the E at Varanasi. This featureless and flat plain, stiflingly hot, dry and dusty in summer, is drained by the Ganga and its many tributaries.

The final region comprises the northern margins of the Peninsula. This runs along the S edge of the state and includes the Vindhya hills in the SE which rise to more than 600m in places.

Rivers and Lakes

The major river of UP and N India, the Ganga is not only sacred to the Hindu population but invaluable for irrigating large areas. Nearly all the other rivers are part of the Ganga system. Second most important is the Yamuna which has its source in the Garhwal Himalaya at Yamunotri, flows through Delhi and Agra and joins the Ganga at Allahabad. The Ghaghra, Gomti, Ramganga and Kosi are other major rivers. There are no lakes on the plains and only a few in the mountains. Situated at 1830m, the largest, Nainital is 1.5 km long and 300m wide.

Climate

From Dec to Feb temperatures range from 7°C min to 27°C max. Between Apr and Jun temperatures range from 22°C min to 42°C max with extremes of 45°C not uncommon. A hot dry wind often blows from the W. The monsoon lasts from mid-Jun to mid-Sep, during which time the maximum temperature is reduced a few degrees, humidity increases and 80% of the annual rainfall is received. The hill region differs from the plains insofar as its highest peaks are permanently under snow, and the daily and seasonal temperatures are lowered according to altitude and aspect.

All of UP receives most of its rain between Jun and Oct. Rainfall totals generally decrease from E to W across the state, but in the hill stations of Nainital and Mussoorie, for example, winter precipitation falls as snow.

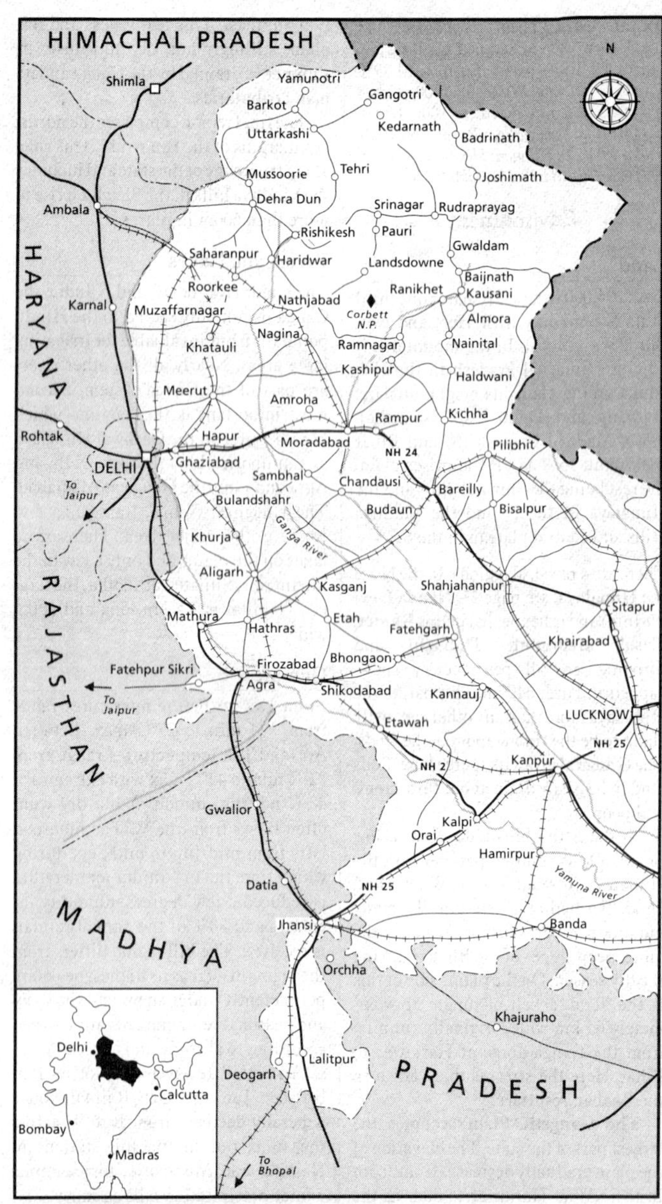
HIMACHAL PRADESH
N
Shimla
Yamunotri
Barkot
Gangotri
Kedarnath
Uttarkashi
Badrinath
Tehri
Joshimath
Mussoorie
Dehra Dun
Ambala
Srinagar
Rudraprayag
Rishikesh
Pauri
Gwaldam
Saharanpur
Haridwar
Landsdowne
Baijnath
Roorkee
Ranikhet
Kausani
Nathjabad
Corbett N.P.
Karnal
Muzaffarnagar
Almora
Nagina
Ramnagar
Nainital
Khatauli
Kashipur
Haldwani
Meerut
Amroha
Rampur
Kichha
Rohtak
Hapur
Moradabad
NH 24
Pilibhit
DELHI
Ghaziabad
Sambhal
Chandausi
Bareilly
To Jaipur
Bulandshahr
Budaun
Bisalpur
Khurja
Ganga River
Aligarh
Kasganj
Shahjahanpur
Sitapur
Mathura
Hathras
Etah
Fatehgarh
Khairabad
Firozabad
Bhongaon
Fatehpur Sikri
Agra
Shikodabad
Kannauj
To Jaipur
LUCKNOW
Etawah
NH 25
Kanpur
NH 2
Gwalior
Kalpi
Orai
Hamirpur
Datia
NH 25
Yamuna River
Jhansi
Banda
Orchha
Khajuraho
Lalitpur
Deogarh
To Bhopal
HARYANA
RAJASTHAN
MADHYA
PRADESH
Delhi
Calcutta
Bombay
Madras

History

For an outline of the early history of UP, see pages 34-66.

Culture

The People

The majority of the population are Hindu but 16% are Muslim, concentrated between Aligarh and Faizabad in what is called 'The Muslim Belt'. At Sarnath near Varanasi the Buddha first preached his message of the Middle Way. Today, however, adherents of Buddhism, Jainism, Christianity and Sikhism together constitute less than 3% of the state's population.

Language

The main language of the state is Hindi, but Urdu is still quite widely used among Muslims. There are numerous local dialects. A broad division can be made between those on the plains and the *Pahari* (hill) dialects. This distinction also applies to ethnic origins. On the plains the inhabitants exhibit Aryan features, northwards giving way to strong Mongoloid features on the border with Tibet.

Modern Uttar Pradesh

Government

UP has the same administrative structure as other Indian States. The head of state is the governor who is appointed by the President for a 5 year term. The 425 seat legislative assembly is at Lucknow, the state capital. UP has 85

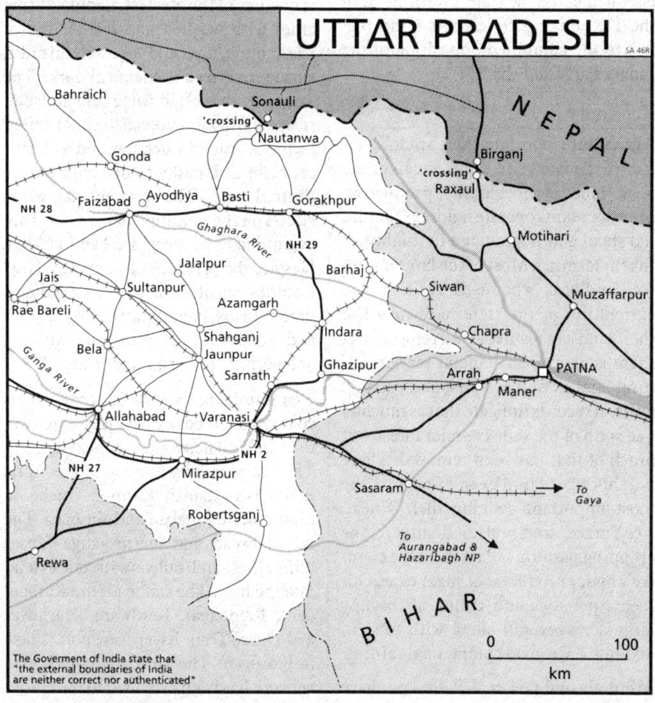

seats in the Lok Sabha (Lower House) and 34 seats in the Rajya Sabha (Upper House), more than any other. It is regarded as the political heartland and has produced most of India's prime ministers since Independence, including Jawaharlal Nehru, his daughter Indira Gandhi and grandson Rajiv Gandhi. In only 2 of the elections to the State Assembly since Independence has the Congress Party failed to win an overall majority in the state. The first was in 1977, immediately following Mrs. Gandhi's Emergency Rule and the second in Dec 1989. In 1991 the BJP took control of the state assembly. The destruction of the Babri Mosque on 6th December 1992 by Hindu zealots backed by the BJP, and the ensuing communal riots, led the Indian Prime Minister to dismiss the state government. In the December 1993 elections the BJP lost to the combined opposition of the Janata Party and the BSP.

Economy

Agriculture Despite the enriching effect of the Ganga in flood, much of the farm land is not highly productive. Many peasants operate holdings that are too small and fragmented for highly efficient farming. Most of the large absentee landlords who used to dominate agriculture of the state have now lost their land as a result of land reforms, but there is enormous demand for agricultural land as well as forest and pasture. Official records indicate that as much as one sixth of the state is under forest, but much of that has been removed. There is a shortage of timber and firewood, the most important cooking fuel. Wheat, rice, maize and pulses dominate the cropping pattern. UP is one of the country's major producers of sugar cane. Oilseeds, potatoes and cotton all occupy large acreages and along with tobacco and jute have good commercial returns.

Minerals and power UP does not have lucrative mineral resources. Limestone and silica are extracted on a large scale and magnesite and phosphatic shale are also mined. There are coalfields in Mirzapur district. Thermal power is the most important source of electricity. The potential for harnessing some of the Himalayan rivers for hydro-electric power is great and some schemes are under way, although the fact that the Himalayan valleys are in one of the world's great earthquake belts makes development both more expensive and more hazardous. The Tehri Dam Project, for example, has faced enormous problems since its inception over a decade ago, and is still unfinished.

Industry Cotton mills were first established in **Kanpur** in 1869 making it one of the older industrial cities of India. It is now one of the greatest manufacturing cities with woollen and leather industries, cotton, flour and vegetable oil mills, sugar refineries and chemical works. The State Govt has established cement factories near **Mirzapur**, precision instrument factories around Lucknow and a chemical plant at **Bareilly** to diversify the industrial base. The severely damaging effects on the pollution of the Ganga are beginning to be recognised and tackled. Despite the presence of some very large factories small-scale enterprises dominate industry, including weaving, leather and woodwork, ceramics, silk weaving and perfumery are all important.

Communications Travel across UP is comparatively easy. There is an extensive road and rail network, very heavily used. The main railway junctions are Agra, Allahabad, Jhansi, Kanpur, Lucknow, Mathura, Moradabad and Varanasi. The use of broad and metre gauge causes difficulties, and railways do not extend into the hills. The railheads are Kathgodam, Ramnagar, Kotdwara, Haridwar and Dehra Dun. River transport is now insignificant. The surprisingly good road network has been extended to the border with Tibet/China to facilitate troop movements. It has undoubtedly benefitted the local population and the annual 300,000 pilgrims travelling from all parts of India to worship at the mountain shrines. However, because of the fragility of the hillsides and the removal of natural vegetation for cultivation, fuel and commercial forest products, landslips are common and disrupt traffic flows, especially during the monsoon.

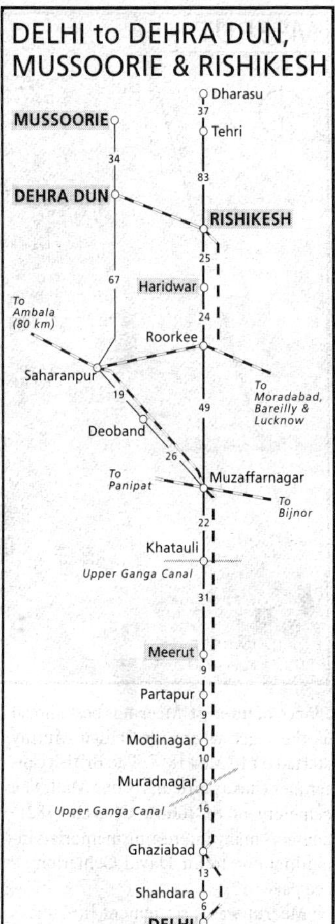

DELHI TO DEHRA DUN, MUSSOORIE, RISHIKESH

From Delhi to Dehra Dun the road runs across the fertile plains between the Ganga and the Yamuna Rivers. Irrigated by canals for over 150 years, the land is intensively cultivated. The journey from **Haridwar** along the Pilgrim Rd that follows the Ganga to **Badrinath** and **Kedarnath** and finally to its source at **Gangotri** is – one of Hinduism's great pilgrimages. Every devout Hindu tries to make the journey at least once. Today the early section of the route passes through a rapidly industrialising extension of Delhi, the 'trans-Yamuna'. Air pollution is often appalling, the air dusty and acrid. Up to Ghaziabad massive apartment blocks and industrial units illustrate the speed of Delhi's growth. Only after Ghaziabad does the road enter a more traditional rural region.

ROUTES From Delhi the main road N crosses the river by the new dual carriageway Yamuna Bridge and continues E as the NH24 to Ghaziabad (19 km) after crossing the railway at Shahdara (6 km). Take the left turn for Meerut. Pass through Muradnagar (17 km) to Modinagar (11 km).

Modinagar

(*Pop* 125,000, *STD Code* 01232) The town has developed around the Modi family conglomerate's industries. A very large sugar mill near the town centre is supplied by long queues of tractors and bulllock carts delivering cane.

ROUTES To the N of Modinagar you cross the Upper Ganga Canal. The road goes through Partapur (9 km) to Meerut (9 km).

Meerut

(*Pop* 850,000; *STD Code* 0121) An important marketing, commercial and administrative town, Meerut has a number of attractive broad streets.

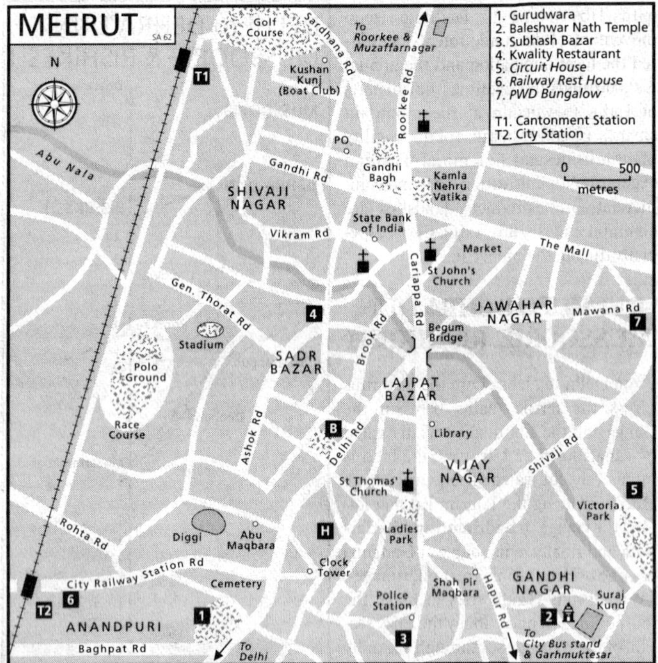

Places of interest Meerut is best known as the place where the Indian Mutiny started on 10 May 1857. The British cantonment has a particularly fine **Mall**. The cemetery of **St John's Church** (1821) contains many interesting memorials including one to Sir David Ochterlony – see page 612.

Meerut was a settlement in Asoka's time and contains various Hindu and Muslim buildings from the 11th century onwards. The **Baleshwar Nath Temple** is pre-Muslim, and several other old Hindu shrines surround the **Suraj Kund** tank built in 1714 by Jowalbhir Mal and fed by a canal from the Ganga. The **Jama Masjid** (1019) was built by Mahmud of Ghazni's *Wazir*. Although later restored by Humayun, it is one of the oldest mosques in India. The red sandstone **Shah Pir Maqbara** (1628) on Hapur Rd, was built by the empress Nur Jahan and further W on Delhi Rd is the **Abu Maqbara**, with a large tank. Qutb-ud-din Aibak is believed to have built the **Maqbara of Salar Masa-ud Ghazi** (1194). Other mausolea and mosques indicate strong Muslim influence. Meerut lies in what has been termed the Muslim belt, and tension between Muslims and Hindus has periodically erupted into violent conflict.

Local festival

Mar: *Nauchandi Mela*, a big fair.

• **Accommodation** **D** *Shaleen* and **D** *Quality* are in the Begum Bridge area.

ROUTES Continue N from Meerut. At Lawar, 18 km N of Meerut, a left turn goes to Sardhana.

Sardhana

The town is associated with an 18th century Strasbourg mercenary, Walter Reinhardt, who was given Sardhana District by the Nawab of Bengal for putting 160 prisoners, including 60 servants of the East India Company, to death in 1763. According to the District Gazetteer of the time the gift was to protect the Nawab's NW borders against the Sikhs. His wife, a Kashmiri dancing girl, inherited his territory in 1778, married a French mercenary, but in 1805 Sardhana was taken under British control, when the Begum died in 1836. The Begum's Palace (Kothi Dilkusha), described by Murray as 'a modern English mansion built in 1834', standing in a large garden, became a Roman Catholic school and orphanage in 1893. It houses a number of pictures. The 2nd Palace, in the town, belongs to a royal family of Afghan descent, and has a mosque and tomb in the complex. St John's Roman Catholic cathedral and college is S of town.

ROUTES Just over half way between Meerut and Muzaffarnagar you cross the Upper Ganga Canal at **Khatauli** (95 km from Delhi). The Canal (built c1840 by the British engineer Cautley), is nearly 70m wide. On the N bank of the canal on the N edge of town is *Cheetal*, a very pleasant café in Forest Dept grounds with shaded open-air seating and a small 'zoo'. Highly rec as a refreshment stop. The main *Cheetal Restaurant* is 200m from the canal (closed Sun). Continue to **Muzaffarnagar** (51 km; *STD Code* 01312) with *Hotel Natraj* and UP Tourism's *Midstream* nr Kamla Nehru Vatika, T 8564 which has 6 rm and Restaurant. You then pass through **Deoband** (*STD Code* 01336) where in the late 19th century the Ulama created a form of Islam which enabled Muslims to do without the State. He spread it by expanding the traditional *madrassa* (school) education. The road goes direct to Saharanpur (54 km) and Dehra Dun (67 km).

Saharanpur

(*Pop* 375,000; *STD Code* 0132) Founded in 1340, named after the Muslim saint Shah Haran Chisti, Saharanpur was a summer retreat for the Mughals. It continues to attract Muslim and Hindu pilgrims. During the British period it became an important military base, especially during the Gurkha War, but the Govt also set out **Botanical Gardens** in 1817. The Eastern Yamuna Canal, one of the first great 19th century canals to irrigate the Ganga-Yamuna doab transformed the landscape of what had been a heavily overpopulated region. It has become a particularly important source of fruit trees for the whole of India. The *Mango Festival* is held in Jun/Jul when hundreds of mango varieties are displayed. **Accommodation D** *Swagat*, nr Clock Tower Chowk, modest business hotel. *Sheetal Restaurant*, W of town, on canal bank in attractive setting.

Nolji

Nearby, is the small town from which the trigonometrical survey of the Himalaya was extended in 1835, see page 824. 30 km from Saharanpur is the *Duck Chick Restaurant*. Pleasant setting, good value snacks. Very popular in season. The main road runs W from Saharanpur across the Yamuna to Yamunanagar and Thanesar or Ambala and Chandigarh (see page 492).

Dehra Dun

Population: 370,000. *Altitude*: 695m. *STD Code*: 0135. From Rishikesh a road runs NW to Dehra Dun (42 km). Dehra Dun (*dera*– camp; *dun* – valley, pronounced doon) lies in a wooded valley in the Shiwalik Hills, and because of its comparatively equable climate, is a popular retirement town, particularly among army officers.

History

In Hindu legend it formed part of Kedarkhand (see Kedarnath above), and was Siva's stamping ground, hence the name Shiwaliks. Rama and his brother are said to have done penance for killing Ravana and the 5 Pandavas stopped here on their way to the high, snowy mountains.

During 17th-18th century it changed hands several times. Guru Ram Rai retreated here from the Punjab after failing to succeed his father. Najib-ud-daula Mughal Governor of Saharanpur, occupied it from 1757 to 1770. The Gurkhas also overran it on the westward expansion from Kumaon to Kangra finally ceding it to the British in 1815. An Asoka rock inscription found in 1860 near Kalsi suggests the area came under the Emperor's rule in the 3rd Century BC.

Places of interest

Dehra Dun was developed by the British as a centre of education and research. The **Forest Research Institute** was established in 1914 in a fine setting in the lawns and forests surrounding the impressive red-brick building. This was followed in 1922 by the **Royal Indian Military College** in quaint mock Tudor style. 10 years later the **Indian Military Academy** was opened with 40 cadets; today it can take 1200. Modelled on Sandhurst, all officers in the Indian army undergo their initial training here. India's first, and one of India's most prestigious public schools, **The Doon School**, is here. The **Survey of India** (founded 1767, whose Surveyor Generals included Sir George Everest) has its headquarters here. It is a pleasant place to relax in or stop en route to Mussoorie. The cantonment across the Bindal Rao is spacious and well wooded. The Mussoorie road is lined with very attractive houses. Main shopping areas are Rajpur Rd, Paltan Bazar and Astley Hall, selling handwoven woollens, brassware and jewellery. The **Tapkesvar Cave Temple** 5 km NW, is in a pleasant setting with Shahasradhara's cool sulphur springs for bathing, nearby. Open sunrise to sunset. Simple Indian café nearby.

Robber's Cave (8 km), **Lakshman Sidh** (12 km), the snows at **Chakrata** (9 km) and sulphur springs at **Shahasradhara** (14 km) are also within easy reach.

Museums

Forest Research Institute's 6 museums

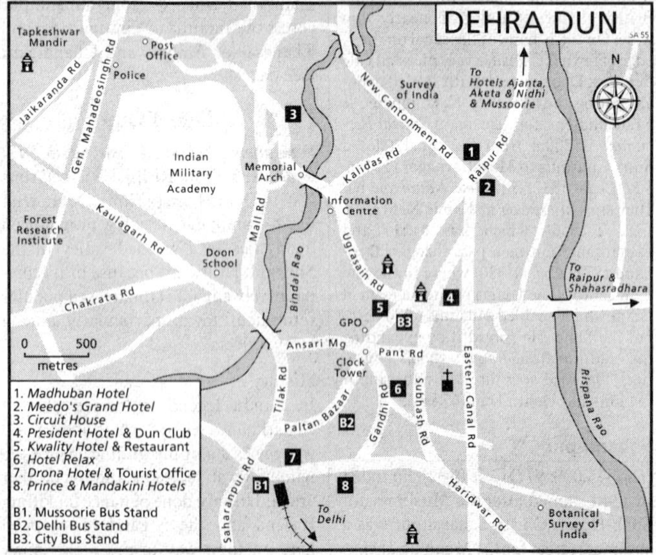

and the Wadia Institute of Geology are open 0900-1730.

Local festivals

Feb/Mar: *Jhanda Festival* in honour of Guru Ram Rai, 5 days after Holi and a large fair at Tapkesvar Temple on Sivaratri.

Local information

● Accommodation

Most 2-4 km rly. Some offer good discounts out-of-season (Aug-Feb). **B** ***Madhuban***, 97 Rajpur Rd, T 24094, F 23181, 42 rm, good restaurants (Indian classical singing, evenings), pleasant garden, clean, comfortable though characterless, but good value business hotel.

C ***Nidhi***, 74-c Rajpur Rd, T 24611, 24 rm, good restaurant, rec; **C** ***Ajanta Continental***, Rajpur Rd, T 29595, 30 rm, good restaurant, pool; **C** ***Inderlok***, 29 Rajpur Rd, T 288113, 50 rm, good restaurant; **C** ***Hilton***, 54 Haridwar Rd, T 29591, 36 rm, restaurant, bar; **C** ***Shipra***, 74C Rajpur Rd, T 22769, 24 rm with balcony, restaurant, bar, modern, clean, business hotel; **C** ***Meedo's Grand***, 28 Rajpur Rd, T 27171, 35 rm, restaurant, bar, coffee shop, exchange, travel, modern, attractive, pleasant atmosphere, friendly service; **C** ***Shahenshah***, Rajpur Rd, T 28508, F 22731, opened 1991, good, modern style hotel, restaurant, bar, coffee shop, exchange, travel.

D ***Niresh***, Chakrata Rd, T 24970, 30 rm, veg restaurant; **D** ***President***, 6 Astley Hall, Rajpur Rd, T 270882, F 28210, 18 rm, good restaurant, bar, coffee shop, exchange, travel, golf and riding arranged, pleasant, central, good service, excellent value; **D** ***Aketa***, 113/1 Rajpur Rd, T 26608, 30 rm, restaurant, exchange, travel; **D** ***Deepshikha***, Rajpur Rd, fairly small, pleasant, modern; **D** ***Kwality***, 19 Rajpur Rd, T 27001, 20 clean rm, some a/c, good restaurant, bar. Newer **D** ***Drona***, 45 Gandhi Rd, T 24371, F 22794, 68 rm, some a/c, dorm (men only), restaurants (good Indian food), bar, travel, shops, large, busy, convenient location for buses and rly, good value, Tourist Office in compound; **D** ***Mandakini***, 1 Haridwar Rd, T 27860, 24 rm, rm service, bar.

E ***Relax***, 7 Court Rd, T 27776, 32 clean rm, restaurant, bar permit, 24 hr coffee shop; **E** ***Meedo's***, nr Rly, quieter rm at back, some with bath; **E** ***Prince***, 1 Haridwar Rd, T 27082, 21 rm with bath, restaurant (Indian), unfriendly, not too clean, overpriced.

● Places to eat

Indian outside hotels, small inexpensive restaurants, serve surprisingly good food. The ***Vegetarian*** and ***Osho*** are especially rec for N Indian. Several bakeries in Paltan Bazar incl ***Grand*** and ***Ellora*** sell fresh bread and biscuits and the local sticky coffee toffee!

● Tour companies & travel agents

Adventures Adventure Holidays, PO Box 7, T 29172; ***Hill Tourism***, 75 Rajpur Rd, T 25121.,GMVN, 74/1 Rajpur Rd, T 26817. Tours arranged to Chandrapuri Tent Camp and Auli Ski Resort. See page 236.

● Tourist office

Regional: *Hotel Drona*, T 23217. **GMVN**: 74/1 Rajpur Rd, T 26817.

● Transport

On State Highway 45. Buses to all major centres of interest.

Local Road City buses: from Rajpur Rd, nr clocktower. **Taxis** and **autorickshaws**.

Air Jolly Grant air strip is on the Dehra Dun-Rishikesh road, 24 km away. See under Rishikesh. Coach (3/4 hr, Rs 25, T 27776), taxi transfers or UP Roadways buses which stop at the gate.

Train Lucknow: *Doon Exp* 3010, daily, 1945, 12½ hr; *Dehra Dun-Varanasi Exp* 4266, daily, 1830, 13¾ hr.

Road Delhi Bus Stand, Gandhi Rd, T 23482 for most destinations. **From Shimla**: HP Roadways run 4 buses to Dehra Dun. 2 deluxe buses, dep 0700, 0900. Rs 75. 2 ordinary, last dep 1030 (10 hr), Rs 50. **From Delhi**: UP Roadways operate 2 buses, dep 0515, 2230 (7 hr), about Rs 75. **To Mussoorie**: frequent buses from rly station, T 23435. Private buses from City Bus Stand, Parade Ground.

ROUTES The 34 km winding drive from **Dehra Dun to Mussoorie** is in stark contrast to the similar uphill climb from Haldwani to Nainital. Whereas much of the latter is through rich forest with splendid views of forested hills, here the hillsides are virtually bare of trees due to exposure to prevailing winds and deforestation by humans.

Mussoorie

BASICS *Population*: 30,000. *Altitude*: 1970m. *STD Code*: 01362. *Climate*: Summer Max 32°C, Min 7°C. Winter Max 7°C, Min 1°C. Monsoons end Jun/end Jul to

Sep. Winter showers and snowfalls in Dec/Jan.

Places of interest

Another self-styled Queen of the Hills, Mussoorie is spread out over 16 km along a horseshoe-shaped ridge. Off this runs a series of buttress-like subsidiaries. In this respect it is like Shimla but it lacks fine buildings. Nevertheless it is an extremely popular destination among Indian tourists especially as it is the nearest hill station to Delhi. The credit for its establishment goes to a Captain Young who built the first British residence in 1826 (in Landour), followed by the Mall, Club, Anglican Church (1837) and library. The early visitors came by road to Raipur, about 10 km E of Dehra Dun, and were then carried up via Barlowganj.

At the E end of town, a narrow spur leads to **Landour** (2270m) and the old barracks area. The winding road through the crowded Bazar leads up to the site of Capt Young's large house. There are lovely walks, and the extra 300m height above Mussoorie here appears to offer cleaner, pine scented air. **Woodstock** International School, (with a sister school at Kodaikkanal) and an International Language School take advantage of the magnificent location.

To the W is Convent Hill and **Happy Valley** where Tibetan refugees have settled and the pleasant **Municipal Garden**. Mall Road connects **Kulri** and **Library Bazars**. Camel's Back and Cart Roads also connect the two, but more circuitously. Like other hill stations, Mussoorie is best for walks. **Lal Tibba** and nearby **Childe's Lodge** on the highest hill is 5 km from the Tourist Office. There is a 400m ropeway to **Gun Hill** (so called because prior to Independence, a mid-day gun fire enabled residents to set their watches!) can be reached by bridle path in 20 min from the Kutchery on The Mall. The view of the snow capped peaks is stunning and best at sunrise. The **Camel's Back Road** starts from Kulri and ends at Library and is a very pleasant 3 km walk with the Camel's Rock en route.

Excursions

Kempty Falls 15 km on the Chakrata road, is pretty and a popular picnic spot.

Dhanolti has the Surkhanda Devi Temple nearby **C** *Dhanolti Breeze* provides comfortable accommodation. 5 km from the temple, 40 km from Mussoorié at **Kanolta** **C** *The Filigree Hermitage*, Rauslikhal, provides comfortable accommodation, rm and family suites, with views, good lawns and restaurant. Reservations for both in Delhi, T 6886909, F 6886122.

Tours

Operated by GMVN. **Kempty Falls**: half day (1100 and 1400). Rs 16. **Kempty Falls, Yamuna Valley and Lakhamandal**: Sun, full day (0730). Rs 60. Run only when coach is full. **Dhanolti-Surkhanda Devi Temple**: full day (0900). Rs 33.

Local information

● Accommodation

Several centrally located hotels, some old-fashioned but full of character. Prices based on high season tariff; some offer big off-season discounts. Restaurants may be closed out-of-season, and to non-residents. Some only offer room-service. **A** *Dunswik Court*, Baroda Estate, T 2680, 48 rm.

B *Savoy*, The Mall, Library, T 2010, 121 rm, best upstairs with balcony, good restaurant (all meals incl) open to non-residents, old library, S facing, superb mountain views, spacious, extensive grounds, originally the site of a school, the hotel opened in 1902, one of India's largest hill-station hotels, it retains a great deal of character, although modernised in some respects; **B** *Solitaire Plaza*, Picture Palace, Kincraig Rd, T 2937, F 6439133, 30 rm; **B** *Shining Star*, opp Vasu Theatre, The Mall, T 2500, 25 rm, restaurant, exchange, travel.

C *Holiday Inn*, The Mall, T 2794, 20 rm, no restaurant, modern, clean, excellent views; **C** *Carlton's Plaisance*, Charleville Rd, T 2800, 10 rm, good restaurant (incl Tibetan), very Victorian with period furniture, lacks views but peaceful orchard, spacious, charming and attentive service; **C** *Mussoorie International*,

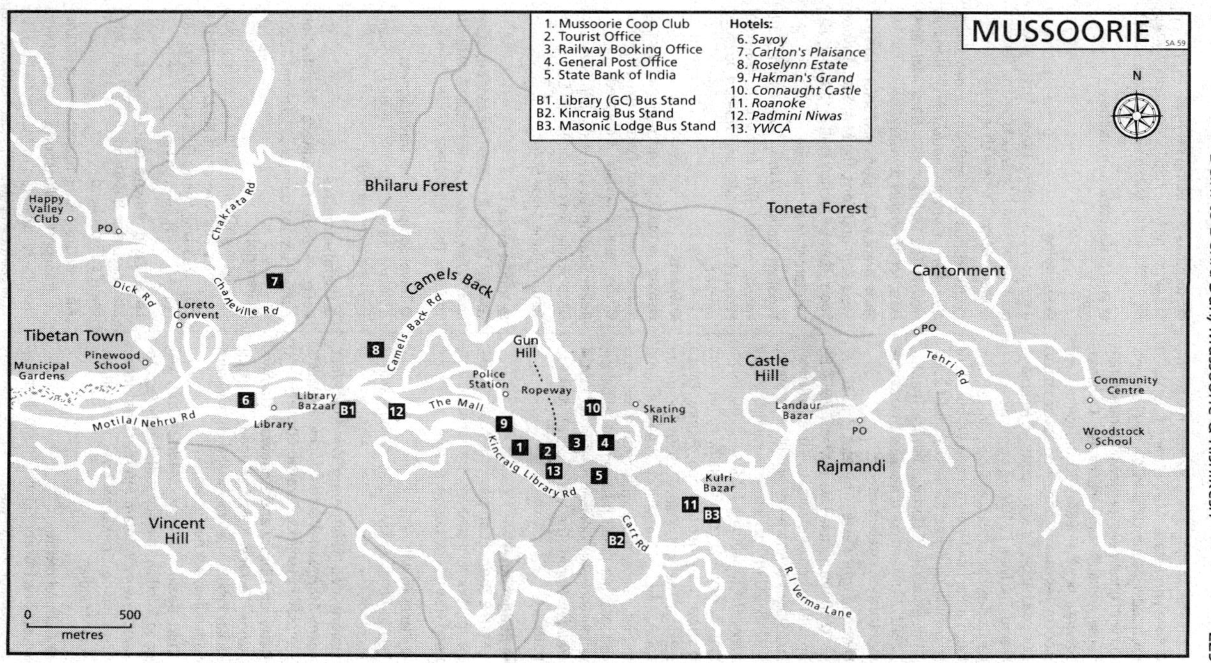
MUSSOORIE
SA 59
N
1. Mussoorie Coop Club
2. Tourist Office
3. Railway Booking Office
4. General Post Office
5. State Bank of India
B1. Library (GC) Bus Stand
B2. Kincraig Bus Stand
B3. Masonic Lodge Bus Stand
Hotels:
6. Savoy
7. Carlton's Plaisance
8. Roselynn Estate
9. Hakman's Grand
10. Connaught Castle
11. Roanoke
12. Padmini Niwas
13. YWCA
Happy Valley Club
PO
Chakrata Rd
Bhilaru Forest
Toneta Forest
Cantonment
Dick Rd
Loreto Convent
Charleville Rd
Camels Back
Camels Back Rd
Tibetan Town
Pinewood School
Municipal Gardens
Gun Hill
Police Station
Ropeway
Castle Hill
PO
Tehri Rd
Community Centre
Library Bazaar
The Mall
Skating Rink
Landaur Bazar
PO
Motilal Nehru Rd
Library
Woodstock School
Kincraig Library Rd
Rajmandi
Kulri Bazar
Vincent Hill
Cart Rd
R I Verma Lane
0
500
metres

Kulri, The Mall, T 2943, 22 rm, restaurant; **C** ***Roselynn Estate***, Mall, Library, T 2201, 20 rm, good restaurant (Indian, Chinese) on rooftop with good views, bar, lawns, former estate house, retains some character; **C** ***Shilton***, Gandhi Chowk, T 2842, 50 rm, central and modern, restaurant, coffee shop, ice cream parlour, exchange, travel, sports; **C** ***Hakman's Grand***, The Mall, T 2105, 32 a/c rm, restaurant, bar, coffee bar, exchange, shops, cinema, very much a Raj hotel with good views but needs renovating; **C** ***Filigree***, Camel's Back Rd, T 2380, 18 rm, restaurant; **C** ***Garhwal Terrace***, The Mall, T 2682, 24 rm and dorm, restaurant, reasonable maintenance, excellent views.

D ***Connaught Castle***, The Mall, T 2538, 27 rm; **D** ***Shipra***, Picture Palace, Mall, T 2662, 88 rm with balcony, restaurants, 2 min walk from Bus Stand; **D** ***Roanoke***, nr Kulri Bus Stand, T 2215, 20 rm, garden restaurant; **D** ***Valley View***, The Mall (Kulri), T 2324, 13 rm, restaurant, bakery and confectionery, coffee shop; **D** ***Shiva Continental***, opp Picture Palace parking, The Mall, Kulri, T 2980; **D** ***Padmini Nivas***, Library, The Mall, T 2793, 24 rm in former palace, some with good views, also cottages, not grand but pleasant ambience, restaurant (veg) open in season; **D** ***YWCA Holiday Home***, The Mall, T 2513, meals to order.

● Budget hotel

GMVN **E** ***Tourist Complex***, The Mall, T 2984, 24 rm, Dorm, restaurant, rm service, clean, good views, basic but good value.

● Places to eat

Best in hotels *Savoy*, *Roselynn* and *Carlton's Plaisance*.

Library area: *Whispering Windows*; *Jeet*; *Laxmi Mishtaan Bhandar* for Indian sweets, samosas and snacks; *Caravan Corner*.

Between Library and Ropeway: *Garhwal Ashok Terrace*, sells fast foods (bhelpuri, chaat, kababs, ice cream, also chicken curry with pulao, kulchas, dosas).

Kulri Bazar: *Kwality*; *Madras Café*, very good S Indian, friendly staff, highly rec; *Apsara*; *Tavern*; *Neelam International*, Indian and Chinese; *Shakahari Kutir*, S Indian and some N Indian.

● Cultural centre

Mussoorie Library: Gandhi Chowk. Membership available Rs 10/month

● Hospitals & medical services

St Mary's, The Mall, T 2845. *Community Hospital*, T 2653 and *Civil Hospital* at Landour, T 2589.

● Post & telecommunications

GPO: Kulri.

● Shopping

4 main shopping areas; Library, Kulri and Landour Bazars, and Shawfield Rd nr Padmini Niwas. *K.Main*, Chinese shoe maker.

Crafts, curios and antiques: *Inder Singh*; *Nirankari Cottage Industries*; *Banaras House*, The Mall, for silks; *Baru Mal Janki Dass*, for tribal silver jewellery.

Photography: *Computerised Colour Lab* and *Mela Ram and Sons*, The Mall; *Star Walking Sticks*, The Mall for handcrafted sticks.

Tibetan: stalls on roadside.

Woollen items: *Natraj Wool and Knitwears*, *Anand Gift Emporium*, *Garwhal Wool House*, nr GPO and *Tibetan outdoor market*.

● Sports

Fishing: in the Aglar and Yamuna Rivers for mahseer and hill trout. Permit from Div Forest Officer, Yamuna Division is required.

Roller Skating: at The Rink, Kulri Bazar and Disco Skating Rink behind Tourist Office.

Tennis: at the *Savoy Hotel*.

● Tourist office

GMVN, The Mall, T 2863; Library Bus Stand and *Tourist Bungalow*, The Mall, T 2948. **UP Tourism**, The Mall, T 2863.

● Travel companies & travel agents

Kulwant Travels, Masonic Lodge Bus Stand, T 2717 also rec for tours.

● Useful addresses

Police: T 2682. **Foreigner's Registration**: Kotwali next to Courts, opp Hakmans, T 2205.

● Transport

Accessible via Dehra Dun from State Highways to Nahan, and Meerut off **NH22** and **NH24**. Delhi (263 km); Shimla (234 km); Dehra Dun (34 km); Haridwar (100 km).

Local Road Private Taxi: *Kulwant Travels*, Masonic Lodge Bus Stand, T 2717. To Dehra Dun, Rs 35 per head.

Air Jolly Grant is the nearest airport, 60 km.

Transport to Mussoorie: Coach to Dehra Dun (Rs 20), then taxi to Mussoorie (Rs 150), or taxi all the way (Rs 275). Agent in Mussoorie,

Savoy Hotel, T 2510.

Train Varanasi: *Doon Exp* 3010, daily, 1945, 20½ hr; *Dehra Dun-Varanasi Exp* 4266, daily, 1830, 24 hr.

Road Enquiries at Mussoorie; Kincraig, T 2691; Library, T 2258; Masonic Lodge, T 2259. Frequent service from Dehra Dun through Ghat roads (1¾ hr). Also buses from Saharanpur Rly and from Tehri.

Muzaffarnagar to Rishikesh

ROUTES From Muzaffarnagar the alternative route is via Roorkee and Haridwar to Rishikesh.

Roorkee

(*Pop* 90,000; *STD Code* 01332) This is India's first 'canal town', near the headworks of N India's first great experiment with really large scale river diversion. On entering Roorkee, the Rural Development Training Centre is on your left. It has developed a very high reputation as an engineering centre. The **Thomason Engineering College** (1847) was transformed into a university specialising in technical sciences. **Accommodation C** *Motel Polaris*, on NH, nr Central Bus Stand, T 2648, 14 decent a/c rm, restaurant, bar, exchange, pleasant lawns, rec.

ROUTES The road leaves Roorkee and passes through Bahadurabad (17 km) and Jawalpur before reaching Haridwar (7 km).

Haridwar

(*Pop* 190,000; *STD Code* 0133) Haridwar is where legend has placed Vishnu's footprint on the bank of the holy river giving it its sanctity. One of the 7 holy cities of Hinduism – see Hindu Holy Sites, page 71. Various episodes from the *Mahabharata* are set here. Every 12th year the Kumbh Mela is held in Haridwar (and Ardha Kumbh every 6 years) – see Allahabad page 281.

Situated at the base of the Shiwalik Hills, Haridwar is where the River Ganga passes through its last gorge and begins a 2000 km journey across the plains, irrigating vast expanses of land. Water is drawn off for the Upper Ganga Canal system and there is also a hydro-electric power station.

It is a very old town and was mentioned by the Chinese traveller Hiuen Tsang. Its Haridwar attracted the attention of Timur who sacked it in Jan 1399 (see page 45). The name Haridwar 'Door of Vishnu (Hari)' dates from about 1400.

Places of interest

The town is situated on the W bank of the river and centres on **Hari-ki-Pairi**, the place where Vishnu is believed to have left his footprint. Part of the Ganga has been diverted here and this later becomes the canal. Bathing here is believed to cleanse all sins. Each evening you can witness priests performing *Ganga Arati* at sunset. Near the steps is a modern clocktower and some temples, none particularly old. Further down along the waterfront are more bathing ghats, numerous sheds where *pandas* of various castes and sects dispense wisdom to the willing. Along the banks you will see *sadhus* who have made make-shift homes under trees. Food stalls and shrines line alleyways leading off into the bazar. There are 5 bridges to take you across the river where it is quieter. Although the religious focus is Hari-ki-Pairi ghat, the main centre of town is nearer the Railway Station and Bus Stand.

Moti bazar along the Jawalapur-Haridwar Road is interesting, colourful, invariably crowded and surprisingly clean and tidy. Stalls sell coloured powder piled high in carefully made cones (used to make the *tika* and sect marks). Others sell saris, jewellery, brass and aluminium pots and, of course, sweets and snacks.

Mansa Devi Temple is worth visiting for the view. Set on the southernmost hill of the Shiwaliks, it is accessible on foot or by chairlift (about Rs 10 return).

Excursions

Kankhal, 3 km downstream, is where Siva's wife Sati is believed to have burnt herself to death because her father Daksa failed to invite Siva to a *yagna*. Prof Wendy Doniger vividly summarises the story as told in the *Puranas*: "Daksha, a son of Brahma, gave his daughter Sati in marriage to Siva, but he did not invite Siva to his sacrifice. Sati, in anger, burnt herself to death. Siva destroyed Daksa's sacrifice and beheaded Daksa, but when the gods praised Siva he restored the sacrifice

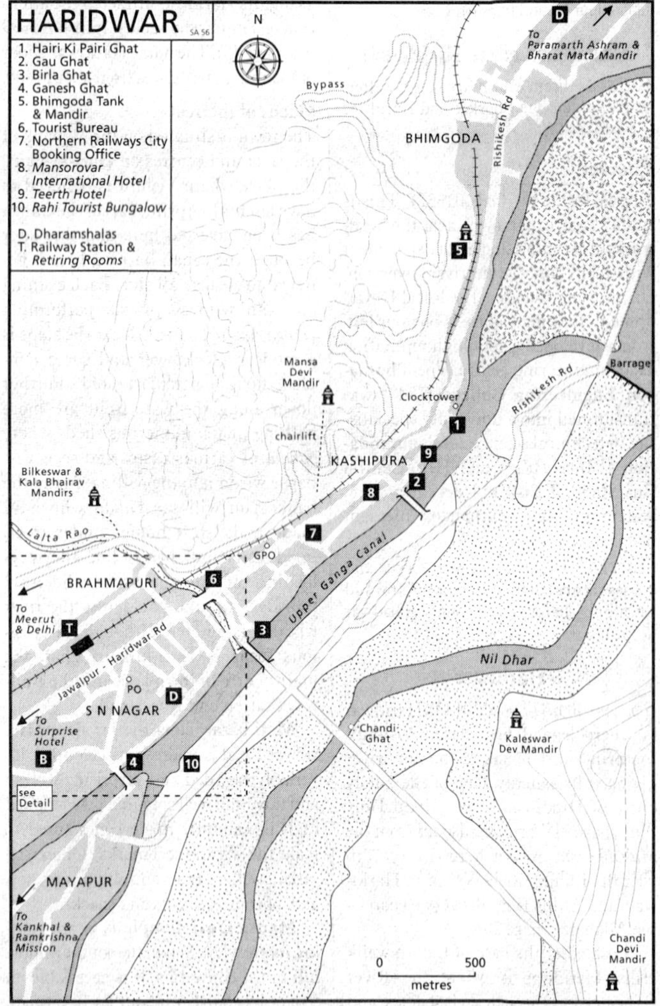

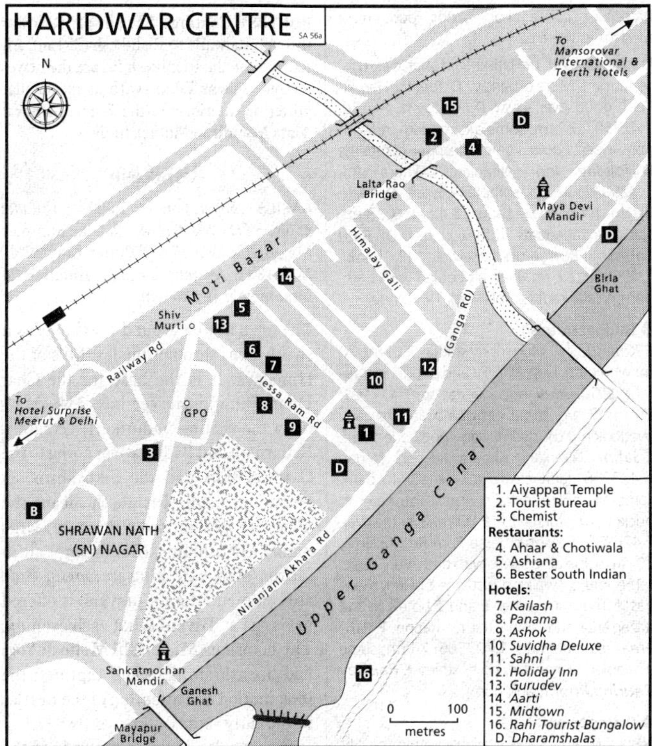

and gave Daksa the head of a goat. When Siva learned that Sati had killed herself, he took up her body and danced in grief, troubling the world with his dance and his tears until the gods cut the corpse into pieces. When the *yoni* fell, Siva took the form of a *linga*, and peace was re-established in the universe." At Kankhal there is the **Temple of Daksehwara.**

Local festivals

Thousands of pilgrims visit the city, the numbers increasing to almost 100,000 when the birth of the river (*Dikhanti*) is celebrated in spring. During the *Kumbh Mela* (next in 1998) over 2 million devotees throng the confined area near Hari-ki-Pairi to bathe in the waters. In the past there have been many deaths due to the great congestion and occasional violence. Elaborate security preparations and extraordinary efforts to provide basic sanitation have helped to minimise the risk. Non-Hindus are advised to view from the opposite bank.

Local information

● Accommodation

Most are between Jawalpur-Haridwar Rd and the Ganga. Many offer off-season discounts outside June/July. Some check out at 1200. **C** ***Suvidha Deluxe***, SN Nagar, T 427423 (Delhi, T 5410894), 29 rm, some a/c, restaurant, modern, very clean, central but quiet, excellent value, highly rec; **C** ***Surprise***, Haridwar-Delhi Rd, Jawalapur, 1.5 km, T 421146, 55 rm, some a/c, restaurants (Non-veg continental, Indian on roof-top and barbecue), coffee shop, shops, pool, most modern in the area.

D *Mansarovar*, nr Hari-ki-Pairi ghat, clean rm, restaurant. More expensive **D** *Teerth*, Hari-ki-Pairi, good river view; **D** *Midtown*, Rly Rd, T 427507, 33 rm, some a/c, modern, reasonably clean, quite quiet despite centrality; **D** *Holiday Inn*, Niranjani Akhara Rd, T 425017, 32 rm, some air-cooled; **D** *Aarti*, Rly Rd (1st Fl, above shops), T 427456, 33 rm, some a/c, adequate if unexciting; **D** UP *Rahi Tourist Bungalow*, Belwala (E bank), T 426379, 22 rm, best air cooled with bath, dorm, restaurant (simple veg), TV lounge.

● Budget hotels

E *Kailash*, Shiv Murti nr rly station, T 6789, 70 rm with bath, best with TV and phone, restaurant; **E** *Gurudev*, opp Rly Station, T 427101, 30 rm, 7 a/c, some with bath and balcony overlooking courtyard, veg food, adequate; **E** *Sahni*, Niranjani Akhara Rd, SN Nagar, T 427906, fairly clean rm, some with bath, some air-cooled (extra charge), hot water in buckets, helpful service; **E** *Vikrant*, nr the river, T 426930; **E** *Ashok*, Jessa Ram Rd, 427328, 29 rm, some air-cooled, with bath, very basic, rather dark, "walking distance of Holly Gangas"! There are other **E** and **F** hotels in the bazar area and round the rly station. **F** *Panama*, Jessa Ram Rd, T 427506, 26 rm, some air-cooled, very basic, noisy street. **E** *Railway Retiring Rooms* and dorm.

● Places to eat

NB: Only veg food is available within the city. On Rly Rd: *Ahaar*, Punjabi meals; *Bestec*, S Indian; *Aashiana*; *Chotiwala* opp Tourist Office. Atmospheric.

● Bank & money changers

State Bank of India, Station Rd, 1000-1400.

● Post & telecommunications

Post Offfice: Upper Rd, 1000-1630.

● Tourist office

Lalta Rao Bridge, T 6019 and Counter at rly station.

● Transport

Train **Old Delhi:** *Dehra Dun Exp* 9020, daily, 1250, 10 hr; *Mussoorie Exp* 4042, daily, 2250, 7 hr. **Dehra Dun:** *Dehra Dun Exp* 9019, daily, 1455, 2 hr; *Mussoorie Exp* 4041, daily, 0650, 1¾ hr. **By bus**: regular services to Haridwar from Delhi (4 hr), Dehra Dun (1¼ hr) and other state centres. Cycle rickshaws are available – fares negotiable.

ROUTES Continue NE out of Haridwar through Raiwalla to Rishikesh (25 km). After 5 km on the Rishikesh Rd are the newer temples. **Pawan Dham** with its spectacular glittering interior and the 7-storey **Bharat Mata Mandir** to Mother India.

Rishikesh

BASICS *Population*: 72,000. *Altitude*: 356m. *STD Code*: 01364. *Climate*: Summer Max 41°C, Min 37°C. Winter Max 32°C, Min 18°C. Average annual rainfall 1524 mm, mostly Jun to Sep.

The town nestles around the Ganga as it swiftly runs through the last hills of the Himalaya. It is the base for the **Char Dham Piligrimage**, see box, 234, (May-Nov) for visiting Yamunotri, Gangotri, Kedarnath and Badrinath or going to the Garhwal hills and the Sikh shrine at Hemkund Sahib. Rishikesh means the 'Place of Sages' and today there are a large number of ashrams. (Beware, not all in saffron/orange clothing are *sadhus*; some are con-men!) *Aarati* (prayers) is offered to Ganga at **Triveni Ghat** each evening. The notorious **Maharishi Mahesh Yogi** had his ashram here and captured the imagination and attention of the Beatles in the early sixties.

The secular business centre is on the W bank of the river and is noisy and dirty. The spiritual haven of the various ashrams are on the other side at **Pauri.** Geoffrey Moorhouse has described it as a cross between Blackpool and Lourdes. The Ganga has 2 suspension bridges – **Lakshman Jhula** along the old Yatra route (where you may be troubled by rhesus monkeys), and **Sivananda** (or Ram) **Jhula** (between Sivananda Ashram and Swargashram). The **Lakshman Jhula** area is very picturesque with the best views, and quieter than the town centre (which has little of interest). Walk NE along the river for secluded beaches. **Muni-ki-Reti** is the area along the Chandrabhaga river which also has some temples.

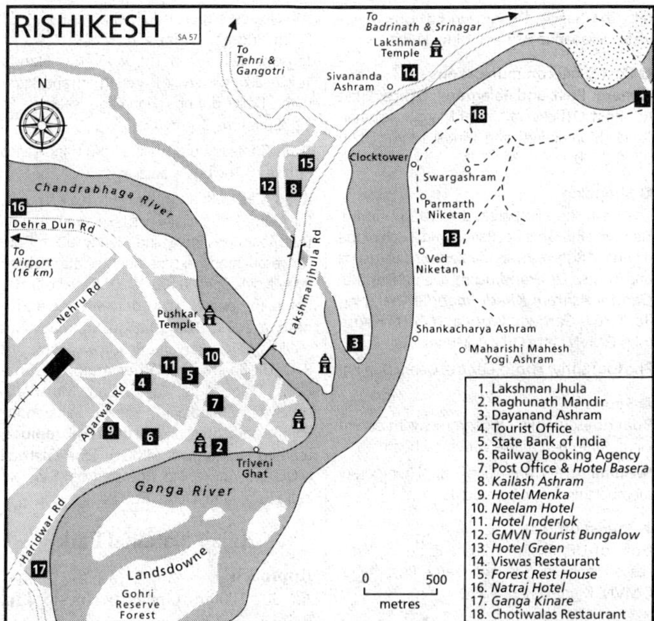

Local information

● Accommodation

Mostly central, some across the river. **C** *Natraj*, Dehra Dun Rd, T 1099, 75 a/c rm, restaurant (veg), exchange, travel, shops, pool, modern, free airport transfer; **C** *Basera*, 1 Ghat Rd, T 767, 39 rm, some a/c, restaurant (veg), exchange, roof top terrace garden; **C** *Ganga Kinare*, 16 Virbhadra Rd, on riverside, T 566, 36 rm, central a/c, pleasant restaurant, evening *aarati* ceremony; **C** *Mandakini International*, 63 Haridwar Rd, T 781, 31 rm, restaurant (veg), travel.

D *Shipra*, T 30533, 24 rm in modern hotel, restaurant; **D** *Inderlok*, Railway Rd, T 555, 52 clean rm, some a/c, with balconies, restaurant (veg), terrace lawn, older hotel, but well kept and with pleasant ambience and mountain views.

● Budget Hotels

E *Tourist Complex Rishilok*, Badrinath Rd, Muni-ki-Reti, T 372, some rm with bath in cottages, dorm and restaurant, reasonable. Across the river, **E** *Green* nr *Parmarth Ashram*, some a/c rm with bath, clean, quiet; **F** *Shikar*, Lakshman Jhula, good, clean rm, some with bath (order hot water), very good restaurant and superb views from rooftop; **F** *Tourist*, Town centre, off Dehra Dun Rd, opp *Padam Confectioners*, relaxed, very friendly, family run, highly rec. There are also several **F** hotels nr Roadways Bus Stand incl *Menka*, Agarwal Rd, T 285 with simple rm. Rm-service. *Dharamshalas* and Ashrams mainly for pilgrims: *Ved Niketan*, *Yoga Niketan*, *Swargashram* (100 cottages), *Parmarth Ashram* (600 beds) and Geeta Bhavan (500 beds). Warning from recent traveller: rooms in some ashrams can be filthy and about Rs 40.

● Places to eat

Rishikesh is a vegetarian temple town. Meat and alcohol are prohibited and even eggs are eaten only in private. Indian: *Darpan*, Railway Rd; *Viswas*, Muni-ki-Reti. *Chotiwala*, Sivananda Jhula, attracts local crowds. Plenty of atmosphere and inexpensive.

● Banks & money changers

Punjab National, Haridwar Rd, and **State Bank of India**, Railway Rd, and others.

● Hospitals & medical services

GD Hospital, Dehra Dun Rd, T 96. *Rajkiya Ma-*

hila Chikitsalaya, Dehra Dun Rd. *Govt Ayurvedic*, Sivananda Ashram, Muni-ki-Reti.

● Post & telecommunications

General Post and Telegraph Office: Ghat Rd. **Post Offices**: at Hiralal Marg, Lakshman Jhula, Muni-ki-Reti and Hiralal Marg. Open 0700-2200.

● Shopping

The main shopping areas are Dehra Dun Rd, Haridwar Rd, Ghat Rd, Railway Rd. Each of the 4 parts of Rishikesh has markets for daily needs and curios. *UP Handlooms*, Dehra Dun Rd. *Gandhi Ashram Khadi Bhandar*, Haridwar Rd, T 367. *Garhwal Wool and Craft House* (opp GMVN Yatra Office), Muni-ki-Reti.

Photography: *Photo Centre*, Dehra Dun Rd.

● Sports

Boat rides: on the Ganga from Swargashram Ghat. Rates negotiable with local boatmen.

Swimming: at *Hotel Natraj's* pool (temporary membership for non-residents).

● Tourist offices

Govt of UP, Rly Rd, T 209 and during Yatra season only at Samyukt Yatra Bus Stand. GMVN, Muni-ki-Reti, T 372.

● Tour company & travel agent

Garhwal Mandal Vikas Nigam (GMVN), Muni-ki-Reti, T 372, organises trekking, mountaineering and allied sports activities from Rishikesh.

● Useful addresses

Police: T 100. **Fire**: T 101, 140.

● Transport

Rishikesh is connected by road via Haridwar and Dehra Dun to various parts of the country. From: Delhi (238 km); Dehra Dun (42 km); Haridwar (24 km); Mussoorie (77 km); Yamunotri (288 km); Gangotri (258 km); Uttarkashi (154 km); Kedarnath (228 km); Badrinath (301 km); Chandigarh (252 km).

Local Unmetered taxis: are available from Garhwal Mandal Taxi Chalak Sangh. Haridwar Rd, T 413 or at various taxi stands, bus stands and rly station. Rates negotiable. **Auto-rickshaws** and **Vikrams** available everywhere. Generally on fixed route point-to-point. Min fare Rs 1/stage. **Cycle-rickshaws** and **Tongas** freely available. Rates negotiable. Constant shuttle between town centre and Lakshman Jhula. **Ferry Service**: at Ghat nr Sivananda Jhula for river crossing.

Air Nearest airport is Jolly Grant (16 km). To Delhi: **Indian Airlines**, daily, 0810, ¾ hr. **Jagsons**, daily (except Th), 0835, ¾ hr. **Nanda Tels**, helicopter service to Kedarnath and Badrinath. Daily during pilgrimage season, Rs 12,750 return, ¾ hr.

Train There is a branch line from Haridwar to Rishikesh. The bus is quicker.

Road Car: with a stop en route (eg *Khatauli*), the journey from Delhi will take about 4½ hr. **Bus**: Roadways Bus Stand, Haridwar Rd, T 66. No reservations except during Yatra season (May-Nov), open 0400-1900. Reserve a day before the journey. **To Kedarnath and Badrinath** takes 3 to 4 days. Various State Govt bus services (DTC, Haryana Roadways, Himachal RTC, UP Roadways). **Other major destinations**: Delhi, Agra, Dehra Dun, Mussoorie, Haridwar, Chandigarh, Patiala, Saharanpur, Shimla, Sarkaghat. **To Northern Hill regions**, serviced by Garhwal MMOU, Tehri Garhwal MOU and Yatayat Ltd, operate from Samyukt Yatra Bus Stand, Dehra Dun Rd.

Rajaji National Park

Approach

Alt 302-1000m. Open 10 Nov-15 Jun, daily between sunrise and sunset.

Background

UP's largest park, consolidated the wildlife sanctuaries at Chilla, Motichur and Rajaji (named after the nationalist leader C Rajagopalachari, the only Indian to hold the post of Governor General). The park covers 820 sq km in the lesser Himalayan foothills, where they meet the Indo-Gangetic plains and is particularly interesting for its location. The Shiwaliks, with its claybeds, sand and loam conglomorates present rugged and precipitous S facing slopes. The vegetation ranges from riverine, broadleaf mixed to *Chir* pine forests interspersed with areas of scrub and pasture which support a wide variety of fauna with over 23 mammal and 180 birds species.

Wildlife

The park is well known for the large number of elephants which together with the rarely seen tiger are at the NW limit of their distribution in India; other mammals include leopards, spotted deer, sambar, muntjac, nilgai and ghoral. Along the tracks it is easy to see wild boar, langur and macaque; the Himalayan yellow-throated marten and civet are rare. Birdlife includes peacocks, jungle fowls and kaleej pheasants in the drier areas; cuckoos, hornbills, woodpeckers, warblers, finches, rollers, oriole, bee-eaters, minivets and nuthatches, while waterbirds attracted by the Ganga and the Song rivers include many kinds of geese, ducks, cormorant, teal and spoonbill among others. For information, entry permit and reservation contact Director, Rajaji National Park, 5/1 Ansari Marg, Dehra Dun, T 23794.

Park information

● Accommodation

D/E *Forest Rest Houses* nr all the gates. Those at Motichur, Raniipur, Chilla and Kunnao have at least 2 suites with electricity and water supply.

● Transport

The park has 8 entry gates. Haridwar 9 km by road from 4 gates (Motichur, Ranipur, Chilla and Satyanarain), Rishikesh is 6 km from Kunnao Gate (via private bus route on Rishikesh-Pashulok route; tongas, auto-rickshaws, taxis also available), Dehra Dun is 14 km from Ramgarh Gate (Delhi-Dehra Dun Highway via Clement Town). Mohand Gate is a 5 hr drive from Delhi.

GARHWAL & THE PILGRIMAGE (YATRA)

Up until the 14th century Garhwal (Land of the Forts) comprised a number of petty principalities, each no larger than a valley. Ajai Pal (1358-70) consolidated these and became the Raja of Garhwal. The Mughals showed little interest in acquiring the region but it was a popular plundering ground for Sikh brigands from the Punjab and the Rohillas – see Rampur (page 241). The Gurkhas overran it in 1803 and treated the population harshly, taking men, women and children into slavery and conscripting males into their army. Compelled to action by Gurkha encroachments on the territory around Gorakhpur, the British expelled the Gurkhas from Garhwal and Kumaon in 1814, took the eastern part of Garhwal as British Garhwal and returned the western part, Tehri Garhwal to the deposed Raja.

Garhwal's fragmented political history gives no clue as to the region's religious significance. The sources of the Yamuna and the Ganga and some of Hinduism's holiest mountains lie in the heart of the region. Hinduism's early myths and epics identify a number of sites as particularly holy, and since the 7th century Tamil saint Sankaracharya travelled north on his mission to re-invigorate Hinduism's northern heartland, some have been watched over permanently by Hindu priests. The most famous is the Rawal – head priest – at the Alaknanda temple in Badrinath, who to this day comes from Kerala. Today the shrines of Kedarnath and Badrinath are visited by hundreds of thousands of Hindu pilgrims each summer, the latter being one of the four *dhams* 'holy abodes' of the gods. Along with Dwarka, Puri and Ramesvaram, they mark the cardinal points of Hinduism's cultural geography. Best time: Apr to Jun, mid-Sep to early Nov are best, Jul to mid-Sep being the rainy season when landslips may occur. Trekking routes are open Apr-Oct. Recommended "Peaks and passes of the Garhwal Himalaya" published by Alpinists Club, 1990.

NB: It is essential for *Yatra* tourists to register with State Govt Yatra Office at Yatra Bus Stand, Rishikesh, T 383. Open 0600-2200. You will also need to produce a current innoculation certificate covering immunisation against cholera and typhoid.

After a ritual purificatory bathe in the

Ganga at Haridwar and, preferably, Rishikesh as well, the pilgrim begins the 301 km journey from Haridwar to Badrinath, one of the 4 holiest places in India for Hindus. The purpose is to worship, purify and acquire merit. Roads go all the way to Gangotri and Badrinath, and to within a few km of Yamunotri and Kedarnath. The correct order for Char Dhams pilgrims is to visit the holy places from W to E: Yamunotri, Gangotri, Kedarnath and Badrinath. **Accommodation** The regional tourism organisation *GMVN* has established a string of moderately priced basic lodges for travellers along the routes. Some have 'deluxe' rooms which are still basic, with bath and hot water.

Haridwar to Yamunotri and Gangotri

Yamunotri (3291m) can be reached from Rishikesh or from Dehra Dun via Yamuna Bridge and Barkot. The former is the more popular. It is 83 km to Tehri (165 km via Deoprayag).

Tehri

The capital of the Princely State will eventually be submerged by the waters behind the controversial and still unfinished Tehri Dam.

ROUTES From here the road goes to **Dharasu** (37 km) where it divides. The left turn leads to Barkot, Hanuman Chatti and Yamunotri (102 km).

Yamunotri

Dominated by **Banderpunch** (6316m), Yamunotri, the source of the **Yamuna**, is believed to be the daughter of Surya, the sun, and the twin sister of Yama, the Lord of Death. Anyone who bathes in her waters will be spared an agonising death. To reach the temple you must walk from **Hanuman Chatti** (13 km), the roadhead, usually with an overnight stay halfway along the trail at **Janki Chatti**.

The trek along the riverbank is exhilarating with the mountains rising up on each side, the last 5 km somewhat steeper. The source itself is a difficult 1 km climb from the 19th century **Yamunotri Temple**, with a black marble deity; open 0600-1200, 1400-2100. The modern temple was rebuilt this century after floods and snow destroyed it. There are hot springs nearby (the most sacred

THE CHAR DHAM PILGRIMAGE: PURIFICATION AND PIETY

There are 2 types of pilgrimage aim: purification from bad *karma* (impurity as a consequence of bad actions in previous births) or the performance of specific rituals usually associated with death. See page 69. Belief in the purifying power of certain precisely performed rituals is often based on the analogy between physical and moral impurity. The purifying power of a sacred river is stronger at the source, at the confluence of rivers and at the mouth. There are *Panch Prayags* (5 confluences) in the Himalayan section of the Ganga. From Rishikesh they are Deoprayag, Rudraprayag, Karnaprayag, Nandaprayag and Vishnuprayag. On the plains, Allahabad is the most important confluence of all, where the Yamuna, the Ganga and the mythical underground river, the Sarasvati, all meet.

Piety Hardship enhances the rewards. It is common to see *sadhus* dressed in the characteristic saffron robes, carrying a staff and a brass pitcher, walking along this road. The really devout prostrate themselves for the whole distance – lying face down, stretching the arms forwards, standing up, moving up to where their fingertips reached and then repeating the exercise, each one accompanied by a chant. This act of extreme piety is more rarely seen nowadays and most pilgrims prefer to make the journey by bus or, if they are fortunate enough, by car.

being Surya Kund) in which pilgrims immerse potatoes and rice tied in a piece of cloth. The meal, which takes only a few minutes to cook is then offered to the deity and later distributed as *prasad*. On the return to Hanuman Chatti, you can visit the **Temple of Someshwar** at **Kharsali**, 1 km across the river from Jankichatti. The temple is one of the oldest and finest in the region and there are excellent views of the mountains. **Accommodation E** *Tourist Rest Houses*, Hanuman Chatti, Janki Chatti and Barkot with clean, simple rm; hot water in buckets. Reserve at GMVN, Rishikesh. Availability very difficult during the Yatra season unless you book a GMVN organised tour.

ROUTES From Dharasu, the road to the right leads to Uttarkashi (26 km) and Gangotri (100 km).

Uttarkashi

On 10 Oct 1991 an earthquake recording 7 points on the Richter scale had its epicentre near Uttarkashi, causing enormous damage. You can trek to **Dodital**. The *Nehru Institute of Mountaineering* here offers courses. Accommodation: E *Tourist Rest House*, Uttarkashi, T 36. 33 rm with bath. Veg meals at *Satyam*. Other hotels, incl *Kailash* are clustered nr the bus stand. Shops sell provisions.

Gangotri

Gangotri (3140m), 248 km from Rishikesh, is the 2nd of the major shrines in the Garhwal Himalaya. A high bridge now takes the road across the Bhagirathi river which rushes through narrow gorges, so buses travel all the way. The 18th century granite **temple**, is dedicated to the Goddess Ganga, where she is believed to have descended to earth. It was built by a Gurkha commander, Amar Singh Thapa in the early 18th century and later rebuilt by the Maharaja of Jaipur.

Hindus believe that Ganga (here Bhagirathi) came down from heaven after King Bhagirath's centuries-long penance. He wanted to ensure his dead relatives' ascent to heaven by having their ashes washed by the sacred waters of the Ganga. When the tempestuous river arrived on earth, the force of her flow had to be checked by Siva who received her in the coils of his hair, lest she sweep all away. A submerged lingam is visible in the winter months.

Rishikund with hot sulphur springs suitable for bathing, nr **Gangnani** (55 km from Uttarkashi) has a 15th century temple above. The **Gaurikund waterfall** (different from the more famous Gaurikund, S of Kedarnath) is one of the most beautiful in the Himalaya.

Bhojbasa (3500m, 17 km) and **Gaumukh** (Cow's Mouth, 3970m, 4 km) are on a gradual but nevertheless scenically stunning trek – see page 254. Gaumukh is the snout of the Gangotri Glacier and the present source of the Bhagirathi River. There are 2 *ashrams* and a small permanent population of *sadhus* who brave the elements throughout the year. Like the other shrines, Gangotri is effectively closed over winter. **Accommodation E** *Tourist Rest House*, 20 rm, and dorm. Meals. *Lodges* have rm, mainly without bath and electricity for under Rs 80. Numerous tea and food stalls nr the Temple.

Rishikesh to Kedarnath and Badrinath

From **Rishikesh** the 30 km of the road follows the west bank of the Ganga and quickly enters forest. The section up to **Deoprayag** (68 km) is astonishingly beautiful. The folding and erosion of the hills can be clearly seen on the mainly uninhabited steep scarps on the opposite bank. Luxuriant forest runs down to the water's edge which in many places is fringed with silver sand beaches. In places the river rushes over gentle rapids. After the truck stop village of **Beasi** the road makes a gradual ascent to round an important bluff. At the top, there are fine views down to the river. Villages now become more common. The way that small pocket handkerchief-sized fields have been created by terracing is marvellous.

NB: It is an offence to photograph sensitive installations, troop movements and bridges on most routes. Offenders can be treated very severely.

Deoprayag

This is the most important of the hill *prayags* because it is at the junction of the **Bhagirathi** and **Alaknanda** rivers. Gangotri is the source of the Bhagirathi and Badrinath is near the source of the Alaknanda. Below Deoprayag, the river becomes the Ganga proper. The town tumbles down the precipitous hillside in the deeply cut 'V' between the junction of the 2 rivers, houses almost on top of one another. Where the rivers meet is a bathing ghat, artificially made into the shape of India. Here pilgrims bathe and to prevent them being swept downstream there are chains to hold on to. **Accommodation** On hillside, outside the village **E** *Tourist Rest House*, T 33. 4 rm, some with bath (Indian). Meals. Other tea-stalls nr bridge.

ROUTES From Deoprayag, the road is relatively flat as far as Srinagar (35 km, not to be confused with its Kashmiri namesake) and for much of the way you pass through well cultivated land. At Kirtinagar the road crosses the river to the E bank. The valley is quite wide here and is known as the **Panai pasture**.

Srinagar

(*Pop* 18,000) This is the old capital of Tehri Garhwal. It was devastated when the Gohna Lake dam burst during an earthquake in the mid-19th century, hence there is little of antiquity. The most attractive part of Srinagar, which is a development centre and university town, runs from the square down towards the river. There are some typical hill houses with elaborately carved door jambs. **Accommodation** Nr Bus Stop in central square, **E** *Tourist Rest House*, T 99, with 90 rm, deluxe with bath, dorm and restaurant. Clean and quiet. Rec. Opp is the **E** *Alka*.

The next stretch is from Srinagar to **Rudraprayag** (700m, 35 km), again mostly through cultivated areas. Roughly half way there is an enormous landslip indicating the fragility of the mountains. Approx 5 km before reaching Rudrapayag, in a grove of trees by a village, is a tablet marking the spot where the "man-eating leopard of Rudraprayag" was finally killed by Jim Corbett – see Corbett National Park (page 248). Rudraprayag is strung out along a fairly narrow part of the Alaknanda valley. **Accommodation** On a hill, **E** *Tourist Rest House*, T 46. 25 rm, deluxe with bath and dorm. **E** *Chandrapuri Camp*, N of town, by the river, has 10 safari type tents for 4.

Kedarnath

For Kedarnath, you leave the Pilgrim Road at Rudraprayag, cross the Alaknanda river, go through a tunnel before following the Mandakini Valley (the tributary) through terrace cultivation and green fields. The road goes past the first town Tilwara (9 km), then Kund, to **Guptakashi** where Siva proposed to Parvati. If time permits stop at **Sonprayag** (26 km) a small village at the confluence of the Mandakini and Son Ganga rivers, to visit the Triyuginarayan Temple (where the gods were married). Find the view point here before continuing to **Gaurikund** (4 km) where the motorable road ends. **Accommodation** At Gaurikund, T 2, with 10 rm; at Guptakashi, T 21, with 6 rm. The hot sulphur springs are recommended for a refreshing bath.

From here you either trek (early start rec) or ride a mule to Kedarnath (14 km). The ascent is fairly steep at first through forests and green valleys to Jungle Ghatti and Rambara (over 1500m); the latter part goes through dense vegetation, ravines and passes beautiful waterfalls. Beyond Rambara the ascent to Kedarnath is gentler. At intervals tea stalls sell refreshments.

Kedarnath (3,584m)
77 km from Rudrapayag. The area around Kedarnath is known as Kedarkhand, the *Abode of Siva*. Kedarnath has one of the 12 *jyotirlingas* – see page 78. In the *Mahabharata*, the Pandavas built the temple to atone for their sins after the battle at Kurukshetra (see page 493).

The **Kedarnath Temple** is older (some claim, originally over 800 years old) and more impressive than Badrinath. Built of stone, unpainted but carved outside, it comprises a simple, squat, curved tower and a wooden roofed *mandapa*. Set against an impressive backdrop of snow capped peaks, the principle one being the Kedarnath peak (6,970m) the view from the forecourt is ruined by ugly 'tube' lights. At the entrance to the temple is a large Nandi statue. Pujas held at 0600 and 1800. **Accommodation E** *Tourist Rest House*, 16 rm, some with bath, and dorm.

Vasuki Tal (5,200m) about 2 km across, the source of Son Ganga, is to the W up along a goat track, with superb views of the Chaukhamba peak (7,164m). A short distance NW is the beautiful Painya Tal where through the clear water you can see the rectangular rocks which form the lake bottom. **NB**: A guide is necessary.

The Panch Kedars There are 5 temples visited by pilgrims: Kedarnath, Madhmaheshwar, Tungnath, Rudranath and Kalpeshwar. These vary in altitude from 1,500-3,680m in the Rudra Himalaya and is quite an arduous circuit so now the majority only visit Kedarnath. Kedarnath and Badrinath are only 41 km apart and there is a tiring *yatra* (pilgrim route) between the two; most pilgrims take the longer but easier way round by bus or car.

The myth of the '5 Sivas' relates how parts of the shattered Nandi Bull fell in the 5 places – the humped back at Kedarnath, the stomach at Madhmaheswar, the arms at Tungnath, the face at Rudranath and the hair at Kalpeshwar. Since all but Kalpeshwar are inaccessible in the winter, each deity has a winter seat in a temple at Ukhimath where the images are brought down in the autumn. They are returned to their principal temples in the spring.

Panch Kedar trek If you wish to undertake the 170 km 14-day trek, you can start at Rishikesh, visiting Kedarnath first (see above). Return to Guptakashi and proceed to Ukhimath to start the 24 km trek to **Madhmaheswar** from Mansuna village. It is possible to stop overnight at Ransi and continue following the Ganga through the Kedarnath Wildlife Park with its contrasting grassland and dense wooded hillsides. From near the temple at 3,030m which has 3 streams flowing by it, you can see Chaukhamba peak (7,164m).

Tungnath (3680m), the highest temple, is surrounded by picturesque mountains (Nanda Devi, Neelkanth, Kedarnath). It is reached by trekking from Chopta (37 km trek from Ukhimath), passing through villages, fields and wooded hills before reaching meadows with rhododendrons. The 4 hr climb of 7 km, though steep, is not difficult since it is along a rocky path with occasional benches.

For **Rudranath** (3,030m) you can get to Gopeshwar by road and then on to **Sagar** (5 km) for the 24 km trek covering stony, slippery ground through tall grass, thick oak and rhododendron forests; musk deer and Himalayan bear are not far away. Landslides are quite common. The grey stone Rudranth temple has the Rudraganga flowing by it. The views of the Nandadevi, Trisul, Hathi Parbat peaks and down to the small lakes glistening in the surrounding are fantastic. **Kalpeshwar** (2,100m) near Joshimath, is the only one of the Panch Kedars accessible throughout the year. Its position overlooking the Urgam valley offers beautiful views of the Garhwal's most fertile region with its terrace cultivation of rice, wheat and vegetables.

Rudraprayag to Badrinath

Along the Pilgrim Road, about midway between Rudraprayag and Karnaprayag you pass **Gauchar**, famous locally for its annual cattle fair. The valley is wider here providing the local population with very good agricultural land. The beautiful Pindar River joins the Alaknanda at **Karnaprayag** (788m, 17 km), while **Nandaprayag** is the confluence with the Mandakini River. All these places have GMVN accommodation.

Chamoli (960m, 40 km) is the principal market for the Chamoli Dist though the HQ is Gopeshwar on the hillside opposite. The valley walls are now much higher and steeper and the road twists and turns more. Troop movements up to the border with Tibet/China are common and military establishments are a frequent site on the Pilgrim road. From Chamoli onwards the road is an impressive feat of engineering.

Joshimath (1,875m, 243 km) is at the junction of 2 formerly important Trans-Himalayan trading routes. Beyond Badrinath is the Mana Pass. To your right along the valley of the **Dhauliganga** is the **Niti Pass**. **NB**: Niti Valley is partially open to group tourists; permits required. The route over the Niti Pass (5,067m) into W Tibet leads to the **Mount Kailas** (6,890m), sacred to Hindus and Buddhists, and **Lake Manasarovar**.

12 km and a steep downhill stretch brings the road from Joshimath to **Vishnuprayag** at the bottom of the gorge – the winter headquarters of the Rawal of Badrinath. Vishnuprayag is the confluence of the Alaknanda and Dhauliganga rivers. **Accommodation** Above the town, **E** *Tourist Rest House*, T 81. 15 rm, some deluxe with bath, and dorm.

Buses for Badrinath, along the narrow hair-raising route start around 0600, the one-way flow regulated by police. You travel through precipitous gorges, past another Hanuman Chatti with a temple and climb above the treeline to reach the most colourful of the *Char Dhams*, in the valley.

The **Bhotias**, a border people with Mongoloid features and strong ties with Tibet – see page 669 – live along these passes. The women wear distinctive Arab-like headdress. Like their counterparts in the E Himalaya, they used to combine high altitude cultivation with animal husbandry and trading, taking manufactured goods from India to Tibet and returning with salt and borax. When the border closed following the 1962 Indo-Chinese War, they were forced to seek alternative income and some were resettled by the government.

Auli, (2,519m) 16 km from Joshimath, and a 5 km trek. The extensive meadows at Auli on the way to the Kauri Pass had been used for cattle grazing by the local herders. After the Indo-China War (1962) a road was built from Joshimath to Auli and in the 1970s a Writer Craft Centre was set up for the Indo-Tibetan Border Police at Auli. With panoramic views of mountains and good slopes it is being developed as a skiing resort by GMVN and UP Tourism. India's 1st ski lift (150m) was opened here in Feb 1993. **Transport**: Local jeeps/ taxis from Joshimath to Auli; a cable car to take people up from Joshimath has been commissioned recently. Also regular buses from Rishkesh (253 km), Haridwar (276 km).

Badrinath

Badrinath (3150m) is 301 km from Haridwar. The Hindu *Shastras* enjoin that no pilgrimage would be complete without a visit to Badrinath, the abode of Vishnu. Along with **Ramesvaram**, **Dwarka** and **Puri** it is one of the 4 holiest places in India – see page 71. According to the *Skanda Purana* "There are many shrines on earth, heaven and hell, but none has been, nor will be, like Badrinath". Guarding it are the Nar and Narayan ranges and in the distance towers the magnificent Nilkanth (6558m) peak. The word *Badri* is derived from a wild fruit that Vishnu was said to have lived on when he did penance at Badrivan, the area which covers all 5 important temples including Kedarnath. Shankaracharya, the monist philosopher from S India, is credited with establishing the 4 great pilgrimage centres in the early 9th century AD. See page 70.

The main **Badrinath Temple** is small and brightly painted in green, blue, pink, yellow, white, silver and red. The shrine is usually crowded with worshippers. The *Rawal* (Head Priest) hails from a Namboodri village in Kerala, the birthplace of Shankaracharya. Badrinath is snowbound over winter and open from late Apr to Nov. After worshipping in the temple and dispensing alms to the official (and wealthy) temple beggars outside, it is customary to bathe in **Tapt Kund**, a hot pool nearby, below the temple. This is fed by a hot sulphurous spring in which Agni (the god of fire) resides by kind permission of Vishnu. The temperature is around 45°C. **Accommodation E** *Devlok*, T 12. 30 large rm. Restaurant. Best in the trekking area. For pilgrims: *dharamshalas* and *chattis* (resthouses) here as elsewhere.

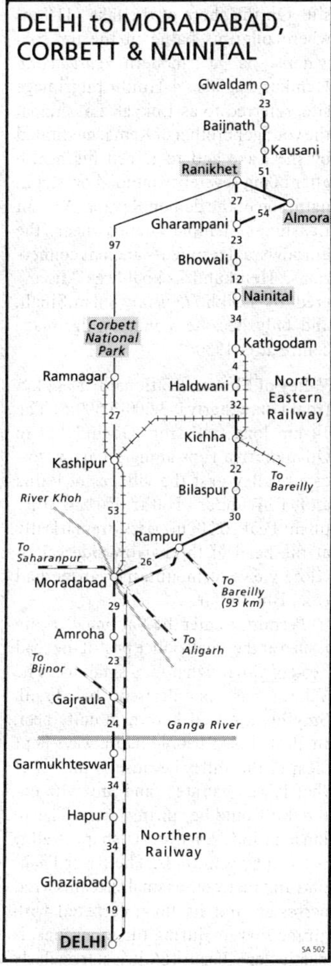

Hemkund and the Valley of Flowers

From **Govindghat** (1,828m), 20 km from Joshimath on the road to Badrinath, a bridle track leads to the Valley of Flowers (19 km) and short diversion from the main track goes to Hemkund Sahib. You can trek or hire mules for the 2-day journey. The 1st day is a 14 km walk to **Ghanghariya** (3,048m). **Accommodation** At Govindghat and Ghanghariya Forest Rest House and a Sikh *gurudwara* offering free accommodation and food to all travellers (donations accepted). Along the route are several tea-stalls.

Hemkund (4 km, 4,329m) Leave the main Valley of Flowers track, up a path to the right. Guru Gobind Singh – see page 92 – is believed to have sat here in meditation during a previous incarnation. It is an important Sikh pilgrimage site. On the shore of the lake (4340m) where pilgrims bathe in the icy cold waters, is a modern *gurudwara*. Hemkund is also a Hindu pilgrimage site, referred to as Lokpal. Lakshman, the younger brother of Rama, meditated by the Lake and re-gained his health after being severely wounded by Meghnath, son of the demon Ravana. A small Lakshman temple stands near the gurudwara. Despite its ancient connections, Hemkund/Lokpal was 'discovered' by a Sikh *Havildar*, Solan Singh, and only became a major pilgrimage centre after 1930.

Valley of Flowers National Park (4 km from Ghanghariya; 3,000-3,600m) The 14 km long trail from Govindghat to Ghanghariya runs along a narrow forested valley past the villages of Pulna and Bhiyundar. Hathi Parbat (Elephant Peak, 6,700m) rises dramatically at the head of the narrow side valley. Close views of mountains can be had from Bhiyundar.

Permits to enter the National Park are issued at the small police post at the road head of Govindghat for a small fee. The Valley was popularised by **Frank Smythe**, the well known mountaineer, in 1931. Local people had always kept clear of the Valley because of the belief that it was haunted, and any who entered it would be spirited away. The 10 km long and 2 km wide 'U' shaped valley is laced by waterfalls. The River Pushpati and many other small streams wind across it, and its floor, carpeted with alpine flowers during the monsoons, is particularly beautiful. It is particularly popular because of its accessibility. **NB:** camping overnight in the valley (or taking pack animals) is prohibited.

Satopanth is a glacial lake, 25 km from Badrinath which takes a day to reach. **NB:** restricted entry. You follow the track along the Alaknanda valley, a gentle climb up to **Mana** village, (6 km N) inhabited by Bhotias. Nearby is the cave where Vyasa is said to have written commentaries on the epic poems of Hinduism. The track disappears and you cross a snowbridge, trek across flower-filled meadows before catching sight of the impressive 44m **Vasudhara Fall**. The ascent becomes more difficult as you approach the source of the Alaknanda near where the Satopanth and Bhagirath Kharak glaciers meet. The remaining trek takes you across the **Chakra Tirth** meadow and over the steep ridge of the glacier till you see the striking green Satopanth Lake. According to legend its 3 corners mark the seats of Brahma, Vishnu and Siva. The peaks of Swargarohini (7898m) from which the glacier flows, Nilkanth (6558m) and Chaukhamba (7164m) make a spectacular sight.

DELHI TO NAINITAL, ALMORA & RANIKHET

If you travel E from Delhi you can visit the hill stations of **Nainital**, **Almora** and **Ranikhet** and the Kumaon region of the UP Himalaya. The road goes through irrigated farm land before climbing to the hills and lakes. Roads are often very busy.

ROUTES Leaving Delhi on NH24, you cross the Yamuna river to Ghaziabad (19 km).

Ghaziabad

(*Pop* 520,000) This is a modern satellite town for Delhi of tall blocks and low-rise buildings – low-cost housing, all made of brick or reinforced concrete, with little or no aesthetic appeal. Even the most modest houses now have TVs. Beyond Ghaziabad is countryside, an area where 2 crops are cultivated each year, mostly rice in the monsoon and wheat in winter, but also sugar cane. Countless bullock carts trundle along the highway and line up outside the refineries. **Accommodation D** *Shipra*, T 8714165. 21 rm. Modern, business hotel.

Hapur

(34 km, *STD Code* 0122) A typical market centre. The main streets are lined with small shops, street artisans, fruit sellers and vegetable stalls.

The road crosses the Ganga just after passing **Garmukhteswar** (34 km, *Pop* 25,000). The small town, with some typical N Indian temples, stands on the W bank, with riverside ghats. According to the *Mahabharata*, this is where King Santanu met the Goddess Ganga in human form. Each year at the full moon in Oct/Nov, thousands of pilgrims converge to bathe in the holy waters. From the road bridge you may see turtles swimming around in the green-brown waters below.

Gajraula

Just beyond the river is Gajruala (24 km), a popular truck stop. The centre of this one street town has a number of restaurants. The best is the *Hi-Way Café* on the right by the petrol pumps. For those wishing to stop the night, the **C** *Highway Motel* has comfortable rm. Can reserve in Delhi, T 6886808, F 6886122. There is a respectable toilet behind the filling station. Carry on through Gajraula and Amroha (23 km) to Moradabad (29 km).

Moradabad

(*Pop* 435,000; *STD Code* 0591), a large provincial town, railway junction and traffic bottleneck, especially around the bus stand near the station. It was founded in 1625 by the Mughal general Rustam Khan, who named it after Prince Murad Baksh, one of Shah Jahan's 4 sons. The **Jama Masjid** (1634) lies N of the ruined fort which is by the **River Ramganga**. There is also the **Tomb of Nawab Azmat-ulla Khan**, a former governor, and the **American Church** (mid 19th century). Moradabad is noted for its inlaid tin, brass and bell metal. **Accommodation D** *Maharaja* Station Rd, T 24283. 20 rm (4 a/c). Restaurant, BA booking agent, exchange, shop. *Loveena Restaurant*, 500m beyond bus stand.

ROUTES Leaving Moradabad, you have the choice of continuing on **NH24** to **Haldwani** and **Kathgodam** and then up to **Nainital**, or turning left and driving N via Kashipur to Ramnagar and the **Corbett National Park**, see page 248. From Corbett there is a direct road to Ranikhet, and if you backtrack to Ramnagar you can reach Nainital via Kaladhungi by an attractive metalled forest road. Continuing along the **NH24** the road passes through Rampur (26 km).

Rampur

(*STD Code* 0595) This town was founded in 1623 by Shah Alam and Hussain Khan, 2 Afghan Rohillas who had sought service with the Mughals. Under Shah Alam's grandson, Ali Muhammad Khan, the Rohillas were united in what was to become known as *Rohilkhand* and later expanded their empire to Almora in the N and Etawah in the S. On the death of Najib-ud-daula in 1772 the region was invaded by the Marathas. With the Nawab of Oudh's and British support the Marathas were beaten off but afterwards the Rohillas fell foul of Oudh and in the ensuing Rohilla War (1773-4) the empire was lost and later dismantled. The Nawab of Rampur remained loyal to the British during the Mutiny and supported them in the 2nd Afghan War and was rewarded with a grant of new territory.

Places of interest

There is an extensive **palace** and **fort**. The **State library** has oriental manuscripts and an excellent collection of 16th-18th centuries portraits, including a contemporary painting of Babur and a small book of Turki verse with notes by both Babur and Shah Jahan.

Local information

● Accommodation

D *Modipur*, Modipur (5 km rly), T 4047. 22 rm. Restaurant, tennis.

E *Tourist*, Station Rd, T 4644. 34 rm. Restaurant.

ROUTES In Rampur take the left fork to **Bilaspur** (30 km; *Pop* 26,000; *STD Code* 07752), one of many sites in the upper Ganga valley which have revealed Painted Grey Ware pottery, see page 300. It was an essentially Iron Age culture. Continue to **Kichha** (22 km) where the main road turns N to **Haldwani** (32 km, *STD Code* 05946891), an important market town and transhipment centre at the foot of the hills. Accommodation: D *Saurabh Mountview*, Haldwani. T 05946891 51. 49 rm. Restaurant, bar.

The land between Rampur and Haldwani used to be covered in jungle known as the *terai*. This once extended unbroken from the gorge below Haridwar to the NE corner of Bihar and was approximately 50 km wide. Under natural conditions it consisted of tall elephant grass and thick *sal* (*Shorea robusta*) forest and was both malarial and tiger infested. It was largely impenetrable and provided an effective natural barrier to communication between the hills and plain. It was only cleared after Independence in 1947. Large numbers of refugees – especially Sikhs – settled here following Partition and converted the forest into good agricultural land. The Corbett National Park and Dudhwa National Park are the last extensive tracts of terai in India. As you drive across this belt the Himalayan foothills appear out of the haze.

Kathgodam

(4 km from Haldwani) This town is the railhead for Nainital (34 km). The climb from Kathgodam to Nainital is dramatic, rising 1300m over 30 km. The road follows the valley of the Balaya stream then winds up the hillsides. Forest and small villages are interspersed. After the long drive the town appears suddenly. It is situated round the lake (*tal*), the land S and on the plains side falling away quite steeply so you only see the lake when you are at its edge.

Nainital

BASICS *Population*: 31,000. *Altitude*: 1,938m. *STD Code*: 05942. *Season*: Apr-May (May and Jun are very busy) and Oct-Nov. Nainital is 306 km NE of Delhi. The nearest airport is Pantnagar (71 km) on the plains.

Set around the 1.5 km long and 500m wide Naini Lake is the charming hill station of Nainital. Lawns with villas, bungalows and larger buildings occupy the tree covered hillsides encircling the lake. 150 years ago there was a small hamlet which was 'discovered' in 1841 by a P Barron, a sugar manufacturer from Saharanpur. He was impressed by the lake and returned with a sailing boat a year later, the boat being carried up in sections from the plains. The spot was developed as a Hill Station, in due course becoming the summer capital of the then United Provinces (see also Shimla, page 515). An old legend of Siva and Sati (see page 228) associates this place as where Sati's eyes fell (hence *naina*). The lake (*tal*) is surrounded by 7 hills, the *Sapta-Shring.*

On 18th Sep 1880, disaster struck the township. At the N end of the Lake, known now as Mallital (the southern part is Tallital) stood the *Victoria Hotel*. In 2 days nearly 1000 mm rain fell leading to a landslip at 1000m which crushed some outhouses, burying several people. At 1330 the cliff overhanging the hotel

CLIMATE: NAINITAL

	Jan	Feb	Mar	Apr	May	Jun	Jul	Aug	Sep	Oct	Nov	Dec	Av/Tot
Max (°C)	10	13	17	21	24	24	21	21	21	19	16	13	18
Min (°C)	2	4	8	12	15	17	17	16	15	10	6	3	10
Rain (mm)	117	44	54	25	75	273	769	561	331	305	7	35	2496

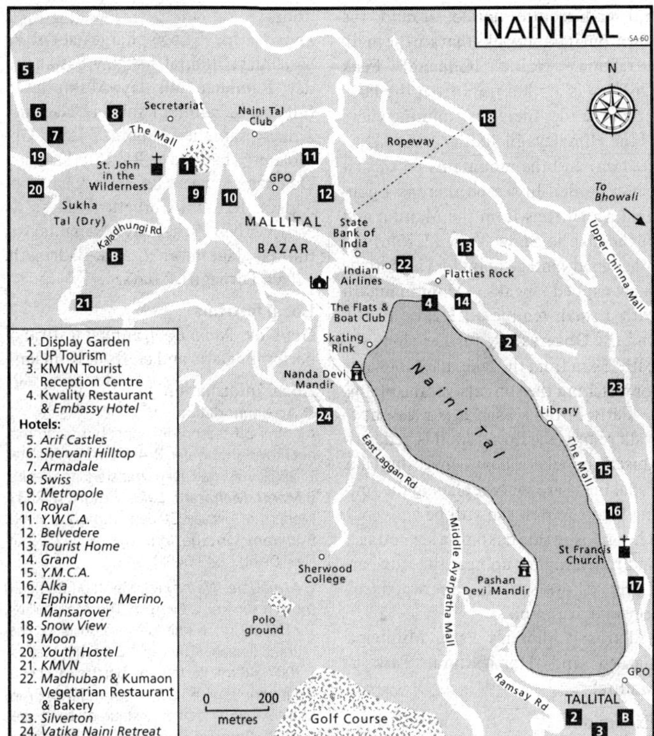

collapsed, burying the soldiers and civilians engaged in rescue work and making it impossible to save the 150 buried. Later the area was levelled, became known as The Flats and was used for public meetings, festive occasions and impromptu games of football and cricket. Today it is more a bus park in the tourist season.

Nainital is popular, especially in May, Jun, Sep and Oct, when accommodation is difficult and prices soar. Congestion and pollution is taking its toll; the Tal, now ⅓ its original size is unable to cope with the increased tourist traffic which has seen a building boom around it. The pony riders, curio-sellers and snack stalls increase in number while the lake water becomes unable to support fish. Out of season Nainital is pleasanter; the town has some attractive walks and there are only a few foreign tourists.

Places of interest

There is little of architectural interest other than the colonial style villas overlooking the lake. The **Church of St John in the Wilderness** (1846), one of the earliest buildings, is beyond Mallital below the Nainital Club. The most distinctive building is **Government House** (1899, now the Secretariat) which was designed in stone by FW Stephens who also responsible for VT and Churchgate Stations in Bombay.

There are other examples of colonial

hill architecture dotted around the town, but it is the walks that are the main attraction. **Naina (Cheena) Peak** (2610m) is a 5 km walk from the lake. From the top, there are stunning views of the Himalaya including Nanda Devi (7816m) and the mountains on the Tibetan border. In season there is a gondola which runs from the Mallital end of the lake to **Snow View** (2270m) another good vantage point for viewing the snow-capped peaks. **Hanumangarh** with a small temple off Haldwani Rd, and the **Observatory** further along the path (3 km from the lake) have lookouts for watching the sun set over the plains.

Early in the season it is pleasant to walk round (the Lower Mall is pedestrianised) or take a boat across the lake. Pedal boats are sadly replacing the rowing boats. March can still be very cold. The opposite side has only a few cottages and much higher up near the ridge are 2 private boys' schools – Sherwood College and St Joseph's.

Parks Children's Park, Municipal Garden and Horticultural Park at Mallital.

Excursions

The Nainital region is called the Switzerland of Asia because of the presence of so many lakes. Govt Tourist Reception Centres (TRCs) offer basic accommodation (see under hotels below). **Sat Tal** (21 km) has 7 lakes. The best known is the jade green Garud Tal after Vishnu's vehicle, followed by the olive green Rama Tal and Sita Tal.

• **Accommodation**: Sita Tal has a 4 roomed **E** *Tourist Bungalow* (KMVN).

Bhim Tal (23 km) is a large lake in an amphitheatre of hills with a wooded island which is a popular picnic spot. Restaurant, boating and fishing.

Naukuchiya (26 km) is a lake with 9 corners, hence the name. Row and paddle boats available.

Tours

Parvat Tours, T 2656 charges about Rs 60-80/day; Bhimtal, half day; Sattal, full day; Ranikhet, full day; Mukteshwar, full day; Kaladhungi, full day; Kausani, 2 days; Ranikhet/Almora, 2 days; Observatory, half day (Rs 15); Kumaon Darshan, 3 days (Rs 330); Chaukori, 3 days; Kausani/Corbett, 3 days (Rs 350); Corbett Park, 2 days; Nanakmatta, full day; Jageshwar, 2 days; Badrinath, 4 days; Purnagiri, 2 days.

Local festivals

Oct/Nov: *Naini Devi*, annual festival of performing arts and crafts of Kumaon.

Local information

• Accommodation

All offer off-season discounts but some may not provide hot water. **B** *Arif Castles*, Mallital. T 2801. 66 rm. Jeep transfers to centre. **B** *Manu Maharani Lake Resort*, T 2531. Modern nr Display Garden with good views. **B** *Vikram Vintage Inn*, Mallital. T 2877 (in New Delhi, T 643 6451). 34 rm.

C *Armadale*, Waverly Rd, Mallital. T 2855. 20 rm. Rm service. **C** *Everest*, The Mall, Tallital. T 2453. 47 rm in unimpressive building. Restaurant (Indian, Chinese). **C** *Royal*, Mallital. T 2007. 46 rm. Restaurant, bar, travel, sports. Indifferent service. **C** *Shervani Hilltop Inn*, Mallital. T 2504. 20 rm. Restaurant, bar, travel, heating. **C** *Vatika Naini Retreat*, Ayarpattha Slopes, T 2105. 31 rm, some with good views. Good restaurant, bar. Quiet. **C** *Belvedere*, above Bank of Baroda, Mallital, T 2082. Comfortable rm with good views of the lake, in former Raja's summer palace – a colonial building with pleasant garden. Restaurant. Quiet. May reserve in Delhi T 6886909, F 6886122.

D *Alka* and *Annexe*, The Mall, Tallital. T 2220. 72 rm. Floating restaurant on lake. **D** *Belvedere*, above Mallital Bazar, T 2082. Faded glory. However, some rm have good views. **D** *Swiss*, Mallital. T 2603. 18 rm. Dining hall, travel, guides for wildlife viewing, garden. **D** *Grand*, The Mall nr Flatties Rock, T 2406. Colonial style. **D** *Silverton*, Sher-Ka-Danda, T 2249. 27 rm in 'chalet', some with good views. 2.5 km centre, peaceful. Veg restaurant. **D** *Empire*, Tallital, T 2325. Clean, friendly, rec.

Kumaon Tourism's **D** *Tourist Reception Centres (TRCs)* nr Sukhatal Bus Stand, T 2374. 20 rm with bath, some with TV. Restaurant, gardens. Good value. One nr Tallital Bus Stand, T 2570, has 8-bed dorms. Hot water, good value.

● **Budget hotels**

TRCs at locations nearby, offer **E/F** accommodation, incl dorm: Bhimtal, T 25, Sattal, T 47, Bhowali, T 74, Kathgodam, T 2245, Kashipur, T 86392, Tanakpur, T 108 and Nanakmatta, T 39. All have restaurants or rm service. **E** ***Madhuban***, Mallital nr Ropeway, T 2295. Some reasonable rm with bath.

F ***YWCA***, nr Mallital Bazar, T 2657. **F** ***Youth Hostel***, W of Mallital Bazar, T 2353. 2 rm, 5 and 8-bed dorms. Open to non-members, book 15 days ahead. **F** ***Moon*** before the YH has good value rm, some with bath. Veg restaurant. Only drawback is distance from the lake (30 min on foot).

● **Places to eat**

Most are at the N end of the lake, on the Mall. Out of season, some offer a limited menu. *Kwality*, serving good Indian food is ideally located on the lake. Opp, the popular *Nanak* serves Western fast food. *Purohit* nearby is rec for veg menu, as is *Sher-e-Punjab*, Mallital Bazar. A little further towards Ropeway *Kumaon Farm Products* is good. Also the bakery nearby. **Indian and Continental**: *Capri* and *Embassy*, Mallital; **Indian**: *New Sher-e-Punjab*; *Tandoor*, Tallital; **Vegetarian**: *Apar Vihar*; *Thal*; *Paradise*, Mallital. **Chinese**: *Heritage*.

● **Banks & money changers**

Several on the Mall.

● **Hospitals & medical services**

BD Pande Govt Hospital, Mallital, T 2012; *GB Pant Hospital*, Tallital, T 2388.

● **Mountaineering & trekking**

Equipment can be hired from the *Nainital Mountaineering Club* and *KMVN*, Tourist Reception Centre, Mallital. The Club organises rock climbing at Barapathar, 3 km away.

● **Post & telecommunications**

Head Post Office: Mallital; Branch at Tallital.

● **Shopping**

Bazars at Tallital and Mallital, the latter being more extensive. Souvenir shops on the Mall: *UP Brassware*, Mallital; *Garud Woollens*, Mallital; *UP Handlooms*, The Mall; *Gandhi Ashram*, Mallital. Along the far edges of the Flats are Tibetan refugee stalls selling woollen and acrylic shawls. *Kumaon Woollens* in the Mallital Bazar sell shawls and locally made tweed – see also Almora, below.

Photography: *Kala Mandir*, The Mall.

● **Sports**

Fishing: permits for Nainital Lake from Executive Officer, Nagar Palika. For other lakes Fisheries Officer, Bhimtal. Boat hire from Boat Club, Mallital.

Yacht hire: from Yacht Club.

● **Tour companies & travel agents**

Kumaon Tourism's *Parvat Tours*, Tallital nr Rickshaw Stand, T 2656; Several others on the Mall.

● **Tourist offices**

UP Govt, Mallital, T 2337; **Information Centre**, (KMVN), Dandi House, Tallital, T 2656; **KMVN**, Secretariat Bldg, Mallital, T 2543.

● **Useful addresses**

Police: T 2424; **Fire**: T 2626; **Ambulance**: T 2012.

● **Transport**

Nainital is connected by good all-weather roads to major centres in N India. During the monsoon (Jun-Sep) landslips are fairly common. Usually these are promptly cleared but in the case of severe slips requiring days to clear, bus passengers are transferred. From Delhi (322 km); Bareilly (141 km); Lucknow (401 km); Almora (66 km); Ranikhet (60 km); Kausani (120 km); Corbett (Dhikala 128 km). **Warning** The hill roads can be dangerous. Flat, straight stretches are extremely rare, road lighting does not exist and villagers frequently drive their animals along them or graze them at the kerbside. Wherever possible, avoid night driving.

Local Ropeway carriages: run by KMVN from Poplars, Mallital (nr GB Pant Statue) to Snow View. Summer 0800-1800, Winter 0930-1600. Return fare Rs 30. **NB:** Some claim its anchorage is weak. **Cycle-rickshaws, horses, boats and dandis**: rates negotiable. **Coaches and taxis**: are available from Parvat Tours, Tallital, T 2656. Coach full day Rs 900 (120 km); about Rs 6/km in hills (less in plains). **Taxis**: full day Rs 300 (120 km), about Rs 3/km.

Air The nearest airport is Pantnagar (71 km). Parvat Tours run transfer coaches to Nainital (2 hr). Reservations: KMVN, T 2570. 1000-1600.

Train The nearest railhead is Kathgodam (34 km) on metre gauge. Reservations: UP Roadways, Tallital, T 2518. **Lucknow**: *Nainital Exp* 5307, daily, 1935, 11 hr. **Bareilly Junc**: *Kumaon*

Exp 5312, daily, 1750, $3^{1}/_{4}$ hr. **Agra Fort**: *Kumaon Exp* 5312, daily, 1750, $12^{3}/_{4}$ hr. **For Delhi**: travel to Bareilly Junc.

Road UP Roadways, Tallital, for major inter-city services, T 2518. 0930-1200, 1230-1700; DTC, *Hotel Ashok*, Tallital, T 2180. Kumaon Motor Owners' Union (KMOU), bus stand nr TRC, Sukhatal, Mallital, used by private operators. Regular services to Lucknow, Bareilly, Delhi, Haridwar, Dehra Dun, Almora, Ranikhet and Ramnagar. A/c night coaches from Delhi.

Almora and Baijnath

ROUTES From Nainital it is an attractive 66 km drive to Almora passing through **Bhowali** (12 km W of Nainital). The road winds through attractive pine mixed forest with good views down towards Kathgodam and the plains. Bhowali is a small subsidiary market well known in the past for its sanatorium and apple orchards. There is a direct road from Haldwani to Bhowali which by-passes Nainital, convenient for travellers bound for Almora. Below Bhowali in the valley of Kosi River is **Gharampani**, a popular refreshment stop. The road then runs along the the Kosi passing refreshing rock pools, riverside terraced fields and small meadows, before beginning the long gradual climb to Almora. About 5 km before you reach the town proper there is a toll barrier and just beyond is the Almora by-pass forking off to the left. Take this to avoid the town's congested main street.

Almora

(*Pop* 27,000; *Alt* 1646m; *STD Code* 05962) 66 km from Nainital, Almora was founded by the Chand dynasty in 1560. The Chands ruled over most of Kumaon which comprises the present districts of Nainital, Almora and Pithoragarh, and Almora still claims to be the cultural capital of the area. Traces of the old Chand fort, paved roads, wooden houses with beautifully carved façades and homes decorated with traditional murals reflect its heritage. Overrun by the Gurkhas in 1798, it suffered heavy bombardment by the British as they endeavoured to expel the Gurkhas in the Gurkha Wars of 1814-15. Now it is an important market town and administrative centre with an agricultural research station.

Places of interest

The picturesque old part of the town is along the ridge. The main thoroughfare runs around the horse-shoe shaped ridges about 100m below the ridgeline. Swami Vivekenanda came to Almora and gained enlightenment in a small cave at **Kasar Devi** on Kalmatiya Hill, 6 km outside the town. Good views. Another vantage point for sunrise and sunset is Bright End Corner, 2 km. The **Udyotchandesvar Temple** houses Kumaon's presiding deity, Nanda Devi, whose festival is in Aug/Sep.

Almora's *Tamta* artisans still use traditional methods to work with copper. Copper metallurgy was known to the people here as early as the 2nd century B.C. and is associated with the Kuninda Dynasty who traded in copper articles. The handbeaten copper pots are 'silver plated' in the traditional way (*Kalhai*). Visit *Ashok Traders* on LR Shah Rd. Just above the *Holiday Home* there is the factory for Kumaon Woollens which produces and sells tweed in the Harris Tweed style. Locally knitted jumpers and the traditional Panchmarhi shawls ('5 weave') in soft wool are popular. Gold and silver jewellery and bowls carved out of salwood from Piltoragarh are particularly fine.

Museums

Govt Museum, nr Bus Stand. 1030-1630, closed Mon. Contains archaeological pieces from 11th century Katyuri and the Chand era.

Excursions

Katarmal, 17 km, has a Katyuri sun temple with exemplary sculpture. **Jageswar**, 34 km, famous for the 164 ornamented temples built by the Chand rajas, has one of the 12 *jyotirlingas*.

Local information

● Accommodation

E *Holiday Home* (KMVN), T 2250. 7 cottages and 18 rm with bath. Restaurant. Overlooking Kosi valley, good mountain views. 2 km bus stand, nr Kumaon Woollens factory. TV lounge. Rec. **E** *Savoy*, T 2329, has 15 rm. Also **F** *Forest Rest House*, T 2065.

● Services

Civil Hospital, T 2322. **Banks** with foreign exchange facilities. **Head Post Offfice** on The Mall. UP **Tourist Office**: T 2180. **Foreigners' Registration Office**: Police Station nr Almora Inter-College.

ROUTES Leaving Almora, the road descends to cross the Kosi river where there is a turnoff for Ranikhet. If you are proceeding N and further into the hills, the road follows the river, crosses the broad fertile valley at **Someswar** with its fine Siva temple in the Katyur style, then climbs to Kausani.

Kausani

(1890m, 51 km from Almora). Kausani sits on a narrow ridge among pine forests. From here there are excellent 300 km wide views of the **Nanda Devi** group of mountains, especially at sunrise. You may trek from here to Bageswar, Gwaldam and the Pindari Glacier. Mahatma Gandhi spent 12 days here in 1929 during which time he wrote his commentary on the Gita-Anashakti Yoga. The guesthouse where he stayed is now the Anashakti Ashram. Hindi poet-laureate Sumitra Nandan Pant was born at Kausani.

Local information

● Accommodation

E *Tourist Bungalow* (KMVN), T 26, 2 km from town. 6 cottages and dorm. Restaurant. Compass on the lawn to spot the peaks. **E** PWD *Guest House*.

F *Uttarkhand* is highly rec as excellent value. Other cheap hotels incl *Neelkanth Tourist Lodge*, *Prashant* and *Amar Holiday Home*.

Baijnath (1125m) From Kausani, the road descends to Baijnath (17 km) and Garur. The small town with its distinctively carved 12th and 13th century Katyuri temples by the Gomti River, now mostly ruined, has houses with intricately carved wooden doors and windows, – see also Kulu Valley (page 523). The main 10th century temple houses a beautiful image of Parvati. The confluence of the Gomti and Garur Ganga is where Siva and Parvati are believed to have married. The valley was named Katyur after their son, Kartikeya; the Katyur dynasty ruled here for over 500 years. **Accommodation** KMVN *Tourist Bungalow*, and Irrigation *Inspection House*.

Just out of **Garur** is the turning for **Bageshwar** – a pilgrimage centre at the confluence of the Gomti and Sarayu rivers, and **Bharari** – see Gwaldam under Roopkund Trek, below. **Bageshwar** (named after Siva as Lord of Eloquent Speech) is Kumaon's most important pilgrimage centre and has several temples and 2 sacred pools. *Uttarayani Fair* (Jan) draws crowds from local villages who bring their handicrafts to sell. **Accommodation** KMVN *Tourist Bungalow*, T 34. 20 rm, where you can hire trekking equipment. Restaurant. If you carry on, after 30 km you will cross into Garhwal and reach Gwaldam.

Gwaldam (1950m), a small market strung out along a ridge surrounded by orchards. The British established tea plantations which have since been abandoned. **Accommodation** Garhwal Tourism's *Tourist Bungalow*. Splendid views from garden, especially at dawn and dusk, of Trisul (7120m) and Nanda Ghunti (6310m). Gwaldam, one of the starting points for the trek to Roopkund (see page 258), overlooks the beautiful Pindar River which the road follows down to its confluence with the Alaknanda River at **Karnaprayag**. The road joins the Pilgrim road. The Pilgrim Road runs from **Rishikesh** and **Haridwar** to **Badrinath**, see page 235.

Pithorgarh (*Pop* 22,000; *Alt* 1650m; *STD Code* 05964) E of Almora and 188 km by road from Nainital, sits in a small valley with some fine temples built by the Chands. It is overlooked by hill forts dating from times when the town was at the cross roads of trade routes. The district, separated from Almora in 1962, borders Nepal and Tibet and has a number of high peaks such as **Nanda Devi** East (7434m) and West (7816m) and offers trekking to many glaciers including **Milam**, **Namik**, **Ralam** and **Panchuli**. Panchuli (the 5 'chulas' or stoves of the 5 Pandavas!) whose last meal, according to legend, was cooked on these 5 fires before they departed for the heavens. The area is now completely open to individual trekkers; no permits required. Good views from Chandak (1890m, 7 km). It is also on the pilgrim road to Mt Kailash and Mansarovar Lake. The Mt Kailash trek starts from Askot and is organized jointly by Indian and Chinese authorities. **Accommodation** UP Tourism *Tourist Rest House*, T 2434. Restaurant. Also some basic hotels.

DELHI TO MORADABAD & CORBETT

The road gives an excellent view of the almost flat, fertile and densely populated Ganga- Yamuna doab, one of the most prosperous agricultural regions of UP and of N India. The Corbett National Park with its abundant wildlife is one of the finest in India.

ROUTES Leave Delhi over the Yamuna Bridge and follow the NH24 to Moradabad (see entry above). Only 1-2 km out of Moradabad travelling E turn left for Ramnagar (134 km).

Much of the way is across farmed land but the final stretch is through remnants of the terai. **Ramnagar** has little to commend it other than there being a branch railway line to Moradabad, the Project Tiger Office for Corbett National Park reservations and a night halt. If you are travelling to the Park without reserved accommodation, you must call here first to make a booking, otherwise you will not be admitted to the Park. The very good **E** *Tourist Reception Centre* (KMVN) with some a/c rm with bath and restaurant is ideal overnight accommodation.

ROUTES From Ramnagar it is 50 km to **Dhikala**, 32 km of which is inside the Park. Night driving is not allowed in the park.

Corbett National Park

Approach

Altitude: 400m – 1200m. *Area:* 500 sq km, of which 350 sq km is core reserve. A 900 sq km extension of the buffer zone is planned. Best season Jan-Jun. Summer is the best time for seeing the larger mammals which are bolder in forsaking the forest cover and coming to the river and water holes, early summer for scenic charm and floral interest. For bird-watching, Dec-Feb is best. Closed 15 Jun-15 Nov.

The main gate at Dhangarhi is approx 16 km N of Ramnagar on the Ranikhet road. Foreigners about Rs 20 per day, Indians Rs 12, students Rs 3. Vehicle charge: light (car, jeep) Rs 10, heavy (coach) Rs 50. Cine camera fee Rs 50. There is no entry to the Park from the Kalagarh side. From March 1st until the monsoon all roads around Dhikala except the main approach road are closed between 1100 -1500, and no visitors are allowed to move about the forest. Entry at any time is at the visitor's own risk.

NB: Only visitors who are staying overnight may enter Dhikala. 100 day visitors per day may enter Bijrani and Dhela (permits from Ramnagar before 1100 hr). Prior reservation is highly desirable for day visits. A reservation at the Bijrani or Dhela Forest rest Houses does not entitle visitors to enter by the Dhangari gate.

Background

Corbett is India's first national park and one of its finest. It is notable not only for its rich and varied wildlife and birdlife but also for its scenic charm and magnificent sub-montane and riverain views. Set up in 1936, in large part due to the efforts of Jim Corbett, this wildlife reserve was named Hailey National Park after the Governor of United Provinces. On Independence it was renamed the Ramganga National Park and later still the Corbett National Park.

The park comprises the broad valley of the **Ramganga River** backing onto the forest covered slopes of the Himalayan foothills which rise to 1210m at Kanda Peak. Longitudinal ridges separate ravines and uplands. A dam at Kalagarh has created a large reservoir at the W end of the park. The Ramganga itself runs through high and narrow banks in places. The only perennial source of water, it meanders to the NW, creating a beautiful scene from Dhikala.

Wildlife – flora

There is an immensely rich flora – 110 species of trees, 51 species of shrubs, 33 species of bamboos and 27 species of climbers. The valley floor is covered with tall elephant grass (*Nall* in the local terminology), lantana bushes and patches of *sal* and *sheesham* (*Dalbergia sissoo*) forest, whilst the enclosing hills on both sides are completely forest covered, with *sal*, *bakli (Anogeissus latifolia)*, *khair (Acacia catechu)*, *jhingan (Lannea coromandelica)*, *tendu (Diospyros tomentosa)*, *pula (Kydia calycina)* and *sain (Terminalia tomentosa)*. Charas (cannabis) grows wild in the fields.

Nullahs and ravines running deep into the forests are dry for much of the year, but there are swift torrents during the monsoon. These hold brakes of bamboo and thick scrub growth. Rainfall varies, being heavier in the higher hills: on average the valley receives 1550 mm, the bulk from July to mid-Sep. Summer days are hot but the nights quite pleasant. Winter nights can get very cold and there is often a frost and freezing fog in the low lying tracts.

TIGER, TIGER, BURNING BRIGHT....

Jim Corbett was born in 1875 into the large family of Christopher Corbett, the postmaster at Nainital. Jim, the 8th child, was a 'domiciled' European. From childhood he was fascinated by the jungles around Nainital. This developed into a considerable knowledge of the ecosystem's workings. Like most ***pukka sahibs*** (proper gentlemen) he learnt to shoot and became a superb shot, killing his first leopard when he was eight. Tigers were his most sought after prey, followed by leopards which were very difficult to sight, let alone shoot.

This interest was sustained during his working life in the Bengal NE Railway and later as an advisor to the army. But from the mid-1920s he ceased to shoot tigers for sport and instead photographed them except to track and kill the man-eating leopards and tigers that terrorised the Kumaon hills from time to time. Later in life he recounted his exploits in a series of books about maneaters and the jungle: *The Man Eating Leopard of Rudrapayag, The Man-eaters of Kumaon* and *Jungle Lore*. For a biography of Corbett see *Carpet Sahib: The life of Jim Corbett* by Martin Booth.

Project Tiger Jim Corbett has always been an inspiration to India's conservationists, typified in Project Tiger. India's tiger population, estimated at 40,000 at the beginning of the century, dwindled to little over 1800 in 1972. On 1 April 1973, with World Wildlife Fund backing, Project Tiger was inaugurated in 9 parks, the aim being to preserve the rapidly dwindling population of tigers in India. The scheme was later extended to over 18 reserves. The results have been encouraging and the Indian tiger population has stabilised at nearly 4000. Corbett has over 80.

Wildlife – fauna

The fauna is as rich as the flora. The park has always been noted for its tigers which are seen quite frequently. There are leopards too but they are seldom seen. Sambar, chital, para (hog deer) and muntjac (barking deer) are the main prey of the big cats and their population fluctuates around 20,000. Some like the chital are highly gregarious whilst the large sambar, visually very impressive with its antlers, is usually solitary. The 2 commonly seen monkeys of N India are the rhesus (a macaque – reddish face and red brown body) and the common langur (black face, hands and feet and silvery coat). Elephants are now permanent inhabitants following the building of the dam and the inundation of their old trekking routes. There are now a few hundred and they are seen quite often. Other animals include porcupine, wild pigs (often seen around

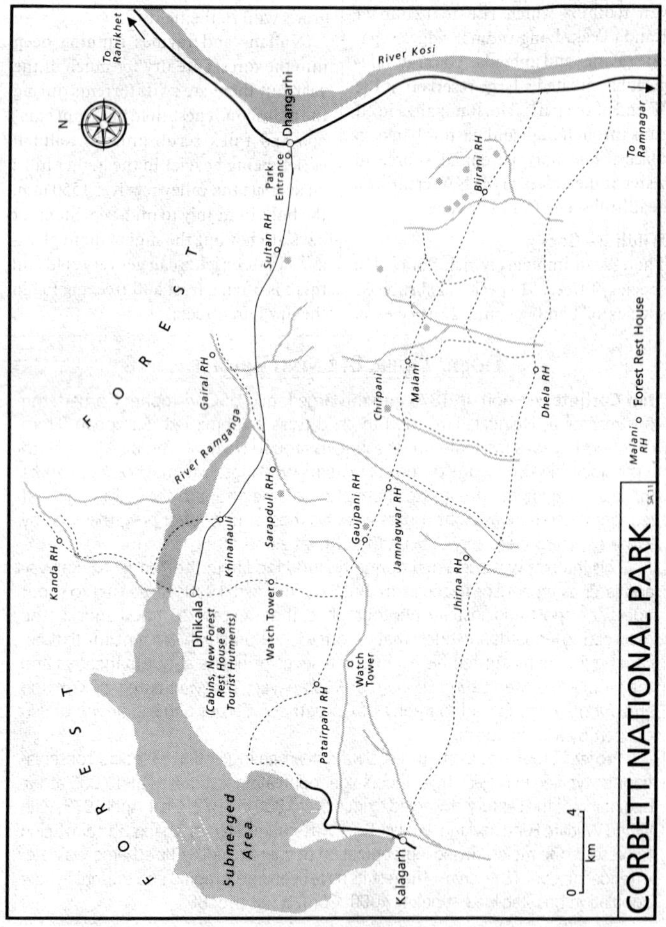

Dhikala) and fox. In total there are over 50 species of mammal alone. However, the Ramganga Dam is reputed to have caused significant losses. The last Swamp deer was seen in March 1978, and the loss of habitat has been keenly felt by the cheetal, hog deer and porcupine, all of which appear to be declining.

In certain stretches of the river and in the Ramganga lake are the common mugger crocodile (*Crocodylus palustris*), the fish eating gharial (*Gavialis gangeticus*), soft shelled tortoises in the streams, and otters. The river has mahseer, rohu, malli and gonchu. The python is quite common.

Wildlife – Birds

The birdlife is especially impressive with over 600 species and this includes a wide range of water birds, birds of prey such as the crested serpent eagle, harriers, Pallas' fishing eagle, osprey, buzzards and harriers. Vultures (the solitary black or king, cinereous and the Himalayan long-billed) are present. Woodland birds include: Indian and Great Pied hornbills, parakeets, woodpeckers, drongos, pies, flycatchers, laughing thrushes, babblers and cuckoos. Doves, bee-eaters, rollers, bulbuls, warblers, finches, robins and chats are to be seen in the open scrub.

Viewing

Elephant rides are available from Dhikala (Park has 6). This is the best way to see the jungle and the wildlife. Morning and evening, 2 hr, Rs 25 (foreigners), Rs 10 (Indians). Book at Dhikala Reception. Cars and jeeps may drive round part of the park but the jeep here is often under repair! Check with Reception.

NB: Apart from the immediate area around Dhikala, **do not go walking in the park**. Tiger and elephant attacks are not unknown.

Park information

Dhikala is the park centre and has accommodation. You can also use a good **library** on payment of a deposit. Wildlife films are also shown. Ramnagar is HQ of Corbett's Project Tiger and is an obligatory point for visiting the park. From Ramnagar it is 50 km to Dhikala. Night driving is not allowed in the park. If you have not reserved accommodation in the Park, you must call at Ramnagar first to make a booking.

NB: During the rainy season the park is closed; the 32 km road to **Dhikala** from the gate at **Dhangarhi** is almost impassable.

Conducted Tours

Garhwal Tourism run 3-day tours from Delhi departing every Fri in season. Reservations: UP Tourist Office, Chandralok Building, 36 Janpath, New Delhi. T 3322251.

● Accommodation

B *Corbett Jungle Resort* (Quality Inns), Kumeria Reserve Forest, T 85520, is about 10 km from the Dhangarhi entrance. Small, purpose-built cottages and tents, in pleasant surroundings on the edge of the Ramganga River. Full board only. Roof-top restaurant. Elephant rides (about Rs 200) are very pleasant but expensive.

C *Corbett Riverside Resort*, at Garija, PO Ramnagar, a few minutes' drive from the park. The resort is by the Kosi river, with comfortable rooms and suites. Meals included, TV in lounge, pleasant garden. Jeep and elephant safaris, mahaseer fishing, swimming and some watersports. Reservations, Dehli T 6886909, F 6886122.

Stay, if possible, in the park at Dhikala. **Note** Indians pay less. **At Dhikala**: **D** *New Forest Resthouse*, 4 suites, **E** *Old Rest House*, 5 suites. Reservations, Chief Conservator of Forests, 17 Rana Pratap Marg, Lucknow, T 246140. **D** *Annexe*, 7 suites and **D** *Cabin 3* with 2 suites. Reservations, UP Tourist Office, Chandralok Bldg, 36 Janpath. **D** *Cabin 1 and 4*, 3 suites each, **E** *Tourist Hutment*, 5 suites, **F** *Green Hut*, 1 4-bed suite and **F** *Loghuts*, 24 bunks. Reservations, Field Director, Project Tiger, Ramnagar. There is an extra charge for blankets. The restaurant is reasonably priced but has limited choice.

At Khinanauli: **D** *Forest Rest House*, 3 suites. Reservations, Chief Conservator of Forests, 17 Rana Pratap Marg, Lucknow, T 246140.

At Bijrani, Sarapduli, Sultan, Gairal: there

are good **F** *Forest Rest Houses* but some have no catering. Bring sleeping bag and food. All accessible by afternoon bus except Gairal. Bijrani involves a 6 km walk but the double rm have bath and the staff are very friendly and helpful. Catering available. Free blankets, though you pay for electricity, so bring candles if you want to economise. Reservations, Field Director, Project Tiger, Ramnagar.

New hotels are planned outside the park. Reserve early with Chief Wildlife Warden, 17 Rana Pratap Marg, Lucknow, T 246140. Enquiries: Field Director, Project Tiger, Corbett National Park, Ramnagar, T 853189 or UP Tourism, Janpath, New Delhi.

● Transport

Air Nearest Phoolbagh airport is at Pantnagar (130 km) with services to Delhi. Transport to Corbett is difficult and lengthy. **Avoid this route**.

Train Nearest station is at Ramnagar (50 km), for connections with Moradabad and Lucknow.

Road Dhikala from Delhi (300 km) passes through Moradabad (turn left at 7th km after Moradabad, towards Kashipur and Ramnagar). **Bus**: Ramnagar has one afternoon bus to Moradabad and Ranikhet by metalled road, and to Dhikala by unmetalled road. Also buses to Delhi and Lucknow. Contact KMOU or UP Roadways Bus Stands at Ramnagar.

CORBETT TO NAINITAL& RANIKHET

It is possible to reach **Nainital** from Corbett via **Ramnagar** and **Kaladhungi** on a picturesque road.

Drive from Dhikala to Dhangarhi gate, on to Ramnagar and turn left. The road crosses the river which has a barrage and skirts along the edge of the hills. At **Kaladhungi** visit **Jim Corbett's house**, now a small museum. Turn up the road opposite and continue up into the hills, travelling along a delightful and well engineered metalled road that winds its way up the hillsides through *chir* pine (*Pinus longifolia*) forest and the occasional village. There are impressive views of the plains. You enter Nainital at the N (Mallital) end of the lake.

ROUTES If Ranikhet is your destination, go from Dhikala to Dhangarhi and turn left. Buses will pick up passengers for Ranikhet and intermediate points without you having to return to Ramnagar. This drive is very attractive as the road gradually climbs up to the first ridges of the Himalaya. The forest jungle looks drier and more open here than nearer Nainital but is just as impressive.

Ranikhet

(*Altitude* 1800m, *STD Code* 05966) No one knows the name of the queen whose field gave Ranikhet (The Queen's Field) its title. In 1869 the land was bought from local villagers and the British established a summer rest and recreation settlement for their troops, made it a cantonment town governed by the military authorities and developed it as a quiet hill station. Set along a 1800m high ride, Ranikhet sprawls out through the surrounding forest without having a proper centre. This is one of its attractions and there are many enjoyable walks.

At one time, Lord Mayo, Viceroy of India, was so enchanted with the place that he wanted to move the army's Summer Headquarters away from Shimla. That did not happen but Ranikhet became and still is the Regimental Centre for the Kumaon Regiment. The views from the ridge are magnificent and the twin peaks of Nanda Devi (7816m and 7434m) can be clearly seen. At **Upat** (6 km) there is a beautifully located 9-hole golf course, and **Chaubatia** (10 km) has a Govt Fruit Garden and Research Station. **Dwarkaghat** (38 km) has 55 architecturally interesting temples.

Local information

● Accommodation

D *West View*, MG Rd. T 2261. 19 rm. 5 km centre. Restaurant, exchange, golf club nearby.

E *Tourist Bungalows* (KMVN), T 2297. Pleasant rm with bath. Restaurant (mostly Indian). Attractive location in the upper cantonment with good views. Also **E** *Moon*, T 2382 and *Natraj*, in Sadar Bazar and **E** *Norton's* in Mall Rd.

● Services

All on the Mall: *Civil Hospital*, nr UP Roadways Bus Stand, T 2422. **Banks**: with foreign exchange facilities. **General Post Office**. UP **Tourist Office**: T 2227.

● Transport

Road Bus: regular buses to Ramnagar, Almora and Nainital operated by KMOU, T 2214, and UP Roadways, T 2516, with bus stands at each end of the Mall, and well connected by all-weather roads.

TREKKING IN THE GARHWAL AND THE KUMAON HIMALAYA

This region contains some of the finest mountains in the Himalaya and is highly accessible and yet surprisingly very few westerners visit it, many preferring to go to Nepal. Of the many treks available, 8 routes are included here which offer some of the most spectacular walking and scenery. See also 114

Exploration in Garhwal and Kumaon

This region had been open since the British took over in 1815 but it was abandoned by explorers in favour of the more mysterious Nepal. Much of the early Himalayan exploration was undertaken here. **Trisul** (7120m), after it had been climbed by Dr Tom Longstaff in 1906, remained the highest mountain climbed for the next 30 years. Famous mountaineers of the 1930s like Bill Tilman, Eric Shipton and Frank Smythe all marvelled at the beauty of the region and Edmund Hillary's first Himalayan peak was Mukut Parbat in Garhwal. Later climbers like Chris Bonington, Peter Boardman and Mick Tasker used alpine techniques to conquer Changabang and Dunagiri.

The scenic splendour of these mountains lies partly in the fact that the forests around the big peaks are still in marvellous condition and the local population are unaffected by the ravages of mass tourism. Also in Garhwal and Kumaon there are ranges that you can easily get among, enabling a greater feeling of intimacy with the alpine giants. The mountains have been described as 'a series of rugged ranges tossed about in the most intricate confusion' (Walton, 1910).

Trekking

Trekking in this region is not highly organized. There are now Govt regulation of porter's rates but traveller's accommodation is not widespread so you need to be well prepared. It is possible to do some treks (eg The Pindar Glacier trek) without a tent, but on other routes this will be very limiting. Communication is a problem as very few villagers speak English. The rewards for the well-equipped trekker who has planned carefully are great, especially the feeling of being far from the madding crowd.

Accommodation If you are travelling in small groups of 3-4 persons, it is often possible to get overnight accommodation in villagers' houses but despite their hospitality, this is uncomfortable. GMVN and KMVN *Tourist Rest Houses*, where available, provide rustic but clean rm (some deluxe rm with bath). Caretakers cook simple meals.

Best season

Feb/Mar: at lower altitudes for the spectacular rhododendrons; **Apr/May** at higher altitudes, though it can get very hot; and **Oct/Nov**, when temperatures are lower, the skies clearer and the the vegetation greener following the monsoon. The monsoon is good for alpine flowers but wet, humid and cloudy for much, though not all, of the time.

Trekking areas

Around **Gangotri and Yamunotri** in Garhwal there are a number of very good treks, some suitable for the independent or 'go-it-alone' trekker. **Nanda Devi** is the other area and this is mostly in Kumaon. There are far more treks than those indicated here. **NB:** you will not be allowed to go beyond Badrinath. Lower part of the Niti Valley is open to groups with requisite permits.

Gangotri and Yamunotri area

Gangotri to Gaumukh

The best known trek here is to **Gaumukh** (The Cow's Mouth) and, if desired, beyond onto the Gangotri Glacier. To Gaumukh can easily be undertaken in 3 days with minimal equipment (carry provisions), see below.

From Gangotri (3046m) follow the well-defined, gradually ascending path to **Bhojbasa** (3800m, 17 km, 5 hr), see page 235. **Chirbasa**, 4 km before Bhojbasa has a rustic *Forest Rest House*. Another at Bhojbasa has 4 rm and a dorm (bring sleeping bags). This, however, is more expensive and often full. You may hire 2-person tents for Rs 160/night (good value). There is an *ashram* where trekkers and pilgrims can stay. The 5 km to **Gaumukh** across boulder scree and moraine takes about 2 hr so it is quite feasible to go from Bhojbasa to Gaumukh, spend some time there then return the same day. There are plenty of tea houses en route. Gaumukh, the main source of the Ganga is at the mouth of the Gangotri glacier where blocks of glacier ice fall into the river and pilgrims cleanse themselves in freezing water. There are breathtaking views. Basic tent accommodation at Bhojbasa (not at Gaumukh).

Beyond Gaumukh (3969m) more care and camping equipment is required. The Gangotri Glacier is situated in an amphitheatre of 6500-7000m peaks which include Mana Parbat (6758m), Satopanth (7084m), Vasuki (6792m), Bhagirathi (6556m), Kedar Dome and the prominent trio of Bhagirathi I, II and III; Shivling (6543m), standing alone is one of the most spectacular peaks in the entire Himalaya.

Tapovan (4463m, 5 km) a grassy meadow on the E bank of the Gangotri glacier is the base camp for climbing expeditions to the stunningly beautiful Shivling (6543m), Siva's lingam and the 'Matterhorn of the Himalaya'. Accommodation in tiny *ashram*. You can either return the same way or make a round trip by crossing over the glacier to Nandanvan (4400m, 3 km) and going up to Vasuki Tal (6 km) beneath Vasuki peak (6792m); since the glacier crossing is fairly risky, it is recommended only for the experienced trekker. The return is via Nandanvan the W bank of the Gangotri glacier crossing the Raktvarn Glacier to Gaumukh; Raktvarn (red clothed) so called because of the rust coloured boulders in its moraine.

Gangotri to Kedartal

This is an excellent short trek with scenic variety and spectacular views but you must be aware of the problems associated with altitude and allow time for acclimatisation, (see Trekking, page 120). It requires a tent, stove and food. It is 17 km to Kedartal (5000m), a small glacial lake surrounded by Meru (6672m), Pithwara (6904m) and Bhrigupanth (6772m).

Leaving Gangotri you proceed up the gorge of the Kedar Ganga, Siva's contribution to the Bhagirathi river. It is 8 km to Bhoj Kharak and then a further 4 km to Kedar Kharak passing through some beautiful Himalayan birch forest (*Betula utilis*) en route. The bark from the trees (*bhoj* in Garhwali) was used by sages and hermits for manuscripts. From Kedar Kharak, where you can camp, it is a laborious 5 km ascent to Kedartal. Besides the peaks surrounding the lake you can also see the Gangotri range.

The return to Gangotri can be the same way or over the ridge separating the Kedartal from the Rudugaira Gad (river). This ridge is 700m above Kedartal and at least 5 hr should be allowed for the crossing. **Rudugaira Kharak** is the base camp for the peaks at the head of this valley. Coming down towards Gangotri you must cross to the opposite bank to avoid the cliffs on the W bank. Nearer Gangotri cross back to the W bank.

Gangori to Yamunotri via Dodital

This is a beautiful trek between Kalyani and Hanuman Chatti, a distance of 49 km. You can do a round trip from either end, allowing 5 days.

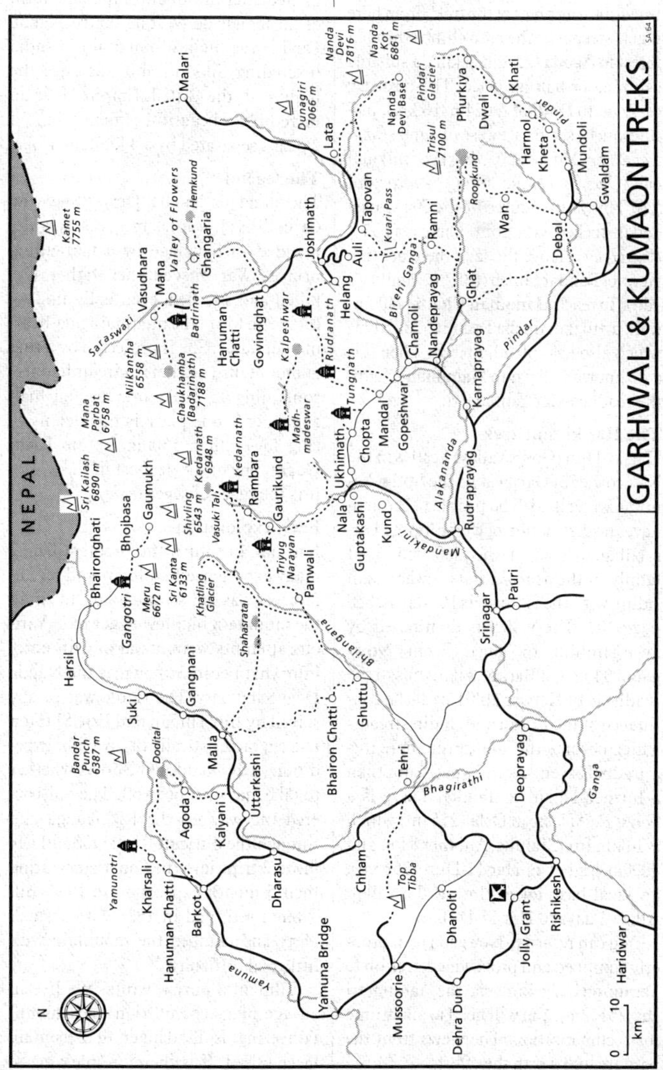

From Uttarkashi take a local bus to Gangotri and get off at **Gangori** (3 km) or walk it. Here take the track to your left up to **Kalyani** (1829m, motorable in dry weather) with its fish hatchery, the recognised starting point of the trek. From here it gets steeper as the path climbs through forest to **Agoda** (2280m, 5 km), a suitable camping or halting place. The next day carry on to **Dodital** (3024m, 16 km), picturesquely set in a forest of pine (*Pinus wallichiana*), deodar (*Cedrus deodara*) and oak (*Quercus dilatata* and *Q. semecarpifolia*). This is the source of the Asi Ganga and is stocked with trout. There is a *Forest Rest House*. Above the lake there are fine views of Bandar Punch (6387m, Monkey's Tail). To reach **Hanuman Chatti** (2400m) walk up to the Aineha Pass (3667m, 6 km) which also has splendid views. Then it is a 22 km walk down to Hanuman Chatti, the roadhead for Yamunotri.

The Har-ki-dun Trek

Har-ki-Dun (God's Valley) nestles in the NW corner of Garhwal nr the Sutlej-Yamuna watershed. The people of the area have the distinction of worshipping Duryodhana, head of the defeated royal family in the *Mahabharata*, rather than siding with the victorious Pandavas. See page 102. The valley is dominated by Swargarohini (6096m). From **Nowgaon**, 9 km S of Barkot, take a bus to the roadhead of Netwar (1401m) at the confluence of the Rupin and Supin streams which become the Tons. From here it is a gradual ascent over 12 km to Saur then a further 11 km to Taluka. There is a *Forest Rest House* at Osla (2559m) which is 11 km from Taluka. Another 8 km and 1000m higher is Har-ki-Dun (3565m), an ideal base for exploring the valley. Allow 3 days to Har-ki-Dun.

You can return to Nowgaon or, if properly equipped and provisioned, trek on to **Yamunotri** (29 km) via the Yamunotri Pass (5172m). You will need to allow time for acclimatisation. The views from the pass are well worth the effort.

The Nanda Devi Area

Dominating the Garhwal and Kumaon Himalaya is the Nanda Devi Group of mountains with **Nanda Devi** (7816m), named after the all-encompassing form of the female deity, at its centre. Nanda Devi is the highest mountain in India (excluding Sikkim) and was once the highest in the British Empire. It is an incredibly beautiful mountain of 2 peaks separated by a 4 km long ridge.

The legend

The hand of Nanda Devi ('She who Gives Bliss'), a local princess, was demanded in marriage by a marauding prince. War ensued, her father was killed and she fled, eventually finding refuge on top of the mountain now bearing her name. She is protected by a ring of mountains, 112 km in circumference, containing 12 peaks over 6400m high and in only one place is this defensive ring lower than 5500m, at the **Rishi Gorge**, one of the deepest in the world. It is the place of sages (*rishi*).

Early exploration

For half a century, the problem facing many experienced explorers and mountaineers was not so much how to climb the mountain but how to get to it. Various attempts were made to gain entry into what became known as the Nanda Devi Sanctuary. The riddle was finally solved by Bill Tilman and Eric Shipton in a characteristically lightweight expedition (they would agonise over whether to take one shirt or two!). They discovered the way up the Rishiganga and through the difficult Rishi Gorge. They made 2 trips into the Sanctuary during their 5 month expedition in 1934. Bill Tilman returned in 1936 with a small party and climbed the mountain with little real difficulty.

Tilman, a purist, wrote "We live in an age of mechanisation and...mountaineering is in danger of becoming mechanised. It is therefore pleasing to

record that in climbing Nanda Devi no climbing aids were used, apart, that is, from the apricot brandy we took. Our solitary oxygen apparatus was fortunately drowned, pitons were forgotten at base camp and crampons were solemnly carried up only to be abandoned." (W.H. Tilman, *The Ascent of Nanda Devi*).

In 1936 the monsoon was particularly heavy. The Pindar River, which is fed by the glaciers of Nanda Kot (Stronghold of Nanda) and Trisul (Siva's Trident), both mountains in the protective ring, rose dramatically. In the village of Tharali 40 lives were lost on 29 Aug, the day that Tilman's party reached the summit. Some say the anger of the Goddess was provoked by the violation of her sanctuary.

NB: The National Park established in 1980 was closed until 1994. Contact Director of the Park at Chamoli before planning a trip. Although declared 'open' by the Central Govt, the UP State Govt is reluctant to allow unrestricted entry. The situation is unclear at present; it is likely that organised trek groups will be allowed in after obtaining necessary permits.

The Pindari Glacier Trek

This is along the S edge of the Nanda Devi Sanctuary and is an 'out and back' trek, ie you return by the same route. **Accommodation** UP Tourism's Travellers *Lodges* (some with only 4 beds) are dotted along the route so this trek can be done with little equipment, although a sleeping bag is essential. Book accommodation early or take your own tent. The trek is 66 km from Song, which has the last bus terminus.

From **Bageshwar** – page 247, get a local bus to **Bharari** (1524m) which has a PWD *Rest House* and a cheap hotel. From here you can walk 16 km along the Sarju valley to **Song** or take another bus. It is just over 1.2 km further to **Loharkhet** (1829m) which also has a PWD *Bungalow* in the village and a basic KMVN *Travellers Lodge* overlooking it. Good views of the hillside opposite and the head of the Sarju Valley. It is 11 km from Loharkhet to **Dhakuri** via the Dhakuri Pass (2835m) which has a wonderful view of the S of the Nanda Devi Sanctuary including Panwali Dhar (6683m) and Maiktoli (6803m). The walk to the pass is mostly through forest on a well graded path. About 100m below the pass on the N side is a clearing with a PWD *Bungalow* and a KMVN *Travellers Lodge*. Great views, especially at sunrise and sunset.

In the Pindar Valley you descend to **Khati** (2194m, 8 km) first through rhododendron, then mixed forests dominated by stunted oak. Khati is a village with over 50 households situated on a spur that runs down to the river, some 200m below. There is a PWD *Bungalow*, KMVN *Travellers Lodge* and a village hotel. You can buy biscuits, eggs and chocolate, brought in by mule from Bharari.

From Khati follow the Pindar to **Dwali** (2580m, 8 km) which is at the confluence of the Pindar and the Kaphini Rivers. Here there is a Govt *Rest House* and a run down PWD *Bungalow*. If you have a tent, camp in front. The next halt is **Phurkiya** (3260m, 6 km) which also has a KMVN *Travellers Lodge* and a poor PWD *Bungalow*. This can be used as a base for going up to Zero Point (4000m) and the snout of the **Pindari Glacier**, which is a steep, 'falling' glacier. On either side there are impressive peaks, including Panwali Dhar (6683m), Nanda Kot (6876m). Return to Bharari the same way.

From Dwali, however, a side trip to the **Kaphini Glacier** is worthwhile. Alternatively, you could trek up to **Sundar Dhunga Glacier** from Khati. Including either of these, the trek can be accomplished in a week but for comfort allow 9 days.

Roopkund Trek

Roopkund (4800m, *kund*, lake in Garhwali), nestles in the lap of Trisul (7100m) and Nanda Ghunti (6310m). 30 years ago the Indian anthropologist DN Majumdar discovered hundreds of skeletons around this small mountain tarn. They were either the remains of a party of pilgrims on a Trisul *yatra* who died when bad weather closed in, or, they may have been the remains of the Dogra Gen Zorawar Singh's army from Jammu which tried to invade Tibet in 1841 but was forced back to return home over the Himalaya. The mystery remains, though carbon-dating suggests the bones are 600 years old.

This is a highly varied and scenic trek which can be undertaken by a suitably equipped party. A week is sufficient – 9 days if you want to take it more comfortably with a rest day for acclimatisation. You can usually get porters at Gwaldam or Debal.

From **Gwaldam** (1950m) (see Almora above) walk down through attractive pine forest, cross the River Pindar and continue to **Debal** (1350m, 8 km) where there is a *KMVN Travellers Lodge*, a *Forest Rest House* and *dharamshalas*. From here you can either walk 12 km along a dirt road through villages with views of Mrigthuni (6855m), or go by cramped jeep taxi to **Bagrigadh** which is 500m below the **Lohajung Pass** (2350m) where there is an attractive *KMVN Travellers Lodge* right on the ridge beside a pretty shrine. Good views here of Nanda Ghunti. If time is at a premium, you can save a day by going by bus from Gwaldam to Tharali, taking another bus to Debal, catching the jeep-taxi to Bagrigadh and walking up to Lohajung in one long day.

From **Lohajung** you walk down through stunted oak forest and along the *Wan Gad* (river) to the village of **Wan** (2400m, 10 km) which has a *Forest Rest House* and *KMVN Travellers Lodge*. From Wan it is essentially wilderness travel as you make the ascent to Roopkund, first walking through thick forest to **Bedni Bugyal** (*bugyal* – meadow) which is used as summer pasture. This is at 3550m and has good views of Trisul and the Badrinath range to the N. There are some stone shepherds' huts which you may be able to use but it is better to take a tent.

From Bedni it is a gradual 7 km climb along a well defined path over the 4500m **Kovali Pass** to more shepherds' huts at **Bhagwabasa** (4400m), the base for the final walk up to Roopkund. This is not a good camp site as water is some way off. A stove is necessary for cooking. From here, it is 2-3 hr up to **Roopkund.** In the final steep part, the ground can be icy. From the 4900m ridge approx 50m above Roopkund, is a magnificent view of the W face of Trisul rising over 3500m from the floor of the intervening hanging valley to the summit. Return to Gwaldam by the same route or via **Ali Bugyal** which bypasses the village of Wan.

The Curzon/Nehru Trail

The Curzon/Nehru trail is an incomparably beautiful trek. It was the route followed by Tilman and Shipton on their way to the Rishi Gorge, and by other mountaineers en route to the peaks on the Indo-Tibetan border. The crossing of the Kuari (Virgin) Pass is a fitting conclusion to a trek that takes in 3 lesser passes and 5 major rivers – the Pindar, Kaliganga, Nandakini, Birehiganga and Dhauliganga. The trail was named after Lord Curzon, a keen trekker, and the path may have been specially improved for him. After 1947 it was renamed the Nehru Trail.

This trek begins at **Gwaldam** and ends at **Tapovan** in the Dhauliganga Valley on the Joshimath-Niti Pass road, after crossing the **Kuari Pass** (3600m), one of the finest vantage points in the Himalaya.

From Gwaldam proceed to **Wan** as in the previous itinerary. Then, go over the **Kanol Pass** (2900m) through thick mixed forest to **Sutol** (2100m, 10 km) in the Nandakini valley. There is a good camp site by the river. The next 2 stages follow the Nandakini downstream to Ramni (2500m, 20 km) via Dhar, taking the higher trail, where the path leads up over the rhododendron forest clad **Ramni Pass** (3100 m) with a good view of the Kuari Pass – the lower trail goes to the nearby roadhead at Ghat from where you can also start the trek. To reach Ramni, however, is a good 3 day walk, down through lush forest to cross the Birehiganga River by an impressive suspension bridge, up around the horse-shoe-shaped hanging valley around Pana village, over an intervening spur and into the forested tributary valley of the Kuari nallah. There is no settlement here; *bharal* (mountain goats) and the rarely seen Himalayan black bear in-habit the rich forest. Waterfalls tumble down over steep crags. There is a good camp (about 1 hr) below the pass at **Dhakwani** (3200 m).

Leave early to get the full effect of sunrise over the peaks on the Indo-Tibetan border. Some of the mountains seen are Kamet, Badrinath (7040m), Dunagiri (7066m), Changabang (6863m) and Nanda Devi herself (7816m). There is a wonderful wooded campsite with marvellous views about 300m below the pass. From here it is down to **Tapovan** and the Joshimath – Niti road. There is a hot spring here and a bus service to Joshimath. Allow 10 days for the trek. A shorter trail leads from the campsite along a scenic ridge to Auli and a further 4 km down to Joshimath.

DELHI TO GORAKHPUR AND NEPAL

There are several possible routes across the Ganga plains. The more northerly route via Moradabad and Bareilly goes through Lucknow, scene of some of the bloodiest fighting during the 1857 mutiny.

ROUTES From Delhi to Moradabad is described in the Delhi to Nainital route – see page 240. In Moradabad keep on NH24 due E to Bareilly (96 km).

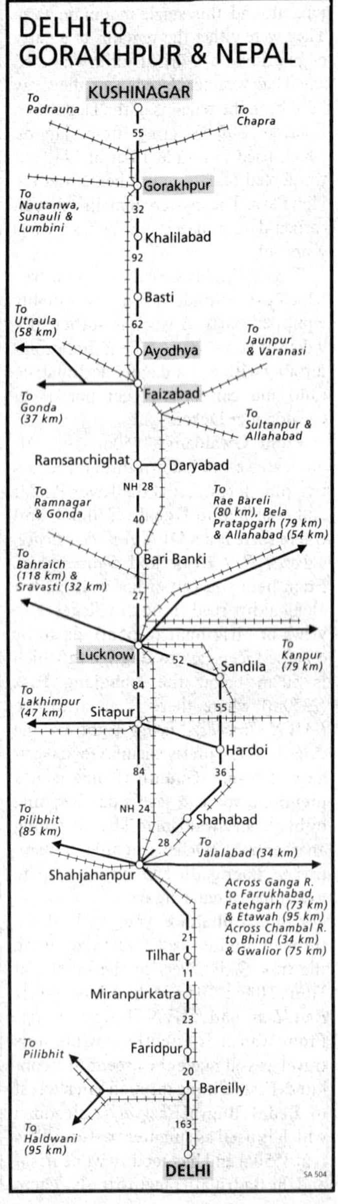

Bareilly

(*Pop* 607,000; *STD Code* 0581) This was the capital of Rohilkhand and was founded in 1537 by the Bas Deo and Barel (hence Bareilly) Deo brothers. Traces of their fortress remain. It was ceded to the British in 1801 and also contributed to the drama of the Mutiny. The important mosques are **Mirza Masjid** (1600), **Jami Masjid** (1657) and the **Mosque of Ahmad Khandar**, and 2 churches, Christ Church and St Stephen's. Bareilly is known for its iron industry and its gold *zari* work. It is a transfer point for rail travel to Haldwani and Nainital.

• **Accommodation D** *Oberoi Anand* and Annexe, 46 Civil Lines, T 70838, 75728. 78 rm, some a/c. Central. Restaurant, exchange, shops, lawns. **E** *Civil and Military Hotel*, Station Rd, T 75879. 22 rm, some a/c. Central. Restaurant, TV, garden.

• **Transport Train** Kathgodam and Nainital: *Kumaon Exp* 5311, daily, 0600, 4 hr. **Road Bus**: extensive local bus routes and connections with all major cities on the plains.

ROUTES The road continues out of Bareilly through Faridpur (20 km), Miranpur Katra (23 km) and Tilhar (11 km) to Shahjahanpur (21 km).

Shahjahanpur (*STD Code* 05842) named after the Mughal Emperor by its founder, Nawab Bahadur Khan in 1647. It came under British control and experienced the Mutiny when residents were attacked in the church.

ROUTE The main road to the right out of Shahjahanpur goes to Jajalabad (34 km), Fatehgarh (73 km) Etawah. Continue straight on for the main road to Lucknow (180 km) through a succession of small towns and villages.

Lucknow

Lucknow, the capital of UP, sprawls unattractively along the banks of the Gomti river in the heart of eastern UP. Although the discovery of Painted Grey Ware and Northern Black pottery demonstrates the long period over which the site has been occupied, its main claim to fame is as the capital of the Nawabs of Oudh (*Avadh*), and later the scene of one of the most remarkable episodes in the Mutiny of 1857. Now it is a major administrative centre and market.

BASICS *Population*: 1.65 mn. *Altitude*: 123m. *STD Code*: 0522. *Area*: 79 sq km. *Languages*: Hindi, Urdu.

History

Early settlement It is not clear when Lucknow was first populated. When the Mughals conquered N India in the 16th century it was rapidly developed under Akbar's patronage. In the 18th century, Nawab Sadat Ali Khan founded the Oudh dynasty. The builder of 'modern' Lucknow was Nawab Asaf-ud-Daula who shifted his capital here from Faizabad in 1775. He intended to build a city of wonderful buildings. Certainly some are remarkable, like the Great Imambara with the largest vaulted apartment in the world. However, he also emptied the regal coffers with his ambitious building and personal extravagance. In Kipling's Kim "no city – except Bombay, the queen of all – was more beautiful in her garish style than Lucknow", famous for its silks, perfumes and jewellery. The buildings themselves are a disappointment, the style of most being aptly described by Tillotson as debased Mughal.

CLIMATE: LUCKNOW

	Jan	Feb	Mar	Apr	May	Jun	Jul	Aug	Sep	Oct	Nov	Dec	Av/Tot
Max (°C)	23	26	33	38	41	39	34	33	33	33	29	25	32
Min (°C)	9	11	16	22	27	28	27	26	23	20	13	9	19
Rain (mm)	24	17	9	6	12	94	299	302	182	40	1	6	992

The British takeover In the mid-1850s under Lord Dalhousie, the British annexed a number of Indian states. Percival Spear suggested that Dalhousie considered British rule so superior to Indian that the more territory directly administered by the British the better it would be for Indians. He evolved a policy of lapse whereby the states of Indian princes without direct heirs could be taken over on the ruler's death. Chronic mismanagement was also deemed just cause for takeover, the justification given for the annexation of Oudh.

The famous Indian novelist Premchand in the *Chess Players* attributes the fall of Oudh to the fact that "small and big, rich and poor, were dedicated alike to sensual joys... song, dance and opium". History suggests that Nawab Wajid Ali Shah continued with his game of chess even as British soldiers occupied his capital. There was considerable resentment at what was regarded as a British breach of faith. A strong British presence was established in the city as it became a key administrative and military centre. Satyajit Ray's film adaptation is excellent.

The mutiny In 1857, when the mutiny broke, Sir Henry Lawrence gathered the British community into the Residency which rapidly became a fortress. The ensuing siege lasted for 87 days. When the relieving force under Sir Colin Campbell finally broke through, the once splendid Residency was a blackened

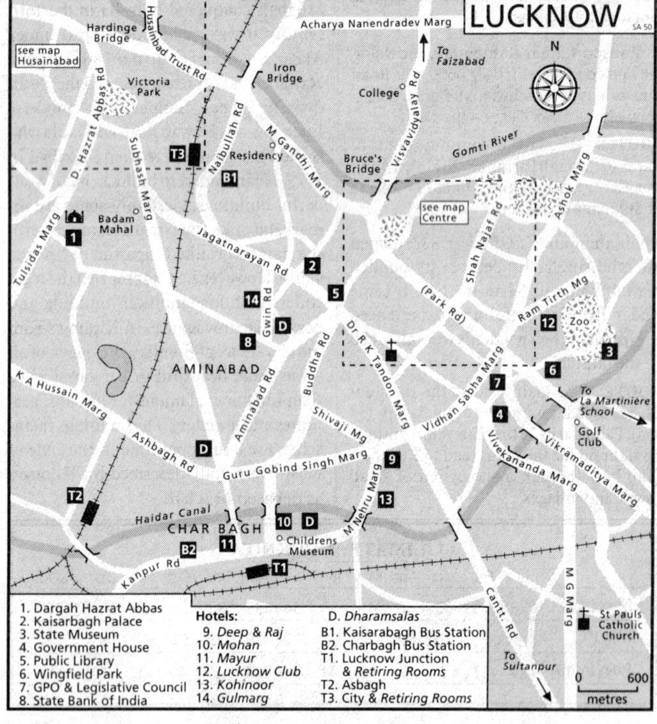

Jobs For The Boys?

In 1784 Lucknow and its region suffered an appalling famine, and thousands of starving people flocked into the city from the countryside. In a spectacular example of 'food for work' – pre-Keynes Keynesian economics – Asaf ud Daula decided to build the Great Imambara. He offered work night and day, reputedly employing 22,000 men, women and children. However, in order to ensure that the task was not finished too quickly, he divided it into two parts. During the day, normal building proceeded. At night the workmen destroyed one quarter of what had been built the previous day. Nobles were allowed to work at night to spare them the embarrassment of being seen as having to labour to survive. To the labourers this act of charity must have seemed of greater importance than any architectural demerits the building may have.

ruin, its walls pockmarked and gaping with cannon ball holes. Today it is a mute witness to a desperate struggle.

Culture

Under the Nawabs, Lucknow evolved specialised styles of dance, poetry, music and calligraphy. Formal mannerisms, the rendering of poetry, the Lucknowi *gharana* (house) of music and the shadow-worked embroidery are reminders of its splendid past. It is a regional cultural capital, though according to Muzaffar Ali "its streets are thronged with cycles and rickshaws. A number of garden roads such as the Kaiserbagh quadrangle which were at one time pleasant walks are thick with the fumes of heavy lorries. In the 1920s the city had seen some of the most outstanding cars the world had known. Today of the vintage modes of travel, only the *ekka* (one-horse carriage) has survived".

Places of interest

The original centre of the city is believed to be the high ground crowned by the Mosque of Aurangzeb on the right bank of the Gomti. Here at Lakshman Tila a family from Bijnor built a fort at the end of the 13th century. It then passed through a number of hands, including the Sharqi kings of Jaunpur (1394-1476), Sher Shah of Delhi (1540-5). The first Nawab, Sadat Khan Burhan-ul-mulk (1724-9) was made governor of Oudh in 1732 by Aurangzeb. His successor, Safdarjang (1739-53) was buried at Delhi, see page 173.

Tillotson suggests that the major buildings of Asaf-ud Daula, constructed after 1775 – the **Bara Imambara**, the **Rumi Darwaza** and the mosque between them, for example – dramatically illustrate the degeneration of Mughal style. He argues that though the individual architectural forms employed are those that appear in mature Mughal buildings, their treatment has been altered, diminishing rather than enhancing their power – "The cusped or foliated arches, the onion domes, the tapering minarets, the small domed kiosks or chhattris, and many other features, all have their prototypes in the Mughal architecture of the preceding century; but here they are deployed in a new, less skillful manner." Note for example the continuous row of tiny chhattris or the replacement of Mughal decorative inlay work with crude stucco.

The monuments (usually open 0600-1700) have been divided into 3 main groups:

W and NW of the City station

This is a circular walk, going anti-clockwise from the City Station. Walk N along Nabiullah Rd. The **Iron Bridge** (1798) designed by Sir John Rennie lay for over 40 years on the river bank before it was assembled for Amjad Ali Shah. Husainabad Trust Rd leads to **Hardinge Bridge**

(1914). To the left is King George's and Queen Mary's Medical Hospital and College (1912) designed by Sir S S Jacob – see page 402.

Machhi Bhavan 'Fish House' fort enclosure is across to your left (Safdarjang was permitted to use the fish insignia by the Mughal Emperor). On the W slope of this is the **Bara (Great) Imambara** (1784), a huge vaulted hall which like all imambaras serves as the starting point for the Muharram procession. The hall (50m long and 15m high), built by Asaf-ud-Daula for famine relief, is one of the largest in the world. There are excellent views of Lucknow from the top. Inside is a five storeyed *baoli*, or step-well, connected directly with the River Gomti. Legends suggest that secret tunnels connect the lower steps, which are always under water, with a treasure stored beneath the Imambara itself. As the well has never been drained, neither the tunnels, nor the map of the treasure trove or the keys to it, which are widely believed to have been thrown into the well, have ever been found.

At the end of the avenue leading up to the Imambara from the river is the **Rumi Darwaza** (1784, Turkish Gate). Just beyond is **Victoria Park** (1890) with several British tombs nearby. S of the Park is the **Chowk**, the Old City bazar where there are some interesting old buildings. Further along Girdharilal Mathur Rd and on your right is the 19th century Gothic, 67m high Husainabad Clocktower (1880s) designed by Roskell Payne, which contains the largest clock in India. Next to it is the attractive octagonal Husainabad Tank (1837-42), around which is the Taluqdar's Hall and the incomplete Satkhanda (1840) 7-storeyed watchtower.

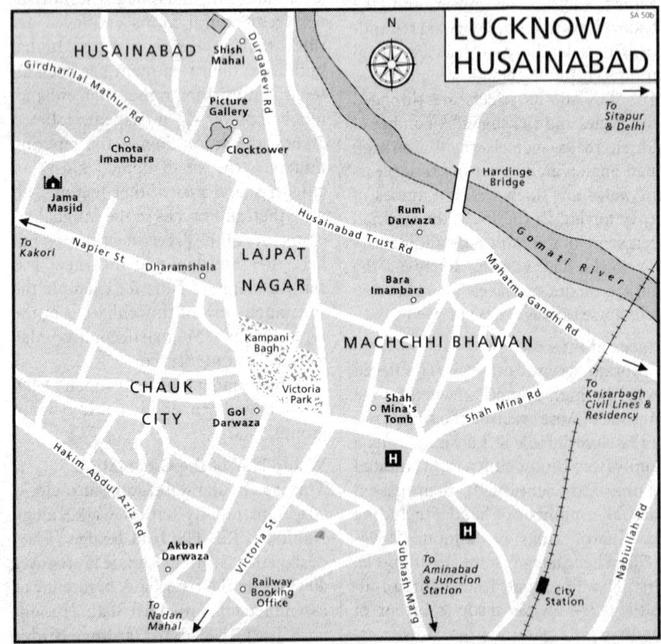

The **Husainabad Imambara** (Chhota Imambara) containing a silver throne (1837) is illuminated during Muharram. Further W is the **Jami Masjid** begun by Muhammad Shah and finished by his wife in the mid-1840s. From here you can return to the city station by walking down Napier St into Khunkhunji Marg. Alternatively, turn right down Dargah Hazrat Abbas Rd to see the **Dargah of Hazrat Abbas** which contains a relic (a metal crest from the battle at Kerbala). Down Hakim Abdul Aziz Rd, across Tulsidas Marg and down Nadan Mahal Rd is the **Badam Mahal** (c1600), the tomb of Shaikh Abdur Rahim, Akbar's Governor of Oudh. This is a fine building, built in the Mughal style and faced with red sandstone. Abdur Rahim's father was Ibrahim Chishti whose tomb is nearby to the E. Allow 2-3 hr for this tour.

The Residency and Hazratganj area

The Residency's 3000 mostly European occupants, hastily brought there by Sir Henry Lawrence, came under siege on the evening of 30 June 1857. Two days later Lawrence was fatally injured. After 90 days Generals Sir Henry Havelock and Sir James Outram appeared through the battered walls with a column of Highlanders. However, the siege was intensified and sepoy sappers (engineers) began tunnelling to lay mines to blow the place up.

From quite early on the beleaguered community of Britons and Indians loyal to the crown ran short of food. Disease was rife. Sir Henry Lawrence's belongings were auctioned off almost as soon as he was buried. As rations dwindled and prices rose, smallpox, cholera and scurvy set in. Surgeons amputated limbs without chloroform. Havelock was slowly dying of dysentery. The heroic Irishman, Henry Kavanagh, had sat in the tunnels and shot mutineers as they wriggled forward to lay more mines. He now volunteered to run the gauntlet through the enemy lines to find Sir Colin Campbell's relieving force, which he did by swimming the Gomti. On 17 November, Lucknow was finally relieved. Of the 3000 Indians and British who had sought refuge in the Residency, only 1000 marched out.

This was one of the great heroic struggles of the Mutiny which was to drag on elsewhere for a few months more. It seemed to bring out all the extremes of human nature – courage, daring, heroism, stupidity, loyalty, bewilderment and if the records are to be believed, only very rarely cowardice. 2 books about the Mutiny, particularly at Lucknow: *The Great Mutiny: India 1857* by Christopher Hibbert (Penguin), a factual history; *The Siege of Krishnapur* by J.G. Farrell, a novel.

The Residency Compound E of the City Station within its scarred walls, is now a historic monument with well tended gardens. You enter through the Baillie Guard gateway to the E. The Treasury on your right served as an arsenal while the grand Banquet Hall next door housed the wounded during the Mutiny. On the lawn of Dr Fayrer's House to your left stands a stone cross to Sir Henry Lawrence, while the Begum Kothi behind belonged to Mrs Walters who married the Nawab of Oudh.

The Residency (1800) to the NE, built by Saadat Ali Khan, has *tykhanas* (cool underground rooms for summer use). There is a small Museum on the ground floor. The graves of Lawrence, Neill and others are in the Church Cemetery. To balance the scene, just outside the Residency on the banks of the Gomti river is a white obelisk erected to commemorate 'The Nationalist Insurgents' who lost their lives in 1857. **Warning** The grounds are popular with courting couples and school-boy onlookers who may harrass unacompanied women visitors; be vigilant and do not visit the cemetery alone.

SE of the Residency is the **Kaiser-**

bagh Palace (1850) conceived as a grand château. In the grounds are the almost twin **Tombs of Saadat Ali Khan** (1814) and **Khurshid Begum** is the larger, paved with black and white marble slabs. The Archaeological Museum is housed in the Lal Baradari to the E, a red sandstone building which was once the Nawabs' Coronation Hall.

To the E again is the **Nur Bakhsh Kothi** (Light Giving Palace). **Tarawali Kothi** (House of Stars, 1820s) was the observatory of Colonel Wilcox, the royal astronomer. To the N is the **Khurshid Manzil** (House of the Sun, 1800-1810) on raised ground, begun by Saadat Ali Khan, finished by his son and used by the army until the Mutiny. It is now La Martinière Girls' School. To the NE, near the River, is the **Moti Mahal** (Pearl Palace) named after its original pearl-like dome, now destroyed. Once a library, also built by Saadat Ali Khan, it was complemented with 2 additional buildings by his son. The royal insignia decorates the Italian wrought iron gates.

Due W, the 2 **Chattar Manzils** (1820s) were royal pavilions, the larger having *tykhanas* underneath.

The southern group

Near the Gomti lies the **Shah Najaf**, the tombs of Ghazi-ud-Din Haidar (r1814-27) and his 2 wives, with its white dome and elaborate interior decorations. It was used by Independence fighters as a stronghold in 1857. Wajid Ali Shah's (r1847-56) pleasure garden Sikanderbagh is just to the W.

To the S of these are **Wingfield Park**, laid out by the Chief Commissioner of Oudh (1859-66), which contains a marble pavilion and some statues. **Christchurch** (1860), a memorial to the British killed during the Mutiny is nearby, along with the imposing **Legislative Council Chamber** (1928) and **Raj Bhawan** (Government House), enlarged in 1907.

Some distance further to the W is **Dilkusha** (Heart's Delight), a Royal Shooting Lodge located in what was once a large deer park. There are graves of soldiers who died in the grounds during the Mutiny. To the E is the abandoned **Wilaiti Bagh** (English Garden) which was laid out by Nasir-ud-Din Haidar (r1827-37) for his ladies.

Finally, there is **Constantia,** now La Martinière's School, planned as the country residence of Major-Gen Claude Martin (1735-1800) a French soldier of fortune. He served both the Nawabs and the British and ended a wealthy man through his success in the indigo business and money-lending. The main building has 5 storeys with extensive wings and shows a curious juxtaposition of styles. It was completed after Martin's death, from the endowment set aside by him for a school here and at Calcutta for 'Anglo-Indians' (Kipling's Kim being one of them). In the central room there is a bust of Martin who is buried in the crypt. Not officially open to the public but you may ask to look around.

NB: MG Marg refers to Mahatma Gandhi Marg.

Museums

State Museum, Banarsi Bagh, T 235542. 1030-1630, closed Mon. The oldest in UP and one of the richest in India. 1st-11th century exhibits of Hindu, Buddhist and Jain works including stone sculptures from Mathura, busts and friezes from Allahabad and Garhwa. Also marble sculptures, rare coins, paintings, natural history and anthropology (an Egyptian mummy). Relics of the British Raj removed at the time of Independence to be replaced by others, are in the backyard, by the scooter stand. Archaeological Section, Lal Baradari, Kaiserbagh. Antiquities from UP. 1030-1700, closed Mon. Motilal Nehru Children's Museum, Balvidya Mandir, Motilal Marg. 1030-1730, closed Mon. Special collection of dolls. Gandhi Museum and Library, Gandhi Bhawan,

Kaiserbagh. Geological Survey of India Museum, MG Marg. 1000-1600. Picture gallery, Hussainabad. 1000-1630, Closed Sun.

Parks & zoos

Botanical Gardens, Shah Najaf Imambara.

Tours

UP Tours and Travels, from *Hotel Gomti*, T 232659. Shah Najaf Imambara, Picture, Clock Tower, Rumi Darwaza, Shaheed Smarak, Residency, Bara Imambara. Enjoyable and good value. 0930 (Pick-up from *Gomti Hotel* and others from 0830). Rs 45.

Local festivals

All major Hindu and Muslim festivals are celebrated, some distinctively in Lucknow, eg a great national kite flying competition at the Patang Park, MG Marg the day after Diwali in Oct-Nov. Each Feb the UP Govt organises a 10-day festival with special emphasis on Indian classical music – song, drama and dance, processions, boating and *ekka* races.

Local information

● Accommodation

A *Taj Palace*, Vipin Khand. 112 rm. New luxury hotel.

B *Clarks Avadh*, 8 MG Marg. T 236500, F 236507. 98 rm. Very good restaurant and shops. *Falaknuma* for regional dishes. Indian classical music, some tables with good view; *Gulham* for continental, modern, clean, comfortable, attentive service.

C *Kohinoor*, 6 Station Rd, T 235421. 52 rm. Restaurant. Clean and good service. **C** *Carlton*, Shah Najaf Marg, T 244021. 66 large a/c rm. Restaurant, bar, exchange, lawns. Palatial but neglected inside.

D *Capoor's*, 52 Hazratganj, T 243958, Fax 234023. 24 a/c rm. Restaurant, travel. Old world and a little neglected. UP Tourism **D** *Gomti*, 6 Sapru Marg, T 240624. 30 rm, some a/c. Restaurant, bar. Clean, attentive service, good value. **D** *Mohan*, Char Bagh, T 52251. 75 rm, some a/c. Restaurant, exchange, travel. **D** *Charan International*, 16 Vidhan Sabha Marg, T 247221 52 rm, some

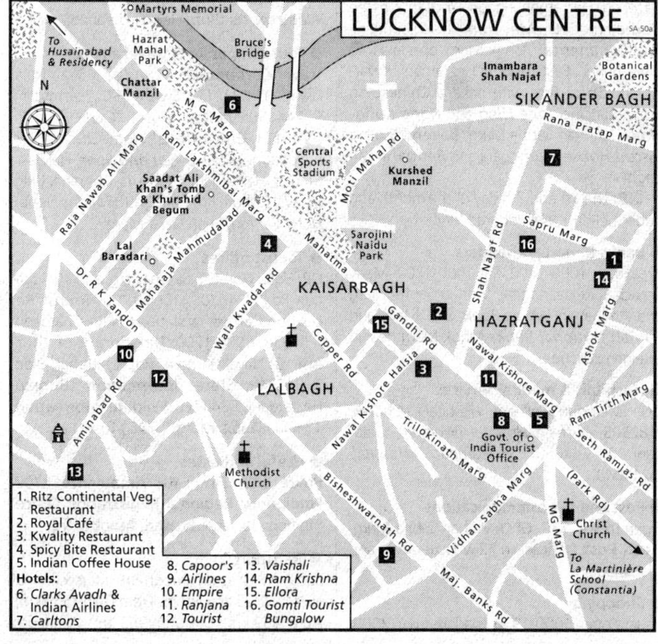

a/c with TV. Restaurant, travel. **D** ***Ellora***, 3 Lalbagh, T 231307. 22 a/c rm. Restaurant. Overpriced. **D** ***Deep Avadh***, Naka Hindola Aminabad Rd, T 236442. 79 rm, some a/c with TV. Restaurant. **D** ***Gulmarg***, Dr BN Verma Rd, Aminabad. T 231227. 53 rm, some a/c. Restaurant (snacks), travel. **D** ***Deep***, 5 Vidhan Sabha Marg, T 236441. 52 rm, some a/c with TV. Restaurant, bar. **D** ***Raj***, 9 Vidhan Sabha Marg, T 249483. 40 rm, some a/c. Rm service.

● Budget hotels

E ***Central***, Jhandewala Park, Aminabad, T 242525. 54 rm, some with bath. **E** ***Mayur***, opp rly station, Charbagh, T 50464. 16 rm, some a/c. Rm service. **E** ***Ram Krishna***, opp Jawahar Bhawan, Ashok Marg, T 249827. 25 rm. Rm service. **E** ***YWCA***, Bairow Rd, T 243409.

F ***YMCA***, Rana Pratap Marg, T 247227. **F** ***Rly Retiring Rooms***, Charbagh station.

● Places to eat

The better hotels serve good Lucknowi food – rich *biryanis, roomali roti* and *kebabs* and *kulfis* to end the meal. Special *Dum Phukt* (steam cooked) dishes are worth trying. **Indian**: ***Royal Café***, in Hazratganj, good. ***Indian Coffee House***, nr GPO; ***Mayuram*** in Hussunganj. ***Ritz Continental***, Ashok Marg, opp Jawahar Bhavan. Rec. **Fast food**: in Hazratganj, ***Kwality*** and ***Spicy Bite*** with bakery. **Chinese**: in Hazratganj incl ***Jone Hing*** and ***Hong Kong-Simon***, Vidhan Sabha Marg. **Bakery**: ***Burma Biscuit House***, Hazratganj and ***Bengal*** in Lalbagh.

NB: The 1st and 7th day of the month and public holidays, are declared 'dry'.

● Banks & money changers

Weekdays 1000-1400, Sat 1000-1200. Many branches in Hazratganj, Vidhan Sabha Marg and Aminabad. ***State Bank***, MG Marg and ***Punjab National Bank***, Ashok Marg deal in foreign exchange.

● Hospitals & medical services

KG Medical College Hospital, Chowk, T 82303. *Dufferin Hospital (Women)*, Golaganj, T 244050. *Balrampur Hospital*, T 244040.

● Post and telecommunications

Open 0930-1730. **GPO**: Vidhan Sabha Marg. **Head Post Offices**: in New Hyderabad and Mahanagar.

● Shopping

Usually open 1000-1930, markets up to 2000.

NB: Hazratganj, Janpath closed on Sun; Aminabad, Chowk, Sadar, Super Bazar on Th; Nahri, Mon; Nishatganj, Wed. Lucknow is famous for *chikan* work, embroidery, silversmiths, gold zari and sequin work. Available from ***Lal Behari Tandon*** Chowk and ***Nath Industries***, 6B Murli Nagar, 1st Gate, 2nd Fl, Cantt Rd. Main shopping areas are Hazratganj, Aminabad and Chowk. **Hazratganj**: ***Gangotri***, UP Handicrafts, ***UPICA***, ***Khadi Gram Udyog Bhawan***, ***Haryana Emporium***, ***Maharashtra Handlooms***, ***Co-optex***, ***Kashmir Government Arts Emporium***. Try ***Kannauj*** and ***Asghar Ali***, nr Chowk, for *attar* (Indian perfumes) and ***Advani***, Hazratganj. Visit **Nakhas** in old Lucknow to see the birdsellers.

Books: ***Universal Booksellers***, Hazratganj.

Photography: ***Kala Mandir***, The Mall. ***C Mull***, Ashok Marg; ***Kapoor Studio***, Hazratganj; ***Gulati***, Aminabad.

● Sports

Golf Course: Kalidas Marg.

Race Course: Cantt.

Swimming: pools at KD Singh Baba Stadium and *Hotel Clarks Avadh*.

Watersports Club: New Hyderabad.

● Tour companies & travel agents

Travel Corporation of India, 3 Shah Najaf Marg, T 233212. ***Swan***, 50 Hazratganj, T 244150. ***Janta***, *Hotel Clarks Avadh*, T 246171. ***Civica Travel***, *Hotel Charan International*, T 232516. ***Iyer and Sons***, Halwasia Market, Hazratganj. ***UP Tours***, Chitrahar Bldg, 3 Naval Kishore Rd, T 248349, ***Holiday Nepal***, *Hotel Carlton*, Shah Najaf Marg.

● Tourist offices

UP, *Hotel Gomti*, 6 Sapru Marg, and 10/4 Station Rd, T 246205. 1000-1700. **Tourist Reception Centre**, rly station (N Rly), Charbagh, T 52533. 1000-1700. **Directorate of Tourism**, 3 Naval Kishore Rd, Chitrahar Bldg, T 247749. **State Information Bureau**, Hazratganj, T 244728. **Wildlife Information**, 17 Rana Pratap Marg, T 246140.

● Useful addresses

Police: T 100. **Fire**: T 101. **Ambulance**: T 102. **Foreigners' Regional Registration Office**: 5th floor, Jawahar Bhavan, Ashok Marg.

● Transport

Lucknow is at an important intersection of NH24, NH25 and NH28. From Delhi (569 km); Agra (369 km); Calcutta (963 km); Allahabad

(237 km); Kanpur (79 km); Khajuraho (320 km); Varanasi (286 km).

Local Taxi: no metered yellow-top taxis. Private taxis from Lucknow Car Taxi Owners Assoc, Station Rd, and hotels and agencies. Full day (8 hr, 80 km) about Rs 150. **Rickshaws and tongas**: tempo-rickshaws on fixed routes are convenient and cheap. Cycle-rickshaws and Horse Tongas are widely available. Agree rates. **City Bus Service**: extensive network and cheap. UP Roadways bus stands: mostly local and some out-of-town from Char Bagh (opp Rly station), T 242066.

Air Amousi airport is 14 km from city centre. **Indian Airlines**: enquiries T 244030 (1000-1730, ticketing 1000-1300,1400-1630); airport T 256327. Daily flights from Delhi (1 hr) and M,Tu,Th,Sa to Bombay (2 hr), Tu,Th,Sa to Calcutta (1½ hr).

Train Lucknow is serviced by the Northern and NE railway networks. Charbagh Station is 3 km from town centre. **N Rly**: enquiries T 131; reservations 1st Class T 51833, 2nd Class T 51488. **NE Rly**: enquiries T 51433; reservations T 51383. City Station T 242411. Weekdays 0830-1530, 1600-1930, Sun 0830-1530. **Warning** Take special care of belongings at the station as several thefts have been reported by passengers in transit.

Old Delhi: *Avadh-Assam Express* 5609, daily, 0540, 9 hr. From Old Delhi: *Avadh-Assam Express* 5610, daily, 0850, 9 hr. **New Delhi:** *Lucknow Mail* 4229, daily, 2200, 8¾ hr *Gomti Express* 2419, daily except Tue, 0515, 8¼ hr. **Bombay (VT)**: *Kushi Nagar Express* 1016, daily, 1125, 28½ hr. **Calcutta** (H): *Amritsar-Haora Express* 3050, daily, 1155, 28 hr; *Amritsar-Haora Mail* 3006, daily, 1120, 21¾ hr; *Doon Express* 3010, daily, 0850, 23½ hr. **Agra Fort** *Avadh Express* 5063, daily, 2150, 7¾ hr. From Agra Fort: *Avadh Express* 5064, daily, 2202, 8½ hr. **Agra Cantt** *Ganga-Yamuna Express* 4283/4213/1187, daily, 2035, 8 hr. **Jhansi** *Pushpak Express* 2134, daily, 2010, 6½ hr; *Chhapra-Gwalior Mail* 1144, daily, 070, 7 hr; *Kushi Nagar Exp* 1016, daily, 1125, 5½ hr. **Allahabad** *Nauchandi Exp* 4012, daily, 0610, 4¾ hr; *Ganga-Gomti Exp* 2416, daily, 1800, 4 hr. **Dehra Dun** *Doon Exp* 3009, daily, 1915, 12¾ hr; *Varanasi-Dehra Dun Exp* 4265, daily, 1955, 13¾ hr.

Bhopal *Pushpak Exp* 2134, daily, 2010, 11¼ hr; *Kushi Nagar Exp* 1016, daily, 1125, 12 hr. **Varanasi** *Kashi Vishwanath Exp* 4058, daily, 2320, 7¾ hr; *Lucknow-Varanasi Varuna Exp* 2428, daily, 1815, 4¾ hr. **Kanpur** *Sabarmati Exp* 9166, daily, 2150, 2¾ hr; *Ganga-Yamuna Exp* 4283, M,W,Th,Sa, 1950, 3½ hr; *Ganga-Yamuna Exp* 4213, T,F,Sa, 0110, 1½ hr. **Jabalpur** (for Kanha): *Chitrakot Exp* 5010, daily, 1625, 16¾ hr. **Kathgodam** (from Nainital): *Nainital Exp* 5308, daily, 2135, 11 hr. **Gorakhpur** (for Nepal): *Vaishali Exp* 2554, daily, 0350, 5 hr; *Sabarmati Exp* 9165, daily, 0550, 5 hr; *Kushi Nagar*, 1115, daily, 1550, 5¼ hr.

Road Regular services to major tourist centres in the region. Reservations: UP Roadways bus stands, for most **local** and some out-of-town, Char Bagh, T 242066; **long distance,** Kaiserbagh, T 242503.

Dudhwa National Park

Approach

Altitude: 164m. *Area* 613 sq km. *Climate*: Temp. Summer, Max. 35°C, Min. 10°C, Winter, Max. 30°C, Min. 4°C. Annual rainfall 1500 mm; most Jun-Sep. *Best Season*: Mar-May (open mid Nov to mid-Jun). In Apr-Jun it becomes very hot, dry and dusty.

Background

Dudhwa is 238 km N of Lucknow and was designated a National Park in 1977. The area was a reserve since 1879 which had been declared a sanctuary in 1965. The terrain and vegetation is that of the *terai*. Bordering the Sarda River in the Terai, it is very similar to the Corbett National Park. It has *sal* forest (in addition to *sheesham*, *asna*, *khair*, *sagaun*), tall savannah grasslands and large marshy areas which are watered by the Neora and Sohel rivers.

Wildlife

The swamps covered with thick tall grass are the ideal habitat of the **Barasingha** (swamp deer with 12 tined antlers, *Cervus duvanceli*), best seen in the Sathiana and Kakraha blocks. The tiger population in Dudhwa is believed to be ⅓ of the official census of 104 (there have been reports of maneaters). Dudhwa also has sambar, nilgai, some sloth bears (*Melursus ursinus*), fishing cats and a few leopards; the one-horned rhino has been introduced from E India. The 400 species of avifauna includes Bengal floricans, pied and Great Indian hornbills and king vultures. It also attracts a great variety of water birds (swamp partridge, eastern white stork) in addition to birds of prey (osprey, hawks, fishing eagles). Open 15 Nov-15 Jun. **Best season** for viewing large game: Mar-Jun. **NB**: Occasionally disturbed due to political activists; check latest position with Field Director. Night driving is not allowed in the park so arrive before sunset.

Viewing

Entry for 3 days, Rs 100, extra Rs 50 per day. Indians and students pay reduced rates. Camera fee Rs 50, video Rs 500. Road fee, Rs 50 per day for light, Rs 100 per day for heavy vehicles. **Jeep Hire** (6-seater) or minibus (10-seater), from Park Office at Dudhwa, Rs 20 per km. Elephants are rec, available at Dudhwa only. Rs 50 per person for 2½ hr. Each elephant carries 4 persons (hence min charge Rs 200). Book elephant ride on arrival at park.

Park information

● Accommodation

All basic, few a/c rm (foreigners pay more). Advance booking advisable; 15 days notice and full payment (bank draft/ postal order) is needed. Bedding is available at Dudhwa and Sathiana complexes. Generators for electricity on request at Sathiana, Sonaripur and Belrayan.

At Dudhwa: **D** *Forest Resthouse*, 4 suites and at Sathiana: **D** *Forest Resthouse*, 2 suites. Reservations: Chief Conservator of Forests, UP, 17 Rana Pratap Marg, Lucknow, T 246140. At Bankatti: **E** *Forest Resthouse*, 4 suites, **F** Dorm. Reservations: Director, Project Tiger Dudhwa National Park, Lakhimpur Kheri, T 2106.

Sonaripur, Belrayan and Kila: also have *Forest Resthouses*.

● Places to eat

Only *Dudhwa* has a canteen serving meals and snacks. Other places have cooking facilities (crockery and utensils). Provisions must be brought in. Palia (10 km) has eating places.

● Other Services

Medical facilities: at Dudhwa (dispensary) and Palia (basic health centre), a **Bank** and **Post and Telegraph office**: at Palia.

● Tourist Office

Reception Centre, Dudhwa National Park, Lakhimpur Kheri, nr Dist Magistrate's residence, T 2106. Wildlife Warden, Dudhwa National Park, Palia, T 185. Tours available in season.

● Transport

Air Nearest airports are Lucknow (219 km) and Bareilly (260 km) in India, and Dhangari (35 km) in Nepal.

Train Dudhwa is on the NE Railway metre gauge line and is connected with Lucknow and Moradabad, via Mailani (45 km from the park). A branch line from Mailani links places in the park. Transport is not always available at Dudhwa Station. Advisable to detrain at Palia (10 km) and take the hourly bus or taxi. The Tourist Complex is 4 km from Dudhwa rly station, 10 km from Palia and 37 km from Mailani.

Road UP Roadways and private buses connect Palia with Lakhimpur Kheri and Lucknow (219 km), Shahjahanpur (107 km), Bareilly (260 km) and Delhi (420 km).

Sravasti

150 km NE from Lucknow, Sravasti was an important city during the time of Buddha who lived and preached at the monastery of **Jetavana**. After his death the monastery enjoyed royal patronage, particularly from Asoka, and it remained active until the 11th century. Remains of the city and monastery are around the villages of Maheth and Saheth which are no more than 500m apart. **Maheth**, on the banks of the Achiravati River, consists of an earthen embankment and the ruins of 2 stupas and temples. **Saheth** contains the remains of the Jetavana monastery. The nearest centres for rail travel and accommodation are Bahraich to the W and Balrampur to the E. **Accommodation** At Balrampur: **D** *Maya*, a TCI hotel, and a *Tourist Bungalow*. At Sravasti: several pilgrim guesthouses (all **F**) *PWD Inspection Bungalow*, Burmese Temple Rest House, *Chinese Temple Rest House*, *Jain Dharamshala*.

Lucknow to Gorakhpur

ROUTES To continue the route from Lucknow take the NH28 E go on to Ramsanchi Ghat (40 km) across the River Kalyani to Faizabad (67 km).

Faizabad

(*Pop* 180,000; *STD Code* 05272) On the S bank of the Ghaghara River, Faizabad was once the capital of Oudh. Shuja-ud-Daula (1754-75), the 3rd Nawab of Oudh built Fort Calcutta here after his defeat by the British at Buxar in 1764. The 42m high white marble **Mausoleum of Bahu Begum** (c1816), his widow, is particularly fine. Its design was probably influenced by the Gulab Bari (Mausoleum of Shuja-ud-Daula, c1775) nearby, which contains the tombs of his mother and father. **Accommodation F** *Circuit House* nr Bus Stand.

ROUTES The road continues E from Faizabad to Ayodhya.

Ayodhya

(6 km), now regarded by many Hindus as the birthplace of Rama and where he once reigned. The historian Romila Thapar stresses that there is no evidence for such a belief. Jains believe that it is the birthplace of the 1st and 4th Tirthankaras, and the Buddha is also believed to have stayed in the town. The town's name means 'that which cannot be subdued by war'. Situated on the banks of the Ghaghara River, Ayodhya is one of the 7 holy Hindu cities – see also Mathura, Haridwar, Varanasi, Ujjain (MP), Dwarka (Gujarat) and Kanchipuram (Tamil Nadu). In view of the special significance of the site to Hindus, the Archaeological Survey of India and the Indian Institute of Advanced Study started on a project in 1978 to explore the town's origins which is still continuing.

The ancient site

Little remains of the ancient settlement. The ruins have a circumference of between 4 and 5 km, rising at some places to 10m above the ground. The excavations carried out so far, according to the Project Director, Professor BB Lal, suggest that "the site came under occupation at a time when the Northern Black Polished Ware of a very high quality and in a variety of shades – steel grey, blue, silvery and golden – was in use. It is now possible to distinguish at least 2 stages in the history of this ware, and the first occupation at Ayodhya would belong to the earlier stage...The houses were made of wattle and daub or of mud. The use of kiln-burnt brick for house construction was not in evidence. Both iron and copper were in use. Although no Carbon 14 dates for the earliest levels at Ayodhya are yet available those available from other sites suggest that...the beginning of the Northern Black Polished Ware may go back to circa 7th century BC if not earlier."

At later levels finds include a Jain figure from the 4th-3rd century BC, possibly the earliest Jain figure found in India. Houses during this period were built in kiln-baked brick, and various coins have been found from periods up to the 4th century AD. Some of the finds in this latter period suggest extensive trade with E India. There is no evidence of occupation between the 5th and 10th centuries AD, although both Fa-Hien and Hiuen Tsang are said to have visited it in the 5th and 7th centuries respectively. BB Lal goes on: "Since the medieval times the site has struggled on in one way or another, many of the now standing temples having been erected during the past two centuries only."

In accordance with Muslim practice elsewhere, a number of temples were razed and mosques were built on the site, often using the same building material. In recent years Ayodhya has become the focus of intense political activity by the *Vishwa Hindu Parishad*, an organisation which wants to assert a form of militant Hinduism. Violence between Muslims and Hindus flared in Ayodhya in 1990 because the VHP and the BJP, its leading party political ally, claimed that Ayodhya was 'Ramajanambhumi' – Rama's birthplace.

The holy site is beneath the remains of the **Babri Mosque** built by Babur, then deserted now for many years. The demands that a temple should be built on the spot caused widespread tension between the Hindu and Muslim communities from 1991 to 1993. Other sites associated with Rama are **Janam Sthana** where the god was raised and **Lakshmana Ghat** where Rama's brother committed suicide. **Hanuman's Fortress** takes its name from the Hanuman and Sita temple and the massive walls surrounding it. Other temples are Kala Rama and Kanak Bhavan.

NB: On 6 Dec 1992 the Babri Mosque was destroyed by militant Hindus. This was followed by widespread disturbances resulting in over 2500 deaths across the country. The Government has stated that it intends to re-build the mosque. Although the situation had quietened down in 1994 it was still a potential flashpoint. Check if you plan to visit.

Local information

● Accommodation

E *Tourist Bungalow* and **F** *Saket*, Station Rd. Rm and dorm. **F** *Railway Retiring Room*. Also

A Region Of Myths

The region around Faizabad is rich in myth, and many of the stories in the Ramayana are supposed to have taken place here. Guptar Park, for example, is where **Rama** is believed to have disappeared. The story of his birth illustrates how his origins have been traced back to **Vishnu**. Rajagopalachari summarises the account of how Rama's father, **Dasaratha**, unable to have children by any of his wives, was instructed to perform a great sacrifice in order that his wives might conceive. At the same time there was great trouble in the home of the gods, for **Ravana**, the king of the demons, had been assured by Brahma that he could never be harmed by a human, or by "devas and other supernatural beings". As a result he was causing havoc on earth. When the gods learned of this promise they turned to Vishnu and begged him to be born as a man so that he could put an end to Ravana and his trouble-making. Vishnu agreed that he would be born as 4 sons of Dasaratha, who was then performing his sacrifice.

Rajagopalachari goes on: "As the ghee was poured into the fire and the flames shot up to meet it, from out of the flames came a majestic figure, resplendent like the noonday sun, holding a bowl of gold. Calling King Dasaratha by name, the figure said: 'The Devas are pleased with you and are answering your prayer. Here is *payasam* sent by the gods for your wives. You will be blessed with sons if they drink of this divine beverage.' With joy unbounded, Dasaratha received the bowl as he would receive a child and distributed the payasam to his 3 wives, Kausalya, Sumitra, and Kaikeyi. He asked Kausalya to drink a half of the payasam and he gave half of what remained to Sumitra. Half of what was then left was drunk by Kaikeyi, and what remained was given to Sumitra again. Dasaratha's wives were happy, even as a beggar suddenly coming upon buried treasure. And in due course all of them were expectant mothers. In course of time" the story goes on "Dasaratha's sons were born. Rama, of Kausalya and Bharata of Kaikeyi. Sumitra gave birth to twins, Lakshmana and Satrughna, she having drunk the divine payasam. In proportion to the quantity of payasam drunk by the respective mothers, the sons are traditionally considered to be parts of Vishnu. Rama was thus half Vishnu."

Birla, T 41 and *Kanak Bhavan* Dharamshalas, T 24.

● **Transport**

Train Varanasi: *Ganga-Yamuna Exp* 4284, Tu,W,F,Su, 1055, 3¾ hr; New Delhi-Varanasi Exp 2450, M,Th,Sa, 0910, 3 hr.

From Ayodhya the road passes through Khalilabad (92 km), to Gorakhpur (32 km).

Gorakhpur

(*Pop* 600,000; *STD Code* 0551) Gorakhpur, at the confluence of the Rapti and Rohini rivers, is the last major Indian town travellers bound for Nepal pass through. The British and the Gurkha armies clashed nearby in the early 18th century. Later it became the recruitment centre for Gurkha soldiers enlisting into the British and Indian armies. It is a delightful centre, noted as a major railway maintenance town and now with a University. The **Gorakhnath Temple** attracts Hindu pilgrims, particularly *Kanfata sadhus* who have part of their ears cut. Unusual terracotta pottery figures and animals are made here. A tourist complex with a Buddha Jayanti Park, a luxury hotel and floating restaurant, is being completed at **Ramgarh Lake** SE of town.

Local information

● **Accommodation**

Mainly for the budget traveller. Groups may contact the International Geographical Union, Univ of Gorakhpur for assistance with booking to avoid paying large commissions to agents. **D** *Ganges*, Gatashanker Chowk. Well managed with some a/c rm. Good restaurant and ice cream parlour. Rec. **D** *Bobina*, Gatashanker Chowk, Nepal Rd, T 336663. 38 rm, some a/c. Restaurant, bar, exchange, travel, lawn. Drab and run-down despite reputation. **D** *Upvan*, Nepal Rd, T 336503. Some a/c or air-cooled rm. Indian restaurant. Clean, efficient rm-service, good air-cooling. Highly rec (ask rickshaw to go next door to *Bobina Hotel*). **D** *President*, in Golghar, T 337654. Best rm, a/c with TV. **D** *Avantika*, Mohaddipur, Airport Rd (NH28), beyond crossroads. **D** *Eelora*, opp station, T 330647. Some a/c rm. Restaurant serves Indian snacks, lacks atmosphere, relatively expensive. Clean rm, suitable for overnight stay, but stuffy and noisy. **D** *Marina*, has some a/c rm.

● **Budget hotels**

Simple hotels nr the rly station incl **E** *Modern*; **E** *Siddharth*. Some a/c or air-cooled rm. **E** *Tourist Bungalow* and **F** *Gupta Tourist Lodge*, opp station. **E** *Railway Retiring Rooms* upstairs, some a/c rm (best deluxe) and 3 dorms. Restaurant. Also NE Rly *VIP Guest House*. Others nearby are similar: **E** *Kailash Dharamshala*, Bazar, 1 km from rly station, T 336404. All air-cooled rm, clean linen and bath, good management. No restaurants nearby. **E** *York*, Golghar, city centre. Some a/c rm with bath. **E** *Amber* is similar. **F** PWD *Inspection Bungalows* and *Dak Bungalows*.

● **Post & telecommunications**

Telephone: ISD and Fax services from *Door Sanchar*, The Target, opp Vijay Cinema.

● **Tourist Offices**

UP, Park Rd, Civil Lines, T 335450; Counter on Platform 1, Rly Station.

● **Transport**

Air Airport 7 km. Currently **Indian Airlines** services are suspended.

Train Gorakhpur Junc, NE Rly HQ station, has Tourist information, left luggage and computerized reservations. **Delhi**: *Vaishali Exp* 2553, daily, 1730, 14 hr, (4¾ hr to Lucknow); *Barauni-Amritsar Exp* 5207, daily, 1245, 16¾ hr; **Lucknow**: *Gorakhnath Exp*, daily, 2230, 6¼ hr; *Sabarmati Exp* 9166A, daily, 1515, 6 hr½ hr. **Varanasi**: *Exp* 3020/5449, daily, 1515, 6¼ hr; *Triveni Exp* 5206/5405, daily, 1920, 6¾ hr; *Fast Passenger*, 1143/81, daily, 0305, 8½ hr. **Bombay (to VT)**: *Kusinagar Exp* 1016, daily, 1845, 30 hr (5¼ hr to Lucknow); *Dadar Exp* (via Varanasi-Allahabad) 1028, daily, 0530 (5¼ hr to Varanasi). **Calcutta (H)**: *Haora Exp*, 3020, daily, 1500, 21 hr; *Purvanchal Exp* 5048, T,Th,Sa,Su, 1025, 16 hr.

Road Bus: the bus station is 3 min walk from rly. City buses meet most main trains. Services to Lucknow (6-7 hr), Varanasi (from Katchari Stand, 205 km, 6 hr), Patna (10 hr), Kusinagara (55 km, on the hr) and other regional towns.

● **Transport to Nepal**

Many travellers choose buses to cross into Nepal. The usual route is to go N to Nautanwa, crossing the Nepal border at Sonauli (though via Pharenda is shorter, but road may be closed). You can visit **Lumbini** (109 km) just across the Nepal border, the birthplace of the

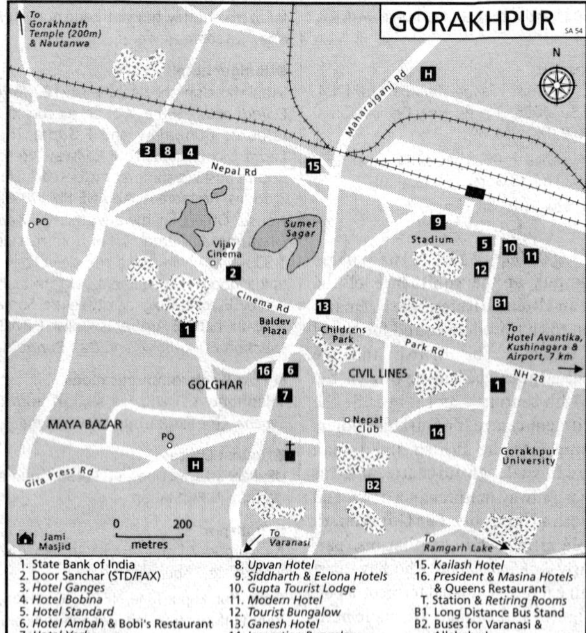

Buddha.

Train (metre gauge) from Gorakhpur Junc. **Nautanwa**: The most convenient are 2 *Fast Passenger* trains. 95, daily, 0615, 2¼ hr (return dep Nautanwa, 96, daily 0910); 93, daily, 1230, 3¼ hr (return 94, daily, 1700). You can usually obtain tickets on day of departure (Cl I, Rs 100, Cl II Rs 35) .

By bus: several from bus stand nr rly station. UP Govt buses (green and yellow) are 'Express' and usually depart close to schedule. Other private buses (sometimes deluxe with air-cooling or a/c up to Kathmandu and Pokhara) leave from opp the rly station. However, it is often difficult to distinguish between them. Services from 0500, for **Nautanwa** (95 km, 3¼ hr), or **Sonauli**, just beyond, on the border (102 km, Rs 20, 3½ hr). It often takes longer.

At Sonauli you need to fill in a small blue form and obtain your Exit Visa stamp at the Indian Immigration office. You then proceed to the Nepalese Immigration counter to get your Entrance Visa stamp (which is noted as your starting date of the visa); the counter is open from 0530-2100. There is little help available to find these offices. If you leave Gorakhpur after 1400 you will arrive at Sonauli after 1700 and will probably do better to stay overnight on the Indian side and walk across (or get a rickshaw for NRs 5) in the morning to maximize Visa days. From there you can take a bus/local taxi (Rs 3) to **Bhairawa** in Nepal (6 km) where onward buses and flights are available.

Air (and bus) connections by Nepal Airways, Sidhartha Nagar (nr bus stop), Bhairawa T 20667. Rec for good value. Flights to **Kathmandu** (US$75) **Pokhara** (US$35), **Nepalganj** (US$77)

Buses to **Kathmandu** (Rs 95, 12 hr) **Pokhara** (Rs 75, 10 hr), **Nepalganj** (Rs 115) or **Narayanghat** (Rs 32 for National Park). Most dep at 0700. Local buses every ½ hr to **Lumbini** (Rs 9 for day trip) and **Butwal** Rs 8. There are different bus stands depending on the destination.

Warning: Beware of ticket touts in Gorakhpur (Private buses opp Rly Station) and Nepal border. Some overcharge, others demand excessive 'luggage charge', incl Rs 10 to put bags on roof-rack. When buying a ticket, make absolutely sure which bus, what is included in ticket (meals, overnight accommodation), when and from where it departs (may be 2 hr delay). Avoid *International Tourism Agency* opp rly station; their buses are very poorly maintained. Nepalese buses from Sonauli are OK.

Excursions from Gorakhpur

Two of Buddhism's 8 holy places are visited from Gorakhpur: Kusinagara (55 km), Lumbini (109 km) and Sravasti. The 8 events, which are repeatedly represented in Buddhist art, are associated with: **Lumbini**, his birth place; **Bodh Gaya**, where he attained enlightenment; **Sarnath** deer park, where he preached his 1st sermon; **Rajagriha**, where he tamed a wild elephant; **Vaishali**, where a monkey offered him honey; **Sravasti**, associated with his great miracle; **Sankasya**, where he descended from heaven and **Kusinagara**, where he died.

Kusinagara

(*Pop* 14,000) 3 km SW of **Kasia** (55 km E of Gorakhpur on NH28), Kusinagara is celebrated as the place where the Buddha died and was cremated and passed into *parinirvana*. Originally known as Kushinara (the actual site is unknown), it is one of 4 major Buddhist pilgrimage sites. Monasteries established after the Buddha's death flourished here until the 13th century.

Mukutabandhana Stupa According to legend it was built by the Malla dynasty to house the Buddha's relics after the cremation. 1 km to the W, the core of the smaller **Nirvana stupa** possibly dates from Asoka's time. The large recumbent figure of the dying Buddha in a shrine in front may have been brought from Mathura by the monk Haribala during King Kumargupta's reign (413-455 AD). The stupas, chaityas and viharas, however, were 'lost' for centuries. The Chinese pilgrims Fa Hien, Hiuen Tsang, and I Tsing, all recorded the decay and ruins of Kushinagar between 900 and 1000 years after the Buddha's death. The stupa and the temple were rediscovered only in the 1880s.

Excavations were begun by the Archaeological Survey of India in 1904-5, following clues left by the Chinese travellers. A shaft was driven through the centre of the stupa "which brought to light a copper plate placed on the mouth of a relic casket in the form of a copper vessel with charcoal, cowries, precious stones and a gold coin of Kumaragupta I." The whole area was occupied until the 11th century. In all there are 8 groups of monasteries, stupas and images, indicating that Kushinagar was a substantial community. *Kusinagara* by Dr DR Patil is published by ASI.

● Accommodation

ITDC **E** ***Travellers' Lodge***, opp main site. 8 rm. UP Tourism ***Pathik Niwas***, nr ASI office, T 7138. PWD ***Inspection Bungalow***, LRP ***Inspection House*** and ***Birla Hindu-Baudh Dharamshala*** which has a Tourist Bureau.

● Transport

There are buses and taxis from Gorakhpur (½ hr).

DELHI TO VARANASI

This route follows the historic **Grand Trunk Rd** through the heart of the flat Ganga-Yamuna doab. It passes through Kanpur on its way to Varanasi, India's most sacred city, on the bank of the Ganga.

The UP Gazetteer of 1908 described the landscape as: "a level plain, the monotony of which is broken only by the numerous village sites and groves of dark olive mango trees which meet the eye in every direction. The fields are never bare except in the hot months, after the spring harvest has been gathered. Even the grass withers, and hardly a green thing is visible except a few patches of garden crops near the village sites, and the carefully watered fields of sugar cane. With the breaking of the monsoon the scene changes as if by magic; the turf is re-

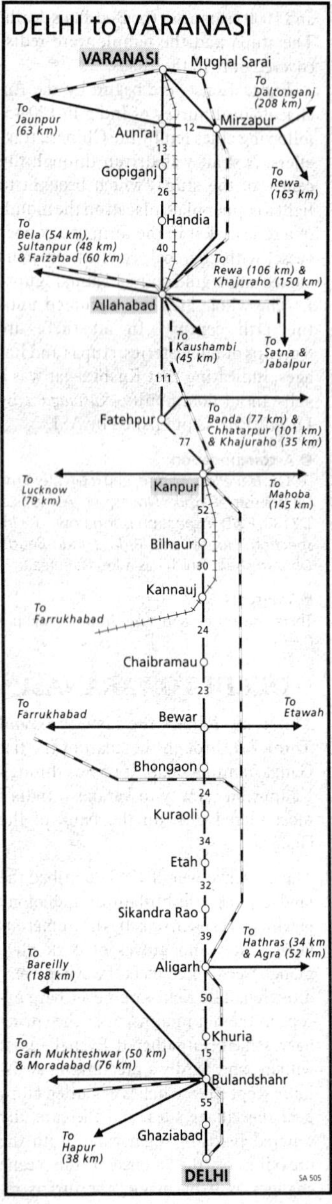

newed, and tall grasses begin to shoot in the small patches of jungle. A month later, the autumn crops – rice, the millets and maize – have begun to clothe the naked fields till late in the year, and are succeeded by the spring crops – wheat, barley, and gram. In March they ripen and the great plain is then a rolling sea of golden corn, in which appear islands of trees and villages."

ROUTES There are 2 main routes to Kanpur by road. It is probably quicker to take the **NH2** to Agra. The GT Rd crosses the Yamuna and goes through Firozabad and Etawah and then across the doab to Kanpur. Alternatively, cross the Yamuna in Delhi and travel S from Ghaziabad to Aligarh. The road crosses the *doab* to the Ganga, which you finally see a few km beyond Kannauj (356 km).

Aligarh

(*Pop* 480,000; *Alt* 200m; *STD Code* 0571) Originally a Rajput stronghold from 1194, Aligarh ('high fort') was administered by Muslim Governors appointed by the King of Delhi. The Fort built in 1524 was subsequently reinforced by French and then British engineers. After the Mughals, it fell into Jat, Maratha and Rohilla hands before being taken by the British under Lord Lake in 1803. The Mutiny of 1857 quickly spread from Meerut when the 9th Native Infantry left to join the rebels at Delhi. The British regained control 5 months later.

There are several **mosques** and the **Aligarh Muslim University**, founded by Sir Saiyad Ahmad Khan in 1875 as the Anglo-Oriental College, modelled on the Oxford and Cambridge collegiate system.

- **Accommodation** on GT Rd: **D** *Ruby*, opp Roadways Bus Stand nr rly, T 25713, 25 rm, some a/c. Restaurant, exchange. *Shahensha*, Banna Desi.

ROUTES From Aligarh the road continues to Etah (69 km, *Pop* 78,000), a district headquarters. Then across the flat plains through a series of small towns to Gursahaiganj (113 km). 17 km beyond, turn left to Kannauj (3 km).

Kannauj

(*Pop* 60,000; *STD Code* 05694). Kannauj was Harsha's capital in the 7th century and later that of the Tomar and Rathor Rajputs. Mahmud of Ghazni sacked the town in 1018. Qutb-ud-din-Aibak took it in 1194 forcing the Rathors to flee to Rajasthan. There is little of interest except the **Archaeological Museum** (sculptures dating from the 1st and 2nd centuries AD), the Shrine of Raja Ajaipal (1021) and the **Jama Masjid** (between the town and the station) which was converted from a Hindu temple by Ibrahim Shah of Jaunpur (early 15th century). Kannauj used to be on the banks of the Ganga. Now it is several km to its S.

ROUTES The road continues SE to **Kanpur** (82 km).

Kanpur

(*Population:* 2.1 mn. *STD Code*: 0512). The largest city of UP, Kanpur is the most important industrial centre in the state. Cotton mills were first established in 1869, some of the first in India. It is now one of the major industrial cities with aviation, woollen and leather industries, cotton, flour and vegetable oil mills, sugar refineries and chemical works.

History

Under the British Kanpur was one of the most important garrisons on the Ganga. During the Mutiny in Delhi, the insurgents turned towards 'Cawnpore' as the British called it. Here they rallied under a princeling, Nana Sahib, who bore a grievance against the British because he had received only a small pension, and laid siege to the British community of around 1000. After a few weeks the defenders were reduced to a few hundred through gunshot wounds, starvation and disease. Nana Sahib then offered a truce and arranged for boats to take the survivors downstream to Allahabad. When they were boarding these at Satichaura Ghat, they were raked with fire and hacked down by horsemen. One boat escaped. The survivors were either butchered and thrown down a well or died of cholera and dysentery.

The reprisals were as horrible. General Sir James Neill "was seized with an Old Testamental vision of revenge when he saw the mangled bodies down the well" (Moorhouse). To break a man's caste, pork and beef were stuffed down his throat, thus condemning him to eternal damnation. More often than not, persons suspected of belonging to the Mutineer army were bayoneted on sight, regardless of whether they were armed or not. Nana Sahib escaped after pretending to commit suicide in the Ganga and is believed to have died of fever in Nepal in 1859.

Places of interest

The principal British monuments are in the SE of the city in the old cantonment area. Stone posts mark the lines of the trenches near **All Soul's Memorial Church** (1862-75), a handsome Gothic style building designed by Walter Granville with a fine stained glass W window and interesting memorials. A tiled pavement outside marks the graves of those executed on 1 July 1857 soon after the

CLIMATE: KANPUR

	Jan	Feb	Mar	Apr	May	Jun	Jul	Aug	Sep	Oct	Nov	Dec	Av/Tot
Max (°C)	23	26	33	38	42	40	34	32	33	33	29	24	32
Min (°C)	9	11	16	22	27	29	27	26	25	20	12	9	19
Rain (mm)	23	16	9	5	6	68	208	286	202	43	7	8	881

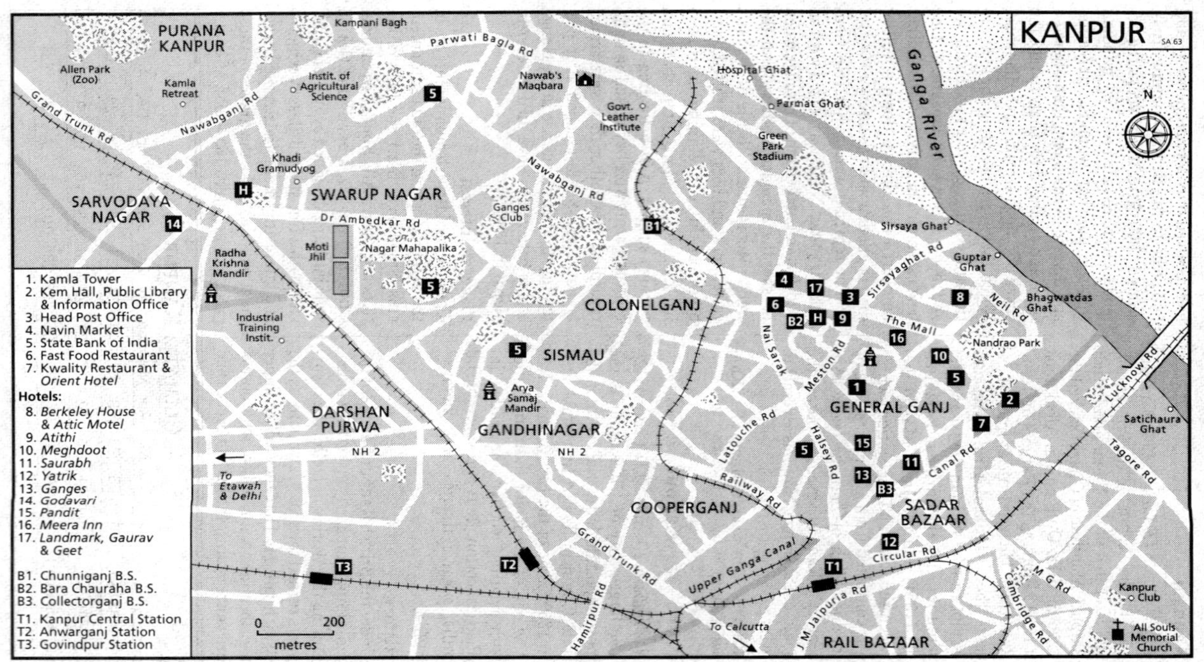
KANPUR
SA 63
PURANA KANPUR
Kampani Bagh
Parwati Bagla Rd
Allen Park (Zoo)
Kamla Retreat
Instit. of Agricultural Science
Nawab's Maqbara
Hospital Ghat
Parmat Ghat
Govt. Leather Institute
Green Park Stadium
Ganga River
N
Grand Trunk Rd
Nawabganj Rd
Khadi Gramudyog
SWARUP NAGAR
Nawabganj Rd
Ganges Club
SARVODAYA NAGAR
Dr Ambedkar Rd
Moti Jhil
Nagar Mahapalika
Sirsaya Ghat
Sirsayaghat Rd
Guptar Ghat
Bhagwatdas Ghat
Neil Rd
Radha Krishna Mandir
Industrial Training Instit.
COLONELGANJ
The Mall
Nai Sarak
Meston Rd
Nandrao Park
Lucknow Rd
SISMAU
Arya Samaj Mandir
GENERAL GANJ
Satichaura Ghat
DARSHAN PURWA
GANDHINAGAR
Latouche Rd
Halsey Rd
NH 2
To Etawah & Delhi
Canal Rd
Tagore Rd
Railway Rd
COOPERGANJ
SADAR BAZAAR
Grand Trunk Rd
Upper Ganga Canal
Circular Rd
M G Rd
Cambridge Rd
Kanpur Club
Hamirpur Rd
To Calcutta
J M Jaipuria Rd
RAIL BAZAAR
All Souls Memorial Church
0 200 metres
1. Kamla Tower
2. Kem Hall, Public Library & Information Office
3. Head Post Office
4. Navin Market
5. State Bank of India
6. Fast Food Restaurant
7. Kwality Restaurant & Orient Hotel
Hotels:
8. Berkeley House & Attic Motel
9. Atithi
10. Meghdoot
11. Saurabh
12. Yatrik
13. Ganges
14. Godavari
15. Pandit
16. Meera Inn
17. Landmark, Gaurav & Geet
B1. Chunniganj B.S.
B2. Bara Chauraha B.S.
B3. Collectorganj B.S.
T1. Kanpur Central Station
T2. Anwarganj Station
T3. Govindpur Station

Satichaura Ghat massacre. To the E, the **Memorial Garden** has a statue by Marochetti and a screen designed by Sir Henry Yule which were brought here after Independence. Originally, the memorial statue stood where the bodies of British women and children had been thrown into a well after the massacre. The infamous **Satichaura Ghat**, 1 km NE of the church by the Ganga has a small Siva temple. In the city centre there is the King Edward VII **Memorial Hall** and **Christ Church** (1848).

The higher grade hotels are along the Mall, some within reach of Meston Rd with its interesting, though faded, colonial architecture and cheap leather goods shops.

Museums

Kamla Retreat Museum, historical and archaeological. Visits only with prior approval. Shyam Hari Singhania Art Gallery.

Local information

● Accommodation

B/C *Meghdoot*, 17/3B The Mall. T 311999, F 310209. 99 rm. Specialist restaurants and fast food, pastry shop. Once the best, now run down.

C *Landmark*, 10 The Mall, T 317601, F 315291 (Delhi T 6471035. Restaurants, casual coffee lounge, bar, poolside barbeque, health club, business facilities, station/airport pickup. **C** *Grand Trunk*, 84/79 GT Rd, T 245435. 30 rm. Restaurant, bar, travel, pool.

D *Atithi*, 17/11 The Mall (1 km from rly), T 311607. Some a/c rm. Restaurant rec, travel. Modern hotel with good view of Mall. **D** *Attic*, 15/198 Civil Lines, 7 a/c rm some with TV. **D** *Gaurav*, 18/54 The Mall, T 269599. 33 a/c rm. Restaurant, garden. **D** *Geet*, 18/174-5 The Mall (opp Phoolbagh), T 311024. 40 a/c rm. Restaurant rec, exchange. Slightly cheaper **D** *Meera Inn*, 37/19H The Mall (opp Reserve Bank of India), T 319972. Some a/c rm with TV. Restaurant (Indian snacks, drinks). Clean, good value, rec. **D** *Orient*, opp Heer Palace, The Mall, T 366130. Some a/c (switched on in summer). Basic Indian restaurant, ice cream parlour below. Once a popular, colonial guest house, now a bit shabby and run down, but run by charming family. Well located nr Meston Rd. Popular business hotel, book in advance. **D** *Saurabh*, 24/54 Birhana Rd, T 61725. 22 a/c rm. Good restaurant, exchange, travel. **D** *Swagat*, 80 Feet Rd, T 241923. 19 a/c rm. Central. Restaurant (Indian, Chinese), exchange, travel. **D** *Yatrik*, 65/58A Circular Rd, T 260373. 15 rm, some a/c with TV. Nr rly. Restaurant, travel.

● Budget hotels

E *Ganges*, 51/50 Nayaganj, T 69185. 80 rm some with bath. Nr rly. Indian restaurant. **E** *Godavari*, 3A Sarvodaya Nagar, T 217126. 9 a/c rm. Restaurant, bar. **E** *Pandit*, 49/7 General Ganj. T 67166. 45 rm, some a/c. Restaurant (Indian veg, Chinese), exchange. **E** *Shivoy*, Shivoy Tower, The Mall. T 212664. A/c rm. Restaurant, travel.

● Places to eat

The Mall has a ***Kwality***, ***Shang-hai*** and ***Fu-Tu*** for Chinese. In Sarvodaya Nagar: ***Kabab Corner*** and ***Sarovar***. Also ***Hamso*** in Swaroop Nagar and ***Upvan***, Cantt. **Fast food** on The Mall: ***Hot Trak***, 9 Som Dutt Plaza; ***Shalaka***, in shopping arcade opp *Landmark Hotel* for pizzas, chips, S Indian snacks.

● Banks & money changers

Usually open 1000-1400. **ANZ Grindlays**, 16 MG Rd, rec for exchanging TCs; **Allahabad Bank**, MG Rd. Others on Bara Chauraha and The Mall.

● Hospitals & medical services

Cantonment General Hospital, T 60540. *Dufferin Hospital*, T 62500. *KPM Hospital*, T 60351. *Guru Nanak Hospital*, T 20156.

● Post & telecommunications

Head GPO: Bara Chauraha, T 60324, (open 24 hr).

● Shopping

Main shopping areas are The Mall, Birhara Rd and Navin Market. Kanpur is famous for cotton and leather products (shops along Meston Rd). ***UPICA***, UP Handlooms, ***Phulkari***, Punjab Emporium; ***Tantuja***, Bengal Emporium are on The Mall. **Photography**: ***Chitra Studio***, Meston Rd, T 63954. ***Chetan's Studio***, The Mall.

● Sports

Cricket: Green Park Stadium.

Golf: Jajmau.

Swimming: pools, in hotels *Meghdoot* and *Grand Trunk*.

Tennis: Kanpur Tennis Club.

● **Tour companies & travel agents**
Several on the Mall: ***Jet Air***, 24/1, LIC Bldg, 1st Fl, T 312787 (GSA for several foreign airlines). Very efficient, rec; ***Sita***, at 18/53 for Indian Airlines.

● **Tourist offices**
UP, 26/51 Birhana Rd (Back Lane of Bazar), opp Post Office. **Dist Information Office**, KEM Hall, Phool Bagh.

● **Useful addresses**
Police: T 100. **Fire**: T 44444. **Ambulance**: T 62500.

● **Transport**
On **NH2** and **NH25**, Kanpur is connected to all parts of the country by good roads. Lucknow (79 km); Allahabad (193 km); Varanasi (329 km); Khajuraho (389 km); Agra (296 km); Jhansi (222 km); Bhopal (369 km); Delhi (438 km); Calcutta (1007 km); Bombay (1345 km); Madras (1998 km).

Local Taxis: there are no yellow-top taxis. Private taxis are available from Canal Rd taxi stand, hotels and agencies. Full day (8 hr) about Rs 180. **Rickshaws & tongas**: tempo-rickshaws operate to all parts of the city. Auto-rickshaws, cycle-rickshaws and horse tongas are available, rates negotiable. **Bus**: City Bus Service is cheap with extensive network.

Air Transport to town: by taxi, Rs 90; from town Rs 70. **Indian Airlines**, opp MG College, Civil Lines, T 211430. Airport, T 43042. Services 5 times a week from Delhi to Kanpur returning via Lucknow.

Train Kanpur is on the main Broad Gauge Delhi-Calcutta line and also has lines from Lucknow, Agra and Central India. **Agra Fort**: *Avadh Exp* 5063, daily, 2335, 6 hr; *Udyan Abha Toofan Exp* 3007, daily, 0835, 5½ hr. **New Delhi**: *Shatabdi Exp* 2003, M-F, 1700, 4¾ hr; *Haora-Danapur Exp* 3031, daily, 0015, 6½ hr; *Gomti Exp* 2419, daily except Tu, 0705, 6¼ hr. **Calcutta (Haora)**: *Rajdhani Exp* 2302, daily except Th and Su, 2215, 12½ hr; *Kalka-Haora Mail* 2312, daily, 1505, 17½ hr; *Haora Exp* 3012, daily, 0635, 23¾ hr. **Patna**: *Northeast Exp* 2522, daily, 1240, 8½ hr; *Tinsukia Mail* 2456, daily, 0130, 9 hr. **Varanasi**: *Neelachal Exp* 8476, Tu,Th,Su, 1220, 6½ hr; *Ganga-Yamuna Exp* 4284, Tu,W,F,Su, 0605, 8¾ hr; *Ganga-Yamuna Exp* 4214, M,Tu,Sa, 0605, 8¼ hr. **Lucknow**: *Ganga-Yamuna Exp* 4284, Tu,W,F,Su, 0540, 2¼ hr; *Ganga-Yamuna Exp* 4214, Mo,Th,Sa, 0540, 2¼ hr; *Gomti Exp* 2420, daily except Tu, 2050, 2 hr; *Sabarmati Exp* 9165, daily, 0240, 2½ hr.

Road UP Roadways and the SRTCs of neighbouring states connect Kanpur to Lucknow, Allahabad, Varanasi, Agra, Unnao, Rae Bareli, Kannauj and Jhansi. UP Roadways Bus Stand, Collectorganj, T 63259; Chunnyganj, T 63603.

ROUTES Leave Kanpur on the **NH2** to Fatehpur (77 km).

Fatehpur

At the end of the 18th century Fatehpur District was waste land. Land revenue settlements in 1814 encouraged its further growth from a Mughal market town. The Islamic monuments are the **Tomb of Nawab Ali Khan** (late 18th century), a minister at the court of the Nawabs of Oudh, the **Jami Masjid** and **Mosque of Hakim Abdul Hasan** of Kara. Four pillars erected by a Mr Tucker who was later killed in the Mutiny, stand by the road. They have the Ten Commandments and quotations from St John's Gospel carved on them in Urdu and Hindi.

ROUTES From Fatehpur continue down the **NH2** to Allahabad (116 km).

Allahabad (Prayag)

(*Population:* 860,000. *Altitude:* 98m. *STD Code*: 0532). There are several early historical sites in the city. Draupadi Ghat, for example, has revealed signs of extensive habitation and considerable quantities of Northern Black Pottery Ware of the type found across N India to Taxila and beyond, dated between 1100 and 800 BC. Two other sites in the city have revealed similar finds. On the present site of the Bharadwaj ashram were remains of the Kushan period. 500 years later Hiuen Tsang visited the city in 643 AD. The Muslims first conquered it in 1194 and renamed it Allahabad in 1584. It later became the HQ of the British Govt of the NW Provinces and Oudh, and here the transfer of government from the East India Company to the crown was announced by Lord Canning in 1858. The first Indian National Congress was held in Allahabad in 1885. Anand Bhavan, the

Nehru family home is here. Today Allahabad is a rapidly growing commercial and administrative city.

The confluence
For Hindus Allahabad is particularly sacred because it is at the junction ('sangam'), of the Ganga and the Jamuna – hence its other name, **Prayag** ('confluence'). The purifying power of a sacred river is strengthened at a confluence just as the physical power is. In addition, the mythical underground river of enlightenment, the **Sarasvati**, is also believed to surface here. The *sangam* itself is a narrow spit of land where the rivers gently mingle and is quite shallow and muddy. Bathing in the rivers at the prayag is auspicious at all times of the year, more so at *Magh Mela* which occurs every year for 15 days (Jan/Feb) and longer at the **Kumbh Mela**. In 1989 the *Kumbhayog*, or most auspicious time for bathing and washing away of a lifetime's sins, was on 4 Feb when 13 million are estimated to have bathed in the rivers.

The story behind the Kumbh Mela is that Hindu gods and demons vied for the pot (*kumbha*) that held the nectar of immortality (*amrit*). During the fight for possession, which lasted 12 days, Vishnu was running with the pot and 4 drops of *amrit* fell to earth, making 4 sacred places Allahabad, Haridwar (UP), to Ujjain (MP) and Nasik (Maharashtra). Holiest of all is Allahabad, the site of the Maha (Great) Kumbh Mela. This festival moves every 3 years returning to Allahabad every 12th year.

Places of interest
The Mughal Period For a town of such antiquity, Allahabad has few monuments pre-dating the Muslim period. The **Fort** begun in 1583 as the largest of Akbar's forts. It has 3 massive gateways and 7m high brick walls, seen to advantage from across the river. The Marathas held it from 1739 to 1750 when it was taken by the Pathans, and then by the British in 1801. Most of the fort is closed to tourists, including the *zenana* (harem) and the 3rd century BC Asoka pillar, which was moved to the fort from Kausambi under Akbar's orders. Under the fort's E wall, reached through a door, is the Undying Banyan Tree (*Akshai vata*), from which pilgrims threw themselves to achieve salvation in death.

Khusrau Bagh Prince Khusrau was murdered in 1615 by his own brother, later the Emperor Shah Jahan (r1627-1658). After staging an unsuccessful rebellion against his father Jahangir (r1605-1627) in 1607, Khusrau spent the next year in chains. Two of his closest associates were sewn into the skins of a freshly slaughtered ox and ass, mounted the wrong way round on donkeys and paraded through the streets of Lahore. The hot sun dried the skins and one died from suffocation. Khusrau himself was forced to ride an elephant down a street lined with the heads of his supporters. When freed, he encouraged a plot to assassinate his father but was discovered. He was blinded, though he did regain partial sight and spent the rest of his life as a captive.

The typical Mughal garden enclosure is entered through an 18m high archway and houses the handsome tomb. The burial chamber is underground with-

CLIMATE: ALLAHABAD

	Jan	Feb	Mar	Apr	May	Jun	Jul	Aug	Sep	Oct	Nov	Dec	Av/Tot
Max (°C)	24	26	33	40	42	40	33	32	33	32	28	24	32
Min (°C)	8	11	16	22	27	28	27	26	25	19	12	8	19
Rain (mm)	23	15	15	5	15	127	620	254	213	58	8	8	1361

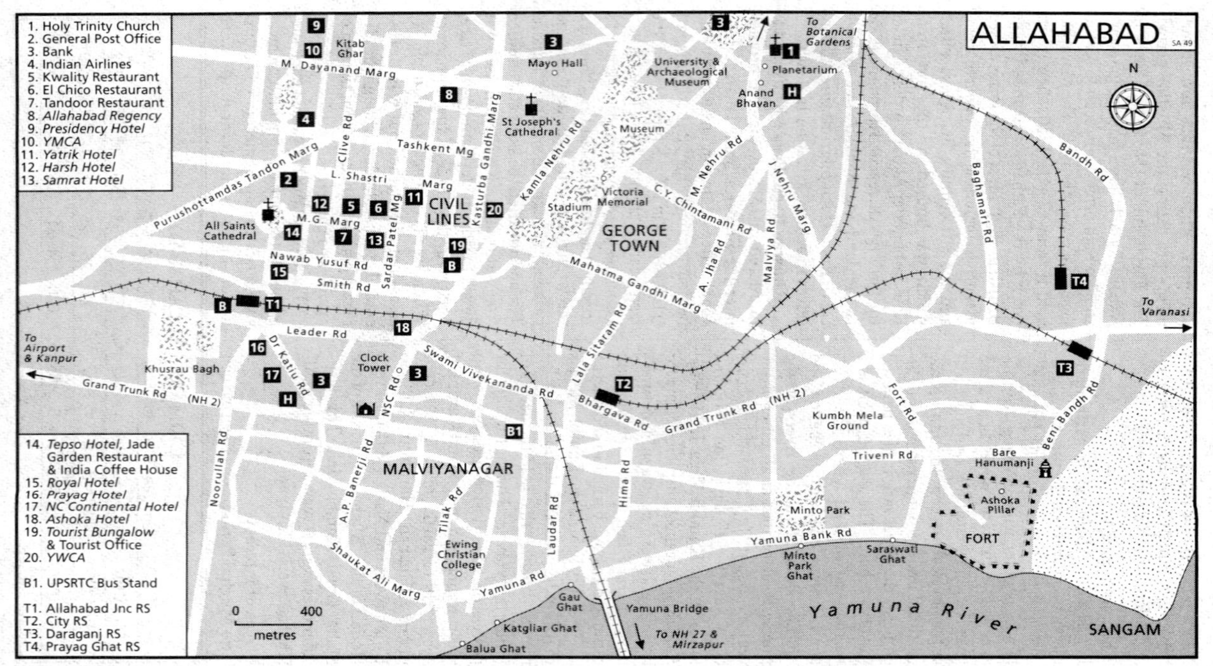
ALLAHABAD
SA 49
N
1. Holy Trinity Church
2. General Post Office
3. Bank
4. Indian Airlines
5. Kwality Restaurant
6. El Chico Restaurant
7. Tandoor Restaurant
8. *Allahabad Regency*
9. *Presidency Hotel*
10. *YMCA*
11. *Yatrik Hotel*
12. *Harsh Hotel*
13. *Samrat Hotel*
14. *Tepso Hotel*, Jade Garden Restaurant & India Coffee House
15. *Royal Hotel*
16. *Prayag Hotel*
17. *NC Continental Hotel*
18. *Ashoka Hotel*
19. *Tourist Bungalow* & Tourist Office
20. *YWCA*
B1. UPSRTC Bus Stand
T1. Allahabad Jnc RS
T2. City RS
T3. Daraganj RS
T4. Prayag Ghat RS
Kitab Ghar
M. Dayanand Marg
Mayo Hall
University & Archaeological Museum
To Botanical Gardens
Planetarium
Anand Bhavan
St Joseph's Cathedral
Clive Rd
Tashkent Mg
Kasturba Gandhi Marg
Kamla Nehru Rd
Museum
M. Nehru Rd
J Nehru Marg
Baghamari Rd
Bandh Rd
Purushottamdas Tandon Marg
L. Shastri Marg
CIVIL LINES
Victoria Memorial
Stadium
C.Y. Chintamani Rd
All Saints Cathedral
M.G. Marg
Sardar Patel Mg
GEORGE TOWN
A. Jha Rd
Malviya Rd
Nawab Yusuf Rd
Smith Rd
Mahatma Gandhi Marg
To Varanasi
Leader Rd
Lala Sitaram Rd
To Airport & Kanpur
Khusrau Bagh
Dr Katju Rd
Clock Tower
Swami Vivekananda Rd
NSC Rd
Grand Trunk Rd (NH 2)
Bhargava Rd
Fort Rd
Kumbh Mela Ground
Beni Bandh Rd
Noorullah Rd
A.P. Banerji Rd
MALVIYANAGAR
Tilak Rd
Laudar Rd
Hima Rd
Triveni Rd
Bare Hanumanji
Ashoka Pillar
Minto Park
FORT
Yamuna Bank Rd
Ewing Christian College
Minto Park Ghat
Saraswati Ghat
Shaukat Ali Marg
Yamuna Rd
Gau Ghat
Yamuna Bridge
Yamuna River
SANGAM
0 400 metres
Katgliar Ghat
Balua Ghat
To NH 27 & Mirzapur

decorative plasterwork. The tomb to the W is thought to be his sister's. Further W is the 2-storey tomb of his Rajput mother.

Buildings from the British Period Canning Town, opp Junction Railway Station, was laid out on a grid in the 1860s. Within it are the Old High Court and Public Offices, classical style buildings from the late 19th century including the Gothic style **All Saint's** Cathedral. At the E end of the Civil Lines is Alfred Park (now Chandra Sekhar Azad Park), N of which stands **Muir College**, a fine example of 'Indo-Saracenic' architecture. It was later established as the University of Allahabad. W of this is **Mayo Hall** with **St Joseph's** Roman Catholic Cathedral (1879) to its S, with its accompanying schools. The **Holy Trinity** Church (early 19th century) on J Nehru Marg, contains memorials from the Gwalior Campaign (1843) and the Mutiny (1857). W of the fort is **Minto Park** where the Royal Proclamation of the Assumption of Rule by the Crown in 1858 – Curzon's 'Magna Carta of India'.

Excursions

Bhita, 22 km SW of Allahabad, the site of a trading community well before 350 BC. A series of mounds were excavated by Marshall in 1910-11. Brick structures belonging to 5 periods were identified but below these lie a series of deposits which include Northern Black Polished Ware, proving its very early historical origins.

Museums

The Allahabad Museum, Chandra Sekhar Azad Park, Kamla Nehru Rd. 18 galleries. 1015-1700. Closed Mon. Re 0.50. Contains a wide range of stone sculptures (2nd century BC from Bharhut and Kausambi, 1st century AD Kushana from Mathura, 4th-6th century Gupta and 11th century carvings from Khajuraho). Also a fine collection of Rajasthani miniatures, terracotta figurines, coins and paintings by Nicholas Roerich.

Anand Bhavan. 1000-1700, closed Mon. Small charge for upstairs. The former Nehru family home contains many interesting items, Motilal Nehru (1861-1931), active in the Independence movement, Jawaharlal Nehru (1889-1964), Independent India's 1st Prime Minister, Indira Gandhi (1917-84) Prime Minister (1966-77, 1980-4) and her sons Sanjay Gandhi who died 1980 and Rajiv Gandhi who died 1991. Next to it stands Swaraj Bhawan, given to the nation by Motilal Nehru.

Kausambi Museum, Univ of Allahabad. Various artefacts from Kausambi (see Excursions) including pottery, terracotta figurines, coins, beads and bangles.

Local festivals

Jan/Feb: *Magh* and *Kumbh Mela* – see Introduction.

Local information

● Accommodation

MG Marg is Mahatma Gandhi Marg. **C** *Allahabad Regency*, 16 Tashkent Marg. T 601519. 13 rm a/c. Restaurant, coffee shop, pool, pleasant garden. **C** *Presidency*, 19 D Sarojini Naidu Marg, T 624097. 10 a/c rm. Restaurant, pool, exchange.

D *Yatrik*, 33 Sardar Patel Marg, Civil Lines, T 601509. 37 rm, 30 a/c rm. Restaurant, pool, travel. Excellent value. Clean and comfortable, first class pool, good service. **D** *Samrat*, 49A MG Marg, T 604854. 30 rm, 16 a/c. Restaurant, exchange. Indian style hotel. UP Tourism **D** *Tourist Bungalow*, 35 MG Marg, T 53640. Some a/c rm. Restaurant, bar, coffee shop. **D** *Prayag*, 16A, Noorullah Rd, T 604430. 30 rm with bath, some a/c. Indian restaurant.

E *Continental*, Dr Katiu Rd. Simple. **E** *Harsh*, 14 MG Marg. Some rm with bath and a/c. Restaurant. Old; once had character.

F *Tepso*, Civil Lines, T 3635. Restaurant. **F** *Royal*, S Rd, T 2520. Large house with big rm. **F** *Jal Nigam Rest House*, Sangam area. **F** *YWCA*, Kasturba Gandhi Marg. **F** *Railway Retiring Rooms* and dorm.

● Places to eat

UP Tourism *Tourist Bungalow*, 35 MG Marg has a bar and restaurant. The better hotels have reasonable restaurants. Others in Civil Lines, especially on MG Marg: For a wide choice *El*

Chico at 24, *Kwality* at 20, and *Vyanjan*. ***Hot Stuff*** for fast foods and ice-cream. **Indian:** *Tandoor*, *Tripti* on Katiu Rd and ***Pallav*** in Ashok Vihar.

● Banks & money changers

Several in the commercial areas including **State Bank of India**, KYT Rd, T 53250.

● Entertainment

Prayag Sangeet Samiti is an important music and dance training institution with indoor and outdoor auditoria. Cultural and musical programmes are held in the evenings.

● Post and telecommunications

Sarojini Naidu Marg, Cantt, just N of All Saints Cathedral.

● Shopping

The main shopping areas are Civil Lines, Chowk and Katra.

Photography: *BR Tandon*, ***Flashlight*** and *Kohli* all in the Civil Lines.

● Sports

Mayo Hall Sports Complex is one of the largest sports training centres in India with facilities for table tennis, basketball, badminton and volleyball.

● Tourist offices

Regional Tourist Office, 35 MG Marg, Civil Lines, T 51543. **Wildlife Warden**, Vindhya Area, 174 C/2 Mehdauri.

● Useful addresses

Foreigners' Regional Registration Office: 2A Mission Rd, Katra. **UP Automobile Association**: 32A, MG Marg, Civil Lines, T 51543.

● Transport

Distances to important towns: Varanasi (122 km), Patna (368 km), Lucknow (237 km), Agra (433 km), Jhansi (375 km), Nagpur (618 km), Bhopal (680 km), Delhi (643 km), Calcutta (799 km), Hyderabad (1086 km).

Local Yellow top taxis, **auto-rickshaws** and **cycle rickshaws** are all widely available. Fares negotiable.

Air Indian Airlines, Tashkent Rd, T 2832. Services suspended.

Train Allahabad is on the major broad gauge route from Delhi to Calcutta. It is also linked to other cities in N, E and central India by broad and metre gauge lines. Enquiries: Allahabad Junction, T 50815, 54057; Prayag (Broad gauge for trains for Kanpur and Lucknow), T 52349; Allahabad City (for most trains to and from Varanasi), T 52202; Daraganj (metre Gauge). **New Delhi**: *A.C. Exp* 2381, Tu,Th,Sa, 0030, 10¼ hr; *A.C. Exp* 2303, M,W,F,Su, 0030, 10¼ hr; *Prayag Raj Exp* 2417, daily, 2100, 9¾ hr. **Bombay (VT)**: *Mahanagri Exp* 1094, daily, 1510, 23¾ hr; *Bombay Mail* 3003, daily, 1110, 24¼ hr; *Varanasi-Bombay Ratnagiri Exp* 2166, Tue, Th, Fri, 2105, 26½ hr. *Bhagalpur Exp* 3417, M,W,Th,Su, 0820, 28¼ hr. **Calcutta (Haora)**: *Kalka-Haora Mail* 2312, daily, 1800, 16½ hr; *Udyan Abha-Toofan Exp* 3008, daily, 2245, 19½ hr; *Haora-Janata Exp* 3040, daily, 0700, 22½ hr. **Jhansi**: *Bundelkhand Exp* 1108, daily, 1825, 14½ hr.

Lucknow: *Nauchandi Exp* 4011, daily, 1730, 4¾ hr; *Ganga-Gomti Exp* 2415, daily, 0600, 3½ hr. **Patna**: *Udyan Abha-Toofan Exp* 3008, daily, 2245, 6¾ hr; *Haora Exp* 3012, daily, 1055, 7½ hr; Tisukia Mail 2456, daily, 0420, 6¼ hr. **Varanasi**: *A.C. Exp* 2382, Tu,Th,Sa, 0230, 2¾ hr; *Mahanagri Exp* 1093, daily, 0035, 3½ hr; *Varanasi Exp* 1027, daily, 0845, 3½ hr. *Sarnath Exp* 4259, daily, 1310, 3 hr; *Bundelkhand Exp* 1107, daily, 0625, 3¾ hr. **Jabalpur** *Varanasi-Tirupati/Cochin Exp* 7492,7490, Tues,Fri, Sat, 1030, 5¾ hr – from Varanasi and via Allahabad, Lucknow, Kanpur and Satna; *Ganga-Kaveri Exp* 6040, M,W, 2105, 6¼ hr.

Road UP Roadways and RTCs of neighbouring states link Allahabad with various centres in the region: Lucknow, Varanasi, Meerut, Delhi, Patna, Muzaffarpur, Rewa, Sasaram, Kanpur, Gwalior and Jhansi. Roadways Bus Stations: Civil Lines, T 53443; Zero Rd, T 50192; Leader Rd, 2718. **Private Operators** bus stands are at Ram Bagh and Leader Rd.

Excursion from Allahabad: Kausambi

ROUTES Take the **NH2** W out of Allahabad to Bamrauli (10 km), then the left turn which leads past the airport to Kausambi (35 km) on the Chitrakoot Rd.

The enormous ruins are spread through several villages. Two – **Kosam-Inam** and **Kosam-Khiraj** – have names suggesting their links with the ruins of the city of Kausam. According to the epics, Kausam was founded by a descendant of the Pandavas who left Hastinapur when it was destroyed by floods from the Ganga. In the Buddha's time it was the capital of the Vatsa king Udayana, and is one of the earliest historical cities of the region. According to Hiuen Tsang the Buddha preached here and 2 *viharas* (monasteries) were built to commemorate the event.

The site The site is demarcated by the remains of a wall with bastions at regular intervals. The ramparts, which form an approximate rectangle over 6 km in perimeter, still average more than 10m above field level, while the bastions tower up to nearly 23m. Originally made of mud they were later surfaced with bricks. There was a moat filled with water from the Yamuna river. The town was occupied continuously from c 8th century BC to 6th century AD. In the SW corner are possibly the remains of a palace. The main **stupa** (5th Century BC) measured 25m in diameter and 25m in height. There is also the damaged shaft of a sandstone column, probably erected during the rule of the Mauryan Emperor Asoka. Another column was removed to Allahabad Fort by the Mughals. When Kausambi was first discovered by Cunningham, coins and terracotta figurines were scattered over the surface.

Recent discoveries Excavations have now been made by GR Sharma of the University of Allahabad at 4 main areas on the site. The earliest excavations made near the Asokan pillar suggested that the first of the 3 periods of settlement of the site came immediately before the Northern Black Polished Ware period. The second period dated back to 300 BC and included the first brick building, a road and finds of coins with the typical Kausambi 'lanky bull' motifs. In the third period of occupation, (175 BC to 325 AD) the coins found testify to a succession of rulers; Mitras, followed by Kushan kings and then by Maghas. The road evidently continued in use up to about 300 AD and the site itself was occupied until about 400 AD. Sharma suggests that excavations in the defence area have pushed back the dates of earliest settlement as far as 1165 BC while the site appears to have been occupied as late as 580 AD. Ghosh argues that these early dates are probably unreliable as there is no hard evidence. The importance of the site itself and the remarkable evidence of enormous defensive structures is not denied.

Ghosh writes that "The terracottas of Kausambi have a special place in the history of clay art of India. On the basis of manufacturing technique they can be grouped into 1. early handmade; 2. moulded; and 3. later partly hand-modelled and partly moulded. The first group has grey and dull-red pieces, sometimes with applied decorations. The second group, of the 2nd-1st century BC represents conceptional rather than realistic portrayal of figures and reflects the traits of contemporary art in dress, ornamentation etc. The third group, in the round, recalls the features of contemporary Kushan art, particularly in facial features. Important are those with elaborate decorations, mother goddesses, reclining women, dancers and drummers with peaked caps indicating Saka-Parthian influence...The handmade cum moulded plaques as usual belong to the early centuries of the Christian era."

Many of the coins and terracottas discovered here are now on display in the Allahabad City Museum and Kausambi Museum at the University of Allahabad.

ROUTES From Allahabad there are 2 routes to Varanasi. The NH2 goes straight to the N of the Ganga via Handia and Gopiganj. The more southerly route crosses the Yamuna over the Yamuna Bridge (NH27 to Rewa) then turns left immediately after the bridge and runs along the S bank of the Ganga. The bridge over the Tons River (30 km) is 363m long and was constructed in 1864.

Mirzapur

(58 km, *STD Code* 05442) This was the largest grain and cotton market on the Ganga before the opening of

the East Indian Railway. Good quality sandstone is quarried nearby and it has an attractive river front with ghats and temples. The town is noted for its brass industry and manufacture of woollen carpets. Approximately 7 km from Mirzapur is a Kali temple once used as a rendezvous for *Thugs*.

Chunar

(35 km E) Chunar sandstone is famous as the material of the Asoka pillars, highly polished in a technique said to be Persian. It is also noted for its **fort** built on a spur of the Kaimur Hills. It stands 53m above the surrounding plain, was of obvious strategic importance, and changed hands a number of times. Akbar recovered it in 1575 and the Mughals held it until 1750 when it passed to the Nawabs of Oudh. The British stormed it in 1764, Warren Hastings retreating to it after Raja Chait Singh's rebellion in 1781.

ROUTES From Chunar it is about 30 km to **Ramnagar** which also has a **fort**, then 7 km to Varanasi, entering it from the S.

VARANASI

(*Population:* 1.03 mn. *Altitude:* 81m. *STD Code*: 0542). Varanasi is situated on the W bank of the Ganga at a point where it sweeps in a great bend N before resuming its SE course to the sea. India's most sacred city, it was probably already an important town by the 7th century BC when Babylon and Nineveh were at the peak of their power. The Buddha came to it in 500 BC and it was mentioned in both the *Mahabharata* and the *Ramayana*. It derives its name from 2 streams, the Varuna on the N side of the city and the Assi, a small trickle on the S. **Banaras** is a corruption of Varanasi. It is also called **Kashi**, ('The City of Light') by Hindus, who as a mark of respect add the suffix *-ji* to it. It is one of the 7 Sacred Cities of Hinduism, see page 71. Each year well over one million pilgrims visit it while about 50,000 Brahmins are residents.

Varanasi is said to combine all the virtues of all other places of pilgrimage, and anyone dying within the area marked by the Panch Kosi road is transported straight to heaven. Some devout Hindus move to Varanasi to end their days and have their ashes scattered in the holy Ganga. The city also has some of the disadvantages of pilgrimage centres, notably rickshaw drivers who seem determined to extort as much as possible from unsuspecting visitors. It is worth trying to check the fare to your destination by asking a local person before hiring a rickshaw, then negotiating. Rickshaws waiting near hotel gates are the worst, so walk a little before hiring.

Early settlement

The earliest inhabitants of Varanasi were the Aryans who made it a centre of culture, education, commerce and craftsmanship. It was raided by Mahmud of Ghazni's army in 1033. In 1194 Qutb-ud-din Ghuri defeated the local Raja's army and Ala-ud-din Khalji, the King of Delhi (1294-1316) destroyed temples and built mosques on their sites. For a brief period in the 18th century it was known as Mohammadabad. Despite its early foundation hardly any building dates before the 17th century and few are more than 200 years old.

CLIMATE: VARANASI

	Jan	Feb	Mar	Apr	May	Jun	Jul	Aug	Sep	Oct	Nov	Dec	Av/Tot
Max (°C)	23	37	33	39	41	39	33	32	32	32	29	25	32
Min (°C)	9	11	17	22	27	28	26	26	25	21	13	9	204
Rain (mm)	23	8	14	1	8	102	346	240	261	38	15	2	1058

A centre of learning

Varanasi stands as the chief centre of Sanskrit learning in N India. Sanskrit, the oldest of the Indo-European languages, is one of learning and religious ritual and has been sustained here long after it ceased to be a living language elsewhere. The **Sanskrit University**, for example, has over 150,000 rare manuscripts. Hindu devotional movements

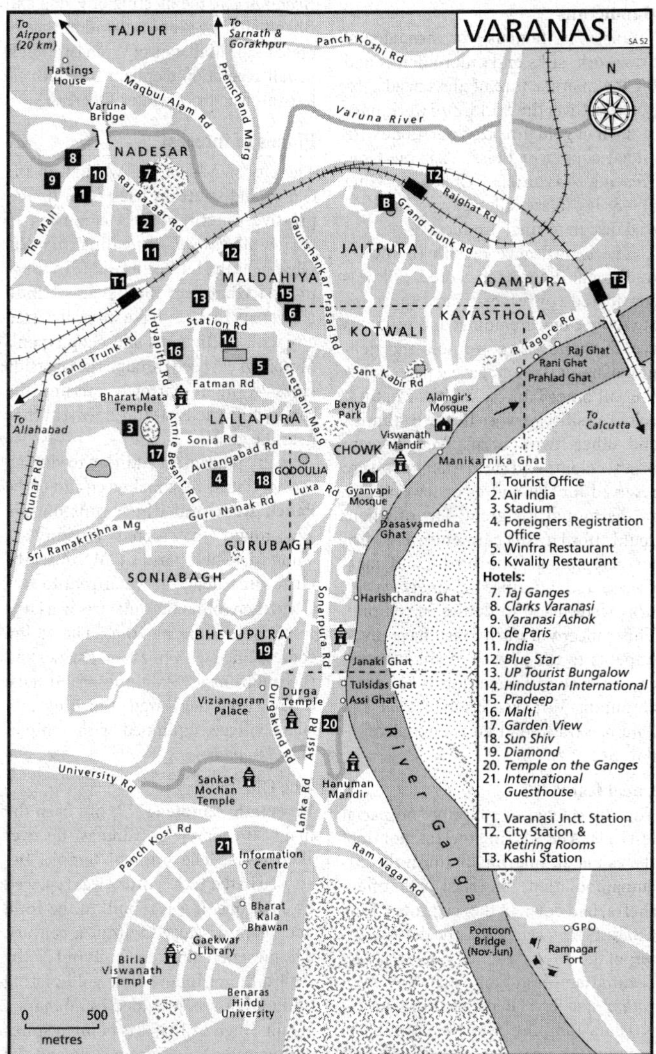

flourished here, especially in the 15th century under Ramananda, and Kabir, one of India's greatest poets, lived in the city. Tulsi Das translated the Ramayana from Sanskrit into Hindi.

Handicrafts

Varanasi is famous for ornamental brasswork, silks and embroideries and for the manufacture of glass beads, exported all over the world. *Zari* work, once of silver or gold thread, is now done with gilded copper or brass. Visit the Govt Weaving Centre, Chauka Ghat (T 43834) to see silk weaving from initial design to final product.

The significance of **silk** in India's traditional life is deep-rooted. Silk was considered a pure fabric, most appropriate for use on ceremonial and religious occasions. Its lustre, softness and richness of natural colour gave it precedence over all other fabrics. White or natural coloured silk was worn by the Brahmins and other 'twice born'. Women wore bright colours and the darker hues were reserved for the Sudras or lowest caste in the formal hierarchy, few of whom could afford it. Silk garments were worn for ceremonials like births and marriages, and offerings of finely woven silks were made to deities in temples. This concept of purity may have given impetus to the growth of silk-weaving centres around ancient towns like Kanchipuram, Varanasi, Bhubaneswar and Ujjain, a tradition that is kept alive today. See page 638.

Local festivals

The city celebrates a number of special festivals. **Apr** During the 1st month of the calendar, pilgrims perform the circumambulation of Kasi Dharmakshetra, laid down in the scriptures. **May** *Ganga Dasara* celebrates the day the waters of the Ganga reached Haridwar. **Oct** *Dasara* Ramlila at Ramnagar. **Nov** *Nagnathaiya* at Tulsi Ghat enacts the story of Krishna jumping into the Yamuna to overcome *Kalija*, the king of the Serpents. Also a fair at Chetganj to remember the occasion when Rama's brother, Lakshmana, cut off Ravana's sister's nose when she attempted to force him into a marriage – *Nakkataiya*! At Nati Imli, *Bharat Milap*, the meeting of Rama and Bharat after 14 years' separation is celebrated – the Maharaja of Varanasi attends in full regalia on elephant back. Music festivals usually in winter, **Dec-Feb**.

Places of interest

The city stands on the W bank of the Ganga and stretches back from its impressive waterfront in a confusion of narrow alleys (*gali*), extending from **Raj Ghat** near the Dufferin Bridge in the N to **Assi Ghat** near the Banaras Hindu University in the S. It is a very congested city with traffic-jams and people-jams. Motor-bikes speed through the riverside lanes by night narrowly missing the cows, while packs of stray dogs scavenge near the ghats.

Every pilgrim, in addition to visiting the holy sites, must make a circuit of the **Panch Kosi** road which runs outside and round the sacred territory of Varanasi. This starts at Manikarnika Ghat, runs along the waterfront to Assi Ghat, then round the outskirts in a large semi-circle to Barna Ghat. The 58 km route is lined with trees and shrines and the pilgrimage is supposed to take 6 days, each day's walk finishing in a small village, equipped with temples and *dharamshalas*.

The Old Town

Visvanath Temple (1777) has been the main Siva temple in Varanasi for over 1000 years. The original temple, destroyed in the 12th century, was replaced by a mosque. It was rebuilt in the 16th, and again destroyed within a century. The present temple was built in 1777 by Ahilya Bai of Indore. The gold plating on the roof was provided by Maharaja Ranjit Singh in 1835. Its pointed spires are typically N Indian in style and the

POLLUTION

All along the Ganga, the major problem of waste disposal (of human effluent and industrial toxins) is being addressed by GAP (Ganga Action Plan) set up by the Govt in 1986. The diversion and treatment of raw sewage in the 7 main cities is planned. In Varanasi however, the 17th century sewers, the inadequate capacity of the sewage works, the increased waterflow during the monsoons and the erratic electricity supply (essential for pumping) have all remained problems. In addition, although most Hindus are cremated, an estimated 45,000 uncremated or partially cremated bodies are put in the Ganga each year. This is being dealt with by introducing a breed of scavenger turtles which dispose of rotting flesh.

Surprisingly, although the Ganga may be one of the world's most polluted rivers, it is also one that can cleanse itself; it can reoxygenate very quickly and is a very efficient re-aerator. Scientists had discovered the river's exceptional property in the last century. The cholera microbe did not survive 3 hours in Ganga water whereas in distilled water it survived 24 hours. Furthermore, that property was lost on boiling. Water from the river remains fresh for long periods; ships could sail with Ganga water from Calcutta (where at the mouth, the water is exceptionally dirty) and it would remain fresh right through the voyage. It is not surprising that a Jaipur maharajah should carry the pure water in urns for his trip to England, see page 406.

exterior is finely carved. 0400-2300. Only Hindus are allowed inside. Views from roof-top opp, Rs 5. The 18th century **Annapurna Temple** (*anna* food; *purna* filled) nearby, built by Baji Rao I, has shrines dedicated to Siva, Ganesh, Hanuman and Surya.

The **Gyan Kup** (Well of Knowledge) next door is said to contain the Siva lingam from the original temple – the well is protected by a stone screen and canopy. Its water is said to 'indicate the highest spiritual illumination' (Rushbrook Williams). The **Gyanvapi Mosque** (Great Mosque of Aurangzeb) with 71m high minarets shows evidence of the original Hindu temple, particularly in the foundations, the columns, and at the rear.

The 17th century **Alamgir Mosque** (Beni Madhav ka Darera) on Panchganga Ghat was Aurangzeb's smaller mosque. It was built on the original Vishnu temple of the Marathas, parts of which were used in its construction. See enclosure walls.

The back lanes

The maze of narrow lanes (or *galis*) along the ghats through the old quarters exude the smells and sounds of this holy city. They are fascinating to stroll through though easy to get lost in! Some find it all too over-powering. Near the Town Hall (1845) built by the Maharaja of Vizianagram, is the **Kotwali** (Police Station) with the Temple of **Bhaironath,** built by Baji Rao II in 1825. The image inside is believed to be of the Kotwal (Superintendent) who rides on a ghostly dog. Stalls sell sugar dogs to be offered to the image. In the temple garden of **Gopal Mandir** near the Kotwali is a small hut in which Tulsi Das is thought to have composed the *Binaya Patrika* poem.

The **Durga Temple** (18th century), to the S along Durga Kund Rd, was built in the Nagara style. It is painted red with ochre and has the typical 5 spires (symbolising the elements) merging into one (Brahma). Non-Hindus may view from rooftop nearby. Nextdoor in a peaceful garden, the **Tulsi Manas Temple** (1964) in white marble commemorates the medieval poet Tulsi Das. It has walls engraved with verses and scenes from the *Ramcharitmanas*, composed in a Hindi dialect, instead of the conventional Sanskrit, and is open to all (closed 1130-1530). Good views from the 2nd Fl of 'Disneyland style' animated show. **Bharat Mata Temple**, S of Cantt Station which was opened by Mahatma Gandhi, has a relief map of 'Mother India' in marble. Good bookshop, but not worth a detour.

The river front

The hundred and more **ghats** on the river are the main attraction for visitors to Varanasi. Visit them at first light (before sunrise, 0430 in summer, 0530 in winter), when Hindu pilgrims come to bathe in the sacred Ganga, facing the rising sun, or at dusk, when leaf-boat lamps are floated down the river. Start the river trip at Dasasvamedha Ghat where you can hire a boat quite cheaply. You may want to go either upstream (S) towards Harishchandra Ghat or downstream to Manikarnika Ghat. You may notice floating bundles covered in white cloth; children, and those dying of high fever (or smallpox in the past), are not cremated but put into the river. This avoids injuring *Sitala* the goddess of smallpox.

For photographs, visit the riverside between 0700-0900 (beware of the cows!). The foggy sunshine early in the morning often clears to produce a beautiful light.

Dasasvamedha Ghat Named as the 'Place of Ten Horse Sacrifices' performed here by Brahma, God of Creation. Some believe that in the age of the gods when the world was in chaos, Divodasa was appointed King of Kashi by Brahma. He accepted, on condition that all the gods would leave Varanasi. Even Siva was forced to leave but Brahma set the test for Divodasa, confident that he would get the complex ceremony wrong, allowing the gods back into the city. However, the ritual was performed flawlessly, and the ghat has thus become one of the holiest, especially at eclipses. Bathing here is regarded as being almost as meritorious as making the sacrifice.

Next is **Munshi Ghat**, where some of the city's sizeable Muslim population (25%) come to bathe. The river has no religious significance for them. Adjacent are the **Ahiliya Bai Ghat** and **Rana Mahal Ghat**, the latter built by the Maratha Rani and the Maharana of Udaipur. Professional washermen work at the **Dhobi Ghat**. There is religious merit in having your clothes washed in the sacred Ganga. Brahmins have their own washermen to avoid caste pollution. The municipality has built new washing facilities away from the ghat.

Narad and **Chauki Ghats** are held sacred since the Buddha received enlightenment here under a *peepul* tree. **Raja Ghat** is associated with the Raja of Pune and here the high-water levels are recorded. The flood level (marked in Jul 1967) is difficult to imagine when the river is at its lowest in Jan/Feb. **Mansarovar Ghat** leads to ruins of several temples around a lake. **Kedar Ghat**, is named after Kedarnath, a pilgrimage site in the UP Himalaya, with a Bengali temple nearby.

The **Harishchandra Ghat** (no photography) is particularly holy and is dedicated to King Harishchandra. It is now the most sacred *smashan* or cremation ghat (Manikarnika is more popular). Behind the ghat is a *gopuram* of a Dravidian style temple. The **Karnataka Ghat** is one of many regional ghats. These are attended by priests who know the local languages, castes, customs and festivals.

The **Hanuman Ghat** is where Vallabha, the leader of a revival in the Krishna bhakti cult is believed to have been born at the end of the 15th century. **Shivala Ghat** or Kali Ghat is privately owned by the ex-ruler of Varanasi. **Chet**

Singh's Fort, Shivala, stands behind the Ghat. The fort, the old palace of the Maharajas, was taken by the Muslims and retaken by Chet Singh. The British imprisoned him in his own fort for not complying with Warren Hastings' orders, but he escaped by climbing down to the river and swimming away. **Anandamayi Ghat** is named after the Bengali saint Anandamayi Ma ('Mother of Bliss') who died in 1982. Born into a poor family, she received 'enlightenment' at 17 and spent her life teaching and in charitable work. One of her ashrams is here. **Tulsi Ghat** commemorates the great saint-poet Tulsi Das who lived here (see Tulsi Manas Temple above). Furthest upstream is the **Assi Ghat**, where the river Assi meets the Ganga, one of the 5 that pilgrims should bathe from in a day. The order is: Assi, Dasasvamedha, Barnasangam, Panchganga and Manikarnika. Upstream on the E bank is the Ramnagar Fort, the Maharaja of Varanasi's residence (see below). Here the boat will turn to take you back to Dasasvamedha Ghat.

From Dasasvamedha Ghat you can go downstream past the following ghats. **Man Mandir Ghat** was built by Maharajah Man Singh of Amber in 1600 and is one of the oldest in Varanasi. The palace was restored in the last century with brick and plaster. The stone balcony on the NE corner gives an indication of how the original looked. Maharaja Jai Singh of Jaipur converted the palace into an observatory in 1710 – see also Jaipur (page 403). Near the entrance is a small Siva Dalbhyeshvara Temple whose shrine is a lingam immersed in water. During droughts, water is added to the cistern to make it overflow for good luck. Dom Raja's House is next door. The **Doms** are the Untouchables of Varanasi who are integral to the cremation ceremony. As Untouchables they can handle the corpse, a ritually polluting act for Hindus. They also supply the flame from the temple for the funeral pyre. Their presence is essential and also lucrative since there are fees for the various services they provide. The Dom Raja is the hereditary title of the leader of these Untouchables. **Mir Ghat** leads to a sacred well and **Lalita Ghat** to the Nepalese temple of Vishalakshi.

Manikarnika Ghat NB: no photography. Above the ghat is a well into which Siva's dead wife Sati's earring is supposed to have fallen when Siva was carrying her after she committed suicide – see page 228. The Brahmins managed to find the jewel from the earring (*manikarnika*) and returned it to Siva who blessed the place. Offerings of *bilva* flowers, milk, sandalwood and sweetmeats are thrown into the tank where pilgrims come to bathe. Between the well and the ghat is *Charanpaduka*, a stone slab with Vishnu's footprint. The adjoining **Jalasayin Ghat** is the principal burning ghat of the city. **Dattatreya Ghat** is named after a saintly Brahmin who has a temple dedicated to him. **Scindia Ghat** was originally built in 1830 but it was so large that it collapsed. **Ram Ghat** was built by the Maharaja of Jaipur.

Five rivers are supposed to meet at the magnificent **Panchganga Ghat** – the Ganga, Sarasvati, Gyana, Kirana and Dhutpapa. The stone column can hold a 1000 lamps at festivals. The impressive flights of stone steps run up to the Alamgir Mosque (see above). At **Gai Ghat** there is a stone statue of a sacred cow whilst at **Trilochana Ghat** there is a temple to Siva in his form as the 'Three-eyed' (*Trilochana*). Two turrets stand out of the water. **Raj Ghat** is the last on the boat journey. The site of ancient **Kashi** excavations have revealed that there was an 8th century BC city situated on a grassy knoll near here. Raj Ghat was where the river was forded until bridges were built across the river.

Kite fights Kite flying is a popular pastime, as elsewhere in India, especially all along the river bank. The serious competitors endeavour to bring down other flyers' kites and so fortify their twine by coating it with a mix of crushed light bulbs and flour paste to make it razor sharp! The quieter ghats (eg Panchganga) are good for watching the fun – boys in their boats on the river scramble

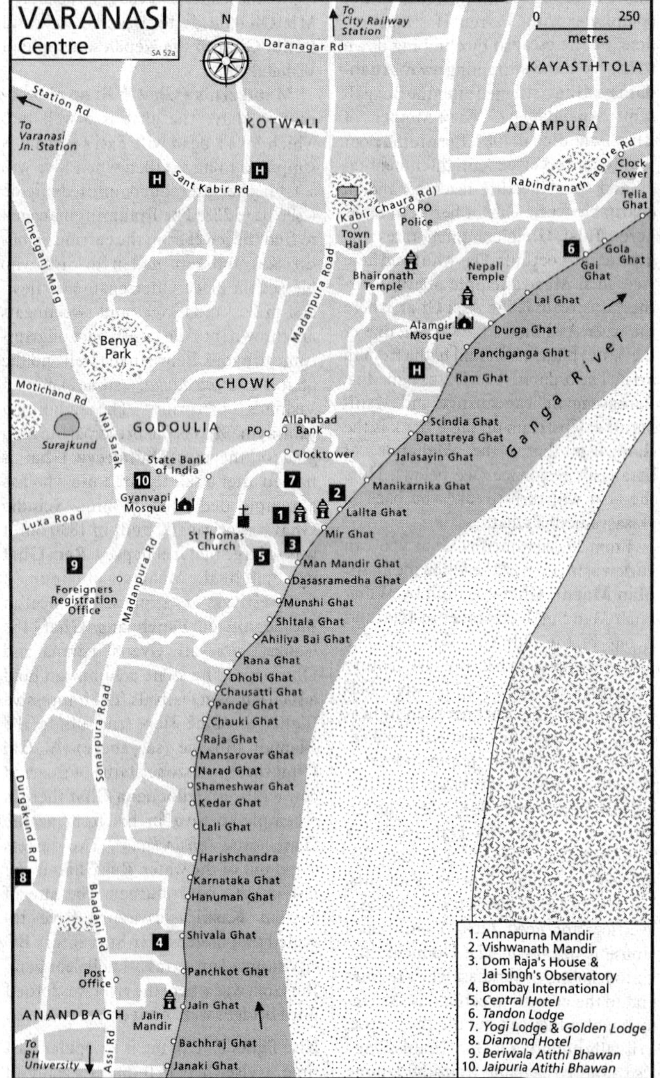

to retrieve downed kites as trophies that can be re-used, even though the kites themselves are very cheap.

Other places of interest

Benares Hindu University (BHU) is one of the largest campus universities in India to the S of the city, almost opp Ramnagar Fort on the other bank. Founded at the turn of the century, it was originally intended for the study of Sanskrit, Indian art, music and culture and has the **Bharat Kala Bhawan Museum** (see below). The **New Visvanath Temple** (1966), one of the tallest in India, is in the university semi circle and was financed by the Birla family. It was planned by Madan Mohan Malaviya (1862-1942), Chancellor of the university, who believed in Hinduism without caste distinctions. The marble Shiva temple modelled on the old Visvanath Temple, is open to all. The 17th century **Ramnagar Fort**, across the river, was the home of the Maharaja of Varanasi; the Durbar Hall houses a **museum** (see below). Beautiful situation, surrounded by narrow, crowded streets, but the Fort is run down. Ramlila performances during Dasara.

Museums

Bharat Kala Bhavan, BHU. Summer 0800-1200, Winter 0930-1630; Closed Sun and holidays. Exhibits include various pieces representative of historic Varanasi plus sculptures from Mathura and Sarnath, and miniature paintings. Ramnagar Fort across the river. 0900-1200, 1400-1700; closed Fri. Small fee. The Durbar Hall is now a Royal Museum containing palanquins, elephant *howdahs*, costumes, arms and furniture. Daily, Summer 0530-1145, Winter 0600-1215.

Conducted Tours

UP Roadways Tour I: River trip, temples, Benaras Hindu Univ. Tour II: Sarnath and Ramnagar Fort. Daily, Summer 1430-1825, Winter 1400-1755. Starts from *Tourist Bungalow*, picking up from Govt of India Tourist Office, The Mall. Tickets on bus. Rec. *Varuna Travels*, Pandey Haweli, also organise tours, mainly from Sep to Mar, T 52173.

Local information

● Accommodation

Price guide
AL Rs 3,000+ **A** Rs 2,000-3,000
B Rs 1,200-2,000 **C** Rs 600-1,200
D Rs 250-600 **E** Rs 100-250 **F** Up to Rs 100.

Varanasi has few top class hotels; most are in the Cantonment area and the Chowk, Lohurabir and Godaulia just outside the old city. Be prepared for power cuts; usually the large hotels have their own generator. There is a large range of very cheap lodging houses. Beware, some can be nasty. **NB:** Auto-rickshaws try to take you where they get commission and pretend others do not exist.

A *Clarks Varanasi*, The Mall. T 46771, F 323186. 140 big rm, cavernous bath. Large and bustling, good facilities and situation; good, if expensive, restaurants. Pool open to non-residents, Rs 175. Best hotel in town. **A** *Taj Ganges*, Nadesar Palace Ground, T 42485. 104 rm. Restaurant drinks expensive (many top hotels appear to use powdered milk), limited facilities (1 large shop, bank, pool closed in winter).

B *Varanasi Ashok*, The Mall, T 46021. 84 rm, some a/c, quieter at back. Restaurant (Indian music at dinner), quite pricey, food and service could be better. Best bookshop in town (also buys books), coach to airport. One of the better *Ashok* hotels but slow and indifferent service only speeds up at prospect of tips.

C *Hindustan International*, C 12/3 Maldahiya, T 54075. 52 rm. Restaurant, bar, coffee shop, exchange, travel. Modern, clean and comfortable but food and laundry not rec. **C** *Ideal Tops*, The Mall (next to *Clarks*), T 42591, F 385785. 5 km from centre. 40 well furnished rm with city views in new modern hotel. Restaurants (Indian rec), exchange, travel, business facilities, free airport transfer. Friendly staff, good value (before prices rise); plenty of light creates pleasant atmosphere. Highly rec.

Most D hotels have rm with TV and attached baths. **D** *Pallavi International*, Hathwa Market, Chetganj, T 56939. 55 rm. Central. Some a/c rm. Restaurant, garden. **D** *Diamond*,

Bhelupur, T 310696. 40 rm, some a/c. Central. Restaurant, exchange, gardens. Reasonable value. **D** *India*, 59 Patel Nagar, Cantt, T 54661. 33 rm, some a/c (new rm and Reception added in 1993). Restaurant, bar, travel, good garden. Restaurant, very popular so service can be slow. Rec. Good value. **D** *Hotel de Paris*, 15 The Mall next to UP Tourist Office, T 46601. 50 rm some dark with small windows, some a/c. Large airy restaurant, bar, travel, large lawns, *Clarks'* pool within easy reach. Recently brightened up. **D** *Gautam*, Ramkatora, between rly station and Chowk. T 46450. 37 air-cooled rm with phone. Good restaurant, efficient service. Rec. **D** *Barahdari*, Maidagin nr GPO, T 330581. 16 rm, some a/c. Central. Good veg restaurant, slightly expensive, garden. Simple, clean. Rec. **D** *Bombay International*, Sonarpura, nr Shivala Ghat. T 310621, 38 clean rm, some a/c. Good restaurant, slow service. **D** *Temple on Ganges*, Assi Ghat, T 312340. 26 rm, some with bath and western toilets, cheap dorm beds. 10 new rm on 2nd Fl. Friendly, almost over-helpful management; peaceful location, clean. Roof-top restaurant serves good food (veg only), no alcohol, yoga lessons. Discounts 1 May-31 July. Highly rec. **D** *Malti*, Vidyapith Rd, T 56844. Some a/c rm with balcony. Restaurant. Good, modern hotel. **D** *Surya*, Varuna Bridge Rd, Cantt, behind *Clarks*. **D** *Pradeep*, Jagatganj, T 44963. Clean rm, some a/c but nr noisy junction. Excellent food at *Poonam* restaurant (see below), friendly staff. Nearby, a therapist offers 'Delusion Removal Conversation'! UP Tourism **D** *Tourist Bungalow*, off Parade Kothi, GT Rd, opp rly station. T 43413. 39 rm, some a/c, with bath, 'deluxe suites' and dorm in barrack-style 2-storey building. Restaurant, shady verandah, garden. Simple, clean and efficient; very helpful Tourist Office. Watch out! Scooter taxis may take you to the private 'Tourist Bungalow' nearby which has no garden and is inferior.

● **Budget hotels**

Riverside hotels can be difficult to find, particularly at night. Local people will often show you the way but may expect a commission from the hotel, thus increasing the rate you pay – clarify position before requesting help. **E** *Blue Star*, S14/84 G Maldahiya (fairly close to rly), T 43137. Small garden, rm and dorm, front noisy. One of the cheapest, very basic but good value, friendly welcome, reasonable food. **E** *Central*, Dasasvamedha Rd, T 62776. Basic, can be noisy. Meals available. **E** *Ganges*, Dasasvamedha Rd, T 321097. Rm cleanliness varies, inspect first. Pleasant restaurant on 1st Fl overlooks bazar, popular. **E** *Golden Lodge*, 8/35 Kalika Gali, nr Golden Temple, T 323832. Enthusiastic proprietor, very central, restaurant (Fagin's), some character. Rec. **E** *River View*, Brahma Ghat (well-signposted along river), T 334565. Some rm with bath and hot water. Good view (watch the dawn from front rm). Slow service at mediocre restaurant; occasionally plagued by westerners learning the sitar. Helpful, safe. **E** *Sandhya Guest House* nr Shivala Ghat PO. Rm with bath. New, clean, tours, airtickets. Rooftop restaurant with good views. Homemade brown bread, relaxed atmosphere, pleasant, helpful manager. **E** *Sun Shiv*, D 54/16-D Ravi Niketan, Aurangabad, Jadumandi Rd. T 52468. Modest but clean, airy rm. Good food, good value. Quiet location and personal attention of very knowledgeable owner. Highly rec. **E** *Surya*, nr *Clarks*, Cantt, T 43014. Some a/c rm. Good Chinese restaurant, garden. **E** *Trimurti Lodge*, next to Golden Temple, T 322616. Reasonably clean small rm, some air-cooled with bath. Some top Fl rm have good views. Friendly service, good food. **E** *Yogi Lodge*, D8/29 Kalika Gali nr Golden Temple. T 53986. Simple rm, shared bath, dorm. Meals on roof terrace; good egg and chips. Congested area. 1994 reports poor rooms but still very busy; popular with backpackers en route to Nepal. Rickshaws don't get commission, so will try to put you off. **Warning**: You may be taken to Yogi Guest House, B21/7 Kamachha instead which at first glance looks pleasant and clean. However, strong complaints in 1994 of rude and unscrupulous management. ITDC **E** *Dak Bungalow*, Caravan Park, The Mall, nr TV Tower, T 42182. Good value rm (cheaper rm without hot water), dorm. Good food (esp breakfasts) but slow service, occasional dancing and sitar music (evenings), large garden. Quiet, pleasant atmosphere, out-of-town location, friendly manager with amazing beard! **Camping** in grounds. Several Indian style **E** and **F** hotels in Lohurabir and Parade Kothi. **E** *Garden View*, Sigra Crossing, 64/129 Vidyapith Rd. T 361093. Some air-cooled rm with bath. Good restaurant. Simple but clean, good service. Rec. **E** *Park Villa*, Rathayatra Crossing, T 57050. 14 rm. Atmospheric, decaying, interesting and friendly. Food, poor.

F *Scindia Guest House*, Scindia Ghat, T 320319. Small cheap clean rm, dorm. Superb roof-top views. Food pricey and not rec; staff friendly but may persist on boat rides etc. **F** *Shanti Guest House*, behind Manikarnika

Ghat (well-signposted). Basic rm, dorm. **F** ***Tandon House Lodge***, Gai Ghat, Patan Darwaza, T 53470. Basic rm, few with bath, some renovated. Rec for its peaceful riverside location with superb views, good roof. European style, away from tourist area but popular. Friendly and helpful management. **F** ***Kumiko***, nr Dasasvamedha Ghat. Rm and dorm. Japanese run, friendly. Also **F** ***Railway Retiring Rooms*** at Varanasi Cantt. Some a/c rm and dorm; **F** ***YMCA***, Cantt, T 55895; **F** ***International Guest House***, BHU (enquiries, Registrar).

● Places to eat

City restaurants are not allowed to serve alcohol. Hotels observe 'Dry Days' on the 1st and 7th of each month, and on certain Public holidays. Varied menu in top hotels and also at ***Pallavi***, ***Bombay International***, ***Gaurav***, ***Garden View***, ***India*** and ***Pradeep***. The last has *Poonam* with a wide choice, though a little pricey; ignore the drab beige decor and order banana lassi, masala dishes and finish with *Shahi tukra*! Do not venture into the toilet. **Barhadari's** *Mughal Room*, nr GPO is rec. ***Blue Moon***, nr Yogi Lodge, Old City centre is good value.

Chinese: *Canton's*, *Hotel Surya*, Cantt; ***Winfa***, behind Prakash Cinema, Lohurabir, for good value, authentic dishes. ***Mandarin***, nr Tourist Bungalow, lacks flavour.

Continental: *Konamey*, Dasasvamedha Rd (Deepak Cinema), Bansphatak rec for good food in simple surroundings. ***El Parador***, Maldahyia Rd, behind City Bus Stand. Set breakfasts (0800-1200), quite good value. Wide choice but overrated, expensive "western" food; populated by tourists alone with occasional loud TV backing; sullen, slow service.

Indian veg: *Tulsi*, Chetganj. ***Fagin's***, nr Biswanath Temple. Close to ghats. Good value. Across from GPO, in a basement (cool in summer, though rather dark and gloomy), ***Sona Rupa*** for Indian veg and Chinese. Large tables, quiet, lots of sweets. Good prices and service but "too much chilli in everything. Inedible" for some. ***Street View***, Gai Ghat and ***Jalajog***, Godoulia, do Indian snacks and sweets.

● Banks & money changers

Open weekdays 1000-1400, Sat 1000-1200. Several branches at Bansphatak and Chetgang. **State Bank of India** at Varuna Br, *Hotel de Paris* (Mon 1300-1500, Wed-Sun 1300-1700. Closed Tues) and *Clarks Varanasi* and *Varanasi Ashok*. Also at airport.

● Entertainment

A funfair with big-wheel and other rides (safety not up to international standards) nr the GPO by the roundabout.

● Hospitals & medical services

BHU Hospital, T 66833. *Birla Hospital*, Machhodari, T 56357. *SSPG Hospital*, T 62424.

● Post & telecommunications

Head PO: Bisheshwarganj (parcel packing outside) and Cantt. **Post**: 0930-1730; **Telegraph**: 0930-1630.

● Shopping

Varanasi is famous for silks incl brocades (Temple Bazar, Visvanath Gali), brassware, ivory and gold jewellery, *sitar* making, carpets, and hand block printed goods. Main shopping areas are Chowk, Godoulia, Viswanath Le, Gyanvapi and Thatheri Bazar. ***UPICA***, Nadesar Cantt; ***UP Handlooms***, Lohurabir, Nadesar and Neechi Bagh; ***Tantuja***, Bengal Emporium, Dasasvamedha Rd; ***Mahatex***, Godoulia. ***Oriental Arts Emporium***, 10/252 Maqbool Alam Rd, Chauki Ghat and ***Brijraman Das*** in Visvanath Gali and K37/32 Golghar and ***J Arora***, Cantt have been rec.

Books: *Ashok Hotel* has the best; new and secondhand (particularly coffee-table books), some good value; they will buy books but you may need to bargain in a friendly way.

Photography: *Passi Studio*, Lohurabir. *Bright Studio*, Godoulia.

● Sports

Sports Stadia: *Sampurna Nand Stadium*, Vidyapith Rd and *multi-purpose Stadium*, BHU.

Swimming: pools at hotels *Taj Ganges*, *Varanasi Ashok*, *Hindustan* and *Clarks Varanasi* (Rs 175 for non-residents). Can be used with temporary membership.

● Tour companies & travel agents

ITDC Transport Unit, *Hotel Varanasi Ashok*, T 42565. ***Mercury***, T 312008; ***Travel Corporation of India***, T 46209 and ***Travel Bureau***, T 46621 at *Clarks Hotel*; ***Nepal Travels***, Parade Kothi; ***Sita***, T 43121; ***Varuna***, Pandey Haweli, 323370.

● Tourist offices

Govt of India, 15B The Mall, Cantt, T 43744. 1000-1700; closed Sun. Guides (4 or 8 hr). Well run, very helpful manager and staff; visit highly rec before undertaking a tour. **Information Counter**, Babatpur Airport. **UP**, Tourist Bungalow, Parade Kothi, Cantt, T 43413.

1000-1700; closed Sun. Very helpful; Japanese spoken. **Information Counter**, Varanasi Cantt Rly Station, T 43544. 0600-2000. **Bihar**, Englishiya Market, Sher Shah Suri Marg, Cantt, T 43821. 0800-2000.

● **Useful addresses**

Police: T 100. **Fire**: Chetganj, T 53333, Bhelupur, T 54444. **Foreigners Registration Office**: Sri Nagar Colony, T 62752.

● **Transport**

Varanasi is situated at the junction of **NH2**, **NH7**, and **NH29**. To Agra (565 km); Allahabad (122 km); Bhopal (791 km); Bodhgaya (240 km); Kanpur (320 km); Khajuraho (406 km); Lucknow (286 km); Lumbini (Nepal; 386 km); Patna (246 km); Delhi (765 km); Calcutta (677 km); Bombay (1590 km); Madras (1901 km).

Local Taxis: no metred yellow-top-taxis. Private taxis available from agencies, hotels. Approx rates: Full day (90 km, 8 hr), a/c Rs 450, non a/c Rs 325; Basic rate per km about a/c Rs 5, non a/c Rs 3. **Rickshaws & tongas**: tempo-rickshaws and auto-rickshaws usually on fixed routes. Basic min Re 1 per stage. Cycle-rickshaws and horse-tongas widely used, rates negotiable. **Cycle and motor-cycle hire**: nr *Hotel Hindustan International* Maldahiya.

WARNING Some cycle-rickshaws drivers take advantage of tourists, particularly near hotels. Try to find out the going rate for typical journey from local people and bargain a fair price before starting a journey. It is best to walk a short distance away from hotel. Insist on rickshaw drivers taking you to the hotel of your choice (where they may not get a commission). Threaten reporting to Police if they refuse or they may demand extra money after agreeing a price.

Ferry and Boats: are the best way to enjoy Varanasi. Available from Ghats, charges generally negotiable. Approx rates for sightseeing: big boat (20) Rs 120, small boat (10) Rs 40-60 per hr, river crossing approx Re 1.50 per person. **City buses**: cover most of Varanasi. UP Roadways Bus Stand, opp rly station, Cantt. T 42011. Open 24 hr.

Air Babatpur Airport is 22 km from Varanasi Cantt. **Transport to town**: by bus to Indian Airlines office, Rs 20, (may not go into city centre), Rs 20; reserve through India Tourist Office, T 43744. Transfer by taxi, a/c Rs 230, non a/c Rs 160. **Indian Airlines**, Mint House Motel, Cantt, T 45959, 1000-1300, 1400-1700. Airport Office, T 43742. **Air India**, *Clarks Hotel*, T 46451. Indian Airlines flies daily to **Delhi** via Agra and Khajuraho, 1515, 3 hr (from Delhi, 0815). 5 flights a week from/to Delhi via Allahabad and Patna. From Bombay en route to **Lucknow**, M,Tu,Th,Sa, 1300, ¾ hr. From Delhi en route to **Bhubaneswar**, M,W,F,Su, 1225, 1¼ hr. **Kathmandu**, daily, 1205, ¾ hr. **NB:** because Indian Airlines flights to Varanasi mainly originate in Delhi and stop at intermediate places en route, they are subject to severe delays (especially in Jan and early Feb) when Delhi is often fogbound. Be prepared for a long wait.

Train Warning: An Information Counter at the station run by travel agents charges large commissions for rail tickets. Buy from Rly Reservations. Even there, travellers have been asked for a little 'help'. Computerised Booking Hall, 0800-1400, 1430-2000; reservations available 1 day in advance (advisable). **Allahabad**: *Sarnath Exp* 4260, daily, 1155, 3 hr; *Bundelkhand Exp* 1108, daily, 1310, 4¾ hr. **Bombay (VT)**: *Mahanagri Exp* 1094, daily, 1135, 27¼ hr; *Varanasi-Bombay Ratnagiri Exp* 2166, Tu,Th,F, 1745, 29¾ hr. **Calcutta** (H): *Amritsar-Haora Exp* 3050, daily, 1950, 20 hr; *Amritsar-Haora Mail* 3006, daily, 1725, 14½ hr; *Doon Exp* 3010, daily, 16½ hr. **Dehra Dun**: *Doon Exp* 3009, daily, 1945, 20½ hr; *Dehra Dun-Varanasi Exp* 4265, daily, 0915, 24½ hr. **New Delhi**: *A.C. Exp* 2381, Tu,Th,Sa, 2115, 13½ hr; *Neelachal Exp* 8475, M,W,S, 0735, 13¾ hr.

Gaya: *Dehra Dun Exp* 3010, daily, 1615, 5 hr; **Gorakhpur (for Nepal)**: *Fast Passenger*, 82/1144, daily, 1340, 10½ hr; *Triveni Exp* 5406/5205, daily, 2350, 7¾ hr; *Exp* 5450/5027, daily, 0700, 9 hr. **Kanpur**: *Neelachal Exp* 8475, M,W,Sa, 0735, 7¼ hr; *Ganga-Yamuna Exp* 4283, M,W,Th,Sa, 1245, 9½ hr: *Ganga-Yamuna Exp* 4213, Tu,Th,Su, 1245, 9½ hr. **Mahoba (for Khajuraho)**: *Bundelkhand Exp* 1108, daily, 1310, 12¼ hr (onward bus, 0600). **(for Khajuraho)**: *Mahanagari Exp* 1094, daily, 1135, 6½ hr (from Satna, bus next day, 4 hr). **Lucknow**: *Varanasi-Lucknow Varuna Exp* 2427, daily, 0515, 4¾ hr; *Kashi-Vishwanath Exp* 4057, daily, 1400, 6½ hr. **Madras**: M,W, 1730, 36 hr. Reserve early.

Road UP Roadways Bus Stand, Sher Shah Suri Marg, opp Junc rly station, Cantt, T 42011. Reservations for deluxe buses to Allahabad. Open 24 hr. UP Roadways and MPSRTC connect Varanasi to important centres incl Sarnath, 9 km, Rs 2. Frequent services to

Allahabad, Gorakhpur, Jaunpur. Lucknow (0745, 1515). To **Delhi** Daily service via Khajuraho and Agra. Pvt buses opp rly station.

Transport to Nepal: the journey requires an overnight stay nr the border plus about 18 hr on the road so can be tiring. UP Roadways buses go via Gorakhpur to **Sonauli**. Dep daily, 0300, 0400, 0930, 2130 (9 hr). **Sonauli**, daily, 0600. Pvt buses (agents nr *Tourist Bungalow*) often demand inclusive fares for hotel stay, though you may opt for their deluxe buses to the border. (See page 274.)

Excursion from Varanasi: Sarnath

Sarnath, 10 km E of Varanasi, is one of Buddhism's major centres in India. When he had gained enlightenment at Bodh Gaya, the Buddha came to the deer park at Sarnath and delivered his first sermon (c 528 BC), usually referred to as Dharmachakra (The Wheel of Law). Since then, the site has been revered. Given its great historic importance visitors may be disappointed to find the stupas neglected and the very limited collection in the museum although it houses some superb pieces. Nevertheless, many find the deer park a place of peace and reflection despite distractions of loud transistor radios and young monks running around or playing cricket! Transport: Infrequent bus service but included in coach tours. From Varanasi, bus from opp Rly station (Rs 2), sometimes stops opp Taj Hotel. Auto-rickshaws (Rs 35), Tempo seat (Rs 5). The road is bumpy; cycling is not recommended as trucks travel along it at great speed.

Both the Chinese travellers Fa-Hien and Hiuen Tsang visited Sarnath, in the early 5th century and 640 AD respectively. Hiuen Tsang described the sangharama (monastery) as having 1500

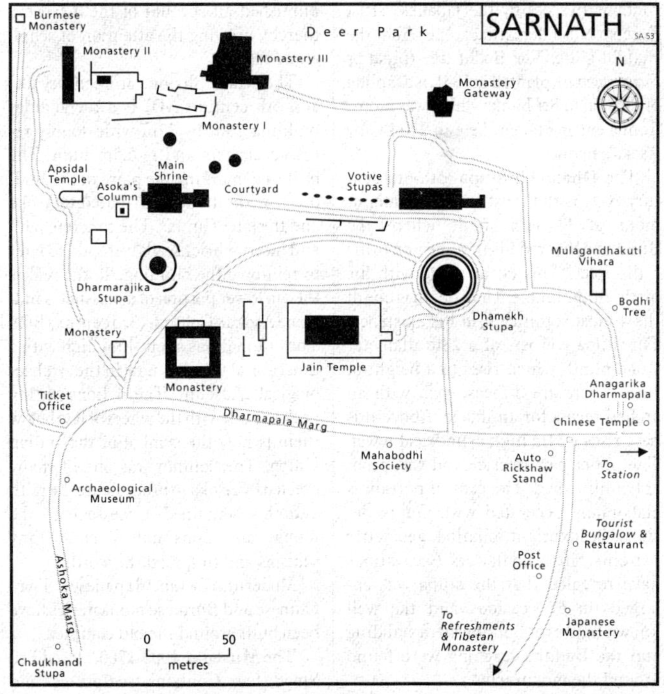

monks, a 65m high vihara, a figure of the Buddha represented by a wheel, a 22m high stone stupa built by Asoka, a larger 90m high stupa and 3 lakes. The remains here and the sculptures now at the Indian Museum, Calcutta and the National Museum, Delhi reveal that Sarnath was a centre of religious activity, learning and art, continuously from the 4th century BC to its abandonment in the 9th century AD. Sarnath was probably destroyed when Muslim armies devastated the region in 1197.

You enter the Deer Park by the E Gateway. On the right is a statue of **Anagarika Dharmapala**, the founder of the Mahabodhi Society which has assumed responsibility for the upkeep of Sarnath and Bodh Gaya – see Bihar (page 781). The modern temple on your right is the **Mulagandhakuti Vihara** (1929-31) which contains frescoes by the Japanese artist Kosetsu Nosu depicting scenes from the Buddha's life. The Bodhi tree (pipal or *Ficus religiosa*), planted in 1931, is a sapling of the one in Sri Lanka which was grown from a cutting taken there in 240 BC by Asoka's nephew.

The **Dhamekh Stupa** (5th-6th century AD) is the most imposing monument at Sarnath, built where the Buddha delivered his first sermon to his 5 disciples. This event along with his birth, enlightenment and death is one of the 4 most significant in his existence. The stupa consists of a 28m diameter stone plinth which rises to a height of 13m. There are 8 faces, each with an arched recess for an image. Above this base rises a 31m high cylindrical tower. The upper part is brick and was probably unfinished. The central portion is elaborately decorated with Gupta designs, eg luxuriant foliation, geometric patterns, birds and flowers. Excavations have revealed that the stupa was enlarged on 6 occasions and the well known figures of Boddhisattva standing and the Buddha teaching were found around the monument.

The Deer Park is holy to Jains because **Shreyamshanatha**, the 11th *Tirthankara* died here. The temple to your left as you move between the stupas commemorates him. The Monastery (5th century onwards) in the SW corner is one of 4 in the Deer Park. The other 3 are along the N edge. All are of brick with cells off a central courtyard. All are in ruins, and there is little evidence of the deer park's earlier attractiveness.

The **Dharmarajika Stupa** (3rd century BC and later) was built by the emperor **Asoka** to contain relics of the Buddha. Like the Dhamekh Stupa this was enlarged on several occasions but was destroyed by Jagat Singh, Dewan of the Maharaja of Benares in 1794 when a green marble casket containing human bones and pearls was found. The British Resident at the Maharaja's court published an account of the discovery thereby drawing the attention of scholars to the site.

The **Main Shrine** (3rd century BC and 5th century AD) is a rectangular building 29m by 27m with doubly recessed corners and is 5.5m high. The building, marking the place of the Buddha's meditation, is attributed to Asoka and the later Guptas. The concrete path and interior brick walls were added later to reinforce the building. To the rear is the 5m lower portion of a polished sandstone Asokan Column (3rd century BC). The original was about 15m high with a lion capital which is now in the Archaeological Museum. The 4 lions sitting back to back with the wheel of law below them is now the symbol of the Indian Union. The column was one of many erected by Asoka to promulgate the faith and this contained a message to the monks and nuns not to create any schisms and to spread the word.

Modern Tibetan, Japanese, Thai, Chinese and Burmese monasteries have been built around the old complex.

The Museum 1000-1700, closed Fri. Small fee. Contains sculptures and pieces from the site, incl the famous lion capital (Asokan Column), a Sunga Period (1st century BC) stone railing, Kushana Period (2nd century AD) Boddhisattvas, Gupta Period (5th century AD) figures, incl the magnificent seated Buddha.

Chaukhandi, ½ km S, has a 5th century Stupa. On top of this is an octagonal brick tower built by Akbar in 1588 to commemorate the visit his father Humayun made to the site. The inscription above the doorway reads 'As Humayun, king of the Seven Climes, now residing in paradise, deigned to come and sit here one day, thereby increasing the splendour of the sun, so Akbar, his son and humble servant, resolved to build on this spot a lofty tower reaching to the blue sky'.

Local Festival May: *Buddha Purnima* marks the birth of the Buddha. A huge fair is held when his relics (which are not on public display at any other time) are taken out in procession.

• **Accommodation** Sarnath can easily be visited in a day from Varanasi which has a good range of hotels. Sarnath has a UP Tourism **E** *Tourist Bungalow*, T 42413. Rm and dorm. Tours. Also ***Birla Rest House*** nr Mulagandhakuti Vihara.

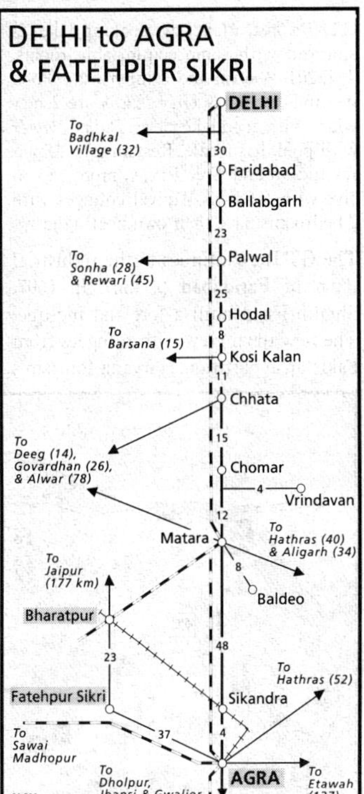

DELHI TO AGRA AND FATEHPUR SIKRI

The best way to see the 3 major sites of Agra on a day trip from Delhi is by using the Shatabdi Express, which gives you 12 hr in the city. By the time you have added in the airport waiting time and possible delays it is often faster than flying.

By bus the journey will take about 5 hr each way. Hired cars can be somewhat faster. If you wish to visit Sikandra and/or Fatehpur Sikri (see **Excursions**) you need to stay at least one night in Agra. This makes it possible to see both the Taj Mahal and Fatehpur Sikri early in the day, which is strongly recommended.

The suggested sequence for viewing the 3 major sites in one day is first the Red Fort, then Itimad-ud-daulah and finally the Taj Mahal.

For the most part the journey passes through agricultural land watered by the Yamuna river. Here, rice and wheat are the principal crops, the former during the *kharif* (rainy) and the latter during the *rabi* (winter) season. The landscape is flat and uninteresting, though there are some low hills at places like Radha Kund and Gobardhan on the W side towards Rajasthan.

ROUTES The **NH2** leaves Delhi along the **Mathura road** and is entirely built up and very busy. 5 km after crossing the **Haryana** border there is a right turn to **Badhkal Village** (32 km) which has motel

C/D *Badhkal Motel*, overlooking lake. 2-storeyed with some comfortable rooms, T 22201. A/c rm and camper huts. Pool, boating. *Garuel* & *Grey Falcon* are 2 new wings with good lake views. *Bath Complex* with pool, has a café. **Restaurants** *Mayur* for Indian and *Grey Falcon*, more expensive with a bar. 2 Minivet cottages with 2 bedrooms have their own boating jetty.

The GT Rd continues to the industrial town of **Faridabad** (4 km). In 1607, Sheikh Farid built a fort and mosque. The new town grew with refugees from Pakistan at partition. Haryana Tourism's attractive motel D *Magpie*, T 288083 with 27 rm, some a/c. Restaurant, bar, garden. The NH2 by-passes **Palwal** (23 km; *Pop* 60,000; *STD Code* 01275), one of many small sites where Painted Grey Ware has been found dating from the end of the Harappan period (see page 37).

The Painted Grey Ware culture A Ghosh has written that the Painted Grey Ware culture was based on agriculture. There is no evidence of towns, and people lived in houses made of wattle and daub or mud and mud bricks. Rice was

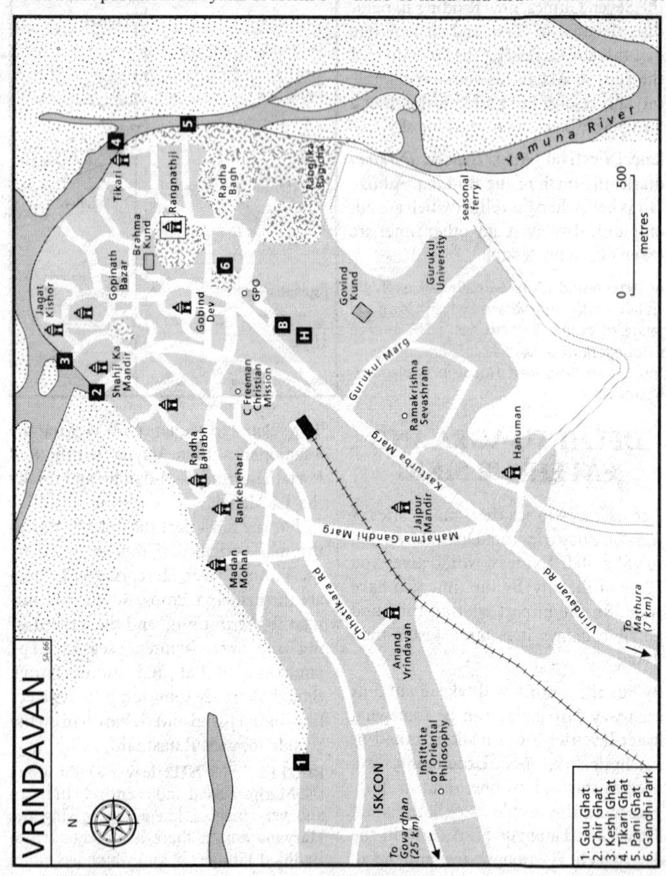

important, and domesticated animals included horses, a favourite animal of the Aryans, cattle, buffalo, pig and sheep. Meat was an important part of the diet, and deer were hunted for food and their antlers, used for making thin pointed tools.

The road continues to **Hodal** (25 km), which has another pleasant Haryana Tourism motel in a 13 acre landscaped site. D *Dabchick*, T 626. 20 rm, 18 a/c, some in cottages and camper huts. Elephant/camel rides, boating. Ruins of medieval *serai*, *baoli* (step well) and a Radha Krishna temple at Pando Ban, nearby. Continue across the state border with UP (6 km) to **Kosi Kalan** (8 km). There is a right turn to **Barsana**, a small town revered as the home of Krishna's wife Radha, lies at the foot of a low range of hills. The 4 prominent peaks are believed to be emblematic of the 4-faced Brahma. Each has a shrine on top. The old town was destroyed when Najaf Khan defeated the Jats in 1773.

Vrindavan

(*STD Code* 05664). The **NH2** continues S from Chhata to Chomar (15 km) and for another 12 km to a road junction. A left turn goes to Vrindavan (4 km) where Krishna played with the *gopis* or cowgirls, stealing their clothes while they were bathing. Here you are entering perhaps the most sacred region of India for Vaishnavite Hindus, where many of the stories surrounding *Krishna* are set (see page 74). Vrindavan – 'Forest of Basil Plants' – is the most famous of the holy sites around Mathura. The temples are open morning and evening.

At the entrance to the town is the 19th century Temple of **Gobind Dev** 1590), the Divine Cowherd, Krishna. Built by Man Singh of Jaipur during Akbar's reign, it was severely damaged by the less tolerant Aurangzeb. Fergusson wrote quite ecstatically on the temple which he said was "the only one, perhaps, from which a European architect might borrow a few hints". Nearby there is a Dravidian style temple dedicated to **Sri Ranganathji** (Vishnu), with 3 *gopura*, each nearly 30m high. There is an annual 10-day *Rath* (car) festival in Mar/Apr. The 16th century **Madan Mohan Temple** stands above a ghat on an arm of the river; there is a pavilion decorated with cobra carvings. Siva is believed to have struck Devi here and made it a place for curing snake bites. The temple has an octagonal tower, similar to the one on the 16th century **Jagat Krishna Temple.** Other temples include: **Gopi Nath** now ruined; **Jugal Kishor** (reputedly 1027), near Kesi Ghat; **Radha Temple** which was partly demolished by Aurangzeb.

ISKCON (International Society for Krishna Consciousness) has a modern marble memorial. The centre runs courses and has a clean D *Guesthouse*, T 82478, with a veg restaurant.

Mathura

History

Mathura, (*Pop* 233,000; *STD Code* 0565) on the W bank of the Yamuna, is one of the most sacred cities of Hinduism dating back to 600 BC. Ptolemy mentioned the town and it assumed importance of a capital city during the 1st-2nd century Kushan Empire. When the Chinese traveller Hiuen Tsang visited it in 634 AD it was an important Buddhist centre with several monasteries. However, Mahmud of Ghazni sacked the city and desecrated its temples in 1017, followed by Sikander Lodi in 1500, whilst the Mughal Emperor Aurangzeb used a local revolt in which his governor was killed as an excuse to destroy the main temples.

Jats and Marathas fought over the city as the Mughal Empire declined, but at the beginning of the 19th century it came under British control. They laid out a cantonment in the S and left a cemetery and the Roman Catholic

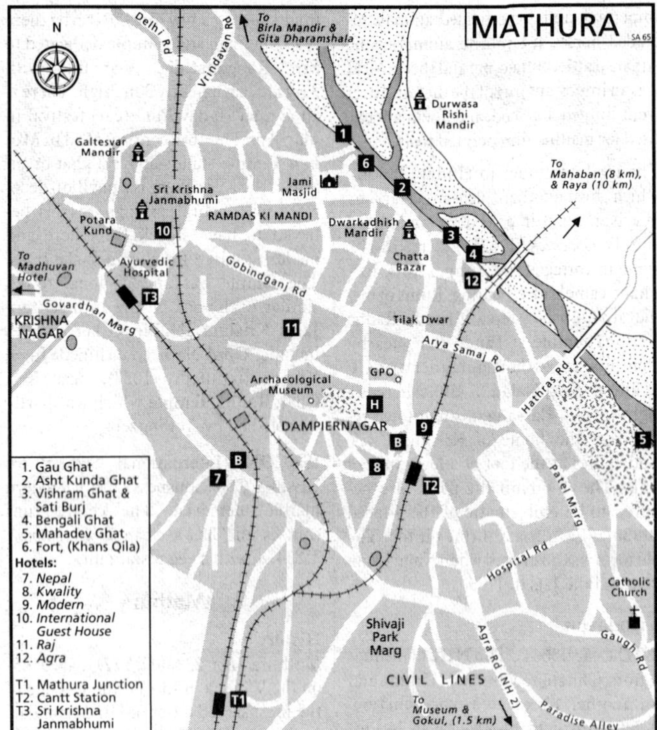

Sacred Heart Cathedral (1870). Today Mathura is an important industrial city. The opening of a big oil refinery on the outskirts of the city in 1975 caused great concern among environmentalists that atmospheric pollution would irreversibly damage the Taj Mahal only 50 km away.

The Vaishnavite city

For Vaishnavites Mathura is perhaps the supremely sacred city of India, being the reputed birth-place of Krishna, the most human aspect of Vishnu. Krishna is widely seen as the embodiment of the ideal lover, soldier, statesman, as well as the adorable baby, or wayward child. Many places are associated with episodes in his life. At Govardhan for example, (see below) Krishna lifted the hill to shelter the people of Brij for 7 days, from the rains sent by Indra. During the monsoon theatrical groups perform the *Banjatra* (Forest Pilgrimage) and act out some of these episodes. Also great celebrations at Holi and Janmashtami. Because of Muslim depredations, almost no monument of antiquity remains in Mathura but its religious association draws thousands of pilgrims.

Places of interest

You enter Mathura by the finely carved **Holi Gate** and in the centre is the **Jami Masjid** (1660-1) with 4 minarets, which was built by Abd-un-Nadi, the governor who was killed. It has a raised courtyard and above the façade which was once covered with brightly coloured enamel tiles, are the 99 names of Allah.

The **Katra** (0.5 km) contains a mosque built by Aurangzeb. This stands over the ruins of one of Mathura's most famous temples, the **Kesava Deo Mandir** which, in turn had been built on the ruins of a Buddhist monastery of the Kushan period. This is considered to be Sri Krishna Janmabhumi (Krishna's birth place). At the rear of this enclosure is a newer **Temple of Kesava**, built by Bir Singh of Orchha – see Orchha, MP page 347). Nearby is the **Potara Kund**, a stepped tank in which Krishna's baby linen was washed. It is faced in the familiar local red sandstone with access for cattle and horses.

The Yamuna The river and its ghats are the focal point for Hindu pilgrims – paved street runs their length. **Vishram Ghat** (reconstructed in 1814) is where Krishna rested after battle with Kamsa. Cows, monkeys and turtles are fed when the Arati ceremony is performed, morning and evening. Best seen from a boat.

The **Sati Burj** (late 16th century), a square, red sandstone tower with a plastered dome, is said to have been built to commemorate the *sati* of the wife of Raja Bhar Mal of Amber. The **Kans Qila** fort was built by Raja Man Singh of Amber and was rebuilt by Akbar but only the foundations remain. Nothing survives of Maharaja Jai Singh's (see page 403) observatory. Shopping in Naya and Chatta bazars and in Tilak Dwar.

Museums

Govt Museum, Dampier Nagar. 1030-1630 except 16 Apr – 30 Jun, when 0730-1230. Closed Mon. An extensive and impressive collection of sculptures, terracottas, bronzes and coins: the 5th century 'Standing Buddha', numerous Gupta figures, a 1st century headless Buddha and Kushana sculptures. Gandhara pieces from the N region of what is now Pakistan discovered at Mathura indicate the links between the 2 regions.

Excursions

Mahaban, 9 km SE of Mathura on the E bank of the Yamuna, means 'a great forest'. There is no forest now, but in 1634 Shah Jahan is recorded as having held a hunt here and killed 4 tigers. The town was sacked by Mahmud of Ghazni and in 1234 was a rendezvous point for the armies of Shams-ud-din Altamish sent against Kalinjar.

Each year in Aug Vaishnavite pilgrims come to the **Palace of Nanda Krishna** where Krishna was believed to have been secretly raised. His cradle stands in the hall, a hole in the wall is where the *gopis* hid his flute, one pillar is polished, apparently by his mother as she leaned against it when churning.

Gokul (2 km) is associated with very early Hindu legends and is where Vishnu first appeared as Krishna. It is approached by a long flight of steps from the river. It is the headquarters of the Valabhacharya Sect who have built some large temples.

Baldeo, 8 km SE of Mathura, another place of pilgrimage, associated with Krishna's elder brother Baladeva, has a temple and Khirsagar tank (Sea of Milk).

Govardhan, 26 km W of Mathura on the Deeg road, lies in the narrow range of the **Girraj Hills**. The story goes that Indra caused a tremendous flood and Krishna raised these hills up above the flood for a week so that people could escape. The **Harideva temple** (by the Manasi Ganga river) was built by Raja Bhagwan Das in the reign of Akbar. On the opposite bank are the *chhattris* of Ranjit Singh and Balwant Singh, both rulers of Bharatpur – (page 418). The small town has 2 lakes, Krishna Kund after the god and Radha Kund after his favourite milkmaid. There are stone ghats on all sides, constructed in 1817. Krishna is believed to have ritually bathed here to purify himself after killing the demon bull Arishta.

On the way to **Radha Kund**, 5 km N, is a cenotaph to Suraj Mal of Bharatpur who attacked Delhi.

Local information

● Accommodation

Largely caters to pilgrims. The western visitor can easily stay in Agra and make a day trip. **C** *Madhuvan*, Krishna Nagar, T 5058. 28 rm, some a/c with bath. Restaurant, exchange,travel, pool.

UP Tourism **E** *Tourist Bungalow*, Civil Lines, By-pass Rd, T 7822. 14 rm. Restaurant, bar. **E** *Nepal*, opp New Bus Stand.

Basic **F** hotels:*Kwality* and *Modern* nr Old Bus Stand, T 3379; *International Guest House*, Katra Keshav Deo, T 5888. Some air-cooled rm. Restaurant; *Agra* nr Bengali Ghat; *Railway Retiring Rooms* at Cantt and Jn Stations. *Gokul* open-air Restaurant and bar, is on the Delhi By-pass Rd.

● Tourist Office

Situated in the Old Bus Stand nr the railway station.

● Transport

Train From Delhi and Agra, the best is: **New Delhi**: *Taj Exp* 2179/2181, daily, 1940, 2¼ hr. **Agra Cantt**: *Taj Exp* 2180/2182, daily, 0900, 50 min. **Sawai Madhopur**: *Paschim Exp* 2926, daily, 1920, 2¾ hr; *Frontier Mail* 2904, daily, 1040, 3½ hr; *Bombay Exp* 9020, daily, 0125, 3¾ hr; *Bombay-Janata Exp* 9024, 1720, 4 hr. **Road** Frequent service to and from Delhi, Agra and neighbouring towns. New Bus Stand is opp Hotel Nepal.

ROUTES From Mathura rejoin the Grand Trunk Rd S.

After 45 km is the **Baradari of Sikander Lodi**, one time King of Delhi, built in 1495, and the 1611 **Tomb of Mariam uz Zamani**, Akbar's Hindu Rajput wife who is said to have been converted to Christianity, though there is little supporting evidence. Beautiful carvings on a red sandstone structure.

Sikandra

(3 km) The GT Rd then passes the tomb of the Mughal Emperor Akbar. Open sunrise-sunset. Rs 2. Parking by Buland Darwaza (main entrance). Large gardens have deer, black buck and monkeys.

Akbar's tomb Following the Timurid tradition, Akbar (r1556-1605) had started to build his own tomb at Sikandra. He died during its construction and his son Jahangir completed it, though not before he had considerably modified the design and had much of the earlier work pulled down. The result is an impressive, large but architecturally confused tomb. A huge gateway, the **Buland Darwaza**, in the style of the massive Victory Gate at Fatehpur Sikri, leads to the great garden enclosure. The decoration on the gateway is strikingly bold, with its large mosaic patterns, a fore-runner of the *pietra dura* technique whereby recesses were cut into the bedding stone of marble or sandstone and pieces set into it. The white minarets atop the entrance were an innovation. They reappear, almost unchanged, at the Taj Mahal. The walled garden enclosure is laid out in the *char bagh* style (in quadrants), with the mausoleum at the centre, and is considerably larger, though less well kept, than that of the Taj Mahal.

A broad paved causeway leads to the tomb which has 4 storeys and is 22.5m high (avoid the monkey captain who likes to sell you a bag of tit-bits for his monkeys). The first 3 storeys of red sandstone are in the style of Fatehpur Sikri. On top of them sits a white marble courtyard containing a finely carved replica sepulchre (the real tomb is below ground level). This 4th storey is very beautiful and points the way to the more extensive use of white marble at the Itimad-ud-Daulah and the Taj Mahal. Visitors are not allowed up to this level.

The lowest storey is 9m high, 97.5m long on each side and contains a massive cloister broken in the centre by a doorway. The one on the S side forms the entrance to the tomb chamber. The vaulted ceiling of the vestibule was ornately frescoed in gold and blue. A section has been restored. The Surah-i-mulk chapter from the Koran runs under the cornice. A gentle ramp leads down through a narrow arched passage to the tomb chamber. You have to remove your shoes or use the over-shoes provided. Off it are sealed bays containing other tombs. In a niche opposite the entrance is an alabaster tablet inscribed with the 99 divine names of Allah. The sepulchre is in the centre of the room, whose velvety darkness is pierced by a single slanting shaft of light from a high window. The holy man there, in expectation of a donation, makes 'Akbaaarrrr' echo around the chamber for 15 secs.

Morning is the best time to visit when few others, apart from guides, are likely to be around; it is an Indiana Jones kind of place – minus giant cobras, fortunately!

ROUTES The GT Rd continues due S to Agra.

4 km S of Sikandra nearly opposite the high gateway of an ancient building called the **Kach ki sarai**, is a sculptured horse, believed to mark the spot where Akbar's favourite horse died. There are also *kos minars* (marking a *kos*, approx 4 km) and several other tombs on the way. You enter Agra through the Delhi Gate, built in Shah Jahan's time (r1627-1658).

Agra

(*Population:* 956,000. *Altitude:* 169m. *STD Code*: 0562). Agra today is one of UP's larger cities with Fatehpur Sikri nearby. Numerous crafts and service industries have flourished, associated with the large tourist traffic – hotels and transport, carpets, *pietra dura* work in marble and soapstone, zari embroidery and leather. It is a vast sprawling city with 7 railway stations. Of these, Agra Cantonment is the most important as it is on the main Delhi-Bombay line, and Agra Fort for traffic from Rajasthan.

Early history

One of the great Mughal cities of S Asia, with minor interruptions, Agra alternated with Delhi as the capital of their empire. Little is known about it before the Muslim conquest. Sikander Lodi seized it from a rebellious governor and made it his capital in 1501. He died in Agra but is buried in Delhi (see page 172). Sikandra owes its name to him. Agra was Babur's capital and he is believed to have laid out a pleasure garden on the E bank of the Yamuna. Humayun built a mosque here in 1530.

Mughal rule

Akbar lived in Agra in the early years of his reign. Ralph Fitch, the English Elizabethan traveller, described a "magnificent city, with broad streets and tall buildings". He also saw Akbar's new capital at Fatehpur Sikri, 40 km W, describing a route lined all the way with stalls and markets. Akbar moved his capital again to Lahore, before returning to Agra in 1599, where he spent the last 6 years of his life. Jahangir left Agra for Kashmir in 1618 and never returned. Despite modifying the Red Fort and building the Taj Mahal, Shah Jahan too moved away to his new city Shah Jahanabad in Delhi from 1638-50, though he returned to spend his last days in Agra as his son Aurangzeb's prisoner. Aurangzeb, the last of the Great Mughals, moved the seat of government

CLIMATE: AGRA

	Jan	Feb	Mar	Apr	May	Jun	Jul	Aug	Sep	Oct	Nov	Dec	Av/Tot
Max (°C)	22	26	32	38	42	41	35	33	33	33	29	24	32
Min (°C)	7	10	16	22	27	29	27	26	25	19	12	8	19
Rain (mm)	16	9	11	5	10	60	210	263	151	23	2	4	764

permanently to Delhi. In the 18th century it suffered at the hands of the Jats, was taken, lost and retaken by the Marathas who, in turn, were ousted by the British in 1803. It was the centre of much fighting in the Mutiny and was the administrative centre of the NW Provinces and Oudh until that too was transferred to Allahabad in 1877.

Places of interest

Warning In late winter and spring, wild bees often nest in the outer walls of some of Agra's major buildings. While there is no cause for alarm, they can be a nuisance under foot at the Taj Mahal and in the Red Fort. Be prepared to take appropriate avoiding action. Con-men, posing as students approach visitors; keep your distance.

The Red Fort

Open daily 0700-1800. Rs 2, Fri free. Allow 1½ hr for a visit. Guide books and good postcards. Reasonable toilets.

On the W bank of the Yamuna River, Akbar's magnificent fort dominates the centre of the city. The site was originally used by the son of Sher Shah, but the present structure owes its origins to Akbar who erected the walls and gates and the first buildings inside. Shah Jahan built the impressive imperial quarters and mosque, while Aurangzeb added the outer ramparts.

There are striking similarities between the Red Fort in Delhi and that in Agra. The outer walls, just over 20m high, faced with red sandstone and topped with pointed merlons, tower above the outer moat. The fort is crescent-shaped, flattened on the E to give a long nearly straight wall facing the river, with a total perimeter of 2.4 km, punctuated at regular intervals by bastions. Like Shah Jahan's fort, the main entrance was also in the centre of the W wall, the Delhi Gate, facing the bazar. It used to lead to the Jama Masjid in the city but is now permanently closed. You can only enter now from the Amar Singh gate in the S. A 3rd entrance, the Water Gate, faces the river. Although only the southern third of the fort is open to the public, this includes nearly all the buildings of interest.

You enter through the **Amar Singh Gate** having had to contend with enthusiastic vendors of cheap soapstone boxes and knick-knacks. If you want to buy something, bargain hard. The admission kiosk is inside the first gate. Guides will offer their services – most are not particularly good.

The fortifications These tower above the 9m wide, 10m deep moat (still evident but containing stagnant water), formerly filled with water from the Yamuna. There is an outer wall on the river side and an imposing 22m high inner, main wall, giving a feeling of great defensive power. The route through the gate is dog-legged. Although it served as a model for Shah Jahan's Red Fort in Delhi, its own model was the Rajput fort built by Raja Man Singh Tomar of Gwalior in 1500, see page 340. If an aggressor managed to get through the outer gate they would have to make a right hand turn and thereby expose their flank to the defenders on the inner wall. The inner gate is solidly powerful but has been attractively decorated with tiles. The similarities with Islamic patterns of the tilework are obvious, though the Persian blue was also used in the Gwalior Fort and may well have been imitated from that example. The incline up to this point and beyond was suitable for elephants and as you walk past the last gate and up the broad brick lined and paved ramp, it is easy to imagine arriving on elephant back.

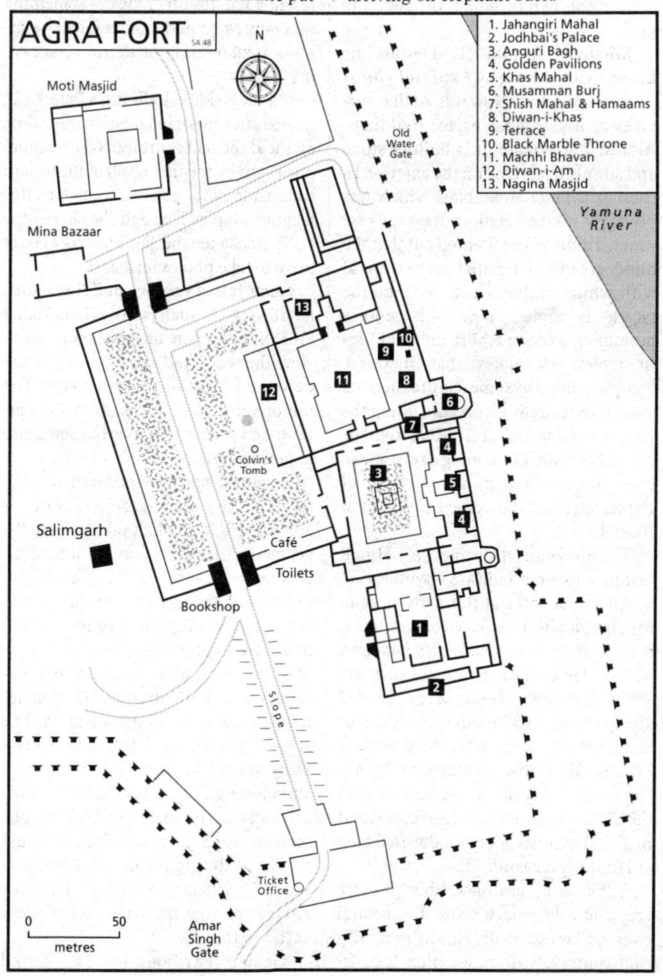

At the top of this 100m ramp is a map and description board on your left, a gate in front and a building and garden on your right. The toilets are round to the right of the gate. There is a shop selling books, postcards and slides in the arcade within the gate and a refreshment kiosk on the right on the other side. The best route round is to start with the building on your right before going through the gate.

Jahangiri Mahal (1) Despite its name, this was built by Akbar (c1570) as women's quarters. Now it is all that survives of his original palace buildings. Almost 75m square, it is built of stone and simply decorated on the exterior. In front is a large stone bowl which was probably used to contain fragrant rose water. Tillotson has pointed out that the blind arcade of pointed arches inlaid with white marble which decorate the façade is copied from 14th century monuments of the Khilji and Tughluqs in Delhi. He notes that they are complemented by some features derived from Hindu architecture, including the balconies (*jarokhas*) protruding from the central section, the sloping dripstone in place of eaves (*chajja*) along the top of the façade, and the domed *Chhattris* at its ends.

The presence of distinctively Hindu features does not indicate a synthesis of architectural styles at this early stage of Mughal architecture, as can be seen much more clearly from inside the Jahangiri Mahal. Here most of the features are straightforwardly Hindu; square headed arches and extraordinarily carved capitals and brackets illustrate the vivid work of local Hindu craftsmen employed by Akbar without any attempt either to curb their enthusiasm for florid decoration and mythical animals nor to produce a fusion of Hindu and Islamic ideas.

Tillotson argues that although there are a few Islamic touches the central courtyard is essentially Hindu, in significant contrast with most earlier Indo-Islamic buildings. In these, he points out, an Islamic scheme was modified by Hindu touches. He suggests therefore that the Jahangiri Mahal marks the start of a more fundamental kind of Hinduisation, typical of several projects during Akbar's middle period of rule, including the palace complex in Fatehpur Sikri. However, it did not represent a real fusion of ideas – something that only came under Shah Jahan – simply a juxtaposition of sharply contrasting styles.

On the S side is **Jodh Bai's Palace** (2), named after one of Jahangir's wives, while on the E the hall court leads onto a more open yard by the inner wall of the fort. In contrast to other palaces in the fort, this is quite simple. Through the slits in the wall you can see the Taj. There is a better place to take photos further on.

Shah Jahan's palace buildings Turn left through to Shah Jahan's Khas Mahal (1636). The open tower allows you to view the walls and see to your left the decorated Mussaman Burj tower. The use of white marble transforms the atmosphere, contributing to the new sense of grace and light.

Anguri Bagh (3, Vine Garden) The formal, 85m square, geometric gardens are on the left. In Shah Jahan's time the geometric patterns were enhanced by decorative flower beds. The Khas Mahal terrace has three. In the middle of the white marble platform wall in front is a decorative water slide. From the pool with its bays for seating and its fountains, water would drain off along channels decorated to mimic a stream. The surface was scalloped to produce a rippling waterfall, or inlaid to create a shimmering stream bed. Behind vertical water drops there are little cusped arch alcoves into which flowers would be placed during the day and lamps at night. The effect was magical. The open pavilion on your right has a superb view across to the Taj.

Golden Pavilions (4) The curved

chala roofs of the small pavilions by the Khas Mahal are based on the roof shape of Bengali village huts constructed out of curved bamboo, designed to keep off heavy rain. The shape was first expressed in stone by the Sultans of Bengal. Originally gilded, these were probably ladies' bedrooms, with hiding places for jewellery in the walls. These pavilions are traditionally associated with Shah Jahan's daughters, Roshanara and Jahanara.

The Khas Mahal (5), the model for the Diwan-i-Khas at the Red Fort in Delhi, has some of the original interior decoration restored (1895) and gives an impression of how splendid the painted ceiling must have been. Underneath are cool rooms used to escape the summer heat. The Khas Mahal illustrates Shah Jahan's original architectural contribution.

These buildings retain some distinctively Islamic Persian features – the geometrical planning of the pavilions and the formal layout of the gardens, for example. They are matched by the normal range of Hindu features such as *chhattris*. However, Tillotson points out that in Shah Jahan's buildings the "Hindu motifs are treated in a new manner, which is less directly imitative of the Hindu antecedents. The temple columns and corbel capitals have been stripped of their rich carving and turned into simpler, smoother forms. The supporting brackets of the *chajja* are similarly not replicas of those on an Indian temple but derived from them. And, as in the Delhi palace, the *Chhattris* have Islamic domes. "Through these subtle changes" he goes on, "the indigenous motifs have lost their specifically Hindu identity; they therefore contrast less strongly with the Islamic components, and are bound with them into a new style. The unity is assisted by the use of the cusped arch and the *Bangladar* roof – forms which had, in various versions, been widely used in India in the past, and so also had no exclusive association".

A true synthesis Seen in this light, the Khas Mahal of Agra's Red Fort achieves a synthesis which eluded Akbar's designs. Tillotson writes: "Shah Jahan's palaces, no less than Akbar's, draw on India's two main traditions; but here the various parts are combined in a new and resolved style. It is that resolution which gives the buildings their appearance of purity. There is no longer an exuberant eclecticism... instead a dignified unity suggesting confidence in a new order. The purity which some writers have supposed to be Persian is in fact Mughal, and in the pavilions of the Anguri Bagh it makes its debut: here Mughal architecture comes of age."

Mussaman Burj (6) On the left of the Khas Mahal is the Mussaman Burj (*Octagonal Tower*, though sometimes corrupted into Saman Burj, then translated as *Jasmine Tower*). It is a beautiful octagonal tower with an open pavilion. With its openness, elevation and the benefit of cooling evening breezes blowing in off the Yamuna river, this could well have been used as the Emperor's bedroom. It has been suggested that this is where Shah Jahan lay on his deathbed, gazing at the Taj. Access to this tower is through a magnificently decorated and intimate apartment with a scalloped fountain in the centre. The inlay work here is exquisite, especially above the pillars. In front of the fountain is a sunken courtyard which could be flooded and in the **Sheesh Mahal** (Mirror Palace) opposite are further examples of decorative water engineering.

From the tower you can appreciate the defensive qualities of the site of the fort and the fortifications erected to take advantage of it. In the area between the outer rampart and the inner wall gladiatorial battles between man and tiger, or elephants were staged. The tower was the Emperor's grandstand seat.

Diwan-i-Khas (7), the Hall of Private

Audience (1637), is next to the Mussaman Burj, approached on this route by a staircase which brings you out at the side. The interior of the Diwan-i-Khas, a 3-sided pavilion, is closed but the fine proportions of the building can still easily be appreciated. The interior was richly decorated with tapestries and carpets. The marble pillars are inlaid with semi-precious stones in delightful floral patterns in *pietra dura*, relieved by carving. It is smaller than the one at Delhi which was modelled on it.

Terrace and Machhi Bhavan In front of the Diwan-i-Khas are 2 throne 'platforms' on a **terrace** (8). The Emperor sat, on the white marble platform facing the **Machhi Bhavan** (9) or Fish Enclosure, which once contained pools and fountains, waiting to meet visiting dignitaries.

Gascoigne recounts how Shah Jahan tried to trick a haughty Persian ambassador into bowing low as he approached the throne by erecting a fence with a small wicket gate so that his visitor would have to enter on hands and knees. The ambassador did so, but entered backwards, thus presenting his bottom first to the Emperor. The **black marble throne** (10) at the rear of the terrace was used by Jahangir when claiming to be Emperor at Allahabad. It is now a popular prop for group photographs. A reddish stain is alleged to be blood.

Nagina Masjid (11) From the corner opposite the Diwan-i-Khas 2 doorways lead to a view over the small courtyards of the *zenana* (harem). Further round in the next corner is the Nagina Masjid. Shoes must be removed at the doorway. Built by Shah Jahan, this was the private mosque of the ladies of the court. Beneath it was a *mina* bazar for the ladies to make purchases from the marble balcony above.

Diwan-i-Am (12) The rooms around the Machhi Bhavan were imperial offices. Go down an internal staircase and you enter the Diwan-i-Am from the side. The clever positioning of the pillars

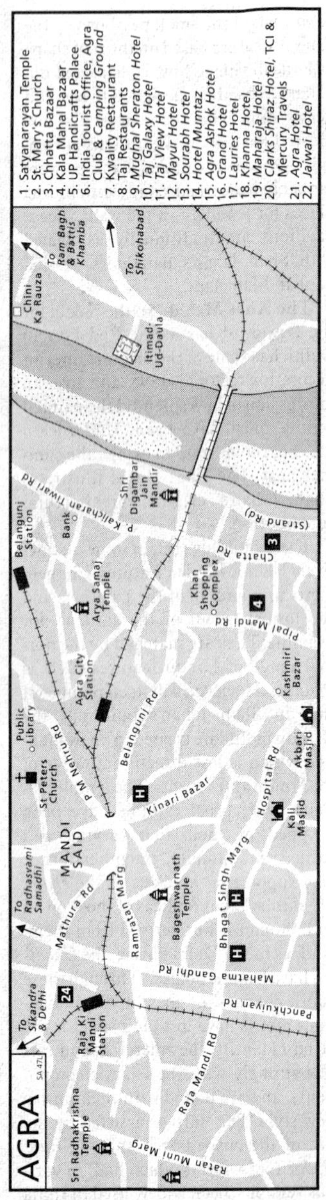

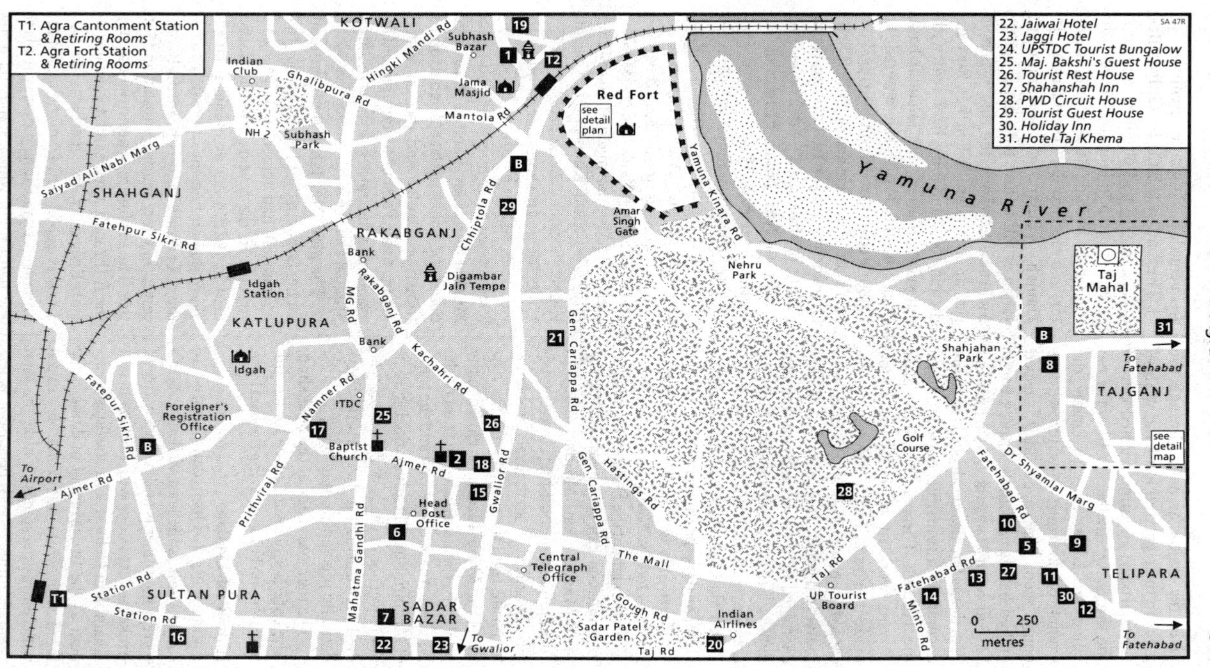
T1. Agra Cantonment Station & Retiring Rooms
T2. Agra Fort Station & Retiring Rooms
22. Jaiwai Hotel
23. Jaggi Hotel
24. UPSTDC Tourist Bungalow
25. Maj. Bakshi's Guest House
26. Tourist Rest House
27. Shahanshah Inn
28. PWD Circuit House
29. Tourist Guest House
30. Holiday Inn
31. Hotel Taj Khema
SA 47R
KOTWALI
Hingki Mandi Rd
Subhash Bazar
Indian Club
Ghalibpura Rd
Jama Masjid
Red Fort
see detail plan
Mantola Rd
NH 2
Subhash Park
Saiyad Ali Nabi Marg
SHAHGANJ
Yamuna Kinara Rd
Yamuna River
Amar Singh Gate
Chhiptola Rd
Fatehpur Sikri Rd
RAKABGANJ
Bank
Nehru Park
Taj Mahal
Idgah Station
Digambar Jain Tempe
Rakabganj Rd
MG Rd
KATLUPURA
Gen. Cariappa Rd
Bank
Kachahri Rd
Idgah
Shahjahan Park
To Fatehabad
TAJGANJ
Fatepur Sikri Rd
Foreigner's Registration Office
Namner Rd
ITDC
Baptist Church
Ajmer Rd
Golf Course
see detail map
To Airport
Ajmer Rd
Prithviraj Rd
Head Post Office
Gwalior Rd
Hastings Rd
Fatehabad Rd
Dr Shyamlal Marg
Mahatma Gandhi Rd
Central Telegraph Office
The Mall
Taj Rd
TELIPARA
Station Rd
SULTAN PURA
SADAR BAZAR
Gough Rd
UP Tourist Board
Fatehabad Rd
Station Rd
Indian Airlines
Sadar Patel Garden
Minto Rd
0 250 metres
To Gwalior
Taj Rd
To Fatehabad

gives the visitor arriving through the gates in the right and left hand walls of the courtyard an uninterrupted view of the throne. On the back wall of the pavilion are *jali* screens to enable the women of the court to watch without being seen. The open-sided, cusped arched hall is extremely impressive; it has 3 aisles of 9 bays and is 64m long and 23m deep. The throne alcove is of richly decorated white marble. It used to house the Peacock Throne, completed after 7 years work in 1634. Its decoration made it extraordinary: "the canopy was carved in enamel work and studded with individual gems, its interior was thickly encrusted with rubies, garnets and diamonds, and it was supported on 12 emerald covered columns" writes Tillotson. When Shah Jahan moved his capital to Delhi he took the throne with him to the Red Fort, only for it to be taken back to Persia as loot by Nadir Shah in 1739.

To the right of the Diwan-i-Am as you look out you can see the domes of the **Moti Masjid** (Pearl Mosque, 1646-53), an extremely fine building closed to visitors because of structural problems. Opposite the Diwan-i-Am are the barracks and **Mina Bazar**, also closed to the public. In the paved area in front of the Diwan-i-Am is a large well and the tomb of Mr John Russell **Colvin**, the Lieutenant Governor of the NW Provinces who died here during the 1857 Mutiny. Stylistically it is sadly out of place.

The tour ends back at the **bookshop**. The **café** is a pleasant place for a drink or ice-cream before leaving the Red Fort.

Itimad-ud-Daulah

Entrance Rs 2. Open daily, sunrise to sunset. This is the least visited of Agra's 3 great monuments and relatively free of trinket sellers. Along with the Chaunsath Khamba in Delhi it set a startling precedent as the first Mughal building to be faced with white inlaid marble (inlaid with contrasting stones). Unlike the Taj it is small, intimate and, because it is less frequented, has a gentle serenity.

The tomb was built for **Ghiyas Beg**, a Persian who had obtained service in Akbar's court. On Jahangir's succession in 1605 he became *Wazir* (Chief Minister) and received the title of Itimad-ud-Daulah ('Pillar of Government'). Jahangir fell in love with his daughter, Mehrunissa, who at the time was married to a Persian. When her husband died in 1607 (and it has been said, without substantiation, that Jahangir had a hand in his death) she entered Jahangir's court as a lady-in-waiting. Four years later Jahangir married her. Thereafter she was known first as **Nur Mahal** ('Light of the Palace'), later being promoted to **Nur Jahan** ('Light of the World') – see page 52.

Her family was almost an extension of the royal family. Her father was *Wazir* and her brother Asaf Khan was Jahangir's second most trusted adviser and later Shah Jahan's (r1627-58) *Wazir*. Her niece Mumtaz married Shah Jahan (r1627-58). Asaf Khan's son, Shaishta Khan, became Aurangzeb's (r1658-1707) *Wazir*. In short, her family provided 2 successive first ladies and 3 successive chief ministers and as the Mughal historian Bamber Gascoigne noted, the 2 most perfect Mughal tombs, Itimad-ud-Daulah and the Taj Mahal, belong to the Persian adventurer and his granddaughter rather than to the great Mughal Emperors themselves.

The plan Nur Jahan built the tomb for her father in the pleasure garden that he himself had laid out. It was constructed in the 6 years after her father died in 1622. 4 km upstream from the Taj Mahal and on the opposite bank of the river Yamuna, it is beautifully conceived in white marble, mosaic and lattice. The enclosure is approached from the E through a red sandstone gateway embellished with marble mosaics. There is a good view from the roof of the entrance. A sandstone pathway leads to the main tomb which stands on a low platform (4m high and 45m square) inlaid with marble decoration. The tomb itself is a low building (21m square) with a dome-roofed octagonal minaret (12m high) at each corner and a central rooftop pavilion in marble tracery. If it has a shortcoming it is that the minarets rather dwarf the central pavilion, making it appear squat, but such a weakness seems somehow irrelevant in the light of the superb decoration. A young Scottish soldier serving in India in 1800, Patrick Macleod, gave a vivid description of a march to Agra and his first sight of the Itimad-ud-Daulah in a letter home. He wrote:

> "This building appeared to me at the time I first beheld it as much more magnificent a structure than I had expected to have seen in Agra, but in this I was afterwards agreeably disappointed. This was a mausoleum in the centre of a large enclosed garden, of a square form, but what constituted its magnificence was its being all faced with high polished white marble inlaid as I then thought in the most masterly style with different coloured marbles forming that kind of ornament called mosaic work. In the interior of the buildings were the tombs of the vizier and his son in a very pretty kind of brown marble. Although there was nothing striking in the architecture of the building, still we could not but contemplate its magnificence as superior to any thing we had yet seen and unanimously agreed, that if we were to view nothing else, this was well worth the trouble of our jaunt."

As he had just marched all the way from Kanpur (300 km) that was no lightly given testimonial.

The development of style Marble screens of geometric lattice work permit soft lighting of the inner chamber. The yellow marble caskets appear to have been carved out of wood. On the top of the woman's tomb is a replica of a slate, the implication being 'here is my heart, clear as a slate, write on it what you will'. On the engraved walls of the chamber is the recurring theme of a wine flask with snakes as handles. This was perhaps a reference by Nur Jahan, the tomb's creator, to her husband Jahangir's excessive drinking. The flanking chambers contain the tombs of other family members. Stylistically, the tomb marks a change from the sturdy and manly buildings of Akbar's reign to softer, more feminine lines. The roof retains a distinctive Hindu influence with its curved roof and broad eaves. In the rooftop pavilion there are replica tombs of the proper one in the main chamber below. This became a popular feature throughout N India (see the Taj Mahal).

Pietra dura The main chamber, richly decorated with mosaics and semi-precious stones inlaid in the white marble, contains the tomb of Itimad-ud-Daulah and his wife. This technique became popular in Europe in the 16th century. Some have argued that the concept and skill must have travelled from its European home of Florence to India. However, there are differences between the two. Florentine *pietra dura* is figurative whereas the Indian version is essentially decorative and can be seen as a refinement of its Indian predecessor, the patterned mosaic (see the S Gateway at Sikandra). See page 185.

Chini ka Rauza

1 km N of the Itimad-ud-Daulah. Literally translated as the 'China Tomb', this is where Afzal Khan, who was in the service of both Jahangir and Shah Jahan, is buried. He died in Lahore in 1639 but was buried in this tomb which had been constructed during his lifetime. The chamber has been severely damaged and the outside is decorated with glazed tiles as were many Mughal buildings in Lahore. The Persian influence is quite strong. It is one of the very few tiled tombs in India to give anything like an idea of what is relatively common in Iran. The glazed surface exfoliated in the Indian monsoon climate. A visit to the roof of the Chini ka Rauza shows how the false dome is carried on a

drum base over the true dome, to aggrandize it.

Ram Bagh

(3 km upstream from Itimad-ud-Daulah), Ram Bagh is believed to be the first Mughal garden in India. Its name is a corruption of the original 'Arambagh' – literally 'garden of rest'. Reputed to have been laid out by Babur (r1526-30) as a pleasure garden, it was the resting place of his body before its internment at Kabul. Now in ruins, it is being cleaned up and its layout restored. The Battis (32) Khamba, a tall octagonal red sandstone cupola, is supported on 32 pillars.

Between the Chinika Rauza and Rambagh is **Zuhara bagh**, another enclosed garden named after Zuhara, one of Babur's daughters. Little remains. It is also possible to visit the unfinished **Radhasvami Samadhi**, 3 km N of the City Station on the Dayal Bagh Rd. It has been under construction for many decades and is an incredible cross between the Taj Mahal and London's Albert Memorial. You can see marble cutting, sculpting and *pietra dura* described above.

The Taj Mahal

Open daily, 0600-1900. Rs 2 except on Fri when it is free (and usually very busy). Rs 100, 0600-0800 and 1700-1900 for viewing at sunrise and sunset, the best times for visiting. Free during Urs (early Jan, commemorating death anniversary of Shah Jahan). Allow 1-2 hr. **NB:** the Archaeological Survey of India explicitly asks visitors not to make donations to anyone in the Taj, including the custodians in the tomb itself, who often ask for money. This request is not very publicly advertised and is enthusiastically flouted by all concerned.

When the Taj Mahal was constructed, the Mughal Empire was already past its prime. The Taj, despite its unquestionable beauty, was an extravagance which the empire could not afford. Because of his profligate overspending of State funds, for the last 8 years of his life Shah Jahan was imprisoned by his son Aurangzeb and confined to his marble palace at the Red Fort.

The state of the Taj declined with the fortunes of the Mughal Empire, the gardens becoming overgrown. In the 19th century the Taj was a favourite place for courting couples and open air balls were held by the British outside the tomb itself. Lord Bentinck, Governor General 1828-35 planned to have the Taj dismantled and sold off in pieces by auction in England. Cranes were even erected in the garden. The plan was only abandoned when a pilot auction of part of Agra's Red Fort

Myths And The Taj

Myths surround masterpieces and the Taj Mahal is no exception. On completion it is said that the Emperor ordered the chief mason's right hand to be cut off to prevent him from repeating this masterpiece. Another legend suggests that Shah Jahan intended to build a replica for himself in black marble on the other side of the river and that the two be connected by a bridge made in alternate blocks of black and white marble. Yet another suggests that the inlaid *pietra dura* work was carried out by Europeans. Historical evidence for these assertions is negligible. Although no one knows who drew up the plans, the overall work is so clearly the result of a flowering of architectural development that had been taking place through the Mughal period, fusing the traditions of Indian Hindu and Persian Muslim into a completely distinct form, that there is no escaping the conclusion that its designers must have had long experience on the developing Mughal tradition, working to meet the demands of their Indian Muslim patron.

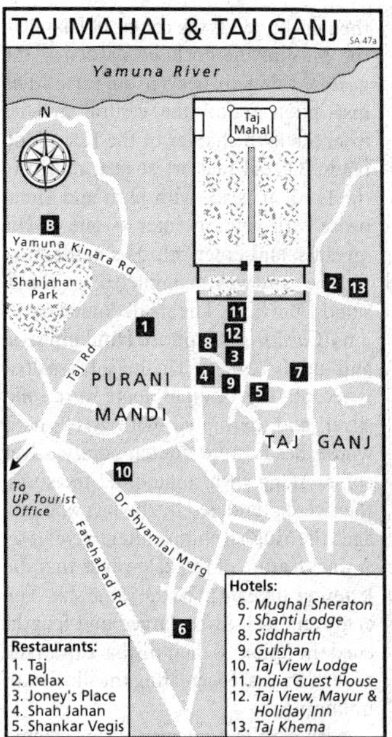

failed to attract enough interest. Fortunately, Lord Curzon, one of Bentinck's successors (1899-1905), repaired much of the damage done over the centuries, reset the marble platform around the Taj, and cleaned up the gardens.

Viewing The best way of viewing the Taj is to do so at different times of the day and year. The white marble of the Taj is extraordinarily luminescent and even on dull days seems bright: the whole building appears to change its hue according to the light in the sky. It is now possible to view it by moonlight in the winter months; at other times see it from outside the compound. In winter (Dec-Feb), it is worth being there at sunrise. Then the mists that often lie over the river Yamuna lift as the sun rises and casts its golden rays over the pearl white tomb. Beautifully lit in the soft light, the Taj appears to float on air.

Entrances You can approach the Taj from 3 directions. The E entrance is often used by groups arriving by coach, the S is from the township that sprang up during the construction of the Taj and the W entrance is usually used by those arriving by car or rickshaw from the Red Fort where there are State Govt emporia selling souvenirs and handicrafts. This used to be an arcade of shops during its construction. On the E approach, the flanking buildings were stables and accommodation for visitors to the Taj. Because of threats to bomb the Taj, visitors now have to enter by a side door to the right of the main gateway. If you have a video camera you are required to hand this in for safe keeping. Entry Rs 2; Rs 100 before 0800 and after 1600. It is worth paying the extra to avoid crowds and take photographs in peace.

The origin of the Taj To the poet Tagore it was "a tear on the face of eternity", a building to echo the cry "I have not forgotten, I have not forgotten, O beloved" (*The Flight of Swans*). The Taj Mahal is an enduring monument to love, with a continually fulfilling beauty. **Shah Jahan** (1618-1666, r1627-58), 5th of the Great Mughals was devoted to his wife **Mumtaz Mahal** (Jewel of the Palace), though he still insisted that she travel with him in all states of health. She died at the age of 39 giving birth to her 14th child. On her deathbed it is said that she asked him to show the world how much they loved one another. It is also said that his hair went grey almost overnight, that he went into mourning for 2 years and lived a very simple life. At the same time he turned away from the business of running an empire and became more involved with his other great love, architecture, resolving to build his wife the most magnificent memorial on earth. It was to be placed along the river Yamuna in full view from his palace at the fort and it was to be known as the **Taj-i-mahal** (The Crown of the Palace).

According to the French traveller Tavernier, the Taj complex took 22 years to build and employed a workforce of 20,000. The red sandstone used was available locally but the white marble was quarried at Makrana, near Jodhpur, 300 km away and transported by a fleet of 1,000 elephants, each capable of carrying a 2.25 tonne block. Precious stones for the inlay came from far and wide: red carnelian from Baghdad, jasper (red, yellow and brown) from the Punjab, green jade and crystal from China, blue lapis lazuli from Afghanistan and Ceylon, turquoise from Tibet, chrysolite (gold) from Egypt, amethyst from Persia, agates in various colours from the Yemen, dark green malachite from Russia, diamonds from Golconda in Central India and mother of pearl from the Indian ocean. A 3.2 km ramp was used to lift material up to the level of the dome and because of the river bank site and the sheer weight of the building, boreholes were filled with metal coins and fragments to provide suitable foundations.

The approach In the unique beauty of the Taj, subtlety is blended with grandeur and a massive overall design is matched with immaculately intricate execution. All contribute to the breathtaking first impression as you pass through the arch of the entrance gateway. You will already have seen the dome of the tomb in the distance, looking almost like a miniature, but as you walk through the arcade of shops and into the open square before the main entrance the Taj itself is so well hidden that you almost wonder where it can be. The glorious surprise is kept until the last moment, for wholly concealing it is the massive red sandstone gateway of the entrance, guarding the enormous wealth inside and symbolising the divide between the secular world and paradise.

In the Koran, the garden is repeatedly seen as a symbol for paradise. Islam was born in the deserts of Arabia. Muslims venerate water, without which plants will not grow and the old Persian word *pairidaeza* means 'garden'. It is no coincidence then that green is the colour of Islam. To the Muslim the enclosed garden is the nearest thing to heaven on earth. The inscription round the central arch is from the 89th chapter of the Koran and reads: "O soul that art at rest, return to the Lord, at peace with Him and He at peace with you. So enter as one of His servants; and enter into His garden".

The gateway, completed in 1648, stands 30m high. The small domed pavilions (*Chhattris*) on top are Hindu in style and signify regality. The huge brass door is recent. The original doors were solid silver and decorated with 1100 nails whose heads were contemporary silver coins. Along with some other treasures, they were plundered by the Jats who ravaged the Mughal empire after its collapse. A final feature of the gateway is that the lettering appears to be the same size. The engravers skilfully enlarged and lengthened the letters as their distance from the ground increased, creating the illusion of uniformity.

Although the gateway is remarkable in itself, one of its functions is to prevent you getting any glimpse of the tomb inside until you are right in the doorway itself. You can still get something of the effect by going from the present entrance straight to what is now the exit. From here only the tomb is visible, stunning in its nearness, but as you move forward the minarets come into view. From here, see how the people walking around the tomb are dwarfed by the 70m high dome.

The Garden "Gardens underneath which rivers flow" is a frequently used expression for the faithful, appearing more than 30 times in the Koran. Four main rivers of paradise are also specified: water, milk, wine and purified honey. This is the origin of the quartered garden (*char bagh*). The watercourses divided the garden into quadrants and all was enclosed behind a private wall. To the Muslim the beauty of creation and of the garden was held to be a reflection of God. The great

Sufi poet Rumi used much garden imagery: "The trees are engaged in ritual prayer and the birds in singing the litany". Thus, the garden becomes as important as the tomb.

The Taj garden, well kept though it is nowadays, is nothing compared with its former glory. The whole of the Taj complex measures 580 x 300m and the garden 300 x 300m. The guiding principle is one of symmetry. The *char bagh*, separated by the watercourses (rivers of heaven) emanating from the central, raised pool, were divided into 16 flower beds, making a total of 64. Each bed was planted with 400 plants. The trees, all carefully planted to maintain the symmetry, were either cypress (signifying death) or fruit trees (life). The channels were stocked with colourful fish and the gardens with beautiful birds. Royal visitors were invited to the tomb – hence the stables and guesthouses. It is well worth wandering along the side avenues for not only is it much more peaceful but also good for framing photos of the tomb with foliage.

The mosque and its jawab On the E and W sides of the tomb are identical red sandstone buildings. On the W (left hand side) is a mosque. It is common in Islam to build one next to a tomb. It sanctifies the area and provides a place for worship. The replica on the other side is known as the **Jawab** (Answer). This cannot be used for prayer as it faces away from Mecca.

The tomb The 4 minarets (41.6m high) at each corner of the plinth provide balance to the tomb. Minarets used in this way first appeared in India with Akbar's tomb at Sikandra. They were used again at Itimad-ud-Daulah and are refined still further here. Each has a deliberate slant outwards – the SW by 20 cm, the others by 5 cm, so that in the unlikely event of an earthquake, they would fall away from the tomb, not onto it. On each pillar is written a letter (R,H,M,N) which together spell the word ar-Rahman (The All Merciful), one of the 99 names of Allah.

There is only one point of access to the plinth (6.7m high and 95m square) and tomb, a double staircase facing the entrance. Here, visitors must either remove their shoes (socks can be kept on) or have cloth covers tied over them. In hot weather the white marble gets very hot. Attendants may request some *bakshish* though strictly payment is not required. The same applies to the attendants inside.

The tomb is square with bevelled corners. Each side is 56.6m long with a large central arch flanked by 2 pointed arches. Each corner smaller domes rise while in the centre is the main dome topped by a brass finial. The dome is actually a double dome and this device, Central Asian in origin, was used to gain height. With the Taj, the Mughals brought to fruition an experiment first tried in Humayun's tomb in Delhi, 90 years earlier. The resemblance of the dome to a huge pearl is not coincidental. There is a saying of the Prophet that describes the throne of God as a dome of white pearl supported by 4 pillars. The exterior ornamentation is calligraphy (verses of the Koran), beautifully carved panels in bas relief and superb inlay work. The last, in the form of large floral sweeps and chevrons is immaculately proportioned.

Inside the tomb The interior of the mausoleum comprises a lofty central chamber, a crypt (*maqbara*) immediately below this, and 4 octagonal corner rooms originally intended to house the graves of other family members. Shah Jahan's son and usurper, Aurangzeb (r1658-1707), failed to honour this wish. The central chamber contains replica tombs, the real ones being in the crypt. It was customary to have a public tomb and a private one. The public tomb was originally surrounded by a jewel encrusted silver screen. Aurangzeb removed this fearing it might be stolen and replaced it with an octagonal screen of marble and inlaid precious stones, the cost being Rs 50,000. It is a stupendous piece of workmanship. The lattice (*jali*) screens are each carved from one block of marble. Even these curved surfaces have been inlaid. If you examine the flowers by placing a flashlight on the surface you can see how luminescent the marble is and the intricacy of the inlay work. Some flowers have as many as 64 pieces making up the petals. By the use of lighter and darker pieces, flowers and foliage are 'highlighted' to give a 3D effect.

Above the tombs is a Cairene lamp whose flame is supposed to never go out. This one was given by Lord Curzon, Governor Gen of India (1899-1905), to replace the original which was stolen by Jats. The tomb of Mumtaz with the 'female' slate, rests immediately beneath the dome. If you look from behind it back to the gateway, you can see how it lines up centrally with the main entrance. Shah Jahan's tomb is larger and to the side, marked by a 'male' pen-box, the sign of a cultured or noble person. Not originally intended to be placed there but squeezed in by Aurangzeb, this flaws the otherwise perfect symmetry of the whole complex. Both tombs are exquisitely inlaid with semi-precious stones. Finally, the accoustics of the building are superb, the domed ceiling being designed to echo chants from the Koran and musicians' melodies. Walk round the outside of the tomb before retrieving your shoes to appreciate it from all sides.

The **museum** above the entrance has a small but interesting collection of Mughal memorabilia, photographs and miniatures of the Taj through the ages. It is worth a brief visit. See under Museums. Open 1000-1700; closed Fri. Free.

Tours

UP Tourism, *Taj Khema*, E Gate, Taj Mahal, T 66140. Coach Tours: Fatehpur Sikri-Taj Mahal-Agra Fort (full day) 1000-1800. Rs 60 (incl guide and entry); Sikandra-Fatehpur Sikri (½ day) 0930-1400, Rs 35; Sikandra-Fatehpur Sikri-Taj Mahal-Agra Fort (full day), 0930-1800; Fatehpur Sikri (½ day) 1030-1400. This only gives 45 min at Fatehpur Sikri. Better take a taxi if you can afford it; UP Roadways, 96 Gwalior Rd, T 72206. Tours start and finish at Agra Cantt Rly Station. Taxi tours possible.

Local festivals

Aug/Sep *The Kailash Fair* at Kailash (14 km). It is believed that Siva appeared in the form of a stone lingam. A temple marks the place.

Local information

● Accommodation

Price guide
AL RS 3,000+ **A** RS 2,000-3,000
B RS 1,200-2,000 **C** RS 600-1,200
D RS 250-600 **E** RS 100-250 **F** Up to RS 100

Most are 5-10 km from the airport and 2-5 km from Agra Cantt Rly. **AL *Welcomgroup Mughal Sheraton***, Fatehabad Rd, Taj Ganj, T 361701. F 361730. 282 rm, ½ with Taj view. 1 km Taj Mahal. *Nauratna* restaurant serves rather bland Mughlai food (good live Indian music), coffee-rm with Taj view, elephant, camel and carriage rides. Beautiful hotel designed in the Mughal tradition (low brick and marble buildings utilising open spaces and gardens) and one of India's finest with "bridge wings" named after Akbar's wives. Won 1980 Aga Khan Award for architecture. The observatory on the roofs offers good views of the Taj.

A *Taj View*, Fatehabad Rd, Taj Ganj. T 361171. 100 rm. Superior rm (even nos) have Taj view. Pleasant, good service. **A *Holiday Inn*** also on Fatehabad Rd is nearby, T 364171. **A *Clarks Shiraz***, 54 Taj Rd. T 361421. 147 rm. Often filled by tour groups. Comfortable restaurant, good shops, pleasant gardens, pool. Comfortable, distant view of the Taj from 4th Fl, excellent roof-top restaurant. **A *Agra Ashok***, 6B Mall Rd. T 361223. 55 a/c rm. 3 km Taj. Typical ITDC – pleasant modern hotel, helpful staff but slow service.

B *Mumtaz*, Fatehabad Rd, Cantt. T 361771. 50 rm, many with view of the Taj, 1 km. Overpriced.

C *Shahanshah Inn*, Fatehabad Rd. T 369119.

24 rm some a/c. Restaurant, pool, travel. **C** ***Amar***, Fatehabad Rd. T 360695. 68 comfortable rm, some a/c. Restaurant, bar, exchange, pool. Chauffeur-driven tourists taken there as drivers get commission. Rm reported dirty and restaurant unable to cope with numbers. Nearby, **C** ***Mayur Tourist Complex***, Fatehabad Rd. T 360310. 30 rm (most a/c) in pleasant bungalows, could be better maintained. Some rm nearest reception spoilt by noise from Holiday Inn's a/c system. Restaurant, bar, pool, garden setting. Good value. Rec. **C** ***Swaagat***, 29 Harinagar, is not rec. Poor rm and service.

D ***New Bakshi House***, 5 Lakshman Nagar, towards airport. T 61292. Best rm has a/c. Good food, courtesy pick-up, car hire. Clean and well run by helpful owners. Rec. **D** ***Grand***, 137 Station Rd, Cantt. T 74014. 58 rm, most a/c with TV in old bungalow. A/c good-value restaurant, bar, exchange, lawns. Popular. Camping. **D** ***Imperial***, MG Rd. T 72500. 8 rm. Indian restaurant, bar, garden. **D** ***Lauries***, MG Rd. T 361019. 28 large rm, some a/c. Restaurant, bar, exchange, pool, lawns. Camping. Old-fashioned but pleasant. **D** ***Major Bakshi's Guest House***, 33/83 Ajmer Rd, T 363829. 12 clean attractive rm. Meals to order, friendly service. **D** ***Ranjit***, 263 Station Rd. T 64446l. 30 rm with bath. Restaurant.

● Budget hotels

E ***Agra***, 165 Gen Cariappa Rd, 500m from Fort, T 72330. 10 large rm, some with Taj view, bath and with a/c. Basic, older hotel, good food, garden. Next door **E** ***Akbar***, Gen Cariappa Rd, is similar. Cheaper rm with basic facilities. Restaurant not so good. Friendly management, good value. **E** ***Jaiwal***, 3 Taj Rd, next to Kwality. T 64141. 17 rm (front better). Central a/c. **E** ***Khanna***, 19 Ajmer Rd, T 66634. Rm with bath around courtyard (front rm noisy). **E** ***Colonel Duggal's Guest House***, 155 Pertabpura (nr Tourist Office). **E** ***Tourist Rest House***, Balugunj nr Dist Board Office, T 363961. Restaurant. Air-cooling inadequate in summer. Fairly basic but excellent value. Often full. **E** ***Tourist Bungalow***, opp Raja-ki-Mandi station, T 72123. A/c rm dearer, dorm and camping. Clean but far from centre. **E** ***Mumtaz Guest House***, 3/7 Vibhav Nagar, T 360865. Rm with bath, TV. Relatively new, clean, pleasant area, friendly, helpful management. Produce Handbook to get 10% discount! **E** ***Siddharth***, 250m S from Taj W Gate, T 360235. Small clean rm. Courtyard and rooftop.

● Very cheap accommodation

S of Yamuna Kinara Rd, nr Taj S Gate, are several cheap guesthouses. **F** ***Gulshan***, is just up the road. Some rm with bath. Good, cheap food, though rather slow service. No commission to rickshaws so drivers may refuse to take you there. **F** ***India Guest House*** just S of Taj Gate, is easy to find. Very basic rm. **F** ***Shanti Lodge***, Chowk Kagjiyan, 150m from S Gate. Air-cooled rm with bath, dearer. Convenient location though monkeys can be a nuisance on rooftop rm. Excellent views of Taj from rooftop and some rooms. Complaints in 1994 of vermin in bathroom and smelly toilets. Restaurant not rec. **F** UP Tourism ***Taj Khema***, E Gate, Taj Mahal. T 360140. 6 rm, 8 camping huts. Restaurant, Tandoori barbecue, travel. Not well-kept. A bit further away: **F** ***Ajay International***, 1 Daresi, nr Agra Fort Rly. T 64427. Cheap and noisy. **F** ***Jaggi Jaiwal***, 183 Taj Rd, T 64142. Rm with bath. Meals and open-air restaurant. Basic. **F** ***Jai Hind***, Naulakha Rd (off Taj Rd). T 73502. Basic, friendly. **F** ***Youth Hostel***, Sanjay Pl, MG Rd, T 65812. **F** ***Railway Retiring Rooms*** at Agra Fort and Cantt Stations, T 72121. For passengers. Advance reservations with money order/draft to Rly Supt, Agra Cantt. Some a/c rm and dorm.

● Camping

In **C** *Mayur*, **D** *Grand, Lauries*, **E** *Agra* and *Tourist Bungalow*; **F** *Taj Khema* and *Jaggi Jaiwal* hotels.

● Places to eat

The larger hotels all have pleasant, multi-cuisine restaurants. On Taj Rd and open all day: ***Kwality*** (a/c) at No 2. Good food, friendly service, reasonable prices, a treat for budget travellers; ***Prakash*** opp, does simple Indian meals. ***Sonam***, at 51, does good Indian and Chinese food, bar. A/c, clean, rec. ***Zorba the Buddha***, below Tourist Office, E13 Shopping Arcade, (off GC Shivhare Rd), Sadar Bazar. Rec for good Indian veg food, reasonably priced. "You may not always get what you order, but it's likely to be good anyway!" Pleasant atmosphere, clean and quiet. ***Chung Wah*** nearby, for Chinese.

Nr Taj: ITDC ***Taj View*** W Gate is convenient, but "uninspiring and seedy"; At the E Gate ***Relax*** has refreshments; ***Taj Khema*** good Indian food (after ordering, ask for chairs to sit out and view the Taj by moonlight while you wait). ***Shankar Vegis***, Chowk Kagiyan, 150m S of Taj Gate, is friendly and rec; excellent banana lassi. ***Shah Jahan***, nearby is very basic, but food edible and very good value. *Joney's Place*, opp, is popular with backpackers.

● Banks & money changers

Andhra, Taj Rd, opp *Kwality's* and others.

● Hospitals & medical services

MG Rd, T 74236, Noori Gate Rd, T 72658 and Hospital Rd, T 72222.

● Post & telecommunications

The Mall (24 hr). At Taj Mahal and elsewhere, 1000-1700. Closed Sun. GPO and Poste Restante, opp India Tourist Office.

● Shopping

The handicrafts Agra specialises in are mostly related to the court, eg jewellery, inlaid and carved marble, carpets and clothes. The main shopping areas for everyday items as well as handicrafts are Sadar Bazar, Kinari Bazar, Gwalior Rd, Mahatma Gandhi Rd, and Pratap Pura. **NB:** tour guides, taxi drivers, rickshaw-wallahs all receive commissions which is built into the price you pay. Go independently to get a better price. You will have to bargain hard anyway. **Warning** You may place an order for a carpet or an inlaid marble piece and have it posted on if you do not find exactly what you want. Reports suggest that what you receive may not be exactly what you ordered. Do not agree to have any jewellery posted.

Books: *Modern Book Depot*, Sadar Bazar stocks a good selection.

Handlooms & handicrafts: Govt emporia in arcade at Taj entrance. *Gangotri* (UP), T 63172. *Kairali* (Kerala), T 62893. *Rajasthali* (Rajasthan), T 73017. *Black Partridge* (Haryana), T 76992. *Kashmir*. Also *UP Handlooms* and *UPICA* at Sanjay Pl, Hari Parbat.

Jewellery: (if you are not visiting Jaipur) try *Kohinoor*, 41 MG Rd; *Munshi Lal* next to UP Handicrafts Palace. Not rec: *Sunrise Jeweller*, 796 Sadar Bazar.

Marble: delicately inlaid marble work by decendants of those who worked on the Taj. *UP Handicrafts Palace*, 49 Bansal Nagar, has a very wide selection from table tops to coasters. Exceptionally high quality and good value. Will collect you from your hotel, T 68214. *Oswal*, 30 Munro Rd, Agra Cantt, is also extremely good. Most other shops stock some marble and soapstones, often of indifferent quality. You may be able to see craftsmen working on the premises here, or at *Krafts Palace*, 506 The Mall.

Soft furnishings: silk, silk/cotton mixed and woollen hand knotted carpets and woven woollen dhurries are all made in Agra. High quality and better prices than in Delhi. *Harish Carpets*, Vibhav Nagar Rd. Wide range and conveniently located for major hotels. An interesting and entertaining experience with non-pushy service. *Bansal Carpets*, Naulakha Market and *Mangalik*, 5 Taj Rd, Sadar Bazar. Closed on Mon. **NB:** artificial silk is sometimes passed off as pure silk.

● Sports

Golf: course on Circuit House campus. Contact *Agra Club*, 191 The Mall, T 74084.

● Tour companies & travel agents

Travel Corporation of India, T 64111 and *Taj*, T 75128 at *Hotel Clarks Shiraz*, Taj Rd. *Ashok*, *Hotel Agra Ashok*, T 76233. *Mercury*, Fatehabad Rd, T 75282. *Sita*, Taj Rd, T 74922. *Aargee*, Fatehabad Rd, T 360529, F 360456.

Tourist offices

Govt of India, 191 The Mall, T 72377. Guides available. Kheria (Agra) Airport counter, during flight times. **UP**, 64 Taj Rd, T 7503 and at *Tourist Bungalow*, Raja-ki-Mandi, T 77035. Counter at Agra Cantt Rly Station, T 66438. **Rajasthan**, T 64582, and **Haryana**, T 65950, at Taj Mahal Shopping Arcade.

● Useful addresses

Police: 200. **Fire**: 201. **Ambulance**: 202. **Foreigners' Registration Office**: 16 Idgah Colony T 74167.

● Transport

Local Bus: City Bus Service covers most areas. Fare Re 0.50-1. From the Taj Mahal area, plenty leave from the Fort Bus Stand. **Rickshaws & tongas**: Auto-rickshaws point-to-point, otherwise rates negotiable. Cycle rickshaws and tongas. Fares negotiable: day hire from Agra Cantt Rly Station (Rs 75 max) for visiting sights, PO, bank etc. **NB:** many earn a commission (as do taxi drivers) by taking tourists to marble/curio/carpet shops; insist on not being rushed away from sights and forced into shops. 'Sabir' outside *Hotel Amar*, rec by reader for outstanding service as rickshaw driver/guide! **Cycle hire**: Saddar Bazar, nr Police station and nr Tourist Rest House. **Taxis**: tourist taxis from Travel Agents, good for visiting nearby sights. Non a/c car Rs 2 per km, full day Rs 240 (100 km), ½ day Rs 110 (45 km). A/c rates negotiable. See Note above.

Air The airport is 7 km from city centre. **Transport to town**: airport bus picks up from major hotels. **Indian Airlines**, Information and reservations: T 360153. Daily flights from Delhi to Agra (3/4 hr), and on to Khajuraho, Varanasi and Kathmandu, returning by same route. **NB:** Long delays in flight departures and arrivals possible especially in winter when Agra and Delhi airports close for periods due to fog. Train travel from Delhi is more reliable and quicker, (see *Shatabdi Express*).

Train Information and reservations: Agra Cantt Rly Station, enquiries T 72515, reservations T 63787, open 0900-1640. Agra Fort Rly Station, T 76161, 72131. Raja-ki-Mandi Rly Station, T 73131. Agra City Rly Station, T 74260. Tundla Rly Station, T 72207. Unless stated otherwise, trains mentioned arrive and depart from Agra Cantt **New Delhi:** *Shatabdi Exp* 2001, daily, 2021, 2 hr; Taj Exp 2179, daily, 1845, 3¼ hr. **Mathura:** *Taj Exp* 2179, daily, 1845, 2 hr. **Jaipur** (from Agra Fort): *Agra Fort Fast Passenger Exp* 9705, daily, 2015, 6½ hr; *Agra-Barmer Exp* 9707, daily, 0815, 11¼ hr; *Agra-Jaipur Exp* 2921, daily, 1700, 5 hr. **Lucknow** (from Agra Fort): *Avadh Exp* 5064, daily, 2202, 8½ hr. **Gwalior:** *Shatabdi Exp* 2002, daily, 0810, 1¼ hr; *Punjab Mail* 1038, daily, 1035, 2¼ hr; Malwa Exp 4068, daily, 2215, 2 hr. **Jhansi:** *Shatabdi Exp* 2002, daily, 0810, 2½ hr; *Punjab Mail* 1038, daily, 1035, 4 hr; *Malwa Exp* 4068, daily, 2215, 3¾ hr.

Mathura *Taj Exp* 2179, daily, 1845, 1 hr. **Bhopal:** *Shatabdi Exp* 2002, daily, 0810, 5¾ hr; *Punjab Mail* 1038, daily, 1035, 10 hr; *Malwa Exp* 4068, daily, 2215, 9 hr. **Bombay (VT):** *Punjab Mail* 1038, daily, 1035, 14¼ hr; 23¾ hr. **Kathgodam (for Nainital from Agra Fort):** *Kumaon Exp* 5311, daily, 2200, 11¾ hr. **Kathgodam and Nainital (via Bareilly Junction):** *Kumaon Exp* 5311, daily, 2200. 11¾ hr. **Calcutta (Haora):** *Udyan Abha Toofan Exp* 3008, daily. 1235, 29¾ hr.

Road Enquiry: UP Roadways Bus Stand, Idgah, T 64198, and at Ram Bagh Crossing (across river Yamuna), T 74141. Information and reservations: T 360153. Most long distance services leave from the **Idgah Bus Station**. Daily Express buses for the following: **Delhi** (204 km via Mathura, 5 hr) from Tourist Office, 0700, 1445. Deluxe, 4 hr; **Jaipur** (240 km via Bharatpur and Mahua, 5 hr); **Khajuraho** (400 km via Jhansi, 0500, 12 hr), Direct 10 hr, 0500; **Lucknow** (357 km via Shikohabad, Etawah and Kanpur), **Gwalior** (119 km via Dholpur and Morena); **Nainital** (376 km via Tundla, Etah, Bareilly and Haldwani, 10 hr).

Fatehpur Sikri

The city's origin

37 km W of Agra. The first 2 Great Mughals, Babur (r1526-1530) and his son Humayun (r1530-1540, 1555-56), both won (in Humayun's case, won back) Hindustan at the end of their lives, and they left an essentially alien rule. Akbar, the third and greatest of the Mughals changed that. By marrying a Hindu princess, forging alliances with the Rajput leaders and making the administration of India a partnership with Hindu nobles and princes rather than armed foreign minority rule, Akbar consolidated his ancestors' gains, and won widespread loyalty and respect.

Akbar had enormous personal magnetism. Though illiterate, he had great wisdom and learning as well as undoubted administrative and military skills. Fatehpur Sikri is testimony to this remarkable character.

Although he had many wives, the 26 year old Akbar had no living heir; the children born to him had all died in infancy. He visited holy men to enlist their prayers for a son and heir. Sheikh Salim Chishti living at Sikri, a village 37 km SW of Agra, told the Emperor that he would have 3 sons. Soon after, one of his wives, the daughter of the Raja of Amber, became pregnant, so Akbar sent her to live with the sage. A son Salim was born, later to be known as Jahangir. The prophecy was fulfilled when in 1570 another wife gave birth to Murad and in 1572, to Daniyal. The Sheikh's tomb is here.

Akbar, so impressed by this sequence of events, resolved to build an entirely new capital at Sikri in honour of the saint. The holy man had set up his hermitage on a low hill of hard reddish sandstone, an ideal building material, easy to work and yet very durable. The building techniques used imitated carvings in wood as well as canvas from the Mughal camp (eg awnings). During the

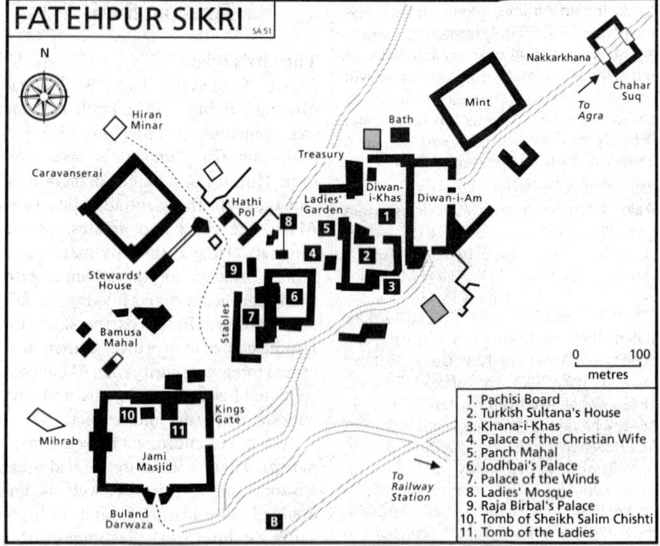

next 14 years a new city appeared on this hill – 'Fatehpur' (town of victory) added to the name of the old village, 'Sikri'. Later additions and alterations were made and debate continues over the function and dates of the various buildings. Over 400 years old and yet it is perfectly preserved, thanks to careful conservation work carried out by the Archaeological Survey of India at the turn of the century.

You enter Fatehpur Sikri through the Agra Gate. The straight road from Agra was laid out in Akbar's time. If approaching from Bharatpur you will pass the site of a lake (32 km circumference) which provided one defensive barrier. On the other sides was a massive defensive wall with 9 gates: Clockwise – Delhi, Lal, Agra, Bir or Suraj (Sun), Chandar (Moon), Gwaliori, Tehra (Crooked), Chor (Thief's), Ajmeri.

Entrance to the city

Entrance Rs 2, sunrise to sunset. It is best to visit early, before the crowds arrive. Allow 3 hr. Carry drinking water and hire 'slippers' where you remove shoes. Hawkers can be troublesome in the mosque and forecourt area. Toilets. **NB**: Most buses and drivers deliver visitors to the main entrance and car park nr the Buland Darwaza which is where the persistent hawkers congregate. It is best to ask to be dropped near the 'hassle-free' entrance by taking the right-hand fork after passing through the Agra gate and taking the road leading up to the original main entrance, where there is now a secondary entrance pay booth and no hawkers. You can then follow the route described below.

From **Agra Gate** you pass the sandstone **Tansen's Baradari** on your right and go through the triple arched **Chahar Suq** with a gallery with 2 *Chhattris* above which may have been a **Nakkarkhana** (Drum House). The road inside the main city wall leading up to the entrance was thought to have been lined with bazars. Next on your right is the square, shallow-domed **Mint** with workshops for other artisans or animal shelters, around a courtyard. Workmen still chip away at blocks of stone in the dimly lit interior. There are 3 sections to the City: The Royal Palace, outside the Royal Palace and the Jami Masjid.

The Royal Palace

Diwan-i-Am or the Hall of Public Audience was also used for celebrations and public prayers. It has cloisters on 3 sides of a rectangular courtyard and to the W, a pavilion with the Emperor's throne, with beautiful *jali* screens on either side separating the court ladies. Some scholars suggest that the W orientation may have had the added significance of Akbar's vision of himself playing a semi-divine role.

This backed onto the private palace. In the centre of the courtyard behind the throne is the **Pachisi Board** (1) or Chawpar. It is said that Akbar had colourfully clothed slave girls moved around as pieces!

The Diwan-i-Khas (Hall of Private Audience) to your right, is a 2-storey building with corner kiosks. It is a single room with a unique circular throne platform. Here Akbar would spend long hours in discussion with Christians, Jains, Buddhist, Hindus and Parsis. They would sit along the walls of the balcony connected to the **Throne Pillar** by screened 'bridges', while courtiers could listen to the discussions from the ground floor. Always receptive to new ideas, Akbar developed eclectic beliefs. The decorative techniques and metaphysical labels are incorporated into Fatehpur Sikri. The pillar, for example, is shaped like a lotus, a Hindu and Buddhist motif, a Hindu Royal Umbrella (*Chhattri*), and the Tree of Life (Islam). The bottom of the pillar is carved in 4 tiers; Muslim, Hindu, Christian and Buddhist designs.

The Throne Pillar can be approached by steps from the outside although there is no access to the upper floor. The design of the Hall deliberately followed the archaic universal pattern of establishing a hallowed spot from which spiritual influence could radiate. In his later years, Akbar developed a mystical cult around himself that saw him as being semi-divine. He appreciated that he could not draw Hindus and Muslims away from their religion but by raising himself to semi-divine status he won the allegiance of Hindus and Muslims alike.

The Treasury In the NW corner of the courtyard is the **Ankh Michauli** (Blind Man's Buff), once believed to have been used for playing the game, comprising 3 rooms each protected by a narrow corridor which were manned by guards. The *makaras* on brackets are mythical sea creatures who guard the treasures under the sea. Just in front of the Treasury is **The Astrologer's Seat**, a small kiosk with elaborate carvings on the 'caterpillar' struts (as seen in Gujarati Hindu/Jain architecture) which may have been used by the court astrologer or treasurer.

The Turkish Sultana's House (2) or Anup Talao Pavilion is directly opposite, beyond the Pachisi Board. Sultana Ruqayya Begum was Akbar's favourite and her 'house', with a balcony on each side, is exquisitely carved. Scholars suggest this may have been a pleasure pavilion. The geometrical pattern on the ceiling is reminiscent of Central Asian carvings in wood while the walls may have been set originally with reflecting glass to create a Sheesh Mahal (Mirror Palace). In the centre of this smaller S courtyard is the **Anup Talao** where the Emperor may have sat on the platform, surrounded by perfumed water. The *Akbarnama* mentions the Emperor's show of charity when he filled the Talao with copper, silver and gold coins and distributed them over 3 years.

In the E corner is the Rose-water Fountain. Next to this is the **Dawlatkhana-i-Khas** (3), the Emperor's Private Chambers. There are 2 main rooms on the ground floor. One housed his library – the recesses in the walls were for manuscripts. Although unable to read or write himself, Akbar enjoyed having books read to him. Wherever he went, his library of 50,000 manuscripts accompanied him. The larger room behind was his resting area. On the first floor is the **Khwabgah** ('Palace of Dreams') which would have had rich carpets, hangings and cushions. This too was decorated with gold and ultramarine paintings. Leaving the Dawlatkhana-i-Khas by the left you enter another courtyard which contained the **Zenana garden** for the ladies, and the 2-storeyed **Sunahra Makan** (4) or Maryam's (the Christian wife's) House for the Emperor's mother, which was embellished with golden murals in the Persian style. The inscriptions on the beams are verses by Fazl, Akbar's poet laureate, one of the '*Navaratna*' (9 Jewels) of the Court.

The Panch Mahal (5) is an elegant, airy 5-storeyed pavilion just N of this, each floor smaller than the one below, rising to a single domed kiosk on top. The horizontal line of this terraced building is emphasised by wide overhanging eaves (for providing shade), parapets broken by the supporting pillars of which there are 84 on the ground floor (the magic number of 7 planets multiplied by 12 signs of the zodiac). The 56 carved columns on the 2nd floor are all different and show Hindu influence. Originally dampened scented grass screens (khuss) which were hung in the open spaces provided protection from the heat and sun, as well as privacy for the women who used the pavilion. From the upper storeys there is a fine view of the rest of Fatehpur Sikri and the adjoining countryside. The impression is that of an encampment in red stone.

Jodh Bai's Palace (6) Jodh Bai, the daughter of the Maharaja of Amber, lived in Raniwas, the spacious palace in the centre, assured of privacy and security by high walls and a 9m high guarded gate to the E. Outside the N wall is the 'hanging' **Hawa Mahal** (7), Palace of Winds, with beautiful screens facing the *zenana* garden which was once enclosed, and the bridge (a later addition) led to the Hathipol. Through the arch is the small **Nagina Masjid** (8) for the ladies of the court. The baths are to the S of the Palace.

The centre of the building is a quadrangle around which were the harem quarters, each section self-contained with roof terraces. The style, a blend of Hindu and Muslim, is strongly reminiscent of Gujarati temples, possibly owing to the craftsmen brought in (see *jarokha* windows, niches, pillars and brackets). The upper pavilions N and S have interesting ceiling structure (imitating the bamboo and thatch roof of huts), here covered with blue glazed tiles, adding colour to the stone buildings.

Raja Birbal's Palace (9) Birbal, Akbar's Hindu Prime Minister was the brightest of Akbar's 'Nine Jewels'. This highly ornamented house to the NW of Jodh Bai's Palace has 2 storeys – 4 rooms and 2 porches with pyramidal roofs below, and 2 rooms with cupolas and screened terraces above. Again the building combines Hindu and Islamic elements (note the brackets, eaves, *jarokhas*). Of particular interest is the insulating effect of the double-domed structure of the roofs and cupolas which allowed the rooms to remain cool, and the diagonal positioning of the upper rooms which ensured a shady terrace. Some scholars believe that this building, *Mahal-i-Ilahi*, was not for Birbal, but for Akbar's senior queens.

S of the Raja's house are the **Stables**, a long courtyard surrounded by cells which probably housed zenana servants rather than the Emperor's camels and horses, though the rings suggest animals may have been tied there.

The Jami Masjid

Leaving the Royal Palace you proceed

The Jewel In The Crown

The 191 carat **Koh-i-Noor diamond** ('Mountain of light') has a long and uncertain history. The earliest reference names Ala-ud-din Khalji as acquiring it from the Raja of Malwa (Rajasthan) whose family had treasured it.

In the "Babur-Nama" the first Mughal Emperor relates how after his victory at Panipat on 21 April 1526 (see page 494) he sent his son and successor Humayun ahead to Agra to secure the treasure there whilst he marched into Delhi. Babur records that "In Sultan Ibrahim's defeat the Raja of Gwalior Bikramajit the Hindu had gone to hell. When Humayun reached Agra the Raja of Gwalior's family had been planning to flee, but Humayun would not allow them to go. They made him a voluntary offering of a mass of jewels and valuables amongst which was the famous diamond which Ala-ud-din Khalji must have brought." Thus was born one of the stories of the diamond's origin near Golconda in the Deccan, see page 1071. Babur went on: " The diamond's reputation is such that every appraiser has estimated its value at 2½ day's food for the whole world. Humayun offered it to me when I arrived in Agra; I just gave it him back."

Thereafter the jewel had a varied history. Some even argue that this was not the true Koh-i-Noor, which it is claimed, was mined at Kollur near the Krishna River and given to Shah Jahan in 1656. Whatever the truth of the jewel's origin, its subsequent history was characterised by repeated violence. Pillaged by Nadir Shah from Delhi in 1739, it passed on his death to the Afghan Ahmad Shah Durrani. His descendents in turn were forced to hand it over to Ranjit Singh, but when the Sikhs were finally defeated by the British in 1849 the jewel was taken to London. The British acquisition lacked lustre and was recut, nearly halving the size, to a brilliant oval crown jewel during Queen Victoria's reign. It was set into Queen Elizabeth, the Queen Mother's, state crown for King George VI's coronation in 1937, and can be seen in the Tower of London.

across a car park to the Jami Masjid and the sacred secton of Fatehpur Sikri. The oldest place of worship here was the **Stone Cutters' Mosque** (10) c1565. It was built near Sheikh Salim Chisti's cell (which was later incorporated into it) by stonecutters who settled on the ridge when quarrying for the Agra Fort began. It has carved monolithic 'S' brackets to support the wide sloping eaves.

The King's Gate (11), the Badshahi Darwaza. This is the entrance Akbar used. Shoes must be left at the gate. The porch is often packed with aggressive salesmen. The 2 other gates on the S and N walls were altered by subsequent additions.

Built in 1571-2, this is one of the largest mosques in India. Inside is the vast congregational courtyard (132m x 111m). To your right in the corner is the **Jamaat Khana Hall** and next to this the **Tomb of the Royal Ladies**. The square nave carries the principal dome painted in the Persian style, with pillared aisles leading to side chapels carrying subsidiary domes. **The mihrab** in the centre of the W wall orientates worshippers towards Mecca. The sanctuary is lavishly adorned with carving, inlay work and painting.

The **Tomb of Sheikh Salim Chishti,** in brilliant white marble, dominates the N half of the courtyard. This is a masterpiece of marble work in India. The Gujarati-style serpentine 'S' struts, infilled with *jali*, do not have structural significance but are highly decorative. The carved pillar bases and lattice screens surrounding the pavilion are stunning pieces of craftsmanship. The canopy over the tomb is inlaid with mother of pearl. On the cenotaph is the date of the saint's death (1571) and the date of the building's completion (1580), though the superb marble screens enclosing the verandah were added by Jahangir's foster brother in 1606. Around the arched entrance are inscribed the names of God, the Prophet and the 4 Caliphs of Islam. The shrine, on the spot of the saint's hermitage, originally had a red sandstone dome which was marble veneered in 1806. Both Hindu and Muslim women pray at the shrine, tying cotton threads, hoping for the miracle of parenthood that Akbar was blessed with. (See page 321 for more about Sheikh Salim Chishti.)

Next to it, within the courtyard, is the larger red sandstone tomb of **Nawab Islam Khan,** Sheikh Salim's grandson and other members of the family.

Buland Darwaza (Triumphal Gate)
Dominating the S wall. It is, however, somewhat out of place. Constructed possibly around 1576 to celebrate Akbar's brilliant conquest of Gujarat, it sets the style for later gateways. The 41m high gate is approached from the outside by a 13m flight of steps which adds to its grandeur. The decoration on this military monument shows Hindu influence but is severe and restrained, emphasising the lines of its arches with plain surfaces. You see an inscription on the right of a famous verse from the Koran:

> Said Jesus Son of Mary (on whom be peace):
> The world is but a bridge;
>
> pass over it but build no houses on it. He
> who hopes for an hour, hopes for
>
> Eternity. The world is an hour. Spend it
> in prayer, for the rest is unseen.

Fatehpur Sikri was only fully occupied for 14 years. When Akbar left, it was slowly abandoned to become 'ruined and deserted' by the early 1600s. Some believe the Emperor's decision was precipitated by the failure of the water supply, but political and strategic motives may also have had a bearing on its desertion. Akbar's change in his attitude towards orthodox Islam and his earlier veneration of the Chisti saints supplanted by a new imperial ideology, may have influenced his decision. In 1585 Akbar moved his court to Lahore and when he did move south again, it was to Agra. But it was at Fatehpur Sikri that Akbar spent the richest and most productive years of his 49 year reign.

Outside the Royal Palace Complex
Between the Royal Palace and the Jami Masjid, a paved pathway to the NW leads to the **Hathipol** (Elephant Gate). This was the ceremonial entrance to the palace quarters, guarded by stone elephants, with its *nakkar khana* and bazar alongside. Nearby are the **waterworks**, with a deep well which had an ingenious mechanism for raising water to the aquaducts above ridge height. The **caravanserai** around a large courtyard fits on the ridge side, and was probably one of a series built to accommodate travellers, tradesmen and guards. Down a ramp immediately beyond is the **Hiran Minar**, an unusual tower studded with stone tusks, thought to commemorate Akbar's favourite elephant, Hiran. However, it was probably an *Akash Diya* ('lamp to light the sky') or the 'zero point' for marking road distances in *kos.* You can climb up the spiral staircase inside it but take care as the top has no guard rail.

This part of Fatehpur Sikri is off the main tourist track, and although less well preserved it is well worth the detour to get the 'lost city' feeling, away from the crowds.

Agra to Gwalior

ROUTES Leave Agra on the NH3 S. The road often shaded with beautiful trees, crosses into Rajasthan, to **Dholpur** (56 km; *Pop* 69,000). A road on the right out of Dholpur leads to **Ramsagar** and the **Vanvihar Wild Life Reserve** (20 km).

There is an abrupt change of scenery as the NH3 crosses the River Chambal (4 km), entrenched in a deep bed. In the dry season it is difficult to imagine that this river can be turned into a vast and turbulent flood. Successive bridges have been washed away or damaged.

To the S begins one of the most notorious regions of India for **dacoity** by castes who make their living from armed robbery. The road climbs through the heavily dissected 'badlands' on the S flank of the Chambal, an arid looking sandy brown for much of the year but converted into a bright green during the monsoon. The river is the boundary between Rajasthan and Madhya Pradesh.

MADHYA PRADESH

Routes

Maps

Madhya Pradesh (the 'Central Provinces'), is at the heart of India. Larger than Germany, the state straddles the country from Rajasthan in the W to Orissa and Bihar in the E. Yet despite its central position it has the character of a marginal territory, containing many of the tribal groups least touched by modernisation, most of India's remaining genuine forest and some of its least densely populated countryside. The W region has been a corridor for the N-S movement of people for over 4,000 years. Today's major towns in MP (Gwalior, Bhopal, Indore) are all in this funnel, as is most of the industrial activity. In contrast, the dense forests to the E have been very difficult to penetrate. However MP has been the home of some of India's earliest settlements. The magnificent paintings and other archaeological discoveries made in rock shelters and caves at Bhimbetka, for example, illustrate the continuity of settlement for over half a million years.

SOCIAL INDICATORS *Population*: 68 mn (Urban 22%, Scheduled Castes, 14%, Scheduled Tribes 23%) *Literacy*: M 57%, F 28%. *Birth rate*: Rural 36:1000, Urban 30:1000. *Death rate:* Rural 14:1000, Urban 8:1000. *Infant mortality:* Rural 145:1000, Urban 79:1000. *Religion*: Hindu 93%, Muslim 5%, Christian 1%, Sikh 0.3%.

MP has been a zone of contact between the N and S core regions of India's cultural development, never the home of a major Indian empire. Rather it has come under a succession of different rulers, most accepting the ultimate sovereignty of a power beyond the region itself. When the British arrived they came relatively late, and left much of the region in the hands of its multitude of princes, often ruling tiny states.

The state has some magnificent historical sites and superb buildings, such as the stupa at Sanchi, the temples at Khajuraho or the splendid fort and palaces at Gwalior. Mandu in Malwa (W MP) occupied a strategic position on the important corridor from Delhi to the western seaboard. Ujjain is one of the 7 holy cities of India and a centre of Hindu pilgrimage. The Kanha National Park is a superb wildlife sanctuary covering the type of country that Kipling based the Jungle Books on.

Communications are only well developed along the N-S corridor in the W, which has hindered MP's industrial development, and some of its richest mineral deposits remain unexploited. MP thus has great potential for sustainable economic growth. Despite its central location, ease of access from Delhi, its wide range of sites and monuments and its freedom from violent political struggles that have afflicted other states, MP is rarely visited by foreigners.

You can now reach **Bhopal** from Delhi in 8 hours by train. There are only a few top class hotels in the region, but there is good accommodation at reasonable prices. MP Tourism has built up an impressive network of tourist complexes at most of the major destinations in the state. These are modest, reasonably comfortable and inexpensive.

Environment

Land

Area 443,000 sq km. MP is India's southernmost landlocked state. Beautiful hill ranges and some of the Peninsula's major rivers, such as the Narmada and the Mahanadi, cross the northern part of the Deccan plateau on which it lies.

The **Vindhya and Kaimur ranges** The magnificent Vindhyans, the most striking hills of the N peninsula, run

Madhya Pradesh – India's Undiscovered Heart

Geographically MP is at the heart of India. Witness to all the major influences which have shaped Indian culture and which continue to contribute to its diversity, today it remains one of the country's least visited regions.

Khajuraho may be the exception that proves the rule, for its temples in the far N of Madhya Pradesh which have become one of India's major tourist attractions are visited by most people en route from Agra to Varanasi. Very few travel further S to the Vindhyan Ranges and the Narmada River, or to the forests and open bamboo grasslands of the SW, with their tribal populations and wildlife reserves.

It is difficult to understand why. In addition to some of India's most beautiful rural scenery it contains sites of outstanding historical interest, magnificent buildings and completely unspoilt areas which it is possible to visit completely without the kind of pressures so common in the popular tourist areas of Rajasthan or UP. There is also outstanding value when it comes to accommodation, from old palace hotels, forest lodges to modern hotels, all at far more modest prices than in the 'high-profile' tourist regions of the N.

Mandu and Ujjain in the far W, a dramatic fortress and one of Hinduism's most revered sites of pilgrimage respectively, give sharply contrasting views of some of India's religious and political history. Yet although Mandu is one of India's most remarkable forts, with commanding views over the Narmada valley, it is possible to wander round its almost deserted buildings totally undisturbed. In contrast, Ujjain retains its own rhythm as one of the most sacred of India's pilgrimage centres, yet untouched by the tourism which has transformed other pilgrimage centres like Pushkar into year-round tourist enclaves.

400 km to the E Kanha and Bandhavgarh, 2 of India's most outstanding national parks, continue to support the natural vegetation which provides the essential habitat for a range of wildlife far beyond that of the much better known but poorer dry savanna parks such as Ranthambor and Sariska.

The explanation for Madhya Pradesh's continued isolation from the beaten tourist track lies in the perception of tour group operators, who account for the travel plans of over 90% of foreign visitors coming to India, that the state is too remote to make comparatively short package tours viable. Bhopal, one of India's most attractive state capitals, is within a comfortable half a day's journey by train from Delhi. It is a journey well worth taking.

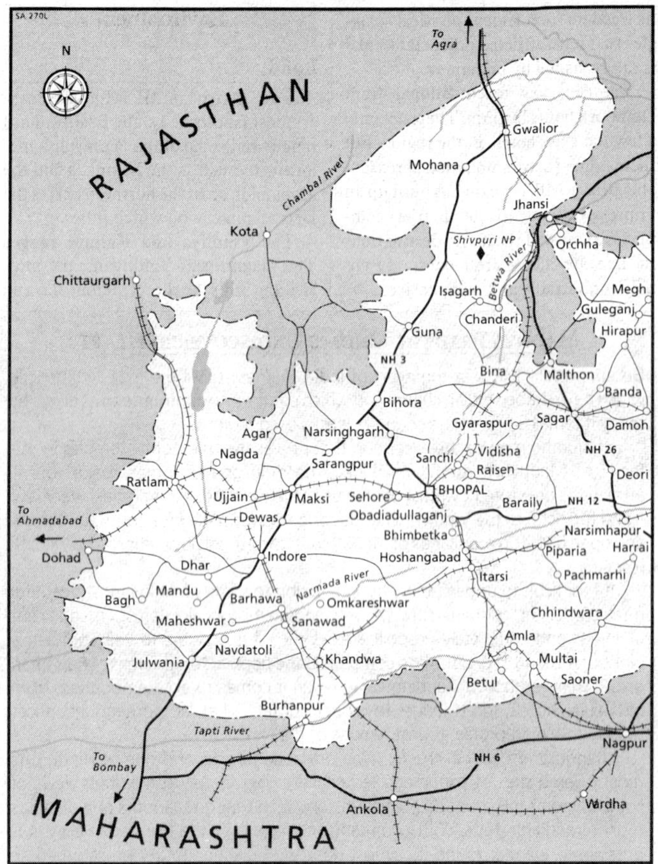

diagonally across the state from around Dhar to Khajuraho. The Kaimur range runs to the N and E through Baghelkhand, overlooking the Gangetic plain around Varanasi and Allahabad in UP. Both are frequently broken by rivers and deep ravines, often covered in forest, and rise to 600m. Behind the Kaimur range at an average height of 300m is the Baghelkhand plateau . Still further E the Hazaribagh range juts into the state, and S of Raipur around Bastar is the plateau behind the E Ghats. To the N of Raipur is the Maikala range.

The **Malwa** region has fertile black volcanic soils but the Narmada Valley with its rich alluvial deposits has the best soils. The Narmada rises in the heart of the state and, along with the Tapti River to its S, it flows W to the Arabian Sea. At Jabalpur it runs through some impressive marble gorges. Along its N edge are the Bhanrer Hills, outriders of the Vindhya Range. In some places, eg between Jhansi and Bina on the railway line from Delhi to Bhopal,

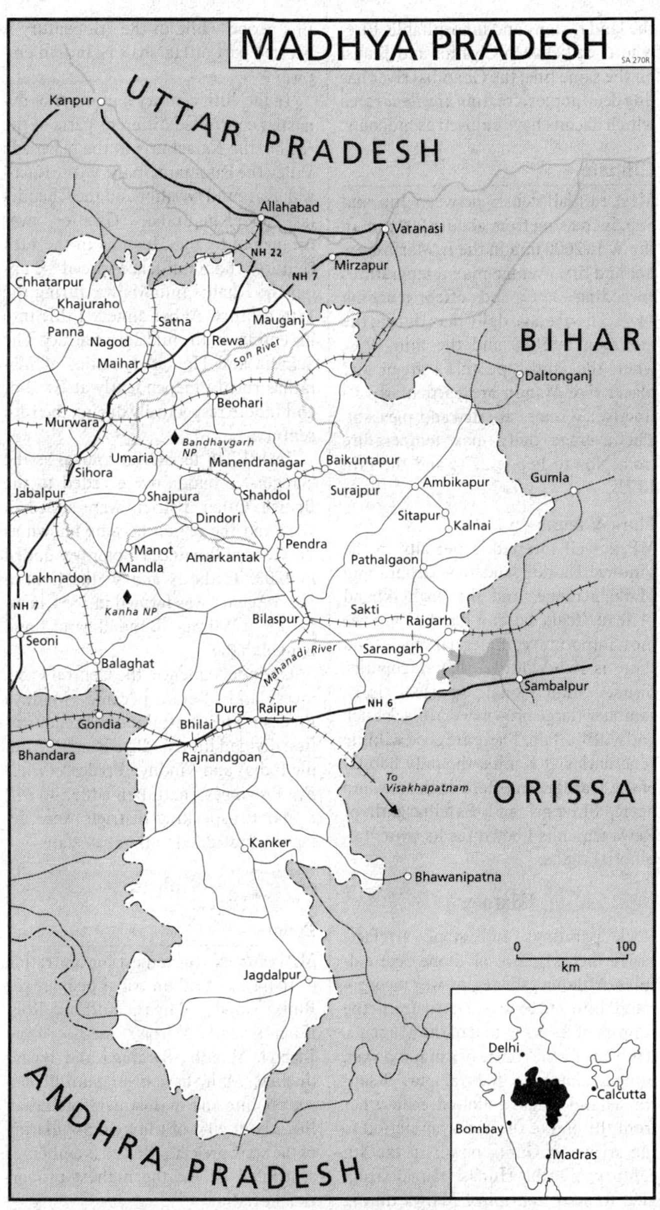
MADHYA PRADESH
SA 270R
UTTAR PRADESH
BIHAR
ORISSA
ANDHRA PRADESH
Kanpur
Allahabad
Varanasi
NH 22
Mirzapur
NH 7
Chhatarpur
Khajuraho
Panna
Nagod
Satna
Mauganj
Rewa
Son River
Maihar
Daltonganj
Beohari
Murwara
Bandhavgarh NP
Umaria
Manendranagar
Baikuntapur
Sihora
Gumla
Jabalpur
Shajpura
Shahdol
Surajpur
Ambikapur
Dindori
Sitapur
Kalnai
Manot
Pendra
Mandla
Amarkantak
Pathalgaon
Lakhnadon
Kanha NP
NH 7
Sakti
Bilaspur
Raigarh
Seoni
Mahanadi River
Sarangarh
Balaghat
Sambalpur
NH 6
Durg
Raipur
Gondia
Bhilai
Bhandara
Rajnandgoan
To Visakhapatnam
Kanker
Bhawanipatna
0
100
km
Jagdalpur
Delhi
Calcutta
Bombay
Madras

the land is stony and inhospitable. Elsewhere, eg between Gwalior and Jhansi on the same line, the Chambal river has dug deep gorges, creating a *badlands* area which dacoits have enjoyed as hideouts.

Climate

Most rainfall comes between Jun and Sep, increasing from about 1000 mm in the W to 2000 mm in the E. Mar-May is hot and dry, average max temperatures exceeding 33°C and often reaching 44°C. The average daily max during the monsoon is 30°C and the min 19°C, when the landscape turns green and places like Mandu are particularly attractive. Winters are dry and pleasant. The average daily max temperature from Nov to Feb is 27°C and the min 10°C.

Flora & fauna

MP is well forested, especially in the Vindhya-Kaimur and the Satpura and Maikala ranges and the Baghelkhand plateau. Teak, sal and bamboo are the most important commercial species and there is rich wildlife: tigers, leopards, bison, chital (small spotted deer), sambhar (large brown deer), black buck and wild buffalo. There are good wildlife sanctuaries at Kanha, the only habitat of the Hardground Barasingha (swamp deer), Shivpuri and Bandhavgarh or Rewa which is known for its white (albinotic) tigers.

History

Rock paintings and stone artefacts prove the existence of Stone Age cultures. Although the region was incorporated into successive states from the Empire of Asoka to that of the Mughals, it was rarely the centre of a major power. Sungas, Andhras, Satavahanas, Ksaptrapas and Nagas followed each other from the end of the Mauryan period to the arrival of Gupta power in the 4th century AD; the Hunas (Huns) struggled to seize control of Malwa during this period while in the 7th century it became part of Harsha's N Indian empire.

In the 10th century a number of dynasties controlled different parts of the region: the Kalachuris in the Narmada Valley, the Paramaras in the W, the Kachwahas around Gwalior and the Chandelas at Khajuraho. Gwalior was conquered by the Muslims in the 11th century, whose influence spread SE under the Khaljis into Malwa during the 13th century. Akbar annexed this into his empire in the mid 16th century. The Scindia and Holkar dynasties of Marathas ruled independently at Gwalior and Indore respectively during the 18th century.

In 1817-18 territories known as the 'Saugor-Nerbudda' were ceded to the British. Other districts were added in 1860 and the region became known as the Central Provinces. Berar was added in 1903. To the N and W the Central India Agency was formed in 1854, comprising Malwa, Bundelkhand and Baghelkhand.

On independence, the Central Provinces and Berar became Madhya Pradesh. The Central India Agency was first divided into Madhya Bharat (Middle India) and Vindhya Pradesh (Vindhya Provinces), and then added to MP. 8 Marathi-speaking districts were detached and added to Bombay state.

Culture

People

MP is home to the largest concentration of India's 22 million tribal peoples the Bhils, Gonds, Baigas, Korkus, Kols, Kamars and Marias, mainly from Jhabua, Mandla, Sarajuga and Bastar districts. Many have been painfully absorbed into the mainstream of Indian life. About 20% of the total population of the state are classified as members of scheduled tribes (the highest proportion in India).

Today the jungle is no longer impenetrable. Travel may be long and dusty but at least you cross the state quite easily, whereas even 50 years ago MP was really inaccessible. Here the tribal people, driven from the comparatively well-watered Gangetic plains by its succession of invaders, took refuge.

Language

Hindi is the most widely spoken language though Marathi is also widespread. Urdu, Oriya, Gujarati and Punjabi are each spoken by sizeable numbers. The Bhils speak **Bhili** and the Gonds **Gondi**, independent in origin of the Indo-European and Dravidian language groups.

Crafts

Textiles are important but MP also has a strong traditional village handicraft industry. Handloom Chanderi and Maheshwar silks are especially sought after. The tribal population produce attractive handicrafts.

Modern Madhya Pradesh

Government

Since it took its present form MP has had a state legislature of 320 seats. With the exception of 1977 and 1989 the Congress Party has always held a comfortable majority of the seats, though the BJP (Bharatiya Janata Party) has always had a strong base of support, winning at least 50 seats in every election after 1967. In the post Emergency election of 1977 the Congress vote slumped from 48% to 36%, but its representation in the Vidhan Sabha fell from 220 seats to 84 seats. It suffered another reversal in the 1989 elections. The State elects 40 members to the Lok Sabha.

In common with the other states of the Hindi belt the Jana Sangh contrib-

The Tribals Of Madhya Pradesh

In the last hundred years the ***Baigas*** of Central India have been forced to abandon shifting cultivation (the burning of forest strips and sowing of seeds in the ashes, the cultivation of crops for a few years on this land and its abandonment for regeneration) and to move from this axe and hoe agriculture to the plough. Most of the 2 to 2.5 million Gonds in MP retain their so-called 'primitive' ways. Traditionally, the tribals were semi-nomadic, some living solely off what they could hunt, others relying on shifting cultivation. Most have now been settled, many it would seem as unhappily as the Australian aborigines. Country liquor and drug dependency are said to be common among the men. Many cling to their older beliefs, such as burying their dead, rather than burning them according to Hindu tradition. Over the centuries, tribal territory has gradually been nibbled away, and everywhere their way of life is under threat.

The **Gonds**, the largest of the tribes, managed to maintain their independence until the last century. From 1200 AD there were as many as 4 Gond Kingdoms. One had an initiation ceremony centred on eating wild orchids. Some tribal traditions, especially mythology and folklore, have been preserved, though they have been exposed to outside cultural influences. The *Pandwani* and the *Lachmanjati* legends are the Gond equivalents of the Hindu *Mahabharata* and *Ramayana* epic poems. Today one of the biggest threats to the tribals comes from that symbol of modernisation, irrigation dams. The proposed building of a succession of dams across the Narmada River in southern MP threatens hundreds of thousands of hectares of tribal forest land. Loud political protests are a feature of the state's current politics.

uted to sweeping the Congress from power in 1977 and again in their reincarnation as the BJP in 1989, when in Dec they won 27 of the 40 seats in the Lok Sabha. In Dec 1993 however the BJP suffered a reverse, the Congress Party winning power again in the State Assembly. In 1994 the Chief Minister was Digvijay Singh.

Economy

Agriculture Nearly half of MP's area is cultivable of which 15% is irrigated. There are 22 major irrigation and power projects with plans to create an irrigation potential of 5.5 million ha. Along with the promotion of Higher Yielding Varieties, the state government is trying to overcome the problem of low agricultural productivity and the use of traditional methods of cultivation. The main food crops are *jowar* (sorghum), wheat and rice and coarse millets such as *kondo* and *kutki*. Pulses (beans, lentils and peas) and groundnuts (peanuts) are also grown. In the E where rainfall exceeds 1270 mm per annum rice is the favoured crop. In the drier eastern areas, wheat is preferred as the principal staple. MP is the largest soya bean producer in India. Important among the commercial crops are oilseeds (linseed and sesame), cotton and sugarcane. The extensive forests are logged for teak, *sal*, bamboo and *salai* which yields a resin used for incense and medicines.

Minerals and power The state is also rich in minerals. The country's largest diamond mine is at Panna near Khajuraho, with recoverable reserves of 1 million carats. Other minerals include high grade limestone, dolomite, iron ore, manganese ore, copper, coal, rock phosphate and bauxite. The state is also the country's only producer of tin ore. Improved communications may help to realise the potential of these resources, and an extensive programme has been undertaken to explore gold deposits in Raipur and Raigarh districts. **Hydro electricity** The 7 major river systems in the state (Narmada, Chambal, Tapti, Son, Betwa, Mahanadi and Indravati) offer good potential for hydro-electric power generation. The Chambal Valley project is jointly run with Rajasthan and other schemes include those at Rajghat, Bansagar, Mahanadi Reservoir, Hasdeo Bango and Bargi.

Manufacturing industry Before the 1950s most manufacturing was around Bhopal. State attempts at regional improvement have led to the establishment of large and medium-scale industries at Indore, Ujjain, Gwalior and Jabalpur. The major industries today are the steel plant at Bhilai, the heavy electrical plant at Bhopal, an aluminium plant at Korba, paper mills at Hoshangabad and Nepanagar, an alkaloid battery factory at Neemuch and numerous cement works.

Communication There are good road and rail communications between Gwalior, Bhopal and Khandwa in the S. In many districts, however, the road network is very poor. The railways, originally laid to connect Bombay with Delhi and Calcutta, and Delhi with Madras, have since been extended to incorporate places like Jabalpur in the heart of MP into the rail network.

BHOPAL

Situated round 2 artificial lakes covering 6 sq km and on gently rolling hills, Bhopal, the state capital, is an attractive city. It achieved international notoriety in 1984 with the Union Carbide disaster. Poisonous gas escaped from the multinational corporation's plant and killed over 1000 people and injured many thousands more.

The city has a good range of hotels and is conveniently located for travel from Delhi (train and air) and to Sanchi. It is a very pleasant city to rest and relax.

BASICS *Population*: 1.06 mn. *Altitude*: 523m. *STD Code*: 0755.

History

Both the origins of the name Bhopal and of the city itself are unclear. Legend suggests that the city stands on the site of an 11th century settlement created by Raja Bhoja, who is believed to have built a dam (*pal*) which resulted in the lakes here. The modern city was developed by Dost Mohammad Khan, one of Aurangzeb's Afghan governors who established himself in power as the Mughal Empire decayed on Aurangzeb's death. He planned to set out wide roads, adorn it with monuments and replant the gardens. After his death Bhopal remained almost an island state in Malwa. It remained loyal to the British through the 18th century. From 1857 until 1926, Bhopal was ruled by women, first Sikander Begum (r1857-1901) and then by Shah Jahan Begum (r1901-1926).

Places of interest

The pink **Taj-ul Masjid** (late 19th century) one of the largest mosques in India, was begun by Shah Jahan Begum (1868-1901), Bhopal's 8th ruler. Work was resumed in 1971. Its 3 white domes, 2 massive minarets, and an impressive hall are are a striking sight. The smaller and earlier **Jama Masjid** (1837) in the bazar, with its minarets topped by gold spikes, was built by Qudsia Begum. The **Moti Masjid** (1860, based on the Jama Masjid in Delhi) was built by Qudsia Begum's daughter, Sikander Begum. At the entrance to the Chowk in old city area is **Shaukat Mahal**, designed by a Bourbon Frenchman, combining Post-Renaissance and Gothic styles. Nearby is the **Sadar Manzil**, the Hall of Public Audience of the former rulers of Bhopal. S of the Lower Lake is the modern **Lakshmi Narayan** (Birla) **Temple** (Vaishnavite). Open 0800-1200, 1400-1800. Entry free. Good views from here and in the evening from Shamla Hills where **Bharat Bhavan** is a national centre of performing arts designed by Charles Correa.

Museums

Below Shamla Hill to the S of the Lower Lake is The State Archaeological Museum which houses sculptures and antiquities and tribal handicrafts. Open daily except Mon. Entry free. On the very pleasant Shamla Hills overlooking the Upper Lake (area 6 sq km) is Bharat Bhawan, centre for creative and performing arts, T 73954. 1400-2000, closed Mon. Small entry fee. Designed by the renowned Indian architect Charles Correa, the low-rise buildings merge with the contours of the landscape. Impressive collection of rural and tribal arts, modern art gallery, crafts gallery, library and theatre. Birla Museum, Vallabh

CLIMATE: BHOPAL

	Jan	Feb	Mar	Apr	May	Jun	Jul	Aug	Sep	Oct	Nov	Dec	Av/Tot
Max (°C)	26	29	34	38	41	37	30	29	30	31	29	26	32
Min (°C)	10	13	17	21	26	25	23	23	22	18	13	11	19
Rain (mm)	17	5	10	3	11	137	499	308	232	37	15	7	1281

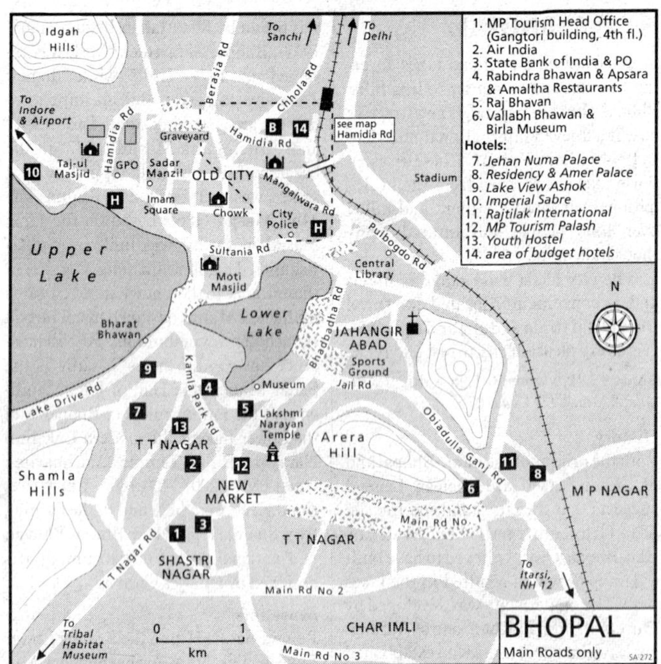

Bhavan. Rare sculptures (7th-12th centuries) and scale model of Bhimbetka. 0900-1700. Closed Mon. **Tribal Habitat Museum**, Shamla Hills. Open-air permanant exhibition of tribal huts.

Parks & zoos

Van Vihar (Bhopal National Park), adjacent to the Upper Lake has tiger, leopard, lion and bear, among others.

Excursions

A cluster of sites to the NE of Bhopal – **Sanchi**, **Vidisha**, **Gyaraspur** and **Udaipur** – can be visited in a day trip from Bhopal. See page 360.

Equally, **Bhimbetka** to the S is particularly well worth visiting, and can be comfortably seen on a day trip combined with visiting **Bhojpur** 28 km from Bhopal, see page 373. If time is restricted but you can hire a car it is comfortably possible to see Bhimbetka in the morning and Sanchi in the afternoon.

Tours

Bhopal Tours on Sun, Tue and Thu, 0900-1600. For tours outside Bhopal, T 65154. Counters at Airport and Rly Station. *MP Tourism* offers a variety of package tours of 3-15 days visiting the principal sights and wildlife parks. Rs 1200-6000.

Local information

● Accommodation

Price guide
AL Rs 3,000+ **A** Rs 2,000-3,000
B Rs 1,200-2,000 **C** Rs 600-1,200
D Rs 250-600 **E** Rs 100-250 **F** Up to Rs 100.

The best are in the quiet Shamla Hills (about 12 km from airport, 5 km from rly and 2 km from centre). In town there are several on Hamidia Rd and Berasia Rd, and less expensive ones on Station Rd. **C** *Jehan Numa Palace*, Shamla Hills, T 540100, F 551912. 60 rm, some in annexe. Restaurant, bar, travel, exchange, shop. Very attractive, central courtyard and gardens, good position but no lake view. Pleasant rooms, friendly and efficient service. **C** ***Lake View***, Shamla Hills, T 541606. 45 rm. Rather bizarre looking modern exterior, but very comfortable. Good restaurant, coffee shop, bar, shops, exchange, modern, clean. Rec. Quiet, good location with views of Upper Lake. **C** ***Imperial Sabre***, Palace Grounds, T 540702. 34 rm. Restaurant, coffee shop, bar. Converted palace guest house in good location. Rec. Several new hotels in the Maharana Pratap Nagar area, near Govt complex under construction. **C** ***Residency***, 208 MP Nagar, T 556001. 48 rm, central a/c. Modern, clean, colour matched rm. Excellent restaurant, pool. **C** ***Amer Palace***, 209 MP Nagar, T 557127. 31 a/c rm. Pleasant modern hotel. **C** ***Rajtilak***, MP Nagar, T 554101. Central a/c, modern hotel.

D ***Mayur***, Berasia Rd, T 540826. Some a/c rm. Dimly lit restaurant. Average. **D** ***President International***, Berasia Rd, T 77291. Some a/c rm. Restaurant, bar. Comfortable, modern. **D** ***Motel Shiraz***, Hamidia Rd, opp Board Office, T 552513. 22 rm, some a/c in cottages. Inexpensive and basic but comfortable. MP Tourism has 2 hotels: **D** ***Palash***, nr '45 Bungalows', TT Nagar, T 553006. 33 rm, 12 a/c. Restaurant, bar. **D** ***Panchanan***, New Market, T 551647. 5 a/c rm. Restaurant, bar. Breakfast included. Both often full. If booking more than 5 days in advance contact Central Reservations, MP Tourism STDC, 4th Flr, Gangotri, TT Nagar, Bhopal. T 554340. Otherwise direct.

Several on Hamidia Rd incl **D** ***Deep***, behind Sangam Cinema, T 75600, some a/c rm. Good for peace and quiet. **D** ***Jyoti,*** No 53, T 76838. Some rm a/c. Restaurant (veg). No alcohol. Clean, popular, good value. **D** ***Pathik***, nr Sangam Cinema, T 77251. 16 rm, some a/c. Rm service only. **D** ***Rajdoot Delux***, No 7, T 75271. 120 rm, some a/c. Restaurant, exchange, travel, car hire; **D** ***Ramsons International***, Hamidia Rd, T 75298. 26 rm. Dirty rm, threadbare carpets, very slow service. " A terrible hotel" by recent accounts. **D** ***Red Sea Plaza***. Nr rly station, T 75551. 60 rm, some a/c. Rm service. Only average. **D** ***Shivalik Gold***, 40 Hamidia Rd, T 74242. Good value. Rec. **D** ***Shrimaya***, 3, Hamidia Rd, T 75454. Modern hotel, some rm a/c. TV. **D** ***Sonali*** T 73990. 21 rm, some a/c. **D** ***Surya*** T 76925, 30 rm, some a/c. Quite reasonable. **D** ***Taj***, 52 Hamidia Rd, T 74769. 48 rm, some a/c. Pleasant roof garden, good view of mosque. Good restaurant, slightly overpriced. Travel. Rec.

● Budget hotels

E ***Rama International***, Radha Cinema Complex, T 543281. 12 rm, some a/c. Little place, tucked back, simple, quiet. **E** ***Sangam***, T 77161. Some a/c rm; **E** ***Samrat***, T 77023.

F ***Pagoda***, nr Bus stand, T 77157, bar and restaurant, very good value, rec; **F** ***Ranjit***, No 3, T 75211, 29 rm with bath. Popular restaurant, bar, TV. Very good value. Rec. **Out of town**: MP Tourism **F** ***Youth Hostel***, TT Nagar, T 63671. Dorm, very basic. **F** ***Railway Retiring Rm***.

● Places to eat

You can sample Gujarati specialities at the ***Jyoti***, Bhopali cuisine at ***Madina,*** Sultania Rd, ***Afgani***, Pir Gate and at ***Hakeem's*** in Jummerati and New Market. ***Amaltha's*** and ***Apsara*** Rabindra Bhavan, in TT Nagar are rec. ***Indian Coffee House*** is in New Market, Hamidia Rd and Sivaji Nagar. Also rec: ***Bagicha*** on Hamidia Rd with garden and bar, and ***Dragon*** next door for Chinese; ***Tapti***, GTB Complex; ***Kwality***, Hamidia Rd and Newmarket: cool and comfortable, reasonably priced. For fast food: ***Doodees***, No 10 Bus Stop, Arera Colony. Inexpensive meals at Rly Station and nr Bus Stand. ***Malwa***, Hamidia Rd for dairy products.

● Hospitals & medical services

Hamidia Hospital, Sultania Rd, T 72222.

● Post & telegraph

Central GPO, TT Nagar T 62465. **GPO**, Sultania Rd T 72095.

● Shopping

The ***Chowk*** and ***New Market*** are the main shopping centres. ***Mrignayanee Emporium***, 23 New Shopping Centre and ***Handicrafts Emporium***, Hamidia Rd stock souvenirs and local handicrafts. ***Women's Coop Zari Centre***, Pir Gate has bags richly embroidered with gold and silver thread, and chiffon saris. ***MP State Emporium***, GTB Complex, TT Nagar, specialises in a local fabric called *chanderi* (a combination of cotton and silk so sheer that the Emperor Aurangzeb insisted that his daughter wear 7 layers of it)! as well as tussar and other raw silks. **Books**: ***Variety books***, 35 Bhadbada Rd; ***Books World***, 33 Bhadbada Rd. **Photography**: Some on Hamidia Rd.

● Sports

Boat Clubs on the Lower and Upper Lakes provide sail, paddle and motor boats.

● Tourist office

MP, Gangotri, 4th Flr, TT Nagar, T 554340.

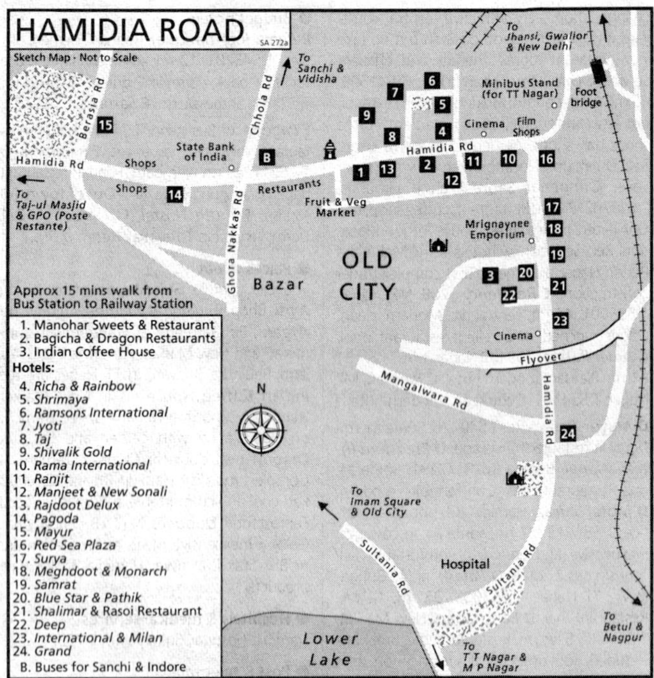

● Useful addresses

Police: T 63939. **Fire**: T 73333. **Ambulance**: T 72222. **Passport Office**: Gangotri, TT Nagar, T 67278.

● Transport

Local Buses, **tempos**, **taxis** (unmetered), **auto-rickshaws** (metered) and **tongas**. **Hire**: MP Tourism has for hire a/c and non a/c cars, buses and mini coaches.

Air The airport is 15 km from centre. **Transport to town**: by taxi, about Rs 200. Indian Airlines bus to airport, daily from City Office, 0700. **Indian Airlines**, City Office, T 550480; Airport T 550142, flies daily to Bombay (2¼ hr) via Indore; daily to Delhi (2 hr) via Gwalior, W,F,Su. **Continental** flies to Bombay, Indore and Raipur on M,W,F. T 554675. **Air India**, GTB Complex, TT Nagar. T 63468.

Train Bhopal is on the main lines between Delhi and Bombay and the southern state capitals of Madras, Hyderabad (Secunderabad), Bangalore and Thiruvananthapuram. There are direct trains to Amritsar and Jammu Tawi in the N and also to major towns in MP. City Booking T 62401. Rly Station, Enquiry T 131, Reservation T 540170. Booking Office on Platform 1. Hamidia Rd is closest from Platform 4 and 5 exit. **New Delhi:** *Shatabdi Exp*, 2001, daily 1440, 7¾ hr; *Punjab Mail*, 1037, daily, 0723, 13 hr; *Jhelum Exp*, 4677, daily, 0930, 12¼ hr; *Malwa Exp*, 4067, daily, 2105, 13 hr. **Bombay (VT):** *Punjab Mail*, 1038, daily, 2042, 15¾ hr. **Calcutta (H):** *Shipra Exp*, 1172, Th,F, 0225, 27 hr. **Lucknow:** *Kushi Nagar Exp*, 1015, daily, 0323, 12 hr; *Pushpak Exp*, 2133, daily, 2215, 11¾ hr. **Jabalpur**: *Amarkantak Exp*, 2854, T,Th,F,Su, 1500, 5½ hr; *Narmada Exp*, 8233, daily, 2235, 7½ hr. **Sanchi**, *Bina Pass*, 1589, 0950, 1 hr. **Ujjain:** *Narmada Exp*, 8234, daily, 0600, 5 hr. **Vidisha (also for Sanchi):** *Jhelum Expr*, 4677, daily, 0942, 45 min;

Road Bus: extensive Bus services (private and state) to cities within the region: **Agra** (NH3 541 km), **Gwalior** (422 km), **Indore** (187 km, good a/c coach, 4 hr, dep 0845, 1430),

Jabalpur, Jaipur (735 km), Kanha (540 km), Khajuraho (387 km, 12 hr), Mandu (290 km), Nagpur (345 km), Sanchi (45 km) hourly from Hamidia Rd Bus Stand, Ujjain (189 km). Roadways Bus Stand, T 540841. Jabalpur, Khajuraho and Ujjain are easier by train.

BHOPAL TO GWALIOR

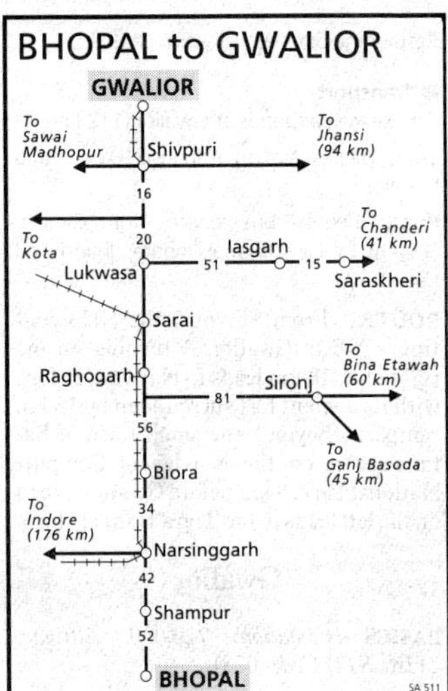

The main route N to Gwalior leaves Bhopal to the NW across the open plateau country immediately to the N of the main range of the Vindhyas. It is attractive countryside, crossing one of the states's driest regions with only about 30 rainy days a year. Although there is little of interest on this route, it is the main NH3 to Agra and Delhi.

ROUTES The road goes W for 5 km towards Dewas, then NW through **Narsinghgarh** (94km) to the NH3 and Biora (34km). The NH3 runs NE to Shivpuri (199 km) with the **National Park**.

Shivpuri National Park

Approach

The dense forests of the Shivpuri or **Madhav National Park** were the hunting grounds of the Mughal Emperors, when great herds of elephants were captured for Emperor Akbar. Now mainly a deer park in forested hill territory, this was also where Maharajas of Gwalior once hunted.

Best season Jan-Mar. After Mar it gets too hot (except early morning and sundown).

Wildlife

The road to Shivpuri passes through the National Park, a 156 sq km dry deciduous forest featuring *dhok* (*Anogeissus pendula*), with Sakhya Sagar, a large perennial lake. Tigers which were once hunted here are seldom seen now. Its main mammals include nilgai, chinkara, chowsingha, sambar, cheetal (the most common deer) and wild pig. The Chandpata lake attracts numerous waterbirds including migratory pochard, pintail, teal, mallard, demoiselle crane and bar-headed geese which remain until May.

In **Shivpuri** the pink Madhav Vilas summer palace (the 'Mahal') was built on a grand scale on a hillock and offers good views. The marble *chhattris* of the Scindia rulers, with fine *pietra dura* inlay and *jali* work, are set in formal Mughal gardens with flowering trees. They synthesise Hindu and Islamic styles with their *sikhara* spires and Mughal pavilions. Curiously, meals are still prepared for the past rulers! Bhadaiya Kund nearby has a spring rich in minerals.

Viewing

Stop where the forest track crosses the stream from the Waste Wier. Good lake views at sunset from George Castle on high ground, once the Scindias' hunting lodge, and from **Burah Koh** watch tower.

Park information

● Accommodation

MP Tourism **D** *Tourist Village*, Jhansi Rd, 3 km from town, Bhadaiya Kund, T 2600. 19 rm in cottages, 5 a/c. Restaurant, bar. Attractive location overlooking lake. **E** *Chinkara Motel*, Agra-Bombay Rd, 8 km from Park, T 2297. 4 rm. Restaurant. **E** *Harish Lodge*, Main Rd.

Restaurant. Simple, well-kept, central.

● **Transport**

Air Nearest airport is at Gwalior (112 km).

Train Nearest station at Jhansi (101 km) and Gwalior.

Road Regular bus services from Gwalior (1½ hr by car), Bhopal, Indore, Jhansi and Ujjain.

ROUTES From Shivpuri the NH3 continues NE to Gwalior. A turning on the right after 18 km leads to **Narwar** (25 km) with its ancient fort surrounded by 13 km ramparts. Beyond, the small town of **Satanwara** is on the N edge of Shivpuri National Park. 9 km before Gwalior a road on the left leads to the **Tigra Dam** (14 km).

Gwalior

BASICS *Population*: 720,000. *Altitude*: 212m. *STD Code*: 0751.

Early history

The colourful hill fort of Gwalior (now in MP), on the N-S corridor from N to W India, was the key to control of the Central Provinces. In legend, Gwalior's history goes back to 8 AD when the chieftain Suraj Sen was cured of leprosy by a hermit saint, Gwalipa. In gratitude he founded and named the city after him. An inscription in the fort records that during the 5th century reign of Mihiragula the Hun, a temple of the sun was erected here. Later, Rajput clans took and held the fort. Muslim invaders like Qutb-ud-din-Aibak (12th century) ruled Gwalior before it passed through a succession of Tomar (Rajput), Mughal, Afghan (Sher Shah), and Maratha hands. During the 1857 Mutiny, the Maharaja remained loyal to the British but 6500 of his troops mutinied on 14th June. Next year, there was fierce fighting round Gwalior, the rebels being led by Tantia Topi and the Rani (Queen) of Jhansi. When the fort was taken by the British, the Rani was found, dressed in men's clothes, among the slain. Although the Maharaja of Gwalior had remained loyal to the British they kept the fort for another 30 years.

Places of interest

The fort contains Jain sculptures, Jain and Hindu temples and the charming sandstone palace. In the town are the palaces, the Moti Mahal and the 19th century Jai Vilas. The Maharaja (Scindia) of Gwalior, an enormously wealthy and powerful man, was one of 5 Maharajas awarded a 21-gun salute by the British.

The Fort

The fort is situated on Gopachal, a sandstone precipice 91m above the surrounding plain, 2.8 km long and 200-850m wide. In places the cliff overhangs, elsewhere it has been steepened to make it unscaleable. The main entrance to the N comprised a twisting, easily defended approach, originally with 7 gates. Seen from the N the 9m high walls present a formidable battlement. On the W is the **Urwahi gorge** and another well guarded entrance.

Apart from its natural defences, Gwalior had the advantage of an unlimited water supply with many tanks on the plateau. It earned the reputation of being one of the most impregnable fortresses of N and C India. The first Mughal Emperor Babur (r1526-30) described it as 'the pearl amongst fortresses of Hind'. If walking, enter by the

CLIMATE: GWALIOR

	Jan	Feb	Mar	Apr	May	Jun	Jul	Aug	Sep	Oct	Nov	Dec	Av/Tot
Max (°C)	23	27	33	39	43	41	34	32	32	33	29	25	33
Min (°C)	7	10	16	22	28	30	27	25	34	18	11	7	20
Rain (mm)	18	7	8	3	9	83	274	259	192	35	2	8	898

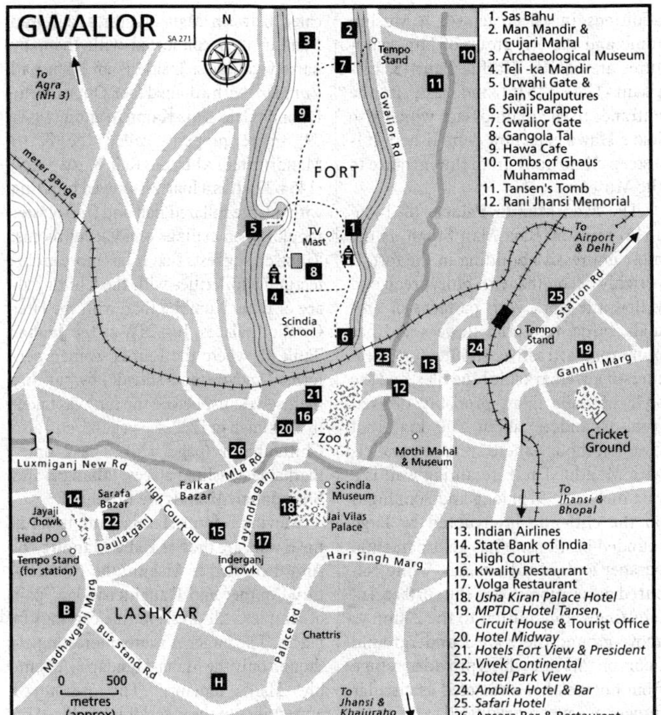

NE entrance, the **Alamgiri Gate**. By car or cycle rickshaw enter by the **Urwahi Gate**, walk to the top and visit the temples in the southern half of the fort area, and the viewpoint. Near the Urwahi Gate are 21 **Jain sculptures** dating from the 7th-15th centuries, some up to 20m tall. An offended Babur ordered their faces and genitalia to be destroyed. Modern restorers have only repaired the faces. The **Dhondha Gate** also on the W side is not in use.

The **NE entrance:** You climb a long, though not unduly steep ramp to approach the main palace buildings and pass through the **Alamgiri** (1660), the first of several gates, most built between 1486-1516. Next is the Badalgarh or the **Hindola** (**1**), because of the swing which was once here. It is (unusually) a true structural arch, flanked by 2 circular towers. The **Gujari Mahal Palace** (c1510) containing the **Archaeological Museum** (**2**) is to the right. Some distance from the fort above, the Gujari Mahal Palace was built by Raja Man Singh for his Gujar queen Mrignayani. The exterior is well preserved. The 3rd gate **Bhairon** no longer exists. The 4th is the simple **Ganesh** (**3**) with a Kabutar Khana (Pigeon House) and a small tank nearby. The mosque beyond stands on the site of an old shrine to the hermit Gwalipa, the present temple having been built later with some of the original material. Before the **Lakshman** Gate (c14th century) is the 9th century Vishnu Chaturbhuja Temple, with later additions, in a deep gap (**4**). A Muslim tomb and the NE group of Jain sculptures are nearby. **Hathia Paur** (**5**, Elephant Gate, 1516) the last, is the entrance to the main palace which also had a **Hawa** gate, now demolished. It is a steep climb down from the entrance to the Museum.

The **Man Mandir Palace** (**6**, 1486-1516) built by Raja Man Singh, is the most impressive building in the fort. It is richly decorated with blue, green and yellow tile-work with patterns of animals, birds, trees and flowers and has numerous attractive architectural features. The remarkable blue tiles, and the style of their inlay, probably derived from Chanderi, about 200 km S of Gwalior, though there are also parallels with Mandu. The E retaining wall is a vast rock face (91m long and 30m high) on the cliff-side interrupted by large rounded bastions. It has an ornamental parapet and gilded cupolas, while coloured decoration covers the surface. Interestingly, in addition to the 2 storeys above-ground there are 2 underground floors on this side which provided refuge from hot weather and acted as circular dungeons when required. Emperor Aurangzeb and his brother Murad were imprisoned here and later executed. The S wall which incorporates the arched Hathi Paur with its guardroom above, is particularly ornate with moulded and colourfully tiled friezes. The beautifully embellished little rooms arranged round 2 inner courts have small entrances, suggesting they were built for the royal ladies. The iron rings here were used for suspending swings and decorative wall hangings. In the SW corner the **Assi-khamba Baoli** (step-well) named '80-pillars' is behind a wall. *Son et Lumière* evenings, Hindi and English, ¾ hr each. No bus; winter evenings can be chilly.

The **Vikramaditya Palace** (7, 1516). Tues-Sun 0800-1100, 1400-1700; 1 April-30 Sept, 0700-1000, 1500-1800. Free. Located between Man Mandir and Karan Mandir, it is connected with them by narrow galleries. Inside is an open hall (*baradari*) with a domed roof. Opposite the Dhonda Gate is the **Karan Mandir** (1454-79), more properly called the Kirtti Mandir after its builder Raja Kirtti Singh (1454-79). It is a long 2-storeyed building with a large pillared hall and fine plaster moulding on ceilings of adjacent rooms. Tillotson suggests that it has more architectural similarities with the Chitor palace of Rana Kumbha than with the later Gwalior palaces. Just NW is the **Jauhar Tank** (**8**) where the Rajput women performed *jauhar* (mass suicide) by burning themselves just before the fort was taken by Iltutmish in 1232, see page 45, and also Chittaurgarh (page 426). The 2 unremarkable Muslim palaces, **Jahangiri** and **Shah Jahan Mahals** are further N.

Moving S from Hathia Paur, towards the E wall, are the **Sas Bahu Mandirs** (**9**). Also dedicated to Vishnu, the 11th century 'Mother and Daughter-in-law' pair of temples still preserve fine carvings in places. The larger is more interesting although only the Maha-Mandapa (Assembly Hall) remains. The 3-storeyed appearance of the exterior is produced by the open galleries surrounding the single high inner hall, the roof of which needed to be supported by 4 large piers due to the limitations of the 'pillar and beam' method of construction. The smaller has an ornately carved base and a vaulted ceiling under the pyramidal roof. To their W is **Suraj Kund** (**10**) a large tank (107m by 55m), first referred to in the 5th century, where Suraj Sen's leprosy was cured (see Early History above).

Teli-ka Mandir (**11**) Guides sometimes incorrectly give the derivation of the name as implying a link with Telangana in modern Andhra Pradesh, and suggest that the temple represents the fusion of Dravidian and N Indian architectural styles. In fact the name means 'oil man's temple', though as Brown says, there is no good explanation for the name. It is the earliest temple in Gwalior, and architecturally has more in common with some early Orissan temples than with those of the S. The unique 25m high Pratihara (mid-8th century) Vishnu Temple, essentially a sanctuary with a *garuda* at the entrance, stands above the rest. The oblong vaulted roof is particularly interesting, somewhat resembling a Buddhist *chaitya* and the Vaital Deul (Bhubaneswar). The highly decorative carvings have been restored. Tillotson records how after the Mutiny the Maharaja "watched the British garrison paying scant respect to the ancient Hindu buildings within the Fort: the great medieval temple, the Teli-ka Mandir, for example was put to service as a soda-water factory and coffee shop. By such acts of desecration the British showed Indian rulers how the ancient Hindu heritage was then regarded by those who laid claim to power and authority". The Katora Tal behind was excavated when the fort was built, like many others here. The Ek-khamba Tal has a single stone column standing in it. **Rani Tal** (**12**) further S was supposedly intended for the royal ladies; it is connected underground to the neighbouring **Chedi Tal**!

The S part of the fort is now a boarding school.

The town

After Daulat Rao Scindia acquired Gwalior in 1809 he pitched camp to the S of the fort. The new city that arose was **Lashkar** (The Camp) with palaces, King George Park (now Gandhi Park), the market (Jayaji Chowk) and the *Chhattris* of the Maharajas.

Jai Vilas Palace (1872-4) Designed by Lt-Col Sir Michael Filose to resemble an Italian palazzo, was completed in 3 years to be ready for the Prince of Wales' visit. The floors resemble marble but are in fact painted sandstone. The Durbar Hall containing crystal furniture is approached by a crystal staircase and in it hang 2 of the world's largest chandeliers. The enormous carpet was made in the Gwalior jail. The silver electric train set transported cigars and port round the dinner table! Part of the palace is the present Maharaja's residence but 35 rooms house the Scindia **museum** (much in need of maintenance).

The other large palace is the **Moti Mahal** nearby which is used as offices. SE of the fort is the spot where **Rani Lakshmi Bai of Jhansi** was cremated, marked by a stirring statue.

The Royal Chhattris are each dedicated to a Gwalior Maharaja. Near the Jayaji Chowk, these ghostly pavillions empty except for a lighted image, are in various stages of neglect.

In the crowded Hazira in the **Old Town**, NE of the fort, is the **Tomb of Ghaus Muhammad**, a 16th century Afghan prince who helped Babur to win the fort. It is in an early Mughal style with finely carved *jali* screens. Hindus and Muslims both make pilgrimage to the tomb. Nearby, in an attractive garden setting, is the **Tomb of Tansen**, the most famous musician of Akbar's court. It is the venue for the annual music festival (Nov/Dec). The present tamarind tree is a recent replacement of the old one which was believed to have magical properties. Gwalior retains a strong musical tradition, and is an influential force in Hindustani classical music. Tansen was an exponent of the *dhrupad* style, and laid the foundations for what in the 19th century became the Gwalior *ghurana* style, noted for its stress on composition and forceful performance. One of the best known contemporary exponents is Amjad Ali Khan, a renowned sarod player.

Excursions

Shivpuri (in MP), summer capital of the Scindia Rulers with a game reserve nearby. See above.

Museums

Gujari Mahal Archaeological Museum, inside Hindola Gate (NE), Fort, T 8641. Pretty palace with interesting collection – sculptures, archaeological pieces, terracottas (Besnagar, Ujjain), coins and paintings, including copies of 2 frescoes from the Bagh caves. Ask curator to see the Shalbhanjika miniature. Good guide book. 1000-1700, Closed Mon. Small fee. **Municipal Corp Museum**, Moti Mahal Rd, T 22819. Collection of armoury and natural history. 1000-1630, closed Mon. Re 1. **Kala Vithika**, MP Kala Parishad. Modern art collection. 0900-1700, closed Sun. Free **Jai Vilas Palace Museum**, 1030-1700, Closed Mon. Maharaja's and Palace memorabilia and decorations. **Scindia Museum**, Jai Vilas Palace, T 23453, 0900-1700, Rs 5.

Tours

To Orchha and Shivpuri Rs 850 (car for 5), same day return. Local sightseeing, Rs 300. Airport transfer Rs 80.

Local information

● Accommodation

B Welcomgroup *Usha Kiran Palace*, Jayendraganj, Lashkar T 323993. 27 rm, some a/c and very large. Maharaja's former guesthouse. Attractive location, excellent restaurant (buffet lunch, good value), beautiful secluded gardens, tennis. Pleasant but over-priced.

C *Gwalior Regency*, New Bus Stand Rd, nr Rly Station, T 29516. 34 rm, some a/c. Restaurant, pool, airport/rly transfer. Not rec.

D MP Tourism *Tansen*, 6A Gandhi Rd, T 21568. 36 rm, some comfortable a/c, with TV. Good restaurant, bar, garden, car hire, airport transfer, Tourist Information. Clean, quiet but slow service. Otherwise rec. **Camping** in garden. **D** *President*, Station Rd, T 24673. **D** *Metro*, Ganesh Bazar, nr Gandhi Market, T 25530. 30 air-cooled or a/c rm with bath. Central. Indian cuisine.

● Budget Hotels

E *Galav Guest House*, nr Roop Singh Stadium, T 27531. 5 rm with bath. Restaurant. **E** *Vivek Continental*, Topi Bazar, T 22938. 30 rm, some a/c with bath (check for cleanliness). Restaurant, convenient for bank, PO and Bazars. On Station Rd: **E** *Safari*, T 21323. **E** *Park-View*, T 21323. 12 rm, some a/c. **E** *Meghdoot*, T 27374. Some a/c rm. Nr Rly Station: **E** *India*, T 24638. On MLB Rd: **E** *Regal*, T 22592. Some rm with bath. Roof-terrace restaurant. **E** *Midway*, T 20316, 11 rm, some a/c. **E** *Fort View*, T 23409. 15 rm, some a/c. Rm service, convenient for town and fort, good views. **E** *Gujri Mahal*, High Court Rd, T 23492. **E** *Bhagirathi*, Falkar Bazar, is rec.

● Places to eat

Usha Kiran Palace, *Motel Tansen*, *India* (Indian Coffee House) are open to non-residents. *Kwality*, and *Wengers*, MLB Rd.

● Entertainment

Son et Lumière, Man Mandir Palace, Gwalior Fort. Ask MP Tourism. A 45 min show, in Hindi first followed by an English version.

● Post & Telegraph

GPO, Jayaji Chowk, T 22642. Birla Nagar, Morar and Residency.

● Shopping

Kothari, Sarafa Bazar. Brocade, *chanderi* (light and flimsy cotton and silk material), silk saris. *MP Emporium* and *MP Khadi Sangh*, Sarafa Bazar. Handlooms. *MD Fine Arts*, Subhash Market. Paintings and objets d'art. *Ganpatlal Krishna Lal* Jewellery and antiques, Sarafa Bazar. These close on Tu. **Photography**: *Akar Studio*, Morar; *Goyal Studio*, Daulat Ganj.

● Tour companies & travel agents

Tourist Taxis/Private Cars available from MP Tourism (see below). *SS Travels*, Usha Kiran Palace, T 26636. *Gooch Travels*, Shivaji Marg, T 24564. *Ambika Travels*, nr Ramakrishna Ashram.

● Tourist offices

MP Tourism, *Motel Tansen*, 6A Gandhi Marg, T 21568.

● Transport

On the NH3, Gwalior is 114 km from Shivpuri and 119 km from Agra.

Local Taxis, Tempos, Auto-rickshaws and Tongas: are available. Fares negotiable.

Air Indian Airlines flights to Delhi and Bombay via Bhopal and Indore, twice a week.

Train Gwalior is on the Central Railways main Delhi-Bombay and Madras-Delhi lines. **New Delhi**: *Shatabdi Exp* 2001, daily 1900, 3¼ hr; *Punjab Mail* 1037, daily, 1415, 6 hr; *Amritsar Exp* 1057, daily, 2325, 7¾ hr; *Jhelum Exp* 4677, daily, 1537, 7½ hr; *Karnataka Exp* 2628, daily, 2320, 4 hr. **Bombay (VT)**: *Punjab Mail*

1038, daily, 1255 (23½ hr). **Bhopal**: *Shatabdi Exp* 2002, daily, 0933, 4½ hr; *Jhelum Exp* 4678, daily, 1548, 6¾ hr; *Punjab Mail* 1038, daily, 1255, 7¾ hr; *Karnataka Exp* 2628, daily, 0336, 5¼ hr. **Jhansi**: *Shatabdi Exp* 2002, daily, 0933, 1 hr; *Punjab Mail* 1038, daily, 1250, 23½ hr; *Karnataka Exp* 2628, daily, 0336, 1¼ hr; *Jhelum Exp* 4678, daily, 1543, 7 hr. **Agra** *Shatabdi Exp* 2001, daily 1900, 1¼ hr; *Punjab Mail* 1037, daily, 1415, 2 hr; *Amritsar Exp* 1057, daily, 2325, 1¾ hr; *Malwa Exp* 4067, daily, 0347, 2 hr. Rly station: Enquiries T 22544, Reservations T 25306.

Road Bus: regular services connect Gwalior with Agra via Morena and Dholpur, **Delhi** (321 km via Agra), **Jaipur** (338 km via Agra and Bharatpur), **Khajuraho** (278 km via Jhansi and Chhatarpur, 9 hr), **Shivpuri** (114 km, 3 hr), Lucknow and other towns in UP, Rajasthan and MP: Rewa, Jabalpur, Panna, Indore and Ujjain.

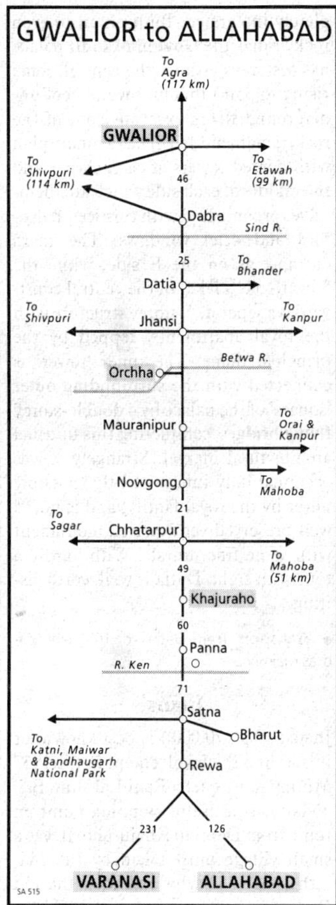

GWALIOR TO ALLAHABAD

The route rises gently onto the plateau from the plains, passing through Jhansi, the fortified palace at Orchha, and Khajuraho, whose temples contain some of the best sculpture in the whole of India.

Gwalior to Jhansi

The route from Gwalior to Khajuraho and Allahabad runs along the northern edge of the Peninsula. Much is now open farmland with occasional scrub or forest, with outcropping rocks and hills. Before Independence it was a land of small Rajput and Muslim states, struggling to maintain and expand their power against the usually greater forces from the plains to the N.

Datia

The first town of significance on the road to Jhansi, 120 km S of Gwalior, is Datia. The Bundela chief Bir Singh Deo built the fortress palace. He supported Salim (later Jahangir) against his father Akbar, and may have been responsible for Abu Fazl's death in 1602. When returning from a Deccan campaign with a camel train of treasure he was ambushed and killed. Bir Singh is believed to have financed much of his building with his ill-gotten gain. His successors, however, were loyal to the Mughals.

The **Palace** (c1620) blends Mughal and Rajput styles beautifully. It was one of the few Indian buildings admired by Sir Edwin Lutyens, architect of much of British New Delhi. Unlike most Moghul palaces, it was conceived as a single unit. Its form and decoration are thus completely integrated. Built on an uneven rocky ridge, the **Govind Mandir** palace has 5 storeys visible (the central dome rising to 35m) though several cool underground floors excavated out of the rock, remain hidden. It has a square plan with domed towers at each corner and the middle of each side which are themselves ornamented with cornices, balconies and oriel windows. The main entrance is on the E side, while the S overlooks a lake. In the central courtyard is a separate 5-storey structure with the royal apartments, topped by the principal dome. The inner 'tower' is connected with the surrounding outer 'square' of the palace by 4 double-storey flying bridges, completing this unusual architectural marvel. Strangely it was occupied only intermittently (possibly never by the royal family) and is now a well preserved yet deserted monument with some fine murals. With hardly a tourist in sight, Datia is well worth visiting.

• **Transport Train** Datia is on the Delhi-Madras main line.

Jhansi

Jhansi (*Pop* 370,000) is best known for its fort and the involvement in the 1857 Mutiny of its queen **Rani Lakshmi Bai**. Today it is a useful stopping point en route from Delhi to Khajuraho. It was a small village until taken by the Marathas in 1742 who extended the old Fort.

History

In 1853 it 'lapsed' (see page 262) to the British (who had gained some control 50 years earlier), when the Raja died without leaving a male heir. The civil station dates from this time. The fort was seized in 1857 by mutineers and most of the occupants slaughtered. The young Rani, who had been denied rule, joined the rebels but had to retire to Gwalior but continued her attempts to return after the British regained control of Jhansi. She was killed in action, on 18th June 1858 at Kotah-ki-Sarai "dressed like a man ... holding her sword 2-handed and the reins of her horse in her teeth ... and fighting with 2 female companions" (Hibbert). See page 343. The British ceded the fort to the Maharaja of Scindia and exchanged it for Gwalior in 1866.

Places of interest

The nucleus of the **Fort** was built by Bir Singh Deo in 1613, with concentric walls, 5.5-9m high, with 10 gates. The breach made by the British in 1858, is between the Sainyar and **Jhirna** gates. **Rani Mahal** once Lakshmi Bai's home is a **museum** with a good sculpture collection (9th-12th century). A road encircles the fort and there are good views from the walls. NE of the railway station is Retribution Hill, which marks the last stand of the Mutineers in 1858.

Local information

● Accommodation

Jhansi lacks top-grade hotels. Best is **D** *Sheesh Mahal* at Orchha, ½ hr taxi or ¾ hr tempo ride away – see Orchha below. **D** *Jhansi*, Shastri Marg, 3 km rly, T 1360. 28 rm, some a/c. Restaurant (expensive), bar, exchange. Good, though faded colonial feel (old oil paintings, Raj silver). **D** *Prakash*, down lane opp Rly station. Decent rm, some a/c. **D** UP Tourism *Viranqana* nr Circuit House, Numaish Maidan, T 2402, 25 rm.Good restaurant.

E *Raj*. Simple, clean rm with bath, some a/c. Rec. **E** *Kannika* has 8 rm. **F** *Central* and **F** *Shipra* are ½ km to left, from station. **F** *Ashok* nr Natraj Cinema. 30 rm. Restaurant, bar. 2 a/c. **F** *Likhdhari Guest House*, T 443167. **F** *Railway Retiring Room* and 6-bed dorm. Small restaurant. Not rec.

● Places to eat

Holiday in the Sadar Bazar serves simple Indian food, clean, inexpensive. Indian sweet shop next door.

● Tourist Office

Railway station has a good MP Tourism counter. UP Tourism often closed.

● Transport

Air The new airport will allow flights from major Indian cities.

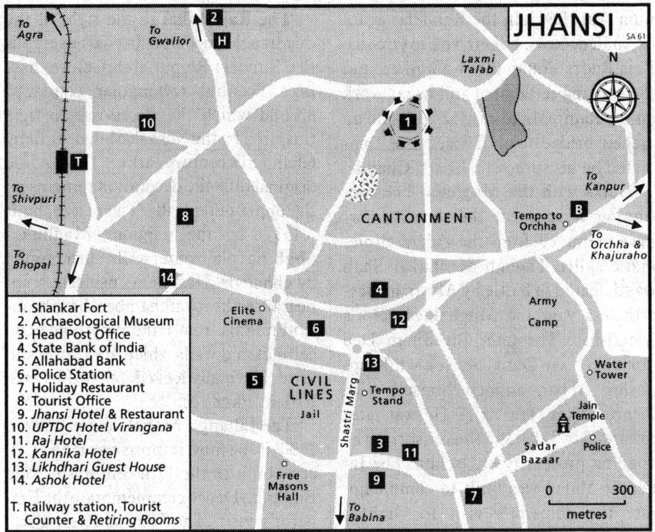

Train New Delhi: *Karnataka Exp* 2627, daily, 0500, 7¼ hr; *Malwa Exp* 4067, daily, 0205, 8 hr; *Amritsar Exp* 1057, daily, 2130, 7½ hr; *Jhelum Exp* 4677, daily, 1410, 7½ hr; *Shatabdi Exp* 2002, daily, 1758, 4 hr; **Bombay (VT)**: *Punjab Mail* 1038, daily, 1500, 21½ hr. **Jabalpur (for Kanha)**: *Mathakosal Exp* 1450, daily, 2235, 10¼ hr. **Lucknow**: *Kushi Nagar Exp* 1015, daily, 0900, 6½ hr; *Gwalior-Chhapra Mail* 1143, daily, 1315, 7 hr; *Pushpak Exp* 2133, daily, 0335, 6½ hr. **Agra**: *Shatabdi Exp* 2002, daily 1758, 2¼ hr; *Punjab Mail* 1037, daily, 1240, 3½ hr; *Amritsar Exp* 1057, daily, 2130, 3½ hr; **Varanasi**: *Bundelkhand Exp* 1107, daily, 1700, 17¼ hr; **Bhopal**: *Shatabdi Exp* 2002, daily, 1047, 3¼ hr.

Road Bus: for Orchha and long distance buses to major N Indian cities from bus stand 3 km E of rly station. Daily Khajuraho UP and MP Roadways a/c coach which connects with the Shatabdi Express from Delhi, leave early from rly station (5 hr). Buy tickets at station tourist office counter. **Orchha**: Tempo from bus stand (suggest you pay for 2 seats to allow for luggage). ¾ hr, Rs 10-15.

ROUTES From Jhansi it is 4 hr by bus to Khajuraho. The road runs along the edge of the hill region of Bundelkhand. Most is through agricultural land but the forested slopes of the hills are quite evident as you cross a number of rivers coming off the plateau, eg the Betwa and Dhasan. Half of the journey is in UP, half MP, but you keep alternating between the 2. It is a very attractive route, through gentle parkland scenery with very little traffic. From Jhansi the road goes E towards Barwar Sagar, Mau Ranipur and Chhatarpur. After 9 km there is a right turn to Orchha (10 km).

Orchha

History

The Bundela chief Raja Rudra Pratap (1501-31) chose an easily defended and beautiful site for his capital. Set on an island on a bend in the Betwa river, it is elevated above the surrounding wooded countryside. Once capital of its own state, Orchha contains 3 palaces, each built by succeeding Maharajas in a similar style and combining to form a complex as imposing as that at Udaipur.

The origins of the dynasty Garhkurar, once capital of the Bundela Rajas, fell to the Tughluqs just as that dynasty was weakening. Into the vacuum that they left, the Bundelas again expanded, moving their base to Orchha. Raja Rudra Pratap threw a wall around the existing settlement and began work on the Ramji Mandir (c1525-32) and an arched bridge to it. These were completed by his successor, Bharti Chand.

Links with the Mughals The continuing fortunes of the dynasty may have stemmed from the rulers' diplomatic skills. Though Madhukar Shah was defeated in battle by Akbar, he nevertheless won the Mughal emperor's friendship. The later Bir Singh Deo (1605-26 – see Datia, above), while opposing Akbar, aligned himself with Prince Salim (Jahangir). He was later rewarded by Jahangir, thus ensuring the ongoing prosperity of Orchha. The Jahangir Mahal was built to commemorate the emperor's visit to Orchha. However, Bir Singh's first son, Jhujan, ran foul of Shah Jahan and, ignoring orders, treacherously killed the neighbouring chief of Chauragarh. The imperial army routed Jhujan and Orchha was pillaged. In 1783 the Bundela capital was moved to Tikamgarh, leaving Orchha to the *dhak* forests, the Betwa river and its guardian eagles. Picturesque Orchha, in the middle of nowhere, abandoned and now somewhat neglected, pays rich rewards to the visitor and is the ideal overnight stop between Gwalior and Khajuraho.

Places of interest

Palace/Fort On a warm moonlit night, the view across the palaces with their chhattris and ornamented battlements is enchanting. Unfortunately, many walls have been desecrated by graffiti. All around, the forest is gradually encroaching on the numerous tombs and monuments. You cross the river by the remarkable granite bridge built by Bir Singh Deo (early 17th century). Audio-cassette from Sheesh Mahal (see Hotel below).

The Raj Mahal to the right of the quadrangle (open 1000-1700) exemplifies Bundela Rajput architecture, having a central rectangular courtyard around which the floors rise in tiers (inspired by the Koshak Mahal, built by Chanderi a century earlier). Some of the original blue tile decoration remains on the upper outer walls. The palace, built (c1537) by the religious **Madhukar Shah**, has plain outer walls, surmounted by chhattris. Despite its neglected appearance, the royal chambers have beautiful murals from Hindu mythology on ceilings and walls which are strong and vivid. Normally locked, opened by custodian. Torch rec.

The **Jahangir Mahal**, (open 1000 to 1700) is the most impressive of the 3 palaces, built in the 17th century by Raja Bir Singh Deo to commemorate the Emperor's visit. The 70m square palace, entered from the S, has a large square interior courtyard around which are the apartments in 3 storeys. Each corner bastion and the projection in the middle of each side, is topped by a dome. These contain apartments with intervening terraces. Hanging balconies with balustrades and wide eaves create strong lines set off by attractive arches and brackets, chhattris and jali screens giving this huge palace a delicate and airy feel. Built at the height of Bundela power it is an excellent example of a medieval fort palace. Within the turreted walls are gardens, gateways and pavilions as well as numerous temples, many near the confluence of the Betwa and Jamni river.

The **Rai Praveen Mahal,** was built by Raja Indramani (r1672-76) for the musician-courtesan who had even enchanted Akbar. The 2-storeyed brick palace with beautifully carved stone niches is built to scale with surrounding trees and the Anand Mandal gardens. The octagonal flowerbeds are watered by 2 wells.

The **Ram Raja Temple** in the village. Following the appearance of Rama in a

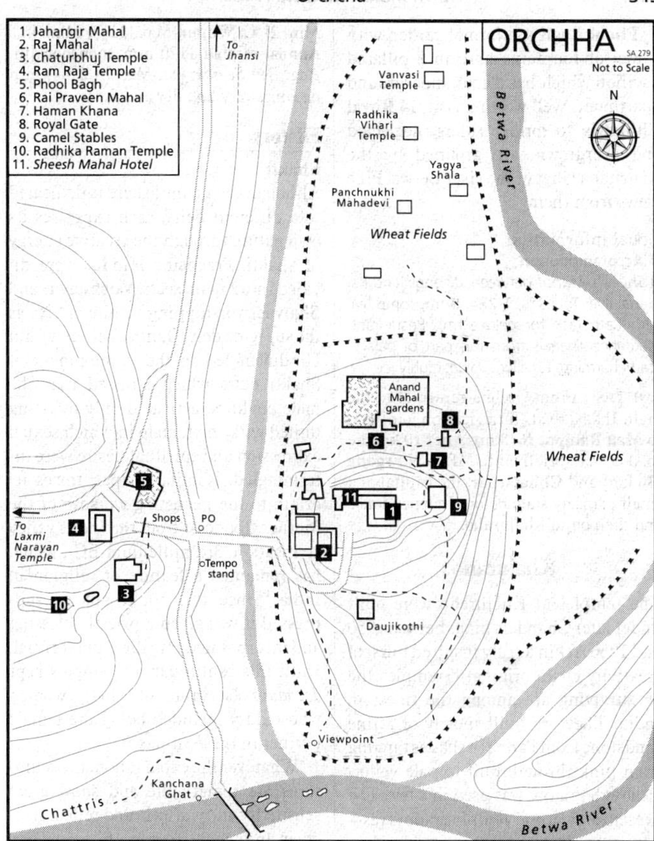

dream, the pious Madhukar Shah brought an image of the god from Ayodhya and placed it in a palace prior to its installation in a temple. However, when the temple was ready it proved impossible to shift the image and the king remembered, only too late, the divine instruction that the deity must remain in the place where it was first installed. It is the only palace-turned-temple in the country where Rama is worshipped as king. Up steep steps, the **Chaturbhuj Temple** which was built for the Rama image stands on a large stone slab.

A stone path through the village links the Ram Raja with the 17th century **Lakshminarayan Temple**, which incorporates elements of fort architecture. The excellent murals (religious and secular) on the walls and ceilings of 3 halls here, are well preserved examples of the Bundela school. If locked, ask at Sheesh Mahal (see Hotels). There is a fine view looking back across the plain to the Chhattris and palace. **Shahid Smarak** in honour of the freedom fighter **Chandrasekhar Azad** houses a museum and library.

Phool Bagh is a formal garden with a row of fountains and an 8-pillared pavilion which has a cool underground apartment. Well worth a visit. 14 **Royal Chhattris** to former rulers, neglected and overgrown, are grouped by the Kanchana Ghat of the river Betwa. Fine views from them.

Local information

● Accommodation

D *Sheesh Mahal* between Jahangir and Raj Mahal (MP Tourism), T 224. 8 rm, some a/c with bath (ask for deluxe rm). Restaurant. Magnificent views from this part of palace. Staff charming. Excellent value, highly rec.

ROUTES From Orchha return N to the main Jhansi road. Turn right on joining it to **Mau Ranipur** (64 km). After 10 km the road crosses briefly into MP to **Nowgong** (30 km) and **Chhatarpur**, the capital of a small princely state before Independence and then on to Khajuraho.

Khajuraho

The temples at Khajuraho were built under later Chandela kings between 950 and 1050 AD in a truly inspired burst of creativity. Of the original 85 temples, the 25 surviving are among the finest in India. They are built mostly of a fine sandstone from Panna in shades ranging from pink through buff to pale yellow although granite was used in a few. The presence of erotic temple sculptures – even though they account for less than 10% of the total carvings – have sometimes been viewed as the work of a degenerate society obsessed with sex. Some believe they illustrate the Kama Sutra, the sensuality outside the temple contrasting with the serenity within. Yet others argue that they illustrate ritual symbolism of sexual intercourse in Tantric belief, see page 78. The Chandelas were followers of the Tantric cult which believes that gratification of earthly desires is a step towards attaining the ultimate liberation or *moksha*.

BASICS *Population:* 6500. *Altitude:* 257m. *Climate*: Temp. Summer, Max. 47°C, Min. 21°C, Winter, Max. 32°C, Min. 4°C. Annual rainfall 1120 mm; monsoon Jul-Aug. *Best Season*: Oct-Mar. In Apr-Jun it becomes very hot, dry and dusty.

History

Shakti

Although each temple here is dedicated to a different deity, each expresses its own nature through the creative energy of Shakti. Practising Hindus were divided into 2 main sects, **Vaishnavas** and **Shaivas**, worshipping Vishnu or Siva as the supreme deity. Tantric beliefs within Hinduism led to the development of Shakti cults which stressed that the male could be activated only by being united with the female in which sexual expression and spiritual desire were intermingled. Romila Thapar, traces its origin to the persisting worship of the Mother Goddess (from the Indus valley civilisation, 3rd millenium BC), which has remained a feature of religion in India. Since this could not be suppressed it was given a priestly blessing and incorporated into the regular ritual. Until this century, many temples kept *devadasis* (servants of God), women whose duty included being the female partner in these rituals.

Whatever the explanation, the sculptures are remarkable and show great sensitivity and warmth, and reflect society in an age free from inhibitions. They express the celebration of all human activity, displaying one aspect of the nature of Hinduism itself, a genuine love of life.

The craftsmen

A.L. Basham suggested that India's art came from secular craftsmen who, although they worked to instructions, loved the world they knew, their inspiration not so much a ceaseless quest for the absolute as a delight in the world as they saw it.

The Gods and demi-gods in temples all over India are young and handsome, their bodies rounded, often richly jewelled. They are often smiling and sorrow is rarely portrayed. Temple sculpture makes full use of the female form as a decorative motif. Goddesses and female attendants are often shown naked from the waist up, with tiny waists and large, rounded breasts, posing languidly, a picture of well-being and relaxation.

The site

These remarkable temples lie in a rich, well watered plain, miles from the nearest large town, with the rocky and forested crags of the Vindhya hills as a backdrop. Mentioned by Ibn Battuta, Khajuraho was formerly the capital of the old kingdom of Jajhauti, the region now known as **Bundelkhand**.

The Chandela Rajputs

The Chandela Rajputs claimed descent from the moon. Hemwati, the lovely young daughter of a Brahmin priest, was seduced by the moon while bathing in a forest pool. The child born of this union was Chandravarman, the founder of the dynasty. Brought up in the forests by his mother who sought refuge from a censorious society, Chandravarman, when established as ruler of the local area, had a dream visitation from his mother. She implored him to build temples that would reveal human passions and in doing so bring about a realisation of the emptiness of desire.

The Chandelas developed into a strong regional power in the early 10th century. Under their patronage Jajhauti became prosperous, and the rulers decorated their kingdom with tanks, forts, palaces and temples, mainly concentrated in their strongholds of Mahoba, Kalinjar, Ajaigarh and also Dudhai, Chandpur, Madanpur and Deogarh (in Jhansi district). They were great patrons of the arts and equally great builders.

With the fading of Chandela fortunes, the importance of Khajuraho waned. For strategic reasons the later kings concentrated their energies on the hill forts of Mahoba, Kalinjar and Ajaigarh. Temple construction continued until the 12th century but at a much reduced pace. Khajuraho can be regarded as the Chandelas' spiritual homeland and, perhaps explains why they chose to build the temples here. Far removed from the political centres of the kingdom, its location minimised the danger of external attack and symbolised its role as a celestial refuge.

Local Festivals

Dance Festival. The publicity rhetoric is sometimes pretentious, but many of the country's most accomplished dancers do perform in the spectacular setting of the Western Group of Temples. Tickets are inexpensive. Buy in advance from Tourist Office. 1995: 3-10 March; 1996: 11-17 March; 1997: 10-17 March.

Places of interest

The temples can be conveniently divided into 3 groups: the western, eastern and southern. Spread over 8 sq km. Allow a day (min 5 hr); entry road-toll Re 1. Of these the western group are the most impressive and the gardens the best kept. If you feel that temple fatigue is likely to set in quickly, then these are the ones to see, especially the **Lakshmana Temple**. Good Archaeological Survey of India booklet by Krishna Deva, available for Rs 5.00. (Detailed book with colour plates, Rs 400). An original interpretation in S Punja (1992) A *Divine Ecstasy*, Viking (Penguin, India).

Temple design

The temples here are compact and tall, raised on a high platform with an ambulatory path around, but with no enclosure wall. Each follows an E-W axis and has the essential sanctum (*garbhagriha*) containing the chief image, joined to the hall for worshippers (*mandapa*) by a vestibule (*antarala*). The hall is approached through a porch (*ardha mandapa*); both have pyramidal towers. Larger temples have lateral transepts and balconied windows, an internal ambulatory and subsidiary shrines. The sanctury is surmounted by a tall *sikhara* (tower), while smaller towers rise from other parts of the temple, imitating mountain peaks culminating in the highest. The sanctum is usually *saptaratha* (7 projections in plan and elevation) while the cubical section below the *sikhara* repeats the number, having 7 bands, *sapta-bada*. The whole, studded with sculptured statues with clear lines of projections and recesses makes most effective use of light and shade. The sculptures themselves are in the round or in high or medium relief depicting cult images, deities, celestial nymphs (*sura-sundaris* and *apsaras*), secular figures and animals or mythical beasts.

In India's medieval period of temple building, stonework techniques replaced previous wooden and brick work. Strict rules on design were laid down in textbooks (*Silpasastra*). The techniques used, though, were comparatively simple. Arches were constructed through corbelling and mortar was rarely used. The holes in places show where iron rods were placed, thus holding together the stones and allowing carved blocks to be attached. Temples were heavily and ornately decorated, but despite this, the impression is one of great mass. Heavy cornices, strong, broad pillars and the wide base of the tower (*sikhara*) give them the feeling of strength and solidity,

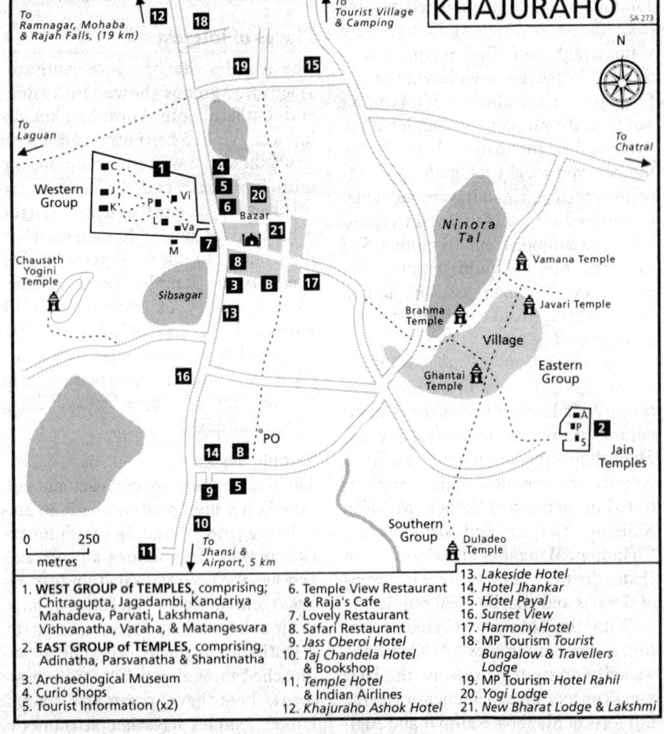

only partly counteracted by the ornate friezes. Records indicate that the area covered by the western group was originally a sacred lake – perhaps a reason for the high plinths.

The Western Group

The temples are in a peaceful setting of a beautiful park. Daily, sunrise to sunset. Free guided tours, 0900. 1430 except Fri and holidays. Guides also from Tourist Office. Entrance is opposite car park, flanked by curio shops and restaurants. Ticket office is to the left; 50p, Fri free. Toilets for emergencies only.

Varaha Temple (early 10th century) a shrine, dedicated to Vishnu in his 3rd incarnation as Varaha, the boar (Vishnu, The Preserver, is usually depicted resting on a bed of serpents, until summoned to save the world from disaster). The rat-demon Hiranyaksha stole the earth and dragged it down to his underwater home. The Gods begged for Vishnu's help. The demon created 1000 replicas of himself to confuse any pursuer, but Vishnu incarnated himself as a boar and was able to dig deep and winkle out the real demon. Thus, Hiranyaksha was destroyed and the world saved.

The huge Varaha is of highly polished sandstone covered with hundreds of deities. He is the Lord of the 3 Worlds – water, earth and heaven and under him is the serpent *Sesha* and the feet of the broken figure of *Prithvi*, the earth goddess. The lotus ceiling shows superb relief carving.

Lakshmana Temple (c950 AD) the earliest, is opposite and best preserves the architectural features that typify the larger temples here. The exterior is richly carved. The platform has friezes of hunting and battle scenes with soldiers, elephants, horses as well as scenes from daily life including the erotic. The basement again has bands of carvings – processional friezes showing animals, soldiers, acrobats, musicians, dancers, domestic scenes, festivities, ceremonies, loving couples and deities. Note the beautifully carved elephants at shoulder height, each one different.

On the walls are the major sculptures of gods and goddesses in 2 rows, with *sura-sundaris* or *apsaras* in attendance on the raised sections and loving couples in the recesses. All the figures are relaxed, resting their weight on one leg, thus accentuating their curves. The bands are broken by ornate balconied windows with carved pillars and overhanging eaves. The nymphs shown attending to their toilet, bearing offerings, dancing, playing musical instruments or as sensual lovers, are executed with great skill and in some ways idealise womanhood. They are graceful and fluid in movement (note the taut muscle or creased skin) with expressive faces and gestures (contentment, serenity, concentration, embarrassment and pleasure). The best examples are seen in the recesses below the main tower.

Some to note among a myriad of fine sculptures, are: On the S façade are a couple of minstrels, their faces express devotional ecstacy, a dancing Ganesh, ladies attending to their toilet, and groups of lovers. Moving to the SW, a *sura-sundari* applies vermillion while another plays with a ball. In the NW corner is a nymph after her bath (note her wet clothes). The S face of the NW shrine has a fine Ganesh panel. On the N face, returning towards the porch, there is a group of *apsaras* accomplished in art and music (one plays the flute, another paints, yet another writes a letter). The E face of the subsidiary shrine in the SE corner has a master architect with his apprentices.

The interior Leave shoes at the entrance and enter through a simple *makara-torana* flanked by gladiators. The circular ceiling of the porch (*ardha mandapa*) is a superbly carved open lotus blossom in 4 concentric circles. In the hall (*mandapa*) is a raised platform possibly used for dancing and tantric rituals. At each corner of the platform are pillars with carved brackets with *apsaras* which are among the finest sculptures at Khajuraho. There are 8 figures on each column, representing the 8 sects of Tantra. The sanctum (*garba-griha*) doorway has a panel showing incarnations of Vishnu while the lintel has Lakshmi with Brahma and Siva on either side. A frieze above depicts the 9 planets with *Rahu*, while Krishna legends, among innumerable carvings of animals, birds and humans, appear on the wall. The *pancha-ratha* sanctum has a 3-headed and 4-armed Vishnu as Vaikuntha and around it are 10 incarnations and 14 forms of Vishnu.

Leaving the temple walk to the rear of the delightful gardens to the 2 temples. The **Kandariya Mahadeva Temple** (c1025-50) is the most developed, the largest and tallest of the Khajuraho temples. Dedicated to Siva, the elaborately carved doorway leads to a dark inner sanctum with a marble linga. The temple roof rises in a series of 7 bands of peaks to the summit of the central 31m high *sikhara*. The 84 smaller, subsidiary towers are replicas of the main *sikhara*. The whole is complex but coherent.

The architectural and sculptural genius of Khajuraho reaches its peak in this temple where every element is richly endowed. The platform is unique in the way it projects to the sides and rear, reflecting the plan of the transepts. It also has the highest and most ornamental basement with intricately carved processional friezes. There are over 800 statues of gods, goddesses, musicians and erotic groupings, carved into its internal and exterior surfaces. The *apsaras* are particulary notable for their slender, sensual form.

Along the same platform, to Kandariya's N is the **Jagadambi Temple** (early 11th century) which is similar in layout and predates the next temple, the Chitragupta. It has a standing Parvati image in the sanctum but was originally dedicated to Vishnu. The outer walls have no projecting balconies but the lavish decorations include some of the best carvings of deities – several of Vishnu, a particularly fine *Yama*, numerous nymphs and amorous couples. In between is the ruined **Mahadeva shrine** (11th century). Little remains except a porch, under which *Sardula* attends a lion-like beast.

The **Chitragupta temple** (early 11th century) 70m N, is the only one here dedicated to Surya, the Sun God. (see page 744) Longer and lower than its companions, it has been much restored (platform, steps, entrance porch, NE façade), occasionally not too sympathetically. Unlike the simple basement mouldings of the Jagadambi, here there are processional friezes; the *maha-mandapa* ceiling too has progressed from the simple square in the former to an ornate octagonal ceiling. The niches outside have numerous deities, *Dikpalas* (directional guardians) and divine couples. The *garbha griha* has Surya driving his chariot of 7 horses, while on the S façade is a statue of Vishnu with 11 heads signifying his 10 incarnations, see page 73.

In the NE corner of the group, is the **Vishvanatha Temple** (1002), dedicated to Siva, and according to the longer inscription on the wall, originally had an emerald linga, in addition to the stone one present today. It was built before the Kandariya Mahadeva and anticipates it – they are similar in design and plan with rising *sikharas* and 3 bands of sculpture on the wall. The high, moulded basement has fine scrollwork and carvings of processions of men and animals as well as loving couples, some of which are again seen in the Kandariya. On the 9 principal basement niches of both are the *Sapta-matrikas* (7 Mothers) with *Ganesha* and *Virabhadra*. The excellent carvings include a fine musician with a flute and amorous couples inside the temple, and divinities attended by enchanting nymphs innumerable poses, (one removing a thorn from her foot) on the S façade.

Only 2 subsidiary shrines of the original 4 remain. Sharing the same raised platform and facing the temple, is the **Nandi Pavilion** with a fine elephant frieze on the basement. It houses a 2.2m polished sandstone Nandi bull (Siva's vehicle). Note the sleeping *mahout* on an elephant by the steps to the S!

Outside this garden complex of temples and next to the Lakshmana temple is the **Matangesvara Temple** (900-925 AD), simpler in form and decoration than its neighbour and unlike all the others, still in everyday use. It has an interesting circular interior which contains a large Siva Linga.

The **Chausath Yogini** (late 9th century) is a ruined Jain temple in coarse granite on a platform. It stands apart from the rest of the W Group beyond the tank. Only 35 of the original *chausath* (64) shrines to the *yoginis* (attendants of Kali), of the 'open-air' temple, remain. The temples in the other 2 Groups are remarkable and pleasing in their own right but not a match for the Western Group.

Eastern Group

S of the village is the ruined **'Ghantai' Temple** (late 10th century). The fine carvings of chains-and-bells (*ghanta*) on the pillars, the richly ornamented doorway and ceiling of the entrance porch are worth seeing. Walk through Khajuraho village to the small **Javari Temple** (late 11th century) with its tall, slender *sikhara*. It has a highly decorative doorway and fine sculptured figures on the walls. About 200m N is the **Vamana Temple** (late 11th century) with a 4-armed Vamana (Dwarf) incarnation of Vishnu in the sanctum. This is in the fully developed Chandela style and has a single tower and no ambulatory. The walls are adorned with sensuous *sura-sundaris* but erotic sculptures are not prominent. Returning to the modern part of Khajuraho, you pass the **Brahma Temple** (early 10th century) on the bank of Ninora-tal, which is one of the earliest. A Vishnu temple, wrongly attributed to Brahma, it has a sandstone *sikhara* on a granite structure.

Three **Jain temples** stand within an enclosure wall (which incorporates some ancient Jain sculptures) about ½ km SE of the Ghantai Temple; others are scattered around the village. The **Parsvanatha Temple** (mid 10th century), is the largest and one of its finest. The curvilinear tower dominates the structure and is beautifully carved. There are no balconies but light enters through fretted windows. Although a Jain temple, there are numerous Vaishnav deities, many of them excellently carved on the 3 wall panels. Some of the best known non-erotic sculptures too are found here, particularly the graceful *sura-sundaris* (one applying kohl on the S façade; another tying ankle-bells on the N façade). The interior is richly carved with elephants, lions, sea goddesses and Jain figures. The temple was originally dedicated to Adinatha, but the modern black marble image of Parsvanatha was placed in the sanctum in 1860.

Next, to the N, is the smaller and simpler **Adinatha Temple** (late 11th century), where only the sanctum (containing a modern image) and vestibule have survived – the porch is modern. The sculptures on 3 bands again depict attractive *sura-sundaris,* the niches have *yakshis,* the corners, *Dikpalas.* The **Santinatha Temple** with its 4.5m statue of Adinatha is the main place of Jain worship. An inscription dating it at 1027-8 is covered with plaster – the thoroughly renovated temple retains its ancient heart and medieval sculptures. There is also a small **Jain museum** here.

Southern Group

The 2 temples stand on open land. The setting, attractive at sunset, lacks the overall ambience of the Western Group but the backdrop of the Vindhyas is impressive. The **Duladeo Temple** (early 12th century), 800m SW of the Jain Temples, is the last the Chandelas built here, when temple building was already in decline. The figures are often repetitive and appear to lack the quality of carving found in earlier temples. The **Chaturbhuja Temple** (c1100) 3 km S of the village, anticipates the Duladeo but lacks erotic sculptures. The sanctum contains an exceptional 2.7m 4-armed *Dakshina-murti* Siva image.

Excursions

At **Rajnagar**, 5 km N, is the imposing ruined 19th century hilltop fort-palace of the Maharaja. Particularly interesting when villagers congregate for the Tuesday market. Possible by auto-rickshaw or car.

Museums

Archaeological Museum, T 2028, nr entrance to W Group Archaeological Park. Ticket to temples allows entry. Mostly sculptures from local Hindu and Jain temple sites; also some Buddhist. 1000-1700, closed Fri. Allow 20 min.

Local information

● Accommodation

Subject to frequent power cuts, especially at harvest time. Big hotels have their own generators. **A** *Taj Chandela*, Chhatrapur, T 2054. 102 rm. Expensive restaurants, best bookshop in town (though pricey), shopping arcades, health club. Attractive, popular with tour groups. Small temple in pleasant garden; camel and elephant rides. **A** *Jass Oberoi*, Bypass Rd, T 2086. 54 rm, quieter away from Reception. Pleasant atmosphere and equally attractive. Good food, pool and gardens, good cultural programmes. Friendly welcome, excellent service though expensive.

2 new Clarks hotels **B** *Clarks Khajuraho* and **B** *Temple* are scheduled to open in 1994; enquiries Delhi, T 3312515, F 3312990. **B** ITDC *Khajuraho Ashok*, T 24. 40 rm, some with temple views. Mediocre restaurant, expensive bar (water Rs 40), small arcade (expensive, though postcards cheap), small bookshop, attractive pool (non-residents pay). Pleasant cool interior; very friendly, ambitious management.

The following MP Tourism hotels are good value: **D** *Payal*, T 2076. 25 decent rm with bath (suspect plumbing), some a/c. Restaurant (good breakfast and tea), bar. Rec. **D** *Jhankar*, T 2063, 19 rm, 5 a/c. Restaurant, bar. **D** *Lakeside*, by Sib Sagar Lake, T 2120. 18 rm and dorm, clean, functional. Beautiful evening views.

● Budget hotels

Many new hotels are being built nr the W Group of temples. **E** *Rahil*, T 2062. 12 rm and dorm. Restaurant, large gardens. **E** *Tourist Bungalow*, N of village, T 2064. 6 rm. Good food but lacks ambiance. **E** *Tourist Village*, away from centre, T 2128. 13 well equipped attractive 2-rm 'ethnic' huts, some with bath. Outdoor restaurant. Quiet, good value, bike useful. *Campsite* nearby. **E** *Temple*, T 2049. Rm with Indian style bath. Airlines offices. Extended in 1994. **E** *Harmony* T 2135. Large rm, some a/c. Small garden, good food, very clean. **E** *Sunset View* well located nr Lake, newish, good value. Rec. **F** hotels include, *Yogi Lodge*, nr Bazar, T 2158, with terrace. Very well run, clean, good food. Rec. *New Bharat Lodge*, nr *Payal*, T 2082. 12 refurbished rm, some with small patio and *Lakshmi*, with smaller rm.

● Places to eat

Western food at *Raja Café*, opp W Group. Swiss managed, shady terrace. Bland food, pricey, yet popular. Small shop, tours, guides. Also at **Temple View Café**, next door. *Safari*, 1st Flr, behind Bank in bazar, overlooking Lake has interesting views of life on waterside and road below. Bizarre pink interior, large helpings (Rs 30-40/ dish); good lassi, amazing Indian muesli! Small cafés nr Museum do S Indian meals. *Lovely*, opp Museum does excellent special *thali* (Rs 15), good curd. Cheap and friendly. Beer is expensive everywhere; Rs 100 min in hotels.

● Shopping

Gift shops selling cheap stone and bronze sculptures, handicrafts and gems (**Panna diamond mines**, the largest in the country are nearby). *MP Emporium* for fixed prices. *Karan Jewellers* for diamonds. W Group has a number of stalls in the square nearby. Tue market at Rajnagar (see above). **Photography**: *Dosaj Photo Centre* and *Bajpai Photo Centre*, in market opp the W Group.

● **Tourist office**

Govt of India (0900-1730, 0800-1230 Sat) opp W Group, T 2047 (bus timetables available) 0900-1730, Sat 0800-1230; Counter at bus stand. Guides available, Rs 100 per day. **Regional Tourist Office**, Tourist Bungalow, T 2051.

● **Useful addresses**

Police: T 2032. **Ambulance**: T 41. **Foreigners' Regional Registration Office**, Superintendent of Police, Chhattarpur. **Post and Telegraph Office**: bus stand, T 2022. **State Bank of India**: opp W Group.

● **Transport**

Local Cycle hire: behind Museum; Rs 10/day, rec mode. **Car hire**: from *MP Tourism* or *Khajuraho Tours*. **Cycle-rickshaws**: are expensive (Rs 30 for shortest journey). Negotiate fare. Most places are within walking distance.

Air The airport is 5 km from the village centre. **Transport to town**: by Taxi Rs 60, occasional auto-rickshaw Rs 35 (overpriced rates but difficult to negotiate down). **Indian Airlines**, flies daily *Temple Hotel*, T 2035. Credit cards not accepted. flies daily from Delhi to Khajuraho (1½ hr) via Agra (¾ hr) and on to Varanasi, returning the same route. Dep to Agra and Delhi (1630), US$ 39 and 53 respectively, and to Varanasi 1150 (¾ hr), US$ 39. **East West Airlines**, at *Temple Hotel*, and Airport, T 2036 offers the same destinations.

Train Railheads are **Jhansi** (176 km, for Agra, Delhi, Bhopal), **Satna** (117 km), best for Varanasi, see below; **Mahoba** (51 km, alternative for Varanasi, but few slow trains daily, small quota).

Road Bus: daily MPSRTC services to **Agra** 391 km, 0900 via Jhansi (10/12 hr); **Bhopal** 350 km, 0600, 0730; **Gwalior** 280 km (9 hr); **Indore**, 480 km, 0600; **Jabalpur**, 210 km, 0730 via Satna; **Jhansi** 176 km, 0530, 0900, 1100, 1245, 1530, 1645 (5 hr); Now an a/c bus *Shatabdi Link* connects with the *Shatabdi Express* (4½ hr); taxis take 3¼ hr. **Mahoba** (stops 3 km from rly station) dep 0800, 0930,1030, 1100, 1430, 1630 (3 hr) and **Satna**, 0830, 0930, 1430, 1530 (see below). UP Roadways runs a service to Agra via Gwalior.

Satna

(*Pop* 160,000, 117 km) This is the main junction for rail travel to/from Varanasi for Khajuraho. It is a busy little town which sprawls along the railway line.

● **Accommodation** Most **D** hotels have some a/c rooms with bath, and do meals. The best, is the newish **D** *USA*, on the edge of town, towards Khajuraho. Reasonably clean. **D** *Khajuraho*, nr rly station in unfinished building. Rickshaws insist on this one; probably get commission. **D** *Savera*, Rewa Rd, T 2231. MP Tourism **D** *Barhut*, over Rly Bridge in Civil Lines, T 2041. 8 rm, some a/c. Restaurant. **E** and **F** generally are not very clean. **E** *India*, 300m to right from rly station, above good veg restaurant.

● **Places to eat** *New India Coffee House*, below Hotel India. Excellent food, cheap comprehensive breakfast menu, special section for 'Ladies and Family'. Good service from turbaned waiters. Rec.

● **Transport Train** For **Varanasi** dep 0035, 0150, 0725, 0845, 1540, 2010, fastest 8 hr; *Bombay Mail*, for **Bombay** dep at 1420 and for **Calcutta**, 1640. Also connects with Allahabad (4 hr), Jabalpur, Lucknow, Madras and Patna. The **Tourist Information** counter at the station has erratic opening hours and little information.

Road Bus: **Khajuraho** The very uncomfortable MPSRTC bus dep 0600, 1000, 1430, 1530 and takes 4 hr (Rs 26); you can buy fruit from market towns en route. In Satna it stops at the railway bridge which is a long walk from the station. Rickshaws charge Rs 5. **Bandhavgarh** Daily bus to Tala, 4 hr (Rs 27).

Khajuraho to Allahabad: northern route

ROUTES From Khajuraho you can drive along the N boundary of MP visiting various Chandela forts and finishing this journey at Allahabad. A northerly route goes via **Mahoba** (51 km), **Banda** (50 km), **Chitrakut** (69 km), **Allahabad** (120 km) and is less interesting scenically, the terrain being flat and tedious. The southerly route is more exciting.

Mahoba and **Charkhari** in UP, approx 50 km N of Khajuraho and Chhattarpur.

'Mahoba' may have been derived from a great sacrifice (Mahotsava) performed by its reputed founder, Raja Chandravarman, in 800 AD. Architectural antiquities of the Chandela period abound in the neighbourhood. The Chandela kings, apparently, desired 2 earthly things after winning Bundelkhand: to build temples for their gods and to bring water to the land. They constructed lakes by damming valleys, mainly for defence. The **Ram Kund** lake marks the place where the dynasty's founder died. **Madan** Sagar, dates from the 12th century, **Vijay** Sagar, from the 11th. The others being **Kalyan** and **Kirat** Sagars. The shores of the lakes and the islands are littered with ruined temples and large rock figures – Buddhist and Jain sculptures left abandoned after Muslim invasions; a dancing Ganesh of whitewashed granite in a mustard field, a sun temple dedicated to Surya, a vast rock-cut Siva and a Siva temple on an island in Madan Sagar.

The hill fort at **Charkhari** is surrounded on 3 sides by water. The landward approach is through an imposing gate with a spiked door to deter elephants. The gradual ascent enabled elephants and heavy guns to be taken higher. The Durbar Hall has portraits of the Charkhari Rajas and within the walls are temple gardens and a step-well. Spectacular views from the fort across the lakes.

Parmadidev, the last Chandela king, was defeated by the Chauhan emperor **Prithviraj** in 1182, who made Delhi his base. **Qutb-ud-Din** (see page 176) took the town in 1195. A number of Muslim remains survive: the tomb of Jalhan Khan built from a ruined Siva temple, and a 1322 mosque founded during the reign of Ghiyas-ud-din-Tughluq (see page 179).

Chitrakut (Chitrakoot)

On the N flank of the Vindhyas where they dip gently beneath the Ganges Plains, Chitrakut's forests and peaceful rivers were home to Rama and Sita in 11 of their 14 years of exile. **Ramghat**, the principal bathing ghat on the banks of the beautiful Mandakini River, is widely revered in India and the site of countless pilgrimages, though scarcely known to foreigners. Like the much more famous waters of the Yamuna immediately to the N at Allahabad or the Ganga at Varanasi further E, the Mandakini is lined with temples. A good way to see the ghats is to hire a boat. Upstream from Ramghat the Mandakini passes through a particularly beautiful stretch of wooded valley. The **Janaki Kund**, where Sita is believed to have bathed, is 2 km from Ramghat, and can be reached easily by boat or road. The surrounding countryside is imbued with many of the Ramayana's legends.

• **Accommodation** MP Tourism **F Tourist Bungalow**, T 5226, 8 rm, nr bus stand. Restaurant. UP Tourism **F Tourist Bungalow**. **F Pramod Van**, dharamshala.

• **Transport Train** The nearest station is **Chitrakut Dham** on the Jhansi-Manikpur broad gauge line. **Road Bus**: regular services to Jhansi, Mahoba, Satna and Chhattarpur.

Khajuraho to Allahabad: southern route

ROUTES From Khajuraho the route crosses the cultivated plain. After 20 km is a popular picnic spot with attractive waterfalls and pools. After crossing the **Ken River** the road climbs the Panna Hills where the forest thins out. The diamond mines are off to the right as is the Panna National Park. The dark grey Kimberlite rocks in the 30 km long belt yield the gems. Not worth visiting as it is difficult to get permission and the wildlife is not very abundant. At **Panna** (40 km) the road goes to Ajaigarh, (80 km from Khajuraho, 26 km from Kalinjar). There is also a shorter direct route from Khajuraho to Ajaigarh by a back road. The Tourist Office will advise on the feasibility if you are driving.

Ajaigarh

(*Alt* 500m) The town lies in rugged country on a granite outcrop and crowned by a 15m perpendicular scarp. 2 of the Forts' original 5 gates are accessible. Virginia Fass notes that although it lies deep in remote and difficult country and is only reached by a stiff 250m climb, the fort repays the effort – large stone steps once helped elephants in their steep ascent. The hill is encircled by a fort wall within which are ruined temples, rock carvings, pillars and sculptures from Hindu and Jain temples, some used by Muslims to reinforce the fortifications. Ajaigarh was a self-contained hill fort, intended to withstand long sieges and to house the entire population of the region. This accounts for its size.

The Chandela kings' main defensive bases were Mahoba and Kalinjar (both now in UP), but as the kingdom expanded these were complemented by other forts such as Ajaigarh. In fact, there are many others in a comparatively small area: Garkhundar, Orchha, Datia, Samthar, Talbehat, Deogarh and Chanderi. The Chandelas, like other kings, donated villages to maintain the families of soldiers who had died in war. This was an effective means of encouraging the continuing flow of soldiers which the system required. Heroic virtues were instilled into a child from birth and any man who shirked combat was held in contempt. Women too were taught to admire men who fought well. A woman had to be ready to die should her husband be killed and *sati* became common practice throughout the region.

As the Chandela's fortunes declined, they lost Mahoba (1182) and Kalinjar (1203) and became confined to the area around **Ajaigarh**. Much later, after the Bundela chief Chattrasal died in the mid-18th century, Ajaigarh fell to the Marathas after a 6-week siege in 1800. In 1808 it was taken by a local chief, Lakshman Daowa who defied the British, precipitating a devastating attack the following year by the British Indian Army. Now the area is being invaded by forests of teak and ebony.

ROUTES From Ajaigarh you can drive directly to Kalinjar (20 km). Ask locally about road conditions or first go to Naraini, then approach Kalinjar from the N (an extra 30 km). Alternatively, miss out Kalinjar and go from Ajaigarh to Atarra Basurg.

Kalinjar

(*Alt* 375m, 53 km S of Banda) The fort stands on the last spur of the Vindhya hills overlooking the Gangetic plains, a plateau with a steep scarp on all sides. One of the most ancient sites in Bundelkhand, referred to by the Greek Ptolemy as Kanagora, it combines the sanctity of remote hill tops with the defensive strength of a natural fortress.

Origins One legend proclaims Kalinjar as the Abode of Siva, the Lord of Destruction (*Kal*= death, *Jar*= decay) but its name is linked with the Chandela kings, and it was one of their strongholds. After the mid-10th century the independent Chandelas joined a Hindu confederacy to repel an Afghan invasion led by Amir Sabuktigin. His son, Mahmud of Ghazni, the 'Idol Breaker', made at least 17 of his almost annual plunder raids into India from 1000-1027. In 1019 he crossed the Yamuna river and approached Kalinjar. Neither side won, but in 1022 he returned and took the title Lord of Kalinjar. Thereafter successive Muslim invasions weakened the fort's defences.

In 1182 the Chandela forces were crushed by the rival Hindu forces of Chauhan. In 1203 Kalinjar fell again to the Muslims and the last Chandela king, Parmadidev, was defeated but was retaken by local chiefs and remained Hindu until 1545. Then the Afghan Sher Shah besieged the fort but was mortally wounded. Akbar took Kalinjar for the Mughals in 1569. Towards the end of Aurangzeb's reign, the Bundela chief Chattrasal took Kalinjar and on his death in 1732 bequeathed it to the Marathas. This was surrendered to the British in 1812.

Places of interest The design of the **Fort** has a mystical significance, giving it a force greater than man's. The only approach is from the N and entry is through **7 gates**. All have barbicans, each corresponding to one of the 7 known planets and stations though which the soul must pass before being absorbed into Brahma. Only some of the names indicate Hindu significance: Alamgir; Ganesh; Chandi, a double gate; Budh Budr, approached by a flight of steps; Hanuman, surrounded by numerous sculptures and inscriptions; Lal and finally Bara Darwaza. At the crest, crumbling Hindu and Muslim monuments stand side by side on the 1.5 km long plateau. Beyond the last gate is a drop of about 3.6m leading to **Sita Sej**, a stone couch set in a chamber hewn from the rock (4th century). Beyond, is a passage leading to Patalganga (underground Ganga) which runs through Kalinjar.

Koth Tirth at the centre of the fort is a 90m long tank with ghats leading down to it. Nearby are the ruins of **King Aman Singh's Palace**. Numerous stone relics are scattered about the site; a dancing Ganesh, Nandi bulls, a model temple complete with figures like a miniature Khajuraho and a reclining Siva. Sati pillars are scattered about the fort, reminders of the tradition of self-immolation by Rajput women, and there are several lingams and *yonis* (female fertility symbols).

The ancient hill of Kalinjar has long been a place of pilgrimage and worship for Hindu sadhus, rishis and pilgrims. It is rarely visited by other travellers.

ROUTES From Kalinjar it is about 150 km to Allahabad via **Chitrakut**, see above. Before reaching Allahabad, visit Kausambi (see Allahabad Excursions).

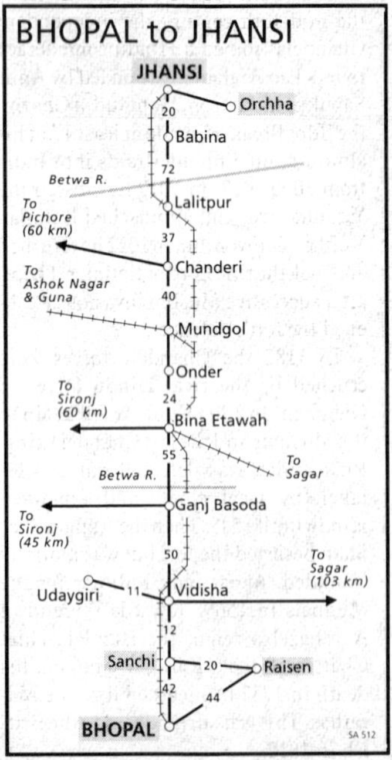

BHOPAL TO JHANSI

A slower route from Bhopal to the N makes it possible to visit a number of Madhya Pradesh's more interesting sites. The route to Sanchi passes occasional low hills, the higher ground all covered in low scrub jungle, the flat lowland cultivated.

Raisen

(14 km; *Pop* 24,000), a hilltop fort. Raisen was a site of a Lower Palaeolithic tool factory and rock shelters. The present settlement has temples, 3 palaces and a large tank. Built around 1200 AD it was later dependent to Mandu (MP), later still declaring its independence before conquest by the Mughal Bahadur Shah. It is a stiff climb.

Sanchi

A peaceful hill crowned by a group of stupas and abandoned monasteries are together one of the most important Buddhist sites in India, included on the World Heritage list in 1989. Although the Buddha himself never came to Sanchi it has a quiet stillness now lost at many of the other famous places of religious pilgrimage yet in keeping with the Hinayana Buddhism that gave it birth.

The surrounding imposing hilltop site has commanding views of the countryside. Sitting under the trees in the bright sunshine, it is easy to slip into quiet meditation and be moved by the Buddhist surroundings and by the fact that comparatively few people visit Sanchi. The rewards of a visit are great.

NB: Sanchi can easily be visited by car for a ½ day trip from Bhopal which has more comfortable hotels. 47 km E of Bhopal, the road follows the rly. You pass the Union Carbide factory in the outskirts. Once in the countryside the Vindhya Hills lie to your right.

Places of interest

Entrance at Main Gate (bottom of hill) – Re 0.50 (also allows entry to Museum). Allow at least 1½ hr. If in a hurry, visit Stupas 1, 2 and 3, Gupta Temple (17), Temple 18, and Monasteries 45 and 51. The Stupa is within walking distance from the rly station. The Archaeological Survey booklet by Debala Mitra describes the site in detail.

History The first stupa was built during Asoka's reign in the 3rd century BC, using bricks and mud mortar. Just over a century later it was doubled in size, a balcony/walkway and a railing were added. 75 years later the gateways were built. Finally in 450 AD 4 images of the Buddha (belonging to the later period) were placed facing each of the 4 gateways. The entrances are staggered. This is because it was widely believed that evil spirits could only travel in a straight line. The wall was built for the same purpose. The **Great Stupa**, one of the largest in India (37m diameter, 16m high), does not compare with the one at Anuradhapura – see page 1336. In India they became taller in proportion to their bases, in other countries the shape was modified further. Around the great stupas were lesser ones, often containing the ashes of monks famous for their piety and learning, plus a whole complex of buildings, eg monasteries, dining rooms, shrinerooms, preaching halls and rest-houses for pilgrims. These can be seen at Sanchi.

From the 14th century Sanchi lay half buried, virtually forgotten and deserted until 'rediscovered' by General Taylor in 1818, the year before the Ajanta caves were found. Amateur archaeologists and treasure hunters caused considerable damage. Some say a local landholder, others say General Taylor, used the Asoka Pillar to build a sugar cane press, breaking it up in the process. Sir John Marshall, Director General of Archaeology from 1912-1919, ordered the encroaching jungle to be cut back and extensive restoration to be effected, restoring it to its present condition. See page 351 for an account of the origins and significance of Buddhist stupas.

Construction Originally, the brick and mortar domes were plastered and shone brilliant white in the tropical sunlight. The earliest decorative carving was done on wood and ivory but the craftsmen at Sanchi readily transferred their skills to stone. Here, the yellow sandstone lends itself to such intricate carving.

The **carvings** illustrate scenes from the life of Buddha, events in the subsequent history of Buddhism and scenes from the *Jataka* stories, legends about the Buddha's previous lives. The gateways have been so finely carved and with such inspiration that they are regarded as the finest of all Buddhist *toranas*.

The Gateways The basic model consists of 2 pillars joined by 3 architraves (cross beams) built as if they actually passed through the upright posts. The East Gateway shows the young prince Siddhartha Gautama, leaving his father's palace and setting off on his journey towards enlightenment. It also contains the dream his mother had be-

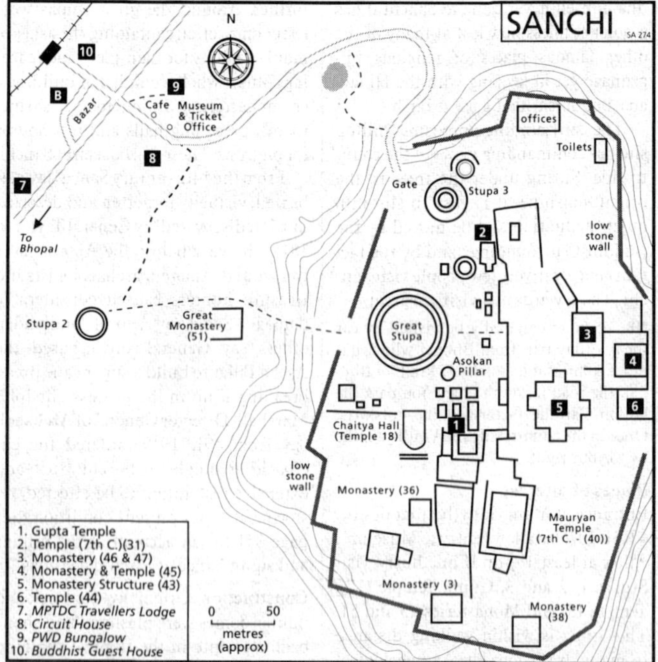

fore Gautama's birth. The West Gateway portrays the 7 incarnations of the Buddha. The North Gateway, crowned by a wheel of law, illustrates the miracles associated with the Buddha as told in the Jatakas. The South Gateway reveals the birth of Gautama in a series of dramatically rich carvings. Just to the right of the S gate is the stump of the pillar erected by Asoka in the 3rd century BC. The capital, with its 4 lion heads, is in the local museum. It recalls the one in the Sarnath Museum, of superior workmanship, that was adopted as the national symbol of Independent India.

Monastery 51 is reached by steps opposite the W gateway of the Great Stupa. It is well preserved with thick stone walls faced with flat bricks and is typical in plan. A raised, pillared verandah with 22 monastic cells behind, surrounds a brick-paved courtyard. The discovery of charred wood suggested that roofs and pillars may have been constructed with wood. There was possibly a chapel at the centre of the W side; the massive 'bowl' beyond the W gate was caused by extraction of a large boulder which you can see on your way to Stupa 2.

Stupa 2 stands on a terrace down the slope. The original balustrade has been dated to the 2nd century BC with later additions. The decoration, though interesting, is much simpler than on Stupa 1, especially when dealing with the human form. The relic chamber of the stupa contained valuable relics of 10 saints belonging to 3 generations after the Buddha's immediate disciples which may explain the choice of this site, below the main terrace.

The **Gupta Temple** (5th century) is one of the early structural temples of India, built of stone slabs with a flat roof. It has a square sanctuary and a pillared portico and shows the sobre decoration and symmetry typical of its style. **Temple 18** (7th century) built on the site of an earlier apsidal temple has only 9 of its 12 pillars still standing which resemble those found in the Buddhist cave temples of W India. **Monastery and Temple 45** (7th-11th centuries) on the E edge shows a more developed style of a N Indian temple. The monastery is built around a courtyard with a ruined temple of which only the core of the carved spire remains. The ornamental doorway and the Buddha image in the sanctuary with an decorative oval halo, are still visible.

Museum

Archaeological Museum, nr entrance to monument. Exhibits include finds from the site (caskets, pottery, parts of gateway, images) dating from the Asokan period. Archaeological Survey guide books to the site and museum available. 0900-1700. Closed Mon.

Excursions

In the area around Sanchi there are a number of minor sites, some of which are Buddhist. Only worthwhile for real enthusiasts with time to spare.

Local information

● Accommodation

Hotels are quite modest. MP Tourism's **D** ***Traveller's Lodge*** is the most comfortable. 8 rm, 2 a/c. Restaurant. Very neat, clean, pleasant airy garden, at foot of stupa hill. Within walking distance of rly station and monuments.

F ***Railway Retiring Rm,*** 2 large rm. Rec. **F** ***Buddhist Guest House***, nr rly station, T 39. 20 non a/c rm, also dorm. Simple. Contact Bhikku-in-charge, Mahabodhi Society. The *New Rest House* is often unavailable.

● Places to eat

Traveller's Lodge (non-residents, with advance notice). Also cafeteria by the Museum and food stalls by the crossroad.

● Tourist office

MP, *Travellers Lodge*, Bhopal run tours to Sanchi.

● Transport

47 km from Bhopal where you can hire a taxi (or book in advance in Delhi). Allow Rs 500 for the visit and approx 1¼ hr each way.

Train Trains on the Jhansi-Itarsi section of the Central Rly, stop in Sanchi. *Pathankot Exp* dep from Bhopal 1530 (1 hr). **NB**: The *Shatabdi Exp* does not stop at Sanchi. 1st Class passengers travelling over 161 km and 2nd class passengers (min group of 10) travelling over 400 km may request a stop at Sanchi on the *Punjab Mail*. Enquire and arrange this in advance.

Road Bus: hourly service from Bhopal (2½ hr) from Hamidia Rd.

Vidisha, Udaygiri Caves and on to Udaypur

ROUTES From **Sanchi** the road follows the railway line NE to Vidisha (6 km).

Vidisha (Besnagar)

(*Pop* 93,000, *STD Code* 07592) In the 5th-6th centuries BC Vidisha (known as Besnagar in Pali) was an important trade centre of the Sunga dynasty where Asoka was governor in the 3rd century BC. Tradition has it that he married a local princess, establishing his contact with Sanchi. The use of lime mortar in the construction of a shrine dedicated to Vishnu, dating from the 2nd century BC, suggests this was one of the first structures in India to use 'cement'. Located at the junction of the Betwa and Bes Rivers, Vidisha was once governed by Asoka before he became emperor. The citizens of Vidisha were patrons of the monuments at Sanchi. Deserted after the 6th century AD, it came into prominence again as Bhilsa between the 9th-12th centuries. It later passed on to the Malwa Sultans, the Mughals and the Scindias. The ruins of the **Bijamandal Mosque** and **Gumbaz-ka Makbara**, both dating from the Muslim period with remains of votive pillars nearby. The small **museum** contains some of Besnagar's earliest antiquities.

Heliodorus Pillar

3 km after crossing the Betwa river. The **Heliodorus Pillar** ("Khambha Baba"), a monolithic, free-standing column, similar to Asokan pillars but much smaller in size has been dated to 140 BC. The inscription states that it was a Garuda pillar erected in honour of Vasudeva by Heliodorus, a resident of Taxila (now in Pakistan) who had been sent as an envoy to the court of Bhagabhadra. This is part of the evidence which shows that relations existed between the Greeks in the Punjab and the kings of this area and that Heliodorus had become a follower of Vishnu.

• **Transport Train** Vidisha is on the main line from Bhopal, and is the most convenient station for Sanchi. **Bhopal:** *Jhelum Exp*, 4678, daily, 2143, 1 hr; *Kota Bhopal Pass*, 1593, daily, 0728, 1½ hr.

Road Car: from Bhopal add-on Rs 125 to the car hire to Sanchi to include Vidisha and Udaygiri. **Bus**: from Sanchi regular service (Bhopal-Vidisha and Raisen-Vidisha). Approx hourly, Rs 3.

ROUTES From Vidisha cross the railway line and go N to the Udaygiri Caves (6 km).

Udaygiri Caves

4 km from Vidisha. A group of rock-cut sanctuaries are carved into the sandstone hillside, an inscription in one indicating that they were produced during the reign of Chandragupta II (382-401 AD). The caves possess all the distinctive features that gave Gupta art its unique vitality, vigour and richness of expression: the beautifully moulded capitals, the design of the entrance, and the system of continuing the architrave as a string-course around the structure. The caves have been numbered, probably in the sequence in which they were excavated.

Cave 1 has a frontage created out of a natural ledge of rock. The row of 4 pillars bear the 'vase and foliage' pattern about which the art historian Percy Brown wrote: "the Gupta capital typifies a renewal of faith, the water nourishing the plant trailing from its brim, an allegory which has produced the vase and flower motif, one of the most graceful forms in Indian architecture". The shrines become progressively more ornate. **Cave 5** depicts Vishnu in a massive carving in his Varaha (Boar) incarnation holding the earth goddess Prithvi aloft on one tusk. Another large sculpture is of the reclining Vishnu. Both reflect the grand vision and aspirations of the carvers. **Cave 9** is notable for its 2.5m high pillars, its long portico and pillared hall.

• **Transport Road** From Vidisha take a tonga or auto-rickshaw (about Rs 40, incl waiting charge).

Udaypur

60 km from Udaygiri. The colossal **Neelkantheswara** temple is the centre-piece, an outstanding example of 11th century Paramara architecture. Its beautifully proportioned spire is delicately carved. Some regard the spire as being unequalled. Built of red sandstone and standing on a high platform, the temple consists of a *garbha-griha* (shrine room), a *sabha mandap* (hall) and 3 *pravesha mandaps* (entrance porches). See section on Khajuraho for terms.

• **Transport Train** From **Bhopal Pathankot** Exp (1530) to **Basoda** (1830; the station is **Ganjbasoda**), then take a bus (Rs 6) or tonga (Rs 25) to **Udaypur**.

North to Jhansi

From Basoda you can travel N to Shivpuri and Gwalior or to Jhansi and Orchha. The road to **Shivpuri** goes through Isagarh (100 km, see page 339).

The road to Jhansi passes through Bina-Etawa (35 km; *Pop* 51,000), an important rly junction, to the NH 26 and to Lalitpur (45 km). Painted Grey Ware has been found at **Lalitpur** (*STD Code* 05176), indicating its early origins as a settlement.

From Lalitpur you can travel W to **Chanderi** (37 km; *Pop* 19,500), an important town under the Mandu sultans. Chanderi is famous for the fine Chanderi saris and brocades and the Koshak Mahal. The road climbs steeply in the approach to Chanderi itself. It is attractively placed in an embayment in the hills overlooking the Betwa, river, though the old town is 8 km N of the present town and is buried in jungle. It contains ruined palaces, market places, mosques and tombs, and Jain temples dating from the 10th century. The town is dominated by its hill fort. Jain statues have been carved in the Khandar Hill. There is a *Dak Bungalow*. The **NH26** continues N from Lalitpur to Jhansi (92 km) through areas of jungle, now increasingly cleared for cultivation.

BHOPAL TO ALLAHABAD

This route goes though farmland, then attractive hilly parkland.

Gyaraspur

64 km NE of Bhopal, Gyaraspur is an attractive and important site of Jain and Hindu activity during the medieval period. The 10th century **Mahadevi Temple**, on the hill above the village, is the most striking of the remains with the ruins of a stupa to its W. Partly rock cut, at different periods it has served as both a Hindu and a Jain shrine. The ruins of an 8-pillared temple, *Athakhambe* (= "8 pillars") and a 4 pillared *Chaukhambe* date from the 9th and 10th centuries.

Sagar

(77 km; *Pop* 237,000, *STD Code* 07582), is the centre of Sagar district, founded by the Bundela Raja Udaussa (17th century). He began work on the fort in 1660, which was completed by the Marathas in 1780. In 1829 it was used as a prison for *thugs*. Today it is a university town and an important route centre. **Accommodation E** *Tourist Bungalow* nr Rest House T 34025 rm, restaurant.

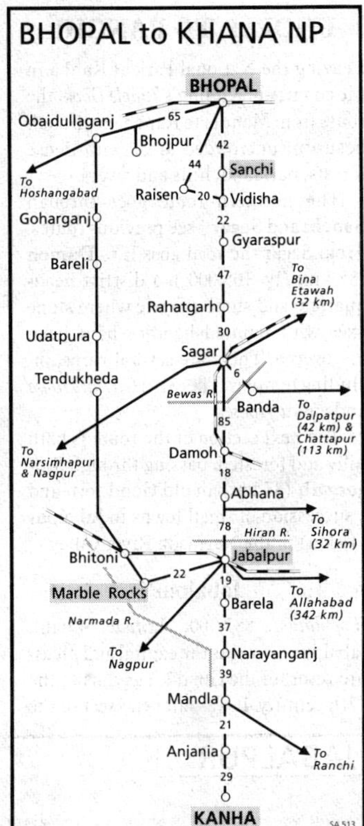

In Sagar the road goes E to Banda and **Dalpatpur** (42 km; *alt* 680m). The road passes through stretches of open farmland alternating with forest northwards with a succession of small towns and villages to **Chhattarpur** (113 km, *STD Code* 07682).

ROUTES For the route onwards to Allahabad, see page 358.

BHOPAL TO RANCHI

Leaving the National Park at Kanha in the country of Kipling's *Jungle Book*, the route from Mandla to Ranchi is through beautiful uncrowded areas with dense forests, parkland, hills and rivers.

The northern route goes through **Sanchi** and **Sagar** – see previous routes. From Sagar the road goes E to **Damoh** (85 km; *Pop* 105,000), a district headquarters and stone age site where stone axes with pointed handles have been discovered. There are several ruins, including temples. There is a *Circuit House* and a *Rest House*.

The next section of the route is both hilly and forested, passing through **Singorgarh** (37 km) an old Gond fort, and a succession of small towns to **Jabalpur** (41 km) in the Narmada River valley.

Jabalpur

(*Population*: 887,000; *Altitude*: 496m). Jabalpur town was the capital and pleasure resort of the Gond kings during the 12th century. It was later the seat of the Kalchuri dynasty until it fell to the Marathas. The British took it in 1817 and left their mark with the cantonment residences and barracks. Jabalpur today is an important regional centre.

Places of interest

The **Madan Mahal Fort** (1116), built by the Gond ruler Madan Shah, the **Rani Durgavati Memorial**, the **Museum**, which houses a collection of sculptures and prehistoric relics, and the **Tilwara Ghat** where Mahatma Gandhi's ashes were immersed in the Narmada, are all places of interest. There are also Jain temples.

Excursions

The **Marble Rocks** (Bherdaghat) 22 km W of Jabalpur can be reached by bus or car. Capt J Forsyth wrote of them: "The eye never wearies of the effect produced by the broken and reflected sunlight, glancing from a pinnacle of snow-white marble reared against the deep blue of the sky and again losing itself in the soft bluish greys of their recesses". These white rocks with views of black/dark green volcanic seams rise to 30m on

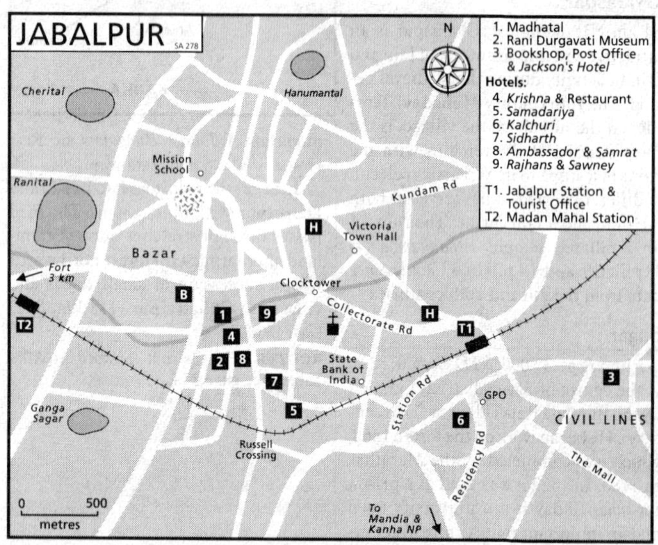

either side of the Narmada river and in moonlight produce a magical effect. Recently, floodlights have been added. Boats for hire (Nov-May), including moonlight boating. Cheap soap-stone carvings are available at the site.

Other sights are the **Dhaundhar Falls** ('smoke cascade') where the Narmada plunges through a narrow chasm, **Hathi-ka-paon** (Elephant's Foot Rock) and **Monkey's Leap** ledge. Nearby is the **Chausath Yogini Mandir,** a 10th century temple with stone carvings. Legend suggests that it is connected to the Gond queen Durgavati's palace by an underground passage. Approached by a long flight of steps, there is an excellent view of the Narmada from the top.

Excursions

Jabalpur is the most convenient base for visiting **Kanha** (173 km) and **Bandhavgarh National Parks** (170 km).

Local information

● Accommodation

C *Jackson's*, Civil Lines, T 322320. 44 rm, some a/c with bath. Restaurant, exchange, trips to Kanha, Khajuraho and Marble Rocks arranged. Rec.

D *Samadariya*, Russell Crossing. Modern, quiet, with a/c rm (some cheaper). Woodlands restaurant. **D** *Ambassador*, Russell Crossing, T 21771. 40 rm, some a/c with bath and TV. Central. Restaurant, travel. Nearby **D** *Samrat* has some rm with bath and a/c. **D** *Sidharth*, Russell Crossing, T 27580. Some a/c rm. Modern. MP Tourism's **D** *Kalchuri*, Wright Town, nr rly, T 321491. 30 rm, some a/c with bath. Restaurant, bar. **D** *Ashok*, Wright Town, T 22167. 45 rm, some a/c with bath and TV. Central. Restaurant, bar, garden. Rec. **D** *Krishna*, nr Rani Durgavati museum, Napier Town, T 28984. Restaurant.

● Budget hotels

F *Raja Gokuldas' Dharamshala*, nr rly station. **F** *Rajhans* and *Sawhney*, T 2495, opp High School, at Naudera Bridge are basic. Other inexpensive hotels around the rly station.

● Places to eat

Jackson's and *Samadariya Hotels* serve good food. *Indian Coffee House*, nr Clock Tower does good snacks and coffee.

● Bank

State Bank of India.

● Tourist office

At rly station, T 22111.

● Transport

Air Jabalpur airport is 23 km from the city. Scheduled flights discontinued but may resume.

Train Jabalpur is on the Bombay-Allahabad-Calcutta rly line. **Allahabad**: *Ganga-Kaveri Exp*, 6039, M,Sa, 2300, 6¼ hr; *Cochin/Tirupati-Varanasi Exp*, 7489/7491, W,Th,Su, 1235, 4¾ hr. **Bhopal**: *Narmada Exp*, 8234, daily, 2215, 7¼ hr; *Amarkantak Exp*, 2853, M,W,F,Sa, 0250, 7 hr. **Delhi (Hazrat Nizamuddin)**: *Mahakoshal Exp*, 1449, 1030, 28 hr. **Lucknow**: *Chitrakoot Exp*, 5009, daily, 1840, 16 hr.

Road Services to Allahabad, Khajuraho, Varanasi, Bhopal and other main centres.

Kanha National Park

Approach

Area: 1945 sq km. *Altitude*: 450-950m. *Climate*: summer Max 43°C, Min 11°C; winter Max 29°C, Min 2°C. Annual Rainfall: 1250 mm; monsoon July-Sep. *Best season*: Jan (when barasingha are in rut) to June. Closed 1 July to 31 Oct. Rec min stay, 2 nights.

Background

This is the country about which Kipling wrote so vividly in his "Jungle Books". The same abundance of wildlife and variety of species still exists today and the park which forms the core of the Kanha Tiger Reserve (1945 sq km) within the game reserve, created in 1974 also protects the rare hard-ground-adapted barasingha (swamp deer). George Schaller, the zoologist, conducted the first ever scientific study of the tiger here and research is also being done on deer and langur habitat.

Wildlife

The park has deciduous hardwoods including *sal* (Shorea robusta) and stands of bamboo (Dendrocalamus strictus), rolling grasslands and meandering streams of the Banjar river. It lies in the

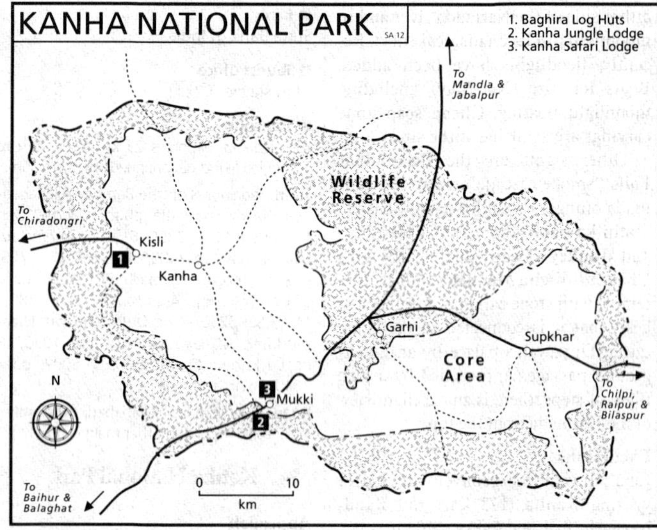

Mandla district in the Maikal hills in the eastern part of the Satpura range. Originally the area was famed as a hunter's paradise but now the valley has been well developed as a national park.

Mammals: Kanha has 22 species and the most easily spotted are 3-striped palm squirrel, common langur monkey, jackal, wild pig, cheetal, barasingha and blackbuck. Less commonly seen are tiger, Indian hare, *dhole* or Indian wild dog, sambar and gaur. Rarely seen are Indian fox, sloth bear, striped hyena, panther (leopard), nilgai (blue bull), Indian porcupine, wolf (outside park proper) and the Indian pangolin (sometimes called a scaly anteater).

Birds: Kanha has 230 species recorded; more to be found. Good vantage points are in the hills where the mixed and bamboo forest harbours many species. Commonly seen species are: leaf warblers, minivets, black ibis, common peafowl, racket-tailed drongo, hawk eagle, red-wattled lapwing, various species of flycatcher, woodpecker, pigeon, dove, parakeet, babbler, mynah, Indian roller, white breasted kingfisher and grey hornbill.

Viewing

Entry fees: Minibus, van or station wagon (for up to 15): Cars, Rs 10. Diesel vehicles, motorcycles and bicycles are not allowed in the park. *Gypsy 4-wheel hire* MPSTDC jeeps from the Baghira Log Huts, Kisli in the park (for max 6), Rs 8 per km. Petrol is often not available at Kisli; nearest *Petrol pumps* at Mandla. Book previous day. *Camera charges*: 8 mm and 16 mm movie camera – Rs 15-60, 35 mm movie camera Rs 250. Films from Baghira Log Huts, Kisli. Forest Dept guides accompany visitors around the Park on mapped out circuits enabling visitors to see a good cross-section of wildlife from a jeep. Here, and in Bandhavgarh, elephants are available only from 1600; in the morning they are used for tiger tracking and if one is spotted, visitors are taken there either from the Lodge or a nearby point reached by jeep.

The *sal* forests do not normally allow good viewing. The best areas are the meadows around Kanha. Bamni Dadar (Sunset Point) affords a view of the dense jungle and animals typical of the mixed forest zone: sambar, barking deer and chausingha (4-horned antelope). Early morning and late afternoon are ideal times and binoculars are invaluable. *Machans* (viewing platforms/ observation towers) are available for use during daylight; those above waterholes (eg *Sarvantal*) are rec.

Park information

● Accommodation

B ***Kanha Jungle Lodge***, Balaghat-Raipur Rd, just S of Mukki, outside the park, 12 km from Baihar and main road. Pick-up on request. 15 simple clean, comfortable rm with hot shower surrounded by *sal* forest. Restaurant, bar. Rates incl meals, audio-visual programmes, discussions, park tours. Also visits to villages and markets. In a woodland setting, good birdwatching. Contact Tiger Resorts, 206 Rakesh Deep, 11 Commercial Complex, Gulmohar Encl, N Delhi, T 666770, F 686 5212.

D ***Baghira Log Huts***, Kisli, 16 rm, restaurant, bar and cheaper canteen. **D** ***Kanha Safari Lodge***, Mukki, T 34. 30 rm (some a/c) and dorm. Contact Wildlife Adventure Tours, 606 Akashdeep, Barakhamba Rd, New Delhi, T 3312773.

E ***Jungle Camp***, Khatia. ***Tourist Hostel***, Khatia. Dorm. Gangotri, 4th Flr, TT Nagar, Bhopal, T 462003. **NB:** reservations over 5 days: Central Reservations, Tours Division, MP Tourism. Less than 5 days: manager of the unit. Contact Dynamic Tours, Delhi for trips to Kanha and Bandhavgarh. Own accommodation. New hotel near Kipling Camp, **D** ***Krishna Hotel***, 30 rm, pool. Booking *Hotel Krishna*, T Jabalpur 28984.

● Camping

Tents and chalets at ***Kipling Camp*** through Bob Wright, Tollygunge Club, Calcutta or ***Sita Travels*** in major cities. Well located, pleasant ambiance, friendly and rec.

● Places to eat

Baghira Log huts, Kisli, ***Kanha Safari Lodge*** and ***Kanha Jungle Lodge***, Mukki and ***Jungle Camp***, Khatia have restaurants attached to them. The canteen at Kisli serves meals and snacks to guests staying at the Tourist Hostel. Ask for boiled water specifically; water served at the lodges is generally filtered. Cold drinks are usually available but fresh fruit is not.

● Shopping

Daily necessities at Baghira Log Huts. Markets at Mocha (Wed), Sarekha (Fri), Tatri (Tue) and Baihar (Sun).

● Banks

You cannot cash TCs at Kanha, Kisli, Mukki or Mandla, nor at any of the lodges. The nearest bank dealing in foreign exchange is in Jabalpur.

● Tourist offices

MPSTDC, Jabalpur Rly Station, T 22111. Can arrange car hire. For Bookings: MPSTDC, Gangotri, 4th Flr, T.T. Nagar, Bhopal, T 63552; 74 World Trade Centre, Cuffe Parade, Bombay, T 214860; Kanishka Shopping Centre, Asoka Rd, New Delhi, T 3321187.

● Useful addresses

Basic **Hospitals** Mandla Civil Hospital and Katra Mission Hospital. Only basic first aid at Mukki, Mocha and Baihar. **Post Offices** at Mocha and Mukki, **Telegraph** Offices and **Telephones** at Katia (non-STD); nearest STD at Mandla.

● Tranport

Air: nearest airport is at Nagpur (226 km); no flights to Jabalpur at present. **Indian Airlines** flies to Nagpur from Bombay, Calcutta and Bhubaneswar, Hyderabad, Delhi and Bhopal.

Train: **Jabalpur** (173 km) on the Bombay-Allahabad-Calcutta, Delhi-Jabalpur and Madras-Varanasi main lines or **Raipur**, 230 km. A delightful, if spartan narrow gauge (diesel) train runs between Mandla and Jabalpur.

Road: Kanha is connected with Jabalpur, Nagpur and Bilaspur by motorable roads. **Daily bus service** connects Jabalpur with Kisli via Mandla and Chiraidongri (dep 0700) which takes approx 7 hr, fare Rs 40. Either stay on bus to Khatia, or stop overnight at Kisli as vehicles are not permitted within the park after dark. 1100 bus from Jabalpur to Mukki (see above). If coming from Nagpur or Raipur enter via Mukki Gate.

Bandhavgarh National Park

Approach

This compact park of 105 sq km is in the Vindhya hills, (*Alt* 800m). The park is set in extremely rugged terrain with many hills. The marshes which used to be perennial now support a vast grassland savanna. *Best time*: Feb-June. Closed 1 July-31 Oct. Temp range: 42°C to 2°C.

Rainfall: 1,500 mm.

Wildlife

Bandhavgarh (pronounced Bandogarh) is not very far S of **Rewa**, famous as the place in which the (albino) white tiger originated. Now it is only found in zoos. Before becoming a National Park in 1968, it was the game preserve of the Maharajas of Rewa. Though it involves quite a journey, it has a wide variety of game and has a longer 'season' than Kanha. Its main wild beasts are tiger, leopard, sloth bear, gaur, sambar, chital, muntjac, nilgai, chinkara, wild pigs. In 1990 a census revealed that the tiger population had grown from 9 in 1969 to 59, sambar from 111 to over 4,500 and spotted deer from 78 to over 7,000. The tigers, whilst elusive, are increasingly seen. The flowering and fruit trees attract woodland birds, which include green pigeon, Jerdon's leaf bird, crested serpent eagle and variable hawk eagle. There are also interesting cave shrines scattered around the park, with Brahmi inscriptions dating from the 1st century BC. You can visit the archaeological remains of a fort believed to be 2,000 years old where you may spot crag martins and brown rock thrush.

The management has embarked on a programme of conservation. Protection from disease, fire, grazing and poaching have all been factors in its recovery as a wildlife area.

Viewing

Jeeps are available from dawn to 1000 and 1600 until dusk when the animals are most active. Visitors must be accompanied by a Forest Dept guide. The short round is 18 km, the long, 37 km. The Fort, 18 km away, requires a 4-wheel drive vehicles (ask at the *White Tiger Forest Lodge*). Forest Dept elephants are available from 1600. Viewing machans are available during the day; *Bhadrashila Watch Tower* attracts *gaur*.

Park information

● **Accommodation**

Bandhavgarh Jungle Lodge, within walking distance of the Park gates. 10 comfortable cottages and a 4-rm house with modern facilities (hot and cold showers and toilets) in an Indian theme vilage setting incl mud huts, thatched roofs and inner courtyard. Good for birdwatching. Thatched dining room, library, resident naturallist, jeep and animal excursions, visits to local villages. Reserve through Tiger Resorts, 206 Rakeshdeep, 11 Commercial Complex, Gulmohar Enclave, New Delhi, T 666770, F 686 5212. ***Jungle Camp***. Reservations: Tiger Tops Mountain Travel, 1/1 Rani Jhansi Rd, New Delhi. ***Forest Rest House*** and **D** ***White Tiger Forest Lodge***, raised lodge, overlooking the river, T 308, 26 rm. Reservations: MP Tourism, Gangotri, TT Nagar, Bhopal, T 66383.

● **Transport**

Air Not possible at present through Jabalpur (see Kanha above). Khajuraho airport then by road (250 km).

Train **Umaria** (35 km) is the nearest station (1 hr by road), on the Katni-Bilaspur sector.

Direct train from Umaria to Delhi: *Utkal Express*, 8478, 1940, 18 hr. To Puri and Bhubaneswar, *Utkal Express*, 8478, 0606, 25 hr. From Katni to Jabalpur, *Mahakosal Exp*, 1450, 0855, 1½ hr. From Katni to Varanasi, *Sarnath Exp*, 4259, 0825, 7½ hr. Local bus or jeep to park (you can arrange a 4-wheel drive "Gypsy" through MP Tourism in Delhi).

Road From **Jabalpur** drive to Shajpura (144 km) then take a country road to Umaria. **Rouk**: From Shajpura the terrain is more hilly. It can also be reached from Satna (129 km) or by bus from Katni Rail Jn. Taxis available from Satna (but the road to the Park is poor), Jabalpura, Katni and Umaria. From **Khajuraho** (237 km), the 5 hr drive takes you across Ken River (parts declared a crocodile sanctuary with fish eating gharials), and past the diamond mines at Panna.

Jabalpur to Ranchi

ROUTES From Jabalpur the main road runs SE along the Narmada valley to Mandla (97 km).

Mandla

The capital of the ancient Gond Kingdom of Garha-Mandla early in the Christian era, Mandla is of great historical significance to the Gond tribal peoples. The Gond Queen Rani Durgavati took her life here when her army was cornered by Mughal forces under Asaf Khan in 1564.

Places of interest The **fort** was built in the 17th century and is surrounded on 3 sides by the Narmada River. It passed to the Marathas and then to the British in 1818. The jungle has since taken over the ruins (only a few towers remain) though there are some temples and ghats in the town.

Excursions The Gond Raja Hirde Shah built a large **Palace** in a commanding site nearby in **Ramnagar** (15 km) of which little remains. Kanha National Park is about 40 km from Mandla (see above)

Kawardha

Just E of the Maikala Range (up to 1100m) to the SE of Kanha National Park, Kawardha is a small town in the Chhattisgarh ('34 forts') region of MP. In this remote area Maharaja Vishwaraj Singh has recently opened his palace to visitors. It provides a delightfully quiet unspoiled contrast with India's big cities and with the much busier tourist circuit of Rajasthan's 'palace circuit'. Kawardha is in the centre of the Baiga tribe, who live in the forests surrounding the town. The Radha Krishna family temple with underground rooms and the Holy Water Tank are nearby. Other 11th century temples in the immediate region have some beautiful carving.

• **Accommodation** **B** *Palace Kawardha*, Kawardha 491995, Dt Rajnandgaon, MP. 4 large suites. Built between 1936-39, the stone-built palace with Italian marble facing is in 4 ha of gardens. A unique experience, with opportunities for visiting tribal settlements, temples, wildlife (including Kanha National Park). Price includes meals and local jeep excursions. Short treks into the hilly surroundings (incl tribal villages) arranged, 5-8 km, 2-5 hr. Bookings and payment for groups of more than 4, must be made 30 days ahead.

• **Transport Air** Raipur has the nearest airport (with flights to Delhi and Nagpur), and also the nearest rly station. **Road Bus**: express buses run from Raipur (117 km) and Bilaspur (124 km), where cars can also be hired. Alternatively the Palace will arrange to pick up from either city (2½hr) or Kanha National Park (3½ hr); approx Rs 900.

Mandla to Ranchi

From Mandla to Ranchi is 800 km, the road crossing some of the least densely populated parts of the peninsula. You need to be prepared for the journey, but it contains some beautiful scenery, dense forests and open parkland, and the source of the River Narmada, one of peninsular India's most sacred rivers. There are only a few small towns along the way and accommodation is only available in spartan *Rest Houses* and official Bungalows.

ROUTES The route out of Mandla keeps N of the Narmada for 31 km where it is crossed by bridge at **Manot**. The confluence of the Narmada and Burhner Rivers is at **Deogaon** then on to **Dindori** and up to **Kabirchabutra** (1040m) in the Maikala Range. **Amarkantak** (1050m) where there is a *Dharamsala* and temple at the source of the Narmada River, is just S of the main road. **Keonchi** has an *Inspection Bungalow*.

The higher hills in this region are over 1100m. The road goes through **Pendra** (29 km) to **Mahendragarh** (85 km) before crossing the River Hasdeo, (18 km). There is a *Forest Rest House*.

The road passes through periodic forested ghat sections and scattered villages and small towns, including **Ambikapur** and **Sitapur** before reaching the River Mand. It then crosses the Mainpat Hills (highest point 1127m) to **Pathalgaon** (also known as Dharmjaygarh and Habkob). In Pathalgaon the road goes NE to **Bandarchuan** and across the **River Ib**. The road to Ranchi runs NE, close to the watershed between the N flowing rivers draining into the Ganga system and the S flowing rivers which run into the Mahanadi. The River Ib flows S to the Hirakud Dam in Orissa – see page 755.

The road to Sundargarh for Rourkela or Sambalpur goes through **Kunjara** (18 km) and **Tapakera** (18 km) which has a *Forest Rest House*. After 13 km the road passes an *Inspection Bungalow* on the banks of the River Ib at Lawkera before reaching the Orissa/Madhya Pradesh border, and **Sundargarh**.

ROUTES If you are going to Ranchi continue NE through Jashpurnagar and across the MP-Bihar border to **Gumla**. Ranchi is then 103 km NE on NH 23. See page 784.

BHOPAL TO NAGPUR

The route from Bhopal to Nagpur follows the Delhi-Madras railway for much of the way. S of Bhopal it crosses the Malwa plateau then cuts through the Vindhyas, crossing the Narmada River at Hoshangabad, then over the Mahadeo Range of the Satpura Hills to Betul before turning SE to Nagpur.

ROUTES The road to Obadiadullaganj passes SE through fields of wheat and vegetables, and orchards scattered across the flat unirrigated land. A turn to the left leads to Bhojeshwar Temple of Bhojpur, while 11 km further S is the Bhimbetka Hill, with its magnificent collection of rock caves and shelters. The rock shelters can be clearly seen from the train just to the W of the main line about 45 km S of Bhopal.

Bhojpur

Bhojpur is famous for its 2 massive ruins, its Siva temple signifying the religious importance of the site, sometimes referred to as the 'Somnath of the East'

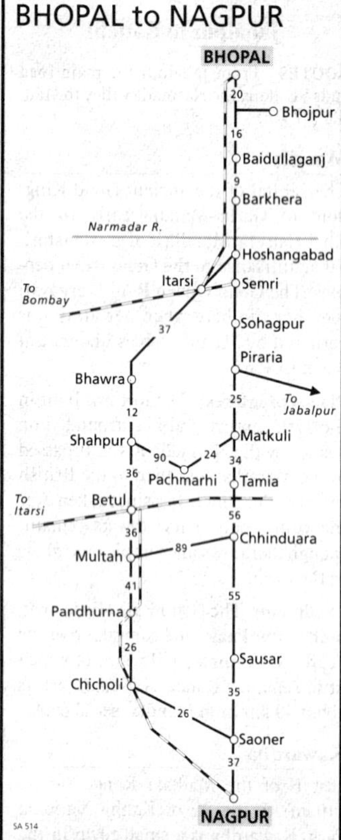

– see page 1276 – and its dams, a testimony to the crucial importance of irrigation water for agriculture in this region. Both the religious and civil functions implicit in these buildings owed their origin to the 11th century Parmar King of Dhar, Raja Bhoj (1010-1053), who was noted not only as a great builder but as a scholar.

The **Bhojeshwar Temple** is a simple square with sides of just over 20m. Surmounted by a corbelled dome, typical of pre-Islamic domes in Indian architecture, the lower doorposts are plain while the upper sections have rich carvings. Two finely carved figures guard the entrance. On a raised platform over 6m square is the focus of the whole temple, a polished stone lingam over 2m high and nearly 6m in circumference.

The temple was never completed, but retains a particular interest in that the traditional medieval means of building the towering structures of great Hindu temples is still visible in the earth ramp, built as a temporary expedient to enable large stones to be raised to the height of the ever rising wall, yet never cleared away. There is a Jain shrine nearby which include a 6m high statue of Mahavir and 2 smaller ones of Parsvanatha.

Cyclopean dams The huge lake once stored by 2 massive stone and earth dams has now disappeared. Built between two hills, the dams were up to 100m thick at the base and retained a lake of over 700 sq km, but in 1430 Hoshang Shah of Malwa demolished the dams. The Gonds believe that it took 3 years to drain, and that the local climate underwent a major change as a result of its drying out.

Bhimbetka Hill

Bhimbetka has S Asia's richest collection of prehistoric paintings and many other archaeological discoveries. The site was discovered by VS Wakanker of the Vikram University, Ujjain, in 1957. Digging at the site has continued since 1971. In the middle of a dense deciduous forest, there are over 30 species of trees with edible fruit, flowers seeds and tubers – a vital food for tribal people even today. There is also still a rich wildlife including several species of deer, wild boar, sloth bear, antelope, leopard, jackal, scaly anteater and a very wide range of bird species. Perennial springs provide the essential year round water supply. This is the setting for a total of more than 1000 shelters stretching for 10 km from the village of Kari Talai in the E to Jondra in the W. Over 500 of them contain prehistoric and later paintings and a smaller number have evidence of Stone Age habitation from the Lower Palaeolithic period to the late Mesolithic.

The earliest settlement

Acheulian period Dating of the occupation is far from complete. In the bottom layers of the settlement sequence were a few pebble tools. There was a thin layer of bare material above this, followed by a thick layer of Acheulian deposits – see page 35. Over 2.5m of accumulated material were excavated in Cave III F-23 for example, bringing to light successive floors paved with stone, and large quantities of stone implements that were clearly being made in the cave. This period is dominated by flake tools – blades, scrapers, cleavers and handaxes. Many were damaged, suggesting that they were not only made on site but used there as well. Some of the core tools were found to weigh up to 40 kg and the high level of skill suggests that they come from the end of the Acheulian period.

This level is followed in many caves by **Middle Palaeolithic** materials (approximately 40,000 to 12,000 years before the present), and the evidence suggests that this culture developed on the same site out of the preceding Acheulian culture. The same raw materials are used, although the tools are generally smaller. The **Upper Palaeo-**

lithic period (approximately 12,000 to 5,500 years before the present) was even shorter than the Middle, again growing out of it. Short thin blades made their appearance for the first time.

Mesolithic period It was in the period immediately following the Upper Palaeolithic that the largest number of caves were occupied. A Ghosh suggests that during this Mesolithic period there was a huge increase in population, and much more can be learned about the culture because there are many remains both of foodstuffs and of skeletons, and some of the cave paintings can be correlated with this period. There may have been improvement in the climate, although there is evidence for climatic change even within the Mesolithic period, which at Bhimbetka has been Carbon-14 dated as running from 5500-1000 BC.

A brand new technology was introduced. Tiny stone tools – microliths – were made by blunting one or more sides into an enormous variety of specialised shapes for specific purposes – knives, arrow heads, spearheads and sickles. Hard, fine grained rocks like chert and chalcedony were the basic material.

An imported technology Ghosh suggests that the technology was clearly introduced from outside the region and gradually supplanted the older technology. The raw materials for the new industry had to be brought in – the nearest source is near Barkhera, 7 km to the SE. From the skeletons that have been discovered it is clear that the dead were buried in caves still occupied by the living, usually though not always in a crouched position with the head to the E, with grave goods like antlers and stone tools buried alongside them. In the middle level of the deposits are copper tools and pottery, and at the very top early historical pottery.

Regular habitation seems to have come to an end at the end of the Mesolithic period, probably by the end of the 1st millennium BC. However, there are several circular structures on the hills around which have been interpreted as much later stupas. 20 km W of Bhimbetka an Asokan inscription has been found recently which supports this view.

- **Transport Road Bus**: if travelling to Bhimbetka by bus from Bhopal you can take the Hoshangabad bus and ask to be dropped at the Bhimbetka turning. The caves are 4 km from the turning, approx 45 min walk. However, it is difficult to get buses to stop on the way back. Better to take bus to Obadiadullaganj, 7 km N of Bhimbetka turning, and hire a bicycle. No facilities or drinks at the caves, so take plenty with you.

Barkhera

7 km SE of Bhimbetka and one of the richest open air Stone Age sites in S Asia. On the S edge of the road there are thousands of Acheulian tools scattered in the thick teak forest, and fields on the N side of the road are equally rich in tools. Ghosh concludes that it is clear that Barkhera was a large camp site of the final Acheulian hunter-gatherers.

Cave paintings By far the most striking remains today, however, are the paintings covering walls and ceilings in over 500 shelters and in rocky hollows. Some are quite small, while some are as much as 10m long. Red and white are the dominant colours used, but green and occasionally yellow are also found. These were obtained from manganese, haematite, soft red stone and charcoal, sometimes combined with animal fat and leaf extract. The paintings belong to 3 periods. The prehistoric phase is dominated by wild life paintings – cattle, boar, tiger, deer, engaged in various activities, and varying from tiny miniatures to life size – and often very lifelike – representations. Hunting is a common theme, the humans during this period being shown simply as 'stick men'. Some women are shown, occasionally pregnant. This period was followed by what Ghosh terms a 'transitional period'. Men are shown grazing or riding animals, but animals lose their proportions and naturalism. The later period probably dating from the early centuries AD, is quite different, showing battle scenes with men riding on elephants and horses with spears, bows and arrows.

ROUTES The road continues through an attractive and densely forested area and across the Narmada River to **Hoshangabad** (29 km; *Pop* 71,000; *STD Code* 07574). Hoshangabad, named after the Mandu ruler Hoshang Ghori (1406-35), was built to defend the Mandu kingdom against the Gonds. **Itarsi** (18 km; *Pop* 86,000; *STD Code* 07572), is an important railway junction. From here the road passes through a forested and hilly region, to **Bhawra** (31 km).

Diversion to Pachmarhi

Between Bhawra and Shahpur is a left turn to Pachmarhi (90 km) a hill resort on the N slopes of the **Satpura** range which forms the northern border of the Deccan.

Pachmarhi

(*Pop* 12,000) In 1857 Capt Forsyth of the Bengal Lancers "discovered" the spot, allegedly at the head of a column of troops but in fact accompanied by just 2 others. The beautiful landscape of the plateau of the Satpura range (*Alt* 1100m) impressed him with its tranquil forests of wild bamboo, *sal*, *yamun*, *amla* and *gular* trees, interspersed with deep pools fed by the streams that ran across the red sandstone hills. Later, acting on Forsyth's advice, the British developed Pachmarhi as a sanatorium and hot weather resort. Today, their legacy remains in MP's only hill station. There are several view points, water falls, rock pools and hills to climb within easy reach.

Pachmarhi is an ideal place from which to escape the heat of Central India. There are numerous walks, requiring varying degrees of exertion, into the countryside. Short 1-day treks are possible to Mahadeo and Dhupgarh peaks.

Places of interest

Caves and rock paintings In the neighbouring **Mahadeo Hills** there is an astonishing wealth of rock paintings. Several have been found in Panchmarhi itself, and others at **Tamia**, **Son Bhadra** and **Jalai** .

Gordon, who studied the paintings between 1935 and 1958, was reluctant to put a Stone Age date to any of them, but more recent studies suggest that the earliest may belong to the Mesolithic period. Ghosh points out 'a Gilgamesh figure' subduing 2 wild animals at Monte Rosa and a scene of rare humour in which a monkey standing on its hind legs plays on a flute while a man lying on a cot too small for his size has raised arms, as if to keep time with the flute. This is in the so-called **Upper Dorothy shelter**.

Ghosh visited the Pachmari shelters in 1940 and discovered 2 additional important ones he called **Bansia Beria** and **Dhuandhar**, near the waterfall. In the Bansia Beria cave, "among other subjects is depicted a large cross around which is a group of men, most of them holding in their hands what may be raised umbrellas. The cross may be a primitive or conventionalised svastika. One of the cows appearing below the cross has her belly cut open to reveal a calf in a crouching position inside. In the same cave there is another painted cross composed of small triangles which look like having been made out of a stencil." Most of these have been dated between 500-800 AD but the earliest are an estimated 10,000 years old.

Priyadarshini Point This outlook point from which Captain Forsyth is believed to have first viewed the Pachmarhi region still gives a commanding view over the town and the region.

Picnic spots There are several delightful picnic spots in and around Pachmarhi. They include the small natural bathing pool known as the **Apsara Vihar**, which can be reached from Jai Stambh. The pool has a broad shallow edge, suitable for children to paddle. There is a short scramble from Apsara Vihar to the top of **Rajat Pratap**, the 'big fall' – a waterfall over 110m high. There are other falls on the river which make attractive outings, including Jalawataran (**Duchess Fall**), 3 km along the path from Belle Vue. It is a strenuous 4 km walk to the base of the first cascade, but the fall has the reputation of being the most attractive in Pachmarhi.

Local information

● Accommodation

MP Tourism has several of reasonable quality. **D** ***Panchvati Cottages***, nr Tehsil offices, T 2079. 5 cottages and non-a/c huts. Restaurant. **D** ***Satpura Retreat***, Mahadeo Rd, T 2097. 6 rm. Restaurant. **D** ***Amaltas***, nr Tehsil, T 2098 4 rm. Restaurant, bar. **E** ***Holiday Homes***, nr Bus Stand, T 2099. 40 rm. Restaurant. **E** ***PWD Hotels***, Old and New blocks, T 2017. SADA accommodation incl **E** *Nilambar*, T 2004, *Vansthali*, T 2129 and *Nandan Van*, T 2018.

● Tourist Office

MP Prashthal Bungalow, T 2100.

● Transport

Train The nearest railhead for Pachmarhi is Itarsi which can be reached from Allahabad, Bangalore, Bombay, Delhi, Gwalior, Indore and Lucknow. The nearest station is Pipariya (47 km) on the Bombay-Haora mainline.

Road **Bus**: daily bus services to Pachmarhi from Bhopal and Itarsi. Taxis are available from **Pipariya**, where there is an MP Tourism *Tourist Motel*, on Pachmarhi Road behind rly station, T 22299. 4 rm. Restaurant.

Bhawra to Nagpur

If you do not make the diversion to Pachmarhi the main road goes S through Shahpur (12 km, *STD Code* 0252711) to Betul (36 km, *STD Code* 07141), where it turns SE through forested and ghat sections to Multai (48 km), and the MP border with Maharashtra (63 km). The market town of **Saoner** is a further 23 km, with ruins of a fort and temples. The road continues to Nagpur (36 km) – see page 1161.

BHOPAL TO AHMADABAD

It is a 3-4 hr drive to either the ancient city of Ujjain (199 km) or the palaces and tombs of Indore (198 km) across a broad, cultivated plain. In the distance to your left are the flat topped Vindhya Hills.

At **Sehore** (37 km E of Bhopal, *STD Code* 07562) there is the *Paradise Restaurant* which is quite attractive. Farmland gradually gives way to open scrub towards Dewas

Dewas

(152 km; *Pop* 164,000, *STD Code* 07272) Where E M Forster 'worked' in the court of the Raja of Dewas Senior in 1921, having visited it earlier in 1912. Forster came to regard his stay in this dusty town, as the 'great opportunity' of his life and used this experience to good effect with the autobiographical *The Hill of Devi* and his most famous novel *A Passage to India*. It is worth going up the 'Hill of Devi' overlooking the town for the views. You can drive all the way to the temple at the top.

ROUTES At Dewas a road turns right for Ujjain (see below) or left for Indore. Alternatively you can go from Bhopal to Ujjain to see the town and then continue to Indore (55 km), where there is better accommodation.

Indore

Indore is a textile town on the banks of the rivers Sarasvati and Khan, and is the largest in MP. Its cotton textile industry is the 4th largest in India. It is also famous for its bangles, and is a notable centre of Hindustani classical music.

BASICS *Population:* 1.1 mn. *Altitude:* 567m. *STD Code* 0731. *Climate*: Temp Summer Max 40°C, Min 22°C; Winter Max 29°C, Min 10°C. Annual Rainfall 1050 mm, mostly Jul-Sep. *Best season*: Oct-Mar, or Jun-Sep if proceeding to Mandu.

History

The area was given to Malhar Rao Holkar in 1733 by the Maratha Peshwas (see page 1155) in appreciation of his help in many of their battles. Malhar Rao left much of the statecraft in the capable hands of his widowed daughter-in-law who administered the area well and succeeded him

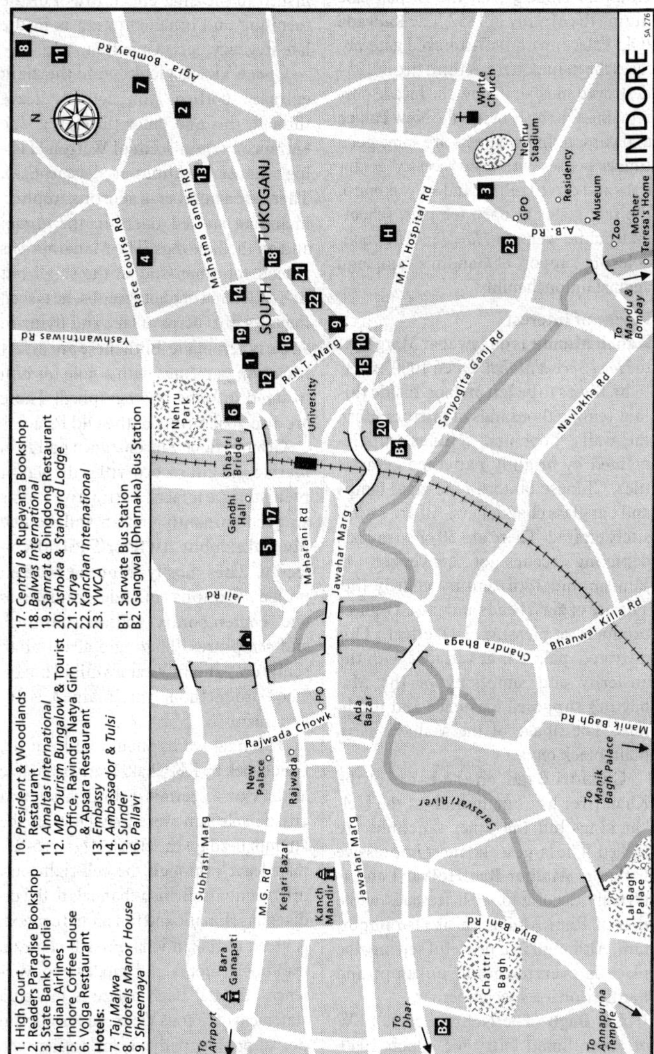

to the throne. Indore was destroyed in 1801 but recovered and was the British headquarters of their Central India Agency. The ruling family of Indore, the House of Holkar, took the British side during the Mutiny in 1857. The **Rajwada** (Old Palace) with its 7-storeyed gateway, faces the main square. A third fire in 1984 destroyed most of it; now the façade only remains. On the N of it is the **New Palace** and garden. In the streets are some good timber houses with deep recessed verandahs and carved pillars. Indore was one of the first states to open temples, schools and public wells to *Harijans* (Untouchables) in support of Gandhi's campaign against untouchability.

Places of interest

Kanch Mandir is on Jawahar Marg next to *Hotel Sheesh Mahal*. Open 1000. Allow ½ hr. Shoes to be left at door. Inside this Jain temple thousands of mirrors adorn the walls, floor and ceilings, supplemented by brightly patterned ceramic tiles, Chinese lantern-type glass lamps and cut glass chandeliers. All are exquisitely crafted. There are 50 or so murals depicting scenes of conversion to Jainism and 19th century courtly life. The use of glass beads and raised figures produces a pleasing 3-D effect. This mirrored palace is at variance with the austerity and simplicity of the Mahavira's supposed existence and teachings. The image of the Mahavir is in plain black onyx.

Chhattri Bagh, on the banks of the Khan river has 7 memorials of the Holkar kings but the inner sanctums are locked. The largest and most impressive is that of **Malhar Rao Holkar I** and is lavishly decorated with frescoes while that of Rani Ahilya Bai is also important. Although in a peaceful setting, the place is overgrown and unkempt and hardly worth a special detour.

Lal Bagh (The Nehru Centre), SW of town. Small entry fee. Open 1000-1700. Once the residence of the Maharaja, built and decorated in a confusion of styles, it is now a museum and cultural centre named after Jawaharlal Nehru. The rooms have been restored and furnished to pleasing effect. Much of the furniture and ornamentation is in the late Regency, early Georgian style.

Queen Victoria looks on to the main entrance portico (you actually leave through this and enter through a side entrance), reminiscent of Warren Hasting's house at Alipur (see page 617). There are a number of sporting trophies including stuffed tigers in the *atrium* and on the landings. The Maharaja was a keen sportman and in the small but fine collection of photographs, he is seen rowing a boat across a lake and flying in an early aeroplane. Both these are in fact backdrop paintings with a hole for him to stand in to be photographed! There are also good prints of the Old Palace.

Ground floor The entrance hall is in marble and gilt rococo with a display of prehistoric artefacts. 2 attractive rooms are predominantly 'Indian' and include Mughal exhibits. 1st floor The coin collection dates mostly from the Muslim period. Exhibits include miniatures and contemporary Indian paintings and sculptures. There are also Italian sculptures and intricately inlaid boxes. The Garden, though maintained, is dry and dusty.

The final words should be from the Guidebook by KK Chakravarty, available at the exit: "a certain hybridisation and artistic solecism were inevitable in the attempt to adapt the classical Graeco-Roman legacy through the self-righteous, interventionist British channels to the indigenous climatic and functional context. A blend of Italian villa, French chateau, traditional motifs and modern conveniences, the Lal Bagh palace is indeed a statement of riotous Victorian eclecticism not surprising, perhaps, for a ruler who supported the British"!

Museums

Central Museum (Archaeological). Bombay-Agra Rd, nr GPO. 1000-1700, closed Mon. Free. Guides available. Allow ½ hr. It has 2 main galleries: **Gallery I** Artefacts from MP's prehistoric period, c 50,000–4,000 BC and some from W Malwa. including stone tools, quartz sickles, ornaments and items of domestic use. Extensive excavation in the Chambal valley have revealed many rock shelter, see **Bhimbetka** above. Also a model of the first Hindu temple – at Barhut (another, slightly better is on display at the Lal Bagh Palace Museum). Thought to be the earliest free-standing building (c3rd century BC) – a small round hall made from brick and wood of which little but the foundations remain. **Gallery II** contains Hindu mythological carvings. Also sculptures in the grounds, said to have been a battlefield during the Mutiny.

If time is precious the Museum can be missed in favour of the riotously varied, but nevertheless fascinating Lal Bagh which has a selected range of early artefacts as well.

Tours

Mandu, Wed, Fri, Sat and Sun; **Omkareshwar** and **Maheshwar** (see Excursions), Mon and Thu. Both dep from Tourist Bungalow, 0730, return 1900. Cost: Mandu Tour Rs 70 (incl lunch and tea); Omkareshwar-Maheshwar Rs 50 (exclusive of meals). Tours are also organised for Mandu by both *Vijayant* and *Trimourti Travels* every Sun.

Local Festivals

Nov: *Sanghi Samaroh*, classical dance and music. *Mandir Festival* for Kathak and Dhrupad.

Local information

● Accommodation

C *President*, 163 RN Tagore Marg, T 433156, F 32230. 65 rm, some a/c. New, clean, friendly service. Rec. Woodlands restaurant (veg only). **C** *Taj Malwa*, 585/2 MG Rd, Palasia, T 433884. 39 rm, some cheaper. Good restaurant, bar, exchange, shops, garden. Clean, modern, family atmosphere, pleasant lobby, good value. 0900 check-out. Easily the best. Rec. **C** *Indotels Manor House* (formerly *Suhag*), Agra-Bombay Rd, T 31645, F 432250. 66 rm, central a/c. Odd numbered rooms are at back and quiet. Bar with TV part of restaurant, can be noisy. Pastry shop, exchange, pool under construction. Comfortable, but far from centre and overpriced.

D *Amaltas International* Agra-Bombay Rd, T 30569, F 492250. 30 rm, some a/c, all small. Restaurant claustrophobic but good value. Bar, garden. Far from centre. **D** *Ambassador*, 11/5 Nath Mandir Rd, Sth Tukoganj, behind High Court, T 33216. Small new hotel, 35 rm, a bit tatty. Restaurant clean, good value. **D** *Balwas International*, 30/2 Sth Tukoganj, T 433124. 40 rm, some a/c. Quiet location, Good restaurant. Popular with tours from Gulf and Pakistan. Good value. **D** *Central*, Rampurawala Bld, 70 MG Rd, T 38541. 41 rm, 12 a/c. Front rm very noisy, rm service only. Above shopping arcade on main rd, old fashioned, popular with budget travellers, good value. **D** *Kanchan International*, 12/2 S. Tukoganj, Kanchan Bagh, T 33395. 28 rm, some a/c with bath. Central. Restaurant. **D** *Lantern*, 28 Yashwant Niwas Rd, T 35327. 26 rm, some a/c. Nr rly. Restaurant, bar. **D** *Pallavi*, 1/1 Sth Tukoganj, T 31707. 22 rm, some a/c. Good value, small, simple, modern. **D** *Paras Regency*, 5 Murai Mahalla, Kibe Compound, T 460179. 38 rm, some a/c with bath. Veg restaurant. **D** *Samrat* 18/5 MG Rd, T 433889. 48 rm, some a/c. Restaurant, ice cream parlour. Popular hotel, good value, but in league with rickshaw drivers. **D** *Shreemaya*, 12/1 RN Tagore Marg, T 34151. 52 rm, half a/c with bath. Nr rly. V good, popular cafeteria style restaurant (S Indian), exchange. Good Indian style hotel. Highly rec. **D** *Sunder*, 17/2 Sth Tukoganj, T 33314. Small, modern, restaurant, bar. **D** *Surya*, 5/5 Nath Mandir Rd, Tukoganj, T 38465. 28 rm, some a/c with TV. Restaurant, bar.

● Budget hotels

E *Embassy*, 9/1/3/ MG Rd, T 36574. 30 rm, some a/c. Small, no frills. Rec. Nearby hotels have good restaurants. MP Tourism's **E** *Tourist Bungalow*, behind Ravindra Natya Griha, RN Tagore Marg, T 38888. 6 rm, 2 a/c with bath. Rooms 4 & 5 are good size with desk. Breakfast only. Central, 10 min rly, 15 min bus stand. Safe, peaceful. Tours can be organised from **Tourist Office** in same complex. Good value.

Rec. The inexpensive **F** hotels close to the rly and bus station can be quite noisy. ***Standard Lodge*** opp bus station, T 63522. ***Ashoka***, on road parallel to and opp Sarawate bus station, T 68341. Clean, pleasant.

● Places to eat

Several nr bus stand and rly station for Indian meals. The better hotels have their own restaurants – *Indotels Manor House* and *Shreemaya*. ***Mehfil***, 36 Sneh Nagar, Main Rd, has a bar and good Indian food. ***Indore Coffee House***, MG Rd; ***Jaiswal***, nr GPO; ***Hong Kong***, Palasia Chowk; ***Volga***, MG Rd.

● Banks

Exchange at State Bank of India, Agra-Bombay Rd.

● Hospitals & Medical Services

Chemists: several in Maharani Rd, incl *Anil Medical Stores* and *Cash Chemists*. **Hospitals**: *Pushpkunj*, PO Kasturbagram, T 63353. *M Y Hospital*, Agra Rd, T 23201.

● Shopping

Sarafa Market specialises in savoury snack foods and antique jewellery. ***Kasera Bazar*** in metalware. Try ***Cheap Jack***, Prince Yashwant Rd and ***The Gallery***, 2-C Tukoganj, T 7741 for antiques and curios. On MG Rd: ***Kilol Fabrics***, Chetak Arch, ***Avanti***, MPLUN, and ***Rupmati*** sell handloom cloth and Chanderi and Maheshwari saris; ***Gift House***, ***Sweet House*** and ***Mrignayani Emporium*** have handicrafts and ***Recent and Decent***, leather garments. **Books** ***Rupayan Bros***. **Photography** ***Anant Photo Stores***, MTH Compound; ***Gopal Studio***, 30 Rajawada Chowk, T 32396.

● Tour companies & travel agents

MP Tourism, Tourist Bungalow, T 38888. ***Sharma Transport***, T 39199. ***Sanghi Travels***, T 7361. ***Vijayant Travels***, T 39771. ***Sindh Travels***, T 39467.

● Tourist office

MP, Tourist Bungalow, behind Ravindra Natyagrih, T 38888.

● Useful addresses

Police: T 100, 35550. **Fire**: T 101. **Ambulance**: T 23201.

● Transport

Local Unmetered taxis, tempos, auto-rickshaws and cycle rickshaws: are available.

Air The airport, T 33161, is 9 km from the city centre. **Transport to town**: at airport ask IA officer or police to fix taxi or rickshaw rate with driver into town. Rickshaw approx Rs 40, Taxi Rs 60. **Indian Airlines**, city office, T 7069; airport, T 31244. **Bombay**: daily except W & Su, 2005, 1 hr 10 min; W & Su, 1155; **Delhi**: M,Tu,Th, F, Sat, 1155, 2¼ hr; **Bhopal**, daily, 1155, 35 min; **Gwalior**, M, F, 1155, 1hr 50min. **Damania**: **Bombay**: daily exc. Sun, 1¼ hr;

Train Indore is on a spur of the Bombay-Delhi line to Ujjain. There is also a metre gauge line to Ajmer and Chittaurgarh (N) and Khandwa, Nizamabad and Secunderabad (S). MPTC bus to city centre. Rec. Rly Enquiries, T 23284, Reservations Office in front of Railway Hospital, T 36185. **New Delhi**: *Indore-New Delhi Malwa Exp*, 4067, daily, 1505, 19 hr. **Bombay Central**: *Indore-Bombay Exp*, 1962, daily, 2030, 15 hr. **Calcutta (H)**: 1172, Th,F, 1915; **Bhopal**: daily, 2120; **Kochi**: 7082, daily, 1330; **Ujjain**: daily, 0805; **Ujjain**: daily, 1230. Reservations office in front of railway hospital. **Bilaspur**: *Narmada Exp*, 8233, daily, 1520, 26¼ hr. **Secunderabad**: *Meenakshi Exp*, 7569, daily, 0501, 13¼ hr. **Jaipur**: *Meenakshi Exp*, 7570, daily. 2226, 15¼ hr. **Ujjain**: *Narmada Exp*, 8234, daily, 1520, 1¾ hr.

Road Bus: buses to **Ujjain** (55 km), **Bagh** and **Mandu** (100 km, Deluxe rec) several times daily, and hourly to **Bhopal** (187 km). Direct bus to Mandu dep 1530 from Sarawate Bus station, 4 hr, Rs 18, (helpful enquiry desk; no timetables in English). Some buses returning from Mandu stop at Gangwal Bus Stand; easy transfer by local bus or rickshaws to town centre. Daily buses to **Udaipur** (Rajasthan) 12 hr and direct to **Aurangabad** (for Ajanta and Ellora caves). Sarawate Bus station, T 65788, Gangwal, T 65688.

ROUTES The direct road from Indore to Ujjain (55 km) via Sanwer passes mainly through farming country.

Ujjain

(*Population*: 367,000. *Altitude:* 492m. *Best season*: Oct-Mar). This comparatively quiet provincial town was one of the best known cities of ancient India and one of Hinduism's 7 sacred cities (see page 71). It is one of the 4 centres of the triennial *Kumbh Mela*, see page 281. Up to 3 million pilgrims converge on it every 12 years. At other times, there is a constant stream coming to bathe in the river Shipra and worship at the temples.

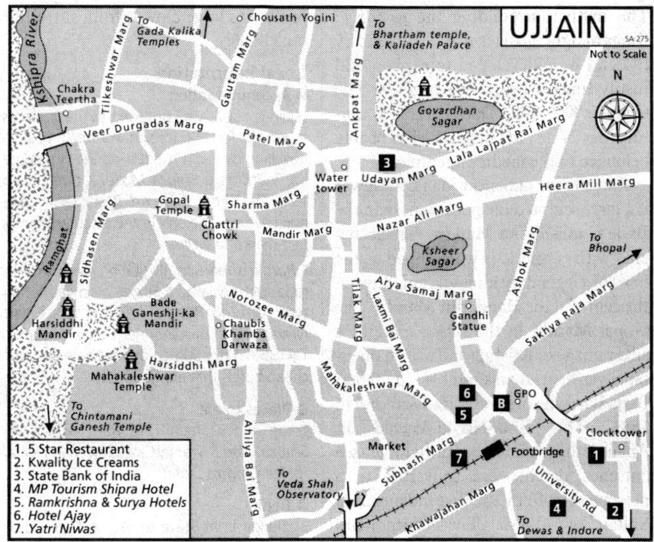

Despite its sanctity and its age, it has few remarkable buildings.

History

Legend has it that Siva commemorated his victory over the demon ruler of Tripuri by changing the name of his capital from Avantika to Ujjaiyini (One who Conquers with Pride). It is also believed that Vikramaditya, greatest king of a Hindu golden age, held court in Ujjain.

Many dynasties ruled over this prosperous city – the Sakas, Guptas, Paramaras, the governors of the Slave Dynasty of Delhi, the Mughals and the Marathas. It is said to have been the seat of the viceroyalty of Asoka in 275 BC. His sons were born here, and it was from here that they set out to preach Buddhism. The poet Kalidasa, one of the *Nava Ratna* (9 Gems) of Hindu literature, wrote some of his works here, where legend holds that the god Krishna studied.

Ujjain stands on the first meridian of longitude for Hindu astronomers, who believed that the Tropic of Cancer also passed through the site. This explains the presence of the **Vedha Shala** observatory, SW of town, built by Raja Jai Singh II of Jaipur around 1730 when he was the Governor of Malwa under the Mughal Emperor Muhammad Shah. Even today the *Ephemeris* tables (predicted positions of the planets) are published here. It is very small compared with Jai Singh's other Jantar Mantars in Delhi and Jaipur and contains only 5 instruments.

In its heyday, Ujjain was on a trade route to Mesopotamia and Egypt and, consequently, trade flourished. Nowadays, it is little more than a provincial town. There are a reasonably large number of sites in Ujjain, reflecting its long history.

Places of interest

Mahakaleshwar Temple, rebuilt by Marathas in the 18th century, dominates the skyline (closed to non-Hindus). Dedicated to Siva, the temple lingam is one of the 12 *jyotirlingas* in India, believed to be *swayambhu* (born of itself).

The myths surrounding the *jyotirlinga* (linga of light) go back to the 2nd century BC and were developed to explain and justify linga worship, see page 78. The Chaubis Khambha Darwaza (c11th century) has 24 carved pillars which probably belonged to the medieval temple.

Close to the tank near Mahakaleshwar is a large sculpted image of Ganesh in the **Bade Ganeshji- ka Mandir**. A rock covered with turmeric is worshipped as the head of a legendary king Vikramaditya in the centre of the **Harsiddhi Mandir**. The **Gopal Mandir** in the Bazar contains a silver image of Krishna and an ornamental silver door. It was built by Maharani Baija Bai (wife of Daulat Rao Scindia) in 1883. The **Bina-Niv-ki-Masjid** in Anantpeth, originally a Jain temple (see entrance porch), was converted to a mosque (c1400) by the first independent Sultan of Malwa. The **Chintamani Ganesh Temple**, across the river is believed to have ancient medieval origins. There are other smaller temples and shrines along the river and the atmosphere at these is generally very restful and relaxed.

Ujjain is an interesting town to wander around – the riverside temples and ghats are worth visiting. About 8 km N, past the British built jail, is the 15th century **Kaliadeh Palace**, built on an island on the Shipra river. This once imposing building with a hall surrounded by galleries and interesting fountains, was built on the site of an earlier Sun temple, by one of the Malwa sultans. Akbar stayed here in 1601. The riverside buildings are quite attractive but the palace, now used as a storeroom, is badly neglected. Except during the monsoon, the river level is quite low.

Local festivals

The triennial *Kumbh Mela* takes place here every 12 years (see page 281). The next one is in 2004. Mar *Mahasivaratri Fair* is held at the Mahakaleshwar Temple. Nov *Kartik Mela*. The month-long fair draws large crowds from surrounding villages.

Local information

Accommodation

Ujjain is not as well provided as many places, especially for the foreign visitor. If you are travelling by car, it is better to stay in Indore. MP Tourism's **D** ***Shipra Motel***, University Rd, T 29628. 30 good size rm. Restaurant, travel, quiet garden. The only hotel/restaurant for the mid-market traveller.

F *Ramkrishna* opp Rly Station. Basic rm. Veg restaurant. Nearby **F** *Surya* is similar. **F** *Railway Retiring Rooms*. MP Tourism's **F** *Yatri Niwas*, new building, left out of station, T 41363. 4 rm, 60-bed dorm. There are some cheap hotels that are good value.

Places to eat

Some nr Rly Station incl *Ramkrishna* and *Shipra*. Also *5 Star* by Clock Tower and *Kwality Ice Creams* S of it.

Bank

Exchange from **State Bank**, nr Water Tower after 1030.

Shopping

The region is famous for its Maheshwari saris, a unique weave introduced to Maheshwar by Rani Ahilyabai. They are mostly woven in cotton with reversible borders.

Transport

Local Unmetered taxis, auto-rickshaws (charge 50% above meter reading), **tempos, cycle rickshaws and tongas**: are widely available. **Hire**: plenty of bicycles for hire.

Air Nearest airport is Indore (53 km), connected by regular flights with Delhi, Gwalior, Bhopal, Bombay and Raipur.

Train **Ahmedabad:** *Bhopal-Rajkot Exp*, 1270, daily, 2350, 9¼ hr; *Sabarmati Exp*, 9186, daily, 2030, 10½ hr. **Bhopal:** *Narmada Exp*, 8233, daily, 1735, 4¾ hr. **Bombay Central:** *Indore-Bombay Exp*, 1962, daily, 2230, 12½ hr. **Indore:** *Narmada Exp*, 8234, daily, 1130, 2¼ hr. **New Delhi:** *Malwa Exp*, 4067, daily, 1655, 15 hr.

Road Bus: regular bus services connect Ujjain with **Indore** (53 km), **Ratlam**, **Gwalior**, **Mandu** (149 km), **Dhar**, **Kota** and **Omkareshwar**. Direct bus to Bhopal (6 hr). **NB**: Bus timetables all in Hindi.

ROUTES Leave Indore and drive W. The road first crosses a cultivated plain and then the headwaters of the Chambal river.

Dhar (65 km), was originally the stronghold of the Paramara dynasty and the capital of Raja Bhoj from Ujjain. It has a number of ruined mosques dating from the 15th century and an imposing fort on the edge of the town. Leaving Dhar, the road gradually climbs on to a more open plateau which is still farmed though less intensively. The final ½ hr of the 2½ hr drive is spectacular as the road reaches the N limits of the Western Ghats. Here and there the land falls steeply away and from the tops of ravines there are stupendous views of the lowland country to the W and SW. The road entrance to Mandu is along a short razor back ridge dividing 2 deep valleys.

Mandu

BASICS *Population:* 5,000. *Altitude:* 634m. *Climate*: Temp, summer max 36°C, min 28°C; winter max 22°C, min 7°C; rainfall 1050 mm. *Best time:* during the monsoon when the tanks are full and the rain turns the entire countryside a verdant green. Good Oct-Feb. Spend 2-3 days.

History

Perched along the Vindhya ranges at 600m, Mandu was fortified as early as the 6th century but gained prominence in the 10th century as Mandavgarh, the fort capital of the Paramara rulers of Malwa. Later, in the early 14th century it came under the sway of the Delhi Sultans under whom it was named Shadiabad (City of Joy); Hoshang Shah made it his capital. Humayun captured Mandu in a brilliant campaign in Malwa in 1534, and it became a pleasure resort, its lakes and palaces the scenes of magnificent festivities. However by the end of the Mughal period it had effectively been abandoned and in 1732, it passed into Maratha hands.

The fine architecture of the buildings, spread over the naturally defensible plateau (21 sq km) with a sheer drop towards the Namar plains to the S and waterfalls flowing into the Kakra Khoh gorge, exude a grace compatible with Mandu's other name. Its rulers built exquisite palaces ornamental canals, baths, pavilions and the outstanding Jama Masjid and Hoshang Shah's Tomb. Architecturally, Mandu represents the best in a provincial Islamic style; most of the structures were built between 1401 and 1526, initially using stone salvaged from desecrated local Hindu temples. The architects disdained the use of elaborate exterior ornamentation and a little imagination is therefore required to picture many here as buildings for pleasure. Mandu can be visited by car as a day excursion from Indore, but it would not do it justice. It makes a peaceful break to spend a couple of days.

Places of interest

The 45 km parapet wall with 12 gates was built from rubble and boulders. Most notable is **Delhi Gate** (1405-7), the main entrance to the city and testimony to the fort's history of violent sieges, approached through a series of well fortified subsidiary gates such as Alamgir and Bhangi Darwaza (the only one now open). The present road is along this route. There are 6 groups of buildings at Mandu, the first 3 being the most important. The return trip taking in Roopmati's Pavilion is about 14 km. The Archaeological Survey of India guide to Mandu by DR Patil (Rs 4.50) is excellent.

The Royal Enclave

The **Mosque of Dilwar Khan** (1405) is the earliest Islamic building, comprising a central colonnaded courtyard. There are Hindu influences in the main entrances. The **Hathi Pol** (Elephant Gate) is the main entrance to the royal enclosure. The **Hindola Mahal** (Swing Palace, c1425) built on a 'T' plan, was the audience hall, acquiring its name from its inward sloping walls which give the impression of swaying. Behind and to the W of the Hindola Mahal is a jumble of ruins which was once the palace of the Malwa Sultans.

Here is the 6.5m deep **Champa Baoli**, an underground well (its water is said to have smelt like the *champak* flower), cool vaulted *tyhkhanas*, (rooms for summer use), a Hammam (hot bath) and a water pavilion.

The late 15th century **Jahaz Mahal** (Ship Palace) reflects the spirit of romantic beauty characteristic of the palace life of the Muslim rulers of India. 122m long and only 15m wide, it was built between 2 artificial lakes, Munj and Kapur Talaos. Its shape and kiosks give it the impression of a stately ship. Built to house Ghiyasu'd-Din's increasing *harem*, it was 'crewed' entirely by women, some from as far off places as Turkey and Abyssinia, and consists of 3 great halls with a beautiful bath at the N end.

Other places of interest in this enclave are **Taveli Mahal** (stables and guardhouse), from which there is a wonderful panorama of the ruins of Mandu, 2 large wells – the *Ujala* (bright) and *Andheri* (dark), Baolis and Gada Shah's Shop and Palace, Kesar Kasturi Mahal. The last, in ruins, retains the romance of its second name – Gada Shah taking pity on a group of gypsies trying to sell their perfumed *kesar* and *kasturi* which had been ruined by a downpour, bought their wares and then had to use it all in his palace since it was unsalable.

The Central Group

Hoshang Shah's Tomb (c1440) in Mandu Bazar is India's first marble monument, a refined example of Afghan architecture. It has a well proportioned dome, delicate marble latticework and porticoed courts and towers. The square base of the interior changes to an octagon through being raised by arches to the next level, and then becomes 16-sided further up. Shah

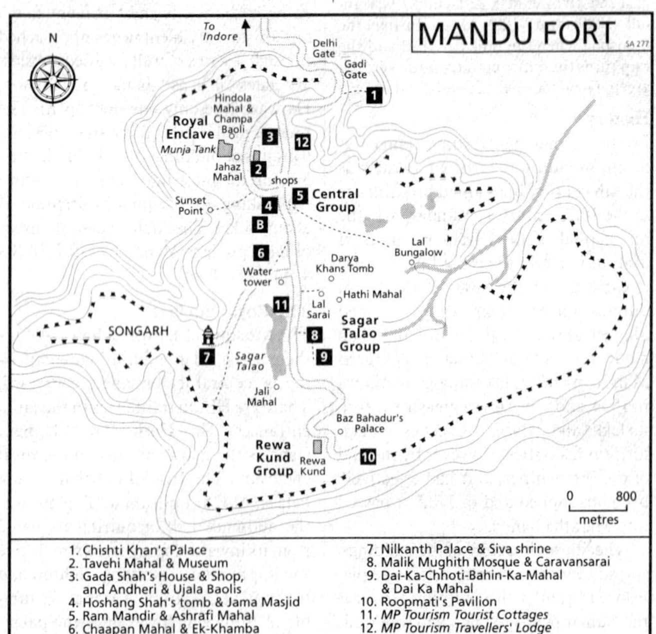

Jahan sent 4 of his architects, including Ustad Ahmed, who is associated with the Taj Mahal, to study it for inspiration. The adjoining **Jama Masjid** (1454) which took 3 generations to complete, was inspired by the great mosque at Damascus. Conceived by Hoshang Shah on a grand scale on a high plinth (4.6m) and a large domed porch ornamented with jali screens and bands of blue enamel tiles set as stars. The courtyard is flanked by colonnades. The western one is the Prayer Hall and is the most imposing of all with numerous rows of arches and pillars which support the ceilings of the 3 great domes and the 58 smaller ones. The central niche (*mihrab*) is beautifully designed and ornamented along its sides with a scroll of interwoven Arabic letters containing quotations from the Koran.

The **Ashrafi Mahal** (Palace of gold coins, c1436-1440), now a ruin, was conceived as the first *madrassa* of Persian studies. Its builder Mahmud Shah Khilji (1436-69) built the 7-storeyed tower to celebrate his victory over Rana Khumba of Mewar (Udaipur). Only one storey has survived. Also in ruins is the tomb, intended to be the largest building in Mandu.

The Sagar Talao Group

Between the village and Sagar Talao is the **Hathi Mahal** (Elephant Palace) which stands to the E of the road and takes its names from its stumpy pillars supporting the dome. It was probably a *baradari* (pleasure pavilion) turned into a tomb with a mosque by it. Traces of old tile work can still be seen. The **Tomb of Darya Khan** (c1526) is a red masonry mausoleum, once embellished with rich enamel patterns. More ruins lie nearby.

In the large group of monuments around the picturesque **Sagar Talao** (lake) is the **Malik Mughith mosque** built in 1432. It has a W wall retaining blue tile decoration in carved niches. In front is the **caravansarai** (also 1432) an open courtyard with 2 halls with rooms at both ends, probably for storage of goods while the halls provided living accommodation. The **Dai-ka-Mahal** (Gumbad) to the S is a tomb which may first have been a house belonging to the wet nurse of a Mandu Prince, and was later converted to her tomb. Alongside, the ruins of a pretty mosque has a fine octagonal base to the dome, decorated with small kiosks.

Rewa Kund Group

This group is 3.2 km S of the village. **Rewa Kund** is a sacred tank whose waters were lifted to supply the **Palace of Baz Bahadur** (1508-9), the musician prince, on the rising ground above. The palace was built before Baz Bahadur, the last Sultan of Malwa (1555), came to occupy it. The main portion of the palace consists of a spacious open court with halls and rooms on all sides and a beautiful cistern in its centre. On the terrace above are 2 *baradaris* (pavilions) from which there is an enchanting view of the surrounding countryside.

Beyond the palace and on higher ground at the S edge of the plateau is **Roopmati's Pavilion**, originally built as a military observation post but later modified and added to as a palace so that Baz Bahadur's mistress could have her *darshan* (view) of the sacred Narmada river, seen 305m below winding like a white serpent across the plains. The shepherdess Roopmati the story goes, so impressed Baz Bahadur with her singing that he captured her. She agreed to go to Mandu with Baz Bahadur when he promised that she would live in a palace within sight of her beloved river! He built the Rewa Kund so that she could practice her Hindu rites. The pavilions, square with hemispherical domes, are the latest additions and these have added distinction to the building. Sunrise and sunset are particularly beautiful.

Other Palaces

On the edge of the plateau is the **Lal Mahal** (Red/Ruby Palace) or **Bungalow**, once used as a royal summer retreat. **Chishti Khan's Palace**, now in ruins, may have been a retreat during the monsoon. W of Sagar Talao (1 km from the Jama Masjid) is the Islamic **Nilkanth Palace**, built for Akbar's Hindu wife and contains the Nilkanth (siva) shrine. On the scarp of one of the great ravines, reached by steps and commanding a magnificent view of the valleys below, it was used by the Mughals as a water palace. On one of the outer room walls is an inscription recording Akbar's expeditions into the Deccan and the futility of temporal riches.

The **Lohani caves** and temple ruins are near Hoshang Shah's Tomb. Approached by steep rockcut steps, they are a maze of dark and damp caverns in the hillside. Panoramic views of the surroundings from **Sunset Point** in front of the caves.

Local information

● Accommodation

MP Tourism's **D** *Tourist Cottages*, Roopmati Rd, 20 min walk from Bus Stand, T 3235. 10 (20 rm) spacious cottages with small lounge, 4 a/c. No 16 best a/c, No 18 best non-a/c; (avoid 1,2,7 and 8). Restaurant (low seats), veg dishes rec, bar, gardens. Peaceful setting by Sagar Talao lake. Rec. MP Tourism's **D** *Travellers' Lodge*, T 3221 is less expensive. 8 rm, some a/c. Restaurant, bright and cheerful. Nearer bus stand, very pleasant, excellent view of plateau. Both may be reserved more than 5 days ahead through Tourism office; otherwise contact direct.

E *SADA Guest House*, T 3234. 7 rm. Simple. **F** *Taveli Mahal Guest House* (Archaeological Survey of India), nr Jahaz Mahal, T 3225. 2 rm in a doctor's house. **F** *PWD Rest House*. Contact Exec Engineer, PWD, Dhar. **NB**: severe water shortage is likely, before the monsoon. Supply may be restricted to a few hours in the morning; buckets provided.

● Places to eat

Simple places (*dhabas*), in the bazar and nr the bus stand. Fruit and vegetable market opp Jama Masjid.

● Tourist offices

MP Tourist Cottages and Travellers Lodge, T 235. Archaeological Survey of India, T 225.

● Useful addresses

No foreign exchange facilities. The Govt **Hospital** is basic.

● Transport

Mandu lies just off NH3 from Agra to Bombay. It is most accessible from Indore.

Local Mandu is essentially a small village spread across a few kilometres. Everything worth visiting can be reached on foot. No taxis. Auto-rickshaws, cycle rickshaws and bicycles are available.

Air Nearest airport is at **Indore** with Indian Airlines connections to Bhopal, Gwalior, Jaipur, Bombay, Delhi and Raipur.

Train The most convenient railheads are **Ratlam** (124 km) on the Bombay-Delhi line, and **Indore** (99 km) on a branch route. Ratlam has connections from Bombay, Delhi, Allahabad, Vadodara, Jaipur, Ajmer, Bhopal, Kanpur, Lucknow, Varanasi, Amritsar and Gwalior.

Road Bus: regular bus services connect Mandu with **Indore**. Direct bus to Indore, 0700, 1700; dep Indore at 1500, 4 hr, Rs 18. Also with **Dhar** (35 km, 1½ hr), first dep 0530; change for Indore and Ujjain. Indore has better choice for other destinations, **Indore** (99 km – 4-5 hr), **Ratlam** (124 km), **Ujjain** (152 km) and **Bhopal** (286 km). Tours from Bhopal and Indore.

Maheshwar to Ahmadabad

ROUTES Return to the main road at **Gujri** (42 km) and turn right to travel S. In **Dhamnod** (11 km) turn left for Maheshwar (13 km).

Maheshwar

Pop 15,000. On the N bank of the Narmada, Maheshwar has been identified as Mahishmati, the ancient capital of King Kartivirarjun, a spectacular temple city mentioned in the *Ramayana* and *Mahabharata* epics. The Holkar queen Rani Ahilyabai of Indore (d1795) was responsible for revitalising the city by building temples and a fort complex.

The queen was widely revered, as was testified by Sir John Malcolm: "She sat every day for a considerable period in open durbar transacting business". Known for her "moderate assessment and an almost sacred respect for native rights... she heard every complaint in person ... Her charitable foundations extend all over India ... She had the courage to watch her own daughter become *sati*, after vainly seeking to dissuade her."

The town is renowned for its **Maheshwar saris** woven in a unique way for over 200 years. Woven in cotton and silk, the 'body' of the sari may be plain, checked or striped. The *pallu* (end section) is distinctive with 5 stripes (3 coloured and 2 white) while the reversible borders have floral designs.

Places of interest The palace inside the fort contains exhibits of the Holkar family treasures and memorabilia including the small shrine on a palanquin which is carried down from the fort during the annual Dasara ceremony. There is also a statue of the Rani seated on her throne. The **Peshwa**, **Fanese** and **Ahilya Ghats** on the river bank are interesting to visit to watch the daily rituals of ordinary villagers. Lining the banks are stone memorials to the *sati's*. The temples to see are **Kalshwara**, **Rajarajeshwara**, **Vithaleshwara** and **Ahileshwar**.

Navdatoli, opposite Maheshwar on the S bank of the Narmada is an important archaeological site. Since its first exploration in 1950, when painted pottery and microliths were found, a broad sequence of cultures have been discovered from the Lower Palaeolithic period up to the 18th century. The third period of occupation during the Chalcolithic has been dated at between 1500 BC and 1200 BC. House plans from this period have been excavated which show either circular or rectangular buildings, the circular houses having a circumference of about 3m. The walls and roof, made of split bamboo covered in mud, were supported by wooden poles.

Burnt grains of wheat and rice, legumes and oil seeds have all been found along with large numbers of bones of domesticated animals which show that the people ate beef, pork and venison. A wide range of ornaments has also been discovered from this third period. It ended with a great flood, and the site was abandoned temporarily. During the succeeding period a small stupa was built though probably left incomplete.

- **Accommodation** All basic. *Ahilya Trust Guest House, Govt. Rest House* and *dharamshalas*.

- **Transport Road Bus**: regular bus services from Barwaha, Khandwa, Dhar and Dhamnod. The nearest railhead is Barwaha (39 km) on the Western Railway.

Omkareshwar (Mandhata)

61 km E, a sacred island shaped like the holy Hindu symbol 'Om' at the confluence of the Narmada and the Kaveri, has drawn pilgrims for centuries. Over 2 km long and 1 km wide the island is divided N to S by a deep gully. The ground slopes gently along the N edge but in the S and E there are cliffs over 150m high forming a gorge. The village spreads to the S bank from the island, now linked by a new bridge, and the river between is reputedly very deep and full of crocodiles.

Places of interest

The **Sri Omkareshwar Mahadeo temple** has one of the 12 *jyotirlinga* in India, natural rock features that are believed to be representations of Siva. The oldest temple is at the E end of the island. The **Siddhnath Temple** on the hill is a fine example of early medieval temple architecture, its main feature being a frieze of elephants over 1.5m high carved on a stone slab at its outer perimeter. Craftsmen have carved elaborate figures on the upper portion of the temple and its roof. Encircling the shrine are verandahs with columns carved in circles, polygons and squares. A gigantic Nandi bull is carved of the hillside opposite the temple to **Gauri Somnath** at the W end of the island.

The temples were severely damaged after the Muslim invasions of Mahmud of Ghazni. Every dome was overturned and the sculptured figures mutilated. They became completely overgrown, and *Murray's Guide* records that when the Peshwa Baji Rao II wanted to repair the temple it could not be found, so he built a new one. Subsequently repairs were carried out to the part that was discovered.

Other places in or near Omkareshwar are the **24 Avatars**, a cluster of Hindu and Jain temples, the 10th century **Satmatrika Temples** (6 km) and the **Kajal Rani Cave** (9 km), a picturesque scenic spot with a panoramic view of the gently undulating landscape.

Local Information

● Accommodation

Holkar Guest House, run by Ahilyabai Charity Trust, Omkareshwar Temple and ***dharamshalas***.

● Transport

Road Bus: Omkareshwar is connected to Indore, Ujjain, Khandhwa and Omkareshwar Road rly station (12 km) by regular bus services. The railhead is on the Ratlam-Khandwa section of the Western Railway.

ROUTES **To Ahmadabad** From Guyri a road turns off the NH3 to Dhar (44 km), then runs W to Dohad (120 km), just across the border of Gujarat. From Dohad it continues W through Godhra (70 km) and Nadiad (82 km) to Ahmadabad (58 km), see page 1240.

RAJASTHAN

Contents

Maps

SOCIAL INDICATORS *Population*: 44 mn (Urban 23%, Scheduled castes 17%, Scheduled Tribes 12%); *Literacy*: M 55%, F 21%. *Birth rate*: Rural 35:1000, Urban 29:1000. *Death rate:* Rural 11:1000, Urban 8:1000. *Infant mortality*: Rural 105:1000, Urban 60:1000. *Religion*: Hindu 89%, Muslim 7%, Christian 0.1%, Sikh 1.5%, Jain 1.8%.

Environment

The regions of Rajasthan

Rajasthan is bounded on the W and NW by Pakistan, Punjab and Haryana in the North, UP in the E, MP in the E and SE and Gujarat in the S and SW. It is almost exactly the same size as Germany.

Land

Area: 342,000 sq km. Rajasthan comprises 3 areas:

Aravalli Hills One of the oldest mountain systems in the world, the Aravallis run across the S, forming a series of jagged, heavily folded synclines, stretching from Mt Abu in the SW (1720m) to Kota and Bundi in the E. Their northernmost ridges break the surface of the plain in the Delhi Ridge on which New Delhi's government buildings now stand. Mt Abu itself is granite but the range has a mixture of rocks. Small quartzite hills are nearly buried under the Ganga alluvium. Rajasthan is also the source of the glittering white Makrana marble used in the Taj Mahal and the Victoria Jubilee Memorial in Calcutta. The route from Delhi to Jaipur gives an excellent view of the approach to the Aravallis, whose hill tops are often dominated by massively impressive forts such as Chittaurgarh, Kota, Bundi, Kumbhalgarh.

Thar Desert In the NW is the arid and forbidding Thar Desert, with its shifting sand dunes and high summer temperature. **Jaisalmer** and **Bikaner** are important settlements on overland routes to the W whose trade has been severely disrupted by Partition from Pakistan. **Jodhpur** lies on the edge of this arid tract, the link between the true desert and the semi arid but cultivable regions to the E.

The East Rainfall and soil fertility increase eastwards. Around Jaipur and

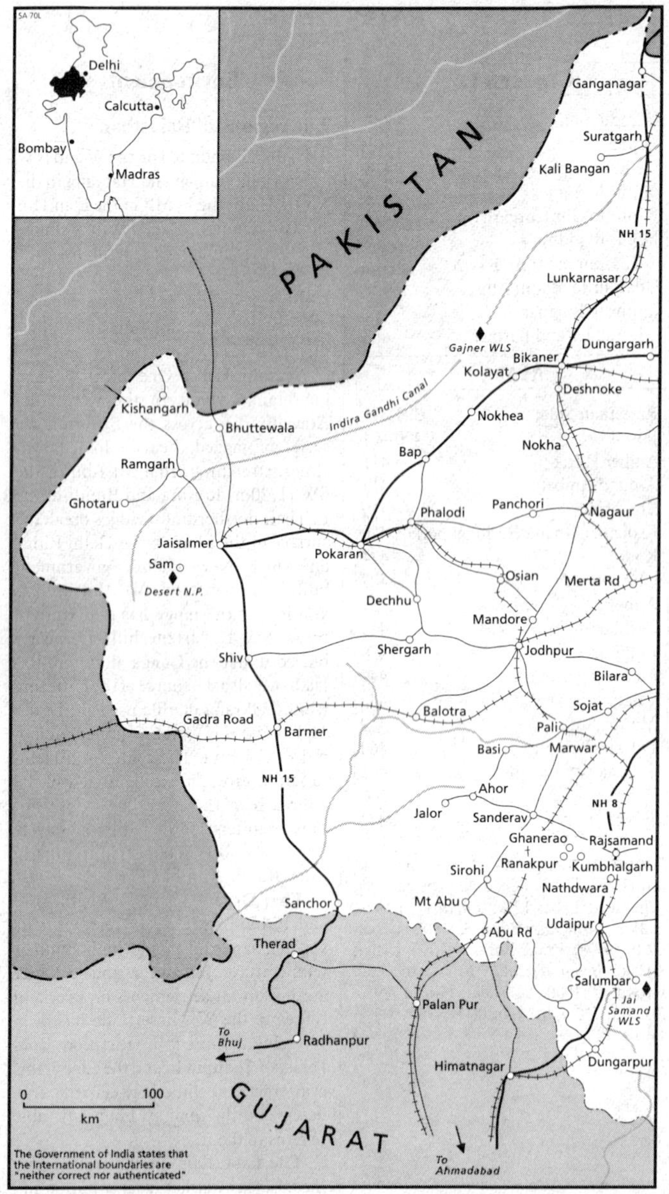
SA 70L
Delhi
Calcutta
Bombay
Madras
PAKISTAN
Ganganagar
Suratgarh
Kali Bangan
NH 15
Lunkarnasar
Gajner WLS
Dungargarh
Bikaner
Kolayat
Deshnoke
Nokhea
Nokha
Indira Gandhi Canal
Kishangarh
Bhuttewala
Ramgarh
Bap
Ghotaru
Phalodi
Panchori
Nagaur
Jaisalmer
Pokaran
Sam
Desert N.P.
Osian
Merta Rd
Dechhu
Mandore
Jodhpur
Shergarh
Shiv
Bilara
Sojat
Balotra
Gadra Road
Barmer
Pali
Basi
Marwar
NH 15
Ahor
Jalor
NH 8
Sanderav
Ghanerao
Rajsamand
Ranakpur
Kumbhalgarh
Sirohi
Nathdwara
Mt Abu
Sanchor
Udaipur
Abu Rd
Therad
Salumbar
Jai Samand WLS
Palan Pur
To Bhuj
Radhanpur
Dungarpur
Himatnagar
0
100
km
GUJARAT
To Ahmadabad
The Government of India states that the International boundaries are "neither correct nor authenticated"

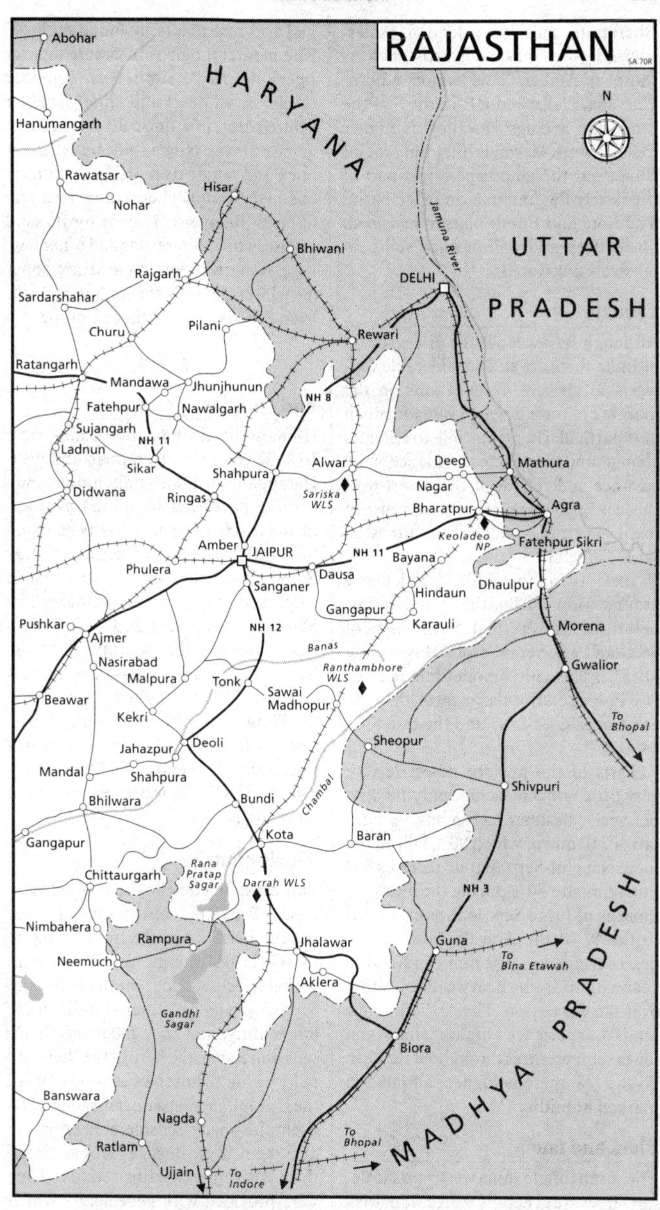
RAJASTHAN
SA 70R
N
HARYANA
UTTAR PRADESH
MADHYA PRADESH
Abohar
Hanumangarh
Rawatsar
Nohar
Hisar
Bhiwani
Jamuna River
DELHI
Rajgarh
Sardarshahar
Pilani
Churu
Rewari
Ratangarh
Mandawa
Jhunjhunun
NH 8
Fatehpur
Nawalgarh
Sujangarh
NH 11
Ladnun
Sikar
Alwar
Deeg
Mathura
Shahpura
Nagar
Didwana
Ringas
Sariska WLS
Bharatpur
Agra
Keoladeo NP
Fatehpur Sikri
Amber
JAIPUR
NH 11
Bayana
Phulera
Dausa
Hindaun
Dhaulpur
Sanganer
Gangapur
Karauli
Pushkar
Ajmer
NH 12
Morena
Banas
Nasirabad
Ranthambhore WLS
Gwalior
Malpura
Tonk
Sawai Madhopur
Beawar
To Bhopal
Kekri
Sheopur
Jahazpur
Deoli
Mandal
Shahpura
Shivpuri
Bundi
Bhilwara
Chambal
Gangapur
Kota
Baran
Rana Pratap Sagar
Chittaurgarh
Darrah WLS
NH 3
Nimbahera
Rampura
Jhalawar
Guna
Neemuch
To Bina Etawah
Aklera
Gandhi Sagar
Biora
Banswara
Nagda
To Bhopal
Ratlam
Ujjain
To Indore

Bharatpur, cultivated land is interspersed with rocky outcrops such as those at Amber. This region adjoins Haryana, Delhi and UP. In the S of the range the average elevation is higher (330-1150m). Mewar is hilly, but around Bharatpur the landscape forms part of the nearly flat Yamuna drainage basin. The Kota and Bundi plateau has good, black, deep and well drained soils, intensively cultivated.

Climate

Although Rajasthan is the driest region of India there are still considerable contrasts in climate. Its locations on the margins of pure desert has made much of it particularly susceptible to climatic change, and there is clear evidence of the advance and retreat of the desert over the last 5,000 years from the presence of fossil sand dunes which reach almost as far E as Delhi.

Except in the hills, particularly around Mount Abu, the summer temperatures are very high with a max of 46°C and an average from May to Aug of 38°C. The daily summer min is 25°C. In winter the daily max in most low lying areas is 22°C to 28°C and the min 8°C-14°C.

Parts of the western desert receive very little rain, on average only 100 mm per year. Jaisalmer has an annual rainfall of 210 mm of which 90% falls in the monsoon (Jul-Sep). Jaipur receives 650 mm annually, 80% during the monsoon months of Jul to Sep. Jodhpur, situated to the W of the Aravallis and on the desert fringe has 380 mm of rainfall a year with the same heavy concentration over the wet season. The Aravalli range tends to experience a higher rainfall and lower temperatures throughout the year. To the SW there is higher rainfall and marked humidity.

Flora and fauna

The scrub jungle thins westwards to desert. Trees are generally scarce. Tamarisk and arid zone plants are found in the W. The natural jungle is ideal territory for tigers, leopards, sloth bear, sambhar (large brown deer) and chital (smaller spotted deer) now normally restricted to game reserves. Nilgai (blue bulls), black buck and ravine deer are fairly numerous on the plains. There is a great variety of birds. Bikaner is famous for its sand grouse, whilst Bharatpur and other low-lying swampy places in the SE are popular winter grounds for migratory birds from Siberia and Northern Europe.

History

Early origins

Humans lived along the Banas river 100,000 years ago. Harappan and post-Harappan (3rd-2nd millennium BC) cultures have been discovered, as at Kalibangan where pottery has been dated to 2700 BC, while rock inscriptions near Bairat reveal that the emperor Asoka controlled this part of the state. The Mauryas were succeeded by the Bactrian Greeks (2nd century BC), the Sakas (Scythians, 2nd-4th centuries AD), the Guptas (4th-6th centuries) and the Huns (6th century). Rajput dynasties rose from the 7th to the 11th centuries and until the end of the 12th century, control of N India was concentrated in their hands.

The Rajputs

Rajputs claimed to be the original *kshatriyas* – warriors – of the ancient *varna* system, born out of the fire offering of the Gods on Mount Abu. They were probably descended from the Huns and Scythians who had entered India in the 6th century, and they modelled themselves on Rama, the hero of the *Ramayan* epic, seeing themselves as protectors of the Hindu *dharma* against invaders. The Brahmins made considerable efforts to give them royal lineages and accorded them *kshatriya* (warrior) status. They were provided with genealogies which connected them with either the solar or lunar race eg Udaipur.

Previous dynasties had ruled irrespective of their caste status and were accepted by the high castes simply because they were the rulers. The Rajputs, however, went to great lengths to insist on their *kshatriya* status, thereby seeking some religious sanction for their rule, a means of demonstrating to their subjects that not only was it foolhardy but also sacreligious to oppose their authority. Associated with this was promotion of those qualities or attributes ascribed to the martial castes, eg chivalry, bravery and unquestioning loyalty.

Between 800 AD and 1200 AD villages were based on a self-sufficient economy. Any surplus wealth was spent on richly ornamented palaces and magnificent temples, a powerful lure to invaders. The king granted some of the revenue from land to his office holders, who in turn leased land to peasant cultivators who handed over a fixed share of their produce to the landowner. Part of the land revenues was sent to the king.

A feudal landowner was bound to express his loyalty to the king in various ways, from being called upon to give his daughter in marriage to the king to using the king's currency. Attendance at court on certain occasions, such as the king's birthday, was obligatory. In return he was permitted the use of a title and various symbols of dignity. He was expected to supply troops when required and to send them of his own accord when the king declared war. These obligations tended to strengthen the martial aspect of the system which lent itself admirably to the rise of the Rajput clan system.

The Mughals and the Rajputs

Rather than engage in costly campaigns to crush the Rajputs, the Mughal emperor Akbar (r1556-1605) sought conciliation. Many Rajput princes were given high office in return for loyalty and Akbar sealed this important strategic alliance by marrying a Rajput princess, Jodh Bai, the daughter of the Maharaja of Amber. The relationship between the Rajput princes and the Mughals did not always remain so close, and in the later Mughal period several Rajput princes sought to secure their autonomy from Mughal rule. Such autonomy was brought to an end by the spread of British colonial power. With the settlement that followed the defeat of the Marathas in 1818 the Rajput princes were confirmed in their status. However, there continued to be rivalries, and attitudes to British rule varied. After the quelling of the Mutiny in 1858 and the establishment of the British Indian Empire the Rajput Princely States gained in the appearance and show of power, with 21 gun salutes, royal polo matches and durbars, just as they lost its reality.

Culture

People

Rajasthan's population, includes many tribals. who today constitute 12% of the state population, nearly double the national average. The Bhils and Minas are the largest groups, but the less well known Sahariyas, Damariyas, Garasias, Gaduliya Lohars and Bhil-Minas are all important. The tribes share common traits which seem to link their pasts together but it is the differences in their costumes and jewellery, their gods, fairs and festivals that set them apart from one another. The tribals are slowly being absorbed into the mainstream of Indian life and losing their distinctive character. You may see one or more of these communities, possibly without realising it. There is an Institute of Tribal Research near Shastri Circle, Udaipur, and the W Zone Cultural Centre in Udaipur (see Udaipur entry) has further details.

The **Bhils** comprise 39% of Rajasthan's tribal population and are concentrated in the S. Their stronghold is Banswara. The generic term derives from *bil* (bow) which describes their original talent and strength. The Hindu epic the Mahabharata mentions the Bhils and their archery skills. Today, the accepted head of all the Rajput Clans of Rajasthan – the Maharana of Udaipur – is crowned by anointing his forehead with blood drawn from the palm of a Bhil chieftain, affirming the alliance and loyalty of his tribe.

The Bhils maintained their numbers by mingling with rebellious outcaste Rajputs. Rajput rulers came to value the guerrilla tactics of the Bhils and Muslim and Maratha attacks could not have been repelled without their active support. However, they always remained a minority and offered no real threat to the city-dwelling princes and their armies. Physically, they are short, stocky and dark with broad noses and thick lips. They marry within a narrow kinship group and the tribe has a patrilineal system of inheritance. The Bhils used to live off roots, leaves and fruits of the forest and the increasingly scarce game. Most now farm land and keep cattle, goats and sheep, while those who live near towns often work on daily wages to supplement their incomes.

Imperfectly absorbed into Hinduism, the Bhils have their own deities. *Nandevro*, a deity who presides over the corn, *Gwali*, the god of milk and *Hir Kulyo*, the god of agriculture, are 3 of the most important. The fact that these gods are worshipped indicates how much the Bhil way of living has changed from their original hunting and gathering existence. Thousands congregate near the confluence of the Mahi and Som rivers in Dungarpur district for the Baneshwar fair in Jan/Feb.

The **Minas** are Rajasthan's largest and most widely spread tribal group. They may have been the original inhabitants of the Indus Valley civilisation. The *Vedas* and the *Mahabharata* mention them, and it was the Kachhawaha Rajputs who finally dispersed them and forced them into the Aravallis. The Minas have a tall, athletic build with sharp features, large eyes, thick lips and a light brown complexion. The men wear a loincloth tied loosely round the waist, a waistcoat and a brightly coloured turban. The women wear a long gathered skirt (*ghaghra*), a small blouse (*kurti-kanchali*) and a large scarf.

Most Minas are cultivators and measure their wealth in cattle and other livestock. They worship Siva and have built temples decorated with stone carving. Other deities worshipped include Sheeta Mata, the goddess of smallpox. Like other tribal groups they have a tradition of giving grain, clothes, animals and jewellery to the needy. The forest dwellings, *Mewas*, comprise a cluster of huts called *pal* and each pal constitutes a family unit. The marriage ceremony performed round a fire is similar to a Hindu one. Divorce, though, is not uncommon or particularly difficult. A man wishing to divorce his wife tears a piece of his clothes and gives this to the woman who leaves carrying 2 pitchers of water. Whoever helps her unload the pitchers becomes her new husband!

The **Gaduliya Lohars**, named after their beautiful bullock carts (*gadis*), are nomadic blacksmiths, said to have wandered from their homeland of Mewar because of their promise to their 'lord' Maharana Pratap. who was ousted from Chittaurgarh by Akbar. This clan of warring Rajputs, vowed to re-enter the city only after the victory of Maharana Pratap who was, however, unfortunately killed on the battlefield. Despite the late Prime Minister Jawaharlal Nehru's efforts to urge them to return to Chittaurgarh, most of them prefer a nomadic life.

The **Garasias** (under 3% of Rajasthan's tribals), have an interesting custom of marriage through elopement, which usually takes place at the annual Gaur fair held during the full moon in Mar. After the elopement, which can be spontaneous or pre-arranged, a bride price is paid to the bride's father. Should the arrangement not work out, the woman returns home. Widows are forced to remarry, since their children – and not they – are given a share in the husband's property.

The **Sahariyas** are jungle dwellers, their name possibly deriving from the Persian *sehr* (jungle). The Sahariyas are regarded as the most backward tribe in Rajasthan and eke out a living as shifting cultivators and by hunting and fishing. More recently, they have also undertaken menial and manual work on daily wages. In most respects their rituals are those of Hindus. One difference is that polygamy and widow marriage (*nata*) are permitted, though only to a widower or divorcee.

The small tribal community of **Damors** probably migrated N from their original home in Gujarat to settle in Dungarpur and Udaipur districts. They are mainly cultivators and manual labourers.

Religion

Nearly 90% of the population are Hindus, Muslims making up the largest minority. Jainism is also significant and was often tolerated by rulers as it was particularly popular with merchants and traders. Islam extended into Rajasthan with the conquest of Ajmer in the 12th century. The saint Khwajah Mu'inuddin Chishti had his refuge at Ajmer, now a popular pilgrimage place. Sikhs and Christians form a very small minority.

The Aryan invaders were often in conflict with tribal groups and gradually forced most of them back into the remote craggy and forested Aravallis. Successive invasions of the Sakas, Kusanas, Abhiras and Huns affected the region but the aboriginal tribes, whilst assimilating some of the ways and manners of the intruders nevertheless managed to preserve a clearly distinct culture.

Language

The principal language is *Rajasthani*, a close relative of Hindi, the 4 most important dialects being *Marwari* in the W, *Jaipuri* in the E, *Malwi* in the SE and *Mewati* in the NE. *Hindi* is rapidly replacing Rajasthani as the lingua franca.

Crafts

Bandhani This ancient technique of tye-dying is common throughout Rajasthan and Gujarat. The fabric is pinched together in selected places, tied round with twine or thread and then dyed. Afterwards the cords are removed to reveal a pattern in the original or preceding colour (the process can be repeated a number of times on a single piece of fabric so long as the dyeing sequence goes from light to dark colours). The commonly used colours are yellow for fertility and Spring, blue or indigo for Lord Krishna, pale blue for water, and saffron for renunciation.

Lacquered Brassware This is a combination of engraving and lacquering of bowls, dishes, vases, trays and goblets. Many are highly coloured and richly engraved.

Leatherwork Decorated and embroidered camel skin slippers, water bottles, handbags and purses.

Pottery The best known in Rajasthan is the Jaipur blue pottery. This uses a coarse grey clay that is quite brittle even when fired. This is then decorated with floral and geometric patterns along Persian lines utilising rich ultramarines, turquoise and lapis colours on a plain offwhite/grey background. Worth purchasing but a problem to carry. In the villages, the common pot is made from a combination of earth, water and dung. The coarse pots are thrown on a simple stone wheel, partially dried then finished with a hammer before being simply decorated, glazed and fired. Stalls selling these attractive terracotta pots are common in the small towns and villages and whilst quite rough they are incredibly cheap. The tendency nowadays is for villagers to use vessels made of more durable materials, eg aluminium, brass and plastic.

Block-printing This is very popular in Gujarat, Rajasthan and S India. Hand-held wood blocks are carefully cut to enable patterns in different colours to be printed and up to 5 blocks enable very elaborate designs to be finished. The most sophisticated of the designs are very fine indeed and good examples can be seen in the City Museum in Jaipur. Much of the block making is done with great manual dexterity. Children are apprenticed to block makers and printers; they master the craft by the age of 14 or 15. The colours used are traditionally based on vegetable dyes but nowadays, although those running emporia will insist on the authenticity of the process, many use chemical dyes. Printing on the great lengths of cotton is done in a long shed and after the block printing is complete, the fabric will be boiled to make the dye fast. There are places between Jaipur and Amber that demonstrate the technique and tour guides and drivers will be pleased to take you. Just S of Jaipur, **Sanganer** is regarded as the capital of block-printing. Delightfully unspoilt, a trip there is worthwhile (see Excursions from Jaipur).

Khari is embossed printing using gold and silver. Skirt borders, blouses, sari ends and the like can be done, floral patterns being the most common. Other crafts that are practised in Rajasthan are dhurri weaving, screen printing, cotton weaving and paper making.

Miniature paintings (often copies) using natural colours (minerals, rocks & vegetables) executed on paper or silk are becoming very popular. The use of old paper sometimes gives the impression of these 'modern' paintings being authentic antiques. Sometimes whole village families are employed in producing these.

Modern Rajasthan

Government

Recent political developments Before Independence in 1947, the state comprised 18 princely states, 2 chiefships and the small province of Ajmer-Marwar which the British administered. After Independence the princely states were gradually absorbed into the Provinces and then states of the Indian Union. The state assumed its present name and form on 1 Nov 1956. The region still maintains its individuality and the people show a loyalty and respect to the successors of royal families. The palaces, many of them converted to hotels, with varying degrees of success, maintain the memory of princely India. The influence of some of Rajasthan's royal families on politics since Independence has been very strong. Rajasthan now sends 25 members of the Lok Sabha. In 1984 the Congress captured over half the vote and won every seat.

In the 1989 elections there was a resurgence of support for the BJP across Rajasthan, continued in the 1991 elections. The key to the BJP's success was its campaigning on the issue of building a temple on the supposed site of Ram's birthplace at Ayodhya – the Ram Janmabhoomi issue. The recent revival of *sati* in the state has caused widespread controversy. The BJP state government was dismissed by the Central Government in Dec 1992 for the complicity of the BJP nationally with the destruction of the Babri Mosque. State Assembly elections in December 1993 saw a resurgence in support for the Congress at the expense of the Janata Dal and other parties, but the BJP was returned to power by a narrow margin.

Economy

Rajasthan is one of the least densely populated and poorest states in India. Primarily an agricultural and pastoral economy, it does have good mineral resources. Tourism makes a large contribution to the regional economy.

Agriculture The total sown area is about 20 million ha of which about 20% is irrigated. It has a low and erratic rainfall and most of the crops are rainfed: wheat, hardy *bajra* (pearl millet) in the more arid areas; *jowar* (sorghum), maize and pulses (peas, beans and lentils) elsewhere. High Yielding Varieties (HYVs) of rice have been introduced on irrigated land. Cotton is important in the N and S of the state. Rajasthan receives water from the Punjab rivers in the N, the Narmada in the S and from the Gurgaon and Agra canals from Haryana and UP respectively. It shares waters from the Bhakra Dam project with Punjab, and the Chambal Valley project with MP. With improved management techniques over 30% of the sown area could be brought under irrigation. The enormously ambitious Rajasthan canal is working much less efficiently than had originally been planned. Many of the areas too dry for cultivation are none the less used for grazing. Rajasthan has a very large livestock population and is the largest wool producing state. It also breeds camels.

Minerals Rajasthan accounts for India's entire output of zinc concentrates, emeralds and garnets, 94% of its gypsum, 76% of silver ore, 84% of asbestos, 68% of feldspar and 12% of mica. It has rich salt deposits at Sambhar and elsewhere and copper mines at Khetri and Dariba. The white marble favoured by the Mughal builders is mined at Makrana near Jodhpur.

Industries The main industries are textiles, the manufacture of rugs and woollen goods, vegetable oil and dyes. Heavy industry includes the construction of railway rolling stock, copper and zinc smelting. The chemical industry also produces caustic soda, calcium carbides and sulphuric acid, fertiliser, pesticides and insecticides. There is a rapidly expanding light industry which includes precision instrument manufacture at Kota and television assembly. The principal industrial complexes are at Jaipur, Kota, Udaipur and Bhilwara. Traditional handicrafts such as pottery, jewellery, marble work, embossed brass, block printing, embroidery and decorative painting are now very good foreign exchange earners.

Tours

It is certainly worth organising your own tour to see something of rural Rajasthan, quite easily done from several towns. The half-day and full day tours offered in many places are very variable and tend to go on well worn paths. In many villages you can see traditional housing, often simply but beautifully decorated, rural handicrafts and farming.

The best known organised tour is the new spacious broad gauge "Palace on Wheels" which has replaced the old nostalgic train with refurbished carriages belonging to former Maharaja's of the Princely States of India, hauled, over a section by the 'Desert Queen'. It ran for 11 years attracting large numbers of foreign tourists but was discontinued from April 1994. The new train is expected to be more comfortable with a/c coaches, modern facilities including cellular phones.

Scheduled are weekly departures (Wed) from Oct to mid-Apr costing about US $200 per night. The itinerary includes Jaipur and Amber Fort, followed by night travel to Chittaurgarh, Udaipur (*Lake Palace Hotel*), Jaisalmer, Jodhpur (*Umaid Bhawan Palace*) and Bharatpur ending with visits to Fatehpur Sikri, Agra and Delhi. Each saloon has its own sleeping accommodation in 2/4 berth cabins, plus a lounge, kitchenette and mini-bar, bathroom and telephone link with the train superintendent. There are also 2 dining cars serving continental and Indian cuisine and a library/ lounge/ observation car with bar.

For those interested in seeing a great deal in a short space of time and travelling in style in a fair degree of comfort. It is also expensive. On the negative side, it is a whistle-stop tour giving only a

RAJASTHAN'S PALACE HOTELS: A WIDENING CHOICE

Although several other regions in India have magnificent palaces, Rajasthan is widely thought of as the real home of the traditional Maharajas and their often exotic homes. The Lake Palace in Udaipur and the Rambagh Palace in Jaipur are just two which have captured the imagination. In their conversion to hotels they have given visitors the opportunity of sampling briefly something of the now lost lifestyle of the earlier princes. The image of luxury conjured up by such palaces has often been deliberately cultivated, and some of these hotels have become among the best in the world. However, they are also increasingly expensive, and the image they have created of opulence beyond the reach of the few has concealed a rapidly widening range of choice.

The recent designation of the new class of "heritage hotels", in which Rajasthan plays a leading part, highlights some of these developments. Indian palaces are as varied as the princely system of which they were one expression. At Independence in 1947 there were over 500 princely states, many in the region of Rajputana, varying in size from the area of France to that of the smallest English county. In addition there was a 'nobility' of landowners who had been granted priveleges of various kinds, and many of whom had sizeable country estates.

Many of these houses are now being opened to visitors, sometimes simply as hotels, sometimes taking paying guests. Many have all the exotic character of the much more expensive hotels but retain a far greater degree of their original style and charm, and often at incredibly low prices. In Rajasthan it used to seem that if you wanted to stay in a palace you had to pay the price of hotels such as the Jai Mahal, recently superbly re-furbished and presented, or some of the more modern imitations, such as the new Rajputana Palace. Yet those looking for a less aseptically packaged version of the old world can now look to at least half a dozen excellent and very modestly priced hotels in and around Jaipur alone.

Often still family run by their original owners, such palaces retain a character which has often been lost elsewhere. Sympathetic modernisation in palaces such as that at Samode have made it possible to stay comfortably in one of the most beautifully designed and decorated old family castles, itself set in the heart of an apparently largely untouched village. In the far south of the state, the holiday hill station of Mount Abu, with its magnificent Dilwara Jain temples, became the summer resort for Rajas from all over Rajasthan. A number of their summer retreats, such as the Bikaner Palace designed at the end of the 19th century by Sir S.S. Jacob, are often readily accessible despite being off the beaten tourist track, and very modestly priced. Or there are opportunities to see genuinely rural India from a castle such as that at Ghanerao, on the route between Udaipur and Jodhpur. On the edge of a small wildlife reserve, Ghanerao and its outlying lodges offers a remarkable chance to enjoy the peace and quiet of rural Rajasthan while still being surrounded by its colour.

All these developments are making it more attractive than ever to discover comfortably, safely,and enjoyably something of India's regal traditions for as little as Rs 500 a night for a double room.

brief introduction to the places in Rajasthan. On Day 7 for example, you will visit 3 places – Bharatpur Bird Sanctuary, Fatehpur Sikri and Agra. A day in each of these places would allow much better viewing, 2 in the case of Agra. All your time is accounted and you are only able to pursue independent daytime activities if you are prepared to forego the tours. Travelling by night means that you do not see much of the countryside between the cities.

Accommodation Jaipur, Jodhpur and Udaipur are well provided with hotels. Other towns such as Bikaner have a very narrow range. Expect variations in the quality and type of accommodation. Some of the converted palaces (see box) have excellent service and facilities. However, even in the most expensive of the conversions, while some rooms may have excellent views others have little or none. Some places, especially in more remote rural areas, remain very simple. Physical facilities may be rudimentary, and despite efforts at their control, pests like rats are sometimes found. **NB**: if you are carrying food, keep it stored in sealed containers. The Heritage Hotels Assoc, 9 Sardar Patel Marg, C Scheme, Jaipur, T 382214, can supply a list of member hotels which are particularly attractive.

Festivals

Rajasthan celebrates a number of festivals of its own as well as the main Hindu festivals. At the festival of *Urs* in Ajmer, hundreds of Muslim pilgrims congregate at the mosques.

Mid-Jan: The *kite flying festival* in Jaipur is spectacular. **13-15 Feb 1995**: *Desert Festival* at Jaisalmer is essentially a commercial phenomenon with no established tradition. There are camel races, camel polo and desert music and dance. **Mar-Apr**: *Gangaur* in about 2 weeks after Holi is a festival of fertility, see page 406. **Jul-Aug**: *Teej*, a fertility festival celebrating of the reunion of Siva and Parvati, is celebrated at the onset of the monsoon. At Jaipur, there is a big procession with ornately dressed elephants. In the villages everybody seems to join in making music and dancing, and the women wear green striped veils. Women and children play on swings decorated with flowers. **Jul-Aug**: *Nag Panchami*, at Jodhpur, is in honour of the serpent king Naga and women visit the snake charmers for worship. **Nov-Dec**: *cattle and camel fair* at Pushkar, famous.

JAIPUR

Jaipur (City of Victory) was founded in 1727 by Sawai Jai Singh II, the Maharaja of the Kachhwaha clan of Rajputs, who ruled from 1699-1744. Today it has become the most popular tourist destination in Rajasthan, making one corner of the 'Golden Triangle' (Delhi-Jaipur-Agra).

BASICS *Population:* 1.51 mn. *Altitude:* 431m. *STD Code*: 0141.

History

Jai Singh had inherited a kingdom under threat not only from the last great Mughal emperor Aurangzeb but also from the Maratha armies of Gujarat and Maharashtra. Victories over the Marathas and diplomacy with the Aurangzeb won back the favour of the ageing

CLIMATE: JAIPUR

	Jan	Feb	Mar	Apr	May	Jun	Jul	Aug	Sep	Oct	Nov	Dec	Av/Tot
Max (°C)	22	25	31	37	41	39	34	32	33	33	29	24	32
Min (°C)	8	11	15	21	26	27	26	24	23	18	12	9	18
Rain (mm)	14	8	9	4	10	54	193	239	90	19	3	4	647

Mughal so that the political stability Maharaja Jai Singh was instrumental in creating was protected, allowing him to pursue his scientific and cultural interests. Jaipur is very much a product of his intellect and talent.

The charming story of the encounter between the Emperor Aurangzeb and the 10 year old Rajput prince tells of the reply made by the child when asked what punishment he deserved for his family's hostility and resistance to the Mughals. The boy answered 'Your Majesty, when the groom takes the bride's hand, he confers lifelong protection. Now that the Emperor has taken my

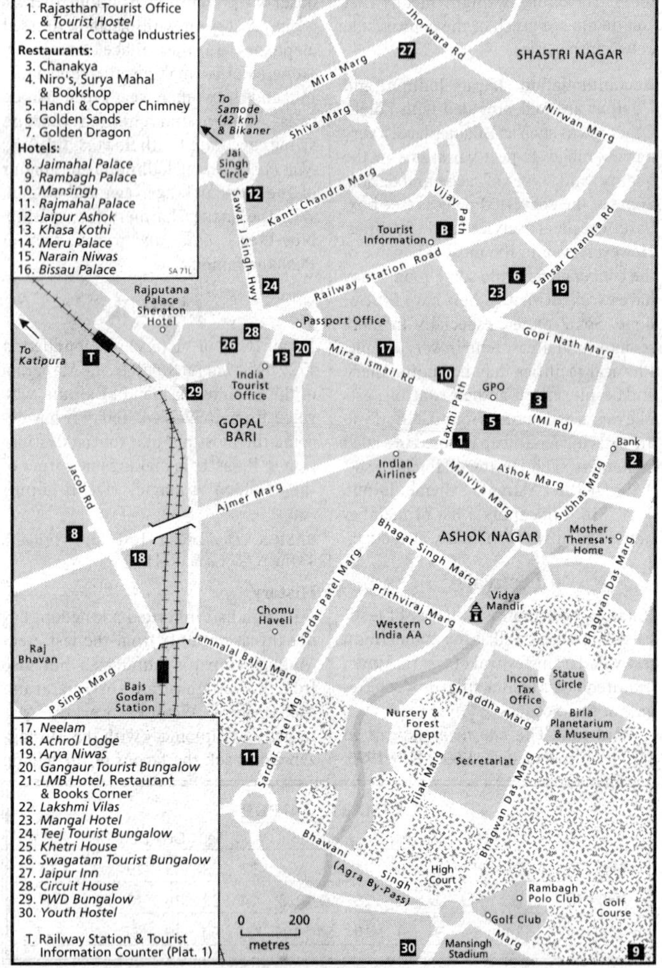

hand, what have I to fear?' Impressed by his tact and intelligence, Aurangzeb bestowed the title of *Sawai* (one and a quarter) on him, signifying that he would be a leader.

Astronomy and science Jai Singh loved mathematics and science. A brilliant Brahmin scholar, Vidyadhar Bhattacharya from Bengal, worked in association with him to design the city. Jai Singh also studied ancient texts on astronomy, had the works of Ptolemy and Euclid translated into Sanskrit, and sent emissaries to Samarkand where Mirza Beg, the grandson of Tamerlane, had built himself an observatory in 1425.

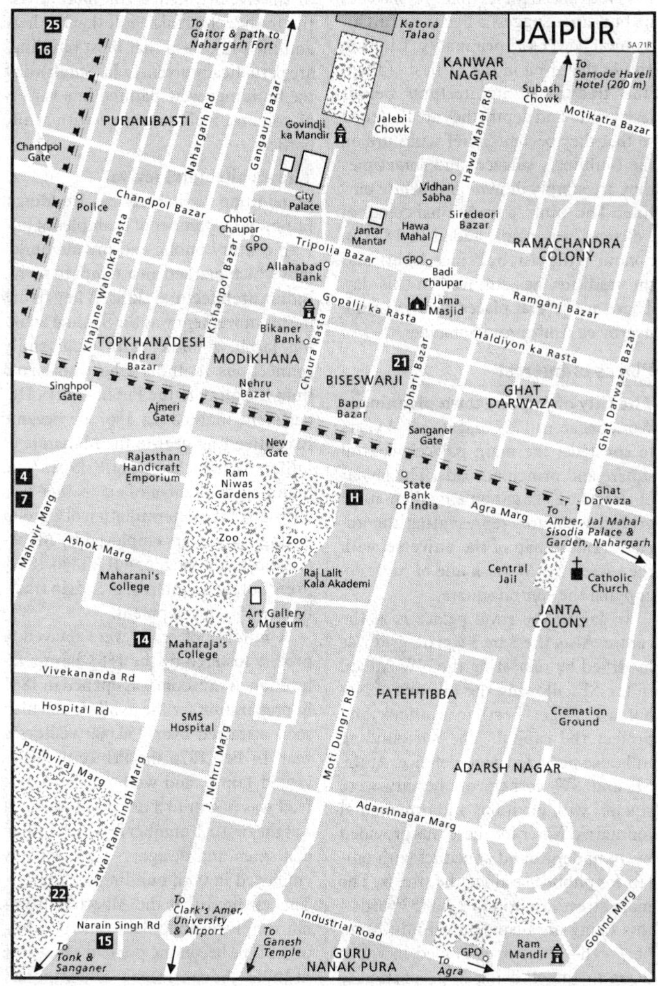

When his throne was secured he spent much of his time studying astronomy, constructing masonry observatories at Delhi, Varanasi, Ujjain and Mathura, and most impressively at Jaipur.

A declining glory? Jaipur is a highly distinctive city. Built with ancient Hindu rules of town planning in mind, it was advanced for its time. Yet many of its buildings suggest a decline in architectural power and originality. Tillotson argues that even in the earliest of them "the traditional architectural details lack vigour and depth; they are flattened so that they become relief sculpture on the building's surface, and sometimes they are simply drawn on in white outline". The 'pink', a traditional colour of welcome, was paint, added in 1853 in honour of the visit by Prince Albert, and the tradition has survived to this day. There are several places worth visiting nearby eg Amber and Sanganer.

Places of interest

The City of Jaipur – town planning

Work began in 1727 and it took 4 years to construct the main palaces, central square and principal roads. The layout of streets was based on a mathematical grid of 9 squares representing the ancient Hindu map of the universe, with the sacred Mt Meru, home of Siva, occupying the central square.

In Jaipur the royal palace is at the centre. Also, the 3 by 3 square grid was modified by relocating the NW square in the SE, allowing the hill fort of Nahargarh (Tiger Fort) to overlook and protect the capital. The surrounding hills also provided good defence. At the SE and SW corners of the city were squares with pavilions and ornamental fountains. Water for these was provided by an underground aqueduct with outlets for public use along the streets. The main streets are wide – 30m (33 yards – this being an auspicious Hindu number) – the lesser ones graded in width down to 4m, all being in proportion to one another. The sidewalks were deliberately wide to promote the free flow of pedestrian traffic and the shops were also a standard size.

Jaipur differs from most Indian cities which were subject to haphazard growth; here town planning was carefully practiced. The result is a highly distinctive city, made all the more attractive by the colourful people that live here and the pink wash that most buildings are periodically given. In Jai Singh's day, the buildings were painted in a variety of colours, including grey with white borders.

The architectural revival

In addition to its original buildings, Jaipur has a number of examples of late 19th century public and private buildings which marked an attempt to revive Indian architectural skills. A key figure in this movement was Sir Samuel Swinton Jacob, a soldier with long family connections in India who transferred from the army to the Public Works Department in 1862. In 1867 he became Executive Engineer to the Maharaja of Jaipur, living there until 1902. The founding of a school of art in 1866 was one sign of the determination of a group of English officers employed by Maharaja Sawai Madho Singh II (r1880-1922) to encourage an interest in Indian tradition and its development.

A number of crafts were revived, a process fostered by the 1883 Jaipur exhibition. A museum was opened in 1881 in preparation for the exhibition which soon attracted over 250,000 visitors a year. In Feb 1876 the Prince of Wales visited Jaipur, and work on the Albert Hall was begun to a design of Jacob. It was the first of a number in which Indian craftsmen and designers were actively employed in both building and design. This ensured that the Albert Hall was not simply an Indo-Saracenic building of the type becoming popular elsewhere in India, though Jacob's contemporary

De Fabek did build the Mayo Hospital in the same style. However, the new opportunities for training provided under Jacob's auspices encouraged a new school of Indian architects and builders. One of the best examples of their work is the Mubarak Mahal (1900), designed by Lala Chiman Lal, director of the State Department responsible for palace buildings.

Jantar Mantar (Observatory)

Literally "Instruments for measuring the harmony of the heavens", the Jantar Mantar was built between 1728 and 1734. Not content with brass, Jai Singh wanted things on a grand scale and chose stone with a marble facing on the important planes. Each of the instruments serves a particular function and each gives an accurate reading. The observatory is a fascinating and attractive site to walk round, but it gets extremely hot in the middle of the day. Clockwise they are:

1. Small Samrat Yantra This is a large sundial (the triangular structure) with flanking quadrants marked off in hours and minutes. The arc on your left will show the time from sunrise to midday, the one on the right midday to sundown. Read the time where the shadow is sharpest. The sundials are constructed on Lat. 27 degrees N (Jaipur's Lat.) and give solar time. To adjust the reading to Indian Standard Time (IST), between 1 min 15 secs to 32 mins must be added according to the time of year and solar position. There is a board indicating the right adjustment.

2. Dhruva Yantra locates the position of the Pole Star at night and those of the 12 zodiac signs. The graduation and lettering is in Hindi and is based on a different system to that employed nowadays. The traditional unit of measurement is the human breath calculated to be of 6 seconds duration. Thus: 4 breaths = 1 pala (24 secs), 60 palas = 1 gati (24 mins), 60 gatis = 1 day (24).

3. Narivalya Yantra sundial with 2 dials: S facing for when the sun is in the S hemisphere (Sept 21 – Mar 21) and the N facing for the rest of the year. At noon the sun falls on the N-S line. The time is read in the normal way.

4. Observer's Seat (Jai Singh's).

5. Small Kranti Yantra, used for the direct measurement of the longitude and latitude of the celestial bodies.

6. Raj Yantra (King of Instruments). Used once a year to calculate the Hindu calendar, all the details of which are based on the Jaipur Standard as they have been for 250 years. A telescope is attached over the central hole. The back of the Yantra is fitted with a bar for sighting purposes. The plain disk is used as a blackboard to record observations.

7. Unnathamsa Yantra is used for finding the altitudes of the celestial bodies. Round the clock observations can be made and the sunken steps allow any part of the dial to be read.

8. Disha Yantra points to the North.

9. Dakshina Yantra, a wall aligned along the N-S meridian and used for observing the position and movement of heavenly bodies when passing over the meridian.

10. Large Samrat Yantra. Operating on the same principle as the Small one (1) but 10 times larger and thus accurate to 2 secs. instead of 20 secs. The sundial is 27.4m high and the observer climbs the steps to make the reading. This instrument is used on guru purnima, a particularly holy full moon in Jul/Aug, to predict the length and heaviness of the monsoon for the local area.

11. Rashivalayas Yantra. Twelve sundials for the signs of the zodiac and operated in the same way as the Samrat Yantras. The instruments enable readings to be made at the instant each zodiacal sign crosses the meridian. Hindus embrace the universe and believe that their fated souls move to its rhythms. The matching of horoscopes is still an

FAMILY HOUSES OF JAIPUR

The design of the houses recognised the joint family as the common social unit. The normal building was the *haveli* (originally Persian for 'enclosed space'), a 3 to 5-storeyed house built around a shaded communal courtyard. To counter the heat and glare, the shops and houses were deep rather than broad. Large eaves and awnings provided shade. An outer gate and walls provided security and privacy, thus clearly delineating the private from the public world.

A number of havelis usually formed a *mohalla* (district) and about 400 of these a *chokra* (section). Each district housed a particular trade, reflecting the occupational divisions existing in Indian society. Muslim jewel cutters still live in Johori Bazaar, marble workers in Chandpol Bazaar and Hindu cloth merchants in Nehru Bazaar. Originally, an area known as Brahmapuri housed royal scholars and priests.

essential part in the marriage arrangements and the selection of partners. Astrologers occupy an important place in day to day life and are consulted for all occasions and decision-making.

12. Small Ram Yantra. A smaller version and a similar purpose.

13. Jai Prakash Yantra. This acts as a double check on all the other instruments. It measures the rotation of the sun and the 2 hemispheres together form a map of the heavens. The small iron plate strung between grosswires indicates the sun's longitude and latitude and which sign of the zodiac it is passing through.

14. Chakra Yantra. This gives the angle of an object from the equator.

15. Large Ram Yantra. As with the Small Ram Yantra (12), this is used to find the altitude and the azimuth (arc of the celestial great circle from Zenith to horizon).

16. Diganta Yantra. Another instrument for measuring the azimuth of any celestial body.

17. Large Kranti Yantra. The same as the Small Kranti Yantra (5).

The City Palace (1728-1732) and Nahargarh

The city palace occupies the centre of Jaipur, covers 1/7th of its area and is surrounded by a high wall. Entry Rs 20, Camera Rs 10 (doorkeepers expect tips when photographed). Entering by the main gate you find yourself in a large courtyard with a building in the centre. This was the **Guest Pavilion** and has a very attractive white marble frontage. On the 1st Fl is the **Textile and Costume Museum**. When Jai Singh moved his court from Amber to the new palace, 4 out of the 36 imperial departments were devoted to costumes and textiles. In this collection are fine examples of fabrics and costumes from all over India as well as musical instruments and toys from the royal nursery.

In the NW corner of the courtyard is the **Arms and Armour Museum** containing an impressive array of weaponry – pistols, blunderbusses, flintlocks, swords, rifles and daggers. This was originally the common room of the harem. Moving now to the gate to your right after leaving the museum you come to the gates to the inner courtyard. The gate itself is flanked by 2 elephants each carved from a single block of marble. Behind these are beautifully carved alcoves with delicate arches and jali screens. There is a fine pair of patterned brass doors.

Hall of Private Audience

Once through this fine gateway, directly opposite you and in the centre of the courtyard is the large Hall (c1730). In it are 2 huge silver urns. Sawai Madho Singh, the present Maharaja's grandfather was an extremely devout Hindu. Any physical contact with a non-Hindu was deemed to be ritually defiling, so any contact with the British carried awkward ritual problems. Whenever required to meet a Britisher, including the Viceroy, the Maharaja would wear white gloves, and after any meeting would ritually purify himself in a bath of Ganga water and have the clothes he wore burnt. When he went to England to celebrate Queen Victoria's Diamond Jubilee he had a P&O liner refitted to include a Krishna temple and carried sufficient Ganga water with him, in these two 309 kg urns, to last the trip. Sawai Singh's picture is beyond the Krishna door.

Art gallery & museum

Entrance in the right hand corner of the inner courtyard. This was the Hall of Public Audience (c1760). Today it houses a picture gallery with a fine collection of Persian and Indian miniatures, some of the carpets the Maharajas had made for them and an equally fine collection of manuscripts. Across the courtyard you enter through the **Ganesh Pol** to the **zenana** and the 7 storey palace of the Maharaja. In this courtyard are some extremely attractive doors, rich and vivid in their peacock blue, aquamarine, amber and other colours. Each doorway has a small marble figure of a Hindu god watching over it.

Chandra Mahal

In the NE corner of the courtyard is the Krishna door, its surface embossed with scenes of the deity's life. The door is sealed in the traditional way with a rope sealed with wax over the lock. Near this and along the corridor is the portrait of Sawai Madho Singh mentioned above. Along the NE side of the zenana courtyard is the **Chandra Mahal** (c1724-34) with its **Chamber of the Privy Council** where the Maharaja would sit in consultation with his ministers. The early 18th Century Govindeoji Temple, which was probably built as a residence, has been restored by an ancient technique using molasses, curd, coconut water, fenugreek, rope fibres and lime.

The furniture is European – Bohemian glass chandeliers, furniture – the decoration Indian. Following the steps around you will see a *mandala* (circular diagram of the cosmos), made from rifles around the royal crest of Jaipur. The ceiling of this hall is in finely worked gold. Further on are the beautiful Mughal style fountains and the Jai Niwas gardens (1727), laid out as a *charbagh*. The view extends across to the Maharaja's private Krishna temple and beyond the compound walls to the Nahargarh (Tiger Fort) on the hills beyond.

Hawa Mahal

Forming part of the E wall of the palace complex and best seen from the street outside the palace, is this 'Palace of the Winds' (c1799). Possibly Jaipur's most famous building, this is in part simply a pink sandstone facade. Built for the ladies of the harem by Sawai Pratap Singh, the 5-storeys stand on a high podium with an entrance from the W. It contains 953 small casements in a huge curve, each with a balcony and crowning arch. The windows enabled cool air (hence the name) to circulate and the ladies to watch processions below without being seen.

Mubarak Mahal

Originally a guest house for the Maharaja and now part of the Palace Museum, Mubarak Mahal is a small 2-storied building S of the palace, immediately opposite the Jantar Mantar. It is designed on the same cosmological plan in miniature as the city itself – a square divided into 9 x 3 square grid. Tillotson suggests that the "greater beauty of the design derives from the delicacy and depth of the façades...achieved by a number of devices: by the variation in the basic plan, with a verandah projecting in the centre of each side; by the cantilevered balconies, which project yet further; by the roof parapet, which rises above those balconies but is separated from them by a deep recession; by the pierced balustrade and the open arcade of the upper gallery. The open space above each arch in the gallery, an arrangement copied from traditional courtyard houses in the city," he goes on "make the building's roof appear to float weightlessly above it. The lightness and the depth are typically Rajput features."

Nahargarh (Tiger Fort, 1734)
Small entry fee. The small fort stands guard over Jaipur, on a sheer rockface nearly 2 km from the city centre, dominating the skyline. The immense walls and bastions are well preserved. You have to walk 1.5 km up a winding path or take an auto rickshaw to reach the top. Beautifully floodlit at night. Much of the original fort is in ruins but 19th century additions survive including rooms furnished for maharajas . This is a ' real fort' – not busy, so very pleasant. Visit rec. You can get excellent views of the city from Rajasthan Tourism *Durg* café which sells snacks and drinks (in 1994, the café had little to offer and had very slow service). Nice walk back to the main Jaipur road.

You can combine this visit with the Jaigarh Fort, 6 km away, (part of the same defensive network), along the flat-topped hill. A good road, originally a military one, connects the 2. A covered aquaduct brought water to Jaigarh over the same distance. Taxis available or you can walk.

Museums
Man Singh II Museum, City Palace. 0930-1645. Closed on holidays. Rs 20. Excellent display of paintings, miniatures, textiles, costumes, armoury, maps, objects from royal court (16th-19th centuries). Incl gigantic silver vessels to carry Ganga water for the Maharaja's visit to England. **Central Museum**, Albert Hall, Ram Nivas Gardens. 1030-1630. Closed Fri, Mon free. Re 1. Mainly excellent metal ware displaying techniques of decoration and miniature portraits among other art pieces in beautiful building. Also Rajasthani village life displayed through costumes, pottery, woodwork, brassware etc. Gallery of Modern Art nearby. SRC **Museum of Indology**, 'Nilambara', Prachya Vidya Path, 24 Gangwal Park. 0900-1800. Collection of folk and tantra art incl mss, textiles, paintings. **Dolls Museum**. Small entry fee. **Hawa Mahal Museum**, closed Fri. Small entry fee. Mon free.

Parks & zoos
Zoological Garden, Ram Niwas Gardens. Entry Re 1. Crocodile farm.

Tours
Rajasthan Tourism: dep Tourist Office, Platform 1, Rly Station. *City Sightseeing, half day*: 0800-1400, 1130-1730, 1300-1900, Central Museum, City Palace, Amber Fort and Palace, Gaitore, Nawab ki Haveli, Jantar Mantar, Jal Mahal, Hawa Mahal. Rs 40; *City Sightseeing, full day*: 0900-1800, incl places above plus Nahargarh Fort, Indology Museum, Dolls Museum, Galta, Sisodia Rani Garden. *Jaigarh Tour*: 1430-1900, Gaitore, Jaigarh, Nahargarh, Jal Mahal. **Ashok Travels and Tours** offers City Sightseeing, half day. Full day, Rs 50.

Local festivals
All the Hindu festivals are celebrated plus: *Makar Sankranti* (**14 Jan**) the kite flying festival is spectacular. Everything closes down in the afternoon and kites are flown from every rooftop, street and even from bicycles! The object is to bring down other kites, attempted to the deafening cheers of huge crowds. See page 291. During *Holi* (**Mar/Apr**), the festival of colours, elephants process in fancy dress. *Gangaur* (Mar/Apr). Ishar and Gangaur are the mythical man and wife who embody marital harmony. The Gangaur festival is held about a fortnight after Holi in honour of Parvati, the consort of Siva. Colourfully dressed

young women carrying brass pitchers on their heads make their way through the streets to the temple of Gauri (another name for Parvati). Here they ceremonially bathe the deity who is then decked with flowers. The women pray for husbands 'such as the one you have been blessed with', and the long life of their husbands. The festival ends with rejoicing for it is also believed that if a woman is unhappy while she sings she will be landed with an ill-tempered husband. The festivities are concluded when Siva arrives, accompanied by elephants, to escort his bride Gauri home.

Teej (**Jul/Aug**) welcomes the monsoon rains to the parched land. The women dress in bright costumes and flock to swings hung from the branches of trees. There is a procession of Parvati through towns and villages signifying her departure from the parental home to take up residence with her husband Siva. The special celebrations in Jaipur have elephants, camels and dancers joining in the processions.

Local information

● Accommodation

Price guide
AL Rs 3,000+ **A** Rs 2,000-3,000
B Rs 1,200-2,000 **C** Rs 600-1,200
D Rs 250-600 **E** Rs 100-250 **F** Up to Rs 100.

Palace and *Haveli* hotels have character; some are reasonably priced. **Note** MG Rd is Mahatma Gandhi Rd, MI Rd is Mirza Ismail Rd, MD Rd is Moti Dungri Rd. **AL** Taj *Jaimahal Palace,* Jacob Rd, Civil Lines, T 68381, F 65237. 120 rm. Tennis, horse riding. Imaginative hotel development around small palace (completely refurbished in 1991). The highest quality rooms, good restaurants and excellent service but snack bar inadequate. Gardens especially lovely. **AL** *Rajputana Palace Sheraton*, Palace Rd, T 360011, F 367848. Very modern *haveli*-style 220 rm luxury hotel, set around 6 royal *chowks* (courtyards), a lush garden, and an open courtyard for live entertainment. Vast impersonal Jaigarh lobby (evoking the fort) but immaculate standards. **AL** Taj *Rambagh Palace*, Bhawani Singh Rd, T 541241, F 521098. 110 rm. Maharaja Ram Singh's (1835-80) hunting lodge. Extensively modified by Madhu Singh II (1880-1922). Some excellent rm (royal suites), others can be cramped. Rms in main palace overlooking garden better than in new wing – choose by arriving early. Sometimes hosts large tour groups. Good food, superb gardens, good shops.

A *Mansingh*, Sansar Chandra Rd. T 78771. 100 rm. Rooftop restaurant (lunchtime buffet), highly rec. Central – excellent location for shopping. Modern. Open-air theatre, good puppet show. No garden or pool. **A** Taj *Rajmahal Palace,* Sardar Patel Marg, T 521676. 11 rm. Once the British Residency. Limited facilities include restaurant, bar, exchange. **A** *Clarks Amer,* J Nehru Marg, T 550616. 118 rm. 8 km centre. All amenities, less 'exotic' since it didn't start out as a palace. Tall building in the middle of the desert, with friendly service, good shops, garden and pool. Food occasionally inspired ('Tourist menu' boring), but rm a/c erratic. A favourite with tour groups. **A** *Jaipur Ashok*, (ITDC), Jai Singh Circle, Bani Park, T 75121. 99 rm. Modern, quite comfortable but unimaginative. Good food. Given the alternatives, not the best value.

C *Samode Haveli*, Gangapol, NE of city, T 42407. 20 rm in charming 19th century *haveli*, with beautiful decorations, magnificent dining room. Good views over city at dawn and sunset, from above. Outstanding value. **C** *Khasa Kothi*, MI Rd. T 75151. 36 rm, some a/c. 1 km rly. Restaurant (mediocre), bar, helpful Tourist Office, exchange, pool. Govt run with most rm in need of attention and unsatisfactory service. Lawns and quiet location small compensation. **C** *Meru Palace*, Sawai Ram Singh Rd. T 61212, F 563767. 48 rm. 1 km centre. Veg restaurant, coffee shop, bar, shops, exchange. New marble building, not a palace but pleasant. **C** *Narain Niwas*, Kanota Bagh, Narain Singh Rd. T 563448. 24 rm, some a/c. Indian restaurant, pleasant 1st Fl courtyard, pool. Narain Singh's *haveli* with many 19th century regal trappings – huge rooms, some rather dark, but full of character. Rec.

Some interesting reasonably priced places: **D** *Bissau Palace*, Chandpol Gate. T 310371/320191, F 317628. Heritage Hotel. 30 rm, individual a/c. 1 km centre. Restaurant, pool, shops, library and royal museum. Built in 1919, home of the Rawal of Bissau, with superb public rooms, lovely decor (flags, guns, swords on the walls); right at foot of Nahargarh Fort walls. Delightful atmosphere, excellent service, very highly rec. **D** *Diggi Palace*, Hospital Rd behind *Meru Palace*, T 74265. Pleasant rm, cottages (Rs 150). Good restaurant. Rec. **D** *Megh Niwas*, C9 Jai Singh Highway, Bani Park, T 74018. 20 rm. **D** *Neelam*, Motilal Atal Rd. T 77773. 52 rm, some a/c with TV. Veg restaurant, shops. Decor may not be to your liking! **D** *Achrol Lodge*, Civil Lines, T 72254. 6 rm. Breakfast and Indian evening meals, exchange, lawns. **D** *Arya Niwas*, Sansar Chandra Rd, behind Amber Towers. T 73456. 60 rm. Good veg restaurant, exchange, travel. Part of hotel was an old palace, now modernised. Clean, friendly and helpful management. Rec. Rajasthan Tourism **D** *Gangaur Tourist Bungalow*, MI Rd, T 60231. 63 rm, some a/c. Restaurant, good coffee shop, travel. Convenient for bus and rly. **D** *Rajasthan Palace*, 3 Peshwa Gardens, Moti Doongri Rd. Pool garden. Reasonable rm but could be cleaner, very poor restaurant (hire car drivers receive commission). Not rec.

D *LMB*, Johari Bazar in Old City, T 565844. 33 rm, some a/c in incongruous, modern building. Excellent veg restaurant, travel, exchange. Monkeys may be a nuisance! **D** *Lakshmi Vilas*, Sawai Ram Singh Rd, T 521567. 21 rm, some a/c. Indian veg restaurant, travel. Quiet. large open grassy court. **D** *Mangal*, Sansar Chandra Rd, T 75126. 65 rm, some a/c. 1 km rly. Veg restaurant, bar, travel. Roof terrace with nightly barbecue. **D** *Kaiser-i-Hind*, off MI Rd, nr Station, has large rm and good management. **D** *Natraj*, Motilal Atal Rd, nr *Man Singh*, T 61348. 19 rm, some a/c. Restaurant, travel. Good veg. restaurant. **D** *Teej Tourist Bungalow*, Collectorate Rd, nr bus and rly, T 74206. 48 rm, some a/c. Restaurant, bar, travel. **D** *Mandawa House*, D 257 Devi Marg, Bani Park, T 77293, F 67760. Old haveli. 18 rm. Air cooled, rm service, good location.

● Budget hotels

E *Broadway*, Agra Rd, T 41765. 22 rm, some a/c. 2 km centre. Restaurant, coffee shop. **E** *Kantichandra Palace*, Station Rd, T 60973. Some rm with bath in an interesting old palace. Restaurant, very pleasant garden, central. A bit run down but clean. Rec. **E** *Rose*, B6 Subhash Nagar, Chandpol Gate, T 77422. Clean rm and dorm. Quiet location with small garden. Meals available. **E** *Khetri House*, outside Chandpol Gate. T 69183. 16 a/c rm in large old palace, not always clean. Restaurant, large gardens, a lot of potential, but property under dispute. Cannot be rec until ownership clarified. **E** *Purohit*, 16 Vanathali Marg, T 61974. 27 rm, TV in some. Indian veg food. **E** *Rajdeep*, Farsoia Market, Bapu Bazar, T 49141. 37 rm, non a/c. Restaurant (Indian, Continental). Rajasthan Tourism **E** *Swagatam Tourist Bungalow*, Station Rd, T 67560. 35 rm. Restaurant, tours. Not rec. Rajasthan Tourism **E** *Tourist Hostel*, MI Rd, T 69013. Rm with bath. Restaurant, tours. **E** *Jaipur Inn*, Bani Park, off Shiv Marg, T 66057. Has been popular and good value, some reports of deterioration. Camping available. **E** *Ever Green Guest House*, Chameliwala Market, opp GPO, MI Rd, T 63446. Good restaurant, travel, garden. Clean rm on new 1st Flr, with showers; others not rec. Reported as not taking Indian visitors.

F *City Centre*, nr Sindi Camp Bus Station. Rickshaws reluctant to go (no commission). Good size, clean room, Western toilet, hot showers. Good value. **F** *Shakuntala*, 157 Durga Marg, Bani Park, T 79225. Family run new guest house, attentive service. Meals available. **F** *Marhudara*, nr Jaipur Inn. Garden. Friendly service, restaurant. Rec. *Rly Retiring Rooms*. The *Youth Hostel*, T 67576, is some way out of town. Discounts for YHA members.

● Camping

D *Achrol Lodge* (see above). Toilet and power connections in large lawns in peaceful setting. **E** *Jaipur Inn*, Bani Park, Shiv Marg, Bani Park. T 66057. See above.

● Places to eat

The following hotels serve very good veg meals: *LMB* with sweets and *kulfis* outside, *Natraj*, *Meru Palace* and *Mangal*.

Restaurants on MI Rd: outside hotels, Indian veg food is highly rec at *Chanakya* and at open-air, canteen style *Handi*, Maya Mansion; *Copper Chimney* (formerly Kwality, and with the same staff) for good, generous helpings; *Chandralok* offers Rajasthani specialities; *Niros* is good with pleasant decor, but more pricey; for inexpensive Indian vegetarian, *Surya Mahal* next door, is rec (try *paneer butter masala*; *Golden Dragon*, Arvind Marg, by Niro, does Chinese; *Atithi* and *Deluxe* do good snacks and confectionery. *Indian Coffee House*, 200m from Kishon Pol, lacks atmosphere but is good value for light meals. *Golden Sand*, Sansar Ch Rd, opp Amber Towers, offers a wide choice.

● Theme villages

On the outskirts, these provide an alternative setting for sampling local veg cuisine (Rs 50).

Choki Dhani 19 km is one which has recreated a 'bazar' atmosphere and offers local entertainment (folk songs, dances, puppet shows) and has a folklore collection. ***Apna Gaon*** on the Jaipur-Sikar Rd, is similar (claims to be more authentic) and *The Village* nr Sanganer airport (Rs 60) has a wider veg menu. Nahargarh Fort's *Durg* café combines sightseeing (see above).

● Banks

Several branches on MI Rd, open 1000-1400, 1430-1630. State Bank of India, International Div outside Sanganeri Gate, not very high tech. Much easier and quicker to change TCs in hotel; rates are very similar.

● Entertainment

Ravindra Rang Manch, Ram Niwas Garden, T 47061, sometimes hosts cultural programmes and music shows. There are also theme villages on the outskirts – see under excursions below for details.

● Hospitals & medical services

SMS, T 72222. Santokba Durlabhji, T 68251.

● Post & Telegraph

Offices on MI Rd. Rly Mail Service, Jaipur Rly Station.

● Shopping

Bazars: the traditional bazars and small shops are well worth a visit; cheaper than MI Rd shops but do not accept credit cards. Most open 1030-1930. ***Bapu Bazar*** (closed Mon) specialises in printed cloth, ***Johari*** (Goldsmiths) ***Bazar*** (closed Tues) for jewellery and ***Khajanewalon-ka-Rasta*** off Chandpol bazar, for marble and stone ware. Try ***Maniharon-ka-Rasta*** for lac bangles which the city is famous for, ***Tripolia Bazar*** at the 3 gates for inexpensive jewellery and ***Chaupar*** and ***Nehru Bazars*** for textiles. ***Ramganj Bazar*** has leather footwear while opp ***Hawa Mahal*** you will find the famous featherweight Jaipuri *rezais* (quilts).

Antiques: In Chomu Haveli *Art Palace* specialises in 'ageing' newly crafted items – alternatives to antiques; also found around *Hawa Mahal*. Fabrics & Handicrafts: Jaipur also specialises in printed cotton, handicrafts, carpets and durries, along the Amber Rd. Also embroidered leather footwear and blue pottery. Try ***Rajasthali***, Rajasthan Govt Handicrafts, MI Rd, Ajmeri Gate. ***Handloom House***, Rituraj Bldg, MI Rd. ***Handloom Haveli***, Lalpura House, Sansar Chandra Rd (various handloom emporia under one roof). ***Rajasthan Fabrics & Arts*** between City Palace gate and the nearby temple for exquisite textiles. ***The Reject Shop***, Bhawani Singh Rd, for 'Shyam Ahuja' durrie collections. You may also watch ***Durrie*** weavers at ***Art Age***, Plot 2, Bhawani Singh Rd. ***Kripal Kumbha***, B-18, Shiv Marg, Bani Park, T 62227, for the world famous exclusive blue pottery. ***Ambika***, Naila House, MD Rd.; ***Art India***, B-180, Mangal Marg, and ***Neeta***, B-50 Ganesh Marg, Bapu Nagar and ***Anokhi***, 2 Tilak Marg, opp Udyog Bhawan (for block-printed cloth, clothing, linen and jewellery). ***Silk Road Bazar***, out-of-town on Amber Rd, is an expensive craft centre, a favourite of tourist coach drivers. Not rec.

Jewellery: Jaipur is famous for its jewellery and gem stones (particularly emeralds, rubies, sapphires and diamonds, but the last requires special ceritification for export). *Kundan* work uses uncut gemstones to set in gold and *meenakari* enamelling which often complements the setting on the reverse side of the pendant, locket or earring. **Note** For a fee (about Rs 30) you can have gems valued at the *Gem Testing Laboratory* nr New Gate. *Gem Palace* and *Lall Gems and Jewels* on MI Rd and ***Beg Gems***, Mehdi-ka-Chowk, nr Hawa Mahal, are rec. You may be able to see craftsmen at work in Johari Bazar (closed on Tues), especially in ***Gopalji-ki-Rasta***, between nos 264 and 268, at ***Bhuramal Rajmal Surana*** in ***Haldiyon ka Rasta***. Similar work on silver and semi-precious stones, is more affordable; however, sterling silver items are rare in India and the content varies widely. For Silverware: ***Amrapali Silver Shop***, Chameliwala Market, opp GPO, MI Rd. ***Arun's Emporium***, MI Rd.***Balaji's***, Siredeori Bazar (off Johari Bazar). ***Silver and Art Palace***, and ***Manglam Arts***, both on Amber Rd. The latter also sells modern miniature paintings; also sold at ***Mona Lisa***, Hawa Mahal Rd and ***Nawalgarh Haveli***, nr Amber Fort Bus Stop.

Books: *Book Corner*, MI Rd by Niro's Restaurant, has a good selection ***Arvind, Best Books*** and ***Usha*** are W of Chaura Rasta. Photography: *Tak Studio*, Chaura Rasta. ***Pictorials***, MI Rd.

● Sports

Most hotels will arrange golf, tennis, riding and squash. Polo enjoys a special place in the city's life: Spring (Mar) is the polo season when 5 polo tournaments are held. Matches are organised at Polo Ground nr Rambagh Palace. Just before the *Holi* festival in the spring, you may even see elephant polo!

● **Tour companies & travel agents**
Sita World Travel, Station Rd. ***Travel House***, Rajputana Palace Hotel. ***Rajasthan Tours***, Rambagh Palace. ***Karwan Tours***, Bissau Palace Hotel, Chandpol Gate; very helpful. ***Mayur Travels***, 10 Park St, off MI Rd. ***Rajasthan Travel Service***, Station Rd, T 65408. ***Aravalli Safari and Tours***, MI Rd.

● **Tourist offices**
Govt of India (T 72200) and Ashok Travels and Tours (ITDC) T 68461, *Hotel Khasa Kothi*. Very helpful. Dept of Tourism, Art & Culture, 100 JL Nehru Marg, T 73873. **Rajasthan**, *Tourist Hostel*, MI Rd, T 370180. Counters at rly station and Sindhi Camp Central Bus Stand.

● **Useful addresses**
Police: T 100. **Fire**: T 101. **Ambulance**: T 102. **Foreigners' Registration Office**: Hazari Garden, behind Hawa Mahal.

● **Transport**
Jaipur is on **NH8** (Delhi-Ahmadabad-Bombay) and **NH11** (Agra-Bikaner) and is connected to all parts of India by black top roads. Some distances from Jaipur are: **Calcutta**, 1472 km; **Bombay**, 1176 km; **Bhopal**, 735 km.

Local Bus: city buses in and around Jaipur, fares low. **Taxis**: tourist taxis available, but no yellow top taxis. 4 hr Rs 300 (40 km), 8 hr Rs 480 (city and Amber). Out of city Rs 4 per km. Other transport includes **3-wheelers**, **cycle rickshaws** (which are not always well-maintained), **tongas** and **mini buses**. **Coach and car hire**: *ITDC*, Hotel Khasa Kothi, T 65451. Rajasthan Tourism, *Gangaur Tourist Bungalow*, T60231-8. *Rajasthan Tours*, Hotel Rambagh Palace, T 76041. *Travel House*, Hotel Mansingh, T 78771.

Air Sanganer airport is 13 km away. **Transport to town**: taxi transfer takes about ½ hr, Rs 125. ***Indian Airlines***, Nehru Pl, Tonk Rd, T 74500; Airport, T 550222. **Delhi**, Daily, 1020, 2120, 40 min; **Jodhpur**, daily, 1820,(¾ hr); **Udaipur**, daily, 0720 (¾ hr), 1820 (1¾ hr); **Aurangabad**, daily, 0710, 2hr 20min); **Bombay**, daily, 0710 & 1820,, 2hr 20 min. ***East West Airlines*** Bombay, daily exc. Mon, 2035, 1½hr.

Train Old Delhi: *Pink City Exp*, 2902, daily, 1700, 5¼ hr; *Delhi Mail*, 9902, daily, 0030, 7 hr; *Chetak Exp*, 9616, daily, 0645, 7½ hr; *Ashram Exp*, 2906, daily, 0435, 5½ hr. **Agra Fort**: *Agra Fort Fast Passenger Exp*, 9706, daily, 0100, 6½ hr; *Barmer-Agra Exp*, 9708, daily, 0730, 12 hr; *Jaipur-Agra Fort Exp*, 2922, daily, 0610, 4¾ hr. **Ahmadabad**: *Ashram Exp*, 2905, daily, 2345, 11½ hr; *Ahmadabad Exp*, 9903, daily, 1750, 16¼ hr; *Ahmadabad Mail*, 9901, daily, 0500, 4¼ hr. **Bharatpur**: *Marudgar exp*, 5314, daily, 1355, 4 hr; *Agra Fort Fast Passenger Exp*, 9706, daily, 0100, 4½ hr; *Jaipur-Agra Fort Exp*, 2922, daily, 0610, 3¼ hr. **Bikaner**: *Bikaner Exp*, 4737, daily, 2105, 10 hr. **Indore**: *Meenakshi Exp*, 7569, daily, 1350, 15 hr. **Chittaurgarh**: *Meenakshi Exp*, 7569, daily except Sun, 1350, 7½ hr; *Garib Nawaz Exp*, 2915, daily, 1125, 6½ hr; *Chetak Exp*, 9615, daily, 2055, 8¼ hr. *Mt Abu Ahmadabad Exp*, 9903, daily, 1750, 11 hr; *Ahmadabad Mail*, 9901, daily, 0500, 10¼ hr. **Jodhpur**: *Mandore Exp*, 2461, daily, 2345, 6 hr; *Agra-Barmar Exp*, 9707, daily, 2230, 7¾ hr; *Marudhar Exp*, 5313, daily, 1415, 7¼ hr. **Udaipur**: *Garib Nawaz Exp*, 2915, daily except Sun, 1125, 10 hr; *Chetak Exp*, 9615, daily, 2055, 12¼ hr. **Ajmer**: *Garib Niwaz Exp*, 2901, daily, 1125, 2¼ hr; *Delhi-Ahmadabad Mail*, 9901, daily, 0500, 3¼ hr; *Delhi-Ahmadabad Exp*, 9903, daily, 1750, 3½ hr; *Ashram Exp*, 2905, daily, 2345, 3 hr. **Indore**: *Meenakshi Exp*, 7569 (Jaipur-Secunderabad), daily, 1350, 15 hr.

Road Bus: Rajasthan Roadways, Haryana Roadways and ITDC run deluxe buses between Jaipur and other major towns in the area. **Delhi** (261 km, ½ hourly, 5 ½ hr); **Agra** (230 km, 4 hr, via Bharatpur); **Jodhpur** (332 km, frequent, 7 hr); **Udaipur** (374 km, 12 hr); **Ajmer** (131 km, ½ hourly, 3 hr); **Bikaner** (321 km); **Jaisalmer** (654 km, 14 hr via Jodhpur). *Rajasthan Roadways*, Sindhi Camp, Jaipur. Deluxe, T 75834, Express, T 66579 (24 hr).

Short excursions from Jaipur

Amber (Amer)

11 km N of Jaipur, Amber was the ancient capital of the Kachhawaha Rajputs from 1037 until Sawai Jai Singh II moved to the newly-created Jaipur. The building of the fort-palace was begun by Raja Man Singh, a noted Rajput general in Akbar's army, in 1600, and was later added to by successive rulers. The architecture shows distinct Mughal influence. The route there is very attractive, leaving Jaipur and travelling first across the surrounding plain. To your left are rocky outcrops, to your right is the **Man Sarobar** lake (often dry) with the exotic and attractive but now abandoned **Jal**

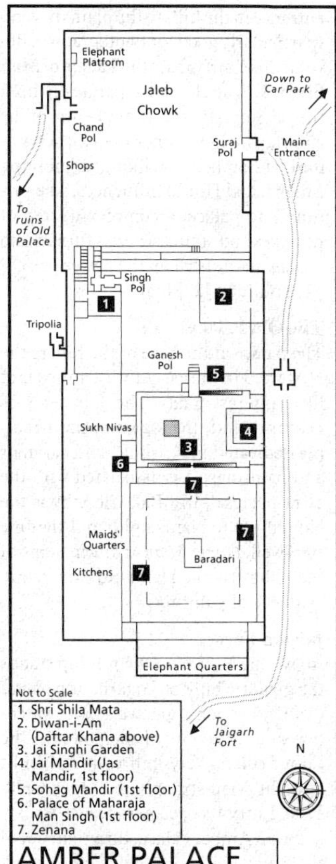

Mahal (Water Palace, 1735) at its centre. During the monsoon the lake is transformed from a huge grassy field into a beautiful water hyacinth-filled lake. Opposite the lake at **Gaitore** are the marble and sandstone *chhattris* of the rulers of Jaipur, set in landscaped gardens. The road climbs through a number of small but defensible rocky gaps before entering the area of flat ground below Amber Fort.

Amidst a cluster of buildings is the first gate and ramp up to the palace. There are often a lot of people waiting around the elephant stand. It is crowded with vendors who can be very persistent but are probably best gently ignored. In the high season there is a continuous train of colourfully decorated elephants walking up and down the ramp. From the side of the road a little further along you get a dramatic view of the hilltop palace. Across the **Maota Lake** to its N is Dilaram Bagh, a formal garden connected to the **Jaigarh Fort** by a path that joins the old military road running up the steep escarpment alongside a powerful defensive wall, to the long, narrow fort running along the top.

ELEPHANT RIDE From the start of the ramp you can either walk or ride by elephant in the style of medieval royalty (10 min journey)! If you have no head for heights this can be somewhat unnerving when the elephant comes close to the edge of the road, but it is perfectly safe; an elephant ride is now an infrequent opportunity outside the Wildlife Parks. You will have to buy a 'return ticket' (Rs 250) even if you wish to walk down after seeing the palace. Sometimes it is difficult to find the right animal for the return journey! You can refuse a demand for *bakshish* when you get off. Once on the elephant's back you will not be immune from people trying to sell you something, be it postcards, a mahout's stick or a photograph of you on the elephant. From the hill top there is a superb view of the gorge and hills around. **NB**: the monkeys here may try to steal any food you have. It may be possible to visit Amber on elephant back from Jaipur (mornings only); enquire at Tourist office.

The entrance After passing though a series of 5 defensive gates, you reach the first courtyard of the **Raj Mahal** built by Man Singh I in 1600, entered through the **Suraj Pol** (Sun Gate). Here you can get a short ride around the courtyard on an elephant, but bargain very hard. There are some toilets near the dismounting platform. On the S side of this Jaleb Chowk with the flower beds, is a flight of steps leading up to the **Singh Pol** (Lion Gate) entrance to the upper courtyard of the palace. Entry Rs 6.

On your right after climbing the steps is the green marble-pillared temple to **Shila Mata** (Kali as Goddess of War) which contains an image Man Singh I brought back from Jessore (now in Bangladesh; the chief priest has always been Bengali). The silver doors were added by his successor. In the left hand corner of the courtyard, the **Diwan-i-Am** (Hall of Public Audience) was built by Raja Jai Singh I in 1639. Originally, it was an open pavilion with cream marble pillars supporting an unusual striped canopy shaped ceiling, with a portico with double red sandstone columns. The room on the E was added by Sawai Ram Singh II. The **Ganesh Pol** (c1700-1725), S of the chowk, colourfully painted and with mosaic decoration, takes its name from the prominent figure of Ganesh above the door. It separates the private from the public areas.

This leads onto the **Jai Singh I** court with a formal garden. To the E is the 2-storeyed cream coloured marble pavilion – **Jai Mandir** (Diwan-i-Khas or Hall of Private Audience) below and **Jas Mandir** (1635-40) with a curved Bengali roof, on the terrace above. The former with its marble columns and painted ceiling has lovely views across the lake. The latter has colourful mosaics, mirrors and marble *jali* screens which allow in cooling breezes. Both have **Shish Mahals** (Mirror Palaces) faced with mirrors, seen to full effect when lit by a match. To the W of the chowk is the **Sukh Niwas,** a pleasure palace with a marble water course to cool the air and doors inlaid with ivory and sandalwood. The Mughal influence is quite apparent in this chowk.

Above the Ganesh Pol is the **Sohag Mandir**, an octagonal chamber with beautiful latticed windows and rectangular rooms to each side. From the rooftop there are stunning views over the palace over the town of Amber, the long curtain wall surrounding the town and further N, through the 'V' shaped entrance in the hills to the plains beyond (particularly good for photographs). Beyond this courtyard is the **Palace of Man Singh I**. A high wall separates it from the Jai Singh Palace. In the centre of the chowk which was once open, is a **baradari** (12-arched pavilion), combining Mughal and Hindu influences. The surrounding palace, a complex warren of passages and staircases, was turned into *zenana* quarters when the newer palaces were built by Jai Singh.

The Old Palace

The palace at the base of the hill, to the N, started in the early 13th century, is of little interest today. The Jain temples nearby include the **Jagatsiromani Temple** dedicated to Krishna, with carvings and paintings; it is associated with the saint-poetess Mira Bai. Close by is the old temple to Narasinghji and the fine step-well, *Panna Mian-ki-Baoli.* Some of the chhattris on Delhi Rd still retain evidence of paintings.

Jaigarh Fort

Above the Palace on the hill top stands the gigantic bulk of Jaigarh, its *parkotas* (walls), bastions, gateways and watchtowers a testimony of the power of the Jaipur rulers. Very impressive when lit at night. Visit strongly rec. Open 0900-1700. Entry Rs 6, camera fee Rs 10.

From Amber Palace, turn right out of the Suraj Pol and follow a stone road, past the old elephant quarters. This is the start of the ascent– a steady climb of about 25 min. The road is protected throughout its length by a strong wall which zigzags up the hill to the fort's main gate. What appears at first to be 2 adjoining forts is in fact all part of the same structure which follows the contour of the hilltop.

The forbidding medieval fort was never captured and so has survived virtually intact which makes it particularly interesting. In the 16th century well-planned cannon foundry you can see the pit where the barrels were cast, the cap-

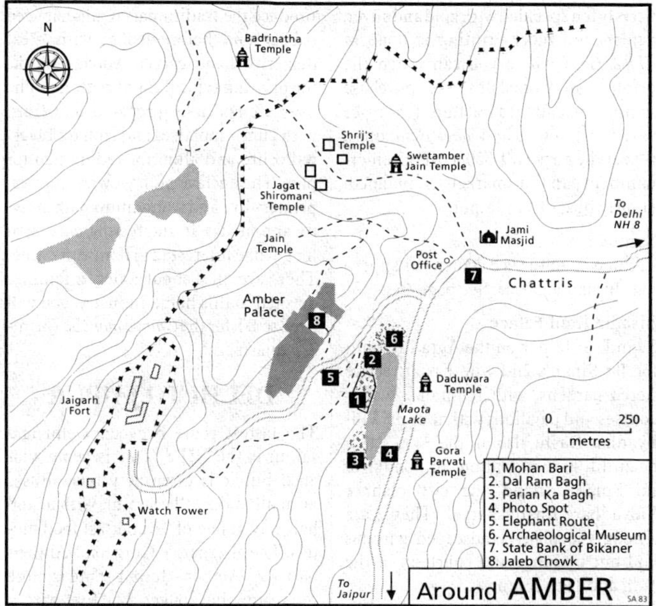

stan-powered lathe which bored out the cannon and the iron-workers' drills, taps and dies. The **armoury** has a large collection of swords and small arms, their use in the many successful campaigns having been carefully logged. Interesting photograph collection too. There is a small *café* outside the armoury.

There are gardens, a granary, open and closed reservoirs; the ancient temples of Ram Harihar (10th century) and Kal Bhairava (12th century) are within the fort. You can explore a warren of complicated dark passageways among the palaces. Many of the apartments are open and you can see the collections of coins and puppets (shows on demand).

The other part of the fort, at a slightly higher elevation, has a tall watch tower. From here there are tremendous views of the surrounding hills. The massive 50 tonne **Jai Ban cannon** stands on top of one tower. Allegedly the largest cannon on wheels in the world, with an 8m barrel, it had a range of around 20 km, but it was never used. 6 km further along the top of the hill is the smaller Nahargarh Fort overlooking Jaipur itself. See page 406.

The Old Palace of Amber (1216) lies at the base of Jaigarh fort. A stone path (currently being restored) from the Chand Pol in the first courtyard of Amber Palace leads to the ruins.

Other excursions

Sanganer 12 km SW of Jaipur. The road into this small town passes through 2 ruined triple gateways, beyond which is the ruined palace and old Jain temples. The old walls with its 4 gates are also in ruins. The greater attractions of Sanganer are paper-making and block-printing. **Paper-making** is practised in the *kagazi mohulla* and uses waste cotton and silk rags which are pulped, sieved, strained and dried. The finished product is often speckled with gold and silver. Screen and block-printing is done in *Chipa Basti* where you can watch the printers in workshops and purchase samples, usually at a fraction of the price asked in Jaipur. *The Village Restaurant*, is near the airport, T 550860. Folk entertainment and a market is planned. Hourly buses from Jaipur.

Samode
42 km NW towards Bikaner, has superb havelis and a palace. See page 463.

Sisodia Rani Palace
8 km E of Jaipur on the Agra Rd, built for Jai Singh's 2nd wife has attractive tiered gardens, with fountains, watercourses and pavilions with murals. **Vidhyadhar Bagh**, also on the Agra Rd, a beautiful garden laid out in honour of Jai Singh's friend and city planner Vidyadhar Bhattacharya. These are among the many landscaped gardens laid out by kings and courtiers in the 18th and 19th centuries.

- **Choki Dhani** Resort, 19 km (see Restaurants above). 35 deluxe cottages being built, T Jaipur 522034.

Ramgarh Lake
33 km NE (45 min drive) has a royal hunting lodge with a museum and library, surrounded by hills, overlooking a large artificial lake. Accommodation-Taj Group A *Ramgarh Lodge*, T Jaipur 521241. 11 rm (2 enormous suites), furnished appropriately. Hunting trophies and art objects in public rooms. Restaurant offers modest menu. Delightful walks. The ruins of the old Kachhwaha fort stands nearby.

Bagru
(35 km SW) with its ground level fort on the Ajmer road by the river Sanjaria, is where the *Chipa* printers are reviving a tradition of hand held block printing over 3 centuries old. They use natural dyes and treat the cotton cloth with Fuller's earth obtained from the riverside, and soak it in turmeric water to produce the traditional cream-coloured background before using, with great dexterity, hand carved wooden blocks for printing typical floral patterns. The dyes are specially prepared and fixed with gum – molasses and iron for black; red ochre and alum for red; indigo for blue. The enclave of the town where the printers live and work, hums with activity and makes an interesting excursion for anyone interested in textile printing. There are only about 3 dozen families devoted to this home-industry; you will need to ask for the *Chippa mohalla* (printers' quarter).

DELHI TO JAIPUR

The fastest route between Delhi and Jaipur is the NH 8. This is being widened but it is often very busy. Buses normally take at least 5 hr, with a stop half way at one of several fast food motels. The alternative Gurgaon – Alwar – Sariska – Amber – Jaipur route is more interesting but longer. The first part of the journey skirts along the N side of the Aravallis but at Tijara the road climbs into the hills.

Gurgaon (*Pop* 131,000; *STD Code* 0124), is a District HQ in Haryana. The road goes S across the plains. To the S **Sohna** is known for its hot springs. Haryana Tourism has an attractive D *Barbet Motel*, T 56. A/c rm and camper huts. Restaurant, pool. **Daruhera** (90 km SW of Delhi) has Haryana Tourism's D *Jungle Babbler Motel*, T 2186. 9 rm, 7 a/c. Restaurant, fast food centre, bar, gardens, camel rides.

Just across the Rajasthan border (100 km from Delhi), 3 km W of the NH8 on a rocky outcrop just above the unspoilt village, is the beautiful **Neem Rana Fort Palace**, converted into a hotel (A, T 4625214 or Delhi T 616145). It is highly accessible but quiet. 22 rm (some more expensive suites), individual decor, furnished with collectors' pieces. Indian and French cuisine. Reservations essential. Highly rec.

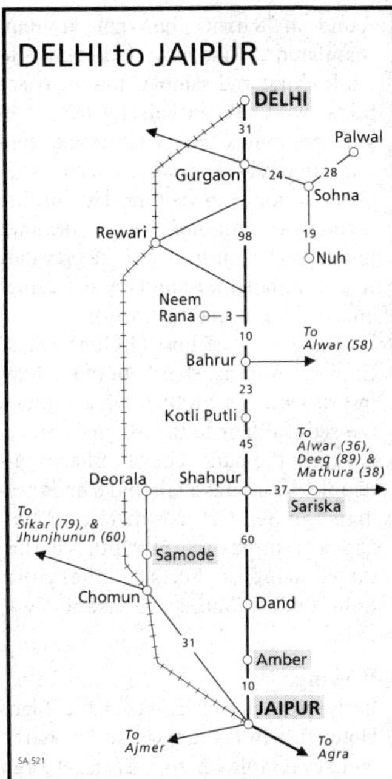

170 km from Delhi the northernmost outcrop of the Aravallis can be seen rising from the arid plain. From Shahpura, 200 km from Delhi and a pleasant rest stop, a road goes W to Samode (see page 463) and E to Alwar, Deeg , Mathura and Bharatpur. (see below)

Alwar

(*Pop* 211,000; *Alt* 250m; *STD Code* 0144) As Mughal power crumbled Rao Pratap Singhji of Macheri founded Alwar as his capital in 1771. It is protected by a hilltop fort 308m above the town from which there is a splendid view of the surrounding countryside. In the fort lie the remains of the palaces, 15 temples and 10 tanks built by the first rulers of Alwar. The fortifications extend 3 km along the hilltop. At Siliserh, 14 km to the W runs an aqueduct which supplies the city with water. The lake, a local picnic spot has boats for hire. The lakeside palace is now a hotel.

Places of interest

The walled city has 5 gates. The **Vinai Vilas Mahal** (City Palace, 1840) contains government offices on the ground floor, and a fine **Museum** with over 7,000 manuscripts (part in the Oriental Research Institute also in the Palace) and miniature paintings, armour, textiles and musical instruments. Collection includes a solid silver dining table and a 73m illustrated scroll. Open Sat-Th, 1000-1700. Small entry fee. The building itself is very fine and successfully blends Mughal proportions with Rajput decoration. The stables could hold 3,000 horses, while the treasury with the crown jewels had a cup carved out of a single diamond.

On the S side of the tank is the **Cenotaph** of Maharaja Bakhtawar Singh (1781-1815) which is of marble on a red sandstone base. The gardens are alive with peacocks and other birds. To the right of the main entrance to the palace is a 2-storey processional Elephant Carriage designed to carry 50 people and be pulled by 4 elephants.

The **Yeshwant Niwas**, built by Maharaja Jai Singh in the Italianate style, is also worth seeing. Apparently on its completion he disliked it and never lived in it. Instead he built the **Vijay Mandir**, 10 km from Alwar, in 1918. The royal family still live in part of this 105-room palace beside Vijay Sagar. Part is open to the public, but prior permission is needed from the secretary.

Local information

● Accommodation

D *Lake Castle Tourist Bungalow*, Siliserh (14 km), T 3764. 11 rm, 3 a/c. Restaurant. Modest but superb location. **E** *Alka* Station Rd. T 2696, **E** *Asoka* T 2027 and *Rly Retiring Rooms* T 2222 are all basic.

● Transport

Train Old Delhi *Delhi Mail*, 9902, daily, 0340, 3¾ hr; *Delhi Exp*, 9904, daily, 1423, 4 hr; *Ashram Exp*, 2906, daily, 0647, 3¼ hr;

Ahemdabad-Jodhpur Exp, 9965, daily, 1909, 3 hr.

Road Bus: there are regular buses from Delhi and Jaipur.

ROUTES A road S climbs into the Aravallis to **Sariska**, the gateway for the Sariska National Park. It is a pleasant, quiet place to stay and relax. Excursions by jeep are possible to forts and temples nearby. **Bhangarh**, (55 km) on the outskirts of the reserve, is a deserted city of some 10,000 dwellings established in 1631. It was abandoned 300 years ago, supposedly after it was cursed by a magician.

Sariska Tiger Reserve

Approach

The princely shooting reserve of the Maharajah of Alwar in the Aravallis was declared a sanctuary in 1955 and is a tiger reserve under Project Tiger. The 480 sq km sanctuary comprises dry deciduous forest of *ber, dhok* and *tendu* among others, set in a valley surrounded by the barren Aravalli hills. *Climate:* Temperature Summer Max 47°C Min 24°C; Winter Max 31°C Min 3°C. Rainfall: 650 mm. Best season: Nov-Apr.

Wildlife

Open all year round. During the monsoon the vegetation is very lush and travel through the forest may be difficult. The place is then alive with birds but many animals move to higher ground. In the dry season, when the streams disappear, the animals become dependant on man-made water holes at Kalighatti, Salopka and Pandhupol, where there are hides. You may arrange to sit out in the *machans* (tree platforms), dawn and dusk being the best times for viewing game, or drive through the park.

The **rhesus** and **langur** monkeys here have become used to humans, so come very close to visitors. **Warning** It is not safe to play with them. The main rhesus population live at Talvriksh, whilst at Brat-Hari you will see many langurs. The *chowsingha*, or 4-horned antelope, is found at Sariska but not at Ranthambhor, 250 km away. Other deer include chital and sambar. You many see nilgai, wild boar, jackals, hyenas, hares and porcupines, though tigers and leopards are rarely seen, since the reserve is closed at night to visitors. The birdlife includes ground birds such as peafowl, jungle fowl, spur fowl and the grey partridge. Babblers, bulbuls and treepies are common round the lodges.

The Kankwari Fort (20 km), where Emperor Aurangzeb is believed to have imprisoned his brother Dara Shikoh, the rightful heir to the Mughal throne, is within the park. The old Bhartrihari temple (6 km) has a fair and 6 hr dance-drama in Sep/Oct. Neelkanth (33 km) has a complex of 6th-10th century carved temples. Further information from Wildlife Warden, Sariska, T Alwar 2348.

Viewing

Early morning jeep trips from the Palace Hotel run into the park as far as the monkey temple where you can get a cup of tea whilst watching the monkeys and peacocks before returning to the hotel for breakfast. Jeep-hire with drivers possible, for non-standard trips in the reserve.

Park information

● Accommodation

C *Sariska Palace*. T Sariska 014652-4247 (Delhi 732365). 40 km from Alwar rly. 31 rm, 14 a/c. Restaurant (set menu good, Rs 120), exchange, jeep hire, extensive gardens. A former Maharaja's hunting lodge. Wonderful building full of hunting photographs and stuffed tigers, rather like a stately home. Cool, high-ceilinged, basic but comfortable rooms (candelabras in case of power failure). Log fires (winter) and good Indian music under the stars on the terrace, delightful staff. Highly rec. **C** *Kushalgarh Palace*, 6 km before Sariska Palace, T 269, Delhi T 6886909, F 6886122. The former Raja's hunting lodge, 34 km from Alwar, is in a splendid setting with large grounds. Good restaurant, camp fire, naturalist services. Jeep Safari (3 hr, Rs 300 per person). Pool planned.

RTDC **E** *Tiger Den Tourist Bungalow*, in the sanctuary, T 42. Avoid at weekends when it is overcrowded. RTDC **F** *Forest Rest House*.

● **Transport**

Air Nearest airport at Jaipur (110 km).

Train Nearest at Alwar (36 km), with buses to the sanctuary.

ROUTES From **Shahpura** the road winds through the arid ridges of the Aravallis to **Amber** (50 km) and **Jaipur** (10 km).

JAIPUR TO AGRA

The second side of the tourist triangle runs 230 km from Jaipur to Agra via **Bharatpur** (best known for its bird sanctuary but also a splendid city) and **Fatehpur Sikri** in UP. It takes about 4 hr by car, 5-6 hr by coach. The road passes through flat cultivated areas for virtually the whole distance. Midway point **Mahua** has a fastfood restaurant, toilets, basic motor repair facilities and simple rooms.

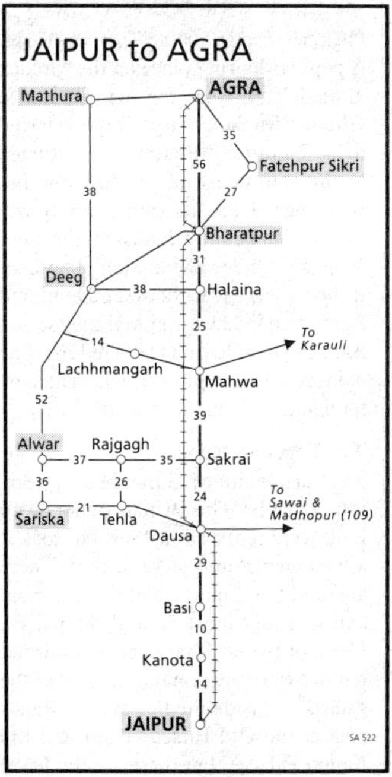

From Jaipur the road E along the **NH11** runs to **Kanota** (14 km). The 200 year old C *Royal Castle*, has been converted into a distinctive and comfortable hotel. Restaurant, garden, museum of armaments and carriages and a library of rare books, manuscripts and paintings and a traditional royal welcome. Horse and camel rides arranged. Rec. Contact *Narain Niwas*, Jaipur, T 563448. The NH11 then goes through a series of small towns and villages to **Sakrai** (77 km) where there is a good roadside Rajasthan Tourism *Restaurant*.

Deeg

(*Pop* 38,000) The fort and pleasure palace are of major architectural importance. Badan Singh (1722-56), a Sinsini Jat, began the development of the town as capital of his newly founded Jat kingdom. The central citadel was built by his son Suraj Mal in 1730. In the late 18th century the town reverted to the Raja of Bharatpur. The British stormed the fort in Dec 1804, after which the fortifications were dismantled.

Places of interest

The square **Fort** with rubble and mud walls is strengthened by 12 bastions and a wide, shallow moat and has a run-down *haveli* (palace) within. Though rather dilapidated now, it still makes an interesting visit. The entrance is over a narrow bridge across the moat, through a gate studded with anti-elephant spikes. Negotiating the thorny undergrowth, you can climb the ramparts which rise 20m above the moat; some large cannons are still in place on their rusty carriages. You can walk right around along the wide path on top of the walls and climb the stairs to the roof of the citadel for good views all round including Deeg's bustling streets below.

The **'Monsoon' Pleasure Palaces**, to the W of the Fort were begun by Suraj

Mal. Open 0800-1200 and 1300-1900. Entry free.

The palaces are flanked by 2 reservoirs, Gopal (W) and Rup Sagar (E), and set around a central square formal garden in the style of a Mughal *char bagh*. The main entrance is from the N, through the ornamental, though unfinished, Singh (Lion) Pol; the other gates are Suraj Pol (SW) and Nanga Pol (NE). The impressive main palace **Gopal Bhavan** (1763), bordering Gopal Sagar, is flanked by Sawon and Bhadon pavilions (1760) named after the monsoon months (mid-Jul to mid-Sep). Water was directed over the roof lines to create the effect of sheets of monsoon rain. Outside, overlooking the formal garden is a beautiful white marble *hindola* (swing) which was brought as booty with 2 marble thrones (black and white), after Suraj Mal attacked Delhi.

To the S, bordering the central garden is the single-storey marble **Suraj Bhavan** (c1760), a temple and **Kishan Bhavan** with its decorated façade with 5 arches, and fountains. The water reservoir to its W was built at a great height to operate the fountains and cascades effectively. It held enough water to work all the fountains for a few hours though it took a week to fill from 4 wells with bullocks drawing water up in leather buckets. Now, the 500 or so fountains are turned on once a year for the Monsoon festival in August. All these are gravity fed from huge holding tanks on the Palace roof with each fountain jet having its own numbered pipe leading from the tank. Coloured dyes are inserted into individual pipes to create a spectacular effect.

The (old) **Purana Mahal** beyond, with a curved roof and some fine architectural points was begun by Badan Singh in 1722. It now houses government offices but the surviving wall paintings in the entrance chamber of the inner court are worth seeing in spite of their simplicity.

Keshav Bhavan, a *baradari* or garden pavilion, stands between the central garden and Rup Sagar with the **Sheesh Mahal** (Mirror Palace, 1725) in the SE corner. **Nand Bhavan** (c1760), N of the central garden, is a large hall 45m long, 24m wide and 6m high, raised on a terrace and enclosed by an arcade of 7 arches. There are frescoes inside but it all has a deserted feel. The pavilion took the monsoon theme further; the double-roof was ingeniously used to create the effect of thunder above! Water channelled through hollow pillars rotated heavy stone balls which made the sound. On a sunny day the fountains are believed even to have produced a rainbow!

Local information

● Accommodation

F *Dak Bungalow*, Agra Rd, T 2366, basic and cheap.

Bharatpur

(40 km S; *Pop* 157,000; *STD Code* 05644) A popular halting place on the 'Golden Triangle' famous for its **Keoladeo Ghana Bird Sanctuary** (simply referred to as *Bharatpur*). Bharatpur is situated at the confluence of the Ruparel and Banganga rivers. Its ruling family was Jat and constantly harassed the later Mughals. Under Badan Singh they controlled a large tract between Delhi and Agra, then led by Suraj Mal they seized Agra and marched on Delhi in 1763. The old fort of Bharatpur is rarely visited by foreign travellers but is worthwhile.

The Fort and Palace

The fort, built by Suraj Mal appears impregnable. The British under Lord Lake were repulsed in 1803, but took it after a month-long siege in 1825. There are double ramparts, a 46m wide moat and an inner moat around the palace. Much of the wall has been demolished but there are the remains of some of the gateways. Inside the fort are the Raja's palace, the Old Palace (1733) and the Kamra Palace. N of these are the Jewel

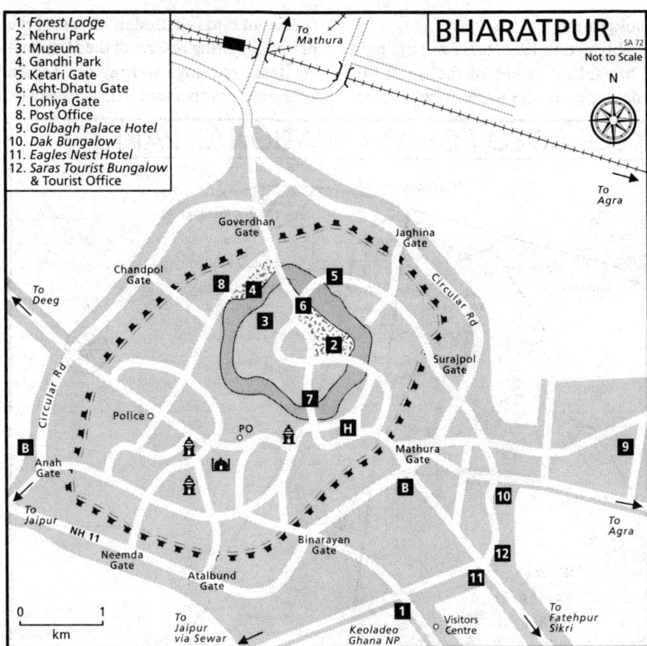

House and Court of Justice. **Golbagh** (c1905), the Maharaja's palace, is 1.6 km E of the city and is what Davies has described as a 'beautiful piece of Victorian eclecticism executed in local sandstone'.

Local information

● Accommodation

D *Golbagh Palace*, off Agra Rd, T 3349. 18 rm, some a/c. Restaurant, bar. Former palace, modernised without losing its character. Good food and service. Rec.

E *Falcon Guest House*, some rm with bath and a/c. Owned by naturalist, full of information, bike hire, very helpful management. Highly rec. Good off-season discount. Numerous **E/F** lodgings and tent camps.

● Transport

Air Nearest airport is at Agra (55 km).

Train Bharatpur town has a Rly station. **Jaipur**: *Marudhar Exp*, 5315, daily, 0936, 4 hr; *Agra Fort Fast Passenger Exp*, 9705, daily, 2155, 4¾ hr; *Agra-Jaipur Exp*, 2921, daily, 1805, 3¾ hr. **Sawai Madhopur**: *Paschim Exp*, 2926, daily, 1953, 2½ hr; *Frontier Mail*, 2904, daily, 1115, 3 hr; **Delhi**: *Paschim Exp*, 2925, daily, 0622, 5hr; *Bombay-Firozepur Janata Exp*, daily, 0813, 4½hr.

Road Bus: bus services from Jaipur (175 km, 5 hr, Rs 28), Delhi (185 km) and Agra (55 km).

Bharatpur-Keoladeo Ghana Bird Sanctuary

Approach

Better known as Bharatpur, this is a UNESCO World Heritage site. Entry Rs 25, Camera fee Rs 10 (professional video camera Rs 1,500). **Warning** Make a note of entrance fees, boat rides at entrance, to avoid being overcharged once inside. **Note** Winters can be very cold and foggy, especially in the early morning. Temp range: 49°C to 2°C. Rainfall: 650 mm.

Background

Established in 1956, this 29 sq km piece of marshland is one of the finest bird sanctuaries in the world with over 360 species of birds. It used to be part of the private shooting reserve of the Maharaja of Bharatpur and during the season enormous numbers of birds were shot by

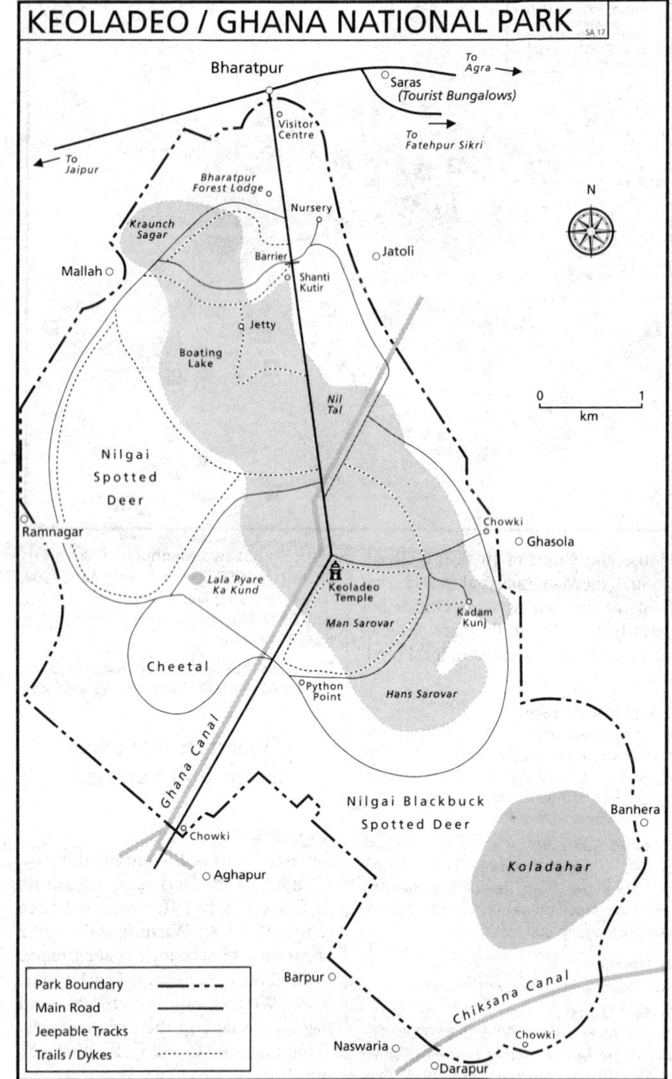

him and his guests.

Wildlife

It is especially good from Nov to Feb when it is frequented by Northern hemisphere migratory birds. The rare Siberian Crane failed to arrive in late 1993; it is possible that the ancient migratory system believed to be 1,500 years old, may be lost since young cranes need to learn the route from older birds (it is not instinctive). These cranes are disappearing – eaten by Afghans and occasionally employed as fashionable "guards" for protecting Pakistani homes (they call out when strangers approach). Sep-Oct is the breeding season but its worth visiting any time of the year.

Among many other birds to be seen are egrets, ducks, coots, storks, kingfishers, spoonbills, Sarus cranes and several birds of prey, including laggar falcon, greater spotted eagle, marsh harrier and Pallas' eagle. There are also chital deer, sambar, nilgai, feral cattle, wild cats, hyenas and wild boar whilst near Python Point, there are usually some very large rock pythons.

FURTHER INFORMATION It is worth buying the *Collins Handguide to the Birds of the Indian Sub continent* (available at the Reserve and in hotel bookshops and booksellers in Delhi, Agra, Jaipur etc). Well illustrated. Also *Pictorial Guide to the birds of the Indian Sub-Continent* by Salim Ali and S Dillon, Ripley and *Bharatpur: Bird Paradise* by Martin Ewans, Lustre Press, Delhi, are also extremely good.

Viewing

The S of the reserve is better for viewing. Dawn, which can be very cold, and dusk are the best times; mid-day may prove too hot "so take a book and find a shady spot". Carry a sun hat and plenty of drinking water. Many prefer to use a bicycle to travel to and around the reserve. Best to hire one the previous day for an early start next morning. You can hire one in town, or nr *Saras Tourist Bungalow* or from your own hotel. About Rs 30/day. Alternatively, hire a cycle-rickshaw (2 passengers) at the entrance. Well worthwhile because some rickshaw-wallahs have binoculars which they are very willing to lend (not hire) and are very knowledgeable about the birds and their location. A small tip is appropriate. A boat ride is highly recommended for viewing too; boatmen are equally knowledgeable. Hire one from *Rest House* nr jetty.

Local information

● **Accommodation**

2.5 km inside the sanctuary: **B** ***Bharatpur Forest Lodge*** (ITDC), T 2760. 8 km rly and bus stand. Book in advance. 17 rm, 10 a/c with balconies. Restaurant (mediocre food), bar, boats for bird watching. Animals such as wild boar wander into the compound. **Note** Convenient for Reserve but residents must pay park entrance fee for car each time (Rs75). Very comfortable. Also cheaper **E** ***Shanti Kutir Rest House***, nr boating jetty, T 2265. Outside: Rajasthan Tourism **D** ***Saras Tourist Bungalow***, Fatehpur Sikri Rd, T 2169. 20 simple clean rm, some a/c (limited hot water), dorm. Restaurant (indifferent food), bar, lawns, tours. Camping. Rather dull, popular with backpackers.

ROUTES 12 km from Bharatpur the road crosses the Rajasthan/UP border, historically a frontier between Rajput and Mughal territory. Continue straight on for Agra (35 km), see page 305.

JAIPUR TO CHITTAURGARH

The route from Jaipur through E Rajasthan via Sawai Madhopur, Ranthambhor and Shivpuri National Parks is very attractive. From Jhansi you can drive to **Orchha** and **Khajuraho** (see page 350). The first part is an alternative route from Jaipur to Udaipur, allowing you to see several interesting sites in SE Rajasthan on the way.

Jaipur to Kota

ROUTES From Jaipur the road S through Sanganer (see above) passes some attractive scenery to the **River Banas**, which has given its name to the post-Harappan culture of the region.

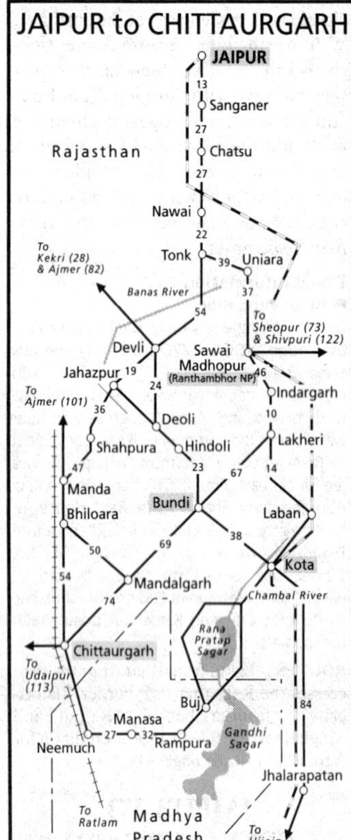

Tonk

(*Pop* 100,200; *STD Code* 01432). Before Independence Tonk was a tiny Princely State ruled by Muslim Nawabs. The **Sunehri Kothi**, a late 19th century addition to the palace built by the Nawab, is a mixture of predominantly local architectural styles with European style additions such as imitation Ionic columns and false marbling of the columns. Some of the 'doors' are also simply painted. The **Amirgarh Fort** built by Amir Khan.

ROUTES From Tonk you have the choice of taking the SE route to Sawai Madhopur (*Pop* 78,000) and Ranthambor National Park, Shivpuri and Gwalior or Jhansi, or the SW route to Bundi, Kota and Chittaurgarh.

Ranthambhor National Park

Approach

Ranthambhor, covering 410 sq km, runs from the easternmost spur of the Aravallis to the Vindhya range. It has both the old fort and the wildlife sanctuary also known as **Sawai Madhopur** and comes under the Project Tiger scheme. Temp range: 49°C to 2°C. Best time: Nov-Apr.

Background

The Chauhan **Ranthambhor fort** situated on a 215m high rock 12 km NE of Sawai Madhopur, was built in 944 and over the next 6 centuries changed hands on a number of occasions. Qutb-ud-din Aibak captured it in 1194 and later handed it back to the Rajputs. Ala-ud-din Khalji took it in 1301 and Akbar in 1569. It later passed to the house of Jaipur. You approach the park along a narrow valley from the W. The path to the fort zig-zags up the steep outcrop in a series of ramps and through 2 impressive gateways. The fort wall runs round the summit and has a number of semi-circular bastions. This combined with the natural escarpment produces sheer drops of over 65m in places. There are 2 tanks, a palace and pavilion and a few temples inside the walls. All are in various states of disrepair but there are good views out over the surrounding countryside to warrant the effort of reaching the fort and it is a wonderfully peaceful place.

Wildlife

Set in dry deciduous forest featuring *Anogeissus pendula*, the area covers rocky hills and open valleys dotted with small pools and fruit trees, this became the private tiger reserve of the Maharaja of Jaipur. Tigers can occasionally be seen in the daytime, particularly Nov-Apr. Sadly poaching has increased with the demand abroad for skins and bones and the tiger population has decreased (only 17 counted in May '92). It provides a fine habitat for sambar; there are also a few leopards, nilgai, sloth bear, jackal, crocodile, the occasional rare caracal and a rich variety of birds.

Viewing

The park has good roads and tracks so it is best to explore by jeep, visiting Nal Ghati, Lahpur, Bakaula, Anantpur and Kachida valley. Padam Talao adjacent to the Jogi Mahal hunting lodge is the park's favourite water source; there are also water holes at Raj Bagh and Milak.

Park information

● Accommodation

D ***Castle Jhoomar Baori***, T 2495, and ***Forest Lodge***, T 620. A former hunting lodge for guests of the Maharaja of Jaipur. Few rm, all large and airy. Book in advance. Good location on hilltop. 7 km rly.

E ***Hunting Lodge***. Once the Maharaja's personal lodge. 3 km rly. **E** ***Jogi Mahal***. Small lodge inside the park, on edge of a Padam Talao lake, covered with water-lilies is overlooked by the fort. Only veg food. 15 km rly.

D ***Anurag Resort***, Ranthambhor Rd, T 07462 2451. Comfortable rm with TV and bath. Restaurant, naturalist, cultural programmes, jungle excursions, large lawns. Pool proposed. Reservations, Delhi T 6886909, F 6886122.

● Transport

Train Sawai Madhopur (14 km) is on the main Delhi-Bombay W Railway. **New Delhi, via Bharatpur & Mathura**: *Paschim Exp*, 2925, daily, 0355, 6½ hr; *Frontier Mail*, 2903, daily, 1255, 6 hr; *Dehra Dun Exp*, 9019, daily 2143, 8 hr; *Firozpur-Janata Exp*, 9023, daily, 0430, 8 hr. **Bombay Central**: *Paschim Exp*, 2926, daily, 2225, 16¾ hr; *Frontier Mail*, 2904, daily, 1423, 16¼ hr; *Bombay Exp*, 9020, daily, 0518, 23¼ hr; *Bombay-Janata Exp*, 9024, 2210, 22¼ hr. **Kota**: *Paschim Exp*, 2926, daily, 2225, 1¼ hr; *Frontier Mail*, 2904, daily, 1423, 1½ hr; *Bombay Exp*, 9020, daily, 0518, 2 hr; *Bombay-Janata Exp*, 9024, 2210, 2¼ hr.

Road The park is midway between Bharatpur and Kota so if you have a car it is worth stopping. **Bus**: bus connections with Sawai Madhopur, not satisfactory, see page 422.

ROUTES For Udaipur a road goes S from Sawai Madhopur to Kota. The first part of the journey runs along the Aravalli ridge (around 500m) to Lakheri (40 km) and on to Kota (55 km).

Kota

(*Pop* 537,000; *STD Code* 05662). Situated on the E bank of the Chambal river below a deep gorge, Kota was on a major trade route from Delhi to Gujarat. It is now a rapidly expanding industrial area for processing chemicals, with hydroelectric and nuclear power plants nearby. Formerly a small state, its fortunes varied inversely with those of its more powerful neighbours. Never militarily strong, it prospered under the guidance of the able 19th century ruler Zalim Singh, but then declined on his death. The British reunited the territory in 1894 and imposed stability.

Places of interest

At the S end of the town near the barrage is the city palace and fort. Entrance by S gate. The **fort** (1625-) lacked an overall plan. The city palace within the fort, part of which is now the excellent **Madho Singh museum** (open daily except Fri, 1000-1700, small entry charge), contains some striking buildings and was built on a huge scale. The **Bhim Mahal**, a large Durbar Hall (early 18th century) is covered with Rajput miniatures documenting the town's periods of expansion and recording Kota's legends. **The Hathi Pol** (Elephant Gate 1625-48) had murals added to it at a later stage, one of which depicts a royal wedding procession. The exterior of the palace has robust fortifications and delicate ornamental stonework. The **Akhade Ka Mahal** (1723-56) was added to the W of the inner court (enlarged 1888-1940). The **Hawa Mahal** (1864) is modelled on its famous namesake in Jaipur. The small Government Museum is on the 1st Fl of the Entrance Gateway.

The **Umaid Bhawan** (New Palace 1904) N of town, was built for the Maharao Umaid Singh II and designed by

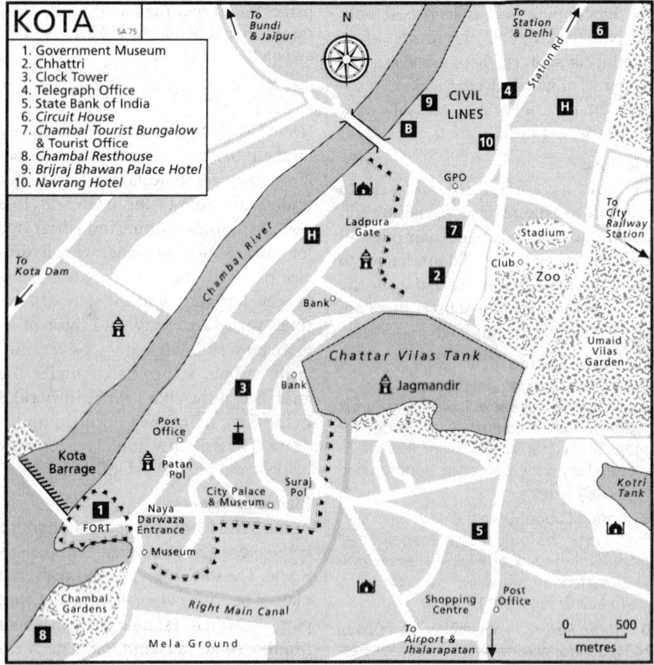

Sir Samuel Swinton Jacob in collaboration with Indian designers. The buff-coloured stone exterior with a stucco finish has typical Rajput detail. The interior, however, is Edwardian with a fine drawing-room, banquet hall and garden.

The Chambal Gardens at Amar Niwas, S of the fort, are popular for picnics. The pond is well stocked with gharial crocodiles, shared by flamingoes. Upstream at **Bharatiya Kund** is a popular swimming spot whilst the Kota **barrage** controls the river level and is the headworks for an irrigation system downstream.

Excursions

Jhalarapatan, 85 km SE of Kota has several fine 11th century Hindu temples, the **Surya Temple** being the best. This is Central Indian in style and has a curvilinear tower adorned with miniature tower-like motifs with a large *amalaka* at the crest. 2 km to the S is the ruined site of 7th century **Chandravati**. Here there are broken sculptures and derelict temples. Many of the sculptures have been removed to **Jhalawar** which is nearby.

Local information

● Accommodation

D *Brijraj Bhawan Palace*, Civil Lines, T 23071. 7 rm, air cooled. Restaurant, travel. A palace in small grounds by river, though homely and relaxing and with regal memorabilia. Used by small tour groups. Rec. **D** *Navrang*, Civil Lines, Nayapura, T 23294. 21 rm, some air-cooled (cheaper without). Rajasthan Tourism **D***Chambal Tourist Bungalow*, nr bus stand, T 26527. 49 rm, some a/c. Restaurant (limited menu), Tourist Office. Clean, simple but pleasant and good value. There is also the *Payal*, T 5401 at Nayapura and the *Rly Retiring Rooms*.

● **Transport**

Train From Kota Junction station. **New Delhi**: *Rajdhani Exp*, 2951, daily except Mon, 0420, 5½ hr; *Paschim Exp*, 2925, daily, 0220, 8 hr; *Dehra Dun Exp*, 9019, daily, 1940, 10 hr; *Frontier Mail*, 2903, daily, 1125, 7½ hr. **Bombay (Central)**: *Paschim Exp*, 2926, daily, 2358, 15 hr; *Frontier Mail*, 2904, daily, 1610, 14¾ hr; *Bombay Exp*, 9020, daily, 0800, 20½ hr; *Bombay-Janata Exp*, 9024, 0035, 19¾ hr. **Sawai Madhopur**: *Paschim Exp*, 2925, daily, 0220, 1½ hr; Frontier Mail, 2903, daily, 1125, 1½ hr; *Dehra Dun Exp*, 9019, daily 1940, 2 hr; *Firozpur-Janata Exp*, 9023, daily, 0244, 1½ hr. *Awadh Exp*, 5064, daily, 1420, 1¾ hr. **Bharatpur**: *Nizamuddin Exp*, 9301, 0525, 3½hr; **Mathura**,*Nizamuddin Exp*, 9301, 0525, 4½hr.

Kota to Chittaurgarh via Rana Pratap Sagar

From **Kota** a picturesque route skirts the Rana Pratap Sagar and Gandhi Sagar lakes to the SW. It is a 236 km round trip but the views are very attractive and there are some beautiful picnic spots along the way. It is 180 km to **Neemuch** and a further 56 km to Chittaurgarh.

Bardoli

On the way to Rana Pratap Sagar, has some of the finest examples of 10th century Pratihara temples in India. They are now rather dilapidated but include the **Ghatesvara Temple**, the best preserved and finest example. It consists of an elaborately carved curvilinear towered sanctuary with a pot finial and a columned porch. Inside are sculptures of Siva dancing flanked by Brahma and Vishnu with river goddesses and dancing maidens beneath. Within the sanctuary is a square pedestal with 5 stone lingas, the central one being an upturned pot or *ghata* which gives the temple its name. The **Mahishamardini Temple** is immediately SW and also has a finely carved curved tower. A smashed image of Durga is in the sanctuary. **Trimurti Temple** to the SE is derelict but houses a large triple-headed Siva image. The temple complex is about 100m to the E of the bus stand.

Kota to Chittaurgarh via Bundi

ROUTES An alterative route goes NW out of Kota to Bundi (37 km), a very picturesque little town and former capital of a small state of the same name.

Bundi

(*Pop* 65,000; *STD Code* 0747). Bundi, in a beautiful narrow valley above which towers the Taragarh Fort, is best visited on a day trip from Kota, which has better hotels. The drive into the town is particularly pleasing as the road runs along the hillside overlooking the valley opposite the fort. Off the beaten track, it is completely unspoilt. The state was founded in 1342. Neither wealthy nor powerful, it nevertheless ranked high in the Rajput hierarchy. The founding family belonged to the Hara Chauhan clan, one of the 4 Agnikula created by Vishnu at the fire-pit at Gaumukh (Cow's Mouth) on Mount Abu.

The town lies on the side of a steep hill and the palace (several small palaces), situated by a lake with little islands, was begun around 1600. Former rulers lived in the Taragarh Fort (1342, see below). **The Chatar Mahal** (1660) is of green serpentine rock and is pure Rajput in style. A steep ramp provides access which is through the **Hazari Darwaza** (1,000 Gate) where the garrison lived. The palace entrance is through the **Hathi Pol** (Elephant Gate, 1607-31), which has two rampant elephants carved at the top of the archway.

The Chitra Mahal, an open courtyard with a gallery running around a garden of fountains, has a splendid collection of miniatures showing scenes from the *Radha Krishna* story. The 18th century murals are some of the finest examples of Rajput art. There is supposed to be a labyrinth of catacombs in which the state treasures are believed to have been stored. Each ruler was allowed one visit but when the last guide died in the 1940s the secret of its location was lost.

Sukh Niwas, a summer palace is on the **Jait Sagar** lake. The square artificial **Nawal Sagar** lake has in its centre a half-submerged temple to Varuna, the god of water. The lake surface beautifully reflects the entire town and palace. W of the Nawal Sagar is **Phool Sagar** palace, started in 1945 but unfinished.

Taragarh is a 20 min difficult climb (very hot and not recommended in summer; good shoes needed). The square fort has large corner bastions, the E wall has a gate which is crenellated with high ramparts. The main gate to the W is flanked by octagonal towers and the approach was difficult. The **Bhim Burj** tower dominates the fort and provided the platform for the **Garbh Ganjam**, a huge cannon. A pit to the side provided shelter for the artillerymen. The **Sabirna-Dha-ka-Kund** (1654) is a square stepped water tank. Overall, the fort is a sombre contrast to the beauty of the town and the lakes below.

Local information

● Accommodation

D *The Rothi*, Ishwari Niwas, opp Circuit House, T 2541. 14 rm, some with bath and hot water. Old mansion belonging to Raja family; friendly, good restaurant (home cooking). Rec. At **E** *Circuit House* and **F** *Dak Bungalow* nr bus stand, Govt officers have priority.

● Transport

Road Bundi is only accessible by road. From Ajmer (165 km) about 5 hr; Kota (37 km) 1 hr. **Buses**: also to Chittaurgarh and Udaipur.

ROUTES At **Menal** (48 km), en route to Chittaurgarh, there is a complex of Siva temples (Gupta period). At **Bijolia**, 16 km further on is another group; only 3 of the original 100 still stand, one with a large statue of Ganesh. At **Begun**, 10 km S of Katoda, Thakur Hari Singh has recently converted his old haveli into a palace hotel.

Chittaurgarh (Chittor)

(*Pop* 72,000; *STD Code* 01472). This is one of the oldest cities in Rajasthan, founded in 728 by Bappu Rawal, who according to legend was reared by the Bhil tribe.

History

2 sites near the River Berach have shown stone tools dating from the Lower Palaeolithic. Buddhist relics from a few centuries BC. From the 7th century it was occupied by a succession of rulers. Invading Muslim armies saw the strategic importance of the imposing fort sited on a rocky outcrop of the Aravallis, and from the 12th century when it became the centre of Mewar.

Excavations in the Mahasati area of the fort have shown 4 shrines with ashes and charred bones, the earliest dating from about the 11th century AD. There was a paved platform over which was a *sati stone*, commemorating the self immolation of a widow, and 2 other loose sati stones were also discovered.

The fort dominates the city and is itself 280 ha in area. Until 1568 the town was situated within the walls. Today the lower town sprawls to the W of the fort and straddles the Berach and Gambheri rivers.

Places of interest

The fort stands on a 152m high rocky hill rising abruptly above the surrounding plain. The great length of the walls (5 km), however, makes the elevation look lower than it really is. The ruins are deserted and the slopes are covered with scrub jungle. The modern town lies at the foot of the hill and is surrounded by a wall. Access is across a limestone bridge of 10 arches over the Gambheri river. The winding 1.5 km ascent to the fort is defended by 7 impressive gates: the Padal Pol (**1**) is where Rawat Bagh Singh, the Rajput leader, fell during the 2nd siege; the Bhairon or Tuta (broken) Pol (**2**) where Jaimal, one of the heroes of the 3rd siege was killed by Akbar in 1567 (*chhattris* to Jaimal and Patta); the Hanuman Pol and Ganesh Pol; the Jorla (Joined) Gate whose upper arch is con-

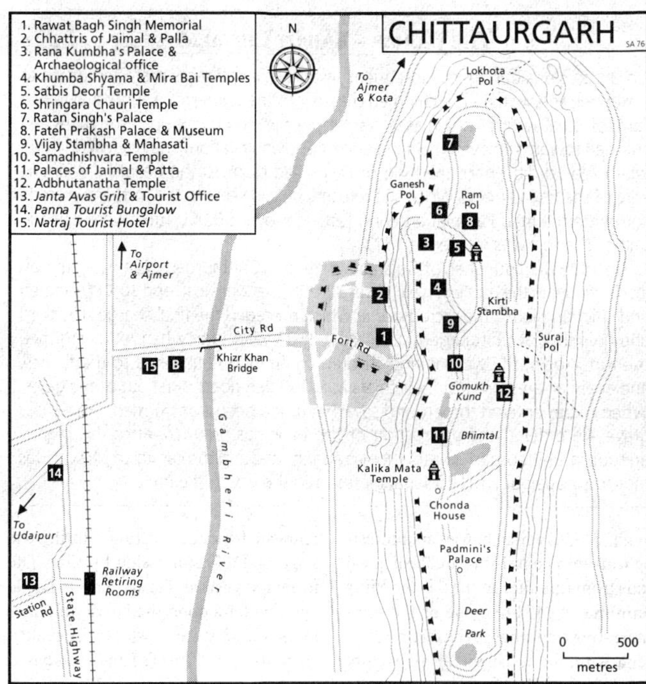

nected to the Lakshman Pol; finally the Ram Pol (1459) which is the main gate. Inside the walls is a village and ruined palaces, towers and temples.

Rana Kumbha's Palace (**3**) On the right immediately inside the fort are the ruins of the palace (1433-68), originally built of dressed stone with a stucco covering. It is approached by 2 gateways, the large **Badi Pol** and the 3-bay deep **Tripolia**. Once there were elephant and horse stables, the *zenanas* (recognised by the *jali* screen), and a Siva temple. The *jauhar* committed by Padmini and her followers is believed to have taken place beneath the courtyard. The N frontage of the palace contains an attractive combination of canopied balconies. Across from the palace is the archaeological office and the **Nau Lakha Bhandar** (The Treasury; *nau lakha*–900,000). The **temple** to Rana Kumbha's wife **Mira Bai** (**4**) who was a renowned poetess is visible from the Palace and stands close to the Kumbha Shyama Temple (both c1440). The older 11th century Jain **Sat Bis Deori Temple** (**5**) with its 27 shrines, is nearby. The **Shringara Chauri Temple** (**6**) c1456, near the fort entrance, has sculptured panels of musicians, warriors and Jain deities.

Rana Ratan Singh's Palace (**7**) is to the N by the Ratneshwar Lake. Built in stone around 1530 it too had stucco covering. Originally rectangular in plan and enclosed within a high wall, it was subsequently much altered. The main gate to the S still stands as an example of the style employed.

To the E of Rana Kumbha's Palace is the early 20th century **Fateh Prakash Palace** (**8**) built by Maharana Fateh

The Jauhar – Rajput Chivalry

On 3 occasions during its subsequent history its inhabitants preferred death to surrender, the women marching en masse into the flames of a funeral pyre in a form of ritual suicide known as *jauhar* before the men threw open the gates and charged towards an overwhelming enemy and annihilation. The first was in 1303 when Ala-ud-din Khalji, the King of Delhi, laid claim to the beautiful Padmini, wife of the Rana's uncle. When she refused, he laid siege to the fort. The women committed jauhar, Padmini entering last, and over 50,000 men were killed in battle. The fort was retaken in 1313.

In 1535 Bahadur Shah of Gujarat laid claim to Chittaurgarh. Every Rajput clan lost its leader in the battle in which over 32,000 lives were lost, and 13,000 women and children died in the sacred *jauhar* which preceded the final charge. The third and final sack of Chittaurgarh occurred only 32 years later when Akbar stormed the fort. Again, the women and children committed themselves to the flames, and again all the clans lost their chiefs as 8,000 defenders burst out of the gates. When Akbar entered the city and saw that it had been transformed into a mass grave, he ordered the destruction of the buildings. In 1567 after this bloody episode in Chittaurgarh's history, it was abandoned and the capital of Mewar was moved to Udaipur. In 1615 Jahangir restored the city to the Rajputs.

Singh (d1930) which houses an interesting **museum** containing archaeological finds from this site. To the S is the **Vijay Stambha** (**9**)1458-68 , one of the most interesting buildings in the fort, built by Rana Kumbha to celebrate his victory over Mahmud Khilji of Malwa in 1440. Visible for miles around, it stands on a base 14m square and 3m high, and rises 37m. The 9-storeyed sandstone tower which has been restored, was covered with sculptures from the Hindu pantheon; the upper section retains some of the original. For Re 0.50 you can climb to the top for good views. Nearby is the **Mahasati** terrace where the ranas were cremated when Chittaurgarh was the capital of Mewar. There are also numerous *sati* stones. Just to the S is the **Samadhishvara Temple** (**10**) to Siva, dating from 11th and 15th centuries with some good sculptured friezes. Steps down lead to the deep **Gomukh Kund**, where the sacred spring water enters through a stone carved as a cow's mouth (hence its name).

Proceeding along the path to the S, the **Palaces of Jaimal and Patta** (**11**), renowned for their actions during the siege of 1567, stand side by side. The former's austere façade has a single opening for a door; the horizontal lines mark out 3-storeys where, in reality, there are only 2! Patta's Palace was based on the *zenana* building of Rana Kumbha's Palace, and is more interesting. You then pass the **Bhimtal** before seeing the **Kalika Mata Temple** (originally an 8th century Surya temple, rebuilt mid-16th) with exterior carvings and the ruins of **Chonda's House** with its 3-storey domed tower. Chonda did not claim the title when his father, Rana Lakha died in 1421.

Padmini's Palace further S, originally late 13th century, was rebuilt at the end of the 19th. The small pleasure palace sited in the middle of the lake has pretty gardens around it. Ala-ud-din Khilji is said to have seen Padmini's beautiful reflection in the water through a mirror on the palace wall. This striking vision convinced him that she had to be his.

You pass the deer park on your way round to the **Suraj Pol** (Sun Gate) you pass the **Adbhutanatha Temple** to Siva

(**12**) before reaching the 2nd tower, the **Kirti Stambh** (**13**) , a Tower of Fame (13th, 15th centuries). Fergusson has described it as one of the most interesting Jaina monuments of the age. Smaller than the Vijay Stambha (23m) with only 7 storeys, it is dedicated to Adinath, the 1st Jain Tirthankara. Naked figures of Tirthankaras are repeated several hundred times on the face of the tower. A narrow internal staircase goes to the top.

Of particular interest are the number of tanks and wells in the fort that have survived the centuries. Water, from both natural and artificial sources was harnessed to provide uninterrupted supply to the people. The good management of water was achieved by keeping animals (for grazing or bathing) away from the source of drinking water.

NB: A tour of the fort must be on foot; the circuit from the town is about 7 km. Allow 4 hr. The views from the battlements and towers justify the effort. The Archaeological Survey Office in the Fort is opp Rana Kumbha's Palace, where guide books are not always available; ask at *Panna Tourist Bungalow*.

Local festivals

Mira Utsav 19-20 Oct 1994; 8-9 Oct 1995; 26-27 Oct 1997; 16-17 Oct 1998.

Local information

● Accommodation

Chittaurgarh has few hotels. If you want comfort then stay in Udaipur and make a day trip to Chittaurgarh. **D** *Padmini*, Chanderiya Rd, nr Sainik School. T 2708. 20 rm, some a/c with TV. Restaurant, airport transfer from Udaipur. Rajasthan Tourism **D** *Panna Tourist Bungalow*, Udaipur Rd, nr rly. T 3238. 24 rm, some a/c, plus dorm. Veg dining hall, bar. Basic and clean. Best rm with view of fort.

E *Janta Avas Grih*, Station Rd, T 2009. 4 a/c rm with bath. Restaurant, Tourist Office. Spartan. **F** *Natraj*, by bus station, T 3009. Basic. **F** *Sanvaria*, nr rly, T 2597. Very basic. Also *Railway Retiring Rooms*, T 2008. Book in advance.

● Tourist information & tours

Rajasthan Janta Avas Grih, Station Rd, T 2009. 0800-1200, 1500-1800. They run 2 daily tours, 0800-1130, 1500-1830. Summer (May-Jun), 0700-1030, 1600-1930. Rs 15.

● Transport

Local The fort is over 6 km from station. **Rickshaws**: unmetered auto-rickshaws and cycle rickshaws are available in the town. Fares negotiable. **Bicycles**: for hire nr rly station.

Train A 117 km branch line runs from **Chittaurgarh to Udaipur**. At **Mavli Junction** (72 km) another branch runs down the Aravalli scarp to **Marwar Junction** (150 km). The views along this line are very picturesque indeed. By taking this route you can visit Udaipur, Ajmer and Jodhpur in a circular journey. **Old Delhi**: *Garib Nawaz Exp*, 2916, daily except Sat, 0920, 13 hr; *Chetak Exp*, 9616, daily, 2210, 16 hr. **Jaipur**: *Meenakshi Exp*, 7570, daily, 0540, 8 hr; *Garib Nawaz Exp*, 2916, daily, 0920, 6¾ hr; *Chetak Exp*, 9616, daily, 2210, 7¾ hr. **Ajmer**: *Meenakshi Exp*, 7570, daily, 0540, 4½ hr; *Garib Nawaz Exp*, 2916, daily except Sat, 0920, 4 hr; *Chetak Exp*, 9616, daily, 2210, 4½ hr. **Indore**: *Exp*, 9671, daily, 0125, 9¼ hr; *Fast Passenger*, 581, daily, 1427, 11¼ hr; *Meenakshi Exp*, 7569, daily, 2150, 7 hr.

Road Bus: there are daily buses to Bundi, Kota, Ajmer and Udaipur.

ROUTES From Chittaurgarh you can travel N to Ajmer (167 km) or W to Udaipur (N route via Fatehnagar 116 km, S route via Mangarwar 113 km). This is a picturesque drive. Along the way you might see fields of pink and white poppies, grown legally for opium. Just before you reach Udaipur you can stop at the remains of the ancient city of **Ahar** – see page 450.

JAIPUR TO JODHPUR, UDAIPUR & MT ABU

It is a very pleasant drive along the NH8 from Jaipur to Udaipur with a number of interesting places en route. After crossing relatively low lying land to Kishangarh the road enters the Aravallis. The road to Jodhpur leaves the NH8 just S of Beawar, and the direct railway line from Jaipur to Jodhpur passes by the Sambhar salt lake. The NH8 passes through **Makrana**, where the white marble used in the Taj Mahal was quarried. Small objects of polished marble can be

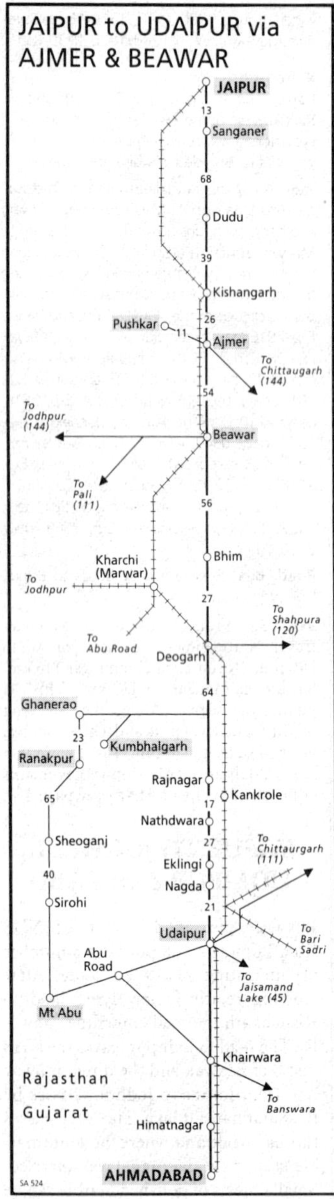

bought at the roadside. There are easy routes from both Jodhpur and Udaipur to Mt Abu, the charming hill station in the southern Aravallis.

ROUTES Leave Jaipur to the SW on **NH8** to Ajmer via Kishangarh.

Kishangarh

(102 km; *Pop* 22,000) was a small princely state within Amber territory, founded by Kishan Singh in 1603. It is chiefly known for its school of miniature painting noted for faces with sharp features and elongated almond-shaped eyes. On the shores of **Lake Gandalan**, the fort palace with its Hathi Pol (Elephant Gate) have walls decorated with fine murals. Though partly in ruin, you can see battlements, courtyards with gardens, shady balconies, brass doors and windows with coloured panes of glass. The temple houses a very fine collection of miniatures.

ROUTES From Kishangarh you continue on **NH8** to Ajmer (27 km). If you are travelling by car, it is worth breaking the journey at Ajmer, seeing the town, making the short drive to nearby **Pushkar**, then proceeding on to Jodhpur the following day. An afternoon drive will bring you to Jodhpur before dark.

Ajmer

The city is situated in a basin at the foot of Taragarh Hill (870m) and is surrounded by a stone wall with 5 gateways. It is said that 7 pilgrimages to Ajmer equal one to Mecca. Every year, especially at the annual Islamic festivals of Id and Mohurram thousands of pilgrims converge on this ancient town on the banks of the Ana Sagar Lake in Rajasthan. Ajmer is renowned throughout the Muslim world as the burial place of Mu'inuddin Chishti who claimed descent from the son-in-law of Mohammad. Born in Afghanistan in the middle of the 12th century, when Islam was on the verge of spreading to India, he visited Ajmer in 1192. He died here in 1235

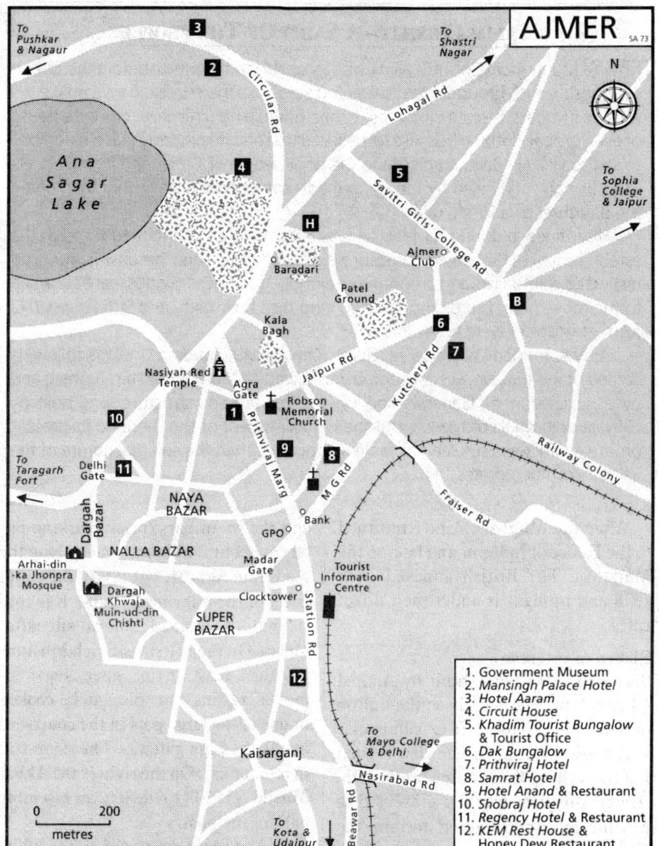

and his tomb became a place of pilgrimage. Mosques, pavilions and other tombs were subsequently erected.

BASICS *Population:* 401,000; *Altitude:* 486m; *STD Code* 0145). *Climate:* Summer Max 44°C Min 38°C; Winter Max 23°C Min 16°C.

Early history

According to tradition it was founded in 145 AD by Raja Ajaipal, one of the Chauhan kings. In the 11th and 12th centuries if suffered attacks from Mahmud of Ghazni and Muhammad Ghuri. The houses of Mewar, Malwa and Jodhpur each ruled for a time until the Mughals. Akbar annexed it in 1556 and made the dargah a place of pilgrimage. He built a palace, later occupied by Jahangir who laid out the beautiful Daulat Bagh garden by the artificial lake Ana Sagar, built by Anaji Chauhan between 1135-1150 AD. Jahangir also received the first British ambassador from King James I in 1616. Shah Jahan followed and adorned the garden with 5 fine marble pavilions.

Salim Chishti – A Saint Of The People

Khwaja Mu'inuddin Chishti (Salim Chisti) probably came to India before the Turkish conquests which brought Islam sweeping across northern India. A sufi, unlike the Muslim invaders, he came in peace. Tirmizi has told how he never owned a house or even proper clothing because he believed that private property was a hindrance to spirituality. He devoted his life to the poor people of Ajmer and its region. He was strongly influenced by the Upanishads; some reports claim that he married the daughter of a Hindu raja.

His influence during his lifetime was enormous, but continued through the establishment of the Chishti school or *silsila*, which flourished 'because it produced respected spiritualists and propounded catholic doctrines.' Hindus were attracted to the movement, but did not have to renounce their faith, and Sufi *khanqah* (a form of hospice) were accessible to all.

Almost immediately after his death Khwaja Mu'innuddin Chishti's followers carried on his mission. His early tomb was visited by Muhammad bin Tughluq and by a succession of Generals and rulers. The present structure was built by Ghiyasuddin Khalji of Malwa, but the embellishment of the shrine to its present ornate character is still seen as far less important than the spiritual nature of the Saint it commemorates.

After the Mughals, Ajmer returned to the House of Jodhpur and later to the Marathas. The British annexed it in 1818 and brought it under their direct rule.

Places of interest

Taragarh (Star Fort), built by Ajaipal Chauhan in 1100, stands on the hilltop overlooking the town. It is rectangular with walls 4.5m thick. The view is good but the walk up the winding bridle path, tiring. Along the way is a graveyard of Muslim 'martyrs' who died storming the fort.

The **Dargah of Khwaja Mu'inuddin Chishti** (1143-1235) is the tomb of the Sufi saint (also called 'The Sun of the Realm') which was begun by Iltutmish and completed by Humayun. Set in the heart of the old town, the entrance is through the bazar. Access to the main gate is on foot or by tonga or auto. The Emperor Akbar first made a pilgrimage to the shrine to give thanks for conquering Chittor in 1567, and the second for the birth of his son Prince Salim. From 1570 to 1580 Akbar made almost annual pilgrimages to Ajmer on foot from Agra, and the *kos* minars (brick marking pillars at about 2-mile intervals) along the road from Agra are witness of the popularity of the pilgrimage route. It is considered the second holiest site after Mecca. On their first visit, rich Muslims pay for a feast of rice, ghee, sugar, almonds, raisins and spices to be cooked in one of the large pots in the courtyard inside the high gateway. These are still in regular use. On the right is the **Akbar Masjid** (c1570), to the left, an assembly hall for the poor.

In the inner courtyard is the white marble **Shah Jahan Masjid** (c1650), 33m long with 11 arches and a carved balustrade on 3 sides. In the inner court is the **Dargah** (tomb), also white marble, square with a domed roof and 2 entrances. The ceiling is gold-embossed velvet, and silver rails and gates enclose the tomb. At festival times the tomb is packed with pilgrims, many coming from abroad.

Nearby is the **Mazar** (tomb) of Bibi Hafiz Jamal, daughter of the saint, a small enclosure with marble lattice-work. Close by is that of Chimni Begum, daughter of Shah Jahan. She never married, refusing to leave her father during the 7 years he was held captive by Aurangzeb. She spent her last days in Ajmer, as did another daughter who probably died of tuberculosis. At the S end of the Dargah is the **Jhalra** (tank).

The **Arhai-din-ka Jhonpra Mosque** ("The Hut of 2½ days"), which lies beyond the Dargah in a narrow valley. Originally a Jain college built in 1153, it was partially destroyed by Muhammad of Ghori in 1192, and in 1210 turned into a mosque by Qutb-ud-din-Aibak who built a massive screen of 7 arches in front of the pillared halls, allegedly in 2½ days (hence its name). The temple pillars which were incorporated in the building, are all different. The mosque measures 79m x17m with 10 domes supported by 124 columns and incorporates older Hindu and Jain masonry. Much of it is in ruins though restoration work was undertaken at the turn of the century; only part of the 67m screen and the Jain prayer hall remain.

Akbar's Palace is in the city centre near the E wall and the railway station. It is a large rectangular building with a fine gate. Today it houses the **Ajmer museum**.

The ornate **Nasiyan Jain Temple** (Red Temple) on Prithviraj Marg has a remarkable museum (Open 0800-1700) alongside the Jain shrine, which itself is open only to Jains. Ajmer has a large Jain population (about 25% of the city's total), and the Shri Siddhkut Chaityalaya, was founded in 1864 in honour of the 1st Jain Tirthankar, Rishabdev, by a Jain diamond merchant, Raj Bahadur Seth Moolchand Nemichand Soni (hence its alternative name, the Soni temple). The opening was celebrated in 1895. Behind a wholly unimposing exterior, on its first floor the Svarna Nagari Hall houses an astonishing reconstruction of the Jain conception of the Universe, with gold plated replicas of every Jain shrine in India. Over 1000 kg of gold is estimated to have been used, and at one end of the gallery diamonds have also been placed behind decorative coloured glass to give an appearance of backlighting. Encased in a huge room behind glass, the whole can be seen from different external galleries. The holy mountain, Sumeru, is at the centre of the continent, and around it are such holy sites as Ayodhya, the birthplace of the Tirthankar, recreated in gold plate, and a remarkable collection of model temples. Suspended from the ceiling are *vimanas* – airships of the gods – and silver balls. On the ground floor, beneath the model, are the various items taken on procession around the town on the Jain festival day of Nov 23rd each year. The trustees of the temple are continuing to maintain and embellish it. The walls and ceilings of the main hall have been completely re-painted in traditional style since the late 1980s, and the surrounding galleries are undergoing a similar programme of renovation. Visit strongly recommended.

Mayo College (1873), 4 km from centre, was founded to provide young Indian princes with a liberal education, one of 2 genuinely Indo-Saracenic buildings designed by De Fabeck in Ajmer, the other being the **Mayo Hospital** (1870). The College was known as the 'Eton' of Rajputana and was run along the lines of an English Public School. It is now open to all.

Ana Sagar, an artificial lake (c1150) was further enhanced by Emperors Jahangir and Shah Jahan who added ther *baradari* and pavilions. The **Foy Sagar**, 5 km, another artificial lake was a famine relief project.

Museum

In the octagonal building of Akbar's palace, built in 1570 and restored in 1905.Very good collection of old Rajput and Mughal armour, coins and some fine sculpture from 6th to 17th centuries. 1000-1630, closed Fri. Photography prohibited.

Excursions

Ajmer is a good base from which to visit Pushkar (11 km W). Buses leave from outside the railway station.

Local festivals

The *urs* festival commemorating *Khwaja Mu'inuddin Chishti's* death in 1235 is celebrated with 6 days of almost continuous music, and devotees from all over India and the Middle East make the pilgrimage. *Qawwalis* and other Urdu music developed in the courts of rulers can be heard. Roses cover the tomb. On the final day, women wash the tomb with their hair, then squeeze the rose water into bottles as medicine for the sick. The urs festival itself is fixed according to the Islamic calendar. It starts on sighting the new moon in *Rajab*, the 7th month of the Islamic year, and celebrations continue for 6 days. The peak is reached on the night between the 5th and 6th days of Rajab when tens of thousands of pilgrims pack the shrine. At 1100 on the morning of the 6th day pilgrims and all visitors are banned from the dargah and the *khadims*, who are responsible through the year for the maintenance of worship at the shrine, dressed in their best clothes approach the shrine with flowers and sweets.

Local information

● **Accommodation**

NB: prices rise sharply – as much as 10 times – during the week of the Pushkar mela. Many hotels are booked well in advance. **A *Mansingh Palace***, Ana Sagar Circular Rd, Vaishali Nagar, T 50855. 60 rm. 1 km centre. Modern hotel, good restaurant and service. Folk entertainment on request. Ajmer's best hotel. **D *Regency***, Delhi Gate, T 30296. 28 rm, some a/c. Central position, in very crowded area but set back from road. Good restaurant. **D *Ajaymeru***, Ana Sagar Circ Rd, T 20089. 30 rm. Restaurant, shops. **D *Prithviraj***, Jaipur Rd, T 23297. 25 rm, 2 a/c. Modest. **D *Samrat***, Kutchery Rd, T 31805. Some air-cooled rm.

● **Budget hotels**

E *Aaram* LIC Colony, T 50272. 22 rm, air/cooled.Restaurant, small garden. Decent modern hotel. **E *Khadim Tourist Bungalow***, Savitri Girls' College Rd, nr bus station, T 20490. 49 rm, 11 a/c, and dorm. Good restaurant, bar. Pleasant setting. Popular and good value. **E *Anand***, Prithviraj Marg, T 23099. Clean rm with shower, some renovated. Friendly service. Rec. **E *Bhola***, Prithviraj Marg, T23844. Simple rm. Veg restaurant. **E *Shobraj*** Delhi Gate, T 23488. 22 rm, 5 a/c. Centre of old town in busy area, clean and acceptable. Popular restaurant.

There is a group of **F** category hotels offering rm with bath, by the rly station: ***King Edward Memorial (KEM)***, Station Rd, T 20936. Very popular with pilgrims, basic, but clean and acceptable with a few larger rm. Very close to rly station. ***Nagpal***, Cinema Rd, T 21603; ***Malwa***, Jaipur Rd, T 23343. Basic rm, better in front.

● **Places to eat**

Honey Dew, almost opp rly station. Good veg food, pleasant shady garden. Open all day. Also *Kwality. Italia, Vikram*

● **Banks**

State Bank of India at the Collectorate and others.

● **Shopping**

Fine local silver jewellery, tie-and-dye textiles and camel hide articles are best buys. The shopping areas are Madar Gate, Station Rd, Purani Mandi, Naya Bazar and Kaisarganj. ***Arts and Art's***, Bhojan Shala, nr Jain Temple.

● **Tourist office**

In the Khadim Tourist Bungalow, T 21626. Approved guide and tourist taxi hire. Information counter at rly station, nr 1st Cl main gate.

● **Transport**

Train Enquiries, T 131. **Old Delhi**: *Aravalli Exp*, 9932, daily, 1905, 10½ hr; *Delhi Mail*, 9902, daily, 2040, 10¾ hr; *Delhi Exp*, 9904, daily, 0710, 11¾ hr; *Ashram Exp*, 2906, daily, 0135, 8½ hr. **Agra (Fort)**: *Agra Fort Fast Passenger Exp*, 9706, daily, 2000, 10½ hr. **Ahmadabad**: *Agra Fort Fast Passenger Exp*, 9705, daily, 0740, 20½ hr; *Ahmadabad Exp*, 9903, daily, 2150, 12¼ hr; *Ahmadabad Mail*, 9901, daily, 0835, 11¾ hr; *Aravalli Exp*, 9931, daily, 0315, 13 hr; *Ashram Exp*, 2905, daily, 0250, 8½ hr. **Beawar**: *Ahmadabad Exp*, 9903, daily, 2150, 1 hr; *Ahmadabad Mail*,

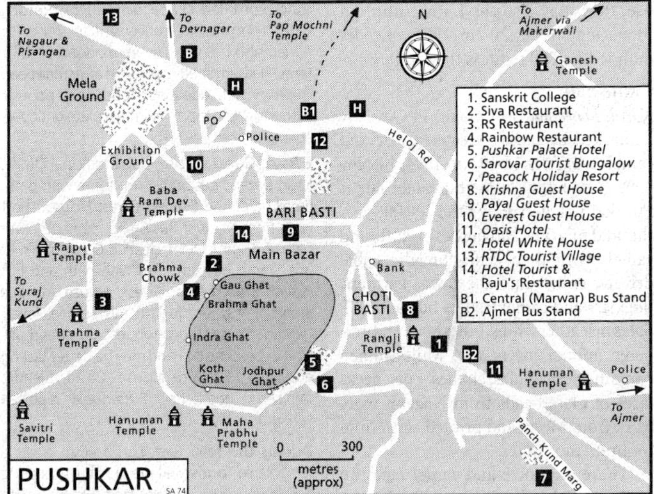

9901, daily, 0835, 1 hr; *Aravalli Exp*, 9931, daily, 0315, 1 hr. **Jaipur**: *Pink City Exp*, 2916, daily except Sat, 1350, 2¼ hr; *Delhi-Ahmadabad Mail*, 9902, daily, 2000, 3½ hr; *Delhi-Ahmadabad Exp*, 9904, daily, 0710, 3¾ hr; *Ashram Exp*, 2906, daily, 0137, 2¾ hr. **Udaipur**: *Garib Nawaz Exp*, 2915, daily, 1358, 7½ hr; *Chetak Exp*, 9615, daily, 0030, 8¾ hr.

Road Bus: enquiries, T 20398. Buses every ½ hr to Jaipur (3 hr). 2 daily to **Jodhpur** (198 km) 5 hr; 3 to **Bikaner** 7 hr; **Chittaurgarh** (190 km), **Udaipur** (302 km) via Chittaurgarh, **Kota** (200 km) via Bundi and Bikaner. Also buses for Agra and Delhi. Buses for Pushkar (Rs 4) are very crowded. **Jeeps**: (Rs 5) better but difficult to get.

Pushkar

(*Pop* 11,500) For most of the year Pushkar is a gentle and peaceful lakeside village on the edge of the desert, though it has been transformed by the year-round presence of large numbers of foreign tourists and backpackers. The road from Ajmer passes the village of Nausar and a striking 2 km long pass through the Nag Pahar (Snake Hills) which divides Pushkar from Ajmer. Pushkar lies in a narrow dry valley overshadowed by these impressive rocky hills. There are spectacular views of the desert at sunset from the hills around the village.

Places of interest

Pushkar lake is one of India's most sacred. Ghats lead down to the water to enable pilgrims to bathe. Fa Hien, the Chinese traveller who visited Pushkar in the 5th century AD commented on the number of pilgrims. However, though several of the older temples were subsequently destroyed by Aurangzeb, many remain. The only Brahma temple in the country, at the farther end of the lake, is believed to have sprung from a lotus flower dropped by Brahma. It is a particularly holy shrine since it is believed to mark the spot where Brahma was incarnated. Pilgrims still come throughout the year. Pandas – priests with responsibility for particular families or local communities – meet pilgrim buses and arrange the necessary rituals, keeping records of who has attended. **NB:** if you receive a "blessing", temple priests may charge for a coconut they use; they may also ask for a minimum "donation" of Rs 20 (in 1994, one demanded Rs 200 to bless the family).

Cattle Fair

Kartik Poornima (full moon) in Oct/Nov is marked by India's greatest cattle and camel *mela* (fair). 15-19 Nov 1994, 4-8 Nov 1995. The huge cattle and camel fair is Pushkar's biggest draw. Over 200,000 visitors and pilgrims and hordes of cattle and camels with their semi-nomadic tribal drivers, crowd into the town. Farmers, breeders and camel traders buy and sell. Sales in leather whips, bits, shoes, embroidered animal covers soar, while women bargain over bangles, clothes, pots, necklaces of glass beads from Nagaur, ivory work from Merta and printed cloth from Jodhpur and Ajmer.

There are horse and camel races on all days and betting is heavy. The Ladhu Umt is a race in which teams of up to 10 men will cling to the camel and one another in a hilarious and often chaotic spectacle. There are also sideshows of jugglers, acrobats, magicians and folk dancing. At nightfall, there is music and dancing outside the tents, around friendly fires. Pilgrims bathe in the lake, the night of the full moon being the most auspicious time, and launch boats of marigold and rose petals in the moonlight. **NB**: the official Fair programme is not always correct.

Local information

● Accommodation

NB: during the fair, hotel charges rise dramatically. Booking in advance for *mela* essential for all the better guest houses and hotels. **D** ***Pushkar Palace***, T 2001. A renovated old palace. 45 rm, best on lakeside with a/c and bath; some small cheaper rm and dorm. Pleasant garden, good food (alcohol prohibited), travel desk arranges camel and horse safaris. Highly rec. Nearby Rajasthan Tourism **D** ***Sarovar Tourist Bungalow***, on lake nr Ajmer Bus Stand, T 2040. 36 clean rm (best with lake view, in old part); some air-cooled with bath and dorm. Set around courtyard in former lakeside palace, some rm have splendid views. Veg restaurant, attractive gardens. Alcohol prohibited. **D** ***Peacock Holiday Resort***, T 18. 1 km centre, convenient for buses to Ajmer. Also has very cheap rm, dorm beds or tents. Pleasant shady courtyard and small pool. Friendly staff, adequate food, very popular with travellers, less than immaculate but bearable amenities.

E ***Payal Guest House***, opp Municipal Office, Main Bazar. Reasonable rm, some with bath. Small garden. **E** ***Everest Guest House***, short walk from Marwar Bus Stand. Some rm with bath and dorm. Quiet, clean. **E** ***Oasis***, nr Ajmer Bus Stand, has some rm with bath and hot water. **E/F** ***Krishna Guest House***, nr Bus Stand, T 43. Rec for friendly service, lovely garden, pleasant roof-top restaurant and unlimited breakfasts! Food may be better tasting elsewhere. **F** ***White House***. Clean, friendly, family-run hotel. Rec. **F** ***Rainbow*** reported very unfriendly, with dirty pool.

During the fair Rajasthan Tourism erects a remarkable **Tourist Village**, a tent city housing 100,000 people. Deluxe tents (Rs 600, with meals), ordinary/dorm tents (Rs 30-50 per bed). Beds and blankets are provided; there is some running water and only Indian toilets. All meals are served in a separate tent. Advance reservation essential: Central Reservation Office, Chandralok Bldg, 36 Jan Path, New Delhi 110001, T 32180 or through a travel agent. ***Royal Camp***, Set up by Maharaja Resorts, Umaid Bhawan Palace, Jodhpur, T 33316, F 35373. 35 comfortable tents capturing the style of Royal Safaris, with baths. Separate dining and reception tents. Nightly campfire with local entertainment laid on. ***JP's Tourist Resort*** at Ganahera. Rural atmosphere, desert orchard among dunes. 28 rm in 'traditional' thatched houses decorated with mandanas (paintings) on doors and windows.

● Places to eat

Take special care during the fair: eat only freshly cooked food and drink bottled water. There are a number of inexpensive to mid-price restaurants. ***RS Restaurant*** opp Brahma Temple, has an open air kitchen with an interesting view of the food preparation. ***Siva*** does unlimited breakfasts and veg *thalis* (about Rs 20) but buffets not rec. ***Sunset Caf*** by *Pushkar Palace Hotel* overlooking lake, rec for breakfast. ***Poppins Rooftop*** is run by an effervescent lawyer. Only 2 tables, slow service but *Malai kofta* rec. Reasonable choice, good value. ***Natraj*** has good views from rooftop. ***Raju's Garden*** excellent Indian and Western (eg tomato/cheese *nan*); very reasonable; unlimited breakfast Rs

20! *Venus*, offers a-la-carte instead of the usual buffet.

● Shopping
Shops selling clothes and handcrafted items cater for young foreigners; bargain. **Books**: Shop around as prices vary markedly.

● Tour companies & travel agents
Tourist Tours and Travels, at *Pushkar Palace Hotel*.

● Transport
Road Bus: frequent service from Ajmer (see above). From Pushkar, direct buses go to Jodhpur via Merta (8 hr); it is quicker to return to Ajmer and take an express bus (4-5 hr) from there. 'First class' passengers travel on the roof!

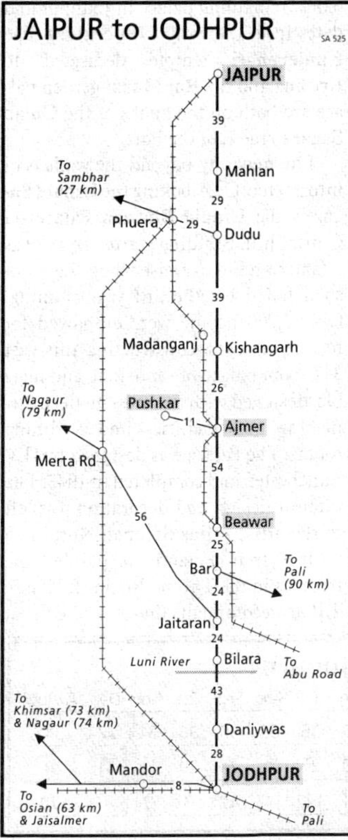

Ajmer to Beawar

ROUTES The route S follows the NH8, still a comparatively quiet road with several resting places. The first is the *Rajasthan Tourist Motel*, 40 km S of Ajmer, just E of the NH8.

Beawar

(54 km S of Ajmer; *Pop* 107,000; *STD Code* 01462). Founded by Colonel CG Dixon, Superintendent of Merwara (1836-48) who planned its layout. His tomb (1857) was once treated as a local shrine and was worshipped by the Mers. It provided the origin for Kipling's story *The Tomb of His Ancestors*. Today the tomb has been replaced by a lamp-post in the middle of the crossroads at the town centre, though local people still know the story. The town is by-passed by the NH8.

● Accommodation E *Vikrant* On W of town near the colourful bazar and Bus Stand, T 21664. 21 Rm, 2 a/c, air-cooled. Modest, centrally placed, adequate.

● Transport Train To Ajmer *Aravalli Exp*, 9932, daily, 1705, 1½ hr; *Delhi Mail*, 9902, daily, 1843, 1½ hr; *Delhi Exp*, 9904, daily, 0520, 1¼ hr.

ROUTES From Beawar the NH8 continues S to Udaipur. See page 447.

Beawar to Jodhpur and Bikaner

Just after leaving Beawar the road crosses the Aravallis and passes from the catchment area of E flowing rivers which join the Ganga, ultimately to flow into the Bay of Bengal, and the W flowing rivers which flow into the Arabian Sea. It also passes into the increasingly arid land of the the Thar desert.

Jodhpur

The second city of Rajasthan, once the capital of Marwar, sprawls around the impressive Meherangarh Fort built on a 122m sandstone bluff.

BASICS *Population:* 648,000. *Altitude:* 216m. *Area*: 23 sq km. *STD Code:* 0291.

Development of the state

The Rathore Rajputs had moved to Marwar – the "land of the dead" – in 1211 after their defeat at Kanauj by Muhammad Ghori, but in 1459 Rao Jodha, forced to leave the Rathore capital of Mandor, 8 km to the N, chose this as his capital because of its strategic location on the edge of the Thar Desert. The Rathores subsequently controlled wide areas of Rajasthan. Rao Udai Singh of Jodhpur (d1581) received the title of Raja from Akbar, and his son, Sawai Raja Sur Singh (d1595), conquered Gujarat and part of the Deccan for the Emperor, an example of the government in partnership that Akbar succeeded in achieving. Maharaja Jaswant Singh (d1678), having supported Shah Jahan in the Mughal struggle for succession in 1658, had a problematic relationship with the subsequent Mughal rule of Aurangzeb, and his posthumous son Maharaja Ajit Singh was only able to succeed him after Aurangzeb's own death in 1707. In addition to driving the Mughals out of Ajmer he added substantially to the Meherangarh Fort in Jodhpur. His successor, Maharaja Abhai Singh (d1749) captured Ahmadabad, and the State came into treaty relations with the British in 1818.

Jodhpur lies on the once strategic Delhi-Gujarat trading route and the Marwaris managed and benefitted from the traffic of opium, copper, silk, sandalwood, dates, coffee and much more besides. They provided the essential economic base for the military power of the state.

Places of interest

NB: Jodhpur is well worth visiting. If you can spare no more than a day, try to see the Umaid Bhavan Palace, Meherangarh Fort and Museum and the nearby *chhattris*.

The Old City is surrounded by a huge 9.5 km long wall which has 101 bastions and 7 gates, above which are inscribed the name of the place to which the road leads. Some of the houses and temples are of richly carved stone, in particular the red sandstone buildings of the Sadar Bazar. Here the **Taleti Mahal**, one of 3 concubines' palaces in Jodhpur, has the unique feature of jarokhas decorated with temple columns. Although it was added to by Ajit Singh, it is probably the oldest remaining palace in Jodhpur and dates from the early 17th century. The **Kunjebehari** temple dedicated to Krishna and the **Raj Mahal** garden palace are both on the banks of the **Gulab Sagar** to the E of the Fort.

The new city beyond the walls is of interest too. Overlooking the **Umaid Sagar** is the **Umaid Bhawan Palace** on Chittar hill. Building started in 1929 as a famine relief exercise when the monsoon failed for the 3rd year running. Over 3,000 people were employed for nearly 14 years, constructing this vast 347 room palace of sandstone and marble, designed with the most modern furnishing and facilities and 8 dining rooms. The Palace was designed by H.V. Lanchester and completed in 1943. The interior design and decoration was left to the artist Julius Stephan Norblin, a refugee from Poland; he painted the frescoes in the Throne Room (E Wing). Tillotson comments that it is "the finest

CLIMATE: JODHPUR

	Jan	Feb	Mar	Apr	May	Jun	Jul	Aug	Sep	Oct	Nov	Dec	Av/Tot
Max (°C)	25	28	33	38	42	40	36	33	35	36	31	27	34
Min (°C)	9	12	17	22	27	29	27	25	24	20	14	11	20
Rain (mm)	7	5	2	2	6	31	122	145	47	7	3	1	378

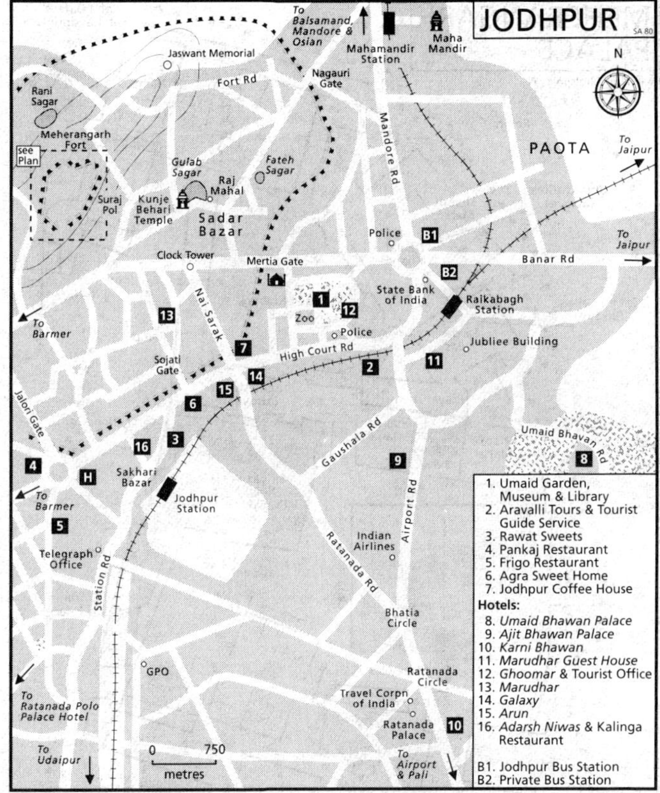

example of Indo-Deco...The forms are crisp and precise, and the bland monochrome of the stone makes the eye concentrate on their carved shapes. The details of the exterior are mostly of Indian origin, and they evoke the spirit of art deco simply through their sculptural treatment and consequent chill elegance." It is now a luxury hotel (see Hotels), and the interior, based strongly on western models, produces a remarkable sensation of separation from the Indian environment in which it is set. There is a subterranean swimming pool decorated with signs of the zodiac; the murals are Norblin's.

Whereas much British inspired building at the end of the 19th century had deliberately gone back to Mughal and Islamic idioms, cultivating the Indo-Saracenic style on the grounds that this was recapturing and developing the best of Indian traditional architecture, Lanchester deliberately avoided such a style on the grounds that Rajasthan had never been fully under Muslim influence. Thus the "dripstones or *chajjis* are ribbed, recalling those of ancient Indian temples" and the dining hall is "a reinterpretation of a Buddhist Chaitya hall".

The **Ratanada Palace**, now used by the military, is S towards the airport.

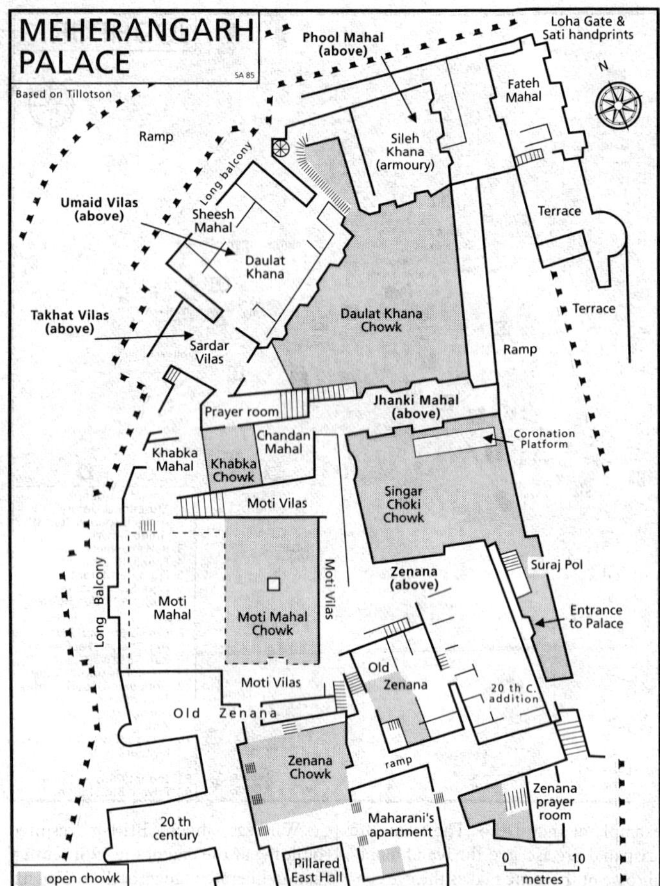

Just SE of Raikabagh Station are the **Raikabagh Palace** and the **Jubilee Buildings**, public offices designed by Sir Samuel Swinton Jacob in the Indo-Saracenic style. 2 km to the N on the Balsamand Rd is the **Mahamandir**, a very large temple set in a housing colony. 3 km further N is the **Balsamand Lake**, surrounded by gardens laid out in 1936 with a European style late 19th century pleasure pavilion a 'Lake Palace', on the bund. Although its internal structures are in a European style it has entirely traditional and beautifully carved red sandstone facings. Plans under way to restore the pavilion.

Meherangarh

The 'Majestic Fort' sprawls along the top of a steep escarpment with a 37m sheer drop at the S end. Originally started by Rao Jodha in 1459, it stands high above the plains, with walls which, in places, are 36m high and up to 21m wide. Most of the fort which stands today dates from the period of Maharajah Jaswant Singh (1638-78), a contemporary of Shah Jahan whose relationship with the Mughal court was often squally. On Jaswant Singh's death in 1678 Aurangzeb occupied the fort, bringing the first major period of fort extension to an end. However, after Aurangzeb's death Meherangarh came back under the Rajput control of Jaswant Singh's posthumous son Ajit Singh. The royal family had been in residence here for over 500 years until the Umaid Bhavan Palace was built in 1943.

The summit is divided into 3 areas: the palace (NW), a wide terrace to the E of the Palace and the strongly fortified area to the S edge of the cliff. The approach is by a winding path up the W side which is possible by rickshaw. Extensive views from the top. En route there is the cremation ground of the former rulers. Distinctive among their memorials is the white marble **chhattri** to Jaswant Singh II (1899). Summer 0800-1730, Winter 0900-1430. Entry Rs 25 (includes attendant/ guides and local musicians), Camera Rs 35. Video Rs 75. Allow at least 2 hr.

The gateways There were originally 7: The 1st, (Fateh Gate) is marked with cannon shots and heavily fortified with spikes and a barbican that forces a 45 degree turn. The smaller Gopal Gate is followed by the Bhairon Gate, with large guardrooms. The 4th, Toati Gate, is now missing but the 5th, Dodhkangra Gate stands over a turn in the path and has loopholed battlements for easy defence. In the NE of the Palace is the Amarti Gate, a long passage flanked by guardrooms. The last, Loha (Iron) Gate, controls the final turn into the fort and has the 31 handprints of royal *satis*, the wives of Maharajas, see page 104. It is said that 6 queens and 58 concubines became *satis* on Ajit Singh's funeral pyre in 1724. Though illegal since 1829, there have been *satis* in Jodhpur in the last decade. *Satis* carried the Bhagavad Gita with them into the flames and legend has it that the holy book would never perish. The climb to the top is quite stiff. Within the fort area are 2 small tanks: the **Rani Talao** (Queen's) and the **Gulab Sagar** (Rose-Water).

The Old Palaces From the **Loha Gate** the ramp leads up to the **Suraj Pol** (Sun Gate), which gives onto the **Singar Choki Chowk**. This is the main entrance to the Museum, and a guide takes visitors round the inner buildings.

Used for royal ceremonies such as the anointing of rajas, the N, W and SW sides of the Singar Choki Chowk date from the period immediately before the Mughal occupation in1678. Tillotson points out that the SE wing is later, having pillars topped by imitative Ionic capitals that were typical of Maharajah Ajit Singh's period between 1707-1724. The upper storeys of the chowk were part of the zenana, and from the **Jhanki Mahal** ("glimpse palace") on the upper floor of the N wing the women could look down on the activities of the courtyard. The upper storeys of the Jhanki Mahal itself comprise a long gallery whose arcades are flanked by a further narrow gallery from which balconies (*jarokhas*) project over the courtyard. Thus the chowk below has the features characteristic of much of the rest of the zenana, *jarokhas* surmounted by the distinctive Bengali style eaves, also incorporated into Mughal fort architecture as in Agra and Delhi, and beautifully ornate *jali* screens. These allowed cooling breezes to ventilate rooms and corridors in the often stiflingly hot desert summers.

Also typical of Mughal buildings was the use of material hung from rings below the eaves to provide roof covering, as in the columned halls of the **Daulat Khana** and the **Sileh Khana** (the armoury), which also date from Ajit Singh's reign. The collection of Indian weapons in the armoury is unequalled, with remarkable swords and daggers, often beautifully decorated with calligraphy, and a wide range of other weapons. **Abai Singh's** tent from his highly successful Deccan campaign is also displayed. Along the ramparts antique cannonry can be seen. Shah Jahan's (later Aurangzeb's) red silk and velvet tent, lavishly embroidered with gold thread, used in the Imperial Mughal campaign, is in the **Tent Room**. The **Jewel House** has a wonderful collection of jewellery, including diamond eyebrows held by hooks over the ears. There are also palanquins, howdahs and ornate royal cradles, all marvelliously preserved and maintained.

The **Phool Mahal** (Flower Palace), above the Sileh Khana, was built by Abhai Singh (1724-49) as a hall of private audience. Although the stone jali screens are original and there are striking portraits of former rulers, a lavishly gilded ceiling and the Jodhpur coat of arms displayed above the royal couch, the murals of the 36 musical modes are a late 19th century addition.

The **Umaid Vilas**, which houses Rajput miniatures, is linked to the **Sheesh Mahal** (Mirror Palace), built by Ajit Singh between 1702-24. The room, which has characteristic large and regularly sized mirror work, unlike Mughal "mirror palaces", looks out to the NW. Immediately to its S, and above the Sardar Vilas, is the **Takhat Vilas.** Added by Maharajah Takhat Singh (1843-73), it has wall murals of dancing girls, love legends and Krishna Lila, while its ceiling has 2 unusual features: massive wooden beams to provide support and the curious use of colourful Belgian Christmas tree balls.

The **Ajit Vilas** has a fascinating collection of musical instruments and costumes. On the Grd Fl of the Takhat Vilas is **Sardar Vilas**, with to its S the **Khabka and Chandan Mahals** (sleeping quarters), which also have the Ionic columns typical of Ajit Singh's period. The **Moti Vilas**, wings to the N, E and S of the Moti Mahal chowk, date from Jaswant Singh's reign. As in the Singar Choki Chowk women could watch proceedings in the courtyard below through the jali screens of the surrounding wings. Tillotson suggests that the **Moti Mahal** (Pearl Palace), although placed in the zenana of the fort, was such a magnificent building that it could only have served the purpose of a Diwan-i-Am, or hall of public audience. He argues that its common attribution to Sawai Raja Sur Singh (1595-1629) is a century too early, the real builder being Ajit Singh, who probably had to demolish buildings on the W of the square to make room for it. The Moti Mahal, one of the most brilliant rooms of the palace, is fronted by excellently carved 19th century woodwork, while inside waist-level niches housed oil lamps whose light would have shimmered from the mirrored ceiling.

From the windows of the palaces you can see the town below; the blue-wash Brahmin houses stand out among the white. For the Rajput princes the Brahmins represented a vital avenue to authentic power, for in exchange for recognising the Brahmins' place at the head of Hindusim's religious hierarchy they in turn granted the Rajputs' right to be regarded as genuine kshatriyas, a status all Rajput leaders were keenly anxious to be accepted. Like all the most spectacular Rajput Palaces and forts, Jodhpur provides a very picturesque and memorable balance between the exigencies of defence and the flamboyance of prosperity.

Museums

Mehrangarh Fort Palace Museum in a series of palaces, beautifully designed and decorated windows and walls. Magnificent collection of the Maharajas' memorabilia – superbly maintained and presented (See above). **The Old Fort Museum** is fascinating. Palanquins, royal *howdahs* lavishly upholstered and one of silver, a golden throne, pearl encrusted shoes, paintings and mirrors among the exhibits. Summer 0800-1800, Winter 0900-1700. Usually tours with English speaking guides included in price.

Umaid Bhawan Palace Museum, *Umaid Bhawan Palace Hotel*. This fine museum includes the Durbar Hall with the flaking murals. A good collection of miniatures, armour and old clocks. 0900-1700. Govt **Museum**, Umaid Park. 1000-1700. A time-capsule from the British Raj (little added since Independence). Some moth-eaten stuffed animals and featherless birds, model aeroplanes, images of Jain *Tirthankars*, textiles, local crafts, miniature portraits and antiquities. A small zoo in gardens has a few rare exotic species.

Parks & zoos

Umaid Park, High Court Rd. Mandore Gardens – see Excursions.

Excursions

Village Safaris These are becoming quite popular and is recommended for those who are not travelling around Rajasthan by car. **NB**: there are some unscrupulous tour operators. It is best to go through a reputable agency or a good hotel, eg *Ajit Bhawan Hotel*.

Mandor 8 km N of Jodhpur the old 6th century capital of Marwar is set on a plateau over the Mandor Gardens. The gardens are set around the former cremation ground of the Rathor rulers' dark red sandstone *chhattris*; very popular with Indian tourists, especially at weekends. The **Shrine of the 33 Crore** (330 Million) **Gods** is a large hall containing huge painted rock-cut figures of heroes and gods. The largest ***deval***, a combination of temple and cenotaph architectural design, is Ajit Singh's (d1724). In common with the other Mandor memorial buildings this has far more in common with the temple design than with the simpler memorial chhattris, though the towering shrine which in a temple would have housed the presiding deity was left empty. Ajit Singh also had a pleasure palace built. A small **Museum** contains 5th-9th century sculptures. There are also the remains of an 8th century Hindu temple on a hilltop nearby.

● **Transport Road Bus**: frequent dep, 100m from Jodhpur Tourist Office.

Tours

City Sightseeing: ½ day (0830-1300, 1400-1800). Fort and palaces, Jaswant Thada, Mandor Gardens, Govt Museum.

Local festivals

In addition to the common Hindu festivals, there are a number especially popular in Rajasthan, eg *Teej* (see Jaipur page 406). **Jul/Aug**: *Nag Panchami*. Reverence for the cobra (*naag*) is shown by people all over the country. The festival day is dedicated to *Sesha*, the thousand-headed god or *Anant* ('infinite') Vishnu, the great god of preservation who is often depicted reclining on a bed of serpents in between great acts or incarnations (*avatars*). In Jodhpur huge effigies of the mythical serpent are displayed in a colourful fair. In other parts of India, idols of hooded serpents are fed with milk and sweets.

Local information

● **Accommodation**

Price guide
AL Rs 3,000+ **A** Rs 2,000-3,000
B Rs 1,200-2,000 **C** Rs 600-1,200
D Rs 250-600 **E** Rs 100-250 **F** Up to Rs 100.

AL Welcomgroup *Umaid Bhawan Palace*, T 22316. 96 a/c rm, AL suites. 3 km centre. Unusual pool. Private museum (Grd Flr, S. Wing), the royal family still occupy part of the palace. Luxurious ambience. Non-residents may have the excellent, though pricey, buffet lunch in the magnificent dining hall (Rs 375). Terrace cover-charge (Rs 250), to discourage day-trippers.

C *Ratanada Polo Palace*, Residency Rd (nr airport), T 31910, F 33194. 50 rm. Restaurant, bar, pool. Only one with central a/c but lacks character. Poor management, over-priced. **C** *Ajit Bhawan*, Airport Rd, nr Circuit House, T 20409. 50 air-cooled rm with bath, best in stone cottage units, tastefully and individually furnished in the local style, some period furniture; few cheaper small rm. Indian restaurant (Buffet Rs 130; order in advance), garden, sports, 'Village safari' by jeep to see the 'real Rajasthan' (Rs 350). May be fully booked by tour groups, so book in advance. Charming family house of Maharaja Swarup Singh; considered superb by some. However, reports of reservation not honoured; back-packers treated with indifference and made to feel unwelcome. Nearby, **C** ***Karni Bhawan***, Defence Laboratory Rd, Ratanada, T 20157. 15 rm. Restaurant (campfire suppers), peaceful lawns, pleasant ambience. Good value. Extra charge for folk-dance and roof-dinner evenings.

D ***Adarsh Niwas***, opp rly station, T 26936. 26 air-cooled rm, with bath and TV, suites best. Good *Kalinga* restaurant. Rajashtan Tourism **D** ***Ghoomar Tourist Bungalow***, High Court Rd, T 21900. 60 rm, dorm. Restaurant, coffee shop, Tourist Information, travel, garden. Not very clean, especially dorms; rather dull; "super deluxe" a/c rm slightly better. **D** ***Marudhar***, 12 Nai Sarak, T 27429. 17 rm, some a/c. Rm service. Another cheaper ***Marudhar International***, opp KN Hall, Raikabagh, T 23208. Simple rm with bath, some a/c, around garden. **D** ***Shanti Bhawan***, opp rly station, T 21689. Better rm with air-cooler, bath and TV (check first), cheaper without bath. Indian veg restaurant. **D** ***Govind***, Station Rd, 200m to right from rly station, opp GPO, T 22758. 14 clean rm, all air-cooled, most with bath, dorm. Good rooftop restaurant with spectacular view of fort, Umaid Palace and city. Helpful staff. Rec.

● Budget hotels

E ***Akshey***, behind station, opp Raikabagh Palace, T 21549. Some a./c rm, cheap dorm. Meals in rm or pleasant garden. **E** ***Galaxy***, nr rly bridge by Sojati Gate, opp Tempo stand, T 25098. 60 rm, some air-cooled, with bath; dorm. Indian veg restaurant. Noisy. **E** ***Godawan Guest House***, Paota, 'C' Rd, nr All India Radio, (3 km centre), T 25001. Some rm with bath and balcony (1st Fl better). Quiet location, garden, friendly. Rec. **E** ***Maharaja Kenya***, Nai Sarak, T 28242. Rm could be cleaner, rate negotiable. **E** ***New Tourist***, Lakshmi Bhavan, nr Jalori Gate. Simple rm (best on roof). Indian veg food, pleasant rooftop, friendly. Tailor opp rec. **E** ***Arun***, Sojati Gate, T 20238. Bank of Baroda useful. **F** ***Rly Retiring Rooms***, Jodhpur Rly Station. Rm and dorm. Reasonable restaurant. See note on *Waiting Room* under Transport. **E** ***Priya***, Nai Sarak. Simple rm.

Guest Houses and cheaper **E** and **F** hotels often have shared baths; some in Jodhpur Station area. **E** ***Raj***, Station Rd, T 28447. 27 basic rm. Rm service, travel. Tourist Office has a list of Paying Guest accommodation.

● Places to eat

Millets are basic to local cooking. ***Sogra*** (thick chapattis) are very popular, served with ghee. Mutton cooked with millet – *Sohita* and mutton kebabs cooked over charcoal – *sulla*, rabbit *Khud khar ghosh*, *Krer kumidai saliria* (beans cooked with cumin and chillies) are also favourites. *Mawa-ki-kachori* is a particularly rich dessert consisting of pastry stuffed with nuts and coconut and smothered in syrup.

The best restaurants (non-residents should reserve) are in hotels: ***Ajit Bhawan***, excellent meal outside with evening entertainment in pleasant surroundings; ***Umaid Bhavan's***, palatial, formal Marwar Hall, also occasional barbecues. A/c ***Kalinga***, below *Adarsh Niwas Hotel*, opp Jodhpur station is popular for W Rajasthani and Mughlai food.

Uttam on High Court Rd and ***Jodhpur Coffee House***, Sojati Gate do good S Indian snacks. Also ***Frigo***, Sardarpura and ***Sheetal***, Chopasi Rd. ***Kashmiri*** nr Anand Cinema serves hot and spicy Indian food. ***Pankaj*** and ***Shundar*** are veg restaurants in Jalori Gate; the latter does a variety of sweets too, rec. ***Agra Sweet Home*** nr Sojati Gate and ***Mishrilal*** do splendid, creamy and saffron flavoured *makhania lassi*. ***Rawat Mishtan Bhandar*** nr the Clock Tower has tempting Indian sweets and drinks. ***Softy 'n Softy***, Nai Sarak opp *Priya Hotel* does excellent icecreams – a sundae is a meal!

● Bars

In *Umaid Palace, Ashok* and *Ghoomar*.

● Shopping

Jodhpur is famous for its Jodhpuri coats and once popular *jodhpurs* (riding breeches), *safas* (turbans), *badle* (water bottles), tie-and-dye fabrics, embroidered camel leather footwear, lacquer work, cast toys and decorations. The main shopping areas of the city are **Sojati Gate** for gift shops and emporia, **Station Rd** for jewellery, **Tripolia Bazar** for handicrafts, **Khanda Falsa** for tie and dye, **Lakhara Bazar** for lac bangles, shoes from **Mochi Bazar**. **Sardarpura** and **Clock Tower**. *Bandhanas* are mostly made by Muslim families in Bambamola; also 'factories' around **Siwanchai** and **Jalori Gates**. Also numerous antique shops. *Durries* are woven at **Salavas** village, 18 km away.

Rajasthan Khadi Sangathan, BK ka Bagh, and in the Industrial Area is rec. ***Khadi Sangh***, Station Rd. ***Bhagatram Ishwarlal, Lucky Silk Shop*** and ***Prakash Silk Stores*** are good. ***Abani Handicrafts***, nr Tourist Bungalow and Umaid Bhawan Palace (good but pricy). ***Arvind Handicrafts, Haswani Handicrafts*** and ***Lalji Handicrafts,*** Umaid Bhawan Rd (very good for local crafts). Several craft shops in the Fort. **Books**: ***Universal Book Depot***, Jalori Gate has a reasonable selection incl City guide book. **Photography**: Shops in High Court Rd, Sojati Gate and in Jalori Gate.

● Banks
1000-1400. **State Bank of India**, High Court Rd. **Bank of Baroda,** Arun Hotel, Sojati Gate for TC encashment. **Bank of Bikaner**, nr Jalori Gate.

● Hospital & medical services
In Jalori Gate, T 24479 and Sivanchi Gate Rd, T 22567; Dispensary, Paota, Residency. 0800-1200, 1700-1900; Sun 0800-1200.

● Post & telegraph
GPO, S of Jodhpur station, 1000-2000, Sat 1000-1600; **Telegraph office**, Sardarpura. 24 hr.

● Tour companies & travel agents
Rajasthan Tours, *Tourist Bungalow*, T 27464. ***Tourist Guide Service***, 15 Old Public Park. ***Peacock Travels*** and ***Aravalli Safari and Tours***, 2 Raikabagh, T 27176. ***Travel Corp of India***, *Ratanada Polo Palace Hotel*. ***Poly Travels***, nr Paota Bus Stand (10D). Rec for friendly and helpful service.

● Tourist offices
Rajasthan, *Ghoomar Tourist Bungalow*, High Court Rd, T 25183. 0800-1200, 1500-1800. Railway Tourist Bureau with waiting room (for passengers only), T 25052.

● Useful addresses
Police: T 20200; **Fire**: T 101; **Ambulance**: T 102.

● Transport
It is 275 km by road from Jodhpur to Jaisalmer, scenically quite tedious. There are day and night buses, but faster and probably better than the train. Jodhpur is linked by State Highways to **NH8** (Delhi-Jaipur-Ahmadabad-Bombay), **NH11** (Agra-Jaipur-Bikaner) and **NH15** (Pathankot-Amritsar-Jaisalmer-Samakhiali).
A convenient bus route links Jodhpur with Ghanerao and Ranakpur, Kumbhalghar and Udaipur. Some distances: **Mt Abu** (292 km); **Bikaner** (256 km); **Kota** (360 km; **Delhi** (594 km); **Bombay** (1,077 km).

Local Taxis: tourist taxis from taxi stands at rly station, *Ghoomar Tourist Bungalow*, Sojati Gate, etc. Fixed tariffs for popular destinations, other rates negotiable. ½ day, usually Rs 125, full day Rs 200, Tourist Officer, T 25183. **Autorickshaws**: all over town. **NB**: Rly station to Fort should be about Rs 10-15 but driver may demand Rs 40; walk away and try another. **Mini-buses**: on fixed routes. **Cycle-rickshaws and tongas**: rates negotiable.

Air The airport is 5 km from town centre. **Transport to town**: by taxi, Rs 120-150. **Indian Airlines,** City Office, nr Ajit Bhawan, Ratanada Rd, T 28600. 1000-1300, 1400-1700. Airport T 20617. **Jaipur**, daily, 2010, ¾ hr; **Udaipur**, daily, 1935, ¾ hr; **Delhi**, daily, 2010, ¾ hr; **Bombay**, daily, 1935, 2¼ hr. **East West**: **Jaipur**, W-Su, 1925, ¾ hr.

Train Enquiries: T 32535. 0800-2400. Reservations: T 20842. 0900-1300, 1330-1600. Tourist Office counter open long hours. Jodhpur is on the W Railways' metre gauge line. Helpful Rly Tourist Bureau, T 25052 (0500-2300) with *International Tourist Waiting Room* for passengers in transit (Grd Fl) has western toilets, showers and armchairs; free. **Agra**: *Barmer-Agra Exp*, 9708, daily, 2200, 21½ hr. *From Agra: Agra-Barmer Exp*, 9707, daily, 0815, 22 hr. **Mt. Abu** *Surya Nagri Exp*, 2907, daily, 2245, 4½ hr; *Ranakpur-Marwar Exp*, 4727, daily, 0725, 6¾ hr. **Old Delhi**: *Mandoe Exp*, 242, daily, 2145, 12¼ hr; *Jodhpur Mail*, 4894, 1545, 14 hr; **Jaipur**: *Mandor Exp*, 2462, daily, 2145, 6¾ hr; *Marudhar Exp*, 5314, daily, 0630, 7 hr. **Jaisalmer**: *4 JPJ Exp*, 2305, daily, 2235, 9 hr; *2 JPJ*, 4791, daily, 0820, 9¾ hr. **NB**: The day train can be a irritatingly slow, hot, dusty and dirty experience. It can also get quite cold travelling across the desert at night in the winter months, so a sleeping bag or blanket is recommended. Take your own if possible, as the bedding provided by the railways on this line is notoriously dirty. To obtain bedding it is essential to order in advance. Arrival at Jaisalmer at dawn can be a tremendously exciting experience. **Udaipur** *Jodhpur-Udaipur Passenger*, 251, daily, 2035, 10¼ hr.

The Maharaja's railway carriages: In 1886 the Jodhpur Railway first introduced camel drawn trains until steam engines were acquired. The railway network had expanded to cover 2,400 km by 1924, stretching from

Jodhpur to Hyderabad, Sind (now in Pakistan) across the desert. The Maharaja's luxurious personal saloons which date from 1926, beautifully finished with inlaid wood and silver fittings may be chartered to run between Jodhpur and Jaisalmer. The carriages have been adapted to provide comfortable coupés for 20. Reserve through Maharaja Resorts, Umaid Bhavan Palace, T 33316, Ext 231, F 35373. You may be able to see them at the station.

Road Bus: Jodhpur Bus Stand, nr Raikabagh rly station, T 22986. 1000-1700. SRTCs of Rajasthan and neighbouring states connect Jodhpur to regional centres with several buses daily: Ahmadabad, 526 km (11 hr); Jaipur, 340 km (8 hr); Abu Road (7 hr); Ajmer, 208 km (4 ½ hr); Jaisalmer, 300 km (8 hr); Udaipur, 275 km (8-10 hr). RT coach service between Jaisalmer and Jodhpur: dep Jodhpur 0630, dep Jaisalmer, 1400, (5-6 hr). Rs 80. **Private Operators**: *Sun City Tours, Hotel Shanti Bhawan* and *Sethi Yatra*, both opp Rly Station. Private companies run deluxe video coaches between Jodhpur and Delhi, Ahmadabad, Jaipur, Bikaner, Bhilwara and Jaisalmer. Earplugs are rec!

Jodhpur to Mount Abu

ROUTES The road goes through **Sirohi** (182 km, *STD Code* 02972) where a country road leads to Mount Abu, saving 50 km. The main road from Sirohi goes to **Pindwara** (23 km), then **Abu Road** (40 km) and finally up to **Mount Abu** (27 km). The shorter route is about 220 km, the longer, 270 km. Allow nearly a day.

Jodhpur to Bikaner

ROUTES There are a number of interesting places to visit if you are travelling by road to Bikaner. Alternatively, they can be treated as day trips from either Jodhpur or Bikaner. For Bikaner see page 468.

Osian

63 km N from Jodhpur is an ancient town in the Thar desert and contains the largest group of 8th-10th century Hindu and Jain temples in Rajasthan. The typical Osian Pratihara-dynasty temple is set on a terrace whose walls are finely decorated with mouldings and miniatures. The sanctuary walls have central projections with carved panels and above these rise curved towers. The doorways are usually decorated with river goddesses, serpents and scrollwork. The 23 temples are grouped in several sites N, W and S of the town. The southern group of small Hindu temples includes one to Harihara. The W group contains a mixture of Hindu temples, including the **Surya Temple** (early 8th century) with beautifully carved pillars. 200m further, the Jain **Mahavira Temple** (8th, 10th centuries) on a hillock, the best preserved of the temples here, rises above the town. The **Sachiya Mata Temple** (11th-12th century), is a living temple of the Golden Durga.

- **Transport Road Bus**: 4 daily from Jodhpur, 2 hr. Worth visiting; allow 1 hr there.

Khimsar

73 km N of Jodhpur (130 km N via Osian) is a remote 15th century Rajput fort in the desert where Aurangzeb is believed to have stayed. The moated castle was built as a fortified home by Karam Singh, the 5th son of Rao Jodha. Accommodation: B/C Welcomgroup *Royal Castle*, T 28. 25 rm, some a/c, with bath. For atmosphere, ask for Old Wing. Restaurant (Mughlai, Rajasthani, Continental), outdoor barbecue. Camel and jeep safaris. Particularly interesting when owner is in residence. Reservations: *Umaid Bhawan Palace*, Jodhpur.

Nagaur

(*Pop* 67,000 *STD Code* 01582). 137 km N of Jodhpur. The dull stretch of desert is enlivened by Nagaur's fort (said to date from the 4th century), palace and mosque. Akbar built the Mosque and there is a shrine of the disciple of Mu'inuddin Chishti of Ajmer (see page 432). A very popular **cattle fair** is held just outside the town in Jan/Feb (6-11 Feb, 1995) during which there are camel races, cock fights, folk dancing and puppet shows. There is no suitable hotel so you may wish to stay at Khimsar. Maharaja Resorts' *Royal Camp* is set up with 35 comfortable tents with baths. Separate dining tent (Rajasthan's cuisine) and open reception tent. Campfires, local entertainment. Reserve through T Jodhpur 33316, Ext 231, F 35735.

70 km N of Nagaur (31 km S of Bikaner) on the main Jodhpur-Bikaner road, **Deshnoke** has the bizarre rat-inhabited Karni Mata Mandir – see page 470.

Tilwara near **Balotra** (127) km SW of Jodhpur is where the annual Mallinathji Cattle Fair is held. Over 80,000 animals are brought (making it Rajasthan's largest) including Kapila cows associated with Lord Krishna and the famous Kathiawari horses.

Beawar to Udaipur

ROUTES The NH8 passes S through dry rocky hills, with occasional date palms and open savanna or agricultural land. Just S of **Bhim** the *Hotel Vijay* is modest but quite clean, and there is a clean F *Rajasthan Motel* at **Deogarh**, 30 km S of Bhim. Reasonable refreshments. At **Kankroli**, 56 km N of Udaipur on the NH8, is the Rajsamand Lake.

Rajsamand Lake

The **Nauchoki Bund** is over 335m long and 13m high, with ornamental pavilions and toranas, all of marble and exquisitely carved. Behind the masonry bund is an 11m wide earthen embankment, erected in 1660 by Rana Raj Singh who had defeated Aurangzeb on many occasions. On the SE side of the lake is the town of **Kankroli** with a beautiful temple.

Udaipur

(*Population:* 308,000. *Altitude:* 577m. *STD Code*: 0294). Set in the Girwa valley amidst the Aravalli hills of S Rajasthan, **Udaipur** is a beautiful city, regarded by many Indians and foreign visitors as one of the most romantic in India. In contrast to some of its desert neighbours it presents an enchanting image of white marble palaces, placid blue lakes and green hills that keep the wilderness at bay. It is an oasis of colour in a stark and arid region.

The city of sunrise

The legendary Ranas of Mewar who traced their ancestry back to the Sun, first ruled the region from their 7th century stronghold Chittaurgarh. In 1586, Maharana Udai Singh founded a new capital on the shores of Lake Pichola and named it Udaipur, the 'abode of Udai' or 'the city of sunrise'. On the advice of an ascetic who interrupted his rabbit hunt, Udai Singh built a temple above the lake and then his palace around it.

In contrast to the house of Jaipur, the rulers of Udaipur prided themselves on being independent from other more powerful regional neighbours, particularly the Mughals. In a piece of local princely one-upmanship, Maharana Pratap, heir apparent to the throne of Udaipur, invited Raja Man Singh of Jaipur to a lakeside picnic. Afterwards he had the ground on which Man Singh had trodden washed with sacred Ganga water, and insisted that his generals take purificatory baths. Man Singh reaped appropriate revenge by preventing Pratap Singh from acceding to the throne. Udaipur, for all its individuality remained one of the poorer princely states in Rajasthan, a consequence of being almost constantly at war. In 1818, Mewar, the kingdom of the Udaipur

CLIMATE: UDAIPUR

	Jan	Feb	Mar	Apr	May	Jun	Jul	Aug	Sep	Oct	Nov	Dec	Av/Tot
Max (°C)	24	28	32	36	38	36	31	29	31	32	29	26	31
Min (°C)	8	10	15	20	25	25	24	23	22	19	11	8	18
Rain (mm)	9	4	3	3	5	87	197	207	120	16	6	3	660

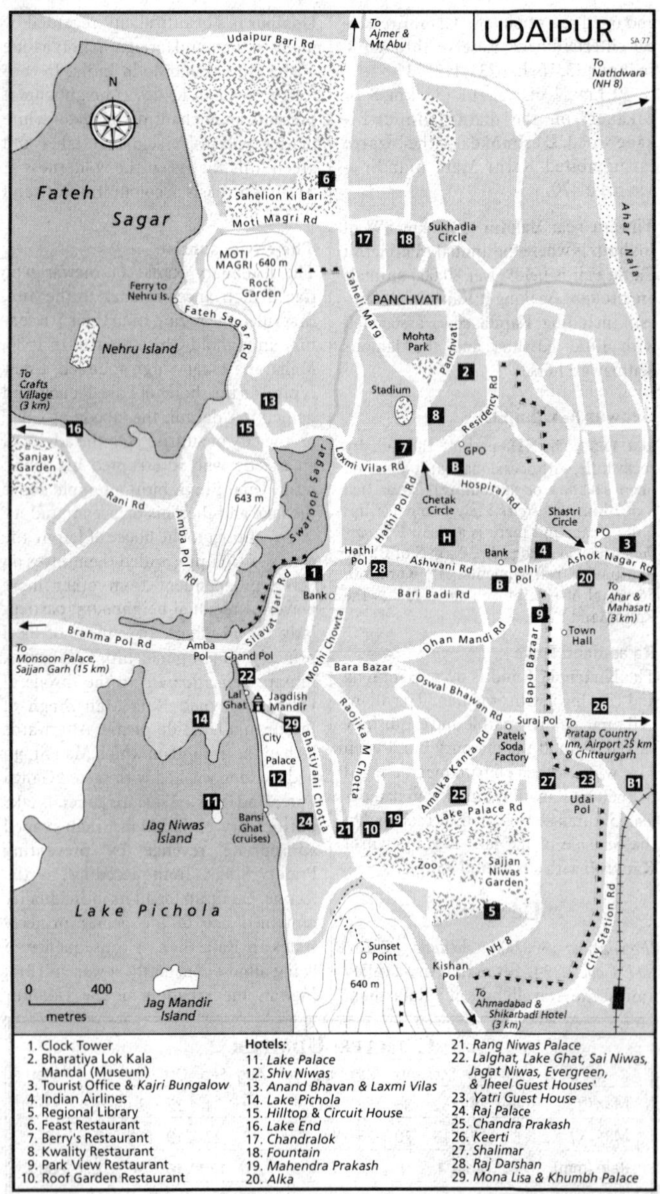

1. Clock Tower
2. Bharatiya Lok Kala Mandal (Museum)
3. Tourist Office & *Kajri Bungalow*
4. Indian Airlines
5. Regional Library
6. Feast Restaurant
7. Berry's Restaurant
8. Kwality Restaurant
9. Park View Restaurant
10. Roof Garden Restaurant

Hotels:

11. *Lake Palace*
12. *Shiv Niwas*
13. *Anand Bhavan & Laxmi Vilas*
14. *Lake Pichola*
15. *Hilltop & Circuit House*
16. *Lake End*
17. *Chandralok*
18. *Fountain*
19. *Mahendra Prakash*
20. *Alka*
21. *Rang Niwas Palace*
22. *Lalghat, Lake Ghat, Sai Niwas, Jagat Niwas, Evergreen, & Jheel Guest Houses'*
23. *Yatri Guest House*
24. *Raj Palace*
25. *Chandra Prakash*
26. *Keerti*
27. *Shalimar*
28. *Raj Darshan*
29. *Mona Lisa & Khumbh Palace*

Maharanas, came under British political control but still managed to avoid almost all British cultural influence.

Fort palaces

Udaipur is a traditionally planned walled city, its bastioned rampart walls pierced by 5 massive gates, each studded with iron spikes as protection against enemy war elephants. High on the hill overlooking the lake stands the massive palace of the Maharanas, probably the largest in Rajasthan. From its rooftop gardens and balconies, you can look out over the Pichola Lake, with the Jag Niwas summer Palace, 'adrift like a snowflake' in its centre. Around the lake, the houses and temples of the old city stretch out in a pale honeycomb.

Places of interest

The Old City was built in the 17th century on undulating ground, and surrounded by a large wall with 5 main gates: Hathi Pol (Elephant Gate-N), Kishan Gate (S), Delhi Pol (NE), Chand Pol (Moon Gate-W) and the Suraj Pol (Sun Gate-E). The W side of the town is bounded by the beautiful Pichola Lake and the E and N sides by moats. To the S is the fortified hill of Eklingigarh. The main street leads from the Hathi Pol to the City Palace (1567 onwards) which stands on a low ridge overlooking the Lake Pichola. This actually comprises a number of palaces that despite variations in design and ornamentation are integrated into an impressive whole. It is built on a massive scale, with a blend of Rajput and Mughal influences.

The old city is a maze of narrow winding lanes flanked by tall whitewashed houses with doorways, decorated with Mewar folk art, windows with stained glass or jali screens, majestic havelis with spacious inner courtyards and shops. Many of the houses within the city were given by the Maharana to retainers – barbers, priests, traders and artisans. Many rural landholders, titled *jagirdars*, had a townhouse conveniently located near the palace. One of the grandest of these is the **Bagor ki Haveli**, all glass work and a succession of cool shady courtyards which is the W Zone Cultural Centre (see Museums).

The **Jagdish Mandir** 150m N of the palace (1651) was built by Maharana Jagat Singh. The temple is a fine example of the Nagari style though a little run down now. A shrine with a brass *Garuda* stands outside and stone elephants flank the entrance steps, within is a black stone image of Vishnu as Jagannath, the Lord of the Universe.

City Palace Entry Rs 8, students Rs 4. Camera fee Rs 15. Guide books available. Guide Rs 50 for at least 1 hr. The entrance to its vast plaster façade is through the **Bari Pol** (Great Gate, 1600) which leads on to the **Tripolia Gate** (1725). Between them are 8 **toranas**, (arches) under which the rulers were weighed against gold and silver on their birthdays, which was then distributed to the poor. Beyond the Tripolia the **Ganesh Deori Gate** leads S to the fine **Rai Angan** (Royal Courtyard, 1571), adjoined on the E side by the Jewel Room. From here you can wander through a number of palace enclosures, some beautifully decorated, all comparatively small and picturesque. Here and there are pretty views over the city or the lake. The **Chhoti Chitra Shali** has interesting blue tiles and the **Manak Mahal** (Ruby Palace) with a central garden, has been filled with figures of porcelain and glass. The **Moti Mahal** (Pearl Palace) is decorated with mirrors and the **Chini ki Chitra Mahal** (1711-34) has fine ornamentation of Dutch and Chinese-made tiles counterpointed with mirror work. The **Bari Mahal** or **Amar Vilas** (1699-1711) has a pleasant garden.

On the W side of the Tripolia are the **Karan Vilas** (1620-28) and **Khush Mahal**, a pleasure palace for European guests with a 'grotesque mixture of European, Rajput and Mughal detailing' (Davies), whilst to the S lies the

Shambhu Niwas Palace. Maharana Fateh Singh added the **Shiv Niwas Palace** to this. (Now a small hotel, one room has crystal furniture.)

Museums Half of the City Palace is still occupied by the royal family and is not accessible. There is a **Palace Museum** in the 'open' part, with some beautiful views across the lake. Well worth a visit. It includes the **Mor Chowk**, with its beautiful late 19th century peacock mosaics. There is also armour worn by Pratap Singh, narrative wall paintings, royal cradles, toys etc. The **Government Museum** within the palace complex has a bizarre collection of exhibits which include a stuffed kangaroo and Siamese twin deer.

Lake Pichola Fringed with hills, gardens, havelis, ghats and temples, Lake Pichola is the scenic focus of Udaipur. Set in it are the Jag Niwas and the Jag Mandir Palaces. The **Jag Mandir** in the S is notable for the **Gul Mahal**, a domed pavilion built during the reign of Karan Singh (1621-28). Prince Khurram (later Shah Jahan), lived on this island when he was in revolt against his father Jahangir. Refugee European ladies and children were also given sanctuary there by Maharana Sarap Singh during the Mutiny. It is now abandoned. A very pleasant 'Boat Cruise' around the lake has no stopover. With a short stop on Jagmandir island it costs more (Rs 90, 1½ hr) and is not as worthwhile. Both leave from the Lake Palace jetty.

The Lake Palace The **Jag Niwas** island (1.5 ha) to the N has the older **Dilaram** and **Bari Mahal** Palaces. They were built by Maharana Jagat Singh II in 1754 and cover the whole island. Once the royal summer residences (now a hotel), they seem to float like a dream ship on the blue waters of the lake. The courtly atmosphere, elegance and opulence of princely times, the painted ceilings, antique furniture and stained glass windows combined with the truly magical setting make it one of the most romantic in India. Superb views. Non-residents: ticket with buffet meal Rs 400. Tour operators make block bookings, so it can be necessary to book well in advance. 1230-1430 Lunch, 1500-1800 Tea, 1930-2030, dinner. Rs 175-300. Some have found the buffet meals disappointing.

The **Jal Burj** is on the water's edge, S of the town. A pleasant walk past the *Jal Burj Caf* leads to the gardens on the wall with good views; pleasant place to relax.

Other sights within the City

The **Fateh Sagar** Lake, N of Lake Pichola, was constructed in 1678 during the reign of Maharana Jai Singh and modified by Maharana Fateh Singh. There is a pleasant lakeside drive along the E bank but, overall, it lacks the charm of the Pichola. The Nehru Park with a restaurant and the W Zone Cultural Centre are here.

Pratap Samak 0900-1800. Entry Re 1. Overlooking the Fateh Sagar is the **Moti Magri** (Pearl Hill) on which is a statue of Maharana Pratap on his famous horse Chetak. Local guides claim that he jumped an abyss of extraordinary width in the heat of the battle even after losing one leg! The path to the top winds through some attractive gardens.

Sahelion ki Bari Gardens. 0900-1800. Entry Re 0.50. This 'Garden of the Maids of Honour' is a small ornamental pleasure garden in the N of the city and contains an elegant lotus pool, gushing fountains, beautiful black marble kiosks on the corners of the pool and stunning bougainvilleas covering the walls of the enclosure. A very attractive place. In what was a pavilion opposite the entrance is a small 'children's' museum which has a curious collection of exhibits.

Ahar 3 km E of the city are the remains of the ancient city which contains some chhattris (cenotaphs) and a small **museum**. The chhattris are in the Jain style and set on high plinths in the Mahasati (royal place of cremation). The museum contains pottery sherds and terracotta toys dating from the 1st Millennium BC plus exhibits from subsequent periods, eg 10th century sculptures. In the vicinity are the temples of Mira Bai (10th century), Adinatha (11th century) and Mahavira (15th century). Nearby is the village of Ahar.

Museums

Bharatiya Lok Kala Museum, charged with the preservation of folk arts, which abound in Rajasthan, has an interesting collection including dresses, dolls, masks, musical instruments, paintings and puppets (0900-1800). There are regular puppet shows at 1800 (1 hr.). Rs 10. Highly rec. **W Zone Cultural Centre and Village** on Fateh Sagar (6 km from City Palace). Open during office hours. A village created with huts from Rajasthan, Gujarat, Maharashtra and Goa faithfully replicated. Collection of colourful folk art. Free, no guide books. Rec. City **Palace Museum**. Entered through the Deoria Gate. 0930-1600. Entry Rs 15 plus Camera Fee Rs 15. Extensive, a little geared to the tourist but worth a visit.

Parks & zoos

Nehru Island Park in Fateh Sagar and **Sahelion ki Bari** (see above). **Gulab Bagh** a rose garden on Lake Palace Rd. Also contains a zoo (unremarkable) and toy train.

Excursions

Monsoon Palace 15 km W. Fantastic views from deserted, run down palace on hilltop, now a radio transmitting centre. The unfinished building on Sajjangarh (335m) was planned by a Maharana to be high enough to see his ancestral home, Chittaurgarh. 3-4 hr round trip by taxi or auto rickshaw.

Tours

Rajasthan Tourism tours from *Kajri Tourist Bungalow*, T 23509. **City Sightseeing**: ½ day (0800-1300), Pratap Smarak, Fateh Sagar, Sahelion-ki-Bari, Lok Kala Mandal, Sukhadia Circle, City Palace, Jagdish Mandir, Gulab Bagh. Rs 30. **Excursion**: ½ day (1400-1900), Haldighati, Nathdwara, Eklingji. Rs 55.

Local festivals

Mewar Festival 3-4 Apr 1995; 22-23 Apr 1996; 10-11 Apr 1997. All the popular Hindu festivals are celebrated but Mar/Apr: *Gangaur* is especially popular in Udaipur – see Jaipur page 406.

Local information

● Accommodation

Price guide
AL Rs 3,000+ **A** Rs 2,000-3,000
B Rs 1,200-2,000 **C** Rs 600-1,200
D Rs 250-600 **E** Rs 100-250 **F** Up to Rs 100.

Most are 25 km from airport, 4 km from rly and 1-2 km from centre. **AL** ***Lake Palace***, Pichola Lake, T 23241. 85 rm, best with lake view. Superb situation (see under places of interest); now catering largely for package tours. An experience; see above for visiting. Some dislike the 'cattle-market' atmosphere of visits; food poisoning cases reported after buffet meal in 1993.

A ***Shiv Niwas***, in the City Palace (turn right after entrance gate), T 28239, F 0294-23823. 31 rm, expensive suites, cheaper but good rm without lake view. Excellent restaurant, lovely pool, tennis, squash, billiards. Garden and boating. Former Royal guesthouse of the Maharana. Palatial, but dull, unimaginative decor. Poolside bar/rest open to non-residents, but charge of Rs 250 for use of the pool. **A** ***Laxmi Vilas Palace*** (ITDC), T 24411. On hill above Fateh Sagar Lake, 27 km airport, 5 km station, 1 km centre. 54 rm (45 a/c). Built as royal guest house by Maharana Bhupal Singh—still atmospheric.

C ***Lake Pichola***, Chandrapol, T 29197. 20 rm, some a/c. Restaurant, bar, exchange, shops, occasional cultural shows. New but in the traditional style, good views, boat rides. Rec. "As good as Lake Palace, at half the price"! **C** ***Shikarbadi***, Govardhan Vilas, Ahmadabad Rd (5 km from centre), T 83200. 25 rm. Not central a/c. Restaurant (incl Marwari and Rajasthani), cultural shows, pool, deer park and riding. Attractive turn of the century forest hunting lodge owned by the Maharaja. Good gardens. Rec. **C** ***Anand Bhawan***, Fateh Sagar Rd, T 23256, 24 a/c rm. Restaurant, bar, exchange. Hilltop location with spectacular views. Another royal guesthouse. **C** ***Chandralok***, Saheli Marg, T 29011. 14 a/c rm. Restaurant, car. Folk dances and puppet shows on request. Well-kept rm. **C** ***Hilltop***, 5 Ambavgarh, T 28708. 55 rm. Restaurant, bar, exchange, shops. Folk dances and puppet shows on request. **C** ***Rajdarshan***, 18 Pannabai Marg, inside Hathipol, T 29671. 52 rm. Restaurant, bar, exchange, shops, pool. Folk dances and puppet shows. Balconies and good views. **C** ***Lake End***, Alkapuri, Fateh Sagar, T 23841. 78 rm, some a/c. Dining hall, bar, shops, pool. Modern with lakeside garden. Reasonably attractive rm with balconies. Reservations, Delhi T 688 6909, F 688 6122.

D ***Sai Niwas***, Lallghat. Redecorated in Rajasthani style. Rm with bath. Good restaurant, beautiful roof-terrace with good views of lake. Rec. for imagination and value. **D** ***Jagat Niwas***, 25 Lallghat, overlooks lake. Best rm have balcony; in old building, beautifully restored. Good restaurant. Rec. **D** ***Fountain***, 2 Sukhadia Circle. T 28291. 30 rm, some a/c. Restaurant, travel. Garden, folk dances and puppet shows. Rajasthan Tourism. **D** ***Kajri Tourist Bungalow***, Shastri Circle, T 23509. 38 rm, some a/c and dorm, Deluxe best. Restaurant, bar, travel, gardens. Rm overlooking garden pleasanter. Restaurant rather dull and food mediocre. Tourist Office nr entrance. **D** ***Damanis***, nr Telegraph Office, Madhuban, T 25675. 25 rm, some a/c. Restaurant, exchange, travel, puppet shows. **D** ***Alka***, Shastri Circle, opp Tourist Bungalow, T 28611. 55 rm, some air-cooled with bath. Restaurant. **D** ***Pratap Country Inn***, Airport Rd, Titadhia Village, T 23638. 33 rm, few a/c. 6 km centre. Free transfer from rly station. Restaurant, horse and camel safaris, riding, pool (sometimes empty). Old royal country house. **D** ***Lakshmi Vilas*** , T 381567, Ram Singh Rd. Former palace, set round grassy courtyard, now rather run-down. **D** ***Mahendra Prakash***, Lake Palace Rd, T 29370. 12 large but simple rm, some air-cooled. Friendly, excellent service. Rec.

Budget hotels The 3 on Lake Palace Rd are rec: **E** ***Rang Niwas Palace***, T 23891. 14 rm, some more expensive with a/c, with bath, also dorm. Restaurant, gardens. Very helpful staff. Old-world and charming. Good value; **E** ***Haveli***, T 28294. Some rm with bath tub. Courtyard. Clean, very helpful manager; Nearby **E** ***Shambhu Vilas***, T 27338. Air-cooled rm with hot shower, travel. Good rooftop *Palace View* restaurant. **E** ***Lake Ghat***, 4/13 Lallghat, behind Jagdish Mandir has some good rm. Clean, friendly,—good view. **E** ***Lallghat Guest House***, 33 Lallghat, T 25301. Best rm with bath. Cheaper rm (no window) and dorm. Restaurant food mediocre, but snacks and drinks fine. Good views from balconies and rooftop; very relaxed atmosphere. Literally next door **E** ***Evergreen***. 7 rm with bath (rm vary, inspect first). Rooftop restaurant overlooking lake, with good views, only snacks and *thalis* rec. Clean, quiet and relaxed; discounts possible though recent visitors found others better value. Western visitors only welcome. Staff can be off-hand; not rec for tours or safaris. **E** ***Jheel Guest House***, 56 Gangor Ghat (behind Jagdish Temple), T 28321. 8 pleasant rm, overlooking Lake, some with bath. **E** ***Raj Palace***, 103 Bhatiyani Chotta (behind City Palace), T 28092. Rm with bath (ask for best) and dorm. Restaurant. Old building with lovely garden. Highly rec for clean rm, comfortable beds, excellent service and good food (pricey). Will organise city tour, Rs 120. **E** ***Yatri Guest House***, 3/4 Panchkuin Rd. Helpful and knowledgeable owner, good value.

F ***Badi Haveli***, nr Jagdish temple. 8 rm with bath, some good. Pleasant terrace, good rooftop views. **F** ***Chandra Prakash***, Lake Palace Rd (nr Sajjan Niwas Garden), T 28109. Some rm with bath. Clean, quiet, food good value. Helpful manager. Rec. **F** ***Ghunghru Guest House***, College Rd, behind the *Keerti Hotel*. Reasonable. Garden. **F** ***Keerti***, Sarasvati Marg, nr Suraj Pol, T 3639. Some rm with bath. Popular. **NB**: *Keerti Tourist Hotel* is not as good. **F** ***Mona Lisa***, City Palace Rd, Bhatina Chotta. Some rm with bath. Not on lake but pleasant and quiet. Good breakfast, garden, newspaper, good value. Rec. **F** ***Ratnadeep***, Lake Palace Rd, T 24730. Few a/c rm. Several basic hotels nr the bus stand incl **F** ***Shalimar***, Udaipol Rd, T 26807, good value. ***Railway Retiring Rooms***. Inexpensive ***Paying Guest*** accommodation with families is another option. List available from the Tourist Office.

● Places to eat

First 3 are highly rec: ***Sai Niwas***, Lallghat ("with marvellously attentive service and very fresh food"); ***Park View***, opp Town Hall, City Station Rd; ***Rooftop Palace View***, Lake Palace Rd. Clean, good food. Very good views, excellent value, esp buffet dinners (***Roof Garden***, has had its view blocked by buildings). ***Kumbha Palace***, Bhatina Chotta, next to *Mona Lisa Hotel*, run by English woman, rec for Indian and western food – try chocolate cake and pizzas. ***4 Seasons*** for Western & Indian food (mild, unless you ask for spicy). ***The Coffee House***, Chetak Circle has good coffee and Indian snacks. Open 0730-2200. ***Berrys***, Chetak Circle and ***Kwality***. Open 1000-2300 and ***Delhi Darbar***, Hathipol. Snack bar outside City Palace is reasonably priced.

● Bars

The larger hotels have bars; an evening drink at the Shiv Niwas is especially pleasant.

● Banks

Numerous branches all over town, some with foreign exchange facilities.

● Entertainment

Rajasthan Tourism's cultural programmes from Sep-Mar. Details from Tourist Information, Kajri Tourist Bungalow, T 23605. Hotels also run cultural shows, notably folk dances and puppet shows. See Lok Kala Museum.

● Hospitals & medical services

General Hospital, Chetak Circle, T 233319. Several **Chemists** on Hospital Rd.

● Post & telegraph

GPO, Chetak Circle and **Poste Restante**, Shastri Circle.

● Shopping

The main shopping centres are Chetak Circle, Bapu Bazar, Hathipol, Palace Rd, Clock Tower, Nehru Bazar, Shastri Circle, Delhi Gate, Sindhi Bazar, Bada Bazar. **Handicrafts**: the local handicrafts are wooden toys, colourful portable temples (kavad), *Bandhani* tie-and-dye fabrics, embroidery and *Pichchwai* paintings. Paintings are of 3 types: miniatures in the classical style of courtly Mewar; *phads* or folk art; and *pichchwais* or religious art, (see Nathdwara below). ***Rajasthali*** Govt Emporium, Chetak Circle, ***Jagdish Emporium***, City Palace Rd and shops nr the temple sell traditional Udaipur and Gujarati embroideries. The more expensive ones are 'old' – 20-30 years – and are in beautiful dusky colours. The cheaper ones are brighter. ***Uday Arts***, Lake Palace Rd and ***Apollo Arts***, Hathipol, have good quality, moderately priced paintings. **Clothing**: good in Hathipol but shop around; prices vary. **Photography**: Some on City Station Rd and Bapu Bazar.

● Sports

Golf: ***Field Club***, Fatehpur.

● Tour companies & travel agents

Godwar Tours and Trekking, Ghanerao House, behind Hill House, Ambagadh, Udaipur. T 27849. Opening up new trekking opportunities. Reliable. ***Rajasthan Tours***, *Garden Hotel*, T 23030 (Lake Palace branch, T 25533). ***Tourist Guide Service***, Chetak Circle, T 23526. ***Mayur***, 59 Polo Ground, T 23482. ***Alka Service***, *Hotel Damanis*, T 22567. ***Lake End Tours***, opp Shastri Circle, T 23611 and others on City Station Rd. **Rajasthan Tourism**, *Kajri Tourist Bungalow*, Shastri Circle, T 23509.

● Tourist offices

Rajasthan, *Kajri Tourist Bungalow*, T 29535. 1000-1700. Information Centre, Mohata Park, Chetak Circle, T 24924. 1000-1700. Counters at City Rly Station, T 25105. 0800-1200 and at Dabok Airport, T 23011 at flight times.

● Useful addresses

Police: T 3000. **Fire**: T 27111. **Ambulance**: T 23333.

● Transport

Udaipur is on NH8. **Jaipur** (405 km); **Jodhpur** (275 km); **Ajmer** (274 km); **Ahmadabad** (252 km); **Mount Abu** (270 km); **Indore** (635 km); **Bhopal** (765 km); **Delhi** (635 km); **Bombay** (802 km); **Calcutta** (1755 km); **Varanasi** (1078 km).

Local Taxis: Rajasthan Tourism tourist taxis from *Kajri Tourist Bungalow*, Shastri Circle. Private taxis from airport, rly station, bus stands and major hotels. Unmetered, so negotiate rates. ***Taxi Stand***, Chetak Circle, T 25112. ***Tourist Taxi Service***, Lake Palace Rd, T 24169. **Auto-rickshaws**: are unmetered. 'Dinesh' from *Kumbh Palace Restaurant*, Bhatiani Chotta, rec. **Bicycles for hire**: try shops nr *Kajri Tourist Bungalow*. Main State Bus Stand, nr rly line opp Udaipol, T 27191. Lake tours Rs 30 for ½ hr.

Air Dabok airport is 25 km from centre. The security check is thorough. No batteries or knives allowed in hand luggage. **Transport to town**: taxis, approx Rs 120-30 (35-45 min). **Indian Airlines**, Delhi Gate, T 28999. 1000-1315, 1400-1700. Airport, T 23011, Enquiry T 142. **Delhi:** daily, 0905 & 1900, 2 hr; **Bombay:** daily, 0825, 2¼ hr, 2045, 1hr 10 min; **Jaipur:** daily, 0905 & 1900, 50 min; **Jodhpur:** daily, 1900, 40 min; **Aurangabad:** daily, 0825, 1 hr.

Train Rly station, 4 km, T 131. **Ahmadabad:** *Udaipur-Ahmadabad Exp*, 9643, daily, 1845, 10 hr. **Old Delhi:** *Pink City Exp/Garib Nawaz Exp*, 2902/2916, daily except Sun, 0530, 16¾ hr; *Chetak Exp*, 9616, daily, 1815, 20 hr. **Jaipur:** *Garib Nawaz Exp*, 2916, daily except Sun, 0530, 10¾ hr; *Chetak Exp*, 9616, daily, 1815, 11¾ hr. **Jodhpur:** *Udaipur-Jodhpur Passenger*, 252, daily, 1615, 11¾ hr. **Ajmer** *Garib Nawaz Exp*, 2916, daily except Sun, 0530, 7¾ hr; *Chetak Exp*, 9616, daily, 1815, 8¼ hr.

Road Bus: State Transport Bus Stand, City Station Rd (NH 8), Udiyapol. Enquiries, T 27191, Reservations open 0700-2100. The Rajasthan, Gujarat, UP and MP SRTC operate buses to Udaipur from Agra, Ahmadabad, Bharatpur, Bhopal, Bikaner, Brindavan, Delhi, Jaipur, Jodhpur, Mathura, Ratlam, Surat, Ujjain and Vadodara. Private bus companies also operate to/from destinations in the region. Luxury coaches run at night.

Udaipur to Mt Abu via Kumbhalgarh and Ghanerao

Little known Kumbhalgarh (63 km) is one of the finest examples of defensive fortification in Rajasthan. In addition to the palace you can wander round the many temples and along the walls to savour the great panoramic views. It is an afternoon's drive, 2 hr N of Udaipur through the Rajasthani countryside, often passing camel trains, and groups of colourfully dressed Rajasthani women and children returning to their villages. The small fields are well kept, wherever possible irrigated from the streams, Persian wheels and tanks that are dotted across the landscape. In winter, wheat and mustard are growing in the fields, and the journey there and back is just as magical and fascinating as the fort itself.

At **Nagda**, 21 km out of Udaipur, are 3 temples: the ruined 11th century Jain temple of **Adbhutji** and the Vaishnavite **Sas-Bahu** ('Mother-in-law'/'Daughter-in-law') temples. The complex, though comparatively small, has some very intricate carving on pillars, ceiling and *mandapa* walls. You can hire bicycles in Eklingi (1 km) to visit them.

Eklingji Hourly buses go from Udaipur to Eklingji village which has a basic *Guest House*. Eklingji and Nagda are set in a deep ravine containing the Eklingji lake. The white marble **Ekalinga Temple** with a 2-storey *mandapa* to Siva, the family deity of the Maharanas, dates from 734 AD but was rebuilt by Raimal in the 15th century. There is a silver door and screen and a silver *nandi* facing the black marble Siva. Open 0500-0700, 1000-1300 and 1700-1900. Evenings draw crowds of worshippers (few tourists). No photography. Nearby is the large but simple **Lakulisa Temple** (972), and other ruined semi-submerged temples. Lots of waterbirds – and very quiet.

Nathdwara, (48 km) is a centre of the Krishna worshipping community of Gujarati merchants who are followers of Vallabhacharya (15th century). Non-Hindus not allowed inside the temple containing a black marble Krishna image, but the outside has interesting paintings. Bazar sells temple hangings (*pichchwais*) illustrating the Krishna legend which originated here. These are painted on cloth with natural colours and are popular with pilgrims. Accommodation: F *Gokul Tourist Bungalow*, T 285. 6 rm and cheaper dorm.

Kumbhalgarh Fort

(*Alt* 1,087m) was the 2nd most important fort of the Mewar Kingdom after Chittaurgarh. Built mostly by Maharana Khumba (c1485), it is situated on a W facing ridge of the Aravallis, commanding a great strategic position on the border between the Rajput kingdoms of Udaipur (Mewar) and Jodhpur (Marwar). It gives superb views over the lower land to the NW, standing over 200m above the pass leading via Ghanerao towards Udaipur. This is where Prithviraj died and the young Udai Singh was saved by his nurse Panna Dai; she sacrificed her own son

Elopement Marriages

The Garacias practise 'elopement marriage'. Young couples are expected to elope at the end of special tribal celebrations. Once they have 'disappeared' they have to remain hidden in the jungle for 3 days while the rest of the tribe hunts for them. If caught during that period they are severely beaten and forcibly separated. However, if they have proved their skills in survival and in remaining hidden their marriage is recognised and they return to live with the rest of the tribe. Today many of the tribal peoples are increasingly integrated into the modern economy. Many women and children regularly collect firewood from the national parks – illegally – to sell in the neighbouring villages and towns.

by substituting him for the baby prince when, as heir to the throne, Udai Singh's life was threatened.

Off the beaten tourist track, it is still accessible enough to make a visit practicable. The final dramatic approach is across deep ravines and through thick scrub jungle. 7 gates guarded the approaches while 7 ramparts were reinforced by semicircular bastions and towers. The 36 km-long walls were built to defy scaling while their width enabled chariots to be driven along. The walls enclose a large plateau containing the smaller Katargarh Fort inside which has the decaying palace of Fateh Singh, a garrison, 365 temples and shrines, and a village. The occupants (reputedly 30,000) could be self-sufficient in food and water (and enough storage to last a year), and the fort's dominant location enabled defenders to see aggressors approaching from a great distance. Kulmbahlgarh is believed to have only been taken once; and that too because the water in the ponds was poisoned by enemy Mughals during the reign of Rana Pratap.

The 1st gate **Arait Pol**, is some distance from the main fort; the area was once thick jungle harbouring tigers and wild boar. Signals would be flashed by mirror in times of emergency and danger. **Hulla Pol** (Gate of Disturbance) is named after the point reached by invading Mughal armies in 1567. **Hanuman Pol** contains a shrine and temple. The **Bhairava Pol** records the 19th century Chief Minister who was exiled. The 5th gate, the **Paghra** (Stirrup) **Pol** is where the cavalry assembled; the Star tower nearby has walls 8m thick. The **Top-Khana** (Cannon Gate) is alleged to have a secret escape tunnel. The last, **Nimbu** (Lemon) **Pol** has the Chamundi temple beside it.

The palace It is a ½hr walk (fairly steep in part) from the car park to the roof of the Maharana's durbar hall. Tiers of inner ramparts rise to the summit, and the appropriately named **Badal Mahal** (19th century) or Palace in the Clouds, with the interior painted in pastel colours. A *chaukidar* holds the keys to the small palace and he will show you round (Rs 10 tip is appropriate). The views from the palace, over the walls to the jungle-covered hillsides (now a wildlife reserve) and across the deserts of Marwar towards Jodhpur, are stunning. The palace rooms are decorated in a 19th century style and some have attractive coloured friezes, but are unfurnished. After the maze-like palace at Udaipur, this is very compact. The **Maharana's palace** has a remarkable blue durbar hall with floral motifs on the ceiling. Polished chunar – lime – is used on walls and window sills, but the steel ceiling girders give away its late 19th century age. A gap separated the merdana (men's) palace from the zenana (women's) palace. Some of the rooms in the **zenana** have an attractive painted frieze with elephants, crocodiles and camels. A circular Ganesh temple is in the corner of the zenana courtyard. A striking feature of the toilets was the ventilation system which allowed fresh air into the room while the toilet was in use. The Neelkantha, Kumbhaswami temples and Raimal's *chhattri* nearby, are worth visiting. The **Mahadeva Temple** (1458) in a gorge below, contains black marble slabs inscribed with the history of Mewar.

Kumbhalgarh Wildlife Sanctuary

Mostly W of the fort, the sanctuary has enabled the endangered wolf to breed, and support leopard, sloth, chowsingha, sambar, hyena, flying squirrel, crocodiles and a variety of birds. *Best seasons*: Mar-Jun, Sep-Nov for the Wildlife Reserve. The monsoons bring on the attractive flora and the autumn, the russet colours. The **tribal** Bhils and Garacias (the latter found only in this belt) can be seen here, living in their traditional huts.

• **Accommodation** C *Aodhi* ('Watchtower') *Lodge* T Kelwara 222 or Udaipur 28239, F 23823. 21 rm. New tourist complex run by one of Mewar's old noble families. Completely isolated, 2 km from fort gate. Delightful stone cottages, tastefully decorated. Restaurant serving authentic Mewari food, horse safaris to fort and surrounding areas. Very pleasant. **E** PWD *Rest House* at Kumbhalgarh.

Ghanerao

5 km beyond the Reserve, founded in 1606 by Gopal Das Rathor of the Mertia clan, Ghanerao has numerous old temples, *baolis* and marble *chhattris*. The village was of great strategic importance, lying at the entrance to one of the few passes through the Aravallis between the territories held by the Rajput princes of Jodhpur and Udaipur. The first Thakur received a grant of 50 villages in 1606, and a guarantee of protection from Jaipur in exchange for his willingness to serve as a front line of defence against Jodhpur's potential – and actual – aggression. It retained a degree of autonomy until Independence in 1947. The present Thakur Sahib Sajjan Singh has opened his medieval castle, hunting lodge and summer house to paying guests, and organises 2-3 day treks (walking, horse or camel back) visiting Ranakpur temples and Kumbhalgarh Fort 18 km (50 km by jeep). This part of Rajasthan has remained essentially rural. It is a delightful place to experience the best of rural hospitality and the rich enjoyment of an unspoiled environment, shared not just by the Rajputs but by Jains and Muslims and by local tribes like the Bhils and Garacias.

• **Accommodation** C *Royal Castle*, Dist Pali, T 02934 7335. The castle stands over the village, with red sandstone *havelis*, marble pavilions and wall paintings. 20 rm with bath. Restaurant. Walks to view village incl crafts. An excellent break for 2 or 3 days, or longer to explore the surrounding Jain and Hindu sites and the Khumbhalgarh Wildlife park. The Mahavir Jain Temple, 5 km from the village, is a beautiful small 10th century temple, set in a shaded grove. Alternatively, stop overnight between Jodhpur and Udaipur. The hotel can put you in touch with a village guide and artist, S M Yunus. Tribal dances. **D** *Ajit Bagh*, the garden resort surrounded by orchard and fields, 5 min walk from Castle. 4 cottages. Only available for longer stays, normal min one week. 4 km away is the hunting lodge **E** *Bagha-ka-Bagh* (Tiger's Den) among tall grass jungle in the wildlife sanctuary. 10 rm and dorm (shared facilities, no electricity) in a "sturdy fortress against the backdrop of the Aravalli Range".

Ranakpur

25 km SW of Kumbhalgarh as the crow flies, Ranakpur can be approached through the wildlife reserve, 1½ hr. One of 5 holy Jain sites, it has one of best known Jain temple complexes in the country. It is particularly noted for the grandiose scale of its architecture. While the carving is not as fine as that in the Dilwara temple in Mt Abu, the complexity of elaborate ornamentation

here demonstrates the W Indian style in full flower. The secluded wooded setting, home to peacocks, langurs and numerous birds, complements the buildings wonderfully.

There are 3 temples worth visiting: The **Adinatha** (1439), the most noteworthy was built by Dharanshah during Rana Kumbha's reign, dedicated to the 1st Tirthankara. The sanctuary is symmetrically planned around the central shrine and is within a 100m square raised terrace enclosed in a high wall with 66 subsidiary shrines lining it each with its spire; the gateways consist of triple-storey porches. The sanctuary with a clustered centre tower, contains a *chaumukha* (4-fold) marble image of Adinatha. The whole, including the extraordinary array of engraved pillars (1444, and all different), carved ceilings and arches are intricately decorated, often with images of Jain saints, friezes of scenes from their lives and holy sites. The beautiful lace-like interiors of the corbelled domes are especially noteworthy as a feature of W Indian temple style.

The **Parsvanatha** and **Neminath** are 2 smaller Jain temples facing this, the former with a black image of Parsvanatha in the sanctuary and erotic carvings outside. The star-shaped **Surya Narayana Temple** (mid-15th century) is nearby.

• **Accommodation** Simple Rajasthan Tourism **E** *Shilpi Tourist Bungalow* on a hillock. 12 rm and dorm. Adequate restaurant. *Dharamshala* with some comfortable rm. Simple veg meals. 4 km N, **E** *Maharani Bagh* Ranakpur Rd, Sadri, T 3750. 12 rm in charming bungalows, with baths. Comfortably furnished in lovely gardens full of bougainvillaea and mangoes. Garden restaurant (Rajasthani), pool. Cultural programmes, jeep safaris and horse riding. Reserve direct or through Maharaja Resorts, T Jodhpur 33316 Ext 231, F 35373.

• **Transport Train** Ranakpur is 39 km from Palna Junction on the Ajmer-Mt Abu line. **Road Bus**: from Udaipur, 6 buses daily (0530-1600), slow journey. Also from Jodhpur and Mt Abu.

ROUTES From Ranakpur a road runs via Sanderau and Pali to Jodhpur. **Rohet** 30 km N of Pali on the Jodhpur road, Thakur Siddharth Singh 27, has opened his fort *Rohetgarh* as a hotel. 25 rm in the renovated palace. Restaurant, pool, riding. Charmingly painted façade with decorative *jharoka* windows.

Sardar Samand The lake of Sardar Samand nearby (NE of Pali) is a beautiful setting for the royal Hunting Lodge which with its annexe provides 16 comfortable rooms. Extensive grounds, pool, Rajasthani restaurant. Pool, tennis, squash, riding, fishing and boating. The lake attracts pelicans, flamingos, cranes, egrets and kingfishers. The wildlife sanctuary has black buck, gazelle, and nilgai. Reserve at Sardar Samand Palace, Dist Pali, Rajasthani or through Maharaja Resorts, T Jodhpur 33316 Ext 231, F 35373.

Sheoganj, 73 km S of Pali on the Jodhpur Mt Abu Rd, has a PWD Resthouse, while **Mansarovar** has a decent *Midway Motel*. Just S of **Sirohi** is a large zinc smelting factory, while across to the E can be seen the almost camouflaged walls of a fort, another in the chain which marked the borders of Marwar and Mewar territory. The road between Ghanerao and Abu Rd passes through dry hills, with broad dry river beds, thorny scrub and eucalyptus scattered on the dry land and granite hills rising from the plains.

Jaisamand Lake, 52 km SE of Udaipur, was constructed in the late 17th century. Before the building of huge dams in S Asia (eg Tarbela or Hirakud), it was the 2nd largest artificial lake in Asia (15 km by 10 km) and is surrounded by the summer palaces of the Ranis of Udaipur and by low hills stretching as far as the eye can see. The highest 2 hills are topped by palaces – the **Hawa Mahal** and **Ruti Rani**. Empty but worth visiting for the architecture and the view. Accommodation: Rajasthan Tourism E Bungalow. 4 rm with enormous bath. Also dorm. Ideal for overnight stay.

UDAIPUR TO MOUNT ABU

ROUTES From Udaipur a road goes SW through the Aravallis to Mt Abu. Most of the road journey is through hill country. It is a slow winding road (192 km). It does not pass through any towns of note.

Mount Abu

Mt Abu is Rajasthan's only hill resort and is very popular locally; many come from Rajasthan and Gujarat to escape the heat and in the case of some Gujaratis to escape their own state's prohibition on alcohol. The hill station stretches along a 20 km long plateau and is approached from Abu Road in the SE. The shops and restaurants are clustered in the compact centre. There is attractive countryside to explore as it is well wooded with flowering trees with numerous orchids during the monsoon and a good variety of birdlife.

Mount Abu, known as *Nandivardhan* (Place that Increases Joy) was the home of the legendary sage Vasishtha. One day Nandini, his wish-fulfilling cow, fell into a great lake. Vasishtha requested the gods in the Himalaya to save her so they sent *Arbuda*, a cobra who carried a rock on his head, dropped it into the lake, displacing the water and saving Nandini. The place became known as Arbudachala 'The Hill of Arbuda'. Indian and Khotanese variants of this story include one set in the Vale of Kashmir. Vasishtha also created the 4 powerful 'five-born' Rajput tribes, including the houses of Jaipur and Udaipur, at a ritual fire ceremony on the mount.

BASICS *Population:* 15,600, though swells considerably during season. *Altitude:* 1720m. *Climate:* Mt Abu benefits from lower temperatures and cooling breezes. Summer: 32-34°C on the plains below; 27-28°C in Mt Abu. Winter (Nov-Feb): Max 22°C, Min 10°C.

History

Abu was leased by the British Government from the Maharao of Sirohi and was used as the HQ for the Resident of Rajputana until 1947 and as a sanatorium for troops. Many of the rulers from surrounding princely states had summer houses here. The main part of the town is around **Nakki Talao** (Lake) sacred to Hindus. which was, in legend, scooped out by fingernails (*nakki*) by gods attempting to escape the wrath of a demon. There are boats for hire (try rowing) and a pleasant walk around the lake past the Raghunath Temple. The Toad Rock is here too; the other rock formations (Nandi and Camel) are not as obvious.

Places of interest

Dilwara Jain Temples 5 km from town centre and set in beautiful surroundings of mango trees and wooded hills, the temples have superb marble carvings. Open 1200-1800. Free. No photography of images. Leather items not allowed. 1 hr's walk from town or shared Jeep, Rs 2 each. Some guides are excellent. The complex of 5 principal temples is surrounded by a high wall, dazzling white in the sunlight. There is a rest-house for pilgrims on the approach road.

Chaumukha temple, the grey sandstone 3-storey building, is approached through the entrance on your left. Combining 13th and 15th century styles, it is generally regarded as inferior to the 2 main temples. The colonnaded hall (Grd Fl) contains 4-faced images of the Tirthankara Parsvanatha (hence *chaumukha*), and figures of *dikpalas* and *yakshis*. Along the entrance avenue on the right is a statue of Ganesh. Some renovation has taken place.

Adinatha Temple (Vimala Shah Temple) lies directly ahead. Open 1200-1800 for non-Jains, cameras Rs 5, the oldest and most famous of the Dilwara group. Immediately outside the entrance to the Temple is a small portico known as the *Hastishala* (elephant hall), built by Prithvipal in 1147-59 which contains a figure of the patron, Vimala Shah, the Chief Minister of the Solanki King, on horseback. Vimala Shah commissioned the temple dedicated to Adinatha in 1031-32. The riders on the 10 beautifully carved elephants that surround him were removed during Alauddin Khilji's reign; the damaged elephants were restored in 1991-2. Dilwara belonged to Saivite Hindus who were unwilling to part with it until Vimala Shah could prove that it had once belonged to a Jain community. In a dream the goddess Ambika (Ambadevi or Durga) instructed him to dig under a *champak* tree where he found the huge image of Adinatha and so won the land. To the SW, behind the hall, is a small shrine to *Ambika*, once the premier deity, now of secondary importance.

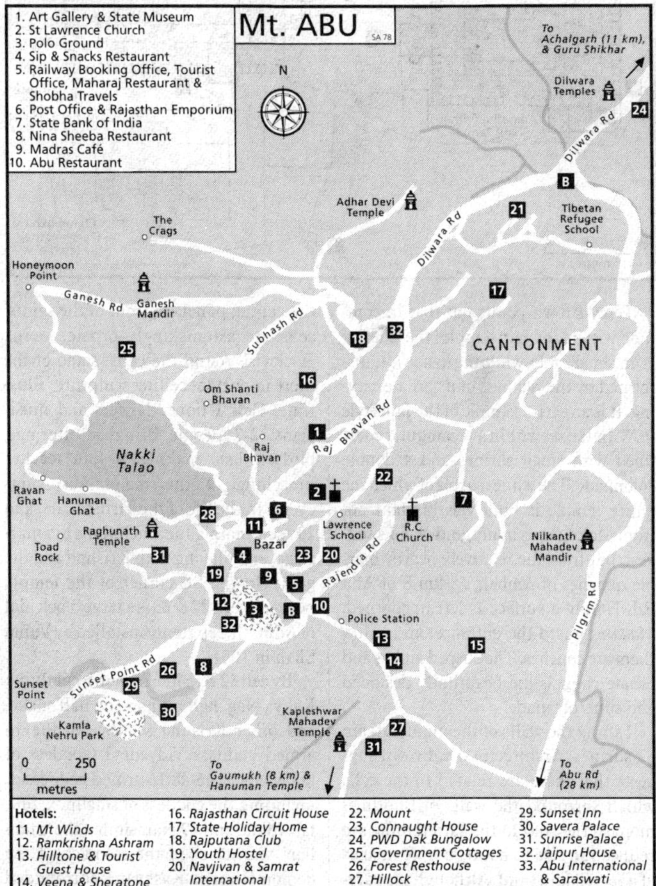

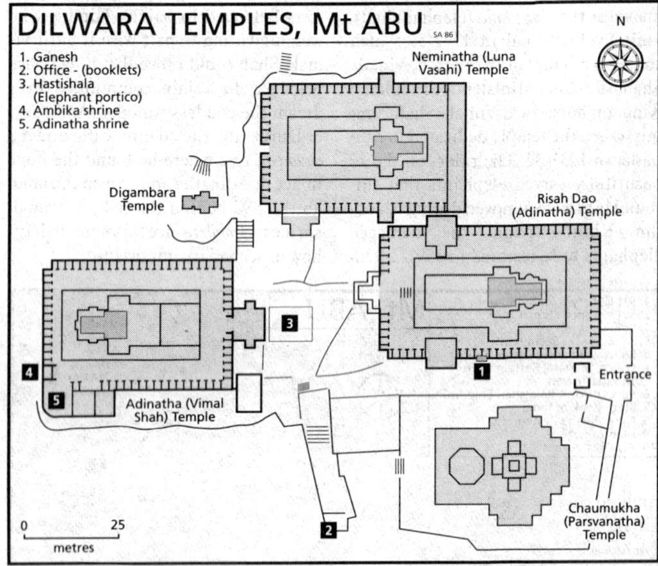

Percy Brown points out that in common with many Jain temples the exterior is unremarkable, while the inside is transformed by the richness of its ornate carving. It is an early example of the Jain style in W India, set within a rectangular court lined with small shrines and a double colonnade. The white marble of which the entire temple is built was brought not from Makrana, as many guide books suggest, but from the relatively nearby marble quarries of Ambaji, 25 km S of Abu Rd. Hardly a surface is left unadorned. *Makaras* guard the entrance, and below them are conches. The cusped arches and ornate capitals are beautifully designed and superbly made.

Lining the walls of the main hall are 52 shrines. Architecturally, Brown suggests that these are related to the cells which surround the walls of Buddhist monasteries, but in the Jain temple are reduced in size to house simple images of a seated Jain saint. Although the carving of the images themselves is simple, the ceiling panels in front of the saints' cells are astonishingly ornate. Going clockwise round the cells, some of the more important ceiling sculptures illustrate: **Cell 1** lions, dancers and musicians; **2-7** people bringing offerings, birds, music making; **8** Jain teacher preaching; **9** the major auspicious events in the life of the Tirthankars; and **10** Neminath's life, including his marriage, and playing with Krishna and the gopis. In the SE corner of the temple between cells **22** & **23** is a large black idol of Adinath, reputedly installed by Vimal Shah in 1031.

By cell **32** Krishna is shown subduing Kaliya Nag, half human and half snake, and other Krishna scenes; **38**, the 16 armed goddess Vidyadevi (goddess of knowledge); **46-48** 16 armed goddesses, including the goddess of smallpox, Shitala Mata; and **49** Narasimha, the 'man-lion' tearing open the stomach of the demon Hiranya-Kashyapa, surrounded by an opening lotus.

As in Gujarati Hindu temples, the main hall focuses on the sanctum which contains the 2.5m image of Adinatha, the first Tirthankara. The sanctum with a pyramidal roof has a vestibule with entrances on 3 sides. To its E is the *Mandapa*, a form of octagonal nave nearly 8m in diameter. Its 6m wide dome is supported by 8 slender columns; the exquisite lotus ceiling carved from a single block of marble, rises in 11 concentric circles, carved with elaborately repeated figures. Superimposed across the lower rings are 16 brackets carved in the form of the goddesses of knowledge.

Risah Deo Temple, opposite the Vimala Visahi, is unfinished. It encloses a huge brass Tirthankara image weighing 4.3 tonnes and made of *panchadhatu* (5 metals) – gold, silver, copper, brass and zinc. The temple was commenced in the late 13th century by Brahma Shah, the Mewari Maharana Pratap's chief minister. Building activity was curtailed by war with Gujarat and never completed.

Luna Vasihi or **Neminatha Temple** (1231) to the N of the Adinatha Temple, was erected by 2 wealthy merchants, Vastupala and Tejapala, and dedicated to the 22nd Tirthankara; they also built a similar temple at Girnar. The attractive niches on either side of the entrance were for their wives. The craftsmanship in this temple is comparable to the Vimala Vasahi; the decorative carving and *jali* work are excellent. The small domes in front of the shrine containing the bejewelled Neminatha figure, the exquisitely carved lotus on the *sabhamandapa* ceiling and the sculptures on the colonnades are especially noteworthy.

There is a 5th temple for the **Digambar** ('sky-clad') Jains which is far more austere.

Adhar Devi, 3 km from town, is a 15th century Durga temple carved out of a rock and approached by 220 steep steps. There are very good views.

Sunset Point, Nakki Lake and Honeymoon Point Sunset Point and Honeymoon Point give superb views across the plains to the W. They can both be reached by a pleasant walks from the bus stand, about 2 km. The route to Honeymoon Point goes past the Nakki Lake.

Museums

Art Museum and Gallery, Raj Bhavan Rd. Small collection which includes some textiles and stone sculptures (9th-10th centuries). 1000-1700, closed Fri. Free.

Excursions

The Aravalli Hills, part of the subcontinent's oldest mountain range look more like rocky outcrops, in places quite barren save for date palms and thorny acacias. From Mt Abu it is possible to make day-treks to nearby spot.

Achalgarh (11 km) has superb views. The **Achaleshwar Temple** (9th century) is believed to have Siva's toeprint, a brass Nandi and a deep hole claimed to reach into the netherworld. On the side of Mandakini tank near the car park is an image of Adi Pal, the Paramara king and 3 large stone buffaloes pierced with arrows. In legend, the tank was once filled with *ghee* and the buffaloes (really demons in disguise), came every night to drink from it until they were shot by Adi Pal. A path leads up to a group of carved Jain temples (10 min climb). The whole site is quite picturesque.

Guru Shikhar (Alt 1720m), 15 km, is the highest peak in the area and there is a road almost to the the top. To get to the small Vishnu temple you need to climb 300 steps or hire a palanquin. Good views especially at dawn. Taxis from Mt. Abu take about 1 hr.

Gaumukh (Cow's Mouth), 8 km SE, on the Mt Abu-Abu Road. A small stream flows from the mouth of a marble cow. There is also a Nandi bull, and the tank is believed to be the site of Vasishtha's fire from which the 4 great Rajput clans were created. An image of the sage is flanked by ones of Rama and Krishna.

The **Arbuda Devi Temple** carved out of the rocky hillside is also worth walking to for the superb views over the hills.

Tours
Rajasthan Tourism runs daily tours to Dilwara, Achalgarh, Guru Shikhar, Nakki Lake, Sunset Point and Adhar Devi. 0800-1300, 1400-1900. Gujarat Travels, T 218, organise jeep tours.

Local festivals
Diwali is especially popular.

Local information
● Accommodation
Prices quoted by hotels are high season, but are reduced sharply off-season. Discounts of between 30% and 50% are available. Peak rates apply at Christmas and mid-Apr to early Jun, though some hotels have longer high seasons. **C** ***Palace Hotel*** (Bikaner House), Dilwara Rd, 3 km NE of town centre, T 3121. 38 large rm. Heritage Hotel. Restaurant, exchange. Built 1893 to design by Sir SS Jacob. Imposing granite and sandstone Maharaja's hunting lodge with antique furnishings, atmospheric public rooms very sympathetically renovated. Very quiet, in a large garden with lake, tennis. Book in advance. Highly rec for distinctively civilised character and excellent value. **C** ***Sunrise Palace*** Old Bharatpur Kothi, nr petrol pump. T 3214, and Ahmadabad 443658, Baroda 540461. 16 rm. Good small restaurant, open air barbeque. Converted palace hotel, on hill with excellent views over town. Full of character, warm welcome. Rec. **C** ***Hillock***, opp petrol pump. T 3467. 35 rm. Restaurant, exchange, garden. Central, very modern, clean and well presented if slightly anonymous. Good restaurant, service. Rec. **C** ***Hilltone***, set back from road nr bus stand, T 3112. 46 rm (4 a/c), some cottages. Good restaurant, exchange, pool, garden. Quiet, good service. **C** ***Connaught House***, Rajendra Marg, uphill opp bus stand, T 3360. Jodhpur Maharaja's summer residence, charming colonial bungalow in terraced garden. 14 rm with period furniture, few a/c. New annexe quieter, old part has more character. Indian restaurant. **C** ***Mount Winds***, Raj Bhawan Rd, nr GPO. 14 rm, modern, small hotel. Clean, enthusiastic service, but overpriced. **C** ***Savera Palace***, Sunset Rd. T 3354. 24 rm. Restaurant, pool. Garish, can be noisy, not very clean.

D ***Mount***, Dilwara Rd. T 3150. 7 rm with unmodernised bath in a British officer's bungalow. Charm very faded, none too clean. **D** ***Samrat International***, nr Bus Stand, T 3173. 50 rm. Indian veg restaurant, exchange, travel. Shares reception area with slightly cheaper **D** ***Navjivan***, T 3153. **D** ***Madhuban***, nr Bus Stand nr Hilltone, T 121. 10 comfortable rm. **D** ***Abu International***, opp Polo Ground. T 3177. 43 rm. Simple, clean. Indian restaurant. **D** ***Sunset Inn*** Sunset Rd, 1 km centre. T 3194. 40 rm. Airy, spacious, clean, pleasant wooded site. Rec. Rajasthan Tourism **D** ***Shikhar Tourist Bungalow*** , T 3129. 82 rm with bath, some 'deluxe' in annexe and cottages and dorm. Basic, but excellent views. Old rm less good, 3 new cottages good value but heavily booked. **D** ***Aravalli*** opp, T 216. 18 rm. Well maintained, terraced garden.

● Budget hotels
E ***Sheratone*** nr Bus stand. T 3544. 42 rm. Modern hotel, clean, characterless, but enthusiastic owner manager. Good value. **E** ***Lake View*** 15 rm, 13 attached bath, with some rm facing Lake. Pleasant situation. **E** ***Saraswati***, W of Polo Ground. Better rm in annexe; simple, clean. Indian meals. **E** ***Tourist Guest House***, T 160, below it, is better. Clean rm, garden, rm service for meals. **F** ***Youth Hostel***, nr bus stand has a cramped dorm.

● Places to eat
Handi at *Hilltone Hotel*, specialises in Indian dishes. Bar 1000-2300. Plenty of choice for good cheap Gujarati, Punjabi & S. Indian food. S. Indian at *Woodlands*, also at Hilltone. Rec. Try ***Madras Caf*** with a garden and the ***Parmar Omlette Centre*** nr Polo Ground where eggs are cooked (any style) at bargain prices. Small coffee shops in the bazar. ***Maharaja***, nr Bus stand. Excellent value thalis. ***Sip & Snacks*** Raj Bhawan Rd. Immaculately clean, tiny fast food restaurant. ***Veena*** nr Taxi Stand. V clean. Snacks and S Indian. ***Kanak***, nr Taxi Stand. Good Gujarati food.

● Banks
State Bank of India is on Raj Bhavan Rd.

● Shopping
There are numerous stalls selling trinkets and ready-made clothing, the latter particularly good value; ***Saurashtra Emporium*** rec. ***Rajasthan Emporium***, nr State Bank, Raj Bhavan Rd, opp Bus Stand and ***Khadi Gramudyog***, opp pony hire have handloom, trinkets, carved

agate boxes, marble figures. *Chacha Museum* has odd curios. ***Roopali***, nr Nakki Lake sells silver. Some open 0900-2100 daily.

● Post & telegraph
GPO is on Raj Bhavan Rd.

● Tour offices
Rajasthan Tourism, opp bus stand, T 51. 0800-1100,1600-2000 (1000-1700 out of season). Supplies guides. ***Shobha Travels***, Chetak Circle. Private company, runs daily service to Udaipur, Ahmadabad and Bombay.

● Transport
Local Taxis: with posted fares for sightseeing. **Buses**: for Dilwara and/or Achalgarh. Check timing. *Baba garis* ('prams'), the oddities of Mt Abu, are small carts used to transport goods (and occasionally children!).

Air The nearest airport is at Udaipur, 165 km to the E.

Train Abu Road is the railhead with many direct buses to Mount Abu. **Jodhpur**: *Marwar-Ranakpur Exp*, 4728, daily, 1220, 6¾ hr; *Surya Nagri Exp*, 2908, daily, 0048, 5¼ hr. **Jaipur**: *Delhi Mail*, 9902, daily, 1308, 10¾ hr; *Delhi Exp*, 9904, daily, 2250, 11½ hr; *Ashram Exp*, 2906, daily, 2030, 8 hr. **Agra Fort**: *Agra Fort Fast Passenger Exp*, 9706, daily, 0650, 24¾ hr. *From Agra Fort: Agra Fort Fast Passenger Exp*, 9705, daily, 2020, 23¾ hr. **Old Delhi**: *Aravalli Exp*, 9932, daily, 1105, 18½ hr; *Delhi Mail*, 9902, daily, 1308, 18¼ hr; *Delhi Exp*, 9904, daily, 2250, 20¼ hr; *Ashram Exp*, 2906, daily, 2030, 13½ hr. **Ahmadabad**: *Ahmadabad Exp*, 9903, daily, 5.05, 5 hr; *Ahmadabad Mail*, 9901, daily, 1525, 4¾ hr; *Aravalli Exp*, 9931, daily, 1016, 6 hr; *Surya Nagri Exp*, 2907, daily, 0335, 3½ hr.

Road Bus: extensive service from Mount Abu. It is often quicker to take a bus all the way to your destination rather than go to Abu Road and then take the train. The local bus takes about 1 hr for the 27 km climb from Abu Road, Rs 8. Passenger tax into Mt Abu, Rs 5, taxis Rs 10. Private bus company runs daily services to Udaipur (165 km), Ahmadabad (250 km) and Bombay. Ask ***Shobha Travels*** in town centre.

JAIPUR TO BIKANER, JAISALMER & BARMER

Bikaner is a full day's drive from Jaipur. The journey can be broken by staying at the magnificent palace at Samode or by visiting the Shekhavati region and staying overnight at one of the towns listed below. **Shekhavati** is the homeland of many Marwari families. The 'garden of Shekha' was named after Rao Shekhaji of Amarsar (1433-88) who challenged the Kachhawahas, refusing to pay tribute to the rulers at Amber, though many of the paintings for which the region is famous date from the mid-19th century.

Samode

1 hour's drive (42 km NW) from Jaipur, the village of Samode is on a former caravan route and although not strictly in the Shekhavati region it is well worth the short detour. The village with its local artisans producing printed cloth and glass bangles, nestles within its old walls, in the dry rugged hills of the northern Aravallis. The old havelis and their paintings are still full of character; at the head of the enclosed valley is the remarkable **Samode Palace** now converted into a hotel. The palace is fabulously decorated with 300 year old fine Shekhavati style wall paintings (hunting scenes, floral motifs etc) which still look almost new. Around the first floor of the Durbar Hall are magnificent kiosks, decorated like *shish mahals*. From here you look down through *jali* screens, as the royal ladies would have done, into the grand Durbar Hall itself with its huge chandelier suspended from 4 large rings in the ceiling.

On a hill immediately above the palace is **Samode Fort**, the Maharajah's former residence, reached in times of trouble by an underground passage. The old stone zig-zag path has been replaced by 300 steps which you climb to see the fort. Though dilapidated, there are excellent views from the ramparts; a care-

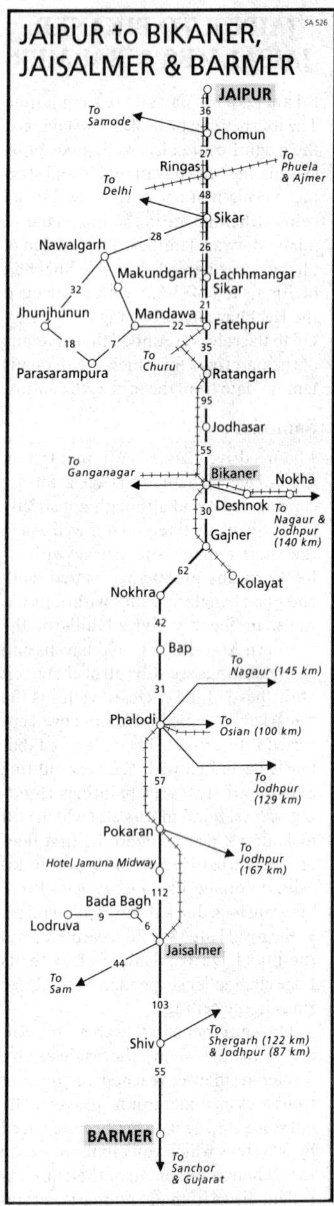

taker has the keys. The main fort gate is the starting point of some enticing walks into the Aravallis. 3 km from Samode, en route to the main Jaipur-Agra road is Samode Bagh, a large formal garden which is being restored (often used as a film set).

• **Accommodation** C *Samode Palace*, T 01423 4114, F 01423 4123. 30 rm. Gardens, royal museum. Magnificent setting. Tastefully modernised without losing any of the charm, friendly, helpful. One of the really remarkable hotels of Rajasthan for its setting, its atmosphere and its value. Highly rec for a memorable experience. At Samode Bagh, 3 km away **C** *Luxury Tents*. Round, carpeted tents equipped as hotel rm, each with its bathroom in the old walls.

Shekhavati

Shekhavati remained independent from 1471 to 1738. This lawless bandit area in the early 19th century was brought under control but the merchants migrated when burdened with taxes and tolls by the British East India Company. The magnificent painted *havelis* in present-day Sikar and Jhunjhunun Districts are open to visitors. They are often occupied by family members or retainers who will happily welcome your visit.

ROUTES From Jaipur take the NH11 NW to Ringas (63 km) and Sikar (48 km). Ideally you should spend 3-4 days in the region but if your time is limited you could do a shorter circuit visiting Sikar, Nawalgarh, Dundlod, Mandawa, Fatehpur, Lachhmangarh, returning to Sikar.

Sikar District

Sikar (*Pop* 148,000 *STD Code* 01572) The late 17th century fort was built when Sikar was an important trading centre and the wealthiest *thikana* (feudatory) under Jaipur. You can visit the old quarter and see the Wedgwood blue Biyani (1920) and Mahal (1845), the Murarka and Somani *havelis* and murals and carvings in Gopinath, Raghunath and Madan Mohan temples.

26 km further on is **Lachhmangarh** (*STD Code* 014923) founded in the early 19th century, and based on Jaipur's model town plan; this can be seen by climbing up to the old fort. The fine *havelis* here with every day scenes include one the area's grandest – Ganeriwala with Char Chowks (4 courtyards). Visit the Rathi haveli nr the Clock Tower in the market; other interesting examples can be seen by walking from Murlimanohar temple to the Chowkhani.

The road goes straight to **Fatehpur** (21 km), founded in the mid-15th century by a Kayamkhani Nawab, which has very attractive havelis found along the main road and by walking in the direction of Sikar and turning right. Visit in particular the Devra (1885), Singhania (c1880) on the Churu Rd, the Goenka (c1880) and Saraogi. Later, amusing frescoes can be seen in the Jalan and white Bhardia (1929) *havelis.* The town also produces good tie and dye fabrics. Hotels Taj Group are planning to open a hotel in late 1994.

You can visit **Ramgarh** a little further N, settled by the Poddars in the late 18th century. In addition to their *haveli* and that of the Ruias, visit the *chhattris* with painted entrances nr the Bus Stand, the temples to Shani (with mirror decoration) and to Ganga. Look for handicrafts and antiques here.

Danta 48 km S of Sikar, originally a part of Marwar, was given to Thakur Amar Singhji in the mid-17th century and became a part of Shekhavati. 2 *kilas* (forts) and the residential wing (early 18th century and now a Dera Heritage hotel) combine Mughal and Rajput art and architectural styles. Danta can also be reached from Ringas (42 km) or Renwal (25 km) by train; transport available from stations.

Jhunjhunun District

Mandawa (*Pop* 16,000) At Fatehpur, turn right down a country road for 22 km. Founded mid-18th century, it has interesting murals in the large rugged fort (c1755) built by Thakur Nawal Singh, which is now a hotel with excellent views. The Goenka havelis worth visiting include Ladhuram Tarkesvar (1878) and Dedraj Turmal (1898); the Ladia havelis – Gulab Rai (1870) and Sneh Ram (1906), Murmuria (1935), Newatia (1910) and the Saraf (1870) havelis are interesting. The Siva temple here has a rock crystal lingam. Visit Harlalka *baoli* (a working step well) early in the morning to watch oxen at work on the ramp to raise water.

Mukundgarh (10 km S) has a good handicrafts market and the Jhunjhunwala (1859) haveli with Krishna stories and Sukhdev (c1880). The 18th century fort is now a hotel.

Nawalgarh (SE, 8 km from Mandawa. *STD Code* 015954) Founded in 1737 by Thakur Nawal Singh. The town has a colourful bazar and 2 forts (c1730); the Bala Kila has a kiosk with beautiful ceiling paintings. It also has the Roop Nivas Palace (now a hotel) and numerous havelis worth visiting, particularly those of Puranmal Chhauchhariya (1875), Poddars (1920, now a school), Bhagats, Dangaiches and Jandgid (1922) . There are also interesting temples in town including Ganga Mai nr Nansa Gate.

Parasarampura is 7 km E with its decorated *chhattri* to Sardul Singh (1750) and the adjacent Gopinath temple (1742); these are the earliest examples of Shekhavati frescoes painted with natural pigments. Caretaker has keys.

Dundlod W of Nawalgarh, has the best murals in the 1750 *kila* (fort/ castle) surrounded by a moat (now a Dera Heritage hotel). You enter the fort by the Suraj Pol and proceed through the Bichla Darwaza and Uttar Pol (N) before arriving at the court yard. Steps lead up to the magestic Diwan Khana furnished with period furniture, portraits and hangings; there is a library with a collection of rare books of Indian history and the *duchatta* above which allowed the ladies in *purdah* to watch court ceremonies, unobserved. Ask for the key to the painted family *chhattris* nearby. The Goenka haveli nr the fort has 3 painted courtyards, and the Satyanarayan temple, religious paintings. The interesting 100m deep stepwell now has an electric pump. Mukundgarh is the nearest station; jeeps and taxis available.

Jhunjhunun or Jhunjhunu (25 km E of Mandawa; *Pop* 72,000, *STD Code* 01592), was a stronghold of the Kayamkhani Nawabs until defeated by the Hindu Sardul Singh in 1730. Worth seeing are the Modi (1896), Tibriwala (1883) and the Muslim Nuruddin Farooqi havelis devoid of figures, the *Chhe* (6) Haveli complex, Khetri Mahal (1760) and Bihariji temple (1776). The Rani Sati temple commemorates Narayana Devi who is believed to have become a sati; her stone is venerated by many of the wealthy *bania* community and an annual Marwari fair is held. In 1988 women's groups organised demonstrations against the fair since it was seen as glorifying the practice of *sati.*

Since 1947, 29 cases of *suttee* have been recorded in the Sikar and its 2 neighbouring districts; the latest, in 1987 in Deorah village caused a national uproar.

Bissau (15 km NW) founded 1746, has painted *chhattris* and a fort. The Sigtia, Khemka, Tibriwala and Kedla havelis are worth visiting. **Mahansar** (founded mid-18th century) S of Bissau, has the Poddar haveli of Son – Chand, the Rama Temple (ask for the key to the Golden Room; no photography) and the large Raghunath Temple with some of the finest paintings of the region.

Churu (35 km NW) 120 villages of Churu Dist once belonged to Shekhavati. The town is known for its Kanhaya Lal Bugla (1870), Kothari (1915) and the 6-storeyed Surana haveli with over 1100 doors and windows.

Alsisar and Malsisar (founded late 18th century) are N of Jhunjhunun, each with a fort. Here the paintings are more angular using unusual hues. Alsisar has Jhunjhunwala havelis and a well complex while Malsisar has temples and houses along the main road.

Chirawa NE of Jhunjhunun, past **Baggar** with a reservoir off the main road, is at a strategic crossroad. The Dalmias and Kakraniyas grew wealthy on trade and built large rambling havelis.

Khetri, S of Chirawa (founded mid-18th century), was the second wealthiest *thikana* under Jaipur and has the Bhopalgarh fort and Raghunath Temple with paintings.

● Accommodation

Danta: **C** *Kila*, T 89362, (a Dera Heritage hotel, T Jaipur 366276, F 41763). 12 rm in residential wing below the 2 old forts. Amenities incl good restaurant, horse riding, camel rides (Rs 175/hr, Rs 400/3 hr) on request. Horse safaris (see under Transport below), Jeep safaris (min 4 persons), Rs 1200 each/day. Special "royal welcome" and folk dance performances arranged for groups.

Dundlod: **C** *Kila* T 2519, (a Dera Heritage hotel, T Jaipur 366276, F 41763). 25 charming rm (each unique) with terraces and a reasonably priced good restaurant. Exchange, swimming. Rides, safaris and entertainment as at Danta above. Full of atmosphere and good murals.

Fatehpur: Simple Rajasthan Tourism **E** *Haveli*.

Jhunjhunun: **D** *Shiv Shekhavati*, Muni Ashram, T 2651. Simple clean rm, a/c or air-cooled, some with bath. Good veg restaurant, Tourist Information Bureau.

Mandawa: **C** *Castle Mandawa*, T Mandawa 224, (Jaipur 75358). 14 km Mukundgarh rly. 49 air-cooled rm with modern baths all round the castle. Excellent restaurant (very spectacular torchlight procession when liveried servants bring in dinner), riding, camel safari, folk dances, puppet shows. Book well in advance. Keshri Singh, 'the Maharaja', also runs **D** *Desert Camp*, T 251, 1 km away. Unique "village huts" with modern amenities are very imaginatively decorated (potters', farmers', weavers'). Swimming pool, shady trees in garden, camel rides. Reserve through Mandawa House, Jaipur T 75358. A newer, **D** *Rath*, T 240, on town's edge. 25 simple rm with bath. Dining hall.

Mukundgarh: New **C** *Mukundgarh Fort*, now a Heritage Hotel with 46 rm, restaurant, bar, garden and pool.

Nawalgarh: **C** *Roop Nivas Palace*, T 01594 22008 or Jaipur T 368726. 1 km from town. 25 comfortable rm, some air-cooled, with baths. Good food, large gardens, billiards, pool. Camel rides, Rs 200/hr–Rs 800/day; horse rides Rs 250/hr–Rs 1,750/day. Also organises 'safaris', see under Adventure Sports in Information for Visitors and page 112. The palace building combines European and Rajput styles with old-fashioned interior furnishings. **D** *Jangid* Haveli behind hospital, T 129. Good veg restaurant, tours, jeep/ cycle hire, camel rides, cultural shows. Helpful, knowledgable owner. Quiet, clean, welcoming guest house. These lack age and character of the fort hotels.

Sikar: *Natraj* Restaurant, Main Rd, does good meals and snacks. Clean, reasonable.

PWD or Electricity board **F** *Dak Bungalows* at **Churu**, **Sikar**, **Jhunjhunun** and **Khetri**, with simple rm and bath, may be available when unoccupied by officials. Meals to order.

● Transport

Train *Shekhavati Exp* (Delhi-Jaipur): To **Mukundgarh**: 3 at night, 1 day, from Delhi 7 hr; from Jaipur, 0935, 1650, 2010, 4¾ hr. To **Nawalgarh**: from Delhi, 2230, 8½ hr. To **Jhunjhunun**: from Delhi, dep 2245, 7¾ hr, arriving in Sikar after 2 hr; from Jaipur, dep 1715, 6 hr, and continues to Delhi, 6 hr. To **Sikar** from Bikaner, dep 2000, 10 hr.

Road Bus: regular buses from Jaipur to principal Shekhavati towns, but these are crowded. To **Nawalgarh**: from Delhi, best from ISBT daily 0800, also 2200, 2300, 8 hr. From Jaipur frequent buses from 0630-1830 (Express in the morning). Also to Sikar from Jaipur and 5 daily from Bikaner.

Horse & Jeep safaris: 1-7 day safaris visiting a number of Shekhavati towns are offered by Dera Heritage hotels (Dundlod and Danta *Kilas*), min 6 persons, Rs 3,000 each /day covering transport, accommodation, meals and entertainment.

ROUTES From Fatehpur it is 35 km to Ratangarh, a market town with a *Rest House*. The NH11 continues to Bikaner (127 km).

Bikaner

Bikaner takes its name from Rao Bhikaji, the 6th son of the Rathor Rajput prince Rao Jodha, the founder of Jodhpur. Bhika set up his independent kingdom in 1488. Like Jaisalmer, it developed as a centre of the cross-desert caravan trade, but a defensive site was necessary to give its ruling princes protection. The rocky outcrop in the desert provides a dramatic setting for the Junagarh Fort, and the merchant houses, palaces and temples in the old city immediately to its SW. The Bikaner area is chiefly agricultural and a fine wool is obtained from its sheep. The Bikaner Gang Canal (1925-7) enabled an area of 285,000 ha of previously arid scrub to be irrigated. Camel rearing is also practised and there is a government breeding station near the city. Bikaner's Marwari traders are noted throughout N India for their business acumen.

BASICS *Population:* 415,000. *Altitude:* 237m. *STD:* 0151. *Climate:* Temperature Summer Max 41°C Min 28°C; Winter Max 23°C Min 10°C. Annual rainfall 440 mm, mostly Jun-Sep.

Places of Interest

Junagarh Fort (1588-93) was started by Raja Rai Singh (1571-1611) but had palaces added for the next 3 centuries. 1000-1600. Closed Fri. The light red sandstone 1 km perimeter wall is surrounded by a moat while the Chowks have beautifully designed palaces with balconies, kiosks and fine *jali* screens with richly decorated interiors and lacquered doors.

You enter by the yellow sandstone Suraj Pol (Sun Gate, 1593). The fort and the palaces within are all superbly preserved. The walls of the **Lal Niwas,** the oldest are elaborately decorated in red and gold. **Karan Singh** commemorated a victory over Aurangzeb by building the **Karan Mahal** (1631-9, durbar hall) on the opposite side of the Chowk. Successive rulers added royal apartments above: the **Gaj Mandir** (1745-87) with its shining Shish Mahal and the Chatra

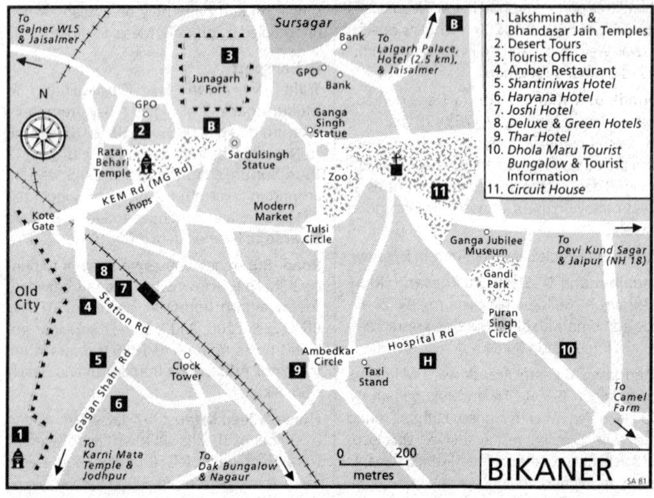

Merchants And Their Havelis

The ***Marwaris*** form one of the most important merchant and business groups in India. Originally from Marwar, further W, they developed their business acumen on the trade routes between Delhi and the coast and between India and Central Asia. Anxious to serve their rulers and be protected by them, they were often the Maharaja's financiers and extravagant patrons of the arts. In the 19th century, they made their fortune, trading from the large British ports of Calcutta, Bombay and Madras and repatriated much of their wealth back to their homeland in the Jhunjhunun and Sikar districts.

Many built grand *havelis* in the 360 villages of Shekhavati which they elaborately decorated with murals depicting scenes from myths, epics, folklore, history and glimpses of everyday village life. They are fascinating social documents particularly as the fashion to be "Westernised" emerged in the awkward juxtaposition of rural life with portrayal of early trains, motor cars, telephones, aircraft and even *sahibs* and *mem-sahibs* accompanied by pet dogs. In addition to their homes, the merchants lavished their money on temples, *chhatris, dharamsalas* and wells, an important focus for people in the desert. .

The *havelis* had the *Baithak* (reception area) beyond the main entrance and courtyard which was impressively decorated, with the inner courtyard leading to the women's section. The upstairs bedrooms projected outwards like a canopy, protecting the paintings on the façade. Usually the exteriors were decorated by local artists but often, specialist painters were brought in for the highly ornamented interiors. The earlier *fresco buono* technique (1830-1900) painted with natural colours on wet plaster are far finer than the later (1900-1930) using imported chemical dyes from Germany executed on dry plaster. The colours used were bright yellows, blues, greens, reds and even silver and gold leaf. The finest plasterwork perfected the application of colour with limepaste and curds, which would be polished with coconut fibre, to look like marble.

The wealth of wall paintings have come to the attention of travellers fairly recently so only a few places have reasonably comfortable accommodation although most towns have basic dharamshalas and official *Dak Bungalows*.

Niwas (1872-87) with its pitched roof has English 'field sport' plates decorating the walls.

Mirror work, carving and marble decorate the ornate **Chandra Mahal** (Moon Palace) and the **Phul Mahal** (Flower Palace), built by Maharaja Gaj Singh. The magnificent Coronation Hall, richly adorned with plasterwork, lacquer, mirror and glass, is in Maharaja Surat Singh's **Anup Mahal** (1788-1828). The decorative facades around the Anup Mahal Chowk, though painted white, are in fact of stone. The fort also includes the **Chetar Mahal** and **Chini Burj** of Dungar Singh (1872-87) and the **Ganga Niwas** (built by Ganga Singh (1898-1943) who did much to modernise his state and also built the Lalgarh Palace to the N. The old biplane here was his Highness's personal aircraft before WW II. The fort itself contains a fine **library** of Sanskrit and Persian books and an armoury which includes the Maharajas' palanquins. The well nearby is reputedly over 130m deep. **Har Mandir** is the royal temple, dedicated to Siva where their birth and wedding ceremonies were celebrated.

The red sandstone 20th century **Lalgarh Palace** with its superb carvings, particularly in the fine lattice work, stands out in the city, surrounded by rocks and sand dunes. Part is now a hotel; the banquet hall is full of hunting trophies and photographs. The bougainvillaea and peacocks add to the attraction of the gardens in which the Bikaner State Railway Carriage is preserved. The **Sadul museum** is on the first floor. 1000-1700, closed Wed. The **Anup Sanskrit Library** is open on request. Contact hotel manager.

Museums

Ganga Golden Jubilee Museum, Public Park. 1000-1700. Closed Fri. A fine small collection of pottery, paintings and weapons. Some pre-Harappan exhibits and a group of terracottas from the Gupta (4-5th century) and Kushan periods. Separate section of local crafts and a gallery of artefacts. Junagarh Fort. 1000-1630. Closed Fri. Rs 4, Camera fee Rs 10. Sadul Museum, Lalgarh Palace, Civil Lines. 1000-1700. Closed Wed. Rs 2.

Parks & zoos

Ganga Nivas Public Park nr Modern Market. 0800-1800. Ratan Bihari Temple Park nr Shopping Centre. Bhawan Palace Park nr Bus Stand. Nathji Park nr Museum.

Excursions

Bhand Sagar (5 km), a group of colourful temples of which the 16th century Jain temple is the most important. Guides from city only. A little difficult to find on your own and numerous steps but wonderful views. Entry Rs 5. **Devi Kund** (8 km) is the site of the Bhika rulers' *devals*, marking the funeral pyres, notably that of Surat Singh with its ceiling decorations of Rajpur paintings.

Karni Mata Mandir (33 km at **Deshnoke** on the Jodhpur Rd). Entry Rs 10 plus camera fee. No guides. Mice and rats, revered and fed in the belief that they are reincarnated saints, swarm over the temple around your bare feet. The 17th century temple with massive silver gates and white marble carvings on the façade which were added by Ganga Singh (1898-1943), who dedicated the temple to a 15th century female mystic Karniji, revered as an incarnation of Durga. Closed 1200-1600. Buses every hour from Bikaner (Rs 7) or taxi (about Rs 150 for return). Train dep 1000, returns 1230.

The road S from Bikaner goes to **Jodhpur** through **Nokha** (51 km) and **Nagaur** (48 km) totalling 236 km. It is served by buses. For excursions on the road to Jodhpur, see page 446.

Camel Breeding Farm (10 km). Claims to be the only one in Asia. Rides available. Camels returning from grazing at sunset are especially picturesque.

Local festivals

Desert Festival for 2 days in Nov. Folk music and dance. Fire Dance is the special attraction in the evenings. *Gangaur Dasara* and *Diwali* are especially spectacular in Junagarh Fort, in the Old City near Kote Gate and some smaller palaces.

Local information

● Accommodation

A *Lalgarh Palace*, T 3263. 40 clean, large, a/c rm. Restaurant, bar, pool, museum. Mediocre and overpriced.

Rajasthan Tourism **D** *Dhola Maru Tourist Bungalow*, nr Puran Singh Circle, T 5002. 26 rm with bath and dorm. Restaurant, bar, shop. Adequate but out of town. **D** *Joshi*, Station Rd, T 6162. 40 rm. A/c. restaurant, terrace garden. **D** *Karni Bhawan Palace*, T 3308. 10 a/c rm. 9-hole golf course. **D** *Thar*, Ambedkar Circle, T 7180. 24 clean rm with bath. Indian veg restaurant, coffee shop. Good service.

Cheaper hotels are very basic, have rm, usually with shared bath and often serve Indian veg food only.

On Station Rd: **E** *Deluxe*, Station Rd, T 23292. Some air-cooled rm with bath. Pleasant restaurant. Eager-to-please management. Popular, clean, can be noisy. **F** *Inder*, further along, 3rd lane on right, opp petrol station. Good value. On Ganga Shahr Rd: **E** *Shantiniwas*, T 5025. **F** *Haryana*, T 5282. **F** *Railway Retiring Rooms*. Reservations, T 4660.

● Places to eat

Veg restaurants on Station Rd: *Amber*. Tasty Indian, some western dishes, good value;

Joshi, and *Anand*. On rd to right: *Ganesh* is cheap. Try the local speciality – *Bikaneri Bhujia* a spicy snack made out of gram and pulses.

● Shopping

Bikaner is famous for *Usta* work (camel leather wares painted in colours) which includes footwear, purses and cushions. You can also get local carpets and woodwork. The main shopping centres are on KEM Rd which starts from nr the Fort, and the nearby roads and lanes, Kote Gate in the Old City and Mahatma Gandhi Rd, Modern Market. ***Cottage Industries Institute***, nr Junagarh Fort. **Rajasthali** counter at Information Centre. **Photography**: ***Studio India*** and ***K Studio*** on MG Rd.

● Banks

State Bank of India in Dauji Rd. Bikaner in Court Rd.

● Hospitals & medical services

PBM Hospital, Hospital Rd. T 4175.

● Post & telegraph

GPO behind Junagarh Fort. **Telegraph Office**, behind Collectorate, Public Park.

● Tour companies & travel agents

Rajasthan Tours, Daudsar House, T 4834. ***Mayur Travels***, 148 Sadul Ganj. ***Desert Tours***, behind Head Post Office, Mangal Niwas. ***Victorian Travels***, Ganga Shahr Rd, T 5626.

● Tourist offices

Rajasthan, Suraj Pol, Junagarh Fort main entrance, T 5445. 1000-1700. **Information Centre**, Old Ghinani Area, T 4595; Dhola-Maru Tourist Bungalow, Poonam Singh Circle, T 5445. 0800-1800, Oct-Mar.

● Useful addresses

Police: T 3840. **Ambulance**: T 4175.

● Transport

From **Delhi** (435 km); **Jaipur** (330 km); **Jodhpur** (250 km); **Jaisalmer** (320 km); **Ajmer** (280 km); **Bombay** (1250 km).

Local Taxis: tourist taxis available at rly station, opp Dak Bungalow or at Bus Stand, S End, Junagarh Rd, or through hotels and agencies. Rates negotiable. **Auto-rickshaws**: easily available. Rates negotiable. **Cycles**: for hire nr Amber Rest.

Train Jaipur: *Bikaner Exp*, 4738, daily, 2000, 10 hr. **Old Delhi**: *Bikaner-Delhi Exp*, 4790, daily, 0845, 11 hr; *Bikaner-Delhi Mail*, 4792, daily, 1930, 11½ hr.

Road Bus: ***Rajasthan Roadways*** run daily deluxe bus services connecting Bikaner to Jaipur, Jodhpur, Ajmer, Sriganganagar, Jaisalmer (8-9 hr), Udaipur, Kota, etc. Daily buses to all district headquarters, daily. 2 daily buses connect Delhi to Bikaner via Hissar. ***Rajsthan Tourism*** runs a deluxe coach service between Jaipur and Bikaner. Central Bus Stand, KEM Rd, T 6688. Reservations 0600-2200. *Dhola-Maru Tourist Bungalow*, T 5002.

Camel: to Jaisalmer by camel usually takes 12 days. Ask tour company.

Bikaner to Jaisalmer

Gajner (30 km). The old hunting lodge is now the Hotel C *Gajner Palace*, T 39, with 22 rm. The **Gajner National Park** harbours nilgai, chinakara, blackbuck and Imperial sand grouse.

Pokaran (165 km from Jodhpur, *Pop* 15,000). The magnificent yellow sandstone **fort** built by the Marwar *thakur* Rao Maldeo (1532-84) with some masonry from an older Satelmer Fort nearby (now in ruins), overlooks a confusion of streets in the town below. The fort has a small **museum** with an interesting collection. Pokaran is the site of India's first nuclear test explosion on 18 Mar 1974. Accommodation: Pokaran Fort. 2 large rm with bath. **NB:** the locomotive is moved from the front to the back for the final leg of the train journey to Jaisalmer, so don't be alarmed! The road out of Pokaran to Jaisalmer (112 km) passes the new *Hotel Jamuna Midway* with 4 huts and a thatched restaurant where you can stop for a meal. Pool, clean toilet. A good stopping point.

Jaisalmer

Jaisalmer is the westernmost town of any significance in India and has an extraordinarily medieval feel, with its crenellated golden sandstone walls and narrow streets lined with exquisitely carved buildings. All, including new structures, are built out of the local honey-coloured sandstone. 275 km from Jodhpur, the final approach to it across the hot barren desert is magical as the city shimmers like a mirage.

BASICS *Population:* 39,000. *Altitude:* 250m. *STD:* 02992.

History

Founded by Prince Jaisal in 1156, Jaisalmer grew to be a major staging post on the trade route across the forbidding Thar desert from India to the W. The merchants prospered and invested part of their wealth in building beautiful houses and temples with the local yellow sandstone. The growth of maritime trade between India and the W caused a decline in trade across the desert which ceased altogether in 1947. However, the wars with Pakistan (1965 and 1971) resulted in the Indian government developing the transport facilities to the border to improve troop movement. This has also helped visitors to gain access. Today, the army and tourism are mainstays of the local economy. The region also has a reputation for harbouring smugglers.

The town is mostly on the N side of the Fort, enclosed by a wall built in 1750. There are 4 major gateways to the city: **Malka Pol** (N), **Amar Sagar Pol** (W), **Baron-ki-Pol** and **Gadisagar Pol** (SE). 2 other gateways have been sealed. You enter through the Amar Sagar Pol; on your right is the former ruler's 20th century palace, **Badal Mahal** with a 5-storeyed tower, which has fine carvings.

Places of interest

Take a walk through the narrow streets often blocked by the odd goat or cow, and see how even today about a thousand of the ordinary people live in tiny houses inside the fort, yet often with beautiful carvings on doors and balconies. It is easy to get lost!

The Fort On the somewhat triangular Trikuta Hill, the fort stands 76m above the town, enclosed by a 9m wall with 99 bastions (mostly 1633-1647). About a quarter of the town's people live within it. You enter the Fort from the E. The inner, higher fort wall and the old gates up the ramp (Suraj, Ganesh, Hawa and Rang Pols) provided further defences. The Suraj Pol (1594), once an outer gate, is flanked by heavy bastions and has bands of decoration seen in local textiles.

As with many other Rajput forts, within the massive defences are a series of palaces, the product of successive generations of rulers' flights of fancy. Often called the Golden Fort because of the colour of the sandstone, it dominates the town. The stone is relatively easy to carve and the dry climate has meant that the fineness of detail has been preserved through the centuries. The *jali* work and delicately ornamented balconies and windows with Bengali style eaves break the solidity of the thick walls which afforded protection from the heat, while the high plinths of the buildings, kept off the sand. Even today new buildings in the town conform to the same material and style.

Royal apartments You arrive at the 7-storey palace first. Open 0800-1300, 1500--1700, Rs 6. The **Juna Mahal** (c1500) with its *jali* screens is one of the oldest Rajasthani palaces. The rather plain *zenana* block to its W, facing the *chauhata* (square) is decorated with false *jalis*. Next to it is the men's quarters (*mardana*) includes the **Rang Mahal**

CLIMATE: JAISALMER

	Jan	Feb	Mar	Apr	May	Jun	Jul	Aug	Sep	Oct	Nov	Dec	Av/Tot
Max (°C)	24	28	33	38	42	41	38	36	36	36	31	26	34
Min (°C)	8	11	17	21	25	27	27	25	25	20	13	9	19
Rain (mm)	2	1	3	1	5	7	89	86	14	1	5	2	216

above the Hawa Pol, built during the reign of Mulraj II (1762-1820) which has highly detailed murals and mirror decoration. **Sarvotam Vilas** was built by Akhai Singh (1722-62) and is ornamented with blue tiles and glass mosaics. The adjacent **Gaj Vilas** (1884), stands on a high plinth. The **Moti Mahal,** another of Mulraj II's buildings, has superb floral decoration and carved doors.

The open square beyond the gates, has a platform reached by climbing some steps; this is where court was held or royal visitors entertained. There are also fascinating **Jain temples** (12th-16th centuries). 0700-1200; leather

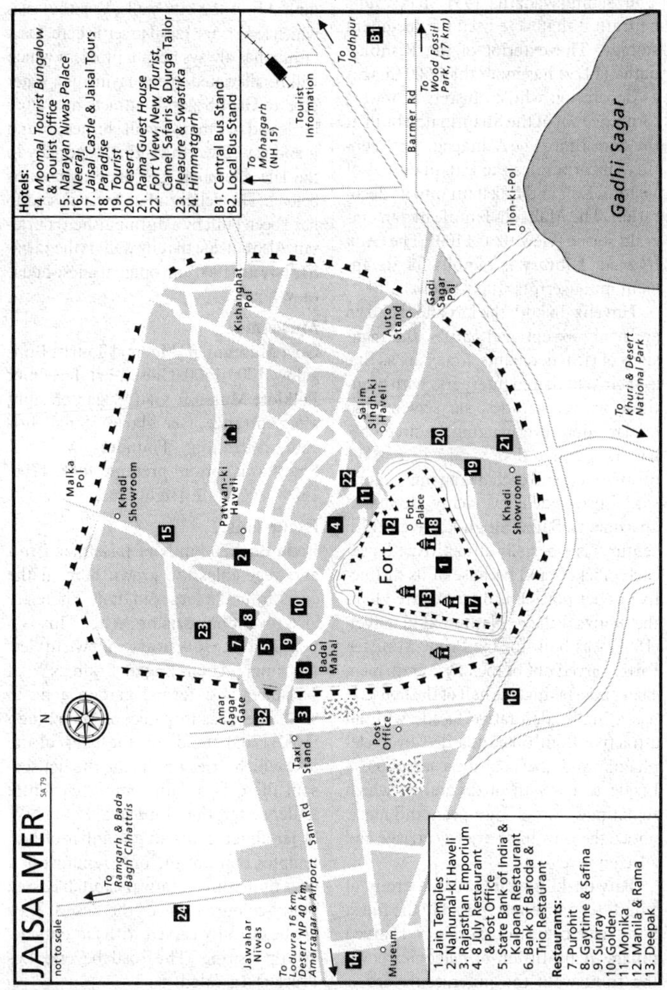

articles not permitted inside; no photography. Whilst the Rajputs were devout Hindus they permitted Jainism to be practised. The Parsvanatha (1417) has fine gateway, an ornate porch and 52 subsidiary shrines surrounding the main structure. The brackets are elaborately carved as maidens and dancers. The Sambhavanatha(1431) has vaults beneath it that were used for document storage. The exterior of the Rishbhanatha (1479) has more than 600 images as decoration whilst clusters of towers form the roof of the Shantinatha built at the same time. The Ashtapadi (16th century) incorporates the Hindu deities of Vishnu, Kali and Lakshmi into its decoration. The Mahavir Temple has an emerald statue (view 1000-1100). The *Gyan Bhandar* **Library** is famous for its ancient manuscripts. 1000-1100.

Havelis In both the fort and the town are many exceptional *havelis*, the mansions of rich merchants. Many are as fine as their Venetian counterparts, with beautifully carved facades, *jali* screens and oriel windows overhanging the streets below. The ground floor is raised above the dusty streets and each has an inner courtyard surrounded by richly decorated apartments. **Salim Singh-ki haveli** (17th century) is especially attractive with peacock brackets and because of its distinctive upper portion is often referred to as the Ship's Palace. **Nathumal-ki haveli** (1885) was built for the Prime Minister. Partly carved out of rock by 2 craftsmen, each undertaking one half of the house. It has a highly decorative façade with an attractive front door, guarded by 2 elephants (mid-afternoon best for photos). Inside is a wealth of decoration which sometimes shows European influence; notice the tiny horse drawn carriage and a locomotive!

Patwon-ki haveli (1805), a group of 5 built for 5 brothers, possibly the finest here, have beautiful murals and carved pillars. A profusion of balconies cover the front wall; the inner courtyard is surrounded by richly decorated apartments. 2 buildings are open 1030-1700. Where the *havelis* are occupied, you may be allowed in on a polite request. Otherwise, your guide (not necessarily an official one) will help you gain access into one or more of these, often at no cost.

The **Gadi Sagar** (Gadisar or Gharisar) tank, SE of the city walls, was the oasis which led Prince Jaisal to settle here. Lack of rain has always been a problem which will be alleviated by the laying of a water pipe to Gadi Sagar. It attracts migratory birds and has many small shrines around it and is well worth visiting, especially in the late afternoon (see under Museums below). The delightful archway is said to have been built by a distinguished courtesan. Also outside the city walls is the **Jawahar Niwas** (1900), an opulent guest-house (now hotel).

Museums

Govt Museum, nr Moomal Tourist Bungalow. 1000-1600. Closed Fri. Jaisalmer Folklore Museum, Gadi Sagar, on right after entrance, (see above). Small private collection. Founder, Mr NK Sharma is often present. 0900-1200, 1500-1800. Rs 2. Highly rec.

Excursions

Bada Bagh, 6 km N of Jaisalmer. Fruit and vegetables are grown here in the oasis around a large old dam. There are also royal **chhattris** or *devals*. This is a popular place to visit at sundown to view Jaisalmer. **Amar Sagar**, 5 km NW of Jaisalmer is a formal garden gone to seed. The pleasure palace of Amar Singh (1661-1703) stands on the bank of the lake which dries up during the hot season; there is a Jain temple currently under restoration. **Lodruva**, 15 km NW of Jaisalmer, contains a number of Jain temples that are the only remains of a once flourishing Marwar capital. Rising honey-coloured out of the desert, they are beautifully carved with *jali* outside. Worth visiting. The road beyond Lodruva is unsealed.

CAMEL SAFARIS

The charming desert outpost of Jaisalmer is the starting point for camel safaris into the surrounding wilderness. These can be one day, one week or longer, eg an 11-day trek to Bikaner. Beware, some find a camel's back very painful after a few days and have to give up. A trip is easy to arrange though it pays to choose carefully, especially if you are planning a longer trip. All the camels are privately owned; the hotels and agents act as middlemen. The larger hotels have reputations to maintain and you may pay more for that, but reports indicate that many small hoteliers do organise good outings. *Narayan Niwas Hotel*, and *Fort View Hotel* safaris are recommended; open to non-residents. Rs 200-250 per day. 3-day/2-night safari costs about Rs 650 (Rs 200 more for a tent). More expensive in Shekhavati, see page 112.

There are day long trips which usually include the Sam sand dunes, see page 475 where Rajasthan Tourism's *Sam Dhani* has 8 huts and a dorm. The usual tours take 4 days and 3 nights and are on a circuit around Jaisalmer via Mool Sagar, the Sam sand dunes and Lodruva. En route you will pass through a few Muslim, Rajput and tribal villages, occupied and abandoned. You will see fields of hardy millet and come across flocks of sheep and goats with their tinkling bells. Some organisers cover a lot of ground in 2½days by taking you one way by jeep with a guide, eg *Adventure Travel*.

Meals and camping equipment are usually provided but check beforehand. On safari there will probably be 1 camel per person plus 1 each for luggage. The camel may be led, you may 'steer' or the driver will sit behind you on the fodder bags. Warning: some travellers reported bad experiences when camel drivers get drunk – and of some hotels organising sub-standard safaris eg Adventure Tours at *New Tourist Hotel*.

A lot depends on individual camel drivers – if you are lucky he will be a conscientious driver and a good cook. If you are cheated, go to the police who may be able to reclaim some money. 'Rival operators are willing to help make the complaint', some have found. NB: make sure your camel is fitted with adequate stirrups – without them the trip will be very uncomfortable! Radios are usually taken, for contact with the police is important in this sensitive border area.

The following are useful: fruit (citrus); water bottle with a shoulder strap or string; (a recent traveller used Glucose-D powder for energy); sunblock; sun-glasses; chapstick; sunhat, turban or/and large scarf as a headcloth (or to keep your turban on!); a cushion (riding on a swaying camel for 20-30 km per day can render your bottom tender); talcum powder helps; cash to tip the camel driver; a shirt with pockets in front for easy access to small things.

Mool Sagar, 9 km W of Jaisalmer on the road to Sam is another small garden around a tank. **Sam** (also *Sain*), 40 km W of Jaisalmer. Popular with camel treks as there are proper sand dunes.

Khuri, 40 km SW of Jaisalmer, is a small picturesque desert village of decorated mud thatched buildings which has ruled by the Sodha clan for 4 centuries. Visitors are attracted by shifting sand dunes, some 80m high, and beautiful sunsets. Local accommodation for 40 and Rajasthani meals accompanied by folk entertainment; half to 2-day camel rides are available. Best months Nov-Feb. Buses from Jaisalmer take 1½hr. **Note** Foreign tourists were not being given permits to visit the area from 1993 for security reasons. Enquire at Dist Commissioner's Office, Jaisalmer.

The Thar Desert National Park is near the village. Enquire in Jaisalmer Tourist Office about permits. You can visit it by jeep and take a short camel ride, visiting desert villages. Superb sunsets.

Thar Desert National Park SW of Jaisalmer (36 km) was created to protect 3,000 sq km of the Thar Desert, the habitat for drought resistant, endangered and rare species which have adjusted to the unique and inhospitable conditions of extreme temperatures. Temp range: 50°C to -4°C. Rainfall: 150 mm. The desert has undulating dunes and vast expanses of flat land where the trees found are mostly leafless and thorny and often have very long roots, eg *khejri* (*Prosopis cineraria*) which dominates. There is also *khair* (*Acacia katechu*), *thor* and *rohira*. The Bishnois who inhabit the area protect the chinkara, black buck and desert fox. Among the birds which include various eagles, the **Great Indian bustard** which can weigh up to 14 kg and reaches a height of 40 cm has made its home here. Best season: Oct-Mar. **Accommodation** *Rest Houses*. Contact Director of Research, Desert National Park, Jaisalmer.

Wood Fossil Park About 14 km S of town on the road (**NH15**) towards **Barmer,** then 3 km on jeepable road, you can see parts of 180 million year old fossils of trees.

Tours

Rajasthan Tourism, T 2392. City Sightseeing: ½ day, 0930-1230. Fort, havelis, Gadisagar Lake, Sam sand-dunes, ½ day, 1530-1930. Rs 30.

Local Festivals

Holi (**Feb/Mar**) is especially colourful in Rajasthan. The *Desert Festival* (13-15 Feb 1995, 2-4 Feb 1996) is a recent Tourism Dept promotion. There is a *son et lumière* amid the sand dunes at Sam, folk dancing, puppet shows and of course camel races, camel polo and camel acrobatics at the 3-day event. Also an opportunity to see craftsmen at work. Rail bookings and hotel accommodation can be difficult.

Local information

● Accommodation

The few good hotels get booked early by package tours. A car is useless inside the city wall making it necessary to carry your luggage some distance. Some hotels do not have the wonderful views often claimed. On arrival by train, hotel touts will harrass you. Take a jeep (no rickshaws usually) to a hotel and decide afterwards. **NB:** the very reasonable prices of rooms often mean you are expected to book their camel safari as well as at *Anand Vilas, New Tourist* and *Deepak*.. Refusal to comply may mean changing hotels. New **B *Heritage Inn***, Sam Rd. 36 rm. Restaurant, bar. **B *Narayan Niwas Palace***, opp Jain Temple, Malka Rd, T 2408. 38, some a/c rm. Good restaurant (buffets), bar, travel, tours and safaris, exchange, occasional cultural shows. Converted old caravansarai with camels stable. Modern extension, pool proposed. Very popular with affluent visitors and tour groups. Reservations, Delhi T 688 6909, F 688 6122.

C *Himmatgarh Palace*, 1 Ramgarh Rd, T 2213. 35 rm in bungalows, a/c in tower. Restaurant (full board), shops, travel, camel safaris, jeep tours, exchange, occasional cultural shows. **C *Jawahar Niwas Palace***, Amar Sagar Rd, T 2208. 15 rm, smaller in modern block and dorm. Restaurant, open-air coffee shop, billiard room, tours, cultural show. Beautiful old haveli with spacious rm, high ceilings, big bathrooms and plenty of atmosphere. Partially renovated but maintenance questionable; appears run down in 1994. Large open grounds (you might catch sight of curious 'desert rats' in a corner!).

Rajasthan Tourism **D *Moomal Tourist Bungalow***, Amar Sagar Rd, T 2392. 51 rm, comfortable, a/c, some cheaper in round huts and dorm. Restaurant, bar, tours, Tourist Office. Modern, outside city walls. Restaurant. Management friendly and helpful. Half day camel safaris. Rec. **D *Neeraj***, Station Rd opp State Bank of Bikaner, T 2442. 24 rm. Dining room, travel, tours and safaris, occasional cultural shows. **D *Rama***, Salim Singh-ki Haveli Marg, Dibba Para, T 2570. 12 rm. Indian restaurant, travel, safaris, check-out 0900. Good views from rooftop. **D** ***Jaisal Castle***, Fort, behind Jain Temple, T 2362. 20 rm (11 overlooking desert, inspect first, best on upper Fl). Small restaurant (cold beer), evenings on rooftop, travel, safaris, exchange. Excellent position, but not easy to reach carrying luggage, and a recent report suggests dirty rm, poor food, bad management. **D** ***Haveli***, Station Rd, Dibba Para, T 2552. 16 rm. Restaurants, travel, occasional cultural shows.

● **Budget hotels**

There are a number of family run, basic but good value **E** and **F** hotels in and around the Fort and some nr the rly station. It is best to check rm beforehand. **E** ***Suraj***, Old Haveli behind Jain temple (Fort), next highest after fort. 5 rm with bath, some with views. Restaurant, travel, camel and jeep safaris. Highly rec. Excellent service. **E** ***Paradise***, Fort, opp Royal Palace, T 2569. 19 rm, most with balconies and views. 24 hr rm service (breakfast, drinks and snacks), safaris, check-out 0900. Rec.

F ***Deepak Rest House***, behind Fort Jain Temple, T 2665. Clean rm, dorm, good atmosphere, local veg food, views from rooftop. Rec. Safaris compulsory. **F** ***Rainbow Guest House***, with decent rm and good roof terrace. Friendly staff. Rec. **F** ***Tourist***, Ward 16, Dibba Para, T 2484. Simple, rm with bath, camel safaris. **F** ***Fort View***, Gopa Chowk, 50m from Fort entrance, T 2214. 20 rm, some with bath, cheap dorm. Restaurant, camel safaris. **F** ***Raj Palace***, nr Fort, T 3264. 8 clean rm (4 more planned). Restaurant serves snacks, camel and jeep tours. Newly opened. Cheerful, young manager, very helpful. **F** ***Sri Nath Palace***, Haveli opp Jain Temple, Fort. Avoid top floor without WC. **F** ***Laxmi Niwas***. In quiet part of fort. 4 simple rm. Warm welcome, clean, good food. **F** ***Pleasure***, Gandhi Chowk, clean rm. Rec; **F** ***Rama***, opp SBBJ, Silvatapara. Pleasant, relaxed. Rec; **F** ***Madhuvan***, Side rd opp Bank of Baroda. Some good rm, but women have had bad experiences. **F** ***Swastika Guest House***, opp State Bank of India, nr Amar Sagar Pol, T 2483. 8 clean, well kept rm with bath and dorm. Rm service, travel. Rec.

● **Places to eat**

All in the fort area. A varied menu, but keen to cater for western palate but often serving up soggy chips. ***Trio***, Gandhi Chowk, Amar Sagar Pol. Partly open-air, tented restaurant with small terrace from which you can watch bread being cooked (meals Rs 50-60). Excellent "proper" tea, Good atmosphere and food; friendly service, comical head-waiter. Dancers and musicians at dinner, usually crowded. Rec. Also rec ***Kalpana*** nearby, towards the Fort Gate. Open-air, is equally good and charges about half the price. ***Treat*** opp Salim Singh Haveli, ***Monika*** Asni Rd, (rec for good Rajasthani *thalis*) and ***8th July*** opp Main Gate and inside fort, have pleasant rooftop seating, good for fruit juice, breakfast, pizzas and icecreams; Australian 'Vegemite' usually available! Nearby ***Mohan Juice Centre*** (nr *Sumil Bhatia Rest House*) delicious lassis, good toasts, cheap. Also rec for breakfast. ***Sky*** a bit more expensive, but large helpings. Mainly Indian, 'English' breakfasts and some Italian. Rajasthani dancers and musicians, colourful and noisy! ***Fort View***, does good snacks. Vyas Meal Service, nr Jain Temple in fort. Good Rajasthani food.

● **Shopping**

Jaisalmer is famous for its handicrafts – stone carved statues, leather ware (incl slippers), embroidery work on fabrics, brass enamel engraving specially on camel Palan (camel seats), Heerawal Pattu shawls, tie-and-dye word on woollen shawls and cotton fabrics, block printing on fabrics, Barmer-style furniture. Usually 1000-1330 and 1500-1900. In Gandhi Chowk: ***Rajasthali*** Govt Emporium, (closed Tue); ***Rajasthan Handloom.*** (closed Sun);***Gandhi Darshan Emporium*** and ***Krishna Jewellers***. Also look in Sadar Bazar, Sonaron Ka Bas and the narrow lanes of the old city inc ***Khadi Parishad***, ***Kamal Handicrafts*** and ***Damodar*** in the Fort. **Tailor**: ***Mr Durga 'tourist tailor'*** working from a small shop nr fort entrance, between *New Tourist* and *Sri Lekha Hotels*. Good prices, excellent workmanship. **Paintings**: ***Hari Ram Soni***, an artist in Taloti Vyaspara. **Photography**: ***Ajanta Studio***, Bhatia Market.

● **Banks**

State Bank of India and **Baroda**, Gandhi Chowk, Amar Sagar Pol. **Rajasthan**, nr Patwon-ki Haveli. **Bikaner and Jaipur**, Air Force Rd. 1000-1400, Mon-Fri, 1000-1200, Sat. Closed Sun.

● **Hospitals & medical services**

SJ Hospital, Gandhi Marg, T 2343.

● **Post & telegraphs**

Nr Badal Vilas, Kotwali, T 2407.

● **Tour companies & travel agents**

Rajasthan Tours, Gandhi Chowk, Amar Sagar Pol, T 2561. ***Tourist Guide Service***, nr Patwon-ki Haveli, T 2450. ***Adventure Tours***.

Variable reports; some claims of cheating, others say camel safaris are satisfactory. They encourage travellers to stay at the very unsatisfactory *Mona Lisa Hotel*. ***Jaisal Tours***, *Hotel Narayan Niwas*. **NB**: some travellers have been cheated when buying bus/train tickets. Check ticket to make sure it is not just a Reservation slip. Also see Camel Safaris box.

● **Tourist offices**

Rajasthan, *Moomal Tourist Bungalow*, Amar Sagar Rd, T 2392. 0800-1200, 1500-1800. Counter at rly station.

● **Useful addresses**

Police: T 23322. **Fire** (Civil Defence): T 2352.

● **Transport**

Jaisalmer is on **NH15** (Pathankot-Samakhiali. The distances are: **Jodhpur** (285 km); **Bikaner** (330 km); **Ajmer** (500 km); **Delhi** (897 km); **Jaipur** (638 km); **Jodhpur** (300 km); **Udaipur** (663 km); **Bombay** (1465 km); **Calcutta** (2110 km); **Madras** (2762 km); **Thiruvananthapuram** (2963 km); **Agra** (868 km).

Local Scooter rickshaws, jeeps and tongas are easily available, but few **tourist taxis**. Negotiate rates. **Bicycle hire**: Central Market.

Train Transport to town: jeeps (often shared) and rickshaws; see also Hotels above. Foreign Tourist Bureau with armchairs in waiting room, T 2354. The single line from Jodhpur offers a very limited service on often poorly maintained trains. Bedding on hire for the overnight journey is often dirty. **Jodhpur**: *3 JPJ*. daily, 2115, 9¾ hr; *JPJ Passenger*, 1, daily, 0900, 9½ hr.

Road Bus: Rajasthan Tourism coach service (T 2392) between Jaisalmer and Jodhpur. Buses depart Jaisalmer, 1400, (5-6 hr), depart Jodhpur 0630. Rajasthan Roadways buses connect Jaisalmer with Jaipur, Jodhpur, Barmer, Bikaner and Ajmer. Mt Abu takes 12 hr; carry drinking water (unavailable on the road). Private operators run deluxe coach services to Jodhpur and Bikaner. *Marudhara Travels*, opp Notified Area Committee Office, Station Rd, T 2351. *National Tours,* Hanuman Choraha, T 2348. **Camel**: to Bikaner usually takes 12 days. Ask tour company.

Jaisalmer to Mount Abu

ROUTES It is a long (400 km), hot, dry and dusty road journey to Jaisalmer and one of little interest unless miles of desert hold an appeal. The road goes via Barmer (158 km).

Barmer, is on the disused railway line from Jodhpur to Hyderabad in Pakistan. It is a centre for wood carving (surprisingly in a desert region), carpets, embroidery and block printing. Suitable accommodation along this route is non-existent and it is a very long way to travel in a day. If you must, take some emergency supplies, eg water, food, blankets/sleeping bags.

HARYANA AND PUNJAB

Contents

Maps

North India's history was decisively influenced on the flat plains NW of Delhi. Kurukshetra, the Krishna's battlefield in the *Mahabharata*, and Panipat where Muslim power was established, lie close to each other. The Jat Sikh community of Punjab still has a strong martial tradition established by the sixth Sikh Guru, Hargobind, when looking for ways of protecting the Sikhs from Mughal attacks. In the summer Haryana and Punjab are hot, dry and monotonous, yet through extensive irrigation it has become one of the most productive regions of India.

Warning In the last decade it has been difficult to travel around Punjab unhindered. Terrorist violence continued in 1992, but peace was beginning to return by early 1993. It is too early to predict whether this improvement will last. Applications for entry permits (when required) are through Indian High Commissions/Embassies worldwide.

Agricultural conditions have improved greatly with the development of canal and tube well irrigation, and the promotion of modern crop technologies. Now, Haryana and Punjab are one of India's most important agricultural regions. In the countryside around Delhi you see traditional Indian village life; festivals, building styles and house decoration, regional handicrafts and cuisine.

Despite its vital role in India's cultural and religious history, the region has few great monuments. However, even though it is not a major tourist attraction, the Haryana state tourist department has done a great deal to provide for tourist's interests and needs. It has developed an extensive chain of tourist complexes, named after different species of birds, modestly priced, all well run and easily accessible.

The major towns and cities of the region are mostly route centres associated with the **Grand Trunk Road**, the great highway from Peshawar to Calcutta. Rudyard Kipling described this as "the backbone of all Hind" and "such a river of life as nowhere else exists in the world" on which he saw "all castes and kinds of men...all the world going and coming". Much of *Kim* was set along it.

SOCIAL INDICATORS **Haryana**: *Population*: 16.3 mn (Urban 26%, Scheduled Castes 19%, Scheduled Tribes nil). *Literacy*: M 68%, F 41%. *Birth rate*: Rural 36:1000, Urban 30:1000. *Death rate*: Rural 9:1000, Urban 7:1000. *Infant mortality*: Rural 100:1000, Urban 62:1000. *Religion*: Hindu 89%, Sikh 6%, Muslim 4%, Christian 0.1%. **Punjab**: *Population*: 20 mn (Urban 32%, Scheduled Castes 27%, Scheduled Tribes nil). *Literacy*: M 64%, F 50%. *Birth rate*: Rural 29:1000, Urban 28:1000. *Death rate*: Rural 9:1000, Urban 7:1000. *Infant mortality*: Rural 82:1000, Urban 53:1000. *Religion*: Hindu 37%, Sikh 61%, Muslim 1%, Christian 1%.

Environment

Land

Haryana *Area:* 44,200 sq km. **Haryana** is roughly triangular in shape. Rajasthan and Punjab border it to the S, W and NW, Himachal Pradesh and Uttar Pradesh to the N and E, with Delhi also on its eastern side. Apart from a small portion of the state in the N which lies in the Shiwalik Hills, Haryana is on the Gangetic plain, lying at a height of

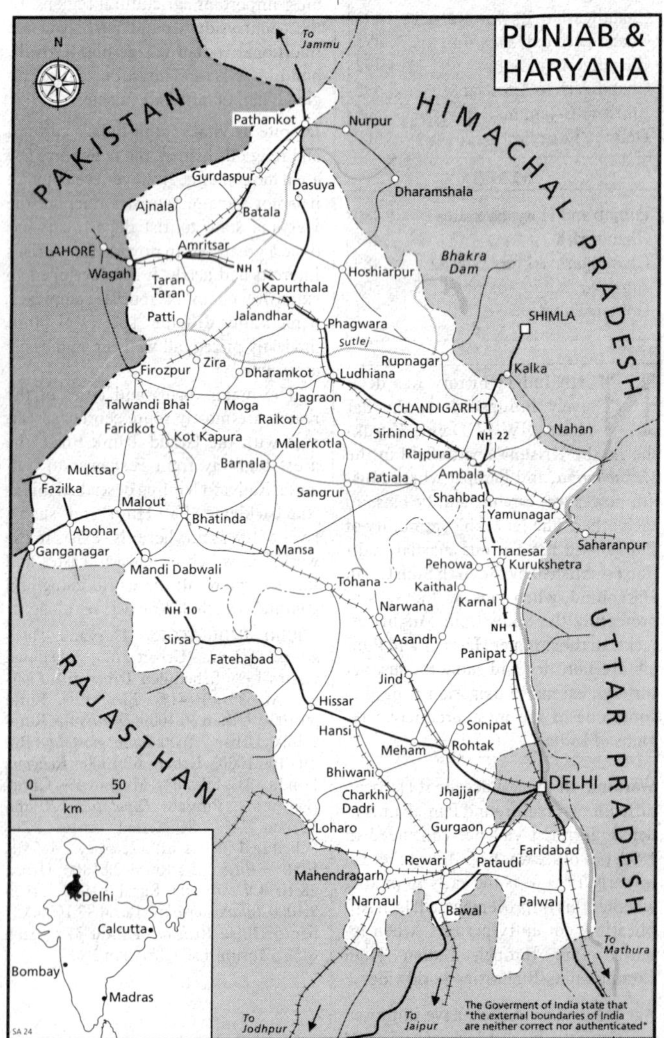

between 220-270m. The river Yamuna forms the eastern boundary of Haryana and its waters feed the extensive irrigation network. A number of small rivers, including the Ghaggar, flow S across it from the foothills of the Himalayas.

Punjab *Area*: 50,300 sq km. **Punjab** occupies a strategic position on India's border with Pakistan. The Punjab is a gently sloping plain, highest in the NE at 275m and falling to 170m in the SW. There are 3 regions. The **Shiwalik Hills** in the NE vary in altitude from 275m to 915m. Between the hills and the plain is a narrow **transitional zone** of gently undulating foothills, broken up in places by seasonal streams. Most of the state is on the low-lying, well watered and highly fertile alluvial soils which make up **the plains**. The 2 major rivers are the Sutlej and the Beas which rise in the Himalaya. In the SW, near the border with Rajasthan, there are sand dunes.

Climate

Haryana and Punjab have an inland continental climate. The winters are quite cold. Between Nov and Feb, daily minimum temperatures range from 5°C to 9°C, occasionally it reaches freezing point,while the daily maximum temperatures are 19°C to 27°C. Humidity at this time is usually low, but depressions moving in from the W sometimes bring rain and a chill dampness to the air. The summers are hot. In May and Jun the average daily temperature is 40°C although it can reach 45°C on extreme days. Amritsar, situated very near the border with Pakistan receives 650 mm rainfall per annum, of which 70% is during the monsoon months of Jul, Aug and Sep. Annual rainfall totals are higher in the Shiwaliks.

Flora & fauna

Nearly all the natural vegetation cover has gone. The Shiwaliks once supported tropical deciduous forests of *shisham* (a valued building and furniture timber), pipal, jujube, *kikar* (gum arabic) but are now covered in bush and scrub. Wild animal life is correspondingly rare and includes the occasional nilgai (blue bull), wild boar, rabbits, jackals, foxes and various species of deer. The birdlife is richer and includes heron, cranes and geese. Like Haryana, Punjab receives migratory birds from the Northern hemisphere over the winter. Cobras, vipers and kraits are all poisonous snakes and relatively common in summer (May and Jun).

History

Early settlement

The **Ghaggar Valley**, running from the Shiwaliks down to the Rajasthan desert, was the home of fortified urban settlements before 3000 BC and the rise of the Harappan civilisation. After approximately 1700 BC, it came under the influence of successive waves of Aryan invaders. The territory became the region in which the Vedas took shape. Incorporated into the Mauryan Empire during the 3rd century BC, it became a vital region for the Muslim kings of the Delhi Sultanate 1500 years later and was part of the Mughals' core region of power. It has long been famous as a battleground. Culturally it is a region of legends. The Pandavas and Kauravas fought at Kurukshetra and Krishna instructed Arjuna at Karnal. See page 104.

The Sikhs

The community of Sikhs or 'disciples' (from the Sanskrit *shishya*) began with the preaching of the Hindu ascetic Nanak who lived in the Punjab from 1469 to 1539, see page 91. Aurangzeb tried to put down Sikhism by force, encouraging the Sikhs to become militant. The Punjab experienced several periods of extreme violence. In 1799 Ranjit Singh set up a Sikh confederacy which governed until the late 1830s. Two wars with the British ended in 1849, after which the Sikh community played an important role in British India, see page 90.

Jallianwallah Bagh

Relations with the British soured in 1919. *Hartals* (strikes) became a common form of demonstration. The Punjab which had supplied 60% of Indian troops committed to the First World War was one of hardest hit economically in 1918 and tension was high. The Lieutenant Governor of the province decided on a 'fist force' to repulse the essentially non-violent but vigorous demonstrations. Some looting occurred in Amritsar and the British called in reinforcements. These arrived under the command of General Dyer.

Dyer banned all meetings but people were reported to be gathering on Sun, 13 Apr 1919 as pilgrims poured into Amritsar to celebrate *Baisakhi*, a holy day in the Sikh calendar. That afternoon thousands were crammed into Jallianwala Bagh, a piece of waste ground popular with travellers, surrounded on all sides by high walls with only a narrow alley for access. Dyer personally led some troops to the place, gave the crowd no warning and ordered his men to open fire, leaving 379 dead and 1200 wounded.

Other brutal acts followed, such as the flogging of 6 youths suspected of beating an English woman who escaped only because a Hindu family treated her injuries and smuggled her into British hands, compounded matters. Related to this incident (modified in Paul Scott's *Jewel in the Crown* epic novel) was Dyer's order that every Indian who lived in the street where she was attacked must go down it on all fours.

The British response The Jallianwala Bagh massacre was hushed up and the British Government in London only got to know of it 6 months later at which time the Hunter Committee was set up to investigate the incident. It did not accept Dyer's excuse that he acted as he did to prevent another insurrection throughout India on the scale of the Mutiny of 1857. He was asked to resign, and returned to England where he died in 1927. However, he was not universally condemned. A debate in the House of Lords produced a majority of 126 to 86 in his favour and the *Morning Post* newspaper launched a fund for 'The Man who Saved India'. Over £26,000 was raised to comfort the dying General.

India was outraged by Dyer's massacre. Gandhi, who had called the nationwide *hartal* (strike) in Mar, started the non-cooperation movement, which was to be a vital feature of the struggle for Independence. This was not the end of the affair. O'Dwyer, the Governor of the Province was shot dead at a meeting in Caxton Hall, London by a survivor of Jallianwala Bagh who was hanged for the offence.

Partition

The next bloody chapter in the Punjab's history occurred during Partition in 1947. In the atmosphere of increasing intransigence and communal violence, the Radcliffe Commission was set up to draw a boundary separating those districts with a Muslim majority from the remainder. The Punjab was divided in two, leaving over 5 million Sikhs and Hindus in Muslim W Pakistan and 40m Muslims in predominantly Hindu India. Many of these groups, terrified by the prospect of losing all that they had worked for, turned on each other in frenzied rage. All across the state villages and bazars were reduced to rubble as men, women and children were butchered.

Amritsar, 24 km from the border, witnessed some of the worst carnage. It is the principal railway station on the line between Delhi and Lahore. All that summer the roads and trains were filled with refugees. Decimated by cholera, the situation was further aggravated when the long overdue monsoon broke causing extensive flooding. In 6 terrible weeks from Aug to mid-Sep it is estimated that half a million people died, maybe more. During Partition, there was a movement of 13 million people across the new borders of India and Pakistan.

After Independence

Sikh political opinion in Punjab continued to stress the need for a measure of autonomy within India's federal constitution. The creation of linguistic states in 1956 encouraged the Sikh Akali Dal to press for the further division of Punjab on the basis of the distinctiveness of Punjabi from Hindi. Punjabi agitation in 1966 resulted in the further sub-division of the Punjab into the present states of Punjab (predominantly Sikh), Haryana (predominantly Hindu) and Himachal Pradesh (a purely mountain state, 96% Hindu).

Sikh fundamentalism and party politics

Despite economic success, political discontent simmered. Some orthodox Sikhs bitterly opposed the liberalism which they saw as a threat to Sikh identity. They attacked the extent to which 'modern' habits of dress and behaviour, such as smoking and drinking alcohol, were being adopted. However, the main causes of Sikh unrest were party political. The Akali Dal party had a majority in the State Assembly between 1969-72 and again between 1977 and 1980. However, in 1980 it was routed by the Congress when Mrs Gandhi returned to power on a national landslide. The disheartened Akali Dal was torn by factionalism as well as by opposition to the Congress Party.

The Akali demands The Akalis presented a list of demands to the central government. First, Amritsar, home of the Golden Temple, the Sikh Holy of Holies should be recognized as the holy city of the Sikhs. Second, Article 25 of the Constitution should be amended to recognize Sikhism as an independent religion and not an offshoot of Hinduism. Third, there should be a daily 90 minute broadcast of readings from the Granth Sahib, the Sikh holy book, over national radio. Fourth, Chandigarh should become the exclusive administrative capital of Punjab. Fifth, certain Sikh lands given by Central Govt to Haryana should be returned and sixth, the restoration of water rights from the Ravi and Beas rivers which had been diverted to Haryana and Rajasthan.

Operation Blue Star

In order to head off mainstream Sikh oppostion to her government Mrs Gandhi encouraged extremist elements among young Sikhs to oppose the traditional Sikh political leadership and to try and split the Sikh Akalai party, the main threat to the Congress in the state. In doing so she sowed the seeds of a fundamentalist movement of which she rapidly lost all control. Their violence made hopes of conciliation fade the longer the agitation persisted. Through 1983 and early 1984 the Sant Jarnail Singh Bindranwale, Mrs. Gandhi's creation as a political force, began to store armaments in the Golden Temple and launched a crusade against all moderates and against the New Delhi government. In July 1984 Mrs Gandhi initiated 'Operation Blue Star' instructing the army to capture the Golden Temple. In the brief but fierce fighting that followed 259 Sikh militants and 59 soldiers died, 90 Sikhs and 110 troops were wounded and 450 militants were arrested. Although the action gained the support of many Hindus, Sikhs were appalled and outraged at the desecration. Two months later, on 31 Oct 1984, Mrs Gandhi was shot in the grounds of the Prime Minister's residence in Delhi by 2 Sikh bodyguards. That was immediately followed by what many saw as officially sponsored attacks on Sikhs in many cities, especially Delhi, resulting in at least 3,000 deaths.

Culture

People

The inhabitants of the Haryana and Punjab are mainly descended from the Aryan tribes that invaded NW India from around 1500BC. Successive invaders became assimilated with the early Aryans. The Jats, Rajputs and most others are a product of this movement of peoples. Punjab is the homeland of the Sikhs and the only state where they form the majority.

Haryana was created when the state of Punjab was divided in 1966. 90% of the population are Hindu, the majority living in rural areas. By South Asian standards there are no large cities, although many of the smaller market towns have grown rapidly as Delhi's industrialization has spilled over into the surrounding states. All the Hindu festivals are important in this region. See page 197.

Punjabi culture

This is influenced by Hinduism and Islam yet it displays a distinctive character of its own. Its literature has strong connections with Sufism. Guru Nanak used the Punjabi language as a medium for poetry. Typically Hindu celebrations and festivals such as Dasara and Diwali are enthusiastically observed as are the birth and death anniversaries of the gurus and saints. Sikh music, much of it like the Mughal *ghazal* and *qawwali* is immensely popular.

The Punjabi *salwar kamiz*, a long *kurta* (shirt) and baggy trousers drawn in at the ankle are traditional and popular forms of dress with men and women, women usually having an accompanying *dupatta* (long scarf). Sikh men are distinctive for their turbans and beards. See page 90.

The Sikhs are often thought of as practical people, using machines from tractors to tubewells, threshing machines to grinders. They are now found driving buses, taxis, and hire cars (they were the drivers in the Indian army and have maintained this role ever since).

Language

Two-thirds of the 21 million people in Punjab speak **Punjabi**, an Indo-Aryan language which is a close relative of Hindi. The remainder speak Hindi.

Modern Haryana and Punjab

Recent political developments

Punjab's trauma may be nearing its end. Elections were held in Feb 1992, and although they brought little immediate sign of change by early 1993 new local level elections were held in a completely different atmosphere. Turnout was high, and although they were non-Party elections, suggested that the state was gradually returning to normal political activity. In 1994 an atmosphere of steady and peaceful progress to normality had returned, though the depth of previous bitterness and the scale of terrorist activity left continuing fears that it could return.

Government

Punjab has 13 seats in the Lok Sabha (Lower House) and 7 seats in the Rajya Sabha (Upper House) in the national parliament in New Delhi. In recent years Punjab has had several periods of direct rule from New Delhi.

In 1947, the Indian government built Chandigarh as the modern administrative capital for the Punjab. When Haryana was created in 1966 Chandigarh became the capital for both states. Arbitration was promised to decide its ultimate allocation, but the political upheavals in Punjab have made it impossible to reach acceptable agreement.

Haryana has 10 seats in the Lok Sabha (Lower House) and 5 seats in the Rajya Sabha (Upper House) in New Delhi. The capital, shared with Punjab, is

Chandigarh which is a Union Territory like Delhi.

The state has undergone several major changes in government. The Congress Party held 7 of the 9 Lok Sabha seats in 1967 and 1971, taking about 50% of the vote. However, it was particularly severely affected by Sanjay Gandhi's campaign of enforced sterilisation during the emergency of 1975-77, and the Congress Party won only 18% of the vote in 1977. Rajiv Gandhi came back to win all 10 seats with 55% of the vote in 1984, but the Jats are a powerful political force in the state and the Congress suffered another big defeat at the hands of the peasant dominated Janata Dal in 1989 and 1991.

Economy

Agriculture The state governments have invested heavily in developing farming. The canal irrigation network and deep well irigation, powered by over half a million electric or diesel pumpsets, have encouraged the rapid adoption of modern crop technologies. Irrigation works implemented since 1947 include the Bhakra Nangal multipurpose river valley project, the largest of its kind in Asia, and the Madhopur-Beas and the Sutlej-Beas Links for the redistribution of water. Now 91% of the total area is cultivated, with wheat, gram, barley and mustard grown over the winter (the *rabi* season) and rice, millet, maize, sugarcane and cotton over the summer (the *kharif* season). The state is also known for the quality of its bullocks and dairy cattle. Cotton and sugar processing have developed into important agro-industries.

Together Punjab and Haryana accounted for 33% and 11% of India's wheat and rice production respectively. It is a myth that this is simply due to Sikh progressiveness. Punjab, Haryana and Western UP have all seen particularly dynamic growth, as has Pakistani Punjab across the border. What they have in common, in addition to a keen interest in the land and the receipt of large scale remittances from family members abroad which has greatly increased agricultual investment, is the benefit of huge irrigation resources. In addition to canals using perenniel rivers this entire region has the benefit of great groundwater resources. These have been extensively tapped by tube wells. As a result today over 90% of Punjab's land is irrigated. The figure is over 60% for Haryana, and compares with a national average of under 25%.

The result has been the widespread adoption of new crop technologies (the 'Green Revolution') which have turned the region into the breadbasket of India. Landholdings average 15-20 ha, large enough to sustain capital-intensive farming, but small enough to spur farmers to maximise returns. Major cash crops are oilseeds, sugar-cane, cotton and potatoes. The consolidation of holdings and the formation of cooperative societies and community development programmes has made the agrarian class the most affluent in India. Higher per capita incomes, increased spending power and reinvestment has promoted the development of agriculture-related and non-farm industries.

Minerals Punjab and Haryana have practically no mineral resources. Industrial development is associated with agriculture and the production of consumer goods. Bicycles and bicycle parts, sewing machines, tools, auto parts, electronic equipment, surgical goods, leather goods, hosiery, knitwear and textiles are all manufactured in Punjab. Ludhiana accounts for 90% of the country's woollen hosiery industry, Jalandhar is an important centre for the production of sports goods and Batala is noted for its manufacture of agricultural implements. Haryana has no heavy industry but a major light industrial zone has been established around Faridabad and it is the largest producer of automobile spare parts in India.

Tourism The 2 states have set up 43 tourist complexes, motels and camping sites in landscaped gardens many of which provide comfortable accommodation with a/c rooms. The State is encouraging adventure tourism, in particular mountaineering, river-rafting and trekking.

Punjab also has large remittances sent from abroad and elsewhere in India.

Communications The state is well served with roads and railways, facilitating the collection and distribution of agriculture produce as well as promoting social mobility. Amritsar is well connected with Delhi and other N Indian centres. There is also a rail link with Pakistan which is 24 km to the W of Amritsar.

CHANDIGARH

(*Population:* 575,000. *Altitude:* 320m. *STD Code:* 0172). In 1947 the Punjab was divided between Pakistan and India and its former capital Lahore was allocated to Pakistan. The Indian government decided to build a new capital for the Indian state of the Punjab, just as later the Pakistan government decided to build a new national capital at Islamabad. The result is Chandigarh which now serves as the administrative centre for both Punjab and Haryana.

The plans

The initial plans were drawn in New York by Albert Mayer and Matthew Novicki. When the latter died in an air crash in 1950 the work was entrusted to the internationally renowned architect le Corbusier. He supervised the layout and was responsible for the grand buildings whilst Maxwell Fry and Jane Drew designed the residential and commercial areas. They laid out the city adopting the latest principles of town planning.

It shares with Jaipur, Fatehpur Sikri and New Delhi the merit of having avoided the unwanted products of haphazard organic growth that typify most Indian cities. Yet many regard it as a failure and characterless. The style of buildings is post-war modernism. In marked contrast to the attractively landscaped and planted open areas in New Delhi too many spaces have been allowed to go to waste. The impression gained by many is that ugly buildings have been carefully laid out in a grid fashion on an unimproved site. It is not a delightful garden city and has not taken advantage of its location on the edge of Shiwalik hills. For all that, Chandigarh is a pleasant enough place to stop en route to Shimla.

Places of interest

The city's major works areas are: the **capitol complex** consisting of the Secretariat, Legislative Assembly and High Court to the N with the Shiwalik Hills as a backdrop; Sector 17, the central **business district** with administrative and state government offices, shopping areas and banks; a **Cultural Zone** for education which includes a museum, campus university with institutions for engineering, architecture, Asian studies and medicine.

The city was planned to accommodate 500,000. Informal housing has

CLIMATE: CHANDIGARH

	Jan	Feb	Mar	Apr	May	Jun	Jul	Aug	Sep	Oct	Nov	Dec	Av/Tot
Max (°C)	20	23	29	34	38	39	34	33	33	31	27	22	29
Min (°C)	7	9	14	19	24	26	24	23	22	17	10	7	17
Rain (mm)	56	25	26	10	13	62	277	263	226	82	5	18	1063

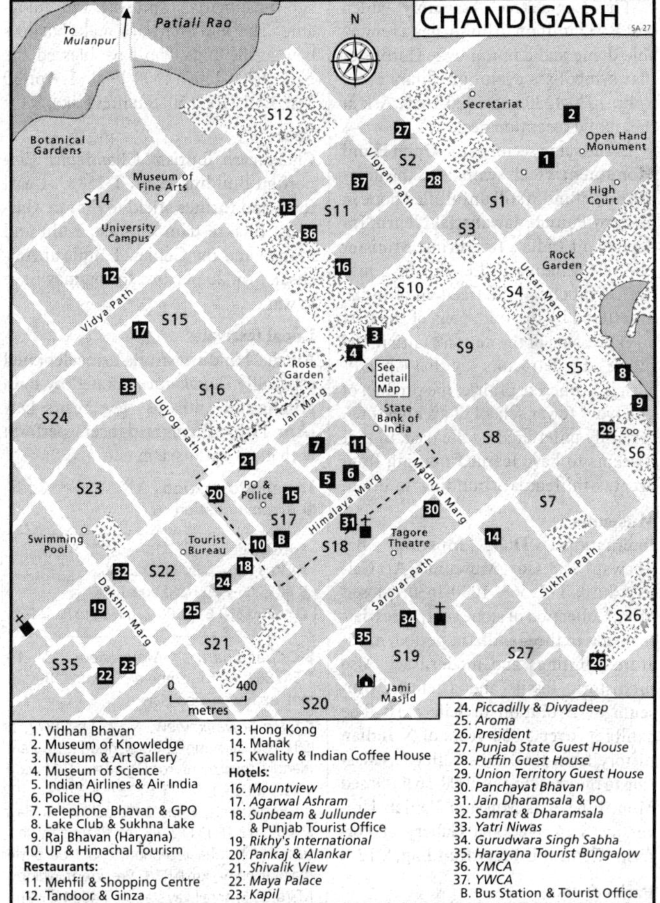

already helped to take the total past that figure. There are 14 categories of housing for ministers down to the lowest-paid government employee. Each sector was built to cater to the community's immediate needs. In this sense they are like traditional Indian villages. Villagers seeking work in Chandigarh live outside the town.

The Government buildings The Govt complex is at the city's N end. The elongated **Secretariat** cost Rs 14 million to build. Tours are given every ½ hr. Ask at the Main Reception. From the rooftop there is a good panorama of the city and the hills and plain beyond. The multi-pillared **High Court** stands nearby with a reflective pool in front. Primary colour panels break up the vast expanses of grey concrete but it all looks rather dated. Its cost was Rs 6.5 million.

The **Legislative Assembly** which cost Rs 12 million to build, has a removable dome and a mural by le Corbusier that symbolises evolution. Tours every ½ hr, 1030-1230 and 1420-1630. Ask at the public reception desk.

In the same sector is the **Open Hand Monument** which symbolises the unity of humankind, a still unfulfilled hope in modern Punjab. Jawaharlal Nehru, Independent India's first Prime Minister said of Chandigarh "Let this be a new town symbolic of the freedom of India, unfettered by the traditions of the past an expression of the nation's faith in the future". Its detractors say that Chandigarh is a concrete prairie, the product of 'the ivory tower school of architecture', certainly unfettered by the past, in that it seems to have learned nothing from over two millennia of building tradition.

Museums

International Dolls Museum, Bal Bhawan, S 23. **Govt Museum & Art Gallery** S 10, T 25568. 1000-1630, Closed Mon. Collection of stone sculptures dating back to the Gandhara period, miniature paintings and modern art. Also prehistoric fossils and artefacts. **Museum of Evolution of Life** S 10. The exhibits cover 5,000 years of N Indian history from the Indus Valley Civilisation to the present day. 1000-1630, closed Mon. **Fine Arts Museum** Punjab University, S 14. **National Gallery of Portraits** Central Library Building, S 17.

Parks & zoos

Raj Bhawan Mini Zoo, S 7. **Rose Gardens**, S 16. Containing over 1,000 varieties of roses, it claims to be the largest in Asia. **Rock Garden** or *Garden of Nek Chand*, S 1. Described as "a concrete maze with a lot of rocks and very little garden". A large number of interesting statues and sculptures made out of discarded items of everyday use, eg bottle tops, fluorescent lights, mud guards. The creation of Nek Chand who began these interesting sculptures 30 years ago. Imaginative, amusing and enjoyable. The low archways make visitors bow to the gods who have blessed the park. 0900-1300, 1500-1900. 1 Apr-30 Sep. Entry Re 0.50. **Sukhna Lake**, S 1.

Tours

Chandigarh Tourism, Chandigarh Emporium Building, S 17, T 25839. Local tours and further afield to Pinjore Gardens, Bhakra dam, Shimla, Kulu and Manali and the Golden Temple at Amritsar. Min 20 persons so you may have to wait.

Local festivals

All the Hindu festivals are celebrated especially *Baisakhi*, celebrated by both Hindu and Sikhs as New Year's Day (**Apr 13th**). Bhangra dancers perform with great enthusiasm.

Local information

● Accommodation

Price guide
AL Rs 3,000+ **A** Rs 2,000-3,000
B Rs 1,200-2,000 **C** Rs 600-1,200
D Rs 250-600 **E** Rs 100-250 **F** Up to Rs 100.

B-C *Chandigarh Mountview*, S 10, T 547862, 69 rm, some a/c. Central. Restaurant, exchange, pool, lawns.

C *Citco Shivalik View*, S 17, T 544877, nr ISBT. Popular business hotel, good restaurant, friendly service, nr rose garden. **C** *Shivalik View*, (CITCO), S 17T 67131, F 32094. 102 rm. Restaurants, shops. **C** *Piccadilly*, Himalaya Marg, S 22, T 43112. 48 rm. Restaurant, bar, travel. Unhelpful reception, could be better maintained. ½ km ISBT. **C** *President*, Madhya Marg, S 26, nr railway station, T 40840. 20 rm. Restaurant, coffee shop, bar, bookshop. **C** *Sunbeam*, Udyog Path, S 22B, corner Himalaya Marg opp ISBT, T 41335. 57 rm. Restaurant, bar. **C-D** *Maya Palace*, S 35 B, T 600547. 28 a/c rm. Restaurant, bar.

D *Aroma*, S 22, T 44434, 27 rm, some a/c. Restaurant, bar travel. **D** *Chandigarh*, SCO 2459, S 22 C, T 41708. Some a/c rm. **D** *Chandigarh Yatri Nuwas*, S24, T 54904, 48 rm, some a/c, clean and reasonable. **D** *Divyadeep*, S 22, T 43191, 15 rm, some a/c. Neat and clean, good a/c veg restaurant, busy at lunchtime. **D** *Kapil*, 303 S 35-B, T 33366.

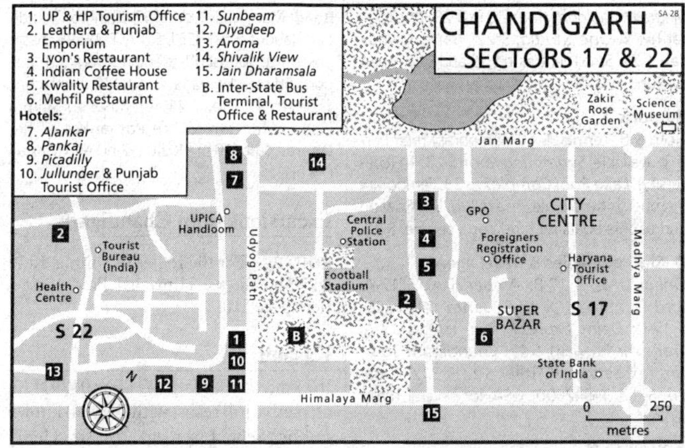

13 rm. Central a/c. Restaurant (Chinese, Indian), bar. Owned by the Indian test cricketer Kapil Dev. **D** *Pankaj*, S 22A, T 41906. 14 rm some a/c rm with bath. Central. Restaurant, bar, exchange, golf by arrangement. Comfortable. **D** *Puffin Guest House*, S2, T 540321, 8 rm. **D** *Southend*, S 35, T 607935, 14 rm, some a/c. Haryana Tourism's **D** *State Guest House*, S 3, nr Sukhna Lake and Rock Garden, opened in 1992. 16 rm. Restaurant, garden. **D** *Union Territory Guest House*, S 6, T 27231. 12 a/c rm. Reservations: Director of Tourism, UT, S 16. **D-E** *Jullunder*, S 22, opp ISBT, T 20777, 16 rm, Indian restaurant.

● Budget hotels & guesthouses

Reserve direct or contact on arrival, Tourism Officer, 1st Floor, ISBT, T 544614. **D** *UT State Guest House*, S 6, nr lake, T 540961, 27 rm, some a/c, quiet pleasant area. Several **E** Hotels in S 22 with some a/c rm and restaurant: *Himalaya Marg* and *Alankar*, Udyog Path. Most guesthouses are basic and have shared bath. Often very good value. **D-E** *Panchayat Bhavan*, S 18, T 44385, 18 rm, some a/c, dorm Rs 12. Restaurant, Busy area. **F** *Vrindavan*, nr Bus Stand, T 3147. Some rm with bath, Indian restaurant. Pleasant, clean rm, but eat elsewhere. **F** *Tourist Rest House*, S 17, 2nd Floor, ISBT, T 544614, 4 bed family rm, only convenient for early morning dep. **F** *Youth Hostel*, Old Panchpulla (18 km on Pinjmerd).

● Places to eat

Tandoori food is particularly good. Many in S 17 incl: *Mehfil*; *Kwality*; *Ghazal*; *Indian Coffee House*; *Mahak* (multi-cuisine). *Mamamia*, S 35-B. Chinese: *Shangrila*; *Mandarin*;*Ginza*, S 14 (University Campus); *Hong Kong*, S 11. Fast Food: *The Hot Million*; *Lyon's*; *Terminal One*; *The Chef* (CITCO), Inter State Bus Terminal, also at lake; *Lyon's*; *Sindhi Sweets*. 24 hr coffee shops: at Hotels *Mountview*, *Shivalik View*, *Aroma* and *Piccadilly*. Indian sweets: at *Sindhi*, S 17, also at S A1 and S 22.

● Banks & money changers

All the banks are in S 17 incl **State Bank of India**.

● Entertainment

Tagore Theatre, S 18, T 26533.

● Hospitals & medical services

General Hospital, Naubharat S 16, T 44697. *PG Medical Institute*, S 12, T 22513. Both hospitals have 24 hr chemists. *Chemists* S 17 and 22.

● Post & telecommunications

GPO: S 17.

● Shopping

The main shopping centres are in Sectors 17 and 22. 1000-1330, 1530-1945. S 17: *Black Partridge* (Haryana), *Chandigarh* (CITCO), *Co-Optex* (Tamil Nadu), *Gram Shilpa Khadi Ashram*, *Handloom Emporium*, *Kashmir Arts*, *Rajasthan* Handicrafts, *The Weaver* (Haryana Govt), UP Handloom, Punsup Clothes (Punjab Govt), *Chamra Shilpa* (footwear), Super Bazar. S 22: *Haryana State Handlooms*, *Punjab State Handloom*, *SEAVCO*, *UPICA* Handloom, *Leathera* (Punjab Govt), *Bharat Leather*. -

Madras Handloom House is in S 28. **Photography**: ***A-One Studio***, S 22; ***Batra Colour Lab***, S 27. Small centres in S 19 and S 22, open on Sun.

● **Sports**

Golf: S 6. **Tennis:** S 10. Temporary membership available. ***Swimming Pool***, S 23, 14 (University). ***Lake Pool Complex***, S 23. Temporary membership available. ***Boat Club***, S 1. Rowing and paddle boats for hire. **Yoga centre**: S 23.

● **Tour companies & travel agents**

Onkar (JAL), S 17-B; ***Amber*** (PIA), S 17-A; ***Bird*** (Lufthansa), S 17-C; ***Janta*** (Air India), S 17-C; ***Delhi Express*** (Thai, PIA), S 17-A; ***Trans Air*** (Kuwait), S 17. ***Chandigarh Tourism Taxi Service***, (CITCO), S 22, T 31256. ***Bajaj***, S 17, T 542000, GSA for several major airlines.

● **Tourist offices**

Chandigarh, 1st Flr, Main Bus Terminal, S 17, T 22548. **UP**, S 22, T 41649. **HP**, opp Bus Stand, S 22, T 26494. **Punjab**, S 22-B, T 43570. **Haryana**, S 17, T 21955.

● **Useful addresses**

Police: 25600. **Ambulance**: 26165. **Fire**: 101. **Foreigners' Registration Office**: Town Hall Bldg, S 17.

● **Transport**

Local Taxis: private taxis (un-metered) stands in S 22, S 17, 35. **Auto rickshaws**: officially metered with a min fare, but always negotiable. **Bus**: The Chandigarh Transport Undertaking (CTU) runs a reasonably good bus service. **Cycle rickshaws**: are widely available. Fares negotiable.

Air The airport is 11 km from the city centre. **Indian Airlines**: Reservations, City Office, S 17, T 40539, 1000-1630. Airport, T 43304. Services connect Chandigarh with Delhi, Jammu, Srinagar and Leh.

Train New Delhi: *Himalayan Queen*, 4096, daily, 1722, 4½ hr; *Shatabi exp*, 2006, daily, 0630, 3¼ hr; **Old Delhi:** *Kalka-Haora Mail* 2312, daily, 0050, 5¾ hr. **Shimla**: *Himalayan Queen* 4095 (Change at Kalka to Express 257), daily, 1030, 6¾ hr; *Haora-Kalka Mail* 2311 (Change at Kalka to Mail 253), daily, 0505, 7¼ hr. The railway station with clean waiting rm is 8 km from the town centre; regular bus transfer. Enquiries, T 22105. Reservations, T 22260, 1000-1700; City Booking Office, 1st Flr, Inter-State Bus Terminal, S 17, T 32696, 0900-1600.

Road Many daily from ISBT, Delhi to Chandigarh (about 5 hr). ISBT, S 17, T 32696, has a post office, tourist office and restaurant. Transport offices: Haryana, T 26370, Himachal, T 20946, Punjab, T 24940. Buses to **Shimla** (5 hr), **Amritsar** (6 hr), **Pathankot** (7 hr), **Dharamsala** (10 hr), **Kulu** (12 hr) and **Manali** (14 hr).

Excursions from Chandigarh

ROUTES For the routes to Shimla, Kulu and Manali, see Himachal Pradesh section, page 510.

Kasauli

(67 km, *Alt* 1927m, *STD Code* 01793) An attractive hill resort with the well known Public School set up by Sir Henry Lawrence. It is only 16 km hike from Kalka (35 km by road). Monkey Point, 4 km from town, gives good views over the plains. **Sanawar**, famous for its school is nearby. Accommodation: HP Tourism D *Roscommon*, T 2005, with restaurant and D *Tourist Bungalow Annexe*.

Pinjore (Pinjaur)

(20 km on Kalka road) The Mughal gardens were laid out by Aurangzeb's foster brother Fidai Khan, who also designed the Badshahi Mosque in Lahore. Within the charbagh gardens are a number of palaces in a Mughal-Rajasthani style: Shish Mahal, which has mirror-encased ceiling and is cooled by water flowing underneath (remove a slab to see!), the Rang Mahal, an arched pavilion, highly decorated with traditional *guldasta* motif, the Jal Mahal set among cool fountains. Cool and delightful. A popular picnic spot. A mini-zoo, camel rides and fair-ground attractions to tempt city dwellers. **Accommodation**: D *Budgerigar*, Yadavindra Gardens, T Kalka 2855. Deluxe Motel with a/c rm. Restaurant, shops. **Restaurants**: *Golden Oriole* next to Rang Mahal has a bar. The Jal Mahal has a small *café*. Several kiosks outside the gardens sell snacks and ice cream.

ROUTES Kalka, beyond Pinjore, is the starting point for the beautiful mountain railway to Shimla. See page 521.

CHANDIGARH TO BHAKRA NANGAL

Anandpur Sahib

Leaving the NH 22 in Kalka a minor road leads to the important Sikh centre of Anandpur Sahib ("the city of divine bliss"), on the E bank of the River Sutlej. A better alternative route from Chandigarh is on the NH 21 to **Ropar** (**Rupnagar**, 50 km; *STD Code* 01881) and **Bilaspur**, where a state highway leads to Anandpur Sahib up the left bank of the Sutlej. In the small town of Ropar there is the pleasant Punjab Tourism *Pinkcassia Tourist Complex* with the Boat Club, T 3097. 20 rm. On the banks of the Sutlej River. Pleasant.

Bilaspur

The town was established by the 9th Guru, Tegh Bahadaur, in 1664, when the Sikhs had been forced into the foothills of the Himalaya by increasing Mughal opposition. It is in a picturesque setting at the foot of the Shiwalik Hills. Guru Tegh Bahadur himself was executed at Chandni Chowk in Delhi, and his severed head was brought to Anandpur Sahib to be cremated. This event contributed to the determination of the 10th Guru, Gobind Singh, Tegh Bahadur's son, to forge a new body to protect the Sikh Community. The Khalsa Panth was thus created on Baisakhi Day in 1699. Anandpur Sahib became both a fortress and a school of Sikh learning. *Hola Mohalla* is celebrated the day after Holi when battles are re-enacted using old weapons. There is a small **museum** dedicated to the memory of Guru Tegh Bahadur recounting the history of the Sikhs in a series of paintings.

• **Accommodation** Punjab Tourism's **E** *Champa Tourist Huts*, on rd between Gurudwara Keshgarh Sahib and Anandgarh Fort, T 46. 4 double rm huts with kitchenette. Snack bar at roadside.

• **Transport Train** To Ambala, *Passenger*, 1338, 5hr; *Express*, 4554, 2050, 4¼hr. **To Nangal Dam**, *Express*, 4553, 0536, 1hr; *Passenger*, 1005, 1hr. **Road Buses**: from Chandigarh and Rupnagar.

Bhakra-Nangal Dam

The dam on the **River Sutlej**, is a further 30 km NW, in Himachal Pradesh. It is claimed to be the highest dam in the world at 225m. The multi-purpose river-valley project (electrical energy and irrigation) is certainly the largest irrigation system of its kind in Asia, and was built as part of the Indus Waters Treaty between India and Pakistan, signed in Sep 1960 and financed by the World Bank.

The Treaty allocated the water of the Rivers Sutlej, Beas and Ravi to India. The building of the Bhakra Nangal Dam, which had already been agreed in 1959, was supervised by the American dam builder Harvey Slocum. It provides electricity for Punjab, Haryana and as far away as Delhi. It is also the source for the Rajasthan Canal project, which is designed to take water over 1500 km S to the Thar desert, a scheme which is still far from complete. The sharing of the water between Punjab, Haryana and Rajasthan remains a problem which successive governments have failed to solve and which has been made more complicated by the crisis in the Punjab. Accommodation: Punjab Tourism's *Kadamba Tourist Complex*, nr Main Market, Nangal, T 2122. 16 rm, some a/c, dorm. Restaurant, beer bar, garden. Haryana Tourism's *Motel* is at **Abub Sahar**.

CHANDIGARH TO DEHRA DUN

The route crosses a rich agricultural area, irrigated by tubewells and canals. The best route follows the NH 22 S to

Ambala, then takes a narrower and quieter state road through villages and the small towns of Saha (13km) and Chhappar (22 km) to Jagadhri (15 km), the Yamuna River and UP. The shorter more northerly route shown on some maps is very poor. Although some local buses take it, it is not recommended.

Jagadhri

In Jagadhri there is a modest hotel on the main road. E *Samrat*, Court Rd, T 21044. 13 rm, some a/c. Small but acceptable. 12 km out of Jagadhri in Yamunanagar the road joins the Thanesar road and in 2 km crosses the Yamuna.

ROUTES Travelling from Saharanpur to Ambala the turning to Jagadhri is almost invisible. An unsignposted and unmade track goes off to the right through a narrow bridge under the railway line just under 2 km after crossing the Yamuna.

A bridge crosses the Yamuna River at Kalanaur and into UP. There is a small town and truck stop at Sarsawa (8 km), the road then passing through rich fields of sugar cane. On the outskirts of **Saharanpur** on the W bank of the canal is the bankside *Sheetal Restaurant*. For the route on to Dehra Dun, see page 219..

CHANDIGARH TO DELHI

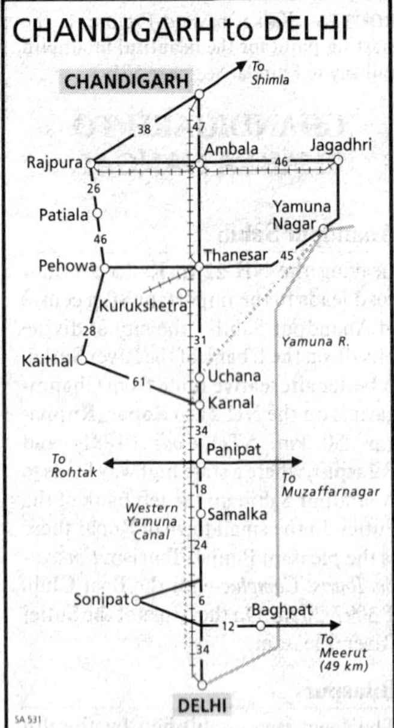

The intensively cultivated fields show the benefits which can come with irrigation. From Dec to Mar the fields are green with wheat. The small brick huts built to house electric or diesel irrigation pumps in the fields are a common sight. Towards Delhi many of the fields are now planted with vegetables for the Delhi market. The **Grand Trunk Road** itself has long stretches lined with magnificent trees, all numbered, for the products of the trees are extremely valuable and villagers have to buy rights to the leaves and wood. Today the road is one of the busiest in India, and increasingly long stretches have been widened into dual carriageway.

Chandigarh to Ambala

ROUTES The NH22 runs due S to Ambala. The NH1 to Ludhiana and Amritsar goes NW from Ambala. See page 495.

Ambala

(*Pop* 120,000; *Alt* 274m; *STD Code* 0171) Ambala became a large British cantonment, laid out from 1843 onwards in grid fashion. The famous Gupta iron pillar now at the Qutb Minar in Delhi was originally on the hill just outside Ambala town before being moved by the Muslim rulers to its present position. **Paget Park** on the N side of the city is a pleasant open space with the shell of St Johns Cathedral, designed in 14th century Gothic style. It was bombed in the 1965 Indo-Pakistan war. The city is the headquarters of the district and an important wheat market.

• **Accommodation and places to eat** Haryana Tourism **D** *Kingfisher*, T 443732. 13 rm (2 a/c). Restaurant, bar, attractive gardens and pool. Excellent value. Outside rly station, several open-air restaurants prepare good local meals. Station restaurant has a curious collection of antique furniture!

• **Transport Train** New Delhi: *Shatabi Exp*, 2006, daily, 0726, 2½ hr. Frequent trains to Chandigarh. N rly connects Shimla trains with those from Jammu Tawi and Lucknow.

ROUTES The road S to Karnal passes through the village of Pipli (34 km), the turn off point to Kurukshetra.

Kurukshetra

The battlefield where Arjuna learned the meaning of dharma has left no trace. See page 104. The flat plain around Kurukshetra is described in Sanskrit literature as '*Brahmavarta*' (Land of Brahma) and is particularly sacred. Like many other sacred sites it becomes the special focus of pilgrimage at the time of exceptional astronomical events. In Kurukshetra eclipses of the sun are marked by special pilgrimages, when over 1m people come to the tank from across N India. It is believed that the waters of all India's sacred tanks meet together in the Kurukshetra tank at the moment of eclipse, giving extra merit to anyone who can bathe in it at that moment. Remarkable arrangements are made to maintain basic health standards.

Places of interest

Brahmasar or Kurukshetra Tank, 1 km W. The lake is about 1 km long. Many pilgrims come and bathe, but it is also visited by a wide range of wildfowl, particularly during the winter (Dec-Feb). The tank is surrounded by temples and *ghats* (steps) leading down to the water's edge. The modern temple can best be described as kitsch, an artificial reproduction of earlier temple styles. But the site is important for its influence on the development of Hindu ideas, not Hindu architecture. There are also the remains of a **Muslim Fort**, including the **Tomb of Shaikh Chilli Jalal** (d1582) and **Lal Masjid**, a small red sandstone mosque. The carving on the domes is similar to that at Fatehpur Sikri.

• **Accommodation**
D Haryana Tourism *Parakeet Motel*, T 250. A/c rm. Restaurant, camping facilities.

Thanesar

Thanesar near Kurukshetra, is an ancient town and birthplace of the ruler Harsha Vardhana (590-647 AD). Thanesar (originally known as *Sthanvisvara*) became the launching pad for Harsha's campaigns. Harsha's father, a local chief, had fought off the Huns besides feuding with his neighbours.

Harsha was 16 years old when he came to the throne. His father had already begun to establish his power in the key strategic region between the Rivers Yamuna and Sutlej. In his 41 year rule Harsha earned a reputation for fairness and an open-handedness. Unlike many other Indian kings Harsha's reign was very fully recorded, especially by the remarkable Chinese traveller Hiuen Tsang. From his capital in Thanesar Harsha extended his territory from Bengal to Gujarat, and he received tribute from as far afield as Assam, but many of the regional kings retaining their thrones.

Sati Harsha shared his throne with the widowed sister whom he had rescued from self-immolation on her husband's funeral pyre. This rite, known in the W as *suttee* (a word which simply means a good or virtuous woman, and not the act of self-immolation) is recorded in the *Vedas*, but probably did not become accepted practice until the early centuries BC. Even then it was mainly restricted to those of the kshatriya caste. By Harsha's time sati had become widespread and tantric cults had also begun to grow rapidly, suggesting Buddhism was already on the decline. Harsha however appeared to model himself on Asoka and leaned towards Buddhism. This earned him the opposition of Brahmins and in 647 AD he fell victim to a murder plot organised by a Brahmin minister and carried out by the army. Thanesar became a Hindu pilgrimage centre and was one of the towns sacked by Mahmud of Ghazni in 1011 AD.

• **Accommodation** Haryana Tourism's new **Adventure Club** HQ at **Yamuna Nagar**, NE of Kurukshetra, is at the **D** *Grey Pelican* Tourist Complex, T 28215, designed like a ship with 9 rm, restaurant and bar. At **Hathni Kund D** *Pintail* Motel has 4 simple rm. Restaurant, rafting and wildlife trails.

ROUTES **Thanesar** is a crossroads, the main road E leading to Yamunanagar, Saharanpur and Dehra Dun (see above).

Diversion to Kaithal

From Thanesar it is possible to divert from NH1 SW through the totally uninspiring small town and pilgrimage centre of **Pehowa** (30 km *Pop* 22,000) to **Kaithal** (63 km; *Pop* 71,000). This was quite an important town during Akbar's reign (r1556-1605) and is located by the picturesque man-made **Bidkiar Lake**. Bathing steps lead down into the tank. In 1767 it passed to the Sikh leader Bhai Desu Singh whose descendants, the Bhais of Kaithal, achieved some prominence on the Indian side of the Sutlej before the British acquired the territory in 1843. The old ruined fort of the Bhais overlooks the lake. **Accommodation:** Haryana Tourism D *Koel Motel*, T 2170. Restaurant, bar, shops.

ROUTES From Kaithal you can re-join the NH1 at Karnal.

Karnal

(34 km; *Pop* 176,000; *STD Code* 0184) Legend suggests that Karnal was founded by one of the leaders of the Kauravas in the great battle recorded in the *Mahabharata* (see below). Seized by the Raja of Jind around 1763 it was taken from him by George Thomas in 1797. A British cantonment was established in 1811 but was abandoned in 1841 due to the unhealthiness of the site, caused by the Western Yamuna Canal interfering with natural drainage and promoting malarial fever. The canal was re-aligned in 1875. At nearby **Uchana** (3 km N) Haryana Tourism has created an artificial lake. **Accommodation:** D *Karna Lake*, T 24279. Deluxe huts, Restaurant, bar, boating and D *Oasis*, T 24264. 2 camper huts, cafeteria, shops. Camping.

ROUTES The route to Panipat continues S from Karnal.

Panipat

(80 km; *Pop* 191,000; *STD Code* 01472) Today Panipat is an important industrial town, noted for its textile industry. In 1994 there were an estimated 30,000 looms in the town providing employment for as many families. A high proportion of the cotton products – carpets, curtains and tablewear – is exported to Europe, Japan and the United States. However, historically Panipat is a battlefield town near the old bank of the river Yamuna. It stands on the higher ground made up of the debris of earlier settlements overlooking the old river course. Three great battles were fought here though virtually no evidence remains to suggest their importance.

The first battle On 21 Apr 1526 Babur, the first Mughal emperor, fought Ibrahim Lodi the Sultan of Delhi. Babur had entered India with about 12,000 men (see page 47). By the time he reached Panipat his forces had swelled to perhaps 25,000. Ibrahim's army was said to number 100,000 and 1,000 elephants. Babur dug himself in using a formation which he claimed to have adapted from Turkish practice. As many as 700 carts were strung together with ropes of rawhide. From behind this, the matchlockmen would fire on the advancing enemy. When Ibrahim was finally provoked into attacking, his army came to a grinding halt before the fusillade of musket fire. Babur's cavalry attacked on both flanks in a pincer movement, raining arrows on the Indian army caught on 3 sides. When the battle ceased, about 20,000 of the sultan's army were dead, including their leader. See page 325.

The second battle of Panipat took place on 5 Nov 1556. Akbar, who had just succeeded his father Humayun, and his general-cum-guardian Bairam Khan, defeated Hemu, the general of the Afghan Sher Shah. The battle was going badly for Akbar until Hemu was wounded in the eye by an arrow. The sight of the tiny Hemu slumped in his elephant's howdah caused his troops to flee. Hemu was brought unconscious before Akbar and Bairam Khan and beheaded, the head then being sent to Kabul and the body to Delhi to be hung on a gibbet. There was a mass slaughter of the captives, and in the gruesome tradition of Genghis Khan and Timur a victory pillar was built with their heads plastered in.

The third battle took place on 13 Jan 1761. The remnants of the once great Mughal Empire was threatened from the W by the resurgent Rajputs and from the NW by the Afghans, who sacked Delhi in 1756-57. The distracted Mughal minister called in the Marathas and, according to Percival Spear "the triangular power struggle between the Mughals, Marathas and Afghans became a duel between the Marathas and the Afghans". The Maratha army numbered 15,000 infantry, 55,000 cavalry, 200 guns. These were supported by 200,000 Pindaris and camp followers. The Afghans comprised 38,000 infantry, 42,000 cavalry and 70 guns, besides numerous irregulars. Despite their numbers the Marathas lost and their soldiers fled. However, the Afghan leader Ahmad Shah Durrani was unable to take advantage of his victory as his followers mutinied for the 2-years' arrears of pay he owed them. Thus, the former Mughal empire was denied to both the Afghans and Marathas, leaving N India in a political vacuum which adventurers tried to fill during the next 40 years.

The main old building in Panipat is a shrine to the Muslim saint **Abu Ali Kalandar**. He was said to have banished all flies from Panipat. However, people complained so he ordered 1000 times as many to come back! Accommodation: Haryana Tourism D *Skylark Motel*, T 3579. A/c rm and dorm. Restaurant. Also catering services at Bus Stand.

ROUTES The NH1 (Grand Trunk Road) runs S to Delhi parallel to the Yamuna River which forms the boundary between Haryana and UP. Accommodation: At **Samalkha**, 70 km from Delhi, Haryana Tourism D *Blue Jay Motel*, T 2110. 7 a/c rm. Restaurant (try *sarson-ka-saag* and *makki-ki-roti* in winter), bar, gardens.

CHANDIGARH TO AMRITSAR

The NH1 from Ambala to Ludhiana is a busy road, lined periodically with market towns which are increasingly surrounded by small scale industrial units.

Along the route is a series of Punjab Tourism complexes. At **Shambhu** the *Kachnar Tourist Complex*, on the GT Road, T 8533. 8 rm, some a/c , 2 dorm, good restaurant and bar. Set in pleasant gardens. Rajpura is 6 km beyond Shambhu. **Rajpura** (*STD Code* 01762) has a *Rest House* and a railway station on the main Delhi-Amritsar line. From Rajpura a road runs SW to Patiala.

Patiala

(26 km to the SW of Rajpura; *Pop* 269,000; *STD Code* 0175). Patiala was once the capital of an independent state, along with Jind and Nabha, whose ruling houses were all Sikh. It suffered at the hands of the European Adventurer George Thomas and was later consolidated into the Sikh Empire of Ranjit Singh who included it in treaty arrange-

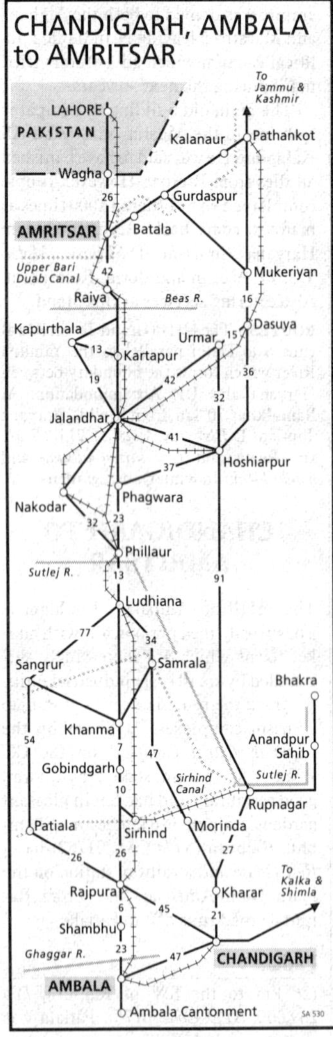

ments made with the British in 1809. Thereafter, the Maharaja remained loyal to the British.

Places of interest The most impressive building in this well-kept town is the huge concentric **fort**, the creation of Maharaja Ala Singh in the late 18th century. Surrounded by a moat, it is 8 km to the NE of town on the Chandigarh road. **Bahadurgarh**, is a good example of a *nara durg*, a large fort built on a plain and capable of housing a garrison large enough to repulse strong attacks such as the unsuccessful but nevertheless fierce Maratha attempt in 1794. It looks majestic from the air and is now surrounded by intensively cultivated fields.

The **Old Motibagh Palace** (late 19th century), in the town, is perhaps one of the largest homes in Asia. The rambling central building is surrounded by lawns and trees. A combination of European, Rajput and Mughal styles, part of it is now the National Institute for Sports. There are 15 dining halls and many outbuildings. The Sheesh Mahal has a **Museum and Art Gallery.** Collection includes ethnography, arms, natural history and miniature paintings. Particularly good laquerware can be found at 94 Bichittar Nagar, New Patiala.

• **Accommodation** D *Green*, Mall Rd, T 4347. 15 rm, 4 a/c. Restaurant.

• **Transport Train** Patiala is on the branch line to Bhatinda and Firozpur. **Road Bus**: daily services to Delhi, other towns in Punjab and neighbouring states.

ROUTES A route W from Patiala goes through a series of small market towns to Bathinda. At **Nidampur**, on the bank of the Ghaggar Canal, is Punjab Tourism's E *Chandni Tourist Complex*, Patiala-Sangrur Highway. 5 rm and dorm. Restaurant and bar. Attractive canal-side setting.

ROUTES From Rajpura the NH1 continues towards Sirhind, which it by-passes 5 km to the S.

Sirhind

This was once capital of the Pathan Sur Dynasty, whose army was defeated by Humayun in 1555. A year later Akbar completed the downfall of the dynasty with his victory at Panipat. There is little left of the fort which commanded the

Sar-i-Hind – the 'Frontier of India'. The town's period of greatest splendour was between 1556 and 1707, ie after the Mughals had wrested control. **Salabat Beg Haveli** is a large and well preserved Mughal house whilst the **Sarai** of the Mughal emperors, in the SW of the town, is now a public hall. There is also a mosque in the N, a number of Mughal tombs and a Gurudwara. For the Sikhs Sirhind is associated with the brutal execution of the 2 younger sons of the 10th Guru, who were bricked up alive in the fort in 1705 for refusing to convert to Islam. Outside Sirhind, Accommodation, Punjab Tourism E *Bougainvillea Tourist Complex*, on GT Rd towards Mandi Gobindgarh, T 170. 8 rm, some a/c. Floating restaurant. Camping and showers for non-residents. E *Queens Flower Tourist Resort,* on Sirhind canal at Neelon, T (Katani Kalan) 32. 6 rm, some a/c. Restaurant, bar, garden. At **Aam Khas Bagh** nearby, E *Mulsari Tourist Complex,* old caravan serai conversion. 4 rm. Restaurant, beer bar, Mughal garden. Archaeological ruins nearby.

The NH 1 continues through Gobindgarh and Khanna to Ludhiana.

Ludhiana

(*Pop* 1,000,000; *STD Code* 0161). A very rapidly growing town on the S bank of the **Sutlej river**, Ludhiana is a major textile (hosiery) and light engineering centre. The rich agricultural area around it supports a large grain market. Founded in 1480 by Lodi princes from Delhi (hence its name), it subsequently passed through a number of hands. Around it at Aliwal, Ferozeshah, Mudki and Sobraon are important battlegrounds from the First Sikh War (1845).

Places of interest

The **fort** (in the NW) includes the Shrine of **Pir-i-Dastgir**, also known as Abdul Kadir Galani. There is an annual pilgrimage of Muslims and Hindus to the Muslim Saint's tomb. There are other tombs belonging to members of Shah Shuja's family while they were in exile from Afghanistan. The town is also the home of the **Christian Medical College Hospital**, which along with the CMC hospital in Vellore, with which it is in partnership, is one of S. Asia's major teaching and research hospitals. The world famous **Punjab Agricultural University** is on the edge of town. It has an excellent **museum**.

Local information

● Accommodation

C *Amaltas*, GT Rd via Netaji Nagar (on outskirts), T 51500. 22 rm some a/c with bath. Restaurants, bar. **C** *City Heart*, T 50240. 44 rm. Nr rly. Restaurant. **C** *Grewals*, 148 Ferozepur Rd, T 50466. 40 rm. Restaurant, travel.

D *Gulmor*, Ferozepur Rd, T 51742. 28 rm. Central a/c. Restaurant, exchange. **D** *Shiraz*, Ferozepur Rd, T 25252. 21 rm, some with TV. Nr rly and centre. Central a/c. Restaurant. **D** *Nanda*, Bhadaur House, T 33618. 28 rm, half a/c.

● Places to eat

Gazebo, 15 Bhadaur House. A/c. *Kabab Corner*, 186 Rani Jhansi Rd, Civil Lines. *Kashmir*, GT Rd, Doraha District.

● Transport

Train There are many local and long distance direct train connections: **To Amritsar**: *Dadar-Amritsar Exp*, 1057, 1505, 3½hr; *Bombay Amritsar Paschim Exp*, 2925, 1640, 3½ hr; **Delhi**: via Saharanpur & Meerut, *Frontier Mail*, 2904, 2340, 9¾ hr; via Kurukshetra Paschim Exp, 2926, 1025, 6½ hr.

Road Bus: daily bus services connect Ludhiana with Delhi and other towns in Punjab and neighbouring states.

ROUTES The direct route from Ludhiana to Firozpur runs W through Jagraon and **Moga**. In Moga, Punjab Tourism E *Kaner Tourist Complex*, Ludhiana-Moga Highway. 8 rm, some a/c, dorms. Restaurant and bar.

ROUTES The **NH1** continues NW out of Ludhiana, crossing the old bed of the Sutlej (14 km, now largely dry) to Phillaur, and **Phagwara** with a Punjab Tourism E *Blue Bell Tourist Complex*, with 5 rm, some a/c, T 61671 Restaurant and bar. Phagwara is the home of JCT Textiles, a widely known trade mark in India. The road is one of the best in India, and many of the small towns show signs of Punjab's rapid industrialisation; steel rolling, textiles, sugar mills, food processing and a whole range of small industrial services from computers to advertising. Jalandhar is 48 km from Ludhiana.

Jalandhar

(*Pop* 520,000; *STD Code* 0181). Formerly Jullundur, Jalandhar is an ancient city of which very little survives. It was sacked by Mahmud of Ghazni and under the Mughals it was an important centre administering the area between the Beas and Sutlej rivers. The **Sarai** (1857) is a comparatively late addition. Today, it is a major road and rail junction. The cantonment area to the SE was established in 1846 to house army units after the treaties signed in Lahore in Mar and Dec 1846 which ended the first Sikh War. It covers an area of 20 sq km. The 'modern' city consists of a number of wards, each originally enclosed by a wall.

Local information

● Accommodation

Most close to centre. **C** *Kamal Palace*, EH-192, Civil Lines, T 58462. 36 rm. Central a/c. Modern and well-presented. **D** *Sky Lark*, Circuit House Rd, T 75682. 72 rm with bath, half a/c. Nr bus stand. Restaurant, bar. **D** *Surya*, 7 Cool Rd, nr Bus Stand, T 3344. 24 rm, some a/c. Restaurant (Indian, Chinese). **D** *Plaza*, Civil Lines, T 73886. 23 rm, some a/c rm with bath. Restaurants, bar. **E** *Ramji Dass*, Model Town Rd, T 3252. 10 rm, some a/c rm with bath. Restaurant.

● Places to eat

In hotels and *Moti Mahal*, GT Rd. Punjab Tourism *Clock Tower*, in Nehru Garden also has a bar.

● Transport

Train The City and Cantt stations are on the same line. There are many trains to Amritsar, and Ludhiana. From City station: **Amritsar**: *Dadar-Amritsar Exp*, 1057, 1620, 2¼hr; *Bombay Amritsar Paschim Exp*, 2925, 1800, 1¾hr; **Delhi via Ludhiana**: and Meerut, *Frontier Mail*, 2904, 2210, 11 hr; via Kurukshetra, *Paschim Exp*, 2926, 0910, 7½ hr. **Calcutta**: via Ludhiana and Varanasi, *Amritsar-Haora Mail*, 3006, 1922, 35 hr.

ROUTES Jalandhar is the focus of several important routes. The NH1A goes N to Pathankot (112 km). Almost half way it passes through **Dasuya**, where there is a small Punjab Tourism E *Tourist Complex*. 4 rm. On bank of a minor canal. Restaurant. The NH1A goes on through Pathankot to Jammu. See below. The main route to Dharamshala from Jalandhar runs NW to **Hoshiarpur**, right on the edge of the plains (*STD Code* 01882). Punjab Tourism D *Lajwanti Tourist Complex*. 14 rm, some a/c, and dorms. Restaurant and bar.

Kapurthala

A short diversion to the S off the NH1 allows you to visit Kapurthala (19 km from Jalandhar).

(*Pop* 63,000; *STD Code* 01822), the capital of the former Sikh princely state and the home town of the Ahluwalia family who conquered it in 1747. Its army fought against the British at Aliwal in the first Sikh War but took the British side during the second Sikh War (1848) and the Mutiny (1857).

Later governed as a model city-state, the French-educated ruler Jagajit Singh, who ascended the throne in 1890, tried to make his capital city a Parisian replica. His palace, the **Jalaukhana**, might have come straight out of the French Renaissance, except that the red sandstone with which it was started had to give way to pink stucco when funds ran out. The palace is now a boys' school. The Maharaja's international preferences changed when he married a Spanish dancer, however, and the **Villa Buona Vista** (1894) has an Iberian flavour.

● **Transport Train** Kapurthala is on the line to Firozpur and can be reached by changing at Jalandhar. **Road Bus**: there are daily services from Jalandhar and Amritsar.

ROUTES The NH1 continues across the River Beas through Jandiala (28 km) to Amritsar (19 km).

En route, at **Kartarpur**, Punjab Tourism has *Magnolia Tourist Complex,* on W edge of town, T 2322. 4 rm. Restaurant, bar, garden. This is a very pleasant point for a break or an overnight stop. 20 km after Kartapur the road crosses the Beas River, about 1 km wide in full spate. It then passes through the small market and canal town of **Raiya**, 15 km from Amritsar. By-pass Amritsar if you do not wish to go into the town.

Amritsar

(*Population:* 709,000. *Altitude:* 234m. *STD Code:* 0183). Amritsar ('Pool of Nectar') is named after the sacred pool in the Golden Temple, the holiest of Sikh sites. Now Punjab's second largest town, Amritsar is only 24 km from the Pakistani border. It is a traditional junction of trade routes and the different people found here – Yarkandis, Turkomens, Kashmiris, Tibetans and Iranians – indicate its connections with the Old Silk Road. Overland travellers have to go through Amritsar for the only land crossing open between India and Pakistan.

Early history

The original site for the city was granted by the Mughal Emperor Akbar (r1556-1605) who also visited the temple and the then Sikh guru, Amar Das (Guru 1552-1574). In 1761 the Afghan Ahmad Shah Durrani sacked the town and destroyed the temple. The temple was rebuilt in 1764 and during the reign of Ranjit Singh was roofed over with gilded copper plates, thereby giving rise to the name 'The Golden Temple'.

Places of interest

The Golden Temple

The spiritual nerve centre of the Sikh faith, every Sikh tries to make a visit and bathe in the holy water. The site has been sacred to the Sikhs since the time of the 4th guru, Ram Das (Guru 1574-1581). In 1577 he heard that a cripple had been miraculously cured while bathing in the pool here. This was enlarged and named **Amrit Sarovar** ('Pool of the Nectar of Immortality'). The Mughal Emperor Akbar granted the land but Ram Das insisted on paying its value to the local Jats who owned it, thereby eliminating the possibility of future disputes on ownership. Ram Das then invited local merchants to live and trade in the immediate vicinity and the subsequent township became Amritsar. Arjan Dev (Guru 1581-1601), Ram Das' son and successor, enlarged the tank further and built the original temple at its centre from 1589-1601.

The Golden Temple suffered twice at the hands of the Afghan Ahmad Shah Durrani, who invaded N India in 1747. The temple was occupied in 1757 and desecrated. The Sikhs united and drove him out, but 4 years later he defeated the Sikh armies at Ghallughara sacking the town and blowing up the temple. After his departure, the Sikhs re-conquered the Punjab and restored the temple and tank. Under their greatest secular leader, Maharaja Ranjit Singh, the roof was gilded. In 1830 he donated 100 kgs (220 lbs) of gold which was applied to the copper sheets on the roof and much of the exterior of the building.

CLIMATE: AMRITSAR

	Jan	Feb	Mar	Apr	May	Jun	Jul	Aug	Sep	Oct	Nov	Dec	Av/Tot
Max (°C)	21	22	28	35	40	41	38	36	36	35	28	23	32
Min (°C)	4	7	12	17	22	26	27	26	23	15	8	4	16
Rain (mm)	43	36	30	26	15	48	142	153	83	10	5	12	598

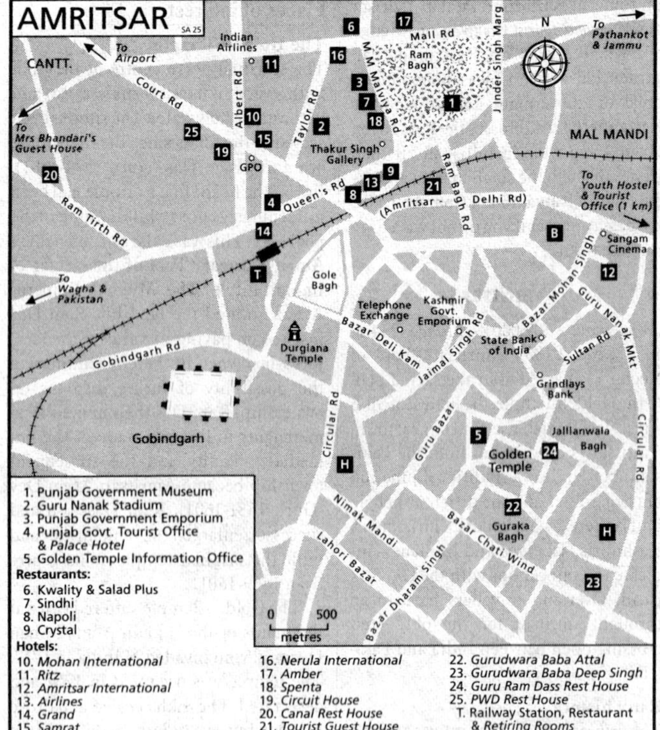

Behaviour in the temple Shoes, sticks and umbrellas are to be left outside at the cloakroom where they are looked after free of charge. Visitors should wash their feet outside the entrance. Socks may not be worn. All visitors should be appropriately dressed and keep their heads covered while in the temple precincts. **NB** Tobacco, narcotics and intoxicants are not allowed to be carried or consumed.

Worship Singing is central to Sikh worship. After building the temple, Arjan Dev compiled a collection of hymns of the great medieval saints and this became the *Adi Granth* (Original Holy book). It was installed in the temple as the focus of devotion and teaching. Gobind Singh, the 10th and last Guru (1675-1708) revised the book and also refused to name a successor saying that the book itself would be the Sikh guru. It thus became known as the *Granth Sahib* (The Holy Book as Guru).

The Temple compound Entering the temple compound through the main entrance or Clock Tower you see the Harmandir, (known by Hindus as the Durbar Sahib) the Golden Temple itself, beautifully reflected in the stunning expanse of water which surrounds it. The atmosphere is particularly powerful from before dawn to early light, when the glistening white marble surrounds to the tank are still cold under foot and the gold begins to shimmer on the lightening water. In winter the marble is really cold for the feet, and the rising sun brings welcome warmth. At 0400 hr in summer and 0500 hr in winter the Guru Granth Sahib is brought in a vivid procession from the Akal Takht at the W end, to the Harmandir, to be returned at 2200.

All pilgrims walk clockwise round the tank, stopping at shrines and bathing in the tank on the way round to the Harmandir itself. The tank is surrounded by an 8m wide white marble pavement, banded with black and

THE SIEGE OF THE GOLDEN TEMPLE: 1984

In the tranquillity of a January morning in the mid-1990s it is difficult to believe that nearly 10 years earlier the Golden Temple had been the site of a 3-day battle between Sikh extremists and Indian armoured forces. Jarnail Singh Bhindranwale and his supporters, having occupied the Golden temple complex for months, had transformed it into a fortress, with machine gun posts on all the vantage points, including the minarets, the Akal Takht and, almost impossible to believe, the Harmandir itself. The Indian army intensified its action. Having pleaded with the occupiers over loud hailers to give up, the army began to fire cannon shells from the Jallianwallah Bagh into the Serais where many insurgents were living. The first Indian troops to enter the central complex were met by a continuous barrage of gunfire. The 3-day siege was only ended when the army brought tanks and armoured vehicles onto the parikrama surrounding the temple tank, firing shells into the Akal Takht where Bhindranwale and his closest associates had their last headquarters. Although the Indian army were under absolute instructions not to fire at the Harmandir itself the Akal Takht suffered extensive damage, which 10 years later is now being restored. Bhindranwale was killed in its basement and the temple finally cleared on 6 June 1984. That however was far from the end of the matter. Mrs Gandhi's assassination 4 months later, and over 8 years of terrorism and civil strife, were just some of the dragon's teeth that sprouted from the blood that had been shed.

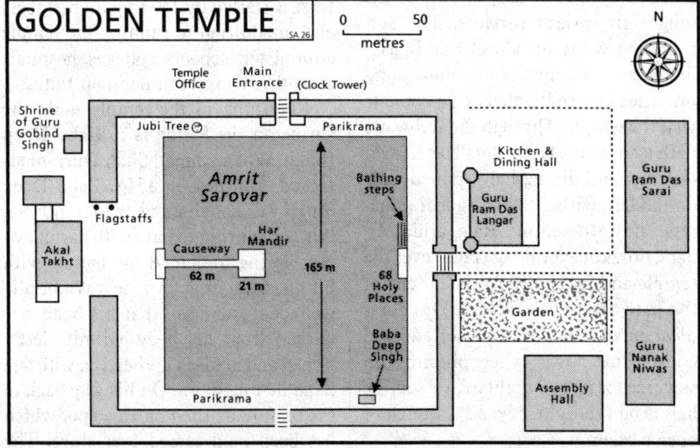

brown Jaipur marble.

The east end To the left from the entrance steps are the bathing ghats at the E end of the tank, and an area screened off from public view for ladies to bathe. Also on the E side are the **68 Holy Places**, a number of shrines and booths, representing 68 Hindu pilgrimage sites. When the tank was built, Arjan Dev told his followers that rather than visit all the orthodox Hindu places of pilgrimage, they should just bathe here thus acquiring equivalent merit.

Also at the E end of the tank is a shrine containing a copy of the **Granth Sahib**. Here and at other booths round the tank the Holy Book is read for devotees. Sikhs can arrange with the temple authorities to have the book read in their name in exchange for a donation. The reader (*granthi*) is a temple employee and a standard reading lasts for 3 hr. A complete reading of the Granth Sahib takes 48 hr. The tree in the centre at the E end of the tank is popularly associated with a healing miracle and many people continue to bring ill relatives hoping for a cure.

Dining Hall, Kitchen, Assembly Hall and **Guest houses** On the E wall of the main complex are numerous plaques commemorating Sikhs who had fought in various services. The surrounding white arcade of buildings – 'bunghas' – are hostels for village communities and individuals who come to visit the temple. Through the archway a path leads to the Guru Ram Das Langar (kitchen and dining hall) immediately on the left, with 2 tall octagonal minarets, the 18th century Ramgarhia Minars, providing a vantage point over the temple and inner city. At the far end of the path are the Guru Ram Das Sarai (*dharamshala* or guest house) and the Guru Nanak Niwas, where pilgrims can stay free for up to 3 nights. An assembly hall is on the right, beyond a stretch of open garden.

Sikhs have a community kitchen where all temple visitors, Sikh, Hindu, Muslims and others, men and women alike can eat together. The 3rd Guru, Amar Das (1552-1574), abolished the caste custom of eating only with others of the same caste, and Sikhs today continue to ignore caste eating prohibitions. Amar Das even refused to bless the Mughal Emperor Akbar unless he was prepared to eat with everyone else who was present, which he accepted. Voluntary service, which continues to be a feature of modern Sikhism, extends to the kitchen staff and workers. The food is paid for out of temple funds. The same practice is found at other Sikh temples and shrines.

The Amritsar kitchen may feed up to 10,000 people a day, with 3,000 at a sitting. It is free of charge and vegetarian, though Sikhs are not banned from eating meat. Lunch is 1100-1500 and dinner 1900 onwards. Next to the Amar Das Langar is the residence of Baba Kharak Singh who is hailed by Sikhs as a saint. His followers are distinguished by their orange turbans. Temple employees and members of the militant Akali sect wear blue or black turbans.

The administrative offices of the temple trust are also in this area. The trust is staffed by 140 unpaid members and in addition to running the temple administers schools, colleges, hospitals and other temples throughout India.

Returning to the temple tank, the shrine on the S side is to **Baba Deep Singh**. When Ahmad Shah Durrani attacked Amritsar in 1758, Baba Deep Singh was copying out the Granth Sahib. He went out to fight with his followers, vowing to defend the temple with his life. 6 km from town he was mortally wounded; some say that his head was hacked from his body. Grimly determined and holding his head on with one hand he fought on. On his way back to the temple he died on this spot which has been held sacred ever since. The story is recounted in the picture behind glass.

The West end The complex to the W has the Akal Takht, the Flagstaffs, and the Shrine of Guru Gobind Singh. The **flagstaffs** symbolise religion and politics, in the Sikh case intertwined. They are joined in the middle by the emblem of the Sikh nation, the 2 swords of Hargobind, representing spiritual and temporal authority. The circle is inscribed with the Sikh rallying call *Ek Omkar* (God is One).

The **Akal Takht** Started when Arjan Dev was Guru (1581-1605), and completed by Guru Hargobind in 1609 the Akal Takht is the seat of the Sikh's religious committee. Today it is largely a mixture of 18th and early 19th century building, the upper storeys being the work of Ranjit Singh. It has a first floor room with a low balcony which houses a gilt covered ark, central to the initiation of new members of the *khalsa*, or brotherhood. It was severely damaged in the 1984 army action and is now being repaired through donations.

Guru Gobind's shrine To the side of the flagstaffs is a shrine dedicated to the tenth and last guru, Gobind Singh (Guru 1675-1708). In front of the entrance to the temple causeway is a square that functions as a gathering place for visitors.

Sometimes you may see **Nihang** (meaning 'crocodile') Sikhs, followers of the militant Gobind Singh, dressed in blue and armed with swords, lances, curved daggers and razor sharp steel throwing irons in their turbans.

The Harmandir (The Golden Temple) At the centre of the tank stands the most holy of all Sikh shrines. Worshippers obtain the sweet *prasad* before crossing the causeway to the temple where they make an offering. The 60m long bridge, usually crowded with worshippers, is built out of white marble, like the lower floor of the temple. The rest of the temple is covered in copper gilt. On the doorways verses from the Guru Granth Sahib are inscribed in Gurumukhi script. Rich floral paintings decorate the walls, and excellent silver work marks the doors. The roof has the modified onion-shaped dome, or inverted lotus, characteristic of Sikh temples, but in this case it is covered in the gold that Ranjit Singh added for embellishment.

The Guru Granth Sahib The ground floor of the 3-storey temple, contains the Holy Book placed on a platform under a jewel encrusted canopy. The Guru Granth Sahib contains approximately 3,500 hymns. Professional singers and musicians sing verses from the book continuously from 0400-2300 in the summer and 0500-2200 in winter. Each evening the holy book is taken ceremoniously to the Akhal Takht and brought back the next morning. The palanquin used for this, set with emeralds, rubies, and diamonds, with silver poles and a golden canopy, can be seen in the treasury on the 1st floor of the entrance to the temple.

Through the day, pilgrims place offerings of flowers or money around the book. There is no ritual in the worship or pressure from temple officials to donate money. The marble walls are decorated with mirrorwork, gold leaf and designs of birds animals and flowers in semiprecious stones in the Mughal style.

The unbroken reading On the 1st floor is a balcony on which 3 respected Sikhs always perform the **Akhand Path** (Unbroken Reading). In order to preserve unity and maintain continuity, there must always be someone practising devotions. The top floor is where the gurus used to sit and here again someone performs the *Akhand Path*.

On the edge of the tank just W of the entrance is the **Tree Shrine**. This gnarled *jubi tree*, 450 years old, is reputed to have been the favourite resting place of the first chief priest of the temple, Baba Buddhaja (meaning 'wise old man'

– there is no connection with the Buddha). Although he was chief priest, he would still do *seva* (voluntary work) and his share of the building work. Women tie strings to the ingeniously supported branches, hoping to be blessed with a son by the primeval fertility spirits that choose such places as their home. It is also a favourite spot to arrange and sanctify marriages, despite the protests of the temple authorities.

The town

The old city is S of the main railway station encircled by a ring road which traces the line of the city walls built during the reign of Ranjit Singh. **Jallianwala Bagh** where General Dyer instigated the massacre is 400m N of the Golden Temple – see page 482. Today the gardens are a pleasant enclosed park. They are entered by a narrow path between the houses, opening out over lawns. A memorial plaque recounts the history at the entrance, and a large memorial dominates the East end of the garden. On the north side is a well in which many who tried to escape the bullets were drowned, and remnants of walls have been preserved to show the bullet holes.

The old town has a number of mosques and Hindu temples, eg the **Durgiana Temple** dedicated to the goddess Durga (16th century), and also the **Lakshmi** and **Narayan Temples** are also found in the city whilst to the SW is **Gobindgarh fort**, built by Ranjit Singh in 1805-1809.

The modern part of Amritsar is NE of the railway station and contains the **Ram Bagh** gardens, **The Mall** and **Lawrence Road** shopping areas. The Ram Bagh Gardens contains a **museum** housing weapons dating from the Mughal times plus some portraits of rulers of Punjab. The building is a small palace built by Maharaja Ranjit Singh. Closed Wed.

Local festivals

Baisakhi, the Hindu solar New Year's Day and is observed over all N India. It is a religious festival when people bathe in rivers and worship at temples to celebrate the day on which the river Ganga is believed to have descended to earth. To the Sikh community, Baisakhi is of special significance because on this day in 1689 Guru Gobind Singh organised the Sikhs into the khalsa or 'pure one' – see page 92. In Punjab, farmers start harvesting with great jubilation. The vigorous *bhangra* dance is a common sight in the villages. The birth anniversaries of the 10 gurus are observed as holy days and those of Guru Nanak, the first (**Oct/Nov**), and Guru Gobind Singh, the last (**Dec/Jan**), are celebrated as festivals. The celebrations are *Akhand Path*, the unbroken recitation of the Guru's verses and processions carrying the Granth Sahib.

Local information

● Accommodation

C *Mohan International*, Albert Rd, T 227801, F 226520. 38 rm. Good restaurants, coffee shop, shops and pool. Rm and public areas need attention; rm not as clean as price suggests. **C** *Ritz*, 45 The Mall, T 226606. 27 rm. Restaurant, exchange, travel, spacious gardens, pool. Pleasant atmosphere.

D *Amritsar International*, City Centre, T 31991. 56 rm. Nr Bus Stand. Central a/c. Restaurant, bar, shops. **D** *Airlines*, Cooper Rd, T 64848. 25 rm. Central. Restaurants, exchange, rooftop garden, Ayurvedic clinic for grey hair and baldness! **D** *Astoria*, 1 Queens Rd, T 66246. 27 rm. Nr rly. Restaurant, travel. **D** *Blue Moon*, The Mall, T 20416. 20 rm, some a/c. Restaurant. **D** *Grand*, Queens Rd, opp rly station, T 612977. 44 rm. Restaurant, bar. **D** *Mrs Bhandari's Guest House*, Cantt, T 64285. Restaurant, pool, camping in garden. Rec for good food and interesting decor – Heath Robinson baths and nostalgic sepia prints of English Lake district.

● Budget hotels

E *Skylark* and *Chinar*, Station Links Rd. Both moderately priced. **E** *Palace*, Station Links Rd. State Tourist Office. **E** *Tourist Guest House*, nr rly station. Guests very unhappy with stay, as well as food in 1994. Not rec. **E** ***Railway Retiring Rooms***, some a/c. **F** ***Youth Hostel***, Mal Mandi, 3 km from centre on GT Rd. Closed in 1994. Now a police post but Tourist Office is functioning.

F ***Vikas Guest House*** and ***Amritsar Majestic***, around the Golden Temple. Some **F** ***Gurudwaras*** in and nr the Golden Temple, and ***Dharamshalas*** offer free accommodation (up to 3 nights) and food (very simple). Please leave a donation. A new block with 150 beds is planned for pilgrims, where upper floor rooms will be available to foreigners. **NB** Tobacco, alcohol and drugs may not be carried or consumed by temple guests. There were reports of mis-behaviour by western tourists in late 1993 resulting in refusal of private rooms to foreigners; only dormitory accommodation was offered.

● Places to eat

Indian, Chinese and Continental: a/c restaurants ***Crystal***, Crystal Chowk; ***Kwality***, Corner of the Mall and ***Salads Plus*** with S Indian snacks under canopy outside; The corner comes alive with ice-cream and fast-food stalls in the evening. ***Amber*** and ***Nerula*** nearby. ***Napoli***, Queens Rd does Tandoori. Very cheap ***Dhabas*** nr the rly station and the temple.

● Shopping

Locally manufactured woollen blankets and sweaters are supposed to be cheaper here than in other parts of India. ***Jaimal Singh Road*** nr the telephone exchange in the old city is a good shopping area.

● Tourist office

Punjab, opp rly station.

● Tansport

Air: *Indian Airlines* **New Delhi:** M,W,F,Su, 1600, 1hr; **Srinagar:** M,W,F,Su, 1305, 34.

Train NB: the station is within 15 min auto rickshaw ride from the Golden Temple. Passengers changing trains with a couple of hours to spare can easily fit in a visit.

New Delhi: *Amritsar-New Delhi Exp* 2460, daily, 0620, 7½ hr; *Amritsar-Dadar Exp* 1058, daily, 0910, 11 hr; *Flying Mail* 4648, daily, 1150, 8¼ hr; *Frontier Mail*, 2904, daily, 2045,10¼hr. **Bombay**: *Frontier Mail*, 2904, daily, 2045,34¼hr. **Calcutta, via Lucknow (17¼hr & Varanasi (23½hr)**, *Amritsar Mail*, 3006, 1755, 39hr. **Pathankot:** *Ravi Exp* 4633, daily, 0910, 2¼ hr.

Road: Daily bus services with **Delhi** (447 km, 10 hr), **Pathankot** (112 km, 3 hr), Chandigarh (230 km, 5 hr), **Jammu** (215 km, 5 hr), **Dharamshala** (250 km, 7 hr), Dalhousie (8 hr).

The border crossing to Pakistan

The road continues W to the Pakistan border. Amritsar itself now sprawls over 12 km from the city centre. Despite the easing in the political situation in Punjab there are numerous police check-posts. If travelling by motor bike or car you may be stopped several times. The police sometimes demand bribes for permission to continue, especially from Indian drivers.

Train The train goes from India to Pakistan with variable frequency. **Lahore** *IP (India-Pakistan) Exp*, 4607, theoretically daily, 0930, 4 hr. This train is seriously affected by the state of political relations between India and Pakistan. It may also be affected by religious pilgrimages. At the end of November when Sikhs visit shrines in Pakistan the train may be restricted to Sikh pilgrims. When running it is a slow, relatively gentle way of entering Pakistan, with sometimes protracted customs and immigration formalities. However, it has often been severely disrupted. Check in Delhi for information before leaving.

Road The road crossing is currently through the Wagha checkpost, 20 km from Amritsar along the attractive and tree-lined GT Road to **Attari**, the last town before the border, just 2 km from Wagha. At **Wagha**, the border checkpoint, Punjab Tourism has the *Neem Chameli Tourist Complex*, *T* 46. 4 air-cooled rm. Restaurant, beer bar, Tourist information, garden. Nominally the Wagha checkpost is open to foot passengers and vehicles between 1000 and 1500, Indian time. **NB:** Pakistan time is 30 mins behind Indian time. The opening times are subject to change.

By private vehicle If you are taking your own vehicle either in or out of India it is essential to have a valid carnet or triptych. You are not allowed to export Indian vehicles without a no-objection certificate, obtainable from the Customs in Delhi, Calcutta, Madras or Bombay. The carnet is valid for 3 months for imported vehicles and can be extended for a further 6 months.

It is best to cross in the morning; allow an hour for formalities. Unless you have your own vehicle you have to walk from the Indian checkpost to the Pakistani checkpost. Indian porters can carry your luggage to the border line, where it is transferred to a Pakistani porter; expect to pay Rs 15 (Indian) and Rs 20 (Pakistani) respectively. There is a bank within the customs area with foreign currency exchange facilities. Beyond Pakistani immigration and customs, there is a taxi and minicab park. It is usually possible to share a cab to Lahore with other travellers (30 km). Amritsar to Lahore usually takes 3-5 hr, though there can be unexpected delays.

AMRITSAR TO JAMMU

The road leaves Amritsar to the NE, one of the first areas in N India to benefit from the enormous irrigation systems built from the late 1830s. Pathankot is the gateway to Jammu Kashmir and to W Himachal Pradesh.

The road crosses the **Bari Doab Canal** (19 km). This part of the canal, which carries water from the Beas River SW into Pakistan, was built by Maharaja Ranjit Singh to fill the tank of the Golden Temple in Amritsar. 'Bari' is a shortened form of the Rivers Beas and Ravi, the *doab* being the land between the 'two waters'.

After crossing the canal the road goes on to **Gurdaspur** (52 km; *Pop* 55,000; *STD Code* 01874). 25 km to the W of Gurdaspur is the small town of **Kalanaur**, where Akbar was proclaimed Emperor. The 13m long, 3m high Jhulna Mahal monument is reputed to sway wildly if sat on. The main road continues NW and crosses the **Upper Bari Doab Canal**. This was one of the first canals to be completed in the new irrigation system of the Punjab. In the early 19th century much of the land to the E of the Amritsar-Pathankot road had been very heavily populated and was suffering declining fertility. After the Anglo-Sikh wars at the end of the 1840s the British decided to try and provide new opportunities for the Sikhs by bringing new land into cultivation further W through extending the canal irrigation system. In doing so they built the system that ultimately transformed the whole of W Punjab from semi-desert into fertile agricultural land. The canal flows across the Pakistan border and through Lahore.

Pathankot

(29 km; *Pop* 147,000; *STD Code* 0186) is a crossroads town and trading centre on the main route from N India to Srinagar. 13 km to the N is the picturesque **Shapur Kandi Fort** (16th Century) on the banks of the Ravi river, once the stronghold of the Rajas of Pathan who fought against and were driven into the hills by the Mughals.

• **Accommodation C/D** *Gulmohar Tourist Bungalow*, Shimla-Pahari, T 20292. 28 rm some a/c, dorm. Restaurant, beer bar. **E** *Shikha International*, Gurdaspur Rd (take a rickshaw if dark). Rm with bath (some rm have no sheets, check beforehand). Excellent restaurant. **F** *Green* and *Imperial Hotels*. **Note** Mineral water is very difficult to find in town.

• **Transport Train** For main connections see Amritsar section. A really spectacular narrow gauge **mountain railway**, built in 1928, runs to Jogindernagar, 56 km NW of Mandi in HP. See page 537. **Baijnath Paprola**, *KV Express*, 0850, 5½hr; **Baijnath & Jogindernagar**, *3PB Passenger*, 0935, 9¾ hr. **Road** the bus and railway stations are 100m apart so transfers are convenient. **Buses**: to all the important destinations nearby. **Taxis**: shared taxis available at the railway station if the prospect of hill bus journeys fails to thrill.

ROUTES From **Pathankot** it is 108 km on **NH1** to **Jammu**, formerly the winter capital of Jammu and Kashmir. The route is along the border between hill and plain, with the Pakistan border always nearby. This is a sensitive, highly strategic area. Accommodation: At **Madhopur** (25 km) D *Coral Tourist Complex*, on NHI, on the bank of the Upper Bari Doab, T 63341. 15 huts and rm, some a/c. Restaurant, bar. The road crosses the Ravi River into Jammu and Kashmir.

DELHI TO FIROZPUR

A route across southern Haryana and Punjab runs from Delhi in the E to Firozpur on the border with Pakistan. For much of the way it follows **NH10**. It allows access to several remote archaeological sites and India's most important early settlement region.

Bahadurgarh, 35 km, a Rathi Jat settlement, was fortified in 1775. Accommodation: Haryana Tourism's D *Gauriyya Tourist Complex, T* 310455. Restaurant, bar, gardens.

Rohtak

(77 km; *Pop* 216,000; *STD Code* 01262) The archaeological sites at Khokhra Kot and Ramala Ala have revealed pottery from pre-Harappan and early historical times after 1500 BC. Coin moulds from the 1st century which have thrown valuable light on the processes of minting coins. In the 18th century Rohtak was a border town between the Sikh and Maratha empires and had a series of local chieftains. Rohtak is well known for its turbans, interwoven with gold and silver thread. Accommodation: Haryana Tourism's D *Myna*, T 77117. Guesthouse and Camper huts in lawns. Restaurant. D *Tilyar*, T 77179. Some a/c rm. Restaurant, bar, boating.

Meham

(30 km) The road W goes on through this small medieval town was built in 1656 by Saidu Kalal, Shah Jahan's mace-bearer. In the war between the Rajputs and Aurangzeb, the town was plundered and fell into decline. It still has high walls, attractive brick houses and an interesting step-well. Despite its small size it achieved notoriety in 1990 as the site of a major election fraud, thugs being used to beat up anyone who showed signs of opposing the then State Chief Minister.

Hansi

(37 km *Pop* 59,000) Dating from the 8th century, was once the capital of the region. Col James Skinner, the son of a Scotsman and a Rajput woman, and founder of the most famous Indian Cavalry regiment, Skinner's Horse, died in the town in 1841. See page 824. Skinner's troops, known as the 'yellow boys' on account of their canary coats, called him Sikander Sahib, likening him to Alexander the Great – see page 190. **Jind** (43 km NE of Hansi) has Haryana Tourism's D *Bulbul*, T 293. 2 good a/c rm in guest house, 2 camper huts. Restaurant.

Hissar

(24 km W; *Pop* 181,000; *STD Code* 01662) Hissar was founded in 1354 by Firuz Shah Tughlaq who constructed a canal to bring water to his hunting ground. This was renovated in the 19th century and incorporated into the W Yamuna Canal. The city was reputedly one of his favourite so he fortified it. The **Gujari Mahal** in the old fort was built from the remains of a Jain temple. The citadel contains the **Mosque of Firuz Shah** (late 14th century) and the **Jahaz** (ship) E of the city, which takes its name from its shape (reminiscent of that at Mandu – see page 384.

- **Festivals** Hissar exports cattle all over India and is widely known for its twice yearly cattle fairs.

- **Accommodation E** Haryana Tourism *Flamingo*, T 2606. Guest House and Camper Huts. A/c rm. Restaurant. Also catering services at the Bus Stand.

Indus Valley "Fossil Fields"

One of the most extraordinary discoveries at Kalibangan has been the unearthing of a field which had clearly been ploughed in two directions. This had been covered by builders' debris. Allchin and Allchin comment that the pattern of having one narrowly spaced set of furrows at right angles to a broader set of furrows, probably made with a wooden plough, is identical to the technique still used in the region for planting 2 crops at once in the same field. Ghosh suggests that the wide range of investigations in the valley that have now been carried out make it possible to distinguish a series of settlement periods, from the pre-Harappan around 3000 BC right through to the early medieval period.

ROUTES You pass the small market town of **Fatehabad** (45 km) and then **Sirsa**(30 km). The site had a settlement from around 1500 BC with pottery known as Rang Mahal Ware. Thus it was clearly occupied long before the traditional date of its founding – the 6th century AD – when it was known as Sarasvati. There is a large cattle fair here in Aug/Sep.

Kalibangan and Harappan sites

Just N of **Sirsa** the road crosses the usually dry bed of the Ghaggar River. This valley was one of N India's most important early settlement regions. Some have identified the Ghaggar with the River Sarasvati, known from early literature. The valley site stretches from the Shimla hills down past the important Harappan sites of Hanumangarh and Kalibangan in Rajasthan, to the S of Bahawalpur in Pakistan and has been explored by archaeologists, notably A. Ghosh, since 1962.

Late Harappan sites were identified in the upper part of the valley, the easternmost region of the Indus Valley civilisation. Sadly in the present state of Indian–Pakistani relations it is not possible to cross the border by land to visit the sites of Harappa 200 km to the NW or Moenjo Daro 450 km to the S. The most impressive of the sites today is that of **Kalibangan**, on the S bank of the Ghaggar River just across the state border in Rajasthan. The site was extensively explored in 1959, and as in Kot Diji in Pakistan it is clear that there were several pre-Harappan phases. The site was a heavily fortified citadel mound, rising about 10m above the level of the plain.

Allchin and Allchin record that the bricks of the early phase were already standardised, though not to the same size as later Harappan bricks. The ramparts were made of mud brick and a range of pottery and ornaments have been found. The early pottery is especially interesting, predominantly red or pink with black painting. It has been possible to date the levels discovered at Kalibangan using radiocarbon dating. The finds in the pre-Harappan phase have been dated at between 2920 to 2550 BC, while a group of 6 dates of between 2550 to 2440 BC for the beginning of the mature Harappan phase are, Allchin and Allchin suggest, "provocatively close to that obtained at Kot Diji" in Pakistan.

• **Transport** Kalibangan is right off the beaten track. **Train** The broad gauge line connects **Suratgarh** with **Anupgarh**, about 15 km from the Pakistan border, where it terminates. Kalibangan is about half way to Anupgarh. The nearest station is Raghunathgarh, but travel from there to Kalibangan is difficult. Best to enquire in Suratgarh or Anupgarh. From **Suratgarh** to **Anupgarh**: *Passenger*, 0620, 2½ hr. Trains from Suratgarh: **Bikaner (Lalgarh Jn)**, 4587, *Chandigarh Exp*, 0830, 3½ hr. **Bhatinda**, 4588, *Chandigarh Exp*, 1930, 3hr. **Road Bus**: local buses run from Suratgarh, which can be reached from Sirsa or Mandi Dabwali and Hanumangarh. The NH 15 connects Suratgarh with Bikaner, which is also a bus route.

Mandi Dabwali

A state border town near the crossing of the Rajasthan Canal, which carries water from the Bhakra Nangal Dam as far S as the Jaisalmer region, another 700 km to the S. The road goes on to the small cross-roads town Malaut (34 km).

Malaut

Accommodation Punjab Tourism's small E *Silver Oak Tourist Complex*, Dabwali Rd offers modest accommodation. 2 rm. Restaurant, bar. Pleasantly situated on bank of Sirhind Feeder Canal.

ROUTES One road runs W to Ganganagar (69 km, just over the border in Rajasthan). The NH 10 goes N to Faridkot and Firozpur.

Faridkot

This was the capital of the small Sikh state dating from the mid 16th century on the site of a much earlier Rajput settlement, whose 700 year old **fort** is still one of the main features of the town. It was captured by Ranjit Singh in 1809, but gained its independence again under the Treaty of Amritsar. Today it is a major agricultural market town.

ROUTES The road to Firozpur (formerly Ferozepur) crosses the Rajasthan Canal.

Firozpur

(*Pop* 78,000; *STD Code* 01632). Firozpur lies very close to the Pakistan border. Although not currently in use the nearby Hussainiwala checkpost has been one of the land border crossings into Pakistan, and could be opened again if political conditions improve. The town was founded during the rule of the Delhi Sultan Firoz Shah in the mid 14th century, but came from Sikh control under the British in 1835. The extension of the Sirhind Canal to the district in the 1880s transformed the previously poverty-stricken agricultural region into a prosperous canal colony. Like the neighbouring lands of Pakistani Punjab across the border, it is a fertile and intensively cultivated region today.

The surrounding area was fiercely fought over during the First Sikh War with the British in 1845-46. The 3 major battlefields at **Mudki** (30 km SE), **Firozshah** (18 km towards Ludhiana) and **Sobraon** (36 km NE) all have commemorative obelisks. There is a British cemetery on the GT Road link to Ludhiana. Firozpur is the terminus of the railway line that used to cross into Pakistan across the Sutlej.

• **Transport Train** From Firozpur Cantt. **Jalandhar**, 4609, *Beas Exp*, 0930, 2½hr; *8JF Passenger*, 1600, 3¼ hr. **Delhi**: *Punjab Mail*, 2138, 2130, 8¾hr; *Janata Exp*, 9024, 0455, 8hr.

HIMACHAL PRADESH

CONTENTS

MAPS

Himachal Pradesh (Himalayan Provinces or HP) is one of India's most beautiful states. Known for its pleasant climate and deliciously cool mountain streams, it supplies India with all its temperate fruit. It also has excellent trekking. The state was created out of the Punjab in 1966 and awarded statehood in 1971. Shimla, a famous British Hill Station, is the state's capital, and worth a visit to see the lengths to which the British went in trying to recreate a part of England on foreign soil. HP is attracting growing numbers of foreigners and Indian visitors alike. Skiing and other adventure sports are being developed along with a widening range of accommodation.

SOCIAL INDICATORS *Population*: 5.1 mn (Urban 9%, Scheduled castes 25%, Scheduled Tribes 5%). *Literacy*: M 75%, F 53%. *Birth rate*: Rural 28:1000, Urban 20:1000. *Death rate*: Rural 9:1000, Urban 6:1000. *Infant mortality*: Rural 100:1000, Urban 62:1000. *Religion*: Hindu 96%, Muslim 2%, Christian 0.1%, Sikh 1%, Buddhist 1%.

Environment

The Land

HP covers 55,673 sq km, one third as much again as Switzerland. It lies between Kashmir (NW) and UP (SE) in the western Himalaya. To the NE is Tibet/China whilst to the SW are Haryana and Punjab. The state is wholly mountainous, stretching from the outer ranges of the Shiwaliks in the S to peaks of more than 6700m. The Dhaula Dhar range runs from the NW to the Kulu Valley. The Pir Panjal is farther N and parallel to it. To the N of these are Lahul and Spiti which are beyond the influence of the monsoon. Consequently they share similar climatic characteristics with Ladakh. High, remote, arid and starkly beautiful, Lahul and Spiti are sparsely populated. They contrast strongly with the well-wooded lushness of HP lying S of the Himalayan Axis.

Rivers The Chenab, Ravi and Beas are the main rivers in the W and the Sutlej and Yamuna in E. Some have been dammed to generate hydro-electricity. The largest lake in the region has been formed by the Bhakra Dam across the Sutlej.

Climate

At lower altitudes the summers can be very hot and humid whereas the higher mountains are permanently under snow. In Shimla, the Kangra Valley, Chamba and the Kulu Valley, the monsoon arrives in mid-Jun and lasts until mid-Sep. As in many hill stations there are often sharp contrasts between sun and shade temperatures, particularly noticeable in spring and autumn when the average temperatures are lower, but the sun can be very warm.

History

Originally the region was inhabited by a tribe called the Dasas who were later assimilated by the Aryans. Parts were occupied by the Muslims. Kangra, for example, submitted to Mahmud of Ghazni and later became a Mughal Province. The Gurkhas of Nepal invaded HP in the early 19th century and incorporated it into their kingdom as did the Sikhs some years later. The British finally took over the princely states in the middle of the 19th century.

Shimla came into existence in 1819 after the Gurkha War. The climate appealed to the British and it rapidly developed into a hot weather resort. In the mid 19th century it became the Summer Headquarters of the government who moved 1,760 km from Calcutta for 4 months each year. After the British, Shimla served as the temporary capital of E Punjab until the new city of Chandigarh was completed. Since 1966 it has been the state capital of HP. Following the Chinese takeover of Tibet, Dharamshala has been the home of the Dalai Lama since 1959.

Culture

People

Hill tribes such as the Gaddis, Gujars, Kinnnaurs, Lahaulis and Pangwalas have all been assimilated into the dominant Hindu culture. The majority is Hindu but the caste system is simpler and less rigid than elsewhere. The tribal peoples in Lahul and Spiti (locally known as Pitians) follow a form of Buddhism, an indication of this region's cultural heritage. The Kinnaur tribals mix Buddhism with Hinduism in their rituals. There are Buddhists elsewhere (many refugees from Tibet), as well as Sikhs, Muslims and Christians.

Their folklore has the common theme of heroism and legends of love and are sung solo, as duets or by groups. *Natti,* the attractive folk dance of the high hills is widely performed.

The state is the least urbanised in India, with under 9% of the total population of 5.11 mn living in towns. Only Shimla has more than 50,000 inhabitants.

Language

The dominant local language is Pahari, a Hindi dialect derived from Sanskrit and Prakrit but largely unintelligible to plains dweller. Hindi is the medium for instruction in schools and is widely spoken.

Handicrafts

Handicrafts include wood carving, spinning wool, leather tanning, pottery and bamboo crafts. Wool products (blankets and clothing) are the most common and it is a common sight in the hills to see men spinning wool by hand as they watch over their flocks or as they are walking along. In the villages, men often knit. Good quality shawls made from the fine hair from pashmina goats, particularly in Kulu, are highly sought after. Fleecy soft blankets called *gudmas*, heavier *namdas* (rugs) and rich pile carpets in Tibetan designs are also produced.

Chappals (leather sandals) are made in Chamba and Chamba *rumals* are beautiful 'handkerchiefs' with scenes embroidered on them imitating the famous miniature paintings of the region. Now, Buddhist *Tankhas*, silver ware and chunky tribal silver jewellery is popular with tourists which are sold in bazars.

Modern Himachal Pradesh

Economy

Agriculture The economy is based on agriculture. Terrace cultivation is practised wherever possible and at higher altitudes farming is supplemented by

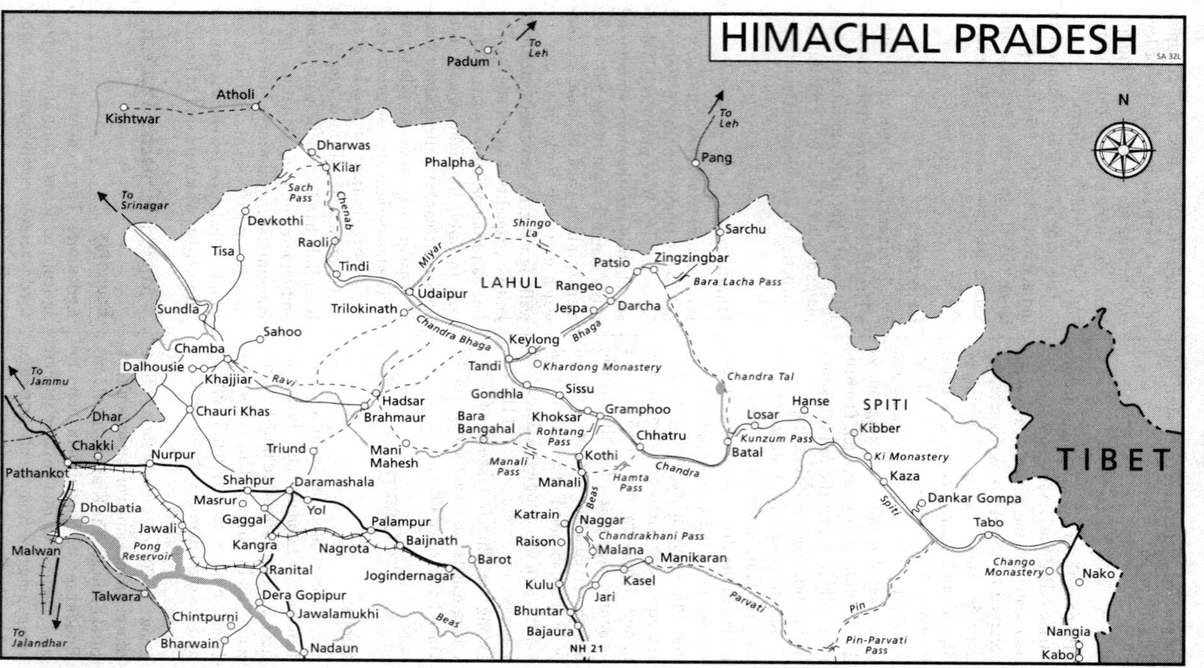
HIMACHAL PRADESH
SA 32L
N
TIBET
SPITI
LAHUL
To Leh
To Leh
To Srinagar
To Jammu
To Jalandhar
NH 21
Padum
Atholi
Kishtwar
Pang
Sarchu
Dharwas
Kilar
Phalpha
Sach Pass
Chenab
Devkothi
Raoli
Tisa
Tindi
Shingo La
Miyar
Zingzingbar
Patsio
Bara Lacha Pass
Rangeo
Udaipur
Jespa
Darcha
Trilokinath
Sundla
Sahoo
Chandra Bhaga
Bhaga
Keylong
Chamba
Dalhousie
Khajjiar
Ravi
Tandi
Khardong Monastery
Chandra Tal
Gondhla
Sissu
Hadsar
Brahmaur
Chauri Khas
Dhar
Chakki
Pathankot
Nurpur
Triund
Mani Mahesh
Bara Bangahal
Khoksar
Rohtang Pass
Gramphoo
Chhatru
Manali Pass
Kothi
Hanse
Losar
Kunzum Pass
Batal
Kibber
Ki Monastery
Kaza
Chandra
Hamta Pass
Manali
Shahpur
Daramashala
Masrur
Yol
Dholbatia
Gaggal
Jawali
Palampur
Baijnath
Kangra
Nagrota
Pong Reservoir
Malwan
Ranital
Barot
Jogindernagar
Katrain
Naggar
Beas
Raison
Chandrakhani Pass
Malana
Manikaran
Kasel
Kulu
Jari
Dankar Gompa
Spiti
Tabo
Chango Monastery
Nako
Talwara
Dera Gopipur
Jawalamukhi
Chintpurni
Beas
Bhuntar
Bajaura
Parvati
Pin
Pin-Parvati Pass
Bharwain
Nadaun
Nangia
Kabo

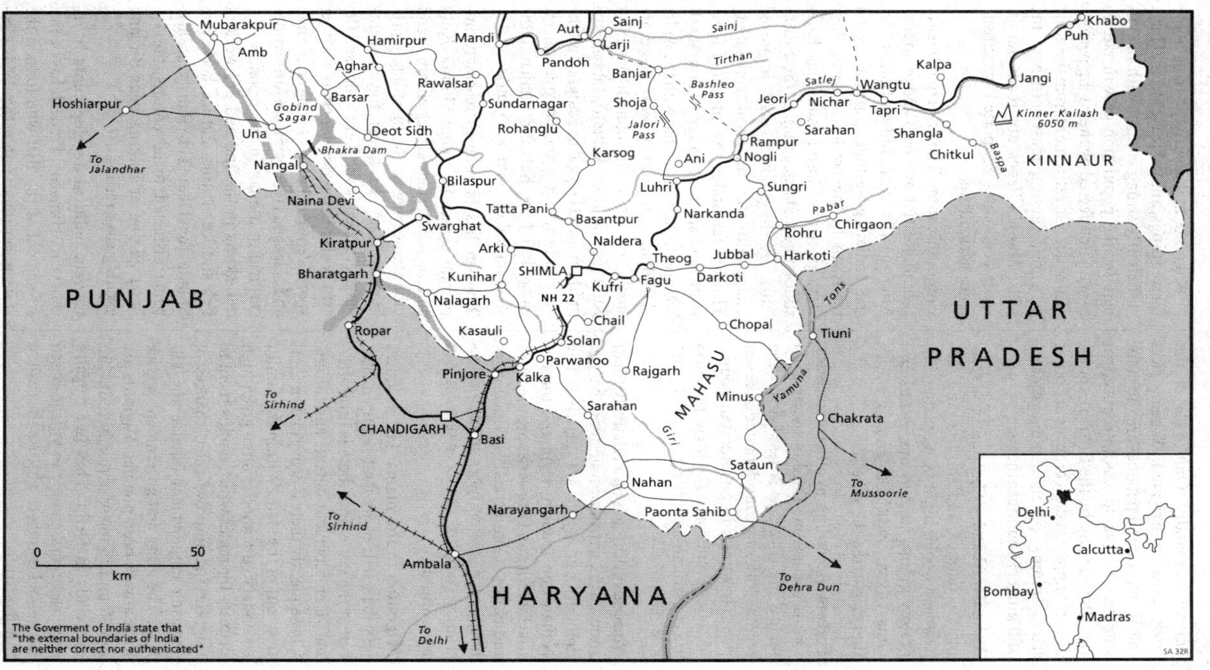

PUNJAB
HARYANA
UTTAR PRADESH
KINNAUR
MAHASU
Mubarakpur
Amb
Hamirpur
Mandi
Aut
Sainj
Larji
Sainj
Pandoh
Tirthan
Aghar
Rawalsar
Banjar
Bashleo Pass
Barsar
Hoshiarpur
Gobind Sagar
Sundarnagar
Shoja
Jalori Pass
Una
Deot Sidh
Rohanglu
Bhakra Dam
To Jalandhar
Nangal
Karsog
Ani
Bilaspur
Naina Devi
Luhri
Narkanda
Tatta Pani
Basantpur
Swarghat
Kiratpur
Naldera
Arki
SHIMLA
Bharatgarh
Kunihar
Kufri
Nalagarh
NH 22
Chail
Kasauli
Solan
Ropar
Parwanoo
Pinjore
Kalka
Rajgarh
To Sirhind
CHANDIGARH
Basi
Sarahan
Giri
Nahan
Narayangarh
To Sirhind
Ambala
To Delhi
0 50 km
The Goverment of India state that "the external boundaries of India are neither correct nor authenticated"
Theog
Fagu
Jubbal
Darkoti
Chopal
Minus
Sataun
Paonta Sahib
Sarahan
Rampur
Nogli
Sungri
Jeori
Satlej
Nichar
Wangtu
Tapri
Pabar
Rohru
Chirgaon
Harkoti
Tons
Tiuni
Yamuna
Chakrata
To Mussoorie
To Dehra Dun
Kalpa
Shangla
Chitkul
Baspa
Jangi
Puh
Khabo
Kinner Kailash 6050 m
Delhi
Calcutta
Bombay
Madras
SA 32R

animal husbandry. Only 15% of the sown area is irrigated. Wheat, rice, maize, barley and potatoes are the main staples. The potato was introduced in the 19th century by the British. Apples are an important cash crop, as are other fruits (plums, peaches, pomegranates and ginger) and mushrooms.

Animal husbandry Sheep and goat rearing is common and the fine and soft *pashmina* wool is highly sought after. Migratory groups such as the Gaddis and Gujars have traditional grazing routes that criss-cross the state.

Forests According to official statistics, forests occupy one third of the area. In reality the coverage is less with some regions suffering considerable deforestation. The forests are an important source of state revenue and the main products are construction timber, fuel wood, gum and resin.

Minerals Mining is on a relatively small scale. Slate, gypsum, limestone, baryte, dolomite and pyrite are quarried. The Nahan iron foundry, resin and turpentine factories and breweries are the main industries. Commercial production of fertilisers has recently begun and an electronics complex has been established near Shimla.

Migration to the plains HP produces less than half of its food requirements, but at the same time there is little alternative employment outside agriculture. Consequently, there is heavy male migration out of the state. Within the family, secondary education is often given high priority for males which equips them to migrate and improve their chances of securing employment outside the village. The army and government service have always been popular. Migrants are now found in towns across N India but especially in Delhi. They live frugally, save and remit money to village-based household members who use the cash to buy foodstuffs.

Migrants make periodic trips home for weddings, annual leave etc. and have sufficiently strong contact with the village for the population growth rate to remain unaffected by their long periods of absence. On retirement from the army or public service, most return to the hills. Many villages are really remittance economies supported by subsistence agriculture.

Communication The principal lines of communication are roads and footpaths. After the 1962 Sino-Indian Border War the Indian government pushed good roads up to the border to serve their strategic needs (during monsoons, landslides may make negotiating these difficult). A by-product was improved accessibility for the local population. This has facilitated the import of foodstuffs and made it easier to migrate. It has also linked Himachal with the wider N Indian economic system. There are small airports at Bhuntar, 10 km S of Kulu (55 km from Manali), Jabbarhatti nr Shimla and Gaggal nr Kangra, and the only railway is the picturesque narrow gauge line from Kalka in Punjab to the state capital of Shimla (96 km).

Tourism has become increasingly important especially round Shimla, Kulu and Manali. Trekking, rock climbing and mountaineering are being strongly promoted. Many Kashmiri travel agents have relocated in the Kulu Valley and the area is also being developed as a winter sports centre. There is skiing in Manali and Narkanda (courses from Jan), winter carnival in Manali in the second week, heli-skiing in the 2nd and 3rd week of Feb and ice skating and ice hockey in Shimla from Dec to Feb. Tourists are also being attracted to adventure sports – hang gliding at Bilking near Bir and exciting river rafting.

Current political developments In recent years Himachal Pradesh has been a stronghold of the BJP, who formed the state government after the 1990 elections, when they won 44 of the 63 State Assembly seats. However, they suffered a major defeat in December 1993, the Congress Party taking power again under the leadership of the new Chief Minister Virbhadra Singh.

SHIMLA

Population: 110,000 approx. *Altitude:* 2213m. *STD Code:* 0177. For the British, the only way of beating the hot weather on the plains in May and Jun was to avoid it. They therefore established a number of hill stations in the Lesser Himalaya and elsewhere (Ooty in the Nilgiris, Mount Abu in Rajasthan, Murree in Pakistan, Darjiling in W Bengal) which became hot weather resorts. These developed some of the features of English county towns or seaside resorts. Bandstands, mock Elizabethan houses with exotic names like Harrow-on-the-Hill and Runnymede, pavilions and picnic spots, churches and clubs and a main street invariably called the Mall.

BEST SEASON Oct and Nov are exceptionally pleasant, with hot days and cool nights. Dec-Feb is cold and there are snowfalls. Mar-Apr is pleasant but the weather can be quite changeable, storms are not infrequent and the air can feel very chill. May-Jun is the height of the Indian tourist season when accommodation is hard to find.

Places of interest

The Town Shimla is strung out on a long crescent-shaped ridge which connects a number of hilltops: Jakhu (2453m), Prospect Hill (2176m), Observatory Hill (2148m), Elysium Hill (2255m) and Summer Hill (2103m). Good views of the snow-capped peaks to the N can be obtained from Jakhu and others. The Mall runs along the ridge, often giving beautiful views. All the walks are lined with magnificent pines and cedars, giving a beautifully fresh scent to the air.

The decaying Raj The wooden buildings look more and more rickety, some of the stone ones are slowly crumbling. Below the British creations strung out along the ridgeline, shabby houses with corrugated iron roofs tumble down the hillside below. As with all 'British' towns in India, although the inspiration and some of the design may have come from the colonial outsiders, much of the town was naturally lived in by local people. Immediately below the ridge is the maze of narrow streets and bazars clinging to the hillside. Throughout the tourist season Shimla is crowded with people up from the plains for a break from the heat.

Jakhu Temple (2455m) Dedicated to Hanuman, the monkey god, and frequented by monkeys. 2 km beyond Christ Church, it is at about the highest spot on the ridge, with excellent views.

Christchurch (1844 onwards) dominates the E end of town. Designed by Col JT Boileau, consecrated in 1857 and later extended with the addition of a clock (1860) and porch (1873). The original chancel window was designed by Lockwood Kipling, Rudyard Kipling's father. No trace remains. Next door is the **Library** (c1910) designed by James Ransome in the Elizabethan style. Where the Mall joins The Ridge is Kipling's *Scandal Point*.

CLIMATE: SHIMLA

	Jan	Feb	Mar	Apr	May	Jun	Jul	Aug	Sep	Oct	Nov	Dec	Av/Tot
Max (°C)	9	10	14	19	23	24	21	20	20	18	15	11	17
Min (°C)	2	3	7	11	15	16	16	15	14	10	7	4	10
Rain (mm)	65	48	58	38	54	147	415	385	195	45	7	24	1481

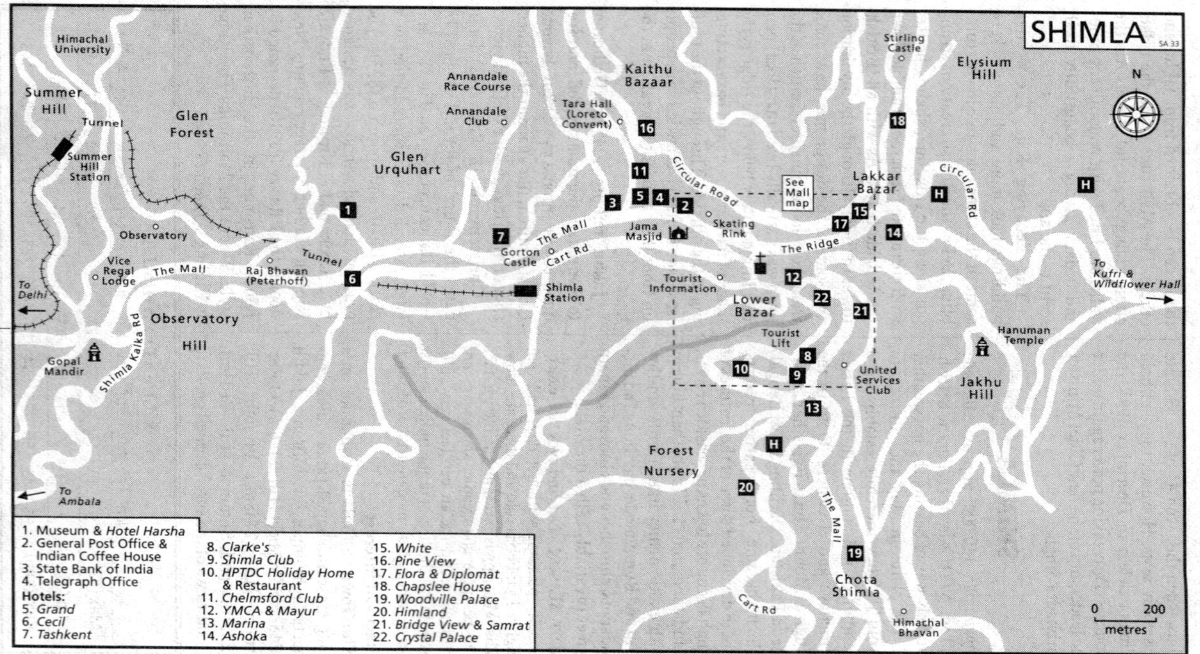
SHIMLA
SA 33
N
Himachal University
Summer Hill
Tunnel
Summer Hill Station
Glen Forest
Glen Urquhart
Annandale Race Course
Annandale Club
Kaithu Bazaar
Tara Hall (Loreto Convent)
Stirling Castle
Elysium Hill
Observatory
Vice Regal Lodge
The Mall
Raj Bhavan (Peterhoff)
Tunnel
To Delhi
The Mall
Gorton Castle
Cart Rd
Shimla Station
Circular Road
Jama Masjid
Skating Rink
See Mall map
Lakkar Bazar
Circular Rd
The Ridge
Tourist Information
Lower Bazar
Tourist Lift
United Services Club
To Kufri & Wildflower Hall
Hanuman Temple
Jakhu Hill
Observatory Hill
Shimla Kalka Rd
Gopal Mandir
Forest Nursery
The Mall
Chota Shimla
Cart Rd
Himachal Bhavan
To Ambala
0
200
metres
1. Museum & *Hotel Harsha*
2. General Post Office & Indian Coffee House
3. State Bank of India
4. Telegraph Office
Hotels:
5. *Grand*
6. *Cecil*
7. *Tashkent*
8. *Clarke's*
9. *Shimla Club*
10. *HPTDC Holiday Home* & Restaurant
11. *Chelmsford Club*
12. *YMCA & Mayur*
13. *Marina*
14. *Ashoka*
15. *White*
16. *Pine View*
17. *Flora & Diplomat*
18. *Chapslee House*
19. *Woodville Palace*
20. *Himland*
21. *Bridge View & Samrat*
22. *Crystal Palace*

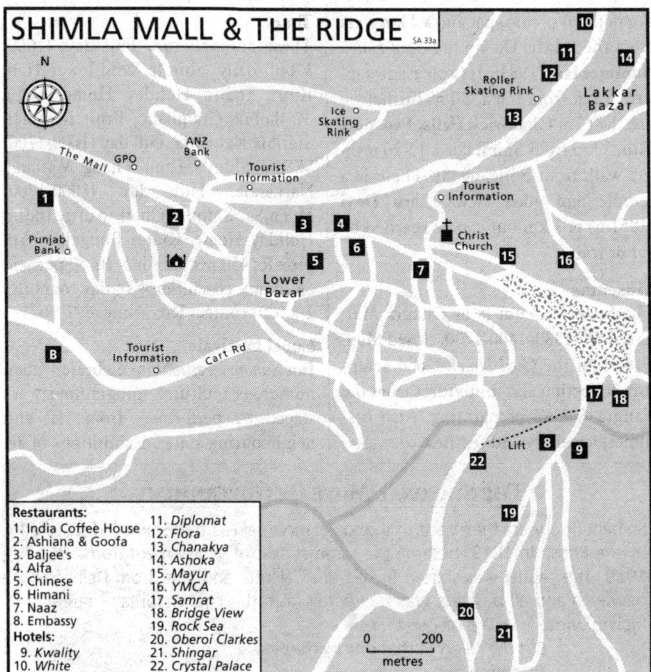

The **Gaiety Theatre** (1887) in the **Town Hall** (c1910) is here, reminiscent of the 'Arts and Crafts' style, as well as the timbered **General Post Office** (1886). Nearby are the YWCA, St Andrew's Church (1885) and the Telegraph Office. Beyond is the *Grand Hotel*. Further down you pass the sinister looking **Gorton Castle**, designed by Sir Samuel Swinton Jacob and much modified during its construction. This was once the Civil Secretariat. A road to the left leads to the railway station, while one to the right goes to Annandale, the racecourse and cricket ground. The road between the Mall and The Ridge is pedestrianized.

The road past the station leads to the Cecil Hotel (1877). Less than 1 km away on Observatory Hill, the watershed, is **Viceregal Lodge** (1888), built for Lord Dufferin, who played a prominent part in its design and building. Henry Irwin, designer of the Madras Law Courts and Mysore's Ambar Vilas Palace – see page 1012 – and Capt HH Cole designed it in the Elizabethan style. Now the **Rashtrapati Niwas,** it houses the Indian Institute of Advanced Study (IIAS). The interior is sombre, the magnificent reception hall, full of heavy teak panelling. It had an indoor tennis court and electric lights. The main reception rooms and the library can be visited, with permission. The gardens, with good views of the mountains, are open. There are still some reminders of its British origins such as a gatehouse, a chapel and the meticulously polished brass fire hydrants imported from Manchester.

Walks

There are a number of pleasant walks in and around Shimla. **The Glen** (1830m) is a popular picnic spot and a 4 km walk from the centre. Go via the *Cecil Hotel*. **Summer Hill** (1983m) is a pleasant 'suburb' 5 km from town. 3 km further on are the 67m **Chadwick Falls. Prospect Hill,** 5 km from Shimla, is a 15-20 minute walk from Boileauganj. There is a temple and good views. **Tara Devi** (1851m) is 7 km but can be reached by car or train.

Museums

The State Museum is nr Chaura Maidan. 1000-1330, 1400-1700, closed Mon. NW from the *Cecil Hotel*. Good sculpture collection and miniatures from the Kangra School of painting. Also costumes, jewellery and textiles.

Tours

These are well run. Full day: (1000-1700), daily: Shimla Wildflower Hall, Kufri, Indira Holiday Home, Fagu, Mashobra, Craignano, Fruit Research Station, Naldehra. Full day (1000-1700) W,F,Su: Shimla, Fagu, Theog, Matiana, Narkanda. Full day (1000-1700) M,Th,Sa: Shimla, Chail, Kufri, Indira Holiday Home, Kiarai Bungalow. Approx Rs 450 per car for 5, Rs 50 per seat on luxury coach.For 4-14 day tours (Rs 2-8,000) contact Ritz Annexe, T 5071.

Local Festivals

Jun *Summer Festival* is celebrated when numerous cultural programmes are staged by performers from HP and neighbouring states. Exhibitions of art

The Seasonal Move Of Government

So beneficial were the effects of the cooler mountain air that Shimla, 'discovered' by the British in 1819, became the summer seat of government from 1865 to 1939. The capital was shifted there from Calcutta and later from Delhi (1912 onwards) and all business was transacted from this cool mountain retreat. As Kipling wrote in *A Tale of Two Cities*:

But the rulers in that City by the Sea
Turned to flee –
Fled with each returning Spring and tide from its ills
To the Hills.

Huge baggage trains were required to transport the mountains of files and the whole operation cost thousands of rupees. At the end of the season back they would all go. Other hill stations, such as Nainital in UP, became summer seats of state governments.

The emphasis was on relaxation and a holiday atmosphere developed. They were places where women heavily outnumbered men, as wives of many British men who ran the empire escaped to the hills for long periods. Army officers spent their leave there. Social life in hill stations became a round of parties, balls, formal promenades along the Mall and brief flirtations.

Colonels of Indian army regiments would not allow their subalterns to go to certain hill stations. Many were said to come down from the hills fighting rearguard actions against the husbands coming up. They became known as 'poodle fakers'. At the height of the Victorian period of propriety in England, Shimla was considered a very sinful place.

The hill stations are still hot weather resorts. As the temperatures on the plains soar, so do the population and room rents in these hilltop retreats. They are best avoided then. Paul Scott's Booker Prize winning novel *Staying On* was set in post Independence Shimla. J G Farell's last unfinished novel *The Hill Station,* set in colonial Shimla of 1871, is also worth reading.

and handicrafts are held and you will get the opportunity to sample different local dishes.

Local information

● Accommodation

Price guide
AL Rs 3,000+ **A** Rs 2,000-3,000
B Rs 1,200-2,000 **C** Rs 600-1,200
D Rs 250-600 **E** Rs 100-250 **F** Up to Rs 100.

In May and Jun, modest accommodation can be difficult to find, especially if you arrive after mid-day, so book beforehand. Some close off-season. Most hotels down to **C** category have a car park. **NB**: some do not accept credit cards. **AL** *Oberoi Clarks*, The Mall, nr Lift, T 212991. 48 rm. Mock-Tudor building where the enterprising Mohan Singh Oberoi started his chain of hotels in 1935. Pleasant, well run with mountain views, good food and bar. Central. **Note**: Indian guests pay rupee price despite AL category. This is an old hotel lacking some of the facilities normally found in this price range. **AL** *Oberoi Cecil*, The Ridge, Mall, Colonial grandeur on the edge of town, with superb views. Reopening Sept 1995 after complete renovation.

B-C *Eastbourne*, Khillini, nr Bishop Cotton School, 5 km from bus stand, T 77260, F 5496. 24 rm. Opened in 1994, in thickly wooded setting, very well furnished, friendly service, rec.

C *Woodville Palace*, Himachal Bhavan Rd, The Mall, T 2763. 11 rm, more expensive suites. Restaurant (rec), gardens. Good views. Spacious palace in large grounds. **C** *Chapslee House*, Lakkar Bazar, T 77319. 7 suites so reserve in advance. Lovely old mansion with character in large grounds with good views. Very good restaurant (price incl full board), excellent personal service. Rec. **C** *Asia The Dawn*, Tara Devi, Mahavir Ghat, T 5858. 37 rm. 4 km from Mall. Restaurant (rec) and terrace barbecue, bar, exchange, shops, regular bus into Shimla. Modern, well managed and in a peaceful setting. HP Tourism **C** *Holiday Home*, Circular Rd, below High Court, nr lift, T 72376. 65 rm, 'Luxury rm' rec. Good restaurants, bar, exchange, tours. Large clean rooms, some with views. Rec. **C** *Meghdoot*, T 78302 is similar. **C** *Honeymoon Inn*, The Mall, T 4967. 20 rm Indian restaurant, indoor sports.

D *Crystal Palace*, Cart Rd (nr lift), T 5088. Some rm with good views. Restaurant, travel. There are numerous less expensive hotels on the Mall and on Circular Rd, Lakkar Bazar. **D** *Surya*, Circular Rd, T 4762. 41 rm. Restaurant, travel. Modern. **D** *Mayur*, The Ridge, T 6047. 32 rm. Good restaurant. Modern and clean; helpful staff. **D** *Pineview*, Mythe Estate, Circular Rd, T 6606. 28 rm. Indian restaurant, exchange. **D** *Shingar*, The Mall, T 2881. 32 clean rm. Restaurant. **D** *Himland East*, Circular Rd, 3 km bus stand, T 3595, F 213041, 24 rm, modest but clean, good views from balconies. **D** *Himland West*, formerly part of *Himland East*, at same address, T 3596, F 6429, 8 rm. Split as a result of family division, but hotels basically similar, good value. **D** *Samrat*, Cambermere Bridge, The Mall, T 78572. Restaurant (Indian, Chinese), travel. **D** *Harsha*, Chaura Maidan, T 3016. 20 rm. Restaurant. Simple but clean; rec for good service. **D** *Gulmarg*, The Mall, T 3168. 48 rm. Restaurant. **D** *Diplomat*, The Ridge, T 3033. 23 rm with bath, some good. Restaurant, travel. **D** *White*, Lakkar Bazar, T 5276. Rm with bath, some with good views. Rec. **D** *Lord St John*, Cart Rd, (nr Capital Hotel) has very clean rm. Friendly staff and rec but if arriving late, knock loudly to be heard!

● Budget hotels

E *Ridge View*, The Ridge, T 4859. 20 rm. Rm service. **E** *Flora*, The Ridge, T 2027. 22 rm. TV, rm service, travel. **E** *Kwality*, The Mall, T 6440. Rm service, travel. **E** *Sharda*, Lakkar Bazar, T 2188. Restaurant. **E** *Marina*, The Mall. T 3557. Dining hall (meals to order), terrace. Older hotel. Several basic **E** hotels on the Mall, some of which have a dining hall, others rm service. Rooms vary, so check first: *Chanakya*, *Bridge View*, Cambermere Bridge, T 78537, *Dalziel* and *Rock Sea*. Some like *Capital*, Cart Rd, T 3581, is favoured by touts where you pay extra for their commission.

F *Tashkent*, lane off Mall, above Victory Tunnel. Very basic. Rm vary, some with bath and TV (possible to bargain down). **F** *YMCA*, The Ridge, above Christ Church, T 3341. Dining hall, TV in common room, quiet location, relaxed atmosphere, popular though institutional. Indoor sports incl gym and billiards. Temp membership Rs 20, electricity extra. Rec.

● Accommodation near Shimla

B *Kufri Holiday Resort*, Kufri, 16 km from Shimla (see below in Excursions). At **Chharabra** HP Tourism **C** *Wildflower Hall*, T 28212, 13 km from Shimla. Main building totally burnt down in Feb 1993. 11 rustic cottages with sitting rooms and kitchens available. Restaurant, outdoor café, bar. Attractive gardens and lovely walks. Also HP Tourism **D** *Log huts* and *cottages*. At Fagu HP Tourism **D** *Peach Blossom* has 6 rm.

● Places to eat

Most offer Indian, Continental and Chinese food. Rec hotel restaurants: *Asia the Dawn* and *Honey Dew,*, excellent; the more intimate *Woodville Palace*, *Chapslee* and *Holiday Home* (reservations advisable, T 72376). **Outside hotels**: *Ashiana* above *Goofa* on The Ridge, circular with good views, rec for Indian and Chinese dishes while *Goofa* is better for pizzas and snacks. *Choice Chinese Food*, Middle Bazar, down steps from the Fire Station – 107 different dishes; highly rec. Several other Chinese restaurants nearby incl *Chung Fa*.

Rec on the Mall:*Indian Coffee House* for cheap S Indian meals and snacks. *Malook's* opp Gaiety Theatre, down steps, for good, cheap Tibetan food; *Fascination* above *Baljee's*; *Alfa*; *Himani*; *Embassy* and *Ajay* opp Telegraph Office. Some of the higher category hotels have **bars**.

● Banks & money changers

Branches of most in the shopping areas incl **State Bank of India**.

● Hospitals & medical services

Kamala Nehru Hospital, T 2841.

● Post & telecommunications

Head GPO: The Mall (nr Scandal Point). Others nr State Bank of India and Cambermere Bridge.

● Shopping

Major shopping areas are The Mall, Lower Bazar, and Lakkar Bazar. On the Mall: *Himachal Emporium*, opp Telegraph Office, for local woollen items. **Books**: on the Mall, *Maria Books* at 78 and *Minerva* at 46, for books, maps and prints.

● Sports

Golf: Naldera, 9-hole. For casual members green fee Rs 15, golf set Rs 10, caddie Rs 10, balls Rs 16-25. **Ice Skating rinks**: below Rivoli. *Roller Skating Rink*, Regal Bldg. **Skiing**: early Jan-mid-Mar. Ski courses at Narkanda (64 km) organised by HP Tourism. 7 and 15-day courses, Jan-Mar, Rs 1,700-3,000. (**E** *Him View Hotel* has 6 rm). See also Manali. **Trekking**: on the Shimla-Kinnaur belt (1-10 days).

● Tour companies & travel agents

Span Tours 'n Travels, 4 The Mall, opp GPO, T 5279, F 201300. Comprehensive and wholly reliable. *Gt Himalayan Travels*, *Devi Travels*, The Mall; *Destinations Inc*, 35 Upper Flat; *Asia and International Travel and Tourist Agencies*, 90 The Mall. *Ambassador Travels*, 58 The Mall, T 4662. *Ibex*, Tara Devi, T 212255. *S E Travels*, Room 7, Masonic Guest House, The Ridge.

● Tourist offices

HP, The Mall, T 78311. 1000-1800. Victory Tunnel, Cart Rd, T 4589. 1000-1700. HP Tourism has a/c and non-a/c cars and luxury coaches. Central Reservations Office, Hotel Holiday Home, Circular Rd, T 72375, F 3887, for advance reservation of transport and accommodation throughout the state.

● Useful addresses

Police: T 100, 2444. **Fire**: T 101. **Ambulance**: T 3464.

● Transport

Kalka (90 km); **Chandigarh** (117 km); **Ambala** (166 km); **Delhi** (370 km); **Dehra Dun** (200 km); **Amritsar** (453 km); **Jammu** (495 km). **Mussoorie** (234 km), 8 hr by taxi, incl shops. A very interesting journey.

Local Taxis: Taxi Union Service, nr Tourist Lift on Cart Rd, T 5123. Private taxis, mini buses and Himachal RTC buses are available for local sightseeing in and around Shimla. **Buses**: from Cart Rd. The Lift, nr *Hotel Samrat*, takes passengers to the Mall.

Air The airport is at Jabbarhatti (23 km). **Archana Airways** now has daily flights to Delhi. **Jagsons**, flies daily except Th, to Delhi, 1120, 2 hr, via Kulu, ½ hr. Office, 58 The Mall.

Train Travel to Shimla involves a change of gauge at Kalka. The delightful narrow gauge train journey is very enjoyable. The **Kalka-Shimla** (2ft 6 in, 0.8m) railway line, completed in 1903, runs 97 km from Kalka in the foothills to Shimla at over 2000m; the magnificent journey takes just over 4 hr. The gradient averages 1 in 33; there are 107 tunnels covering 8 km, and bridges over 3 km. Travel by bus is quicker but requires a stronger stomach.

Chandigarh: *Kalka-Haora Mail* 2312 (change at Kalka to 254), daily, 1745, 6½ hr; *Himalayan Queen*, 4096 (change at Kalka to 258), daily, 1722, 4½ hr. **New Delhi:** *Himalayan Queen*, 4096 (change at Kalka to 258), daily, 1055, 6¼ hr. **Old Delhi:** *Kalka-Haora Mail* 2312 (change at Kalka to 254 Mail), daily, 1745, 12¾ hr. The day train to Delhi rec; women alone may prefer Ladies' carriages which are less crowded.

Road Services to **Delhi** (10-12 hr), **Chandigarh** (4 hr), **Manali** (11 hr), **Dharamshala** (12 hr), **Dehra Dun** (9 hr) and from other places within the state. HPRTC deluxe buses between Shimla and Delhi in the summer (9 hr). **NB**: Reports of unsatisfactory service in 1993. Enquiry, T 2887 (in Delhi, Kashmiri Gate Terminal). You may not be able to avoid the video coach. Remarkably, if the video is not working, you may get a discount.

SHIMLA TO CHANDIGARH

Kalka, 35 km N of Chandigarh, is the terminus for the narrow gauge railway from Shimla and connected by broad gauge to the rest of the country. Kalka is also easily reached by bus or taxi.

ROUTES The road descends rapidly from Shimla to Tara Devi (11 km; 1820m) and continues to Kundarghat.

Chail

(2250m)Iin a superb forest setting with fine snow views 45 km SE of Shimla, Chail is worth a diversion or an overnight stop. Popular with birdwatchers, it was once the Maharaja of Patiala's summer capital built on 3 adjacent hills which claimed to have the country's highest cricket ground! The old palace on Rajgarh Hill has been converted to a comfortable hotel while the old residency 'Snowview' and a Sidh temple stand on the other 2 hills. Accommodation: B/C *Chail Palace*, T Chail 8343. 19 suites in palace, and 10 cottages (1-4 bedrooms), 'Rajgarh' being the most expensive; simple D 'Log Huts' for 2, the cheapest. Restaurant. Modest but full of character. D *Himneel*, is basic.

Solan

(*Alt* 1450m; *STD Code* 01792) The half way point to Shimla on both the road and railway line, Solan is noted for its brewery and mineral water springs. Accommodation: HP Tourism E *Tourist Bungalow*, T 3733.

Parwanoo

In Oct 1992 the hauling rope of the cable-car here snapped and some passengers were stranded for nearly 2 days owing to bad weather, before being rescued by helicopter. Accommodation: C *Timber Trail Resort*, T 497. 25 rm, 10 tents. Restaurant, cafe, bar and good rooms. *Timber Trail Heights*, reached by cable-car, also with restaurant. Excellent setting with gardens. Open 24 hr. Also D *Shiwalik*, T 4222 (HP Tourism).

Kalka

The road enters UP at Kalka (6 km *STD Code* 01733) the end of the ghat section.

• **Transport Train Shimla**: *KS1*, daily, 0400, 5¼ hr; *Rail Car*, 101, daily, 0540, 4¼ hr; *Mail*, 251, 0620, 5¼ hr; 255, *Express*, 1140, daily, 5½hr. **Delhi**: *Shatabdi Exp*, 2006, daily, 0545, 4 hr; *Kalka-Haora Mail*, 2312, 2330, 7 hr; *Himalayan Queen*, 4096, 1640, 5¼ hr.

Pinjore

(*Pop* 8,000) It is worth stopping briefly to see the Mughal summerhouse and garden built by Fidai Khan, see page 490. Chandigarh is a further 20 km.

SHIMLA TO LEH VIA KULU AND MANALI

From Shimla the route runs through the Shiwalik hills to **Bilaspur**, then N to Mandi. The road continues N into Kashmir, though foreigners need Frontline Permits to travel in this region. **Note** During the monsoons (Jul, Aug), landslides may result in very long delays. Carry plenty of water and some food.

ROUTES The road winds its way down for much of the way from Shimla, to Kheri Ghat (19 km; 1280m) then through small villages and hamlets to **Namhol** (33 km) where there is a *Rest House* and a checkpost. After a further 16 km there is a junction. The road to the right goes to Bilaspur (18 km), the left to **Swarghat** (33 km), with a *Forest Rest House*, and to **Naina Devi** (56 km; 910m) with another *Forest Rest House* and a *Tourist Inn*.

Bilaspur used to be the centre of a district in which the tribal Daora peoples panned in the silts of the Beas and Sutlej for gold. Their main source, the Seer Khud, has now been flooded by the Bhakra Nangal Lake, and they have shifted their area of search upstream, some as far as the high reaches in Kinnaur. Bilaspur has the *Lake View Café*, with clean toilets.

ROUTES Go N, cross the River Sutlej, which now feeds into the Govind Sagar lake, and follow the road to **Sundernagar** (18 km; *Pop* 20,000), **Tattapani**, (18 km) where there is a hot spring, and on to Mandi. The *Roadside Milk Bar*, 8 km S of Mandi serves excellent milkshakes.

Mandi

(8 km; *Pop* 23,000; *Alt* 760m; *STD Code* 01905) at the S end of the Kangra Valley (where you enter the Kulu Valley), reached by climbing the narrow and spectacular gorge of Beas river was founded by a Rajput prince (c1527).

Places of interest

The **Triloknath Siva Temple** (1520), built in the Nagari style with a tiled roof, at the centre of a group of sculpted stone shrines (14th-16th centuries), overlooks the river and offers good views. The **Bhutnath Temple** by the river in the town centre has a *nandi* facing the ornamental double arch to the sanctuary. The modern shrines nearby, are brightly painted. There is a 17th century palace and a colourful bazar. In the **Uhl river** valley is a hydroelectric dam with a power station downstream. Although there is little to see, it is worth stopping one night in this quaint town.

Excursion

The small **Rawalsar Lake**, 24 km SE of Mandi, with its floating reed islands, is a popular pilgrimage centre with Hindu, Buddhist and Sikh shrines on the lakeside. The colourful Buddhist monastery with prayer flags and prayer wheels, has a golden image.

Local festival

Feb/Mar: *Sivaratri Fair* is celebrated with a week of dance, music and drama. Temple deities are taken in procession with chariots and palanquins.

Local information

● Accommodation

D *Mayfair*, Seri Bazar, T 2570. 60 a/c or air-cooled with bath. Restaurant, exchange, travel. **C-D** *Manish Resorts*, 3 km bus stand, T 22330, above New Beas Bridge, Rs30 by taxi from bus stand. Lovely views and garden, friendly welcome, very clean, personal service by owner. **D** *Raj Mahal*, nr District Court, Main Bazar, T 2401. 16 rm with bath. Former Maharaja's Palace, has character but in need of attention. Restaurant, bar. **D** *Ashoka Holiday Inn*, nr Chohatta Bazar, Gandhi Chowk, T 2800. Reasonable rm. Restaurant. **D** *Standard*, nr Old Bus Stand, Main Bazar, T 2948. 15 rm with bath. Restaurant, terrace garden. Tourism **D** *Mandav*, nr bus stand, T 22123, 13 rm and good value. Restaurant (clean toilet, if you are driving through). **E** *Beas Guest House*, nr bus stand, T 23409, 4 rm, some very cheap dorm beds. **D** *Holiday Home*, Samkhater Bazar, T 22531, 3 rm. **E** *Shiva*, College Rd, nr old bus stand, T 24211, 12 rm. There are also a number of cheap and basic **F** hotels in town of which the *Adarsh* is quite good. Clean rm with bath.

● Places to eat

HP Tourism *Café Shiraz* nr Bhutnath Temple.

● Shopping

Handicrafts are sold nr Bhutnath Temple and in Seri Bazar.

The Kulu valley: the valley of the gods

From Mandi the road N enters the Kulu Valley, through which the Beas river flows to Mandi from the Rohtang Pass (3,985m). The pass was the gateway to Lahul and the distant lands of Central Asia which traded in wool and borax. It is enclosed to the N by the Pir Panjal range, to the W by the Bara Bangahal and to the E by the Parvati range. The approach is through a narrow funnel or gorge but in the upper part it extends outwards to almost 80 km width. The name Kulu is derived from *Kulantapith* 'the end of the habitable world'. It is steeped in Hindu religious tradition and it seems that every stream, rock and blade of grass is imbued with some religious significance.

For a long time the **Kulu kingdom** was restricted to the upper Beas Valley. The original capital was at **Jagatsukh**, a few km to the S of Manali. In the 15th century it was extended S to Mandi. In the 17th century the capital was shifted to Kulu and the kingdom's boundaries extended into and Spiti and as far E as the Sutlej. Kulu was strategically located on trade routes from N India to Ladakh and beyond, so was bound to attract outside interest. The Sikhs, for example contested Kulu's control of this section of the trade route. In 1847, Kulu came under British control and was governed from Dharamshala.

The **Kulu valley**, famous for its apple orchards, beautiful women, wooden temples and folk music and dance, is one of the most accessible of the Central Himalayan valleys. It is now a popular alternative to Kashmir. Whilst it is not the secluded backwater that it was, it is still a pleasant and restful haven after the rigours of travel. Best Season: mid-Mar to mid-Apr, mid-Sep to mid-Nov.

ROUTES The **NH 21** goes NE to **Pandoh** (19 km) where there is a dam on the Beas. At **Aut** (22 km, 910m; pronounced 'out') there is trout fishing (Season Mar and Apr). The Tourist Office issues licences. From Aut, a road branches off across the Beas into the Tirthan valley leading to the beautiful Rest House in **Shoja** (70 km), then crosses the Jalori Pass (3350m) before descending to the Sutlej Valley and linking up with the main Shimla-Tibet road. From Bhuntar a jeepable road goes off to the right to Jari and Manikaran in the Parvati valley.

Kulu

(*Pop* 14,500; *Alt* 1219m) Also known as Kullu , it is the district headquarters but not the main tourist centre. It sprawls along the W bank of the Beas and the grassy *maidans* on the S side are the sites for annual festivals such as Dasara which is usually vivid and colourful, when the town is well worth visiting. Best seasons mid Mar-Apr, mid Sep-Nov.

Places of interest

Sultanpur Palace contained some fine examples of the Kulu style of miniature painting, characterised by simple rural scenes and the lack of sophistication of the human subject. Most have been removed to Delhi.

The Temples These bulky curvilinear structures seem to resemble the huge boulders found in river beds and on hillsides. A peculiar feature of these Nagari temples is the umbrella-shaped covering made of wood or zinc sheets placed over and around the *amalaka* stone which forms the top of the spire.

The **Raghunathji Temple** is the temple of the principal god of the Dasara festival. The shrine houses an image of Shri Raghunath in his chariot. **Bhekhli**, a 3 km climb away, has excellent views from the **Jagannathi Temple**. There are also superb views from the walk up to the tiny **Vaishno Devi Temple**, 4 km N, on the Kulu-Manali road, where a small cave has an image of the goddess Vaishno. The walk is steep and not always well marked.

Bijli Mahadev is connected by jeepable road, 8 km from Kulu at 2435m. The temple is sited on a steep hill and has a 20m rod on top which is reputedly struck by *bijli* (lightning), shattering the stone *lingam* inside. The priests put the lingam together each time with *ghee* (clarified butter) and a grain mixture, until the next strike breaks it apart again.

Excursions

Bajaura Temple is on the banks of the Beas river, about 200m off the Kulu-Mandi road at **Hat** or Hatta. Some believe its ancient origins make it one of the oldest in the valley. It is a massive pyramidal structure magnificently decorated with images of Durga

Mahishamardini, Vishnu and Ganesh in the outer 3-sided shrines. Floriated scrollwork adorn the exterior walls. Inside this Siva temple is a large *yoni-lingam*. Accommodation: PWD *Rest House* at Bajaura.

Parvati Valley/Manikaran, 45 km can be walked or there is a 'luxury' coach service – details from Tourist Office. This valley runs NE from Bhuntar, 8 km S of Kulu. Attractive orchards and river valley scenery en route. The local legend describes how while Parvati bathed in the river, Naga, the serpent god stole her ear-rings (*manikaran*). At Siva's command he angrily blew them back from underground causing a spring to flow. Manikaran is a hot sulphur spring, purportedly the hottest in the world. The local people cook their food by the springs and there are separate baths for men and women. There is a temple to Rama and a Sikh temple. Unfortunately, this is a popular place for dropouts.

• **Accommodation** HP Tourism **D** *Parvati*, T 35, 12 rm, sulphur baths, restaurant, terraces.

• **Transport Road Buses**: local buses from Kulu via Bhuntar.

Local Festivals

End of Apr. Colourful 3-day *Cattle Fair* attracts villagers from the surrounding area. Numerous cultural events accompany. *Dasara* is a festival sacred to the goddess Durga. Elsewhere in India it is an occasion that tends to be overshadowed by *Diwali* which follows a few

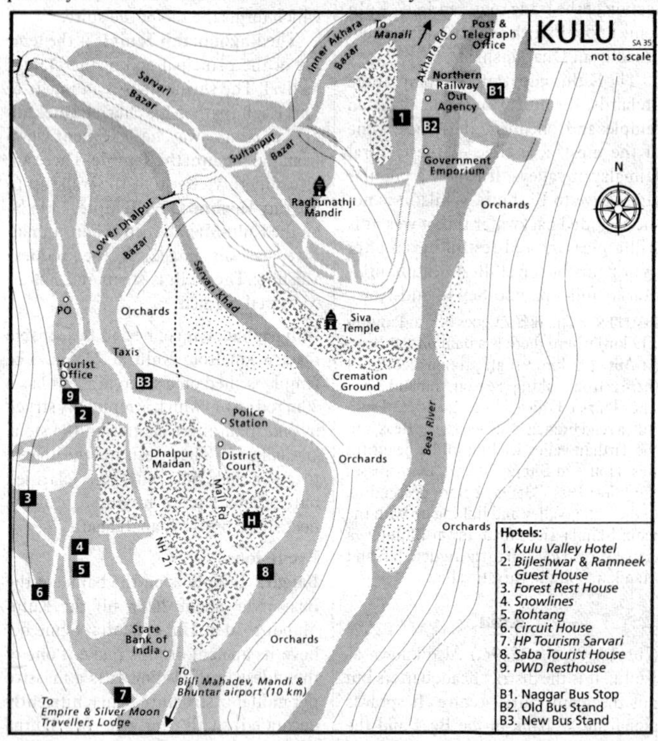

Dasara In Kulu

This festival celebrates Rama's victory over the demon Ravana. Elsewhere Ravana's effigy is burnt. In Kulu it is not. From their various high perches about 360 gods come to Kulu, drawn in their *raths* (chariots) by villagers to pay homage to Raghunathji who is ceremoniously brought from his temple in Kulu. The goddess Hadimba , patron deity of the Kulu Rajas has to come before any other lesser deities is allowed near. Her chariot is the fastest and her departure marks the end of the festivities. All converge on the maidan on the first evening of the festival in a long procession accompanied by shrill trumpeters. Thereafter there are dances, music and a market. During the high point of the fair a buffalo is sacrificed in front of a jostling crowd. Jamlu, the village God of Malana , high up in the hills, follows an old tradition. See page 550. He watches the festivities from across the river, but refuses to take part! On the last day Raghunathji's *rath* is taken to the river bank where a small bonfire is lit to symbolise the burning of Ravana, before Ragunathji is returned to his temple in a wooden palanquin.

NB: in recent years this religious event has become heavily commercialised.

weeks later. In this part of the Himalaya it is a great social event and a get-together of the Gods. Every village has a deity, and they all come to Kulu.

Local information

● Accommodation

Limited choice, most fairly basic. **C** ***Apple Valley Resorts***, Mohal, off the main road on the Beas river, T 4115. Comfortable, well designed modern chalets in landscaped grounds. Excellent food.

D ***Rohtang***, Dhalpur, T 2303. 12 rm with bath. Restaurant (Indian, Chinese). Simple, clean and good value. HP Tourism has two: the small **D** ***Silver Moon Travellers Lodge*** , T 2488 is rec. Perched on a hill, 2 km S from centre. 6 rm with bath and heaters. Good food. The cheaper **D** ***Sarvari***, 10 min walk from New Bus Stand, T 2471. 8 rm. Good dining hall, gardens. Elevated with good views and peaceful.

● Budget hotels

E ***Aroma Classic***, Circuit House Rd, T 3075. **E** ***Empire***, T 97, nr Travellers Lodge. 9 rm. Good food. **E** ***Shoba***, across Dhalpur maidan, T 2800. **E** ***Bijleshwar*** nr Tourist Office is well kept. Rm with fireplace.

F ***Ramneek***, nearby is good value. Also **F** ***Kulu Valley Hotel*** opp Old Bus Stand.

● Places to eat

Silver Moon and ***Rohtang*** have restaurants. Tourist Dept's ***Monal Caf*** nr Tourist Office does simple meals.

● Shopping

Best buys are shawls, caps, *gadmas*. Akhara Bazar has a ***Govt Handicrafts Emporium***, ***HP Khadi Emporium*** and ***Khadi Gramudyog***. ***Charm Shilp*** is good for sandals. ***Bhutti Weavers Colony*** 6 km away, has a retail outlet in town.

● Tourist Office

HP, T 2349, nr Maidan. 1000-1700. Local maps available.

● Transport

Air The airport is at Bhuntar, 10 km S of Kulu. **Transport to town**: buses and taxis at the airport. **Jagson**: **Delhi**, daily except Sun, 1125, 1¼hr. City Office, Dhalpur Maidan, T 2286. Also at *Hotel Amit*, nr Airport, T 122. **City Link**: daily to Delhi, 1200, 2 hr, via Chandigarh, ½ hr. Check schedules with travel agents.

Road Buses: there are several direct buses between Kulu and **Shimla** (235 km, 8½hr). **Dharamshala**, **Chandigarh** (by-passing Shimla, 270 km, 12 hr) and **Delhi** (512 km, 15-18 hr). Most services continue on to **Manali**. For Delhi 3 weekly luxury coaches in season. Use New Bus Stand nr Tourist Office. **Taxi**: between Kulu, Chandigarh and Shimla.

Kulu to Manali

ROUTES The climb continues from Kulu to Manali. There are 2 roads which go through terraced rice field and endless apple orchards. The direct, smoother road runs along the W bank of the Beas. The old road, along the other side is rougher, more circuitous and more interesting. Buses travel both routes, every 2 hr direct, and twice daily by the old road. Avoid the latter if it is wet.

Raison 8 km N of Kulu, is a grassy meadow favoured by trekking groups. Accommodation: HP Tourism E *Tourist Huts* by Beas river. 14 rm and Camping. Peaceful setting. Reserve at Kulu Tourist Office.

Katrain and Naggar, mid-way between Kulu and Manali, are on opposite sides of the river. The widest part of the Kulu Valley this is overlooked by Baragarh Peak (3325m). **Katrain** has good hotels. HP Tourism D *Apple Blossom*. 9 rm in 4 stone cottages, superb views. Spartan inside but with bathrooms. *River View* with family rm, is similar. Book through the Tourist Office, Kulu, T 2349. The expensive A *Span Resort*, Kulu-Manali Highway, T 8338, is very comfortable, but with C category facilities. It is very westernised with little local colour. 8 attractive stone cottages with 24 rm, overlooking the river. Restaurant, bar, travel, sports, riding. Resort dining room and Riverside Restaurant have good views. Trout hatchery nearby ensures good river fishing. Reservations at travel agents or *Span Motels*, GF-7, Surya Kiran, 19 Kasturba Gandhi Marg, New Delhi, T 3311434.

Across the bridge at **Patli Kuhl**, the road climbs through dark *deodar* forests to Naggar.

Naggar

Naggar is situated high above Katrain. The **Castle** is a fine example of timber-bonded building of W Himalaya which withstood the earthquake of 1905. Traditionally believed to have been built by Raja Sidh Singh in the early 16th century it was used as a royal residence and state headquarters until the 17th century when Raja Jagat Singh transferred the capital to Sultanpur (see Kulu). It continued as a summer palace until the British arrived in 1846, when it was sold to Major Hay, the first Asst Commissioner. He Europeanised part of it – fitted staircases, fireplaces etc. This quaint fort is built round a courtyard with verandahs with stunning views over the valley. It is now the very spartan hotel. Below the castle are about 40 *barselas* (sati stones) with primitive carvings.

There are a number of temples around the castle including the 11th century **Gauri Shankar Shiva**, nr the market. Facing the castle is the **Chatur Bhuj** to Vishnu. Higher up are **Tripura Sundari** with a multi-level pagoda roof in the Himachal style. Above that is the **Murlidhar Krishna** at Thawa claimed as the oldest in the valley, has a beautifully carved base. Damaged in the 1905 earthquake, it is now well restored.

Also above the castle is the **Nicholas Roerich Museum**. The views from this fine little museum are excellent. Check at the Kulu Tourist Information Office, T 2349, for opening times.

Roerich was born in St Petersburg in 1874, in a family of eminent jurists. He studied law to please his father but switched to painting and archaeology. In Russia he achieved great renown as an artist and set and costume designer for *Prince Igor* and other ballets (see page 1014). Shortly after the Russian Revolution, he left Russia with his wife and 2 sons visiting Finland, England and America where he earned great admiration. Already fascinated by the East, after meeting Tagore in London he planned his journey to India where he finally arrived in Nov 1923.

Nicholas travelled to Sikkim and Bhutan where while researching Buddhist manuscripts and planning his mammoth expedition across central Asia he began to paint the Himalaya. The family nearly perished on the return Trans-Himalayan expedition in 1929 (suspected for his Russian sympathies the British refused their return to India) and were only saved by being given temporary permission to regain their health in Darjiling, to avoid an 'international incident'. He returned to India where his ailing wife had been given permission to remain and settled in Naggar where the family set up the Urswati Institue of Himalayan Research. He lived here until his death in Dec 1947. His son Yuri was a renowned Tibetologist, while Svyatoslav, who later took up painting, settled in Bangalore.

• **Accommodation D/E** *Castle* with 14 simple rm, dorm. Restaurant (limited). Book in advance through Tourist Office, Kulu, T 2349. **E** *Poonam Fruit Garden* 6 rm in town is comparatively new. Also a *Forest Rest House*.

ROUTES If you are travelling on the old road, 12 km N of Naggar and 6 km S of Manali, is **Jagatsukh**, the capital of Kulu before Naggar. There are some very fine stone temples here including one of the late 13th with good carvings.

Manali

At the N end of the valley, Manali is the main tourist destination of the Kulu Valley but it is not a hill station and there are few Raj-style buildings. In the summer it is packed with Pahari-speaking Kulus, Lahaulis, Nepali labourers, Tibetan refugees and foreign and Indian tourists. The town of Manali is comparatively new and increasingly unattractive as it getting crowded with cheap hotels. Some visitors are disappointed to find yet another place becoming a hideout for a pot-smoking clique. The old village, 2 km away, is pleasanter and worth a visit. Apples are to Kulu what apricots are to Hunza, and Manali is the centre of a flourishing orchard industry. It is also the trailhead for a number of interesting and popular treks.

BASICS *Population*: 2600. *Altitude*: 1926m. *Climate*: Temp. Summer Max 25°C, Min 12°C. Winter Max 15°C, Min 3°C. Average annual rainfall 1780 mm. *Best season*: Spring (Mar-Apr) and post monsoon (Sep-Nov).

Places of interest

2 km pleasant walk from the Tourist Office is the Doongri Temple to **Hadimba Devi** (1553) in a clearing among ancient *deodars*. Built by Maharaja Bahadur Singh, the 27m high pagoda temple has a 3-tier roof and some fine naturalistic wood carving of animals and plants, especially around the doorway. The structure itself is relatively crude, and the pagoda is far from perfectly perpendicular. Massive deodar planks form the roof, but in contrast to the massive scale of the exterior wooden structures the brass image of the goddess Hadimba, enshrined inside, is tiny. To prevent the master craftsman producing another temple to equal this elsewhere, the king ordered his right hand to be cut off; the local legend relates how the artist trained his left hand to master the technique and reproduced a similar work of excellence at Trilokinath nr Udaipur in the Pattan Valley. Unfortunately, his new masters became equally jealous and cut off his head. See page 549. The goddess Hadimba plays an important part in the annual festival at Kulu as well as here in May.

The **Tibetan Monastery** built by refugees, is not old but is attractive and the centre of a small carpet making industry. Rugs and other handicrafts are for sale. The colourful **Market** sells Kulu shawls, caps and Tibetan souvenirs.

Vashisht (3 km N, 2200m), is a small hillside village that can be reached by road or by footpath (30-40 min walk from Tourist Office). Note the carvings on the houses of the wealthy farmers. The village has Vashisht and Rama temples with the sulphur springs to the right of the path before the village. Free hot springs at the top of the hill are very soapy since they are communal baths where you wash in other people's dirty water! The Vashisht **Hot Baths**, half way up the hill, where natural sulphur spring water is piped into a modern bath-house, with the old stone lined pool nearby is rec. Open 0700-1300, 1400-1600, 1800-2200. Rs 24 for ½ hr in a private bath. Caf serves hot and cold drinks, 0700-2200. Rec early morning or after trekking or rigourous road travel.

Walks

An interesting walk is along the N bank of the Manalsu river, W of old village. Relatively easy mule track with more adventureous tracks leading from it. Nehru Kund (6 km) is on the Keylong Rd.

Tours

A/c and deluxe coaches on Delhi-Manali and Shimla-Manali routes in summer and autumn. Book at HP Tourism, T 25. Full day tours daily during season (0900-1600): To Nehru Kund, Rahla Falls, Marhi, Rohtang Pass. Rs 500

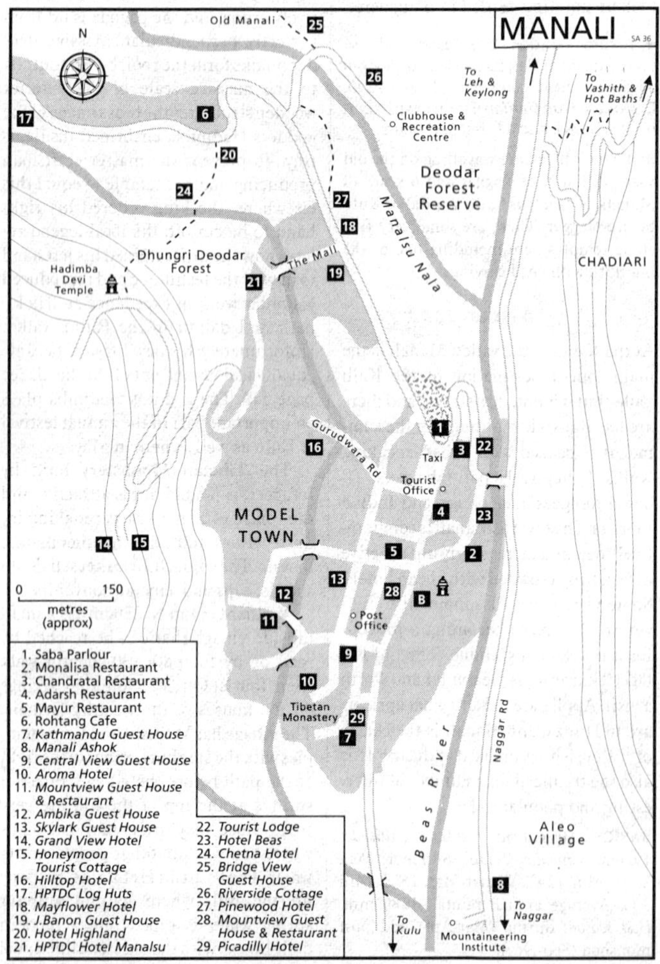

(car for 5), Rs 65 by luxury coach. Also To Naggar. Rs 225 (car for 5), Rs 35 by luxury coach. To Manikaran (0900-1800), Rs 600 (car for 5), Rs 70 by luxury coach.

Local Festivals

Mid-Feb: week-long winter sports carnival. **May**: 3-day colourful *Doongri Forest festival* at Hadimba Devi Temple, celebrated by hill women.

Local information

● Accommodation

Few hotels have a/c since it is not needed, though in winter heating is desirable. There are large discounts in winter. In the peak period (May-Aug) accommodation may be difficult (highest charges in May and Jun). The modest hotels may only provide hot water in buckets; many have a simple, rustic charm. HP Tourism **B** *Log Huts*, T 2134. 12 fully equipped 2-bed rm cottages in beautiful riverside setting. Cafeteria nearby and rm service. Peaceful.

C *Piccadilly*, The Mall, T 2149. 44 rm. Centrally heated. Good restaurant, bar, coffee shop, travel. **C** *Ambassador Resort*, Sunny Side, Chadiyari, overlooking Old Manali, T 2235. 40 rm. Restaurant, coffee shop. Interesting design, good views. Recently refurbished and upgraded. ITDC **C** *Manali Ashok*, Naggar Rd, Aleo, nr Mountaineering Inst, T 2331. 10 rm and suites with bath. Restaurant. Away from centre but quiet, with superb views; good value. **C** *Honeymoon Inn*, Aleo, T 2244. 37 rm. Restaurant, disco, tours. **C** *Preet*, NH21, T 2129. 34 rm. Restaurant, coffee shop. **C** *Panchratan Resorts*, nr Log Huts, T 2160. 30 rm. Centrally heated. Restaurant, bar, coffee shop, travel, car hire. Poor maintenance. **C** *John Banon's Guesthouse*, The Mall, T 2490. 12 rm with snowview. Full board (good western), garden. The Banon family has been in the valley for the last century and many of them are now running guesthouses. Peaceful in orchard, simple and rustic but very pleasant. **C** *Mayflower*, The Mall, T 2104, is similar. Warm welcome in charming guest house. New spacious, woodpanelled rm with log fires.

HP Tourism has several: **D** *Honeymoon Tourist Cottages*, T 2334. 12 fully furnished cottages. Pleasant, good value. **D** *Rohtang Manalsu*, nr Circuit House, The Mall, T 2332. 27 rm. Good restaurant. Covered in evergreen, way from centre but with superb views. **D** *Beas*, nr Tourist Office. 24 rm and dorm. Rm service. Magnificent river view. Cheaper **D** *Tourist Lodge*, on river bank. 4-bed rm with shared bath. Spartan; bring your own towel. Several in **D** category on the Mall. **D** *Holiday Home International*, nr Circuit House, Club House Rd, T 2010. 16 rm. Restaurant, car hire. Good bathrooms and good views. **D** *Pinewood*, The Mall, T 2113. 10 heated rm. Restaurant, gardens. Run by the Banon family. Attractive rooms (best upstairs), good views, quiet. **D** *Rohtang Inn*, opp Bus Stand, The Mall, T 2441. Modern rm, bath tubs. Meals. **D** *New Hope*, The Mall, T 78. 14 rm with phone and some with good mountain views. Restaurant, tours and trekking, winter sports. Simple, rustic, quiet, away from centre. Elsewhere: **D** *Chetna*, nr Log Huts, T 2245. 13 comfortable rm. Good open-air restaurant. TV. Elevated, with beautiful views. **D** *Kalpana* nearby, in forest setting, is cheaper. **D** *Highland*, nr Log Huts, T 2399. 34 rm (20 in new block well appointed), some with balcony. Restaurant, pleasant garden. Stone building with bright rooms, recently upgraded. **D** *Aroma*, Model Town, nr Tibetan monastery, T 2181. 12 rm with bath. Restaurant. **D** *Dev Lok* (Soland Resorts), Hadimba Rd, T 3125. Set in orchard with hill views.

● Budget hotels and Guest Houses

E *Hill Top*, School Rd, T 2140. 9 simple rm. Rm service, hilltop location. **E** *Sunshine*, The Mall, T 20. 10 rm. Restaurant. Away from centre, so quiet. Family atmosphere, rustic but with comfortable sitting rm. Good value. **E** *Mountview*, T 2465. Large rm, shower and western toilet, TV in some and rooftop terrace. Friendly, obliging. Off-season bargain, excellent value. Restaurant serves good pizzas and spaghetti. Rec. Many **E** and **F** hotels on the Mall, School Rd and Model Town offer modest rm, often with shared baths. Some have restaurants, others offer rm service. *Skylark*, *Kathmandu Guest House* and *Ambika*, T 2181, are in Model Town. Inspect rm first. *The Mountaineering Institute*, T 42 has a hostel.

Families in Old Manali take paying guests: **E** *River View*, T 2463, **E** *Bridge View* and **E** *Riverside Cottage* are nr Beas bridge. **F** *Youth Hostel*, on road to Vashisht. Basic, with dorm.

● Places to eat

Hotels may need advance notice from non-residents. The following in the town are rec: *Mehak*, (Indian veg), HP Tourism *Rohtang* , towards Log Huts, and upmarket *Adarsh* on the Mall; HP Tourism *Chandratal*, in town centre (Indian, Chinese) with *Sa Ba* (snack, pizzas) opp ; *Mountview*, Model Town (incl Japanese and Tibetan). Also rec: *Mayur* and the more expensive *Monalisa*. *Ashiana*, The Mall, nr Bus Stand, has good S Indian and Gujarati veg. Some of the hotels have **bars**. *Pete's Wholefood*, just down from State Bank. Delicious quiches, fresh bread, cakes and ground coffee. Rec in spite of flies and eccentric owner. In Old Manali: the more expensive *German Bakery* has good cakes, pizzas and breads. Several cheap good restaurants include *Peace and Freedom*. *Green Forest* with an unimpressive exterior — wooden hut and rickety chairs in front – serves the best fresh grilled trout.

● Banks & money changers
State Bank of India in town centre.

● Clubs
HP Tourism *Club House*, on river bank. Indoor sports and a well appointed restaurant.

● Hospitals & medical services
Mission Hospital, T 2379.

● Post & telecommunications
GPO: is nr Model Town.

● Shopping
Handicrafts and local curios at Main Market, Tibetan Bazar and Tibetan Carpet Centre. Govt shop on the Mall has a good selection. *Bookworm* behind the Taxi Stand.

● Sports
Skiing/Mountaineering: The Mountaineering and Allied Sports Institute (T 42), 1.5 km out of town organises courses in mountaineering, skiing, watersports, high altitude trekking and mountain-rescue courses. 5 and 7-day ski courses, Rs 3,000 for the latter, Jan-Mar. There is a hostel, an exhibition of equipment and an auditorium.

● Tour companies & travel agents
Himalayan Adventure, 1st Flr, Mayflower Guest House, T 2182, is rec. *International Trekkers*, Sunnyside, Chadiyari, T 2372, and *Arohi Travels*, The Mall, T 2139.

● Tourist office
HP, The Mall, T 2325.

● Useful address
Police Station: T 2326.

● Transport
From: **Shimla** (280 km); **Chandigarh** (312 km); **Delhi** (838 km); **Pathankot** (326 km); **Dharamshala** (253 km), **Udaipur** (Himachal, not Rajasthan, 166 km).

Air As for Kulu. Nearest airport at Bhuntar, 50 km. **Transport to town**: buses and taxis at the airport. *Ambassador Travels*, The Mall, T 110. 1000-1700, Jagsons agents.

Train Up to Chandigarh or Shimla and Jogindernagar, and then bus transfers.

Road Buses: deluxe and ordinary buses of various State Transport Corporations offer direct connections to all major towns in the neighbouring states. HRTC Bus Stand, The Mall. Reservations, 1000-1200,1400-1600. HPTDC daily services from **Delhi**: a/c coach, dep 0600, 16 hr, Rs 400; non-a/c Rs 250 (not rec as travellers in 1993 reported: drivers may be drunk and unsafe and crew rude and aggressive). From **Shimla**: non a/c coach, dep 0900, 9 hr, Rs 160. **Rohtang Pass**: day trip with many photo-stops (Rs 80) very worth while for stunning scenery (take a sweater/jacket)

LAHUL AND SPITI

Lahul (also referred to as Lahaul) and Spiti lie N of the Himalayan Axis in a rain shadow area; the terrain is very similar to Ladakh's. Upper Lahul comprises the Bhaga and Chandra valleys, Lower Lahul the region below the confluence. Spiti and Kinnaur lie to the E. The whole region can be approached by road from 3 directions: from **Shimla** via the Spiti Valley, along the road which runs up to the Tibetan border through Kinnaur; from **Manali** over the Rohtang Pass (3985m) into Upper Lahul; and from **Zanskar** and **Ladakh** over the Shingo La and Baralacha La (passes). The Shingo La gives access to Lahul from Zanskar (see Padum-Darcha trek description) while the Baralacha La (4880m) is on the Leh-Manali road and provides access to Lahul from Ladakh. There is a trekking route from Manali to Zanskar.

Lahul

Lying in the transition zone between the green alpine slopes of the Kulu and

Chamba valleys to the S and the dry, arid plateau of Ladakh, Lahul gets enough rain during the monsoon months to allow extensive cultivation, particularly on terraces, of potatoes, green peas and lately, hops for beer making. Lahul potatoes are some of the best in the country and are used as seed material for propagation. Hops, potatoes and rare herbs have brought wealth to the area. Most people follow a curious blend of both Hindu and Buddhist customs though there are a few who belong wholly to one or the other religion.

Spiti

The climate in Spiti is much drier than in the Kulu valley and is similar to the climate of Ladakh. The temperatures are more extreme both in summer and winter and most of the landscape is barren and bleak. The wind can be bitingly cold even when the sun is hot. The annual rainfall is very low so cultivation is restricted to the ribbons of land that fringe rivers with irrigation potential. The crops are chosen for their hardiness and include potatoes, wheat, barley and millet. The local inhabitants farm suitable land, raise goats and traditionally have combined this with some Tibetan trading. The people are of Mongol origin and almost everyone follows a Tibetan form of Buddhism.

Early history

Historically there are similarities between this region and Ladakh since in the 10th century Lahul, Spiti and Zanskar were part of the Ladakh kingdom. The Hindu Rajas in Kulu paid tribute to Ladakh. In the 17th century Ladakh was defeated by a combined Mongol–Tibetan force. Later Lahul was separated into Upper Lahul which fell under the control of Kulu, and Lower Lahul which came under the Chamba Rajas. The whole region came under the Sikhs as their empire expanded, whilst under the British Lahul and Kulu were part of the administrative area centred on Kangra. Spiti was part of the Maharaja of Kashmir's state of Kashmir and Ladakh but was later exchanged for territories formerly belonging to Kangra. The British improved communications but little else since strategic considerations were far more important than economic development.

Manali to Leh

This is the main route for foreigners into the region of Lahul and Spiti. The 530 km highway is usually open from the end of June to mid-Oct. The first 52 km crosses the Kulu valley, then climbs through the Rohtang Pass into Lahul. The journey, which has memorable mountain scenery but some scary roads, is best done with 2 night stops, possible at Keylong (see below), Sarchu and Pang which have campsites with tents on terraces above the river valley. You may continue all the way to Leh (no permits necessary). The highest pass on the route is the 5370m Taglang La.

ROUTES From Manali the road continues N through cultivated tracts and sheltered valleys before climbing steeply through Rahala (Rohla,19 km, 2600m), where there is a 70m high waterfall, to the Rohtang Pass (34 km, 3985m)

Rohtang Pass From the pass you get spectacular views of precipitous cliffs, deep ravines, large glaciers and moraines. In season, HP Tourism runs a daily bus tour from Manali to the pass and back which is popular with Indian tourists who want to see and feel snow. Details from Tourist Office. Manali.

ROUTES The road then descends by steep hairpin bends to Saspol (tea stalls) in the Chandra valley, and a further 18 km to a road junction. The left turn goes to Khoksar (3 km, 3170m) where there is a checkpoint and all passorts must be registered. The road remains at this height all the way to Patsio (92 km). The highway then continues through willows and poplars to Sissu (3130m) where you can cross the bridge over the river to see the attractive waterfall. The villagers cultivate potato and peas, barley and buckwheat on terraces. Gondhla is 15 km away, followed by Tandi, where the Chandra and Bhaga rivers meet to form the Chenab or Chandrabhaga, and then Keylong (116 km from Manali).

Gondhla (3160m) is worth stopping at to see the "Castle" belonging to the local *Thakur* (ruler) built around 1700. The 7-storey house with staircases made of wooden logs, has a verandah running around the top and numerous apartments on the various floors. The 4th Flr was for private prayer; while the Thakur held court from the verandah. There is much to see in this neglected, ramshackle house, particularly old weapons, statues, costumes and furniture. The 'Sword of wisdom' believed to be a gift from the Dalai Lama some time ago, is of special interest. On close inspection you will notice thin wires have been hammered together to form the blade, a technique from Toledo, Spain! The huge rock near the Government School, which some claim to be of ancient origin, has larger-than-life figures of *Bodhisttvas* carved on it.

Keylong

(3350m) The principal town of the district, Keylong is set amidst fields of barley and buckwheat surrounded by brown hills and snowy peaks and was once the home of Moravian missionaries. The local deity 'Kelang Wazir' is kept in Shri Nawang Dorje's home which you are welcome to visit. There is a Tibetan Centre for Performing Arts. Traders and trekkers negotiate the pass out of season.

As in the rest of this region, monasteries abound. **Khardong Monastery** (3.5 km), across the Chandra river, up a steep tree-shaded path, is the most important in the area. It is believed to have been founded 900 years ago and was renovated in 1912. Nuns and monks enjoy equality; married lamas spend the summer months at home cultivating their fields and return to the monastery in winter. The monastery with its 4 temples contain a huge barrel drum, a valuable library and collections of *thangkas*, Buddha statues, musical instruments, costumes and ancient weapons. **Sha-Shur Monastery**, (1 km) has ancient connections with Bhutan and contains numerous wall paintings and a 4.5m thangka. The annual festival is held in Jun/Jul.

• **Accommodation** E *Tourist Bungalow*, now with solar heated pool, rm with bath and 2-bed 'Swiss cottage' tents. Meals to order. Also PWD **E** ***Rest House***. Mainly for officials; rm with shared bath may be available (bring sleeping bag). Reservations, Deputy Commissioner, Keylong.

• **Places to eat** several local restaurants on main road, *Vikrant* rec (good goat curry).

• **Transport** **Road** From Manali takes 7/8 hr.

Around Keylong

At the confluence of the Chandra and Bhaga rivers, **Guru Ghantal** on a hill above Tupchiling village (where there is a caretaker) was founded by Padma Sambhava 800 years ago. The images here are made of wood instead of the usual clay; a black Kali image in stone suggests its Hindu origin. Sadly the damp is taking its toll on the wall paintings in the monastery; Tupchiling now houses some of its treasures. **Tayul Monastery**, above Satingri village, has a 4m high statue of Padma Sambhava, wall paintings and a library containing valuable scriptures and *thangkas*. The mani wheel here is supposed to turn on its own marking specially auspicious occasions, the last time having been in 1986.

Jespa (21km, 3200m) has a camp site and a mountaineering institute.

ROUTES The road continues over the Baralacha La (54 km, 4880m), 107 km from Keylong, at the crossroads of Lahul, Zanskar, Spiti and Ladakh regions before dropping to **Sarchu** (HP border). It then runs beyond **Brandy Nala** by the Tsarap river before negotiating 22 spectacular hairpin bends crossing the Nakli La (4950m) and **Lachalung La** (5065m). It then descends past tall earth and rock pillars, and through **Pang**, a summer settlement in a narrow valley (overnight stops in communal tents only possible) before arriving on the 40 km wide Moray plains (4400m). The road climbs to **Taglang La** (5370m), the highest pass on this road and the 2nd highest in the world, (view point). It descends slowly towards the valley, passing small villages, before entering a narrow gorge with purple coloured cliffs. The road turns left to continue along the Indus basin passing **Upshi** with a sheep farm and a checkpost, and **Thikse**, before reaching Leh. **Note** See under Transport below for road conditions.

SHIMLA TO MANALI-LEH HIGHWAY

Old Hindustan Tibet Road

The road from Shimla to the Tibetan border has now been extended into a loop which connects with the main Manali-Leh highway just N of Manali, following the Sutlej and then the Spiti rivers through Kinnaur and Spiti. It is a fascinating and scenically beautiful route. Accommodation is either in simple *Rest Houses* and *Lodges* or in tents. In some places enterprising local families are opening their modest homes to paying guests. Local village shops often stock canned food and bottled water, and you may be surprised by the advent of television even in remote villages.

NB: 'Inner Line' permits are required for travel close to the Tibetan border. Groups of 4 may obtain a permit but not stay overnight. The 'Inner Line' runs parallel to and 40 km inside the border; all visitors are barred except for places like Kaza which fall within 40 km but are specifically exempt. Overnight stay is not permitted in Puh, Khabo, Sumdo, Dankar Gompa and Tabo. See **Trekking** in Information for Visitors. Rules may be further relaxed, so check with the Tourist Office in Delhi or Shimla on the current position.

ROUTES The road to the Tibetan border (520 km from Shimla) goes E from the bus stand to Dhali (8 km) where there is a road on the left to **Mashobra** (6 km, 2150m). This is an attractive picnic spot with good forest walks. 3 km further on is **Craignano** (2280m) which has a hilltop *Rest House*. Go straight on to Kufri.

Kufri

(Alt 2500m) This is Himachal's best known ski resort, 16 km from Shimla. Best time Jan and Feb, with an annual winter sports festival in the 1st week of Feb. At **Danes Folly** (2550m) 5 km away is a government run orchard. The road continues to Naldera.

• **Accommodation**: **C** *Kufri Holiday Resort*, T 8341. 21 rm in 8 cottages. Modern with facilities of a western holiday resort – restaurant, barbecue, coffee shop, bar, health club, meditation centre. Good for walks. At weekends, the outdoor barbecue has the option of allowing you to cook while they provide! *Rest House* can be booked through Tourist Officer, The Ridge, Shimla.

Naldera

(Alt 2050m) A diversion from the main road 26 km N of Shimla, has a 9-hole golf course which claims to be the oldest in India. The Mahung temple is beautiful.

HUMAN SACRIFICE IN THE HIMALAYA

Human sacrifice was practised for centuries in the original Bhimkali temple in Sarahan. During the 16th and 17th centuries such sacrifice was carried out with elaborate rituals. The sacrificial victim would be kept in the adjoining *Narasimha Temple*. After the ritual offering his blood would be placed on Bhimakali's tongue for her to 'drink' and would then be used to wash the feet of a second deity *Ushadevi*. The priest would also place a mark of blood on the forehead of each worshipper. The sacrificed head would finally be thrown into the Sutlej river and the body into the well, which is now blocked.

In Jun there is the colourful *Sipi Fair* which attracts crowds from the surrounding villages who bring handicrafts to sell.

• **Accommodation**: HP Tourism **E** *Golf Glade*, 12 rm. Restaurant, café. Reserve at Shimla, T 78311.

ROUTES The main road goes through Theog (10 km, 2250 m) and Narkanda (2700m). From Luhri (800m) it follows the Sutlej River, passing through the large district town of Rampur to **Jeori** (Jiuri, 160 km from Shimla).

Rampur, 130 km, is an important market town. It has a Buddhist monastery with a huge prayer wheel and a Hindu temple. The *Lavi Fair* (Nov 11-14) draws large crowds of colourful hill people who bring their produce to the special market and enjoy sporting competitions, dancing and making music. Rampur Palace, erstwhile residence of the Rampur Rajah's built in the 1920s, has interesting carved wooden panels and wall murals, just opposite the Bus Stand.

• **Accommodation** **E** PWD *Rest House*, *Tourist Bungalow* and small hotels.

• **Transport** **Road Buses**: to and from Shimla take 8 hr.

Sarahan

(*Alt* 1850m) 21 km and a steep uphill drive from S of Jeori (½ hr drive) and 40 km E of Rampur, was an important market town for traders of neighbouring regions. An attractive town amidst apple orchards, it has a pheasant breeding centre.

Sarahan was the old capital of the local rulers and has a fort and the strikingly carved wooden **Bhimakali Temple** (rebuilt c1927) in a mixture of Hindu and Buddhist styles. It is dedicated to the worship of Durga as the destroyer of the *asuras* (demons). According to some sources the ancient brick and mortar temple is many centuries old. Closed for safety reasons, it has a silver covered wooden door. The 2 temples stand on a slope among apple and apricot orchards. Plan for an early morning visit to the temple to see morning prayers.

The hilltop Himachali temples differ in style from those on the plains in being dedicated to local gods and goddesses instead of to the major deities, and in being built by local rulers instead of kings. The unusual renovated Bhimakali Temple is 2-storeyed, standing on a tall towerlike base which houses the stairs; the roof shape is borrowed from a Tibetan *gompa*. Built in the traditional style with white-washed stone masonry and horizontal cedar logs, the upper floors have balconies and windows which are clad in superb ornamental woodcarving. The 1st floor has a 200 year old gold image of goddess Bhimkali which is actively worshipped only during the *Dasara* festival, while on the 2nd floor, daily early morning *puja* is carried out to a second image. The 3 other shrines are to Raghunath, Narsingh and Sri Lanka Bir. The place is dominated by Shrikhand Mahadev Peak (5227m) which takes pilgrims 7 days to circle round. Accommodarion: E *Shrikhand*, on a hilltop, overlooks the narrow valley and hills. 30 rm with bath and hot water. Reservations: HP Tourism, Shimla.

Kinnaur

An exciting mountain road through cliffside cuttings along the left bank of the Sutlej, leads from Jeori to **Wangtu** where the river is crossed and vehicles details are noted down. Immediately after crossing the Wangtu bridge a narrow side road goes to **Kafnoo** village (2427m) in the **Bhabha Valley**. It is a 5 hr drive from Sarahan to Kafnoo, which is a camping site and the start for an attractive 10-day trek to the Pin Valley. For **trekking** here, see page 549.

Baspa Valley

ROUTES The road route from Wangtu runs to Tapri (1470m) near where the 'Inner Line' permits are checked, and

Karchham (1899m), where the Baspa river joins the Sutlej.

There is a hair-raising excursion by a precipitous winding rough road to **Sangla** (2680m), a village built up the slope. The old Kamru **Fort** a few km N, occupied by the local rulers for centuries and where the Kinnaur rajas were once crowned, now has a temple to Kamakshi; the idol is from Guwahati, Assam, see page 685. There is a *Rest House* and **C** *Camping Banjava*, superb site, 10 km beyond Sangla, excellent facilities, highly rec. Beyond Sangla, the valley widens and the road passes through wooded hillsides to picturesque **Chitkul** (18 km, 3450m) with small houses, monasteries and temples. There is a *Forest Rest House*. The valley has saffron farms (claimed to be better than at Pampore, Kashmir) and is famous for its apples; the climate is ideal- especially as there is no hail damage.

Another side road to the left from Powari on the National Highway, takes you up to **Recong Peo** (1990m, 7 km) the District HQ. A monastery commemorates the Dalai Lama's Kalachakra Sermon delivered here in August 1992.

The road then climbs steeply to **Kalpa** (2960m, 13 km) and on to Chinni *Forest Rest House* (2 km). The modern building has superb views over valleys and mountain peaks of the Kinner Kailash, including a unique view of Shiva Linga peak.

NB: Travellers are not allowed beyond this point without an 'Inner Line' permit from the District magistrate. Contact District Magistrate's office in Shimla.

The road from Kalpa passes through coniferous forests, though there are apple orchards around the hamlet of Pangi, then bare and rugged hills beyond Morang. **Morang** has impressive monasteries containing wood carvings and sculptures. There is a **F** *Forest Rest House* and a provision store. The road continues to Jangi where there is a checkpost and to Puh. Khabo (2831m), a morning's drive from Kalpa, is at the confluence of the Sutlej and Spiti rivers, just S of Kah which is a steep climb with hairpin bends. The road follows the Spiti while the Sutlej valley disappears to the E towards the Tibet border. **Sumdo**, the last village of Kinnaur at the divide between the Hamrang Valley and the Spiti Valley, has a Border Police checkpost and a tea shop.

Spiti

The 180 km State Highway (SH 30) which joins Sumdo with Batal then passes through an arid valley with small patches of cultivation of peas and barley near the snow melt streams, to Tabo (31 km). For treks in this area, see page 535.

Tabo (3050m), a small town between high hills where there is a checkpost, is rapidly being modernised with paved streets and electric lights. New government offices have appeared alongside traditional mud homes while the local shops sell goods for trekkers the villagers have never seen before.

Tabo Gompa (c996) is regarded as one of the oldest and possibly the most important in the country, noted especially for its colourful wall paintings which some compare to those at Ajanta (natural vegetable dyes and powdered stone colours were mixed with *dzo* milk and yak urine). It houses 60 lamas and has a good collection of scriptures, *thangkas* and art pieces including clay images of the Buddha in 1000 poses. **Note** Carry a torch when visiting gompas. No photography here.

A new monastery outside, furnished in the Tibetan style, also displays wall paintings and more recent works of art. N of the monastery there are several small caves above the road which were once used by the lamas. These are being restored by the Archaeological Survey of India and will be open once work is completed. A Tourist Information counter is planned.

Dankar (25 km), once the capital of Spiti, is a tiny village. It has a beautiful large pond at just under 4100m which is reached by a 2.5 km track. Boating may be possible. On a hilltop the early 16th century fort/monastery **Dankar Gompa** (3890m) once served as a jail. Today it has over 160 lamas in residence, a collection of Bhotia Buddhist scriptures and a four-in-one *Dhyan Buddha* figure. The gompa is a 2 hr steep climb from a point 2 km beyond Sichling on the main road.

About 5 km from Dankar is a sign for the Pin Valley National Park which is on the other side of the river; the Pin river joins the Spiti opposite the village of Lingti. 10 km along the Pin valley, above Attargo, is the **Ghungri Gompa** (c1330) which shows evidence of Tantric Buddhism as practised in this valley. The trek from the Bhabha Valley ends at the road head at Ghungri.

The 60 km long Lingti Valley is famous for its **fossils**; Shilla peak (6300m), one of the highest in HP, is at the northern head of the valley; the highest is Chau Chau Kang Nilda or CCKN (6794m). The road continues to climb to Kaza following the Spiti River which in places makes a very wide valley.

Pin Valley National Park The Pin Valley is described as the "land of Ibex and snow leopard". It adjoins the Gt Himalayan National Park (SW) and Rupi Bhabha Wildlife Sanctuary (S) with the Bara Shigri Glacier forming its N boundary. The park covers 675 sq km with a buffer zone of 1150 sq km mainly to its E where there are villages, and varies in altitude from 3600m to 6630m. Although the scenery in rugged, the summer brings a little more rain here than the rest of Spiti, resulting in a profusion of wild flowers.

The wildlife includes Siberian Ibex, snow leopard, red fox, pika, weasels, lammergeier, Himalayan griffon, Golden eagle, Chakor partridge, Himalayan snow cook and a variety of rose finches. The Siberian Ibex can be sighted at high altitudes, beyond Hikim and Thango village. From July to September the young Ibex kids need protection; the females move up to the higher pastures near cliffs while the adult males concentrate on feeding lower down.

Kaza (3600m) is 13 km from Lingti village with the Ki Monastery, a further 12 km along the road on the hill above, visible from the State Highway. Old Kaza has village homes while New Kaza sports government offices. It is a Bus terminus, has a small market, a basic health centre and jeeps for hire.

• **Accommodation** *Rest Houses* of PWD with 7 rm; *Electricity Board*, 4 rm, and some small hotels. Ideal for camping. Irrigation Dept has a 2 rm *bungalow* at Rangrik (4 km). The local *Rani* hopes to open a modern hotel nearby.

• **Transport Road Buses**: from Manali (201 km) take 12 hr via Rohtang Pass and Kunzum La. From Shimla (412 km) on the route described, it takes 2 days.

From Kaza, a road to the right goes to **Kibber** (4205m), which has a school, post office and a bank. It claims to be highest village in the world connected by road, a claim which would be disputed by similar villages in Peru and Bolivia. **Ki Monastery** (7 km) on the way is the largest in Spiti and houses 300 lamas, rare paintings and sculptures. Lamas receive religious instruction but also take part in singing, dancing and playing horn pipes.

Lalung gompa known for its carved wood panelling is off the SH 30, 22 km from Kaza, reached by 8 km narrow, motorable track. **Losar** (4079m), 55 km from Kaza, the last village in Spiti is reached after driving through fields growing peas and cabbage, among poplars, willows and apple orchards.

The road continues up to the **Kunzum La** (Pass) (18 km, 4551m) meaning "meeting place for ibex", which gives access to Lahul and good views of some of the highest peaks of the Chandrabhaga

(CB) group notably CB 14, 16 and 17 that lie immediately opposite the Kunzum La. The pass has an ancient chorten marker. The new temple to Gyephang, the presiding deity, is circumambulated by those crossing the pass; the giver of any offering in cash which sticks to the stone image receives special blessing.

ROUTES The road does 19 hairpin bends to descend down the rock strewn terrain to the valley of the River Chandra to **Batal**, and on to **Chhota Dhara** and **Chhatru**, (both have 2-rm PWD *Rest Houses*) and **Gramphoo** joining the Manali-Keylong-Leh highway (3 hr journey from the pass). See page 548.

SHIMLA TO KANGRA, DHARAMSHALA AND CHAMBA

You can reach the Kangra Valley from Shimla to the E, Hoshiarpur to the S. Pathankot to the W is linked by a superb narrow gauge mountain railway. The fastest route by road from New Delhi is via Ambala, Ludhiana and Hoshiarpur. For **trekking** in this area, see page 553.

ROUTES From Shimla take the road that goes to Mandi (124 km) – see page 521 and NW to **Jogindernagar** (56 km; 1220m). Accommodation: HP Tourism D *Tourist Bungalow*, on hill out of town, T 2575. 7 rm, best upstairs with balcony, and dorm. Simple, clean and peaceful. Restaurant, bar. The road continues at the same height to Baijnath (22 km) with a PWD *Rest House*.

• **Transport Train** Beautiful journey by narrow gauge rail from Pathankot 0750 and 1220, 9½ hr.

Baijnath

The temples here are old by hill standards, dating from at least 1204. The **Vaidyanatha Temple** (originally c800) which contains one of 12 *jyotirlingas* stands by the roadside on the Mandi-Palampur road, within a vast rectangular enclosure. Originally known as **Kirangama**, its name was changed after the temple was built to Siva in his form as Vaidyanath, the Lord of Physicians. It is a good example of the Nagari style; the walls have the characteristic niches, and the *sikhara* (tower) has an *amalaka* and pot finial at the summit. The niches enshrine images of Chamunda, Surya and Karttikeya and a life-size stone Nandi stands at the entrance. There are miniature shrines and memorial stones. The temple faces W and has an antechamber supported by 4 carved pillars. Note the Lakshmi/Vishnu figure and the graceful balcony window on the N wall.

• **Accommodation E** *Chamunda, Shankar View* and *Tourist Inn*.

Palampur

(1260m; *Pop* 3600), 16 km (40 km from Dharamshala via Yol). A pleasant little town for walking, with beautiful snow views, surrounded by old British tea plantations, thriving on horticulture. The Neughal Khad, a 300m wide chasm through which the Bundla flows is very impressive when it swells during the monsoons.

• **Accommodation Note**: Taxis are needed for first 3 hotels from bys or train station: **C** *Silver Oaks Resort*, Bandla Tea Estate, T 2442. 10 large rm with impressive reception area. Quiet scenic location on hill 3 km from bus stand (past *Masand Hotel*). Furnishing not completed 1994. **C** *Masand*, 2 km bus stand, T 2405, 8 rm, restaurant, clean, on hill away from bazar. **D** *Palace Motel*, in former Taragarh Palace, Al-hilal, few km away, T Baijnath 3034. 12 rm with period furniture. Luxurious suites, tastefully decorated. Good restaurant, lovely gardens and mango orchards. HP Tourism **D** *T-Bud*, (tea-pickers pick 'a bud and 2 leaves') 1 km from bus stand in a beautiful setting, T 2081, adequate, but lacks maintenance. 12 rm and cheaper dorm, hot water. Restaurant, extensive garden. Clean and quiet. **D** *Sawhney*, T 2133. 22 rm. Also **D** *Yamini*, T 2588, in town, decent, cheap dorm, and *Masand Nayar*, T 2415 with 10 rm. Several other good hotels and motels.

• **Transport Air** Nearest airport is at Gaggal, 28 km. **Train** From Delhi via Pathankot. **Road Bus**: via Kangra.

Andretta nr Palampur is a peaceful, attractive village associated with Norah Richards, a follower of Mahatma Gandhi who popularised rural theatre and the artist Sardar Sobha Singh who revived the Kangra School of painting. Today there is a community of artists and a potters' society.

Kangra Valley

The Kangra Valley situated between the Dhaula Dhar and the Shiwalik foothills, starts near Mandi and runs NW to Shahpur near Pathankot. It is named after the town of Kangra, but now the largest and main centre is Dharamshala. From Palampur the road continues winding W, closely following and crossing the railway line.

In 1620 Shah Jahan captured Kangra fort for his father Jahangir, and Kangra became a Mughal province. During Muhammad's invasion, many of the court artists fled to neighbouring Chamba and Kulu and the Rajas submitted to Mughal rule. On its decline the 16 year old **Sansar Chand Katoch II** (1775-1823) recaptured the fort and the Rajas reasserted their independence. Under his powerful leadership Kangra sought to extend its boundaries into the Chamba and Kulu Valleys. This was forestalled when the vigorous and powerful Gurkhas arrived from Nepal and conquered what is now the hill region of UP and HP. With the rise of the Sikh Empire, the valley was occupied until the Treaty of Amritsar. Under the British, Dharamshala was made the administrative capital of the region which led to the decline of Kangra.

Kangra School of Painting Raja Goverdhan Singh (1744-1773) of Guler gave shelter to many artists who had fled from the Mughals, and during the mid-18th century a new style of miniature painting developed based on Mughal miniature painting, but the subject matter was different – the theme derived from Radha/Krishna legends; rajas and the gods were depicted in a local setting. Under Sansar Chand II the region prospered and the **Kangra School** flourished. Kangra fort where he held court for nearly 25 years was adorned with paintings and attracted art lovers from great distances. Later he moved his capital to Nadaun and finally to **Sujanpur Tira** (80 km) and at each place the temples and palaces were enriched by artists. The 1905 earthquake damaged many of these buildings though you can still see some miniature wall paintings. Fortunately thousands of paintings have been preserved in the Museums at Chamba, Chandigarh and Delhi.

Kangra

(450m) 18 km S of Dharamshala, formerly much more extensive, was once the second most important kingdom in the W Himalayas after Kashmir. The capital, Kangra, was also known as Bhawan or Nagarkot, and overlooks the Banganga River and claims to have existed since the Vedic period with historical reference in Alexander's war records. **Kangra fort** (see above) stands on a steep rock dominating the valley. A narrow path leads up to the fort which was once protected by several gates and had the palace of the Katoch kings at the top.

Brajesvari Devi Temple in Kangra Town, achieved a reputation for wealth in gold, pearls and diamonds and attracted many invaders over centuries. Muhammed of Ghazni sacked it in 1008, in 1337 Muhammed-bin-Tughluq plundered it, Sikander Lodi destroyed the idols early in the 15th century and it was sacked yet again by Khawas Khan in 1540. In the intervening years the temple was rebuilt and refurbished several times but in the great earthquake of 1905 both the temple and the fort were badly damaged.

The Devi received unusual offerings from devotees; according to Abul Fazal, the pilgrims "cut out their tongues which grew again in the course of 2 or 3 days and sometimes in a few hours"! The present temple was built in 1920 and stands behind the crowded, colourful bazar; the deity sits under a silver dome with silver *chhatras* (umbrellas). The State Govt maintains the temple; the priests are expected to receive gifts in kind only.

Local information

● Accommodation

E ***Jai Hind***, T 197. 10 rm, dorm. **E** ***Preet***, T 260 has 10 rm. Several others incl ***Anand***, 10 rm and ***Mountview***, 8 rm. ***Gupt Ganga*** Dharamshala has 30 rm and 3 halls. Please leave a donation.

● Transport

Air Gaggal airport is 7 km from Kangra.

Train Narrow gauge **Pathankot**: *Kangra Valley Exp*, 1615, 3½ hr. From Pathankot *Kangra Valley Exp*, 0850, 3½ hr, continues to Baijnath, 2 hr.

Road Dharamshala: a traveller suggests you cross the railway track and follow the path all the way down to the road bridge, way below; stop the bus to Dharamshala on the opposite side of the bridge after it has crossed it.

Excursions

Masrur,

(*Alt* 800m) 15 km S of Kangra (22 km by road), A sandstone ridge to the NE of the village has fifteen 9-10th century *sikhara* temples excavated out of solid rock. Although their remote location protected them from Mahmud of Ghazni and their stone construction prevented severe damage in the 1905 earthquake, they are badly eroded and partly ruined. Even in this state they have been compared with the larger rock cut temples at Ellora in Maharashtra and those at Mamallapuram S of Madras. Their ridge top position commands a superb view over the surrounding fertile countryside, but few of the original *shikharas* stand, and some of the most beautifully carved panels are now in the State Museum, Shimla. The main shrine dominates the centre.

Jawalamukhi

34 km S of Kangra, this is one of the most popular Hindu pilgrimage sites in HP recognised as one of 51 *Shakti pitha*. The **Devi temple** tended by the followers of Gorakhnath is set against a cliff and from a fissure comes a natural inflammable gas which accounts for the blue 'Eternal Flame'. Natural springs feed the 2 small pools of water; one appears to boil, the other with the flame flaring above the surface contains surprisingly cold water. **Note** Emperor Akbar's gift of gold leaf cover of the dome. In Mar/Apr there are colourful celebrations during the *Shakti Festival*; another in mid-Oct. **Accommodation:** HP Tourism D *Jwalaji*, T 2280. Some a/c rm, dorm. Also a PWD *Rest House*. The road N climbs the 18 km to Dharamshala.

Dharamshala

Founded in 1855, Dharamshala has one of the most spectacular settings for a Hill Station. It is built along a spur of the Dhaula Dhar range and varies in height from 1250m at the bazar to 1800m at McLeodganj. Surrounded by *deodar* forests, it is set against a backdrop of peaks rising to over 4750m on 3 sides. Superb views over the Kangra Valley and Shiwaliks, and of the great granite mountains that almost overhang the town.

It was one of the 80 hill stations established by the British between 1815 and 1847, though not quite on a par with Shimla, Nainital and Mussoorie in terms of popularity and size. McLeodganj is 450m higher than Dharamshala. As a result temperatures vary sharply. The distance between them is almost 10 km by road but there is a shorter, steeper path (3 km) that takes about 40 min on foot.

BASICS *Population*: 8600. *Altitude*: 1250-1980m. *STD Code*: 01892. *Climate*: Summer Max 38°C, Min 22°C, Winter Max 15°C, Min 0°C. Annual rainfall 2900-3800 mm, mostly Jun-Sep.

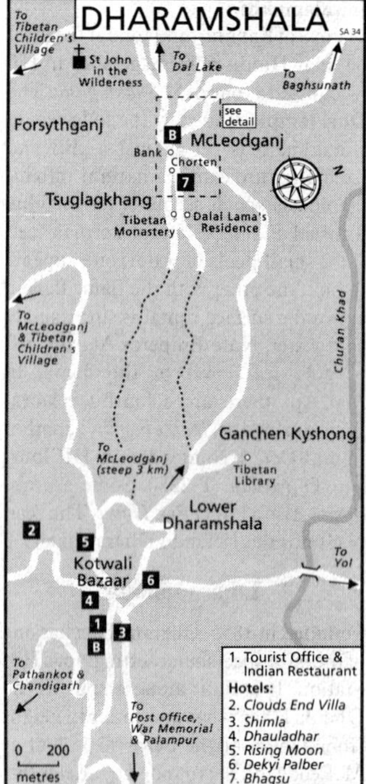

Tibetan influence There is a strong Tibetan influence here although some visitors are disappointed since it lacks a Buddhist feel. The **Dalai Lama** settled here after his flight across the Himalaya following the Chinese invasion of Tibet in Oct 1959. The Tibetan community has tended to take over the hospitality business and provide cheap but clean little hotels and small friendly restaurants serving old favourites like banana pancakes for the western visitor. The hippy community once flocked here in large numbers.

Places of interest

The Church of **St John-in-the-Wilderness** (1860) with attractive stained glass windows, is a short distance below McLeodganj on the way to Forsythganj. Along with other buildings in the area, it was destroyed by the earthquake of 1905 but has been rebuilt. The 8th Lord **Elgin**, one of the few Viceroys to die in office, is buried here according to his wish as it reminded him of his beloved native Scotland.

The **Namgyal Monastery** at McLeodganj with the Centre of Tibetan Studies is known as Little Lhasa. This Tsuglagkhang ('cathedral') opposite the Dalai Lama's residence, resembles the centre of the one in Lhasa. The Tsuglagkhang is a 5 min walk from the main bazar down the 3 km steep motorable road to Dharamshala. Further down is the library and Nechung Monastery in Gangchen Krishong. Dip-Tsechokling Monastery with its golden roof in a wooded valley can be seen from above. The Tsuglagkhang contains large gilded bronzes of the Buddha, Avalokitesvara and Padmasambhava. When in residence the Dalai Lama often leads the prayers. Entry free. It is good place to see Buddhism 'at work'; monks are very friendly. If you wish to have an audience with the Dalai Lama, you need to sign up at the Security Office by Hotel Tibet. **Note** His Holiness is a Head of State and seen as God by many here; please remember to show respect by dressing appropriately (no shorts, sleeveless tops/dirty or torn clothes). One Tibetan's remark on seeing unwashed foreigners – "they look as though they have just finished excercising" is telling; monks are setting up a committee to 'monitor' visitors. See note on Visiting Temples in Information for Visitors on page 134. There is a **Tibetan Library** and small **museum** on the road from Dharamshala. The Library is down the path, S of cottage towards Dharamshala. Good lectures/classes on Tibetan culture and Buddhism. Good range of books, magazines; photocopying facilities. Please leave a donation.

Politicians have been accused of taking advantage of heightened feelings after an unpleasant incident when in April 1994, a Gaddi youth was killed by a Tibetan in a local fight. Communal jealousies came to the surface with anti-Tibetan slogans and demands for the refugees to leave town.

The Dalai Lama reluctantly suggested that he might be forced to relocate the government in exile, possibly to Karnataka where there is already a significant Tibetan settlement in Bylakuppe. However, in July 1994, the Tibetan community seemed set to remain.

The **Tushita Meditation Centre** N of town runs regular courses which get fully subscribed.

Excursions in the Kangra Valley

From McLeodganj there are a number of interesting walks. There is a 2 km stroll to **Bhagsunath** where there is a spring and a temple. The spring, channelled through 3 spouts feeds a small pool; there is an attractive waterfall beyond. You can continue on towards the snowline. In Sep, an annual fair is held at **Dal Lake** (1,837m), 3 km from McLeodganj bus stand is a pleasant

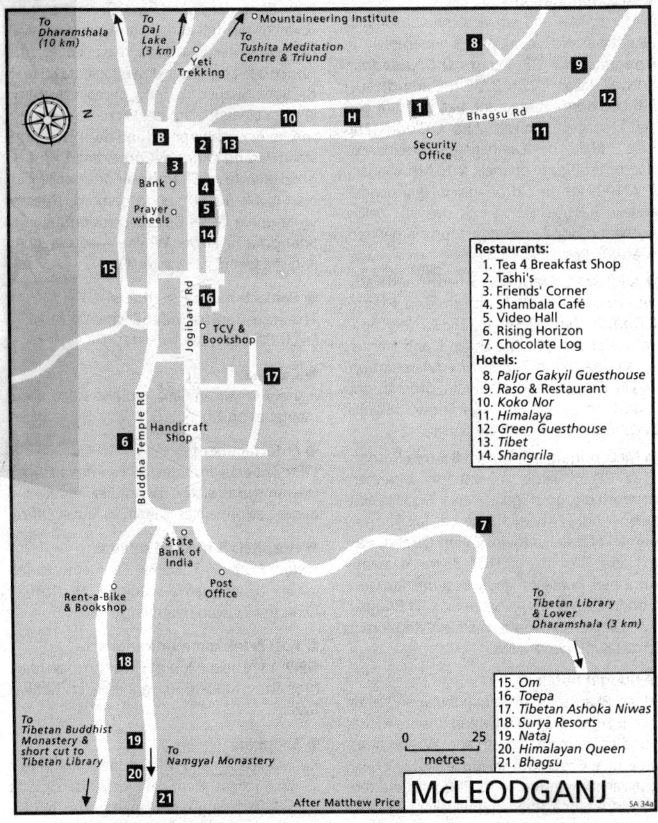

walk, but the lake is no more than a small pond. 1.5 km uphill from the bridge is Naddi with superb views of the Dhauladhar Range. Accommodation includes **D** *Udechee Huts*, occupying a vantage site, rm with bath, some in huts, well kept, pleasantly furnished, friendly service. **Kareri Lake** (3,048m) is further. From Bhagsunath you can also walk to **Dharamkot**, 3 km, has very fine views.

It is an 8 km trek to **Triund** (2,827m) which is at the foot of Dhaula Dhar. A further 5 km brings you to the snowline where there is a *Forest Rest House*.

Local information

● Accommodation

In March, May and Jun, accommodation may be difficult. No a/c rm, as it is unnecessary. **In Dharamshala**: HP Tourism **D** *Dhauladhar*, Kotwali Bazar, T 22109. 23 rm, and cheaper 3-6 bed dorm. Restaurant, bar, pleasant garden. Terrace for meals. Also **C** *Clouds End Villa*, (Raja of Lambagraon's residence), Naoroji Rd, ½ km off main rd to McLeodganj, T 22109. Rm in old bungalow (Raj period); annexe has excellent views over the valley. Authentic local cuisine, tours organised, peaceful. Rec.

D *Jaldhara Cottage* with 3-bed rm and **Kashmir House**, T 23101 with rm and **F** dorm. **E** *Dhauladhar View*, T 22889. New hotel with 9 decent rm. The cheap **E** and **F** hotels are all Tibetan run: *Tibet United Association*, *Deyki Palber* nr the fountain, *Shimla*, opp Tourist Office and *Sun and Snow*, downhill beyond the Bus Stand, are similar.

In McLeodganj: HP Tourism **B** *Surya Resorts*, T 22768. 40 large rm, tastefully furnished, comfortable, quiet, good views. Good restaurant, friendly, 24 hr exchange, bar, fax. The new upmarket hotel in town. **C** *Him Queen*, next to Natraj, T 24361, F 23184, 35 rm. Pleasantly furnished, homely, friendly. Best rm with view. Good seasonal discounts. **D** *Bhagsu*, T 23191. Rm with bath and dorm. Restaurant, large lawns, good views.

● Budget hotels

Along Bhagsu Rd are very popular and often full. **E** *Tibet*, T 22587, behind Bus Stand, has good rm, some with bath and TV, and a restaurant. **E** *Green Guest House* has fairly clean but variable rm (up to Rs 300 with western bath). Restaurant (banana pancakes rec). Likely to be crowded with backpackers, friendly but service has deteriorated and price gone up. **E** *Koko Nor*, T 22011, is basic and cheap. **F** *Ashoka Niwas* has very clean rm with good views; nice owners. Rec. Away from Bhagsu Rd **F** *Om*, on the main street, has good restaurant and is popular.

● Places to eat

Because of western demand and Tibetan enterprise to satisfy it, Dharamshala offers good alternatives to Indian food. You can be adventurous and try Tibetan soups, noodle dishes, fried *momos* and *shabakleb*. **In Dharamshala**: *Café Dhauladhar*, Kotwali Bazar. Terrace with good views. **In McLeodganj**: *Om*. Popular, relaxed and inexpensive; at the friendly, cheap *Tea for Breakfast* huge pancakes (Rs 10), rec. Busy *Tibet*, does good food. *Green* has deteriorated: too full and more expensive "even Bob Dylan records don't make up for it!" *Chocolate Log*, 2 min down Jogibara Rd from the Bank. Shaped like a log, deceptively shack-like is a pleasant surprise. Excellent cakes and snacks, reasonably priced and clean. Nr the bus stand *Pasang's Friends Corner* and *Tashi's* do good breakfasts. *Shambala* does excellent Indian meals (Rs 50); good portions, pleasant atmosphere (Miles Davis records on request). *Shangrila* nr Prayer Wheels is equally good and cheaper (Rs 25 for meal).

● Banks & money changers

The State Bank of India, Dharamshala, Mon-Fri, 1000-1400, Sat 1000-1200.

● Cinemas

3 show American films and also video documentaries on Tibet, Rs 5.

● Entertainment

TIPA (*Tibetan Institute of Performing Arts*), Dharamshala, stages occasional music and dance performances. Details at Tourist Office.

● Hospitals & medical services

District Hospital, T 22333. Of interest to followers of alternative medicine, *Dr Dolma's Clinic* (for Tibetan treatment).

● Post & telecommunications

GPO: 1 km below Tourist Office on main road. Mon-Sat, 1000-1630, another in Kotwali Bazar.

● Shopping

Kotwali Bazar and McLeodganj are major shopping areas. Plenty of Tibetan handicrafts for sale including wool carpets. The Sunday market in McLeodgunj has good handicrafts, handwoven cloth and garments.

● **Trekking**

Equipment can be hired from a branch of the Mountaineering Institute (Manali) at Dharamshala. Best season Apr-Jun and Sep-Nov.

● **Tourist office**

HP, Kotwali Bazar, nr Bus Stand, T 23163. *Hotel Tibet* also has good information.

● **Useful addresses**

Police: T 22303. **Foreigners' Registration Office**, below Dharamshala Bus Stand.

● **Transport**

NB: It is dangerous to drive at night in the hills. The roads are not lit and the risks of running off the edge are great. Few local drivers drive at night. State Highways link Dharamshala to Pathankot and Jalandhar, on NH1, and NH1A. To: Madras (2,678 km); Bombay (1,929 km); Calcutta (1,763 km).

Local Buses and taxis: for various places in and around Dharamshala. Dharamshala to McLeodganj, 10 km, ½ hr bus ride, Rs 3. **Walk**: you can walk by taking the 3 km steep road that passes by the Tibetan Library which takes about ¾ hr.

Air Nearest airport at Gaggal (13 km). Flights between Delhi and Gaggal on Archana Airways 3 times a week.

Train Nearest broad gauge railway station is at Pathankot.

Road Buses: all buses originate at Dharamshala; most leave early. About 4 daily to **Shimla** (317 km, 10 hr) and **Delhi** (521 km); Semi-delux coach dep Delhi Kashmir Gate Bus Station, around 1930 arr Lower Dharamshala about 1000. Rec as best views are in the morning climbing up into the foothills; stops en route (15 hr, Rs 140). Direct and regular State and private services to **Chandigarh** (248 km, 9 hr), **Jalandhar** (197 km, 8 hr), **Pathankot** (90 km, 4 hr), **Kulu** (214 km, 10 hr) and **Manali** (253 km, 13 hr. Best to go to Manali by daylight; stunning views but bus gets overcrowded so avoid sitting by door where people start to sit on your lap! Always keep baggage with you.

Dharamshala to Dalhousie

ROUTES To travel W from Dharamshala or Kangra rejoin the Mandi-Pathankot road at Gaggal. From Gaggal the road drops steadily to Nurpur.

Nurpur

(52 km; *Pop* 8000; *Alt* 420m). Emperor Jahangir named this after his wife in 1622, 2 years after Kangra had been taken from him by his son Shah Jahan. The fort is now in ruins. Some fine carving remains visible along with a Krishna temple, also in ruins. The town is known for its *pashmina* shawls. Nurpur has a *PWD Rest House*.

From Nurpur continue to **Chakki** (13 km; *Alt* 370m). The main road continues to Pathankot (11 km). From Chakki the road climbs to **Dhar** (14 km; *Alt* 680m) where a road to the left leads to **Udhampur** and Kashmir. At Dunera (17 km) there is a barrier gate to keep traffic to a one way system for the next 28 km to **Banikhet** (1,680m). The road continues 8 km to Dalhousie.

Dalhousie

Purchased by the British in 1853 from the Raja of Chamba, Dalhousie, named after the Governor-General (1848-56), sprawls out over 5 hills ranging from 1600-2400m, just E of the Ravi river. Lt-Col Napier (later Lord Napier of Magdala) selected the site. By 1867 it was a municipality and sanatorium and reached its zenith in the 1920s and 30s as a cheaper, but arguably more attractive, alternative to Shimla. Its popularity declined after 1947 and it became a pleasant quiet hill station surrounded by thick pine forests interspersed with oak and rhododendron. Recent years, however, have seen a steady increase in tourist numbers and resultant road traffic. Rabindranath Tagore wrote his first poem here as a boy and Subhash Chandra Bose came secretly to plan his strategies during the second World War, see page 602. Its main importance is due to the number of educational institutions and the presence of the army.

BASICS *Population*: 8600. *Altitude*: 2030m. *Climate*: Temp Summer Max 24°C, Min 16°C. Winter Max 10°C, Min 1°C. Annual rainfall 1500 mm.

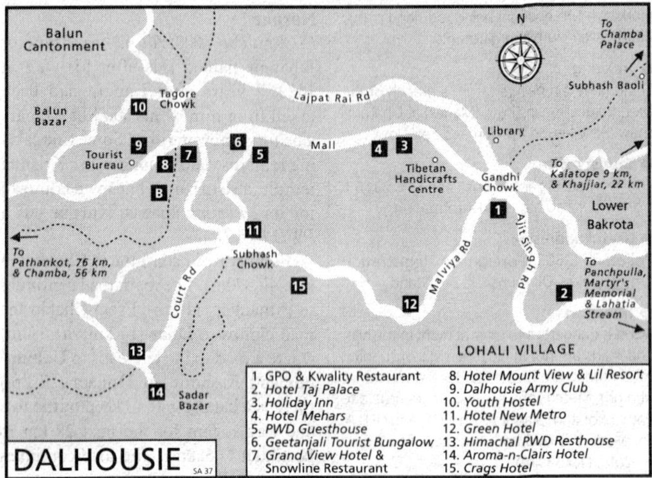

Places of interest

The town centres on **Gandhi Chowk** (formerly Post Office Sq). A number of industrious Tibetans make and sell various handicrafts, woollens, jackets, cardigans and rugs. There are no buildings of great interest but a number of pleasant walks over the 5 hills. Just over 2 km from the square is **Martyr's Memorial** at Panchpulla (5 bridges) which commemorates Ajit Singh, a supporter of Subhash Bose and the Indian National Army during World War II. On the way you can see the **Satdhara** (7 springs) said to contain mica and medicinal properties. **Subhash Baoli** (1.5 km from the square) is another spring. It is an easy climb and offers good views of the snows. ½km away is **Jhandri Ghat**, the old palace of Chamba rulers, set among tall pine trees. For a longer walk try the Barkota Round (5 km) which gives good views of the mountains.

Excursions

Kalatope 9 km (2500m), is a level walk through a forest sanctuary with a E *Tourist Lodge*. The road is jeepable. **Khajjiar**, 22 km (1940m) along a motorable road, is a long and wide glade ringed by cedars with a lake in the centre and a golden-domed Devi temple.

• **Accommodation** HP Tourism D *Devdar* Tourist Bungalow, 11 clean rm, dorm, simple restaurant, horse riding, beautiful setting. Also F *Youth Hostel* and a *PWD Rest House*.

• **Transport Road Buses**: regular buses and more expensive HP Tourism coaches. It is also a day's walk and this can be made into a short trek to Dharamshala over 2 days. A 30 km path through dense deodar forest leads to Chamba.

Tours

Full day (0900-1500) during the tourist season to Khajjiar by HP Tourism. Rs 225 by car for 5 people, Rs 35 per seat by luxury coach.

Local information

● **Accommodation**

Unfortunately some look rundown, often because the cost of maintaining the Raj-built structures is prohibitive, sometimes due to laziness and neglect. Nearly all, however, have good mountain views and offer discounts out-of-season. **C** *Jhandri Ghat Palace*, 2 km E of centre has been converted to a comfortable hotel. Reserve in Delhi, T 6886808, F 6886122. **D** *Aroma-n-Claire*, Court Rd, The Mall, T 2199. 20 rm with bath, large but spartan. Restaurant, exchange, shop. Best available with good views and character. **D** *Moun-*

tview, nr Bus Stand, T 2127. 12 large rm. Restaurant. Better managed than most and has good views. More expensive, **D** *Grand View,* above Mountview, T 2123. 26 rm. Restaurant. Rather run down; overpriced. HP Tourism **D** *Geetanjali*, T 2155. 12 rm with bath. Reservations: Tourist Office, T 2136. **D** *Holiday Inn*.

● **Budget hotels**

E *Circuit House*, Deputy Commissioner, Chamba, T 2121. 3 rm. Meal to order. PWD **E** *Rest House*, has 4 rm.

F *Fairview*, T 2206 and **F** *Mehar's*, T 2179, on The Mall. 43 rm. **F** *New Metro*, Subhash Chowk. **F** *Lill Resort*. Dorm. Good views. Nr the bus stand are cheap and basic. **F** *Youth Hostel* (HP Tourism). T 2159. Good discounts for YHAI Members. Reservations: Tourist Office, T 2136. *Dalhousie Army Club* offers temporary membership and has rm and a self-contained cottage.

● **Places to eat**

Moti Mahal, *New Metro* and *Lovely*, on Subhash Chowk. Several nr GPO incl *Kwality* and *Milan* which are rec for Indian and Chinese food. The latter, very friendly, serves large portions. *Snow Lion*, nr Grandview Hotel does Tibetan dishes.

● **Shopping**

Tibetan Handicrafts Centre, Gandhi Chowk; *Himachal Handicrafts Emporium*.

● **Sports**

Pony hire from Shubhash Chowk and Gandhi Chowk.

● **Tourist office**

HP, nr Bus Stand. T 36. 1000-1700.

● **Useful addresses**

State Bank of India; **Civil Hospital**, T 26; **General Post Office**, Gandhi Chowk. **Police**, T 26.

● **Transport**

Dalhousie is linked by State Highway to Pathankot in Punjab on NH 1A. From: **Pathankot** (78 km); **Delhi** (559 km); **Chandigarh** (336 km); **Shimla** (414 km).

Local Jeeps, **ponies** and *dandis* are available for visiting Khajjiar and other places in and around Dalhousie. Rates may be obtained from the local Tourist Office.

Air Nearest airport at Amritsar (200 km).

Train Nearest rly station at Pathankot, 2 hr by taxi.

Road Buses: state and private buses connect Dalhousie with many towns and cities in the region. From Dalhousie to **Chamba** (56 km, 2 hr), **Pathankot** (80 km, 4 hr), **Dharamshala** (7 hr via Gaggal on the Shimla bus. Change at Gaggal, 30 min from Dharamshala).

Chamba

From Dalhousie it is a very pleasant drive to the medieval town of Chamba (26 km). The higher road, at about 1800m, passes through some beautiful forests and the small town of Khajjiar (see above). The other, winter road, takes a lower route. The distances are similar.

Chamba State occupied the upper part of the Ravi river valley and some of the Chenab Valley. Founded in the 9th century, it was om an important trade route from Lahul to Kashmir and was known as 'The Middle Kingdom'. Though Mughal suzerainty was accepted by the local Rajas, the kingdom remained autonomous though it came under Sikh rule from 1810-46. Its relative isolation led to the nurturing of the arts – painting, temple sculpture, handicrafts and unique *rumal*. The pieces of silk/cotton with fine embroidery imitating miniature paintings (the back and front, the same).

Nomadic pastoralists Chamba is the centre of the **Gaddis**, shepherds who move their flocks of sheep and goats, numbering from a couple of hundred to a thousand, from lower pastures at around 1500m during winter to higher slopes at over 3500m, after snowmelt. They are usually only found in the Dhaula Dhar range which separates Kangra from Chamba. Some believe that these herdsmen first arrived in this part of Himachal in the 10th century; groups of the tribe certainly moved from the area around Lahore in Pakistan before the close of the 18th century, when Islamic power prevailed under the Mughals.

Their religious belief combines animism with the worship of Siva; **Brahmaur** with its distinctive Manimahesh temple, is their principle centre of worship (see below).

Nomadic for a part of the year, they are semi-pastoral; in the winter they can be seen round Kangra, Mandi and Bilaspur and in the small villages between Baijnath and Palampur. Gaddi men traditionally wear a *chola* (a loose white woollen garment) tied at the waist with a black wool rope and a white embroidered cap.

Chamba (760m) is on the S bank of the Irawati (Ravi), its stone houses clinging to the hillside. The river ultimately makes its way past Lahore to join the Chenab. Some see the town as having an almost Italian feel, surrounded by lush forests. In the centre is the Chaugan, or grassy *maidan* (meadow) with a promenade. Sadly, in the last 2 decades, shops have encroached into the open space; an underground shopping complex may be built to save it.

Places of interest

The **Rang Mahal** was built by Raja Umed Singh in the mid 18th-century. He had been a prisoner of the Mughals for 16 years and was obviously influenced by their architectural style. Additions were made by Jit Singh (1794-1804) and Charat Singh (1808-44), neither of which enhanced the original style of the palace. It became the women's residence until 1947. The wall paintings are splendid and represent one of the most extensive hill collections. The theme is usually religious, Krishna stories being particularly popular. The older ones are found in the **Devi-ri-Kothi** temple but the best were in the Rang Mahal. Some murals were removed to the museum after a fire, as well as wood carvings and manuscripts.

The temples There are a number of old temples in Chamba, both to Siva and Vishnu, their great curvilinear stone towers indicating the influence of Central Indian architecture from the 10th century Pratihara period. (Aurangzeb is believed to have ordered them to be knocked down but died before this was carried out). The overhanging wooden roofs are later additions. The **Lakshmi Narayana Temple** (14th century) is opposite the palace of the Chamba rulers and contains several shrines and a tank in 4 courts, each higher than the one before. The Gauri Sankara shrine in the 3rd court dates from the 11th century. There are also large Siva, Parvati and Nandi images of brass inlaid with copper and silver. The **Hariraya Temple**, S of the *chaugan*, is 14th century and contains a fine 338 kg 9th-10th century brass sculpture of Vaikuntha.

Museum

The **Bhuri Singh Museum** in a 3 storey building houses a heritage collection, craft items (incl *roomals*) and fine examples of Chamba, Kangra and Basholi schools of miniature paintings. Daily except Sun, 1000-1700.

Local festivals

Chaugan, is where fairs and festivals are held. Apr: *Suhi Mela* lasts 3 days. **Jul-Aug:** *Minjar*, 7-day harvest festival when people offer thanks to the rain gods. Decorated horses and banners are taken out in procession to mark its start. Sri Raghuvira is followed by other images of gods in palanquins and the festival ends with a procession to the River Irawati for immersion of *minjars* (tassels of corn). Many cultural events take place with the Gaddis, Batlis and Gujjars taking part.

Local information

● Accommodation

HP Tourism **D** *Irawati* nr Bus Stand, T 2671. 12 large rm with bath. Restaurant. **E** *Akhand Chandi*, College Rd, Dogra Bazar, T 2371. 9 rm, some a/c. Restaurant. **F** HP Tourism *Champak* Tourist Bungalow, T 2774. Rm and dorm.

● Places to eat

Apart from the ubiquitous tea shops, 2 hotels have restaurants. Also *Ravi View Cafe*.

● **Shopping**
Rumal embroidery and leather goods from *Handicrafts Centre*, Rang Mahal.

● **Transport**
Train Pathankot, the nearest railhead is 3 hr drive away.

Road Buses: daily Bus service with Dalhousie (2-3 hr). **Jeeps**: for hire but relatively expensive.

TREKKING IN HIMACHAL PRADESH

Trekking from Shimla

From Shimla there are opportunities for short and long treks. Shimla is on the Hindustan-Tibet Highway. **Wildflower Hall**, 13 km beyond Shimla at 2,593m, was the residence of Lord Kitchener, Commander-in-Chief of the Indian Army. The original building was replaced, but its successor, converted into a hotel, was burnt down in Feb 1993. The site is in lovely gardens, surrounded by *deodar* forest and there are some pleasant walks from it. At Naldera, 23 km from Shimla, was Curzon's summer retreat. HP Tourism *Bungalow* (see page 533).

Narkanda

Still further on at **Narkanda**, 64 km from Shimla, is another trek with very good walks, especially up Hattu Peak. From Narkanda the road runs down to the Sutlej valley and enters Kinnaur and Spiti. Foreigners are allowed into Spiti with permits. See **Trekking** section in Introduction

Jalori Pass

From just beyond Narkanda you can trek NW over the Jalori Pass (3350m) in the SARAJ region. Starting from Ani village reached by bus/jeep from Luhri in the Sutlej Valley below Narkanda, you trek into the lower part of the Kulu Valley, joining the Kulu-Manali road at Aut. There is a jeepable road over much of this route. An alternative is to proceed 65 km from Narkanda to Rampur and then trek into the Kulu Valley via the Bashleo Pass (3600m). There are *Forest Rest Houses* en route so a tent is not essential. The pass is crossed on the 3rd day of this 5-day trek. Both treks end at Banjar in the Tirthan Valley from where there are buses to Kulu.

Trekking From Chamba

There are several short and longer treks that can be undertaken from Chamba and Brahmaur in the Upper Ravi Valley. G & M Puri's *Trekking in HP* is recommended.

Season

The Chamba region receives the monsoon rains but the amount is less than in the Kangra Valley to the S. A trek, particularly over the Pir Panjal into Lahul is possible during the monsoon months (Jun-Sep). The ideal season, though, is just after the monsoon.

Pir Panjal

To the N there are 3 main passes over the Pir Panjal into Lahul: the Kalicho, Kugti and Chobia Passes. At least 5 days should be allowed for crossing them as their heights are around 5000m and acclimatization is highly desirable. All the first stages of the walks are along the Budhil River which flows through Brahmaur and is a tributary of the Ravi river. After the first 2 days, the services of a guide or porters are recommended for picking the right trail. Views from the passes are very good both of the Himalaya to the N and the Chenab Valley to the S. The descent from the passes is very steep. On reaching the road you can take a bus from Udaipur or Trilokinath in the Pattan Valley, to the Kulu Valley over Rohtang Pass.

Brahmaur

(1981m), (or Bharmaur) 65 km from Chamba, can also be reached by bus. It was the original capital Brahmapura for 4 centuries and has 8th-10th century Pahari (hill) style temples. The best known are the Lakshminarayan group which is the centre of worship for the semi-nomadic Gaddi tribe. From Brahmaur a 3-day trek is possible to **Manimahesh Lake** (3950m) in the Manimahesh Kailash (5575m), a spur running off the Pir Panjal. The lake is revered by local people as a resting place of Siva; pilgrims arrive at the temple here and take a holy bath a fortnight after *Janmashtami* (Jul/Aug).

Trekking In Lahul, Kinnaur & Spiti

The border areas are being opened to trekkers with permits. At the same time the local tribal people are being exposed to outside influence which started with the introduction of television in these valleys. Now enterprising families open their homes to paying guests, youths offer their services as guides and muleteers and shops stock bottled drinks and canned food; however, anyone trekking in this region is advised to carry food, tents and all essentials.

The 'freedom' walking popular in Nepal is not really feasible and porters and/or horses are required; these are not always easily available and prices fluctuate considerably. A good arrangement is to go on an organised trek with a group. You can do it independently but it requires greater planning. The trek into or from Zanskar is strongly recommended for the vigorously fit. **Note** The area is becoming littered with rubbish so please take care when disposing of any.

Lahul

Lahul (and Zanskar and Ladakh) are ideal trekking destinations during the monsoon as they are not nearly as wet as most other regions. Best Season: mid-Jun to mid-Oct.

You can take a trek from **Darcha** (see page 532) up the valley over the **Shingo La** and on to **Padum**, the capital of the Zanskar region. Padum is linked with Leh. Shingo La is over 5000m so some acclimatization is desirable. The route is well marked.

An alternative route to Zanskar is up the Chandra valley and over **Baralacha La**. This is a more gradual ascent and includes much fine scenery. The route taken from **Manali** is over the **Hamta Pass** with good views of Deo Tibba (6001m) weather permitting, to **Chhatru** village in the Chandra Valley with a *Rest House* with camping in the grounds (4 days' trek from Manali). 2 days along the dirt road brings you to **Batal** (to save time you can take the bus from Manali over the Rohtang Pass). The next stage of both variations is to Chandratal.

Chandratal (4270m), 'the lake of the Moon', is 18 km from Batal. The first section up to Kunzum Pass is on the bus route. The remaining 8.5 km trail is open Jun-Oct and brings you to the beautiful clear blue water lake, about a km long and ½ km wide which lies on a glacial bowl. Carry your own tent and provisions. The lake can also be reached from Manali on a lower but longer trail that directly run from Batal (no regular buses from Manali).

From Chandratal the route goes over the Baralacha La (usually 3 days) then over another pass along the same ridge as the Shingo La, to join the main Darcha-Padum trail. From here you can continue on to **Padum** or return to Darcha in Lahul. This second option makes for a very good circular trek.

A third possibility is to trek down the Chenab Valley and either cross the Pir Panjal by one of a number of passes into the Ravi Valley via Brahmaur, to Chamba or carry on to Kishtwar.

It is possible to trek in **lower Lahul**, using the district town of Udaipur as a base. Udaipur is at the base of the Miyar Nala the upper section of which is glaciated. To the E, high passes lead give access to the Bhaga valley and to the W to the Saichu Nala (Chenab tributary).

Udaipur

The village in the Pattan Valley whose name was changed from Markul about

1695 when Raja Udai Singh gave it the status of a district in his administration, has the unique **Mrikula** (Markula) **Devi temple** (AD1028-63) near the bazar. The temple dedicated to Kali, looks wholly unimposing from the outside with a battered looking wood-tiled 'conical' roof and crude outside walls. However, inside are some magnificent intricate deodar-wood carvings on the doors, walls and ceilings. The silver image of Kali (*Mahishashurmardini*; 1570) is a strange mixture of Rajasthani and Tibetan styles, with an oddly proportioned body. The wood carvings come from two periods. The façade of the shrine, ceiling panels of the mandapa and pillars supporting the ceiling are earlier than those beside the window, the ceiling architraves or 2 western pillars. Scenes from the *Mahabharata* and the *Ramayana* epics decorate the architraves, while the 2 door guardians (*dvarapalas*), which are relatively crude, are stained with the blood of sacrificed goats and rams. Accommodation: E PWD and Forest *Rest Houses.* Book in Keylong.

The Trilokinath temple nearby also has some fine woodcarving.

Trilokinath (2760m), 3 km from Udaipur (8 km off the main road) has a fine Siva temple with a stone *nandi* in the compound. It is in the particular ancient pagoda style of wooden temple building; indeed, parts of the original columns are believed to date from the the 8th century, though the white marble 6-armed image of Avalokiteshvara (Bodhisattva) is from the 12th. Hindus and Buddhists celebrate the 3-day *Pauri Festival* in August. The wood carvings here closely resemble that of the Hadimba Temple at Manali and some believe it was the work of the same 16th century craftsman. See page 527.

Trails run into the Miyar Nullah, renowned for flowers, then over the 5100m Kang La pass to Padum. Alternatively, you can follow the Chandrabhaga river to the scarcely visited Pangi valley with its rugged scenery and then over the 4240m Sach Pass leading to Chamba District.

Pangi valley The Chandrabhaga flows at over 2400m after the 2 rivers meet in this desolate and craggy region. The cheerful and goodlooking Pangiwals keep their unique heritage alive through their singing and dancing. The Mindhal temple to Devi is their focus of worship. **Kilar** is the HQ which has a *Rest House* and the Detnag Temple nearby. From Kilar a wide trail follows the steep slopes above the Chandrabhaga (Chenab) river to Dharwas on the Himachal/Kashmir border and then onwards to **Atholi** in the Paddar region of Kishtwar, known for its sapphire mines.

Kinnaur

Close to the Tibetan border on its E, Kinnaur has the Sutlej flowing through it. Garhwal is to the S, Spiti Valley to the N and Kulu to the W. The rugged mountains and sparse rainfall makes Kinnaur resemble Lahul. The Kinners are Hindu but the Tibetan Buddhist influence is evident in the numerous gompas that can be seen alongside the temples. The *Phulaich* (*Festival of Flowers*) takes place in Sep when some villagers leave for the mountains for 2 days and nights to collect scented blossoms, then return on the 3rd day to celebrate with singing and dancing.

Kinnaur, including the lovely side valleys of Sangla and Bhabha, are now open with permits easily available from the Dist Magistrates in Shimla, Kulu or Keylong. These treks are immensely enjoyable; although there are stone huts and the occasional *PWD* or *Forest Rest House*, always carry a tent in this area. See page 534.

Baspa Valley Starting from **Sangla** (2680m), you can take a fairly level track through thick forest up to Rakcham (8 km, 3130m) and climb gradually to reach **Chitkul** (18 km, 3450m) passing through Mastrang. Another option is to

The Valley Of The Gods

The origin of Malana is difficult to trace. People believe that a band of renegade soldiers who deserted Alexander's army in the 4th century BC, settled here (some wooden houses have soldiers carved on them); it is more probable that their antecedents were from the Indian plains. Their language called Kanashi has no script but is linked to Tibetan. The villagers are directly involved in taking decisions on important matters affecting them thus operating as an ancient democratic 'city state'. Language, customs and religious practices too differ from neighbouring hill tribes, polygamy being permitted.

A charming myth is associated with Jamlu, the principal deity in the valley. Jamlu, possibly of pre-Aryan origin, was carrying a casket containing all the important deities of Hinduism and while crossing the mountains through the Chandrakhani Pass into Kulu, a strong gust of wind blew open the box and spread the deities all over the valley. Since then Malana has been known as 'The Valley of the Gods'.

start at **Morang**, see page 535, which has a bus from Kalpa. The trail follows the Sutlej river bank for a short distance until the Tirung Gad meets it. Here it turns SE and after going through a narrow valley reaches **Thangi** a village connected to Morang by jeepable road where mules are available for hire. The track continues along barren hills to Rahtak (camping possible) before rising steeply to Charang Pass (5266m) then drops down following a mountain stream to Chitkul.

Spiti

Meaning literally 'the place of Mani' Spiti is a high altitude desert, bare rugged and inhospitable, with the Spiti River running from the slopes of Kunzum La (4551m) to Sumdo (3230m). Kunzum La offers seasonal access by road to Kulu from the valley, and it is also directly connected with Shimla via the NH 22 and the SH 30.

Like neighbouring Lahul, Spiti is famous for its **gompas** (monasteries). See page 535 for details. At **Tabo**, 33 km from Spiti, the Buddhist monastery is one of the region's most famous. Permit details are checked here. There is a dispensary and 2 adequate teashops. **NB**: foreigners are not allowed to stay overnight in Tabo although there is a PWD *Rest House* here. There are other important gompas at **Dankar, Ki, Ghungri and Lalung**.

Trekkers interested in **fossils** choose a trail starting at **Kaza** and travel to **Langza** (8.5 km) which has a narrow motorable track. The trek goes to Hikim, the Tangyut monastery, Comic (8 km) and returns to Kaza (6 km).

From Kibber (4205m) there is a 6 km track through alpine meadows to **Gete** (4520m) which claims to be one of the highest permanent settlement in the world only reached on foot.

NOTE Foreigners are now permitted to trek in this region going up to **Kibber**, one of the highest villages in the world. For details of 'Inner Line' permit requirements see Trekking in Information for Visitors.

Trekking in the Kulu Valley

There is a variety of treks in the Kulu Valley in terms of duration and degree of difficulty. There are pleasant walks up the subsidiary valleys from Aut and Katrain with the opportunity to camp in spectacular and high locations without having to spend very long getting there. An easy option is to take the bus up to the Rohtang Pass, 59 km from Manali, which is very spectacular and then walk down. There is a path, and it only takes a few hours. There are also longer treks which offer a wider variety of scenery.

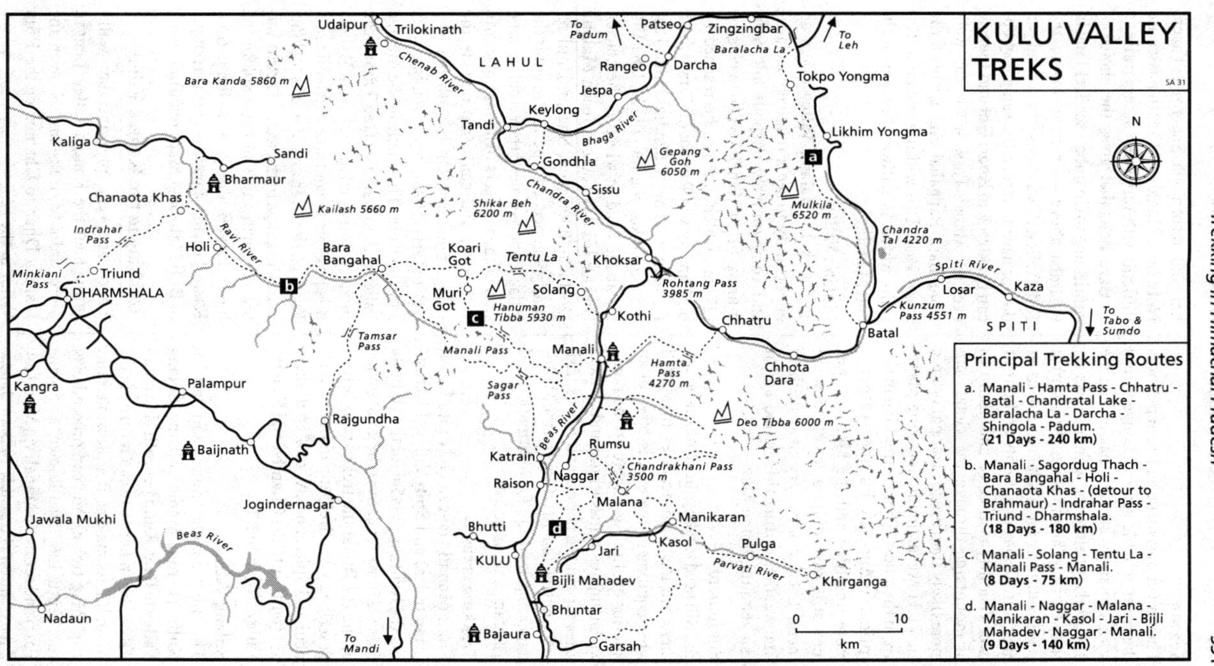
KULU VALLEY TREKS
SA 31
N
Udaipur
Trilokinath
LAHUL
Chenab River
Bara Kanda 5860 m
To Padum
Patseo
Zingzingbar
Baralacha La
To Leh
Rangeo
Darcha
Tokpo Yongma
Jespa
Keylong
Tandi
Bhaga River
Likhim Yongma
Kaliga
Sandi
Bharmaur
Gondhla
Gepang Goh 6050 m
Sissu
Chandra River
Mulkila 6520 m
Chanaota Khas
Kailash 5660 m
Shikar Beh 6200 m
Indrahar Pass
Holi
Ravi River
Chandra Tal 4220 m
Bara Bangahal
Koari Got
Tentu La
Khoksar
Minkiani Pass
Triund
DHARMSHALA
Muri Got
Solang
Rohtang Pass 3985 m
Spiti River
Losar
Kaza
Hanuman Tibba 5930 m
Kothi
Kunzum Pass 4551 m
Chhatru
Batal
SPITI
To Tabo & Sumdo
Tamsar Pass
Manali Pass
Manali
Hamta Pass 4270 m
Chhota Dara
Kangra
Palampur
Sagar Pass
Rajgundha
Beas River
Deo Tibba 6000 m
Baijnath
Rumsu
Katrain
Chandrakhani Pass 3500 m
Naggar
Raison
Jogindernagar
Malana
Manikaran
Jawala Mukhi
Bhutti
Kasol
Pulga
Beas River
Jari
KULU
Parvati River
Bijli Mahadev
Khirganga
Bhuntar
Nadaun
0 10 km
To Mandi
Bajaura
Garsah
Principal Trekking Routes
a. Manali - Hamta Pass - Chhatru - Batal - Chandratal Lake - Baralacha La - Darcha - Shingola - Padum. (21 Days - 240 km)
b. Manali - Sagordug Thach - Bara Bangahal - Holi - Chanaota Khas - (detour to Brahmaur) - Indrahar Pass - Triund - Dharmshala. (18 Days - 180 km)
c. Manali - Solang - Tentu La - Manali Pass - Manali. (8 Days - 75 km)
d. Manali - Naggar - Malana - Manikaran - Kasol - Jari - Bijli Mahadev - Naggar - Manali. (9 Days - 140 km)

Season

The post-monsoon period, ie Sep-Nov is the most reliable season. Longer treks with crossings of high passes can be undertaken before the winter snows arrive. During the monsoon (Jun-Sep) it is wet but the rain is not continuous. It may rain all day or for only an hour or two. Visibility is affected and glimpses of mountains through the clouds are more likely than broad clear panoramic views. However, many flowering plants are at their best. There is trekking in the spring, ie Apr-May, but the weather is more unsettled and the higher passes may still have quite a lot of snow on them. There can be very good spells of fine weather during this period and it can get quite hot in May.

Equipment

You will need to take your own as although there are few good agencies in Manali what equipment there is, is often of an inferior quality. Also, there are no pony-wallah unions as in Kashmir and no fixed rates for guides, porters and horses. Ask at the hotels, Tourist Office and the Mountaineering Institute for information and assistance, see page 530.

Trekking areas

From **Manali** you can go N into **Lahul** (Map trek **a**) and **Spiti** Valleys by crossing the Rohtang (3985m) or the Hampta Pass (4270m). Once over the great divide of the Pir Panjal the treks are as briefly described – see Trekking in Lahul, Kinnaur and Spiti above. W of Manali there are routes into the **Chamba** and **Kangra** Valleys (Map trek **b**).

Solang Valley

The most popular route, and trek in Kulu, is from Manali up the **Solang Valley** to **Beas Kund** beneath Hanuman Tibba. From here you can return via the Manali Pass making it a pleasant 8 day trip (Map trek **c**). You can proceed over the Tentu La) (also known as Solang Pass) and return to Manali via Muri Got. An extention is possible to Bara Bangahal and return via Sagordug Thach. **Note** Both Manali and Tentu passes are difficult with very steep access trails.

Bara Bangahal gives the choice of continuing to Chamba – see Trekking in Chamba above – or returning to the Kulu Valley. If you choose the second you do not have to return the same way but can backtrack to **Koari Got** and then go over the Manali Pass, or you can walk from Bara Bangahal and go over the Sagar Pass. This will return you to Katrain which is halfway between Kulu and Manali.

Malana Valley

The trek to **Malana Valley** offers an opportunity to see a relatively isolated and comparatively unspoilt hill community. From Manali you go to **Naggar** (28 km, which can also be reached by bus) and stay at **Rumsu** (2377m) which is higher. The Chandrakhani Pass (3500m) takes you into the Malana Valley at the head of which is the glacier. On the 3rd day you can reach **Malana** (2650m) 20 km from Naggar. Until recently you needed a permit to enter the village, now you need the verbal permission of the villagers (who may also provide food) and can camp outside the village boundary. On the 4th day you trek to **Jari** (1500m) where you can catch a bus to Kulu. The whole of the Malana Valley is dominated by **Deo Tibba** peak in the N. To extend the trek from Malana it is possible to continue to Manikaran, Kasol on the river, and onwards to Pulga and Khirganga in the scenic Parvati Valley. Alternatively, you can explore the lower Parvati Valley by walking from Kasol, Jari, to Naggar via the Siva temple of Bijli Mahadev (Map trek **d**).

Trekking in the Kangra Valley

There are very pleasant day walks throughout the Kangra Valley. Longer, more arduous treks are N over the Dhaula Dhar to Chamba or the Kulu Valley in the E.

Baijnath, **Palampur** and **Dharamshala** are popular starting points. See page 537. From here you go over the **Dhaula Dhar** at passes such as the Indrahar and Minkiani (both from Dharamshala) and the Waru (from Palampur) then enter a feeder of the Upper Ravi Valley.

Midway up the valley which lies between the Manimahesh Dhar and Dhaula Dhar ranges is Bara Bangahal. From there you can go downstream to **Chamba** or upstream which offers the choice of at least 3 passes for crossing into the Kulu Valley. The northernmost of these is the Solang Pass which passes Beas Kund beneath Hanuman Tibba. In the middle is the Manali Pass whilst the southernmost is Sagar Pass. A good trip which includes the upper part of this valley is the round trip trek from Manali – see Trekking in the Kulu Valley above.

JAMMU AND KASHMIR

CONTENTS

MAPS

Kashmir, the contested jewel of South Asia's northernmost region, has seen its astonishingly beautiful valleys and mountains repeatedly scarred by political dispute. Its lakes, fertile valleys and remote, snow-covered peaks have drawn rulers, pilgrims and ordinary travellers from the Mughals onwards. Fought over in 1948, 1965 and 1971 by India and Pakistan, its territory is still disputed. Politically it is divided by a Line of Control between India and Pakistan. The easternmost part of that boundary across the Siachen Glacier, at over 6,000m, was left undemarcated. It has been the scene of sporadic fighting for over 10 years. NB: In 1993 visitors to India have been advised not to travel to Kashmir. All foreigners entering Jammu and Kashmir are required to register their arrival.

Those who visited the valley in 1993 advise, "speak to other travellers to gauge situation – do not believe touts – not for the faint-hearted".

SOCIAL INDICATORS *Population*: 9 mn (Urban 25%, Scheduled Castes 8%, Scheduled tribes nil); *Literacy*: M 40%, F 20%. *Birth rate*: Rural 33:1000, Urban 23:1000. *Death rate*: Rural 8:1000, Urban 6:1000. *Infant mortality*: Rural 74:1000, Urban 43:1000. *Religion*: Hindu 32%, Muslim 64%, Sikh 2%, Buddhist 1.2%, Christian 0.2%.

Environment

The regions of Kashmir

The State comprises 3 regions: **Jammu**, the mainly Hindu foothills in the S; the **Vale of Kashmir**, predominantly Muslim in the centre; and **Ladakh**, the E highlands of the great Himalayan axis, predominantly Buddhist. Together they comprise the largest of India's Himalayan states and contain over 9 million inhabitants.

Kashmir had been one of the most visited states of India up to the late 1980s. The Vale of Kashmir was always the main focus, with a superb summer climate and glorious scenery. Gulmarg and Pahalgam offer trout fishing and trekking. Adventure sports such as white water rafting are being added to trekking in Ladakh. Most travellers to Ladakh are also attracted by its Buddhist and Tibetan culture. Tragically, the vale of Kashmir has been virtually closed to visitors since 1989. It is essential for foreigners to take advice in Delhi from Indian Tourist Information and from their consulates before leaving.

Land

Area: 222,000 sq km. – slightly smaller than New Zealand. Kashmir is joined to the rest of India by a 30 km long boundary with Punjab and a 300 km boundary with Himachal Pradesh. Its other neighbours are foreign countries: Pakistan to the E, Tibet/China to the N and NE.

Jammu is the borderland with the Punjab, and the transitional zone be-

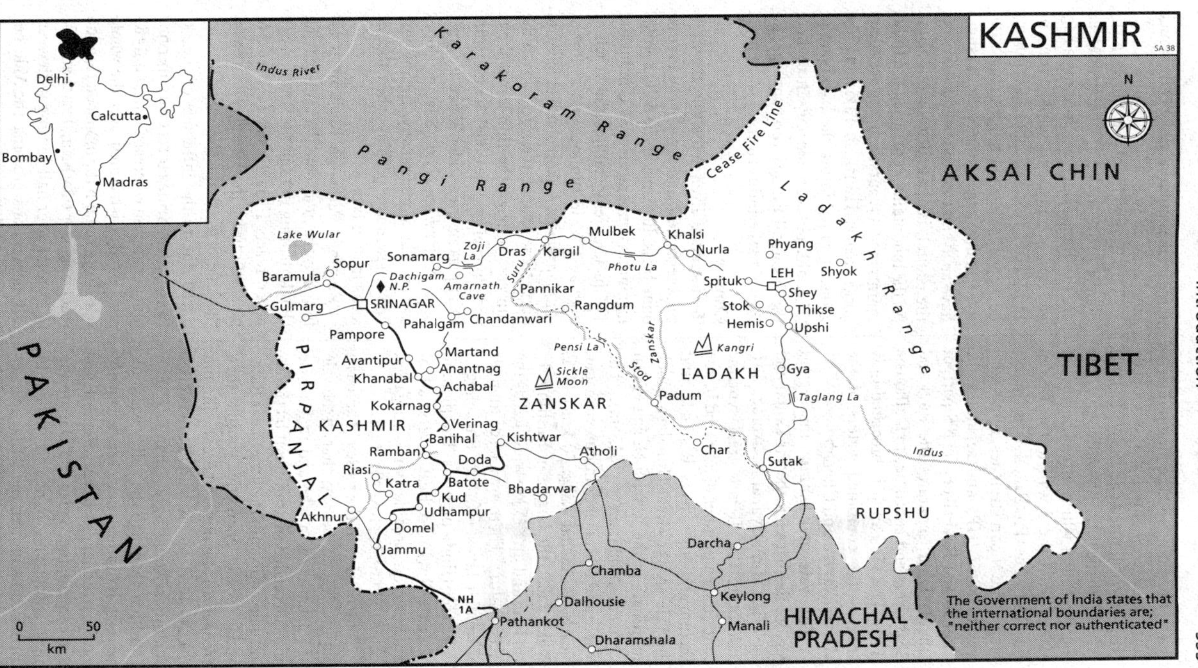
KASHMIR
SA 38
N
Delhi
Calcutta
Bombay
Madras
Indus River
Karakoram Range
Pangi Range
Cease Fire Line
Ladakh Range
AKSAI CHIN
TIBET
PAKISTAN
Lake Wular
Baramula
Sopur
Gulmarg
Sonamarg
Zoji La
Dachigam N.P.
Amarnath Cave
SRINAGAR
Pahalgam
Chandanwari
Pampore
Avantipur
Martand
Anantnag
Khanabal
Achabal
Kokarnag
Verinag
PIR PANJAL
KASHMIR
Banihal
Ramban
Riasi
Katra
Batote
Doda
Kud
Udhampur
Akhnur
Domel
Jammu
NH 1A
Pathankot
Dras
Kargil
Suru
Pannikar
Rangdum
Mulbek
Photu La
Khalsi
Nurla
Pensi La
Sickle Moon
ZANSKAR
Zanskar
Stod
Padum
Kishtwar
Atholi
Bhadarwar
Char
Spituk
LEH
Phyang
Shyok
Shey
Stok
Thikse
Hemis
Upshi
Kangri
LADAKH
Gya
Taglang La
Sutak
Indus
RUPSHU
Darcha
Chamba
Dalhousie
Keylong
Manali
Dharamshala
HIMACHAL PRADESH
The Government of India states that the international boundaries are; "neither correct nor authenticated"
0 50 km

tween the plains and the mountains. Its thin thirsty soils are liable to erosion. Irrigation is limited and the water-table is deep. To the N the Shiwaliks give onto the Pir Panjal which attain heights of 5000m from the S wall to the Vale of Kashmir. The Pir Panjal is a double range. The N part stretches from Kishtwar to Kulu (HP) and separates the Chenab and Ravi rivers. The S part, or Dhaula Dhar, separates the Ravi and Beas rivers and continues to Dalhousie (HP). The Pir Panjal is breached only once by the combined waters of the Marwa-Warvan and Chenab.

The Vale of Kashmir, the second region, lies between the Pir Panjal and the High Himalaya, at an average altitude of 1580m. It is a great syncline containing a number of lakes fed by the Jhelum and other rivers. Rising behind the Vale are the Great Himalaya which culminate in the W with Nanga Parbat ('Naked Mountain' – 8125m). The Nagin and Dal lakes dominate Srinagar. Nearby is Anchar Lake. 30 km NW is Wular Lake, the largest in Kashmir, 17 km long and up to 5 km wide, fed by the river Jhelum. There are a large number of smaller lakes. Of these Sheshnag is sacred for Hindu pilgrims. The Jhelum, Chenab, Ravi and Beas rivers, all of which later provide vital irrigation water to Punjab, cross the state.

The origins of the valley There is a popular legend that says that all the Vale of Kashmir was a lake and that a wise man succeeded in draining it by throwing gold coins into the water near Baramula. Some energetic youths then dredged an opening – where the Jhelum river is now – in order to get the coins. Scientists would agree that less than 1 million years ago the valley was submerged. It drained, however, because of local earthquakes. Today, of the lakes that remain, the Wular and Dal are the most important. When it floods in spring and summer, the Wular reaches 260 sq km in size making it one of the largest lakes in India. Lake Dal is much smaller at 38 sq km.

The Trans-Himalaya Between the Ganga plains and the Tibetan Plateau are the Trans-Himalaya, forming a rugged zone of transition. Across it runs the Indus river, rising in Tibet and running between the Zanskar range to the S and the Ladakh range to the N. Both ranges have an average altitude of 5000m. Leh, the capital, is at an altitude of 3520m. As the mountains were raised the Indus maintained its course, carving very deep gorges, eg at Hunza in Pakistan. The Zanskar range forms the backbone of S Ladakh and is broken only once where the Doda and Tsarap rivers converge and flow N to the Indus river.

Climate

Temperature Even in the Vale, the air in summer is fresh and at night can even be quite brisk. In Srinagar the daily average maximum temperature is 31°C in Jul and 4°C in Jan. Temperatures can reach as high as 37°C in summer and as low as -11°C in winter. A short climb quickly reduces these temperatures. In Ladakh the sun cuts through the thin atmosphere, and diurnal and seasonal temperature variations are even wider. There are great contrasts between N and S facing slopes and even in summer many streams only flow a few hours per day when the ice melts in their beds.

Rainfall Although Kashmir is affected by the monsoon, the rain-bearing clouds drifting in from the Arabian Sea never reach Ladakh, where they are blocked out by the Himalaya. Even in the Vale of Kashmir the rainfall is reduced due to the influence of the Pir Panjal. Still, Srinagar receives over 650 mm per annum whereas Leh has only 85 mm, evenly distributed over the whole year. Even though the monsoon rains do reach Srinagar they bring less than 30% of its total, over half coming with westerly depressions crossing the Vale between Jan and Apr.

Pashmina And Shahtush

Kashmir shawls are world renowned for their softness and warmth. The best are *pashmina* (Cashmere) and *shahtush*, the latter being the warmest, the rarest and, consequently, the most expensive. Prized by Moghuls and Maharajas they found their way to Europe and through Napoleon's Egyptian campaign became an item of fashion in France.

The craft was possibly introduced from Persia in the 15th century. Originally a fine shawl would take months to complete especially if up to 100 colours were used. The soft fleece of the pashmina goat or the fine under hairs of an antelope were used, the former for cashmere shawls, the latter for *shahtush*. The very best were soft and warm and yet so fine that they could be drawn through a finger ring. The designs changed over the years from floral patterns in the 17th century to Paisley in the 19th century. The Mughals, especially Akbar, used them as gifts. However, with the introduction of the Jacquard loom, cheap imitations were mass produced at a fraction of the price. The Kashmir shawls thus became luxury items, their manufacture remaining an important source of employment in the Vale, but they ceased to be the major export.

Flora and fauna

In Ladakh vegetation is very thin and apart from occasional thorny bushes it is confined to the watercourses. In contrast to Kashmir where about 30% of the land is still under forest, Ladakh has few trees. The shortage of timber and fuel are a pressing problem for the local inhabitants. In Kashmir the forests provide the Government with a significant income though there is concern that they are being over-exploited. Among them are the chenar tree (the giant Asian Plane Tree, *Platanus orientalis*), willows and a wide variety of conifers, including the Deodar cedar.

History

For many years Kashmir was ruled by Scythian Hindu princes who were succeeded by Tartars. Shams-ud-din gained possession in 1341 and spread Islam.

The Vale of Kashmir

The origins of the Vale of Kashmir's popularity date back to the Mughals. They found the heat of the Indian plains in summer oppressive. Babur longed for the streams and cool mountain air of North of the Hindu Kush and improvised by laying out gardens, thus starting a family tradition. Akbar first visited in 1586 after its conquest. The journey took 6 weeks, largely because an army of stone cutters and navvies prepared the way for him. On this visit, floating gardens and river palaces were prepared for him. He visited the Valley 3 times and liked to refer to it as his private garden where he would go water-fowling, watch the fields of saffron being harvested or just relax. Jahangir also found this natural paradise captivating; he is responsible for many of Srinagar's finest creations.

Who has not heard of the Vale of Cashmere
With its roses the brightest that earth ever gave
Its temples, and grottoes, and fountains as clear
As the love-lighted eyes that hang over their wave.

Thomas Moore wrote *Lalla Rookh, an Oriental Romance* in 1826 in a sentimental style typical of the Persian poets. His poem captured the English public's imagination of this, the most famous valley in the Himalayas, adored by Mughal Emperors. *Lalla Rookh* sold 85,000 copies and ran to 55 editions before the copyright expired in 1880.

The small trickle of British visitors became a steady stream, laying the basis for making Kashmir India's most popular destination until the political trouble after 1989 virtually closed it to outsiders. In 1588 the Mughal emperor Akbar conquered Kashmir and built the fort on Hari Parbat Hill in Srinagar. His son Jahangir (1605-27) was captivated by the beauty of the Vale of Kashmir, planting *chenar* trees and constructing pleasure gardens. In 1739 it was annexed by Nadir Shah.

The Hindu Misr Chand, who served as a General in the army of the Sikh Ranjit Singh, took it in 1819 and was granted effective control in exchange for his loyal service. At the close of the first Sikh War in 1846 it was assigned to the Maharaja Gulab Singh of Jammu, who founded a dynasty of Dogra Rajputs. Thus, Hindus ruled a mainly Muslim population. Gulab Singh's territory included his home base of Jammu, the Vale of Kashmir, Ladakh, Baltistan and Gilgit.

Jammu

Jammu is the homeland of the Dogras, the Rajput clans of the hill region N of the Ravi River. They are descended from the Katoch branch of the lunar race of Rajputs. These people have a well deserved reputation as a martial caste. Under the Mughal Akbar's policy of conciliation and religious tolerance, the Dogras became loyal feudatories of the Mughal Emperors.

During the rule of the Sikh Ranjit Singh, the Dogras were allowed a large degree of independence. At the close of the Sikh War in 1846 and by virtue of a treaty with the British the resourceful Gulab Singh became the ruler of the combined states of Jammu and Kashmir. He wanted to establish Jammu as a religious centre that compared favourably with Varanasi. He commissioned the Raghunath Temple which was completed by his son Ranbir Singh who in turn commissioned the Rambireshwar Temple. Nearby is the important cave temple of Vaishno Devi – see Excursions. It is often called the City of Temples. At Partition, Hari Singh, the Maharaja of Kashmir, decided to side with India. This resulted in the creation of the state of Jammu and Kashmir.

19th century development

Kashmir became popular with the British – hunters enjoyed the rich wildlife. Visitors stayed in houseboats which came into existence to provide accommodation when non-Kashmiris were forbidden to own land. In peaceful times these are still extremely popular.

Independence

Before Independence Kashmir had already developed a distinct political base, with the secular Congress Party, led in Kashmir by Sheikh Abdullah, establishing itself as the leading democratic political force in the state. Although the Muslim League favoured joining Pakistan, the Congress had a clear preference for joining India, or even of remaining independent of both new states, a wish seemingly shared by the Maharaja. The question was still not resolved when India and Pakistan gained their independence in Aug 1947. In the autumn, tribes in the northern territories of Gilgit and Baltistan revolted and joined Pakistan. In SW Kashmir Muslims rebelled, declared 'Azad Kashmir' (Free Kashmir) and forged links with Pakistan, who then proceeded to invade Kashmir. When the Pakistanis were very near to Srinagar, the Maharaja threw in his hand with India who quickly despatched troops there. Hostilities between India and Pakistan continued until 30 Dec 1948 when a ceasefire was agreed upon. That ceasefire line has become the *de facto* frontier separating the Indian State of Jammu and Kashmir from the Pakistani Azad Kashmir.

The plebiscite After the 1948 war a plebiscite was agreed to by India on condition that the armies of both parties withdrew from all the territories of the former state, and that peace and normalcy were restored first. Those conditions were never met and the plebiscite was never held. When Sheikh Abdullah resurrected the idea of one in 1953, he was imprisoned. The Kashmir Assembly declared the state to be a part of India in 1957. In 1965 President Ayub Khan of Pakistan launched a military attack on India in the hope of capturing Kashmir by force, but the war rapidly ground to a stalemate.

The Simla Agreement The crushing defeat of Pakistan in the 1971 war over Bangladesh led Zulfikar Ali Bhutto, the new Pakistan Prime Minister, to believe that Pakistan could no longer look to take Kashmir from India by force. In 1972 he signed the Shimla Agreement with Mrs Gandhi under which both countries recognised the line of control and agreed that the dispute would be resolved through bilateral negotiations. Following the Simla Agreement Mrs Gandhi released Sheikh Abdullah from prison and allowed elections.

Although Bhutto's power was unchallenged at the time some criticised him for "selling out" Pakistan's interests in Kashmir. Since the uprising in 1989, which India argues and many international observers believe was greatly augmented by Pakistani support, the Pakistan Government has thrown all its weight behind Kashmir's separatists. However, it only supports those who wish Kashmir to join Pakistan, and is strongly opposed to any moves for Kashmir's Independence.

The current political situtation

There is no sign that the Indian government feels it can afford to be pushed into granting independence, though it has given some indications that it would be willing to consider alternative forms of government with greater Kashmiri autonomy. In the meantime India is estimated to have up to 300,000 troops in the Vale. The government has been widely accused of human rights abuses, but in 1994 it showed increasing signs of wilingness to allow foreign as well as the highly critical Indian press into the state, and to take action against any of its forces found guilty of abuse.

Warning In mid 1994 the situation remained tense, and although visitors were travelling into the state the situation was far from normal and was potentially dangerous for travellers as the abduction of British tourists in mid 1994 showed.

Culture

People

The 9 million people are unevenly scattered. The Vale of Kashmir has over half, whilst Ladakh is the most sparsely populated. Culturally Jammu, Kashmir and Ladakh could scarcely be more different from each other. Jammu was traditionally the seat of Dogra power and serves a largely Hindu population. Its affinities are more with the Punjab than with the Vale of Kashmir. Kashmir marks the northernmost advance of Islam in the Himalaya while Ladakh is aptly named 'Little Tibet'. Ethnically the Ladakhis are of Tibetan stock. The early history of Ladakh, is that of Tibet itself as it was a province of Tibet. It was governed in secular matters by an independent prince and in spiritual affairs by the Dalai Lama. Today, in Ladakh 52% of the population are Lamaistic Buddhists. Among the followers of Islam (47% of the total), are immigrant Kashmiris and Dards who speak their own languages.

Language

Kashmiri is influenced by Sanskrit and belongs to the Dardic branch of the Indo-Aryan languages. Linguistically and physically Kashmiris are similar to the tribes around Gilgit in Pakistan. The Ladakhis physically reveal Tibetan-Mongolian and Indo-Aryan origins while their language belongs to the Tibetan-Burmese group.

Cuisine

The rich cuisine of Kashmir is at its best in the ceremonial *wazwan*, a formal meal prepared in the home to mark a special occasion. The *waza* is the chief cook who supervises the serving of up to 2 or 3 dozen specially prepared dishes to guests who are usually seated on the floor in groups of 4, the meal being eaten with the fingers.

Preparations are made days in advance, using the very best of fresh produce and spices and herbs. The meal begins with the passing around of the *Tash-t-Nari* for guests to wash their hands, followed by numerous delicacies – *methi*, *Rogan Josh*, kebabs, vegetables – finishing with the very special *gushtaba* (goat meat balls). The dessert is usually *phirni* and finally a drink of *kahwah*, the green tea, flavoured with saffron, cardamom and almonds.

Handicrafts

Despite the problems in Kashmir, many Kashmiri products are still available outside the State. Kashmir is renowned for its distinctive and finely executed handicrafts. Small-scale handicraft enterprises include carpets, papier mâché objects, woollen shawls, woodcarving and brassware. Many of these developed when Srinagar was an entrepot on the ancient trans-Himalayan trade route. They later grew in response to the demands of the court and to tourism. High quality craftsmanship in S Asia initially owed much to the patronage of the court and Kashmir was no exception. From the 15th century onwards, carpet making, shawl weaving and decorative techniques were actively encouraged. This developed into the tradition that persists today and forms an invaluable part of the local economy. At the end of the 19th century, for example, the estimated population of the Vale was 800,000 of which 30,000 were weavers. At present normal shopping is impossible. Kashmiri handicrafts are still widely available across the rest of India.

Carpets Hand knotted carpets are available in wool (often imported from New Zealand), wool and cotton mix or silk. The patterns tend to the traditional, the Persian and Bukhara styles being especially common, though figurative designs such as The Tree of Life are becoming increasingly popular. Young boys work with a master and it is common to hear them calling out the colour changes in a chant. Child labour in carpet-making across N India is increasingly widely criticised. Government attempts to insist on limiting hours of work and the provision of schooling often seem to be ignored. A large carpet will take months to complete, the price depending on the density of knots and the material used, silk being by far the most expensive. The salesmen usually claim that only vegetable dyes are used and whilst this is true in some instances, more readily available and cheaper chemical dyes are commonplace. After knotting, the pile is trimmed with scissors, loose threads burnt off and the carpet washed and dried.

Papier mâché work is extremely popular and comes in many forms – boxes, trays, egg cups, serviette rings etc. Paper is soaked, dried in a mould, then

CLIMATE: SRINAGAR

	Jan	Feb	Mar	Apr	May	Jun	Jul	Aug	Sep	Oct	Nov	Dec	Av/Tot
Max (°C)	4	8	13	19	25	29	31	30	28	23	15	9	20
Min (°C)	-2	-1	3	7	11	14	18	18	13	6	0	-2	7
Rain (mm)	73	72	104	78	63	36	61	63	32	29	17	36	664

painted and lacquered. The traditional style is on a black background. Often natural colouring is used, eg lapis lazuli for blue, gold leaf for gold, charcoal for black. The patterns can be highly intricate and the finish exquisite.

Other crafts include crewel work (chain stitching) on fabric, fur coats and 'Kashmiri silver' jewellery. The Kashmiri silk industry and woodcarving, particularly on walnut wood, provides employment for many.

Modern Jammu and Kashmir

Government

The state enjoys a special status within the union. As defined in Article 370 of the constitution, since 1956 Jammu and Kashmir has had its own constitution affirming its integrity. The central government has direct control over defence, external affairs and communications within the state and indirect influence over citizenship, Supreme Court jurisdiction and emergency powers. The governor of the state is appointed by the President of India while executive power rests with the Chief Minister and his council of ministers. The state sends 6 representatives to the Lok Sabha and 2 members who are nominated by the governor to the Rajya Sabha.

Economy

Agriculture Only 20% of Jammu and Kashmir is cultivated but this is farmed intensively. Wherever possible irrigation is practised. This is most striking in the starkly beautiful, almost lunar landscape of Ladakh where stream water is carefully tapped by constructing headworks and running channels (*yura*) along the natural contours to fields up to 8 km away. **Rainfed crops** About 80% of the people depend on agriculture. Tiny plots of rice, wheat and maize, the major crops of the region as a whole are often perched on perilous terraces. Barley, *bajra* and *jowar* are grown in some parts, and pulses are also cultivated in market gardens and well-watered areas. A wide variety of temperate vegetables are grown. The floating market gardens of Lake Dal are especially fertile. In the Vale of Kashmir there are large orchards of apples, peaches, pears, apricots, walnuts and almonds. The Vale is also the only S Asian producer of true saffron (*Crocus sativus*), highly prized as a delicate spice.

Minerals Some tin is mined, as is lapis lazuli. Turquoise has traditionally been valued as decoration for Ladakhi head-dresses.

Communication The Indian government has invested heavily in communications for strategic reasons. The Jawahar tunnel which links Jammu with the Vale of Kashmir is one of the longest in Asia. The road from Srinagar to Leh via Kargil is a magnificent piece of engineering and the means by which most people travel between the 2 places. The journey takes 2 days and is a route used heavily by the Indian military who have approximately 200,000 men stationed in Kashmir and Ladakh.

SRINAGAR

(*Population:* 570,000 (1981). *Altitude:* 1730m). Srinagar is beautifully located around a number of lakes, of which Lake Dal is the best known. The city is divided in 2 by the river Jhelum which is crossed by a number of bridges (*kadal*). The city was built by Raja Pravarasen in the 6th century. Its name was once mistakenly thought to be derived from Suryanagar (The City of Surya or the Sun god) but its true derivation is *Sri Nagar* – 'beautiful city'. It had a strategic as well as economic importance as it stands on the ancient trade route to Central Asia. Akbar reinforced the massive fort on Hari Parbat which dominates the surrounding countryside.

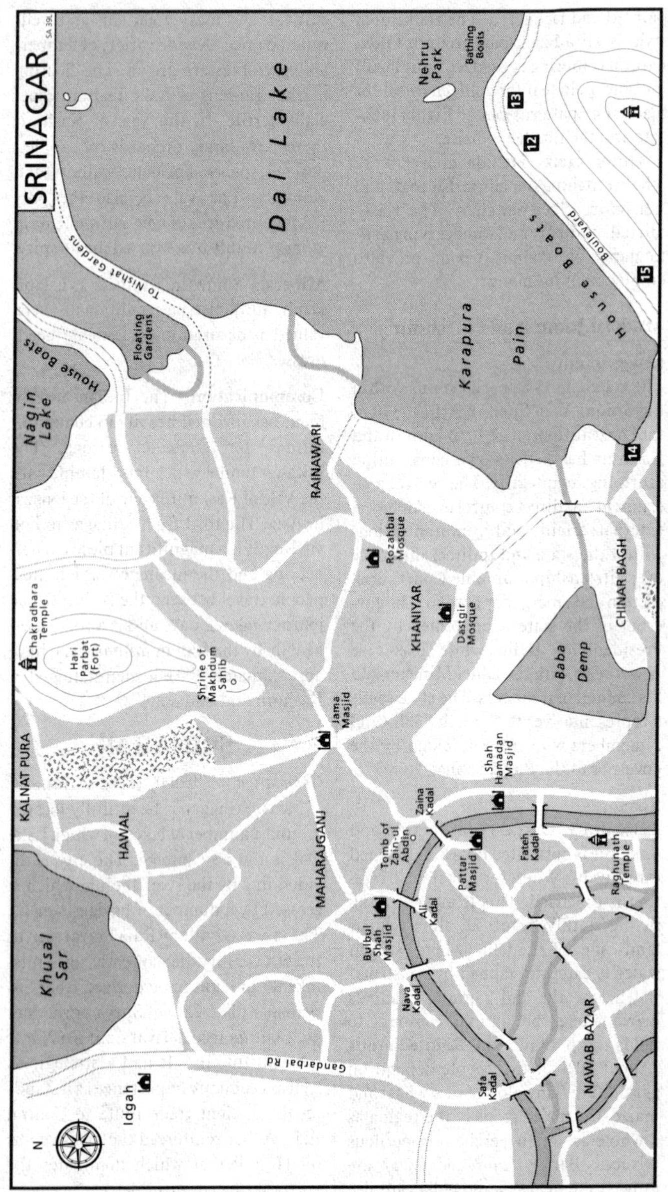
SRINAGAR
SA 39L
Dal Lake
Nehru Park
Bathing Boats
13
12
House Boats
Boulevard
15
To Nishat Gardens
Floating Gardens
House Boats
Nagin Lake
Karapura
Pain
14
RAINAWARI
Rozahbal Mosque
KHANIYAR
Dastgir Mosque
CHINAR BAGH
Chakradhara Temple
Hari Parbat (Fort)
Shrine of Makhdum Sahib
Baba Demp
Jama Masjid
KALNAT PURA
Shah Hamadan Masjid
Zaina Kadal
HAWAL
Tomb of Zain-ul Abdin
Pattar Masjid
Fateh Kadal
Raghunath Temple
MAHARAJGANJ
Bulbul Shah Masjid
Ali Kadal
Khusal Sar
Nava Kadal
NAWAB BAZAR
Gandarbal Rd
Safa Kadal
Idgah
N

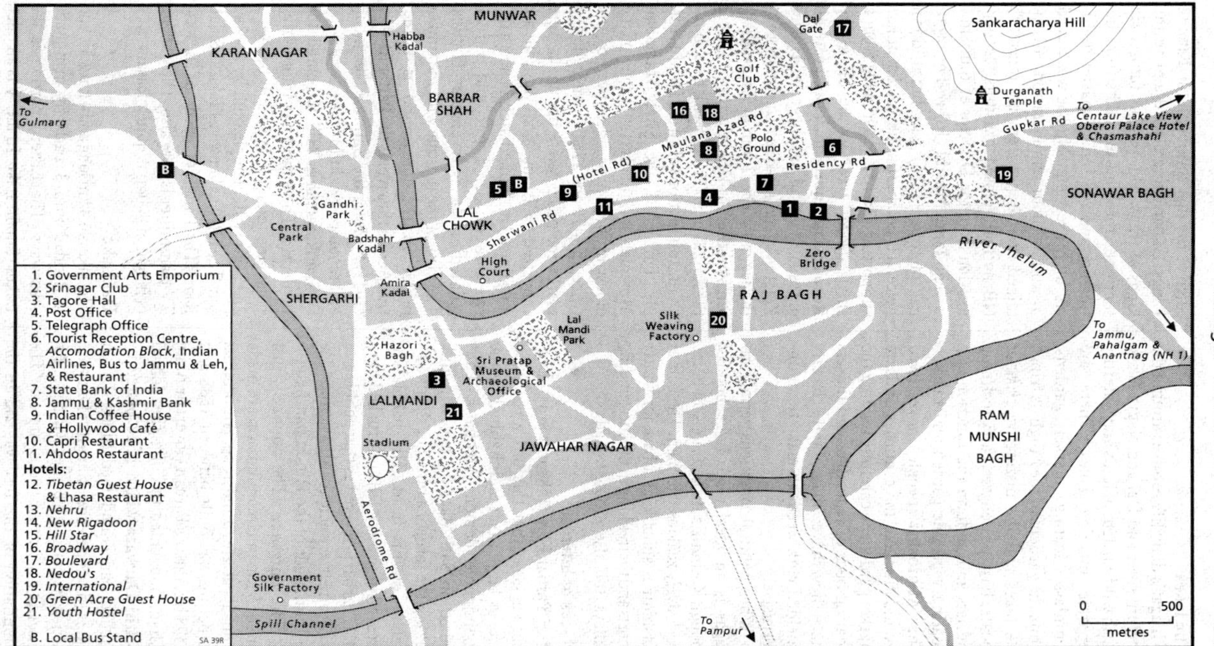

MUNWAR
KARAN NAGAR
Habba Kadal
Dal Gate
Sankaracharya Hill
Golf Club
Durganath Temple
To Gulmarg
BARBAR SHAH
To Centaur Lake View Oberoi Palace Hotel & Chasmashahi
Gupkar Rd
Maulana Azad Rd
Polo Ground
Residency Rd
(Hotel Rd)
SONAWAR BAGH
Gandhi Park
LAL CHOWK
Sherwani Rd
Central Park
Badshahr Kadal
High Court
Zero Bridge
River Jhelum
Amira Kadal
SHERGARHI
RAJ BAGH
Lal Mandi Park
Silk Weaving Factory
To Jammu, Pahalgam & Anantnag (NH 1)
Hazori Bagh
Sri Pratap Museum & Archaeological Office
LALMANDI
RAM MUNSHI BAGH
Stadium
JAWAHAR NAGAR
Aerodrome Rd
Government Silk Factory
Spill Channel
To Pampur
0 500 metres
1. Government Arts Emporium
2. Srinagar Club
3. Tagore Hall
4. Post Office
5. Telegraph Office
6. Tourist Reception Centre, *Accomodation Block*, Indian Airlines, Bus to Jammu & Leh, & Restaurant
7. State Bank of India
8. Jammu & Kashmir Bank
9. Indian Coffee House & Hollywood Café
10. Capri Restaurant
11. Ahdoos Restaurant
Hotels:
12. *Tibetan Guest House* & Lhasa Restaurant
13. *Nehru*
14. *New Rigadoon*
15. *Hill Star*
16. *Broadway*
17. *Boulevard*
18. *Nedou's*
19. *International*
20. *Green Acre Guest House*
21. *Youth Hostel*
B. Local Bus Stand
SA 39R

The lakes

Srinagar's daily life revolves around the Jhelum river and Dal and Nagin lakes. Lush wild gardens of lotus and waterlily separate bustling lanes. There are countless floating market gardens, while the gardens of the Mughals fringe the lakes and the distinctive *shikaras* (boats) ferry passengers, carry reclining tourists and perform the function of a floating vegetable garden and market. The Mihrbahri people have lived around the lake for centuries and are market gardeners, carefully tending the floating beds of vegetables and flowers that they have made and cleverly shielded with weeds to make them unobtrusive.

When political conditions permit Srinagar is an ideal place for a holiday, though Kashmiris are notorious for being excessively zealous salesmen. The Vale of Kashmir is suitable as a base for winter sports and for trekking in the surrounding valleys. It is also a route to Ladakh.

Places of interest

Hari Parbat Fort (1588 onwards). Legend suggests that this hill was once a lake as large as a sea, inhabited by the abominable demon Jalobhava. They called on Sati Mata for her help and, taking the form of a bird, she dropped a pebble on his head. The pebble increased in size as it fell and crushed him. Hari Parbat is revered as that pebble and it became the home for all 33 crore (330 million) gods of the Hindu pantheon.

The entrance The ramparts, just under 5 km in circumference, are made from local grey sandstone. An original structure was built between 1588 and 1598 by Akbar's Pathan Governor Azim Khan. You enter through the domed **Kathi Darwaza** which is decorated by arched panels and medallions. Lesser gates include the Sangin Darwaza which has attractive oriel windows. An inscription on its walls states: "The foundation of the fort was aid in the reign of the just sovereign, the King of Kings, Akbar, unparalleled among the kings of the world, past or future. He sent one crore and ten lakhs from his treasury and 200 Indian master builders, all his servants. No one was forced to work without remuneration. All obtained their wages from his treasury". **NB**: normally closed to visitors. Get permission from the Director of Tourism.

The **Jama Masjid** (1674). The original mosque (1385) was burnt down twice. It is notable for the wooden pillars supporting the roof, each made from a single *deodar* tree. To the SE is the **Rozahbal mosque**, which has the 'tomb of Jesus' (a visitor has suggested Holger Kersten's *Jesus Lived in India* for more of the legend). The **Tomb of Zain-ul-Abdin's mother** (c1430) is by the river near the Zaina kadal (bridge) which was built on the foundations of an old Hindu temple. Further S, the **Shah Hamadan Mosque**, (originally 1395), one of the oldest in the city was destroyed by fire twice, in 1479 and 1731. Some believe it marks the place where brahmans were converted to Islam. Non-Muslims are not allowed in. Immediately beneath the riverside façade, a tree and a rock painted orange is revered by Hindus. The view of the mosque with the timber bridge in the foreground is attractive. Across the river is the **Pattar Masjid** (1623) built for the Empress Nur Jahan and renamed Shahi Mosque.

Shankaracharya Hill is behind the Boulevard. The temple was built during Jahangir's reign but is said to be over a 2nd century BC temple built by Asoka's son. The hill was known as Takht-i-Sulaiman – The Throne of Solomon. The local TV transmitter is here also. The walk up (a height of 400m) is quite pleasant.

Dal Lake

The lake is 6.4 km long and 4 km wide and is divided into 3 parts by man-made causeways. The eastern portion is the Lokut (Small) Lake. In the W is an inlet, the deepest part of the lake. There are some houseboats here. The small islands are willow covered. Around the edges of the Lake are groves of *chinar*, poplar and willow. There are also the pleasure gardens.

Set in front of a triangle of the lake created by the intersecting causeways with a slender bridge at the centre lies the famous **Nishat Bagh** (Garden of Gladness). Sandwiched between the hills and the lake, it was laid out by Asaf Khan, Nur Jahan's brother, in 1632 (see page 312). Its terraces, the splendid *chenar* trees, and the central water channel flowing down to the lakeside complement the natural beauty of the site. Apparently Jahangir, the creator of the nearby Shalimar Bagh was slightly jealous of the landscape gardener's achievement and expressed pained surprise that a subject, albeit his brother-in-law, could produce something so lovely. Piqued, the emperor ordered the water supply to be cut off, but Asaf's faithful gardner, risking royal displeasure, restored the supply.

Shalimar Bagh is about 4 km away and set back from the lake. A channel extends up to their edge. Built by Jahangir for his wife Nur Jahan, the gardens are distinguished by a series of terraces linked by a water channel. These are surrounded by decorative pools which can only be reached by stepping stones. The uppermost pavilion has elegant black marble pillars and niches in the walls for flowers during the day and candles or lamps at night. The water tumbles down to the bottom in a series of waterfalls. The 2 lower pavilions are called the Diwan-i-Khas (Hall of Private Audience – middle) and Diwan-i-Am (Hall of Public Audience – lowest). Jahangir was responsible for choosing the ideal site for the garden and Shah Jahan for the exquisite buildings. In Jahangir's day the emperor would sit with his wife while musicians played to the gentle background of cascading fountains, the air rich with the bouquet of rose water. It was intended that both the gardens were approached by water. The original name of Shalimar was *Farah Baksh* – the pavilions' pitched roofs date from the 18th century.

Chashma Shahi (Royal Spring, 1632) near the *Oberoi Hotel*. This much smaller garden was built around the course of a renowned spring and is attributed to Shah Jahan though it has been much altered over the centuries. Originally, the water bubbled into a marble lotus basin in a central pavilion. This was removed, so the garden has lost its focal point though the siting is superb. Small entry fee. Just above the Chashma Shahi is the **Pari Mahal** (Fairies' Palace), a school of astrology built by Dara Shikoh, Aurangzeb's brother, for his tutor Akhund Mullah Shah. Several levels of the garden have recently been restored. Originally, there was a central building with flanking pavilions. One of the loveliest sites around Srinagar the view down to the Lake and to the hills beyond is captivating.

Hazratbal (Majestic Place) is on the W shore of the lake and commands excellent views. The modern mosque has a special sanctity as a hair of the prophet Mohammad is preserved here. In 1994 the mosque was occupied by rebels and was besieged by the Indian army. The siege created enormous tension among India and Pakistan but finally ended peacefully. Just beyond is the **Nazim Bagh** (Garden of the Morning Breeze), one of the earliest Mughal Gardens and attributed to Akbar. Little remains of the original buildings but some of the trees are believed to be those planted by the Emperor. It is now part of an Engineering College.

Museums

Pratap Singh Museum, Lal Mandi (between Amira Kadal and Zero Bridge). Free (small donation is appreciated). 1000-1700. Closed Mon, Fri lunchtime.

A fine collection of miniature paintings, weapons, tapestries and sculpture rather poorly displayed.

Parks & zoos

Apart from those mentioned above. Nehru Memorial Park, Shirazi Bagh, Nehru Park, Dal Lake, Gandhi Park, nr New Secretariat and the Polo Grounds, between Maulana Azad Rd and Sherwani Rd.

Excursions

Anchar Lake lies 11 km N of Srinagar and is a popular excursion.

Achhabal (Peaceful Place, 1,677m) 58 km on the old route from Jammu to Srinagar. Set into the mountains, the garden is supposedly the work of Nur Jahan. Smaller than the Shalimar and Nishat Baghs it incorporates features of both. The original Mughal buildings have been replaced by Kashmiri style structures; the massive chenars produce an attractive dappled effect of light and shade. The large waterfall gushes into a large tank containing a pavilion with delightful views. The source was renowned for its sweet water and was a place of pilgrimage before the garden was laid out.

Kokernag, 6 km E of Achhabal, has a botanical garden and springs whose water is said to cure indigestion. Across the enclosure are 5 temples. There are *Tourist Huts* and a *Tourist Bungalow*.

Dachigam National Park, can be visited from Srinagar (see below).

Tours

J&KSRTC: City Forest and Shopping Tour – Sankaracharya Hill, Cheshma Shahi Garden and Zeathyar, Central Market, Weaving Factory and Museum. Also to Mughal gardens and Sankaracharya Temple; Daksum via Achhabal and Kokernag; Gulmarg; Pahalgam; Sonamarg; Wular Lake; Yusmarg, Verinag, Shikargah.

Local Festivals

Mar-Apr: *Shab-e-Miraj* The day the Prophet Mohammad departed for heaven. Relics of the Prophet are displayed. *Navratri* The Festival of the Nine Nights marks the beginning of the New Year. **Mid-Apr**: *Baisakhi* This is also known as the 'Blossom Festival' and marks the end of winter and beginning of spring. Large crowds gather in the gardens. **Jul/Aug**: *Amarnath Yatra* An important Hindu pilgrimage when thousands of devotees undertake a 5-day trek to Amarnath in the Lidder Valley to offer prayers to Siva in a cave (3,962m) with an ice *lingam* (see Excursions). **Oct/Nov**: *Id-ul-Milad*, the Prophet Muhammad's birthday, celebrated with prayers and festivities.

Local information

● Accommodation

Price guide
AL Rs 3,000+ **A** Rs 2,000-3,000
B Rs 1,200-2,000 **C** Rs 600-1,200
D Rs 250-600 **E** Rs 100-250 **F** Up to Rs 100.

NB: since the military clampdown in Kashmir it has been impossible to verify changes in hotels. Many major hotels are occupied by military personnel, some have closed. Houseboats provide the alternative especially as prices have been cut. The following is a small selection of possibilities. **A** ***Centaur Lake View***, (Air India) Chashma Shahi, T 75631. 248 rm. 5 km centre. 2 restaurants, coffee shop, travel, pool. **A** ***Oberoi Palace***, Gupkar Rd, T 71241. 101 rm. 6 km centre. Shops. Former palace of the Maharaja with excellent garden but uninspiring buildings. 1st floor rm with lake view best.

B *Broadway*, Maulana Azad Rd, T 75621. 106 rm. 3 km centre. 3 restaurants. Modern, well run.

C *Pamposh*, Regal Chowk, Sherwani Rd, T 75601. 48 rm. Nr bus stand and TRC. Restaurants (one open air), coffee shop, exchange. **C** *Tramboo Continental*, Boulevard, T 73914. 54 rm. 1 km centre. Restaurant. Clean, comfortable, good value. Welcomgroup **C** *Nedous*, Maulana Azad Rd, T 74006. Large rm. Restaurant, good gardens. **E** *Boulevard*, Boulevard, T 77153, 80 rm. **D** *Nehrus*, Boulevard. T 73621. 35 rm. 4 km centre, travel. **D** *Parimahal*, Dal Lake Boulevard (base of hill), T 71235. 35 rm. Restaurant.

Good. **D** ***Gulmarg***, Dal Lake Boulevard, T 71331. 1.5 km centre. 49 rm. Restaurant, bar. Good older hotel. **E** *Tibetan Guest House* Gagrabal Road off Buchwara Road. Good value but no food; you may get woken by the muezzin.

J&KTDC accommodation: Reserve at ***Tourist Reception Centre***, **T** 76107. **D** ***Cheshma Shahi Huts***, T 73688. 55 huts, 1-3 bedrooms with bath, kitchen and sitting rm. Need transport to reach them. **D** *Tourist Reception Centre,* Maulana Azad Rd and Sherwani Rd, T 72644. Hotel Blocks with Deluxe suites and **E** Double rm.

● Budget hotels

E *International*, Sonwar Bagh, T 78604. 60 rm. 2 restaurants. **E** *New Shalimar*, Dal Lake, T 74427. 30 rm. **E** *Surya*, Samir Market, Sherwani Rd, T 78778. 18 rm. **J&KTDC E** ***Tourist Bungalow,*** Nagin Lake, T 76517, with 4 rm and **F** ***Tourist Hostel***, T 77305, for dorm. No bedding.

● Houseboats

These are peculiar to Srinagar and came into existence as a way to circumvent a royal edict which prohibited the ownership of land by non-Kashmiris. The answer was to build on water. Today, there are over 1,000 houseboats moored along the shores of the Dal and Nagin Lakes and along the Jhelum. Each range in length from 25-45m and 3-6m width. Some are delightfully cosy with one bedroom, others are sumptuously deluxe with 2-3 bedrooms and well appointed living areas. The larger ones are therefore capable of accommodating separate groups of guests prepared to share. Built of fragrant cedar planks, the interiors are intricately (some think fussily) carved and display the artistry of the Kashmiri craftsmen. The furnishings tend to take no regard of matching and rugs, bedspreads, walls, curtains, lamps etc all tend to be classically and busily ornate. Houseboats usually come with their own staff, eg a cook and often a boatman for your shikara, who usually live in the adjoining 'kitchen boat'. All meals are included.

Categories The State government has categorised the houseboats into 5 price categories: Deluxe A, B, C and D according to the comfort provided. There is variation in quality and value for money in each. Rec for Nagin Lake ***Roshu Doktoo,*** Suleiman Shipping Corp, Dal Lake, T 74547 and small boats from Abdul Rashid Major, Nagin Bagh. Also rec ***Butts Claremont***, Nasim Bagh, Hazratbal, T 72325. Nr centre ***Siah Group***, Box 76, T 74044. Greater risk and increased inconvenience of travelling in 1993 is balanced by some benefits as some found excellent bargains: Deluxe houseboats charging Rs 100-150 per day, per head (sometimes no others to share!)

C ***Welcomgroup Gurkha Houseboats***, PO Box 57, T 75229. 17 rm. 7 km centre. Each houseboat has a sitting and dining room, sun deck. Meal, shikara rides, sight seeing, folk entertainment. **C** ***Alps Houseboats***, PO Box 390, Dal Lake. T 78669. 6 houseboats. **C** ***California Group of Houseboats***, PO Box 19, Dal Lake, T 73549. 16 houseboats. **C** ***Lion of Kashmir Houseboats***, PO Box 61, Nagin Lake, T 74253. 12 houseboats. **C** ***Meena Bazar Group of Houseboats***, PO Box 433, Srinagar-190 001, T 74044. 25 rm. 5 km centre. Travel. **C** ***Pintail*** has nice rm and good continental food. Inadquate heating in winter. **D** ***White Horse*** Dal Lake (through Gulam Nali Gagroo, T 79107, has nice rm. Rec. **E** ***New Manila*** Dal Lake (through Bashir Ahmad, T 72787 (or Bombay T 3096616, F 3072860). Beautiful houseboat owned by very friendly family who will arrange outings and make travel arrangements. Highly rec. Rs 200 incl 3 meals.

● Places to eat

Restaurants serve *Muslim* meals which may include saffron *pillau, badam pasanda* (meat with almonds) and *gushtaba*. The first 3 hotels listed are the best for comfort and food, but expensive. Transport back into town at night difficult. **Kashmiri**: on Sherwani Rd: ***Mughal Darbar***, next to Suffering Moses. Drab exterior but rec. Reasonable price; ***Adhoo's***, Residency Rd; ***Wazwan*** TRC. **N Indian**: ***Broad View***, New Secretariat Rd. ***Hollywood***, Sherwani Rd and ***Indian Coffee House*** which also does snacks; ***Kwality***, Hari Singh High St. Continental cuisine at ***Solace***, Sherwani Rd. Gujarati food at ***Surti***, Lal Chowk. ***Grand,*** Sherwani Rd, is veg. **Chinese**: ***Lhasa***, Boulevard, and the small ***Alka Salka***, Sherwani Rd. ***Glocken Bakery*** for drinks and snacks. Close by, nr Dal Gate ***Sultan's Bakery*** rec for western delicacies. ***Dimple*** is good for milk shakes.

● Banks & money changers

Usually open 1000-1400. Several branches incl **Grindlays** and **State Bank of India** on Sherwani Rd. The latter also opens 1600-1800 Winter, 1600-1900 Summer.

● **Hospitals & medical services**
Nehru Memorial Hospital.

● **Post & telecommunications**
GPO: The Bund. **Central Telegraph Office**: Maulana Azad Rd, open 24 hr.

● **Shopping**
Major shopping centres are located at the Bund, Boulevard, Dalgate, Lal Chowk, Polo View, Maulana Azad Rd and Sherwani Rd. On Sherwani Rd: ***Govt Arts Emporium***, ***Khadi Bhandar*** and ***Rajasthan Emporium***. ***Arts Emporium,*** Govt Central Market, Boulevard. Exhibition Gr. ***Art Emporium***. Carpets: ***Indo-Kashmir Carpet Factory***, Shah Mollah and ***Roshu Doktoo,*** Dal Gate. ***Shyam Brothers***, Hotel Rd for furs. ***Darson's***, opp Lhasa restaurant, Boulevard Lane II. Walnut woodcarving, shawls and Papier mâché: ***Langoo***. ***Suffering Moses*** is well known for quality goods and is aware of their reputation. Shop shikaras 'patrol Dal lake like sharks'. **Bargain very hard for anything you like. Photography *Preco Studios*. *Mahattas*. *Royal*.**

● **Sports**
Sher-e-Kashmir Sports Complex, Hazuriburg. Excellent facilities. Restaurant and snack bar. **Golf**: *Kashmir Govt Golf Club*, Maulana Azad Rd. 18-hole golf course, temporary membership. **Swimming and boating**: Water Sports Institute, Nagin Lake. *Hotels Broadway* and *Centaur Lake View* have pools.

● **Tour companies & travel agents**
Rec: ***Ladakh Safari*** and ***Tiger Tops Mountain Travel*** Bund; ***Mercury***, Oberoi Palace; ***Sita*** and ***TCI***, Maulana Azad Rd. Others incl: ***Adventure Tours***, ***Reshu Boktoo***, Sulaiman Shopping Complex, and ***MM Butt*** on Dalgate and ***Trade Winds***, Boulevard.

● **Tourist offices**
J&K Tourism, 72449, after hours, T 77303; Tourist Reception Centre, T 77303, 1000-1700. **India**, Vir Marg. 0800-2000. Govt TRC, T 77303. **Kashmir Motor Drivers Assoc**, T 72798, 76504. **Hotel Assoc Booking Counter**, Tourist Reception Centre, T 76631. Also at New Airport.

● **Useful addresses**
Police: T 100. **Fire**: T100, 72222. **Ambulance**: T 74591. **Tourist Police**: T 77303. **Foreigners' Registration Office**, CID Special Branch, Sherwani Rd, nr the Bund. 1000-1600. Also at New Airport, T 31521. **Tourist Reception Centre**, T 76458.

● **Transport**
Srinagar is situated on **NH1A**, which connects to all parts of the country by all-weather roads. From: **Jammu** (293 km) by the narrow mountain road, often full of lorries and military convoys, takes 12 hr; few stops for food and facilities; **Gulmarg** (56 km); **Pahalgam** (96 km); **Sonamarg** (87 km); **Kargil** (204 km); **Leh** (434 km); **Delhi** (876 km); **Chandigarh** (630 km).

Local Auto-rickshaws: are readily available. Fares negotiable. **Matador Mini-Bus**: service covers most areas in the city. Mini fare Re 1. **City Bus service**: main bus stand at Lal Chowk. **Bicycle hire**: from several shops along Boulevard close to Dalgate. **Shikaras**: are water taxis on the lakes and Jhelum river. There are 'Stands' where 'official' fares to most destinations are posted, but these may be difficult to implement. You can hire them by the hour, part of, or all day.

Air The airport is 14 km from City Centre. **Tranport to town**: by taxi or coach. **Indian Airlines**, City Office T 71918, Airport, T 30334, flies daily between Delhi and Srinagar, 3 times a week via Amritsar; 4 times via Jammu.

Train The nearest railhead is Jammu Tawi with coach and taxi transfer. Govt TRC, 0700-1900. City Office, TRC, T 72698 for reservation of 2nd Cl Sleeper and a/c only. Summer 0830-1900, Winter 1000-1800. Also City Booking Office at *Radhakrishnan*, Budhah Chowk, T 72929.

Road J&KSRTC and the STRCs of Punjab, Haryana, Delhi and Himachal Pradesh regularly run to Jammu from major northern cities like Delhi, Chandigarh and Amritsar. Some continue to Srinagar, while there are many connections from Jammu. J&KSRTC, TRC, Srinagar, T 72698. Summer 0600-1800, Winter 0700-1700.

Dachigam National Park

This area of the W Himalayas was the Maharajah of Kashmir's hunting preserve. The 140 sq km park covers the 2 sectors of **Upper Dachigam**, in places above the tree line (over 4,200 m), accessible only in the summer after a hard 2-day trek, and **Lower Dachigam**, at about 1,500m (22 km from Srinagar) with motorable roads and so when political conditions allow, possible to visit even in winter. **Note** Special permits needed from Controller, Tawaza, Srinagar. Best season: May-Sep. Temp range: 32°C to -8°C. Rainfall: 660 mm.

The scenic park with deep ravines, rocky outcrops, conifer covered slopes and alpine glades, supports the endangered hangul (Kashmir stag) a species of red deer, which moves to the Marsar Lake in Upper Dachigam in the summer.

The **Dagwan** river flows through **Lower Dachigam** which has tracts of riverine forest and a heronry. The plentiful supply of fruit trees (peaches, plums, wild cherries) attracts numerous migratory birds (incl monal pheasant, golden oriole, long-tailed blue magpie, Himalayan griffon, pied woodpecker and rubythroat) and the Himalayan black bear in June, after its winter hibernation. There are also Indian horse chestnut, willow, walnut and oak.

- **Accommodation** in Srinagar or *Wildlife Rest Houses* or *Lodges* in Dachigam.

- **Transport Road** By a good road from Srinagar and then **trekking** or by **pony**.

Gulmarg and Khilanmarg

Gulmarg (2730m) is 52 km W of Srinagar on the N side of the Pir Panjal. The road journey from Srinagar is through picturesque rice field and avenues of poplars, passing small villages. Tangmarg marks the end of the valley and the drive ascends through fir covered hills. Gulmarg, originally Gaurimarg, was a favourite of Emperor Jahangir. It stands in a broad upland bowl-shaped meadow– the name means 'flower-filled meadow'. From vantage points you can see the entire Vale of Kashmir and admire the surrounding mountains. It is a good base for treks into the Pir Panjal.

Walks

There are a number of walks around Gulmarg, the best known being the 11 km **Outer Circular Walk**. As its name suggests, this runs right round Gulmarg through pleasant pine forests. Nanga Parbat (8126m), the 8th highest peak in the world is visible to the N and Haramukh (5148m) to the S.

Khilanmarg is a small valley, 4 km uphill from Gulmarg, carpeted with flowers in spring and a ski run in winter. It is an exhilarating steep walk with beautiful scenery, best undertaken in the morning. Further on, 13 km from Gulmarg is **Alpather Lake**(3843m), which lies at the foot of the main Apharwat Peak (4511m). Much of the lake is frozen until mid-Jun. A ridge separates this from the main Gulmarg valley so a walk there entails going over the Apharwat Ridge (3810m). There is a well graded pony track all the way.

Ferozepore Nallah, 5 km from Gulmarg, and reached from the Tangmarg road and the Outer Circular Walk, is a mountain stream that is particularly good for trout. **Ziarat of Baba Reshi** is the tomb (*ziarat*) of Baba Payam-ud-Din, a noted Muslim saint. Before renouncing the world he was a courtier to a 15th century Kashmiri King and is revered by both Hindus and Muslims. The path leads through thick forest.

Local information

● Accommodation

Most open May to mid-Nov; most with electric heaters or *bukharis* (wood-burning stoves in the middle of the room). **B** *Hilltop*, T 245. 35 rm. Shops, health club.

C *Highlands Park*, T 207. 40 rm in bungalows. 1 km centre. Open during skiing season. Lovely building in a fine garden, good views. Restaurant, bar, travel. **C** *Nedous*, T 223. 20 rm, 3 huts. Putting green. Good views, pleasant, with character. **C** *Affarwat*, T 202. 18 rm. Simple but well managed. **C** *Pine Palace*, nr Ski Lift, T 266. 21 rm. Gardens. Simple but good.

D *New Zum-Zum*, T 215. 20 wood-panelled rm with bath and balcony. Restaurant, 24-hr rm service. Rec.

● Budget hotels

J&K Tourism offers huts; gas cylinder hire from Tourist office. **E** *Tourist Huts*, T 239. 14 insulated huts, 1-4 bedrooms with bath, sitting rm and kitchen. Charming wooden insulated huts with heating. Popular, so book very early through Tourist Office, T or travel agent. **E** *New Tourist Bungalow*, T 241. Clean, open all year round. 24 rm with Indian bathrooms. No restaurant. Good value.

● Places to eat

Rec: ***Highlands Park*** is expensive but not exceptional. ***Khailan***, *Affarwat Hotel*, pleasant. Also ***Nedou's, Woodlands*** and ***Yamberzal***. Nr the Bus Stand, ***Ahdoos*** does good meals. Some hotels and the Govt Club have **bars**. Try the lounge bar at the *Highlands Park*.

● Entertainment

Golf 18-hole course maintained by the J&K Dept of Tourism. Claims to be one of the highest greens in the world at 2652m. Temporary membership available; Tourist Office next door has limited equipment and caddies for hire. The course has recently been relaid and now offers a greater challenge. *Golf Club, T* 224. 2 rm for guests.

Ponies can be hired through the Tourist Office (see Local transport below)

Skiing Some of the best slopes in the country are at Gulmarg. However, India is not a skiing nation so do not expect too much. There is a 500m chair lift (allowing a 900m run), and a 200m T-bar, suitable for beginner or intermediate levels. Off-piste possible; advanced skiiers my walk to Apherwat and descend in 30 min. Heli-skiing (helicopters taking skiiers to nearby peaks) is offered in season. Passes, instruction and equipment hire are very cheap (Rs 120 daily). In summer the chair lift is used for sightseeing. Basic ski equipment and toboggans can be hired from the Ski Shop, Tourist Office, T 299. *Indian Institute of Ski and Mountaineering, T* 246.

Trekking Equipment and porters can be hired from the Tourist Reception Centre, Srinagar, T 77305. Nominal charges.

● Tourist Office

J&K, Club Building, Gulmarg, T 239. 0930-1800. Also Tangmarg, T 77303.

● Useful addresses

There is a Police Station, a Govt **Hospital**, State **Bank** of India and a **Post Office**.

● Transport

Local Cars: are restricted. **Ponies**: can be hired through Tourist Offices at Tangmarg and Gulmarg; reasonable fixed rates on daily and hourly basis.

Air J&K Tourism runs a helicopter service to Gulmarg. Frequency depends on weather conditions and demand. Rs 600 return.

Road Bus: J&KSRT offers regular deluxe sightseeing (Rs 46 return) and ordinary bus services (Rs 13 one way, 3 hr) from Srinagar. In winter it is only up to Tangmarg (13 km from Gulmarg); rest by jeep – Rs 150 one way for full load. **Taxi**: full taxi from Srinagar Rs 300 approx. Fix price before departure. As always in Kashmir, bargain hard.

SRINAGAR TO LADAKH

In addtion to the Srinagar-Leh road, there are several trekking routes into Ladakh, the most popular before the clamp-down in Kashmir, being along the **Warvan Valley**. The **Boktol Pass** (4420m) was the most popular pass, another being the Chilung Pass (5200m). If normal trekking becomes possible again, treks to Ladakh should start in mid-Jun with the season continuing until mid-Oct when the passes are blocked with snow. For the current alternative Manali-Leh route. See page 531.

Before going over the passes, time should be allowed for acclimatisation. Basic food supplies can usually be obtained from the larger villages in the Warvan Valley. Ponies are available and also porters if farm labour demands are not too high. From **Sheshnag** (Amarnath trek) you can reach Ladakh via the Gulgali Pass (4500m). Allow 6 days and take a local guide if you are doing this early in the season.

Ladakh

The mountains of Ladakh are not as spectacular as some parts of the high Himalaya. As even the valleys are at an altitude of 3500m the summits are only 3000m higher. Because it is desert there is little snow on them and they look like big brown hills, dry and dusty, with clusters of willows and desert roses along the streams. Yet Ladakh is a completely magical place, remote, with delightful, gentle, ungrasping people.

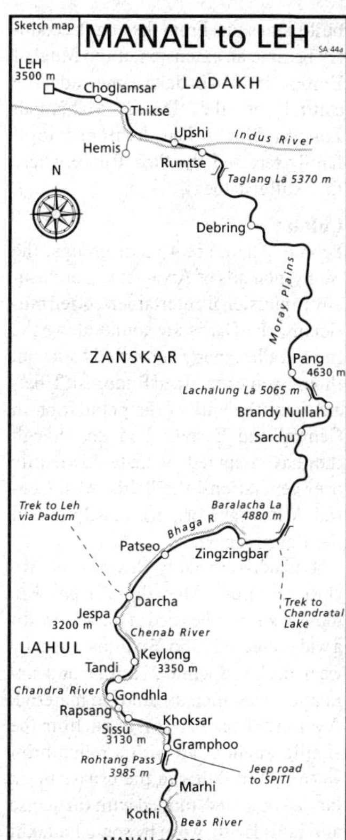

BASICS Approx 98,000 sq km. *Population*: 135,000. *Altitude*: 2500-4500m with passes at 4000-6000 and peaks up to 7500m.

Ladakhi society has generally been very introverted and the economy surprisingly self-sufficient. Ladakh also developed a very distinct culture. Polyandry was common, many men (and in the past, women) became monks. The harsh climate contributed to very high death rates, which resulted in a stable population based on subsistence agriculture. That is rapidly changing. Imported goods are increasingly widely available and more and more people are taking part in the monetary economy. Ladakh and Leh, the capital, have been open to tourists only since 1974. Some argue that already there have been too many.

Travel by road gives you an advantage over flying into Leh as it enables you to acclimatise to a high altitude plateau and if you are able to hire a jeep or car it will give you the flexibility of stopping to see the several sights on the way.

Environment

Land Four mountain ranges cross Ladakh – Gt Himalaya, Zanskar, Ladakh and Karakoram – as do the Indus and its tributaries, Zanskar, Shingo and Shyok. Ladakh also has the world's largest glaciers outside the polar regions, and the large and beautiful lake Pangong Tso, 150 km long and 4 km wide at a height of 4000m.

Climate The temperature goes down to -30°C in Leh and Kargil and -50°C in Dras, remaining sub-zero for 3 months, from Dec to Feb. Yet on clear sunny days, it can be scorching hot and you can easily get sunburnt. Rainfall is only 50 mm annually, the melting snow sustaining life. Sand dunes dot the desert-like landscape in places and there are even occasional dust storms.

Flora & fauna Willow and poplar grow in profusion and provide fuel and timber, as well as fodder and material for basket making. The fragrant juniper is reserved for religious ceremonies. The area supports some rare species of animals and birds – red foxes, wolves, ibex, mouse hare and marmots and among the 100 or so species of birds, black necked cranes, Bactrian magpies, Turkoman rock pigeon, desert wheatears, buntings, larks, kite, kestrel and many kinds of finches, ducks and geese. Some of the mammals are only found in Ladakh, among them the *brong drong* (wild yak), *kyang* (wild horse) and *nyan* (the large-horned sheep). The snow leopard is the rarest wild animal and you are unlikely to see some of the others, like the musk deer, the Tibetan gazelle or the Tibetan antelope which is prized for its fleece which produces *Shahtoosh*, the very best wool.

History of Ladakh

Rock carvings indicate that the region has been used for thousands of years by nomadic tribesmen who include the Mons of N India, the Dards, the Mongols and Champa shepherds from Tibet. The Mons introduced Buddhism and established settlements in the valleys while the Dards from Gilgit introduced irrigation. Kashmir and Ladakh lay on a feeder of the great Silk Road that ran from China to the Mediterranean in Roman times.

Early political development By the end of the 10th century, Ladakh was controlled by the Thi dynasty who founded a capital at Shey and built many forts. Tibetan Lamaistic Buddhism took hold at the same time and over 100 gompas were built. In 1533 Soyang Namgyal united the whole region up to the outskirts of Lhasa and made his capital at Leh. The Namgyal dynasty still exists today. The Rani (Queen) of Stok was elected to the Indian Parliament.

Medieval expansion During the reigns of Senge Namgyal (c1570-1620) and Deldan Namgyal (c1620-60) Ladakh was threatened from the S and W by the Baltis, who had enlisted the assistance of the Mughals. They were beaten back and the Namgyals extended Ladakhi power. The expansionist era came to an end when the fifth Dalai Lama of Tibet, Nawang Lobsang Gyatso (1617-82) persuaded the Mongolians, whom he had converted to Buddhism, to enter a military campaign against W Tibet and Ladakh. The Ladakhis were unable to repel the invading Mongol forces. Delegs Namgyal turned to Kashmir for help. The Mughal Governor of Kashmir sent troops to help the King of Leh regain his throne but in return he had to pay regular tribute and build a mosque. From then on the country became an extension of the Mughal Empire. In 1834 Ladakh came under the control of the Dogra Maharajah Zorawar Singh. The dethroned royal family received the Stok Palace where they still live today.

Culture

People There are 4 main groups: the **Mons**, nomads of Aryan stock, are usually professional entertainers, often musicians; the **Dards** are found along the Indus valley, many converted to Islam, though some remained Buddhist; **Tibetans** form the bulk of the population in Central and Eastern Ladakh, though they have assumed the Ladakhi identity over generations; the **Baltis** with Central Asian Saka origins, mostly live in the Kargil region.

Ladakhis are hardy, cheerful and live close to nature. They dress in *gonchas*, loose woollen robes tied at the waist with a wide coloured band. Buddhists usually wear dark red while Muslims and nomadic tribes often use undyed material. A variety of head dress is worn, from the simple woollen cap with a rolled brim worn by the Baltis to the ornate black lambskin *peraks* studded with turquoise and lapis lazuli, worn by some Ladakhi women.

Religion The majority are Mahayana Buddhists (*Vajrayana*), with a mixture of animistic pre-Buddhist Bon and Tantric influences. W Ladakh also has a large number of Shia Muslims, their mosques influenced by Persian architecture. The Buddhist *gompas* or monasteries are places of worship, of meditation and religious instruction and the structures, often sited on spectacular mountain ridges, add to the attraction of the landscape while remaining a central part of the Ladakhi life. Travellers to Ladakh will find visits to *gompas* a rewarding experience, especially as some are within easy reach of Leh.

Festivals The festivals usually take place in the bleak winter months when villagers gather together, stalls spring up around the *gompas* and colourful dance dramas and masked dances are performed in the courtyard. Musical instruments, weapons and religious objects are brought out during these dance performances. The high priest (the *Kushak*) is accompanied by monks in monotonous recitation while others play large cymbals, trumpets and drums. The serious theme of the victory of Good over Evil is lightened by comic interludes. Although most of the annual festivals are celebrated in Jan and Feb, you may be lucky to be at one of the few that celebrates their's in a warmer month, eg *Lamayuru* (end Apr/early May); *Hemis* (end Jun/early Jul); *Phyang* (Jul); *Thikse* (mid Jul/early Aug). The Festival of Ladakh is held in the 1st week of Aug.

Modern Ladakh

Recent History Following India's independence and partition in 1947 Ladakh, like Kashmir, was divided. Indian and Chinese troops have been stationed on the E border since the Chinese invasion of Tibet in 1950. From the early 1950s Chinese troops were stationed in the Aksai Chin, which India also claimed, and without Indian knowledge built a road linking Tibet with Xinjiang. This was one of the 2 fronts in China's war with India in 1962, which confirmed China's de facto hold on the territory. India still disputes its legality. Since 1962 when trouble with the Chinese flared up, the Indian army has maintained an obvious presence in Ladakh. Whilst this has not produced devastating effects, the strategic requirements of better links with the rest of India have resulted in Ladakh being 'opened up' to some influences from outside.

Economy Out of necessity, the people, particularly the Baltis, are expert irrigation engineers, cutting granite to channel melt water to the fields. Barley is turned into *tsampa* (pancake) after roasting and grinding or *chang* the sour alcoholic drink and tea into *gur gur* which is salted and buttered. Apple and apricots grow well, with the latter being dried for the winter, the kernel yielding oil for burning in prayer lamps. At lower altitudes, grape, mulberry and walnut is grown. Livestock is precious, especially the *yak* which provides meat, milk for butter, hair and hide for tents, boots, ropes, horns for agricultural tools and dung for fuel. Goats, especially in the E region, produce fine *pashm* for export. The Zanskar pony is fast and strong and therefore used for transport – and for the special game of Ladakhi polo!

Ladakhi farming Cultivation in Ladakh is restricted to the areas immediately around streams and rivers. Altitude and topography determine the choice of crop. Barley is the most common and is roasted, ground and combined with water to form the staple or eaten dry. Peas are the most common vegetable and apples and apricots the most popular fruits. Because of the harshness of the climate and lack of rain, the cropping season only lasts from Mar to Nov. Sheep, goats and yaks are taken to alpine pastures at altitudes of 4000m and more over the summer months. From Ladakh and Kashmir is obtained the wool of the Pashmina goats which has achieved international fame as 'cashmere'.

Communication Though the area is virtually cut off for 6 months, it has always retained cultural links with its neighbouring regions in Himachal Pradesh, Kashmir, Tibet and Central Asia and traded in valuable *Pashm*, carpets, apricots, tea, and small amounts of salt, boraz, sulphur, pearls and metals. Animal transport is provided by yaks, ponies, Bactrian camels and the broad backed *hunia* sheep.

SRINAGAR TO LEH

The journey from Srinagar to Leh must be one of the most fascinating road journeys in the world. There are dramatic scenic and cultural changes as you go from Muslim, verdant Kashmir to Buddhist, ascetic Ladakh. The engineering skill employed in constructing the road is stunning as it negotiates high passes and fragile mountainsides. This is a trip to remember – however, see warning below. **NB**: because of political unrest in Kashmir, in 1994-95 the route may not be open to foreign visitors. The alternative route to Leh is from Manali. See page 531.

Sonamarg

('Path of Gold', 2740m, 84 km from Srinagar), is the last major town in Kashmir before the Zoji La and Ladakh. Its name may derive from its past importance as a feeder to the Great Silk Road or, more likely, because of its carpet of spring flowers. The legendary Spring has the power to turn anything into gold. This valley by the Sindh river is a close rival to Gulmarg with its beautiful forests of silver fir and blue pine. **Accommodation**: Open in summer. D *Sonamarg Glacier.* Also, a range of Govt hotels: E *Tourist Huts* with double rm, kitchen and sitting rm, an F *Rest House* nr the Tourist Office, and *Tourist Bungalow* outside the town.

The small village of **Baltal** (43 km), the last Kashmiri settlement, is at the foot of the pass. **Zoji La** (13 km, 3529m) marks the boundary between Kashmir and Ladakh. The road here is unsurfaced, narrow and with steep unprotected drops which can be alarming. This is the first of the passes on the Srinagar-Leh Highway to be blocked by snow each year even though it is not the highest, as those nearer Leh are in a rainshadow area. The approach is a long haul across a slate mountainside which looks as though it might shear off at any moment.

From Zoji la the road descends to **Minamarg** meadow, rich in rare Alpine flora and then on to **Dras** (50 km from Baltal), the first village after the Zoji La pass, where the convoys over the pass terminate. It is also the base for the road clearing gangs. The winter temperatures go down to -50°C, and heavy snow and strong winds cut off the town. The inhabitants are Dard Muslims. There is a bank and a *Tourist Bungalow.* You travel along the Dras river and pass **Kharbu**. Nearing Kargil (30 km), water is channelled carefully to irrigate terraces growing apples and apricots, fields of buckwheat and barley and groves of willow and poplar.

The broad Kargil basin and its wide terraces is separated from the Mulbekh valley by the 12 km long **Wakha Gorge**. Kargil is also the starting point of trekking expeditions lasting 7 to 12 days and mountaineers attempting to climb the Nun and Kun, both over 7000m high, start from here.

Kargil

(*Alt* 2740m) On the bank of the river Suru, Kargil was an important trading post on 2 routes, from Srinagar to Leh, and to Gilgit and the lower Indus Valley. Even today the town has a medieval atmosphere with narrow cobbled streets. The people are mainly Balti Muslims; the 2 mosques show a strong Turkish influence. Before 1990 it was the overnight stopping place of the Srinagar-Leh highway.

Local information

● Accommodation

Price often includes meals. The best is Welcomgroup's **C** *Highlands*, Baroo, T 41. 40 rm. **D** *Caravan Sarai*, nr Tourist Office, overlooking Bazar. Comfortable rm, good food. **D** *Zoji La*, Kargil Ladakh Rd, T 28. **D** *Suru View*, T 103. 40 rm. 2 **E** *Tourist Bungalows*, one nr the main street by the river. Reasonable. Of the **E** hotels, *Greenlands*, Kargil-Ladakh Rd, T 31, has been rec. **E** *International*, T 123. The **F** hotels are basic and dingy – *Argalia, Crown*.

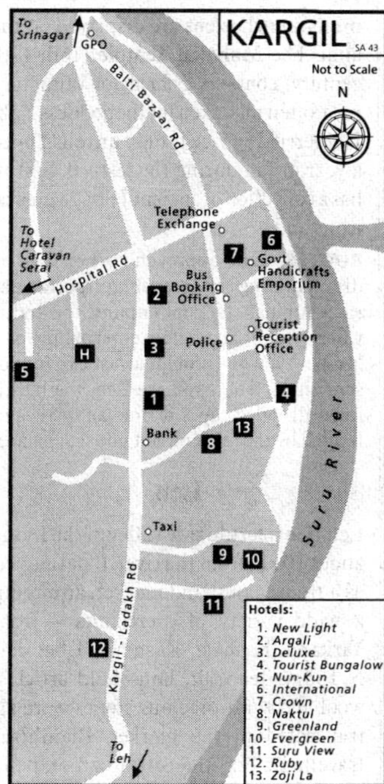

● **Useful services**

There are a couple of **banks**, a **Hospital,** a **Post Office**, **Police** Station and a **Tourist Office**.

ROUTES From Kargil the road goes on to **Shergol** (30 km), the cultural boundary between Muslim and Buddhist areas.

Mulbekh (9 km). Limestone masses are thrust up along fracture zones round the village; monasteries with frescoes perch on hill tops. Just outside the village is the famous huge sculpture of *Maitreya* (8th-9th century AD, though some date it to 1st century BC. 9m high and carved on a solitary finger of rock, it depicts a standing Boddhisattva with 4 arms with a headdress and jewels. The *kharoshti* inscriptions at the back are believed to have been buried. In the village of tidy white-washed houses there are 2 *gompas* and a basic *Tourist Bungalow*.

Namika La (13 km, 3720m), is known as the Pillar in the Sky; Bodh Kharbu, (15 km); Photu La (4093m) is the highest pass on the route. From here you can catch sight of the monastery at Lamayuru. **Khalsi** (36 km) is where the road meets the milky green Indus river which leaves the wide valley of Ladakh and disappears into a deep granite gorge. The village has abundant apricots.

Lamayuru (10 km), the monastery is perched on a crag overlooking the Indus. The complex, which includes a library, thought to be the oldest in the region, was founded in the 11th century and belongs to the Tibetan Kagyupa sect. The present monastery dating from the 16th century was partly destroyed in the 19th. You can still see some of the murals, which mix Indian and Tibetan styles, the 11-headed and 1000-armed Avalokiteshvara image along with the recently redecorated *dukhang* (assembly hall). There are caves carved out of the mountain wall and some of the rooms are richly furnished with carpets, Tibetan tables and butter lamps. Festivals are in Feb/Mar and Jul.

Rizong (53 km), has a monastery and nunnery, which may accommodate visitors. After passing the caves at Saspol you can reach Alchi (7 km) by taking a branch road across the Indus.

Alchi, (70 km from Leh) has a large temple complex and is regarded as one of the most important Buddhist centres in Ladakh and a jewel of monastic skill. There are 5 shrines in the **Choskor** complex (11th century) which has some splendid wall paintings (some liken it to the Byzantine style) and wooden figures; note the painted wooden ceiling of the gate. The ante-room wall shows 2 rowing boats with fluttering flags, a reminder perhaps of the presence in ancient times of lakes in this desert. The flood plain at Alchi is very fertile and provides good and relatively extensive agricultural land.

Lekir (12 km) reached by a scenic journey has the next monastery with huge clay Buddha statues. The beautiful murals are 9th century. You then reach the fortress of **Basgo** (10 km) which contains the ruins of a Buddhist citadel impressively sited on a spur overlooking the Indus Valley. It served as a royal residence for several periods between the 15th and 17th centuries. Tibetan and Mongol armies besieged it. There are 2 Buddhist temples, numerous *chortens* and *mani* walls beyond the village. The Maitreya Temple (16th century) was constructed by the Namgyal rulers which has a large sculpture of Maitreya at the rear of the hall. The Serzang (Gold and Copper) Temple (17th century) is the other and contains murals depicting the Buddha (much damaged by water).

ROUTES From here the road rises to another bare plateau to give you the first glimpse of Leh, 30 km away.

Phyang (20 km from Leh) belongs to the Red Hat sect, with its 16th century *gompa* housing hundreds of statues on wooden shelves and *thangkas*. A traditional monastery, setting for a spectacular religious festival with masked dancing in July.

Spituk (8 km from Leh). The monastery with 3 chapels here was founded in the 11th century but the buildings, in a series of tiers with courtyards and steps, date from the 15th century. The Gelugpa monks created the precedent in Ladakh of building on mountain tops rather than valley floors; this is the seat of the head Lama. The long 16th-17th century *Dukhang* is the largest building and has 2 rows of seats the length of the walls to a throne at the far end. Sculptures and miniature chortens are displayed on the altar. The **Mahakal Temple** (16th-17th century) contains a shrine of Vajrabhairava, often mistaken for the goddess Kali. Her terrifying face is only unveiled once a year in Jan during the festival. Spituk has a collection of ancient Jelbagh masks, icons and arms.

ROUTES The approach to Leh can be disappointing after such a spectacular ride. Amidst stark mountains, the Indus valley widens and before entering the city 'proper' you go through a vast expanse of army huts. Then you see Leh, the buildings all piled up on one another and topped by the ancient, but unused, palace.

Leh

Leh is in a fertile side valley of the Indus about 10 km from the river. It developed as a trading post and market, attracting a wide variety of merchants – from Yarkand, Kashgar, Kashmir, Tibet and N India. Tea, salt, household articles, wool and semi-precious stones were all transacted in the market. Buddhism travelled along the Silk Road and the Kashmir and Ladakh feeder, and so have soldiers, spies, explorers and latter day pilgrims. Today, Leh is important as a military base and a tourist centre, the two contributing most to the urban economy.

BASICS *Population*: 9000. *Altitude*: 3500m. *Clothing*: plenty of layers. When the sun is up it gets quite hot but in the shade it can still be very cold. Protect against sunburn.

WARNING Arriving in Leh (*Alt* 3521m) by plane you need to acclimatise by not exerting yourself too much. If you have travelled by road from Srinagar you will

CLIMATE: LEH

	Jan	Feb	Mar	Apr	May	Jun	Jul	Aug	Sep	Oct	Nov	Dec	Av/Tot
Max (°C)	-3	1	6	12	17	21	25	24	21	14	8	2	12
Min (°C)	-14	-12	-6	-1	3	7	10	10	5	-1	-7	-11	-1
Rain (mm)	12	9	12	7	7	4	16	20	12	7	3	8	117

have acclimatised better. Still, a mild headache is common and can be treated with aspirin or paracetamol. After a couple of days you will feel more energetic as your body adjusts to the changed atmospheric conditions. If you have a heart condition, consult your doctor on the advisability of your going to Leh.

If you want to acclimatise slowly the best way to travel to Leh is to go by road and return by air, weather permitting. The ordinary buses are inexpensive and crowded but an enjoyable experience. The 'Luxury' buses charge considerably more. It is also possible to hitch-hike. Alternatively, you can hire a taxi which works out more expensive than flying but gives you the freedom to stop when you want to, especially to visit *gompas* on the way. The road journey offers breathtaking scenery.

HEALTH WARNING There is no clean water or sewage system for a town which may have a population of 25,000 in the summer. Furthermore, most meat is brought in unrefrigerated lorries from Srinagar, a 2-day journey, so is best avoided. **Many people suffer from stomach upsets. Be very careful about food and hygiene**.

SECURITY As a matter of course, you should carry your passport with you. This is especially so in Ladakh which is a sensitive border region. There are checkpoints on some routes; from Srinagar to Leh via Kargil you pass very close to the *de facto* border with Pakistan.

Places of interest

The town has a wide main bazar street (c1840s) wide enough to accommodate caravans, with 2 old gates at each end. It is an interesting town to walk around. The bazar is colourful gives and gives an insight in to Ladakhi life. The Old Village, with its maze of narrow lanes, sits on the hillside below the Palace. A flashlight is recommended especially if you are visiting the gompas.

Leh Palace in the N has been described as a miniature version of Lhasa's Potala Palace, also built in the mid-16th century, though this was partly in ruins by the 19th. It has 9 storeys, sloping buttresses and projecting wooden balconies. The impression is that it is massively solid yet graceful as it rises up like a mountain. From the town below it is dazzling in the morning sun and ghostly at night. Built by King Singe Namgyal and still owned by the royal family, it is now unoccupied – they live in the palace at Stok. Visible damage was caused during Zorawar Singh's invasion from Kashmir in the last century. Be careful of the holes in the floor.

Inside, it is like the Potala with numerous rooms, steps and narrow passages lined with old *thangkas*, paintings, arms and constitutes a museum. The central prayer room, usually locked but opened on request, is unused but has numerous religious texts lining the walls. From the roof of the palace are magnificent views of the Zanskar Range. Currently being restored by Archaeological Survey of India, so possible to watch work in progress. In summer 0700-0930, and also sometimes 1500-1800.

High above the Palace is the older and even more ruined **Palace/Fort** and the remains of the **Temple of the Guardian of the Deities.** The temple houses a large golden Buddha, many painted scrolls, murals and old manuscripts. Of the monasteries, the **Soma Gompa** (1957) (new monastery) in the Old Village was erected to commemorate the 2500th anniversary of the birth of Buddha. The **Ecological Centre** near *Tsemo La Hotel*, opened in 1984, uses solar energy. Interesting display, library, dehydrated meals for trekkers, and local food in *Restaurant*. Trekkers may dehydrate their own food here.

Tsemo (Red) **Gompa** (15th century-) is a strenuous walk N of the city and has a colossal 2-storey high image of Bodhisattva flanked by figures of Avalokiteshvara (right) and Manjusri (left). It was founded by the Namgyal rulers and a portrait of Tashi Namgyal hangs on the left at the entrance. **Sankar Gompa** (17th-18th centuries), 3 km pleasant walk past the *Himalayan Hotel* through fields, is the only monastery here built at valley level and is the modest residence of the chief Lama of Spituk and 20 lamas. The newer monks' quarters are on 3 sides of the courtyard. There are a number of paintings and sculptures including a 1000-armed Avalokiteshvara. Open 0700-1000, 1700-1900, Prayers at 1800 (before visiting, check at the Tourist Office). The architecturally striking **Leh Mosque** (1594) was built by Singe Namgyal as a tribute to his Muslim mother. It is in the main bazar which itself is worth visiting to see the colourful local people.

From the Radio station there are 2 long **mani walls**. *Rongo Tajng* is in the centre of the open plain and was built as a memorial to Queen Skalzang Dolma

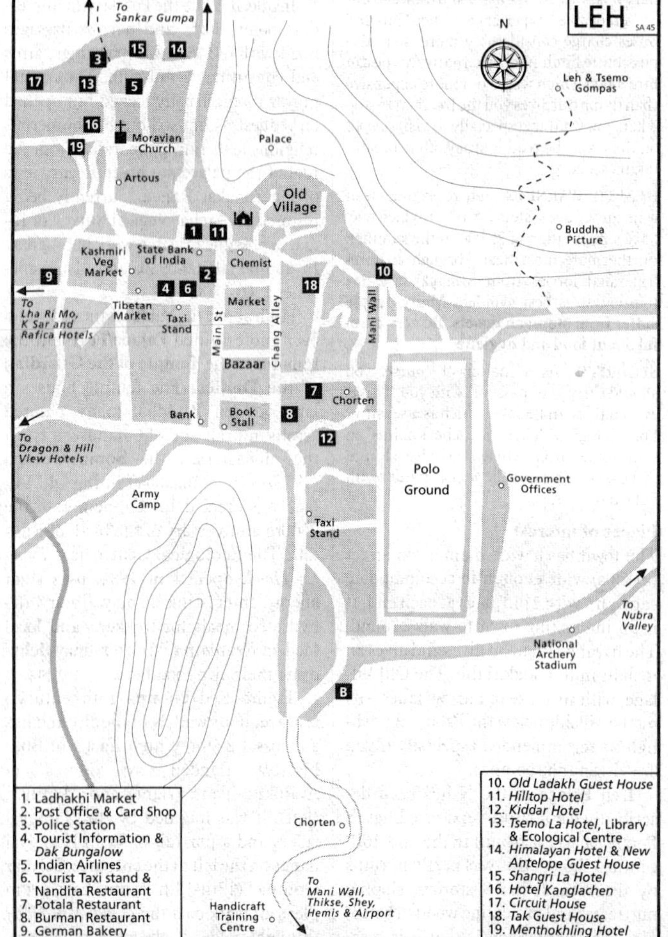

by her son Dalden Namgyal. It is about 500m long and was constructed in 1635. The stones have been meticulously carved. The other, a 350m *mani* wall is down the hill and is believed to have been built by Tsetan Namgyal in 1785 as a memorial to his father the king.

Local festivals

Ladakh's monasteries hold colourful festivals in the summer – see page 573, under Ladakh religion. *Ladakh Festival* in Aug organised by the Tourist Office, and the *Hemis Festival* in Jun, are notable. The latter is held to commemorate the birth of Guru Padmasambhava who is believed to have fought local demons to protect the people. Young and old of both sexes and lamas, take part in masked dance-dramas. Stalls sell handicrafts and other wares. *Losar* which originated in the 15th century, is celebrated in the 11th month of the Buddhist year. It was held before a battle to protect the people.

Local information

● Accommodation

Electricity supply, though much improved, can still be erratic. Usually on from afternoon to 2300. The most expensive in the area is **C** ***Ladakh Sarai,*** Stok, T 181. 11 km. 15 rather fancy circular tents set among willows in a very peaceful location. Convenient for short treks, visiting monasteries and river rafting. Reservations: Tiger Tops Mountain Travels, Srinagar or 1/1 Rani Jhansi Rd, Delhi, T 523057. **C** ***Tsemo La***, Karzoo, T 84. 2 old resthouses, partly refurbished. Clean rm with bath (hot water). Restaurant (rather bland), very pleasant garden, good views. Popular with tour groups. **C** ***Kanglachen,***, nr Bazar, T 144. 24 rm, most with baths. Good restaurant, pleasant garden. **C** ***K-Sar,*** T 148. Large rooms with pleasant views. Restaurant. **C** ***Lharimo,*** T 101. 30 rm with baths, good views from balconies. Restaurant. Attractive, central, rec. **C** ***Shambala***, Skara, T 67. Large rm but run down. Restaurant. Far from centre. **C** ***Indus***, has large rm (hot water in buckets) and good food. **C** ***Kangri,*** Nehru Park, T 51. 22 rm furnished in local style with bath. Restaurant (Indian, Chinese, Ladakhi). Loud generator nearby a nuisance until 2300. **C** ***Rafica,***, behind K-Sar Hotel. 24 rm, those on 1st Flr have good views. Good value.

D ***Bijoo***, T 131. 2-storey white building enclosed by high wall. Rm with bath. **D** ***Dragon Leh***, T 139. 16 rm with bath. Almost always filled with trekking parties (porters camp in garden!). **D** ***Himalayan***, Sankar Gompa Rd, T 104. 16 rm, most with bath. Old building in a quiet, shady willow grove by a stream. Camping. Restaurant. **D** ***Menthokling***, nr Moravian Church. Good rm, large garden, good food. **D** ***Ri-Rab***, Changspa. Clean simple rooms with baths. Restaurant (own fresh garden veg).

● Guest Houses

These are often very basic with cold water only. You should use your own sleeping bags. Fleas and bed bugs can be a problem. Among many: **E** ***Hills View***, nr Tourist Office, T 58. Clean rm some with good views. Pretty garden. **E** ***New Antelope Guest House***, Main St, T 86. 11 simple, clean rm, some with bath. Good food, quiet, shady garden. Quietly situated, ***Bimla*** on road to *Dreamland*, T 185. Welcoming and similar.

F ***Lung Snon***, Sheynam Chulli Chan. Delightful guest house. Clean and friendly, but simple. Earth toilet. **F** ***Two Star Guest House*** nr Tsemo La across the stream. Basic but good, cheap food. **F** ***Larchang***, is cheaper still. 6 clean rm, earth toilets. Cheap meals to order. **F** ***Palace View***, nr Polo Ground, T 161. Rm, cheap but not clean. Govt **F** ***Circuit House*** and **F** ***Tourist Bungalow*** have a few rm with bath (VIP rm best). Book in advance through Tourist Office with 50% deposit.

● Places to eat

Local restaurants serve a variety of cuisines: Chinese, Tibetan, Mughlai, S Indian, Ladakhi. One of the best is ***Mona Lisa***, opp Police Station. Charming, tastefully decorated interior with rattan walls. Excellent food (order the delicately flavoured momos with steamed vegetables in advance); serves alcohol (even champagne). ***Dreamland Restaurant*** (separate from *Hotel Dreamland* next door). Central, good atmosphere, good food and reasonable. ***Menthokling*** Pleasant, inexpensive, tables in garden. Good European and local food. ***Tibetan Friend*** Clean, simple – popular with local people interested in Tibetan politics (entertaining, at the expense of the cooking!). ***Shambala*** is also rec but is more expensive.

Ecological Centre behind Tsemo La has good cakes (may re-open after closure in 1993). German-run ***German Bakery*** sells good bread and excellent cakes and muesli.

● **Banks & money changers**

State Bank of India, slow for changing currency. Better at **AmEx** (1000-1400, Sat 1000-1200). Avoid Bank and market on Army pay-day!

● **Hospitals & medical services**

Sonam Narbu Memorial Hospital, T 14. *Soway Clinic*, T 117. *Kunfan Octsnang Clinic*. ***Ladakh Medicate***, behind Post Office.

● **Post & telecommunications**

Head Post Office and Telegraph Office: Leh. (1000-150). **Post Offices**: at Choglamsar, Thikse, Shey, Sakti, Chemray, Hemis, Karu, Matho.

● **Shopping**

Leh Bazar is full of shops selling curios and knick-knacks. **NB**: there are tight restrictions on the export of anything over 100 years old. Baggage is checked at the airport partly for this reason, but mainly for security purposes. But don't worry; even though most items are antique looking, they are, in fact, fresh from the backstreet workshops. If you walk down the narrow lanes, you will probably find an artisan at work from whom you can buy direct. *Chang* (the local barley brew) and tea vessels, cups, butter churns, knitted carpets with Tibetan designs, Tibetan jewellery, prayer flags are all available. Prices are quite high so bargain vigorously. Try to have lots of small change, there appears to be a shortage in general circulation. It is usually better to buy Ladakhi jewellery and souvenirs from Ladakhis instead of the Kashmiri traders who have moved in.

Curios Chang Alley is worth exploring for curios and local jewellery.***Dragon***. ***Tibetan Arts*** and ***Ladakhi Village Curios*** have a good selection of *thangkas*, inlaid bowls, baubles, bangles and beads. ***Imtaz***, Main Street, is Kashmiri-run and reasonable. **Fruit and nuts**Take a plastic bag for apples and apricots; the recycled paper bags break easily. Peanuts are cheap in season. **Tailor** next to Budshah Inn nr mosque. Excellent shirt maker, made-to-measure Rs 100. **Books**: ***Artou Books***, opp Post Office, Zangsti (the old metal-workers' district). Excellent; also Fax and telephone here. **Photography**: **Ali Shah's Postcard Shop** near Hilltop Hotel is worth a visit. Very interesting display of old photos (copies sold) of personalities, festivals etc.

● **Sports**

Mountaineering: information on mountaineering from Indian Mountaineering Federation, Benito Juarez Marg, New Delhi, T 671211. ***Adventure Institutes in India***, contact the Tourist Office, T 97. **The Polo Club** – the highest in the world – is well worth a visit; a local version is played in summer.

● **Tour compamies & travel agents**

The non-profit making ***SECMOL*** (Students' Educational & Cultural Movement), Karzoo Compound, T 284, offers treks and tours. ***Artou***, T 146. ***Dragon Tours***, Zangsti, T 8. ***Explore Himalayas***, Main Rd, T 2368. Well informed, rec. ***Gypsy***, Old Fort. Also rec. ***Fargo; Kang-chan Trek and Tours; Ladakh Safari Tours; Mamsothong Hing Adventure; Yuva Treks***.

● **Tourist Office**

Tourist Information Centre, 2 km on Airport Rd, T 297.

● **Useful addresses**

Police: T 18 **Ambulance**: T 14. **Foreigners' Registration Office**, Superintendent of Police, T 18.

● **Transport**

Leh is connected to Srinagar, via Kargil, by a State Highway (closed at present) and to Manali via Keylong (closed late Oct-May). Information on road conditions from the Traffic Police HQ, Maulana Azad Rd, Srinagar. From: **Kargil** (230 km); **Srinagar** (434 km); **Jammu** (739 km).

Local Tourist taxis, jeeps, tongas: available with Ladakh Taxi Operators Union, Leh. Fixed fares point-to-point. Ponies and mules, check with Tourist Office, T 97. A day's taxi hire to visit nearby *gompas* costs about Rs 500. **Local buses**: run to Alchi (W,Su), Choglamsar Tibetan Refugee Camp (3 daily), Hemis (daily, 1030), Kargil (daily in summer), Lamayuru (daily, take the Kargil bus), Matho (daily), Phyang (3 daily), Shey (3 daily), Spituk (3 daily), Stok (2 daily), Thikse (3 daily, from 0800). The vehicles are ramshackle but the fares are low.

Air The airport is basic; 11 km along the Srinagar road. *Transport to town*: buses and Jeep taxis available. **NB**: Weather conditions can deteriorate even in the summer, which might lead to flight cancellations (especially outside Jul and Aug) so you should always be prepared to face a delay or take the alternative, that is road transport, out of Ladakh. Furthermore, Indian Airlines fly quite full planes into Leh but can take fewer passengers out because of the high altitude for take-off. That adds to the difficulty of getting a flight out. Book your tickets as soon as possible, at least a month ahead. If you fail to get on the flight you had booked you do not get an immediate refund from the airline but have to reclaim it from the travel agent. It is also essential therefore to have enough money to travel out by road. Allow 4 days to get to Delhi by taxi. Make sure that you are not connecting with an onward flight or train, immediately after your visit to Ladakh. Be prepared to take a taxi if your return is imperative. Occasionally, Srinagar houseboat owners will offer to get 'VIP tickets' at short notice, for which there will be a surcharge of about Rs 60 a ticket. Despite the difficulties, even if you do not have a firm outward booking you may sometimes get on a flight at short notice if weather conditions prove to be better than expected. It is worth asking.

Indian Airlines, City Office nr Dak Bungalow, T 276. Airport, through Army Exchange. Indian Airlines links Leh with Srinagar, 5 times a week (50 min), daily with Delhi (1¼ hr) during peak season (Jul-Sep); less frequently at other times. Also to Jammu and Chandigarh (50 min) twice a week. In winter months, this is the only link between Ladakh and the outside world. The flight over the Himalayas is very spectacular.

Road To Manali takes 2 days. Dep early (0400) arrives Keylong 2200 (18 hr). Next day, 4 hr to Manali. Road conditions worse than to Srinagar but goes over the high Tanglangla (Pass). Some travellers like to travel on the rooftop for a part of the journey! Roadside tents provide food en route and sometimes places for overnight stop (carry good sleeping bag) when breaking journey before Keylong. **NB**: Many travellers find the mountain roads extremely frightening, and they are comparatively dangerous. Perhaps 1 vehicle in 10,000 falls off the road into a river or deep valley. Some of it is cut out of extremely unstable hillsides, usually with nothing between the road's edge and the nearly vertical drop below although it is nothing like as hair-raising as the Srinagar to Leh road. The road is often pot-holed or covered by landslides. It is also a long and uncomfortable journey, but there is some spectacular scenery. **Buses**: HP Tourism runs regular deluxe and ordinary bus services between Manali and Leh, from mid-Jun to Oct, 2 days. The deluxe bus fare is about Rs 300. **Taxi**: between Leh and Manali are expensive, but recommended if you want to stop en route. The one-way hire charge for the 2 day trip is about Rs 3500 (Rs 6000 return). However, it is often possible to find one returning empty to Srinagar which you may be able to hire for as little as a quarter of the regular charge.

Excursions around Leh

If you hire a car or jeep you can visit all the places below in one day. If you are short of time, try to visit Thikse and Hemis, at least. **Note** You must take a local Ladakhi guide as the Lamas can refuse admission if unaccompanied.

Stok

10 km S of Leh on the W bank and close to the Choglamsar Bridge over the Indus. This is the royal palace dating from the 1840s when the King of Ladakh was deposed by the invading Dogra forces. The last king died in 1974 but his widow is still alive and his son continues the royal line and ascended the throne in July 1993. A rambling building where only a dozen of the 80 rooms are used. The small Palace **Museum** occupying 3 rooms is well worth a visit. It is a showpiece for the royal *thangkas* (many 400 years old), royal crown, dresses, coins, precious stones and turquoise head dresses. Open 0700-1800. Rs 25. There is an archery contest in July. A 3 hr walk up the valley behind Stok takes you to some extraordinary mountain scenery dominated by the 6121m high Stok Kangri.

Shey

15 km S of Leh on the E bank of the Indus up a stone path. Open all day; try to be there 0700-0900, 1700-1800 when prayers are chanted. Rs 5. Until the 16th century, Shey was the royal residence, located at an important vantage point in the Indus Valley. Kings of Leh were supposed to be born in the monastery. Shey, along with Thikse, is also regarded as an auspicious place for cremation. The royal family moved to Stok in order to escape advancing Dogra forces from Kashmir who came to exploit the trade in *pashmina* wool. Much of the palace

and the fort high above it, have fallen into disrepair though the soot covered wall paintings in the palace have now been restored. The palace gompa has a 12m-high blue haired Maitreya Buddha which is attended by Drukpa monks from Hemis. It is made of copper and brass but splendidly gilded and studded with precious gem stones. The large victory *stupa* is topped with gold.

There are extensive grounds to the E with a large number of *chortens* in which cremated ashes of the devout was buried. A newer temple houses another old giant Buddha statue. There are several rock carvings; particularly noteworthy is that of 5 *dhyani* Buddhas at the bottom of the hill.

Thikse

25 km S of Leh on a crag overlooking the flood plain on the E bank of the Indus, It is one of the most imposing monasteries in Ladakh and was part of the original Gelugpa order in the 15th century. Entry Rs 10 (most goes towards the monastery's restoration and maintenance). Drinks kiosk at entrance.

The 12-storey red monastery with typical tapering walls has 10 temples, a nunnery and 60 Lamas in residence whose houses cling to the hillside below. The complex contains numerous *stupas*, statues, *thangkas*, wall paintings (note the fresco of the 84 *Mahasiddhas*, high above), swords and a large pillar engraved with the Master's teachings.

Near the entrance the new temple interior is dominated by a giant 15m-high Buddha figure. The Library/principal *dukhang* has holes in the wall for storing religious texts; good views from roof. The temple with the Guardian Deities (which elsewhere may be closed to women) is open to all since parts of the offending figures are covered. The *dukhang* lower down has Tibetan syle wall paintings.

Thikse Monastery is a good place to watch religious ceremonies (usually 0630 or 1200). They are preceded by the playing of large standing durms and long horns similar to *alpenstock;* masked dances are performed during special festivals.

Stakna

Across the valley on a hill is the Drukpa monastery which was built at the same time as Hemis, named 'Tiger's nose' because of the shape of the hill. There are some interesting paintings here.

Hemis

45 km S of Leh on the W bank of the Indus, the Monastery built on a green hillside surrounded by spectacular mountain scenery, is hidden in a gorge. It is the biggest and wealthiest in Ladakh and is a 'must' for visitors. Colourful flags flutter in the breeze from the 4 pillars in the courtyard, against the white walls of the buildings and the clear blue sky. You enter the complex through the E gate which leads into a large 40m x 20m courtyard where sacred dances are performed during the annual festival – see Leh Festivals.

On the N side are 2 assembly halls approached by a flight of steep steps. The paintings and murals depict guardian deities and the Wheel of Life and are in a good state of preservation. At the upper level are a number of shrines, one of the most important being the bust of the first Lama. The *lakhang* (chapel) has a 12th century Kashmiri bronze Buddha and silver *chortens*, an important library of Tibetan style books and an impressive collection of *thangkas*, the largest of which is displayed every 12 years (last display 1992).

- **Places to eat** in a walled garden below the monastery.

- **Transport Road** You can visit Hemis from Leh comfortably in one day by bus, car or jeep. Bus services have improved allowing you to do the trip even in an afternoon. For those wishing to stay on there is a rather grubby but cheap *Tourist Hotel* but many householders have overnight accommodation. Camping permitted.

Hemis High Altitude National Park
Set up in 1981, the park covers 600 sq km in the Markha and Rumbak valleys. The rugged terrain with limited vegetation contains some rare species of flora and fauna, some, like the snow leopard, ibex, *bharal* and *shapu,* are endangered. There are camping sites which you can reserve through the Div Forest Officer, Wildlife Warden, Leh. **Note** Since most of the Park lies within 'Restricted' areas, you need a special Group Permit for entry, also issued in Leh. Contact local travel agent for advice.

TREKKING IN LADAKH

Ladakh can be divided into 3 regions: Little Baltistan (the Suru Dras, Wakka and Bodkarbu Valleys), the Indus Valley and Zanskar.

Little Baltistan

The region just beyond the **Zoji La**, marks the climatic and cultural watershed between Ladakh and Kashmir. It was incorporated into the Dogra Zorawar Singh's Kashmir Empire in the mid 19th century. This was a part of the larger region of Baltistan which was divided on Independence. The Dards were among the earliest settlers who became Buddhist before 500 AD. When Tibetan forces invaded Ladakh a new culture was introduced. In the 15th century, most Dardic communities were converted to Islam, though Buddhist pockets remained. Trade links and cultural ties were stronger with Gilgit than with Kashmir and Ladakh.

Suru Valley

This offers some very good trekking and Kargil is the jumping off point for treks in this region. There is a road along the valley now but this can be avoided for large sections of the trek. The metalled part extends to Parachik which is beyond Pannikher. An unmetalled road runs over the Pensi La (4420m) – see Trekking in Zanskar below. The road to Padum is generally open by the beginning of July.

Sanko
This is a good starting point for a trek. From here you have the choice of continuing along the valley past the Nun Kun Massif to the S and on towards the Pensi La, or going over the Wakka La and Sapi La to Mulbekh. You can also reach Dras via Umba La.

Sanko to Dras
This route goes through some very picturesque villages, especially in spring when all the wild flowers are out. **Umba** is the highest village. From the pass above it (3350m) there are very good panoramas of the Himalaya and Nun Kun. There is an intermediary ridge between the Umba La and Dras. Allow 3 days to do this trek comfortably.

Sanko to Mulbekh
This trek should take about 4 days and could be combined with a Dras-Sanko trek. From Sanko the route follows the **Thargam Valley**. The climb to the **Wakka La** (4930m) is steep. For the sake of acclimatisation, 2 camps are recommended before crossing the pass. Two more stages are necessary for crossing the **Sapi La** and descending to Mulbekh on the Kargil-Leh Highway.

Rangdum to Heniskot

Rangdum is further down the Suru Valley towards the Pensi La and the trek runs NE over the Zanskar range to Heniskot on the Kargil-Leh Highway. The Kanji La (5270m) needs to be approached gradually because of its height and you should acclimatise well. If the ascent is undertaken too quickly there will be little enjoyment. 4 or 5 days should be allowed for the trek.

The first stage follows the valley E of **Rangdum** with a 17th century hilltop monastery. A guide is recommended as the trail divides and that used by yak herders skirts the southern edge of the Zanskar range and goes over the Pingdom La, Kesi La and Netuke La to Lingshet. Camp at the confluence of the 2 rivers in the Rangdum valley. From this plateau camp there is a gradual 4 hr ascent to the pass. In late spring there are snow bridges. By late Sep the going is over scree which can be very tiring.

From the **Kanji La** there are fine views of the Karakoram and Ladakh ranges. Care is needed on the N descent as it is heavily corniced. The camp is near the valley floor. The 3rd stage follows the watercourse downstream and eventually **Kanji village** is reached. Here the path splits again.

It takes another 4 days to cross the **Yogma La**, travel down the **Shilakong Valley** and then on to Lamayuru. From Kanji to **Heniskot** is a spectacular descent through impressive gorges. Unfortunately, there are over a dozen river crossings. As always, extreme care is needed.

The Indus Valley

Leh is the major town in this valley and the destination of many visitors. For trekking in this region, July and August are pleasant months. Go earlier and you will be trudging through snow much of

the time. September and October are also good months though colder at night.

Spituk to Hemis

Another popular trek. Both places are in the Indus Valley, only 30 km apart. A very satisfying 9-10 days can be undertaken by traversing the Stok range to the Markha Valley, walking up the valley and then back over the Zanskar range to Hemis.

There is an interesting monastery at **Spituk**, a short drive from Leh see approach to Leh above). From Spituk proceed SW of the Indus along a trail passing through barren countryside. After about 7 km you reach the **Jinchan Valley** and in a further 5 hr, the beautiful Rumbak village. Camp below the settlement. You can also trek here from Stok which takes 2 days and a steep ascent of the **Namlung La** (4570m).

From Rumbak it is a 5 hr walk to Utse village. The camp is 2 hrs further on at the base of the bleak **Gandha La** (4700m), open, bare and windswept. To go over the pass takes about 3 hrs, then the same time again to negotiate the wooded ravine to Skiu. Here the path meets the Markha Valley. You can make a ½ day round trip from Skiu to see the impressive gorges on the Zanskar River. The stage to Markha where there is an impressive fort, is a 6hr walk. The monastery, which is not particularly impressive from the outside, has some superb wall paintings and *thangkas*, some dating from the 13th century. You need to take a torch.

The next destination is **Hankar** village, whose ruined fort forms an astonishing extension of the natural rock face, an extremely impressive ruin. From here the path climbs quite steeply to a plateau. There are good views of Nimaling Peak (6000m) and a number of mani walls en route. From **Nimaling** it is a 2 hr climb to **Gongmaru La** (5030m) and views of the Stok range and the Indus Valley. The descent is arduous and involves stream crossings. There is a lovely camp site at **Shogdu** and another at **Sumda** village, 3 km further on. The final stage is down the valley to Martselang from where you can walk down 5 km to Karu village on the Leh-Manali road or take a 2 km diversion to visit Hemis monastery. The daily walking time on this trek is 5-6 hr so you must be fit.

Lamayuru to Alchi

This is a shorter trek of 5-6 days. The average daily walking time is 6½ hr so do not imagine that the shortness of the trek means less effort. 3 passes, the **Printiki La** (3500m), **Konke La** (4570m) and **Stapski La** (5200m) are crossed rewarding the exertion of reaching them with excellent views.

The first stage involves walking from the usual camp site just below the monastery down the valley for 2 km then over the Printiki La. You then descend the **Shilakong Valley** and climb to Phangi village, passing huge boulders brought down by a landslide, and impressive irrigation in such a forbidding landscape. From Phangi you walk up the Ripchar Valley to Halsi, crossing the river a number of times. There are a number of small settlements until you reach the summer grazing ground a few km below the pass. The Konke La is a steep 2 hr climb. From here you will see the Zanskar river and gorge and the Stok range. At **Sumdahchenmo** village there is a large wooden statue of the Buddha.

The fourth stage should be with a guide since the trail splits, one leading to Chillung on the Zanskar River, the other to Sumdahchoon, the latter being quite treacherous as it involves many river crossings. About 3 hr below Sumdahchenmo there is a path which climbs the ridge above the river. It is quite easy to miss this, hence the guide. There is a monastery at Sumdahchoon with an impressive statue of the Buddha and some attractive wall paintings. Just beyond the village are some camping areas. The last stage of the trek is long, about 8 hr walking, and takes you over the **Stapski La** to **Alchi**. The views from the top are superb. From Alchi you can get a bus to Leh.

ZANSKAR

Land

Zanskar is a remote area of Ladakh contained by the Zanskar range to the N and the Himalaya to the S. There are 2 subsidiary valleys, the **Stod** (Doda Chu) and the Linak (Tsarap Chu) which converge below **Padum** the capital. The Zanskar river flows along the valley from Padum to Zangla, then cuts through the Zanskar range in a series of impressive gorges to join the Indus. The main valley is approximately 300 km long and is ringed by mountains. Access to it is therefore over one of the high passes. The most important are the **Pensi La** connecting Zanskar with the Suru Valley in the W, the **Umasi La** with the Chenab Valley in the S and the **Shingo La** with Lahul in the E. This makes for very spectacular trekking country. The long Zanskar Valley was 'opened' up for tourism even later than the rest of Ladakh and quickly became popular with trekkers. There is now river rafting on the Zanskar river. The jeep road from Kargil to Padum over the Pensi La is closed for over half the year.

History

Zanskar became an administrative part of Ladakh under Singe Namgya I whose 3 sons became the rulers of Ladakh, Guge and Zanskar/Spiti. This arrangement collapsed after Ladakh's war with Tibet and the Zanskar royal house divided, one part administering Padum, the other Zangla. Under the Dogras, the rulers were reduced to puppets as the marauding army wreaked on the villages, monasteries and population.

Culture

People The Zanskaris are of the same stock as the Ladakhis and because of the sheer isolation of their homeland were able to preserve their Buddhist culture against the onslaughts of Islam. There are some Muslim families in Padum, the capital, dating from the Dogra invasion.

Religion The foundation of Sani in the 11th century is recognised as the 1st monastery in Zanskar. Phugyal and Karsha date from the same period. The sects developed alongside those in Ladakh. The Gelugpa (Yellow Hat) order was established in the 15th century and monasteries at Karsha, Linshet and Mune belong to this. The Drukpa sect set up monasteries at Bardan and Zangla and 'occupied' that at Sani. These have links with Stakna near Leh and the Gelugpa is associated with the Likir monastery.

Traditional Ladakhi and Zanskari life, even today, comes close to Gandhi's idealised vision of life in ancient India: small village 'republics', each self-sufficient, everyone playing a valuable part, with no crime and discrimination with regard to caste or religion and where disparities in wealth would not exist.

Economy

Agriculture An almost total lack of precipitation has meant that cultivation must rely on irrigation. As in Ladakh, the rivers have been harnessed but with difficulty. The deep gorges presented a problem. Headworks were constructed and irrigation channels (yura) were contoured along to the fields, some up to 5 km away. Barley is the most suitable crop as it is very hardy, copes well with poor soils and can be roasted to form the staple *tsampa* (ngamphe) which can be eaten without cooking. This is useful in winter when fuel is scarce. Animal husbandry complements agriculture which only produces one crop per year. Sheep and goats are taken to high meadows in the summer after the snow melt and grazed while the shepherds live in small stone huts.

Padum

Padum has a population of about 1,000 of whom a sizeable minority are Sunni Muslim. On arrival you must report to the Tourist Officer. Accommodation is very limited, being mostly dormitory style. You can camp. Access is either by the jeep road already mentioned, generally open for 4 months (mid-Jun to mid-Oct) with twice weekly bus service from Kargil. The alternative method is to trek in.

Trekking in Zanskar

A road has been constructed over the Pensi La from Kargil to Padum. This tenuous link with the rest of the country can only be used in the summer. Ladakh can be cut off by snow for as much as 7 months each year. This isolation has helped it to preserve its cultural identity, although this is now being eroded. Traditional values include a strong belief in Buddhism, frugal use of resources and population control. For centuries, the Zanskaris have been able to live in harmony with their hostile and yet nevertheless fragile environment.

Trekking in Zanskar is not easy. The paths are often rough and steep, the passes high and the climate extreme. Provisions, fuel and camping equipment should be taken along from Srinagar, Kishtwar, Manali or Leh. You may get necessities such as dried milk, biscuits and sugar from Padum, though probably not at the beginning of the season. In **Padum** you must register at the Tourist Office. The Tourism Officer and Govt Development Officer will be able to advise and maybe even assist in hiring horses. Porters can be hired at **Sani** village for the traverse of the **Umasi La** into Kishtwar. Horses cannot use this pass. In Padum you may be able to hire porters with whom you can traverse rougher terrain.

Pensi La to Padum (3 stages)

You can trek this route before the road opens (Jun-Oct) when it is free of vehicles.

Karsha to Lamayuru (9 stages)

This is a demanding trek which includes 7 passes, 5 of which are over 4500m. The highest is the Singi La (5100m). It is essential to be very fit before starting the trek. Each day's walking should take under 6 hr, but with time for rests and lunch this adds up to a full day. An extra day allows for flexibility.

The 16th century monastery of the Tibetan Gelugpa (Yellow Hat) sect at Karsha is the largest and wealthiest in the Zanskar Valley and is occupied by nearly 100 monks. It is a 2 hr trek from Padum. The first 2 stages more or less follow the Zanskar River. Then it is a steady climb up to the **Purfi La**. The camp site is halfway down the other side. The next pass is the **Haluma La** (4800m) which provides a very good view of the last pass, the **Singi La**, and the distant Stok Range. Then it is a steep descent to **Lingshet** which has a monastery which is similar but smaller (30 monks) to that at Karsha. On the 5th stage you can camp below the Singi La.

This is the highest on the route to Lamayuru and gives a good view of where you have come from and where you are going. On the 7th stage you should cross the Shirshi La then descend through an area that supports abundant wildlife. In the Photang Valley that you reach next, some river crossings may be necessary. The final stage follows the Shiulakong Valley upstream to the Prinkiti La. The descent takes about an hour. The village often has cold beers!

Padum to Leh

This is another demanding trek which also takes about 10 days. Some is through the spectacular gorges between Markha and Zangla. A local guide is recommended as this is truly a wilderness area. The trek involves walking along stream beds and in July there is still too much snow melt to allow safe crossings. Recommended only for Aug/Sep.

It is 7 hr walking from Padum to Zangla and this includes crossing the Zanskar River by a string and twig bridge that spans over 40m. Ponies are not allowed on it and if it is windy sensible humans don't. At **Zangla** you can see the King's palace. The 3rd stage takes you over the **Charcha La** (5200m). On the next stage river crossings are again necessary. This is time consuming and if you are travelling in mid-summer, an extra day may be called for.

You then follow the **Khurna River** to a narrow gorge that marks the ancient border between Zanskar and Ladakh and end up below the Rubarung La. When you cross this you get good views of the Stok range. You then descend into the Markha Valley and from here you can reach Leh in 4 stages, either by going down the Markha Valley and going over the Gandha La and Namlung La to Leh or by crossing the Gongmaru La to Hemis and Leh.

Padum to Darcha

This is a week long trek and starts with a walk along the Tsarap Chu to Bardan which has stupas and interesting idols, and Reru.

After 2 stages you reach **Purni** where you can stay 2 nights and make a side trip to the impressive 11th century **Phugtal monastery**. On a spectacular site, it has been carved out of the mountainside round a limestone cave. Usually there are about 50 monks in attendance. From Purni you continue on to Kargya, the last village before the **Shingo La**. It is still another day's walk to the camp below this high pass (5200m).

The mountain scenery is stunning with 6000m plus peaks all around. Once over the pass you can stop at Rumjack where there is a camp site used by shepherds or you can go further to the confluence of the **Shingo River** and the **Barai River**. By Jul and Aug this is quite a torrent and great care is required when crossing it. From here the trail passes through grazing land and it is about 15 km from the river to Darcha, the end of the trek. Keen trekkers can combine this with a trek from **Darcha** to **Manali**. The average daily walking time of the Padum–Darcha trek is 6 hr so this is also a very full trip. You have to be very fit.

SRINAGAR TO PAHALGAM

Pahalgam is 96 km from Srinagar. The journey, along roads lined with poplar, is very attractive.

Avantipur, 29 km from Srinagar, is famous for its ruined temples. It was the capital of Avantivarman (855-83), the 1st ruler of the Utpala dynasty of Kashmir. Several sculptures from the Avantisvamin and Avantishvara temples (both 9th century) are in the Sri Pratap Museum in Srinagar. The ruins of the **Vishnu Temple**, Srantisvami are very impressive. **Sangram** (35 km) is a centre for the manufacture of cricket bats.

At the foot of the Lidder Valley is **Anantnag** (54 km), a spring town surrounded by a flower garden. A myth associates Anantnag with Indra. Achhabal and Kokarnag (see Excursions above) can be visited as detours.

Martand 8 km from Anantnag in the lower Lidder Valley, is famous for its 8th century **Surya Temple**. Like the town, it is on a plateau which affords a splendid view of the Vale of Kashmir. Lalitaditya (724-60), the best known of the Karkota dynasty, is accredited with building it. Paraspora, NW of Srinagar, is also associated with him, and was his capital. The temple is dedicated to the Sun God and though rather dilapidated, it is an impressive example of the early Kashmir

The Most Expensive Spice In The World

Pampore, 16 km from Srinagar is the centre of Kashmir's saffron industry. Saffron, a species of crocus (*Crocus sativus*), grows here in abundance and in a few other places in the world, and is harvested by hand. Within each purple bloom, the 3 orange-red anthers yield pure saffron. Over 4500 blooms make 1oz (28.3g) of the spice, so the price of this delicate flavouring and colouring in cooking is high, as costly by weight, as gold.

The precious orange coloured dye was used by royalty and the colour saffron was chosen by monks for their robes after the Buddha's death. In 631 AD Hiuen Tsang commented on how rich the country was agriculturally, noting the abundant fruits and flowers as well as the medicinal herbs and saffron. He also admired the Kashmiris' good looks and their love of learning, but also felt that they were too frivolous and given to cunning.

style. It is set in the E half of an 80m by 60m colonnaded courtyard which is mostly in ruins. Originally there were 84 columns, a sacred Hindu number. The sanctuary up a broad flight of steps comprises a main sanctum and 2 minor shrines. Damaged images of Ganga (N) and Vishnu (S) can still be seen. The roof has gone but this may have been gabled in 2 tiers, similar to those found protecting temples in the Western Himalaya as in Chamba, HP (see page 74). Note the corbelled trifoliate arches.

Pahalgam

Altitude: 2130m. One of Kashmir's major resorts, Pahalgam is best visited between mid-Apr and mid-Nov. The town with little more than one main street, is at the confluence of the **Lidder** (sometimes called Aru here) and Sheshnag rivers set amidst pine and fir woods and surrounded by snow-capped mountains. It is a pleasant place to stay away from noisier and busier Srinagar and ideal for short walks. It is also the base for launching a trekking trip – see page 597. The area around Pahalgam is famous for its shepherds who more than anyone are responsible for maintaining the tracks and bridges over much of the trekking country as they herd their flocks from pasture to pasture.

There is trout fishing (fly only) in the river and permits have to be obtained in Srinagar and each year in Jul and Aug the town is thronged with thousands of pilgrims en route to the holy cave at Amarnath. See page 598. Around the town there are luxuriant meadows and groves of poplar, willow and mulberry, the last of which is important for Kashmiri sericulture. The only yellow-flowered colchicuon species grows in profusion here, flowering in Mar-Apr.

The **Mamaleswara Temple** (12th century) dedicated to Siva is 1.5 km downstream, S of town. **Baisaren**, (2438m) 2 km, a small meadow 150m above the valley, surrounded by forest, makes a pleasant walk. **Tulian Lake** (3353m), 13 km further, snow covered most of the year, is a day's trek. The small village of **Aru** (2408m) 11 km up the Lidder River is the first stage for the Kolahoi Glacier trek. The main track is motorable, but it does make a very interesting day's walk through pine forests.

Tours

J&KSTDC runs tours to Wular Lake (dep 0900, Rs 40), Yusmarg in the Pir Panjal range (dep 0900, Rs 40) and Sonamarg (dep 0830, Rs 45). All leave from the Tourist Reception Centre. These are return tickets but you may want to try and get a one-way ticket.

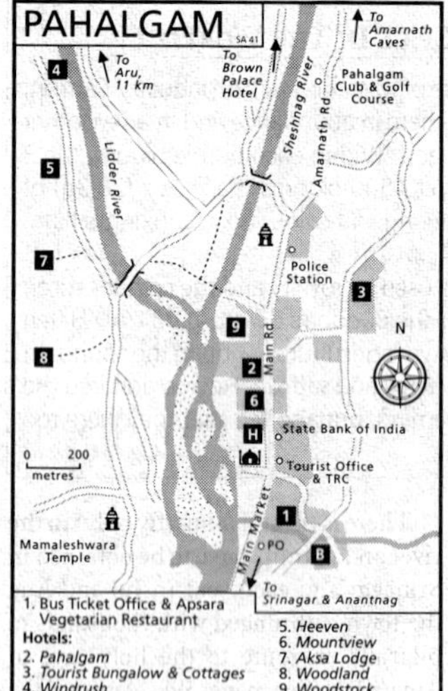

Local information

● Accommodation

Tourist numbers have been severely reduced since 1990. Many hotels are deserted and offer large discounts. **C** *Pahalgam*, Main St, nr Bazar, T 26. 46 rm best with river view. Indoor pool and sauna. **C** *Woodstock*, closer to river, T 27. Good restaurant. Well run, good views of the river. **C** *Heaven*, far side of Lidder River, T 17. 15 rm. Restaurant. Modern, quiet, free transport to town. **C** *Pine View.*, T 70. Garden. **C** *Senator Pine-N-Peak*, T 11. 75 rm. Restaurant, shops.

Out of town on a hill top is **D** *Hill Park*, T 79. 38 rm. Restaurant. **D** *Mansion*. 20 rm. Restaurant. Modern. **D** *Natraj*, T 25. Rm and self-contained cottages. **D** *Plaza*, T 39. 32 comfortable rm with bath. Pleasant views. Restaurant, bar, garden. **D** *Mountview*, T 21. 43 rm. Restaurant. **D** *Tourist Bungalow and Cottages*. 7 pleasant rm with bath. Also 10 huts with bedroom, sitting rm, bath and kitchen. Furnished tents in high season. J&KTDC, TRC, Srinagar, T 76107.

● Budget hotel

D *Aksa Lodge* on the Lidder. Some rm with balconies. Rec **E** *Brown Palace*, N, out of town, T 255. Clean rm with bath and hot water. Good food, free transport from Bus Stand, peaceful. Rec. **E** *Windrush*. Described as "absolutely superb situation, inexpensive good food, lovely garden, but facilities very basic – no showers". Further still is the *White House* on Laripora Rd, by river. Quiet and comfortable. Govt *Pahalgam Club*, T 51. 3 rm for non-members (Temp membership).

● Places to eat

Local Kashmiri food is served in most hotels: *Woodstock*, *Pahalgam*, *Natraj* also do Chinese; *Pineview* and *Mountview* offer continental. *Poornima* is Indian. **Bars** in *Woodstock*, *Pahalgam*, *Plaza*, *Natraj* and Pahalgam Club.

● Pony trekking

Ponies can be hired through the Tourist Office, T 24.

● Services

State **Bank** of India exchanges foreign currency, a **Post Office** (open 1000-1700) and a Govt **Hospital**.

● Shopping

Pahalgam was originally a shepherds' village. Wool products such as *gadbas* and *namdas* (blankets) can be bought in local shops. Many shops in the square have closed. **Photography** *RK, Delhi, Soni, Pitam and Longman Studios.*

● Sports

Golf: The *Govt Pahalgam Club has a golf course open to non-members.* **Fishing**: the Lidder River has some excellent fishing beats. Season: Apr-Sep. Permits at approx Rs 75 per day per rod and for a max of 3 days at a time. Contact Directorate of Fisheries, Tourist Reception Centre, Srinagar, T 72862. Fishing tackle can be hired in Srinagar. Live baits and spinning are prohibited.

● Tourist office

Srinagar Rd, nr the Bus Stand, T 24.

● Transport

Road Buses: from Srinagar (4½ hr, often longer when road is blocked by army). You can take a sightseeing coach to Gulmarg and pay a one-way fare if you intend spending a few nights there. **Taxi**: one way from Srinagar costs Rs 450-500. Return is not much more expensive. Sometimes possible to get a taxi returning empty for about Rs 150.

SRINAGAR TO PATHANKOT

From Srinagar the NH1A follows the River Jhelum upstream across the nearly flat valley floor before climbing up to the Banihal Pass (Jawahar Tunnel), for many years the only road entry into Kashmir.

Verinag (1,876m), 80 km S of Srinagar at the foot of the Banihal Pass, was a stopping place en route to Srinagar from Jammu. This is the most dramatic example of a spring tamed for the use of a Mughal garden. The Bihat River wells up in a clear pool that Jahangir calculated was 14m deep. Originally circular, it was transformed into an octagonal basin in 1620 and surrounded by a brick wall. The waters are a turquoise blue. A 300m channel led off the water to the stream. A set of octagonal pavilions were set around the tank and on its completion, Jahangir is said to have given a party there, plying his guests with alcohol and peaches brought by runners from Kabul. The pool was stocked with carp, some of which had gold rings attached by the emperor and empress. There is a *Tourist Bungalow* here.

The **Jawahar Tunnel** (2200m) is 93 km from Srinagar and 200 km from Jammu. There are 2 passages through the hill and the 2.5 km tunnel was used in David Lean's film *Passage to India*. When you enter the tunnel you leave the verdant Vale of Kashmir for the rugged descent down to the Chenab valley, Udhampur and Jammu.

The NH1A drops steeply from Banihal to Ramban (40 km, 1720m) where the deeply cut River Chenab is bridged (30 km, 675m). Both have *Tourist Bungalows*. On the route up from Jammu Banihal is the last place of consequence before the Jawahar Tunnel and the overnight stop for buses leaving Jammu after the morning trains have arrived. The road climbs rapidly to Batote.

Batote (1560m) 12 km further, a health resort in attractive wooded country has a D *Tourist Bungalow* and dorm and several hotels. Here the NH1B goes E to Kishtwar and Bhadarwa.

Bhadarwa near the border with Himachal Pradesh is in a beautiful valley at 1570m, known for its Naga (snake) temples each of which has black stone images of Wasik Nag, the local snake deity, and Jamuitvahan. The ones in the principal temple in town have particularly fine images. The festivals at the end of the monsoons attract pilgrims to Wasik Kund (lake) at 4240m. Processions, fairs, fire-walking, devotional singing and ecstatic dances accompanied by drumming and playing on serpentines trumpets, mark the festivities.

The NH1A continues S to **Patni Top** (2024m) on a plateau amidst thick forests. It is a popular hill station with an E *Tourist Rest House*, TV and heating. Also an *Inspection Bungalow* and *Youth Hostel*. **Sudhmahadev** nearby attracts pilgrims at full moon in Jul/Aug to the ancient trident associated with the epic *Mahabharata*. **Kud** (38 km, 1738m), a little to the S, is another small hill station and also a popular lunch stop, with an E *Tourist Bungalow*, T Jammu 49554. The **Swamai Hi Bauli** is a well known spring 1.5 km from the road. A side road leads to **Sanasar**. This is in an attractive scooped-out valley at just over 2000m and is a centre for Gujar shepherds each summer. D*Rest House* and *Huts* available from J&K Tourism, T Jammu 49554.

Before descending to Jammu the road drops to **Udhampur** (680m) with its boulder strewn slopes. There is a *Tourist Bungalow*. The National Highway also passes through Jhajhar Kotli, a picturesque little settlement by a clear mountain stream. Springs send cascades of water over the rocks and through a narrow gorge above Jharjhar. A Tourist restaurant was built before Kashmir's political crisis. It already seems run-down. The road to the very important Hindu pilgrimage centre of Vaishnodevi (see page 594) leaves the National Highway about 2 km S of Jhajhar Kotli.

Jammu is the railhead and main entry point for Kashmir. Before the Jawahar tunnel (named after Nehru) was completed, the journey took 2 days with an overnight stop at Batote. Now it can be covered in one long day. The shortest route to Pathankot is via **Samba**. The fastest route follows the NH1 through Jammu itself.

Jammu

The city of Jammu is the second largest in the state and is the winter capital of the government. Until the late 18th century its fortunes were closely associated with events in the Punjab.

BASICS *Population*: 223,361 (1981). *Altitude*: 305m.

Places of interest

Jammu has 2 distinct parts, the hilltop **Old Town** overlooking the Tawi River and the **New Town**.

The **Raghunath Temple** (1857) in the city centre, the focus of the town's religious attentions, is one of the largest temple complexes in N India. The temple consists of 7 shrines each with a tower, the one over the central shrine being curvilinear. Its fluted surface, arches and niches show Mughal influence. The interior is gold plated and the principal sanctuary is dedicated to Rama, Vishnu's 8th incarnation, and the Dogras' patron deity.

Morning and evening *aartis* are ritually attended and there is also a stone lingam here and in the other shrines for this is a centre for Shakti worship. A portrait of Ranbir Singh, the temple patron and a sculpture of Hanuman are at the entrance. The other shrines have images of Vishnu in various incarnations, Siva and Surya. The **Sanskrit Library** here contains numerous rare manuscripts.

The Rambiresvar Temple (1883) opposite the **Dogra Art Gallery**, also centrally located, is dedicated to Siva. It has a 75m tower and extraordinary crystal lingams. It is the largest Siva temple in N India.

On a rock face overlooking the river are the ruined ramparts of the **Bahu Fort**, the oldest remaining building in the region. The original structure was improved and rebuilt as the **Mondi Palace** (c1880) by the Dogra rulers. It is situated in the NE of the city and is entered through a large quadrangle. **Bagh-e-Bahu** gardens has a cafeteria. The **Kali Temple** inside the fort attracts large crowds at a festival held twice a year in Mar/Apr and Sep/Oct. The Old Palace is now the **High Court**.

The **Amar Mahal** (early 20th century), on the bend of the Tawi, just off the Srinagar road, bears the imprint of its French designer with its chateau-like sloping roofs and turrets. The museum has a portrait gallery and royal memorabilia.

Museums

Amar Mahal Palace Museum, T 5676, in superb site above the Tawi river. Winter 1000-1200, 1500-1700, summer 1700-1900. Sun 1000-1200. Closed Mon. Pahari paintings of *Mahabharata* scenes. Dogra Art Gallery, Gandhi Bhawan, opp Old Secretariat. Free. Winter 1100-1700,

CLIMATE: JAMMU

	Jan	Feb	Mar	Apr	May	Jun	Jul	Aug	Sep	Oct	Nov	Dec	Av/Tot
Max (°C)	18	21	26	33	39	40	35	33	33	31	26	21	30
Min (°C)	8	11	15	21	26	28	26	25	24	19	13	9	19
Rain (mm)	71	54	57	25	17	61	321	319	151	29	8	29	1142

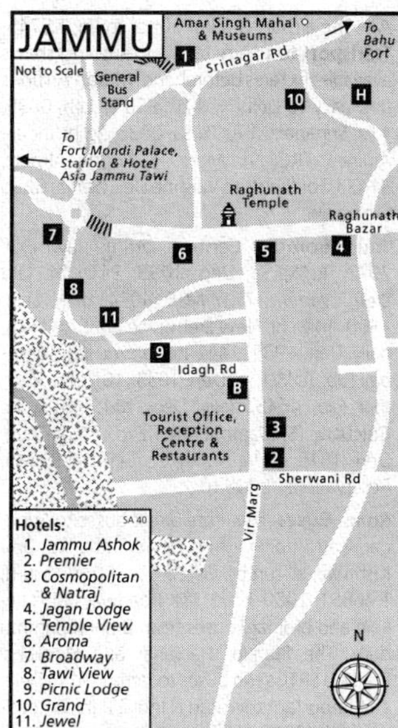

summer 0800-1330. Closed Mon. Fine collection of Pahari miniatures, terracottas, manuscripts and sculptures including 6th century terracotta heads.

Excursions

Akhnoor, 32 km NW of Jammu, is where the Chenab river meets the plains and was on the route to Kashmir in Mughal times. **Surinsar and Mansar Lakes,** 80 km and 42 km E of Jammu. Picturesque forest fringed lakes. *Tourist Bungalow* and *Huts*.

Local festivals

Jan: *Lohri* is an important festival throughout N India and is celebrated with *havan yagnas* in temples and houses. **Apr**: *Baisakhi* is the harvest festival. A large celebration is held at Nagbani temple.

Local information

● Accommodation

Jammu is well provided with hotels (many **E** and **F** category), reflecting its significance as a transit town. Buses which connect with arriving trains often stop at Banihal where there is little accommodation. **C** *Asia Jammu-Tawi*, Nehru Market, N of town. T 49430. 51 rm (expensive suites). Restaurant, shops, exchange, pool. Clean, comfortable. Rec. **C** *Jammu Ashok*, opp Amar Mahal, T 43127. 48 rm. Restaurant, shops, pool.

D *Cosmopolitan*, Vir Marg. T 47561. 28 rm, some a/c. Good restaurant, bar, coffee shop. **D** *Mansar*, Denis Gate. T 46161. 22 rm, some a/c. Central. Restaurant, bar. **D** *Premier*, Vir Marg. T 43234. 21 rm, some a/c. Central. Restaurants, bar. Rec. **D** *Tourist Reception Centre*, Vir Marg. T 42231. 128 rm with bath, a few air cooled, and dorm. Restaurant. Good value with best rm in Blocks NA and A. Dorm not so good. **D** *Jahangir*, Shaheedi Chowk, 47882. 23 rm. **D** *Samrat*, nr General Bus Stand, T 47402. 20 rm. **D** *Vardaan*, J P Chowk, T 43212. 28 rm, some a/c.

● Budget hotels

E *Airlines Lodge*, 299 Canal Rd, T 47002. 20 rm. **E** *Tawi View*, T 43752. Few air-cooled rm. Meals. **E** *City Centre Lodge*, Jewel Chowk, T 43295. 38 rm. **E** *Indra Lodge*, Vinayak Bazar, nr Jewel Cinema, T 46069. **E** *Jagan Lodge*, Raghunath Bazar, T 43243. 16 rm. **E** *Natraj*, Vir Marg, T 7450. **E** *New India Pride*, Rani Mandir, below Gumat, T 49689. 1984 visitor found it dirty. Not rec. **E** *New Naaz*, Shaheedi Chowk. 11 rm. **E** *Picnic Lodge*, Idgah Rd, T 43931. 20 rm. **E** *Standard*, Shaheedi Chowk, T 5455. **E** *Tourist Reception Centre*, Via Marg. One block has a/c and TV. 5 cheaper blocks. T 49554. Dorm not rec.

F *Railway Retiring Rooms*, Jammu Tawi Rly Station. Some a/c rm and dorm. Reservations: Snr Supt, Counter 2, Jammu Rly Station, T 30078. **F** *Retiring Rooms*, Gen Bus Stand, T 47078. Booking: Counter, General Bus Stand. Some bad reports.

● Places to eat

In Hotels: *Asia Jammu Tawi's* outdoor, *Bar-e-Kabab,* evening entertainment. *Cosmopolitan* for Chinese and Kashmiri food. *Premier* and the *Chinese Room* nearby. **On Vir Marg**: *Tourist Reception Centre Canteen*; *Dragon*, Chinese; *Kwality*; *Silver Inn*, Indian. *Rachna*, Shalimar Rd for Veg; *Capri Coffee House*, Old Hospital Rd and *India Coffee House*, Exhibition Gr. For fast food try *Jewel*

● **Banks & money changers**
State Bank of India, Raghunath Bazar and many others in town.

● **Entertainment**
Cultural Academy, Jewel Chowk. Programme from TRC, Vir Marg.

● **Hospitals & medical services**
SMGS Hospital, Jammu City, T 5080.

● **Shopping**
Wool tunics (*pherans*) and woodcarvings are good. Main shopping areas: Raghunath Bazar, Hari Bazar, Upper Gumat, Below Gumat. ***J&K Govt Arts Emporium*** and ***Khadi Gramudyog*** are both on Vir Marg.

● **Sports**
Swimming at *Jammu Tawi Hotel* (temp membership). ***Maulana Azad Stadium Complex*** has a large pool, T 42038.

● **Post & telecommunications**
GPO: Pacca Danga Raja Ram.

● **Tour companies & travel agents**
On Vir Marg: ***Alpine India Travels***, ***Gouri Travels*** and ***India Travels***. Others in town incl Hotels *Gulmour, Diamond* and *Rightway*, both below Gumat and at *Ambassador.*

● **Tourist offices**
J&K Tourism, **Tourist Reception Centre**, Vir Marg, T 48172. **TRC**, Jammu Tawi Rly Station, T 43803.

● **Useful addresses**
Police: T 100. **Fire Service**: T 101. **Ambulance**: T 5080, 442779. **Foreigners' Registration Office**: Supt of Police, Canal Rd, T 42676.

● **Transport**
Jammu is on NH1A (Jalandhar-Srinagar-Uri). It is connected to destinations in Jammu and Kashmir, by all-weather roads, and to Ladakh via Srinagar from May to Oct. From: **Srinagar** (293 km); **Kargil** (497 km); **Leh** (727 km); **Amritsar** (214 km); **Chandigarh** (363 km); **Agra** (786 km); **Jaipur** (847 km); **Patnitop** (112 km); **Kishtwar High Altitude National Park** (248 km); **Delhi** (586 km).

Local Buses: city bus services run frequently on fixed routes. Low fares. Popular **Matador Mini-buses** and **tempos** operate on point-to-point fixed routes. Fare Re 0.50-1. **Taxis and auto-rickshaws**: are easily available but unmetered. The railway station is on the other side of the Tawi River from town. Allow approx Rs 10 by auto rickshaw.

Air The airport is 6 km out of town, T 5745. **Transport to town**: taxis and auto-rickshaws available; fix fares beforehand. **Indian Airlines** flies daily to Delhi 1¼ hr; F,Su to Leh, 0835, 1 hr; Srinagar, M,Tu,Th,Sa, 0835, ¾ hr. Indian Airlines, TRC, Vir Marg, T 42735. Airport, 31433. For flights to Vaishno Devi (Sanjhi Chat) see below.

Train Bombay Central: *Jammu Tawi Exp*, 2972, Tu,W,F,Sa, Dep. 1035, 31½ hr. **Old Delhi**: *Jammu Tawi Mail*, 4034, daily, Dep. 1500, 14¼ hr. **New Delhi**: *Jhelum Exp*, 4678, daily, Dep. 1935, 14¾ hr; *Jammu Tawi-Bombay Exp*, Tu,W,F,Sa, Dep. 1035, 10½ hr; *Shalimar Exp*, 4646, daily, Dep. 1845, 16¼ hr. **Calcutta (S)**: *Jammu Tawi Exp*, 3152, daily, Dep. 1815, 46¼ hr. Rly Enquiries, T 31085, Reservations, T 43836.

Road Buses: there are direct buses to Srinagar, Katra (for Vaishno Devi), Pathankot and Kishtwar, all run by J&K SRTC, TRC, Vir Marg, T 46851. 1000-1700. J&K Roadways runs deluxe and ordinary buses from Delhi to Jammu daily. The Punjab, Haryana, and Himachal Pradesh SRTCs run buses to Jammu from Delhi and important towns in N India. Punjab Roadways, T 42782. All inter-state buses operate from the General Bus Stand, Jammu, T 47078. Super deluxe, deluxe, video and A-class coaches to Srinagar leave from the rly station, usually between 0600 and 0700. B-class buses to Srinagar leave from the General Bus Stand. These go via the rly station, but go to the point of departure to be sure of a seat.

Excursions

Vaishno Devi

61 km N of Jammu, can be visited from Jammu or en route to Srinagar. Vaishno Devi, a cave situated at 1700m, is 30m long and only 1.5m high. It is dedicated to Mahakali, Mahalaxmi and Mahasaraswati, the 3 mother goddesses of Hinduism. According to legend Vaishno Devi used the cave as a refuge when she was fleeing from the demon Bhairon who wanted to marry her. She would have nothing to do with this and killed him. A pilgrimage to the cave should be accompanied by a visit to the temple of Bhairon who was absolved of his sins before he died. The cave is one of the region's most important pilgrim sites.

From **Katra** the arduous climb along the 13 km track to the cave temple has been relaid, widened and tiled, and railings provided. Tea, drinks and snacks are available on the route. Another road from Lower Sanjichat to the Dabba brings you 2 km closer with 300m less to climb. Ponies, *dandies* and porters are available from Katra at fixed rates. As the temple draws near you hear cries of *Jai Matadi* (Victory to the Mother Goddess). At the shrine entrance, pilgrims walk in batches through cold ankle-deep water through the narrow cave entrance to get a glimpse of the deity. The main pilgrimage season is Mar-Jul.

• **Accommodation** Only vegetarian food is available. **F** ***Dormitories*** at Vaishno Devi provide sheets and blankets. Simple rooms at half-way point. At Katra **D** ***Asia Vaishnodevi***. 37 rm. **D** ***Ambica***. 50 rm. J&K Tourism **E** ***Tourist Lodge*** and similar.

• **Transport Air** The airport is at Sanjhi Chat. *Gulf Airways* helicopter service connects with Jammu, daily except W, 0840, 0930, 1020, 1/4 hr. Rs 1750 (one way), baggage 2 kg. From Jammu 0815, 0905, 0955. In Jammu, TRC, T 42672; in Delhi, *Hotel Maurya Sheraton*, T 3010101. **Road Buses and taxis**: leave from General Bus Stand, Jammu (or the rly station at peak season) as far as Katra, 48 km, an attractive town at the foot of the Trikuta Hills.

TREKKING IN KASHMIR

It is currently almost impossible to trek from the Vale of Kashmir, though it is still possible to get into Ladakh. The Government is making great efforts to develop alternatives to Kashmir in Himachal Pradesh, see page 547. The following treks may become practicable again if the political situation improves.

Kishtwar

Kishtwar, approx 226 km NE of Jammu. Kishtwar is an isolated district of Jammu and Kashmir and, despite its physical proximity to Srinagar it is administered from Jammu.

Both Hinduism and Islam are strong. Rajputs controlled the area before the establishment of Islam which gained a firm hold under the Mughals. Zorawar Singh was appointed governor in the 1820s and used it as a base for mounting his Dogra military campaigns in Ladakh and Western Tibet.

Today, this is a spectacular region of mountains in the Pir Panjal, with cascading waterfalls. Good quality saffron is grown on the plateau above the Chenab River and in spring and summer presents a very colourful sight. It is well off the beaten track and has few facilities. The hotels are all around the bus stands and are cheap and 'ethnic'. It takes over 10 hr by bus from Jammu and 15 hr from Srinagar. A jeep road runs from the Vale of Kashmir via the Sythen Pass. Eventually this will be used for bus services which will reduce the journey time by half.

Trekking in Kishtwar

The region offers some very fine trekking which can be undertaken out of Jammu. Supplies of basic foodstuffs and fuel can be obtained in Kishtwar. Horses and porters can also be recruited, the cost varying with the destination. The rates for Zanskar bound routes are almost twice those for Kashmir. There are no foreign exchange facilities so you will have to change enough money in Jammu. You can start trekking from Kishtwar or take buses and trucks further, ie up to the road head at Galhar about 15 km from Kishtwar.

Trekking from Kishtwar to Kashmir

Routes There are 2 routes into Kashmir, either by way of the **Chatru Valley** and Sythen Pass or the **Marwa/Warvan Valleys** and the Margan Pass. From Kishtwar you can bus or walk to **Palmer** village. Suitable camping is a few km further on the road to Ikhala. From Ikhala the mule track passes through forested gorge country before reaching **Sondar** and **Sirshi** villages which are located in the valley at the confluence of the Kiar and Kibar Rivers. This is the northernmost limit of rice cultivation and also Hinduism. From here you can make a satisfying side trip to the base camp of **Brammah** or **Sickle Moon**. Both require 3-4 days for the round trip. If you are going to Brammah you will need porters as horses cannot negotiate the route.

Two relatively short stages go from **Sirshi** to **Yourdu** via Hanzal where a hydro-electric scheme for the lower part of the river are under way. From Yourdu it is a comparatively long walk along the Warvan Valley to Inshin. There are some very attractive camp sites en route for those who do not want to cover the full distance in one day. The ascent to the **Margan Pass** from Inshin is quite steep. The views back down the Warvan Valley to Brammah and Sickle Moon are excellent. This is a long pass and a major route of the goat-rearing *Bakrawallahs* (*bakra* is Hindi for goat), so expect well fertilised camp sites for most of the trek!

There is a jeep track over the pass but you do not need to follow it. From **Lehinvan** you can take the bus to Anantnag and Srinagar. Along the trekking route are *Forest Rest Houses*. Daksum, on the Lehinvan to Anantnag road has a particularly scenic *Rest House*. From Daksum, you can cross the Synthen Pass and return to Kishtwar.

TERRAIN Without the side trips to Brammah and Sickle Moon, this trek can be completed comfortably in a week. Each day's walking is about 6 hr.

Kishtwar to Chamba

A day should be allowed to reach **Padyarna** (6 hr walk) because the bus service is often disrupted. It is a warm day's walk but there are tea stalls along the route. Horses can be obtained in Padyarna or the next village of Galhar though they usually come in multiples, ie it is difficult to get only one at a time. From Galhar it is uphill to Shasho with good views on the **Chenab Valley**. Much of the area is heavily forested and there are a number of gorges. At **Shasho** there is a big waterfall and a pleasant camp site. It is a long day's trek so you may choose to break it up by stopping at **Nunhoto**. **Atholi** is the next destination and is a Hindu and Muslim town. On the opposite bank is Gulabgarh, once a busy centre for the sapphires mined nearby at great heights, whose population includes Buddhist traders from Zanskar. You can stock up with more provisions at Atholi.

From Atholi there are 2 trails, one leading to the **Umasi La** and **Zanskar**, the other continuing up the Chenab Valley to **Chamba** passing through Shoal and Istahari in 2 stages before reaching the border with Himachal Pradesh. It is then 3 stages to the Sach Pass (4400m). There are excellent views of the Pir Panjal on the Kishtwar side and of the distant Dhaula Dhar and the Ravi Valley on the Himachal side. The trek ends at the roadhead at **Tarila**.

TERRAIN This trek can be completed in 10 days though an extra couple of days would make it much more relaxed. The daily walking time is just under 6 hr. It is not as arduous as the treks in Zanskar and Ladakh.

Kishtwar to Zanskar

You follow the same route as above to Atholi. You can hire horses at Gulabgarh from the Ladakhi traders who will make cheerful trekking companions. It is 3 stages up the **Paddar Valley** (the Umasi La is known as the Paddar La by the people of Atholi and Kishtwar) to the base of the pass. Suncham is the last village and 4 km beyond on the plateau above the terminal moraine is the **Hagshu Base Camp**. From here it is a long steady grind and another camp to the pass (5340m).

With such a high crossing, acclimatisation is essential. The last part will be through snow. The views of the Zanskar range are magnificent. The descent, however, is steep and difficult and an ice-axe or stick is essential. If you have hired horses you will have the services of a guide. From the camp at Nabil it is an easy day's walk to Ating in the Zanskar Valley. From there you can continue to Karsha or Padum and catch a bus or truck out over the **Pensi La**. to Kargil.

TERRAIN This trek is certainly spectacular but it is also demanding because you have to cross a high pass. The average daily walking time is 6 hr and the trek can be completed in 10 stages. An extra one or 2 days are recommended to allow flexibility and make it easier.

The Sindh and Lidder Valleys

This is the most popular trekking area in Kashmir and offers a variety of routes from the very easy to the longer yet still not very difficult. It is also the easiest place in Jammu and Kashmir for making suitable trekking arrangements. The season lasts from mid-Jun to late Oct. Jul and Aug are good months but there can be some heavy rainfall even though Kashmir does not receive a 'full' monsoon. Sep and Oct are ideal as the weather is settled, the atmosphere clear and the temperatures not too high.

Making arrangements

There is a pony wallah union in Kashmir and the rates are more or less fixed. Pahalgam is the best place for this and there is a board displaying the rates. You will have to budget for the pony wallah's return journey. Provisions can be obtained in Pahalgam. Basics such as rice, dal and potatoes are generally available at Aru though this cannot be relied upon.

Equipment is not so readily available but enquire at trekking hotels. It is much better to bring your own equipment. You will need some rope in case river crossings have to be made. Be cautious at all times. There are a number of medium length treks worth considering. **NB**: in most trekking areas there has been a problem with litter. Please do not add to it. Unfortunately, there is no official policy on removing, burying or burning garbage and no permit system which would create funds for clean-up operations. The emphasis is on each individual and group being responsible.

The Lidder to Sindh Valley trek via the Yemhar Pass

The Lidder to Sindh Valley trek via the Yemhar Pass leaves from Pahalgam and follows the road almost to Aru. There are excellent views looking back down the valley. The meadow camp site has a number of trekking lodges and some interesting day trips can be undertaken from here.

From **Aru** the trail climbs through pine forest to a Gujar grazing meadow and follows the Lidder River. F *Friends Guest House* is clean and friendly. "Running hot water", advertised on sign comes cold in buckets! There is a *Government Rest House* at **Lidderwat** and a number of other lodges which tend to mar the scenic beauty of the meadow. The F *Paradise Guest House*, was the only one open in 1993. Rm rather dirty and run down but owner is a good cook and very helpful (arranges Kolahoi Glacier trek – guide Rs 50).

The next stage is quite short (3 hr) to **Satlanjan**, the largest Gujar village in the Lidder Valley. From this camp site you can make a long round trip up to the Kolahoi glacier. An early start is essential if you are to get good views. Tiring, but very rewarding. **Sekiwas** is the next camping ground on the trek and can be reached from Lidderwat in only 3 hr.

From mid-Jun onwards there is a profusion of wild flowers, including marsh marigolds, gentians, buttercups and up in the crags, occasionally Himalayan Blue Poppy. There is another side trip to the 2 km by 1 km **Tarsar Lake**, one of the most beautiful in Kashmir. From the ridge beyond the lake you get good views into the Dachigam Sanctuary, see page 568. The round trip from Sekiwas will take about 8 hr including reasonable stops.

From Sekiwas the valley splits into three. The left hand path goes over the **Sonamous Pass** (3960m), the centre one over an unnamed pass (4200m) and the right hand one over the **Yemhar Pass** (4350m). The ascent to the Yemhar should take about 3 hr and from the top there are excellent views. The camping ground is by a small glacial lake. The following day's walk is an easy stretch down to **Kulan** where you can get transport back to Srinagar or Sonamarg.

TERRAIN There are a number of variations to this trek which take in different passes, eg from Sekiwas you can go over the Sonamous Pass – passable when the snow on the Yemhar Pass is too soft. Local shepherds and trekkers will be able to advise. Also there is a route from Aru to Sonamarg via the Harbaghwan Pass (4200m).

The Lidder to Sindh Valley Trek via Mahgunis Pass and Amarnath

(47km, *Alt* 3962m) This is another popular route, and you have to contend with a sizeable Hindu pilgrim traffic. Each year at Jul/Aug full moon in the month of *Sawon*, about 25,000 pilgrims make their way to the cave at **Amarnath**, where Siva explained the secret of salvation and the path to immortality to Parvati. There is an ice lingam (a stalactite formed by water dripping through the limestone roof of the cave, which changes size according to the season.

For pilgrims, the trek takes about **5 days**. Transport can be hired in the form of mules or ponies and *dandies* which are wooden palanquins carried by bearers. The pony rates nearly double, during the season. **Accommodation** is in pilgrim shelters and *Rest Houses*. It is certainly an experience to be part of this *yatra* (pilgrimage) but you have to like noise, crowds, be prepared for cramped conditions and poor sanitation.

Day 1 Pahalgam to the busy village of **Chandanwari** (16 km, 2895m) along a mule track and jeepable road. Day 2 By pony track, in places steps are cut into the mountain side. After a hard climb up to Pissughati, and passing a camp at Zojibal you reach the beautiful glacial lake at **Sheshnag**, (11 km, 3573m) with a campsite above, nearly surrounded by steep mountains. There are shelters and a *Rest House* in **Wawjan** higher up along the track. Day 3 Climb up to the snowbound Mahgunis Pass (4580m) through Poshpathar descend to **Panchtarni** (13 km) in the Sind valley with its long line of tents. Day 4 To **Amarnath** (6 km). From the crowded stalls near the campsite steep rockcut steps lead up to the cave where the ice lingam stands. You can return to Pahalgam on the final day.

TERRAIN The whole trek can be done at other times; recommended if you want to feel more a part of the countryside. It is an attractive and spectacular trek. Go before the annual *yatra* and the camp sites and track will be less polluted with litter.

The Sonamarg to Haramukh Trek

This can be treated as an extension of the Lidder-Sindh Valley Trek. It can be completed in a week and includes wonderful scenery, opportunities for fishing and the chance to get lost. If you are travelling without local guides, you should check your route with shepherds as the trail bifurcates frequently.

You will get views of the Zoji La and of Baltoro and K2 from the Nichinni Bar (4,000m), Nanga Parbat from Vishenagar Pass (4300m), glacial lakes, Gujar shepherd encampments, Gangabal Lake, Haramukh peak (5755m) and the Vale of Kashmir.

TERRAIN Each day's walking will take 5 hr and there are plenty of ups and downs. It is recommended for those with a reasonable level of fitness.

EAST INDIA

CONTENTS

ROUTE MAPS

INTRODUCTION

East India is the least visited region of India, yet it contains some of the country's most beautiful scenery, remarkable religious monuments and vibrant cultural centres. In Calcutta it has India's second largest city, at the same time notorious for its poverty and famous for its cultural contribution to the national life. The Orissan temples of Puri, Bhubaneswar and Konark are among the most striking architectural developments of any period of India's religious building, while in the interior of Orissa and Bihar, as well as in the North Eastern Hill States some tribal societies are only just being brought into contact with the modern world. Finally, the Himalaya to the north are as magnificent as anywhere in their 1500 kilometre length, with Darjiling in West Bengal and Sikkim encapsulating the small independent hill state of Bhutan.

Environment

The regions of East India

East India covers 10 states, containing some of the most striking contrasts in the sub-continent. W Bengal, Bihar and Orissa have over 190 million of the region's total population of 220 million. The much smaller states of the north-east, Assam, and the tribal hill states of Arunachal Pradesh, Manipur, Meghalaya, Mizoram, Nagaland and Tripura, have all received full statehood comparatively recently. The total area of the East region is 673,000 sq km, almost exactly the size of Texas. Calcutta, at its hub, is 1100 km from Assam's N border with China, 960 km from the SE tip of Orissa, and 700 km from the NW tip of Bihar.

Land

The Himalaya

The northernmost section comprises the Himalayan ranges. Darjiling, in northern W Bengal, is dominated by the Himalaya, with Kangchendzonga majestic on the immediate skyline and, weather permitting, Everest visible from Tiger Hill.

The plains

Immediately to the S are the plains of the Ganga (in the W) and the Brahmaputra (in Assam). N Bihar and W Bengal occupy the alluvial plains of the Ganga. The silt brought down by the frequent floods that devastate parts of Bihar and W Bengal has also contributed to the fertility of the soil. Despite the general flatness of the plains they contain a rich variety of colourful landscapes, from the mango forests of Malda to the mangroves of the Sundarbans.

Chota Nagpur plateau
To the S again are the ancient rocks of the Chota Nagpur plateau in S Bihar and Orissa. While the coastal districts of Orissa have broad flat delta landscapes, the interior has hills rising to over 1500m. The forest cover of Orissa, cleared much more recently than elsewhere in the region, is still widely populated by tribal peoples.

NE hill states
Assam and the states that used to comprise the NE Frontier Agency (NEFA) are quite different, physically as well as culturally, from the plains areas of W Bengal and Bihar. In medieval India Assam was regarded as 'foreign' to the rest of India, and it is still distinct today. The distinctiveness of the NE is provided not just by the Brahmaputra Valley or by the scenery to its S of low forest-covered hills, but by the prevalence of Mongoloid tribes, barely assimilated into mainstream Indian culture and life. Many still have strong ethnic connections with Burma and other regions of S E Asia. Many have also converted to Christianity, and in Nagaland and Mizoram, for example, Christians make up the majority of the population.

Brahmaputra
The Brahmaputra, which flows through the Assam valley, is one of the most remarkable rivers in the world. Nearly 3000 km long from its source in the high Himalaya to the junction with the Meghna, it flows from W to E for the major part of its course before taking a hairpin turn to run SW through Assam. The change in direction is almost certainly the result of earth movements. Before reaching Assam proper it passes through gorges over 5000m deep. It is broader 1600 km from the sea than is the Rhine near its mouth. In the snow melt and wet season the river flow increases dramatically. At Guwahati, where the river is nearly 1.5 km wide, it rises between 4 and 5m during the wet season. It often floods, forcing settlements back from its banks.

Climate

Temperature
Between Nov and Feb the weather can be very pleasant, cool at night and warm in the daytime. Both minimum and maximum temperatures are higher the nearer you get to the Tropic of Cancer. Altitude has its cooling effects, though, and around Ranchi in Bihar as well as further S into the Eastern Ghats of Orissa, winter temperatures are also very pleasant. From Mar onwards the temperatures throughout the region rise sharply, and in all the lowlying and coastal areas high humidity makes it extremely uncomfortable. Temperatures can rise to between 40°C and 47°C, with humidity levels at around 80%, but Darjiling and the hills are magnificent through to the end of May. The arrival of the rains brings a slight lowering of the temperatures but a marked increase in humidity.

Rainfall
The E region contains some of the wettest places in the world. Most of its rain comes between Jun and Oct, but amounts vary considerably. Orissa and W Bengal receive between 120 cm and 150 cm, decreasing generally from E to W, so that W Bihar receives less than 100 cm. The whole of Bengal is subject to storms between Mar and May, and cyclones can devastate any part of the coastal region from Orissa round to the state of Tripura and the Burmese coast in May and between Oct and Dec. Altitude makes a tremendous difference to rainfall. Meghalaya ('abode of clouds') is appropriately named since Mawsynram near Cherrapunji has the wettest weather station anywhere in the world. Between Jun and Oct, it receives over 10m of rain on average – and in a wet year, more than double that figure. See page 696.

History

Early history

The eastern region has some of India's most important historical sites. By the 6th century BC the northern plains of modern Bihar were the developing heartland of Indian political power. Here both the Buddha and Mahavir, founder of Jainism, were born into royal families. Within a night's train journey from Calcutta you can reach many of the most sacred sites associated with the Buddha's life.

Two centuries later the plains were the hearth from which the Mauryan Empire expanded to conquer the major part of the sub-continent. Under Asoka (see page 716) the influence of Buddhism spread far beyond its original home. His bloody victory over the Orissan king converted him to non-violent Buddhist beliefs.

The E region was also the hearth of a succession of Hindu kings and emperors. The Guptas of the 4th to 6th centuries AD controlled great areas of N India from the plains of modern Bihar, creating an artistic tradition by which Hindu art has come to be judged. Much later, from the 9th to the 13th century AD, Orissa became the centre of a regional power responsible for some of India's most outstanding architectural and religious monuments, the temple complexes of Bhubaneshwar, Puri and Konarak.

The arrival of the Muslims

That period marked the high water mark of Hindu kingdoms in E India. Very soon after the Delhi Sultanate was established in 1206, Muslim power spread right across the Ganga plains into Bengal. Successive Muslim powers were established in Bengal itself whose influence stretched from Bihar in the W to Assam in the E.

From the 16th century Muslim power was consolidated and the religious balance of population in the region as a whole shifted. Anxious to increase both their revenues and their political security the Mughal emperors offered incentives to clear and settle new lands. The Ganga plains between Delhi and Varanasi were already densely populated and cultivated. Further E great tracts of jungle remained uncleared. Muslim nobles set about clearing and settling forested tracts far into the Ganga delta. Associated with the new settlements Muslim *pirs* set up shrines and carried the word of Islam, that all are equal in the eyes of God, to poor and outcaste Hindus.Thus they created a second core of Muslim population, separated from that in NW India by the Hindu belt of the central Ganga plains.

Periodically there was also a destructive element in the extension of Muslim power across the E. Particularly under Aurangzeb many Hindu temples were desecrated or destroyed, some having mosques built on their sites. The eviction of the Brahmin priests from the major temples in Bhubaneshwar and Puri caused a reaction which is still powerful today, and is reflected in the refusal to allow non-Hindus into the shrines of the Lingaraj and the Jagannath temples.

The British

The arrival of the British rapidly transformed the region's economy and its social character. From the settlement of Calcutta in 1690 to the permanent control of Bengal established after the Battle of Plassey in 1757, the traders of the East India Company developed networks of influence to protect their trading rights and powers. These involved political deals with princes who themselves were trying to protect their local power as the Mughal Empire began to collapse. During the next 100 years the East India Company converted Calcutta into the chief centre of its economic and political power in India. Agriculture was channelled into producing goods, notably indigo, opium and later jute, for sale to Europe, and so produced tax revenue for the support of the Company, its servants and its army.

It was elements of the Bengal army that mutinied first in 1857, though they were stationed in Meerut, far to the NW, and Bengal itself remained unaffected. Calcutta had already been the pre-eminent city of the British East India Company's territories for 150 years. From 1857 it became the first capital of 'British' India, which it remained until 1911, when the capital was moved to Delhi.

The role of Calcutta

By then the economy of E India had been permanently re-shaped. Calcutta developed into India's largest manufacturing city, and much of the eastern region was tributary to it. All railways in the eastern part of the British Indian Empire centred on Calcutta. New lines stretched to the hills of Assam to allow tea to be sold on the Calcutta market. Coal from W Bengal and Bihar supplied the city and passed through it to other Indian destinations. Every fibre of jute grown in E Bengal was either exported through Calcutta or was processed there before export. It was a regional capital par excellence.

Calcutta had also become the centre of the newly emerging educated Bengali elite. The government administration in Assam, Bihar and Orissa was dominated by the new educated class of Bengalis. That was just one element of new population movements encouraged by the economic changes which were the hallmark of the later British period. The massive migration of labour into the tea estates from Bihar and Orissa was another. They led to changes which remain politically important today. Periodically troubles erupted, sometimes as a result of industrial disputes, sometimes because the intellectual Bengali population, kept at a distance by the ruling British, began to feel strongly a sense of discrimination.

The partition of 1905

Troubles were brought to a head by Lord Curzon's 1905 plan to divide the area which included Bengal, Bihar and Orissa. Bengal was divided into E and W, the former being predominantly Muslim. This produced a strong reaction in Calcutta where the call to boycott British goods and buy *Swadeshi* had begun a revolt sustained until Independence in 1947. Bengalis played an increasingly leading role in the movement for independence.

The most prominent was **Subhas Chandra Bose**, who disappeared aboard a Japanese plane but is still revered throughout W Bengal. A one-time President of the Indian National Congress, Bose argued that India should side with the Axis powers and Japan during the Second World War in order to speed up the eviction of the British. After bitter disagreements with Gandhi and Nehru, he left for Japan, returning to Burma to head the Indian National Army alongside the Japanese.

Modern East India

Government

The partition of India and Pakistan created great problems for the economy of Calcutta, cutting off access to supplies of raw jute. The war with China in 1962 opened up the whole of the Brahmaputra Valley to a Chinese invasion, and the Indian army's defeat sent shock waves through the entire region. Following the Pakistan military crackdown on 25 March, 1971, 10 million Hindu refugees fled into India, only returning after the brief war of December 1971 which created the independent state of Bangladesh.

Until the middle 1970s the NE hill states were ruled as a special Frontier Agency of the Government of India. Many of the tribal peoples were fighting guerrilla wars against the Indian army, trying to establish their own autonomy.

Assam has its own individuality. It is one of the very few areas in the whole of S Asia that until very recently had cultivable land to spare. As a result there had been continuous movements of agriculturalists from Bengal into the Brahmaputra Valley. Bengalis colonised much of the lower land, cultivating rice as in the deltas of Bengal from which they came. Land below 1500m above sea level was severely malarial until the 1950s, which contributed to the sparseness of the population. In the late 1970s the native born Assamese mounted huge political protests against the immigrant non-Assamese. The problems have only partially been resolved. Elsewhere in the NE the major tribal groups have now been given their own states. Long periods of violent protest against the central Indian government in Nagaland and Mizoram were brought to an end in the late 1980s, but in 1994 tribal issues remained prominent. In the hill regions of West Bengal an agitation for creating a separate state for Gurkhas, spearheaded by the Gurkha Liberation Front (GLF) continued into 1994, occasionally causing considerable disruption.

Economy

Agriculture

The East is one of India's poorest regions, and although there have been significant developments in some areas there has been little improvement in others, notably in many parts of Bihar. **Tea**, grown in both W Bengal and Assam, is far and away the region's most important cash crop. Indigenous tea plants were discovered in the NE corner of Assam in 1823. The East India Company began to exploit it when it lost the monopoly of the Chinese trade in 1833. As the geographers Spate and Learmonth have said, "the early days of the industry were marked by frantic speculation, non-existent estates in the midst of unmapped jungle being sold over and over again, and the acute shortage of local labour being met by beguiling Biharis and Madrassis with glowing promises, convoying them under guard, and keeping them in what were virtually concentration camps. In 18 months over 18,000 out of 50,000 coolies died or vanished into the jungle." Darjiling tea is now world famous, and production has risen steadily over the last three decades. Although India's share of the world tea market has fallen from nearly 50% at Independence to 25% today, the volume of exports has risen steadily to over 200 million kg in 1994. However, far more Indians are drinking tea now than at any time earlier, and domestic consumption is now over 550 million kg. In the 1990s the tea estates have suffered serious political disturbances which continued into 1994. See page 656.

For most of the region **rice** is the staple crop, cultivated both for subsistence and for sale. W Bengal, Bihar and Orissa account for 30% of India's total rice production. Wheat is much less important, grown as a winter crop while rice is predominantly a monsoon crop. The same land sometimes produces both crops at different times of year. **Jute**, the dominant cash crop in Bangladesh, has also become important on the much less well suited soils of W Bengal and Orissa, to provide raw materials for the jute industry whose supplies were cut off soon after the creation of Pakistan in 1947.

There is obvious pressure on the land. The average farm size in W Bengal and Bihar is under 2 ha and over 20% of the village working population has no land at all. The great majority of people thus remain poor, although there have been important agricultural developments, particularly where irrigation is available.

Manufacturing & resources

The E region has some of India's most vital resources. **Oil** has been exploited in Assam for over 50 years, and it has contributed a major share of India's home produced oil which now accounts for over 30% of total requirements. In Orissa, Bihar and W Bengal are huge reserves of iron ore, coal and **minerals**, which contributed to the decision of Jamshedji Tata, founder of the Tata Iron and Steel Company, to locate India's first steel mill at Jamshedpur in 1908. The region has seen a huge expansion in heavy engineering industry, coal mining, power generation and a range of related activities, making it one of the most important industrial regions of S Asia.

Calcutta played a vital role in this expansion, with 1 m people employed in jute and engineering work, and its port and other transport links, notably rail connections, serving the rest of India and the outside world. In the 1960s and 1970s Calcutta handled nearly half of all India's trade. Its network of railway links make it the pivotal point for the region as a whole, and for over 100 years it has also been a centre for migrants coming from all over India in search of work.

CALCUTTA

Contents

Maps

India's second largest city and the capital of W Bengal is arguably the world's most controversial city. To some it has always been and remains an unequalled centre of poverty, squalor and deprivation. To others it is the proud cultural and intellectual capital of India with an outstanding contribution to the arts, science, medicine, and social reform in its past and a rich contemporary cultural life.

BASICS *Population*: 10.92 mn. *Altitude*: 5.3m.

History

Calcutta was founded by the remarkable English merchant trader **Job Charnock** in 1690. He was in charge of the East India Company factory (or warehouse) in Hugli, then the centre of British trade from Eastern India. Attacks from the local Muslim ruler forced him to flee – first down river to Sutanuti and then 1500 km S to Madras. However, in 1690 he selected the 3 villages where Armenian and Portuguese traders had already settled, leased them from Emperor Aurangzeb and returned to what was to become the capital of British India. Charnock became the first Governor of Calcutta, where he lived with his Indian wife, whom he had rescued from committing *sati* on her first husband's funeral pyre.

Calcutta has inspired passionate views. By 1780 the high quality of the British housing in Calcutta led to the nickname 'village of palaces', but the Indian settlement was already desperately squalid. The traveller William Macintosh wrote in 1782 that "from the western extremity of California to the eastern coast of Japan there is not a spot where judgment, taste, decency, and convenience are so grossly insulted as in that scattered and confused chaos of houses, huts, sheds, streets, lanes, alleys, windings, gullies, sinks, and tanks, which, jumbled into an undistinguished mass of filth and corruption, equally offensive to human sense and health,

Climate: Calcutta

	Jan	Feb	Mar	Apr	May	Jun	Jul	Aug	Sep	Oct	Nov	Dec	Av/Tot
Max (°C)	26	29	34	36	36	34	32	32	32	31	29	27	31
Min (°C)	12	15	20	24	26	26	26	26	26	24	18	13	21
Rain (mm)	13	22	30	50	135	263	320	318	253	134	29	4	1571

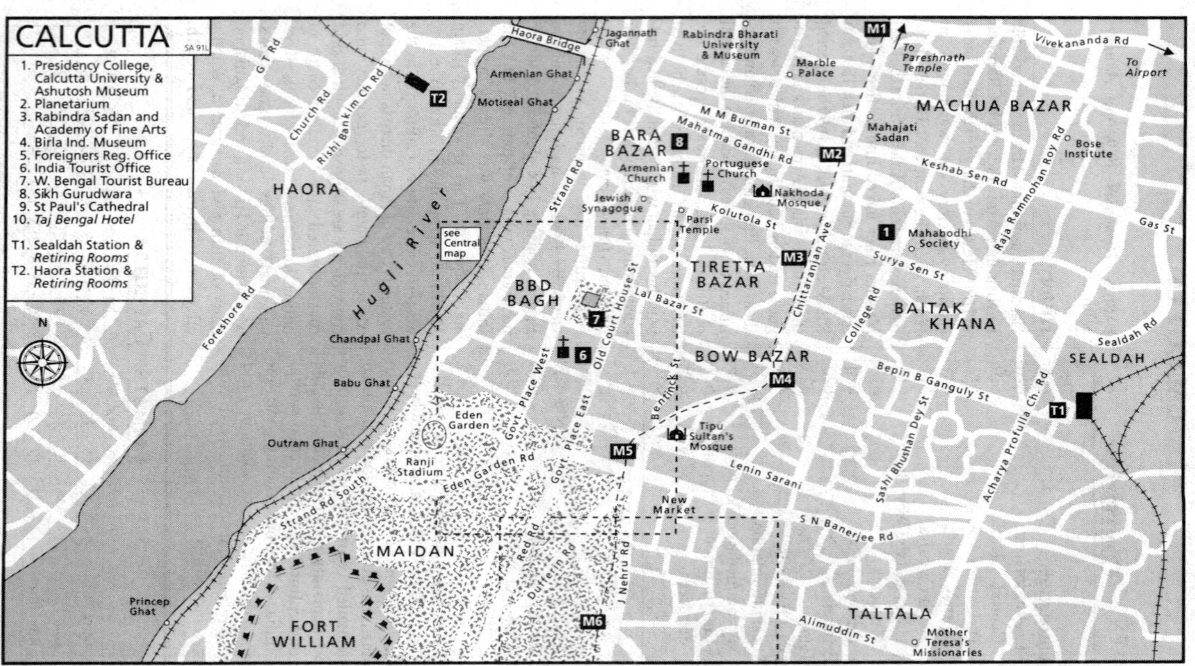
CALCUTTA
SA 91L
1. Presidency College, Calcutta University & Ashutosh Museum
2. Planetarium
3. Rabindra Sadan and Academy of Fine Arts
4. Birla Ind. Museum
5. Foreigners Reg. Office
6. India Tourist Office
7. W. Bengal Tourist Bureau
8. Sikh Gurudwara
9. St Paul's Cathedral
10. Taj Bengal Hotel
T1. Sealdah Station & Retiring Rooms
T2. Haora Station & Retiring Rooms
N
G T Rd
Church Rd
Rishi Bankim Ch Rd
T2
HAORA
Foreshore Rd
Haora Bridge
Armenian Ghat
Motiseal Ghat
Hugli River
see Central map
Chandpal Ghat
Babu Ghat
Outram Ghat
Princep Ghat
Strand Rd South
MAIDAN
FORT WILLIAM
Jagannath Ghat
Rabindra Bharati University & Museum
Marble Palace
M1
To Pareshnath Temple
Vivekananda Rd
To Airport
MACHUA BAZAR
Mahajati Sadan
Bose Institute
M M Burman St
Mahatma Gandhi Rd
BARA BAZAR
8
M2
Keshab Sen Rd
Raja Rammohan Roy Rd
Strand Rd
Armenian Church
Portuguese Church
Nakhoda Mosque
Jewish Synagogue
Kolutola St
Parsi Temple
Gas St
1
Mahabodhi Society
M3
Chittaranjan Ave
Surya Sen St
TIRETTA BAZAR
BBD BAGH
Lal Bazar St
7
College Rd
BAITAK KHANA
Sealdah Rd
SEALDAH
6
Old Court House St
BOW BAZAR
Govt. Place West
Bentinck St
M4
Bepin B Ganguly St
T1
Eden Garden
Govt. Place East
Tipu Sultan's Mosque
Sashi Bhushan Dey St
Acharya Profulla Ch. Rd
Ranji Stadium
Eden Garden Rd
M5
Lenin Sarani
New Market
S N Banerjee Rd
Red Rd
Dufferin Rd
J Nehru Rd
M6
TALTALA
Alimuddin St
Mother Teresa's Missionaries

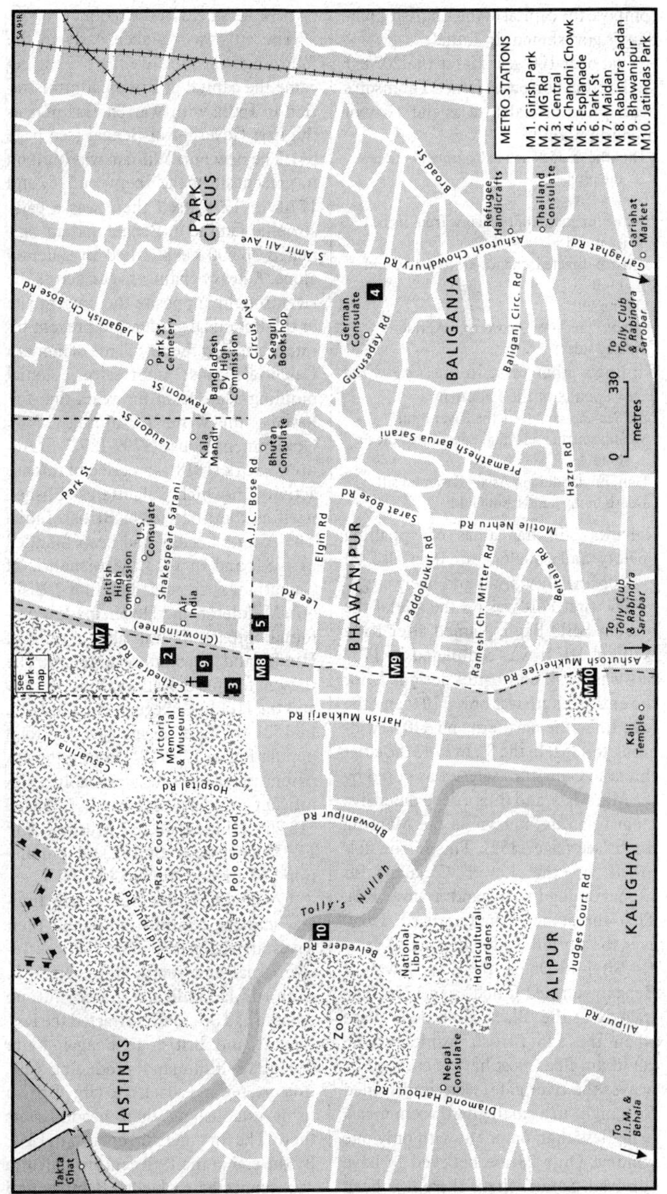
METRO STATIONS
M 1. Girish Park
M 2. MG Rd
M 3. Central
M 4. Chandni Chowk
M 5. Esplanade
M 6. Park St
M 7. Maidan
M 8. Rabindra Sadan
M 9. Bhawanipur
M10. Jatindas Park
PARK CIRCUS
Broad St
Refugee Handicrafts
Thailand Consulate
Gariahat Market
Gariahat Rd
Ashutosh Chowdhury Rd
S Amir Ali Ave
A Jagadish Ch. Bose Rd
Park St Cemetery
Bangladesh Dy High Commission
Circus Ave
Seagull Bookshop
German Consulate
Gurusaday Rd
BALIGANJA
Baliganj Circ. Rd
To Tolly Club & Rabindra Sarobar
0 330 metres
Rawdon St
Laudon St
Kala Mandir
Bhutan Consulate
Pramathesh Barua Sarani
Park St
U.S. Consulate
Shakespeare Sarani
A.J.C. Bose Rd
Sarat Bose Rd
Hazra Rd
Motilal Nehru Rd
British High Commission
Air India
Elgin Rd
Lee Rd
BHAWANIPUR
Paddopukur Rd
Ramesh Ch. Mitter Rd
Beltala Rd
To Tolly Club & Rabindra Sarobar
(Chowringhee)
Cathedral Rd
see Park St map
Ashutosh Mukherjee Rd
Harish Mukharji Rd
Victoria Memorial & Museum
Casuarina Av.
Hospital Rd
Kali Temple
Bhowanipur Rd
Race Course
Polo Ground
Khidirpur Rd
Tolly's Nullah
KALIGHAT
Judges Court Rd
Belvedere Rd
National Library
Horticultural Gardens
ALIPUR
Alipur Rd
Zoo
HASTINGS
Nepal Consulate
Diamond Harbour Rd
To I.I.M. & Behala
Takta Ghat

compose the capital of the English Company's government in India".

Just over 100 years later the 20 year old Kipling borrowed James Thomson's description of Calcutta as the 'City of dreadful night':

Thus the midday halt of Charnock – more's the pity!
Grew a City
As the fungus sprouts chaotic from its bed
So it Spread
Chance-directed, chance-erected, laid and built
On the silt
Palace, byre, hovel – poverty and pride -
Side by side

Kipling's other verse in the *Song of the Cities* speaks of the Calcutta

the Sea-captain loved, the River built,
Wealth sought and Kings adventured life to hold.
Hail, England! I am Asia – Power on silt,
Death in my hands, but Gold!

Calcutta still has areas of appalling poverty and squalor, but it is also an extraordinarily vibrant and lively city.

The first Fort was on the site of the present BBD Bagh. Named after King William III, it was completed in 1707 but was weak and badly designed "for the entire length was only 710 ft and the breadth at the northern end 340 ft, widening to 485 ft in the S". In 1742 the chief threat to Calcutta's safety was posed by the Marathas, and thus a deep defensive moat was dug, known as the Maratha ditch (see page 1155). This is now followed by the Lower Circular Rd (Acharya Jagdish Chandra Bose Rd). That threat never materialised. However, the city fell easily when the 20-year-old **Siraj-ud-Daula**, the new Nawab of Bengal, stormed Calcutta in 1756. The tragedy of the **'Black Hole'** took place when the 146 British residents who could not flee (most having escaped by way of the river gate) were imprisoned for a night in a small guard room measuring less than 6m x 5m with only one window. Only 23 are believed to have survived. Some believe there had been 64 prisoners held in the room.

The city was re-taken early in the following year by Clive. In 1772 it became the capital of British administration in India with Warren Hastings as the first Governor of Bengal (see page 54). The new Fort William was built on its present site to the S between 1757 and 1770. In 1770 itself there was a catastrophic famine in Bengal and an estimated 76,000 people died in Calcutta alone. A heavy chain was run across the river, roughly opposite the present site of the Botanical gardens, to prevent pirates attacking the city. Some of modern Calcutta's most impressive colonial buildings date from the years that followed – the Writer's Building (1780), Government House (1799-1802), St Andrew's Kirk (1818) – a period of intense activity, in which Calcutta established itself as the first city of British India. The Asiatic Society had been founded in 1784, and in 1813 the Bishopric of Calcutta was created. The first 2 Bishops, Middleton and Heber, made a profound impact. It was also a time of Hindu and Muslim resurgence. The present temple to Kali was built in 1809 and the Hindu College opened in 1817. In 1821 the first census gave the total population as 179,917. Despite the apparent precision it was probably a significant underestimate. It showed 118,203 Hindus, 48,162 Muslims and 13,138 Christians. By 1850 the population had already risen to 400,000.

Colonial Calcutta grew as new traders, soldiers, administrators and their wives arrived establishing their exclusive social and sports clubs. Trade in cloth, silk, lac, indigo, rice, areca nut and tobacco had originally attracted the Portuguese and British to Bengal. Later Calcutta's hinterland producing jute, iron ore, tea and coal led to large British firms establishing their headquarters there. The first jute mill opened in 1854. By the end of the 19th century Calcutta was connected to Delhi, Bombay and

Calcutta's Place In The Cosmic Dance

Calcutta's site was particularly holy to Hindus. According to one myth, King Daksa was enraged when his daughter Sati married Siva. He organised a *Yajna* (grand sacrifice) to which he invited everyone in the kingdom – except his son-in-law. Kali was distraught to hear that her husband had been so insulted by her father and threw herself on the sacrificial flames. Siva in turn arrived on the scene to find his wife's body already burnt. Tearing it from the flames, he started his dance of cosmic destruction. All the other gods, witnessing the devastation that Siva was causing in his anguish, pleaded with Vishnu to step in and end the chaos. Vishnu intercepted him with his flailing *chakra* (a discus-like weapon) and, in order to dislodge Kali's body from Siva's shoulder, chopped it into fifty one pieces, which were flung far. The place where each one fell became a place of pilgrimage – a *pithasthana*. Kali's little toe fell at Kali Ghat hence Kalikshetra or Kalikata gave the city its name.

Madras by rail. Roads had improved, a bridge of boats was opened in 1874 to connect it with Haora, the industrial town across the river, and townships grew in the suburbs. In 1876, the Calcutta Corporation began to provide filtered drinking water and a drainage scheme, and Calcutta prospered as the main centre of commerce and trade and the political capital of British India up to 1911, when it was transferred to Delhi. That move dealt a blow to Calcutta's morale which has left a continuing sense of grievance.

Independence and after

The city's economy was dealt a further blow by Partition. When Pakistan closed its borders to trade with India in 1949 Calcutta lost its supplies of raw jute. Although engineering, chemicals and consumer goods industries grew, the loss of several hundred thousand jobs and the failure to attract new investment created critical economic problems.

The difficulties were increased in the late 1960s with outbreaks of violence organised by the **Naxalites**, a revolutionary political movement. The election of the Communist Party of India Marxist (CPM) to power in 1977 has been followed by a period of stability for the city, and there are some signs of renewed growth.

The port of Calcutta has also declined in importance. 150 km upstream from the sea, the Hugli up to Calcutta was always difficult to navigate. The river was silting steadily, with decreasing amounts of fresh water coming down even in the wet season. In the dry season the flow was so low that sea water was travelling many miles upstream of Calcutta at high tide, seriously affecting the city's main drinking water supply. For that reason the Govt of India built a barrage on the Ganga at **Farakka**, over 150 km to the N, so that water could be diverted down the Hugli. The scheme was first put forward by British engineers in the 1850s but wasn't taken up until 100 years later. Completed in 1971, water began to flow down the Hugli in 1975. Although it has helped to alleviate Calcutta's water problems it has caused major disagreements with Bangladesh ever since, as Bangladesh also needs the dry season flow of the Ganga for irrigation.

Local crafts & industries

The trade in jute, tea and the industries that flourished in the city's hinterland owing to the rich deposits of coal and iron continue to play an important role in the economy. Some heavy engineering, car manufacture and ship building continue, but the emphasis is shifting to electronics and lighter consumer industries.

Places of interest

Sightseeing takes time, and outside Nov to early Mar can be very hot. Calcutta traffic is often extremely slow moving, and while the metro and the new road bridge across the Hugli have greatly improved travel S of the Esplanade, the line N to Dum Dum will not be completed until the mid 1990s. Traffic N of BBD Bagh is often seriously held up.

Central Calcutta

BBD Bagh (Dalhousie Sq)

Many historic buildings surround the square. Quietest before 0900. Renamed Benoy Badal Dinesh Bagh after 3 Bengali martyrs, the square was created in the imperial capital with a small artificial lake in the centre fed by natural springs, from which it is thought that Job Charnock obtained drinking water. North, on Strand Rd N, is the dilapidated **Silver Mint** (1824-31) opposite the Mint Master's House, built at the same time in the Greek style.

The **Writers' Building** (1780), designed by Thomas Lyon as the trading HQ of the East India Company, is on the N side of BBD Bagh. Re-faced in 1880 it is now the state Govt secretariat. The classical block with 57 sets of identical windows on 3 storeys was built like a barrack inside. **Mission Row** (now RN Mukharji Rd), Calcutta's oldest street, is one street E of BBD Bagh. The **Old Mission Church**, built by the Swedish missionary Johann Kiernander was consecrated in 1770.

West side of BBD Bagh

On the W side of BBD Bagh is the white-domed **General Post Office** designed by Walter Granville (1868), with its Corinthian pillars, built on the site of the original Fort William. Brass plates mark the position of the walls of the fort, destroyed in 1756 by Siraj ud Daula. The Black Hole of Calcutta was at the NE corner of the Post Office. The commercial quarter of the city is a little further N, and the sight of the **Lyon's Range stock exchange** in full swing, spilling out onto the street, confirms that commercially, Calcutta is still very much alive.

South of BBD Bagh

S of BBD Bagh, at the N end of the Maidan, is the imposing **Raj Bhavan** (1799-1802), now the residence of the Governor of W Bengal, formerly Govt House for British Governors-General and Viceroys. It was modelled on Kedleston Hall in Derbyshire (later to be Lord Curzon's home), and designed by Charles Wyatt, one of many Bengal Engineers who designed several buildings in the city by studying books and plans of famous British buildings. The Govt house with its Ionic façades and its

Calcutta's Changing Names And Numbers

Although many of the city's streets have been re-named over the last 3 decades, the old names still survive in popular use and are more easily recognized by the public at large. Maps and guide books often refer to either of these names, some of which are listed here.

Bowbazar St – Bepin Behary Ganguly St; **Chowringhee** – JL Nehru Rd; **Free School St** – Mirza Ghalib St; **Harrington St** – Ho-Chi-Minh Sarani; **Harrison Rd** – Mahatma Gandhi Rd; **Haora** – Haora; **Kyd Street** – Dr M Ishaque Rd; **Landsdowne Rd** – Sarat Bose Rd; **Lindsay St** – Nelly Sengupta Sarani; **Lower Chitpur Rd** – Rabindra Sarani; **Lower Circular Rd** – Acharya JC Bose Rd; **Theatre Rd** – Shakespeare Sarani; **Wellesley St** – Rafi Ahmed Kidwai Rd.

Telephone numbers Exchange numbers are being altered by area and you may need to check those listed with 44, 46 and 47.

processional staircase, set in grounds of 2.5 ha and topped by a massive dome, was built so that India could be governed from a 'palace'. It is built of brick with cream-washed plaster. The interior is lavishly decorated with stately rooms and the Marble Hall containing several curiosities such as Tipu Sultan's throne, a 'bird cage' lift once driven by steam, and some artistic treasures. Entry is restricted.

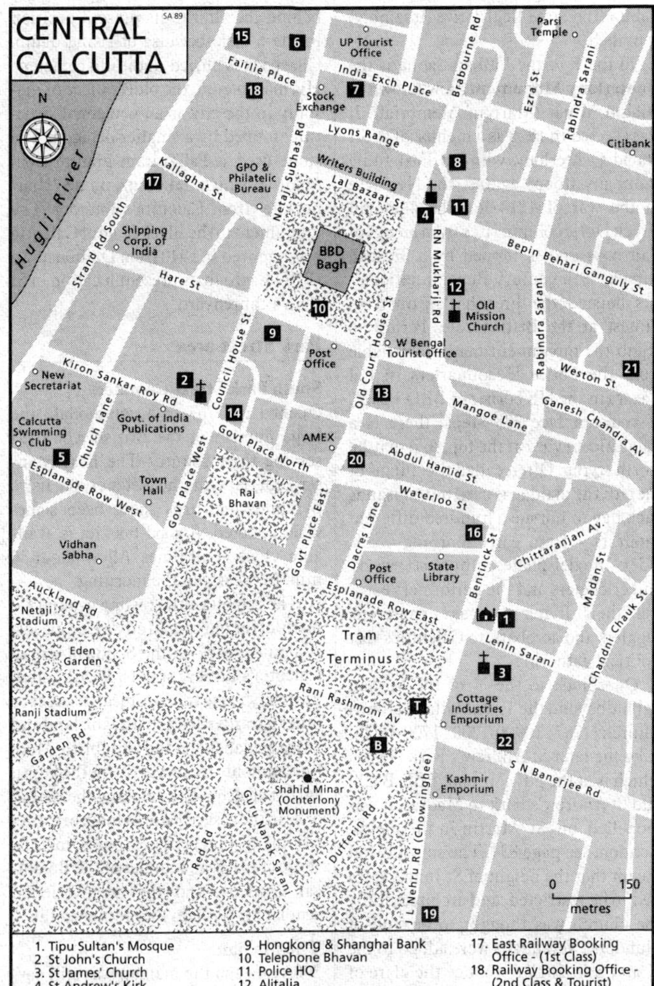

Due W of Raj Bhavan is the **Calcutta High Court**, built in 1872. The 'most important Gothic building in the city' it was modelled on the medieval cloth merchants hall at Ypres in Flanders, it has a 55m high tower. The **Vidhan Sabha** (the State Legislative Assembly) is to its S.

To the E of the Vidhan Sabha is the **Ochterlony Monument**, now known as Shahid Minar (Martyrs' Memorial). It was erected in 1828 as a memorial to Sir David Ochterlony, who led East India Company troops against the Nepalese in the war of 1814-16. The 46m tall Greek Doric column rises from an Egyptian base and is topped by a Turkish cupola. 19th century Bengali nationalists hoisted the French flag on it in protest at the British rule. Permit to climb the monument may be available from the Police Headquarters in Lal Bazar (in the NE corner of BBD Bagh). If you can face 223 steps, there is a magnificent view at the top, so it may be worth trying. Often called the 'lungs' of the city, the maidan is used by thousands each day to pursue a hundred different interests – from early morning yogis, riders, model plane enthusiasts, weekend cricketers and the performers earning their living – snake charmers, jugglers and acrobats, to Calcutta's vast political gatherings.

One block to the N of the Vidhan Sabha, beyond the Town Hall, is St John's Church (1787) (0900-1200, 1700-1800). Like the later St Andrew's Kirk (1818), which is at the NE corner of BBD Bagh, and St Andrew's Kirk in Madras, it was modelled on St Martin-in-the-Fields, London, see page 824. The soft sub-soil meant that the height of St John's spire had to be restricted, and architecturally the church was thought to be 'full of blunders'. Verandahs were added to the N and S in 1811 to reduce the glare of the sun. It contains a desk and chair belonging to Warren Hastings. Memorials inside include that to Major Kirkpatrick, Resident of Hyderabad from 1789-1805 and the tomb of Bishop Middleton, first Bishop of Calcutta. The Last Supper by Johann Zoffany, which shows Calcutta residents dressed as the Apostles, was moved from its original place behind the altar to its present position in the S aisle because of rising damp. Charnock is buried in the old cemetery. His mausoleum, the oldest piece of masonry in the city, is an octagonal structure, topped by a smaller octagon. The stone used is Pallavaram granite from Madras, which takes its name 'charnockite' from Calcutta's founder. The monument to the Black Hole of Calcutta was removed in 1940 from Dalhousie Sq (BBD Bagh) to its present location in St John's churchyard.

Park Street area

South Park Street Cemetery

Opened in 1767 to accommodate the large number of the British who died serving their country. The heavily inscribed, decaying headstones, obelisks, pyramids and urns have been somewhat restored. A good booklet is available. Open at all times. Allow about 30 min. Best early in the morning.

The cemetery, the resting ground for many of the old capital city's Europeans, is a quiet space on the S side of one of Calcutta's busiest streets. Death, often untimely, came from tropical diseases or other hazards such as battles on land and at sea, melancholia and childbirth. More uncommonly there was death through a surfeit of alcohol, or smoking the *hookah* or as in the case of Rose Aylmer, of eating too many pineapples! Tombs include those of Col Kyd, founder of the Botanical Gardens, and the great oriental scholar Sir William Jones among others.

The Maidan

200 years ago the maidan was still covered in dense jungle. Today it is Calcutta's lifeline, a unique 'green', covering over 400 ha in the heart of the

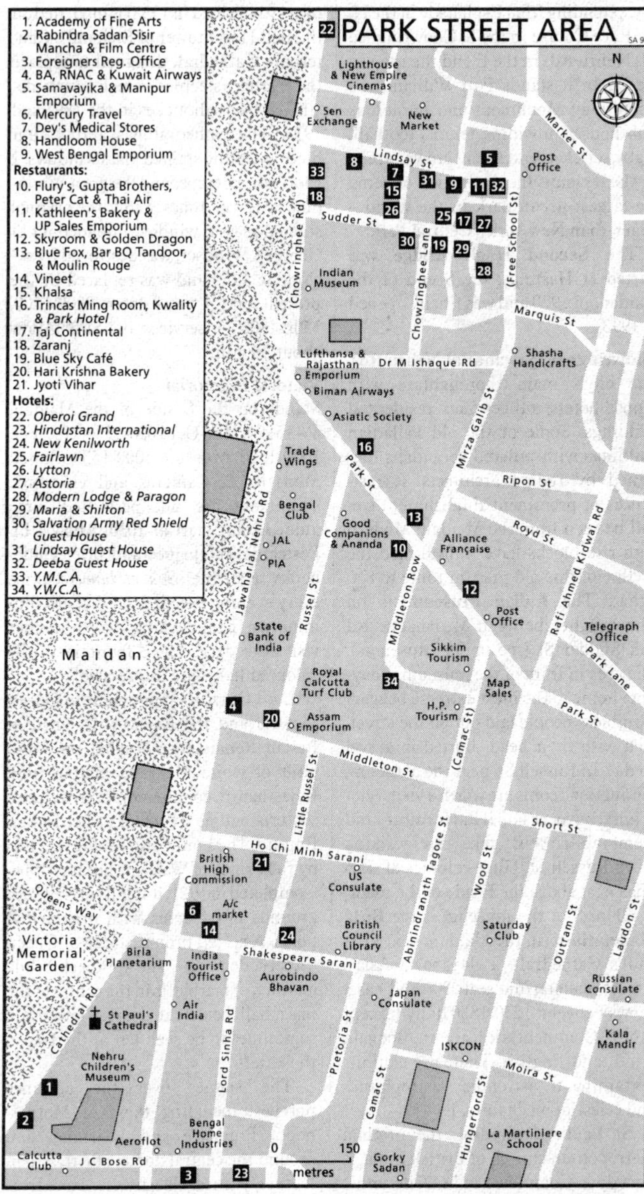
PARK STREET AREA
1. Academy of Fine Arts
2. Rabindra Sadan Sisir Mancha & Film Centre
3. Foreigners Reg. Office
4. BA, RNAC & Kuwait Airways
5. Samavayika & Manipur Emporium
6. Mercury Travel
7. Dey's Medical Stores
8. Handloom House
9. West Bengal Emporium
Restaurants:
10. Flury's, Gupta Brothers, Peter Cat & Thai Air
11. Kathleen's Bakery & UP Sales Emporium
12. Skyroom & Golden Dragon
13. Blue Fox, Bar BQ Tandoor, & Moulin Rouge
14. Vineet
15. Khalsa
16. Trincas Ming Room, Kwality & Park Hotel
17. Taj Continental
18. Zaranj
19. Blue Sky Café
20. Hari Krishna Bakery
21. Jyoti Vihar
Hotels:
22. Oberoi Grand
23. Hindustan International
24. New Kenilworth
25. Fairlawn
26. Lytton
27. Astoria
28. Modern Lodge & Paragon
29. Maria & Shilton
30. Salvation Army Red Shield Guest House
31. Lindsay Guest House
32. Deeba Guest House
33. Y.M.C.A.
34. Y.W.C.A.
Lighthouse & New Empire Cinemas
Sen Exchange
New Market
Market St
Post Office
Lindsay St
Sudder St
(Chowringhee Rd)
Chowringhee Lane
(Free School St)
Indian Museum
Marquis St
Lufthansa & Rajasthan Emporium
Dr M Ishaque Rd
Shasha Handicrafts
Biman Airways
Asiatic Society
Mirza Galib St
Trade Wings
Park St
Ripon St
Bengal Club
Good Companions & Ananda
Royd St
JAL
PIA
Alliance Française
Jawaharlal Nehru Rd
Middleton Row
Rafi Ahmed Kidwai Rd
Russel St
Post Office
State Bank of India
Telegraph Office
Maidan
Sikkim Tourism
Park Lane
Royal Calcutta Turf Club
Map Sales
Assam Emporium
H.P. Tourism
Park St
(Camac St)
Middleton St
Little Russel St
Short St
Ho Chi Minh Sarani
British High Commission
US Consulate
Abinindranath Tagore St
Wood St
Queens Way
A/c market
British Council Library
Saturday Club
Outram St
Laudon St
Victoria Memorial Garden
Birla Planetarium
India Tourist Office
Shakespeare Sarani
Aurobindo Bhavan
Russian Consulate
Air India
Japan Consulate
Cathedral Rd
St Paul's Cathedral
Lord Sinha Rd
Pretoria St
Kala Mandir
ISKCON
Moira St
Nehru Children's Museum
Camac St
Hungerford St
Bengal Home Industries
Aeroflot
La Martiniere School
Calcutta Club
J C Bose Rd
0 150 metres
Gorky Sadan

city, extending from Esplanade in the N, the Race Course in the S, Chowringhee (JL Nehru Rd) in the E and the river to the W. In it stands Fort William, the Ochterlony Monument and numerous club houses providing tennis, football, rugby, cricket and even crown green bowls. It claims the distinction of being the largest urban park in the world – larger, than New York's Central Park!

The **Second Hugli Bridge** was started at Hastings, the S end of the Maidan, in 1970 and was finally opened in 1993.

Chowringhee (Jawaharlal Nehru Rd)
The city's main thoroughfare with shops, hotels, offices and residential buildings. Some of the old Palladian buildings with pillared verandahs (designed by Italian architects as residences of prominent Englishmen) can still be seen from the Maidan. Modern high rise blocks have transformed the skyline of this old pilgrim route to Kalighat. The **Indian Museum** is on Chowringhee between M. Ishaque Rd and Sudder St (see under Museums). The area in front of the museum is daytime home to the most extreme beggars – limbless people laid out on the street, men with their heads buried in gravel all day. In Russell St, near the Museum, the auction rooms are worth a visit. A lot of junk, but occasional Raj furniture and memorabilia. **NB**: take care walking down Russell St. Huge colonies of starlings nest above the E side of the road!

600m S of the museum is the **Birla Planetarium** (in the Maidan, next to St Paul's Cathedral), T 441554. S Asia's largest planetarium seats 500 and has 3 shows between 1230-1830 daily (except Mon). Commentaries are in Bengali, Hindi and English. There are exhibits pertaining to astronomy, astrophysics and celestial mechanics. Rs 5.

St Paul's Cathedral, the original metropolitan church of British India, is next door. Completed in 1847, its gothic tower (dedicated in 1938) is modelled on the Bell Harry tower of England's Canterbury Cathedral, designed to replace the earlier steeples which were destroyed by earthquakes in the 1897 and 1934. The cathedral has a fine altar piece, 3 Gothic stained glass windows, 2 Florentine frescoes and the great W window by Burne Jones. Sadly, the original stained-glass E window, intended for St George's Windsor, was destroyed by cyclone in 1964 and was replaced by the present one 4 years later. 0900-1200, 1500-1800. 5 services on Sun. Allow about 20 min.

Victoria Memorial
Stands on the S side of the Maidan, T 445154. Mar-Oct 1000-1530. Nov-Feb 1000-1630. Museum 1000-1530. Closed Mon. Rs 2. Cameras and electronic equipment are not permitted. Free guided tours start at 1030. Allow 1 hr. Postcards, catalogues and brief guidebooks available. *Son et lumière* twice every evening except Mon. Superb illumination in the evening – worth another visit after dark. The 3 fountains lit by coloured lights are impressive.

Lord Curzon's monument to Queen Victoria and the Raj was designed in Italian Renaissance-Mughal style and built of white Makrana marble from Rajasthan, in commemoration of Queen Victoria and as a symbol of her Indian Empire. The Foundation stone was laid by the Prince of Wales in January 1906. Completed in 1921, it stands in well kept grounds of 64 acres with ornamental pools. A seated bronze statue of Queen Victoria dominates the approach, while another, of marble, is in the centre of the main hall, below the dome. Flowers are sometimes to be seen left at the feet of the latter!

The statues over the entrance porches, including those of Motherhood, Prudence and Learning, and around the central dome, of Art, Architecture, Justice, Charity etc, came from

Italy. The entrance is through large ornate iron gates and it has an impressive 'weather vane' in the form of a 5m. tall bronze winged figure of Victory, weighing 3 tons. There are over 3000 exhibits in 25 galleries, including a wealth of Raj memorabilia; portraits, paintings, sculpture, arms and armoury downstairs, prints of old Calcutta, documents tracing the history of the East India Company and also a wealth of watercolours and engravings of Indian scenes upstairs. Also shown are Queen Victoria's rosewood piano and desk, books, portraits and paintings by Zoffany, the 2 Daniells, Davis and Emily Eden (prior arrangement needed to view). There are also fine miniatures, a rare collection of Persian manuscripts, portraits of national leaders and many reminders of military conflicts. There is a first class reference library. Allow at least 1 hr.

Fort William

After the defeat in 1756 the British built a new massive fort and named it after King William III. Completed around 1781 on the site of the old village of Govindapur and designed to be impregnable, it was roughly octagonal, about 500m in diameter, large enough to house all the Europeans in the city in case of an attack. It stood on the edge of the river Hugli from which water was channelled to fill the wide moat. The church of St Peter, the barracks and stables, the arsenal, prison and strong rooms still stand. The jungle around it was cleared to give a clear field of fire. This became the Maidan. Today the Fort is the Eastern Region's Military Headquarters. Permission needed to enter.

North Calcutta

Dakshineshwar Kali Temple

On the opposite side of the river from Belur Math alongside the Vivekananda Bridge, the temple was built in 1847 by Rani Rashmoni. No priest –*'pujari'* – was willing to serve in the temple because of the Rani's low caste. The Kali temple has 12 spires and 12 other smaller temples in the large courtyard are dedicated to Siva and Radha Krishna. Ramakrishna's elder brother accepted the role and was succeeded by Ramakrishna himself, when Ramakrishna achieved his spiritual vision of the unity of all religions. Non-Hindus are not permitted inside. Accessible by buses from BBD Bagh. Allow about 20 min.

S of the Dakshineshwar Kali Temple is Chitpur and **Kumartuli**. Off Chitpur Rd in N Calcutta are the *kumars* or potters who work throughout the year preparing clay images around cores of bamboo and straw. For generations they have been making life-size idols of gods and goddesses, particularly of Durga on her vehicle the lion slaying the demon Asura, for the pujas or festivals. The images are usually unbaked since they are immersed in the holy river at the culmination of the festival. Often very brightly painted and gaudily dressed, as the time of the pujas approaches, thousands of images are stacked awaiting the final finishing touch by the master painter, before they are ready to be sold. There are also *shola* artists (see page 639) who make images for the pujas and floral decorations for weddings. The material is the pith of Bengal's sponge wood tree.

Immediately to the N of the new Belgachia metro station, on the N side of Belgachia Rd, is the **Paresnath Jain Temple**. This ornate Digambar Jain temple, built in the central Indian style by a jeweller in 1867, is dedicated to the 10th *Tirthankara*, Sitalanatha. The interior is richly decorated in European baroque and Italianate styles, with mirrors and Venetian glass mosaics. The gardens have formal geometric flower beds and a gold fish tank. 0600-1200, 1500-1900. Free. Allow 15 min.

College Street

Running parallel with, but one street to

the E of Chittaranjan Ave is College Street, 'the heart of intellectual Calcutta'. On a short stretch of this street stands the **University** with its various associated institutions, including the old **Sanskrit College** and the highly thought of **Presidency College**. Its Centenary Building was opened in 1817 as the Hindu College to provide 'a liberal education' through the efforts of European and Indian benefactors. The Bloomsbury of Calcutta, this was the centre for Bengali writers, artists, religious and social reformers and thinkers of the 19th century. It was also the spawning ground of the nationalist *Swadeshi* movement at the beginning of this century. The College Sq water tank is to the S of the Hindu School and Sanskrit College, and to the N, in a 3 storeyed building, are the principle book companies, an auditorium and the famous smoke filled 'CoffeeHouse'. Opened in 1944, this has been the haunt of the city's intelligentsia and students ever since. You can still get an excellent cup of coffee and enjoy the atmosphere, watching regulars in their reserved chairs who may spend their whole day arguing, joking and discussing the events of the day. All along are the second-hand book stalls displaying their 'treasure' on wooden shelving which takes up every space along the iron railings.

Marble Palace

46 Muktaram Babu St (travelling N up Chittaranjan Ave, the 3rd turning on the left after crossing Mahatma Gandhi Rd). 1000-1600, closed Mon and Thu. Photography allowed for documentary purposes. Visitors free on obtaining passes from the W Bengal Tourist Bureau, 3/2 BBD Bag, 24 hr in advance. Shoes must be removed before entering the reception hall.

It was built in the *Chor Bagan* or Thieves' Garden area of N Calcutta in 1835, an ornate building with Italianate courtyard, classical columns a large tank with fountain and Egyptian sphinxes. It houses the one-man collection of Raja Rajendra Mullick Bahadur. There is some interesting statuary in the garden with 6 sleeping marble lions gracing the lawns. The entrance is through a courtyard where one is greeted by mynahs and macaws from the aviary. Befitting its name there are said to be 90 different kinds of marble, used to great effect on the patterned floors and cool white walls. The long galleries are crammed with statues, pottery, mirrors, chandeliers and English, Dutch and Italian paintings, disorganised and gathering dust. The Reynolds, Titian and Rubens are not generally on display. Part of the mansion is still lived in by the Raja's descendants, the present owners, who continue to keep up the tradition of feeding the poor at their gates at noon. The rambling museum on 2 floors has curiosity appeal. Allow about 40 min.

Jorasanko & Haora Bridge area

To the N of the Marble Palace is the Tagore family seat at **Jorasanko**, the home of the wealthy merchant Dwarkanath Tagore whose grandson was the gifted Rabindranath (see page 644). This is also the **Rabindra Bharati University and Museum** (see Museums below). Further N on Baghbazar St is the **Girish Mancha**, the new Govt theatre complex. Returning S and across Mahatma Gandhi Rd is the **Nakhoda Mosque** on Rabindra Sarani, able to accommodate 10,000 worshippers. Open 0600 – 2000 daily. Built between 1926 and 1942 of red sandstone, it is a four-storeyed structure reminiscent of Akbar's tomb in Sikandra, near Agra, and has huge blue and white painted domes flanked by two 46m minarets. Near the Mosque and just to the S of Haora Bridge is the **Armenian Church of Holy Nazareth** (1724), a reminder of the important trading role that the small Armenian community played in major Indian cities from the 17th century. On its E side, is the **Roman Catholic Cathedral** (1797), built by the Portuguese.

Haora Bridge ('Rabindra Setu'). Opened in 1943, this single span cantilever bridge replaced the old pontoon bridge which joined the city with its main railway station and Haora. It remains a prominent landmark. To avoid affecting river currents and silting, the two 80m high piers rise from the road level; the span between them is 450m, increasing by a metre on a hot day. The 8 lanes of traffic and 2 foot paths are nearly always packed with vehicles and pedestrians. The second bridge across the river was finally opened in 1993 which has eased the congestion fractionally.

South Calcutta

Kali Temple

(0500-2000) Dedicated to Kali, the patron goddess of Calcutta, who is usually portrayed with blood dripping from her tongue and garlanded with skulls. It was re-built in 1809 over the site of an older temple which marked the spot where the goddess' little toe is said to have fallen when Siva carried her charred corpse in a frenzied dance of mourning and she was cut into pieces by Vishnu's *chakra*. Kalighat remains an important Hindu pilgrimage centre. Only Hindus are permitted inside. In the past human sacrifices are said to have been made but now only goats are offered daily on 2 wooden blocks to the S of the temple. Legend has it that *thugs* would offer their prayers to Kali here before a robbery. Next door is *Nirmal Hriday* the home for the dying started by Mother Teresa. Allow ½ hr.

Mother Teresa's Homes

Mother Teresa was born of Albanian parents in Yugoslavia and as a Loreto Sister came to teach in a Calcutta school in 1931. 19 years later she obtained permission from the Pope to start her Order of the Missionaries of Charity to serve the destitute and dying among the poorest. You may see the nuns always in pairs in their white cotton saris with blue borders busy working in different parts of the city in the many homes, clinics and orphanages. *Nirmal Hriday* (pure heart), near the Kali Temple, the first 'home' was opened in 1952 for the dying among the poorest which is open to anyone who needs a place to find peace. Today there are nearly 300 different homes and refuges. Office at 54A Acharya JC Bose Rd.

National Library

Just S of the Maidan in Alipur, the former winter residence of the Lieutenant Governors of Bengal on Belvedere Rd was originally the property which was given by Mir Jafar to Warren Hastings on which the latter erected an 'ordinary Anglo-Indian building'. Later additions made it more impressive. Built in the Renaissance Italian style, with a double row of classical columns, it is surrounded by 12 ha of wooded grounds. Approached through a triple arched gateway, through a drive between mahogany and mango trees, to the sweeping staircase to the S which is the entrance to the Durbar Hall. The ground floor has 15 km of closed stacks while the reading room in the old Banquet Hall has access to 10,000 reference books and Gazetteers. There is a new annexe with an auditorium and canteen as well as a readers' hostel. The a/c Rare Books Section contains some very rare documents while the Asutosh Mookerjee collection, the world's largest personal collection, is also here (1000-1800 weekdays). The library is the largest in the country, approaching 2 million books and manuscripts, some very rare and includes all published material in India. There are 10,000 bound volumes of newspapers in a Reading Room in Esplanade. 0900-2000 weekdays, 1000-1800 weekends.

Rabindra Sarobar

The lake in S Calcutta is surrounded by shaded walks and palm trees. The city's rowing clubs hold their regattas here and there is a stadium for concerts. To the S is the 'lily pool' and to the SE, the Japanese Buddhist temple.

Haora and the West Bank

North

16 km N of the city across the Ganga from Calcutta is **Belur Math**, the international headquarters of the Ramakrishna Mission, founded in 1899 by Swami Vivekananda who was a disciple of the great 19th century Hindu saint Ramakrishna (see page 930). He preached the unity of all religions. Symbolising its belief the *Math* ('monastery') synthesises Hindu, Christian and Islamic architectural styles. The *Math* houses many temples, the main one housing a statue of Paramhansa Dev. *Kumari Puja* is performed during Durga Puja when a young girl is dressed up as Durga. 0630-1100,1600-1930; winter 1530-1900. Free. Allow 20 min.

South

Botanical Gardens On the W bank of the Hugli, 20 km from BBD Bagh. Founded in 1787 by the East India Company, the gardens cover more than 100 ha. The major attraction is a flourishing 200 year old banyan tree with a circumference of over 380m, said to be the largest in the world. The original trunk was struck by lightning in 1919 and had to be removed, but more than 1500 offshoots form an impressive sight. The tea grown in Darjiling and Assam was developed here. The avenues of Royal Cuban palms and mahogany trees are impressive and there are interesting and exotic specimens in the herbarium, fern, cacti (orchid houses and the 16m domed palm house are no longer there). Though much of it is ill-tended, the pleasant and cool gardens can make a welcome change from the city. Getting there: avoid Sun and public holidays when it is very overcrowded. May be reached by ferry from Fairlie Jetty (rec) Chandpal, Metiabruz or Takta Ghat or by road across Haora Bridge and through Haora which may take an hr. This road journey can be very slow, hot and bumpy. Free. 0700-1700. Permits for cars from Govt of India Tourist Office, 4 Shakespeare Sarani, T 441402.

Museums

Indian Museum 27 JL Nehru Rd, T 299853. Mar-Nov 1000-1700, Dec-Feb 1000-1630. Closed Mon. Re 1. Fri Free. Possibly Asia's largest, founded in 1814 and known locally as Jadu Ghar (magic house). Excellent collection, much – though not all – well displayed. The colonnaded Italianate building completed in 1875 stands opposite the Maidan and surrounds an open grassed area. 36 galleries, about 10,000 items, divided into 6 sections; art, archaeology, anthropology, geology, zoology and economic botany. The last has the interesting section on 'plants in the service of man' with details of herbs, plants and woods. It has a very large geological gallery (Siwalik fossils from lower Himalaya) and an excellent natural history section. Outstanding archaeological exhibits include fine examples of Indian ware from the Harappa and Moenjodaro periods as well as Buddhist art (Barhut gallery to the S of the entrance), a reconstruction of a part of the 180 BC Buddhist stupa and ancient sculptural pieces from Sanchi, Gandhara, Amaravati and Sarnath. The chronological coin collection is exceptional, with over 50,000 coins of gold, silver and other metals, but requires special permission to view; sections displaying miniature paintings and the Art and Textile gallery with ivory, bone, glass and silverware also particularly notable. The new Egyptian gallery boasts a popular exhibit – a partially exposed mummy. Also good dioramas of tribal people and displays of their handicraft. The new a/c Theme Gallery has rare paintings, 200 yr old hand-drawn maps, moving dioramas of Sights and Sounds of Calcutta. There is a good guide book. Some galleries are poorly lit and gathering dust. Best to be selective and allow at least 2 hr. Photography allowed on payment of fee.

Academy of Fine Arts Cathedral Rd. 1500-1800. Closed Mon. Re 1. Founded in 1933, the collection incl Indian miniature paintings, textiles, works of contemporary Indian artists including Jaimini Roy and Desmond Doig and also Tagore's paintings and manuscripts. Guide service and films once a month and photography with permission. Gardens display modern Indian sculpture. Two galleries also hold exhibitions of works of local artists.

Asiatic Society 1 Park St. 1000-2000 weekdays, 1000-1700 weekends. Free. The oldest institution of Oriental studies in the world was described by the founder and great Orientalist Sir William Jones in 1784 as the platform for "Man and Nature, whatever is performed by one or produced by the other within the geographical limits of Asia". Originally restricted to Europeans; opened its doors to Indians in the 19th century. The library was started when a valuable collection from Fort William was transferred together with Tipu Sultan's libraries from Mysore. Today incl a treasure house of books, documents and ancient manuscripts in most Asian languages, some dating back to the 7th century. The museum, opened in 1814, incl a rare collection of coins although much of the original archaeological, geological and zoological exhibits have been transferred to the Indian Museum nearby. Gallery of paintings incl works by Reynolds, Canaletti, Rubens and Guido.

Asutosh Museum Centenary Building, Calcutta University, College St. 1030-1630 weekdays. Sat 1030-1500. Closed Sun and Univ. holidays. Free. Small museum with objects of eastern Indian art and antiquity including textiles and terracotta figures, with particular emphasis on Bengali folk art. Good booklet.

Bangiya Sahitya Parishad 243/1 Acharya PC Rd. 1300-1900. Closed on Th and public holidays. Free. Imposition of English as the medium of instruction by Macaulay in 1834 later led many Bengalis to return to the riches in their own literature and language. In 1894 a group of 30 intellectuals founded the *Parishad.* Collection of books, rare manuscripts, antiques, icons, metal and stone inscriptions. Memorabilia of Rammohun Roy, Vidyasagar and Sister Nivedita.

Birla Academy of Art & Culture 108/109 Southern Ave, T 467843. 1600-2000. Closed Mon. Re 0.50. Mainly medieval and contemporary paintings and sculpture.

Central National Herbarium Botanical Gardens, Haora. 1015-1600. Closed Sundays, 2nd Saturdays and Central Govt holidays. Free. The largest collection of dried plants in S and S E Asia of some 1.5 million specimens and including the collections of eminent botanists of the last 200 years. Centre for taxonomic research in India.

Nehru Children's Museum 94/1 JL Nehru Rd. 1200-2000. Closed Mon. Adults Rs 2 and children under 12, Re 1. Tales from the Ramayana and Mahabharata are depicted in miniature clay figures from Krishnagar. Well displayed in glass cabinets, convenient for children to view. Allow about 30 min.

Netaji Research Bureau Elgin Rd, is in his home which is now a museum of Netaji and the freedom struggle. See page 602.

Rabindra Bharati Museum 6/4 Dwarakanath Tagore Lane. 1000-1700. Sat 1000-1400. Sun and holidays 1100-1400. Free. Located in the ancestral home of Rabindranath Tagore, writer, artist and philosopher who won the Nobel prize for literature in 1913. A major section is devoted to his life and works, and the Renaissance movement in Bengal in the 19th century.

Parks & zoos

Eden Gardens NW corner of the Maidan, named after Lord Auckland's sisters Emily and Fanny Eden. Established in 1836 a part forms the Ranji Stadium, enclosing the Calcutta cricket grounds. The first cricket match was played in 1864, and today Test Matches are played. Usually open for matches only (small tip at Gate 14 gains entry). Contains pleasant walks, an artificial lake, tropical palms and a small Burmese pagoda (about average size for this type of *Pyatthat*).

The Zoo 0600-1700. Re 1. Opened in 1876, the 16 ha grounds house a wide variety of animal and bird life. The white tigers from Rewa and the *tigon*, a cross between a tiger and a lion are the rarest animals. A reptile house, children's zoo and aquarium are across the road. Migratory birds crowd the zoo lakes each winter. There are 4 restaurants; picnics are permitted. Vehicles are only allowed in for the disabled.

Horticultural Gardens by the National Library nr the Zoo. The Horticultural Society was started in 1820 by the Baptist missionary William Carey. 0600-1000, 1400-1700. Closed Mon. Re 0.50. Pleasant and quiet with Flower Show at the beginning of Feb.

Nicco Park Jheel Meel, Salt Lake. New attraction, 1000-2100. Amusements, rides, refreshments. Rs 5.

Excursions

There are several interesting places within reach of a day's outing. However, road travel is very slow in and around the city, so it is best to leave central Calcutta well before 0800 to avoid the worst traffic. To visit places on the W bank of the Hugli from Belur northwards, it is possible to cross the Haora Bridge and join the GT Road. Haora itself is extremely congested. The Barrackpur Trunk Road on the E bank of the river is not much better. It is possible to visit Barrackpur and then to cross the Hugli over the Vivekananda road and rail bridge which runs from the Dakshineshwar Temple. Suburban trains from Haora are fast and frequent. Buses leave Esplanade, but the journey is a lot slower.

Barrackpur

(25 km), a cantonment town of the East India Company, was originally planned as the site for building the extravagant country house of the governor. Only a large 'bungalow' was built on the E bank which is now the hospital. The grounds house the bronze Raj statues which have been removed from their pedestals in Central Calcutta. The tower in the garden was part of the river signalling system. Permission from the Secretariat, Raj Bhavan, Calcutta. Gandhi Ghat is by the river side where there is a museum. There is a pleasant garden in memory of Jawaharlal Nehru. **Accommodation** WBTDC **E** *Tourist Bureau Cottages*, have 8 rm.

Hugli District

The Danish, Dutch, French and Portuguese each had outposts along the river Hugli. Hugli District has a rich history. Some independent kingdoms had considerable achievements in art and architecture, but they fell to Pathan, Mughal and Bargi invaders. When the Mughals lost power several of the ancient seats of past rulers of Bengal became centres of foreign trade. The Portuguese and British settled at Hugli, the Dutch chose Chinsura, the French, Chandernagore, the Danes, Serampore, the Greeks had an outpost at Rishra and the Germans and Austrians one at Bhadreswar!

Serampore (Srirampur)

5 km, *STD Code* 02422. Across the river from Barrackpore is this old Danish settlement, known originally as Fredricnagore, founded in 1616. Serampore became the site of a new Danish colony in 1755, and was home to 19 Danish Governors. The eleventh, Col. Olie Bie, served 40 years and developed

Serampore into a garden city. It was the centre of missionary activity from the beginning of the 19th century until sold to the East India Company in 1845. **Government House**, the **Roman Catholic Church** and **St Olaf's Church** and the **Danish cemetery** retain a feeling of the past. The **College of Textile Technology** at 12 Carey Rd. Weekdays 1000-1630, Sat 1000-1300.

Serampore is particularly well known for the work of the Baptist missionaries Carey, Marshman and Ward who came to the Danish port since they were not welcomed by the English administrators in Calcutta. They set up the Baptist Mission Press, which by 1805 was capable of printing in 7 Indian languages and was responsible for the first vernacular newspaper. **Serampore College**, founded in 1818 and empowered to confer degrees by the Danish King in 1827, stands on the river bank with its imposing 7 columned classical portico. Several interesting portraits hang in the great hall. It was the first Christian Theological college in India though today perhaps only 60 of the 2000 students there read theology. The library has rare Sanskrit, Pali and Tibetan manuscripts, over 40 translations of the Bible into Asian languages, and also the treasured 17th century Persian manuscript of the lives of the apostles. Mon-Fri 1000-1600 and Sat 1000-1300. You can get permission to visit from the Principal.

At nearby **Mahesh**, 3 km away, there is a large Jagannath temple. The annual Rathyatra, 'Car' Festival, which takes place in Jun/Jul, second only to the one in Puri, draws very large crowds.

Chandernagore

A further 4 km N along the river. The former French colony, which dates back to 1673, was one of the tiny pockets of 'non-British India' that did not gain Independence in 1947. It was handed over to India after a referendum in 1950. The French traded from here from 1673 except for 2 periods when the British took control. Attractively laid out with a promenade along the river Hugli, the churches, convents and cemeteries of the French in Chandernagore still remain. The **Bhubanesvari and Nandadulal temples** too are worth visiting, especially when *Jagaddhatri Puja* is celebrated. The Institute Chandernagar at the **Residency** has an interesting collection of documents and relics of the French in India as well as paintings, terracottas and antiques. Weekdays 1600-1830, Sun 1100-1700. Closed Th. The orange-painted Italian missionary Church of the Sacred Heart built in 1726 also stands witness of Chandernagore's European past although the old French street names and shops have given way to Bengali. The church has stained glass windows, and a statue of Joan of Arc in military dress in the garden.

Chinsura

Another 2 km N. Originally given in 1628 by the Nawab of Murshidabad to the Dutch, who built the **Fort Gustavus**. It was later exchanged with Sumatra in Indonesia and became British in 1825. The octagonal **Dutch church** to the N dating from 1678, with its cemetery a short distance to the W and 3 East India Company barracks remain. The Armenian church of **St John the Baptist** was built at the end of the 17th century. The Dutch are still remembered at the **Shandesvar Siva** temple, important to Hindus, on occasions when the *lingam* is decked in western clothes and a sword presented by the former rulers.

Hugli

1 km N of Chinsura. The village was an important trading port in the 16th century and a factory was set up by the Portuguese in 1537. However, Emperor Shah Jahan, who disliked the Portuguese for refusing to help him against his father, took the town after a siege in 1632 and made Hugli a royal port. The British were granted permission to trade

from Bengal in the 17th century under a royal 'firman' and built a factory at Hugli in 1651. Fighting between the Mughals and the British broke out and much of the town was burnt, including Charnock's East India Company factory. After the Mahrattas sacked it Clive regained it for the British in 1757.

The **Imambara of Hazi Mohammed Mohasin**, (1836-1876), belonging to the Shi'a sect, is the principal sight. Muharram is a amjor festival event. The large façade has a central gateway with two 35m minarets on either side. The mosque proper stands on the N side of the quadrangular courtyard which has halls and rooms all around it. Texts from the Koran decorate the walls of the Imambara, while the interior has rich marble inlay, a silver pulpit and elaborate lanterns and chandeliers. The library has a rare collection of old manuscripts. The **Old Imambara** built in 1776 is on the opposite side of the road. The **Amulya Pratnasala Museum** in Rajbalhat village has a collection of Sculpture, coins, terracottas and manuscripts. 1400-2100 daily, closed 2nd and 4th Tue and Wed. In **Chota Pandua** on the outskirts of Hugli are several interesting Muslim buildings including the 14th century Bari Masjid, which though ruined retains elements of Buddhist sculpture. There is a 30m five storey minaret nearby.

Bandel

A further 3 km from Hugli. The Portuguese settlers built **Bandel Church** dedicated to Our Lady of the Rosary around 1660 on the foundations of an older church and monastery built by Augustinian friars. The name Bandel (Portuguese *bandar* – "wharf') testifies to the settlement's original function. Today it is an important railway junction. The keystone of the original church (1599) can be seen on the riverside gate of the monastery. It is believed to be one of the earliest Christian churches in W Bengal. Destroyed in 1640 by Emperor Shah Jahan it was reinstated 20 years later. It always had a close association with the seafaring Portuguese, who believed that the statue of the Virgin, 'Our Lady of Happy Voyages' on top of the church's bell-tower, could work miracles. One story relates how the statue, which was being carried across the river to save it from the Emperor's soldiers, was lost and then in 1842 appeared on the river bank. There are fine cloisters to the S and a priory with an impressive hall dedicated in 1820 to St Augustine. The **Hanseswari Temple** is 4 km away, built of stone and terracotta in the 18th century.

Tribeni

5 km N of Bandel. An ancient seat of culture, it is now a straggling village. Originally known as *Saptagram*, 7 villages, it acquired great sanctity being sited at the confluence of the 3 rivers Ganga, Saraswati and Kunti, and several temples were built in the area. A mound near the river houses several monuments including tombs and a ruined mosque. There appear to have been some structures of Vaishnavite and Buddhist origin of the Pala-Sena period of the 11th and 12th centuries. The remains of the **Mazar of Zafarkhan Ghazi** illustrates the way black basalt sculpture and columns of the earlier temples and palaces were incorporated into the later masonry. It is the earliest mausoleum in E India (1313). The mosque bears the Arabic inscription 1298, possibly the date of the original structure, although it certainly underwent alteration. A group of small temples surrounds the **Benimadhava Temple** near the river bank.

Pandua

Pandua (Hugli District) is a further 20 km up the GT Rd, the seat of a former Hindu ruler. Once a fortified town with a wall and moat, it has several architectural remains of the Pala and Sena periods. Among them are a tower, 2 mosques, a tomb and 2 tanks. The most important of these is the 39m 5 storeyed **Tower** which has a circular base of 18m diameter narrowing to 5m at the top. The outer surface is fluted and the inner walls have enamelled decoration. A circular staircase rises to the top with doorways leading to a narrow balcony on each storey which circles the tower. It has a court house at its base and is believed to have been used by a *muezzin* to call the faithful to prayer. Shah Sufi-ud-din is said to have erected the tower to commemorate his victory over the local Hindu ruler in 1340. Hoards of Kushana and Gupta dynasty gold coins have been found in nearby **Mahanad**.

Antpur

62 km from Calcutta. The 18th century temples for which Antpur is known were mainly built by Krishnaram Mitra, a local zamindar. The **Radha-Govinda temple**, dedicated to the family deity, is the most ornately decorated. The terracotta panels that appear on the front wall as well as walls of the prayer hall or *jagamohan* which forms a part of the large temple structure, depict scenes from the epics as well as contemporary life. Inside, the vaulted ceiling of the *jagamohan* has coloured murals. The whole is on a raised platform with additional sections of the *Dolmancha* and *Rasmancha*. Apart from several other temples, the structure of *Chandimandap* is unique for its artistry in wood. There is also a temple to commemorate the birth place of Swami Premananda of the Ramakrishna Mission in whose home Swami Vivekananda and 8 other disciples took their vows of *sannyasa*.

Tours

ITDC Tours *Departure point*: 4 Shakespeare Sarani, T 441402. 2 tours with 1 hr lunch break. Morning tour: Commercial area, Jain Temple, Dakshineswar Temple, Belur Math and Botanical Gardens. Afternoon Tour: Indian Museum, Nehru Children's Museum, Victoria Memorial, The Zoo and Rabindra Sarobar. These may be booked at Ashok Travel & Tours, 3-G Everest Buildings, 460 JL Nehru Rd, T 440901 or ITDC Airport Counter. *WB Tourism Dev Corp*, 1 Sarat Bose Rd, T 448187.

WBTDC Tours *Departure point*: 3/2 BBD Bagh E, 1st Flr, T 288271 (1000-1330, 1415-1530). Daily coach tours in and around Calcutta. 0730-1140 and 1240-1700. A/c half day ticket Rs 40 and full day Rs 50. **Morning tour**: 0730, Eden Gardens, High Court, Writers' Building, Botanical Gardens, Belur Math, Dakshineswar, Jain Temple and Esplanade. **Afternoon Tour**: 1240, Esplanade, Indian Museum, Nehru Children's Museum, Victoria Memorial, The Zoo, Rabindra Sarobar and Birla Academy. Passengers are required to pay entry fees where applicable. The morning tour goes further and is better value; most of the sights visited in the afternoon are within easy reach of the centre. At weekends and on public holidays only full day tours may run. Check nearer the time if these will be operating. Private tour operators also conduct similar city tours.

Long distance Tourist coaches go to several destinations. Digha. Santiniketan – Bakreswar. Malda – Murshidabad – Gaur – Pandua. Antpur – Bishnupur – Mukutmanipur – Kakrajhore – Jhargram. Shaktapithas. Jairambati – Kamarpukur – Tarakeswar. Mayapur (ISKON) – Krishnagar – Bethuadari Deer Park. Sundarbans – Tiger and Crocodile projects (not Jul-mid Sep). Tourist Guides approved by the Dept of Tourism are available from the WBTDC Tourist Office, the charges varying according to the size of the group, Rs 50 for half day; Rs 100 for full day.

Local festivals

Jan: *Ganga Sagar Mela* is at Sagar, 105 km S of Calcutta where the river Hugli joins the sea. Vast numbers of Hindu pilgrims bathe in the holy water.

Jun-Jul: *The Ratha Yatra* (Jun-Jul) car

Worship Of The Clay Goddess

Durga Puja The most important Hindu festival of Bengal which dates from the 17th century, precedes the full moon in late September, early October. Celebrations of music, dance and drama last for 15 days while Government and other offices remain closed for 4 days of the puja proper. Educational institutions and law courts close for 3 weeks for the 'Puja holidays'.

Images of the 10-armed, 3-eyed Goddess Durga (see page 78) astride her 'vehicle' the lion, portray Durga slaying *Mahisasura,* the evil demon who assumed the form of a buffalo. Durga, shown with her 4 children, is worshipped throughout the city in hundreds of brightly illuminated and beautifully decorated *pandals* (marquees) made of bamboo and coloured cloth. Some of the structures assume enormous proportions and imitate famous buildings. The priests perform prayers at appointed times in the morning and evening (around 2030) while devotees, usually dressed in new clothes, arrive throughout the day to show their reverence with folded palms and spend a while in private prayer. Loudspeakers relay contrasting Indian film songs and devotional music into the small hours. On the 4th and last day of festivities, huge and often emotionally charged processions follow devotees who carry the clay figures to be immersed in the river at many points along the banks. The images ultimately disintegrate, the clay dissappearing into the river; the potters return to collect the raw material once again for the following year. You can see the imagemakers in Kumartuli (see above) a few days earlier and visit the *pandals* early in the evening, before they become crowded. The WB Tourist Bureau offers an all night bus tour (Rs 50) as well as a 2-hr launch trip on the Hugli to watch the immersion ceremony on the last night.

festival at Mahesh, nr Srirampur, is particularly famous, 25 km from Calcutta. *Id* is celebrated by thousands of the city's Muslims in congregational prayer on the Maidan. During *Muharram* (meaning 'the sacred') they process beating their chests, chanting the names of Hassan and Hussain, the 2 murdered grandsons of Muhammad. They carry replicas of the Mecca tombs.

Dec: *Christmas* is also celebrated in a big way. The numerous churches hold special services, including Midnight Mass, and the New Market takes on a new look in Dec as *Barra Din* (Big Day) approaches with temporary stalls selling trees, pre-packed traditional stockings, baubles, streamers, and glitter. All other major religious festivals are observed as elsewhere in India.

Local information

Accommodation & food

● Accommodation

NB: 10% luxury tax, 10% service charge and 20% expenditure tax (not applicable when paying in foreign exchange) are charged at most hotels. In a hotel without central a/c, if you occupy an a/c room without requesting one, the hotel may demand an extra tax payable to the Tax authority. Infants sharing a room with parents (without an extra cot) are usually free. For facilities in AL, A and B categories, see page 137. Most listed hotels are about 15-18 km from the airport. Telephone numbers are being changed across the city.

AL *Oberoi Grand*, 15 JL Nehru Rd, T 292323. 300 rm. 16 km airport, 5 km rly. Centrally sited opp the Maidan, a grand white Victorian edifice exquisitely restored, suites have giant 4-posters, new tea lounge (own blend of tea particularly rec.), international disco. Excellent restaurants, but slow room service. **AL** *Taj Bengal*, 34B Belvedere Rd, Alipore, T 283939, F 281766. 250 rm with contemporary paintings. 10 km rly. Nr Calcutta Race Course and Zoo. Restaurants are plush, imaginative, intimate with good food, but expensive. Excellent *coffee-shop* serving substantial snacks. Poolside barbecue in winter. You can order an unusual Bengali breakfast of '*luchi* and *chholar daal*' (wheat fried 'bread' and a savoury lentil dish). *Incognito* disco, Tu-Sun from 2000 for members, residents and guests over 25 yrs.

A few other good hotels have been extensively improved. Mostly modern, centrally located, efficient and with good restaurants, but lack atmosphere and character. **A** ***Airport Ashok***, Calcutta Airport, T 569111. 152 rm. Modern hotel, soundproofed, restaurant with 'frontier cuisine'. Chief advantage convenience for airport, but unexciting. **A** ***Hindusthan International***, 235/1 A.JC Bose Rd, T 472394, F 472824. 212 rm. 10 km rly. Good buffet lunches, coffee shop, also serves meals; slow service but good value. **A** ***Park***, 17 Park St, T 297336, F 298027. 170 rm. 5 km rly. Lacks style and ambience. Good Chinese restaurant.

B ***Great Eastern***, 1-3 Old Court House St, T 2823311. 200 rm, incl cheaper non a/c. 2 km rly. The old Raj style hotel has lost its former splendour; undergoing reconstruction. Recent visitors found it dusty and dirty. *Shah-en-Shah* serves tandoori dishes; live Indian music. **B** ***New Kenilworth***, 1 & 2 Little Russell St, T 223403. 6 km rly. Good Indian food, open-air barbecue on lawn. Good location, courteous service, good value. Only few credit cards accepted. Rec.

The city centre: about 5 km from the rly, has several medium range hotels with comfortable a/c rooms. **C** ***Rutt Deen***, 21B UN Brahamachari Sarani (Louden St), T 475210. 50 rm. 5 km rly. Open-air restaurant, bar, garden. Friendly service. **C** ***Lytton***, 14 Sudder St, T 291875, F 201747. 59 clean rm. Central a/c. Restaurants, exchange. Rec. **C** ***Fairlawn***, 13/A Sudder St, T 244460. 20 rm some a/c. Trades on its reputation as a relic of the Raj; some find it charming, others old-fashioned, unmodernised, overpriced. Meals at set times (incl in price) are semi-formal. Becoming more of a parody of itself each year. **C** ***Astor***, 15 Shakespeare Sarani, T 226215. 32 rm (annexe not so good). Open-air *Kebab-e-que* with trio of musicians, serves delicious fish, chicken and meat kebabs; good value. **C** ***Shalimar***, 3 SN Banerjee Rd, T 285030. 22 rm. Central but noisy. **C** ***Minerva***, 11 Ganesh Chandra Ave, T 263365. 38 rm some a/c. A/c restaurant, travel, business services. Price incl English breakfast. Popular with business clients and families. **C** ***Executive Tours***, nr Park Circus. Well-furnished rm. Very clean.

There are several moderately priced places to stay. Some include breakfast, others all meals. A few have a/c rooms but unlike the larger hotels which have their own generators, these may suffer from hours of power cuts, especially in the hot season. Most of these are centrally-located and 5 km from the rly. **D** ***Astoria***, 6/2,3 Sudder St, T 241359. 30 a/c rm. Restaurant, travel. Busy area opp. market. **D** ***Lindsay Guest House*** 8B Lindsay St, T 248639. Some a/c rm. Fairly simple, clean and good value. Busy area opp. market. **D** ***Gujral Guest House*** 8B Lindsay St (2nd Flr). 6 rm, T 224 0620. Large rm, clean and excellent value. **D** ***Marble Palace Guest House***, 5 Beck Bagan Row, T 476766. Some a/c rm. **D** ***YMCA***, 25 JL Nehru Rd, T 292192. Large gloomy building but rooms have attached baths and breakfast and dinner are included. Table tennis, snooker and billiard tables in the lounge!

● Budget hotels

E ***Airport Rest Rooms*** in Old Terminal Bldg cheaper. ***Rest House III*** and **E** ***Rest House 1 & 2***, meals at Airport Restaurant. **E** ***YMCA***, 42 SN Banerjee Rd, T 292192. **E** ***YWCA***, 1 Middleton Row, T 297033. 75 rm. For women only. Special wing for married couples. **E** ***Udaychal Tourist Hostel***, (WBTDC) DG Block Sector II, Salt Lake, T 378246. 20 km from centre. Some simple a/c rm and cheap dorm. One meal compulsory.

A large number of simple, cheap hotels (most with dorm) in the Sudder St area are popular with back packers. Salvation Army **E** ***Red Shield Guest House***, 2 Sudder St, T 242895. Few modest rm and 3-5 bed dorms, water supply erratic, no late nights! Breakfast. Will look after non-residents' baggage for Rs 10 per piece/day. **E** ***Deeba Guest House***, Mirza Ghalib St (nr Kathleen's Restaurant), clean rm, friendly service. **E** ***Maria***, 5/1 Sudder St, T 243311. 21 rm, some with bath, and dorm. Basic, could be cleaner; no drugs or alcohol. Some nearby have been suspect. **E** ***Shilton***, T 243613. 5A Sudder St. Rec as good value and friendly service.

F ***Diplomat Travels*** 10 Sudder St, T 242145, F 296077. Shared bath, basic but good atmosphere, popular. Rec. **F** ***Modern Lodge***, Stuart Lane, T 444960. Rec. **F** ***Paragon***, 2 Stuart Lane. Small rm, cheap dorm beds. Upstairs better.

In Haora: **E** *Railway Retiring Rooms* some a/c, at both stations for rail passengers only. **E** *Railway Yatri Niwas*, Haora Station, between old and new stations. 28 rm, many with balconies overlooking Hugli, 8 a/c, 5-7 bed dorms. No reservations. Book in morning, max stay 3 nights, checkout 1000. Left luggage. Only available for Indrail Pass holders or tickets over 200 km. Hotel has *Yatrik Restaurant* . Striking building and good value. **F** *Youth Hostel*, 10J Ananda Dutta Lane, T 672869.

Dharamshalas run by religious foundations provide very simple accommodation (often free) for one or more nights for travellers. Alcoholic drinks not permitted. Some are restricted to Hindus only. One open to all (no smoking) is Bara Sikh Sangat, 172 Mahatma Gandhi Rd, T 385227. Others at 51B Sir Hari Ram Goenka St, 37 Kalakar St, 41 Kali Krishna Tagore St, 242 Kalighat Rd, 15 Hazra Rd, 42 Sarat Bose Rd and 34 Ezra St.

● Club accommodation

It is also possible to stay in one of Calcutta's clubs, each with a character of its own. **NB:** Technically membership of an affiliated club is necessary or an introduction by a member, which is possible at short notice. *The Bengal Club*, 1/1 Russell St. Ideally situated opp the Maidan, comfortable with excellent dining room (try the steak), Chinese restaurant, pastry shop. Estab 1827; a former home of Lord Macaulay. *The Calcutta Club*, 241 Acharya JC Bose Rd. Started for the Indian 'upper classes' in period when the Bengal Club refused them entry (until 1970). Pool, tennis, pleasant public rooms and a very popular bakery. Only male members may stay overnight. Busy at lunchtime. *Saturday Club*, 7 Wood St. Good bar and dining room. Rm well appointed but no phones. *The Tollygunge Club*, 120 Deshapran Sasmal Rd. T 463141, F 741923. 18-hole golf course, riding, tennis and swimming. Away from centre but on Metro and bus; atmosphere, grounds and location compensate for average accommodation and dining room. Former residence of the family of Tipu Sultan after he was killed at Seringapatam, and built on an old indigo plantation site, you need to book well in advance.

● Paying guest accommodation

Contact Govt India Tourism (Shakespeare Sarani) or West Bengal Tourism (BBD Bagh) for details.

● Places to eat

Thurs are 'meatless' days, but chicken and fish are available. Licensed restaurants are allowed to serve alcoholic drinks. As a result some of Calcutta's good restaurants have changed in character. They are no longer very pleasant places to eat since the emphasis is on drink rather than on food. However, there are still a number which provide excellent food and service, though at a price. **NB:** Be prepared for a large surcharge for live music (and sometimes even for recorded music) at a restaurant. This, and other taxes can mean that the bill is often double the price on the menu. Many restaurants, outside hotels, do not accept credit cards.

Multi-cuisine: there are several a/c restaurants in the Park St area and a few further afield. *Skyroom*, 57 Park St (closed Tue). Slightly cramped surroundings were once compensated by excellent food and charming extras. Very run down in 1994. *Blue Fox*, 55 Park St. Bar. Pleasantly quiet, but if you don't order alcohol you may be ignored. *Kwality*, 17 Park St (closed Th) and 2 Gariahat Rd (closed Wed). Famous for ice creams but also for Indian and continental (baked fish, chicken Kiev, vegetable gratin). Usually crowded. Good value. *Kathleen's*, 12 Mirza Ghalib St (closed Th) with the 'Princess' suitable for families. Excellent pastry shop. *Tandoor*, 43 Park St (closed Wed). *Bar-B-Q*, 43 Park St (closed Th). Bar. *Trinca's Ming Room*, 17B Park St. The best of a group of related restaurants on the premises. Not cheap but good. *Oasis*, 33 Park St, 2 Madge Lane, (closed Th). Small, good value, quick lunches. *Peter Cat*, 18 Park St (closed Th). Good Indian food, kebabs and sizzlers, crowded, reasonably priced. Bar. *Blue Sky Café*, 3 Sudder St, is the backpackers meeting place – always full. Refurbished recently, excellent cheap food, exceptional choice of Western food. Very highly rec. *Cosy Nook*, Nr Jodhpur Park Market, S. Calcutta. Dimly lit but good cheap food. Chicken butter masala speciality.

Indian: *Amber*, 11 Waterloo St in the business district is said to be the largest Indian restaurant in the country. Excellent Tandoori dishes; reservations essential. Bar. Not cheap, but fast efficient service, generous helpings. Highly rec. *Shiraz Golden Restaurant*, 56 Park St. Rec for Muslim cuisine. *Badshah*, in the heart of the shopping centre, well known for *Kebab rolls*. Bar. *Rung Mahal*, 15 JL Nehru Rd (closed Mon). *Ji's Shop*, 123B Rashbehari

Ave. Bengali cuisine. ***Lahore***, 140 SN Bannerjee Rd. ***Aminia***, 1 Corporation Place. Largely patronised by men. Excellent biryani and chicken chaap, and mutton pasand kebab. ***Zaranj***, Corner Sudder St & Chowringhee, high quality, exclusive, expensive. ***Sagar***, 1 Meredith St. REec for kebabs. Nearby ***Elfin*** does cheap thalis and Chinese lunches. ***Kebab-e-Que***, Astor Hotel, 15 Shakespeare Sarani. Outstanding kebabs, eaten outdoors or in.

Vegetarian: *Vineet*, 1 Shakespeare Sarani (A/c Market). Live Indian Pop music in the evenings. Good for snacks and ice creams. Slightly expensive. ***Jyoti Vihar***, 3A Ho Chi Minh Sarani, nr British High Comm and ***Vicky's*** Lindsay St (rec) for quick service and good S Indian cuisine. Good value. ***Anand*** Chittaranjan Ave, also rec for S. Indian.***Gupta Brothers***, 18B Park St. *Thalis* and Indian sweets. ***Invader Centre***, 12 Loudon St. ***Friends' Home***, 1 Chowringhee Centre.

Chinese: connoisseurs now travel to S Tangra Rd (off the E Metropolitan Bypass) where many Chinese have moved to from old China Town. Food excellent but surroundings not so pleasant. ***Blue Diamond, Ka Fa Lok*** and ***Sin Fa*** for excellent soups, jumbo prawns and honey chicken. Best to go early (noon for lunch, 2000 for dinner). More central but not as good: ***How Hua***, 10 Mirza Ghalib St and ***Waldorf***, 24B Park St, non a/c, (closed Tue). *Golden Dragon*, 40 Park Mansions, Park St (closed Wed). ***Eau Chew***, P32 Mission Row Extn, upstairs. Unusual dishes; try meal in a soup. ***Chin Wah***, Temple St. ***Chung Wah***, 13 A&B Chittaranjan Ave. Central, very cheap and popular. ***Mandarin***, 217 Landsdowne Rd. ***Mayfair China Bowl***, 122A Meghnad Saha Sarani (closed Th), is a small and intimate restaurant in S Calcutta which offers 'Indianised' – spicy – Chinese and other Far Eastern cuisine. Prawns a speciality. ***Jimmy's Kitchen***, AJC Bose Rd and Shakespeare Sarani crossing. Rec. ***Chinoiserie, Taj Bengal***, 34B Belvedere Rd, Alipore. Very popular, high quality and expensive.

Swiss confectionery: ***Kathleen's***, 12 Mirza Ghalib St. & ***Hari Krishna Bakery*** corner Russell and Middleton Sts, are rec. ***Kookie Jar***, Express Towers, Rawdon St. ***Flury's***, 18 Park St (closed Mon). Traditional English breakfasts, morning coffee, afternoon teas and pastry counter. ***Nahoum***, F 20, New Market. Good pastries.

Fast food: *Super Dooper*, 18C Park St. ***Health Food Centre***, 21 Park St. ***Big Max***, 1 Russell St. ***Garden Café***, Alipore Rd for pizzas and dosas, burgers and Chinese fast food. Highly rec. ***Super Snack Bar***, 14 Old Court House St. Good dosas. ***Corner Café***, Lower Circular Rd for pizzas and burgers. For a difference try the ***Coffee House*** (see N Calcutta above).

The excellent Moghlai *Kathi-kebab* (tender meat on bamboo skewers) in a *paratha* (rich unleavened 'bread'), is hard to beat. Try ***Nizam's*** (22/25 Hogg Market) and stalls in Zakaria St, Park Circus and around the cinemas off Esplanade. Inexpensive snacks in the Sudder St area: ***UP*** and ***Bihar***, ***Taj Continental, Blue Sky, Khalsa Restaurant*** and ***Mughul Durbar***. Others are ***Royal Indian***, 99 Lower Circular Rd and ***Sabir's*** in Chandni Chowk.

Ice Creams: ***Upvan, Sub-Zero*** and ***Tulika*** on Little Russell St and ***Yankee*** in Ballygunge Circular Rd with 42 varieties. ***Scoop***, 71 Strand Rd, Man-o-War Jetty. On riverside with terrace.

Bengali sweets: worth sampling (often very sweet!) are *sandesh*, *roshogolla*, *barfi*, *roshomalai*, *pantua* and *mishti doi* yoghurt made with jaggery. ***Mithai***, 48B Syed Amir Ali Ave. ***Bhim Chandra Nag***, 8 Vivekananda Rd. ***KC Das***, 11 Esplanade E, and 1/433 Gariahat Rd, ***Sen Mahasay***, 171H Rashbehari Ave. ***Girish Chandra Dey***, 167N Rashbehari Ave. ***Jadav Chandra Das***, 127A Rashbehari Ave. ***Ganguram***, 46C JL Nehru Rd. ***Mukherjee Sweets***, 29/1 Ballygunge Place.

Savoury snacks: are also sold fresh every afternoon at most sweet shops from about 1600-1730. Try *singaras*, *kachuris* and *nimkis*. ***Radhu's***, Lake Market serves superb snacks – Bengali *fish fry* and *chicken* or *'prawn cutlet'* (fillets, crumbed and fried), rich *Moghlai paratha* and *aloor dum* (potato curry).

● Bars

In all the larger hotels and up-market restaurants. In addition there are independent bars which are open usually till 2230. Atmosphere is not very sociable (some popular with men only). ***Asoka***, 3B JL Nehru Rd. ***Olympia***, 21 Park St. ***Shenaz***, 2A Middleton Row (also good kebabs). ***Saki***, 177 Lenin Sarani, T 273061. ***New Central***, 99 Chittaranjan Ave. ***Amber***, 11 Waterloo St. Grd Flr.

Entertainment & shopping

● Clubs

The 4 prominent clubs listed under places to stay above are affiliated to a number of clubs in India and some foreign clubs covering the 5 continents, among them Royal Overseas League, Travellers', St James', The National Liberal and United Oxford and Cambridge University Clubs, London, Sind Club, Karachi, Hong Kong Club, Wellington Club, New Zealand, Dubai Country Club, Doha Club, The American Club, Singapore and Columbia Club, Indianapolis. In addition several sports clubs attract a large and active membership.

● Cultural centres & libraries

Alliance Française, Park Mansions, Park St. **British Council** Library, 5 Shakespeare Sarani for newspapers and journals from UK. Day passes at gate. **Max Mueller Bhavan**, Ballygunge Circular Rd. **USIS**, 7 JL Nehru Rd. **Indo-American Society**, 17 Camac St. **Indo-CIS, Gorky Sadan**, Gorky Terrace nr Minto Park.

● Entertainment

Calcutta: this Fortnight is distributed free by the W Bengal Tourist Office. The monthly *Calcutta Skyline* also carries information of all major events in the city. The *Sunday Telegraph* and English language dailies carry a comprehensive list of what is showing.

Auditoria: regular performances of dance, music and theatre at **Rabindra Sadan**, Acharya JC Bose Rd; **Kala Mandir**, 48 Shakespeare Sarani; **Ramakrishna Mission Institute of Culture**, Golpark and **Gorky Sadan**, Gorky Terrace, nr Minto Park. Some of these also put on art exhibitions as at **Academy of Fine Arts**, Cathedral Rd next to Rabindra Sadan, and the Ramakrishna Mission which also has a library, International Guest House and a language teaching centre. **Nandan**, Acharya JC Bose Rd is the Govt film complex with an auditorium and exhibition area. Other venues for Bengali theatre of a high standard are **Children's Little Theatre**, Aban Mahal, **Biswaroopa**, 2A Raja Raj Kissen St, and **Star Theatre**, 79/34 Bidhan Sarani (productions by Bahuroopi and People's Little Theatre are highly rec).

Cinemas: which are a/c and comfortable, showing English language films 3 or 4 times a day mostly off JL Nehru Rd near Esplanade and near Hogg Market. **Elite**, SN Banerjee Rd. **Globe**, Lindsay St. **Lighthouse**, Humayun Place. **Metro**, JL Nehru Rd. **Minerva**, Chowringhee Place. Worth enquiring if a film by one of the top Bengali film-makers (Satyajit Ray, Mrinal Sen, Aparna Sen, Ritwick Ghatak) is showing, although since there would be no sub-titles you would ideally need to be accompanied by a Bengali.

Performing arts: English-language stage productions organized by the **British Council** and local educational institutions. Cultural programmes are also staged by **United States Information Service**, 7 JL Nehru Rd. The **Sangeet Research Academy** nr Tollygunge Metro station, set up in 1970 is a national centre for training in Indian Classical music. On Wed evenings there is a free concert. **Rabindra Bharati University**, 6/4 Dwarakanath Tagore Lane, holds performances, particularly during the winter, of the performing arts including Rabindra Sangeet (songs) and Dance and *Jatras*, the folk theatre of Bengal which is enjoying a revival. *Jatra* is community theatre in the round, highly colourful and exaggerated both in style of delivery and make-up, drawing for its subject either the old romantic favourites from mythology or more up-to-date social, political and religious themes.

● Shopping

Most open 1000-1730 or later (some break for lunch) weekdays and 1000-1300 on Sat.

Art: *Galerie 88*, Shakespeare Sarani is a small gallery for modern art.

Books: *Cambridge Book & Stationery*, 20D Park St. *Oxford Book Shop*, Park St. *Bookmark*, 56D, Free School St. *Survey of India* Map Sales Office, 13 Wood St. A wealth of second-hand pavement bookstalls along *College Street* caters for students but may equally reveal an interesting 1st edition for a keen collector (see under Places of interest). *Dasgupta & Co*, 54/3, College St. One of first bookshops on College St, wide range of English and Bengali books. Widely patronised. *Seagull*, Circus Ave, opp Bangladesh High Commission specialising in fina arts. For a fortnight every Jan the **Calcutta Book Fair** takes over a part of the Maidan nr Victoria Memorial. Stalls sell paperback fiction to antiquarian books.

Boutiques & handicrafts: several in Park St and streets leading off it. *Bengal Home Industries*, 57 JL Nehru Rd, *Good Companions*, 13C Russell St, *Ritu's Boutique*, 46A Rafi Ahmed Kidwai Rd, *Ananda*, 13 Russell St, *Guy's N' Dolls*, 14 Sudder St, *Jete*, Park Centre, Park St and *Women's Friendly Society*, 29 Park Lane are all centrally located and will provide unusual gifts. *Benetton*, 43 Park Mansions, Park St.

Womens' self-help centres which have shops and also give you the opportunity to see techniques such as handloom weaving, batik printing, embroidery, handblock printing being practised are specially rec. Visit ***All Bengal Womens' Union***, 89 Elliot Rd, ***Karma Kutir***, 32 Ballygunge Place (*kantha* making), and ***Nari Seva Sangha*** in Jodhpur Park. ***Sasha***, 27 Mirza Ghalib St (off the Rd). Tue-Sat, 1000-1900; Sun, Mon 1000-1300. Excellent handicrafts by women's voluntary organisation. Cane, bamboo, *Dokra*, *kantha*, leather and crafts from E and NE India.

Government Emporia: are mainly in the town centre and are fixed price shops. ***Central Cottage Industries***, 7 JL Nehru Rd. ***Handloom House***, 2 Lindsay St. ***Khadi Gramodyog***, 28 Chittaranjan Ave. ***Assam***, 8 Russell St. ***Bihar***, 145 Rashbehari Ave ***Cauvery***, 7 JL Nehru Rd. ***Kashmir Art***, 12 JL Nehru Rd. ***Manipur***, 15L Lindsay St. ***Manjusha***, 7/1D Lindsay St. ***Meghalaya***, 9 Russell St. ***Phulkari***, 26B Camac St. ***Rajasthali***, 30E JL Nehru Rd. ***Tripura***, 58 JL Nehru Rd. ***Refugee Handicrafts***, 2A Gariahat Rd. ***U P***, 12B Lindsay St. Also at ***Dakshinapan***, nr Dhakuria Bridge. Mon-Fri 1030-1930, Sat 1030-1300. Very convenient. Excellent selection of quality handloom and handicrafts.

Markets: see map pages 606-607. The ***New Market***, Lindsay St, behind original Hogg Market (largely rebuilt since a fire in 1985), has over 2500 shops covering an area of 5 ha. Be prepared to be pestered by porters insisting on offering their services. It used to be said that you could buy anything from a needle to an elephant (on order) in one of its stalls. Today it is still worth a visit, preferably early in the morning, to watch it come alive. You will find dull mundane everyday needs of the city dweller to the most exotic luxuries.

Calcutta has a number of ***bazars*** each with a character of its own. In ***Bentinck Street*** are Muslim tailors, Chinese shoemakers interspersed with Indian sweet meat shops and tea stalls. ***Gariahat*** market has an enormous range of fish; also very diverse clientele – city businessmen, professors, cooks, servants. Best in early morning. In ***Shyambazar*** the coconut market starts business at 0500 and you will miss it if you arrive 2 hr later. The fragrant flower market is on ***Jagannath Ghat*** on the river bank. There are dozens of others equally interesting. The old ***China Bazar*** no longer exists although a trip to the Tiretta Bazar area still retains its ethnic flavour; exceptional Chinese breakfasts are available off street stalls. In the city centre you can shop in a/c comfort in the ***Market*** on Shakespeare Sarani, ***Park Centre*** on Park St or ***Vardaan Market*** on Camac St.

Photography: camera films, accessories and quality printing services are easily available. Several on Park St at 33, 161, 191. ***Bourne & Shepherd***, 141 SN Banerjee Rd; ***Image***, 10C Ramesh Mitra Rd.

● Sports

There are numerous sports clubs.

Cricket: Eden Gardens is the venue of cricket test matches, and of international tennis tournaments, important football fixtures and other sports championships. Open throughout the year.

Golf: Calcutta has some noted golf courses, including the ***Royal Calcutta Golf Club*** was founded in 1829, and is the oldest golf club in the world outside Great Britain. It moved to its present course in 1910. It took the radical step of admitting women in 1886. Also at ***The Tollygunge Club***, on land that was once an indigo plantation.

Horseracing: ***Royal Calcutta Turf Club***, 1 Russell St. Some visitors enjoy race meetings (Tote, bookmakers available). The first Indian Derby was held in 1843-44, and has a number of other Indian 'firsts': the first licensed bookmaker (1881), photofinish camera (1948) starting stalls (1966) and electronic tote (1989). Racing takes place in the cool season (Nov – first week of April) and monsoon (Jun – Oct). The Derby is in the first week of Jan.

Polo: *Calcutta Polo Club*, 51 JL Nehru Rd.

Racquets: *Calcutta Racquet Club*, Maidan near St Paul's Cathedral.

Rowing: *Calcutta Rowing Club*, ***Bengal Rowing Club*** and ***Lake Club*** (Rowing), at Rabindra Sarobar.

Swimming: *Calcutta Swimming Club*, 1 Strand Rd.

Tennis: *Calcutta South Club*, 1 Woodburn Park. Calcutta is also home to the most famous Indian football teams, ***Mohan Bagan***, ***East Bengal***, and ***Mohammadan Sporting***, all with club grounds on the Maidan. The season starts in May and runs through the monsoon.

Services

● Airline offices

National airlines: **Air India**, 50 JL Nehru Rd, T 442356. Airport, T 572611, Extn 346. **Indian Airlines**, 39 Chittaranjan Ave, T 263390.

Airport Counter, T 572567. Indian Airlines Booking Counters at *Hotel Hindusthan* International, 235/1 Acharya JC Bose Rd and *Great Eastern Hotel*, 1,2 & 3 Old Court House St, T 280324.

International: **Aeroflot**, 58 JL Nehru Rd, T 449831. **Air France**, 41 JL Nehru Rd, T 296161. **Air Lanka**, c/o STIC Travels, *New Kenilworth Hotel*, 1 Little Russell St, T 448394. **Alitalia**, 2/3 Chitrakoot Building, 230A Acharya JC Bose Rd, T 447394. **Biman**, 1 Park St, T 212862. **British Airways**, 41 JL Nehru Rd, T 293430. **Cathay Pacific**, 1 Middleton Row, T 293211. **Druk Air**, 51A Ballygunge Circular Rd, T 434419. **KLM**, 1 Middleton St, T 441221. Kuwait Airways, 230A Acharya JC Bose Rd, T 444697. **Lufthansa**, 30A/B JL Nehru Rd, T 299365. **Pan Am**, 42 JL Nehru Rd, T 443251. **Qantas**, *Hotel Hindusthan International*, 235/1 Acharya JC Bose Rd, T 440718. **Royal Nepal Airlines**, 41 JL Nehru Rd, T 298534. SAS, 18G Park St, T 249696/8. **Swissair**, 46C JL Nehru Rd, T 220291. **Thai Airways**, 18G Park St, T 299846. **Gulf Air, Singapore Airlines, Philippine Airlines** are represented by GSA Jet Air, 230A Acharya JC Bose Rd, T 447783.

● Banks & money changers

Mon-Fri 1000-1400, Sat 1000-1200. **State Bank of India**, 1 Strand Rd, 43 JL Nehru Rd, 1 Middleton St, 11 Shakespeare Sarani. **United Bank of India**, 16 Old Court House St. **United Commercial Bank**, 10 Brabourne Rd. **Central Bank of India**, 13 Netaji Subhas Rd. **Andhra**, 58 JL Nehru Rd. **Allahabad**, 2 Netaji Subhas Rd. **Bank of India**, 15A Hemanta Basu Sarani. **Foreign Banks**: **American Express**, 21 Old Court House St. **Bank of America**, 8 India Exchange Place. **Bank of Tokyo**, 2 Brabourne Rd. **Citibank**, 43 JL Nehru Rd. **ANZ**, 19 Netaji Subhas Rd. **Standard Chartered**, 4 Netaji Subhas Rd. **Algemene Bank Nederlands**, 18A Brabourne Rd. **Banque Nationale de Paris**, 4A BBD Bagh E. **Hong Kong & Shanghai**, 8 Netaji Subhas Rd. 24 hr teller service.

Exchanges: **State Bank of India**, 31 JL Nehru Rd. **RN Dutta**, Stephen House, 4,5, BBD Bagh E; 5 & 7 Kidderpore Dock and Calcutta Airport. **Maneek Lal Sen**, New Market. **RR Sen**, 18 JL Nehru Rd.

● Chambers of Commerce

Bengal Chamber of Commerce, 6 Netaji Subhas Rd. **Bengal National Chamber of Commerce and Industry**, 23 RN Mukherjee Rd. **Bharat Chamber of Commerce**, 8 Old Court House St. **Indian Chamber of Commerce**, 5 Exchange Place. **Calcutta Chamber of Commerce**, 18H Park St. **Merchants Chamber of Commerce**, 3-1 Armenian St.

● Deputy High Commissions & Consulates

Austria, 96/1 Sarat Bose Rd. **Bangladesh**, 9 Circus Ave. **Belgium**, 5/1A Hungerford St. **Bhutan**, 48 Tivoli Court, Pramothesh Barua Sarani. **France**, Park Plaza, Park St. **Germany**, 1 Hastings Park Rd. **Greece**, 41 JL Nehru Rd. **Indonesia**, 128 Rashbehari Ave. **Italy**, 3 Raja Santosh Rd. **Japan**, 12 Pretoria St. **Nepal**, 19 National Library Ave. **Netherlands**, 18A Brabourne Rd. **Norway**, 11 RN Mukherjee Rd. **Spain**, 1 Taratolla Rd. **Sweden**, 5/2 Russell St. **Thailand**, 18B Mandeville Gardens. **Turkey**, 2 Nazar Ali Lane. **UK**, 1 Ho-Chi-Minh Sarani. **USA**, 5/1 Ho-Chi-Minh Sarani. **USSR**, 31 Shakespeare Sarani.

● Hospitals & medical services

Ambulance: *Dhanwantary Clinic*, 1 National Library Ave, T 456265. *Emergency Doctors' Service*, A 165 Lake Gardens, T 466770.

Chemists: *Dey's Medical*, 6/2B Lindsay St; 55 Gariahat Rd; 41/A Block A New Alipore. *Blue Print*, 1 Old Court House St. *King & Co* (Homeopath), 29 Shyama Prasad Mukherjee Rd. *Life Care*, 1/2A Hazra Rd. *Moonlight*, 180 SP Mukherjee Rd (24 hr). *Seetal*, 22A Shakespeare Sarani. *Singh Roy*, 4/1 Sambhunath Pandit St. (24 hr Wed-Sun.) *Sterling & Co* (Homeopath), 91-C Elliot Rd. *Welmed*, 4/1 Sambhunath Pandit St (24 hr Mon, Tue).

Hospitals: **Government**: *Calcutta Hospital & Medical Research Institute*, 7/2 Diamond Harbour Rd, T 453921. *Calcutta National Medical College & Hospital*, 24 Gorachand Rd, T 441012. *Medical College Hospital*, 88 College St, T 359252. *NRS Medical College & Hospital*, 138 Acharya JC Bose Rd, T 243213. *RG Kar Medical College & Hospital*, 1 Belgachia Rd, T 554311. *SSKM Hospital*, 244 Lower Circular Rd, T 449753.

Private: *Belle Vue Clinic*, 9 Dr UN Brahmachari St, T 442321. *Woodlands Nursing Home*, 8/6 Alipore Rd, T 453951. *Park Nursing Home*, 4 Victoria Terrace, T 443586. *Metropolitan Nursing Home*, 18 Shakespeare Sarani, T 432487.

Opticians: *Himalaya Opticals*, 25 Camac St. *Presidency Optical*, 306 Bepin Behari Ganguly St (Lal Bazar).

● **Laundry**
Plenty of dry-cleaners can be found all across the city.

● **Post & telecommunications**
Numerous post offices throughout the city, usually open from 1000-1700. **GPO**: BBD Bagh (W). Post Restante here. **Telex facilities**: at the Philatelic Bureau. **Central Telegraph Office**: 8 Red Cross Place. Open 24 hr for International calls, Telex and cable. **Speed Post**: for foreign and Indian mail is available from major post offices. Park St Post Office, 65 Park St. Telex facilities (0900-2000, Sun and holidays 1000-1700). **International calls**: from many public phones. Park St Telegraph Office, Park Lane off Rafi Ahmed Kidwai Rd and from Telephone Bhavan, BBD Bagh (S). For **international telex, telegrams and Fax services**: go to Business centres at major hotels.

● **Places of worship**
Among many: **Buddhist**: *Mahabodhi Society*, 4A Bankim Chandra Chatterjee St.

Christian: *St Paul's Cathedral*, Cathedral Rd. *St Andrew's Kirk*, 15 BBD Bagh. *St John's Church*, 2/1 Council House St. *The Cathedral*, Portuguese Church St. *St Thomas' RC Church*, 7 Middleton Row.

Hindu: *Kali Temple*, Kalighat Rd. *Ramakrishna Mission Belur Math*, Haora.

Jewish: *Shalome Synagogue*, Synagogue St.

Muslim: *Nakhoda Mosque*, Rabindra Sarani/Zakaria St.

Sikh: Gurdwara Bara Sikh Sangat, 172 Mahatma Gandhi Rd.

● **Tour companies & travel agents**
American Express, 21 Old Court House St. ***Balmer Lawrie***, 21 Netaji Subhas Rd. ***Charson Tours***, 6 JL Nehru Rd. ***Diplomat***, Sudder St (rec for cheap flights to Bangkok). ***Everett***, 4 Govt Place (N). ***Globe***, 11 Ho-Chi-Minh Sarani. ***Indian Air Travels***, 28 Chittaranjan Ave. ***Indo-Culture Tours***, 18 A-C JL Nehru Rd. ***James Warren***, 31 JL Nehru Rd. ***Mackinnon Travel***, 16 Strand Rd. ***Mercury***, 46C JL Nehru Rd. ***Panurge***, 20B JL Nehru Rd. ***Sita***, 3B Camac St. ***Trade Wings***, 32 JL Nehru Rd. ***Travel Corp of India***, 46C JL Nehru Rd.

● **Tourist offices**
The different State Govts have their own Information Centres in the city. **Andaman & Nicobar Islands**, 3A Auckland Place (2nd Flr). **Arunachal Pradesh**, 4B Chowringhee Place. **Assam**, 8 Russell St. **Bihar**, 26B Camac St (1st Flr). **Haryana**, 49 Muktaram Babu St. **Himachal Pradesh**, 25 Camac St (2nd Flr). **Jammu & Kashmir**, 12 JL Nehru Rd. **Madhya Pradesh**, Chitrakoot, 6th Flr, Rm 7, 230A AJC Bose Rd. **Manipur**, 26 Rowland Rd. **Meghalaya**, 9 Russell St. **Mizoram**, 24 Old Ballygunge Rd. **Nagaland**, 13 Shakespeare Sarani. **Orissa**, 55 Lenin Sarani. **Punjab**, 1/425, Gariahat Rd, 4th Floor, Calcutta 68. Rajasthan, 2 Ganesh Ch Ave. **Sikkim**, 5/2 Russell St (4th Flr). **Tripura**, 1 Pretoria St. **UP**, 12A Netaji Subhas Rd.

● **Useful addresses**
Foreigners Regional Registration Office: 237 Acharya JC Bose Rd, T 443301. Permits for Sikkim, 24 hr. **Home Political Dept**: 1st Flr, Block 2 and **Forestry Dept**: (for Sunderbans permit), 5th Flr, Block G, Writers' Building, BBD Bagh.

Transport

● **Transport in Calcutta**
Buses: run by W Bengal State Transport provide a regular service throughout the city and suburbs from 0500-2030; always overcrowded, very cheap; minimum fare Re 0.70. The alternative private maroon minibus service covers major routes; faster, slightly more expensive. New S Bengal minibuses are bigger. They will often stop on request. Very limited headroom!

Ferry: services from 0815-2000 from Chandpal Ghat operate at 15 min intervals except on Sun; can be used to cross the river to Haora station or the Botanical Gardens. Often more comfortable and quicker than Haora Bridge. **Luxury launches** can be hired for short cruises. Tourist Bureau, Rs 2200 for first 4 hr. *Omar Resort*, 135 Canning St, T 251379. Rs 300 per hr. Max 50 people. Candida Customer Services, Mercantile Building, 9/12 Baghbazar St, T 202382. Rs 1500 per weekday, Rs 2000 for holidays. Max 15 people.

Metro: the only city in India to have one and rightly very proud of it. The Metro opened in 1984, is clean, efficient and punctual: music and videos at stations to entertain you while you wait! Only 10 km of the 16.5 km planned of the main N-S trunk route is operational from 0800-2100; Tollygunge to Esplanade and Belgachia to Dum Dum. Further extension due. Outside City Centre, a few **auto-rickshaws** operate, especially as shuttle service to Metro Stations. Rs 3.

Private taxi operators: Rent-a-Car Service, 1/5 Dover Lane, T 467186. **Car Rent Services**,

233/4A Acharya JC Bose Rd. T441285; 1/5 Dover Lane, T 467186. **Durgapur Automobiles**, 113 Park St, T 294044. **Wheels on Road**, 150 Lenin Sarani, T 273081.

Rickshaws: Calcutta is the only city to have hand-pulled rickshaws many of which are hired for the day by the 'pullers'. Can be as expensive as taxis, especially when wet. When the streets are flooded they become indispensable. Supposedly 40,000 rickshaw-pullers would lose their livelihood if these were banned.

Taxis: yellow-top taxis are available throughout the city. Meters show current rates: Rs 5 for first 2 km. Taxis are much cheaper in Calcutta than some other Indian cities. With strong bargaining it should cost no more than Rs 100 from the city centre to the airport. The pre-paid taxi service from the airport costs Rs 65.

Trams: many people's favourite transport: the only Indian city to run them. Extensive network, from 0400-2300. Often crowded except on Sun; very cheap – fares from Re 0.60.

● Long distance connections

Air NB: The pre-paid taxi service from Dum Dum to city is excellent value, if a hair-raising ride. Rs65. Return from city centre costs more – Rs100 if you bargain hard. A bus goes from Indian Airlines city centre Office approx two hourly from 0530. The public bus is a nightmare: strongly not rec.

Domestic: **Indian Airlines**, 39 Chittaranjan Ave, T 260874. Airport, Arr T 5529841; Dep 5529843. **Air India**, City office, T 442356. Airport, T 572031. ***Damania***, T 4756356. Airport, T 5528779. **Modiluft**, T 296257. **East West Airlines**, 39 Chittaranjan Ave, T 260730. Airport, T 572633.

Indian Airlines: **Agartala**, twice daily, 3/4 hr; **Bagdogra**, Tu,Th,Sa,Su, 1 hr; **Bangalore**, M,Tu,W,Th,Sa,Su, 2½ hr; **Bhubaneswar**, W,F,Su, 1 hr, and Tu,Th; **Bombay**, twice daily, 2½ hr; **Delhi**, 4 times daily, 2¼ hr; **Dibrugarh**,Tu,Th,Sa,Su, 1½ hr; **Dimapur**, Tu,Th, 2 hr; **Guwahati**, twice daily, 1 hr; **Hyderabad**, daily except M, 2 hr; **Imphal**, daily except M, 2 hr. **Jorhat**, Tu,Th,Sa, 2½ hr; **Lucknow**, M,W,F, 1½ hr; **Madras**, daily, 2 hr, and Tu,W,Th,F; **Nagpur**, W,F & Su, 3 hr; **Patna**, daily, 2½ hr, and M,W,F; **Port Blair**, Tu,Th,Sa, 2 hr; **Ranchi**, daily, 1 hr; **Silchar**,daily, 1 hr; **Tezpur**, Tu,Th & Sa, 1210, 1¼ hr; **Visakhapatnam**, W,F, 1½ hr.

Damania: **Bombay**, daily, 0915, 2 hr 45; Mon-Sat, 2200; **East West Airlines**: **Delhi**, daily except Su, 1505, 2 hr; **Guwahati**, daily except Su, 0900, 2 hr. **ModiLuft**: **Delhi and Jammu**, daily, 2000, 2hr 10;

International: **Indian Airlines**: **Bangkok**, Tu,Th,F,Sa, 0855, 1½ hr; **Chittagong**, Sa, 1230, 1½ hr; **Dhaka**, M,W,F,Sa, 1330, 1¼ hr; **Kathmandu**, M,W,F,Sa, 1245, 1½ hr. Indian Airlines Enquiries, T 263390. Resrvations, T 260731. **Air India**: flies to Bangkok (F), Singapore (M,F) and Tokyo (F). **International carriers**: connect Calcutta with Amman, Bangkok, Belgrade, Beijing, Chittagong, Dhaka, Dubai, Frankfurt, Hongkong, Kathmandu, London, Moscow, New York, Osaka, Paris, Paro, Singapore, Tokyo. International Flight Enquiry, T 569364.

Train: Calcutta is served by 2 Railway stations, **Haora** and **Sealdah**, and is connected to major cities all over the country. Haora now has a new S station for platforms 18-21. Trains listed here depart from Haora, unless marked **S**. From Haora a/c Expresses (via Gaya) go to **New Delhi** on Tu,W and to **Amritsar** on Sa, and via Patna to New Delhi on Th, and to Amritsar on Su. There are fast trains to Bombay and Madras daily, as well as to numerous other destinations through the week including Darjiling, Ranchi, Guwahati, Puri, Hyderabad, Bangalore, Cochin, **Trivandrum** (Thiruvananthapuram), Ahmadabad and Jammu. **Computerised Booking Office**, 61 JL Nehru Rd. Rly Booking, 6 Fairlie Place, BBD Bagh, T 204025. Haora Station, T 263535. Sealdah Station, T 359213. Tourists are often still automatically told to go to the Tourist Counter at Fairlie Place, which is the upstairs booking hall. However, unless you are travelling on an Indrail Pass or buying a pass, it is worth checking whether seats are available for the trains you want downstairs first, as this can often be much quicker. It is also easier to get a refund if you want to change your ticket as you must always return to the counter of purchase. **Foreign Tourist Quota** If the trains you want are listed as 'Full', it is worth trying the Tourist Counter. Be prepared for **at least** a ½ hr wait, and check when you enter which queue to join for the region you want to travel in. There are separate queues for N and SE Railways. SE Railway Booking and Information, Esplanade Mansion, T 289530. 24-hr railway information for incoming trains, T 203445-203454. Other information, T 203535-203544. For reservations, T 280370 (0900-2100 weekdays and 0900-1400 Sun).

Note There are always lots of taxis at Haora. Do not be browbeaten into going with the first driver who insists on taking you. One way of getting away from the crush is to take the ferry across the river and taking a taxi from the other side.

Delhi (D): *Rajdhani Exp* 2301(AC/CC), 1600, M,Tu,Th,F,Su, 18 hr. *Kalka Mail*, 2311 (AC/II), daily, 1900, 25 hr; *AC Exp*, 2303 (AC/CC), M,W,F,Su, daily, 0915, 25½ hr; **Bombay (VT)**: *Gitanjali Exp*, 2860 (AC/II), 1310, 32½ hr; *Bombay Mail*, 8002 (AC/CC), daily, 2000, 35¾ hr; **Madras (MC)**: *Coromandel Exp*, 2841 (AC/II), daily, 1445, 27 hr; *Madras Mail*, 6003 (AC/II), daily, 2045, 32 hr. **Agra**: *Toofan-Udyanabha Exp*, 3007, daily, 0945, 29½ hr; **Allahabad**: *Kalka Mail*, 2311 (AC/II), daily, 1900, 14 hr; *Bombay Mail*, 3003 (AC/II), daily, 2000, 14¾ hr; **Bhubaneswar**: *Coromandel Exp*, 2841 (AC/II), daily, 1445, 7¼ hr; **Darjiling (H)**: *Kamrup Exp*, 5659 (AC/II), daily, 1735, New Jalpaigunï 13½ hr; connects with 3D, daily, 0715, 8½ hr. (**S**) *Darjiling Mail*, 3143 (AC/CC&AC/II), daily, 1915, NJ, 13 hr; connects with 1D daily, 0900, 8½ hr. (**S**) Kanchenjungha Ex; 5657, daily, 0625, NJ, 11¾ hr; connects next morning with 3D at 0715. 13 hr; **Gaya**: *AC Exp*, 2381 (AC/CC&AC/II), M,W,F,Su, 0915, 7½ hr; *Jammu Tani Exp*, 3151 (AC/II), daily, 1120, 9¼ hr; **Guwahati**: *Trivandrum-Guwahati*, 2601 (AC/II),Sa, 1410, 22½ hr; *Cochin-Guwahati Exp*, 2649 (AC/II), Th, 1410, 22½ hr; *Bangalore-Guwahati Exp*, 2674 (AC/II), M, 1410, 22½ hr; **Patna**: *AC Exp*, 2303 (AC/CC&AC/II), daily, 0915, 9 hr; *Delhi Exp*, 3011, daily, 2045, 10½ hr; **Puri**: *Haora-Puri Exp*, 8007, daily, 2215, 10¾ hr; *Sri Jagannath Exp*, 8409 (AC/II), daily, 1920, 10 hr; **Ranchi**: *Hatia Exp*, 8015, daily, 2115, 9¾ hr; **Trivandrum** (Thiruvananthapuram): *Guwahati-Trivandrum*, 2602 (AC/II), M, 2235, 48 hr; **Varanasi**: *AC Exp*, 2381 (AC/CC&AC/II), Tu,Th,Sa, 0915, 10¾ hr; *Amritsar Mail*, 3005 (AC/II), daily, 1920, 14¾ hr.

Bus: Calcutta is connected by an extensive network of National Highways with the major cities and towns of tourist interest nearby. Calcutta State Transport Corp Booking Office is at Esplanade Bus Terminus, T 281916. The buses operate on routes similar to the tours detailed above under Tourist Offices and Information.

Sea: the **Shipping Corp of India**, 13 Strand Rd, T 232354. It operates steamer services from Calcutta to Port Blair in the Andamans.

WEST BENGAL

CONTENTS

MAPS

West Bengal covers 88,000 sq km, more than double the area of Switzerland, but its population of 68 million makes it India's fifth largest state. It stretches 600 km from the Bay of Bengal to the borders of Sikkim in the North.

SOCIAL INDICATORS *Population*: 71 mn (Urban 28%, Scheduled Castes 22%, Scheduled Tribes 6%). *Literacy*: M 67% F 47%. *Birth rate*: *Rural* 30:1000, *Urban* 18:1000. *Death rate*: *Rural* 9:1000, *Urban* 7:1000. *Infant mortality*: *Rural* 93:1000, *Urban* 52:1000. *Religion*: *Hindu* 76%; *Muslim* 22%; *Christian* 1%; *Sikh* 0.3% Bengali and several minor and tribal languages, eg *Santali*, are spoken. Hindi, English and many regional languages are spoken in Calcutta.

Environment

Land

Most of the state lies on the W delta of the Ganga. In the E the Ganga valley's great alluvial-filled trough which fronts the Himalaya becomes much shallower. The basalt **Rajmahal Hills**, in the centre of the state, are a projection NE of the Peninsula rocks. However, like Bangladesh, which forms the E half of the delta, W Bengal is made up largely of 'new mud, old mud and marsh'. Originally densely forested, now the only jungle that remains is in the mangrove swamps of the **Sundarbans** in the far S and on the slopes of the Himalaya in the N. Elsewhere the plains have been converted into an intensively cultivated rice growing landscape.

Even here there is great variety. Immediately N of Calcutta is the so-called 'moribund delta'. The river's old channels of the Ganga are silted up, often dry in the winter, sometimes with old meanders and shallow cut-off lakes left as wild swamp. Coconut-fringed village ponds break up the scenery and villages often stand surrounded by orchards with mangoes, papayas and palmyra palms.

Rivers

In the Ganga delta the rivers continue to change their course frequently. Over the last 300 years the main course of the Ganga has shifted progressively E, leaving the Bhagirathi-Hooghly as a minor channel. The front margins of the Himalaya are one of the great belts of earth movement, and the shifts in the river courses may have been caused both by earth movements and by silting of the western rivers. Certainly in the 16th century the **Bhagirathi** was the main course followed by the Ganga to the sea. In 1770 the Damodar River, which used to flow from Bihar to join the Bhagirathi N of Calcutta shifted its course 130 km S – one of several major changes of course made by the delta rivers.

The road N and a new railway now cross the **Farakka Barrage**, which diverts the Ganga waters in the dry season back down their old course in order to supply more water for Calcutta and to flush silt from the river bed. It also reopens the rail route to northern W Bengal and Assam which had run across the Hard-

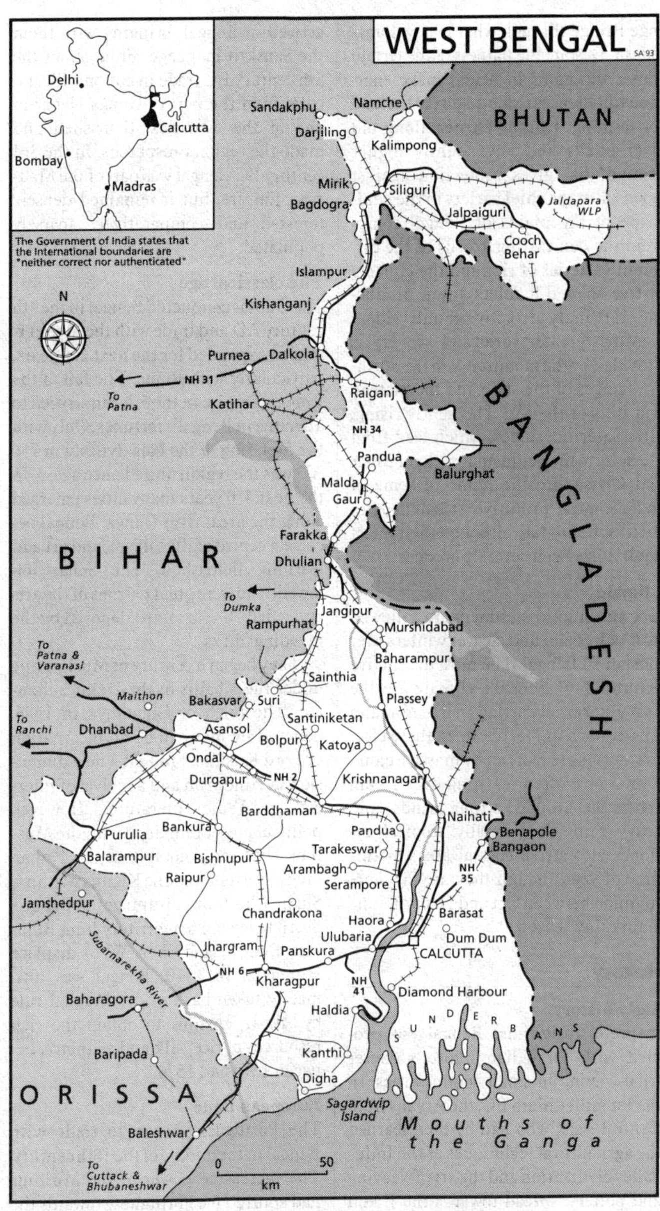
WEST BENGAL
SA 93
Delhi
Calcutta
Bombay
Madras
The Government of India states that the international boundaries are "neither correct nor authenticated"
N
BHUTAN
BANGLADESH
BIHAR
ORISSA
Sandakphu
Namche
Darjiling
Kalimpong
Mirik
Siliguri
Bagdogra
Jalpaiguri
Jaldapara WLP
Cooch Behar
Islampur
Kishanganj
Purnea
Dalkola
NH 31
To Patna
Raiganj
Katihar
NH 34
Pandua
Balurghat
Malda
Gaur
Farakka
Dhulian
To Dumka
Jangipur
Rampurhat
Murshidabad
To Patna & Varanasi
Baharampur
Sainthia
Maithon
Bakasvar
Suri
Plassey
To Ranchi
Dhanbad
Asansol
Santiniketan
Bolpur
Katoya
Ondal
Durgapur
NH 2
Krishnanagar
Barddhaman
Naihati
Purulia
Bankura
Pandua
Benapole
Bangaon
Balarampur
Bishnupur
Tarakeswar
Raipur
Arambagh
NH 35
Serampore
Jamshedpur
Chandrakona
Haora
Barasat
Dum Dum
Ulubaria
Jhargram
Panskura
CALCUTTA
NH 6
Kharagpur
Subarnarekha River
NH 41
Diamond Harbour
Baharagora
Haldia
SUNDERBANS
Baripada
Kanthi
Digha
Sagardwip Island
Mouths of the Ganga
Baleshwar
To Cuttack & Bhubaneshwar
0
50
km

inge Bridge through what is now Bangladesh. Despite the flatness of the terrain minor variations in height make enormous differences to the quality of the land for farming. Houses cluster along old river banks and any slightly higher ground that gives protection against floods. But the chief variety in the landscape of the plains of Bengal comes from the contrasting greens of the different varieties of rice and the clusters of tree-shaded hamlets, often producing startlingly attractive countryside.

Much greater variety of scenery is provided by the mountains on the northern fringes of the state and the plateau and hills of the SW. The gently rising, often lateritic, slopes, which lead from the delta to the peninsular rocks of Bihar and Orissa, are the home of some of India's most primitive tribal peoples such as the Santals, although their forest habitat has been severely eroded.

Climate

Hot and humid summers are followed by much cooler and clearer winters over most of W Bengal. The most distinctive feature of W Bengal's climate are the heavy storms occurring in late Mar and Apr. Known as Nor'Westers, these electric storms are marked by massive cloud formations, often reaching over 15 km above the ground, strong winds, and heavy rain. Occasionally tropical cyclones also strike coastal areas at this time of year, though they are far more common between Oct and Dec, after the main rainy season.

History

Early history

In pre-historic times Bengal was peopled with Dravidian hunter-gatherer tribes, living in small communities. In the 1st millennium BC, the Aryans from Central Asia, who had by then learned the agricultural techniques of the Indus Valley civilization and the art of weaving and pottery, spread towards the E and arrived in Bengal, bringing with them the Sanskrit language. From about the 5th century BC trade in cotton, silk and coral from the port of Ganga Nagar in one of the estuaries, flourished and made the region prosperous. In the 3rd century BC Bengal was part of the Mauryan Empire, but it remained densely forested and comparatively sparsely populated.

The classical age

The Guptas conquered Bengal in the 4th century AD and trade with the Mediterranean expanded for the next 200 years, particularly with Rome. The fall of the Roman Empire in the 5th century led to a decline in Bengal's fortunes. Only with the founding of the Pala dynasty in 750 AD was the region united once again. In the next 450 years many cities emerged along the great river Ganga. Bengal became a centre of Buddhism, and art and learning flourished. The Senas followed, who were great patrons of the arts and ruled 50 years until deposed by the invading Turks.

They began a century of Muslim rule under the Khaljis of the Delhi Sultanate. The birth of Chaitanya in 1486, believed by many to be an incarnation of Lord Krishna, brought a new dimension in Hinduism and a revival of interest in Vedic literature. However, political power remained with the Muslims. The most notable of the Pathan kings who followed the Khaljis was Sher Shah, who took advantage of Babur's death to extend his territory from Bihar into Bengal, and then W to displace Humayun in 1540. Bengal was ultimately taken back under Mughal rule by Akbar, anxious to obtain the rich resources of rice, silk and saltpetre, between 1574 and 1576.

European trade

The Portuguese began to trade with Bengal in the middle of the 16th century. The increasing power of the Muslims had spurred the Portuguese towards the subcontinent but before long they faced competition from the Dutch and the British and in 1632 the attack on their port near Calcutta by Emperor Shah Jahan reduced their merchant power.

In 1634 one of Shah Jahan's daughters was badly burned in a fire. For weeks her life was in danger, but she was finally saved under the guidance of an English surgeon, Gabriel Boughton, who was visiting the court. In gratitude Shah Jahan granted the British permission to trade from Bengal and establish 'factories', or trading posts, there. English surgeons repeatedly played a part in securing more than the health of the Company's servants. 80 years later another surgeon, William Hamilton, cured the Emperor Farukhsiyar of venereal disease, and was granted effective control of trading rights for the Company in Bengal. In 1690 the purchase of the 3 villages which grew into Calcutta enabled the British to build a fort and consolidate their power.

In 1700, Bengal became an independent Presidency and Calcutta prospered. The *firmans* granted were for trading from the ports but the British took the opportunity of gaining a monopoly over internal trade as well. The internal waterways gave them access to rich resources and to the other commodities was added the export of saltpetre to fuel the wars in Europe.

The Mughals ruled from Delhi through the Nawabs they appointed in the distant parts of their Empire. Following the death of Aurangzeb the authority of Delhi slowly crumbled. In 1756, the 20-year old Siraj-ud-Daula, the then Nawab of Bengal, began to take note of Calcutta's growing wealth. Finding the British strengthening the fortifications (apparently against the French, which he chose not to believe), he attacked Fort William, finding little difficulty in capturing the city. This victory was short lived, for within a year Clive took the city back and then defeated the Nawab at Plassey – a turning point for the British in India.

Through the 19th century W Bengal became the economic and political centre of British India. Agricultural raw materials – indigo and opium in the first half of the century, jute in the second – became staples of trade. Manufacturing and processing developed in the late 19th century, along with engineering industries which grew up with Calcutta's port activities and focus as a railway centre.

Religious and social reform

Calcutta also developed as the major centre of cultural and political activity in modern India. Bengali literature, drama, art and music flourished. Religious reform movements such as the Brahmo Samaj, under the original leadership of Raja Ram Mohan Roy in the 1830s, grew out of the juxtaposition of traditional Hinduism with Christian missionary activity, of which Calcutta was a major centre in the early 19th century. At the end of the century and into the 20th, one of India's greatest poets, Nobel Prize winner Rabindranath Tagore (1861-1941), dominated India's cultural world, breathing moral and spiritual life into the political movement for independence from colonial rule.

Until 1905 Bengal had included much of modern Bihar and Orissa, as well as the whole of Bengal. Lord Curzon's partition of Bengal in 1905 created 2 new states; E Bengal and Assam, and W Bengal, Bihar and Orissa. It roused fierce political opposition among Bengalis, and also encouraged the split between Muslims and Hindus which finally resulted in Bengali Muslim support for the creation of Pakistan and partition in 1947. The division into the 2 new states was accompanied by the migration of over 5 million people and appalling massacres as Hindus and Muslims fled. W Bengal was directly affected by the struggle to create Bangladesh in 1971, when about 10 million refugees fled into the state from E Pakistan after 25 Mar 1971. Most of them returned after Bangladesh gained its independence in Dec 1971.

Culture

People

The majority of the people are Bengalis. Tribal groups include Santals, Oraons and Mundas in the plains and the borders of Chota Nagpur, and Lepchas and Bhotias in the Himalaya. Over 85% of the population speak Bengali. Hindi, Urdu, and tribal languages account for most of the remainder.

Cuisine

Bengalis are sometimes said to be obsessed about what they eat. The men often take a keen interest in buying the most important elements of the day's meal, namely fresh fish from the bazar. Typically, it is river fish, the most popular being Hilsa and Bekti or the more widely available shell fish, especially king prawns. Bekti is grilled or fried (tastier than the 'fried fish' of the W as it has often been marinated in mild spices first). The prized smoked Hilsa, although delicious, requires patience as it has thousands of fine bones which are best removed with the help of your teeth and fingers. Fish comes in many forms as *macher jhol* in a thin gravy, *macher jhal* spicy and hot, or prepared with coconut milk and spices to produce *malai curry* 'chop' with a covering of mashed potato and crumbs or *chingri macher* 'cutlet', (flattened king prawn 'fillets', crumbed and fried). 'Chop' and 'cutlet' (as with the *macher* 'fry') are hangovers from the days of the Raj but bear little resemblance to the original!

Bengali cooking uses mustard oil and mustard which grows in abundance, and a subtle mixture of spices. *Panch Phoron*, a mixture of 5 spices (cumin, mustard, fennel, onion seed and fenugreek) is used in some vegetable preparations. You will only find the true flavour of Bengali cooking in someone's home (or a special restaurant; most fight shy of the subtle taste and tend to offer the universally available N Indian cuisine).

Mishti, sweetmeats are another distinctive feature. Many are milk based and the famous sandesh, *roshogolla*, *roshomalai*, *pantua* and *Lady Kenny* are prepared with a kind of cottage cheese. There are dozens on offer with different textures, shapes, colours and taste, but nearly all of them, though delicious, are very sweet. One which needs a special mention is pale pinkish brown *mishti doi*, an excellent sweet yoghurt eaten as a dessert, typically sold in hand-thrown clay pots. If travelling outside Calcutta, try the specialities – *mihidana* and *sitabhog* in Barddhaman, *sarpuria* in Krishnanagar and *Lady Kenny* in Ranaghat.

NB: It is not safe to buy sweets on the road side as they are often covered with flies. However, the good sweet shops have glass display cases or you may catch a sweet-meat maker at work in front of his shop and buy your favourite as it emerges from the boiling syrup!

Crafts

Silk has been woven in India for more than 3500 years and there are references to Bengal and Assam silk in manuscripts of the 2nd century. The tradition continues with the weaving of the natural coloured wild silk called *tassar*. Bengal silk, commonly found as block-printed saris, has had a revival in the exquisite brocade weaving of *baluchari*, produced in the past under royal patronage, and is carried out today in Bankura. The saris are woven in traditional style with untwisted silk and have beautiful borders and *pallu* (the end section), which often depict horses, peacocks, flowers and human figures. Fine cotton is woven into saris, fabrics and articles for everyday use (see page 288).

Kantha embroidery, also typically Bengali, uses a quilting technique of running stitches to make patterns of birds, flowers and animals or scenes from mythology. Several layers of old cotton *dhoti*, the long piece of fine white cloth worn by men, were traditionally stitched together to form the basis for a quilt or shawl which would then be embroidered from the centre outwards with thicker coloured threads retrieved from the borders of old *saris* worn by the women. The outlines of the patterns would be filled in by lines of close stitches, often in another colour, while the ground would have similar stitches in white, the whole reinforcing the old cloth while producing attractive useful articles. Villages developed their distinctive designs, although each item produced would be unique, often the work of several pairs of hands as women sat around to work on a single piece. Today, *kanthas* for sale are new, usually made up into small pictures, cushion covers, bedspreads and *kurtas*.

Other crafts The Bankura horse has become a symbol of pottery in W Bengal which still flourishes in the districts of Bankura (see page 641), Midnapore and Birbhum. Shola pith, the core of the sponge wood that grows in marshy areas of Bengal, is fashioned into delicate flowers, toys and deities by Malakars and are in great demand during festivals. The *Sola Topee* or the pith helmet, so inseparable from the colonial in India, was derived from this *shola*, not the solar of the sun! Soft soap-stone is used for carving out copies of temple images and for making small boxes and plates. Shell craft is another speciality as it is considered auspicious for women to wear conch shell bangles. The ivory carvers produce superb decorative items, a skill developed in the Mughal period and then during British rule for the European market. Ivory export is now banned, and plastic has largely replaced ivory in inlay work. Metal workers produce brass and bell-metal ware while the tribal Dokra casters still follow the ancient *cire perdu* or lost-wax method. High quality jewellery is made, as it has been for centuries, and very fine items of gold and silver are available. In contrast, the Kalighat *pat paintings* are in a primitive style using bold colours and mythological themes. The origin of the pats go back to a time when travelling patuas, painter-story-tellers, went from village to village entertaining folk with their tales, using illustrated scrolls.

Modern West Bengal

Government

W Bengal has 42 seats in the Lok Sabha and a State Assembly of 294 seats. Since the mid-1960s political life has been dominated by the confrontation between the Communist Party of India Marxist (the CPM) and the Congress Party. The CPM has held power in the State Assembly continuously since June 1977. In 1987 it held 187 out of 294 seats. The Congress is the second largest party, winning 40 seats in the 1987 State Assembly elections. It has performed consistently better in the Lok Sabha parliamentary elections.

Economy

Agriculture Rice is the dominant food crop, but there are dozens of varieties suited to the small contrasts in height, soil type and season of growth. Jute (*Corchorus*) has become an important cash crop since Independence. It grows to a height of between 3 and 4m. The best jute grows on freshly deposited river silt, found far more widely in Bangladesh than in W Bengal. Tea is the second major cash crop, see page 656.

Industry & resources Bengal became famous for its jute, which is twisted to produce a variety of household items. Jute production was mechanised in 1855, powerlooms being introduced 4 years later. A large number of prosperous mills were established along the banks of the Hugli. After 1947, and the partition of

E Bengal from the W, the jute mills in the Indian side were separated from the jute growing areas and Pakistan made it impossible to export raw jute to India. This was tackled by increasing production of jute as a cash crop in E India, while Bangladesh has set up its own jute mills.

Across the margins of W Bengal, Bihar and Orissa lie India's richest mineral resources. Coal was first exploited at Raniganj in 1774-75, but has been mined continuously since 1815. The development of the railways boosted demand, in the 1970s accounting for 20% of the total coal output, which by 1994 had reached over 200 m tonnes. In the 1950s the Damodar River was dammed in a scheme to bring wide-ranging, integrated development, modelled on the Tennessee Valley Authority in the USA. Flood control in downstream areas of W Bengal, irrigation and power development have made it a major economic region. A new steel mill was commissioned at Durgapur in 1957, and Asansol, Burdwan and Burnpur have all become important industrial towns.

Alongside the jute industry, Calcutta developed a range of engineering industries, diversifying into production of cars and lorries and more recently into electronics. However, the loss of raw jute supplies from E Pakistan coupled with a very hostile climate for investment in the 1960s and 1970s contributed to very slow overall growth compared to other Indian cities.

Despite the growth of power generation, demand has constantly outstripped supply. Much of W Bengal, including Calcutta, suffers major power cuts (referred to as 'loadshedding'), especially during the summer, often making it almost unbearable.

REGIONAL TOURS

The major places of interest in W Bengal, other than those in and around Calcutta, are in 4 areas; the W, north-central, far N and S. Each of the groups of places described below could make a self-contained tour of 2 or 3 days by train, car or bus, centred on Calcutta, though flying from Calcutta to Bagdogra shortens the time necessary to see Darjiling. In a more extended tour it would be possible to link the groups together without returning to Calcutta.

CALCUTTA TO SANTINIKETAN

The road goes W of Calcutta to Bishnapur, with its Bengal terracotta temples. The modern steel town of Durgapur has massive plants for steel ingots and high-tech alloys. Santiniketan is a quiet contrast, with the Vishva Bharati University ('Abode of Peace') and many local festivities.

ROUTES Immediately W of Calcutta are the flat floodplains of the Damodar River, once ravaged by periodic floods but now protected by the massive Damodar Valley Project scheme. The NH 2 leaves Calcutta travelling due N before turning towards the administrative and industrial town of Barddhaman (formerly Burdwan), Durgapur and Asansol, now the heavy industrial belt of W Bengal. It has a lot of heavy traffic.

There is also a quieter road W which leaves the NH 2 N of Srirampur (Serampore) to Jairambati (103 km) and Kamarpukur (5 km).

Jairambati and Kamarpukur

These small towns are noted as the birth places of Sri Ramakrishna (17 Feb 1836) and his wife Sri Saradamani. The Ramakrishna Mission has an Ashram in spacious gardens at Kamarpukur and the place where Ramakrishna was born is marked by a marble statue. A few kilometres from Kamarpukur are the ruins of the **Garh Mandaran fort**. Ac-

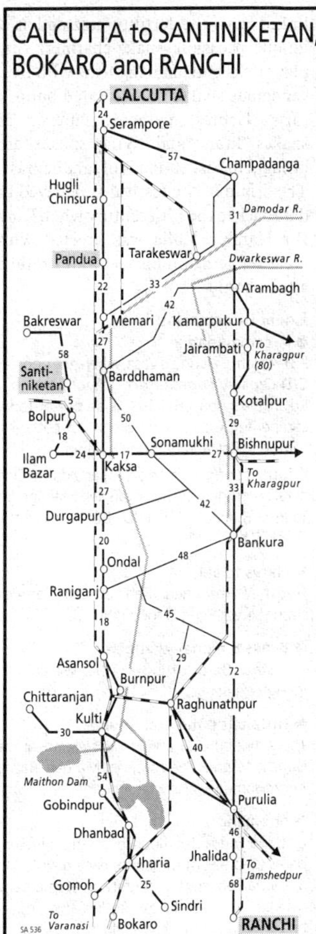

commodation Simple *Mission Guest House*. To reserve contact Secretary. The road continues W to Bishnupur (45 km).

Bishnupur

Pop 56,000; *STD Code* 032442. This was the seat of the Malla Kings, the warrior rulers who administered this part of Bengal from the late 16th century until the British sold it by auction to the Maharajah of Burdwan 200 years later. The Mallas were great patrons of the arts, architecture, sculpture and music. Bishnupur is also the birth place of the Dhrupad style of classical Indian vocal music and is famous for the 17th and 18th century Bengal terracotta temples.

Local industry Local handicrafts include silk, tassar, conch-shell and bell-metal ware and the famous terracotta 'Bankura horse', *Dokra* and also slate statues and artefacts. Bengali sweetmeats and flavoured tobacco are Bishnupuri specialities.

Places of interest

There are more than 2 dozen temples mostly dedicated to Krishna and Radha in Bishnupur. The exceptionally ornamental temple architecture which is distinctive of the Malla's reign survives today. The temples have walls built on a square plan but topped with a gently curved roof like Bengali thatched huts, which are built of bamboo and mud. The style was taken across India by the Mughals and later by the Rajputs, and was used to great effect in forts (eg Lahore and Agra). The temples are usually built of brick but sometimes of laterite. The terracotta tiles depict episodes from the epics Ramayana and Mahabharata, but occasionally there are scenes from daily life. The interior consists of a sanctuary (*thakurbari*) and has a platform (*vedi*) for the image on one side. The upper storey has a gallery topped by 1, 5 or even 9 towers.

Most of the temples are concentrated within the fort (built later by Muslim rulers), while a few stand outside. Distances are from the Tourist Lodge. The **Rasmancha** (3 km) is a unique Vishnu shrine. A squat, stepped pyramid, the *thakurbari* is surrounded by passageways. It was built by Bir Hambir in 1587 as a place for all the local Vaishnavite deities to be brought together in a procession from the other temples during the annual Ras festival. The well preserved cannons, in particular the 4m long **Dalmadal** to the S of the Rasmancha, date back to the Mallas. The **Jor Mandir** (5 km), a pair of hut-shaped structures with a single *sikhara*, built of brick in 1655 by Raghunath Singh, is highly ornamented. The panels illustrate battle scenes from the epics, hunters with wild animals, maritime scenes and life at court.

The **Madan Mohan Temple** (5 km), one of the largest, stands in a compound on a 16m square base with a white façade. It was built of brick with terracotta panels in 1694 by King Durjan. **Shyam Rai Temple** (7 km) also built by Raghunath Singh is perhaps the earliest example of the *pancharatna* style, with 5 towers built together in brick with a fine *sikhara*. Each façade is triple arched and the terracotta panels depict stories from the Ramayana and Lord Krishna's life. The **Lalji** and **Madan Gopal** are 17th century examples of temples built of laterite, the former with a single tower and the latter in the *pancharatna* style.

The **Mrinmoyee Mandir** (3 km) is an ancient place of worship dating from AD 997. The temple deity, Durga, is a clay idol. In the courtyard is the curiosity of 9 trees growing together. The **Malla Kings' Fort** (3.5 km) was built by Bir Singh but little remains. The gate of laterite, *pathar durwaza*, has holes drilled in different directions through which the king's soldiers would fire shots. A stone chariot is believed to date back to the 13th century. The moat which used to be served by 7 lakes is partially dry although the water reservoirs can still be seen.

Museum Jogesh Chandra Pura Kirti Bhavan not far from the Tourist Lodge. 1000-1200, 1400-1800 or by request. Contact Manager, Tourist Lodge.

Local festival

The most famous local festival, *Jhapan* takes place in August in honour of the serpent goddess *Manasa*, the daughter of Siva. A regional harvest festival it is linked with the fertility cult and is a unique occasion; snake-charmers display tricks and amazing feats with live, venomous snakes on decorated bullock carts. Cobras, pythons, vipers, rat snakes, kraits and flying snakes are brought in baskets made of cane or grass. The origin of the festival is believed to date back to the 17th century when King Bir Hambir Malla was greeted with great rejoicing on his victorious return after a battle.

Local information

● Accommodation

23 km from Calcutta is Vasa, where the popular **C/D** ***Omar Village Resort*** Diamond Harbour Rd, T (Bishnupur) 615257, is an out-of-town escape for Calcutta dwellers. 22 cottages, some a/c. Restaurant, pool, boating.

F *Tourist Lodge*. Some a/c rm and dorm. One meal is compulsory. Reservations: Manager or Tourist Bureau, 3/2 BBD Bagh, Calcutta, T 238271.

● Places to eat

Guest N Rest, near Rabindranath Tagore's statue serves Bengali food only.

● Banks & money changers

The **State Bank of India**, T 51, will convert foreign exchange.

● Hospitals & medical services

The Bishnupur Sub-Division Hospital (near the Court); *Vishnu Pharmacy* in Maruee Bazar; *Kiron Homeo Hall* in Matukgunge.

● Shopping

Cottage industries flourish in the different *paras* (quarters of the town) each devoted to a specialized craft – pottery in Kamarpara, *sankha* (conch-shell) cutting in Sankharipara and weaving, particularly Baluchari silk saris in Tantipara. You may purchase silks from ***Silk Khadi Seva Mandal***, Boltala, or Bankura horses, clay dolls and folk toys from ***Terracotta Crafts***, ½ km from the Tourist Lodge. ***Shri Hari Sankha Bhandar*** and ***Ma Durga Sankha Bhandar***, Sankharipara, specialize in conch-shell craft. Camera films from ***Chitriniketan***, Matukgunge.

● Transport

Local Car hire: from the *Tourist Lodge* and Kiron Homeo Hall, Matukgunge. **Cycle rickshaws**: widely available.

Train Trains from Haora (Calcutta): Fast Chair Car to Bankura, daily, 1600, 4 hr. Asansol, Gomoh and Purulia Passenger.

Road Bus: WBSTC buses leave Esplanade Terminus in Calcutta daily at 0745 and 0845. Rs 19. Durgapur State Transport Super Express buses leave Durgapur daily at 1115 (journey 1 hr). Rs 26.

ROUTES To visit Durgapur (72 km) from Bishnupur take the road N to Sonamukhi and Kaksa, which is on the NH 2.

Barddhaman

Pop 245,000; *STD Code* 0342
Barddhaman, an administrative and commercial centre, is between Calcutta and Durgapur. Much of the land on either side of the road is irrigated from the Damodar Valley scheme. The road runs close to the Damodar Canal all the way from Memari to Durgapur. This steel town was built in the mid-1950s within easy reach of the rich belt of coal and iron ore. The steel plant, the thermal power projects, and the Fertilizer and Allied Machinery Corp are the places of interest.

Durgapur

BASICS *Population*: 416,000. *Altitude*: 69m. *STD Code*: 0343 *Climate*: Summer Max 46°C, Min 38°C. Winter Max 32°C, Min 29°C. *Annual rainfall*: 1500 mm mostly from Jun to Sep.

Places of interest

Durgapur is a planned city, with land use zoned for different kinds of use. It is also quite widely spaced out. Distances are given from the railway station. The steel plant (10 km) was commissioned in 1957 and now produces over 1.6 million tonnes of ingot steel, and crude tar, ammonium sulphate and crude benzol from the residual gases. A 176 km gas pipe supplies Calcutta with domestic gas from Durgapur. The AVB Heavy Engineering Plant (6 km) an Indo-British enterprise is the largest in the private sector. A joint Japanese-Canadian venture provided technical cooperation to set up the Alloy Steel Project (10 km). The 692m Durgapur Barrage (3 km), controls the 2500 km canal network in the region. Permits to visit are issued by the Public Relations Office, T 483, personal application only. Visiting: 1030-1230, 1430-1630 on weekdays, 0930-1215 on Sat.

Excursions

Maithan, 66 km away has a massive dam and a hydro-electric project.

Local information

● Accommodation

Govt **E** *Tourist Lodge* (T 5476) with 24 rm, all a/c. Restaurant and a very inexpensive **F** *Youth Hostel* nr rly station. Reserve at WBTDC, 3/2, BBD Bagh (E), Calcutta, T 235917. To reserve the Steel Plant's **E** *Durgapur House*, contact PRO, T 3611, Ext 315 or Manager, T 2517. Some private hotels incl the **E** *Durgapur Lodge*, nr rly station, T 5921.

● Places to eat

The *Tourist Lodge*, has a bar, *Kwality* nr the Steel Plant, and *Qaiser* in Nachan Rd, have restaurants.

● Banks & money changer

There are several in town incl the **State Bank of India**.

● Shopping

The main shopping centres are Benachitti Market, the City Centre and the Sector Market of the township. Handicrafts are available from *Gramin* and *Rehabilitation Industries Corp* both in Benachitti.

● Tourist office

PRO, Durgapur Steel Plant, T 3611, Ext 315 provides information. Tourist Information Bureau at city centre.

● Transport

Durgapur is on the main railway line to Calcutta. There are also frequent buses, both to Calcutta (176 km) and to neighbouring towns, including Santiniketan.

ROUTES To reach Santiniketan return to the NH 2. Turn right, and after 16 km (just before the road crosses the railway line) turn left for Bolpur (Population 53,000), the railway station for Santiniketan.

Santiniketan

BASICS *Population*: 34,600. *Climate*: Summer Max 39°C, Min 34 °C. Winter Max 16°C, Min 12°C. *Annual rainfall*: 1250 mm, mainly June-Sep.

Santiniketan was founded by Maharshi Debendranath Tagore, father of Rabindranath Tagore, the Nobel Laureate, who first started an *ashram* here, later named the 'Abode of Peace'. In 1901 his son started an experimental place of learning with a 'classroom' under the trees, and a group of 5 pupils. It went on to become the **Vishva Bharati University** in 1921 which attracts students from all over the world and aspires to be a spiritual meeting ground in a serene, culturally rich and artistic environment. There are faculties in all major disciplines, although the humanities and performing arts dominate, particularly philosophy, Sanskrit, art, Indian music and drama. It also includes agriculture and cottage industries, thus providing employment within the campus. Satyajit Ray, Indira Gandhi and the Maharani of Jaipur are among the famous who studied here. An interesting feature of Santiniketan is the number of sculptures, frescoes, paintings and murals that are to be found around the campus, particularly paintings by Rabindranath and Nandalal Bose and sculptures by Ramkinkar.

Places of interest

The University, where classes are still held in the open-air, is unique. Among the many *Bhavans* are those concentrating on art (Kala Bhavan), music and dance (Sangit Bhavan). Vinaya Bhavan is the Teachers' Training College. **NB**: sightseeing is permitted only after university hours – summer, 1430-1730, winter 1400-1700 and during vacations 0730-1100. Photography is not permitted. Trained guides for Kala Bhavan Galleries. The **Uttarayan Complex** where the poet lived consists of several buildings in distinctive architectural styles. Sadhana **Prayer Hall**, where Brahmo prayers are held on Wed was founded in 1863 (see page 81). It has a polished marble floor usually decorated with *alpana* designs and is surrounded by glass doors with patterns picked out in stained glass.

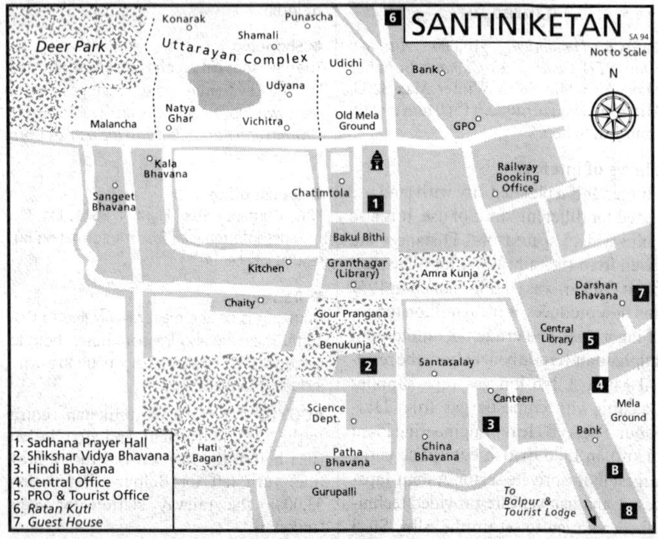

Chhatimtala, where Maharishi Debendranath sat and meditated, is the site at Convocation time of special prayers. In keeping with its simplicity, graduates are presented with a twig with 5 leaves from the *Saptaparni* trees which grow freely in the area. **Sriniketan**, 3 km away, has the Dept of Rural Reconstruction where the country's socio-economic problems are studied and is also a College of Agriculture. Activities include weaving, leather craft, pottery, *Kantha* embroidery and *Batik*. 0800-1000, 1030-1230. Photography with prior permission from the PRO, Viswa Bharati. **NB**: closed on Tue afternoon and Wed.

Museums Rabindra Bhavan (Bichitra), a museum and research centre containing paintings, manuscripts and many objects of interest, including personal belongings which give a picture of Tagore's life and times. 1030-1300, 1400-1630. Closed Tue pm, Wed. No photography. Kala Bhavan Gallery. A rich collection of 20th century Indian art, particularly sculptures, murals and paintings by famous Bengali artists. 1500-1700. Closed Wed. Trained guides. Nandan Museum, Vishva Bharati. 0730-1200, 1400-1600. Closed Wed and Univ holidays. Free. Collection of terracotta, paintings and original tracings of Ajanta murals.

Parks and zoos Ballavpur Deer Park. 3 km. The area of rapidly eroding *khowai* has been reclaimed and now forms a large wooded area with herds of black buck and spotted deer and winter migratory birds. 1000-1600, closed Wed. The Uttarayan Garden is delightful, particularly when the roses are blooming.

Excursions

Bakresvar, 58 km NW of Santiniketan, between Suri and Chinpai. It is known for its sulphurous hot springs, said to have medicinal properties. There are 7 important *kunds* (springs) where the temperature varies from 36°C to 67°C, the hottest being Agnikunda (fire spring). Rare halogen gases have been found here too. Therapeutic qualities of the spring water led the W Bengal Mineral Development Corp to market it under the brand name *Tirtha Salil*. Temples to Siva, Sakti and Vishnu make it a Hindu pilgrimage centre for the 3 principle sects. The 2 important temples are Bakresvar Siva Temple and the Mahishamardini Temple. **Accommodation** W Bengal **E** *Tourist Lodge*, a **F** *Youth Hostel* and an *Inspection Bungalow*. Reservations: Exec Engineer, PWD (Roads), Birbhum, Suri.

Tarapith, 80 km. The Shakti cult has 51 *pithas* (pilgrim sites of special sanctity where the fragments of Kali's body are believed to have fallen). The sage Vashishta is believed to have worshipped the goddess Tara at Tarapith, and Tara's temple is visited from all over the region. It is particularly crowded on the night of the new moon after Dasara. Rail Tarapith is 5 km from Rampurhat Station (bus or cycle rickshaw). Connections to Bolpur.

Local Festivals

Poush Mela (23-25 Dec), is Santiniketan's most important fair. It coincides with the village's Foundation Day and brings thousands of visitors. You have the opportunity not only to see a large number of *Santals*, the tribal group in this region, who may be seen performing dances, but also to hear the *bauls*, Bengal's wandering minstrels. Most are worshippers of Vishnu. They travel from village to village singing their songs, often accompanied by a single string instrument, *ektara*, and a tiny drum. Tribal silver and 'Dokra' metal crafts make attractive buys.

The *Convocation* (Samabartan Utsav) of the University is usually held in Dec when the Prime Minister of India presides, but it is not open to the general public for security reasons. *Magh Mela* at Sriniketan marks the anniversary of the *Brahmo Samaj* and the founding of

Sriniketan. It is an agricultural and rural crafts fair held at the end of Jan. *Vasanta Utsav* in Mar coincides with Holi, *Varsha Mangal* in Jul/Aug during the rainy months and *Saradotsava* in the autumn marks the end of term before the Pujas. Programmes of dance, music and singing are held throughout the year, particularly good during the various festivals.

Local information

● Accommodation

In Bolpur: **D** *Santiniketan Tourist Lodge* with some a/c rm, and **E** and **F** inexpensive dorms (4 and 13 bedded), T 699. **In Santiniketan**: **D** *Mayurakshi*, Prantik. A/c rm. **D** *Aparajita*, Purbapalli, T 828. A/c and non-a/c. Contact 99/5/9B Ballygunge Place, Calcutta, T 756899.

E *Poushali*, Pearsonpalli. 3-7 bedded rm. Restaurant. **E** *Dreamland*, Modrampur Rd, NRI Complex, T 859. Contact KGR Industries, 222 Acharya JC Bose Rd, Calcutta.

Contact PRO, Vishva Bharati, T 751, Ext 6 for **D** *Guest House*, 172 Purbapalli, with a/c rm and **F** *International Guest House* with simple rm, one a/c.

● Places to eat

The *Tourist Lodge, Happy Lodge* and *Poushali* have restaurants but may require prior notice. *Kalor Dokan* is an 'institution' which has become a meeting place for intellectuals and is open all hours. Indian sweet shops have sprung up in its neighbourhood.

● Banks & money changers

State Bank of India in Bolpur and Santiniketan (nr Chitra Cinema) have foreign exchange facilities. Foreign Travellers' Cheques cashed in Santiniketan only.

● Hospitals & medical services

Pearson Memorial Hospital, Santiniketan. *Janata Pharmacy* in Chowrasta, Santiniketan.

● Places of Worship

Brahmo: Prayer Hall, Santiniketan.

Christian: Methodist Church.

● Post & telecommunications

Santiniketan Rd, Bolpur. Santiniketan PO, Chowrasta.

● Shopping

The local embossed leather handbags, purses and belts are particularly popular. Handicrafts are available at *Gramin* and *Sarvodaya Ashram* in Bolpur and the Vishva Bharati *Silpa Sadans* in Santiniketan and Sriniketan.

Books: *Manisha Granthalaya*, Sriniketan Road, Bolpur and *Subarnarekha* in Santiniketan sells rare books.

Photography: Camera films at*Studio Vichitra*, Bolpur and others.

● Tourist office

Tourist Lodge, Bolpur, T 398. PRO, Vishva Bharati Office, T 751. 1000-1700, closed Tue pm, Wed.

● Transport

Local Autorickshaws and **cycle rickshaws**, occasionally **taxis**.

Rail Bolpur is connected to Calcutta by rail from both Haora and Sealdah (147 km). To Calcutta (H): *Shantiniketan Exp*, 3016, daily, 1300, 2¾ hr. Other fast trains from Haora: *Kanchenjunga Exp, Danapur Fast Passenger* and *Viswa Bharati Exp*. Santiniketan, 2 km away, can be reached by taxi or cycle rickshaw.

Road Bus: the road journey on NH2 takes longer (213 km), and can be very slow, but may be a useful way of visiting other places of interest en route.

CALCUTTA TO DARJILING

The northern hill stations have spectacular scenery and views of the Himalaya. Darjiling is the centre for trekking and monasteries can be visited, one of them by the second highest railway in the world. Rhino, elephants, leopards and tigers can be seen in the Jaldapara wildlife sanctuary. NH 34 is the main route N from Calcutta, passing many sites of interest. The first 250 km crosses the Ganga delta to the new Farakka Barrage, then the drier plains of N Bengal to Sikkim, Darjiling and Assam.

Plassey (Palashi)

172 km, became famous after the battle between Robert Clive and Siraj-ud-Daula with his French supporters in 1757, where the British enjoyed their first significant victory, although it was not great in terms of time and lives lost.

CALCUTTA to GANGTOK via DARJILING & KALIMPONG

GANGTOK
27
Namche
Kalimpong
51
Darjiling
29
Kurseong
To Gurumara NP, Jaldapara NP & Guwahati
Tista R.
48
Siliguri
To Guwahati
New Jalpaiguri
103
Kishanganj
31
To Purnea (63 km)
Daleola
68
To Kaliaganj (24 km)
Mahanunda R.
Raiganj
50
To Balurghat (84 km)
Gajol
26
To Pandua (18 km)
Malda
Ingraz Bazar
54
Gaur
Ganga River
Farakka
To Murarai (27 km) & Dumka (80 km)
45
Bhagirathi R.
Jangipur
Murshidabad
6
Baharampur
To Domkal & Jalangi
Palashi
Kaliganj
To Barddhaman (65 km)
50
Jalangi R.
Krishnanagar
19
Shantipur
To Bangaon (74 km) for border crossing
16
Ranaghat
30
Chakdaha
To Bangaon (30 km)
Hugli R.
51
Barasat
To Bangaon & Benapole (53 km)
26
CALCUTTA
SA 537

The monuments on the battlefield include a mound by the river bank which marks the position of the British forces but the meandering Bhagirati river has eroded away much of the site. An *Inspection Bungalow* can be reserved.

ROUTES The NH 34 continues N to Baharampur, formerly an important junction of roads crossing into what is now Bangladesh with routes to the N and W. Leave the NH 34 to travel N for 6 km to Murshidabad (49 km).

Murshidabad

Pop 30,300 Hiuen-Tsang, on his travels in the 7th century described *Karna Suvarna*, the first capital of ancient Bengal, which was nearby. Named after Nawab Murshid Kuli Khan, a Diwan of Bengal, Bihar and Orissa under Emperor Aurangzeb, it became the capital of Bengal in 1705 and remained so up to the time of the battle of Plassey. During the following 3 decades the judicial and revenue functions were moved to Calcutta.

Places of interest

The **Nizamat Kila** on the river bank near the centre of town, encloses the Nawabs' old **Hazarduari** (1000 doors) **Palace** built in the Italian style by one of Mir Jafar's descendants and designed by one of the Bengal Engineers in 1837. It has an imposing domed banqueting hall with mirrored doors, an impressive chandelier and an ivory throne. It is now a splendid museum with a portrait gallery, a circular durbar hall and a library and contains a rare collection of old arms, curios, china and paintings. Closed Fri.

The **Imambara** (1847) within the walls is one of the largest in the region. Also Italianate in style, it is believed to have replaced the original built by Siraj-ud-Daula. The domed, square pavilion with a verandah nearby may be what remains of the original Imambara that reputedly contains earth from the Karbala in Mecca, justifying the inscription found on the new Imambara. There are numerous 18th century monuments in the city. **Jafaragunj Deorhi** known as the traitor's gate was where Mir Jafar, and later his son Miran lived and where the latter is believed to have murdered Siraj-ud-daula. The **Kat-gola** which was the garden-house of a rich Jain merchant houses a collection of curios and has an old Jain temple. The **Palace of Jagat Sett**, one of the richest financiers of the 18th century is 2 km from the Jafargung Cemetery which is to the N of the palace and where lie buried many of the Nawabs. The **Katra Mosque** (1724) outside the city proper, modelled on the Great Mosque at Mecca was built by Murshid Kuli Khan where he lies buried under the staircase. You can still see some of the decorative panels on the outside of the ruins as well as 2 octagonal minarets. It was once an important centre of learning.

3 km S of the city is **Moti Jheel** (pearl lake), an ox-bow lake, and the ruins of **Begum Ghaseti's palace**. Only a mosque and a room remain. Another important sight is **Khosbagh** (Garden of Delight) across the river. There are 3 walled enclosures entered by the outer enclosure, a flower garden, from the E. The 2nd enclosure is the cemetery where Siraj-ud-Daula and Alivardi Khan are buried. The 3rd enclosure has a tank and what was once a 'travellers' rest house'.

Local information

● Accommodation

WBTDC **F** *Tourist Lodge* at Baharampur, 12 km away. 26 rms, some a/c, restaurant. Reservations in Calcutta, T 285917. **F** *Youth Hostels* at Lalbagh and Murhsidabad. Reserve through Youth Services, 32/1 BBD Bagh S, Calcutta, T 280626.

● Shopping

Woven and handblock printed Bengal silk saris, bell metal ware and ivory carving are the main local industries. Murshidabad also produces excellent mangoes, of which there are more than 55 varieties.

● Transport

Train Murshidabad can be reached by the *Lalgola Passenger* train from Calcutta (S).

Road Bus: buses leave the Esplanade Terminus, Calcutta for Baharampur, 12 km; from there you can get a taxi, bus or cycle rickshaw. To hire a tourist car or taxi, contact Tourist Bureau or ITDC.

ROUTES From Murshidabad return to Baharampur to rejoin the NH 34 N. It crosses the Ganga by the Farakka Barrage (95 km). Immediately to the W are the **Rajmahal Hills**, ranging in height from 460 to 575m. They are the north-easternmost extension of the Peninsula, made up of black basalts much used in the building of Malda. The alluvium which makes up the surface of the Ganga Plain is at its thinnest at this point. There is a series of historically important sites on the road northwards. The first of these on the road to Ingraz (English) Bazar (*Pop* 177,000) is Gaur (20 km), followed by Malda and Pandua, both to the N of (Ingraz) Bazar.

Gaur, Malda and Pandua

Gaur

Situated on the ancient site of Lakshanavati Gaur, now almost lost, Gaur was the capital of the Senas where an exceptional complex of basalt buildings once stood. Its situation on the Ganga bank within easy reach of the Rajmahal hills, with their fine black basalt, made it possible for the gifted stone masons to construct both religious and secular buildings of great beauty and architectural skill. It was the capital of King Sasanka in the 7th century, followed by the Buddhist Pala and Hindu Sena kings. Gaur became famous as a centre of education, art and culture during the reign of the latter in the 12th century. Its fortunes fluctuated from the beginning of the 13th century when it was invaded by Bhaktiar Khalji. The Fakhr-ud-din, founders of an Afghan dynasty, captured it in the 14th century and transferred their capital to Pandua for a time, plundering the temples to construct their

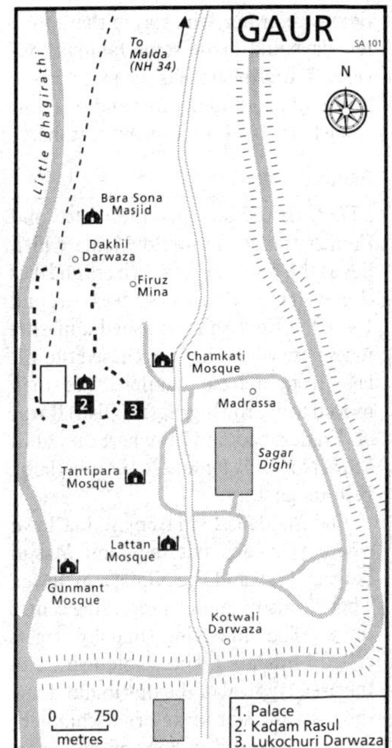

own mosques and tombs, and destroying most of these buildings. Gaur regained its importance in 1500 until it was sacked by Sher Shah Suri in 1537 (see page 49). The city's population was wiped out by plague in 1575.

Places of interest Muslim monuments of the Sultanate period displaying various architectural styles are strewn around the deserted city. The remains of the embankments of the Fort are to the S on the bank of the Bhagirati. The **Dakhil Darwaza**, the main gateway to the fort with its 5-storeyed towers in the 4 corners, was constructed in the early part of the 15th century out of small red bricks embossed with decorations. The façade is broken up by turrets and circular bastions, producing a striking contrast of light and shade, with decorative motifs of suns, rosettes, lamps and fretted borders. During the 15th century, a number of mosques and mausolea were built in the new architectural style. The usual courtyard of the mosque gave way to a covered hall, possibly as a practical measure against monsoon rains. The length of the façade was broken up by several pointed arches, while the interior was divided into arched aisles supported by pillars giving the impression of a church nave. The intersections of the aisles were marked by a dome and the important W wall of the mosque had several recessed *mihrabs*.

Inside SE corner of the Fort is the **Baisgazi Wall** which enclosed the Old Palace. It got its name from its height of '22 yards' (20m). This high brick wall is 5m broad at its base decreasing to about 3m at the top. The **Royal Palace** with its *darbar*, private quarters and *harem* were supposed to have stood within the enclosure. **Kadam Rasul** is to the E of the Palace within the perimeter of the fort. The domed square building with the Bengali thatch style roof was erected in 1513 to house the relic of The Prophet, a footprint in stone. The Royal Eastern Gate or **Lukochuri Darwaza** (hide-and-seek gate) is a large 2 storeyed structure about 20m long and 13m wide although the entrance itself is only 3m across. Believed to have been built by Shah Shuja around 1655 it is in a later Mughal style. The **Kotawali Darwaza** (late 15th century), in the S wall is now in ruins but once had a magnificent archway. It is close to the border with Bangladesh.

1 km or so E from the SE corner of the fort, on the main road, is the **Tantipara Mosque**, built around 1475 in what was probably the *tanti* or weavers' quarter of the town. It is in superbly decorated red brick with 5 entrance arches and octagonal turrets in the corners. Another km S is the **Lattan** or the Painted Mosque built by Yusuf Shah in 1475 although the legend holds that a dancing girl of the Royal Court was responsible for it. It is notable for its elegant structure and the decorative bands

of blue, green yellow and white glazed tiles which were used to adorn it.

About a km outside the fort's E wall is the **Firuz Minar**, probably built as a victory tower by Sultan Firuz Shah in 1486 but also used to call the faithful to prayer. It is about 26m high in 5-storeys and 19m in circumference. The lower 3 storeys are 12 sided while the upper 2 are circular. The striking feature of the tower is the introduction of blue and white glazed tiles which are used in addition to the terracotta and brick. The crude quality of the tiles contrasts with the excellence achieved by the Hindu craftsmen in producing terracotta decorations by that time. A spiral staircase inside leads to the top chamber with its 4 windows.

Bara Sona Masjid, also known as Baroduari, is outside the fort, to the NE, and is the largest of the monuments. The great golden mosque was built in 1526 and is an enormous rectangular structure built of brick with stone facing with a large open square in front. There were arched gateways on 3 sides and you enter through one 8m high and 2m wide. There appear to have been 44 domes over the 4 arched colonnades and you can see the quality of the carving in marble in what remains of the minarets.

The **Chika Mosque** (bat mosque), not far from the Kadam Rasul is a single domed structure which must have freely used Hindu idols in its construction. Although this early 15th century building is in ruins, you can still see evidence of this in the stone work of the doors and lintels. Nearby is the **Chamkati Mosque**, probably built in 1475. The remains still show the vaulted ceiling of the verandah and there are medallions visible between the arches in the main chamber.

Ramkeli not far from the Bara Sona Masjid has the Madan Mohan Jiu Mandir and is of particular religious significance for the followers of **Sri Chaitanya**, the 14th century Bengali religious reformer, who stayed there for a few days and made some famous converts. **Tamaltola** marks the place where he meditated under a tree and pilgrims come here to see a footprint in stone.

Malda

STD Code 03512. Once the Dutch and French traded from Old Malda which lies at the confluence of 2 rivers and was thus well placed to act as a port. Around 1680, the English established a market town here when they purchased the village from a local landlord and then moved to nearby Ingraz (**English**) **Bazar** or (Englezabad) in 1771 where they built a fort. Now only famous for its juicy large Fajli mangoes.

Old Malda is 4 km from Malda Town where you can visit the Jami Masjid built in 1596 and the Nimasarai Tower. There is also a mango processing centre there. The low-lying marshy tracts called **bhils** are a noticeable feature of the area. Typical of the moribund delta, they are formed in deserted channels, cut-off bends and ox-bows of the Ganga. From Nov to mid-Feb they attract a large number of wild fowl including the Siberian goose.

The **Jami Masjid** was built in 1596 out of decorated brick and stone and displays some good carving on the entrance pillars. The 17m tower across the river dating from the same period has strange stones embedded on the outer surface which may have once been used to display beheaded criminals.

Malda museums established in 1937, has a collection of stone images, coins and inscriptions from Gaur and Pandua, the 2 medieval towns nearby.

• **Accommodation D** *Purbanchal*. Reservations: 18 NS Bose Rd, Calcutta, T 224278. **E** *Meghdoot Lodge*, some A/c. **F** *Malda Tourist Lodge*, T 2213. 13 rm, 2 a/c. Restaurant. Reservations: WBTDC, T 285917. **E** *Rly Retiring Rooms* incl a/c, and dorm. Being modernised, helpful staff.

• **Services** Malda has all essential amenities

with several banks, post offices, shops and hospitals.

• **Transport Local Rickshaws** are the common means of transport but buses, taxis and **tongas** are available for visiting Gaur and Pandua. **Taxis**: take you to both Gaur and Pandua for about Rs 200. **Bus**: seats on local buses only cost a few rupees. You can get a taxi or bus to Murshidabad. **Train Calcutta (H)**: *Kanchenjunga*, 2558 (AC/II), daily, 1410, 6¾ hr. **Road Bus**: N Bengal STC operate regular express services to Calcutta, 8 hr. Reservations: Esplanade Terminus, Calcutta or the Malda office on Krishna Jiban Sanyal Rd, T 2465.

Pandua

18 km from Malda, alternated with Gaur as a capital of Bengal between 1338 and 1500, when it was abandoned. Some ruins show clearly how the Muslims made free use of material from Hindu temples near Malda. The old brick-paved road, nearly 4m wide and about 10 km long, passes through the town and most of the monuments stand close to it.

Places of interest The **Adina Masjid** (1369), perhaps the most outstanding mosque of eastern India, sadly in a poor state of repair, gives an idea of Muslim architecture in medieval Bengal, with evidence of 12th century Sena architecture. 154m from N to S and 86m E to W, comparable to the great 8th century mosque at Damascus, it was built between 1364 and 1374 by Sultan Sikander Shah. The space is enclosed by pillared aisles, 5 bays deep on the W sanctuary side and 3 on the others, using 260 pillars in all. In the interior is a screen of 88 arches enclosing an open quadrangle with the mosque to the W. It seems to have incorporated the *sikhara*, a tall ornate tiered structure, and trefoil arches and is remarkable in the absence of a large entrance gateway.

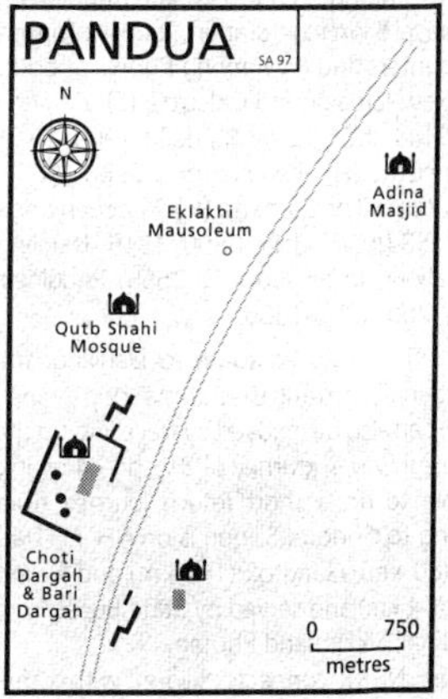

Although the upper part of the building and the arches and domes were built of brick, most of the substructure was of basalt masonry plundered from existing Hindu temples and palaces; in many instances the carved surfaces were inserted into walls. The pillars may have been taken from earlier Hindu structures too. A small doorway in the W back wall of the mosque clearly shows evidence of having been removed from an earlier Vishnu temple which exhibited not only the stone masons' skill but the exceptional advance made by the metal workers of the time.

The **Eklakhi Mausoleum** built of brick around 1412 with a large single dome, has a Hindu idol carved on its front lintel. The octagonal chamber housing 3 tombs, has outer walls decorated with finely carved terracotta bricks and the ceiling inside ribbed and plastered with decorations. The **Qutb Shahi Mosque** also called the *Sona* or golden mosque was built in 1582 in brick and stone and had ten domes. Further along are the **Chhoti and Bari Dargah**, the 17th century shrines to Saint Nur Qutbul Alam and Harazarat Shah Jalal Tabrizi. They are in ruins but within their campus are relics of various quarters, baths, prayer stations, kitchens and the Bibi Mahal.

NB: Percy Brown's volumes on Indian Architecture have detailed descriptions of Bengal's temples and Muslim tombs and mosques.

ROUTES The road route to Darjiling via Siliguri from Ingraj Bazar continues up the NH 34, a distance of 334 km. Alternatively it is possible to travel by air or train (see below).

Siliguri

Population 227,000, *Altitude* 125m *STD Code* 0353 Surrounded by tea plantations, Siliguri has little of interest in itself, but is a base of travel into the hills and to the Jaldapara National Park.

Local information

● Tours

Mirik via Sukna, Rs 50; Dooars, Jalpeswar, Jaldapara via Phuntsholing, Rs 350-450 (weekends); By taxi Jaldapara overnight at *Madarihat Lodge*, Rs 100, *Holong Lodge*, Rs 114. **Note** Hill Cart Rd is officially Tenzing Norgay Rd.

● Accommodation

C *Sinclairs*, Mallaguri, start of airport road, T 22674. 54 rm, some a/c. Good restaurant, bar, pool. Rec.

D *Ranjit*, Hill Cart Rd, T 22056. Some a/c rm. **D** *Gateway*, Sevoke Rd, T 23539. 60 rm, some a/c. Nr bus stand. **D** *Kabira*, Hill Cart Rd, T 22888. 28 rm, some a/c. **D** *Viramma Resorts*, Sevoke Rd, T 26222. 100 rm, some a/c. Nr bus stand.

● Budget hotels

E *Hill Mount View*, Hill Cart Rd, T 25919. Very pleasant, clean. Chinese restaurant. Off-season discount. Rec. **E** *Hikanaya*, rec for clean large rm with bath.

F *Air View*, Hill Cart Rd, T 21160. Restaurant. **F** *Railway Retiring Rooms*, at Siliguri Junc, T 20017, and New Jalpaiguri, T 21199. 4 rm and 6 dorm beds in each.

WBTDC has several: **D** *Mainak Tourist Lodge*, Hill Cart Rd, T 20986. 38 rm, some a/c more expensive. Satellite TV, well-kept gardens. Very good restaurant and bar with live band some nights, car hire, garden. Highly rec. Accommodation can be booked here for Jaldapara Wildlife Sanctuary (*Madarihat Lodge*, see page 653). **F** *Tourist Lodge*, Hill Cart Rd nr Junc rly station, T 21028. 10 rm with bath, dorm. **F** *Youth Hostel*, Kangchendzonga Stadium. 130 beds in dorms. At Khalpara: **F** *Maheshwari Bhavan*, with 200 beds. **F** *Agra Bhawan*, with 100 beds can be reserved through T 21466.

● Shopping

On Hill Cart Rd: Bidhan and Hongkong Markets. AK Choudhary's cane work, Mongaldeep Bldg.

● Tourist office

W Bengal Tourism, 1st Flr, Hill Cart Rd, T 21632. Bhutan and Sikkim, also nr rly station.

● Transport

Air Nearest airport, **Bagdogra** (90 km). **Indian Airlines**: to **Calcutta** M,W,F,Su, 1435, 1 hr; **Delhi**, M,W,F,Su, 1150, 2 hr; **Guwahati**, M,W,F,Su, 0950, 1 hr. Transfer by car or coach adds another 2½-3½ hr. Taxis charge approx Rs 100/ person when carrying 7; the W Bengal Tourism Coach costs Rs 55. Indian Airlines, *Belle Vue Hotel*, Chowrasta, T 2355. Weekdays 1000-1700, Sun 1000-1300. Tourist Information counter.

Train Siliguri, and New Jalpaiguri, 5 km away are the nearest stations to Darjiling. Each is connected by a good network to other parts of the country. The 586 km rail journey from Calcutta to NJ takes about 13 ½ hr. To NJ from Calcutta (**S**), 3143, daily, 1915, 13½ hr from Calcutta. Then taxi or cycle rickshaw (Rs15) to Siliguri for buses to Darjiling or the toy train. Check beforehand if the train is running as services may be disrupted by landslides during rains. Dep NJ station 0715, 0900, 8 hr return from Darjiling 0825, 1000. **NB:** For long distance rail journeys from New Jalpaiguri, first buy tickets at Siliguri (Central Reservations Office, Bidhan Rd nr Stadium; T 23333. NJ, T 20017). For 1st Cl tickets, avoid queueing by going to Chief Res Officer at side of building. Then travel 5 km to NJ station. Tourist Information counters and *Rly Retiring Rooms* at both. From New Jalpaiguri to **Calcutta (S)**: *Darjiling Mail*, 3144 (AC/CC&AC/II), daily, 1900, 13¾ hr; **Calcutta (H)**: *Kamrup Exp*, 5660 (AC/II), daily, 1720, 13 hr. **Calcutta (H)**: *Kanchenjunga Exp*, 2558 (AC/II), daily, 0800, 12½. Darjiling Rly Station: Reservations: T 2555. Enquiries: 1000-1200, 1300-1600.

Road The views en route to Darjiling, the mountain villages and the Batasia Loop ('windy place') can also be enjoyed by travelling up the State Highway, a journey of 3½ hr – 4 hr. It is possible to do a short return journey from Darjiling to Ghoom. Siliguri is on NH 31; Darjiling (80 km), Gangtok (114 km) and Kalimpong (54 km) and served by State Buses from WB, Bihar, Sikkim and Bhutan.

Bus: NH31 connects Siliguri with other

parts of India. You may wish to drive from **Calcutta** (570 km) and visit other places of interest on the way. The overnight N Bengal STC's 'Rocket' bus service is faster than the train, dep 2100, 12 hr, Rs 125, a/c Rs 250. Reserve seats in Calcutta, T 281854 or in Burdwan Rd, Siliguri, T 20531. They can be very full and noisy – not a relaxing way to travel! N Bengal State Transport Corp, Darjiling, T 3133. From **Siliguri to Darjiling**, travel by taxi (Rs 700), W Bengal STC bus (4 hr, Rs 30) or more comfortable Tourist Bus (min 6 passengers). **Darjiling to Siliguri or Bagdogra**, Tourist bus leaves from traffic island nr Keventers. Tickets from Tourist Office (*Bellvue Hotel*). Main taxi stand, Chowk Bazar. One recent visitor claimed that "for thrills and spills, no fairground attraction can rival the narrow hairpinned, switchback road that climbs the Himalayan foothills to Dajilling."

Buses for Kalimpong dep 1130 to 1645 (3½ hr). WBSTC and more comfortable Tourist buses to Darjiling. Bus Stand, Burdwan Rd, T 20531. N Bengal STC Buses, Sevok Rd, T 20531. Taxis opp *Air View Hotel*, Hill Cart Rd and on Sevok Rd, and rly stations to connect with most trains. Buses to Madarihat (for Jaldapara) 10 min walk from *Mainak* leave from bus station on Hill Cart Rd.

Nepal: buses to Kakarbhitta, border town lacking suitable accommodation (see below under Darjiling). From there dep at 0400 or 0500 to arrive at Kathmandu, same evening.

NB: You are advised to arrive in Siliguri or New Jalpaiguri by daylight.

Jaldapara Wildlife Sanctuary

Approach

160 km from Bagdogra airport, 224 km from Darjiling. The Jaldapara Sanctuary covers an area of 116 sq km situated close to Phuntsoling in Bhutan with the river Torsa flowing through and trained elephants are available to take visitors around. Best season Nov-Apr when forest cover is thinner.

Wildlife

The riverine forests of *sal, khair, sheeshu* harbour the one-horned rhino, elephants, wild boar, bison, deer, leopard, gaur and the occasional tiger.

Park information

● Accommodation

Simple and inexpensive, at **Hollong**: **E** *Forest Lodge*, built of timber on stilts deep inside the sanctuary, 6 km from Madarihat. 7 rm (all meals obligatory). The lodge is very popular since it is close to the sanctuary and also en route to Phuntsholing in Bhutan. Book well in advance through Tourist Bureau, Siliguri, T 21632, DFO, Calcutta, T 222774 or Coochbehar, T 247.

At **Madarihat**: **F** ***Travellers' Haven Tourist Lodge***, on park fringe, T 30. 8 rm and restaurant (1 meal obligatory). Reserve direct or through Tourist Bureau, Siliguri, T 21632, Darjiling, T 2050 or Calcutta WBTDC, T 285917.

At **Baradabri**: **F** ***Youth Hostel and Lodge***, 4 km from Hasimara rly station;18 km from Madarihat. 3 rm, 14 beds in 4 dorm. Meagre catering. Reserve through DFO, Jalpaiguri, T 838, Coochbehar, T 247, Tourist Centre, Jalpaiguri, T 183 or WBTDC, Calcutta, T 285917.

At **Hasimara**: **F** ***Nilpara Forest Bungalow***. 2 rm, very basic. Facilities for cooking. Caretaker will prepare a simple meal if requested; remember to take all provisions.

● Transport

Air Indian Airlines has daily flights from Calcutta to Bagdogra (¾ hr) and also from Guawahati and Delhi. From airport, bus to Siliguri and then 4 hr scenic drive through tea gardens to Jaldapara (155 km). There is an airfield at Hasimara.

Train Hasimara Station (4 km from park) has trains from Siliguri Junc.

Road Bus: express buses from Calcutta to Madarihat or Siliguri to Park (128 km). Forest Dept transport to Hollong inside the sanctuary.

Darjiling

Population: 73,000. *Altitude:* 2134m. *STD Code* 0354 Between Jun-Sep the monsoons bring heavy downpours, sometimes causing landslides. Winter evenings are cold.

NB: Darjiling suffers from seasonal water shortages and regular 'load shedding', ie power cuts. After dark the town often has no lights. A torch is essential.

ENTRY REQUIREMENTS Foreigners entry restrictions have been completely withdrawn with regard to travel in the Darjiling area.

Darjiling (formerly 'Darjeeling' which is still in common usage) – *place of the thunderbolt* or possibly *Dorja the mystical*, and the surrounding area once belonged to the Rajas of Sikkim although parts were annexed from time to time by the Bhutanese and Nepalis. The East India Company's intervention and the subsequent return of the territory's sovereignty to the Rajas of Sikkim, however, led to the British obtaining permission to gain the site of the hill-station called *Darjiling* in 1835, in return for an annual payment. It was practically uninhabited and thickly forested – "a worthless, uninhabited mountain", but soon grew into a popular health resort after a road and several houses were built and tea growing was introduced. It is a favourite tourist resort for Bengalis, although in the late 1980s political disturbances greatly decreased its popularity. The situation has now improved and it is recovering from its run down appearance.

Built on a crescent shaped ridge, it faces the Himalaya, the surrounding hills thickly covered with coniferous forests or terraced tea gardens. The upper reaches were originally occupied by the Europeans who built houses with commanding views. Down the hillside on terraces sprawled the humbler huts, tenements and bazars of the Indian town. The Bengal Govt escaped from the Calcutta heat to take up its official summer residence here. The Shrubbery (Govt House) is at the N end on Birch Hill with St Andrew's Church at the highest point.

The railway station is in the lower part of town on Hill Cart Rd, with the taxi and bus stands. The Chowrasta is a focal point with the busy Mall and Nehru Rd leading off it. The lower and upper roads are linked by a series of connecting roads and steps.

The Gurkha National Liberation Front has contiinued to cause sporadic violence.

Places of interest

Believed to be the site of the Mahakala cave, **Observatory Hill** (now known as Chaurashtra), sacred to Siva, offers an excellent viewing point for the twin peaks of Kangchendzonga. A Red Hat Buddhist monastery which stood here was destroyed in the 19th century but gave its name to the hill station. Even during the monsoons it is worth rising before dawn as you may catch a glimpse of the peaks early in the morning. **NB:** beware of the monkeys: they bite.

Aloobari Monastery on Tenzing Norgay Rd is open to visitors. Tibetan and Sikkimese handicrafts, made by the monks, for sale.

Ghoom Monastery 8 km. *Altitude* 2550 m. The Yiga-Choling Gompa, a yellow hat Buddhist Monastery, the most famous in the area, was built in 1875. It has a 5m gilded statue of *Maitreya* (future) Buddha and famous Buddhist scriptures. Visit by 'Toy' train (Apr-Jun, Oct-Nov). Camera fee Rs 10. Attractive village.

Senchal Lake Close to Tiger Hill is the lake that supplies Darjiling with water. It is a pleasant picnic spot. Pass (nominal fee) from entrance.

Tiger Hill 11 km. *Altitude* 2590 m. It is

CLIMATE: DARJILING

	Jan	Feb	Mar	Apr	May	Jun	Jul	Aug	Sep	Oct	Nov	Dec	Av/Tot
Max (°C)	9	11	15	18	19	19	20	20	20	19	15	12	16
Min (°C)	3	4	8	11	13	15	15	15	15	11	7	4	10
Rain (mm)	22	27	52	109	187	522	713	573	419	116	14	5	2759

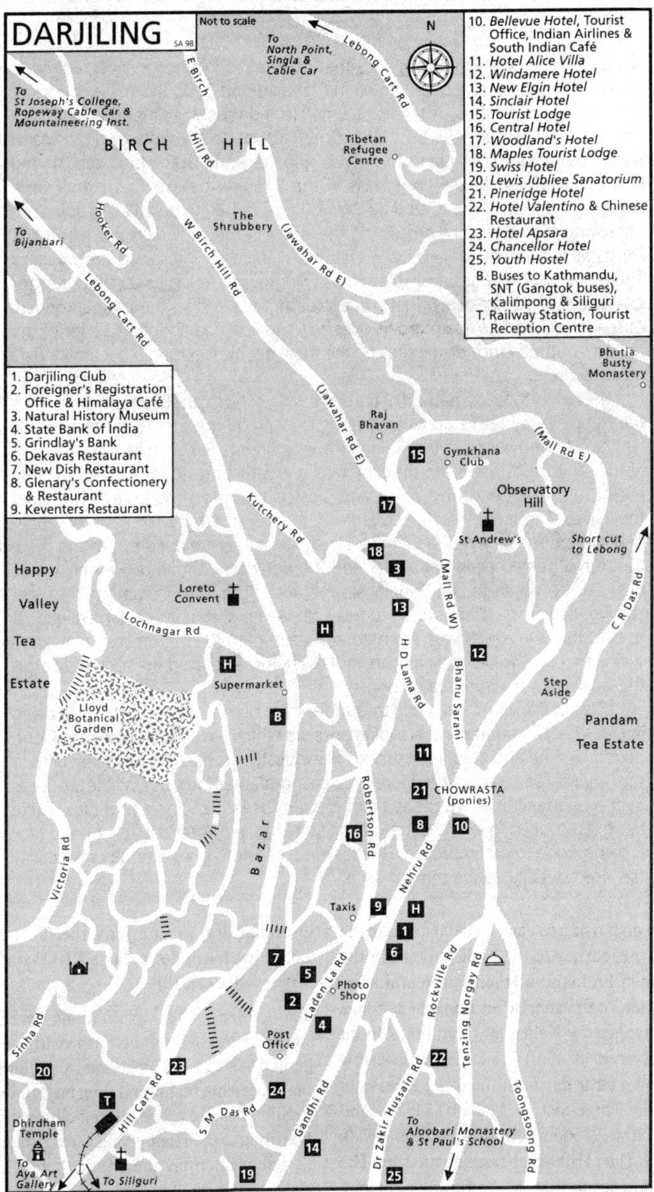

DARJILING
SA 98
Not to scale
N
To North Point, Singla & Cable Car
To St Joseph's College, Ropeway Cable Car & Mountaineering Inst.
To Bijanbari
BIRCH HILL
E Birch Hill Rd
Lebong Cart Rd
Hooker Rd
W Birch Hill Rd
(Jawahar Rd E)
The Shrubbery
Tibetan Refugee Centre
Bhutia Busty Monastery
Raj Bhavan
Gymkhana Club
(Mall Rd E)
Observatory Hill
St Andrew's
Short cut to Lebong
Kutchery Rd
(Mall Rd W)
Loreto Convent
Lochnagar Rd
Happy Valley Tea Estate
Supermarket
Lloyd Botanical Garden
H D Lama Rd
Bhanu Sarani
C R Das Rd
Step Aside
Pandam Tea Estate
CHOWRASTA (ponies)
Robertson Rd
Bazar
Victoria Rd
Nehru Rd
Taxis
Laden La Rd
Photo Shop
Rockville Rd
Tenzing Norgay Rd
Post Office
Sinha Rd
Hill Cart Rd
S M Das Rd
Gandhi Rd
Dr Zakir Hussain Rd
Toongsoong Rd
To Aloobari Monastery & St Paul's School
Dhirdham Temple
To Aya Art Gallery
To Siliguri
1. Darjiling Club
2. Foreigner's Registration Office & Himalaya Café
3. Natural History Museum
4. State Bank of India
5. Grindlay's Bank
6. Dekavas Restaurant
7. New Dish Restaurant
8. Glenary's Confectionery & Restaurant
9. Keventers Restaurant
10. Bellevue Hotel, Tourist Office, Indian Airlines & South Indian Café
11. Hotel Alice Villa
12. Windamere Hotel
13. New Elgin Hotel
14. Sinclair Hotel
15. Tourist Lodge
16. Central Hotel
17. Woodland's Hotel
18. Maples Tourist Lodge
19. Swiss Hotel
20. Lewis Jubliee Sanatorium
21. Pineridge Hotel
22. Hotel Valentino & Chinese Restaurant
23. Hotel Apsara
24. Chancellor Hotel
25. Youth Hostel
B. Buses to Kathmandu, SNT (Gangtok buses), Kalimpong & Siliguri
T. Railway Station, Tourist Reception Centre

TEA

An ancient Chinese legend suggests that 'tay', tea, originated in India, although tea was known to have been grown in China around 2700 BC. It is a species of Camellia, *Camellia thea*. After 1833, when its monopoly on importing tea from China was abolished, The East India Company made attempts to grow tea in Assam using wild 'chai' plants found growing there and later introduced it in the Darjiling area and in the Nilgiri hills in the S. Some believe that plants were smuggled in from China. Certainly, Chinese experts had to be asked to advise on improving the method of processing the leaves in the early days while horticulturists at the Botanical Gardens in Calcutta worked on improving the varieties. There are now varieties available which will grow at much lower altitudes, for example at Bagdogra or in Sylhet in Bangladesh. Today India is the largest producer of tea in the world. Assam grows over half and Darjiling about a quarter of the nation's output. Once drunk only by the tribal people it has now become India's national drink.

The old 'orthodox' method of tea processing, which can still be seen by visiting the Happy Valley Tea Estate near Darjiling, among others, produces the aromatic lighter coloured liquor of the Golden Flowery Orange Pekoe in its most superior grade. The fresh leaves are dried by fans on 'withering troughs' to reduce the moisture content and then rolled and pressed to express the juices which coat the leaves. These are then left to ferment in a controlled humid environment in order to produce the desired aroma. Finally the leaves are dried by passing them through a heated drying chamber and then graded – the unbroken being the best quality, down to the 'fannings' and 'dust'. The more common 'crushing, tearing, curling' (CTC) method produces tea which gives a much darker liquor. It uses a machine which was invented in Assam in 1930. The process allows the withered leaves to be given a short light roll before engraved metal rollers distort the leaves in a fraction of a second.

Most of Darjiling's tea is sold through auction houses, the largest centre being in Calcutta. Tea tasting and blending are skills which have developed over a long period of time and are highly prized. The industry provides vital employment in the hill areas and is an assured foreign exchange earner. India as a whole produces over a quarter of the world's tea and is easily the largest single producer. There has been concern over the deteriorating state of the plantations and a great deal is being done to use improved varieties when replanting. As a result productivity has risen steadily during the last decade.

worth rising as early as 0400 to make the 1 hr journey to the highest point in the area. From the hill there is a breathtaking view of the sunrise on Kangchendzonga flanked by Kabru and Pandim. Mount Everest (8846m) 225 km away, is visible on a clear day with the other 2 peaks of the Three Sisters, Makalu (8482m) and Lhotse (8500m). An alternative is to walk to Tiger Hill which takes about 2 hrs. The return journey can be through Ghoom. Overnight stay in tents only; the Tourist Lodge has burnt down, but a VIP Room serves coffee (Rs 10).

Tea gardens Tea plantations were started in the 1840s. It is worth visiting a garden to watch the pickers at work, tour the processing plants and then buy some locally grown tea. The garden closest to Darjiling is the **Happy Valley Tea Estate** (2 km walk from the Market) which claims to use the old 'orthodox' method of tea production. Visitors 0800-1200, 1300-1630 (best in the morning). Closed Sun, Mon. Particularly worth a visit during the season.

Museums

Natural History Museum nr Chowrasta. 1000-1600. Afternoons only Wed, closed Th. Re 1. Rec. Large collection of fauna of the region. **Himalayan Mountaineering Institute and Everest Museum**, T 2438. Entrance is through the Zoo on Jawahar Rd W. The institute, previously headed by the late Tenzing Norgay who jointly conquered Everest in 1953, trains mountaineers, holds demonstrations during the season and has a hostel for old mountaineers. The Everest Museum traces the attempts to climb the mountain from the first in 1857. The museum has old mountaineering equipment including that used on that historic Tenzing-Hillary climb, a model of the Himalaya and a display of Himalayan flora and fauna. Among the curiosities is a powerful telescope that had been a gift from Adolf Hitler to the Maharajah of Nepal. The Library subscribes to international mountaineering journals. Rec. 0900-1300, 1400-1600. Closed Tue in winter. Re 1 main museum and Re 0.50 Everest Museum. Telescope Re 1. Movie Re 1. **Ava Art Gallery**, Ghoom, T 2469. 0800-1200, 1230-1800. **Hayden Hall**, Laden La Rd is where you can buy woollen goods from local women.

Parks & zoos

The **Lloyds Botanical Gardens** nr the market was laid out on land given by Mr W. Lloyd, owner of the British Lloyd's Bank in 1878. Its 16 ha have an interesting collection of Himalayan and Alpine flora including banks of azaleas and rhododendrons, magnolias, a large collection of orchids and a hot house. The herbarium has rare botanical specimens. 0600-1700. Closed Sun. and bank holidays. Free. Western visitors are often disappointed. Victoria Falls which is only impressive in the monsoons provides added interest to a ½-hr nature trail. The *Zoological Park* next to the Mountaineering Institute has among its high-altitude wildlife Himalayan black bear, Siberian tiger, red pandas, yaks and llama although they are kept in small enclosures. 0800-1630. Re 1. The *Shrubbery* behind Raj Bhawan on Jawahar Parbat (Birch Hill) affords spectacular views of Kangchendzonga.

Trekking

Darjiling has become rightly famous for trekking and offers many options (see below). Details are available from the W Bengal Tourist Bureau on 1 Nehru Rd. See **Treks** below.

Tours

Departure point: Tourist Office **Tour 1**: Tiger Hill, Senchal Lake, Ghoom Monastery, Batasia Loop. 0400-0730 (Min 8). Rs 40. **Tour II**: Local sightseeing. Ava Gallery, Manjusha Bengal Emp, Dhirdham Temple, Himalayan Mountaineering Inst, Zoo, Ropeway, Lebong Race Course, Tibetan Refugee Self-help Centre. 0930-1230, 1330-1630 (Min 8). Rs 40. **Tour III**: Mirik. 0830-1730 (Min 12) Rs 75. **Tour IV**: Gangtok and Kalimpong. (Min 20). 2 days. 0800-1730 following day. Rs 255 for transport only.

Local Festival

Buddha Jayanti in Apr-May, celebrates the birth of the Buddha and is observed with much ceremony in the monasteries.

Local information

● Accommodation

Mostly 90 km from airport, 1 km from rly. Few centrally heated. Many operate American plan only (full board). Quality of service has suffered from town's law and order problems **B** ***Sinclairs***, 18/1 Gandhi Rd, T 3431. 54 rm. No heating, no generator, cold in winter, good service. Restaurant, bar, shops, travel. **B** ***Windamere***, Observatory Hill, T 2397. 27 rm. On the edge of the Mall in an enviable position (good views when clear) with sun terraces, comfortable, with character but old-fashioned with memorabilia. Bathrooms undermodernised, but bedrooms still have log fires. A wonderful place for Christmas! Restaurant not quite what it was. Interesting clientele, rec. **B** ***New Elgin***, HD Lama Rd, T 3314. 23 rm in old bungalow with annexe. Full board only. Restaurant serves good set meals for Rs 110. Rec. **B** ***Central***, Robertson Rd, T 2033. 52 rm. Good restaurant, bar. Full board only. Comfortable rm. Off-season discounts. Popular with tourist groups. **B** ***Darjiling Club***, Nehru Rd has some rooms. The old Planters' Club, a relic of the Raj, allows temporary members. Dining, bar, billiards, tennis. Slightly run down, but log fires, friendly, good service.

C ***Valentino***, 6 Rockville Rd, T 2228. 17 rm. Central heating. Chinese restaurant rec, bar, travel. **C** ***Chancellor***, SM Das Rd, Off Laden La Rd (Opp GPO), T 2228. 27 rm. Central heating. Rather characterless 3-storey brick, cement and glass, but clean, well appointed rm, some with K'junga views. Efficient service, good food. Chinese restaurant rec, bar, travel. Excellent bakery (good cakes).

D ***Bellevue***, The Mall, T 2129. 43 rm. 2 hotels: Both good value but one on Chowrasta cleaner and friendlier and has best views in town incl Kangchendzonga on a clear day. Convenient location. Restaurant, shops, travel, Govt tourist offices, pony rides. **D** ***Alice Villa***, HD Lama Rd nr Tourist Bureau, T 2381. Large clean rm, good restaurant. Cosy bungalow. Rec. **D** ***Tiffany***, 4 Franklyn Prestage Rd (below Gymkhana Club), T 2840. 7 rm (1st flr better). Restaurant, tours. **D** ***Darjiling Tourist Lodge***, Bhanu Sarani (Mall), behind Windamere, T 2611. 15 clean rm (smaller cheaper). Breakfast and evening meals incl (Rs 65). Superb views and warm. **D** ***Polynia***, 12/1 Robertson Rd, T 2705. 34 rm. Indian restaurant. **D** ***Pineridge***, 19 Nehru Rd, T 2094 and ***Cosy Inn***, Nehru Rd, T 2073. 28 rm. Restaurant, travel. **D** ***Apsara***, 61 Laden La Rd. 24 rm. Veg restaurant, travel.

● Budget hotels

Some cheaper **E** and **F** hotels offer 3/4 bedded rm; most have limited menu in restaurants. **E** ***Prestige***, above GPO Laden La Rd, T 3199. Central, clean, attached bath. Very friendly. Rec. **E** ***Dekeling*** 51 Gandhi Rd, T 734101. Dekevas Rest very pleasant, excellent food and snacks. Rec.

F ***Pagoda*** 1 Upper Beechwood Rd. Very friendly, clean but basic. Some problems with water, but central and good valuse budget hotel. Also ***Tara***, 125 Gandhi Rd. 27 rm. Restaurant (Indian and Chinese). ***Broadway, La Bella, Surja Bhawan***, 3 Coochbehar Rd, 29 rm. Good location with roof-top views. ***Purnima***, 2A Coochbehar Rd, 20 rm. ***Springburn***, 70 Gandhi Rd, 12 rm. Indian. Cheaper still are the ***Lewis Jubilee Complex***, Dr SK Pal Rd, T 2127, and the very inexpensive **F** ***Youth Hostel*** on Dr Zakir Hussain Rd, T 2290, for 46 in rm and dorm. No restaurant. Reservations direct or through WBTDC, 3/1 BBD Bagh (E), Calcutta, T 28591 or Tourist Bureau, 1 Nehru Rd, Darjiling, T 2050. Popular, but access difficult. Other cheap guest houses are on Dr Zakir Hussain Rd on the way up to the Youth Hostel. **F** ***Aliment***, 100m below Youth Hostel. Clean rm, hot shower, good food. rec. Owner organizes trips to Tiger Hill. **F** ***Prestige*** Laden La Rd, T 2699. Very clean, friendly. Rec. The Mohanlal Shivlal **F** ***Dharamshala*** is on Cart Rd.

● Places to eat

Hotels with restaurants will usually serve non-residents. Several have **bars**.

Outside hotels: *Glenary's* on Nehru Rd, very good tea-room with excellent confectionery, friendly service. Typical Raj room, first class breakfast. Kalimpong cheese and wholemeal bread for sale. Also refurbished licensed restaurant. ***Keventer's*** on Nehru Rd for breakfast and tea, a well-patronized snack bar, popular with youngsters from public schools. Also serves full English breakfasts, very good cheese omelettes. The terrace above is particularly pleasant. ***Hotel Chancellor's*** pastry shop rec. Good, cheap breakfasts at ***Himalaya Café*** on Laden La Rd, cheap Tibetan at the friendly ***Lhasoo*** and adventurous Chinese rec at ***New Dish*** below. ***Valentino***, Rockville Rd, rec for Continental and Chinese.

Indian: *Gol Ghar*, Main Bazar, serves excellent meat dishes with chapatis, naan and rotis. Open-air ***S Indian Restaurant*** on Chowrasta serves very good veg meals; dosas at ***Hotel Charlie***. Excellent Bengali food at ***Asian***, behind Nehru Rd. Also ***Ghalay's***, Chowk Bazar and ***Narayandas***, Cart Rd. Chinese: ***Chopstix*** nr Rly station, ***Shangrila***, Nehru Road, ***Druk***, Goenka Rd. ***Dekavas***, bottom of Nehru Rd, rec for fast food. ***Lunar***, Gandhi Rd (snacks). At Delo, above Dr. Graham's Home, a new ***Lodge*** has been built with good views.

● Banks & money changers

Grindlays and **State Bank of India**, Laden La Rd.

● Clubs

The old *Gymkhana Club* has indoor sports

THE TOY TRAIN – A MINI MIRACLE

The toy train between New Jalpaiguri and Darjiling,with its 0.6m (2 foot) gauge track and hauled by sparkling tank engines, some originally built in Glasgow, is a rewarding experience. The brainchild of East Bengal railway agent Franklyn Prestage, the train promised to open access to the hills from the sweltering humidity of the Calcutta plains in summer. Following the line of an earlier steam tramway, the name was changed to the Darjeeling Himalayan railway Company in 1881. The first 32 km was opened in March 1880 – for the Viceroy's train only. Fully opened in September 1881, like all transport engineering works the original estimates grossly understated the true bill. Its final cost was Rs 45,000 per km – well over twice the original estimate. Yet it is a stunning achievement, winding its way up the hillside, often with brilliant views over the plains. It travels the 82 km with gradients of up to 1 in 19, in 7-8 hr (Rs 250). At **Ghoom** it reaches 2438m and then descends 305m to Darjiling. Ghoom is sometimes wrongly clamed to have the highest railway station in the world – several in South America are higher including Cuzco, in Peru, which is at an altitude of over 3300m. But do the record books really matter when you have the view over Darjiliing from Batasia?

facilities incl roller skating, snooker (Rs10 per hr), badminton, squash and also tennis courts (all Rs 5 per hr). Temporary membership available Rs 15 for 2 days. Visit rec. Staff excellent.

Hospitals & medical services

Sadar Hospital, T 2218. Shahid Durgamaull, T 2131. Darjiling and Dooars, T 2302.

● Post & telecommunications

GPO: Laden La Rd. **Telegraph Office**: Gandhi Rd.

● Places of worship

St Andrew's Church 0900 every Sunday.

● Riding

Pony rides are popular on the Mall starting at Chowrasta. The Tibetan 'guides' charge approx Rs 20 per hr. Pony races are held during the spring and autumn at the *Lebong Race Course*, one of the smallest and highest in the world.

● Shopping

There are plenty of curio and handicrafts shops which provide you with an overwhelming choice. The main shopping areas are Chowrasta, Nehru Rd, Laden La Rd and Chowk Bazar. The local handicrafts sold widely include Buddhist *tankhas* which are hand painted scrolls surrounded by Chinese brocade, good wood carving, carpets, handwoven cloth, jewellery, copper, brass and white metal religious curios such as prayer wheels, bowls and statues. The Chowrasta shops are closed on Sun and Chowk Bazar on Th. ***The Tibetan Refugee Self-Help Centre*** is on Gandhi Road with its temple, school and hospital. Closed Sun. After the Chinese invasion, thousands of Tibetan refugees settled in Darjiling (many having accompanied the Dalai Lama) and the rehabilitation centre was established in 1959 to enable them to continue to practise their skills and provide an outlet for their goods. It is possible to watch the craftspeople at work (weaving, spinning, dyeing, metalwork) and then buy carpet, textiles, curios or jewellery in the shop. Well worth a visit, though not cheap to buy. At ***Hayden Hall*** in Laden La Rd, colourful woollen goods are sold by local women. The W Bengal Govt's ***Manjusha Emporium*** on Nehru Rd is rec for silk, cotton handloom and handicrafts. The ***Markets*** are very colourful and worth visiting.

Books: ***Oxford Bookshop*** is on Chowrasta. It has old books on India and Tibet.

Photography: ***Darjiling Photo Stores, Singh Studios, Das Studios*** on Nehru Rd. The last sells interesting black-and-white prints from Raj days; order from album (1-2 days).

Tour companies & travel agents

Travel Corp (India), Gandhi Rd. ***Himalayan Travels***, Sinclairs, Gandhi Rd. ***Juniper Tour and Travels***, 14 HL Ghosh Rd. ***Summit Tours***, Indrani Lodge, Chowrasta. ***Singamari Syndicate***, Main Taxi Stand.

● Tourist offices

W Bengal Tourist Office, Belle Vue Complex, 1st Flr, 1 Nehru Rd, T 2050. In season 0930-1730. Off season 1000-1630. Also Rly station, and at New Car Park, Laden La Rd. Darjiling GHC, Silver Fir Bldg, The Mall, T 2524.

● **Useful addresses**
Foreigners' Registration Office, Laden La Rd, T2261. Entry permits for Sikkim (15 days) available. Allow 24 hr.

● **Transport**
Local Bus operators: N Bengal State Transport Corp, T 3133. Gorkha PAKU, Chowk Bazar Bus Stand, T 3487. Darjiling Siliguri Motor Syndicate, Motor Stand. Singamari Syndicate, Main Taxi Stand, T 2820. **Taxis**: private taxis charge approx Rs 3 for Nehru Rd to Top Station. *Clubside Motors*, T 2123 and *Siddique Motors*, T 2370 on Robertson Rd. *Darjiling Transport Corp*, Laden La Rd, T 2074. *Kalimpong Motor Transport Syndicate*, Motor Stand, T 2269. Sikkim SNT agent, T 2101. Tourist Taxis, Landrovers, and Jeeps are readily available for both short or long journeys. Prices vary according to the season; negotiate rates. The **Ropeway Cable Car**: the first of its kind to be built in India to carry passengers, connects Top Station with Tukvar Station in Singla Valley on the Little Rangit River. In season, hourly service in both directions, morning up to mid-afternoon. Rs 20 return.

Air Nearest airport, **Bagdogra** (90 km) – see above. Transfer by car or coach is 2½-3½ hr. Taxis charge approx Rs 100 per person when carrying 7; the W Bengal Tourism Coach costs Rs 55. Indian Airlines, *Belle Vue Hotel*, Chowrasta, T 2355. Weekdays 1000-1700, Sun 1000-1300. Tourist Information counter.

Train Siliguri, which is 80 km away, and *New Jalpaiguri* nearby, are the nearest stations to Darjiling. See above.

Road Bus: NH 31 connects Siliguri with other parts of India. You may wish to drive from **Calcutta** (570 km) and visit other places of interest on the way. The overnight N Bengal STC's 'Rocket' bus service is faster than the train, dep 2100, 12 hr, Rs 125, a/c Rs 250. Reserve seats in Calcutta, T 281854 or in Burdwan Rd, Siliguri, T 20531. Buses can be very full and noisy – not a relaxing way to travel! N Bengal State Transport Corp, Darjiling, T 3133. From **Siliguri to Darjiling**, travel by taxi (Rs 700), W Bengal STC bus (4 hr, Rs 30) or more comfortable Tourist Bus (min 6 passengers). **Darjiling to Siliguri or Bagdogra**, Tourist bus leaves from traffic island nr Keventers. Tickets from Tourist Office (*Bellvue Hotel*). Main taxi stand, Chowk Bazar. One recent visitor claimed that "for thrills and spills, no fairground attraction can rival the narrow hairpinned, switchback road that climbs the Himalayan foothills to Dajilling." **To Kalimpong** Buses are less frequent, slower and not much cheaper. Taxi stand, Robertson Rd/Laden La Rd. Landrovers and buses depart from the Bazar Motor stand.

Nepal Kathmandu to Darjiling: direct bus (N Rs 450). Bus and jeep, 23 hr: Bus to Kakarbhitta (N Rs 230); from Kakarbhitta to Darjiling by bus (Rs 95); to Siliguri by jeep (Rs 25) and Darjiling by bus (Rs 30).

Short excursions from Darjiling

Mirik (1730m, 49 km from Darjiling) with its lake, forests of cryptomeria, orange orchards and cardamom plantations, is an attractive resort accessible by buses from Darjiling (50 km) and Siliguri (52 km). The 3.5 km lakeside promenade is popular – boating. The carpet weaving centre is at Krishannagar. You can trek to Kurseong and Sandakphu.

● **Accommodation** DGHC **E** *Tourist Cottages* has single/ double rm (no catering). DGHC **F** *Tourist Hostel* has 60 beds in rm and dorm. Reserve through DGHC Darjiling, T 2524. WB Tourism *Tourist Tents*; *Day Centre* has a restaurant . Also simple *Mrigaya*, *Vasthan* and *Parijat* Hotels.

● **Transport Road** To/from Darjiling: N Bengal STC and private buses from 0630 to 1500. Jeep and landrover services 1200 & 1330.

Treks

The E Himalaya attract the seasoned trekker as much as the inexperienced as it is possible to walk up to altitudes of 3660m in stages, along safe roads through wooded hills. The best trekking season is in Apr-May or Oct-Nov. In the spring there may be the occasional shower, more than compensated for by the beauty of the magnolias and rhododendrons in full bloom. In the autumn the air is dry and the visibility excellent and although early Dec is not too late, it may turn very cold.

You can do a short trek to **Tiger Hill** about 5 km away (see Darjiling above) but if there is more time, the agents in

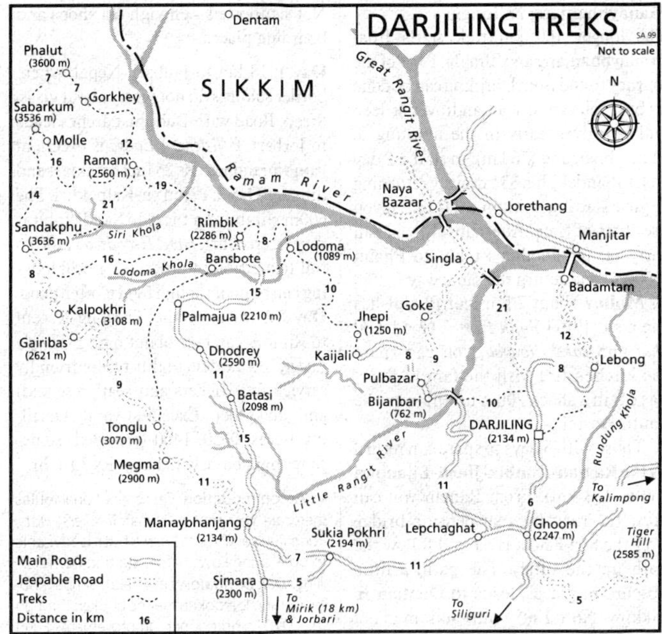

Darjiling can organize 4 to 7 day programmes.

Trekking agents
Clubside Tours, 16 Ladenla Rd, T 2122, are the oldest and best. Highly rec; *Himalayan Travels,* Sinclairs Hotel, T 3431; *Mohit Tours,* HD Lama Rd, T 2020; *Summit Tours,* Indrani Lodge, Chowrasta Rd; *Tushita Treks,* 9/1 Pamu Bldg, TN Rd, T 3120. The *Tourist Bureau* in Darjiling, will provide detailed information, plan the trek and book your accommodation and also obtain necessary equipment (sleeping bag, wind-jacket etc.) and arrange a Sherpa guide. **NB**: Trekking gear can be hired from the *Youth Hostel* where there is a very useful book of helpful suggestions by past trekkers.

Himalayan Mountaineering Institute (see under Museums, Darjiling above) runs some courses for trekkers (about Rs 250 for Indians, Rs 1200 for foreigners).

Phalut
Most trekkers take in Phalut at the junction of Nepal, Sikkim and W Bengal and Sandakphu which offers a fantastic view of 5 of the world's highest peaks – Everest (8846m), Kangchendzonga (8598m), Makalu, Lhotse and Cho Oyu. Everest is 140 km from Sandakphu as the crow flies and you can see about 3700m of its slopes from there. Kangchendzonga, on the Nepal/Sikkim border is the world's 3rd highest peak. **Sandakphu** (3636m), in the Singalila range, is the highest point in the district with panoramic views on a clear day. The route takes you through fragrant forests of conifers with rhododendron, primulas and a great variety of orchids. A bird-watchers' dream – 600 species, including orioles, minivets, flycatchers, finches, sunbirds, piculets, emerald cuckoos, falconets and Hoodson's imperial pigeons.

Manaybhanjang & Tonglu

The longer 160 km trek starts from **Manaybhanjang** and **Tonglu**. Parts of the journey to and from Darjiling can be done by bus. You can hire a Landrover or Jeep and be driven early in the morning to Manaybhanjang (26 km), to start a 2 day trek to Sandakphu, 33 km away returning to your starting point in a day or 2 if you are short of time. Alternatively, you can carry on for another 21 km to **Phalut** (3600m) and return the same way.

Molley about 7 km S of Phalut has the new (1992) *Youth Hostel*. Good *dahl bhat* and *rakshi/tongba*; you can share the kitchen fire with the family. Sherpas eat in a shack 200m uphill from the Youth Hostel.

Those with 5 days to spare can return by the **Raman-Rimbik-Jhepi-Bijanbari** route (153 km). From Raman you can cross the river by a suspension bridge over the Siri Khola river and follow the path up the valley. The path, a little obscure in places, leads to **Dentam** in Sikkim (**Note** Entry into Sikkim is not permitted on this route). The valley makes a pleasant break from the well-trodden route and is rich in birdlife – particularly kingfishers and view of undisturbed forest. From **Bijanbari** (762m) it is possible to return to Darjiling 36 km away, in a Jeep or climb a further 2 km to Pulbazar and then return to Darjiling 16 km away. Those wishing to only go to Rimbik may return to Manaybhanjang via Palmajua and Batasi (180 km), which takes a day.

Manaybhanjang to Rimbik

A 3 day trek from Manaybhanjang (a jeep from Darjiling for 5, about Rs 1000), to Rimbik. In Manybhanjang, *Wangdee Restaurant* gives good trekking information. You can also leave your backpack. You can stay at *Hotel Indica,* Meghma, if you want to share a simple Tibetan home (homemade cheese, hanging from ceiling) but unfortunately dirty. Jeepable track is quiet in evenings. Not signposted – enough tea shops and boarding places.

Day 1: 18 km to Jaubari, Nepal, where border soldiers do not worry about visas. Steep. Road with Buddhist arches leads to Jorbari. F *Teacher's Lodge* is excellent value for money (Rs 25 incl breakfast and dinner). **Day 2**: 19 km via Kalpokhri. The 600m climb from there to Sandakphu is very steep (2 hr). *Hotel Broadway* is often full (extension in progress). Local lodging can be poor though food is often good. **Day 3**: Attractive route. The long descent to Rimbik can take about 6 hr. F *Sherpa Lodge,* in a garden, highly rec for friendly service (bus tickets and seats reserved) and good food. Excellent value. Darjiling buses, 0530, 1400 (crowded, sometimes dangerously driven). Rs 30, 6 hr.

• **Accommodation** On conventional routes there are very simple, cheap *Trekkers' Huts, Bungalows* and *Youth hostels* but it is advisable to book bungalows before starting from Darjiling. ***Dak Bungalows*** at Phalut, Sandakphu, Tonglu and Jorepokhri may be booked through the Dy Commissioner, Improvement Fund Dept. The one at Jhepi should be reserved through the Dist Land Revenue Officer. ***Trekkers' Huts*** at Manaybhanjang, Gairibans, Sandakphu, Phalut, Rimbik and Dhodrey. 1 rm, 13 dorm beds in each (Rs 20). Carry provisions for caretaker to cook to order. Reserve through Tourist Bureau, Darjiling or Siliguri. ***Forest Bungalows*** at Palmajua and Batasi may be booked through the Div Manager, W Bengal Forest Dev Corp while for the ***Inspection Bungalows*** at Bijanbari, applications must be made to the Div Engineer, State Electricity Board, Siliguri. It is not necessary to apply in advance for overnight stays in Raman, Rimbik, Sandakphu and Manaybhanjang youth hostels.

NB: It is advisable, as it saves a lot of time, to ask a local Darjiling trekking agent to arrange reservations for you for a small fee.

Kalimpong

Population: 41,000. *Altitude:* 1250m. *STD Code* 03552 *Best season:* Mar-Jun, Sep-Feb. Passport and visa are checked at

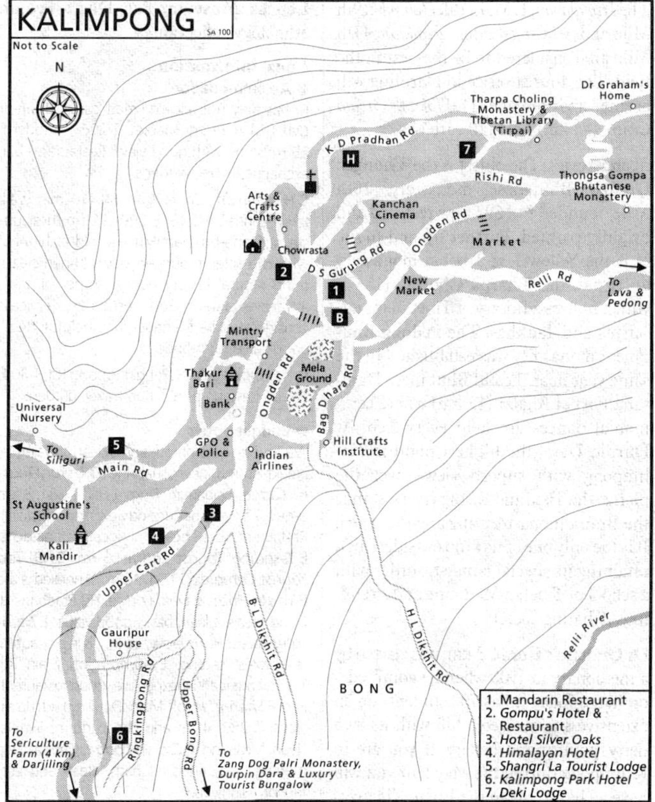

Tista bridge check point; no entry permit needed.

Kalimpong, a remote hill station, has been a meeting point of the once 'three Closed Lands' on the trade route to Tibet, Bhutan and Nepal. The original name meant the stronghold (*'pong'*) of the king's minister (*'kalim'*). The gentle climate has warm summers (around 30°C) and cool winters (down to 7°C), and the beautiful mountain scenery, oak forests and the abundance of flowers makes Kalimpong an attractive resort. The lifestyle of the local people reflect the social influences of its neighbours, Nepal, Tibet, Sikkim and Bhutan.

ROUTES From Darjiling 51 km away, it is possible to make the trip by taxi or Jeep in about 2½ hr, taking in beautiful scenery. The road, which is variable but improves with distance, descends to 200m at Tista where it crosses the river on a single lane bridge. The road winds through the Peshok and Lopchu tea estates and a halt at Lovers' Meet and View Point will give you superb views of the Rangeet and Tista rivers ringed by mountains.

Places of interest

Nurseries Kalimpong excels in producing orchids, amaryllis, roses, cacti, dahlias and gladioli among others for export.

The *Himalayan*, E Main Rd, *Holumba*, 9th Mile and *Sri Ganesh Moni Pradhan*, 11th Mile are considered to be the best in the field. The Tourist office in Darjiling will arrange a visit to one. The *Takdah Orchid Centre* (44 km) sells 110 varieties.

Monasteries The oldest is the **Thongsa Gompa** Bhutanese monastery, 10th Mile, founded in 1692 now restored and brightly painted. Further up and to the N is the Yellow Hat Tibetan monastery at Tirpai, the **Tharpa Choling** (1837), which houses a library of Tibetan manuscripts and Tankhas. The **Pedong** Bhutanese monastery was established in the same year near the old Bhutanese Damsang Fort at Algara (15 km) where ceremonial dances are held every Feb. At Durpin Dara, the highest point in Kalimpong with superb views over the plains, the Tista and Reang rivers, stands the **Brang** monastery at Zang-dog Palri. It is the only one of its kind outside Tibet, retaining its special lamaistic order with a school of Tibetan Medicine and a religious debating society.

Dr Graham's Home, 3 km, was started by a missionary in 1900 when he admitted 6 orphans. Today it has 700 students on an extensive site on Deolo hill with its own dairy, poultry and bakery. If you are in Kalimpong during the May Fair you will have a chance to see the Lucie King cottage. The **Central Sericultural Farm**, 4 km, produces high-grade silk cocoons and nearby is the **Swiss Welfare Dairy** set up by a missionary who started producing cheese in Pedong and then expanded to this large co-operative. You can trek from **Lava** (32 km) or **Lolaygaon** (56 km) which has spectacular views of Kangchendzonga or visit **Mungpo Cichona plantation** (26 km) or picnic on the river beaches at Tista Bazar and Kalijhora.

There are pleasant walks through Tista Road and rice fields to **Chitray Falls**, 9 km, a 3 hr walk to **Bhalu Khop** and a a 1 ½ hr downhill from the Motor Stand to the **Relli River**.

Lepcha Museum, Bag Dhara has an ethnology collection.

Local information

● Accommodation

Hotels may not accept credit cards. **B** ***Silver Oaks***, Main Rd, nr Market, T 296, is modern. 25 rm some with good view. Restaurant, bar, exchange, travel, gardens.

C *Himalayan*, Upper Cart Rd (10 min walk town centre), T 248, F 290. 11 rm (best upstairs). Stone-built family home; old-fashioned, with character, mountain views (when clear), good natural history books (some for sale), attractive gardens. Good restaurant. Service is considerate, the Manager very helpful. Rec – good value for money.

D *Kalimpong Park*, Ringkingpong Rd, T 304, 20 rm. Restaurant rec, bar, travel, garden.

● Budget hotels

WB Tourism accommodation is clean and simple; breakfast and dinner usually incl: **D** ***Luxury Tourist Lodge***, Singamari, Durpin Hill, T 384, 3 km centre. 7 rm with bath (good views from upstairs). Restaurant, bar, beautiful location, gardens. **E** *Tashding Tourist Lodge*, 6 rm. **E** ***Hill Top Tourist Complex***, T 654. 10 rm. Annexed is the **F** *Youth Hotel*. **E** ***Deki Lodge***, HD Pradhan Rd. Good meals. Clean, basic, good value. **E** ***Munsong Forest Bunglaow***, 25 km, is in a beautiful teak forest setting. **E** ***Gompu***, off Main Rd, T 818. Larger and inexpensive, good restaurant. Rec. **F** ***Shangri la***, off Main (Darjiling) Rd, down steps, T 280. 4 rm and cheap dorm. Simple, clean. Meals incl. **F** ***Crown Lodge***. Central. Free morining tea, attached bath, clean and very friendly. Highly rec.

● Places to eat

Gompu's, rear of hotel, is informal with good views. Friendly. Very good food, incl Chinese. *Kalimpong Park*, and *Mandarin*, nr Taxi Stand are also rec. *Maharaja* has good S Indian food. Bakeries sell good bread and cakes.

● Shopping

Tibetan and Nepalese handicrafts and woven fabrics are particularly good. The Market or *haat* every Wed and Sat becomes a meeting place for colourful villagers who sell fruit, vegetables, spices, traditional medicines, woollen cloth, yarn and musk. A place to visit for the atmosphere (even if you do not make purchases) and think back of the times when Kalimpong was the starting point of the trade route to Lhasa. For local appliqué wall hangings and *thangkas,* contact Norden Pempa Hishey, T 435. Co-operative Society and Book Depot on Main Rd.

● **Useful Services**
There are **Banks**, **Hospitals** and **Post Office** nr the Police Station.

● **Transport**
Kalimpong is off the NH 31-A to Gangtok. Landrovers or taxis to Siliguri and Bagdogra; last 1500.

Air Nearest airport at Bagdogra, 80 km, 2¼hr by car (see Darjiling, page 652). IA information, Mintry Transport, T 241. Taxi seat or bus Rs 40.

Train The nearest railhead is New Jalpaiguri/Siliguri station, 67 km, which has direct services to Calcutta, Delhi, Guwahati and Lucknow.

Road Bus: N Bengal STC and private buses to regional centres. Several to **Siliguri**, 0615-1115, (2½ hr); **Darjiling** 0640, 0715 (4 hr); **Gangtok** 0730, 0800, 0830 (3 hr). N Bengal STC Booking Office, Motor Stand, Kalimpong, T 525. Jeeps cost more but are faster.

CALCUTTA TO THE MOUTH OF THE HUGLI

Short trips are possible to the S of Calcutta to the mouth of the Hugli and to the Sundarbans in the Ganga/ Brahmaputra delta.

East bank of the Hugli

Diamond Harbour

Follow the road due S from Calcutta to Diamond Harbour (51 km; *Population* 32,000, *STD Code* 03174) which lies on the bend of the river where it turns S towards the sea. Once the ships of the East India Company anchored here: the ruins of a fort are said to date back to the days of the Portuguese pirates. Today it is a favourite picnic spot for day-trippers. Motor launches take passengers to Sagar island or country boat trips do rounds of the estuary. **Accommodation** WBTDC **E** *Sagarika Tourist Lodge*, some a/c rm and suites, and cheap dorm. **F** *Irrigation Dept Bungalow*. Reservations: Irrigation Dept, 11A Mirza Ghalib St, Calcutta.

Bakkhali

Continue S to Kulpi (18 km) and Kakdwip (26 km) en route. This small village has a pleasant unspoilt palm fringed beach close to the Sunderbans. The beach, however, is very muddy in places. Very few people speak English but are nevertheless very welcoming. A peaceful retreat from a busy Calcutta.

● **Accommodation** WBTDC basic **F** *Tourist Lodge* (T Kakdwip 76). 48 beds in rm and dorm. The beach house and **restaurant** are among casuarina groves. Boat trips to Jambu Dwip.

● **Transport Train** Train to Diamond Harbour, stopping en route at the pleasant Tourist Centre overlooking the widening Ganga and proceed for Bakkhali the following day. **Road Bus**: from Calcutta, you can get as far as Namkhana by bus (3 hr), take a ferry across the Hatania-Doania river and then another bus for 90 min.

Sagardwip

This island at the mouth of the Ganga is where the *Ganga Sagar Mela* is held in mid-Jan. It attracts over half a million pilgrims each year who come to bathe and then visit the **Kapil Muni Temple**. The island has been devastated many times by cyclones and floods often killing large numbers of inhabitants. There is a lighthouse to aid navigation in the SW tip. WBTDC organizes 2 day boat trips with accommodation on board.

● **Accommodation** **F** *Youth Hostel*. *Bharat Seva Sangha* Dharamshala. Free for 3 days.

● **Transport** Bus/taxi to Harwood Point. Ferry crossing to Kochuberia Ghat (Sagar). 30 min Bus across island to where the Ganga meets the Sea.

Sundarbans Tiger Reserve

Approach
Sundarbans ("beautiful forests") derived from Sundari trees (pneumatophoric roots) which predominate. The mangrove swamps and riverine forests,

cover over 2,500 sq km in the Ganga delta and spreads across to Bangladesh. They are said to be the largest estuarine forests in the world. The area has a vast network of creeks and channels with innumerable islands.

Wildlife

The biosphere reserve still preserves the natural habitat of about 200 Bengal tigers which here, have become strong swimmers, and known to attack fishermen. They are bigger and richer in colour than elsewhere in S Asia and are thought to survive on salt water (rainwater is the only source of fresh water in the park). Spotted deer, wild boar, monkeys, snakes, fishing cats, water monitors, Olive Ridley sea turtles and large estuarine crocodiles are the other wildlife to be seen, particularly on Lothian Island and Chamta block. You must be accompanied by armed forest rangers to view the wildlife from watch towers.

Viewing

Season: Nov-Mar. Heavy rains and occasional severe cyclones in Apr-May and Nov-Dec can make a visit impossible so best, Dec-Feb. Temp range: 35°C to 15°C. Rainfall: 1920 mm. Viewing from motor launches which can be hired from Canning, Basanti, Namkhana and Raidighi. Contact: Field Director, Sundarbans Tiger Reserve, Canning, 24 Parganas.

NB: You need a permit (valid 4/5 days) from the Forestry Dept, 5th Flr, G Block, Writers Bldg, BBD Bagh, Calcutta. This may require patience and persistence. Armed with the permit you go to the Tourist Office nearby, (see Calcutta) and book a 1-3 day tour (not run during monsoons, Jul-mid Sep). 2-day trips twice a month or 1-day cruises by 2 luxury launches more frequently. *Sundarbans Cruise* WBTDC 'Chitralekha' (all weather) 1 night – 2 day cruise on the marshy Hugli. Accommodation varies; luxury coach from Calcutta and meals are included. Alternatively make your own arrangements (see below).

Sajnekhali has a famous sanctuary for water birds and can be approached from Canning or Basanti by motor launch.

Park information

● Accommodation

F *Sunder Chital Tourist Lodge*. Simple.

● Transport

Train Canning (105 km).

Road Bus: via Sonakhali. To Basanti, bus from Babu Ghat, Strand Rd, Calcutta, 0600 (3 hr). Then hire a boat to Tourist Lodge.

West bank of the Hugli

Digha

Pop 5000, 185 km from Calcutta on the W bank of the Hugli estuary where it has already become indistinguishable from the Bay of Bengal. Warren Hastings visited Digha nearly 2 centuries ago and called it the 'Brighton of the East'. It is rather difficult to see why, as there is not a pebble for at least 2000 km! The casuarina-lined hard wide beach is very popular with Bengalis.

Junpur Beach 8 km from Contai and 40 km from Digha has a fishing research station and duck breeding centre. **Chandaneshwar** 8 km from Digha has a Siva Temple which can be reached by going to the Orissa border by bus and then completing the last 3 km by rickshaw.

• Accommodation D *Sea Hawk*. Comfortable rm, some a/c. Cottages and cheaper dorm, T 35, Calcutta T 572048. **E** *Dolphin*, BB Ganguly St and WBTDC **E** *Luxury Tourist Lodge*, T 55 are basic.

• Transport Train The nearest railway halts are at Kharagpur (116 km) and Contai Road (151 km) Stations on the SE Rly. **Road Bus**: express buses and Tourist Bureau luxury buses from Calcutta take 6 hr, the route having been shortened by the Norghat Bridge. Calcutta-Digha-Calcutta dep 0700 from Esplanade. Rs 35.

SIKKIM

Contents

Maps

Sikkim is famous for Kangchendzonga (8,586m) the third highest mountain in the world, a rich flora and fauna and a diverse ethnic and cultural population. The original inhabitants, the Lepchas, call the region *Nye-mae-el* ('Paradise'). To the later Bhutias it is *Beymul Denjong* ('The Hidden Valley of Rice'). *Sikkim* is commonly attributed to the Tsong word *Sukhim* meaning New or Happy House.

SOCIAL INDICATORS *Population*: 410,000 (Urban 18%, Scheduled castes 6%, Scheduled Tribes 23%); *Literacy*: M 64% F 47%. *Birth rate*: *Rural* 33:1000, *Urban* 25:1000; *Death rate*: *Urban* 4:1000, *Rural* 10:1000. *Religion*: *Hindu* 67%; *Buddhist* 29%; *Muslim* 1%; *Christian* 2%.

Visiting Sikkim

Tourism is still in its infancy though Sikkim is beginning to attract trekkers too. With 660 species, Sikkim is an orchid-lovers paradise. Orchids are found mostly in tropical regions up to 2100m, though there are some at 3000m.

Permits Free Inner Line Permits for foreigners from Inspector Gen of Police, Gangtok for 15 days to visit Gangtok, Rumtek, Phodong and Pemayangtse. Groups of up to 20 may apply to trek for a max of 15 days. Apply at Indian missions 24 hr in advance or from Ministry of Home Affairs in New Delhi, Calcutta or Siliguri. In Darjiling, allow 3 hr for the 15 day permit. In Darjiling you must go to the Magistrates Court and then Foreigners' Regional Registration Office.

Tour You can stay a few days in Gangtok, making day trips to Rumtek and Phodong then move to Gezing. From there you can walk up to Pemayangtse and catch a bus to Siliguri or Darjiling.

Environment

The Land

Sikkim is in the E Himalaya, sandwiched between Nepal to its W and Bhutan to the E. In the N is Tibet/China. To the S is the Indian state of West Bengal. It is the second smallest state in India (*Area* 7298 sq km), only 112 km length and 64 km width. Flat land is a rarity.

It encompasses the upper valley of the Tista river, a tributary of the Brahmaputra. The watershed forms the borders with Tibet/China and Nepal. The Rangit and Rangpo rivers form the border with W Bengal. The Singalila range separates Sikkim from Nepal to the W and the Dongkya range forms the border in the N and NE. In the E the Chumbi valley lies between Sikkim and Bhutan, a tongue of Tibetan land that gives Sikkim its strategic and political sensitivity.

Sikkim once covered a much larger area but now begins at the foot of the mountains. It is dominated by Kangchendzonga (formerly *Kanchenjunga*), which means the 'Five Treasures of the Great Snows'. According to Sikkimese belief it is the repository of minerals, grains, salt, weapons and holy scriptures. On its W side is the massive 31 km long Zemu glacier. Various explorers and mountaineers have claimed to have seen yeti or their prints in the vicinity of the mountain and its glacier, and in common with other regions of the Himalaya and Karakoram the 'abominable snowman' has its place in folklore.

Rivers and lakes The Tista river valley traverses the whole country from N to S, and allows the monsoon rains to penetrate the northernmost parts. As a result of high monsoonal rainfall, tributaries of the Tista have cut numerous deep valleys out of the soft slate in the S. In the N is an area of rock, glacial debris and snow, with only occasional thin grass cover. This forms the transitional zone between the Himalaya and the Tibetan plateau.

Climate

Temperatures In the lower valleys Sikkim's climate is sub-tropical. Above 1000m the climate is temperate, while the tops of the higher mountains are permanently under snow.

Rainfall Sikkim is one of the wettest regions of the Himalayas. It has the same seasonal rainfall pattern, dominated by the monsoon, as the rest of the E Himalaya. Total rainfall is more than 3000 mm.

Flora & fauna

Vegetation has been influenced by altitude, aspect and rainfall. In the lowest parts there is wet *sal* (Shorea Robusta) forest with 660 species of orchids and 20 species of bamboo. This gives way to tropical evergreen mountain and rain forests (tree ferns, epiphytes, bamboo, oak, beech, chestnut, tree fern, giant magnolia, rhododendron and conifers (firs, pines) up to the treeline at 3600-4200m.

The alpine forests 3900-5000m are characterised by such beautiful flowering plants as primulas, gentians, blue poppies, and wild strawberry, raspberry and rhubarb. Sikkim is a botanist's delight.

Wildlife The animal and bird life is correspondingly rich, with 81 species of mammals, 600 species of birds and 631 species of butterflies – wild asses and yaks in the N, bears, lesser (red) pandas, silver foxes and leopards in the tropical forests. The birdlife is also rich, with pheasants, teal, partridges, cuckoos, babblers and thrushes among many others.

History

The Lepchas claim to be the original inhabitants of Sikkim and call themselves Rongpas. From the 13th century Tibetans immigrated into the area, including the Namgyal clan in the 15th century, who gradually won political control over Sikkim. In 1642 Phuntsog Namgyal (1604-70) became the Chogyal (king). He presided over a social system based on Tibetan Lamaistic Buddhism, and divided the land into 12 *Dzongs* (fortified districts).

In the 18th century Sikkim was much reduced in size, losing land to Nepal, Bhutan and the British. Armies from Bhutan and the newly consolidated Gurkha empire of Nepal invaded and took considerable areas of Sikkim. When the Gurkhas launched a campaign into Tibet and were defeated by the Chinese in 1791-2, Sikkim won back its N territories. The narrow Chumbi valley that separates Sikkim from Bhutan remained with Tibet.

When the British defeated Nepal in 1815, the southern part of the country was given back to Sikkim. However, in the next conflict with Nepal, Darjiling was handed over to the British in return for their assistance. Later in 1848 the Terai region at the foot of the mountains was annexed by the British.

Nepalis migrated into Sikkim from the beginning of the 19th century, eventually becoming more numerous than the local inhabitants. This led to internal conflict which subsequently also involved the British and the Tibetans. When the British refused to stop the influx of Nepalis the *Gyalpos* (Kings, *gyalmos* – Queens) enlisted Tibetan help. The British won the ensuing battles and declared Sikkim a protectorate in 1890. The state was controlled by a British Political Officer who effectively stripped the Gyalpos of executive power. It was many years before the Sikkimese regained control.

Culture

People

Three tribes – the Naong, Chang and Mon are believed to have inhabited Sikkim in prehistoric times.

The **Lepchas**, who have no myths or legends of migration, may have come from Tibet well before the 8th century and brought Lamaistic Buddhism, which is still practised. They completely assimilated the earlier tribes and are now regarded as the indigenous peoples. They are a deeply religious, shy, and peaceful people, but at the same time cheerful. Most have accepted Mahayana Buddhism, while retaining the pre-Buddhist Bon practices.

The government has reserved the Dzongu area in N and Central Sikkim for Lepchas only, now numerically smaller than the later Nepali immigrant population, making up less than 10%. It is a heavily forested region bounded by the rivers Tista and Tolung, and surrounded by the mountain ranges of Kangchendzonga, Pandim, Narsing, Simvo and Siniolchu. Until comparatively recently, the Lepchas were sheltered from outside influence, and their main contact with the outside world was the market-place at Mangan, where they bartered oranges and cardamom, but have now been brought closer to the mainstream of Indian life. Their alphabet was only devised in the 18th century by the king.

There are other minority groups in Sikkim. The **Magar** are renowned as warriors and are mentioned in chronicles as one of the groups that celebrated the coronation of Phuntsog Namgyal, the first Chogyal of Sikkim in 1642.

The **Bhotias** (meaning 'of Bhot/Tibet') (Bhutias) entered Sikkim in the 13th century from Kham in Tibet, led by a prince of the later Namgyal dynasty. Many adapted to sedentary farming from pastoral nomadism and displaced the Lepchas. Some, however, preferred to cling to their older style of existence, and combined animal husbandry with trading over the Trans-Himalayan passes that punctuate the border: Nathula (4392m), Jelepla (4388m), Donkiala (5520m), Kongrala (4809m). Over the years the Bhotia have come into increased contact with the Lepcha and intermarried with them.

Nearly every Bhotia family has one family member who becomes a monk. Traditionally, the priesthood was regarded as the intellectual as well as spiritual elite. Today, with the spread of the Indian educational system into Sikkim and the social mobility that secular employment offers, Bhotia society is in a state of flux. The monasteries remain the repositories of Bhotia culture, and the main social events are the festivals held in them.

Like the Lepchas and the Nepalis, the Bhotias are fond of their *chhang*, a fermented millet, that is the unofficial national drink. They are famous for their weaving, especially hand-woven rugs from Lachen, and are also skilled wood carvers.

The largest migration into Sikkim took place in the 19th century and was from Nepal. The **Newars**, skilled in metal and wood work, were granted the right by the *chogyal* to mine copper and mint the Sikkimese coinage. They were followed by other Nepali groups: the Sherpas, Gurung, Tamang and Rai. All had developed high altitude farming skills in Nepal and settled new lands. As population pressure increased, terraced farming and wherever possible irrigation, were practised with the introduction of rice cultivation. Their houses were built directly on the ground, unlike the Lepcha custom of building on stilts.

The Newars were followed by the Chettris, Bahun and Bishu Karma clans of Nepal, who introduced Hinduism, which became more popular as their numbers swelled. Yet it was Hinduism of the Himalayan type, which included a pantheon of Buddhist bodhisattvas as well as Hindu deities. In Sikkim, as in Nepal, Buddhist and Hindu beliefs have traditionally interacted and amalgamated.

Religion & local festivals

Hindu and Buddhist rituals form the basis for Sikkim's festivals and the same annual *pujas* as in India and Nepal are performed. The animist tradition also prescribes that evil spirits be propitiated. Each ethnic group has an impressive repertoire of folk songs and dances with one for almost every occasion. Since the 22 major festivals are dictated by the agricultural cycle and the Hindu-Buddhist calendar, it is best to check dates with the Tourist office.

Feb: *Losar* Tibetan New Year – preceded by Lama dances in Rumtek.

Jun: *Saga Dawn* A Buddha festival – huge religious processions round Gangtok. *Rumtek chaams* Dance festival in commemoration of the eight manifestations of Guru Padmasambhava, the teacher who is thought to have established Buddhism in Tibet.

Aug/Sep: *Pang Lhabsol* commemorates the consecration of Kangchendzonga as Sikkim's guardian deity, and has its origins in the Lepcha belief of the mountain as their place of birth. However, the actual origin of the festival is said to be the blood brotherhood covenant between theBhotias and Lepchas at Kabi between the Lepcha *bongthing* and the ancestors of the Namgyal royal family. The masked warrior dance is especially spectacular. Kangchendzonga is represented by a red mask and her commander a black one. The warriors who accompany wear traditional armour of helmets, swords and shields. The dramatic entry of *Mahakala* (Protector of the Dharma) is one of the highlights of the festival.

Sep/Oct: *Dasain* and *Deepavali* is the biggest and most important festival celebrated by the Hindu Nepali population. It coincides with *Dasara* in N India and *Durga Puja* in Bengal. See festivals in India, page 152. It begins on the first day of the bright half of the lunar month of *Aswin*. Barley seeds are planted in prayer rooms, invocations are made to Durga and on the 8th day buffaloes and goats are ritually sacrificed. *Diwali* (the Festival of Lights) is celebrated after Dasain.

Nov-Dec: *Losoog* (*Namsoong* to the Lepchas) is the Sikkimese New Year and may also be called *Sonam Losar*, for this is the farmers' celebration of their harvest and beginning of their new cropping calendar. Both Losog and Losar are exuberant family celebrations.

Dec: *Kagyat Dances* enact various themes from the Buddhist mythology and culminate with the burning of effigies made of flour, wood and paper. This symbolises the exorcism of evil and the ushering in of prosperity for the coming year. The dancers of this extremely popular *chaam* are always monks who are accompanied by liturgical music and chanting.

Modern Sikkim

Government

The Indian Government took over effective control of political life in Sikkim in 1950. The Gyalpos lost their power as a result of the new democratic constitution, and the pro-India Nepali population gained the upper hand. Sikkim was formally annexed by India in 1973 and became the 22nd state in the Union through an amendment to the constitution in 1975.

Economy

Agriculture is the main economic activity, and is practised on terraced fields that have been laboriously created from the steep hillsides. Wherever possible irrigation has been introduced. Maize, wheat and barley are grown as winter crops and rice in the summer. Potatoes, oranges and tea are grown in the foothills. Sikkim is the largest producer of cardamom in India. Cardamom is exported, and fruit farming has led to the development of a small canned fruit industry, also for export. Animal husbandry is important in upper Sikkim, with sheep and yak being shepherded to the high pastures over 3500 metres for the summer. Forests cover one third of the state and have enormous economic potential.

Resources and industry Sikkim is rich in minerals and has deposits of copper, lead, zinc, coal, iron ore, garnet, graphite, pyrites and marble, all of which are mined. There are also high grade reserves of gold and silver.

Manufacturing Traditional handicrafts and carpet weaving are important. A distillery was set up in 1956. The Government of India has declared Sikkim an industrially backward area and has set up a flour mill and tannery, watch assembly, tea processing, cable and soap factories.

GANGTOK

The capital of Sikkim lies on a ridge overlooking the Ranipool River. Its name means 'High Hill'. The setting is spectacular with fine views of the Kangchendzonga range, but the town itself has long since lost its quaint charm. It is now rather dusty and uninspiring, and sprawls over the hillside. New and invariably ugly buildings dominate the urban landscape though clean peaceful, flower-filled corners can still be found. There is a high police presence.

BASICS *Population*: 25,000. *Altitude*: 1547m. *STD Code*: 03592. *Clothing*: Summer – light woollens and cotton, Winter – heavy woollens.

Gangtok has only a road connection with the rest of India. The nearest airport is at Bagdogra (124 km), and the nearest railhead at Siliguri (114 km). All the main facilities including hotels, cafés, bazar, bus stand and post office are along the main road from Darjiling which ultimately merges with the old Hindustan-Tibet road.

Places of Interest

At the N end of the town is the **Government Institute of Cottage Industries** where a wide range of local handicrafts are produced, many with a distinctive Tibetan and Chinese look and feel to them, eg woollen carpets, blankets, shawls, dolls, decorative papers and carved and painted wooden tables. Open 0900-1230 and 1330-1530 daily. Closed Sun and every 2nd Sat of the month. Visit recommended.

Enchey Monastery is 3 km to the NE of the main bazar, and next to the Tourist Lodge. Believed to be 200 years old, though the present building dates from 1909. Religious dance performances in Jan.

The **Palace of the Chogyal** is only open once a year in the last week of Dec for the *Pang Lhabsol* festival. Below this is the **Tsuklakhang** or Royal Chapel, standing on a high ridge. This is the major place of worship and has a large and impressive collection of scriptures. Coronations and royal marriages took place here. The interior is lavishly decorated with woodcarving and murals and houses a number of Buddha images. Not always open to visitors and photography prohibited. Moving S along the road you pass the **Secretariat** complex on your left. Beyond this is the **Deer Park,** loosely modelled on the famous one at Sarnath (with a statue of the Buddha, see page 297). The red panda (portrayed in their leaflet) has died; replaced by a vulture!

The unique **Research Institute of Tibetology** on a hilltop was established in 1958 to promote research on Tibet and Mahayana Buddhism. Open 1000-1600 daily except Sun. Free. The library maintains a large and important Buddhist collection. Many fine *thangkas*, icons and art treasures on display.

The **Orchidarium**, and **Saramsa Gardens**,14 km, S of the Institute and lower down, contains over 500 indigenous species in what is more like a botanical garden with large orchidariums. Best time: Mar-May though some visitors have been disappointed in May. The **Deorali Orchid Sanctuary** has 200 species.

CLIMATE: GANGTOK

	Jan	Feb	Mar	Apr	May	Jun	Jul	Aug	Sep	Oct	Nov	Dec	Av/Tot
Max (°C)	14	15	19	22	22	23	23	23	23	22	19	15	20
Min (°C)	4	5	9	12	14	16	17	17	16	12	9	6	11,
Rain (mm)	44	56	142	222	493	644	663	588	476	152	35	15	3530

The **Do-drul Chorten** on one of the southern approaches to Gangtok has the sacred gold-topped stupa with 108 prayer wheels. Nearby is a monastery for young lamas.

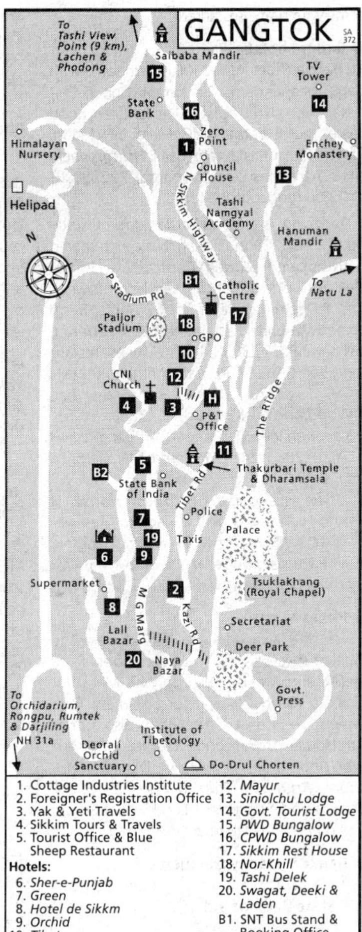

Excursions

Pleasant walks around Gangtok. To Tashi Viewpoint via Enchey Monastery; over Hanuman Top, Ganesh Top, Chandman and back.

Tours

Gangtok *Departure point:* Tourist Information Centre. **Morning Tour** – Govt Institute of Cottage Industries, Deer Park, Chorten, Research Institute of Tibetology, Orchid Sanctuary and Enchey Monastery. In season daily 0930-1230. Rs 25. **Afternoon Tour** – Orchidarium and Rumtek Monastery. In season daily 1400/1430-1700. Rs 35.

Outside Gangtok Phodong Tour. Rs 50. Cars are more expensive. **Package tours to** W Sikkim (min 16), Fri at 1030 returning Sun 1600 (2 nights). Rs 500. Tourist Information Centre, Pemayangtse, organises treks in W Sikkim and helps with information and equipment. **Mountain Flight** to view Kangchendzonga. 35 min. Daily in season weather permitting. Min 12. Fare Rs 350.

Local Festivals

Most of the festivals above are celebrated with great fervour in Gangtok.

Local information

● Accommodation

Because of Gangtok's altitude, a/c is unnecessary. Delux rm in some have excellent views and bath tubs. MG Marg refers to Mahatma Gandhi Rd. **B** *Nor Khill*, Paljor Stadium Rd, T 23186. 35 rm. In old palace, spacious public rm. Good views and gardens. Once excellent but standards slipping.

C *Tashi Delek*, MG Marg, T 22991. 50 rm. Central. Restaurant, bar, exchange, shops, travel (airlines counter), roof garden, free audio-visual programme. Govt **C** *Mayur*, Paljor Stadium Rd, T 22825. 27 rm with bath. Restaurant, bar, tours. Bookings for all Tourism Dept units. Modern.

D *Tibet*, Paljor Stadium Rd, T 22523. 28 rm, with bath. Restaurant (incl Japanese), bar, exchange. Run by Dalai Lama Trust. Peaceful and charming. Govt **D** *Siniolchu Lodge*, nr Enchey Monastery, T 22074. 24 rm, some with bath. Restaurant, bar, tours. **D** *Orchid*, NH 31A, T 23151. 21 rm, some with bath. Restaurant, bar. Clean, good value. **D** *Swagat*, Lall Bazar Rd, T 22991. 16 rm with bath. Indian restaurant. **D** *Green*, MG Marg, T 23354. 45 rm, some with bath. Restaurant.

Budget hotels

E *Lhakpa*, Tibet Rd, T 23002. 3 rm some with bath, cheaper dorm. Restaurant (v good Chinese), bar, roof terrace with views. Clean, good value, rec. **E** *Karma*, MG Marg, nr Gandhi Statue. 17 rm. Restaurant, bar. **E** *Hungry Jack*, NH 31A (nr Bansi Lal petrol pump), T 22353. 10 rm (2 on roof), outside toilet.

F *Denzong*, is rec. **F** *Primula Lodge* Church Rd, T 23599. Central, clean, basic with shared bath, but rec. **F** *Modern Central*, Tibet Rd has clean rm, hot showers, rest. Very helpful owner. Rec. **F** *Deeki*, Lall Bazar Rd, T 23402. 18 rm, some with bath. Restaurant, bar. **F** *Ladenia*, Lall Bazar Rd, T 23058. 10 rm. Chinese restaurant, bar. **F** *Sher-e-Punjab*, Arithang Rd (NH 31A), T 22823. 10 rm. Restaurant, bar. **F** *Woodlands*, MG Marg, T 23361. 16 rm. **F** *Kanchen View*, PO Tadong, Arithang Rd (NH 31A), T 22086. 24 rm. **F** *Doma*, MG Marg. 14 rm.

There is also the CPWD *Rest House*, N Sikkim Highway. 2 very cheap rm. Reservations, CPWD Executive Engineer, Gangtok. Govt **F** *Tourist Lodge*, N end of town, T 474. 23 rm, 4-bed dorms.

Places to eat

Hotels offer a varied menu incl Sikkimese and Tibetan specialties. Specially rec: *Tibet*, *Tashi Delek* and *Mayur*. Also on MG Marg: for Chinese *Khoo Chi* and for Sikkimese *Blue Sheep*, by Tourist Office Bldg; also *Cooks Inn*; *House of Bamboo, Krishna* and *Marwari Bhojanalay*. On NH 31A, Deorali: *Windshore*, *Risur* and *Snip 'n Bite*, Taxi Stand. *Dreamland*, Stadium Rd. Local Sikkimese rum and other spirits are made in Rangpo.

Banks & money changers

Several incl **State Bank of Sikkim**, NH 31A and **State Bank of India**, MG Marg.

Hospitals & medical services

STNM Hospital, NH 31A, opp Hotel Mayur, T 2944.

Important Services

Police: T 2022. **Fire**: T 2001. **Ambulance**: T 2924.

Post & telecommunications

GPO: Stadium Rd and PO in Gangtok Bazar.

Shopping

Sikkim is famous for traditional crafts. Carpets, *thangkas*, traditional jewellery, shirts, boots and fur caps, wood carving all offer good buys. *Cottage Industries Sales Outlet* Mon-Sat 0930-1230; 1300-1530. Also at **Old Bazar**, **Naya Bazar** and **Lall Bazar** (*Haat* on Sun). Closed Tues.

Photography: *Radiant Studio*, Paljor Stadium Rd and others on MG Marg.

Sports

Mountaineering Himalayan Mountaineering Institute based in Yuksom offers climbing courses in stunning surroundings. *Trekking* information from Tourist offices in Gangtok and Pemayangtse for W Sikkim. *River rafting* on Rivers Tista and Rangeel arranged by Tourism Dept and private travel agents.

Tour companies & travel agents

Yak & Yeti Travels, *Snow Lion Travels* and *Sikkim Himalayan Adventures* all organise treks. *Sikkim Tours & Travels*, Church Rd, T22188, F 2707. Some demand US$40-50 per day but will often come down to US$25-35. In Nepal: *President Travels & Tours*, Durbar Marg, Kathmandu, T 226744.

Tourist office

MG Marg, Gangtok Bazar, T 2064. Open in season 0900-1700, off season 1000-1600. No good map but TTK map on sale elsewhere. Also offices in: Hill Cart Rd, Siliguri; Bagdogra Airport; 4C Poonam, 5/2 Russell Street, Calcutta; 14 Panchsheel Marg, Chanakyapuri, New Delhi, T 3015346.

Transport

Gangtok is on the **NH 31A**. Darjiling (139 km) and Kalimpong (81 km).

Local Taxis: fixed rate charts provided, in Gangtok. Rates negotiable for sightseeing. Dept of Tourism, MG Rd, T 2064. **Car hire**: Tarriff per day: Car (max 5 persons) – Rs 500 for travel outside Sikkim, Rs 400 within Sikkim, night halt Rs 200. **Mini-coach**: for 16 (eg Darjiling, Rs 100 per head). **Land Rovers** and **Jeeps** also available.

Air Nearest airport is Bagdogra (124 km), see page 652, under Darjiling. Indian Airlines, Tibet Rd, Gangtok, T 3099. 1000-1600. Taxi to Gangtok, about Rs 125 (Rs 700 for full taxi, max 5 persons) or Snow-Lion mini-bus, 5 hr. **Helicopter**: between Gangtok and Siliguri daily, about Rs 400, one way. Book at Tourist Information Office, MG Rd, T 2097.

Train Nearest railway stations are at Siliguri (114 km) and New Jalpaiguri (126 km) which are well connected with other centres in N and

E India. Reservations: Sikkim Nationalised Transport (SNT), T 2016; 0930-1100, 1330-1430 for transport to stations.

Road The road between Darjiling, Siliguri, Kalimpong and Gangtok is usually motorable through the year. During the monsoons, however, enquire about road conditions at the Sikkim Tourist Office at Siliguri and at the Tista Bridge Check Post. **Bus**: SNT bus services to Darjiling, Kalimpong and Bagdogra (5-6 hr) in N Bengal, and Rumtek, Namchi (which has a Govt 80-bed *Youth Hostel*), Namok, Chungthang and Mangan in Sikkim. Private buses to Kalimpong (6 hr) and 4 daily to Siliguri (6-7 hr). **NB:** You may have to buy tickets 24 hr prior to travel. Ask your hotel if you cannot get it personally. Direct Calcutta-Gangtok, a/c bus Rs 260.

SNT Bus Stand, NH 31A, T 2016. Private buses from West Pt Taxi Stand, NH 31A, T 2858. From Siliguri, N Bengal STC, Burdwan Rd Bus Stand.

Outside Gangtok

Rumtek Monastery

(24 km) Situated in one of the lower valleys, SW of Gangtok, it is the headquarters of the Kagyupa (Red Hat) sect of Tibetan Lamaistic Buddhism. The 16th Gwalpa Karmapa took refuge in Sikkim after the Chinese invaded Tibet. He and his followers brought with them whatever statues, thangkas and scriptures they could and at the invitation of the Chogyal, the Karmapa settled in Rumtek and the lamasery was built. He died in 1982 but the 17th Gwalpa has yet to be identified; a meeting of senior lamas in March 1994 failed to reach a decision. The original monastery built by the 4th Chogyal and destroyed by an earthquake, was rebuilt in the 1960s in the traditional style as a faithful copy of the Kagyu headquarters in Chhofuk, Tibet and now houses the **Dharma Chakra Centre** and the **golden reliquary** of the 16th Gwalpa.

The important *chaam* (religious masked dance) of Rumtek is performed on the 10th day of the 5th month of the Tibetan calendar, and presents 8 manifestations of the Guru Rimpoche. This is highly colourful and spectacular and draws many pilgrims and visitors. Prayers at about 0400 and 1800. Tours in Jul-Aug from Gangtok. Visit recommended.

- **Accommdation E** *Sanjoy*, just outside monastery. Basic but clean, charming, serves meals and is good value.

- **Transport Road Bus**: daily dep Gangtok about 1600 (2 hr) then 30 min walk; return dep about 0800. **Taxi**: Rs 120 for 3.

Phodong

(30 km N) Pleasant walk to gompa, friendly monks show you around. A further walk of 2 km takes you to the older **Labrang** monastery. **Accommodation F** *Yak and Yeti*. Rec as friendly, quiet, clean and good value. **Getting there**: bus from Gangtok, 0900 (2 hr) Rs 30, return dep 1500. Then walk 2 km up to monastery.

Pemayangtse

(140 km W; *Altitude* 2085m) Has Sikkim's 2nd oldest monastery, near the start of the Dzongri trek. A full day's trip by car from Gangtok, Pemayangste (The Perfect Sublime Lotus) was built during the reign of the 3rd Chogyal Chador Namgyal in 1705. The walls and ceilings have innumerable paintings and there is an exceptional collection of religious artworks, including an exquisite wooden sculpture depicting the resting place of Guru Rimpoche.

There are approximately 100 monks in residence and according to tradition they have been recruited from the leading families in Sikkim as this is the 'headquarters' of the Nyingama sect. Annual *chaam* dances, at the end of Feb, 12th month of the Tibetan calendar. Open sunrise-sunset; if closed, ask for key. Good guide. No photography inside.

- **Accommodation** Beautiful views of Kanchendzongha from the comfortable **D** *Mount Pandim* Luxury Tourist Lodge, Pelling (2 km below monastery), T 256. 25 large rm with bath, some with views. Meals incl. Reservations, Tourist Office, Gangtok. **F**

Garuda is an excellent lodge with good food, (roof-top breakfast with mountain views). Helpful staff. Rec. **F** *Rest House* on obtaining prior permission from SPWD, Gangtok. Govt *Trekkers' Hut* has 4 5-bed dorm.

• **Transport Road Bus**: from Gangtok, Rs 40. Onward to monastery, 1000-1430, Rs 10. **Jeep**: shared jeep, Rs 50. From Gangtok starting early enables you to see Tashiding, stop overnight at Gezing or Pemayangtse. Buses can be crowded, esp during Pujas and Diwali. Get ticket on bus if ticket counter is busy. (If you plan to visit **Varanasi** after Gangtok, take the SNT bus to Siliguri/New Jalpaiguri Jn).

Yuksom

(42 km N from Pemayangtse by jeepable road) is where the coronation of the country's first ruler took place in 1641. The wooden alter and throne and a stupa are still here in this beautifully peaceful and picturesque pine forest with a lake. Sikkim's oldest monastery, the simple 'Hermit's Cell' (**Dhubdi**) is uphill (1 hr walk). Dzongri treks start here (see below). **Accommodation** Govt *Trekkers' Hut*.

Gezing

About 100 km from Gangtok (8 hr by car/jeep or bus). **Accommodation** Gezing has basic Guesthouses **F** *Bamboo* where food is available but toilets poor and **E** *Kanchendzonga*. 2 km along the track to Pemayangtse is a **F** *PWD Rest House*. Reservations: CPWD, Gangtok nr Cottage Industries Institute.

From Gezing it is about 6 km (2 hr) climb up to **Pemayangtse monastery**. **Accommodation** Forest Dept **F** *Resthouse*. Bring your own bedding. Local meals available in the town. Reservations: Tourist Office, Gangtok.

Tashiding

W Sikkim. The gold topped monastery was built by the half-sister of Chador Namgyal in 1716 on a spot consecrated by Guru Rimpoche, between the Ratong and Rangit rivers on a ridge overlooking both. Considered to be the most sacred *chorten* in Sikkim, the sight of which is thought to bring blessing. Pilgrims come each spring for the *Bumchu* or water-pot festival in Feb to drink water from the sacred pot which has never run dry for over 300 years.

TREKKING IN SIKKIM

Trekking is in its infancy and many of the routes are through areas that seldom see foreigners. As a consequence, facilities for independent trekkers are poorly developed though the paths are usually clear. Best time mid-Feb to late-May, Oct to early Dec. You do not need previous experience since most treks are between 2000 to 3800m.

MAPS The U 502 sheets for Sikkim are NG 45-3 and NG 45-4. PP Karan published a map at the scale of 1:150,000 in 1969. Price US$3.00, available from the Program Director of Geography, George Mason University, Fairfax, VA 22030, USA. Sikkim Himalaya (Swiss Alpine Club) – Huber 1:50,000. Very detailed. £16.

The **Kangchendzonga National Park** offers trekking routes through picturesque terraced fields of barley, past fruit orchards to lush green forests of pines, oak, chestnut, rhododendrons, giant magnolias. The tracks continue up to high passes crossing fast mountain streams and rugged terrain. Animals in the park include Himalayan brown bear, black bear, sambar, barking deer and the endangered musk deer, flying squirrel, Tibetan antelope, wild asses and Himalayan wild goats. The red panda found between 3000-4000m, lives mostly on treetops. There are about 600 species of birds. **NB** Entry into the Park was restricted in 1994.

It is possible to trek from Pemayangtse (8-15 days) or Naya Bazar (7-8 days) with several options of routing. From Darjiling, a shorter trek goes to Singla and Pemayangtse. See Darjiling Treks, page 660, for details of others.

WARNING Anyone contemplating a trek should aim to be self-sufficient. For this reason, and the likelihood of getting lost and being unable to communicate sufficiently well to re-orientate oneself, the organized group trek is recommended. Foreigners must make up a group of 4 at least before applying for a permit. A Sikkim Police Liaison Officer will usually accompany the group. A number of international companies operate trips to Sikkim. Local agents in Darjiling, see page 659 and Gangtok agents will organize a trek. Govt of India Tourist Offices overseas can often supply a list of tour operators in the country with an accompanying note of special interest tours organized by each.

Trekking agents

Bayul Tours, 27 Supermarket, Gangtok, T 23455, F 22707; *Tashila Tours*, 31A NH, T 22979.

Gangtok – Pemayangtse – Yuksom – Dzongri

The route is from Gangtok to Pemayangtse via Rumtek, then on to Yuksom, Bakhim and Dzongri (described briefly below). Although it is not a long trek there are excellent views throughout as you travel up the Ratong Chu river to the amphitheatre of peaks at the head of the valley. These includes Kokthang (6150m), Ratong (6683m), Kabru Dome (6604m), Forked Peak (6116m) and the pyramid of Pandim (6720m) past which the trail runs.

From Pemayangtse the route passes through terraced fields of rice, barley and corn. After crossing the Rimbi Khola river on a narrow suspension bridge, the road gradually rises to Yuksom.

• **Accommodation** Govt **E** *Trekkers' Huts* with rm and dorm for overnight stops are clean, having been recently built, although the toilets are basic. Bring sleeping bags. Meals are cooked by a caretaker. The huts are in picturesque locations at **Pemayangtse, Yuksom, Tsokha and Dzongri**. An added attraction are that *dzos* (cross between a cow and a yak) will carry your gear instead of porters. The trekking routes also pass through villages which will give an insight into the tribal people's life-style. See Gangtok for Travel Agents.

Yuksom – Thangshing – Gochla La

Yuksom (28 km from Pemayangtse, 2 hr drive) is the base for a trek to the **Gocha La**. This 8-9 day trek includes some magnificent scenery around Kangchendzonga.

Day 1 Yoksum to Tsokha An 8 hr climb to the growing village of Tsokha, settled by Lepcha yak herders and more recently arrived Tibetan refugees. The first half of the climb passes through dense semi-tropical forests and across the Prek Chu on a suspension bridge. A steep climb of 6 hr leads first to **Bakhim** (2740m) which has a tea stall and a *Forest Bungalow*. There are good views back down the trail. The track then goes on through silver fir and cypress to **Tsokha** (2950), the last village on the trek. *Trekkers Hut, Camping ground* and good private *Lodge*.

Day 2 Tsokha to Dzongri (alternatively may be taken as a rest day to acclimatise). Mixed temperate forests gradually give way to rhododendron. **Phedang** is less than 3 hours up the track. Pandim, Narsingh and Joponu peaks are clearly visible, and a further 1 hr climb takes the track above the rhodondron to a ridge. A gentle descent leads to **Dzongri** (4030m, 8 km from Bakhim), where nomadic yak herders stay in huts. There is a *Trekkers Hut* and *Camping ground*. Dzongri is considered specially important for its *chortens* containing Buddhist relics and so attracts occasional pilgrims. From the exposed and windswept hillsides nearby you can get a good panoramic view of the surrounding mountains and see a spectacular sunrise or sunset on the Kangchendzonga.

Day 3 Dzongri to Thangshing A trail through dwarf rhododendron and juniper climbs the ridge for 5 km. Pandim is immediately ahead and a succession of other ridges lead into the heart of Sikkim. A steep drop descends to the Prek Chu again, crossed by a bridge, followed by a gentle climb to **Thangshing** (3900m). The southern ridge of Kangchendzonga is ahead. *Trekkers Hut* and *Camping ground*.

Day 4 Thangshing to Samity Lake The track leads through juniper scrub to a steeper section up a lateral moraine, followed by the drop down to the glacial - and holy - Samity Lake. The surrounding moraines give superb views of Kangchendzonga and other major peaks. You can camp here is at 4250m or stay *Trekkers Hut* with 2 rm and a kitchen.

Day 5 To Chemathang and Gocha La and return The climb up to **Chemathang** (4800m) and **Gocha La** (4900m) gives views up to the sheer face of the eastern wall of Kangchendzonga itself. Tibetans collect sprigs of the scrub juniper growing in abundance here to use in religious rites. It is a vigorous walk to reach the pass, but almost equally impressive views can be gained from nearby slopes. It is rough underfoot as much of the walk is on the moraine with loose boulders.

Day 6 Samity Lake to Thangshing Return to Thangshing. This is only a 2 hour walk, so it is possible to take it gently and make a diversion to the yak grazing grounds of Lam Pokhari Lake (3900m) above Thangshing. You may see some rare high altitude birds and blue sheep.

Day 7 Thangshing to Tsokha The return route can be made by a lower track than that taken on the way up, avoiding Dzongri. Dense rhododendron forests flank the right bank of the Prek Chu, rich in bird life. The day ends in Tsokha village.

NB: See Trekking for detailed advice, see page 112. **Leeches** can be a special problem in the wet season, below 2000m. They can be a nuisance as a bite can become septic. To remove do not pull away but use a spray (eg Waspeeze), some salt, a lighted cigarette or match or, as a last resort, a sharp knife to encourage it to drop off. It is a good idea to spray socks and boot laces well with an insect repellant before setting off each morning.

NORTH-EASTERN HILL STATES

Contents

Maps

The NE is a true frontier region. It has over 800 km of border with Myanmar (Burma) and at least that distance again with China and Bhutan. The NE hill states are a region of transition, with their own distinct cultures and traditions.

Visiting the north east

The NE has been a politically sensitive region since before Independence. **NB:** in 1994 disturbances in the region have continued to make some areas unsafe. The Manas National park is currently closed, and it is essential to take advice about travel locally.

Foreigners visiting Assam, Meghalaya and Arunachal Pradesh must obtain Restricted Area Permits from the Secretary, Ministry of Home Affairs, Govt of India, N Block, New Delhi 110001, 4 weeks in advance (applications may require 2 photos). Foreigners Registration Offices in Calcutta, Delhi, Bombay and Madras are authorised to grant permits to organized groups for visits only to Shillong in Meghalaya. **NB:** the helpful Delhi office of Assam Tourism, B I Baba Kharak Singh Marg, 2nd Flr, can often organize group travel for 4 or more (or help place individuals in groups) within 24 hr. Calcutta is probably the worst place to try and get a permit. Permits cost Rs 260 per person.

Indians wishing to visit the other states, Arunachal Pradesh, Manipur, Mizoram, Nagaland and Tripura require Inner Line Permits from the Ministry of Home Affairs.

Check the political situation and rules before departing as they are subject to change.

Environment

Land

Even this outlying section of the S Asian landmass has elements of all 3 major physical features of the sub-continent. The N mountains are a continuation of the Himalaya, with many peaks over 6500m on both the Indian and Chinese sides of the border. To the immediate S, the Brahmaputra Valley is part of the same trough that, filled with silt, makes up the Ganga basin. To its S lies the Shillong Plateau, now Meghalaya State, which is an outlier of the ancient peninsular rocks of southern India. These became detached in the northwards push of the Indian plate, see page 22, leaving a shallow gap of about 240 km between it and the main peninsular block in Bihar. Through that gap pour the waters of the Brahmaputra and the Ganga. Like the Peninsula, the Shillong Plateau is made up of ancient quartzites, shales, schists, and granites, reaching heights of around 1800m.

These hills marked the sharp end of the advancing Indian plate as it forced itself NE under the Asian landmass. In

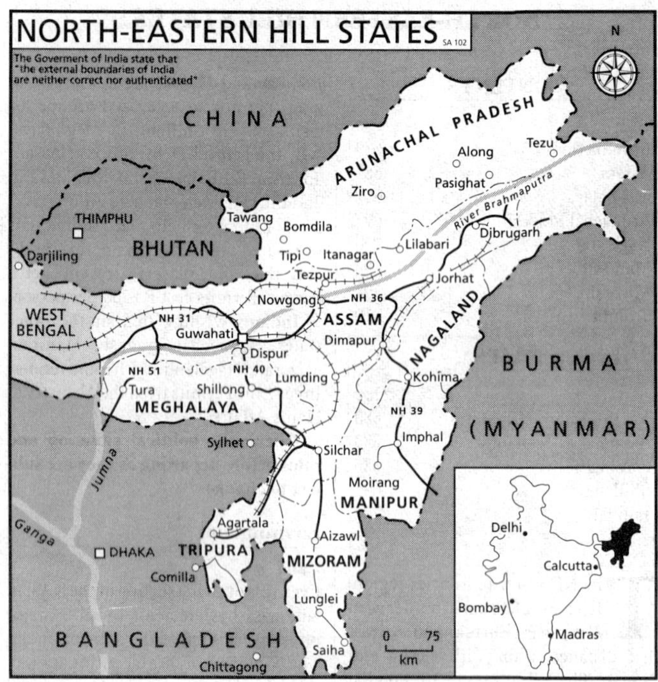

doing so it grossly distorted the easternmost hills of the Arakan so that they now run N-S in parallel ridges. Heights rarely exceed 2100m, although the highest point on the Indo-Burmese border, Saramati (formerly Mount Victoria) is 3810m.

Climate

The region is in one of the wettest monsoon belts in the world. The driest area, a tiny pocket in central Assam, affected by the rainshadow of the Shillong Plateau, has over 1600 mm rain a year. The rest of the Assam Valley has between 1600 mm and 3200 mm a year, while the wettest parts of the Shillong Plateau has received well over double that.

Many of the hills are covered with dense forest, now much degraded. This has stemmed partly from the shifting cultivation practised by tribal peoples who have been forced into ever more intensive use of land by their own increased population, and by the spread of settled agriculture from the plains into the valleys of the hills. On top of these pressures has come commercial forestry. Bamboo forest is common – in places over 10m high. Elsewhere mixed deciduous and evergreen forest is widespread. Assam still has more forest than any other state.

History

After 1947 large parts were governed directly from New Delhi as a special region, the NE Frontier Agency, although Assam has been a state since 1947. In 1962, the year of India's crushing military defeat in its war with China, the Naga Hills district was separated to form Nagaland. Political pressure for autonomy in the tribal areas remained high. 10 years later Meghalaya became a separate state and Arunachal Pradesh and Mizoram became Union Territories. In the 1980s these too were given statehood. Throughout the 1980s Assam was the centre of agitations against the central government in New Delhi, focusing on the issue of immigration from Bangladesh and the eligibility of over 2 million immigrants to vote in elections. In 1994 this was still a vital issue.

Culture

People

The people show strong Mongoloid elements, and the **tribal people** who comprise the overwhelming majority of the region's population have been welded together from Aryan and Mongoloid races who originally came from China, Tibet, Thailand and Burma. They possess distinct cultures with a variety of musical, dance and folk traditions and religious practices with Hindu, Buddhist and animist backgrounds.

A wide range of tribal people – Garo, Khasi, Jaintia in Meghalaya, Nagas and Mizos to the S, have until recently tried to keep themselves to themselves, and have resisted integration into wider Indian life. The local *Ahom* population of the Assam Valley itself has long been intermixed with immigrant Bengalis, Hindus from Calcutta and Muslims from Sylhet and the northern regions of what is now Bangladesh. The towns have minorities from further afield in India, notably Marwari businessmen from Rajasthan, who control trade throughout the region.

Crafts

Handloom weaving is the major cottage industry, women being the principal weavers. A young girl's dowry usually includes a loom. Tribal designs and weaves make the items of clothing and table linen unique. The patterns may reflect the courage and valour of the Naga warrior, the tragic tales in local folklore or the coils of a legendary snake. Wild silks are especially noteworthy, in particular the golden *muga* of Assam as well as the *endi* and *tassar*. It is believed that the finer mulberry silk industry was also already established in Manipur long before the British introduced it into India.

In Manipur, cushions and mats are made of a locally grown spongy reed called *kounaphak*. Cane and bamboo, of which there is a plentiful supply, has led to the hill-states producing a wide range of basketry, both useful and ornamental, including the traditional *sitalpatti* or cool floor covering. Fine wood carving too has an old tradition, especially in Assam.

Dances are performed in locally woven costumes, exotic head dresses of feathers and animal relics, ornaments of cowrie shells and beads and gleaming spears, by many of the 60 or so tribal groups.

Modern NE hill states

Economy

Agriculture The economy of the NE is sharply divided between the settled agricultural economy of the rice growing valleys, notably the Brahmaputra, and the tribal economy of the hills, with its dependence on the forests, and a tradition of shifting cultivation. Increasing population pressure is forcing changes in agriculture, less and less land being available in the hill tracts or in the Brahmaputra Valley for extending land under cultivation.

Industry and resources Oil and natural gas are the most important natural resources, exploited for over 50 years, mainly for export. There is little heavy industry except some engineering work related to the oil industry.

ASSAM

Assam's area of 78,438 sq km, a little smaller than Portugal, makes it the largest of the hill-states in the NE, and its population in 1991 of 22.3 million, dwarfs that of the surrounding ring of tribal states.

SOCIAL INDICATORS *Population*: 24 mn (Urban 11% Scheduled Castes & Scheduled Tribes n.a.). *Literacy*: M 51% F35%. *Birth rate*: *Rural* 30:1000, *Urban* 22:1000. *Death rate*: *Rural* 11:1000, *Urban* 8:1000. *Infant mortality*: *Rural* 103:1000, *Urban* 72:1000. *Religion*: *Hindu* 72%, Muslim 26%, others 2%.

Environment

Land

Occupying the long narrow floor of the Brahmaputra Valley, Assam lies just to the N of 26°N. It stretches nearly 800 kms from E to W but on average is only 80kms wide. The Himalaya to the N and the Shillong Plateau to the S can be clearly seen. The valley floor, even in the rainshadow of the Shillong Plateau, still receives heavy rainfall during the monsoon season of Jun to Oct, often more than 1800 mm. Elsewhere rainfall exceeds 2500 mm.

Assam is dominated by the mighty Brahmaputra, one of the great rivers of the world. It passes through the Assam valley from E to W for over 700 km before entering Bangladesh. Rarely more than 80 km wide, the river valley not only has a fertile alluvial plain growing rice, but is also famous for its tea and for the 2 game reserves at Kaziranga and Manas. The valley floor is covered in recent alluvium, often rather coarse. Earthquakes are common, the 1950 earthquake which had its epicentre on the border between Assam and Tibet being estimated as the fifth largest earthquake in the world.

Flora & fauna

Although most of Assam is low-lying it has some beautiful scenery and some outstanding game reserves. On the banks of the Brahmaputra, the Kaziranga park occupies approximately 430 square km and combines grassland with thorny rattan cane, elephant grass and evergreen forest as well as areas of swampy ground and extensive ponds and lakes. It was declared a game sanctuary in 1926, to save the Indian one-horned rhino which had become threatened with extinction at the turn of the century. The present rhino population has grown to over 1100 although poachers still kill the animal for its horn. The official toll for 1992 was 48, a single horn being valued at US$40,000 in 1994. The park also harbours wild buffalo, bison, sambar, swamp deer, hog deer, wild pig, hoolock gibbon, elephants and tiger. There are otters in the river as well as the long-snouted fish-eating crocodile, the *gharial*.

History

The Ahoms, a Thai Buddhist tribe, arrived in the area in the first part of the 13th century, deposed the ruler and established a kingdom with its capital in Sibsagar. They called their kingdom Assam and later adopted Hinduism. The Mughals made several attempts to invade in the following centuries without success, but the Burmese finally invaded Assam at the end of the 18th century. As a result of these invasions much of the valley became virtually depopulated, and the Burmese held it almost continuously until it was ceded to the East India Company in 1826. The British administered it in name until 1947, though many areas were effectively beyond the reach of normal British government.

Culture

People

The ethnic origin of Assamese varies from Mongoloid tribes to those of directly Indian stock, but the predominant language is Assamese. The Ahom settlers who came into the valley from Burma were Buddhist but most converted to Hinduism. There has been a steady flow of Muslim settlers from Bengal since the late 19th century, a flow which was not stopped by the Partition of India and Pakistan or the creation of Bangladesh. Nearly 90% of the people continue to live in rural areas.

Modern Assam

Modern political development

At Partition, Sylhet district was allocated to Pakistan. Since then Assam has

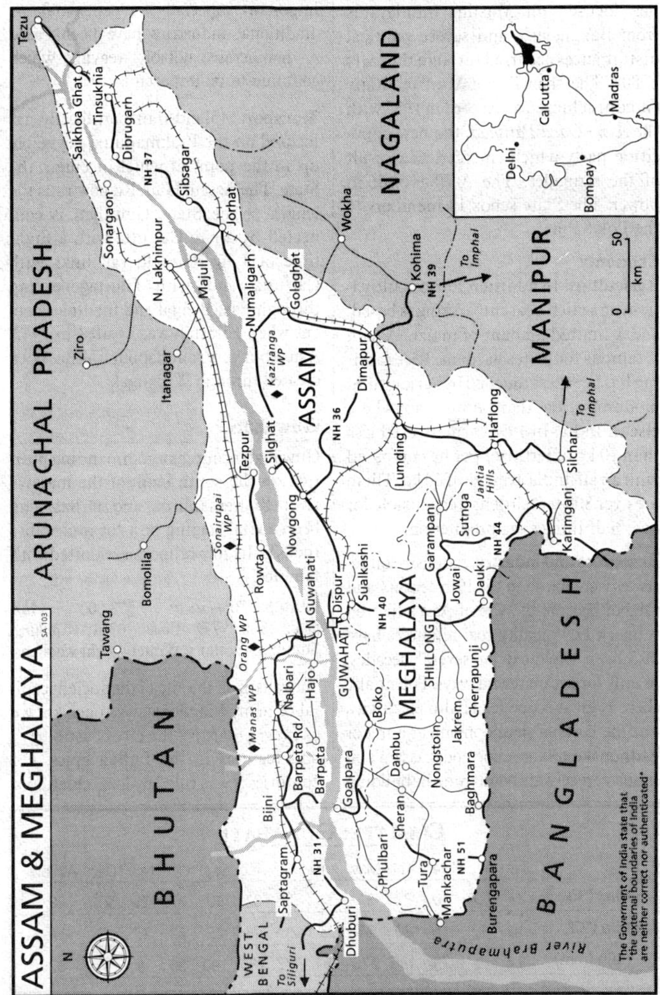

also lost most of its tribal areas which have been given independent statehood. The Assam Valley is in a strategically sensitive corridor for India, lying close to the Chinese frontier. Its sensitivity has been increased by the tension between local Assamese and immigrant groups. Since the late 1970s attention has focused on Muslim immigrants from Bangladesh, and severe political disturbances occurred through the early 1980s. The then Prime Minister Rajiv Gandhi achieved an Accord in 1985 with the *Asom Gana Parishad*, the new opposition party which emerged as a result of the struggles. The AGP is still in power. The State sends 14 members to the Lok Sabha.

Economy

Agriculture In addition to rice cultivation, on which peasant farming is based, and a limited amount of maize, Assam is famous for its tea gardens. Rice farming has been less touched by agricultural modernisation than almost anywhere else in India. In 1991 farmers used less than 10 kg of fertiliser per ha compared with an all-India average of 60 kg. There are over 800 tea gardens, responsible for over half India's tea production.

Resources and industry Extensive oil reserves were found in the 19th century and Digboi became the site of Asia's first oil refinery. Low quality coal resources have also been exploited for several decades, mainly for use on the railways. Potentially there is great scope for Hydro electricity, but the costs of development in a major earthquake area are enormous. Assam's oil industry received a boost from the building of the Guwahati Oil Refinery. The first in the public sector in India, the Noonmati Refinery was erected with Rumanian collaboration in 1961 and produces petrol, light diesel, aviation fuel and furnace oil. The forests continue to provide essential timber, resins and tanning material from tree bark. Bamboo is very important, especially for paper making. Traditional industries have been based on handicrafts, notably weaving, which continue to be important.

Transport Inland transport locally has focused on the Brahmaputra, navigable up to the point at which it enters the State. The Assam High Rd now runs the length of the State. Guwahati is connected by air to Calcutta with a flight time of 1 hr. The old rail links with Calcutta and with Chittagong ran through East Bengal and the links were cut when Pakistan was created in 1947. A new but very roundabout link has been created through W Bengal.

Guwahati

Guwahati occupies a commanding position on the south bank of the massive river Brahamaputra, and it has long been a vital staging post for routes into the NE. Its low hillocks are dotted with temples.

BASICS *Population*: 578,000. *Altitude*: 55m. *STD Code*: 0361. *Clothing*: Summer – cottons, Winter – light woollens.

Guwahati, on the site of the ancient capital of many kingdoms, was once known as *Pragjyotishpur*, ('the city of astrology') and features in the Indian epics. For centuries it was ruled by local chieftains.

CLIMATE: GUWAHATI

	Jan	Feb	Mar	Apr	May	Jun	Jul	Aug	Sep	Oct	Nov	Dec	Av/Tot
Max (°C)	23	27	30	32	31	32	32	32	30	27	25	27	29
Min (°C)	10	12	16	20	23	25	26	26	25	22	17	12	20
Rain (mm)	17	9	73	136	276	351	373	294	190	86	8	7	1820

Since very early times it was a seat of learning and a centre of Hindu pilgrimage. In the 7th century, Hiuen Tsang described its beautiful mountains, forests and wildlife.

Places of interest

Janardhan Temple In the heart of the city atop the hillock Suklesvar the temple was rebuilt in the 17th century having been consecrated in the 10th. It has an image of the Lord Buddha which is an unique blend of Hinduism and Buddhism. **Navagrah Temple** (temple of nine planets), W of Chitrachal Hill was the ancient seat of astronomy and astrology for which Pragjyotishpur was named. **Umananda Temple** dedicated to Siva, stands on Peacock Island in the Brahmaputra as it flows through the city and can be reached by ferry. An Ahom king built the temple in 1594 believing Siva's consort, Uma, to have stayed there.

Kamakshya Temple 8 km NW of Guwahati by bus or taxi. Believed to be an ancient Khasi sacrificial site, the temple on the sacred Nilachal Hill is dedicated to the goddess Kamakshya and has been a well known centre for Tantric Hinduism and worshippers of Sakti. The creative part of the goddess's body (the *yoni*) is said to have fallen here when Siva was carrying her to Mount Kailasa. See page 617. Re-built in 1665 after the original 10th century temple was destroyed by a Brahmin who had become a Muslim convert in the 16th century, it typifies Assamese temple architecture with its distinctive sikhara or spire in the shape of a beehive, the nymph motifs and the long turtle back hall. The hill top also affords a panoramic view of the Brahmaputra. Non-Hindus may not enter the sanctum. The *Ambubachi* in June celebrates the end of Mother Earth's menstrual cycle when the temple draws large crowds and a fair is held.

12 km from Guwahati is the beautifully situated **Basistha Ashram**. The ashram, believed to occupy the site where the sage Vasistha lived, is a natural beauty spot with 3 mountain streams flowing nearby.

Museums

Assam Forest Museum, S Kamrup Div has collections of timber, cane and ivory work, tusks and horns, and models of buildings and bridges. 1000-1600 weekdays, 1000-1330 Sat. Guide service. Assam Govt Cottage Industries Museum. 1000-1600 weekdays,1000-1300 Sat. Assam State Museum has collections of archaeology, sculpture, paintings, metal, ivory and woodwork, costumes and ethnology. 1000-1630, Tue-Sat and 0800-1200 on Sun. Closed Mon and on second Sat. Re 0.50. A small museum, well lit and thoughtfully displayed with notes in Assamese and English where you can get a good idea of Ahom and neighbouring cultures. Guide book available. Guide service and films occasionally. Photography with permission. The Veterinary College Museum, 1000-1600. Closed Sun. Commercial Museum, Guwahati University has collections of art and craft, commercial products, minerals and rocks, coins etc. 1230-1830, Mon-Sat, closed Sun and University holidays. Free. No photography.

Parks & Zoos

Zoo and Botanical Gardens has swamp tapirs, rhinos, tigers, lions, panthers among other species and rich birdlife, particularly interesting because there are animals and birds of NE India which are not often seen elsewhere. It is largely an open-enclosure zoo with landscaped gardens. Restaurants and souvenir shops. Opening times vary but usually Sep-Mar 0700-1600, Apr-Oct 0800-1730. Re 1. Access by bus, taxi and auto-rickshaw.

Tours

State Dept of Tourism runs tours from the Tourist Lodge on Station Rd. *City sightseeing*: Basistha Ashram, Zoo, Museum, Kamakshya Temple, Govt Sales

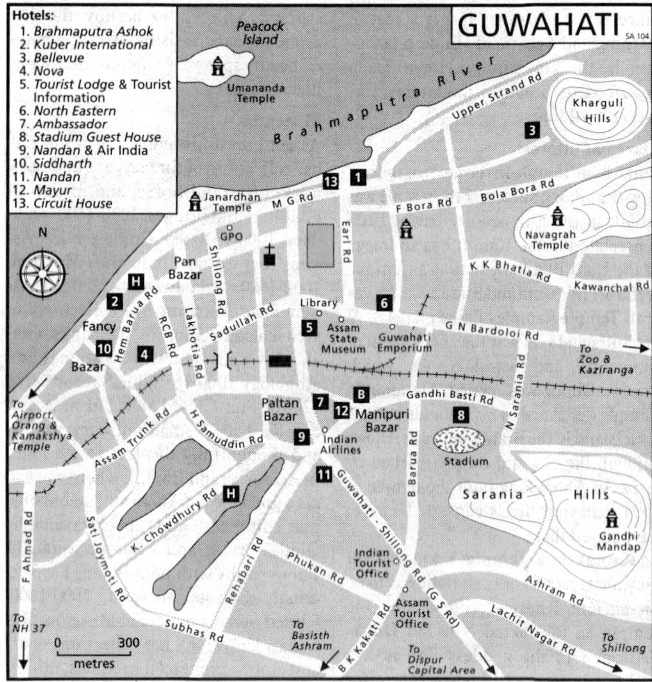

Emporium. Daily on demand, 0700-1800. Rs 30. For other tours see Excursions below.

Local Festivals

Magh Bihu in **Jan** and *Bohag Bihu* and *Rongali Bihu* in mid-**Apr**, the week-long New Year festivities are celebrated with singing and dancing. **Mar** – *Sivaratri* is celebrated on Peacock Island at the Umananda Temple with all night vigil and hymns and prayers. **Sep** – *Manasa Festival* at the Kamakshya Temple in honour of the Snake goddess. You can watch devotees in unusual costumes dancing and going into trances from galleries built for the purpose on the hillside above the temple. Between Nov and April the *Assam Tea Festival* is celebrated with events in various parts of the State. Details from Assam Tourism.

Local information

● Accommodation

Most are close to the railway and about 20 km from airport (except *Urvashi*). **C** *Brahmaputra Ashok*, MG Rd, T 41064. 50 rm. Central a/c. Good restaurant, bar, exchange, shops, travel. Riverside rm best. **C** *Chilarai Regency*, HP Brahmachari Rd, Paltan Bazar, T 26877. 44 large rm, some a/c. Restaurant, bar, exchange. **C** *Prag Continental*, Motilal Nehru Rd, Pan Bazar, T 28201. 62 rm. Public areas and some rm, a/c. Restaurants, one on terrace, *Continental Café*, travel. **C** *Coronet Dynasty*, SS Rd, T 35610. 68 rm. 2 restaurants and bar. **C** *Urvashi*, nr airport, Bonjhar, T 82889. 25 rm. Central a/c. Restaurant for residents, free airport transfer. **C** *Raj Mahal*, AT Rd, Paltan Bazar, T 541125. Very large modern hotel, excellent restaurant for north and south Indian and continental food. Excellent value cheaper rm.

D *Kuber International*, Hem Barua Rd, T 32601. 75 a/c rm. Good restaurant with views, revolving *Orbit* for snacks and icecream, bar, shops. **D** ***Nandan***, Paltan Bazar, GS Rd, opp. IA. T 40856. 55 rm, some a/c. 2 restaurants, *Upavan* snack bar, bar, shops, travel. Luxury buses to other hill states. Rec. **D** ***Belle Vue***, MG Rd, opp Raj Bhawan, T 40847. 45 rm, some a/c. Simple. On river front. Restaurant, permit room, exchange. Elevated and quiet. **D** ***Siddharth***, Hem Barua Rd, Fancy Bazar, opp Taxi Stand, T 40857. 36 rm, some a/c. Restaurant, exchange, travel. **D** ***Samrat***, Assam Trunk Rd, Santipur, T 34542. 24 rm, half a/c. Restaurant and bar, travel. **D** ***North Eastern***, GNB Rd, T 28281. 18 rm, some a/c. Licensed dining room (Indian, Chinese). Many medium priced and budget hotels have some a/c rm and tend to serve Indian meals only. **D** ***Maruti***, Radha Bazar, Fancy Bazar, T 23306. 62 rm, some a/c. Veg restaurant.

● Budget hotels

E ***Mayur***, Paltan Bazar, opp ASTC Bus Stand, T 34385. 158 rm. Restaurant.

F ***Railway Retiring Rooms***. Rm and small dorm. Book at Enquiry Counter. **F** ***Tourist Lodge*** (Assam Tourism), opp rly station, T 24475. 5 rm. Conveniently situated, fairly clean with good toilets. Service indifferent and no catering. Good value for short stay. Contact Tourist Information Officer, Guwahati. **F** ***Nova***, Fancy Bazar, T 23258. **F** ***Stadium Guest House***, 13 Barua Rd, T 23312. **F** ***Circuit House*** and ***Dak Bungalow*** and a ***YMCA Hostel*** on Chhattribari Christian Hospital Compound with double rm. Simple and inexpensive **F** hotels in Paltan Bazar: ***Joydurga***, KC Sen Rd. 30 small rm. Indian meals. ***Rajdoot Palace*** T 22732; ***Sukhmani***, KC Sen Rd; ***Ambassador***, T 28341.

● Places to eat

Assamese *thalis* incl rice, fish and vegetable curry, often cooked with mustard. You might try Veg *Kharoli, Omita* or *Khar* (rice and papaya). Only larger hotels serve Continental food and have bars – ***Kuber International*** is rec. Outside hotels: ***Silpukhuri*** (Assamese *thalis*, Chinese, Indian). ***Paradise***, Sangamari, Moniram Dewan Rd, for *thalis* are rec. ***Piccadilly*** and ***Sunflower*** (a/c) are in Pan Bazar.

● Banks & money changers

State Bank of India, Fancy Bazar and Grindlays Bank, Lakhotia, among others, deal in foreign exchange.

● Entertainment

Regular cultural programmes *Rabindra Bhawan* and the *Dist Library Auditorium* in Ambari.

● Hospitals & medical services

Medical College, Bhangagarh, T 87477. *MM Choudhury Hospital*, Pan Bazar, T 32446. *Chhattribari Christian Hospital*, T 24469.

● Post & telecommunications

GPO: Pan Bazar. **Central Telegraph Office**: Pan Bazar.

● Shopping

Assamese *Muga, Pat and Endi* silks, hats, bamboo and cane baskets, flutes, drums, pipes and ivory carvings are typical of the area (though as elsewhere in S Asia ivory exports are now banned). ***Pragjyotika Assam Emporium*** at Ambari, sells silks, bamboo, wood, brass and ceramics. ***Purbashree***, GNB Rd has traditional craft items from all the NE hill-states. ***Assam Co-op Silk House*** on HB Rd, Pan Bazar has pure silk items including saris with typical geometric patterns in cotton (Rs 500- over Rs 2000). ***Manipur Emporium***, Paltan Bazar; ***Tantuja***, Ulubari for Bengal handloom. You may need to bargain in Panbazar and Fancy Bazar.

Books: Pan Bazar has some bookshops.

Photography: *S Ghoshal*, HB Rd. *Apsara* and *Hara Kamani*, Pan Bazar. *Bombay* and *Photo Concern* in Fancy Bazar.

● Sports

Swimming: *Assam Swimming Club*, Ambari and Pool in Nehru Stadium.

● Tour companies & travel agents

Rhino, Motilal Nehru Rd, Pan Bazar T 40061 and ***BSS***, Fancy Bazar for Indian Airlines, and for tours to game reserves and Shillong. In Paltan Bazar: ***Blue Hill***, Brahmachari Rd (or at *Brahmaputra Ashok*) and ***Assam Valley Tours***, GS Rd are rec. 0700-1900.

● Tourist offices

Govt of India, BK Kakati Rd, Ulubari, T 31381. 0900-1700, Sat 0900-1300. Airport counter, T 82204. **Assam Tourism**, Station Rd, T & F 47102. Information Office, T 24475. Also counters at airport and Rly station. **Meghalaya**, Tourist Information Office, ASTC Bus Stand, Paltan Bazar. 1000-1700 except Sun.

● Transport

1151 km from Calcutta by road, Guwahati is well connected by road to all major centres of the NE region being at the junction of **NH 31, 37** and **40**.

Local Transport to town: transfer by taxi, Rs 150 for 5. Guwahati Taxis, Paltan Bazar, nr

Police Station behind rly. **Auto-rickshaws** also available for city sightseeing. There is a city **bus** service. Assam Tourism has **cars**, **jeeps** and **mini-buses** for hire (Rs 400 per day plus overnight Rs 150). The Inland Waterways Transport Corporation runs a **ferry** to Raja Duar and Madhya Khanda from MG Rd Ferry Station. Re 0.50 one way. Visitors who have been elsewhere in India will be shocked by the cost of autorickshaws – Rs15-20 for the shortest distance.

Air **Indian Airlines**, Paltan Bazar, GS Rd, T 40355. Reservations, T 40398, Airport, T 82235; 0900-1600. Transfer coach Rs 15. **Calcutta**, daily, 1430, 1 hr and M,W,F,Su, 1110; **Delhi**, Tu,Th,Sa, 1215, 2½ hr; **Bagdogra**, M,W,F,Su, 1030, ¾ hr; **Imphal**, W,F,Su, 1135, ¾ hr.

Pawan Hans operates a helicopter service to Shillong and Tura. The airport is 25 km from the centre of town and the IAC transfer coach and Assam Tourism Coach connect with Calcutta flights (Rs 20 per person). Taxis are more expensive (Rs 150 for 5), but can be shared (1 hr). Rhino Travels and *Brahmaputra Ashok* also provide coach transfers. Pawan Hans Agents, Rhino Travels, Motilal Nehru Rd, Pan Bazar. 0900-1800.

Train The town is linked with all parts of the country by broad gauge and metre gauge rly. Enquiries: T 26644. Reservations, T 32288; 0945-1700. **Dibrugarh Town**: *Tinsukia Mail*, 5907, daily, 1315, 17¾ hr; **Calcutta (H)**: *Kanchenjunga Exp*, 2558 (AC/II), daily, 2230, 22½ hr; *Kamrup Exp*, 5660 (AC/II), daily, 0745, 22¾ hr; To **Delhi (D)**: *Tinsukia Mail*, 2455 (AC/II), daily, 1315, 40¾ hr.

Road Bus: State Transport Corps of the neighbouring hill states all provide good links with the capital of Assam with Deluxe and Express buses. Assam STC Bus Stand, Paltan Bazar, T 40208. Reservations 0630-1230,1330-1700. Private coaches and taxi services also operate from Paltan Bazar; they provide extra facilities (waiting rooms, left-luggage counters and snack bars). Private operators run daily services to: **Silchar** 1730. **Shillong** from 0630 to 1730 (3½ hr). **Kohima** 2000, 2015, 2030 (13 hr). **Itanagar** 1830 (11 hr). **Aizawl** 1830 (11 hr). **Imphal** 2000, 2015, 2030. **Siliguri** 1830, 1845, 1900. **Tezpur** 0700.

Distances between Guwahati and some places of interest in the region: Shillong 103 km, Kaziranga National Park 233 km, Manas Wildlife Sanctuary 176 km, Itanagar 401 km, Imphal 579 km.

Excursions

Assam Tourism offers a hill package tour and a north east tour as 6 to 8 day excursions for between Rs1300 and Rs1700 per person, starting from Guwahati Travel Lodge. It also ofers a full day trip to Hajo, Dep. 0930, return 1630, Rs 300. Other tours include: *Shillong*: day trip. W,Su, 0700, arr. Shillong 1030, return 2000. Rs 100. *Kaziranga*: Nov-Apr. Overnight trip departing at 0930, via Nagaon, arr. 1600. Return 1630 on the following day. Rs 300. Also morning bus, dep. 0700 from Assam State Bus Station. 5½ hr

Sanctuary visit on elephant. M,Th,Sa,Su. Oct-May. Rs 265. *Manas*: Nov-Apr. Tiger Reserve, currently closed because of political agitation by the Bodo tribal peoples who have occupied it. See Excursions, below.

Hajo

24 km across the river is a centre for different religions. The **Hayagriba Madhab**, the best known in the group of Hindu temples is believed by a section of Buddhists to be where the Buddha attained Nirvana. It is also a Muslim pilgrimage centre since the mosque known as **Pao Mecca** built by Pir Ghiasuddin Aulia, is supposed to have ¼ (pao) of the sanctity of Mecca. Bell-metal work produced here.

Sualkashi

32 km S, is the famous silk-producing village. Every household is involved with weaving of *Muga*, *Endi* or *tassar* silk; prices 30% cheaper than Guwahati. There are also brass-workers here. Ferry services operate between Guwahati and N Guwahati.

Guwahati to Dibrugarh via Kaziranga

The road from Guwahati runs through forest covered hills, small villages, and low-lying fields with stands of coconut palms before entering tea estates. There are still low-lying shallow-water expanses before the road begins to rise quite sharply as it approaches the **Kaziranga National Park**. The road continues to the S of the Brahmaputra through Jorhat and Sibsagar to Dibrugarh.

Kaziranga National Park

Approach

Guwahati is 215 km from Kohora, the entry point of the Kaziranga Wildlife Sanctuary on the NH37. *Altitude* 65m. *Climate* Temp. Summer Max. 35°C Min. 18°C Winter Max. 24°C Min. 7°C. Annual rainfall 2300 mm, heavy in summer. *Best Season* Nov-mid April. Closed mid Apr-mid Oct during monsoons. *Clothing* Cottons but carry a jacket for sudden cool weather. Woollens in the winter.

Background

On the banks of the Brahmaputra, the park occupies 430 sq km, combining elephant grass with thorny rattan cane, areas of semi-evergreen forest and shallow swamps. The Karbi Anglong Hills rise S of the park, while the river forms its N boundary. There are a number of rivulets which flow down to the flood plain, bringing down rich silt and spreading out into shallow lakes called *bheels**. The habitat varies from marshes to grassland, woodland, rising to moist deciduous forests and finally to tropical semi-evergreen forests.

Wildlife

Kaziranga was declared a game reserve in 1926, to save the Indian one-horned rhino which had become threatened with extinction at the turn of the century. The present ***rhino*** population is over 1100 (although poachers still kill the animal for its horn), and you can easily see them in the marshes and grasslands. The park also harbours wild buffalo, sambar, swamp deer, hog deer, wild pig, hoolock gibbon, elephants, pythons and tiger, the only predator of the docile rhino. There is a rich variety of shallow-water fowl including egrets, pond herons, river terns, black-necked stork, fishing eagles, and adjutant storks which breed in the park and a pelicanry. The grey pelicans nest in tall trees near the village and there are otters and dolphins in the river.

Viewing

Trained *elephants* may be hired for seeing the game reserve. Whereas the elephants cover less ground than motor vehicles, they can get a lot closer to the wildlife, particularly rhinos and buffalo, than the vehicles. Elephants carry 4 and a seat may be booked through the Forest Range Officer for about Rs 25. The Dy Director, Dept of Tourism, Kaziranga has *jeeps* for hire by the hr, the rates take into account a given distance. **NB** Those taking a car or a jeep around the sanctuary **must be accompanied by a Forest Dept guide**, provided free, who can give directions as well as spot wild life. Cars and jeeps are charged an entry fee plus passengers, for forest viewing (about Rs 7, Re 1 for students). Camera fees: Rs 5 for a still camera without telephoto lens rising to Rs 500 for a 35 mm ciné camera.

Park roads open 0800-1100, 1400-1630. Elephant rides between 0500-0600, 0630-0730 and 1530-1630. There are 3 road routes for visiting the park. The *Kaziranga Range* – Kohora, Daflang, Foliomari; the *Western Range* – Baguri, Monabeel, Bimoli, Kanchanjuri; and the *Eastern Range* – Agortoli, Sohola, Rangamatia. The *observation towers* are situated at Sohola, Mihimukh, Kathpara, Foliamari and Harmoti.

Tours from Guwahati

Assam Tourism offers a 2-day tour from Guwahati during the season, starting on Th, Sat and Sun which includes food, accommodation, transport and sanctuary visit on elephant back. Adults Rs 275. Child reductions.

Park information

● Accommodation

D *Wild Grass Hotel*, 21 rm and deluxe camping. T 0377 681737. (In Guwahati: Add. barva Bhavan, 107 M.C. Rd, Uzan Bazar, T 0361 596827, F 091 541186; Calcutta T 9792722) Wonderfully situated by stream in paddy fields and forest. Spotless accommodation, wood floors, cane furniture, superb service. Organises elephant rides, local dancing. Pick up service from Guwahati airport for groups. All facilities, beautiful walks through forests and tea plantations. Highly rec. **D** ***Kaziranga Forest Lodge***, T 29. Some a/c rm. Restaurant with reasonable meals, bar. Best rms with private balconies overlooking the Karbi hills (more comfortable, suitable for elderly or those travelling with children). Reservations: Manager, ITDC. **D** ***Aranya Tourist Lodge*** (Assam Tourism), T 0377681 429. Some a/c rm. There are two other Assam Tourism Tourist Lodges, *Bonani* (T 0377681 423), also with some a/c but slightly cheaper, and the still cheaper and entirely non-a/c ***Bonashree***. Contact through Directorate of Toursim, Guwahati, T 40061.

E ***Kaziranga Tourist Lodge*** has 2 bungalows. No.1 (western style), 5 rm. Upper floor better, some a/c. No. 2 (Indian style) has 7 rm. Surcharge for a/c. Clean, good upkeep and catering. ***Dormitory*** at Kohora. Linen optional. Two 12-bedded rm and two 3-bedded. Reasonably clean but no cupboards or lockers. Shared toilets. Meals, both Indian and Western at Tourist Lodge. Suitable for the young prepared to rough it. Reservations: Dy Director of Tourism, Kaziranga Sanctuary, Sibsagar District. T 23, The Wildlife Society has a **library** of books and magazines and can organise wildlife films for large groups of foreign tourists.

● Post & telecommunications

Post Office: nr the Tourist Lodge and at the Park.

● Transport

Air Jorhat, 88 km away is the nearest airport. Daily Indian Airlines flights to Jorhat from Calcutta via Guwahati. See page 688. **NB**: Groups of foreign tourists may only use Guwahati airport. See page 679.

Train Nearest railway station is at Furkating, 75 km away with a metre gauge line to Guwahati. Buses connect Guwahati with Kaziranga via Golaghat.

Road Kaziranga is on the NH 37 which crosses the Brahmaputra from Goalpara Ghat in W Assam. Assam Road Transport operates buses from Guwahati and Jorhat which stop at Kohora which has accommodation. Private companies operating long-distance coaches make request stops at Kohora. The *Forest Lodge* at Kaziranga has 10 seats reserved on the Express coach between Golaghat and Guwahati.

Manas Wildlife Sanctuary

Approach

NB: In 1994-95 the sanctuary was closed due to political troubles with the Bodo tribal movement. *Alt* 70 m. *Area* 2800 square km. *Climate* Temp. Summer Max. 35°C Min. 18°C, Winter Max. 24°C Min. 7°C. Annual rainfall 410 mm.

Background

Scenically, the Sanctuary is one of India's most beautiful. It lies in the foothills of the Himalaya, SE of the river Manas, which with its associated rivers *Hakua* and *Beki* separate India from the neighbouring kingdom of Bhutan. Over half the area is covered with tall grass and scattered patches of woodland with *simul, khoir, udal, sida, bohera* and *kanchan* trees. This changes to dense semi-evergreen forest in the upper reaches and even to conifer on hills abutting Bhutan.

Wildlife

The forests are home to most of the larger animals found in Kaziranga, most common being wild buffalo, swamp deer, hog deer, sambar and elephant. Some 20 of the animal and bird species are on the endangered list of the IUCN incl the rare capped and golden langur which can be seen among the flowering trees, mostly on the Bhutan side. In addition it also has pigmy hog, the hispid hare, slow lorris, clouded leopard and tiger. The **Manas Tiger Reserve**, a core area of 360 sq km was demarcated in 1977/8 when the preservation programme 'Project Tiger' was launched. The sanctuary is also rich in birdlife (over 400), attracting many migratory flocks including redstarts, forktails, mergansers and ruddy shelduck. Otters are frequently seen in the Manas river; it is possible to take a boat ride. Between Dec and Mar the river fish made it an angler's paradise but this has been banned since 1988. Boats (for 2-8) for hire for 4-8 hr from the Forest Beat Officer, Mothanguri. To see the animals from close range, an elephant ride is best, which starts from Mothanguri, inside the sanctuary. 3 hr ride for 3, Rs 50. 0900-1200, 1400-1700. The visiting arrangements by car, taxi or minibus, and charges for entry and camera fees are similar to Kaziranga (see above). **Note** Manas was closed due to political activism. Latest position from Field Director.

Park information

● Accommodation

F *Manas Forest Lodge* which is built on a hill overlooking the river and the Forest Dept's *Forest Lodge* and *Bhutan Tourist Lodge*, Mothanguri provide very simple and inexpensive accommodation which is clean and well maintained and must be booked well in advance. Cook available but visitors must carry their own provisions. Camp site available for visitors with tents. The prefabricated *Rest House* provides linen but has no electricity. Open Oct-May. Contact Divisional Forest Officer, Wildlife Div, PO Barpeta Rd, Assam, T 19 or Field Director, Manas Tiger Reserve, PO Barpeta Rd, Assam.

● Services

Barpeta Road: is the nearest place with **medical facilities**, a **Tourist Information Office**, **Banks** and a **Post Office**.

● Transport

Air Guwahati, 176 km away is the nearest airport.

Train Nearest railway station at Barpeta Road (40 km) with connections to Guwahati and Calcutta.

Road There is a good fair weather road from Manas to Barpeta which in turn has a very good road to Guwahati.

Jorhat

(*STD Code* 0376) Jorhat is one of Assam's major tea centres and host to the Assam tea festival held in November.

● **Accommodation** Only basic small guest houses and one *Government Tourist Lodge*. Reservations: Asst. Tourist Information Officer, PO Jorhat, Tarajan. T 21579.

● **Transport Air** Jorhat has the main airport for the far Northe East. There are Indian Airlines flights to Calcutta on Tu,Th,Sa, dep 1145. **Road** Guwahati (314 km), Sibsagar (55 km) and Dibrugarh (131 km) are all connected by bus.

Sibsagar

(*STD Code* 03772) District HQ of the largest tea and oil producing area in the North East, Sibsagar was the Ahom Kingdom's capital for 6 centuries before the British took over power. The Ahom Queen Madambika constructed the huge tank on which the town stands in 1734. The tower of the Siva temple on its bank is one of the highest in India.

Places of interest

Kareng Ghar and Talatal Ghar 6 km from Sibsagar centre, the seven storeyed place – three of the storeys being underground – was built between 1696-1714 by King Rudra Singha. Two underground tunnels are popularly believed to have connected the palace with Gargaon's Palace 15 km away and with the Dikhow River. The East India Company is held responsible for their disappearance.

Gargaon Palace 13 km E of Sibsagar, Gargaon was the 16th century capital of the Ahoms, but the present palace dates from 1762 and was built by King Rajeswar Singha.

The Royal Tanks There are 3 major royal tanks and associated temples. The **Joysagar Tank** (1697) at Rangpur, 5 km away, built by King Rudra Singha in memory of his mother Joymoti. He also built the 3 temples on the bank in 1698, the Vishnu Temple (Joydol), Shivadol and Devadol. Queen Phuleswari Devi (1722-91) dedicated the **Gaurisagar Tank** to Durga, while the **Rudrasagar Tank** and its temple were built in 1773 by King Rudra Singha.

Charaideo, 28 km E of Sibsagar, the first capital of the Ahoms kings in 1253 AD.

Local information

● Accommodation

Assam Tourism **F** *Tourist Lodge*. Reservations, Asst Tourist Information Officer, PO Sibsagar, Tarajan, T 2394.

● Transport

Although Sibsagar is on the main road to

Dibrugarh the nearest railway station is at Simaluguri (20 km) and the nearest aiport at Jorhat (60 km). Regular buses from Guwahati.

Digboi

(*STD Code* 0374) The site of the oldest oil wells in India, the oil fields of upper Assam were first exploited in 1879, and refining was attempted between 1879 and 1883. Drilling began at Digboi in 1888 and the first wells came on stream in 1892, the first refinery being opened in 1900. Although Digboi's own resources are now drying up, the region still has considerable potential, though the industry has been severely disrupted by the political troubles of the 1980s and early 1990s.

Dibrugarh

(*STD Code* 0373) Dibrugarh, set in the upper Assam plain, lies in the heart of the tea estate region.

MEGHALAYA

Meghalaya's name, 'abode of the clouds', is appropriate, for the S-facing slopes overlooking Bangladesh are the wettest place on earth. Meghalaya is a compact and isolated state, bordered on the N by Assam and on the S by Bangladesh. It covers 22,500 square kilometres of rolling plateau, and lies in a severe earthquake belt. The entire town of Shillong was destroyed in an earthquake in 1896. One of the smallest States in India, it has only 1 million people.

ENTRY PERMITS Always check before travel as entry regulations often change. See page 679. Applications for permits to visit for up to 10 days from the Under Secretary, Govt of India, Ministry of Home Affairs, Lok Nayak Bhavan, New Delhi. Meghalaya House, 9 Aurangzeb Rd, T 3014417 or 9 Russell St, Calcutta, T 200797, processes applications from groups of 4 or more within a day. Also available from FRRO Bombay and Chief Immigration Officer Madras.

SOCIAL INDICATORS *Population*: 1.8 mn (Urban 19%, Scheduled Tribes 86%). *Literacy*: M 58% F 45%. *Birth rate*: *Rural* 34:1000, *Urban* 19:1000. *Death rate*: *Rural* 13% urban 5%. *Religion*: *Christian* 53%, *Tribal and animist religions* 26%, *Hindu* 18%, *Muslim* 3%.

Environment

Land

Meghalaya has been referred to as the 'Scotland of the East' in view of the similarity of the climate, terrain and scenery with pine clad hills, beautiful lakes and waterfalls. Much of the plateau is made up of the same ancient granites as are found in peninsular India. Its S facing slope, overlooking Bangladesh, is very steep. The hills rise to heights just under 2000m which makes it pleasantly cool despite the fact that it is so close to the tropics. Much is still densely forested.

Climate

The altitude of the plateau at 1500m moderates the temperatures, but also causes tremendously heavy rainfall as the monsoon winds come N from the Bay of Bengal laden with moisture. Cherrapunji has received more than 20,000 mm in one year.

History

The Khasi, Jaintia and Garo tribes each had their own small kingdoms until the 19th century when the British annexed them one by one. The Garos were originally from Tibet. They were animists, and once practised human sacrifice. Since the mid-19th century have stopped displaying human skulls in their houses. The Khasis are believed to be Austro-Asiatic. Jaintias are Mongolian and similar to the Shans of Burma. They believed in the universal presence of god and hence they built no temples. The dead are commemorated by erecting monoliths and groups of these can be seen in Khasi villages in central Meghalaya on your way from Shillong to Cherrapunji.

Similar monoliths erected by ancient

peoples in other parts of the world, as in Brittany, Corsica, Cornwall and Wales are called cromlechs, dolmens or menhirs, the 'men' from the word for 'stone'. Curiously, the Khasi word for stone is also 'men'! In the 19th century many were converted to Christianity by missionaries, although they continued many of their old traditions. They have several distinctive customs. All 3 tribes are matrilineal passing down wealth and property through the female line.

Culture

People

The Garos (who are also found in Bangladesh), the Khasis and the Jaintias account for the majority of the population. Each has their own tribal language. Shillong is the only important town, and 80% of the people live in villages.

Local festivals

Shillong A 2-day folk-dance festival of thanksgiving '*Shad Suk Mynsiem* in Apr; 5-day *Nongkrem Dances* for harvest and Autumn Festival in Oct/Nov. In Ashanagiri near Tura, the harvest is celebrated in Nov with the *Wangala*, the 100 Drums Festival by the Garos. Jowai celebrates the harvest with *Laho* dances and the *Behdeinkhlam* in Jun/Jul when Smit hosts the Khasi *Shed Nongkrem* dance festival.

Modern Meghalaya

Government

The hill-state was created on 21 Jan 1972 out of Assam. The Congress Party came to dominate elections to the Lok Sabha after claiming only 36% of the vote in 1977, winning 74% in 1980 and 62% in 1984. However, it has never won more than 25 of the 60 State Assembly seats, local opposition parties, most recently the Hill Peoples Union, claiming the largest minority of seats.

Economy

The tribal people practise shifting cultivation. They grow oranges and potatoes as cash crops. Rice, maize and vegetables are grown as food crops. There are rich mineral deposits, including mica, gypsum and coal, but they are not yet being used. There is no large scale modern industry. Handicrafts and weaving are as important in Meghalaya as in the other Hill States. Brightly coloured textiles are a speciality.

Shillong

Set in pine forests and heather clad hills Shillong has beautiful lakes and waterfalls, is a popular hill-station which the British favoured and has a famous 18-hole golf course and a polo ground.

BASICS *Population*: 222,000. *Altitude*: 1496m. *STD Code*: 0364 *Climate*: Summer Max 23°C, Min 15°C; Winter Max 16°C Min 4°C. Annual rainfall 2030 mm, mostly Jun-Sep. *Best Season*: Oct to May. *Clothing*: Summer cottons, light woollens, Winter woollens. Umroi airport is 16 km from city centre.

Places of interest

The horse-shoe shaped **Ward Lake** set in a landscaped botanical garden and popular for boating is near Raj Bhavan, a 2 min walk from Police Bazar. The **Botanical Garden** and **Museum** adjoin it and just over a km away is **Lady Hydari Park**, designed like a Japanese

Archery Stakes

The Archery Stakes for which bows and arrows are sold, are unique to Shillong. Bookies' stalls are set up daily under canopies on an open stretch of ground where archers from clubs belonging to the Khasi Archers' Association shoot 1,500 arrows at a cylindrical bamboo target for 4 min. The betters count the number that stick and any who has guessed the last 2 digits of the number of arrows that stick is rewarded with an 8:1 win!

garden where you will see the pine native to the area – *Pinus khasiana*. It is well laid out with its **Mini Zoo**. Mar-Sep 0500-1800, Oct- Feb 0630-1700. The nearby **Crinoline Waterfalls** has a swimming pool surrounded by orchids, potted Bonsais and a rock pool with reeds and water lilies. The Shillong Swimming Club and Health Resort allows membership at a nominal charge but may ask for a medical certificate if you wish to swim! 0600-1400, Fri 0600-0800 Ladies only. **The Butterfly Museum** is at Wankhar and Co, Riatsamthiah, who have started breeding butterflies as a conservation measure and for their commercial activity. They have a good display of mounted butterflies and beetles from India and abroad. 1000-1600: **Bara Bazar** is well worth a visit to see the authentic local colour. It attracts tribal people in their colourful dresses who come to buy and sell produce – vegetables, spices, pots, baskets, chickens and even bows and arrows. The small stalls sell real Khasi food.

Excursions

The other places of interest nearby are mostly accessible by bus or taxi. **Shillong Peak**, 10 km away from which the city derives its name, rises to 1960m. It is revered as the 'abode of the gods' and offers excellent views. Since the area is at present under the Air Force, visitors have to stop at the barrier and enter their names and addresses in a book. **Elephant Falls,** 12 km, is a short diversion from the Cherrapunji road. It is a scenic spot with 2 high falls, surrounded by fern-covered rocks. You can walk down to the lowest pool by wooden steps and bridges and get a good view. However, the mountain stream tends to dry up between Nov and May. **Umiam Lake** (Barapani) 16 km, is an attractive spot for picnics, fishing and watersports. Govt *Orchid Lodge* has rm. Also floating restaurant and bar.

30% of Meghalaya is covered in forest. There are traditional Khasi villages nearby with views into Bangladesh. **Mawsmai**, on the way has high waterfalls, though they tend to dry up in winter. Beautiful scenery and huge caverns add to the interest.

Museums

Central Museum, Lachumiere has ethnographic and archaeological objects. 1000-1600, Mon-Sat. except 2nd Sat and all Govt holidays. Free. Guide service, occasional film shows. No photography. Tribal Research Institute, Mawlai has indigenous specimens and articles of the tribal people. 1000-1600, Mon-Sat. Free. Zonal Anthropological Museum, Lachumiere, T 3459. 1000-1630, Mon-Sat. except 2nd Sat.

Tours

Departure point: Hotel Orchid. City sight seeing 0900-1600. Rs 50. Cherrapunji: 0830-1630. Rs 60. Reserve at Meghalaya Tourist Office, Jail Rd.

Local information

● Accommodation

C *Pinewood Ashok* T 23116. 40 rm some in 8 cottages. Best in old bungalow. Set in spacious elevated grounds but not in the same class as other top ITDC hotels. Rec restaurant, coffee shop and bar, exchange. Ward Lake for boating and golf-course adjoining.

D *Polo Towers*, Polo Rd, T 22863. 40 rm. Restaurant. **D** *Alpine Continental*, Thana-Quinton Rd, T 25361, F 25199. 41 rm. Heating. Restaurant, travel, exchange. **D** *Shillong Club*, Kutchery Rd, T 26938. 14 rm, 2 cottages for temporary members. Indian restaurant, bar. **D** *Magnum*, Police Bazar, T 27797. 14 rm. Restaurant. New MTDC **D** *Crowborough*, 117 rm. Restaurant, exchange, travel. Also 2 Assam Tourism's *Tourist Bungalows* on cliff top. Reservations: Police Bazar office.

● Budget hotels

MTDC **E** *Orchid*, Polo Rd, T 24933. 48 rm and also very inexpensive dorm. Good restaurant (Indian, Chinese), bar. There are several simple hotels charging from around Rs 80-100 for single and Rs 150 for double, some with an Indian restaurant. On GS Rd: *Broadway*, T 26996; *Godwin*, T 26516 and *Monsoon*, T 23316. *Liza*, Malki Point, Lower Lachumiere, T 27328. No restaurant.

● Places to eat
You can try local pork dishes: *dohjem; jadoh* is spicy, cooked with rice and *dohkhleh* is ginger flavoured minced brains at small restaurants in Bara Bazar. Hotels ***Pinewood Ashok*** and ***Orchid*** are rec. Continental at ***Ambrosia***, Red Hill Rd. Also fast food and a pastry shop. Chinese in Bara Bazar – ***Sterling***, ***York*** and ***Abba*** in Lower Lachumiere. *Regal* in Police Bazar serves S Indian specialities. Best **bar** in ***Pinewood Ashok***.

● Banks & money changers
State Bank of India, Gari Khana. Evening Bank at Police Bazar.

● Hospitals & medical services
Civil Hospital, GS Rd, T 24100. *Nazareth Hospital*, Laitumukhrah, T 24052.

● Post & telecommunications
GPO: GB Rd, Police Bazar.

● Shopping
You can get handwoven shawls, canework and beautiful butterflies mounted in glass, handicrafts, orange flower honey. The Khasi women's dress, the 'jainsem' is also suitable as a western dress. The emporia are rec: ***Megha-***

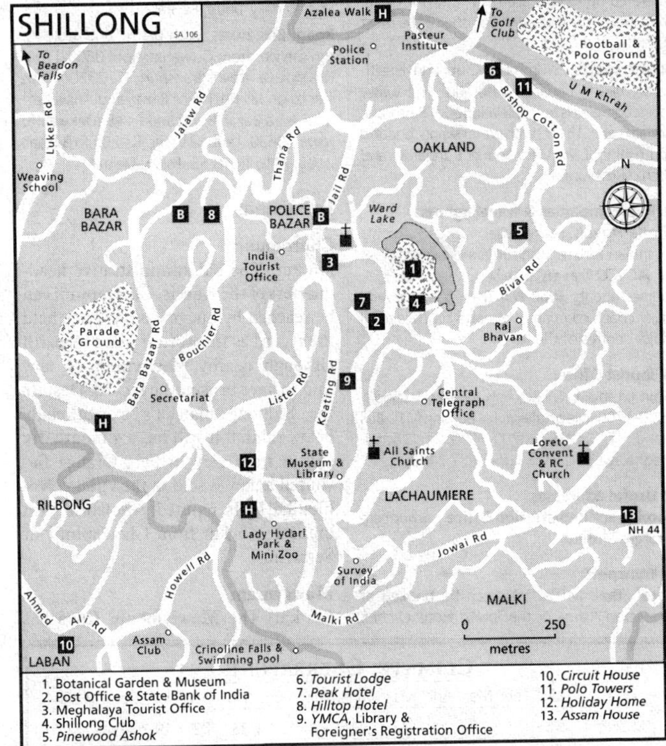

laya Handicrafts, *Purbashree*, *Khadi Gramodyog* and *Manipur Emporium* are on Jail Rd, Police Bazar. Also *Assam Govt Sales Emporium*, GS Rd and *Arunachal Museum*, Cantonment Rd, *Assam Co-op Silk House*, Bara Bazar. The main shopping areas are in Police Bazar, Bara Bazar and Laitumukhra. The *Bara Bazar* market where tribal people gather wearing their traditional costumes, is particularly interesting. They sell attractive Nepali silver and Khasi gold and amber jewellery.

Books: *Modern Book Depot*, Police Bazar.

Photography: camera films from *Photo Studio* and *Assam Studio* are on GS Rd.

● Sports

Golf: the Golf Club has an 18-hole course where competitions are held. Clubs for hire. The course is the wettest but one of the most beautiful in the world.

Water sports: Swimming Club and Health Resort near Crinoline Waterfalls. The water sports complex is being developed at Bara Pani, Umiam Lake (16 km) with water skiing, boating and fishing; *Lake View* Tourist Bungalow and *Orchid* Restaurant.

● Tour companies & travel agents

Sheba Travels, Police Bazar, T 23015. Agents for Indian Airlines and run airport coach service. *ACSCO Travels* at Shillong Club, T 23354. Airlines agents. *Blue Hill Travels* and several other coach companies operate coaches to all major centres of the NE.

● Tourist Office

Govt of India, GS Rd, Police Bazar, T 25632. 1000-1700. **Meghalaya**, Jail Rd, opp MTC Bus Stand, T 26220. 0700-1800, T 26054. Meghalaya TDC, Polo Ground, T 24933.

● Useful addresses

Foreigners' Registration Office: Lachumiere nr State Museum.

● Transport

Local Taxi: MTDC taxis can be booked at *Pinewood Ashok* or the Tourist Hotel *Orchid*. Local sightseeing costs about Rs 80 per hr or Rs 600 for any destination (8 hr, 100 km). Yellow-top taxis also available.

Air Transport to Guwahati airport (127 km): taxi hire Rs 450 (3½ hr), nearly double for dep after 1100, or frequent bus (4 hr) or Meghalaya Tourism coach 0900, Rs 65. *Pawan Hans* occasional helicopter service to Guwahati and to Tura. Contact Meghalaya Tourism, Jail Rd, Police Bazar, T 26054. Taxis available at Umroi airport (31 km).

Train Guwahati (103 km) the nearest railhead is well connected to the rest of the country. Rly Booking Out Agency, MTC Bus Stand, T 23200. Current booking: 0600-1100, 1300-1600. For advance reservations 1130-1300. Meghalaya Tourism coach to Guwahati Rly Station daily, 0800, Rs 30.

Road Bus: buses, both Deluxe and ordinary, run services from Guwahati from 0600-1700. Meghalaya Road Transport, T 23200. Bus stands on Jail Rd, Police Bazar, and Anjali Cinema, Bara Bazar. Rs 30 and Rs 45 (Deluxe). To Jowai, 0630-1200. 2½ hr, Rs 20; To Silchar, 2100, 11½ hr, Rs 55, Rs 95 (Deluxe).

Excursions

Cherrapunji

(56 km) The old administrative headquarters of the Khasis, Cherrapunji can be reached by bus or taxi. It once held the record as the wettest place on earth although nearby Mawsynram is now said to have broken the record. Despite the Shillong plateau's exceptionally heavy rainfall it still has a 4 month dry season from Nov to Feb. Orange flavoured honey is sold in the village. **Nohkalikai Falls,** reputedly the world's 4th highest is 5 km from Cherrapunji nr Serrarim.

Mawsynram

(55 km) The **Mawjymbuin Cave** has

CLIMATE: CHERRAPUNJI

	Jan	Feb	Mar	Apr	May	Jun	Jul	Aug	Sep	Oct	Nov	Dec	Av/Tot
Max (°C)	16	17	21	22	22	22	22	23	23	22	19	17	21
Min (°C)	8	9	13	15	16	18	18	18	18	16	12	9	14
Rain (mm)	18	53	185	666	1280	2695	2446	1781	1100	493	69	13	10799

water dripping from a breast-shaped stone onto what looks like a Siva lingam. The rainfall record (over 1200 cm) has beaten that of Cherrapunji. **Getting there**: from Shillong bus at 1400, 3 hr, Rs 15.

Jakrem

(64 km). There are hot springs. Getting there: bus at 1400, 3 hr, Rs 14.

ARUNACHAL PRADESH

Arunachal Pradesh has a population of under 865,000, scattered very sparsely across over more than 84,000 sq km, twice that of the Netherlands. It is NE India's largest and remotest state, as it has no railways and air services to only 3 of its towns. It has been recently opened to a limited number of visitors through 'Group Travel'.

ENTRY PERMITS Foreigners require Restricted Area Permits. Indian Tourists need an Inner Line Permit. Both are fairly easily available from the Resident Commissioner, Govt of Arunachal Pradesh, Nyaya Marg, Delhi, T 3013956 or Liaison Officer, Calcutta, T 286500. Also from FRROs in Bombay and Chief Immigration Officer in Madras. Foreigners must book tours through an approved Indian Travel Agent who can also arrange entry permit.

SOCIAL INDICATORS *Population*: 865,000 (Urban 13% Scheduled Tribes 64%). *Literacy*: M 51% F 29%. *Birth rate*: *Rural* 36:1000, *Urban* 29:1000. *Death rate*: *Rural* 15:1000, *Urban* 5:1000. *Religion*: *Tribal and Animist* 52%, *Hindu* 29%, *Buddhist* 14% (one of the highest figures in India), *Christian* 4%, *Muslim* 1%.

Environment

Land

On the NE frontier of India, Arunachal Pradesh stretches from the foothills of the E Himalayas to their peaks. The Brahmaputra, known in the state as the Siang River, enters the E of the state from China and flows through a deeply cut valley from N to S.

Flora & fauna

Stretching from the snow capped mountains of the Himalaya to the steamy plains of the Brahmaputra valley, there is an extraordinary range of forests from the Alpine to the sub-tropical – from rhododendrons to orchids, reeds and bamboo. It is an orchid lovers paradise with over 550 species identified. The wildlife includes elephants, clouded leopard, snow leopard, tiger, sloth, bear, Himalayan black bear, red panda and musk deer. The **Namdapha National Park** is located near Miao. The National Park (200 – 4500m) is singular in harbouring all 4 of the cat family – tiger, leopard, snow-leopard and clouded leopard, is on the Indo-Burmese border.

History

The area has remained isolated since 1873 when the British stopped free movement and the policy was continued after Indian independence. In Dec 1992, the Indian Govt decided to open the state to selective tourism for a restricted number but charging substantially for permits.

Culture

People

The Arunachali people are the state's greatest attraction. One account illustrates the diversity of the tribal people who speak over 60 different dialects:

> "There are gentle and cultured Monpas of W Kameng who received Buddhism from Padma Sambhava; The Thongi whose chiefs trace their treaty relationships with the powers in the valley to 1000 years back; the Hrusso who for 30 generations have patronised Vaishnava scholars; the proud Bangni-Nishi and the Tagin typifying the ancient Indian ideal of the honourable warrior; the Adis and Mishmis who are eager to build academic careers; the Apatanis with their marvels of wet-rice cultivation; the Khampti in their magnificent ceremonial robes and peaceful, progressive Nocte, Wancho and Tangsa".

In the capital Itanagar you may see Nishi warriors wearing their hornbill caps, carrying bearskin bags and their knives in monkey-skin scabbards.

The people have a very strong community sense which goes beyond narrow tribalism; there is a strong sense of justice. India's first Prime Minister, Jawaharlal Nehru struck a warning note when he spoke of India's tribal people – "not to treat them as anthropological specimens for study...not to interfere with their way of life but want to help them live it".

Most Arunachalis have an oral tradition of recording their historic and cultural past by memorizing verses handed down through generations. Some Buddhist tribes have however maintained written records. These are largely concerned with the State's Buddhist history, still vibrantly alive and shown in buildings such as the Tawang Monastery (see below).

Modern Arunachal Pradesh

Economy

The main food crop is rice, grown on valley bottoms and on some terraced slopes. There is no large scale manufacturing industry, though some coal and lignite are mined. Forest products, especially bamboo, are vital resources. Weaving is the universal craft as in other parts of the NE, with beautiful, highly coloured fabrics being made largely by women.

Itanagar

BASICS *Population*: 17,300. *Altitude*: 750m. *STD Code*: 03781. *Rainfall*: 2660 mm. *Best season*: Oct-Mar.

The capital, Itanagar has been identified as Mayapur, the capital of the 11th century Jitri dynasty and there is a fort dating back to the 14th or 15th centuries which is believed to have been built by King Ramachandra. Naharlagun and the new capital, Itanagar are 10 km apart but together provide the capital's administrative offices. Itanagar's new light earthquake-proof wooden-framed buildings are mixed with the traditional huts built on the slopes of the hill. On one peak is the Residence of the Governor while on the other there is a new Buddhist temple: in between are shops, bazar, old huts and new administrative buildings.

Places of interest

In Naharlagun (*Pop* 13,700, *Alt* 200m, *STD Code* 03781) The **Polo Park** is on top of a ridge with interesting botanical specimens including the cane thicket, which looks like palm, as well as a small zoo.

In Itanagar The new yellow-roofed **Buddhist Temple** stands in well-kept gardens on top of the hill. The shrine is behind a *stupa* and on one side has a tree planted by the Dalai Lama. The **Gyaker Sinyi** (Gang Lake) is 6 km away and provides a drive through jungle with bamboo, tree ferns and orchids growing on tall trees. When the road reaches the foot of the hill you walk across a bamboo bridge, up steps cut on the red clay of the hill to reach a ridge which looks down on the forest lake (**Ganga Lake** or **Gyaker Sinyi**) which you can row across.

Museum

Jawaharlal Nehru State Museum. Newly opened. Grd Flr. Good coverage of tribal people – collection incl art, wood carvings, musical instruments, religious objects. 1st Flr has archaeological finds from Malinthan, Itafort, Noksaparbat and others, textiles, ornaments and weapons. Open daily, except Mon, Re 1.

● Accommodation

For Govt officers primarily, so reserve at least a month in advance.

In Itanagar: **C** *Donyi-Polo Ashoka* (ITDC), T 2626, 18 rm, 2 deluxe suites, a/c rest. & coffee shop. **E** *Ganga* Ganga Market. 10 rm, some deluxe. Nearby **F** *Himalaya* T 2210, has 9 rm. **F** *Field Hostel*, T 2275. 24 rm. Reservations: Chief Engineer, CPWD, Itanagar, T 2536.

In Naharlagun **E** *Hornbill*, 14 rm, some deluxe, T 4419. **F** *Lakshmi*, T 4111, 19 rm (1st

Flr better). **F** *Inspection Bungalow*. 24 rm. Reservations: Supt Engineer, Naharlagun. **F** *Youth Hostel*, T 4474, 60 beds.

● Useful services

There are **banks** and **post offices** at both Itanagar and Naharlagun. **Hospitals**, Itanagar T 2263, Naharlagun, T 4269.

● Shopping

The cotton textiles are colourful and are beautifully patterned. You can also get wooden masks and figures, and cane belts and caps. The Handicrafts Centre sales section for shawls, *thangkas*, handloom articles, wood carvings, cane and bamboo work and carpets. Next to the show room you can watch tribal craftsmen trimming, cutting and weaving cane.

● Tour companies & travel agents

Arunachal Travels, Itanagar T 4411 are agents for Indian Airlines. *Blue Hills Travels*, Naharlagun runs a night coach service to Guwahati. 1730, Arr Guwahati 0500. Rs 75, T 4438.

● Tourist office

Govt of India, Sector 'C', Naharlagun, T 4328. **Arunachal Pradesh**, Naharlagun, T 4371.

● Transport

Reasonable road connections with other towns in the region. Some distances: Agartala 980 km, Aizawl 901 km, Kohima 350 km, Guwahati 381 km, Imphal 495 km, Shillong 481 km. There is a road from Tezpur to Bomdila and Tawang. The old road to Mandalay ran from Ledo crossing the Burmese border through the Pangso Pass.

Local Buses: frequent service between Itanagar and Naharlagun, 0600-2000. **Cycle rickshaws**: are only available in Naharlagun. **Taxis**: per day, about Rs 500 plus fuel; can be shared between Itanagar and Naharlagun.

Air Nearest airport is Lilabari in Assam, 57 km from Naharlagun, 67 km from Itanagar. Access to the state from Calcutta is through Dibrugarh (1½ hr) by **Indian Airlines**, Tu,Th,Sa,Su, 1300, 1½ hr.

Train The nearest convenient railhead is N Lakhimpur in Assam, 50 km from Naharlagun and 60 km from Itanagar served by Nos 2, 9 and 10 *Arunachal Fast Passenger* and other local trains. Nearest railheads for the bigger towns: **Itanagar**: Harmutty (33 km); **Along**: Silapathar; **Tezu**: Tinsukhia; **Miao-Namdhapa**: Margharita and **Khansa**: Naharkatia. Taxis are available for the connections. Out Agency, T 4209.

Road Bus: State Transport buses run services from Naharlagun Bus Station. **Guwahati**, daily, except Tu, 0630 (8 hr). **Shillong**, W, 0630. Lilabari Airport, daily except M, 0630 (2 hr). **Ziro**, daily 0700 (6 hr) and non-stop service on Tu,Th,Sa, 0800. **N Lakhimpur**, daily 0745, 1100, 1430, 1800. **Bomdila**, M and Th, 0630 (12 hr). *Blue Hills Travels* has an overnight coach to Guwahati 1730 (11½ hr). Enquiries: T 4221.

Excursions

Museums

There are *District Museums* in Along, Bomdila, Khonsa, Pasighat, Tezu and Ziro which hold collections of art and craft objects. 1000-1700. Free. Photography is prohibited.

To reach **Tawang** from Tezpur, 216 km (the nearest airport) travel to Bomdila (160 km) which has a regular bus service. The road passes through low wooded slopes for about 60 km. On the bank of the Bharali River in the upper plains, is **Tipi** (190m), a glass house with more than 7500 orchids. From there the road rises sharply to reach Bomdila.

Bomdila

Altitude: 2530m; *STD Code* 037822 Bomdila has marvellous views of the snow capped mountains. It has a craft centre, apple orchards and Buddhist *gompas*. Good views of Himalayan landscape and hills. **Accommodation E** *Tourist Lodge*, T 249 has 8 rm. Also **F** *Inspection Bungalow*, 4 rm, T 221 and **F** *Circuit House*, 8 rm, T 228. The next stretch of the journey of 180 km passes through the pretty Dirang Valley and pine woods, then climbs to the Sela Pass at 4,215m which presents a far starker view. You see a high-altitude lake and the trout hatchery at Nuranang just below the pass before reaching Tawang.

Tawang Monastery

Set in a breathtakingly beautiful setting at over 3000m, the monastery is one of the largest in India. Built in the 17th century with 65 residential buildings around the main temple structure, it still houses over 500 *lamas* belonging to the Gelugpa or Reformed Sect of Mahayana Buddhist monks. It is where the 6th Dalai Lama was born and houses a very large Buddha and many priceless manuscripts, books and *thangkas*. **Accommodation** **F** *Circuit House*, T 27, 5 rm. Res: Dy Commissioner, Tawang.

Siang District
In the foothills of W Siang, old granite images of Hindu deities were found in **Malinithan** in the lower part of the Siang District while in Dibang Valley the ruins of **Bismaknagar Palace** are thought to date from the 12th century. Direct buses from Itanagar (185 km) and N. Lakhimpur (109 km) to Malinithan where there is an **F** *Inspection Bungalow* with 4 rm. Reservations: Extra Asst Comm., Likabali, W. Siang.

Parasuram Kund
The state is best known for its famous Parasuram Kund, a lake near **Tezu** where at Makar Sankranti in mid-Jan thousands of pilgrims come to the Fair and take a dip in the holy water to wash away their sins. **Accommodation** Spartan accommodation is available in Govt *Tourist Lodge* at Tezu. Book well in advance through Dy Commissioner, Tezu.

Ziro
Altitude: 1475m; *STD Code*: 037892. 150 km from Itanagar, Ziro is in a level valley called Apatani plateau surrounded by pine-covered hills. The area is known for paddy and fish culture. **Accommodation** **F** *Inspection Bungalow* and *Circuit House*, T 30. 8 rm. Reservations, Dy. Comm, Lower Subansiri Dist. **Getting there** Daily buses from Itanagar and Lilabari (100 km).

Namdapha National Park (see 'Land' above) can be reached from Dibrugarh (140 km) connected by air to Calcutta. State buses run from Dibrugarh via Margharita (64 km), the nearest railhead where you can also hire taxis.

NAGALAND

BASICS *Area*: 16,579 sq km. *Altitude*: 900-1200m.

ENTRY PERMITS Foreigners require Restricted Area permits. See above.

SOCIAL INDICATORS *Population*: 1.3 mn (Scheduled Tribes 84%). *Literacy*: M 66% F 56%. *Birth rate*: *Rural* 21:1000, *Urban* 15:1000. *Death rate*: Rural 5:1000, *Urban* 1:1000. *Religion*: *Christian* 80%, *Hindu* 14%, *Animist* 4%, *Muslim* 2%.

Environment

Land
The narrow strip of mountain territory has Assam to the W, Burma to the E, Arunachal Pradesh and Assam to the N and Manipur to the S. From Dimapur which is in the plains, the road leaves the tea gardens and rises up wooded mountains. There are green valleys with meandering streams, high mountains with deep gorges and a rich variety of flora and fauna.

History
The British reached peace with the Nagas at the end of the 19th century and found them useful allies in the war against the Japanese, who reached Kohima before finally retreating from the region. After Indian independence, Nagaland became a separate state on 31 December 1963. A separatist movement continued to demand fully independent status but this was abandoned when in 1975 they accepted the Indian Constitution.

Culture

People
It is almost entirely inhabited by 16 groups of the Tibeto-Burmese tribes among them are the Angamis, Aos, Konyaks, Kukis, Lothas, Semas and Wanchus.

The **Nagas**, who were once head hunters, have been known for their fierceness and the regular raids they made on Assam and Burma. The warring tribes believed that since the enemy's animated soul *yaha* in Wanchu dialect, was to be found at the nape of the neck, it could only be set free once beheaded. However, since the spiritual soul *mio*, resided in the head and brought good fortune by way of prosperity and fertility, it was thought important to add to a community's own store of dead ancestors by acquiring extra *mio* by taking enemy heads. Nagas therefore attempted to carry home the heads of dead comrades while 'welcoming' any alien spirits of enemies killed in battle by ceremonial rituals. Wooden images, masks, jewellery and headgear displayed in several museums across the country, particularly in New Delhi, illustrate Naga culture.

The villages are situated on hill tops and ridges and are protected by stone walls. Often the first building in a village is the *morung*, a meeting house with a single huge cross beam often as much as 20m long and 10m high. This was also used as a boys' dormitory, for storing weapons and displaying the prizes of war in the form of enemy heads, often as many as 150 in any *morung*. Since the longhouses were constructed out of timber, bamboo and thatch, the record in the form of skulls would often be destroyed in a fire, when it would be substituted by carving small replicas to retain the good fortune which otherwise would be lost. The huge sacred drum which stood by each *morung* was hollowed out of a tree trunk and carved appropriately to resemble a buffalo head.

Religion

Originally animists, today 90% of the Nagas are Christians. The Bible was translated into many of the Naga dialects, nearly every village boasts a church, yet the people have retained many of their old customs. There are also remains of the Hindu kingdom of the Cacharis at Dimapur near the present capital Kohima, which was destroyed by the Assamese Ahoms in the 16th century.

Crafts

The ancient craft of weaving on portable looms is still practised by the women. The strips of colourful cloth are stitched together to produce shawls in different patterns which distinguish each tribe, the shawl being a universal garment worn by Nagas all over the state. Ao warriors wear the Tsungkotepsu, a red and black striped shawl with a white band in the middle embroidered with symbols.

Modern Nagaland

Economy

Primarily agricultural, the Nagas have now become dependent on the timber industry. The practice of *jhuming* (shifting cultivation) continues. However, the period between cultivation has diminished to a couple of years and the larger trees which remained untouched are felled for valuable timber. Rice and maize are the dominant crops. Timber is the most important product from the state, but traditional handicrafts are still made.

Kohima

Kohima attracted world attention during the World War II because it was here that the Japanese advance was halted by the British and Indian forces.

BASICS *Population*: 53,100. *Altitude*: 1500m. *STD Code*: 03866.

Places of interest

The **World War II Cemetery** is in a beautiful setting, with well maintained lawns where rose bushes bloom in the season. Two tall crosses stand out at the lowest and highest points. The stone markers each have a polished bronze plaque commemorating the men who fell here. The flowering cherry tree which was used by Japanese soldiers as a snipers' post was destroyed and what you see is what grew from the old stump, marking the limit of the enemy advance. The upper cross carries the following inscription:

> "Here, around the tennis court of the Dy Commissioner lie men who fought in the battle of Kohima in which they and their comrades finally halted the invasion of India by the forces of Japan in April 1944."

At the base of the lower cross, are 4 lines:

> When you go home
> Tell them of us and say
> For your tomorrow
> We gave our today.

The Market outside the Supermarket brings tribal women in their colourful dress who come to buy and sell their produce from farms, rivers and forests. **Kohima Village (Bara Basti)** is the old village which was the origin of Kohima. It has a traditional Naga ceremonial gateway carved with motifs of guns, warriors and symbols of prosperity at the entrance to the village that rise steeply up the hill. The traditional Naga house with its crossed 'horns' on the gables, carved heads to signify the status of the family, a huge basket to hold the grain in front of the house and a trough where rice beer is made for the whole village community.

Museums

Nagaland State Museum, Kohima. 1000-1500. Closed Sun and holidays. Collection of anthropological exhibits of the different Naga tribes. Gateposts, status pillars, jewellery, a ceremonial drum which looks like a dugout war canoe in a separate shed. There is a strong belief that the Nagas' ancestors came from the seafaring nation of Sumatra and retain their link with their island past in their legends, village drums and ceremonial jewellery which uses shells. The basement has birds and animals of the NE Hill states.

Parks & zoos

The Zoo built into a wooded hill side has most of its animals kept in cages. To the left of the entrance are the semi-wild Naga *mithun* bison. There are also golden langurs and the rare tragopan pheasant in a cage at the top of the hill. Summer 0900-1100, 1300-1700. Winter 0900-1100, 1300-1600. Closed Mon.

Local festivals

Feb: *Sekrenyi* is celebrated by Angamis for 10 days when all work in the field cease. The young people sit and sing traditional songs throughout one day. **Mar-Apr**: *Aoling* Konyaks observe the 6-day festival after the sowing is completed. It marks the end of the winter and beginning of spring and the New Year. **May**: *Moatsu*, a similar 6-day festival marking the beginning of the growing season after the hard work of clearing the fields, burning the jungles and sowing of seeds. The different tribes celebrate their special festivals – *Tutuni* and *Naknyulum* in July, the harvest festival of *Metemneo* in Aug, *Amongmong* in Sep, *Tsokum* in Oct and *Tokhu Emong* in Nov. The priests perform ceremonies followed by dancing, singing and drinking of rice beer.

Local information

● Accommodation

C *Japfu Ashok*, PR Hills, T 2721.

D *Ambassador*, D Block, T 444.

E *Pine*, nr Transport Commissioner's Office.

E hotels on NST Rd: *Meyase*, T 402 and

Climate: Kohima

	Jan	Feb	Mar	Apr	May	Jun	Jul	Aug	Sep	Oct	Nov	Dec	Av/Tot
Max (°C)	15	17	21	23	25	24	24	25	24	22	19	10	21
Min (°C)	8	10	13	17	18	19	19	19	19	17	13	10	15
Rain (mm)	18	18	55	63	177	319	382	353	270	143	39	4	1841

Valley View, T 2738.

Govt **F** *Tourist Lodge*, nr Minister's Hill, T 2417. 10 rm. few Indian style **F** category hotels. *Razhu* nr Supermarket. *Travel Lodge*, Assam Rifles Rd, below MLS Hostel, T 2470. *Evergreen* nr Nagaland Emporium.

● Places to eat

Some serve Indian and Chinese food – *Le Baron*, *Relax* opp Emporium and *Midland* which also does Continental.

● Services

There are **banks**, a **post office** and a **hospital**.

● Shopping

Warm and colourful Naga shawls are excellent. You can also get shoulder bags, decorative spears, table mats, wood carvings and bamboo baskets. The *Sales Emporium*, New Market, opp State Bus Station. There are also shops in the Supermarket.

● Tour companies & travel agents

Green Hills Travel, Taxi Stand, Kohima, T 2279 run coaches and do internal flight bookings.

● Tourist office

Kohima, T 607. Also at Dimapur Tourist Bungalow, T 2147.

● Transport

Air Dimapur (74 km) the nearest airport, 3 hr by car (4 hr by bus). Flights to Calcutta: M,Tu,Th,Sa, 14250, 1¼ hr via Guwahati, 1/42 hr.

Train Dimapur has the nearest railhead on the NE Frontier Rly. From Dibrugarh **Guwahati**: *Tinsokia Mail*, 5908, daily, 1745, 18 hr; **Calcutta (H)**: *Kamrup Exp*, 5906 (AC/II), daily, 1000, 18½ hr, change at Guwahati (3¼ hr wait), then *Kamrup Exp*, 5660 (AC/II), daily, 0745, 22¾ hr (total time 44½ hr). From Dimapur **Guwahati**: *Assam Mail*, 5904, daily, 0025, 6½ hr; **Dibrugarh Town**: *Tinsukia Mail*, 5907, daily, 2030, 10½ hr. Guwahati–*Dimapur Exp* No 207. Dibrugarh–*Guwahati Assam Mail* No 3. Calcutta (H)-*Dibrugarh Kamrup Exp* No 5.

Road Nagaland State Transport (NST) runs services from Dimapur to Kohima from 0530-1530 (2½ hr). Bus Station, T 2094. *Blue Hills Travels* runs luxury coaches from Guwahati which connect with Kohima and all other state capitals of the NE Hill states.

Excursions

Dimapur

(STD Code 03862) 74 km from the capital, on the NH 39 is Dimapur, which is the railhead and has the only airport. This old capital of the Kacharis (13th-16th century Hidimbapur) is the state's main trading and commercial centre. The Kachari relics including a huge brick-built arch are 1 km from the NST Bus Station. Nearby are 30 huge mushroom shaped monoliths which lie upside down; their origin is unknown. You can watch women weaving at *Ruth's* and *Haralu* emporia. Handicrafts and shawls for sale. **Accommodation D** *Tourist Lodge*, nr Bus Station, T 2147, has a/c rm.

Trekking

Trek to **Jopfu Peak** (3043m) 15 km S for good mountain views, into **Dzukou Valley** (2462m) through rhododendrons or to **Mount Tiyi.** *Tourist Lodges* and *Rest Houses* in most places.

MANIPUR

Further S from Nagaland is the former princely state of Manipur. Manipur lies about 700 km NE of Calcutta. The 'land of jewels', Manipur shares an international border on its E with Burma and State borders with Nagaland to the N, Assam to the W and Mizoram to the S.

BASICS *Area*: 22,327 sq km (half the size of the Netherlands). *Population*: 1.8 mn.

SOCIAL INDICATORS *Population*: 1.9 mn (Urban 26%, Scheduled Castes 1%, Scheduled Tribes 27%). *Literacy*: M 58% F 39%. *Birth rate*: *Rural* 24:1000, *Urban* 16:1000. *Death rate*: *Rural* 7:1000, *Urban* 6:1000. *Religion*: *Hindu* 60%, *Christian* 30%, *Muslim* 7%.

Environment

Land

Much of Manipur lies above 2000m. However, the heart of the populated area is a low lying basin. In its centre is the reedy Lake Loktak (the largest freshwater lake in the North East), and the flat bottomed basin and river valleys that drain into it are extremely beautiful. There are several large lakes in the central area where the rivers drain southwards. They are used for fishing and duck shooting as well as for special boat races.

History

Manipur has always been quite independent of its neighbouring tribal areas. Although there are few historical landmarks, Bishnupur temple, nearly 30 km from Imphal, was built in AD 1467 during the reign of King Kiyamba. Manipur was often invaded from Burma but it also enjoyed long periods of quite stable government. In 1826 it was brought into India by the Treaty of Yandabo at the end of the Indo-Burmese War, British sovereignty being recognized in 1891. In 1939 a remarkable women's social revolt ('Nupilan' – from 'nupi' – women- and 'lan' – war) led to government action against monopolistic traders. The contemporary party *Nisha Bandh* consists of an all-women patrol which seeks to keep the streets safe at night. The role of women traders can be seen most colourfully in the women's market (see Below). During World War II Imphal was occupied by the Japanese. After Indian independence Manipur became a Union Territory and subsequently achieved statehood in 1972.

Culture

People

The majority of the population are Vaishnavite Hindus. They belong to the *Meithe* tribe and are related to the *Shans* of Burma, who live in the valleys. The 20 or so hill-tribes who constitute about a third of the population are Christian.

Like the Nagas, the **Manipuris** too have a reputation for being great warriors, still practising their skills of wrestling, sword fighting and martial arts. Most of the wars were fought across the border in Burma. They were also keen on sport, and polo, which is said to have originated in Manipur, is the principal sport.

Dance, drama & music

The ancient musical forms of the valley dwellers are closely connected to the worship of Vishnu, expressed in the **Manipuri school of Indian dancing**. The *Rasa* dances usually adopting a Krishna-Gopi theme are performed at every ceremony and are characterised by graceful and restrained movements and delicate hand gestures. The ornate costumes worn by the women are glittering and colourful. The *Sankirtana* dance often precedes the *Rasa*. They are usually performed by men and are vigorous, rhythmic and athletic, requiring them to play on the *pung* (drums) and cymbals while they dance. The tribal ritual dances, some of which are performed by priests and priestesses before deities, are very different and may end in a trance. Others can last several days observing a strict form and accompanied by the drone of a bowed instrument, *pana*.

Modern Manipur

Economy

Subsistence agriculture provides the basis of living for the majority of the rural population. Weaving and other handicrafts are as important in Manipur as elsewhere in the NE. No mineral deposits to speak of have yet been exploited, but as elsewhere in the hill regions forest products are important, and there is a significant local stoneware industry. Women play an active role in the economy, working in the fields, spinning and above all weaving, as well as doing house work. In contrast the men are widely regarded as idle.

Imphal

Imphal, the capital, lies in the heart of an oval shaped valley. It is traditionally thought to have been founded in the 3rd century BC making it one of the oldest state capitals of the country. It derives its name from *yumpham* (homestead).

BASICS *Population*: 200,600. *Altitude*: 785m. *STD Code*: 03852.

Places of interest

The Old Palace In the heart of town, has ruins of the old fortress and a palace. As it is occupied by paramilitary forces, you have to convince the guard that you are visiting the ruins. The **Shri Govindaji Temple** adjoins the palace and is a Vaishnavite centre. It has 2 golden domes and a large raised hall. The presiding deity Vishnu has on one side shrines to Balaram and Krishna and to Jagannath on the other side. Well patronized performances of ceremonial dancing are held there regularly. Overlooking the University (8 km), the historic palace of **Langthaband**, with its ceremonial houses and temples, stands on the hills among formally planted pine and jackfruit trees on the Indo-Burma road.

Khwairamband Bazar ("Nupi Keithel" or "Ima Market") in the town centre is the largest women's bazar perhaps anywhere in the country. Open 0700 – 1900. It is an excellent place for handicrafts and handloom goods, as well as vegetables, fish and other foodstuffs, jewellery and cosmetics. As many as 3000 women gather every day in the Ima Market, supervised it is believed by the Ima Goddess. It represents a form of family work sharing, for while younger mothers stay at home to look after children the older women and grandmothers come to market. The Ima women do not bargain and will be offended if you try to pick through fruit or vegetables, as they take great pride in serving only the best quality at a fair price. Their own union helps to maintain the bazar and is a potent political force.

The War Cemeteries Two cemeteries are maintained by the Commonwealth War Graves Commission, one on the Imphal-Dimapur National Highway and the other on the Imphal-Ukhrul Road. They are beautifully maintained and serenely peaceful sites.

The Konghampat Orchidarium, 7 km from Imphal along the NH 39, has over 300 varieties of orchids, including rare species. Best season Apr-May.

Museums

Manipur State Museum nr Polo Ground, T 220709. 1000-1630 weekdays. Closed Sun and holidays. Nominal entry fee. Collection of art, archaeology, natural history, geology and textiles, and also costumes, portraits and old arms.

Parks & zoos

The **Zoological Gardens** are 6 km away at Lamphelpat to the W. The rare brow-antlered deer, seen in the wild at Keibul Lamjao Sanctuary, can be seen here in captivity. The **Khonghampat Orchid Yard** is 7 km on the NH 39. Set up by the State Forest Dept, it has well over a hundred varieties of orchids including some rare species. Best season Apr-May.

Tours

Manipur Tourism runs day tours to Sri Govindaji Temple, Bishnupur, INA Memorial, Moirang, KL National Park and the Lok Tak Lake. Dep. Hotel Imphal, Sun 0800.

Local festivals

Feb-Mar: *Yaosang* on full-moon night, boys and girls dance the Thabal

CLIMATE: IMPHAL

	Jan	Feb	Mar	Apr	May	Jun	Jul	Aug	Sep	Oct	Nov	Dec	Av/Tot
Max (°C)	21	23	27	29	29	29	28	29	29	29	28	25	22
Min (°C)	4	7	10	15	19	21	22	22	21	17	11	5	15
Rain (mm)	17	31	51	91	231	278	253	189	136	117	28	3	1425

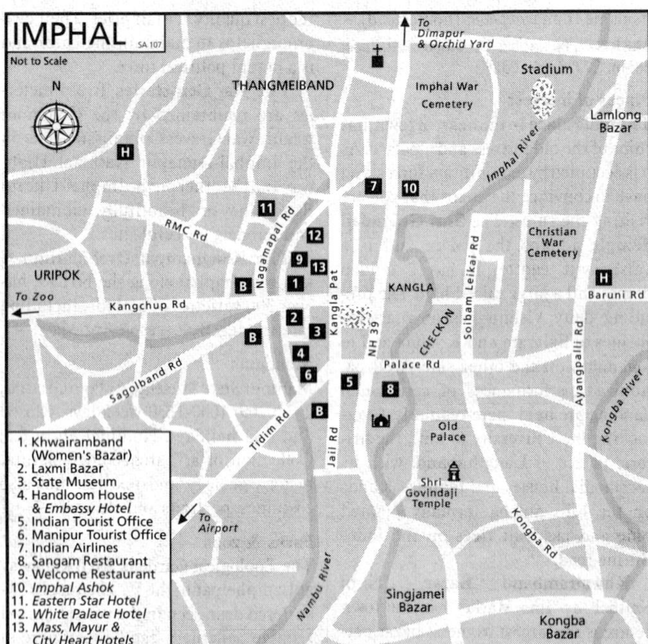

Chongba and sing in a circle in the moonlight. **May-Jun**: is celebrated in honour of forest gods. **Sep**: *Heikru Hitongba* is mainly non-religious, when there are boat races along a 16m wide moat in narrow boats with large number of rowers.

Local information

● Accommodation

D *Imphal* (Manipuri Tourism), with some a/c and modern facilities, Imphal-Dimapur, North AOC, T 220459. 45 rm. Restaurant. **D** *Prince*, Thangal Bazar, T 220587. 22 rm, some a/c. **D** *Pintu*, AT Line, North AOC, T 22743. 8 rm. Restaurant. **D** *White Palace*, 113 MG Ave, T 20599. 26 rm.

F *Tourist Lodge*, inexpensive. Reservations: Director of Tourism, T 459. Very basic. There are a few **F** Indian style hotels – *Grand* in Paona Bazar, T 777 and *Eastern Star* in Thangal Bazar, T 22154, 22 rm. *Diplomat*, BT Road. Also a Marwari *Dharamshala*.

● Places to eat

Manipur is a 'dry' state. The Govindaji Temple prepares local dishes with advance notice. In hotel restaurants, try *iromba* the Manipuri savoury dish of fish, vegetables and bamboo shoots and the sweet *Kabok* made with molasses and rice.

● Services

Banks in Paona Bazar, Thangal Bazar and MG Avenue. There are **Hospitals** at Porompat and Lamphalpat. The **GPO** handles fax, speedpost and STD.

● Shopping

The handloom textiles have a distinct Manipuri design. Paona Bazar is the main area where fixed-price shops make purchases easier – *Manipur Handlooms Sales Emporium*, *Handloom House*, and *Tribal Emporium* Paona Bazar, T 21495. *Sangai Handloom*, nr Gandhi Memorial. Khwairamband Bazar is nearby – see places of interest. Textiles and skirts from *Mother's Market*, Thangal Bazar.

● Tourist office

Director of Tourism, nr Raj Bhavan, T 224603, F 222629. **Manipur information** at Imphal airport open for flights. **Meghalaya Tourism,** Kishampath, T 20802, 0900-1630, closed Sun and 2nd Sat. **Govt of India,** Old Lambulane, Jail Rd, T 21131, closed Sat and Sun.

● Transport

Local Taxi: tourist taxis from Tourist Information Centre. Rest un-metred. **Auto-rickshaws** and **rickshaws**.

Air Indian Airlines: **Calcutta**, W,F, 1300; **Guwahati**, W,F, 0925; **Silchar**, Tu,Th,Sa,Su, 1130. **Indian Airlines,** MG Ave, T 220999. Airport is 6 km from town centre. Coaches between airport and Hotel Imphal.

Train Dimapur on the N Frontier Rly is the nearest railhead.

Road Imphal is well connected by a good network of roads with major centres in the NE, the NH 39 running to Guwahati via Slichar (53 km). Regular buses connect Dimapur with Imphal (8-9 hr). Also Agartala 465 km, Aizawl 374 km, Guwahati 579 km, Itanagar 413 km, Kohima 123 km, Shillong 643 km and Silchar 198 km. **Manipur Golden Travels,** MG Ave, T 221332, runs a/c bus to Guwahati and Shillong. **Green Valley Tours,** Bir Tikendrajit Rd, T 221753, and **Kangleipak Tours,** MG Ave, T 222911, run daily buses to Guwahati.

Excursions

NB: The first 3 places can be visited in a circuit from Imphal.

Bishnupur (Bishenpur)

(27 km) Named after a temple to Bishnu (Vishnu), Bishnupur is a picturesque town at the foot of a hill. Built in AD 1467 during the reign of King Kiyamba, the very thin bricks used are said to have been influenced by the Chinese. There is a significant stoneware industry here.

Moirang

45 km from Imphal, Moirang stands on the W fringe of the Loktak lake, noted for its early Manipuri folk-culture. The ancient love story of Khambha and Thoibi is said to have given birth to traditional folk dance form in this city. There is a temple to the forest god, *Thankgjing*, where garments of the 12th century Moirang kings are preserved. During World War II Moirang was the HQ of the Indian National Army (INA)for a short time, and the Congress flag is believed to have been raised here as a symbol of national independence for the first time on 12 April, 1944. There is an INA memorial and a war museum. **Accommodation** On top of **Sendra Island** in the Loktak Lake is the **F** *Serena Tourist Home*, with a small restaurant attached. Beds are Rs 10. Reservations Dep Director of Tourism Manipur, T Imphal 20802. A very peaceful spot with lovely views of the lake. Fishermen, who live in houses on islands of floating weed, use nets to farm fish and water chestnut – 'singharas'.

Kaina

(29 km) This Hindu pilgrimage centre is associated with Shri Govindaji who was said to have appeared in a dream to his disciple Jai Singh, Maharaja of Manipur. He requested that a temple be built to him enshrining an image carved out of a jackfruit tree. The dream is enacted in ceremonial dances at the *Rasa Mandapa*. **Accommodation F** *Kaina Tourist Home*. Reservations: Dep Director of Tourism Manipur, T Imphal 20802.

Keibul Lam Jao National Park

The park covering 25 sq km, is the only floating sanctuary of its kind in India. It has a small population of thamin (*Sangai*), the brow-antlered deer, one of the most endangered species of deer in the world, hog deer, wild boar, panther, fishing cat and water birds. The swamps around the 65 sq km Lok Tak lake which was the natural habitat of the thamin was reclaimed for cultivation, resulting in the near extinction of this "dancing deer" which led to the formation of the National Park here in 1977. Best time: Dec-May. Temp range: 41°C to 0°C. Rainfall: 1,280 mm.

Large areas consist of mats of floating humus covered with grass and *phumdi* reeds, which feeds the thamin until the rainy season when the deer move to the hills. You can travel through the creeks on small boats. There is an observatory tower on Babet Ching, a small hillock in the park. **Accommodation** *Forest Lodges* at Phubala and Sendra. Contact Asst Conservator of Forests at BPO, Kha-Thinungei, Manipur. **Note** Travel restrictions for foreigners as elsewhere in the NE. **Getting there** Nearest airport and railway station is at Dimapur, 32 km from Imphal.

New Churachandpur
(59 km) This is where the Kuki tribe live, produces attractive handicrafts which can be bought at the market.

MIZORAM

The southern-most of the NE hill states, Mizoram juts down between Burma and Bangladesh. Until 1972 it was known as the 'Lushai Hills', a district of Assam. It has State borders with Manipur, Assam and Tripura to its N, and its western border is with the Chittagong Hill Tracts of Bangladesh.

BASICS *Area*: 21,000 sq km. *Population*: 686,000.

SOCIAL INDICATORS *Population*: *700,000* (Urban 46%, Scheduled Tribes 94%). *Literacy*: M 85% F 79%. *Religion*: *Christian* 94%, *Hindu* 4%, *Muslim* 1%.

Environment

Land

The half a dozen or so parallel N-S ranges of hills rising to over 2000m near the Burmese border are covered in dense forests of bamboo and wild banana. At the bottom of the deep gorges the rivers run in narrow ribbons.

The villages perch on top of the ridges with the chief's house and the *zawlbuk* (bachelors' dormitory) the focal point, in the centre. Houses often have front doors level with streets cut on steep slopes, while the backs stand precariously on stilts. The Mizo people love flowers, and every home proudly displays orchids and pots of geranium, begonia and balsam. Over a thousand varieties of medicinal plants grow wild.

Culture

People

Mizo is derived from *mi* (man) and *zo* (highland), a collective name given by their neighbours to a number of tribes which settled in the area. The different groups of **tribal** people are thought to have originally come from NW China who were gradually pushed S towards Tibet and Burma in the 7th century and finally reached their present homeland less than 300 years ago. The Mizos were originally animists, believing in good and evil spirits of the woodland.

Religion

The raiding of British tea-plantations which carried on until around the end of the last century led to the introduction of Inner Line permits which gave free access to missionaries to visit the area. They not only carried out their religious duties but also introduced literacy which is exceptionally high in this state, the language having adopted the Roman script. The great majority of the self reliant and music loving Mizos are Christian converts and have built up a strong tradition of Western choral singing.

The remainder, mainly nomadic Chakmas along the western border, practise a religion which combines Hinduism, Buddhism and animism. Some Kukis who were once headhunters converted to Judaism.

Modern Mizoram

Economy

Rice and maize are supplemented by shifting cultivation. They provide the chief means of support for about 75% of the population. There are no mineral resources exploited as yet. Handicrafts and handwoven textiles predominate, and there are no large scale industries. The Govt has sponsored some light industrial development in Aizawl.

Aizawl

The town, built on the central ridge, stands out like a citadel and dominates the scenery. The Assam Rifles Centre is an important landmark with the administrative buildings and Raj Bhavan nearby. On the E side is the Zoo with birds and animals from Mizoram, Burma and the Chittagong area in Bangladesh.

BASICS *Population*: 154,000. *Altitude*: 1132m. *STD Code*: 03832. *Climate*: Summer Max 29°C, Min 20°C. Winter Max 21°C, Min 11°C. *Annual rainfall*: 3000 mm.

Places of interest

Bara Bazar, the main shopping centre is on the other side of the ridge, with the steep Zion St lined with stalls selling garments and vendors of Mizo recordings on music cassettes. The main bazar is where the people gather in their traditional costumes to sell produce from farms and homesteads including river crab in little wicker baskets. The **Weaving Centre** is above the Bata shoe shop where you can watch women at their looms weaving traditional shawls which are available for sale. **Luangmual Handicrafts Centre**, 7 km away takes ½ hr to reach by car. The *khumbeu* ceremonial bamboo hat is made here using waterproof wild *Hnahthial* leaves.

Museums

Mizoram State Museum, McDonald's Hill in town centre. Tue-Fri 0930-1600; Mon 1200-1600. Free. Though small it has an interesting collection of historical relics, ancient costumes and traditional implements.

Local festivals

Early Mar: *Chapchar Kut*, a traditional spring festival marking the end of *Jhumming* is celebrated with singing, dancing and feasting. *Mimkur* (Maize Festival) in **Aug/Sep** and *Phawlkur* in **Dec/Jan** are others. *Cheraw* is performed by nimble-footed girls who dance in and out of bamboo poles, clapped together by teams of young men. Similar dances are performed in Myanmar, Thailand and the Philippines. *Khillam* is accompanied by drums and gongs.

Local information

● Accommodation and places to eat

E *Embassy*, Chandmari. 32 basic rm, some in Indian Extn. **E** *Ritz*, Bazar Bungkawn. **E** *Ahimsa*, Zarkawt. **E** *Tourist Lodge*, Chaltlang, 14 rm. Restaurant. Reservations: Director, Tourism, Treasury Sq, Aizawl, T 449. Meals.

F *Shangrila*, Bara Bazar and **F** *Chawlrha*, Zarkawt.

Labyrinth Restaurant in Chandmari serves Chinese and Indian food.

● Banks & money changers

State Bank of India and Mizoram Co-op Apex at Treasury Sq; others in Bara Bazar.

● Hospitals & medical services

The Civil Hospital, Aizawl, T 2318 and at Durtland, T 265.

● Post & telecommunications

GPO: Treasury Sq.

● Shopping

KVI Show Emporium and *Handloom Emporium* Zarkawt, sell handloom and handicrafts (shawls, bags and fine bamboo articles). In Zion St you can buy locally produced music cassettes. See *Weaving Centre* under Places of Interest.

Photography: *Hauhnar Bros*, Zion St.

● Tour companies & travel agents

Thanginkhuma, Khatla, T 2297 and *Omega*, T 2283, are Indian Airlines agents.

● Tourist office

Aizawl, T 2449. Mizoram Houses at Rangir Kharia, Silchar, Assam, T 87091 and at Zoo Rd, Guwahati.

● Transport

NH44 runs from Silchar to Tuipang.

Local Taxi: un-metred taxis charge about Rs 150 for 2 hr sightseeing within the town. **Bus**: buses connect with other towns.

Air Taxi or bus from airport (27 km), 1 hr. Flights from Silchar to Calcutta, daily except Fri, 1025 or 1235m 1 hr.

Road Bus: Mizoram State Transport, T 2226, has bus services to **Silchar**, 180 km, (6 hr) Rs 50; Pvt buses to Guwahati via Silchar and Shillong, Rs 200.

TRIPURA

Tripura is the smallest of the hill states in NE India. Covering just under 10,500 sq km, it is almost surrounded on the N, W and S by Bangladesh. It has over 4000 mm of annual rainfall.

SOCIAL INDICATORS *Population*: 2.8 mn (Urban 11%, Scheduled Castes 15%, Scheduled Tribes 28%). *Literacy*: M 68% F 50%. *Birth rate*: *Rural* 25:1000, *Urban* 17:1000. *Death rate*: Rural 8:1000, Urban 5:1000. *Religion*: *Hindu* 89% *Muslim* 7% *Christian* 1%.

Environment

Land

The N falls into 4 valleys, separated by hills rising to just under 1000m. The more open land of the S is still forested. Indian hardwoods include sal (*Shorea robusta*), which is economically important. There are many small streams. N draining rivers include the Deo, the Khowai and the Dhalai while the Gumti is the biggest river flowing S.

History

Legend has it that Tripura existed in the times of the epic *Mahabharata* but recent history confirms that around the end of the 14th century it came under the rule of the Manikya dynasty of Indo-Mongolian origin. Permanently feuding with her neighbours, particularly the Nawabs of Bengal, the British found a means of gaining influence in the area by coming to the help of the Maharaja and establishing a protectorate separating the princely state from tribal lands outside the control of the Hindu rajas. The Manikyas ruled continuously right up to India's independence when Tripura joined it as a Union Territory later to become a state in 1972. Rabindranath Tagore's play *Visarjan* and novel *Rajarsi* based on the legends of the Manikyas is said to reflect the friendship that existed between the poet and the Maharaja Virehandra Manikya who was a great patron of the arts, see page 644. Tagore's university at Santiniketan found patrons among the royal family.

Culture

People

Tripura remains predominantly tribal, even though the great majority of the population are now described as Hindu. One typical old tribal custom of welcome is to build a bamboo arch and garland the guest, who is greeted with wafting of incense. An egg is held in front of the person which is believed to absorb any evil spirits which is then rubbed in paddy, dipped in water and thrown away.

Modern Tripura

Economy

Rice is the main crop. It is well suited to the marshy conditions of the northern basin. Jute, cotton, tea and fruit are important cash crops. Sugar cane, mustard and potatoes are also grown. There is very little industry, though in the last 10 years the Indian Govt has encouraged small industries. Weaving, carpentry, pottery and basket making are common.

Agartala

In the 1930s Maharaja Bir Bikram made his kingdom more accessible by opening an airport in Agartala. He also designed the college named after him which stands on a hillock by a lake on the E part of the city. The town has well kept gardens, intricately woven cane fences and official buildings of red brick favoured by the royal family. However, evidence of British fondness for white can be seen in a few important structures, notably the one designed to be the palace for the Maharaja in 1901.

BASICS *Population*: 158,000. *Altitude*: 1280m. *STD Code*: 0381. *Climate*: Summer Max 35°C, Min 24°C; Winter Max 27°C, Min 13°C. *Annual rainfall*: 2240 mm, Jun-Aug. *Best Season*: Sep-Mar. Clothing cottons in summer, woollens in winter.

Places of interest

Ujjayant Palace, built in the Mughal style by Maharaja Radha Kishore Manikya in 1901 is now the State Legislative Assembly. Reputedly the largest building in the state (covering 1 sq km) it once stood amidst formal Mughal gardens with pools and fountains. The magnificent tiled floors, the ceiling of the Chinese room and the beautifully carved front doors are particularly notable. The late 19th century **Jagannath temple** is across one of the artificial lakes in front of the palace. It rises from an octagonal base to a striking orange 4-storeyed *sikhara* or tower.

Temple of Chaturdasa Devata 8 km, near old Agartala, is dedicated to 14 gods and goddesses, represented by their heads only. It is built in the Bankura style of Bengali temple architecture but has a Buddhist stupa type structure on top. In July worshippers come from all over Tripura for *Kharchi Puja* which has evolved from a tribal festival.

Museums

Tripura Govt Museum, West. Weekdays 1000-1700. Free. Collection includes rare stone images, old coins, Bengal *kantha* embroidery, archaeological finds from Tripura and adjoining areas. A small museum but sculptures, including 8th-10th century Buddhist sculptures from Pilak, are very well displayed.

Tours

Agartala-Sipahijala-Neermahal, 0800-1930, Sun. Agartala-Kamalasagar Matabari (Tripura Sundari)-Sipahijala, 0800-1930, Tue. Agartala-Bhuvenswari Matabari-Sipahijala, 0800-1930, Fri.

Local information

● Accommodation

Fairly basic and small with a few a/c rm. **D** *Agartala Club*, T 1375. **D** *Broadway Guest House*, Palace Compound, T 3122. 12 rm. Rm service (Indian, Chinese). **D** *Sonali Rest House*, GB Hospital Rd, Kunjaban, T 5322. 12 rm. Indian and Chinese food. **D** *Rajdhani Guest House*, BK Rd, nr City Office. Some a/c rm. **D** *Meenakshi*, Khushbagan, T 5721. Indian food.

● Budget hotels

E *Royal Guest House*, Palace Compound, W Gate, T 526. *Minakshi*, Hawkers Corner, HG Basak Rd, T 1433. **F** *Circuit House*, Tel 41 (Dist Magistrate, Tripura, W) and *Dak Bungalow* (Chief Manager, PWD, Agartala).

● Places to eat

Indian: *OK*, HG Basak Rd; *Ambar*, Sakuntala Rd; *Insrapuri*, Akhaura Rd.

● Banks & money changers

Several on HG Basak Rd: **State Bank of India**.

● Hospitals & medical services

VM Hospital, AK Rd. *GB Hospital*, Kunjaban.

● Post & telecommunications

General Post Office and PO: Chowmuhani.

● Shopping

Tripura is noted for its exceptional bamboo, cane and palm leaf handicrafts, among the finest in India. You can see craftspeople at work at *Purbasha*, MMB Sarani. *Tripura Handicrafts*, Akhaura Rd. *Aithorma* Coop. Handlooms from *Tantumita*.

Photography: Sen and Sen, Kaman Chowmuhani.

● Tourist offices

Gandhighat, T 3839. Also **Tripura Bhavan** at Lachit Nagar, Guwahati.

● Travel agent

Ramkanai Travels, Motor Stand Rd, T 3633.

● Transport

Calcutta 1808 km, Guwahati, 599 km, Shillong 499 km, Imphal 539 km, Kohima 683 km, Silchar 317 km, Itanagar 980 km and Siliguri 1074 km.

Local Rickshaws: auto-rickshaws and Cycle-rickshaws for airport transfer, Rs 35 or Rs 8 per person. Sightseeing is charged by the hr – about Rs 30 and Rs 9 respectively. **Bus**: the city has a bus service. The Directorate of Information has Tourist Cars and coaches. **Taxis**: unmetred taxis from the airport (about Rs 75); for sightseeing and excursions, about Rs 300 per day plus per km charge.

Air This is the only convenient means of travel to Agartala. *Indian Airlines*, Palace Compound, T 5588 and Airport, T 3128. **Calcutta**, twice daily, 0850, 1440, ¾ hr.

Train The nearest rly station at **Dharmanagar**, 200 km, is connected to Lumding Station. Guwahati is connected to Lumding by the *Cachar Exp*, *Kamrup Exp*, *Tinsukia Mail* and *Barak Valley Exp*.

Road Bus: Tripura RTC runs 4 buses from Dharmanagar to Agartala daily, 8 hr. A private tourist coach to Silchar once daily.

Excursions

Sipahijala 33 km. A botanical garden with a small zoo (elephant rides) and a boating lake. **Accommodation F** *Forest Bungalow*. Contact Chief Conservator of Forests, Agartala. **Getting there** Hourly buses from Agartala, 0700-1600.

Neer Mahal

(53 km) A water-palace built for one of the Maharajas in **Rudrasagar Lake** is like a fairytale castle with tower and pavilions, moats and bridges. **Accommodation F** *Sagarmahal Tourist Lodge*. Tourist coaches from Agartala.

Tripura Sundari Temple

(57 km) Known as **Matabari**, the temple in the ancient capital, Udaipur was built on the hillock Dhanisagar in the mid-16th century. Claimed to be one of the 51 holy *pithasthans* mentioned in the *Tantras*. The temple of the Mother Goddess, is served by red-robed priests and is the location of a large fair during Diwali in Oct/Nov. Small hotels and buses from Agartala.

ORISSA

Contents

Maps

Despite the fame of the Sun Temple at Konark and of the Jagannath Temple in Puri, Orissa remains one of the least visited parts of India. Yet Orissa has had a long and distinctive history, and contains some of India's most outstandingly beautiful scenery.

SOCIAL INDICATORS *Population*: 33 mn (Urban 12%, Scheduled Castes 15%, Scheduled Tribes 22%). *Literacy*: M 62% F 34%. *Birth rate*: *Rural* 30:1000, *Urban* 25:1000. *Death rate*: *Rural* 13:1000, *Urban* 8:1000. *Infant mortality*: *Rural* 139:1000, *Urban* 64:1000. *Religion*: *Hindu* 95%, *Muslim* 2%, *Christian* 2%.

Environment

Land

The train or road journey from Calcutta to Bhubaneswar enters Orissa from the NE. The road from Midnapore turns sharply S after entering the State passing to the E of the ancient volcanic Simlipal Massif, which rises to a height of more than 1000m. SW from Balasore the road crosses the rice growing alluvial deltas of the Brahmani and Mahanadi rivers. Just to the N of Cuttack, the old capital of Orissa, the road crosses some of the striking red lateritic soils that run in a band some 40 or 50 km wide from Balasore to Bhubaneswar and beyond. They provided one of the building materials for Bhubaneswar itself.

If you just visit the cities of Bhubaneswar and Puri and the Sun Temple at Konark it is easy to get the impression that Orissa is nothing but a flat alluvial plain. On any of the roads between that famous triangle of sites the view stretches for mile after mile over flat paddy fields. Occasional low mounds of granite, such as the hill at Dhauli on which a new Buddhist stupa now stands, overshadowing the ancient edicts of Asoka carved on a bare outcrop, and the site of the Battle of Dhauligiri, which moved Asoka to become a Buddhist, break the otherwise straight horizon.

The delta stretches nearly 170 km from north to south and is often over 80 km wide. Until the Hirakud dam was completed in 1957, the Mahanadi River used to flood with devastating frequency. The Chilika Lake, in the S is only a few metres deep but covers between 900 and 1200 sq km according to the season, the water alternating between fresh and brackish. But the delta accounts for no more than 10% of Orissa's surface area.

The **area inland of Bhubaneswar** is

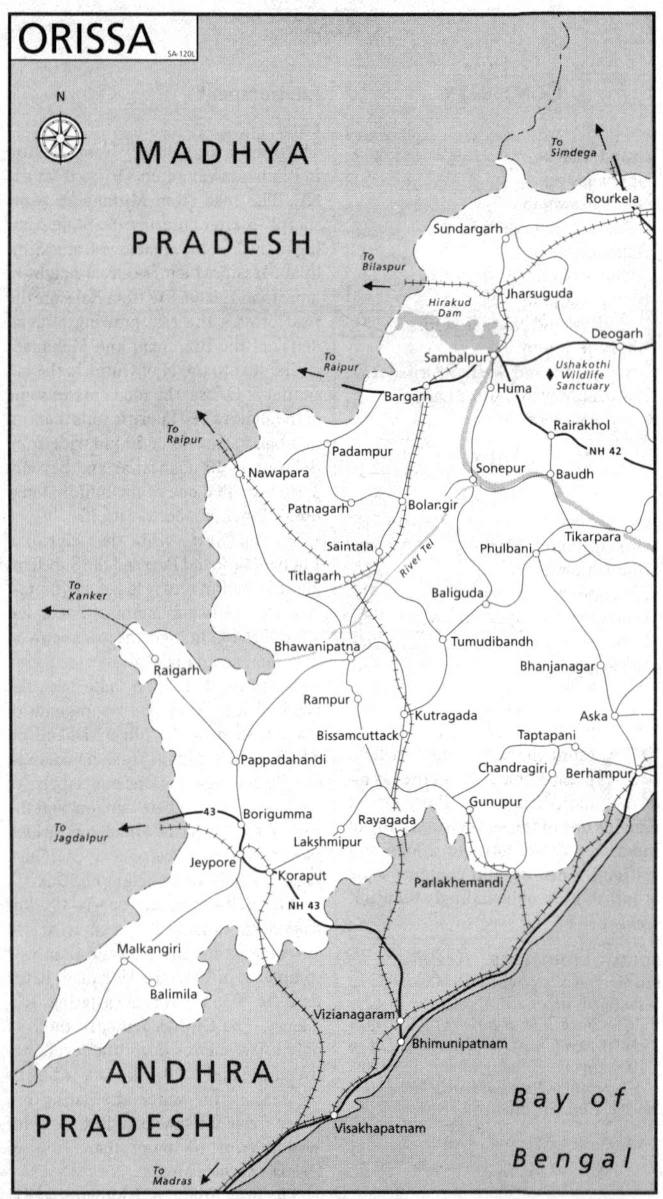
ORISSA
SA-120L
N
MADHYA
PRADESH
To Simdega
Rourkela
Sundargarh
To Bilaspur
Jharsuguda
Hirakud Dam
Deogarh
Sambalpur
To Raipur
Ushakothi Wildlife Sanctuary
Huma
Bargarh
To Raipur
Rairakhol
NH 42
Padampur
Sonepur
Baudh
Nawapara
Patnagarh
Bolangir
Tikarpara
Saintala
Phulbani
River Tel
Titlagarh
To Kanker
Baliguda
Tumudibandh
Bhawanipatna
Raigarh
Bhanjanagar
Rampur
Kutragada
Aska
Bissamcuttack
Taptapani
Pappadahandi
Chandragiri
Berhampur
Gunupur
43
Borigumma
Rayagada
To Jagdalpur
Lakshmipur
Jeypore
Koraput
Parlakhemandi
NH 43
Malkangiri
Balimila
Vizianagaram
Bhimunipatnam
ANDHRA
PRADESH
Bay of
Bengal
Visakhapatnam
To Madras

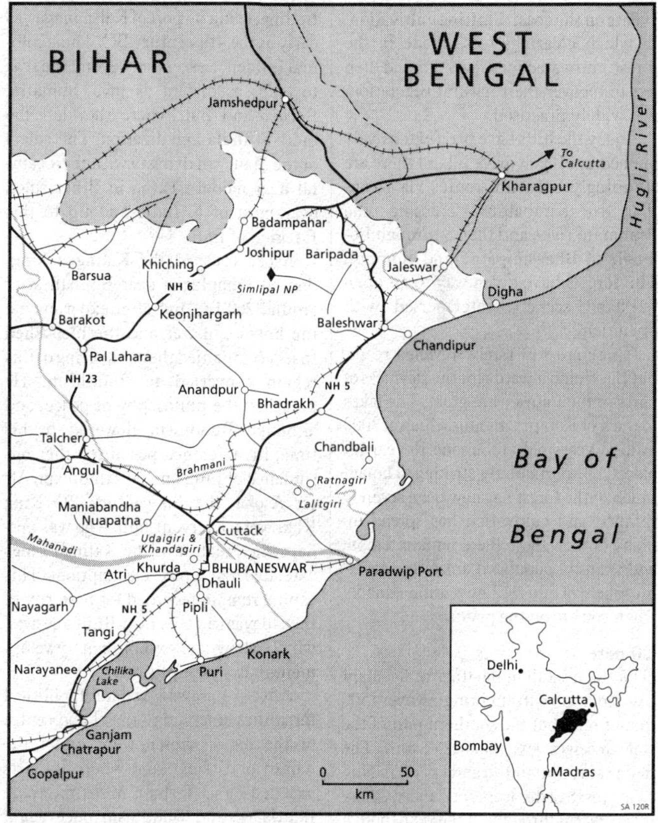

made up of the ancient rocks of peninsular India, among them India's richest mineral resources. Coal is mined in thick seams 100 km NW of Bhubaneswar. Around Bhubaneswar and at several other sites in the interior are important bauxite deposits, which began to be exploited in the 1980s for aluminium smelting. In the far N of the state are enormous reserves of very high grade iron. These are now exploited in the iron and steel mill, built with help initially from Germany, at Rourkela. In addition to these basic mineral resources there are also important reserves of manganese, graphite and mica.

Such a list of resources might suggest an unattractive industrial landscape. In fact until recently much of the State was inaccessible, densely forested hills rising in the SW to over 1500m made inhospitable to settlers from the plains both by the difficulty of clearing the forest and by the devastating prevalence of malaria.

The combination of climate and relief resulted in dense deciduous *sal* forest, peopled only by tribal groups, living in isolation, with a stone age culture, and barely touched by the societies and events on the coast. Shifting cultivation, in which clearings were made in the forest, cultivated for a few years and then left to recover their natural vegetation, was widely practised.

Today the hills have been extensively opened up. If you drive inland there are stunningly beautiful routes via Keonjhar to Sambalpur, crossing the Brahmani river, and then S through Bolangir to Bhawanipatna and Koraput. The forests have given way to an open parkland scenery, interspersed with open fields.

These are still rarely travelled roads, but the scenic rewards for the slowness of parts of the journey are great. The lakes to the S of Koraput, in hills which at 3000 million years old are among the earth's oldest, are particularly striking. Though much of the forest has now been severely thinned and cultivation has spread up many of the valleys there remain remote and sparsely populated areas, and an atmosphere of quiet stillness unimaginable when you are on the plains.

Climate

N Orissa lies full in the track of the main SW monsoon current bringing over 1500 mm of rain, but the southern part of the state receives less than 1250 mm. The main rains start in Jun and tail off in Nov. Lying just S of the Tropic of Cancer, Orissa is very warm throughout the year, though the hills are sufficiently high (1500m) to moderate the temperatures significantly. Most of Orissa has one of the shortest dry seasons in India, only Jan and Feb being virtually rainless.

History

Early history

The coastal plains that were the focus of early settlement and the first development of politically organised kingdoms in the region. Orissa, a part of the ancient kingdom of Kalinga which also comprised of a part of what is now Andhra Pradesh, grew prosperous through trading, using its port of Kalingnagar, as early as the 4th century BC. Their colonial influence extended beyond the seas to lands as distant as Java, Sumatra, Borneo and Bali where they left the mark of Indian civilization. The rulers of the Mauryan dynasty with their capital near modern Patna in Bihar ruled over most of N India and up to this E region of India.

Asoka crushed the Kalingan kingdom at Dhaulagiri near Bhubaneswar around 260 BC, but after experiencing the horrors of war and the bloodshed that accompanied the conquering of this region converted to Buddhism. He preached the philosophy of peace, and although Buddhism flowered in his time, his tolerance permitted the continuance of Jainism and Hinduism. After Asoka, the 1st century BC King Kharavela, a fervent Jain, who was perhaps the greatest of the Kalinga kings extended his empire. Descriptions of his capital remain recorded for posterity in the Udayagiri caves near Bhubaneswar, which show an exceptional development in cave sculpture.

After Kharavela separate political territories emerged to the N and centre of the region which went under the names of Utkal ('land where the arts excelled') and Toshali. Maritime trade flourished and Buddhism once again became a popular religion. The Buddhist caves being excavated in Lalitagiri, Ratnagiri and Udayagiri near Cuttack may date from the early 2nd century and do not, as believed until recently, only go back to around the 5th century.

Ganga dynasty

The greatest period of temple building in Bhubaneswar coincided with the Kesaris (7th-12th century) to be followed by Ganga dynasty (12th-15th century) who were responsible for the Jagannath Temple in Puri (c1100) and the Sun Temple at Konark (c1250). The most significant years were between 750-1250 AD which saw the flowering of the distinctive Northern or Indo-Aryan style of Orissan temple architecture. The affluence of the Gangas, who became rich and powerful on trade, gave them the means to support an ambitious programme of developing temple architecture.

The Mughals

Orissa resisted the annexation of her territory by Muslims. For a time the Afghans held Orissa in the 16th century until finally the powerful Mughals arrived as conquerors in 1592 and during their reign destroyed many of the temples that once stood in Bhubaneswar. It was their violent disruption of temple life in Puri and Bhubaneswar that led the Brahmin community to ban all non-Hindus from the precincts of the Lingaraj and Jagannath temples when they were allowed to return. The Mughals were followed by the Marathas in 1751.

The British

In 1765 after Clive's win at Plassey, parts of Orissa, Bihar and Bengal were acquired by the East India Company with further gains in Cuttack and Puri at the beginning of the following century, thus by 1803 British Rule extended over the whole region.

Art & achitecture

Temple architecture

The temples of Bhubaneswar, along with those of Puri and Konark, represent a remarkably full record of the development of Orissan architecture from the 7th century AD to the 13th century AD. Although some of the temples have suffered structural damage many are virtually intact and some are still in everyday use. These are living shrines, centres of active pilgrimage, worship and faith. Although non-Hindus are excluded from 2 of the most famous, the Lingaraja Temple in Bhubaneswar and the Jagannath Temple in Puri, it is possible to gain some impression of both from views over the external walls. Even with these restrictions the temples that are open provide plentiful opportunity to follow the development of Orissan art and architecture. Furthermore, they are all easily accessible. The temples in Bhubaneswar are within 2 km of each other and are very easy to reach from any of the main hotels on foot, by rickshaw or by car.

Culture

People

Orissa has the 3rd highest concentration of tribals in India. The tribal population, about 25% of the total, live mainly in the Koraput, Phulbani, Sundargarh and Mayurbhanj districts. There are some 62 *Adivasi* ('ancient inhabitants') or tribal groups living in remote hill regions of the state, some of whom still remain virtually untouched by modern civilization and have kept their tribal traditions alive. Each has a distinct language and pattern of social and religious customs.

Although they are not economically advanced and literacy is low, the tribal groups have a high degree of performing and plastic arts. Their artistic skills are expressed through tattooing and painting their bodies, in their ornments made of metal, shell, wood or stones; in their weaving and in decorating their homes with wall paintings. Music and dance form an integral part of life-cycle ceremonies and those marking the agricultural year. There has been a new interest in their rich heritage and the Tourism department is keen to promote visits to tribal areas (see below, page 732).

The **Khonds** who live mainly in the W, are the most numerous (about 100,000) and speak Kuvi, a Dravidian language. They used to practise human 'Meriah' sacrifice mentioned in Fraser's *Golden Bough*, offering the blood to their supreme goddess represented by a rectangular wood or stone, to ensure the fertility of the soil. This has been replaced by animal sacrifice at the time of sowing seeds to ensure a good crop. They

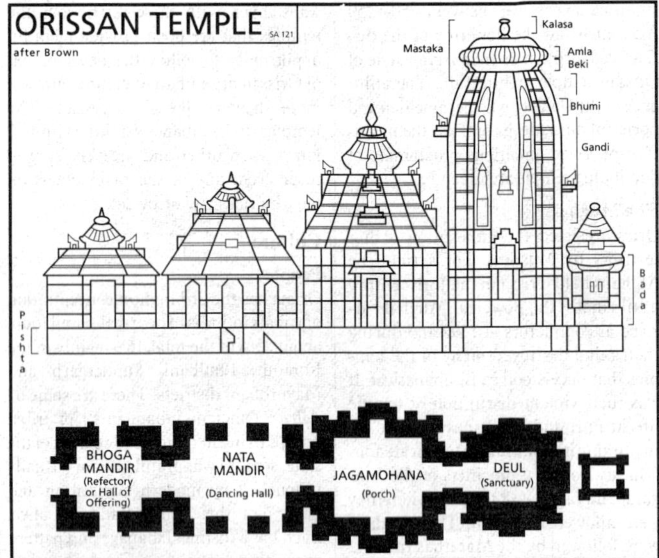

ORISSAN TEMPLES

The most obvious features of Orissan temples are the tall, curvilinear tower or spire, and a much lower, more open structure or porch in front of the entrance to the tower. The taller tower, which rises over the sanctuary, is known as the *deul* (pronounced day-ool) or *rekha deul,* while the porch is usually referred to as the *jagamohana*. The interior of the sanctuary is quite dark and is designed to allow only a glimpse of the presiding deity and to enable priests to conduct ritual worship. It is usually considerably smaller than the more open porch, where worshippers may meditate or simply wait. In later temples 2 further halls were often added, the dancing hall (*nata mandira*) and the hall of offering (*bhoga mandira*), sometimes referred to as *nata mandapam* and *bhoga mandapam*.

The main sanctuary tower and the porch are both normally square in plan. However, the square plan is broken vertically by the inward curving upwards form of the main tower. Furthermore each exterior face of the sanctuary tower is divided by vertical, flat-faced, projections (*rathas*). In the early temples in Bhubaneswar there was just one such projection, dividing each face into 3 parts – giving rise to the term *tri-rathas*. As temples became more ornate with increasing technical and artistic sophistication the number of projections increased, creating 5 or 7 sections (*panch-rathas* or *sapta-rathas*) – or more as in the Rajarani temple, Bhubaneswar.

Both the sanctuary and the porch are divided vertically as well as horizontally. Some Orissan architects likened the structure of the temple to that of the human body, and the names given to the vertical sections correspond to the main parts of the body. Fuller architectural details are given in the Archaeological Survey's publications, but the chief features may be summarised as follows:

still use bows and arrows to defend themselves from wild animals.

The **Santals**, the second most numerous group, come from the N districts of Mayurbhanj and Balasore particularly from around the Simlipal National Park area. They belong to 12 patrilineal clans (*paris* or *sibs*) and marriage is forbidden within the clan. Santali, one of the Munda group of Austro-Asiatic languages, is one of the oldest in India. In the northwestern industrial belt, they have abandoned their aboriginal lifestyle to go and work in the steel mills.

Music and dance, especially at marriages and religious ceremonies, are a common and distinct feature of the tribal life style. Tribal and folk dances are performed throughout the year in the villages but more particularly during festival time in Oct-Nov and Mar-Apr. Santals fear evil spirits; supernatural beings of the forest, hills and rivers have to be appeased by magic. The women carry out witchcraft while the *ojhas* are the medicine men.

The **Bondas** In the S districts, especially Koraput there are about 6000 of the aggressive Bondas, 'naked people' of Tibeto-Burmese origin whose language also belongs to the Mundari group. They come to trade at local markets. They live on high hills, growing rice by shifting cultivation, irrigating and terracing paddy fields and keeping domesticated cows and goats. The women wear a narrow loin cloth woven from the *kerang* fibre collected from the forest mixed with bought yarn. They cover themselves with bead necklaces and striking brass and silver necklets which cover the neck completely. Their shaved heads are decorated with bands and plaits of palmyra leaves.

1. The platform. (pishta) Early temples had no platform; even some important temples are without one. In contrast, in highly developed temples (eg Surya temple at Konark), the platform is a prominent feature, often being built up to a height of more than 3m.

2. The lower storey, (bada) seen as corresponding to the lower limbs. In early temples this was divided into 3 parts, the base (the foot), above which was a perpendicular section corresponding to the shin. This was topped by a set of mouldings. In some mature temples the scale of this section was greatly elongated and was itself then divided into 5 layers.

3. The upper storey (gandi) takes the shape of a curvilinear spire in the case of the sanctuary, or a pyramidal roof in the case of the porch, and is seen as corresponding to the human trunk.

4. The head (mastaka) with crowning features. The head is divided into a series of elements: The 'head' or *mastaka* of the sanctuary developed over time. The first standard feature is the 'neck' (*beki*) a recessed cylindrical portion which is surmounted by the skull *amla*. This is represented by a symbolic fruit, the *amalaka*. On the *amla* rests a 'water pot', which is an auspicious symbol, then on top of all comes the sacred weapon of the deity.

The real distinction between the sanctuary and the porch lies in the development of the upper sections. Over the porch (*jagamohana*), the upper storey tapers rapidly in a pyramidal shape made up of a series of flat layers decreasing in size from the bottom upwards. The upper storey of the main sanctuary (*deul*) tower has a convex curve upwards, very gentle at first but increasing sharply at the top. Occasionally the *deul* has a barrel-vaulted and elongated roof, though it is comparatively rare in Bhubaneswar. This type is called *khakhara*, named after *kakharu*, a local pumpkin. The best example is the Vaital Deul (see page 729).

Girls and boys sleep in separate dormitories and select their partners themselves, later obtaining parental permission. Usually girls select much younger boys for marriage who must pay a bride-price. If they are from a wealthy family they must sacrifice a buffalo.

The **Saoras**, another major tribe, have retained much of their original culture particularly in hilly areas of Parlakhemundi (Ganjam Dt) and Gunupur (Koraput Dt), living in endogamous groups marked by their occupation and locality. The stratified society is organised under a headman who is assisted by a religious leader. Their religion recognizes good and evil spirits as well as watchful deified ancestors who are in communication through *shamans*.

In contrast to organisation into clans, common among the other tribals, Saoras live in extended families, *Birindas*, descended from a common ancestor (marriage within the family is prohibited). Polygamy is common, several wives being the sign of prosperity, implying greater areas of hill cultivation and hence accumulation of grain. Children are given adult status from an early age, being allowed to drink and smoke to attain proficiency in vocational skills and crafts very early. Village houses of mud and stone walls are raised on plinths with high wooden platforms inside, to store grain. The walls are decorated with remarkable paintings, traditional designs now incorporating hunters on aeroplanes and bicycles!

The **Koya** who live in villages in clearings in the middle of dense forest are distinguished by their headgear made of bison horn.

Dance, drama & music

Odissi The region of magnificent temple sculpture gave rise to a classical dance form which shadows the postures, expressions and lyrical qualities of the carved figures. The dance was a ritual offering performed in the *nata mandiras* of temples by the temple dancers (*maharis* in Orissa) resplendent in their costume and jewellery. The Odissi which evolved as a religious dance follows strict rules of position for the body, feet and hands falling into postures and attitudes akin to the figures sculpted in rock centuries ago. A favourite subject for interpretation is Jayadev's *Gita Govinda* dating from the 12th century, which explores the depths of Krishna's love for Radha, and the dancer expresses both the sensual and devotional with great lyricism.

The *folk dances* usually performed during festivals take various forms – day long *Danda Nata* are ritual dances, the traditional fishermen's dance *Chaitighoda* requires a horse dummy, there is a battle dance called *Paika Nritya* and *Chhau* is the masked dance-drama reminiscent of Orissa's martial past. In addition there are tribal dances which are often performed with distinctive head gear made of animal horns shells and colourful costumes, sometimes accompanied by simple string instruments, flutes and drums.

Cuisine

Rice forms the staple food, wheat taking second place. Most meals are accompanied by fairly lightly spiced side dishes prepared from a large variety of vegetables and pulses as well as chutneys and pickles. Fresh sea-food especially prawns and the flat *pomfret* fish are included in the coastal areas. Restaurants will sometimes offer Orissan food in addition to typical N Indian and S Indian dishes. You might try *mohuro* or *sago bhoja* (fried mustard or spinach leaves), *dahi baigono* (aubergines cooked with yoghurt) or the festive *baisoro* (vegetables cooked with mustard seed paste). Continental and Chinese food is frequently available in the larger restaurants in the major cities and towns.

Orissa is particularly noted for its sweetmeats prepared from milk –

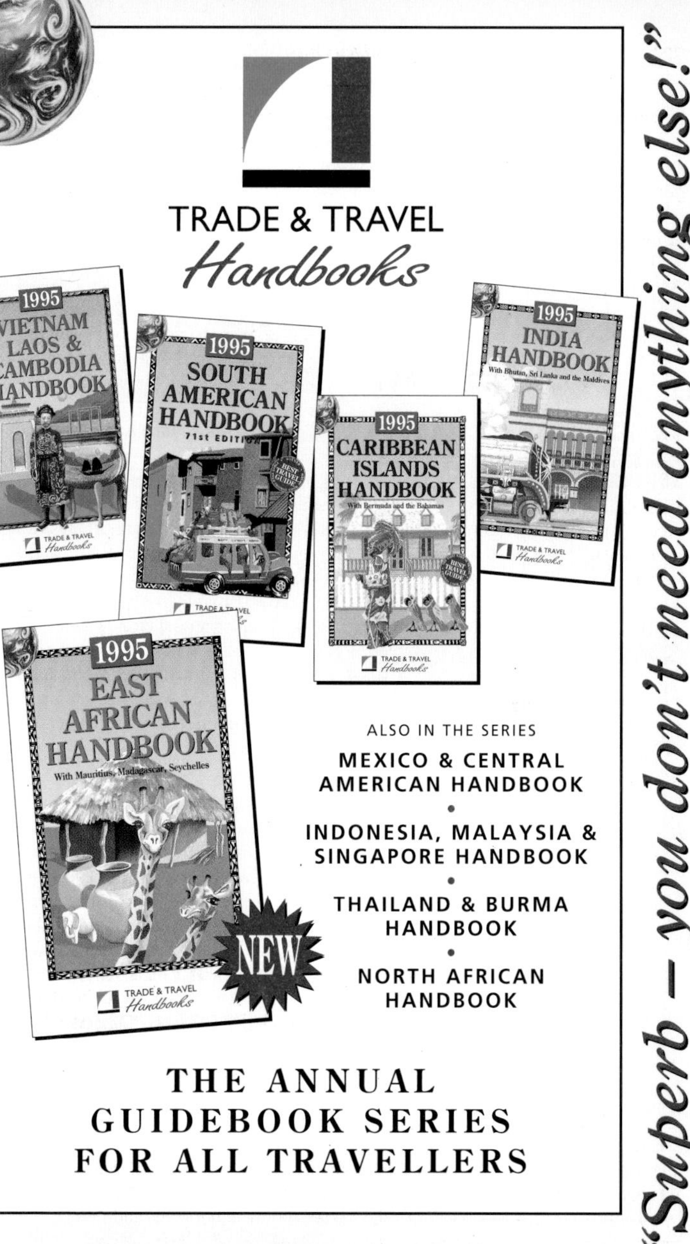
TRADE & TRAVEL
Handbooks
1995
VIETNAM
LAOS &
CAMBODIA
HANDBOOK
1995
SOUTH
AMERICAN
HANDBOOK
71st EDITION
1995
CARIBBEAN
ISLANDS
HANDBOOK
With Bermuda and the Bahamas
1995
INDIA
HANDBOOK
With Bhutan, Sri Lanka and the Maldives
1995
EAST
AFRICAN
HANDBOOK
With Mauritius, Madagascar, Seychelles
NEW
ALSO IN THE SERIES
MEXICO & CENTRAL
AMERICAN HANDBOOK
INDONESIA, MALAYSIA &
SINGAPORE HANDBOOK
THAILAND & BURMA
HANDBOOK
NORTH AFRICAN
HANDBOOK
THE ANNUAL
GUIDEBOOK SERIES
FOR ALL TRAVELLERS
"Superb – you don't need anything else!"
Write to us for more details.

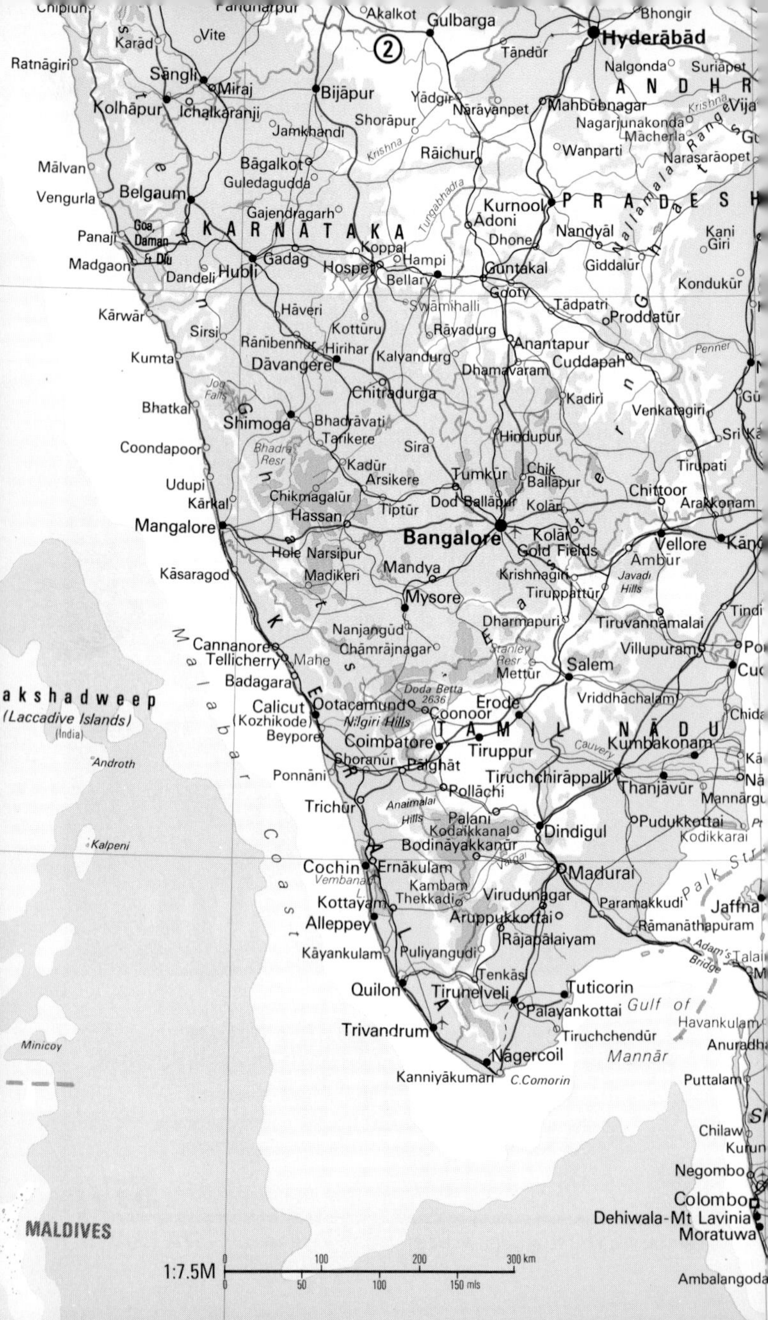

Akalkot
Gulbarga
Bhongir
Hyderābād
Vite
Karād
Ratnāgiri
Sāngli
Miraj
Bijāpur
Tāndūr
Nalgonda
Suriāpet
A N D H R
Kolhāpur
Ichalkaranji
Yādgir
Nārāyanpet
Mahbūbnagar
Krishna
Jamkhandi
Shorāpur
Nagarjunakonda
Macherla
Wanparti
Krishna
Rāichur
Bāgalkot
Narasarāopet
Mālvan
Guledagudda
Vengurla
Belgaum
Tungabhadra
Kurnool
P R A D E S H
Gajendragarh
Ādoni
Nallamala Range
K A R N A T A K A
Goa, Daman & Diu
Panaji
Nandyāl
Kani Giri
Koppal
Dhone
Madgaon
Gadag
Hampi
Hubli
Hospet
Guntakal
Giddalūr
Dandeli
Bellary
Kondukūr
Gooty
Kārwār
Hāveri
Swāmihalli
Tādpatri
Proddatūr
Kottūru
Sirsi
Rāyadurg
Rānibennur
Hirihar
Anantapur
Penner
Kumta
Kalyandurg
Cuddapah
Dāvangere
Dhamavaram
Jog Falls
Chitradurga
Kadiri
Bhatkal
Venkatagiri
Shimoga
Bhadrāvati
Hindupur
Tarikere
Coondapoor
Bhadra Resr
Sira
Kadūr
Tirupati
Chik Ballapur
Tumkūr
Arsikere
Udupi
Chittoor
Kārkal
Chikmagalūr
Dod Ballāpur
Kolār
Arakkonam
Tiptūr
Hassan
Mangalore
Bangalore
Kolār Gold Fields
Vellore
Hole Narsipur
Ambūr
Mandya
Kāsaragod
Madikeri
Krishnagiri
Javadi Hills
Tiruppattūr
Mysore
Tiruvannāmalai
Dharmapuri
Nanjangūd
Cannanore
Chāmrājnagar
Villupuram
Tellicherry
Mahe
Stanley Resr
Mettūr
Salem
Badagara
Doda Betta 2636
Lakshadweep (Laccadive Islands) (India)
Erode
Vriddhāchalam
Calicut (Kozhikode)
Ootacamund
Coonoor
Nilgiri Hills
Malabar Coast
T A M I L N Ā D U
Beypore
Coimbatore
Cauvery
Kumbakonam
Tiruppur
Androth
Shoranūr
Palghāt
Tiruchchirāppalli
Ponnāni
Thanjāvūr
Pollāchi
Mannārgudi
Trichūr
Anaimalai Hills
Palani
Pudukkottai
Kodaikkanal
Dindigul
Kodikkarai
Kalpeni
Bodināyakkanūr
Cochin
Ernākulam
Vaigai
Madurai
Palk Strait
Vembanad L.
Kambam
Kottayam
Thekkadi
Virudunagar
Paramakkudi
Jaffna
Aruppukkottai
Alleppey
Rāmanāthapuram
Rājapālaiyam
Kāyankulam
Puliyangudi
Adam's Bridge
Tenkāsi
Tuticorin
Quilon
Tirunelveli
Palayankottai
Gulf of Mannār
Havankulam
Trivandrum
Tiruchchendūr
Anuradhapura
Minicoy
Nāgercoil
Kanniyākumari
C.Comorin
Puttalam
Chilaw
Kurunegala
Negombo
Colombo
Dehiwala-Mt Lavinia
Moratuwa
MALDIVES
1:7.5M
0
100
200
300 km
0
50
100
150 mls
Ambalangoda

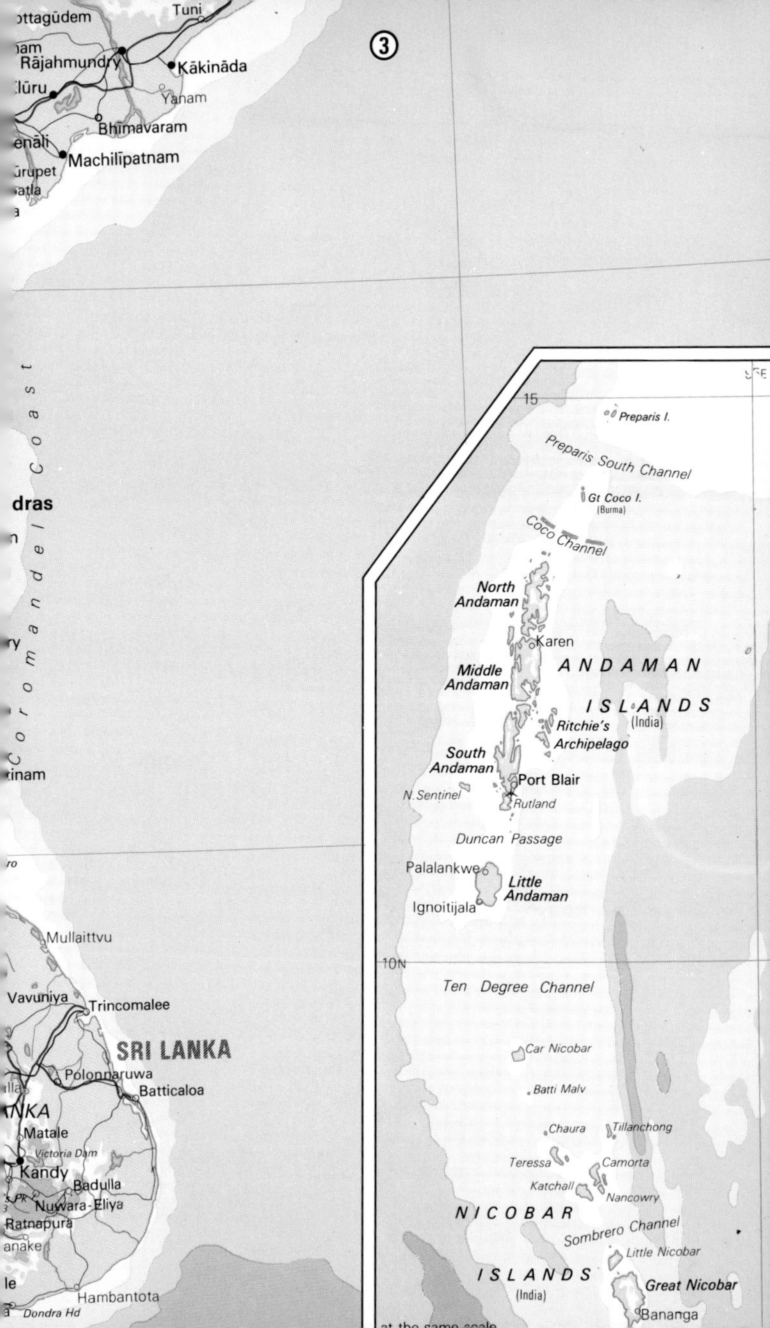

3
Tuni
Rājahmundry
Kākināda
Yanam
Bhīmavaram
Machilīpatnam
Coromandel Coast
dras
Mullaittvu
Vavuniya
Trincomalee
SRI LANKA
Polonnaruwa
Batticaloa
Matale
Victoria Dam
Kandy
Badulla
Nuwara-Eliya
Ratnapura
Hambantota
Dondra Hd
15
Preparis I.
Preparis South Channel
Gt Coco I.
(Burma)
Coco Channel
North Andaman
Karen
Middle Andaman
ANDAMAN ISLANDS
(India)
Ritchie's Archipelago
South Andaman
Port Blair
N. Sentinel
Rutland
Duncan Passage
Palalankwe
Little Andaman
Ignoitijala
10N
Ten Degree Channel
Car Nicobar
Batti Malv
Chaura
Tillanchong
Teressa
Camorta
Katchall
Nancowry
NICOBAR ISLANDS
(India)
Sombrero Channel
Little Nicobar
Great Nicobar
Bananga

R Ā J A S T H Ā N
4
Pokaran
Devikot
Thar
Dausa
Daulpur
Hindaun
Kishangarh
Ajmer
Mālpura
Shergarh
Jodhpur
Bilāra
Beāwar
Tonk
Chambal
Bālotra
Sojat
Kekri
Toda
Sawai Mādhopur
Bārmer
Pāli
Devli
Sheopur
Mārwār
Arāvalli Range
Jālor
Būndi
Shivpuri
Bhīlwāra
Chachro
Sādri
Bārān
Kota
Sirohi
Chittaurgarh
Jhālāwār
Udaipur
Rāmpura
Guna
Nagar Parkar
Gāndhi Sāgar
Bari Sādri
Nīmach
Pālanpur
Khed Brahma
Rādhanpur
Mandsaur
Sironj
Pātan
Siddhapur
Rājgarh
Dūngarpur
Malwa Plateau
Agar
Himatnagar
Mahesāna
Bānswāra
Jaora
Vidisha
Shājāpur
Kadi
Gāndhinagar
Ratlām
Shujālpur
Bhopāl
G U J A R Ā T
Ujjain
Morbi
Dhrāngadhra
Ahmadābād
Dāhod
Dewās
Vindhya
Surendranagar
Nadiād
Godhra
Jhābua
Indore
Hoshangābād
Petlād
Dhār
Mhow
Rājkot
Vadodara
Barwāh
Gondal
Botād
Jasdan
Jambusar
Dabhoi
Narmada
Sanāwad
Harda
Kāthiāwār
Bhāvnagar
Barwāni
Khargon
Khandwa
Betūl
Amreli
Bharūch
Rājpipla
Sātpura Range
Sendhwa
Pālitāna
Gir Hills
Kundla
Nandurbār
Burhānpur
Achalpur
Mahuva
Sūrat
Tāpi
Amalner
Jalgaon
Bhusāwal
Akot
Amrāvati
Gulf of Khambhāt
Dhule
Malkāpur
Akola
Navsāri
Diu
(Goa, Daman & Diu)
Malegaon
Buldāna
Valsād
Ajanta
Khāmgaon
Damān
(G,D. & D.)
Chālisgaon
Kāranja
Silvassa
Ellora
Mehekar
Wāshīm
Nāsik
Manmād
Aurangābād
Deolāli
Kopargaon
Jālna
Pusad
Godāvari
Hingoli
Sangamner
M A H Ā R Ā S H T R A
Thāne
Kalyān
Parbhani
Pūrna
Nānded
Ahmadnagar
Bombay
Bīr
Lonāvale
Parli
Alībāg
Pune
(Poona)
Bodhan
Daund
Udgir
Western Ghats
Lātūr
Mahād
Bārāmati
Mānjra
Shrīvardhan
Wai
Barsi
Phaltan
Bidar
Koyna Resr
Solāpur
Sātāra
Homnābād
Chiplūn
Pandharpur
Akalkot
Gulbarga
Vite
Karād
Tāndūr
Ratnāgiri
Shāhābād
Sāngli
Miraj
Bijāpur
Yādgir
Kolhāpur
Ichalkaranji
Nārāyanpet
Jamkhandi
Shorāpur
Krishna
Rāichur
Bāgalkot
Mālvan
Guledagudda
Tungabhadra
Vengurla
Belgaum
Kurnool
Gajendragarh
Ādoni
Panaji
Goa, Daman & Diu
K A R N Ā T A K A
Dhone
Koppal
Gadag
Hampi

Etāwah
Lucknow
Faizābād
Basti
Gorakhpur
Janakpur
Jaleswar
Motihāri
Madhubani
P R A D E S H
5
Unnāo
Kānpur
Auraiya
Kālpi
Orai
Hamīrpur
Rāe Bareli
Gomati
Sultānpur
Ghāghara
Āzamgarh
Muzaffarpur
Darbhanga
Fatehpur
Bela
Mau
Jaunpur
Ballia
Chhapra
Betwa
Rāth
Bānda
Charkhāri
Allahābād
Vārānasi
Ara
Patna
Barauni
Mokama
Bihār
Orchha
Mahoba
Karwa
Mirzāpur
Sasaram
Dehri
Gaya
Nawāda
Chhatarpur
Khajuraho
Tikamgarh
Panna
Rewa
Satna
Maihar
Sidhi
Son
B I H A
Barhi
Rājmahā
Giridi
Govind Ballabh Paht Sāgar
Garwa
Dāltenganj
Hazārībāg
Dhanbā
Damoh
Murwāra
Katni
Beohāri
Rānchi Plateau
Rāmgarh
Aiyar Resr
Sindri
Sihora
Umaria
Baikunthpur
Lohārdaga
Rānchi
Muri
Tropic of Cancer
Manendragarh
Chotanāgpur
Shahdol
Bishrāmpur
Ambikāpur
Gumla
Jabalpur
Narsimhapur
P R A D E S H
Mandla
Keonchi
Chāibāsa
Korba
Nainpur
Maikala Range
Raurkela
Mungeli
Bilāspur
Sundargarh
Seoni
Kawardha
Chāmpa
Raigarh
Jhārsuguda
Bālaghāt
Keonjharga
Tirodi
Mahānadi
Hirakud Resr
Sambalpur
Tumsar
Gondia
Kāmthi
Durg
Raipur
Bargarh
Bhandāra
Bhilai
Tālcher
Raj Nāndgaon
Mahāsamund
Brāhmani
Angul
Umred
Balāngīr
Dalli Rajhara
Dhamtari
Dhenkānal
Hinganghāt
Phulbāni
Titlagarh
O R I S S A
Cutta
Bhuba
Khurda
Kānker
Chandrapur
Bhawānipatna
Puri
Chilka Lake
Aska
Kondagaon
Eastern Ghats
Chatrapur
Berhampur
Kotapad
Rāyagada
Jagdalpur
Belampalli
Jeypore
Parvatīpuram
Sironcha
Dantewāra
Koraput
Parlākimidi
Manchērāl
Bījāpur
Bobbili
Sukma
Sālūr
Karīmnagar
Godāvari
Sabari
Srīkākulam
Warangal
Vizianagaram
Siddipet
Vishākhapatnam
Narsīpatnam
Anakāpalle
Yellandu
Bhadrāchalam
Bhongir
Kottagūdem
Tuni
Hyderābād
Khammam
Nalgonda
Suriāpet
Rājahmundry
Kākināda
ANDHRA PRADESH
Elūru
Krishna
Yanam
Vijayawada
Macherla
Guntūr
Bhīmavaram
Tenāli
Narasarāopet
Machilīpatnam
Chilakalūrupet
Nallamala Range
Bāpatla
Chīrāla
Kani Giri
Ongole
1:7.5M
0
100
200
300 km
0
50
100
150 mls

6
Quetta
Khost
Loralai
Gowārān
Nushki
Hamun-i-Lora
Dalbandin
Ras Koh 3008
Kharan
Kalat
Gandava
Dadhar
Sibi
Kohlu
Kahan
Bhag
Dera Bugti
Sui
P A K I S T A N
B A L U C H I S T A N
Washuk
Khuzdar
Wad
Nagha Kalat
Hingol
Bela
Uthal
Sonmiani
Sonmiani Bay
Karachi
Korangi
Mouths of the Indus
Keti Bandar
Tatta
Kirithar Range
Sehwan
Dadu
Moro
Moenjodaro
Larkana
Shadadkot
Jacobabad
Shikarpur
Sukkur
Rohri
Khairpur
Indus
KHAIRPUR
Nawabshah
Sanghar
S I N D
Tando Adam
Mirpur Khas
Kotri
Hyderabad
Nat. Gas
Tando Muhammad Khan
Badin
Naokot
Umarkot
Chachro
Sartanahu
Muzaffargarh
Dera Ghazi Khan
Jampur
Multan
Khanewal
Shujaabad
Bahawal
Lodhran
Bahawalpur
Uch
Rajanpur
Mithankot
Chachran
BAHAWALPUR
Khanpur
Rahimyar Khan
Sulaiman
Fort Abba
Bijnot
Kishangarh
Rāmgarh
Jaisalmer
Pokaran
Phalod
Devikot
Sartanahu
Shergarh
Jodhp
Bālotra
Bārmer
THAR
INDIAN DESERT
RĀJ
Jāl
Sirohi
Nagar Parkar
Rann of Kachchh
Rādhanpur
Pālanpur
Pātan
Siddh
Mahesāna
Kadi
Kāvda
Lakhpat
Kori Ck.
Tropic of Cancer
Bhuj
Gāndhīdhām
Māndvi
Navlakhi
G. of Kachchh
Morbi
Dhrāngadhra
G U J A R
Surendranagar
Nadiad
Petlād
Okha
Jāmnagar
Dwārka
Rājkot
Gondal
Jasdan
Botād
Jambusar
Kāthiāwār
Bhavnagar
Porbandar
Dhoraji
Amreli
Pālitāna
Jūnāgadh
Gīr Hills
Kundla
Māngrol
Verāval
Mahuva
Diu
(Goa, Daman & Diu)
Gulf of Khambhāt
Sūrat
Navsā
Valsā
Damār
(G.D. & D.
ARABIAN SEA
1:7.5M
0
100
200
300 km
0
50
100
150 mls
Thāne
Bombay
Alībāg

Abohar
Bhatinda
Sangrur
Narendranagar
Pauri
Simikot
Mānsa
Haridwar
7
Roorkee
Almora
Ganganagar
Kaithal
Kali
Baitadi
Sirsa
Narwāna
Karnāl
Muzaffarnagar
Nagina
Naini Tal
Silgarhi
HARYĀNA
Haldwāni
Sūratgarh
Jind
Pānīpat
Bijnor
Kāshīpur
Dandeldhura
Nohar
Hisār
Rohtak
Sonīpat
Meerut
Rāmpur
Pīlībhīt
Dhangarhi
Hānsi
Moradābād
Bhiwāni
Delhi
Gauri Phanta
Rājgarh
New Delhi
Ghāziābād
Sambhal
Sardarshahr
Gurgaon
Bulandshahr
Bareilly
Nepalganj
Rewāri
Khurja
Chūru
Budaun
Ratangarh
Palwal
Lakhīmpur
Nānpāra
Jhunjhunūn
Nārnaul
Aligarh
Shāhjahānpur
Yamuna
Sujāngarh
UTTAR
Lādnūn
Sīkar
Alwar
Mathura
Hāthras
Sītāpur
Ganga (Ganges)
Dīdwāna
Bharatpur
Firozābād
Nāgaur
Sandila
Makrāna
Jaipur
Āgra
Mainpuri
Bāra
Dausa
Lucknow
STHĀN
Etāwah
PRA
Daulpur
Unnāo
Rāe Bareli
Hindaun
Morena
Merta
Bhind
Kānpur
Kishangarh
Auraiya
Ajmer
Mālpura
Gwalior
Chambal
Kālpi
Orai
Hamīrpur
Fatehpur
Beāwar
Tonk
Sind
Toda
Kekri
Sawai Mādhopur
Datia
Rāth
Devli
Sheopur
Bānda
Betwa
Allahābād
Charkhāri
Karwa
Būndi
Shivpuri
Jhānsi
Orchha
Bhīlwāra
Mahoba
Kota
Bārān
Chhatarpur
Khajuraho
Chittaurgarh
Tikamgarh
Rewa
Jhālāwār
Panna
Satna
Lalitpur
Rāmpura
Guna
Maihar
Gāndhi Sāgar
Bari Sādri
Nīmach
Bina-Etawa
Sironj
Mandsaur
Garhākota
Damoh
Katni
Rājgarh
Murwāra
Dūngarpur
Malwa Plateau
Agar
Sāgar
Umaria
Sihora
Bānswāra
Jaora
Shājāpur
Vidisha
Tropic of Cancer
Ratlām
Shujālpur
Bhopāl
Shahdol
Jabalpur
Ujjain
Dewās
Narsimhapur
Dāhod
Godhra
Jhābua
Indore
MADHYA PRADESH
Hoshangābād
Mandla
Dhār
Mhow
Mahadeo Hills
Barwāh
Nainpur
Harda
Narmada
Dabhoi
Sanāwad
Chhindwāra
Seoni
Barwāni
Khargon
Betūl
Bālāghāt
Khandwa
Tirodi
Sātpura Range
Sendwha
Gondia
Maikala Range
Tumsar
Nandurbār
Burhānpur
Achalpur
Kāmthi
Durg
Tāpi
Bhandāra
Bhusāwal
Akot
Amrāvati
Nāgpur
Raj Nāndgaon
Amalner
Jalgaon
Dhule
Akola
Wardha
Dalli Rajhara
Malkāpur
Umred
Buldāna
Malegaon
Ajanta
Khāmgaon
Hinganghāt
Chālisgaon
Kāranja
Yavatmāl
Ellora
Mehekar
Wāshīm
Rājura
Manmād
Nāsik
Aurangābād
Chandrapur
Deolāli
Kopargaon
Pusad
Jālna
Hingoli
Penganga
Godāvari
Ādilābād
Sangamner
MAHĀRĀSHTRA
Nānded
Kalyān
Parbhani
Pūrna
Nirmal
Belampalli
Ahmadnagar
Bīr
Sironcha
Jagtial
Parli
Mancherāl
Lonāvale
Pune (Poona)
Bodhan
Nizāmābād
Udgir

9
Baxoi
Bomi
Namjagbarwa Feng
7756
Rawu
Nyang Qu
Doilungdêqên
Lhasa
T
Dagzê
Nyingchi
Mêdog
Qüzü
Yarlung Zangbo Jiang
Nêdong
Yamzho
Yumco
Nang
Xian
Zayü
Mishmi Hills
Kadusam
5108
Lhozhag
Arunāchal
Pradesh
Sadiya
Cona
N
G
E
Dapha Bum
4578
Punakha
Tongsa
Dibrugarh
Tinsukia
Hāpoli
Bomdila
Digboi
Ledo
BHUTAN
Tashigang
Itānagar
Sibsāgar
Naga Hills
Chhukha
Manas
Dewangiri
Brahmaputra
Jorhāt
Hukawng
Valley
Tezpur
Mariāni
Alīpur Duār
Mairābāri
Golāghāt
Kumon Range
Mokokchūng
ASSAM
Barpeta
Gauhāti
Nowgong
NĀGĀLAND
Dhuburi
Singkaling
Hkamti
Goālpāra
Hojāi
Diphu
Dimāpur
Kohīma
Lumding
Tura
Shillong
Jowai
Mogaung
MEGHĀLAYA
Chilmari
Khasi - Jaintia Hills
Cherrapunji
Ukhrul
Jāria Jhānjail
Chhātak
Hāflong
Mohanganj
Karimganj
Imphāl
Jamalpur
Silchar
Homalin
Netrakona
Sylhet
MANIPUR
Gangaw Range
Mymensingh
Meghna
Hailākāndi
Banmauk
Habiganj
Dullabchara
Katha
Mangin Range
Churāchāndpur
Tamu
BANGLADESH
Dhākā
(Dacca)
Brahman-
Barra
TRIPURA
Wuntho
Pabna
Agartala
Āīzawl
Narayanganj
Mawlaik
Tagaung
MIZORAM
Letha Range
Manipur
Faridpur
Padma
Comilla
Mizo
Hills
Shweli
Bhātāpāra
Ghāt
Kalewa
Mogok
Chandpur
Madaripur
Karnafuli
Resr
Ponnyadaung Ra.
Yeu
Falam
Maijdi
Barisal
Lunglei
Haka
Chindwin
Shwebo
Noakhali
Bagherhat
Rangamati
BURMA
Madaya
Patuakhali
Chittagong
Saiha
Monywa
Maymyo
Myinmu
Mandalay
Gangaw
Sagaing
Amarapura
of the Ganga (Ganges)
Kyaukse
Kutubdia I.
Myingyan
Maiskhal I.
Pakokku
Myittha
Kaladan
Mt Victoria
3053
Cox's Bazar
Paletwa
Thazi
Meiktila
Heho
Teknaf
Lemro
Yamethin
Y
OF
Minbu
Magwe
Sittwe
1:7.5M
0
100
200
300 km
Pyinmana
50
100
150 mls
Kyaukpyu
ENGAL
Ramree I.
Prome

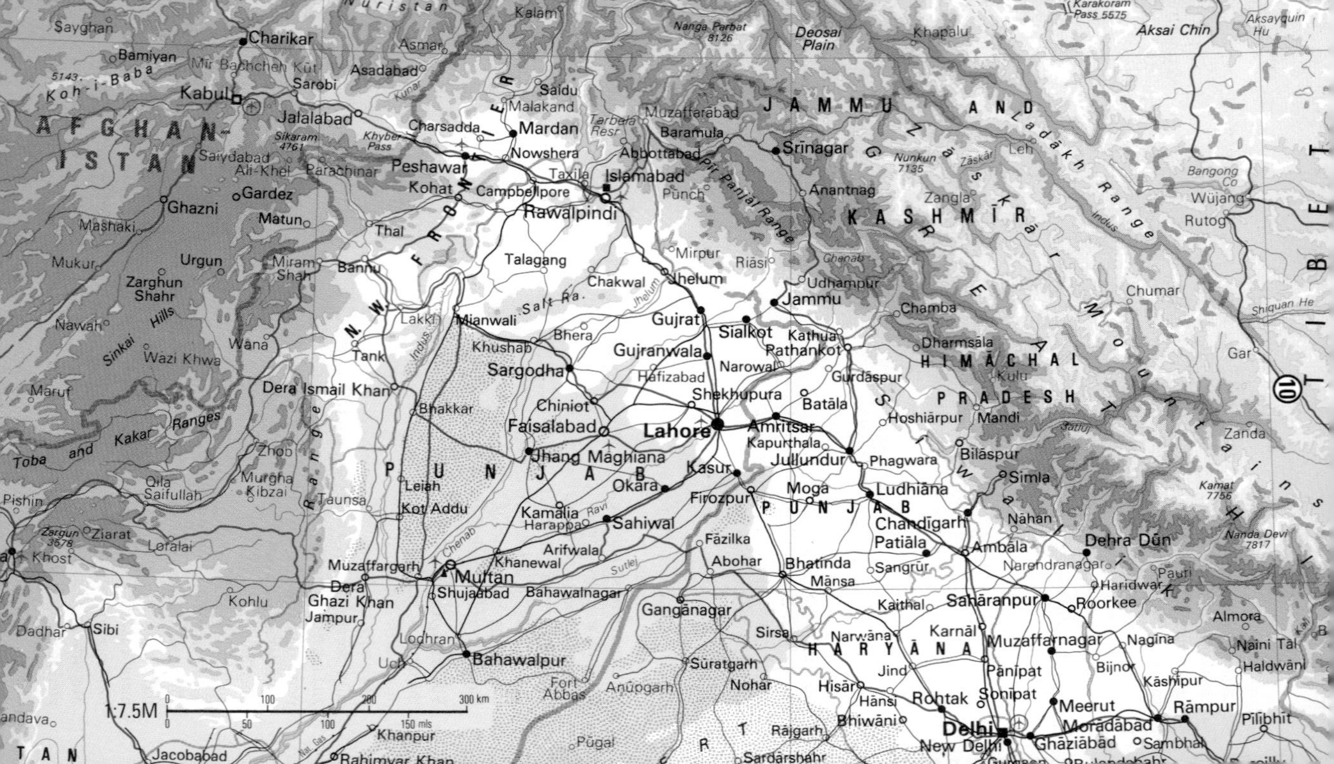

Nuristan
Kalam
Karakoram Pass 5575
Aksayquin Hu
Aksai Chin
Saygham
Charikar
Nanga Parbat 8126
Deosai Plain
Khapalu
Bamiyan
Mir Bachchen Kut
Asmar
Asadabad
5143
Koh-i-Baba
Kabul
Sarobi
Saidu
Malakand
JAMMU AND
Ladakh Range
Jalalabad
Charsadda
Mardan
Tarbela Resr
Muzaffarabad
Baramula
AFGHANISTAN
Sikaram 4761
Khyber Pass
Nowshera
Abbottabad
Srinagar
Nunkun 7135
Zaskar
Leh
Bangong Co
Wujang
Saiydabad
Ali-Khel
Parachinar
Peshawar
Taxila
Islamabad
Pir Panjal Range
Gardez
Kohat
Campbellpore
Punch
Anantnag
Zangla
KASHMIR
Indus
Rutog
TIBET
Ghazni
Rawalpindi
Mashaki
Matun
Thal
Mirpur
Riasi
Chenab
Mukur
Urgun
Miram Shah
Bannu
Talagang
Chakwal
Jhelum
Udhampur
Chumar
Zarghun Shahr
Salt Ra.
Jammu
Shiquan He
N.W. FRONTIER
Nawah
Hills
Lakki
Mianwali
Gujrat
Sialkot
Chamba
Wana
Khushab
Bhera
Kathua
Pathankot
Dharmsala
HIMACHAL
Gar
Sinkai
Wazi Khwa
Tank
Gujranwala
Narowal
Kulu
Sargodha
Hafizabad
Gurdaspur
10
Maruf
Dera Ismail Khan
Shekhupura
Batala
PRADESH
Chiniot
Hoshiarpur
Mandi
Bhakkar
Ranges
Faisalabad
Lahore
Amritsar
Satluj
Zanda
Kakar
Zhob
Kapurthala
Bilaspur
Toba and
Jhang Maghiana
Jullundur
Phagwara
Simla
PUNJAB
Kasur
Qila Saifullah
Murgha Kibzai
Leiah
Okara
Moga
Ludhiana
Kamat 7756
Pishin
Range
Taunsa
Kot Addu
Firozpur
Kamalia
Ravi
Harappa
Sahiwal
Chandigarh
Nahan
Zargun 3578
Ziarat
Loralai
Fazilka
Patiala
Dehra Dun
Nanda Devi 7817
Khost
Arifwala
Ambala
Muzaffargarh
Khanewal
Abohar
Bhatinda
Narendranagar
Pauri
Multan
Sutlej
Mansa
Sangrur
Haridwar
Dera Ghazi Khan
Shujabad
Bahawalnagar
Kohlu
Ganganagar
Kaithal
Saharanpur
Roorkee
Jampur
Almora
Dadhar
Sibi
Sirsa
Karnal
Narwana
Nagina
Lodhran
HARYANA
Muzaffarnagar
Naini Tal
Bahawalpur
Suratgarh
Jind
Panipat
Bijnor
Haldwani
Uch
Kashipur
Fort Abbas
Anupgarh
Nohar
Hisar
Hansi
Sonipat
Meerut
1:7.5M
0
100
200
300 km
Rohtak
Rampur
50
150 mls
Pilibhit
Bhiwani
Moradabad
andava
Rajgarh
Delhi
Khanpur
New Delhi
Ghaziabad
Sambhal
TAN
Jacobabad
Pugal
Rahimyar Khan
Sardarshahr
Nat. Gas
Kunar
Kali

rasagolla, rasamalai, chenapodapitha, khiramohan, rajbhoga, rabidi, jilabi and *kalakhanda. Khiri* is prepared with milk and rice (similar to rice pudding) or semolina or vermicelli for festive occasions. There are also the *pithas* which are often filled with sweetened coconut.

Although tea is the common drink, coffee is freely available in hotels and restaurants. Fruit juices (mango, sugar cane, bel) and the very refreshing green coconut 'milk' is worth trying, often sold on the roadside – safe and ready-to-drink.

Crafts

Stone carving has been highly developed in Orissa for over 2000 years. The artistry that produced the early sculptures and the superb carvings on Orissan temples in Bhubaneswar, Puri and Konark is still alive in modern craftsmen. Sculpting in stone, which reached such magnificence in the temples nearly a 1000 years ago, can be seen today in the delicate images, bowls or plates carved out of soft soapstone, hard konchila or multicoloured serpentine from Khiching. In Puri the sculptors' quarter is in Pathuria Sahi or Stone carvers' Street. Orissa also has a tradition of hornwork in Parlakhemundi and Cuttack, buffalo horn being carved into the usual small flat figures of animals and birds.

Silver filigree, *Tarkashi* is perhaps one of the most distinctive and exquisite works of the Cuttack jewellers who turn fine silver wire into beautiful, fragile objects with floral patterns. Small boxes, trays and most of all jewellery are the popular items. The silver used is close to sterling silver which is drawn through finer and finer holes.

Everyday domestic utensils are widely available in brass and bell-metal. The same craftsmen also produce small figurines, vases and plates. The tribal metal casting in the *dokra* style by the lost wax process is carried out in the Mayurbhanj district. A clay shell is created around a wax core and molten metal is poured into the shape, displacing the wax.

Wood carving and inlay work on wood is still practised, brightly coloured replicas of the deities in the Jagannath temple, and other figures of animals and birds being common. Ivory inlay, now replaced by plastic inlays, was traditionally carried out for making gifts for the Puri temples by rich patrons and also for making illustrated wooden covers for narrow palm leaf manuscripts. The tradition of using papier-mâché masks of deities and animal characters, to tell stories from the epics also comes from Orissa.

The **chitrakars** (picture makers), particularly from the village of Raghurajpur near Puri, paint the *pattachitras* on specially prepared cloth, coated with earth to stiffen it and finally finished with lacquer after painting, producing not only pictures but attractive playing cards in the form of discs. Old sets of *ganjapa* consisted of 96 cards. The bold curved and angular lines and vibrant colours which traditionally came from earth, stone, leaves and flowers, depict the tales from the Vedas and Puranas, but mainly of Radha, Krishna and Lord Jagannath. The best *chitrakars* hold the coveted post of painting the Puri temple deities and their 'cars' each year. They also produce fine murals for the temples and manuscripts on paper and palm-leaf, commissioned by the rich. However, what is commonly available in the bazars are cruder examples for pilgrims to take home as mementos.

Palm leaf etching is another skill that is still practised. An iron stylus is held stationary while moving the leaf to produce illustrated manuscripts. It was a technology that helped to give the Oriya script its rounded form. Manuscripts from the 16th century have been found, most of which are secular. The leaves had to be prepared by drying, boiling, drying again and flattening before coating with shell. After inscribing, the grooves would be rubbed with soot or powdered charcoal while colour was added with a brush. The leaves would be stacked and strung together and placed between decorative covers made of wood. The artists who work on *pattachitras* in Raghurajpur have also revived this art form.

Appliqué Pipli, a small town about 32 km SW of Bhubaneswar on the Puri road is famous for its colourful appliqué work, one of the centres for production of a special kind of brightly coloured embroidered cloth probably originally designed for use in the Jagannath temple. The shops on the road side sell items for the house and garden – sun umbrellas, canopies, cushion covers, wall-hangings and heart-shaped cloth shields called *tarasa*, which use primary colours to make patterns of animals, birds and flowers on a backcloth. Unfortunately the attempt to churn out goods for a growing market has resulted in the loss of attention to detail of the original fine Pipli work which picked out motifs of appliqué by cleverly stuffing sections of the pattern. The best pieces now tend to be sent away to the Govt emporia in Bhubaneswar and New Delhi.

Textile weaving has been a traditional handicraft throughout Orissa for generations and thousands are still employed in this cottage industry in different parts of the state. In common with other parts of India which have developed a textile of its own, it is one of the few regions producing *ikat* – see also page 1069 – the technique of 'resist-dyeing' the warp or weft thread, or both, before weaving, so that the fabric that emerges from the loom has a delicate enmeshed pattern. The favourite designs include rows of flowers, birds and animals (particularly elephants) as well as geometric shapes, using either tussar or cotton yarn. Berhampore, Sambalpur, Mayurbhanj and Naupatana are all prominent centres producing silk and cotton saris. Some also produce tapestry, bedspreads and embroidered fabric.

Crafts villages There are several villages where craftsmen are grouped together. In **Raghurajpur** (12 km from Puri) you can watch villagers painting the *Pattachitras* in bright folk-art style or etching palm leaves. **Pipli**, on the Bhubaneswar-Puri Road, specialises in appliqué work, **Belakati** (10 km from Bhubaneswar) in bell-metal, and there is a community of Tibetan carpet weavers at **Chandragiri** near the Taptapani Hot Springs in tribal country. Adjacent to the Buddhist site of **Lalitagiri** is a stone-carvers' village, while master-weavers work at their looms in the Buddhist villages of **Nuapatna** and **Maniabhanda** (70 km from Bhubaneswar) or down the narrow streets next to the temple at **Berhampur**. Cuttack remains famous for silver filigree work.

Modern Orissa

Economy

Agriculture Shifting cultivation used to be widely practised. Even in the 1960s it was estimated that over 3 million hectares of forest was cut every year by shifting cultivators. Today the hills have been extensively opened up to settled farming. In the S colonisation schemes have been introduced for Indian emigrants returning from Burma and Sri Lanka. Rice is grown on 90% of the fertile plains of the Mahanadi delta. There are also small areas of jute, ragi, oilseeds and gram.

Resources and industry Coal is mined in thick seams at Talcher, 100 km to the NW of Bhubaneswar. Around Bhubaneswar itself and at several other sites in the interior are important bauxite deposits, exploited first in the 1980s for aluminium smelting. In the far N of the state, especially between Keonjhar and Rourkela, are enormous reserves of very high grade iron, frequently occurring as outcropping hills of almost solid iron ore. In addition to these basic mineral resources there are also important reserves of manganese, graphite and mica. Mining began only after Independence in 1947. A new port was built at Paradwip to handle the export of minerals from Orissa and an expressway was constructed from the mines at Daitari.

In the last 20 years Orissa has seen major developments of industry. There has been increasing investment from within India, but some of the development has taken place with the help of foreign aid and commercial investment. Despite recent growth, Orissa still provides only 3% of India's factory employment.

BHUBANESWAR

Bhubaneswar ('The Lord of the Universe') is the capital of Orissa, chosen in 1948 in place of Cuttack some 29 km to the NE. One of the reasons for the decision lay in the antiquity of Bhubaneswar's role as capital of the Kalinga Empire. It is the architectural legacy of that period which remains Bhubaneswar's greatest attraction.

BASICS *Population*: 411,500. *Altitude*: 45m. *STD Code*: 0674. *Languages*: Oriya, Hindi and English.

History

There are several sites in the vicinity which testify to the importance of the region far earlier than the 7th to 11th centuries when the Kalinga kings ruled Orissa and regions beyond. Both Jain and Buddhist shrines give clear evidence of important settlements around Bhubaneswar in the first 2 centuries BC, and one of the most complete edicts of the Mauryan Emperor Asoka, dating from between 272-236 BC, remains carved in rock just 5 miles to the SW of the modern city. The remains of a ruined moated city, Sisupalgarh (opposite the Dhaulagiri battlefield and Asoka edicts), have been excavated to show that it was occupied from the beginning of the 3rd century BC to the middle of the 4th century AD. According to Mortimer Wheeler the pottery shows Roman influences.

Places of interest

The Bindusagar tank was once reputed to be surrounded by 7000 temples, and Bhubaneswar still attracts pilgrims and tourists to the 500 that survive.

The Parasuramesvera Temple

This is an excellent place to start a tour. It is easily found, 200m down a lane to the right off the main road to Puri, 1 km S of the museum. In order to reach it you pass the Muktesvara Temple, to which you should return.

The temple dates from the 7th century. Small but highly decorated, it is the best preserved – though not the oldest – of the early Bhubaneswar temples. Its early date is indicated partly by the nature of the porch, rectangular rather than square, and with a stepped roof rather than a pyramidal structure typical of later development. Even so, the porch was probably built after the sanctuary itself, as is suggested by the rather crude junction between the two.

The early date of the temple is also illustrated by the building technique used, in which masonry was kept in place by weight and balance without any cement. Another feature which marks this out as an early temple is the carving of a goddess and two sea-monsters on the lintel over the doorway into the sanctuary. Traditionally this entrance is topped by carvings of the 9 planets, but in the Parasuramesvara temple there are only eight.

The temple marks an important stage in the development of Hindu power at the expense of Buddhism in 7th century Orissa, illustrated by the frequent representation of the figure of **Lakulisa**, the 7th century priest responsible for Hindu proselytism, sculpted in Buddha-like form, often surrounded by disciples. A second illustration is the use made of distinctive window-shaped motifs developed earlier in Buddhist

CLIMATE: BHUBANESWAR

	Jan	Feb	Mar	Apr	May	Jun	Jul	Aug	Sep	Oct	Nov	Dec	Av/Tot
Max (°C)	29	32	35	38	38	35	31	31	31	31	29	28	32
Min (°C)	16	19	22	26	27	26	25	25	25	23	18	16	22
Rain (mm)	12	25	17	12	61	223	301	336	305	266	51	3	1612

chaitya halls, such as those at Ajanta, described as *chaitya* windows. On the front of the sanctuary tower the central section has 2 obvious examples. The lower shows Siva tackling Ravana, with Ravana, the demon king of Lanka, desperately trying to root out Mount Kailasa, Siva's home. Ganesh and

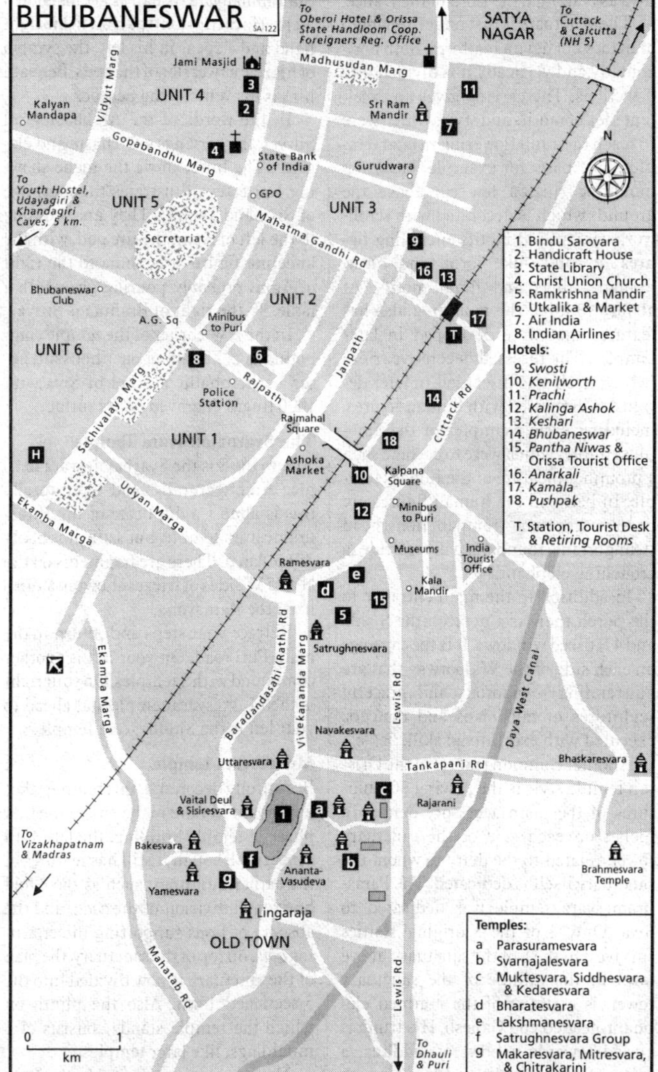

Karttikeya are ready to fight while Siva is comforting his wife, Parvati. This story is still widely known by Hindus today. The upper *chaitya* window shows Siva as Nataraja, the Lord of the Dance.

The sanctuary is just under 13m high and does not have a platform. Both horizontally and vertically it is divided into 3 sections. The carving gives an excellent idea of motifs and styles which were to reach their full flowering in later temples. The base, for example, has a top moulding (just a few cm above the ground) which is decorated with scrollwork, tiny round motifs encircling figures in cameo-like form, and birds, human beings and floral motifs. At about eye level, the moulding also has features that were developed in later temples. The recessed decorative frieze (which itself was discarded in later designs) is embossed with human figures, including early examples of the amorous couples which were to become such a prominent feature of the Konark temple. In between the human figures are panels with *vyalas* – rampant lions, head swung right round, usually astride a crouching elephant.

In addition to the main entrance to the porch there is a door on the S side and 4 latticed windows. It is the carvings on each side of the W doorway that are outstanding – vigorous and graceful sculptures of musicians and dancers, executed with exceptional skill.

Another common feature of the Orissan temple style is the placing of sculptures of the main accessory deities in niches on each side of the sanctuary tower, related to the deity to whom the sanctuary itself is dedicated. The Parasuramesvara temple was dedicated to Siva. Only 2 of the 3 original deities survive. On the S of the sanctuary, at eye level in the middle of the sanctuary tower, is a statue of the 4-armed elephant-headed god Ganesh. His trunk is curled towards a bowl of laddhus, a sweet of which tradition has it Ganesh was particularly fond. In his upper left hand he holds a hatchet. In the S niche is the 2 armed brother of Ganesh, Karttikeya, known in S India as Subrahmanya. His hair is arranged in 3 locks. He carries a citrus fruit in his right hand and a spear in his left, the symbol of his role as warrior of the gods. Beneath him is his vehicle, the peacock.

In the words of the Archaeological Survey, the carvings are 'chaste and elegant'. The lintel above the niche showing Karttikeya illustrates the marriage of Siva and Parvati. They are standing to the left of Agni, the fire god, with the kneeling figure of Brahma to the right of Agni, probably pouring ghee with a ladle. To the right of Brahma is Surya.

In the NW corner of the temple compound is a 'lingam of one thousand *lingas*' – the phallic symbol of Siva with 1000 lingas engraved on its surface.

The Svarnajalesvara Temple

50m to the S is the Svarnajalesvara temple. Architecturally and sculpturally this is almost a duplicate of the Parasuramesvara temple, but sadly it is badly dilapidated. There are fragments on the N and W sides of friezes showing stories from the Ramayana.

Retrace your steps and return to the main Puri road. On your left is another compound with 2 temples. On your right is the Muktesvara temple and ahead to your left is the Siddhesvara temple.

Muktesvara temple

Beautifully decorated, this temple takes us forward in time to the end of the first phase of temple building, the late 10th century. Although it still has features of the earlier buildings, such as the 3 fold horizontal division of the *bada*, and the absence of lions supporting the crowning *amla* on top of the sanctuary, the plan of the sanctuary is now divided into the 5-sectioned form. Also the plinth on which the temple stands consists of 5 mouldings, like later temples.

New designs are in evidence, with

graceful female figures and *pilasters* carved with snake figures – *nagas* and *naginis*. Most strikingly, the porch is taking on a new and more dramatic layered form, although the pyramidal roof is not yet topped with the full range of elements. To set the seal on the transition, Ketu has been introduced as the ninth planet and Ganesh is joined by his mount, the mouse, unlike his depiction in the Parasuramesvara Temple.

The first impression of the Muktesvara temple is given by the unique gateway arch or *Torana*, which has been dated at about AD 900. Although the upper portion of the arch is restored, the original skill can still be seen in the graceful female figures. But the compactness of the temple is also very striking. The rectangular tank at its E end, in use today by priests and devotees, and the well on the S side of the compound into which women still toss coins in the hope of curing infertility, symbolise the continued holiness of the site. On the door frame of the well is carved the figure of a local saint, Lakulisa, whose image is found on several of Bhubaneswar's early temples, for he played a major part in replacing Buddhist with Hindu worship in the region.

But it is the carvings which make the sharpest impression. The *chaitya* windows carved in the vertical *rathas* of the sanctuary are crowned by a decorative motif showing the grinning face of a lion. A string of beaded tassels often comes out of the lion's mouth, and the whole is flanked by 2 dwarves in an ensemble that is known as a *bho* motif. It finds its finest expression in the Muktesvara Temple.

The decoration of the porch walls imitates some of the scenes from the main vertical section of the sanctuary. On the N and S walls is a diamond-shaped latticed window. Notice the monkey scenes on the outer frame. There is also an unusual degree of carving on the interior of the porch.

Siddhesvara Temple

Immediately to the NW of the Muktesvara Temple is the later Siddhesvara Temple. It shows the mature Orissan temple form almost complete. Unlike the earlier temples, the vertical lower section is now divided into 5 parts and the *amla* on top of the sanctuary is supported by 4 squatting figures. However, the overall effect is comparatively plain, as sculptures which were marked out on the rock were never executed, a feature evident also in the porch of the Rajarani temple.

The **Gauri temple** to the S probably dates from a similar period to the Muktesvara temple. However, not only is it built in the *khakhara* form, like the Vaital Deul (see below) but it has been substantially repaired. The porch was rebuilt in the early years of this century, but there are a few original sculptures of real merit. Note the girl shown leaning against a post, on which is perched a bird, on the S face of the eastern projection of the sanctuary. On the W projection there is an equally beautiful sculpture of a girl removing her anklets.

The Rajarani Temple

Go back up the main road towards Bhubaneswar a very short distance, then follow the road to the right. The entrance to the Rajarani Temple is about 300m on the right. The Brahmesvara Temple is a further 1 km down the same road. The Rajarani temple is set back 200m from the road in an open space. Both are representatives of later styles, the Rajarani being early 11th century and the Brahmesvara precisely datable to AD 1060. However, the Rajarani Temple no longer has an image of the presiding deity in the sanctuary and it is therefore out of use, while the Brahmesvara continues to be an active temple for worship.

Even approaching the Rajarani temple, the form of the sanctuary is striking, for the main tower, nearly 18m high, is surrounded by 4 miniature copies. These give the sanctuary an almost circular appearance, which perhaps detracts from the impression of the heavenwards projection of the main sanctuary. The example was not followed in other temples. They have the further effect of concealing the diagonal placing of the sanctuary against the porch in a form which is not uncommon elsewhere in India but which is unique in Orissan temples. The diagonally placed square plan of the sanctuary is further concealed by the intricacy of the carving which gives it an almost circular appearance.

The porch, or *jagmohana*, is comparatively plain, even though it has the mature style of pyramidal roof. This simplicity reflects the fact that much of the sculpture was unfinished. However, it is possible to see the way in which Orissan sculptors started their work by cutting the stone into sections ('blocking out') which were then roughly shaped ('boasted'), to be finished later by the master sculptor. The finished work is visible in the sculpture of the main sanctuary which is extremely fine.

Perhaps the best preserved features of the temple, not nearly as clearly visible on the other temples, are the statues of the 'guardians of the 8 cardinal directions', the *Dikpalakas*. These are the deities whose responsibility it is to protect the central shrine from every quarter. They are placed in pairs about 3m above ground level, carved in the lower section of the main sanctuary tower.

If you approach the main sanctuary tower by passing to the left (S) of the porch you come across them in the following order:

1. Facing E is Indra, the Guardian of the E. He holds a thunderbolt and an elephant goad, and has his vehicle, the elephant, beneath.

2. At right angles to Indra, facing S, is the pot-bellied and bearded figure of Agni, god of fire and Guardian of the SE. He rides a ram.

3. Moving a few yards along the wall, on the far side of the projection, is the S facing figure of Yama, holding a staff and a noose. In the staff is a skull, a symbol associated with Tantrism, as is his vehicle the buffalo.

4. Again at right angles to the figure of Yama is the W facing figure of Nirritti, Guardian of the SW. Nirriti, the god of misery, holds a severed head and a sword over a figure lying beneath.

5. Again facing W, but on the N side of the sanctuary's central projection, is the image of the Guardian of the W, Varuna. He holds the noose associated with fate or destiny in his left hand, while his right hand is in the gesture of giving.

6. At right angles to Varuna, facing N, is Vayu (meaning 'wind'), Guardian of the NW. He holds a banner, clearly fluttering.

7. The last pair of guardians are on the further side of the central projection, on the N and E facing sides respectively. First you come to **Kubera**, Guardian of the N, pot-bellied to signify prosperity, and placed above 7 jars of precious stones.

8. Isana, Guardian of the NE, is shown as was customary with an erect phallus and accompanied by an emaciated figure.

The Brahmesvara Temple

Still in use today. As you enter from the N you pass through the 2 enclosure walls, the inner one of which forms a compact surround for the temple complex which is raised on a platform. Immediately facing you on the N wall of the porch you see a well-oiled image of Lakshmi, covered in cloth, with incense sticks burning in front of it. The sanctuary itself houses a Siva linga, and it is from an inscription, now missing, that the precise date of the temple's building is known. In addition to the main central sanctuary you see 4 minor shrines, one in each corner of the compound.

The sanctuary tower is over 18m high. The vertical wall follows the pattern of mature temples in having a 5-fold division. Looking at the base and at the top of the wall (the *pabhaga* and the *varanda*) you see the rich carvings with which they are decorated. The wall itself is divided into upper and lower sections by a single broad moulding. The lower section is decorated alternately by miniature representations of the *khakhara* style temples, such as the *Vaital Deul* which you may visit next. Alternating with these sculptures are those showing rampant lions. Although the central niches of the miniature temple carvings which decorate the corners of the lower section have the guardians of the cardinal directions, they are less prominent than in the Rajarani temple.

In the corresponding spaces of the upper section are miniature representations of the normal temple sanctuary towers, and graceful women. These are not deities but are secular images. The scenes in the niches of the miniature temples of the upper section are mainly erotic couples and female figures. A Nataraja playing on a vina above a bull, shown on the W face, is one of the rare depictions at this level of a deity.

The Satrughnesvara group
(Mohini, Uttaresvara, Gauri-Sankara-Ganesh and Paschimesvara temples). Despite their ruined state, with only the cores remaining visible, the first 3 temples deserve mention as almost certainly the oldest in Bhubaneswar, dating from the late AD 6th century. The southernmost temple in the group has been rebuilt by the Archaeological Dept of Orissa.

Vaital Deul
Return towards the main temple complex surrounding the tank. 2 features mark out this small, late 8th century, temple. The first and most obvious is its form. Seen from the road the semi-cylindrical shape in section of the *deul* (which is just over 11m high) is immediately distinct. As such, its *khakhara* style derives as Percy Brown says, from a quite different tradition than the Parasamesvara temple. The shape of the tower is similar to that of the gopurams of Dravida temples in S India. Like them, it takes this shape originally from the Buddhist chaitya halls referred to above. Yet the porch, with its miniature 'sanctuary towers' at each corner suggests that the Vaital Deul was a forerunner of the 5-shrined type of temple common later in N India.

The second is its tantric associations, marked by its presiding deity, Chamunda (a form of Durga) and by other features visible on closer viewing. The first external view of Durga can be obtained from the carving on the N face of the *bada* where she is shown as the 8 armed *Mahishasuramardini* (slayer of the buffalo demon). She holds a snake, a bow, a shield, a sword, a trident, a thunderbolt and an arrow, and she is piercing the neck of the buffalo demon.

There are excellent carvings elsewhere on the exterior. On the E face of the *deul* there are 2 *chaitya* windows. The lower of these has a beautifully carved figure of the sun god Surya, with Usha and Pratyusha shooting arrows on either side of him while Aruna (goddess of the dawn) drives a chariot in front. It has a certain incongruity in view of the image within the sanctum itself. The upper *chaitya*-window has a 10 armed Nataraja, or dancing Siva.

Further evidence of the tantric basis of the temple comes from the stone post to which sacrifices were tethered, just in front of the jagamohana, but more importantly from the image of the deity Chamunda in the central niche of the deul. This is extremely difficult to see without artificial light, though very early morning sun penetrates the gloom of the interior. In Mitra's words "The sanctum is pervaded by a weird atmosphere, the image of the 8-armed Chamunda is depicted in her most terrifying aspect conceivable. Seated on a corpse with an owl on the right and a jackal on the left, she has an emaciated body with only skin and bones, a shrunken belly, an open mouth and sunken eyes and decorated with a garland of skulls." There are numerous other figures, the most chilling being that of "a male figure on the N wall in the attitude of rising from the ground after filling his skull-cup with the blood of a person whose severed head lies on the right; on the pedestal is an offering of 2 more heads on a tray resting on a tripod, flanked by a jackal feasting on a corpse on the right and a woman holding a head on the left".

The Lingaraja Temple

Along with the Jagannatha Temple at Puri the Lingaraja Temple represents the peak of achievement of the Orissan middle period. Built in 1000 AD, 100 years before the Jagannath Temple, Brown suggests that the Lingaraja Temple is one of India's most remarkable architectural achievements. Although non-Hindus are not allowed inside it is possible to get an impression of the main features of the temple from a specially constructed viewing platform outside the N perimeter wall. An inscription states that the temple, which had fallen into disrepair and disrepute, was restored and then managed by the British Indian Civil Serivce. An Indian civil servant is still the chief administrator. If you wish to take photographs, note that early morning and late afternoon are by far the best times.

Even from a distance the sanctuary's 54m high tower (known here as the *Sri Mandir*) dominates the landscape. From the viewing platform you can see that it is just one of the 4 main buildings in the temple compound, though there are many other subsidiary shrines. Immediately to the left of the tower is the pillared hall of the *Jagamohan*, then the *Nata Mandir* (dance temple) and finally the *Bhoga Mandir* (hall of offering). Although they all lie on the same E-W axis the latter 2 buildings were added a century after the sanctuary and the porch.

The tower itself is a monumental piece of work. In plan it is just under 17m square, although the projecting faces take its form out of the true square. Approximately ⅓ of its height is vertical. From 15m above ground level the sanctuary tower begins to curve inwards, gently at first and then rapidly at the top to produce a graceful parabolic curve at 37.5m above ground level. The *amla* head is supported by 4 mythical gryphons, surmounted by the pot-shaped pinnacle, in turn carrying the trident of Siva. According to Brown the inner sanctuary is highly unusual. Just under 6m sq, the small chamber housing the deity has no ceiling, but rises like a chimney up the centre of the tower, only capped by the top of the sanctuary tower itself. Externally the middle section is textured by horizontal mouldings, the background to individual motifs which stand in sharp relief. These comprise a vertical line of miniature towers. On each of the 4 sides there is massive protruding sculpture of a lion crushing an elephant – a common symbol in Orissan architecture.

This section relies on the excellent account given by Debala Mitra in the Archaeological Survey of India's booklet on Bhubaneswar. Copies are available from the Archaeological Survey of India and from the Orissa State Museum in Bhubaneswar.

Ekamra Kanan

In Nayapally (N of the town) the Government has opened a new botanical research and conservation centre on a 200 ha site. It includes a large rose garden, lawns, woods and flowerbeds, and a large lake which has become home to migratory birds.

Museums

Orissa State Museum, Gautam Nagar. 1000-1700. Closed Mon and govt holidays. The collection includes archaeological exhibits of stone inscriptions and tools, copperplates, coins, sculptures from temples, portraits and models, musical instruments and particularly, rare palm leaf manuscripts. The Harijan and Tribal Research Institute's **Tribal Museum of Man**. 1000-1700 except Sun. Collection of tribal dress, weapons and jewellery and tribal dwellings. **Handicrafts Museum**, Secretariat Rd, T 50484. 1000-1700 except Sun. Large collection of traditional art and crafts including stone sculptures, *pattachitras*, brass and horn ware, toys, masks, playing cards, silver filigree and dowry boxes.

Tours

OTDC: by luxury coach from Panthanivas. **Nandankanan-Khandagiri and Udayagiri-Temples and Museum-Handicraft Emporium-Dhauli**. 0900-1730. Daily except Mon. Rs 60 (no guide). **Puri-Konark** with guide. 0745-1800. Daily. Rs 80. 20 min stop at Pipli village for appliqué. Rec. Also a number of package tours (min 30 people). Rates often include accommodation at a Panthanivas and should be booked 1 month ahead. **Bhubaneswar-Puri-Konark**: 2 days. Rs 190. **Bhubaneswar-Chilika-Gopalpur**: 2 days. Rs 240. **Bhubaneswar-Puri-Konark**: 3 days. Rs 280. **Bhubaneswar-Puri-Konark-Chilika**: 3 days. Rs 275; 5 days. Rs 480; 6 days. Rs 550. Children, half price.

Swosti Travels, by a/c car: ½ day: City temples, Rs 1000. **Konark and Puri**: Rs 2500. **Konark or Puri**: Rs 1600. **Temples and caves**: Rs 1400. Chilika, Rs 2700. **Udayagiri, Ratnagiri, Lalitgiri**: Rs 3000. A round trip by car visiting Konark and Puri from Bhubaneswar takes 6-8 hr depending on time spent in Puri. About Rs 1500 for non-a/c car and driver. Allow at least 1 hr for Konark. It may be possible to obtain lower quotes from other agents.

Local Festival

Asokashtami The Lingaraja Car Festival when the image of Lord Siva (Lingaraja) is drawn on a chariot from his own temple to visit the Ramesvara temple for 4 days takes place in **Mar/Apr** on the 8th day of the waxing moon in the month of 'Chaitra'. The *Tribal Fair* at the end of **Jan** is attended by tribal groups from different regions. There are excellent performances and crafts exhibitions.

Local information

● Accommodation

Principal hoteliers in the city belong to HRAO, an association to promote tourism; good communication between hotels. Report complaints to their President JK Mohanty at *Swosti Hotel*. New telephone exchanges have resulted in recent changes (often '5' replaced with '40'). Please check.

A *Oberoi Bhubaneswar*, Nayapalli, T 56116, F 56269, nr Ekambara Kanan (Botanical Gardens). 70 rm. 5 km centre. Luxury hotel in temple architecture style, tastefully decorated using Orissan handicrafts, set in well kept gardens, tennis.

C *Kalinga Ashok*, Gautam Nagar, ITDC, T 53318. 64 rm. Restaurant (slow service), bar and coffee shop overlooking lawn, exchange, shop. Unsatisfactory management, tatty around the edges. **C** *Kenilworth* (was *Konark*), 86A-1 Gautam Nagar, T 54330, T 56147. 72 rm (front busy, quieter at back). Central a/c. Refurbished good restaurant with occasional live music (small portions), pleasant bar, coffee shop with *pattachitras* and *Pipli* appliqués, exchange, travel, book shop. Avoid pool (no filter system). Lacks garden; 1st Flr barbecue terrace overlooks main road. Nr Museum, Tourist office, Temples and rly. Well-managed, helpful staff, very good value. Rec. **C** *Swosti*, 103 Janpath, 5 min walk from Rly station, T 404178, F 407524. 60 large rm (some can be noisy). Restaurant, bar, coffee shop, exchange, travel. Dimly lit restaurant, low seating, generous portions, good value. Very popular with local businessmen. Do not be put off by frontage on road. Rec. **C** *Prachi*, 6 Janpath, T 402328. 48 rm, some a/c (refurbished rm better, others overpriced). Restaurant (excellent Chinese), terrace barbecue, exchange, travel, shops, large well-kept gardens, hard tennis court, good size pool among palm trees.

D *Bhubaneswar*, Cuttack Rd nr Rly, T 51977. 42 rm, 4 a/c. Clean. Simple Indian style hotel, good value. Rec. **D** *Keshari*, 113 Station Sq, T 408801. 40 simple rm, some a/c with view of parks. Restaurant, bar, travel, CC. Overpriced, inexperienced management. **D** OTDC *Pantha Niwas*, Jayadev Marg (Lewis Rd), T 54515. 72 rm, some a/c, others cheaper (use own padlock) – modest but clean. Mediocre restaurants, Tourist information and tours behind complex. Good value, friendly service, conveniently situated for temples out-of-town. **D** ***Safari International***, 721 Rasulgarh and ***Jajati***, Station Sq, Unit III are not rec.

● Budget hotels

Other simple **E** hotels: ***Anarkali***, 110 Kharavel Nagar, Unit III, T 404031. 22 rm. Restaurant, bar, travel. Small compact hotel, walk from Rly station.

F ***Kamala*** Old Station Bazar (20m W of rly station) T 56132. Clean and convenient. **F** ***Pushpak***, Kalpana Sq, T 50896. 22 rm a few a/c. Could be cleaner. Restaurant (good S Indian). **F** ***Janpath***, Bapuji Nagar (Nr Rly station) T 401147. Basic, but friendly and clean. **F** ***Youth Hostel***, Khandagiri 8 km from centre. Enquire at Tourist Office.

● Places to eat

Rec in Hotel: ***Kenilworth*** 1st Flr, *Prachi* for Chinese, ***Prachi*** for S Indian. ***Swosti***, and ***Panthaniwas*** incl local specialities. Others: ***Hare Krishna*** Smart, modern, veg, food highly rec.***Venus Inn***, 217 Bapuji Nagar (2nd Flr) nr Ashok. Good S Indian veg. ***Swapanpuri***, Sahid Nagar, (Indian). ***New Ganguram Sweets***, Brit Market, Station Sq for delicious Indian sweets and snacks. Oberoi, Kenilworth, Swosti and Panthaniwas have comfortable **bars**.

● Banks & money changers

Close on Mon. **State Bank of India**, by Capital Police Station opp Capital Market, International Banking on 2nd Flr.

● Entertainment

Programmes of Odissi and folk dances and folk drama are staged regularly and worth seeking out. *Rabindra Mandap*, nr GPO and *Suchana Bhavan* nr Bus Stand.

● Hospitals & medical services

Capital Hospital, Unit 6, T 50688.

● Post & telecommunications

General Post and Telegraph Office: Sachivalaya Marg.

● Shopping

See Introduction for Orissa's rich heritage of art and craft. The capital is a good place to shop if you are unlikely to travel to the special villages where the skills are practised, sometimes exclusively. Many shops close on Th and take a long lunch break. The Market Building shops have fixed prices. Rec. ***Utkalika***, (E Tower), sells Orissa handloom and handicrafts. ***Orissa State Handloom Co-op Soc***, (W Market), and ***Kala Mandir***, T 52456 (Closed Sun) are very good for saris and handloom fabrics. You can buy gifts and stationery from ***Lalchand***.

Books: *Modern Books*, Station Sq has a good selection on the region's history and art.

Photography: *Neel Kamal*, W Tower Market, Rajpath, ***Sujata***, Sahid Nagar, ***Orissa Colour Lab***, Bapuji Nagar and ***Sonali***, Lewis Rd.

● Sports

Bhubaneswar Club, Unit-6, Rajpath, T 52277. Table tennis, billiards, badminton and bridge. Contact Secretary for temporary membership.

● Tourist offices

Orissa (OTDC), 5 Jayadev Marg nr Panthanivas, T 50099. 1000-1700, closed Sun. Airport counter, T 404006. Rly station counter, T 54715. A large Tourist Map of Orissa, available from **Bhubaneswar Tourist Office** (Pantha Niwas) or from the Delhi office at Baba Kharak Singh Marg, is very helpful as it lists typical Orissan crafts and textiles and indicates where they are produced. **Govt of India**, B 21, Kalpana Area, T 54203.

● Travel agents & Tour operators

Larger hotels have helpful travel counters. ***Swosti***, 103 Janpath, T 404178, F 407524. They have the only a/c coach. Offer city sightseeing and other specialist tours such as tribal, architectural and wildlife tours and beach resorts. ***Sita*** in Kenilworth, T 53330. ***Mercury*** in *Oberoi*, T 54216. ***Arya*** in *Prachi*, T 402380. ***Kalinga*** 29 E Tower, Market Bldg, T 55845.

● Useful addresses

Foreigners Registration Office: Supt of Police, Bureau, Sahid Nagar, T 51816.

● Transport

Bhubaneswar is on NH 5 which links Calcutta and Madras and has good connections by road to other important regional centres. Some distances to other tourist centres are: Calcutta 480 km, New Delhi 1745 km, Madras 1225 km, Bombay 1691 km, Bangalore 1430 km, Ahmedabad 1829 km. Within Orissa: Cuttack 32 km, Several to Puri, 62 km, 1 hr (non-stop), Konark, 65 km, 1 ½, Chilika Lake 130 km.

Local Rickshaws: auto-rickshaws and cycle-rickshaws are widely available. Negotiate rates in advance. **Bus**: city buses are inexpensive and cover major routes charging Re 0.50 up to 3 km and Re 1 for longer journeys. OTDC (Transport), T 55515, hires out non-a/c and a/c **Taxis**: tourist taxis, Rs 50-75 for 1 hr/10 km and rises to Rs 400 to Rs 700 for 8 hr/80 km within the city. Outside Bhubaneswar charges range from about Rs 4 to 5.50 per km. No metred taxis. They were permitted to remove meters by the governor and now charge Rs 50 even for short journeys. **Coaches** and **mini-buses** both with and without a/c are also available for hire. It is also possible to hire **motor launches** and **yachts** at the seaside resorts and for Chilika Lake at the Panthanivas, Barkul.

Air Transport to town: Taxi transfer Rs 60-70. **Indian Airlines**, Airport, T 401084; City, T 400544; Reservations, T 402380. Flights to: **Calcutta**, Tu-F, Su (1 hr), **Delhi**, daily (3 hr), **Hyderabad**, W,F,Su (2¾ hr) via Nagpur (1¼ hr), **Madras**, Tu,Th.

Train Rly station, Reservations, T 402042; Enquiry, T 402233; Tourist Information Counter T 54715. Auto and cycle rickshaws for transfer. 'Superfast' connections link Bhubaneswar with major regional centres. **Calcutta (H)**: *Dhauli Exp*, 2822 (AC/CC), daily, 1345, 7½ hr; *Haora Mail*, 6004 (AC/II), daily, 2215, 8½ hr; **Madras**: *Coromandal Exp*, 2841 (AC/II), daily, 2200, 19½ hr; *Guwahati-Trivandrum Exp*, 2602 (AC/II), Tu 0626, 21¾ hr; **Bangalore**: *Haora-Bangalore Exp*, 2611 (AC/II), W, 0626, 21¾ hr; *Guwahati-Bangalore Exp*, 2674 (AC/II), M,Th, 0626, 21¾ hr; **Cochin**: *Haora/Patna-Cochin Exp*, 2652 (AC/II), F,Sa, 0626, 21¾ hr; *Guwahati-Cochin Exp*, 2650 (AC/II), Su, 0626, 21¾ hr; **Cuttack**: *Puri-Haora Exp*, 8008, daily, 2100, 1 hr. **Cuttack** 1725. **Puri**: Not rec as it takes too long. *Kalingutkal Exp*, 8478 (AC/II), daily, 0538, 2¼ hr; also 0925, 1305, 2220. **Delhi (ND)**: *Puri-New Delhi*, 2815 (AC/II), M,W,Th,Sa, 1052, 30 hr; *Neelachal Exp*, 8475 (AC/II), Tu,F,Su, 1052, 34½ hr.

Road Bus: the bus station has moved to 10 km from centre. For Puri, it is better and quicker to get a minibus from Rajpath (the end farthest from Rly station) nr old bus stand, or by petrol station opp *Ashok Hotel*. Do not travel at the end of the working day. T 400540.

Udayagiri and Khandagiri caves

6 km from Bhubaneswar, the hills are very easy to visit by car, public transport, rickshaw or bicycle from Bhubaneswar. Access to the caves is now controlled and entry is only permitted between 0800-1800. Allow ½ day. Auto-rickshaws, Rs 50 return (negotiate before). Many teastalls at entrance. **NB:** please do not buy peanuts to feed monkeys; they will pester you all the way to the caves. An Amenities Centre is being opened to include the new Sulabha Sauchalaya and an improved *Youth Hostel*.

The caves on the 2 low hills of **Udayagiri** and **Khandagiri** bear witness to the Jain and Buddhist occupation of the region at least by the 2nd century BC. A narrow valley winds between the hills, the route of an early Buddhist pilgrim track leading to a stupa which probably stood on the present site of Bhubaneswar.

The coarse-grained sandstone which forms Khandagiri ('broken hill') and Udayagiri ('hill of the sunrise') rises nearly 40m above the surrounding lateritic and infertile plain. The crumbling nature of the sandstone into which the caves were dug has exposed them to severe damage over time. The Archaeological Survey of India has done extensive work repairing vital supporting features of the caves and protecting the most important carvings. While some of these works have a rather crude effect their necessity is obvious. The Archaeology Dept has now numbered the caves.

History

The Jain caves are among the earliest in India. Furthermore, the inscriptions found on some of the rock surfaces, especially that above *Hathi Gumpha*, the elephant cave (No 14), provide historical evidence of a dynasty known as the Chedis who ruled the region of Kalinga from their capital. This is probably identifiable with the site of present-day Sisupalgarh, 9 km SE of Khandagiri.

Kharavela, according to his own record, took the power of the Kalingas across a large part of N, central and S India. He also devoted great efforts to civil works at home. Among these were the improvements of canals, rebuilding his capital city of Kalinganagara, and, in his 13th year of rule, excavating some of the caves for Jain ascetics at Udayagiri-Khandagiri. Probably all the caves now visible were constructed in the 150 years preceding the birth of Christ. They were designed for the ascetic life of Jain monks, with no concessions to any form of comfort other than an attempt to provide dry shelter. Too low to stand, the cells are nothing more than sleeping compartments, cramped even for that purpose.

Although the Jainess did not enjoy royal patronage after the fall of Kharavela's dynasty, Jain occupation was continuous throughout successive Buddhist and Hindu periods in Bhubaneswar and the region. The Parsvanatha temple on top of Khandagiri was built at some time in the early 19th century, while the Hindu temple was built in the 1970s.

Visiting the caves

It is simplest to follow the route indicated in the plan below, as the numbering of the caves is then easiest to follow. First follow the path up towards Udayagiri, to the right of the hills as you face them.

Udayagiri

Cave 1, the *Rani Gumpha* is on the path to the right. This is the largest and most impressive of the caves, a double-storeyed monastery cut on 3 sides of a quadrangle. Some of the pillars have now been restored. Note particularly the sculptured wall friezes. On the lower storey the right hand wing is flanked by 2 sentries. The pilasters at the entrance to the cell and the arches are very richly carved, illustrating both religious and royal scenes. The whole series of sculptures in the main central wing of the caves celebrates the king's victory

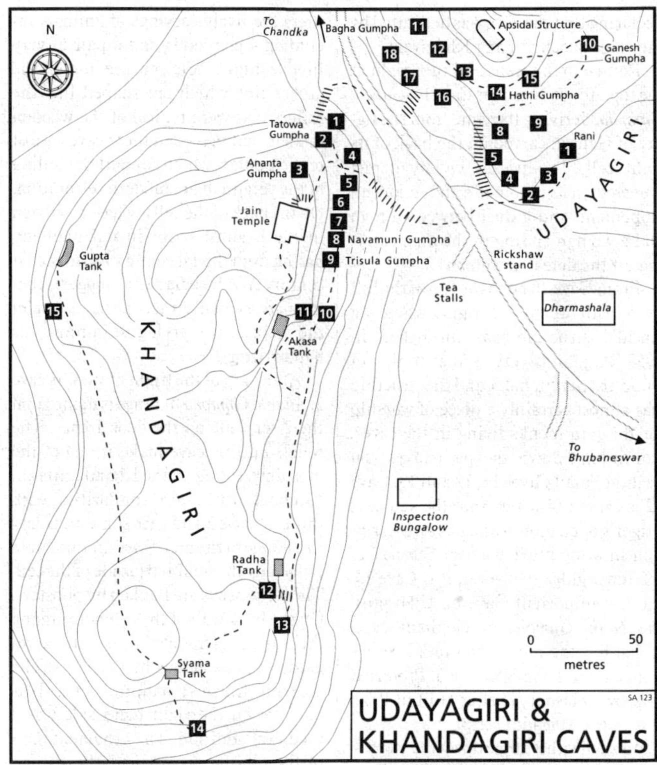

march. 2 small guard rooms with richly decorated outer faces are placed where the right and the left wings meet the main wing. 7 of the pillars of the upper storey are modern replacements. As in the lower storey the doorway arches to the cells are ornately carved. Auspicious Jain symbols like the snake and the lotus are common, and the friezes vigorously depict stories which seem to have little religious content.

Retrace your steps. Cave 3, above and to the left of Cave 2, has 3 elephants carved on either side. Cave 4 has 2 cells one above the other, the upper cell reached by a flight of steps in front of Cave 5. The pillars are mainly modern, though the inner brackets are original with good carvings – including a lion with prey and an elephant entwined by a serpent. As in several caves the floor of Cave 6 has been lowered significantly (perhaps by as much as a metre) by comparatively recent quarrying. Cave 8 is unusually high-ceilinged. Behind it and up to the right is Cave 9. The lower storey has 2 wings, guarded by armed doorkeepers carved against the pilasters. The caves include a badly damaged relief showing the worship of a Jain religious symbol by figures including a king. On the roofline of the lower storey is a royal inscription. The upper storey carries an important 3 line inscription declaring that the cave was dedicated by the chief queen of King Kharavela.

Return to the steps and turn right at the top. About 50m on is **Cave 10**, *Ganesh Gumpha*, deriving its name from the figure of Ganesh carved on the back of its right cell. The friezes vividly depict scenes such as a woman's abduction, an elopement, and a duel between a man and a woman ending in the man carrying off the defeated woman.

From Cave 10 go to the top of the hill by a path up to the right, where an **Apsidal structure** was unearthed in 1958. Its plan is very similar to that of Buddhist *chaitya* halls, and the structure was almost certainly a place of worship for the Jain monks living in the caves. Continuing down the path takes you past the small **Caves 11, 12 and 13**. Cave 12 is carved bizarrely into the shape of a tiger's open mouth and has an inscription showing it to have been the cave of the town judge. However, it is **Cave 14**, the last important Cave on Udayagiri, the *Hathi Gumpha* or elephant cave, which has the most important inscription, that of King Kharavela. Protected now by a masonry shelter built in 1902, it is in the Magadhi script.

You can either come down the steps in front of Cave 17 to the main road or down the flight of steps in front of caves 2 to 7. The first route goes across the road and up the footpath to cave 1 of Khandagiri. The steps opposite the main entrance take you up between caves 5 and 6.

Khandagiri

Caves1 and 2 are known as *Tatowa Gumpha* from the parrots carved on the arches of their doorways. 2 sentries wearing dhotis guard the entrance to cave 1, and between the arches a short inscription names the cave as that of Kusuma. The modern steps lead up to Cave 2 on the left, which is larger and more elaborately carved. It has 3 doorways which have arches and pilasters. The pilasters have octagonal bases, and there are lively carvings of animals including 4 elephants and a pair of very lifelike bulls. You can see under the arches ribs which are shaped like the rafters that were typical of the wooden models that preceded these caves. Most of the 2 pillars which support the ceiling of the verandah are modern restoration. On the back of the cell are letters written in the Brahmi script in red pigment, dating from the 1st century BC to the 1st century AD. Debala Mitra suggests that they are evidence that "perhaps one of the recluses was trying to improve his handwriting"!

At the top of the flight of steps is **cave 3**, *Ananta Gumpha*, taking its name from the 2 serpents on the door arches. The reliefs on this cave make it one of the most interesting on the Khandagiri hill. Although there are similarities with those in Cave 2 and with some on Udayagiri some of the motifs are unique. Note especially the sculpted façade of the cell. The 4 doorways are flanked by pilasters. On the back wall of the cell note among the various symbols the svastika, regarded as auspicious by the Jains. The partially finished sculpture of a Tirthankara on the right hand side was a medieval addition. The ornamentation of the pilasters is particularly distinctive. The faces of the arches have numerous carvings. The central arches have a frieze of boys chasing lions, bulls and other animals. The first arch has rosettes in loops of garlands while the fourth has a line of 12 geese carrying a lotus in their beaks "as if to offer it to the sacred tree depicted below the arch" as Mitra says.

The tympanums also have unique motifs, including royal elephants, a turbaned royal person, identified as Surya the sun God, attended by a woman with a fly whisk. The next tympanum shows Lakshmi in the lotus lake, lotus stalks round her arms and elephants holding pots from which she is bathing. A fourth tympanum shows a sacred tree with a woman worshipping, a man and 2 dwarfs. An inscription on the outside of the architrave between the left pilaster and the first pillar of the verandah says that the cave belonged to Dohada.

You can follow the footpath on up the hill to the Jain temple at the top, or you can retrace your steps to Cave 2 and then follow the path round to the right past caves 4 and 5. Cave 4 is a single small cell with 2 entrances, while Cave 5 at the top of the modern flight of steps from the road is called **Khandagiri** from the cracks (khanda) in it. Both its cells are damaged. The path continues past caves 6,7,8 and 9, in a row facing an artificial terrace. Cave 7, *Navamuni Gumpha*, gets its name from the 9 Tirthankaras (munis) carved on the back and right walls. It has been substantially modified since it was first formed as a residential cell. The last of the 5 inscriptions in the cell mentions Subhachandra, a renowned teacher of the 11th century. On the back wall of what was originally the right hand cell are sculptures of 7 Tirthankaras in high relief. There are 2 reliefs on the right wall of the cave, one of Parsvanatha (last but one of the 24 Tirthankaras) and the other of the sage Rishabanatha. Parsvanath sits under the 7-hooded canopy on either side of which is a flying figure holding a garland. Rishabanatha has a halo and beneath his seat is a bull.

Cave 8 has 2 12-armed figures on the side walls of the veranda. Again, originally it was a dormitory but was converted into sanctuary by carving images. At the same time as this was done the floor was scooped out. The pillars are modern, replacing old ones. The 24 are sculpted, with Parsvanatha being shown twice. Adjoining this is Cave 9, the *Trisula Gumpha*. The figures carved are much later than those in cave 7, probably from the 15th century at the earliest. The masonry altar at the back of the chamber has 3 chlorite images of Rishabhanatha. Mitra suggests that "the facial expression of the figures is highly pleasing; so also is the youthful modelling of the body. Particularly noteworthy is their coiffure where the artist has lavished all his skill."

Caves 10-15 Little to see, only worth detour for exercise and views. Caves 10 and 11are a further 40m S, both almost destroyed by large scale quarrying though some carvings are still visible. Other minor monuments are found 200m further on and on the other side of the hill. You can reach the **Jain temple** on top of the hill either by taking the steep path up past cave 10 or by going back to cave 5 and climbing the steps. The temple was built in the first quarter of the 19th century by Manju Chowdhury and his nephew Bhavani Dadu of Cuttack. The central white marble image in the shrine, dedicated to Rishabanath, was placed there quite recently, probably in the 1930s. There was a much earlier temple on the site.

It is well worth climbing to the temple to get the view both of Udayagiri and of the plains surrounding Bhubaneswar. The modern peace pagoda at **Dhauli** is clearly visible about 10 km away, built on the hillock next to one of Asoka's rock edicts (see below).

Atri

42 km W of Bhubaneswar, is famous for the hot sulphur springs whose temperature remains at 55°C and is supposed to cure skin disorders. There is a shrine to Hatakesvara. The drive through avenues of *neem*, peepul and plantains is picturesque.

REGIONAL TOURS

Orissa has a great deal to offer if you have more time and the state is promoting **Tribal tours** in a big way. N and W Orissa remain largely unvisited, yet they are quite accessible by car or bus and offer a tremendous contrast to the densely populated towns of the coastal plain. Suggested tours take Bhubaneswar as the starting point. After describing the

Bhubaneswar, Puri, Konark triangle they are grouped into northern, western and southern Orissa. A number of places of interest can be visited in day trips from Bhubaneswar. In a more extended visit it is possible to link the longer tours together.

BHUBANESWAR TO PURI AND KONARK

The journey to Puri is most rewarding for the Jagannath Temple, one of the 4 holiest Pilgrimage centres for Hindus, and the superb beaches. Konark, one of the world's wonders according to Mark Twain, is amongst the most vivid architectural treasures of Hindu India.

ROUTES The route S from Bhubaneswar to Puri passes through Dhauli (8 km S of Bhubaneswar).

Dhauli

It was here that the horrors of the Kalinga war led Asoka to acknowledge the value of Buddhist teachings. The 2 'Kalinga Edicts' differ from others which expound Buddhist principles. The rock edicts at the bottom of the hill (and the other at Jaugada) dating from c260 BC suggest that the conquered area may have had two administrative headquarters. They give detailed instructions to his administrators to rule his subjects with gentleness and fairness. "... You are in charge of many thousand living beings. You should gain the affection of men. All men are my children, and as I desire for my children that they obtain welfare and happiness both in this world and next, the same do I desire for all men..." Above the inscription you can see the front of an elephant carved out of an enormous rock. It may have been placed there to mark the position of the edicts. All around there is a magnificent view, even better from the hill now topped by the **Peace Pagoda**, of the flat rice growing landscape. This is particularly attractive in the early morning or late evening.

Now the rock edicts are almost ignored by the bus loads of tourists who are taken on up the hill to the Buddhist Peace Pagoda and the Hindu temple beyond. Known as the **Shanti Stupa** the Pagoda was built in the early 1970s by the Japan Buddha Sanga and Kalinga Nippon Buddha Sangha. The old temple of Lord Dhavaleswar which was reconstructed in 1972 is also on the hill top here.

Pipli

(15 km S) is famous for its appliqué work, and houses and shops are covered in samples of the brightly coloured work. See page 722.

Puri

BASICS *Population*: 125,000. *Altitude*: Sea level. *STD Code*: 06752.

The Sabaras, an *adivasi* tribal group who predated the Dravidian and Aryans, were believed to have inhabited the thickly wooded area around Puri. The ancient site of Dantapura, 'town of the Tooth', is believed to be in the region of Puri although no proof exists. Its name was derived from the left canine tooth of The Buddha which was for a time enshrined there before being taken to Sri Lanka.

CLIMATE: PURI

	Jan	Feb	Mar	Apr	May	Jun	Jul	Aug	Sep	Oct	Nov	Dec	Av/Tot
Max (°C)	27	28	30	31	32	31	31	31	31	31	29	27	30
Min (°C)	18	21	25	27	27	27	27	27	27	25	21	18	24
Rain (mm)	9	20	14	12	63	187	296	256	258	242	75	8	1440

See page 1350. Mahatab believes that the Puri Jagannath temple was originally a Buddhist stupa. According to Murray, in Japan and Sri Lanka the Tooth Festival of Buddha was celebrated with 3 cars and the similarity with the *Rath Yatra* at Puri further strengthens the theory that the deities in Puri evolved from Buddhist symbols. The temple of Jagannath, the Lord of the Universe, attracts thousands on feast days and particularly at the time of the *Rath-Yatra*.

Places of interest

Jagannath Temple The temple to the 'Lord of the Universe' is the major attraction of Puri. To remain here for 3 days and 3 nights is considered particularly rewarding and the fact that in the eyes of Jagannath there are no caste distinctions, has made Puri a very popular destination with the devout. The wooden figures of the 3 deities, Jagannath, Balabhadra and Subhadra (returned to their shrines in May 1993 after restoration work) stand in the sanctuary garlanded and decorated by the priests. The extraordinary form that Jagannath takes, according to legend, is the unfinished work of the craftsman god Viswakarma, who in anger left this portrayal of Lord Vishnu incomplete. Small wooden replicas of the 3 images are available around the temple.

The temple, referred to by some as the 'white pagoda' (the Konark temple being the 'black pagoda') is only open to Hindus. Records suggest that a victory pillar was erected by the conqueror of Kalinga, Chora Ganga, in 1030 which was consecrated nearly a century later and possibly the temple was only completed at the end of the 12th century. The

RATH-YATRA

The festival is believed to commemorate Krishna's journey from Gokul to Mathura. Each is brightly decorated and take on the shape of a temple sanctuary. Lord Jagannath's 'car', 13m tall on a base which is more than 10m sq and with 16 wheels each 2m in diameter, is the largest and most impressive. Loud gongs announce the boarding of the deities onto the chariots with the arrival of the Raja of Puri accompanied by bedecked elephants. The Raja still plays an important religious role in representing the old rulers. On this occasion he fulfils his role as the 'sweeper of the gods', symbolizing that all castes are equal before God. He sweeps the floor of the *raths* with a ceremonial golden broom and sprinkles holy water and the procession then starts, led by the one carrying Balabhadra followed by Subhadra's and lastly Lord Jagannath's. The *dahuka* (charioteer) is expected to sing, often bawdy, songs before the *raths* start on their journey. The fabrics used to decorate the different *raths* are red with blue, black and yellow respectively. About 4,000 are needed to draw each chariot, which is accompanied by devotional dances and music.

During the week away, the deities are treated to *padoapitha,* special rice cakes and are dressed in new garments each day before returning home to their own temple. After a week the journey is retraced with a similar procession. Before being permitted to re-enter the temple, Jagannath has to implore Lakshmi (his consort) who had to remain behind and now bars his way, to allow him in! The ceremonies and the fairs attract more that 200,000 devotees to Puri each year. In the past some were said to have thrown themselves under a massive wheel to die a blessed death. The journey is slow and the short journey may take as much as 24 hrs. After the festival, the *raths* are broken up and bits are sold to pilgrims as relics. The massive 'car' has given the English language the word *juggernaut*.

original temple built in the Kalinga style, consisted of the *deul* or sanctuary and the *jagamohan* or audience hall in front of it. It was only in the 14th or 15th century that the '*nata mandir* (dance hall) and the *bhoga mandir*' (hall of offerings) were added in alignment, in the style of other Orissan temples, making it 95m in length and 25m in width. The *nata mandir* is unusual in that it has 16 pillars in 4 rows to support the large ceiling. There are signs of decline in the quality of craftsmanship by the time of the later additions, and to deal with the deterioration of the original stone work plaster was used to carry out the restoration in the last century which has inevitably masked the finer details. The Archaeological Survey of India has undertaken to restore the temple.

The site is a virtual 200m sq enclosed within an outer wall 6m high. Within is another concentric wall which may have acted as fortification, inside which

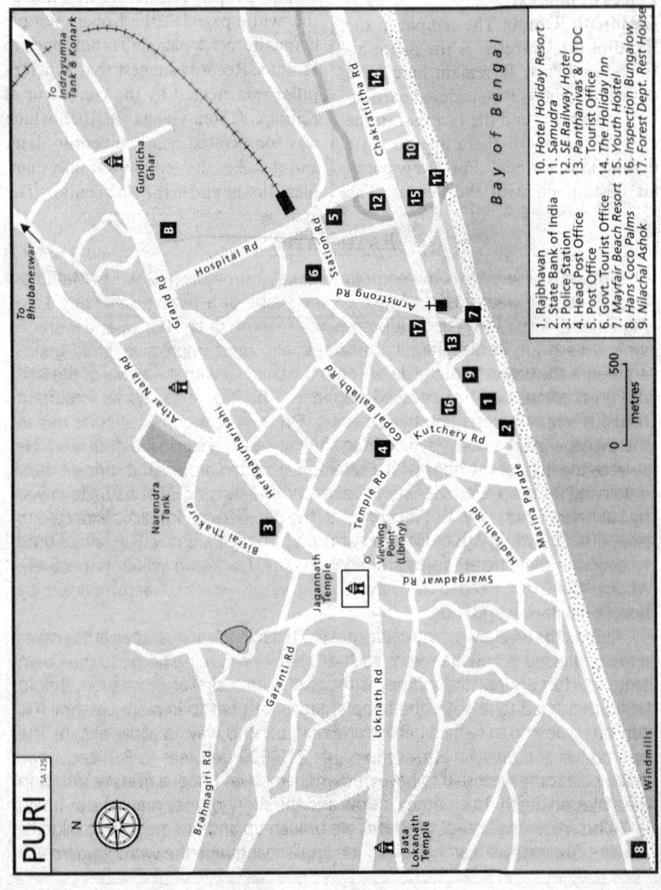

stands the tallest temple in Orissa, reaching a height of 65m where it is crowned by the wheel of Vishnu and a flag. On the higher ground in the enclosure are 30 small shrines, including those to Vimala, Vishnu and Lakshmi, much in the Buddhist stupa tradition. Pilgrims are expected to visit these smaller temples and even those with limited time must visit 3 before proceeding to the main temple. According to Percy Brown, its elevated position gives it added eminence and has led some to conjecture that it is indeed the site of Dantapura, which for a time was sanctified by the holy Buddhist relic.

The outer wall has a gateway with pyramidal roofs on each side with 2 lions guarding the main Lion entrance. On this E side there is an intricately carved 10m high free-standing stone pillar with a small figure of *Aruna*, the charioteer of the Sun. This once stood in front of the *Nata Mandir* at Konark but was moved to its present site about 200 years ago by the Raja of Khurda, see page 744. To the left of the main entrance is the temple kitchen which daily prepares 56 varieties of food making up the *Bhogas* for the deities which are offered 5 times a day and this *mahaprasada* is then distributed from the *Ananda Bazar* to thousands. At festival times as many as 250,000 visitors can be served daily.

There are vantage points from which tourists may view the temple, such as the roof of the Raghunandan Library opp the main entrance to the E or from the Jaya Balia Lodge nearby. A small donation is expected in return. The temple is supposed to be a self-sufficient community, served by some 6000 priests and more than 10,000 others who depend on it for their livelihood.

The 4 sacred *tanks* in Puri provide thousands of pilgrims with the opportunity to take a holy dip. The Narendra Tank is particularly famous since the deities are taken there during the *Snana Yatra*.

Gundicha Ghar, the terminus of the Rath Yatra, where the deities from the Jagannath Temple spend a week at their 'aunt's house'. Open to Hindus only it is an example of the Orissan style demonstrating the unique and ingenious use of wrought iron to form a framework to support the laterite lintels of the massive structures of the other temples. The great blocks of laterite used in construction were finely balanced by means of counterpoise. Stone lintels were used which had to be reinforced with metal bars, some of which, as in the case of the Jagamohan in Konark, measured 10m in length and nearly 20 cm in thickness.

The Beach

The other major attraction is the long stretch of golden beach, shallow enough to walk out a long distance, with superb surf. Sunrise is particularly striking. The currents can be treacherous at times but you can swim safely on your own if you take care. The customary *nulia*, fisherman turned life-saver in a distinctive conical hat, may offer his services for either half or full day at a small price for those not used to bathing in the sea. The best hotels have a stretch of clean sand.

The beach can get unpleasant underfoot away from the tourist hotel area as many sections are used as open latrines. It is interesting to walk to the nearby fishing villages along the coast to watch the fishermen set out in their colourful boats, but you have to be prepared to pick your way carefully.

Sakhigopal, a pilgrim centre, 22 km from Puri has a temple with a charming image of Gopal or Child Krishna who in legend was called here as witness in a dispute between 2 Brahmins. The myth says that the god followed the Brahmins as long as they did not look round. When one looked round the god turned into a statue, so Sakhi Gopal = Gopal the witness.

Atharnala Bridge If you are interested in an ancient engineering marvel, go and see the 85m bridge over the Madupur stream. It was built in the 13th century and is still in use.

Tours

Orissa Tourism and private tour operators conduct daily sightseeing tours (except Mon) to Konark, Pipli, Dhauli, Bhubaneswar temples, Nandan Kanan biological park, Udayagiri and Khandagiri, Sakshigopal. Approx Rs 80. The Chilika Lake tour, Mon, Wed and Fri costs Rs 100.

Local festivals

Jun/Jul *Rath-Yatra* takes place each year in June/July when massive *raths* or 'chariots' carrying wooden images of Jagannath, his brother Balabhadra and his sister Subhadra process through the streets to spend 7 days at Gundicha Ghar, or Garden House, a temple 1.5 km away.

Apr: *Chandan-Yatra* coincides with the Hindu new year in mid-April when the images of Jagannath accompanied by his brother and sister are taken in decorated boats with swan-heads on a daily ride in the Narendra tank for 21 days. The festival derives its name from the use of sandal paste, *chandan*, to anoint the deities and the celebrations include music, dancing and singing of devotional songs. *Snana Yatra* follows the *Chandan Yatra* and marks the ritual bathing of the 3 deities from the temple, on a special barge. For 4 days the gods are said to convalesce out of sight and is a period when worshippers must be satisfied with praying before paintings or *pattachitras*. This festival which precedes the *Rath-Yatra* is missed every so many years (the number being decided by astrological calculations) when new images of the deities are carved from specially selected trees and the old ones are secretly buried by the temple priests.

Local information

● Accommodation

Beach Resort status of Puri means prices are higher than normal. **B** *Mayfair Beach Resort*, Chakratirtha Rd, T 4041, F 4242 (opened 1993). 16 rm (to be increased) with sea view, balconies and private lawn and shaded seating. Restaurant with terrace (excellent Chinese, non-alcoholic cocktails and kebabs), bars, pools. Very clean and well maintained grounds with small Hindu temple. Free pick-up from Bus and Rly stations, if arranged in advance. Best in Puri. **B** *Toshali Sands* – Orissa's Ethnic Village Resort, Konark Marine Dr, T 2888, F 57365. 62 a/c rm in cottages, villas and thatched tents (some close together). 8 km from Puri. A comfortable and innovative style of resort in 30 acres of palm grove, spoilt by lots of inane 'witty' sign posts along footpaths. A very peaceful location but 2 major drawbacks – not close to beach (private forest land and Konark Rd in between), and the distance from Puri removes choice of eating place. Forced to use hotel restaurant – pricy for nothing special. Free transport to Bus and Train stations only if arranged in advance. *Camping*, luxury tents in season.

C *Hans Coco Palms* formerly *Prachi*, Swargadwar, Gourbari Sahi, T 2633 (in Delhi *Hans Plaza*, T 3316868, Calcutta T 228377). 36 refurbished rm with balconies to sea, Grd Flr rm have beach access. Central a/c. Palm filled restaurant, bar, exchange, pool, putting green. Friendly staff; manager has extensive local knowledge. Free pick-up from Bus/ Rly station; arrange in advance. Popular in season; Reserve 15 days ahead. Highly rec. Potentially the best in Puri without luxury trappings. Stay here and eat at the Mayfair. **C** *Nilachal Ashok*, next to Raj Bhawan, VIP Rd, set back from beach, T 3639. 36 simple rm, some a/c, most without sea views. Restaurant, bar, coffee-shop, exchange, travel. Well kept front garden where no one sits! Access to beach by path approached through barren basement and scrubby ground.

D *SE Rly Hotel*, Chakratirtha Rd, T 2063. 36 rm, few with a/c and bath (1st Flr rm offer greater privacy, verandahs overlooking sea). Restaurant, bar. 200m from beach, well-kept gardens. Siestas encouraged with silence expected from co-operating residents from 1400-1600! A curiosity with old-world atmosphere with courteous service, although it has lost its old grandeur and superb cuisine; now more English boarding school menu. No credit cards. **NB:** Raw sewage in sea opp. **D** *Vijaya International*, Chakratirtha Rd, T 2701. 44 rm, half a/c. Good seafacing restaurant, travel.

Quiet. **D** ***Holiday Resort***, Sandy Village, Chakratirtha Rd, T 3580. 75 rm and 24 small cottages, some a/c. A/c restaurant (good seafood – owner made money in prawn and shrimp exports), bar, exchange, travel. Colourful fountains in gardens. Large complex overlooking beach, Spanish Costa style! Very popular with local people, not for those seeking peace.

E ***Holiday Inn***, Chakratirtha Rd, T 3782. 20 basic rm with own cooking space; sea-facing rm have no view – several blocks between hotel and beach. Restaurant.

● Budget hotels

Reasonable beachside hotels with restaurants, few a/c rm. Many shops and eating places nearby: **E** ***Panthanivas***, T 3329, 48 rm (some a/c), and the smaller ***Mahodadhinivas*** (Panthabhawan), T 3526, 9 rm. Both have restaurant and travel. The Panthanivas has large rm in the old wing but those in the new wing are better and closer to the sea. Also bar and coffee shop. Reservations: Manager, with a day's room rent in advance. **E** ***Z***, NE end of beach, in an old mansion, T 2554. 13 rm. Some rm with seafacing terrace, clean shared bath. Good food, garden. Now at upper end of price category; still very popular, and rec – apart from non-Indian policy. Note: beach behind hotel is used as a public toilet. **E** ***Puri***, T 2114. 127 rm some a/c (cheaper in old section). Restaurant. Popular Indian family hotel, quiet clean.

The very inexpensive **F** ***Youth Hostel***, T 2424, has segregated pleasant dormitories, some for 2 or 3, but guests are expected to be in by 2200. Dining room. **F** ***Railway Retiring Rooms*** are equally inexpensive. There are some ***Dharamshalas*** in the town and a ***camping*** at *Toshali Sands* in coconut grove between Puri and Konark. There are also many **F** hotels near the beach near the village east of the town.

● Places to eat

It is usual to dine in your hotel but the larger hotels will accommodate extra diners. The abundance of fresh fish is worth taking advantage of although an unaccustomed stomach might well object to daily intake of seafood. ***Chandu's*** Chakratirtha Rd is rec; try pancakes! ***Chungwah***, behind *Puri Hotel*. ***Peace Restaurant***, nr *Z Hotel*, is very good. The 3 govt run hotels and Holiday Resort have Bars.

● Entertainment

Classical *Odissi* dances and folk dances and drama which are always performed for festivals are also staged from time to time and are worth seeking out.

● Hospitals & medical services

District HQ Hospital, T 2062. *ID Hospital*, Red Cross Rd, T 2094. *Gopabandhu Ayurvedic Hospital*, Armstrong Rd, T 2072.

● Shopping

Handicrafts: are available at ***Utkalika*** and ***Crafts Complex*** at Mochi Sahi Sq and at ***Sun Crafts*** in Tinikonia Bagicha while ***Sudarshan*** on Station Rd specialises in stoneware. Handlooms are sold at the ***Weavers' Co-op Society*** on Grand Rd and at *Odissi* in Dolamandap Sahi.

You can get very good buys in the vast ***bazar*** around the Jagannath Temple, along Bada Danda and Swargadwara, but prices there are not fixed and you are expected to spend time bargaining. ***Hawkers*** on the beach sell shells and bead jewellery (often passing on glass beads for coral!). If you have more time, a visit to the villages and neighbourhoods where the craftsmen and weavers can be seen at work will be rewarding. In Puri itself, Pathuria Sahi is the area where the stone carvers live and nearby, Raghurajpur produces *pattachitras* and etchings on palm leaf (see page 721).

Photography: ***Photo Life*** on Grand Rd and ***Metro Studio***, Mochi Sahi.

● Tour companies & travel agents

Tribe Tours, CT Rd, T 3781. ***Konark***, Sea Beach, T 3435. ***Travel Care***, Grand Rd, T 2956.

● Tourist office

OTDC, Pantha Bhawan, T 2507. **Govt of Orissa**, Station Rd, T 2131 (1000-1700, closed Sun). Tourist Counter, Rly station, T 3536.

● Useful addresses

Police: T 2039.

● Transport

The distance from Puri to Calcutta is 541 km, and from Madras 1285 km.

Local Cycle hire: rec. Some from opp Z Hotel, NE end of beach. **Cycle-rickshaws**: freely available but bargain and fix fare in advance. **Taxis**: tourist taxis from larger hotels, from *Dullu Tours* (T 2171) and from Taxi Stand (T 2161). Daily rates Rs 300-Rs 500 depending on whether a/c, and the distance travelled.

Air Bhubaneswar 60 km, is the nearest airport. See Bhubaneswar page 733. **Indian Airlines**, Airport T 401084, Bhubaneswar City

T 400544, Reservations T 400533. **Transport to town**: mini-bus to Puri, 1 hr, Rs 10.

Train The main Calcutta-Madras broad gauge line branches to Puri linking it to all parts of country by Express trains. New Delhi and Calcutta have direct trains while Hyderabad, Madras and Bombay have fast train connections at Bhubaneswar. **Calcutta (H)**: *Puri-Haora Exp*, 8008, daily, 1800, 11½; Sri *Jagannath Exp*, 8410 (AC/II), daily, 2045, 11 hr; **Bhubaneswar**, *Puri-New Delhi Exp*, 2815 (AC/II), M,W,Th,Sa, 0915, 1½ hr; *Neelachal Exp*, 8475 (AC/II), Tu,F,Su; 0915, 1½ hr; **Bombay**: *New Delhi Exp*, 2815, AC/II, M,W,Th,Sa; 0915, 7½ hr and *Neelachal Exp*, 8475 (AC/II), Tu,F, Su; 0915, 7½ hr change at Kharagpur (5½ hr wait), then *Bombay Mail*, 8002, daily, 2155, 33¾ hr; (total time, 46½ hr); **Madras**: *Coromandal Exp*, 2841, daily, 2200, 19½ hr; **Delhi (ND)**: *Puri-New Delhi*, 2815, (AC/II), M,W,Th,Sa; 0915, 31¾ hr. For further details see Bhubaneswar section, page 733. Puri Railway Station T 2065 which is about 2 km N of the town.

Road Bus: Bhubaneswar (2 hr), Konark (1 hr, minibuses and taxis ¾ hr) and Cuttack, Visakhapatnam and Calcutta.

Konark

ROUTES The 35 km drive takes nearly 1 hr, but there are very attractive views. The recently-built road runs close to the coast across the thin, lateritic soils, overlain by sand in places, which are being brought into use by extending cashew, casuarina and eucalyptus plantations in between the cultivated fields. There are some excellent deserted beaches along this coast road. You can cycle to Konark and bring the bike back on the bus. It is also possible to get to Konark from Bhubaneswar (65 km). OTDC run tours by 'luxury' coach from both towns; or you can hire a car. (Details in Bhubaneswar section, see pages 731 and 742). **NB:** Few places for drink en route so carry water.

Konark (or Konarak) is one of the most vivid architectural treasures of Hindu India. It no longer stands as a landmark on the sea shore since the land has risen and the sea is now some 3 km away. Despite the fact that the 'black pagoda' as it was called by European sailors, to distinguish it from the whitewashed 'pagoda' of the Jagannath temple in Puri, now lies in ruins, the remaining porch or *jagamohana* and the other structures in the complex are still magnificent, the culmination of Orissan art. It is best to see it after visiting the temples in Bhubaneswar, to appreciate in full the development both of style and of technical skill which the Surya temple of Konark represents.

History

One legend surrounding the building of the temple relates the story of Samba who, cursed by his father Lord Krishna, suffered from leprosy for 12 years before being cured by the Sun god and so built a temple to *Surya*. It was in fact built by King Langula Narasimha Deva in the 13th century, although there may have been an older 9th century temple to the Sun god here. Built of *khondalite*, it is said to have taken 1200 masons 16 years to complete.

It was only in 1906 that the first tentative steps were taken to reclaim the ruins of the temple from the encroaching sand. By that stage not only had the sanctuary or *deul* collapsed but a number of the statues had been removed, notably in the 1830s by the Hindu Raja of Khurda, who wanted them to decorate temples he was building in his own fort about 100 km away and at Puri. Kittoe, an English visitor, wrote in 1838 that:

> "The Kurda Raja has demolished all 3 entrances and is removing stones to Puri; the masons pick out the figures and throw them down to take their chance of being broken to pieces (which most of them are); such they leave on the spot, those that escape uninjured are taken away. The elegant doorway called the Navagriha has been completely destroyed."

In recent years there has been substantial renovation, some of it protective, some replacing fallen stone work and sculptures, so that the appearance of the whole temple complex is now very different from that of even a few years ago.

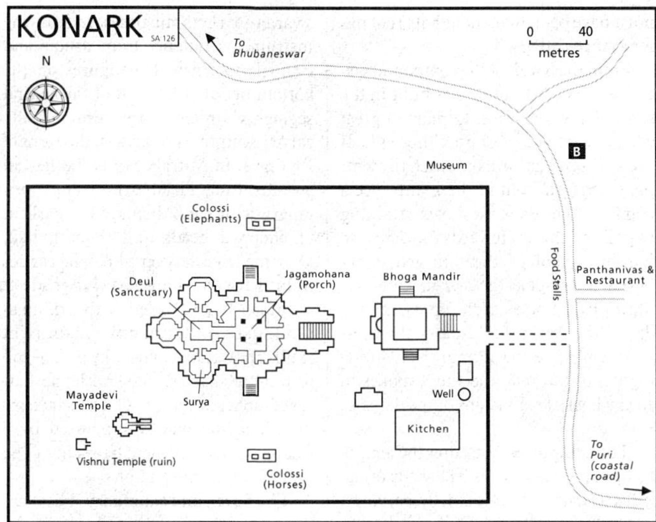

GUIDES Konark is the focus of rapidly growing tourist interest. Archaeological Survey approved guides are available for tours lasting under an hour. Unofficial guides (*pandas*) will also press their services, but can be unreliable.

The **Surya temple** is set back some 180m from the road and is reached by a wide laterite path. There are plenty of places to buy soft drinks and snacks on the way in and out of the temple. The image of the deity has long since been removed and the sanctuary is no longer regarded as a holy place. Shoes may thus be worn throughout. The exception is in the small modern building in the NE corner of the compound which houses the old doorway arch showing the 9 planets, removed from the temple. In recent years these have become objects of veneration, and Brahmin priests are now in charge of this building as a place of worship. The path to the temple is lined with beggars, as is common in major centres of Hindu pilgrimage.

The temple compound The temple is set in the middle of a spacious compound which lies about 2m below the surrounding land. It is easy to see how the lower parts of the ruins were covered with wind blown sand. The overall scale of the buildings and their layout can be gauged by walking round the outer perimeter wall, which also gives excellent views for photographs.

At the E entrance to the complex of buildings is the *bhoga mandir*, an isolated hall with massive pillars, raised on a richly decorated platform. There is some debate as to whether this was a dancing hall (nata-mandapa); there is certainly no other special building for this purpose. To its W is an open space, leading to the porch, or *jagamohana*. This still rises magnificently to its original height of 39m, and is now the dominant building in the temple complex. To its E is the massive lower section of the original sanctuary, or *deul*. Estimates based on its known architectural style and existing base suggest that originally it was over 60m tall. Walking round the compound wall it is possible to get some sense of what the original sanctuary must have been like, though its roof has long since collapsed.

From the S wall of the compound you can see that the temple was built in the form of a war chariot. 12 pairs of great wheels were sculpted on either side of the 4m high platform on which the temple stands. In front of the E entrance a team of 7 horses were shown straining to pull the chariot towards the dawn. In Hindu mythology the Sun god is believed to traverse the sky in a chariot drawn by 7 horses each representing a day of the week; the 12 pairs of wheels may symbolize the 12 months (24 fortnights) of the year and the 8 spokes in each wheel, the divisions of the day into 8 *prahars*.

The sculptures You enter the temple compound from the E. The walls of the *bhoga mandir* are covered by carvings, but as Debala Mitra writes, you "rather feel tired with the monotonous over-ornamentation, lack of balanced composition and mediocre quality in the sculpture." The platform gives an excellent view of the whole E front of the main temple. It is the best place to see the E doorway of the porch and the large and remarkably vivid sculptures, carved in the round, on the terraces of its pyramidal roof, unique in Orissan architecture. See page 412.

The sculptures draw for their subject from every aspect of life – dancers, musicians, figures from mythology, scenes of love and war, of court life, hunting, elephant fights – the list goes on. Since the temple was conceived to reflect a rounded picture of life and since *mithuna* or union in love is a part of that, a significant section of the sculpture is erotic art. Konark is unusual in that the carvings are found both on the outer and inner surfaces.

The roof of the porch is divided into 3 tiers, separated by terraces. Above the bottom and middle tiers is a series of some life-sized and some larger than life-sized musicians, vividly captured in a variety of rhythmic poses, and playing instruments ranging from drums and cymbals to vinas. The figures on the bottom tier at either end of the central segments (*rahas*) are dramatically carved sculptures of Siva in the form of Bhairava. In Mitra's words "he has an awe-inspiring facial expression, open mouth with teeth displayed, a garland of chopped heads and flaming hair. Dancing in ecstasy on a boat, he carries in his left hand a mace, a club made of a human bone headed with a human skull, and a kettle drum and in the right skull cap, a trident and a wheel." The top of the porch is crowned with the flattened spheres typical of Orissan temples. The top one is supported by 8 figures seated on their haunches. The lower is held up by 8 lions.

The porch and sanctuary These are designed as an integrated whole. Although there is a wealth of detail the broad structures are clear. One of the remarkable features of the temple is that the skill and quality of the craftsmanship is displayed down to tiny details of stone carving. It is impossible to see everything of note in a short visit. Mitra estimates that on the narrow plinth alone, at the base of the platform, are carvings of over 1700 elephants – each different!

The plinth (upana), a few cm high, runs right round the base of the temple, and is decorated with a variety of friezes – elephants, notably wild elephants being trapped, military marches, hunting, journeys, and a variety of other animals, including, on the S side, crocodiles and a giraffe.

The platform is divided into the same 5 horizontal layers that characterise the temple itself. It is carved in magnificent detail. Above the plinth is a series of 5 horizontal mouldings, connected at intervals of every metre or so by vertical bands. These are richly decorated with creepers and scrolls, and end with tiny motifs of *chaitya* windows.

Along the lower mouldings are spaced miniature temple-like façades – *khakhara-mundis* – which contain niches. Set into these are a variety of figures, often young women – caressing a bird, washing hair, playing the *vina* and so on. The slabs between are sculpted with a further variety of figures. Some are erotic, some are *nagas* or *nagis*, each with a human head but with the tail of a snake. Others are sexually provocative women, or miscellaneous figures illustrating a wide variety of scenes.

The middle of the platform has 3 horizontal mouldings at about eye level. Above these are the 2 remaining sections, the *upper jangha* and the *verandah*. The former is as richly sculpted as the lower section, sometimes with religious scenes such as the gods *Mahishasuramardini* (or the Goddess of destruction, Durga) and *Jagannatha*, enshrined in a temple. Other sculptures show royal or simple family scenes. Along the top of the platform is the verandah, consisting of 2 mouldings separated by a narrow recess. These are severely damaged, but even these mouldings are decorated with friezes.

While going round the platform it is well worth examining the wheels. Intricately carved, each 16-spoked wheel is shown with its axle, a decorated hub, and an axle pin. Floral motifs, creepers and the widely shown chaitya windows cover the stonework. Medallions with gods like Surya and Vishnu, erotic figures, noblemen, animals – all add immense life to the structure.

The sanctum sanctorum Although the *jagmohana* is now the dominant building of the complex, the scale of the sanctuary is still evident, and the climb up the outer walls and then down into the sanctuary itself, which is possible for the reasonably agile, allows you to see at close quarters both the remarkable chlorite statues of Surya on the outer S wall and the interior of the sanctuary. This is particularly interesting as it gives an almost unique opportunity to see the inside of a temple sanctuary in full light.

It is best to climb up the main E steps of the porch and to walk round it to the left, or S side. The E door of the porch is the best preserved. Each door jamb is divided into 8 facets, all carved with a variety of reliefs which repay a close examination. Climbing up to the more than life-sized statue of Surya it is possible to see clearly how even the larger sculptures show an attention to minute detail. Made of grey-green chlorite which stands in sharp contrast with the surrounding yellowish orange *khondalite* stone, Surya stands on a chariot drawn by his 7 horses, lashed by Aruna, the charioteer, shown down to the waist. Shown around the central figure of Surya are two 4-armed gods, a pot-bellied Brahma on the right and possibly Vishnu on the left. Below them are 4 women, possibly the wives of Surya.

The original approach was through the porch. A recent flight of steps from the W end of the temple leads down into the holy of holies. The route is clearly indicated.

The main feature inside is the chlorite platform at the western end of the 10m square room which used to support the presiding deity. Even when the debris from the fallen tower was cleared the pedestal was empty, for the image had already been moved to the Jagannath Temple at Puri. It is possible that it is now in the Virinchi temple within the complex at Puri, but can only be seen by Hindus. The platform which remains is none the less outstanding; some of the central carvings almost certainly show the king, the donor of the temple, in the company of priests. The hollows on top of the platform's E edge were caused by the placing of pots over a long period.

The temple grounds: the colossi Originally each of the 3 staircases to the porch was guarded by a pair of colossi. The E stairway had 2 rampant lions on top of a crouching elephant, the N 2 fully harnessed and decorated elephants, and the S 2 war horses. Those on the N and S sides have been remounted a short distance from their original sites. The lions have been put in front of the E steps up to the *Bhoga mandir*, nr the entrance.

Museum

The Archaeological Museum, nr Travellers' Lodge, T 222. 0900-1700, closed Th. Free. Small collection includes many important pieces of loose sculpture from the Sun Temple complex. Exhibitions with lectures and film shows are held occasionally. Archaeological Society publications on Konark and other monuments for sale.

Local information

● Accommodation

Most visitors only visit for the day. 3 major hotel chains (*Taj*, *Oberoi* and *Clarks*) have obtained land to build hotels on the beach about 3 km from Konark but still await permission from the Ministry. Good for tourism but may spoil an already crowded and popular site **E** ***Panthanivas***, T 231, opp the temple. 9 rm. Restaurant and fast food counter. Clean, good value. **E** ***Ashok Travellers' Lodge***, towards Museum, T Konark 223. Very simple, 4 large a/c rm.

F ***PWD Inspection Bungalow***, T 34, available only when unoccupied by officials. Camping in grounds. **F** ***Labanya Lodge***, Chandrabagha road, 150m on left from Bungalow. Good value clean rm.

● Tourist Office

Panthanivas, T 221.

● Useful addresses

Police: T 225.

BHUBANESWAR TO CUTTACK AND THE NORTH EAST

The road from Bhubaneswar passes Nandankanan, a large well laid-out zoo, to Cuttack, the medieval regional capital. Amid the idyllic hillsides of Ratnagiri and Lalitgiri, ancient Buddhist sites are being excavated.

Nandankanan

The 'Pleasure Garden of the Gods' is 20 km out of Bhubaneswar on the road to Cuttack and is a zoological park and botanical garden set in 400 hectares in the dense Chandaka forest. There are tigers, including the rare white ones, a lion safari, rhinos, panthers, leopards and a variety of wild fowl and reptiles in their natural surroundings. It has also succeeded in breeding black panthers and *gharials* in captivity. The botanical gardens with its cactus house and rosarium are across the lake which separates it from the zoo. There is a *Guest House* and a lakeside cafeteria where you can get refreshments. Open 0730 – 1730 (summer), 0800–1700 daily except Mon. Entry Rs 2.

Cuttack

30 km N of Bhubaneswar along the NH 5 is the medieval capital Cuttack, one of the oldest towns in Orissa. Founded by Nripati Kesari (r920-935) it remained the administrative centre until the end of the British Raj and was the state capital until 1956. It occupies an important strategic position in relation to the network of canals in the region. Situated at the head of the Mahanadi delta and surrounded by the great river and its tributary the Kathjuri, the town is almost an island.

BASICS *Population*: 439,300. *STD Code*: 0671.

Places of interest

The ancient stone embankment to the S was built in the 11th century by the Kesari ruler to protect the town from flooding by the Kathjuri river in spate. It still stands as a reminder of the engineering skills which went into its construction 900 years ago.

The blue granite 13th century **Barabati Fort** is in ruins. Its wide moat, a gateway and a mosque inside can still be seen although the 9-storeyed palace is no longer there. Probably built by one of Ganga rulers in the 14th century, it was

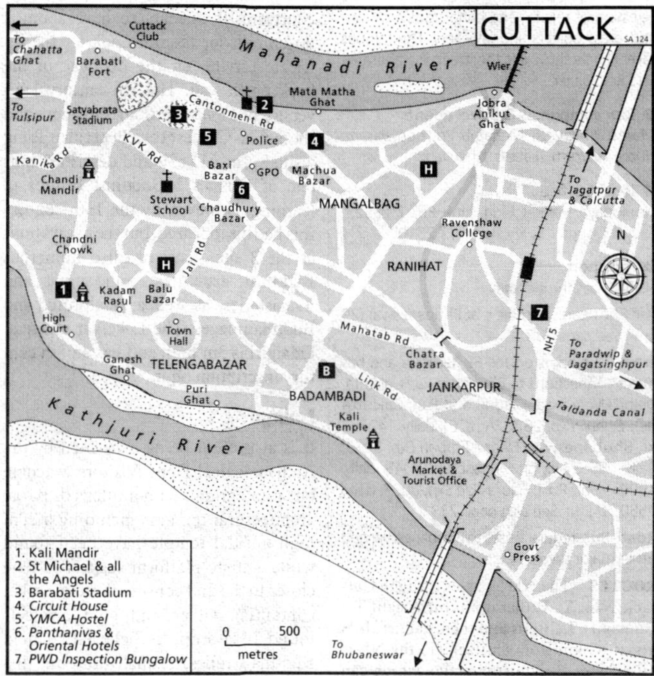

in Marhatta hands when it was taken by the British in 1803. Close to the fort is the vast Barabati Stadium where major sporting and cultural events are held.

The **Qadam i Rasul** (Kadam Rasul) in the centre of the city has three 18th century mosques with beautiful domes and a music gallery within a walled enclosure with towers at each corner. The Muslim shrines contain relics of the Prophet Mohammad as well as the Prophet's foot print carved on a circular stone. It is visited as a shrine by both Muslim and Hindu pilgrims.

The Church of North India **Church of St Michael and all the Angels**, by the river, is worth a visit. Typical of Raj style church buildings.

Local information

● Accommodation

D *Trimurti International*, Link Rd, T 22918. 38 rm. Central a/c. Restaurant, bar, travel. **D** *Akbari Continental*, Dolmundai, Haripur Rd, nr Rly, T 25242. 30 rm. Central a/c. **D** *Asoka*, Ice Factory Rd, College Sq, T 25708. 50 rm, some a/c. **D** *Neeladri*, Mangalabag, T 23831. 28 rm, some a/c. **D** *Orienta*, Tinikonia Bagicha, T 24249. 55 rm. some a/c. Restaurant, bar, exchange, travel. OTDC **D** *Panthanivas*, Baxi Bazar Chouk, T 23867. 30 rm (6 a/c). A/c restaurant, bar, central.

E *Anand*, Ranihat Canal Bank Rd, Ranihat, T 21936. 32 rm, some a/c with bath. Restaurant.

● Budget hotels

There are several cheap hotels. Among the **F** category in the College Sq area are: *Vijaya*, Ice Factory Rd, College Sq, T 23560. 50 rm. Restaurant and coffee shop. **F** *Cuttack* , College Sq, T 23845. 15 rm (some under Rs 50). Veg. restaurant. **F** *Ambika*, College Sq, T 21437. 58 rm, some a/c. Restaurant.

● Shopping

Utkalika on Jail Rd, T 21961, has a very good

selection of textiles and handicrafts incl horn and brass objects and jewellery. The famous silver filigree shops line the streets in Nahasarak and Balu Bazar.

● **Tour companies & travel agents**
Majestic Travels, Mahatab Rd, opp *Basanti Hotel*. *Tirupati Travels*, Chauliaganj.

● **Tourist office**
Arunodaya Market Bldg, Link Rd, T 23525. Tourist Counter at Rly station, T 25107.

● **Transport**
NH5 passes through city.

Air The nearest airport is at Bhubaneswar (29 km). See page 733.

Train Cuttack is on the SE Railways and has direct connections to Bhubaneswar, Calcutta, Delhi, Hyderabad, Madras and Puri. **Calcutta (H)**: *Dhauli Exp*, 2822 (AC/CC), daily, 1425, 7 hr; **Bhubaneswar**: *Haora-Tirupati Exp*, 8079, daily, 0855, 1¼ hr; *E Coast Exp*, 8045, daily, 1900, ¾ hr; **Puri**: *Haora-Puri Exp*, 8007, daily, 0550, 3¼ hr. See also page 733.

Road Bus: regular buses to Bhubaneswar and other major towns nearby.

ROUTES The NH 5 passes through Cuttack NE. At Patharajpur turn right for Ratnagiri, Lalitgiri and the Udaigiri Hills about 65 km from Cuttack. To the NE is an ancient Buddhist complex which can only be reached by rough road. You can take a car to the bottom of the Lalitgiri and Udaigiri hills and climb to the sites.

Ratnagiri

The site, which has produced the best finds, is more difficult to reach since you must cross a narrow river by ferry and spend another ¼ hr on a rickshaw. Cuttack is 70 km, Bhubaneswar 90 km. It is possible to do a day excursion from there, but allow at least 2 hrs each way. Extensive remains have been excavated, which show an excellence in the quality of sculpture combining different coloured stones; from blue-green chlorite with the purple-red garnets in brownish silver khondalite. The finds include 3 monasteries, 8 temples and several stupas believed to date from the 7th century. The largest monastery is 55m sq with a surrounding verandah with 60 pillars built around a courtyard. It appears to have about 2 dozen cells for monks. Look for the intricate carving on the doorway of the back porch wall. The 7th century University of *Pushpagiri* flourished here and the famous Chinese traveller Hiuen Tsang visited it in AD 639 and described it as one of Orissa's 2 Buddhist centres of learning. However, by the 13th century this had disappeared, but the excavations at the 3 sites have revealed numerous Buddhist structures, both stupas and monasteries, as well as sculptures and Buddha images. The Lokesvar image at **Udaigiri** is 3m high and has an 8th century inscription on it.

Lalitgiri

It is at present being excavated by the Archaeological Dept. Visitors welcome but photography is not allowed. Large architectural remains including a 20m high apsidal temple have been found while a stone platform suggests a date closer to the 2nd century. A stone casket containing silver and gold artefacts found in a stupa is believed to hold Buddha's relics; a small museum displays some of the finds. There is the stone-carvers' village at the base of Lalitgiri which traces its connections back to ancient times and produces excellent pieces of sculpture. Worth a visit.

The whole area with its hills rich with excavated Buddhist remains is in an idyllic situation, surrounded by green fields. **Accommodation** *Panthasala* at Patharajapuram, and an OTDC Tourist Complex is planned.

Paradwip

94 km from Cuttack on the NH 5. Today Paradwip is a pleasant beach resort and active port at the mouth of the Mahanadi river. Thousands of giant sea turtles migrate from as far afield as S America every year to lay their eggs and then return. However, perhaps as much as 2500 years ago Orissan sailors regularly set sail for Indonesia and mainland South East Asia

from this point – a journey that was re-enacted by the small Indian Navy Sailing vessel Samudra which sailed to Bali in November 1992. **Accommodation** **D** *Aristocrat*, nr Bus Stand, T 2091. 30 rm, 10 a/c. The best available. **Getting there** There are regular buses from Cuttack and Bhubaneswar.

BHUBANESWAR TO SIMLIPAL AND NORTHERN ORISSA

In visits of between 3 and 7 days it is possible to visit several places of historic and religious interest in N and NW Orissa as well as to see outstandingly beautiful scenery and the Simlipal National Park. Some accommodation offers excellent value en route (particularly at Chandipur), though in places it is very basic. Travel either by bus or car. Arrange car hire (with driver) in Bhubaneswar.

Baleshwar (Balasore)

(*STD Code* 06782) Lying on the NH 5 (NE from Bhubaneswar), this medieval maritime trading port was first established by the British in 1642 with subsequent competition from the French who called it *Farasidinga* and the Dutch *Dinamardinga*. Ruins of **Dutch tombs** can still be seen and traces of **canals**, up which ocean going ships were hauled inland.

• **Accommodation** **D** *Torrento*, Remuna Golei, NH 5, T 3481. Some a/c rm. **E** *Veena*, Nayabazar, T 06782. 30 rm, some a/c. Restaurant, coffee shop. The rest are basic **F** hotels. *Moonlight Lodge* is on Naya Bazar, T 2443, The *Circuit House* (T2120) and *Dak Bungalow* (T 2043) are on Station Rd, and an *Inspection Bungalow* (T 2066) on NH 5.

Turtles In Peril

Bhitarkanika Wildlife Sanctuary nr Paradwip. The mangrove forests covering 65,000 ha contains virtually every species of the tree. The swamps harbour estuarine crocodiles, water monitors and cobras but it is particularly known for the Olive Ridley turtles (*Lepidochelys olivacea*) which have mysteriously arrived each year in vast numbers to lay eggs on a 10 km stretch of Gahirmatha beach, bordering the sanctuary.

Sea turtles are believed to return to nest where they hatched so the cycle continues. They arrive at night, for a fortnight around the full moon from October to May, with a spectacular *arribadas* (the 'coming') in February, when record numbers find their way from the Indian Ocean or from Australia, via the Pacific. In 1993 an estimated 610,000 came, making it one of the largest in the world (Costa Rica has a comparable *arribadas*). They lay their eggs in nests excavated in the sand, a safe distance above the waterline and shed a salty "tear" afterwards (giving up excess salt). The eggs hatch about 2 months later, the incubation temperature deciding the sex; clutches are male around 24-26° C and female around 30-32, mixed when temperatures are in between.

Now the Talchua fishing complex (not far from the existing fishing jetty at Dhamara across the Brahmani River) and the relocation of cyclone-affected villagers, sanctioned by the Orissa Govt, threatens to affect the ancient pattern and will probably bring an end to the migration of these large sea turtles. The 80 km road with 3 bridges being built through the sanctuary at present between Rajnagar and Talchua is already disturbing the delicate ecosystem while the turtles compete for food with the fishermen from Dhamara, and already thousands have met their death when trapped by their nets. Marine conservationists are attempting to call a halt to the development.

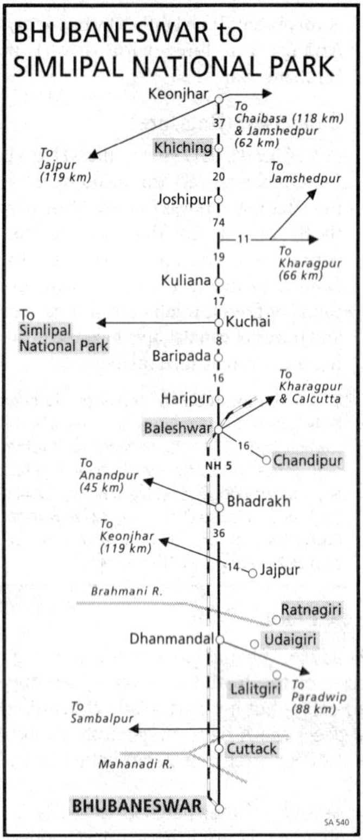

BHUBANESWAR to SIMLIPAL NATIONAL PARK

Keonjhar
To Chaibasa (118 km) & Jamshedpur (62 km)
37
To Jajpur (119 km)
Khiching
20
To Jamshedpur
Joshipur
74
11
19
To Kharagpur (66 km)
Kuliana
17
To Simlipal National Park
Kuchai
8
Baripada
16
To Kharagpur & Calcutta
Haripur
Baleshwar
16
Chandipur
NH 5
To Anandpur (45 km)
Bhadrakh
To Keonjhar (119 km)
36
14
Jajpur
Brahmani R.
Ratnagiri
Dhanmandal
Udaigiri
Lalitgiri
To Paradwip (88 km)
To Sambalpur
Cuttack
Mahanadi R.
BHUBANESWAR
SA 540

• **Tourist Office** SPA Marketing Complex, Block B, Station Sq, T 2048.

• **Transport Train** It is on the SE Rly between Calcutta and Madras. For Chandipur, leave train at Baleshwar and take a scooter taxi (Rs 45), or walk 1/2 km to town centre and catch the occasional bus. **Road Bus**: regular buses from Bhubaneswar and Calcutta.

Chandipur

(*STD Code* 06785) On the coast and 16 km from Baleshwar. It has one of Orissa's finest beaches with the tide receding 5 km daily. The sand dunes and casuarina groves make it particularly attractive. It makes an excellent stopping place and is a good point from which to go on to Simlipal and Khiching. Next to the PWD Bungalow is the **rocket range** where India test fires its latest surface to air missiles. There is strong local opposition to the central Govt's plan to extend the rocket range on environmental grounds (damage to fishing and wildlife) and because it would affect tourism.

• **Accommodation** **D** *Pantha Nivas*, T 2251. 10 rm, 2 a/c and cheap dorm. On the beach, is very well run with helpful staff and good food (freshly caught sea fish a speciality). Buy from fishermen at the harbour, 3 km walk along the beach to N of Chandipur. Look out for sea eagles cruising overhead. **D** *Shubam* is clean and friendly. Garden lobby. **E** *Chandipur*, opp is basic. **F** *PWD Bungalow* on a promontory overlooking beach. Reserve at PWD office, Baleshwar. Bring your beer from Baleshwar!

Mayurbhanj District

ROUTES The **NH 5** turns N in Baleshwar and enters Mayurbhanj District after approx 20 km. Do not take the right turn to Kharagpur 10 km N of Baleshwar, but follow road to Baripada.

The district is thickly forested, with hills, waterfalls and streams and is the home of much of India's wildlife which can now be seen at Simlipal. There are also prehistoric sites at Kuchai, Kuliana, Khiching, Baripada and Haripur, where the Bhanja rulers have left their mark, which are also interesting. The area produces excellent tussar silk, carvings of images and utensils on multi-coloured translucent serpentine stone from Khiching and tribal metal casting of toys and cult images. The tribal people have enriched the culture of the district particularly with their traditional dances. **NB:** accommodation throughout the district is very basic.

Haripur

16 km SE of Baripada. Previously called Hariharpur, it was founded by Maharaja Harihar in 1400 as the capital of the Bhanja dynasty. A later king built the

magnificent **Rasikaraya Temple** which, though now in ruins, stands as a unique example of a brick built Orissan temple. The area is still fascinating as it has several other historic buildings in the vicinity of the temple. The ruins of Ranihamsapur, the inner apartment of the queen, can be seen to the N of the courtyard. To the E are the remains of the Durbar Hall with its beautiful sculptured stone columns and arches. The brick-built **Radhamohan Temple** and 14th century **Jagannath Temple** are architecturally interesting although the deities were moved and are now worshipped in a neighbouring village **Pratapur**. Getting there: there is a regular bus service.

Baripada

(*STD Code* 06792) The district HQ. **Museum** Baripada Museum. Summer 0700-1200, Winter 1000-1700. Closed Mon and Govt holidays. Free. Collection of stone sculpture, coins, seals, terracottas, inscriptions.

Festival Mar/Apr: *Chhau* dance festival is held at the palace. The *Rath Yatra* (car festival) is unique because the chariot carrying *Subhadra* is drawn by women.

• **Accommodation** *Circuit House*. Reservations: the Dist Magistrate. *PWD Inspection Bungalow* Contact Exec Engineer (R and B). Also some simple private lodges. **F** *Ganesh Bhavan*, T 2784. 33 rm, some attached bath. **F** *Kichaka*, T 2557. 38 rm, restaurant, 24 hr coffee shop.

• **Useful services** **Hospital**, **Post Office**, **State Bank of India** and shops selling local handicrafts and handloom (Central Tussar Depot). **Tourist office**: T 2710.

• **Transport** **Road Bus**: services connect all major towns in the region but you can also hire private taxis or travel by deluxe coaches to visit the sights.

8 km N from Baripada on the road to Simlipal, **Kuchai** has been excavated to reveal a prehistoric site yielding pottery and neolithic and microlithic implements. **Kuliana**, 17 km further N, is rich in palaeolithic finds.

Simlipal National Park

Approach

Best time: Nov-Apr (monsoons from Jun). Temp range: 45°C to 5°C. Rainfall: 2000 mm.

Background

Simlipal is Orissa's principal wildlife sanctuary extending over 2750 sq km at the heart of which is one of the country's earliest tiger reserves covering about 300 sq km. The area has majestic *sal* forests interspersed with rosewood and flowering trees (*Champak and kadamba*), expanses of grassland, waterfalls, gorges and valleys through which run 12 rivers and streams which attract the animals.

Wildlife

The fauna includes tiger, elephant, leopard, wolf, chital, sambar, deer, gaur, flying squirrel and a large variety of birds including mynas, parakeet and peacocks. The *Barehapani* waterfall with a drop of 400 m and the *Joranda* Falls, 150 m, are both very impressive as are the Bachhuriachara grassland, where you might see a herd of elephants and the 1158 m peak of Meghasani. Best to travel by jeep within the park. However, logging disturbance and dense vegetation makes viewing difficult.

Viewing

Prior permission is required before visiting Simlipal. Contact the Assistant Conservator of Forests, Joshipur, Dt. Mayurbhanj. The Field Director, Simlipal Tiger Reserve, Baripada is able to issue Restricted Permits for visiting Barehapani and Joranda waterfalls and the *Chahala* woodland and *Nawana* valley which are situated in the core area. Jeeps with spotlights can be arranged through the Assistant Conservator of Forests, Joshipur.

Park information

● Accommodation

Spend 2-3 days to make the visit worthwhile. The *OTDC Tourist Complex* at Lulung about 10 km inside the park is completely run on solar power in order to retain its natural ecology. The stone lodges with catering facilities are more comfortable than the very spartan ***Forest Rest Houses***. These are at Chahala, Nawana, Joranda, Barehapani with a view of the waterfall, Jenabil and Upper Barkamra. Reservations through the Field Director, Simlipal Tiger Reserve, PO Baripada well in advance. Others: at Gudgudia, Jamuari, Dhudruchampa (log house), Kachhida and Talabandha, through Simlipal Forest Dev Corp, PO Karanjia; and Lulung Rest House and ***Panthasala***, Bangriposi, through Tourist Officer, Baripada. Take your own food; the caretaker/cook will help to prepare the meal. Alternatively you can visit the park as an excursion from the beach resort **Chandipur** near Balasore, see page 752 above.

● Transport

Train: the nearest stations on the SE Railways at Tatanagar and Balasore. **Road:** the park can be reached from Baripada by road via Lulung, 30 km W, which has a regular bus service. However, it is also possible to enter directly from the NH 6, either at Bangriposi via Talabanda or at the Joshipur entrance, where there is a **crocodile breeding centre**.

Khiching

Approximately 20 km W of Joshipur along the NH 6. The capital of the Bhanja rulers in the 10th-11th century, Khiching is just N of the NH 6 nearly half way between Kharagpur in W Bengal and Sambalpur. You can combine it with an excursion to Simlipal from Chandipur near Balasore as mentioned above.

The local deity **Kichangesvari,** once the family goddess of the Mayurbhanj royal family, has a unique temple built entirely of chlorite slabs. The reconstructed 20th century temple which has fine carvings is believed to have used the traditional temple building skills which date back to the 8th century. Nearby there are a number of other temples built in the Kalinga style, some of which are still in use.

Museum Khiching Museum, PO Sukruli. Summer 0700-1200, Winter 1000-1700. Closed Mon and Govt holidays. Free. Though small, it has a rare collection of art, sculpture and pottery.

• Accommodation *PWD Inspection Bungalow*. Reservations: Exec Engineer (R and B). PO Baripada. ***Revenue Rest Shed***, PO Sukruli. Contact Dist Magistrate, PO Baripada.

• Shopping *Khiching Stone Workers Society* sells the locally produced carvings from translucent coloured serpentine stone.

• Transport By rail: the nearest station is Rajrangpur 96 km away, but it is better to get down at Balasore, 210 km, which has a fast service on the SE Railway. **By bus**: regular buses from Baripada, 150 km.

BHUBANESWAR TO SAMBALPUR AND WESTERN ORISSA

The route passes through Sambalpur, famous for its textiles, dance and music. The gigantic Hirakud Dam can be visited as well as the densely forested Ushakothi Wildlife Sanctuary. The road to the steel town of Rourkela runs by the Brahmini river through glorious scenery.

It is possible to travel directly to Sambalpur, Hirakud and the NW from Bhubaneswar by crossing the Mahanadi at Cuttack and taking the State Highway through Denkanal and Angul to Sambalpur. If you have already visited Khiching it is also easy to continue W along the NH 6.

Sambalpur District

This part of Orissa to the NW of the state was settled in ancient times. An undeciphered pictograph found at Vikramkhol, N of the Hirakud reservoir, is evidence of such settlement. The region also features in Ptolemy's text of the 2nd century and was once the centre for trading in diamonds. In the 8th century King Indrabhuti became a Buddhist and a preacher of the Vajrayana sect. Its present name probably comes from the presiding deity Samalesvari to whom a temple was built by the Chouhans in the mid-16th century.

Sambalpur

Population 193,000 *STD Code* 0663
Sambalpur is famous for its textiles, particularly Sambalpuri saris from Bargarh, its tie and dye work, folk dance and music. It also produces some of the finest rice in the country and trades in *kendul* leaves and *sal* seeds. 20 km away at Hirakud is one of the longest mainstream dams in the world and the vast reservoir can be seen if you climb the Gandhi Minar or the Jawahar Minar in Sambalpur town. Good views from Budharaja Hill and the *Panthanivas*.

• **Accommodation D** *Uphar*, VSS Marg, T 21558. 13 rm, 6 a/c. Restaurant. **D** *Panthanivas*, T 21482. 24 rm, half a/c. Restaurant, bar, tours. **D** *Sujata*, VSS Marg, T 21403. 24 rm, 7 a/c. Restaurant. Inexpensive **E** *Tribeni*, VSS Marg, T 21301. 26 rm, 2 a/c. Restaurant. **D** *Li-n-ja*, next to Ashoka Talkies, T 21403. 27 rm, 2 a/c. Restaurant. Inexpensive **F** hotels: *Nataraj*, Gole Bazar, T 22223. 23 rm. *Chandramani Lodge*, VSS Marg, T 21440. 63 rm. Restaurant. *Ashoka*, opp Police Station, T 21010. The *Inspection Bungalow*. Cook will prepare meal if you take provisions. Reservations: Exec Engineer (R and B), Sambalpur.

• **Tourist office** Orissa Tourist Bungalow, T 20318. Rly station counter, T 1661.

• **Transport** At the junction of NH 6 and 42. **By rail**: SE Rly has 2 stations which connect with Calcutta, Madras and Tata. **By bus**: regular buses to Raipur, Ranchi, Rourkela, Bhubaneswar, Puri etc.

Ushakothi Wildlife Sanctuary

48 km E of Sambalpur on the NH 6, is densely forested and covers 130 sq km. Wild elephant, leopard, tiger, bison, wild boar and chital, barking deer inhabit the sanctuary. Best time: Nov-June, at night (2000-0200). Take a guide with search lights and see the wildlife from the watch-towers sited near watering points to which the animals come. Open hooded jeeps recommended. Permits to visit from the Forest Range Officer, PO Badrama. Very basic (no electricity) *Forest Rest House*, Badrama, 3 km away. Reservation: Divisional Forest Officer, Bamra, Sambalpur.

Hirakud Dam

The Mahanadi created enormous problems every year through devastating floods of the delta region. In order to combat these the Dam was built some 20 km NW of Sambalpur. The key section is an over 1100m long masonry dam, with a further earthen dam of over 3500m. It is over 60m high and drains an area of 133,000 sq km, twice the size of Sri Lanka. Since it was completed in 1957 there have been no serious floods in the Mahanadi delta. The dam has a 270 MW hydro electric power station and also allows the irrigation of nearly 750,000 ha of high quality land. Some of this is on the right bank of the Mahanadi S of Sambalpur and the remainder in the delta itself. Contact the Deputy Supt of Police, Security Force, Hirakud before visiting. Accommodation: there is a good Guest House, *Ashok Nivas* at one end of the dam. Contact Supt Engineer, Hirakud Dam Circle, Burla, Sambalpur. You get an excellent view from the revolving tower, Gandhi Minar at the other end. Getting there: regular buses from Sambalpur.

Huma

About 32 km S of Sambalpur is Huma, where there is a famous **Leaning temple** on the bank of the Mahanadi, dedicated to Lord Siva. The temple (and auxilliary temple to the N) leans southwards but the pinnacle is vertical. The colourful **Kudo fish**, easily seen from Jan to Jun, which thrive in the river are believed to belong to the deity so is never caught by fishermen. Visitors may feed them grain. Country boat rides available at a small fee.

Sundargarh District

To the N of Sambalpur is Sundargarh District. In the tribal heartland it is an area of undulating hills with the richest deposits of mineral wealth in the state. Cave paintings are evidence of the existence of early man in this region. Once relatively untouched by modern civilisation and with a rich tribal culture, notable for many dances, the district was chosen for the siting of the first public sector **steel plant** at Rourkela. The route from Sambalpur to Rourkela runs E 115 km to Barakot, then N up the E bank of the Brahmani River. It passes through some glorious scenery. The Brahmani itself flows along a wide rocky and sandy bed, a torrent in the monsoon, with forested hills on either side.

Rourkela

Pop 399,000, *STD Code* 0661 A large industrial town girdled by a range of hills and encircled by rivers, Rourkela was selected for its prime position, as a steel plant in 1955 and has a Fertilizer Complex attached to it. The power for the steel plant comes from Hirakud. Both plants can be visited with permission from the PRO. The Gandhi Park and Zoo are the other attractions.

• **Accommodation** The western style *Rourkela House* T 5076 is best. *Ispat Guest House*, Sector 2 and *Atithi Bhavan*, Sector 4 are alternatives. Reservation: PRO, Rourkela Steel Plant. **D** *Mayfair*, Panposh Rd, T 4649. 18 rm. Restaurant and 24 hr coffee shop. Pool. **D** *Radhika*, Main Rd (Madhusudan Chowk) opp Rly station. T 7930. 86 rm. Restaurant and 24 hr coffee shop. **D** *Shyam*, Bisra Rd. T 3367. 110 rm. Restaurant and 24 hr coffee shop. **D** OTDC *Panthanivas*, Sector 5, T 6549, modern, with 16 rm, 8 a/c with TV. Restaurant, bar.

• **Budget hotels** There are several small hotels and *dharamshalas* as well as *PWD Inspection Bungalows* in Sector 4 and Panposh. For the last 2, contact Exec Engineer, R&B Div, Uditnagar, Rourkela.

• **Services** The town is well provided with banks, post offices, shops and hospitals. *Orissan Handicrafts*, Sector 5 is worth visiting for stone statues, shell ornaments, horn craft, silver filigree, clay and wooden toys and silks. **Tourist Office** at UGIE Sq, Uditnagar, T 3923. Rly station counter, T 4150.

• **Transport** Within the township there are buses, taxis, auto-rickshaws and cycle-rickshaws. **By rail**: direct trains from Bhubaneswar, 470 km away. **By bus**: regular services from Bhubaneswar and Sambalpur 192 km away.

BHUBANESWAR TO CHILIKA LAKE AND SOUTHERN ORISSA

Chilika Lake is India's largest, and has an abundance of bird and marine wildlife. Several excursions to the hills and coast can be made from Berhampur, a trading centre for silk fabric.

Chilika Lake

NH 5 passes SW across the narrowing coastal plain of the Mahanadi before reaching Chilika Lake about 100 km SW of Bhubaneswar en route to Berhampur. Chilika, in the heart of coastal Orissa, is the largest inland lake in the country. It covers an area of 1100 sq km stretching across the Puri and Ganjam districts and forms an enormous lagoon as it is joined to the Bay of Bengal with a narrow mouth, a sandy ridge separating it from the sea. The lake has a number of lush green islands and is the winter home of migratory birds, particularly on Nalabana island, some flying great distances from Persia and Siberia. During the winter months when it is best to visit Orissa, you can watch white bellied sea eagles, ospreys, golden plovers, sandpipers, flamingoes, pelicans and gulls.

Its aquatic fauna has made it a rich source for fishermen who come in search of prawn and crab. The presiding deity of the lake has a shrine at the Kalijai temple on one of the tiny rock islands. Barkul now has a water sports complex with kayaking, rowing, surfing and waterskiing.

Local information

● Accommodation

OTDC **E** *Panthanivas* Rambha, T 346. 2-storeyed building with restaurant, 11 rm, 2 a/c. **D** *Panthanivas*, Barkul, T Balugaon 240, 18 (6 a/c) very small rm and dorm. Restaurant, bar. Watersports complex. 2 hotels in Balugaon, *Asoka*, T 8 and *Chilka* T 68.

● Boating

OTDC motor launches for cruising on the lake through the marshes and backwaters, are available from Barkul and launches belonging to the Revenue Dept at Balugaon. Country boats can be hired from private operators from Barkul, Rambha and Balugaon at Rs 350-400 for 4/5 hr. ML *Sagarika* (34 seater) can be chartered for Rs 300 per hr or Rs 10 per seat. The smaller ML *Paryataka* (8 seater) can be chartered for Rs 40 per hr or you pay Rs 10 per seat when there are at least 4 passengers. A 2 hr cruise goes to the Kalijai Temple and a 4 hr one to Nalabana Island. Reservations through Manager, Panthanivas, Barkul, T Balugaon 60.

● Services

There is an OTDC Tourist Office at Rambha, T 44, as well as a post office and a Govt dispensary.

● Transport

It is easiest to reach by road from Barkul, 6 km N of Balugaon or Rambha, at the S end of the lake. Both are on the Madras-Calcutta NH 5. The Calcutta-Madras rail route touches the Lake at Balugaon, Chilika, Khallikote and Rambha.

Ganjam District

Travelling S of Chilika Lake is Ganjam District. It takes its name from the Persian Ganj – Am, meaing granary of the world, a testimony to its agricultural fertility. Much of the district is covered in dense forest. Settled in prehistoric times, it also came under the influence of Emperor Asoka's rule. The handicrafts of the region include brass and bell-metal ware, horn work, wood carvings, silks and carpets.

Ganjam

(*STD Code* 068114) Ganjam was the District HQ, but the administration moved to Chatrapur due to its unhealthy location. Its chief interest is the small East India Company fort by the sea. An interesting excursion can be taken from the NH5 inland to Aska (52 km) and Bhanjanagar (35 km).

Aska

(*Pop* 19,400) was famous as the centre of the sugar trade. Raw sugar was distilled, especially for rum production. The original owner's mansion is now the Govt Secondary School. Sugar was exported through Gopalpur.

Bhanjanagar

(*Pop* 17,100) originally named Russell Konda (Russell's Hill) after the Commissioner Russell who subdued the Konds in the 2 wars of 1836-38 and defeated the local raja of Gunsoor-Upendrabhanja. However, he had the last laugh as the name of the town was changed to Bhanjanagar. The local reservoir was dug out by Kond prisoners of war.

Berhampur

(*STD Code* 06812) On the NH 5, a trading centre for silk fabric, is the major commercial town of Ganjam District. An important station on the SE Railway where there is an OTDC Tourist counter (T 3870, 0500-2100), it is on the Madras-Calcutta highway and has a good bus network to other towns in the region.

Places of interest

The **Thakurani, Jagannath, Nilakanthesvar Siva temples** are worth visiting. It is also a good place to shop for silks.

Museum

Berhampur Branch Museum. Summer 0700-1400, Winter 1000-1700. Closed Mon and Govt holidays. Free. Collection of sculpture, armoury, anthropological and natural history specimens. No photography.

Local information

● Accommodation

The only accommodation is cheap. There are many small lodges and hotels. **F** *Moti*, Gandhinagar Rd, Gandhinagar Rd, T 2345.**F**

Berhampur Rest House, Convent School Rd, T 2244. **F** *Udipi*, Fire Station Rd, T 2196. 38 rm. Restaurant & ice cream parlour. **F** *Municipal Guest House*, Town Hall Rd, T 3318; *Circuit House* on Station Rd, and an *Inspection Bungalow* (Revenue) on Engineering School Rd. Reservations for last 2: Sub-Div Officer, T 2103. *PWD Inspection Bungalow*, Courtpetta. Contact SE Southern Circle, T 2082. There is also a 1 rm *Railway Retiring Rm* and a dormitory.

● **Services**

The **State Bank of India** has a branch among others and there are several shops, **post offices** and a **hospital**.

● **Tourist office**

OTDC, Old Christian St, T 3226. Tourist Counter at the Rly station, T 3870.

● **Transport**

Local Private cars and taxis: for excursions to places like Gopalpur-on-Sea, Jaugada and Taptapani.

Train Bhubaneswar: *Haora Mail*, 6004 (AC/II), daily, 1855, 3¼ hr; **Vijayawada**: *Coromandal Exp*, 2841 (AC/II), daily, 0011, 10¼ hr; *Haora Mail*, 6003 (AC/II), daily, 0705, 12½ hr; **Madras (MC)**: *Coromandal Exp*, 2841 (AC/II), daily, 0011, 17½ hr; **To Calcutta (H)**: *Coromandal Exp*, 2842 (AC/II), daily, 0119, 10¼ hr.

Gopalpur-on-Sea

Offers a seaside alternative to staying in Berhampur. 16 km E of the town, Gopalpur was an ancient sea port from which early settlers from Kalinga sailed as far as Java, Bali and Sumatra. In more recent times it was a port for the export of Aska sugar and coolie labour to Assam tea gardens. British India ships called regularly. It became a popular seaside resort offering a beautiful sandy beach which has a regular bus service from Berhampur. Though it has the rather faded feeling and appearance of many seaside resorts, almost as if it were permanently out of season, it has its attractions. Sand dunes, groves of coconut palm and casuarinas separate the small town from the beach on the Bay of Bengal. The backwaters, creeks and lagoons give some variety.

● **Accommodation B** *Oberoi Palm Beach*, T 8123. 20 rm, 4 a/c. Good restaurants, bar, private beach, surfing. Run like a British country house. The **F** *Youth Hostel* for 16 (members only). Some inexpensive hotels are **E** *Sea View Lodge*, 6 rm, **E** *Sea Breeze*, T 56, **E** *Holiday Home*, 11 rm, T 49, **E** *Motel Mermaid*, on the beach with restaurant, T 50 and *Kalinga*, T 33.

Excursions from Berhampur

It is possible to visit a number of places of interest in the neighbourhood of Berhampur. **Taptapani**, 50 km along the state highway to the NW is at an altitude of 500m, and has a regular bus service from Berhampur and Koraput. There is also a direct bus from Bhubaneswar 240 km away. Water from the very hot sulphur springs which were discovered in a forest setting are channelled to a pond for bathing. There is a shrine to goddess Kandhi inside the original *kund*. The sulphurous spring is believed to cure infertility, and tribal women enter the hot water in the pool by the rest house and try to pick up a seed pod from the mud at the bottom of the pool.

● **Accommodation** Piped sulphur spring water also supplies hot water to the govt's **E** *Panthanivas*, T Pudamani 431. 8 rm, 2 a/c, with bath. This is bearable, but the smell of sulphur can make you feel quite nauseous. Wildlife is advertised as aproaching the hotel, but rarely seems to oblige. 2-storeyed Travellers' Lodge has a restaurant and some a/c rm, T Digapahandi 21. **F** *Youth Hostel*. Reservations: Secretary.

Chandragiri

32 km S of Taptapani in the tribal hills, the Tibetan carpet weavers have settled in a refugee colony after fleeing from Tibet in the 1950s. The temple and Buddhist prayer flags lend a distinctive atmosphere. The carpets and handicrafts can be seen being woven; prices are very reasonable.

Jaugada

35 km N of Berhampur, is in the Malati Hills, famous for one of Asoka's 'Kalinga Edicts' (see Dhauli above) found inscribed in granite, which was discovered in the early 19th century but the shelter was built only in 1975. It is more difficult

to get to but can be reached by a jeepable road from Purusottampur which has a regular bus service from Berhampur. Emperor Asoka's doctrine of conquest through love instead of the sword and his declaration "All men are my children" appear here. Sadly, neglect and possibly unskilled restoration of the monument has led to the disappearance of the inscriptions, in places. The old fort which is believed to date back to the 6th century contains images of the 5 Pandavas in stone which are worshipped in the temple of Guptesvar.

There are several other interesting sites nearby especially those in **Buguda**, a few km away, where there is the **Viranchinarayan Temple** with its beautifully carved wooden *Jagamohan* and its murals depicting stories from the epic Ramayana. Also, close by in **Buddhakhol** are Buddhist sculptures and shrines to Siva.

TRIBAL AREAS

Orissa's rich tribal heritage has survived among the hills and forests across the districts of Koraput, Phulbani, Kalahandi, Ganjam, Keonjhar, Dhenkenal and Mayurbhanj. See page 717. The state government is actively promoting tourism in some of these districts.

It is possible to visit some of the areas by booking a tour at least a month ahead to obtain permission to visit tribal territories. The area only provides very basic accommodation and some camping is necessary when trekking. Itineraries are adjusted to allow visitors to attend festivals and markets. Transport is by non-a/c car, jeep or minibus. **NB:** photography is prohibited in Bonda and Dongariya territories.

Tours

A typical 9-day tour covers about 2000 km. Best season Sep-Mar. Book tours through *Swosti Travels*, 103 Janpath, Bhubaneswar, T 404178.

Day 1 From Bhubaneswar to **Baliguda**. En route visit roadside villages to be aware of the differences between tribal and common villages in terms of organisation, materials used, size etc. Night at *Hotel Sanosh Bhawan*.

Day 2 Via **Rampur** to **Rayagada** visiting Kuttiya Kondh tribal villages and a market. Overnight at *Hotel Swagat* or *Hotel Kapilash*.

Day 3 Drive to **Chatikona**. Trek 8-10 km visiting Dongariya Kondh tribal villages. Overnight at *Hotel Swagat* or *Hotel Kapilash*, Rayagada.

Day 4 To **Jeypore**. En route visit some Parajas and Kondh tribal villages. Overnight at *Hotel Apsara* or *Hotel Madhumati*.

Day 5 Drive to **Malkangiri** visiting Koya tribes and somes villages and markets. Overnight at *Hotel Apsara* or *Hotel Madhumati*, Jeypore.

Day 6 Drive to **Onukudelli** visiting **Gadaba** tribal village. Overnight at *Hotel Apsara* or *Hotel Madhumati*, Jeypore.

Day 7 Drive to **Mudulipada** visiting Bonda highlands and trek about 4-5 km to tribal villages. Overnight at *Hotel Swagat* or *Hotel Kapilash*, Rayagada.

Day 8 Drive to **Puttasingh** visiting **Langia Soura** tribal villages. Overnight at *Panthanivas*, Taptapani (see above).

Day 9 Return to Bhubaneswar, en route visiting **Chilika**, Asia's largest saltwater lake (see above).

It is quite possible and much cheaper to organise your own tour from Jeypore rather than from Bhubaneswar. An evening train (1800 hr) to Vizianagaram (arr 0100) then bus (or taxi) to Jeypore. It is reportedly easier to get permits to visit tribal areas in Koraput than in Bhubaneswar. In Jeypore a local travel agent, *Travel Care*, Sardar Patel Marg, Jeypore, T 06854 2291, will organise tours for individuals or groups. They supply good guides and will obtain permits if given notice. They also organise tribal tours in Madhya Pradesh. The Manager is extremely helpful.

BIHAR

Contents

Maps

Bihar took its present form at Independence, and apart from losing Purnea and Manbhum districts to W Bengal was unaffected by the states' reorganisation. *Area*: 174,000 sq km. *Population*: 86.3 mn; half the size of Germany.

SOCIAL INDICATORS *Population*: 91 mn (Urban 12.5%, Scheduled Castes 15%, Scheduled Tribes 8%). *Literacy*: M 53% F 23%. *Birth rate*: *Rural* 35:1000, *Urban* 28:1000. *Death rate*: *Rural* 13:1000, *Urban* 8:1000. *Infant mortality*: *Rural* 116:1000, *Urban* 60:1000. *Religion*: *Hindu* 83%, *Muslim* 14%, *Christian* 1%. *Languages*: Hindi, Maithili, Santali, Mundari, Kurukh.

Environment

Land

Bihar is a region of transition from the wet lowlands of Bengal to the much drier and now more prosperous alluvial plains of W Uttar Pradesh, Haryana and Punjab. It is a landlocked state, surrounded by W Bengal, Orissa, Madhya Pradesh and Uttar Pradesh and sharing an international boundary with Nepal to the N. From that boundary on the Siwalik foothills of the Himalayas it stretches 600 km S to the forests of the Chota Nagpur plateau.

The River Ganga runs from W to E through the heart of the plains. It is joined by its N tributaries from the Nepal Himalaya. To the N of the Ganga are the scars of old river beds which often form chains of lakes during the monsoon. These provide a vital source of fish. N Bihar is India's biggest producer of freshwater fish, over half of which is sold to Calcutta. Torrential rain in the Himalayan foothills and the flatness of the Ganga valley floor cause some of the rivers, like the Kosi, to flood catastrophically. Over a period of 130 years the Kosi has moved over 110 km westwards. It also deposits vast quantities of coarse silt which, unlike the fine silts deposited in the Bengal delta, destroy previously fertile land. About 100 km N of Monghyr old indigo factories have been almost completely buried under the new silt, deposited as the river has flooded.

History

The name Bihar is derived from *vihara* ('monastery'), suggesting its wealth of religious monuments. All the major religions of India have left a mark, most notably Buddhism and Jainism. The world's first university of Buddhist learning was founded at Nalanda (now an easy bus ride 50 km SE of Patna).

Bihar was settled from the W as Aryan tribes moved down the Ganga valley, clearing the forest and developing cultivation. Agriculture provided the base for the Magadhan kings who ruled from the 6th to the 4th centuries BC. Some of these kings were clearly outstanding administrators. Bimbisara, for example, travelled widely through his kingdom, maintained good relations with neighbouring states and contacts as far afield as Taxila in the NW and Tamil Nadu in the S. He was deposed and murdered in about 490 BC, 7 years before the Buddha died.

The early Magadhan kings had their capital at Rajagriha, 100 km SE of modern Patna. It was surrounded by stone walls with a perimeter of about 40 km, which can still be seen. Later they moved their capital to Pataliputra, the site of modern Patna. From that base the last of the Magadhan kings, the unpopular tyrant Nalanda, was overthrown by Chandragupta Maurya, some time between 324 and 313 BC. Bihar thus became the centre of the first empire to unite most of India under one ruler. Pataliputra had already taken much the shape of modern Patna, a long narrow city, strung about 12 kms along the S bank of the Ganga.

The Guptas, who played a central role in the flowering of Hindu culture of the classical period, rescued Magadha in the 4th and 5th centuries AD from more than 600 years of obscurity. They were followed by the Palas of Bengal who ruled until defeated by the Muslims in 1197. The Delhi sultans and a succession of Muslim rulers independent of Delhi controlled the region until the Mughals brought it into their territory. A variety of Muslim place names such as Aliganj and Hajipur are evidence of 5 centuries of Muslim political dominance. 14% of the population today is Muslim. Babur overran the Lodis in 1529. When Akbar re-took it from the Afghan Sher Shah the Mughals retained it until the British won the Battle of Buxar in 1764. Subsequently Bihar was separated from Bengal and became a province under British rule until India's independence in 1947.

Culture

People

There is a sharp division between the plains of N Bihar, with about ¾ of the total population, and the Chota Nagpur plateau to the S. The plains are peopled largely by Hindus, though 12% are Muslims, and in N Bihar Muslims account for about 17% of the total. Aboriginal **tribal peoples** account for over 60% of the total population in districts such as Ranchi; Santal, Oraon, Munda and Ho tribes are particularly numerous. Some of the tribal populations have converted to Christianity in large numbers, over 50% of the Kharias, and about 25% of the Mundas and Hos being Christian.

Silt

Recent research suggests that the silt deposits result from the rapid uplift of the Himalayan mountains rather than from deforestation. A protective embankment was built in 1960 to limit the flooding and westward movement of the river, protecting 265,000 ha of agricultural land. Attempts to control the Kosi by building dams in Nepal are still under consideration, but the very large amounts of silt, the fact that the Himalayan foothills are a zone of major earthquakes, and the difficulties of the political relationship between India and Nepal, makes projects extremely difficult to implement effectively.

To the S of the Ganga is another stretch of alluvium, much shallower than that to the N of the river and about 150 km wide. When the Ganga is in full flow it is higher than the tributaries which join it from the S, so it is also subject to severe floods between Jul and Oct. The alluvium barely covers the ancient rocks of peninsular India which form the Chota Nagpur plateau, emerging in broken hills to the S. There is beautiful open parkland scenery in Chota Nagpur itself, much of the original forest having been cleared.

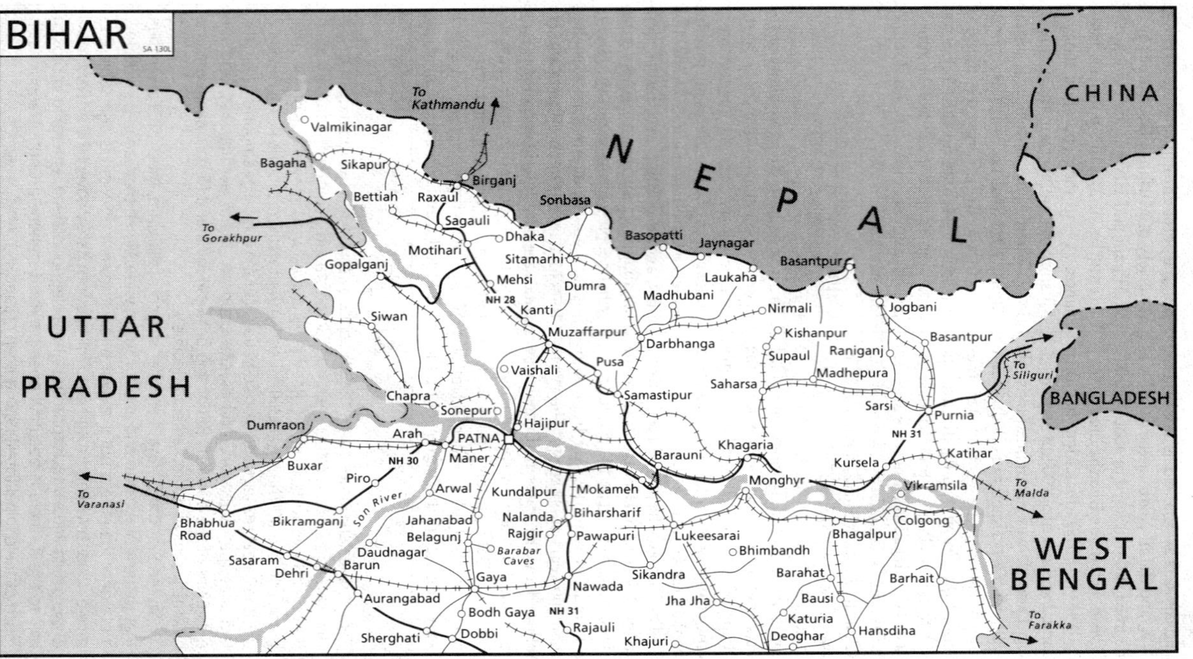
BIHAR
SA 130L
CHINA
NEPAL
BANGLADESH
WEST BENGAL
UTTAR PRADESH
To Kathmandu
To Gorakhpur
To Varanasi
To Siliguri
To Malda
To Farakka
Valmikinagar
Bagaha
Sikapur
Bettiah
Raxaul
Birganj
Sagauli
Motihari
Dhaka
Sonbasa
Sitamarhi
Mehsi
Dumra
Gopalganj
NH 28
Kanti
Muzaffarpur
Siwan
Vaishali
Pusa
Basopatti
Jaynagar
Laukaha
Basantpur
Madhubani
Darbhanga
Nirmali
Kishanpur
Supaul
Raniganj
Madhepura
Saharsa
Jogbani
Basantpur
Sarsi
Purnia
NH 31
Samastipur
Chapra
Sonepur
Hajipur
Dumraon
Arah
PATNA
Maner
NH 30
Buxar
Piro
Barauni
Khagaria
Kursela
Katihar
Monghyr
Vikramsila
Colgong
Mokameh
Kundalpur
Arwal
Son River
Bhabhua Road
Bikramganj
Jahanabad
Nalanda
Biharsharif
Rajgir
Pawapuri
Belagunj
Lukeesarai
Bhimbandh
Bhagalpur
Daudnagar
Barabar Caves
Sasaram
Dehri
Barun
Gaya
Nawada
Sikandra
Barahat
Barhait
Aurangabad
Jha Jha
Bausi
Bodh Gaya
NH 31
Katuria
Rajauli
Sherghati
Dobbi
Khajuri
Deoghar
Hansdiha

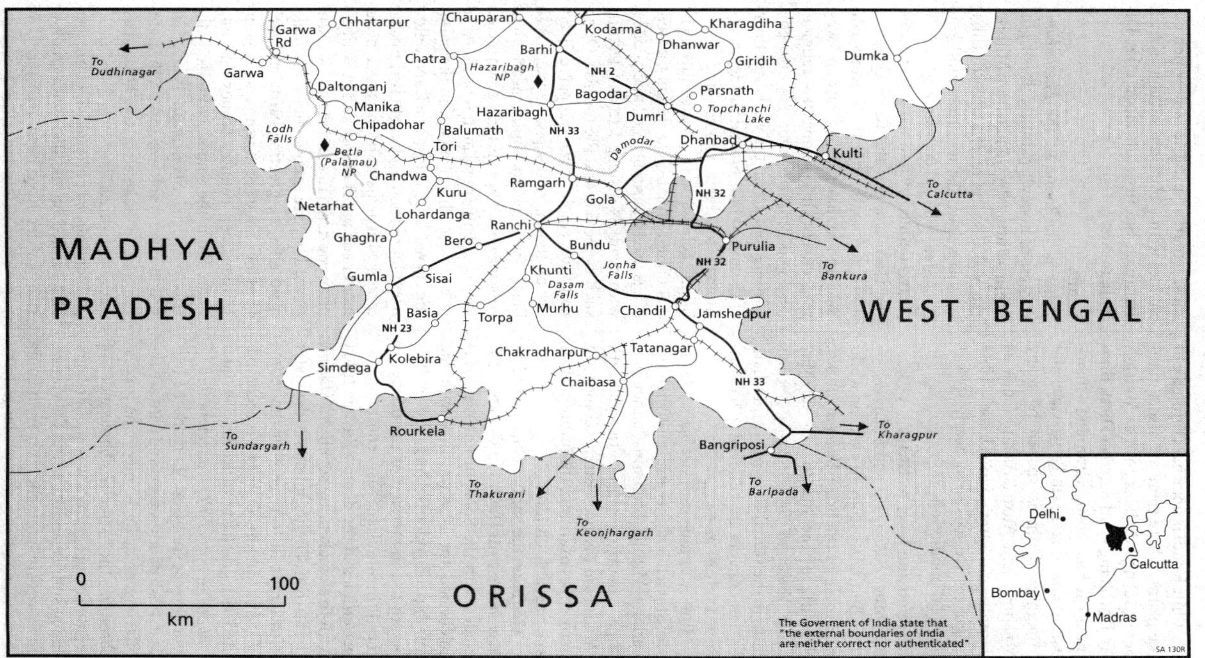
MADHYA PRADESH
WEST BENGAL
ORISSA
To Dudhinagar
Garwa Rd
Garwa
Chhatarpur
Chauparan
Kodarma
Kharagdiha
Dhanwar
Giridih
Dumka
Barhi
Chatra
Hazaribagh NP
NH 2
Bagodar
Parsnath
Topchanchi Lake
Daltonganj
Manika
Chipadohar
Hazaribagh
Dumri
Lodh Falls
Balumath
NH 33
Dhanbad
Betla (Palamau) NP
Tori
Damodar
Kulti
Chandwa
Ramgarh
To Calcutta
Kuru
Gola
NH 32
Netarhat
Lohardanga
Ranchi
Ghaghra
Bero
Bundu
Purulia
Gumla
Sisai
Khunti
Jonha Falls
NH 32
To Bankura
Dasam Falls
Basia
Torpa
Murhu
Chandil
Jamshedpur
NH 23
Kolebira
Chakradharpur
Tatanagar
Simdega
Chaibasa
NH 33
To Sundargarh
Rourkela
To Kharagpur
Bangriposi
To Thakurani
To Baripada
To Keonjhargarh
0 100 km
The Goverment of India state that "the external boundaries of India are neither correct nor authenticated"
Delhi
Calcutta
Bombay
Madras
SA 130R

While Hindi is dominant throughout the plains, where there are also a number of related dialects such as Maithili (in Darbhanga and Saharsa Dist), Bhojpuri (in Shahabad, Saran and Champaran) and Magahi (in Patna, Gaya and Monghyr). Urdu is spoken by many Muslims, and Austro-Asiatic (such as Santali) and Dravidian (Oraon) tribal languages are spoken by nearly 10% of the total population.

Religion and local festivals

Apr/May: *Bodh Gaya* and *Rajagriha* attract Buddhists from all over the world who come to celebrate *Buddha Jayanti*, the birth of the Buddha in Apr/May while *Mahavira Jayanti* in Apr brings Jains to the sacred Parasnath Hill where 22 tirthankaras are believed to have attained salvation.

Jun: A unique *marriage market* takes place for a fortnight each June when the nation's Mithila Brahmins gather in a large mango grove in Saurath (Madubani district). Parents come with horoscopes to arrange the future of their marriageable children.

Oct/Nov: the annual *Pataliputra Festival* starts with Dasara in Oct and concludes with the Sonepur fair. *Dasara* is celebrated for 10 days, first with the worship of goddess Durga for 9 days before the immersion of the image on the 10th. Simultaneously enormous paper effigies of the demon Ravana filled with fire-crackers are set alight. *Diwali*, the festival of lights, follows 20 days later with lamps lit to remember the return of Rama after his exile and is accompanied with grand fireworks. Six days later *Chhath* or *Surya Puja* is celebrated to worship the Sun God. To mark the harvest, fresh paddy, sweets and fruit are the offerings made by devotees who process through the streets. Thousands of women, waist deep in water, offer homage at sunrise and sunset in the Ganga. *Sonepur Fair* across the river from Patna is the scene of one of Asia's largest and most remarkable cattle fairs which coincides with a Hindu festival at Kartik Purnima, the first full moon after Diwali, in Nov.

Crafts

Bihar is the home of the *Madhubani* ("forest of honey") painting. Its origins are in paintings by women from Mithila, the 60,000 sq km region of north Bihar who pass down the skill from mother to daughter. The 60,000 sq km area is clearly defined by four natural features: the Himalaya and the River Ganga to north and south, and the Rovers Gandaki and Mahananda on east and west respectively. On ceremonial or religious occasions centuries ago, they created a striking folk art on the walls and floors of their mud huts often drawing on mythology for their subject and using bright colours with strong lines. The elaborate Kobhar Ghar design for weddings used figures of a god and goddess with symbols of long life and fertility such as the fish and the tortoise. Originally vegetable dyes prepared from leaves, flowers and sap were used, with black from the soot underneath their cooking pots. The rules laid down meant they could not spend money on material or use any edible plants. Now the paintings in red, blue, green, black and yellow use coloured powder bought in the bazar mixed with goats milk and are done on handmade paper or fabric. The white is often powdered rice and the black, burnt straw. They are unique items and make good gifts, eg greeting cards and wall hangings showing Krishna with gopis (milkmaids), country scenes and animals. From the same Madhubani district a special *Sikki grassi* is dyed in bright colours and woven with the natural grass to make attractive boxes, baskets and figures.

Floral *alpana* patterns which are usually painted on the floor with chalk or rice powder have been transferred to paper, cloth or wood to sell as decorative items. Around Bodh Gaya, *miniature paintings* on leaves or paper depicting the lives of the Buddha or Mahavira are sold to pilgrims and tourists. Bihar is also well known for wooden toys, small white metal figures and leather goods. Wood inlay is another ancient craft which has been practised in the Patna region. The craftsman uses different woods, ivory, metal and horn to create inlaid designs for table tops, trays and wall plaques.

Cuisine

Bihar does not have a particularly distinctive style of cooking. The typical meal consists of boiled rice, unleavened bread, lentils and vegetables cooked with hot spices. *Sattoo*, a combination of grains, is made into a dough and eaten either as a savoury or a sweet when mixed with sugar or jaggery. The mixture can also be taken as a drink when mixed with milk or water and flavoured with cardamoms and cloves. *Puri-aloo,* deep fried Indian bread with potatoes cooked with onions and garlic, and *kachoris* made with wheat and lentil flour and served with *kala chana* (black gram) are tasty snacks.

Modern Bihar

Modern political development

From its pre-eminent position in the culture and politics of early and classical India, Bihar has declined today to one of India's poorest and most badly administered states. Throughout the 1980s there have been outbreaks of caste-based violence in the countryside. Many of the tribal peoples have been under pressure from agricultural settlers from the plains. Often in desperation the poor have moved to cities like Calcutta and Bombay or to work on tea estates. Hundreds of thousands of Biharis also migrate seasonally to regions like Punjab, Haryana and Nepal to work in harvesting periods.

Bihar has 54 seats in the Lok Sabha and 324 seats in its State Assembly. After long periods of Congress rule the present administration was formed in 1991 by the Janata Party.

The Economy

Resources and industry Bihar has 40% of India's mineral wealth in coal, mica, copper, bauxite and iron, located in the Chota Nagpur plateau in the S. They have been the basis of rapid industrial expansion in towns like Jamshedpur, Ranchi and Dhanbad. Jamshedpur was founded as the location of India's first integrated iron and steel mill, opened by Jamshedji Tata in 1908.

Since Independence major industrial projects have been undertaken by the Govt of India. Bokaro steel mill in the Damodar Valley project area was one of such developments. Bharat Heavy Electricals at Ranchi is another, built with Soviet aid in the 1960s.

India is the world's leading **mica** producer, Bihar accounting for 50% of that production, but the decline in world demand for mica has hit the industry hard. Production dropped from 15,000 tonnes in 1971 to under 3500 tonnes in 1992. The industry is focused on Hazaribagh, about 70 km N of Ranchi, where women and children work at splitting the mica sheets, reportedly to thicknesses of $\frac{1}{25}$ mm. In the same period bauxite production has more than doubled. It is mined in laterites at Lohardaga, 50 km W of Ranchi and moved to Luri, S of the Damodar River, for processing.

PATNA

Modern Patna stretches along the S bank of the Ganga for about 15 km. Divided in 2 by the Maidan, a large open park, it has some open suburbs, but the central city is crowded, dusty and with little of architectural interest or merit. It is one of the poorest large cities in India. Thousands sleep on the streets and there are few street lights at night. However, around the station food stalls are beautifully set out and illuminated, and it can be interesting to take a cycle rickshaw round by day or night. Many tribals come into the town, often working on roads or building sites. Children sometimes perform tightrope walking at the station, but there are very few tourists and people are generally friendly without pestering. Some streets have been renamed although they often continue to be referred to by their old names, eg Fraser Rd now Nazharul Huque Path and Exhibition Rd now Braj Kishore Path, although Beer Chand Patel Marg has replaced Gardiner Rd. Bailey Road has become J Nehru Marg. The new Mahatma Gandhi Bridge across the Ganga has speeded up the route north. Modern custom now holds that it is lucky to drive in the middle and make a wish – possibly to reach the other side! In the monsoon Patna sometimes suffers severe flooding. Black marks on the walls of some village stone houses near the river testify to the flood depth.

BASICS *Population*: 1.1 mn. *Altitude*: 53m. *STD Code*: 0612.

At the confluence of the rivers Son, Punpun and Ganga, Patna's history can be traced back 2500 years. Ajatasatru, the second Magadha king who ruled from Rajagriha, built a small fort at Pataligrama. Later Chandragupta Maurya founded the Mauryan Empire with Pataliputra as its capital, see page 39. Buddhist histories suggest that it was here that Asoka usurped the throne of his father, Bindusara, murdering all his rivals and starting a reign of terror, before a conversion 8 years later. It marked the beginning of perhaps the greatest reforming kingship the world has known. The Greek ambassador Megasthenes was deeply impressed by the efficiency of the Chandragupta's administration and the splendour of the city. Ruins can be seen at Kumrahar, Bhiknapahari and Bulandhi Bagh with its 75m wooden passage. Excavations date the site back to the pre-Mauryan times of 600 BC. In the 16th century the Pathan Sher Shah Suri established the foundations of a new Patna, building a majestic mosque in 1540 which dominates the skyline. See page 49.

Places of interest

Patna's buildings reflect its administrative and educational functions. The collectorate, Judge's court, Medical College and Hospital, Patna College, the University, the Law College and the College of Engineering are all close to the river banks in the western part of the city. Also on this side lies the Governor's state house, Raj Bhavan, the Maharaja's palace, the High Court and the Museum as well as the better residential quarters. To the E is Old Patna with its bazars, the old mosques, Har Mandir and Padri-ki-Haveli or St Mary's, the oldest Roman Catholic church in Patna, which was built in 1775.

Golghar The *Gola* or round house is the extraordinary 29m high bee-hive shaped structure between the Maidan and the Ganga. It was built of stone slabs in 1786 by Capt John Garstin of the Bengal Engineers, as a grain store for the British army in case of a famine similar to that of 1770. It has a base 125m wide where the wall is 3.6m thick, with 2 brick staircases which spiral up the outside. Never completed, it was intended to hold 137,000 tons of grain. The grain was to be carried up the one side, poured in through the hole at the top and then the workforce was to descend the other staircase to collect more. The last line of the inscription 'First filled and publicly closed by___' was never completed. Although now empty, it is well worth climbing the steps for an excellent view of the city and the Ganga. It is sometimes possible to go inside and listen to the remarkable echo. Between Jul and Sep the river can be over 5 km wide at this point with a current of 8 to 10 knots in places.

Har Mandir is in the Chowk area of old Patna. The gurdwara built by Maharaja Ranjit Singh is the 2nd of the 4 great *takhts* or thrones in the Sikh world and consecrates the birth place of the 10th Guru Gobind Singh. The shrine of white marble with kiosks on the terrace above has a **museum** on the ground floor exhibiting photos, holy scriptures and personal possessions of the Guru.

Qila House or Jalan Museum. Across the road from Har Mandir, the private house was built over the ruins of Sher Shah's fort and is a museum containing Chinese paintings, a valuable collection of jade and silver filigree work of the Mughal period. Prior permission must be obtained from the owner. **Saif Khan's Mosque** or Pather-ki-Masjid. It is situated on the bank of the Ganga and was built in 1621 by Parwez Shah, the son of the Mughal Emperor Jahangir.

Kumrahar Excavations at the site of the ancient capital on the bypass between Patna Sahib and Patna Junction stations, have revealed ruins enclosed within a high brick wall. These date back to 600 BC, the first of 4 distinct periods up to AD 600. The buildings were devastated by a fire and lay hidden in the silt. The more recent 5th phase dates from the beginning of the 17th century.

The most important finds are rare wooden ramparts and a large Mauryan assembly hall with highly polished sandstone pillars which date back to 400-300 BC. In the 5th century AD, when the Chinese pilgrim Fa-hien visited the area, he commented on the brilliant enamel-like finish achieved by the Mauryan stone-cutters and wrote of it "shining bright as glass". The excavations suggest that the immense pillared hall was 3-storeyed and covered an area of 77m sq. There were probably 15 rows of 5 pillars, each 4.6m apart. From the single complete column found they are estimated to have been about 6m high. The fact that much of the building was wooden explains why so little has survived after the fire. The excavations also point to the possibility of one of the ceilings having been supported by immense *caryatid* figures which, taken together with the use of numerous columns, show a marked similarity with the palaces at Persepolis in S Iran. The pleasant garden site has little to show today other than the remaining intact pillar. The site of the hall is sometimes flooded, and the tiny museum had its small collection of valuable finds almost invisibly shut away in a dark room.

Gulzaribagh About 8 km E of the Golghar near Kumrahar is the former East India Company's principal opium *godown* (warehouse), now a Govt printing press. Strategically placed by the river, the 3 long buildings with porticoes on each side were easily accessible to boats which would carry the opium

CLIMATE: PATNA

	Jan	Feb	Mar	Apr	May	Jun	Jul	Aug	Sep	Oct	Nov	Dec	Av/Tot
Max (°C)	24	26	33	38	39	37	33	32	32	32	29	25	32
Min (°C)	11	13	19	23	26	27	27	27	26	23	16	12	21
Rain (mm)	21	20	7	8	28	139	266	307	243	63	6	2	1110

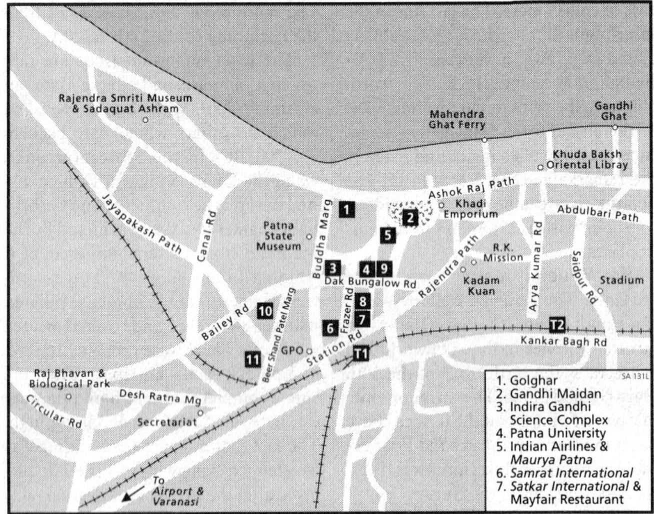

down to Calcutta from these N Indian headquarters. The old opium godowns, ballroom and hall are open to visitors.

Museums

Khuda Baksh Oriental Public Library. One of the largest one-man collections of books and rare Persian and Arabic manuscripts was founded in 1900. It also contains Mughal and Rajput paintings and the only books rescued from the Moorish University of Cordoba in Spain and an inch-wide Koran. It is now one of India's national libraries. **State Museum**, Buddha Marg. 1030-1630. Closed Mon. Free. Bags may not be permitted. Avoid toilets. Collection of coins, paintings, terracotta, bronze and stone sculptures including the famous Mauryan Didarganji Yakshi (c200 BC), Jain sculptures (2nd, 3rd centuries) and finds from Bodh Gaya, Nalanda and Kukrihar. It has Chinese and Tibetan sections and a 15m long fossil tree. The presentation is uneven, there are few if any labels, and the whole museum has a rather dog-eared feel. There are oddities like having lots of moth balls in the moth cabinet and a mutant stuffed kid goat labelled 'a freak of nature'. However, the first floor gallery is well lit, with a collection of terracotta heads from the 3rd century BC, and there is also an interesting collection of Tibetan thankas on the mezzanine floor. **Rajendra Smriti Museum**, Sadaquat Ashram. Summer 0700-1100, 1400-1900, winter 0800-1200, 1400-1800. Closed Mon. Free. A small museum containing the former Indian President Rajendra Prasad's personal belongings. The ashram itself is the seat of Bihar Vidyapith, the national university established in 1921. **Indira Gandhi Science Complex** Corner of Buddha Marg and Bailey Rd. Includes a planetarium. Opened April 1993.

Parks & zoos

Gandhi Maidan is often crowded. The **Vir Kunwar Singh Park** is on Station Rd. The **Sanjay Gandhi Biological Park** is a zoo and botanical garden; open sunrise to sunset, closed Mon.

Tours

City sightseeing: *Bihar Tourism (BSTDC)*, *Ashok Travels & Tours* and

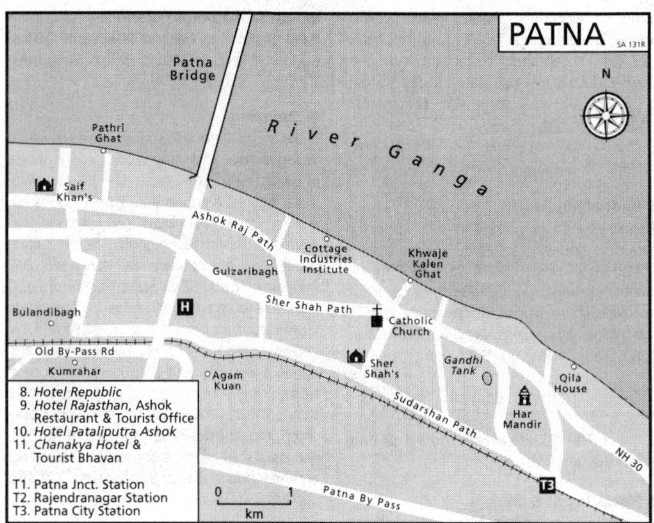

Patna Tours. Oct-Mar, Rajgir, Nalanda and Pawapuri, usually 0800-2200. Rs 50. **Longer tours**: *Bihar Tourism* runs tours to Vaishali, Bodh Gaya, Buxar and Sasaram. A minimum number is needed for the tour to run. Buses can be slow and uncomfortable. *Travel Corporation of India* and *Ashok Travels* hire non-a/c cars (4 passengers) with driver for touring (eg 5 days Chitwan, Pokhara and Kathmandu, Rs 5500 or similar for Buddhist sites, incl Bodhgaya, Rajgir and Nalanda, Sahet, Mahet, Kushinagar and Varanasi). Also a/c cars from TCI. **River cruises**: *Bihar SRTC* runs an hour-long cruise on the river from Mahendra ghat on its floating restaurant *Sagarika*.

Local information

● Accommodation

A *Maurya Patna*, Fraser Rd, S Gandhi Maidan, T 222060, F 222069. 80 rm. Modern, clean, 2 restaurants (expensive), excellent pool, poolside barbecue. Attentive service. Being renovated floor by floor. Easily Patna's best. **B** *Pataliputra Ashok*, Beer Chand Patel Path, T 226270. 45 rm. Travel. Tourist Office. Day rms for half-day use. Large lobby but slightly run-down maintenance and dingy rm, but helpful management. Good food, and excellent kebabs, though sometimes slow service. **C** *Chanakya*, Beer Chand Patel Marg, T 223141. 40 rm. Restaurant. Clean and modern, much used by political clientele. **C** *Samrat International*, Fraser Rd, T 220560. 68 rm. 2 restaurants (roof-top barbecue), bar, coffee shop, exchange. Dominated by political clients. **D** *Satkar International*, Fraser Rd, T 220551 F 220556. 50 rm. central a/c. Minimal spending on maintenance. Mainly business clientele. Nalanda Restaurant pleasant atmosphere, good food. **D** *Republic*, Lauriya Bagh, Exhibition Rd, T 55021. 35 rm some a/c. Dining hall, exchange, roof garden. Very good veg. meals. **D** *Marwari Awas Griha*, Fraser Rd, T 31866. 42 rm, some a/c, some much cheaper rm. Virtually all Indian guests. Small but very good veg. dining hall – according to some, "the best veg. food in Bihar". **D** *Mayur*, Fraser Rd, T 23333. New hotel, basic rm, some with attached bath, clean. Restaurant. **D** *Jayasarmin*, Kankarbagh Rd (5 min walk Patna Jct station) T 354281. Large rm, a/c or aircooled, clean linen and rm. Good rm service. Jasmine restaurant serves good veg and non-veg food, but slow service. **D** *Avantee*, opp Dak Bungalow, Fraser Rd, T 220540. 40 rm, some a/c. Restaurant. **D** *President*, off Fraser Rd, T 220600. 36 rm, some a/c. Restaurant, travel. **D** *Rajasthan*, Fraser Rd, T 25102. 20 rm some a/c. Good veg. meals. Travel. **D** *Chaitanya*, Exhibition Rd, T 55123. 48 rm, some a/c. Rm acceptable, restaurant not rec. **D** *Anand Lok*, Just opp Patna Jn Rly Station, T 223960. 43 rm, some a/c. **D** *Paryatan Bhawan* (BSTDC), Beer Chand Patel Path, T 25320. 44 rm, some a/c. Cheap dorm. Restaurant, exchange, travel.

● Budget hotels

Also several inexpensive hotels especially on Fraser Rd and Ashok Rajpath. Some have a restaurant and few, a bar. **E** *Railway Retiring Rooms* at Patna Junc, small, stuffy, some a/c rm, cheap dorm. Not rec. Reservations: Enquiry Supervisor. *Dharamshalas* Pataliputra and Birla Mandir are at Subji Bagh. Ram Piari Kunwar is at Kadam Kuan and Arya Athithi Grih at Naya Tola. **F** *Tourist Bhawan*, Beer Chand Patel Marg, T 25320. Clean, simple. Some dorms. **F** *The AA of Eastern India*, Dak Bungalow Rd. Good value.

● Places to eat & drink

Amrali Beer Chand Patel Marg (in same building as Hotel Kautilya Vihar), T 225969. Excellent vegetarian Indian food, quick service, dimly lit. Highly rec. Indian Restaurants on Fraser Road – *Ashok* (1st Flr) is dimly lit but serves good food. *Palji* at Krishna Chowk. *Chef*, good Chinese. *Mayfair*, inexpensive snacks and ice creams. *Vasant Vihar*, Maurya Lok Complex, Buddha Marg.

● Banks & money changers

State Bank, Gandhi Maidan for exchange. **Bank of India**, Main branch, Fraser Rd. Also at Beer Chand Patel Path, T 226069.

● Cultural centres & library

British Library, Bank Rd, nr Gandhi Maidan. 1030-1830 Tue-Sat. Very good collection and helpful staff.

● Entertainment

Cinemas: in Gandhi Maidan and on Exhibition Rd and 3 auditoria in Gandhi Maidan – Kalidas Rangalay, Sri Krishna Memorial Hall and Prem Chand Rangalay. Bharatiya Nritya Kala Kendra at Fraser Rd.

● Hospitals & medical services

Patna Medical College Hospital, Ashok Rajpath E, T 52301. *Nalanda Medical College Hospital* and *Upadhyaya Nursing Home*, T 52203 on Kankar Bagh Rd. *Getwell Nursing Home*, Jamal Rd, T 34183. Chemists on all main roads.

● Post & telecommunications

GPO: Station Rd. **Central Telegraph Office**: Buddha Marg, T 31000. **Telex Enquiries**: T 26858.

● Shopping

Patna and its surrounding villages are known for **wooden toys and inlay work**, silver jewellery in beaten rustic style, tussar silk, beaten white metal figures, bamboo and leather goods (including shoes). Madhubani paintings, lacquerware and papier mâché goods are other good buys. The Govt emporia are *Amrapali*, Dak Bungalow Rd and *Bihar State Handloom and Handicrafts* on E Gandhi Maidan, *Bihar Khadi Gramodyog Kendra* and shops at Patna Market, New Market, Maurya Lok Complex and Boring Canal Rd. Govt *Lacquerware Productions*, Maghalpura for lacquer on wood. **Books**: The S half of Fraser Rd has several bookshops. *Tricel International* is the best of very limited range, but *Reader's Corner* has a mix of old and new books. **Photography**: Foto Daffodils, opp Maurya Lok Complex, on Bailey Rd.

● Sports

Golf: Golf club on Bailey Rd. **Swimming**: Swimming pool in *Hotel Maurya* (Rs 150/- per day non-residents) with a poolside barbecue.

● Tourist offices

Govt of India, Rm 151, Paryatan Bhawan, Beer Chand Patel Path, T 226721. 1000-1700. Excellent service. Arranges local tours and excursions. Well worth visiting. **Bihar**, *Hotel Kautilya*, Fraser Rd, T 225411. 0800-2200. Airport counter, T 23199. *Hotel Ashok* counter, T 26270. Also at Patna Jn Rly Station.

● Travel agents & tour companies

Ashok Travels & Tours, *Hotel Pataliputra Ashok*, Beer Chand Patel Path, T 223238, T 26271; In *Maurya Hotel* complex, S. Gandhi Maidan: *Travel Corporation of India*, T 221699 See above. Nearby is *Swan Travel* on Biscauman Bldg, T 223700. *Tourist Bureau* in *Hotel Menka*, Kadam Kuan. *Patna Tours*, Fraser Rd, T 226846. *Pataliputra Tours*, Fraser Rd, T 222798.

● Transport

Patna is on NH 30. Distances by road to major cities: Delhi 1011 km, Calcutta 595 km. Other important tourist sites are Bodh Gaya 105 km (short route via Jahanabad) 3 hr, Gaya (via Rajgir) 174 km, Nalanda 90 km, Rajgir 107 km, Sasaram 152 km, Betla National Park 316 km, Ranchi 326 km and Varanasi 246 km.

Local Transport **Car hire**: (See also Tours above) *Travel Corporation of India*. Competitive rates, including longer tours. *Ashok Travels and Tours* for car and coach hire. Car hire vary from about Rs 400 (4 hr) to Rs 800 (8 hr). Out-of-town touring (600 km) eg Bodhgaya, Rajgirh, Nalanda Rs 2300 (a/c). Also a/c coaches for hire. **Taxis**: no yellow-top taxis. Private un-metered taxis available from the airport, railway station, some hotels and important tourist sites. Fix rates beforehand. The same applies to auto rickshaws, cycle-rickshaws and horse-drawn tongas. There is a city bus service.

Air: *Transport to town:* Coach from Airport to Indian Airlines City Office (7 km) stops at various hotels, T 63354. Rs 10. *Indian Airlines*, S Gandhi Maidan, T 222554. Airport Office, T 223199. 1000-1300, 1400-1600 **Delhi**, daily, 0950; 1½ hr; Via Lucknow, M, W, F, 1925, 2¼ hr; daily, 0845, ¾ hr; **Calcutta**, daily (via **Ranchi**, 0845, 2½ hr; M,W, F, 2010, 55 min.

Train: Patna Junc Rly Station: Enquiries, T 22012. Reservations: Class I, T 22016 and Class II, T 23300. Express trains, a few a/c, run from Patna Junc to Delhi, Calcutta, Varanasi, Bhagalpur, Amritsar, Jammu Tawi, Guwahati, Bombay and Madras among others. **Calcutta (H)**: *AC Exp*, 2304, M,Tu,Th,Sa, 0815, 9¾ hr; *Amritsar-Haora Mail*, 3006 (AC/II), daily, 2208, 10 hr; **Delhi (ND)**: *NE Exp*, 2521 (AC/II), daily, 0500, 15¼ hr; *AC Exp*, 2303, M,W,F,Su; 1820, 16¼ hr; **Varanasi**: *Amritsar Mail*, 3005, daily, 0520, 4¾ hr; **Gaya**: *Palamu Exp*, 3348, daily, 1910, 3¼ hr; **Guwahati**: *NE Exp*, 2522 (AC/II), daily, 2120, 21 hr; **Bombay (VT)**: *Chapra-Bombay Exp*, 5114 (AC/II), M,Th,Sa, 2345, 37 hr; **Madras (MC)**: *Patna-Madras Exp*, 6044, Sa, 1535, 43¼ hr. **Gaya Jn**: *Patna Express*, 8624, daily, 2125, 2½ hr; *Patna-Hatia Express*, 8625, daily, 1010, 2hr. Many other trains.

Road: Bihar, W Bengal and UPSRTC run Luxury and Exp bus services between Patna and their regional centres, including Calcutta, Siliguri, Bhagalpur, Ranchi, Hazaribagh, Monghyr and Gumra. Bihar STRC, Bus Stand, Gandhi Maidan, opp GPO. Enquiries, T 53898. Reservations: 1030-1800. Private bus companies also have services to neighbouring towns and tourist sites.

Transport to Nepal Several STRC and private buses run daily from Hardinge Park Bus Stand to Raxaul, (5-7 hr, Rs 50). However, timings are difficult and the buses extremely crowded and uncomfortable. Night buses reach the border in early morning. Morning buses from Patna connect with the night bus to Kathmandu. Either way you have to have at least one night bus journey unless you stay at Birganj – an unenviable option, though there are 2 modest hotels. Raxaul is even worse.

You can cross the border to Birganj by rickshaw/tempo; in Raxaul the tempo stand is S of the railway line and the Immigration and Customs office. In Birganj the tempo stand and Bus Park are in Adarsh Nagar, to the S of town. In the morning, buses depart from the Bus Stand E of the Clock Tower, to **Tandi Bazar** (4 hr, for Chitwan, Rs 40), **Pokhara** (11-12 hr, Rs 70) and **Kathmandu** (11-12 hr, Rs 75). Even Express buses are slow and packed. 'Tourist' Minibuses are the only moderately comfortable option. For Entry formalities, see below.

From Nepal When travelling to India via Patna it is best to stay overnight in Hetauda and catch the 0530 bus from the Bus Park (arrive at 0500 to get a seat) to Birganj (3 hr). At Birganj walk or get a horse-drawn rickshaw (rather expensive) to the auto-tempo stand at 2nd crossroads. From there travel to Raxaul on the Indian side.

Obtain an Exit stamp from Nepalese Immigration counter before crossing the border and an Entry stamp in Raxaul from the Indian Immigration office which is difficult to find (round the corner, and across the road from the Customs office). You may require Customs clearance first. Occasionally an additional fee is demanded by immigration personnel for "extras" eg Registration card.

Short excursions from Patna

The 7.5 km **Mahatma Gandhi Bridge**, one of the world's longest river bridges, crosses the Ganga to the E of Patna. **Note** Even recent maps often do not show this road connection, opened in 1983. Bihar is divided by the Ganga, but the new bridge has made both the road route to Nepal and short excursions to the N of the river much more practicable by bus or car.

Sonepur

(*STD Code* 0622484) 22 km across the Ganga, near its confluence with the Gandak, Sonepur has a station on the NE Railway. Sonepur witnesses Asia's biggest cattle market which begins on

Kartik Purnima, the first full moon after Diwali (Oct/Nov). The month long fair which accompanies the trading in livestock and grain draws thousands to the magic shows, folk dances and contests of skill and stalls selling handicrafts and handlooms. According to legend Sonepur was the site of a battle between *Gaj* (elephant), the lord of the forest and *Garh* (crocodile), the lord of the waterways. Elephants (as well as camels, horses and birds) are still bought and sold at this fair but their numbers are dwindling. The *Harihar Kshetra Mela* commemorates the coming together of devotees of Siva and Vishnu who perform their Puja at **Hariharnath Temple** after bathing in the river on full moon day. **Accommodation:** Bihar Tourism sets up a Tourist Village a week before the Fair. 'Swiss Cottage Tents' are furnished and have attached baths.

Vaishali

55 km N of Patna, about 1 hr by car or bus. Even including Sonepur it makes a comfortable day excursion. The road crosses the Ganga on the Mahatma Gandhi Bridge and goes via Lalganj (not the state highway to Muzaffarpur). Vaishali's name is derived from King Visala, mentioned in the epic Ramayana, and its history dates back to the 6th century BC when it was a flourishing city of the Lichchavis. Reputedly it was one of the first cities in the world to adopt a republican form of government. It was visited by the great Chinese travellers Fa-hien and by Hiuen-Tsang, who took back a piece of sculpture from one of the stupas. The Buddha preached his last sermon there announcing his approaching Nirvana. A century later, in 383 BC, it was the venue of the 2nd Buddhist Council, when 2 stupas were erected. Jains of the Svetambara sect believe that Mahavir was born in Vaishali in 599BC. Today the district is part of the Mithila region famous for Madhubani paintings on the walls of village houses.

Also at Vaishali is the **Asoka Pillar** at **Kolhua**, also known as Bhimsen-ki-Lathi (stick), a single piece of very highly polished red sandstone with a bell-shaped inverted lotus capital, 18.3m high which has a life size lion carved on top. Asoka pillars or *stambhas* were un-ornamented shafts with a circular section which tapered like the trunk of a palm tree. It suggested that columns of this sort were forerunners of temples, developed from the ancient form of worshipping in the forest. The idea of sacred sites developed as early as Vedic times when rocks, trees and water, having a powerful significance, would be made more prominent by cutting and defining them. The Mauryan capitals bear some resemblance to those found in Persepolis, while the practice of obtaining high polish by rubbing, shows the influence of the Greeks. Many of the pillars were erected in places sanctified by the Buddha, or they marked the ancient royal route northwards from Pataliputra to the border region of Nepal. This is one of 2 Asoka pillars which remain *in situ*. Of the 30 or so monoliths that the Emperor was believed to have erected, remains of about 10 have been found and those with capitals have been moved to the Indian Museum. The Wheel of the Law which tops many of the pillars is the mark of the social and political order laid down by the Emperor, who drew a distinction between that and the Buddhist Law.

Ramkund

Also known as Monkey Tank as, according to legend, it was dug by monkeys who offered the Buddha a bowl of honey. The 2 Buddhist **Stupas** are said to hold urns containing the Buddha's ashes, the second only having been excavated in 1958. The ancient **Coronation Tank** or Kharauna Pokhar, contains holy water which was used for anointing the ruler of Vaisali at his coronation. The 500m long **Lotus Tank** nearby was said to be a picnic spot in the 6th century BC.

Miranji-ki-Dargah Muslim tombs, containing the relics of Sheik Muhammed Qazin, celebrated local saint of the 15th century, built over a ruined brick stupa.

Raja Vishala ka Garh The ruin occupies an area enclosed by a wall about 1 km long and 2m high. The moat surrounding the ancient Parliament House which could hold an assembly of 7707 representatives is 43m wide. The temples include the 4th century **Chaumukhi Mahadeva**, the 4-faced Lord Siva at Kamman Chapra. Another is at

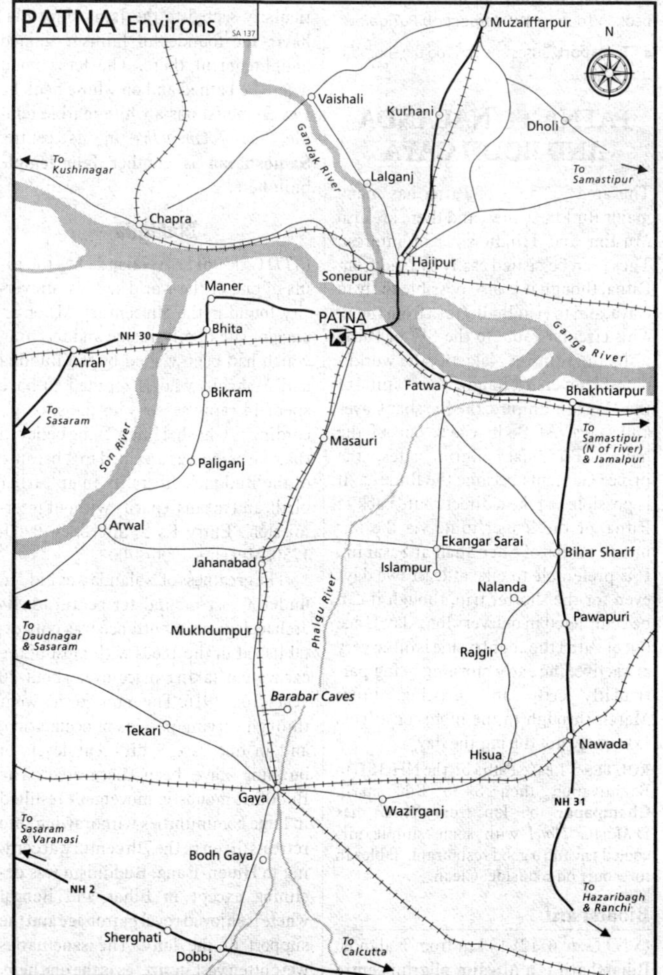

Basarh, by Bavan Pokhar an ancient tank, which was built in the Pala period and enshrines beautiful images of Hindu deities.

Museum Vaishali Archeological Museum. 1000-1700; closed Fri. Free. The collection includes terracottas, pottery, seals, coins, sculpture and antiquities.

- **Accommodation** *Tourist Bungalow*, 10 beds and dorm. *PWD Inspection Bungalow*.
- **Transport** Buses and taxis do the short trip from Patna.

PATNA TO NALANDA AND BODH GAYA

The area to the S of Patna has many major Buddhist sites, and there are also Muslim and Hindu sites of interest. These can be visited easily by road from Patna, though it is also possible to fly to Gaya, and to visit Bodh Gaya from there. This circular route to the SW of Patna visits the ruins of Nalanda, the world's oldest University, Rajgir, royal capital of the Magadh Empire, the Barabar Caves and Gaya. At Bodh Gaya, one of the holiest Buddhist pilgrim sites, the prince Gautama became the Buddha. It is possible to take a direct route back to Patna, or the longer route via the immense tombs of Sher Shah at Sasaram. It is preferable to take at least two days even for the shorter trip, though it can be completed in one very long day. Once out of Patna the countryside is often very attractive, the early morning being particularly crisp and inviting. From March through to the monsoon it gets extremely hot during the day.

ROUTES Leave Patna on the NH 31 E to Bakhtiyapur, then S to Biharsharif. **Champapur** (50 km from Patna) has D *Mamta Hotel* with some simple air-cooled rm and a good restaurant. Tables in forecourt on roadside. Clean.

Biharsharif

(*STD Code* 6112) 13 km from Nalanda, Biharsharif is a Muslim pilgrim centre particularly during the annual Urs fair. The *dargah* (tomb) of Mukhdoom Shah, a 13th century Muslim saint and Malik Ibrahim Baya are sited here. It remained an Islamic cultural centre up to the 16th century.

Pawapuri

(Also **Apapuri** – 'sinless town'), is particularly sacred to the Jains since Mahavir, the founder of Jainism, gained enlightenment there. The lotus pond where he bathed and on whose bank he was cremated has a white marble temple, the *Jalamandir*, in its centre. **Samosharan** is another Jain temple built here.

Nalanda

(*STD Code* 061194) Nalanda has the ruins of one of the world's oldest university, found in the 5th century AD on an ancient site of pilgrimage and teaching which had been visited by the Buddha and Mahavir, who is reputed to have spent 14 rainy seasons on the site. According to Ghosh, Hiuen Tsang believed that the name was ascribed to it because of the Buddha's liberality in an earlier birth, and means 'charity without intermission'. Entry Rs 5. Site open 0900-1750, Museum 1000-1700.

The greatness of Nalanda was hidden under a vast mound for centuries. Its archaeological importance was only established in the 1860s with most of the excavation taking place over about 20 years from 1916. The monasteries went through varying periods of occupation, and in one case 9 different levels of building have been discovered. The Buddhist monastic movement resulted in large communities withdrawing into retreats. Even in the 7th century, according to Hiuen-Tsang, Buddhism was declining except in Bihar and Bengal where it enjoyed royal patronage and the support of the laity. The sanctuaries were often vast in size, as is the one here, which is nearly 500m in length and 250m in width.

Places of interest

The remains of 11 monasteries and several *chaityas* (temples) built by kings of different periods mainly in red brick, have been found as well as a large stairway, a library, lecture halls, dormitories, cells, ovens and wells. The buildings are in several storeys and tiers on massive terraces of solid brick, with stucco decorations of the Buddha as well as Hindu divinities, and secular figures of warriors, dancers, musicians, animals and birds. Several of the monasteries are aligned S to N, with a guarded entrance on the W wall with the monks' cells around a central quadrangular courtyard with a wide verandah which was replaced by a high wall in some cases. Opposite the entrance, a shrine is found in the centre of the E wall which must have contained an impressive image. Drains are found which carried sewage to the E and there are staircases giving access to the different storeys. The row of temples to the W of the monasteries left an open space where there were possibly smaller shrines.

The monasteries are numbered from 1 to 11 from S to N, the path from the gate entering between monasteries 1 and 4 at the S end of the site. The path goes W, across an open space to the largest of the temples, **No 3**. Almost certainly this was originally constructed by Asoka, but his stupa was enlarged several times. The earliest temples were small structures, completely incorporated into the successively larger mounds. It is believed that the N facing shrine chamber on top once contained an enormous Buddha image. The top gives a commanding view over the remains as a whole, particuarly impressive in the evening light.

Returning E, Monasteries **1, 1A** and **1B** are the most important of the monastery group. Ghosh suggests that the lower monastery was built by a Sumatran king in the reign of the third king of the Pala dynasty, Devapala, between AD 810-850. The excavated cells demonstrate the existence of an earlier monastery underneath, probably after the earlier walls had at least partially collapsed. It is possible to walk around all three of these southern monasteries. **Monastery 4**, immediately to the N of the entrance path, was also built on an

The First Monasteries

It is assumed that the Gupta Emperors were responsible for the first monasteries. In the 7th century Hiuen-Tsang spent 12 years, both as a student and a teacher, at Nalanda which once had over 3,000 teachers and philosophers. The monks were supported by 200 villages, and a library of 9 million manuscripts attracted men from countries as far flung as Java, Sumatra, Korea and Japan and China. Great honour was attached to a Nalanda student and admission was restricted with 7 or 8 out of 10 applicants failing to gain a place.

I-Tsing, another Chinese scholar, arrived here in AD 673 and also kept detailed records, describing the severe life-style of the monks. The divisions of the day were measured by a water-clock, and the syllabus involved the study of Buddhist and Brahmanical scriptures, logic, metaphysics, medicine and Sanskrit grammar. Asoka built a monastery, King Harshavardhana donated a 26 m high copper image of the Buddha, and Kumaragupta endowed a college of fine arts. The University flourished until the 12th century when the Afghan Bhaktiar Khalji sacked it in 1199, burning and pillaging and driving the surviving residents into hiding. It was the end of living Buddhism in India until the modern revival.

earlier collapsed monastery.

There are several interesting features in the other monasteries: double rows of cells in **Monastery** 5, brick courtyards and two sets of double ovens in the upper courtyard of **No 6**, and the evidence of 3 successive monasteries built on the same site at **No** 7. There is an imposing shrine and unique doorway in **No 8**, striking drains in **No 9** and arched doorways in **No 10**. The fragments of 25 stone pillars were recovered from the ruins of **No 11**, which stood 1m apart and at a height of more than 2m. Ghosh suggests that fire was a recurrent hazard, and every monastery was deserted and re-occupied.

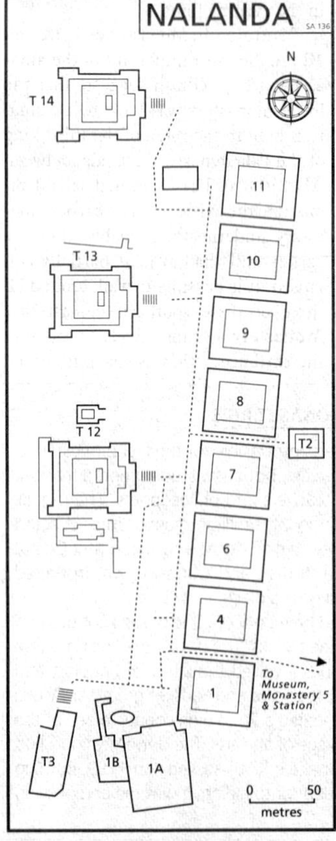

In addition to the monasteries and the main temple, 4 other temples have been excavated. **Temples 12, 13 and 14** are in a line stretching N from the main temple. They all have a square outline, and originally had large Buddha images, now destroyed. On the N of **Temple 13** a brick smelting furnace was discovered, while the niches of the pedestal of the image in **Temple 14** contain the only example of mural painting in Nalanda. Little remains.

Temple site 2, E of Monasteries 7 and 8, and reached by a path between them, has a sculpted dado with over 200 panels showing a wide variety of scenes depicting Hindu deities. The panels probably date from the 6th or 7th centuries AD, and may have been brought in from another temple.

In addition to the monasteries and temples there are several images, including the Buddha, and Marachi (the Buddhist goddess of the dawn).

New excavations to the NE in **Sarai Mound** show evidence of a brick temple with frescoes of elephants and horses of the Pala period. The villages of **Bargaon** and **Begampur** to the N and **Jagadishpur** to the SW contain several impressive Buddhist and Hindu images.

FURTHER READING The Archaeological Survey's booklet by A Ghosh gives excellent detailed description of the site and the Museum.

Nava Nalanda Mahavihar

2 km from the principal site, is a post-graduate institute for research into Buddhism and Pali literature set up by the Govt of Bihar and has many rare manuscripts. It is now the site of the Indira Gandhi Open University. There is a colourful **Thai temple** built in the 1980s. **Kundalpur** 1.6 km N of Nalanda, is believed by the Digambara sect of Jains to be the birth place of Mahavir.

Museum

Archaeological Museum. 1000-1700. Rs 5 for complex. It has a good collection of antiquities, Buddhist and Hindu stone sculptures, terracottas and bronzes particularly of the Gupta and Pala periods and also includes coins, inscriptions, plaques, seals, pottery and samples of burnt rice found in the ruins at Nalanda as well as Rajgir. Nalanda was the centre of a tantric cult, well-represented in the sculpted remains.

Local information

● Accommodation

Hotels are better in Rajgir. **D** *Gautam Vihar* Bihar Tourism. Some a/c and dorm. Simple but the best. **E** *Tathaghat Vihar*. Modest ordinary rm. **F** *Ajatashatru Vihar*. Very basic, dorm only. **F** PWD *Rest House*. Very spartan rm. Reservation: Div Officer, PWD. **F** *Inspection Bungalow*,. Meals to order. Contact Supt, Archaeological Survey of India, Eastern Survey, Patna. Also **F** *Burmese Rest House*, beyond museum, **F** *Youth Hostel* and rm at the *Pali Institute*.

● Tourist Office

In Bargaon, Nava Nalanda, nr Bus Stand.

● Transport

Local: Cycle-rickshaws and tongas outside the Tourist Information Centre. **Bus**: Nalanda has regular bus services from Patna (90 km N) with the nearest airport, and Rajgir from (15 km) with the nearest railway station.

ROUTES Continue S out of Nalanda to Rajgir (15 km) or Rajagriha (Royal Palace). The road passes through **Shilau**which is famous locally for *Khaja*, a sweetmeat (pastry soaked in syrup).

Rajgir

(*Pop* 24,000) The capital of the Magadhan empire before Pataliputra, Rajgir was occupied from around 800 BC. Encircled by forested hills it is held sacred by both Buddhists and Jains for its association with the Buddha and Mahavir, who taught here for many years.

Places of interest

The Buddha is believed to have converted the Magadhan King Bimbisara on **Gridhrakuta**, the 'Hill of Vultures'. It was one of his favourite places, and he delivered many important sermons there. The old stone road leading up the hill is attributed to Bimbisara. It was used by Hiuen-Tsang in the 7th century and still provides the best access. Rock-cut steps lead to the 2 natural caves; plaques and Buddhist shrines were found in the area, now in Nalanda Museum. The first Buddhist Council was held in the **Saptaparni Cave** on Vaibhara Hill, 6 months after the Buddha's death, and his teachings were written down for the first time. On the way to the Saptaparni Cave is the **Pippala stone house** or *Machan* (watch tower), an extraordinary structure built of blocks of stone. It is about 24m sq and 7m high. On all sides there are small cells which may have been shelters for guards later used by monks.

The 40 km cyclopean dry stone wall that encircled the ancient city is in ruins as is the 5th century BC **Ajatasatru Fort**. The outer wall was built with blocks of stone, 1m to 1.5m long, with smaller boulders in its core. In places it was 4m high and 5.5m wide, finished at the top with smaller stones. Bastions strengthened the wall on the outer side while on the inner side there were ramps giving access to the top with watch-towers added later. Of the 32 large gates (and 64 small ones) mentioned in ancient texts, only one to the N can be seen. Of the inner city wall which was about 5 km long and roughly pentagonal, only a section to the S survives with 3 gaps through which the old roads ran. A part of the deep moat which was cut into the rock can also be seen. In the valley is a circular brick structure, about 6m high, decorated with stucco figures all around it, which had an old Jain shrine called **Maniyar Math.**

Nearby is **Venuvana**, the bamboo grove where the Buddha spent some time. Excavations have revealed a room and some stupas, and the Karanda Tank where he bathed, now a deer park with a small zoo. Also some Muslim graves. There is little to see. To the S of Venuvana there are Jain and Hindu temples. Ruins of Buddha's favourite retreat within the valley, the **Jivakamarvana Monastery** (4th-3rd century BC) with elliptical walls have been found with remains of 4 halls and several rooms.

The **Visva Santi Stupa** was built by the Japanese on top of **Ratnagiri**. Dedicated to world peace, the large white monastery has 4 golden statues of the Buddha representing his birth, enlightenment, preaching and death. Cable car (0.6 km) to the **Nipponzan Myohoji**. (when working). Usually 0900-1300, 1500-1700. Rs 6 return. Good views.

Mahavir spent 14 rainy seasons in Rajagriha and the 20th Tirthankara was born here so today Rajgir is also a major Jain pilgrimage centre, with temples on most of the hill-tops. It has also become a popular resort, the hot springs being a special attraction. Non-Hindus are not allowed into the temple near the baths. The Kund Market nearby where buses stop, has shops, stalls and local eating places.

Local information

● Accommodation

A *Centaur Hokke*, primarily for Japanese pilgrims. 110 comfortable rm. Impressive building, 1 km from Bus Stop. Open Nov-Mar. Near by Bihar Tourism has built a new **D** *Tourist Hotel* with 90 simple rm. Open Nov-Mar. 2 Govt *Tourist Bungalows*, rm with bath. Contact Bihar State Tourism Information Centre, Fraser Rd, T 25295. **F** PWD *Rest House* and *Youth Hostel*. **D** *Dist Board Rest House* and *Inspection Bungalow*, 1 km SW of rly station. Reservations: Board Engineer, Biharsharif. Several *Jain Dharamshalas* nr the station.

● Places to eat

Green Hotel in the corner is the only one rec. Very simple – tables in verandah with fans better than indoors.

● Tourist Information Centre

2 Kund Market, T 36.

● Transport

Bus: to Patna (105 km) and Gaya. Auto-rickshaw or Tonga to Nalanda.

ROUTES From Rajgir to Hasua, then turn right along the State Highway to **Gaya** (92 km). **Bajidgunj**, en route, has extraordinary granite outcrops which mark the N edge of the peninsula where it sinks below the alluvium of the Ganga. Sunday fair at the temple here.

Gaya

(*Pop* 294,000, *STD Code* 0631) Gaya is the city which Vishnu is said to have blessed with power to absolve all temporal sins in the same way as Varanasi is sanctified. It draws believers to the many sacred shrines, especially during the monsoon in Sep-Oct at Pitrapaksh Tarpan, where prayers are offered for the dead before pilgrims take a dip in the seasonal holy river Phalgu, having brought with them *pindas* or funeral rice cakes and sweets. Cremations take place on funeral pyres in the burning ghats along the river. The town is on slightly raised ground in the valley between the Ramsila and Pretsila Hills.

Places of interest

There are several old Buddhist temples and monastery remains around Gaya. In the centre of the town is the **Vishnupad Temple** supposed to have been built over Vishnu's footprint which is imprinted on a rock inside set in a silver basin.

The 30m high temple has 8 rows of beautifully carved pillars which support the mandapa or pavilion which were refurbished in 1787 by Rani Ahalyabai of Indore. Hindus only are permitted into the sanctum. Within the temple grounds stands the immortal banyan tree *Akshayabat* where the final puja for the dead takes place. It is believed to be the one under which the Buddha meditated for 6 years. 1 km SW is Brahmayoni Hill with its 1000 stone steps which lead to a vantage point for viewing both Gaya and Bodh Gaya.

The **Surya temple** at **Deo** 20 km away, dedicated to the Sun God, attracts large crowds in Nov when *Chhatt* Puja is celebrated.

Excursion

Barabar Caves (35 km N). The 22 km track leading to the caves in the impressive granite hill turns E off the main road to Patna (short route via Jahanabad) at **Belagunj** (½ hr from Gaya, 2 hr from Patna) where buses stop. From here allow 4 hr to walk up (45 km by 4-wheel drive). The caves inspired the setting of EM Forster's *A Passage to India*. They date from the 3rd century BC and are the earliest examples of rock-cut sanctuaries. With the tolerance required by Buddhism, Asoka permitted non-Buddhists to practise their religion. They created these rock-cut temples.

The whale-backed quartzite gneiss hill stands in wild and rugged country. Inscriptions reveal that, on instructions from Asoka, 4 chambers were excavated, cut and chiselled to a high polish by the stone masons, retreats for ascetics who belonged to a sect related to Jainism. Percy Brown pointed out that the extraordinary caves, particularly the *Lomas Rishi* and the *Sudama*, are exact copies of ordinary beehive shaped huts built with bamboo, wood and thatch. The barrel-vaulted chamber inside the *Sudama* is 10m long, 6m wide and 3.5m high which through a doorway leads to a circular cell of 6m diameter. The most impressive craftsmanship is seen on the façade of the *Lomas Rishi* which replicates the horse-shoe shaped gable end of a wooden structure with 2 lunettes which have very fine carvings of lattice-work and rows of elephants paying homage to Buddhist stupas. Excavation is incomplete as there was a possibility of the cave collapsing. There is also a Siva temple on the Siddheshwar peak.

Nagarjuna Hill 1 km NE from Barabar there are 3 further rock-cut sanctuaries. The *Gopi* (Milk-maid's) cave has the largest chamber measuring 13.5 x 6m and 3m in height. Inscriptions date these to about 50 years after the excavations at Barabar and clearly indicate that they were cut when Asoka's grandson Dasaratha acceded to the Mauryan throne.

Museum

Gaya Museum 1000-1700, closed Mon. Free. Collection of sculptures, bronzes, terracottas, paintings, arms and manuscripts.

Local information

● Accommodation

Mostly very basic with non a/c rm. **D** *Siddharth International*, off Station Rd, T 21254. Some a/c rm. Modern, but already slightly shabby, noisy and overpriced. Despite the picture of the fasting Buddha emblazoned on rm service menu, the food is probably the best in Gaya; cheap breakfast. "Art and queer gift shop" on 1st flr. Despite oddities, still easily the best hotel. **E** *Surya*, Swarajpuri Rd, between Samrat Hotel and bus stand. T 24004. Some rm with bath and hot water. Cleanest of the cheap hotels, and quieter as it is away from the extremely noisy railway station. **F** *Ajatshatru*, opp Rly station, T 22514. Gloomy and noisy, but popular ground fl restaurant has large menu, cheap but good basic food.*Sri Kailash Guest House*, N Azad Park. *Shyam*, Ramna Rd, T 22416; *Samrat*, Swarajpuri Rd, T 20770. *Pali Rest House*l Some rm with bath. *Railway Retiring Rooms* at Gaya Jn. 6 rm, 2 a/c. Several large *Dharamshalas* for pilgrims.

● Places to eat

Sujata in *Hotel Ajatsatru* is the best; *Station View* and *Punjab* on Station Rd (Indian).

● Tourist office

Bihar Govt, Gaya Jn Rly Station Main Hall, T 20155. 0600-2100.

● Travel agent & tour company

Sakun Tourist View, Shyam Bazar, Ramna Rd, T 22416, offers tours.

● Transport

Local: Tourist **taxis** from *Sri Kailash Hotel*, *Hotel Shyam* and Ramna Rd, T 22416. Negotiate rate before journey (major sites have fixed rates). **Auto-rickshaws, cycle-rickshaws** and horse-drawn *tongas* easily available. The buses, mini-buses and auto-rickshaws which run services to Bodh Gaya from the Zila School Bus Stand are always very crowded. Bus, Rs 5, auto-rickshaw, Rs 12. Six seater rickshaw at Rs 3 per seat better value than bus at Rs 2.50. You may prefer a cycle rickshaw for Rs 40-50 if you can persuade a driver to take you. It's worth it for the relative peace and comfort. No transport to Bodh Gaya after 1900.

Train: Superfast and express trains connect the city to other regions of the country as it is on the Grand Chord line of the Delhi-Calcutta section of E Railway. **Calcutta (H)**: *AC Exp*, 2382 (AC/CC&AC/II), W,F,Su; 0930, 8½ hr; *Kalka-Haora Mail*, 2312 (AC/II), daily, 2340, 9 hr; *Rajdhani Express*, 2302 (AC/CC&AC/II), M,Tu,W,F,Sa; 0451, 6¼ hr; **Varanasi**: *AC Exp*, 2381 (AC/CC&AC/II), Tu,Th,Sa, 1659, 4 hr; **Delhi (ND)**: *Rajdhani Express*, 2301 (AC/CC&AC/II), M,Tu,Th,F,Su; 2151, 12 hr; *Puri-New Delhi Exp*, 2815 (AC/II), Tu,Th,F,Su, 0129, 15½ hr; *Haora-Kalka Mail*, 2311 (AC/II), daily, 0247, 20 hr; **Patna**, *Palamau Express*, 3347,daily, 0410, 2¼ hr; *Hatia Patna Express*, 8626,daily, 1424, 2¼hr; **Puri**, *Neelachal Express*, 8476,Tu,F,Su, 2310, 19¼ hr; **Agra**, *Chambal Express*, 2159, Sa,Su, 0011, 20½ hr; Gaya Jn Rly Station. Enquiries and Reservations: T 20031. 0900-1600.

Bus: Bihar STC buses operate services to Patna and other tourist centres at Rajgir, Ranchi and Hazaribagh from the Bus Stand opp Gandhi Maidan. Private coaches run to Calcutta.

ROUTES Continue S from Gaya to reach Bodh Gaya, (13 km).

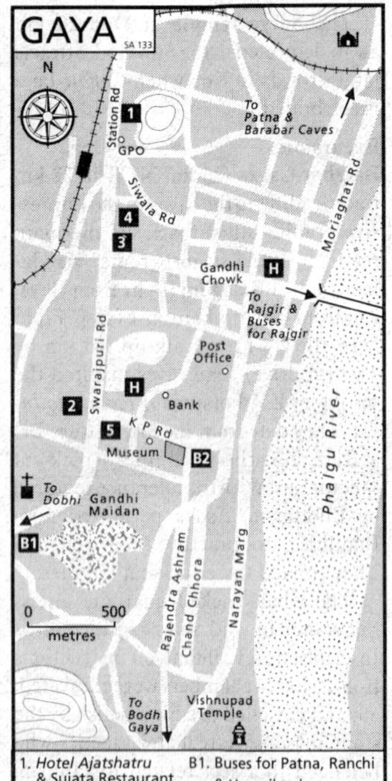

Bodh Gaya

Bodh Gaya, a quiet village near the river Niranjana (Phalgu), is one of the holiest Buddhist pilgrimage centres since it was under the Bo tree here that Gautama, the prince, attained enlightenment to become the Buddha. The road S into the small town runs along the broad sandy river bed, shaded by Kahua, mango and tamarind trees. The site itself is very flat, while around the village are date palms, still cut into distinctively notched shapes to collect sap for making local sugar. Land values in town are astonishingly high – up to US$250,000 per ha in the town centre.

BASICS *Population*: 22,000. *Altitude*: 113m. *Climate*: Summer Max 47°C, Min 28°C; Winter Max 28°C, Min 4°C. *Annual rainfall*: 1860 mm.

When the Tibetans arrive *en masse* in January the area N of the bus station resembles a spiritual rock festival or medieval army camp. Informal camps spring up, with tents serving as restaurants and accommodation. The food is smokey and there are long waits, but it is full of colour. Unfortuunately the air is heavily polluted by badly serviced buses, making a walk along the road like a stroll along the M25 at Heathrow.

Places of interest

The original **Bodhi tree** was said to have been destroyed by Asoka before he was converted, and others which replaced it also died, although the present tree is believed to have grown from a sapling from the original stock, see page 1336. The story of Prince Mahinda, the Emperor's son describes him carrying a sapling from the sacred Bo or pipal tree to Sri Lanka when Buddhism spread there, which in turn produced a sapling which was brought back to Bodh Gaya. The red sandstone slab, the **Vajrasila**, under the tree marks the place where Gautama sat in meditation. Today pilgrims tie pieces of coloured cloth on its branches when they come to pray.

Mahabodhi Temple Entry Rs 5, Cameras Rs 5. Asoka erected a shrine near the Bodhi tree which was replaced by this temple in the 2nd century which in turn went through several alterations. The temple on a high and broad plinth, with a soaring 54m high pyramidal spire with a square cross-section and 4 smaller spires, houses a gilded image of the Buddha in the *asana* (pose) signifying enlightenment. The smaller spires appear to have been added to the original when Burmese Buddhists attempted extensive rebuilding in the 14th century.

An ornately carved stone railing in *bas relief,* once believed to have been erected by Asoka, surrounds the temple on 3 sides and several carved Buddhist stupas depict tales from the Buddha's early life. Unlike earlier circular railings this had to conform to the quadrangle of the temple structure and its height of 2m and lighter proportions together with the quality of its carving suggests that it was constructed in the Sunga period in the early part of 1st century BC. The entrance is through a *torana* or ornamental archway on the E side. The lotus pond where the Buddha may have bathed is to the S of the temple. To the N is the *Chankramana*, a raised platform dating from the 1st century with lotus flowers carved on it, which marks the consecrated promenade where the Buddha walked back and forth while meditating on whether he should reveal his Message to the world. This appears to have been later converted into a covered passage with pillars of which only one survives. Numerous attempts to restore the temple have obscured the original. Fragments are now housed in various museums.

Animeshlochana is another sacred spot where the Buddha stood to gaze in gratitude at the Bodhi tree for a week. The temple also attracts Hindu pilgrims since the Buddha is considered to be one of the *avatars* or incarnations of Vishnu. Pilgrims from many lands have built their own temples here so there are Tibetan, Thai, Japanese Chinese, Bhutanese and Burmese shrines to visit.

Buddha Statue A giant stone statue 20m tall on a 5m base stands at the end of the road, beyond the Japanese Temple. It was 'opened' by the Dalai Lama in 1989. The modern 2-storey, spotless **Japanese Temple** with beautiful polished marble floors has gold images of the Buddha. Open 0700-1200, 1400-1800. The **Tibetan Temple and Monastery** next door, (1938) is ornately painted and has a *Dharma Chakra* or wheel of law which must be turned 3 times when praying for forgiveness of sins. A large 2m metal ceremonial drum in red and gold is also on display. Opposite is the Nipponji Temple Complex with a free clinic, monastery and a Peace Bell (rung from 0600-1200 and at 1700). Returning to the Mahabodhi Temple you will pass the Bhutan Temple, a typical pagoda style Thai Temple and a Bangladesh Temple under construction.

Magadha University, an international centre for studies in history, culture and philosophy is less than 1 km from the Mahabodhi Temple.

Museum

Archaeological Museum. 1000-1700 but closed Fri. Free. The collection of antiquities includes sculptures and fragments of railings and posts from the original temple as well as gold, bronze

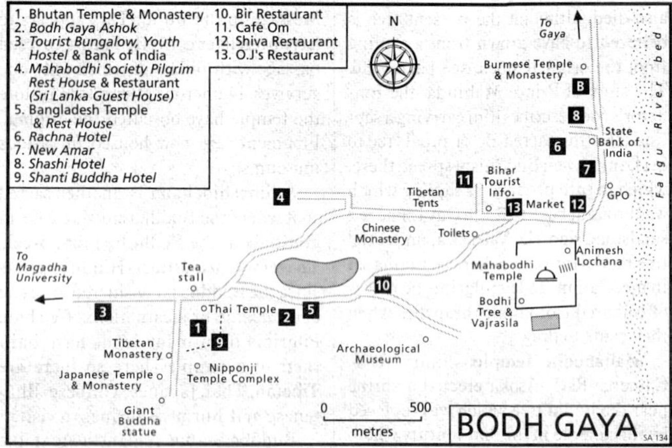

and stone images of the Buddha and Hindu deities.

Local information

● Accommodation

B *Bodh Gaya Ashok* nr Museum, T 22708 (Gaya). 30 rm, 20 a/c. Good food in the restaurant, pleasant building, far from luxurious and no pool. BSTDC **D** *Tourist Bungalow II*, nr Thai Temple. 7 rm. Meals on order. **E** *Shanti Buddha* is off the main rd behind the Bhutan monastery. Small **E** *Bangladesh Resthouse* under construction. **E** *Bhutan Monastery* (Druk Do Nagcholing Monastery). 18 rm in guest houses. **E** *Burma Vihar*F255D Dble and dorm, Very cheap, mosquito nets provided. Eat at Pole Pole opposite. **E** *Mahabodhi Society Pilgrim Rest House* (Sri Lanka GH), T 42. 6 rm, 3 dorm. Veg canteen. **F** *Tourist Bungalow* I, nr Thai Temple, 9 small clean dorm with 6 to 8 beds each.

The **Burmese and Japanese monasteries** also provide spartan accommodation primarily for pilgrims from their respective countries. All the religious organisations expect guests to conform to certain rules of conduct and good behaviour. Res: Contact Monk-in-Charge. On Main Rd nr the Temple there are a few very simple hotels: *Rachna*, *New Amar* and *Shashi*.

● Places to eat

The *Ashok Hotel* has a good restaurant. On the road up to the Ashok a good tent restaurant does a limited but very good Indian menu. Opens late, excellent hot breads. You can get good simple western food at the popular *Shiva*, in the market, diagonally opposite entrance to stupa, but food not special. Indian at *Kalpana* nr Mahabodhi Temple. Also clean is the *Pole Pole*. Excellent management, good though not exceptional food. Rec. Far and away the best Tibetan restaurant is the *Cafe Om*. Really excellent cakes and cheesecakes, and a stall selling very cheap attractive items. Very highly rec. *Gautam's*, tent opposite Burmese Vihar, has apple strudel and cinnamon rolls. *Roberto's*, next to the Tibetan tent, sells Italian food. There is a good clean little *Orange Juice stall* opposite the stupa. Chinese food at the Sri Lanka Guest House.

● Services

There is a **bank, post-office** and **police station** on the Main Road. The Post Office is open M-Sat, 1000-1700. The **Bank of India** in the Tourist Bungalow changes cash (up to US$100) M-F 1030-1430, Sat 1030-1230. A few autorickshaws and plenty of cycle-rickshaws and tongas are available.

● Shopping

Miniature paintings are specially prepared to be sold as mementos. **Mahabodhi Temple Market Complex** and the **New Tibetan Market** have a number of shops selling the softstone articles handcrafted in Patthalkatti nearby. Also small images of the Buddha, Hindu divinities and some tableware.

● Tourist office

Govt of Bihar, 34-35 Mahabodhi Temple Market Complex, T 26. 1000-1700.

● **Transport**

Note If you are travelling to Bodh Gaya via Gaya and arrive in Gaya after dark, the Government recommends you stay in Gaya and travel in daylight because of robbery. Dobbi, 22 km away is on the Delhi-Calcutta NH2. Calcutta, 482 km, Patna 125 km to the N. **Air**: Patna, 125 km, is the nearest airport with regular flights to all major cities by Indian Airlines. Calcutta, 482 km, has an international airport. Buses (Rs 5) and auto-rickshaws (Rs 12) which take about ½ hour from Gaya are usually very crowded. **Train**: Gaya, 16 km away has the nearest station. **Bus**: Bihar SRTC has bus services to Gaya, Patna, Nalanda and Rajgir. The main bus stand is opp the Mahabodhi Temple.

Muslim sites

A round tour from Patna can continue by visiting Sasaram and Maner. Continue S from Bodh Gaya about 20 km to Sherghati on NH 2. Turn right and travel W approx 100 km. You reach Sasaram 19 km after crossing the River Son.

Sasaram

(*STD Code* 06184) The driving force behind the erection of the tombs at Sasaram was **Sher Shah Suri** who around 1535 obtained the services of the master-builder Aliwal Khan to construct a tomb for his father **Hasan Khan**. This laid the foundations for the second tomb for Sher Shah himself – see page 49. The first imitated the octagonal structure and walled enclosure of the earlier Lodi tombs but lacked a plinth and had rather a plain appearance without any ornamentation in its middle storey. What followed however was extraordinary not only in its size, which was 75m wide at its base and 45m high, but also in its conception and execution. The mausoleum was set in an artificial lake 430m sq so it appeared to float while it cast its reflection on the water. It is approached by a causeway through first entering a guard room on the N bank. This may have been an afterthought as it would appear that the original plan may have been for visitors to approach by barge from the ghat on the E side of the tank.

Percy Brown describes the construction in 5 stages, starting with the lower 2 on a square plan rising out of the water and forming a terrace with pillared pavilions in each corner with steps down to the water. The third is octagonal with 3 arches on each side with doorways to enter the mausoleum except to the W where the *mihrab* is positioned, the whole being surrounded by a verandah. The storey immediately above follows the same horizontal plan with its simple plainness broken by ornamental kiosks

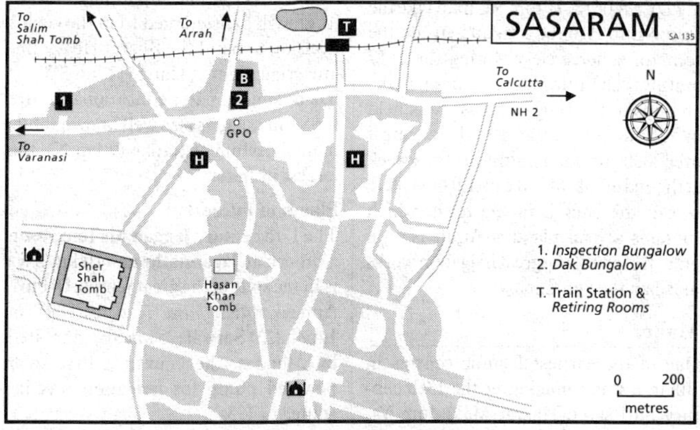

at each of the 8 angles. The final stage is the dome itself which cleverly loses the angles and arises circular leading up to the lotus at the top. The tomb chamber which is 20m wide thus rises to a height of 27.5m without a break. A curious fact is that the base itself was not correctly positioned for the faces of the structure to coincide with the points of the compass but with a clever correction of 8 degrees, the planned orientation of the upper storeys was achieved!

The use of fine grey sandstone for construction, quarried at Chunar nearby gives the tomb a fitting sense of gravity. However, a closer examination reveals that geometrical patterns in red, yellow, blue and white adorned the exterior in places and the dome itself was painted white with a golden lotus at its crown.

The third tomb for Sher Shah's son **Salim** was to have been even larger and again set within a lake, but was never completed because of his untimely death. There is a memorial to the architect Aliwal Khan and a further tomb to Bhakiyar Khan in **Chainpur** nearby.

• **Accommodation** F *Shershah Vihar* Some single and dorm.There are 2 *Rest Houses*, a Govt *Youth Hostel* and small hotels. **Tourist Information Centre**, T 203.

Arrah

(*STD Code* 06182) From Sasaram take the road NE to Piro (60 km) and Arrah, the scene of a fierce siege during the 1857 mutiny. The Little House at Arrah, in the grounds of the Judge's House, was held by 50 Sikh and 12 English soldiers against over 2000 attacking mutineers for a week at the end of Jul 1857. It can still be visited, as can the church in the town, which contains several plaques. Arrah is on a branch of one of the great irrigation works in Bihar, the Son Canals.

Maner

One of the earliest Islamic centres in Bihar, it was named after the 13th century Sufi saint, Hazrat Makhdum Yahiya Maneri. His tomb known as the Badi Dargah is a very sacred shrine. The Chhoti Dargah, a mausoleum commemorating the Muslim saint's disciple Shah Daulat is famous for its architectural interest. An annual *Urs fair* is held here. From Maner it is 30 km to Patna.

SOUTH BIHAR AND THE CHOTA NAGPUR PLATEAU

Ranchi, the area's main town, is in beautiful countryside with many waterfalls and lakes. The Betla and Hazaribagh Wildlife Sanctuaries support tiger, leopard, elephant and many other species. There are several lakes, some suitable for boating and swimming.

Ranchi

Population: 614,000. *Altitude:* 658m. *STD Code:* 0651 Once the summer capital of Bihar, the town still attracts holiday makers for its location on higher ground in the heart of the Chota Nagpur tribal country and its proximity to beautiful waterfalls and lakes. Like many middle ranking Indian towns it has been growing very fast in the last 20 years, though it has few of the public buildings which might be expected to accompany its size and present importance. Part of its growth has stemmed from the Govt's decision to build the Bharat Heavy Engineering plant at Hatia (11 km SW). It has become a major educational centre for S Bihar and is also well known for its mental asylum at Kanke (9 km N), the largest in India.

Places of interest

The 17th century **Jagganath Temple** on a hillock at **Jagannathpur**, (10 km SW) is in the style of the great temple in Puri. Annual *ratha yatra* (car festival) in Jun/Jul. At **Sarwal** (25 km SE) inhabited by Mundas, the country's first solar powered pump for irrigation was installed in 1981.

Excursions

There are several very attractive short excursions that can be made from the town. The Subhanarekha River, which rises SE of the town, is interrupted by several impressive waterfalls, within easy range of Ranchi. **Hundru Falls** (45 km E of Ranchi) is formed by the 100m drop of Subarnarekha river, particularly impressive just after the monsoons. You can picnic and bathe in the pools at the bottom. The other falls in the area include **Johna Falls** (40 km E on the Purulia road) and **Dassamghagh Falls** (34 km). A local Munda belief holds that the god of the waterfall demands sacrifices. Irrespective of the truth of that belief, it is dangerous to bathe here, and several people have drowned. There is a teahouse at the Falls.

Museums

Ranchi Museum, Tribal Research Institute Bldg, Morabadi Rd, T 21160. 1030-1700. Closed Sun. Free. Collection of stone sculpture, terracottas and arms as well as ethnological objects at the Institute itself. Ranchi University, Dept of Anthropology, T 23695. 1100-1700. Closed Sun and Univ holidays. Free. Ethnographic collections of central Indian states and Andaman and Nicobar Islands.

Local information

● **Accommodation**

C *Ranchi Ashok*, Doranda, T 300037. 30 rm. Central a/c. Typical ITDC middle range hotel. Service can be slow. **C** *Kwality Inns*, Station Rd, T 26821. 36 rm most a/c. Restaurant, bar, exchange. **C** *SE Railway Hotel*, across Narrow Gauge lines. 22 rm in cottages. Restaurant, lawns, Tennis. Old-world feel. **C** *Yuvraj Palace*, Doranda, T 300805. 25 rm. Central a/c. Restaurant, bar, exchange, travel. **D** *Hindustan*, Makhija Towers, Main Rd, T 27988. 36 rm, some a/c. Central. Restaurant, shops, exchange, travel. **D** *Arya*, HB Rd, Lalpur, T 20355. 32 rm, some a/c. Good a/c restaurant with live music, travel,TV. **D** *Yuvraj*, Doranda, T 300403. 45 rm half a/c. A/c restaurant, exchange, travel. **D** *Chinar*, Main Rd, T 28867. 43 rm, some a/c. Restaurant, exchange. **D** *Raj*, 57A Main Rd, T 22613. 18 rm, some a/c. Central. Veg restaurant, snack bar, garden.

● **Places to eat**

Kwality on Main Rd is licensed.

● **Tourist Information Centre**

Court Compound, Circular Rd, T 20426.

● **Transport**

The distance by road is 598 km from Calcutta on the NH 33. **Air**: *Indian Airlines* has daily connections to **Patna**, 0815, ¾ hr, and on to **Delhi** (3¼ hr). To **Calcutta**, 1020, 1 hr. Indian Airlines, Main Rd. **Train**: to **Calcutta (H)**: *Hathia-Ranchi Haora Exp*, 8016, daily, 1659, 4 hr.

Wildlife sanctuaries

There are game reserves set in often stunningly beautiful and remote scenery on the Chota Nagpur plateau which can be easily reached from Ranchi.

This is one of the poorest areas of Bihar with extensive missionary activity.

Palamau National Park

Approach

Also known as the **Betla National Park**, in the Chhotanagpur plateau, it covers an area of 930 sq km of dry deciduous forest, mainly of *sal* and bamboo. *Climate:* Temp range: 48°C to 3°C, rainfall: 1200 mm. Open throughout the year. Best time: Oct-Apr.

There has been considerable deforestation. It is said to be a hunting ground of slavers who kidnap young children (often tribal) for the carpet weaving industry which needs their agile fingers. (Anti-Slavery Society estimate there are 100,000 slaves in India).

Wildlife

It is the 2nd major wildlife sanctuary in Bihar which was once the home of the extinct Indian **cheetah**. It is in the Project Tiger scheme and the world's first tiger census was taken here in 1932. The wildlife also includes leopard, gaur, sambar, muntjac and nilgai as well as the Indian wolf. The N Koel river and its tributary run through the park but in the summer animals become dependent on waterholes. The Flame of the Forest (*Butea monosperma*) and *mahua* flower also attract wildlife. The **Hathibajwa** wooden tower and Madhuchuhan hide, 'Tree Top' and 'hides' at **Kamaladah** are good vantage points. Elephants can be seen after the monsoons and until the waterholes begin to dry up in Mar. Over 200 species of water and woodland birds, the remains of two 16th century **forts** of Chero kings who once ruled from here, and hot springs, add to the interest.

Viewing

Jeeps for viewing the animals can be hired from the Forest Dept.

Park information

● Accommodation

Rest Houses at Kehr and Kechki provide basic but the new a/c ***Forest Lodge*** at Betla is more comfortable. Good deer viewing. Recent reports of no electricity or food. Reservations: Field Director, Project Tiger, Palamau, Daltonganj. For *Rest Houses* at Mundu, Garu, Chhipadohar and Baresand, contact Div Forest Officer, S Forest Div, Daltonganj. **E** ***Debjon***, is a newish hotel. Food available. Contains a large polystyrene model of Calcutta's Victoria Memorial!

● Transport

Air: through Ranchi (115 km). **Train:** from Daltongunj (25 km) or Chhipadohar (80 km). **Road:** take the road WNW out of Ranchi for Kuru (57 km), in Kuru fork right to Tori, then towards Daltonganj.

Hazaribagh wildlife sanctuary

Approach

Alt 615m, *STD Code* 06546 Named 'thousand gardens' and set amidst hilly and still forested country, visitors also use it as a base to see the wildlife sanctuary, waterfalls and the Tilaiya Dam (55 km) and Konar Dam (51 km).

Background

(*Alt* 550m) Set in hilly terrain, it is a part of the Chhota Nagpur plateau in tribal territory, forested with grass meadows and deep waterways and covering an area of 186 sq km. Best time: Feb–Apr.

Wildlife

The park supports some sambar in addition to nilgai, deer, chital, leopard, tiger, wild boar and wild cat. Roads permit easy access to large sections of the forest; the NH 33 takes you to the Pokharia gate (16 km from Hazaribagh). There are 10 watch towers for viewing but accommodation in *Forest Rest Houses* at Rajdewra and Harhad within the sanctuary area is very spartan. Reservations: Div Forest Officer, Hazaribagh.

Park information

● Accommodation

Tourist Lodge, Rajderwa, T 236. Reservations: Tourist Information Centre, Govt of Bihar, Hazaribagh or Bihar STDC, Beerchand Patel Path, Patna. ***Inspection Bungalow*** through the Collector, PWD, Hazaribagh. Inexpensive Indian style hotels with restaurants in the town centre nr the bazar. ***Magadh, Ashok*** and ***Standard***.

● Transport

Air: from Ranchi (115 km). **Train:** Hazaribagh Road Station (66 km). **Road:** N from Ranchi on the NH 33 through Ramgarh to Hazaribagh (26 km). NH 33 takes you up to the main gate at Pokharia.

INDUSTRIAL TOWNS OF BIHAR

Jamshedpur

Population 835,000, *STD Code:* 0657 130 km SE of Ranchi is a flourishing steel town, established as a planned township by the Parsi industrialist Jamshedji Tata in 1908. The first ingots from the Tata Iron and Steel Company (TISCO) rolled out in 1912. Located close to rich iron and coal deposits, there are also limestone quarries and some magnesite. Other industries in the town include locomotives and boilers, agricultural machinery and wire, chassis and tin plate. Visitors are permitted around some of the industrial complexes. The **National Metallurgical Laboratory** is a premier research institute. The town has retained much of its natural attraction, with its lakes and rivers enclosed by the Dolma hills, in spite of the pollution from its heavy plants. The town is split in two by the steel plant and rail sidings. **Keenan Stadium** in Bistupur, N end of town, is the venue for international cricket matches.

• **Accommodation** Several are 2-3 km from centre. **C** *Centre Point*, 2 Inner Circle Rd, Bistupur, T 21666, F 26759. 52 rm. Restaurant (residents only) in basement is rather gloomy, exchange, travel, good gym. Spacious lobby but indifferent service. **D** *Castle Guest House*, Contractors Area, Rd 2, T 23606, F 25435. 25 rm (some a/c). Rather cramped, rm service only. 24 hr checkout. **D** *Boulevard*, Sakehi Boulevard, Main Rd, Bistupur, T 25321, F 27743. 43 a/c rm. Restaurants (Indian, Chinese), bar, old fashioned, run down and noisy. **D** *Nataraj*, Sakehi Boulevard, Main Rd, Bistupur. *TISCO Guest House*, 7 B Rd mainly for company guests. Restaurant. In green residential area, very comfortable Country Club style. **E** *Sahu*, Gowshala Chowk, off Station Rd, nr Market. Simple, clean, Indian style hotel. Some a/c rm. Rm service only. There is also a *Circuit House*, *Dak Bungalow*, *Forest Rest House* and a *Lake House* on Dimna Lake. Several small hotels along Station Rd – turn right out of station.

• **Places to eat** *Kwality*, Main Rd, Bistupur, is the town's only good licensed restaurant which also sells confectionery.

• **Transport Local**: Autorickshaws (unmetered) charge inflated prices, eg Rly station to Bistupur Rs 35. **Train**: Tatanagar station is on the SE Rly on the Calcutta (Haora)-Bombay line. **To Calcutta**: *Steel Exp*, 8014, 0600. *Ispat Exp*, 8012, 1735. *Haora Mail*, 8001, 0327. **Puri** *Nilachal Exp*, 8476, M,W,Sa, 0725. **Patna** (Superfast) 8183, 0500. **Ranchi**, *Hatia Exp*, 8015, 0225. **Alleppey**, *Alleppey Exp*, 8189, 1530. **Bombay** *Haora-Bombay Exp*, 8019, 1020. *Getanjali Exp*, 2860, 1637. **Ahmedabad** *Haora-Ahmedabad Exp*, 8034, 0045.

Damodar Valley

Other centres have emerged along the Damodar Valley which cuts through the Chota Nagpur plateau through rocky, thickly wooded areas which are the home of the many aboriginal tribal people of Bihar. The Santals, Bedia, Khond, Munda and Oraon were the original inhabitants and though a few still live in isolated villages, most have been influenced by developments in the region to abandon their old lifestyle and many have joined the workforce in the industrial townships. The river valley has a number of hydro-electric power stations and with them large dams as at Maithon, Panchet and Tilaiya, run by the Damodar Valley Corporation. These have become centres offering recreational water-sports.

Tilaiya Dam This is a small dam, producing only 4000 kw, but it was the first to be built by the DVC for flood control. It is in a picturesque setting with its hills and reservoir with motor boats, swimming, terrace gardens and deer park. Accommodation: there is a fairly comfortable *Rest House* (6 rm) and

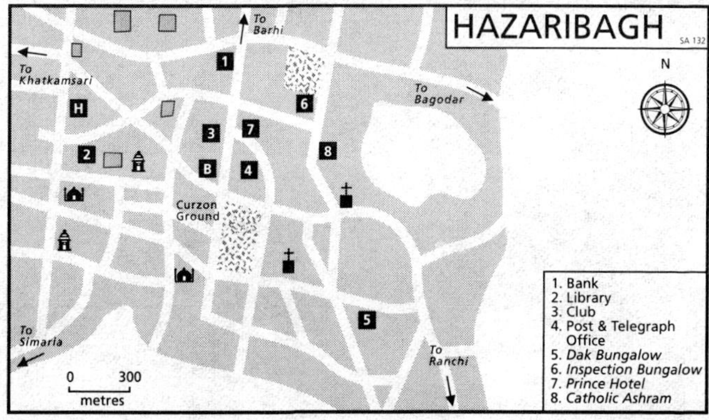

a simple *Tourist Bungalow* (8 rm). Reservations: Asst. Engineer, DVC, Tilaiya Hydel Station, Hazaribagh. Getting there: on the Patna-Ranchi Rd, it is 17 km from Barhi. Kodarma is the nearest rly station from where you can get a bus.

The main centres of activity in the Damodar Valley region are Dhanbad for coal, Chittaranjan for locomotives and Bokaro for steel.

Dhanbad

Population 818,000, *STD Code* 0326 Dhanbad has the highest concentration of mineral wealth in India with collieries, technical and research institutions in the town. Little to recommend it for the sightseer. The DVC Maithon and Panchet dams are within easy reach (about 50 km) and Topchanchi Lake is 37 km away.

Maithon Dam

This was designed for flood control but has the unique underground power station, the first in S Asia. Permits to visit are obtained from Assistant PRO for guided tours.

- **Accommodation** *Inspection Bungalow* 10 rm (6 a/c) or *Rest House* with 12 rm. Reservations: Exec Engineer, Maithon Div, DVC.

Panchet Dam 6 km with a hydro electric power station. Accommodation: The DVC *Inspection Bungalow* (4 rm) can be booked through PRO, DVC, Anderson House, Calcutta 700027. Getting there: the nearest convenient rly station for both is at Barakar (8 and 12 km away). There are buses or taxis from there, and from Dhanbad and Asansol (35 km).

ANDAMAN AND NICOBAR ISLANDS

CONTENTS

MAPS

The islands have brilliant tropical flora and are thickly forested with evergreen, deciduous rainforest and tropical trees, with mangrove swamps on the water's edge. Hilly in parts, they have superb palm-fringed white sand beaches and coral reefs. The sparkling clear water is excellent for snorkelling. The Andamans are also a bird-watchers' paradise with 242 species recorded and the wild life includes 46 species of mammals and 78 of reptiles.

SOCIAL INDICATORS *Population*: 188,700 (Urban 26%, Scheduled Tribes 12%). *Literacy*: M 74% F 66%. *Birth rate*: *Rural* 22:1000, *Urban* 16:1000. *Death rate*: *Rural* 7:1000, *Urban* 3:1000. *Religion*: *Hindu* 29%, *Christian* 4%, *Muslim* 1% *Animist* 66%.

Brilliant tropical flora and dense evergreen and deciduous tropical forest cover the sometimes hilly islands. Mangroves and palm-lined white sandy beaches lead down into coral filled seas whose crystal clear waters are ideal for snorkelling. The Andamans are also a bird-watchers' paradise, with 242 species recorded, while the islands also contain 46 species of mammals and 78 of reptiles.

Entry regulations

Foreigners arriving by air with tourist visas for India are allowed a maximum stay of 30 days on arrival at Port Blair, the principal harbour and capital but may not visit tribal areas or restricted islands including Nicobar. Permits are obtainable from Indian Missions abroad or the Ministry of Home Affairs (ANL Div.), Govt of India, N Block, 2nd Flr, New Delhi, 110 001, which may take up to 6 weeks by post. A personal visit may cut it down to 48 hours. Alternatively, Foreigners' Regional Registration Offices in Delhi, Calcutta and Bombay and the Chief Immigration Officer, 9 Village Road, off Nungambakkam High Rd, Madras can grant permits.

If you travel without a permit you must get your passport endorsed on arrival by the Duty Officer whom you may have to ask to see. Permits are given to individual foreigners to visit Port Blair, Havelock, Long Island, Neil Island, Mayabunder, Diglipur and Rangat, and stay overnight. Day visits are allowed to Jolly Buoy, Red Skin S Cinque Island, Mount Harriet and Madhuban. Ross Island, Chiriya Tapu and Wandoor are also open to day visitors. Check whether the rules have been relaxed for visiting the restricted islands.

Indians may visit the Andamans and Nicobars without a permit but must obtain a permit for restricted areas on arrival at Car Nicobar or from the Dy Commissioner (Nicobar) at Port Blair.

Environment

Land

Area 8249 sq km. The Andaman and Nicobar group is made up of a string of about 300 islands formed by a submarine mountain range which divides the Bay of Bengal from the Andaman Sea. The islands lie between latitudes 6° to 14° N (about level with Madras and longitudes 92°-94° E, a span of 725 km). The Andamans to the N are separated from

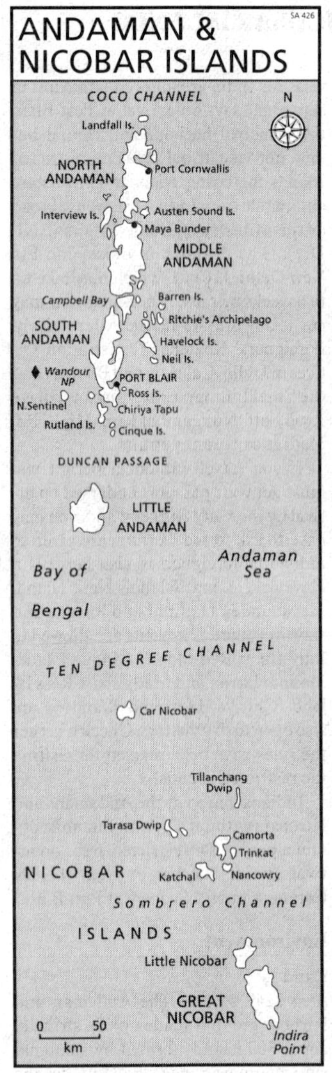

the Nicobars by a 90m deep 150 km strait. The Andamans group has 204 islands with its 3 main islands of North, Middle and South, which are separated by mangrove-fringed islets and are together called **Great Andaman** as they virtually join each other. Only 26 of these are inhabited. The **Nicobar Islands** comprise 12 inhabited and 7 uninhabited islands including the 3 groups, **Car Nicobar** in the N, **Camorta** and **Nancowry** in the middle and the largest, **Great Nicobar** in the S. The land rises to 730m (Saddle Peak), formed mainly of limestones, sandstones and clays.

Climate

Tropical. *Temperature*: 20°C to 32°C. *Annual rainfall:* 2540 mm. Monsoons – mid-May – mid-Sep and Nov – mid-Dec. *Best Season*: mid-Dec – mid-May. The island climate has no extremes, the main contrasts coming with the arrival of the monsoon, and tropical storms in late summer can cause damage.

History

Lying on the trade route between Burma and India the islands' existence was known to early sailors. They appeared on Ptolemy's 2nd century map and were also recorded by the Chinese traveller I-Tsing in the 7th century. At the end of the 17th century the Mahrathas established a base there to attack the trading British, Dutch and Portuguese ships. Dutch pirates and French Jesuits had made contact with the islands before the Danish East India Company made attempts to evangelise the islands in the mid-18th century. The reputation of ferocity attributed to the Nicobarese may have been partly due to Malay pirates who attacked and killed sailors of any trading vessel that came ashore (some anthropologists believe that inspite of common belief, the aboriginals themselves were not cannibals). The first British attempt to occupy the islands was made in 1788 when the Governor Gen of India sent Lt Blair (whose name was given to the first port) and although the first convicts were sent there in 1794, it was abandoned within a couple of years.

After the Mutiny in 1857 the British

gained control of most of the islands and used them as a penal colony for its prisoners (who until then had been sent to Sumatra) right up to Indian Independence with a short break from 1942-45, when the Japanese occupied the Nicobar islands. However, political prisoners were sent in large numbers only after the completion of the Cellular Jail in 1910. The British used it primarily as a penal colony to send the Indian freedom-fighters and criminals for life imprisonment. Each revolt on the mainland resulted in the transportation of people from various parts of India, hence the presence of Bengalis, Malayans and Burmese among others. Subhas Chandra Bose, the Indian Nationalist first raised the Indian tricolour here in 1943. The name *Kalapani* or 'black water' by which the islands were known referred to the blood shed by the nationalists.

Culture

People

Sir Arthur Conan Doyle in 1890 described the islanders as "perhaps...the smallest race upon this earth...fierce, morose and intractable". In the mid-19th century, the British guessed the tribal population was around 5000 but the number has been steadily dwindling. Today most of the inhabitants are Indians, Burmese and Malays – some, descendants of the criminals who were transported here. Since the 1950s, refugees from E Pakistan (now Bangladesh), Burma and Indian emigrants from Guyana have settled on the main islands to be followed more recently by Tamils from Sri Lanka. The largest concentration is around the capital, Port Blair, with the majority of the tribal people (about 15% of the population) living in the Nicobars.

Language

Hindi, Bengali, Tamil, Malayalam, English. The **Andamanese Language** which bears no resemblance to any other language uses prefixes and suffixes to indicate the function of a word and is extraordinary in using simply 2 concepts of number, 'one' and 'greater than one'.

Crafts

Mother-of-pearl jewellery, shell and exotic woods (including the *paduk*, resistant to termites; ebony and teak) crafted for the tourist trade, palm mats and beautiful natural shells.

Modern Andaman & Nicobar

Economy

Local seafood (lobsters, prawns and sea fish) is good. Tropical fruit like pineapples, variety of bananas and the extra sweet papaya is plentiful and the green coconut water very refreshing. Rice is also cultivated.

Resources and industry Tourism is rapidly becoming the Andamans most important industry. Forests represent an important resource. The government has divided 40% of the forests into Primitive Tribal Reserve areas which are only open to Indian visitors with permits and the remaining 60% as Protected Areas from which timber is obtained for export as plywoods, hardwoods and matchwoods. Rubber and mahogany have been planted in addition to teak and rosewood which are commercially in demand.

PORT BLAIR

The small town has changed in the last 3 decades from one which saw a ship from the mainland once a month if the weather permitted, to a place connected by flights from Madras, Delhi, Bhubaneswar and Calcutta several times a week. It now has a hospital, a co-operative stores, schools, a college of higher education and a few museums, in addition to resort hotels and water sports facilities. The central area of Aberdeen Bazar is where you will find most of the hotels, the bus station and shops. The airport is a few km S of Port Blair.

BASICS *Population*: 75,000. *STD Code*:

03192. The capital is 1255 km from Calcutta and 1191 km from Madras.

Places of interest

There are only a handful of sights in Port Blair but as a tourist you will find enough to do particularly if you enjoy a beach holiday with its related water sports, especially the fascinating marine life on the reefs, or bird watching and fishing.

Cellular Jail N of Aberdeen Jetty, it was built between 1886-1906 by the British to house dangerous criminals. Subsequently it was used to place Indian freedom fighters until Independence in 1947. Open 0900-1200, 1400-1700. Mon-Sat. **Son et lumière**: English on Wed, Sat, Sun at 1915, Hindi daily, 1800. Once it could hold 698 solitary prisoners in small narrow cells. There is a site museum, photographs and lists of 'convicts' held, a 'death house' and the gallows,

The Tribals Of Andaman And Nicobar

The origin of the name Andaman may be linked to the monkey god *Hanuman* who is believed to have arrived there on his way to Lanka (Sri Lanka) in search of Sita (see page **103**). The islands have been inhabited by Aboriginal tribes (some Negrito) for thousands of years but remained unexplored because anyone attempting to land would be attacked. Up to the mid-19th century tribal people lived a Stone Age existence. Today there are only a few **Andamanese** who once inhabited the Great Andamans, some **Onges** in Little Andaman who traditionally painted their naked bodies, the fierce **Jarawas** on S Andaman and the **Sentinelese** on N Sentinel. Car Nicobar (Carnic) is inhabited by the mongoloid **Nicobaris**, the most numerous group and **Shompens** who may have been of pre-Dravidian stock, live in Great Nicobar.

The islanders practised hunting and gathering, using bows and arrows to kill wild pigs; and fishing with nets, and catching turtles with harpoons from dug-out canoes. The iron for the arrowheads and harpoons came from the metal collected from wrecks. The **Shompens** used digging sticks for agriculture. Some tribes made pottery but the **Andamanese** particularly were exceptional since they had not discovered fire-making. The Anthropological Survey of India and the Andaman Administration have been jointly trying to establish friendly contact with the Jarawas and Sentinelese since the '60s. Five **Jarawas** first appeared in Port Blair in the late 1960's but have not made much contact with the civilised world since.

The **Sentinelese** consistently repelled groups of explorers with poisoned arrows. More recently, some have picked up coconuts (which do not grow on their island) which were left on the beach as a gesture of friendship by anthropologists. In Jan 1991, Triloknath Pandit, with other Indian anthropologists succeeded in landing on N Sentinel and in Feb, a few Sentinelese boarded a lifeboat to accept gifts of coconuts. He now makes regular visits but must do so after removing most of his clothes in order to be accepted. The 400 or so Sentinelese do not appear to have a hierarchical social structure; they are naked, painting their bodies with chalk and ochre and wearing bead and bone ornaments.

The attempt to rehabilitate some friendly tribals and encourage them to fish for sea slugs and collect edible birds' nests for the Chinese market did not succeed. The Govt of India keeps the Primitive Tribal Reserve Areas out of bounds though Indian tourists may seek permission to visit some islands. However, you may get a chance to see aboriginals who have been integrated into the immigrant population, who now dress up in their tribal costume and perform dances for tourists.

where you can get an impression of the conditions within the prison in the early 1900s and the implements used in torture. 3 of the original 7 wings which extended from the central guard tower survive. Allow about 1½ hrs.

Chatham Saw Mill One of the oldest in Asia employing 1000 workers. Tours take you through the different processes of turning logs into 'seasoned' planks. Photography is not allowed. You can also visit the museum (listed below). Allow about 1 hr.

Mini Zoo has specimens of unusual island fauna including a sea crocodile farm. Open 0700-1200, 1300-1700, daily except Mon.

Sippighat Farm (14 km) Govt demonstration farm where you can see cash crops such as spices and other plants being propagated. Open 0600-1100, 1200-1600, daily except Mon. A water sports complex has been developed.

Excursions

Corbyn's Cove is to the S of South Andaman, 10 km from Port Blair and 4 km from the Airport where the Andaman Beach Resort is situated and where you can get a snack. The water is warm, clear with gentle surf and the white sand beaches are clean and palm fringed. Rs 35 taxi from Aberdeen Bazar.

Chiriya Tapu (Bird Island) 30 km 1 hr drive, on the S tip of S. Andaman is very picturesque. Rich in butterflies in addition to birdlife, it has a beach covered in interesting shapes of driftwood. You may visit it if you get a permit to visit Cinque Island, which takes 2 hr by boat.

Wandoor Beach (28 km) on the W coast is particularly good for snorkelling and diving where you can get a boat to uninhabited Jolly Buoy (1 hr). The National Marine Park includes Jolly Buoy, Red Skin and several other islands. See below.

Madhuban (14 km) is on the seaside on the E side where young elephants are trained for forestry and **Burma Nalla** (17 km) where they are used for lumbering.

Mount Harriet is opposite Chatham Island and rises to 365m. It is possible to climb it to get good views of Port Blair. By car, it is 2 hrs from Port Blair, or 10 min by ferry from Marine to Hope Town and then a ½ hr walk to the top.

Museums

Anthropological Museum Small but very informative on tribal life with model villages, artefacts, records of exploratory expeditions. Open 0900-1200, 1300-1600, weekdays. Publications on sale. Comprehensive Research Library with books and periodicals on the islands on the second floor which is open until 2000. Allow 1 hr. A visit is strongly rec. Marine Museum with collection of corals and display of 350 species of marine life including tropical fish, sea crocodiles, barracudas, pearl oysters and dolphins (which you may also be lucky enough to see on a boat trip). Open 0830-1600, weekdays. Allow ½ hr.

Forest Museum, Haddo near the Saw Mill has unusual local woods including red paduk, satin and marble woods and shows the use of different woods in the timber industry and the methods of lumbering and finishing. Open 0830-1600, daily. Allow ½ hr.

Tours

Half-day sightseeing of Port Blair and on Sun to Corbyn's Cove. Daily Harbour cruises from Cholunga Wharf at 1500 (2 hr) including Viper Island. Marine Department trips to Jolly Buoy from Wandoor Beach usually in the morning returning around 1500. Also to Car Nicobar with special permit, visiting Karchal, Nancowry and Campbell Bay in Gt Nicobar. The Andaman Beach Resort can arrange trips to Wandoor National Park (min 4). Travel agents also arrange tours.

Local information

● Accommodation

Many offer discounts in low season (Apr-Sep) and charge extra for a/c rm. **B** *Bay Island* (Welcomgroup), Marine Hill, 2km, T 20881. 48 rm most with balconies, some a/c and some

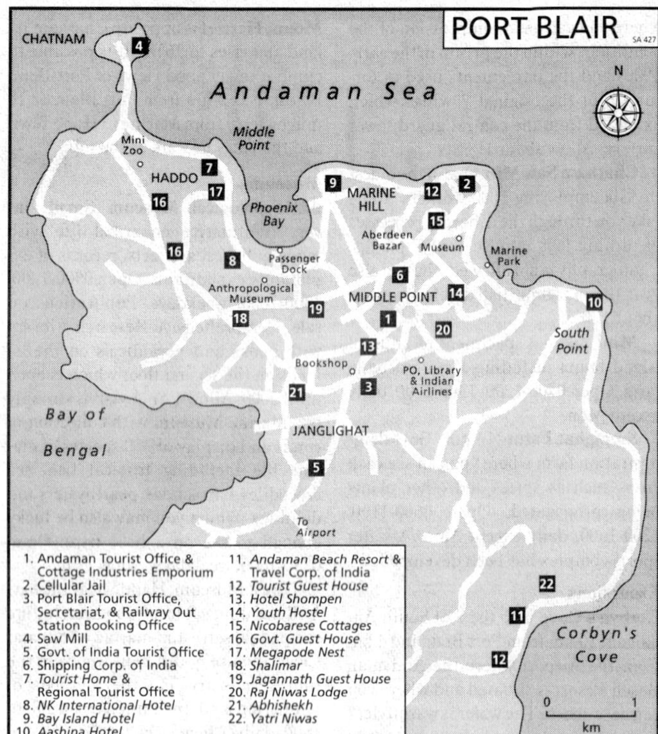

A suites. On a steep hill with superb views but not too close to beach. Rooms imaginatively designed to imitate local huts, facilities in main building. Good open-air restaurant and bar, travel, video, sea-water pool (at bottom of hill) and watersports (snorkelling and fishing). The most expensive on the islands.

C *Andaman Beach Resort* (TCI), Corbyn's Cove, 4km, T 21462. 52 rm, beautiful gardens, restaurant, bar, good travel counter, car hire, most watersports, sailing, tennis. White sandy beach with shady palms.

D *Aasiana*, S. Point, T 20937. 23 rm. Resort hotel in elevated location on road to Corbyn's Cove but not nr beach. **D** *Shompen*, 2 Middle Point, T 20360. 45 rm. These 2 have some a/c rm (harbour facing with balconies), restaurants, some facilities and free airport transfer.

● Budget hotels

Simpler Govt accommodation is good value. **E** *Guest House*. Good location at Corbyn's Cove, past Andaman Beach Resort. E *Megapode Nest*, T 20207, has 10 rm, and **E** *Nicobarese Cottages* have thatched roofs. Both are at Haddo, have superb views, some a/c rm and are rec. 2 **F** *Tourist Homes*: One at Haddo, 20 min walk from centre has the Regional Tourist Office, T 20380. 18 simple rm. Another on Marine Hill (T 20365). 6 rm (better in new section, with bath and sea view balcony). Reservations: Dy Director of Tourism, Port Blair.

In Aberdeen Bazar, inexpensive simple **E** hotels and guest houses offer good off-season discounts. **E** *Dhanalaxmi*, Aberdeen Bazar, T 21306, 16 clean rm with bath, some a/c. Restaurant. **E** *NK International*, T 21066. Some a/c rm with bath. Some in **F** category are very basic and not always clean: *Tourist Cottage*, Babu Lane, (T 21021) *Ram Nivas Lodge* (T 21026), *Sampat* (T 21752), and *Central Lodge*, Goalghar (T 21632). **F** *Youth Hostel*,

Gymkhana Ground, nr Aberdeen Bazar, T 20459. Also 2 *Guest Houses* but be prepared to rough it. Reservations: Exec Engineer, Port Blair Div.

Chiriya Tapu in the S of the island and **Wandoor Beach**, have very cheap *Forest Rest Houses*, though most people visit them on a day excursion.

Middle Andaman: *Rest Houses* at Betapur, and Kangal and N Andaman at Aerial Bay, Diglipur, Kundantala, Mayabunder, Parangara and Tugapur.

● Places to eat

Seafood and venison are fresh and plentiful. Most hotels down to **E** grade have restaurants offering mainly spicy S Indian. Larger hotels offer continental, Indian, Chinese and Burmese food. *Dhanalaxmi* and *Annapurna Café* (Aberdeen Bazar) are rec. Govt guest houses are also open to non-residents. Meals (most ingredients have to be brought from the mainland), and drinks, are expensive.

● Entertainment

Occasional dance performances for tourists.

● Post & telecommunications

Post Office: nr centre, by Indian Airlines office. 0700-2200 weekdays, 0800-1800 weekends.

● Shopping

Cottage Industries Emporium next to Tourist Office. Open 0900-1300, 1330-1700. Closed Mon and Fri. Small selection of souvenirs in wood and shell. *Aberdeen Bazar* is a good place with small shops selling local crafts where you can bargain.

● Sports

Swimming: is excellent. The best spot is the crescent shaped Corbyn's Cove or one of the uninhabited islands which tourists may visit for the day. A variety of water sports are offered by the resort hotels where some equipment is available. It is best to bring your own mask and snorkel.

Snorkelling and skin diving: are particularly good in the Wandoor National Marine Park.

● Tour companies & travel agents

Island Travel, Aberdeen Bazar. Good for excursions and hire of water sports equipment. *Travel Corp of India*, Andaman Beach Resort. *Shompen Travels*, 2 Middle Pt.

● Tourist office

Govt of India, Super Shoppe, Junglighat VIP Rd, T 21006 (on way to airport). Dy Director, Information, Publicity and Tourism, Secretariat, T 20694. **Port Blair Tourist Office** at the Secretariat. Regional Tourist Office at Tourist Home, Haddo, T 20380. The Regional Office screens occasional films about the islands (1730 on Mon, Wed, Fri).

● Useful addresses

PRO, Andaman and Nicobar Administration, T 20694. Also Resident Commissioner, Curzon Rd Hostel, F105 Kasturba Gandhi Marg, New Delhi, T 387015 and 3A Auckland Place, Calcutta, T 442604.

● Transport

Local Bicycles: on hire (about Re 1/hr) but you need to be very fit to manage the hilly island. The hire shop is between Aberdeen Bazar and the Bus Stop. **Bus**: tours are cheap and do the capital's sights and Corbyn's Cove. **Ferry**: 3 services daily around S. Andaman, Neil and Havelock islands, operated by the Marine Dept. Local boat hire from Oceanic Company, MG Rd, Middle Point or Marine Dept. Inter-island ships for visiting the Nicobars. **Helicopters**: for island hopping if you have a permit to visit. Services from Port Blair to Rangat, Mayabunder, Hut Bay, Car Nicobar, Kamotra, Diglipur and Campbell Bay. **Taxis**: on hire through hotels or by contacting Taxi Stand, open until 2000.

Air Indian Airlines, G55 Middle Point, Port Blair. **Transport to town**: hotel taxis sometimes available, or private taxi from stand; fix the fare before starting (around Rs 30). Indian Airlines from **Calcutta** to Port Blair on Tu,Th,Sa departing 0640 (2 hr) returning back at 0820. Also from **Madras** on W,F departing 0640 (2¼ hr) returning at 0925.

Sea Sailings from Calcutta and Madras which run to a schedule of sorts (usually fortnightly) and occasional ships from Visakhapatnam. Journey time 2-3 days (allow about 10 days for round trip). Deluxe a/c Cabin: up to Rs 1300 (plus Rs 50 for meals per day and Port Toll Tax) with cheaper cabins in A, B and C Class. The least expensive is an 'Ordinary Bunk' for about Rs 400. Contact Shipping Corp of India at 13 Strand Rd, Calcutta 700001, T 282354, Port Trust, Old Warehouse Building near Customs House, Rajaji Salai, Madras 600001, T 514401, or Aberdeen Bazar, Port Blair T 21417. In Madras: KPV Sheik Md. Rowther and Co., 41 Linghi Chetty St, T 510346; in Vishakapatnam: Bhanojiraw and Guruda, Pattabirmaya, PB 17.

WANDOOR NATIONAL MARINE PARK & THE OFF ISLANDS

The coral beds and underwater life is exceptional off some uninhabited islands. **Cinque** can be reached by boat from Port Blair (3½ hr), **Chirya Tapu** in the S (2 hr) and **Jolly Buoy** which is now a part of the Marine Park.

Wandoor National Marine Park

About 30 km SW of Port Blair the marine park is well worth visiting. It is a group of about a dozen islands with deep blue waters separating them. It includes Grub, Redskin, Jolly Buoy, Pluto, Boat Island, with Tarmugli on the W, Kalapahar or Rutland to the E and the Twins to the S. It is very rich not only in marine life but also in the variety of tropical flowers and birds. The dense forests come down to the beach where the mangrove thrives on the water's edge.

You will see a rich variety of tropical fish, including angelfish, green parrot, yellow butterfly, black surgeon and blue damsel fish. There are also silver jacks, squirrel, clown fish and sweetlips as well as sea cucumbers, sea anemones, starfish and a variety of shells – cowries, turbots, conches and the rarer giant clam which can be as much as a metre wide. There are turtles, sharks and barracudas on the outer reefs and beautiful corals of many different varieties including the brain, finger and antler coral, the colours derived from the algae that thrive in the living coral. **NB: coral and shell collecting is strictly forbidden.** Fishing can be rewarding and you can get your catch grilled on the beach.

Jolly Buoy is at the centre of the park and is encircled by a coral reef. The boat lands visitors on the beach in the N and it is possible to see some sea life in the tidal pools but the best is underwater on the reefs. Only supervised diving is advised because of the strong currents.

Redskin has a colony of spotted deer introduced by the British, with caves to the rocky N and mangrove swamps to the S and E but with sandy beaches on the W coast where you will probably land.

Tarmugli is good for snorkelling and diving, with a stretch of coral reef on the SW while the tiny island of **Grub** has good sandy beaches.

Ross Island, once the island with the British Residence, is now only inhabited by peacocks and spotted deer. It has ruins of the Government House, churches, clubs, dungeons, bungalows and bakeries. Ferries from Phoenix Bay. **NB**: remember to pack lunch and drinks for the day.

Viper Island nr Haddo Wharf is at the mouth of Port Blair harbour where convicts were interned before the Cellular Jail was built, with its gallows. Indian nationals can apply to visit **Dugong Creek** where Onges have been rehabilitated in wooden huts.

The Ministry of Tourism is to release Amkunj Beach in **Middle Andaman** and Radha Nagar in **Havelock Island** for development as beach resorts with A grade hotels and water sports facilities.

NICOBAR ISLANDS

It is now possible to visit parts of the islands on an inter-island cruise – **Katchal** with a large rubber plantation; **Nancowry** harbour, **Indira Point**, India's southernmost tip and **Campbell Bay** (Gt Nicobar). The friendly Nicobarese enjoy singing and dancing, wrestling, fishing, swimming and canoe racing. The huts, which look like large thatched domes, are raised on stilts, about 2m high and must be entered through the floor.

SOUTH INDIA

Contents

MAPS

Introduction

South India is made up of the 4 states of Andhra Pradesh, Karnataka, Kerala and Tamil Nadu. Geologically they are formed of the same ancient granites found further N, many over 3,000 million years old. See page 22.

Environment

Land

Western Ghats

The Ghats are at their highest in South India, where in the Nilgiri Hills they reach heights of over 2500m. The Indian plateau falls away to the E, and as a result all the major rivers of South India rise within 100 km of the W coast but reach the sea in the Bay of Bengal. Here the Krishna, the Godavari and the Kaveri have created broad alluvial deltas which contrast sharply with the higher land of the interior, often covered with dry, thin red soils. Where the possibility of irrigation has been exploited, the alluvial soils have supported rich rice cultivation. In the far S the Kaveri and Tamraparni deltas were the centres of major southern kingdoms while the river valleys of the centre, such as the Krishna, had been the focus of highly developed Buddhist kingdoms in the Nagarjunakonda region.

In places extraordinary outcrops of granite boulders create a bizarre landscape, especially when they are interspersed with small patches of bright green paddy growing.

Eastern Ghats

The slope from the Ghats to the E coast is also interrupted by massive outlying blocks of hills, from N Andhra Pradesh (an extension of the Orissa Hills) to S

Tamil Nadu. Sometimes called the Eastern Ghats, these are essentially a disconnected series of hills, the highest rising to over 1500m, which have often enjoyed sufficient isolation and distinctive climate to produce quite distinct micro regions.

Climate

Best Time

Nov through to Mar is the best time to visit the S. Even then you need to be prepared for the heat, which in the daytime can be oppressive.

NB: The height of the Western Ghats and the southern position of the 4 states have a major influence on local climates.

Temperature

All of South India is S of the Tropic of Cancer. Thus even in places like Kodaikkanal, at an altitude of more than 2000m, daytime temperatures in the coldest months remain above 15°C. At sea level mean temperatures in Jan are around 26°C and 28°C. Cooling breezes from the sea and much greater cloud cover help to keep summer temperatures at sea level in the low 30s. On the coast these temperatures are accompanied by very high humidity, making the climate from Mar through to Oct uncomfortable except where altitude brings greater freshness. Even Bangalore, at a height of just under 1000m, is noticeably cooler and fresher for most of the year than coastal places like Madras.

Rainfall

In most of the region the dry season lasts from Jan through to May. The SW monsoon reaches the southernmost point of Kerala in mid-May, gradually moving N towards Bombay into Jun. The warm, wet winds, having crossed over 3000 km of the Indian Ocean, are suddenly forced to rise and cool by the mountains near the coast. As a result, on the W coast and the Ghats very heavy rain falls, often for several days at a time. Total rainfall is often more than 4000 mm a year. Such rain can produce spectacular results – the 250m high Jog Falls at Shimoga, in W Karnataka, are a magnificent sight in full spate.

The picture immediately to the E of the Ghats is very different. Protected by the rainshadow effect of the mountains, strong winds sweep down across the plains to the E through the early monsoon period, warming and becoming drier as they descend. The contrasts with the W coast are often striking, the extreme SE experiencing almost semi-desert conditions. The journey by land from Tiruvananthapuram to Madurai round India's southern tip illustrates the dramatic effects on vegetation and agriculture of this sudden decrease in rainfall.

Retreating Monsoon

Tamil Nadu has an exceptional rainfall pattern, receiving most of its rain in the retreating monsoon. From Oct to Dec depressions move across the E coast around Madras from the Bay of Bengal. They bring heavy rains, often accompanied by storms, to the coastal belt, decreasing inland and southwards from Madras. Cyclonic storms, originating much further to the E and SE over the eastern Indian Ocean, may also strike any part of the South Indian coast as they move first W and then N up the Bay of Bengal. Such cyclones can cause enormous disruption, damage and loss of life.

History

Pre-History

South India as a whole has long been the home of distinctive cultural traditions within India. There were stone age settlers nearly a million years ago. By the 2nd century BC, South India was the home of Iron Age megalithic cultures, and **megalithic burial sites** are common in several parts of the region. Recent analysis of skeletons discovered near Hyderabad on 16 Dec 1931, has shed

Left And Right-Handed Castes

In the 11th century a major social division developed spread across S India, remaining powerful into the 19th century under the labels "right hand" and "left hand" castes, given the Tamil names ***Valangai*** and ***Idangai*** respectively. An account of 1072 records a fight between 2 groups which says that "in the second year of the King Kulottunga I there was a clash between the right-hand and left-hand communities in which the village was burnt down, the sacred places destroyed, and the images of deities and the treasure of the temple looted." Probably originating in Tamil Nadu, the division spread across Karnataka and Andhra Pradesh. Both the origins and the functions of the division are imperfectly understood. At some periods and places, as for instance 17th century Madras, the division was a major feature of the social organisation of communities, where in common with much earlier periods the left hand groups were identified with particular types of artisan activity, in contrast with the right-handed groups more commonly engaged in agricultural work.

Burton Stein quotes an inscription dated AD 1218 found at the ***Uttamacholan Temple*** 25 km N of the Kaveri River near Trichy which vividly illustrates the incorporation of a group into the Idangai division: "In order to kill the demons that disturbed the sacrifices of Kasyapa (the priest of Visvakarma, the patron god of artisans) we were made to appear from the sacrificial fire pit and while we were thus protecting the said sacrifice, Chakravartin Arindama honoured the officiating priests by carrying them in a car and led them to a Brahmana colony. On this occasion we were made to take our seats on the back of the car and to carry the slippers and umbrellas of these sages. Eventually with these Brahman sages we were made to settle down in the same villages...We received the clan

new light on the life style, illnesses and causes of death of the early megalith builders. The skeletons of 4 males and 6 females from Raigir, nr Hyderabad, were found by chance in the wardrobe of an elderly Londoner on 17 Oct 1983. It has been shown from studying the pattern of wear and disease on the teeth that the megalithic peoples of the area after 1100 BC were settled food producers. Since at least the 4th millennium BC, the S had been inhabited by the Dravidians who now make up the great majority of its people.

Early political development

By the 4th century BC Tamil Nadu was under the rule of 3 dynasties. The Cholas occupied the coastal area E of Thanjavur and inland to the head of the Kaveri Delta at Tiruchi. Periodically they were a strong military power, one of their princes, Elara, for example conquering the island of Sri Lanka in the 2nd century BC. The centre – Madurai, Tirunelveli and a part of S Kerala were under the Pandiyas while the Cheras controlled much of what is now Kerala on the W coast of the peninsula. The 3 kingdoms are mentioned in Ashokan edicts of c257 BC, although not a great deal is known other than that the Pandiyas had good relations with the Mauryan Emperor.

From a very early period South Indians used the sea to trade. Chinese records from the 2nd century BC identify Kanchipuram as an important trading centre. Western classical sources mention ports such as Kaveripatnam, Pondicherry, Malakkanam and Masulipatnam. Indian merchants organised themselves in guilds, trading with the Kra Isthmus and other SE Asian ports.

name Idangai because the sages (while they got down from their cars) were supported by us on their left side. The ancestors of this our sect having lost their credentials and insignia in the jungles and bushes, we were ignorant of our origins. Having now once learnt it, we the members of the 98 subsects enter into a compact, in the fortieth year of the king Kulottunga III that we shall hereafter behave like sons of the same parents and what good and evil may befall any one of us, will be shared by all. If anything derogatory happens to the idangai class, we shall jointly assert our rights until we establish them. It is understood that only those who, during their congregational meetings to settle communal disputes, display the insignia horn, bugle, and parasol shall belong to our class. Those who have to recognise us now and hereafter, in public, must do so from our distinguishing symbols – the feather of the crane and the loose hanging hair. The horn and the conch shell shall also be sounded in front of us and the bugle blown according to the fashion obtaining among the idangai people. Those who act in contravention of these rules shall be treated as enemies of our class. Those who behave differently from the rules thus prescribed for the conduct of the idangai classes shall be excommunicated and shall not be recognised as members of the community. They will be considered slaves of the classes opposed to us."

The designation left and right for the two groups embraced many different castes across the region. The impurity associated with left-handedness may suggest ritual connections, though why those called "left-handed" should have accepted such a damaging description is not clear. Stein suggests that perhaps the usefulness of the label came to outweigh the underlying stigma of its associations, but that to disadvantaged groups of both poorer agriculturalists and artisan-traders alliances across wide regions gave a measure of security and political leverage.

Literature

From around the 2nd century AD a poets' academy known as the **Sangam** was established in Madurai. From the beginning of the Christian era a development began to take place in Tamil religious thought and writing, transforming Krishna from a remote and heroic figure of the epics into the focus of a new and passionate devotional worship – bhakti. Jordens has written that this new worship was "emotional, ardent, ecstatic, often using erotic imagery". From the 7th to the 10th century there was a surge of writing new hymns of praise, sometimes referred to as 'the Tamil *Veda*'. Attention focused on the "marvels of Krishna's birth and infancy and his heroic and amorous exploits as a youth among the cowherds and cowherdesses of Gokula". In the 9th century Vaishnavite Brahmans produced the *Bhagavata Purana*, which, through frequent translation into all India's major languages, became the vehicle for the new worship of Krishna, see page 302. Its tenth book has been called "one of the truly great books of Hinduism". There are over forty translations into Bengali alone.

Religious orders

Followers of both Siva and Vishnu (*Saivites* and *Vaishnavites*) formed religious orders. Monks travelled all over India, preaching and converting, giving the lie to the widely held view that Hinduism is not a proselytising religion. The Vaishnava mystic and saint **Ramanuja** is believed to have lived between 1017 and 1137 (the earlier date is probably too early). He was the first and perhaps the greatest of these. Fleeing from the Saivite Cholas in Tamil Nadu he founded the *Srivaishnava* sect. It developed a strong following in Karnataka as well as in Tamil Nadu; the whole of the S was involved in the new movement. Madhva, a Kanarese Brahmin, founded the Madhva sect in the 13th century. The Telugu Brahmins Nimbarka (13th century) and Vallabhacharya (1479-1531) carried the message to Varanasi.

The facts of South Indian religious development are often surrounded in myth. It is said for example that Tamil literature was put through an extraordinary test, see page 917. Books would be thrown into the sacred tank of the Minakshi Temple at Madurai and those that floated would be deemed worthy, while those that were useless would sink! (This might suggest that this would produce a very small body of worthy literature, but books were written on leaves of the Palmyra palm!) See page 103. The writings of the Sangam literature suggest that life in Tamil society had a different system of hierarchy from that in North India, with the sages at the top, followed by peasants, hunters, artisans, soldiers, fishermen and scavengers – quite different from the caste system that existed in the rest of the subcontinent.

Political Development

In the early centuries of the Christian era South India thus experienced its own religious development. Politically too it saw the rise of regional powers. The **Pandiyas** became a great maritime trading power who had connections with the Roman Empire up to the time of Nero and well beyond. Later they returned to power in the Tamil area after the decline of the Cholas and ruled from 1175 to 1300. In the 13th century, international trade flourished under their control and was only superseded by the rise of Vijayanagar.

The Telugu speaking area, was under the rule of the **Andhras** from about 230 BC. They reigned for 450 years and traded with many nations from Rome in the W to the countries of SE Asia in the E. Buddhism flourished under their patronage, as did art and craft. The Amaravati stupa in their second capital is attributed to them, but the work of their craftsmen travelled round the world, illustrated by an ivory carving found in the ruins of Pompeii.

To the S of the Andhras, the **Pallavas** of Kanchi, during whose reign the sage poets flourished, came to power in the 4th century AD. They held power over much of the S for 4 centuries. They are thought to have come from the N and may have had connections with Parthians. Mamallapuram (*Mahabalipuram*) became an important port and naval base in the 7th century, when the famous *rathas* were carved, followed in the next century by the building of the Mamallapuram shoretemple, during the reign of Narasimhavarman II. He also built the great Kailasanatha temple at Kanchipuram which for 150 years was not only the administrative centre but also a literary and artistic capital where Sanskrit and the Vedas were studied.

The **Chalukyas** (543-755) The Chalukyas with their fortified capital at Badami, ruled the Deccan for 2 centuries from around the middle of the 6th century and at their peak controlled the vast region between the Narmada and the Kaveri rivers including present-day Maharashtra, Karnataka and western Andhra Pradesh. Warriors and temple builders, the Chalukyas have left some of their finest works at Badami, Aihole and Pattadakal.

The **Cholas** returned to power with the decline of the Pallavas in 850 and were a dominant political force until 1173. Within a century, during the reign of Rajaraja I, they defeated the Pandiyas and the Cheras (whose home base was in Kerala) and their great empire at one time expanded to cover the whole Tamil area, Sri Lanka, the region of the

Andhras, southern Karnataka and the islands of Laccadives and the Maldives. Further expansion followed during the 11th century during the reign of *Rajendra Chola* (1013-44) which covered Kerala and the Pandiya lands and to the NE across Orissa and up to the Ganga in Bengal. His naval expeditions to the Malayan Peninsula resulted in Chola domination over the trade routes in that entire area of the Indian Ocean and control of the sea routes to Java, Sumatra and China. The control over such a vast area continued for nearly a century until the Pandiyas became powerful again and in Karnataka the Hoysalas emerged as a strong power at the beginning of the 11th century.

The **Hoysalas** (1022-1342) extended their empire from the Krishna to the Kaveri rivers and during the 12th century, after the conversion of King Vishnuvardhana from Jainism to Vaishnavism by the saint Ramanuja, great temples were built. These include the finest in the kingdom at Belur and Halebid. They failed to organise effectively to resist the spread of Muslim power from the N in the mid 14th century and the empire collapsed.

The arrival of the Muslims

The **Muslims** (1296-1347) The Delhi Sultanate's advance was led by Malik Kafur who conquered first the N Deccan establishing strongholds in Devagiri and Warangal. Later they took control of the Tamil lands. However, in 1347 the Muslim officers in what is now N Karnataka and Andhra Pradesh rebelled against Delhi. Their leader Hasan Kangu set up the independent Bahmani Kingdom after adopting the name Ala-ud-din Hasan Bahman Shah. Myths about his origins continue to circulate. The court genealogists were persuaded to trace his ancestry back to the Iranian king Bahman Isfander, while another myth asserted that he was the servant of Gangu Brahmin of Delhi. In fact he was the nephew of one of the Delhi sultanate's greatest generals, Hizabru'd Din Zafar Khan.

Ala-ud-din founded the **Bahmani dynasty** (1347) setting up their first capital in Gulbarga where a great mosque was built. He extended his control over much of N and central Karnataka and Andhra Pradesh, a process of expansion consolidated by his successor Muhammad I (1358-1375). A succession of 5 sultans ruled after Ala ud Din's death in 1375 up to 1397. The early Muslim rulers encouraged immigration from Iran and Arabia, but the high positions occupied by many such immigrants often caused intense jealousy and conflict, being resented both by local people and by immigrants from North India. Such tensions encouraged divisions within the ruling family, and the sultanate was constantly fighting against the rising power of the Vijayanagar Empire and against internal factions. In 1422 Ahmad I (1422-36), having won one such battle over the Raja of Warangal, N of Hyderabad, moved the capital to Bidar. However the gains he made were frittered away by his son and successor Ala ud Din, and the dynasty continued to be beset with internal and external conflicts.

Rizvi quotes the Russian traveller Athanasius Nikhitin, who visited the Deccan between 1469 and 1474, illustrating the nature of life at the Bahmani court. "The Sultan of Bedar is a little man, 20 years old, in the power of the nobles. Khorassanians rule the country and serve in war. There is a Khorassanian Boyar, Melik-Tuchar, who keeps an army of 200,000 men; Melik Khan keeps 100,000; Kharat Khan, 20,000, and many are the khans that keep 10,000 armed men. The Sultan goes out with 300,000 men of his own troops. The land is overstocked with people; but those in the country are very miserable, whilst the nobles are extremely opulent and delight in luxury. They are wont to be carried on their silver beds, preceded by some 20 chargers caparisoned in gold, and followed by 300 men on horseback and 500 on foot, and by horn-men, 10 torchbearers and 10 musicians."

The kingdom split up at the end of the 15th century resulting in the formation of 5 independent states of Berar, Ahmednagar, Bijapur, Golconda and Bidar.

Vijayanagar Empire (1336-1565)

See page 46. At the same time as the Muslim sultanates were pressing S the Vijayanagar Empire was re-asserting Hindu political power from its capital, Hampi in Karnataka. The last Hindu Empire was named after its capital on the Tungabhadra river. It rose out of the break away from Delhi by the Madurai Sultanate in Tamil Nadu, the separation of power into smaller Muslim sultanates and the resistance to Islam by the Hindu kingdoms which soon came to include the Hoysalas. Under the founder of the Empire, Harihara I, the region S of the Kaveri river came under the rule of a single king which was to extend over the whole of the S.

For the next 2 centuries the Vijayanagar kings flourished and for a time their influence spread as far as Orissa. They were patrons of a vigorous expansion of temple building across South India. Although they were frequently at war with the Muslim kingdoms to their N they capitalised on the rivalries between the Muslim sultans, periodically siding with one or other of the 5 kingdoms as self interest suggested prudent.

Between 1559-61 Bijapur and Vijayanagar were on one side against the sultanate of Ahmadnagar, but the Vijayanagar king Ramaraja so disgusted his allies by playing off one kingdom against another that the Muslim states formed a coalition to take on the Vijayanagar forces. For the first and only time they came together as an effective force on 24 December 1564. They marched to fight the Vijayanagar army on 23 February 1565 at Talikota. Ramaraja himself was captured and executed, the Vijayanagar army comprehensively defeated and the capital city pillaged. Even after their forces were routed by a confederacy of the Muslim states of the Deccan in 1565 their kings continued to rule from further S into the next century.

The Deccan sultanates held on to their independent states until the arrival of the Mughals under Aurangzeb while the Tamil areas broke up into independent principalities to be fought over by foreign empires attempting to establish first their trading bases and then colonies. The advent of the Muslims in North India had less impact in this part of the subcontinent but its history changed after 1639 with the arrival of the British as a trading company.

The Europeans

The fall of the Roman Empire in the 5th century AD ended the direct trade between Europe and India which had flourished for 6 centuries. The Arabs, Byzantians and Venetian and Genoese traders acted as middle men before goods reached Europe. The hunger for spices and exotic goods increased so Vasco da Gama sailed from Lisbon for the East

The Portuguese were the first to establish trade with the Vijayanagars, arriving at the port of Kozhikode in 1498 in search of 'Christians and spices', thus ending the long-held Arab monopoly of sea trade with India. It was to be a bloody takeover in the fighting that followed the attacks on Kozhikode over the next few years. In 1510, the seizure of Goa by Alberquerque established the Portuguese empire. He built many forts at strategic places along the coast and dominated sea trade in the Indian Ocean for the next half century until the fall of Vijayanagar in 1565. During this period St Francis Xavier was sent by the Society of Jesus 'to convert the Indians'.

He arrived in Goa in 1542, spending a few years before going further E to Malacca. He returned briefly to Goa in 1547 and again in 1551 before going further E again. His name lives on in the several Jesuit educational institutions to be found all over India.

Up to the end of the 16th century the sailors had depended on the monsoon winds to traverse the Indian Ocean. In 1595 the Dutch published navigation maps which made sailing eastwards quicker. The Dutch East India Company was set up in 1602 in Amsterdam and they subsequently established themselves in Surat, the Mughal port N of Bombay and later seized Pondicherry from the French in 1693 only to return it in 6 years. They, however, unlike the other European trading companies had not sought to establish an empire in India.

The English In 1620 the Danes arrived in Tranquebar on the E coast, between Karaikal and Pondicherry, but their activities remained very limited. In 1600 the English merchants' companies in London obtained permission to hold monopoly of trade with the Indies from Queen Elizabeth I. The East India Company's first counting house was set up in Surat in 1619, followed by settlement near Madras with the building of Fort St George in 1639. A century later the French under Dupleix seized Madras and held it for 3 years until the treaty of Aix-la-Chapelle forced its return to the English in 1749. In 1751 Clive's victory over the French in Arcot was a turning point and following the French example he placed his own Indian agent on the throne there. Trouble for the English emerged with the coming to power of Haidar Ali on the throne of Mysore in 1761.

Haidar Ali was exceptional as a military strategist on both land and sea and as a patron of the arts. He defeated the English and their ally the Nizam of Hyderabad in the first Mysore war. He and his son **Tipu Sultan** won many battles against the English with the help of the French at vast expense, during the Second Mysore War which started in 1780. The victories extended the rule of the Sultan of Mysore over most of South India including Malabar (Kerala). However, Haidar Ali was defeated in 1781 and died the following year when his son acceded to the throne. But the Treaty of Versailles in 1783 brought the French and English together and Tipu was forced to make peace. The English took Malabar in 1792 and finally marched on Tipu's capital in Srirangapatna (Seringapatam) near Mysore where the Sultan was killed in his fort in 1799. In 1801, Lord Wellesley brought together most of the S, with the exception of Hyderabad and Mysore, under the Madras Presidency, see page 1011.

The French established their East India Company in 1664, their ships arriving at the port of Surat to set up the first counting house where the English and the Dutch had already established themselves. This was followed by the acquisition of land at Pondicherry in 1673 and Masulipatnam, 14 years later. In 1742, Dupleix who had been administering Chandernagore near Calcutta in East India was named Governor of the French India Company and took up residence at Pondicherry. He seized Madras within a few years but was forced to fight against the Nawab of Arcot who demanded its return. Having won his victory he made grand plans for the empire by installing his chosen men on the thrones of the Nawabs of Arcot in the S and Nizams of Hyderabad in the N of the region.

However, in 1751 Clive attacked Arcot. His victory was the beginning of the end of the French in India. The Treaty of Paris brought their Empire to a close in 1763 although they retained 5 counting houses. Louis XIV and Louis XV had not shown any interest in the Orient so the English gained an increasing advantage in trade which made them the foremost colonial

Temple Worship

David Shulman gives an excellent idea of the way in which a pilgrim approaches the temple. He writes: "There is often to begin with, the long, uncomfortable journey to the shrine, which may be defined as a form of asceticism, *tapas*. The journey is, however, only the prelude to a deeper sense of self-sacrifice. Once the pilgrim arrives at the shrine, he sees before him the towering gopuras or gates set in the walls that enclose the sacred area. He leaves his shoes outside the gate; he will also usually undergo an initial purification by bathing, which prepares him for contact with the powerful forces inside. Once the pilgrim goes through the gopuram the real journey begins. This is a journey of the self, and backwards in time. The tall gopurams of the S Indian temple create a sense of dynamism, of movement away from the gate and towards the centre, which is locked inside the stone heart of the main shrine. There lies the sacred force contained within the walls, rendered accessible only through the strong ties that bound it, and through the ritual ordering of the universe within."

So the physical form of the temple has direct spiritual significance. Shulman goes on to illustrate how the pilgrim approaches the central shrine. "The worshipper first circles around the temple compound, offering obeisance at minor shrines, always keeping the main sanctuary on his right; he circumscribes the centre in an individual act of demarcation, just as the stone walls forever mark its limits. At length he will penetrate into the recesses of the main shrine and come to rest before the *garbhagrha*, where the image of the deity is located. Here he has arrived at the farthest reach of his wandering; hidden away in stone and darkness, as in a cave in the bowels of the earth, lies the symbol of the god, which is imbued with the divine power whose deeds are related in myths. Knowledge, or truth, is, in the eyes of the Hindus, by nature esoteric; it is buried, lost, to be recovered from the depths of the sea or from the darkness of the earth. The temple expresses in its very structure this search for hidden wisdom: the *gopuras* point us inward, to the cave. But the *garbhagrha* is, literally, a 'house of the womb'; at this spot the pilgrim is conceived afresh, to be reborn without taint, with all the powers latent in the newborn child. He is not, indeed, alone in this experience; the very deity whom he worships also suffers in this site a new birth preceded by violent conception. Life enters the womb in darkness, out of the disintegration into chaos and death of an earlier existence."

He goes on to ask what pilgrims hope to achieve by their pilgrimage. Usually there is a very practical aim – the worshipper comes into contact with a power that helps him in his ordinary life. By offering his own sacrifice to the god, he hopes that the god will reward him by meeting his wishes – for good health, for a suitable husband or wife, for the birth of a child, for prosperity. As Shulman says "It is important to realise that no one in Tamil Nadu goes on pilgrimage in order to attain release from this world (*moksha*). What has happened in the Tamil tradition is that the world-renouncing goal of the ascetic has been re-defined as equivalent to *bhakti* (worship and praise). Pilgrimage came to be a substitute for *sannyasa*." The Hindu *bhakti* movements which developed personal worship and praise of a personal Lord, often directed the worshipper back to the world in which they live rather than to seek release from it. For further information, see page 71.

power in India. English power spread from Madras northwards up the coast of modern Andhra to Visakhapatnam and the borders of Orissa, southwards to include the whole of modern Tamil Nadu and westwards to the coast at Mangalore.

South Indian Temple architecture

Tamil Nadu has been at the heart of South Indian religious development for 2000 years, although other regions have made important contributions to the development of temple styles. Temple building was a comparatively late development in Hindu worship, see page 717. Long before the first temple was built shrines were dotted across the land, the focus of pilgrimage, each with its own mythology. Even the most majestic of South Indian temples have basic features in common with these original shrines, and many of them have simply grown by a process of accretion around a shrine which may have been in that spot for centuries.

Mythology The myths that grew around the shrines were expressed first by word of mouth. Most temples today still have versions of the stories which were held to justify their existence in the eyes of pilgrims. There are several basic features in common. David Shulman has written that the story will include "the (usually miraculous) discovery of the site and the adventures of those important exemplars (such as gods, demons, serpents, and men) who were freed from sorrow of one kind or another by worshipping there". The shrine which is the object of the story nearly always claims to be supreme, better than all others. Many stories illustrate these claims of superiority: for example, we are often told that Ganga herself is forced to worship in a South Indian shrine in order to become free of the sins deposited by evildoers who bathe in the river at Benares.

Early Architecture Through all its great diversity Hindu temple architecture repeatedly expresses these beliefs, shared though not necessarily expressed, by the millions who make visiting temples such a vital and living part of life for Hindus today. In architecture as in religious philosophy, the S has derived much from its northern Hindu relations. The Buddhist *chaitya* hall with its apsidal plan had been the common form of most religious shrines up to the time of the Chalukyans in Karnataka, who in the 6th century started experimenting with what the Guptas in the N had already achieved by elaborating the simple square plan of earlier shrines. Developments at Aihole, Badami and Pattadakal led to the divergence of the 2 styles of Hindu temples and this became obvious in the shape of the spire. In the N, the *sikhara* was a smooth pyramidal structure, rising to a rounded top with a pointed end, while in the S the *vimana* was more like a stepped pyramid, usually square in plan and had at its top a rounded cupola. You can see examples of both types of tower at Aihole and Badami.

The **Dravida** or Dravidian style underwent several changes during the reign of the different dynasties that held sway for about 1000 years from the time of the Pallavas who laid its foundations. In Mamallapuram, rock-cut cave temples, *mandapas* or small excavated columned halls and the *rathas* or monoliths in the shape of temple chariots, were carved out by the early Pallavas in the 7th century. These were followed by structural temples and bas relief sculptures on giant rocks, which added another dimension. The Shore Temple (see page 851) built in the 8th century and the Kailasanatha at Kanchipuram (page 904) were structural expressions of the Pallava style with the distinctive 'lion pillar' which became a hall mark of the period, as well as the rectangular enclosure. The Ekambaranatha Temple in Kanchipuram shows the evolution of the Dravidian style – the shrine with its pyramidal tower, the separate *mandapa* all within the courtyard with its high enclosure wall made up of cells. Six centuries later the 2 separate structures were joined by the covered hall or *antarala*. In the Kailasanatha, whereas the substructure was solid granite the upper portion was in sandstone which allowed more freedom to the sculptor. A large subsidiary shrine there which took the place of an entrance gateway also hinted at the later *gopuram*.

Various dynasties fought for the Tamil lands until the *Cholas* gained supremacy in the 9th century and established their kingdom in the Kaveri river valley later extending their realm to become rulers over a vast area from the Ganga to Sri Lanka. They did away with the rampant lion pilasters, introduced high relief, half-size sculptures of deities and the gryphon motifs. Their greatest architectural achievements are seen in the early 11th century temples at Gangaikondacholapuram and at Thanjavur with huge pyramidal towers on high vertical bases with exquisitely carved figures in niches on the walls. The Cholas are also remembered for the fine bronzes which adorned their temples.

Development of Gopurams The Pandiyas succeeded the Cholas a century later and although no outstanding changes were made they introduced the practice of building tall and prominent watch towers, the *gopurams* and concentric, often battlemented fortress walls which enclosed the courtyards with shrines. Percy Brown observes that the reason for this change may have been due to the inability of the Pandiyas structurally to alter or remove any insignificant holy shrine which they found to be of no artistic merit but in order to draw attention to them and give them prominence they constructed the high walls and massive, richly ornamented gateways.

The *gopuram* took its name from the 'cow gate' of the Vedic village, which later became the city gate and finally the monumental temple entrance. This type of tower is distinguished from the *vimana* by its oblong plan at the top which is an elongated vaulted roof with gable ends. It has pronounced sloping sides, usually 65°, so that the section at the top is about half the size of the base. Although the first 2 storeys are usually built solidly of stone masonry, the rest is of lighter material, usually brick and plaster. You can see examples of Pandiya gopurams at Jambukesvara near Tiruchirappalli and in Chidambaram and Tirumalai, see page 864. The Airavatesvara Temple at Darasuram in Thanjavur District built in the 12th century, towards the end of Chola rule under King Rajaraja II, is a more complete example of the period, see page 869. Not only does it have the central temple with its tower but the enclosure also includes a number of smaller shrines. The lion pilasters and the gryphons of the earlier periods reappear here, only to be replaced by the horses and dragons in later temples. In the Ramesvaram region on the coast in S Tamil Nadu, open courtyards, trefoil arches and chariot forms became distinguishing features.

From the 13th century Muslim conquerors pentrated ever deeper into the S, bringing a halt to large scale temple building for 200 years. However by the 15th century the Vijayanagar kings established their empire across much of South India, building their fortressed city at Hampi. Their temples were carved out in harmony with the rock, the flat-roofed halls having numerous distinctive highly sculpted pillars. Changes in temple design reflected the changes in the ceremonial observances in worship. There was a proliferation of special purpose buildings within the temple enclosure. Around the central temple, a subsidiary shrine was built (usually to the NW) to house the consort of the main deity and to celebrate their marriage anniversary, a many-pillared open hall with a central altar, or *kalyana mandapa*, made its appearance close to the E entrance. The temples at Kanchipuram, Tadpatri, Srirangam, Lepakshi and Vellore are also in the Vijayanagara style. The development of the temple complex with several shrines to different deities in the courtyard, the tradition of building *gopurams* in each of the 4 enclosure walls and the remarkable use of the horse motif (and sometimes lions or dragons), mark the Vijayanagara period. The *kalyana mandapas* of the temples at Vellore and Kanchipuram make particular use of hippogryphs in their pillars. In the Srirangam temple it reaches its full expression in the *Seshagiri mandapa* or 'Horse Court'.

17th century After the defeat of Vijayanagar by the Muslim sultans of the Deccan, the Hindu rulers were pushed further S. The Nayakas emerged in the 17th century with their capital at Madurai and continued to build temple complexes with tall *gopurams*. These increased in height to become dominating structures covered profusely with plaster decorations. Madurai and Srirangam have a profusion of defensive walls, lengthy colonnades of the 'thousand pillar' halls and towering *gopurams*. The tall *gopurams* of Vijayanagara and *Nayaka* periods may have served a strategic purpose, but they moved away from the earlier *Chola* practice of giving the central shrine the tallest tower. The *kalyana mandapa* or marriage hall with a 'hundred' or 'thousand' pillars, and the temple tank with steps on all 4 sides, were introduced in some southern temples, along with the *Nandi* bull, Siva's 'vehicle', which occupies a prominent position at the entrance to the main Saivite shrine. In some temples you will see the sacrificial altar with a pole which may have small bells attached.

In Karnataka, at Belur, Halebid and Somnathpur, the Hoysalas from the 12th century developed their own style. The temples had a high star-shaped platform, providing an ambulatory around a pillared hall with hand-lathe turned and intricately carved columns, and parallel bands of exquisitely carved friezes and figures of deities around the exterior walls. The quality of the craftsmen in stone reached a peak during this period.

Kerala developed its own style of temple architecture resulting from the need to keep off the heavy rain. The temple roof imitated the functional tiled house roof and sometimes these were covered in metal sheets, occasionally golden as in the case of Guruvayur. The pagoda type tiered roof with gable windows are distinctive of the style as is the circular plan of some Kerala temples.

Culture

Dance, drama and music

Indian music

Changes constantly occurred in different schools of music within the basic framework of *raga-tala-prabandha* which was well established by the 7th century. From the 13th century the division between the *Hindustani* or the northern system (which included the western and eastern regions as well) and the *Carnatic* or the southern system, became pronounced. The southern school has a more scale-based structure of *raga* whereas the northern school has greater flexibility and thus continued to develop through the centuries. The *tala* too is much more precise. It is also nearly always devotional or didactic where the northern system also includes non-religious, everyday themes which are sometimes sensuous. The language that lends itself naturally to the southern system is Telugu and the only bowed instrument that is used to accompany vocal music is the violin, imported from the West but played rather differently.

The fundamental form in **Carnatic music** is the *varnam*. This is like an étude which conforms to phrases and melodic movements of a particular *raga*. They all have lyrics. The complex structure reaches its height in the *kritis* which are usually devotional, particularly in the 18th century with singers like Shyama Shastri and Tyagaraja. Unlike some North Indian musical forms in which the melody became more important than the lyric, *kriti* restored the balance between words and music.

Dance

Bharata Natyam is thought to be the oldest from of classical dance in India having started with the temple dancers in the S. Originating in Tamil Nadu, it is essentially a highly stylised solo feminine dance which combines movement, music and mime with *nritta* (pure dance) and *nritya* (expression), usually on the theme of spiritual love. The opening *alarippu* shows the dancer unfolding her body in strict rhythm and order, accompanied by the *mridangam* (drum) and the singing of the *nattuvanar* (conductor) and the dancer's own ankle bells, while the middle section *varnam* allows her to display her greatest skill and is very demanding, physically and emotionally. The 2 related dance forms, the *Bhagavata Mela*, performed by men in some important temples and the *Kuravanji*, a dance-opera for women for certain temple festivals also come from Tamil Nadu. Institutions excelling in the teaching of this form are Kalakshetra, Madras, Darpana, Ahmadabad, Rajarajeswar Kala Mandir, Bombay, MS University, Baroda and Triveni Kala Sangam, New Delhi.

Dance Drama

Rhythmic singing naturally leads to dancing. The *tillana* is like abstract dance while the *padams* tell a story by attitudes, gestures and facial expression. **Kuchipudi** takes its name from a village in Andhra Pradesh where it started as a religious dance-drama performed by men (although women now take part) where acting and speaking are also a part of the performance. The most important in this form is **Kathakali** which comes from Kerala and in its traditional form relates stories from the epics Ramayana and Mahabharata and is accompanied by shrill music with the performance lasting the whole night. It may appear rather strange and exaggerated with the highly elaborate make-up in green, red and white, with stylised beards made of rice paste and head dress giving the impression of a mask. The eyes convey the subtlest of expressions. The dancers are all male taking the part of gods and demons with make up and costumes (including large skirts) conforming to strict convention. Being based partly on traditional martial arts, the dancers sometimes carry weapons and the dancing is expressive and vigorous requiring long and rigorous training, see page 946.

The simpler **Ottan Thullal** combines classical with folk. Kerala has several institutions specialising in Kathakali – Kala Mandalam, PSW Natya Sangam, Unnayi Warrior Kala Nilayam. New Delhi has the International Centre, Calcutta Rabindra Bharati and Viswa Bharati in Santiniketan near Calcutta. **Mohiniyattam**, a secular dance has combined elements of both Kathakali and Bharat Natyam and the dance of an enchantress. Karnataka has its own folk theatre style of dance-drama in **Yakshagana** and is considered by some to outdo Kathakali in make up and costume! Its theme draws from strength, valour and anger in contrast to other forms which concentrate on the gentler emotions, the *nava rasas* (the 9 sentiments). Details in Introduction to the different states.

Percussion The unusual southern percussionists' contest takes place during the *Tala Vadya Kacheri* when instrumentalists compete with each other while keeping within the framework of a rhythm and finally come together in a delightful finale.

Cuisine

South India excels in vegetarian food. Strict South Indian Brahmins are strictly vegetarian and their meals avoid the use of garlic and onion and in some cases even tomatoes. The cuisine reflects what grows in abundance in the S – particularly coconut, chillies, tamarind and bananas. Although many Tamilians are vegetarians there are also many in South India who are not. However, the choice of vegetarian food is particularly wide. Favourites for breakfast or 'tiffin' (snack) include *dosai* (thin crisp pancakes, plain or 'masala' when stuffed with potatoes), *idli* (soft steamed fermented rice cakes), delcious rice-based *pongal* (worth searching out) and *vadai* (savoury lentil doughnuts), all served with a coconut chutney and *sambhar* (a spicy lentil and vegetable broth). *Dosais* and *idlis* have become universally popular and you may now find it on the menu of restaurants all over India.

Try a typical meal at a Lunch Home or Udipi restaurant. *Thalis* here are served on a stainless steel plate or more commonly on green plantain leaf. An unlimited quantity of boiled rice will be accompanied by *rasam* (a clear peppery lentil soup), 2 or 3 vegetable preparations often cooked with yoghurt and coconut, and *sambar*, plain yoghurt and chutney. The dessert usually is *payasam* (similar to rice or vermicelli pudding, prepared with thickened milk). Coffee is freshly roasted and ground, filtered and served mixed with hot milk, frothy and aromatic as it is poured from tumbler to a bowl.

Hyderabadi cuisine remains distinct because of its history of Muslim rule. Specialities include an aubergine dish *baghara baigan*, and *haleem*, a mutton and wheat preparation. Other non-vegetarian specialities include Mughlai dishes of *biriyani* (rice cooked with meat), *paya*, a soup, egg *paratha*, the rich unleavened bread and spicy pepper chicken *Chettinad* style.

Handicrafts

The southern states are particularly famous for both silk and cotton handloom products such as Kanchipuram silk, Bangalore silk and *ikats* from Andhra Pradesh. Apart from traditional saris these fabrics can be bought by the metre. Lacemaking by women, which was introduced by the British, is a flourishing cottage industry in the Godavari delta area.

Palms grow in profusion and cane, reed and coir are transformed into furniture, mats and baskets. Wood inlay and carving is carried out with rosewood and sandalwood, the latter also being used to produce soap, incense and perfume. Handcarved wooden blocks are also produced for printing fabrics to produce Machlipatnam (Masulipatam) *kalamkari*. In Kalahasti, they practise the traditional method of using a *kalam* (bamboo pen) to introduce the dyes on the material.

Bidri work which comes from Hyderabad in Andhra Pradesh has silver damascening on a dark metal alloy and you can buy small bowls, boxes, vases or items of jewellery. The leather industry is highly developed from Bangalore to Madras, producing shoes, bags and cases as well as being a centre for exporting garments. Channapatna, also in Karnataka, has long been famous for its wood-turning industry. You can purchase delightful and colourful traditional toys there: miniature carts, swings, roundabouts and furniture.

Modern South India

Government

At Independence the old province of Madras which included Andhra Pradesh and part of Kerala in addition to present day Tamil Nadu, became the State of Madras. In 1969, the name was changed to Tamil Nadu. Sixteen years earlier Andhra Pradesh itself had become the first state to be re-organised on the basis of a common language when the coastal districts of Andhra were joined with the interior districts of Telangana. Kerala was formed out of the former Princely States of Travancore and Kochi joined with some of the western coastal districts of Madras Presidency. Similarly Karnataka was formed by a re-grouping of districts which had previously been in different states, uniting all those districts where Kannada was the majority language.

The Economy

Agriculture

Rice is the most important crop in all the coastal regions of the 4 southern states, supplemented in some irrigated areas by sugar. Inland millets such as *ragi* (finger millet) and *sorghum* (known in Hindi as *jowar* and in Tamil as *cholam*) are supplemented by cash crops such as groundnuts and cotton on the plains, and tea, coffee, cardamom, ginger and pepper in the hills.

Resources and industry

There are important deposits of iron ore in Tamil Nadu, Andhra Pradesh and Karnataka, now being exploited for the manufacture of steel, magnesite, coal and lignite, and gold and gemstones from the Kolar Gold Fields northwards. Modern industrialisation can be traced back to the late 19th century in Madras, and the textile industry expanded rapidly in Coimbatore and Madurai before the Second World War. Since Independence Bangalore and Hyderabad have developed a widening range of high technology industries, especially in the field of communications, computing and aeronautics.

MADRAS

Contents

Maps

Madras was founded by the East India Company trader, Francis Day, in 1639, but some of the villages on the site – Triplicane, Mylapore, Tiruvottiyur, Pallavaram – go back over 2000 years.

BASICS *Population*: 5.36mn; *Altitude*: Sea level; *STD Code*: 044.

History

Before the arrival of the British, there was a Portuguese settlement in the San Thome area and Armenian traders. In 1639, Francis Day, a trader with the East India Company, negotiated the grant of a tiny plot of sandy land to the N of the Cooum River as the base for a warehouse or 'factory' which consisted of a mere strip '3 miles long and a mile at its widest'. By 1640 a few thatched houses had been built, close to the beach, protected by walls on 4 sides. Since it was completed on 23 April, St George's Day, it was christened Fort St George. There was no natural harbour, and there was nothing in the site of Madras itself to attract a settlement. Its choice was dictated partly by local politics – Francis Day's friendship with Dharmala Ayyappa Nayak provided a useful lever with the Raja of Chandragiri, the last in the line of Vijayanagar chiefs who still controlled that section of coast – but more importantly by the local price of cotton goods, which was better than anywhere else along India's eastern seaboard.

By 1654 the settlement had grown and been fortified. Fort St George had a church and English residences and it came to be known as 'White Town' or Madraspatnam. To its N was what the British referred to as 'Black Town', which the local people called Chennapatnam after Nayak's father. The 2 towns merged and Madraspatnam grew with the acquisition of neighbouring villages of *Tiru-alli-keni* or Lily Tank (Triplicane) in 1676. In 1693, Governor Yale (founder of Yale University in the USA) acquired Egmore, Purasawalkam and Tondiarpet from

Climate: Madras

	Jan	Feb	Mar	Apr	May	Jun	Jul	Aug	Sep	Oct	Nov	Dec	Av/Tot
Max (°C)	29	31	33	35	38	37	35	35	34	32	29	28	33
Min (°C)	20	21	23	23	28	28	26	26	25	24	23	21	24
Rain (mm)	24	7	15	15	52	53	83	124	118	267	309	139	1216

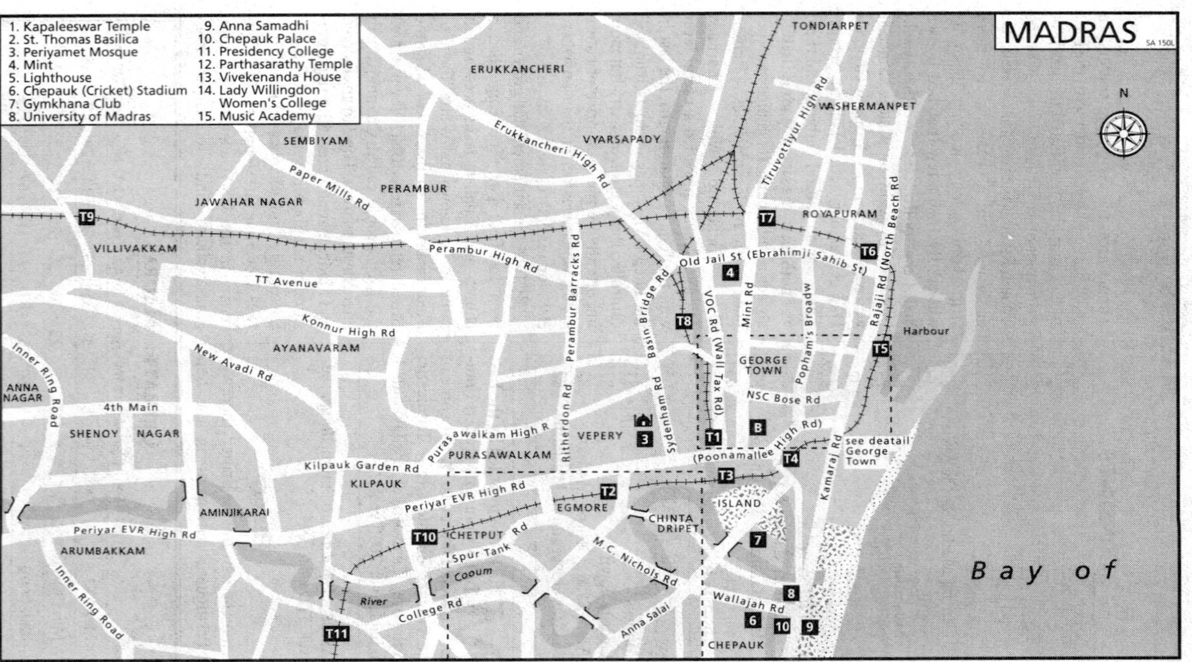
MADRAS
SA 150L
1. Kapaleeswar Temple
2. St. Thomas Basilica
3. Periyamet Mosque
4. Mint
5. Lighthouse
6. Chepauk (Cricket) Stadium
7. Gymkhana Club
8. University of Madras
9. Anna Samadhi
10. Chepauk Palace
11. Presidency College
12. Parthasarathy Temple
13. Vivekenanda House
14. Lady Willingdon Women's College
15. Music Academy
N
TONDIARPET
ERUKKANCHERI
WASHERMANPET
Tiruvottiyur High Rd
SEMBIYAM
Erukkancheri High Rd
VYARSAPADY
Paper Mills Rd
PERAMBUR
JAWAHAR NAGAR
ROYAPURAM
Rajaji Rd (North Beach Rd)
VILLIVAKKAM
Perambur High Rd
Perambur Barracks Rd
Old Jail St (Ebrahimji Sahib St)
TT Avenue
Basin Bridge Rd
VOC Rd (Wall Tax Rd)
Mint Rd
Popham's Broadw
Harbour
Konnur High Rd
AYANAVARAM
New Avadi Rd
GEORGE TOWN
NSC Bose Rd
Inner Ring Road
ANNA NAGAR
4th Main
SHENOY NAGAR
Purasawalkam High R
Ritherdon Rd
VEPERY
Sydenham Rd
(Poonamallee High Rd)
Kamaraj Rd
see deatail George Town
PURASAWALKAM
Kilpauk Garden Rd
KILPAUK
Periyar EVR High Rd
EGMORE
ISLAND
CHINTA DRIPET
AMINJIKARAI
Periyar EVR High Rd
ARUMBAKKAM
CHETPUT Rd
Spur Tank
Cooum
M.C. Nichols Rd
Inner Ring Road
River
College Rd
Wallajah Rd
Anna Salai
CHEPAUK
Bay of
T1
T2
T3
T4
T5
T6
T7
T8
T9
T10
T11
B

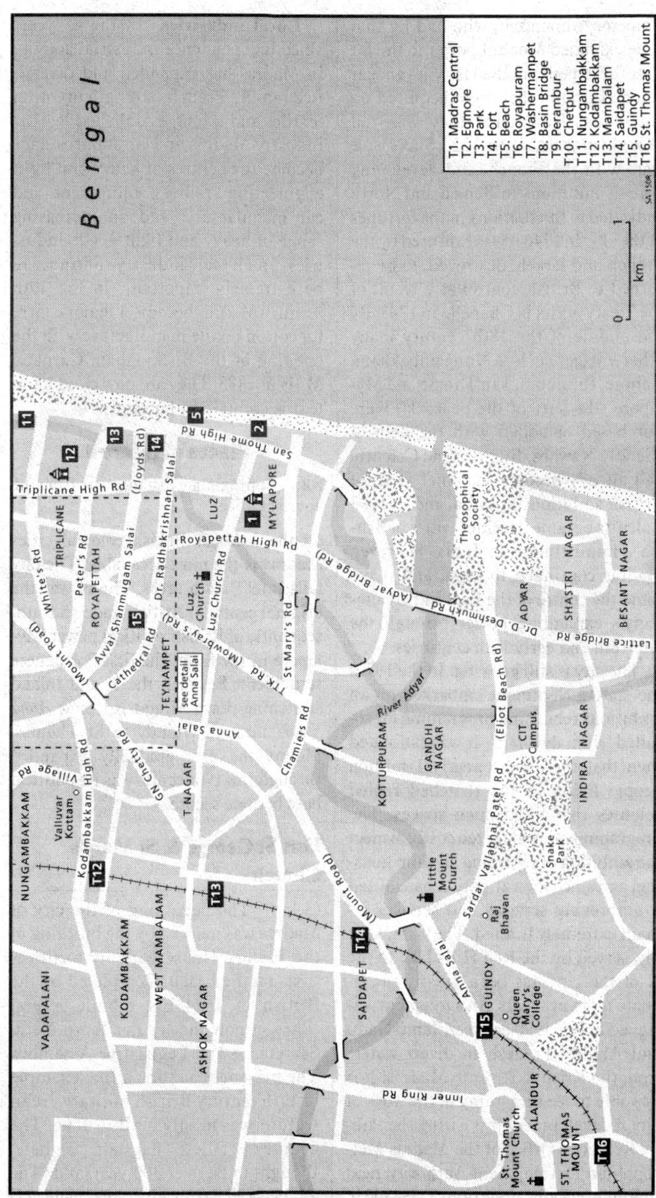
Bengal
T1. Madras Central
T2. Egmore
T3. Park
T4. Fort
T5. Beach
T6. Royapuram
T7. Washermanpet
T8. Basin Bridge
T9. Perambur
T10. Chetput
T11. Nungambakkam
T12. Kodambakkam
T13. Mambalam
T14. Saidapet
T15. Guindy
T16. St. Thomas Mount
0
1
km
Triplicane High Rd
San Thome High Rd
TRIPLICANE
White's Rd
Peter's Rd
ROYAPETTAH
(Lloyds Rd)
Dr. Radhakrishnan Salai
Avvai Shanmugam Salai
(Mount Road)
Cathedral Rd
TEYNAMPET
see detail Anna Salai
LUZ
MYLAPORE
Royapettah High Rd
Luz Church
Luz Church Rd
(Mowbray's Rd)
TTK Rd
St Mary's Rd
(Adyar Bridge Rd)
Dr. D. Deshmukh Rd
Theosophical Society
ADYAR
SHASTRI NAGAR
BESANT NAGAR
Lattice Bridge Rd
(Eliot Beach Rd)
CIT Campus
INDIRA NAGAR
River Adyar
Chamiers Rd
Anna Salai
KOTTURPURAM
GANDHI NAGAR
Village Rd
NUNGAMBAKKAM
Valluvar Kottam
Kodambakkam High Rd
GN Chetty Rd
T NAGAR
Sardar Vallabhai Patel Rd
Snake Park
Little Mount Church
Raj Bhavan
(Mount Road)
KODAMBAKKAM
WEST MAMBALAM
SAIDAPET
VADAPALANI
ASHOK NAGAR
Anna Salai
GUINDY
Queen Mary's College
Inner Ring Rd
ALANDUR
St. Thomas Mount Church
ST. THOMAS MOUNT

Emperor Aurangzeb, who had by that time extended Moghul power to the far S, at the expense of the last Vijayanagar rulers. Initially they were acquired on an annual lease until they were all brought in to the city in 1720. Successive wars with the French, and developing British ambitions in Bengal and North India, led to fluctuations in the fortunes of the city. In 1746 it was captured by the French and largely destroyed, to be returned to British control as a result of the Treaty of Aix la Chapelle in 1748. By the middle of the 18th century many other villages such as Nungambakkam, Ennore, Perambur, San Thome and Mylapore (the 'city of the peacock') were purchased or added with the help of friendly Nawabs. By this time Calcutta had already become the chief focus of British ambitions in India, and in 1793 Calcutta became the chief centre of British administration in India. However, Madras continued to grow, and it became the centre of the East India Company's expanding power through the late 18th and early 19th centuries.

The city is still growing. In the 1970s the state government embarked on an ambitious rehousing programme for so-called 'slum dwellers'. It was estimated then that there were nearly 1 million people living in the thatched roofed colonies that filled open spaces. The programme proved far too costly to meet the ambition of replacing all slum housing, and since then attention has shifted to improving services, but services remain extremely limited. The water supply, served by the Red Hills lake to the N of the city, has been grossly inadequate for many years. An agreement was signed in Feb 1990 between Tamil Nadu and Andhra Pradesh to divert waters from the Krishna River to Madras. It is possible to see something of the work of city redevelopment by visiting the Public Relations Office of the Madras Metropolitan Development Authority, next to Egmore Railway station, T 834855.

Local industries In the 45 years since Independence industrial activity in Madras has expanded and diversified rapidly. From its strength in cotton textiles and a long established leather industry Madras and its suburbs have become the centres of heavy and light engineering, railway equipment and car manufacture, and an increasing range of heavy and light goods industries. Small scale industry continues to be extremely important. In the 19th century Madras became a major centre for cotton textile manufacture with the opening of the Buckingham Carnatic Mills in 1885. They are now closed, but textiles remain important.

Places of interest

NB: Approximate distances are from the Tourist Office.

Of the 3 major British colonial cities Madras is the most accessible. The city falls into 3 main areas. The N was the original centre of British trade and subsequently of British political power. Mylapore in the S was the first Portuguese settlement. Between the 2, and inland stretching down Mount Rd (now *Anna Salai*) through Guindy to St Thomas' Mount the city gradually expanded through the 19th century as its political base became secure.

Fort St George & St Mary's Church

(3 km) The beginning of the city of Madras was marked by the building of the Factory House with its fortifications on the beach. Completed by the British in 1654 but rebuilt several times, it now houses the Tamil Nadu Secretariat and Legislative Assembly. The present structure, a fine example of 17th century British military architecture, was mostly built in 1666. The country's tallest flagstaff is here, thought to be over 300 years old. The 24 black Charnockite (see page 22)

pillars are those reclaimed by the British in 1762 of the original 32 which once formed the colonnade of the present Secretariat building (the French had carried them off to Pondicherry after their victory in 1746).

The State Legislative Hall has fine wood work and black and white stone paving. You can also see the old barracks and officers' quarters including the house occupied by Lord Clive which he rented from an Armenian merchant and where you can see one room; Clive's Corner has small exhibits.

Inside the Fort is **St Mary's Church** (3 km). Built 1678-80 by Streynsham Master in solid masonry to a simple plan of 3 aisles with semi-circular cannon-proof roofs and 1.3m thick walls. It was the safest building in the Fort and in times of siege was used as a military dormitory and store house. The first English church in India, it was entirely re-built in 1759 after being severely damaged in a siege. A fluted spire was added and the tower and belfry which were originally detached were linked to the main church. Well-known people associated with the church include Robert Clive, who married Margaret Maskelyne here in 1753, and Governor Elihu Yale, who was also married here, later founded Yale University and gave a plate to the Church in 1687. The most remarkable monument is the one erected by the East India Company to the famous missionary Schwartz, at one time the intermediary between the British and Haidar Ali. He is shown dying on his bed surrounded by a group of friends. The church now has an active congregation in membership with the Church of South India. The original black granite font has been in continuous use. Job Charnock, who founded Calcutta, is thought to have had his 3 daughters baptised here in 1689. The painting of the Last Supper over the altar is attributed to the school of Raphael and was originally believed to have been looted by the British from a French church in Pondicherry. The teak balustrade in the W gallery has curious oriental carvings.

George Town

Re-named after the future King George V on the occasion of his visit to India in 1905, George Town has long been the centre of Madras's commercial activity. Lying to the E and NE of the Central Railway station, it had been a densely packed labyrinth of lanes and gullies in the late 18th century. Then a dramatic change was brought about by the lawyer Stephen Popham, who was in Madras from 1778-95. By this time the city had been a major centre for over a century. One estimate put its population in 1690 at over 300,000, and although its destruction by the French in 1746 had caused a mass evacuation it rapidly regained its former size. Popham had already laid the basis for setting up a police force in the city, but was particularly enthusiastic about improving the city's housing and sanitation. He argued that main drains should be constructed in the Black Town to carry away the stagnant waters. The scheme could be realised when the Governor finally insisted on the removal of a low hill just inland of Fort St George, then known as Hog Hill, which was thought to threaten the security of the Fort. The work was carried out, and the earth used to infill the low-lying marshy land immediately to its N. Here Popham laid out what was to become Madras's main commercial street throughout the 19th century, still known as **Popham's Broadway**.

In Popham's Broadway itself is the **Wesleyan Church** (1820, now Church of South India). In **Armenian Street** to its E is the beautiful **Armenian Church of the Holy Virgin Mary**, built in 1772. The solid walls and massive 3m high wooden doors conceal the spotless open courtyard inside. The church stands on the site of an ancient cemetery and in

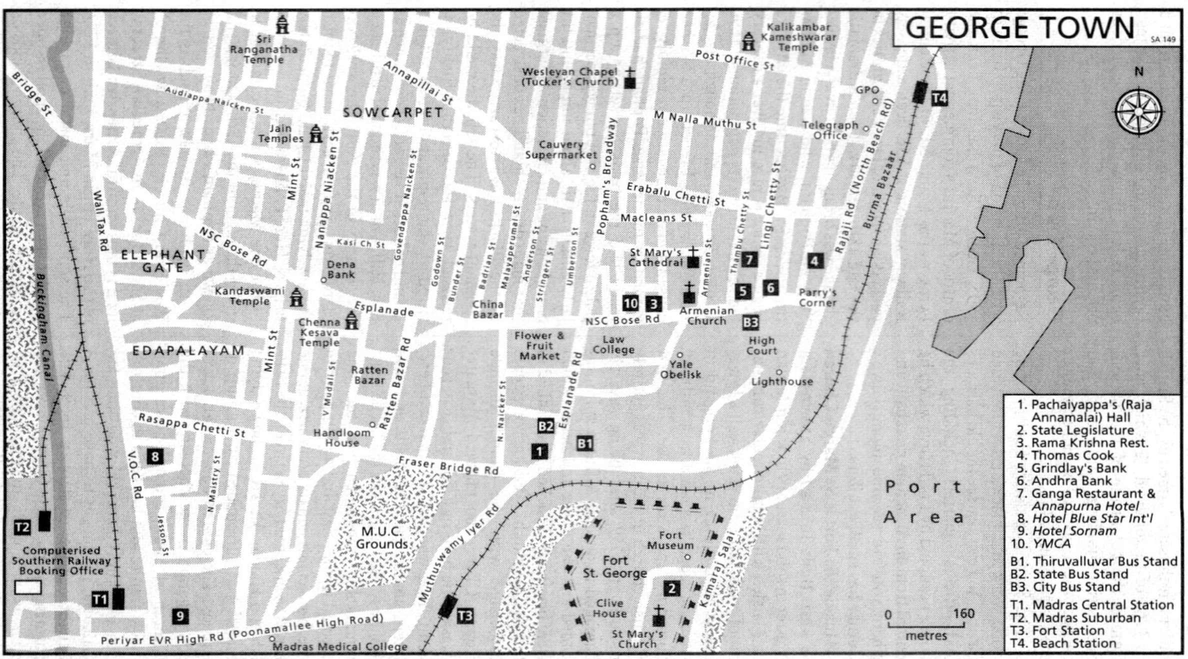
GEORGE TOWN
SA 149
N
Sri Ranganatha Temple
Kalikambar Kameshwarar Temple
Post Office St
Wesleyan Chapel (Tucker's Church)
GPO
T4
Bridge St
Annapillai St
Audiappa Naicken St
SOWCARPET
M Nalla Muthu St
Telegraph Office
Jain Temples
Cauvery Supermarket
Popham's Broadway
Rajaji Rd (North Beach Rd)
Burma Bazaar
Wall Tax Rd
Mint St
Nanappa Niacken St
Govendappa Naicken St
Erabalu Chetti St
Macleans St
Thambu Chetty St
Lingi Chetty St
NSC Bose Rd
Kasi Ch St
ELEPHANT GATE
Dena Bank
Godown St
Bunder St
Badrian St
Malayaperumal St
Anderson St
Stringers St
Umberson St
St Mary's Cathedral
Armenian St
Buckingham Canal
Kandaswami Temple
Esplanade
China Bazar
NSC Bose Rd
Armenian Church
Parry's Corner
Chenna Kesava Temple
Flower & Fruit Market
Law College
High Court
EDAPALAYAM
Ratten Bazar Rd
Ratten Bazar
V Mudali St
Yale Obelisk
Lighthouse
Esplanade Rd
N. Naicker St
Rasappa Chetti St
Handloom House
V.O.C. Rd
Fraser Bridge Rd
Port Area
N Maistry St
Jesson St
M.U.C. Grounds
Muthuswamy Iyer Rd
Fort Museum
Fort St. George
Kamaraj Salai
Computerised Southern Railway Booking Office
Clive House
St Mary's Church
Periyar EVR High Rd (Poonamallee High Road)
Madras Medical College
0 160 metres
1. Pachaiyappa's (Raja Annamalai) Hall
2. State Legislature
3. Rama Krishna Rest.
4. Thomas Cook
5. Grindlay's Bank
6. Andhra Bank
7. Ganga Restaurant & Annapurna Hotel
8. Hotel Blue Star Int'l
9. Hotel Sornam
10. YMCA
B1. Thiruvalluvar Bus Stand
B2. State Bus Stand
B3. City Bus Stand
T1. Madras Central Station
T2. Madras Suburban
T3. Fort Station
T4. Beach Station

the red-brick paved courtyard are several tombstones. The first Armenian church was built in 1712, but the oldest Armenian tombstone dates from 1663, and the community of Armenian traders grew steadily. The East India Company valued their 'sober, frugal and wise' style of life and they were given the same rights as English settlers in 1688. The most famous Armenian in Madras was Coja Petrus, who made a series of charitable gifts to benefit the city, including the first bridge across the Adyar, used by Anna Salai today. A plaque commemorates the gift. The present church has a separate white belfry with 6 bells, the largest in Madras. On the walls of corridors outside the church sanctuary now hang some beautiful pen and ink portraits and pictures of Armenia drawn by the present – and last remaining – Armenian sexton.

Immediately to the N of the Armenian Church is the Roman Catholic Cathedral, **St Mary of the Angels**, built in 1675 with the help of a grant sanctioned by Governor Elihu Yale. The date 1642, inscribed at the entrance to the Church, is the date when the Capuchin monks built their first church in Madras. The present sanctuary contains oil paintings of the Crucifixion and Mary Magdalene.

To the E again is **Parry's Corner**, named after the company founded by Thomas Parry in 1790. The corner plot on which Dare House stands was bought by Parry in 1803. Then the sea washed right up against the building's walls. The group is now controlled by Nattukkottai Chettiars from Ramanathapuram District – see page 912. Other famous commercial names are also found in the same area, including Binny, established as early as 1682.

The **High Court** (5 km) built in 1892, is to the N of the Fort in the Indo-Saracenic style of the late 19th century architects such as Henry Irwin, who was also responsible for the National Art Gallery. It stands on the site of the old 'Esplanade Park', which was made in 1757 when the original Black Town was finally demolished. The red judicial building (believed to be second only in size to London's), has a number of domes, minarets and spires above and a labyrinth of vaulted corridors within. You are allowed to visit the courtrooms in the lawcourts by using the entrance on the left. A fine example is Court No 13 which has stained glass, fretted woodwork, carved furniture, silvered panels and a painted ceiling. Contact Registrar for visit and guide. 1045-1345, 1430-1630. Mon-Sat.

The huge red central tower nearly 50m tall built like a domed minaret to serve as a **lighthouse** can be seen 30 km out at sea. It took over from the Esplanade lighthouse in 1894 as the city's third lighthouse and was in use until 1977 when the new one was built on the Marina. You can climb to the top of the lighthouse for a good view. The **Esplanade Lighthouse** SE of the High Court is in the form of a large Doric pillar which took over from the Fort lighthouse in 1841. It is used as the standard bench mark for Madras.

W of the High Court is the **Law College** with its twin minarets which stands on the site of the old cemetery of Fort St George. Behind it is the **Yale Obelisk** which marks the grave of Elihu Yale's 4 year old son and his wife's first husband Edward Hynmers.

To the W of the Law Courts are the Law College (opened in 1892 on the site of the European settlers' first burial ground) and the **Pachaiyappa's Hall**, built in 1850 and modelled on the Athenian Temple of Theseus. Pachaiyappa Mudaliar was a Hindu who was one of the first Indians to leave a will. Born in 1748 in a destitute family, he had made a fortune by the age of 21. He wished a major share of his wealth to go to charity, and his will was contested for 47 years after his death in 1794. In the event the court decided that Rs 450,000 should be held in trust to provide education for poor Hindus. The trust now administers charities across India, sponsoring 6 colleges, a polytechnic and 16 schools in Tamil Nadu.

The 19th century growth of Madras can be traced N from Parry's corner. **First Line Beach** (N Beach Rd), built on reclaimed land in 1814, was the road fronting the beach. The **GPO**, designed by Robert Fellowes Chisholm, was finished in 1884. By then the first harbour pier had been in use for over 20 years, and the harbour which was to transform the economy of the city was begun in 1876. The whole structure was washed away in a catastrophic cyclone in 1881, but the work was renewed, to be completed in 1896.

There are several reminders of the wealth of the 18th century city. Major commercial expansion took place between First Line Beach and **Mint Street**. The Mint from which the road takes its name was first opened in 1640, from the end of the 17th century minting gold coins under licence for the Mughals, though it did not move to Mint St until 1841-2.

Today the Mint is part of the Government Printing Press. S. Muthiah writes that in 1699 Thomas Salmon had written of the 'Black Town' that "the streets are wide, and trees planted in some of them; and having the sea on one side and a river on the other, there are few towns so pleasantly situated or better supplied; but except for some few brick houses the rest are miserable cottages, built with clay and thatched and not so much as a window to be seen on the outside... but I must say, notwithstanding all their appearance of poverty, I never was in a place where wealth abounded more, or where ready money was more plentiful about 20 years ago... Beyond the Black Town are gardens for half a mile together planted with mangoes, coconuts, guavas, oranges, where everybody has the liberty of walking and may purchase the most delicious fruit for a trifle". Standing on the banks of the Buckingham Canal today it is difficult to imagine that it could ever have been an attractive scene.

Immediately to the N runs **Wall Tax Road** (now called **VOC Road**). It takes its original name from an unsuccessful plan to raise money by taxation to pay for the defensive wall constructed between 1764-69 to ward off the attacks of Haider Ali. At **Basin Bridge** it reaches one of the early experiments to provide Madras with a secure drinking water supply, Charles Trevelyan's 'basin' dug out to act as a reservoir.

'Interior' George Town is much the same now as the early 19th century town, except, as Muthiah says, "it just keeps getting more and more congested". He goes on to say "in the northern half there still remain the country-tiled houses with pillared verandahs, short and heavy doors inches thick and 'caste marks' at the entrance. The southern half, mainly in Peddanaickanpet, is Madras's wholesale market, street after street, narrow and crowded, specialising on street level in particular goods, with palatially equipped homes often occupying the upper reaches of these same dingy buildings". Paper in Anderson St, fireworks in Badrian St, fruit in Bunder St, vegetables in Malayaperumal St, turmeric and *kumkum* powder, silk thread for charms, false hair, glass and mica in Devaraj Mudali St. The list of specialist wholesalers is seemingly endless. The pavements of the main streets are now lined with trinket sellers, though a new wholesale market has been opened at Koyambedu, W of Annanagar.

Central Madras and the Marina

Triplicane and **Chepauk** contain some of the finest examples of late 19th century Indo-Saracenic architecture in India, focused on the University of Madras just to the S of the Cooum. South Beach Rd (now *Kamarajar Salai*, after the well

American Ice For Madras Heat

The first ice arrived in Calcutta from New England in 1833, and followed on the discovery by Frederic Tudor of Boston that ice would remain frozen if covered in sawdust. Tudor organised the cutting and storing of ice blocks during the New England winter and their transport around the world. The "ice house" in Madras was built in the early 1840s. The business survived for 30 years, until refrigeration was invented. The building then changed hands several times before becoming the home for a few months of Swami Vivekenanda in 1892 hence its modern name, Vivekenanda House.

known Tamil Congress politician), laid out in 1846, runs 3.5 km due S to Mylapore. The Governor of Madras Mountstuart Elphinstone Grant-Duff (1881-86) decided to develop the Marina, especially as a promenade. Ever since it has been a lung for the city and a favourite place for thousands of city dwellers to walk on Sun evenings. Over a century before that the **Chepauk Palace** had been built for Wallajah Muhammad Ali, Nawab of the Carnatic. It marked the move of the Nawab to Madras and became the focus for a growing Muslim population in the city which remains focused on Triplicane and Wallajah Rd. See below.

Marina Beach and Aquarium (3 km)
The fine sandy beach stretches to about 5 km from the harbour to St Thome. Its width is artificial, for until the harbour was built to the N at the end of the 19th century the sea washed up close to the present road. The N drifting current has progressively widened the beach since the harbour walls were constructed out into the sea in 1876.

On the beach itself is the **Anna Park** named after the founder of the DMK, CN Annadurai and the Chief Minister of its first administration in 1967. The **MGR Samadhi** commemorates MG Ramachandran, the film star and charismatic Chief Minister during the 1980s. The latter has become a focus of pilgrimage from all over Tamil Nadu.

The **Sunday afternoon Market** on the beach is worth visiting. There is an **aquarium**, described by one Madras resident as something "Madras should be ashamed of". The swimming pools are not rec. 1400-2000 weekdays, 0800-2000 holidays. Small fee.

WARNING Swimming unattended along Marina beach is dangerous.

The University Building and Presidency College

The University of Madras was incorporated in 1857 and is one of India's oldest modern universities. In 1864 Chisholm won a competition to design the University and Presidency College buildings. The 2-storeyed Presidency College, 'combining Italianate with Saracenic' styles, making full use of red brick, was completed in 1870. The Senate House was begun in 1874 and completed 5 years later. The Senate Hall was built to seat 1600 people. In the words of S Muthiah "the ceiling is elaborately carved and the stained glass windows were, in their day, the finest in Madras".

Chepauk and Beach Road

Chepauk Palace (4.5 km) on the Beach Rd was the residence of the Nawab of Carnatic and now houses the Public Works Department. Designed by Philip Stowey in 1768, it is one of the city's earlier Mughal style buildings. Originally built in 2 sections, the 2-storeyed Khalsa Mahal with 4 small domes and the Humayun Mahal with the grand *durbar* hall, a tower was built between the two after the Govt took over the palace in 1855. The original building is now hidden from the road by the modern PWD building, *Ezhilagam*.

Immediately behind is the **Chepauk cricket ground** where test matches are played. Lining the S Beach Rd is a succession of University buildings, including the Lady Willingdon Teacher Training College and Queen Mary College. This women's college was founded in 1914.

Almost next door to the Lady Willingdon Teacher Training College is the unimpressive-looking **Vivekenanda House**. Despite its looks, it has an interesting history, for it was Madras's first 'ice house', built for storing ice imported from abroad. On the other side of the beach is the sculpture "the Triumph of Labour" the work of KCS Pannicker. He was the successor to the architect Robert Fellowes Chisholm as Principal of the School of Industrial Art. When he retired in 1966 he founded the Cholamandal artists colony. Running N-S immediately behind the University buildings is the Buckingham Canal, which runs right through the city on its 500 km course up the E coast to Andhra Pradesh. In Madras it is nothing more than an open, mosquito-infected stinking sewer.

The Island and Anna Salai (Mount Road)

Immediately to the S of Fort St George is the Island, created between 1696 and 1705. First the grounds for a Governor's residence, it later became a military camp, and it has retained its military ownership ever since. In the SW corner is the **Gymkhana Club**, and a range of sporting facilities including a golf course. Beyond the Willingdon Bridge is the bronze statue of the former governor Sir Thomas Munro, cast in 1839. Shown on horseback, it has the curious feature that he is shown riding without stirrups.

Near the Round Thana is the Banqueting Hall of the old Government House, now known as **Rajaji Hall**. Set back from Anna Salai where it crosses the River Cooum, it was built on the instruction of Robert Clive's son Edward to mark the British victory over Tipu Sultan. It is in a very attractive setting and was used as a banqueting hall. Designed in the Greek temple style by Danish astronomer, Goldingham, who had been working with the East India Company since 1786, it was completed in 1802 (altered in the mid 19th century). The surrounding compound is often used for trade fairs and exhibitions.

Parthasarathi Temple (3 km) On Triplicane High Rd and the tank which gives its name to the locality is the oldest temple structure in Madras. Built in the 8th century by Pallava kings, it was renovated in the 16th by Vijayanagara rulers. Dedicated to Krishna as the royal charioteer, it shows 5 of Vishnu's 10 incarnations and is the only one dedicated to Parthasarathi whose legend is told in Tamil and Telugu inscriptions on the outer wall. 0600-1200, 1600-2200.

Wallajah Mosque (3.5 km) On Triplicane High Rd, the 'Big Mosque' was built in 1795 by the Nawab of the Carnatic to house thousands. There are 2 slender minarets with golden domes on either side and a wide set of steps. There is an excellent view of the mosque from the roof of the *Broad Lands Hotel*.

Chintadripet, Egmore and the western inner suburbs

Almost enclosed by a loop on the S side of the Cooum River, just to the S of the Central Railway station, **Chintadripet** is one of Madras's earliest suburbs. Today it is a densely packed collection of single and double storey houses, enclosing courtyards. Founded in 1734, it was set up as a weavers' settlement when the East India Company was finding it difficult to get enough good cloth to meet the demand in England. The Tamil words *chinna tari pettai* mean 'village of small looms', and by 1737 over 230 weaving families were settled in the suburb. The area remains a centre of small scale industry. A Jain shrine was built in 1985.

Egmore A bridge across the Cooum at Egmore was opened in 1700. In the last quarter of the 18th century the area to the S of the Poonamallee High Rd between the bends of the Cooum became a popular new residential area. Pantheon Rd, laid out in the late 1780s, became the centre of Madras's social and cultural life for 200 years. Now focussing

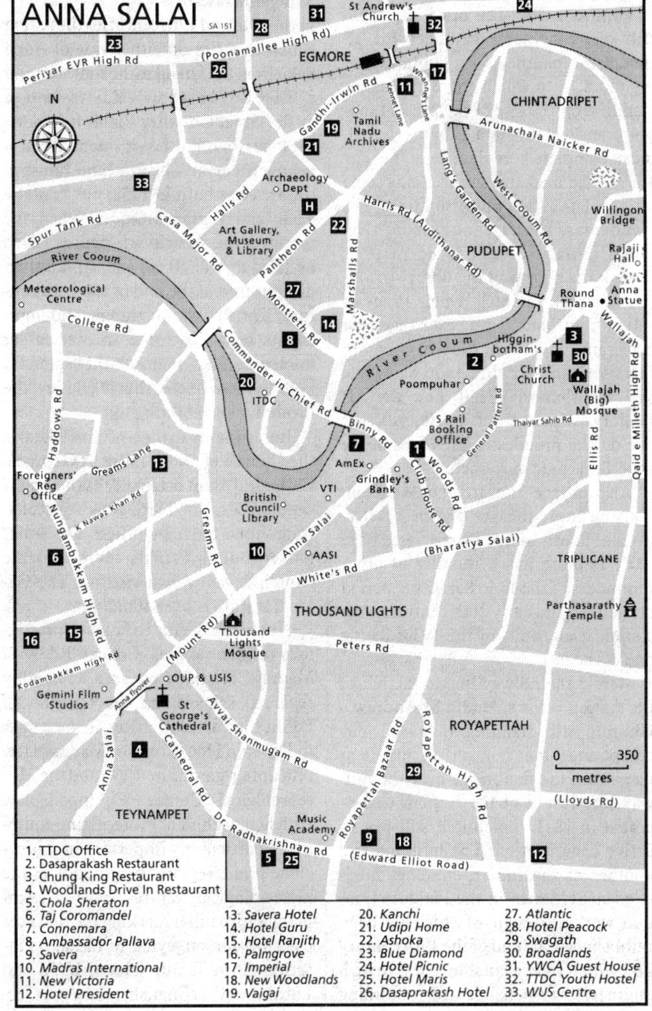

on the metre gauge railway station connecting Madras with stations to the S, Egmore was first developed in 1715 with the construction of a 'garden house' for Richard Horden. In the 100 years after 1720 all the major roads of contemporary Egmore were laid out, some taking their names from senior army officers.

Pantheon Rd The most important still keeps the name Pantheon Rd, although the 'pantheon' – or public assembly rooms – to which the name refers, standing on the site of the present museum and Connemara Library, was almost completely replaced in the late 1880s. The museum site contains some striking late 19th century buildings. The **Connemara Library**, one of India's National Libraries, was opened in 1896, though the origins of the library in Madras go back to 1662, "when a bale of calico from Madras was exchanged for books in London". At the SW corner of the site stands Irwin's Indo-Saracenic Victoria Memorial Hall, now the **Art Gallery**, which Tillotson describes as one of "the proudest expressions of the Indo-Saracenic movement".

Also on the site are the **Museum**, housing one of the world's finest collections of South Indian bronzes (see page 827). Egmore has a number of other reminders of the Indo Saracenic period of the 19th and early 20th centuries, the station itself, built in the 1930s, being one of the last.

Across the railway line to the NE of the station is the splendid **St Andrew's Church**, still standing in a spacious compound. You can get an excellent view from the footbridge over the railway line just E of the station. Consecrated in 1821, the church still has an active congregation. The building was another of the Indian churches modelled on St Martin-in-the-Fields in London, working designs of which had been published at the end of the 18th century and which were available to the British engineers responsible for building churches for the British community in India in the early 19th century. However, apart from the façade the church is essentially circular, 25m in diameter, and has a magnificent shallow-domed ceiling. The spire is 51m high.

Thousand Lights & Nungambakkam

In the 18th and 19th centuries the region which now lies on either side of Anna Salai from the Island to the southern end of TTK Rd (Mowbray's Rd) was known as the Great Choultry Plain. It became the focus for high class residential European settlement. The first large house in the area was built in 1758, just N of the Thousand Lights Mosque. When the threat to the security of Madras posed by Haidar Ali and his son Tipu Sultan disappeared at the end of the 18th century British administrators and merchants began to move in ever larger numbers, and many built splendid houses, including Arthur Wellesley, the future Duke of Wellington.

Immediately to the S of Anna Salai is the Church of South India **St George's Cathedral**, built originally as the Anglican cathedral in 1816. Now concealed from Anna Salai by offices and other modern buildings in the compound, the church is well worth visiting. The Cathedral spire is over 40m high.

Nungambakkam today is a prestigious residential area. College Rd, with Madras Christian College, a very highly regarded school, and the Director of Public Instruction's offices are next door to Doveton House (one of Madras's few remaining 'garden houses') and the **Meteorological Centre**. Equipped now with high technology forecasting equipment, particularly important in this cyclone prone region, the grounds of the meteorological centres have a commemorative pillar marking the first ever base line for surveying in India. Its inscription, in Tamil, Telugu, Urdu and Latin as well as English, reads "the Geodetic position (Lat 13° 4'3" 0.5N Long 80° 14'54" 20E) of Col William Lambton is primary original of the Survey of India. Fixed by him in 1802, was at a point 6 feet to the S and 1 foot to the W of the centre of this pillar. The centre of the meridian circle of the Madras Observatory was at a point 12 feet to the E of the centre of this pillar". From that minutely precise beginning spread the extraordinary undertaking of surveying S Asia from the southern tip of Kanniyakumari to the heights of Mount Everest, named after the surveyor George Everest who completed the first survey. Here too are India's earliest bench marks.

The Thousand Lights Mosque is a landmark on the corner of Anna Salai and Peters Rd. The old mosque was built by the Wallajah family in the early 17th century but had to be replaced by the new 5-domed mosque, as it was unsafe. The name recalls the 1000 oil lamps that used to be lit in the old mosque.

Valluvar Kottam (4 km) was built in 1976 as a memorial to a Tamil poet and philosopher Thiruvalluvar. He wrote the great Tamil classic Thirukkural in 1330 verses which is inscribed on 133 granite slabs mounted on 67 pillars. It has a vast auditorium with a capacity of 4000 and is one of Madras's important cultural centres. A special feature is the 2700 tonne 35m granite replica of the temple chariot of Tiruvarur which carries a statue of the poet. Its pale pink dome which is reflected in the 2 large pools in the terrace garden can be seen from a long distance. 0900-1900.

South Madras

The **Basilica of San Thome** (6 km) at the S end of Marina Beach, surrounded now by the tenement re-housing scheme of a fishermen's colony. The church is claimed as one of very few churches to be built over an apostle's tomb. St Thomas Didymus (Doubting Thomas) is believed to have come to India in AD 52. According to one legend, having landed on the W coast, he travelled across the peninsula, arriving in **Mylapore** ('town of peacocks') where he lived and preached. To escape persecution he took shelter in Little Mount (see below). An alternative story recalls how he was invited to visit the King Gondophernes in Taxila, where he converted the king and his court before moving to South India.

A few 100m to the W is the **Kapaleeswarar Temple** (4 km) off Kutchery Rd. It is a 16th century Siva temple with a 40m *gopuram*, built after the original was destroyed by the Portuguese in 1566 on an older site which may date back to the 7th. It is very sacred to Tamil Saivites so non-Hindus are only allowed in the outer courtyard where there are several bronze statues. There is also a shrine to a saint with a sculpture of the miracle of bringing back a dead girl to life. 0600-1200, 1600-2200.

From the temple in the heart of Mylapore you can go W along Luz Church Rd to the **Luz Church**, probably the oldest church in Madras. It was built by the Portuguese in 1516, according to the inscription, in honour of Our Lady of Light. The actual date is probably between 1547 and 1582. The Tamil name for the church, *Kattu Kovil*, means 'jungle temple', and a story suggests that Portuguese sailors were rescued from a storm by following a light. They traced it on shore, where it disappeared, and on the spot they built the church. The neighbourhood has become a busy shopping centre. From the church you can continue W, then S to the **Madras Club**. This is housed in a late 18th century house owned then by George Mowbray, and is surrounded by very attractive gardens. Admission is no longer restricted to European men, but you still need to be invited by a member.

Cross the Adyar River by the Elphinstone Bridge, built to provide work during the catastrophic famine in South India in 1876-78. The river itself has a sailing club, but capsizing is not recommended. A survey of pollution in the Adyar River has suggested that it is 98% effluent, and all 3 waterways of Madras – the Adyar, the Cooum and the Buckingham Canal – remain appallingly heavily polluted.

On the S banks of the river are the world HQ of the **Theosophical Society** (8 km), in 120 ha gardens. These contain several shrines of different faiths and a Serene Garden of Remembrance for the founders, Madam Blavatsky and Colonel Olcott who founded the society in New York in 1875 and moved its HQ to Madras in 1882. The 400 year old magnificent banyan tree is of particular interest. Its roots were disturbed in a storm in 1990, but it is now recovering. The garden also has exotic shrubs and trees and several species of birds and wildlife. There are several buildings, including the Olcott Memorial School, the press, a child welfare centre, a museum, the Adyar Library and Research Centre and a Hall of Meditation.

3 km due W of the Theosophical Society is the old **Government House,** built in 1817 in the style of a Raj bungalow. It is now **Raj Bhavan**, the Governor's house. It has superb grounds, now a national park.

Little Mount, on the S bank of the Adyar where St Thomas is believed to have spent some time. You will see 2 churches, the older, with its small vaulted chapel having been built by the Portuguese in 1551. The modern circular church was built in 1971. To the SW of the city is **Great Mount** where the apostle is believed to have been martyred and bled to death in AD 52. Some believe he was accidentally killed by a hunter's arrow. On top of the 90m high 'mount' is the **Church of Our Lady of Expectation**, where the altar marks the spot where Thomas fell and the cross one of which he had himself carved. The Madonna and Child over the altar is said to be one painted by St Luke. It is believed that the original church was built by Armenians in AD 530 but was replaced by the Portuguese in 1523. The latter forms the core of the present church which was subsequently extended.

The **Armenian Christians** who came from Persia are believed to have found St Thomas's grave and built a tomb and a church over it. The village was called San Thome. One school of thought says that the original burial site and the church have disappeared under the sea. Marco Polo in his travels recorded the chapel and a monastery on a hill to the N where the apostle was put to death. In 1523, when the Portuguese started to rebuild the church they discovered the tomb containing the relics consisting of a few bones, a lance head and an earthen pot containing bloodstained earth. The church was replaced by the neo-Gothic structure which has 2 spires and was granted the status of a basilica in 1956. The relics are kept in the sacristy and can be seen on request. There are 13th century wall plaques, a modern stained glass window, a 450 year old Madonna brought from Portugal and a 16th century stone sundial.

The **Snake Park** at Guindy is in the grounds of the Guindy national park, the Raj Bhavan Estate. Quite a wide collection of snakes and other reptiles. The cages are poorly lit and some wrongly labelled but still interesting. There is an hourly display from 1000 nr the entrance, with an inaudible recording in English, Tamil and Hindi. Brave visitors may be allowed to handle one! Government has banned 'milking'. 0830-1730. Small fee. Trains from Egmore or Beach Rly station or buses from town centre. Also has deer park (see under Parks and Gardens below).

NB: Snake skins are sold by hawkers but Indian Government does not allow it and most countries have banned import of articles made from snake skin.

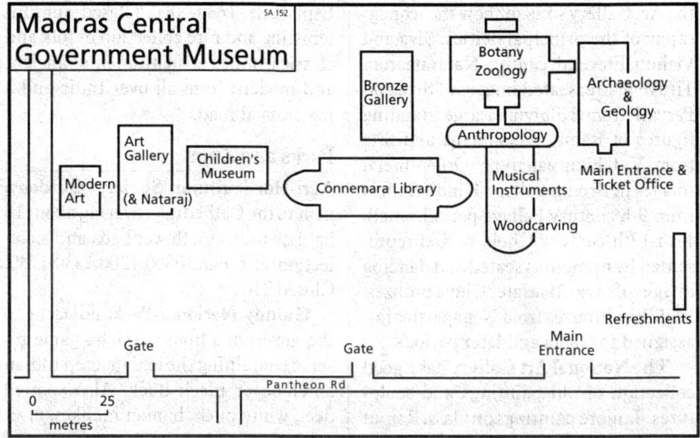

Museums

The Government Museum and Art Gallery, Pantheon Rd. 0900-1700. Closed Fri. Entry Free. The Pantheon had been a 'place of public entertainment and balls' in the late 18th century. The museum is a circular red-brick rotunda surrounded by an Italianate pillared arcade. Started in 1851 as Museum of Practical Geology and Natural History it comprises 3 separate buildings: Archaeology, Art, Bronzes. Look for the excellent collection of bronzes and the interesting exhibits of Stone and Iron Age hunting and cooking implements which have been excavated locally. There is also an excellent numismatic collection and sections on botany (500 year old teak and engineering designs inspired by plants), zoology (18.5m whale skeleton) and arms and armoury. There is a separate children's gallery with a model railway.

Archaeology This features early stone sculptures from the Deccan and the beginnings of Buddhist artistic traditions. Fragments from Jaggayyapeta (in Andhra Pradesh, between Vijayawada and Hyderabad), including the depiction of a royal figure (10). There is a long frieze of Vessantara Jataka from Goli. Both are dated from the 2nd and 3rd centuries and are carved in limestone. Amaravati is represented by a large number of damaged limestone panels, posts and railings from dismantled stupa. Several figures date from 2nd century BC include a representation of a multi-storey tree shrine with flying celestials (IB.11). Remainder mainly 2nd and 3rd centuries. Episodes in life of Buddha – Master subduing elephant (IIIA.15) and the bowl of the Buddha uplifted by devotees (IIIA.6). Jataka stories also illustrated. Elaborate lotus medallions and garlands, and picture of the stupa itself. Also some rare free-standing Buddha figures, wearing finely fluted robes. There are numerous Hindu images from later periods of South India. Tenth century sculptures from Kodambalur – Siva and the Goddess 'fine examples of the early Chola style'. Contemporary sculptures part of panel from Hemavati (104.38) and Siva and Parvati together in elliptical frame from Penukonda. Hoysala style represented by an ornate doorway. Sage leaning on staff (Tadpatri) and figure of Durga standing on buffalo are Vijayanagar period.

Bronzes The largest and finest collection in India, excellently displayed in the Art Gallery so as to show the iconography of the principal deities, Siva and Vishnu. Eleventh century Nataraja from Tiruvengadu; seated images of Siva and Parvati from Kilaiyur. Large standing figures of Rama, Lakshmana and Sita from Vadakkuppanaiyur. Other metal images in Bronze gallery. Hindu figures from 9th century Pallava period, small, 11th-12th century Chola period represented by numerous seated and dancing images of Siva. Also later Chola bronzes. Buddhist bronzes from Nagapattinam – assigned to Chola and later periods.

The National Art Gallery has a good collection of old paintings and sculptures. Tanjore paintings on glass, Rajput and Mughal miniatures, 17th century Deccan paintings, 11th and 12th century handicrafts, metalware and ivory carvings. Fine 13th and 14th century bronzes are housed in a separate building at rear.

The Gallery of Modern Art has a permanent collection of contemporary art with temporary exhibitions on the first floor.

Fort Museum, S Beach Rd (within Fort St George). The 18th century building houses exhibits from 300 years of British Indian history. Includes prints, documents, paintings, sculpture, arms (medieval weapons with instructions on their use) and uniforms. Indo-French gallery has some Louis XIV furniture and clocks. Clive Corner which includes letters and photographs particularly good. 0900-1700. Closed Fri. Entry free.

Development Centre for Musical Instruments, 86 Mundakanni Koil St, Mylapore. Ancient and modern instruments which you may touch and play. Some curiously ornamental (sitars and veenas carved into fish and peacock shape) and some modern experiments (violin made out of a walking stick). Of special interest are those reconstructed with the help of ancient literary texts and temple sculptures. Tamil Isai Sangam, Raja Annamalai Hall (2nd floor), Esplanade. 1630-2000. Closed Sun. Interesting and rare collection of folk and classical musical instruments, ancient and modern from all over India and a few from abroad.

Parks and Zoos

Agri-Horticultural Society Gardens, next to the Cathedral, covering about 10 ha. Lawns, trees, flower beds and a collection of *bonsai*. 0800-1200,1330-1730. Closed Th.

Guindy National Park, adjacent to the governor's house. 231 ha game reserve containing the endangered Indian antelope or black buck. Also spotted deer, white buck, bonnet monkey, civet cat, jackals and common mongoose and many species of birds.

Excursions

Anna Zoological Park

Vandalur. 32 km. 520 ha. Attempts to provide a natural environment and breed some endangered species. Hippos, zebras, chimpanzees, elephants, Nilgiri langurs, Rhesus macaque, jackals and spotted deer among 28 species of mammals and includes a nocturnal animal house. Also 61 species of birds include macaw parrot, blossom headed parakeet and Manila duck and 8 species of reptiles. There is a ropeway and monorail, and a lion and bison safari park. Small battery operated 'cars' and bicycles for hire. 0800-1700, daily except Tues. Camera fee Rs 3.

Cholamandal Artists' village

T 412892. 20 km out of Madras on the road S and close to the sea. Started in 1969, the community of artists who live and work here, exhibit and sell their paintings, graphics, sculptures, pottery and batik. Occasional dance performances in small open-air theatre. Stop for a short visit. daily 0600-2000.

Muttukadu

30 km is being developed as a rowing, boating and wind surfing resort.

Covelong

This fishing village and beach is 38 km away, the road having branched off at Kelambakkam (16 km). You may wish to stop for a drink and snacks at the Taj Group's *Fisherman's Cove Hotel*.

Crocodile Bank

Continuing S, 42 km from Madras is the **Crocodile Bank** where Indian and African species are bred in addition to native species of turtle. It was set up in 1976 by Romulus Whittaker who was also founder of Guindy Snake Park and has saved the endangered *gharial* and marsh crocodile. One of the largest crocodiles in the world, over 7m long is here. Entry – Re 1. Cameras Rs 5. Allow ½ hr.

NB: A shop has crocodile skin articles for sale but you may not export it.

ROUTES The Madras to Tiruchirappalli coastal route takes you to Mamallapuram and beyond. See page 848.

Tirukkalukundram

60 km from Madras and 16 km from Mamallapuram on the Chingleput road, Tirukkalukundram (Pakshitirtham) has a small finely carved Siva temple dedicated to Bhaktavatsleesvara on the hill top with its *gopuram* or gateway standing out like a beacon. About 400 steps take you to the top of the 160m hill and at 1000 you will see 2 Neophran vultures (*Pharaoh's chickens*) fly down to be fed by the priests. The tank is considered holy and said to produce a conch every 12 years. The temple here and the larger Siva temple in the village below have made this a Hindu pilgrim centre. A range of small shops in the village, cold drinks available. Good views from hill top.

Vedanthangal Bird Sanctuary

On the Trichy Rd, 87 km from Madras and 60 km from Mamallapuram. The sanctuary is said to have been in existence as a protected area for about 250 years. A marshy 30 ha site attracting numerous water fowl, has a small lake and a grove of *Kadappamaram* (Barringtonia acutangula) trees part of which remains submerged in the rainy season and provide the main nesting site for the birds. Visitors and residents include crested cormorants, night herons, grey pelicans, sand pipers, grey wagtails, open-billed storks, white ibis, egrets, little grebe and purple moorhens.

Viewing from observation tower near the small lake. You can walk along a shaded raised path along the W bank of the lake to see the nesting colonies of birds from late Oct until Feb. Best season: Nov-Feb for migratory birds which include blue-winged teals, pintails, shovellers, numbering about 100,000. Best time dawn and 1500-1800. **Accommodation** A long day-trip from Madras is possible; otherwise the very simple **F** *Forest Rest House* has suites of rooms with electricity, bath and running water. The cook will prepare an Indian meal to order. Reservations: Wildlife Warden, 49, 4th Main Rd, Adyar, Madras, T 413947. Advance payment for rm and food to Forester in Charge of the Rest House, Vedanthangal. **Getting there**: **Train**: to Chingleput (28 km) and then bus 20 km to sanctuary. **Road**: from Madras (75 km) by car or bus from the Broadway Bus Stand, Madras (only weekends) or one from Mamallapuram. It is also included in some of the coach tours.

Tours

These are on deluxe coaches and accompanied by a guide. **Tamil Nadu Tourist Development Corporation** (**TTDC**) *Departure points and reservations*: Sales Counters at 143, Anna Salai, T 849803 and at Express Bus Stand nr High Court compound, T 560982 (0600-2100). Reservations also from Tourist Information Centre, Central Rly Station, T 563351 (24 hr). City sightseeing: *half-day*. Daily 0830-1330, 1400-1800. Fort St George, Govt Museum, Valluvar Kottam, Snake Park, Kapaleeswarar Temple, Elliot's Beach and a drive along Marina Beach. (Govt Museum closed on Fri.) Fare Rs

40. *Full-day*. Daily 0810-1900. Drive along Marina Beach, Kapaleeswarar Temple, Snake Park, Vallavur Kottam, Museum, Fort St George, St Mary's Church, Birla Planetarium, Muttukadu Boat House and VGP Golden Beach. Fare Rs 60 (includes veg meal). Excursions: there are separate day tours to Mamallapuram (strongly rec) and Tirupati. Weekend Tour: Dep Fri 2100, Arr Sun 1930. Covers Thanjavur, Velankanni, Nagore, Tirunallar, Poompuhar, Vaitheeswaran Koil, Chidambaram (night at hotel), Pitchavaram, Pondicherry. Fare: Twin sharing Rs 180, Single Rs 210. Longer tours cover sites in Tamil Nadu and Karnataka and also Goa.

India TDC Tours *Reservations*: ITDC, 29 Victoria Crescent, C-in-C Rd, T 478884. Booking counters at 154 Anna Salai, T 478884, Express Bus Stand, Esplanade, T 561830, Central Rly Station, T 566438. Garage, 5-6 Chamiers Rd, T 454056. City Sightseeing: daily 1330-1830. Fort St George, St Mary's Church, Fort Museum, Government Museum, National Art Gallery, Vallavur Kottam, Gandhiji, Rajaji and Kamaraj Memorials, Children's Park, Snake Park, Kapaleeswarar Temple, Marina Beach. On Fri the Government Museum and Art Gallery are closed so the visit includes the Botanical Garden and Parthasarathi Temple. Fare Rs 30. Excursions: also offers Kanchipuram, Tirukalikundram, Mamallapuram Tour (0730-1900). Fare: a/c coach Rs 110, Non-a/c Rs 80. Tirupati, Tiruchanur Tour (0630-2030). Fare: a/c coach Rs 240, Child Rs 195. Non-a/c Rs 170, Child Rs 140 (includes Darshan Fee at Tirumala, breakfast and lunch). Longer tours: the 5-day South India Panorama Tour covers Bangalore, Mysore, Mudumalai, Ooty, Coimbatore, Salem and Tiruvannamalai. Dep. Sun 0630, Arr. Th 2030. Fare: Twin sharing Rs 950, Single Rs 1050, Child Rs 750 which does not include meals. The 8-day South India Safari Tour covers Tiruchirappalli, Kodaikkanal, Kanyakumari, Tiruvananthapuram, Madurai, Rameswaram, Tanjore, Kumbakonam, Chidambaram and Pondicherry. Dep. Fri 0630, Arr. Fri 2030. Fare: Twin sharing Rs 1295, Single Rs 1395, Child Rs 995.

Local information

Accommodation & food

● Accommodation

Price guide
AL Rs 3,000+ **A** Rs 2,000-3,000
B Rs 1,200-2,000 **C** Rs 600-1,200
D Rs 250-600 **E** Rs 100-250 **F** Up to Rs 100.

NB: All **A** class hotels collect an extra 15-20% of the rate quoted as Luxury Tax. In most hotels *Permit Room* refers to the bar. Most are 12-15 km from airport. A number of new **C** and **D** category hotels are coming up along the Poonamallee High Rd, W of the *Dasaprakash Hotel*.

Mount Road (Anna Salai): a number of hotels, including all the most expensive, are strung out within 1 km either side of Mount Road.

AL *Taj Coromandel*, 17 Nungambakkam High Rd, T 474849, F 470070, 240 rm, possibly the best modern luxury hotel, excellent restaurants (evening Bharat Natyam dance recitals) but buffet lunch reported mediocre and expensive, good pool, good location, high quality shops nearby, MH Taxi, Travel and Transport Service is rec; **AL** *Chola Sheraton*, 10 Cathedral Rd, T 473347, F 478779, 135 rm, rooftop restaurant, superb views, good food; **AL** *Park Sheraton*, 132 TTK Rd, T 452525, F 455913, 160 rm, *Dakshin* restaurant (South Indian inc 'Chettinad' style), pool side barbecue.

A *Connemara*, Binny's Rd (Off Anna Salai), T 860123, T 8257361, after major renovation, retains splendid art deco features, extremely comfortable, excellent location, outdoor *Rain Tree* specialises in excellent South Indian 'Chettinad' cuisine (evenings) with South Indian music and dance in a very attractive garden setting, one of the best pools in the city, good bookshop, heavily booked Dec-Mar; **A** *Trident*, 1/24 GST Rd, T 2344747, F 2346699, 172 rm, very useful 12-hr rate, restaurants all rec, elegant garden setting; **A** *Ambassador Pallava*, 53 Montieth Rd, T 862061,

F 8268757, 120 rm, Chinese restaurant, rec, overpriced.

B *Savera*, 69 Dr Radhakrishnan Rd, T 474700, F 473475, rec for location, pool and excellent restaurants: roof top, good views, very good Kashmiri and Mughlai food, North Indian music; **B** *Ramada Madras*, St Thomas Mount (nr airport), 174 rm.

C *Residency*, 49 GN Chetty Rd, T 8253434, F 8250085, 112 very comfortable rm on 9 Flr, 4th upwards have good views, excellent restaurant (good buffet lunches), bar, coffee shop, exchange, travel, shop, highly rec, better rm and service than some higher priced hotels; **C** *Madras International* (Indian style), 693 Anna Salai, T 861811, F 861520, 66 comfortable rm, restaurant, bar, exchange, travel, quiet and clean (usual hazard of cockroaches).

D *Sindoori*, 24 Greames La, Greames Rd, T 471164, 89 rm, central, a/c, restaurant, shops; **D** *Shrilekha Inter-Continental*, 564 Anna Salai, T 453132, 200 rm, some a/c, restaurant, bar, exchange; **D** *President*, 16 Dr Radhakrishnan Rd (E Elliots Rd), T 832211, F 832299, 144 rm, some a/c (when functioning), restaurant, bar, pool, shops, exchange, travel, seaview, poor value for money; **D** *Ranjith*, 9 Nungambakkam High Rd, T 470521, 51 rm, some a/c, restaurant (good non-veg continental), shops, travel, exchange; **D** *Palmgrove*, 5 Kodambakkam High Rd, T 471881, 80 rm, some a/c (some cottages), restaurant (veg), bar, exchange, travel; **D** *Transit House*, 26 Venkataraman St, T Nagar, T 441346, some a/c rm, snack bar and pleasant garden; **D** *New Woodlands*, 72/75 Radhakrishnan Rd, T 473111, 172 rm, some a/c rm, restaurant excellent for South Indian, exchange, small but pleasant pool, good value; **D** *Shrilekha*, 49 Anna Salai, T 830521, 77 rm, some a/c, restaurant, bar, exchange, travel; **D** *Kanchi*, 28 C-in-C Rd, T 471100, 75 rm, some a/c, roof top restaurant (Indian veg), bar, exchange, travel, good value and modern; **D** *Peninsula*, 26 GN Rd, T Nagar, T 8252700, F 8254745, 127 rm, some a/c, restaurant (Indian), bar, exchange, travel; **D** *Ganpath*, 103 Nungambakkam High Rd, T 471889, 55 rm, some a/c, restaurants, bar; **D** *Harrisons*, 154/5 Village Rd, T 475271, some a/c rm, restaurant (South Indian/Chinese), bar; **D** *Swagath*, 243-4 Royapettah High Rd, T 868422, 137 rm, some a/c, restaurant, exchange, travel; **D** *Himalaya*, 54 Triplicane High Rd, T 847522, 45 rm with nice bath, some a/c, Modern, welcoming, clean, bright, no food, but available from *Hotel Gandhi* next door; **D** *Broad Lands*, 16 Vallabha Agraharam St, T 845573, set around lovely shady courtyards, it is clean with good service, reasonably quiet and extremely popular, 50 rm, a few with baths, often necessary to book, giving arrival time. Rm will be let out if you arrive late, best rm at top of building, helpful management but operate a "no-Indians" policy; some say it is over-rated, overpriced but convenient. **D** *Blue Diamond*, 934 Poonamallee High Rd, T 6412244, 33 rm, some a/c, quieter at rear, restaurant, exchange, travel, no credit cards; **D** *Picnic*, 1132 Poonamallee High Rd (nr Madras Central Rly), T 588809, 55 rm, some a/c, restaurant, bar, exchange, travel; **D** *Maris*, 9 Cathedral Rd, T 470541, 70 rm, some a/c, restaurant, bar, travel, exchange.

Budget Hotels **E** *Tourist Hostel*, Andhra Mahila Sabha, 3B Adyar Bridge Rd, T 416001, some a/c rm, veg restaurant, good guest houses in this category; **E** *Krishna* 159 Peters Rd, T 868997, F 865037, with cheap rm, some with bath; **E** *YMCA (1)*, 14 Westcott Rd, Royapettah, T 811158. The **Automobile Assoc of South India** (Anna Salai) has a guest house for members.

Egmore Many hotels are clustered around Egmore Station (which serves the S) and the Poonamallee High Road, an auto-rickshaw ride away to the N of the railway line. They include many of the best budget hotels. Many hotels in the **D** category also have cheaper rooms.

C *Breeze*, 850 Poonamallee High Rd, T 6413334, 6413301, 40 rm, restaurant, bar, exchange. Fairly new, modern.

D *New Victoria*, 3 Kennet La, Egmore, T 8253638, 50 a/c rm, restaurant good value, bar, exchange, travel, 200m from Egmore Station, quiet in spite of busy area, clean with generally good service, rec; **D** *Merryland Inn*, 815 Poonamallee High Rd, T 6411343, some a/c rm with bath, restaurant, roof garden, fairly new, set back from main road; **D** *Pandian*, 9 Kennet Lane, Egmore, T 8252901, F 834728, 90 rm, some a/c, a/c restaurant (lacks atmosphere), bar, travel, shop, clean but Spartan, helpful staff, expensive rm service; **D** *Peacock*, 1089 Poonamallee High Rd, T 39081, 72 rm some a/c, quieter at rear, restaurant, exchange, travel.

Some hotels in the same category are significantly cheaper. They often have veg restaurants. When on the main road they may have a problem with noise except at rear of the building. **D** *Vaigai*, 3 Gandhi Irwin Rd, Egmore, T 834959, F 835774, 58 rm, some a/c, restaurant, exchange, travel, good value; **D** *Udipi Home*, 1 Halls Rd, Egmore, T 8251875, 89 rm, some a/c, restaurant; **D** *Madras Hotel Ashoka*, 33 Pantheon Rd, Egmore, T 8253377, 168 rm, some a/c, 1 km rly, restaurant, bar, travel, exchange, nothing to do with the ITDC Ashoka hotels; **D** *Imperial*, 14 Whannels Rd, Egmore, T 8250376, 70 rm, some a/c, best at rear, 4 restaurants, good food, reasonable price, bar, travel, friendly; **D** *Dasaprakash*, 100 Poonamallee High Rd, T 8255111, 100 rm, some a/c, rec restaurant (veg), bar, exchange, no credit cards, travel, good grounds and public area but in need of refurbishing. **NB**: non-veg food and alcohol not allowed on premises and suggests "No tipping" for service; **D** *Atlantic*, 2 Montieth Rd, Egmore, T 860461, 116 rm, some a/c, restaurant (poor food and service), exchange, shops, travel; **D** *YWCA International Guest House*, 1086 Poonamallee High Rd, T 39920, restaurant (rate includes breakfast), 60 rm, with bath, few a/c, ror men and women, small membership fee, popular so book early, very good value, also *camping ground*, Res Secretary. Also within the compound is the **F** *Laharry Transit Hostel*, for women under 30 only, very cheap and good value.

Budget hotels and Youth hostels **E** *YMCA (1)*,(2) at 17 Ritherdon Rd, Vepery, T 32831 where there are **D** rm with bath. Nearby **E** *Salvation Army's Red Shield Guest House* has clean **D** rm with bath and dorm (for men) at 15 Ritherdon Rd, Vepery, T 38148, contact Warden. Other dorm beds are at **F** *Youth Hostel*, Indira Nagar, T 412882, reservations, Warden. Also at **F** *World University Service Centre*, Spur Tank Rd, T 663991, some rm with bath, dorm, International Students' cards needed, couples not allowed to share a room, reservations: Director, very good value, reasonable canteen and well located for Egmore and S central Madras; **F** Egmore Station, T 848533.

George Town The heart of the old city and the area round the Central Station and Thiruvalluvar Bus Stand has some budget accommodation. Most are not as good as those in Egmore.

Budget hotels **E** *Sornam International*, 7 Stringer St, T 563063, CCTV, rooftop veg restaurant, large modern hotel; **E** *Blue Star*, 108 VOC Rd (Wall Tax Rd), T 30005; **E** Central Station *Railway Retiring Rooms*, T 32218, some a/c rm, cheaper dorm; **F** TTDC *Youth Hostel*, EVR Rd, Park (nr Central Rly Station), T 589132, reasonably quiet; **F** *YMCA*, NSC Bose Rd, T 583941, opposite City bus stand.

● Places to eat

The greatest choice is in South Indian veg food. Those serving non-veg dishes are often the more expensive especially in the top hotels. Most open 1200-1500, 1900-2400. *Dasaprakash*, Anna Salai, next to Higginbotham's Bookshop. One of the best, reasonably priced modern restaurants. Spencer's *Fiesta*, (Continental and Chinese) has a dance floor, recorded music, fast food counter. Rec. This and some others open almost throughout the day incl the less expensive *Mayur* at *Hotel Ganpat* and *Madras International's* *Shangrila*. *Blue Diamond*, 934 Poonamallee High Rd, good for breakfasts (0700-2400). *Buhari's*, 83 Anna Salai has a terrace and a/c dimly lit dining room with unusual decor. Good food; try crab curry, egg rotis and Muslim dishes. Another branch in Park Town nr Central Station. *Maharaja*, Triplicane High Rd, 100m from *Broadlands* rec for Indian meals; popular with backpackers. Opp, Woodland's *Mathura*, Tarapore Towers, 2nd Flr, Anna Salai, lacks style but does good Udipi dishes. *Dasaprakash*, 100 Poonamallee High Rd (0900-2400) and *Woodlands Drive-In Restaurant*, 30 Cathedral Rd (0600-2100) are rec for South Indian veg. The former has a very good salad bar. Others: *Eskimo*, 827 Anna Salai and *Pals*, 42 Anna Salai.

Chinese: particularly good at *Golden Dragon* (*Taj Coromandel*), *Shanghai* (*Trident*), also *Chopsticks* (*Ambassador Pallava*) and *Sagari* (*Chola Sheraton*). *Chungking*, 67 Anna Salai (opp Anna Rd Post Office), (1030-2200) where lack of atmosphere (dim lighting) is compensated by good food. Also *China Town*, 74 Cathedral Rd, (a/c) and *Dynasty* at *Harrison's Hotel*, rec. The last 3 are less expensive and very popular.

Thai: *Cascade*, Kakani Towers, 15 Khaderi Nawaz Khan Rd (inc Chinese, Japanese and Malay).

Fast food places are: *Cakes 'n' Bakes*, 22 Nungambakkam High Rd; *Chit Chat*, 557 Anna Salai; *Maratha* (*Trident*) and *Snappy*, 74 Cathedral Rd; *Cake Walk* and *Hot Breads*. *Avin* is a milk bar on Anna Salai. You can get good Indian sweets and savoury snacks from *Nala's* on Cathedral Rd and *Naga's* in Village Rd.

● **Bars**
It is possible to obtain alcoholic drinks without any difficulty despite local restrictions on sale of alcohol. Regulations change periodically, however, and All India Liquor Permits are available from either an Indian mission or a Govt of India Tourist office abroad or in one of the regional capitals.

Entertainment and shopping

● **Clubs**
Temporary membership at most, sometimes for sports only. ***Madras Gymkhana Club***, Anna Salai. Tennis, swimming, cricket, billiards, library, bar. Golf at Guindy Race Course. ***Cosmopolitan Club***, Anna Salai. Tennis, billiards, golf, library, bar. ***Madras Boat Club***, Adyar. Bar. ***Madras Cricket Club***, Chepauk. Tennis, swimming, cricket, billiards, bar. ***Madras Riders Club***, Race View, Race Course, Velachery Rd. Riding (including lessons) throughout the year except June. *Radio Hams*, Call sign: VU2 MU.

● **Cultural centres**
Bharatiya Vidya Bhavan, 38/39 R E Mada St, T 74674. Some of the foreign cultural centres have libraries and arrange film shows. ***Alliance Française***, 3/4 A College Rd, Nungambakkam. ***American Centre***, 220 Anna Salai. Library 0930-1800, closed Sun. ***British Library*** (British Council Division), 737 Anna Salai. 1000-1900, closed Mon. ***Max Mueller Bhawan***, Express Estate. 0900-1900, closed Sun. ***House of CIS Culture***, 27 Kasturi Rangan Rd.

● **Entertainment**
Cinemas Show foreign (usually English language) films are mostly in the centre of town on Anna Salai. They are a/c and quite comfortable and you may appreciate a break on a hot day!

Music and Dance *Madras Music Academy* auditoria is the scene of numerous performances of Indian music, dance and theatre, not only during the prestigious 3 week Music Festival in from mid-Dec but right through the year. ***Sabhas*** are membership societies that offer cultural programmes 4 times a month to its members, but occasionally tickets are available at the door. There are several other auditoria: ***Raja Annamalai Hall, Mylapore Fine Arts Club, Narada, Brahma and Krishna Gana Sabhas*** and the little ***Sittraragam***.

● **Shopping**
Shopping in Madras has been changing rapidly in the last 5 years. The old Moore Market, has been re-built behind the new Railway Central Reservation Office. A range of new shopping centres has been developed both in the 2 central parts of the city (Parry's corner and Anna Salai) and in a number of suburbs. Although there are no large department stores there are many new specialised shops both on Anna Salai and in complexes around. Most shops are open Mon to Sat 0900-2000 with a lunch break from 1300-1500 although some remain open throughout the day. Weekly holidays may differ for shops in the same locality. You should ask for a receipt and check what you buy carefully because it may be difficult to return or exchange goods. There are often discount sales during the festival seasons of Pongal, Diwali and Christmas.

Bookshops: books are often extremely good value in India. Books in English are widely available, often at much lower prices than abroad. Most open 0900-1900. ***Higginbothams***, 814 Anna Salai and F 39 Anna Nagar E, nr Chintamani Market. ***Landmark*** in Apex Plaza, 3 Nungambakkam High Rd, often has discounted books. Many publishing houses have bookselling departments: ***Oxford Book House*** in Cathedral Grounds (Anna Salai) and ***Allied Publishers*** (off Anna Salai) have extensive collections. The *Taj Coromandel*, *Sindoori* and *Adyar Park Sheraton Hotels* have branches of ***Danai Bookshops*** open 0830-2400. Also rec, ***Giggles*** at *Hotel Connemara*.

Crafts: for many years it has been possible to obtain excellent South Indian handicrafts (wood carving, inlaid work, ivory, sandalwood) at very reasonable (fixed) prices from the Govt-backed ***Victoria Technical Institute***, Anna Salai nr *Connemara Hotel*. The Govt's craft store ***Poompuhar***, Anna Salai, specialises in first class bronzes. Other rec shops are the excellent ***Cane & Bamboo***, 26 C-in-C Rd, ***Firdusi***, Fountain Plaza (miniature paintings), ***Jamal's Corner Shop***, 44 Devraja Mudali St (antiques, bric-a-brac), ***Cottage Industries Exposition*** opp *Taj Coromandel Hotel* and ***Contemporary Arts and Crafts*** off Cathedral Rd. ***Kalakshetra*** at Thiruvanmiyur excels in kalamkari and traditional weaving; also good household linen. ***Meyerson's Carpet Museum***, 152 Anna Salai, (and *Walnut Willies*, 14 Jaffar Syrang St, nr Harbour) is a family firm specialising in carpets, gems, jewellery and crafts. Also undertakes bulk exports.

Department Stores: such as *Mini Cauvery*, 21 Madloy Rd, *Supermarket*, 112 Davidson St and TNHB Building, Annanagar (closed Fri), *Harringtons*, 99 Harrington Rd, Chetput and *Five Stars*, 60 Pantheon Rd, Egmore have made shopping easier. Most open 0900-2000, some close 1330-1600.

Jewellery: traditional South Indian jewellery in gold or with diamond and stone setting is best Also available is the 'Madras Diamond' which is zircon jewellery and the larger than life artificial stone products used by dancers and stage performers. Some rec shops for gold are *Thangamaligai*, T Nagar, *Bapalal*, 24/1 Cathedral Rd and *Fashion 'n' Gems*, 9 Nungambakkam High Rd. *Vummidi Bangaru Kanna*, Anna Flyover. *Taj Gems* in *Hotel Taj Coromandel* and *Gem Palace* in *Hotel Adyar Park* are good for stone set jewellery.

Silks, cottons and clothes: Madras was founded because of the excellence and cheap prices of the local cotton. Today some of India's best silk comes from Kanchipuram, 65 km away, and can readily be bought in the city. Both Govt run and private retailers have excellent stocks of traditional Indian clothes, including some of the best silk and silk saris available in India, and some Western fashioned clothes. The Govt's *Co-optex* all over Madras have a wide variety of handloom silks and cottons while their *Khadi* (handspun and handwoven cotton) stores specialise in the rather coarse but lightweight cotton.

It is now possible to buy good clothes at shopping centres in various parts of the city. However, 3 shops are still regarded as particularly good for silks in terms of quality and value. *Radha Silk Emporium*, 1 Sannathi St, Mylapore, is nr the Sri Kapaleshwarar Temple, *Kumaran* and *Nalli Chinnasami Chetty* (opp Panagal Park), both in Theagaraya Nagar (universally known as T.Nagar). *Amrapali* in Fountain Plaza and Adyar and *Shilpi*, and *Urvashi* on Mowbrays Rd are good for cottons. *Handloom House* is in 7 Rattan Bazar while *India Silk House* and a number of Government Emporia are along Anna Salai. They are at numbers 121 Andhra Pradesh; 700 Haryana; LIC Building, Karnataka; 42 Kashmir;138 Kerala; 189 N E Region; 818 Tamil Nadu; 834 W Bengal.

Photography: *GK Vale*, 107 Anna Salai. *India Photo Co*, 129 Greams Rd. *Photo Art*, 181 Luz Church Rd, Mylapore.

● Sports

Facilities in clubs (addresses in Clubs section above) are for members only. You can either go as a guest or take out temporary membership on being rec by a permanent member. Your country's Foreign Representation may be able to help. Some hotels allow facilities to be used on payment of a fee.

Boating: Muttukadu Boat House, Injambakkam has facilities for windsurfing and also has boats for hire. Yachting is possible at Ennore. Contact Captain, Royal Madras Yacht Club. The Taj Group's *Fisherman's Cove Hotel* in Covelong has windsurfing, yachting and sailing.

Fishing: Madras offers ample opportunity for good fishing especially in Chetpet Lake, YWCA International Guest House grounds, backwaters of Ennore and Covelong but it is not possible to hire equipment.

Swimming: few hotels open their pools to non-residents; *Ambassador* is an exception. Madras Cricket Club has an excellent pool (less crowded before noon); you need an introduction. Others open to the public are at Marina Beach and the YMCA pool at Saidapet. Sea bathing is safe, though no longer attractive, at Elliot's Beach.

Tennis: Clubs allowing members' guest and temporary members to use courts are Madras Club, Gymkhana Club, Cricket Club, Cosmopolitan Club, Presidency Club and Lady Willingdon Club. YMCA at Saidapet also has courts.

Services

● Airline offices

Most are open 0930-1730 Mon-Fri, 0930-1300 Sat. **Air India**, 19 Marshalls Rd, T 474477. Airport T 474488. **Air France**, 769 Anna Salai, T 88377. **Air Lanka**, 758 Mount Chambers, Anna Salai, T 861777. **British Airways**, Alsa Mall, Khalili Centre, Montieth Rd, T 477388. **Indian Airlines**, 19 Marshalls Rd, T 478333. **Iraqi Airways**, 1-30 Pantheon Rd, T 811740. **Lufthansa**, 171 Anna Salai, T 81483. **Malaysian Airlines**, 189 Anna Salai, T 868625. **NW Airlines**, 1 Whites Rd, T 87703. **Qantas**, Eldorado Building, Nungambakkam High Rd, T 478649. **Sabena**, Regency House, 250 Anna Salai, T 451598. **Singapore Airlines**, 167 Anna Salai, T 862871. **Swissair**, 40 Anna Salai, T 82583.

Several Airlines operate through a General Sales Agency (GSA). **Air Canada, Air Kenya, Garuda Airways, Japan Airlines** are all c/o Global Travels, 733 Anna Salai, T 87957. **Alitalia** and **Zambia Airways**, c/o Ajanta Travels, Kavraj Mansion, 738 Anna Salai, T 810936. **Bangladesh Biman, Philippines Airways**, c/o Jet Air Transportation, 55 Monteith Rd, T 861810. **Cathay Pacific** and **KLM**, c/o Spencer & Co., *Hotel Connemara*, Binny's Rd, T 811051. **Ethiopian Airlines, Iberian Airways, LOT Polish Airways** and **Royal Nepal Airlines**, c/o STIC Travels, *Hotel Chola Sheraton*, 10 Cathedral Rd, T 473347. **Egypt Air** and **Yemen Air**, c/o BAP Travels, 135 Anna Salai, T 849913. **Kuwait Airways**, c/o National Travel Service, Embassy Towers, 50 Monteith Rd, T 811810. **Maldive Airways**, c/o Crossworld Tours, 7 Rosy Tower, Nungambakkam High Rd, T 471497. **Pakistan International Airways**, c/o Swaman, 63 Pantheon Rd, T 810619. **Pan Am**, c/o Indam Travels, 163 Anna Salai, T 811209. **Saudi Arabian Airlines**, c/o Arajaath Travels, 3 Monteith Rd, T 811370. **Thai International**, c/o Swan Travels, Kodambakkam High, T 812775. **TWA**, c/o Air Transportation, Hardevi Chambers, 68 Pantheon Rd, T 812775.

● Banks & money changers

Most open 1000-1400 on weekdays; 1000-1200 on Sat. Closed Sun, national holidays and June 30 and Dec 31. Most deal in foreign exchange upto 1300 but it is tedious and time consuming; some refuse to cash TCs. In Madras, deal direct with Exchange Offices (Amex, Thomas Cook). Most big hotels will cash TCs and a few have 24-hr banks.

American Express offers a full Travel Service. G-17, Spencer Plaza, Anna Salai. Includes full range of foreign exchange and travellers' cheque services. **Bank of America**, 748 Anna Salai. **Citibank**, 768 Anna Salai. **Grindlays**, 19 Rajaji Salai, and 164 Anna Salai (only Visa TCs). **Hong Kong and Shanghai**, 30 Rajaji Salai. **Standard Chartered**, 58 NSC Bose Rd. **Andhra**, 265 TTK Salai. **Central Bank of India**, 803 Anna Salai. **Indian Overseas**, 762 Anna Salai;109 Nungambakkam High Rd, (0900-1300, Sat 0900-1100) and 15 Hunters Rd (0830-1230, Sat 0830-1030). **State Bank of India**, 103 Anna Salai (Foreign Ex in Tower Bl at rear. Good rate but only encash some TCs). **Union Bank of India**, 35 Anna Salai.

NB: Some banks have extended hours **Grindlays**, 3A Padmanabha Nagar, Adyar, (0830-1230, Sun 0830-1030, closed Mon), nr *Tourist Hostel*. **Indian Overseas**, 473 Poonamallee High Rd (0830-1530, Sat 0830-1230). **Indian**, Puraswalkam High Rd (nr *Hotel Picnic*), (0830-1230, 1600-1800, Sat 0830-1030, 1600-1800).

Exchange: facilities at International (0630-2400) and Meenambakkam Airport. **Thomas Cook**, 112 Nungambakkam High Rd.

Credit cards: **American Express**, c/o Binny Ltd, 16 Armenian St. **Diners Club**, Greenmore, 16 Haddows Rd.

● Chambers of Commerce

Southern India Chamber of Commerce and Industries, Esplanade, T 562228. **Andhra Chamber of Commerce**, T 583798. **Hindustan Chamber of Commerce**, T 586394. **National Chamber of Commerce**, T 583214. **Indo-German Chamber of Commerce**, 5 Kasturi Ranga Rd, T 454498.

Others: **All India Manufacturers' Organisation**, 69 NH Rd, T 471966. **Clothing Manufacturers' Association of India**, 2 Errabalu St, T 581042. **Cotton Textiles Export Promotions Council**, 26 Stringer St, T 583681. Gem and Jewellery **Export Promotion Council**, High Towers, NH Rd, T 476188. **Federation of the Association of Small Industries of India**, 10 GST Rd, T 433413.

● Deputy High Commissions and Consulates

Most open 0830-1330. Mon-Fri. **Austria**, 114 Nungambakkam High Rd, T 472131. **Belgium**, 1/E Spur Tank Rd, Chetput, T 665495. **Brazil**, 1B 1st Main Rd, Gandhi Nagar, T 412397. **Czechoslovakia**, 31A Haddows Rd, T 479754. **Denmark**, 8 Cathedral Rd, T 85116. **Finland**, 762 Anna Salai, T 867611 (1000-1700). **France**, 111 Flr, 26 Cathedral Rd, T 476854 (0930-1700). **Germany**, 22 C-in-C Rd, T 471747. **Greece**, 9 Harley's Rd, Kilpauk, T 869194. **Hungary**, 3A Sivaganga Rd (off Sterling Rd), T 478803. **Italy**, 5th Flr, 86 Chamiers Rd, T 452329 (1000-1700). **Japan**, 60 Spur Tank Rd, Chetput, T 865594. **Malaysia**, 287 TTK Rd, T 453580. **Norway**, 44-45 Rajaji Salai, T 517950. **Philippines**, 86 Radhakrishnan Rd, T 470160. **Romania**, 27 Khadar Nawaz Khan Rd, T 478387. **Russia**, 14 San Thome High Rd, T 71112. **Singapore**, 2nd Floor, Apex Plaza, 3 Nungambakkam High Rd, T 473795. **Spain**, 8 Nimmo Rd, San Thome, T 72008. **Sri Lanka**, 9D Nawab Habibulla Ave, off Anderson Rd, T 472270 (0900-1700). **Sweden**, 6 Cathedral Rd, T 472040 Extn 60.

Turkey, 202 Linghi Chetty St, T 25756. **UK**, 24 Anderson Rd, Nungambakkam, T 473136 and 470658 (0830-1600). **USA**, 220 Anna Salai, T 473040 (0830-1715).

● Hospital & medical services

Ambulance: *Government*, T 102; *St John's Ambulance*, T 864630. 24-hr.

Chemists: at *Apollo Hospital*, 21 Greams Rd, T 476566; *Devaki Hospital*, 148 Luz Church Rd, Mylapore, T 73935; *National Hospital*, 2nd Line Beach Rd, T 511405; *SS Day & Night Chemists*, 106 D Block, 1st Main Rd, Anna Nagar, T 615263.

Hospitals: *Govt Dental College*, T 564341; *Kilpauk*, Poonamallee High Rd, T 8255331; *General Hospital*, Park Town, T 563131.

● Post & telecommunications

Poste Restante: at the GPO, Rajaji Salai; other major post offices which accept Speed Post Mail are in Anna Salai, Pondy Bazar, T Nagar, Meenambakkam, Nungambakkam High Rd, Flower Bazar and Adyar. Opening times vary, first 3 open 0800-2030. CTO, Rajaji Salai (nr Parry's Corner). Computerised ISTD booths all over town, some open 2400.

NB: Beware of con-men claiming to be Sri Lankan refugees needing help to pay for a telegram 'home to Sri Lanka'. Many people have lost money.

Courier services: *DHL Express Centre*, 13, Sunkurama Chetty St, Georgetown. T 583548, 0930-1800; *DHL*, 44/45 Pantheon Rd, Egmore. T 8254102, 0930-1800. *Skypak*, 19 Rutland Gate, T 474237, and 173 Kodambakkam High Rd, T 474271, 24 hr.

Fax: contact Videsh Sanchar Bhavan, Adams Rd, T 566315. Overseas, Rs 110-125.

● Places of worship

Hindu: there are several temples in the city apart from the famous *Kapaleeswarar* in Mylapore and *Parthasarathi* in Triplicane detailed under Places of interest above.

Muslim: in addition to *The Big Mosque* and *Thousand Lights Mosque* listed under Places of interest, there is also the *Perimet Mosque* in Sydenhams Rd.

Christian: **Church of South India**: *St Mary's*, Fort St George; *St George's Cathedral*, Cathedral Road; *St Andrew's*, Poonamallee High Road, Egmore. **Roman Catholic**: *St Thomas' Cathedral Basilica*, 24 San Thome High Rd; *St Mary's Cathedral*, 2 Armenian St; *St Theresa's*, Nungambakkam.

● Tour companies & travel agents

Ashok Travels, 34 Pantheon Rd; ***Cox & Kings (India)***, A15 Kodambakkam High Rd; ***Mercury Travels***, Mohan Mansion, 191 Anna Salai; ***Orient Express***, 150 Anna Salai; ***Richfield Agencies***, Trade Centre, 100 Wallajah Rd, T 840135; ***Sheriff Travel***, 22 Second Line Beach; ***Sita World Travel***, Fagun Mansion, 26 C-in-C Rd, T 478861; ***Thomas Cook (Travel & Foreign Exchange)***, Eldorado Building, 112 Nungambakkam High Rd, T473092; ***Trade Wings***, 752 Anna Salai, T 864961; ***Travel Corporation of India***, 734 Anna Salai, T 868813.

● Tourist offices

Govt of India Tourist Office (GITO), 154 Anna Salai, T 88685/6, weekdays 0900-1800, Sat 0900-1300. Domestic Airport Counter, T 431686, 24 hr and International Airport Counter, open at flight times. **India Tourism Development Corporation** (ITDC), 29 Victoria Crescent, C-in-C Rd, T 478884, weekdays 0600-2000, Sat and Sun 0600-1400. **Tamil Nadu Tourist Office**, 143 Anna Salai, T 830390, weekdays 1000-1730, central advance booking for all TTDC accommodation possible at this office. **Tamil Nadu Tourism Development Corporation** (TTDC) Tours and Travels, 143 Anna Salai, T 830390 and at Central Rly Station, T 563351 (Sales Counter on Sun only).

State Government Tourist Bureaux and Information Centres are open from 1030-1700 on weekdays, closed on Sun and 2nd Sat. **Haryana**, 700 Anna Salai. **Himachal Pradesh, Kerala, Rajasthan** and **UP** are at 28 C-in-C Rd. **Jammu and Kashmir**, 1st Flr, 837 Anna Salai, W Bengal, 787 Anna Salai.

● Useful addresses

Foreigners Registration Office, 9 Village Rd, Nungambakkam, T 478210. Good for visa extensions.

Local transport

● Bus

The city has a cheap and convenient bus service, and apart from the rush hour not as crowded as in most Indian cities. The buses offer a realistic alternative to autorickshwas and taxis. Pallavan Transport Corp (PTC), Anna Salai, T 566063, runs an excellent network of buses from 0500-2300 and a skeleton service through the night (timetables from major bookshops). Monthly bus pass available at a bus depot. Avoid the rush hr (0800-1000, 1700-1900) when buses are very crowded, and make sure you know route numbers as most bus signs are in Tamil. '**M**' Service on mini-buses are good for the route between Central and Egmore stations and journeys to the suburban rly stations. The '**V**' service operates fast buses with fewer stops and have a yellow board with the route number and LSS (Limited Stop Service). PTC has a ½ hourly "luxury" mini-bus service between Egmore Station, Indian Airlines, Marshalls Rd office and Meenambakkam Airport picking up passengers from certain hotels (inform time keeper at Egmore in advance, T 561284. The fare is about Rs 20.

Major Bus routes within Madras: Between **Airport and Parry's, via Mount Rd**, 18R, 18RR (limited stop); 52, 52A, B, D, E, G, 55A, 60, 60A. **Between Egmore and Central Station/ Parry's**, 4B, 9, 9A, 9B,10, 17E, T, K, 28A, M4. **Between Egmore and Anna Sq (the Marina)**, 27, 27B, 29A. **Between Egmore and Adyar**, 23, A, B, C, E, G, J. **Between Central Rly Station and Poonamallee High Rd (Dasaprakash)**, 15, 15B, C, D, G, 50, 53, 53A, B, C, E, G, K, 71, 71C. **Between Parry's/ Broadway and Gemini**, 17B, C. **Between Parrys and St Thomas's Mt**, 18, 18A, 52, 54C, G, K, T, 55A. **Between Parry's/ Broadway and Adyar**, 19M, 21B, E, F, K. **Between Anna Sq and Gemini, Guindy**, 25C, E, 45B. **Between Anna Sq and San Thome**, 12R.

● Taxis

Yellow top taxis are increasingly hard to find. From a hotel, ask the bell-boy to call one and insist on using the meter (check it is cleared first and ask to see a chart before paying any supplementary charge). Some absolutely refuse to go a short distance, or go a long distance after 2000! Others may demand a 20% surcharge between 2200-0500. Drivers often refuse to use meters, and their first asking price can be 4 or 5 times the metered fare.

● Car hire

Chauffeur driven a/c or ordinary cars are good value and convenient for sightseeing, especially for short journeys out of the city, when shared between 3 and 5 people, otherwise costly. Ashok Travels, ITDC, Transport Unit, 29 Victoria Crescent Rd, C-in-C Rd, T 478884. Bajaji Tourist, 270 Anna Salai, T 453628. Balakrishna Tourist Taxi, 882 Poonamallee High Rd, Egmore, T 663340. Ganesh Travels, 36 Police Commissioner's Office Rd, T 561941. Travel Wings, 98 Alagappa Rd, T 666344. TS Narayanan, 1/35 Luz Church Rd, Mylapore, T 72883. TTDC, 143 Anna Salai, T 849803, Time Central, T 583351. Wheels, 499 Pantheon Rd, T 568327.

● Cycle Rickshaws

Often no cheaper than autorickshaws. Fix the fare first.

● Auto Rickshaws

Three-wheeler scooter taxis take 2 adults and a child, extra passengers negotiable. Usual extra night charge of 25% between 2200-0500. Rs 4.40 for first km. Insist on using the metre. If they refuse or claim their's does not work, walk away. There are plenty available.

● Metro

A **Metro** is being built but will take some time to complete.

● Suburban Railway

Inexpensive but very crowded at peak times. Stops between Beach Rly Station and Tambaram (5 min in rush hr) are Fort, Park, Egmore, Chetpet, Nungambakkam, Kodambakkam, Mambalam, Saidapet, Guindy, St Thomas Mount. Also serves suburbs of Perambur and Villivakkam.

NB: Convenient stop at Tirusoolam for Meenambakkam Airport, 500m walk from the terminals.

Long distance connections

● Air

Airport connections: Madras has an international airport with 2 terminals, Meenambakkam International (15 km) and Domestic (17 km). Pre-paid taxis are available from national and international airports to anywhere in the city. In mid 1994 the listed rate to Madras Central or Egmore was approx Rs 100. Egmore *Pallavan Transport Corp* (PTC) runs coaches to Egmore Rly Station via the big hotels. This can be a very slow way of getting into town, on a very roundabout route. Fare Rs 25. Airport, T 432534. Egmore, T 561284 (see Local Transport above). The cheapest way into town is from the Tirusoolam suburban line station to Egmore and Fort.

Free Fone: in the main concourse, after collecting baggage in the International Airport, you can use this phone to ring hotels. Railway Bookings 1000-1700.

Domestic: **Indian Airlines**: Reservations: 19 Marshalls Rd, T 478333 (0630-1900). Enquiries: T 477977. Flight information: Airport, T 2345144. Mini Booking Offices: Mena Building, 57 Dr Radhakrishnan Rd, T 479799. Umpherson St (nr Broadway), T 583321, 57 Venkatanarayana Rd, T Nagar, T 447555. Reservations and Cancellations 24 hr. Ticketing 0900-1700. **Delhi**, daily, 0600, 3¾ hr; **Bombay**, daily, 0620, 1050, 1¾ hr; **Bangalore**, daily, 0610, 1100, ¾ hr; **Calcutta**, daily, 2020, 3 hr; **Ahmedabad**, W,F,Su, 1400, 3¼ hr; **Coimbatore**, Tu,Th, 1440, 2 hr via Bangalore; **Madurai**, M,Tu,Th,Sa, 0700, 1¾ hr via Tiruchirappalli; **Poona**, M,W,F, 1500, 2¾ hr via Bangalore; **Tiruvananthapuram**, daily, 1100, 2¾ hr via Bangalore; **Kochi**, M,W,F,Su, 0830, 2 hr via Bangalore; **Port Blair**, T,W,F, 0640, 2 hr; **Hyderabad**, daily, 0600, 1845, 1 hr.

East-West Airlines: Mootha Centre, Grd Flr, 9 Kodambakkam High Rd, T 477007, F 865538. **Bombay** twice daily, 0830, 2015, 1¾ hrs; **Delhi**, daily, 0630, 2¾ hr.

Jet Airways: **Bombay**, daily, 1925, 1½ hr.

Modiluft: T 8269572. **Delhi**, daily, 0920, 2¾ hr, on to **Jammu** except Su, 4¾ hr; **Hyderabad**, Tu,Th,Sa, 1545, 1 hr.

International: **Air India** flies once a week to New York, Kuwait and Jeddah, twice a week to London and Kuala Lumpur, 5 times a week to Singapore. **British Airways** flies to London twice a week. **Singapore, Air Lanka, Malaysia** have several weekly flights to their capital cities.

● Train

Madras has 3 rly stations, **Madras Central** for broad gauge trains to all parts of India and **Egmore** for metre gauge trains to other towns in the southern region. The 2 have a mini-bus link (taxi journey 5 min). Beach Station is for suburban services.

Madras Central: General Enquiry, T 563535. Train Arrival, T 567575. Current Reservations: 1st Class, T 563545; 2nd Class, T 564455. Advance Reservations Centre, Southern Rly, is in a separate new building by station, open 0700-1300, 1330-1900. Sun 0700-1300. You can also order bedding. Separate Ladies' Counter. Indrail Passes and booking facilities are available here to foreigners and Indians resident abroad, on the 1st Flr. **Egmore**: Enquiry and Current Reservations, T 566565; 1st Class, T 564010; 2nd Class, T 566555/7.

There are several *Southern Rly Booking Offices* in addition to the ones at the stations. Annanagar, T 615132. Anna Salai, T 849642. Esplanade, T 563672. George Town, T 23553. Guindy, T 431319. Ambattur, T 653387. Mylapore, T 72750, T Nagar, T 441491. Triplicane, T 842529. Meenambakkam Airport has a Rail Booking Counter. You may reserve 60 days in advance, except for Inter-city Day Expresses to Bangalore, Coimbatore, Madurai, Mysore, Tirupati and Tiruchirappalli which can only be reserved 30 days in advance. A number of extra trains have been introduced for the 3 summer months from April. They include a Delhi-Madras Rajdhani Expresss 3 tier a/c sleeper.

From **Madras Central**: **Bangalore**: *Madras-Bangalore*, 6023 (AC/II), daily, 1330, 7¼ hr; **Bombay (VT)**: *Madras-Bombay Mail*, 7010 (AC/II), daily, 2220, 30½ hr; **Bombay (Dadar)**: *Madras-Dadar Exp*, 6512 (AC/II), daily, 0915, 26¾ hr; **Calcutta (H)**: *Coromandal Exp*, 2842 (AC/II), daily, 0810, 27¼ hr; *Haora Mail*, 6004 (AC/II), daily, 2230, 33¼ hr; **Delhi (ND)**: *Tamil Nadu Exp*, 2621 (AC/CC and AC/II), daily, 2100, 33¾ hr; *Grand Trunk Exp*, 2615 (AC/II), daily, 2115; 36¾ hr; **Hyderabad**: *Madras-Hyderabad*, 7053 (AC/II), daily, 1530, 16 hr; **Guntakal** (for Hospet) Bombay Mail 7010, daily, 2200, 10 hr; **Kochi**: *Madras-Kochi Exp*, 6041 (AC/II), daily, 1935, 14 hr; **Mysore**: *Shatabdi*, daily except Tu, via Bangalore, 0600, 7½ hr; **Thiruvananthapuram**: *Trivandrum Mail*, 6319 (AC/II), daily, 1855, 16¾ hr.

From **Egmore**: **Kollam via Kodi Rd & Madurai**: *Quilon Mail*, 6105, daily, 1930, 19½ hr; **Madurai via Tiruchirapalli**: *Vagai Exp*, 2635, daily, 1225, 7¾ hr; **Madurai via Kodi Rd**: *Pandyan Exp*, 6717 (AC/II), daily, 1905, 11 hr (this connects with the bus service at Kodaikkanal reaching at mid-day; **Rameswaram**: *Rameswaram Exp*, 6101, Daily, 2020, 16¾ hr; **Tiruchirappalli**: *Pallavan Exp*, 2605 (AC/II), daily, 1225, 7¾ hr.

● Road

The National Highways are motorable, the state Highways are reasonably well-maintained but condition of other roads vary. You can hire cars (usually with driver) through ITDC or a private car-hire company (see under Local Transport above) or take the Tourist offices' coach tour. Distances to some major towns in the region: Bangalore 334 km, Kochi 669 km, Coimbatore 486 km, Hyderabad 620 km, Kanchipuram 75 km, Madurai 461 km, Mamallapuram 64 km, Mysore 465 km, Periyar 554 km, Pondicherry 162 km, Ramesvaram 613 km, Salem 326 km, Tirupati 143 km, Tiruchirappalli 319 km, Tiruvananthapuram 710 km, Visakhapatnam 800 km.

Bus: Thiruvalluvar Transport Corporation (TTC) offers good connections within the whole region and the service is efficient and inexpensive. Best to take a/c coaches or super deluxe a/c. Buses originate from Express Bus Stand, Esplanade, T 561835, picking up from T Nagar, Egmore, T 561284, Broadway, T 561144 and Basin Bridge, T 519527. Bookings 0700-2100.

Other state and private companies cover the region but you may wish to avoid their video coaches which make listening, if not viewing, compulsory as there are no headphones! Interstate Bus Depot, Broadway Bus Stand handles enquiries and reservations. Computer reservations are now made on long distance routes. Andhra Pradesh (APSRTC), T 560735. Booking hours 0430-2100.

From Tamil Nadu State Bus Stand (Broadway). The listings given are for route number, departure time, distance and journey time. **Coimbatore**: No 462, 500 km, 1800. **Kanniyakumari**, 282; 0830, 1315, 1800, 2115, 700 km. **Kumbakonum**: 305, 8 daily, 0600-2000, 289 km, 6½ hr. **Madurai**:137, 22 daily, 0330-2245, 447 km, 10 hr. **Pondicherry, Chidambaram and Nagapattinam**: 326, 14 daily, 0530 and 2300. **Nagercoil**: 198, 10 daily, 0530-2300, 682 km, 14 hr. **Ooty**:465, 1730, 565 km, 13hr. **Thanjavur**:323,14 daily, 0530-2350, 320 km, 8hr. **Tiruchirappalli**:123, 23 daily, 0300-2330, 320 km and Route 124 8 daily, 0030-2100, 7 hr. **Yercaud**: 434, 0715,360, 8 hr. **Bangalore (via Vellore and Krishnagiri)**:831 12 daily, 0530-2300, 360 km, 8 hr. **Bangalore (via Kolar)**: 8 daily, 0830-2330, 350 km, 7½hr. **Mysore via Bangalore** 863, 2000, 497 km, 11 hr:**Pondicherry**: 803, 20 daily, 0420-2330, 160 km, 4 hr. **Tirupati via Kalahasti**: 802, 0815, 1530, 2030, 150 km, 3½ hr. Also 17 Andhra Pradesh State Transport Corp buses to Tirupati daily. APSTC runs daily buses to many others towns in the state. **Mamallapuram**: No 19C, 119A down the coast road (via Covelong); 188, 188A, B, D, K on the less attractive inland road (the coast road allows you to get off at the hotels immediately N of Mamallapuram, which can save some effort if staying there) (see page853); 108B goes via Meenambakkam airport, (2/3 hr).

From TTC Bus Stand, Parry's Esplanade, Enquiries, T 566351.

● Sea

Regular passenger ships to the Andaman and Nicobar Islands charge from about Rs 600 for a/c Deluxe Cabins down to Rs 400 for C Class. Agents: The Shipping Corporation of India, Rajaji Salai, T 514401. A passenger line is reputed to be opening to Singapore. Check with a local travel agent for details.

TAMIL NADU

Contents

Maps

Tamil Nadu is in the SE corner of India. Lying between latitudes 8°N and 14°N, to its E and S is the Bay of Bengal and the Indian Ocean. Across the Palk Straits in the SE is Sri Lanka. To its N and W are Andhra Pradesh, Karnataka and Kerala. The state covers an area of 130,000 sq km, approximately the same size as England Tamil Nadu has over 2000 years of continuous cultural history. Tamil is one of the oldest literary languages in India, some of its poetry dating back before the birth of Christ. Tamil Nadu also has some of the most remarkable temple architecture in India, and a living tradition of music and dance.

BASICS *Population*: 55.6mn (Urban 35%, Scheduled Castes 18%, Scheduled Tribes 1%); *Literacy*: M 75% F 52%; *Birth rate*: *Rural* 22:1000, *Urban* 16:1000; *Death rate*: *Rural* 8:1000, *Urban* 6:1000; *Infant mortality*: *Rural* 90:1000, *Urban* 48:1000; *Religion*: *Hindu* 89%, *Muslim* 5%, *Christian* 6%.

Environment

Land

The W flank is dominated by the Western Ghats, the Nilgiris in the N and the Palani, Cardomom and Anamalai hills in the S. The Nilgiris cover an area of about 2500 sq km, formed of rocks over 3000 million years old, and rising to heights of over 2500m. Dodabetta is the second highest mountain in S. India. To the E of the hills are the plains. In the N of the State isolated blocks like the Shevaroy and Javadi hills reach heights of over 1500m. The coast itself is a flat alluvial plain, with deltas at the mouths of major rivers.

Rivers and lakes

The Kaveri (formerly Cauvery) which rises in Karnataka is vital to the irrigation of the Thanjavur delta. It is used so effectively that it is possible to walk across it ankle deep at its mouth. Other rivers include the Palar in the N and the Tamramparni in the S. Like all rivers in peninsular India they are often dry, reflecting the seasonal nature of the rainfall pattern. Tamil Nadu's biggest lake is that created behind the Mettur Dam. This was built in 1926 to improve the efficiency of use of the River Kaveri.

Climate

Protected by the rainshadow effect of the mountains, Tamil Nadu is much drier than Kerala to its W. The districts around Madurai, for example, receive less than 750 mm annually. Tamil Nadu, and particularly the area around Madras receives the bulk of its rain in what is sometimes called the retreating monsoon from Oct to Dec. See page 799.

History

Early history

Although there is much evidence of Stone and Iron Age settlements, Tamil Nadu's cultural identity has been shaped by the Dravidians, who had inhabited the S since the 4th millennium BC. Tamil, its oldest language, developed from the earlier and unknown languages of people who are generally believed to have been displaced from N Asia by the Aryans from 2000 BC to 1500 BC.

Tamil Nadu was under the rule of 3 dynasties from the 4th century. The Cholas occupied the coastal area E of Thanjavur and inland to the head of the Kaveri Delta at Tiruchi. Periodically they were a strong military power. One of their princes, Elara, for example conquered the island of Sri Lanka in the 2nd century BC. Madurai, Tirunelveli and a part of S Kerala, were under the Pandiyas. The Cheras who controlled much of what is now Kerala also penetrated S Tamil Nadu.

From around the 2nd century AD a poets' academy known as the **Sangam** was established in Madurai. The writings describe life in Tamil society as belonging to a different system of hierarchy from that in the N. In Tamil Nadu the sages were at the top, followed by peasants, hunters, artisans, soldiers,

THE TERRIFYING GUARDIAN DEITIES

Many Hindu villagers in Tamil Nadu believe in guardian deities of the village. NVR Swamy has written how they go under several names: Ayyanar, Muneeswaram, Kaliamman, Mariamman and many more. It is common to see groups of larger than life images of these guardians on the outskirts of many villages, built of brick, wood or stone and covered in brightly painted lime plaster – *chunam*. Sometimes they are on horseback, to ride through the night. They are deliberately terrifying creatures, designed to frighten away evil spirits from village homes, but villagers themselves are also very frightened of these gods and try to keep away from them. Among the evils which the deities are supposed to prevent are epidemics, but if an epidemic does strike special sacrifices will be offered, both of rice and of animals, though the latter has largely disappeared. Firewalking, often undertaken in fulfilment of a vow, is a feature of the special festivals at these shrines. Disease is also believed to be held at bay by other ceremonies, including the piercing the cheeks and tongue with wire and the carrying of *kavadis*. These special carriages or boxes are sometimes designed like a coffin. Swamy says that those who undertake vows may then be bathed, dressed in a cloth dipped in turmeric and carried through the village streets as though dead, to "come to life" when the procession enters the temple.

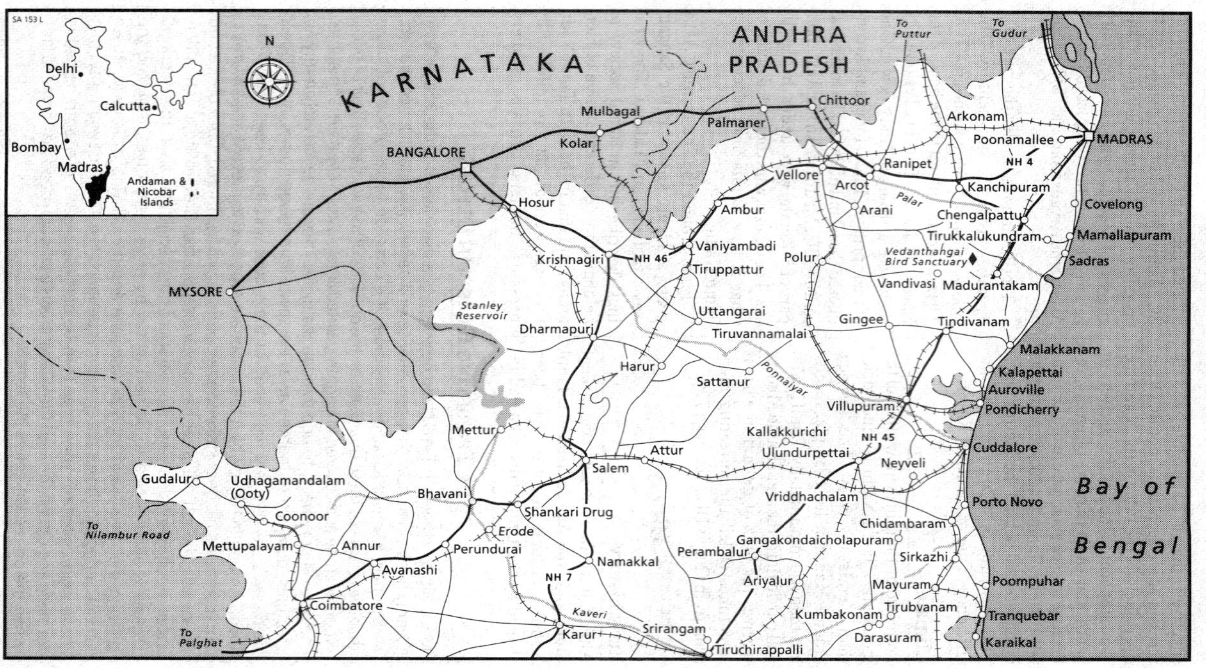
SA 153 L
Delhi
Calcutta
Bombay
Madras
Andaman & Nicobar Islands
N
KARNATAKA
ANDHRA PRADESH
To Puttur
To Gudur
Chittoor
Mulbagal
Palmaner
Arkonam
Poonamallee
MADRAS
Kolar
BANGALORE
Ranipet
NH 4
Vellore
Arcot
Kanchipuram
Palar
Hosur
Ambur
Arani
Covelong
Chengalpattu
Tirukkalukundram
Mamallapuram
Vaniyambadi
Krishnagiri
NH 46
Polur
Vedanthangai Bird Sanctuary
Sadras
Tiruppattur
MYSORE
Vandivasi
Madurantakam
Stanley Reservoir
Uttangarai
Gingee
Tindivanam
Dharmapuri
Tiruvannamalai
Malakkanam
Harur
Ponnaiyar
Sattanur
Kalapettai
Auroville
Villupuram
Pondicherry
Mettur
Kallakkurichi
NH 45
Attur
Ulundurpettai
Cuddalore
Salem
Neyveli
Gudalur
Udhagamandalam (Ooty)
Bay of Bengal
Bhavani
Vriddhachalam
Porto Novo
Shankari Drug
Coonoor
To Nilambur Road
Chidambaram
Erode
Mettupalayam
Annur
Perundurai
Gangakondaicholapuram
Perambalur
Sirkazhi
Namakkal
Avanashi
NH 7
Ariyalur
Mayuram
Poompuhar
Coimbatore
Tirubvanam
Kaveri
Kumbakonam
Tranquebar
Srirangam
To Palghat
Karur
Darasuram
Karaikal
Tiruchirappalli

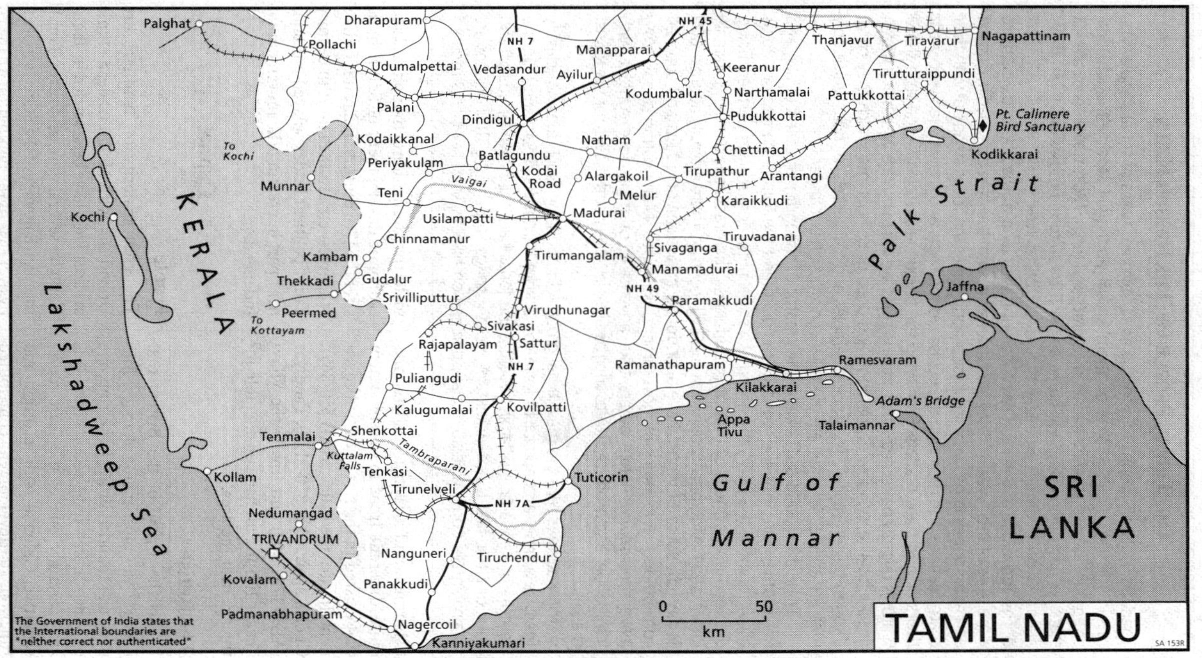
Palghat
Pollachi
Dharapuram
NH 7
Manapparai
NH 45
Thanjavur
Tiravarur
Nagapattinam
Udumalpettai
Vedasandur
Ayilur
Keeranur
Tirutturaippundi
Kodumbalur
Narthamalai
Pattukkottai
Palani
Dindigul
Pudukkottai
Pt. Calimere
Bird Sanctuary
Kodaikkanal
Natham
Chettinad
Kodikkarai
To Kochi
Periyakulam
Batlagundu
Kodai Road
Alargakoil
Tirupathur
Arantangi
Vaigai
Munnar
Teni
Melur
Karaikkudi
Palk Strait
KERALA
Kochi
Usilampatti
Madurai
Chinnamanur
Tiruvadanai
Sivaganga
Kambam
Tirumangalam
Manamadurai
Thekkadi
Gudalur
NH 49
Jaffna
Srivilliputtur
Paramakkudi
Peermed
Virudhunagar
To Kottayam
Sivakasi
Sattur
Rajapalayam
Lakshadweep Sea
NH 7
Ramanathapuram
Ramesvaram
Puliangudi
Kilakkarai
Kalugumalai
Kovilpatti
Adam's Bridge
Appa Tivu
Talaimannar
Shenkottai
Tenmalai
Kuttalam Falls
Tambraparani
Tenkasi
Kollam
Tuticorin
Gulf of Mannar
SRI LANKA
Tirunelveli
NH 7A
Nedumangad
TRIVANDRUM
Nanguneri
Tiruchendur
Kovalam
Panakkudi
0 50 km
Padmanabhapuram
Nagercoil
Kanniyakumari
TAMIL NADU
SA 153R
The Government of India states that the international boundaries are "neither correct nor authenticated"

The Tribal People Of The Nilgiri Hills

There are isolated groups of as many as 18 different types of tribal people who live in the Nilgiri Hills. Some of them are of aboriginal stock although local antiquities suggest that an extinct race preceded them. Most travellers to the hill stations, particularly Ooty, will come across *Toda* culture, but besides them there are a few other groups who lead their own distinct lives.

- The **Todas'** life and religion revolve around their long-horned buffalo which are a measure of their wealth. They are pastoralists, with the men occupied in grazing and milking their large herds. In physical appearance the Todas stand out with their sharp features, the men with their close cropped hair, and the women who wear theirs in long shiny ringlets. Both wrap the traditional *puthukuli* toga style shawl which is brightly patterned. Their small villages are called *munds* with half a dozen or so igloo-like, windowless bamboo and dried grass huts into which they crawl through tiny entrances. The animist temples and 'cathedrals' or *boa*, which only men are allowed to enter, are of similar construction but larger.

Their chief goddess 'Tiekirzi', the creator of the indispensable buffalo, and her brother 'On', rule the world of the dead and the living. Marriage customs allow for loose ties and 'fatherhood' is a social requirement, with partners being changed on payment of a price in buffaloes. The practice is declining, female infanticide having been stopped in the 19th century. There are only about 1,000 Todas left, some of whom have abandoned their traditional huts and adopted conventional dwellings with government assistance. Many young people now leave their *munds* while others take advantage of their close contact with 'civilisation' and produce articles such as silver jewellery and shawls for the tourist market.

- The **Badagas** are the main tribal group (although the Govt does not classify them as a tribe) and appear to have come from Karnataka. Their language is a mixture of Kannada and Tamil, (whereas the Todas have their own language) and their oral tradition is rich in folktales, poetry, songs and chants. Their villages are mainly in the upper plateau, usually perched on hillocks, with rows of 3-roomed

fishermen and scavengers. This was quite different from the caste system that existed in the rest of the subcontinent. In turn the Pallavas (AD 550-869), Cholas again (AD 850-1173), Pandiyas (AD 1175-1300) and finally the Vijayanagar Empire all had considerable influence over the area.

The British

It was the arrival of the British that brought the most major changes. Madras, was founded in 1639. It is thus one of South India's most recent cities. It is also certainly one of the least representative. Colonial both in origin and function, its development contributed to the transformation of the political and economic development of South India after the 17th century. Today it is India's 4th largest city. In the late 19th century Tamil political leaders played a prominent part in creating the movement for Independence.

Culture

People

The great majority of Tamilians are Dravidians, with Mediterranean ethnic origins. They have been settled in Tamil Nadu for several thousand years. Tamil, the main language of the State, is spoken by over 85% of the population. In the N,

houses. They are principally agriculturists growing mainly potatoes, although many have branched out to tea and vegetable cultivation, often working in the plantations. They are worshippers of Siva and observe special tribal festivals including an unusual fire feast in honour of the gods of harvest. Progressive and adaptable, they are being absorbed into the local community faster than the others.

- The **Kotas** who live mainly in the Kotagiri/Tiruchigadi area are particularly musical and artistic, and are distinguished by their colourful folk dances. Their villages are also on the upper plateau, with a few detached huts or rows of huts, each with a living and sleeping area with the place of worship in a large square with a loose stone wall. They preceded the Badagas but also speak a language derived from Kannada and Tamil. Being the artisan tribe, they are the blacksmiths, gold and silver smiths, carpenters, potters and tanners to the other groups. Their musicians play at Badaga funerals.
- The **Kurumbas** live in the lower valleys and forests in villages called *'mothas'* under the control of headmen and speak a corrupt form of Tamil and Kannada. They collect fruit, particularly bananas, honey, resin, medicinal herbs and also hunt and trap big game. Their major festivals are in honour of tribal deities. Most of their dead are buried in a sitting position, except the very old who are cremated. In the past they had a reputation for practising black magic when they could conjure up elephants and tigers at will and reduce rocks to powder with their magic herbs, so were murdered by the other tribes. Today many have become employees in the plantations and have given up their tribal ways.
- The **Irulas** are the second largest group after the Badagas and in many ways similar to the Kurumbas. They live on the lower slopes in huts made of bamboo and thatch cultivating small areas to grow *ragi*, and fruit like plantains, oranges, pumpkins and jackfruit. They also hunt and ensnare wild animals. They take produce such as honey, beeswax, gum, dyes and fruit, down to towns in the plains to trade. The Irulas are worshippers of Vishnu, especially in the form of Rangaswamy, and their temples are simple circles of stone which enclose an upright stone with a trident. In common with other tribal people they wear a large number of ornaments but like the Kurumbas also have a reputation for witchcraft.

especially around Madras are many Telugu speakers, who make up a further 10% of the population. Hindus make up nearly 90% of the population. Over 5% are Christian, a group especially strong in the S where Roman Catholic and Protestant missions have been active for over 500 years. However, the origins of Christianity in the S traditionally go back to 52 AD, when St Thomas the Apostle is believed to have come to India and to have been martyred in Mylapore, now a suburb of Madras. There are also small but significant minorities of Muslims, Jains and Parsis.

Modern Tamil Nadu

Government

There are 18 administrative districts. Tamil Nadu sends 39 Members to the Lok Sabha. It elects 234 Members to its own Legislative Assembly and a further 63 to its Legislative Council. Tamil Nadu took its present form as a result of the States Reorganisation Act of 1956. Until 1967 the Assembly was dominated by the Indian National Congress. However, after an attempt by the central government to impose Hindi as a national language the Congress Party was routed in 1967 by a regional party, the Dravida Munnetra Kazhagam (the

DMK) under its leader CN Annadurai.

Annadurai was almost universally respected and indeed revered in Tamil Nadu. He had helped to convert the original Dravida Kazhagam from its position of atheistic Tamil Nationalism, committed to absolute independence for a Tamil state, into a political party within the broad Indian mainstream struggling for social and economic reform while insisting on the primacy of regional Tamil culture. After his death the party split and either the DMK or the splinter party, the All India Anna DMK, has been in power in the State.

Neither party has any constituency beyond Tamil Nadu and thus at the all India level each has been forced to seek alliances with national parties. For most of its existence the AIADMK has been aligned with the Congress Party. When the Congress Party has been weak at the centre the AIADMK has used its bargaining power to advance its own cause, while the DMK has normally been allied with oppostion parties. Since the late 1960s the AIADMK, which has controlled the State Assembly for most of the time, has been led by 2 film stars. The first, MG Ramachandran, known lovingly by his initials MGR by millions of his film fans and political supporters, was a charismatic figure, who even after a stroke which left him paralysed remained the Chief Minister until his death. In 1993, Jayalalitha, his successor and a film actress who had starred in many of MGR's films, broke off the AIADMK's alliance with the Congress Party nationally, hinting that it would move towards the BJP. In fact, as the BJP has lost support in the N and Prime Minister Narasimha Rao has regained popular support, in 1994 the AIADMK has shown signs of returning to an alliance with the Congress.

The Economy

Agriculture There are great contrasts between irrigated agriculture and dry farming. Irrigation has been practised in the region for over 2000 years.

Tanks – large, shallow reservoirs – were built as early as the 8th century AD in the areas around Madras. Further S the River Kaveri has been used for irrigation for over 1000 years. There are over 20,000 km of irrigation channels (known in Tamil as 'anicuts') in Tamil Nadu. In both regions rice is the most important crop, Tamil Nadu accounting for over 10% of India's rice production. Sugar cane is also a vital cash crop, as are groundnuts and other oilseeds. Cotton and bananas are also grown for market. In the hills of the Western Ghats tea makes a major contribution to exports and domestic consumption. The hills are also famous for cardamom, pepper, ginger and other spices. Potatoes are widely grown in the Nilgiris for sale in India's big cities. Fishing is increasingly important, about one fifth of India's seafood exports, including prawns, crab, squid and oysters, come from Tamil Nadu.

Resources and industry There are extensive deposits of lignite, exploited at Neyyveli, iron ore is now being used in the steel mill at Salem, and magnesite has been mined for many years in Salem district, but Tamil Nadu does not have rich mineral resources. The E facing slopes of the Western Ghats have also offered considerable potential for the development of hydro electricity. Tamil Nadu is one of India's most industrialised states. The state's first industrial venture was a small steel mill at Porto Novo in 1820. That failed, and the only successful venture in the next 50 years was the setting up of sugar mills, converting *gur* into white sugar in S Arcot District.

The biggest development was in cotton milling. The disruption to Europe's cotton supplies caused by the American Civil War led to a great expansion of the area under cotton in Tamil Nadu. However, when the war ended and American supplies were resumed there was a glut of raw cotton on the market, and both

British and Indian investment looked to setting up mills in India. Mills were built in, Tuticorin, Madras and Coimbatore in the 1870s and early 1880s. During the same period the sugar industry expanded and the leather industry grew rapidly from its traditional small scale base. All 3 industries remain pillars of the modern Tamil Nadu economy. In the 1930s hydro-electricity was developed in the hills of the SW, and Coimbatore rapidly became a major industrial centre for the textile industry. By Independence Tamil Nadu had over 80 cotton textile mills, 5 sugar factories and over 300 leather manufacturing units.

Rapid industrialisation followed. Tamil Nadu has become a centre of engineering works making cars, buses, lorries and railway rolling stock, alongside motorbikes and precision tools. Leather is one of India's major export earners and 70% of the country's tanning capacity is in Tamil Nadu, which accounts for over 40% of all India's leather exports. Madras ranks third behind Delhi and Bombay for garment manufacture, exporting to Australasia and the fashion markets of Europe. One of the major growth areas has been the export of granite, especially to Japan, where in polished form it is highly valued as a finished surface for buildings as well as for furniture such as tables. There are also oil refining and fertiliser industries while chemical industries rose to second position by the early 1990s, with fertilisers accounting for nearly 50% of their value. Over half the fixed industrial capital in Tamil Nadu is concentrated in the 3 districts of Coimbatore, Madras and Salem, though an industrial estate at Hosur (about 30 km from Bangalore), one of several set up by the state government in the early 1970s to stimulate growth in backward districts of Tamil Nadu, has become a major industrial centre.

Among the innovations now being implemented are an India-Singapore Trade Corridor, the Madras Industrial Park, in which a wide range range of technical services will be provided.

Power At Independence two-thirds of Tamil Nadu's total installed electric capacity came from hydro schemes, the remainder being coal fired power stations. Production capacity has gone up from 156 MW then to over 4500 MW in 1994. Of this hydro still contributes a major share, over 1400 MW. However, demand has risen so fast that there remain major shortages. A nuclear power station was commissioned in the late 1980s at Kalpakkam, 70 km S of Madras, but it is still not producing to its 500 MW capacity.

Transport Tamil Nadu has some of the best road and rail connections in India. The broad gauge rail system links Madras with Bangalore, Kochi, Bombay, Delhi, Calcutta and the N. The metre gauge system serves the S. Tamil Nadu has the second highest road density in the country.

ROUTES The routes outlined below are suggestions as to convenient ways of seeing some of the state's most interesting places, but it is easy to find alternatives as bus transport goes within range of virtually every village.

MADRAS TO THANJAVUR

The suburbs of S Madras give way to casuarina groves along the road to Mamallapuram. Crossing the attractive salt flats to Tirukkalukundram, the quiet district road then passes through fascinating villages and the coconut fringed coast to Pondicherry.

The road out of Madras via **Tiruvanmiyur** goes past the Cholamandalam Artists colony, in the suburbs of S Madras, the VGP *Golden Beach Resort* (a tacky commercial 'fair'), and Fisherman's Cove. **Accommodation D** *VGP Golden Beach Resort*, E Coast Rd, Injabakkam, T 412893, F 458674, restaurant, bar, exchange, very gaudy, popular with Indian day tourists.

Tiruvanmiyur is noted for its temple dedicated to the Goddess Tripurasundari, who is believed to have been worshipped here by one of Tamil Nadu's most revered poets, *Valmiki*. The temple is packed with worshippers on Fridays, and the temple has 108 Sivalinga images. Through Tiruvanmiyur are numerous small temples and shrines and a number of modern small industries. Coconut and casuarina trees are common on both sides. The casuarina plantations provide firewood and scaffold timbers for Madras. The poor sandy soils produce an extremely valuable harvest. The round concrete buildings are cyclone shelters, a reminder that this coast is subject to catastrophic cyclones. Some are used to house Tamil refugees from Sri Lanka. Inland of Covelong the road crosses a shallow lagoon and across salt pans. Traditional picottah wells can still be seen.

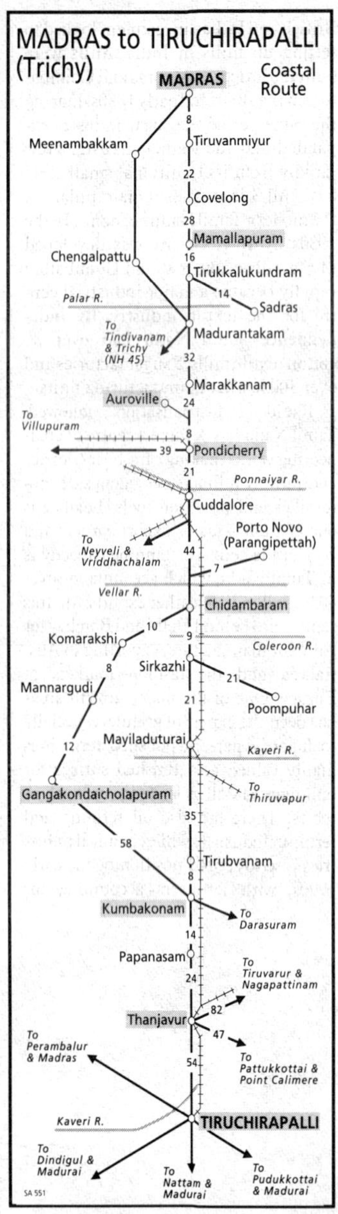

Approaching Mamallapuram are attractive views to right across extensive paddy fields. and the outline to the W of Tirukkalukundram hill – the first glimpse of the 3000 million years old Charnockite rocks that outcrop across Tamil Nadu. The town of Mamallapuram is still a rather scruffy little place, though there are comfortable places to stay.

Mamallapuram

58 km from Madras; *Population*: 9,500; *STD Code*: 04113. Previously called Mahabalipuram after the legend of Vishnu conquering the giant Mahabali, it has been renamed as the town of 'Mamalla' (great wrestler) the name given to Narasimhavarman I Pallavamalla (r630-668) the Pallava ruler who made the port famous in the 7th century and was largely responsible for the temples. There are 14 cave temples and 9 monolithic *rathas* (shrines in the shape of rathas or temple chariots), 3 stone temples and 4 relief sculptured rock panels. The nature of the area with its 2 vast natural granite-gneiss mounds lent itself to rock cut architecture although there were also structural temples in this spot.

Another characteristic feature of the temples here was the system of water channels and tanks, drawn from the Palar river, which made it particularly suitable as a site of religious worship apart from providing water supply for household use. The *naga* or serpent cult associated with water worship can be seen given prominence at Arjuna's Penance.

Local Festivals

Jan 10-day dance festival.

Mar *Masi Magam* attracts large crowds of pilgrims.

Apr-May *Brahmotsava* lasts for 10 days.

Oct-Nov The *Palanquin Festival* is held at the Salasayana Perumal Temple.

Places of interest

NB Distances from Bus Stand

Bhagiratha's Penance (Descent of the Ganga), sometimes referred to as Arjuna's Penance, is a bas relief sculpted on the face of 2 enormous adjacent rocks, 29m long and 7m high. It shows realistic life size figures of animals, gods and saints watching the descent of the river from the Himalayas. Bhagiratha, Rama's ancestor is seen praying for Ganga. A contrived water fall fed from a collecting chamber above, issued from the natural crack between the 2 rocks. Some see the figure of an ascetic (on the upper register of the left hand side rock, near the cleft) as representing Arjuna's penance when praying for powers from Siva though some authorities dispute this. The animals are particularly curious; for example, a cat imitates the solemn posture of a saint in meditation while rats dance around him (bottom of right hand rock nr elephant's trunk). The 2 large elephants are remarkable and there are also scenes from the fables in the *Panchatantra* and a small shrine to Vishnu.

Mandapas There are 10 cave temples or *mandapas* (of which 2 are unfinished) on the hill which are cut out of rock to make shallow halls (porticos). They are very distinctive architecturally and show a progression in the Dravidian temple style. The pillared halls are a means of providing space for the sculptures depicting tales from mythology, but they are also superbly executed. The temples are fairly small – mostly 8m wide and 8m deep and about 6m high with pillars 3m tall and 50 cm in diameter.

A path goes N from Bhagiratha's Penance to the **Ganesh mandapa**, a rectangular shrine with pillars which have lions at their base. It is double-storeyed and has a vaulted roof. An active shrine, Ganesh is clothed. To the W are the **Valayankuttai** and twin **Pidari** rathas which are small monolithic temples.

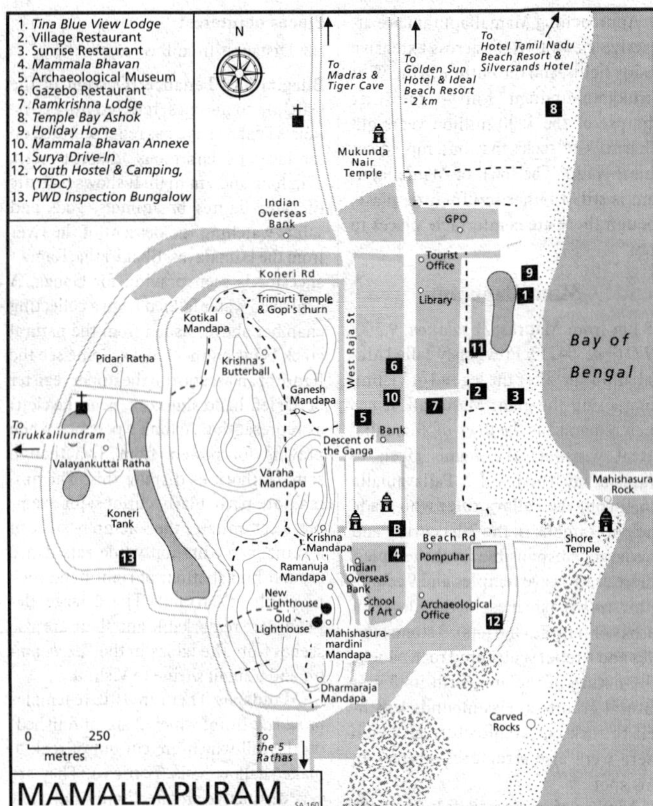

One path turns sharply left onto the hill. The path N goes past the extraordinary isolated rock, **'Krishna's butterball'**, through some huge boulders at the N end of the hillock to the **Trimurti Temple** caves, which have 3 shrines to Brahma, Vishnu and Siva, the last with a lingam. On the S is a Mamalla style Durga niche, 630-660, while next door is the 'Gopi's churn', a Pallava cistern. A path runs back to the S along the spine of the hill. Walk back S along the ridge, passing Krishna's butterball on your left. A number of boulders show signs of incomplete work. The **Varaha Mandapa** (640-674 AD) on the left of the ridge, is just SW of the Ganesh temple. It shows 2 incarnations of Vishnu – Varaha (boar) and Vamana (dwarf), among other scenes of kings and queens and has the distinctive architectural feature where the base forms a narrow receptacle for water for pilgrims to use before entering the temple. From the Varaha you can walk to the top of Bhagiratha's Penance. The water channel is clear.

The **Krishna Mandapa** (mid-7th century) has a bas relief scene of Krishna lifting Mount Govardhana to protect a crowd of his kinsmen from the anger of the Rain God, Indra. The **Kotikal Mandapa** may be the earliest of the mandapas, (the beginning of the 7th century), roughly carved with a small shrine with no image inside. Immediately NE, the **Ramanuja Mandapa** was originally a triple cell Siva temple, converted later into a Vaishnava temple.

S of the new lighthouse is the early 7th century **Dharmaraja** cave which is simpler and contains 3 empty shrines. To its W is the Isvara Temple, or **Old Lighthouse**, a truncated Siva temple still standing like a beacon on the highest summit, with a view for miles around. To the S you see across the 5 rathas to the nuclear power station of Kalpakkam, to the W across the flat lagoon and the original port of Mamallapuram at the small village of **Punjeri**. You can take photos from here, though not from the top of the new lighthouse, which is open from 1400-1600 on weekdays (entry Re 1). Immediately below the old lighthouse is the **Mahishasuramardini Mandapa** (mid-7th century) which has particularly fine bas relief and finely carved columns which show the introduction of the lion to the base of the pillars. It is named after the scene of the goddess Durga slaying the buffalo demon Mahishasura which is beside 1 of the 3 shrines. Another shows Vishnu lying under the hood of Adishesha the 7-hooded serpent. These panels are outstanding examples of Pallava art.

The **Five Rathas** (1.5 km), **Pancha Pandava**, are monolithic temples to the S, sculpted out of the rock in the mid-7th century and influenced by Buddhist architecture in resembling the *vihara* (monastery) and *chaitya* hall (temple). The overall shape of the original granite hill can be clearly seen from the SW or NW corner of the compound. They point to the evolution of different kinds of Dravidian temples with *gopurams*, *vimanas* and *mandapas*. The purpose of imitating in granite temple structures that were built of wood is not known.

Named after the 5 Pandava brothers, the heroes in the epic *Mahabharata* and their wife Draupadi. The largest is the domed **Dharmaraja**, then the barrel vaulted **Bhima** which is followed by another dome shaped ratha **Arjuna**. The **Draupadi** ratha is the smallest and simplest and in the form of a thatched hut rising about 6m. The base is covered by sand, concealing the lion in front as though carrying it, which may suggest that it is a replica of a portable shrine. Immediately E is a Nandi. To its W is the apsidal **Nakula Sahadeva** ratha with a free-standing elephant nearby. The Dharmaraja and Arjuna are particularly well sculpted. Bhima, Sahadeva and Ganesh rathas follow the form of the Buddhist *chaitya* hall, and are oblong in plan and built to 2 or more storeys, a precursor to the *gopuram*, the entrance gateway.

The Shore Temple (1 km) now has an enormous protective sea wall barrier of granite boulders about 50m out to sea. The space has been filled in and is being grassed. The gardens are being re-designed according to descriptions of the original layout from ancient texts. It is a world heritage monument. There are very large numbers of tourists coming through from early morning. A compact temple with 2 spires, built at the end of the 7th century by king Rajasimha, it is based on the Dharmaraja Ratha and is unusual in that it has shrines to both Siva and Vishnu. Its position on the sea shore and the decision to make the altar face E to catch the rising sun as well as provide a lamp light (a stone pillar to hold the beacon for sailors is evident) at night meant there was no space for a forecourt or entrance gateway. Two additional shrines were built to the W, asymmetrically. The 2nd smaller spire adds to the unusual structure of this temple.

This early temple shows the introduction of the lion figure at the base of *pilasters* – an architectural style which was to become significant. Some of the temple has been reclaimed from the sea and it seems that the central shrine could be surrounded by water by the flooding of the outer enclosure. The outer parapet wall has lines of *nandi* or sacred bulls and lion pilasters. Good postcards from hawkers.

5 km N of Mamallapuram, on the coast, is the excavated temple at **Saluvankuppam** which has the **Tiger Cave** mandapa with carvings of tigers' heads. The cave is not signposted from the beach. Secluded and very peaceful – a lovely place for a picnic. On the way you will see the **Mukunda Nayar Temple**.

NB: Check about safety of swimming in the sea. One visitor writes "If you're white, female and wearing shorts, you have to be prepared to star in lots of photos".

Excursions

Sadras (30 km) can be reached through Tirukkalukundram (see below). The ruined Dutch fort is close to the sea and a cemetery going back to 1679. In line with many other small European territories in India, its fate depended largely on events outside India. Sadras was taken by the British in 1781, but given back to the Dutch in 1818. It was finally ceded to the British in exchange for British-held territories in Sumatra.

Museum

The small **Archeological Museum** on W Raja St, nr the Ganesh Ratha, has granite sculptures and fragments which have been found nearby.

Tours

(TTDC) to Kanchipuram and Mamallapuram. 0500-1900. Tiring, but good value if you do not mind being rushed. It also includes a stop at the appallingly garish *VGP Beach Resort*.

Local information

● Accommodation

A *Fisherman's Cove*, Covelong, T 6268 (Madras T 474849), 80 rm, some a/c cottages, and with sea view, between Madras and Mamallapuram, pool, bar, excellent value, on a beautiful site with very good facilities.

C *Silversands Beach Village*, Covelong Rd, 2 km N of town, T 283, F 280, (Madras T 477444), 65 a/c rm, some with balcony (best on beach with sea view), more expensive suites, very good, friendly restaurant, travel, cultural shows, open-air Disco, free transfer from Madras for long-stay visitors; **C** ITDC *Temple Bay Ashok*, T 251, 23 a/c rm, restaurant, occasional barbecue, bar, travel, small pool, some cottages with kitchenette and fridge, 'Resort hotel'.

D *Golden Sun*, 59 Covelong Rd, 3 km N, T 245, F 4444 (Madras T 841020), 69 a/c cottages, restaurant, bar, exchange, shop, car hire, garden, pool, fairly simple but in pleasant surroundings. **NB** Visitors are charged for access to sea although half is coupon for food and drink at stalls. Sewer runs into sea; **D** *Ideal Beach Resort*, Covelong Rd ($3^1/_2$ km N), T 2240, F 2243, 15 rm in cottages, some a/c, restaurant (generous portions, good quality), barbecue, exchange, travel, pool and gardens, reduced rate May-Aug, immaculately clean, comfortable, friendly and relaxed, highly rec; **D** TTDC *Shore Temple Beach Resort*, T 235, 48 cottages, some a/c, with telephones and TV (newer split-level 2-rm cottages on beach, best), restaurant, bar, travel, good pool, clean, very good value.

● Budget hotels

E *Mamalla Bhavan Annexe*, 105 E Raja St, T 260, 20 rm, 12 a/c, excellent Indian veg restaurant, spotless, pleasant atmosphere, friendly service, cultural show at weekends; **E** *Silver Inn*, (Silversands) rm with shower and huts, away from beach; **E** *Surya Drive-in*, nr beach and Tourist Office, T 290, cottages, very clean, some a/c with seaview, in quiet shaded gardens, a/c restaurant, occasional live entertainment, car hire, sculptures by owner in small garden, camping site.

F *Mamalla Bhavan* opp Bus Stand, T 250, 20 rm, some with bath, clean, simple, pleasant, good restaurant (South Indian veg); **F** *Ramakrishna Lodge*, 8 Ottavadai St, nr Tourist Office, rm with shower, restaurant, basic but clean and very good value; **F** *Uma Lodge*, 21 rm, rm service, friendly staff; **F** *Tina Blue View Lodge*, 25 rm, nr fisherman's colony on sea shore, highly praised food, sometimes slow but friendly service, cottages for long term rent.

There are also some cheap guest houses nr the Bus Stand and on E Raja St and the **F** *Nemmeli Alavander Naicker Dharamsala* nr Bus Stand, T 229.

● **Youth Hostel & Camping**

F TTDC *Shore Temple Youth Hostel and Camping Site*, Shore Temple Rd, T 287, 18 cottages, dorm, restaurant, bar, exchange, clean, good value, (no mosquito nets), well placed though not on beach, rec; *Drive-in Camp Site*, 1 Thirukula St, T 290, 8 cottages, 2 rm, camping, restaurant, travel.

● **Places to eat**

The best are in the hotels. Beachside café at *Silver Sands*, popular and rec, especially attractive in evenings; *Sunrise Restaurant*, Shore Temple Rd, simple, under thatch, serves good fish dishes; *Village Restaurant* nr Bus Stand (rec for sea food).

Others: *Tina Blue View*, Othavadai St (breezy balcony upstairs with views), rec; On *Honeyfalls*, *Gazebo* E Raja St, Shore Temple Rd; *Ashok* and *Youth Camp* have snack bars; Also rec, *Sea Queen*.

● **Banks & money changers**

Indian Overseas Bank, nr the Tourist Office.

● **Library**

There is a small library nr the Tourist Office

Post & telecommunications

Post office: The Sub Post Office is nr the Tourist Office. **Telephone**: several ISD phones on E Raja St.

● **Shopping**

Poompuhar, nr the Shore Temple and shops nr the 5 Rathas complex sell small statues in soapstone and metal, shell jewellery and trinkets and palm leaf baskets. *Govt School of Sculpture* nr the Bus Stand continues to practise the skills which flourished centuries ago. 0900-1300, 1400-1830. Closed Tue.

● **Tourist office**

Tamil Nadu, E Raja St, T 232, 1000-1730. TTDC guides can be hired from Madras. The *Archaeological Survey of India Office*, S of Bus Stand, has a guide/ lecturer (free) who can guide visitors on request.

● **Transport**

Local Bicycle hire: to get to Tirukkalukundram – from Dec-Feb a comfortable and very attractive ride.

Train The nearest station is Chingleput, 29 km away, T 004113.

Road Bus: Several regular daily buses from Madras which also go to Tirukkalukundram and Pondicherry. Nos 19C, 68, 119A. Note that buses that take the coast road may stop at hotels which are to the N of the town. **Taxi**: Taxis charge Rs 700-1000 1-day excursion.

ROUTES The road to Tirukkalukundram (16 km) first crosses salt flats and the Buckingham Canal, which stretches over 350 km into Andhra Pradesh. Patches of land under rice cultivation are irrigated by wells visible from the roadside. This attractive landscape illustrates the contrasts between wet and dry land in much of South India. Small wells – the water table here is very high – and tanks allow irrigation of low lying areas; slightly higher land or land beyond the range of such irrigation is uncultivated. Hilltops, springs, trees, are all imbued by Hindus with special significance as places where the divine has been revealed.

FROM THORN SCRUB TO TREE PLANTING

A feature common throughout India is the numbering of trees, indicating their value – for fuel, fodder, building and other purposes. On the dry land a thorn scrub, *Prosopis juliflora*, is now very common. Introduced at the turn of the century as a fencing plant to keep cattle off fields by an enthusiastic Dist Collector, this has run riot on dry, thin soils. In some areas it is now being used to make charcoal.

On the road between Mamallapuram and Tirukkalukundram is an experimental tree-planting scheme for tribal women. There are now many such schemes sponsored both by the Govt and by Non-Governmental Organisations. Much of this re-afforestation has been with eucalyptus, introduced to India from Australia a century ago. There are examples on both sides of the road between 5 and 6 km S of Tirukkalukundram on the road to Madurantakam. Such plantations have attracted fierce criticism from some experts, who believe that they take a lot of water from the soil and that they do not supply the products needed by poor people available from local varieties of trees.

Tirukkalukundram

(*Population*: 23,300) The dramatic potential of hilltop sites for temples is well illustrated here. It has a small finely carved Siva temple dedicated to Bhaktavatsleesvara on the hill top with its *gopuram* or gateway standing out like a beacon. About 400 steps take you to the top of the 160m hill and at mid-day you will see 2 Neophran vultures (*Pharaoh's chickens*) fly down to be fed by the priests. The tank is considered holy and said to produce a conch every 12 years. The temple here and the larger Siva temple in the village below have made this a Hindu pilgrim centre. A range of small shops in the village, cold drinks available. Good views from hill top.

ROUTES The road goes straight to Madurantakam (14 km; *Population*: 26,600), crossing the broad, sandy bed of the **Palar** river approximately halfway. The Palar rises in Andhra Pradesh and flows through Vellore and past Kanchipuram. Though it rarely has surface water its bed is tapped along its length for ground water, now seriously polluted, particularly by the leather tanning industry. Join briefly the NH 45 at **Madurantakam** (see page 876).

Turn E along a quiet district road with a moderate surface. Unlike the NH 45 there is little heavy traffic, though some local buses come this way. Follow it down to **Marakkanam** (12 km), mentioned in Roman records as an important port in the 1st century AD. The village has an ancient, quite well-worked, Siva temple, with many inscriptions. Along the coast are communities of fishermen who live along the beach itself, selling their catch at small markets inland. From Marakkanam the road follows the coast again, passing through some fascinating villages and beautiful scenery. The coast is coconut fringed, and the glimpses of azure water through the trees are captivating.

Approaching Pondicherry you pass the University of Pondicherry buildings and 8 km from Pondicherry the turning to Auroville (see below under Excursions). Inland is a clear view of the sharp ridge of red soil, raised from the sea since the ending of the last Ice Age. These bright red soils, typical of much of S Arcot Dist, provide a striking contrast with the golden sands of the shoreline. 5 km out of Pondicherry the road passes under a canopy of coconut trees, sheltering scattered thatched village huts. In Jan and Feb, when the rice is being harvested, you drive across the straw spread out across the road to winnow the chaff. Enter Pondicherry down Anna Salai, the W Boulevard.

Pondicherry

Population: 401,000; *Altitude*: Sea Level; *STD Code*: 0413. The town, also known as Puducherry planned in a grid, acquired a distinct French atmosphere amidst the surrounding Tamil country. French was spoken and street names were in French. Except for short periods when the colony passed into Dutch and British hands, it was retained by the French until 1954. It was then voluntarily handed over to the Indian Govt and became the Union Territory of Pondicherry together with Karaikal, the other French enclave in the state, Mahe in Kerala and Yanam in AP.

Pondicherry is believed to be the site of ancient Vedapuri where *Agastya muni* (sage) had his hermitage in 1500 BC. In the 1st century AD Romans traded from nearby Arikamedu and in the 9th century a Sanskrit University flourished. The small fishermen's village called Pulicheri which existed in 1673 was set up as a trading post by the French and renamed it Pondicherry.

Today, many visitors are attracted by the Ashram founded by Sri Aurobindo and the Mother. Sri Aurobindo Ghosh was a Bengali revolutionary and philosopher who struggled for freedom from British colonial power, see page 80. In 1910 he left Calcutta as it proved too difficult for him to continue with his political activities, and was welcomed by this far corner of French territory. He had a vision of an age of the super mind and developed a system of 'integral yoga' combining the ancient yogic philosophy with what he knew of modern science. He started the Ashram where he could put into practice his ideals of a peaceful community living. In this aim he found a lifelong French companion in the Mother, who helped, supported and guided him from 1920 until his death in 1950 and then continued as the spiritual successor and charismatic figure of Pondicherry until her death in 1973. Auroville, 'City of Dawn', was set up in 1968 as a tribute to Sri Aurobindo (see under Excursions).

The grid pattern of the planned town has the waterfront to the E, along which runs Goubert Salai or Avenue, sometimes called Beach Rd, with a good beach over 1 km long. A statue of Mahatma Gandhi is among the 8 carved pillars of the War Memorial commemorating those who died in World War I. On the other 3 sides, the main town is contained in a semicircular boulevard with a NS canal along Gingee St. Most of the accommodation is on the W. To the E are most of the public buildings, Govt Place, Ashram offices and the International Guest House. It retains much of its former attraction. The NH 45A enters the town past the bus station through Lal Bahadur St while the Rly Station is to the S off S Boulevard.

Local festivals

Feb/Mar *Masi Magam* On the full moon day of the Tamil month of Masi, pilgrims take a holy dip in the sea when deities from about 40 temples from the surrounding area are taken in colourful procession to the seaside for a ceremonial immersion. 'Fire walking' sometimes accompanies festivals here, 3 or 4 times a year.

Local crafts and industries

Dolls of papier mâché, terracotta and plaster are made and sold at Kosapalayam. Local grass is woven into *Korai* mats. Craftsmen at the Ashram produce marbled silk, hand dyed cloths, rugs, perfumes and incense sticks. It is well worth visiting the Sri **Aurobindo Hand made paper** 'factory', 44 Patel St, N Boulevard. There is an excellent, highly informative guided tour, and a shop selling attractive products. Enquiries at the Ashram.

Places of interest

Sri Aurobindo Ashram has its main centre in rue de la Marine where you can see the marble *Samadhi* where Sri Aurobindo's and the Mother's remains are kept, as well as their houses. The International Centre is across the road which has occasional films, lectures and other performances (free) and also several Ashram shops and workshops scattered around the town.

Ecole Française d'Extrême Orient nearly 100 years with centres all over Asia has 3 departments in Pondicherry for Sanskrit, Tamil and Archaeological studies. **The French Institute** rue St Louis, close to the N end of Goubert Salai, was set up in 1955 for the study of Indian culture; the Scientific and Technical Section for ecological studies produces soil and vegetation maps. Superb library overlooking the sea (reference only), many books in French and English. The colonial building is worth seeing.

CLIMATE: PONDICHERRY

	Jan	Feb	Mar	Apr	May	Jun	Jul	Aug	Sep	Oct	Nov	Dec	Av/Tot
Max (°C)	28	29	30	32	34	36	35	34	33	31	29	28	32
Min (°C)	21	21	23	26	26	26	25	25	25	24	23	22	24
Rain (mm)	13	6	52	21	45	28	62	74	135	327	380	210	1351

Churches and temples The French Catholic influence is evident in a number of churches, notably the Jesuit church, *Notre Dame de la Conception*, the Cathedral, begun in 1691 but only finished 74 years later. The Eglise de notre dames des anges (1855) is noted for an oil painting of Our Lady of Assumption given to the Church by King Louis Napoleon III. The Church of the Sacred Heart of Jesus is another 19th century building, the central gable being flanked by 2 gothic towers. One of the oldest Christian shrines, the 17th century Chapel of Our

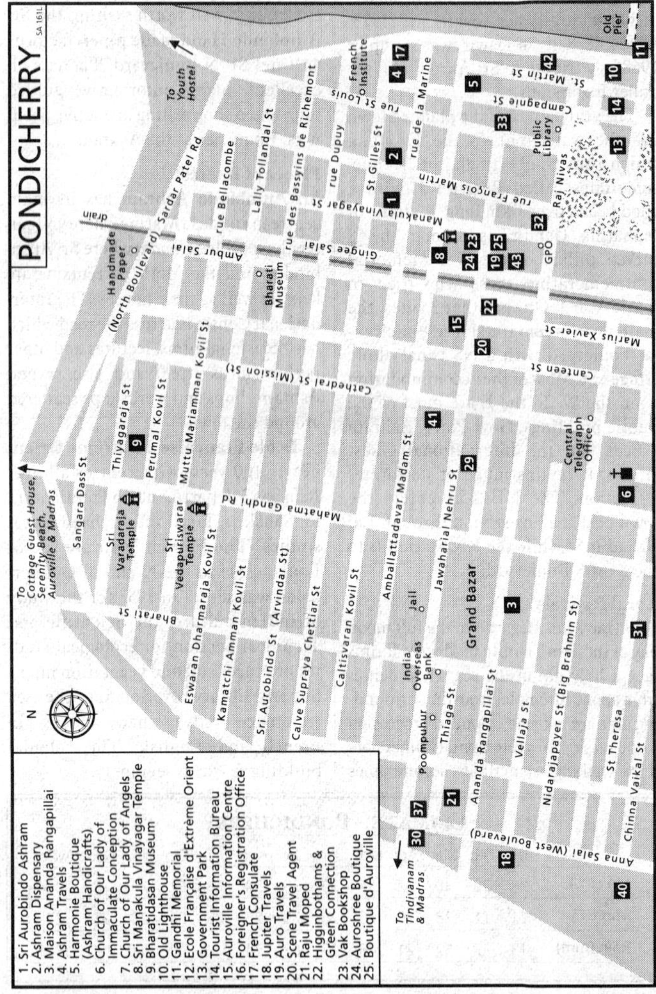

Sisters of Cluny, is 4 km S at Ariyankuppam (see below). Although there are no Hindu temples of architectural note the *Vedapureswar Temple* (Easwran Koil St), dedicated to Ganesh, is much visited, especially on Friday evenings. There is also a *Big Mosque* on Mullah St.

Beaches The beaches in town look attractive in places, but are best avoided; the one near the New Pier is used as a public toilet. **Serenity Beach**, within bike range from the town centre to the N is much better; very pleasant with few spectators.

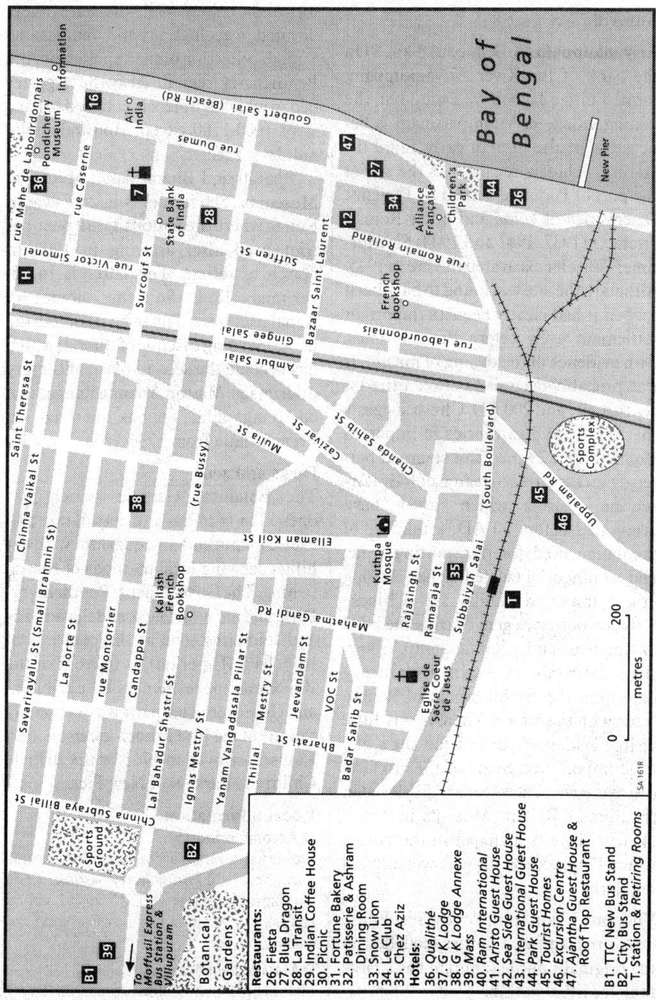

Excursions

Boat trips to see dolphins can be booked through the *Seagulls* restaurant. Approx Rs 350 per hr for a trip on a converted fishing boat. The boat leaves the commercial fishing harbour, 15 min bike ride away. Best in early morning for chance to see dolphins. Rec.

Auroville See page 861.

Ariyankuppam (Arikamedu) 3 km S On the bank of the River Ariyankuppam, formed into a lagoon by a sand bar, the fishing village of Virampattinam is believed to be the *Virai* of early Tamil literature. Scholars regard it as the site of the port of Podouke named by Ptolemy. Discoveries of coins and other Roman artefacts (1937, 1941 and 1944) Sir Mortimer Wheeler excavated the site in 1945. Although the site was found to have been robbed it had clearly been an important settlement even before Roman times, with evidence of the dyeing of muslin. It was probably occupied between the 1st century BC and 200 AD. Ghosh suggests that there are 3 categories of imported Roman ware: 29 pieces of stamped pottery from the Arrezzo region of Italy ('Arrentine' ware), which must have originated before 50 AD; a number of amphorae used for transporting wine; and a number of faceted dishes. Among other imported finds are Chinese Celadon pottery, a gem bearing the head of Augustus and a Roman lamp. Ghosh suggests that the settlement's origin may date from the establishment of Roman trade with the region. There is very little visible evidence today of the site's historic importance. Some of the artefacts discovered here however are displayed in the Romain Rolland Museum in Pondicherry. There is a chapel in the village where Dupleix and his wife worshipped regularly.

Villianur 12 km from Pondy. The Eglise de Notre Dame de Lourdes modelled on the original Lourdes church, has a large tank for ritual bathing

Museums

Pondicherry Museum S of Govt Park has a good sculpture gallery with items from the Pallava, Chola and Vijayanagara periods and a section of archaeological finds from the Roman settlement at Arikamedu including pottery and burial urns. The French gallery charts the history of the colony while there are others devoted to geology, art and handicrafts. Superb collection of snail shells from the Pondicherry region. Also the 4-poster bed in which Dupleix is believed to have slept. 1000-1700, except Mon and public holidays. Free.

Bharati and Bharatidasan Memorial Museums. The former is in 20 Eswaran Koil St where the famous Tamil poet-patriot lived after arriving in 1908 in search of refuge. The latter is in 95, Perumal Koil St, the home of Kanakasubburatnam who adopted the name meaning disciple of Bharati which has become the second place of literary pilgrimage. **Maison Ananda Rangapillai** on Rangapillai St has material on French India from 1736-1760.

Parks and zoos

The **Botanical Gardens** which was opened in 1826 has a variety of rare and exotic plants and an aquarium with exhibits showing local methods of coastal fishing. The **Government (Pondicherry) Park**, laid out with lawns and flower beds and fountains (one at the centre is of Napoleon III period), is in front of the Raj Niwas, the residence of the Lieutenant Governor. The park was originally the site of the first French garrison, Fort Louis, destroyed in 1761 by the British. **Children's Park**, N of New Pier.

Local information

● Accommodation

Western style hotels are fairly comfortable and have a/c rm. **C** *Pondicherry Ashok*, Chinnakalapet, T Kalapet 460, 20 rm, 12 km rly, central, a/c, restaurant, bar, coffee shop, exchange, travel.

D *Mass*, Maraimalai Adigal Salai, T 27221, just off the NH 45A, nr the New Mofussil Bus Stand,

35 rm, 2 restaurants, bar, exchange, travel, shops, mediocre; **D** ***Sea Side Guest House***, 10 Goubert Salai, T 26494, very central, 8 large rm in an old building, with bath, like all the ashram accommodation, it closes by 2230, so if you are later you will be locked out, restaurant, rec; **D** ***Qualithé***, 2 rue Mahé de Labourdonnais, opp Governor's House and park, T 24325, airy rm with bath, restaurant, bar.

NB *Grand Hotel d'Europe* – you may hear of this formelry well-known hotel, but it is now closed.

● Budget hotels

The Aurobindo Ashram has several guest houses which are primarily for official visitors to the Ashram but also open to others (not to 'hippies'). No alcohol and no smoking and do not be put off by the presence of pictures of the founders.

E ***International Guest House***, Gingee Salai, nr Head Post Office, T 26695, 57 very clean and airy rm, huge for the price, central and very popular, book in advance, non-a/c rm much cheaper. Also, **E** ***Park Guest House***, T 24412, Goubert Salai, 80 clean simple rm with sea view and dorm, veg meals, pleasant garden, rec, good value; **E** ***Ram International***, 212 W Boulevard, N of Botanical Gardens, T 27230, 53 rm, some a/c with phone and TV, excellent and cheap veg restaurant, shop; **E** ***Aristo Guest House***, 50A Mission St, T 26728; **E** ***Ajantha Guest House***, 22 Goubert Salai, T 38927, ask for Beach Rd, as there are other Ajanthas, clean rm, more expensive sea facing, very helpful management, food pleasant, excellent staff, restaurant service better in evening, rec; Govt **E** ***Tourist Homes*** at Uppalam Rd, T 26376, 12 rm some a/c and VIP suites, in a garden. Next door, ***Excursion Centre*** with very cheap bunk-beds in dorm, suitable for groups, S of town, clean and quiet, very good value. Another in Indira Nagar, opp JIPMER in suburb NW of the town, T 26145.

Also **F** ***GK Lodge***, 47 Anna Salai, T 23555, quite central, simple, modest but acceptable; **F** ***Railway Retiring Rooms*** for passengers, quieter than most stations! These are all about 20-30 min walk from the centre but easier if you hire a bicycle. **F** ***Palm Beach Cottages***, by Serenity beach, N of town, very basic, concrete beds with mattress, friendly staff, excellent food, esp fish, good for travellers with bikes or motor bikes; **F** ***Cottage Guest House***, Periarmudaliarchavadi, on beach, 6 km N of town, rm in cottages, french food, bike and motorcycle hire, peaceful, good beach under palm and casuarina trees.

● Youth Hostel

F *Youth Hostel*, Solaithandavan Kuppam, T 23495, N of town has cheap beds; close to the sea among fishermen's huts. Bicycle or transport essential.

● Places to eat

Le Café Pondicherry Goubert Salai, by the Gandhi memorial statue, pleasant spot with waves lapping around the base of buliding, good snacks (daytime only); ***Sea Side Snack Bar*** offers French cuisine; ***Le Club de l'Alliance Française***, (open evenings), is smart, more expensive, but good; ***Mass, Ram International***, ***Bon Ami***, ***Aristo*** (rooftop) are all rec; ***Blue Dragon***, (Chinese), 30 rue Dumas nr the New Pier (S end of Goubert Salai) has excellent food while surrounded by antique furniture. Tibetan at ***Snow Lion***, 22 rue St Louis (nr Raj Bhavan) and Vietnamese at ***Chez Azis***. ***La Transit***, Romain Roland St, closes out-of-season. ***Indian Coffee House***, 41 Nehru St serves non-veg fare throughout the day.

For a simple veg meal in an unusual setting, try the ***Ashram Diningroom*** N of Govt Place, where you will be seated on cushions, at low tables (buy ticket for 3 meals), farm grown produce, non-spicy and non-greasy; ***Picnic***, Kamaraj Salai is veg.

Fortune, 13/9 rue St Thérèse, nr Nehru St, is an excellent bakery; ***La Patisserie***, 39 Rangalillai St.

● Bars

In larger hotels listed above.

● Banks & money changers

Several branches of National banks including **State Bank**, 5 Suffren St; **Indian Bank**, 65 Mission St and **Canara Bank**, 16 Nehru St

● Consulate

French Consulate, 2 Marine St.

● Cultural centres

French Institute, rue St Louis, close to the N end of Goubert Salai, and ***Alliance Française*** at the S end of Goubert Salai for cultural programmes.

● Entertainment

Cinemas: on Kamaraj Salai and Vallabhai Patel Salai. Ask at Ashram or Auroville offices for programmes. **Alliance Française**, 33 rue Dumas, has a library, organises French cultural programmes incl films, private restaurant. Register as a temporary member.

● Hospitals & medical services

General Hospital, rue Victor Simone. *Ashram Dispensary*, Depuis St, nr seaside.

● Post & telecommunications

Head Post Office: NW corner of Govt Place. **CTO**: Nidarajapayer St.

● Shopping

Books: *Vak*, Nehru St, *French Bookshop*, 38 St and the large ***Kailash French Bookshop***, 87 Lal Bahadur St. ***Higginbothams***, JVS Bld, 14B Ambur Salai.

Boutiques: several on Nehru St, some belonging to the Ashram, incl ***d'Auroville*** at no 12, ***Auroshree*** at no 2D, ***Harmonie Boutique***, ***Ashram Exhibition Centre***, ***Aurocreation*** and ***Handloom Centre***. For handmade paper see Local crafts above. The shopping areas are along Nehru St and Mahatma Gandhi Rd.

Crafts: several handicraft emporia selling local crafts including ***Co-optex*** at 28 and ***Poompuhar*** at 51 Nehru St, ***Khadi and Village Industries***, 10 Amber Salai and ***Tibetan Handicrafts*** at 22 Colas Nagar.

Food: health food from ***Green Connection***, Nehru St.

Market: *Pondicherry market* off MG Rd. Excellent, worth visiting any day but especially on Mon.

● Sports

Boating: Chunnambar river through the Boat Club, 10 km away.

Sports Complex: S of the town nr the Govt Tourist Home.

Swimming: pools in *Hotel Blue Star* and *Calva Bungalow*, Kamaraj Salai open to non-residents for a fee.

Yoga: Ananda Ashram on Yoga Sadhana Beach, 16A, BMettu St, Chinamudaliarchavadi, Kottakuppam. They run courses 1, 3, 6 month courses starting from Jan, Apr, Jul and Oct.

● Tour companies & travel agents

Auro Travels, Karikar Bldg, Nehru St, T 25128, efficient, quick service; ***Scene***, 3rd Flr, 11 JN St, for unusual locations.

● Tourist Offices

Tourist Information Bureau, Old Secretariat in Compagnie St, E of Govt Place, has limited information. **Auroville Information Centre**, 12 Nehru St, W of the canal. **Pondicherry Tourism**, (PTDC), Goubert Salai, T 23590, town maps and some other info. **Ashram Reception Service**, Main Building, rue de la Marine, T 24836.

● Useful addresses

Foreigners' Regional Registration Office, Goubert Salai.

● Transport

Local City buses, **cycle rickshaws** and **auto rickshaws**: negotiate fares in advance for the last 2. **Taxi**: taxis available, particularly along the canal. *Jupiter Travels*, 170A Anna Salai, has luxury taxis. **Bike hire**: *Super Snack*, Nehru St opp Information Centre; *Jaypal*, Gingee Salai; also an un-named hire shop just off Subbaiyah Salai (S Boulevard). Charge, about Rs 20 per day.

Air No flights at present. *Air India* office is on Goubert Salai.

Train connects by metre gauge only with Villupuram which is on the main line and in turn has connections to Madras, Madurai, Tiruchirappalli. Two trains a day from Pondy: 0815 (arr 0925), 2030 (arr 2200). The evening train connects with the *Pandyan Exp* 6717, from Madras to Trichy, Kodai Road and Madurai (dep 2225), and the *Quilon Mail* 6105 from Madras to Trichy and Kollam.

NB: The ½ hrly bus to Villupuram, stops 100m from station and connects with other trains from Villupuram. Rly Station, Enquiries: 0900-1200, 1500-1800. It is possible to make reservations from Pondy station to any other station. Pondy has its own quota on major trains leaving from Madras Central.

Road Bus: Thiruvalluvar (TTC) buses run from its own bus stand on NH 45A, a short distance W of the traffic circle, T 26513. Computerised Reservations: 0700-2100. The Moffusil (New) Bus Stand, further W, serves all other bus companies, State and Private, which run services to the major cities in the region. Thanthai Periyar Transport (Tpy) Corp Enquiries: T 26919, 0430-1230, 1330-2130. Pondicherry Tourism Corporation (Pt), T 23590, also runs long distance services. Timiings below must be checked.

Madras: TTC No 803, 20 buses a day, 0045-2330; Tpy Non-stop, 8 buses, 0440-1910; **Bangalore**: TTC No 822, 0830, 2200; Pt 2330; **Chidambaram**: frequent buses by all companies; **Coimbatore**: TTC No 842, 0700, 1300, 2130, No 839 0930, 2000; **Ernakulam via**

Trichy: TTC No 882, 1730; **Kanniyakumari** No 880, 2130; **Kannur and Mahé** TTC No 889, 1745; **Madurai**: TTC No 847, 1000, 1445, 1645, 1830, 1900, 1930, 2130; **Mamallapuram**: Tpy No 188, 0315, 0620, 0900, 1145, 1300, 1420, 1645. **Ooty**: TTC No 860, 1930; **Ramesvaram** TTC No 853, 0730, 1930; **Thiruvananthapuram via Thanjavur**: TTC No 886, 1645; **Tiruchchirappalli** TTC No 852, 0545.

Auroville

Auroville can be visited by taking either of the 2 roads N from Pondicherry to Madras. Taxi or bicycle hire in Pondicherry. In Pondicherry *La Boutique d'Auroville*, 12 Nehru St can give you directions. There are conducted tours to Auroville 3 times a week.

The Mother

As Sri Aurobindo Ghose's chief disciple Mirra Alfassa was universally known, died at the age of 93 in 1973. She had hoped that Auroville would be a centre for world brotherhood and a major focus for meditation and spiritual regeneration. Futuristically designed, the layout of the city and its major buildings, notably the Matri Mandir, were to reflect the principles of Sri Aurobindo's philosophy. The Charter says "To live in Auroville one must be a willing servitor of the Divine Consciousness" and describes it as belonging "to humanity as a whole...the place of an unending education, of constant progress...a bridge between the past and the future...a site of material and spiritual researches". Development since 1968 has been very slow. It was planned in the form of a spiral nebula, symbolising the universality of its faith. The central meditation building remains incomplete and the crystal of meditation which is to be placed in its centre is ready for installation. The city itself is largely unfinished.

Sri Aurobindo and the Mother hoped to achieve the ideal international commune. The Mother's Agenda, now published in 13 volumes, states that "Mother's prodigious exploration into the body's cellular consciousness...as narration of 23 years' experimentation strikes deep into the most recent discoveries of modern physics. Step by step we uncover what may well be Man's passage to the next species upon earth: how to change the law of death and the old genetic programme of cells".

The population in 1990 was still less than 700, drawn mainly from a range of European nations. Designed by a French architect, Auroville has over 50 settlements spread across about 50 sq km; you will come across names like Sincerity, Shanti (peace), Grace, Verité, Horizon, Transition, Recueillement, Gratitude, Fertile etc. Activities include village work, education, 'Green work' (17 different kinds of windmills, afforestation), food growing, dairies, alternative technology and handicrafts. The settlements are widely spaced out and can only be visited comfortably by cycle or by car.

The **Matrimandir** at the centre is a 30m high globe with the lotus bud shaped foundation urn where 124 young people put soil from their own country on 28th Aug 1968, within a small '**amphitheatre**'. The **Nursery** nearby is nurturing saplings and orchids while **Bharat Nivas** is a furturistic auditorium to be used for cultural performances with the Secretariat and Boutique nearby. The *Centre Guest House* is also near the amphitheatre. To the W, a short distance away is **Kottakarai**, the village with a frequent bus service from Pondicherry Town Bus Stand.

From Matrimandir, the road towards the sea goes to **Auroson**, the residential area with a Kindergarten. Beyond this, turning right at the crossroads towards Edianchavadi village brings you to the **Udavi** community and the incense factory *Aurosikha* followed by **Auro Orchard** before joining the Madras highway. If you go S at the crossroads near Auroson you will get to **Forecomers** the ecological commune, beyond which a path leads you back to town. The road left at the crossroads, towards the sea, lkeads to Koilapalayam village with **Aspiration** the largest residential community beyond and the handicraft making community **Fraternity** to the left. Continuing towards the sea, and after crossing the old Madras road, **Aurobeach** is beyond the village of Chinamudaliarchavadi with the Yoga Ashram.

The area of Green Belt N of the the Matrimandir is yet to be connected to electricity and water supply where communities live a very rustic life.

Visiting The community at Auroville welcomes visitors who have a genuine interest in the philosophical basis of the community, though it does not encourage general sightseeing. There are 3 **E** Guest Houses ***Fraternity***, ***Swagatham*** and ***Utility Repose*** where food is included in rm charges. Since accommodation is limited it is best to make enquiries in advance; if you propose to spend a night or participate as a guest in a community, contact Boutique d'Auroville, in Pondicherry or Bharat Nivas in Auroville. Tourist facilities are very limited with a restaurant at Bharat Nivas (open Tue, Thur, Sat evenings; reserve in advance), tea shops, a bank, a post office and 2 shops.

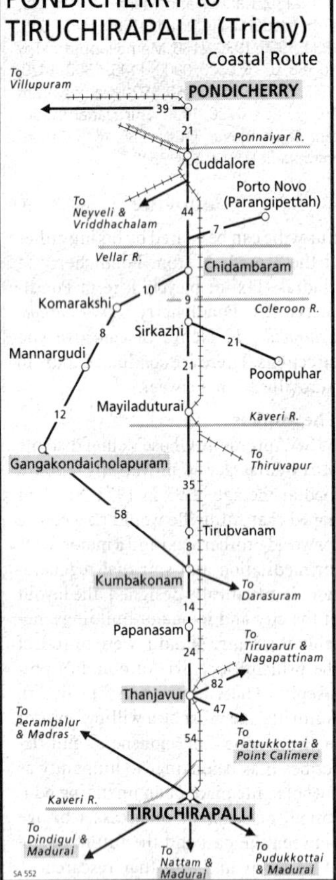

PONDICHERRY TO POINT CALIMERE via Thanjavur

Early morning is an excellent time to travel in most places in India, but especially in the S. The air is fresh and cool, the light limpid. Southwards from Pondy on the road to Cuddalore there are alternating groves of casuarina trees, many recently planted, with coconut and palmyra palms. In Jan-Feb at harvest time there is also a delightful scent of fresh straw in the air. Paddy, groundnut and sugar cane are all found in the fields along the road to Cuddalore, and S Arcot district is one of the main sugar producing districts of South India.

Development is taking place fast along the roadside. The road passes a small steel rolling mill (E Coast Steel) on the left. The second wide river to be crossed is the ***Ponnaiyar***, which rises nearly 500 km to the N W just N of Bangalore. Its flow is now controlled by the Sathanur Dam just W of Tiruvannamalai, but it remains very variable, coming down in short floods which rapidly dry up. It is held to be a sacred river, especially during the first 5 days of the Tamil month of *Tai*, when bathing in it is thought to be particularly meritorious. There are beautiful views crossing the river early in the morning and again in late afternoon.

Cuddalore

(21 km; *Population*: 144,000; *STD Code*: 04128) Signs of the changing economic face of Tamil Nadu are evident here with the presence of shops selling motor bikes, electric pumpsets, even videos. There are not many signs of its origins as an East India Company trading settlement in 1684, nor of **Fort St David** which was built soon after but destroyed by the French General Lally in 1758. All that remains is the ditch, and some ruins of walls. The oldest part of the town is the commercial centre, at the junction of the 2 rivers the Gadilam and the Uppanar, from which the town took its name. The second oldest section is 4 km to the NW, followed by the district of Manjikuppam, the official city centre, where today's district offices are located.

In the middle is an open maidan, referred to in old records as the lawn or the green, recalling images of village England, surrounded by shaded avenues and the old Collector's house, completed in 1733. Fort St David is the most recent sector. Soon after their arrival the traders of the English East India Company began to set up new suburbs (*pettahs*) for weavers, some of whom were brought in from as far afield as Kalahasti nearly 100 km N of Madras. Brookespettah and Lathomspet are 2 examples of such late 18th century settlements. At one time the 'new' town of Tiruppapuliyur was a major Jain centre. The present large temple enshrines the deity Patalesvara, and there are several Chola inscriptions. It has been richly endowed by the *Nattukkottai Chettiars* (see page 912) and houses a silver car and a gold palanquin.

Between 43 km and 29 km from Chidambaram, the land becomes a totally flat plain, but the irrigated rice fields make it a beautiful sight. Tamarind trees line much of the road – all carefully numbered, along with all the other trees on the roadside. The rich fertile irrigated soils alternate with much poorer land. The difference lies in the availability of irrigation. Land slightly above the irrigation channels or beyond their reach remains sparsely cultivated or waste. Soon after dawn the roads begin to fill with pedestrians, cyclists, lorries and buses. Villages and towns come alive – and are much slower to get through.

You can take a short detour back to the coast again to visit **Porto Novo** (21 km), a port established by the Portuguese in 1575, the first Europeans to land on the Coromandel coast. They were followed by the Dutch, who occupied it in 1643 with a 2 year gap, until 1781. War having broken out in Europe between the British and Dutch the British captured it (along with all the other Dutch factories along the Indian coast) and made it a trading post. On 1 July 1781 the British military commander Sir Eyre Coote won a battle for the port over Haidar Ali of Mysore that in the view of some historians ensured the possibility of British expansion in South India. It changed hands twice more before finally being ceded to the British in 1824. Today the town has a large Muslim population, mainly involved in sea based trade. 10 km N of Chidambaram the road crosses the Vellar River ('white river').

Chidambaram

(15 km; *Population*: 69,000; *STD Code*: 04144) The capital of the *Cholas* from AD 907 to 1310, Chidambaram lies on the N edge of the Coleroon River, which in itself marks the N limit of the Thanjavur delta. In Tamil Nadu Chidambaram is regarded as a holy town of great importance, and has been the home of noted Tamil poets and saints.

Local festivals
Jun/Jul *Ani Tirumanjanam* Festival.
Dec/Jan *Markazhi Tiruvathirai* Festival.

Places of interest

The **Nataraja Temple** is dedicated to the dancing Lord Siva, a favourite deity of the Chola kings. One legend surrounding its construction suggests that it was built by 'the golden coloured Emperor', Hiranya Varna Chakravarti, who suffered from leprosy. He came to Chidambaram on a pilgrimage from Kashmir in about 500 AD. After bathing in the temple tank he was reputed to have recovered from the disease, and as a thank-offering rebuilt and enlarged the temples. Enter the temple by the E gate. Shoes can be left with the door keeper just outside. A slow walk round takes about 1 hr, though you could spend much longer. Written notice boards outside the inner sanctum say that non-Hindus are not allowed, especially at times of Puja, but that rule seems to be readily waived. Groups or individuals may be taken straight in. 0400-1200.1630-2100.The evening puja at 1800 is interesting.

This is a highly active temple, with Brahmins at every shrine – though they all belong to a local Brahmin community, unrelated to the 3000 Brahmins Hiranya Varna Chakravarti is reputed to have brought with him from Kashmir. Some of them make repeated and insistent requests for donations. Although this can be irritating it needs to be understood against the background of the very unusual form of temple management. The S

Chidambaram – Centre Of The Universe?

One of the most basic ideas of Hinduism "is the identification of a sacred site with the centre or navel of the universe, the spot through which passes the axis connecting the heavens, the earth and the subterranean world of *Patala*" writes David Shulman. **Siva** is quoted as saying: "The day I danced in the forest of Tillai while **Vishnu** looked on, I saw the spot that could not support me... But there is a site which can sustain the dance... the world is analagous to the body. The left channel (of the 'subtle body') goes straight to Lanka, and the right channel pierces the Himalaya. The central channel goes directly through the great *Tillai*, the site of the original linga." This myth refers back to the story of the founding of Chidambaram, for Tillai is the ancient name of Chidambaram, "where Siva performed his dance of joy; so powerful is this dance, which represents the entire cosmic process of creation and dissolution, that it can be performed only at the very centre of the cosmos.... Chidambaram, which sees itself as the heart of the universe, locates an invisible Akasalinga in its innermost sanctum, the Chitsabha ("room of consciousness"). The centre thus proclaims its identity as the centre which, like the hidden source of life within man, is directly linked to the infinite."

The imagery goes back to the myth of the origin of the Chidambaram temple itself. The S Arcot Dist Gazetteer recounts it as follows: "In the forest of Tillai was an ancient shrine to Siva and another to the Goddess **Kali** which was built where the Nritta Sabha now stands. Siva came down to his shrine to manifest himself to 2 very fervent devotees there, and Kali objected to his trespassing on her domains. They eventually agreed to settle the question by seeing which could dance the better, it being agreed that the defeated party should leave the site entirely to the winner. Vishnu acted as the umpire, and for a long time the honours were evenly divided. At length Vishnu suggested to Siva that he should do his well known steps in which he danced with one leg high above his head. Kali was unable to imitate or beat this style of dancing, Siva was proclaimed the winner and Kali departed outside the town, where her temple is still to be seen."

Arcot Dist Gazetteer explains: "The Chidambaram temple has never had landed or other endowments, and it belongs to a group of Brahmans called *Dikshitars* ('those who make oblations'). They are peculiar to Chidambaram and are regarded locally with very high respect. You may notice that they have the single Brahmin style tuft of hair at the front rather than the back of their heads, and they marry only among themselves. Temple ritual is more like family worship than normal temple ritual.

Theoretically all the married males have a say in the running of the temple. They support it by going round the district asking for alms and offerings for themselves. Each has his own particular clients, and in return for the alms he receives he undertakes to make offerings at the shrine of his benefactors. From time to time he will send them holy ash or an invitation to a special festival. 20 *Dikshitars* are always on duty at the temple, each of the males doing the work which is divided into 20 day rotas. The 20 divide themselves into 5 parties of 4, each of which is on duty for 4 days at 1 of the 5 shrines at which daily puja is made, sleeps there at night and becomes the owner of the routine offerings of food made at it. Large presents of food made to the temple as a whole are divided among all the *Dikshitars*. The right to the other oblations is sold by auction every 20 days to one of the *Dikshitars* at a meeting of the community. These periodical meetings take place in the Deva Sabha".

At each shrine the visitor will be daubed with *vibhuti* (sacred ash) and paste. It is not easy to see some of the sculptures. All Hindu temples are very dark inside and it takes time for eyes to adjust. If you are accompanied by a tour guide and are going round in a group you are less likely to be pressed by others to accept their services, but you may need patience and persuasive powers if you want to take your own time. The effort will be repaid. Although some of the buildings date from the late Chola period the group as a whole was built over several centuries. There are definite records of its existence before the 10th century and inscriptions from the 11th century. At the N, S, E and W are 4 enormous **gopurams**, the N and S ones being about 45m high. The E gopuram, through which you enter the temple, is the oldest, being erected in 1250 AD. Large sculptures in the upper niches are of Saiva deities. The N gopuram has an inscription which shows that it was built by the great Vijayanagar king Krishna Deva Raya (1509-30). The temple compound of over 12 ha is surrounded by 2 high walls, outside which run the streets used for the temple car processions, nearly 20m wide.

On entering the E gate you see immediately in front and to the right the large **Sivaganga** tank, with still further to the right the **Raja Sabha**, a 1000 columned hall or *mandapa*, built between 1595 and 1685. In the NW of the compound are temples dedicated to **Subrahmanya** (late 13th century), and to its S, the 12th century shrine to **Sivakumasundari** or Parvati, the wife of Siva. According to Michell this is the oldest building in the complex, though other authorities suggest that it is a 14th century building. The ceiling paintings are 17th century.

At the S end of this outer compound is what is said to be the largest shrine to **Ganesh** in India. The next inner compound has been filled with colonnades and passageways, some used to store images used in processions. In the innermost shrine are 2 images of Siva, the Nataraja and the lingam. A later Vishnu shrine was added to Govindaraja by the Vijayanagar kings.

The **inner enclosure** is the most sacred and contains 4 important **Sabhas** (halls), the **deva sabha**, where the temple managers hold their meetings; the **chit sabha** or *chit ambalam* (from which the temple and the town get their names), meaning the hall of wisdom; the **kanakha sabha**, or golden hall; and the **nritta sabha**, or hall of dancing. Siva is worshipped in the *chit ambalam*, a plain wooden building standing on a stone base, in his form as Lord of the Dance, Nataraja. The area of the shrine immediately over the deity's head is gold plated. Immediately behind the idol is the focus of the temple's power, the 'Akasa Lingam'. It represents the invisible element, 'space', and hence is itself invisible. Known as the 'Chidambaram secret', it is believed to be situated immediately behind the idol. A curtain and a long string of golden *bilva* leaves are hung in front of it.

Local information

● Accommodation

Budget hotels **E** TTDC *Hotel Tamil Nadu*, Railway Feeder Rd, T 2323, some a/c rm, restaurant, not very clean. Also **F** *Youth Hostel* dorm; **E** *Saradharam*, 19 VGP St, nr rly, T 2966, 21 rm, some a/c, with bath, TV, unreliable plumbing, very good food in evening at the open air 'garden restaurant'. Other simpler and cheaper hotels are in the centre of town, further from the station.

F *Ramanathan Mansions*, 127 Bazar St, rm with bath, quieter than most, away from the busy temple area, good value; **F** *Star Lodge*, 101 S Car St, T 2743, nr Bus Station, basic but clean; **F** *Raja Rajan*, 163 W Car St, T 2690, has rm with bath. Also **F** *Railway Retiring Rooms*.

● Places to eat

Non-veg meals at *Hotel Tamil Nadu*, *Mahalakshmi* or *Udipi Hotel*.

● Banks & money changers

State Bank of India in Pava Mudali St; **Central Bank**, 62/63 Bazar St and **Indian Bank**, 64 S Car St.

● Post & telecommunications

Post office: The Head Post Office is in N Car St.

● Shopping

The Shopping area is around the Nataraja temple.

● Tourist office

Govt of Tamil Nadu Tourist Office in Railway Feeder Rd.

● Transport

Train The metre gauge railway links Chidambaram with Madras, Kumbakonam, Thanjavur and Tiruchirappalli among others.

Road **Bus**: there are also daily buses to the above cities and to Nagapattinam and Pondicherry.

Chidambaram to Kumbakonam

ROUTES Travelling S from Chidambaram to Kumbakonam you enter the Thanjavur delta some 10 mins S of Chidambaram. After 9 km you cross the Coleroon River, the northern edge of the delta proper. A large modern rice mill on the left illustrates the present day importance of this area to the economy of the state. Sugar cane and paddy remain dominant, but the landscape is quite heavily wooded. Scattered village ponds are often filled with beautiful lotuses, and there are occasional wayside shrines where drivers will often stop to make an offering to their chosen deity.

From Chidambaram take right turn out of town to Komarakshi, Mannargudi and Gangakondaicholapuram (30 km).

Gangakondaicholapuram

This, the capital of the Chola King Rajendra (1012-1044) has now all but disappeared, though recent archaeological work suggests that interesting remains lie buried, especially at the site of the palace less than 2 km from the temple. The 5 km long 11th century reservoir embankment also survives.

In 1942 Percy Brown wrote "this fine structure now stands in solitary state, except for the mud huts of a village straggling around it, as centuries ago the tide of life receded from these parts, leaving it like a great stranded shell. Nature with artistic hand has endeavoured to veil its abraded surfaces, not always to its structural good, with festoons of foliage, so that it appears as a lovely grey-green pile slumbering amidst the tangled verdure of a wide neglected garden".

The whole site has now been restored, although it is still in an isolated backwater of Tiruchirappalli Dist. It is well worth visiting. The **temple** which Rajendra built to celebrate his victory march up the Ganga Valley remains a magnificent testimonial to the skill of his Chola architects and builders. The name itself means 'The city of the Chola who conquered the Ganga', reference to his supposedly filling the temple tank with water brought from the Ganga. (It was an achievement that recent governments of Tamil Nadu have planned to emulate with proposals for a World Bank funded project to build a canal from the Ganga to the Kaveri.) The temple was built to rival the Brihadisvara temple built by Rajendra's father Rajaraja in Thanjavur. The 2 temples have important similarities, though the temple here has not been as extensively repaired or altered by subsequent builders as happened at Thanjavur. The enclosure is even larger than that at Thanjavur and was surrounded by a wall that may have had defence at least partly in mind. Note the bastion at the SE corner.

You enter the rectangular compound by the ruined E gopuram and see the huge Nandi placed facing the mandapa and sanctuary. Unlike the Nandi in Thanjavur this is not carved out of 1 block of stone. As in Thanjavur the mandapa and sanctuary are raised on a high platform, orientated from W to E and climbed by steps at the right and left sides. The whole building is over 100m long and over 40m wide. Two massive doorkeepers (*dvarapalas*) stand guard at the entrance to the long closed mandapa, its roof supported by comparatively ordinary slender pillars. (This hall is the first of the many subsequent mandapas which expanded to 'halls of 1000 pillars'.) The plinth of the mandapa is original. The narrow colonnaded hall linking the entrance mandapa and the shrine (the *mukha-mandapa*) are similarly guarded, as is the shrine itself.

On the E side of this hall are various carvings of Siva such as bestowing grace on Vishnu, who worships him with his lotus-eye, and Kalyanasundara-murti (going out for his marriage attended by goblins) and many others. On the NE is a large panel, a masterpiece of Chola art, showing Siva blessing Chandikesvara (the steward of Siva's household). The temple, though not as highly decorated as the Brihadisvara Temple in Thanjavur, has many similar figures and many single figure subjects. Dancing Nataraja is shown in a panelled recess of the SW corner, Siva within a flaming lingam on the W, Ganesh on the S.

At the centre of the shrine is a huge lingam on a round stand. As in Thanjavur there is a magnificent pyramidal *vimana* (tower) above the sanctuary, nearly 55m high. Its vertical base has 2 sections, succeeded upwards by 8 tiers. Unlike the austere straight line of the Thanjavur temple, however, here gentle curves are introduced. The space on the temple base below the frieze is covered in inscriptions. Immediately to the N of the mandapa is a shrine dedicated to Chandikesvara, with an excellent carving showing the steward of Siva's household. To N and S are 2 shrines dedicated to Kailasanatha, erected by 2 of Rajendra's queens. There are excellent sculptures on the walls. In the SW corner is a small shrine to Ganesh.

From Gangakondaicholapuram take the road due S across the Coleroon. If you go straight from Chidambaram to Kumbakonam you follow the road through Sirkazhi (9 km after crossing the Coleroon) where there is a good *Inspection Bungalow*. A minor road goes S from here to Poompuhar.

Poompuhar

A popular excursion among many Tamil tourists is to Poompuhar, at the mouth of the Kaveri. At this point the flooding waters of the Kaveri are reduced to a trickle as they enter the sea. As Kaberis Emporium, it had trading links with the Romans in the 1st century AD; it was also visited by Buddhists from the Far East. An important port of the Cholas, later most of the city of Kaveripoompattinam (as it was then called) was lost under the sea. Excavations have revealed an ancient planned city. The name Poompuhar has been adopted for Tamil Nadu Govt emporia throughout the country.

There is a good beach. The Govt of Tamil Nadu has built a tourist complex with a number of bizarre buildings in modern South Indian style or art imitating kitsch. A 7-storeyed Art Gallery built in the traditional style illustrates the Tamil classic, *Silappadikaram* (Story of the Anklet), in stone carvings. Set in Poompuhar it tells the story of Kannagi the exemplary Tamil woman, Kovalan her princely husband and Madhavi. Next door, TTDC.

• **Accommodation & food** **F** TTDC *Tourist Bungalow*, *shell* and *conch* cottages, T Sirkazhi 39. TTDC *Restaurant*.

• **Transport Road** From Sirkazhi, Chidambaram or Thanjavur.

Tiruvenkadu, 2 km, is where Chola bronze statues have been found. South along the coast is Karaikal, once a French settlement and Tranquebar.

Tranquebar

Known as Tharangampadi, the Danish King Christian IV, received permission from Raghunath Nayak of Thanjavur to build a Danish Fort here in 1620. The Danish Tranquebar Mission was founded in 1706. The town, with the **Danesborg fort** and the old **church** still survive. The Danes spread Christianity and education, attracted trading contacts from other European countries, and also set up the first Tamil printing press; the Tamil script was altered to make the casting of type easier. The Danish connection resulted in the National Museum of Copenhagen today posessing a remarkable collection of 17th century Thanjavur paintings as well as valuable Chola bronzes. There is a **Museum** and a good beach. Further reading: Georgina Harding's '*Tranquebar: a season in South India*'. London, Hodder and Stoughton, 1993.

The main road from Chidambaram to Thanjavur goes to Tirubvanam and Kumbakonam.

Kumbakonam

(54 km; *Population*: 151,000; *STD Code*: 0435) Named from the legend where Siva was said to have broken a *kumbh* (water pot) after it was brought here by a great flood, the water from the pot is reputed to have filled the Mahamakam Tank. Today Kumbakonam is a very busy town.

Local industries

Local industries include textiles, gold and silver jewellery.

Places of interest

There are 18 temples in the town centre (closed 1200-1630) and a monastery of the Kanchipuram Sankaracharya here. The oldest is the **Nagesvara Swami Temple**, a Saivite temple begun in 886 AD. It had several later additions and has been repainted fairly recently. The small Nataraja shrine on the right before you reach the main sanctum is designed to look like a chariot being pulled by horses and elephants. There are some superb statues on the outside walls of the inner shrine; Dakshinamurti (exterior S wall) Ardinarisvara (W facing) and Brahma (N) are in the central panels. They have been described as among the best works of sculpture of the Chola period, and are worth a visit in themselves. Above the sanctuary is a pyramidal tower.

Sarangapani is the largest of Kumbakonam's 18 shrines. Dedicated to Vishnu, the temple is dominated by its 11-storey main *gopuram*, 44m tall. The mandapa, built during the Nayaka period, is inside the first court, which then leads through a second, smaller gopuram to a further mandapa. There is a

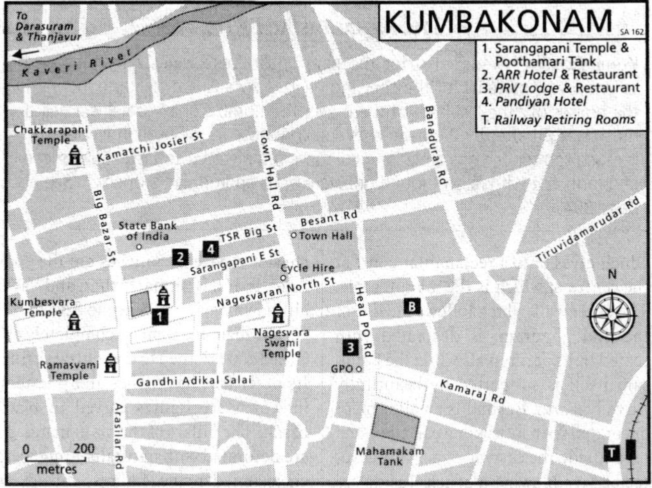

small vaulted shrine to Lakshmi, Vishnu's consort, on the N. The main central shrine is the oldest, dating from the end of the Chola period. In common with a number of other shrines such as those in Chidambaram or distant Konarak, it resembles a chariot, with horses and elephants carved in relief. The shrine is covered by a vaulted roof and the walls are richly carved.

The **Kumbesvara** temple dates mainly from the 17th century and is the largest Siva temple in the town. It has a long colonnaded *mandapa* and a magnificent collection of silver *vahanas* (vehicles) for carrying the deities during festivals. The **Ramasvami** temple is another Nayaka period building, with beautiful carvings in its pillared mandapa. The rearing horses are typical of the Vijayanagar sculptures, and the frescoes on the walls depict events from the Ramayana. The Navaratri Festival is observed with great colour.

NB: The temples in this region contain some exceptional pieces of jewellery which can be seen on payment of a small fee.

The **Mahamakam Tank**, towards the rly station, is visited for a bathe by huge numbers of pilgrims every 12 years when 'Jupiter passes over the sign of Leo', and the Ganga is believed to flow into it. On 18 Feb 1992 as many as 2 million pilgrims were estimated to converge on the tank. 60 pilgrims were crushed to death by a collapsing wall as they tried to see the Tamil Nadu Chief Minister Jayatalitha make her pilgrimage to the tank.

Excursions

Darasuram, 5 km S of Kumbakonam has the **Airavatesvara Temple**, the 3rd of the great Chola temples, after Thanjavur and Gangakondaicholapuram, built during the reign of Raja Raja II between 1146-72. Originally named Rajarajesvaram, most of the temple is constructed out of granite. Open sunrise to sunset. See C Sivaramamurti's booklet on the Chola Temples (Archaeological Survey of India) available from the Brihadisvara Temple in Thanjavur.

The entrance to the temple is through 2 gateways. The upper part of the outermost gopuram has now been lost. Inside this 1st gateway is a small inner gateway

The Aphrodisiac Betel

Kumbakonam is renowned for the high quality betel vines grown here, the essential raw material for the chewing *paan*. AVM's Guide to South India sings the praises of "the last item of the meal...The Kumbakonam betel is a delicacy much sought after by the paan-chewing connoisseurs in South India because it is much too tender, has a pleasing colour and is pleasant to taste. Lovers love it and munch it with relish though unaware of its aphrodisiac property". See also page 894.

which gives onto a rectangular court at the centre of which is the main temple. The outer wall, which follows the line of the 2nd gopuram, is decorated with seated bulls at intervals while the gopuram itself is supported by beautifully carved *apsaras*. Beyond is an altar place decorated with lotus petal carvings, and on one side the carving of a dwarf devotee of Siva blowing a conch. Inside are friezes full of lively dancing figures and musicians. The entrance is flanked by crocodiles – *makara* – often portrayed as guardians. Inside is a mandapa which is best entered from the S, though there were steps on the E and W. Though the steps have now gone the balustrades which lined them still show their decoration on the outer side. Note the elephant being ridden by dwarfs whose trunk is lost down the jaws of a crocodile.

Architecture You can see evidence of the development of style in the late Chola period from the capitals of the pillars in the mandapa, which show the first signs of being carved into flower corbels, typical of the later Vijayanagar style when they were developed into full lotus patterns. The rectangular sections of the pillars show mythological stories such as the penance of Parvati and Siva's marriage. On either side of the extension of the mandapa through which you enter are superbly carved galloping horses. The front base of the extension has more decorated panels illustrating stories such as that of Siva burning Kama who had dared to attack him with his bow, and Siva fighting the Tripuras from a chariot. Above in 5 niches are the gods Agni, Indra, Brahma, Vishnu and Vayu, all shown paying homage to Siva.

The main mandapa is completely enclosed and is joined to the central shrine. Its outer face has niches and pilasters, in which are figures carved in black basalt. The pillars of the main mandapa are decorated with naturalistic creepers enclosing dancing figures, musicians and deities. The ceilings are also richly decorated, and the capitals of the pillars show the same development of flower emblems as in the outer mandapa. Moving through from the outer mandapa towards the main shrine are niches which have some outstanding sculptures. Some of the openings in the main mandapa have been bricked up in recent years. The sculpted guardians on the N are particularly well carved.

At the entrance to the main shrine is a nandi, smaller than that at the entrance to the main mandapa itself. The sculpted door-keepers have massive clubs. Some of the niches inside contain superb early Chola sculptures, including a unique sculpture of Ardhanarisvara with 3 faces and 8 arms; a 4-armed Nagaraja, easily recognised from the snake-hoods above his head, and a very unusual sculpture of Siva destroying Narasimha (seen by climbing a small flight of steps). Other sculptures include Durga with 8 arms and seated on the severed head of the buffalo and Siva carrying an axe, deer, bow and arrow. The sides of the main shrine have a long frieze on the lower half of the base. The sculptures are all of polished black basalt.

Exterior The outer walls are also highly decorative. Siva as Dakshinamurti on the S wall, Brahma on the N wall and Siva appearing out of the linga on the W wall are all accompanied by appropriate figures. The inner wall of the encircling walkway (*prakara*) is divided into cells, each of which used to house a deity. Some have disappeared. The corners of the courtyard have been enlarged to make 4 mandapas, again with beautiful decoration. There is a small **museum** in the NE corner, but the mandapa in the NW corner probably has the best collection of sculptures. This appears to have been the mandapa reserved for dance, the *nata mandapa*, which according to Sivaramamurthy probably housed a bronze Nataraja. Immediately to the W is a group of large sculptures representing Siva as a beggar, and a number of attendants. Beyond are Siva saints with their names and a short description inscribed.

Tirubvanam (8 km) has another famous 13th century Chola temple dedicated to Kampahareswara which has a remarkably high base. The spacious Mahalingasvami temple has a sacred tank. The *gopuram* is modelled on the one at the Thanjavur temple.

Local information

● Accommodation

E *ARR*, 21 Big St, T 21234, simple, some a/c rm with bath, reasonably good veg restaurant.

F *Pandiyan*, Sarangapani E Sannadi St, T 20397, clean rm, restaurant, good value; **F** *Karpagam*, T 21086. Some a/c rm with bath; **F** *PRV Lodge*, 32 Head Post Office Rd, towards Tank, T 21820, best rm with bath, restaurant (veg); **F** *Railway Retiring Rooms*.

● Banks & money changers

The **State Bank of India**, Big St, nr *ARR Hotel*.

● Post & telecommunications

Post office: nr Mahamakham Tank on Head Post Office St.

● Transport

Local Cycle hire: opp *New Diamond Lodge*, Nagesvaran N St.

Train Station 2 km from town centre. Trains to Madras, Chidambaram (3 ½ hr), Thanjavur (3 hr) and Tiruchirappalli.

Road Bus: TTC buses to Madras, No 305, several daily (7½ hr); ½ hourly to Thanjavur.

Thanjavur (Tanjore)

Capital of the great Chola Empire and later of the *Thanjavur* Nayaka and Maratha rulers. The Chola kings built the majority of Thanjavur's 93 temples. The treasures gained from defeating the Chalukyas were used to enrich the temple. Stein wrote that "The Brihadisvara Temple was built and maintained through the demands by Raja Raja I upon villages throughout the Kaveri Delta core of Chola power as well as from the 'booty in the conquests of Chera, Pandiya...and Chalukya kings. Such warfare tended to enhance the prestige of a few warriors, and this was an important secondary objective of the activity, but it also brought fame and fortune to the groups who made up the armies led by such warriors – soldiers of the left and right divisions of castes, certain artisan groups, guilds – thus it strengthened the vigorous corporate structure of South Indian political relations at least until the 14th century". The Chola kings were great patrons of the arts and while they lavished their wealth to build temples, they encouraged the belief in the divine right of kings. The practice of donating a part of one's wealth to the temple for spiritual gain was encouraged, a practice still in evidence.

BASICS 38 km; *Population*: 200,200; *Altitude*: 59m; *STD Code*: 04362; *Climate*: Summer: Max 37°C, Min 33°C; Winter: Max 24°C, Min 23°C; *Annual rainfall*: 940 mm.

Local crafts and industries

Stone carving, particularly in granite, is an ancient craft that is being revived by the Govt through centres which produce superbly sculpted images and columns for Hindu temples. Blocks of stone are cut, chiselled, rubbed and polished,

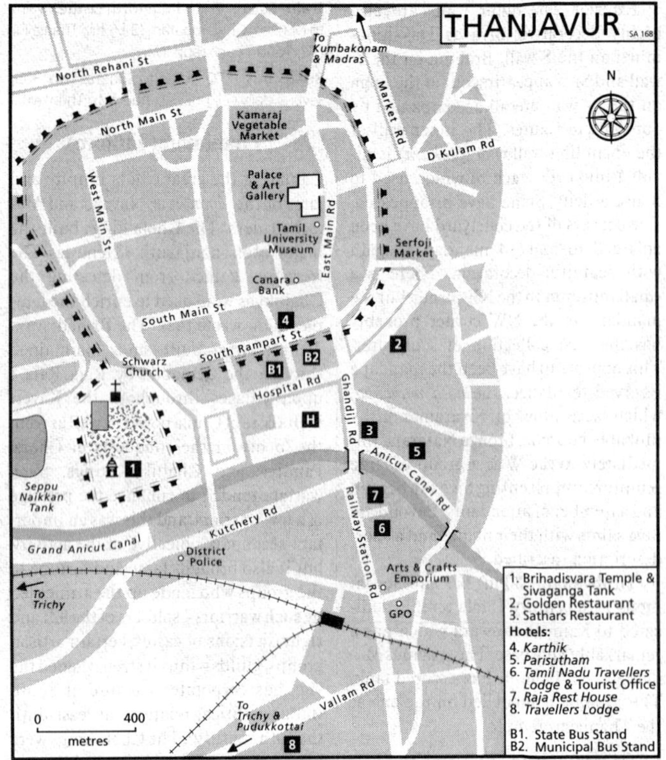

which takes months to produce the finished work of art. Also wood carving, bronze and brass casting, decorative copper plates with silver and brass patterns in relief (repoussé) or inlaid; Chola style bronzes are still made in Swamimalai. Papier mâché dolls and paintings on wood and on glass.

Places of interest

The **Brihadisvara Temple**, known as the big temple, is the achievement of the Chola king **Rajaraja I** (r AD 985-1012). It is one of the World Heritage monuments. With its tank, fortified by a wall and moat, the temple stands to the SW of the old town, near the Grand Anicut Canal. The main temple is Chola and is one of the most magnificent in the country, with a 14-storey, 62m high *vimana* (the tallest in India) topped by a dome carved from a block of granite, the whole so cleverly designed that it never casts a shadow at noon, throughout the year. The 80 ton block is believed to have taken a 6.5 km ramp to raise it to the top.

After crossing the moat you enter through 2 *gopurams*, the second guarded by 2 guardians (*dvara palakas*). This design is representative of the early Chola period, when the gopuras on the outer enclosure walls were dwarfed by the scale of the *vimana* over the main shrine.

Shulman has suggested that "in cases such as this the pilgrim's passage toward the central shrine is a form of ascent – as of course, it is in the many shrines built upon hills or mountains. Yet even here the *garbhagrha* remains remote, in the chamber of stone, and the worshipper seems to enter and re-emerge from a womb". An enormous *Nandi* which too is carved out of a single block of granite 6m long, guards the entrance to the sanctuary. It is the second largest in the country. According to one of the many myths that revolve around the image of a wounded *Nandin*, the Thanjavur Nandi was growing larger and larger, threatening the temple, until a nail was driven in its back. The same idea of dangerous growth was applied to the Siva linga. The architecture, sculpture and painting are all exceptional. Built mainly with large granite blocks there are superb inscriptions and sculptures of Siva, Vishnu and Durga on 3 sides of the massive plinth. To the S there are images of other deities. To the N, W and S of the sanctuary are 3 huge sculptures of Siva in 3 forms, the dancer with 10 arms, the seated figure with a sword and trident and Siva bearing a spear. The carvings of dancers showing the 81 different Bharat Natyam poses are the first to record classical dance form in this manner.

The main shrine has a large *lingam*. In the inner courtyard are Chola frescoes on walls prepared with lime plaster, smoothed and polished, then painted while the surface was wet. These were hidden under later Nayak paintings. Chambers 7 and 9 are well preserved and have fresco paintings of kings, queens and musicians. 0600-1200, 1600-2030. One of the unique records inscribed on the walls of the temple lists gifts from the royal family, details of how the temple was to be maintained including the payments granted to certain shepherds who would be responsible for providing clarified butter for the temple lamps.

The permanent exhibition in the temple complex has reproductions of the paintings and a record of the Archaeological Survey of India's conservation programme. 0900-1200, 1600-2000. Since music and dance (this being the cradle of Bharat Natyam) were a vital part of temple life and dancing in the temple would accompany the chanting of the holy scriptures which the community attended, Raja Raja also built 2 housing colonies nearby to accommodate 400 *deva* (temple dancers). Subsidiary shrines were added to the main temple at different periods. The Vijayanagara kings built the Amman shrine, the Nayaks the Subrahmanya shrine and the Marathas the Ganesh shrine.

The Palace Though part in ruins, this is one of the principal buildings which once stood within the fort, built by the Nayakas in the mid-16th century, and later completed by the Marathas. You enter from E Main St, proceed towards the police station and the entrance is to your left. The evidence of the splendour of the original palace can be seen in its ornate Durbar Hall (left of Library) which has some bronzes on display, long corridors and towers which are worth climbing for a good view; one tower has a whale skeleton washed up in Madras! The **Art Gallery**, **Sangeeta Mahal** with excellent acoustics, **Saraswati Mahal Library** and the **Tamil University Museum** are here, together with some Govt offices.

The **Schwarz Church** (1779) is just N of the Sivaganga Tank (known for its sweet water) next to a landscaped garden. It is dedicated to the Danish missionary FC Schwarz (also commemorated in St Mary's Church, Madras) who died in 1798. There is a particularly striking marble bas relief sculpture at the W end of the church by Flaxman of Schwarz on his deathbed, showing him surrounded by the family of Raja Serfoji to whom he was tutor.

Museums

Raja Raja Museum and Art Gallery in Thanjavur Palace. Large collection of Chola sculptures in bronze (lost wax process) and granite, lithic pieces. Look for Bhairava, Umasahita Siva, Kali, Somaskanda and the Rama Lakshmana group. 0900-1200, 1500-1800, closed Fri. Also in the Palace buildings is the Saraswati Mahal Library containing over 40,000 rare books, several 1st editions and about 8000 palm leaf manuscripts. One of the country's major reference libraries, it contains books and manuscripts in many foreign languages (incl French, German, Italian, Greek and Latin) covering Literature, Art, Philosophy, Music, Astrology, Sciences and particularly Medicine. 1000-1300, 1400-1700 except Wed. **Tamil University Library** has a numismatic section and a collection of old musical instruments.

Local festivals

Jan *Thyagaraja Music Festival* to commemorate one of the 3 most important personalities of Carnatic music at Thiruvaiyaru, 13 km away. Buses from Thanjavur.

Oct *Raja Raja Chola's* birth anniversary celebrations.

Local information

● Accommodation

Best is **C *Parisutham***, 55 Grand Anicut Canal Rd, T 21466, 36 rm, some a/c, also deluxe, 15 min airport, nr rly, modern hotel, very good inexpensive restaurants (Indian and Chinese), *thali* rec, bar, coffee shop, exchange, travel, shop, garden.

TTDC has 2: **D *Tamil Nadu I***, Gandhi Rd, T 21421, comfortable rm, some a/c, with bath, in pleasant setting around a cool inner courtyard, restaurant rather simple, bar, Tourist Office, heavily booked, very good value. Slightly cheaper **D *Tamil Nadu II***, Trichy Rd, T 20365, some rm with bath, mediocre restaurant, garden, clean, but inconvenient.

The Govt's **F *Raja Rest House*** is behind *Hotel Tamil Nadu I*, quiet, a little run-down. Both about 10 min walk from station and Bus Stands. **F *Karthik***, 73 S Rampart, T 22116. Very nr bus station. Restaurant. Basic but clean.

● Places to eat

A/c ***Golden Restaurant***, Hospital Rd is rec for veg food; ***Sathars*** nr the Bus Stand serves good Tandoori food until midnight. For traditional meal off a banana leaf try ***Karthik***, 73 S Rampart St

● Banks & money changers

The Canara Bank, S Main St. **State Bank of India**, Hospital Rd.

● Hospitals & medical services

The *Govt Hospital*, Hospital Rd, S of the old town.

● Police

The Dist Police Office is S of the Big Temple between the canal and the rly.

● Post & telecommunications

Head Post and Telegraph Office are S of the old city off the Rly Station Rd.

● Shopping

Poompuhar Arts and Crafts Emporium, Gandhiji Rd, nr *Hotel Tamil Nadu*. ***Govt Industrial Sales Centre*** and other shops sell crafts in the Gandhiji Rd Bazar.

● Tourist office

The Tourist office, Gandhiji Rd (*Hotel Tamil Nadu Complex*). 0800-1100, 1600-2000 except Mon.

● Transport

Local Un-metred and tourist **taxis**, **auto rickshaws** and **cycle rickshaws** and a **city bus** service.

Train **Tiruchirappalli**: *Cholan Exp*, 6153, daily, 1800, 1¼ hr; *Madras Tirunelveli Janata Exp*, 6179, daily, 2210, 1¼ hr; **Madras (ME)**: *Cholan Exp*, 6154, daily, 0845, 8¾ hr; *Rameswaram Exp*, 6102, daily, 2042, 9½ hr.

Road Bus: Thiruvalluvar (TTC) service runs 12 buses daily to Madras (8 hr) and others daily to Pondicherry, Madurai and Tirupathi. The TTC Bus Stand is N of Hospital Rd, S of the old town, T 175. While opp the Municipal Bus Stand runs a frequent service to Kumbakonam (1 hr) and Tiruchirappalli (1¼ hr).

Thanjavur to Kodikkari

Tiruvarur

The Thyagaraja Temple at Tiruvarur, one of the ancient Chola capitals, 55 km on the road to Nagapattinam, is one of the largest in South India. The palace had a 'calling bell' hung which any citizen could ring in an emergency and gain the attention of the King for justice. The legend of the prince running over a calf with his chariot relates how the Chola king sought to deliver justice on the bell being rung, by ordering that a chariot run over his own son. Happily, Siva intervened and revived both the calf and the prince. The stone chariot of Tiruvarur is famous.

The Tyagaraja temple was built over a period of more than 3 centuries from the 13th century. Founded by the Cholas, it was added to periodically, the most important additions being those made by the Nayaka kings in the 17th century. There are magnificent gopurams in the outer enclosures, the N and W gateways being late additions of the Vijayanagar and Nayaka periods. Just inside the second enclosure wall on the S side is the 10th century shrine of Achalesvara.

The W facing temple follows the early Chola pattern, with a simple base, pilasters on the walls and a pyramidal tower. The roof is hemispherical. The name *Achalesvara* means 'immovable Lord' because Siva promised never to abandon it. The story goes that the king Samatkara "performed *tapas* and, when Siva appeared to him, begged him to be present forever in the holy site. The god said that he would remain, immovable, in that place. The king set up a linga, and a voice from heaven announced: "I will dwell eternally in this linga; even its shadow will never move". So it happened: the shadow of the Achalesvara linga is ever stationary. Only he who is to die within 6 months is unable to perceive this marvel. As David Shulman points out, "the miracle is made secure by terror – he who doubts it will die!". In the innermost court are the shrines of *Vanmikanatha* and *Tyagaraja*, both E facing. Most of the external plaster decoration on the former is a late addition to what is mainly a 10th century shrine. The latter dates from the 13th century.

Tiruvarur celebrates a *car festival* to continue the tradition when the 23m high old temple chariot needed 10,000 devotees, led by the King, to pull it. Today the chariot is smaller and no longer needs thousands of devotees to pull. This is also the birth place of the saint Tyagaraja (1767-1847), 1 of the 3 music composers of note who lived in Tamil Nadu in the 18th century.

Nagapattinam was an important port in the Chola period (10-11th century) attracting trade from many nations. During the British period it became a prominent Chrisitian centre and regained its status as a trading port with a new railway connection. Sikkal and Sembian Madevi temples are nearby. **Accommodation E** TTDC *Tamil Nadu*, Thonitturai Salai, nr Rly Station, T 2389, some a/c rm, good value.

Point Calimere (**Kodikkarai**) 80 km from Thanjavur to the SE and 11 km from Vedaranyam.

Point Calimere Bird Sanctuary

The sanctuary on the coast, is open throughout the year. Best season – Nov to Feb for flamingoes. It is famous for its migratory water birds and covers 17 sq km, half of which consists of tidal swamps. Known as the Great Swamp, it attracts one of the largest colonies of flamingoes in Asia, numbering between 5000 and 10,000 during the season.

In the spring when the berries are available on the trees and shrubs, the green pigeons, rosy pastors, koels, mynahs and barbets can be seen. In the winter the availability of vegetable food and insects attracts paradise fly catchers, Indian pittas, shrikes, swallows, drongos, minivets, blue jays, woodpeckers, robins among others. Spotted deer, black buck, feral horses and wild boar are also supported.

- **Accommodation** *Poonarai Rest House* (10 suites) and **F** *Calimere Rest House* (4 suites). Reservations: District Forest Officer, Thanjavur Div.

- **Transport Road** From Thanjavur (80 km).

MADRAS TO TIRUCHIRAPPALLI (TRICHY) via NH 45

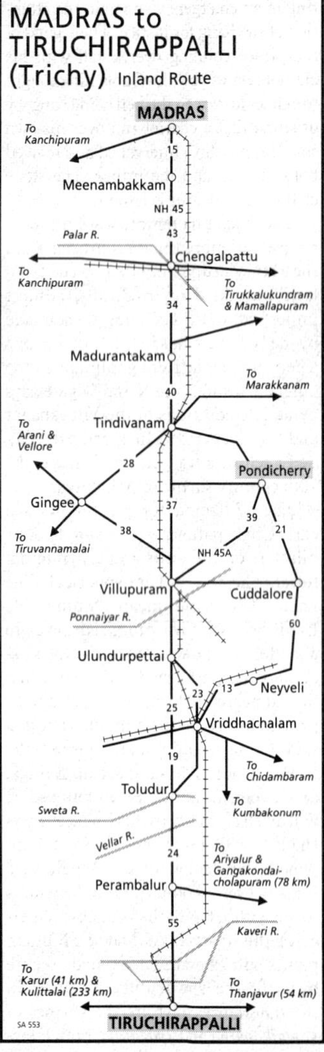

ROUTES The NH 45 runs direct from Madras to Tiruchirappalli (320 km). In a modern car this can be done comfortably in under 4 hrs driving, but the road can be busy and slow. Allow up to 5 hrs travel time.

Chengalpattu or Chingleput (58 km; *Population*: 54,000; *STD Code*: 04144). The fort was built by the Vijayanagar king Thimmu Raya after his defeat at the Battle of Talikota in 1565. After 1687 it was absorbed into the Mughal Empire. In 1750 it was taken by the French, who held it until it was captured by Clive in 1752. Its control in British hands was not finally established until the defeat of Haidar Ali in 1781. Although the fort is now almost totally destroyed (the railway runs through the middle of it) the **Raja Mahal** ('King's Palace') remains. It is an extraordinary design, having been modelled on the temple car in Kanchipuram. The 5-storey structure was said to be particularly tall so that Thimmu Raya's queens could worship at midday within sight of the great gopuram of the Kanchi temple. Some of the architecture was 'Islamised' during the Muslim control. The bus stand has the usual array of fruit stalls and tea and coffee shops.

Immediately S of Chengalpattu cross the Palar River, a stretch of sand over 1 km wide, usually with no running water visible on the surface. Just outside Chengalpattu is one of South India's largest tanks, a beautiful sight and an invaluable source of irrigation water, built in the 8th century. **Accommodation E** *Kanchi*, modern, clean hotel with restaurant, on NH 45 at junction with Mamallapuram road.

Driving S to **Madurantakam** (*Population*: 26,700) a new road by-passes the town along the *bund* of another great tank. Madurantakam is a typical medium sized town strung out along the roadside. Tea/coffee stalls around the bus stand. The road goes through **Tindivanam** (40 km; *Population*: 61,700) to **Villupuram** (37 km; *Population*: 89,000; *STD*

Code: 04146), just to the S of which the road crosses the Ponnaiyar River. The branch railway line from Pondicherry joins the main line at Villupuram. To the W, between the Ponnaiyar and Velar Rivers is the distant block of the Kalrayan Hills. **Neyveli** (*Population*: 126,500), where lignite has been mined open cast since 1961 as part of an integrated power and fertilizer production scheme, is off to the E just S of **Ulundurpettai**. **Accommodation E** TTDC *Tamil Nadu*, T 258, some a/c rm.

Diversion
A diversion (23 km S) brings you to the attractive temple town of **Vriddhachalam** (*STD Code*: 04143) where there are several temples with excellent carving. The **Vriddhagireesar Temple**, the most important here, with the presiding deity and his 2 consorts, attracted the devotion of local Hindu rulers. A 10-day *temple car festival* is held at Adi Puram. It is a Rly Junc on S Rly. Take the road W to rejoin the NH 45 which crosses the Velar river before reaching **Perambalur** (69 km; *Population*: 26,500; *STD Code*: 04328). Visible on the right are the Pachamalai and Kollamalai Hills. Rising from the plains to the S is the dramatic rock, over 70m high, on which Tiruchirappalli fort stands.

Tiruchirappalli

Population: 711,100; *Altitude*: 88m; *STD Code*: 0431. Known as **Trichy** or **Tiruchi** for short, Tiruchirappalli, in the heart of Tamil Nadu, is at the head of the Kaveri delta. The land around Tiruchirappalli in the kaveri delta is very fertile, though as the land rises slightly to the SE it presents an astonishingly bleak and windswept contrast, thin and dry red soils supporting the tinnest of vegetation cover.

The town was mentioned by Ptolemy in the 2nd century BC. A Chola fortification from the 2nd century, it came to prominence under the Nayakas from Madurai who built the fort and the town, but saw the ravages of war through the centuries because of its important strategic position. The Muslims ended Chola rule in the 14th century, and it also saw the Maratha Wars and the wars between the British and the French for over 100 years. In legend its name is traced to a 3-headed demon Trisiras who terrorised both men and the gods until Siva overpowered him in the place called Tiruchi.

The railways came to Tiruchirappalli in 1862 and it became an important junction. It was the headquarters of the privately owned South Indian Railway until nationalisation. There are 4 stations – The Town, The Golden Rock, Palakkarai and The Junction, the last being the most important. Most of the hotels, restaurants and offices needed by the tourist are in the Junction or Cantonment area to the S, near the Junction Rly Station. The sights are near the Town Station 1.5 km to the N. The Golden Rock area is an industrial suburb.

Local crafts and industries
With the industrial district of Coimbatore to the W and the agricultural one of Thanjavur to the E, Tiruchirappalli gains advantage from both. Handloom textiles are manufactured in Woraiyur and Karur. **Cigar making** became prosperous between the 2 World Wars, while the indigenous *bidis* continue to be made here, following a tradition started in the 18th century. More importantly Tiruchirappalli is the country's largest centre manufacturing **artificial diamonds** having taken over from centres in Switzerland and Rangoon in Burma which provided most of the artificial gems until the Second World War. Cleaving, shaping, faceting and polishing the synthetic gems is carried out in and around the city (Jaffersha St is commonly known as 'Diamond Bazar') providing employment for thousands of local people including a large number

of women. They are not only used in everyday jewellery but also to produce the brilliant ornaments worn by dancers and are also in demand abroad. In addition the town produces glass bangles, carpets, mats, palm leaf boxes and high quality string instruments, particularly *veenas* and *violins*.

Heavy engineering includes the Boiler Plant (Bharat Heavy Electricals Ltd) at Tiruvembur 11 km away, steel mills and the old established **Railway**

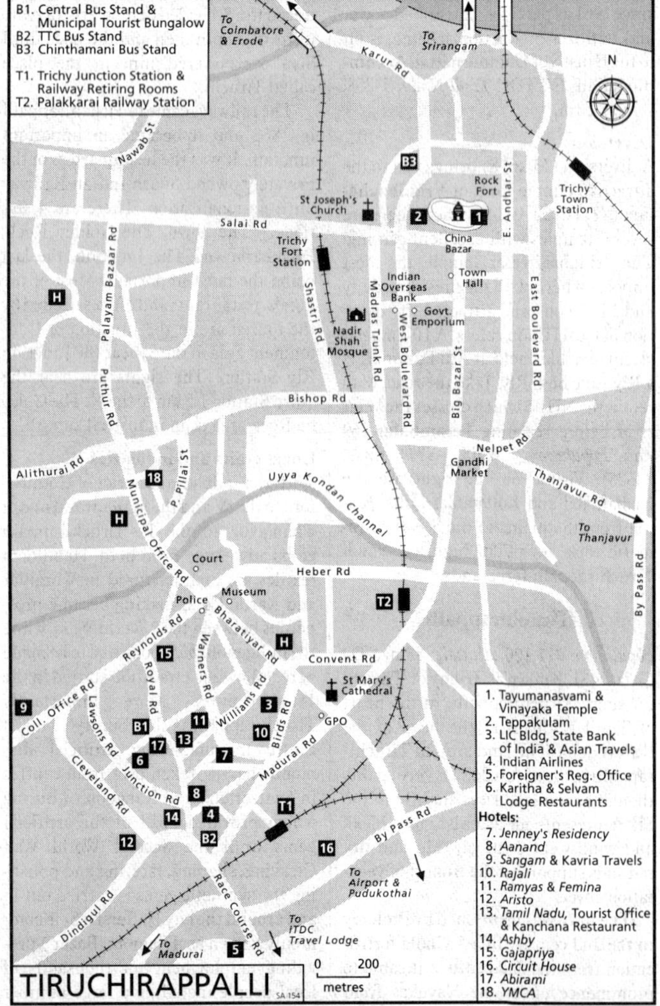

Workshop at Golden Rock. Sembattu, nearby, is an important centre for leather tanning.

Places of interest

The **Rock Fort** was built on an 84m high rock in the centre of town in about 1660. The **Vinayaka Temple** or Ucchi Pillayar Koil with a shrine to *Ganesh* is at the highest point from which you get marvellous views although you need to climb 437 rock cut steps to reach it. 0600-2000. On your way up you come to the main 11th century defence line and the remains of a thousand pillar hall which was destroyed in 1772, at the top of the first flight of steps. Further up is a hundred pillar hall where civic receptions are held. At the end of last flight is the **Tayumanasvami Temple** dedicated to Siva which has a golden *vimana* and a lingam which is carved out of the rock on which the temple stands. There are also other 7th century Pallava cave temples which have beautifully carved pillars and panels. It is worth while discovering the old city on foot, particularly **Big Bazar Street** and **China Bazar**.

Teppakulam at the foot of the rock is a large artificial *tank* surrounded by colourful stalls and a flower market. Among the dozen or so mosques in the town, the **Nadir Shah Mosque** near the Teppakalum and city railway station stands out with its white dome and metal steeple. Chanda Sahib who is said to have built it with material taken from a Hindu temple is buried there. **St Joseph's College Church** (Church of our Lady of Lourdes) is one of many Catholic churches in Tiruchirappalli and was designed as a smaller version of the Basilica at Lourdes in S France. Its unusual sandalwood altar is interesting. The 18th century **Christ Church** in the Fort, N of the Teppakulam is the first English church built through raising money from the British officers, by Schwarz the Danish missionary.

The **Museum** is on Bharatiyar Rd, 19/2 Promenade Rd, Cantt. Display of sculpture, art, archaeology, handicrafts, numismatics, geology and science. 0900-1230, 1400-1700. Closed Fri. Free.

Local festivals

Mar The *Festival of Floats* on the Teppakulam when the temple deities are taken out onto the sacred lake on rafts. Several at Srirangam (see Excursions below).

Local information

● **Accommodation**

The most expensive is **C** ***Sangam***, Collector's Office Rd, T 25202, 58 comfortable a/c rm, nr rly, good a/c restaurants, bar, exchange, shops, spacious lawns.

D ***Jenney's Residency***, 2/14 Macdonalds Rd, T 41301, 78 comfortable rm, most a/c, nr rly, good restaurant, rec for service and value; **D** ***Femina***, 14C Williams Rd, T 41551, 72 rm, 42 a/c, nr rly, restaurants, bar, travel; **D** ***Ramyas***, Williams Rd, T 31470, nr Bus Stand, some a/c rm; **D** ***Gajapriya***, 2 Royal Rd, T 41444, some a/c rm, restaurant, bar; **D** ***Tamil Nadu***, Macdonalds Rd (Cantonment) opp Bus Stand, T 40383, 12 rm, some a/c with bath, nr bus and rly, restaurant rec, bar and Tourist Office, basic, dirty sheets and mosquitoes reported.

● **Budget hotels**

E ***Aristo***, 2 Dindigul Rd, T 41818, 31 rm (including 'theme' cottages), some a/c with bath, nr rly, 4 km centre, restaurant, exchange, travel, shops, attractive lawns, large clean rm, very good value; **E** ***Abirami***, 10 Macdonalds Rd, opp Central Bus Stand, T 40001, 55 rm, some a/c with bath, good a/c restaurant (veg), exchange, travel, shops. TTDC has **E** ***Ashby***, Junc Rd, T 23652, 11 rm, 8 a/c, with bath, nr rly, restaurant, bar, old fashioned, with Raj character and can be a little noisy; **E** ***Aanand***, 1 Racquet Court Lane, Cantt, T 26545, 71 rm, some a/c with TV and bath, nr rly, restaurant (South Indian veg), lawn; **E** ***Lakshmi***, 3A Alexandria Rd, Cantt, T 25298, 48 rm, 7 a/c, nr rly, restaurant, coffee shop, Air Lanka office, car hire; **E** ***Sevana***, 5 Royal Rd, Cantt, T 31201, 44 rm, some a/c with phone, TV and bath, a/c restaurant (Indian) and bar; **E** ***Midland Lodge***, 20 Macdonalds Rd, Cantt, T 23911; **E** ***Tamil Nadu***, Race Course Rd, Kajahmalai, T 23498, 4 rm, some a/c.

F ***Mayaram Lodge***, 87 Vanapattrai St, T 24089, nr the Rock Fort; **F** ***Municipal Tourist Bungalow***, Central Bus Stand, T 27680; **F** ***Railway Retiring Rooms***, some a/c, reputed to be one of the best in India.

● **Places to eat**

In hotels: ***Jenney's Residency***, highly rec Chinese, reserve; ***Sangam's*** Indian, Continental (pizzas rec) and ***Abbirami's***, rec for veg.

Outside hotels: Very good inexpensive Indian veg restaurants in China Bazar, esp ***Vasantha Bhavan***; another branch opp Tourist Office. Rec for *thalis* and good service. Also ***Sree Ranga Bhavan***, with local character. Nr Tourist Office, ***Kanchana*** serves non-veg. At corner of Junc Rd and Williams Rd, a/c ***Kavitha***, rec for veg *thalis*. ***Skylord*** is on Municipal Office Rd.

● **Banks & money changers**

State Bank of India, Dindigul Rd, N of Jenney's Residency.

● **Shopping**

Artificial diamonds, cigars, wood and clay toys, bangles and textiles make attractive buys. You will also find pith temple models in Big Bazar St. In the Srirangam Temple precinct, there are shops selling brass figures and handicrafts. Govt Emporia – ***Poompuhar***, nr Main Guard Gate and ***Khadi Kraft*** opp Rly Station.

● **Tour companies & travel agents**

Asian Travels, LIC Building, Cantt, T 27660.

● **Tourist offices**

Information office at the *Hotel Tamil Nadu Complex*, Cantt, T 25336, 1030-1730, closed Sun. Also counters at the Airport and the Tiruchirappalli Railway Junc Station. 0700-2100.

● **Transport**

Good road connections to all major towns in the S. Chidambaram 156 km, Coimbatore 205 km, Kumbakonam 92 km, Madras 330 km, Madurai 161 km, Palani 152 km, Kanniyakumari 396 km.

Local Bus: good City Bus service. From airport Nos 7, 63, 122, 128, take 30 min. The State Bus Stand is across from the Tourist Office (No 1 Bus passes all the sights). **Taxi**: unmetered taxis, and tourist taxis from Kavria Travels, *Hotel Sangam*, Collector's Office Rd, T 25202. **Cycle rickshaws** and **auto rickshaws**.

Air The airport is 8 km from the centre. ***Indian Airlines***, Rly Cooperative Mansion, Dindigul Rd opp *Aristo Hotel*, T 23116. **Madras** via Madurai M,Tu,Th,Sa, 0815. ***Air Lanka***, *Hotel Lakshmi*, 3a Alexandria Rd, Cantt, T 27952.

Train An important railway junction connecting the city with major towns in the region. **Madurai**: *Vaigai Exp*, 2635 (AC/CC), daily, 1745, 2¼ hr; *Pandyan*, 6717 (AC/II), daily, 0300, 3¼ hr; **Madras (ME)**: *Pallavan Exp*, 2606 (AC/II), daily, 0615, 5¼ hr; *Vaigai Exp*, 2636 (AC/CC), daily, 0911, 5¼ hr; **Madras (via Thanjavur, Kumbakonum and Villupuram)** *Rameshwaram Exp*, 6102, daily, 1925, 10½ hr; **Kollam (via Madurai and Tuticorin)**: *Kollam Mail*, 6105 (AC/II), daily, 0330, 11¼ hr; *6161 Exp*, daily, 1610, 12¼ hr. **Pudukkottai and Ramesvaram**, *Madras-Rameshwaram Exp*, 6101, daily, 0700, 1hr and 6½ hr. **Bangalore**, *Bangalore Exp*, 6531, daily, 2145, 11½ hr. **Mangalore (via Erode, Coimbatore and Kozhikode)**: *6531 Express*, 6531, daily, 2050, 16½ hr; **Erode via Karur (broad gauge)**, *Kochi Exp*, 6565, daily, 19355, 1½ hr and 3hr.

Road Thiruvalluvar buses (T 23680) – 30 daily to Madras (8 hr), 2 daily to Kanniyakumari (9 hr) and Tirupati (9½ hr). Others go to Coimbatore, Kodai, Madurai, Nagercoil, Ramesvaram and Nagapattinam and major inter-state destinations.

Around Tiruchirappalli

Srirangam

(*Population*: 70,0001; *STD Code*: 0431) Three km to the N, on an island in the Kaveri is the temple town of Srirangam surrounded by 7 concentric walled courtyards, with magnificent gateways and several shrines reached by an arched bridge. The **Ranganathasvami Temple**, one of the largest in India, is dedicated to Vishnu.

NB: Some guides appear to be in collusion with priests demanding large donations.

The original small temple built by Raja Dharma Varman was enlarged by Chola, Pandiya and Vijayanagara kings. The fact that it faces S, unlike most other Hindu temples, is explained by the legend that Rama intended to present the image of Ranganatha to a temple in Sri Lanka but this was impossible since the deity became fixed here but it still honours the original destination.

The temple is famous for its superb sculpture, the 21 impressive *gopurams* and its rich collection of temple jewellery. The 'thousand' pillared hall (904 columns) stands beyond the 4th wall, and in the 5th enclosure there is the unusual shrine to Tulukka Nachiyar the God's Muslim consort. Some of the pillars have beautiful carvings out of a single block of stone. It lacks any grand plan since it was expanded by different rulers, mainly between the 14th and the 17th centuries, each of whom left the central shrine untouched but competed with their predecessors by building further walls with taller *gopurams*. The restoration of the deteriorating granite walls and the unfinished 7th *gopuram* was undertaken with the help of UNESCO and completed in the 1980s. Non-Hindus are not allowed into the sanctuary but can enter the 4th courtyard where the famous sculptures of *gopis* (*Radha's* milk maids) in the Venugopala shrine can be seen. Shoes must be left here. Guides available. Camera fee.

A small 1-room **Museum** has a negligible display of copper plates, ivory sculptures, bronze casting, weapons and coins. From the top of the wall you can get an excellent view. The **festival** of *Vaikunta Ekadasi* in Dec/Jan draws thousands of pilgrims who witness the transfer of the image of the deity from the inner sanctum under the golden *vimana* to the *mandapa*. In the same period the car festival is also celebrated.

Tiruvanaikkaval

(So named because a legendary elephant worshipped the lingam) is 6 km E of Srirangam. It has the architecturally finer **Jambukesvara** temple with its 5 walls and 7 *gopurams*. It is one of the oldest and largest Siva temples in Tamil Nadu where the unusual lingam under a *jambu* tree, always remains under water. There are special festivals in Jan and the Spring. In Aug, *Pancha Piraharam* is celebrated in *Panguni* the images of Siva and his consort Akhilandesvari exchange their dress.

A major Siva temple in the heart of Vaishnava territory, the temple here, according to the noted architectural historian Percy Brown, gives a clearer "idea of the Dravidian style at its best" than any other temple in South India. 0600-1300, 1600-2130. Non-Hindus are not allowed into the sanctuary. Nominal fee, Cameras Rs 10.

There are many Chola temples in the area. **Kothamangalam** at **Thiruthavathurai** with its Chola temple was renamed Lalgudi by the Muslims, ('Lal' red, 'gudi' temple).

The **Grand Anicut Barrage** near Tiruchirappalli was built in the 2nd century by the Chola king Karikalan. Reinforced by successive kings it still functions as a 320m long barrage across the river Kaveri. Nearby at **Chittanavasal** are Jain cave temples with famous frescoes where Jain monks took shelter when they fled from persecution in the N. The *Brahmi* inscriptions date from the 2nd century BC.

About 20 km N of Tiruchirappalli on the Turaiyur road, is the small village of **Tiruvellarai** which has a Pallava temple on top of rocky hill. It has an ancient well and rock walls and the steps are cut in the form of a swastika. There are several other Pallava monuments including a rock cut Siva temple to the E.

Kulittallai 37 km W at Tanninpalli, Dom Bede Griffiths, who died in May 1993, set up a Christian Ashram, *Shantivanam*, where you can find peace. The *Ananda Ashram* opp has slightly more expensive accommodation if you would like solitude in your own hut.

Karur (*STD Code*: 04324) Karur may have been the ancient capital of the Cheras of the *Sangam* Age. The Amaravati river bed nearby has yielded artefacts including Roman amphora, Roman and Chera gold and silver coins, portrait fig-

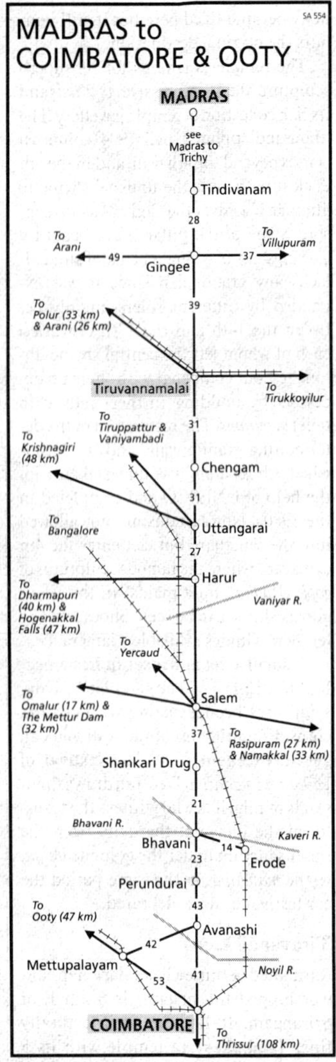

ures and stone inscriptions bearing the Brahmi script. The larger hoards (once as many as 500 silver Roman coins) were found mainly in the 19th century. More recently gold signet rings bearing Tamil inscriptions (in Brahmi) with identifiable personal names have been dated to the 1st and 2nd century AD. Also found were rings with typical Roman animal motifs. Karur appears to have been the centre for gold jewellery making and gem setting, the gold having been imported mainly from Rome.

MADRAS TO COIMBATORE AND OOTY

ROUTES The shortest route to Coimbatore and Ooty from Madras follows the NH45 to Tindivanam (119 km), see page 876.

Gingee to Salem

Gingee A road runs W from Tindivanam to **Gingee** and the 15th century Vijayanagar fort. If you are going by bus to Gingee take a rickshaw from the bus stand to the hills. It should not cost more than Rs 25 for the round trip. Although it had Chola foundations, the 'most famous fort in the Carnatic', was almost entirely re-built in 1442. It is set on 3 Charnockite hills, all strongly fortified and connected by walls 5 km round. In places the hills on which the fort stands are sheer cliffs over 150m high. The highest is *Rajagiri* ('king's hill') which has a S facing overhanging cliff face, on top of which is the citadel. The fort was protected on the N by a deep narrow ravine, crossed by a wooden bridge. The citadel is approached from the E through a series of defensive lines, 2 of which have impressive triple arches. In all there are 7 gateways, some with large courtyards between them.

There are several interesting remains in the fort itself; 2 temples and a square court used by the women of the Governor's household known as the **Kalyana Mahal**. On top of the citadel is a huge gun, a smooth granite slab known as the Raja's bathing stone. An extraordinary stone about 7m high and balanced precariously on a rock, surrounded by a low brick wall, is referred to as the prisoner's well. The fort was intensely contested by successive powers. The Vijayanagar king lost it to the Sultan of Bijapur in 1638, 18 years before the catastrophic defeat of the Vijayanagar Empire at the Battle of Talikota in Karnataka, see page 1058. In 1677 it was taken by the Marathas under Sivaji, see page 1154, but they only held it for 13 years before it was captured for the Mughals by Zulfikar Khan. It was taken by the French in 1750 who held it until it was taken by an East India Company force in 1762.

Tiruvannamalai

(37 km; *Population*: 119,000; *STD Code*: 04175) Continue on the road due W from Gingee to Tiruvannamalai, one of the holy towns of Tamil Nadu and widely thought of in the region as the home of Siva and his consort Parvati. As such it is a major pilgrimage centre, and its location at the foot of the rocky **Arunachala Hill** gives it a striking setting.

The Tamil scholar Arunachalam describes the mythical origins of the hill: "Brahma and Vishnu quarrelled over who was superior. Siva appeared to them in a linga of fire. Vishnu tried to find its base by digging in the form of a boar, while Brahma became a goose and flew towards the top. Neither could find any limit to the linga. They recognised it as a form of Siva, who made the fiery linga into the mountain Tiruvannamalai".

Places of interest

There are over 100 temples in the town below the hill, but by far the most important, and possibly the largest in South India, is the **Arunachala Temple** itself, approx. One km SE of the railway station. Built mainly in the 16th and 17th centuries under the patronage of

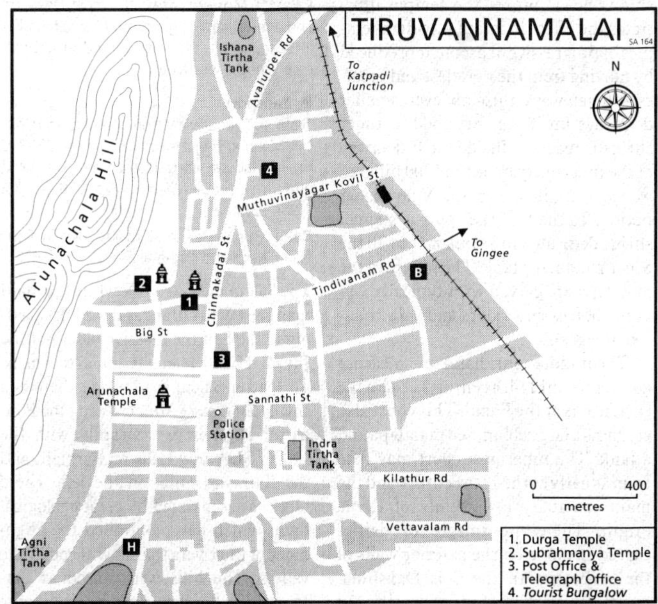

the Vijayanagar kings, its massive gopurams, the tallest of which is 66m high, dominate the centre of the town. It is dedicated to Siva as God incarnate as Fire.

The temple has 3 sets of walls forming a series of nested rectangles, built at quite different periods and illustrating the way in which many Dravidian temples grew by accretion rather than by overall design. The E end of each is extended to make a court, and the main entrance is at the E end of the temple. The lower parts of the gopurams date from the late Vijayanagar period but have been added to subsequently. As is common with Dravidian temples, their lower sections are built of granite while the upper 10 storeys and the decoration are of brick and plaster.

There are some remarkable carvings on the gopurams. On the outer wall of the E gopuram, Siva is shown in the centre of the N wall while in the S corner he is shown dancing with an elephant's skin. The design of the temple illustrates the effect in later Dravidian temples of progressive abasement produced by moving from the grandest and greatest of gateways through ever smaller doorways until the very modest inner shrine is reached. Inside the E doorway of the first courtyard is the 1000 pillared *mandapa* built late in the Vijayanagar period. To the S of the court is a small shrine dedicated to *Subrahmanya*. To the S again is a large tank. The pillars in the mandapa are carved with typically vigorous horses and riders and *yalis* (lion-like images).

The middle court has 4 much earlier gopurams (mid 14th century). Again the entrance is at the E end. This court also contains a large columned mandapa and a tank. The innermost court may date from as early as the 11th century and the main sanctuary is certainly of Chola origin. There are images of deities carved in stone on the exterior walls of the sanctuary. In the S is Dakshinamurti, the W shows Siva appearing out of a lingam and the N has Brahma. The outer porch has small shrines to Ganesh and Subrahmanya. In front of the main shrine are a brass column lamp and the *Nandi* bull.

The much-visited ashram of the **Guru Ramana Maharishi**, who died in 1950 is on the edge of town.

Excursions

Sathanur Dam, a small power project 35 km to the W on the Ponnaiyar River, has attractive gardens and is a popular picnic and day outing site.

Local festivals

Karthikai Deepam Full moon day in Nov-Dec. A huge beacon is lit on top of the hill behind the temple. The flames, which can be seen for miles around, are thought of as Shiva's lingam of fire, joining the immeasurable depths to the limitless skies.

Local information

● Accommodation

F *Park*; F *Modern cafe* with simple, clean, rm and a restaurant, is good value. Small market in building sells ultra-pasteurised milk, processed cheese, pasta etc.

● Transport

Train To Tirupati via Vellore, Katpadi and Chittor: *Madurai Tirupati Exp*, 6800, daily, 2253, 6 hr; To Madurai via Chidambaram, Thanjavur and Trichy: *Tirupati Madurai Exp*, 6799, 2123, 12 hr 3/4 hr.

Road Bus: buses to all major cities in Tamil Nadu, Keral and Karnataka.

The Salem road goes SW while the main road goes W to **Uttangarai** (62 km), passing to the S of the massive blocks of the **Javadi Hills**. There it joins the main Tirupattur-Salem road where there is a small *Rest House*. After crossing the Ponnaiyar River it rises steadily, with the 1100m **Shevaroy Hills** on the right and the **Kalrayan Hills** on the left. These blocks are separated by great geological faults which have controlled the alignment of the rivers that flow through the valleys. The hills were raised as flat-topped *horsts*, pushed up possibly some

300 million years ago. Some experts suggest that it took place at the same time as the Western Ghats were raised along the fault line from the Arabian Sea. The Javadis and the Shevaroys still have forest cover on some of the steep slopes. Until very recently these were the scene of shifting cultivation.

The gently rolling tops of the hills are intensively cultivated, though their height alters the climate enough to allow crops such as coffee to be grown in the Shevaroys. Ragi, gram, *sorghum* are the most common crops, and forest products have also been an important source of income. Particularly striking is the development of cattle breeding in the districts of Dharmapuri and Salem. Dharmapuri-Krishnagiri cattle are famous throughout South India and are the main source of heavy draught cattle from Kerala to southern Andhra Pradesh. "The breeding herds live on the forests for the greater part of the year, where they are kept in pens at night time. They are brought back to the village at harvest, when the harvested fields provide grazing for some time, and the cattle supply the necessary manure for the succeeding ragi crop.... The breeders cannot be considered *ryots* (farmers). They certainly grow crops for their own requirements but by profession they are breeders of cattle, dependent on the sale of their calves for their livelihood... A good number of breeding bulls live in a semi-wild state." Littlewood's description of the situation in the mid 1930s still applies.

On the low land of the valley floors small scale irrigation has always been important. You may notice wells being operated by bullocks moving up and down a ramp, pulling a large bucket from a well. This kavalai system is widespread in northern Tamil Nadu, and it can be operated by only 1 man. The most important crop is groundnut.

ROUTES The road S to **Harur** (27 km; *Population*: 20,000; *Rest House* available) passes through a small area of forest. A turn in Harur crosses the Vaniyar River and leads up onto the Reserved Forests of the westernmost block of the Kalrayan Hills. The Salem Rd leaves the town to the SW (58 km).

Salem

Population: 573,700; *Altitude*: 280m; *STD Code*: 0427. The road passes the impressive Shevaroy Hills on the right. The town is at the junction of roads from Bangalore to the N and Tiruchirappalli to the S, and is surrounded by the Shevaroy and Nagaramalai Hills to the N, the Jerumumalai Hills to the S, the Godumalai Hills to the E and the Kanjamalai Hills to the W. Salem is divided in 2 by the River Manimutheru, the old town being on the E bank, Shevapet being on the opposite side. One tradition holds that the town takes its name from *Sela* or *Shalya*, a corruption of Chera, named because a Chera king from the S was believed to have rested at Salem. The town is also one of many places held to be the birthplace of the Tamil poetess Avvaiyar.

It is pleasanter to stay in Yercaud and visit Salem for the day.

Local industries

Salem is a rapidly growing industrial town. It is an important textile centre, with over 130 textile cooperatives in the town. Walk along Bazar Street in the evening and you will get a sense of the importance and range of the weaving industry. Cotton carpets made in nearby Bhavani and Komarapalayam are sold in the Bazar. The All India Institute of Weaving and Handloom Technology has its headquarters in the city. A new iron and steel works was opened in the 1980s at Kanjamalai, near Salem Junc, using the haematite iron ores found immediately to the W of the town to make stainless steel and other special steels. In the region immediately around Salem are important mineral resources – magnesite, bauxite, limestone and

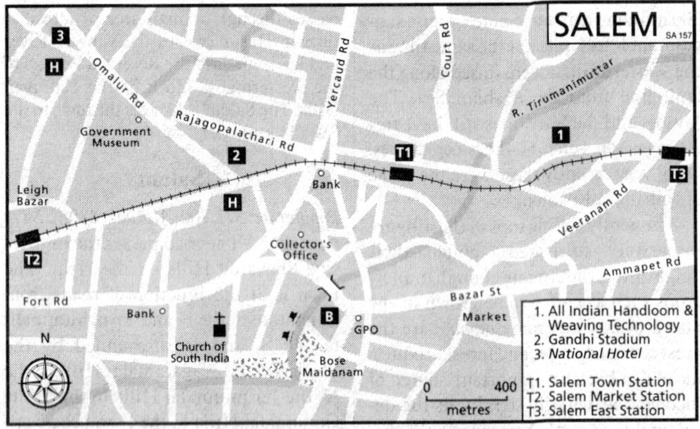

iron ore as well as many other minor deposits. There are now literally hundreds of small scale sago plants, using the tapioca which is one of the district's most important agricultural products. The chief product is starch, used in the textile industry and exported largely to Bombay and Ahmadabad.

Places of interest

Salem was once a defensive site. The **fort**, of which only the E wall remains, is the oldest part of the town. Situated on the right bank, a bridge crosses the river from its NE corner. The main administrative buildings such as the Collector's Office and the Town Hall are just N of the fort, near to Christ Church, which was consecrated in 1875. A seated Jain figure is opposite the old Collector's bungalow known at the *Talaivetti Muniappan*, or 'Muniappan with the broken head'. Devotees bring offerings of the blood of goats and chickens. Near the Jain statue is a shrine to Tipanja Amman which contains a stone slab with a round top on which are carved 2 human figures. It reputedly commemorates 2 women who burned themselves on the spot when they learned of their husbands' death in battle.

Also near the centre of the town are the compound of the old **London Missionary Society**, now part of the Church of South India, and to its W the market of **Shevapet**. This takes its name from the Tamil word Sevvai, the name for the planet Mars. The market is held on Tue (Mars' day) every week and is still attended by thousands of people from all around the town.

There are several important temples. The **Siva** temple is dedicated to **Sukavaneswara**, the 'Lord of the Parrot Forest', though one inscription describes him as the 'parrot coloured Lord'. The main entrance to the temple has a pillared portico. N of the portico is a *kalyanamandapa* named after the British Collector who gave it, WD Davis. To the N of the hall is a deep round well called 'the **frogless spring**', because it is said that all the frogs were frightened away by Adisesha who once visited the well. In addition to the temples there are several mosques, the oldest of which is in the fort. A Friday Mosque was built by Tipu Sultan on the bank of the river. The mosque in Shevapet was built in 1882, causing riots among objectors.

S of Shevapet is **Gugai** which "takes its name from a cave, the entrance to which is marked by the Muniappa temple. The cave is said to have been the abode of a Hindu hermit who for some inscrutable reason was petrified into the idol of Muniappan. The idol is seated cross-legged in the attitude of meditation and at its feet is seated a bearded devotee in a similar posture". (S Arcot Dist Gazetteer) To the N of the town the Yercaud road leads from Christ Church through the mainly European area, with spacious compounds and attractive avenues. There was once a race course near the houses of the District Judge and the London Mission. Two km N of the jail is a garden with an attractive bathing tank.

Among other features of interest are the **cemetery** next to the Collector's office with some interesting tombstones. To the SE of the town on a ridge of the Jerumalai Hills is a highly visible *Naman* painted in chunam and ochre. The temple on the nearby hill was built in 1919 by Karuppanasvami Mudaliar and is particularly sacred to the community of weavers. 600 steps lead to the top and there is an excellent view over the town. There is a huge boulder at the foot of the hill known as **Sanyasi Gundu**, below which is a cave believed once to have been the home of a Muslim hermit. This is reputed by some Hindus to be linked with another cave in Gugai by an underground tunnel. The boulder has marks believed to be the imprints of the foot and 2 hands of the saint who stopped the boulder when it came rolling down the hill. This story is very similar to that surrounding a Muslim shrine near Attock in Pakistan, where Guru Nanak, the founder of Sikhism, is also believed to have left his hand print on a boulder.

Museums

Government Museum, Omalur Rd, 0900-1230, 1300-1700. Closed Fri, 2nd Sat and national holidays. The collection has archaeological, zoological and botanical exhibits; a good life-size portrait of Gandhi by VRL Ramalingam. There is a library, guide service, lectures and films. **Planetarium** The South's 1st planetarium, housed in the Govt College of Engineering. Fixed shows; apply at the college.

Local information

● Accommodation

D *National*, Omalur Rd, nr TVS, T 54100, 90 rm, 40 a/c, 10 cottages, 3.5 km rly, restaurant, a/c bar, travel, roof garden; **D** *Hema International*, 70 Chittukoil St.

E *Woodlands*, Five Rds, T 7272, 40 rm, some a/c, 2 km centre, a/c restaurant (Indian); **E** *Maduthi*, T 64214, some a/c rm; **E** *Gokulam*, Meyyanur Rd, T 7071, some a/c rm; **E** *Apsara*, 19 Car St, T 63075, 37 rm, 3 a/c, nr rly, restaurant (Indian, Continental), coffee shop, exchange.

3 **F** *Railway Retiring Rm*, noisy.

● Shopping

Handlooms and jewellery (silver and gold chains) are best buys at *Agrahram*.

● Transport

Air Coimbatore is the nearest airport with commercial services.

Train Salem Junction, the main station, is broad gauge and metre gauge, the other being metre gauge only. **Madras (MC)**: There is a daily train originiating from Cochin, dep 1745, 6 hr; also *West Coast Exp*, 6028, 0805, 6 hr. *Kovai Exp*, 2676, daily, 1640, 5¼ hr; **Coimbatore**: *W Coast Exp*, 6027, daily, 1725, 3¼ hr; F85MAlappuzha via Coimbatore and Ernakulam: *Bokaro-Alleppey Exp*, 8689, daily, 1040, 10 hr.

Road Bus: the new bus station is N of the Hospital, off Omalur Rd. Salem is well connected by bus with all major towns in Tamil Nadu, Kerala and S Karnataka. TTC buses, T 62960.

Excursions from Salem

Mettur Dam

Built between 1925-1934, the dam is still one of the world's largest. Its reservoir holds 3 times as much water as the Aswan Dam on the River Nile, over 2600 million cu m. The dam is 1.6 km long and 54m high, and the lake it impounds is over 155 sq km. The water provides irrigation to Salem and Coimbatore and the Mettur Hydroelectric Project is situated here. It can be visited by leaving Salem at the Salem Junc Rly station, and via Taramangalam to Pottaneri. There are also regular buses from Salem. There are 2 **F** *Circuit Houses*. Reservations: Sub-Divisional Officer, PWD, Stanley Dam, Sub Division, PO Mettur Dam.

Shevaroy Hills

Salem is an excellent base from which to visit the Shevaroy Hills.

Yercaud

BASICS 33 km; 1515m; *STD Code*; 04281; *Climate*: Summer: Av 29°C, Winter: Av 13°C; Annual rainfall 168 cm; *Clothing*: Summer: cottons, Winter: woollens; *Season*: throughout the year, busy Apr-Jun.

Yercaud claims to be the least expensive of India's hill stations and is pleasant for a quiet holiday though as a hill station it is definitely second best to Kodaikkanal or Ooty. The drive up the steep and sharply winding ghat road from Salem is beautiful. Those wishing to see Salem are advised to stay here.

There are several points of interest within 3 km. There is a small artificial **lake** with Anna Park nearby. Some attractive though unsignposted walks start here, but there are no shops or restaurants. Just outside the town is **Lady's Seat**, which overlooks the Ghat road and gives wonderful views across the Salem plains. In May there is a special festival focused on the **Shevaroyan Temple**, on top of the 3rd highest peak in the hill range. Many tribal people take part, but access is only possible on foot. Ask for details in the Tamil Nadu Tourist Office in Madras. Near the Norton Bungalow, the oldest bungalow in Yercaud on the Shevaroyan Temple Rd, is another well known local spot, **Bear's Cave**. Formed by 2 huge boulders, it is now occupied by huge colonies of bats. The whole area is full of botanical interest, the altitude of over 1500m allowing a quite different range of species to grow from those common on the intensively cultivated plains below. There is an **Orchidarium-cum-Nursery** and a **Horticultural Research Station**, many varieties of flowers flourish in the relative coolness, along with pear, jack and orange trees.

The main bazar area has little to recommend it. A few very dirty and dingy restaurants, local mine blasting from PA Systems from 0500 to midnight.

• **Acommodation** Most offer off-season discounts Jul-Mar. **D** *Shevaroys*, Main (Hospital) Rd, nr lake, T 636601, 20 rm, 11 newer cottages with Western baths, restaurant, bar, good views; **D** *Sterling Resort*, nr Lady's Seat, modern, excellent views, rec; **D** *Tamil Nadu* (TTDC), Salem-Yercaud Ghat Rd, nr Lake, behind Panchayat Union Office, T 2730, 12 rm, some a/c, restaurant, Tourist information, garden.

• **Budget hotels** Inspect rm first in those nr Bus Stand: **E** NGGO *Holiday Home*, opp Bus Stand, when not booked by officials. T Salem 3605; **E** *Select*, nr Bus Stand, T 296. *Youth Hostel*, dorm (one a/c), simple, good value. Reservations: Manager, Hotel or TTDC, 143 Anna Salai, Madras, T 830390. **E** *Hill View*, Main Rd, nr bus stand, T 2446. The view is the only feature to recommend it.

• **Banks** Dealing in foreign exchange are on Main Rd.

• **Hospital & medical services** *Govt Hospital*, 1 km from Bus Stand; *Providence Hospital*, on road to Lady's Seat.

• **Post & telegraph**
The Post Office is on the Main Rd.

• **Tourist office** At Rajaram Nagar, T 66449.

• **Transport Local Bus**: no local buses but some from Salem continue through town and connect with nearby villages. **Train** Nearest stations are at Salem. **Road** From Salem, 1 hr.

Namakkal

(*Population*: 45,000; *STD Code*: 04286) The ruins of this extraordinary hilltop fort 50 km S of Salem dominate the busy market town below. It was believed to have been built by Tipu Sultan. Namakkal is equally famous in Tamil Nadu for its Vishnu temple. Opposite the temple is a huge statue of Hanuman worshipping. The bare rock to the N of the main tank (*Kamalalayam Tank*) covers 2 ha. The district played a leading part in the Indian independence movement, and Mahatma Gandhi addressed a huge meeting from this spot in 1933. Within the shrine of the **Narasimhasvami Temple** there are 4 particularly remarkable Pallava bas reliefs.

Salem to Coimbatore

From Salem join the NH 47 SW to **Shankari Drug** (35 km), passing the 750m high rock fort on the right. Haider Ali was reputed to have kept hoards of gold in the rock fort at the top of the hill, 500m above the plain. Magnificent views over the Shevaroy Hills and to the Kaveri River from the top. The fort has various gruesome associations. It is said that 'undesirable persons' were rolled down the almost vertical 500m cliff on the SW side of the hill. The hill has several springs with medicinal properties, the most famous being the *Maan Sunai* or Deer Spring which is never touched by the sun's rays. The main road crosses the Kaveri at **Bhavani** (21 km; *Population*: 97,000; *STD Code*: 04256) which straddles the rocky banks of the river just above its confluence with the Bhavani River. The town is a centre of pilgrimage, especially from Palakkad. The Nayaka **Sangamesvara Temple** at the confluence of the 2 rivers has bathing ghats. Six km to the W of Bhavani is an open cast mica mine, yielding good quality green mica.

ROUTES From here the route enters a region of great historical importance as an area of contact between the plains of Tamil Nadu to the E, the plateaus of Mysore to the N and the coastal plains of Kerala, reached through the Palakkad gap to the S. The frequency with which the word *palayam* ('encampment') occurs in place names indicates the extent to which this was also a region of conflict between the *Cholas*, the *Pandiyas* and the *Cheras*. From Bhavani the main road goes SW to **Perundurai** (23 km). Asbestos is mined nearby.

Erode

(*Population*: 357,400; *STD Code*: 0424) Noted as the home of the great Tamil nationalist, social reformer and political leader Periyar EV Ramaswamy Naicker, the town is also famous for its handloom products. The road from Bhavani W crosses some of the district's most fertile areas, the 'granary of Kongu country'. Paddy, sugar cane, groundnut, cotton, turmeric, tobacco, bananas, and various millets are all grown in what is regarded as one of the most progressive agricultural areas of Tamil Nadu. Today Erode is a busy, hot and dirty industrial railway town.

• **Accommodation** Erode is not a place to stay unless you have to. One possibility is **E** *Brindhavan*, 1499 EVN Rd (Mettur Rd), in front of bus stand, T 61731, quite good veg restaurant, but bar dingy and "full of gamblers and heavy drinkers".

• **Transport Train** Erode is an important railway junction on broad and metre gauge lines. Direct connections to Bangalore, Thiruvanandapuram, Mangalore, Hyderabad, Calcutta and Delhi, as well as frequent local trains to Tiruchirappalli, Salem and Coimbatore.

Avanashi

(*Population*: 17,000; *STD Code*: 04296), has a widely visited Siva temple, dedicated to Avinasisvara, noted partly for its colossal Nandi. The outer porch of the temple has 2 stone alligators, each shown vomiting a child. They recall a story which told how a local saint, Sundaramurti Nayanar, interceded on behalf of a child who had been swallowed by an alligator, and the infant was disgorged unhurt. There is a shrine to the saint inside the temple and on the bund of the Tamaraikulam tank (pond of lotuses). The temple gopurams were renovated in 1756, but inscriptions indicate that the temple goes back to at least the early 13th century. The biggest temple tower lost its top 5 storeys in 1860. To some local chiefs it was known as the *Kasi* (Varanasi) of the S.

If you are going direct to Ooty take the right turn a few km out of Avanashi on the Coimbatore road to Mettupalayam via Annur. Frequent local buses.

Tirupur Just S of Avanashi, on the main railway line to Coimbatore, Tirupur is a rapidly growing industrial town. Tamil Nadu's textile industry now accounts for 25% of India's cotton textiles, and Tirupur has become one of India's industrial boom towns. Between 1991-92 alone its output grew by nearly 50%, specialising in knitwear. It accounted for nearly two-thirds of India's knitwear exports, most of them going to the US and the European Community.

Coimbatore

Population: 1.135mn; *Altitude*: 425m; *STD Code*: 0422. The city owes its rapid growth in the last 50 years to the development of Hydro Electricity from the **Pykara Falls** in the 1930s. This led to a boom in cotton textile milling, Coimbatore often being called the Manchester of South India.

The cotton textile industry had started in 1888 with 2 mills, but until electric power became available it could not compete with the much larger scale production in Bombay and Gujarat. Related industries have also developed, including pump sets for irrigation, motor parts and assembly. The centre of a rich agricultural area, Coimbatore has a noted agricultural university. The nucleus was an Agricultural Demonstration Farm started on the outskirts of Madras in 1868. This was shifted to Coimbatore in 1907 and became an internationally known centre of agricultural research. It is a centre for seed breeding experiments. Advertisements for seeds in fields and on walls, with the prefix 'CO' and a number, indicate their origin in the Coimbatore Agricultural University. The Textile Research Institute SITRA has recently invented a new fibre 'palf' from pineapple leaves.

Places of interest

The Tamil Nadu Agricultural University **Botanical Garden**. On the W edge of Coimbatore, the garden has grown from 3 ha in the early 1900s to over 300 ha now. Surrounded by fields and with the backdrop of the Nilgiris behind it is in a most attractive setting. Open to the public. It includes formal gardens, such as the to piary section with casuarina groves and rose gardens as well as informal areas with a wide variety of trees, including a recently developed section of flowering trees.

Museums

College Museum, Tamil Nadu Agricultural Univ, Open 0900-1200, 1400-1700. Closed Sun and Govt holidays. Special collections of minerals, rocks, insects, pests, fungal diseases, snakes, silver and gold medals. Guide service. **Gass Forest Museum**, Southern Forest Rangers' College and Research Centre, Coimbatore. 1900-1300, 1400-1630. Closed Sun, second Sat and public holidays. Exhibits of forestry and forest products. Library.

Climate: Coimbatore

	Jan	Feb	Mar	Apr	May	Jun	Jul	Aug	Sep	Oct	Nov	Dec	Av/Tot
Max (°C)	30	33	35	35	34	31	30	31	32	31	29	29	32
Min (°C)	19	19	21	23	23	22	22	22	22	22	21	19	21
Rain (mm)	7	4	5	70	76	35	37	18	42	127	127	25	573

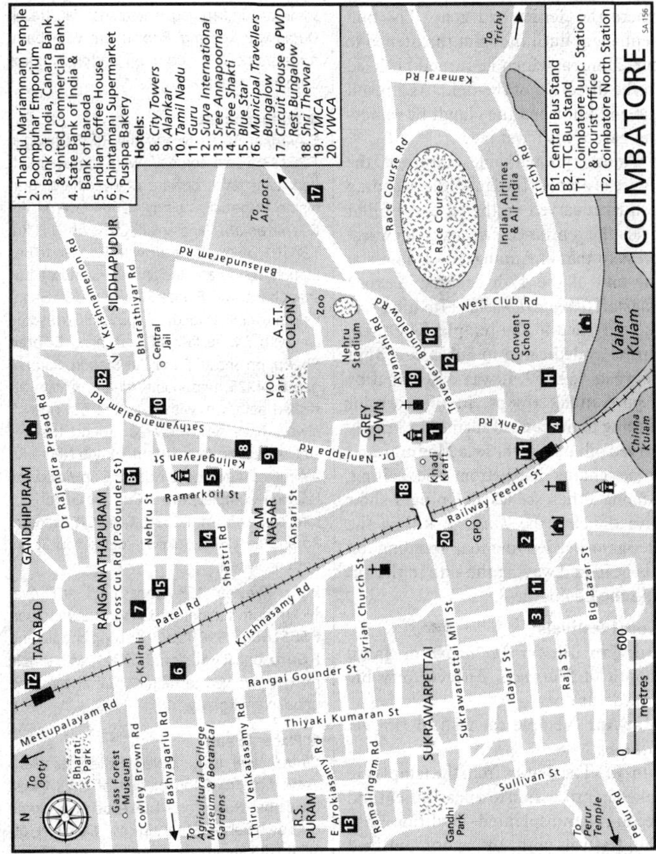

Parks and zoos

The VOC Park and Zoo nr the Stadium has a toy train circuit. Bharati Park, Main Rd, 1 Sai Baba Colony. Botanical Garden, nr Agriculture University.

Excursions

Perur (*Population*: 9,200) Now a suburb of Coimbatore, 6 km W of the city centre, Perur has 1 of 7 *Kongu Sivalayams*, a temple of great sanctity. The outer buildings were erected by Tirumala Nayak of Madurai between 1623-1659, but the inner shrine is much older. The stone image of the Nandi in front of the temple illustrates a story which is traditionally believed to lie behind one of the temple's festivals.

The saint Sundaramurti Nayanar came to Perur but the deity in the shrine was unwilling to see him and left the temple with the goddess, disguised as outcastes. Before leaving, the god warned the Nandi not to disclose his whereabouts to Sundaramurti. Unable to find the god, Sundaramurti returned to the temple and asked the Nandi where the deities had gone. The bull kept silent until the saint threatened to curse him, at which he turned his head in the direction of the field. As a result the god punished the Nandi by removing part of his lower jaw.

Another remarkable feature is the figure of a *sepoy* (Indian soldier) loading a musket carved on the base of a pillar near the entrance, wearing identical dress to that of Aurangzeb's soldiers at the end of the 17th century. A stone flagstaff (*dhvaja stambha*) 11m high is at the entrance to the temple. The main shrine is dedicated to *Sabhapati*. Built between 1623-59, it was desecrated by Tipu Sultan's troops. In the corridor leading to the central shrine are 8 richly carved pillars like those in Madurai, and stone chains hang from the ceiling. Among other scenes the pillars show Siva dancing the *Tandava*; killing the elephant-headed demon, treading on his head and waving the skin in the air; and the lion of the S.

Local festivals

Dec-Jan *Arudra Darsanam* in Tamil month of *Margazhi*. Attracts very big crowds, as does—

Mar-Apr Temple car festival *Panguni Uttaram*.

Jun-Jul The deities from the temple are taken in procession to a nearby field and seeds are transplanted. Tradition links the festival with the story outlined above.

Local information

● Accommodation

C-D ***City Towers***, Dr Nanjappa Rd, Gandhipuram, T 37681, 97 pleasant rm some a/c, 2 restaurants (good on rooftop; Grd Flr basic, no alcohol), car hire, popular with businessmen, rec.

D ***Surya International***, 105 Race Course Rd, T 37751, 44 rm, 37 a/c, restaurant, bar, exchange, travel, shops, lawn; **D** TTDC ***Tamil Nadu (Star)***, Dr Nanjappa Rd opp Bus Station, T 36310, 49 rm, some a/c with TV (charge), restaurant, bar, rec; **D** ***Sree Annapoorna***, 47 E Arokiasamy Rd, RS Puram, T 33053, 56 rm some a/c, Indian veg restaurant, bar, travel; **D** ***Railway Retiring Rooms***, rm with bath, some a/c, noisy, the dorm off platform 1 is less expensive, restaurant.

● Budget hotels

E ***Alankar*** 10 Dr Sivaswamy Rd, Ramnagar, T 26293, 57 rm, some a/c with TV, restaurant, dark bar, travel, beware of overcharging in dining 'special', dingy and overpriced; **E** ***Janaranjani***, Janaranjani Cross off N H Rd, T 34101, 36 rm, some a/c with TV, close to Bus Station, restaurant (Indian veg, Chinese), bar, snack bar, travel; **E** ***Blue Star***, Nehru St, Gandhipuram, nr Bus Station, T 26395, 50 rm, some a/c with TV, restaurant, car hire; **E** ***Shree Shakti***, on Shastri Rd nr Bus Station, Ramnagar, T 34225, reasonable, clean rm with attached bath, rm 'with TV' extra but doesn't always have set! The area around the bus stations, particularly Shastri Rd and Nehru Rd are full of inexpensive hotels. **E** ***Sri Lakshmi***, Lakshmi Complex, Cross Cut Rd, Gandhipuram, some a/c rm, T 3330; **E** ***YMCA*** Avanashi Rd and **E** ***YWCA***, Sukrawarpettai Mill St are both nr Flyover.

F ***Shri Thevvar***, 153 Avanashi Rd, nr Flyover ½ km from station, T 23341, restaurant, bar; **F** ***SBS Lodge***, 996 Raja St, just opp airport, and **F** ***Guru***, opp Rly Station, T 30341, with simple rm over a/c veg restaurant, are cheap, and good in emergency.

● Places to eat

Cloud Nine (City Towers Hotel), excellent views from roof top of one of city's tallest buildings. Good food but expensive. Some outside hotels are "best in city" ***Dakshin***, off DB Rd, RS Puram, very smart and good food; Moderately priced '***Solai Drive-in***', Nehru Stadium, nr VOC Park for ice creams, drinks, Chinese and Indian food; ***Richy Rich***, DB Rd does good milk shakes; On Arts College Rd: ***Annapoarna*** has good cheap S Indian; ***Dasa*** (a/c) for veg, pricey, though good icecreams. ***Gem Continental*** has a good menu but mediocre atmosphere and interior. ***Udhayam***, Nehru St, Gandhipuram; ***China Restaurant***, 410 Trichy Rd; ***Sri Sampoorna***, Gandhipuram for S Indian; the ***Royal Hindu*** nr the station is an Indian veg restaurant while ***Top Form*** offers non-veg meals; ***Indian Coffee House***, Ramar Koil St; ***Pushpa Bakery*** is not far from the *Blue Star Hotel*.

● **Banks & money changers**
Bank of India, Canara Bank, United Commercial Bank all on Oppankara St. **State Bank of India**, T 36251 and **Bank of Baroda** are on Bank Rd.

● **Entertainment**
Cinemas: Central, Mettapalayam Rd, shows English films, top price Rs 10.

● **Hospitals & medical services**
Govt Medical College and Hospital is on Trichy Rd.

● **Post & telecommunications**
Head Post Office and Telegraph Office, nr flyover, Rly Feeder Rd. Fax service available.

● **Shopping**
Famous for handloom and handicrafts. ***Poompuhar Emporium***, off Big Bazar St, ***Kairali*** off Mettapalayam Rd and ***Khadi Kraft*** on Dr Nanjappa Rd. Several other shops along the street, handloom in Shukrawarpettai and Gandhipuram. Asoka Plaza and Laxmi Complex, corner of Trichy Rd.

● **Sports**
Yoga: Integral Yoga Institute, 116 Bashyakaralu Rd (W) off DB Rd, RS Puram. Run by American women 'swamis', courses/classes in meditation, breathing, chanting – all in English.

● **Tourist office**
Coimbatore Junc Rly Station, weekdays 1000-1900, Sat and Sun 1000-1700.

● **Transport**
Coimbatore is on the NH 47 and there are good roads to other towns in the region. Bangalore 312 km, Kochi 184 km, Kanniyakumari 469 km, Kodaikkanal 172 km, Madras 492 km, Madurai 227 km, Ooty 90 km, Tiruvananthapuram 400 km.

Local Bus: City Buses run a good service. No 12 connects the Bus Stations with the Coimbatore Junc Rly Station, No 20 with the airport (Rs 20). Central (Cheran) Bus Stand. **Taxi**: Tourist Taxis and un-metred yellow top taxis at the Bus Station, Rly Station and Taxi stands. About Rs 40 per hr. Out-station hill journeys more expensive. **Auto rickshaws**: negotiate fare before journey, min Rs 3.

Air Sulur Airport (30 km centre). **Transport to town** Cheran Transport runs an airport coach to several hotels and parts of the city, Rs 20; Taxis Rs 100; Auto-rickshaw Rs 50. **Indian Airlines** and **Air India** Office, Trichy Rd. Enquiries T 22743, Reservations T 22208. 1000-1300, 1345-1730. Airport T 73396. **Bangalore and Madras** Tu,Th, Sa Su 1405, 2 hr. **Bombay**, daily, 0910, 2 hr. **East-West Airlines**, City Office Gowthan Centre, 1055 Avanashi Rd, T 210286, Airport T 573445. **Bombay**, daily, 0745, 1¾ hr. **Jet Airlines**: **Bombay**, daily, 1520, 1¾ hr.

Train Junc Rly Station **Madras**: *Kovai Exp*, 2676 (AC/CC), daily, 1415, 8¾ hr; *Tiruvananthapuram-Guwahati Exp*, 2601, Th, 2215, 7¾ hr; **Bangalore**: *Nagercoil-Bangalore Exp*, 6525 (AC/II), daily, 2055, 9½ hr; **Kochi (HT)**: *Tiruchirappalli-Kochi Exp*, 6365, daily, 0045, 5½ hr; *Haora/Patna-Kochi*, 2652/2610 (AC/II), Tu,Sa,Su, 1315, 5¼ hr; *Guwahati-Kochi*, 2650 (AC/II), F, 1315, 5¼ hr; **Delhi (ND)**: *Mangala Link Exp*, 2625/2625A (AC/II), daily, 1925, 43 hr. **Madurai** (5½ hr) and **Ramesvaram** (12 hr), *Ramesvaram Exp*, daily. *Kanniyakumari Exp*, daily, 13½ hr. Other trains: *W Coast Exp (Madras – Coimbatore – Kozhikode – Bangalore)*, daily to Kozhikode (4½ hr) and Bangalore (9 hr). **Ooty**: train at 0630 connects with narrow gauge train from Mettupalayam. **Mettupalayam**: to Coimbatore dep 0815; to Madras, 1930. Coimbatore Junc Rly Station. Enquiries, T 37716. Reservations, T 24157, 0700-1300, 1400-2030.

Road Bus: TTC and the SRTCs of the neighbouring states and private companies run regular services to many cities. Frequent buses to Ooty (5 hr) between 0400 and 2400. TTC also runs frequent buses to Madurai and Tiruchirappalli (5½ hr) and 5 daily to Madras (12 hr). The 2 Bus Stands for out-station services are in the Gandhipuran area on Dr Nanjappa Rd. TTC Bus Stand, Cross Cut Rd, T 25949. Computerised reservations 0700-2100, T 26700. Corporation Bus Stand: Reservations 0900-1200, 1600-1800, T 27086. Central (Cheran) Bus Stand, T 26309.

Coimbatore to Coonoor

From Coimbatore there is an excellent road N to **Mettupalayam** (53 km, *Population*: 63,200; *STD Code*: 042254), a centre of the *areca* nut trade, and between the town and the bottom of the ghat road up to Coonoor and Ooty the road passes through magnificent groves of tall slender areca nut palms. These are immensely valuable trees, and the nut is used across India wrapped in betel vine leaves as 2 of the essential ingredients in India's universal after-meal digestive agent, *paan*. The town is the starting point of the ghat railway line up to Ooty (see page 898). On the banks of the Bhavani river, it has also become the centre for new industrial units, notably producing synthetic gems.

- **Places to eat** *Karna Hotel* in the bus station is good for *dosas*. The ghat road up to Coonoor (32 km) is one of the most famous in India, giving superb views over the plains below.

Coonoor

The second largest of the 3 Nilgiri hill stations, it is much less developed and has a milder climate than Ooty. It is a very pleasant place to relax. The recent increase in population is partly due to the arrival of Tamils from Sri Lanka. The town is physically divided into upper and lower Coonoor.

BASICS *Population*: 99,600; *Altitude*: 1800m; *STD Code:* 04264; *Climate*: Summer: Max 24°C, Min 14°C, Winter: Max 19°C, Min 9°C; Annual rainfall 130 cm; *Best season*: Apr-June, Sep-Oct; *Clothing*: Summer: light woollens, Winter: woollens.

Places of interest

At its heart is **Sim's Park** which was founded in the mid-19th century as an amusement park for Coonoor and the Cantonment at Wellington nearby. Named after JD Sim, a secretary to the Madras Club in 1874, the 12 ha park in Upper Coonoor is on the slopes of a ravine and has been developed into a botanical garden partly in the Japanese style. It has over 330 varieties of roses. The fruit and vegetable show is held in May, after the Flower Show in Ooty. Coonoor also has the **Pomological Station** where the State Agricultural Dept researches on fruits including persimmon, apricot and pomegranates. Surplus fruit is sold to the public. There are 2 other research stations in the Nilgiris, at Burliar and Kallar. The **Pasteur Institute** opp the main entrance to Sim's Park was established in 1907, researches into rabies and manufactures polio vaccine. You can take a tour with a guide on Sat between 1030 and 1115. Otherwise you may visit with permission of the Director. Next door is the **Silkworm Rearing Station** of the Central Silk Board. Contact the United Planters' Association of Southern India (UPASI), Glenview if you wish to visit tea and coffee plantations. There are several view points nearby some of which can be reached by road.

Lamb's Rock 6 km away is on a high precipice from which you can see the plains of Coimbatore and the coffee and tea estates on the slopes. **Dolphin's Nose** (12 km), is another, 10 km away, from which you can see Catherine Falls, and **Droog** (13 km) which has ruins of a 16th century fort used by Tipu Sultan as an outpost, requires a 3 km walk. **Law's Falls** (5 km), is near the junction of Coonoor and Katteri rivers on the road to Mettupalayam. There are several very attractive local shady walks here including Tiger's Hill, Walker's Hill and Brookland's Road.

Excursion

Wellington (3 km; *Population*: 19,600). The barracks which is the raison d'etre for the town, were built in 1852. It is now the HQ of the Indian Defence Services Staff College. It is also the HQ of the Madras Regiment, over 250 years old and the oldest in the Indian Army. Follow the road up to Ooty (17 km).

Tours

TTDC Coonoor-Kotagiri Rs 95, 6 hr; visiting Valley View, Sim's Park, Lamb's Rock, Dolphin's Nose, Kodadu view point. Reservation, Tourist Office, T 3977 or Hotel Tamil Nadu, T 4370.

Local information

- **Accommodation**

Out-of-season discounts possible. **B** *Taj Garden Retreat* (formerly Hampton Manor), T 219241, 31 rm, good restaurants; **D** *Ritz*, 14

Orange Grove Rd, T 620084, 24 rm, with bath, some with TV, good restaurant, bar, garden, rec; **D *Blue Hills***, Mount Rd, T 20103, 40 rm, good restaurant, fairly basic, good value.

● Budget hotels

There are also Indian style hotels: **E *Vivek Tourist Home***, Figure of 8 Rd, nr UPASI, T 7292, 60 rm with bath, restaurant; **E *Lakshmi Tourist Home***, Kamrajpuram, Rockby, T 21022, 35 rm, Indian restaurant, car hire and TV lounge; **E *YWCA Guest House***, Wyoming, nr Hospital, 12 large rm, dining hall, garden, "a superb place to stay". **F *Venkateswara Lodge***, Cash Bazar nr Bus Stand, T 6740, 40 rm.

● Hospital & medical services

Govt Lawley Hospital, Mount Rd, T 2223. *Emmanuel Eye Hospital* has an excellent reputation.

● Shopping

Bazar full of activity, highly recommended. ***Mission Arts and Crafts*** and ***Spencer's***, Figure of 8 Rd, ***Variety Hall***, Jubilee Bridge and ***Shanthi Mahal*** nr the Bus Stand. ***Issu Book Centre***, Bedford.

● Tour company & travel agent

MB & Co, Belmont, T 6207.

● Transport

Local Taxis: MB, Belmont, T 6207. **Rickshaws**: charge whatever they think they can get.

Train A Mountain Rly connects Coonoor with Coimbatore via Mettupalayam. See below under Ooty.

Road Bus: frequent buses connect Coonoor with Ooty (every 10 min) some via Sim's Park and many via Wellington. Also regular services to Kotagiri and Coimbatore through Mettupalayam.

Ooty (Udhagamandalam)

Near the junction of Tamil Nadu, Karnataka and Kerala, Ooty was mentioned in the Madras Gazette of 1821 as 'Wotokymund'. It had been inhabited by *Toda* tribal people who lived in villages or 'munds' consisting of a handful of huts. See page 844. The origin of the name is disputed. Some think it comes from the Tamil word *votai*, a dwarf bamboo, *kai* meaning vegetable or unripe fruit, and the Toda word *mund*. Others believe it is 'one-stone-village' in the Toda language. The English shortened it to 'Ooty'. The 'Queen of the Blue Mountains', along with Kotagiri and Coonoor nearby, is famous for its rolling hills covered in pine and eucalyptus forests and its coffee and tea plantations. Because of its climate it was developed by the British as a summer retreat after a Collector from Coimbatore, John Sullivan, 'discovered' it. A Government House was built, and the British life style developed with cottages and clubs – tennis, golf, riding – and teas on the lawn. The Indian Maharajahs followed, built their grand houses and came here to shoot.

The centre of town is unpleasant (see Budget hotels below). To curb unplanned growth of new building a temporary ban was imposed in 1993.

BASICS *Population*: 81,700; *Altitude*: 2286m; *STD Code*: 0423; *Climate*: Summer: Max 25°C, Min 10°C, Winter: Max 21°C, Min 5°C; Rainfall 121 cm; *Season*: Apr-Jun; *Languages*: Tamil, English, Kannada, Malayalam, Hindi; *Clothing*: light woollens in the day, occasionally. Warm woollens in the evenings and during the monsoons.

Local crafts and industries

Many large and small tea estates clothe the hillsides to produce the famous Nilgiri tea with about 65 large factories and 94 others catering for the 20,000 'small growers'. The Cordite factory, in the Aravankadu Valley off the Ooty-Coonoor road, was set up in 1904. Served by its own HEP station at Katery Falls it manufactured explosives. The Hindusthan Photo Films Unit (largest of its kind in S Asia), 8 km away in the Wenlock Downs, on the Gudalur Bus route, is a Govt of India enterprise undertaken in 1960, now in collaboration with Dupont. Products incl special films for CAT scanners and space photography and magnetic tape. Visits with prior permission. The Needle factory in Yellanhalli village (8 km) at a height of over 2200m was started in 1949 with production of the simple hand sewing needle. It has become a leader in the field producing the highest quality needs for medicine, exporting know-how to the Far East. Also units producing gelatine, mushroom and the more common vegetables and fruit, and a cottage industry extracting **Eucalyptus Oil** as well as oils from citrioda, lemon grass, camphor and vetiver.

Places of interest

The **Botanical Gardens**, 2 km E of Rly station, over 20 ha planted with more than 1000 varieties of plants, shrubs and trees including orchids, ferns, alpines and medicinal plants among beautiful lawns and glass houses. There is a small lake with a 20 million-year-old fossil tree trunk by it. Originally the kitchen garden of a few residents, the Gardens were developed by the Marquis of Tweeddale in 1847 who got a Kew gardener to transform it into an ornamental garden. Ten years later was taken over by the Govt in Madras. To the E of the garden in a Toda *mund* is the Wood house made of logs from which you can get good views. The Raj Bhavan is next door. The Annual Flower Show (mainly exotics) with its accompanying exhibition is held in the third week of May. Unless you are attending the flower show, Ooty is best avoided at this time. It cannot cope with the thousands of extra visitors.

Ooty Lake was constructed between 1823 and 1825 through the initiative of the Collector Mr. John Sullivan as an irrigation tank. Although artificial, the winding lake looks beautifully natural. It has been shrinking for decades and is now about 2.5 km long and between 100 and 140m wide. Part of the land which was under water in the last century has been reclaimed to provide recreational facilities, including the race course. The Tourism Dept hires out boats from the Boat House, 0800-1800. Rec. The lake had become very polluted and water hyacinth covered over ⅘ of its 26 ha until cleaning up commenced in 1992; being one of the fastest vegetative reproducers, given ideal conditions just 10 plants can multiply to cover ½ ha of water in a month! By early 1994 there was some success in curbing the menace from the weeds after volunteers worked day and night for several months. Other measures have also been taken: the ponies are officially restricted to enclosures and sewage is to be pumped out to Kandal where a new treatment plant is being set up.

Raj Bhavan Built by the Duke of Buckingham and Chandos in 1877, when Governor of Madras, in the style of his family home at Stowe. The Government House, now the Raj Bhavan, is superbly positioned on the Dodabetta Ridge to the SE of Ooty and is approached through the Botanical Gardens. The grounds are very well maintained and open to visitors, though the building is not; now only occasionally used for official entertaining.

Stone House The first bungalow built here by John Sullivan is the residence of the principal of the Govt Art College which has its campus opposite. The house which gives its name to the hill above the market place where it stands, was called *Kal Bangla* (stone bungalow) by the tribals.

Kandal Cross Three km W of the rly station is a Roman Catholic shrine considered the 'Jerusalem of the East'. During the clearing of the area as a graveyard in 1927 an enormous 4m high boulder was found and since then a cross was erected. Today, a relic of the True Cross brought to India by an Apostolic delegate is shown to pilgrims every day. The annual feast is in May.

St Stephen's Church Ooty's first church, built in the 1820s in a Gothic style, occupies the site of a Toda temple. Much of the wood is said to be from Tipu Sultan's Lal Bagh Palace in Srirangapatnam, after his final defeat, which had to be hauled up by elephants from the plains up Sigur Ghat. The clock tower and gallery were added in 1851 and the 9 tubular bells in 1894. Unimpressive from the outside, the inside of the church and the graveyard (with its poignant colonial plaques and head stones) at the rear are worth seeing.

Palaces Maharajahs and Nawabs built their summer palaces and mansions, the most impressive being those of the rulers of Baroda, Hyderabad, Jodhpur and Mysore. Many have been turned into hotels, such as **Fernhill**, built by the Maharajah of Mysore and

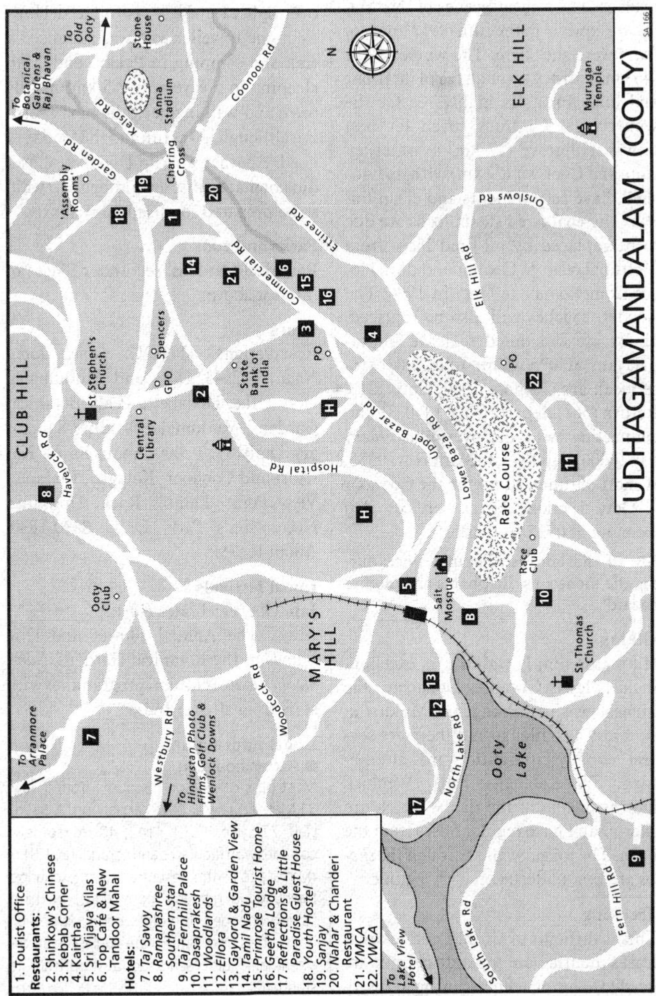

Arranmore Palace built by the Maharaja of Jodhpur and now a Govt Guest House, *Tamizhagam*. Open to visitors.

The **Blue Mountain Railway** The delightful narrow gauge Mountain Railway in its blue and cream livery goes from Mettupalayam to Ooty via Coonoor negotiating 16 tunnels and 250 bridges. The railway scenes of the 'Marabar Express' in the film of *A Passage to India* were shot here. The whole 4½ hr (46 km) journey through tea plantations and lush forests is highly rec for the scenery (1st Cl front coach for best views). Hillgrove (17 km) a 'watering' stop, and Coonoor (27 km) with its Loco shed, have refreshments and clean toilets. The coal-fired steam locos are due to be replaced by oil-fired locos from Mettupalayam to Coonor and diesel locos from Coonor to Ooty in 1996. The wooden coaches will also be replaced. Trains are scheduled to leave Mettupalayam at 0750 (Apr-June has extra service), arr Coonoor 1040, Ooty 1210. Return (561) departs Ooty, 1450, 3¼ hr, connecting with the overnight *Nilgiri Exp* (6006) dep 1915, to Madras arr 0555. If short of time just try the the Coonoor – Ooty section. Extra services dep Coonoor at 0725 and 1635.

NB: Landslides can disrupt services during the monsoons. Elephants are another hazard!

Hiking

Hiking or simply **walking**, is excellent in the Nilgiris. Climbing Dodabetta, the highest peak in the range and Mukurthi, is hardly a challenge and there are several equally straightforward alternatives. Try Kalahatti Falls, Wenlock Downs or one of the dams, which are shorter and have regular buses from the town. The longer walks through the *sholas* are best undertaken with a guide.

Trekking

This is difficult to arrange and takes at least a month. Four separate permits are needed, any of which can be refused. Treks of up to 7 days are arranged with permits requiring 1 month's notice, by the Nilgiris Trekking Association, Kavitha Nilayam, 31-D Bank Rd, Ooty, F 2572. NR Ayyapan, the President is very knowledgeable about trekking in the area.

One day treks without a permit and overnight camping is also offered. However, one traveller who was promised a trek and camping in Pykara ended up sleeping in a cave only 2.5 km outside town and walking back the next morning although it was fun and the food very good. Another walk to Dodabetta Peak did not materialise even after a 5 hr wait, so be prepared for disappointment.

Parks and zoos

Botanical Gardens, see under Places of interest above.

Tours

Reservations TNTDC, *Hotel Tamil Nadu*, T 2543. **Ooty and Mudumalai:** Ooty Lake, Dodabetta Peak, Botanical Gardens, Mudumalai Wildlife Sanctuary. Daily 0830-2000. About Rs 70. **Kotagiri and Coonoor:** Kotagiri, Kodanad View Point, Lamb's Rock, Dolphin's Nose, Sim's Park. Daily 0830-1830. About Rs 75.

Local festivals

Jan Ooty celebrates *Pongal*.

May The Annual Flower and Dog Shows in the Botanical Gardens. *Summer Festival* of cultural programmes with stars from all over India.

Local information

● Accommodation

Most offer off season discounts from 1 July-31 Mar. Virtually all have car parking. **A** *Savoy* (Taj), 77 Sylkes Rd, T 4142, 40 rm, some in cottages with fireplaces and verandahs, 1.5 km rly, close to centre, restaurant, bar, exchange, travel, good gardens, pony rides, trekking, fishing arranged, the old section supposedly has timbers from Tipu Sultan's palace in Srirangapatnam! old fashioned atmosphere, Taj standards.

B Comfort Inn *Jothi Park*, 'Victorian' architecture in large landscaped grounds with superb views over Ooty "from the point the resort was discovered", 84 rm in the only centrally heated hotel in town; **B** Ramanashree *Southern Star*, 22 Havelock Rd, T 3601, 67 rm, some refurbished, restaurant (over-attentive service!), bar, tea garden, exchange, travel, shops, health club. Good, clean, comfortable; attracts filmstars on location; **B-C** Taj *Fernhill Palace*, T 3910, 47 rm, half renovated in 1994, good restaurant (rec), expensive bar, exchange, travel, lawns, horse riding, built in 1842 in wooded surroundings, as the Mysore Maharajahs' summer retreat, has many prints of Ooty Hunt which met here, service greatly improved since Taj group takeover and is good value.

D *Regency Villas*, Shooting Lodge of *Fernhill Palace*, 100m away, under separate management, large rm, clean and comfortable, small restaurant, tea gardens, rec, good value; **D** *Dasaprakash*, S of Racecourse, T 2434, 100 rm, nr rly, Bus Stand, off season 15 June-10 Apr, student group discounts, 2 restaurants (veg), coffee shop, exchange, travel, garden, comfortable, quiet location; **D** *Lake View*, W Lake Rd, T 3904, 117 rm in cottages most without a 'view', restaurant, bar, exchange, travel, riding arranged, rec; **D** *Nahar*, 52 A Charing Cross, T 2173, 88 rm with heaters, 1 km rly, off season discounts; restaurant (Veg *thalis*), bakery, travel, shops; **D** *Snowdon Inn*, Snowdon Rd, T 2138, 12 rm, restaurant, exchange, travel, golf and pony rides arranged. There are several middle range hotels in the Charing Cross area, nr the Post Office. **D** Karnataka Tourism's *Mayura Sudarshan*, Fern Hill, T 3828. Also the Karnataka State Tourism information office and tour booking agency. **D** TTDC *Tamil Nadu*, Charing Cross, up steps by Tourist Office, T 4010, rm and penthouse, restaurant, bar; **D** *Woodlands*, S of Race Course Rd, T 2550, some rm in old colonial house, some in cottages, quiet, comfortable.

Budget hotels & youth hostels

Most are centred around Commercial Rd and Ettines Rd; many are filthy and noisy flea pits which charge inflated rates; the area has overflowing sewers, too much traffic and too many beggars and touts. Avoid it if you can and try the outskirts which are still pleasant, quiet and much more preferable. A selection is listed here; few have running hot water (usually supplied in buckets).

E *Apsara*, avoid this, designed like a prison block, no ventilation, very noisy next to a mosque and large bed bugs, friendly management let down by abysmal premises; **E** *Ellora*, rm with bath (Indian toilet), an old tiled bungalow, rm a little shabby but some have fireplace and old "Victorian" furniture, garden with lawns overlooking Ooty and lake; **E** *Garden View*, Lake Rd, opp Bus and Rly stations, T 3349, 26 rm with bath, deluxe, with better views and hot tap, restaurant, good size rm, a little tatty but clean; **E** *Gaylord*, connected to *Garden View*, T 2378, rm with bath overlooking a quiet geranium-filled courtyard, cheap dorm (24 beds), good, clean roof-garden restaurant, tours, pony rides, old tiled bungalow overlooking Rly Station, amazing home-made boiler dispenses hot water! **E** *Little Paradise Guest House*, N Lake Rd, rm with bath, not very clean, smelly, overpriced; **E** *Primrose Tourist Home*, Commercial Rd, T 3848, 18 rm with bath, dorm, 2 good restaurants, modern building with no views but central, noisy at times, rates vary according to demand; **E** 4 *Railway Retiring Rooms*, T 2246; **E** *Reflections*, N Lake Rd, T 3834, 6 rm, clean, homely guest house with good views, friendly owners, pleasant dining room, not rec for females travelling alone; **E** *Sanjay*, Charing Cross, T 3160, rm with spacious balcony, restaurant, travel, clean, sometimes noisy at night, excellent rm service, rec; **E** *YWCA*, Ettines Rd, T 2218, rm, cottages, dorm, popular with the young, though not central, restaurant.

F *Geetha*, T 4186, 13 very clean rm, cheap dorm, shared Indian toilet, central but fairly quiet, best value for money; **F** *Youth Hostel* nr Tourist Office, T 3665, dorm, restaurant.

● Places to eat

In hotels: *Savoy*, highly rec for its relaxed atmosphere and good, not too spicy food, buffets are more affordable; *Fernhill Palace*, rec for reasonably priced Indian and Continental; *Ritz*, hotel, good, inexpensive food, excellent lemon sodas. Good veg thalis at *Nahar*. Several inexpensive restaurants on Commercial Rd: *New Tandoor Mahal*, smart, serving meat and chicken dishes, good veg curries, over-attentive waiters; *Top Café* next door below *Primrose Tourist Home* does Indian veg and has icecream parlour; *Kabab Corner* opp with upmarket, Western decor does good curries and naan. Inexpensive non-veg food at *Kaveri* and at *Blue Hills* in Charing Cross; *Sri Vijaya Vilas* opp rly station does very cheap veg meals and dosa, clean, fast service, popular with Indians, rec.

Chinese: *Shinkow's*, 42 Commissioner's Rd (nr Collector's Office), good authentic dishes, reasonably priced – popular, especially late evening; *Chung Wah*, Commercial Rd, less good; *VK Bakery*, 148 Commercial Rd is rec.

● Bars

In larger hotels. *Southern Star*, rec, though expensive.

● Banks & money changers

State Bank of India on Bank Rd. Several national banks deal in foreign exchange. You can also change money at the TTDC *Hotel Tamil Nadu* on Charing Cross Rd.

● Entertainment

The recently renovated 100 year old **'Assembly Rooms'**, Garden Rd, T 2250, shows Western films. Most of the annual events take place in May – Summer Festival, Dog Show, Flower Show, Vegetable Show in the Botanical Gardens, Boat Race and Pageant on the lake.

● Hospitals & medical services

Govt Hospital, Hospital Rd.

● Post & telecommunications

Post office: Head Post Office, Collectorate, and Telegraph Office, Town W Circle. **International direct dialling and fax facility**: Post Office at Charing Cross.

● Shopping

Most open 0900-1200, 1500-2000. The smaller shops keep longer hours. *Poompuhar* and *Kairali Emporia*. Charing Cross has the *Toda Showroom* which sells silver and tribal shawls. *Kashmir Emporium*, Garden Gate and *Kashmir House*, Charing Cross sell mainly Kashmiri handicrafts but also stock Toda jewellery. Municipal Market and Coop Super Market and Upper and Lower Bazar Roads are other shopping areas. *Nilgiri Dairy Farms* outlets sell quality milk products. *Variety Hall* in Silver Market for cloth/silk. Takes some credit cards.

Books: *Higginbotham's Bookshop*, Charing Cross, 1000-1300, 1550-1930.

● Sports

Gymkhana Club, T 2254, allow temporary membership for a fee. Beautifully situated in the middle of the 18-hole Golf course which is superbly maintained. *Ootacamund Cricket Club*, T 2846. Anna Stadium has good facilities for badminton and table tennis. *Lawley Institute*, T 2249, for tennis, badminton, billiards, bridge. Boating and rowing on Ooty Lake.

Fishing: is good at Avalanche, 25 km away, where there is a trout hatchery. Forestry Guest House for overnight accommodation. Licenses for hired tackle from Assistant Director of Fisheries, Fishdale, T 2232.

Trekking: see note above.

● Tour companies & travel agents

Blue Mountain Travel, Nahar Shopping Centre, Charing Cross, luxury coach bookings to neighbouring states; *George Hawkes*, 52 C Nahar Complex, Charing Cross, T 2756, for tourist taxis; *MB Travel*, Commercial Rd, next to *Higginbothams*.

● Tourist offices

Tourist Office, Super Market Building, Charing Cross, T 3964. Attempts to be helpful without succeeding.

● Transport

Good road connections to other towns in the region. Ghat roads have numerous hairpin bends which can have fairly heavy traffic at times. The Gudalur road passes through Mudumalai and Bandipur sanctuaries. See page 1018. You might see an elephant herd and other wildlife especially at night. From Bangalore, the road is via Mysore.

Local Taxis and the cheaper **cycle rickshaws** can take you to your hotel. **Autorickshaws** are unmetered. **Cycle hire**.

Air Nearest airport, Coimbatore, 105 km. Taxis available.

Train The *Nilgiri Express* (6005) travels overnight from Madras (dep 2105) via Coimbatore to Mettupalayam (0720) and from there you can reach Ooty by road or rail. The Blue Mountain Railway (562) departs ½ hr later. For details, see above.

Road Bus: frequent services to Coonoor (every 10 min) and Coimbatore (every 20 min from 0600-2100), taking 3½ hr, about Rs 15. Several to Bangalore (5 from 0630-2000), Mysore (5 from 0800-1530) and Kozhikode (8 from 0530-1515), Mettupalayam (frequent, 2 hr), and daily buses to Kannur (0900, 2030), Hassan (1130), Kanniyakumari (1630), Kodaikkanal (0830, 2030), Madras (1600), Madikere (0700), Palani (0810), Pondicherry (1700) with connection to Kodaikkanal.

Around Ooty

Wenlock Downs

8 km from the station on the Gudalur road, the area of about 8000 ha of grassland with *sholas* or 'gallery forests' is described in the Madras Gazetteer of 1908. "In the *sholas* grow rhododendron, ilex, ferns of many varieties, bracken, tree-orchids with delicate blossoms, the hill gooseberry, blackberries, the sweet scented Nilgiri lily, the alpine wild strawberry.... Hedges are often made of heliotrope, fuchsia, and geraniums". It has changed since those days with the planting of eucalyptus and wattle forests to provide firewood and siting of factories in a part of the downs, but it is very pleasant for walks especially if you can get well into the interior (it is possible to take a car in). The 'Ooty Hunt' with horses, hounds and the jackal and the Hunt Ball, is still resurrected but not in quite the style of the past. The downs are also where the golf links are situated.

Mount Dodabetta

About km 10 E of the rly station, off the Kotagiri road, the 'big mountain' reaches 2638m, the second highest in the Western Ghats sheltering Coonoor from the SW monsoons when Ooty gets its heavy rains and vice versa during the NE Monsoon in Oct and Nov. Easily accessible by road, on a clear day you can see as far as the Coimbatore plain and the Mysore plateau. The top is often shrouded in mist. There is a viewing platform at the summit which is covered by red-flowered Rhodendron arboretum, truly wild and not a 'garden escape'.

Mukurti Peak

(36 km) Turn left off the Gudalur road after 25 km which brings you to the Hydro-Electricity Board's *Inspection Bungalow* and another km to the right, Mukurti Lake, which is surrounded by high hills and is 6 km long. The name is derived from 'muku' (nose) and 'ardha' (half) suggesting a severed nose for the shape of the peak. The Electricity Dept and Nilgiris Game Association *Bungalows* are on the S side of the lake, half way along, and you can go fishing and boating is permitted. You need to book the Bungalows early as they are popular as an excellent place to escape for walking and view the occasional wildlife. Mukurti Peak, not an easy climb, is to the W. The Todas believe that the peak is sacred as from it the souls of the dead and the sacrificed buffaloes leap to the next world.

Avalanche

(24 km) The 'avalanche' in 1823 gave the valley its name. A beautiful part of the *shola* with plenty of rhododendron, magnolia and orchids and a trout stream running through. Excellent for walking and superb scenery. Forestry Dept *Guest House*, clean with good food. Avalanche Top is 4 km from bungalow.

Pykara

(19 km) You can get there by car, bus or bicycle. The river has a dam and power plant. Breathtaking scenery. The Falls, about 6 km from the bridge on the main road, are best in July, though it is very wet then, but are also worth visiting from Aug to Dec.

Kotagiri

(29 km; *Population*: 37,800) is the oldest of the 3 Nilgiri hill resorts and sits on the NE crest of the plateau overlooking the plains. At 1983m it is milder than Ooty but more bracing than Coonoor, and is also protected by the Doddabetta range from the worst of the SW Monsoon rains. The name comes from Kotar-Keri, the street of the *Kotas* who were one of the original hill tribes and have a village to the W of the town (see page 845).

There is a **Handicrafts Centre** of the Women's Welfare Dept. You can visit some scenic spots – St Catherine Falls (8 km) and Elk Falls (7 km), or one of the peaks – Kodanad Viewpoint (16 km) which you reach through the tea estates or Rangaswamy Pillar which is an isolated rock and the conical Rangaswamy Peak.

• **Accommodation F** *Queen's Hill Christian Guest House*, very clean, bath, hot water, beautiful surroundings, friendly, superb breakfasts, highly rec; **F** *Blue Star*, next to Bus Station, rm with shower and toilet in new modern building; **F** TTDC *Hotel Tamil Nadu* and *Youth Hostel*, well sign-posted beyond bus station, rm dirty and crowded with noisy tea-pickers.

• **Transport Road Bus**: There are regular bus services from Mettupalayam Rly Station, Ooty and Coonoor.

MADRAS TO BANGALORE (Northern Route)

ROUTES The N route to Bangalore follows NH 4 all the way. For the first 150 km the road crosses the Coromandel coastal plain through Chingleput district into N Arcot. It leaves the much more densely populated southern route at Ranipet, enters Andhra Pradesh and then climbs gently up the plateau.

The road out of Madras to the W is now extremely busy. It runs along the Cooum River before passing through the village of **Poonamallee** (*Population*: 28,300) and into open country. Chingleput and N Arcot districts are typical 'tank' country, each having over 3000 of the shallow reservoirs, irrigating over 260,000 ha. Some date back to the Pallava period of the 6th to 8th centuries AD, and many were added by the Chola kings. The smaller tanks are fed by rainwater, but some have springs or streams flowing into them.

• **Accommodation & food** 8 km W of Poonamallee are 2 small modern hotels/restaurants. **E** *Motel Highway*, 89 Bangalore Trunk Rd, T 57240, some a/c rm, attractively laid out open air restaurant, excellent South Indian breakfasts and snacks, 24 hr meals; **E** *Village Motel*, a little W of the Motel Highway, T 434546, restaurant also serves good snacks.

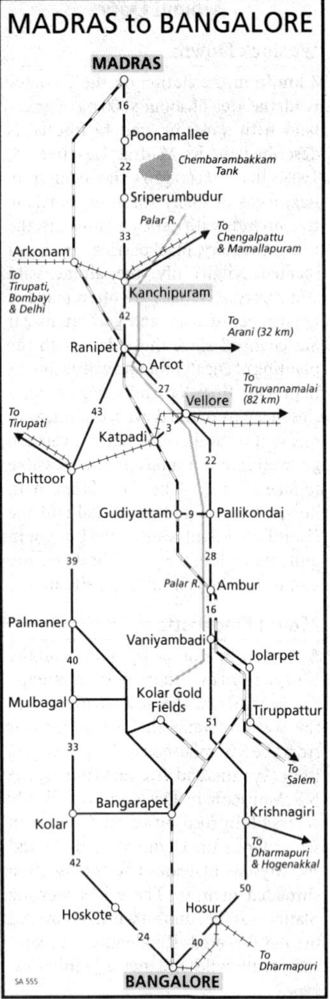

The NH 4 forms the W boundary of the **Chembarambakkam Tank**, one of the biggest in the region and one of India's most ancient. It is fed by the Palar River. The water is dammed by an embankment of nearly 9 km running from some high ground in the N to bare rocky soils in the

S. It often has water throughout the year, though its surface area fluctuates enormously. When it is full it is nearly 10 km long and has an area of over 2500 ha, but its shallowness and the great surface area result in over half the stored water being lost through evaporation. In 10 km the road passes through the small town of **Sriperumbudur**, the birthplace of the 11th century Hindu philosopher Ramanuja, where Rajiv Gandhi was assassinated on 21 May 1991. In the 3 years since Sriperumbudur has become something of a boom town, based partly on the tourist generated by the assassination. A new hotel is under construction to cater for the many official visitors who come to the memorial which has been erected on the spot of Rajiv Gandhi's death, and a number of motels have spring up on the Madras-Sriperumbudur road. Not all the growth is due to macabre interest. Just beyond the outer suburbs of Madras, the town had already a thriving modern industrial base, with distilleries, electrical goods, leather and car parts. **Irungattukottai** a few km away, has a racing circuit where the All India Grand Prix is held in Feb.

Kanchipuram

Population: 170,000; *Altitude*: 20m; *STD Code*: 04112. The history of 'The golden city of a thousand temples' can be traced back to the early Cholas in the 2nd century, although Buddhism is believed to have reached here in the 3rd century BC. However, none of the 3rd century BC Ashokan stupas which were supposed to have existed, now remain. Successive dynasties made it their capital and built over a hundred temples, the first as early as the 4th century with the best examples dating from the 6th and 7th centuries. It is one of Hinduism's 7 most sacred cities (see page 71). In addition to being a pilgrimage centre, it was a centre of learning, culture and philosophy. Sankaracharya and the Buddhist monk Bodhidharma lived and worked here.

From the 16th century the silk weavers have used high quality mulberry silk from neighbouring Karnataka and pure gold thread woven in beautiful colours and patterns on their handlooms. Nowadays, about 20,000 work with silk and another 10,000 with cotton. To visit the weavers at work in their spotless huts, contact Weavers' Service Centre, 20 Railway Station Rd, T 2530. The main town is W of the rly.

Local Festivals

At temples throughout the year; important ones are mentioned under each temple.

Places of interest

Temples Only a few of the 70 or so temples can be seen in a day's visit; most open early but close 1200-1600.

Ekambaresvara Temple is in the NW of the town between W and N Mada St about 1 km from the Bus Stand. Nominal charge for entry. Cameras: Rs 2, still; Rs 5, movie. **Festivals**: *Panguni Uthiram Festival* in Mar-Apr. The temple's historical connections include Clive's Arcot campaign when it served as a fortress. Non-Hindus are not allowed to enter the sanctum sanctorum. It is the largest of the temples covering an area of 9 ha and has 5 enclosures and a 'Thousand-pillared Hall' (actually 540). Dedicated to Siva in his ascetic form it was first built by the Pallavas, developed by the Cholas with further additions by the Vijayanagara King Krishna Deva Raya. At the beginning of the 16th century he built the high stone wall which surrounds the temple and the 59m tall *rajagopuram* or main tower (one of the tallest in South India) on which are sculpted several figures of him and his consort. Some find the temple rather eerie, with decaying statues, lots of bats and a feeling of being trapped in time.

The main sanctuary has a *lingam* made of earth (Siva as one of the elements) and the story of its origin is told

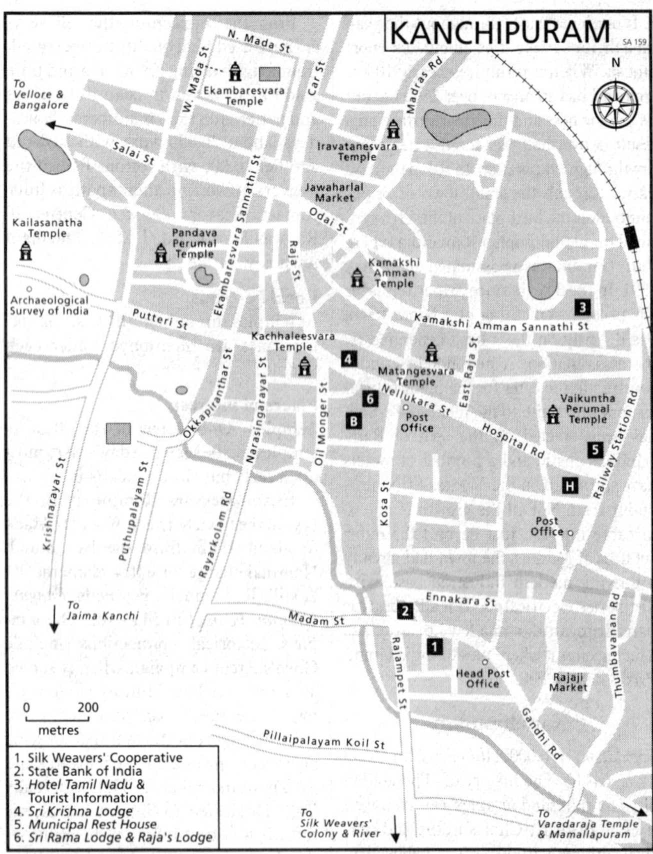

on a carved panel. The teasing Parvati is believed to have unthinkingly covered her husband Siva's eyes for a moment with her hands which resulted in the earth being enveloped in darkness for years. The incident enraged Siva and he ordered Parvati to do severe penance during which time she worshipped her husband in the form of an earth *lingam* which she created. When Siva sent a flood to test her, she clung to the lingam with her hands until the waters subsided. Some devotees claim they can see her finger prints on the temple *lingam*. The old mango tree in one of the enclosures is claimed to be 1000 years old (2500 according to some!) and still bears fruit.

Kailasanatha At the W end of the city (1.6 km), this is considered the most beautiful of the town's temples. It was built of sandstone in the early 7th century by the Pallava King Narasimha Varman II with the front completed by his son Mahendra III. The outer wall has a dividing wall with a shrine and doorways, separating a large courtyard from a smaller. The unusual enclosure wall has 58 small raised shrines with a *nandi* in each pavilion; some frescoes have survived. The 7 shrines in the temple complex are similar to the *rathas* in Mamallapuram and have images of different forms of Siva. The intricately carved panels on the walls depict legends about Siva with accompanying text in ancient Grantha script. Archaelogical Survey of India Office has limited opening hours. **Festivals**: *Mahashivaratri* in Feb.

Vaikuntha Perumal Temple (1 km) SW of the station. Dedicated to Vishnu this was built in the 8th century by the Pallava king Nandivarman just after the Kailasanatha and illustrates the progress of Dravidian temple architecture. As Percy Brown points out, the 2 temples (and the Shore Temple at Mamallapuram) are examples of dressed stones being used for structural temples. Here too the sanctuary is separated from the *mandapa* by an open space. The cloisters are built out of lines of lion pillars. Panels of bas relief accompanied by lines in old Tamil, trace the history of the wars between the Pallavas and Chalukyas. There is an unusual *vimana* (tower) with shrines in 3 tiers with figures of Vishnu in each.

Varadaraja (Devarajasvami) (3 km) SE of town. Built by the Vijayanagara king (c16th century), it has superb sculpture in its marriage hall (96 pillars). Note the rings at each corner and the massive flexible chain supposedly carved out of 1 piece of granite although they are no longer in one piece. The mutilation of the figures and the chains is attributed to Muslim invaders and particularly to Haider Ali. The main shrine is on an elephant shaped rock, Hastagiri. There are also small shrines in the courtyard with painted roofs. The 2 tanks in the temple enclosures have granite steps sloping down. Entry Re 0.50, Camera fees Rs 2 for still, Rs 5 for movie. **Festivals**: *Float Festival* in Feb and Nov, *Brahmotsavam* in May, *Garuda Sevai* in June.

Kamakshi Amman on Odai St in the centre of town built probably initially before the 7th century and later by the Cholas in the 14th century. It is dedicated to Parvati and is 1 of the 3 holiest places of *shakti* worship, the others being Madurai and Varanasi. There is a shrine to Sri Sankara who founded a monastery and a golden *gopuram*. The 'Amai' *mandapa* is beautifully sculpted. **Festivals**: The annual *'car' festival* when other deities are drawn to this temple in their wooden temple chariots, draws large crowds in Feb-Mar.

Anna Memorial comemorates the scholar/ statesman CN Annadurai who was born here.

Jaina Kanchi is just SW of town. The 2 temples worth visiting are **Vardhamana Temple** with beautiful paintings and the smaller **Chandraprabha**.

Local informaion

● Accommodation

Budget hotels **E** TTDC *Tamil Nadu*, 78 Kamakshi Amman Sannathi St, T 2953, 20 rm, 4 a/c, restaurant, garden, bike hire, very clean, good value, rec; **E** *Sri Rama Lodge*, 19-20 Nellukkara St, nr Bus Stand, T 3995, has some fairly basic a/c rm, veg restaurant, CCTV; *Rama Lodge* next door is similar.

Across the road, **F** *Sri Krishna*, 68A Nellukara St, T 2831, is cleaner; **F** *Municipal Rest House*, Rly Station Rd, is basic (no food), when not required by govt officers, advance booking with payment to Commissioner, Kanchipuram Municipality, T 2301.

● Places to eat

Hotel Tamil Nadu has a reasonable restaurant but service can be slow. Others are small *Thali Bhawans* in the centre of town nr the Bus Stand, inexpensive veg *thali* meals.

● Banks & money changers

State Bank of India, Gandhi Rd.

● Post & telecommunications

Head Post Office, 27 Gandhi Rd. Others on Rly Station Rd and near the Bus Stand.

● Shopping

Silk and cotton fabrics with designs of birds, animals and temples or in plain beautiful colours sometimes 'shot', are sold by the metre in addition of course to saris. Weavers do not sell directly but it is best to buy from Govt shops or Co-operative Society stores. ***Srinivas***, 135 Thirukatchi Nambi St (cont of Gandhi Rd), ***Thiruvalluvar Co-Op Soc***, 207 Gandhi Rd, ***Co-Optex***, 182 Gandhi Rd, ***BM Silks***.

● Tourist information
at *Hotel Tamil Nadu*, 78 Kamakshi Amman Sannathi St, T 2461.

● Transport
Local Cycle-rickshaws and **autorickshaws** for visiting temples.

Train Trains to Madras Beach Station and to Arakkonam on the Madras-Bangalore line.

Road Bus: direct Thiruvalluvar (TTC) buses to Madras (No 828), Bangalore (No 828), Kanyakumari (No.193), Pondicherry (109 km, No 804) and Tiruchirappalli (No 122). To get to Mamallapuram (65 km), either take a direct bus or quicker still take a bus to Chingleput (35 km) which are frequent and catch one from there. Other buses go to Tirupati, Tiruttani and Vellore.

Kanchipuram to Chittoor

Ranipet and Arcot

Ranipet (42 km, *Population*: 42,700, *STD Code*: 04172) Founded by the Nawab of Arcot in 1771, takes its name from the Rani Desingh of Gingee. Her husband, Raja of Gingee, had refused to pay tribute to the Nawab of the Carnatic, was killed in battle, and his widow performed *sati* on her husband's funeral pyre. The town was established as a mark of respect by the victorious Nawab. It was an important East India Company cantonment, later becoming a centre of Christian mission work, notably a hospital. Today it is has a large industrial estate built in the 1980s. Enfield Motorbikes are among the modern industrial products of the town, which has received significant Tamil Nadu Govt aid under its programme for developing 'backward areas'. **Accommodation** TTDC's **E** *Hotel Tamil Nadu*, T 84012.

Arcot (*Population*: 45,200) Five km away on the S bank of the Palar River is this historically important town which was formerly the capital of the 18th century Nawabs of Arcot. Virtually nothing of the old town remains except the Delhi gate, on the banks of the Palar. The moat which used to surround the citadel is dry and filled with trees. Beyond the Jami Masjid to the W are the ruins of the palace of the Nawabs. Yet in these now insignificant surroundings Robert Clive made his reputation, capturing and then holding the fort during a siege which lasted nearly 2 months until 15 Nov 1751 – some 6 years before the Battle of Plassey.

Chittoor and Palmaner

In Ranipet the NH4 turns N to **Chittoor** (43 km; *Population*: 133,200; *Altitude*: 315m). A monument at **Narsingh Rayanpet**, near Chittoor, marks the place where Haidar Ali died on 7 Dec 1782. The cemetery in the town contains a number of striking tombs. The road passes through some of the least densely populated parts of S Andhra Pradesh. To the right are the S limits of the Vellikonda Ranges, terminating very strikingly in Nagari Nose, an escarpment visible on a clear day even from Madras 90 km away. Light brown soils are cultivated with millets. The road passes through some extraordinary landscapes of huge outcropping granite boulders.

In the 19th century **Palmaner** (39 km; *Population*: 35,500; *Altitude*: 700m) was regarded almost as a hill station. Before the Nilgiris were opened up officials from Madras and others visited the town to provide a break from the intense heat of the lower plains. The road goes on to Kolar (73 km; *Population*: 83,200; *STD Code*: 08512, see page 1001) and Bangalore (66 km).

MADRAS TO BANGALORE (Southern Route)

ROUTES The S route follows the NH 46 via Ambur to Bangalore. Although only about 30 km longer than the N route via Chittoor and Kolar it is very much slower, passing through the densely populated **Palar valley**. It is a route of considerable historical interest. The Vijayanagar Empire left one of its finest temples, albeit a miniature, in Vellore. The whole valley became the scene of Anglo-French-Indian contest at the end of the 18th century. Today it is the centre of South India's vitally important leather industry, especially the towns of Ambur and Vaniyambadi.

For the section to **Ranipet and Arcot** see the previous route above. The road approaches Vellore along the S bank of the dry bed of the Palar River. The region has experienced rapid agricultural development since the early 1970s. The effectiveness of well irrigation has been increased by the use of electric pumpsets, which has encouraged farmers to invest in new varieties of seeds, especially of paddy. Improved varieties of rice had been introduced as early as the 1930s. Today every farm plants cross-bred high yielding varieties, usually with considerable inputs of fertiliser. This is one of the centres from which the Govt hoped to spread "green revolution" technology to Indian farming. There is a widening range of small scale industries and shops selling consumer goods that would have been completely unavailable 20 years ago – from soap to torch batteries.

Vellore

27 km; *Population*: 304,700; *Altitude*: 220m; *STD Code*: 0416. Vellore is a thriving market town. The fort is a major attraction, but Vellore is now world famous for its Christian Medical College and Hospital, the best place for treatment in South India.

Local industries

Vellore specialises in making 'Karigari' glazed pottery in a range of traditional and modern designs. Vases, water jugs, ashtrays and dishes are usually coloured blue, green and yellow. The local automatic fruit processing unit dealing with mangoes, tomatoes and other fruit, was set up with technical assistance from Czechoslovakia.

Places of interest

Vijayanagar architecture is beautifully illustrated in the temple at **Vellore Fort**, a perfect example of military architecture and a *jala durga* or water fort. The main rampart of the small fort, believed to have been built by the Vijayanagara kings and dating from the 14th century, is built out of imposing blue granite. It has round towers and huge gateways along its double wall which has Hindu motifs. The moat, still filled with water by a subterranean drain, followed ancient principles of defence with a colony of crocodiles. Defenders could flood the causeways at times of attack. A wooden draw-bridge crosses the moat at the SE. It was the scene of many battles and sieges.

In the 17th century it fell to the Muslim Adil Shahis of Bijapur and then to the Marathas. Vellore came under British control in 1768 who defended it against Haidar Ali in 1782. After the victory in Seringapatnam in 1799, Tipu Sultan's family was imprisoned here and a *sepoy* mutiny of 1806, in which many British and Indian mutineers were killed, left many scars. In the fort is a parade ground, the CSI church, the Temple and 2-storeyed *mahals* which are used as Govt offices. The moat was refilled and is used for fishing and swimming. The wide promenade between the lower outer wall and inner wall contains a tennis court.

Jalakantesvara Temple (enter from the S). Considerable restoration work has been undertaken in recent years, especially to the 7-storeyed granite gopuram, over 30m high. Inside on the left, the *kalyana mandapa* (wedding hall) one of the most beautiful structures of its kind, has vivid sculptures of dragons and 'hippogryphs' on its pillars. The central pillars show the much older motif of the seated lion, a Pallava symbol from the 7th century, but elaborated to match its Vijayanagar surroundings. Note the impressive stepped entrances and the free hanging chains. Surrounding the temple is a high wall, embossed with small but immaculately carved animal figures. The temple consists of a shrine to Nataraja in the N and a lingam shrine in the W. The *nandi* bull is in the courtyard. Typical giant guardians stand at the door of the main shrine. Although the temple was not touched by the Muslim occupiers of the fort, it was used as a garrison by invading forces and was thus considered desecrated. Since 1981 worship has been resumed and free access is allowed to non-Hindus. The Archaeological Survey of India is in charge.

The **Christian Medical College Hospital** was founded by the American missionary Ira Scudder in 1900. Started as a one-room dispensary, it extended to a small hospital through American support. Today it is one of the country's largest hospitals with over 1200 beds and large out-patients Dept which caters for over 2000 patients daily. The College has built a reputation for research in a wide range of tropical dis-

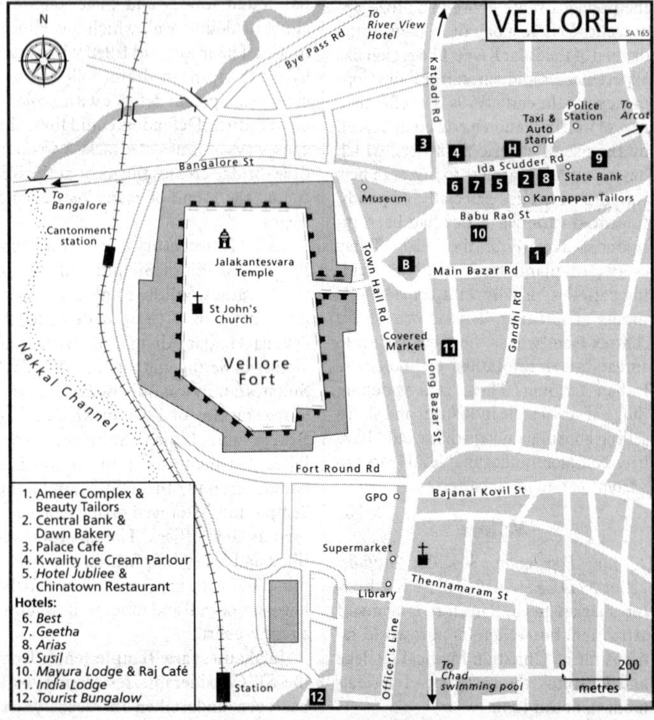

eases. One of its earliest and most lasting programmes has been concerned with leprosy work and there is a rehabilitation centre attached. In recent years it has undertaken a wide ranging programme of social and development work in villages outside the town to back up its medical programmes. The hospital serves people from all over S and SE Asia and has the support and financial assistance from nearly 100 church organisations throughout the world.

Museums

There is a small museum in the Fort. Closed 2nd Sat every month and Hindu festivals. Interesting collection of wood and stone carvings, sections on anthropology, painting, handicraft, coins and nature.

Excursion

35 km S of Vellore, half way to Tiruvannamalai, is the small market town of Polur, famous for its Jain rock carvings. These are found in the Tirumalai temple, which also houses the tallest Jain image in Tamil Nadu.

Local information

● Accommodation

The best **D *River View***, Katpadi Rd, T 25768, 1 km N of town, nr Nakkal Channel, 31 rm, some a/c, restaurants, clean, good value. Inexpensive hotels, are mainly nr the hospital on Babu Rao St and a few in Ida Scudder St.

F *YWCA*. In CMC Hospital Avenue. Very basic Indian canteen; **F *Mayura Lodge***, 85 Babu Rao St, T 25488, clean rm, very good value; **F *India Lodge***, inexpensive rm and *Raj Cafe*, good veg restaurant downstairs; **F *Municipal Tourist Bungalow*** is close to the Vellore Rly Station.

● Places to eat

Three restaurants at *Hotel River View*, Katpadi Rd; ***Palace Cafe***, 21 Katpadi Rd, (Indian) 0600-2200. Several others serving South Indian food.

On Ida Scudder Rd, nr the hospital: *Best* Some meals very hot, nice parathas; open 0600 for excellent breakfast; ***Geetha*** and ***Susil***, rooftop or inside, good service and food, reasonable prices.

On Gandhi Rd: *Nanking*, (Chinese); ***Chinatown***, a/c, small, friendly (play your own music tapes) – excellent food, good service, very reasonable prices, highly rec; ***Jubilee***, rooftop restaurant – best early in evening, but service can be very slow; ***Dawn Bakery*** is rec for fresh bread and biscuits, wide range of cakes, also sardines, mineral water, fruit juices. Other bakers at *Long Bazar*. ***Bavarchee***, fast food, reasonable pizzas. ***Shimla***, tandoori, nan. Very good.

● Banks & money changers

Central Bank and **State Bank**, Ida Scudder Rd, E of CMCH exit. Central Bank is usually at least 10 min faster at changing travellers' cheques than the State Bank.

● Post & telecommunications

Post office: *CMC Hospital* has PO, stamps and parcels.

● Shopping

Most of the shops are along Main Bazar Rd and Long Bazar St with a large covered market S of the Bus Station. ***Poompuhar***, 48 Commissary Bazar Rd.

Shoes: ***Rolex Footwear*** made to measure leather sandals, Rs 120, next day.

Tailors: delivery from all tailors may be slower than promised – may need prompting. *Beauty*, Ameer Complex, Gandhi Rd. Cheapest good quality tailoring. The lady in charge speaks good English and can design from sketches. *Mr. Kanappan*, Gandhi Rd. Very friendly, good quality, a little more expensive. More expensive still is *Velan*, next to *Mr. Kanappan*.

● Sport

Swimming: at CHAD (Community Health and Development), excellent private pool Rs 250 per week. Popular with CMC medical students. Open early morning to late evening, closed lunch. Very good snack bar.

● Transport

Train Katpadi Junc to the N of town is on the broad gauge line between Madras and Bangalore. Buses into Vellore. **Madras (MC)**: *Bangalore-Madras Exp*, 6024 (AC/II), Daily, 1202, 2½ hr; *Brindavan Exp*, 2640 (AC/CC), daily, 1743, 2 hr; **Bangalore (C)**: *Brindavan Exp*, 2639 (AC/CC), daily, 0915, 4½ hr; *Madras-Bangalore Exp*, 6023 (AC/II), daily, 1558, 4¾ hr; it is also on the metre gauge line to **Villupuram** to the S, with daily passenger trains to **Tirupathi**, **Tiruvannamalai** and **Pondicherry**. The Cantonment Station is about a km S of the GPO.

Road Bus: the Bus Station is off Long Bazar St, E of the Fort. Buses to Tiruchirappalli, Tiruvannamalai, Bangalore, Madras, Ooty, Thanjavur and Tirupathi. The regional state bus company PATC run frequent services to Kanchipuram from 0500 (2½ hr) and also several a day to Madras and Bangalore.

Vellore to Bangalore

Ambur

50 km; *Population*: 75,700; *STD Code*: 04176. This is an important centre of the leather tanning industry. There is also a large sugar milling co-operative, and sugar cane is widely grown. Ambur is the headquarters of the Syrian and Orthodox Apostolic Church of the Indies. There is a large Muslim population throughout the Palar valley and a significant Christian minority. Churches, mosques and madrassas are common sights.

The NH 45 passes SW through the intensively cultivated valley of the Palar River. To the S and E are the rising mass of the Javadi Hills and their outliers, reaching up towards Vellore. Shortly after passing **Vaniyambadi** (16 km; *Population*: 92,100), another major centre of the leather industry, there is a left turn to the railway junction of Jolarpet and the district market town of **Tiruppattur** (*Population*: 55,000). Just S of Jolarpet is the tiny hill 'resort' of **Yelagiri** (Elagiri), in the Javadi Hills. The hills themselves are still relatively isolated and populated by tribals. The hamlet of Yelagiri is at the foot of the hills, but the winding road up to the top gives superb views, and the flat topped hills have a completely different feel from the plains below. **Accommodation F** TTDC *Hotel Tamil Nadu*.

The NH 45 turns W to **Krishnagiri** (51 km; *Population*: 60,200) famous for cattle. **Accommodation E** TTDC *Hotel Tamil Nadu*, T 2079, some a/c rm with bath (day tariff available), restaurant.

Excursion to Hogenakkal

ROUTES The route S to the district capital of Dharmapuri is the most convenient way of getting to the remote Hogenakkal Falls on the Kaveri. If you are looking for peace and quiet and an undisturbed day or 2, the falls provide an ideal spot, the point at which the Kaveri takes its last plunge down the plateau edge to the plains, 250m above sea level. There is a beautiful forested drive down from Pennargaram to the falls, where the water drops 20m through a long zig zag canyon. **Hogenakkal** ('smoke that thunders' in Kannada) is an apt description. **Accommodation D** *Hotel Tamil Nadu*, Pennagaram, T 47, some a/c rm, with bath, with restaurant and **D** *Youth Hostel*, clean and very good value.

Hosur

From Krishnagiri the road goes NW to Hosur (50 km; *Population*: 37,200; *STD Code*: 04344). Until the early 1970s Hosur was a sleepy town in a backward district. Since then a huge industrial estate has been opened by the Tamil Nadu Govt, bringing large scale industrial investment from other parts of India and abroad. The town has grown rapidly, benefitting partly from the nearness of Bangalore (40 km) (see page 997). Many managers still commute from Bangalore. **Accommodation E** TTDC *Hotel Tamil Nadu*, Hosur, a small, non-a/c complex, basic.

TIRUCHIRAPPALLI TO MADURAI (Eastern Route)

ROUTES There are several options for travelling S from Tiruchirappalli to Madurai. The eastern and central routes are much less busy than the national highway which runs through Dindigul and to the W of the beautiful Sirumalai Hills. The eastern route goes through the former small princely state of Pudukkottai and the district known as **Chettinadu** (the land of the Chettiars), a trading community that has the reputation as one of India's wealthiest clans. Remarkable houses remain in the district (see below).

Leave Tiruchirappalli past the aerodrome, cutting straight across the unirrigated land beyond the reach of the Kaveri canals. Industries are growing on

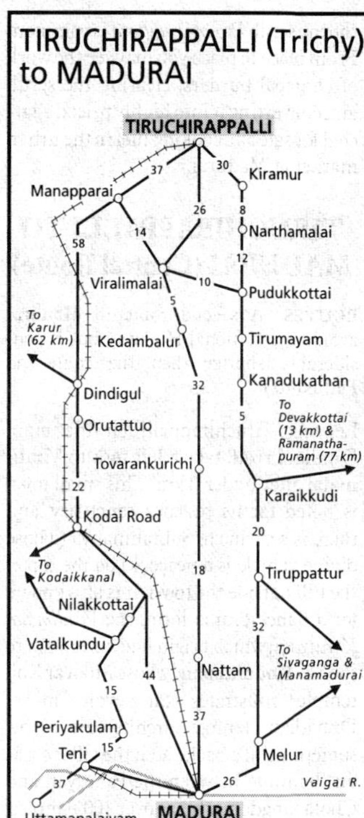

either side. Close by Kiranur (30 km) is the Kunnandarkoil cave temple, built in the 8th century AD, with the later addition of a Vijayanagar mandapa. Some of the bronzes in the temple are also excellent. Straight on to Narthamalai (8 km), which has an important Chola temple. The most significant stone figures are in the Govt museum in Pudukottai. In the hills near Narthamalai are some Jain caves.

Pudukkottai

(12 km; *Population*: 98,600; *STD Code*: 04322) The capital of the former princely state ruled by the Tondaiman Rajas, founded by Raghunatha Raya Tondaiman in 1686. At one entrance to the town is a ceremonial arch raised by the Raja in honour of Queen Victoria's jubilee celebrations. The town's broad streets suggest a planned history. The temple is at the centre, with the old palace and a tank. The new palace has become the office of the District Collector.

Local industries There is a TVS bus factory, making luxury buses for export.

Places of interest The natural rock shelters, caves and Neolithic burial sites show that there was very early human occupation. ***Sittannavasal*** where Jain monks found refuge nearby, is rich in Pallava finds, especially the very fine frescoes in the shrine. The triangle *Pudukottai-Kiranur-Kodumbalur* has a number of early Chola and late Pallava monuments.

Museum The museum has a wide range of exhibits, including sections on geology, zoology and the economy as well as sculptures and the arts. The archaeology section has some excellent sculptures from nearby temples, including those from Narthamalai. There is a notable carving of Siva as *Dakshinamurti* and some fine bronzes from Pudukottai itself.

Local festivals Jan-Feb The area has bullock races (*manju virattu*).

• **Transport Train** Madras (ME): *Sethu Exp*, 6114, daily, 2101, 9¼ hr; **Ramesvaram**: *Ramesvaram Exp*, 6101, daily, 0751, 5½ hr. **Road** Pudukkottai is well connected by bus with Tiruchirappalli, Thanjavur, Madurai, Ramnad and Ramesvaram.

Chettinad country

Karaikkudi (*Population*: 110,500; *STD Code*: 04565) is in the heart of Chettinad country. Many of the villages that were once the homes of fabulously wealthy merchant families are now semi-deserted. **Kanadukathan** (*Population*: 6,500) for example, 5 km N of Karaikkudi, has a number of magnificent mansions, some of them empty except for bats, monkeys – and antique dealers. It has been estimated that the Burma teak and satinwood pillars in just one of the village's Chettiar houses weighed 300 tonnes. The plaster on the walls is made from a mixture of lime, eggwhite, powdered shells and myrobalan fruit (the astringent fruit of the tree *Phyllantles emblica*), mixed into a paste which, when dried, gave a gleaming finish. One of the specialities of the houses was the quality of their woodcarving, notably on the doors. Traditionally in the jewellery and trading business, Chettiars now own a variety of large companies. The existence of 11 banks in the town illustrates the wealth that has flowed into it. Some of that money continues to be channelled back to this remote region, but there is an air of decay and dilapidation about many of the finest houses.

Local industry Karaikkudi is quite an important industrial centre. Processing betelnuts and chewing tobacco. There are noted diamond cutters and goldsmiths, over 2000 handlooms and several dyeing factories, and a wide range of food processing industries. The modern Electro Chemical Research Institute is open to visitors.

• **Transport Train** The *Rameswaram Exp* connects Madras with Pudukottai. **Road Bus**: bus routes link the town with every part of the State.

The road goes W to **Melur** (*Population*: 32,800; *STD Code*: 04548) across open agricultural land. Bright red soils are common – generally the result of deep weathering of the iron-rich gneiss underneath. During the rains it becomes very marshy but bakes hard as rock during the long hot and dry periods. There are patches of laterites, almost impossible to cultivate and giving rise to expanses of bare flat land. Isolated tanks, such as the particularly beautiful tank W of Melur, add light, colour and coolness to an otherwise often dry landscape. On the land beyond the reach of reliable irrigation, thorny scrub *Prosopis juliflora* is common. From place to place you may see the work of charcoal burners, clearing the scrub and converting it into highly priced charcoal for sale as a cooking fuel in the urban market of Madurai.

TIRUCHIRAPPALLI TO MADURAI (Central Route)

ROUTES A second route to **Madurai** avoids the National Highway but is considerably shorter than the route via Pudukottai.

Leaving Tiruchirappalli on the main Dindigul road, take a left fork to **Viralimalai** after under 2 km. This small town is noted for its peacock sanctuary, and there is a shrine to Subrahmanya (whose divine vehicle is a peacock) on the top of the hill outside the town. It is also known for a dance drama form, the *Viralimalai Kuravanji*, which originated here. 5 km to the S is **Kodumbalur**, whose Moovar Koil temple illustrates the evolution of Dravidian temple architecture. Now something of a backwater, the village was on the route between the Pandiyan and Chola kingdoms. It has over 100 temples, and was once the capital of the Irukkuvel dynasty.

The road passes through quiet, attractive open country. It passes through Tovarankurichchi and Natham, where drinks and fruit are available at the bus stand. The road continues over the rolling country and unirrigated farm land to Madurai. The local bus ride over the whole route is easy and often quite uncrowded, and gives an interesting view of an area off the beaten track. The road from Natham crosses the Periyar Main channel about 6 km after passing through the village of Chattrapatti. It enters Madurai in the NE at the *Pandiyan Hotel* and *Tamil Nadu Tourist Complex*.

TIRUCHIRAPPALLI TO MADURAI (Western Route)

ROUTES From Tiruchirappalli the NH45 goes SW to **Manapparai** (*Population*: 31,800; *STD Code*: 04332), famous for its cattle fairs and markets, held on Wednesdays. The cattle are often highly decorated, with bells and painted horns.

Dindigul

(56 km; *Population*: 182,300; *Altitude*: 300m; *STD Code*: 0451) Now a large market town, it commands a strategic gap between the Sirumalai Hills to its E and the Palani Hills to the W, both formed out of Charnockite rising from the plateau of granite. The market handles the produce of the Sirumalai Hills, mainly fruit. Sirumalai and the Palanis used to be famous for a particular variety of hill banana with a pinkish skin and a very distinctive flavour. Growing at a very limited range of altitude, their production has been decimated by disease.

Local industries
Tobacco, tanning and cotton industries are all important. Dindigul is particularly known for its cheroots. Iron safes and locks are also made in the town.

Places of interest
The fort The massive granite rock towers over 90m above the plain. Under the first Nayaka kings the near vertical sides were fortified, controlling the western province of the Nayaka kingdom. The importance of the site encouraged the Mysore army to attack and capture it in 1745 and Haidar Ali was appointed Governor in 1755. He used it as the base from which to capture Madurai itself, and is reputed to have disposed of the prisoners he took by throwing them over the side of the cliff. It changed hands with the British twice in the late 1780s before being ceded to the British under the Treaty of Seringapatam. There are magnificent views of the town, the valley and the hills on either side from the top of the rock fort. **Our Lady of Dolours Church**, one of several churches in the town, is over 250 years old and was rebuilt in 1970.

- **Accommodation & food** Several tea shops and small restaurants nr the bus stand.

- **Transport Train** Madras (ME): *Vaigai Exp*, 2636 (AC/CC), daily, 0745, 6¾ hr; Tiruchirappalli: *Vaigai Exp*, 2636 (AC/CC), daily, 0745, 1½ hr; **Madurai**: *Vaigai Exp*, 2635 (AC/CC), daily, 1900, 1¼ hr. Now broad gauge to **Karur**, 1700, 2 hr. **Road Bus**: good and frequent bus service to Tiruchirappalli, Madras, Salem and Coimbatore as well as longer distance connections.

From Dindigul the NH 45 goes S to **Orutattu** with the 500m *Rishimalai* ('Rishi Hill') hill on the right. From **Kodai Road** Railway station buses leave for Kodaikkanal. It then runs through beautiful and lush countryside, irrigated by the **Peranai Main channel** which the road crosses near the village of Andipatti.

This channel, built in 1897, was made possible by the Periyar River Scheme at Thekkadi. A scheme of reversing the flow of the Periyar by digging a tunnel under the top of the Cardamom Hills was first mooted at the beginning of the 19th century. It diverted water that would otherwise have flowed to the W coast eastwards down the channel of the Vaigai. When completed it irrigated over 50,000 ha mainly in Madurai District. The water has the unusual quality of being almost entirely silt free. In the 1960s a new dam near Periyakulam has helped to regulate the flow still further and to increase the irrigated area.

The **Vaigai River**, on which much of the agriculture to the E partly depends, has always been notoriously unreliable. The Ramnad Dist Gazetteer for 1910 reported the flow of the Vaigai with repeated comments like "No water in the Vaigai" (1823-24, 1834-35, 1885-86) or alternatively "Vaigai full – filled all the tanks in the district" (1841-42). That kind of variability has always been a handicap, and the benefits of increased control can be seen from the fields around Madurai which receive the channelled water. The alluvium of the Vaigai reaches up the valleys from the sea almost as far as Madurai and NE in a broad band across the low tableland inshore from the sea. To the right of the road after Andipatti is the long spine of *Nagamalai* (snake hill), a ridge of pink granite running SE towards Madurai (63 km).

Madurai

(*Population*: 1.094mn; *Altitude*: 100m; *STD Code*: 0452) Madurai's main claim to fame is as a temple town, though it has become a major industrial city. The greatest of the Nayaka rulers, Tirumalai (r 1623-55) was responsible for building the *gopurams* of the temple. After the Carnatic Wars the British destroyed the fort in 1840, filling in the surrounding moat now followed by the 4 Veli streets. They still mark the boundary of the old city, which lies to the S of the river Vaigai. The Nayakas laid out the old town in the pattern of a lotus with narrow streets surrounding the Minakshi Temple at the centre. The streets on the 4 sides of the central temple are named after the festivals which take place in them and give their relative direction, eg S Masi St, E Avanimoola St and E Chitrai St.

History

Madurai is situated on the banks of the river Vaigai. Its history goes back to the 6th century BC when it traded with Greece and Rome. According to legend drops of nectar fell from Siva's locks on this site, so it was named 'Madhuram' Madurai, or the nectar city. Ancient Madurai was a centre of Tamil culture, famous for its writers, poets and temple builders and was the literary and cultural centre during the last of the 3 *Sangam* periods (Tamil Academies) nearly 2000 years ago (see page 841). The Pandiyas made it their capital and held it for several centuries against their neighbours, the Pallavas and Cholas to the E, and the Cheras to the W, becoming a major power from the 6th to the beginning of the 10th century. They remained in their capital Madurai until the 14th century although they were subservient to the Cholas who gained control over the area from the beginning of the 10th century and ruled for nearly 300 years, after which the Pandiyans returned to power. Malik Kafur completely destroyed the city in 1310, following which there was a short period when it became a Sultanate. In 1364 it was captured by Hindu Vijayanagar Kings, who retained power until 1565. Their local governors the Nayakas then asserted their independence.

The Nayakas have been seen essentially as warriors, given an official position by the Vijayanagar Govt. The term *nayaka* was used in Karnataka at least 300 years before the Vijayanagar empire was established, but in origin it is a Sanskrit term applied to someone of prominence and leadership. Although in the mid-16th century there may have been as many as 200 nayakas, throughout the Vijayanagar period only 27 have been mentioned in inscriptions. As Burton Stein comments, "the history of the Vijayanagara state is essentially the his-

CLIMATE: MADURAI

	Jan	Feb	Mar	Apr	May	Jun	Jul	Aug	Sep	Oct	Nov	Dec	Av/Tot
Max (°C)	30	32	35	36	37	37	36	35	35	33	31	30	34
Min (°C)	21	22	23	25	26	26	26	25	25	24	23	22	24
Rain (mm)	26	16	21	81	59	31	48	117	123	179	161	43	905

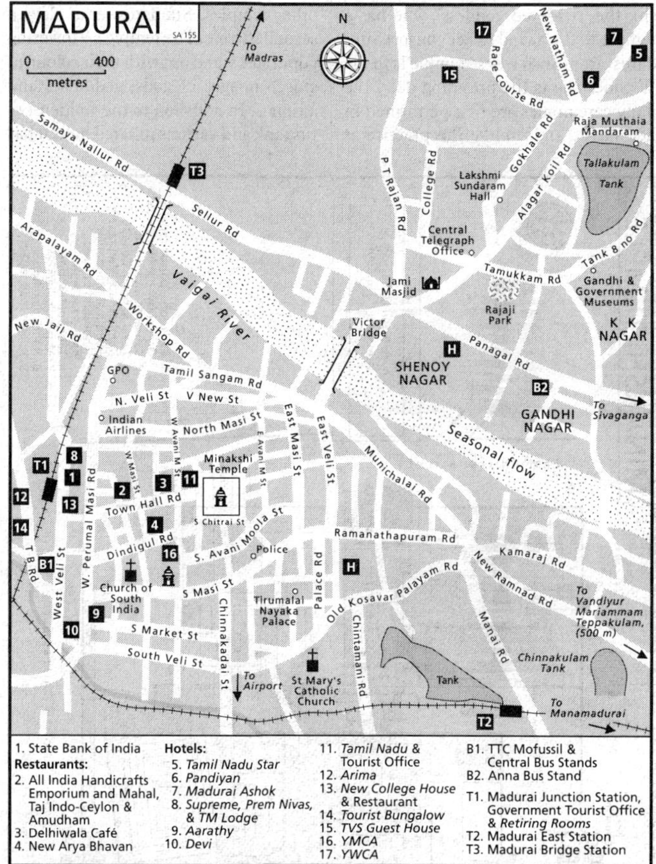

tory of the great Telugu Nayakas, their formidable military capabilities, their patrimonial power, and their relations to religious leaders in a new level of authority everywhere in the S peninsula". The Vijayanagar kings were great builders and preserved and enriched the architectural heritage of the town.

Local industries

Several spinning mills produce a variety of yarn for the handloom and industrial sectors – fine cottons, embroidery threads, sophisticated blends for medical sutures, tyre cord and fibres for parachutes. Other engineering industries include sugar and chemicals.

Places of interest

The **Minakshi Temple** is an outstanding example of Vijayanagar temple architecture. The massive gopurams are profusely decorated (some say with as many as 33 million carvings, including an encyclopaedia of dancing poses). It is dedicated to the consort of Siva, Minakshi, the 'fish-eyed goddess', who has a temple to the S, and to her consort Sundaresvarar (Siva) whose temple is to the W. Since she is the presiding deity the daily ceremonies are first performed in her shrine and, unlike the practice at other temples, Sundareswarar plays a secondary role. The temple's 9 towering gopurams stand out with their colourful stucco images of gods, goddesses and animals. In addition to the Golden Lotus tank and various pillared halls it has

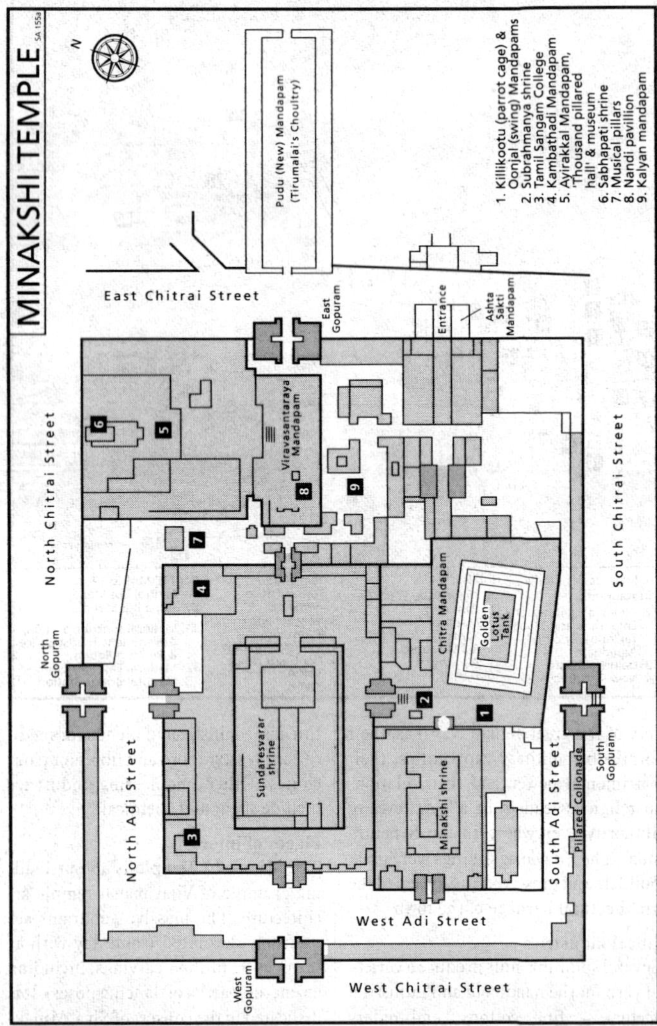

5 vimanas over the sanctum sanctorums.

NB: Inner Temple open 0430-1230, 1600-2130.

The main entrance to the temple is through a small door (porch of the 8 goddesses) which projects from the wall, S of the E *gopuram*. Inside, to your left is the sacred tank of the Golden Lotus, with a lamp in the centre, surrounded by pillared cloisters and steps down to the waters. The *Sangam* legend speaks of the test that ancient manuscripts had to undergo – they were thrown into the sacred tank, if they sank they were worthless, if they floated they were considered worthy! (See page 802). The N gallery has 17th century murals, relating 64 miracles said to have been performed by Siva, and the southern has marble inscriptions of the 1330 couplets of the *Tamil Book of Ethics*. To the W of the tank is the *Kulikka* or *Yali Mandapa*, the pavilion leading to the Minakshi shrine. Here the pillars are carved in the form of the mythical beast *yali* which recurs in temples throughout the region. You will also see parrots, Minakshi's green bird which brings luck, in cages hanging from the ceiling. The Minakshi shrine stands in its own enclosure with smaller shrines around it. To the N of the tank is another enclosure with smaller *gopurams* on 4 sides within which is the Sundareswarar shrine. The sculpture of the divine marriage of Minakshi and Sundareswarar being blessed by Vishnu and Brahma and Siva in his 24 forms are in the *Kambathadi Mandapa* (19th century), around the flagstaff in front of the Sundareswarar Shrine.

The 'thousand pillared hall' in the NE corner dates from the mid-16th century. Each column is exquisitely carved. Note Siva riding a peacock, Parvati as a huntress playing the *vina*, a gypsy leading a monkey. The museum exhibits temple art and architecture, fine brass and stone images, friezes and photos. The labelling could be improved. Open 0800-2000. Re 1, Camera Rs 25 at the Temple office nr the S tower. Near the N *gopuram* are 5 clusters of pillars each set carved out of a single stone. Each produces a different note which vibrates when tapped. Nayaka musicians could play these as an instrument. The *Nandi* pavilion is to the E and is often occupied by flower sellers. The long *Pudu Mandapa* (New Mandapa), with its beautiful sculptures of *yalis* and Nayaka rulers and their ministers, is outside the enclosure wall, between the E tower and the base of the unfinished *Raya Gopuram* which was planned to be the tallest in the country.

The temple is a hive of activity, with a colourful temple elephant, flower sellers, and performances by musicians, who are often excellent, from 1800-1930, 2100-2200. At 2115 an image of Sundareswarar is carried from the shrine near the E *gopuram* to Minakshi to sleep by her side, which is returned the next morning. Camera fee Rs 10 at the temple office near the S Tower. Good views from the top of the S Gate when open.

About 1 km SE of the Minakshi temple is the **Tirumalai Nayaka Palace**, built in 1636 in the Indo-Mughal style. Its 15 domes and arches are adorned with stucco work while some of its 240 columns rise to 12m. Its *Swarga Vilasam* (Celestial Pavilion), an arcaded octagonal structure, is curiously constructed in brick and mortar without any supporting rafters. Special artisans skilled in the use of traditional lime plaster and powdered sea shell and quartz have been commissioned by the Archaeological Dept for renovation. The original complex had a shrine, an armoury, a theatre, royal quarters, a royal bandstand, a harem, a pond and a garden but only about a quarter survives since Tirumalai's grandson removed sections to build another palace in Tiruchirappalli. Open 0900-1300, 1400-1700. Ten min walk from Temple. Bus 17, 17a, 11, 11a. (For Museum and Sound and Light Show, see below under Museums and Entertainment). **Vandiyur Mariam-**

mam **Teppakulam** to the SE of town, which has a small shrine in its centre where the annual *Float Festival* takes place in Jan/Feb. Buses 4 and 4A take 10 min from the Bus Stand and Rly Station.

Museums

Best of 3 is the excellent Gandhi Museum, Old Palace of Rani Mangammal built 300 years ago. Contains an art gallery, memorabilia (Gandhi's *dhoti* when he was shot), traces history of Independence struggle from 1800, also Quit India exhibition; same management as one at Delhi and is equally good; Also a Khadi and Village Industries Section and one of South Indian handicrafts. 0900-1300, 1300-1830, closed Wed. Government Museum in the same complex was opened in 1981. 1030-1300, 1400-1730, closed Fri. Bus No 1, 2 and 3. Thirumalai Nayak Palace Museum concentrates on the history of Madurai with galleries on the famous Nayaka King and the art and architecture of Tamil Nadu. Bus No 4.

Parks and zoos

Rajaji Park opp Temkum Ground.

Excursions

There are some excellent walks and scrambles around Madurai. One of the most accessible is up **Yanai Malai** (elephant hill), the gneiss outcrop to the E of Madurai that looks like a seated elephant. Take the road out of Madurai across the Vaigai and turn right immediately. The road leaves Madurai and runs along the S edge of the hill. Approx 1 km after reaching the W end of the hill a road turns sharp left straight to a village at the bottom of the hill. Approach for first 15 min is up cut out steps – last 15 min is a steep climb up a very precarious slope (as demanding as Uluru, ie Ayers Rock!). The top gives superb views across the cultivated plain below. It is a beautiful early morning outing between Dec and Mar, but gets very hot later in the day.

NB: Only for the fit and active; wear boots or gripping shoes.

Koodal Alagar Temple 20 km to the W of Madurai (Bus No 44) is an ancient Vaishnavite Temple with beautiful sculptures of Vishnu.

Tour

Apr-Jun TTDC *Kodaikkanal*. 0700-2100.

Local festivals

Jan/Feb At Vandiyur Mariammam Teppakulam. The annual *Float Festival* marks the birth anniversary of Thirumalai Nayak, who originated it. Many temple deities in silks and jewels, including Minakshi and Sundaresvarar, are taken out on a full moon night on floats colourfully decorated with hundreds of oil lamps and flowers. The floats carry them to the central shrine to the accompaniment of music and chanting. The *Jallikattu Festival* (Taming the Bull) is held in Jan.

Apr/May *Chithrai Festival* The most important at the Minakshi Temple is the 10-day festival which celebrates the marriage of Siva and Minakshi in the Kalyana Mandapa, when pilgrims come to the banks of the river.

Aug/Sep The *Avanimoolam* is the Coronation Festival of Siva when the image of Lord Sundareswarar is taken out to the river bank dressed as a worker.

Local information

● Accommodation

The better hotels are N of the river, about 3 km from centre. Auto rickshaws, about Rs 15, but ask for more. Alternatively, City Buses will take you there.

A *Taj Garden Retreat*, Pasumalai Hills, 6 km town centre, T 88256, F 88601, 30 rm, the best in town.

C *Pandiyan*, Race Course, T 42471, 57 comfortable rm, testaurant, pleasant garden; **C** *Madurai Ashok*, Alagarkoil Rd, T 42531, 43 rm, central, a/c, restaurant, pool.

D *Supreme*, 110 W Perumal Maistry St, T 36331, 69 rm, some good a/c, central, nr rly, restaurants (meals at veg *Rooftop* with good views, open in evening, rec), exchange, travel, shops, 24-hr international phone from basement, rec; **D** TTDC *Tamil Nadu Star*, Alagarkoil Rd, nr Collector's Office, T 42461, 51 rm, some a/c, restaurant, bar, exchange, travel, shop, not conveniently placed, though quiet.

E ***Prem Nivas***, 102 W Perumal Maistry St, T 37531, clean rm with bath, some a/c, restaurant, basic but good value; **E** ***Aarathy***, 9 Perumalkoil W Mada St, T 31571, nr Bus Station, clean, comfortable rm, some a/c with balcony, all with bath, restaurant, friendly staff, rec; **E** ***Arima***, 4 TB Rd, T 23261, 37 rm, some a/c; **E** ***TM Lodge***, 50 W Perumal Maistry St, T 31481, 57 rm, some a/c, some with TV; **E** ***Tamil Nadu***, W Veli St, T 37470, 44 rm, some a/c, central, nr Bus Stands, restaurant, bar, exchange, travel, rather dingy rms, can be noisy. ***YMCA***, Dindigul Rd, T 33649; ***YWCA***, Vallabahi Rd, T 24763.

● Budget hotels

Several other inexpensive hotels on W Perumal Maistry St and Town Hall Rd, in the heart of town, W of the temple, with plenty of places to eat in the locality. **E** ***Railway Retiring Rooms***, Madurai Junc Station, 1st Flr above Platform 1, 13 double rm, some a/c, can be very noisy; **E** ***New College House***, 2 Town Hall Rd, T 24311, 193 rm, some a/c (better rm on upper Flr), restaurant (Indian veg) rec, travel, basic, reasonably clean but gets crowded and noisy. Nearby **E** ***Sree Devi 20*** W. Avanimoola St, T 36743, has rm with bath (avoid noisy Grd Flr), no meals but good value, clean, modern towerblock, superb views from rooftop. Behind the Rly Station there is a Municipal **F** ***Tourist Bungalow***, 33 rm.

● Places to eat

Hotels particularly good on South Indian veg dishes, include ***Pandiya***, ***Madurai Ashok***, ***Tamil Nadu Star*** and ***New College House***. Good Indian restaurants are W of the temple, mainly along Town Hall Rd and W Veli St. On Town Hall Rd, the a/c ***Mahal*** and ***Amudham*** are rec. Also ***Taj***. Non-veg (*paratha* and mutton curry) at ***Muniyandi Vilas*** outlets and at ***Indo-Ceylon Restaurant***.

● Bars

There are **bars** in some of the hotels listed above.

● Banks & money changers

Branches of national banks with several on E Avanimoola St. Also **Central Bank of India**, 15 Minakshi Koil St. **State Bank of India**, 6 W Veli St

● Entertainment

Sound and Light Show: at Thirumalai Nayaka Palace (TTDC), it tells the story of *Silappathikaram* and the life of the Nayaka King Thirumalai. Timings: English 1845-1945. Tamil 2000-2100. Rs 3. During the day there are performances of dance drama and concerts in the courtyard.

Auditoria: ***Raja Muthaia Mandaram***, opp District Court. ***Lakshmi Sundaram Hall***, Tallakulam.

Several cinemas in Satamanglam and Muthuramalingam.

● Hospitals & medical services

Christian Mission Hospital, E Veli St. *Govt Rajaji Hospital*, Panagal Rd. *Grace Kennet Foundation Hospital*, 34 Kennet Rd.

● Post & telecommunications

Post office: the town GPO is at the N end of W Veli St. In Tallakulam there is another Head Post Office and the Central Telegraph Office, on Gokhale Rd.

● Shopping

Best buys are textiles, carvings in wood and stone, brass images, jewellery and appliqué work for temple chariots. Most of the shops are on S Avanimoola St (for jewellery), Town Hall Rd and Masi St, in and around the Temple, where you will find the ***All India Handicrafts Emporium*** at 39-41 Town Hall Rd. ***Poompuhar Sales Emporium***, ***Khadi Gramodyog Bhandar*** and ***Surabhi*** (Kerala Handicrafts) on W Veli St. Also ***Cooptex*** shops on W Tower St and S Chitrai St and ***Pandiyan Co-op Supermarket***, Palace Rd. ***Hajee Moosa***, 18 Chitrai St, nr E Gate, is a large textile Department Store. Tailoring in 8 hr. Other facilities at the store include exchange, export enquiries, hotel and travel reservations and laundry! They also have a Cutpiece Centre at 15 Chitrai St and Readymades at ***Shabnam***, No 17. Another similar store selling textiles, clothing and gifts is ***Femina***, 10 W Chitrai St. They invite you to take aerial view photos of the Minakshi Temple from their rooftop. Near the new ***mandapa*** there are tailors' shops where you can choose some material and have a made-to-measure garments sewn up in a few hours.

Sweets ***Delhiwala Sweets***, W Tower St for delicious cheap sweets and snacks.

● Sports

Swimming: public pool nr Gandhi Museum, Rs 10 per hr. **TTDC Children's Park**: Vandiyur Kanmoy with restaurant, toy train and boating.

● **Tour companies & travel agents**
Trade Wings, 279 N Masi St, T 30271; *South India Travel Agency*, W Veli St, T 22345.

● **Tourist offices**
Tamil Nadu, W Veli St, T 22957, 1000-1750, closed Sun, 2nd Sat, Govt holidays, useful maps. Also at Madurai Junc Rly Station, Main Hall, 0630-2030. Information Counter at the Airport is open during flight times. Guides are available through the Tourist Office.

● **Transport**
The NH 45 and 7 cross at Madurai providing it with good links to the rest of the region. Bangalore 427 km, Coimbatore 227 km, Kanniyakumari 242 km, Madras 447 km, Ramesvaram 167 km, Tiruchirappalli 128 km, Tiruvananthapuram 259 km.

Local Bus: Pandiyan Roadways Corp has a good network within the city and the suburbs. **Taxi**: Unmetered taxis hire about Rs 250 per day plus km charge. For 5 km: Taxis charge approx Rs 50. **Rickshaw**: Cycle-rickshaws Rs 10 and auto rickshaws Rs 15; bargain first.

Air Airport to city centre (15 km) by Pandiyan Roadways Corp transfer coach (calls at top hotels) or autorickshaw. *Indian Airlines*, Office, 7A W Veli St, T 22795. 1000-1300, 1400-1700; Airport T 37433. **Madras**: daily, except Mon, 0840, 1 hr. *Air India*, opp Rly Station, W Veli St. *East West Airlines*: Office119, 1st Fl West Perumal Maistrya rd, T 24995, airport T 37433: **Bombay** via Tiruvananthapuram, daily, 1150, 3 hr.

Train Madurai Junc Rly Station, W Velit, Enquiries, T 37597. Reservations: I Class T 23535, II Class T 33535. 0700-1300, 1330-2000. **Madras (ME)**: *Vaigai Exp*, 2636 (AC/CC), daily, 0645, 7¾ hr; *Pearl City*: 6104 (AC/II), daily, 2045, 11 hr; **Ramesvaram**: *Tirupati-Ramesvaram Exp*, 6799, daily, 1030, 4¾ hr; *Ramesvaram Fast Pass*, 6115, daily, 0520, 6 hr; **Kollam**: *Kollam Mail*, 6105 (AC/II), daily, 0650, 8 hr; *6161 Exp*, daily, 2035, 8 hr; **Tirupati**: *Ramesvaram Exp*, 6800, daily, 1040, 18½ hr. *Tirupati Madurai Exp*.

Road Bus: State and Private Bus Companies such as TTC, MPTC, PRC run services to other cities. There are 4 main Bus Stations. The 3 Bus Stands for TTC, Mofussil and Central are in the centre on W Veli St. Buses to **Kodai** leave from outside New College House, 2 Town Hall Rd. Arrive early in Apr-Jul, 4 hr, Rs 60. The Anna Bus Stand is 3 km from centre. TTC Enquiries, T 25354. Reservations: 0700-2100, T 41730. Computerised reservation, Anna Bus Stand, T 43380. Mofussil Bus Stand Enquiries, T 36818. Periyar Bus Stand, T 35293. Pandiyan Roadways Corp, Anna Bus Stand, T 43622. Rani Mungammal Transport, T 33740.

MADURAI TO RAMESVARAM

Seen from the air the plains of the **Vaigai River** form one of the most remarkable landscapes in India, for there are over 5000 tanks, and irrigation has been so widely developed that scarcely a drop of water is wasted.

The coastal districts of Ramnad have their own highly distinct economy and society. Both Hindu and Muslim communities have long established trading links across the Bay of Bengal – to Malaysia and SE Asia and to Sri Lanka. Small towns and villages along the coast such as Kilakkarai have long been associated with smuggling. The civil war in Sri Lanka had made it a sensitive region.

Between Madurai and Manamadurai the road crosses and re-crosses 1 of the 96 canals which take off from the Vaigai river. Although the Vaigai is often dry by the time it reaches Madurai, the canals serve the vital function of leading flood water both directly to the fields and into the tanks for storage. When full the Vaigai presents a beautiful and imposing sight.

Manamadurai

(45 km; *Population*: 22,800) Takes its name from the story of the Ramayana, which tells how Hanuman the monkey god stopped here with his monkey allies on his way to Lanka to rescue Sita. In the **Perumal Temple** Hanuman is enshrined, with the highly unusual feature of a crown on his head, reflecting the local belief that Hanuman was crowned here before leaving for Lanka. According to one account the name of the town is derived from this visit, which in Tamil is described as *Vanara Veera Madurai*, which has been corrupted to become Manamadurai.

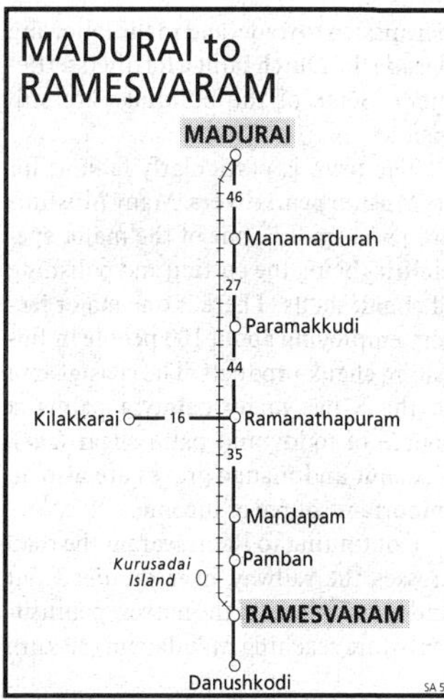

The crowned Hanuman is enshrined nr the entrance of the Vaishnavite Veera Alagar Koil temple on the E bank of the river. The bridge which crosses the river at this point was opened in 1927. Of the 3 large temples here, the biggest is the Somanathasvami temple, built by 2 brothers between 1783-1801, which has a gopuram of 15m. Inside, the *Nandimandapa* and the *Kalyanamandapa* were added in 1900.

The town is particularly noted for its **ceramics**, the red clay soil being well suited to pottery, tiles and bricks. Along the road you may well see bricks being fired in the local way, which is to build a large hollow pile of bricks, as large as a big house, covered with thatch and with wood and charcoal underneath. This is then set fire and burns for many hours until the bricks are baked. Modern industries include cement pipe manufacture and brass ware. There are several small restaurants, the best veg.

The road continues SE to **Paramakkudi** (*Population*: 72,000), probably taking its name ('embankment town') from its position on the Vaigai. There are small restaurants and tea shops and a traveller's bungalow, post and telegraph office. The road and rail run through a scatter of villages. Tanks remain vital to the success of agriculture. Although this remote part of SE Ramnad is widely regarded as one of South India's most backward districts, the area has opened up dramatically in the last 30 years. The frequent bus service has brought all the villagers within easy reach of Madurai, and Ramnad has become an important market. Many farmers are now able to take their crop direct to market.

As a result there have been big changes in the cropping pattern. East of Paramakkudi is one of the driest regions of SouthEast India – though if you are travelling in Oct or Nov you might not believe it, as 500 mm of rain has been known to fall in 24 hrs. However, beyond the reach of tank irrigation crops have to resist drought. Traditionally that meant growing varieties of rice that would survive long periods without water and still give some return. Now however it is common to find oilseeds and millets being grown for market as quick growing crops for sale in the market. Another important crop in this area is chillies, again bringing a very good cash return from sale in the cities. An additional problem for the farmers is that although many could now afford pumpsets the groundwater is very salty in many areas, and therefore unusable for drinking or irrigation.

Ramanathapuram (Ramnad)

(*Population*: 52,600; *Altitude*: 10m; *STD Code*: 04567) The nearest market, is only 16 km from the sea, and now a bustling market town, with shops, restaurants and cinema. It is the terminus for several bus routes. After the eruption of the civil war in Sri Lanka the district became the centre for Tamil refugees from Sri Lanka. Between 1985 and 1987 there were over 160,000 refugees in camps through the district. Those numbers decreased sharply after the Indo-Sri

Lankan Accord of July 1987, but then rose again. Ramnad will continue to be affected as long as the political crisis in northern Sri Lanka remains unresolved.

Local industry Coarse cloth is made in the town and there is a recently built spinning mill. Palm leaf products are made as a cottage industry, and Ramnad is centre for the chilli trade.

Places of interest Between 1674 and 1710 Raghunatha Setupati, a local chieftain, built a **fort** of brick and stone (a commodity in short supply in these alluvial plains) nearly 2 km W of the present town, but it now lies in ruins. In the centre was an extensive palace with high stone walls, still visible, along with some of the artillery. **Christ Church** (now CSI) was built by Colonel Martinez, a French Catholic army officer, but handed over and dedicated as a Protestant Church in 1804 under the governorship of Lord William Bentinck. **Accommodation** There is a comfortable 3-rm **F** *Traveller's Bungalow*.

Kilakkarai

(*Population*: 29,800) is a strikingly distinct small coastal settlement, reached by the road that goes due S from Ramnad town. The entire coastline here has been emerging steadily from the sea, perhaps by as much as 15m. Fossils of various species of oysters, which now live at depths of 10m, are found inland at heights of up to 5m. The uplift is responsible for converting the living coral into solid rock, and made the link between Ramesvaram and Pamban Island. (This was followed by the railway line until a catastrophic cyclone and storm surge destroyed it in 1963) The name *Kilakkarai* simply means 'East coast'. The majority of the population is Muslim and there are 12 mosques in the town as well as a 16th century temple dedicated to Siva, and a number of other temples. From 1759 the Setupati chiefs gave the Dutch East India Company permission to trade, and in the following decade the Dutch built a fortified settlement. Some of the buildings are still visible.

The town is particularly famous for its Muslim **pearl divers**. Many Muslims are jewel traders, one of the major specialities being the cutting and polishing of chank shells. There is one major factory employing about 100 people in finishing chank products. The coastal area to the S has many palmyra palms, a source of toddy and palm sugar (*gur*). Coconut and mango groves are also an important source of income.

Continuing to Ramesvaram the road crosses the railway, over the dead flat and marshy land of the narrow peninsular before reaching Mandapam (30 km).

Mandapam

(*Population*: 20,400) Since the mid 1960s this has been the main port of entry for Tamil tea estate workers from the central highlands of Sri Lanka who have been repatriated to India under the agreement signed between the Indian and Sri Lankan govts in 1965. There was a Sri Lankan Govt quarantine **camp** here. As a result of the Sri Lankan crisis access to Mandapam, one of the main crossing points from Sri Lanka and camps for 'returnees' is now strictly controlled.

It is predominantly a Muslim **fishing** village, the long Ramesvaram island providing sheltered fishing even during the strong NE monsoon. The main catch is silverbelly, a non-edible variety of fish converted into fish meal. An Indo-Norwegian project has established a plant that sells fish meal across the country. Prawns have also become an important source of foreign exchange. The Marine Biological Research Centre is also here. To the S lie a chain of small coral islands, one of the few coral areas of India. **Kurusadai Islands** W of the Pamban bridge, between the mainland and Ramesvaram can be reached via Mandapam. They are surrounded by coral reefs and the shallow waters harbour a wealth of marine life of interest to scientists – starfish, crabs, sponges, sea cucumbers, algae and sea cow. Approach the Fisheries Dept for permission.

Museum Central Marine Fisheries Research Institute has a museum and aquarium at Mandapam, which includes seaweeds, corals, sponges, fishes and a pair of live sea cows (*dugongs*). **Accommodation F** TTDC *Youth Hostel*, T 92, with a dorm at Mandapam. Reservations: Manager or TTDC, 143 Anna Salai, Madras, T 830390.

Ramesvaram

(*Population*: 32,700; *STD Code*: 04573) A pilgrim to Varanasi is expected to visit Ramesvaram next where Rama worshipped Siva.

The Ramayana tells how the monkey king Hanuman built the bridges linking Ramnad to Pamban and Danushkodi (the spot where Rama is believed to have bathed; the name means 'Rama's bow', taken probably from the gently curving shape of the shoreline) in order to help rescue Sita from the demon king Ravana. When he returned he was told by the *rishis* that he must purify himself after committing the sin of Brahmanicide, for *Ravana* was the son of a Brahman. To do this he was advised to set up a lingam and worship Siva.

The red image of Hanuman N of the main E gate illustrates this story. According to popular belief the marks visible on the lingam today resulted from Hanuman's struggle. In order to pacify him Rama asked Hanuman to fix his lingam a little to the N of that made by Sita and ordered that all pujas should be offered first to the Hanuman lingam. Some say that as the Ramayana has been dated to the 3rd century BC the lingams must be over 2200 years old. Certainly the original shrine long predates the present great Ramesvaram temple, though there is no evidence as to the real age of the lingams. It is one of India's most sacred shrines, being visited by pilgrims from all over India and one of the 14 sacred temples of the Pandiyas. The temple benefitted from enormous donations from the Rajas of Ramanathapuram, the 17th century *Setupatis* ('guardians of the causeway', who derived their wealth from the right to levy taxes on crossing to the island). The island on which the temple stands is covered in low acacia shrubs, coconut palm and umbrella pines, and the temple stands on slightly higher ground, surrounded by a freshwater lake.

Places of interest

The **Ramalingesvara temple** (also known as Ramanathasvami temple) was founded by the Cholas but most of the temple was built in the Nayaka period (16th-17th centuries). It is a massive structure, enclosed by a huge rectangular wall with gopurams in the middle of 3 sides. Entrances through the E wall are approached through columned mandapas and the E gopuram is on the wall of the inner enclosure rather than the outer wall. Over 45m high, it was begun in 1640 but left incomplete until recently. The W gopuram is comparatively recent. In contrast the N and S gopurams were built by Keerana Rayar of the Dec-

CLIMATE: RAMESVARAM

	Jan	Feb	Mar	Apr	May	Jun	Jul	Aug	Sep	Oct	Nov	Dec	Av/Tot
Max (°C)	28	29	32	33	33	32	32	32	32	31	29	28	31
Min (°C)	24	24	25	27	27	27	26	26	26	26	24	24	26
Rain (mm)	66	23	18	46	25	3	13	15	28	216	297	193	943

Rama, Hanuman And The Lingam

Rama, the story goes, fixed an auspicious time and sent Hanuman to Mount Kailasa to fetch a ***lingam***. Hanuman failed to return on time, so again on the advice of the *rishis* he set up a lingam made by Sita. Soon Hanuman returned with a lingam, but was dejected to discover a lingam already in place; his journey had been in vain. He threatened to kill himself because of the dishonour shown him by Rama. Rama instructed him in the virtue of detachment; then he told the monkey that he could remove the linga fashioned by Sita and install in its place the one he had brought. Hanuman took hold of the sand linga with his hands and tried to move it; it would not budge. Then he wrapped his tail around it, touched the earth with his hands and jumped high in the heavens. The earth with its mountains and islands shook, and the monkey fell senseless near the lingas, his mouth, eyes, nostrils, ears and anus streaming with blood. Sita wept over the fallen monkey. Rama picked up his body and stroked it as he wept, covering Hanuman with his tears. Hanuman awoke from his faint, and seeing Rama in this state, sang his praises and those of Sita. Rama said: "This act of violence was committed by you in ignorance. None of the Gods could move this linga; you fell because you offended against Siva. This place where you fell will be known by your name; the Ganga, Yamuna and Sarasvati will unite there, and whoever bathes there will be free of evil. At Rama's command Hanuman set up the linga he had brought. The other linga still bears the marks of the monkey's tail." – David Shulman.

can in about 1420 AD.

The most remarkable feature of the temple is its pillared mandapas. In total these have been estimated to stretch for 1200m. The longest corridor is over 200m long. The pillars, nearly 4m tall, are raised on moulded bases and the shafts decorated with scrollwork and lotus motifs. They give an impression of almost unending perspective, those on the N and S being particularly striking. There are 2 gateways on the E side which give access to the Parvati and Ramalinga shrines at the centre. The masonry shrine is probably the oldest building on the site, going back to 1173.

On entering the E gate you see the statue of Hanuman, then the Nandi flanked by statues of the Nayaka kings of Madurai *Visvanatha* and *Krishnama*. The *Sphatikalinga Puja* is performed daily at 0500. Worshippers take a holy bath in the sea in a very calm bay 25 km away, where the waters are believed to wash away their sins. Fishermen occasionally offer to take visitors for a boat ride.

NB: Non-Hindus are not allowed beyond the first enclosure.

Gandhamadana Parvatam Just over 2 km N of Ramesvaram is an unimpressive looking single storeyed building on a low sand hill about 30m high, reached by a black top road from the temple. Its name is derived from the Sanskrit words *gandha* (fragrance) and *mad* (intoxicate), 'highly fragrant hill place'. Dedicated to Rama's feet, this is the spot from which Hanuman is believed to have surveyed the area before taking his leap across the narrow Palk strait to Sri Lanka. You can get an excellent view from the top of the mandapa.

Kotandaramasvami Temple (8 km) The 1964 cyclone completely washed away the southernmost tip of the Dhanuskodi island but the temple was untouched. The legend marks it as the spot where Ravana's brother Vibhishana surrendered to Rama hence the images of Rama, Sita, Lakshmana, Hanuman and Vibhishana.

Local information

● Accommodation

Budget hotels D TTDC *Tamil Nadu*, T 277, 18 rm, some a/c, clean, balconies overlook the sea, restaurant, sea bathing is possible nearby (when calm). **F** *Youth Hostel* with dorm. Both, especially the hotel, are heavily booked so you should book well in advance. Res: Manager, *Hotel Tamil Nadu*, Ramesvaram or Commercial Manager, TTDC, 143 Anna Salai, Madras, T 830390.

E *Maharaja's*, 7 Middle St, W of the Temple, T 271, 30 rm, some a/c with bath, travel, temple music broadcast on loudspeakers, otherwise rec; **E** *Santhya Lodge*, 1 W Car St, T 329, 22 double rm, some a/c, with bath, travel. *Devasthanam Lodges and Cottages*, T 241, 115 cottages some of which are **E** category, modern with a/c rm. Res: Executive Officer, Devasthanam, Ramesvaram, T 223.

F *Railway Retiring Rooms*, T 226, 9 rm and dorm. Several other small Indian style hotels without restaurants, some of which offer triple or family rm on W Car St, N Car St, S Car St and Bazar St. In addition there are *dharmasalas* most of which cater for religious groups.

● Places to eat

Hotel Tamil Nadu, restaurant open to non-residents but you may need to order in advance. The *Devasthanam Trust* has a canteen opp the E gate of the temple. For Indian veg food, some specialising in food from Gujarat, Rajasthan and Andhra try *Ashok Bhawan* and *Vasantha Vihar* on W Car St and *Vasantha Bhawan* at the Central Bus Stand. Others are *Arya Bhawan* and *Lakshmi Mess*.

● Banks & money changers

State Bank of India on N Car St and **Indian Bank**, W Car St.

● Hospitals & medical services

Govt Hospital nr the Rly Station.

Post & telecommunications

Office is on Mela St. 0930-1730.

● Shopping

Local crafts include conch shells, beads and articles made of banana fibre and palm leaf can be bought from shops near the E Gate of the Temple. *Khadi Kraft*, E Car St, close to the temple; *Cottage Industries* and *Sea Shell Industries*, Middle St. Tamil Nadu Handicrafts Dev Corp shop, *Poompuhar* operates during festival time.

● Tourist office

Tamil Nadu, E Car St, T 371. 1000-1700. Rly Station Counter. Open (with breaks) 0700-2030.

● Transport

Mandapam (19 km) is connected by road to various towns in the S. The Indira Gandhi road bridge across the Pamban Strait, opened in 1988, has made Ramesvaram accessible by road from other parts of the S via the NH 49.

Local Bus: services of the Marudhu Pandiyan Transport Corporation (MPTC) cover the town and its surrounding area. The Bus Station is 2 km W of the town. You can get a bus from the Rly Station to the Ramalingesvara Temple, to Pamban via the temple or to Dhanushkodi via the temple. Also services from outside the Temple's main E Gate to Dhanushkodi roadhead every 1½ hr and to Gandhamadhana Parvatham every 2 hr. **Taxis**: a few cars and jeeps are available from the Rly Station and hotels. **Tongas**, **Cycle rickshaws** and **Auto rickshaws** are easily available. You can hire a **bicycle** by the hour from W Car St.

Air Madurai (154 km) has the nearest airport.

Train Ramesvaram Rly Station, Enquiries and Reservations, T 226. Open 0800-1300, 1330-1730. **Madurai**: *Ramesvaram Exp*, 6800, daily, 0600, 4½ hr; *Coimbatore Fast Pass*, 6116, daily, 1610, 5¾ hr; **Madras**: *Sethu Exp*, 6114, daily, 1545, 14½ hr; **Tiruchirappalli**: *Ramesvaram Exp*, 6102, daily, 1230, 6½ hr; **Coimbatore**: *Coimbatore Fast Pass*, 6116, daily, 1610, 12¼ hr; **Tirupati**: *Ramesvaram-Tirupati*, 6800, daily, 0600, 23 hr.

Road Bus: the State owned TTC, MPTC and private bus companies run regular bus services via Mandapa to several towns in the region. There are frequent buses to Madurai, 173 km, (4 hr), 2 to Pondicherry and one to Thanjavur. Other services include Kanniyakumari 300 km, Madras 592 km, Ramanathapuram 37 km, Tiruchendur 205 km and 6 daily to Tiruchirappalli 258 km (3½ hr). The Central Bus Stand is 2 km from the main temple gate. TTC Reservations, N Car St. 0700-2100. MPTC, Central Bus Stand, Kartupilyar Kovil, no reservations.

MADURAI TO TIRUVANANTHAPURAM (Eastern route)

ROUTES The NH 7 crosses the central part of southern Tamil Nadu, the heart of the Pandiyan kingdoms from the 8th century. It passes through the major educational centre of Tirunelveli, with 4 centuries of Christian missionary activity and a large Christian population.

Almost on the outskirts of Madurai are the Pandiyan rock cut shrines of the 8th century AD, and the much later Nayaka Hindu temple at **Tiruparankunram** (*Population*: 30,000), with a wide range of Hindu gods carved on the walls. The Subrahmanya cave temple (773 AD) has a shrine dedicated to Durga, with the figures of Ganesh and Subrahmanya on either side. Other carvings show Siva dancing on the dwarf on the right hand side and Parvati and the Nandi with musicians on the left.

In **Tirumangalam** (*Population*: 34,500), a busy market town, the NH 7 forks left to Virudhunagar.

Virudhunagar (*Population*: 70,900). Meaning 'city of banners'. The town has a considerable history of civic pride and self-awareness. The municipality changed its name to Virudhunagar from *Virudhupatti* ('hamlet of banners') in 1915, and was upgraded to a full municipality in 1957, reflecting the upwardly mobile social status of the town's dominant local caste, the Nadars. Originally low caste toddy tappers, the Nadars have established a wide reputation as a dynamic and enterprising group. Their best known political leader was Kamaraj Nadar, the powerful Congress leader chiefly responsible for Mrs. Gandhi's selection as Prime Minister. Virudhunagar has become a very important commercial and industrial town – cotton ginning, textile mills, a steel rolling mill, paper and match factories have been joined by a range of new industries.

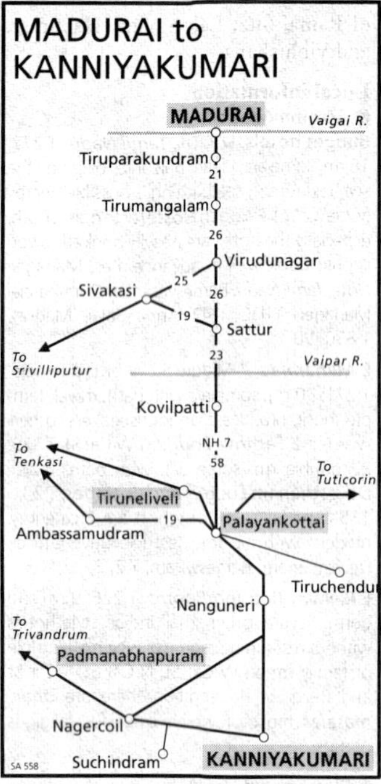

It makes an excellent base for visiting neighbouring temple towns. **Accommodation F** *Amyon Lodge*, 200m from Bus Stand opp Police Station, modern, clean, good value, rec. Also *Coronation Hotel*.

The road continues S through **Sattur** (*Population*: 29,200; *STD Code*: 04572), a district HQ, situated on the banks of the Vaipar River. Occasional floods devastate the town. 21 km S is **Kovilpatti** (*Population*: 78,000; *STD Code*: 04632) in the heart of the southern black cotton soil district. To the E is the driest region in the whole of South India, with as little as 550 mm rain a year in the port city of Tuticorin. The black soils (known as *regur*) around Kovilpatti are developed not from lavas but from the underlying gneiss, and are well suited to the common rotation of cotton, *bajra* and *sorghum*, which provide both foodgrain and fodder for animals. Cotton is widely irrigated, and electrification has encouraged the use of electric pumps to increase the efficiency of well irrigation.

The road to Tuticorin and the coast from Kovilpatti crosses the startlingly red soils leading to the *teri* of the coast. Much is just waste, but the *palmyra palm* is everywhere. One estimate suggests that there may be 10 million palmyra palms in Tirunelveli district alone. They are a vital resource for village economies. The broad fan-shaped leaves were used for writing early Tamil literature, but today they still serve for thatching, fencing, sunshades, basket making and mats. The fibres of the stem are used for making string, rope or brushes. The extremely sweet sap is sometimes drunk fresh, but more commonly it is allowed to ferment into the potent *toddy* or converted into sugar, or *jaggery*. The red *teri* soils are wind blown sands, though the dunes on the coast have often been fixed. They form small rolling plateaus, often occurring as thin deposits over the underlying sandstones which occur at heights of about 60m, suggesting that since the last Ice Age the land may have risen by this amount. They are a rich source of stone age tools.

Tuticorin (*Population*: 284,200; *STD Code*: 0461), is an important industrial port. It is also the centre of the pearl fishing industry and marketing. Settled originally by the Portuguese in 1540, who were establishing themselves in Ceylon at the same time, it experienced the same succession of foreign control as the island to the S. The Dutch captured it in 1658 and the East India Company took it over in 1782. The British control was short lived, only finally coming back into their hands in 1825. The Portuguese built the most important church in the town. Its dedication to Our Lady of the Snows can only have been the result of a strong sense of irony or perhaps of deprivation. Today the Church is the scene of an annual Golden Car Festival every August.

6 km S of Kovilpatti, just after passing through the village of Nalattinputtur a road turns right off the NH 7 to **Kalugumalai** (also Kazhugumalai, 20 km; *Population*: 13,000) which has a profusion of magnificent 5th century bas-relief Jain figures on a huge rock and an unfinished monolithic cave temple to Siva (c950 AD). These carvings are well worth the detour.

NB: The Jain temple is to the N of the rock and is not easily noticed.

Tirunelveli and Palayamkottai

Tirunelveli (*Population*: 135,700; *STD Code*: 0462) is now joined with the twin settlement of Palayamkottai (*Population*: 97,700; *STD Code*: 0462), located on the banks of the only perennial river of the

The Pearl Fishers Of Tuticorin

The shallow waters and islands off the SE coast of Tamil Nadu are an ideal breeding ground for pearl-bearing oysters, which develop in shoals over a 4 year period. The Department of Fishing monitors the growth of shoals, and announces a pearl fishing season in the appropriate areas. The fishing season lasts for up to 5 weeks, usually in March. Teams of up to 70 small boats, each with 10 divers, leave the shore at midnight in order to start fishing at dawn. The divers work without oxygen, being lowered to the bottom with the help of a weight. Working in pairs to keep watch for sharks or other dangers, the divers normally stay down for up to 80 seconds, though some have stayed down for several minutes. Opportunities for pearl fishing are relatively rare, sometimes as infrequently as once in 10 years. The pearl market in Tuticorin is an extraordinary sight when the season is on.

S, the **Tamraparni**. The irrigation from the river has created 'a splash of green in the naturally dull brown of the vegetation map' of the area. Rising only 60 km to the E at an altitude of over 1700m, the river benefits from both the SW and the SE monsoons. It tumbles down to the plains and follows a narrow strip of land which itself gets more rain – an annual average of about 850 mm – than the belts on either side. Thus a narrow strip of rich paddy growing land has been created.

Places of interest

Tirunelveli is a market town and one of the oldest Christian centres in Tamil Nadu. St Francis Xavier settled here to begin his ministry in India in the early 16th century, but it has also been a centre of Protestant missionary activity. In 1896 it became the head of an Anglican diocese, now Church of South India. **Kanthimathi Nellaiyappar temple**, a twin temple with the N dedicated to Siva (Nellaiyappar) and the S to Parvati (Kanthi), is worth visiting. Each section has an enclosure over 150m by 120m. The temples have sculptures, musical pillars, valuable jewels, a golden lily tank and a 1000 pillared mandapa. *Car festival* in Jun/Jul. **Palayamkottai** has **St John's Church** (Church Missionary Society) with a spire 35m high, a landmark for miles around. The town produces palm-leaf articles.

Excursion

Tiruchendur (*Population*: 75,400; *STD Code*: 04639), 32 km SE of Tirunelveli, has a famous shore temple dedicated to Subrahmanya (see page 1023) (1 of his 6 'abodes') and a cave with rock cut sculptures. **Accommodation E** *Tamil Nadu*, nr the temple, T 268, some a/c rm.

To the S is **Kulasekharapatnam**, which was once a port and has a good beach; the *Dasara* celebrations at Mutharammam Temple attracts folk dancers from all across Tamil Nadu. Next is Manapad.

Manapad (18 km from Tiruchendur) is a predominantly Roman Catholic coastal village where St Francis Xavier is said to have landed and lived in a cave near the headland. The Holy Cross Church (1581) close to the sea is believed to house a fragment of the True Cross from Jerusalem.

Festival

Sep 1st-14th Thousands of pilgrims visit the church.

Local information

● **Accommodation & food**

Budget hotels Several are clustered nr Junc Rly Station. Rm usually with Western toilet and shower. **E** *Tamil Nadu*, T 24268, has some a/c rm with bath and a restaurant; **E** *Aryaas*, 67 Madurai Rd, T 23361, 57 rm, with hot shower, terrace, some a/c, restaurants, permit rm, TV, modern Indian hotel, best in town. Similarly priced **E** *Sri Janakiram*, 30 Madurai Rd nr bus stand, T 24451, 70 rm, with hot shower, some a/c, restaurants, lift. Smart, clean, brightly lit; **E** *Barani*, 29 Madurai Rd, T 23234, 40 rm, with hot shower, some a/c, veg restaurants (1 a/c), TV, busy hotel in large, 4-storey modern block; **E** *Sakuntala International*, Trivandrum High Rd, T 71760, rm with hot shower, a/c with TV more expensive, good veg restaurants (1 a/c), in modern 6-storey Indian style hotel, good value.

F *Blue Star*, 36 Madurai Rd, T 24495, rm with cold shower, a/c more expensive, good veg restaurant, Indian style, modern; **F** *Sri Narayan Tourist Lodge*, Trivandrum High Rd (nr small bridge), T 24451, rm with cold shower, Indian toilet, very basic but clean, no English spoken, popular with truck drivers; **F** *Railway Retiring Rooms* and dorm.

● **Banks & money changers**

There are banks on Trivandrum High Rd.

● **Hospitals & medical services**

In High Ground, Palayamkottai.

Post & telegraph

Post office: the GPO is on Trivandrum High Rd.

● **Shopping**

Shops are on Trivandrum High Rd and nr the Bus Stand.

● **Tourist Information**

counter at Junc Rly Station, T 26235.

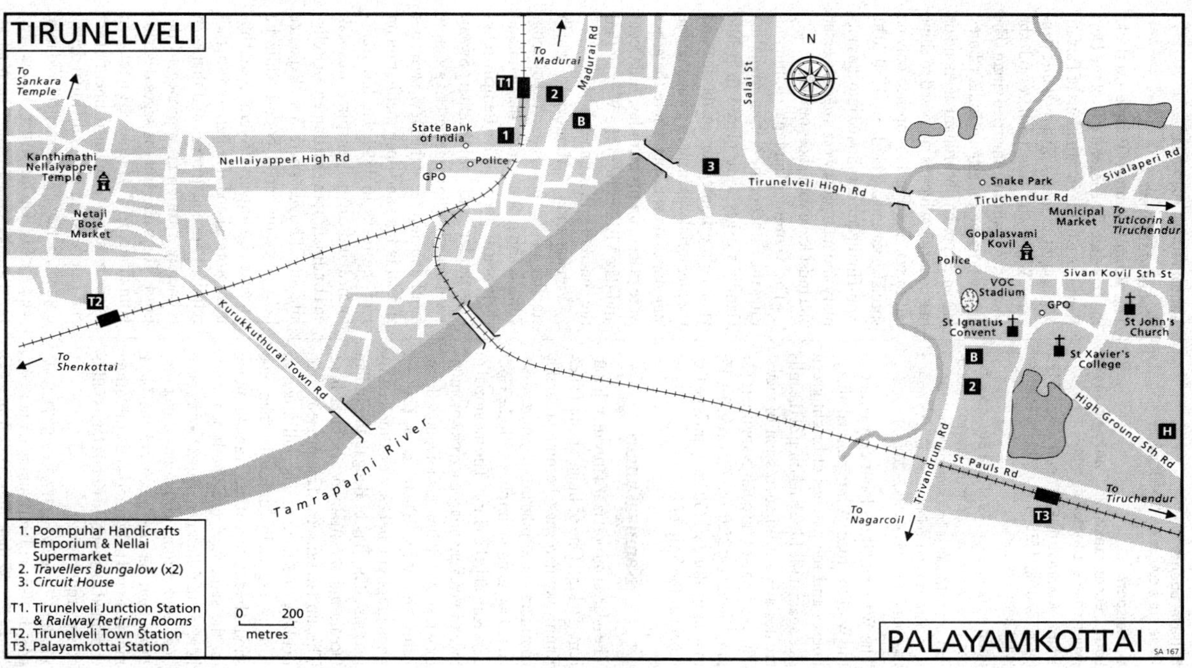
TIRUNELVELI
To Sankara Temple
To Madurai
Madurai Rd
Salai St
N
T1
2
B
1
State Bank of India
Police
GPO
Nellaiyapper High Rd
Kanthimathi Nellaiyapper Temple
Netaji Bose Market
3
Tirunelveli High Rd
Snake Park
Sivalaperi Rd
Tiruchendur Rd
Municipal Market
To Tuticorin & Tiruchendur
Gopalasvami Kovil
Police
Sivan Kovil Sth St
VOC Stadium
GPO
St Ignatius Convent
St John's Church
St Xavier's College
B
2
High Ground Sth Rd
H
T2
To Shenkottai
Kurukkuthurai Town Rd
Tamraparni River
Trivandrum Rd
St Pauls Rd
To Nagarcoil
To Tiruchendur
T3
1. Poompuhar Handicrafts Emporium & Nellai Supermarket
2. Travellers Bungalow (x2)
3. Circuit House
T1. Tirunelveli Junction Station & Railway Retiring Rooms
T2. Tirunelveli Town Station
T3. Palayamkottai Station
0 200 metres
PALAYAMKOTTAI
SA 167

● **Travel agents**
There are a couple on Madurai Rd.

● **Transport**
Local Buses, **taxis** and **auto-rickshaws** (which charge extortionate rates).

Train Madras (ME): *Nellai Exp*, 6120 (AC/CC), daily, 1735, 15 hr. Also to Madurai and Kanniyakumari.

Road Information in Tamil only. **Bus**: good bus connections to Kanniyakumari, Tiruvananthapuram, and to Madurai, Tiruchirappalli and Madras. For Courtallam, go to Tenkasi (Rs 12, 1½ hr) and take bus to Courtallam (Rs 2, 20 min).

The Western Ghats loom ever larger to the W of the road. White painted village houses and the patches of bright green rice against the blue backdrop of the hills creates a beautiful succession of views. The road passes through Nanguneri (31 km; *Population*: 25,000; *STD Code*: 04635) to Kanniyakumari (50 km), or Cape Comorin at the S tip of India.

Kanniyakumari

The nearest airport is at Tiruvananthapuram (86 km). One of India's holiest sites, Kanniyakumari has become a highly commercialised pilgrimage centre, associated as its name implies with the Goddess Kumari, the virgin. The memorial to Swami Vivekenanda, on a rocky promontory just over 400m offshore, now dominates the view. There is a ban on photography of the best views 'for security reasons'. The Bay of Bengal, the Indian Ocean and the Arabian Sea meet here. The sunrise, sunset and moonrise are particularly spectacular. The full moon in Apr is especially unusual when you should be able to see the sun and the moon on the same horizon. The beach sands here are of different colours, having been deposited from different directions. Prominent on the beach are the black monazite and red garnet sands, the former exploited further N in Kerala for its radioactive properties.

BASICS *Population*: 17,200; *STD Code*: 04653; *Climate*: Temp Summer: Max 39°C, Min 22°C, Winter: Max 33°C, Min 20°C; Annual rainfall 1020 mm.

Places of interest
The **Kanniyakumari Temple** overlooks the shoreline. The legend tells of the Devi Kanya, one of the incarnations of Parvati, who sought to marry Siva by doing penance. When she was unsuccessful she vowed to remain an unmarried virgin. The deity who is the 'protector of India's shores' has an exceptionally brilliant diamond on her nose ring which is supposed to shine out to sea. The E gate is opened only on special occasions. 0430-1130, 1730-2030. Non-Hindus are not allowed into the sanctuary and men must wear a *dhoti* to enter. You must leave your shoes outside.

The **Gandhi Mandapa** commemorates the Father of the Nation. Mahatma Gandhi's ashes were placed in public view before immersion in the sea and the memorial was built in a way that the sun shines on the spot where the ashes were placed, on his birthday, 2nd Oct at mid-day. Visitors from the W may find the concrete rather unaesthetic.

Vivekananda Memorial which stands on 1 of 2 rocks separated by about 70m, is about 500m from the mainland (half-hourly ferry). The Bengali religious leader and philosopher Swami Vivekananda who came here as a simple monk and devotee of the Devi, swam out and sat in long and deep meditation on 1 of the rocks in 1892. He left transformed and divinely inspired to speak on Hinduism at the Parliament of Religions in Chicago. There his eloquence held every one spell bound while he preached for universal tolerance and human brotherhood. He believed that all religions are equally true and that each is merely a different approach to the Lord. "He is one, but the sages describe Him differently." He looked on religion as the most powerful instrument of social regeneration and individual development, believing in practical Vedanta, see page 618. On his return, he founded the Ramakrishna Mission in Madras,

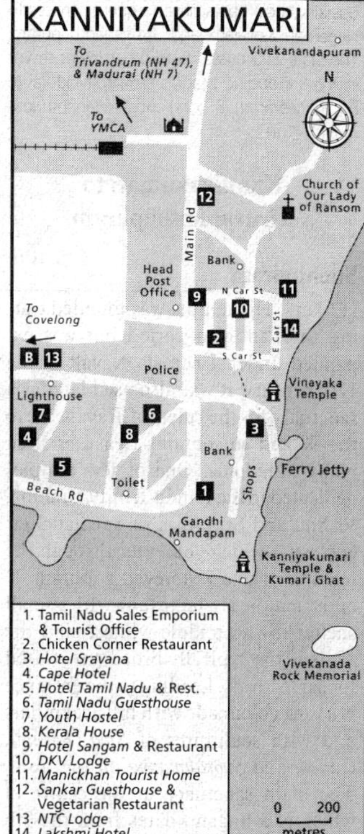

which now has spread across the world. The rock was renamed Vivekananda Rock and a memorial was built in 1970. The design of the *mandapa* incorporates different styles of temple architecture from all over India and now also houses a statue of Vivekananda. People also come to see Sri Pada Parai, the 'foot print' of the Devi where she did her penance on the rock (divine foot prints are believed to be raised when enshrined on rock). Smoking and eating prohibited. Wear thick socks as you must take off shoes before entering. Open daily except Tues, 0700-1100, 1400-1700. Entry Rs 3, Ferry Rs 5. Excellent views from **Lighthouse**. 1500-1900. Small entry fee. No photography.

At **Vivekanandapuram** 1 km N, Yoga Kendra, runs yoga courses. There's a pleasant sandy beach 3½ km on Kovalam Rd.

A gigantic 40m-high statue of Thiruvalluvar will be in place on Vivekananda rock in 1994.

Museums

Govt Museum, Main Rd, nr Tourist Office. 0900-1300, 1400-1700. Very simple, showing aspects of Indian life. **'Wandering Monk'** Exhibition, Main Rd.

Local festivals

Apr usually 2nd week. *Chitra Purnima* is a special full moon celebration at the temple; sunset and moonrise can be seen together.

Oct 1st week. Special *Navarathri* celebrations.

Local information

● Accommodation

The hotels are in heavy demand especially State Tourism hotels on the beach; book well in advance. The better hotels have rm with attached facilities (cold showers, hot tap and Western toilets).

D *Samudra*, Sannathi St, T 71162, seafacing rm with bath (prices vary), restaurant, clean, modern and fairly new, rec; TTDC **D** *Cape Hotel*, W of Kerala House, T 71222; **D** TTDC *Tamil Nadu Guest House*, in Travancore Maharaja's palace, T 71257, 45 rm, some a/c, twin cottages, dorm cheaper; **D** Kerala Tourism *Kerala House*, in 3-storey building (largest in town) designed to resemble an aeroplane from the air, T 71229, 11 rm, every one with a view of sunset and sunrise (Sep-Feb), restaurant, exterior looks run down and scarcity of water evident in the garden, but attracts VIPs to experience the proximity of the *sangam* of 3 oceans.

● Budget hotels

E *Lakshmi Tourist Home*, E Car St, T 71333, some a/c rm with views and bath, restaurant, 24-hr coffee shop, travel, STD facilities, TV; **E** *Manickan Tourist Home*, N Car St (nr sea), T 71387, some a/c rm with bath. Restaurant, travel, TV. Most others have rm with fan and cold showers only: **E** *Sangam*, Main Rd opp the Post Office, T 71351; **E** *Sankar's Guest House*, Main Rd towards Rly station, T 71260, some large seaview rm with balcony, good veg restaurant; **E** ***NTC Lodge***, Bus Station, Kovalam Rd, some good, clean rm with sea view and cheaper dorm (men only), good restaurant, good value.

F ***DKV Lodge***, comfortable rm; **F** ***Rly Retiring Rm***, T 71247; **F** TTDC *Youth Hostel*. Reservations: Manager, *Cape Hotel* or TTDC, 143 Anna Salai, Madras, T 830390; **F** ***Parvati Nivas Lodge***, nr Museum has cheap rm in an old Kerala style colonial house, but is basic and dirty.

● **Places to eat**

TTDC *Restaurant* (non-veg), which looks like a barrack, serves excellent Indian meals. Non-veg at ***Manickam Tourist Home***. The 2 ***Saravanas***, Rock Rd, nr Jetty and on Sannathi St, serve good veg. ***NTC*** at Bus Station, good value.

● **Banks & money changers**

Branches of **Canara Bank, State Bank of India** and **State Bank of Travancore**.

● **Post & telecommunications**

Post office: Head Post Office, Main Rd. Branches at Vivekandandapuram. 1100-1600 and in Sannathi St, 1000-1400.

● **Shopping**

Tamil Nadu Co-optex Sales Emporium nr the Gandhi Mandapa; ***Khadi Krafts***, S Car St; ***Indco Products***, Beach Rd; ***Poompuhar Handicrafts Emporium***, Sannathi St.

● **Tourist office**

At *Hotel Tamil Nadu* Complex, T 276, on Beach Rd nr the Gandhi Mandapa.

● **Transport**

Local Taxis and **cycle rickshaws** are available. **Ferry**: the ferry service to the Vivekananda Rock is half-hourly and runs from 0700-1100, 1400-1700. Fare Rs 3.

Train The Station to the N off the Trivandrum Rd, is large and well organised. **Madras**: *Him Sagar Exp*, 6017, Th, 2330, 24 hr. If you take this train to its ultimate destination of Jammu the journey lasts 3 days 14 hr, the longest in India. **Bombay (VT)**: *Kanniyakuman*, 1081 (AC/II), daily, 1535, 47 hr; **Delhi (ND)**: *Him Sagar Exp*, 6017, Th, 2330, 72 hr; **Tiruvananthapuram**: *Him Sagar Exp*, 6017, Th, 2330, 2¼ hr *Kanniyakuman*, 1082 (AC/II), daily, 0515, 2¼ hr.

Road Bus: the Bus Station is to the W of town, about 15 min walk from the centre. It has a restaurant, waiting room and ***Retiring Rooms*** upstairs. Local buses have frequent services to Nagercoil, Kovalam and Tiruvananthapuram. The State TTC buses go to other major towns in the S including Madras (16 hr), Madurai (6 hr), Ramesvaram (8½ hr) and Tiruvananthapuram (2½ hr).

Kanniyakumari to Tiruvananthapuram

Suchindram

(12 km) The temple was founded during the Pandiyan period but was expanded under Tirumala Nayak in the 17th century. It was also used later as a sanctuary for the rulers of Travancore to the W and so contains treasures from many kingdoms. One of few temples dedicated to the Hindu Trinity, Brahma, Vishnu and Siva, it is in a rectangular enclosure which you enter through the massive ornate 7-storeyed gopuram. N of the temple is a large tank with a small shelter in the middle while round the walls is the typically broad street used for car festivals. Leading to the entrance is a long colonnade with musical pillars and with sculptures of *Siva*, *Parvati*, *Ganesh* and *Subrahmanya* on the front. The main sanctuary, at the centre of which is a lingam, dates from the 9th century, but many of the other structures and sculptures date from the 13th century and later. There are special temple ceremonies at sunset on Fridays.

Nagercoil

(19 km; *Population*: 189,500; *STD Code*: 04652) The landscape begins to feel more like Kerala than Tamil Nadu. Nagercoil is set with a stunning backcloth of the Western Ghats, reflected from place to place in the broad tanks dotted with lotuses. It is an important railway junction and bus terminal. The old town of **Kottar**, now a suburb, was a centre of art, culture and pilgrimage. The temple to Nagaraja, after which the town is named, is unique in that although the presiding deity is the Ser-

The Nadars – A Caste On The Rise

The history of the Nadars is illuminating. In 1874 Nadars tried to enter the Minakshi temple in Madurai, but were refused permission. In 1876 they tried to enter the Tirumangalam temple, but again were refused. In 1899 they petitioned to gain entry to the *Visvanathasvami* temple in Sivakasi but were turned down once more. They then tried to gain entry to temples wherever they were numerous enough. High caste Hindus began to object strongly, and on 26 April 1899 Sivakasi Nadars burnt 55 houses belonging to a higher caste group, the *Maravars*. As a reprisal, on 6 June 1899 the Maravar community organised a huge demonstration which led to widespread rioting. Nadar houses were looted and set on fire and police and the army had to be called from as far afield as Trichy. 1,958 people were arrested, 552 were convicted and 7 were executed.

pent God *Naga,* there are also shrines to Siva and Vishnu as well as images of Jain *Tirthankaras*, Mahavira and Parsvanatha on the pillars. The 'snake' temple is alive with snakes during some festivals. Christian missionaries played an important part in the town's development and have left their mark in schools, colleges, hospitals and of course churches of different denominations. There is also a prominent Muslim community in Kottar which is reflected in the closure of shops on Fri, remaining open on Sun.

The NH 47 continues past Padmanabhapuram (15 km), see page 954, to Tiruvananthapuram (53 km), page 948.

MADURAI TO TIRUVANANTHAPURAM (Western Route)

ROUTES A much shorter route from Madurai to Tiruvananthapuram runs to the W of the NH 7 through the Western Ghats at the Shenkottai gap. In addition to beautiful scenery as the road climbs through the ghats there are some interesting towns en route, quite off the beaten track.

The road journey is much more interesting than the long rail trip to Kollam from Madurai. The night train is best. Although it is shorter, overall the road is no quicker than the comparatively straight and flat main route. On the Kerala side of the border the road is busy and slow, running through the rubber plantations of S Kerala to Tiruvananthapuram.

Srivilliputtur

(53 km; *Population*: 68,500; *STD Code*: 04568) One of 108 sacred Vaishnavite sites, the gopuram of the **Vishnu Vadabadrasaikoil** in Srivilliputtur towering nearly 60m is a landmark for the whole district. Built of wood, brick and plaster it comprises 13 storeys excluding the superstructure forming its roof. The superstructure is, in the words of Percy Brown, an "excessively tall composition resembling a hall with a chaitya roof, elaborately ornamented with a great *suraj mukh* ('sun face') above its gable end and a row of huge pinnacles along its ridge". It has a slightly concave curvature, emphasising its grace while lessening the feeling of power and strength. There have been increasing signs of stress. In 1904 major cracks were noticed, and by the early 1970s 25 cracks had opened up from the foundations to varying heights. The NW corner of the tower seems to have settled more than 15 cm. The whole tower is supported by a timber frame of teak, built on foundations that go no deeper than 2.3m. An enormous temple car is associated with the temple, built over 100 years ago, which takes 3000 people to pull it. Srivilliputtur is revered throughout Tamil Nadu as the birthplace of the Tamil poetess and devotee Andal. In the town is an **old palace of Tirumala Nayak**, partly converted into the *Taluk* office.

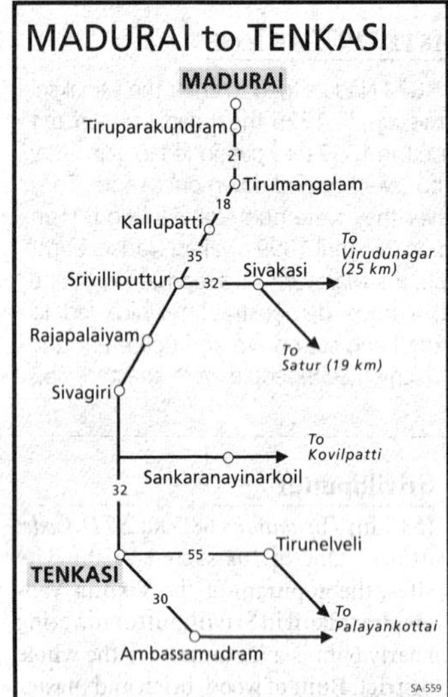

There is an important handloom industry, and brass and other utensils are made.

Excursions

The **Srivilliputtur Reserved Forest** has a wild life sanctuary which is the only known habitat in the world of the grizzled squirrel. There is no guarantee that you will see one! 19 km SE of Srivilliputtur is the important industrial town of **Sivakasi** (*Population*: 102,100). On the main Tiruvananthapuram-Madras railway line and well connected by road, Sivakasi is famous for modern industries such as litho printing, but it is also notorious for the extensive use of child labour in its match and firework factories, see page 560. There are over 70 fireworks factories in the town, and most of the *firecrackers* used in India are produced in Sivakasi. At the turn of the 20th century there was great rivalry between the low caste Nadar community and the higher castes, reflected in the continuing struggles today over caste discrimination in India.

Rajapalayam (*Population*: 114,000; *STD Code*: 04563) owes its origins to the dispersal of the Vijayanagar families after 1565, see page 994. The Western Ghats rise to heights of over 1200m immediately behind the town. Wild elephants continue to come down through the forests, causing devastation to farm land. The town is a centre of small scale industries, including engineering and food processing.

• **Accommodation & food** F *Bombay Lodge*, 885 Tenkasi Rd, 300m left out of bus station, T 20907, very clean inexpensive rm with Western toilet and cold water, a/c and delux rm more expensive but still good value, new Indian style very well run hotel, excellent Indian veg restaurant, highly rec.

• **Transport Road Bus**: to Sankaracoil, Rs 5, ¾ hr; from there to Kalugumalai, Rs 3, ½ hr. Buses to and from Tenkasi, Rs 10, 2 hr.

ROUTES The road over the Ghats is narrow and winding, though nowhere particularly steep. It passes through **Puliangudi** (39 km; *Population*: 54,000) to **Tenkasi** (37 km; *Population*: 55,000; *STD Code*: 04633), the nearest town to the Courtallam (6 km). Tenkasi means literally the Kashi (Varanasi) of the S. The temple flagstaff is beleived to be 400 years old

Courtallam

An extremely popular health resort, especially between Jun and Sep. There are 9 waterfalls (Kutallam Falls), including the Main Falls where the River Chittar cascades over 92m. With average temperatures of 22°-23°C, the waters are widely believed to have great curative powers. The tranquil village at the base of forest clad hills is empty out-of-season when some services close. The Thirukutralanathar Temple contains old inscriptions while the small **Chitra Sabha Temple** nearby, 1 of 5 *sabhas* (where Siva as Nataraja is believed to have performed his cosmic dance) contains religious murals.

• **Accommodation & food** Over 30 lodges (nearly every building) take in guests. **F** *Sri Venkateswara*, rm with Indian toilet, cold water tap, in old-fashioned Indian style hotel; **F** *Township Bungalow*, T 2128, contact Exec Officer 15 days ahead; **F** PWD *Tourist Bungalow*, T 2123, contact Dist Collector, Tirunelveli; **F** Forest Dept *Rest House*, contact, District Forest Officer, Shencottah. *Hotel Tamil Nadu* (restaurant only), serves tasty and cheap veg meals through the year.

- **Shopping** Several handicrafts stalls nr Main Falls.

- **Banks & money changers** On the main rd.

- **Post & telecommunications** **Post Office**: at Bus Station and Main Falls.

- **Tourist office** Seasonal Tourist office at Bus Station.

ROUTES From Tenkasi the road heads NW through **Shenkottai** (10 km; *Population*: 25,800; *STD Code*: 04631) to the pass across the Ghats. The town has major saw mills using timber from the surrounding hills. There are magnificent views from this road as it approaches the narrow pass. Stretched out is a panoramic view of intensively cultivated and lush green paddy fields, interspersed with irrigation tanks, leading down onto the open plains below. From **Tenmalai** (21 km) you can either take the direct but slow road through Nedumangad (51 km) to Tiruvananthapuram (18 km) or the longer alternative route from Tenmalai via Punalur (21 km) to Tiruvananthapuram (101 km).

MADURAI TO KOCHI (COCHIN) via Thekkadi and Kottayam

ROUTES The most direct route from Madurai to Kochi (Cochin) crosses the Western Ghats at the Periyar-Thekkadi game reserve, then either down through **Peermed** and **Kottayam** or S to Tiruvananthapuram. Allow 3 hrs by road up to Thekkadi. In all the small towns there are tea shops and cold drink stalls.

From Madurai the NH 7 goes W to Usilampatti (39 km; *Population*: 26,400), skirting the N end of the Andipatti Hills. At Teni (35 km; *Population*: 66,000), an important market town at the head of the lake created by the **Vaigai Dam**. A road turns left up the Kambam Valley. It passes through a succession of market towns. Irrigation supports paddy and sugar cane as well as some cotton on the rich valley-floor soils. Away from the river the soils are thinner and poorer, and on the dry land sorghum, bajra, groundnut and cotton are grown. The Suruli River is supplemented by the waters of the Periyar, which were diverted E through the crest of the Ghats by the Periyar scheme, completed in 1897. Chinnamanur (22 km; *Population*: 35,400), and Kambam (17 km; *Population*: 52,000) lie on the valley floor, but from Gudalur (10 km; *Population*: 36,600) the road rises steeply up the Ghat.

The Ghat section of the road continues for 70 km across to Mundakayam in Kerala. It gives wonderful views on the 14 km stretch up to Kumili and Thekkadi (*Altitude*: 1000m), a left turn 1 km after passing through Kumili. See page 987. The road through Kerala passes down through tea (on the higher slopes) and rubber plantations (at middle levels). Cardamom is grown in lightly shaded areas, often on small holdings, as is ginger, coffee and pepper. On flat land, even at high altitude, rice is grown. After 33 km the road passes through Peermed (*Altitude*: 1130m). The ghat road continues to Kottayam (77 km) through gardens of areca nut, coconut, banana, pepper and cashew (see page 983), and Kochi is 38 km, see page 969.

MADURAI TO KOCHI via Kodaikkanal, Palani and Thrissur

ROUTES The route follows the NH 45 NW to Kodai Road, then branches off to Batlagundu. It moves from the fertile and shaded irrigated lowlands around Madurai, to the upper dry land on the land to the N of the Vaigai River.

Kodai Road (40 km) is just a railway halt; change here if travelling from Madras to Kodai. **Vattalkundu** (20 km; *Population*:

20,000) is an attractive small town, with an active market. Surrounded by irrigated land, with sugar cane and rice occupying the best land, just outside Vattalkundu is a boys' orphanage (*Boys' Town*) which supports itself by producing a range of products from foodstuffs and spices to handcrafts. Their products are widely available.

The ghat road begins about 20 km out of Vattalkundu. It is one of the most rapid ascents anywhere across the Ghats. Take some warm clothing, particularly if you are travelling between Dec and Mar, and if you are going up in the late afternoon. The views are stunning, and there are several excellent places to stop, though the buses usually only stop occasionally. In the lower reaches of the climb you look down over the Kambam valley, the Vaigai Lake and across to the Varushanad Hills beyond. The road twists and winds up through rapidly changing vegetation, but generally wooded slopes to Kodaikkanal (40 km).

Kodaikkanal

BASICS 40 km; *Population*: 27,500; *Altitude*: 2343m; *STD Code*: 04542; *Clothing*: Summer: light woollens, Winter: warm woollens.

Today Kodai is growing fast as a resort centre for South Indians on holiday. The small artificial lake, created in 1910 by the building of a dam just below the International School (established in 1901), acts as a focus for the town. The 5 km walk around its perimeter gives beautiful and contrasting views across the water and into the surrounding woods, with a variety of species including pine and eucalyptus. Best late Sep-early Oct. Avoid May when it is crowded and expensive.

The **Palani Hills** were first surveyed by British administrators in 1821, but the surveyor's report was not published until 1837 – 10 years after Ooty had become the official 'sanitorium' for the British in South India. A proposal to build a sanitorium was made in 1861-2 by Colonel Hamilton, who noted the extremely healthy climate and the lack of disease. Despite the warmth of that recommendation the sanitarium was never built because the site was so difficult to get to. It was the freedom from malaria that was the greatest incentive to opening a hill station there. The American Mission in Madurai, established in 1834, had lost 6 of their early missionaries within a decade. It looked as if the Sirumalai Hills, at around 1300m, might provide a respite from the plains, but it was soon discovered that they were not high enough to eliminate malaria. The first 2 bungalows were built by Jun 1845.

The early route was extraordinarily difficult. For 5 km of zig-zag on the steepest section the path was less than 1m wide, and the average width was only 2m for the whole journey. Despite the obstacles, the permanent population had reached over 600 by 1883. Seven years later it stood at 1,743. These changes had come about partly because Europeans began to spend their long periods of leave in Kodai, and some civil servants and missionaries retired there rather than to Europe. The most influential was Sir Vere Henry Levinge, and in the words of the American geographer Nora Mitchell "it was ac-

Climate: Kodaikkanal

	Jan	Feb	Mar	Apr	May	Jun	Jul	Aug	Sep	Oct	Nov	Dec	Av/Tot
Max (°C)	18	19	20	20	21	18	15	17	18	19	19	18	19
Min (°C)	5	6	8	10	11	11	11	10	10	10	9	7	9
Rain (mm)	43	21	73	231	169	96	129	122	157	263	237	123	1664

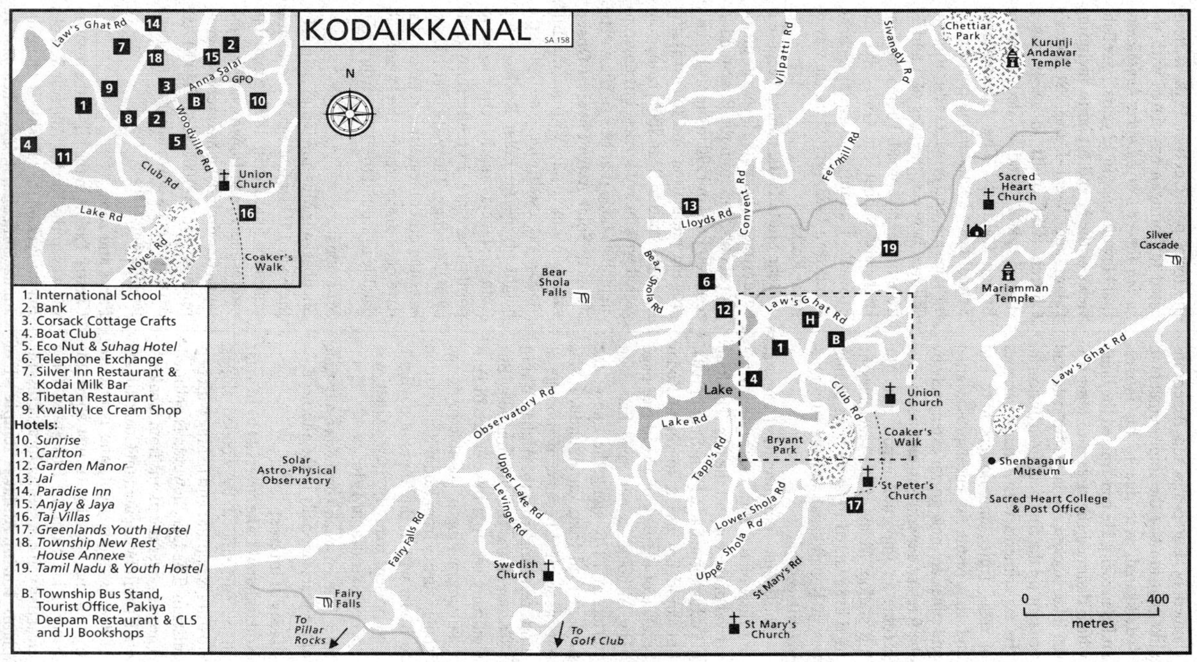
KODAIKKANAL
SA 158
N
Law's Ghat Rd
Anna Salai
GPO
Woodville Rd
Club Rd
Union Church
Lake Rd
Noyes Rd
Coaker's Walk
Vilpatti Rd
Sivanady Rd
Chettiar Park
Kurunji Andawar Temple
Fernhill Rd
Convent Rd
Lloyds Rd
Bear Shola Rd
Bear Shola Falls
Sacred Heart Church
Silver Cascade
Mariamman Temple
Law's Ghat Rd
Lake
Club Rd
Union Church
Coaker's Walk
Observatory Rd
Lake Rd
Bryant Park
Tapp's Rd
Shenbaganur Museum
Sacred Heart College & Post Office
St Peter's Church
Solar Astro-Physical Observatory
Upper Lake Rd
Levinge Rd
Lower Shola Rd
Upper Shola Rd
St Mary's Rd
Fairy Falls Rd
Swedish Church
Fairy Falls
To Pillar Rocks
To Golf Club
St Mary's Church
0
400
metres
1. International School
2. Bank
3. Corsack Cottage Crafts
4. Boat Club
5. Eco Nut & *Suhag Hotel*
6. Telephone Exchange
7. Silver Inn Restaurant & Kodai Milk Bar
8. Tibetan Restaurant
9. Kwality Ice Cream Shop
Hotels:
10. *Sunrise*
11. *Carlton*
12. *Garden Manor*
13. *Jai*
14. *Paradise Inn*
15. *Anjay & Jaya*
16. *Taj Villas*
17. *Greenlands Youth Hostel*
18. *Township New Rest House Annexe*
19. *Tamil Nadu & Youth Hostel*
B. Township Bus Stand, Tourist Office, Pakiya Deepam Restaurant & CLS and JJ Bookshops

claimed by Europeans and Americans alike that most of the improvements in Kodaikkanal were due to his interest and generosity. He constructed the bund which dammed the stream to form Kodai lake, stocked the lake with fish, and brought up the first boat from Tuticorin. His experiments with foreign varieties of trees, fruits, and flowers have had enduring results as eucalyptus, wattle, and pines are now grown extensively by the forestry department, and pears have become an important export from the hill station. Many of the vegetables he tried are planted today in large quantities in Kodaikkanal and the surrounding villages".

The major transformation came at the turn of the 20th century with the arrival of the car and the bus. The Raja of Pudukkottai had a French car in 1904, but could not use it to get to Kodai because of the lack of a road (see page 911). Although a new road had been started in 1876, along the line of the present road from Vattalkundu, it was left incomplete because of shortage of funds resulting from the Afghan War in 1876. In 1905 the Trichinopoly Bus Company set up a bus service to Periyakulam, making it possible to do the whole journey from Kodai Road station to Kodai within the hours of daylight. The present road, up 'Law's Ghat' was opened to traffic in 1916.

NB: The mist can come down any time of the year, especially in the afternoon.

Places of interest

Kodaikkanal Lake covers 24 ha in a star shape surrounded by wooded slopes. Boating is popular and fishing with permission. The lake, however, is polluted. The view over the plains from **Coaker's walk** (built by Lieutenant Coaker in the 1870s), is magnificent, and is reached from a signposted path just above the bazar, 1 km from the Bus Stand. On a clear day you can see Madurai across the plains. **Kurinji Andavar Temple** NE of the town, past Chettiar Park, is dedicated to Murugan associated with the *kurinji* flower (*Strobilanthes kunthianus*) that blossom once in 12 years. Excellent views of the N and S plains, including Palani and Vagai Dams. **St Peter's Church** (CSI) built in 1884, has a stained glass window dedicated to Bishop Caldwell. **The International School** has a commanding position on the lakeside, and provides education for children between the ages of 5 and 18 from India and abroad. There is also the Highclere School for Girls and the Bhavan's Gandhi Vidyasram School, founded in 1983, located on the way to Pillar Rocks.

Bear Shola Falls, named because it once attracted bears, is a favourite picnic spot about 2 km from the Bus Stand. A reservoir built in 1990 to supply Kodai's growing population and tourist traffic led to the road to Bear Shola being congested with heavy lorries, but environmentalists hope that this traffic will be stopped. **Solar Astro-Physical Observatory**, 6 km to the W from the Bus Stand, was established in 1899 at a height of 2347m. **Pillar Rocks**, 7 km from the lake, is another striking viewpoint. There are 3 granite formations over 120m high. There are over 100 *dolmens* and other megalithic remains that have been discovered in the Palanis, all datable to around the 2nd century AD.

Museums

Shenbaganur Museum is maintained by the Sacred Heart College, a theological seminary founded in 1895. Small but interesting. In addition to local flora and fauna (inc orchids) it has archaeological remains. Open 1000-1130, 1500-1700. Attractive walk down hill from the town passing waterfalls.

Parks and zoos

Chettiar Park is in the NE of the town on the way to the Kurinji Andavar Temple. Bryant Park on the lakeside is where the annual horticultural show is held in May.

Excursions

Berijam Lake A road runs W past the golf course and Pillar rocks to Berijam Lake (15 km). which has beautiful views, especially over the Lake, before running down to it. Apart from timber lorries the road is little used. The road to **Munnar**, one of the most attractive routes in the whole of South India, has been made impassable to ordinary cars by the heavy traffic of the timber lorries. A 4-wheel drive vehicle is essential to complete the journey across the highest road in peninsular India.

Local Festivals

May *Summer Tourist Festival*: Boat Race, Flower Show and Dog Show and other entertainments.

Local information

● Accommodation

Most offer off-season discounts (1 Jul-14 Oct, 15 Jan-31 Mar). The majority have rm with bath in the **B** to **D** categories, only a few have single rm. The more expensive hotels are some distance from the centre.

B *Carlton*, Boat Club Rd, T 561, 91 rm, restaurant (excellent especially buffet lunch), tennis, golf, billiards, and boating arranged, excellent position overlooking lake.

C *Sornam Apartments*, Fernhill Rd, T 431, 6 apts, restaurant (Indian), coffee shop. Also 40 beds in 4 *Youth Hostels*. **C** *Suhaag* Woodville Rd, overlooking bus station, T 41143, small dingy overpriced rm.

D *Kodai International*, 55 rm, with bath, restaurant; **D** *Garden Manor*, Lake Rd, T 525, restaurant, good lakeside location; **D** *Paradise Inn*, Laws Ghat Rd, T 774, 38 rm, with bath, restaurant; **D** *Sterling Resorts*, 44 Gymkhana Rd, T 636, 40 cottages, restaurant, exchange, travel; **D** *Raku International*, Upper Lake Rd, reasonable rm but poor service, no restaurant; **D** *Jai*, Lloyds Rd, T 344; **D** *Taj Villas*, Coakers Walk nr the centre has pleasant rm in an old building, popular.

● Budget hotels & youth hostels

E *Sri Bala and Co*, nr Hilltops Tower, stone cottages, some self-contained with kitchen and bath, cottages variable, but you can self-cater, beautiful grounds, short-cut through grounds to Lake; **E** TTDC *Tamil Nadu*, Fernhill Rd, T 481, 15 min walk from Bus Station (away from most interesting walks), restaurant and bar, with cheap **F** *Youth Hostel*. Reservations: Manager, or attached *Youth Hostel*, 143 Anna Salai, Madras, T 830390. **E** *Anjay*, Anna Salai, T 489; **E** *Jaya*, Anna Salai nr Bazar.

F *Youth Hostel*, Greenlands, end of Coakers Walk, very basic but superb views, dorm and 2 rm with bath; **F** *Township New Rest House Annexe*, Poet Thyagaraja Rd; **F** *Township Bus Stand Rest House*, Anna Salai; **F** *Taj Lodge*, end of Coaker's Walk, very primitive and rustic, but friendly staff.

● Places to eat

Best at the *Carlton Hotel*, set in very pleasant grounds overlooking Lake. *Garden Manor* and *Tamil Nadu* and *Sornam* (Indian). *Pakiya Deepam* opp the Bus Stand and *Apna Punjab* in 7 Rd are Indian restaurants. On Hospital Rd are *Silver Inn*, the *Kodai Milk Bar*, *Tibetan Restaurant* and *Kwality Ice Creams* opp Kodai International School. There are a few bakeries – *Jacob* in the Main Bazar, PO Rd, *Vasu* on Lake Rd nr the Telephone Exchange, and the tiny *Manna Bakery* on Bear Shola Rd which also serves pizzas and Western veg food. *Philco's Cold Storage*, opp Kodai International School for confectionery, cakes, frozen foods, delicatessen.

● Banks & money changers

State Bank of India and others on Anna Salai. *Hotel Tamil Nadu* has an exchange counter.

● Hospitals & medical services

Government Hospital, T 292. *Van Allan Hospital*, T 273.

● Post & telecommunications

Post office: Head Post Office on Post Office Rd. Others in Main Bazar, Observatory, Lake View, Anantha Giri, Pambapuram and Shenbaganur. **Telephone**: you can make STD calls from the Telephone Exchange, the Boat Club and the kiosks being introduced in most larger towns.

● Shopping

Excellent vegetables available in the town market off the bazar. Also *Eco-Nut*, Woodville Rd, above AMS Chicken Broiler Shop, opp Bus Stand. Good whole foods, brown bread, muffins, cheese, yoghurts. Very tasty. *Kashmir Handicrafts Centre*, 2 N Shopping Complex, Anna Salai for shawls, jewellery, brass, leather, marble, bone and walnut wood articles and 'Numdah' rugs. *Khadi Emporium, Handloom Cooperative*

Stores, Travancore Craft Works, Post Office Rd. *Govt Sales Emporium* nr Township Bus Stand is only open during the season. *Cottage Crafts Shop*, Anna Salai (Council for Social Concerns in Kodai) is run by volunteers. **Books** *CLS Bookshop*, Anna Salai.

● Sports

Boating: *Kodaikkanal Boat Club* which allows daily membership with club facilities.

Golf Club

Riding: Ponies for hire near the Boat House; may have to bargain down price.

● Tourist office

Tamil Nadu, Township Bus Stand, Rest House Complex. 1000-1700, Mon-Fri.

● Transport

Local Taxi: unmetered taxis available. Tourist Taxis only from Madurai. **Bicycles**: can be hired at the top of the Bazar.

Train Reservations for Kodai Road Station trains from agents at Jayaraj Hall, Coakers Walk Rd.

Road Bus: direct buses to Dindigul (90 km), Kodai Road (80 km), Madras (497 km), Madurai (120 km), Palani (65 km), Tiruchirappalli (197 km), Coimbatore (171 km) during the season, among others. Frequent service to Madurai (3-4 hr journey) and several to the other destinations. Also 1 daily to Kumili for the Periyar Wildlife Sanctuary, 4½ hr. Bangalore has an overnight service by the Karnataka SRTC. RMTC Bus Stand.

Kodaikkanal to Kochi

The ghat road to Palani, opened in the 1970s, is not heavily used, and gives superb views of the lower Palani Hills. It passes through coffee, orange and banana smallholdings some of which have seen major improvements and investment in the last decade. Interplanting of crops such as pepper are further increasing the yields from what can be highly productive land, even on steep slopes. The dangers of incautious cultivation however are of greatly increased erosion. This road was built in part with money given by the Palani Temple Fund (*devasthanam*).

Palani

(35 km; *Population*: 76,000; *STD Code*: 04545) The hill top shrine to **Murugan** is a very important site of pilgrimage. At full moon in Jan-Feb pilgrims walk from up to 80 km around to the shrine. Many carry shoulder-poles with elaborate bamboo or wooden structures on each end, living out the myth which surrounds the origin of the shrine. See *Agastya and the demon* box. **Accommodation** In **F** *Sri Venkateswara Lodge*, Adivaram; **F** *Devasthanam Rest House*, Dandapani Nilayam.

ROUTES The route to the W coast continues through Pollachi and Thrissur (90 km); S down NH 47 to Kochi (75 km). A highly picturesque alternative is from Udumalpet via Munnar (87 km), Perumbavur (97 km) and Aluva (15 km) to Kochi (21 km).

Pollachi (61 km; *Population*: 127,200; *STD Code*: 04259) has been an important trading centre for over 2000 years, as is witnessed by the finds of Roman silver coins bearing the heads of the Emperors Augustus and Tiberias. Today it still occupies an important position on the route from E to W through the Palakkad Gap. It is also the gateway to the small but very attractive sanctuary.

Parambikulam Sanctuary

35 km to the SW. Sheltered by the Neelampathi Ranges on its W and by dense forests, access to the sanctuary is only by public bus. Entry only between 0700 and 1900. The journey traverses the thin scrub of the lowland through bamboo groves around Sethumadai and moist deciduous forests near the reserve itself. Parambikulam itself has rich tropical rain forest. The reserve is particularly rich in birdlife, but also has one of the earliest managed teak forests in the world, going back to 1845. Some of the trees are reputed to be over 400 years old. If trekking beware of leeches. The sanctuary contains 3 dams, and the

dammed waters are home to a variety of endangered species, including crocodiles, otter and turtles.

Annamalai National Park

The park (1400m), near Pollachi, covers an area of 960 sq km in the Western Ghats. Open round the year. Best time: Dec-June. Wildlife includes Nilgiri langur, lion-tailed macaque, elephant, *gaur*, tiger, panther, sloth, wild boar, birds (incl pied hornbill, drongo, red whiskered *bulbul*, black-headed oriole) and a large number of crocodiles in the Amaravathi reservoir. Jeeps available.

• **Accommodation F** *Forest Rest Houses* at Top Slip, Mt Stuart, Varagaliar, Sethumadai and Amaravathinagar. Reservations: District Forest Officer, Coimbatore S Div, Mahalingam Nagar, Pollachi, T 2508.

• **Transport Air** Nearest airport at Coimbatore (90 km). **Train** From Pollachi (35 km). **Road** Connections with Pollachi and Coimbatore.

COIMBATORE TO BANGALORE via Palakkad

ROUTES The major route to Bangalore is along NH 47 and NH 7. The shortest route is across the Nilgiris via Ooty and Mysore. However, there is another very attractive alternative via the Palakkad gap, Kodagu and Mysore.

Coimbatore to Palakkad

(48 km) This important route town commands the most important gap through the southern part of the Western Ghats which has been used by traders since before Roman times. The railway line from Karnataka and Tamil Nadu to Kerala passes through Palakkad.

• **Transport Train** Coimbatore: *Kerala-Mangala Link Exp*, 2625/2625A (AC/II), daily, 1800, 1¼ hr; Madras: *Madras Exp*, 6042 (AC/II), daily, 2015, 10 hr; **Ernakulam Junc**: *Kerala-Mangala Exp*, 2626 (AC/II), daily, 0845, 3 hr; **Kochi**: *Guwahati/Haora Exp*, 2650/2652 (AC/II), M,Sa,Su, 1440, 4 hr.

ROUTES Routes from Palakkad are described separately under the routes from Kochi to Kannur and Bangalore.

AGASTYA AND THE DEMON

David Shulman tells how the sage ***Agastya*** "was given two hills, *Shivagiri* and *Shaktigiri*, as sites of worship, with permission to take them S. One day he met the demon, Itumpan... Seeing he was of a good nature, Agastya sent him to bring the hills. When Itumpan arrived at the hills, a shoulder-pole appeared, and the eight serpents which support the world took the form of ropes so he could tie the hills to the support. In this way he lifted the mountains and carried them S until he reached Palani. Suddenly he felt faint; he put the hills down and rested, but when he tried to lift them again he could not move them. Puzzled and sorrowful, he climbed one of the trees, and there he noticed a child under a tree. "Go away" he said to the child, and added that he was a murderous demon. "This is my home," said the child; "pick it up if you can!" "You may be small in size but you tell big lies," cried Itumpan as he leaped at the boy. But the child was ***Murugan***, playing his games; he killed Itumpan at a stroke. When Itumpan's wife Itumpi heard of her husband's death, she prayed to Murugan, who revived him. Agastya came to worship Murugan at that spot, and he ordered the demon to serve Murugan there for his salvation."

KERALA

Contents

Maps

The name Kerala is recorded in Asoka's edicts before the start of the Christian era, over a thousand years before the Malayalam language of contemporary Kerala took shape, and was applied to the area known in Tamil as *Seranadu*. For many this is India's most idyllic state. India's most densely populated region, it has a distinctive charm which belies the statistics which suggest that it is also one of India's poorest states. High levels of education and health care have given Kerala an enviable reputation elsewhere in India, and its unique balance of Hindu, Muslim and Christian sets it apart even from next door neighbours Tamil Nadu and Karnataka.

BASICS *Population*: 29mn (Urban 28%, Scheduled Castes 10%, Scheduled Tribes 1%); *Literacy*: M 95% F 87%; *Birth rate*: *Rural* 18:1000, *Urban* 18:1000; *Death rate*: *Rural* 6:1000, *Urban* 6:1000; *Infant mortality*: *Rural* 32:1000, *Urban* 24:1000; *Religion*: *Hindu* 58%, *Muslim* 21%, *Christian* 21%.

Environment

The land

Area: 39,000 sq km. Kerala's coastline stretches over 550 km from Karnataka to within 100 km of the S tip of India, but nowhere is it more than 120 km wide. The discovery of coral formations several km inland proves that the narrow coastal fringe has been raised in recent geological time from the sea. On the coast is a narrow band of alluvium. Immediately inland are low, rolling hills of laterite, then inland again the ancient gneisses of the Peninsula which form the backbone of the Western Ghats.

The state's palm-fringed "backwaters" along the coastline are a special attraction, see page 964. The Silent Valley National Park in the Western Ghats, 46 km E of Mannarghat (restricted entry) has the only substantial area of evergreen rain forest in the country

Climate

Kerala has an almost equatorial climate. Maximum temperatures rarely rise above 32°C. Minimum temperatures at sea level are never below 20°C. The annual range at Kochi is 6°C. The Western Ghats receive over 3,000 mm of rain a year, mainly from May to Nov. Although Kerala is strongly affected by the monsoon it does not have the extended dry season characteristic of the rest of India, over a quarter of its rain falling between Dec and May.

Fauna & flora

There are 2 National Parks (Eravikulam and Silent Valley) and a number of small wildlife sanctuaries in the state. In addition to the wildlife typical of S India described in the introduction, Kerala has a distinctive and beautiful range of butterflies. Among the most striking are: Commander (*Moduza procris*): the com-

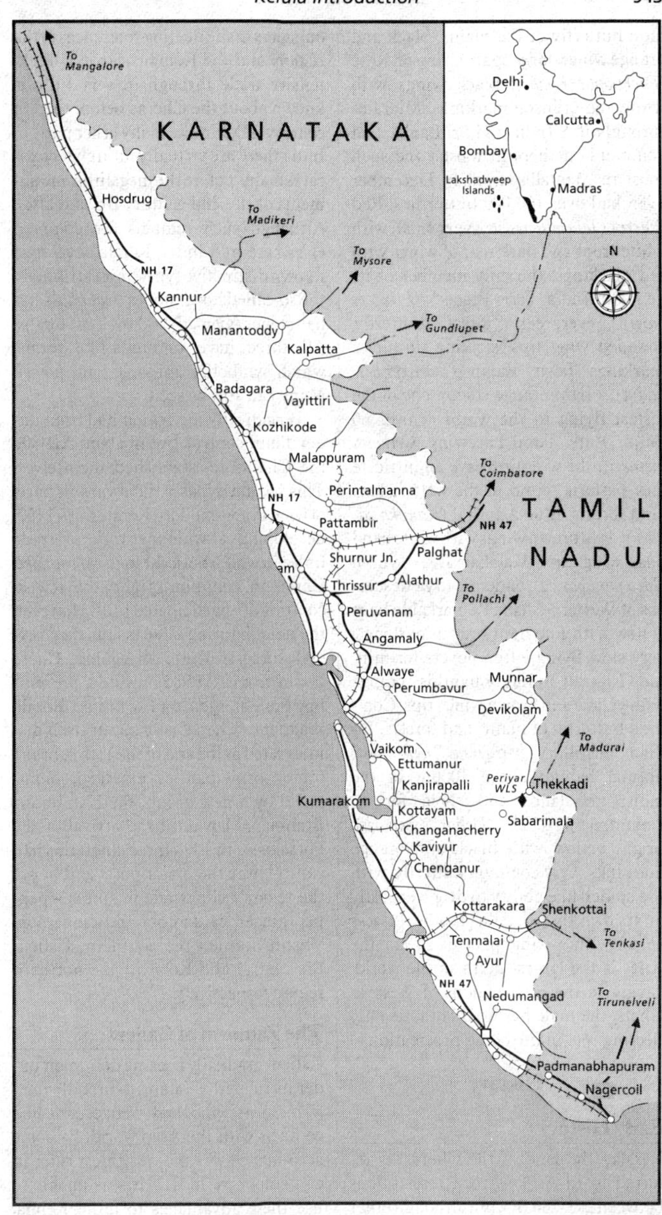
To Mangalore
KARNATAKA
Delhi
Calcutta
Bombay
Lakshadweep Islands
Madras
Hosdrug
To Madikeri
To Mysore
N
NH 17
Kannur
Manantoddy
To Gundlupet
Kalpatta
Badagara
Vayittiri
Kozhikode
Malappuram
To Coimbatore
Perintalmanna
NH 17
TAMIL NADU
Pattambir
NH 47
Shurnur Jn.
Palghat
Alathur
Thrissur
To Pollachi
Peruvanam
Angamaly
Alwaye
Munnar
Perumbavur
Devikolam
To Madurai
Vaikom
Ettumanur
Periyar WLS
Kanjirapalli
Thekkadi
Kumarakom
Kottayam
Sabarimala
Changanacherry
Kaviyur
Chenganur
Kottarakara
Shenkottai
To Tenkasi
Tenmalai
Ayur
NH 47
Nedumangad
To Tirunelveli
Padmanabhapuram
Nagercoil

mon butterfly of the plains, black and orange wings, large span. Crimson Rose (*Pachliopta hector*): black wings with white and crimson markings. Migrates throughout S India and Sri Lanka, and commonly gathers in roosts; one such roost in Mamallapuram in December 1985 had over 100,000 butterflies. Red Pierrot (*Talicada nyseus*): very small with white front and dark rear of wings with red markings; the only member of its genus in India. Paris Peacock (*Princeps paris*): evergreen forest butterfly, rounded wing tips, striking turquoise markings. Tawny Rajah (*Charaxes bernadus*): a light orange colour, one of the fastest flying in the world at over 60 kmph. Rare. Tamil Lacewing (*Cethosia nietneri*): the wingtips have an intricate lacy pattern; found in the wettest lowland forests. Blue Admiral (*Kaniska canace*): dark brown wings with white band near wing tips. Malabar Tree Nymph (*Idea malabarica*): endemic to wettest areas of Western Ghats. Remarkable light yellow with fine light brown markings; very slow flying, often hovers for minutes. *Rustic* (Cupha erymanthis): orange with yellow and brown wings tips. Common butterfly of plains and forests. Indian Fritillary (*Argyreus hyperbius*): normal habitat above 1000m in the moist grasslands and shola forests. Common Jezebel (*Delias eucharis*): bright yellow with black and orange markings. Very common butterfly, with the spider-like ability to drop vertically on its own thread. Atlas moth (*Atttacus atlas*): with a wing span of 24 cm the Atlas is the largest moth in the world. Living in the high regions of Western Ghats, the male has no mouth, its only fleeting role in life being procreation.

History

Early History

Kerala, 'the land of the Cheras' is referred to in Asoka's rock inscriptions between 273-236 BC, but although other outsiders made fleeting references to the region, and the Romans carried on extensive trade through it, very little is known about the Cheras before the 8th century AD. Unlike many other parts of India there are virtually no archaeological remains before the megalithic monuments of the 2nd century BC and after. Although such remains are common elsewhere in S India, Kerala developed its own distinctive types, most strikingly the so-called hood-stones (*kudaikal*) and hat-stones (*topi-kal*) and rock cut tombs. All three have umbrella-like forms, which symbolize authority and power. Many can still be seen.

Periodically the region had been under Tamil control, but in about AD 800 the Cheras re-established themselves. This second dynasty ruled various parts of what is now modern Kerala until 1102, developing a wide network of trade links, in which both the long established Christian community and the Jewish community participated fully. However, the neighbouring Cholas launched several successful attacks against Chera power from AD 985 onwards, preventing the emergence of a united Kerala kingdom. When Chola power itself disintegrated at the end of the 11th century, minor principalities emerged, dominated by a new group, the Nambudiri Brahmans. Up until the arrival of the Portuguese in 1498 three chieftains had control over the major ports and hence the region's vital trade in spices – pepper, ginger, cardamom and cinnamon. Venadu formed the southern, Calicut the central and Kolattiri the northern region respectively.

The Zamorin of Calicut

Calicut gradually became dominant under its ruler, the Zamorin (literally *Lord of the Sea*), who had well established contacts with the Arab world. By some accounts he was the wealthiest ruler in contemporary India. He was unable to use these advantages to unite Kerala, and during the 16th century the Portuguese exploited the rivalry of the Raja of Kolattiri with the Zamorin of Calicut, being granted permission to trade from Kochi in 1499. Over the following century there was fierce competition and sometimes open warfare between the Portuguese, bent on eliminating Arab trading competition, and the Zamorin of Calicut, whose prosperity depended on that Arab trade. The competition was encouraged by the rulers of Kochi, in the hope that by keeping the hands of both tied in conflict their own independence would be strengthened. After a century of hostility the Dutch arrived on the W coast. The Zamorin of Calicut seized the opportunity of gaining external support, and on 11 November 1614 concluded a Treaty giving the Dutch full trading rights. In 1615 the British E India Company was also given the right to trade by the Zamorin. By 1633 the Dutch had captured all the Portuguese forts of Kollam, Kodungallur, Purakkad, Kochi and Kannur. The ruler of Kochi rapidly made friends with the Dutch, in exchange having the new Mattancherry Palace built for him, and inevitably facing renewed conflict with Calicut as a result.

Travancore and the British

In the decade after 1740 Raja Marthanda Varma succeeded in uniting a number of petty states around Thiruvananthapuram and led them to a crushing victory over the Dutch in the Battle of Kolachel in 1741. By 1758 the Zamorin of Calicut was forced to withdraw from Kochi, but the Travancore ruler's reign was brief. In 1766 Haidar Ali had led his cavalry troops down onto the W coastal plain, and he and his son Tipu Sultan pushed further and further S with a violence that is still bitterly remembered. In 1789, as Tipu was preparing to launch a final assault on the S of Travancore, the British attacked him from the E. He withdrew his army from Kerala and the Zamorin and other Kerala leaders looked to the British to take control of the forts previously held by Tipu's officers. Tipu Sultan's first defeat at the hands of Lord Cornwallis led to the Treaty of Seringapatam in 1792, under which Tipu surrendered all his captured territory in Malabar, the N part of Kerala, to direct British rule. Travancore and Kochi became Princely states under ultimate British authority.

Culture

People

Kerala is the first state in India to obtain 100% literacy. Infant mortality is less than ¼ of the national average. Women enjoy a high social status, perhaps partly a reflection of the matrilineal system common in pre-modern times. Yet in the hills are some of India's most primitive tribes, and on the coastal plains there remain too few economic opportunities for the growing population. Very large numbers of Malayalis have emigrated to find work, in recent years to the Gulf. It is one of the 2 Indian states, along with W Bengal, where Communists have played a major part in Govt for several periods since Independence.

Religion

Although Hinduism is still dominant, as much as a quarter of the population is Christian, the majority tracing their Christian roots back at least 1,500 years. There is also a significant Muslim population. Religious communities have often lived amicably together. There is no conflict between the varying Hindu sects, and most temples have shrines to each of the major Hindu divinities. Christianity, which is thought to have been brought by St Thomas the Apostle to the coast of Kerala at Kodungallur in AD 52, has its own very long tradition. The Portuguese tried to convert the Syrian Christians to Roman Catholicism, but although they established a thriving Catholic Church the Syrian tradition survived in various forms. The equally large Muslim community traces its origins back to the spread of Islam across the Indian Ocean with Arab traders from the 7th century, and is particularly strong in the N of the state. In the last 15 years the Muslim community responded quickly to the new opportunities in the Gulf. It suffered correspondingly from the dramatic repatriation of Indian workers in 1990-91 but is now recovering.

Local festivals

Kerala has several distinctive festivals:

Jan-Feb *Ulsavam* is celebrated for 8 days at the Ernakulam Siva Temple. An elephant procession and folk dance and musical performances are staged. In Guruvayur this festival is celebrated at the end of Feb.

Apr-May *Vishukani* celebrates the start of the rainy season and the sowing of the main paddy crop. The fire crackers exploded to ward off evil spirits can be quite terrifyingly loud. On the eve of the festival families place a large bell metal container between 2 lamps, filled with rice and *Nava Dhanyas* (9 kinds of grain) each in a banana leaf cup, a picture of a favourite goddess, cash, jewellery and fruit. Next day, at dawn the family first look at the gifts of nature, in the hope that it will bring prosperity through the year.

Aug-Sep The biggest and most important festival is *Thiruvonam* (*Onam*), a harvest festival, celebrated throughout Kerala in the month of *Chingom* (Aug/Sep) and lasts 4 days. According to legend it is on the first day that the good Asura king Mahabali who once ruled Kerala, comes from exile to visit his beloved people. Homes are prepared for his visit, decorated with flowers. It is accompanied by elephant processions, Kathakali dances, fire works, water carnivals and *vallam kalli*, the famous snake boat races, sometimes with over 100 oarsmen per boat. The festival is held at several places, including Alappuzha, Kottayam, Kochi, Aranmula and Payipad. In 1995 it will be celebrated between 5th-11th Sep.

Kerala Tourism organises several festivals specifically for tourists. The most important are:

Jan 17-20 *Great Elephant March* Tourists have the chance to feed and ride on elephants. A boat race in Alappuzha is included the elephant festival is also held in Thrissur and Thiruvananthapuram.

Nishangandhi Dance Festival All the important types of Indian dance are performed by leading artistes at Nishagandhi open-air auditorium, Kanakakkunnu Palace.

Aug-Sep *Onam Tourist Week* Art and folk presentations at over 20 venues in Thiruvananthapuram.

Language

Malayalam, the State language, is the most recent of the Dravidian languages, developing from the 13th century. However, the region has been distinct from its neighbours for far longer.

Dance

Kathakali See page 810. The special dance form of Kerala has its origins in the *Theyyam*, a ritual tribal dance of N Kerala, and *kalaripayattu*, the martial arts practised by the high-caste Nayars, going back 1,500 years. In its present form of sacred dance-drama, Kathakali has evolved over the last 400 years. The performance is usually out of doors, the stage is bare but for a lamp (now helped by electric lighting), with the drummers on one side and the singers with cymbal and gong, who act as narrators, on the other. The art of mime reaches its peak in these highly stylised performances which last through the night. For the performers the preparations begin several hours in advance, since putting on the elaborate make-up and costumes is very time consuming. The final application of a flower seed in the lower eye-lid results in the red eyes you will see on stage.

This classical dance requires lengthy and hard training to make the body supple, the eyes expressive. 24 *mudras* express the nine emotions of serenity, wonder, kindness, love, valour, fear, contempt, loathing and anger. Dancers must learn all the major character parts of the core repertoire of about three dozen plays and be able to change roles frequently. The gods and mortals play out their roles and chaos brought about by human ambition but ends in peace and harmony restored by the gods.

Every 12 years N Malabar village communities organise a *Theyyam* festival in which the dancer wears a 9m tall head dress made of decorated cloth stretched over a bamboo framework. The ancient rituals at a *kavu* shrine preceding the performance, gives the dancer a divine significance even though they all come from a group of *Untouchables*, and the festival of dancing and singing ends with the scattering of rice and blessings and a final feast. *Kavus* were once dedicated to ancient animistic deities.

Mohiniyattam performed by women, is known as the dance of the charmer or temptress and is particularly sensuous. It evolved through the influence of Tamil dancers who brought Bharata Natyam to the Kerala royal courts. It is performed solo as in Bharata Natyam with a similar core repertoire and musical accompaniments but with the addition of *idakkai*, a percussion instrument. **Tullal**, again peculiar to Kerala, is another classical solo dance form which comes closer to contemporary life, and is marked for its simplicity, wit and humour. In addition there are a number of dance forms which are special to each locality and in general all are performed in very colourful, often gaudy, costumes and ornaments, and accompanied by singing and drumming.

Kalaripayattu is still practised in *kalaris* or gymnasia which teach this Keralan form of martial arts of unarmed combat which is accompanied by scientific body massage. Some believe that karate originated in this form and was taken to SE Asia by a Buddhist monk.

Ayurvedic Medicine

Ayurveda (science of life/ health) is the ancient Hindu system of medicine – a naturalistic system depending on diagnosis of the body's 'humours' (wind, mucus, gall and sometimes, blood) to achieve a balance. In the early form, gods and demons were associated with cure and ailments; treatment was carried out by using herbs, minerals, formic acid (from ant hills) and water, and hence was limited in scope. Ayurveda classified substances and chemicals compounds in the theory of *panchabhutas* or 5 'elements'. It also noted the action of food and drugs on the human body. Ayurvedic massage using aromatic and medicinal oils to tone up the nervous system, has been practised in Kerala for centuries. Interest has been revived in this form of medicine and there are now holidays offered by Kerala Tourism which include a 'rejuvination programme'. Nirmala Ayurvedic Hospital is in Thiruvananthapuram.

Handicrafts

Temples and palaces have excellent carving, and rose wood is still inlaid with other woods, bone or plastics (to replace the traditional ivory). Wooden boxes with brass binding where plain or patterned strips of brass are used for decoration are also made, as are carved models of the 'snake boats'. Kerala produces astonishing *masks* and *theatrical ornaments*, particularly the *Krishnattam* masks which resemble the mask-like make up of the Kathakali dancers. *Conch shells* which are also available in great numbers are carved out in relief.

Modern Kerala

Government

The reorganisation of the Indian States

in 1956 brought together the Malayalam language area of Kerala into one political unit. It comprises all except some of the Kanniyakumari districts of Travancore, Kochi, Malabar and a part of S Kanara District from Karnataka. Kerala politics has been dominated by the struggle between the Communist Party Marxist and the Congress, and the State government has often been formed by coalitions.

Economy

By some economic indicators Kerala is only a middle ranking Indian State – 9th in the mid 1980s. In the 1970s the flow of migrants from Kerala to the Gulf increased rapidly, and remittances played an increasing role in the lives of many villagers. Kerala accounted for over half the total Indian emigration to the Gulf up to the end of the 1980s. Ironically, the greater the flow of remittances, the slower has been Kerala's economic growth, particularly in the productive sectors of the economy. There are some exceptions, the most notable being banking and insurance and transport and communications. Most migrants came from the coastal districts such as Thiruvananthapuram and Thrissur. In these areas land prices rocketed tenfold in the years 1975-86. The Gulf War in 1991 caused a severe drop in remittances and the return of thousands of migrants. However, it is the first state to obtain 100% literaracy and get every village on the phone.

Although unemployment has remained extremely high, in some semi-skilled areas there have been labour shortages that have pushed up wage rates and encouraged migrants to come in from neighbouring states, especially Tamil Nadu. Most of the new money from remittances has gone on consumption. Strikingly it is the poorer families who have benefited most, even though there has been a significant drain of skilled workers as well. Most of the increases in demand for consumer goods in Kerala have been met by imports from other states of India – rice, pulses, sugar, medicine, clothing, cosmetics and construction materials. That trade has produced a huge State financial deficit. Ironically Kerala's trade overseas – tea, cardamom, ginger, rubber – produces big surpluses.

Industry & resources The coir industry which has supported the Malabar coastal economy still thrives. The coconut palm is used in a dozen different ways. Annually, each palm produces around 80 nuts. The fibrous outer covering is removed and the fibres soaked in water for some months, dried and beaten with a stick, to form coir. This is woven into mats or twisted into rope. Each part of the tree is put to use, the trunk for building houses or boats, the leaves for thatching or basket making, the 'milk' for drink, fresh or fermented. The fleshy white kernel is eaten or used for oil or soap making and the hard outer shell dried to be turned into bowls or pots or simply burnt as fuel. Kerala is also India's most important cocoa growing region, accounting for nearly 12,000 ha of the country's total of 17,000 ha in 1994.

THIRUVANANTHAPURAM (Trivandrum)

BASICS *Population*: 825,700; *STD Code*: 0471; *Airport*: 6 km.

Thiruvananthapuram is 87 km from the S tip of India. It became the capital of the Raja of Travancore in 1750 when the then Raja moved from Padmanabhapuram. The name is derived from *Tiru Ananta Puram*, the abode of the sacred serpent *Ananta* upon whose coils Vishnu lies in the main temple. It is a peaceful, attractive city built on low hills by the sea, very relaxed for a state capital. Away from the centre, you can walk through narrow winding streets with whitewashed houses with red tiled roofs in cool, green gardens. The typical gabled pagoda-like roof style is unique to Kerala and coastal Karnataka. Despite its size it still has the feel of an overgrown village or market town and is a good place to get an impression of Kerala town life.

Local crafts & industries

Ivory carving used to be carried out until restrictions imposed by the govt. Wood carving (sandal and rosewood).

Places of interest

Sri Padmanabhasvami Temple Only open to Hindus: 0415-0515, 0615-0650, 0815-1000, 1130-1200, 1715-1915. Kerala Brahmins are often stricter than those in Tamil Nadu. They have rules of clothing even for male Hindus who must enter wearing only a white *dhoti*. According to legend the temple was built in stages to house the statue of Vishnu reclining on the sacred serpent *Ananta*, which was found in the forest. It was rebuilt in 1733 by Raja Marthanda Varma who dedicated the whole kingdom, including his rights and possessions, to the deity. Unusually for Kerala, it is in the Dravidian style with beautiful murals, sculptures and 368 carved granite pillars which support the main pavilion or *Kulashekhara Mandapa*. You can see the 7-storeyed *gopuram* with its sacred pool from outside. The **Kanakakunnu Palace**, 800m NE of the Museum, now belongs to the Govt. **Museum** and **Botanical Gardens, Art Gallery** and the **Zoo** are described below. **Shankhumukham Beach** near the airport has a stretch of clean sand, but is unsuitable for sea bathing.

Veli Tourist Village 10 km from the city, boating on a lake and restaurant in well-landscaped gardens with sculptures.

Museums

The Napier Museum. N of city, in park grounds nr zoo and art galleries, 400m E of Indian Airlines. 1000-1700 except Wed, 1300-1645. Closed Mon. A spectacular wooden building designed by R.F. Chisholm in traditional Kerala style and completed in 1872, it is a landmark. See page 821. It has a famous collection of mainly 8th-18th century S Indian bronzes; some superb. Rules for sculpting deities such as Siva, Vishnu, Parvati and Lakshmi were laid down in the *Silpa Sastras*. Sculpture in Kerala was strongly influenced by Tamil styles, but there are distinctive features. Most of the 400 bronzes are from Chola, Vijayanagar and Nayak periods; a few Jain and Buddhist sculptures. Also excellent wood carvings, for which Kerala is particularly famous. Ceilings, gables and doors of both homes and temples were usually built of wood and richly decorated. Ivory carvings and Kathakali costumes also displayed. Printed guide available.

Natural History Museum, E of Napier Museum. Natural history and a small ethnographic collection.'Includes a beautifully made replica of a typical Kerala Nayar wooden house (*nalukettu*) describing principles of its construction. These houses were particularly common in N Travancore among wealthy Nayar families, a highly regarded Hindu warrior caste whose members inter-married with Brahmins. The Nayars were noted for their matrilineal pattern of descent.

Sri Chitra Art Gallery Excellent

CLIMATE: THIRUVANANTHAPURAM

	Jan	Feb	Mar	Apr	May	Jun	Jul	Aug	Sep	Oct	Nov	Dec	Av/Tot
Max (°C)	31	32	33	32	31	29	29	29	30	30	30	31	31
Min (°C)	22	23	24	25	25	24	23	22	23	23	23	23	23
Rain (mm)	20	20	43	122	249	331	215	164	123	271	207	73	1838

THIRUVANANTHAPURAM (TRIVANDRUM)
SA 181
To Quilon (NH 17)
To Zoo
Indian Airlines
PMG Circle
LMS Jn.
Kanakakunna Palace
Vazhangodu Circle
Museum of Science & Technology
Main Central Rd
Museum Rd
Observatory
Kerala Tourist Office
Handicrafts Design Centre
N
Public Library
Nandavanam Rd
Palayam Jn.
PO
Tagore Theatre
Forest Museum
VAZHUTHACUD
KUNNUKUZHI
M G Rd
Central Survey Office
General Hospital Circle
Spencer Jn.
Bakery Jn.
To Youth Hostel, Beach & Airport
Statue Rd
State Bank of India
Air Lanka
Vazhuthacud Rd
Yoga Centre
Panavilla Circle
Secretariat
Foreigner's Registration Office
Pulimudu Jn.
Maldive Airways
SMSM Handicrafts
PO
Press Rd
Childerns Museum
Mahatma Gandhi Rd
THYCAUD
VANCHIYUR
Aristo Rd
S S Coil Rd
Thycaud Hospital Rd
GPO & Post Restante
A College Jn.
Manjalikulam Rd
THAMPANOOR
Mettukkada Mukku
Thycaud Jn.
Chettikulangara Rd
Bank
Tourist Office
Central Station Rd
Hospital Rd
Thampanoor Jn.
Thakaraparambu Rd
VALIYASALA
SRI KANTESWARAM
Verma Travels
Padmavilasam Rd
Padmanabhasvami Temple
FORT
Bhajanpura Palace
Handicrafts Design Centre
To Airport
Post Office
0 300 metres
To Kovalam (16 km)
1. Napier Museum, Open Air Theatre, & Natural History Museum
2. Sri Chitra Art Gallery
3. Vellayambalum Palace
4. Cosmopolitan Club
5. Swimming Pool
6. Victoria Jubilee Market
7. Kairali Handicrafts Emporium
8. Antiquarts
9. Air India
10. Kalandriya Restaurant
11. Indian Coffee House
12. Arul Jyoti Restaurant & Telegraph Office
13. Nalukeltu Restaurant
Hotels:
14. Luciya Continental
15. Mascot
16. Pankaj
17. Horizon
18. Shanti Woodlands & Annapurna Restaurant
19. Chaithram
20. Highlands
21. Bhaskara Bhavan Tourist Paradise
22. Omkar Lodge & Safari Rest.
23. Rajdhani Tourist Home
24. Magnet & Jaihind Travels
25. South Park & Kerala Travels
26. Geeth
27. Jas
28. Government Rest House
29. Residency Guest House
30. PWD Rest House
31. YMCA
32. YMCA & Brit Council Library
33. Mas
34. Pravin Tourist Home
35. Manacaud
B1. KSRTC & TTC Bus Stand
B2. Fort Bus Station
B3. Buses to Kovalem
T. Railway Retiring Rooms

collection of Indian art with examples from early to modern schools. Paintings by Raja Ravi Verma and paintings from Java, Bali, China and Japan, Mughal and Rajput miniature paintings, and Tanjore paintings embellished with semi-precious stones. 1000-1700. Closed Mon and Wed mornings. Rs.2. Well worth a visit, as is the new gallery devoted to modern art next door.

Museum of Science and Technology Nr the *Mascot Hotel*. Highlights science, technology and electronics. 1000-1700, closed Mon. Small entry fee. **Children's Museum**, Thycaud. Dolls, masks, paintings. 1000-1700. **Oriental Research Institute and Manuscripts Library**, University, Kariavattom. Literary treasures including vast collection of palm leaf manuscripts.

Parks & zoos

Botanical Gardens and Zoo. 0900-1645. Closed Mon. Rs.2, Video/cine cameras Rs 5. Entrance at SW corner of park, 400m E of Indian Airlines. Set in wooded hilly parkland the zoo is spacious and offers delightful shaded walks. It has a wide collection of animals, including several species of monkey, lions, tigers, leopards, giraffes, deer, zebra. Sadly some do not look well cared for. The park Botanical Gardens are here with many trees clearly labelled.

Other parks and gardens in the city – around the Secretariat, Gandhi Park, Waterworks Gardens and at Veli Tourist Village. **NB** The Aquarium nr the beach has closed.

Tours

Kerala Tourism: Dep from Thiruvananthapuram: **1** *City tour*: 0800-1900, incl Kovalam Beach (125 km), Rs 50 daily; **2** *Kanniyakumari*: 0730-2100, incl Kovalam, Padmanabhapuram and Kanniyakumari (200 km), Rs 70 daily; **3** *Ponmudi*: 0830-1900, daily, Golden Valley and Ponmudi (125 km), Rs 50; **4** *Thekkadi Wild Life*: Sat 0630 return Sun 2100 (520 km); **5** *Kodaikkanal*: 3-day tour including Thekkadi and Kanniyakumari, Sat 0630 return Mon 2100 (800 km), Rs 270; **6** *Courtallam*: Sat, Sun, Rs 70; **7** *Periyar*: 2-day tour; Sat, Rs 150. **8** *Kodaikkanal*: 3-day tour; last Sat, Rs 250. If pressed for time these can be worth considering, but they can be very exhausting and the amount of time given to stops at sites of interest, is often very limited. Particularly true of the Thekkadi tour, most of which is spent in the bus (9 hr each way), so is not rec. New 'Health & Fitness' and 'Body, Mind and Soul' packages for women, 7-14 days at Kovalam or Thiruvananthapuram. *Gt India Tour Co*, Grd Flr, Mullassery Towers, Vanross Sq, T 331516. Also does afternoon City tour daily

Local festivals

Mar *Chandanakuda* at Beemapalli when local Muslims process to the mosque, holding incense sticks and pots. Marked by sword play, singing, dancing, elephant procession and fireworks.

Mar/Apr *Ulsavam* Celebrated at Padmanabhasvami Temple for 10 days with music and dance and procession of elephants. *Arat* Image of Vishnu is taken to the sea for immersion. Also in Oct/Nov.

Sep/Oct *Navaratri* at the special mandapam in Padmanabhasvami Temple. Several concerts which draw famous musicians. *Thiruvonam week* 15-21 Sep 1994 ; 5-11 Sep 1995. Many other fairs and festivals are organised by different agencies throughout the year.

Local information

● Accommodation

Price guide
AL Rs 3,000+ **A** Rs 2,000-3,000
B Rs 1,200-2,000 **C** Rs 600-1,200
D Rs 250-600 **E** Rs 100-250 **F** Up to Rs 100.

(See also under Kovalam) The central area (about 5 km from airport) and the railway station have many very cheap hotels, some excellent value. Even the better hotels are very reasonably priced compared with larger cities elsewhere in India. Attached bath often indicates showers.

C *Luciya Continental*, E Fort, T 73443, F 73347, 104 rm, some a/c, large 'fantasy suites' with Keralan, 'Old English', unusual Chinese and Arab decor, the Kerala Suite particularly rec, good restaurant (and outdoor barbeque), exchange, travel, shop, another good value hotel, rather more expensive than the *Mascot* or *Pankaj*; **C** Kerala Tourism ***Mascot***, Mascot Sq, T 438990, 42 rm, some a/c, dark and sombre appearance inside, though mostly of modern construction, restaurant, 24 hr coffee shop, pool., competent without being exciting, but very good value for money, open-air Barbecue (evenings only), close to Museum and Tourist Office; **C** ***South Park***, Spencer Junc, MG Rd, T 435422, 82 rm, restaurant (inc good buffet lunches), bar, modern, marble and glass, some business facilities, but pricey; **C** *Fort Manor*, Power House Junc, T 70002, 60 a/c rm, restaurant, bar, shops.

D *Horizon*, Aristo Rd, T 66888, F 446859, 47 rm, some a/c with showers, central, good restaurants (roof-top, open weekend evenings), bar, bookshop, comfortable though simple; **D** *Amritha*, Thycaud, ½ km rly, T 63091, pleasant; **D** ***Pankaj***, MG Rd, opp Govt Secretariat, T 76667, 50 rm, some a/c, 2 good restaurants (1 roof-top), bar, exchange, central (can be noisy), excellent value for money; **D** Kerala Tourism ***Chaithram***, Station Rd, Thampanoor, T 75777,. 88 rm, some a/c, good restaurants, bar, exchange, modern, very clean, next to rly and bus stand; **D** ***Highlands***, Manjalikulam Rd, Thampanoor, T 78440, 85 comfortable rm, some a/c, central, good value; **D** *Jas*, PO Box 431, Thycaud/ Aristo Junc, T 64881, 50 rm, some a/c, roof-garden restaurant rec, quiet, good value, rec.

● **Budget hotels & guest houses**

E *Geeth*, off MG Rd, nr GPO, Pulimood, T 71941, 50 rm, some a/c, good value, roof-top restaurant rec; **E** *Mas*, Over Bridge Junc, nr SL Theatres, town centre, T 78566, F 72380, clean, pleasant, well-maintained, restaurant, but sometimes effectively shut; **E** *Ganesh*, Ambujavilasam Rd, Opp P.R.S. Court, dirty and dingy rm, a really badly run hotel. **E** *Pravin Tourist House*, Manjalikulam Rd, 750 m from Thampanoor Rd, clean, quiet, no restaurant. **E** *Manacaud*, Manjalikulam Rd, 500 m from Thampanoor Rd. Adequate.

F *Bhaskara Bhavan Tourist Paradise*, nr Ayurveda College, T 79662, 40 rm, sombre but clean, good value; **F** ***Taurus Lodge***, Statue Rd, has rm with bath, kitchenette, v clean, quiet and helpful service; **F** ***Omkar Lodge***, MG Rd, opp SMV School, T 78503, 15 clean rm, rec; **F** *Rajdhani Tourist Home*, E Fort, T 73353, 50 rm; **F** Govt ***Yatri Niwas***, Thycaud, T 63711, extremely cheap, very busy; **F** ***Thopil***, TC4/370 Palayam, T 62256, welcomes 6 guests in a dorm and **F** *Jose Villa*, University Rd, T 77557, has a rm to spare.

● **Youth Hostels**

F *YWCA Guest House*, Palayam is behind Secretariat, T 68059; **F** ***Youth Hostel***, Veli, T 71364, rm and dorm, pleasant site, boating on the lake at leisure complex (see above), good Indian restaurant, 10 km from centre, reached by bus and taxi, perhaps the cheapest in Thiruvananthapuram!, even cheaper than **F** *Railway Retiring Rooms*, dorm.

● **Places to eat**

In hotels: *Luciya Continental* (S Indian), *Horizon* and *Pankaj* (with sweet stall-cum-restaurant at its entrance) are rec.

Others: *Kalandriya*, on MG Rd (N Indian), nr the Overbridge Junc. ***Azad Hotel***, MG Rd, Statue Junc, specialises in Muslim dishes and ***Arul Jyoti***, MG Rd, opp Secretariat, Statue Junc, in good S Indian veg. ***Indian Coffee House*** has 2 branches on MG Rd, one nr YWCA, N of the Secretariat and the other nr E Fort nr bus stand. The last, designed by an English architect, spirals upwards – worth seeing. Excellent coffee and cheap snacks. ***Kalpakavadi***, YMCA Rd, new non-veg restaurant, modern and smart, rec. ***Nalukettu***, a little out of the way in Vazhuthcud Rd, offers inexpensive Kerala thalis, T 69287. ***Karthika***, at *Hotel Ganesh*, Ambujavilasam Rd, Opp PRS Court, in town centre.

● **Bars**

Several of the hotels and the larger restaurants have bars.

● **Air offices**

Air Lanka, Geetanjali Bldg, Ganapathikoil Rd, Vazhuthacud, T 68767. **Gulf Air**, Jet Air, Panavila Junc, T 67514. **Kuwait Airways**, National Travel Service, Panavila Junc, T 634301. **Saudi Airways**, Arafath Travels, Pattom, T 78101.

● **Banks & money changers**

Banks in Kerala are open 1000-1400, Mon to Fri, and 1000-1200, Sat. Otherwise, the Airport now has a bank (usually 24 hr). **State Bank of India**, nr Secretariat. Others on MG Rd, Spencer Junc, Ayurveda College Junc and Statue Junc.

● Clubs

Trivandrum Club, Vazhuthacud. **Automobile Assoc of S India**, VJT Hall Rd.

● Cultural Centres

British Library, nr Secretariat. **Alliance Française**, Vellayambalam. **Indian Council of Cultural Relations**, Vellayambam.

● Entertainment

Cinemas: several especially nr Station and Overbridge Junc on MG Rd some showing English language films.

● Hospitals & medical services

Chemists: a few nr Statue Junc. *Lakshmi Medical Stores*, MG Rd and *Krishna Medicals*, E Fort.

Hospitals: *General Hospital*, Vanchiyoor. *Cosmopolitan Hospital*, Maurinja Palayam. *Ramakrishna Mission Hospital*, Sasthamangalam. *Nirmala Ayurvedic Hospital*, Taliyal (SE of town).

● Post & telecommunications

GPO: Palayam, in a narrow street just W of MG Rd opp the **Central Bank of India**. Poste Restante, 0800-1800. Also PO at Thampanoor, opp Manjalikulam Rd. **Telegraph office**: Statue Rd, 200m to its N, T 61494. Open 24 hr. **Rly Mail service**: nr Central Statiion, Thampanoor. **Couriers**: *DHL*, Vellayambalam, T 65863. *Corporate Couriers*, Bakery Junc, T 6 9125.

● Shopping

Usually open 0900 to 2000, though some take a long lunch break. Although ivory goods have now been banned carving of wood and marquetry using other materials such as plastic continue to flourish, and are the hallmark of traditional Kerala handcrafts. These and items such as *Kathakali* masks and traditional fabrics can be bought at a number of shops, including the Govt run ***SMS Handcrafts Emporium*** behind the Secretariat. ***Natesan Antique Arts*** and ***Gift Corner*** on MG Rd have a wide collection of high quality goods including old dowry boxes, carved wooden panels from old temple 'cars' or chariots, miniature paintings, old ivory carvings and bronzes. ***Kairali*** opp the Secretariat in MG Rd. Items of banana fibre, coconut, screw pine, mainly utilitarian. Also excellent sandalwood carvings and bell-metal lamps, utensils. ***Gram Sree*** for excellent village crafts. Also ***Spencers*** supermarket, MG Rd. Shopping areas include the Chalai Bazar, the Connemara market and the Main Rd from Palayam to the E Fort.

Books: ***Higginbothams***, ***Pai & Co***, ***India Book House***, all on MG Rd. ***Macmillan***, in Pulimood. ***National Book Stall*** and ***Current***, at Statue Junc.

Photography: several on MG Rd and Rly Station Rd, at Pulimood and Aristo Junc.

● Sports

Trivandrum Golf Club and ***Tennis Club***, both in Kowkidar; ***Indoor Recreation Centre***, Shankumugham.

Swimming: ***Waterworks*** pool nr Museum. 0430-1000, 1015-1200, 1400-1530, 1815-2000. Closed Mon. Also at ***Mascot Hotel***.

● Tour companies & travel agents

IATA approved agencies include: ***Air Travel Enterprises***, New Corp Bldg, Palayam, T 67627; ***United*** Pulimood, MG Rd; ***Jai Hind*** Samrias Centre, PMG Junc; ***Kerala Travels*** LMS Bldg, Museum Junc; ***Swastik***, Swastik Bldg, MG Rd; ***Aries***, Ayswarya Bldg, Press Rd; ***Gt India Tour Co***, Grd Flr, Mullassery Towers, Vanross Sq, T 331516; ***Chalukya Tours***, Vadayakadu, Kunnukzhy, T 444618, run unique and expensive tours and treks incl 3-day trek through forest staying in bamboo tree-houses and living with bamboo cutteres; the 3rd day ends with river rafting return. Also 2-day elephant or bullock cart 'safari' through village areas, and 3/ 4-day treks around Munnar or Kodaikkanal. Very well organised.

● Tourist office

Govt of India and **Kerala Tourist Information Counter**, Thiruvananthapuram Airport, T 71085. Also counters at the Rly station and bus station T 67224. **Kerala Tourism (KTDC)**, Tourist Reception Centre, Thampanoor, nr Bus Station, T 75031 and Mascot Sq, T 63476. The main Kerala Tourist Information Centre, Park View, opp Museum, T 61132. 1000-1700, closed Sun. The Kerala Tourist offices are particularly well supplied with leaflets and information sheets and are very helpful.

● Useful address

Visa extension: City Police Commissioner, Residency Rd, Thyacaud, T 60486; Superintendent of Police (Rural), Kowkidar, T 61296. The former is a better bet. Allow up to a week, though it can take less. Open 1000-1700 Mon-Sat.

● Transport

Thiruvananthapuram is the centre of a good

network of roads since several National Highways connect with it other cities in the S. NH 7 (Kanniyakumari to Varanasi), NH 17 (Thrissur to Bombay), NH 45 (Dindigul to Madras) and NH 47 (Kanniyakumari to Salem). Some distances: Kanniyakumari 85 km, Kochi 219 km, Coimbatore 410 km, Madurai 307 km, Thekkadi for Periyar 271 km.

Local Buses: are extremely crowded but an easy and very cheap way of getting about. Frequent buses to Kovalam leave from the Fort Bus Depot – see below. **Taxis**: charge about Rs 2.50/km. **Car hire**: luxury cars and Tourist Taxis can be hired through several firms – ITDC Transport Section, Chettikulamkara, T 61783. Verma Travels, E Fort, T 71400, Blaze Car Rentals, E Fort, Airport Rd, T 71622. Jai Hind Travels, *Hotel Magnet*, Thycaud, T 64445. Kerala Travels, LMS Building, T 63212. **Auto-rickshaws**: charge min Rs 3; it is often necessary to bargain in the evening.

Air Thiruvananthapuram airport is located on the beach 6 km away. There are new terminal buildings. Handling of domestic flights is straightforward, though international flights, especially to the Maldives, can be more difficult. Even with confirmed international bookings it pays to arrive in good time. Individually the staff are usually very helpful. If in doubt, ask frequently. **Transport to town**: by local bus No 14 is very cheap. Alternatively you can get a taxi or auto rickshaw – about Rs 30.

International: **Indian Airlines**, Mascot Junc, T 66370, Airport T 72228, Enquiries T 73537, Duty Officer T 71470. **Colombo**: M,Th,Sa, 1950, ¾ hr (**Air Lanka** flies there other days); **Male**: M,Tu,Th,Sa, 1610, ½ hr. **Air India**, Velayambalam, T 64837, Airport T 71426, Duty Officer T 70281. Flights to London, New York, Frankfurt and Paris and several destinations in the Gulf.

Domestic: **Indian Airlines Madras**: daily, 1840, 1 hr; W,F,Su (+ 1 other), 1730, 1 hr; **Bombay**: daily, 1500, 2 hr; **Bangalore**: daily, 1840, 1 hr. **East West Airlines**: **Bombay**: daily, 1245, 2 hr. **Air India**: **Bombay**: M,Tu,Th,F (2), Su.

Train Thiruvananthapuram Central Enquiry, T 62966, after 1800 T 63066. Reservations open 0700-1300,1330-1930, Sun 0900-1700. **Bangalore**: *Kanniyakumari-Bangalore Exp* 6225, daily, 1025, 18½ hr. **Madras**: *Trivandrum-Guwahati Exp* 2601 (AC/II), Th, 1250, 16¾ hr; *Madras Mail*, 6320 (AC/II), daily, 1330, 16¾ hr; **Calcutta (H)**: *Trivandrum-Guwahati Exp* 2601 (AC/II), Th, 1250, 49 hr; **Delhi, via Vijayawada, Nagpur & Bhopal (ND)**: *Kerala Exp* 2625 (AC/II), daily, 0945, 54½ hr; **Bombay (VT)**: *Kanniyakuman Exp* 1082 (AC/II), daily, 0725, 45½ hr. **Kollam via Varkala**: 12 trains daily, 0725-2035, 1¼ hr; **Mangalore**: *Malabar Exp* 6029, daily, 1740, 16 hr; *Trivandrum-Mangalore Parsuram Exp* 6349, daily, 0610, 15 hr.

Road Bus: Kerala State Road Transport Corp (KSRTC) operates a comprehensive service from Thiruvananthapuram, throughout the state and Tamil Nadu. Central Bus Station, Thampanoor, T 63886. **Kanniyakumari** via Nagercoil or direct, 10 daily, frequent dep, 2½ hr. Buses to **Kochi** via Kollam start at 0730, 5 hr (Exp), 6½ hr. It is possible to get from Thiruvananthapuram to Kochi in a day and include a section of the backwaters. **Kozhikode**, 10 hr (Exp) and **Thrissur**, 7 hr (Exp) also have a Superfast service.

Thiruvalluvar Transport Corp (TTC) and Tamil Nadu Govt Nesamony connects the city with many other centres – Coimbatore, Cuddalore, Erode, Kanniyakumari, Madurai and Madras. The Termini are opp Thiruvananthapuram Central Rly station. TTC, T 67756.

Short excursions from Thiruvananthapuram

Leave Thiruvananthapuram on NH 47 S to Nagercoil and Kanniyakumari. It is a slow and busy road, heavily wooded, to Marthandam (46 km) then passing through gently rolling countryside the 17 km to Padmanabhapuram, capital of the kings of Travancore from 1550 until 1750.

Padmanabhapuram

Excellent day trip from Thiruvananthapuram or Kovalam to the old palace of the Rajas of Travancore at Padmanabhapuram, their former capital. (*Padma*, lotus; *nabha*, navel; *puram*, town; the name refers to the image of the lotus coming from the navel of Vishnu.) The palace is beautifully kept and contains some fascinating architecture and paintings.

From the 9th century this part of Tamil Nadu and neighbouring Kerala were governed by the Ay dynasty, patrons both of Jainism and Hinduism. However, the land was always contested by the Cholas, the Pandiyas and the Cheras. By the late 11th century the new Venadu dynasty emerged from the Chera rulers of Kerala and took control of Kanniyakumari District in 1125 AD under Raja Kodai Kerala Varman. Never a stable kingdom and with varying degrees of territorial control, Travancore State was governed from Padmanabhapuram between 1590-1790, when the capital was shifted to Thiruvananthapuram. Although the Rajas of Travancore were Vaishnavite kings, they did not neglect Siva, as can be seen from various sculptures and paintings in the Palace.

The King never officially married, and the heir to the throne was his eldest sister's oldest son. This form of 'matrilineal descent' was characteristic of the earlier Chera empire (who ruled for 200 years from the early 12th century). The palace shows the superb craftsmanship, especially in woodworking, that has been characteristic of Kerala's art and architecture. There are also some superb frescoes and excellent stone-sculpted figures.

Open: 0900-1700 (last tickets 1630), closed Mon. Entry Rs 2, still cameras Rs 5, video Rs 500. **NB** It is difficult to photograph in the palace without flash or fast film. It is compulsory to take the tour with a guides who are available at the entrance to the main building and are very competent.

1. The main entrance A granite bed (notably cool) is in one corner and ceremonial bows line one wall. The carving on the royal chair is Chinese, illustrating the commercial contact between China and the Kerala kings. 90 different flowers are carved in the teak ceiling. **2.** 1st floor, the **durbar hall** where the king met with his ministers. The floor is made of egg-white, cement and lime, coconut water, charcoal, river sand, giving a smooth, hard, black finish. It is very well ventilated with wooden slatted surrounds, and has some coloured mica in windows. **3**. An enormous 2-storeyed hall (19m x 34206m), designed as a **dining hall** where 2,000 Brahmins were fed free once daily. Its long low cross-beams make it rather like an enormous old English barn in appearance. Downstairs are granite tubs – cool – for curds and buttermilk. **4**. The *Thaikottam* – 'Mother palace' – is the original structure. It was built in 1550. There is a *puja* room for the worship of Durga, with a jackfruit tree column. The woodwork is stained teak, with whitewashed stone

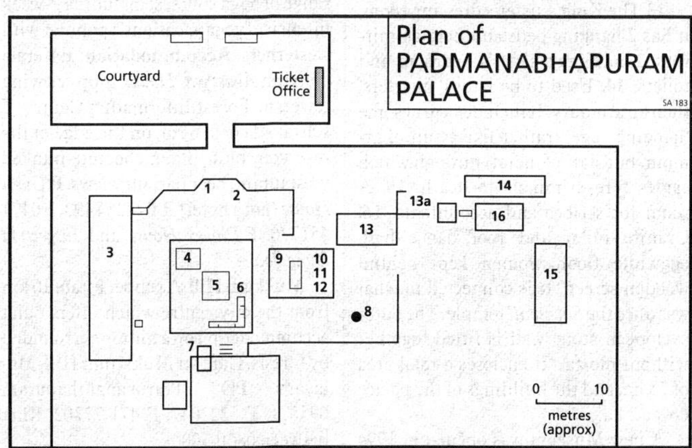

work below. **5**. A small **courtyard** (open to the sky). This is typical of Keralan domestic architecture. There is an **underground secret passage**, which is said to run from another palace 2 km away. **6**. Houses large urns for pickle for Brahmins' meals: lime, mango, gooseberry, and a list of others. **7**. Steps down to bath, room above for oil massage. **8**. The 38 kg stone standing on a pedestal in the courtyard at chest height had to be lifted 101 times consecutively over head as qualification to join the king's army. The potential recruit was watched from room 10. **9**. The **Treasury** on the ground floor. **10. King's bedroom** contains a four poster medicinal bed of 64 ayurvedic healing woods eg sandalwood, presented by the East India Company. It has the serpent of Hippocrates at its head.

11. King's special bedroom for fasting times, balcony all round. **12. Vishnu's bedroom** (teak beds) vegetable oil tints and frescoes of deities on every wall, 2 hanging brass lanterns lit continuously since the 18th century. Coconut oil is added twice daily, a cotton wick once a week. The room has a balcony all round. **NB** Rooms **11** and **12** are currently closed to the public for renovation. If you are lucky the guide might open up.

13 The King's sister's **dressing room**; it has 2 hanging beds and Belgian mirrors. **13a. King's sister's bedroom** and toilets. **14.** Used to be ladies' quarters, then an **armoury**. It includes a gruesome 'hanging cage' (rather like a suit of armour, but slats of metal) through which eagles tore criminals to death. **15.** A room for scribes and accountants. **16.** Granite pillar and roof dance hall, eggwhite floor, women kept behind wooden screen. It is connected to what was once the *Sarasvati* temple. The outer cyclopean stone wall is fitted together without mortar. It encloses a total area of 75 ha, and the buildings of the palace cover 2 ha.

A new **Museum** was opened in 1994 directly opposite the Ticket Office. It contains some excellent wooden sculptures and copies of the murals. **Getting there** Regular buses to Tiruvananthapuram and Kannyiakumari. Less frequent buses to and from Kovalam. From Kovalam, dep approx 0940 to Thuckalai. Rickshaw to Padmanabhapuram. Return buses from Thuckalai dep 1445, 1530. Taxi: Day tours from Kovalam including Padmanabhapuram, Suchindram and Kanniyakumari cost approx Rs 650.

Neyyar Dam and Wildlife Sanctuary

30 km E, at the foot of the Western Ghats makes an interesting trip through impressive landscape. The vegetation moves from grassland to tropical wet evergreen. Wildlife includes elephants, gaur, sloth bear, Nilgir Tahr, jungle cat, Nilgiri langur. There is a crocodile rearing farm.

The Dam area is painted rather artificially and the gardens decorated with larger-than-life statues. There is boating on the reservoir.

The International Sivananda **Yoga Vedanta Dhanwantari Ashram**, has a 5 ha site here. The ashram offers a wide range of Yoga courses, including 2-week intensive "yoga vacations"; popular with westerners. **Accommodation E** Kerala Tourism *Agasthya House*, opp viewing tower, nr Forest Information Centre, T Kattakada 660, 6 rm, on the edge of the reservoir, built like a concrete bunker, yrestaurant, beer parlour, views. **F** *Guest House* (not a hotel), T 047254493, F 0471 451776. **F** *Project House* and *Inspection Bungalow*.

Mukkuni Hill A rubber estate 10 km from the city centre which offers quiet accommodation on a hilltop surrounded by forests. Contact Mukkunni Hill, Malayam PO, Thiruvananthapuram 695571, T 5222047, F 471 77702. Ring between 0800-1000.

ROUTES To Kovalam No 11 and many local buses from E Fort, MG Rd (S of the Central Bus Station) for Kovalam Beach about every ½ hr, from 0630 to 2100, Rs 3. Also taxis and auto rickshaws, but they wait to fill up with passengers and have no fixed charge. Pay about Rs 25 each. If going by cycle, motorbike or car from Thiruvananthapuram follow signs (not always clear) for Kovalam or Vizhinjam. The road, which is quite hilly, has been enormously developed in the last 5 years. The laterite has been cut back and back to create building plots. *Hotel Samudra*, N of Kovalam is the first sign. (**NB** Vizhinjam is S of Kovalam, not N as shown on many maps.)

Kovalam

(*Population*: 2,500; *STD Code*: 04723). 16 km from Thiruvananthapuram (½ hr from Thiruvananthapuram airport). Once just a series of sandy bays separated by rocky promontories, deserted except for the scattered fishing villages under the coconut palms, it is becoming one of the Govt's major tourist centres. Despite the development, it is still better than Goa and has a superb beach. It caters very much for the western backpacker who can get away from the chaos of the larger cities and liver here cheaply "discovering themselves". The Govt has recently widened the beach by 100m, pushing back the line of small restaurants and shops from the beach edge. A new road has been built from the hospital down to the centre of Lighthouse beach.

There are 4 main stretches of beach, each about a 400m long, with a rocky promontory, on which stands Charles Correa's award-winning *Ashok Hotel*, dividing them into N and S sections. The hotel has its own small section of beach immediately to the N of the promontory, giving the most sheltered bathing and the clearest water. The S beaches are much more populated; Lighthouse beach is a long line of bars, cafés and vendors selling fruit, clothes, crafts and sometimes, drugs. Though there are now life guard patrols you need to be careful when swimming. The sea can get rough, particularly between Apr and Oct with swells of up to 6m. From mid-May the sea-level rises reducing the beach width considerably, the golden beach is covered with black scum and swimming becomes hazardous owing to undercurrents. *Best season*: Dec-Mar; even at the end of Mar it can get very hot around mid-day. Only a handful of thatched parasols were available in 1994.

Excursions

Just S of Kovalam beach is the small village of **Vizhinjam**, the capital of the later *Ay* rulers who dominated S Travancore in the 9th century AD. In the 7th century they had faced constant pressure from the Pandiyans of S Tamil Nadu, who kept the Ay chieftains under a firm control for long periods. During this period rock cut temples were constructed using a number of Tamilian features.

Local information

● Accommodation

There is now a wide range of accommodation. Rates are highly seasonal, although the definition of 'season' varies from hotel to hotel. Cheaper hotels tend not to distinguish between Peak and High season. Long power cuts are common, so although hotels on the hill are further from the beach they often get cooling breezes. The area behind the lighthouse beach is now full of hotels with a range of rm from the most basic (Rs 25) to an average of Rs 600 with all facilities. *Peak season*: 20 Dec to 10 Jan; *High season*: 1 Dec-19 Dec, 11 Jan-28 Feb; *Season*: Mar, Apr, Aug-Nov.

A *Ashok Beach Resort*, T 0471 68010, 85 rm, 40 cottages, 64 rm now added on the promontory, now has new generator, so protected from power cuts, reports in mid 1994 suggest that both food and service have improved, stunning location and clean, comparatively isolated private beach, overpriced for standard of rooms and range or quality of services.

B *Samudra*, Samudra beach, T 62089, 50 rm, with bath, some a/c, best with balcony overlooking sea, good beach front, garden and roof-top, pleasant, comfortable, slightly "old Soviet" feel; **B** *Kadaloram Beach Resort*, GV

Raja Rd, T 0471 62721, F 62762, quite plush western style rm, overlooking lagoon but a little isolated, opened 1993.

C *Swagath Holiday Resorts*, next to Upasana Hospital, T 54421, new time-share accommodation also acting as hotel, smart modern style rm with all facilities; **C** *Raja*, T 62080, off-beach location, large modern Indian style hotel, all rm sea facing, recently re-furbished, some a/c rm, but rm quite small and "balconies" more like open air passageways, restaurant; **C** *Moonlight*, Kovalam Beach, T 375, large modern rm, guaranteed water supply, used by tour groups, Hotel arranges local and backwater tours Rs 500 for 2 people; **C** *Neptune*, Light House Beach, T 222, 37 rm, some a/c, simple meals, patio garden, occasional Kathakali shows; **C** *Sea Weed* Light House Rd, T 391, F 60806, 36 rm, modern, clean, airy rm, views from roof restaurant, shady courtyard, ice cream parlour; **C** *Rockholm*, Lighthouse Rd, T 306, F 607, 17 rm, with bath, excellent position on S end of beach just above lighthouse, excellent restaurant, beautiful views, especially early morning, money changing for guests, rec; **C** *Aparna*, Light House Rd, T 74367, 8 rm with large baths, in modern

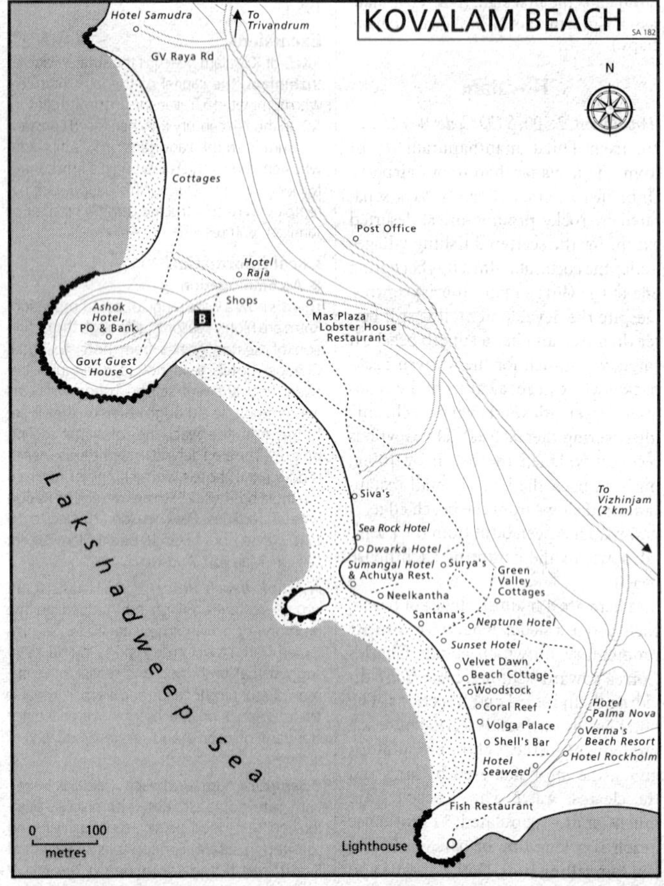

multi-storey building, clean, private sea facing terrace, very pleasant; **C** ***Palmanova***, Lighthouse Rd, T 494, F 496, 19 rm, some a/c from 1995, with bath, restaurant, marble foyer, sea facing balconies, semi-private beach.

D ***Kovalam Tourist Home***, nr Bus stand, T 441, some a/c rm, but basic concrete boxes, grim atmosphere; **D** ***Al Italia Beach Resort***, Samudra beach, T 319, secluded beach front, quiet, breezy, shady restaurant, delicious food, friendly service, "a pleasant break from the pumping acid house and *lungi* sellers of Light House Beach"; **D** ***Sea Rock***, on the beach, nr Lighthouse, clean, sea-facing rm are twice the price (no mosquito nets or wall sockets), good restaurant.

● Budget accommodation

There are numerous cottages and rm to let. Many have scouts out at the bus stand to greet arrivals, but you may pay considerably more if you use their services. Long stays can win big reductions in price – it pays to bargain. You will find several small hotels (rooms behind bars and restaurants), by walking from the *Sea Rock* towards the lighthouse. Inexpensive, clean though simple.

E ***Blue Sea***, nr Telegraph office, T 401, roof-top terrace rm more expensive but superb views, converted Kerala-style family home in large garden with pool, very pleasant and excellent value; **E** ***Achutta***, with restaurant, rec for good clean rm, "best bed in India" and good food; Siva's Moon **E** ***Beach Cottages***, have clean, comfortable rm with bath, rec; **E** ***Paradise Rock***, Light House Rd, T 658, large rm, hot showers, close to beach, good views and breeze; **E** ***Thiruvathira***, Light House Rd, T 657, 8 rm, modern hotel, large, breezy sea-facing terraces, *Anu Massage Centre* for traditional Ayurvedic massage (and 30-day martial arts) courses. **E** ***Wilson Tourist Home***, in a large garden, 20 rm with bath, prices vary – more expensive rm with western toilet and hot shower, open-air restaurant, accepts VISA, clean, safe and well run, rec.

F ***Swami Tourist Home***, with good clean rm and friendly service; **F** ***Sergeant Guest House***, Light House Beach, lots of character and style, good restaurant, run by charming retired sergeant, very popular, close to beach, nr lighthouse; **F** ***Shangri-La House, Lighthouse Beach. Attractive setting, nr beach and lighthouse. Restaurant and library.***

It is also possible to rent rooms in private houses cheaply, especially for longer stays. Several on the Samudra Beach and GV Raja Rd (Samudra Rd) area.

● Hotels near Kovalam

The Government and private companies are beginning to develop accommodation on beaches within 10 km of Kovalam. 5 km from Kovalam, just off the Thiruvananthapuram road is the **D** Kerala Tourism ***Lagoona Beach Resort***, Pachalloor, T 0471 443738, 4 rm, completed 1993. The Pozhikkara Beach runs NW from the *Samudra Hotel* at Kovalam past the Lagoona resort, which is idyllically located where the backwaters reach the sea. Completely unspoilt location, and deliberate policy of keeping simple. No TV, video or western music, and not much western food. Delicious Kerala meals in the restaurant. 2 hr backwater tours in country boats organised (Rs 100 per person), visiting villages completely informally but with excellent guide. A chance to see coir making, cashew, pepper, ginger and a wide variety of other tropical plants. Tours at 0800 and 1600. Special trips also arranged. Rowing boats for hire.

Between 8 and 10 km S of Kovalam are 2 new beach resort hotels. The **A** ***Surya Samudra***, Pulinkudi, Mullur PO, T 413, F 0471 77702, has a number of houses and cottages, access by taxi or rickshaw, old Kerala houses are re-assembled and modernised on the site to provide large airy rm, bathrooms are open air, with banana plants etc growing in them, exclusive atmosphere, secluded beach, stunning setting, very special, built and run with German co-operation. Can book in Germany via Toptour GMBH, Piusallee 108, GD-48147 Münster T 0049 251 235559, F 0251 235216. **A** ***Somatheeram Beach Resort***, Chowara PO, 10 km S of Kovalam, T 04723 600, F 0471 77702 Attn Somatheeram. Nearing completion in 1994. Rm prices vary. An ayurvedic health resort has been incorporated into the traditional-style (but new) cottage setting. Also a superb location, luxurious, and a wide range of specialist ayurvedic treatments offered (see Culture in Introduction above). The ordinary massage usually takes ½ hr with another 10 or 15 min for the body to absorb the medicated oils before a hot bath is taken.

● Places to eat & bars

Midway Restaurant at the *Al Italia Beach Resort*, is rec. ***Sea Rock***, quite slow service but varied menu, excellent food. ***Rockholm*** is rather pricy but excellent. Also rec ***Swami*** for tandoori and snacks. Others towards the lighthouse – ***Palm Beach*** and ***Island View***, which does good pastas, popular with Italians. ***Velvet Moon*** and ***Shell's Bar*** for excellent BBQ fish. ***Achhutha*** for excellent food. ***Santana*** rec for atmosphere, music, backgammon, chess, good food (but very slow service), as in ***Coral Reef***. ***Lonely Planet*** (was *Siva's No 1*) is the only veg restaurant; serves excellent Indian cuisine (not too spicy), in good location overlooking paddy fields and coconut palms. Cheap *thalis* rec.

Videos are shown free nightly at several restaurants, though the bonus sometimes has to be set against poorer food: they include ***Dwarkas***, ***Neelkantha*** with comfortable seats and a generator to overcome regular power cuts and ***Hawah Beach*** where veg dishes taste of fish! Also at ***Shell's Bar, Siva's Moon*** and ***Flamingo***; the last does very good tandoori (try barracuda).

Ashok's Bar is open to non-residents. Beach bars are far cheaper and sell beer, rum and occasionally spirits.

● Banks & money changers

State Bank of India branch in *Ashok Hotel* changes money and TCs for non-residents after 1045.

● Hospitals & medical services

Emergency assistance either through *Kovalam Hotel* or from the *Govt Hospital* in Thiruvananthapuram. *Upasana Hospital*, next to the *Lobster House*, has a good English speaking doctor.

● Shopping

Numerous craft shops, including Kashmiri and Tibetan shops selling a wide range of goods. The majority are clustered around the bus stand at the gate of the *Ashok Hotel* with another group to the S around the lighthouse. It is possible to get good quality paintings, metalwork, carpets, woodwork at reasonable prices. Tailoring at short notice is very good value.

Books: several bookshops sell or 'rent' (Rs 10) English paperbacks.

● Sports

Fishing can readily be arranged through the hotels, as can excursions on traditional catamarans or motor boats.

● Tour companies & travel agents

Western Travels, opp bus stand, Kovalam. Open 0800-2400. Taxi day trips to Kollam (Rs 325) including backwater boat trip, Kanniyakumari tour (Rs 625) and Thiruvananthapuram City (Rs 550). ***Karuvayal Tours***, at Mooonlight Tourist Home and the Rockholm Hotel. Organise special country boat backwater tours from Thiruvallam, dep 073 and 1500.

● Tourist office

Kerala Tourism office is at the entrance to the Ashok Hotel driveway. Very helpful manager, prepared to go out of his way to look for any information requested.

● Transport

Local Bus: frequent buses into Thiruvananthapuram from bus stand outside *Ashok Hotel* gate. **Auto rickshaws** and **taxis** from this point, and from above the lighthouse outside the *Rockholm Hotel*.

Road Bus: Theoretically the following bus times apply though not entirely reliable. To **Kochi & Kollam (Quilon)**, at 0700. **Kochi via Kottayam**, 0900; **Kanniyakumari**, 0940, 1645; **Nagercoil**, 0950, 1800; Varkala,1650; **Thodopuzha via Kottayam**, 1700.

To take a backwater trip from Kollam you can take a shared taxi (approx Rs 50 each). The boat jetty is very near the bus station. Boat leaves at 1030, arrives Alappuzha (Alleppey) 1830. There are very frequent buses from there to Kochi.

Longer tours from Thiruvananthapuram – Kerala hill stations

Kerala's hill stations are much less well kown than those of neighbouring Tamil Nadu or of the Himalaya, yet the state has several small towns set in beautiful scenery that many a wonderful break from the damp heat of the lowland forests or the beaches. Much of highland Kerala is now put to commerical use – for tea, cocoa, rubber and a wide range of spices, but although there is virtually no natural forest left and even the hills are densely populated they still offer a calm and green environment, ideal for a short break or for a brief diversion while travelling between Kerala and Tamil Nadu.

The hill stations are stretched in a string along the edge of the Ghats. From

Ponmudi in the furthest S to Munnar in the N, they experience the full force of the wet monsoon winds from May to November, often being covered in cloud. The hills offer lovely country for walks and treks.

WARNING Particularly in the wet season be prepared for leeches when walking through the forest. See page 119.

Ponmudi

(*Altitude*: 1,000m) Ponmudi is the nearest hill station to Thiruvananthapuram (65 km), 2 hr away. **Accommodation E** Kerala Tourism *Ponmudi Tourist Complex*, T 330, 24 rm and 10 cottages, stand in attractive gardens surrounded by wooded hills, spartan facilities, food must be booked in advance. The complex serves as a good base for trekking, birdwatching and visiting the nearby deer park. **Peppara Wildlife Sanctuary** (50 km) on the road to Ponmudi, accessible from Vithurai covers 53 sq km on the ghats. The forests and eucalyptus plantations attract a variety of birds and harbours elephants, sambar and lion-tailed macaque.

Peermade

(*Altitude*: 914m; *STD Code*: 04869) On the main road from Kottayam to Thekkadi and Madurai, Peermade is often simply passed through on the way to the much better known wildlife reserve of Periyar 43 km away. Although it is considerably lower than Thekkadi (Periyar), it is surrounded by tea, rubber and cardamom plantations. It can be a pleasant brief halt. **Accommodation F** *Govt Guest House*, T 32071; **F** Kerala Tourism *Sabala Motel*, Kuttikanam, T 32250. Both basic but acceptable.

Munnar

(*Altitude*: 1,520m; *STD Code*: 04865) The rains from Jun -Sep are very heavy (annual total 270 cm). A major centre of Kerala's tea industry, and close to Anaimudi, at 2695m the highest peak in S India, Munnar is the nearest Kerala comes to a genuine hill station. It is surrounded by about 30 tea estates, among the highest in the world, and forest that is still rich in wildlife despite the increasing commercial use of the hills. Despite the appearance of calm the town has witnessed catastrophes, notably the 1924 flood which destroyed the whole settlement. It is possible to visit a working tea factory. Contact the Manager, *Govt Guest House* for information. There is an Indo-Swiss dairy project 13 km away. Open to visitors.

The tea plantations can be visited by contacting the Tata office in Munnar; you can watch tea pickers at work and how tea is processed; tea is also available for sale.

Excursions

Lockhart Gap, 20 km, has superb views, and it is possible to row on the Mattupetty Lake (13 km). On working days it is possible to visit the Pullivasal Hydro Electric Project (19 km). Permission from the Executive Engineer, Kerala State Electricity Board, Chittirapuram.

Eravikulam/ Rajmalai National Park 16 km away, set up to preserve the endangered Nilgir Tahr (Nilgiri Ibex) (*Hemitragus hylocrius*) has resulted in the park now supporting the largest population of the species in the world. The sure-footed wild goat which inhabits the steep black rocky slopes of Anaimudi mountains live in herds. They are brownish, have short flat horns, with the male carrying a thick mane, and can be easily seen around the entrance; the Forest Rangers make sure there is a salt lick near the gate which attracts the herds around mid-day. There are also elephants, sambars, gaurs, macaque and the odd leopard and tiger. The park is approached by road up to Rajmalai and the remainder on foot.

Park information

● **Accommodation**

High Range Club, T 53, colonial style planters'

club, members only (or those with reciprocal arrangements) may stay, lunch and dinner available for non-members, if booked in advance. **D** *Edassery East End*, Temple Rd, T 30451, brand new, marble and chrome, very clean, also some cottages, excellent restaurant, rec – but totally unreliable travel information; **D** *Hillview*, T 30567, 35 rm with bath, TV and phone, cheap dorm, restaurant; slightly cheaper **D** *Royal Retreat*, Kannan Deven hills, T 30240, restaurant, modern building, rm with balcony upstairs.

F *SN Lodge*, T 212, 29 rm; **F** *Govt Guest House*, T 385; attractive old bungalow **F** *PWD Rest House*.

● **Places to eat**

In **D** hotels and *Pandyan Coffee House*, *Munnar*, *Brothers*, and *Azhakathu* all serve meals in town.

● **Banks & money changers**

State Bank of India and State Bank of Travancore.

● **Transport**

Road Jeeps/taxis go to the National Park. **Bus**: to Kottayam (148 km) and Kochi (133 km).

Thattekad Bird Sanctuary

This is approached from Kothamangalam (20 km away) on the Kochi-Munnar Rd. The sanctuary is surrounded by the Periyar river (shallow most of the year). It attracts water birds and other indigenous birds including Malabar grey hornbill, rose and blue-winged parakeet, egret, heron and mynah while rarer birds like Ceylon frog-mouth and rose-billed rollers are also found.

Devikolam (Devikulam)

The last settlement on the road across the Western Ghats to Bodinayakkanur, Kodai and Madurai in Tamil Nadu. There is an alternative shorter route to Kodai via Top Station, but the road is often washed out or damaged by heavy logging trucks, and is normally only passable to 4-wheel drive vehicles. Jeep hire for the journey is approx Rs1300, but the road is appalling and bribes are sometimes necessary to get through. The town is near the Devikulam lake from which it takes its name, and there are extensive and beautiful views over the highest ranges of the Western Ghats. There is an **F** *Govt Guest House*.

THIRUVANANTHAPURAM TO KOCHI (The Coastal Route)

There are 2 main routes through Kerala from Thiruvananthapuram. They run nearly parallel and very close to each other so it is possible to make detours to places of particular interest from one route to the other if you wish. Road transport can be very slow. The NH 47 tends to by-pass more of the small towns and villages. The inland route is slower, but both pass through some beautiful scenery.

The **NH 47**, leaves Thiruvananthapuram from the Indian Airlines Offices and the *Mascot Hotel* along the Quilon Rd, a winding and very busy town street. It crosses low rolling hills covered in coconut, jack, eucalyptus, cashew, mangoes, papaya, and under the wood cover cassava. 18 kms from Thiruvananthapuram the road crosses a toll bridge. In **Attingal** (25 km; *STD Code*: 04726; capital of the Travancore Tamburetti princes until 1758) take a left turn off the NH 47 to **Anjengo** (5 km). Initially held by the Portuguese, this massive laterite fort has an English cemetery, the earliest tomb of which is dated 1704. An English warehouse and trading post had been set up 20 years earlier, but was abandoned in 1810. For a coast line fringed almost its entire length with coconut palms it is slightly ironical that Anjengo should mean 'five coconut trees'. Return to the NH 47.

The lateritic rocks surface from time to time, and there are views of a succession of low ranges, no more than 15m to 30m, but with a regular succession of rice growing, flat river valleys with wooded slopes. The better-off rice

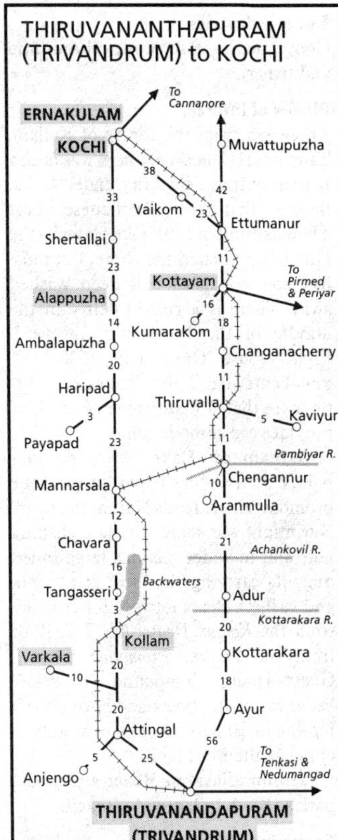

farmers live in the valley bottoms, while only 30m or so up the slope live the much poorer (and mainly Christian) peasantry. Occasional rubber plantations stretch as far down towards the coast as NH47, but most lie further inland. 20 km N of Attingal a left turn leads to the superb beach at Varkala.

Varkala

(10 km; *Population*: 39,000; *STD Code*: 04724) Unlike Kovalam, there are still relatively few tourists here, though it is rapidly becoming better known. There are mineral water springs on the cliffs. Wonderful for sunbathing and unwinding – perhaps until the new Taj Group **AL** *Hotel* is opened on the almost deserted clifftop site.

Local information

● Accommodation

Most hotels are on the beach, though there are 2 nr the rly station 2 km inland. It is also possible to stay with local families. **NB** Some thefts and a mugging reported in early 1994. Take care with personal possessions.

D *Varkala Marine Palace*, closest to the beach, modern, simple and comfortable restaurant, overlooking beach is good value, restaurant, good food, slow service, geared towards the young, highly rec. Much cheaper rm available; **D** *Hill Top Beach Resort*, N end of cliffs, brand new building, clean, overlooks beach and bay, very quiet, rather limited restaurant and slow service; **D** *Akshay Beach Resort*, Beach Rd, T 2668, some a/c rm, bright, new clean and smart; TV lounge, rec – probably the best available.

F *Mamma Home*, 100m beyond *Akshay*, shared toilet, well water, but good food, a very picturesque converted Kerala farmhouse; immediately opp is the **F** *Beach Palace*, in a good position but very basic, good value restaurant, tables set on stilts in small pond; **F** ITDC *Tourist Home*, basic, but clean and very cheap; **F** *Govt Guest House*, towards Taj hotel site, has 8 rm in an old house, former summer residence of Maharaja, very charming, reserve in advance, T 2227. *Paying-guest* accommodation is available with families if you ask around.

In Varkala: **E** *Babuji*, nr centre, T 72243, new building, badly maintained, overpriced, poor value.

F *Anandan Tourist Home*, opp Rly station, T 2135, 32 rm, some a/c, restaurant, clean modern building, noisy in early mornings as next door to temple, good value; **F** *JA Tourist Home*, Temple Junc, T 2453, 11 rm, modern Indian hotel, good value, also excellent roof restaurant, reasonably priced, delicious food though slow if friendly service.

● Places to eat

In Varkala: *Sri Padman restaurant*, Temple Junc, good cheap food incl excellent western breakfasts, overlooks temple water tank.

● Banks & money changers

State Bank of Travancore will exchange TCs

and payments on Visa cards, but will not change cash.

● Services

Scientific School of Yoga and Massage 10-day yoga and massage course, professionally explained by English speaking doctor T 695141. Also shop selling ayurvedic oils, soaps, shampoo etc.

● Transport

Local Motorcycle: hire from next door to *JA Tourist Home*, Temple Junc.

Train To **Tiruvananthapuram**: 0445, then 0713, 0805, 1043, 1447, 1748, 2838, 2107; to **Kanniyakumari**: 1110, 1405.

Road Bus: frequent buses to **Alappuzha** and **Kollam**, and several long distance connections.

Kollam (Quilon)

Kollam is a shaded town on the side of the Ashtamudi Lake, though it has a growing industrial activity and at times it can be very busy. It is one of Kerala's most ancient settlements, going back to the 9th century AD. The Malayalam calendar is calculated from the founding of the town, possibly by Raja Udaya Marthanda Varma, which was the capital of the Venad kingdom in the 9th century. It was also associated with the early history of Christianity. Its traditional industries include cashew nut processing and fisheries but modern industries are booming. If you're familiar with autorickshaws in other parts of India the hard-topped autorickshaws with roof-racks come as a surprise. The District HQ, Kollam has been an important centre of Travancore administration under successive different rulers.

Known to Marco Polo (as *Koilum*) its port traded with Phoenicians, Persians, Greeks, Romans and Arabs as well as the Chinese. Superb chinaware has been found in the area. It is the S end of Kerala's backwaters.

BASICS *Population*: 362,400; *STD Code*: 0474; *Climate*: Temp Summer: Max 35°C, Min 25°C; Winter: Max 34°C, Min 24°C; *Annual rainfall*: 2,800 mm; *Best Season*: Oct-Mar; *Clothing*: cottons.

Local industries

Coir, ceramics, cashew nuts, aluminium and fisheries.

Places of interest

Three km from the centre of Kollam, **Tangasseri** (*Changana Cheri*) was once a British outpost, covering under 40 ha. Before that the Portuguese Fort Thomas, built in 1503, taken later by the Dutch, dominated the shore, but most has now collapsed and been washed away. There is a ruined belfry in the middle of the Protestant graveyard. Light House. Open daily 1530-1730. Small entry fee. Today Tangasseri is little more than a shanty town. *Hotel Vani* provides accommodation.

Ashtamudi Lake with coconut palms on its banks and picturesque promontories extends N from the town. You might see some 'Chinese' fishing nets and in wider sections large-sailed dugouts carrying the local coir, copra and cashew. Boats for hire for cruising from the *Kollam Boat Club*, T 2519 or from the *Tourism Promotion Council*, Guest House Compound, T 76456. Pedal or rowing boats and speed boats for 4, 8 or 10 persons. The boat jetty is opposite the Bus Stand.

Thirumullavaram Beach and model park at **Kochupilamoodu Beach**.

Excursions

The **Backwaters** give an almost uniquely quiet view of Kerala village life, impossible to get simply from the road. Agriculture in Kerala has always taken advantage of the comparatively long rainy season. While coconuts provide a vital economic resource, the land underneath is often intensively cultivated. From the boat you see papaya, mangoes, jack fruit and cassava (*tapioca*). As tapioca was only introduced to Kerala in 1920 its popularity is particularly striking, and reflects the fact that it gives remarkably high yields from lateritic soils that are about 'as fertile as railway ballast'. Boat cruises along the

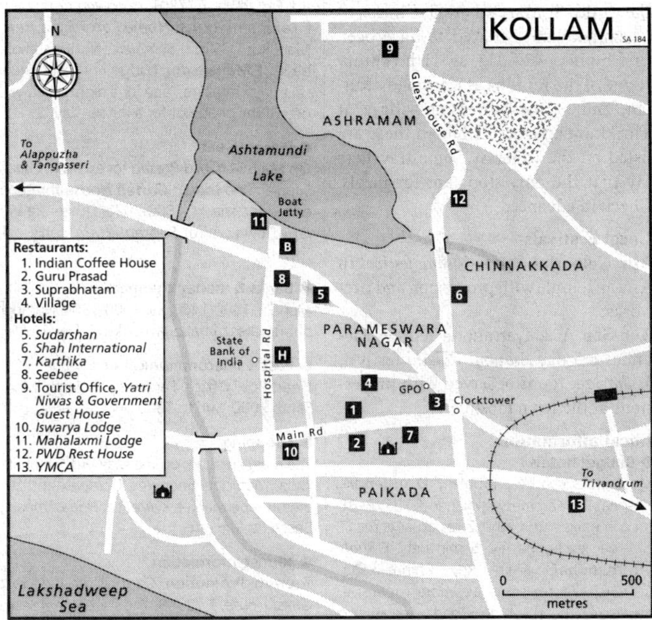

backwaters provide one of the most delightful tours in India. Some people find the full journey too long. Shorter trips are possible, either round trips returning to Kollam or by picking up the trip closer to Alappuzha. Changanacherry and Kottayam are alternatives.

Short trips to **Kapapuzha** (2 daily) and **Guhanandapuram** across lake (2 hr, several daily), Rs 3 are very scenic. Daily trip to Alappuzha in each direction takes over 8 hr with 2 stops (Rs 10, dep Kollam at 1030), but can be very interesting if you have the time.

Vallikkavu The ashram of Ma Math, 10 km N of Kollam on the backwaters, sandwiched between the sea and the river. *Darshan* on Thur and Sun, attended by large numbers of villagers and western tourists. **Accommodation** and good Western canteen available for those who wish to stay in the ashram. Donations expected.

NB: Even in the coolest times of year (Dec-Feb) this journey during daytime can get very hot. **TIPS**: Sometimes there are 2 options. **1** The 'luxury' ATDC boat (Tue and Sat, dep 1015) costs Rs 80, even if you join half way, 2 stops for food. **2** The local ferry costs Rs 10 (when it runs), many travellers strongly recommend it. **WARNING** Timings, prices and services change. It is necessary to enquire for up to date details.

Tours

Day tour arranged on request for groups of 10 or Backwater cruise for 20 to Alappuzha, Rs 70, 8 hr. ATDC 8 hr cruise, Tue, Th & Sat, 1015, Rs 80. Arrives in Alappuzha at 1815. En route the trip may call at several places of interest.

These include the longest snake boat in the world, St Mary's Forane Church at Champakulam, believed to have been first built in 427 AD, an 11th century statue of the Buddha at Karumady Kuttan, and a coir processing village at Thrikkunnapuzha. Although these are listed on the itinerary, some travellers say that the only stops are for meals. Check in advance.

Local Festivals

Apr Colourful 10 day *Vishnu festival* in Asram Temple with procession and fireworks.

Aug-Sep Avadayattukotta Temple celebrates a 5 day *Ashtami Rohani* festival. *Muharram* too is observed with processions at the town mosque.

Local information

● Budget hotels

Mosquitoes can be a problem. **D** *Sudarsan*, Hospital Rd, Parameswar Nagar, T 75322, 38 rm some a/c with baths, 2 restaurants rec (1 a/c), bar, exchange, TV, 5 min jetty. **E** *Shah International*, Main Rd, Chinnakkada, T 75362, 72 rm some a/c more expensive, mediocre hotel but good restaurant; **E** *Karthika*, Paikada (Main) Rd, T 76241, 40 rm with bath, some a/c, restaurant, bar, backwater trips arranged, mediocre; **E** *Neela*, Kollam Cantt, T 73616, some a/c rm; **E** *Prasanthi*, T 75291, has some a/c rm; **E** *Seebee* Hospital Rd, nr Jetty Bus Stand, T 75371.

F Kerala Tourism *Govt Guest House*, Ashramam, T 76456, 8 large rm and restaurant, fine 200-year-old building with garden on edge of lagoon, now looking a little like "a run down Club House in search of a golf course", former British Residency and an "amazing place" with assault course, roller skating rink, boating, small pool and a children's park by the lake, excellent value for money, rec; 1½ km rly and bus stand, centre, is a disadvantage; **F** *Yatri Nivas*, Guest House Compound, Ashramam, T 78638, 15 rm and 2 6-bed dorm, restaurant, beer, Tourist Office, boating; **F** *PWD Resthouse*, Chinnakkada, just beyond Bridge on Guest House road, T 77838, old colonial building with large clean rm but indifferent service, often reserved for Govt officers, reservation: Exec Engineer, PWD; **F** *YMCA*, T 76933 and *YWCA*, T 77010, reservations: Gen Secy; **F** *Iswarya Lodge*, Main Rd, E of town, T 77801, good veg restaurant; **F** *Lakshami Tourist Home Parry & Co Junc*, Main Rd, T 70167. Some a/c. Nr bus station, basic; **F** *Mahalaxmi Lodge*, nr Ashtamudi Lake, very small rm, 'fine for a night when you get off the boat, not for a longer stay'.

● Places to eat

On Main St *Guru Prasad* for excellent cheap S Indian and *Indian Coffee House* for good coffee and snacks, 0800-2030. Others are *Village* (Town centre), *Suprabhatam* (opp Clock Tower).

● Banks & money changers

Mon-Fri, 1000-1400, Sat 1000-1200. Number of branches of national banks.

● Post & telecommunications

Head Post Office, Parameswar Nagar. Mon-Sat to 2000, Sun to 1800.

● Shopping

The main areas are on the Main Rd. Chinnakkada, Municipal Shopping Complex and Supreme Supermarket. *Kairali*, at *Hotel Ambadi*, Beach Rd for crafts.

● Tourist information

Tourism Promotion Council, at the *Govt Guest House*, T 72558. The staff do not seem very keen to give out information

● Transport

Local Buses and **auto rickshaws** are plentiful. **Bikes** for hire.

Train Kollam Junc rly station N of town, is about 3 km from Boat Jetty and Bus Station. **Thiruvananthapuram**: *Kerala-Mangala Exp* 2626 (AC/II), daily, 1530, 1¼ hr. **Madras (MC)**: *Madras Mail* 6320 (AC/II), daily, 1457, 16¼ hr. **Madurai**: *Quilon Mail* 6106 (AC/II), daily, 1220, 7¾ hr.

Frequent services to **Thiruvananthapuram**; every ½ hr to **Kochi (140 km, 3 ½ hr) and Alappuzha** (85 km, 2 hr) and other towns on the coast. Daily bus to **Kumily** village for Periyar National Park, (change at Kottayam), 1000, 7 hr. Also buses to **Kanniyakumari**. To **Varkala** take a bus to Kollambalam and change. It is easier to take the train as all southbound trains stop at Varkala.

ROUTES Rejoin the NH 47.

Chavara *STD Code*: 047593. *Kerala Minerals and Metals*' Titanium Oxide Pigment Plant makes use of the radioactive ilmenite and monazite sands which were found along the beach in the early part of this century. The concentrations are very high, containing 8% to 10% thorium oxide. Known reserves exceed 1.5mn tonnes. Titanium from the ilmenite sands is used for some highly specialised electrical and chemical industries – electrodes, tracer bullets, and as a catalyst. The monazite sands of the Kerala coast are particularly important for India's nuclear power programme. An enormous slick of pollutants drifts S from the factory down the coast. There is also an Indo-Norwegian Fishing project.

Between Kollam and Alappuzha the road passes through more coconut groves and jack fruit, mango, and eucalyptus along road sides. There is an atmosphere of prosperity quite different from the neighbouring states. 4 km N of Chavara is one of several new mosques, built with money sent to Kerala by migrants working in the Gulf. The area suffered considerable retrenchment after the Gulf War but is now picking up again. The road goes through **Mannarsala** which has a Nagaraja Temple in the forest. **Haripad** has a Subrahmanya Temple and there is a Snake Boat Race at **Payipad** (3 km by bus) for 3 days. *Jalotsav* during Onam. Boat processions on first 2 days followed by competitive races on 3rd day. Entry by ticket in Aug and Nov/Dec. **Ambalapuzha** The temple dedicated to Krishna celebrates 10 day festival in March-April when a number of dances from Kerala are performed.

Alappuzha (Alleppey)

Alappuzha is a major centre for backwater cruises and also the state's coir industry. A large network of canals pass through the town and there is a long sandy beach.

BASICS *Population*: 264,900; *STD Code*: 0477; *Climate*: Temp Summer: Max 35°C, Min 22°C; Winter: Max 32°C, Min 22°C; *Annual rainfall*: 250 mm; *Best Season*: Dec-Mar.

Local industries

The headquarters of Kerala's coir industry, cashew nuts.

Places of interest

The **backwaters** Alappuzha is the starting point of backwater boat trips to Kollam, Kottayam and Kochi, and the main centre for cruises on the backwaters. This is one of the main tourist attractions. ATDC 8 hr cruise to Kollam (see also above), dep 0945, Mon, Wed, Fri, Rs 80. There are several others: to **Champakulam**, 16 km (see below), 1½ hr, 9 dep from 0430-2300; **Changanachery**, 3½; **Chengannur**, 5 hr; **Kochi**, 5½ hr; **Kottayam**, 29 km, 8 dep from 0500-2100, Rs 3, local ferry, 2½ hr; Rs 50, Tourist boat, 3½ hr takes more scenic route. Some visitors feel that this trip is so different from the Kollam-Alappuzha trip that it is worth doing both. The journeys in the daytime are obviously much more interesting for watching unspoilt village life of Kerala.

If you wish to hire a motor boat for a short time, the best hourly rate is offered by the *State Water Transport Dept*, Contact Traffic Supt. *Vembanad Tourist Service*, Akkarakalam Buildings, Jetty Rd, and *Kuttanadan Travels*, Boat Jetty, charge 2 to 3 times the rate but may offer larger boats. The Alappuzha Tourism Dev Co-op Society (ATDCS) has started a new backwater cruise on Big Country Boats (Kattuvallam). Built in the Keralan style of houseboat. This is punted around the backwaters. A 2 day/one night tour costs Rs 2200 for two, incl. meals. Cheaper if you can get deck space. The gentle pace and quiet contribute to making this an exccellent tour.

Excursions

Some places of interest can be visited either on the backwaters or by road.

Champakulam The Syrian Church dates only from 1870, but is on the site of churches going back to 470 AD. The English speaking priest is happy to show visitors round. Nearby the St Thomas Statuary makes wooden statues of

Christ for export round the world. A 2 m statue of Jesus costs approx $450. Champakulam is particularly attractive because there is no traffic other than the occasional cycle and canoes. Visit rec.

• **Transport Sea** Take the Alappuzha-Changanacherry bus (every ½ hr) to Moncompu (Rs 4), then rickshaw to Champakulam (4 km, Rs 12). Alappuzha-Edathna ferry leaves at 0615 and 1715 and stops at Champakulam. In Edathna you can visit the early Syrian St George's Church.

Krishnapuram Palace 47 km, at Kayamkulam Typical of Kerala architecture with gabled roof, dormer windows and narrow corridors, the palace (c1740s) is ascribed to Raja Marthanda Varma. It contains a large mural, covering over 5 sq m, relating the story of Gajendra Moksha. The **Museum** displays bronzes, sculptures and paintings. **Accommodation F** Kerala Tourism *Motel Araam*, has simple rm (2 hr use available).

Local Festivals

Jan *Cheruppu* is celebrated in the Mullakkal Devi Temple with procession of elephants, music and fireworks. *Champakulam Boat Race* takes place 16 km ferry ride away on 'Moolam' day (check with Tourist Office).

Jul (3rd Sat) *ATDC Boat Race* in the backwaters.

Aug Alappuzha is the site of one of Kerala's most famous boat races. The Nehru Cup, inaugurated in 1952, is the largest *Snake Boat Race* in the state. It takes place on the 2nd Sat in Aug at Punnamada kayal. As many as 40 'snake boats', with highly decorated and carved prows, are rowed by several dozen oarsmen before huge crowds. Naval helicopters do mock rescue operations and stunt flying. Entry by ticket.

Local information

● Accommodation

D *Alleppey Prince*, on AS Rd (NH 47), 2 km N of centre, T 3752, Hotel uses local woods and coir in its furnishings, central, a/c, 30 rm with bath and phone, good restaurant, pool (not well-maintained), rec as good value, luxury boat for backwaters trips, rate negotiable.

● Budget hotels

E *Komala*, nr Municipal Maidan, opp Jetty N of canal, T 3631, some a/c rm, recently refurbished, has one of the best restaurants in town, friendly management; **E** *Narasimhapuram Lodge*, Cullen Rd, Mullakkal, T 62662, some a/c rm.

F *Kuttanad Tourist Home*, between Jetty and Bus station, T 4354, fairly new with clean rm, some a/c; **F** Kerala Tourism *Motel Araam*, T 4460, 2 simple rm with bath, restaurant; **F** PWD *Rest House*, Beach Rd, 4 km Bus Stand, T 3445, excellent value, cheap, reasonable food (order in advance) but indifferent service, reservations: Dist Collector, Collectorate, Dist HQ, Alappuzha; **F** *Karthika Tourist Home*, SDV Rd, N of canal, opp Jetty, T 5524, clean, some large rm with baths, good value, Alappuzha Tourism office. Also *YWCA*, T 3313. **F** *St George Lodge*, CCNB Rd, A-5, T 61620, terrace restaurant, good value, popular with backpackers; **F** 2 *Raillway Retiring Rooms* and Snack bar.

● Places to eat

Arun in *Komala Hotel* and *Prince Hotel's Vemanad* are highly rec. Try *Indian Coffee House*, 1.5 km S of Jetty for non-veg, almost opp the *Aryas* (formerly *Gokul*), Mullakal Rd (Main St). *Vijaya*, Jetty Rd for good veg S Indian.

● Banks & money changers

Nr the Post Office and the Telegraph Office.

● Post & telecommunications

Head Post Office: off Mullakal Rd in town centre. **Telegraph office**: on corner of NH 47 and Beach Rd, just over canal.

● Shopping

Coir mats a local speciality. Mullakal Rd and Market Rd are the shopping centres.

● Tourist office

Karthika Tourist Home, T 2554; Collectorate, T 2549.

● Transport

On NH 47, with good road connections with important cities in the S.

Local Tourist and other **taxis**, and **auto-rickshaws**. **Boat hire**: see 'Backwaters' in **Places of interest** above.

Train The station is 3 km from the Jetty with occasional buses between the two. New broad gauge line from Ernakulam to Thiruvananthapuram. To **Madras** via Madurai: *Exp* 6041, 0530.

Road Bus: bus services to Kollam (every ½ hr, 2 ½ hr), Thiruvananthapuram (several, 4 hr), Kochi (every 20 min from 0630-2330, 1 ½ hr), Kanniyakumari, Calicut, Thrissur. **NB**: That here as elsewhere in Kerala 'Non-stop' buses are faster than 'Express' buses.

ROUTES From Alappuzha the NH 47 goes N through Shertallai to Kochi.

Kochi-Ernakulam

Kochi (Cochin) is one of the most interesting towns in S India. Today Ernakulam and Kochi are dynamic cities. During the day the city centre streets are packed with pedestrians and the traffic into the cities is often reduced to a crawl.

BASICS *Population*: 1.14mn; *STD Code*: 048; *Clothing*: Cottons.

A trading port since at least Roman times, it was on the main trade route between Europe and China. The town is in 3 main parts. **Fort Kochi** (Fort Cochin) occupies the S promontory on the seaward side of the Bay. **Willingdon Island** was created in the 1920s by dredging the bay to increase the depth of the entrance to the harbour to over 11m. It is the HQ of the Southern Command of the Indian Navy, and has the airport, the railway terminus and at its N tip the Malabar Hotel. Across the causeway from Willingdon Island is **Ernakulam**. Immediately opposite the jetty at Ernakulam is **Bolghatty Island**, strictly speaking a long narrow peninsula, and beyond it **Vypeen Island** (also a peninsula).

From 1795 until India's Independence the long outer sand spit, with its narrow breach leading to the wide bay inland, was under British political control. The inner harbour was in Kochi State, while most of the hinterland was in the separate state of Travancore. The division of political authority delayed development of the harbour facilities until 1920-23, when the approach channel was dredged to allow any ship that could pass through the Suez Canal to dock safely, opening the harbour to modern shipping.

Local industries

Kochi is famous for its coir products. Now the centre of a ship repair industry there is a growing range of engineering industries, making Kochi-Ernakulam the centre of Kerala's industrial economy.

Places of interest

Most of the historic buildings are in **Fort Kochi**. The Portuguese fort, founded 1503, is now in ruins. **Mattancherry Palace** Open 1000-1700. Closed Fri and national holidays. Entrance free, no photography allowed. It is very dark inside; you need fast film to get any worthwhile photos. The palace was built by the Portuguese in 1557 as a gift for the Raja of Kochi in exchange for trading rights. In 1663, it was substantially rebuilt by the new occupants of Kochi, the Dutch. The palace is on 2 floors built round a quadrangle. The plan follows the traditional Kerala pattern known as *nalukettus* ('four buildings'). See Thiruvananthapuram Museum (page 949). It has a central courtyard, in common with most well constructed houses in Keralan architecture. The temple in the centre is dedicated to *Bhagavati*. To the S of the palace is another temple complex dedicated to *Siva* and *Vishnu*. The palace is surrounded by high walls, with gates in the E and W.

Although the Palace has exhibits of

CLIMATE: KOCHI-ERNAKULAM

	Jan	Feb	Mar	Apr	May	Jun	Jul	Aug	Sep	Oct	Nov	Dec	Av/Tot
Max (°C)	31	31	31	31	31	29	28	28	28	29	30	30	30
Min (°C)	23	24	26	26	24	24	24	24	24	24	24	23	24
Rain (mm)	9	34	50	139	364	756	572	386	235	333	184	37	3099

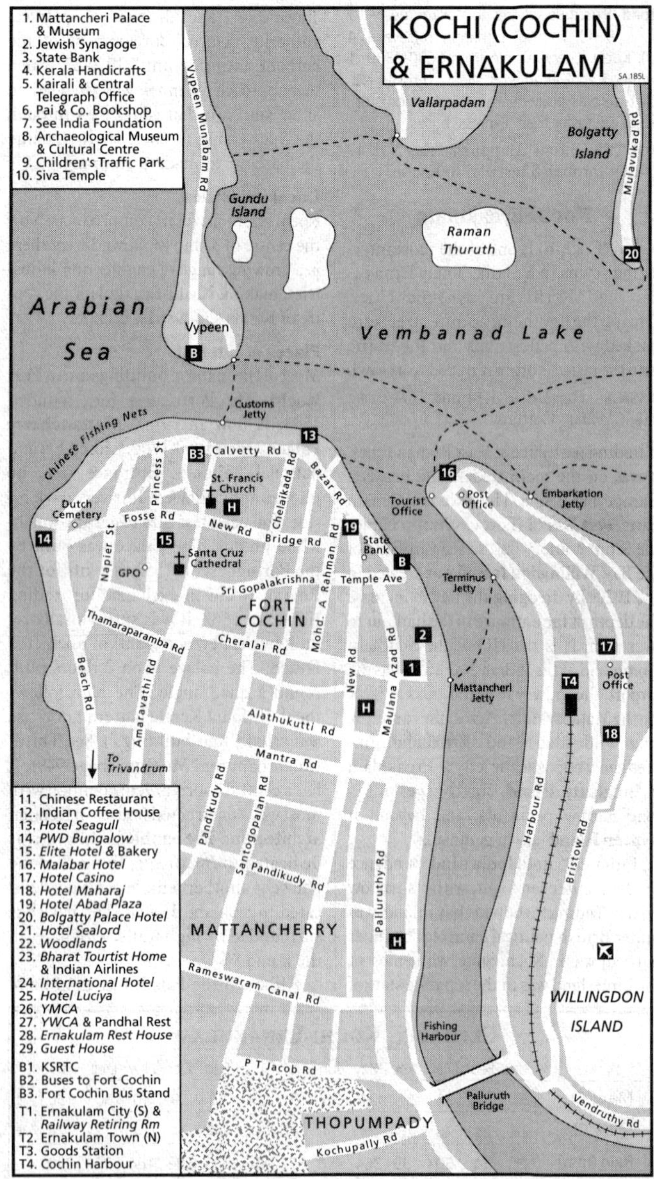
KOCHI (COCHIN)
& ERNAKULAM
SA 185L
1. Mattancheri Palace & Museum
2. Jewish Synagoge
3. State Bank
4. Kerala Handicrafts
5. Kairali & Central Telegraph Office
6. Pai & Co. Bookshop
7. See India Foundation
8. Archaeological Museum & Cultural Centre
9. Children's Traffic Park
10. Siva Temple
11. Chinese Restaurant
12. Indian Coffee House
13. Hotel Seagull
14. PWD Bungalow
15. Elite Hotel & Bakery
16. Malabar Hotel
17. Hotel Casino
18. Hotel Maharaj
19. Hotel Abad Plaza
20. Bolgatty Palace Hotel
21. Hotel Sealord
22. Woodlands
23. Bharat Tourtist Home & Indian Airlines
24. International Hotel
25. Hotel Luciya
26. YMCA
27. YWCA & Pandhal Rest
28. Ernakulam Rest House
29. Guest House
B1. KSRTC
B2. Buses to Fort Cochin
B3. Fort Cochin Bus Stand
T1. Ernakulam City (S) & Railway Retiring Rm
T2. Ernakulam Town (N)
T3. Goods Station
T4. Cochin Harbour
Vallarpadam
Bolgatty Island
Mulavukad Rd
Vypeen Munabam Rd
Gundu Island
Raman Thuruth
Arabian Sea
Vypeen
Vembanad Lake
Customs Jetty
Chinese Fishing Nets
Calvetty Rd
Princess St
St. Francis Church
Chelaikada Rd
Bazar Rd
Tourist Office
Post Office
Embarkation Jetty
Dutch Cemetery
Fosse Rd
New Rd
Bridge Rd
Mohd. A Rahman Rd
State Bank
Napier St
Santa Cruz Cathedral
GPO
Sri Gopalakrishna
Temple Ave
Terminus Jetty
FORT COCHIN
Thamaraparamba Rd
Cheralai Rd
Maulana Azad Rd
New Rd
Mattancheri Jetty
Beach Rd
Amaravathi Rd
Alathukutti Rd
Mantra Rd
To Trivandrum
Pandikudy Rd
Santogopalan Rd
Pandikudy Rd
Palluruthy Rd
Harbour Rd
Bristow Rd
MATTANCHERRY
Rameswaram Canal Rd
WILLINGDON ISLAND
Fishing Harbour
P T Jacob Rd
Palluruth Bridge
THOPUMPADY
Kochupally Rd
Vendruthy Rd

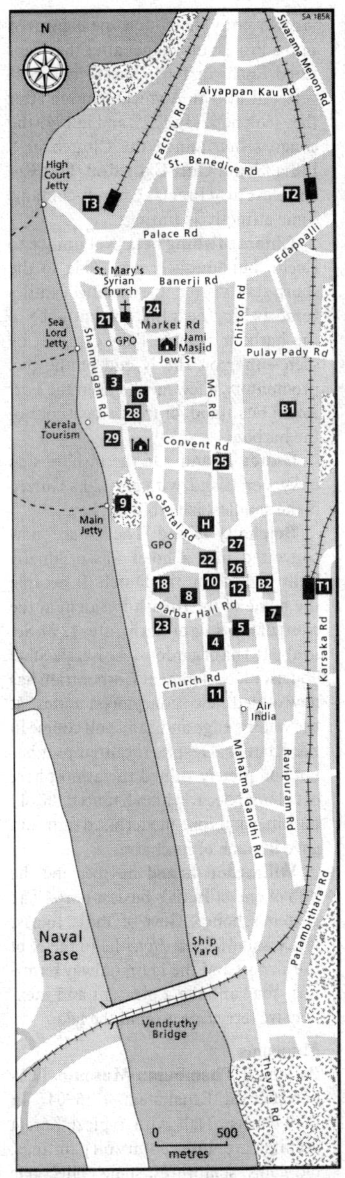

the Rajas of Kochi (clothes, palanquins, weapons, furniture) the main feature is the series of murals painted on the wooden walls. These are remarkable, matched only by those in the Padmanabhapuram Palace S of Thiruvananthapuram (see page 954). The 'royal bedroom' immediately to the W of the Coronation Hall (*palliyara*) has low wooden ceilings and walls covered in about 45 paintings illustrating the *Ramayana*, from the beginning to the point of Sita's return from captivity. These paintings date from the late 16th century. Every cm of space is covered with darkish colour. White is very rarely used and blue is used very sparingly. To the S of the Coronation Hall is *kovinithilam* (staircase room), which has six 18th century large murals including the coronation of Rama. (The staircase led downstairs to the women's bedroom on the ground floor.) The pictures have no theme, and they are lighter in tone than those of the royal bedchamber. The room to the N of the *kovinitilam* has a painting of Vishnu. Other rooms upstairs have more exhibits of the royal house. 2 of the women's bedrooms downstairs have 19th century murals, much less congested than those upstairs, with details more clearly shown. In the words of H. Sarkar, "shadings produce tonal effects and realistic colours have been employed, thus minutely delineating even minor features like nails, fingers, folds of clothes and so on. Figures are comparatively slimmer with attenuated waist... All the panels here, like Siva dallying with Mohini, Krishna and Gopis, and others breathe an air of freedom, charged with an undercurrent of sensuousness in spite of the fact that the themes are mythological." One of the rooms shows the poet Kalidasa's story of *Kumarasambava*, while the other has 5 large murals relating themes from the *Puranas*.

Jewish Synagogue Open 1000-1200 and 1500-1700. Closed Sat and Jewish holidays. Entrance Re 0.50. The Jews quarter is in S Mattanchery, next door to the Mattancherry Palace. The story of the Kochi Jews is fascinating. For several centuries there were 2 Jewish communities. The older was that of the 'black' Jews. According to one source they claimed to have settled in 587 BC. The earliest evidence of their presence and importance is a copper inscription dated AD 388 (possibly as much as a century later) by the Prince of Malabar. The White Jews came much later, and eventually in larger numbers, possibly totalling as many as 4,000 at their peak. The synagogue of the White Jews is next to the Mattancherry Palace. Stepping inside is an extraordinary experience of light and airiness, given partly by the flooring of 18th century light blue Cantonese ceramic tiles, hand made and each one different. In addition to the trade with China, the Jewish community may also have had strong links with Babylonian Jews. It is possible to see the Great Scrolls of the Old Testament and the copper plates on which privileges were granted to the Jewish community by the Kochi rulers. Since Indian Independence and the founding of the State of Israel the Jewish community has shrunk to fewer than 50, and the second Jewish synagogue (in Ernakulam) is deserted.

St Francis Church Originally named Santo Antonio, St Francis Church is the first church to have been built in the new, European influenced tradition. In Fort Kochi, the original wooden building (1510) was soon replaced by the present stone building. (There is no authority for the widely quoted date of 1546.) Vasco da Gama died on the site in 1524 and was originally buried in the cemetery. 14 years later his body was removed to Portugal. The church has an impressive façade; inside, the chancel is separated from the nave by a plain arch. The use of the arch is in sharp contrast to traditional Indian use of flat overlapping slabs, or *corbelling*, to produce gateways. The church was taken over by the Dutch and converted into a Protestant chapel after they captured Kochi in 1663. The British converted it into an Anglican church after they took power in 1795, and in 1949 the congregation joined the Church of S India. **Santa Cruz Cathedral**, Fort Kochi, close to St Francis Church, contains some attractive paintings.

Chinese fishing nets Not unique to Kochi, but uniquely accessible to the short stay visitor, the fishing cantilevered fishing nets line the entrance to the harbour mouth. They can best be seen either on the N end of the fort promontory, a few metres from the Fort Kochi bus stand, or from a boat tour of the harbour.

Gundu Island On the inshore side of Vypeen island, with only 2 ha Gundu is the smallest island in the bay.

Bolghatty Island The 'palace' now converted into a hotel was originally built in 1744 by the Dutch. It became the home of the British Resident at the court of the Raja of Kochi after 1799. Set in about 3 ha of gardens, the Kerala State Tourism Development Corporation has now added new "honeymoon suites" at the water's edge and has a golf course in the grounds. Despite the attempt it has not completely ruined the atmosphere of colonial decay which haunted the old building in its pre-modernised form and gave it much of its charm.

Willingdon Island has become the hub of one of India's busiest ports. The custom's house, Govt of India tourist office and *Malabar Hotel* lie to the N of the airport and the main railway terminus. You can take a pleasant and inexpensive ferry ride around the lake.

Museums

Parishath Thamburan Museum, Darbar Hall Rd, Ernakulam, T 369047. In Old Durbar Hall with typical Kerala architecture. 19th century oil paintings, old coins, sculptures, some collections from Kochi Royal family. Open 0930–

1200 and 1500-1730, closed Mon and national holidays. **Hill Palace Museum**, Tripunithura, T 857113. Royal exhibits, paintings, carvings, arms. Open 0900-1700, closed Mon. Small entry fee, extra for car. **Kerala Fine Arts Society**, Fine Arts Ave, T 352730. **Museum of Kerala History and its Makers**, Edappally, Kochi. Open 1000-1600, closed Mon and national holidays. Starting with Neolithic man through St Thomas, Vasco da Gama and historical personalities of Kerala are represented with sound and light. Entry Rs 2, Child Re 1. **Archaeological Museum**, Mattancherry Palace. Ornaments, weapons, clothes and paintings. Open daily 1000-1700. Closed Fri. Entry free.

Parks & zoos

Children's Traffic Park and Subhas Chandra Bose Park in Ernakulam and Nehru Memorial Children's Park in Fort Kochi.

Excursions

Kalady *STD Code*: 04857. 45 km from Kochi, Kalady, on the bank of the Periyar River, is the birthplace of one of India's most influential philosophers, Sankaracharya. Living in the 8th century, Sankaracharya founded the school of *advaita* philosophy (see page 70) which spread widely across S India. There are now 2 shrines in his memory, one as *Dakshinamurti* and the other to the Goddess Sarada, open 0530-1230, 1530-2000. The management of the shrines is in the hands of the Math at Sringeri in Karnataka. See page 1031. The Adi Sankara Kirti Stambha Mandapam is a 9-storeyed octagonal tower, 46m high, and details Sri Sankara's life and works and the Shan Maths or 6 ways to worship. Open 0700-1900. Small entry fee. Kalady can easily be visited in an afternoon from Kochi. **Accommodation** Sri Sankaracharya *New Guest House* which is basic and cheap, T 345. *Ramkrishna Mission Guest House*. Also *PWD Rest House*, apply to Asst Engineer, PWD, Angalamlai.

Tours

Daily *Kerala Tourism* offers: *Boat Cruise and Sightseeing* tours visiting Dutch Palace, Jewish Synagogue, Francis Church, Chinese Fishing Nets, Gundu Island, Bolghatty Island. *Dep from Boat Jetty opp Sealord Hotel*, Shanmugam Rd, Ernakulam. 0930-1300, 1400-1730. Mornings cooler. Rs. 40. Highly rec. **Overnight** *Thekkadi Wildlife Tour* by coach visiting Kadamattam Church, Moolamattom Power House, Idukki Dam, Periyar. *Dep from Tourist Reception Centre*, every Sat 0730 returning 2000 Sun. Rs.150 plus food and hotel. **3-day** *Velankanni Tour* by coach visiting Thanjavur, Madurai and Thekkadi. *Dep from Tourist Reception Centre*, first Fri every month 0800 returning following Sun 2100. Rs 250 plus food and hotel. Reservations through Kerala Tourism. *Visitinda Tours & Travels* organise a delightful boat tour along Kochi's backwaters in a dugout, paddled and engine-less. Through very peaceful shady waterways, led by an excellent guide. Contact Mr Ajith Edassery, Visitinda, Public Library Buildings, Convent rd, Ernakluam, Kochi 682035. T 365078, F 484 370073. Rs 270 per half day. Highly rec. *Tours India*, Cochin, backwaters houseboats based on the Kettuvallam (rice boat) with modern facilities. Ernakulam to Kuttanad and return. Rs 3000 per head, Rs 300 meals.

Local festivals

Jan/Feb *Ulsavam* is celebrated at the Siva Temple in Ernakulam for 8 days and at Tripunithura Temple in Nov/Dec. There are elephant processions each day and folk dance and music performances.

Aug/Sept *Onam*.

Local information

● Accommodation

Most hotels are in Ernakulam, with very limited accommodation in Fort Kochi. Outside Kochi, the Govt *Guest House* in Aluva is one of the most attractive in Kerala (see under Aluva below).

Willingdon Island: **A** Taj *Malabar*, T 340010, F 69497, 100 rm, 12 km centre, excellent hotel and service, superb setting with lawns on the waterfront, range of facilities being developed, beautifully furnished rm – those on upper floors have sitting areas, suites in Kerala and Chinese styles, Malabar's ***Rice Boats*** is excellent but expensive, waterfront café, excellent buffet snacks on the lawn, regular ferry service from Ernakulam to its own jetty.

C *Casino*, T 668221, F 668001, 71 rm, better in the older building, close to rly, central a/c, restaurants (inc outdoor seafood restaurant), exchange, travel, shops, outdoor pool in large garden, not on the water front.

D *Island Inn*, Bristow Rd, T 666816, rm quite large and airy, facing in to courtyard, pleasant atmosphere, very good food.

Budget hotel: **F** *Maruthi Tourist Home*, next to *Casino hotel*, T 6365, 26 rm, Indian business style hotel, quite good value, if a little run down, good veg meals.

Bolghatty Island: **D/C** *Bolghatty Palace*, Mulavukad, T 355003, former British Residency, built by Dutch in 1744, in peaceful, spacious grounds has 11 rm some a/c, restaurant, bar, lawns on the waterfront, small golf course, Kathakali Show, 1830 (1 hr), Rs 25 ('amateurish but good fun'), enormous old fashioned 'suites' with large marble floored bathrooms, but some run-down, in addition, good waterside tree house (beware of mosquitoes), 'honeymoon' cottages with round beds and own staircases, ferries every 20 min from High Court Jetty and frequent sightseeing boat tours.

Ernakulam: **C** *Presidency Ashok*, 47 Paramara Rd, Ernakulam Town, T 363100, 47 rm, deluxe with fridge, central, central a/c, restaurant, bar, coffee shop, exchange, travel; **C** *Abad Plaza*, MG Rd, T 361636, F 369729, 41 rm, central, central a/c, restaurant (seafood specialities), bar, exchange, travel, shops.

D *Dwaraka*, MG Rd, T 352706, 92 rm, some a/c, modern Indian style hotel, dingy, slightly tacky bar, reasonable value; **D** *Sealord*, Shanmugam Rd, Ernakulam, T 352682, 40 rm, central a/c, restaurant (check bill for extra taxes); **D** *Grand*, MG Rd, Ernakulam, T 353211, 24 rm, some a/c, central, a/c restaurants, bar, exchange, travel, garden, comfortable with good food; **D** *International*, MG Rd, Ernakulam, T 353911, 26 rm, central a/c, restaurant (Kerala specialities), bar, coffee shop, exchange, travel; **D** *Woodlands*, MG Rd, Ernakulam, T 351372, 65 rm, 21 a/c with bath, nr rly, very central, a/c veg restaurant, good value; **D** *Bharat Tourist Home*, Durbar Hall Rd, Ernakulam, T 353501, 92 rm some a/c, close to Ernakulam Junc Rly, a/c restaurants (Indian veg), coffee shop, exchange, good value; **D** *Gaanam*, Chitoor Rd (behind Sangeetha),T 367123, 40 rm, modern, very clean, veg and non veg meals, free breakfast, good restaurant.

Budget hotels: **E** *Biju's Tourist Home*, Market Rd, nr Canon Shed Rd corner, Ernakulam, T 369881, 28 large rm, few a/c, no restaurant, but rm service, good position, clean and comfortable, friendly; **E** *Sangeetha*, Chitoor Rd, T 368736, 48 rm some a/c, close to rly, central, unimaginative design but pleasant service, trad Indian breakfast included in price, a/c veg restaurant; **E** *Blue Diamond*, Market Rd, Ernakulam, T 353221, 42 rm some a/c, restaurant, a/c bar, roof-garden; **E** *Modern Guest House*, opp rm with bath, clean, well-maintained, friendly staff, rec; **E** *Piazza Lodge*, nr S rly station, Ernakulam, T 367408, F 370136, a/c rm, lovely rm, clean, excellent value; **E** *Luciya*, Stadium Rd, nr Bus Station, Ernakulam, T 354433, 106 rm with bath, some a/c, best with balcony, good restaurant and bar. Friendly and helpful. Other inexpensive non-a/c accommodation **E** *Bosoto Lodge*, Press Club Rd, nr jetty, drably decorated, friendly staff, beware of mosquitoes and bed bugs.

F *Railway Retiring Rooms*, 5 rm, contact Station Master; **F** *Govt Rest House*, opp Guest House, Ernakulam, T 361265, reservations: Dist Collector, Trikkakara, large rm but run down, reservations: Exec Engineer, PWD (B & R), Ernakulam; **F** *Hakoba* Shanmugam Rd, T 353933, 12 rm, good sea views from some, clean, friendly, popular; **F** *Sea Shells* Shanmugam Rd, T 353807, 9 rm, some a/c, very simple though sea facing rm have excellent views, cheap and reasonable meals; **F** *YMCA*, Chittor Rd, Ernakulam, T 355620, reservations: Gen Secy.

Fort Kochi: **D** *Sea Gull*, Calvetty Rd, Fort Kochi, NE between the 2 ferry stops, T 352682, 8 rm, ask for a/c, restaurant, bar, exchange, converted old warehouses and houses on the waterside, between the 2 ferry stops; **D** *Abad* Chullickal, Mattancherry, T 28211, 20 comfortable a/c rm, good restaurant for seafood, coffee shop, rec.

E Kerala Tourism *Subala*, Mattancherry, overlooking fishing nets, restaurant, comfortable, good value; **E** *Elite* nr St Francis Church, T 25733, some cheaper rm though the bedrooms are quite a walk from the toilets, which in some circumstances can be a disadvantage, rm at rear quieter, its *Sabala Restaurant* is inexpensive, popular and good, pleasant atmosphere, good ice creams opp hotel.

F *Princess*, opp Elite, cheap, but very dirty, hot and the moquitoes multiply, but being renovated, so may improve; **F** *Tharavadu Tourist Home*, Quiros St, behind Head PO, T 363100, 8 clean rm, with bath, good value, rec; **F** PWD *Inspection Bungalow*, nr Fort Kochi beach, T 25797; **F** *Ninan's*, located in the bus station, doubles with bath, rec.

● Places to eat

Ernakulam: offers a good choice. Rec hotels: *Sealord's*, roof-top (good fish dishes and Chinese); Abad Plaza's *Regency* (inc Chinese), *Grand* (inc Japanese dishes) and *Presidency Ashok*. Other restaurants serving non-veg food: *Chinese Garden*, off MG Rd, (a/c) rec as serving authentic Chinese cuisine; *Pandhal*, on MG Rd which is also good for snacks. *Whizz*, Abad Plaza Complex, MG Rd; *Malabar*, Market Rd, though gloomy inside, serves excellent, inexpensive S Indian food. *Yuvrani*, Jos Junc, MG Rd, specialises in seafood platters.

Jancy's Café, Shanmugam Rd, good snacks. *Bimbi's*, nr corner of Durbar Hall and MG Rd has fast-food, *Khyber*, meals upstairs. *Indian Coffee Houses*, opp Bimbi's and at corner of Park Av and Canon Shed Rd for good coffee and snacks. *Ceylon Bake House*, Ernakulam. Very good fish and chips, excellent service – lovely place. *Chariot Beach*, Children's Park Junc, on corner of Princess Rd and River Rd. Fort Kochi quite an upmarket outdoor cafe feel, meals about Rs 100. Very popular with Indians and Western tourists. Ice creams at *Snow Ball*, Rajaji Rd, nr Muthoot Towers and *Caravan*, Broadway, S end.

● Bars

Rec in major hotels only, although prohibition is not in force.

● Airline offices

On MG Rd: **Air India**: Ernakulam, T 351295; **British Airways**: Nijhwan Travels, Kochi, T 364867; **Cathay Pacific & KLM**: Spencers, Kochi, T 369165; **Japan Airlines**: Global Travel, Kochi, T 350544; **Singapore Airlines and Swissair**: Aviation Travels, Ernakulam, T 367911.

● Banks & money changers

Most open till 1500, a few stay open until 1700, and also Sat afternoon for 2 hr. **Union Bank**, Panampilly Nagar, opens Sun. Several banks on MG Rd, Shanmugam Rd and on Broadway, Ernakulam. Branches of **Chartered, Grindlays** and **State Bank of India** on Willingdon Island. Others in Mattancherry and on Palace Rd, Kochi Rd.

● Entertainment

Daily performances of *Kathakali* at centres where you can arrive early to watch the extraordinary make-up being applied. Nr Junc Station, See **India Foundation**, XXX/111 Kalathiparampil Lane off Chittoor Rd, behind Laxman Theatre, T 369471. Now a/c. Devan Gurukalam's "great evening of dance". Make up from 1800, Performance with excellent English commentary, 1900-2030. Rs 50. T 368471. **Art Kerala Theatre**, XXXV/346, Kannanthodath Lane, Valanjanbalam. Very good daily performance (make-up demonstration) Rs 50. **Kochi Cultural Centre**, (XXXV/1521 Sangamom, Manniath Rd, Ernakulam). At Darbar Hall Grounds by the Museum Theatre. Demonstration with explanations 1830-2000. Rs 50. Check with Tourist Office for date of monthly performance at Kathakali Club, Layam Rd, Ernakulam. Also highly recommended is the Kathakali Dance Centre, next to *Seagull Hotel*, Fort Kochi, Dance 1330-1930 every evening. Rs 50. Can watch make-up being put on. Main dancer does excellent ayurvedic massage for Rs 100.

● Hospitals & medical services

General Hospital, Hospital Rd, Ernakulam, T 360002 (nearby *Oriental Pharmacy*, Market Rd open 24 hr); *Govt Hospital*, Fort Kochi, T 24444; *Maharaja's Hospital*, Karuvelipady, Kochi, T 24561. Ernakulam Private: *Lissie Hospital*, Lissie Junc, T 352006; *Lourdes Hospital*, Pachalam, T 351507. On MG Rd: *City*, T 368970, and *Medical Trust Hospital*, T 352303, have 24-hr pharmacies.

● Post & telecommunications

Post office: Ernakulam Head PO, Hospital Rd, (0800-2000, Sun 1000-1800); Kochi Main PO, Mattancherry (for Poste Restante), 0800-2000, Sun 0930-1700). N End PO, Willingdon Island. **Central Telegraph Office**: (24 hr) Jos Junc Bldg, 2nd Flr, MG Rd, Ernakulam and Mattancherry, Kochi.

● Shopping

Coir products (eg mats), Carvings on rosewood, buffalo horn, ivory and models of snake boats. Several Govt Emporia on MG Rd, Ernakulam, including ***Kerala State Handicraft Emporium, Kairali, Khadi Bhavan, Handloom House and National Textiles*** (which also has a shop in Banerji Rd). Other shopping areas are in Broadway, Super Bazar, Anand Bazar, Prince St and New Rd. ***Curio Palace***, MG Rd sells gift.

Books: *Bhavi Books*, Convent Rd.

● Tour companies & travel agents

Govan, Hospital Rd, T 354970; ***Gt India Tour Co***, 1st Flr, Pithru Smarana, Srikandath Rd, Ravipuram, T 369246, F 351528; ***Harrison Malayalam***, Willingdon Island, T 6007; ***Travel Corp of India***, Telstar Bldg, Ravipuram, T 351646. Several on MG Rd. Ernakulam: ***Jai Hind***, T 361011; ***Kerala Travels***, Jos Junc, T 367738; ***Sita***, T 367672. ***Olympus Travel***, bottom of MG Rd, Ernakulam, nr Little Kingdom shop. Very competent and helpful.

● Tourist offices

Govt of India Tourist Office, next to *Malabar Hotel*, Willingdon Island, T 6045, where you can pick up maps and small booklets. Very helpful. **Kerala Tourism**, Old Collectorate, Park Avenue, Ernakulam. Kerala Tourism, Shanmugam Rd, Ernakulam, T 353234 where you can get a small booklet 'Kerala Travel Facts' with useful listings and 3 rather small scale maps. 0800-1800. *Guides* are available through the Govt of India Tourist Office. Rates vary: For up to 4 persons, half day (4 hr) Rs 50 and full day (8 hr) Rs 100. For journeys outside the city additional charges are made of about Rs 50. **Tourist Desk**, by the main Boat Jetty, Ernakulam. PJ Verghese, the Organising Secretary, helps tourists plan itineraries round Kerala on a voluntary basis. Very helpful.

● Useful address

Automobile Association of S India MG Rd (opp Hotel Dwaraka), T 351369. **Visa extension**, City Police Commissioner, Shanmugam Rd, T 360600.

● Transport

Kochi is at the junction of NH17 (to Panvel, Bombay) and NH47 (to Kanniyakumari). Other major highways lead to Bangalore, Madras and other cities beyond. Distances to some are Madras 675 km, Bombay 1,400 km, Alappuzha 64 km, Thiruvananthapuram 223 km, Kanniyakumari 309 km, Ooty 312 km, Kodaikkanal 330 km, Thekkadi (Periyar National Park) 190 km, Thrissur 80 km and Madurai 324 km.

Local Ferries: are the best way of getting about between the islands – faster, cheaper and much more comfortable than buses or autos. Ferry stops are clearly named. Fort Kochi 'Customs' (main stop) with a separate one for Vypeen Island, Willingdon Island 'Embarkation' to the N and 'Terminus' on W side towards Mattancherry. From **Ernakulam** to Fort Kochi Customs, Willingdon Terminus and Mattancherry: half-hourly from 0630 to 2130. To Bolghatty Island: every 20 min from High Court Jetty from 0600-2200. To Vypeen Island via Willingdon Embarkation: ½-hr or more, from 0530-2230. From **Fort Kochi** Customs to *Malabar Hotel*, ½-hr approx and to Vypeen Island, very frequent with about 2 car ferries an hour. To Varapusha, 0740, every 40 min till 1500. An alternative to a long backwater trip. **Buses**: fairly frequent and cheap in Ernakulam. Journeys between Ernakulam, Willingdon and Fort Kochi useful after ferries stop running. **Taxis**: yellow top and Tourist taxis, both luxury and ordinary, can be hired by the hour or on a charge based per km. Extra charges for waiting. On MG Rd, Ernakulam: Corp Taxi Stand, T 361444; Ensign Taxis, T 353080; Piazza's, S Rly Rd, Kochi, T 367408 and Princy, nr N Overbridge, Kochi, T 352751, among others. Kerala Tourism, Tourist Reception Centre, Shanmugham Rd, Ernakulam, and Princey Travels, nr N Overbridge, Ernakulam, also offer coach hire. **Auto-rickshaws**: usually ask for a min charge. Approaching Police Check Pt outside Rly Station make meters work!

Air Airport on Willingdon Island, 5 km from Ernakulam. **Transport to town**: taxis from airport to Ernakulam centre about Rs 30. **Indian Airlines**, Durbar Hall Rd, nr Bharat Hotel, T 353901. Airport, T 6486. **Bombay**: daily, 0915, 1¾ hr and Tu,Th,Sa, 1215; **Delhi** via Goa: daily except M, 1010, 4 hr; **Madras** via Bangalore: M,W,F,Su, 1105, 2 hr. **East West Airlines**, L Links, Badriya Trent Complex, MG Rd, Ernakulam, T 355242; Kochi, T 355242, F 355639. **Bombay**: daily, 0745 and 1220, 2 hr. **Jet Airways**, MG Rd, Kochi, T 369423. **Bombay**: daily, 1130, 1¾ hr. **Modiluft**, Chandrika Bldg, MG Rd, Kochi, T 367740. **Bangalore**: Tu,Th,Sa, 1055, ¾ hr; on to Hyderabad, 2½ hr.

Train Kochi is on the broad gauge line joining the Thiruvananthapuram to Mangalore, Bangalore and Madras lines. Trains from the important cities in the N stop alternately at Kochi and Ernakulam Junc, the latter continuing to Thiruvananthapuram. Enquiries: Kochi

Harbour Terminus, T 6050. Ernakulam Junc, T 353100, Public Information, T 369119. Trains stop at Ernakulam Town station, T 353920, when incoming trains bypass Kochi HT. **Ernakulam to Thiruvananthapuram**: *Vanchinad Exp* 6303, daily, 0600, 4¼ hr; *Venad Exp* 6301 (AC/CC), daily, 1710, 4¾ hr. **Kochi to Madras (MC)**: *Madras Exp* 6042 (AC/II), 1620 (from Ernakulam 1655), 14 hr. **Ernakulam to Delhi (ND)**: *Kerala Mangala Exp* 2625/2625A (AC/II), daily, 1440, 47¾ hr. **Kochi to Bombay (VT)**: *Netravati Exp* 2136 (AC/II), Mon, Wed, Fri, 1725 (from Ernakulam 1750), 36¼ hr. **Ernakulam to Bombay (VT)**: *Kanniya Kumari Exp* 1082 (AC/II), daily, 1330, 39½ hr. **Ernakulam to Mangalore**: *Thiruvananthapuram-Mangalore Exp* 6349 (AC/-CC), daily, 1100, 10 hr.

Road Bus: Kerala SRTC run Express and Fast services from Ernakulam Bus Terminus to other major cities within Kerala and into the neighbouring states with reciprocal services from other STCs. Enquiries: Bus Terminus, T 352033. To **Alappuzha**, 1½ hr, Rs 15; **Devikolam**, 6 hr, Rs 30. **Kannur**, 7 hr (Exp), 8½ hr, Rs 55. **Kottayam**, 2¼ hr, Rs 15. **Kozhikode**, 5 hr (Exp) Rs 48, 6½ hr, Rs 40; **Thekkadi**, 3 daily, 6¾ hr, Rs 40. **Thiruvananthapuram**, , 5 hr (Exp) Rs 50, 6½ hr, Rs 40. **Thrissur**, 1¾ hr (Exp), Rs 18.

Interstate of SRTCs: **Bangalore** via Kozhikode, Battery and Mysore, 5 daily from 0600-2000, 14 hr, Rs 155. **Coimbatore**, 5 hr (Exp), Rs 45. **Kanniyakumari Exp**, daily, 9 hr, Rs 70. **Madras** via Coimbatore, Erode, Salem, daily, 1530, 21 h; 16½ hr (Exp), Rs 132. **Madurai**, 9¼ hr (Exp), Rs 66. **Mysore**, 11 hr, Rs 115.

Private operators: from Kalloor and S Bus stands. Indira Travels, DH Rd, T 360693 and SB Travels, Ensign Agencies, MG Rd, opp Jos Annexe, T 353080, run overnight video coaches to Bangalore (12 hr) and to Kottayam, every ½hr from main bus station. Also to Madras and Coimbatore.

Sea Cruises to Lakshadweep organised by SPORT, Harbour Rd, Willingdon Island, T 69755.

KOCHI TO KANNUR

Initially going inland, this route goes through Kerala's most sacred pilgrimage centre at Guruvayur and the many megalithic monuments around the western end of the Palakkad gap. It rejoins the coast at the major town of Kozhikode (Calicut) and along the attractive coastline to Kannur.

Aluva (Alwaye)

STD Code: 04854. Aluva, 21 km N of Ernakulam, is an important industrial town; the radioactive monazite sands of the beach here are processed. Other industries include chemicals, glass, aluminium, rayon, tyres, fertilisers. Despite its industrial activity the Periyar River on which it stands is still very attractive, and good for river swimming. There is a Siva lingam on the sand bank. **Accommodation** Govt **E** *Guest House*, with 10 rm, which also has Tourist Information, T 3637, this is one of the best Govt *Guest Houses* in Kerala, an old palace on the banks of the river, it has a beautiful circular verandah, large rm and efficient staff. Apply to Manager; **E** *Periyar Ltd*, New By-Pass Rd, T 5465, 10 rm, some a/c. Cheaper **F** *Rest House* which you can reserve through the District Collector, Ernakulam or direct.

Kodungallur (Cranganore)

STD Code: 0488. The Syrian orthodox church here blends early Christian architecture in Kerala with surrounding Hindu traditions. Thus the images of Peter and Paul are placed where the *dvarapalas* (door-keepers) of Hindu temples would be found, and a portico is placed in front of the church for pilgrims. H Sarkar of the Archaeological Survey of India suggests that "the church architecture in Kerala evolved out of an indigenous building tradition, and basically the same trend continued until recently despite the impact of later ecclesiastical architecture of Europe."

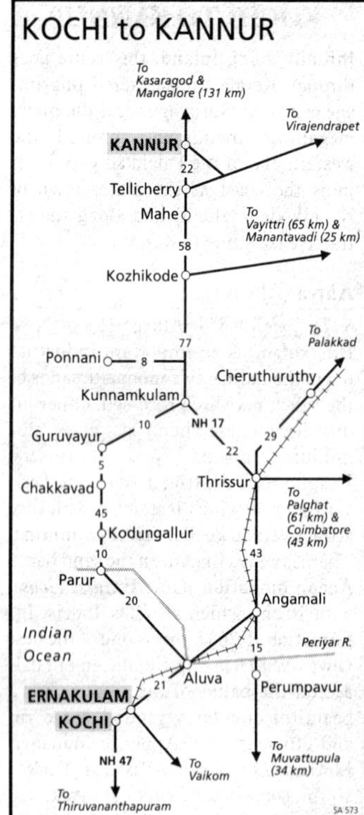

At one time Kodungallur was the W coast's major port, and the capital of the Chera king Cheraman Perumal. **Muziris**, on the shore, is the point at which St Thomas is believed to have landed. It is worth visiting the Tiruvanchikulam Temple, the Bhagavati Temple and the Portuguese fort. Kodungallur is also associated by tradition with the arrival of the first Muslims to reach India by sea. Malik-ibn-Dinar is reputed to have built India's first mosque here. There is no evidence that the present mosque can be dated as early as the 7th century AD, but it does have some interesting features. The outer walls have a moulded base similar to that of Brahmanical temples, for example.

The **Bhagavati Temple** is the site of the spectacular and controversial annual *Bharani festival*, held in the Malayalam month of Meenom (Mar-Apr). The temple, which dates from the Chera period, is the focus of Shakti worship. Intoxicated devotees process to the temple singing obscene songs, celebrating the expulsion of 'foreigners' (possibly Buddhists) from the temple. On the 1st day of the month of Aswathi pilgrims run madly around the temple compound, watched by spectators jammed into any available vantage point. So-called 'oracles' associated with the temple, dressed in scarlet, enter the temple in a frenzied and ecstatic state, often flailing themselves. Some earlier rituals, such as the sacrifice of cocks, was abandoned under government pressure in 1954, and the whole festival still causes local controversy.

• **Budget hotels E** *Indraprastham*, E Nada, T 2678, *Kairali*, Kattapuram, T 2770 and *Polakulath*, N Nada, T 2602, are simple but have some a/c rm. **F** *Parsanthi*, T 2939, is more basic; **F** PWD *Resthouse*. Apply direct or to Dist Collector, Thrissur.

ROUTES Continue N through Chavakkad to one of Kerala's most sacred pilgrimage centres, to Guruvayur.

Guruvayur

STD Code: 0487. The **Sri Krishna Temple** which probably dates from at least the 16th century makes this a very sacred place and an important pilgrimage centre. The image of Krishna has 4 arms with the conch, the discus, the mace and the lotus. One devotee has written that "Adorning himself with the divine tulais garland and pearl necklace, the Lord here appears in all his radiance. His eyes stream forth the milk of compassion and kindness. To millions, *Gurvayurappan* is a living deity who answers all their prayers. He is *Sri Krishna*, the divine cowherd who played his flute in Gokulam and Vrindhavan and enchanted the whole world with his music. It is not only the gopis or milkmaids who yearn for oneness with him, but all men and women who wish to be liberated from *samsara*".

In the outer enclosure there is a tall gold plated flagpost and a pillar of lamps. The sanctum sanctorum is in the 2-storeyed *srikoil,* with the image of the 4 armed Krishna garlanded with pearls and marigolds. **Punnathur Kotta**, 4 km away, houses the 40 temple elephants. An unusual feature of the temple at Guruvayur is the timing of the rituals. The sanctum opens at 0300 and closes at 2100. Except between 1300 and 1600, when it is closed, a continuous series of pujas and processions is performed. The darshan at 0300 is believed to be particularly auspicious. It is called the *nirnalaya* darshan, when the image is decked out with the previous day's flowers. Non-Hindus are not allowed inside the Sri Krishna Temple, where the devotional poet Melpattur Narayan Bhattathiri composed a famous Sanskrit devotional poem, *Narayaniyam*.

Festivals

Feb/Mar *Ulsavam* 10 days of festivities start with an elephant race and continue with colourful elephant processions and performances of Krishattam dances. Details of the timing can be obtained from Kerala Tourist offices.

Nov-Dec Guruvayur is famous for its recitals of classical music at the temple.

• **Accommodation** Accommodation in a/c rm in the **E** category available in *Ayodhya*, W Nada, T 566226; **F** *Elite Tourist Home*, T 6215 in E Nada; **F** *Vanamala Kusumam*, S Nada, T 566702. Cheaper rm at: **F** *Surya*, T 566505; **F** *Maharaja*, T 566369; **F** *Namaskar Tourist Home*, W Nada, T 566355; **F** Kerala Tourism *Nandanam*, E Nada, nr Garuda Statue & rly station, T 566266; **F** *Mangalya*, nr Sri Krishna Temple, E Nada Gopuram, T 556267, 7 (4 to 6-bed), non-a/c rm; *Panchajanyam*, (Guruvayur Devaswom) S. Nada, T 6535. Also a VIP Guest House *Sreevalsam*, reservations: Administrator.

• **Places to eat** In the hotels listed. Also an *Indian Coffee House* and *Ramakrishna Lunch Home*.

Kunnamkulam

STD Code: 04889. The road goes inland to Kunnamkulam (10 km). This area is noted for its wide range of **megalithic monuments**. On the W side of the Palakkad gap, it has been one of the few easy routes through the Ghats for 3,000 years. Megalithic cultures spread from the Tamil Nad plains down into Kerala, but developed their own local forms. The small villages of Eyyal, Chowanur, Kakkad, Porkalam, Kattakampala and Kadamsseri, between Guruvayur and Kunnamkulam, have *hoodstones*, *hat-stones*, *dolmens*, *burial urns* and *menhirs*. **Chovannur** in particular has many *Topikals* (hat stones), one of the particularly distinctive iron age megalithic remains of Kerala. Nearby **Porkalam** has a wide range of monuments side by side within an area of less than 1 ha. Hoodstones (kudaikal) are made of dressed granite and are like a handleless umbrella made of palm leaf used locally. It is shaped into a dome and covers a burial pit. The hat-stones, made of dressed laterite, have a circular top stone resting on four pieces of stone placed upright in an almost circular form, looking like a giant mushroom. They did not have any burial chamber.

ROUTES Continue N. The road keeps away from the coast, to Kozhikode (77 km).

Kozhikode (Calicut)

BASICS *Population*: 800,900; *STD Code*: 0495: *Climate*: Temp Summer: Max 35°C, Min 23°C; Winter: Max 32°C Min 22°C; *Annual rainfall*: 2,500 mm; *Best season*: Nov-Mar.

Kozhikode (meaning literally 'cock crowing') was the capital of the Zamorin Rajas. According to the early 19th century historian Buchanan-Hamilton "when Cheruman Perumal had divided Malabar, and had no principality remaining to bestow on the ancestors of the Tamuri, he gave that chief his sword, with all the territory in which a cock crowing at a small temple here could be heard. This formed the original dominions of the Tamuri, and was called Colicudu, or the cock crowing". That romantic derivation of the name is not unchallenged, but the story is suggestive of the tiny states that existed in medieval Kerala. In 1498 Vasco da Gama landed at the port, starting a turbulent, often violent, 150 years of contact with European powers.

When the Portuguese arrived Calicut was under the control of the Vijayanagar Empire (see page 1044), based in Hampi over 500 km to the NE. After a decade of violent raids the local Zamorin made peace with the Portuguese and gave them trading rights and the right to build a fort. It remained a centre of Portuguese economic and political power and influence for over a century. In 1766 the city was threatened not by Europeans from the sea but by the Muslim Raja from Mysore, Haidar Ali. The Zamorin offered peace, but when the offer was rejected barricaded himself and his family in the palace and burnt it to the ground. Although Haidar Ali soon left, his son Tipu Sultan returned twenty three years later and devastated the entire region. British rule was imposed in 1792 by the Treaty of Seringapatam.

Its name during the British period, Calicut, was given to the *calico* cloth, a block printed cotton exported round the world. Today Kozhikode is a major commercial centre for N Kerala.

Local industries

The major centre for Kerala's timber industry. Boat building is also important. The textile mill started by the Basel Mission in the 19th century is now state owned.

Places of interest

Kallai (6 km from centre) is the main centre of the timber industry; the yard is said to be the second largest in the world. Elephants are still widely used for hauling timber.

Museums

Pazhassiraja Museum 5 km on E Hill. The Archaeological Department Museum, located at E Hill. Exhibits include copies of original murals, plus bronzes, old coins and models of the different types of megalithic monuments widespread in the area. **The Art Gallery** and **Krishna Menon Museum** (named after the Kerala politician who became a leading left wing figure in India's post-Independence Congress Govt). Located next door to the Pazhassiraja Museum, it has an excellent collection of paintings by Indian artists and also wood and ivory carvings. A section of the museum is dedicated to the personal belongings of VK Krishna Menon. Open 0930-1230, 1430-1730. Daily except Mon. Entry free.

Excursions

There is a very picturesque journey over Western Ghats to Ooty and Mysore 214 km (5½ hrs). This goes up through **Vayittiri** (65 km) and **Manandavady** (Manantoddy – 25 km; *Altitude*: 750m; *STD Code*: 04962) 3 km before Manandavady is the Vallurvaku or "fish pagoda", dedicated to Durga. The tank has sacred carp. **Accommodation F** *Deluxe Tourist Home*, 'clean, comfortable but not deluxe!', it has a fairly good restaurant, rm have attached and clean, en-suite Indian toilets.

A branch road 10 km from Vayittiri leads to **Sultan's Battery** (now spelt Sultan's Batary, but formerly known as Ganapathivattom, 'the fields of Ganapathi', 22 km; *STD Code*: 04968), an 18th century fort built by Tipu Sultan in the heart of the Wynad coffee and cardamom growing region. Not much of the fort itself remains. 6 km E of the fort is a natural deep crack in the rock on which four inscriptions have been carved and some crude drawings. **Accommodation D** *The Resort*, has some a/c rm, restaurant. **F** *Modern Tourist Home*, quite modern and reasonable. Also **D** Kerala Tourism *Motel Araam*, very basic ((2 hr rate, Rs 25).

Local festival

Feb *Ulsavam* at Srikantesvara Temple for 7 days during Sivaratri week. Elephant processions, exhibitions, fair and fireworks.

Local information

● Accommodation

Jail Rd is Maula Md Ali Rd, Mavoor Rd is Indira Gandhi Rd. **D** ***Malabar Palace*** GH Rd, T 64974, a/c rm, good restaurant and ice cream; **D** ***Seaqueen***, Beach Rd, T 60201, 27 rm, 15 a/c, 1.5 km rly, good restaurant, a/c bar, exchange; **D** ***White Lines***, Kallai Rd, T 65211, some a/c rm, others cheaper; **D** ***Paramount Tower***, Town Hall Rd, T 54623, some a/c rm, restaurant.

● Budget hotels

E Kerala Tourism ***Malabar Mansion***, Kerala Tourism Corner, SM St, 1 km rly station, T 76101, 30 rm, some a/c, restaurant, beer parlour, travel; **E** ***Beach***, Beach Rd, T 73852, 14 rm, some a/c, restaurant, bar; **E** ***Hyson***, Bank Rd, T 54623, 51 rm, some a/c, 1 rm some a/c with bath and phone, 1 km rly, central, restaurant, bar, garden, credit cards; **E** ***Alakapuri Guest House***, Maulana Md Ali (Jail) Rd, T 73361, restaurant, bar, exchange; **E** ***Kalpaka Tourist Home***, Town Hall Rd, nr rly, T 62371, 100 rm, some a/c, with bath, restaurant (S Indian); **E** ***NCK Tourist Home***, Mavoor Rd, above *India Coffee House*, T 65331, 54 rm, some a/c, with bath, good veg restaurant, good value; **E** ***Govt Guest House***, is on W Hill with a/c rm, T 51520, contact Manager. ***Rest House*** is cheaper, reservations, District Collector. **E** ***YMCA***, nr Rly Gate No 4, T 55740; **E** ***YWCA***, Kannur Rd, T 54604. Several **E/F** 'Tourist Homes' on Mavoor and Kallai Rd, some with simple a/c rm.

● Places to eat

Some in hotels as above; several others on Beech Rd, and Mavoor (Indira Gandhi) Rd. ***India Coffee Houses*** on Kallai and Mavoor Rd, ***Woodlands*** Mavoor Rd. Snack bars, including ***Mammas & Pappas*** French Bakery on Beech Rd, ***Park*** open-air, Mananchira, and ***Royal Cakes*** on Bank Rd, highly rec.

● Banks & money changers

State Bank on Bank Rd. Several on Cherooty Rd.

● Post & telecommunications

Head Post Office: nr Mananchira. **Central Telegraph Office**: 24-hr ISD and Fax.

● Shopping

Local handicrafts are rosewood, ivory, buffalo horn carvings, coir products and model snake boats. ***Supermarket***, Mavoor Rd, ***CSI***, Mananchira and ***Big Bazar***, SM St.

Books: ***TBS***, next to Malabar Palace Hotel. Good range, rec. ***Pai***, Kallai Rd.

● Sports

Yoga: Kerala Yogasanam, New Rd. Others in Gandhiigram and Maulana Md Ali Rd.

● Tour companies & travel agents

Ravel Tours, Bank Rd; ***Gt India Tour Co***, League House, Red Cross Rd, T 55248, F 53727; ***Harrisons***, Beach Rd.

● Tourist office

Kerala Tourism, KTDC Corner, T 76101. **District** Information Office, Civil Station, T 73096.

● Transport

Well connected to other important towns in Kerala and neighbouring states, including Mangalore 246 km, Kochi 225 km, Thiruvananthapuram, Bangalore, and Madurai.

Local Tourist **taxis**, Yellow top taxis, **autorickshaws** and SKS Luxury **Buses** from Maulana Md Ali (Jail) Rd.

Air Airport is 25 km from centre. **Indian Airlines**, Bank Rd, T 55233. Air India, Bank Rd, T 55659. **Bombay**: daily, 0845, 1½ hr; **Sharjah (Gulf)**: daily, 1730, 3 hr. **East West Airlines**, Zam Zam Bldg, Mavoor Rd, T 64883. **Bombay**: daily, 0755 and 1220, 1¾ hr.

Train Trains to Mangalore 3 hr, Ernakulam about 5 hr, Thiruvananthapuram about 10 hr. Also to Madras and Bangalore and Coimbatore.

Road Bus: KSRTC services from Mavoor Rd Bus Stand to **Thiruvananthapuram** via Thrissur, Ernakulam, Alappuzha, Kollam, 0630-2200, 10 hr.

Kozhikode to Kannur (Cannanore)

ROUTES The NH 17 runs N along the coast. **Mahe** (*STD Code*: 04983) is just one more village in the apparently endless palm fringed beach of Kerala. It was named after M. Mahe de Labourdonnais, when he captured it for the French in 1725. A tiny settlement of 7 sq km, Mahe is beautifully positioned on a slight hill overlooking the river. From the neighbouring hill where the Basel Mission house was built are very attractive views of the Wynad hills inland. It is still part of Pondicherry. **Accommodation F** *Arena*, T 2421, has simple rm.

The coast road often gives attractive views of the sea, glimpsed between the coconut palms and thatched roofed village houses.

Thalassery(Tellicherry; 6 km; *STD Code*: 04984) set up by the British E India Company in 1683 to export pepper and cardamom. In 1708 the Company obtained permission to build a fort. It survived a siege laid by Haidar Ali and today is still standing on a rocky promontory about 15m above sea level. The population is largely Moplah (Kerala Muslims). There are some very attractive old buildings, including some within the Fort citadel. The town is on a beautiful site and is a very pretty fishing village, with good swimming (protected by an off-shore reef) and a fascinating and colourful bazar. Few visitors come to the town but it is well worth seeing. **Accommodation E** *Pranam*, T 20634, restaurant.

Kannur (Cannanore)

(*Population*: 464,000; *STD Code*: 0497) The centre of the Moplah community, a group of Arab descent, was also the capital of the N Kolathiri Rajas for several hundred years. Their palace is at **Chirakkal**, 6 km away. The town stands on low hills with cliffs at the sea face, no more than 10m to 15m above sea level. At the end of the NW promontory is the Fort St Angelo, built by the Portuguese in 1505, later taken over by the British as their most important military base in the S. A massive building, constructed out of laterite blocks, it is surrounded by the sea on 3 sides and a dry ditch on its landward side. The British cantonment area was on the NW side of the bay while the highly picturesque Moplah town is round the bay to the S of the fort. There is a good beach.

Excursion

Madayi, 22 km away, has a famous 12th century mosque built by Malik Ibn Dinar with white marble, claimed to be from Arabia.

Parassinikadavu Snake Farm 16 km from Kannur. Several poisonous and non-poisonous snakes are bred. Remote and attractive rural setting. 2 km away on the banks of the Valapatnam River is a shrine to Muthappan in the Saivite Parassinikadavu Temple. The deity is offered the locally appropriate though highly unusual gift of toddy and dried fish.

• **Accommodation C/D** *Kamala International*, SM Rd, T 66910, has some a/c rm. Several **Budget hotels E** *Omar Inn*, Station Rd, T 68957, *Savoy*, Beach Rd, T 66910, *Centaur*, MA Rd, T 68270, *Choice Seaside*, Cantt, T 68317, and *Kavitha*, SN Park, have a few a/c rm, others with fan are cheaper. **F** Kerala Tourism *Motel Araam* with simple rm (2 hr rate, Rs 25); **F** *Yatri Nivas*, nr Police Club, T 69700, some a/c rm but quite basic.

• **Tourist office** Dist Tourism Promotion Council, T 64242.

• **Transport Train Mangalore**: *Mangalore Mail* 6001 (AC/II), Daily, 1020, 3 hr; *Thiruvananthapuram-Mangalore Exp* 6349 (AC/CC), daily, 1805, 3 hr. **Palakkad**: *Kerala-Mangalore Exp* 2625/2625A(AC/CC), daily, 1140, 6 hr; *Madras Mail* 6002 (AC/CC), daily, 1515, 5¼ hr. **Coimbatore**: *Kerala-Mangala Exp* 2625/2625A (AC/II), daily, 1140, 7½ hr; *Netravati Exp* 2136 (AC/II), Mon, Wed, Fri, 1600, 6½ hr. **Madras (MC)**: *Madras Mail* 6002 (AC/II), daily, 1515, 15¼ hr.

ROUTES Leave Kannur by NH 47 – the coast road continues N to Kasargod (85 km) and Mangalore (131 km).

Kasaragod (*STD Code*: 04995) is the northernmost town in Kerala. **F** *Motel Araam*, in Kunjathur has basic rm. On the way the road passes **Ezhimala** (55 km), famous for its ayurvedic herbs. A new naval academy is being built. 16 km to the N is the ancient fort of **Bekal**, the largest and best preserved in Kerala. Bekal has a beautiful, and in mid-1994, still undeveloped beach. Kerala Tourism has plans to develop it soon into "a resort of international standards". **Budget accommodation** Recently built **F** *Tourist Rest House*, inside the Fort, very good value.

THIRUVANANTHAPURAM TO THRISSUR AND PALAKKAD

The two routes N are never widely separated, and it is possible to divert from one to the other at several places according to time and interest. The road N out of Thiruvananthapuram winds through apparently endless settlements, villages without beginning or end. Through all the hours of daylight people are visible on every section of road. Some parts of this route run through rubber plantations, and the lush vegetation makes it very attractive.

115 km N of Thiruvananthapuram is **Chengannur** (*STD Code*: 047812) which has a small Narasimha temple dating from the 18th century. The **Mahadeva Temple** uses the base of an older shrine as its *kuttambalam* (a building where dance, music and other rituals are performed). It illustrates the elliptical shape that was found again in the early Siva temple at Vaikom 60 km to the N. In the heart of the town is a famous *Bhagvati* temple, described by the arch over its main entrance as the *Mahadeva* temple, on the W side of the Thiruvananthapuram-Aluva road. The shrine is dedicated to Parvati (facing W) and Parameswara (facing E).

Aranmula10 km from Chengannur has the Parthasarathi Temple. The festival, on the last day of Onam is celebrated with the *Boat Race*. It takes the form of a water festival, instead of being purely competitive, boats and boatmen being very colourfully turned out.

Kaviyur (5 km from Thiruvalla, E of the main Rd) is noted for the best preserved rock cut cave in Kerala, dating from the 8th century. The small shrine, dedicated to Siva, is decorated with strikingly well carved reliefs. The cave has a shrine and *linga*, with a pillared hall immediately in front of it, all aligned E-W. The walls of the pillared entrance hall have reliefs showing either a chieftain or donor of the temple, a bearded ascetic, a 4-armed *Ganesh* and at the entrance the 2 doorkeepers. The chieftain is an impressive, strong-looking figure, standing with arms folded. The temple is a link between the Pandiyan kingdom of S Tamil Nadu and that of S Kerala, having much in common with temples in Ramanathapuram and Tirunelveli Districts.

Kottayam

Population: 166,200; *STD Code*: 0481. Kottayam is the main Christian centre in Kerala. Kottayam is surrounded by some of the most fertile and beautiful scenery in Kerala, with the hills to its E and backwaters to the W. The foothills of the Ghats are intensively cultivated with cash crops, notably rubber, tea, coffee, cardamom and pepper, while the valley bottoms are given over to paddy. Despite very low yields when compared with Malayan rubber production the area planted to rubber has grown dramatically.

The Christians in Kerala largely owed their allegiance to the Orthodox Syrian tradition until the arrival of the Portuguese. Indeed, bishops continued to be sent out from Syria to lead the church. After the Inquisition was introduced in 1560 the Portuguese tried to encourage the conversion of Syrian Christians to Roman Catholicism. One of the cruder means was by intercepting ships carrying Syrian bishops and preventing them from joining their churches in Kerala. At the same time efforts were made to train Indian priests, and in 1599 the Thomas Christians were allowed to use the Syriac liturgy. A formal split occurred in the Syrian church in 1665 (the year of London's great

The Chengannur Mystery

KR Vaidyanathan recounts a widely believed legend about the image of Parvati enshrined in the temple as follows: "There is a legend describing how Siva and Parvati came to reside in Chengannur. It was the wedding of Parvati and Parameswara at Mount Kailas. All the 33 crores of *devas* and *asuras* had assembled for the occasion. It looked as though the earth would tilt towards the N because of the undue weight that side. Siva grew anxious. He summoned the sage Agastya and requested him to proceed to the S to maintain the balance.

Sage Agastya felt sorely disappointed that he would miss the celestial wedding. Parameshwara understood his feelings. He assured him that he would see everything through divine sight. Further, he promised that after the marriage ceremony he with his consort would come to the S and grant him *darshan* – **see page 68**. Accordingly sage Agastya journeyed towards the S and selected that part of the Sahyadri Hills called Sonadri for his meditation. True to his word, Siva went there with Parvati and blessed Agastya. While there, the goddess had her period. The divine couple therefore stayed here for 28 days after the purificatory bath." Vaidyanathan goes on to tell the development of the story. "Wonder of wonders," he writes, "even today the deity which is cast in *panchaloha* gets her periods, a phenomenon which is not heard of in any other temple." He reports that the head priest of the temple describes what happens as follows. The head priest or his assistant "on opening the shrine in the early morning removes the previous day's decoration and hands it over to the attendant along with the white petticoat without looking at it. The attendant examines the dress closely and if there are signs of bleeding sends it to the home of the temple *tantri*. There the lady of the house scrutinises the cloth again and confirms the period." He goes on: "The petticoat, after the occurrence, is available for sale to the public. Though the rate fixed by the temple management is only Rs 10, due to its being a rarity it is grabbed by devotees paying hundreds of rupees, booking it well in advance. Among the dignitaries who bought this, we are told, are the late Sir C P Ramaswami Aiyer and ex-President VV Giri." The Tamil scholar John Marr has described this as "a fascinating example of myth appropriation, as this story is a variation of the Tamil myth of Agastya and Podiyilmalai, which recounts how the sage came S (for the same reason of maintaining balance) and taught the first Tamil grammar!"

Vaidyanathan recounts the story of a sceptical British adviser to the Raja of Travancore between 1810-14, Col Munro. "When carrying out his duty of checking the temple accounts to regulate their expenses Col Munro found expenses relating to replacement of garments soiled by the period. He is reported to have laughed at the naivete of the people. How can a metal deity get its periods? he mused. It is not only absurd but obscene he said, and cut out the budget provision with a stroke of his pen. At the same time the goddess had her period. But the Colonel learnt his lesson. His wife started to have heavy bleeding and their children took ill." Fortunately he is reported to have repented of his doubts and ensured the full recovery of all his family.

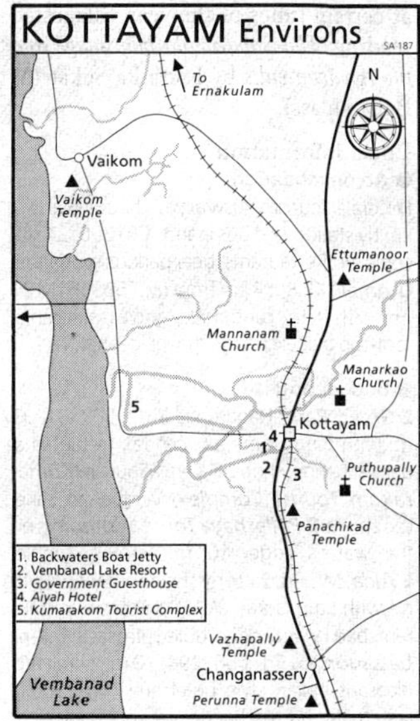

plague) when the Roman Syrians split from the Syrian Christians under their Bishop Mar Gregory. He was a Jacobite, which resulted in the name Jacobite Christians being applied to his branch of the Syrian Church. Subsequent divisions occurred in the 18th and 19th centuries, but several of the Protestant Syrian churches came back together when the Church of S India was formed in 1947.

Local industry

The town is the centre of Kerala's rubber industry.

Places of interest

Two of the Syrian churches 50m apart, are a little away from the town centre on a hillock 5 km out of town. They give an indication of church architecture of the period. The 450 year old **Cheria Palli** (Small Church) which has beautiful vegetable dye paintings over the alter. The **Vallia Palli** (Big Church) was built in 1550. Here, 2 'Nestorian' crosses are carved on plaques inserted behind two side altars. One has a Pahlavi inscription on it, the other a Syriac. The cross left of alter is the original and may be the oldest Christian artefact in India; the one to the right is a copy. By the altar, there is an unusual small triptych of an Indian St George slaying a dragon. Note the interesting Visitors Book 1898-1935 – paper cutting reports "the church has attracted many European and native gentlemen of high position". Mass at Vallia Palli at 0900 on Sun, and Cheria Palli at 0730 on Sun and Wed. The Malankara Syrian Church has its headquarters at Devakolam.

Excursions

The middle of Kottayam is a noisy, busy and increasingly polluted place, but the outskirts are much pleasanter. Kottayam is also a good place to take a trip on the **backwaters**. It takes under 3 hr to Alappuzha, the 1st boat leaving at 0630. Shorter trips are also possible, and the route is very attractive.

Kumarakom *STD Code*: 048192. A Kerala Tourism development on an old rubber plantation set around the Vembanad lake, now also a bird sanctuary. 16 km from Kottayam, ½hr, under Rs 3 by bus, which goes to the Kumarakom Tourist Centre. Open 0900-1800. Entry Re 1. A path goes through the swamp to the main bird nesting area, and the Island in the middle of the lake (*Pathiramanal* – 'midnight sands') can be reached by boat. Best season for bird life Jul-Dec. **Accommodation** Some luxury at **A** *Taj Garden Retreat*, T 048192 377, or **A** *Coconut Lagoon*, T 668221, F 668001, "ethnic type" accommodation, good restaurant. Cheaper at **E** Kerala Tourism *Kumarakom Tourist Complex*, Vembanad Lake, T 564866, 4 rm with bath, restaurant (limited menu), set in large woodland on the shores of the lake, the 50 year old mansion has simple rm overlooking the lotus pond, the woodland attracts a variety of birds, 1 km path through the woods to the lake; you can hire a boat for about Rs 70/hr, popular so book in advance, rec. It is possible to continue by ferry from Kumarakom to the village of Muhama (1/2 hrly from 0630-2100), a 40 min journey. You can then go to Alappuzha by bus.

Sabarimala *STD Code*: 04739 Many Hindu pilgrims make the journey to the forest shrine dedicated to Sri Aiyappan at Sabarimala (191 km N of Thiruvananthapuram) on a route through Kottayam. Aiyappan is a particularly favoured deity in Kerala and there are growing numbers of devotees. The pilgrims are readily visible in many parts of S India as they wear black dhotis as a symbol of the penance they must undergo for 41 days begins at *Deepavali*, before they make the pilgrimage. In addition to the black dress pilgrims must take 2 baths daily and only eat food at home during this period. The pilgrimage is only for males and pre-pubescent and post-menstrual females, in order to avoid the defilement believed to be associated with menstruation.

The pilgrimage in January itself is deliberately hard, writes Vaidyanathan, because "the pilgrimage to the shrine symbolises the struggle of the individual soul in its onward journey to the abode of bliss and beatitude. The path of the spiritual aspirant is always long, arduous and hazardous. And so is the pilgrimage to Sabarimala, what with the observance of severe austerities and trekking up forested mountains, risking attacks from wild animals." The route from Kottayam goes through Erumeli, where thousands of Hindu pilgrims worship at a mosque. This is dedicated to Vavr who is regarded as having been a contemporary of Ayyappa, now worshipped as a deity. The route then goes on to Chalakkayam and Pamba (5 km from the temple). There is then a steep 2 hr walk through the jungle to the shrine (914m). Pilgrims carry their own food, and there are only temporary sheds provided. **NB** The temple is only open at certain times of the year. Suggested reading: *The Sabarimala pilgrimage and the Ayyapan cults* by Radhika Sekar (M Banarsidass).

Local information

● Accommodation

D Kerala Tourism ***Aiswarya***, Thirunakkara, 2 km rly station and bus stand, T 61250, 34 rm, some a/c, Restaurants, beer parlour, exchange; **D** ***Anjali***, KK Rd, 4 km from rly, T 563661M 27 rm, with bath, central a/c, good restaurants, roof-top bar, exchange, travel, central, rec.

● Budget hotels

E ***Green Park***, Nagampadam, T 563331. 33 rm with bath, some a/c, central, restaurants, bar, exchange, shops; **E** Kerala Tourism ***Kumarakom Tourist Complex***, Vembanad Lake, see above; **E** ***Pallathaya Tourist Complex***, on the water's edge, 10 rm 'motel', simple; **E** ***Aida***, MC Rd, 2 km rly station, T 568391, 40 rm with bath, some a/c, 5 km centre, restaurant, bar, TV, very clean, quiet, pleasant; **E** ***Ambassador***, KK Rd, T 563294, 18 rm, some a/c, pleasant Indian style hotel and comfortable restaurant, bar, exchange, very good value.

F ***Kaycees Lodge***, YMCA Rd, T 563440, good quality for the price, and clean; **F** PWD ***Rest House***, reservations: Dist Collector, Kottayam or Exec Engineer, PWD Kottayam; **F** ***Venad Tourist Complex***, Ancheril Bldg, nr State Bus Stand, T 61383, modern building, clean, restaurant, rec; **F** ***Railway Retiring Rooms***.

● Places to eat

Sabala. Pallathaya Tourist Complex Restaurant is rec with its outdoor setting by the lake. ***Kumarakom Tourist Complex*** on the lake for simple food. ***The Indian Coffee House***, TB Rd opp bus station. ***Black Stone***. Good veg.

● Tour operators & Travel agents

Concord Manorama Junc, GS Rd, T 560350; ***Moti*** Sastri Rd, T 564919; ***Olympus World Tours***, opp. rly station, T 563154, F 484 360031; ***Seeland***, Padinjarekkara Chambers, KK Rd, T 560337.

● Transport

Local Auto-rickshaws: to boat jetty, 2 km.

Train Kollam: *Mangalore-Thiruvananthapuram Exp* 6350 (AC/CC), daily, 1518, 2 hr; *Vanchinad Exp* 6303, daily, 0705, 2 hr. **Thiruvananthapuram**: *Vanchinad Exp* 6303, daily, 0705, 3¼ hr; *Guwahati-Thiruvananthapuram Exp* 2602 (AC/II), Wed, 1908, 3¼ hr.

Road Bus: fast and frequent bus connections with Thiruvananthapuram, Kochi, Thekkadi and 3 buses a day to Madurai. This takes 7 hrs and goes over the Thekkadi pass, with superb views down the E side of the Ghats onto the Tamil Nad plains. The bus station in Kottayam has been described as "especially chaotic, even for India, and there is a mad scramble to get on the Periyar bus". Direct bus to Thekkadi dep 0900, otherwise buses every 2 hr to Kumily between 0900 -2250. Change at Kumily. The route from Thekkadi to Kottayam is described on page 935.

Sea Boat: to Alapuzha, State boats dep 0730, 1000, 1130, 1300, 1730, 2030 & 0100. Rs 4.50, 2½ hr. Very busy in peak season. To Champakulam, 1600, 4 hr.

Periyar Wildlife Sanctuary, Thekkadi

BASICS *Area*: 777 sq km; *Climate*: Temp Summer: Max 29°C Min 18°C; Winter: Max 21°C, Min 16°C; *Annual rainfall*: 2,600 mm; *Season*: Dec-May, *Best*: Mar-May. Crowded in mid-Jan for Makar Sankranti festival; *Clothing*: Summer – cottons, winter – light woollens.

Approach

Set on attractive lake side, the 780 sq km sanctuary was created by the old Travancore State govt in 1934 and can easily be reached from Kottayam. The drive goes up through Kanjirapalli, Mundakayam and Peermed (where there is a *Traveller's Bungalow*). The road rises from the plains, through tropical evergreen forests, rubber and spice plantations, pepper on the low land gives rise to tea and cardamom plantations. Be prepared for a rapid change in temperature. Above 1,000 m the air freshens and you may need warm clothing. In 1895 the lake was created by building a dam which covered 55 sq km of rich forest. A 180 m long tunnel led the water which had flowed W into the Arabian Sea E into the Suruli and Vaigai Rivers, irrigating extensive areas of Ramanathapuram and Madurai districts. To see the dam, no entry fee but permission from Executive Engineer, PWD Periyar Project, Tallakulam, PO Madurai.

Wildlfe

The sanctuary, near the border with Tamil Nadu, is in a beautiful setting and was designated a part of **Project Tiger** in 1973, though it is better known for its elephants. Most bulls here are tuskless (makhnas). Best to avoid weekends and holidays. Ideal times are dawn and dusk, so stay overnight. Motor launch trip on the lake recommended – but "**not** the one for about 60 people, which is too noisy, scaring animals away". Book a boat for 8-12 people from the Aranya Nivas Hotel (where the buses terminate). You can usually find other tourists wanting to share it with you. Rs 10 each plus camera fees.

The elephants, bison, sambar, wild boar and spotted deer are common and in periods of drought when the forest water holes dry up, on rare occasions a tiger or leopard is sighted. There are plenty of water fowl which perch on the dead trees in the lake, and woodland birds, owls and hornbills in the forests and smaller animals including black Nilgiri langurs and flying squirrels.

Viewing

The forests have special viewing platforms which you can use if you prefer to walk with a Game Ranger who can act as guide (about Rs 7). Can get hot so carry water. Elephant rides are readily available (Rs 30 per elephant). Book at Information Centre by lake. 1 hr ride allows you to see much more wildlife than the boat trip.

Park information

● Accommodation

At Thekkadi, with Kerala Tourism accommodation nearest the lake. Book well in advance through any Kerala Tourist office. Telephone numbers are Kumily exchange.

B *Spice Village*, Thekkadi-Kumily Rd, T 22315, F 22317, booking also through *Casino Hotel*, Willingdon Island, Kochi, T 0484 668221, double thatched cottages only, pine furniture, terrace overlooking spice garden, pool and superb restaurant, luxurious, green and quiet.
B *Lake Palace*, T 22023, 6 rm, restaurant with

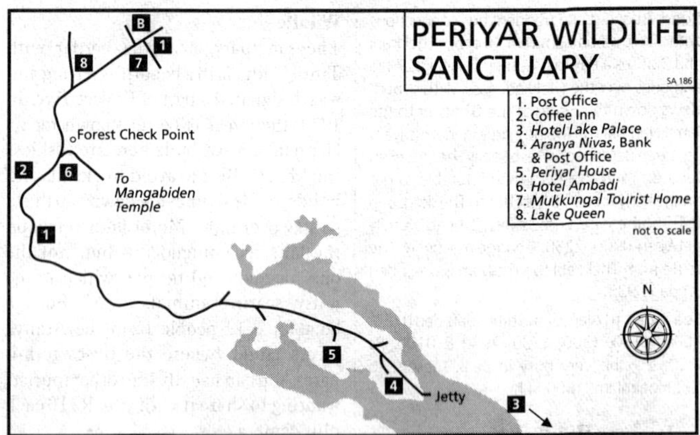

fixed, uninspired menus (meals obligatory) – Indian dishes better, non-residents should give advance notice, former hunting lodge in idyllic island setting with superb views, attractively re-decorated 1992, well into the park and accessible by free ferry (20 min) from the Aranya Nivas jetty (last trip 1600).

C *Aranya Nivas*, by lake, T 22023, 26 rm of different categories, cheaper ordinary to a/c VIP. Old stone building re-decorated – simple, comfortable and modern. Restaurant (fairly basic), bar, exchange, small shop and post, pool planned, cycle hire.

D *Ambadi*, T 22192, some a/c rm and cottages, new double-storey units – ornate wood decoration, mirrors over the beds, but basic cottages still good value, nr the Forest Checkpost at the entrance (2 km), reasonable restaurant; **D** *Leelapankaj Resort*, new 1994, very small cottages, very expensive for quality and service offered.

● Budget Accommodation

E Kerala Tourism *Periyar House*, 5 min walk from lake, T 22026, F 22282, 48 rm, some with bath, simple, very pleasant, clean and comfortable, dorm, reasonable if slightly dingy restaurant. Charming Govt **E** *Forest Rest House*, 3 rm, which is well placed for walks and listening to the animals at night, rec, but book well ahead.

F *Rolex Lodge*, Thekkadi Junc, T 22081, very basic concrete rm.

At Kumily village, 3 km away, are some cheap hotels: **F** *Holiday Home*, T 22016, large rm with good views; **F** *Mukkungal Tourist Home*, T 22070, veg restaurant, rm at rear noisy; **F** *Rani Lodge*, T 2033 and *Lake Queen*, in centre, T 22084.

● Places to eat

Thekkadi hotel restaurants welcome non-residents. *The Coffee Inn*, about ½ km outside the park from the check post, half way between Kumily village and the lake, serves good food (0700-2200) but is expensive, as most others in Kumily attracting tourists.

● Services

There is a **post office**, a **bank** and **hospitals** at Kumily.

● Transport

Local Buses: between Kumily and Thekkadi. Jeeps are more costly although you can share one. **Bicycles**: for hire in Kumily village or walk the 3 km. On the lake, **motor launches** for 2 hr trips are inexpensive but you may need to wait for the boat to fill on a quiet day although they are scheduled to start every 2 hr from 0700-1500. Aranya Nivas also has boats for private hire (for 60, 40 or 30 persons). Contact Manager, Aranya Nivas, or Wildlife Preservation Officer, Thekkadi. Small charge in addition to boat hire plus camera fees.

Air Nearest airports with road connections are Madurai (140 km) and Kochi (208 km).

Road Bus: regular buses run between Kumily and other important towns nearby. Kottayam 116 km, has 6 daily (4 hr), Rs 30, 4 daily to Madurai (4 hr). 3 daily to Trivandrum, 285 km (8 hr) and Kochi/Ernakulam (6 hr), and one daily to Kodaikanal (4½ hr) and Kovalam (9 hr). Kerala Tourism 2-day tours from Ernakulam, Sat dep 0730, ret 2000, Rs 120. Buses from Kumily go down to Aranya Nivas on the lake-side; daily late afternoon Kollam bus (4½ hr) also from Aranya Nivas.

ROUTES The road from Kottayam goes through Ettumanur (11 km) and **Vaikom** (*STD Code*: 04829), which has a famous Hindu temple (non-Hindus are not normally allowed inside). Then across the flat marshy and backwater terrain of the Kochi backwaters to Kochi (45 km) – see page 964. The NH 47 leaves Kochi for Alavu, and Angamaly. Between Kochi and Thrissur is a beautiful backwater, and the journey can be made by boat. By road Peruvanam is 33 km, then a further 10 km to Thrissur.

Thrissur (Trichur)

Thrissur is on the W end of the Palakkad gap through the low pass between the Nilgiri and the Palani Hills. Thus it has been on the most important route into Peninsular India since pre-Roman times. Once the capital of Kochi State, it was captured by the Zamorin of Calicut and in the 18th century by Tipu Sultan. It is particularly famous for its annual Pooram festival (Apr-May)

BASICS *Population*: 275,000; *STD Code*: 0487; *Climate*: Temp Summer: Max 35°C, Min 23°C; Winter: Max 32°C, Min 20°C; *Annual rainfall*: 2540 mm.

Local crafts & industries

Cotton spinning, weaving and textile industries, silk saris and brass lamps.

Places of interest

Thrissur is built round a hill on which stands the **Vadakkunnatha Temple**, a multi-shrined complex with 3 principal shrines dedicated to Vadakkunnatha (Ten-Kailasanatha) where the Mahalingam is covered by centuries of offerings of *ghee* (clarified butter), Sankaranarayana and Rama. The shrine to Sankaranarayana has superb murals depicting stories from the Mahabharata. Apparently renovated in 1731. Other subsidiary shrines were added, including the apsidal Ayyappan shrine and the shrine dedicated to Krishna. It is a classic example of the Kerala style of architecture with its special pagoda-like *gopura* roof which is richly decorated with fine wood carving. Open 0400-1030, 1700-2030. Non-Hindus are not permitted inside. The large and impressive **Lourdes Church** with an interesting underground shrine. **Town Hall** which is an impressive building housing an art gallery with murals from other parts of the state.

Museums

State Museum, Chembukkavu, T 20566. 1000-1700. Closed Mon. Free. **Art Museum**, Zoo compound has a collection of wood carvings, metal sculptures, an excellent collection of traditional lamps and old jewellery. Open daily 1000-1700, closed Mon.

Parks & Zoos

Thrissur Zoo, nr the Art Museum is reputed to have one of the best snake collections in India. Open 1500-1715. Small entry and camera fee. Filming only with prior permission of the Director of Museums and Zoos, Govt of Kerala, Thiruvananthapuram. There is an **Aquarium**. nr Nehru Park which is open daily 1500-2000.

Excursions

Cheruthuruthy 29 km N of Thrissur nr Shornur Junc. Famous for the Kerala Kalamandalam which led to a revival of Kathakali dancing. Centre for teaching music, drama and Mohiniyattam and Ottam Thullal in addition to Kathakali. You can watch training sessions from 0430-0630!, 0830-1200 and 1530-1730. Closed Sat, Sun and 31 Mar, 15 June and public holidays. The centre is closed in Apr and May. Entry free.

- **Accommodation** Some simple Hotels incl **F** Govt *Guest House*, T 498; **F** PWD *Rest House*, here and at Shornur, T 514.

- **Transport Road/Rail** Frequent private buses from Thrissur to Shornur (1 hr), which is also served by rail, then 3 km to Cheruthruthy.

Peechy Dam has accommodation, boating facilities and you may on occasions see wild elephants in the sanctuary there.

• **Transport Road Bus**: Frequent buses from Thrissur.

Local festivals

Apr-May *Pooram* Festival in the Tekkinkadu maidan outside the temple is marked by huge, colourful and very noisy processions. 30 elaborately bedecked elephants carrying priests and deities are taken through streets specially decorated with lamps and palm leaves, with the accompaniment of music and terminating with a grand display of fireworks.

Aug/Sep The district also celebrates *Kamdassamkadavu Boat Races* at *Onam*.

Local information

● Accommodation

D *Casino*, TB Rd, T 24699, 25 rm with bath, 11 a/c, nr rly, restaurant, bar, Pastry shop, exchange, shop; **D** *Luciya Palace*, Marar Rd, T 24731; **D** *Elite International*, 22 Chembottil La, T 21033, 90 rm with bath, some a/c, nr rly and centre, a/c restaurants, bar.

● Budget hotels

E *Skylord*, Municipal Office Rd, T 24662, 10 rm with bath, some a/c, 1 km rly, central, restaurant; **E** Govt *Ramanilayam Tourist Bungalow*, Palace Rd, T 20300, some a/c rm in a modern building (old palace for govt officers), roof-garden restaurant; **E** *YMCA* Palace Rd, T 21190 and *YWCA* in Chemukkavu, T 21818; **E** *Alukkas*, Railway Station Rd, nr Bus Stand, T 24067, has clean rm, some a/c, good value; **E** Kerala Tourism *Yatri Nivas*, Stadium Rd, nr Indoor Stadium, T 332333, 16 rm, 1 a/c.

F *Railway Retiring Rooms* and a PWD *Rest House*. Reservation: Dist Collector.

● Places to eat

Most **D** hotels have good restaurants: *Casino* is in large garden with coloured fountains! others are simple. *Bharat* serves good S Indian food.

● Shopping

Kerala State Handicraft Emporium *Surabhi*, and shopping areas in Rounds S, W, N and MO Rd, High Rd and MG Rd.

● Tourist office

In the Govt *Guest House*, Palace Rd, T 20300, and opp Town Hall.

● Transport

Local Yellow top and tourist **taxis**, **autorickshaws** and **buses**.

Train Connections to coastal cities in Kerala and through Coimbatore and Salem to Madras. Even Express trains stop at Thrissur. **Kochi**: *Madras-Kochi Exp* 6041 (AC/II), daily, 0705, 2½ hr. **Madras (MC)**: *Madras Exp* 6042 (AC/II), daily, 1840, 11½ hr; **or**: *Kochi-Gorakhpur Exp* 5011 (AC/II), Mon & Fri, 1155, 11½ hr.

Road Bus: KSRTC and private buses connect to major towns in the state with direct services to Palani, Madurai, Bangalore, Mysore, Erode and Madras.

Palakkad (Palghat)

The strategically placed town marks a low point in the Ghats and hence has been know as the Palakkad Gap through which the road crossed from W to E. It is still the road and rail route from Kerala to Coimbatore and Madras. The area is notable for tobacco and rice cultivation and processing and its textile industry. Haidar Ali's old fort here was built in 1766 which the British took in 1790. **Accommodation D** *Indraprastha*, English Church Rd, T 24641 and *Kandath Inn*, TB Rd, T 24662, have some a/c rm and a restaurant. The rest are **Budget** and incl **E** *Fort Palace*, W Fort Rd, T 24626; *Surya*, T 28338 and *Devaprabha*, T 23383, both on TB Rd, and *Kairali*, Shornur Rd, T 24611. **F** The cheaper *Kandath*, Head PO Rd, T 23388 and Kerala Tourism *Motel Araam* in Erimayur, Alathoor.

Malampuzha Dam 14 km away in the foothills, across Baharathpuzha river, has landscaped gardens, swimming pool, children's park and boats. **Budget accommodation E** Kerala Tourism *Garden House*, 300m bus stand, T 5217. 16 rm, some a/c, restaurant, panoramic views of dam and gardens. Other hotels incl: **F** Govt *Guest House*, nr Hermit's End, T 5207. They have a ropeway between them.

KARNATAKA

CONTENTS

MAPS

BASICS : 45mn (Urban 33%, Scheduled Castes 15%, Scheduled Tribes 5%); *Literacy*: M 67% F 44%; *Birth rate*: *Rural* 27:1000, *Urban* 16:1000; *Death rate*: *Rural* 10:1000, *Urban* 7:1000; *Infant mortality*: *Rural* 70:1000, *Urban* 45:1000; *Religion*: *Hindu* 86%, *Muslim* 11%, *Christian* 2%.

Environment

Land

Area 192,000 sq km. Karnataka has a lush coastline, 320 km long. The Western Ghats, called the Malnad or hill country, have beautiful forests with waterfalls and wildlife parks. To the E stretches the Mysore Plateau. 3 great rivers originate in the Ghats – the **Kaveri**, the **Tungabhadra**, and the **Krishna**. Some, like the short westward flowing **Sharavati**, have very impressive waterfalls, Jog Falls being one of the highest in the world. Parts of N Karnataka are barren, rocky and covered with scrub.

History

Early History

Some of the earliest settlements in peninsular India have been found in the region between the **Tungabhadra** and the **Krishna Rivers**. At one site just N of the Krishna these go back over 500,000 years. More than 300 artefacts have been discovered at **Rangampet** and evidence of hunter gatherer communities has been found at several sites. By the Middle Stone Age there was already a regional division appearing between the black cotton soil area of the N and the granite-quartzite plateaus of the S. The division appears between the Krishna and Tungabhadra Rivers in the modern districts of **Raichur** and **Bellary**. In the N hunters used pebbles of jasper taken from river beds; to the S quartz tools were developed.

The first agricultural communities of the peninsula have also been identified from what is now N Karnataka. Located in the region of black cotton soils with islands of granite hills, the Neolithic communities of N Karnataka lived at roughly the same time as the early Indus

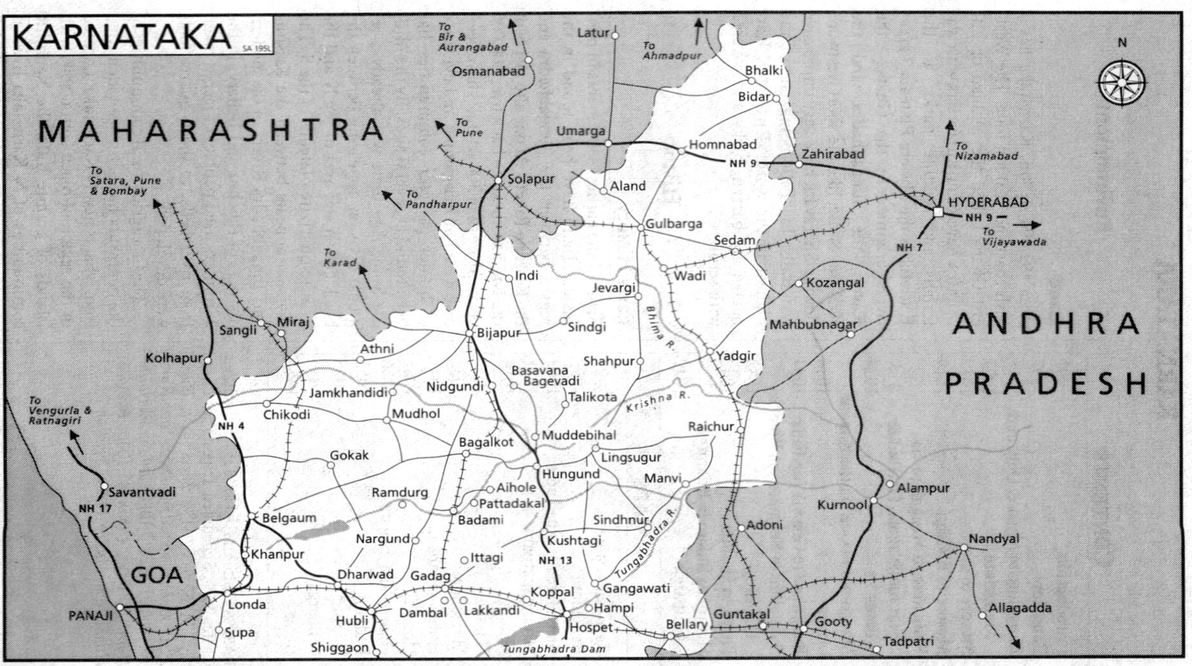
KARNATAKA
SA 195L
N
MAHARASHTRA
ANDHRA PRADESH
GOA
To Bir & Aurangabad
Osmanabad
Latur
To Ahmadpur
Bhalki
Bidar
To Pune
Umarga
Homnabad
NH 9
Zahirabad
To Nizamabad
HYDERABAD
NH 9
To Vijayawada
NH 7
To Satara, Pune & Bombay
Solapur
Aland
Gulbarga
To Pandharpur
Sedam
Wadi
To Karad
Indi
Jevargi
Kozangal
Sangli
Miraj
Bijapur
Sindgi
Bhima R.
Mahbubnagar
Kolhapur
Athni
Shahpur
Yadgir
Basavana Bagevadi
Jamkhandidi
Nidgundi
Talikota
Krishna R.
To Vengurla & Ratnagiri
Chikodi
Mudhol
NH 4
Muddebihal
Raichur
Bagalkot
Lingsugur
Gokak
Hungund
Manvi
Aihole
Alampur
Savantvadi
Ramdurg
Pattadakal
Kurnool
NH 17
Belgaum
Badami
Sindhnur
Adoni
Nargund
Kushtagi
Tungabhadra R.
Nandyal
Khanpur
Ittagi
NH 13
Dharwad
Gadag
Gangawati
Koppal
Londa
PANAJI
Dambal
Lakkandi
Hampi
Alagadda
Hubli
Hospet
Guntakal
Supa
Bellary
Gooty
Shiggaon
Tungabhadra Dam
Tadpatri

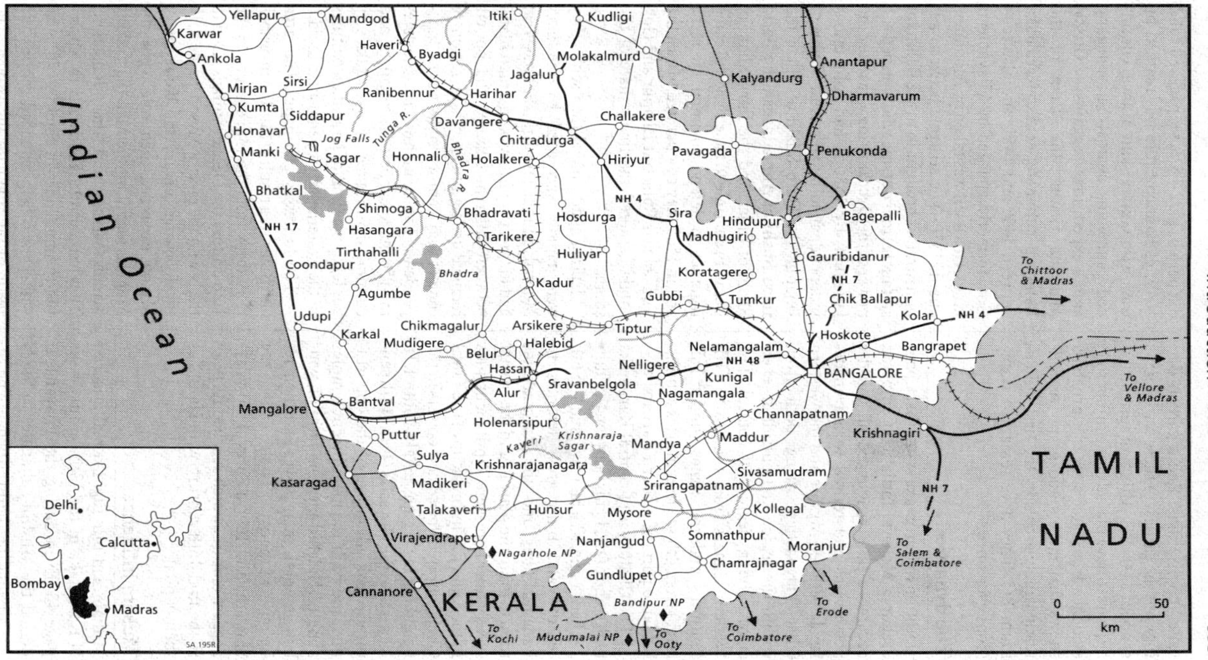

Indian Ocean
TAMIL NADU
KERALA
Yellapur
Mundgod
Karwar
Ankola
Haveri
Byadgi
Itiki
Kudligi
Molakalmurd
Jagalur
Anantapur
Kalyandurg
Dharmavarum
Sirsi
Mirjan
Kumta
Ranibennur
Harihar
Siddapur
Honavar
Davangere
Challakere
Jog Falls
Tunga R.
Chitradurga
Manki
Sagar
Honnali
Bhadra R.
Holalkere
Hiriyur
Pavagada
Penukonda
Bhatkal
NH 4
Shimoga
Bhadravati
Hosdurga
Sira
Hindupur
Bagepalli
NH 17
Hasangara
Tarikere
Madhugiri
Tirthahalli
Huliyar
Gauribidanur
Coondapur
Bhadra
Koratagere
NH 7
To Chittoor & Madras
Kadur
Agumbe
Gubbi
Tumkur
Chik Ballapur
Udupi
Kolar
NH 4
Chikmagalur
Arsikere
Tiptur
Karkal
Hoskote
Mudigere
Halebid
Nelamangalam
Bangrapet
Belur
NH 48
Nelligere
Kunigal
Hassan
BANGALORE
To Vellore & Madras
Alur
Sravanbelgola
Nagamangala
Mangalore
Bantval
Channapatnam
Holenarsipur
Puttur
Krishnaraja Sagar
Maddur
Krishnagiri
Kaveri
Mandya
Sulya
Krishnarajanagara
Sivasamudram
Kasaragad
Madikeri
Srirangapatnam
NH 7
Delhi
Talakaveri
Hunsur
Mysore
Kollegal
Calcutta
Virajendrapet
Nanjangud
Somnathpur
Nagarhole NP
Moranjur
To Salem & Coimbatore
Bombay
Chamrajnagar
Gundlupet
Cannanore
Madras
Bandipur NP
To Erode
0 50
km
To Kochi
Mudumalai NP
To Ooty
To Coimbatore
SA 195R

valley civilisations. Radio carbon datings put the earliest of these settlements at about 3,000 BC. Although agriculture appears to have played only a minor role, evidence from later sites in Karnataka shows that millets and gram were already widely grown by the first millennium BC. They have remained staple crops ever since.

The dynasties

Tradition in Karnataka states that **Chandragupta Maurya**, India's 1st emperor, became a Jain, renounced all worldly possessions and retired to Sravanabelagola between Mysore and the Western Ghats. Dynasties, rising both from within the region and outside it, exercised varying degrees of control. The **Western Gangas** from the 3rd to 11th centuries and the **Banas** (under Pallavas) from 4th to 9th centuries controlled large parts of modern Karnataka.

The **Chalukyas** of central Karnataka took some of the lands between the Tungabhadra and Krishna rivers in the 6th century and built great temples in Badami. They and the **Rashtrakutas** tried to unite the plateau and the coastal areas while there were Tamil incursions in the S and E. The break up of the Tamil Chola empire allowed new powers in the neighbouring regions to take control. In Karnataka the **Hoysalas** (11th–14th centuries) took advantage of the opportunity, and built the magnificent temples at Belur, Halebid and Somnathpur, symbolising both their power and their religious authority. Then came the Sangama and Tuluva kings of the **Vijayanagara** empire, which reached its peak in the mid-16th century, with Hampi as their capital.

Muslim influence

Muhammad bin Tughlaq had attacked N Karnataka in the 13th century – see page 45. Even during the Vijayanagar period the Muslim sultanates to the N were extending their influence. The Bidar period (1422-1526, see pages 803 and 1049) of **Bahmani rule** was marked by wars with Gujarat and Malwa, continued campaigns against Vijayanagara, and expeditions against Orissa. **Mahmud Gawan**, the Wazir of the Bahmani sultanate, seized Karnataka between 1466 and 1481, and also took Goa, formerly guarded by Vijayanagar kings. Goa itself was taken by **Albuquerque** in 1510. The struggle between administrators brought in to the Bahmani sultanate from outside who usurped the power of the Deccani king weakened the kingdom. By 1530 it had split into 5 independent sultanates: **Adil Shahis** of Bijapur, the **Qutb Shahi** of Bidar, the **Imad Shahi** of Ahmadnagar, the **Barid Shahi** of Bidar, and the **Imad Shahi** of Berar. From time to time they still came together to defend common interests, and in 1565 they co-operated to oust the Vijayanagar Raja, but Bijapur and Golconda gathered the lion's share of the spoils.

Falling apart among themselves they were rapidly succeeded by the later Mughals and then the British. Thus what had for most of history been a marchland between different cultures and powers retained its significance as a region of contact and conflict right up to Independence. The creation of linguistic states in 1956 made explicit the linguistic and cultural significance of Karnataka's N border as the limit of Dravidian cultures in the western part of peninsular India.

The fortresses of Bijapur, Gulbarga and Bidar are a result of **Muslim** invasions from the N from the 13th century. In the 16th century the **Deccan Sultans** ruled in the N with the rajas of Mysore in the S. In the following century the **Wodeyars** of Mysore expanded their rule while the Mughals fought off the Marathas, taking Srirangapatnam and then Bangalore. They lost control to **Haidar Ali**, the opportunist commander-in-chief in 1761 who with French help extended control and made Srirangapatnam the capital. The

Mysore Wars followed and with Haidar Ali's, and then his son Tipu Sultan's death in 1799, came the British who re-established rule of the Wodeyars. The Hindu royal family from Mysore (with the exception of a 50 year period from 1831 when a British Commissioner was appointed) continued to administer the state even up to the reorganisation of the state in the '50s when the Maharaja was appointed State Governor.

Art & architecture

Karnataka's role as a border territory was illustrated in the magnificent architecture of the Chalukyan dynasty from 450 AD to 650 AD. Here, notably in **Aihole**, were the first stirrings of **Brahman temple design**. A mixture of Jain temples illustrates the contact with the N of India which continued to influence the development of the Dravidian temples which grew alongside them. Visiting this small area of N Karnataka it is possible to see examples in Pattadakal alone of 4 temples built on N Indian "**Nagari**" principles and 6 built on S Indian "**Dravida**" lines. Nothing could more clearly illustrate the region's position as a major area of contact. That contact was developed through the Hoysalas 4 centuries later. In **Belur, Halebid** and **Somnathpur**, the star-shaped plan of the base and the shrine, with the bell-shaped tower above and exquisitely crafted exterior and interior surfaces became a hall-mark of their temples, a distinctive combination of the 2 traditions.

The Chalukyas were followed by the Vijayanagara kings who advanced temple architecture to blend in the rocky, boulder ridden landscape at **Hampi**. Flat-roofed pavilions and intricately carved pillars characterised their style.

Bijapur has some of the finest Muslim monuments on the Deccan, from the austere style of the Turkish rulers to the refinement in some of the pavilions and the world's 2nd largest dome at the Gol Gumbaz.

Culture

People

While the Lingayats are the dominant caste group in N Karnataka a peasant caste, the **Vokkaligas**, is dominant in the S. Their rivalry still runs through Karnataka politics. Karnataka has its share of tribal people. The nomadic **Lambanis** live mostly in the N and W, one among several tribal peoples in the hill regions.

Language & literature

Most people speak the Dravidian language **Kannada** (Kanarese). However, there has been a lot of intermixture with speakers of Indo-Aryan languages, evident in the N of the state. The other southern languages are spoken in the border regions while Hindi is often used for business and trade.

Kannada has the 2nd oldest Dravidian literary tradition. The earliest classic known is *Kavirajamarga* which dates from the 9th century. A treatise on the writing of poetry, it refers to several earlier works which suggests that the language had been in existence for some centuries. Kannada inscriptions dating from 5th and 6th centuries support this view. Early writings in both Telugu and Kannada owe a lot to Jain influence. Kannada made a distinctive contribution in its very early development of prose writing.

From the 10th to the 12th centuries a mixed poetry and prose form was developed by the writers **Pampa, Ponna** and **Ranna** – the "three gems of Kannada literature". Towards the end of the 12th century the Saivite saint **Basava** started a new Hindu renaissance. He disliked Brahmins and didn't believe in transmigration of souls; he didn't support child marriages or the veto on widow-remarriage. His sect, the **Lingayats**, used simple rhythmic prose, the *vachanas*, to spread its teaching. Jordens gives the following example: "Oh pay your worship to God now – before the cheek turns wan, and the neck is wrinkled, and the body shrinks – before the teeth fall out and the back is bowed, and you are wholly dependent on others – before you need to lean on a staff, and to raise yourself by your hands on your thighs – before your beauty is destroyed by age and Death itself arrives. Oh now worship Kudala-sangama-deva." The Lingayats started as a reforming and egalitarian group, becoming highly influential especially across N Karnataka.

The Hindu-Sanskrit tradition was greatly strengthened by the rise of the Vijayanagar Empire. One of their greatest kings, **Krishna Deva Raya** (r 1509-29), was also a poet in Telugu and Sanskrit, though through his influence poetry reflected the life of the court rather than of the people outside. From the 16th century onwards Vaishnavism produced a rich crop of devotional songs. However after the fall of the Vijayanagar Empire, the quality of literature declined. Muslim power encouraged Hindu art forms almost to go underground, and expressions of Hindu devotion and faith became associated with song and dance for popular entertainment – the *Yakshagana* in Kannada, and the remarkable *Kathakali* in Kerala, see page 946.

Dance, drama & music

Open-air folk theatre or *Bayalata* of Karnataka has developed from religious ritual and is performed in honour of the local deity. The plays evolve and are improvised by the actors on an informal stage. The performances usually start at night and last often into the early hours. The famous *Yakshagana* or *Parijata* usually has a single narrator while the other forms of Bayalata have 4 or 5 assisted by a jester. The plots of the *Dasarata* which enacts several stories and *Sannata*, which elaborates one theme, are taken loosely from mythology but sometimes highlight real-life incidents and are performed by a company of actors and actresses. There is at least one star singer and dancer in each company and a troupe of dancers who not only perform in these dance-dramas but are also asked to perform at religious festivals and family celebrations.

The *Doddata* is less refined than the *Yakshagana* but both have much in common, beginning with a prayer to the god Ganesh, using verse and prose and drawing from the stories of the epics *Ramayana* and *Mahabharata*. The costumes are very elaborate with fantastic stage effects, loud noises and war cries and vigorous dances. It all amounts to a memorable experience but requires stamina as you will have to sit up all night!

Modern Karnataka

Government

There are 19 districts which are grouped into 4 divisions of Bangalore, Mysore, Belgaum and Gulbarga. The state legislature, which has its assembly hall, the remarkable Vidhana Soudha, in Bangalore, has a legislative assembly of 208 directly elected members and a legislative council of 63 indirectly elected members. Chief Minister assisted by a council of ministers.

The Economy

Karnataka has the benefit of abundant hydroelectricity. In the early years of Independence this allowed it to produce enough to sell to neighbouring states. In recent years the growth of industrial demand has been so rapid that at the end of the 1980s it had a higher deficit than any other Indian state, over 27% of demand. It also has extensive forests, is India's chief source of gold, 90% of its coffee production, and most of the world's sandalwood. The western **'Malnad'** forests yield teak, bamboo and sandalwood (the oil being a major export), and also gum, lac and dyes for the tanneries. Some of these resources are also under enormous stress. The harvesting of sandalwood, for example, is now illegal except under direct Government monitoring. The price is so high that there is a highly profitable black market trade. Agriculture still accounts for over 50% of the state's income. The coastal plains intensively cultivated, rice being the main food crop and sugar cane a major cash crop. Cultivation in the E allows sugarcane, rubber, bananas and oranges.

Mining & industry There are rich deposits of manganese, iron, mica, chromite, copper, and small amounts of bauxite. The Kolar gold fields, with mines over 3000m deep, produce 85% of the country's gold. There has been an iron and steel industry at **Bhadravati** since the 1920s and heavy engineering works in Bangalore. Cotton milling, sugar processing and cement and paper manufacture, provide employment. The silk industry in Mysore and Bangalore takes advantage of the cultivation of *Tuti* trees, on which the silk worm feeds, and which produces very fine silk. In the last decade there has been a rapid expansion of high technology communication industries in and around Bangalore.

Transport through the W Ghats is still difficult. The only railway line directly down to the Karnataka coast from the plateau is to Mangalore, closed in the monsoon season. There are 2,700 km of m gauge and 150 km of narrow gauge line, with Bangalore as the main focus. Bangalore is connected by broad gauge line to Madras and to Mysore. Mangalore connects with Kerala in the SW. Although there is an extensive road network surfaces are sometimes poor, and the W is often impassable during heavy rains.

BANGALORE

State capital and today India's 6th largest city. It is one of the fastest growing, but it is also rightly called 'The Garden City' with its numerous parks and avenues of jacaranda, gulmohur and cassia. The old part of the city is to the S of the City Railway Station with most of the sights further S, while the Cubbon Park area with Mahatma Gandhi Rd to its E is where you will find the Tourist office, Government buildings and the bigger hotels and restaurants, book shops and Government emporia. MG Road is very pleasant to wander round, with excellent shops, eating and drinking places.

BASICS *Population*: 4.09mn; *Altitude*: 920m; *STD Code*: 080.

Kempe Gowda, a Magadi chieftain (1513-1569) founded Bangalore in 1537, building a mud fort and marking the limits of the city by his 4 watch towers and called it Bengaluru. His statue stands in front of the City Corporation Buildings. It was extended by **Haidar Ali** and **Tipu Sultan** becoming a fortified city. When the British gained control after 1799 they installed the **Wodeyar** of Mysore as the ruler and the Rajas developed it into a major city.

In 1831 the British took over the administration for a period of 50 years, making it a spacious garrison town, planting impressive avenues and creating parks, building comfortable bungalows

CLIMATE: BANGALORE

	Jan	Feb	Mar	Apr	May	Jun	Jul	Aug	Sep	Oct	Nov	Dec	Av/Tot
Max (°C)	28	31	33	34	33	30	28	29	28	28	27	27	30
Min (°C)	15	16	19	21	21	20	19	19	19	19	17	15	18
Rain (mm)	4	14	6	37	119	65	93	95	129	195	46	16	819

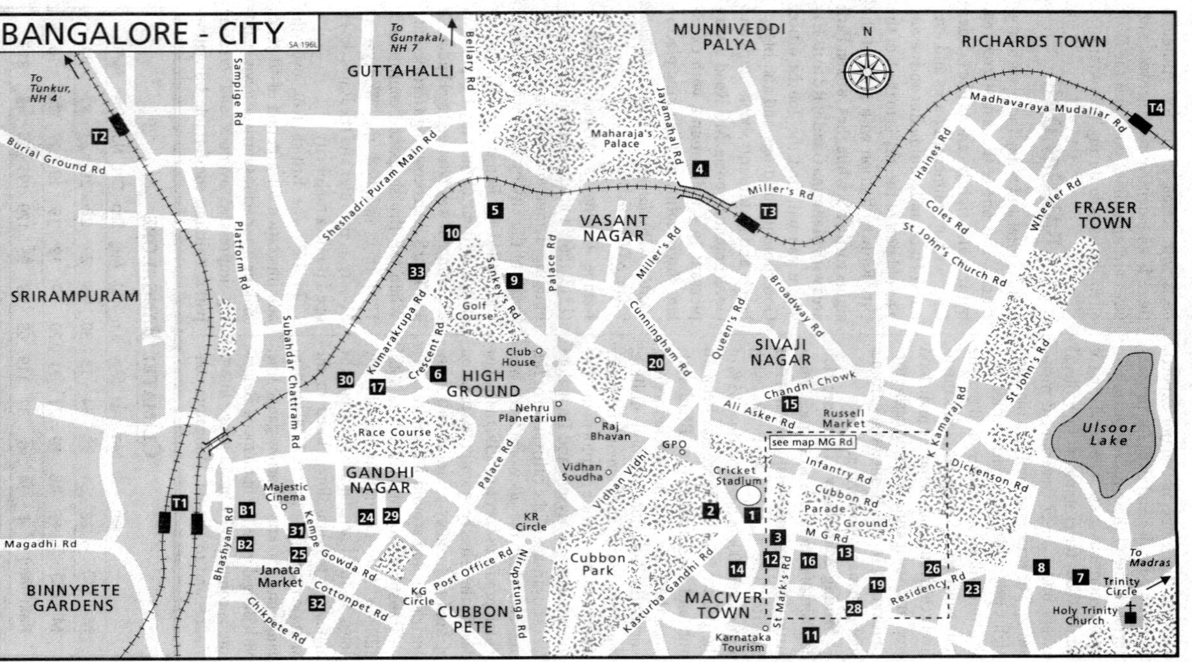
BANGALORE - CITY
SA 196L
To Tunkur, NH 4
To Guntakal, NH 7
GUTTAHALLI
MUNNIVEDDI PALYA
N
RICHARDS TOWN
Sampige Rd
Bellary Rd
Maharaja's Palace
Jayamahal Rd
Madhavaraya Mudaliar Rd
Burial Ground Rd
Sheshadri Puram Main Rd
Haines Rd
Miller's Rd
Coles Rd
Wheeler Rd
FRASER TOWN
VASANT NAGAR
Platform Rd
St John's Church Rd
SRIRAMPURAM
Miller's Rd
Palace Rd
Sankey's Rd
Golf Course
Kumarakrupa Rd
Cunningham Rd
Queen's Rd
Broadway Rd
SIVAJI NAGAR
St John's Rd
Subahdar Chattram Rd
Crescent Rd
Club House
HIGH GROUND
Chandni Chowk
Ali Asker Rd
Russell Market
Nehru Planetarium
Raj Bhavan
Race Course
K Kamaraj Rd
Ulsoor Lake
see map MG Rd
GPO
Vidhan Soudha
Vidhan Vidhi
Cricket Stadium
Infantry Rd
Dickenson Rd
GANDHI NAGAR
Palace Rd
Majestic Cinema
Cubbon Rd
Parade Ground
KR Circle
M G Rd
Magadhi Rd
Bhashyam Rd
Kempe Gowda Rd
Janata Market
Post Office Rd
Cubbon Park
Kasturba Gandhi Rd
St Mark's Rd
Residency Rd
To Madras
Trinity Circle
BINNYPETE GARDENS
Cottonpet Rd
KG Circle
CUBBON PETE
Nirupatunga Rd
MACIVER TOWN
Holy Trinity Church
Chikpete Rd
Karnataka Tourism
T1
T2
T3
T4
B1
B2

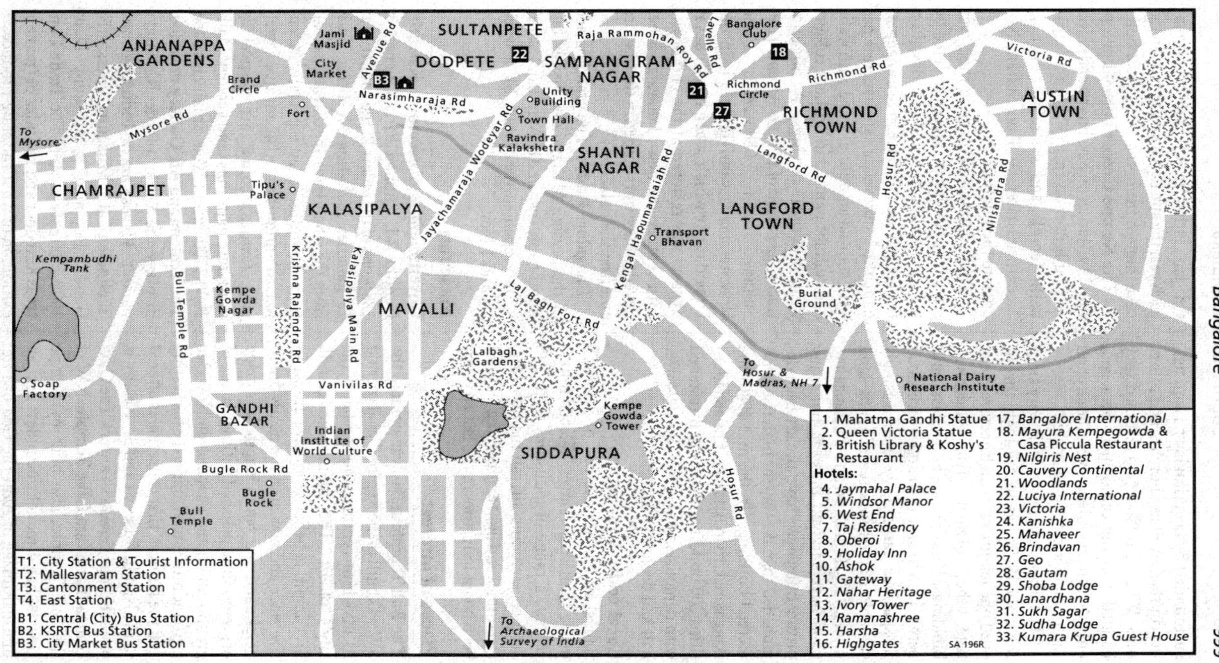
ANJANAPPA GARDENS
SULTANPETE
DODPETE
SAMPANGIRAM NAGAR
RICHMOND TOWN
AUSTIN TOWN
CHAMRAJPET
KALASIPALYA
SHANTI NAGAR
LANGFORD TOWN
MAVALLI
GANDHI BAZAR
SIDDAPURA
Jami Masjid
City Market
Brand Circle
Fort
Avenue Rd
Narasimharaja Rd
Raja Rammohan Roy Rd
Lavelle Rd
Bangalore Club
Richmond Circle
Richmond Rd
Victoria Rd
Unity Building
Town Hall
Ravindra Kalakshetra
Mysore Rd
To Mysore
Tipu's Palace
Jayachamaraja Wodeyar Rd
Kengal Hanumantaiah Rd
Langford Rd
Hosur Rd
Nilsandra Rd
Transport Bhavan
Burial Ground
Kempambudhi Tank
Bull Temple Rd
Kempe Gowda Nagar
Krishna Rajendra Rd
Kalasipalya Main Rd
Lal Bagh Fort Rd
Lalbagh Gardens
To Hosur & Madras, NH 7
National Dairy Research Institute
Soap Factory
Vanivilas Rd
Indian Institute of World Culture
Kempe Gowda Tower
Bugle Rock Rd
Bugle Rock
Bull Temple
To Archaeological Survey of India
T1. City Station & Tourist Information
T2. Mallesvaram Station
T3. Cantonment Station
T4. East Station
B1. Central (City) Bus Station
B2. KSRTC Bus Station
B3. City Market Bus Station
1. Mahatma Gandhi Statue
2. Queen Victoria Statue
3. British Library & Koshy's Restaurant
Hotels:
4. *Jaymahal Palace*
5. *Windsor Manor*
6. *West End*
7. *Taj Residency*
8. *Oberoi*
9. *Holiday Inn*
10. *Ashok*
11. *Gateway*
12. *Nahar Heritage*
13. *Ivory Tower*
14. *Ramanashree*
15. *Harsha*
16. *Highgates*
17. *Bangalore International*
18. *Mayura Kempegowda &*
Casa Piccula Restaurant
19. *Nilgiris Nest*
20. *Cauvery Continental*
21. *Woodlands*
22. *Luciya International*
23. *Victoria*
24. *Kanishka*
25. *Mahaveer*
26. *Brindavan*
27. *Geo*
28. *Gautam*
29. *Shoba Lodge*
30. *Janardhana*
31. *Sukh Sagar*
32. *Sudha Lodge*
33. *Kumara Krupa Guest House*
SA 196R

surrounded by beautiful lawns with tennis courts as well as churches and museums. When the Wodeyars returned they handed over the cantonment area, and only after Independence were the city and cantonment areas amalgamated.

The dramatic growth of the city since the early 1950s has increasingly threatened one feature of its architectural heritage, the colonial style "residency' buildings. Many private bungalows, built between 1830 and 1940 and which stood in spacious gardens, were increasingly valuable islands in a sea of rising land prices. The High Court and the Bangalore Club have survived thus far, but many private bungalows have already been demolished to make way for high rise commercial buildings. In the mid 1980s the Bangalore Urban Arts Commission identified 200 buildings that were threatened with demolition or neglect. By 1994 over half had been destroyed.

Local crafts & industries

Bangalore has become one of S India's major industrial centres. Telecommunications, a range of industries related to defence, including aircraft manufacture, electronics and light engineering, have all been boom industries in the last 20 years.

Places of interest

The Bull Temple at Basavanagudi in the SW, was built in the Kempe Gowda period in mid-16th century, and is one of the city's oldest. The monolithic Nandi, Siva's bull, is believed to have grown in size since and now measure nearly 5m in height and over 6m in length. It is made of grey granite polished with a mixture of groundnut oil and charcoal. In Nov/Dec a groundnut festival marks the harvesting and the farmers' first collection is offered to the Nandi. Buses 34 and 37. Nearby is one of Kempe Gowda's 4 towers. The **Gavi Gangadharesvara Cave Temple**, NW of the Bull Temple, also built by Kempe Gowda, has 4 monolithic pillars and an unusual image of Agni the God of Fire. On Jan 14th/15th (*Makara Sankranti*) each year the sun lights up the deity in the cave through the horns of the great bull.

The Kempe Gowda Fort, 4 km S of the City Market on Krishnarajendra Rd, was built of mud in 1537 with a Ganapathi Temple, and was rebuilt in stone 2 centuries later by Tipu Sultan. Not open to the public.

Tipu's Summer Palace to the S was started by Haidar Ali and completed by his son Tipu Sultan in 1789. Based on the Daria Daulat Palace in Srirangapatnam, the 2-storeyed ornate structure has a substantial amount of wood with walls and ceilings painted in brilliant colours with beautiful carvings. A museum traces the period of Haidar Ali and Tipu Sultan, open 0800-1800. The Venkataramanasvami Temple is in the Dravida style which, when the Wodeyar dynasty was restored at the end of the 18th century, the new Maharajah is believed to have worshipped in first, before entering the palace.

Bangalore Palace The grand palace of the Mysore Maharajahs, visibly but improbably inspired by Windsor Castle, is only open to the public for a week around 1 Nov.

Museums

Government Museum, Kasturba Gandhi Rd, Cubbon Park. Opened in 1886, one of the oldest in the country has 18 galleries including Neolithic finds from the Chandravalli excavations, and from the Indus Valley, especially Moenjodaro antiquities. Also antique jewellery, textiles, coins, art (especially miniature paintings) and geology. Daily 1000-1700 except Wed. Small entry fee. The **Venkatappa Art Gallery** next door displays the works of the Karnataka painter. **Visveswaraya Industrial and Technological Museum**, Kasturba Gandhi Rd, next to Museum. Daily 1000-1700 except Mon. The **Trade Centre** is next door and includes permanent exhibition of what the state produces.

Parks & zoos

Lalbagh Gardens The superb 100 ha Botanical Gardens were laid out by Haidar Ali in 1760 while his son Tipu Sultan added a wealth of plants and trees from many countries. It has a very good collection of tropical and subtropical and medicinal plants with over 1,800 species and a Floral Clock. The Glass House, based on London's Crystal Palace, is a venue for exhibitions. Flower Shows in Republic Day (26 Jan) and Independence Day (15 Aug) weeks. One of Kempe Gowda's four Towers built in 1537 is here. 0800-2000.

Cubbon Park, a 120 ha wooded site was laid out in the Cantonment in 1864 with flower beds and lawns. Fountains, a bandstand and statues were added and so were a number of official buildings which included **Attara Kacheri**, the High Court (finished in red stucco with an Ionian facade), the State Library and the museums. The Vidhan Soudha is on the N boundary, a post Independence granite building in the neo-Dravida style which houses the State Legislature and Secretariat. The Cabinet Room has a huge sandalwood door. The gardens are open to the public but you need prior permission to enter the Legislature and Secretariat.

Bal Bhavan, is a children's park with pony rides, boat rides and other attractions. Toy train rides, 0930-1800 Sun, 0930-2000 Public holidays. Closed Mon, 2nd Tue of month. The **Aquarium** on Kasturba Gandhi Rd in a circular building has a good collection. 1000-1730. Small entry fee.

Excursions

Bannerghatta National Park 21 km on Anekal Rd, covering over a 100 sq km, has a lion and tiger safari, a crocodile and snake farm and offers elephant rides. Picturesque scenery and a temple. Open daily except Tues. Small entry fee.

- **Place to eat** Karnataka Tourism **Mayura Vanashree**, T 42.
- **Transport Road Buses**: from Bangalore – No 366 from City Market, 365 from City Bus Stand, 368 from Sivajinagar.

Kolar Gold Fields 98 km has the world's deepest gold mines, some 2,400m below the surface, the oldest and largest in the country. Open to visitors with prior permission on Mon, Wed and Sat only. Children under 10 are not allowed.

- **Accommodation** *PWD Guest House*.
- **Transport Road Buses**: from KSRTC Bus Stand in the city go via NH 4.

Silvapura Turbonahalli Jyoti Sahi, the painter and a small artistic community are at 'Vishram', a Christian Ashram. There is a small school for untouchables run by Mrs Sahi.

- **Transport Road Buses**: from Bangalore, Main Bus Stand, 1½ hr.

Muthyala Maduvu – Pearl Valley 45 km due S of Bangalore on the road to Anekal is the 90m high waterfall. There is an interesting Siva temple nearby.

Hesaraghatta Lake 10 km out of Bangalore along the NH 4 to Tumkur a road follows the right bank of the Arkavati River N to the Hesarghatta lake. The lake now has a boat club with windsurfing facilities. Fishing permits can also be obtained, and there is an Indo-Danish dairy development project which is open to visitors.

Whitefield 16 km due E of Bangalore centre on the airport road, Whitefield is now known for its **Sai Baba** Ashram.

Tours

Karnataka Tourism tours from Badami House, NR Sq: *Bangalore City Sightseeing*: Tipu's Palace, Bull Temple, Lalbagh, Ulsoor Lake, Soap Factory, Vidhana Soudha, Museums, also stops at Govt Emporia. ½-day, 0730-1330 and 1400-1930. Rs 50. Unlike some city day trips this is recommended.

There is a large choice of trips out of the city. **1-day** *Nandi Hills*, daily during summer; *Sravanabelagola, Belur and Halebid*, daily, 0730-2200, Rs 200; *Mysore* daily, 0730-2300, Rs 200 incl meals; *Mysore* and *Tirupati* every Fri; at weekends to *Muthyalamlavedu and Bannerghatta* and *Sivangange and Devarayanadurga*. **2-day** *Jog Falls*, every 2nd Sat; *Subramanya and Dharamsthala*, every Sat. **3-day** *Mantralaya, Tungabhadra Dam and Hampi*, Fri and *Ooty and Mysore*, Mon and Fri, Oct-Jan. Longer: **4-day** *Goa*, Th. **5-day** *Bijapur, Badami, Aihole, Pattadakal, Hampi and Tungabhadra Dam*, Fri from Oct-Jan, Rs 600 inc hotels, and a **10-day** South India tour, Fri, Rs 1,800. **NB** Details and prices change, so check with Karnataka Tourism, 8/3 Parklamutt Building, Tank Bund Rd, Bangalore, T 75072.

Local Festivals

Apr *Karaga* Sakti (Mother Goddess) worshipped as Draupadi, the daughter of Fire. To test one's strength of character, a number of pots are balanced, one on top of the other. In the main temple procession, held on a moonlit night, a priest dresses as a woman and carries a pot on his head. The procession includes a number of followers – *Veerakumars* – who wave swords in the air in a vigorous display.

Nov-Dec *Kadalekaye Parishe* (Groundnut Fair), at the Bull Temple includes a groundnut eating competition.

Local information

● Accommodation

Price guide
AL Rs 3,000+ **A** Rs 2,000-3,000
B Rs 1,200-2,000 **C** Rs 600-1,200
D Rs 250-600 **E** Rs 100-250 **F** Up to Rs 100.

Luxury hotels are nearly as expensive as Delhi and Bombay and can charge up to 25% in taxes. Several hotels are clustered around the MG Rd area, nr the centre. Restaurants, cinemas and shops are also nearby. Most are about 10 km from the airport, and some 3-4 km rly. One traveller found some hotels in this rather snobbish city turn people away, saying they are full, unless they look relatively smart.

AL Taj *West End*, Race Course Rd, nr rly, T 269281, F 200010, 135 rm, rm with verandahs around lawn better than in new block, rm nr entrance dismal, so view first, spacious site (8 ha) with superb lawns, good restaurants (incl outdoor food-complex) and pool, riding and golfing arranged, highly rec; **AL** Taj *Residency*, 14 MG Rd (Trinity Circle), T 5584444, F 5844748, 180 rm, modern exterior, but tastefully conceived public areas, *Southern Comfort* serves South Indian specialities among others, balconies with bougainvilleas; **AL** *Welcomgroup Windsor Manor*, 25 Sankey Rd, T 269898, F 264941, 140 rm, 8 km rly, deluxe suites up to Rs 5,000, in plush Indian/Regency style, good restaurants (inc NW Frontier cuisine) where buffets are rec (Rs 180), poolside barbecue and 'English' bar; new **AL** *Oberoi*, 37-39 MG Rd, T 585858, F 5585860, 130 rm with private sit-outs, landscaped Japanese gardens with waterways.

A *Holiday Inn*, 28 Sankey Rd, T 269451, F 267676, 182 rm, nr golf, overpriced, food uninspired; **A** ITDC *Ashok*, Kumara Krupa High Grounds, T 269462, F 260033, 187 rm, 3 km Cantonment Rly (**NB** Get off there if travelling by train), suites up to Rs 4,000, spacious grounds with tennis courts (golf nearby), very central but service can be slow, avoid rm immediately below *Mandarin Restaurant* if you want a quiet evening.

B *Gateway*, 66 Residency Rd, T 544545, 96 rm some a/c, 6 km rly, restaurant, bar, coffee shop, pool.

C *Central Park*, 47 Dickenson Rd, off MG Rd. T 5584242, F 5587609, 130 rm, modern "American style' hotel, good value; **C** *Nahar Heritage*, 14 St Mark's Rd, T 213233, F 261468, new hotel with friendly service, good value; **C** *Ivory Tower*, on Penthouse Fl of Barton Towers, 84 MG Rd, T 5589333, F 5588697, spectacular views over the city and parade ground, central, spotless, good value if you like heights; **C** Comfort Inn *Ramanashree*, 16 Raja Rammohan Roy Rd, nr Richmond Circle, T 2235250, F 2584703, 67 rm, rec restaurants, roof-top garden, good value; **C** *Rama*, 40/2, Lavelle Rd (off MG Rd) nr Cubbon Park, T 213381, F 580357, 40 rm, 20 a/c, central, restaurant and bar on 1st Flr, good food but 'disco' music, travel, shabby exterior but pleasant inside with good clean rm, popular with Indian businessmen, good value (breakfast incl).

D *Harsha*, 11 Venkataswamy Naidu Rd, Sivajinagar, T 565566, F 563249, 80 clean rm, 40 a/c, central, a/c restaurants, bar, exchange, pool; **D** *Highgates*, 33 Church St, T 589989,

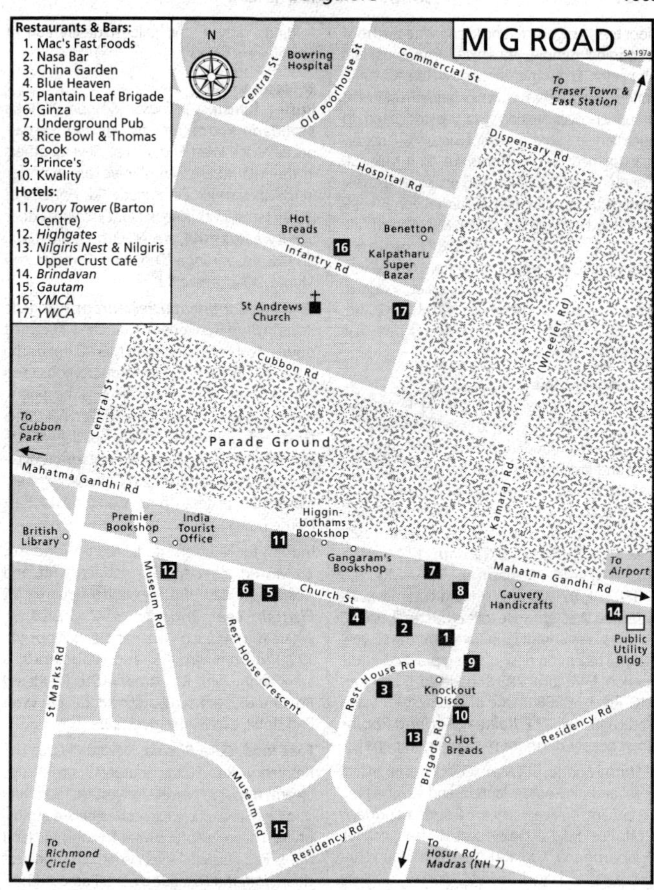

F 260174, 40 rm, central a/c, very modern, light airy, central, very pleasant atmosphere, excellent value; **D** *Bangalore International*, 2A-2B Crescent Rd, High Grounds, T 268011, 57 rm, some a/c, 2 km rly, restaurant, travel; **D** Karnataka Tourism *Mayura Kempegowda*, Dhanvantri Rd (nr bus stand), T 71606, large, clean rm, with balcony, good service, rec, nr rly and centre; **D** *Nilgiris Nest*, 171 Brigade Rd, T 588401, 24 rm, 14 a/c on upper Flr, very central, restaurant, bar, exchange, travel, dairy farm shop below, busy location, clean, comfortable, good value; **D** *Cauvery Continental*, 11-37 Cunningham Rd, T 266966, 59 rm and cottages, some a/c, restaurant, exchange; **D** *Ashraya International*, 149 Infantry Rd, T 261921, 72 rm; **D** *Woodlands*, 5 Sampangi Tank Rd, T 225111, 247 rm, some a/c and cottages, with attached baths and fridge, a/c restaurant, bar, coffee shop, exchange, travel, TV in deluxe rm, large but pleasant Indian style hotel, good value; **D** *Luciya International*, 6 OTC Rd, T 224148, F 239898, 66 rm, 15 a/c, a/c restaurant and bar, exchange, TV, popular; **D** *New Victoria*, 47-48 Residency Rd, opp Mayo Hall, T 570336, F 213281, 21 rm, 1 a/c, very central, garden, built as bungalows in 1890s (some new), dining room with Italian floor tiles, teak beams and Mangalore tiled roof all original, simple, attractive furnishings, real character. Economy rm good value. Clean in spite of cockroaches! Outdoor garden restaurant or under-cover seating, Sat live trio band to entertain at table. Pleasant grounds, friendly management, rec; **D** ***Kanishka***, 2, II Main St, Gandhinagar, T 265544, 106 rm, some a/c, restaurant (Indian, Chinese); **D** ***Mahaveer***, 8/1 & 9 Tank Bund Rd, Opp bus station & 3 min S of City rly station, T 2870774, F 2269843, modern 5 storey hotel, clean, basic rm at front can be very noisy, larger deluxe rm at back quiet, spacious, good value; **D** *Brindavan*, 108 MG Rd, T 573271, spacious rm with shower, superb *thali* restaurant, good value, rec.

● Budget hotels

The Majestic area due E of the Bus stand towards the Race Course is a good area for budget accommodation. Hotels here are quieter and less likely to be full than the MG Rd hotels. **E** ***Geo***, 11 Devganga Hostel Rd (nr Richmond Circle), T 221583, modern, Western bath, restaurant slow but reasonable food, clean business hotel; **E** ***Gautam***, 17 Museum Rd, T 577461; **E** *Ajantha*, 22A MG Rd, T 584321, 62 spacious rm and cottages with attached Western style toilets but no showers, 7 km rly, restaurant (S Indian veg), travel, very helpful reception desk offering practical information; **E** ***Vellara***, 283 Brigade Rd, 1 km from MG Rd, T 565684. One of the best for value and centrality; 23 **E** ***Railway Retiring Rooms*** and cheaper dorm for passengers in transit.

F *Shoba Lodge*, 5th Main, Gandhinagar, Indian toilet and shower/tap, laundry and attached veg restaurant, quiet and cheap; **F** ***Sudha Lodge***, 6 Cottonpet Rd, T 605420, central, clean, helpful; **F** *Janardhana*, Kumara Krupa High Grounds (nr bus stand and rly), T 264444, spartan but clean rm, restaurant, popular with local people, Indian business hotel.

● Youth Hostels

F *City YMCA*, Nrupathunga Rd, T 211848. *Guest House* and Programme Centre provides beds for Youth Hostels Assoc of India (Office at 4 Obalapa Garden, B 82, T 611292). Also *Bourdillon Guest House* at 65 Infantry Rd, T 572681. *YWCA Guest House*, 86 Infantry Rd, T 570997. **F** *YMCA* (for families only) 57 Millers Rd, T 57885; **F** ***Students Christian Movement***, 2E Unity Bldg, Mission Rd, T 223761. Other *Guest Houses* and *Dharamsalas* (for short stays only) are fairly inexpensive. Avoid ***New Citizens Lodge***, Lady Curzons Rd – 'dingy, dirty' is the mildest description of some recent visitors.

● Places to eat

Buffet lunches: *Windsor Manor*, Ashok's ***Mandarin Room*** (for Chinese) and the barbecue at the *West End* are rec. Several others in the MG Rd area, mostly a/c, are open for lunch and dinner. On Brigade Rd: ***Prince's*** at No.9, 1st Flr, with *Knock Out Disco* next door and ***Kwality's*** at 44, are rec. Others: ***Blue Fox***, 80 MG Rd, Shrungar Shopping Complex and ***Shipla***, 40/2 Lavelle Rd.

Chinese: ***Continental Restaurant***, 4 Brigade Rd, and ***Blue Heavens*** on Church St. Rec. ***Rice Bowl*** nr corner Brigade and MG Rd run by the Dalai Lama's sister, serves large portions (also Tibetan) but is expensive, lively atmosphere, friendly, western music, good chilled beer. Rec. ***Ginza***, 43 Church St, Chinese specialities. ***Ullas***, MG Rd, 1st Flr verandah restaurant overlooking MG Rd, Indian and Chinese veg, very reasonable prices. ***China Garden***, 44 Rest House Rd.

Indian: for N Indian specialities try ***Tandoor***, 28 MG Rd, ***Khyber***, 17/1 Residency Rd, and ***Koshy's***, St Mark's Rd. For good S Indian try ***RR Plantain Leaf Brigades***, 55/1 Church St, where you can eat off a banana leaf; ***Woody's***, 177/178 Commercial St and ***Woodlands***, 5 Sampanghi Tank Rd. ***Amarvathi***, Residency Rd. ***Chalukma***, Race Course Rd, next to West End Hotel, excellent veg restaurant.

Fast food: ***Casa Piccola***, Devatha Plaza, 131 Residency Rd. Pizzas, burgers, steaks, ice creams desserts. "excellent western food, very good hygiene, European coffee house atmosphere, cheap; helpful owner." Highly rec (and note, 'Raga of Gifts' – very good gift shop next door). ***Indiana Fast Foods***, 9 St Patrick's Complex, Brigade Rd, serves American fast foods, all day. On MG Rd: ***Indian Coffee House*** for snacks; ***Chit Chat*** and ***Lake View*** for ice-creams. Opp Kwality's, on Brigade Rd, ***Nilgiris Upper Crust Café*** sells snacks, breads, pastries and cheeses, slightly expensive but good, clean toilets. ***Mac's Fast Food***, Church Rd (off Brigade Rd) has separate section for women and families, disappointing food, clean toilets. New ***Wimpy*** nearby, quite expensive but good (esp veg) and the atmosphere – "Like something out of 'Grease'!" ***Hot Breads***, Infantry Rd, Residency Rd and Brigade Rd, good for pastries. ***Sukh Sagar Food Complex***, nr Majestic Cinema, 6 S.M. Rd, Majestic Sq, 3 Flr, each serving different styles of food, fresh fruit juice, excellent Indian and Chinese snacks, very clean, modern, a/c.

● Bars

Bars generally open from 1900-2300, but some open 1100-2300. The larger hotels and *Kwality's*, *Tandoor* and *Khyber* restaurants have bars. Other Restaurants with bars are ***Fiesta***, MSIL Complex, opp HAL Airport, and ***Napoli***, Gupta Market, Gandhi Nagar.

Pubs: ***The Pub*** off MG Rd. English style, with wooden bar and beer on tap for reasonable prices – "a real treat". ***Nasa***, 1/4 Church St, built like a space shuttle, hi-tech laser show, latest western dance sounds, video movies, loud, trendy, smart. ***The Underground***, 65 Bluemoon Complex, MG Rd. London Tube theme, bar very popular with the young, couples' bar and disco. ***Downtown***, Residency Rd, looks like modern English pub, nice atmosphere, 2 snooker tables (crowded).

● Airlines offices

Air India, Unity Bldg, JC Rd, T 224143; **Indian Airlines**, City Office, Karnataka Housing Board Bldg, T 567525; **Air France**, St Mark's Rd, T 214060; **British Airways**, TT Travels, Sophia Complex, St Marks Rd, T 214034; **Cathay Pacific, KLM**, *West End Hotel*, T 29745; **JAL**, 9/1, 2 Residency Rd, T 215416; **Lufthansa**, Ulsoor Rd, T 570740; **Alitalia**, Ajanta Travels, St Patrick's Complex, Residency Rd, T 215416.

● Banks & money changers

Usually open 1000-1400, Mon-Fri. Several on Kempe Gowda Rd.

● Clubs

Bangalore Club, Residency Rd. Badminton, table tennis, lawn tennis, squash, swimming, library and bar. See also under **Sports.**

● Cultural Centres

Alliance Française, Millers Tank Bund Rd, Off Thimmaiah Rd, opp Cantonment Rly Station. ***American Cultural Centre, British Library,*** St Mark's Rd, corner of MG Rd and Kasturba Gandhi Rd (next to Koshy's Restaurant). 1030-1830, Tues-Sat. ***Max Mueller Bhavan***, Almas Centre, 87 MG Rd. ***Bharatiya Vidya Bhavan***, Race Course Rd. ***Indian Council for Cultural Relations***, 1, 12th Main Rd, Vasanth Nagar. ***Karnataka Sangeeta Nataka Academy***, Canara Financial Corp Complex, Nrupathunga Rd.

● Entertainment

A/c cinema: *Santosh* on Kempe Gowda Rd shows English films.

● Hospitals & medical services

Chemists: at City Market, corner of Krishnaraja Rd and Narasimharaja Rd and Pancha Shila Medical Store on Brigade Rd. *Siddique Medical Shop*, opp Jamia Masjid, nr City Market, is open 24 hr.

Hospitals: *Bowring and Lady Curzon Hospital*, Hospital Rd, T 570782 is N of Cubbon Park. *Victoria Hospital* opp City Market, T 606575.

● Post & telecommunications

GPO: Raj Bhawan Rd. Brigade Rd Post and Telegraph Office and Museum Rd Post and Telegraph Office. Branch Post Offices at several locations in the city.

● Shopping

Shops and markets open early and close late (about 2000) though they remain closed from 1300-1600. Brass, copper, soapstone statues, sandalwood and rosewood carvings, ivory and coloured wood inlay work. Sandalwood oils and soaps, incense sticks, lacquer work, ceramics, carpets. Also fabrics (silk, cotton, georgette), watches and silver jewellery.

MG Rd (especially in Public Utility Bldg): ***Cottage Industries Emporium***, ***Manjusha***, ***Cauvery***, and ***Shrungar***. New ***Mota Shopping Complex*** on Brigade Rd; also ***Nilgiris*** Dept Stores. Residency Rd and Avenue Rd also have several shops. ***Khadi Gramudyog Bhavan*** is Silver Jubilee Park Rd, nr City Market, ***Karnataka Silk Industries Corp*** in Gupta Market on Kempe Gowda Rd, ***Mysore Silk Showroom***, Leo Complex, MG Rd, ***UP Handlooms***, 8 Mahaveer Shopping Complex, Kempe Gowda Rd, and ***Janardhana Silk House***, Unity Bldg, JC Rd. ***Vijayalakshmi Silk Kendra***, Kempe Gowda Rd, will also make shirts. ***Raga of Gifts***, A-13, Devatha Plaza, 131 Residency Rd. Very attractive gift shop.

Books: ***Gangarams***, MG Rd, has a wide ranging and expanding collection; ***Higginbothams*** and ***International Book House*** also on MG Rd. ***Premier***, 46/1 Church St. A small shop with a good selection of specialist and academic books.

Market: to see a colourful local market, with plenty of atmosphere, selling fruit, vegetables and flowers, try *City Market* or *Russell Market*.

Silver and Goldsmiths: have shops in Commercial St with ***NS Narayana*** and ***S Baba Prasad of Suryanarayan*** at No 28. Also ***KR Market***, Residency Rd and ***Jayanagar*** Shopping Complex.

● **Sports**

Golf: *Bangalore Golf Club* celebrated its centenary in 1976. The new International Championship Golf Course (Karnataka Tourism and Golf Association) is nr the airport. 0600-1800, closed Mon.

Horse racing: Bangalore is also famous for horse racing and stud farms. *Bangalore Turf Club*, Race Course Rd. The racing season is May-July and Nov-Mar.

Swimming: there are pools in *Hotel Ashok*, Kumara Krupa High Grounds, *Harsha*, Shivaji Nagar and *Windsor Manor Sheraton*, Sankey Rd. Pools at Corp Office premises, nr Square, Kensington Park Rd, nr Ulsoor Lake, Sankey Tank, Sadhiv Nagar, Jayanagar 3rd Block.

Tennis: *Bangalore Tennis Club*, Cubbon Park.

● **Tour companies & travel agents**

Bharat, St Mark's Rd, T 572251; *Mercury*, Infantry Rd, T 577730; *Sita*, St Mark's Rd, T 578091; *Thomas Cook*, 55 MG Rd; *Trade Wings*, Lavelle Rd, T 574595; *Travel Corp of India*, Richmond Circle. *Tee Gee Tours Clockwork*, 17 St Mark's Rd, T 218668, F 218751, is rec.

● **Tourist offices**

Govt of India, KFC Bldg, 48 Church St, T 579517. 1000-1800 Mon-Fri, 0900-1300, Sat. Helpful. **Directorate of Tourism**, F Block, 1st Flr, Cauvery Bhavan, KG Rd, T 215489. **Karnataka STDC**, 10/4 Kasturba Gandhi Rd, 2nd Flr, Queen's Circle, (nr MG Rd Corner), T 212091. Also at Badami House, Narasimharaja Sq (opp Corp Office), T 215883 where tours originate. Tourist Information Counter, 64 St Mark's Rd. 0900-1900. City Rly Station Counter, T 213139. 0700-2100. Airport Counter, T 571467. 0700-2030.

● **Useful addresses**

Visa extensions: Commissioner of Police, Infantry Rd, T 75272.

● **Transport**

Situated at the intersection of 3 National Highways, Bangalore is at the centre of a good road network: NH 4 (Bombay – Pune – Madras), NH 7 (Varanasi – Nagpur – Kanniyakumari), NH 48 (to Mangalore). It is well connected by air and rail (both broad gauge and metre gauge).

Local Auto rickshaws: metered, widely available, similarly priced. **Bus**: City Buses run a frequent and inexpensive service throughout the city. **Taxis**: at Rly stations. **Private car hire**: firms for city and out-of-town sightseeing. ***Ashok Tourists***, 6 First Main Rd, Sampangiramnagar, T 645653. Very reliable and competitive rates. Marutis and Ambassadors. Highy Rec. **Europcar** Office in Windsor Manor Hotel. Rates for standard saloon Rs430 per 8hr/80 km or Rs1060 per full day/250km. ***Karnataka Tourism Transport Unit***, *Hotel Mayura*, Kempegowda, T 71759.

Air Airport enquiries, T 566233. **Transport to town**: (8 km) by taxi, 20 min, Rs 120 (pre-paid taxi available); auto-rickshaw, Rs 70. KSRTC coach from airport to major hotels, MG Rd and bus station, Rs 10. **To airport**: special bus leaves from Sivajinagar Stop (nr *Hotel Harsha*).

Indian Airlines, Cauvery Bhavan, Kempe Gowda Rd, T 211211, Airport T 566233. **Delhi**: daily, 0745 and 1850, 2½ hr; **Bombay**: daily, 0945, 1630, 1950, 1½ hr; **Calcutta**: M,W,Th,Sa,Su, 0935, 2½ hr; **Madras**: daily, 0910, 2035 and others, ¾ hr; **Hyderabad**: daily, 0850, 1 hr; **Goa** Tu,Th,Sa, 1015, 1 hr; **Mangalore**: Tu,Th,Sa, 0915, ¾ hr; **Coimbatore**: Tu,Th, 1555, ½ hr; **Kochi**: W,F,Su, 0945, ¾ hr; **Ahmedabad**: W,F,Su, 1515, 2 hr; **Thiruvananthapuram**: daily, 1235, 1 hr; **Pune**: M,W,F, 1615, 1½ hrs. **Jet Airways**: **Bombay**: daily, 1900, 1½ hr. **Damania Airways**: T 588866. **Bombay**: daily, 2000 and daily except Sun, 0830, 1½ hr. **Modiluft**: **Delhi**: daily, 1905, 2¾ hr; **Hyderabad**, Tu,Th,Sa, 1215, M,W,F,Su, 1535, 1 hr; **Kochi**, Tu,Th,Sa, 0935, 50 min; **Goa**, M,W,Th,Sa, 0935, 1 hr;

Train Several Express trains connect Bangalore on the broad gauge line with important cities in the rest of India. On the metre gauge line there are connections with other cities in the S. Pre-paid taxi service available at City Station. Autorickshaw to MG Rd, Rs 15. City Rly Station. Computerised booking. **NB**: No 1 is Foreigners' Counter (also for disabled) in the new building. Enquiries: T 77918; Arr and Dep: T 74173. Reservations, T 76351 for 1st Class; T 74172/4 for 2nd Class. Disembark at Cantt Station for some hotels. Station: T 27000.

Madras: *Brindavan Exp* 2640 (AC/CC), daily, 1355, 6 hr; *Bangalore-Madras Exp* 6024 (AC/II), daily, 0725, 7 hr. **To Maddur, Srirangapatnam & Mysore**: *Kaveri Exp* 6222, daily, 0605,3 hr. **Bombay (VT)**: *Udyan Exp* 6530 (AC/II), daily, 2030, 24 hr. **Calcutta (H)**: *Bangalore-Guwahati* 2674 (AC/II), Sat, 2330, 24¼. **Hyderabad**: *Bangalore-Hyderabad Exp* 7086 (AC/II), daily, 1715, 16 hr. **Goa** (Vasco-da-Gama): *6201 Mail*, daily, 1710, 20 hr.

Road Bus: the Central (City) Bus Station, opp the City Rly Station is extremely busy but well organised. Karnataka (KSRTC), Andhra (APSRTC) and Tamil Nadu (TTC, T 76974) run efficient, frequent and inexpensive services to all major cities in S and Central India from KSRTC Bus Station (just to the S) the KSRTC Bus Station (first to the S). Very frequent service to Mysore No 4 (3 hr), several to Madras (9 hr), 8 to Madurai (10 hr) and to Hassan, 6 daily to Hyderabad, 4 daily to Mangalore (8 hr). Bombay (24 hr). Purnima Travels run to Madikeri from outside the City Rly Station; 7 hr, but timing not guaranteed. Private bus operators offer Deluxe or Ordinary coaches which are usually more comfortable though slightly more expensive, but the Video Coaches can be noisy and very tiring.

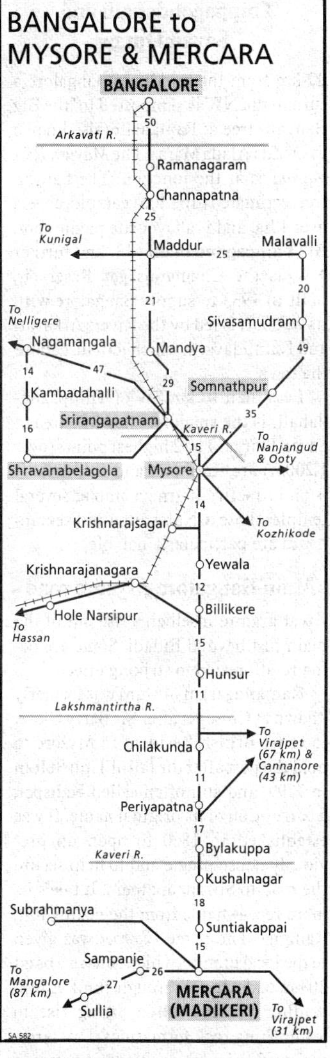

BANGALORE TO MYSORE, OOTY & MANGALORE

There are 2 routes to Mysore. The southern route through Kanakapura and Malvalli is longer. The more northerly road to Mysore is relatively good and quick. It crosses the open parkland of the Mysore *maidan*. The ancient rocks of some of the oldest granites in India give reddish or brown soils, often outcropped by extraordinary hills and boulders. These plateaus are the highest in Karnataka, rising to over 1,200m. To the S of Mysore the road climbs through the forests of the N slopes of the Nilgiris, now heavily cut and replanted with non-local species. Historically the open plateau of the Mysore *maidan* was fiercely contested. Several towns show the marks of their successive rulers, from Vijayanagar temples to Muslim Forts and British settlements.

The Mysore road leaves Bangalore past the City Market. It passes the Bharat Heavy Electricals factory 8 km from the city centre and the Bangalore University Campus. Signs of Bangalore's dramatic urban and industrial growth can be seen in the sprawl of houses and a heavily polluted river which runs to the S of the road. There are attractive small towns and villages mixed with new industrial units - distillers, pharmaceuticals, fruit processing and a Pepsi factory. There are also beautiful views to the SE over the Maidan.

Thippagondahalli and Savan Durga

22 km from the middle of Bangalore a turn to the NW is signposted to "the Big Banyan" tree at Ramahalli (also known as Dodda Alada Mara). The *Mayura Restaurant* is at the junction. The banyan tree, estimated to be 400 years old, covers over 1 ha, and is a favourite picnic spot. At **Thippagondahalli**, 13 km further NW, is the Chamarajsagar Reservoir, built in 1933 to supply Bangalore with its water. It is fed by the Rivers Arkavati and Kumudavathi which join just above the town.

Less than 10 km SW of Thippagondahalli is the small forested hill area of Savan Durga. The 2 highest points (over 1,200m) are Karibetta and Bilibetta. It is an attractive journey; among several temples those to Narasmiha and Veerabhadra are particularly notable.

Main Bangalore-Mysore road

Great granite inselbergs rise out of the plain just beyond Bidadi. Some are being re-afforested to striking effect.

Ramanagaram (48 km) was formerly known as Closepet after Sir Barry Close, the first British Resident in Mysore to hold the post after the fall of Tipu Sultan in 1799, and still often called **Kalispet**, a corruption of its original name. It was established in 1800 to open up previously dense jungle and to help secure the road to Srirangapatnam. It takes its more recent name from the nearby hill, Ramgiri. The name *Closepet* was given to the local granite, which runs in a band 20 km wide due N through Tumkur into Andhra Pradesh, often giving rise to astonishing rock formations. Dry farming predominates on flat land between the bizarre granite boulders, with ragi (*finger millet*), other millets and gram common. There are several small tea shops and restaurants, but none are clean.

Ramanagaram to Mekedatu (Goat's Leap Falls)

3 km S of Ramanagaram the main road crosses the Arkavati River. A left turn follows the right bank of the river to Kanakapura (26 km), where it crosses the southern route between Bangalore and Mysore. A minor district road continues S through Dodda Alahalli, on the edge of the quite dense state forest, to the Sangameshwara Temple, an attractive picnic spot at the confluence (sangam) of the Kaveri and Arkavati Rivers. There is a PWD *Rest House*. A track leads about 5 km SE along the left bank of the Kaveri to Mekadatu, or 'goat's leap', where the Kaveri is forced through a narrow gorge. The stretch of the Kaveri here is famous for its fishing, including mahseer, carp and other species. Fishing trips can be arranged in Bangalore. Contact: *Jungle Lodges and Resorts*, 348/349 Brooklands, 13th Main Rd, Rajmahal Vilas, T 362820. If you are travelling on to Mysore you have to return to Satnuru, and follow the road through Malavalli to Mysore. Local buses cover the whole route.

Main road: Ramanagarm to Maddur

15 km S of Ramanagaram the road crosses the Kangal River and passes the new Hanumantayya Temple, built by a recent and eponymous Chief Minister of Karnataka. Entering Channapatna the tree-lined road passes the large Police Training School and the Sericulture Training School. **Channapatna** (10 km; *Population*: 55,200; *STD Code*: 08113), entered along the tank bund, is a busy market town, known particularly for its lacquer ware. Small dolls with nodding heads are a speciality. From the late 1980s the World Bank was giving assistance to producers, along with external design guidance. Steel strings are also made for musical instruments. Tipu

Sultan's religious teacher is buried in one of the 2 large Muslim tombs just N of the town. The ruined fort in the town was built by Jagadura Rai in 1580. Indian emperors and kings often granted land to minor chiefs for services performed on their behalf. **Jagadura Rai** was given land around Channapatna by the Vijayanagar King in gratitude for his military support in defending Penukonda in 1577 – see page 1111. The buses stop on the main road in the town centre, where there are small tea stalls but no really good restaurants. In the town centre the **Karnataka Silk Industries Corporation** has a retail show room, while on the road SW of the town it has a factory and show room.10 km S of Channapatna the *Kavitha Restaurant* is quite good.

Maddur (19 km) New industrial development is taking place around the town which is on the banks of the River Shimsha. It was briefly the HQ of a Vijayanagar Viceroy. There are 2 Vaishnava Temples dedicated to Narasimhasvami and Varadaraja. The brick bridge was built in 1850. 2 km N of Maddur on the main road is the *Tiffany's Restuarant*. 300m N of Maddur rly station. Superb S and N Indian meals, freshly prepared. Very clean and extremely tasty food. If you are travelling by train between Bangalore and Mysore it is worth considering getting off at Maddur for an hour to sample the very simple but excellent food. The town bus stand has been moved onto the by-pass road.

• **Places to eat** Karnataka Tourism *Hotel Mayura*, near the bus stand, is a clean and airy restaurant.

• **Transport Train** See **Bangalore** (above) and **Mysore** (below), for trains which stop at Maddur.

Sivasamudrum Falls, Talakad and Somnathpur

The road goes due S through irrigated rice fields and sugar cane to **Malvalli** (23 km), the battlefield on which Tipu Sultan was defeated in March 1799, leading to his retreat and ultimate death at Srirangapatnam. After just over 10 km there is a left turn to the falls at **Sivasamudram** on the edge of the plateau region. The Kaveri plunges over 100m into a series of wild and inaccessible gorges. At the top of the falls the river divides around the island of Sivasamudram, the Barachukki channel on the E and the Gaganchukki on the W. The hydro electricity project was completed in 1902, the first HEP scheme of any size in India. During the wet season the falls are an impressive sight, water cascading over a wide area in a series of leaps. The discharge at peak flow can be as high as 12,000 cubic m per sec although the average flow is less than 10% of this figure. In front of the Gaganchukki fall are the water pipes which feed the generators 125m below. **Accommodation** *Guest Houses* may be reserved through Executive Engineer, KEB and Asst Executive Engineer, PWD at Bluff, Malavalli Taluk, Mandya Dist. Food to be ordered in advance. Tea stalls available.

WARNING The notorious sandalwood smuggler Veerappan has been successfully holding out against the police for several years, occasionally attacking police posts and kidnapping and murdering local people. The forest area is highly sensitive, and visitors' papers are checked. Entry to the falls, Shimsha power station and the Rest Houses may be restricted.

The road to Sosale (28 km) and Somnathpur (7 km) keeps N of the Kaveri. The narow country road passes through the pleasant little tree-shaded village of Belakavadi (5 km). Two km beyond Belakavadi a left turn goes to **Talakad** (10 km). Once an ancient temple town on the banks of the Kaveri, Talakad is now almost deserted. The Kritti Narayana (Vaidyeshwara) **Temple** comes to life once every 12 years during the Panchalinga Darshan, when the temple on the wide sandy banks of the Kaveri is the focus of a colourful and busy festival.

In Sosale the left turn goes to Tirumakudal Narsipur where a bridge crosses the Kaveri leads to the shortest route to Mysore. A right turn goes to Somnathpur.

Somnathpur

This tiny village has one of the best preserved and the only complete one of approx 80 **Hoysala** temples in the Mysore region. The small **Kesava Temple** (1268) is in gardens maintained well by the Archaeological Dept. Excellent ceilings shows the distinctive features of the late Hoysala style, and its roof is intact where other famous temples have lost theirs. It has 3 sanctuaries with the *trikutachala* (triple shrine) and stands in the middle of its rectangular courtyard about 70m long and 55m wide with cloisters containing 64 cells around it. From the E gateway there is a superb view of the temple, standing on a raised platform in the form of a 16-pointed star, with an ambulatory. The pillared hall in the centre with the 3 shrines to the W give it the form of a cross in plan. Walk around the temple to see the bands of sculptured figures which are particularly fine. The lowest of the 6 shows a line of elephants, symbolising strength and stability, then horsemen for speed, followed by a floral scroll. The next band of beautifully carved figures (at eye level) is the most fascinating and tells stories from the epics. Above is the *yali* frieze, the monsters and foliage possibly depicting the river Ganga and uppermost is a line of *hamsa*, the legendary geese.

Open daily 0900-1730. Guide book on the Hoysalas by Mishra, available from custodian. Karnataka Tourism *Restaurant* in the garden. Allow at least 1 hr. **Accommodation** At Bannur (7 km) Karnataka Tourism *Mayura Keshava*, T 85. There is a small Vishnu temple in the village. The road crosses the Kaveri (5 km) before entering Mysore (20 km)

Maddur to Mysore

At **Maddur** the direct road to Srirangapatnam enters a landscape transformed by canal irrigation from the Krishnarajasagar Dam, W of Mysore – see page 1014, where sugar cane becomes the dominant crop.

Krishnarajasagar Dam

The main benefits of the Krishnarajasagar Dam (1927) were greatly increased cash returns on farming and a boost to local processing industries. 100 years ago the land that now looks so fertile was largely unirrigated. By the time the new canal irrigation was established nearly 80% was irrigated by a canal that guaranteed water from 1 Jun to 30 Nov. From 1 Dec to 31 May the villages receive water in rotation, 10 days with water and 4 days without. The low yielding but hardy crops like millets were rapidly replaced by rice and sugar cane, which takes a year to mature, so guaranteed water supply is essential. However, poor drainage often led to increases in malaria, which stopped population growth until 1950 and much of the village's land was left fallow because there was not enough labour to work it. Malaria was not tackled effectively until DDT was introduced after World War II.

Since the early 1950s use of chemical fertilisers, high yielding varieties of rice, and electric pumpsets has grown dramatically. Villagers have been willing to experiment. The Japanese method of transplanting rice seedlings in straight lines was tried in the 1970s as against intensive but random transplanting. Although it increased yields, the benefit was more than offset by the increased costs of labour, so the experiment was abandoned.

Mandya (16 km; *Population*: 120,000; *STD Code*: 08232) The road passes through Mandya, an important market town, especially for sugar. It became the centre of the Mysore Sugar Company, which has made refined sugar and spirit since 1930. Tea and coffee shops, cold drinks, S Indian meals are available in the town centre.

Srirangapatnam (Seringapatam)

(23 km *STD Code*: 08236) The name comes from the temple of Vishnu Sri Ranganathasvami, which is far older than the fort or the town. The town has played a crucial part in the region since its origins in the 10th century. The great Vaishnavite philosopher and reformer **Ramanuja** (see page 73), who had fled from the Saivite Chola kings in Tamil Nadu, settled in 1133, and the site was frequently a focal point in S India's political development. The fort was built under the Vijayanagar kings in 1454. 150 years later the last Vijayanagar king handed over authority to the Hindu Wodeyars of Mysore, who made it their capital. In the 2nd half of the 18th century it became the capital of **Haidar Ali**, who defended it against the Marathas in 1759, laying the foundations of his expanding power. He was succeeded by his son **Tipu Sultan**, who also used the town as his HQ.

Colonel Wellesley, the future **Duke of Wellington**, established his military reputation in the battle in which Tipu Sultan was finally killed on 4 May 1799, see page 56. Tipu Sultan died in exceptionally fierce fighting at the N gate of the Fort, "shot dead by a British soldier who fancied the jewel in his turban" according to the Duke of Wellington's biographer Elizabeth Longford. She also records that in his pocket book was found a prayer: "I am full of sin; thou art a sea of mercy. Where thy mercy is, what became of my sin?" For Wellesley it was the beginning of a 5 year governorship of Seringapatam before he returned to Europe.

The **fort** and town lie on a low rocky island 5 km long and 1 km wide in the middle of the **Kaveri River**. It has triple fortifications, but the British destroyed most of the fort. The **Jama Masjid**, built by Tipu Sultan, has delicate minarets, and there are 2 Hindu **temples**, Narasimha (17th century) and Gangadharesvara (16th century). 1 km to the E of the fort is the beautiful **Daria Daulat Bagh** (Splendour of the Sea), Tipu Sultan's summer palace built in 1784, in its lovely garden. There are colourful

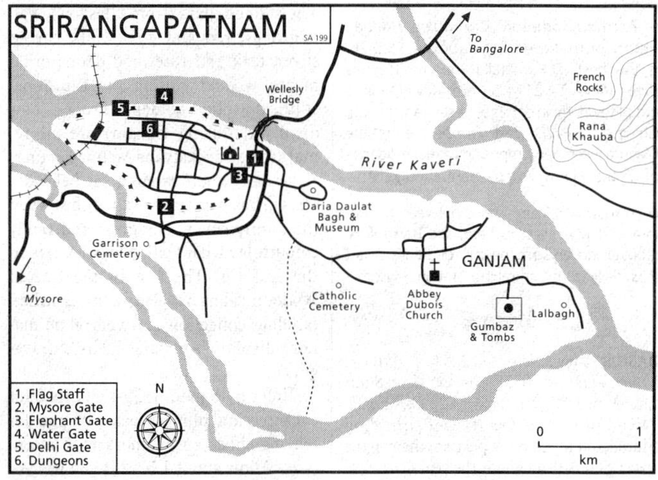

frescoes of battle scenes between the French, British and Mysore armies, ornamental arches and gilded paintings on the teak walls and ceiling which are full of interesting detail. The W wall shows Haidar Ali and Tipu Sultan leading their elephant forces at the battle of Polilur (1780), inflicting a massive defeat on the British. As a result of the battle Colonel Baillie, the defeated British commander, was a prisoner in Srirangapatnam for many years. The murals on the E walls show various palace durbars at which Tipu is shown offering hospitality to neighbouring princes. The small museum upstairs has 19th century European paintings and Tipu's belongings. Open daily. Excellently maintained by the Archaeological Survey of India.

The family mausoleum, 3 km, was built by Tipu in remembrance of his father. The ornate white domed **Gumbaz** which has beautiful ivory-on-wood inlay and Tipu's tiger stripe emblem. Some of his swords and shields are kept here. **Getting there** To visit the sights there are tongas and rickshaws. Also bicycle hire from shops on the main road.

• **Accommdodation** **C** *Amblee Holiday Resort*, on the Kaveri river, PO Box 17, T 52326, is the best. **D** Karnataka Tourism *Mayura River View*, T 52114 on river Kaveri, a little out of town, rm in cottages, restaurant (Indian, Chinese). **F** *PWD Rest House*, beside the Mayura River View, imposing former residence of George Harris, very pleasant, though basic.

• **Transport** **Train** Trains between Bangalore and Mysore stop here; see **Bangalore** (above) and **Mysore** (below) for details. **Road Bus**: daily from Central Bus Station, Mysore.

Mysore

BASICS *Population*: 652,200; *Altitude*: 776m; *STD Code*: 0821; *Climate*: Temp Summer: Max 28°C, Winter: Max 22°C; *Rainfall*: 74 cm; *Best season*: Oct (*Dasara Festival*) to March, but much more pleasant than on the lower plains throughout the year.

The former capital of the Princely State, Mysore is Karnataka's 2nd largest city. The city of royal palaces (there were 5 plus a dozen mansions), sandalwood and a centre for the manufacture of incense sticks. An attractive and clean city with a pleasant climate, it has beautiful parks and shady avenues. The scent of jasmine, for which the city is famous, fills the air in the spring.

Local crafts & industries

Sandalwood, rosewood carving. Sandalwood oil, incense, soaps, ivory inlay on wood. *Agarbatti* (incense sticks). Women and children produce *agarbatti* at home, producing thousands each day with thin bamboo sticks covered with putty and powdered incense. Silk weaving.

Places of interest

Amber Vilas, the City Palace, was designed by **Henry Irwin** and built in 1897 as the new palace after a fire which burnt down the old wooden one. It is in the **Indo-Saracenic** style in grand proportions, with domes, arches and colonnades of carved pillars and shiny marble floors. One of the largest palaces in the country with some art treasures, it is beautifully restored and maintained. The stained glass (from Glasgow), wall paintings, red and gold walls, carved silver, teak and rosewood doors, ornamental wooden ceiling and the stone-studded solid golden throne (now displayed during Dasara) are all remarkable. The **Kalyana Mandap** or marriage hall, where women sat behind a screen, has paintings of the times when the family ruled. The great and richly colourful **Durbar Hall** (47m x 14m) is on the 2nd Flr. The last in the line of Wodeyar rulers has also put his families' fabulous collection of jewels on permanent display. "Amazing in its extravagance."

Enter by S gate. 1030-1730. Rs 2 for each section plus 25 paise charge for leaving shoes and camera with attendant. Allow about 1 hr, 2 if you wish to

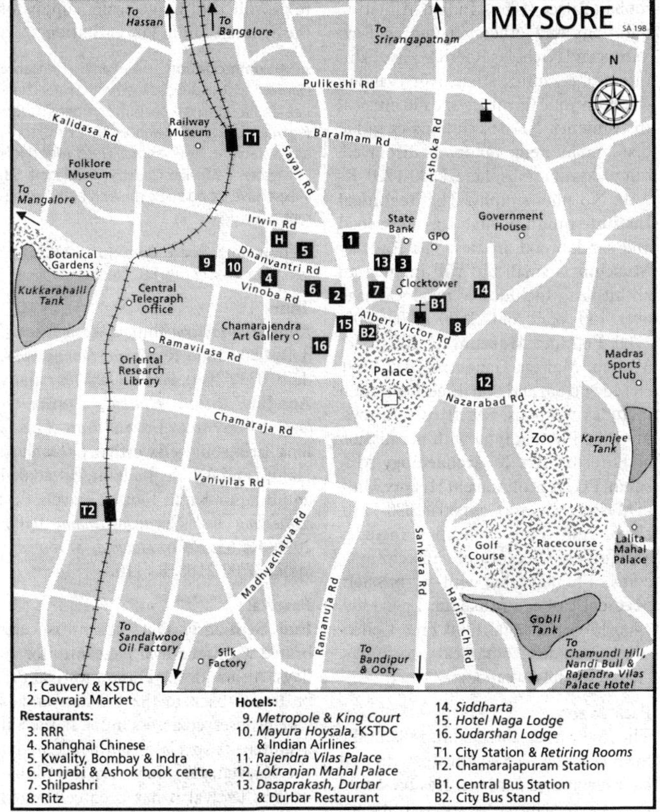

see everything. No photography indoors. Downstairs is fairly accessible to the disabled. On Sunday nights and during festivals it is lit by 50,000 light bulbs. Can be very crowded at weekends although Sun illuminations well worth seeing (after 1900).

Chamundi Hill The hill immediately to the SE of the town has a temple to Durga (Chamundeswari) celebrating her victory over the buffalo god. She became the guardian deity of the Wodeyars. On the road to the top is the giant Nandi, carved in 1659. Beautiful views on a clear day, otherwise little of interest. Worth taking a bus up and walking down.

With prior permission you can visit the Govt **Sandalwood Oil Factory** you can see the extraction of oil and how incense is made. The factory produces more than half the country's output. Sales counter. 0900-1100, 1400-1600, but oil not always available. Also **Silk Factory**, Manathandy Rd, T 21803, where weavers produce Mysore silk saris. 0900-1100, 1230-1630 on weekdays.

Museums

Chamarajendra Art Gallery at Jaganmohan Palace (1861). Indian Miniature paintings and others, including Ravi Varma and Nicholas Roerich. Also exhibition of ceramics, stone, ivory, sandalwood, antique furniture and old musical instruments. No descriptions or guide book; many items randomly displayed, but pleasant atmosphere. 0800-1700. Rs 2.50. No photography. The **Technical Institute** produces high class rosewood and sandalwood articles. The **Railway Museum** is small but will interest an enthusiast. Includes a royal carriage over 100 years old. 1000-1300, 1500-1700. **Folklore Museum**, University of Mysore, Manasa Gangotri. 1030-1730, closed 2nd Sat and Sun. Free. Collection includes weapons, jewellery, folk toys, utensils. Photography with permission of Director. **Art & Archaeology Museum**, PG Dept of Ancient History, Univ of Mysore, Manasa Gangotri. 1030-1730, closed Sun. Free. Collection includes antiquities, sculpture, inscriptions, coins. Photography with permission. **Medical College Museum**, 1830-1300, 1400-1700. Sun 0800-1300. Free. Collection includes botanical paintings, charts, models, weapons.

Park & zoo

The Zoo was established in 1892 in the town centre on a 5 sq km site with well kept lawns and gardens. Has bred wild animals in captivity especially tigers. Well managed in spacious enclosures. 0900-1400, 1500-1800, weekdays. 0900-1800, Sun. Rs 2. Camera charge extra. Accessible to the disabled.

Excursions

The **Brindavan Gardens** (for Krishnarajasagar dam, see page 1010). 19 km from Mysore. Closed due to bomb threats in 1992-93, tha dam and its attractive gardens were re-opened to visitors in late 1993. It makes a very popular day out for Indian tourists. The 2 km, rock-filled dam is one of the biggest in India and forms a 130 sq km lake. It was built by Maharaja Krishnaraja Wodeyar to provide continuous water supply for the Sivasamudram Power Station.

• **Accommodation** **A** *Oberoi Brindavan Gardens*, 130 rm, landscaped with water channels and fountains – beautiful gardens. **C** *Ritz Krishnaraja Sagar*, T Belagola 22, 22 rm, some a/c, restaurant, reservations: *Hotel Metropole* in Mysore. **F** *Mayura Cauvery*, T Belagola 52, inexpensive, good value rm with bath, restaurant.

• **Transport Road Bus**: No 150 every 30 min from Mysore City Bus Stand.

Tours

Karnataka Tourism Tours: *City sightseeing*: daily 0800-1800, Rs 60; incl *Somnathpur*: daily 0730-2030, Rs 95. *Ooty Tour*: daily Apr-July. *Belur, Halebid, Sravanabelagola*: 1-day tour, Fri and Sun. This is long, tiring but well worth it. *Other tours*: Hampi and Aihole, Badami, Pattadakal and Bijapur. Kiran Tours & Travels: *City sightseeing incl Srirangapatnam*: 0800-2030, Rs 65. *Belur, Halebid, Sravanabelagola*: 0700-2100, Rs 110.

Festival

End Sept-early Oct *Dasara* is celebrated with medieval pageantry for 10 days. Although the Dasara festival can be traced back to the Puranas and is widely observed across India, in the S it achieved its special prominence under the Vijayanagar kings. As the Mahanavami festival it has been celebrated every year since it was sponsored by Raja Wodeyar in late Sep 1610 at Seringapatam. It symbolises the victory of goddess Chamundeswari (Durga) over the demon Mahishasura.

Today the festival is still enormously colourful. On the last day, with the sound of guns and bands, colourfully bedecked elephant with a golden *howdah* carrying the statue of Bharatmata starts from the palace to process with palace chariots and units of the army through the city to Banni Mantap about 5 km away where the Banni tree is worshipped. The temple float festival takes place at a tank at the foot of Chamundi

Hill and a car festival on top. In the evening there is a torchlight parade by the mounted guards who provide an exciting display of horsemanship and the night ends with a great display of fireworks. A good time for cultural programmes particularly at the Palace Durbar Hall and Exhibition Grounds which with other public buildings, are ablaze with illuminations during this period.

Other local festivals

Mar-Apr *Temple car festival* with a 15 day fair, at Nanjangud 23 km; *Vairamudi festival* which lasts 6 days when deities are adorned with 3 diamond crowns, at Melkote Temple, 52 km.

11th Aug *Feast of St Philomena*, in Mysore, the statue of the saint is taken out in procession through the city streets ending with a service at the cathedral.

Local information

● Accommodation

NB: In the higher class hotels Sales Tax on food, Luxury Tax on rooms plus a Service Charge can increase the bill significantly. In May, the most important wedding month, hotels get booked in advance.

AL (ITDC) ***Lalitha Mahal Palace***, T Narasipur Rd, T 27650, F 33398, 54 rm, 8 km rly, built in 1931, in superb gardens for the Maharaja's non-veg foreign guests! Central dome modelled on St Paul's Cathedral, London, grand and old-fashioned, main palace rooms have verandahs, some have original baths with extraordinary system of spraying!, for nostalgia stay in the old building, sports inc billiards, badminton, tennis and table tennis, attractive pool in lovely garden, possibly the best managed ITDC hotel in 1994.

A Taj ***Rajendra Vilas Palace***, Chamundi Hills, T 20690, 29 a/c rm, inc Royal suite, built in 1939 as Majarajah's to escape from the city, newly refurbished, out-of-town hilltop situation attractive but 30 min to city centre; **A** Quality Inn ***Southern Star***, 13-14 Vinobha Rd, T 27217, F 32175, 108 rm, nr rly, speciality restaurant, new smart hotel in convenient location, rec for excellent restaurant, pool and friendly staff, though evening entertainment mediocre.

C ***Ritz Metropole***, 5 Jhansi Lakshmibai Rd, nr Indian Airlines, T 20681, F 31869, 22 rm, 4 a/c, old, full of character, reasonable restaurant (dim atmosphere but pleasant service), travel, large, comfortable rm, excellent service, attractive Victoriana, very pleasant gardens but some traffic noise, very good value, highly rec; **C** ***Highway***, New Bannimantap Extn, T 21117, 40 rm some a/c, 2 km rly; **C** ***Dasaprakash Paradise***, 104 Vivekananda Rd, Yadavgiri, T 26666, 2 km rly station, 90 rm, 36 a/c with bath, very clean hotel, highly rec restaurant (veg); **C** ***Kings Kourt***, Jhansi Lakshmi Bai Rd, T 25250, F 32684, 60 rm, central a/c, nr rly, very central, modern hotel, pleasant; **C** ***Ramanshree Comforts***, T 63136, F 27273, 68 a/c rm, new, spotlessly clean, airy and light, excellent.

D ***Lokranjan Mahal Palace***, Lokranjan Mahal Rd, T 21868, 31 rm part a/c, pool.

● Budget hotels

The **Gandhi Square** area has some Indian style hotels which are clean and good value. Several in Dhanvantri Rd incl clean and comfortable **E** ***Ashraya***, T 27088, nr the market. **E** ***Dasaprakash*** Gandhi Sq, T 24444, 145 rm, most with bath, few a/c, clean, fresh looking, attractive courtyard, quite quiet, veg, restaurant, rather dark, ice cream stand, travel, rec. (In case you are uncertain as to your future the resident astro-palmist will take a photocopy of your palm print and give appointments for subsequent consultation: Rs 100 for brief oral summary, Rs 200 for detailed written analysis.) **E** Karnataka Tourism ***Mayura Hoysala***, 2 JLB Rd (opp *Hotel Metropole*), T 25349, 21 large rm with bath in colonial mansion, nr rly in city centre, good restaurant, bar, good tours, good value, rec; **E** ***Maurya Palace***, 2716-2-3-7, Sri Harsha Rd, T 35912, 27 large clean rm, some a/c with TV, restaurant, travel, restaurant reasonably priced – good food and service though a bit dark, rec, popular hotel so reserve ahead, bus and railway nearby; **E** ***Siddharta***, 73/1 Guest House Rd, Nazarabad, T 26869, 76 rm some a/c, nr centre, restaurant (Indian veg), exchange, new, clean, good value; **E** ***Calinga***, 23 KR Circle (opp City Bus Stand), T 31310, 80 rm (some with 3 tier cot!), with baths (occasional hot water) and Indian toilets, restaurant (Indian veg), travel, phone, TV, fairly basic, clean, central and popular; **E** ***Railway Retiring Rooms*** are reasonable, dorm beds very inexpensive; **E** ***Park Lane***, 2720 Curzon Park, Sri Harsha Rd, nr Bus Stand and Palace, T 30400, 8 rm, beautiful and very well-kept, lovely, architecturally interesting, if cramped, rooms, management friendly, very attractive courtyard restaurant and good food, though quite expensive. **E** ***Sudarshan Lodge***, opp Jaganmohan Palace, T 26718. Central, clean rm and dorm. Very friendly owners, rec though area not too pleasant and hotel has unattractive exterior.

F ***Green's Boarding***, N of Palace, T 22415, large clean rm with bath, restaurant cheap but limited, helpful staff, popular hotel, excellent value; **F** ***Durbar***, Gandhi Sq, T 20029, rm are quiet, away from road and face a small courtyard full of plants, pleasant non-veg roof-garden restaurant, open in evenings, good travel information; **F** ***Indra Bhavan***, Dhanvantri Rd, T 23933, quiet central courtyard, good veg restaurant, popular; **F** ***Sangeeth***, 1966 Narayanashastri Rd, nr Udupi Sri Krishan Mandir, T 24693, clean Indian style hotel, fairly quiet, nr rly station, no food, but nr the excellent *Kwality Restaurant*; **F** ***Youth Hostel*** is rather inconvenient, 5 km NW of city centre.

● Places to eat

On Sayaji Rao Rd: *Bombay Indra Bhavan* and ***Paras***, a/c, S and N Indian veg dishes, rec. ***Gaylord*** and ***Kwality***, Dhanvantri Rd are rec. The *Kwality* does superb buttered *naan*. ***Govardhan Hotel***, Sri Harsha Rd, nr Palace does good *thalis* and confectionary. ***Ritz***, Bangalore-Nilgiri Hill Rd, Nr Central Bus Station has inexpensive, good food and excellent lime-sodas! For veg food try ***Dasaprakash*** serving excellent, as-much-as-you-can-eat 'meals'. Good Chinese food at Hotels *Metropole*, *Rajendra Vilas*, *Southern Star*, *King's Kourt*, *Lokranjan Mahal Palace*, also at ***Shanghai Chinese*** on Vinobha Rd. ***Sampar*** (N Indian), rec. ***Gun Hill Imperial***, Bangalore-Nilgiri Hill Rd and ***Punjabi Bombay Juice Centre***, 397 Dhanvantri Rd are also rec. ***RRR*** MG Sq, 200m from Shilpashri Rest, excellent food, rec.

● Bars

Best in the hotels: *Lalitha Mahal Palace*, *Lokranjan Mahal Palace* and *Gun Hill Imperial*.

● Airline offices

Indian Airlines, *Hotel Hoysala*, JLB Rd, T 21846. There are no direct flights from Mysore.

● Banks & money changers

State Bank of Mysore, corner of Sayaji Rao Rd and Sardar Patel Rd. **Mysore Bank**, opp GPO in city centre.

● Entertainment

Cinema: there are 2 cinemas showing English language films.

● Post & telecommunications

GPO: on corner of Ashok Rd and Irwin Rd. Poste Restante mail here. **Central Telegraph Office**: open 24 hr, is E of Maharajah's Palace.

● Shopping

Superb carved figures, sandalwood and rosewood items, silks, incense-sticks, handicrafts. The main shopping area is Sayaji Rao Rd which runs N from the centre, just N of the Maharaja's Palace. ***Cauvery Arts & Crafts Emporium*** for sandalwood, ivory and rosewood items. ***Devaraja Market***; lanes of stalls selling spices, perfumes and much more. ***Sri Lakshmi Fine Arts & Crafts*** (opp the zoo) also has a factory shop at 2226 Sawday Rd, Mandi Mohalla. Also rec: ***Ancient Curios*** at 12, and ***Ganesh*** at 532 Dhanvantri Rd. For reasonably priced silks try ***Dulhan Silk Emporium***, 1751 Sayaji Rao Rd, which has a good selection. ***Karnataka Silk Industry's*** shop is on Visweswara Bhavan, RKR Circle. You can watch machine weaving at the factory shop on Mananthody Rd, 0730-1130. 1230-1630, Mon-Sat.

Books: ***Geetha Book House***, KR Circle and ***Ashok Book Centre***, Dhanvantri Rd.

● Sports

Madras Sports Club, Lalitha Mahal Palace Rd, just before the hotel.

● Hospitals & medical services

Medical College, corner of Irwin and Saiyaji Rao Rd. *KR Hospital*, S of Irwin Rd. *Mary Holdsworth Hospital* (in a striking building dating from 1906 which was established as a Methodist Mission Hospital).

● Travel agents & tour operators

Karnataka Tourism Transport Wing, *Hotel Mayura Hoysala*, Jhansi Lakshmi Bai Rd, T 25349; ***Kiran Tours & Travels***, 21/1 Chandragupta Rd, T 24083; ***Shri Raghavendra***, Narayanshastri Rd.

● Tourist offices

Regional Tourist Office, Old Exhibition Bldg (corner of Irwin Rd). T 22096. 1000-1730. Rly Station, T 30719.

● Transport

Mysore has a number of state highways radiating to major cities and towns in Karnataka, Tamil Nadu and Kerala and connects to NH 48.

Local Bus: frequent city buses to the Govt Silk Weaving Centre and the Sandalwood Oil Factory (No 1A, to both). No 150, every 30 min to Krishnarajasagar Dam and Brindavan Gardens.

No 101 to Chamundi Hill. To Manasagangotri No 30. To Srirangapatnam No 210. **Autorickshaws**: are also easily available.

Train Enquiries, T 20100. **NB**: Because the rly to Mysore has now been converted to broad gauge there are new through trains to other cities. The newest fast train is the *Shatabdi Express* to Madras, but others are scheduled to be brought in. To **Bangalore (non-stop)**: *Tipu Exp* 6205, daily, 1020, 3hr. **Madras via Bangalore**: *Shatabdi*, daily, 1400, 7½ hr. **Bangalore via Srirangapatnam, Mandya & Maddur**: *Chamundi Exp* 6215, daily, 0615, 3½ hr; *Nandi Exp* 6211, daily, 1300, 3¼ hr; *Tirupati Exp* 6213, daily, 1630, 3½ hr; *Kaveri Exp* 6222, daily, 1800, 3½ hr.

Road Bus: timings occasionally change. For more important centres with 1 or 2 hrly service the times of first and last buses are shown. Check at KSRTC Bus Station, T 20853. SRTC buses of Karnataka, Tamil Nadu and Kerala run regular daily services between Mysore and other major cities. In addition, private companies operate on long distance routes, eg Kiran Tours, Ooty night service daily at 2400. They are sometimes faster and marginally less uncomfortable.

Bangalore: every ¼ hr, 0545-2130, from Non-stop platform. Semi-deluxe approx every ¾ hr, 0630-2130.

From **Platform 1**: Mandya: approx hrly, 0600-2030; Maddur: 0900, 1100, 1400, 2045; Kolar Gold Fields: 0530, 0715, 0900, 1300. **Platform 2**: Chitradurga, Tumkur, Hassan, Raichur. **Platform 3**: Belgaum, Hubli, Davangere, Hassan, Periyapatna, Bellary, Hospet & Badami, Sravanabelagola (0730, 1045, 1230, 1600). **Platform 4**: Sringeri, Dharmasthala (0830, 1000, 1045, 1130, 2200, 2230), Hassan (0215, 1515-2000); Shimoga (0800, 0945, 1015). **Platform 5**: Mangalore (0515, 0830-2230); Madikeri (0100, 0130, 0945-1800); Virajpet (0100, 0215, 0910-1915; Nagarhole (0615, 1315); Hunsur (0900-1620). **Platform 6**: Gundlupet (0600, 1030, 1445). **Platform 7**: Karnakapura (1130-1900), Mallavalli (0800-2200), T Narsipur (1100, 1500). **Platform 8**: Bandipur (1430, 1215, 1715). **Platform 9**: Ooty (0115, 0615-1500); Coimbatore (0715); Madras (1800, 1900); Madurai (1845, 2100, 2230); Vellore (1000, 2100, 2200); Salem (1600, 1000, 1315, 1515, 2130); Kanniyakumari (1430); Kozhikode (Calicut, 0430, 0600-2230); Kannur (Cannanore, 0800-2230); Ernakulam (0800, 1630, 2130, 2230); Thrissur (Trichur: 0530, 0800, 2030); Hyderabad (1730), Panaji (1600); Tirupati (1800, 2130); Vijayawada (1230).

MYSORE TO UDHAGAMANDALAM (OOTY)

From Mysore the Bangalore – Ooty road continues S to the small town **Nanjangud** (23 km; *STD Code*: 08221), famous throughout Karnataka for the 3 day temple-car festival held in March. The temple itself is over 110m long and is supported by 147 columns. The road crosses the railway and continue S to **Gundlupet** (35 km).

From Gundlupet the road S goes to the **Bandipur** and **Mudumalai Wildlife Sanctuaries**. Bandipur is in Karnataka while Mudumalai is in Tamil Nadu, but they are extensions of the same forest reserve which also stretches W to include the Kerala reserve of Wynad.

Bandipur National Park

BASICS *Altitude*: 780-1,455m; *Area*: 874 sq km; *Temp range*: 30°C to 18°C; *Rainfall*: 1,000 mm; *Best season*: Jun-Sep, Jan-Mar; *Open*: 0600-0900, 1600-1800; Camera fees (high for movie).

Background

Bandipur, set up by the Mysore Maharajah in 1931. It has a mixture of subtropical moist and dry deciduous forests (predominantly teak and Anogeissus) and scrubland in the Nilgiri foothills. The wetter areas support rosewood, sandalwood, silkcotton and *jamun*.

It was the first park in S India to be chosen for the Project Tiger scheme. You should easily spot *gaur*, *chital* (spotted deer), elephant and sambar, but tigers and leopards are rare. Also good variety of bird life incl crested hawk and serpent eagles and tiny-eared owl.

Viewing

Jeeps and vans available through Forestry Dept (Rs 12) and viewing is from *machans* (raised platforms) near watering places. Elephant rides, Rs 25 per hr.

Park information

● Accommodation

Inexpensive but good value, under shady trees. Simple **F** ***Forest Lodges, Guest Houses*** with attached baths, and 3 ***Wooden Cottages*** for 12 in Kakanhalla, Mulehole and Kalkere. A couple of VIP lodges – Rajendra I and II, and ***Swiss Cottage*** tents. Cooks prepare food to order (cooking in rm prohibited). Also **F** ***Venuvihar Lodge***, in beautiful Gopalaswamy Hills (20 km), take all provisions, book in advance through Asst Conservator of Forests, Bandipur National Park, T 21 or Forest Officer, Forest Dept, Woodyard, Ashokpuram, Mysore (S of Mysore city, Bus No 61 from city centre) or through Field Director, Project Tiger, Govt House Complex, Mysore, T 20901.

● Transport

Air Mysore (80 km) has the nearest airport with Vayudoot connections with Bangalore, Hyderabad and Tirupati.

Train Through Mysore to Ariskere, Bangalore and Hassan. Nanjungud (20 km).

Road See Mudumalai below. Last bus for Mysore (80 km) dep 1515.

The road climbs through Bandipur to one of the highest parts of the Mysore Plateau before dropping sharply into the deeply cut Moyar Valley, the floor of which is only between 300 and 500m above sea level. The River is the boundary between Karnataka and Tamil Nadu, and the N edge of the Nilgiri Hills.

Mudumalai Wildlife Sanctuary

Background

The sanctuary (in Tamil Nadu) adjoins **Bandipur** beyond the Moyar river, its hills (885 -1,000 m), ravines, flats and valleys being an extension of the same environment. Open through the year. *Best season*: Sep-Oct, Mar-May. When the undergrowth dies down, it is easier to see the animals, particularly when they are on the move at dawn.

Wildlife

The sanctuary has large herds of elephant, gaur, sambar, barking deer, wild dog, Nilgiri Langur, bonnet monkey, wild boar, 4-horned antelope and the rarer tiger and leopard. There are also smaller mammals including the scaly anteater, pangolin, mouse deer, civet, giant Malabar flying squirrels and a rich variety of bird life (jungle fowl, peacock, Malabar hornbill, woodpeckers, Malabar whistling thrush, paradise flycatchers, warblers, babblers and a number of birds of prey and nocturnals). Reptiles include python, saw-scaled viper, Hamadryad (King cobra) and large monitor lizards.

Elephant Camp at **Kargudi**, 5 km, is particularly interesting. Here wild elephants are tamed and some are bred in captivity and trained to work for the timber industry. You can see baby elephants do acrobatics (and *puja* at the temple at 1800!) and watch them being fed in the late afternoon, learn about each individual elephant's diet and specially prepared blocks of food. In the wild, elephants spend most of the day foraging, consuming about 300 kg of green fodder daily over a large area, but in captivity they have to adapt to a totally alien life style.

Viewing

You can hire a jeep or van but must be accompanied by a guide. Elephant rides from 0600-0800 and 1600-1800 (Rs 35 each). The elephant rides are normally better value than the 46-seater coaches. With patience you can see a lot, the park is one of the more popular and the park is trying to limit numbers to restrict disturbance to the elephants. *Machans* are located near waterholes and salt licks.

Park information

● Accommodation

Advance booking essential during season. Best nr Masinagudi (11 km). **D** ***Jungle Hut Guest House***, T Masinagudi 240 via Ooty, 12 clean, simple rm with bath in 3 stone cottages in valley, phone for pick-up, food and service excellent, jeep hire, highly rec; **D** ***Bamboo Banks Farm Guest House***, T Masinagudi 222 via Ooty, 6 clean rm, some in cottages in pleasant garden, good food, jeep hire; **D** ***Jungle Trails Guest House***, T Masinagudi 256, 4 clean rm in a bungalow close to elephant trail.

Several Forest Dept **F** Forest Houses: Theppakkadu ***Log House***; Abayaranyam ***Sylvan Lodge*** and ***Annexe***; Masinagudi ***Log House*** and ***Rest House***; Kargudi ***Rest House*** and ***Annexe***, ask for deluxe rm. There is also a **F** TTDC ***Youth Hostel*** at Theppakadu, T 259; **F** ***Dormitories Peacock***, beds only Rs5, food excellent. (Also *Minivet and Morgan*). Reservations: Wildlife Warden, Kargudi, T 26 or Reception Range Officer, Mudumalai Wildlife Office, Theppakadu, Coonoor Rd, T 4098.

● **Transport**

Air Coimbatore (152 km).

Train Ooty (64 km) or Mysore.

Road Bus: on Mysore-Ooty bus route. From Mysore, services from 0615. Also from Gudalur (Kerala). Bandipur (14 km) has the same service.

From the Moyar River the road climbs to **Gudalur** (49 km) at the base of the hills, then left up to **Naduvattam** (10 km) through mixed woodland, managed through this century by the Forest Dept. Many imported species have been experimented with, including fragrant and medicinal trees such as eucalyptus and chinchona, the bark of which was used for extracting quinine. The drive often gives beautiful views, and as with all the hill climbs in India the rapid change in altitude quickly brings a freshening coolness. Udhagamandalam (25 km) is set in rolling downland on the plateau top of the Nilgiris – see page 895.

MYSORE TO KODAGU

It is possible to make a very pleasant 2 or 3 day excursion to the beautiful wooded hills of Kodagu (Coorg) District, which also lies on the routes to Mangalore or northern Kerala. The road is a major bus route travelled frequently by local and express buses to the west coast and a number of towns scattered along the Ghats. Madikere, the capital of Kodagu, is 120 km SW of Mysore and 24 km N of the Nagarhole National Park. The forests are still home to wild elephants and other wildlife, while the Kodava people are very proud of their martial traditions and their hospitality. It also has a highly distinctive cuisine, in which pork curry (*Pandhi curry*) and rice dumplings (*Kadumbuttu*) are particular favourites.

The road leaves Mysore past the University at Manasagangotri through an open but industrial area, with factories making bricks, plywood and electrical goods. After 8 km there is a turn to the Krishnarajsagar Dam, open again in 1994 after a period of being closed to visitors. In Yelwala a road leads directly to Srirangapatnam. 17 km from Mysore the *Dewdrop Inn* is a very good restaurant and a convenient stop.

The road pases through several villages scattered across the rolling plateau. It is well signposted in English, Hindi and Kannada. 29 km from Mysore a right turn leads to KR Nagar and Hassan, and in a further 15 km reaches Hunsur.

Hunsur (*STD Code*: 08222) The bus stop is on the by-pass. **Accommodation & food** There are small hotels on the E side of Hunsur at the junction with the by-pass. **F** *Brindavan*, modest but acceptable; **F** Karnataka Tourism *Kingsway*, adequate for brief stay; in the centre of town the Karnataka Tourism **F** *Deviprasad*, BM Rd, T 3224, small clean rm, Indian toilet, noisy in very early morning, good veg canteen, new building, best in town. There is a very good restaurant right by the bus stand.

ROUTES In Hunsur a road runs S to Nagarhole.

Nagarhole National Park

Background

Nagarhole (*nagar* snake, *hole* streams) Once the Maharajas' reserved forest, became a National Park in 1955. Covering gentle hills bordering Kerala, it includes swampland, streams, moist deciduous forest, stands of bamboo and valuable timber in teak and rosewood trees. The Kabini river which is a tributary of the Kaveri flows through the deciduous forest where the upper canopy reaches 30 m. A number of tribesmen, particularly Kurubas (honey-gatherers), live here. There were greatly exaggerated rumours of devastating fire damage to the National Park in 1992 and some suggested that the Park would not recover for many years. In fact fires are not untypical of savannah forests, and Nagarhole had recovered by 1993.

Wildlife

Includes elephants, *gaur* (Indian bison), *dhole* (Indian wild dogs), wild cats, 4-horned antelopes, flying squirrels, sloth bears, monkeys, sambar and panthers. Many varieties of birds including the rare Malabar *trogon*, great black woodpecker, Indian pitta, pied hornbill, whistling thrush and green imperial pigeon. Also waterfowl and reptiles.

Viewing

Entry Rs 2 plus camera fees. Jeeps, vans and guides through the Forest Dept. 1 hr tour at 1715. Viewing from *machans* near water holes. Trekking possible with permission. You can also visit the Govt's Elephant Training Camp at Haballa. Organised tours are available on 15 and 26 seater coaches – not particularly suitable vehicles for the purpose.

Park information

● Accommodation

From Sep-June, **B** Karnataka Tourism ***Kabini River Lodges***, nearby at Karapur on reservoir bank, 14 rm in 2 new buildings, good restaurant, bar, exchange, partly, Mysore Maharajas' 18th century *Hunting Lodge* and the *Viceregal Bungalow*, package includes sailing, rides in buffalo-hide coracles on the Kaveri but only jeep, minibus at Nagarhole and Murkal complex. **NB**: Prices for foreigners are double those for Indians. Reservations: Jungle Lodges and Resorts, 348/9 Brooklands, 13th Main, Rajmahal Vilas Extn, Bangalore, T 362820.

E ***Cauvery Lodge*** and ***Gangotri Lodge*** in Park, 2-4 bedrm with bath and services of cook, simple but comfortable. Reserve through Asst Conservator of Forests, Wildlife Sub-Div, Aranya Bhavan, Ashokpuram, Mysore, T 21159. **NB**: Book at least 10 days in advance.

● Transport

Train Through Mysore (96 km). See **Bandipur** above.

Road Bus: from Mysore (96km, Exp, 3hr, Rs 35) via Hunsur; from Madikere, 1000. Bus to Bangalore Dep 1000, 6hr.

Hunsur to Madikeri

Five km out of Hunsur the road crosses the Lakshmantirtha River, which drains N into the Krishnarajsagar Reservoir. Soon after the road forks, the right going to Madikeri and the left to Kannur. The Kannur road goes through **Virajpet** (Virajendrapet, 59 km), while the Madikeri road forks right through Chilakunda Village, which has a radio transmitter. Virajpet is a small place of limited charm, with a few very basic hotels – no windows, sheets or fans, and shared Indian toilets.

Buses go N to the important pilgrimage town of Dharamsthala. Passing small tracts of tank-irrigated land and the Vishnu Textile Mills at Kinalapura, the road goes to **Piriyapatna**. There is very simple accommodation at the *Pravani Mandir Guest House*. Just E of the bus stand the *Sindhnur Hotel* serves decent meals. Buses go to Madikeri and Chikballapur. Piriyapatna has an attractive little street market on Saturdays.

Travelling W you enter the more heavily wooded land approaching the ridge of the Western Ghats. White painted, thatched-roofed houses are tucked away in the forest, surrounded by coffee bushes among the taller trees.

Bylakuppa A ridge running parallel with the road illustrates the increasing forest cover travelling westwards. The Tibetan camp at Bylakuppa is bustling with activity and has quite a prosperous air. There is a Syndicate Bank in the village. The basis of the settlement's economic life, as for many Tibetan communities, is carpet weaving and the manufacture of *thangkas* for sale. A large section of forest was made available for the Tibetan refugees, who now number over 15,000. They have established several monasteries, and live in scattered villages, having built homes which retain certain Tibetan features. They have their own schools and craft workshops and have become self-reliant through farming maize, rice and millet.

Increasing communal tension in Dharamsthala, in 1994 led to the Dalai Lama's reluctantly voicing a possible transfer to Karnataka, of his headquarters of the Tibetan Govt in exile.

Kodagu (Coorg)

Set in water meadows even Kushalnagar, at the very edge of Kodagu territory, shows the district's distinct identity. Graffiti on some walls illustrate the modern demands by some for a separate state. Although there were early references to Kodagu people in the Sangam literature of the Tamils 2000 years ago, the earliest inscriptions in Kodagu date from approximately the 8th century. They seem to have retained a degree of independence from major powers such as the Cholas and subsequent dynasties who ruled areas to the East, but the foundations of modern political rule was established by the Lingayat caste of minor Nayak rulers, the Haleri Rajas of Kodagu. The founder of the dynasty was Virarajendra, and their capital was at **Haleri** 10 km from the present district capital of Madikeri. Most of the Kodagu Rajas were Hindus. The later Kodagu rajas were noted for some bizarre behaviour. Dodda Vira (1780-1809) was reputed to have put most of his relatives to death, a pattern followed by the last king, Vira Raja, before he was deposed by the British in 1834. The economic character of the state was quickly transformed. Coffee, which has become the staple crop, was introduced soon afterwards. In 1852 the last Lingayat ruler of Kodagu, Chikkavirarajendra Wodeyar, became the first Indian prince to sail to England. Kodagu was incorporated into Karnataka after the States' reorganisation in 1956.

Kushalnagar and Nisargadhama On the upper reaches of the River Kaveri, 5 km W of Bylakuppa, Kushalnagar is the easternmost town in Kodagu.

- **Accommodation & food** *Kwality*, at the bus stand. Small hotel offering basic boarding and lodging. ***Ganesh Lodge*** and ***Shanti*** are veg restaurants, both quite reasonable.

- **Transport Road Buses**: to Madikere (Rs 10, ¾ hr) and Mysore (Rs 25) every 30 min.

Nisargadhama is a small island reserve in the Kaveri River, 2 km from Kushalnagar. It consists mostly of bamboo thickets and trees, including sandalwood, and is very good for seeing parakeets, bee eaters and woodpeckers and a variety of butterflies. It is a very quiet spot, hardly visited and very clean. Only open to day visitors between 0900-1800. A very pleasant and unusual place, completely untouched by tourism.

- **Accommodation F** Karnataka Tourism ***Cottages***, built largely of bamboo have simple rm, some, including the dining room, standing on stilts over the water, some brick built cottages have electricity, but no fan or hot water.

- **Transport Rickshaw**: from Kushalnagar Rs10.

From Kushalnagar the road climbs through the quite different scenery of Kodagu. Occasionally you can see elephants working in the teak forests, and after about 10 km the road passes through coffee estates, scattered with beautiful poinsettias, and with neatly trimmed hedges along the roadside. Pepper vines are interpsersed through the estates, and in places towering silver oaks form a shady canopy. 6 km before Madikere the road passes through the *chinchona* plantation of Suntiakappai.

Madikeri (Mercara)

BASICS *Population*: 30,000; *Altitude*: 1,525m; *STD Code*: 08272; *Climate*: Temp Max (May) 29°C, Min Jan 9°C; *Annual rainfall*: 3,250 mm, wettest months Jun-Sep. In winter there is often hill fog at night, making after dark driving dangerous.

The capital of Kodagu District, Madikeri is an attractive small town in a beautiful hilly setting surrouned by the forested slops of the Western Ghats.

Places of interest

The **Omkareshwara Temple**, dedicated to both Vishnu and Siva, was built in 1820. The tiled roofs are typical of Kerala Hindu architecture, while the domes show Muslim influence. The **fort** with its 3 stone gateways, built between 1812-14 by Lingarajendra Wodeyar II, is on high ground dominating the town. It has a small museum in St Mark's Church (open 1000-1730) as well as the town prison, a temple and a chapel while the palace houses govt offices. The **'Rajas' Tombs'** (Gaddige), built in 1820 to the N of the town, are the memorials of Virarajendra and his wife and of Lingarajendra. Although the rajas were Hindu, their commemorative monuments are Muslim in style; Kodagas both bury and cremate their dead.

The Friday Market near the bus stand, is very colourful as all the local tribal people come to town to sell their produce. On Mahadevped Rd, which leads to the Rajas' tombs, is a 250 year old Siva temple with an interesting stone façade. Madikeri has an attractive 9-hole golf course.

Excursions

A comfortable day trip can include Bhagamandala, at the confluence of the Kaveri, Kanike and Suiyothi Rivers, and Talacauvery, the source of the Kaveri itself.

Bhagamandala (36 km), where the Triveni bathing ghat is at the confluence of the 3 rivers. Among many small shrines the Bhandeshwara temple is particularly striking. It stands in a large stone courtyard surrounded by Keralan style buildings on all 4 sides.

- **Accommodation** *Sri Laxmivilasa*, 'fooding and lodging' is very basic.

- **Transport Road** Rama Motor Serivc runs a tour from the private bus stand, dep 0830, with ½ hr stop.

Talacauvery, 8 km further, has been 'developed' so that what was a small temple in the forest is now a disintergrating concrete complex on a barren hillside. Steps lead up from the spring which is the Kaveri's source to the summit of the hill, commanding superb views. The spring is contained in a small and unspectacular pool of brown water. *Sankaramana Day* On one day in Oct, the spring gushes at a particular and foretold moment; a bath in the water then is considered to be particularly beneficial.

Abbi Falls Within 30 min rickshaw ride of Madikeri (Rs80 round trip) the ride to the falls through forests and coffee plantations is pleasant and interesting. The falls themselves are less so – recent visitors describe them as littered in rubbish with excreta everywhere.

Tadiyenda Mol A well known hill top. Buses depart hourly from the State bus stand from 0645 to 1900 to Napoklu. It is then a 10 km trek to the summit.

Nagarhole (100 km) For a longer excursion, Shakti Motor Service bus leaves for the national park at 1000 daily from the private bus stand (see above).

Local information

● Accommodation

D *Coorg International*, Convent Rd, T 27390, 27 rm, restaurant, good for Chinese and Indian, avoid 'western specialities' eg 'vegetables fried in Branston pickle'!. Wide range of facilities incl good bookshop, tours and trekking, modern, western style, tastefully decorated and very comfortable, young, enthusiastic and friendly staff, reserve direct or in Madras, Alsa Mall, III Fl No. 9-A, Montieth Rd, Egmore, T 8273824; **D** *Capitol Village*, 5 km from town, 7 rm, a traditional Keralan building with tiled roof and wooden beams, set in a coffee, cardamom and pepper estate, very quiet, outdoor restaurant shaded by trees, single-hole 'golf course', fishing in small lake, rickshaw from twon centre Rs 40, book 10 days in advance through *Hotel Cauvery*, Madikeri.

● Budget hotels

Many really cheap hotels are virtually homes for semi-permanent Indian guests, so never seem to have rooms available. **E** *Cauvery*, School Rd, T 26292, rm (no fans) with bath, restaurant does cheap standard Indian meals; **E** *Chitra*, Main Rd, T 27311, nr bus stand, modern, being extended by 50 rm with western toilets, hot shower, rm simple but clean, good value, restaurant serves excellent, reasonably priced Indian meals, highly rec. **NB**: Do not confuse with *Chitra Lodge*, opp, very cheap and not rec. **E** *Coorg Side*, Daswal Rd, T 26789, 20 clean rm, hot water, veg canteen, quiet, away from bus station, overlooking Madikeri, best of the cheap hotels; **E** *East End*, Gen Thimaya Rd, T 26496, 7 rm, restaurant, bar, charming traditional style local hotel, courtyard with views over Madikeri, clean and neat, but limited accommodation can often mean it is fully booked, good restaurant, excellent dosas; **E** Karnataka Tourism *Mayura Valley View*, Raja's Seat, T 26387, 19 rm, restaurant, good value, perched on clifftop, outstanding views over town and across the rolling forests, looks very run down outside, but inside the rm are airy, desperately needs some investment but friendly staff, tranquil and hassle free atmosphere, book direct or at Karnataka Tourism, 10/4 Mithra Towers, Kasturba Gandhi Rd, Bangalore; **E** *Vinayaka Lodge*, 25m from bus stand, T 26230, 50 rm, but only 4/5 ever let to visitors, attached bath, hot water buckets, TV lounge, clean and quiet, despite its unpromising external surroundings of open sewer and bus stand.

F *Tourist Bungalow*, Munnar Rd, T 26580, very basic, tourist office next door.

● Banks & money changers

State Bank of India, College Rd. **Indian Overseas Bank** and **Canara Bank**, Main Rd.

● Post & telecommunications

Post Office: behind the private bus station.

● Tour companies & travel agents

Kamadenu Travels above Private Bus Stand, T 27024, for booking Super Deluxe bus with Purnima Travels.

● Tourist office

Munnar Rd, next to Tourist Bungalow.

● Transport

It is only possible to reach Kodagu by road.

Road Bus: express buses ½ hrly to **MysoreF255D, 0630-2300; Bangalore**, 0600-2300; **Mangalore**, 0615-2030; **Thalassery**, 0530-1730; **Kannur**, 0530-1715; **Chikmagalur**, 0700-1430. Every 1½ hr to **Hassan** , 0650-1930. Purnima Travels bus to Bangalore, 0745. Bus tours are available from Bangalore and Mysore. Ordinary buses run regularly between Kannur or Thalassery on the Kerala coast and Virajpet and Madikeri (Mercara) and on to Mysore and Bangalore. In addition Madikeri is connected by direct buses with Madurai, Coimbatore and Ooty.

Madikeri to Mangalore

ROUTES The road drops quickly down the ghats through rubber, coconut and new cocoa plantations, forests and a series of small towns and villages. A number of bus routes follow this road.

Sampanje, 27 km from Madikeri, is a very attractive village built in the W coast style, in a valley at the foot of the Ghats. There is a lovely river crossing, and hedges are still common. In a further 4 km the road crosses the Kodagu-S Kanara border to the village of Kalugulli, where there is a coffee shop. The road continues down the valley, lined with mature rubber plantations interspresed with dense forest, and spices such as cloves and cinnamon. The road runs along the right bank of the River Chandragiri through mixed teak and coconut forests to Sullia (21 km).

Sullia The village is a long and busy street. There are several small hotels and bars. To the N of the bus stand are the modest *Gopika*, *Supari* and Annapurna Woodlands hotels. There is also an *Inspection Bungalow*. The road from Sullia to Puttur continues to descend through mixed forests. There are some striking outcrops of bright red lateritic soil, and occasional cocoa plantations.

Subrahmanya Four km W of Sullia

a road runs to the important pilgrimage centre associated with Subrahmanya, an ancient Dravidian folk-god known in Tamil as Murugan, "divine child". See page 941. He was later identified with Skanda the God of War, but is known by a wide variety of names and in S India in particular is believed to have power over illness. The shrine in these quiet forested hills marks a spot where the nagas (cobras) are believed to have sought Subrahmanya's protection which he provided in local caves. At the shrine he is worshipped in the form of a snake. There is a huge 150 year old temple car (*ratha*) which is processed during the Nov-Dec fair, when thousands of people congregate at the temple.

Puttur (*STD Code*: 08251) Typical of many minor towns along the SW coast, Puttur is strung out along a narrow winding road constantly humming with different activities. It shows all the signs of thriving business and rapid modernisation, including computer software firms, electronics, and share investment advisers. When the by-pass is completed it will reduce some of the pressure. Note the autorickshaws in this region of coastal Karnataka which all have a small boot for luggage. The Madre Deus Church near the town centre witnessess to the presence of a sizeable Christian community.

- **Accommodation** In several hotels and Guest houses. **E** *Rama*, GL Complex, Main Rd, (N side of town), T 7060, 33 rm (better at back), 1 a/c, modern, clean, good veg restaurant.

- **Transport Road Bus**: Puttur is served by express buses linking Mangalore with Bangalore, Mysore, Madikeri and several other long distance destinations.

ROUTES Puttur the road joins the NH 48 at Mani and crosses the Netravathi River over a one-way bridge at Panemangalore. There are beautiful views from here of the Netravathi estuary. **Buntwal** (26 km from Puttur) has the small hotel *Rajesh* less than 100m from the bus stand. The road continues along the N bank of the Netravathi through Adyar village to Mangalore.

BANGALORE TO MANGALORE via Sravanabelagola, Halebid & Belur

This route crosses the open plains of the Mysore plateau, intensively cultivated where irrigation is possible from tanks or occasionally wells. It is the land of the Vokkaliga caste, the dominant agricultural community of S Karnataka, traditionally at loggerheads with the reformist Lingayats of the N districts. The NH 4, the main route to Bombay, is lined with banyan and eucalyptus, with broad views across parkland scenery.

Nelamangala (26 km; *STD Code*: 08118) is an important market town. The Mangalore road (NH 48) leaves the NH 4, and after 20 km the road passes through the S end of the Devarayadurga hills (highest point 1387m), formed out of the underlying Closepet granites.

Kunigal (45 km; *Population*: 23,200; *STD Code*: 08132), is a bustling town with the stud farm of the Bangalore Turf Club, a college and tile factories. In Nelligere (35 km) mulberry is grown for the silk industry. Turn off the NH 48 to the 10th century Jain shrines at Kambadahalli which also has a horse stud farm.

Kambadahalli

(15 km) The shrines at Kambadahalli have many features in common with the contemporary Chola temples in Tamil Nadu; clearly defined mouldings on the base, walls divided by pilasters, and shrines with stepped towers rising above them. The Panchakutu Basti has 3 shrines, housing *Adinatha* (the father of the Jain saint Gommateshwara) in the S shrine, *Neminatha* in the E and *Santinatha* in the W (note the high relief carvings on the ceiling). There are many excellent sculptures, including a seated Jain figure.

A visit to Kambadahalli can serve as an hors d'oeuvre to seeing one of the

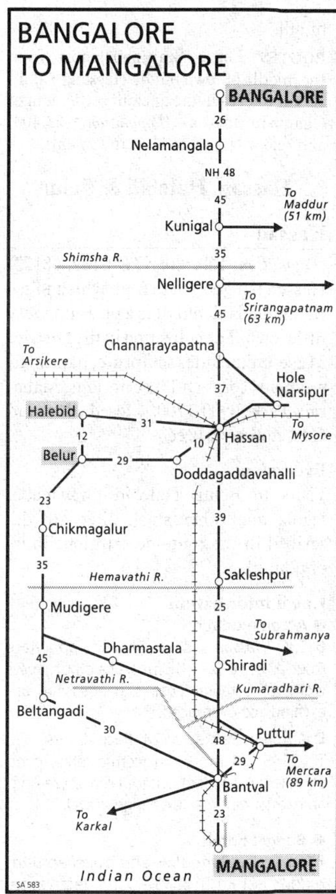

marvels of Jain sculpture, the colossal monolithic statue of Shri Gommatesvara at Sravanabelagola, one of the most visited pilgrimage sites in India and a centre for Digambara Jains.

Continue from Nagamangala towards Channarayapatna. Sravanabelagola (20 km) lies between 2 bare granite hills.

Sravanabelagola (Shravanabelgola)

(*Altitude*: 930m) The statue of **Gommatesvara** stands on **Vindhyagiri** (sometimes known as Indrabetta or Indragiri) to the S, rising 150m above the plain while **Chandragiri** to the N (also known as *Chikka Betta*) is just under half that height. The statue was erected at some time between AD 980 and 983. Just over 17m high, it represents the saintly prince **Bahubali**, son of the first Tirthankara, after he had gained enlightenment. Having fought a fierce war with his brother Bharata over the rights to succession, Bahubali accepted defeat when he had won the battle because he recognised its futility. Passing on his kingdom to his defeated brother, Bahubali adopted a life of meditation. The statue is nude (possibly as he is a Digambara or 'sky clad' Jain) and captures the tranquillity typical of much Buddhist and Jain art. The depth of the saint's meditation and withdrawal from the world is suggested by the spiralling creepers shown growing up his legs and arms, and by the ant hills and snakes at his feet. He is shown standing on a lotus. While the features are finely carved, the overall proportions are odd, with greatly enlarged shoulders, lengthened arms but shortened legs.

To reach the statue climb up nearly 700 steps carved in the steep granite slope, starting near the village tank. (Shoes must be removed. The granite gets extremely hot; thick socks are rec. Dholis are available at the foot of Indragiri to carry visitors up the steps.) The path up gives excellent views. There are several small shrines on the way to the statue on top. In order these are the **Odeagal Basti**, the **Brahmadeva mandapa**, the **Akhanda Bagilu** and the **Siddhara Basti**, all built in the 12th century except the Brahmadeva Mandapa which is 200 years older. Several are intricately carved.

Sravanabelagola is often crowded with visitors. Every 12th year it is the focus for Jain pilgrims from across India to celebrate the **Mastakabhisheka** – the 'magnificent anointment', or sacred head-anointing ceremony. The night before the ceremony 1008 pots – 'kalashas' – holding sacred water are sold by auction to devotees. The pots are left at the statue's feet overnight, and the following morning the water is poured over the statue's head from specially erected scaffolding. The water is followed by *ghi*, milk, coconut water, turmeric paste, honey and vermilion powder. Some even sprinkle gold dust. Unlike many festivals in India, the event is watched by the thousands of devotees in complete silence. The next celebration will be between 2006-2008.

In the town itself is the **Bhandari basti** (1159 and added to later), about 200m to the left from the path leading up to the Gommatesvara statue. Inside are 24 images of Tirthankaras in a spacious sanctuary. There are 500 rock-cut steps to the top of the hill and it takes about 30 min to climb. It is safe to leave luggage at the Tourist Office branch at the entrance (closed 1300-1415). There are 14 shrines on **Chandragiri** and the Mauryan Emperor Chandragupta, who is believed by some to have become a Jain and left his Empire to fast and meditate, is buried here. The temples are all in the Dravidian style, the Chamundaraya Basti, built in 982 AD being one of the most remarkable. There is a good example of a freestanding pillar or *mana-stambha* in front of the Parsvanathasvami Basti. These pillars, sometimes as high as 15m, were placed at the temple entrance. Here, the stepped base with a square cross-section transforms to a circular section and the column is then topped by a capital. **Accommodation** All facilities are very basic. **F** *Tourist Canteen cum Rest House*, 50 rm, reserve direct or at Karnataka Tourism, 9 St Mark's Rd, Bangalore, T 579139; **F** *Travellers Bungalow*, reservations: Chief Exec Officer, Taluk Board, Chennarayapatna, Hassan Dist. Several tea and coffee shops, cold drink stalls. Canteen at the bus station. Veg restaurants and **F** *Shriyans Prasad Guest House*, a pilgrim's guest house, at foot of hill.

ROUTES Leave Sravanabelagola from the middle of town on the Hassan road. In 10 km you reach the ancient settlement of Channarayapatna (*Population*: 23,400) and rejoin NH 48 to Hassan (36 km).

Hassan, Halebid & Belur

Hassan

(*Population*: 108,500; *STD Code*: 08172) Hassan is a good base from which to see Belur and Halebid. It is a pleasant, busy little town. The collection in the **District Museum** includes sculpture, paintings, weapons, coins and inscriptions. Maharaja Park. 0900-1700. Closed Mon and Govt holidays. Free.

Excursions

Visits to Belur, Halebid, Sravanabelagola and other small sites are described in the route description. Tours organised.

Local information

● Accommodation

B ITDC *Hassan Ashok* BM Rd, opp Race Course Rd, T 68731, 46 rm, half a/c (not always working), restaurant, bar, exchange, shop, unexciting and overpriced.

D *Amblee Palika*, 4724 Race Course Rd, T 67145, 34 rm, clean, comfortable, good value (esp cheaper rm without carpet), reasonable restaurant, bar, exchange, travel.

● Budget hotels

F *Inspection Bungalow and Travellers Bungalow*, BM Rd, T 68437, 7 rm, reservation: Exec Engineer, PWD, Hassan Div, BM Rd, T 68437, no facilities, but cheap, mainly for Govt officials; **F** *Vaishnavi Lodging*, Harsha Mahal Rd, E of bus station, T 67413, clean, spacious, good veg restaurant; **F** *Satyaprakash Lodge*, Bus Stand Rd, T 68521, S of bus station, excellent value; **F** *New Abhiruchi* BM Rd, W of city circle, T 68885, very good veg restaurant downstairs. Very clean, walking distance of Bus Stand, excellent value, rec; **F** *Railway Retiring Room*, 1 rm only (2 km from centre).

● Places to eat

Several reasonable places, mainly S Indian and veg food, all grouped close by 200m S of bus

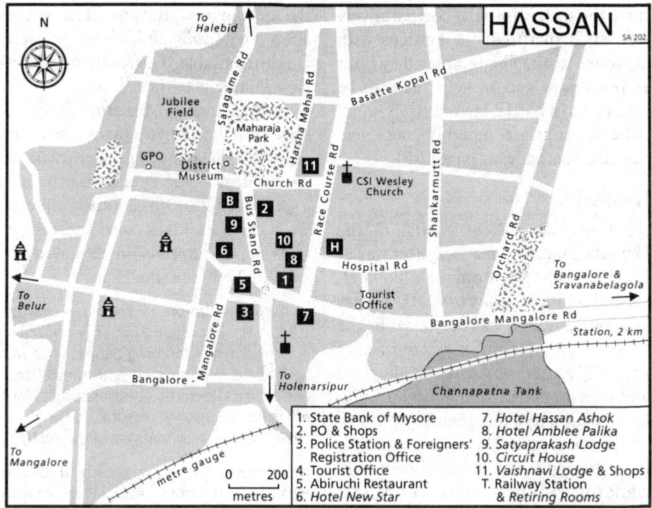

station. *Hassan Ashok*, the most expensive, good *thalis*, otherwise mediocre. *Abiruchi*, (N Indian, Chinese); *New Star* (non-veg Indian), cheap but good; *Shantala*, nr Bus Station, (good S Indian meals); a/c *Prasanna* (N Indian).

● Banks & money changers

State Bank of India, Aurobindo Complex. Others on Narasimharaja Circle.

● Post & telepgraph

Post Office: 100m from town centre bus stand.

● Hospitals & medical services

General Hospital, Hospital Rd and *Mission Hospital*, Race Course Rd.

● Travel agents & tour companies

Cauvery Tourist Centre, Race Course Rd, T 68026. The Govt Tourist Office has daily conducted tours from Bangalore and thrice weekly from Mysore.

● Tourist office

Vartha Bhavan, BM Rd, T 68862.

● Transport

Local Buses: The Bus Stand, T 68418. **Taxis**: Private Tourist Taxis can be hired from Cauvery Tourist Centre, Race Course Rd, T 68026. **Tongas**: are also available.

Train Trains to Bangalore, Mangalore and Mysore.

Road Bus: regular buses to Sravanabelagola, Belur and Halebid and Bangalore (every ½ hr, 4½ hr), (Goa 14 hr), Hampi, Mangalore, Mysore (hourly, 3 hr) and others.

ROUTES Leave Hassan on NH 48, turn right for Doddagaddavahalli (10 km) on the Belur road.

Doddagaddavahalli

The comparatively plain **Lakshmidevi Temple**, built in 1113 in the early Hoysala style, is contemporary with the Belur temple but has virtually no sculpture on the outside. 4 shrines lead off a common square mandapa. The N shrine has an image of Kali, followed clockwise by Mahalakshmi, Bhairava (a form of Siva) and Bhutanatha. Continue NW to Belur (20 km).

The Hoysalas who ruled a large kingdom between the rivers Krishna and the Kaveri, made Belur and Halebid their capital. Although great warriors, culture and art were also patronised. The artisans were encouraged to rival each other and even sign their names on their work of art. Steatite gave the sculptors the opportunity to work with intricate detail since the rock is initially comparatively soft when quarried but hardens with exposure to air. The temples they built as prayers to god to help them to be victorious in battle, are relatively small structures but are superbly conceived. See also Somnathpur page 1010.

Halebid

(25 km) The ancient capital of the Hoysala Empire is reached after travelling through picturesque hilly landscape. Founded in the early 11th century as **Dvarasamudra**, was destroyed by the armies of the Delhi Sultanate in 1311 and 1327, after which it was deserted and later renamed Halebid (Old Capital). Fortunately the great temple survived. The famous Hoysalesvara temple is to the right, but it would be worthwhile first visiting the 12th century **Jain Bastis** about 1 km S. These are remarkably plain, with lathe-turned and multi-faceted columns but are interesting. Several bastis in a garden enclosure, which you can walk around and see the dark interiors with carved ceilings within 15 min.

The **Hoysalesvara Temple** set with lawns around, has 2 shrines, one dedicated to Siva and the other to Santeleswara with a *Nandi* bull facing each. The largest of the Hoysala temples, it was started in 1121 but remained unfinished 86 years later. In structure it is similar to the one at Belur, but its superstructure was never completed. There are extraordinary half life-size statues of Hindu deities, with minute details of each, all around the temple. These, and the 6 bands of sculpture below, show the excellence of the artisans' craft. The lines of elephants at the base, followed by lions and then horsemen, a floral scroll and then most impressive of all, at eye level, stories from the epics and the Bhagavata Purana. This frieze relates incidents from the Ramayana and Mahabharata among them Krishna lifting Mount Govardhana, Rama defeating the demon god Ravana. The friezes above show *yalis* and *hamsa* or geese. Guides available. The smaller Kedaresvara Temple is to the SE.

Archaeological Museum 1000-1700, closed Fri. Free. There is a small museum on the lawn near the S entrance where the Archaeological Survey of India maintains a gallery of 12th-13th century sculptures, wood carvings, idols, coins and inscriptions. Some sculptures are displayed outside. To the W is a small lake.

• **Accommodation** F *Tourist Cottages*, T 24, in the Inspection Bungalow compound in nice garden overlooking temple, 4 rm with fan and mosquito nets and bath, simple, modern, limited kitchen facilities, restaurant. *Travellers Bungalow*, reservations: Asst Engineer, PWD, Halebid. Also some tea stalls nearby.

• **Services** There is a branch of **Canara** Bank, a **Post Office**, and a **Photography** shop.

• **Transport Road Bus**: Karnataka SRTC bus connections with Hassan and from there to Bangalore, Mangalore and Mysore. Bus Stand, 2km from temples.

Belur

(12 km; *Population*: 16,800) On the banks of the Yagachi river, Belur was the capital of the dynasty before it was moved to Halebid. The temples stand in a courtyard with the **Chennakesava Temple** (1116) near the centre. One of the earliest of its type, started during the period when the great cathedrals of Europe such as Lincoln and Rheims were built, took a century to complete. It celebrated the Hoysala victory over the Cholas at Talakad. Dedicated to Krishna it stands in a courtyard surrounded by a rectangular wall, built on a star shaped platform with an ambulatory. The winged figure of **Garuda**, Vishnu's carrier, guards the entrance, facing the temple with joined palms.

At first glance the temple is unimpressive because the superstructure has been lost. However, exquisite sculptures cover the exterior with the friezes. The line of 650 elephants (each different) surround the base, with rows of figures and foliage above. The detail of the 38 female figures is perfect. Look at the young musicians and dancers on either side of the main door and the unusual perforated screens between the columns. 10 have typical bold geometrical patterns while the other 10 depict scenes from the *Puranas* in its tracery. Inside superb carving decorates the hand-lathe-turned pillars and the bracket-figures on the ceiling. Each round filigreed pillar is different and bears witness to individual sculptors producing a masterpiece in competition with each other. The unique Narasimha pillar at the centre of the hall is particularly fine and originally could be rotated. The detail is astounding. The jewellery on the figures is hollow and moveable and the droplets of water seem to hang at the ends of the dancer's wet hair on a bracket above you. On the platform in front of the shrine is the figure of Santalesvara dancing in homage to Lord Krishna. The annual *Car Festival* is held in Mar-Apr. To the W is the **Viranarayana Temple** which has some fine sculpture and smaller shrines around it. It is worth visiting the **Jain Bastis** a few km away although the decoration is incomplete on most.

• **Budget hotels** **E** Karnataka Tourism *Mayura Velapuri*, T 9, 2 simple, clean rm, reservations: Direct or through Karnataka Tourism, 10/4 Kasturba Gandhi Rd, Bangalore, T 578901. Other very inexpensive and basic accommodation in **F** *Vishnuprasad*, Main Rd, T 63, 12 rm and **F** *New Gayatri*, Main Rd, T 55, 7 rm.

• **Banks & money changers** On Temple Rd.

• **Transport Road Bus**: to Mysore, Mangalore, Mercara, Ariskere and Bangalore among others.

Over the Ghats to Mangalore

Chikmagalur

(23 km; *Population*: 60,800; *STD Code*: 08262). From Belur continue to the hill station of Chikmagalur (meaning literally 'younger daughter's town' – as it was the legendary gift (dowry) for the younger daughter of a local chieftain). In addition to the Hoysala style **Kodandarama temple** there are mosques, the moated fort and the new St Joseph's Roman Catholic Cathedral.

The town is at the centre of one of India's major **coffee** growing areas. To the N of Chikmagalur in the Baba Budan Range, coffee was first grown in 1670; the Central Coffee Research Institute, set up in 1925, now covers 120 ha. The district has curing works for the processing of raw coffee. Mar-Apr is the coffee flowering season, a beautiful time of year in the hills. Baba Budan Giri itself (1,895m) is 28 km N of Chikmagalur. Mullaiyanagiri, the highest point in the hills (1,926m), is one of the highest peaks S of the Himalaya. 3 large caves on the hill are widely believed to be sacred, and there is an annual pilgrimage.

The road NE from Chikmagalur to Kadur passes the beautiful tank built by Rukmangada Raya and renovated in 1156 during the Hoysala period at Ayyanakere. Receving a regular water supply from the Baba Budan Hills, the tank irrigates over 1,500 ha.

12 km SE of Chikmagalur on the Belur road is the small Hoysala temple village of **Marle**. The most important of the temples is the Chennakeshava, dating from 1150 AD. 10 km E of Halebid itself at **Belavadi** is the Veeranarayana temple, another superb example of Hoysala temple architecture.

From Chikmagalur the road runs SW along the E facing slopes of the Western Ghats rising to heights of over 1800m. **Mudigere** (35 km; *Population*: 7,800) The founder of the Hoysala dynasty, Sala, is believed to have killed a tiger in the Mudigere neighbourhood, which then became an emblem in the Hoysala crest.

The Mangalore road turns sharply W to cut through the hills, one of the wettest regions of India, and the road enters dense tropical forest. Wildlife abounds. Langur monkeys hang in the trees and squat by the roadside. Occasionally King cobras up to 3m in length slide across the road. The narrow strip of true tropical evergreen forest – no more than 20 km wide – is rich in varied species. Giant bamboos, often 40m high, arch gracefully, and even in the dry season the forest feels comparatively cool and damp.

A district road drops quite steeply down to **Beltangadi** (45 km) where it enters the small embayment around Mangalore formed by the Netravati River, which rises just N of Madikeri, and crosses a low laterite plateau between 50 and 120m above sea level, giving the bright red soils. The Netravathi has laid some alluvium over the ancient granites, but these break the surface from place to place. Rice becomes the dominant crop again but forestry is vital to the district as a whole. Teak, mainly as a plantation crop, and other timbers, plus bamboos, canes, honey and wax are important products. Cashew nuts, introduced by the Portuguese in the 16th century, grow wild as well as cultivated. The nuts are exported and processed for a variety of industrial uses – in paints and varnishes and for caulking boats. On the laterites, which are not fertile enough for rice, ragi and pulses are common. Just outside Beltangadi a road runs S to the important pilgrimage centre of Dharmasthala.

Dharmasthala

(Formerly Kuduma) 75 km from Mangalore, Dharmasthala is noted for both its shrine to Sri Manjunatha, and for the catholicity of its management. Served by Madhva Vaishnava priests, the Saivite temple is administered by a Jain trustee. The Jains have recently installed a massive, 12m-high monolith of Bahubali. The temple is also noted for its free distribution of meals to all visitors and pilgrims. During the festival of *Laksha Deepotsava* 100,000 lamps are lit. Pilgrims bathe in the River Netravathi, 3km away. The temple authorities run a museum, car museum and aquarium and several charitable trusts. Darshan for visitors to the shrine: 0630-1300; Darshan and Mahapuja 1900-2000.

From Beltangadi a minor road runs NW to **Venur** and Mudabidre. Both are famous Jain centres. Venur has a Gommateshwara 12m statue built in 1604 by Veera Thimanna Ajila IV

Mudabidri

Population: 25,000 Mudabidri (Moodabidri), sometimes described as the Jain Varanasi, has 18 Jain bastis, although Jains themselves are a tiny minority of the population. The 1000 pillar **Chandranatha Basti** (1429, dedicated on 18 January 1431), also known as Savira Kambada Basti, is a powerful presence in the centre of the town. 3 *mandapas* lead to the main sanctuary; they have a series of sloping tiered roofs, adapted to the heavy monsoon rainfall of the region, and the sanctuary itself is surmounted by a gabled roof. The main entrance, which faces E, opens onto a superb monolithic pillar (*mana-stambha*) in front of the main doorway. The temple has a valuable collection of metal , jewel-encrusted images of Jain tirthankars and superb monolithic columns, each in the Jain tradition, with a different carving. Although such columns are a common feature of Chalukyan architecture, the columns in the Mudabidri temple are extraordinary, being elaborately carved in astonishingly fine detail. There is a 2 m high *panchaloha* image of Chandratha.

The Jain *Math* (monastery) 100m E of the main temple entrance, has a library with some beautiful 12th and 13th century palm leaf manuscripts. Booklets on Mudabidri in English, Hindi and Kannada are available. The 17th century **Chowta Palace**, which is still occupied by descendents of the Royal Family, is also worth visiting for its beautifully carved wooden pillars, ceilings and screen.

Karkala, 17 km from Mudabidra has the 4th of the great monolithic statues of Gommateshwara in S India – the only ones in the world. It is now floodlit.

Sringeri

This is a small town surrounded by dense forests near the ridge of the Western Ghats and the source of the Tunga River, which joins the Bhadra to become the Tungabhadra, one of the great rivers of peninsular India. Sringeri is associated with Shankaracharya, the 7th century Advaitin philosopher, who established a monastery here. See page 70. The leaders of the modern *math* are widely revered by modern followers of Shankaracharya's philosophy, as authorities.

The **Vidyashankar temple** has a large courtyard. 12 pillars represent the signs of the zodiac, a huge lion being carved on the front of each; each has a large moveable stone ball in its mouth. The pillars are arranged to catch the rays of the sun during the appropriate period of the zodiac. The smaller Sharada Devi (Saraswati) temple on the left bank of the Tunga contains a much admired statue of the deity standing on a *Sri Chankra* (a *yantra*). This is the main focus of activity in the town. **Transport** Buses link Sringeri with Udupi and Chitradurga and many long distance destinations including Mangalore, Bangalore and Mysore.

ROUTES The road runs through Bantval (30 km; *Population*: 34,000) to Mangalore (23 km) between the Hassan-Mangalore railway and the right bank of the Netravathi River.

Mangalore

Population: 425,800; *STD Code*: 0824 Capital of S Kanara District, Mangalore is a minor port, but handling 75% of India's coffee exports and the bulk of its cashew nuts. The modern port is 10 km N of the town.

In the 14th and 15th centuries Mangalore traded with Persian and Arab merchants and was fought over by the Nayaka princes and the Portuguese. In the 18th century its control was contested by **Haidar Ali** (who made it his centre for shipbuilding) and his son Tipu Sultan on the one hand, and the British on the other. Its modern economy is dominated by agricultural processing and port related activities. Cashew nuts are brought from many coastal areas for processing and export (notably from Kerala, where 90% of India's cashews are grown, and there is a national cashew Research Centre at Puttur, inland. Mangalore's other claim to fame is that it produces Ganesh **Bidis** (the cheap alternative to cigarettes), a few pieces of tobacco wrapped in a leaf tied with thread. The leaf varies, one used is from the Camel's Foot Tree (*Bauhinia*).

Places of interest

St Aloysius College Chapel on Light House Hill is sometimes referred to as 'the Sistine Chapel' of S India. The 19th century frescoes painted by the Italian trained Jesuit priest Moscheni, cover the walls and ceilings in a profusion of scenes, though some might feel the comparison with Michelangelo a little stretched. The town has a sizeable Roman Catholic population (about 1/5).

The tile-roofed low structure of the 10th century **Mangaladevi Temple** is named after a Malabar Princess, Mangala Devi, who is believed to have given her name to Mangalore. **Kadri Caves** and **Sri Manjunatha Temple** are set in attractive gardens, now partly an amusement park for children. The temple dates back to 1068, and its central image of Lokeshwara is a remarkable bronze.

There are also lakes which have water with medicinal properties, and the Old Lighthouse dating from the 18th cen-

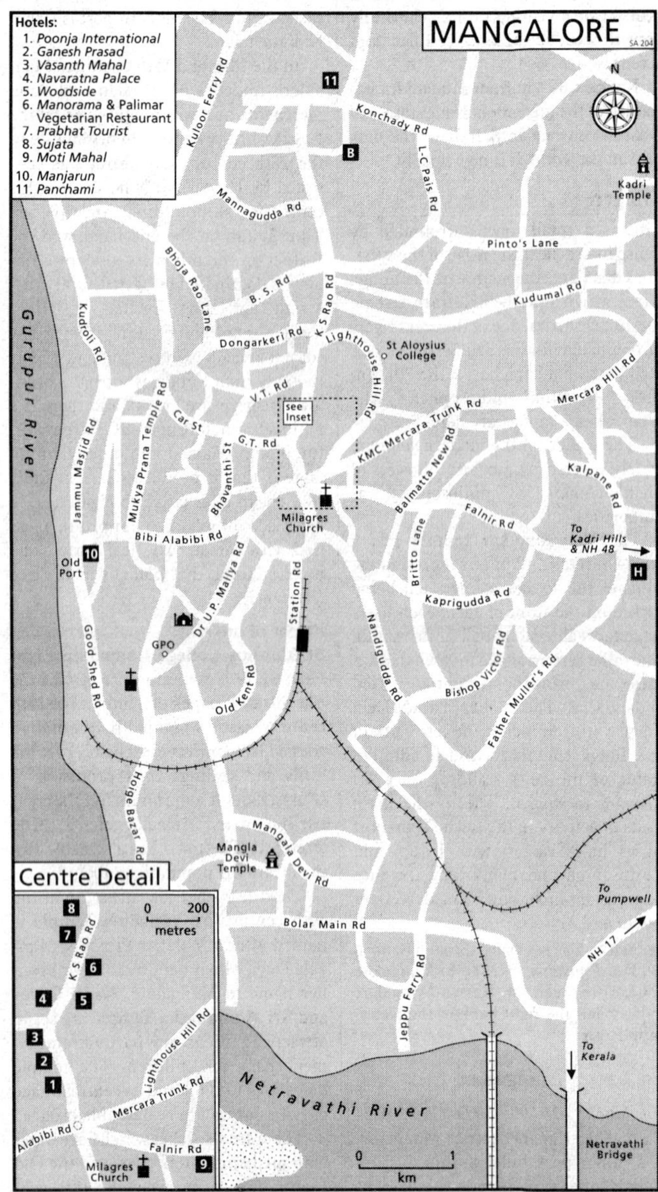
MANGALORE
SA 204
Hotels:
1. Poonja International
2. Ganesh Prasad
3. Vasanth Mahal
4. Navaratna Palace
5. Woodside
6. Manorama & Palimar Vegetarian Restaurant
7. Prabhat Tourist
8. Sujata
9. Moti Mahal
10. Manjarun
11. Panchami
Kuloor Ferry Rd
Konchady Rd
L-C Pais Rd
Kadri Temple
Mannagudda Rd
Pinto's Lane
Bhoja Rao Lane
B. S. Rd
K S Rao Rd
Kudumal Rd
Gurupur River
Kudroli Rd
Dongarkeri Rd
Lighthouse Hill Rd
St Aloysius College
Mercara Hill Rd
V.T. Rd
Mukya Prana Temple Rd
see Inset
Mercara Trunk Rd
Jammu Masjid Rd
Car St
G.T. Rd
KMC Mercara Trunk Rd
Balmatta New Rd
Kalpane Rd
Bhavanthi St
Milagres Church
Falnir Rd
Bibi Alabibi Rd
To Kadri Hills & NH 48
Old Port
Britto Lane
Station Rd
Dr U.P. Mallya Rd
Kaprigudda Rd
Nandigudda Rd
Good Shed Rd
GPO
Bishop Victor Rd
Father Muller's Rd
Old Kent Rd
Hoige Bazar Rd
Mangala Devi Rd
Mangla Devi Temple
Bolar Main Rd
To Pumpwell
NH 17
Jeppu Ferry Rd
To Kerala
Netravathi River
Netravathi Bridge
0 1 km
Centre Detail
0 200 metres
K S Rao Rd
Lighthouse Hill Rd
Mercara Trunk Rd
Alabibi Rd
Falnir Rd
Milagres Church

tury. It is generally believed to have been built by Hyder Ali, who built a naval dockyard in Mangalore. Just to the E is an Idgah. You can take a trip out to the sand bar at the river mouth to watch fascinating boat building and river traffic on the Netravathi River. Mangalore Port is now India's 9th largest cargo handling port. In addition to exporting coffee from the hills inland it imports a variety of goods, including tropical timber from SE Asia for furniture making, a necessity since India placed major restrictions on its own teak felling.

Excursion

Suratkal Beach, 15 km from the town centre, is near the promontory on which the new lighthouse stands. A steep path connects the lighthouse to the Sadasiva Temple. The beach is very popular with Mangaloreans, especially on holidays. **Transport** The beach is on the bus route Nos 40, 41 and 45.

Museums

Shremmanti Bai Memorial Museum 0900-1700, closed Mon. Free. Collection includes archaeology, ethnology, porcelain and wood carvings. **Mahatma Gandhi Museum**, Canara High School. 0930-1230, 1400-1730, closed Sun and holidays. Free. Collection includes zoology, anthropology, sculpture, art, coins and manuscripts.

Local information

● Accommodation

C *Manjarun* (formerly Welcomgroup), Old Port Rd, T 420420, 103 rm, some with sea view, restaurant, bar, pool, wide range of facilities, 5-min drive from rly, nr sea and harbour, friendly service.

The older **D** *Moti Mahal*, Falnir Rd, T 22211, F 33097, 90 rm, 53 a/c, a/c restaurant and bar, coffee shop, shops, pool, reasonable value; **D** *Poonja International*, KS Rao Rd, T 440171, 154 rm, central a/c, wide range of facilities, new multi-storey hotel, spotlessly clean, excellent value; **D** *Srinivas*, Ganapathi HS Rd, T 22381, 50 rm, 23 a/c, 1 km rly, restaurant, bar, exchange, travel, shops, indoor games; **D** *Swagath's Panchamahal*, Kodialbail, T 36003, 56 rm, restaurant, central; **D** *Summer Sands Beach Resort* at Chotamangalore, Ullal (10 km), T 6400, 128 rm, 49 a/c in cottages and bungalows, restaurant, bar, travel, good pool, imaginatively designed in the local style with a superb beach, good value.

● Budget hotels

E *Navaratna Palace*, KS Rao Rd, T 441104, 56 rm, 13 a/c with TV, a/c restaurant, bar, exchange, travel, very central, immaculate, excellent value; **E** *Manorama*, KS Rao Rd, T 440306, 65 rm (TV extra); **E** 3 good *Railway Retiring Rooms* with cheaper dorm beds.

F Karnataka Tourism *Mayura Netravati*, Kadri Hills (3 km), T 24192, 18 rm and dorm, restaurant, bar; **F** *Vasanth Mahal*, KS Rao Rd, T 441311, 73 rm, very cheap – and very cramped and basic; **F** *Panchami*, opp entrance to bus stand, simple, basic but adequate, convenient one-night stop.

● Places to eat

Embers for open-air dinners by the pool and *Galley* at *Manjarun Hotel*, both expensive but good, reservations rec. *Taj Mahal* and *Navratna* both nr the Bus Stand, serve very good veg meals. The big hotels have **bars**.

● Sports

Sailing, boating and tennis at the *Summer Sands Beach Resort* at Chotamangalore.

● Transport

Air Bajpe airport is 25 km out of town. **Indian Airlines**: **Bangalore & Madras**: M,Tu,Th,Sa, 1015, ¾ hr & 2 hr; **Bombay**: daily (+ 1 other), 0755, 1¼ hr; **Madras**: daily. Indian Airlines office, Moti Mahal Hotel, T 4669. **East West**: **Bombay**: daily, 1255, 1¼ hr. **Jet Airways**: **Bombay**: daily, 1110, 1¼ hr.

Train Mangalore is at the N end of the broad gauge line which goes down the coast to Kozhikode and then inland to Coimbatore, connecting with all major destinations. **Madras, via Kannur & Kozhikode**: *Mangalore Mail* 6002 (AC/II), daily, 1240, 18 hr.

Road Bus: the Mangalore bus stand , 3 km N of town centre, is clean and well-organised. The booking hall at the entrance has a computer printout of the full timetable in English, and the main indicator board has a colour scheme for different categories of bus: red – ordinary; blue – semi-deluxe; green – super-deluxe. Bus connections to the E and N are much shorter and quicker than train. **Bangalore &**

Mysore: 405 km & 296 km, ½ hrly. The route through Madikeri is the most pleasant; **Madras**: 717 km, 1345; **Madurai**: 691 km, 1500. Express buses can be reserved up to 7 days in advance.

MANGALORE TO GOA via the Kanara coast

The road up what the Karnataka Tourist Board now calls "the sapphire coast" to Goa is one of the least travelled scenic routes in India. This is partly because the coast road crosses numerous broad estuaries, many of which have only recently bridged. Furthermore, a part of the colonial legacy was the absence of any direct coastal rail link north from Mangalore to Bombay. This is now being rectified by the building of the new Konkan Railway, work on which is well under weigh, although parts of the route have still to be finalised. The route runs through some strikingly beautiful country. The Western Ghats are never far away to the east, while the road frequently skirts the Arabian Sea, in the north passing some magnificent beaches.

The road N passes through Mangalore's suburbs to Kullur and the New Mangalore Port. Kullur has a good, modern hotel. **D** *Cauvery International*, on NH 17 nr Katarqa Chowk, T 414861, 50 rm, restaurant. For several kilometres the National Highway runs through the rapidly industrialising outskirts of the Mangalore, including the Kudremukh Iron Works, processing ore from 80 km inland, the timber and granite export yards of Panambor and the marble and stone works around Kollai Village.

Suratkal At the junction with the road to Mangalore airport in the new **D** *Hotel Lalitha*, modern and reasonable. After 5 km the road crosses the River Paranje. In Mulki (7 km) there is a turn to the Durga Parameshwari Temple. 6 km fter crossing the River Shambari another road leads into the Ghats and Kudremukh. At this point is a signpost to Bombay – 1002 km.

Katpadi The small roadside village is famous for its Mangalore Maliga Maylur – beautiful flowers widely used for garlands. There are usually women selling the flowers by the roadside. 4 km before reaching Udupi the road crosses the River Papanashini.

Udupi

(*Population*: 117,700; *STD Code*: 08252) Udupi (also known as Udipi) is one of Karnataka's most important pilgrimage sites being the birthplace of the 12th century saint Madhva, who set up 8 sanyasi *maths* (monasteries) in the town. See page 70.

Sri Krishna Math, Car Street. According to one legend the statue of Krishna once turned to give a low caste devotee darshan. The temple, set in the heart of the town, is a low building set around a large and attractive tank, the Madhava Sarovar, into which devotees believe that the Ganga flows every 10 years. A boat is used on the tank for major ceremonies, notably the biennial *Paraya Mahotsava* (festival), held on 17 or 18 Jan every even-numbered year, when the temple management changes hands. The priest-in-charge is the head of each of the 8 *maths* in turn. Thousands of pilgrims visit the temple for the occasion. In common with a number of important Hindu temples it is of far greater religious than architectural importance, and receives a succession of highly placed political leaders.

Sri Ananthasana Temple, where Sri Madhvacharya is believed to have dematerialised while teaching his followers, is in the centre of the temple square. The 8 important *maths* are around Car St: Sode, Puthige and Adamar (S); Pejawar and Palamar (W); Krishna and Shirur (N); and Kaniyur (E). Udipi is almost as well known today as the home of a family of Kanarese Brahmins who have established a chain of coffee house/hotels across S India.

Museum Rashtrakavi Govind Pai Museum, MGM College, **Manipal**, 5 km from Udupi. It has a collection of sculpture, bronze, inscriptions and coins and is famous throughout Karnataka as the centre of the Yakshagana dance drama, which like Kathakali in Kerala is an all night spectacle.

• **Accommodation D** *Kediyoor*, Shiribeedu, nr bus stand, T 22381, 54 rm, some a/c, clean modern hotel, good restaurant. **F** *Mallika*, KM Marg, nr Sanskrit College, T 21121, 40 rm (3 more expensive a/c), restaurant, fairly modern and reasonable value; **F** *Sindhnur Palace*, on road into town, nr *Hotel Mallika*, 30 rm, T 20791, not a palace, but adequate basic accommodation. **E** *Karavali*, W of the by-pass nr Malpe turning, a large, clean and modern hotel; **E** *Sharada*, E of by-pass, another modern hotel. **In Manipal**: **E** *Valley View*, T 20285, 50 rm; **E** *Green Park*, T 20851, 38 rm.

• **Banks & money changers** State Bank of India, opp Affan Complex.

• **Transport Road Bus**: frequent service to Mangalore. Also mornings and evenings to Bangalore and Mysore (1st bus 0600); Hubli, approx hrly from 0900; Dharmasthala, frequent from 0600-0945, 1400-1830; Bombay 4 buses daily, 1120, 1520, 1700, 1920.

Malpe, 5 km W of Udupi, is one of the best port sites in S Karnataka. Across the bay is the island of Darya Bahadurgarh and 5 km to the SW is **St Mary's Isle**, composed of dramatic hexagonal basalt. Inaugurating a new era for S Asia, Vasco da Gama made his first landfall in India on this island and set up a cross. Malpe is an important fishing port today. Although some tourist brochures say it is an ideal place to swim, there is usually a powerful smell of fish.

From Udupi a road goes inland to Sringeri and the Jain temples at Karkal and Mudabidri. See page 1030.

The coast road north from Udupi

ROUTES The road N from Udupi crosses the Swarna Bridge. In the village of Brahmavara a road runs E to Sringeri, while the NH 17 continues over the River Seeta to Khumbashi and Kundapura.

Kundapura (formerly Coondapur), another small port, served the Rajas of Bednur about 50 km inland. The 16th century Portuguese fort survives. **Accommodation E** *Sharon*, NH 17, S of town at junc of by-pass and city road, nr Tourist bus stop, T 6623, 54 rm, some a/c, modern, spacious, airy and clean, good restaurant, rec.

Two km N of Kundapura is a large tileworks, one of several while provide roof tiles for much of S India. There are lovely views of the ghats to the E, and the road passes mangrove swamps and crosses the Kollur and Uppunda Rivers. Just N of the village of Byndoor the road rises sharply to cross a laterite plateau with an landscape dominated by sparse scrub.

Bhatkal (*STD Code*: 08385) There is one of the many bullock cart tracks that used to be the chief means of access from the coast over the often apparently impenetrable Western Ghats from **Bhatkal**. Now only a small town with a predominantly Muslim population, in the 16th century it was the main port of the Vijayanagar Empire. It also 2 interesting small temples. From the N the Jain Chandranatha Basti (17th century) with 2 buildings linked by a porch, is approached first. The use of stone tiling is a particularly striking reflection of local climatic conditions, and is a feature of the Hindu to its S, a 17th century Vijayanagar temple with typical animal carvings.

• **Accommodation F** *Vaibhav Lodge*, very basic.

• **Transport Road Bus**: direct bus to Jog Falls at 0600 from the bus station (2 hr). Later buses take 3 hr.

The road N along the coast is followed for long stretches by the new Konkan railway, still under construction in 1994. Just N of Shirali a road leads down to the shore temple of Sri Murdeshwar, and 12 km further N reaches Manki and the Sharavathi River (a further 13 km). Jog Falls is just 20 km inland, accessible from this point only to 4-wheel drive vehicles, and even then with difficulty from **Manki**. The 1½ km long road bridge was damaged in 1982 and buses and heavy traffic have to take the ferry. Two km N of the bridge is the excellent *Kamat Restaurant*, serving veg meals. Buses stop just outside.

Honavar (18 km; *Population*: 16,200) The W coast has a long wet season and high total rainfall, as shown by the figures for Honavar. The contrast with the peninsula, as shown by Bellary (see page 1110), is striking.

Kumta (20 km) is raised on another laterite plateau, but unlike Bhatkal is surrounded by green vegetation, with a wide variety of trees including commercially grown cashew nuts. Kumta itself has another excellent *Kamat Restaurant* on the NH 17, which crosses the River Haganashini. There are superb views along the river. A turn inland at Mirjan goes to Sirsi (50 km) and Hubli (156 km).

North from Mirjan to Ankola, Karwar and Goa

Gokarna After another 19 km a turn to the W leads 2 km to another shore temple, dedicated to Siva, on an attractive site at Gokarna. The temple is famous for its Atmalinga, which Ganesh is believed to have fooled the demon Ravana into putting down on the spot where it now stands. As Ravana was unable to lift it again once he had put it down the linga is known as Mahabala (the strong one). The Tambraparni Teertha is widely regarded as a particularly sacred river in which to put the ashes of the dead. Today Gorkarna is a centre of Sanskrit learning. **Accommodation** Tourist Dept **F** *Guest House*, on hill top overlooking the sea.

The coastal region is noted for its salt production. 3 km N of the Gokarna turning the Gangavli River cuts through a deeply incised valley in the laterite plateau, and travelling north the Western Ghats begin to approach very close to the road.

Ankola (30 km; *Population*: 13,600) Ankola has the remains of a fort and a beautiful beach.

Karwar (37 km; *Population*: 51,000; *STD Code*: 08382) Also has beautiful beaches to rival those of Goa less than 100 km to the N, but still deserted. From the Hattikari Bridge to Karwar (28 km) the road runs through alternating sections of forested hills and bays, sometimes with fantastic views. The road runs along the coconut fringed W coast, studded with inlets and bays. Karwar has a deep-water port, now being developed for naval use, and superb beaches. It is the administrative headquarters of N Kanara Dist on the banks of the Kalinadi River. From 1638 to 1752 there was an English settlement, surviving on the pepper trade. The Portuguese held it for nearly 50 years from 1752 before the old town was destroyed in 1801. **Accommodation** **D** *Bhadra*, on NH 17 4 km N of Karwar, T 5212, 20 rm, some a/c, lovely views over estuary, a modern hotel on the main road.

CLIMATE: HONAVAR

	Jan	Feb	Mar	Apr	May	Jun	Jul	Aug	Sep	Oct	Nov	Dec	Av/Tot
Max (°C)	29	29	31	32	32	31	29	28	28	29	30	29	30
Min (°C)	21	22	24	26	27	25	24	24	24	24	23	21	24
Rain (mm)	2	2	2	18	66	752	793	404	241	97	33	5	2415

The road crosses the Kali River (car toll of Rs5) then reaches the Goa border and checkpost (8 km). In Goa the NH 17 becomes a narrow and winding wooded road to the small town of Maxem (10 km). It passes through the small towns of Bhatpal (12 km) and Canacona (4 km). There is a vegetarian *Udupi Restaurant* in town. **Palolem Beach** , 2 km off the main road, is an attractive little campsite with minimal facilities and right off the beaten track, set in a lovely bay overlooking an island. Buses from Chauri to Margao. See page 1226. It is 40 km to Margao.

BANGALORE TO GOA via Jog Falls

Two roads lead to Shimoga and Jog Falls. The better and quicker route take the NH 48 to Hassan, then goes N via Belur to Chikmagalur, Tarikere and Bhadravati. The shorter but slower route, sometomes with very poor road surfaces, takes the NH 4 to Tumkur, then follows district roads through Gubbi, Arsikere and Kadur to Tarikere. After the open plains of the Mysore plateau, the route passes the Baba Bhudan hills where coffee was first grown in 1670 and the impressive Jog Falls. A short diversion leads to some beautiful, unspoilt beaches, whilst the coastal road goes through several historic ports.

NW to Jog Falls

Bhadravati (*Population*: 150,000; *STD Code*: 081826) An industrial town, is on the edge of the **Baba Bhudan Hills**. Scenically beautiful, the hills are an important sources of iron ore and the centre of a major coffee growing region. The Mysore Iron and Steel Co set up a plant here in 1923, making extensive use of charcoal. As a side process it had one of Asia's biggest wood-distillation plants, producing 136,000 litres of distillate every day, the source of calcium acetate, methyl alcohol and formaldehyde. The plant has expanded into production of ferro-manganese, iron castings and pipes, steel ingots and tar products.

Shimoga (16 km; *Population*: 192,600; *STD Code*: 08182) It is worth asking at the Dist Commissioner's Office whether there is accommodation available at the *Inspection Bungalow* at Jog Falls. This is often heavily booked and best reserved in advance. The road from Shimoga runs in the lee of the Western Ghats but close enough to the ridge to benefit from higher rainfall than the plateau to the E. Open woodland and rice cultivation on gently terraced slopes are common. They give way to some magnificent forest, often with bamboo. In **Sagar** (77 km; *Population*: 42,200) turn left to visit the 16th century temples at **Ikkeri** (3 km), for a brief period the capital of an independent Nayaka kingdom. The largest and most interesting is the Aghoresvara Temple. The influence of Vijayanagar style is evident in the vigorously sculpted animals rearing up, but Muslim influence can be seen in the parapets of some of the smaller buildings. It is a centre for sandalwood carving. Jog Falls (30 km) can be reached via Sagar.

Jog Falls

At the start of the cool season just after the rains have finished the Falls are a magnificently spectacular sight. The 50 km long Hirebhasgar Reservoir now regulates the flow of the Sharavati River in order to generate hydro-electricity, but there is still an enormous difference between wet and dry season flow. The Mysore Power Corp releases water to the falls every 2nd Sun from 1000-1800. Often during the monsoon the falls are shrouded in mist. Dampness envelopes everything, water drips or pours from the trees, leeches seem to attach themselves to you at every step if you walk down the paths to the base of the falls, and rooms in the guest houses have a permanently musty smell. In the dry season the water is often reduced to a trickle. Best time to visit: definitely late-Nov to early-Jan.

There are 4 falls. The highest is the **Raja**, with a fall of 250m and a pool below 40m deep. Next to it is the **Roarer**, while a short distance to the S is the **Rocket**, which spurts great shafts of water out into the air. In contrast the **Rani** (once called the White Lady or Dame Blanche) cascades over the rocks. The walk to the bottom of the falls is highly recommended for the fit. The Inspection Bungalow has excellent views.

• **Accommodation F** *Inspection Bungalows*, nr the Falls and in the colony, are often heavily booked for officials and hence difficult to reserve. The alternatives are unexciting. **F** *Woodlands*, T 22, simple, poorly maintained, poor food and service; The Tourist Dept's **F** *Jog Falls Guest House*, reservations: Resident Manager; **F** *Tunga Tourist Home* is very basic; **F** *Guest House*, nr the Falls, reservations: Supt Engineer (Elec), Mahatma Gandhi Hydro-electric Works, Jog Falls.

• **Transport Train** Jog is 16 km from the railway at Talguppa. Bangalore train has one coach for Mysore; choose the right one! **Road** To Karwar daily, leaving Jog in the morning. Also many other destinatios, including Sirsi (2 hr) , Sagar the S.

ROUTES From Jog Falls roads run SE to Shimoga or N to Siddapur and Sirsi. One route to Goa runs down to join the NH 17 on the coast at Mirjan, another continues through the Ghats to Yellapur and Londa, joining the NH4A between Dharwad and Panaji.

Mundgod Lying on the road between Sirsi and Hubli, Mundgod became the home to a Tibetan colony in1971. The original settlement of 216 monks has now grown to more than 10,000, with three monasteries of Drepung, Ganden and Tsera accounting for nearly 3000.

BANGALORE TO BELGAUM via Bombay Highway

The **NH 4** runs from Bangalore to Hubli-Dharwad, Pune and Bombay across the high open country E of the crest line of the Western Ghats, following one of the main routes for trade and military movement over centuries. Even before the spread of cultivation the forest was comparatively light and easy to penetrate. Bullock cart tracks came up from the small W coast ports through the dense jungles of the ghats to the plateau.

In **Dobbspet** a road runs 5 km S to Sivaganga and the cone-shaped Sivaganga Hill, which reaches 1347m. At the top is the cave shrine to Gangadareshwar and a temple to Honna Devi. It is a stiff climb to the top. To the N of Dobbspet are the **Devarayadurga Hills** and state forest, covered in quite dense scrub. There are 2 hilltop temples to Yoganarasimha and Bhoganarasimha (*Altitude*: 1,190m).

Tumkur (72 km; *Population*: 179,500; *STD Code*: 0816) is an important market town and road junction. From Tumkur the NH 4 goes NW to Hiriyur.

Hiriyur (96 km; *Population*: 37,500; *STD Code*: 0819312) The town is on the right bank of the River Vedavati. The Teru-Malleshwara Temple has a 14m-high lamp pillar which holds enough oil for the lamp to be re-lit only once a year. You can climb the pillar by the slightly projecting steps. There is a very large temple car festival in Jan-Feb each year when images of Siva, Parvati and Uma-Maheshwar, seated on the *nandi*, are processed through the streets. 15 km to the SW is the Vanivilasapur dam and reservoir. Built at the end of the 19th century it was Mysore's first modern dam, and the lake is in an attractive setting. **Getting there** Local buses run from Hiriyur to Hosdurga.

Molakalmuru A district road also

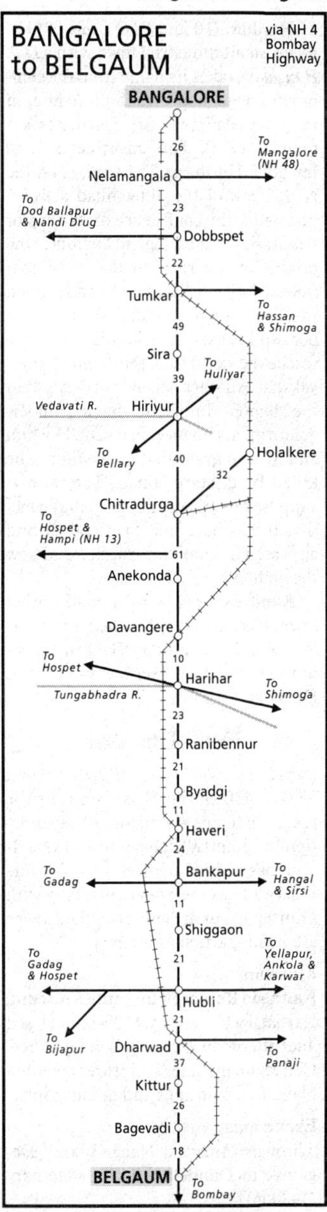

runs due N from Hiriyur to Bellary, pasing on the way Molakalmuru (92 km; *Altitude* 560m), an important centre for making pure silks. The town has an attractive traditional reservoir. It lies approx 10 km S of **Siddapur**, the site of 3 Asokan rock edicts at **Brahmagiri** Asokan edicts on a large boulder, on the Chinna Hagari River banks. Although they are relatively minor, they represent some of the southernmost discoveries of Asoka's empire. They were discovered in 1891 by BL Rice.

The N side of the granite hill has subsequently revealed evidence of settlements dating at least 5 periods. The finds include terracottas beads, pottery, semi-precious stones and metal, and date from early stone age Stone age site periods up to the Hoysala. In the first period, the Polished Stone Axe culture, the oldest remains are the remnants of grinding stones and houses. The culture's most distinctive feature of triangular polished stone axes, made of dolerite. There was a very limited use of metal including some for ornaments. Ghosh suggests that human skeletal remains of both adults and infants from the later Bronze Age have shown that dead infants were folded up and interred in an urn, while adults were laid out with the head towards the E. Burial furniture always included a spouted vessel.

Later cultures included the Megalithic pit culture Megalithic site in which iron became common, sickles were used for agriculture and the pottery changed dramatically. Among the most important articles were hemispherical deep bowls and tulip-shaped bowls. The burial customs also changed, making use of stone burial chambers covered in enormous slabs. The Megalith periods also underwent successive developments before giving way to the Andhra culture when a sophisticated pottery began to make its appearance. Dating of this last period has been made reasonably accurate by the discovery of Roman coins of the Augustan and Tiberian period (minted between 2BC-37AD) at the neighbouring site of Chandravalli.

The landscape on the road NW from Hiryur is marked by often thin soils, and periodically bare outcrops of granite break the surface. There are gold and copper mines just S of the fast growing town of Chitradurga (40 km).

Chitradurga

(40 km; *Population*: 103,300; *Altitude*: 976m; *STD Code*: 08194) Chitradurga is at the foot of a group of granite hills, rising to 1175m in the S. The Fort of Seven Rounds was built in the 17th century by Nayak Poligars, semi-independent landlords who fled S after the collapse of the Vijayanagar Empire in 1565. They were crushed by Haidar Ali in 1779 who captured the fort and scattered the population. Haidar Ali replaced the Nayaka's mud fort with stone and Tipu built a palace, mosque, granaries and oilpits in it. There are 4 secret entrances in addition to the 19 gateways, and ingenious water tanks which collected rainwater. There are also 14 temples, including a cave temple to the W of the wall. They are placed in an extraordinary jumble of outcropping granite rocks, a similar setting to that of Hampi 300 km to the N. The Hidimbeshwara temple is the oldest temple on the site.

ROUTES The NH 13 joins the NH 4 just beyond the NW end of the Chitradurga by-pass, leading to Hampi and Bijapur. See page 1044.

Anekonda Heavy rains have exposed small gold coins in the past. There is a very small Hoysala temple dedicated to Ishvara which has beautifully worked carvings on the doorways.

Davangere (61 km; *Population*: 287,000; *STD Code*: 08192), an important market town for cotton, groundnut, sugarcane and millets. The cotton markets are piled high with huge mounds of snowy white cotton, brought in by tractors and lorries as well as the traditional bullock carts.

Harihar, (10 km; *STD Code*: 08197), now a small industrial town with a *Dak Bungalow*, takes its name from the combined image, half Siva, half Vishnu, in the Hoysala style Sri Harihareswara temple (1223). This enshrines a 1.3m image of Harihara. The town is on the right bank of the Tungabhadra River, just below the confluence of its 2 major tributaries. A local legend attributes the origins of the river to the sweat that flowed down Vishnu's tusks and formed two streams when he took the form of a boar and engaged in a heroic struggle to rescue the world from the demon Hiranyaksha. Another legend suggests that the demon Gulhasura, having undergone a great penance, persuaded Vishnu and Siva to grant that he would not be killed by either of them. The town is supposed to take its name from the fact that it was here that Siva and Vishnu appeared in a joint incarnation and slew the demon.

Ranibennur (23 km), a small market town, has a rocky hill to the S known as Scorpion Hill, and the NH 4 then goes to the twin city of Hubli (110 km) and Dharwad (21 km).

Hubli-Dharwad

(*Population*: 647,600; *Altitude*: 600m; *STD Code*: 0836) Hubli is a centre for the textile industry is a major railway junction for Bombay, Bangalore and Goa. It also has a big medical school while Dharwad has the State University with a museum, but in themselves the 2 towns are not of particular interest.

Museum

Kannada Research Institute Museum, Karnataka University. 1100-1800, closed Tues afternoon and Univ holidays. Free. Collection includes sculpture (notably a Nataraja), paintings and manuscripts.

Excursions

Through Alnavar, Nangad and Degamve to **Dandeli Wildlife sanctuary** (142 km).

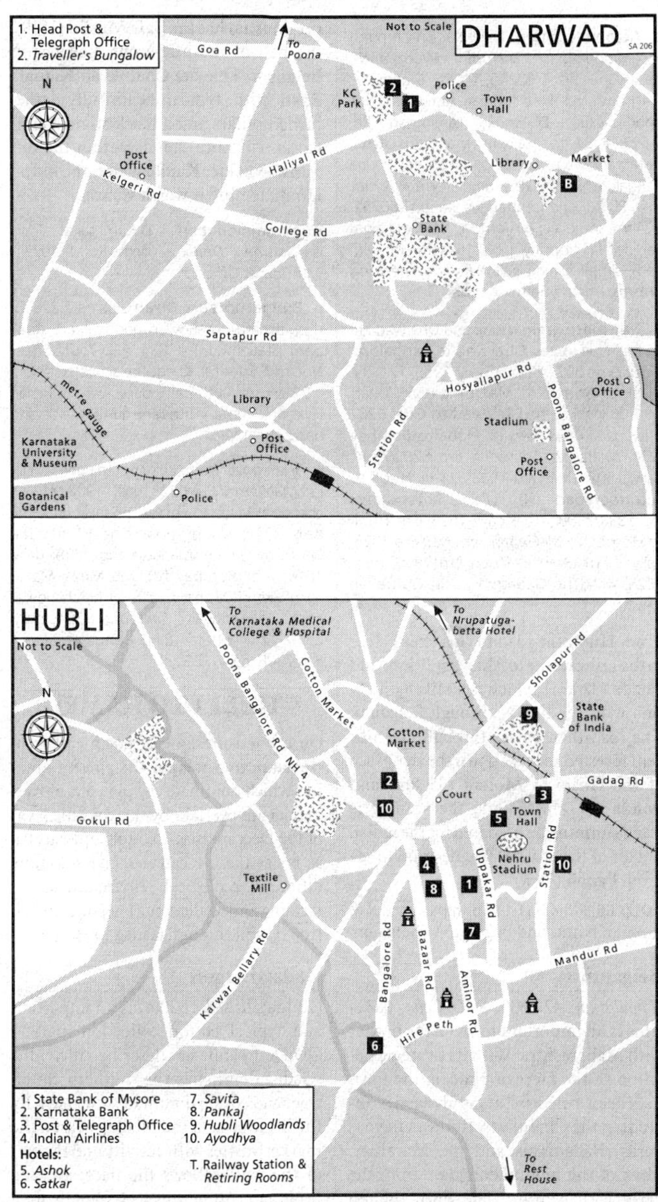

DHARWAD
SA 206
Not to Scale
1. Head Post & Telegraph Office
2. Traveller's Bungalow
N
Goa Rd
To Poona
KC Park
Police
Town Hall
Post Office
Haliyal Rd
Kelgeri Rd
Library
Market
B
State Bank
College Rd
Saptapur Rd
Hosyallapur Rd
Post Office
metre gauge
Library
Stadium
Station Rd
Poona Bangalore Rd
Karnataka University & Museum
Post Office
Post Office
Botanical Gardens
Police
HUBLI
Not to Scale
To Karnataka Medical College & Hospital
To Nrupatuga-betta Hotel
Poona Bangalore Rd NH 4
Cotton Market
Sholapur Rd
State Bank of India
Cotton Market
Gadag Rd
Court
Town Hall
Gokul Rd
Nehru Stadium
Station Rd
Uppakar Rd
Textile Mill
Bangalore Rd
Bazaar Rd
Aminor Rd
Mandur Rd
Karwar Bellary Rd
Hire Peth
To Rest House
1. State Bank of Mysore
2. Karnataka Bank
3. Post & Telegraph Office
4. Indian Airlines
Hotels:
5. Ashok
6. Satkar
7. Savita
8. Pankaj
9. Hubli Woodlands
10. Ayodhya
T. Railway Station & Retiring Rooms

• **Accommodation** Hubli has only modest accommodation. **D** *Hubli Woodlands*, Keshwapur Rd, T 62246, 50 rm, 6 good a/c with bath, nr rly, a/c Indian restaurant, bar, good value; **D** *Ashok*, Lamington Rd, T 62271, 87 rm, 1 a/c, nr rly and Bus Stand, restaurant (veg), exchange; **D** *Shree*, Poona Bangalore NH, T 2015, some a/c rm. **E** *Ayodhya*, PB Rd, opp Central Bus Stand, T 66251, 104 rm, some a/c; **E** *Ajantha*, Jaichamarajnagar, not far from rly, T 62216, some rm with bath, simple dining hall. **F** *Railway Retiring Rooms*, rm and dorm.

• **Transport Train** Hubli and Dharwad are on main rail routes. **Dharwad to Bangalore**: *Kittur Exp* 1007 (AC/CC), daily, 1955, 12½ hr. **Hubli to Goa**: *6201 Mail*, daily, 0555 (Dharwad 0631), 7¼ hr. **Dharwad to Goa**: *6201 Mail*, daily, 0631, 6¾ hr. **Hubli to Bombay (VT)**: *Mahalaxmi/Sahyadhri Exp* 6203/7304, daily, 1505 (Dharwad 1538), 21 hr. **Hubli to Secunderabad (H)**: *Vijaynagar/Venkatadri Exp* 7830/7598 (AC/II), daily, 1625, 6 hr. **Hubli to Hospet**: *Hubli-Guntur-Amravati Exp* 7826, daily, 1215, 3½ hr. *Vasco Exp* 7830, daily, 1625, 4 ½ hr. **Gadag**: 1½ hr; **Guntakal**: 6¼ hr.

From Hubli the road to Goa keeps close to the railway line to Alnavar (29 km) and Londa (32 km), which is a railway junction with the line N through Belgaum. The road then passes through magnificent forested scenery down the steep face of the Ghats to **Molem** (35 km) and **Ponda** (37 km). While the scenery is often stunning be prepared for the moist, hot air of the coast as you descend to sea level. **Panaji** (34m).

ROUTES The NH 4 to Bombay goes NW through Kittur and Bagevadi to Belgaum.

Belgaum

(*Population*: 420,000; *STD Code*: 0831) This is an important town on the border with Maharashtra. With its strategic position in the Deccan plateau, the town had been ruled by many dynasties including the Chalukyas, Rattas, Vijaynagaras, Bahamanis and the Marathas. Most of the monuments date from the early 13th century. The **Fort**, though pre-Muslim has the **Safa Masjid** (1519), the best of the numerous mosques in Belgaum. The late Chalukyan **Kamala Basti** with typical beautifully lathe-turned pillars and a black stone Neminatha sculpture, stands within the fort walls. Outside, **Kapileswara**, the oldest Hindu temple is worth visiting.

• **Accommodation** **D** Karnataka Tourism *Sanman Delux*, College Rd, T 20777, with Tourist Office.

• **Budget hotels** **E** *Milan* Club Rd, T 22535, rm with bath (hot shower), good value; **E** *Anupam*, Station Rd, T 22834. Also *Tourist Rest House*. **F** *Sheetal*, Khade Bazar nr bus station, T 29222, rm with bath, prices vary, in Indian style, noisy, hotel in busy and quite entertaining bazar street, rec.

• **Transport Train** Belgaum to Pune via Miraj: *Mahalaxmi Exp* 6203, daily, 1900, 2¾ hr, change at Miraj (1¾ hr wait): *Sahyadhri* 7304, daily, 2340, 7¼ hr; (total time 12 hr). **Goa** (Vasco-da-Gama): *Mandovi Exp* 7898, daily, 1015, 7 hr. **Bombay (VT) via Miraj**: *Mahalaxmi Exp* 6203, daily, 1900, 3 hr, change at Miraj (1¾ hr wait): *Sahyadhri* 7304, daily, 2340, 12½ hr (total 18 hr). **Bangalore**: *Kittur Exp* 7808, daily, 1655, 16½ hr.

HUBLI TO HAMPI

On a line running east north east from **Belgaum** to **Sholapur** the ancient granites which dominate the plateaus of Karnataka are overlain by the volcanic lavas of the Deccan. Black 'cotton' soils stretch as far as the eye can see, giving a quite different ecological environment for farming and settlement. The route runs E from Hubli through Gadag to Hospet.

Gadag-Betgeri

(23 km; *Altitude*: 620m) is an important and typical cotton collection market. CD Deshpande has described it vividly: "Gadag dominates the southern cotton tract and cotton dominates the town. By the beginning of the picking season the market bustles with activity and the rest of the town follows the pace; ginning mills and cotton presses lying idle for a

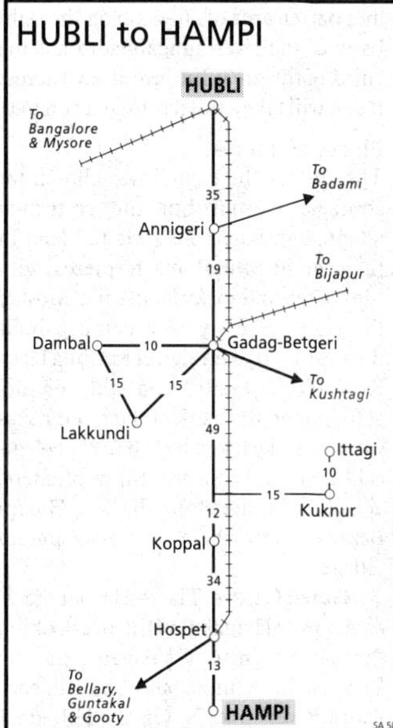

long time are now set to work; cotton finds its way out in a well-graded form to Bombay or for export. By the middle of June this activity is at its zenith, then settles down to a quiet life during the next 8 months".

Places of interest

The **cotton market** is well worth a visit. A **Vaishnavite temple** in the NW corner has a 15m high gopuram. The **fort** at Gadag has a Saivite temple of Trimbakeshwar, "Lord of the Three Peaks", elaborately carved, and an enormous carved bull. An inscription dates the temple at AD 868. Behind the main part of the temple is a shrine to Saraswati. The porch is perhaps the best feature of the temple. The black hornblende pillars have been smoothed to a remarkable finish with superbly detailed carving, sharp and clear.

Excursion

It is possible to take a diversion to the SE to visit the 12th century Dodda Basappa temple at **Dambal** (10 km). This is a late Chalukyan temple with a plan similar to the Hoysala temples further S. There is a highly polished *nandi* at the E end. The sanctuary has a multi storeyed tower above it, and there is some decoration on the otherwise polished stone work. **Services** Gadag, a railway junction, has tea stalls, cold drinks and simple restaurants and a Dak Bungalow. **Transport Train** Guntakal: *Hubli-Guntur-Amravati Exp* 7826, daily, 1350, 4¾ hr (via *Hospet*, 1 ¾ hr). Hubli: *Link Exp* 7837, daily, 2045, 1½ hr. Solapur: *Golgumbaz Exp* 6542, daily, 2300, 7½ hr. Bijapur: *Bijapur Exp* 7789, daily, 1555, 4¾ hr.

Lakkundi (15 km)

Return to Gadag and turn right to visit the 17 Hindu and Jain **temples** (11th, 12th centuries). The stone used for the temples in Dambal, Gadag and Lakkundi is the schist brought from Dharwad. The sculpture was carried out at the quarry and the near finished work then transported to the temple. In this the method used differed from that in Orissa, for example, where raw stone was moved to the temple site before sculpting. Basements are moulded, walls have pilasters and there is remarkable detail on the ceilings. The late 11th century Jain basti is the largest of the temples, with a 5-storeyed pyramidal tower and square roof. Especially fine carving is found on the incomplete Kasivisvesvara Temple, dating from the 12th century. Both temples are near the tank in the SW of the town, which is no more than 1 km across. There is a small museum between them.

To the N of Lakkundi are 2 more sites with temples of the same period, **Kuknur** and **Ittagi** (10 km). The Mahadeva temple in Ittagi (1112 AD) has similarly finely finished columns with beautifully finished miniature carvings. The Navalinga complex, dated at the late 9th century has 9 shrines, originally dedicated to female deities. The 2 gateways are Vijayanagar. The **Kallesvara Temple** (10th century) has a square sanctuary topped by a 3-storey tower. Ganesa and Durga are enshrined. They represent the transition from a Rashtrakuta style to a Chalukyan style.

Return to the main Hospet road to **Koppal** (37 km), noted for 2 impressive forts. On the margins of Maratha, Hyderabad and Mysore power, this territory was once under the control of the Nizams of Hyderabad and Koppal was given to Salar Jung, one of the Nizam's nobles, as a *jagir* (a land gift). The upper fort is over 120m above the plains while the lower one was rebuilt by French engineers when it had been captured by Tipu Sultan from the Marathas. The road continues to Hospet.

Hospet & Hampi-Vijayanagara

Hospet (*Population*: 135,000; *Altitude*: 480m; *STD Code*: 08394) is used as a base by many visitors to Hampi since it offers a variety of accommodation and is the nearest station (see below under Hampi). The remains are very scattered and need at least one whole day (2 better) to see fully.

Hampi (*Altitude*: 467m; *Best season*: Oct-Mar) 'The town of victory', **Vijayanagara**, is 13 km ENE of Hospet town . Hampi was once the seat of the Vijayanagara Empire and a great centre of Hindu rule for 200 years from its foundation in 1336, although there may have been a settlement in the area as early as 1000 years before then.

The city was enormously wealthy, 'greater than Rome', with a market full of jewels and palaces plated with gold, having held a monopoly of trade in spices and cotton. It was very well fortified and defended by a large army. With the defeat in 1565 at Talikota at the hands of the Deccan Sultans, the city was largely destroyed. Today the stark and barren area of 26 sq km on the right bank of the river Tungabhadra has the ruins of the great Empire strewn across it and will take a full day to cover on foot.

Places of interest

The site for the capital was chosen for strategic reasons but the craftsmen adopted an ingenious style to blend in their architectural masterpieces with the barren and rocky landscape. Most of the sites are early 16th century, built during the 20 year reign of Krishna Deva Raya (1509-1529) with the **citadel** standing on the bank of the river. Excavations undertaken by the Archaeological Survey of India are still in progress. You enter the area from the W at **Hampi Bazar** or from the S at **Kamalapuram** village.

Sacred Centre The road from the W comes over **Hemakuta Hill**, overlooking the sacred centre of Vijayanagara, the Virupaksha Temple and the Tungabhadra River to its N. On the Hill are 2 large Ganesha monolithic sculptures and some small temples. Good views. The road runs down to the village, in the once world-famous **Market Place**, where you can now only see the wide pathway running E from the towering **Virupaksha** (*Pampapati*) **Temple** with its 9-storey *gopuram*, along the river where the bazar hummed with activity. Before entering the precinct, foreigners are expected to sign a book at the office on the left. Rs 2. 0800-1230, 1500-1830. The temple is still in use; note interesting painted ceiling of *mandapam*. The monkeys here can be aggressive.

You can walk along the river bank (2 km) to the famous Vitthala Temple. The path is easy and passes several interesting ruins. (Alternatively, a motorable road skirts the Royal Enclosure to the S, and goes all the way to the Vitthala Temple) After passing **Achyuta Bazar**, which leads to the Tiruvengalanatha Temple 400m to the S, the riverside path goes near **Sugriva's Cave**, where it is

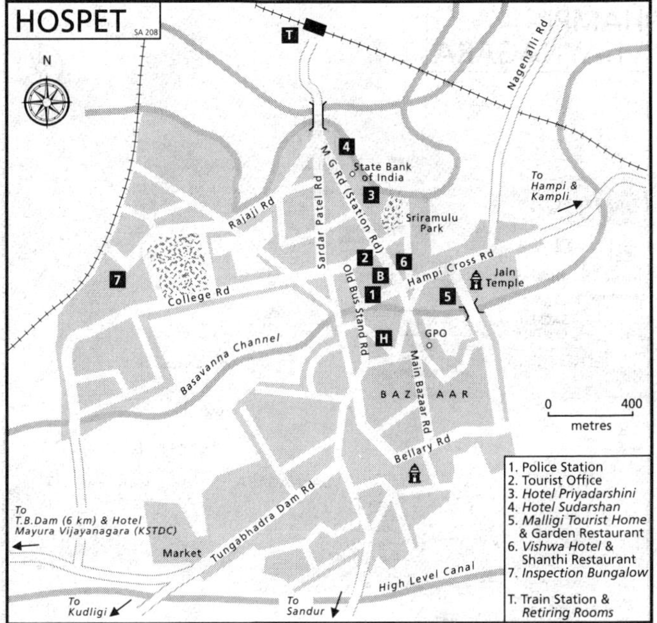

said that Sita's jewels, dropped as she was abducted by the demon Ravana, were hidden by Sugriva. There are good views of the ancient ruined bridge to the E, and nearby the path continues past the only early period Vaishnavite shrine, the 14th century **Narasimha Temple**. The **King's balance**, is at the end of the path as it approaches the Vitthala Temple. It is said that the rulers were weighed against gold, jewels and food, to be distributed to Brahmins.

The **Vitthala Temple**, a World Heritage Monument, is dedicated to Vishnu. It stands in a rectangular courtyard, enclosed within high walls. Probably built in the mid-15th century, it is one of the oldest and most intricately carved, with its *gopurams* and *mandapas*. The *Dolotsava mandapa* has 56 superbly sculpted slender pillars which can be struck to produce different musical notes. It has elephants on the balustrades and horses at the entrance. The other 2 ceremonial mandapas, though less finely carved have some interesting carved pillars, eg Krishna hiding in a tree from the gopis, a woman using a serpent twisted around a stick to churn a pot of buttermilk. In the courtyard is a superb chariot carved out of granite, the wheels raised off the ground so that they could be revolved!

On the road between the Virupaksha bazar and the Citadel, you pass **Krishnapura**, Hampi's earliest Vaishnava township with a Chariot Street 50m wide and 0.6 km long, which is now a cultivated field. The Krishna temple has a very impressive gateway to the E. Just SW of the Krishna temple is the colossal monolithic statue of akshmNarasimha in the form of a 4-armed man-lion with fearsome bulging eyes sheltered under a 7-headed serpent, Ananta. It is over 6m

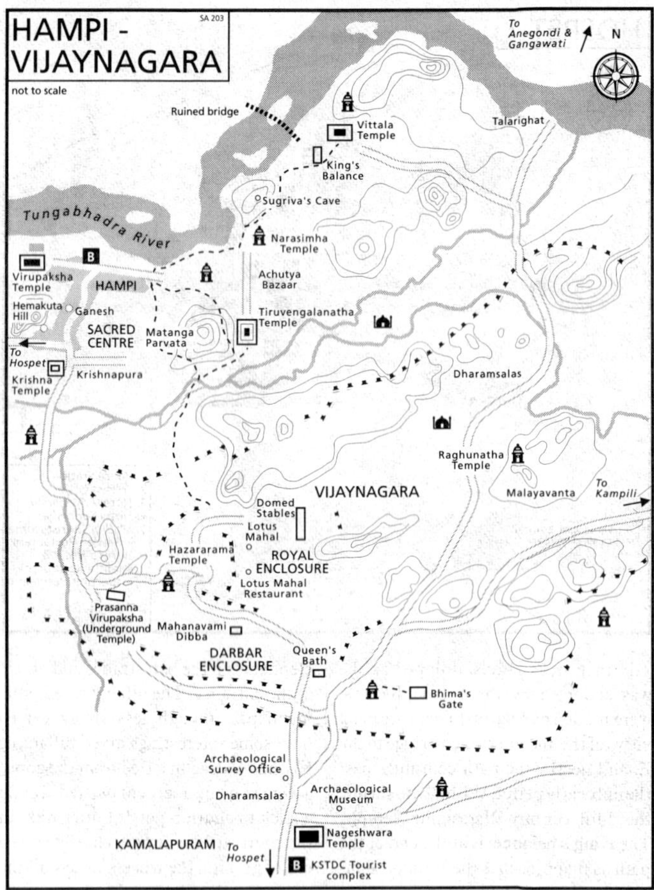

high but sadly damaged. The road S towards the Royal Enclosure passes the excavated **Prasanna Virupaksha** (misleadingly named "underground") and interesting watchtowers.

Royal Enclosure At the heart of the Metropolis, is the small **Hazara Rama Temple**, the Vaishanava 'chapel royal' (*hazara* meaning 1000). The outer enclosure wall to the N has 5 rows of carved friezes while the outer walls of the *mandapa* has 3. The episodes from the epic, *Ramayana* are told in great detail, starting with the bottom row of the N end of the W *mandapa* wall. The 2-storeyed **Lotus Mahal** is in the **Zenana** or ladies' quarter, screened off by its high walls. The watch tower is in ruins but you can see the domed stables for 10 elephants with a pavilion in the centre and the guardhouse. Each stable had a wooden beamed ceiling from which chains were attached to the elephants' back and neck. In the **Durbar Enclosure** is the

VIJAYANAGAR'S NAVA RATRI

It is not difficult to imagine the magnificence of the Vijayanagar court or of some of its special occasions. Burton Stein describes the *Mahanavami festival*, an annual royal ceremony of the 15th and 16th century "occurring from mid Sep-mid Oct". The festival lives on across S India today, now often known as *Nava ratri*. It provided a ritual through which the power of the Vijayanagar Kings was given validity. Many Persian and Portuguese travellers visited the court. Paes called suggested all activity centred around the "House of victory" – the *mahanavami dibba,* and the King's Audience Hall. Now they are just vast granite platforms, which almost certainly carried wooden buildings. Through the festivities Stein records that the King sometimes shared his throne, or sat at its foot while it was occupied by a richly decorated processional image of the god, while at other times he was alone.

"In front were constructed a number of pavilions which contributed to the aura of wealth and sumptuousness of the festival as a whole. They were elaborately decorated, in among other ways, with 'devices', symbols of the grandee occupants. ...There were 9 major pavilions for the most illustrious notables, and each military commander also had to erect one in the broad space before the palace. Access to the guarded, central arena of festival activity," he goes on, "was gained by passage through several gates enclosing wells of the temple precincts....What was viewed was a combination of great durbar with its offerings of homage and wealth to the King and return of gifts from the King – exchanges of honours; the sacrificial re-consecration of the King's arms – his soldiers, horses, elephants – in which hundreds of thousands of animals were slaughtered; ***darshana*** and ***puja*** of the King's tutelary – the goddess – as well as his closest kinsmen; and a variety of athletic contests, dancing and singing processions involving the King's caparisoned women and temple dancers from throughout the realm, and fireworks displays. The focus of these diverse and magnificent entertainments was always the King as glorious and conquering warrior, as the possessor of vast riches lavishly displayed by him and his women (queens and their maids of honour) and distributed to his followers."

specially built decorated platform of the **Mahanavami Dibba**, from which the royal family watched the pageants and tournaments during the 9 nights of *dasara* festivities. The 8m high square platform originally had a covering of bricks, timber and metal but what remains still shows superb carvings of hunting and battle scenes, as well as dancers and musicians.

The exceptional skill of water engineering is displayed in the newly excavated system of aquaducts, tanks, sluices and canals, which could function today. The 22m square **Pushkarini** is the attractive stepped tank at the centre of the enclosure. The road towards Kamalapura passes the **Queen's Bath**, in the open air, surrounded by a narrow moat which had scented water fill the bath from lotus shaped fountains. It measures about 15m by 2m and has interesting stucco work around it.

Museum

The **Archaeological Museum** at Kamalapuram has a collection of sculpture, paintings, copper plates and coins. The Archaeological Survey booklet is on sale and there is a scale model of Hampi in the courtyard. 1000-1700, closed Fri.

Excursion

The Tungabhadra Dam 6 km further where the 2 km Dam is 49m high and offers panoramic views. One of the largest masonry dams in the country it was completed in 1953 after 8 years of construction work to provide electricity for irrigation in the surrounding districts. **Accommodation** **E** *Vaikunta Guest House*, Tungabhadra Dam, T 8241, beautiful hill-top site, but out of town above the dam so own transport needed, usually occupied by officials, book 15 days in advance. **F** *Indrabhavan*, Munirabad, 5 km N of Dam; also **F** *Lake View Guest House*, Munirabad, difficult to reserve. **Getting there** Bus tours to Hampi include a visit to the Dam. State Tourist Office will arrange trips but several local bus services daily do the trip (¼ hr).

Local festivals

Hampi Jan-Feb Virupaksha *Temple Car festival*. Also annual Purandaradasa Aradhana *Music festival* at Vithala Temple.

Hospet There is a significant Muslim population in Hospet and *Muharram* is celebrated with vigour. Firewalkers walk across burning embers and there are noisy celebrations, a custom which may go back to long before Islam arrived. Villagers still celebrate events such as the beginning or end of migrations to seasonal feeding grounds with huge bonfires. Cattle are driven through such fires to protect them from disease. The archaeologists Allchin and Allchin suggest that Neolithic ash mounds around Hospet could have resulted from similar celebrations over 5,000 years ago.

Local information

● Budget hotels

Hospet: Station Rd has been re-named Mahatma Gandhi Rd (MG Rd). **E** Karnataka Tourism *Mayura Vijayanagara*, T 8270, 3 km W of centre on TB Dam Rd, basic with fans, mosquito nets and bath, simple dining hall, good *thalis*; **E** *Malligi Tourist Home*, Bellary Rd, T 8101, 64 rm, 2 a/c with bath, good restaurant (try *Malai kofta*) with breakfast on order, exchange, travel, well-maintained large rm, good value, though stay over 3 days not encouraged, over-attentive service (described as "constant hassle") so be firm; **E** *Sudarshan*, MG Rd, T 8574, few a/c rm.

F *Priyadarshini*, 45A MG Rd, T 8838, some a/c rm; **F** *Railway Retiring Rooms*, T 360; **F** *Vishwa*, MG Rd, opp bus station, new style S Indian hotel, clean and excellent value.

Hampi: **E** Karnataka Tourism *Tourist Complex*, 27 rm; **E** *Hampi Power Station Inspection Bungalow*, T 8272, 3 km climb from Kamalapuram, pleasant spot but fairly basic, reservation: Supt Engineer, HES, Tungabhadra Dam, Hospet, meals to order. *Inspection Bungalow* at Kamalapuram.

● Places to eat

Hospet: two at *Malligi Hotel*, one open-air with bar. Also many nr Bus Station, eg *Shanbag Cafe*, do good *thali* meals.

Hampi: several simple places serve veg meals in the Hampi Bazar area. Karnataka Tourism has the *Lotus Mahal Restaurant* nr Hazara Rama Temple among the ruins.

● Shopping

Hampi: **Books**: *Aspirations Bookshop* in the Bazar has an interesting selection of books (Longhurst's "Hampi Ruins", Settar's "Hampi"), postcards, crafts from *Aurobindo Ashram* in Pondicherry and soft drinks.

● Useful services in Hospet

Bank: **State Bank of India**, next to Tourist Office. **Post office**: opp vegetable market. **Telegraph office**: in *Hotel Sudarshan*. **Tourist office**: Karnataka, MG Rd, nr Bus Stand. Free map and leaflets and occasionally guides for the sites.

● Transport

Local transport to Hampi **Cycle rickshaws**: from rly station to Bus Stand about Rs 10. **Bus**: frequent local buses to Hampi's 2 entry points (Hampi Bazar, 13 km, Rs 3 and via Kamalapuram and Museum, Rs 3.50), from 0630; last return from Hampi around 2000, ½ hr. Also from Tungabhadra Dam, ¾ hr. **Cycle rickshaw**: **Cycle hire**: Bikes available in Hospet to visit Hampi (13 km) but check condition carefully. A bike is very useful in Hampi as the site is very spread out. Bikes, which some consider essential, may not be available in Hampi itself. **Taxi**: also for sharing.

Hospet to Hampi **Train** Secunderabad via Guntakal: *Tungabhadra Exp* 7508, daily, 2015, 2¾ hr, change at Guntakal (1½ hr wait): *Venkatadri Exp* 7598, daily, 0030, 9 hr (total 14¼ hr); **Guntakal**: *Hubli-Guntur-Amravati Exp* 7826, daily, 1545, 4 hr. **Bangalore**

via **Guntakal**, *Hospet-Bangalore Hampi Exp* 6591, daily, 2015, 1-½ hr; **Guntakal and Narasaraopet**, *Tungabhadra Exp* 7598, daily, 2000, 3 hr; *Hubi-Guntur Amaravati Exp* daily, 1540, 3 hr.

Road Bus: Express buses from **Bangalore**, 12 daily from 0700. Overnight Karnataka Tourism luxury coach.

HAMPI TO BIDAR via Bijapur & Gulbarga

An extended tour of northern Karnataka can be made from Hampi across classic "marchlands" territory.

Some of peninsular India's earliest Neolithic settlements are found near the rivers which cross the plateau. Ever since, the relatively open forests of the open plateaus have provided a major route between the power centres of N and S India. From the 4th to the 8th centuries AD the **Chalukyas** ruled over this part of the Deccan making the cities of Aihole, Badami and Pattadakal their capitals. They became among the northernmost centres of Dravida temple architecture. The villages are very attractive and unspoilt, and the sites themselves are well preserved and maintained in attractive gardens, close enough to each other to be visited over 2 to 3 days by making either Aihole or Badami the base. Buses connect the villages.

History The region was a historic battleground between the Hindu Vijayanagar Empire immediately to its S and the Muslim sultanates to the N. The **Bahmani Dynasty** was the most powerful in the Deccan, ruling from **Gulbarga** from 1347 until 1422, then making **Bidar** the capital. The founder, Ala'u'd-Din Bahman Shah, divided the kingdom into 4 quarters (*taraf*) and assigned each one to a trusted officer (*tarafdar*). The **Raichur doab** (the land between the Krishna and the Tungabhadra rivers) was contested between the Vijayanagara and the Bahmani rulers. In the reign of Firuz Shah Bahmani (1397-1422) the 2 powers fought 3 times without disturbing the status quo. Firuz developed Chaul and Abhol as ports trading in luxury goods not only from the Persian, Arabian, and African coasts, but also (through Egypt) from Europe. Persians, Turks, and Arabs were given a ready welcome by the Bahmanids, ultimately producing conflicts between locals and the foreigners (*pardesis*).

The Bidar period (1422-1526) was

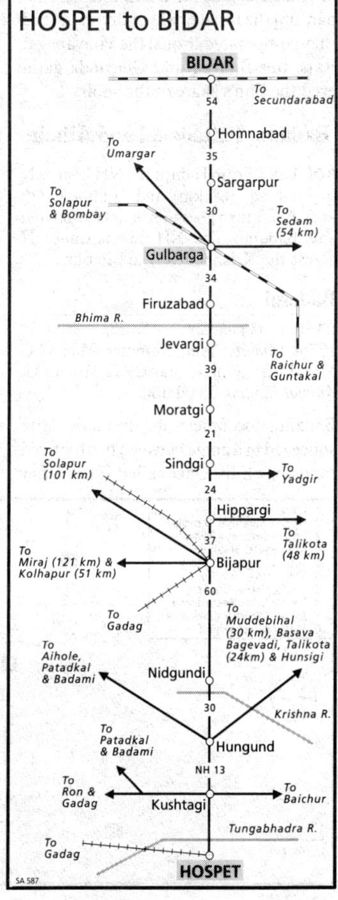

marked by wars with Gujarat and Malwa, continued campaigns against Vijayanagara, and expeditions against Orissa. Mahmud Gawan, Wazir of Bahmani sultanate, seized Karnataka between 1466 and 1481, and then Goa, formerly guarded by Vijayanagar kings. But the kingdom, weakened by the struggle between *pardesis* and Deccani kings, split into 5 independent sultanates by 1530: the Adil Shahi of Bijapur, the Qutb Shahi of Bidar, the Imad Shahi of Ahmadnagar, the Barid Shahi of Bidar, and the Imad Shahi of Berar. In 1565 they co-operated to oust the Vijayanagar Raja, but Bijapur and Golconda gathered the lion's share of the spoil.

Badami, Pattadakal and Aihole

ROUTES From Hampi the NH 13 goes N to Kushtagi (68 km) and Hungund (39 km). A left turn goes to Aihole, Pattadakal and Badami. The NH 13 continues N across the Krishna River to Bijapur.

Badami

BASICS *Population*: 15,023; *Altitude*: 177m; *Climate*: Temp Summer: Max 38°C Min 23°C, Winter: Max 29°C Min 15°C; *Annual rainfall*: 5,000 mm.

Badami occupies a dramatic site squeezed in a gorge between two high red sandstone hills. Once called *Vatapi*, after a demon, Badami was the Chalukyan capital from 543 – 757AD. The ancient city has several Hindu and Jain temples and a Buddhist cave. For a short time the Chalukyas lost control of Badami to the Pallavas in the mid-7th century and were finally defeated by the Rashtrakutas. They were followed by the Western Chalukyas, the Yadavas, the Vijayanagaras, the Bijapur emperors and the Marathas.

Places of interest

South Fort is famous for its cave temples, 4 of which were cut out of the hill side in the second half of the 6th century. You climb 40 steps to get to Cave 1, the oldest. There are several sculpted figures, including Harihara, Siva and Parvati, and Siva as Nataraja with 18 arms seen in 81 dancing poses. Cave 2, a little higher than Cave 1, is guraded by *dvarapalas* (door-keepers). Reliefs of Varaha and Vamana decorate the porch. Cave 3, higher still, is dedicated to Vishnu. It was excavated in 578 AD (from a Kannada inscription). It has numerous sculptures including Narasimha (man-lion), Hari-Hara (Siva-Vishnu), a huge reclining Vishnu and interesting friezes. Note the frescoes and the carved ceilings and brackets. Cave 4, probably about 100 years later than the 3 earlier caves,

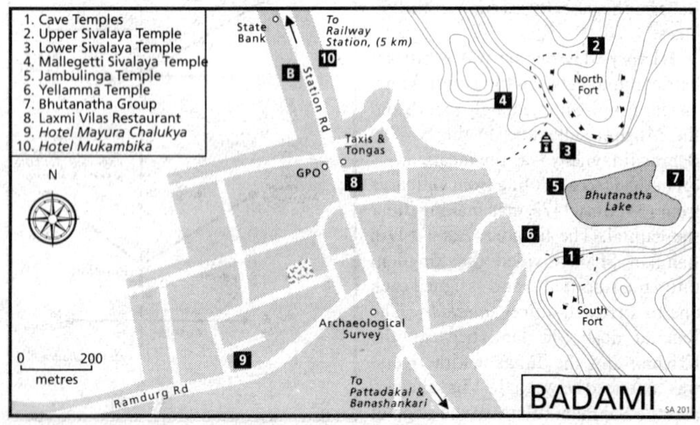

is the only Jain cave. It has a statue of the seated Parsvanatha.

Jambulinga Temple This early temple is in the centre of the town near the rickshaw stand. Dating from 699, as attested by an inscription, and now almost hidden by houses, the visible brick tower is a late addition from the Vijayanagar period. However, its 3 chapels, dedicated to Brahma, Vishnu and Siva, contain some fiine carving. It is the carvings here, especially that of the Nagaraja in the outside porch, which has helped to accurately date the Lad Khan temple in Aihole (see below). Opposite the Jambulinga temple is the 10th century Virupaksha temple.

The **Buddhist temple** is in the natural cave near the ancient artificial Bhutanatha Lake, where the mossy green water is considered to cure illnesses. The Yellamma has a female deity while of the 2 Saivite temples, one is to Bhutanatha (God of souls); in this form, Siva appears angry in the dark inner sanctuary.

The **North Fort** temples, mainly 7th century, give an insight into Badamis history. Steep steps, almost 1m high, take you to 'gun point' at the top of the fort which has remains of large granaries, a treasury and a watchtower. The **Upper Sivalaya Temple**, though damaged, still has some friezes and sculptures depicting Krishna legends. The village with its busy bazar has whitewashed houses clustered together along narrow winding lanes up the hill side.

There are also scattered remains of 18 stone inscriptions (6th-16th century).

Museum
Archaeological Survey's **Medieval Sculpture Gallery** N of the tank has fine specimens from Badami, Aihole and Pattadakal and a model of the natural bridge at Sidilinapadi, 5 km away. 1000-1700, closed Fri. Free.

• **Accommodation** **E** Karnataka Tourism *Mukambika*, opp Bus Stand, T 67, fairly clean spartan rm with bath, simple veg restuarant; **E** *Mayura Chalukya*, 1 km on Ramdurg road, T 46, 10 rm with baths, well placed, in wooded surrounding, basic restaurant with poor food, hotel reported run down and dirty, new building planned. *Inspection Bungalow* opp has 2 suites, reservation rec. PWD *Guest House* and *Malaprabha* Irrigation Dept *Bungalow*. Better *Circuit House* at Bagalkot, 38 km (see below).

• **Places to eat** A few serve snacks nr the Tonga Stand. *Laxmi Vilas*, rec for veg meals.

• **Transport** **Train** Station 5 km on the Hubli-Solapur metre gauge route. Bijapur, 2 daily, 4 hr; Bombay, 18½ hr and Madras, 20 hr (change at Hotgi for both). **Road** **Bus**: local buses are frequent. For details of road transport see Bijapur (below).

On the road to Pattadakal there is a village named after the goddess **Banasankari**. At the temple with its unusual 3 levels and its slender tower, you can see her rather terrifying black image riding a fierce golden lion. She was said to have been transformed into the lake alongside the temple.

Local festival
Jan-Feb 20 day fair at the Temple.

Pattadakal

(15 km) On the banks of the Malaprabha river, Pattadakal was the second capital of the Chalukyan kings between the 7th and 8th centuries and the city where the kings were crowned. Ptolemy referred to it as 'Petrigal' in the 1st century AD. Two of their queens imported sculptors from Kanchipuram. Most of the temples cluster at the foot of a hill, built out of the pink-tinged gold sandstone, and display a succession of styles of the southern Dravida temple architecture of the Pallavas (even miniature scaled-down models) as well as the N Indian Nagara style, vividly illustrating the region's position at the crossroads of N and S Indian traditions. With one exception the temples are dedicated to Jains. Most of the site is included in the archaeological park. Megalithic monuments dating from the 3rd-4th

centuries BC have been found in the area. Pattadakal is a World Heritage centre. Open sunrise to sunset.

Places of interest

Immediately inside the entrance are the very small **Jambuliinga** and **Kadasiddheshvara Temples** (8th century). Now partly ruined, the curved towers survive and the shrine of the Jambulinga temple houses a figure of the dancing Siva next to Parvati. The gateways are guarded by dvarapalas.

Just to the E is the 8th century **Galaganatha Temple**, again partly damaged, though its curved tower characteristic of N Indian temples is well preserved, including its *amalaka* on top. A relief of Siva killing the demon Andhaka is on the S wall in one of 3 original porches.

The **Sangamesvara Temple** dating from the reign of Vijayaditya (696-733) is the earliest temple. Although it was never completed it has all the hallmarks of a purely Dravidian style. Beautifully proportioned, there are mouldings on the basement and pilasters divide the wall. The main shrine, into which barely any light is allowed to pass, has a corridor for circumambulation, and a lingam inside. Above the sanctuary is a superbly proportioned tower of several storeys.

To the SW is the late 8th century North Indian style **Kashi Vishveshvara Temple**, readily distinguishable by the *nandi* in front of the porch. The interior of the pillared hall is richly sculpted, particularly with scenes of Krishna.

The largest temples, the **Virupaksha** (740-44) with its 3-storeyed *vimana* and the **Mallikarjuna** (745), typify the Dravida style, and were built in celebration of the victory of the Chalukyan king Vikramaditya II over the Pallavas at Kanchipuram by his wife, Queen Trailokyamahadevi. The king's death probably accounted for the fact that the Mallikarjuna temple was unfinished, attested by the failure to do more than mark out some of the sculptures. However, the king's victory over the Pallavas enabled him to express his admiration for Pallava architecture by bringing back to Pattadakal one of the chief Pallava architects. The Virupaksha, a Saivite temple, has a sanctuary surrounded by passageways and housing a black polished stone Siva linga. A further Saivite symbol is the huge 2.6m high chlorite stone Nandi at the entrance, contrasting with the pinkish sandstone surrounding it. The 3-storeyed tower rises strikingly above the shrine, the outside walls of which, particularly those on the S side, are richly carved. Many show different forms of Vishnu and Siva, including some particularly striking panels which show Siva appearing out of a linga. Note also the beautifully carved columns inside. They are very delicate, depicting episodes from the *Ramayana*, *Mahabharata* and the *Puranas*, as well as giving an insight into the social life of the Chalukyas. Note the ingenuity of the sculptor in making an elephant appear as a buffalo when viewed from a different side.

In the 9th century the Rashtrakutas arrived and built a Jain temple with its 2 stone elephants a short distance from the centre. The carvings on the temples, particularly on the **Papanatha** near the village which has interesting sculpture on the ceiling and pillars, synthesises N and S architectural styles.

Further reading: *A guide to Pattadakal Temples* by AM Annigeri, Kannada Research Institute, Dharwar, 1961.

Local festivals

Jan *Nrutytsava* in Jan draws many famous dancers and is accompanied by a Craft Mela.

Mar-Apr *Temple car festivals* at Virupaksha and Mallikarjuna temples.

• **Accommodation** No suitable accommodation. Stay either in Badami, Aihole (see above) or **Bagalkot** where there is a good **E** *Circuit House* with a/c rm, 5 km from centre on Bijapur Rd.

Aihole

19 km from Pattadakal, Aihole was the first Chalukyan capital, but the site was developed over a period of more than six hundred years from the 6th century AD and includes important Rashtrakuta and Late Chalukyan temples, some dedicated to Jain divinities. It is widely regarded as the birthplace of Indian temple architectural styles, and the site of the first built temples, as distinct from those carved out of solid rock. Most of the temples were originally dedicated to Vishnu, though a number were subsequently converted into Saivite shrines.

Places of interest

There are about 140 temples – half within the fort walls– illustrating a range of developing styles from Hoysala, Dravida, Jain, Buddhist, Nagara and Rekhanagara. All the roads entering Aihole pass numerous temple ruins, but the road into the village from Pattadakal and Bagalkot passes the most important group of temples which would be the normal starting point for a visit. The main temples are now enclosed in a park. Open sunrise to sunset. Flash photography prohibited.

Durgigudi temple The 'Durga' temple is named not after the Goddess Durga but because it is close to the *durga* (fort). Dating from the late 7th century, it has an early *gopuram* structure and semi-circular apse which imitates early Buddhist chaitya halls. It has numerous superb sculptures, a series coontained in niches around the ambulatory: walking clockwise they represent Siva and Nandi, Narasimha, Vishnu with Garuda, Varaha, Durga and Harihara.

Lad Khan Temple Until quite recently one of the oldest structures was believed to be the Lad Khan Temple, though recent research suggests that it dates not from the 450 AD as suggested by the first Archaeological Survey of India reports in 1907, but from approximately 700 AD. This is suggested by the similarity of its some of its sculptures to those of the Jambulinga temple at Badami, which has been dated precisely at 699 AD. Originally an assembly hall and *kalyana mandapa* (marriage hall) it was named after Lad Khan, a pious Muslim who squatted in the temple at the end of the 19th century. A stone ladder through the roof leads to a shrine with damaged images of Surya, Vishnu and Siva carved on its walls. It bears a striking resemblance to the megalithic caves which were still being excavated in this part of the Deccan at the beginning of the period. The roof gives an excellent view of the village.

Gaudar Gudi Temple Near the Lad Khan temple is this small, rectangular Hindu temple, probably dating from the 7th century. It has a rectangular columned mandapa, surrounded on 3 sides by a corridor for circumambulation. Its roof of stone slabs is an excellent example of N Indian architecture.

Beyond the Gaudar Gudi temple is a small temple decorated with a frieze of pots, followed by a deep well. There are othersl in various states of repair. To see the most important of the remaining temples you leave the main park. Excavations are in progress, and the boundaries of the park may sometimes be fenced. Turning right out of the main park along the Bagalkot road leads to the **Chikki Temple**. Similar in plan to the Gauda Gudi, the Chikki temple has particularly fine carved pillars. The beams which support the platform are also well worth seeing.

Ravan Phadi Cave temple Formerly known as the Brahman cave, from the main park entrance turn left to get to the temple, about 300m from the village. The cave itself is artificial, and the 6th century temple has a variety of carvings of Siva both outside and inside. One of his figures is in the Ardhanarisvara form, half Siva, half Parvati; and Siva dancing between Parvati and Ganesh. There is a huge lotus carved in the centre of the hall platform. There are 2 small 8th century temples at the entrance, the one to the NW dedicated to Vishnu and that to the S, badly weathered, may have been based on an older Dravidian style temple.

The Buddhist temple There is a rather plain 2-storyed Buddhist temple on a hill beyond the end of the village on the way to the Meguti temple. It has a serene smiling Buddha with the Bodhi Tree emerging from his head, on the ceiling of the upper floor. Further uphill is the Jain temple, a plain structure lacking the decorations on the plinth, columns and no gopuram as found on some of the Hindu temples. It has a statue of Mahavira in the shrine within. Climb up through the roof for a good view of Aihole.

The **Meguti Temple** (634 AD) From the Buddhist Temple a path leads down to a terrace, where the left hand route takes you to the foot of some stairs leading to the top of a hill which overlooks the town. This is the site of what is almost certainly the oldest building in Aihole and one of the oldest dated temples in India. Its 1634 date is indicated by an inscription by the court poet to the king Ravikirtti. A Dravidian style temple, it is richly decorated on the outside, and although in origin it has elements which suggest Saivite origins, it has an extremely impressive seated Jain figure, possibly Neminath, in the sanctuary, which comprises a hall of 16 pillars.

The Kunti Group To visit this group of 4 Hindu temples (7th-9th centuries) you have to return down to the village. The oldest is in the SE. The external columns of its mandapa are decorated with *mithuna*, or erotic couples. The NW temple has beautifully carved ceiling panels of Siva and Parvati, Vishnu and Brahma. This temple is a little later than the SE temple, while the other 2 date from the Rashtrakuta period.

Beyond these temples is the **Hucchappayya Math**, dating from the 7th century, which has sculptures of amorous couples and their servants, while the beams inside are beautifully decorated.

Museum

Archaeological Museum 1000-1700, closed Fri. Free. Collection includes early Western Chalukyan sculpture of 7th-8th century. Photography with permission.

Local festivals

Feb-Mar *Ramalinga Temple Car Festival.*

• **Accommodation** **E** Karnataka Tourism *Tourist Lodge*, T Amingad 41, close to the temples, 11 rm, some with bath, simple food on giving prior notice, helpful staff, you may request a meal even if you are not staying.

ROUTES From Aihole a road rejoins the NH 13 at Hungund. This now takes a new direct route to Bijapur (not shown on any maps), crossing the Krishna S of Nidgundi.

Bijapur

Population: 193,000; *Altitude*: 550m; *STD Code*: 08352. The Chalukyas who ruled over Bijapur were overthrown at the end of the 12th century. In the early years of the 14th century the Delhi Sultans took it for a time until the Bahmanis, with their capital in Gulbarga, ruled through a governor in Bijapur who declared independence in 1489 and founded the Adil Shahi dynasty. Of Turkish origin, they held power until 1686. Bijapur has the air of a N Muslim city with its mausolea, masjids and palaces.

Places of interest

The Jama Masjid is one of the finest in the Deccan with a large shallow, onion-shaped dome and arcaded court. It was built by Ali Adil Shah I (r1557-79) during Bijapur's rise to power and displays a classic restraint. During his reign the citadel was built with its moat as well as palaces, pleasure gardens and a conduit system. The Emperor Aurangzeb added a grand entrance to the Masjid and also had a square painted for each of the 2250 worshippers that it can accommodate. The **Citadel** with its own wall has few of its grand buildings intact. One is the Durbar Hall, **Gagan Mahal**, open to the

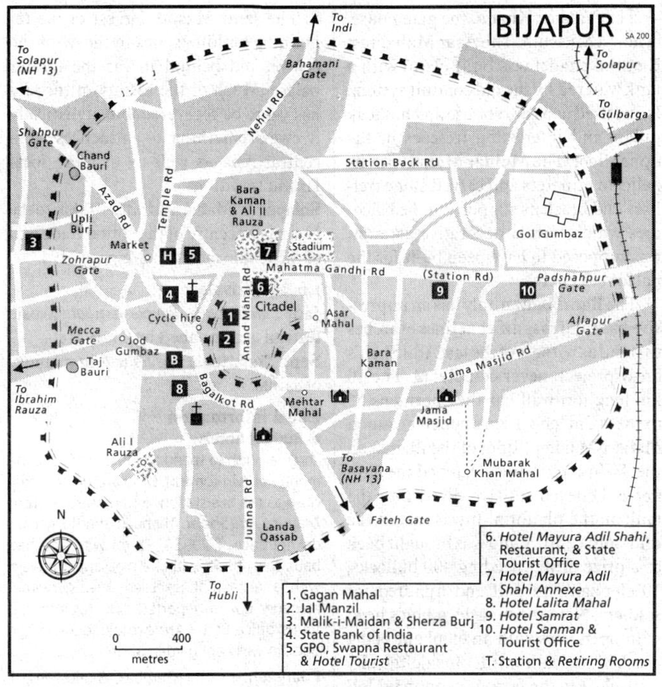

N so that the citizens outside were not excluded. It had royal residential quarters on either side. Another worth visiting is the **Jal Manzil** or the water pavilion, a cool sanctuary.

Ibrahim Rauza, the palatial 17th century tomb outside the city wall to the W, is beautifully proportioned. It has slender minarets and carved decorative panels with lotus, wheel and cross patterns as well as bold Arabic calligraphy, bearing witness to the tolerance of the Adil Shahi dynasty towards other religions. Built during the dynasty's most prosperous period when the arts and culture flourished, it also contains the tomb of Ibrahim Adil Shah II (r1580-1626) who had it built for his wife but died first. Near the Rauza is a huge tank, the Taj Bawdi, built by Ibrahim II in memory of his wife. The approach is through a giant gateway flanked by two octagonal towers.

Gol Gumbaz To the E of the city near the Rly Station is the vast tomb of Mohammad Adil Shah. The world's second largest dome (unsupported by pillars), its wide **whispering gallery** carries a message across 38m which is repeated 11 times. However, noisy crowds make hearing a whisper quite impossible. Quietest in early morning. Numerous narrow steps in one of the 50m high, 7-storeyed corner towers, lead to the 3m wide gallery which can seat 1000. It is believed that the plaster was made out of eggs, cowdung, grass and jaggery. Excellent view of the city with its walls, from the base of the dome. Adil Shah is buried here with his wife, daughter and favourite court dancer. 0600-1800. Small entry fee except Fri, free.

The **Nakkar Khana**, the gate house, is now a Museum. The **Asar Mahal** just E of the citadel was built c1646 with a tank watered by the old conduit system. It was used as a court house and has teak pillars and interesting frescoes in the upper floor. The **Mehtar Mahal** with its delicate minarets and carved stone trellises and brackets supporting the balconies which form a decorative gateway, was supposed to have been built for the palace sweepers.

The **Bara Kaman** only has an impressive base and magnificent lines of arches to stand as witness of the last Adil Shah's great project, never completed. The 10 km long fort wall has the enormous 55 tonne, 4.3m long, 1.5m diameter cannon Malik-i-Maidan (Ruler of the Plains) on the W. To avoid being deafened the gunner is believed to have dived into the tank on the platform! It was cast in the mid-16th century and was brought back as a prize of war needing 400 bullocks, 10 elephants to pull and hundreds of soldiers. Note the muzzle, a lion's head with open jaws with an elephant being crushed to death inside. Inside the city wall, close to the famous cannon is **Upli** (or Haidar) **Burj**, the 24m high watch tower on high ground with its long guns and water tanks. You can climb up the winding staircase outside to get a good view of Bijapur.

Museum

The **Archaeological Museum** in the gatehouse of the Gol Gumbaz has an excellent collection of Chinese porcelain, parchments, paintings, armoury, miniatures, stone sculpture and old Bijapur carpets. 1000-1700, closed Fri. Free.

Excursions

Firuzabad (34 km S of Gulbarga) From Bijapur the road to Gulbarga passes E to these ruins. On a bend in the Bhima River where it takes a U turn from N to S, the massive stone fort walls enclose the old city of Firuzabad on the E, N and S. The **Jami Masjid**, largest of the remaining buildings, lies to the W of the centre, and behind it was the former palace. Much of the history of the city has yet to be recovered, but stylistically it owes something to influences from central Asia as well as to more local Hindu traditions.

Solapur (in Maharashtra) is 101 km to the N, a major centre of the cotton trade and of the textile industry. See page 1194.

Local festivals

Jan *Siddhesvara Temple festival*. Music festival accompaned by Craft Mela.

Sept *Asar Mahal Urs festival* in memory of saints.

Local information

● Budget hotels

You may wish to spend a night here to see the monuments in comfort. Most are located fairly close to the bus station. **E** Karnataka Tourism *Mayura Adil Shahi*, Anandamahal Rd, nr citadel entrance, T 20934, 15 rm with attached bath, fairly basic, within a pleasant courtyard with a restaurant, excellent meals, helpful manager but rm reported dirty, rat infested, tourist office. Better *Annexe* (old Tourist Lodge opp), in well kept garden, 4 rm.

F *Sanman*, nr Gol Gumbaz, Station Rd, T 21866, 24 simple rm, noisy in front, restaurant, local Tourist Office; **F** *Tourist*, MG Rd by Post Office, T 20655, simple rm with bath. Both good value. **F** *State Guest House* nr Sainik School and *Inspection Bungalow*, Station Rd, are primary for official, reservations: Exec Engineer, PWD, Bijapur Div; **F** *Railway Retiring Rooms* and dorm; nearby **F** *Samrat*, Station Rd, T 21620, basic clean rm with bath, good veg restaurant; **F** *Lalita Mahal* nr Bus Station, T 20761, rm at rear quieter.

● Places to eat

Mayura Adil Shahi and *Samrat* do good S Indian *thalis* and *Swapna*, MG Rd nr PO with good veg downstairs.

● Banks & money changers

The State Bank is in the citadel, others in the city outside.

● Shopping

Handlooms, toys and Lambadi gypsy jewellery.

● Tourist office

Mayura Adil Shahi Hotel, 1030-1330, 1415-

1730, Mon-Sat.

● Transport

Local Local bus service: between station (2 km E) to W end of town.

Train Bijapur has a train to Badami which takes about 3½ hr. **Bombay & Hyderabad via Solapur**: Regional timetable: 1506, 3½ hr, change at Solapur (4¼ hr wait); *Bombay-Hyderabad Exp* 7031 (AC/II), daily, 2245, 7¾ hr (total time 15½ hr). **Hospet via Gadag**: *Bijapur Exp* 7790, daily, 0615, 4¾ hr.

Road Bus: buses are frequent between Bijapur and Bidar, Hubli, Belgaum and Solapur (3 hr). There are daily services to Hospet and Badami, Bangalore and Hyderabad.

To visit Badami, Aihole and Pattadakal It is possible to visit Badami, Aihole and Pattadakal by public bus from Bijapur, but it takes a half day to see Badami and does not allow a detour to Mahakuta. If possible it is well worth hiring a car in Bijapur which allows you to see all the sites quite comfortably in one day. If travelling by bus it is best to visit Badami first, followed by Pattadakal and Aihole. By car it is best to start at Aihole and end at Badami.

Bijapur to Raichur and Adoni

ROUTES Take the main road E out of the city centre to Sedam (54 km) which is on the main rail link between Hyderabad and Bangalore. Continue to Yadgir and Raichur (120 km).

Raichur

(*Population*: 170,500; *STD Code*: 08532) For 200 years in the medieval period Raichur dominated the central plateaus of the **Krishna-Tungabhadra doab**. It is still at a crossroads of the regional cultures of Karnataka, Andhra Pradesh and Maharashtra. As Kannada is the dominant language it was allocated to Karnataka after the reorganisation of the states in 1956. Now it is an important market town in the middle of a cotton growing area. Cotton takes up more than 20% of the sown area, followed by groundnuts.

Places of interest

The site of the **fort's citadel** at Raichur gives magnificent views over the vast open spaces of the Deccan plateau nearly 100m below. Built in the mid 14th century Raichur became the first capital of the Bijapur kingdom when it broke away from the Bahmani Sultans in 1489. Much of the fort itself is now in ruins, but there are some interesting remains. The N gate is flanked by towers, a carved elephant standing about 40m away. On the inner walls are some carvings, and a tunnel reputedly built to enable soldiers access to barricade the gate in emergency. Near the W gate is the old palace.

The climb to the citadel begins from near the N gate. In the citadel is a shrine with a row of cells with the Jani Masjid in the E. Its eastern gateway has 3 domes. The top of the citadel is barely 20 sq m. There are some other interesting buildings in the fort below the hill, including the **Daftar ki Masjid** (Office Mosque), built around 1510 out of masonry removed from Hindu temples. It is one of the earliest mosques in the Deccan to be built in this way, with the bizarre result of producing flat ceilinged mosques with pillars carved for Chalukyan temples. The **Ek Minar ki masjid** ("the one minaret mosque") is in the SE corner of the courtyard. It has a distinctively *Bahmani* style dome. **Accommodation** The *Railway Retiring Rooms* offer a choice of accommodation in its rooms and dormitory.

From **Raichur** continue S through Madhavaram (where the road crosses the Tungabhadra River into Andhra Pradesh).

Adoni (80 km *Population*: 135,700; *STD Code*: 08512) a major cotton market. After the Battle of Talikota in 1565 Malik Rahman Khan, the Abyssinian, was appointed Governor by the Sultan. He remained for 39 years. His tomb on the Talibanda Hill is a pilgrimage centre. The lower fort and Jami Masjid were built by his adopted son. The fort was captured by one of Aurangzeb's generals in 1690 after fierce fighting, and in 1740 it fell to the Nizam of Hyderabad, Asaf Jha. Its position at the borders of warring regional powers exposed it to a turbulent history, which culminated in its capture by Tipu Sultan in 1786 and its demolition, ultimately to be returned to the Nizam and then to the British in 1800. The citadel is built on 5 hills, rising 250m above the plateau. There is an excellent tank halfway up the rocks that is reputed never to run dry.

Bijapur to Hungund, Gulbarga and Bidar

ROUTES From Hungund the NH 13 runs N across the Krishna River at Dhanur. An unmetalled road goes E from Dhanur along the S bank of the Krishna River to the hamlet of Amaravadgi (12 km) and a track continues 5 km E to the site of the Battle of Talikota, where the Vijayanagar Empire was swept aside by the combined force of the Deccan Sultanates in 1565. No visible signs remain of the battle site which lies on the S bank of the Krishna River just upstream of the massive Narayanpur Dam (1982) which supplies irrigation water for the left bank of the Krishna. There are attractive gardens at the dam site.

The NH 13 crosses the Krishna to Muddebihal (*Altitude*: 584m), a small market town. A minor road goes SE to Nalatvad and Narayanpur, close to the Jaldurg Falls, where the Krishna, forced between rocky embankments, shoots down a 12m cascade. Part of the river runs through a cave. Nearby is Chhaya Bhagavati, an important riverside pilgrimage centre.

In Muddebihal a route leaves the NH 13 to go NE to **Talikota** on the Don River. 50 km to the E of Talikota is **Hunsigi** (Hunasagi), where some of earliest remains of human settlement have been found, and on to the Lingsugur-Shorapur road.

Shorapur (Surpur; *Altitude*: 400m) is an attractively sited town, surrounded by hills. The fort stands on a hill-top at 567m. The mid 19th century Venkatappa Nayak, Raja of Shorapur, was one of the few S Indian princes to support the 1857 mutiny against the British. The town is noted for the residence of Col Meadows Taylor, still known for his historical novels, but appointed to Shorapur as Political Agent between 1841-53 when he was responsible for Venkatappa Nayak's education. Meadows' house, 'Taylor's Manzil', has excellent views over the town. The Gopalaswamy shrine is the site of a big annual fair.

Sonthi (Sannathi) is an important pilgrimage centre, the **Chandralamba temple** being built at an auspicious point on the banks of the Bhima River where it turns briefly from its southerly direction to flow N. Meanders on the rivers of the Peninsula had long been valued as settlement sites. Not only do they provide protection on 3 sides, but water accumulates in the deep area of a meander bend and tends to remain throughout the dry season, making them not only a source of water for humans but a constant attraction for wildlife.

The Chandralamba temple, probably of Chalukyan origin and dedicated to Siva, has huge mandapas on each side of the main entrance, while the inner courtyard enshrines 12 lingas and statues of Mahakali, Mahalakshmi and Saraswati. There are several others temples, and excavations are showing how Sonthi was once an important Buddhist centre, with the remains of stupas and Buddhist sculptures.

Sonthi was the site of a series of archaeological expeditions in the late 1980s carried out by the British Society for South Asian Studies and the Archaeological Survey of India. An area of 86 ha on the S bend of the river is enclosed by a 4m high wall, frequently interspersed with bastions and gaps which probably corresponded with gateways. Inside is what Howell has described as probably an inner citadel of some 16ha. 3 mounds outside the city are now known to have been Buddhist stupas, which formerly had sculpted relief panels (now in the State Government Museum at Gulbarga). The stupas may have been systematically robbed, and relatively few sculptures or other ornamentation has been discovered from the 1st stupa. The 2nd stupa was associated with large quantities of pottery and over 50 coins dating from the 2nd century AD. Beads, rings and copper ornaments along with glass, shell and terracotta are common. The extent of the discoveries as well as the scale of the fortifications suggest that Sonthi was a major city during the period of Buddhist expansion in the Krishna region and the sculptures are similar though less refined than those at Amaravati and Nagarjunakonda. The whole site may be inundated by a new Government irrigation project.

Gulbarga

(*Population*: 310,000; *STD Code*: 08472) The road N to Gulbarga crosses the undulating black soils of the Deccan lavas. The town was the 1st capital of the Bahmani kingdom (from 1347-1525). It is also widely known among S Indian Muslims as the home of Saiyid Muhammad Gesu Daraz Chisti (1320-1422) who was instrumental in spreading pious Islamic faith in the Deccan. The annual *urs festival* in his memory attracts up to 100,000 people.

Places of interest

The most striking remains in the town are the fort, with its citadel and mosque, the Jami Masjid, and the great tombs in its eastern quarter – massive, fortress-like buildings with their distinctive domes over 30m high.

The **fort** is just 1 km W of the centre of the present town. Originally built by Ala-ud-din Bahmani, 14th century ruler of the Bahmani dynasty, most of the outer structures and many of the buildings are in ruins, although the outer door of the W gate is still intact. The Bala Hissar (citadel) remains almost intact. It is a massive structure. A flight of ruined steps leads up to the entrance in the N wall, and the citadel has turrets at the sides and corners.

The Jami Masjid The whole area of 3500 sq m is covered by a dome over the *mihrab*, 4 corner domes and 75 minor domes, making it unique among Indian mosques. It was built by Firoz Shah Bahmani (1397-1432). Similarities with the great Spanish mosque of Cordoba have contributed to the legend that it was designed by a North African architect from the Moorish court who used the Cordoba mosque as a model.

The tombs of the Bahmani sultans are in 2 groups. One lies 600m to the W

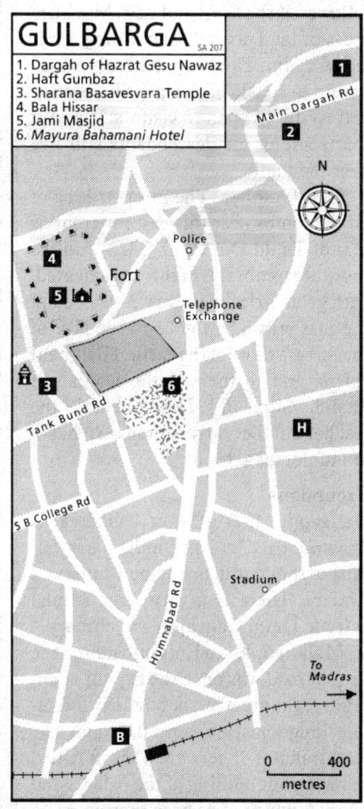

of the fort, the other on the E side of the town. The tombs of the E quarter have no remaining exterior decoration, though the interiors show some evidence of decorative finishing. The tomb of the Chishti saint Gesu Daraz, the Dargah of **Hazrat Gesu Nawaz,** (also known as Khwaja Bande Nawaz) who came to Gulbarga in 1413 during the reign of Firoz Shah Tughlaq, is open to visitors – see page 44. It is surrounded by a complex of buildings. The tomb is 2-storey with a highly decorated painted dome. There is a mother of pearl canopy over the grave which was a late addition. It is reputed to have been built during the reign of Mahmud Adil Shah. Firoz Shah Tughlaq's brother was a devoted follower of the saint and gave him huge areas of land, as well as building a college for him. The Dargah library which has up to 10,000 books in Urdu, Persian and Arabic is open to visitors. It is said that some of his descendants still live near the tomb.

Haft Gumbaz The most striking of all the tombs near this eastern group is that of Taj ud Din Firuz (1422). Unlike the other tombs it is highly ornamented, with geometrical patterns developed in the masonry. The tombs to the NW of the fort are those of the earliest Bahmani rulers, and to their N the Dargah of Shaikh Suraj ud Din Junyadi, the teacher of the early sultans. It has a monumental gateway.

Excursions

Gangapur, 40 km W of Gulbarga, is known for its Sri Narasimha Saraswati *math* at the confluence of the Bhima and Amjera. There is a very large annual yatra to Deval Gangapur in February.

Malkhed, 40 km E of Gulbarga on the Sedam road was once the capital of another of the great but now largely forgotten kingdoms of central India, the Rashtrakutas. There are a few fortified remains, but nothing of the palaces and temples which were once prominent.

• **Accommodation** **F** Karnataka Tourism *Mayura Bahmani*, Public Gardens, T 20644, is probably the best of several small hotels. *Railway Retiring Rooms* for passengers in transit.

• **Transport** Gulbarga is 190 km from Hyderabad in neighbouring Andhra Pradesh. There are regular train and bus connections to Hyderabad and Solapur. **Train Hyderabad**: *Bombay-Hyderabad Exp* 7031 (AC/II), daily, 0050, 5¾ hr. **Secunderabad**: *Minar Exp* 2101 (AC/II), daily, 0745, 4½ hr. **Solapur**: *Kanniyakumari* 1082 (AC/II), daily, 1633, 1½ hr. **Bombay (VT)**: *Udyan Exp* 6530 (AC/II), daily, 0905, 11¼ hr; or: *Minar Exp* 2102 (AC/II), daily, 2010, 10 hr. **Bangalore**: *Karnataka Exp* 2628 (AC/II), daily, 0415, 11 hr. **Madras (MC)**: *Dadar-Madras Exp* 6063 (AC/II), M,W,Th,F,Sa, 0617, 13¾ hr.

ROUTES From Gulbarga the road runs N to Homnabad, where it crosses the Bombay – Hyderabad National Highway, and continues to Bidar.

Bidar

(*Population*: 130,900; *Altitude*: 673m; *STD Code*: 08482) The walled fort town, on a red laterite plateau in N Karnataka, once the capital of the Bahamanis and the Barid Shahis, remained an important centre until it fell to Aurangzeb in 1656 – see page 803. The Bahamani Empire fragmented into 4 kingdoms, and the 9th Bahamani ruler, Ahmad Shah I, shifted his capital from Gulbarga to Bidar in 1424, rebuilding the old Hindu fort to withstand cannon attacks, and enriching the town with beautiful palaces and gardens. With the decline of the Bahamanis, the Barid Shahi dynasty founded here ruled from 1487 until Bidar was annexed to Bijapur in 1619.

Places of interest

The impressive **fort** is still intact and the town sprawls within and outside its crumbling walls, in places retaining its old medieval charm. The palaces and tombs provide some of the finest examples of Muslim architecture in the Deccan. The intermingling of Hindu and

Islamic styles has been ascribed to the use of Hindu craftsmen, skilled in temple carving in stone, particularly hornblende, who would have been employed by the succeeding Muslim rulers. They transferred their skill to Muslim monuments, no longer carving human figures, forbidden by Islam, but using the same technique to decorate with geometric patterns, arabesques and calligraphy, wall friezes, niches and borders on the buildings for their new masters. The pillars, often of wood, were intricately carved and then painted and burnished with gold to harmonise with the encaustic tiles.

The Persian influence in the decorations and tilework may be attributed to the presence of artists and designers from the North, after the mass migration forced by Muhammad-bin-Tughluq, from Delhi to Daulatabad (see page 1172). The preference for brick over stone is evident and in order to create large domes, a light brick was fired using sawdust with clay. The resulting spongey brick was light enough to float!

The **Inner Fort** built by Muhammad Shah out of the red laterite and dark trapstone was later embellished by Ali Barid. The steep hill to the N and E provided natural defence. It was protected to the S and W by a triple moat (now filled). A series of gates and a drawbridge over the moat to the S formed the main entrance from the town. The 2nd gate, the **Sharaza Darwaza** (1503) has tigers carved in bas relief on either side (Shia symbols of Ali as protector), tile decorations on the walls and has the *Nakkar Khana* (Drum gallery) above. Beyond this is a large fortified area which brings you to the 3rd gate, the huge **Gumbad Darwaza**, probably built by Ahmad Shah Wali in the 1420s which shows Persian influence. Note the decorated *gumbad* (dome).

You will see the triple moat to the right and after passing through the gateway, to your left are steps leading to the **Rangin Mahal** (Coloured Palace) where Muhammad Shah moved to, after finding the nearby Shah Burj a safe refuge in 1487 when the Abyssinians attacked. This small palace (an indication of the Bahamanis' declining years) was built by him, elaborately decorated with coloured tiles, later enhanced by Ali Barid with mother-of-pearl inlay on polished black granite walls as well as intricate wood carvings. If locked, ask at Museum for key.

The old banyan tree and the **Shahi Matbak** (once a palace, but served as the Royal Kitchens) are to the W, with the **Shahi Hammam** (Royal Baths) next to it, which now houses a small **Museum**. The exhibits include Hindu religious sculptures, stone age implements, cannon balls filled with bits of iron. 0800-1700.

The **Lal Bagh**, where remains of water channels and a fountain witness to its former glory, and the *zenana*, are opposite the Hamman. The **Sola Khamba** (16 column) or Zanani Mosque is to the W (1423). It is the oldest Muslim building in Bidar and one of the largest in the Deccan. The adjacent **Tarkash Mahal** (part of the zenana enclosure possibly refurbished by the Barid Shahis for the harem), to the S of Lal Bagh, is in ruins but still retains some tilework. From behind the Mosque you can get to the **Gagan Mahal** (Heavenly Palace) which once carried fine decorations and carvings and is believed to have allowed the ladies to watch animal fights in the moat below from the back of the double hall. Good view from the roof. The **Diwan-i-Am** (Hall of Public Audience) is to the NW of the Zenana which once held the 'Takhti-Firoza' (turquoise throne). Little remains of the splendid tiles and stonework. The black hornblende steps and bases of wooden columns survive, which possibly supported a wooden ceiling. To the N stands the **Takht Mahal** with royal apartments, audience hall and swimming bath. The tile decorations and stone carvings are

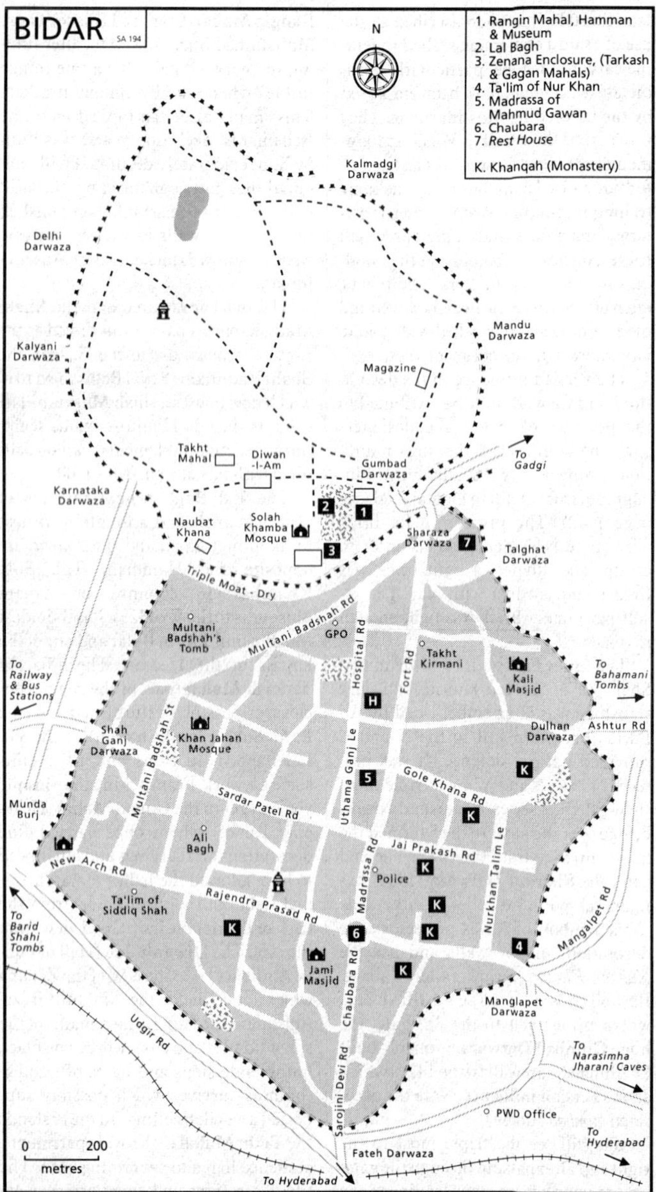
BIDAR
SA 194
N
1. Rangin Mahal, Hamman & Museum
2. Lal Bagh
3. Zenana Enclosure, (Tarkash & Gagan Mahals)
4. Ta'lim of Nur Khan
5. Madrassa of Mahmud Gawan
6. Chaubara
7. Rest House
K. Khanqah (Monastery)
Kalmadgi Darwaza
Delhi Darwaza
Mandu Darwaza
Kalyani Darwaza
Magazine
Takht Mahal
Diwan -I-Am
Gumbad Darwaza
To Gadgi
Karnataka Darwaza
Naubat Khana
Solah Khamba Mosque
Sharaza Darwaza
Talghat Darwaza
Triple Moat - Dry
Multani Badshah's Tomb
Multani Badshah Rd
GPO
Hospital Rd
Fort Rd
Takht Kirmani
Kali Masjid
To Bahamani Tombs
To Railway & Bus Stations
Shah Ganj Darwaza
Multani Badshah St
Khan Jahan Mosque
Uthama Ganj Le
Dulhan Darwaza
Ashtur Rd
Gole Khana Rd
Sardar Patel Rd
Munda Burj
Ali Bagh
Jai Prakash Rd
Nurkhan Talim Le
Madrassa Rd
New Arch Rd
Police
Ta'lim of Siddiq Shah
Rajendra Prasad Rd
Mangalpet Rd
To Barid Shahi Tombs
Jami Masjid
Chaubara Rd
Manglapet Darwaza
Udgir Rd
To Narasimha Jharani Caves
Sarojini Devi Rd
PWD Office
To Hyderabad
0 200
metres
Fateh Darwaza
To Hyderabad

particularly fine. Good views of the 'lowlands' from the windows of the royal apartment to the W. The steep staircase will take you down to underground chambers.

S of the Royal Apartments is the well which supplied water to the fort palaces through clay pipes. Of the so called **Hazar** (thousand) **Kothri**, you can only see a few underground rooms and passages which enabled a quick escape to the moat when necessary. Further S, the **Naubat Khana** probably housed the fort commander and the musicians. The road W from the Royal Apartments leads to the encircling Fort Wall (about 10 km) with bastions carrying vast canyons, the one to the NW being the most impressive. The wall is interrupted by various *darwazas* and *burges* and gives a view of the moat. You can see the ammunition magazine inside the Mandu Darwaza to the E before returning to the main Fort entrance.

Old Town

As you walk S from the fort you can see the ruins of the **Madrassa of Mahmud Gawan**, (1472). The great warrior/statesman/scholar increased the power and extent of the Bahamani kingdom and introduced administrative and military reforms, but these cost him his life. His gift to the country of his exile was the fine Madrassa with its valuable collection of manuscripts. See page 994. Once a famous college which attracted Muslim scholars from afar, it was badly damaged by lightning in 1695 and from an accident when Aurangzeb's soldiers used it to store gunpowder. It is a fine example of his native Persian architecture and still bears signs of the once brilliant green, white and yellow tiles which covered the whole façade with swirls of floral patterns and bold calligraphy. Percy Prior points out that lead sheets were used in the foundation, much like a damp-proof course, to reduce moisture damage to the tiles. Here "instead of decoration being subordinate to the construction, it dominates it".

The **Chaubara** is a 23m circular watch tower at the crossroads, S of the town centre (good views from the top). S of this is the **Jami Masjid** (1430) which bears the Barid Shahis' typical chain and pendant motif. The **Kali Masjid** (1694), S of the Talghat Darwaza, is made of black trapstone. It has fine plaster decorations on the vaulted ceiling. There are also a number of **Khanqahs** (monasteries).

To the E of town, outside the walls, are the **Habshi Kot** where the palaces of the important Abyssinians were. From the Police Station, a road leads to the **Narasimha Jharani** underground cave temple (1.5 km). The natural spring requires devotees to wade through water to the sanctuary.

The road E from the Dulhan Darwaza, opp the General Hospital, leads to the 8 **Bahamani tombs** at **Ashtur**. 0800-1700. These are best seen in the morning when the light is better for viewing the interiors. **NB** The attendant can use a mirror to reflect sunlight but it is best to carry your own flash light.

The square tombs, with arched arcades all round have bulbous domes. The exteriors have stone carvings and superb coloured tile decoration showing strong Persian influence, while the interiors have coloured paintings with gilding. The tomb$of **Ahmad Shah I**, the 9th Bahamani ruler (see above), is impressive with a dome rising to nearly 35m, and has a particularly fine interior with coloured decorations and calligraphy in the Persian style, highlighted with white borders. To the E and S are minor tombs of his wife and son. The tomb of **Alauddin Shah II** (1458) is possibly the finest. Similar in size to his father's, this has lost its fine painting inside but enough remains of the outer tilework to give an impression of its original magnificence. The flat surface of the walls are broken by black stone borders to the colourful tiled panels. Some of the tombs were never completed, and that of 'Humayun the Cruel' was rent apart by lightning, revealing in cross-section the use of light bricks in order to create a large dome (see above). **Muhammad Shah**, who ruled for 36 years, was able to complete his own tomb. Its interest lies in the arched niches.

On the way back, is the **Chaukhandi of Hazrat Khalil-Ullah** which is approached by a flight of steps. Most of the tilework has disappeared but you can see the fine carvings at the entrance and on the granite pillars.

The **Barid Shahi tombs** each of which once stood in its garden, are on the Nanded Rd to the W of the old town. That of Ali Barid is the most impressive, with the dome rising to over 25m, with granite carvings, decorative plasterwork and calligraphy and floral patterns on the coloured tiles, which sadly can no longer be seen on the exterior. Here, abandoning the customary *mihrab* on the W wall, Ali Barid chose to have his tomb left open to the elements. A prayer hall, music rooms, a combined tomb for his concubines and a pool fed by an aquaduct are nearby. There are fine carvings on the incomplete tomb to his son Ibrahim Barid, to the W. You can also see 2 sets of granite Ranakhambas (lit battleposts) which may have been boundary markers. Other tombs show the typical arched niches employed to lighten the heavy walls which have decorative parapets.

The road N from Ali Barid's tomb, descends to **Nanak Jhera**, where a *gurdwara* marks the holy place where Sikhs believe a miracle was performed by Guru Nanak (see page 91) and the *jhera* (spring) rose.

Local information

● Accommodation

Best is the **D** *Bidar International*, Udgir Rd; **D** Karnataka Tourism *Mayura Barid Shahi*, Udgir Rd, nr Bus Station, T 20571, 20 rm, restaurant, beer bar.

E *Hubshi Kot Guest House* and *Orient House* may be booked through Exec Engineer, Bidar.

F PWD *Travellers Bungalow*.

● Shopping

Excellent *bidriwork* (see page 1068) here, where it is said to have originated, particularly shops in Siddiq Talim Rd. You can see craftsmen at work in the narrow lanes.

● Transport

Local Autorickshaws: are the most convenient.

Train Bidar is on a branch line from Wadi Jet to Secunderabad.

ANDHRA PRADESH

CONTENTS

MAPS

BASICS *Population*: 66mn (Urban 30%, Scheduled Castes 15%, Scheduled Tribes 6%); *Literacy*: M 56% F 34%; *Birth rate*: *Rural* 24:1000, *Urban* 22:1000; *Death rate*: *Rural* 10:1000, *Urban* 7:1000. *Infant mortality: Rural* 86:1000, *Urban* 50:1000; *Religion*: *Hindu* 88%, *Muslim* 9%, *Christian* 3%.

Environment

Land

Area 275,000 sq km. Andhra stretches over 1,200 km along the eastern seaboard of India from Berhampur (just in Orissa) almost to Madras. Along the coast is a long, narrow and flat strip of land. The alluvial soils can be very fertile when they are irrigated, as in the deltas of the Godavari and Krishna Rivers. However, the deltas are subject to some of the worst cyclones in S Asia. Protective measures have now been taken to provide sheltered housing, but severe storms still cause heavy damage. Immediately inland is a series of hill ranges running nearly parallel with the coast. The ancient rocks of the Peninsula inland generally give very thin red soils.

Rivers For much of the year many areas of Andhra look hot, dry and desolate although the great delta of the Krishna and Godavari Rivers retains its lush greenness by virtue of their irrigation water. The **Godavari** and the **Krishna** cross the state, dominating its drainage pattern. The Godavari, rising less than 200 km N of Bombay and flowing nearly 1,500 km SE across the Deccan Plateau, is the largest of the peninsular rivers. The Krishna rises near **Mahabaleshwar** at an altitude of 1,360m. It then flows 1,400 km to the Bay of Bengal.

After the Ganga these 2 rivers have the largest watersheds in India, and between them they irrigate nearly 6 million ha of farm land. The much smaller rivers of the **Pennar** and **Cheyyar** are important locally, but are often dry. The Nagarjunasagar Dam on the Krishna impounds AP's largest lake. On the delta between the Krishna and the Godavari the *Kolleru Lake* covers nearly 260 sq km during the wet season and is now a bird sanctuary.

Climate

AP is hot throughout the year. The interior of the state is in the rain shadow of the Western Ghats and receives less rainfall than much of the coast. All regions have most of their rain between Jun and Oct, although the S gets the benefit of the retreating monsoon between Oct and Dec.

History

The first historical evidence of a people called the 'Andhras' came from Emperor Asoka. The first known Andhra power,

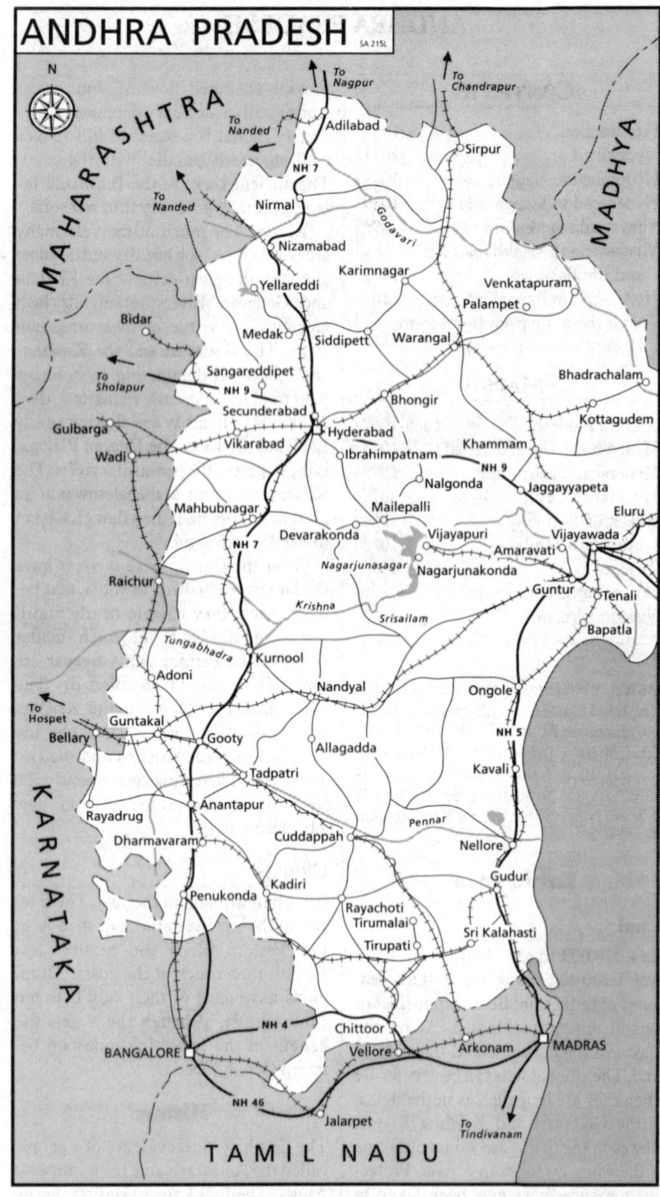
ANDHRA PRADESH
SA 215L
N
MAHARASHTRA
MADHYA
KARNATAKA
TAMIL NADU
To Nagpur
To Chandrapur
To Nanded
To Nanded
To Sholapur
To Hospet
To Tindivanam
Adilabad
Sirpur
NH 7
Nirmal
Godavari
Nizamabad
Karimnagar
Yellareddi
Venkatapuram
Palampet
Bidar
Medak
Siddipett
Warangal
Sangareddipet
NH 9
Bhadrachalam
Bhongir
Secunderabad
Kottagudem
Gulbarga
Hyderabad
Vikarabad
Khammam
Wadi
Ibrahimpatnam
NH 9
Nalgonda
Jaggayyapeta
Mahbubnagar
Mailepalli
Eluru
Devarakonda
Vijayapuri
Vijayawada
NH 7
Amaravati
Nagarjunasagar
Nagarjunakonda
Raichur
Guntur
Tenali
Krishna
Srisailam
Bapatla
Tungabhadra
Kurnool
Adoni
Nandyal
Ongole
Guntakal
Bellary
Gooty
NH 5
Allagadda
Kavali
Tadpatri
Anantapur
Rayadrug
Pennar
Dharmavaram
Cuddappah
Nellore
Gudur
Penukonda
Kadiri
Rayachoti
Tirumalai
Sri Kalahasti
Tirupati
NH 4
Chittoor
MADRAS
BANGALORE
Vellore
Arkonam
NH 46
Jalarpet

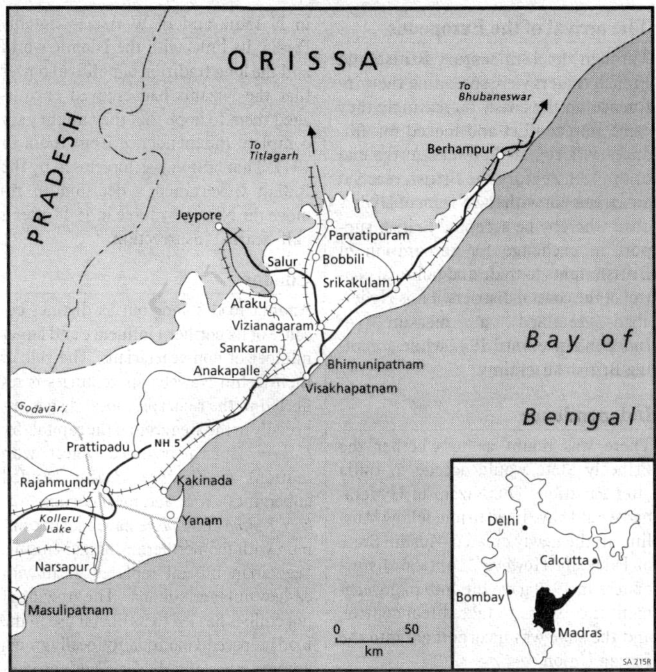

the Satavahanas, encouraged various religious groups including Buddhists. Their capital at Amaravati shows evidence of the great skill and artistry of early Andhra artists and builders. In the 50 years before AD 200 there was also a fine university at Nagarjunakonda.

Vijayanagar

In 1323 Warangal, just to the NE of the present city of Hyderabad, was captured by the armies of Muhammad bin Tughlaq. Muslim expansion further S was prevented for 2 centuries by the rise of the Vijayanagar Empire, itself crushed at the Battle of Talikota in 1565 by a short-lived federation of Muslim States, and the cultural life it supported had to seek fresh soil.

The Muslim states From then on Muslim rulers dominated the politics of central Andhra, the region now known as **Telangana**. The Bahmani kingdoms in the region around modern Hyderabad controlled central Telangana in the 16th century. They were even able to keep the Mughals at bay until Aurangzeb finally forced them into submission at the end of the 17th century. Hyderabad was the most important centre of Muslim power in central and S India from the 17th to the 19th centuries. It was founded by the 5th in line of an earlier Muslim dynasty, Mohammad Quli Qutb Shah, in 1591. His tomb, standing outside Hyderabad next to Golconda Fort, is an impressive testimony to the power in the region. Through his successors Hyderabad became the capital of a Princely State the size of France, ruled by a succession of Muslim Nizams from 1724 till after India's Independence in 1947.

The arrival of the Europeans

Through the 18th century British and French traders were spreading their influence up the coast. Increasingly they came into conflict and looked for alliances with regional powers. At the end of the 18th century the British reached an agreement with the Nizam of Hyderabad whereby he accepted British support in exchange for recognition of British rights to trade and political control of the coastal districts. Thus Hyderabad retained a measure of Independence until 1947 while accepting British suzerainty.

Independence

There was doubt as to whether the Princely State would accede to India after Partition. The Nizam of Hyderabad would have liked to join fellow Muslims in the newly created Muslim State of Pakistan. However, political disturbances in 1949 gave the Indian government the excuse to take direct control, and the state was incorporated into the Indian Union.

Culture

People

Most of Andhra Pradesh's 67 m people are Dravidians. Over 85% of the population speak Telugu. However, there are important minorities. Tamil is widely spoken in the extreme S, and on the border of Karnataka there are pockets of Kanarese speakers. In Hyderabad there are large numbers of Urdu speakers who make up 7% of AP's population.

Religion

Hyderabad, the capital of modern AP, was the seat of government of the Muslim Nizams. Under their rule many Muslims came to work in the court, from N India and abroad. The Nizam's capital was a highly cosmopolitan centre, drawing extensively on Islamic contacts in N India and in W Asia – notably Persia. Its links with the Islamic world and the long tradition of political power that the Nizams had enjoyed encouraged them to hope that they might gain complete Independence from India in 1947. That option was foreclosed by the Indian Government's decision to remove the Nizam by force in 1948 after a half-hearted insurrection.

Cuisine

Andhra food stands out as distinct because of its northern influence and larger number of non-vegetarians. The rule of the Muslim Nawabs for centuries is reflected in the rich, spicy local dishes, especially in the area around the capital. Try *Haleem* (spiced pounded wheat with mutton) or *Baghara Baigan* (stuffed aubergines). Rice and meat *Biryani*, *Nahari*, *Kulcha* and *Kababs* have a lot in common with the northern Mughlai cuisine. Vegetarian biryani replaces meat with cashew nuts and sultanas. The growing of hot chillies has led to its liberal use in the food prepared. Good quality locally grown grapes (especially *Anab e Shahi*) or khobani (puréed apricots) provide a welcome neutralising effect.

Craft industries

Andhra's **Bidriware** uses dark matt gunmetal (a zinc and copper alloy) with silver damascening in beautiful flowing floral and arabesque patterns and illustrates the Persian influence on Indian motifs. The articles vary from large vases and boxes, jewellery and plates to tiny buttons and cuff links. The name is derived from Bidar in Karnataka and dates back to the Bahmani rulers. **Toys** Miniature wooden figures, animals, fruit, vegetables and birds are common subjects of **Kondapalli** toys which are known for their bright colours. **Nirmal** toys look more natural and are finished with a herbal extract which gives them a golden sheen, **Tirupati** toys are in a red wood while Ethikoppaka toys are finished in coloured lacquer. Andhra also produces fine figurines of deities in sandalwood. **Jewellery** Hyderabadi jewellers work in gold and precious stones which are often uncut. The craftsmen can often be seen working in the lanes around the Char Minar with shops selling the typical local bangles set with glass to the W. Hyderabadi cultured pearls and silver filigree ware from Karimnagar are another speciality.

Textiles The state is famous for **Himru** shawls and fabrics produced in cotton/silk mixes with rich woven patterns on a special handloom. Silver or gold threads produce even richer 'brocade' cloth. A young boy often sits with the weavers 'calling out' the intricate pattern. The art of weaving special **Ikat** fabrics (see page 722) has been revived through the efforts of the All India Handicrafts Board in the villages of Pochampalli, Chirala, Puttapaka and Koyyalagudem among others. The practice of dyeing the warp and weft threads before weaving in such a way as to produce a pattern, additionally used oil in the process when it was woven into pieces of cloth *Teli rumal* (literally oil kerchief) to be used as garments. Other towns produce their own special weaves. **Kalamkari paintings** (*kalam* refers to the pen used) produced in Kalahasti in the extreme S of Andhra, have a distinctive style using indigo and vegetable dyes extracted from turmeric, pomegranate skin etc, on cloth. Fabric is patterned through the medium of dye, then glued. The blues stand out markedly from the otherwise dullish ochre colours. Originally designed to tell stories from mythology (Mahabharata and Ramayana), they make good wall hangings. *Pallakollu* and *Masulipatam* were particularly famous for printing and painting of floral designs. In addition hand block printed textiles are also produced. **Carpets** are produced in Warangal and Eluru and are known as 'Deccan rugs' with designs that reflect a Persian influence.

EARLY ANDHRA SATIRE

Although the name Andhra was well known the Telugu language did not emerge until the 11th century AD. There developed a vigorous literary tradition, not always simply in the hands of the Brahmin priesthood. Two writers dominated. Potana (1400-75) was a poor man who lived in the countryside. His translation of the Bhagavata, immediately popular, combined simple language with deep devotion. Vemana (15th century) was a low caste Saivite, an individualist and a revolutionary. J.T.F. Jordens has pointed out that "His sataka (century) of gnomic verse is known to all Telugus and to most S Indians. His verses bristle with sarcastic attacks on the Brahmans, on polytheism, idolatry, and pilgrimages.

> The solitariness of a dog! the meditation of a crane!
> The chanting of an ass! The bathing of a frog!
> Ah, why will ye not try to know your own hearts?
>
> What are you the better for smearing your body with ashes?
> Your thoughts should be set on God alone;
> For the rest, an ass can wallow in dirt as well as you.
>
> The books that are called the Vedas are like courtesans,
> Deluding men, and wholly unfathomable;
> But the hidden knowledge of God is like an honourable wife.
>
> He that fasts shall become (in his next birth) a village pig;
> He that embraces poverty shall become a beggar;
> And he that bows to a stone shall become like a lifeless image."

Modern Andhra Pradesh

Government

In 1953 AP was created on the basis of the Telugu-speaking districts of Madras Presidency. This was not enough for those who were demanding statehood for a united Telugu-speaking region. One political leader, Potti Sreeramulu, starved himself to death in protest at the government's refusal to grant the demand. Finally, in 1956, AP took its present form. It was the first State to be re-organised when the Indian Government decided to re-shape the political map inherited from the British period. In 1956 all Telugu-speaking areas were grouped together in the new State of AP. This brought together the eastern parts of the old Nizam's territories and the coastal districts which had formerly been in Madras Presidency became the capital of the new state.

Despite the growth in the economy many areas of the state remain extremely poor. Some regions have continued to see political unrest. The Naxalite movement, which started in Bengal, has a hold in NE Andhra Pradesh. AP was regarded as a stronghold of the Congress Party until 1983 when a regional party, the Telugu Desam, won a crushing victory in the State Assembly elections. The Leader of the Telugu Desam, NT Rama Rao used his fame as film star playing popular gods as a stepping stone to political power, and in the late 1980s his hold seemed unbreakable. However, the Congress continued to do well in Lok Sabha elections, and in the 1989 elections the Telugu Desam suffered its own resounding defeat. On June 20th 1991, PV Narasimha Rao became the first ever South Indian Prime Minister.

AP elects 42 members to the Lok Sabha, the lower house of Parliament in New Delhi. It has a Legislative Assembly of 294 seats and a Legislative Council as a 2nd chamber elected by university graduates, representatives of local bodies and Members of the Legislative Assembly. It has 23 administrative districts.

The Economy

Agriculture Rice is the dominant crop, but some cash crops like sugar cane are also important in the deltas of the Godavari and Krishna. In the dry interior farming is much more difficult. Rainfall is around 1000 mm a year, but evaporation rates are very high and the concentration of rainfall in 3 or 4 months of the year greatly limits its effectiveness. In the Telangana region of central AP only between 20% and 40% of the area is cultivated. Millets, sorghum and gram are grown on the unirrigated land. Oil seeds are the most important cash crop, especially groundnuts and castor. On the areas brought under well, tank or canal irrigation rice predominates. Valley floors are often intensively cultivated while the surrounding hills and slopes are completely barren. The comparatively harsh 'dry land' environment contributed to the United Nations' decision to set up the *International Centre for Research in the Semi Arid Tropics* (ICRISAT) just outside Hyderabad in the early 1970s. This has now become the world's leading research centre for dryland tropical agriculture.

Hyderabad also grows a special variety of grape which was discovered growing in a garden in the early part of the 20th century, believed to have been introduced originally from the Middle E, by *Haj* pilgrims. Its flavour so impressed the Nizam that he named it the King of *Grapes* or *Anab-e-Shahi*. Its high productivity has led to a flourishing viticulture industry.

Industry and Resources The state's most important *mineral resources* are coal, mined in the Singareni field along the lower Godavari valley, and high quality iron ore in the far N, which is not yet developed as fully. Some believe, one of the most famous diamonds in the world, the Koh-i-Noor, was found at Golconda, W of Hyderabad. Diamond mines are being opened up again after a long period of closure. Iron ore, copper, asbestos and barytes are found, but are too scattered to be of great economic value.

AP has nearly 10% of India's total industrial employment. High tech industries have grown up fast around the capital Hyderabad. Shipbuilding, heavy engineering and iron and steel are important in the coastal belt, especially at Visakhapatnam. In addition, over 60,000 people are employed in small scale units.

Transport Hyderabad is on main railway lines to Bombay and Madras, and is linked via Warangal with Delhi. There are over 2,500 km of national highway and over 50,000 km of state and minor roads, but most of these are unsurfaced. Hyderabad and other major towns are connected by air to the national network. Visakhapatnam has been greatly expanded as one of the country's major ports. It has facilities for shipbuilding and is the Indian Navy's Eastern HQ.

HYDERABAD

Population: 4.28mn; *STD Code*: 0842; *Altitude*: 537m. Approaching Hyderabad from the air it is often possible to obtain magnificent views of the extraordinary landscape in which Hyderabad is at the heart. Over 400 km E of the crest line of the Western Ghats, Hyderabad lies in the rain shadow of the hills. It is built on the ancient granites and gneisses of the Peninsula, which outcrop in bizarre shapes on hills in many parts of the city and its surrounds, and which provide building stone for some of the city's most impressive monuments, such as the pillars of the Mecca Masjid in the old city centre. Within the rocks lay some of the region's most valued resources, gem stones. The Golconda kingdoms which preceded those of Hyderabad and whose capital lies just 8 km from the present city, produced magnificent diamonds, including the **Koh-i-Noor**. This legendary jewel was given to the Mughal Emperor Humayun after the Battle of Panipat, subsequently to be cut and dispersed, a part into the English royal crown. See page 325.

Hyderabad was the most important centre of Muslim power in central and S India from the 15th to 19th centuries. Even though the population was always predominantly composed of Telugu-speaking Hindus, Hyderabad was ruled by a succession of Muslim Nizams from 1724 when the Nizam-ul-Mulk ('Regulator of the Land') Asaf Jah, seized power from the Mughal Governor of the Deccan district of Khandesh, founding the dynasty that included some of the 'richest men in the world'. Hyderabad had been founded by the 5th Sultan of Golconda of an earlier Muslim dynasty, Muhammad Quli Qutb Shah, in 1589, under the original name of *Bhagnagar*. The founders were apparently famous for their beautiful 'monuments, mosques and mistresses' and also for their diamond markets. Hyderabad stood on the S bank of the river Musi, in a prime military position.

Unlike other Mughal cities, it was

CLIMATE: HYDERABAD

	Jan	Feb	Mar	Apr	May	Jun	Jul	Aug	Sep	Oct	Nov	Dec	Av/Tot
Max (°C)	29	31	35	37	39	34	30	29	30	30	29	28	32
Min (°C)	15	17	20	24	26	24	22	22	22	20	16	13	20
Rain (mm)	2	11	13	24	30	107	165	147	163	71	25	5	763

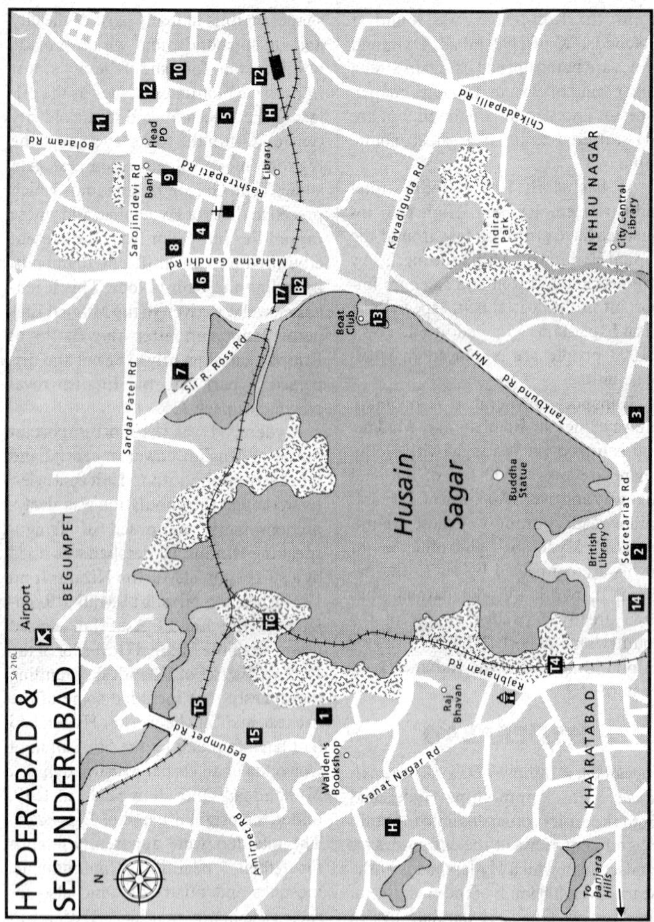

planned in a grid pattern with enormous arches and the Char Minar was built in 1591 by the Sultan as the city's prime monument. The streets were lined with stone buildings which had shops below and living quarters above (many are still standing). If you come out through the western arch of the Char Minar you enter Lad Bazar where shops sell the typical Hyderabadi glass embedded bangles while to the N you will find the jewellers including those with pearls, and cloth merchants. To the S the craftsmen in their tiny shops still prepare thin silver 'leaf' by pounding the metal.

During the Asaf Jahi rule the city expanded N of the river. Then in the early 19th century, during the reign of Sikander Jah(1803-30), the cantonment of Secunderabad was developed by the

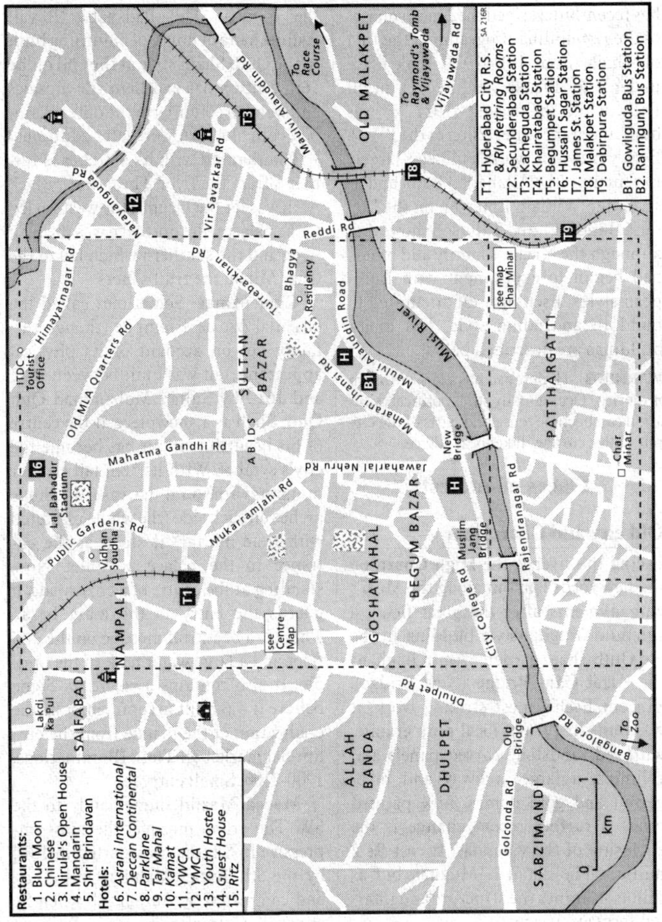

British, further up river. Close to the Salar Jung Museum, you can see examples of Asaf Jahi architecture. N of the river are the Asafia State Library and Osmania General Hospital and on the S bank the City College and the High Court. Other typical examples are in the Public Gardens behind the Archaeological Museum, where you will find the Ajanta Pavilion, the elaborate Jubilee Hall, the State Assembly Hall and the Health Museum.

In 1908 several lowlying parts of the city were totally destroyed by floods of the River *Musi*, and a devastating plague followed in 1911. These disasters were followed by programmes of urban renewal initiated by Nizam Osman Ali Khan, with a series of new public buildings dating from this period. Tillotson has recently described the 2 main phases of the re-building programme, the first of which, from 1914-1921, took place under the British architect Vincent Esch, while the second (1921-36) was built under the supervision of the PWD. Esch's previous work had been largely in Calcutta (the Allahabad Bank and as second to William Emerson on the Victoria Building), and Tillotson shows that although the Nizam's family and others had begun to experiment with European styles, Esch himself attempted to build in an Indian style. His major buildings are described below.

WARNING Hyderabad has a large Muslim minority. Occasionally the political situation can become tense and parts of the city put under curfew. Take local advice.

Places of interest

Old city and Charminar

Facing the river is the **High Court**, on the new roads laid out along the Musi's embankments after the great flood, a splendid Mughal-style building in the old Qutb Shahi gardens, Amin Bagh, nr the Afzal Ganj Bridge (New Bridge). Vincent Esch's most striking work, it was built in 1916 of local pink granite, with red sandstone carved panels and columns, a large archway and blue-glazed and gold domes, now painted pink. A further recent change is the enclosure of the verandas. It cost Rs 2 million. The detail is Mughal, but as Tillotson argues the structure and internal form are Western.

Next door to the High Court is Esch's **City College** (1917-20), originally built as the City High School for boys. Built largely of undressed granite, there are some distinctive Indian decorative features including some marble *jalis*. Esch deliberately incorporated Gothic features, calling his style 'Perpendicular Mogul Saracenic'.

Going S, on Mahboob Shahi Rd you will see one of the oldest imambaras in the country. The Badshahi (Royal) **Ashurkhana** or house of mourning built in the Qutb Shahi style at the end of the 16th century has excellent tile mosaics and wooden columns in the outer chamber, both of which were later additions.

Charkaman with its 4 arches is further S from the river. The eastern Black Arch was for the Drums, the western led to the palaces, the northern was the Fish Arch and the southern which led to the Char Minar, the fruit sellers.

Char Minar Sometimes called the Oriental Arc de Triomphe (though certainly not on account of its physical appearance), it was built between 1591 and 1612 by Sultan Mohammad Quli Qutb Shah as a showpiece at the centre of his beautiful city; it has become the city's symbol. With its 56m tall slender minarets with spiral staircases and huge arches on each side (the whole plastered with lime mortar) it stood at the entrance to the palace complex. Now, standing at the centre of a crossroads, it guards the entry to the main bazar. There is a beautiful mosque on the 2nd floor and a large water tank in the middle. It also contains a *madrassa*. Some believe it was built to commemorate the eradication of the plague from the city. Special market on Thur. Illuminations, 1900-2100. Small entry fee.

Mecca Masjid immediately to the SW. The grand mosque, the most impressive in S India, was started in 1614 by the 6th Sultan Abdulla Qutb Shah and completed by Aurangzeb when he annexed Golconda in 1692. Built of enormous black granite slabs quarried nearby it has tall pillars, stucco decorations and red bricks on its entrance arches believed to have been made from clay from Mecca mixed with red colouring. The vast mosque, one of the largest in India, can accommodate 10,000 at prayers. The tombs of the Asaf Jahi rulers, the Nizams of Hyderabad, are in a roofed enclosure to the left of the courtyard. To the NE also on the E of Sardar

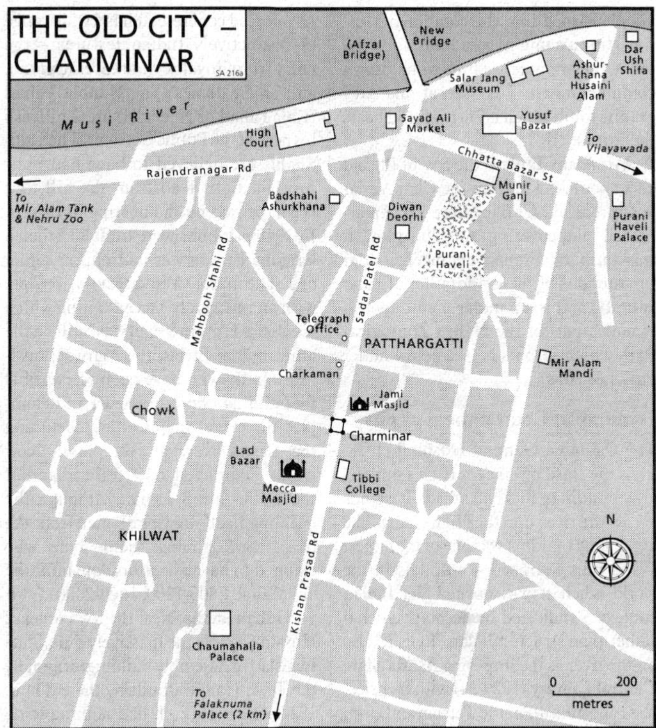

Patel Rd, the **Jami Masjid** in a narrow lane was the 2nd mosque built in the old city at the end of the 16th century.

To the W of the Char Minar the **Lad Bazar** area has interesting buildings with wood and stone carvings and the pink elephant gates. You arrive at the **Chowk** which has a mosque and a Victorian Clock Tower. SE of the Lad Bazar is the huge complex of the palaces which were built by the different Nizams, including the grand **Chaumahalla Palace** around a quadrangle.

About 2 km S along Sardar Patel Rd and Kishan Prasad Rd, on Kohi Tur Hill, stands the **Falaknuma Palace** (1873), originally a rich nobleman's house, built in a mixture of classical and Mughal styles. Bought by the Nizam in 1897, it has a superb interior (particularly the state reception room) with marble, chandeliers and paintings. The palace houses oriental and European treasures, including a collection of jade, crystal and precious stones and a superb library. Prior permission is required to visit.

North East of Char Minar is the **Purani Haveli** (Old Palace) which is a vast mansion, worth visiting (prior permission required).

The **Tomb of Michel Raymond** is off the Vijayawada Rd, about 3 km from the Oliphant Bridge. The Frenchman joined the 2nd Nizam's army in 1786 as a common soldier and rose to command 15,000 troops. His popularity with the people earned him the combined Muslim-Hindu name 'Moosa Ram' and even today they remember him by holding a commemorative *Urs* fair at his grey granite tomb which is 7m high and bears the initials 'JR'.

Mir Alam Tank to the SW of the old city, about 2.5 km from the Char Minar is approached by Bangalore Rd. An artificial lake covering over 20 sq km, it was built by French engineers under instructions of the grandfather of Salar Jung III and is a popular picnic spot. It is now a part of the **Nehru Zoological Park** which is to its N (see below under **Parks & zoos**).

Hyderabad Centre: the new city

The **Osmania General Hospital** (1918-21)is the third of Vincent Esch's impressive buildings in Hyderabad. It stands across the river, opp the High Court. The 200m long building was one of the largest – and best equipped – hospitals in the world when it was opened. Its Indian context is indicated by decorative detail rather than structural plan. To its E, also on the river, is the imposing **Asafia State Central Library** (1929-34) with its priceless collection of Arabic, Persian and Urdu books and manuscripts. The Library was designed by anonymous architects of the PWD. Tillotson states that "Its main front facing the river is dominated by the huge arch of the entrance portal. This is a powerful and also an original motif: round, rather than the usual pointed form, it is rendered Indian by the mouldings on the intrados and by the *chajja* which sweeps over the top."

The **Public Gardens** in Nampally, N of Hyderabad Station, are the largest in Asia and contains many important buildings including the Archaeological Museum and Art Galleries and the State Legislative Assembly (Vidhan Sabha). The **City Railway Station** (1914) was intended by Esch to be pure Mughal in style but built entirely of the most modern material then available – pre-cast, re-inforced concrete. It has a wide range of distinctively Indian features – the chhattris of royalty, wide eaves (*chajjas*), and onion domes. The **Naubat Pahad** (Kala Pahad or Neeladri) are 2 hillocks to the N of the Public Gardens. The Qutb Shahis are believed to have had their proclamations read from the hill tops accompanied by the beating of drums. In 1940 pavilions were built and then a hanging garden was laid out on top of one. The marble **Venkatesvara Temple** with an intricately carved ceiling which overlooks Husain Sagar, was built on the other by the Birlas, the Marwari business family who have been responsible for building important new Hindu temples in several major cities, including the Laxmi Narayan Temple in New Delhi. Completed in 1976, the images of the deities are S Indian, although the building itself drew craftsmen from the N as well, among them some who claimed to have ancestors who built the Taj Mahal. 0800-1200, 1600-2000.

Vidhan Sabha Near the SW corner of Husain Sagar is the massively built State Legislative Assembly building, originally the Town Hall, wasbuilt by the PWD in 1922. Although Esch had nothing to do with its design Tillotson records that he greatly admired it for its lightness and coolness, even on the hottest day. He suggests that both the Town Hall and the State Library marked a move away from a Hyderabadi style to a more universal "Indian" approach to design.

The **Jubilee Hall** (1936), behind the Vidhan Sabha, is another remarkable PWD building, with clear simple lines. Tillotson notes the irony in the fact that official contemporary descriptions of these works claim that they represent the natural re-development of a Hyderabadi style, when the PWD architects themselves appear to have been aiming for something more genuinely pan-Islamic.

Husain Sagar is further N. The lake was built in the 16th century and named to mark the gratitude of the Qutb Shahi

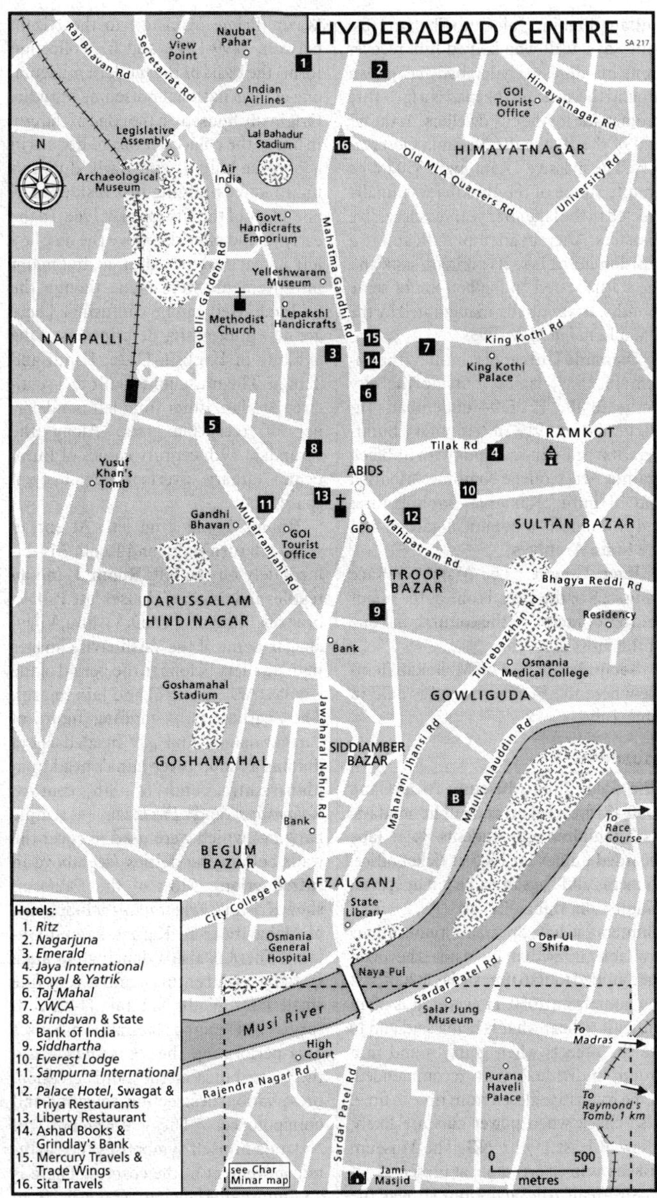
HYDERABAD CENTRE
SA 217
Raj Bhavan Rd
Secretariat Rd
View Point
Naubat Pahar
Indian Airlines
Himayatnagar Rd
GOI Tourist Office
Legislative Assembly
Lal Bahadur Stadium
HIMAYATNAGAR
Old MLA Quarters Rd
University Rd
N
Archaeological Museum
Air India
Govt. Handicrafts Emporium
Mahatma Gandhi Rd
Public Gardens Rd
Yelleshwaram Museum
Methodist Church
Lepakshi Handicrafts
NAMPALLI
King Kothi Rd
King Kothi Palace
RAMKOT
Tilak Rd
Yusuf Khan's Tomb
ABIDS
Gandhi Bhavan
Mukarramjahi Rd
GOI Tourist Office
GPO
Mahipatram Rd
SULTAN BAZAR
TROOP BAZAR
Bhagya Reddi Rd
DARUSSALAM
HINDINAGAR
Turrebazkhan Rd
Residency
Bank
Osmania Medical College
Goshamahal Stadium
GOWLIGUDA
Jawaharal Nehru Rd
SIDDIAMBER BAZAR
Maharani Jhansi Rd
Maulvi Alauddin Rd
GOSHAMAHAL
To Race Course
Bank
BEGUM BAZAR
City College Rd
AFZALGANJ
State Library
Osmania General Hospital
Dar Ul Shifa
Naya Pul
Sardar Patel Rd
Salar Jung Museum
Musi River
To Madras
High Court
Rajendra Nagar Rd
Sardar Patel Rd
Purana Haveli Palace
To Raymond's Tomb, 1 km
0 500 metres
see Char Minar map
Jami Masjid
Hotels:
1. Ritz
2. Nagarjuna
3. Emerald
4. Jaya International
5. Royal & Yatrik
6. Taj Mahal
7. YWCA
8. Brindavan & State Bank of India
9. Siddhartha
10. Everest Lodge
11. Sampurna International
12. Palace Hotel, Swagat & Priya Restaurants
13. Liberty Restaurant
14. Ashad Books & Grindlay's Bank
15. Mercury Travels & Trade Wings
16. Sita Travels

Sultan, Ibrahim Quli Qutb Shah to Hussain Shah Wali who helped him recover from his illness. Hyderabad has grown around the lake and the *bund* is a favourite promenade for the city dwellers. At the far end of the lake is the Nizamia Observatory. The massive 17.5m high, 350 tonne granite statue of the Buddha was finally erected in the lake after years of successive disasters. After an attempt to float it to a position in the lake its pontoon sank and the statue rested on the bottom for some months. It was finally inaugurated by the Dalai Lama in May 1993.

Osmania University, built by the Nizam in 1939, is just outside the city limits to the E of Secunderabad. Inaugurated in 1917 in temporary buildings, its sprawling campus with its black granite Arts College combines Moorish and Hindu Kakatiya architectural styles. There is a botanical garden and the **State Archives**.

Race Course The Malakpet Race Course, S of the river, is one of the major centres of racing in the country and one of the most modern.

Secunderabad The Mahakali Temple where the *Bonalu* festival is held in June/July.

Museums

The Salar Jung Museum, Afzal Ganj. 0930-1715, closed Fri and public holidays. Rs 2, Children and students Re 1. Tape recorded guides for Rs 5 at ticket office. Cameras and bags must be left at special counter on right. Tickets (Rs 2) from counters on left. Specialist publications available immediately inside the door. Free guided tours 6 times a day at half past the hour, from 1030. However, it is often difficult to hear what is being said and to see the objects when going round in a group; individual visit recommended. Some rooms are closed from time to time. Also check when power cuts are likely. Allow at least 1½ hr. **NB** The Museum upkeep is in a sorry state at present.

Sir Yusuf Ali Salar Jung III was the Wazir (Prime Minister) to the Nizam between 1899-1949, and his collection forms the basis of the modern museum, one of the 3 national museums in India. Originally housed on the edge of the city in one of the palaces, it was re-housed in a purpose-built if singularly dull and unattractive building just inside the N boundary of the city in early 1968. In the early period after the move the displays left a great deal to be desired, but major improvements were made though the building itself can be confusing. There are now informative descriptions of the exhibits in English, Urdu, Hindi and Telugu. The museum is built to a semicircular plan. Enter from left hand corner of reception area. Along the verandah, 19th century copies of European statuary overlook small open space.

Rooms 1 and **2** on left. At end of verandah turn right, and Room 3 is immediately on the left. **Room 3** **Indian textiles and bronzes** Houses late Pallava bronzes, 9th century AD, Vishnu, Vijayanagar. Some of the Vaishnavite images in this gallery belong to the period of the Cholas (AD 846-1216) and Jain images. The earliest is a standing figure of Parthavananda and a 9 headed cobra holding a canopy over Jaina's head from Maharashtra, end of 8th century. *Kalamkaris* and *Picchwais* – temple hangings which were used to cover the walls behind the deities (see above in **Introduction**). Most of the *Picchwais* show Krishna. *Jain statues* include some of Mahavira from Karnataka and Gujarat. There is also a dancing Nataraja (S India 14th century), and a very fine small Tamil Nadu Nataraja (14th century). The Dancing Nataraja symbolises Siva performing the *Anandatandava* – the 5 attributes of the Lord: creation, preservation, destruction, salvation and omnipotence. The movement of Nataraja himself symbolises the rhythmic movement of the cosmos. There is an unusual dancing Ganesh from

Mysore (15th century). **Room 3a** Indian sculpture opp **Room 3**. Early development of the plastic arts in India. Stone carving from rock pillars (Asokan edicts), Sungan art developments, abounding with the organic forms of nature, through Gupta period. Amaravati and Nagarjunakonda had a soft grey limestone, popularly known as *Palna* marble. An early Gupta *Mukhalinga* (3rd century AD) is given pride of place in the room. **Room 4** Minor arts of S India Wood carving – one of most ancient crafts of the S – sandalwood and rose wood. Temple carving. **Room 6** Printed fabrics and glass Temple cloths in Rajasthani freehand designs with glued appliqué work, wood block printing and scrolls used as visual aids by itinerant "preachers" and storytellers. Some clothing, including 18th century Dhaka muslin. There is some attractive Mughal glass characterised by gilt paint, flowers, coniferous trees. Go through **Room 6**. At other end the small open space is **Room 7**. Turn right. The small open space on the right with large pots counts as **Room 8**. Return. On the right as you retrace your steps are **Rooms 9**, **10**, **11** Children's sections. **Room 12** is a very shallow porch with stags, deer etc in glass cabinets. The children's sections contain some very crude models, but they also contain some toys that are real collectors' pieces. Possibly the only model flying boat left in the world, brought out by W Bristow's in 1939, is in the collection. From a collectors' point of view, many of these exhibits have been devalued by the museum numbers, and some suffer from the usual metal-fatigue that attacks pre-war zinc alloy 'Mazah'! **Room 14** The ivory room Ivory chairs, inlaid tables. Delhi, Mysore, Travancore and Visakhapatnam are current centres. The cuckoo clock is a great attraction. **Room 16** Armaments 17th century chain mail, Blunderbusses, matchlock guns etc. Persian swords 17th century. Amazing variety and enormous quantity of old arms, including firearms. **Room 15** Metal ware There are some excellent examples of Bidri ware, local to the region. **Room 17a** Modern Indian painting 19th & 20th century with some examples of leading Indian artists such as Ravi Varma, Abanindranath Tagore, Sunil Prakash. **Room 18** Indian miniatures Representatives of major schools, Mughal Deccani, Rajasthani, Mewar, Amber and Jain palmleaf manuscripts.

Upstairs **Room 20** European art Nothing of great interest. A Landseer is perhaps the best in a mediocre collection. 21 European porcelain Examples from Dresden, Sèvres and Wedgwood, as well as some Italian and Austrian porcelain. A porcelain mirror, belonging to Marie Antoinette is displayed. **Room 25** Jade Some outstandingly beautiful examples of Indian and Chinese jade. **Room 26** European bronzes All 19th century copies of classical sculpture. **Room 28** Clock room Some bizarre examples, many French. Some English grandmother clocks. **Room 29** Manuscripts This includes some magnificent early Islamic scripts. A 9th century Qu'ran, a script on Unani medicine. No 6 is the oldest in collection. A copy of the Qu'ran, written in 1288, has signatures of Jahangir, Shah Jahan and Aurangzeb. Also a large copy of Qu'ran written in Arcot. **Room 31** Far Eastern Porcelain Sung Dynasty. (Marco Polo compared pottery to Porcella, the white shell). Celadon – brought to Europe in the 12th century, was replaced by cobalt-derived blue ('Mohammadan blue') from Persia and Baluchistan. **Room 32** Kashmiri room **Room 33** Far Eastern statuary Various Buddhist sculptures recounting the birth of Buddha at Lumbini.

Other Museums

Govt Archaeological Museum Public Gardens. Small museum, located by Lal Bahadur Stadium. 10 min by car from Banjara Hills hotels, 2 min from Ritz.

1030-1700. Small entry fee. Closed Mon and public holidays. Publications section, but nothing on archaeology! Opened in 1930 in the specially constructed 2-storeyed, semi-circular building. Sections on pre-historic implements, sculptures, paintings, inscriptions, illuminated manuscripts, coins, arms, bidri ware, china, textiles and the crowd drawing 4,000 year old Egyptian mummy. Behind the museum, in the Ajanta Pavilion are life size copies of Ajanta frescoes while the Nizam's collection of rare artefacts are housed in the Jubilee Hall. The Public gardens open daily except Mon.

Birla Archaeological Museum, Malakpet. Collection of finds from excavations of historic sites, housed in Asman Ghad Palace, 9 km away. Open daily. **Birla Planetarium** Believed to be 'the most modern planetarium in the country'. Naubat Pahad. 6 shows daily, 8 on Sat, Sun and holidays. Rs 5. **Khazana Museum** On the way to Golconda – stone sculptures (see **Excursions**).

Parks & zoos

Nehru Zoological Park occupies 13 ha of a low hilly area with remarkable boulders. The animals are kept in natural surroundings. One of the best zoos in India. Also a lion safari park and a nocturnal house. The Natural History Museum, Ancient Life Museum, Pre-historic Animals Park, a Lion Safari Park and a children's train are here. 0900-1800, closed Mon. Small entry fee. Cars Rs 10. **Nampally Public Gardens** N of the Station, close to the Lal Bahadur Stadium, is the largest in Asia. Lotus ponds and Children's Playground. There are municipal parks in Tank Bund Rd, Club Rd, Secunderabad, Indira Park below Tank Bund Rd and Public Gardens in Saifabad.

Tours

APTTDC City sightseeing: half or full day. Rather unsatisfactory as it allows about an hr at the Fort and includes sights which could be omitted. *Hyderabad-Pochampalli*: Sat, 0800-1300. *Yadagirigutta*: twice daily for Yadagirigutta Laxmi Narayan Temple. *Nagarjunasagar*: daily 1-day tour to Nagarjunasagar Dam and Museum, Ethipothala Falls and Nagarjunakonda, 0630-2230. 4 hr each way. *Mantralayam*: 2-day for Sri Raghavendra temple, Alampur and Srisailam for Mallikarjuna Svami Temple, Pathal Ganga falls, Sikharam Power House. Sat 1000-Sun 2100, 7 hr each way. Others offer a range of options lasting 3-15 days.

Local festivals

Mid-Jan *Makara Sankranti*, usually 13th-15th. Houses bring out all their collection of dolls.

Mar-Apr *Ugadi* New year in Andhra Pradesh – *Chaitra Sudda Padyami*. *Muharram and Ramzan* are celebrated distinctively in Hyderabad.

Local information

● Accommodation

Price guide
AL Rs 3,000+ **A** Rs 2,000-3,000
B Rs 1,200-2,000 **C** Rs 600-1,200
D Rs 250-600 **E** Rs 100-250 **F** Up to Rs 100.

Hyderabad In Rd 1, Banjara Hills: **AL** Oberoi *Krishna*, T 222121, F 223079, 274 rm, 5 km centre, very luxuriously appointed, 3 restaurants, looking out on an artificial waterfall, large swimming pool and beautiful gardens, immaculately kept.

A Taj *Gateway Banjara*, T 222222, F 222218, 124 rm, 5 km centre, service and food excellent, esp local cuisine and lakeside barbecues; **A** *Bhaskar Palace*, T 226202, F 222712, 222 rm, rec restaurant.

B Holiday Inn *Krishna*, T 223467, F 222684, 152 rm; Quality Inn **B** *Green Park*, Begumpet, Greenlands, T 224455, 160 rm.

C *Ritz*, Hillfort Palace, T 233571, 40 rm, central, central a/c, restaurants rec, bar, exchange, travel, pool, tennis, pleasant lawns, old palace now very run down, grd Flr rm in main wing best and retains character.

D *Nagarjuna*, 3-6-356 Basheerbagh, T 237201, F 236789, 60 rm, central a/c, restaurants (esp Mughlai, Chinese), travel, shop, pool, on a busy main road; **D** ***Sampurna International***, Mukramjahi Rd, T 40165, 120 rm, central, central a/c, restaurants rec (esp Indian veg), bar, travel, shop; **D** ***Rock Castle***, Rd 6, Banjara Hills, T 33541, 22 rm, some a/c in cottages with phone, restaurant, bar, large delightful gardens, has character, but is not central; **D** ***Emerald***, Chirag Ali Lane, Abids, T 202836, F 233902, 69 rm, central, central a/c, restaurant, shop; **D** ***Jaya International***, Bank St, Abids, T 232929, 75 rm, 18 a/c, central, travel, reasonable but no restaurant; **D** ***Ashoka***, 6-1-70 Lakdi-ka-pul, T 230105, 90 rm, 50 a/c, a/c restaurant (N and S Indian veg), exchange, travel, shop, good value.

Secunderabad: **C** ***Baseraa***, 9-1, 167/168 Sarojini Devi Rd, T 823200, 75 rm, central, central a/c, restaurants rec, bar, exchange, travel; **C** ***Asrani International***, 1-7-179 MG Rd, T 842267, 65 a/c rm with phone, central, restaurants rec (esp Indian, Mughlai), bar, exchange, travel.

D *Deccan Continental*, Minister Rd, T 840981, 70 rm, nr airport, central a/c, restaurant, pool, good value; **D** ***Karan***, 1-2-261/1 SD Rd, T 840191, 44 rm, nr centre, central a/c, restaurants, coffee shop, exchange, travel, roof-garden; **D** ***Parklane***, 115 Park Lane, T 840466, 47 rm, central, central a/c, restaurants, exchange, travel, shop.

● Budget hotels

Hyderabad: **E** *Taj Mahal*, H-1-999 Abid Rd, corner of King Kothi Rd, T 237988, 69 rm, 20 a/c with baths, central, restaurant (S Indian veg), travel, roof-garden, TV. There are several inexpensive **F** category hotels in the Abids Circle area, nr Hyderabad Rly Station.

Secunderabad: **E** Andhra Tourism *Yatri Niivas*, SP Rd, Secunderabad, T 843931, 16 rm, some a/c. Rly Station has **F** *Retiring Rooms* for passengers.

● Youth hostels

Very cheap **F** *Youth Hostel*, behind Boat Club, Secunderabad, T 220121, with 51 beds, pleasant position but far from the centre. There are *Dharamsalas* in Nampally and also at Grain Bazar in Secunderabad. *Municipal Sarai*, Nampally, T 220930.

● Places to eat

Rec in hotels: *Gateway*, *Krishna*, *Bhaskar*, *Palace*, *Ritz*, *Asrani International*, *Baseraa*, *Nagarjuna* and *Sampurna International*. Outside hotels there are several licensed a/c restaurants – ***East and West***, Saifabad opp Telephone Bhavan and ***Manju Cafe***, 4-1-873 Tilak Rd.

Chinese: on Abid Rd, ***Palace Heights*** (8th floor of tall building) and ***Golden Deer*** nearby and ***Golden Dragon*** nr Park Lane Hotel off MG Rd, Secunderabad, are highly rec. Also ***China Regency***, Airport Rd, Begumpet.

Hyderabadi: in Nampally, ***Asian***, ***Aziza***, ***Parvaz*** are rec. Also ***Mughal Durbar*** and ***Nilgara***, Basheerbagh Rd. Nr High Court: ***Diwan*** and ***Shadah***. ***Akbar***, MG Rd, ***Garden***, Sarojini Devi Rd.

Western style Fast foods: Himayatnagar Rd: Nirula's ***Open House***, (corner of Basheerbagh), ***Pick 'n Move***, Amrutha Estates. Also ***Varun***, Begumpet opp Police Station. ***Liberty's***, Bank St (Abids) for Continental and Chinese. Also ***Kwality's*** at 103 Park Lane, Secunderabad.

● Bars

City has no prohibition. There is a wide range of bars, most in the larger hotels.

● Airline offices

Air India, 1st Flr, Samrat Complex, Secretariat Rd, T 232858. **Air France**, Nasir Arcade, Secretariat Rd, T 236947. **British Airways**, Chapel Rd, T 234927. **Cathay Pacific**, Spencers Travel Division, 89 SD Rd, Secunderabad, T 840234. **Egypt Air**, Safina International, Public Garden Rd, T 230778. **Kuwait Airways**, National Travel Service, United House. **KLM**, Gemini Travels, Chapel Rd, T 236042. **Lufthansa**, 86 Shantinagar, T 220352. **Saudia**, Arafath Travels, Basheerbagh, T 238175. **Singapore Airlines** and **Swissair**, Regency Buildings, Begumpet. **Thai**, Swan Travels, Chapel Rd, T 236042.

● Banks & money changers

1000-1400, Mon-Fri,1000-1200, Sat. In Hyderabad, several banks on Bank St (incl **State Bank of India**), Sultan Bazar and Moazam Jahi Market and in Secunderabad on Rashtrapati Rd.

● Clubs

Flying Club, Begumpet. ***Riding Club***, Saifabad. ***Boat Club***, Kavadiguda and *Golf Club*, Bolarum.

● Cultural centres & librairies

Alliance Française, T 220296. ***British Library***, Secretariat Rd. ***Max Müller Bhavan***, Ramkote, T 43938. ***Bharatiya Vidya Bhavan***, King Kothi Rd, T 237825.

● Entertainment

Son et lumiere at Golconda Fort. A spectacular

show, with narrative by the famous Indian film star Amitabh Bachchan, inaugurated in August 1993. Details from Golconda Fort or **AP Travel and Tourism Dev Corp** (see below). The *Charminar* is also floodlit in the evenings. The city claims to have the largest number of cinemas in the country, most screening 4 times daily. Check papers for English language films. *Ravindra Bharati* stages dance, theatre and music programmes, *Lalit Kala Thoranam*, Public Gardens, free film shows daily and *Max Mueller Bhavan*, Eden Bagh, theatre and film shows.

● Hospitals & medical services

Several are open to foreigners. Most have out-patients from 0900-1400, Casualty 24 hr. *General Hospital* in Nampally, T 234344.

Post & telecommunications

In Hyderabad: **GPO** and **Central Telegraph Office**, Abids.

In **Secunderabad**: **Head Post Office** in RP Rd and **Central Telegraph Office** on MG Rd.

● Shopping

Most open 1000-1900, some close on Fri. Pearls, Bidriware, Crochet work, Kalamkari paintings, filigree work, inlaid wood work, himroo and silk saris, Kondapalli toys and Hyderabadi bangles nr Charminar (see above). Shopping areas in Hyderabad – Abid Rd, Nampally, Basheerbagh and Sultan Bazar and in Secunderabad, Rashtrapati Rd. Fascinating ***bazar*** around the Char Minar with colourful stalls where you can imagine Hyderabad in past centuries. Down the alleys, silver craftsmen work in their tiny rooms.

Antiques: ***Govind Mukandas***, Bank St, ***Humayana*** at Gateway, ***Rizvi***, Darus Shafa.

Books: ***A A Hussain***, MG Rd, good guide books. ***Waldens***, Raj Bhavan Rd, Begumpet, opp *Blue Moon Hotel*, good general books. ***Haziq and Mohi***, Lal Chowk, interesting antiquarian bookshop.

Handicrafts: Govt Emporia – ***Nirmal Industries***, Raj Bhavan Rd; AP's ***Lepakshi***, Gun Foundry; Kerala's ***Kairali***, Saifabad; ***Coircraft***, Mayur complex, Gun Factory. ***Cooptex***, Abids; ***Tantuja*** (W Bengal), nr Telephone Bhavan, Saifabad and UP's ***Gangotri***, Abids. APCO ***Handloom Houses*** on Mukharam Jahi Rd, Abids, MG Rd, Amerpeth Kothi among others. ***Khadi Bhandar***, Sultan Bazar. ***Khadi Crafts***, Municipal Complex, Rashtrapati Rd, Secunderabad. Privately owned ***Jewelbox***, SD Rd, ***Baba Handicrafts***, MG Rd, Secunderabad, ***Canaud House***, Shastri Stadium, ***Sheelas***, Lal Bahadur Shastri Stadium and ***Bidri Crafts***, Abids.

Jewellery: ***Mangatrai Ramkumar*** at Gateway and Pathergatti, ***Sri Jangadamba Pearls***, MG Rd, Secunderabad, ***Tibrumal***, Basheebagh and ***Totaram Sagarlal***, Abids.

Photography: *Ganrys*, Abids, ***Murthy***, Nampally, ***Byas***, Basheerbagh, ***Jyothi***, Secunderabad.

● Sports

Swimming: *BV Gurumoorthy Swimming Pool*, Sardar Patel Rd, and ***Hanuman Vyayamshala***, Sultan Bazar. Some hotels have pools – *Ritz*, *Parklane*, *Nagarjuna* and *Deccan*.

● Tour companies & travel agents

Mercury, Public Gardens Rd, T 234441; ***Sheriff***, Basheerhagh, T 237914; ***Thomas Cook***, Saifabad, T 222689; ***TCI***, Regency House, Somajiguda; ***Trade Wings***, Public Gardens Rd, T 230545; ***Travel Express***, Saifabad, T 234035.

● Tourist offices

Govt of India, Sandozi Building, 26 Himayatnagar, T 668777. **AP Travel and Tourism Dev Corp** (APTTDC), Gagan Vihar (opp Indianoil), 5th Flr, MJ Rd, (Nampally High Rd) T 557531, for tours. Also at *Yatri Nivas*, SP Rd, Secunderabad, T 843929; tours T 843943. Information centres at Hyderabad Rly Station, T 221352, Secunderabad Rly Station, T 70144 and Begumpet Airport, T 848944.

● Useful address

Foreigners' Regional Registration Office, Commissioner of Police, Purani Haveli, Hyderabad, T 230191.

● Transport

Hyderabad and Secunderabad are on the NH 7 and NH 9. Aurangabad 599 km, Bombay 739 km, Bangalore 566 km, Madras 704 km, Nagpur 468 km, Tirupati 651 km, Vijayawada 271 km, Visakhapatnam 637 km.

Local Buses: City buses are very crowded in rush hours. Gowliguda Bus Station is on Maulavi Alauddin Rd, N Bank of river, E of Afzalgunj Bridge. No 1: Afzalgunj to Secunderabad Station (No 7 does return journey); No 80 goes to Golconda Fort. No 8: Secunderabad Station to Char Minar. No 87: Char Minar to Nampally. Nos 119, 142: Nampally to Golconda Fort. **Taxis**: unmetered taxis or metered **Auto rickshaws**: (Rs 4 per 2km) and cheaper **cycle rickshaws**. **Car hire**: tourist taxis and luxury cars from AP Tourism,

Gagan Vihar, 1st Fl, MG Rd, T 557531, *Ashok Travels*, Lal Bahadur Stadium, T 230766, *Travel Express*, Saifabad, T 234035. About Rs 400 per day.

Air The airport is at Begumpet, Secunderabad. **Transport to town**: pre-paid taxi, unmetered Tourist taxi or auto-rickshaw transfer (Banjara Hills about ½ hr; Rs 85 and Rs 25).

Indian Airlines: enquiries: Saifabad, T 236902, Airport T 844422. **Delhi**: daily, 0750, 1850, 2 hr; **Madras**: daily (+ 1 other), 0850, 1 hr; **Bombay**: daily, 0640, 1120, 1600, 1¼ hr; **Calcutta**: daily via Bhubaneswar, W,F, 1630, 2¾ hr; **Nagpur**: W,F,Sa, 1630, 1 hr; **Bangalore**: daily, 0700, 1 hr; **Nagpur**: W,F,Su, 1630, 1 hr; **Visakhapatnam**: M,W,F, 0900, 1 hr. **Continental Aviation**: **Bangalore**: Tu,Th,Sa, 0920; **Bombay** via Pune: daily except Su, 1820. **East West Airlines**: Secunderabad, T 77080. **Bombay**: daily, 0740, 1640, 1¼ hr; **Delhi**: Tu,Th,Sa, 1300, 2 hr. **Jet Airways**: **Bombay**: daily, 1825, 1 hr. **Modiluft**: T 243783. **Bangalore**: daily, 1715, 1 hr; **Kochi via Bangalore**: daily, 0935, 1 hr; **Madras**: Tu,Th,Sa, 1400, 1 hr. **East West**: **Visakhapatnam**: daily except Su, 0740, ¾ hr; **Bombay**, daily except Su, 1020, 1¼ hr.

Train The broad gauge lines Delhi-Madras, Calcutta-Madras and Bombay-Madras all serve the city. From **Hyderabad**: Reservations: T 231130. **Bangalore**: *Hyderabad Exp* 7085 (AC/II), daily, 1750, 17 hr. **Bombay (VT)**: *Hyderabad-Bombay Exp* 7032, daily, 1935, 17¼ hr. **Madras (MC)**: *Charminar Exp* 6060 (AC/II), daily, 1830, 14¾ hr. **Tirupati**: *Rayalaseema* 7429 (AC.II), daily, 1700, 16¼ hr. **Vijayawada**: *Godavari Exp* 7008 (AC/II), daily, 1715, 6½ hr. From **Secunderabad**: Reservations: T 75413. Centralised Enquiries: T 131. **Aurangabad**: *Ajanta Exp* 7551 (AC/II), daily, 1830, 12¼ hr. **Bombay (VT)**: *Minar Exp* 2102 (AC/II), daily, 1535, 14½ hr. **Delhi (ND)**: *AP Exp* 2723, daily, 0635, 26 hr. **Guntakal**: (for Hospet and Hampi) *Venkatadri Exp* 7598, daily, 1530, 9 hr. Connects with *Vasco Exp* 7829, daily 0300, 2 ½ hr. **Tirupati**: *Venkatadri* 7597, daily, 1530, 18 hr. **Vijayawada**: *Godavari Exp* 7008 (AC/II), daily, 1745, 6 hr.

Road Bus: APSRTC, Musheerbad, T 64571. Main bus station, Gowliguda covers the state. Private coaches run services to Aurangabad, Bangalore, Bombay, Madras and Tirupati. Reservations: Royal Lodge, Entrance to Hyderabad Rly Station.

Short excursions from Hyderabad

Golconda

(11 km) was the capital of the Qutb Shahi kings who ruled over the area from 1507 to 1687. Originally built of mud in the 12th century by the Hindu Kakatiyas, the fort was reinforced by masonry by the Bahamanis who occupied it from 1363. The massive fort, built on a granite hill, was surrounded by 3 walls. One encircled the town, another the hill on which the citadel stood and the last joined huge boulders on the high ridge with parts of masonry wall. The citadel's double wall had 87 bastions with cannons and 8 huge gates with outer and inner doors and guardrooms between. The total circumference of the outer curtain wall is 5 km. Each of the gateways carries relief ornamentation of birds and animals, and some of the guns of the Qutb Shahis are still on the walls. The *Fateh Darwaza* or Victory Gate made of teak, with a Hindu deity engraved, is studded with iron spikes as a defence against war elephants.

The fort had an ingenious system of laminated clay pipes and huge *Persian Wheels* to carry water to cool the palace chambers and up to the height of 61m where there were hanging gardens. It also had superb acoustics which enabled a drum beat or bugle call or even a clap under the canopy of the *Fateh Darwaza*, to be heard by someone at the palace at the very top. The famous diamond vault once held the **Koh-i-noor** and the **Hope diamonds**. The fort fell to Emperor Aurangzeb after 2 attempts, an 8 month siege and the help of a Qutb Shahi General who turned traitor. The English traveller Walter Hamilton described it as being almost completely deserted in 1820 "the dungeons being used by the Nizam of Hyderabad as a prison for his worst enemies, among whom were several of his sons and two of his wives."

There are still mosques, temples, the 3-storeyed armoury, the harem, the Hall of Public Audience and the Rani Mahal with its royal baths. The central hill, the **Bala Hissar**, is over 110m high. There are fortifications at various levels on the way up. As you enter the gate you see the remains of the **armoury** and the women's palaces on the left. About half way up is a large water tank or well, near the **King's storehouse**. A Persian inscription on black basalt states that the **Ambar khana** was built during the reign of Abdullah Qutb Shah (1626-72), and to the N is what was once the most densely populated part of the city. Near the top of the fort the path passes the Hindu **Mahakali temple** on the way to the **Durbar Hall** on the summit. Another of S Asia's supposed **underground tunnels** is believed by some to run from a corner of the summit about 8 km to Gosha Mahal. It is well worth climbing the stairs onto the roof of the Durbar Hall. The path down is clearly signed to take you on a circular route through the ruins back to the main gate. The old mint on the road to Golcogical Department which exhibits stone sculptures.

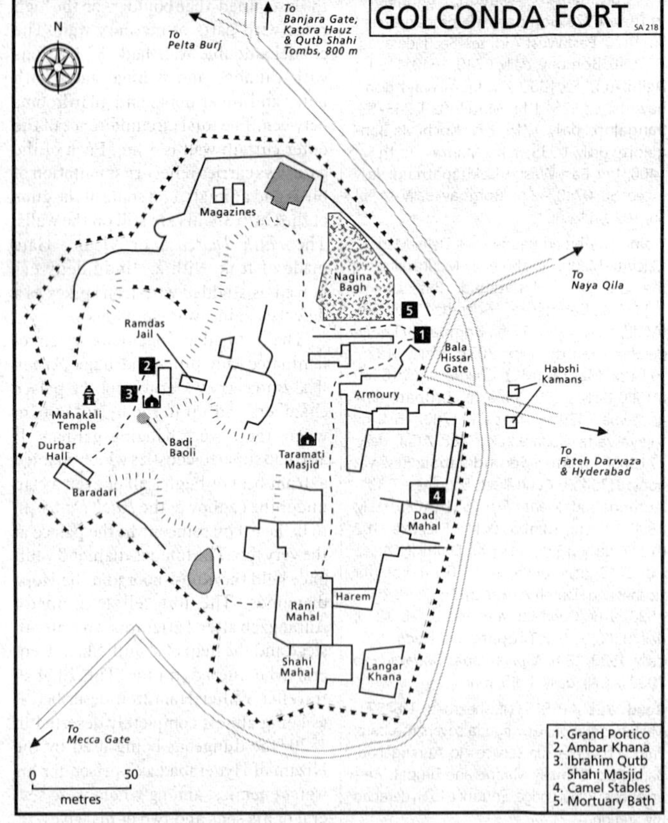

Qutb Shahi Tombs

One road leaves Golconda Fort to the N through the Banjara Gate. 800m NNW of the fort on a low plateau, are the Qutb Shahi Tombs, each of black granite or greenstone with plaster decoration, built on a square or octagonal base, with a large onion dome and arches with fine sculptures, inscriptions and remains of glazed decoration. The larger tombs have their own mosque attached which usually comprises an eastward opening hall with a *mihrab* to the W. The sides have inscriptions in beautiful Naksh script, and remnants of the glazed tiles which used to cover them can still be seen in places. The tombs of the rulers were built under their own supervision. They fell into disrepair and the gardens ran wild until the end of the 19th century when Sir Salar Jang restored them and replanted the gardens. It is now managed and kept in an excellent state of repair by the Archaeological Survey of India. It is a popular place to visit, and from 1000 can get busy. Allow half a day for a leisurely exploration. Guidebook available. The bus (Nos 119 or 142) takes an hour from Nampally, Hyderabad. Nizam-ul-Mulk repossessed it in 1724 and restored it to its former glory for a time. 0900-1630 except Fri. Re 0.50, camera fee Rs 2.

The road from Golconda fort goes N, passing **1** the tomb of **Abdullah Qutb Shah** (1626-1672) as it approaches the entrance to the tombs, which is at the E gate of the compound. On the left hand side of the road just outside the compound is **2** the tomb of **Abul Hasan Tana Qutb Shahi** (r1672-1687). He was the last of the kings to be buried here as the final king in the line of the Qutb Shahi dynasty, Abul Hasan, died in the fort at Daulatabad in 1704, see page 1172. To the right of the entrance are **3** the tomb of **Princess Hayat Baksh Begum** (d1677), the daughter of Ibrahim Qutb Shah, and a smaller mosque, while about 100m directly ahead is **4** the granite tomb of **Muhammad Qutb Shah** (r1612-1626). Tucked away due N of this tomb is **5** that of **Pemamati**, one of the mistresses of Muhammad Qutb Shah, dating from 1663. The path turns S and W around the tomb of Muhammad Qutb Shah. About 100m to the S is a tank

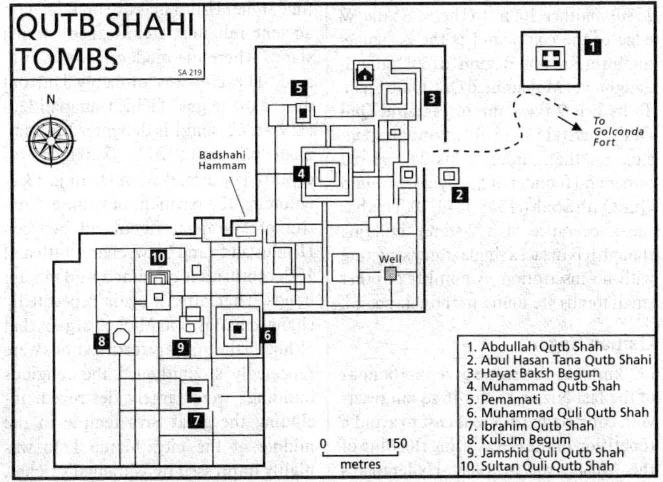

which is still open. The ramp up and down which the bullocks walked to draw the water is typical of those found in villages across S India where *kavalai* irrigation is practised. The path turns right again from near the corner of the tank and runs W to the oldest structure in the compound, the *Badshahi Hammam*, the 'bath' where the body of the king was washed before burial. You can still see the channels for the water and the special platforms for washing the body. The Badshahi kings were Shi'a Muslims, and the 12 small baths in the Hammam stand symbolically for the 2 imams revered by the Shi'a community.

To the S of the Hammam is a series of major tombs. The most striking lies due S, **6** the 54m high mausoleum of **Muhammad Quli Qutb Shah** (r1581-1612), the poet king founder of Baghnagar (Hyderabad). It is appropriate that the man responsible for creating a number of beautiful buildings in Hyderabad should be commemorated by such a remarkable tomb. The underground excavations here have been turned into a Summer House. You can walk right through the tomb and on to **7** the tomb of the 4th king of the dynasty, **Ibrahim Qutb Shah** (r1550-1580) another 100m to the S. At the W edge of the compound is the octagonal tomb **8** of **Kulsum Begum** (d1608), granddaughter of Mohammad Quli Qutb Shah. To its E is **9** the tomb of **Jamshid Quli Qutb Shah** (r1543-1550), who was responsible for the murder of his 90 year old father and founder of the dynasty, **Sultan Quli Qutb Shah** (r1518-1543) **10**. This has the appearance of a 2-storey building though it is in fact a single storey structure with no inscription. A number of other small tombs are found in the compound.

Osman Sagar

(22 km) was the name given in honour of the last Nizam to the 46 sq km reservoir, constructed at great cost to avoid a repetition of the devastating flooding of the Musi river in 1908. Hyderabad's water supply comes from this lake, also known as Gandipet. Very pleasant landscaped gardens and a swimming pool. **Accommodation** *Guest Houses Sagar Mahal* and *Visranti*, dormitory can be reserved through AP Tourism. **Himayat Sagar**, an 85 sq km lake named after the Nizam's eldest son, close to Osman Sagar, can only be reached by a separate road 22 km from Hyderabad. **Accommodation** *Dak Bungalow* with a cook available, reservations: Supt Engineer, PWD, Water Works, Gosha Mahal, Hyderabad, T 48011.

Vanasthalipuram Deer Park

13 km on the Hyderabad-Vijayawada road. 125 ha park also known as Mahavir Harin Vanashtali is also a wildlife sanctuary with spotted deer, black buck, chinkara, wild boar, porcupines and python and over a hundred species of birds.

Warangal and surroundings

Warangal (*Population*: 466,900; *STD Code*: 08712) 140 km N of Hyderabad, was the capital of the Hindu Kakatiya Empire in the 12th and 13th centuries. The name is derived from the Orugallu (one stone) Hill, a massive boulder with ancient religious significance which stands where the modern town is situated. The city was probably laid out during the reigns of King Ganapatideva (1199-1262) and his daughter Rudrammadevi (r until 1294). Warangal was captured by armies from Delhi in 1323, enforcing the payment of tribute. Control of Warangal fluctuated between Hindus and , and between the 14th and 15th centuries it remained in Bahmani hands. Thereafter it again repeaqtedly changed hands, and Michell argues that although the military fortifications were repeatedly strengthened the religious buildings were largely destroyed, including the great Siva temple in the middle of the city. Marco Polo was highly impressed by Warangal's riches, and it is still famous for the remains of its temples, its lakes and wildlife, and for its 3 circuits of fortifications.

The site At the centre is a circular area approximately 1.2 km diameter – the 'fort'. Most is now farm land with houses along the road. Near the centre are the ruins of the original huge Siva temple, the chief remaining feature of which are the carved stone entrance gateways, one on each side of the almost square enclosure, 130m E-W, 144m N-S, aligned along the cardinal directions. They are beautifully decorated. The top of the lintel is nearly 30m above the ground. Michell observes that "of the temple itself nothing remains except overturned slabs and smashed columns, brackets and ceiling panels: a more vivd picture of wilful destruction can hardly be imagined." This is now an archaeological site being excavated.

Nearby Siva temples are still in use, and to the W is the Khush Mahal, a massive royal hall used by the Muslim Shitab Khan at the beginning of the 16th century for state functions, before his defeat in 1510 at the hands of the Vijayanagar empire. Michell suggests that it may well have been built on the site of earlier palaces, near its geometric centre, arguing for 'a symmetrical distribution of temple and palace about the north-south axis of the city.' Some still unidentified structures in the central area may have been granaries.

From the centre 4 routes radiate along the cardinal directions, passing through gateways in the 3 successive rings of fortification. The innermost ring is made of massive granite blocks, well-fitted and up to 6m high, with bastions regularly spaced along the wall. The middle wall is of unfaced packed earth, now eroded, while the outermost circuit, up to 5m high, is also of earth. The 4 main roads pass through massive gateways in the inner wall, and there are also gateways in the second ring of fortifications, though they are less complete. Some of the original roads that crossed the city have disappeared.

Michell suggests that the plan of Warangal implies fixed rules of design conforming to early Hindu principles of town planning, which include specifications for '*swastika* towns' as especially suited for royalty, the *swastika* plan being achieved by the layout of the buildings symmetrically rotated with respect to the 4 axial roads. The centre of the city was its most powerful site, and he suggests that 'the diagram of concentric circles and *swastikas* that underlies Warangal's plan is identical to that which regulates *mandalas* and *yantras*. Thus the city may be seen as a miniature representation of the universe, the power of god and king recognised symbolically and in reality at the centre. **Accommodation F** *Tourist Rest House*, Kazipet, T 6201, simple rm, Tourist information.

Hanamakonda The Chalukya style '1,000-pillar' Siva *Rudresvar* temple on the slopes of the **Hanamakonda Hill** (Hanumankonda) to the N has beautiful carvings, with subsidiary shrines to the N and S, a low, compact temple, built on several stepped platforms. There are subsidiary shrines to Vishnu and the Sun God *Surya*, rockcut elephants, a large superbly carved *nandi* in the courtyard and an ancient well where villagers have drawn water for 800 years. The **underground passage** which is believed to have connected the temple with the Fort 11 km away, cannot be seen. The hill top Bhadrakali Temple overlooks a shallow lake.

Excursions

Ramappa, Pakhal, Lakhnavaram and Ghanpur lakes are a result of the Kakatiya rulers' management of water resources in the 12th and 13th centuries. They created the artificial lakes by building earth dams across the valleys.

Pakhal (50 km), **Ethurnagaram** and **Lakhnavaram Game sanctuaries** are nearby. This is the richest area for wildlife in the state with tiger, panther, hyena, wild dogs, wild boars, gaur, foxes, spotted deer, jackals, muntjacks, sloth bears and pythons. There is also a large variety of water birds and fish, otters and alligators in the vast lakes. Pakhal lake is superb for bird-watching and occasional crocodile spotting. Tigers and panthers live deep in the forest and are rarely seen. Forest rangers might show you plaster casts of tiger pug marks. **Kothaguda** about 10 km further is a Banjara tribal village. Subjected in recent years to unregulated tree-felling – also activities of political extremists.

• **Accommodation** **F** *Forest Rest House*, at entrance to Wildlife Sanctuary, facing the lake, Colonial style bungalow, 2 large rm with verandah, keep door and windows shut to stop monkeys stealing food!; APTTDC **F** *Sarovihar* is 2 km along dirt track, on top of dam, idyllic situation, popular with groups so can be noisy, both good value, bring provisions; staff will cook a meal for a small fee, reserve at Warangal Tourist Office.

• **Transport Road Bus**: from Hanamkonda or Warangal Bus Station to Narsampet. Regular service from Narsampet to Pakhal Lake.

Palampet (64 km) lies close to the Ramappa Dam. The **Ramappa Temple**, dedicated to Siva as Rudreswara, was built in 1234 and is one of the finest medieval Deccan temples. The black basalt sculpture and paintings are excellent (even richer than those at the thousand-pillar temple) with famous Mandakini figures of female dancers which appear on brackets at the 4 entrances. The base of the temple has the typical bands of sculpture, the lowest of elephants, the 2nd, a lotus scroll, the 3rd which is the most interesting depicting figures opening a window on the life of the times and finally another floral scroll. More fine sculpture inside, some displaying a subtle sense of humour in common with some of the figures outside, and paintings of scenes from the epics on the ceiling. **Accommodation** APTTDC **F** *Vanavihar Tourist Rest House* nearby, also overlooking the lake, serves snacks, there are 4 simple and clean rm, cook available but bring own provisions.

• **Accommodation** **D** *Ashok*, Main Rd, Hanamkonda, T 85491, 8 km rly (Rs 20 auto rickshaw or bus), 40 clean a/c rm and good restaurant, bar, friendly service. 4 km away, **E** *Govt Tourist Rest House*, Kazipet Rd beyond Forest Dept, T 6201, renovated, 4 a/c rm. Other **F** hotels in town.

• **Tourist Office** here for booking Rest Houses at Pakhal Wildlife Sanctuary.

• **Transport Train** Many Express trains stop here. **Nagpur**: *Tamil Nadu Exp* 2621 (AC/CC&AC/II), daily, 0653, 7 hr. **Delhi (ND)**: *Tamil Nadu Exp* 2621 (AC/CC&AC/II), daily, 0653, 23¾ hr. **Vijayawada**: *Kerala-Mangala Exp* 2626 (AC/II), daily, 1154, 3¼ hr; *GT Exp* 2616 (AC/CC&AC/II), daily, 2032, 3¼ hr. **Madras (MC)**: *Kochi-Bilaspur Exp* 7058 (AC/II), Th, 1323, 11¾ hr. **Secunderabad**: *Konark Exp* 2119 (AC/II), daily, 1204, 3 hr; **or** *Golconda Exp* 7201 (AC/CC), daily, 1005, 3¼ hr.

ROUTES FROM HYDERABAD

All the routes from Hyderabad are off the major tourist track. This does not mean that they are inaccessible or difficult, though accommodation is often limited and basic, but there are attractive and very lightly travelled roads.

HYDERABAD TO NAGPUR

The route from Hyderabad to Nagpur runs almost due N across the granite Telangana plateau, with its thin red soils, rock strewn landscape and scattered vegetation, then across the black Deccan lavas. The road crosses the boundary into Maharashtra at the Penganga River, a tributary of the Godavari. The road NH 7 goes through several small towns to **Kondapur**, the town of mounds (90 km) with the remains of a great Buddhist complex. Nearly 2000 coins have been discovered – gold, silver, copper and lead – as well as fine glass beads, coming from as far afield as Rome.

Medak (96 km; *Population*: 35,800; *STD Code*: 08452), 10 km W of NH 7, has an extraordinary Gothic style cathedral, complete with stained glass windows and a spire over 60m high, begun in 1914 and completed 10 years later; it can hold 5000. Nizam Sagar, a further 30 km NW, covers 130 sq km and irrigates rice, sugarcane and turmeric.

If you want to continue N from Medak return to the NH 7 at Ramayampet. From time to time the road passes through forest of teak and sal, now often broken up by cultivated land. **Kamareddi** (*STD Code*: 08468) has important iron ore deposits, in common with several areas immediately to its N. NH 7 goes on to the market town of **Nizamabad** (26 km; *STD Code*: 08462). **Getting there Rail** Secunderabad: *7592 Exp*, daily, 1340, 3¾ hr. Aurangabad: *Ajanta Exp* 7551 (AC/II), daily, 2225, 8 hr.

From Nizamabad the road continues N across the Godavari River to **Nirmal** (52 km; *STD Code*: 08734). Nirmal became famous in the 16th century for its wood painting. Today the painters and craftsmen of Nirmal are making furniture as well as painting portraits and pageants for which they are more commonly known.

11 km from Nirmal are the 46m **Kuntala Falls** on the River Kadam, a tributary of the Godavari, an impressive sight immediately after the monsoon. To the E are the important coal reserves of **Singareni**.

Once across the Godavari the focus of economic life is N towards Nagpur. **Adilabad** (81 km; *Population*: 84,200; *STD Code*: 08732) is the last major town before crossing the Penganga into Maharashtra. The road goes to **Hinganhat** (118 km; *Population*: 78,700) before reaching the turning left to **Wardha** (36 km; *STD Code*: 07152), the centre of the Gandhi ashram movement. It is possible to go direct from Hinganghat to Nagpur (74 km).

HYDERABAD TO VIJAYAWADA

The road route from Hyderabad to Vijayawada is off the beaten tourist track, although parts are heavily used by goods traffic. The route along the NH 9 from Hyderabad to Madras descends gently eastwards down the Telangana plateau slope to the flat rice-growing delta of the Krishna, with Vijayawada at a vital crossing point. It passes through a series of small towns to Vijayawada (269 km), approximately 4 to 5 hr driving. There are regular and frequent buses between all the towns along the route, as well as express buses linking the major cities. An interesting though longer route can be taken via Nagarjunakonda (172 km).

Nagarjunakonda

One of India's richest Buddhist sites, Nagarjunakonda now lies almost entirely under the lake created by the Nagarjunasagar Dam, completed in 1960. Rising from the middle of the artificial lake is the Nagarjuna Hill (*konda* is the Telugu word for hill) which had been nearly 200m above the floor of the secluded valley in which the remains of a highly cultured Buddhist civilisation had remained almost undisturbed for 1600 years until their discovery by AR Saraswati in March 1926. A full account of Nagarjunakonda is available from the Archaeological Survey of India Guide published in 1987. While the scale of archaeological work that was carried out was remarkable, don't imagine that the visual effect of the reconstruction is remotely on a scale to match that of the Egyptian reconstruction above the Aswan Dam. The reconstructed buildings are on a comparatively small scale, in a peaceful setting on top of the hill top fort, now an island.

The valley lies in the N ranges of the **Nallamalais** ('black hills') which surround it on 3 sides. On the 4th side was

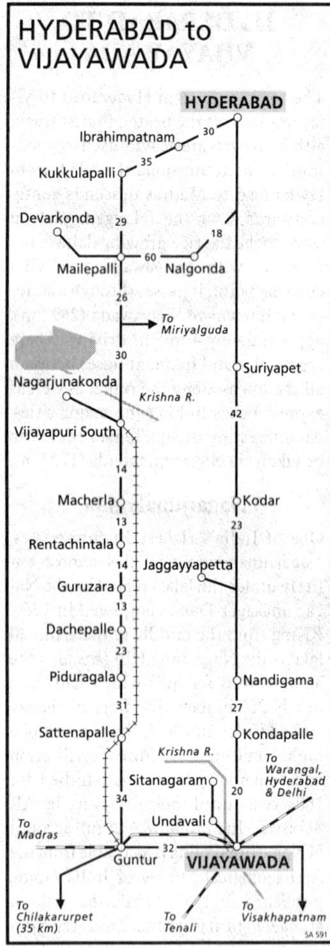

the great River Krishna, superimposed on the hills as it flows towards the Bay of Bengal. Early archaeological work showed the remnants of Buddhist monasteries, many limestone sculptures and other remains. In the early 1950s the government decided to build the Nagarjunasagar Dam. The archaeological site had by that time barely been touched, and the Archaeological Survey of India carried out a 6 year programme of fully excavating the sites in the valley before they were to be covered by the rising waters of the lake. The excavations discovered more than 100 distinct sites ranging from the prehistoric early stone age period to the late medieval. Some of the most important remains have been moved and reconstructed. 9 monuments have been rebuilt in their original form and there are 14 large replicas of the excavated ruins shown on what is now the island hill-top.

History

The valley site has probably been occupied for almost 200,000 years. Crude stone tools were found – points, scrapers and handaxes, made out of quartzite pebbles – on the banks of the Krishna. In the 3rd millennium BC rural settlements began to take shape. One of the sites excavated showed a Neolithic cemetery, suggesting permanent settlement, and many pits. From around 400 BC Megalith builders appeared, leaving stone circles under which were pits for the dead, often buried in groups. Just a few had any ornamentation. One site showed the bodies of women, one of which had gold spiral earrings and a necklace. In all 19 skeletons were discovered.

After a 400 year gap the **Ikshvakus** made Nagarjunakonda the centre of extraordinary artistic activity from the 3rd century AD. Inscriptions suggest that their first king, *Chamtamula* followed the Hindu god of war, *Karttikeya*. However, his sister, Chamsatri, supported Buddhism, creating the first Buddhist establishment found at Nagarjunakonda. The support of both Buddhism and Brahmanism side by side throughout the reign of the Ikshvaku rulers encouraged the building of monuments and development of art which reflected both traditions at the same site. It would seem that the supremacy of the Ikshvakus in the region was unchallenged over a long period. Datable records show that the building of monuments in the valley started in the sixth year of the reign of Virapurushadatta and ended abruptly in the 11th year of Rudrapurushadatta's reign.

In the mid 4th century AD the Pallavas pushed N from Tamil Nadu and eclipsed the Ikshvaku kingdom, reducing Nagarjunakonda to a deserted village. However, during the Chalukya period between the 7th and 12th centuries AD a Saiva centre was built at Yellaswaram, on the other bank of the Krishna.

In the 15th and 16th centuries the hill became a fortress in the contest for supremacy between the Vijayanagar, Bahmani and Gajapati kings. After the fall of the Vijayanagar Empire both the hill and the valley below lost all importance.

The site

The Ikshvakus capital was a planned city on the right bank of the Krishna – **Vijayapuri** ('city of victory'). The citadel had rampart walls on 3 sides with the river serving as protection on the 4th. The buildings inside included houses, barracks, baths and wells. The buildings were probably destroyed by a great fire. Most people lived outside the citadel in houses made of rubble bound by mud. An inscription near a goldsmith's house showed that there were guilds of craftsmen – sweet makers, masons, artisans. There was a shell cutting industry near the Brahman shrines, and many fragments of shell bangles were discovered. The most striking secular building was the amphitheatre which could seat about 1000 people, possibly to watch the wrestling scenes depicted in some of Nagarjunakonda's art. Dice, game boards and dancing were all common. The 9 temples show the earliest developments of Brahmanical temple architecture in S India. The Vishnu temple (AD 278), housed an 8-armed wooden statue. Two beautifully carved pillars were recovered from its site. 5 temples were dedicated to Siva or Karttikeya.

Two km upstream was a shrine clearly associated with a **burning ghat**. One sculpture recovered shows a woman as if lying in state while a 2nd seems to show *sati* taking place – a woman throwing herself onto her husband's funeral pyre. The main bathing ghat on the banks of the Krishna was remarkable, and has been moved to its new site above the lake. The river bank was dotted with **Brahmanical shrines**. The largest temple complex was nearly 150 m sq, with an apsidal sanctuary, and was clearly a centre of pilgrimage for long after the decline of the Ikshvaku kingdom. The Brahmanical temples of this period had not developed a standard form. Some had a single shrine, others more than one, each with a pillared hall in front of it. Oblong, apsidal and square shrines are all found, and while brick was used for the shrines, stone was prominent in the construction of the *mandapas*, which were flat roofed.

There are over 30 **Buddhist buildings** throughout the valley, spanning a period of about 100 years.The earliest structure in the whole of Nagarjunakonda, the *Maha chaitya*, was in the centre of the site, and was built between the 6th and 18th years of King Virapurushadatta's reign. It was a stupa with a wheel shaped plan with a diameter of over 27m. It had a tooth relic among other relics, and the inscription refers to the bodily remains of the Buddha. In their earliest phases none of the stupas had image shrines, and there were several small stupas unconnected with other buildings. However, some later monasteries did have shrines. There were 9 monastic buildings around the citadel itself and a further 10 in the NE part of the valley. These were later, and show 2 new trends; the development of circular image shrines, and a memorial pillar opposite a *stupa-chaitya* which was put up in honour of the Queen's mother.

Both the early **Hinayana Buddhism** and the later **Mahayana** schools were represented, see page 86. The Hinayana schools never introduced images into worship and therefore resisted also the development of temple forms which allowed and encouraged image worship. The early Buddhist monasteries had simply a stupa and a vihara for the monks to live in. Apsidal shrines were introduced later, possibly from the NW. The Gandharan sites in modern Pakistan had innovations that clearly came before they were introduced at Nagarjunakonda – quadrangular monasteries, square or oblong image shrines, a pillared hall for the congregation, miniature stupas and a square platform for the stupa. The most striking development within Nagarjunakonda itself was that of the wheel-shaped plan of stupas, the architects transforming a Buddhist symbol into an architectural plan. This too may be a Gandharan development, as the Dharmarajika stupa at Taxila is so constructed. The other development in Nagarjunakonda's stupa architecture was that of building *ayaka platforms* at the cardinal directions. Each platform was designed to have 5 pillars symbolising the 5 stages of the Buddha's life – Birth, Great Renunciation, Enlightenment, First Sermon and Extinction.

Nagarjunakonda excavations also revealed some of India's finest early **sculptures** and **memorial pillars**. Over 20 pillars were raised in the memory not just of rulers and nobles but also of artisans and religious leaders. The sculptures represent the final phase of artistic development begun further E at Amaravati and Jaggayyapeta in the 2nd century BC. The first phase included carvings on drum slabs and a few memorial pillars. The Buddha was always represented by symbols – wheel, feet, column of fire, throne with a swastika and others. Later figures have much greater boldness, rhythm and clarity, and capture pathos, joy and sorrow. The major themes were all taken out of a dozen *Jataka* stories of Buddhist literature, but there were probably several different groups of sculptors at work. Particularly striking is the amount of secular art, including the carvings on memorial pillars. They may relate simply to the deeds of an individual, and battle scenes are particularly popular. One shows an elephant with its rider, and the most vivid description of a battle is on 3 minutely carved pillars from Site 37.

The **hill fort** dates from the first part of the 14th century and has remnants of the Vijayanagar culture. The ruins run the entire length of the hill. The main entrance was from the NE, near where the ferry now lands on the island. In places the walls are still over 6m high, with regular bastions and 6 gateways. There are 2 temples in the E, where the museum now stands. After the foundation by the Reddi kings of Andhra, it was taken over by the Gajapatis of Orissa before falling to the Vijayanagar kings. The present layout of the fort probably dates from as recently as 1565, the year in which the Vijayanagar Empire was crushed at the Battle of Talikota. The earliest of the 3 temples remaining in the fort was probably built in the mid 14th century. Near the rebuilt Maha stupa, it was originally a Jain shrine, and was then converted to a Vaishnavite temple. The image of a Jain *Tirthankara* in black stone remains just outside the temple. There is another Jain Tirthankara near the bathing ghat, shown seated.

Museum

0900-1600. Closed Fri. Most of the reconstructed buildings are around the museum on the hill fort, now an island in the lake planted with low trees. There are several important and beautiful exhibits. They include beads, coins, relic caskets and a variety of ornaments, but most importantly, the sculptures. A 3m high standing Buddha, put together from several fragments, is one of the few figures carved in the round. Also prehistoric and protohistoric remains and several panels and friezes depicting Buddhist scenes.

The island is 11 km from Vijayapuri. 2 ferries daily from jetty, 0930 and 1330. Other ferries serve APTTDC tours organised locally or from Hyderabad (Tours Rs 75).

The **Nagarjunasagar Dam** project is one of the largest in India. The dam is constructed out of stone masonry, both cheaper and more labour intensive than concrete. Now completed, the scheme generates 400 MW of electricity, and feeds nearly 800 km of canals. 2 tunnels are said to be among the longest irrigation tunnels in the world. The Jawahar Canal (right bank) has an overall length of 12 km, while the Lal Bahadur Canal (left bank), is 3 km long with an internal diameter of 9m. They are named after India's first 2 Prime Ministers.

• **Budget hotels** No Western style, but a few inexpensive, basic hotels. **E** APTTDC *Soundarya Tourist Annexe*, Hill Colony, 8 rm, a/c or air-cooled and **F** *Vijaya Vihar Complex*, 8 a/c rm, restaurant, reservations: Asst Manager, T 69; **F** APTTDC *Project House*, T 2133, 25 rm on ground floor, 18 rm upstairs cheaper; **F** *River View Rest House*, on Rght Bank. Also furnished cottages on Hill Colony which are a little more expensive and cheaper cottages on the Right Bank. **F** *Youth Hostel* has 12 rm, contact the Exec Engineer B & R Hill Colony, T 2672, Res 2635.

• **Services Banks** and **Post Offices** at Hill Colony and Pylon (4 km). **Tourist Office** at AP Tourism, Project House, Hill Colony, T 2133 (Office), T 2134 (Residence). There is one guide available through this office. Others from the Hyderabad Tourist Office.

The largest of the State's Wildlife Sanctuaries is near **Nagarjunasagar** at **Srisailam Wildlife Sanctuary** (201 km from Hyderabad).

Nagarjunasagar Srisailam Wildlife Sanctuary

BASICS *Altitude*: 200-900m; *Temp range*: 42°C to 12°C; *Rainfall*: 1,500 mm.

Background

The largest of the state's national parks named after the reservoir (201 km from Hyderabad) which is also India's largest tiger reserve, covers 3,560 sq km in 5 neighbouring districts. The sanctuary cut by deep gorges of the Nallamalai hills has areas of mixed deciduous and bamboo forest as well as semi-desert scrubland in the NE. Best time: Oct-Jan.

Wildlife

There are tiger, leopard, a large colony of Indian pangolins, panther, wild dogs, civet, hyena, jackals, wolves, giant squirrels, crocodiles, lizards, python, vipers, kraits and over 150 species of birds.

Fort and temple

Srisailam also attracts visitors to its fort and temple (originally, c 2nd century AD) with one of 12 *Jyotirlinga* in the country, see page 382. The ancient **Mahakali Temple** on a hill rising from the Nallamalai forest contains a rare *lingam* which draws large crowds of pilgrims daily and especially at *Sivaratri*. The walls and gates have carvings depicting stories from the epics. Non-Hindus are allowed into the inner sanctuary to witness the daily puja ceremony. To avoid the long queue in the middle of the day, it is best to arrive early – first prayers at 0545! **NB**: At times disturbed due to political activists. Check latest position with Forest Officer.

• **Accommodation** AP Tourism **F** *Saila Vihar*, 3 *Rest Houses* and **F** *Temple cottages*.

• **Transport Air** From Hyderabad (150 km). **Train** Marchelna (13 km). Hire Jeep beforehand.

Amaravati

En route to Guntur from Nagarjunakonda, it is possible to take a short diversion to the capital of the medieval Reddi kings of Andhra. 1500 years before they wielded power it was a great Mahayana Buddhist centre (see page 86). Initially the shrine was dedicated to the Hinayana sect but under Nagarjuna was changed into a Mahayana sanctuary where the Buddha was revered as Amareswara.

The **Great Stupa** (Maha Chaitya), supposed to have been 32m in height and 32m diameter, larger than that at Sanchi, see page 360. Its origins go back to the 3rd-2nd centuries BC, though it was enlarged between the 1st and 4th centuries AD when the 5m wide ambulatory path and 4.5m high railings were added. The dome was faced with intricately carved marble slabs. At festival time, pilgrims circled the Stupa, carrying lamps which gave rise to its other name 'Deepaldinne' (dome of light). Very little remains. Excavations began in 1797 and most of the magnificent sculpted friezes, medallions and railings have been removed, the majority to the museums at Madras (see Amaravati Gallery which has finds from excavations from 1797-1905) and Calcutta. Half of the finds went to the British Museum, London.

The **Archaeological Museum** on site contains panels, mainly broken, railings and sculptures of the Bodhi Tree, *chakras* and caskets containing relics. Episodes from the life of the Buddha are common, and there are some free standing images of the Buddha. Some of the sculptures are exquisitely carved. Also galleries containing pottery, coins, bangles and terracotta. Apart from items excavated since 1905, there are some exhibits from other sites in the Krishna and Visakhapatnam Dist. 0900-1700 except Fri. Free. **Accommodation F** *PWD Guest House.*

Vijayawada

BASICS *Population*: 845,300; *STD Code*: 0866; *Climate*: Summer: Max 41°C, Min 29°C; Winter: Max 30°C, Min 20°C.

At the head of the Krishna delta 70 km from the sea, the city is surrounded by bare granite hills. During the hot dry season these radiate heat and temperatures of over 45°C are not uncommon in April and May. The Krishna cuts through a gap less than 1,200m wide in the bare ridge of gneissic rocks. The Krishna Delta canal scheme, one of the earliest major irrigation developments of the British period in S India, completed in 1855, now irrigates nearly 1 million ha, banishing famine from the delta and converting it into one of the richest granaries of the country. The dam Prakasam Barrage, over 1000m long, carries the road and railways.

Places of interest

The name of this city, over 2,000 years old, is derived from the goddess Kanakdurga, the presiding deity of the city, also called Vijaya. There is a temple to her on a hill along the river. There are several sites with caves and temples with inscriptions from the 1st century AD. The **Mogalarajapuram Temple** has an *Ardhanarisvara* statue which is thought to be the earliest in S India. There are two 1,000 year old **Jain temples** and the **Hazratbal Mosque** which has a relic of the Prophet Mohammad. The Qutb Shahi rulers made Vijayawada an important inland port. It has retained its importance as a commercial town, and has capitalised on its position as the link between the interior and the main N-S route between Madras and Calcutta.

The **Victoria Jubilee Museum** contains a colossal granite statue of the Buddha, one of the reminders that the site of the modern town was an important Buddhist religious centre even before the 7th century AD, when it was visited by Hiuen Tsang.

Museums

Victoria Jubilee Museum, Bandar Rd. Collection includes sculpture and paintings. 1030-1700 except Fri. Free. Camera Rs 3.

Excursions

20 km out of Vijayawada, just N of the NH 9 to Hyderabad, is the famous toy-making centre of **Kondapalli**. The toys are usually made of light wood and laquered in brilliant colours. Craftsmen can be seen working on carvings of human, animal and religious figures.

A rock temple close to the village of **Sitanagaram** and a 5-storeyed Brahman cave temple at **Undavali**, dating from the 5th century, were discovered in 1797. The upper storeys are set back, while the lowest storey has 3 rows of pillars partly cut out of the rock. They probably date from the same period as the Mamallapuram shore temples. One compartment has a shrine cell with an altar, another has a relief of Vishnu and his wives. There are friezes of geese, elephants and lions. The 3rd storey has a hall over 15m by 10m, with a figure of **Vishnu** seated on the snake Ananta. Another shows **Narayana** on the snake Sesha. The top storey has barrel vaulted roofs. To reach the temple, cross the barrage going S out of Vijayawada, then turn right up the course of the river for nearly 3 km beyond and W of Sitanagaram.

Local information

● Accommodation

Nr the centre: **D** *Kandhari International*, MG Rd, T 471311, 73 a/c rm, a/c restaurants, bar, coffee shop, travel, shops; **D** *Swarna Palace*, Eluru Rd, T 67222, 50 rm, most a/c, restaurants, bar, travel; **D** *Raj Towers*, Congress Office Rd, T 61311, 50 rm, some a/c, restaurants, bar; **D** *Mamata*, 45-15-478 Eluru Rd opp Bus Stand, T 61251, 59 rm, most a/c with bath, a/c restaurants (one roof-top), bar. Alternative is cheaper *Sri Durga Bhavan*, 42 rm, veg restaurant. **D** *Manorama*, 27-38-61 Bander Rd, T 77221, 69 rm, 19 a/c, a/c restaurants, exchange, shops. AP Tourism *Krishnaveni*, Sitanagaram (nr Barrage), T 75382, restaurant, Tourist office, car/coach hire, shop; **D** *Tilotthama*, nr Bus Stand, Governorpet, T 73201, 53 rm, some a/c with phone, restaurant (veg).

E *Chaya*, 27-8-1 Governorpet, T 61336, 39 rm, 12 a/c with phone, restaurant (S Indian veg), travel; **E** *Sree Lakshmi Vilas*, Besant Rd, Governorpet, T 62525, 50 rm some with bath, a/c restaurant.

There are several inexpensive hotels nr the Bus Stand on Bandar Rd and a few nr the Rly Station. **F** *Railway Retiring Rooms* and reasonable *Station restaurant* opens at 0600; **F** Govt *Guest Houses*, Surya Rao Pet, T 61241 and on Bandar Rd – **F** *Canal Guest House*, **F** *R & B Guest House* and **F** *Zila Parishad Guest House*.

● Places to eat

Kandhari and *Mamata* hotels are rec. Garden restaurants are very pleasant, esp ***Greenlands***, 40-17-191/1 Bhavani Gardens, Labbipet, 7 huts, in lawns.

● Banks & money changers

Several branches inc **State Bank of India**, Babu Rajendra Prasad Rd.

● Post & telecommunications

Head Post Office: Kaleswara Rao Rd, T 75645.

● Shopping

Local Kondapalli toys and Machilipatnam Kalamkari paintings are especially popular. The emporia are in MG Rd, Governorpet and Eluru Rd. ***Apco***, Besant Rd, ***Aptex***, AP Handlooms, Eluru Rd, ***Handicrafts Shop***, *Krishnaveni Motel*, ***Lepakshi***, Gandhi Nagar are rec.

Photography: ***Bombay Studio***, Park Rd, ***Veeranna***, Kaleswararao Rd.

● Sports

Water sports & boating: K L Rao Vihara Kendram, Bhavani Island on Prakasham Barrage Lake offers a variety of water sports including rowing, canoeing, water scooters, pedal boats. 0930-1830. Rs 5-15. Contact Asst Manager, Water Sports Unit, *Krishnaveni Motel*, T 75382.

● Tourist office

27-23-294 Gopal Reddy Rd. Gpveruorpet, opp Old Bus Stand, T 75382. 0600-2000. Full Day tour. AP Tourism counter at RTC Bus Stand, Machilipatnam Rd, T 61220.

● Useful Services

Foreigners' Regional Registration Office, Superintendent of Police, Bandar Rd, T 77772.

● Transport

Linked to other regions by NH 5 and 9. Bangalore 638 km, Bombay 1,012 km, Calcutta 1,193 km, Delhi 1,724 km, Hyderabad 270 km, Madras 444 km, Nagpur 679 km, Tirupati 380 km, Visakhapatnam 366 km.

Local Tourist **taxis**, **auto rickshaws**, **cycle rickshaws** and **tongas** are available. Very few metered yellow-top taxis. **Bus**: Good network of city buses but overcrowded. **Ferry**: service to Bhavani Islands, 0930-1730. Tourist Taxi hire from AP Tourism, Krishnaveni Motel, Seethanagaram, T 75382.

Air Transport to town: Tourist taxi from airport (20 km), 40 min, Rs 100-150.

Hyderabad: daily except Su, 0940, 1 hr.

Indian Airlines have an office opposite Old RTO Office, Bandar Rd, T 472218. 1000-1315, 1400-1700.

Train Vijayawada is an important junction and is connected to most major cities by express and superfast trains. **Bhubaneswar**: *Coromandel Exp* 2842 (AC/II), daily, 1520, 12¾ hr; *Konark Exp* 2120 (AC/II), daily, 1900, 14¼ hr. **Calcutta (H)**: *Coromandel Exp* 2842 (AC/II), daily, 1520, 20¼ hr. **Madras (MC)**: *Tamil Nadu Exp* 2622 (AC/CC&AC/II), daily, 0110, 6¾ hr; or *Coromandel Exp* 2841 (AC/II), daily, 1045, 6¾ hr. **Delhi (ND)**: *Tamil Nadu Exp* 2621 (AC/CC&AC/II), daily, 0350, 27 hr; *Kerala Mangala Exp* 2625 (AC/II), daily, 1035, 28 hr. **Secunderabad**: *Konarak Exp* 2119 (AC/II), daily, 0845, 6½ hr. **Hyderabad**: *E Coast Exp* 8045, daily, 1200, 7 hr. Vijayawada Rly Station Enquiries, T 67771. Reservations, A/c and I Class, T 74302, II Class T 73555. 0800-1300, 1300-2000. Tokens issued ½ hr earlier.

Road, **Bus**: AP, Karnataka, MP SRTC Buses offer Vijayawada a good service to and from cities in the 3 states. New Bus Stand, Bandar Rd Hwy, nr Krishna river. Enquiries T 73333. Reservations 24 hr.

Sea Services between Krishnaveni Motel and Amaravati. Daily 0800. Rs 50 return. Reservations: AP Tourism, Krishnaveni Motel, T 75382 or Counter at RTC Bus Station.

VIJAYAWADA TO MADRAS

In Vijayawada the NH 9 joins the main Calcutta-Madras NH 5. It becomes much busier, and is slow moving, particularly around Vijayawada and Guntur and between Nellore and Madras in the S. About 7 hr by road to Madras. You can divert to Tirupati before completing the short journey to Madras.

The journey becomes extremely uncomfortable during the hot weather from early Mar, and in Oct-Nov the eastern coastline is subject to severe cyclones. **NB** If you are travelling at that time of year check the weather forecasts. The deltas and the flat coastal plains are fringed with palmyra palms and occasional coconut palms, rice and tobacco. Inland barely 40% of the land is culti-

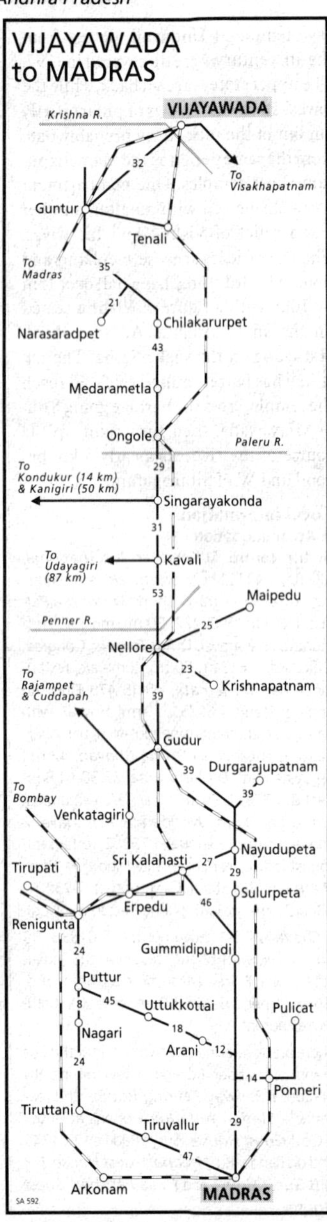

vated. The coast itself is either fringed by mangroves or lined with wind blown dunes and casuarina trees. About 120 km to the W of the road run the Vellikonda ranges, only visible in very clear weather, and in the S sections of the route where they come closer to the coast.

Guntur

(32 km; *Population*: 471,000; *STD Code*: 0863) From Vijayawada the road crosses the barrage (giving magnificent views over the Krishna at sunset) to Guntur , a major commercial town. It lies at the junction of the ancient charnockite rocks of the Peninsula and the alluvium of the coastal plain. It is also a junction for the rail line crossing central AP to Guntakal. In the 18th century it was important as the capital of the region known as the Northern Circars, and was under Muslim rule from 1766 under the Nizam of Hyderabad.

• **Accommodation** **F** *Railway Retiring Rooms*.

• **Transport Train Secunderabad**: *Golconda Exp* 7201 (AC/CC), daily, 0525, 8¼ hr. **Hospet**: *Hubli-Amravati Exp* 7825, daily, 2010 (via Guntakal, 10 ¼ hr) 14 hr. **Calcutta via Vijayawada**: *Golconda Exp* 7201 (AC/CC), daily, 0525, 55 min, change at Vijayawada (15 min wait), then *Howrah Mail* 6004 (AC/II), daily, 0635, 15½ hr (total time 16¾ hr). **Madras via Vijayawada**: *Golconda Exp* 7201 (AC/CC), daily, 0525, 55 min, change at Vijayawada (4 hr wait), then *Coromandel Exp* 2841, daily, 1025, 7¼ hr (Total time 14¼ hr).

ROUTES The road S through Ongole (113 km) and Kavali (60 km) to Nellore (53 km) runs across the stony lateritic coastal plain, often covered with thin scrub and occasional palmyra palms.

Nellore

(*Population*: 316,400; *STD Code*: 0861) is another administrative and commercial town. Along the roadside are some good S Indian restaurants – excellent coffee, dosai, idli and puris available near the bus stand.

• **Transport Train Madras (MC)**: *Bokaro-Madras Exp* 8689, daily, 0456, 4¼ hr; **or** *Navjivan Exp* 2641 (AC/II), Tue, Wed, Sat, Sun, 1405, 3¼ hr. **Vijayawada**: *Navjivan Exp* 2642 (AC/II), Mon, Wed, Th, Sun, 1310, 4 hr. **Secunderabad**: *Charminar Exp* 6059 (AC/II), daily, 2127, 10½ hr.

ROUTES The NH 5 continues S to Naidupet (54 km) where it is possible to take a diversion to Sri Kalahasti (27 km) and Tirupati (27 km). The main road to Madras goes through Gudumallam, Puttur and Arani.

Diversion to Sri Kalahasti

(Or Kalahasti; *STD Code*: 08578) is very attractively sited on the banks of the Svarnamukhi River at the foot of the extreme southern end Vellikonda Ranges, known locally as the Kailasa Hills. The **Kalahastisvara Temple** dominates the town with its gopuram facing the river. It is built in the Dravida style like the world-famous Sri Venkatesvara temple of Tirumalai. The town and temple, built in the 16th and 17th centuries, developed largely as a result of the patronage of the Vijayanagar kings.

The magnificent detached gopuram was built by the Vijayanagar emperor Krishnadeva Raya. Although it does not compare with the neighbouring centre of Tirumalai, it is still a considerable pilgrimage town. The bathing ghats of the Swarnamukhi (golden) river and the temple have a steady flow of pilgrims, but in addition to its function as a pilgrim centre the town is known throughout S India for its production of *Kalamkaris*, the brightly coloured hand painted textiles used as temple decoration. There are fine examples in the Salar Jung Museum in Hyderabad, see page 1078.

The temple is set within 4 high walls with a single entrance in the S wall. The temple is particularly revered for the white stone Siva lingam in the western shrine, believed to be worshipped by *sri* (spider), *kala* (King Cobra) and *hasti* (Elephant). The Nayaka style is typified by the columns carved into the shape of rearing animals and the riders. The temple to the Wind God *Vayudeva* is the only one of its kind in India. A further 27 km from Sri Kalahasti is Tirupati.

Tirupati and Tirumalai

BASICS *Population*: 189,000; *STD Code*: 08574; *Altitude*: 152m; *Climate*: Temp Summer: Max 40°C, Min 22°C; Winter: Max 32°C, Min 15°C; *Annual rainfall*: 710 mm, mainly Oct-Dec.

The Tirumalai Hills provide a picture-book setting for the famous temple. The main town of **Tirupati** lies at the bottom of the hill where there are several temples, some centres of pilgrimage in their own right. The 7 hills are compared to the 7 headed Serpent God Adidesha who protects the sleeping Vishnu under his hood.

Local crafts

Copper and brass idols are produced at **Perumallapalli** Village 8 km away. Wooden toy-making is also a local industry.

Places of interest

The main destination of pilgrims, the **Sri Venkatesvara Temple**, is in **Tirumalai** (*Population*: 17,000; *STD Code*: 08577; *Altitude*: 860m) 22 km away at the top of the ghat road. It is believed to have been dedicated by Ramanuja in the 11th century. In the N the temple complex is called Balaji and in the S, Srinivasa Perumalai. Pilgrims usually walk up the wooded slope to the top of the hill through mango groves and sandal wood forest chanting "Om namo Venkatesaya" or "Govinda, Govinda". A road runs all the way with a bus stand at the top.

Of all India's temples, this draws the largest number of pilgrims. Order is maintained by providing 'Q sheds' under which pilgrims assemble. Two types of queues for *Darshan* or special viewing are allowed. 'Sarvadarsan' is open to all while 'Special darshan' is offered to those paying Rs 25 who are allowed to join a separate shorter queue. The actual *darshan* itself lasts a precious second and a half even though the 'day' at the temple lasts 21 hr. Every day is festival day with shops remaining open 24 hr. Sri Venkatesvara's image is widely seen across S India, in private homes, cars and taxis and in public places, and is instantly recognisable from its black face and covered eyes, shielded so that the deity's piercing gaze may not blind any who look directly at him. In the temple the deity's body is anointed with camphor, saffron and musk. The holy *prasadam* or consecrated sweet is distributed to around 50,000 pilgrims on an ordinary day, and many more for a festival.

Sri Venkatesvara is a form of Vishnu. Theoretically the inner shrines of the Tirumalai temple are open only to Hindus. However, foreigners may be invited to sign a form stating that they are Hindus, and if they are willing to do that they are allowed in. The Tourist Information publicity leaflet states that "All are welcome. The temple welcomes all devotees regardless of formal religions. The only criterion for admission is faith in God and respect for the temple's conventions and rituals."

The Venkatesvara Temple dates from the 10th century, with later additions. The atmosphere is unlike any other temple in India. Turnstiles control the flow of pilgrims into the main temple complex, which is through an intricately carved gopuram on the E wall. Much of the gopuram is rebuilt. There are 3 enclosures. The 1st, where there are portrait sculptures of the Vijayanagar patrons, including Krishnadeva Raya and his queen and a gold covered pillar and the *vahanas* or sacred 'vehicles'. Several rituals are performed daily. The outer colonnades are Vijayanagar; the gateway leading to the inner enclosure may be of *Chola* origin. The 2nd enclosure has more shrines, a sacred well and the kitchen. The inner enclosure is

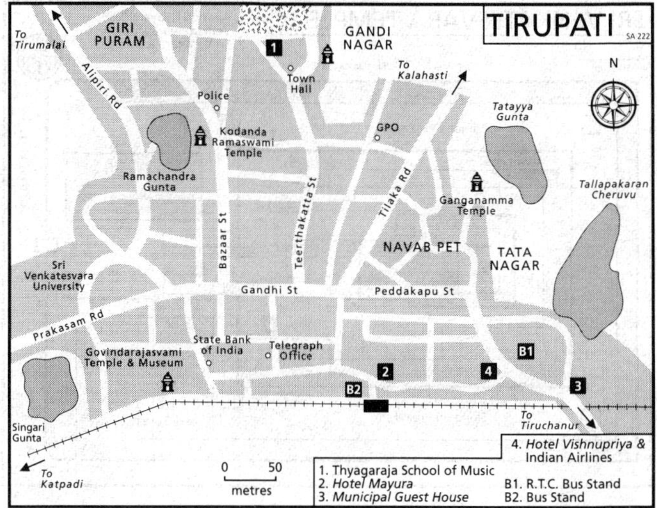

opened only once every year. The main temple and shrine is on the W side of the inner enclosure.

The sanctuary (9th-10th centuries), known as 'Ananda Nilayam', has a domed *vimana* entirely covered with gold plate, and gold covered gates guard the sanctum sanctorum. The image in the shrine is a standing Vishnu, richly ornamented with gold and jewels. The 2m high image stands on a lotus, 2 of his 4 arms carry a conch shell and a *chakra* or discus and he wears a diamond crown which is said to be the most precious single ornament in the world. It is flanked by *Sridevi* and *Bhudevi*, Vishnu's consorts. There is a small **museum** with a collection of stone, metal and wooden images (see below).

Govindarajasvami Temple (16th-17th centuries), is the most widely visited in Tirupati itself. Built by the Nayakas, the successors to the Vijayanagar Empire, the temple has an impressive outer gopuram. Of the 3 gopurams the innermost is also the earliest, dating from the 14th-15th centuries. The main sanctuaries are dedicated to Vishnu and Krishna. The other temple is **Kapilesvarasvami** in a very attractive setting has a sacred waterfall Kapilateertham.

Other excursions

One km away are strange rock formations in a naturally formed arch, resembling a hood of a serpent, a conch and a discus, are thought to have been the source of the idol in the temple. There is a sacred waterfall **Akasa Ganga** 3 km S of the temple. The Papa Vinasanam Dam is 5 km N. **Chandragiri** (11 km) became the capital of the Vijayanagaras in 1600, after their defeat at the battle of Talikota 35 years earlier. The Palace of Sri Ranga Raya, built in 1639 witnessed the signing by Sri Ranga Raya of the original land grant to the East India Company of Fort St George, but 7 years later the fort was captured by Qutb Shahi from Golconda. The fort was built on a 180m high rock where earlier fortifications may date from several hundred years before the Vijayanagar Kings took over. You can still see the well preserved fortifications and some palaces and temples. Visit the Rani Mahal and Raja

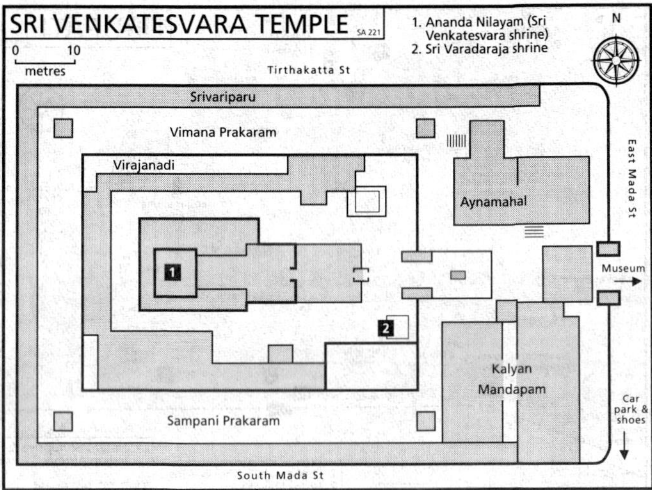

Mahal with its pretty lily pond. Museum, in Raja Mahal, contains Chola and Vijayanagar bronzes. **Tiruchanur** 5 km SE has the temple to Parvati, the consort of Venkatesvara.

Museums

At Tirupati, the TTD **Sri Venkatesvara Museum** of Temple art at the Sri Govindarajasvamy Temple compound. 0800-2000. Re 1. An interesting collection of Indian musical instruments at the entrance to the temple in Tirumalai. 0800-2000. Re 1. Sri Venkatesvara University Oriental Research Institute. Collection includes images of stone, wood and metal, pottery, coins, inscriptions. 1000-1630. Free. At Tirumalai a small museum, **Hall of Antiquities**, opp Sri Venkateswara Temple. 0800-2000. Re 1.

Tours

AP Tourism, Rm 15, Srinivasa Choultry, T 20602. *Local sightseeing Tour* starts at the APSRTC Central Bus Stand at 1000. Rs 30. Tirupati, Kalahasti, Tiruchanur, Chandragiri and Srinivasamangapuram.

Local festivals

May/Jun *Govind Brahmotsavam*.

Sep *Brahmotsavam* is the most important, especially grand every 3rd year when it is called *Navarathri Brahmotsavam*. On the 3rd day the Temple Car Festival *Rathotsavam* is particularly popular. Many others.

Local information

● Accommodation

Thousands of pilgrims are usually housed in well maintained Temple Trust's *choultries* which can accommodate about 20,000. They vary from Luxury suites, well-furnished cottages, dormitories to unfurnished accommodation (some free). Contact PRO, TT Devasthanams, T 2753 or Reception Officer 1, T 2571. TTD ***New Guest House, Travellers' Bungalow, Modi Bhavan, Shriniketan, India, Balakuteeram, Padmavati, Gokulam Guest Houses*** are graded as Deluxe. An Indo-American collaboration is to open a **B** category, 141 room hotel, 30 km from Tirupati.

D Karnataka Tourism ***Mayura Saptagiri***, Pravasi Mandir, T 7285, 65 rm, some a/c with phone, restaurant (S Indian veg), exchange, travel; **D** ***Sri Oorvasi International***, Renigunta Rd, T 20202, 78 rm, some a/c with TV, 1 km rly, restaurant (veg), travel; **D** ***Vishnu Priya***, opp APSRTC Central Bus Stand, T 20300, 134 rm, some a/c, restaurants, travel (Indian Airlines office), exchange, shops; **D** ***Bhimas Deluxe***, 34 G Car St, T 20121, 60 rm, 40 a/c, nr rly and centre, a/c restaurant (Indian), travel; **D** ***Bhimas***, 42 G Car St, T 20766, 59 rm, some a/c, nr rly, central, restaurant (South Indian veg), roof-garden.

● Places to eat

at the better hotels are reasonable. Outside hotels, veg restaurants: ***Laxmi Narayan Bhawan*** and ***Dwarka***, opp RTC Bus Stand and the ***Konark*** on Rly Station Rd and ***New Triveni***, 139 TP Area have been rec. The Tirupathi-Tirumalai Devasthanams Trust (TTD) provides free veg meals at its guest houses. In Tirumalai particularly, the Trust prohibits non-veg food, alcohol and smoking. Near the TTD Canteen and the APSRTC Bus Stand: ***Indian Coffee House*** and a ***Tea Board Restaurant***. There is also a ***Woodlands*** in the TB Area.

● Banks & money changers

Most of the banks are on Gandhi Rd. **State Bank of India**, opp APSRTC.

● Shopping

The brass and copper idols and utensils for which the area is famous and also wooden toys can be bought at the Handicrafts Emporia ***Poompuhar*** (Tamil Nadu) on Gandhi Rd and ***Lepakshi*** (AP) in the TP Area.

● Tourist offices

AP Tourism Regional, 139 TP Area, nr III Choultry, T 23208. **AP Govt State Information Centre**, Govindraja Car St, T 4818. **Karnataka Tourism & Tours**, Hotel Mayura Saptagiri (see above). **TTD Information Centres**, 1 New Choultry, T 22777 and also at Rly Station and Airport.

● Useful address

Foreigners' Regional Registration Office, Inspector Intelligence, 499 Reddy Colony, T 20503.

● Transport

Tirupati is on the NH 4 and NH 5: Bangalore 247 km, Hyderabad 617 km, Madras 172 km.

Local Bus: APSRTC Bus Service between Tirupati and Tirumalai every 3 min from 0330 to 2200. Padmavati Bus Stand, opp Rly Station for passengers with through tickets to Tirumalai; Enquiries: 3rd Choultry, T 20132. Sri Venkatesvara Bus Stand in TP Area, T 20203. Long queues for buses but buying a return ticket from Tirupati (past the Rly foot bridge) saves time at the ticket queue. The journey up the slow winding hill road takes about ¾ hr. In Tirumalai, arrive at Kesavanagar Bus Stand, nr Central Reception area, ½ km SE of temple; walk past canteen and shop. Dep from Rose Garden Bus Stand, E of the temple. **Taxi**: tourist taxis from the Bus Stand and Rly Station. Taxi sharing is common between Tirupati and Tirumalai and can cost about Rs 30 per person. Auto rickshaws point-to-point fares fixed and displayed. **Cycle rickshaws**: fares negotiable.

Tirupati Hair Cuts

Architecturally Sri Venkatesvara temple is unremarkable, but in other respects is extraordinary. It is probably the wealthiest in India, and the *devasthanam* (or temple trust) now sponsor a huge range of activities, from the Sri Venkatesvara University at Tirupati to hospitals, orphanages and schools. Its wealth comes largely from its pilgrims, on average over 10,000 a day but at major festivals many times that number. All pilgrims make gifts, and the *hundi* (offering) box in front of the shrine is stuffed full with notes, gold ornaments and other gifts.

Another important source of income is the **haircutting service**. Many pilgrims come to Tirupati to seek a special favour – to seek a suitable wife or husband, to have a child, to recover from illness – and it is regarded as auspicious to grow the hair long and then to offer the hair as a sacrifice. You may see many pilgrims fully shaven at the temple when appearing before the deity. Lines of barbers wait for arriving pilgrims. Sometimes, when coaches unload their pilgrims, one barber will line up customers and shave one strip of hair off as many heads as possible in order to maximise the number of customers committed to him before he returns and finishes off the job! The hair is collected, washed and softened before being exported to the American and Japanese markets for wig making.

Air Tirupati Airport is 15 km from the city centre. **Transport to town**: RTC coach between airport and Tirupati (Rs 8) and Tirumalai (Rs 15). **Indian Airlines**, *Hotel Vishnupriya* opp Central Bus Stand, T 22349. 1000-1730. No flights at present.

Train Good rail links with rest of the region. Broad gauge trains: **Madras (MC)**: *Tirupati-Madras Mail* 6054, daily, 1025, 3¼ hr. **Hyderabad**: *Rayalaseema Exp* 7430 (AC/II), daily, 1530, 16½ hr. **Bombay (VT) via Madras (MC)**: *Saptagiri Exp* 6058, daily, 1810, 3½ hr, change at Madras (¾ hr wait), then *Madras-Bombay Mail* 7010 (AC/II), daily, 2220, 30½ hr (total time 34¾ hr). **Guntakal**: *Rayalaseema Exp* 7430 (AC/II), daily, 1530, 7½ hr. **Mysore**: *Tirupati Mysore Exp*, daily, 2200, 12 hr.

Road Bus: The State Road Transport Corps of AP, Tamil Nadu and Karnataka connect Tirupati with other cities in the neighbouring states. APSRTC, Central Bus Stand Enquiries, T 22333.

VIJAYAWADA TO VISAKHAPATNAM AND BHUBANESWAR

From Vijayawada the NH 5 crosses the lush and fertile delta of the Krishna and Godavari to Rajahmundry and then the narrowing coastal plain with the beautiful hills of the Eastern Ghats rising sharply inland. Rice and sugar cane dominate.

The whole pattern of life contrasts sharply with that to the S. Higher rainfall and a longer wet season, alongside the greater fertility of the alluvial soils, contribute to an air of prosperity. Village house styles are quite different, with thatched roofed cottages and white painted walls, distinctive house types and equally distinctive bullock carts. The canals of the delta are also important.

The area was brought under Muslim rule by the Golconda kings of the Bahmani Sultanate in 1575 and ceded to the French in 1753. In 1765 the Mughal Emperor granted the whole area to the East India Company, its first major territorial acquisition in India. The region is also the most urbanised part of AP, with a dozen towns with more than 100,000 people. Most are commercial and administrative centres with neither the functions nor the appearance of industrial cities, but they serve as important regional centres for trade, especially in agricultural commodities, and they are the homes of some of the wealthiest and most powerful families in Andhra.

Although the building of dams on both the Krishna and the Godavari has eliminated the catastrophic flooding common until the mid-19th century, it is still prone to **cyclones**. In 1864 a cyclone claimed over 34,000 lives. The totally flat delta, lying virtually at sea level, was completely engulfed by a tidal wave in 1883 when the volcano of Mount Krakatoa blew up 5000 km away. In 1977 a cyclone just E of Vijayawada resulted in over 25,000 deaths. You may notice the increasing number of small concrete buildings on raised platforms along the roadside designed to give temporary shelter to villagers during cyclones. **NB** Read weather forecasts before travelling.

For much of the way to **Eluru** (63 km; *Population*: 212,900; *STD Code*: 08812) the road runs sandwiched between the Kommanur canal on the right and the railway on the left. The canal (becoming the Buckingham Canal) stretches 100 km S of Madras. Eluru is a trading and administrative centre with little by way of industry apart from carpet making. The nearby Kolleru Lake has been a site visited by migrating water birds for many years and is now a sanctuary.

Rajahmundry

(67 km; *Population*: 403,700; *STD Code*: 0883), the capital of the Eastern Chalukyas, was captured by the Muslims from the Vengi kings in 1471, then returned to the Orissan kingdom in 1512. The Deccan Muslims re-took it in 1571 and

it was repeatedly the scene of repeated bitter hostilities until being granted to the French in 1753. It is remembered for the poet Nannayya who wrote the first Telugu classic *Andhra Mahabharathamu*. Every 12 years the Pushkaram celebration is held by the river bank. The **Markandaya** and **Kotilingeswara Temples** on the river bank draw pilgrims. Rajahmundry is noted for its carpets and sandalwood products and as a convenient base from which to visit the coastal districts.

Excursions

It is one of 2 points along this route where you can divert towards the hills of the Eastern Ghats. 80 km NW of the town the Godavari cuts through a gorge a succession of stunningly beautiful lakes, reminiscent of Scottish lochs rather than India. You can take boat trips on the lakes.

15 km E of Rajahmundry is the small 10th century Chalukyan temple of **Samalkot**. It is unusual, being arranged on 2 levels. A 2-storey tower with a dome roof rises above the roof. There is no sculpture on the walls but some of the columns have figures.

Kadiam, (25 km, 1 hr drive) has flourished since the earlier 1980s when a social forestry programme helped to set up plant nurseries. Today there are 250 nurseries covering 325 ha employing 600 people. Plants grown for sale, mainly in Delhi and Jaipur, include crotons, hybrid roses, royal and table palms and Ashoka trees. About 1 mill plants are sold monthly and there are spin-offs into pottery.

Museums

Sri Rallabandi Subbarao Govt Museum, Godavari Bund Rd. 1030-1700. Closed Fri and AP Govt holidays. Free. Collection of coins, sculpture, pottery, palm leaf manuscripts and inscriptions. Photography with permission. Sri RSR Govt **Museum,** Ullithota St. Collection of Archaeological material and sculpture. 1030-1700. Closed Fri and Bank holidays. Camera fee Rs 3.

• **Transport Air** To Vijayawada: daily except for Su, 0855, ½ hr. **Train Vijayawada**: *Coromandel Exp* 2841 (AC/II), daily, 0747, 2¾ hr; *Guwahati-Thiruvananthapuram Exp* 2602 (AC/II), Tue, 1825, 2½ hr. **Calcutta (H)**: *Coromandel Exp* 2842 (AC/II), daily, 1750, 17¾ hr. **Visakhapatnam**: *Coromandel Exp* 2842 (AC/II), daily, 1750, 3¼ hr; or *Haora Mail* 6004 (AC/II), daily, 0935, 4 hr; or *E Coast Exp* 8046, daily, 1645, 3¾ hr.

ROUTES The NH 5 passes through **Jaggampetta** (48 km), Thamayapeta (32 km), to **Talapalem** (99 km), the road being increasingly hedged in by the hills. The scenery is often outstandingly attractive, with the flat-floored valleys, planted with rice, surrounded by steep hills. The road finally passes through low hills into the very rapidly growing industrial port of Visakhapatnam (49 km).

Visakhapatnam

Population: 1.05mn; *STD Code*: 0891. Set in a bay with rocky promontories, *Vizag* has become one of India's most rapidly growing cities. It is already India's 4th largest port, and in addition to its role as Eastern Headquarters of the Indian Navy it has developed ship building, oil refining, fertiliser, petrochemical, sugar refinery and jute industries as well as one of India's newest and largest steel mills. On the Dolphin's Nose, a cliff rising 174m from the sea, is a lighthouse whose beam can be seen 64 km out to sea. The airport is 12 km from the centre.

Its twin town of **Waltair** to the N used to be thought of as a health resort with fine beaches, though increasing atmospheric pollution is a problem. The good beaches are Ramakrishna Beach, along the 8 km Lawson's Bay and below the 300m Mt Kailasa 6 km away. **NB** Do not swim at the harbour end of the beach.

Places of interest

The **Andhra University** founded in 1926 is in the Uplands area of Waltair. The red stone buildings are built like a fortress and are well laid out on a large campus. The country's major **Ship Building Yard** at Gandhigaram makes all types of ocean going vessels – passenger liners, cargo vessels as well as naval ships. The **Zoo** is large and attempts to avoid cages, keeping its animals in enclosures which are close to their natural habitat.

Each of the 3 hills here is sacred to a different religion. The Hindu Venkateswara temple on the the Venkateswa Konda was built in 1866 by the European Captain Blackmoor. The Muslims have a mausoleum of the saint Baba Ishaq Madina on the Darga Konda, while the highest Rose Hill has a Roman Catholic Church. A Buddhist relic was discovered at **Dhanipura** nearby.

The **Borra Caves** in the nearby limestone hills have stalactites and stalagmites. Here the village stream disappears into the hillside and reappears in the gorge, 90m below. Since there is little of tourist interest, you might walk about the old part of town between the State Bank and fishing port. Good views of town and port from Kanya Mary Church, approached by steep steps or gentler concrete road.

Tours

AP Tourism, to *Amaravati*, full day, Rs 30 and Manginapudi Beach. Full day *local sightseeing*, Rs 40, Araku Valley Rs 75.

Local information

● Accommodation

B Taj *Residency Visakhapatnam*, was *Sea Pearl*, Beach Rd, T 474849, 100 narrow sea-facing rm, spacious, light restaurant with sandlalwood blinds (pricy but generous), bar, exchange, travel, best in town, refurbished, located at centre of bay, unremarkable public beach across road; **B** *Park*, Beach Rd, T 54861, 64 renovated rm, expensive suites, restaurant, bar, exchange, travel, bookshop, clean pool, well kept gardens, facilities average, slick management, overpriced but better value than former, best for direct beach acceess (beware of rocks when swimming), popular with German and Czech expatriates.

C *Dolphin*, Dabagardens, T 64811, F 63737, 147 rm, central, popular restaurants and coffee shop, bar, exchange, travel, shops, pool, TV, rec, roof-top restaurant highly rec, reserve with good views ahead, band plays Beatles and early '70s music, family run with excellent service, drawback, distance from beach, stay on the beach and eat here!

Late night arrivals are quoted high prices by auto-rickshaws to beachside. Stay overnight at simple hotel (walk right from Rly Staion) and move next morning. **D** *Apsara*, 12-1-17 Waltair Main Rd, T 64861, 130 rm, central a/c, restaurants, bar, coffee shop, exchange, travel, shops, very helpful and friendly staff; **D** *Sea Rock*, 49 Daspalla Hills, T 66244, 27 a/c rm, restaurant, travel; **D** *Daspalla*, Suryabagh, T 64862, 72 rm, central a/c, 2 good restaurants (western and *thalis)*, bar, exchange, travel, set back from road, rec by some, but no check-in if you arrive late at night; **D** *Ocean View Inn*, Kirlampudi, T 54828, 48 rm, some a/c rm, a/c restaurant, clean and comfortable, location at N end of the beach spoilt by new high-rise flats, 2 min walk to beach, quiet end of town; **D** *Palm Beach*, Beach Rd (next to Park), Waltair, T 54206, 34 rm, 30 a/c, restaurant, beer garden, pool, CC, pleasant location with shady palm grove but run-down building, rec for inexpensive beach break; **D** *Meghalaya*, Asilametta Junc, T 55141, F 55824, some a/c rm, dull veg restaurant (non-veg on rm service, Amercian chop-suey rec), spacious lobby with murals, greenery, pleasant roof garden. Central, back-of-town, 5 min walk from Bus Stand, short auto-rickshaw ride from Rly, friendly and helpful, popular with Indian tourists, best value in category, hightly rec.

● Budget hotels

E *Lakshmi*, next to St Joseph's Hospital, Maryland, 10 rm a/c, some with bath and TV, clean

Climate: Visakhapatnam

	Jan	Feb	Mar	Apr	May	Jun	Jul	Aug	Sep	Oct	Nov	Dec	Av/Tot
Max (°C)	28	29	31	33	34	34	32	32	32	31	29	28	31
Min (°C)	17	19	23	26	28	27	26	26	26	25	21	18	24
Rain (mm)	7	15	9	13	53	88	122	132	167	259	91	17	973

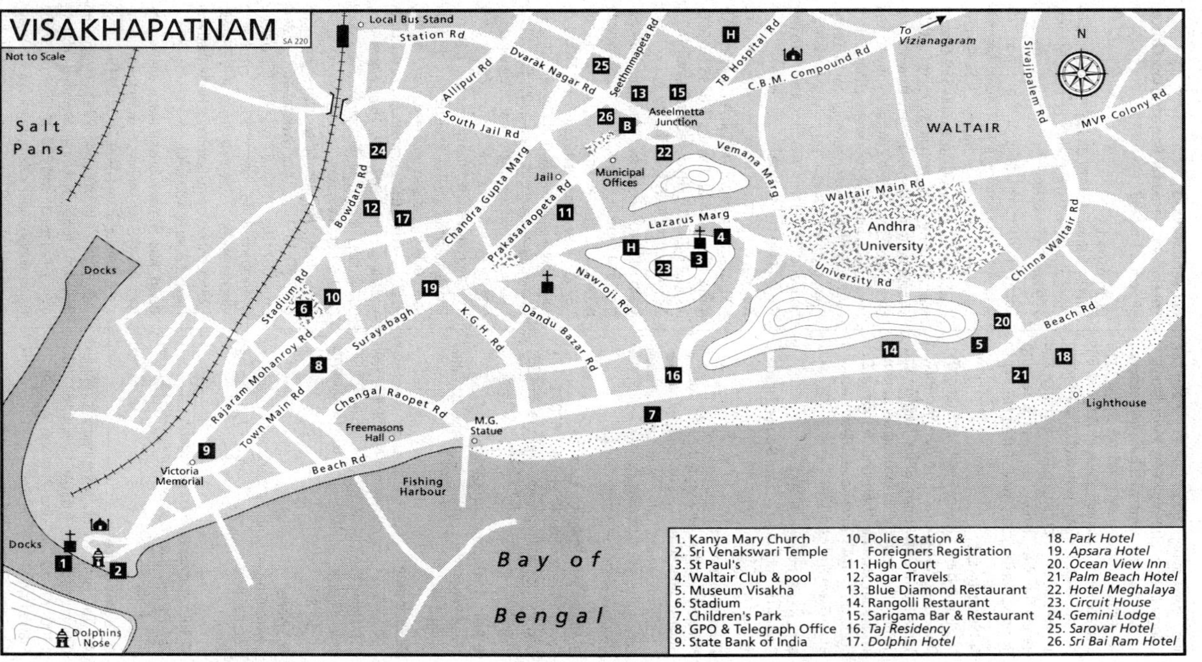
VISAKHAPATNAM
SA 220
Not to Scale
Local Bus Stand
Station Rd
Dvarak Nagar Rd
Seethmmapeta Rd
TB Hospital Rd
C.B.M. Compound Rd
To Vizianagaram
Sivajipalem Rd
N
MVP Colony Rd
Allipur Rd
South Jail Rd
Aseelmetta Junction
WALTAIR
Salt Pans
Vemana Marg
Jail
Municipal Offices
Chandra Gupta Marg
Bowdara Rd
Prakasaraopeta Rd
Waltair Main Rd
Lazarus Marg
Andhra University
Chinna Waltair Rd
Docks
University Rd
Stadium Rd
Nawroji Rd
Dandu Bazar Rd
K.G.H. Rd
Surayabagh
Rajaram Mohanroy Rd
Beach Rd
Town Main Rd
Chengal Raopet Rd
Freemasons Hall
M.G. Statue
Lighthouse
Victoria Memorial
Beach Rd
Fishing Harbour
Docks
Bay of Bengal
Dolphins Nose
1. Kanya Mary Church
2. Sri Venakswari Temple
3. St Paul's
4. Waltair Club & pool
5. Museum Visakha
6. Stadium
7. Children's Park
8. GPO & Telegraph Office
9. State Bank of India
10. Police Station & Foreigners Registration
11. High Court
12. Sagar Travels
13. Blue Diamond Restaurant
14. Rangolli Restaurant
15. Sarigama Bar & Restaurant
16. *Taj Residency*
17. *Dolphin Hotel*
18. *Park Hotel*
19. *Apsara Hotel*
20. *Ocean View Inn*
21. *Palm Beach Hotel*
22. *Hotel Meghalaya*
23. *Circuit House*
24. *Gemini Lodge*
25. *Sarovar Hotel*
26. *Sri Bai Ram Hotel*

and welcoming, good Indian restaurant; **E** ***Saga Lodge***, off Hospital Rd towards beach, rm with balcony, some with bath and seaview, no restaurant but very good rm service, rec; **E** ***Viraat***, Indira Gandhi Stadium Rd, Old Bus Stand, T 64821, 42 rm with bath and TV, some a/c, central, a/c restaurant and bar, exchange and travel. The Bus Station has good **E** ***Retiring Rooms***. The Rly Station has a **F** ***Rest House***.

● Places to eat

Most have **bars**. Outside hotels, on Station Rd: ***Diwanjee***, ***Imperial*** and ***Golden Phoenix***. In Surya Bagh: ***Sky Room, Black Dog*** (nr Jagdamba Theatre) and in Dabagardens: ***Omar Khayyam***, ***Pink Elephant*** and ***Shangrila***. ***Delight*** on 7-1-43 Kirlampudi, Beach Rd and ***Blue Diamond*** opp RTC.

● Banks & money changers

Several on Surya Bagh. **State Bank of India** is at Old Post Office.

● Entertainment

Theatre: *Andhra University* has an open-air theatre and 2 other auditoria at Waltair, T 63324. *Gurjada Kala Mandir* nr Collector's Office and *Samba Murti Kala Mandir* in Port Grounds stage live performances.

● Hospitals & medical services

Seven Hills, Rockdale Layout, T 63081. *King George*, Hospital Rd, Maharani Peta, T 64891. *St Joseph's*, Maryland, T 62974.

● Post & telecommunications

Head Post Office: Vellum Peta. Also at Waltair Rly Station.

● Shopping

The main areas are Jagadamba Junc and Waltair Uplands, Main Rd. The AP Govt Emporium ***Lepakshi***, Hospital Down Rd. ***UP Handlooms***, Saraswati Centre.

● Sports

Swimming: in *Hotel Park* and *Palm Beach* are open to non-residents. *Waltair Club* also has a pool.

● Tour company & travel agent

Taj Travels, *Meghalaya Hotel*, T 55141, ext 222, F 55824.

● Tourist office

AP Tourism, 1st Flr, Nehrunagar Complex, China Waltair Rd, T 63016, T 63016, 1000-1700, closed Sun and 2nd Sat. Also at Rly Station nr city centre. Transport Unit, 8 RTC Complex, Dwarka Nagar, T 61985.

● Useful services

Foreigners' Regional Registration Office, SP Police, T 62709.

● Transport

On NH 5: Bangalore 1,004 km, Bombay 1,376 km, Calcutta 879 km, Delhi 1,861 km, Madras 799 km, Puri 442 km.

Local Taxi: tourist taxis at the airport, rly station or from hotels (eg ***Taj Travels***, *Meghalaya Hotel*). For non-a/c and a/c: 5 hr, 50 km, Rs 250-300; 10 hr, 100 km, Rs 400-550. Longer trips: Rs 3-Rs 5; night halt Rs 75-100. **Rickshaws**: auto rickshaws are very common but cycle rickshaws in the centre. Happy to use meter if you offer Rs 2 over meter-charge; night fares exorbitant. Rates negotiable for all. **Ferry**: operates from 0800-1700 between the Harbour and Yarada Hills. You can take one to visit the Dolphin Lighthouse.

Air Airport is 12 km from city centre; Taxi (Rs 120) or auto-rickshaw. **Indian Airlines** and **Air India** agent, Sagar Travels, T 64353. 1000-1300, 1345-1700. **Hyderabad**: M,W,F, 1425, 1 hr. **Calcutta** M,W,F, 1030, 1¼ hr.

Train Well connected by broad gauge line Express and Superfast trains, it is on the main route between Calcutta and Madras. Enquiries, T 69421. Reservations T 46234. 0900-1700. Advance Reservations, left of building (facing it). Computer reservations close 2100, Sun 1400. Counter system avoids crush at ticket window. City Rly Extension Counter at Turner's Chowltry for Reservations. **TIP**: Trains are often delayed. Phone station in advance if catching a night train as it could be delayed until next morning. Taxi, Rs 50. **Calcutta (H):** *Coromandel Exp* (Calcutta – Madras) 2135, 2842, daily, 13 hr; *Haora Mail*, 6004, daily, 1400, 17 hr; *Tirupati Exp* 8080, daily 0600, 22 hr; *Bangalore – Haora Exp* 2673, Su, 2115, 14 hr; *Thiruvananthapuram – Guwahati Exp* 2601, Fri, 2115, 14 hr. **Hyderabad**: *Godavari Exp* 2602, Tue, 1510; *E Coast Exp* (Calcutta – Hyderabad) 8045, daily, 0530; *Konark Exp* (Bhubaneswar – Secunderabad) 2119, daily, 0225. Connections to Bombay at Hyderabad and Nagpur (Fare Rs 180-590).

Road Bus: the new bus station is well organised. APSRTC run services to main towns in the state. Amalapuram (1900, 2000, 2115), Araku Valley, Guntur (0930, 1545, 2045), Hyderabad (638 km, 1630), Kakinda, Mamby (175 km, 1745), Paderu (from 1730-0230), Puri (0700), Rajahmundry, Srikakulam, Tendi (1630), Vijayawada (1945, 2015), Vizianagram (57 km, many 0610-2130). APSRTC Enquiries, T 65038. Reservations 0600-2000.

Sea Occasional service to Port Blair in the Andaman Islands. Announcements in the press but sometimes giving short notice.

HYDERABAD TO BANGALORE

For much of the way this route follows NH 7 N across the boulder covered plateau of the ancient peninsular granites and gneisses. On either side reddish or light brown soils are cultivated with millets or rice on the patches of irrigated land. There are broad views across the gently rolling plateau.

Hyderabad to Kurnool

ROUTES The route from Hyderabad to Kurnool follows the railway line across the Telangana Plateau to Farooqnagar to Badepalli. The National Highway bypasses the important commercial town of Mahbubnagar (*Altitude*: 650m; *STD Code*: 08542). The NH 7 continues S, passing through Kottakota and crossing the incised Krishna River just S of the tiny village of Rangapuram and the Tungabhadra River about 40 km later, just N of Kurnool. The confluence of the Krishna and Tungabhadra is 30 km E.

Kurnool

(*Population*: 274,800; *Altitude*: 300m; *STD Code*: 08518) Between 1950-56 Kurnool was capital of the state of Andhra Desa before Hyderabad was chosen as the capital of the new state of Andhra Pradesh in 1956. Located at the junction of the Hindri and Tungabhadra rivers, it was an administrative centre for the Nawabs of Kurnool. Muslim influence is still evident in the **ruined palace** of the Nawabs on the steep bank of the Tungabhadra.

- **Accommodation** D *Raviprakash*, Railway Station Rd (1/2 km from rly), T 21116, 46 rm and bungalows, some a/c with attached baths, restaurants (Indian), conveniently located with lawns.

- **Transport Train** Kurnool Town to Ma-

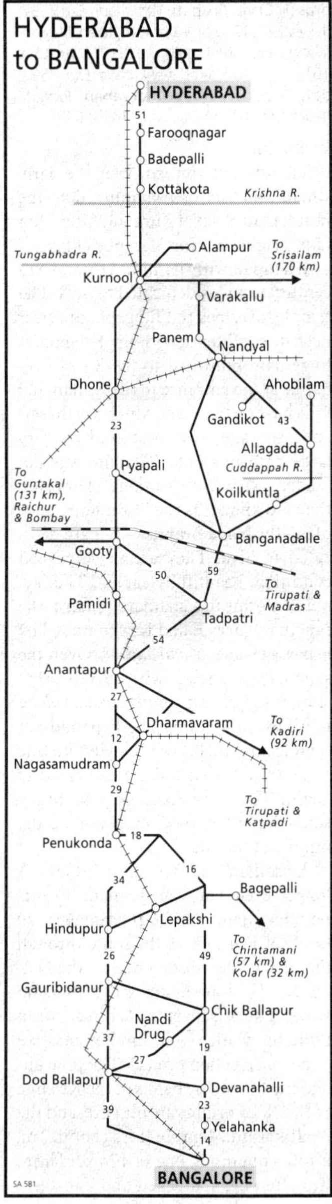

dras (MC) via Tirupati: *Venkatadri Exp* 7597, daily, 2122, 12¼ hr + 1 hr wait; then *Tirupati-Madras Exp* 6054, daily, 1025, 3¼ hr (total 16½ hr). Guntakal: *Venkatadri Exp* 7597, daily, 2122, 2¾ hr. Secunderabad: *Tungabhadra Exp* 7058 (AC/II), daily, 1415, 6 hr.

Excursion

From Kurnool you can visit the early Chalukyan site of Alampur. Take the minor road N out of Kurnool. After 6 km take a right turn for Alampur (4 km).

Alampur with its nine 7th and 8th century **temples** dedicated to Siva. The temples overlook the Tungabhadra river near its confluence with the Krishna. A huge dam built just to the SE of Kolhapur at the entrance to the Nallamalai hills has created a lake which has threatened the site, now protected by very large embankments. The site was defended with fortifications. However, they are known as the '9 Brahma' temples – the **Nava Brahma** – but are dedicated to Siva. They are in very good condition, beautifully carved. The layout conforms to a standard pattern: the sanctuary faces E and is surrounded by a passage and a *mandapam*. Over the sanctuary is a tower with curved sides, similar to Orissan temples. An *amalaka* motif caps the tower. The **Papanatham** temples are Chalukyan in style with fine stone trellis work and are dedicated to Yogini (Shakti). Alampur also has a small but very good **museum** in the middle of the site.

Srisailam (*STD Code*: 085195) A longer excursion can be made to this popular site of Saivite pilgrimage, 170 km E of Kurnool on the route through Doranala. The wooded hills of the Nallamalai Hills are home to the Chenchu tribes. The Srisailam township has been built for workers on another massive dam construction project. The pilgrimage site lies on the banks of the Krishna to the N. Its origins are obscure, and the **Mallikarjuna Temple** (14th century) on a hill, containing one of 12 *jyotirlingas*, has often been attacked and damaged. It is surrounded by a 5m wall 300m long (dated to 1456). The outer face is richly decorated with carved figures. These include a portrait of Krishna Deva Raya, the Vijayanagar Emperor who visited the site in 1514. *Mahasivaratri Festival* draws large crowds. Srisailam can also be reached straight from Hyderabad (200 km) across the wide open **Telangana Plateau**.

ROUTES From **Nandyal**, where a hoard of Roman coins was found in 1932, the road goes on to Gandikot, with the so-called "fort of the gorge", Allaguda and Ahobilam.

Gandikot

Built in 1589 at a height of more than 500m above sea level, Gandikot fort proved far from impregnable, falling in succession to the Golconda kings, to the Nawab of Cuddappah, to Haidar Ali and finally to the British. The remains hang precariously, just to the W of the flat Nandyal Valley through which the Kurnool River flows S to join the Pennar. It is part of a route that has always been strategically significant.

From Gandikot the road continues to Allaguda and Ahobilam.

Ahobilam

Ahobilam is an important Hindu pilgrimage centre. The **temples** are dedicated to Narasimha, where according to local legend the man-lion incarnation of Vishnu actually took form to defeat the demon Hiranyakasipu. There are 2 main sets of temple complexes: in town, and in Upper Ahobilam (8 km). In the heart of the limestone region, there are many natural caves, some of which are used for temples. The 14th century shrine in the town of Lower Ahobilam was developed and completed by the Vijayanagar kings. "The inner gopuram, which is the better preserved of the two, has its outer walls adorned with elongated pilasters. The successive storeys of the steeply rising pyramidal tower and also the vaulted capping form with arched ends have been renovated recently" (Michell). In Upper Ahobilam the Narasimha temple has been made in a natural cave. It is entered from the E or W sides. There is a well known Vaishnav *Math* here. **Getting there** Local buses connect with Kurnool and Tadpatri.

ROUTES From Allagadda the road goes SW and crosses the Cuddappah River (often dry) to Koilkuntla and Banganapalle (*STD Code*: 08516), formerly the capital of a small Muslim princely state and which has some noted diamond mines. One road goes S, first through the gap between the Seshachalam Hills to the S and the Erramalai Hills to the N, then along the Penner River, to Tadpatri.

Tadpatri

(*STD Code*: 08558) Founded in 1485 under the Vijayanagar Empire, Tadpatri has 2 interesting temples. The **Ramalingesvara temple**, on the S bank of the Pennar River, is the more impressive of the two, according to Fergusson, who wrote that "The wonders of the place are the 2 gopurams belonging to the Rameshwara temple, which is now deserted on the banks of the river. One of these was apparently quite finished." This houses a Siva lingam in a stand filled with spring water. There are 2 sanctuaries in the S temple of the complex with images of Parvati and Rama, Lakshmana and Sita. "The architectural elements include double basements, pilastered walls, niches framed by multi-lobed arches or surmounted by tower like pediments, and pilasters standing in pots. All of these are encrusted with friezes of jewels and petals, scrollwork and miniature animals and birds..... the resulting sculptural density is unparalleled." (Michell) About 1 km to its S is the equally highly decorated Venkataramana Temple. The **Venkataramana Temple** is about 1 km NE of the bus station, and the Ramalingesvara Temple a further 1 km N. The main shrine of the Venkataramana Temple (mid 16th century) is dedicated to Vishnu. Sculptures relate stories of Krishna, Rama and Sita. The gopuram is partly ruined but still impressive.

From **Tadpatri** the road runs SW through Singanamalla and the N tip of the **Seshachalam Hills**. Formed of massive quartzites, but with layers of slates and volcanic lavas, they present a steep scarp face to the W. Crossing the scarp towards Tadpatri you enter a region of limestones and shales, the westernmost line of a dramatic, crescent shaped range of hills. To their E, out of sight though clearly visible from the air on the flight from Hyderabad to Madras, are the **Nallamalais** and the **Vellikondas** in the N and the **Pallikondas** in the S, stretching down to the famous temple town of Tirumalai.

Although the region is dry for much of the year the major rivers – the **Pennar**, the **Cheyyaru** and the **Krishna** – have cut deep gorges through the hills on their course to the E coast. Of these only the Krishna rises in the Western Ghats, guaranteeing it much more reliable water supply for at least 6 month a year. The others are often completely dry. The hills themselves are thinly wooded, much of it destroyed by overgrazing an area with under 1,000 mm rainfall a year.

Gooty

(50 km; *Altitude*: 355m; *STD Code*: 08553) Gooty has a dramatic **Vijayanagara Fort** on an isolated granite outcrop 300m high. In the 18th century the fort fell into the hands of the Maratha chief Murari Rao Ghorpade. It was captured in 1776 by Haidar Ali after a siege of 9 months. Sir Thomas Munro, Governor of Madras died nearby in 1827. The town (4 km from the rly station) has no tourist accommodation, but situated at a major crossroads it is a market town and truck stop. A new bypass has taken many of the hundreds of lorries that used to pass through the town every day round its outskirts, leaving it once more as a typically pedestrian-dominated Indian market town.

• **Transport Train** Guntakal: *Madras-Bombay Mail* 7010 (AC/II), daily, 07.55, 40 min; *Madras-Dadar Exp* 6512 (AC/II), daily,

1803, 1/2 hr. **Madras (MC)**: *Dadar-Madras Exp* 6511 (AC/II), daily, 0803, 8 1/2 hr.

From Gooty you can go W through the major railway junction town of Guntakal and Bellary to visit Hampi and Hospet (see page 1044).

Guntakal

Altitude: 260m; *STD Code*: 08552 Guntakal is a medium sized town but an important railway junction.

- **Accommodation** There is an excellent value **F** hotel with an adjacent S Indian Restaurant. Local rickshaw wallahs will take you there if you have to spend the night.

- **Transport Train Madras (MC)**: *Dadar-Madras Exp* 6511 (AC/II), daily, 0738, 9 hr; **or** *Chennai Exp* 6063 (AC/II), daily except Tu,Su, 1140, 8 1/4 hr. **Bangalore**: *Karnataka Exp* 2628 (AC/II), daily, 0939, 5 1/2 hr; **or** *Ahmadabad-Bangalore Exp* 6501 (AC/II), daily, 1108, 6 3/4 hr. **Hospet**: *Vasco Exp* 7829, daily, 0300, 2 1/2 hr; *Hubli Pass* 221, daily, 1920, 3 1/2 hr; *Hubli-Amaravati Exp* 7825, daily, 0745, 2 1/2 hr; *Guntakal-Chalukya F. Passenger* daily, 1000, 2 3/4 hr; *Guntur-Hubli-Amaravati Exp* daily, 0745, 2 1/2 hr; *Vijayanagara Exp* 7829, daily, 0300, 2 1/2 hr. **Secunderabad**: *Venkatadra Exp* 7598, daily, 0030, 9 hr. **Hyderabad**: *Rayalaseema Exp* 7430 (AC/II), daily, 2303, 9 hr. **Bombay (VT)**: *Udyan Exp* 6530 (AC/II), daily, 0315, 17 1/4 hr; **or** *Netravati Exp* 2136 (AC/II), M,W,F, 1236, 17 1/4 hr. **Goa (Vasco-da-Gama)**: 7829, 0300, 16 1/4 hr. **Hubli**: *Guntur-Hubli Amravati Exp* 7825, daily, 0745, 6 1/2 hr. **Kochi (HT)**: *Ahmadabad Kochi Exp* 2637, Th, 1108, 20 3/4 hr.

Bellary

Altitude: 460m; *STD Code*: 08392 The first agricultural communities of the peninsula lived around Bellary. The climate is typical of the central peninsula.

The black cotton soils are pierced by islands of granite hills, and the Neolithic communities here lived at roughly the same time as the early Indus valley civilisations. Radio carbon datings put the earliest of these settlements at about 3000 BC. Hill tops were favoured for settlement, and caves or rock shelters were used for living space. A distinctive feature has been the discovery of ash mounds at 4 places in this area, close to the confluence of the **Krishna** and **Tungabhadra**, and to the S of Bellary. The mounds are where cattle were herded together. Some of the pens are near permanent settlements but others are isolated. They looked very like the traps used for catching wild elephants much nearer to the modern period. Although agriculture appears to have played only a minor role, evidence from later sites in Karnataka shows that millets and gram were already widely grown by the first millennium BC. They have remained staple crops ever since. **Transport Train** Gadag: *Guntur-Hubli Exp* 7825, daily, 0845, 3 1/2 hr. **Guntakal**: *Hubli-Guntur Exp*, daily, 1720, 1 1/4 hr.

Anantapur (*STD Code*: 08554) is on the E edge of a quite distinct geographical region, the Anantapur-Chittoor basins and the hill ranges of Cuddapah. An important East India Company town when the Nizam of Hyderabad ceded control of the three southern districts of Bellary, Kurnool and Cuddappah in 1800, Anantapur was closely associated with its first collector Thomas Munro.

The Seshachamal Hills are clearly visible to your left travelling S from Anantapur. In the hills to the W are deposits of corundum, mica and gold. The main road crosses the railway after Nagasamudram and continues S. To the

CLIMATE: BELLARY

	Jan	Feb	Mar	Apr	May	Jun	Jul	Aug	Sep	Oct	Nov	Dec	Av/Tot
Max (°C)	31	34	37	39	39	34	32	32	32	32	31	29	34
Min (°C)	17	19	23	26	26	24	24	23	23	22	19	17	22
Rain (mm)	3	5	5	20	48	43	41	61	125	107	51	3	512

left is the railway junction and silk producing town of **Dharmavaram**, connected by rail with Tirupati and Katpadi (for Vellore). The road cuts through the granite hills towards **Nagasamudram**.

Penukonda (*STD Code*: 088196) It is possible to climb Penukonda (Literally 'big hill'; *Altitude*: 932m) by a steep path that goes to the top. At the base E of the hill are huge walls and gateways of the old fortifications. The Jain **Parsvanatha Temple** has a sculpture of Parshvanatha, naked in front of an undulating serpent (11th century) in late Chalukyan style. There are also 2 granite Hindu temples from the early Vijayanagar period dedicated to Rama and Siva, the mosque of Sher Ali, built about 1600, and the **Gagan Mahal** (Ancient Palace). This has Islamic style arches, plaster decoration and features that are derived from temple architecture. Penukonda became the headquarters of the districts ceded to the E India Company by the Nizam of Hyderabad in 1800. There is a well carved stambha 10m high in the compound of the sub-collector's office.

Lepakshi

Approaching Lepakshi from Chilamattur you see a massive sculpture of Siva's bull (*Nandi*), carved out of granite boulder, 5 m high and 8m long. This tiny village, has a temple of outstanding interest for its murals. The **Virabhadra Temple**, built in 1538 under the Vijayanagar emperor Achutyadeva Raya, has well preserved Vijayanagara sculptures, but the mural paintings are particularly striking, depicting popular legends from the *Puranas* (see page 105) and epics. They show "Elegant linework and vibrant colours (mostly browns and ochres) and details of costumes and facial types are of outstanding interest" (Michell). On an outcrop of gneiss, the main temple is entered from the N through 2 gopurams, with unfinished brick towers. There are pyramidal brick towers over the main sanctuary and Vishnu shrine. Inside are large sculptures of Nataraja and Bhikshatanamurti on columns of the central bays. Narrative reliefs on the S walls illustrate Siva legends, including Arjuna's penance. In the principal sanctuary is a life size image of Virabhadra, decked with skulls and carrying weapons, appropriate to this form of Siva, bent on revenge.

ROUTES From **Chikballapur** it is possible to divert 10 km to the granite hill of Nandidurg.

Nandidurg

(*Altitude*: 1,418m; *STD Code*: 08156) Literally 'the fort of Nandi', Nandidurg was named after Siva's bull in the Nandi Hills. Regarded as a minor hill resort today, Nandidurg was once a summer retreat for Tipu Sultan, who thought it would be impossible to capture. Guarded on 3 sides by almost sheer cliffs, on one side over 300m high, Tipu massively fortified the western approach. There are superb views from the top. The temple at the foot of the hill is an important example of the Nolamba style which then had extensions built during the Vijayanagar period. The **Bhoganandisvara Temple** (9th & 16th centuries) is entered from the E side. The gopuram at the entrance was built during the Vijayanagar period. The 2nd gate leads to a colonnaded enclosure with twin Siva shrines. The early style is suggested by the plainness of the walls, but the stone windows have carvings of Nataraj and Durga. The Bhoganandishvara shrine has pyramidal towers and an octagonal roof.

• **Accommodation D** Karnataka Tourism *Mayura Pine Top*, T 8624, contact Manager or Karnataka Tourism, 10/4 Kasturba Gandhi Rd, Bangalore, T 212901. **F** *Rest Houses*, Dept of Horticulture, Govt of Karnataka, T 21, reservations: direct, or Director of Horticulture, Lalbagh, Bangalore, T 602231.

• **Transport Road** Dep Bangalore, from 0830 in the morning. The hills can be visited as a day excursion from Bangalore.

LAKSHADWEEP, MINICOY & AMINDIVI ISLANDS

BASICS *Population*: 51,700; *Climate*: Temp Summer: Max 35°C, Min 25°C; Winter: Max 32°C, Min 20°C; *Annual rainfall*: 1,600 mm, SW monsoon mid-May to Sep. Hottest Mar-May; *Best season*: Oct-Mar when tours are conducted.

Entry regulations

You can only visit the islands on a package tour as individuals may not book independently. The Society for Promotion of Recreational Tourism and Sports (SPORTS) organises trips. Their offices are at Kavaratti, Lakshadweep and Harbour Rd, Willingdon Island Kochi, T 69775. Entry permits from The Liaison Officer, Lakshadweep Office, F 306 Curzon Rd Hostel, Kasturba Gandhi Marg, New Delhi 110001, T 386807. Bangaram and Suheli Islands have been opened to foreign tourists and are being developed. You can get information from the Travel Agents listed below.

History

The islands were mentioned by a 1st century Greek sailor as a source of tortoise shell which was obtained by the Tamils. He had been taken off course by the monsoon winds and discovered a route from the Arab ports to the peninsular coast by chance.

The ruling dynasties of the S, the Cheras, Pandyas and Cholas, each tried to control the islands, the last succeeding in the 11th century. However, from the beginning of the 13th century the powerful Muslim family of Kannur, the Arakkals, for a time controlled the islands by appointing administrators. The Portuguese 'discovered' the islands in 1498 and built a fort, guarding their rights over the island's coir production by keeping an army. There was, however, an uprising led by the islanders in 1545. After the Treaty of Srirangapatnam in 1792, the southern group was allowed to be administered by the local chiefs. It was only in 1854 that the British East India Company replaced them by *amins*, chosen from the ruling families on the Laccadive Islands. In 1908 a Resident Administrator in Calicut was given authority over the islands. The islands became a Union Territory in 1956 and were renamed Lakshadweep in 1973. The original name meant 'one *lakh* islands' (a *lakh* being a hundred thousand), and referred to the chain including the Maldives to the S. Minicoy retains its Maldivian character even today.

People

Up to the 10th century, Hindus from 3 castes from the Kannur area settled the groups are distinguishable even today – Koya (land owners), Malmi (sailors) and Melachery (farmers). With the exception of Minicoy, most of the people speak a sort of Malayalam (the language of Kerala). Minicoy (Maliku) is populated by Maldivian speakers whose ancestors were Buddhists up to the 12th century. The Moplahs (mixed Indian and Arab descent) are nearly all Muslims having been converted around the 9th century Local legend claims that in the middle of the 7th century, Ubeidulla was shipwrecked on Amini Island on returning from pilgrimage to Mecca, and performed miracles which led the population to convert to his faith.

Agriculture and Economy

Sea fishing (especially tuna), with coconut production provide the main income for the islanders. Palm trees and jack fruit trees abound. Bananas, grains, pulses and vegetables are also grown. There is also some fruit canning and a small amount of dairy and poultry farming. **Tourism** is the latest industry to take advantage of the islands' unspoilt

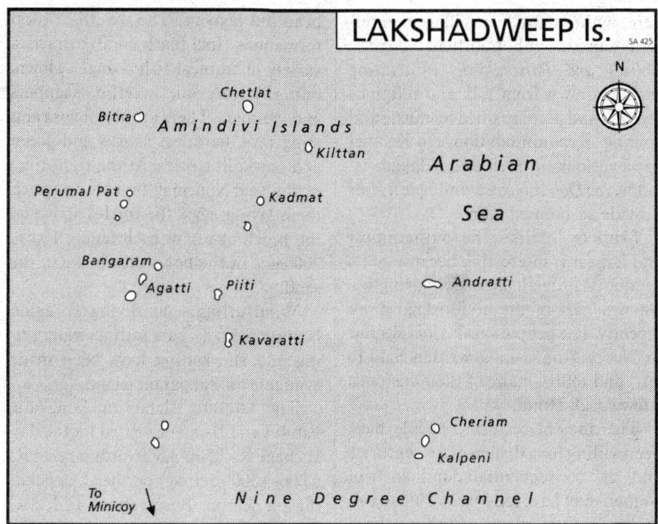

beauty, lagoons, coral reefs and the possibility of offering watersports. **Watersports** such as kayaking, motor and sailing boats, glass-bottomed boats and water skiing are available on Kavaratti, Kalpeni, Kadmat and Minicoy; Bangaram has extra facilities. **NB DO NOT REMOVE CORAL.**

THE ISLANDS

Foreign tourists may only visit the uninhabited Bangaram Island and Indians, Kadmat, Kavaratti, Kalpeni and Minicoy. Thinakkara and Cheriyam are being developed.

Kavaratti, the administrative capital, is in the centre of the archipelago and has a bank. The Ajjara and Jamath mosques (of the 52 on the island) have the best woodcarvings and the former has a particularly good ceiling carved out of driftwood; a well within is believed have medicinal water. The Aquarium with tropical fish and corals, the lake nearby and the tombs are the other sights. The wood carving in the Ajjara is an example of the superb craftsmen and masons who inhabit Kavaratti. **Accommodation** *Dak Bungalow*, basic, with 2 rm and a *Rest House* with 4 rm may be reserved through the Administrator, Union Territory of Lakshadweep, Kozhikode 1.

Some of the other islands in the group are, **Androth**, one of the largest which was first to be converted to Islam, **Agatti**, the only one with an airport, which neighbours Bangaram and also has a beautiful lagoon, **Piiti** which is tiny and only has birds, **Cheriam** and **Kalpeni** which have suffered most from storm damage.

Kalpeni with its group of 3 smaller uninhabited satellite islands is surrounded by a lagoon rich in corals, which offeres excellent water sport facilities including snorkelling and diving. The raised coral banks on the SE and E shores are remains of a violent storm in 1847; the Moidin Mosque to the S has walls made of coral. A walk through a village is interesting. The islands are reputedly free from crime; the women dressed in wrap-around *lungis* (sarongs) wear heavy gold ornaments here, without any fear. Villagers entertain tourists with traditional dances, *Kolkali and Parichakkali*, illustrating themes drawn from folk and religious legends and accompanied by music and singing. **Accommodation** On Koomel bay overlooking Pitti and Tilakam islands, the *Dak Bungalow* and *Tourist Huts* provide accommodation.

Minicoy (Maliku) the southernmost and largest is interesting because of its unique Maldivian character having become a part of the archipelago more recently. The people speak *Mahl* similar to *Dhivehi* (the script is written right to left) and follow many of their customs; a few speak Hindi.

The ancient seafaring people have been sailing long distances for centuries and the consequential dominance of women may have led Marco Polo to call this a "female island". Each of the 9 closely knit matrilineal communities lives in an *athir* (village) and is headed by a *Moopan*. The village houses are colourfully furnished with carved wooden furniture. Tuna fishing is a major activity and the island has a cannery and ice storage. The superb lagoon of the palm-fringed crescent shaped island is enclosed by coral reefs. Good views from the top of the 50m lighthouse built by the British.

The **Amindivi** group consists of the northern islands of *Chetlat*, *Bitra* the smallest (heavily populated by birds, for a long time a rich source of birds eggs), *Kiltan* where ships from Aden called en route to Colombo, *Kadmat* and the densely populated, *Amini*, rich in coconut palms, which was occupied by the Portuguese.

Kadmat has a fine beach and lagoon ideal for swimming. The tourist huts shaded by palms are away from the local village.

Bangaram, an uninhabited island, (together with Suheli) **is the only one open to foreign tourists**. The teardrop shaped island has superb beaches and beautiful lagoons. The wealth of coral formations (incl black coral) attracts a variety of tropical fish – angel, clown, butterfly, surgeon, sweetlip, snappers and groupers. There are also manta and sting rays, harmless sharks and green and hawkbill turtles. At the right time of the year you may be able to watch them laying eggs, the turtles arrive on the beach at night, each laying 100 to 200 eggs in the holes they make in the sand.

Windsurfing, scuba diving (Poseidon Neptun School), para sailing, water skiing and snorkelling have been made available on Bangaram island.

The satellite islands of Tamakara, Parali I and II can be visited for the day. Package Rs 2,500-3,600 (ordinary) to Rs 6,000-9,500 (deluxe) per head, depending on season. Reservation: TCI, MG Rd, Ernakulam, Kochi (opp Kavitha Theatre), T 31646 or at TCI's Bombay office at Chander Mukhi, Nariman Point, T 231881. Also *Casino Hotel*, Willingdon Island, Kochi, T 340221, F 340001.

Package Tours

Tourism is still in its infancy and facilities are limited on the islands you will be allowed to visit. The relatively expensive package tours (the only way to visit) operate from Oct-Apr and only go to **Kadmat, Minicoy, Kavaratti** and **Kalpeni** for Indian tourists and to **Bangaram**, for foreigners. **NB** Schedules may change, so allow for extra day when booking onward travel.

Kadmat: *Silver Sands*, 6 days (incl 2 day sailing, stay in *Kadmat Cottages* or *hostel*), Rs 3-4,000. **Kalpeni**: *Coconut Grove* (incl 2 days sailing, stay in *huts*), Rs 2,700-3,500. **Kavaratti**: *Taratashi*, 6 days (incl 2 days sailing, stay in *Family Huts*), Rs 3,500. **Minicoy**: *Swaying Palms*, 6 days (incl 2 days sailing, stay in *Tourist Huts*, Minicoy), Rs 3,100- 3,500. **Minicoy, Kavaratti, Kalpeni**: *Coral Reef*, 5-day cruise visiting islands, stay on board ship, Rs 2,700- 3,800; *Lakshadweep Special*, 3 days (inc helicopter/ speedboat between islands and flight from Kochi), stay in *cottages*, Kadmat, Rs 6,700-7,200.

Local information

Accommodation

Usually in basic Tourist cottages which resemble local huts with tiled roofs and coconut palm matting. Each hut has 1 or 2 bedrooms, mosquito nets, fans and attached baths. Electricity is from diesel generators.

On Bangaram: *Centaur Bangaram Beach Resort*, 30 rm in 8 bungalows with modern facilities, restaurant (buffet meals, varied menu incl local specialities), bar.

Kadmat: 10 Executive and Tourist *Cottages* and *Youth Hostel* for 40.

Kalpeni: *Family Huts*.

Kavaratti: 3 *Family Huts*.

Minicoy: *Tourist Huts*

Alternatively, on board comfortable ship, see below under **Transport**.

Food

Meals are served on the beach and is similar to Keralan cuisine using plenty of coconut. Breakfast might be *idlis* or *pooris* with vegetables. Lunch and dnner might be rice and vegetable curry, *sambhar*, meat, chicken or fish curry. Vegetarian meals available on request. Bangaram offers international menu.

Alcohol

Alcohol is available on board ship and on Bangaram Island (tourists are requested not to take in alcohol).

Tour companies & travel Agents

Tours should be booked at least 2 months ahead. In **Bombay**: *Raj Travels*, 27 B Panchratna, Grd Flr, Opera House, Mama Parmanand Marg, T 8117000; *Lakshadweep Travelinks*, Passport Studio, Jermahal 1st Flr, Dhobitalo, T 254231, F 14412220.

Calcutta: *Ashok* (ITDC), T 220901 and *Mercury* both in Everest Bldg, 46 JL Nehru Rd, 223555.

Madras: *Island Tours*, T 523124; *Mercury*, 191 Mount Rd, T 869993.

New Delhi: *Ashok* (ITDC), Kanishka Plaza, 19 Ashok Rd, T 3324422 Extn 2321, F 360233; *SITA*, F 12 Connaught Place, T 3311133, F 3324652.

Bangalore: *Clipper Holidays*, *Airlines Hotel Complex*, 4 Madras Bank Rd, T 217054.

Kozhikode: *Lakshadweep Tours and Travels*, Hi-Bon Plaza, I Gandhi Rd, T 75552.

Kochi: *SPORTS*, Lakshadweep Office, Indira Gandhi Rd, Willingdon Island, T 340387, F 340155; *Lagoon Travels*, Shop 44, Kadavanthara Shopping Complex, T 353170.

Mangalore: *Lakshadweep Foundation*, Lighthouse Hill.

Pune: *Leonard Travels*, 5 MG Rd, T 668647.

Thiruvananthapuram: *Kerala Tourism*, Mascot Sq, T 68627.

Useful address

Secy to the Administration, Lakshadweep, Harbour Rd, Kochi 3.

Transport

Air No flights at present.

Sea For Indians, MV Tippu Sultan/Bharat Seema sails from Kochi for Kavaratti. 26 passengers in 1st and Exec class have 2 and 4-berth a/c cabins with washbasins, shared toilets, Rs 3,000; 120 passengers in 2nd class in reclining seats in a/c halls, Rs 2,500. Ship anchors 30-45 min away from each island; passengers are ferried from there. Total travel time from Kochi can take up to 30 hr.

WEST INDIA

CONTENTS

ROUTES

ENVIRONMENT

The states of West India

Gujarat, Maharashtra and Goa, cover an area the size of Spain, 507,000 sq km. Goa, formerly the Portuguese territory of Goa, Daman and Diu, covers only 3814 sq km while Maharashtra, with 308,000 sq km, is the third largest. Bombay is the dominant city of the region and the commercial capital of the country.

Land

Kachchh

Kachchh is a transitional region between the Indian peninsula and the Indus delta in Pakistan. The **Rann of Kachchh**, is an apparently limitless stretch of tidal mudflats, occasional patches of white salts lightening the otherwise dark surface. In it is India's most remote and inhospitable wildlife sanctuary. Here wild asses share the same terrain with Indian army units patrolling the sensitive border with Pakistan. To the N the mud and sand merge imperceptibly. In the monsoon, as the floodwaters rise, the upland area between the Great Rann and the Little Rann becomes an island, literally a world apart.

The Kathiawad peninsula

With its central core of low lying hills and a long coastline, Kathiawad is a highly distinctive region. Immediately to the S is Saurashtra, while Gujarat proper lies to the E, with the more fertile alluvium deposited by the rivers Narmada, Sabarmati and Mahi. The Govt plans to build at least 30 dams along the 1000 km long Narmada River and 41 of its tributaries, submerging 2.5 million ha and displacing perhaps as many as 1 million people. By comparison the Tennessee Valley Authority flooded 1.6 million ha and displaced 70,000 residents. The World Bank committed US$450mn to the project but withdrew in 1993 under intense political pressure. It is still proving a highly controversial scheme but the Indian Govt remains committed to it.

Economically the most important geological feature in West India is the series of oil bearing tertiary sediments in the Gulf of Cambay. These run from inland S to some distance from the shoreline in an area known as the Bombay High.

The Konkan

Lying to the S again, a coastal lowland stretching from around Surat as far as Goa. Only 50-80 km wide, it is broken up by hills. Short rivers run straight from the mountains to the sea. Rising dramatically behind them is the wall of

The Ghats

The Western Ghats and the Deccan plateau form a striking mountain wall, rising dramatically to over 1,300m in places. On the seaward side they present steep-sided ravines and deep canyons. On the landward side flat-topped spurs are intersected by valleys so gentle that sometimes the slopes are imperceptible. In places there are still patches of dense forests of teak. Interior Maharashtra dips gently E from the scarp of the Western Ghats. The Krishna and Godavari have their sources in the Western Ghats and have broad gently undulating valleys. There are often tremendous views across what sometimes seems a treeless plain.

the Western Ghats. Coconut palms fringe much of the coast all the way down to Kerala, and play an important part in the economy. **Bombay**, built on the site of 7 former islands but now linked together by draining and filling the marshes, is the geographical focus of the region. Near the northern boundary of Goa the Deccan lava gives way to the ancient Archean rocks of the Peninsula, a change marked by a series of breaches in the mountain wall. South from Ratnagiri laterite is more common and is very noticeable in Goa where you can go the 100 km length of the state alternating between red-crusted barren looking uplands and lush green deltaic lowlands.

Climate

Just S of the Tropic of Cancer, West India's climate is dominated by the monsoon.

Temperatures

Temperatures vary much less than they do further N in India. The greatest contrast is between the N and S. Minimum winter temperatures in N Gujarat may be as low as 10°C, though daytime temperatures are twice that, while Goa has minimum winter temperatures of 20°C and daytime temperatures throughout the year of at least 28°C. The W coast as a rule does not suffer the stiflingly humid heat of the E coast.

Rainfall

The coast is extremely wet during the monsoon. Heaviest rainfall is between Bombay and Goa, total amounts diminishing N towards the deserts of Rajasthan. East of the Western Ghats rainfall diminishes rapidly, though the monsoon season is still humid, overcast and often windy. The tops of the hills themselves are often shrouded in mist and cloud from Jun to Oct.

HISTORY

Early History

The Indus Valley (Harappan) Civilisation influenced the NW corner of the region. Very few historic monuments belonging to this period are preserved, although there is a growing number of significant archaeological sites which are revealing important details of the pattern of development and decline of the earliest Indian civilisation. Lothal, 80 km S of Ahmadabad in Gujarat, dates from the 3rd millennium BC and displays many characteristic features of the Harappan culture. Junagadh, on the Saurashtra peninsula, also dates from pre-Harappan times. Kaira, 32 km SW of Ahmadabad dates from 1400 BC.

Buddhism & Jainism Buddhism and Jainism flourished in the western region. From an early period Jains became influential in trade and commerce in Gujarat and Maharashtra, being restricted to those activities as the least likely to harm any form of life. Asokan Edicts indicate western India's importance in 250 BC, and under the Satavahanas (200 BC-200

AD) the first Buddhist temples were constructed at Ajanta and Bhaja in Maharashtra. The later Kshatrapas (100-300 AD) were patrons of the cave dwelling monastic communities at Karli, between Bombay and Pune. More Buddhist cave development occurred at the Maharashtrian sites of Ajanta, Aurangabad and Ramtek under the Vakatakas (300-500 AD) when Mahayana Buddhism had become popular.

Hindu sites One of the earliest examples of Hindu temple design is at **Gop**, 50 km NE of Porbandar in Gujarat. The caves on the island of Elephanta were excavated during the Kalachauri period (500-600 AD), and there are 17 Hindu cave temples and monasteries at Ellora dating from 600-900 AD. From 900-1200 AD the Solankis emerged as the most powerful rulers in Gujarat and S Rajasthan. Patan, Prabhas Patan, Modhera and Girnar, all in Gujarat, developed under their patronage. Patan, 130 km N of Ahmadabad was the 8th century capital of the Hindu Kings of Gujarat and once had over 100 Jain temples. A distinctive West Indian architectural style emerged, beautifully displayed in the temples and step wells (*baolis*) at Modhera and Patan. Later *baolis* had cool pavilions incorporated into the wells. Dwarka, on the tip of the Kathiawad Peninsula in Gujarat, was closely associated with the Krishna legend, and is regarded as one of the 4 holy abodes of the gods – see page 71. The present town and 12th century temples are built on the sites of 4 former cities.

The Muslims

11th century Muslim raids under Mahmud of Ghazni caused much damage to important religious monuments. By the 14th century most of the region had come under Muslim control. Khalji Sultans of Delhi established themselves in the coastal towns, demolishing earlier Hindu temples and using the materials for their own mosques and buildings (see Qutb Minar, Delhi, page 175). Ahmadabad was founded in 1411 and became a Muslim stronghold flourishing in the second half of the 15th century. It now contains the largest concentration of Muslim buildings in West India.

The Bahmani Sultans dominated the Deccan until the late 15th century when they split into 5 kingdoms – Ahmadnagar, Berar, Bidar, Bijapur and Golconda. The Bahmanis of Maharashtra (1390-1485) had strong links with the Hindu kingdom of Vijayanagar. The Ahmad Shahis were dominant in Gujarat over the period 1451-1526. Early buildings are the mosques at the important ports of Surat and Broach and also at Patan.

Trade with the West

India's W coast naturally had far more contact with the maritime trading regions to the West than with the East. It has many small sheltered havens, but only a narrow immediate hinterland and few well defined routes into the interior. However, its W facing shoreline made it readily accessible to trading Arabs and later to the Europeans, and the monsoon wind system brought Arab dhows and early European traders across the Arabian Sea and the Indian Ocean.

The Portuguese Trade with the Middle East, the spread of Islam from Arabia, and later European interest in the Indies all had an impact on West India. In the 16th century the Portuguese established themselves at Daman, Diu and Goa, bringing a distinctive Mediterranean flavour to the W coast. The Portuguese lost their maritime supremacy to the Dutch in the East Indies and to the British in the Indian Ocean. Thereafter, Goa became a 'somnolent colonial backwater', past its prime, a foreign enclave on Indian soil until Jawarharlal Nehru ordered the Indian Army to take over in 1961, ending 4½ centuries of Portuguese influence.

The Mughals

At the same time as the Portuguese were establishing their small settlements on the coast the Mughals were expanding their territories in the interior. Gujarat was taken in 1534-5 by Humayun who subsequently lost it. It was retaken by Akbar in 1572 and remained firmly in Mughal hands for the next 180 years. By Akbar's death in (1605) the region up to the Godavari river had been absorbed (see page 47).

The Deccan states The Muslim States of the Deccan were successors of the Bahmani Kingdom, in turn a splinter of the Delhi Sultanate. The Mughals could claim little justification in seeking to annex these territories, but the most orthodox of the emperors, Aurangzeb, was also the most implacable of annexers. It took him nearly to the end of the 18th century to extinguish the last Deccan Muslim Kingdom, capturing Ahmadnagar, Bijapur and Golconda, which fell in 1686 and 1687 – see page 47. Thereafter, Aurangzeb campaigned against the Marathas until his death in 1707.

The Marathas under their leader Shivaji played an often dominant role in the region from the mid-17th century until the arrival of the British. See page 1155. However, it was never an uncontested dominance, a fact illustrated by the existence of approximately 175 forts in Maharashtra alone. Many are associated either directly or indirectly with Sivaji, who is believed to have built 111 of them.

The British

Like the Portuguese, the early activities of the British were confined to the coast. Their first factory was at Surat, although their first well-established foothold was in Madras. As the East India Company extended its trading influence from Eastern India it needed to link the 3 Presidencies of Bombay, Bengal and Madras. With territorial acquisition and the elimination of Maratha power, communications across the Deccan improved.

From the 1850s railway lines were pushed inland and the hinterland of Bombay was dramatically expanded. Mahabaleshwar was established as a hill station and the old Maratha capital of Pune became a fashionable summer retreat. The British garrison was across the river at Kirkee.

Gujarat was never fully absorbed into British India but fragmented into 200 petty princely states which included Porbandar, Morvi, Wankaner, Rajkot, Jamnagar, Bhavnagar and dominant Baroda (Vadodara). Outside Bombay British buildings are comparatively few in Gujarat and Maharashtra. There are palaces at all the places mentioned above as well as Surat.

Independence

Mohandas Karamchand Gandhi was born in Gujarat. The beliefs he espoused were in part influenced by the pacifism inherent in Buddhism and Jainism. Both had an enduring influence on the region's development. The Salt March which he led from his ashram at Ahmadabad to the coast in protest against not only the law enacted by the British against domestic production of salt, but against foreign rule in India, drew world-wide attention to the non-violent movement in the struggle for independence.

After independence the old Princely States were absorbed into the new federal structure of Independent India. The creation of linguistic states in 1956 led to the separation of Gujarat and Maharashtra. Goa, Daman and Diu were forcibly absorbed into the Indian Union after Portugal had declined to recognise the end of an era initiated by Vasco da Gama and Alfonso Albuquerque.

MODERN WEST INDIA

Economy

The railways opened up the Deccan Plateau to commercial cotton growing in the second part of the 19th century, which stimulated cotton production for export and for milling in India. Long before that much of the coastal economy of the region was geared towards overseas trade. Surat, Goa, Daman, Diu, Cambay and Broach were all important ports, some like Surat as much for their role in the annual Muslim pilgrim traffic to Mecca as for trade. Many areas have seen rapid industrial development since Independence.

Agriculture

This sector employs the largest number of people. Irrigation is comparatively restricted, and today the Indian Govt is caught up in fierce arguments over proposals to build the world's largest irrigation system through constructing a series of dams on the Narmada River (see above).

Wheat, cotton and bananas, irrigated by a complex of rivers, dominate the N, while in coastal Maharashtra and Goa, rice becomes the dominant crop, with bananas and coconuts important cash crops. Sorghum (*jowar*), pearl millet (*bajra*), wheat and pulses are common in the drier interior. Coconuts, copra and fish are all coastal products, along with groundnuts, cashew nuts and bananas.

Cash crops Interior Maharashtra and eastern Gujarat have ideal climatic and soil conditions for cotton growing and the Indian cotton textile industry, centred on Ahmadabad and Bombay, developed on the strength of it. Tobacco is grown in Gujarat whilst the forests of northern Maharashtra yield teak. The British used it to build their first warships outside England in the dockyards of Bombay.

Energy

Exploration in West India for oil and natural gas started in 1955 with the setting up of the Oil and Natural Gas Commission. Extensive finds have been made both onshore in Gujarat, around the head of the Gulf of Cambay, and offshore to the S. Development has remained below early expectations, but both gas and petroleum are now being extracted on a significant scale, meeting approximately half of India's current demand. Some coal is mined in E Maharashtra, and West India has been in the forefront of nuclear power development. The atomic power station at Tarapur was India's first nuclear power plant.

Manufacturing

Manufacturing is centred on Bombay, Thane, Kolhapur and Sholapur in Maharashtra and Ahmadabad, 'the Manchester of India', in Gujarat. Maharashtra alone accounts for a quarter of the nation's industrial output by value. Ahmadabad is the region's second most important industrial city. Maharashtra has a particularly vigorous programme for encouraging industrial development in 'backward areas'.

BOMBAY

Contents

Maps

During the British period the Gateway of India, built to commemorate the Prince of Wales' visit in 1911, was the point of disembarkation. Appropriately, the Taj Mahal hotel, one of India's finest, is located immediately behind it. Bombay has a wide range of accommodation, but prices tend to be high. There are not many really cheap hotels or guest houses suitable for travellers on very tight budgets.

Bombay is well connected with other parts of the country by air, road and rail. The 2 major railway stations are Bombay Central and Victoria Terminus.

BASICS *Population*: 12.57mn; *STD Code*: 022; *Languages*: Marathi, Gujarati, Hindi and English. There is also a sizeable Tamil speaking population.

History

Origins

300 years ago, the area occupied by this great metropolis was 7 islands inhabited by Koli fishermen (from whom we have the word 'coolies') and their families. With land reclamation the islands were connected, so that now Bombay occupies a thin isthmus. The British acquired these marshy and malarial islands for a pittance. Mumbadevi or Mumbai (from which Bombay gets its name), was part of Catherine of Braganza's marriage dowry when she married Charles II in 1661. Four years later, the British took possession of the remaining islands and neighbouring mainland area and in 1688 the East India Company leased the whole area for £10 sterling per year.

Originally Bombay was rivalled by Surat in Gujarat where the first English headquarters in India had been established in 1612. Until the early 19th century, Bombay's fortunes rested on the shipbuilding yards established by progressive Parsis. Durable Malabar teak was used, and the yards received the first orders for ships placed outside England.

Bombay before the Suez Canal

Bombay remained isolated by the sharp face of the Western Ghats, the difficult terrain inland and the constantly hostile Marathas. However, Bombay thrived on

Climate: Bombay

	Jan	Feb	Mar	Apr	May	Jun	Jul	Aug	Sep	Oct	Nov	Dec	Av/Tot
Max (°C)	31	32	33	33	33	32	30	29	30	32	33	32	32
Min (°C)	16	17	20	24	26	26	25	24	24	23	20	18	22
Rain (mm)	0	1	0	0	20	647	945	660	309	117	7	1	2707

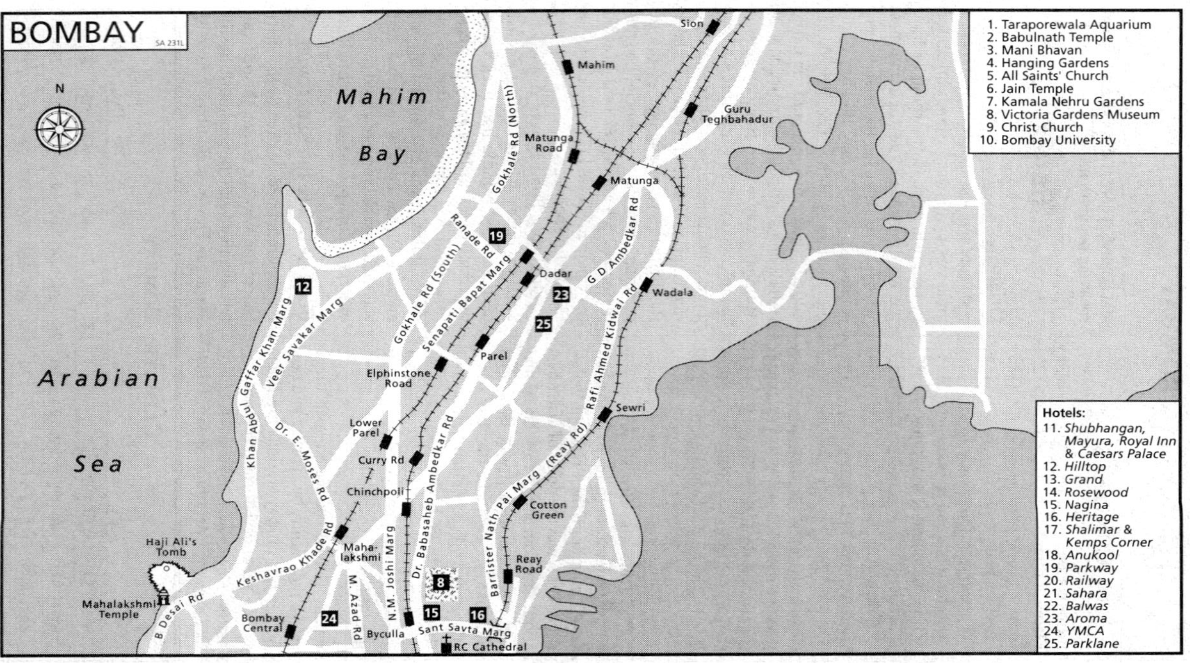
BOMBAY
SA 231L
N
1. Taraporewala Aquarium
2. Babulnath Temple
3. Mani Bhavan
4. Hanging Gardens
5. All Saints' Church
6. Jain Temple
7. Kamala Nehru Gardens
8. Victoria Gardens Museum
9. Christ Church
10. Bombay University
Hotels:
11. Shubhangan, Mayura, Royal Inn & Caesars Palace
12. Hilltop
13. Grand
14. Rosewood
15. Nagina
16. Heritage
17. Shalimar & Kemps Corner
18. Anukool
19. Parkway
20. Railway
21. Sahara
22. Balwas
23. Aroma
24. YMCA
25. Parklane
Mahim Bay
Arabian Sea
Sion
Mahim
Guru Teghbahadur
Matunga Road
Matunga
Wadala
Sewri
Dadar
Parel
Elphinstone Road
Lower Parel
Curry Rd
Chinchpoili
Cotton Green
Reay Road
Maha-lakshmi
Bombay Central
Byculla
Gokhale Rd (North)
Ranade Rd
Gokhale Rd (South)
Senapati Bapat Marg
G D Ambedkar Rd
Rafi Ahmed Kidwai Rd
Barrister Nath Pai Marg (Reay Rd)
Dr. Babasaheb Ambedkar Rd
N.M. Joshi Marg
M. Azad Rd
Sant Savta Marg
RC Cathedral
Veer Savakar Marg
Khan Abdul Gaffar Khan Marg
Dr. E. Moses Rd
Keshavrao Khade Rd
B Desai Rd
Haji Ali's Tomb
Mahalakshmi Temple

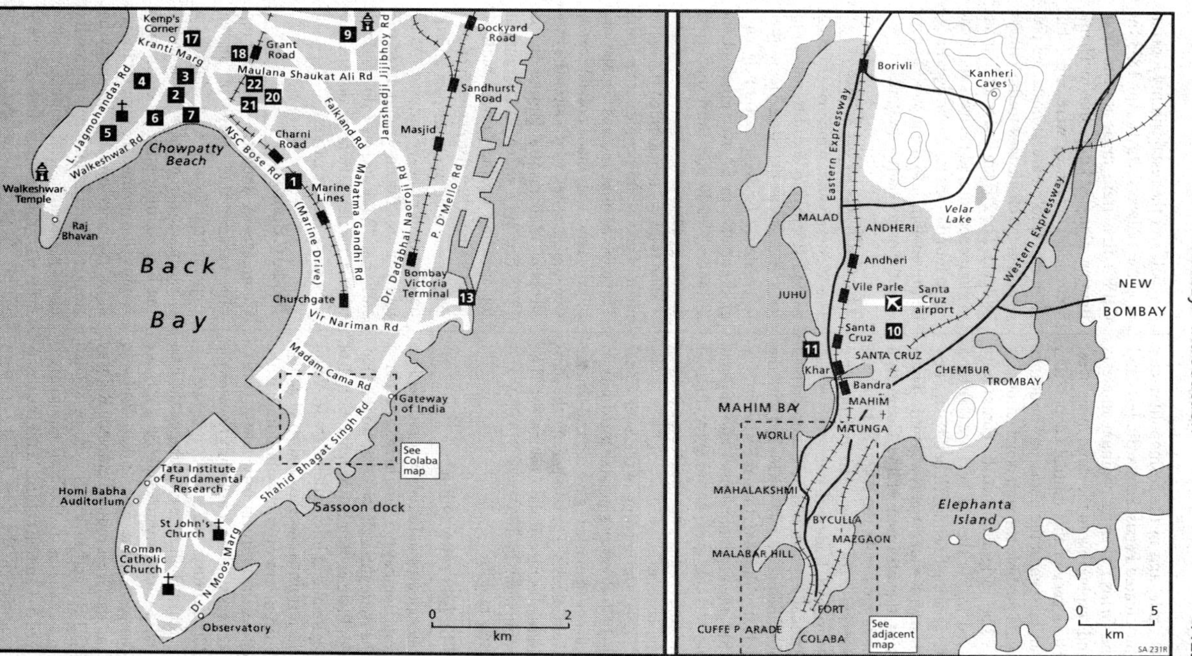
Kemp's Corner
Kranti Marg
L. Jagmohandas Rd
Walkeshwar Rd
Walkeshwar Temple
Raj Bhavan
Chowpatty Beach
Back Bay
Grant Road
Maulana Shaukat Ali Rd
Charni Road
NSC Bose Rd
Marine Lines
(Marine Drive)
Churchgate
Falkland Rd
Mahatma Gandhi Rd
Jamshedji Jijibhoy Rd
Dr. Dadabhai Naoroji Rd
P. D'Mello Rd
Masjid
Sandhurst Road
Dockyard Road
Bombay Victoria Terminal
Vir Nariman Rd
Madam Cama Rd
Gateway of India
See Colaba map
Shahid Bhagat Singh Rd
Sassoon dock
Tata Institute of Fundamental Research
Homi Babha Auditorium
St John's Church
Roman Catholic Church
Dr N Moos Marg
Observatory
0 km 2
1 2 3 4 5 6 7 9 13 17 18 20 21 22
Borivli
Kanheri Caves
Eastern Expressway
Velar Lake
Western Expressway
MALAD
ANDHERI
Andheri
Vile Parle
Santa Cruz airport
NEW BOMBAY
JUHU
Santa Cruz
10
11
SANTA CRUZ
Khar
CHEMBUR
TROMBAY
Bandra
MAHIM
MAHIM BAY
MATUNGA
WORLI
MAHALAKSHMI
BYCULLA
MAZGAON
Elephanta Island
MALABAR HILL
FORT
CUFFE P ARADE
COLABA
See adjacent map
0 km 5
SA 231R

its trade, and in the cosmopolitan city this created Parsis, Sephardic Jews and the British sharing common interests and responding to the same incentives. The legacy of this mutual cooperation can be seen in the numerous buildings made possible through benefactions.

The original British community lived within the old Fort area. After a devastating fire on 17th Feb 1803, a new town with wider streets was built. Then, with the abolition of the Company's trade monopoly, the doors to rapid expansion were flung open and Bombay flourished. Trade with England boomed. Annual exports of raw cotton trebled over the period 1809-1816, and with the defeat of the Marathas at Kirkee in Nov 1817, the economic hinterland of Bombay was able to expand along revitalised old trade routes onto the Deccan plateau and beyond.

After the opening of the Suez Canal in 1870 Bombay's greater proximity to European markets gave it an advantage over Calcutta. The port became the commercial centre of the Arabian Sea. The population in 1864 was 816,000, and grew rapidly.

The first railway line

The opening of India's first railway line from Bombay to Thana in 1854 prepared the route through the Ghats to the Deccan Plateau. Bombay became the hub of regional and international trade. Victoria Terminus was the product of a magnificent era of railway building at the end of the 19th century when the British Raj was striding confidently towards the 20th century.

Lord Dalhousie encouraged the East India Company to establish 2 private companies, the East Indian Railways and the Great Indian Peninsula Railway (GIPR), and investors were persuaded to buy shares on the basis of a guaranteed 5% annual return. With the disappearance of the East India Company after the Mutiny, the government of India took over the responsibility for running the railways. On 16 Apr 1853 the GIPR's first train made its run from Bombay along 32 km of line to Thana. Subsequent advances were rapid but often incredible natural obstacles presented great challenges to the railway builders. The 263 km line from Bombay to Surat encountered 18 rivers and some of the foundations for the bridges had to be driven 45m into the ground to cope with the monsoon floodwaters.

The challenge of the Ghats

The Western Ghats which rise to 800m behind Bombay posed different problems. As many as 40,000 navvies worked to create 22 bridges, 25 tunnels on a gradient of 1 in 37 over much of the distance. Nearly one third died from disease or accidents.

The railways transformed the movement of goods and people across India. This enabled more Indians to make long pilgrimages. They made possible extensive famine relief, which after the catastrophic Maharashtra famine in the 1870s became a widely used argument for speeding up the railway building programme. They also encouraged cash crop production and transport and the development of heavy industry. As the journalist Sir Edwin Arnold noted very early on: "Railways may do for India what dynasties have never done ... they may make India a nation".

Modern Bombay

Commerce & industry Bombay rapidly became the centre of an entrepreneurial as well as a commercial class, drawing from the Parsi as well as the Bania Hindu business community. Bombay has become the home of India's stock exchange and HQ for many national and international companies. It is also a major industrial centre. A cotton mill was established here in 1854. Within 30 years there were nearly 50, employing over 30,000 workers. The expansion of the railway system into the cotton producing areas of Maharashtra was a strong stimulus not only to milling but to engineering industries. Originally these were concentrated round the ports and railway facilities, but have become more diversified with the growth of light and medium engineering installations. This, in turn, has made Bombay more resistant to national recession than Calcutta, for example, with its strong reliance on the jute industry. Other important activities are printing, furniture manufacture, ceramics, food, pharmaceuticals, tobacco and jewellery.

The pressures of growth With population pressure in the surrounding agricultural hinterland, Bombay is still growing fast. One third of the population live in Bombay's desperately squalid *chawls* of cramped, makeshift and miserable hovels. There are also many thousands of pavement dwellers. Even those who live in what look like temporary huts often pay high 'protection money' to local strong men to make sure that they are not removed by force. Due to heavy demand for building space, property values are exceedingly high. Far more crowded than Delhi, which has opportunities for almost limitless spatial expansion, the alleys between the houses can scarcely be seen.

Poverty & planning Bombay's planners have been trying to decentralise the metropolitan region and create more living space. The Maharashtra government has promoted industrial dispersal since the 1960s and this has had a strong impact. They have also developed a massive market complex (Bandra-Kurla) in the N part of Bombay Island. Also, New Bombay across the Thana Creek and Bombay Harbour is being developed to ease the pressure on the isthmus.

Despite the extreme poverty Bombay remains a city of hope. Like Delhi, it is full of contrasts. It has none of the old monuments which are scattered across Delhi. 'Bombayites' are far more westernised and it has a mass rapid transit system, all be it often desperately overcrowded. There is a heavily used suburban train network, a good bus service and only in the suburbs will you see the autorickshaws, which buzz like flies all around Delhi. Bombay often claims to be the most modern and cosmopolitan of India's cities.

Film capital Bombay produces over 300 films per year, making "Bollywood" the world's second largest film maker after Hong Kong. The stars live in sumptuous dwellings, many of which are on Malabar Hill, Bombay's Beverly Hills, and despite the spread of videos their popularity seems undiminished.

Recent political development After the shock of a series of thirteen bomb explosions within a few hours in March 1993, Bombay life returned to its normal business as the commerical capital of India. Politically, attention shifted to a stock market scandal, which for a time seemed to threaten the programme of economic liberalisation embarked on by the government, and the political life of India's Prime Minister. By early 1994 that scandal too had given way to renewed optimism that the dynamic expansion of India's economy, from which Bombay is a major beneficiary, was resuming.

PLACES OF INTEREST

Apollo Bunder and the Gateway of India

The Indo-Saracenic style Gateway of India (1927), designed by George Wittet to commemorate the visit of George V and Queen Mary in 1911, is modelled in honey-coloured basalt on 16th century Gujarati work. The great gateway comprises an archway with halls on each side capable of seating 600 at important receptions. The arch replaces an earlier, lighter building. The present structure, though heavy in appearance, when viewed from the sea looks quite distinctive set against the imposing *Taj Mahal Hotel*. It was the point from which the last British regiment serving in India signalled the end of the Empire when it left on 28 Feb 1948. The area around the Gateway is popular among Bombayites for evening strolls and is a pleasant place to visit at sundown. A short distance behind the Gateway is an impressive statue of **Sivaji**, erected in 1960. See page 1154.

The Taj Mahal Hotel is one of India's modern institutions. The original red-domed hotel, has been adjoined by a modern skyscraper (called the *Taj Mahal Inter-Continental*). Jamshedji Tata, a Bombay Parsi, was behind the enterprise and the hotel, designed by W Chambers, is now one of the world's leading hotels.

Colaba

S of the Gateway of India is the crowded S section of Shahid Bhagat Singh Marg (S Bhagat Singh Marg) which leads 3 km down to Colaba and the S tip of the peninsula. ('Shahid' means martyr. The

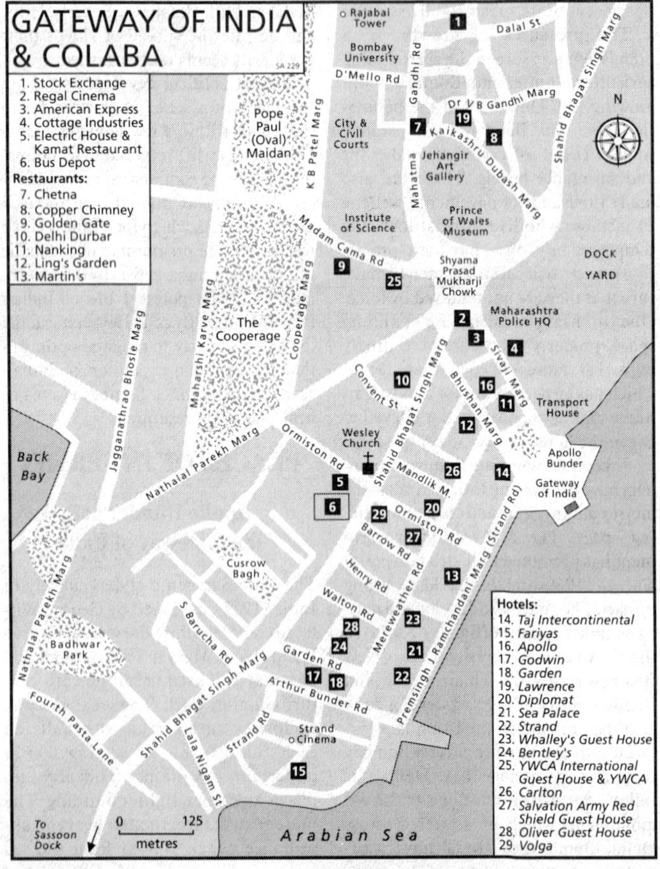

road is named after Bhagat Singh.) **The Afghan Memorial Church of St John the Baptist** (1847-58) is at the N edge of Colaba itself. Early English in style, with a 58m spire, it was built to commemorate the soldiers who died in the First Afghan War. Fishermen still unload their catch early in the morning at **Sassoon Dock**, the first wet dock in India. Photography is prohibited. Beyond the church near the tip of the Colaba promontory lie the **Observatory** and **Old European cemetery**.

Central Bombay

The area stretching back up the peninsula from Colaba Causeway to Victoria Terminus is the heart of British Bombay. Most of the buildings date from the period after 1862, when Sir Bartle Frere became Governor (1862-7), and under whose enthusiastic guidance Bombay became a great civic centre. It is an extravaganza of Victorian Gothic architecture, modified by the Indo-Saracenic influences. From the Gateway of India, proceed along Sivaji Marg to Mahatma Gandhi Rd and you will see many of these buildings, most still in use as offices.

Just behind the **Prince of Wales Museum** in S Bhagat Singh Marg (Marine St) is **St Andrew's Kirk** (1819), a simple neo-classical church. The steeple, irreparably damaged by lightning in 1826, was rebuilt a year later. Next door there used to be a circular building (1840) for storing imported American ice (see page 822). Local ice plants appeared in the 1880s. At the S end of Mahatma Gandhi (MG) Rd is the Renaissance style **Institute of Science** (1911) designed by George Wittet. The Institute, which includes a scientific library, a public hall and examination halls, was built with gifts from the Parsi and Jewish communities.

The Pope Paul (Oval) Maidan

Immediately to the N, on the E side of Baburao Patel Marg (Mayo Rd) and the Pope Paul (Oval) Maidan, is a series of striking buildings, bringing together a range of European styles from the early English Gothic to the Romanesque. From S to N they are the old Secretariat, the University Library and Rajabai Clocktower, the High Court and the Public Works Office.

The Venetian Gothic style old **Secretariat** (1874) is 143m long, with a façade of arcaded verandahs and porticos faced in buff-coloured Porbander stone from Gujarat. Decorated with red and blue basalt, the carvings are in white Hemnagar stone. The **University Convocation Hall** (1874) to its N was designed by Sir George Gilbert Scott in a 15th century French Decorated style. Scott also designed the adjacent **University Library** and the 79m high **Rajabai Clocktower** (1870s) next door, based on Giotto's campanile in Florence. The sculpted figures in niches on the exterior walls of the tower were designed to represent the castes of India. Originally the clock could chime 12 tunes such as Rule Britannia.

The High Court (1871-9), in Early English Gothic style, has a 57m high central tower flanked by lower octagonal towers topped by the figures of Justice and Mercy. The Venetian Gothic **Public Works Office** (1869-72) is to its N. Opposite, and with its main façade to Vir Nariman Rd, is the former General Post Office (1869-72). Now called the **Telegraph office**, it stands next to the original Telegraph Office adding Romanesque to the extraordinary mixture of European architectural styles. Both buildings are in honey-coloured sandstone from Kurla.

NB: The old buildings of the centre are floodlit after 1900 hrs.

Horniman Circle

Turn right at the Flora (or Frere) Fountain (1869), now known as **Hutatma Chowk**, along Vir Nariman Rd to the

Old Custom House, Town Hall and Mint on the imposing Horniman (Elphinstone) Circle. By Bombay standards the **Custom House** is an old building and is believed to incorporate a Portuguese barrack block of 1665. Over the entrance is the crest of the East India Company. Parts of the old Portuguese fort's walls can be seen; more exist in the Naval Dockyards (inaccessible to tourists). Many Malabar teak 'East Indiamen' ships were built here.

The Mint (1824-9), built on the Fort rubbish dump, has Ionic columns and a water tank in front of it. The **Town Hall** (1820-3) has been widely admired as one of the best neo-classical buildings in India. The Doric columns that give the Town Hall its grandeur were shipped from England. The original idea of paired columns was abandoned as being too monumental and half the imported columns were used at Christ Church, Byculla. The Corinthian interior houses the Assembly Rooms and the Bombay Asiatic Society.

Horniman Circle was laid out in 1860. On the W edge are the Venetian Gothic **Elphinstone Buildings** (1870) in brown sandstone. Immediately to their W is the **Cathedral Church of St Thomas**, begun in 1672, opened in 1718, and subject to a number of later additions. Inside are a number of monuments forming a heroic 'who's who of India'.

Behind Horniman circle on the water's edge lies the **Old Castle**. Entry is not permitted. Proceeding N to Victoria Terminus you pass the **Port Trust Office** on your right, while a little farther on, to your right by the station is the **General Post Office** (1909), based on the architecture of Bijapur (Karnataka) in the Indo-Saracenic style.

The Victoria Terminus area

Immediately N of the General Post Office is the **Victoria Terminus** (1878-87), the most remarkable example of Victorian Gothic architecture in India, opened during Queen Victoria's Golden Jubilee year, and known today as 'VT'. Over half a million commuters use the station every day.

The frontage is symmetrical with a large central dome flanked by 2 wings. The dome is capped by a 4m high statue of Progress by Thomas Earp, who also carved the Imperial lion and Indian tiger on the gate piers, nearly all executed by the Bombay School of Art. The booking hall with its arcades, stained glass and glazed tiles was inspired by London's St Pancras station.

The first train in India left from this terminus for Thane in 1853, well before the present station was opened. It was built at a time when fierce debate was taking place among British architects working in India as to the most appropriate style to develop for the buildings increasingly in demand. One view held that the British should restrict themselves to models derived from the best in Western tradition, as the British were to be seen as a 'civilising force' in India. Others argued that architects should draw on Indian models, trying to bring out the best of Indian tradition and encourage its development. By and large, the former were dominant, but as Tillotson argues, the introduction of Gothic allowed a blending of Western traditions with Indian (often Islamic Indian) motifs, which became known as the Indo-Saracenic style.

At the junction of Dadabhai Naoroji Marg (Dr DN Marg) and Mahapalika Marg are the grand Municipal Buildings (1893), built by Stevens. The tower is 78m high and the statue crowning the gable is designed to represent 'Urbs Prima in Indis' (*The first city in India*). More British buildings are in Mahapalika Marg (Cruickshank Rd). On your right you will see the **Police Courts** (1888), **Cama Albless Hospital** which has interesting Gothic windows with conical iron hoods to provide shade, **St**

THE "DABBAWALLAHS"

If you go inside Churchgate station at mid-morning or after lunch, you will see the *dabbawallahs*, members of the Bombay Union of Tiffin Box Carriers. Each morning, the 2,500 dabbawallahs call on suburban housewives who pack freshly cooked lunch into small circular aluminium or stainless steel containers – "dabbas". They are divided into about 4 compartments, stacked one on the other and held together by a clip with a handle (they are widely available in general stores and bazaars). Typically the *dabbawallah* will collect 30-40 tiffin boxes, range them out on a long pole and cycle to the nearest station. Here he will hand them over to a fellow *dabbawallah* who will transport them into the city for delivery to the consumer.

Over 100,000 lunches of maybe *sabze* (vegetable curry), *chappattis, dal* and pickle, make their way daily across town to the breadwinner and back again. The service which costs a few rupees a week, is a good example of the fine division of labour in India, reliable and efficient for the *dabbawallahs* pride themselves on never losing a lunch. It enables the family to rest knowing that carefully prepared 'pukka' (proper) food has not in any way been defiled.

Xavier's College founded in 1867 and **Elphinstone High School** (1872) MG Rd, among the trees. On the opposite side of the road is the **Maidan**, popular with cricketers of all ages.

Turning right into Lokmanya Tilak Marg (Camac Rd), on your right is **St Xavier's School**, and **Gokuldas Tejpal Hospital** (1877) built by Parsi benefactors. On the SE and SW faces are medallions by Rudyard Kipling's father Lockwood Kipling.

Immediately to the N is **Crawford Market** (1865-71; officially Phule Market), at the junction of Lokmanya Tilak Marg and Dadabhai Naoroji Rd. Designed by Emerson in the 12th century French Gothic style, over the entrance is more of Lockwood Kipling's work. The paving stones are from Caithness! The market is divided into sections for fruit, vegetables, fish, mutton and poultry. From Crawford Market you can return to the Gateway of India or take a taxi to either the **Victoria and Albert Museum** at Byculla or **Malabar Hill** (now officially 'Malbar', but in some tourist offices this spelling or pronunciation is never used).

Between Crawford Market and Bombay Central Railway Station is **Falkland Road**, the centre of Bombay's red-light district. Prostitutes stand behind barred windows, giving the area its other name 'The Cages'. Many of the girls and women are sold or abducted as forced labour from various parts of India and Nepal. Recent medical reports suggest that AIDS is now very widespread.

Marine Drive and Malabar Hill

You can do an interesting half day trip from Churchgate Station, along Marine Drive to the Taraporewala Aquarium, Mani Bhavan (Gandhi Museum), the Babulnath temple, past the Parsi Towers of Silence to Kamla Nehru Park, the Hanging Gardens and the Jain Temple. If you wish you can go further towards Malabar Point to get a glimpse of Raj Bhavan and the Walkeshwar temple, before returning N via the Mahalaxmi Temple and Haji Ali's tomb on the W shore.

Churchgate Station (1894-6) designed by FW Stevens for the Bombay, Baroda and Central India Railway, is at the W end of Vir Nariman Rd. Stevens was a great protagonist of the Indo-Saracenic style. With its domes and façades Churchgate station is Byzantine in flavour. The statue on the W gable shows a figure holding a locomotive and wheel, symbols of technological progress.

Marine Drive and Chowpatty Beach The long stretch of white sand beach looks attractive from a distance, but on closer examination is polluted. Swimming here is not recommended. Like Juhu Beach there is a lot of beach activity.

Chowpatty has witnessed some significant events in India's contemporary history as it was the scene of a number of important 'Quit India' rallies during the Independence Movement. Also, at important festivals like *Ganesh Chaturthi* and *Dasara* (see Festivals), it is thronged with jubilant Hindu devotees.

Netaji Subhash Rd, better known as Marine Drive, runs round **Back Bay** along Chowpatty from just below the Hanging Gardens on Malabar Hill to Nariman Pt. At night, lined with lights, it is a very attractive sight from Malabar Hill, a view which gave rise to the description of it as 'Queen Victoria's Necklace'.

Towards the N end of Back Bay is the **Taraporewala Aquarium**, 1100-2000, closed Mon. Re 1. One of the best aquariums in India for fresh and salt water fish. The latter has water piped from Back Bay. Shells and shell crafts on sale. A western visitor may be disappointed.

Gandhi Museum Further N just SW of Nana Chowk is the Gandhi museum

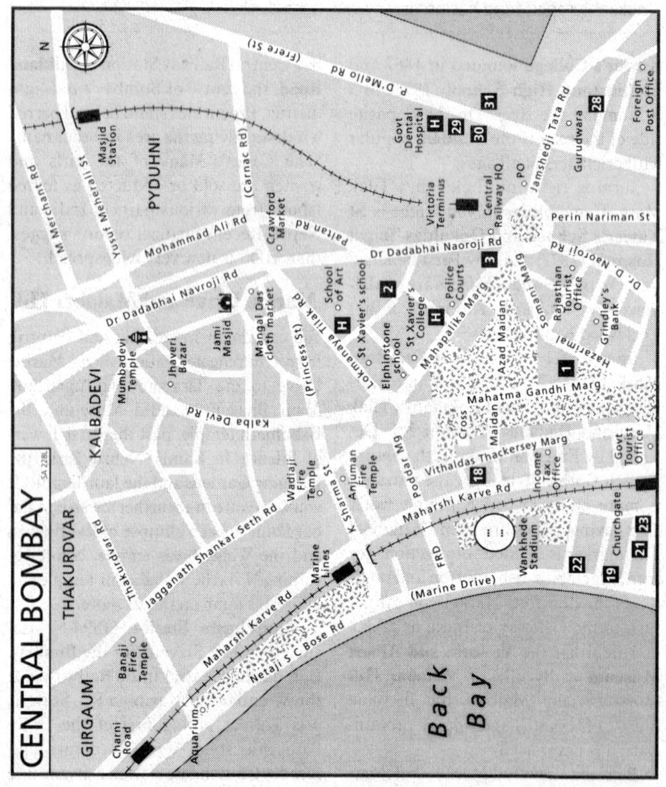

at **Mani Bhavan**. The nearest station is Grant Rd. See **Museums** below.

The Towers of Silence are in secluded gardens 500m to the W of the Gandhi Museum. This very private place is not accessible to tourists but it can be glimpsed from the road. Sir Jamshetji Jeejeebhoy gave a large area of land around the towers, thus affording them privacy and allowing the creation of a tranquil garden. Parsis believe that the elements of water, fire and earth must not be polluted by the dead, so they lay their 'vestments of flesh and bone' out on the top of the towers to be picked clean by vultures. See page 95. Some guides claim that the reason the Hanging Gardens were created was to protect Bombay's water supply from being polluted by half-eaten corpses dropped by vultures. There is no truth in this.

The Hanging Gardens (Pherozeshah Mehta Gardens) immediately S of the Towers of Silence, in the centre of a low hill, are so named since they are located on top of a series of tanks that supply water to Bombay. These formal gardens have some interesting animal topiary and good views over the city.

Nearby is the Church of North India **All Saints' Church** (1882). Across the road from the Hanging Gardens is the

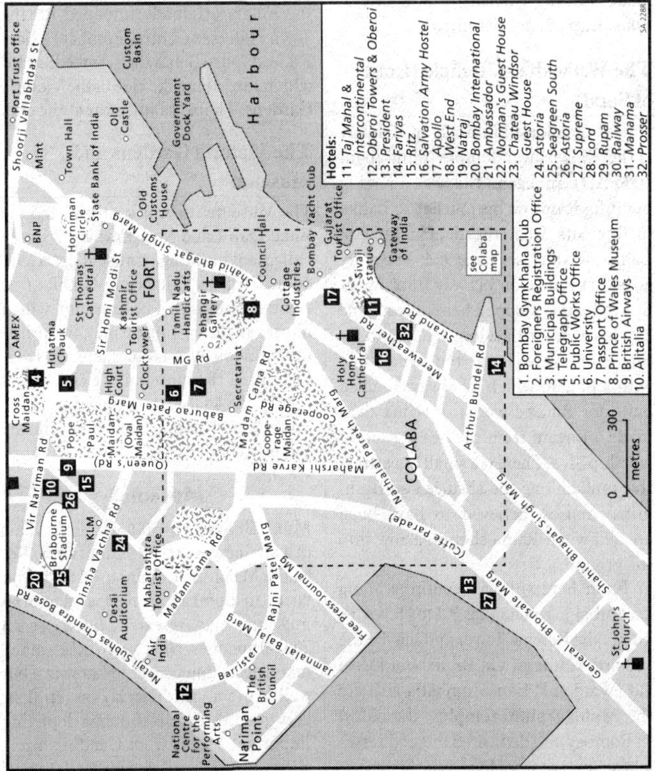

Kamla Nehru Park, laid out in 1952 and named after the wife of India's first Prime Minister. Very good views over Back Bay. The *Naaz* café is next door (awaiting restoration after arson in Dec 1992) and the top terrace is a particularly good vantage point.

Jain Temple (1904) Built of marble and dedicated to the first Jain *Tirthankar*. Much of the decoration depicts the lives of the Tirthankars but overall the temple is not of great interest.

Raj Bhavan (Government House) is the Governor's official residence. Sir Evan Nepean (1812-1819) was the first to live there and succeeding Governors made various extensions and alterations. Entry is not permitted.

The Walkeshwar Temple (Lord of Sand)

One of the oldest buildings in Bombay is the Walkeshwar Temple (built about 1000 AD). In legend this was a resting point for Rama on his journey to Lanka to free Sita from the demon king of Lanka, Ravana, see page 923. The story goes that Rama, on his way from Ayodhya to Lanka, stopped here to rest. One day his brother Lakshman failed to return from Varanasi at the usual time with a lingam which he always fetched daily for Rama's worship. Rama then made a lingam from the beach sand to worship Siva. There is a small but attractive tank among the shrines and Brahmins' houses, believed to have been created when Rama shot an arrow into the ground.

From here you can continue along Laxmibai Jagmohandas Rd to Haji Ali's Tomb, the Rajabai Tower and maybe the Victoria Gardens. On Bhulabhai Desai Rd (Warden Rd) on Cumballa Hill are the **Mahalakshmi temples**, the oldest in Bombay and dedicated to 3 goddesses whose images were found in the sea.

Haji Ali's Tomb

The tomb and mosque are devoted to a Muslim saint who drowned here. They are reached by a long causeway usable only at low tide. Note the moneychangers are willing to exchange 1 rupee coins into individual paise coins, enabling pilgrims to make many individual gifts to beggars rather than 1 large one, thereby reputedly increasing the merit of the gift.

From Haji Ali's Tomb go along Keshavrao Khade Rd to SG Maharaj Chowk (Jacob's Circle). Go down Maulana Azad Rd then turn left into Clare Rd. On your right is **Christ Church, Byculla** (1835), which incorporated half the pillars originally intended for the Town Hall (see Central Bombay). Clare Rd leads onto Babasaheb Ambedkar Rd which runs along the side of the Victoria Gardens. There is a juice bar at the end.

The Victoria Gardens and Museum

The Museum (now officially named the Bhau Daji Laud Museum) is a 2 storey Palladian building, unusual in a city dominated by Victorian Gothic (see Central Bombay). The museum, which houses an interesting display on the history of Bombay, was completed in 1872. In front of the museum is a clocktower (1865), the 4 faces show morning, noon, evening and night. Next door are the Victoria Gardens.

Museums

Mani Bhavan 0930-0600. Free. This private house, at 19 Laburnum Rd, where Mahatma Gandhi used to stay on visits to Bombay, is now a memorial museum and research library with 20,000 volumes. Not easy to find – many taxi drivers don't seem to know it – but well worth a visit. Display on top floor very good, especially diorama depicting important scenes from Gandhi's life – slides of it are available for Rs100 at the entrance – you will have to mount them yourself. Cards, pamphlets etc at the door. Allow 1 hr.

Victoria and Albert Museum North end of MG Rd. Closed Wed. Mon, Tue, Fri, Sat 1030-1700, Th 1000-1645, Sun 0830-1645. Small fee. This was inspired by the Victoria and Albert Museum in S Kensington, London. Financed by public subscription, it was built in 1871 in a Palladian style. Sir George Birdwood, a noted physician and authority on Indian crafts, was the driving force behind it and became its first curator. The collection covers the history of Bombay and contains prints, maps and models.

In front of the Museum is a Clocktower (1865) and a stone statue of an elephant found by the Portuguese in the harbour. Elephanta Island was named after it. The gardens are very attractive. A list at the entrance indicates which trees and shrubs are in blossom. A stroll in Victoria Gardens is very much a part of Bombay life.

Prince of Wales Museum South end of MG Rd. Closed Mon. 1015-1730 (Oct-Feb), 1015-1800 (Jul-Sep), 1015-1830 (Mar-Jun). Rs 3, Tue free for students. Camera fee Rs 15 (no flash or tripods). Good guide books, pamphlets, cards and reproductions on sale. Citywide bus connections; ask at Inspectors' Booth outside. Designed by George Wittet to commemorate the visit of the Prince of Wales (later King George V) to India in 1905. A bronze statue of the king stands outside and an equestrian statue of Edward VII on the other, all set in a landscaped garden. The dome of glazed tiles has a very Persian and Central Asian flavour. The whole is Indo-Saracenic, and thus in keeping with the Gateway of India which was built at the same time.

There are 3 sections. The archaeological section has 3 main groups: Brahminical, Buddhist and Jain, Prehistoric and Foreign. The Indus Valley section is well displayed. The art section includes an excellent collection of Indian miniatures and well displayed *tankhas*. There are also works by Gainsborough, Poussin and Titian as well as Indian silver, jade and tapestries and a collection of arms. The **Natural History** section is based on the collection of the Bombay Natural History Society founded in 1833 and includes dioramas.

Jehangir Art Gallery Closed Mon. 1030-1800. Within the complex of the Prince of Wales Museum. Bombay's principal art gallery, often staging exhibitions of modern art. The 'Samovar' café is good with a terrace overlooking the museum gardens. Public phones and toilets. **Gallery Chermould** on 1st Floor.

Nehru Planetarium, Dr Annie Besant Rd, nr Haji Ali, Worli. Closed Sun. Rs 5. Shows in English at 1500 and 1800, closed Mon. In the same grounds, **Nehru Science Museum**, Lala Lajpat Rai Rd, T 493266. Science Park and permanent gallery. Closed Mon. **National Maritime Museum**, Middle Ground off Gateway of India. Sat, Sun and holidays. Ask at boat operators at Gateway.

Parks & zoos

Marine Drive, Chowpatty Beach and the **Hanging Gardens** are open expanses but afford little shade in the heat of the day. The **maidans** in the centre of town are quiet in the early morning but crowded at other times. There are large gardens at the **Willingdon and Gymkhana Clubs** but temporary membership is required (see under **Clubs**). The **Victoria Gardens** are very pleasant. There is a small zoo there. Open sunrise to sunset, usually 0800-1800. Closed Wed. Small fee. Elephant, camel and pony rides are available for children. **Kamla Nehru Park**, Bal Gangadhar Kher Rd, Malabar Hill.

Tours

City sightseeing

Several tour operators offer city sightseeing. The City Tour usually includes visits to The Gateway of India, Aquarium (except Mon), the Prince of Wales Museum (closed Mon), Jain temple, Hanging Gardens, Kamla Nehru Park and Mani Bhavan (Gandhi Museum). Some tours stop during the monsoon. The Suburban Tour includes Juhu Beach, Tulsi Lake National Park, Kanheri Caves and Lion Safari Park (closed Mon). Some visitors have described the tour as 'awful'.

ITDC, Nirmal Bldg, Nariman Pt, T 2026679. Booking also at 123 Maharshi Karve Rd, T 213144. City Tour: daily except Mon, 0900-1300 and 1345-1745, Rs 35. **Maharashtra Tourism**, Madam Cama Rd, Opp. LIC Building, T 2026713. City Tour: daily except Mon, 0900-1300 and 1400-1800, Rs 50. Suburban Tour: 0915-1815, Rs 85. **Travel Corp of India (TCI)**, Chander Mukhi, Nariman Pt, T 2021881. City Tour: daily 1430-1630, Rs 45. **'BEST' Undertaking**, Transport House, S Bhagat Singh Marg, Colaba Causeway, T 240601. Suburban Tour: Sun only, 0830-1730.

Elephanta

(see Excursions) Tours by **Elephanta Jal-Vahatuk Sahakari Sanstha Maryadit** and **Orient Charters** from the Gateway of India, departures every hr from 0900 until 1400. If you wish to sightsee independently with a guide, the Tourist Office can arrange this.

Ajanta and Ellora

Maharashtra Tourism runs a tour to the famous caves at Ajanta and Ellora. Daily departures for 4 day tour. Dep 0830, return 0800 4 days later. About Rs 900 for transport, entry fee and guide charges, meals and accommodation at good hotels (Rs 765 for lower category hotel). One-way fare also possible. Reservations and further information: T 2023343. For details of caves see page 1172. If you want to see the caves at your leisure, it is much better to make your own arrangements.

Adventure Tourism

Maharashtra Tourism has been active in encouraging adventure tourism (incl Jungle Safaris and Water sports) by introducing 'Rent-a-Tent' and hiring trekking gear. Some sites provide electricity, linen, bathrooms and authentic cuisine in rustic restaurants. It has also set up 27 **'Holiday Resorts'** providing cheap accommodation at hill stations, beaches, archaeological sites and scenic spots. Details of packages from Tourist offices.

Local festivals

In addition to the national Hindu and Muslim festivals there are:

Mar *Jamshed Navroz* This is New Year's Day for the Parsi followers of the Fasli calendar. The celebrations which include offering prayers at temples, exchanging greetings, alms-giving and feasting at home, date back to Jamshed, the legendary king of Persia.

Jul-Aug *Janmashtami* celebrates the birth of Lord Krishna. Boys and young men form human pyramids and break pots of curd hung up high between buildings.

Aug *Coconut Day* The angry monsoon seas are propitiated by devotees throwing coconuts into the ocean.

Aug-Sep *Ganesh Chaturthi* Massive figures of Ganesh are worshipped and immersed in the sea on several days following the festival.

Sep *Mount Mary's Feast* celebrated at St Mary's Church, Bandra. A fair is also held.

Sep-Oct *Dasara* During this nationwide festival, in Bombay there are group dances by Gujarati women in all the auditoria. There are also Ramlila celebrations at Chowpatty Beach. *Diwali* (The Festival of Lights) is particularly popular in mercantile Bombay when the business community celebrate their New Year and open new account books.

25 Dec *Christmas* Christians across

Bombay celebrate the birth of Christ. A pontifical High Mass is held at midnight in the open air at the Cooperage Grounds.

Local information

Accommodation & food

● Accommodation

Most are concentrated in the central area (Marine Drive, Nariman Pt, Apollo Bunder and Colaba) and in Juhu out of town. Prices tend to be high but there are several relatively cheap hotels immediately behind the Taj.

Juhu is convenient for the airport especially early morning departures. Here the **B** and **C** category hotels lack character. Juhu Beach used to be quite an attractive and relaxed seaside area. It has now been absorbed into the metropolis. The sea is polluted and the beach is not pleasant enough for sunbathing but there is a lot happening on Sun evenings when it has a fairground atmosphere. For services in **AL**, **A** and **B** hotels, see page 137. **Hotlink**, India's first on-line reservation system, links 300 medium to top class hotels, T 6152394.

NB: Accommodation in Bombay is usually heavily booked. Whenever possible make reservations in advance. If you have not, arrive as early in the day as possible.

Price guide
AL R 3,000+ **A** Rs 2,000-3,000
B Rs 1,200-2,000 **C** Rs 600-1,200
D Rs 250-600 **E** Rs 100-250 **F** less than Rs

● Juhu Beach hotels

Virtually all less than 10 km from the airport and approximately 20-25 km from the centre. Most are close to a suburban railway station. Many down to **D** category offer free coach transfer to/from airport. Beach activity provides a constant distraction.

AL *Leela Kempinski*, Sahar, T 8363636, F 6360606, 280 rm, excellent restaurants include Chinese-Hunan, but slow service in coffee shop, good sports facilities; **AL** Welcomgroup *Sea Rock Sheraton*, T 6425454, 398 rm, 6 restaurants (incl *NW Frontier*, *Seafood*, *Far-eastern* on revolving rooftop), live entertainment and dancing, squash, tennis and courtesy coach, not well located for the city but on water's edge and excellent for a relaxing stay or for an overnight stop from the airport, best views from upper floors.

A *Centaur Juhu Beach*, Juhu Tara Rd, T 6113040, F 6116343, 370 rm, on beach front; **A** *Holiday Inn*, Balraj Sahani Marg, T 6204444, F 6204452, 210 rm, 2 pools, windsurfing, squash, tennis, courtesy coach to town, typical Holiday Inn, reliable but no special character; **A** *Ramada Inn Palm Grove*, T 6112323, F 6142105, 113 rm, some single rm Rs 1200, full facilities plus windsurfing; **A** *Sun-n-Sand*, 39 Juhu Beach, T 6204945, 118 rm, comfortable though cramped poolside, good restaurant; **A** *The Resort*, 11 Madh Marve Rd, Malad (W), T 882331, 58 rm, 15 km N of airport, 42 km centre, wide range of sports.

B *Sea Princess*, 969 Juhu Beach, T 6116080, 72 rm; **B** *Horizon*, 37 Juhu Beach, T 6148100, 161 rm, facilities incl disco, good but no sea view; **B** *Sands*, 39/2 Juhu Beach, T 6206448, 40 rm, excellent restaurant, rec.

C *Ajanta*, 8 Juhu Rd, Juhu, T 6124890-1, 32 a/c rm, restaurant.

D *Atlantic*, 18B Juhu Tara Rd, T 6122440-1, 27 a/c rm, restaurants, bar, exchange, travel; **D** *King's*, 5 Juhu Tara Rd, T 6149775, 47 a/c rm, restaurant, bar; **D** *Seaside*, 39/2 Juhu Rd, T 6200923, 36 a/c rm, rm service, no sea view!

Budget hotel E *South End*, 11 Juhu Tara Rd, Juhu, T 6125213, 38 rm, some a/c, light refreshments.

● Airport hotels

A *Centaur Airport*, Bombay Airport, T 6116660, F 6113535, 260 rm, reasonable, good service, very close to domestic airport, damaged in the Mar 1993 bombing the hotel is fully functioning again, often very heavily booked.

C *Airport International*, Plot No 5/6, Nehru Rd, Vile Parle, T 6122891, very close to domestic terminal, 27 rm, modern business hotel, clean, comfortable; **C** *Atithi*, 77A, B Nehru House, Vile Parle, T 6116124, 47 rm (15 permanently occupied), modern comfortable hotel, 5 min walk domestic terminal, free courtesy coach, very popular and heavily booked – give at least 10 days notice; **C** *Airport Kohinoor*, JB Nagara, Andheri-Kurla Rd, Andheri (E), T 6348548-9, 48 rm, central a/c, restaurant; **C** *Jal*, Nehru Rd, Ville Parle (E), T 6123820, 40 a/c rm, nr domestic airport, restaurant (Veg Indian and Chinese), coffee shop; **C** *Kamat Plaza*, 70C Nehru Rd, Santa Cruz Airport, T 6123390, F 6105974, 68 rm, 5 min walk from domestic terminal; **C** *Kumaria Presi-*

dency, Andheri-Kurla Rd, facing International Airport, Marol Naka, Andheri (E), T 6042025, 32 a/c rm, 8 km Bandra, restaurant, coffee shop, 24-hr exchange, travel; **C *Parle International***, Agarwal Market, Ville Parle (E), T 6144335, 39 a/c rm, restaurant, bar, exchange; **C *Shubhangan***, 711 1st Rd, Chitrakar Dhurandar Marg, Khar (W), good veg restaurant, modern, rec; **C *Royal Inn***, opp Khar telephone exchange, Linking Rd, Khar (W), T 6495151, 23 a/c rm, central, restaurant, exchange, travel; **C *Transit***, Off Nehru Rd, Ville Parle (E), T 6121087, 46 a/c rm, restaurant, bar, exchange, shops.

D *Caesars Palace*, 313 Linking Rd, Khar, T 542311, 20 a/c rm, restaurants, bar, exchange; **D *Jay Shree***, 197 Dayaldas Rd, Ville Parle (E), T 6146787, 30 a/c rm, travel; **D *Mayura***, 352 Linking Rd, Khar, T 6494416, 28 a/c rm, restaurants, bar, exchange, travel, pretty basic and run-down; **D *Metro Palace***, Junction of Hill Rd and Waterfield Rd, Bandra (W), T 6427311, 34 a/c rm, bar, 24-hr rm service, travel; **D *Samraj***, Chakala Rd, Andheri (E), T 6349311, 32 a/c rm, restaurant, exchange.

Budget hotels The less expensive hotels often have no restaurant but some will provide meals in rm. **E *Galaxy***, 113 Prabhat Colony, Santa Cruz (E), T 6125223, 24 rm, some a/c,

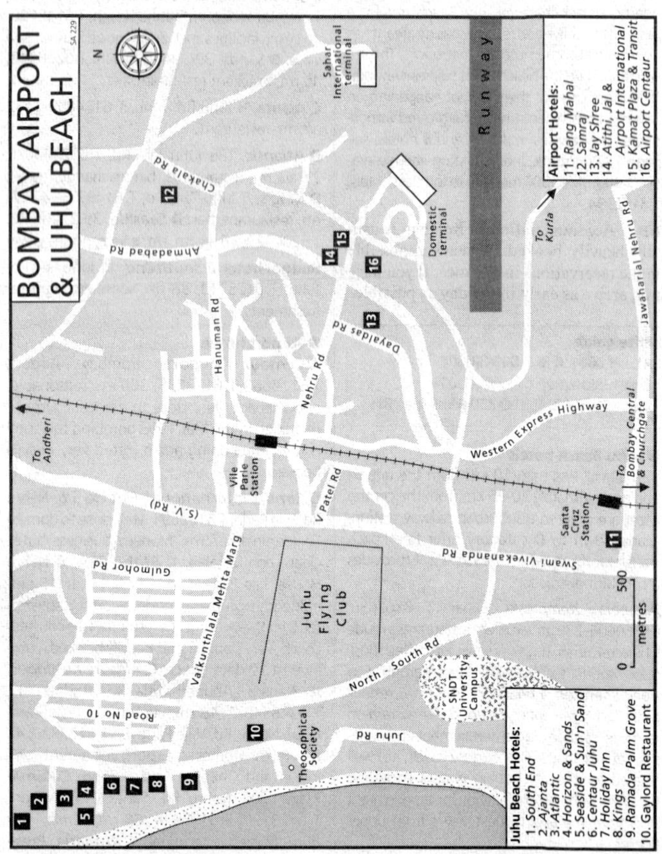

rm service; **E** *Manali*, Manchhubhai Rd, Malad (E), T 6881392, 44 rm, some a/c; **E** *Rang Mahal*, Station Rd, Santa Cruz, T 6490303, 22 rm, rm service (Indian).

Town hotels

All 25-30 km from airport, close to Victoria Terminus Rly, with central locations.

AL *The Oberoi*, Nariman Pt, T 2025757, 337 large rm, the newer Oberoi combining modern technology with period furniture, excellent restaurants; **AL** *The Oberoi Towers*, Nariman Pt, T 2024343, 594 rm, excellent views from higher floors, garden pool, excellent shopping complex; **AL** *President*, 90 Cuffe Parade (Taj Grp), T 2150808, F 4151201, 299 rm, every facility, good service, informal but lacks character, business hotel but equally comfortable and welcoming to others.

A *Ambassador*, Churchgate Extn, Vir Nariman Rd, T 2041131, 127 rm, all facilities, including revolving restaurant and pastry shop, slightly run down feel.

B *Natraj*, 135 Netaji Subhash Rd, T 2044161, 83 rm, some with views over bay, but not worth the price; **B** *Ritz*, 5 Jamshedji Tata Rd, T 220141, 72 rm, some a/c, nr Tourist Office and Churchgate Rly station.

C *Grand*, 17 Sprott Rd, Ballard Estate, T 268211, 72 a/c rm, restaurant, exchange, bookshop, old fashioned, built around a central courtyard but relaxing; **C** *Shalimar*, August Kranti Marg, T 8221311, 74 a/c rm, restaurant, bar, exchange, bookshop; **C** *West End*, 45 New Marine Lines, T 299121, 80 a/c rm, restaurant, bar, exchange, shops.

D *Astoria*, 4 JT Rd, Churchgate, T 221514, 70 a/c rm, restaurant, bar; **D** *Heritage*, Sant Savta Marg, Byculla, T 8514981, 84 a/c rm, restaurant (good Parsi), bar; **D** *Nagina*, 53 Dr Ambedkar Rd, Byculla, T 8517799, 52 a/c rm, exchange; **D** *Rajdoot*, 19 Jackeria Bunder Rd, Cotton Green, T 8514442, 56 rm, some a/c, restaurant; **D** *Railway Hotel*, P D'Mello Rd, nr GPO, T 2616705, very good value, rec; **D** *Rosewood*, 99C Tulsiwadi, opp A/c market, T 4940320, 50 rm, central a/c, restaurant, exchange; **D** *Sea Green South*, 145A Marine Drive, T 222294, 34 rm, some a/c, with sea view best; **C-D** *Chateau Windsor Guest House*, 86 Vir Nariman Rd, next to *Ambassador Hotel*, T 2043376, 36 rm, (some a/c); some very small and dark, friendly, (occasionally, unwelcome attention) clean, good value; **D** *Lord Hotel*, 301 Mangalore St, Fort, nr P D'Mello Rd, T 2610077, 36 good rm, beer parlour; **D** *Supreme*, 4 Pandey Rd, nr *President*, T 215623, clean rm with bath, good service but a little noisy. **D** *Railway Retiring Rooms*, T 3077292, some a/c with bath and deluxe.

Budget hotels **E** *Manora*, 243-245 PD Mello Rd, T 2616650, 54 rm, some a/c with TV; **E** *Norman's Guest House*, 2 Firdaus, 127 Marine Dr, T 294234, 6 rm, some a/c, avoid noisy front rm; **E** *Pals*, Reay Rd, Cotton Green, Kalachowki, T 8511951, 59 rm, a/c restaurant; **E** *Rupam*, 239 P D'Mello Rd, Victoria Terminus, T 2616225, 37 rm, some a/c with phone, clean, friendly, comfortable beds; **E** *Sea Green South*, 145A Marine Drive, T 221613, 36 rm, some a/c, TV lounge; **E** *Railway Hotel*, Raja Rammohan Rd, T 351028, 31 rm, non a/c rm, beer parlour, very basic; **E** *Residency*, 26 Gunbow St, corner Dr DN Rd, Fort, opp City Bank and Khadi Bhandar, Hornby Rd, T 2625525; **E** *Sahara*, 35 Tribhuvan Rd (above Sher-e-Punjab restaurant), T 361491, 31 rm, some a/c; **E** *Seashore*, T 2874237, has good rm, facing sea; **E** *YWCA* at 34 Motibai St, Byculla, T 372744.

Very cheap hotels *Social Service Centre*, 122 Maulana Azad Rd, Byculla, T 241824; *Carlton*, 12 Mereweather Rd, T230642.

Dadar & Bombay Central area

B *Midtown Pritam*, Pritam Estates, Dadar, T 4300019, 63 rm, terrace garden.

C *Hilltop*, 43 Pochkanwala Rd, Worli, T 4930860, 70 a/c rm, restaurant.

D *Kemps Corner*, 131 August Kranti Marg, T 8224646, 35 a/c rm, breakfast only, travel; **D** *Parkway*, Sivaji Park, Ranade Rd, Dadar, T 456531, 15 a/c rm; **D** *Park-Lane*, Hind Rajasthan Bldg, 95 Dadasaheb Phalke Rd, 200m N of Dadar Central Rly Station, T 4114741, 23 rm, some a/c, on 5th Flr of apartment block, run down, rooms dirty, not good value; **D** *Anukool*, 292-8 Maulana Skaukatali Rd, corner of Grant Rd, T 392401, 23 rm, some a/c, coffee shop, good value.

Budget hotels **E** *YMCA International House and Programme Centre*, 18 YMCA Rd, nr Bombay Central, T 891191, shared bath, meals incl, temp membership – Rs 40, very good value, often booked up 3 months ahead; **E** *Aroma*, 190 Dr Ambedkar Rd, Dadar, T 4111761, 37 rm, some a/c, terrace garden; **E** *Balwas*, 323 Maulana Shoukat Ali Rd, Grant Rd, T 363313, 27 rm, some a/c.

● **Gateway of India & Colaba**

AL *Taj Mahal* and *Taj Mahal Intercontinental*, Apollo Bunder (Gateway of India), T 2023366, F 2822711, 599 rm, every facility with restaurants (inc French), excellent shopping parade and pastry shop, visit if you are not staying, the former, for style and character, the latter is a plush, modern, world class, 5-star hotel. Indian dance performance (evenings) open to non-residents, very good, Rs 50, 1 hr.

C *Fariyas*, 25 Arthur Rd, off Bunder Rd, Colaba, T 2042911, 80 rm, good restaurants, 'pub', roof garden; **C** *Apollo*, 22 Lansdowne Rd, Colaba, behind *Taj Intercontinental*, T 2873312, 32 rm, some a/c, best with sea view, restaurant, bar, comfortable; **C** *Ascot*, 38 Garden Rd, T 240020, 26 a/c rm, some with bath, restaurant (Indian); **C** *Diplomat*, 24-26 BK Bonam Behram Marg, Colaba, T 2021661, 52 a/c rm, restaurants, bar, exchange, behind Taj, quiet and homely, good value; **C** *Godwin*, 41 Garden Rd, Colaba, T 241226, 48 large, clean a/c rm, restaurant, bar, rooftop garden, highly rec. **C-D** *Shelley's*, 30 Ramchandani Marg, Colaba (opp Radio Club), T 240229, large comfortable, bright airy rm with TV and fridge, some sea-facing (less expensive, when not), helpful and friendly owners, rec.

D *Garden*, 42 Garden Rd, Colaba, T 241476, F 2871592, 32 large a/c rm, restaurant; **D** *Bentley's*, 17 Oliver Rd, nr the Harbour, Colaba, T 241474, 37 rm, some a/c, breakfast incl in rate, exchange, good value; **D** *Sea Palace*, 26 PJ Ramchandani Marg (Strand Rd), T 241828, 48 rm, some a/c, restaurant; **D** *YWCA* (for men and women), 18 Madam Cama Rd (entrance on side), Fort, T 2020445, 34 clean, pleasant rm with bath, breakfast incl, temp membership – Rs 25/month, deposit with advance reservations in writing.

Budget hotels E *Lawrence*, Rope Walk La, behind Prince of Wales Museum, T 243618, tiny, usually full, good value; **E** *Whalley's Guest House*, Jaji Mansion, 41 Mereweather Rd, T 221802, 25 rm, some a/c with balcony and bath, inc breakfast, accepts TC; **E** *Prosser*, Curzon House, 2-4 Henry Rd, corner of PJ Ramchandani Marg, T 241715. Not too clean, poor value.

Also many **F** category are clustered around the *Taj Mahal Hotel*. *Salvation Army Red Shield Hostel*, 30 Mereweather Rd, T 241824, mostly dorm, some double rm, restaurant (meals included), lockers, check out 0900, book in advance or be there early, check in as others check out, rec as convenient, friendly, good value; *Oliver Guest House*, Walton Rd. On Arthur Bunder Rd, Colaba, there are several, often on upper floors, usually shared facilities, cold water only, some rm have no window, arrive early and inspect rm first: *India*, *Seashore* and *Gateway Guest Houses*. *Volga*, above Citywalk Shoes, Colaba Causeway, simple but acceptable.

Paying Guest accommodation Contact Govt of India Tourist Office, 123 M Karve Rd, T 293144.

● **Places to eat**

Recommended restaurants outside hotels are marked with an *. Buffet Lunches at the bigger hotels are good value. Usually about Rs 100-200 excluding beverages.

Airport & beach restaurants

Continental & Indian: *Green House*, Rao Apt, Nehru Rd, Vile Parle (E), restaurant and bar, good value; *Oasis*, Andheri W, modern, good value; *Patio*, Vile Parle (W), modern, rec.

Mughlai & Tandoori: *Manjit da Dhaba**, corner of W and Main Ave, opp Grindlays Bank, Linking Rd, Santa Cruz, simple atmosphere – eating around a mango tree on rush seats round simple wooden tables, emphasis on authentic North Indian food, many dishes served in *handis*, quite expensive, reservations essential, popular with the young; *Daavat**, 21-25 Natasha Shopping Centre, 52 Hill Rd, Bandra, nr *Searock Hotel*, look for small sign on dark door, marble floor and pleasant garden, authentic traditional North Indian food, quite expensive; *Gazebo*, Bandra; *Sheetal Samudra**, 648 Khar Pali Rd, excellent sea-food esp tandoori crab; *Sheetal Bukhara*, on same Rd, nr Khar Telephone Exch, has good kebabs.

Goan: *St Mary Hotel**, 120 St Mary Rd, Mazgaon, T 868475, small inexpensive upstairs restaurant, chutney fish fry and beef tongue, specialities; *Goa Portuguesa*, is one of the newer ethnic restaurants, it brings authentic dishes to a comfortable restaurant where you can try *sungto* (prawn) served between *papads*, *kalwa* (oyster), *teesryo* (shell) and clams and to end the meal *bibinca*, lobsters cooked with tomatoes, onions and spices. Others are *O Balcao* and *Saayba**, Bhatiya Bldg, opp Bandra Masjid, SV Rd, mainly seafood, closed Mon; *Woodland's Garden Café**, Juhu Scheme, Vaikuntial.

In town

Chinese: Some close for 3 days over Chinese New Year. *China Garden**, 123 August Kranti

Marg, bar, interesting, imaginative menu, incl Thai and Japanese, reasonably expensive, service can be slow; ***Chinatown***, 99 August Kranti Marg, Kemps Corner, upstairs more comfortable, Szechwan, Cantonese and Mandarin dishes, 27 soups to choose from; ***Chinese Palace***, Tardeo A/c Market; ***Chopsticks****, 354 Vithal Bhai Patel Rd (Linking Rd), W Bombay, mainly Cantonese, some tables in garden, generous helpings; ***Chopsticks****, 90 A Vir Nariman Rd, Churchgate, good food, moderately priced, offering unusual dishes, eg taro nest, date pancakes and toffee bananas, other branches at Jewel Mahal A/c Shopping Complex and 7 Bungalows, Versova; ***Flora***, Worli Seaface, A Gaffar Khan Rd, nr *Hilltop Hotel*, over 200 dishes; ***Golden Gate***, Madam Cama Rd; ***Kamling****, 82 Vir Nariman Rd, Cantonese, simple and good, often busy, wide selection of ice creams; ***Ling's Garden****, 19/21 KC College Hostel Bldg, Landsdowne Rd, behind Regal Cinema, new, with stylish decor, good atmosphere and delightful service, colourful menu, generous helpings, highly rec; ***Mandarin****, Dhanraj Mahal, Sivaji Maharaj Marg, Apollo Bunder, excellent food and service (also cold beer), rec; ***Nanking****, Apollo Bunder, nr Gateway of India, good choice of very good Cantonese dishes, expensive, fish ball soup, Pomfret Nanking, pickled fish and beef with watercress.

Continental & Indian: most are open daily, 1230-1500, 2000-2400. ***Delhi Durbar****, Holland House, S Bhagat Singh Marg, Colaba, also in Falkland Rd, good and cheap; ***Gaylord***, Vir Nariman Rd, Churchgate, tables inside and out, with barbecue, pleasant, good bar; ***Talk of the Town***, 143 Netaji Subhash Rd, mainly continental, also Indian dishes, band nightly for dancing except Mon, pleasant outdoor cafe for coffee and snacks, 1100-2400; ***George***, 20 Apollo St, Fort (nr Horniman Circle), pleasant quiet atmosphere, faded colonial feel, good service, lunchtime *biriyanis* and *thalis* good value.

Mughlai & Tandoori: ***Khyber****, Kala Ghoda, Fort, for an enjoyable evening in beautiful surroundings (paintings by Hussain and AE Menon), excellent food, especialy lobster and *reshmi* chicken kebabs, try *paya* soup (goat's trotters!); ***Balwas***, Maker Bhavan, 3 Thackersey Marg, New Marine Lines, inexpensive, well-prepared food; ***Berry's***, Vir Nariman Rd, nr Churchgate Station, Tandoori specialities, good *kulfi**, reasonable prices; ***Copper Chimney****, Annie Besant Rd, Worli, window into kitchen, very good food, from extensive menu, reasonable prices; ***Copper Chimney****, K Dubhash Marg, behind Prince of Wales Bldg (different management), subdued lighting and quietly tasteful, good N Indian dishes, kitchen visible; ***Delhi Durbar****, 197 Falkland Rd, nr Regal, good biryanis; ***Gulshan****, Palton Rd, Crawford Market, downstairs for men, popular for breakfasts; ***Kabab Corner****, *Natraj Hotel*, kebabs a speciality; ***Kwality***, has branches at 252C, Dr Annie Besant Rd, India House, Kemps Corner, and Worli.

Indian & Continental – Medium priced: ***Santoor***, Maker Arcade, Cuffe Parade, nr *President Hotel*, small, mughlai and Kashmiri specialities, chicken *malai* chop (with cream), *chana* peshawari (*puri* with chickpeas), Kashmiri soda made with salt and pepper rec; ***Sapna***, Vir Nariman Rd, very traditional Mughlai delicacies, bar, some tables outside, attentive service, good value; ***Sher-e Punjab****, 389 B Dr DB Marg (Lamington Rd), wide choice of Tandoori, Mughlai and Continental dishes, pleasant, also at 261/4 S Bhagat Singh Marg, good food in simple surroundings, try *makai ki roti*, *saag* and *tandoori* chicken; ***Yogi*** 403 KST Rd, Chembur; ***Vaishali***, Govandi Rd (1st Flr), opp rly station, Chembur.

Goan: ***Martin's****, 21 Glamour House, Strand Rd, Colaba for simple, inexpensive, authentic food, excellent sea food and pork Sorpotel, very busy; ***Trishna***, with bar, behind Kala Ghoda, next to Old Synagogue, good seafood, particularly crab; ***City Kitchen***, 301 S Bhagat Singh Marg, Fort Market, closed Sun.

Gujarati & Western Indian: ***The Village***, Poonam Intercontinental, nr Mahalaxmi racecourse in 'Gujarati village' setting, sea views, good food, for authentic Maharashtrian; *Sindhudurg*, RK Vaidya Rd, Dadar, try seafood *thali* and fish fry; ***Rajdhani****, nr Crawford Market; ***Chetna****, 34K Dubash Marg, opp Jahangir Art Gallery, veg dishes; ***Thacker's****, corner M Karve Rd and 1st Marine St, good *thalis*. Home cooked specialities at ***Thaili****, Tara Baug Estate, Charni Rd.

Parsi: see 'Cuisine' in **Introduction to Maharashtra** below. ***Piccolo Café****, 11A Sir Homi Mody St, 0900-1800, closed Sat pm and Sun, profits to charity, homely, clean, good *dhansak*; ***Landmark***, 35 S Patkar Marg, also run by Ratan Tata Institute but the latter is a fully fledged restaurant, closed Mon, Parsi and Continental, try kid *gosht* cooked with cashew nuts in coconut milk or the vegetarian stew *lagasara*. Takeaway shop next door. Another is ***Bombay A1****, 7 Proctor Rd (Grant Rd Junc), cheerful, varied cuisine, incl *Patrani machli*. Two family-run restaurants are also rec – ***Britannia and Goa****, Wakefield House, Sprott Rd, Ballard Estate and ***Paradise****, Sindh Chambers, Colaba Causeway (closed Mon), (not a/c) excellent dhansak but also serves other cuisines, spotless. On MG Rd (N end), you can have a good traditional breakfast, often as early as 0600 at ***Bastani***, ***Kyani*** or the ***Sassanian Restaurant***.

South Indian: *New Indian Coffee Shop*, Kittridge Rd, Sassoon Dock, good Kerala breakfast; ***Woodlands****, Mittal Chambers, Nariman Pt, nr *Oberoi Towers*, closed Sun, excellent *idli* and *dosai* and good *thalis*, busy at lunchtime; ***Kamat****, Electric House, S Bhagat Singh Marg (Ormiston Rd corner), very inexpensive *thalis* and veg snacks.

Vegetarian: *Landmark*, S Patkar Marg; ***Kamats Restaurant****, Navrose Mansion, Tardeo Rd; ***Dasaprakash***, at Bristol Grill, Sir PM Rd (S Indian Buffet); ***Purohit****, Vir Nariman Rd, excellent *thalis*, also Parsi; ***Rasna****, Churchgate Reclamation, J Tata Rd, closed Sun; ***Samarambh***, by BEST House, S Bhagat Singh Marg, good *thalis*, *chola battura*, a *puri* topped with spiced chickpeas; ***Samrat****, Prem Court, J Tata Rd, Churchgate, large Gujarati *thalis*; ***Satkar***, Indian Express Bldg, Churchgate, delicious, a/c section more expensive; ***West Coast****, Rustom Siduha Rd, around the corner from Strand Bookshop off Sir PM Rd for very good, cheap meals; ***Woodlands***, Nariman Pt, Madras style *thalis*.

Out of town: *Revival**, Chowpatty Sea Face, classy, slightly expensive, good buffets and desserts, ice cream, rec.

Fast food

Pizzas & Burgers: *Gazebo Open House*, 537 VB Patel Rd (Linking Rd), burgers, pizzas, confectionery and ice creams, also branch at Vir Nariman Rd, opp Churchgate station; ***New Yorker***, 25 Chowpatty Sea Face, pizzas, sandwiches and Mexican fast food, ice cream; ***Pizza King***, Nylor House, 245 Dr Annie Besant Rd, Worli and 6 Tirupati Shopping Centre, Warden Rd; ***Waikiki***, 16 Murzban Rd, clean and cheerful, burgers and ice creams. Others at ***Kobe Sizzlers,*** Hughes Rd nr Sukh Sagar and ***Sundance Café***, Eros Bldg, Churchgate (also Mexican and Continental food); ***Akbarally's Snack Bar***, Vir Nariman Rd.

Indian Snacks: *Indian Fast Food,* Vithal Bhai Patel (Linking) Rd, opp the National College; ***Swaati,*** Tardeo Rd for clean bhelpuri and chaats; ***Fountain Dry Fruit Stall,*** Flora Fountain, *badami* (rich almond collection), *pedah* (milk and sugar sweet) and nuts; ***Rasna***, nr KC College, Churchgate, Indian, Chinese and vegetarian snacks, garden cafe, packed lunches; ***Chimney Restaurant and Bar***, Filka Bldg, Daftary Rd nr E Bombay Rly Station, also does snacks and packed lunches. Behind *Taj Mahal Hotel*, ***Sheekh Kabab Stall**** on Tulloch Rd, does excellent Muslim snacks, opens 1900.

24-Hr Coffee Shops: in all the biggest hotels.

● Bars

All major hotels and restaurants have bars; others may only serve beer. The *Ambassador* has excellent all-round views, as do the *Taj* and *Oberoi* hotels, but at a price. Beer at the ***Naaz Café***, Hanging Gardens on Malabar Hill (burnt down in Dec 92, awaits restoration) or the small Irani restaurants in Churchgate or Fort.

Pubs and Cafés are the craze: ***Leopold's***, Colaba is full of young backpackers who throng here for good value meals (large portions), a wide choice of dishes and beverages, and friendship; ***The Tavern***, *Hotel Fariyas*; ***Rasna***, Churchgate (J Tata Rd) and ***Gokul's***, Apollo Bunder, behind *Taj* are all more bars and pubs.

Out of Town: *Prithvi Theatre*, Juhu, has open-air bar (sells snacks) with pleasant atmosphere.

Entertainment & shopping

● Art Galleries

Commercially run art galleries that have works for sale: ***Taj Art Gallery***, *Taj Mahal Hotel*; ***Centaur Art Gallery***, *Hotel Centaur*, ***Pundole Art Gallery***, Hutatma Chowk; ***JJ Art Gallery,*** Dadabhai Naoroji Rd; ***Aakar*** and ***Cymroza Art Galleries***, Bhulabhai Desai Rd.

● Clubs

Bombay Gymkhana Club, M Gandhi Rd. **Cricket Club of India,** Brabourne Stadium, Dinshaw Wacha Rd, temp membership for 15 days, contact Secretary, affiliated clubs are the Royal Overseas League, London and the Caledonian Club, Edinburgh, cricket, badminton, tennis, pool, squash, table tennis and cards, central with large and pleasant grounds. **Royal Bombay Yacht Club,** Apollo Bunder, temp membership for 10 days, contact Secretary, library, billiards, table tennis, pleasant garden. **Willingdon Club**, Haji Ali Rd.

● Entertainment

Many hotels have local information.

Discotheques: Hotels are open to non-residents who have to pay for admission. Residents often pay a nominal fee. Typically drinks are quite expensive.

Theatres: Western India has a strong creative tradition much like that in W Bengal. Plays are performed in English, Hindi, Marathi and Gujarati. Performances usually begin at 1815-1900. Check *Bombay* or *This Fortnight* for details.

● Shopping

Most shops are open 1000-1900 weekdays; the bazars sometimes staying open as late as 2100. Best buys in Bombay are textiles, particularly tie and dye from Gujarat, hand-block printed cottons, Aurangabad and 'Patola' silks, and gold bordered saris from Surat and Khambat. Wood carving, brass ware and handicrafts of all kinds make good gifts. Jewellery and leather goods also attract the Western shopper. The hotel arcade shops often stock a good selection of high quality goods but prices are usually higher than you would pay elsewhere in the city.

Specialist shops

Bazars: *Crawford Market*, MR Ambedkar Rd (fun for bargain hunting). Other shopping streets are S Bhagat Singh Marg, Mangaldas Market, M Karve Rd and Linking Rd, Bandra. For a different experience try *Chor (Thieves') Bazar*, on Maulana Shaukat Ali Rd in central Bombay, full of finds – from Raj left-overs to precious jewellery. Some claim that the infamous name is unjustified since the original was 'Shor' (noisy) bazar! On Fridays 'junk' carts sell less expensive 'antiques' and fakes. *Phillips Antiques*, Indian Merchants Mansions, Madame Cama Rd opp Regal Cinema is an Aladdin's Cave of bric-a-brac and curios.

Books: the bookshop at the Domestic terminal of the airport (not the shop near the entrance) is very good and cheap. *Nalanda* in the *Taj Mahal Hotel* is one of the best for art books. The *Oberoi* bookshop charges higher prices. *New Secondhand* Bookstore, Kalbadevi and *Strand Books*, off PM Rd nr HMV have an excellent selection. Will also arrange shipping (reliable), and offer 20% discount on airfreight. *Bharatiya Vidya Bhavan*, Chowpatty.

For **Antiquarian** books and prints try *Jimmy Ollia*, Cumballa Chambers (1st Flr), Cumballa Hill Rd. Along Churchgate St and nr the University are lines of second-hand book stalls. Religious books at *Chetna* Restaurant, 34K Dubash Rd, Rampart Row.

Clothes for men: *Cotton World*, Colaba and *Raymonds*, Warden Rd (also tailoring) are rec.

Silks & Saris: *Kala Niketan*, MG Rd and Juhu Reclamation and *Sheetal*, Grant Rd and *Vama*, in Kanchenjunga (Peddar Rd, next to Kemp's Corner). Tailoring possible.

Western: Warden Rd, Dr Dadabhai Naoroji Rd ("Dr DN Rd"), Colaba Causeway shops starting nr the *Taj Mahal Hotel*. Cheapest at Fashion St opp Bombay Gymkhana, Shahid Bhagat Singh Marg, but check quality (often export surplus) and bargain vigorously.

Government emporia: all good for handicrafts and textiles at fixed prices. Most representative of the region is *Gurjari*, 27 Khaitan Bhavan, JN Tata Rd, particularly good for textiles, furnishings, wood carving and brassware. *Central Cottage Industries Emporium*, Apollo Bunder, represents a nationwide selection, especially Kashmiri embroidery, South Indian handicrafts and Rajasthani textiles; *Handloom House*, Dr DN Rd; *Bihar Emporium*, Dhun Nur, Sir PM Rd; *Kairali*, Nirmal, Nariman Pt; *Kashmir Govt Arts Emporium*, Co-op Insurance Bldg, Sir PM Rd; *Purbashree*, Khira Bhavan, Sandhurst Bridge; *UP Emporium*, Sir PM Rd for silks, cottons and brocades; *Black Partridge* (Haryana), Air India Bldg, Nariman Pt; *Gangotri* (UP), *Mrignayanee* (MP) and *Phulkari*, *Shikha* and *Trimurti* (Maharashtra) are all at World Trade Centre, Cuffe Parade. *Khadi and Village Industries*, D Naoroji Rd.

Jewellery: you can buy **silver** by weight at the *silver bazar*, Mumbadevi and gold jewellery at *Zaveri Bazar*.

Leather: try *Dhaboo St bazar* for bargains, or pay higher prices at arcade shops in top hotels. *Oberoi* shopping centre will make you a jacket in 1-2 days. 'Bhendi Bazar' (ask taxi driver) for good quality and wide selection at a fraction of the price. *Rasulbhai Adamji*, Colaba Causeway, behind *Taj* has excellent handbags, cases, wallets.

For **shoes**: *Oberoi* Centre and Colaba Causeway. Out of town, Linking Rd, Khar has several *Metro*, rec.

Musical instruments: Govt approved shops are *RS Mayeka* at No 386, *Haribhai Vishwanath* at No 419 and *Ram Singh* at Bharati Sadan, all on Sardar V Patel Rd.

Photography: several in Dr DN Rd. Films available in big hotels.

● **Sports**

Cricket: *Bombay Cricket Association*, Wankhede Stadium, Churchgate.

Cycling: *National Sports Club*, Lajpatrai Marg.

Golf: *Bombay Presidency Golf Club*, Chembur.

Gymnasia: *Talwakars Gymnasium Club*, Charni Rd; *Talwakars Gymnasium*, Gohil House, Jamshetji Rd, T 457548.

Hockey: *Bombay Hockey Association*, Charni Rd.

Horse racing: the Mahalaxmi Race Course, opp Haji Ali, season Nov-Mar, Sun and Public holidays, 1400-1700. The course is delightful and many of India's top races are held here, including the Derby in Feb/Mar. The original Bombay race course was established at Byculla in 1800. The Mahalaxmi course was opened in 1878. Bombay used to be famous for horse trading, especially Arab horses but was banned in 1948 thus encouraging the development of a local breeding industry. India today has around 80 studs.

Squash: *Cricket Club of India*, Brabourne Stadium, Dinshaw Wacha Rd, also billiards, snooker and badminton.

Tennis: *Maharashtra State Lawn Tennis Association*, Cooper, Colaba.

Yoga: *The Yoga Institute*, Praghat Colony, Santa Cruz East; *Yoga Training Centre*, 51 Jai hind Club, Juhu Scheme; *Yoga Vidhya Niketan*, Sane Guruji Marg, Dadar.

Services

● **Airline offices**

Santa Cruz Airport, T 6144433. Sahar Airport, enquiries, T 6329090, 6329293.

Domestic: **Damania Airways**, 17 Nehru Rd, Vakela, St Cruz E, T 6102525, F 6102544, Airport T 6102454. **East West Airlines**, T 2620646, F 2617320. **Indian Airlines**, Air India Bldg, Nariman Pt, Enquiries, T 2023131, Reservations, T 2023031, Airport T 6144433. **Modiluft**, T 3631921.

International **Air India**, Air India Bldg, 1st Flr, Nariman Pt (Counters also at Taj Mahal Hotel, Centaur Hotel and Santa Cruz), T 2024142, Airport T 6329090. **Aeroflot**, 241-2, Nirmal Bldg, Nariman Pt, T 221743, Airport T 6320178. **Air Canada**, Oberoi Towers Hotel, Nariman Pt, T 2021111, Airport T 6435653. **Air France**, Taj Mahal Hotel, Apollo Bunder, T 2025021, Airport T 6328070. **Air Lanka**, Mittal Towers, C Wing, Nariman Pt, T 223288, Airport T 6322829, 6327050. **Air Mauritius**, Air India Bldg, Nariman Pt, T 2028474, Airport T 6366767. **Alitalia**, Dalamal House, 206 Nariman Pt, T 223112, Airport T 6329082. **Al Yemda**, F-99, Shopping Arcade, 2nd Flr Oberoi Towers Hotel, Nariman Pt, T 2024229, Airport T 6320700 Ext 522. **Bangladesh Biman**, Airlines Hotel, 199 J Tata Rd, Churchgate, T 224580, Airport T 6366700 Ext 524. **British Airways**, 202-B Vir Nariman Rd, T 220888, Airport T 6329061. **Canadian Pacific**, 15 World Trade Centre, T 2185207, Airport T 6321965. **Continental**, **Eastern**, **Iberia** and **MAS**, STIC Travel & Tours, 6 Maker Arcade, Cuffe Parade, T 2181431. **Delta**, Taj Mahal Hotel, T 6324769. **Egypt Air**, Oriental House, 7 J Tata Rd, T 224580. **Emirates Airlines**, T 2871649. **Gulf Air**, Maker Chambers, 5 Nariman Point, T 2021626.

JAL, No 3 Raheja Centre, Nariman Pt, T 233136. **KLM**, 198 JN Tata Rd, Khaitan Bhavan, T 221372. **Lufthansa**, Express Towers, Nariman Pt, T 2023430, Airport T 6321485. **PIA**, Oberoi Towers Hotel, Nariman Pt, T 2021480, Airport T 6300328. **Philippines Airlines**, 199 J Tata Rd, Churchgate, T 224580. **Qantas**, 42 Sakhar Bhavan, Nariman Pt, T 2029297, Airport T 6127219. **Royal Jordanian**, 199 J Tata Rd, T 224580. **Sabena**, Nirmal Bldg, Nariman Pt, T 2022724, Airport T 6348847. **Saudia**, Express Towers, Nariman Pt, T 2020199, Airport T 6323126. **SAS**, 15 World Trade Centre, Cuffe Parade, T 215207. **Singapore Airlines**, Air India Bldg, Nariman Pt, T 2023835, Airport T 6327861. **Swissair**, Maker Chambers, 220 Nariman Pt, T 222402, Airport, 6326084. **Thai Airways**, 15 World Trade Centre, Cuffe Parade, T 215207.

● **Banks & money changers**

Most are open 1000-1400, Mon-Fri and 1000-1200, Sat. Closed on National holidays, 30 Jun and 31 Dec. Best to change money at the airport and in Air India Bldg, Nariman Pt. **Thomas Cook** can be slow.

American Express, Dr DN Rd. **Bank of America**, Express Towers, Nariman Pt. **Bank of Tokyo**, Jeevan Prakesh, PM Rd. **Banque Nationale de Paris**, 62 Homji St. **Barclays**, Maker Tower F, Cuffe Parade. **Chartered Bank**, 25 MG Rd. **Citibank**, 239 Dr DN Rd. **Grindlays**, MG Rd. **Hongkong and Shanghai**, 52 MG Rd.

State Bank of India, Bombay Samachar Marg (at *Centaur Airport Hotel* until 2200) and

Churchgate, behind India Tourist Office, among others. **Reserve Bank of India**, Foreign Exchange Dept, New Central Office Bldg, S Bhagat Singh Marg. **ABN Bank**, 19 Vir Nariman Rd. **Andhra Bank**, 18 Homi Modi St, Fort. Bank of India, Express Towers, Nariman Pt. **Union Bank of India**, 239 Backbay Reclamation, Nariman Pt.

Credit Cards: **American Express**, Majithia Chambers, 276 Dr DN Rd. **Diners Club**, Raheka Chambers, 213 Nariman Pt. **Mastercard**, Bank of America, Express Towers. **VISA**, ANZ Grindlays Bank, 90 MG Rd.

● Chambers of Commerce

Bombay Chamber of Commerce and Industry, Mackinnon Mackenzie Bldg, 4 Shoorji Vallabhdas Marg, Ballard Estate, T 2614681. **Maharashtra Chamber of Commerce**, Oricon House, 6th Flr, 12K Dubash Marg, Fort, T 244548.

● Deputy High Commissions & Consulates

Australia, Maker Tower E, 16th Flr, Cuffe Parade, T 2181071. **Austria**, Taj Bldg, Dr DN Rd, T 2042044. **Belgium**, Morena, 11 Dahanukar Marg, T 4939261. **Russia**, 42 L Jagmohandas Marg, T 8223627. **Egypt**, 12/B Maker Tower, 1st Flr, Cuffe Parade, T 2182425. **France**, Datta Prasad, NG Cross Rd, T 4949808; **Germany**, 10th Flr, Hoechst House, Nariman Pt, T 232422. **Indonesia**, Lincoln Annexe, S Barodawala Marg, T 368678. **Italy**, Vaswani Mansion, D Wachha Rd, T 222192. **Japan**, 1 ML Dahanukar Marg, T 4933857. **Netherlands**, The International, 16 M Karve Rd, T 242042. **Philippines**, Industry House, J Tata Rd, T 2026340. **Spain**, 6 K Dubash Marg, T 244644. **Sweden**, Indian Mercantile Chambers, R Kamani Marg, T 2612583. **Switzerland**, 90 Vir Nariman Rd, Churchgate, T 2043550. **UK**, 2nd Flr, Mercantile Bank Bldg, MG Rd, T 274874. **USA**, Lincoln House, Bhulabhai Desai Rd, T 8223611. **Yugoslavia**, Vaswani Mansion, D Wachha Rd, T 222050. Others can be obtained from the Bombay telephone directory.

● Hospitals & medical services

The larger hotels usually have a house doctor, the others invariably have a doctor on call. Ask hotel staff for prompt action. The telephone directory lists hospitals and General Practitioners.

Chemists: several around the city. *Kemps, Taj Mahal Hotel*, Apollo Bunder open until late. *Wordell*, Stadium House, Churchgate; *New Royal*, New Marine Lines; *Dilip*, *Nanavati Hospital*, Vile Parle (W); *Gohil*, Vile Parle (E); *Badri*, Khara Tank Rd; *National*, Sarvakar Rd, Mahim; *Navjivan*, Malad.

● Post & telecommunications

Usually open 1000-1700. Sahar Airport 24 hr. Post offices all over the city and most 5 star hotels.

GPO: Nagar Chowk. Mon-Sat, 0800-2000 (*Poste Restante* facilities 0800-1800) and Sun 1000-1730.

Central telegraph office: Hutatma Chowk, Churchgate PO, 'A' Rd. Colaba PO, Colaba Bus Station and also at Mandlik Rd, behind *Taj Mahal Hotel*. Foreign PO, Ballard Pier. Counter at Santa Cruz.

Couriers: *EMS Speedboat*, GPO, T 2621671; *DHL*, Maker Chambers V, Nariman Pt, T 2044055; *Skypak*, Marol, Andheri E, T 6368181. *Infotek*, Express Towers, Nariman Pt, 223092 have international phone, fax, telex and other business services under one roof.

● Places of worship

Buddhist: Temple at Worli.

Christian Roman Catholic: *Pro Cathedral*, N Parekh Marg, Colaba.

Hindu: *Walkeshwar*, Malabar Hill; *Laxmi Naryan Temple*, Madhav Devi.

Jewish: *Knesseth Ellyahoo*, Fort; *Magen David*, Byculla; *Magen Hasidim*, Abdul Hamid Ansari Marg, nr Jacob Circle; *Tifereth Israel*, Clerk Rd, nr Jacob Circle.

Muslim: *Jama Masjid*, Mahatma Phule Rd; *Zakaria Masjid*, Zakaria St.

Parsi: Anjuman, Banaji, Wadiaji Fire Temples.

Protestant: *St Thomas' Cathedral*; *All Saints Church*, Malabar Hill; *St John's (Afghan Memorial)* Colaba.

Sikh: *Guru Govind Singh Sabha*, Kalbadevi; Dadar Gurudwara.

● Shipping offices

Mughal Lines, Shipping House, N Cama Rd, T 234861. **Anchor Line**, Neville House, JN Heredia Marg, Ballard Estate, T 262294. **British India Steam Navigation**, 4 Vallabhas Marg, T 268021. **Forbes Campbell**, Forbes Bldg, Charanjit Rai Marg, T 2048081. **P&O**, c/o Mackinnon Mackenzie, 4 Ballard Estate, T 268081. **Patel Volkart India**, Volkart Bldg, 19 JN Heredia Marg, T 266751. **Scindia Steam Navigation**, Scindia House, Ballard Estate, T 268161. **Shipping Corp of India**, Shipping

House, Madame Cama Rd, T 2026666. **United Liner Agencies**, Mahindra Spicer Bldg, JN Heredia Marg, T 266451.

● Tour companies & travel agents

Some well established agents: ***American Express***, Majithia Chamber, 276 Dr DN Rd, T 2048949; ***Cox and Kings***, PO Box 398, Grindlays Bank Bldg, Dr DN Rd, T 2043065; ***Everett***,1 Regent Chambers, Nariman Pt, T 245339; ***Mercury***, 70VB Gandhi Rd, T 273275; ***Sita***, 8 Atlanta, Nariman Pt, T 233155; ***Thomas Cook***, Cooks Bldg, Dr DN Rd, T 258556, which has opened its domestic tours division *India Alive*; ***Trade Wings***, 30 K Dubash Marg, T 2043434; ***Space Travels***, 4th Flr, Sir PM Rd, T 2864773, offer discounted flights and special offers for students, Mon-Fri, 1000-1700, Sat 1030-1500; ***Orient Express***, 359 Dr DN Rd, T 2871047; ***Raj Travels***, 27 Panchratna, Mama Parmanand Marg, Opera House, T 8117000; ***Trans Travel***, 4 Jain Chambers, 557 SV Rd, Bandra, T 6425411; ***Travel Corp***, Chandermukhi, 1st Flr, Nariman Pt, T 2021881.

● Tourist offices

Govt of India, 123 M Karve Rd, T 293144, Mon-Sat 0830-1730 (closed every 2nd Sat of month from 1230). Counters open 24 hr at Sahar and Santa Cruz airports, and at the *Taj Mahal Hotel*, Mon-Sat 0830-1530 (closed every 2nd Sat from 1230). Helpful staff who can also issue Liquor Permits (essential for Gujarat). **Maharashtra Tourism**: CDO Hutments, opp LIC Bldg, Madam Cama Rd, T 2026713; Express Towers, 9th Flr, Nariman Pt, T 2024482. **Gujarat**, Dhanraj Mahal, C Sivaji Rd, T 243886. **Goa, Daman and Diu Counter**, Bombay Central Station, T 396288. **Rajasthan**, 230 Dr DN Rd, T 267162. **Madhya Pradesh**, 74 World Centre, Cuffe Parade, Colaba, T 214860 Ext 299. **Maharashtra Tourism**, Information and Booking counters: counters at international and domestic terminals. Also: opp LIC Building, Madam Cama Rd, T 2026713; Koh i Noor Rd, nr Pritam Hotel, Dadar T 4143200; VT Rly Station, T 262 2859; Chhatrapati Sivaji Marg, Gateway of India, T 241877.

● Useful Addresses

Police Emergency: T 100. **Fire**: T 101. **Ambulance**: T 102. **Foreigners' Regional Registration Office**: Annex 2, Police Commissioner's Office, Dadabhai Naoroji Rd, nr Phule Market, T 268111. **Passport Emigration Office**: T 4931731.

Transport

Bombay is connected by good motorable roads to all major regional tourist and business centres: **Pune** (163 km), **Mahabaleswar** (239 km), **Aurangabad** (392 km), **Vadodara** (432 km), **Ahmadabad** (597 km), **Panaji** (Goa – 597 km), **Hyderabad** (711 km), **Bangalore** (998 km), **Madras** (1367 km), **Delhi** (1460 km), **Calcutta** (2081 km).

Travel Times for trains and planes are published each Sat in the *Indian Express* newspaper.

Local transport

Taxis (yellow top): easily available. Metered charge about Rs 4 for first 1.6 km, additional fare as per revised tariff card carried by driver. Much more in times of trouble. By Sep 1993 half the taxis will be using Compressed Natural Gas, an environment friendly substitute fuel which is cheaper and will lower the tariff!

Private car hire: min for 8 hr or 80 km: Luxury cars, a/c Rs 800, non a/c, Rs 600; Ambassador: A/c Rs 600, non a/c, Rs 400. **Makson Auto Hirers**, Sagar Kunj, L Jagmohandas Marg, T 8121701; **Auto Comforts**, T 4936581; **Bhuta Travels**, Nagardas Park, Old Nagardas Rd, Andheri (E), T 6325334; **Blaze**, Eucharistic Congress Bldg, No 2, 3rd Flr, Colaba, T 2020073; **Budget**, T 4942644 and **Hertz** cars, with or without drivers. **Wheels**, T 4948168.

Auto-rickshaws: not available in central area. Metered charge about Rs 2.50 for first 1.6 km, revised tariff card held by the driver. **Victorias** (Horse drawn carriages), available at Bombay Central, Chowpatty and Gateway of India. Rates negotiable.

Buses: Bombay Electrical Supply Co (BEST) buses are available in most parts of Greater Bombay. Special buses operating within the Central Business Dist are marked 'CBD'. Maharashtra Tourism have introduced Holiday **Caravans** with driver, T 2024627, Re 1/km/person.

Trains: suburban electric trains are economical. Trains start from Churchgate for the W suburbs and Victoria Terminus for the E suburbs. They are often desperately crowded. Trains leaving central Bombay often have seats at the terminus but fill up at the next 3 or 4 stops.

NB: Avoid the rush hr, and keep a tight hold on valuables. The difference between 1st and 2nd class is not always obvious although 1st class is more than 10 times as expensive. Inspectors fine people for travelling in the wrong class. Note the class on the side of the compartment.

Air The airport is 26 km from central Bombay. Allow an hour by taxi. **NB**: At peak traffic hours it can take much longer. **Indian Airlines**, Air India Bldg, Nariman Pt, T 2021441, 2021626. **Transport to & from the airport**: EATS (Ex-servicemen's) bus connects both domestic (Santa Cruz), Rs 30, and international (Sahar), Rs 35, terminals with the city. Drop-off and pick-up points in town are Air India and Indian Airlines offices, *Taj Mahal Hotel* and Prince of Wales Museum. From the city, the bus starts from Air India, Nariman Pt, from 0400 to 0100. **Prepaid taxis** into town best, from counter at the international terminal. Retain your receipt as the driver requires this at the end of the journey. Small additional charges for luggage. To Nariman Pt, about Rs 120.

Indian Airlines: **International connections**: Karachi (1½ hr). **Domestic Ahmadabad**: 0545 and 1800, 1 hr; **Aurgangabad**: daily, 0725, ¾ hr; **Bangalore**: daily, 0715, 1400, 1730, 1½ hr; **Bhavnagar**: M,Tu,Th,Su, 1150, 1 hr; **Bhopal** (via Indore): daily, 0550, 2¼ hr; **Bhuj**: W,F,Sa, 1150, 2 hr; **Calcutta**: daily, 0540, 1600, 2¼ hr; **Kozhikode**: daily, 1440, 1 hr 40 mins; **Kochi**: daily, 0650, 1½ hr; **Delhi**: daily, 0615, 0910, 1700, 1900, 2035, and others; **Goa**: daily, 1230, 1 hr; **Gwalior**: W,F,Su, 0550, 3½ hr; **Hyderabad**: daily, 0855, 1335, 1815, 1¼ hr; **Jaipur**: daily, 0725, 1715, 3½ hr; **Jamnagar**: M,Tu,Th,Su, 1440, 1 hr; **Jodhpur**: daily 1715, 2½ hr; **Lucknow**: M,Tu,Th,Sa, 0700, 3¾ hr; **Madras**: daily, 0900 and 1315, 1¾ hr, and 1 other; **Mangalore**: daily, 0610, 1¼ hr; **Nagpur**: daily, 1850, 1¼ hr; **Rajkot**: W,F,Sa, 1150, 1 hr; **Tiruvananthapuram**: daily, 1210, 2 hr; **Udaipur**: daily, 0725, 1715, 2½ hr; **Vadodara**: daily, 1500, 1 hr; Varanasi, M,Tu,Th,Sa, 0700, 2 hr.

Damania Airlines: flies daily to **Bangalore**: 0630, except Su, 1800; **Calcutta**: 0600, except Su, 1700, 2½ hr; **Goa**, 1530; **Indore**: except Su, 1045, 1¼ hr; **Pune**: daily except Su, 0715, 1815, ¾ hr.

East-West Airlines: daily flights to: **Ahamadabad**: 1830; **Aurangabad**: 1600; **Bangalore**: 1730; **Vadodara**: 0630; **Bhavnagar**: 1010; **Calcutta**: (except Su) 0530; **Kozhikode**: 0545, 1010; **Kochi**: 0525, 1000; **Coimbatore**: 0530; **Delhi**: 0600, 1515, 1830; **Goa**: 1500, **Hyderabad**: 0600, 1500; **Jaipur**: 1830, 1½ hr; **Madras**: 0600, 2005; **Madurai**: 0930; **Mangalore**: 1100; **Pune**: 1900; **Rajkot**: 0900; **Tiruvananthapuram**: 0930.

Jet Airways: flies daily to **Ahmadabad**: daily, 0600, 2010 (except Sun); **Kozhikode**: 1000; **Kochi**: 0915; **Coimbatore**: 1310; **Delhi**: 0700, 1750; **Goa**: 1400; **Hyderabad**: 1645; **Madras**: 1715; **Mangalore**: 0925; **Vadodara**: 0630.

Train Bombay is the HQ of the Central and Western Railways. **Enquiries**: Central Rly, T 131/132; Western Rly, T 134/135. **Reservations**: Central Rly, Victoria Terminus, Bori Bunder, T 264321, 0900-1230, 1300-1630; Western Rly, Churchgate, T 291952 and Bombay Central, T 375986; 0800-1345, 1445-2000. All for 1st Class bookings and Indrail Passes. **Foreign tourists**: Tourist Quota counter on mezzanine flr behind Tourist Office opp Churchgate Station (ask for Kamal Singh). Railway Tourist Guides at VT and Churchgate can assist.

NB: The trains included below are generally the fastest available, have daily departures and do not involve changing trains en route. For all trains, book as early as possible. All leave from **Victoria Terminus** (VT) unless stated. VT has TV screens showing availability of seats 3 days in advance. For reservation and travel the same day do not queue in reservation area but buy tickets from booking office, then queue at booth on Platform, 1 hr before departure.

Ahmadabad: *Bombay-Gandhidham Kachchh Exp* (from **Central**) 9031, daily, 1715, 8 hr; *Gujarat Exp* 9011, daily, 0600, 9¼ hr; *Bombay-Ahmedabad Janata Exp* 9007, daily, 1935, 9 hr; *Gujarat Mail* 9001, daily, 2130, 9 hr. **Allahabad**: *Haora Mail* 3004, daily, 2110, 23½ hr; *Mahanagiri Exp* 1093, daily, 2355, 24 hr; *Bombay-Bhagalpur Exp* 3418, Tu,Th,F,Su, 1935, 27¾ hr. **Agra**: *Punjab Mail* 1037, daily, 1615, 23¾ hr. **Aurangabad**: *Jalna Exp* (for Ellora and Ajanta) 1003, daily, 2230, 9 hr. **Bangalore**: *Udyan Exp* 6529, daily, 0755, 24¼ hr. **Kochi**: *Netravati Exp* 2135, Tu,Th,Su, 2015, 35½ hr. **New Delhi**: *Punjab Mail* 1037, daily, 1615, 28 hr; From Bombay Central: *Rajdhani Exp* 2951, daily except M, 1700, 16¼ hr; *Paschim Exp* 2925, daily, 1130, 23 hr; *Frontier Mail* 2903, daily, 2115, 21¾ hr. **Bhopal**: *Punjab Mail* 1037, daily,

1615, 15 hr. **Gorakhpur (for Nepal)**: *Kushi Nagar Exp* 1015, daily, 1120, 33¾ hr. **Guntakal**: (for Hospet) *Madras Mail* 7009, daily 2315, 19¼ hr. **Gwalior**: *Punjab Mail* 1037, daily, 1615, 21¾ hr. **Calcutta (Haora)**: *Gitanjali Exp* 2859, daily, 0605, 32¼ hr; *Haora Exp* 8029, daily, 2130, 41¾ hr; *Calcutta Mail* 8001, daily, 1910, 35¾ hr; *Haora Mail* 3004, daily, 2110, 40 hr. **Lucknow**: *Kushi Nagar Exp* 1015, daily, 1120, 28 hr. **Allahabad**: *Haora Mail* 3004, daily, 2110, 23½ hr; *Mahanagri Exp* 1093, daily, 2355, 24 hr; *Bombay-Varanasi Ratnagiri Exp* 2165, M,W,Th, 0500, 24¼ hr. **Madras Central**: *Bombay-Madras Mail* 7009, daily, 2315, 30½ hr. *Dadar-Madras-Chennai Exp* (from **Dadar**) 6063, daily, 1950, 24 ¼ hr. **Pune**: *Bombay-Madras Mail* 7009, daily, 2315, 4¼ hr; *Udyan Exp* 6529, daily, 0755, 4 hr; *Deccan Queen Exp* 2123, daily, 1710, 3½ hr; *Bombay-Hyderabad Exp* 7031, daily, 1235, 4¼ hr; *Sinhagad Exp* 1009, daily, 1435, 4½ hr. **Ujjain (from Central)**: *Bombay-Indore Exp* 5064, daily, 2000, 12¼ hr. **Secunderabad/Hyderabad**: *Minar Exp* 2101, daily, 2155, 14¼ hr. **Tiruvananthapuram**: *Kanniyakumari Exp* 1081, daily, 1535, 44¾ hr. **Varanasi**: *Mahanagiri Exp* 1093, daily, 2355, 28 hr; *Bombay-Varanasi-Ratnagiri Exp* 2165, M,W,Th, 0500, 27½ hr.

Road Bus: Maharashtra Road Transport Corporation operates bus services to all the major centres and Dist HQs in the state as well as to Ahmedabad, Bangalore, Goa, Mangalore, Indore, Vadodara and Hyderabad in other states. Information on services from MRTC, Central Bus Stand, Bombay Central or Parel Depot. Private buses also travel long distance routes. Some long distance buses also leave from Dadar. Information and tickets from Dadar Tourist Centre, just outside Dadar station, T 4113398. There is a wide range of travel agents at Dadar.

Sea Mughal Lines operates an occasional service between Bombay and Goa, normally suspended during the monsoon season. Check with Mughal Lines, Shipping House, N Cama Rd, T 234861.

Excursions from Bombay

The Hindu caves of Elephanta and the earlier Buddhist caves of Kanheri, are within easy reach. You can also cross the bay to Chaul or go N to the old Portuguese fort of Bassein, and further afield to Bombay's hill station of Matheran (171 km, see page 1172).

Chaul

This group of Moorish and Portuguese forts lie to the S at the mouth of Bombay harbour. On the N side of the creek, it was taken in 1522 by the Portuguese. Although it is similar to Bassein and has a very attractive fort it never equalled it in importance. The Marathas took it in 1739 and in 1818 it passed into British hands.

Little remains of the settlement apart from ruined churches and broken walls. If you look across the creek you will see the hilltop Muslim fort of Korlai. From the New Ferry Wharf it is a 90 min trip to Revas. From there you can take a 30 km bus ride to Chaul and then continue by road to Mahabaleswar or join the Bombay-Pune road.

Cave sites

More than 1,200 cave sites have been discovered across India. The vast majority of these were purpose-built as temples and monasteries. They were still excavated and decorated long after building techniques were developed that allowed substantial and durable structures to be erected on the ground, being excavated over the period from 3rd century BC to the 10th century AD. Jain, Buddhist and Hindu caves often stand side by side in the same rock formation. Although Ajanta and Ellora in Maharashtra are the most highly developed, the Elephanta caves are also well worth visiting.

The setting of the Elephanta caves is symbolically significant; the sea is the ocean of life, a world of change (*Samsara*) in which is set an island of spiritual and physical refuge. The journey to it was also important. In the rough seas of the monsoon it could be both difficult and dangerous. It was therefore a voyage of determination as well as discovery.

Elephanta Caves

The caves are 10 km by boat from the Gateway of India. An earlier name for the island was Gharapuri – city of forts – but the Portuguese re-named it after the colossal sculpted elephants when they captured Bombay from the Sultan of Gujarat in 1535. Attractive but not as splendid as the caves at Ajanta and Ellora. It is an extremely popular day trip for Bombayites so avoid the weekend rush. It is quite a stiff climb of about 125 sloping steps from the old landing place on the S of the island. Today boats normally land in the NW, about 400m from the caves, which are at a height of 75m. Palanquins available. The island is formed of 2 parallel ridges separated by a valley. The highest point is 173m.

NB: Maharashtra Tourism normally organises a festival of classical music and dance on the island in the 3rd week of Feb.

Transport Maharashtra Tourism tour launches with guides leave the Gateway of India, hourly from 0900 until 1400 and lasts 4 hr (journey 1 hr each way). Adult Rs 30, child Rs 20. Not during monsoons (Jun-Sep). Reservations, T 2026384. Small private boats without guides, (adult Rs 25, child Rs 15) continue during the monsoon when the seas can be very rough. The service is sometimes suspended.

The temple cave on Elephanta island, dedicated to Siva, was probably excavated during the 8th century by the Rashtrakuta dynasty which ruled the Deccan from 757 to 973 AD. The Portuguese stationed a batallion on Elephanta who reportedly used the main pillared cave as a shooting gallery. They are also believed to have removed an important stone panel which probably gave more precise information on the cave's excavation and ornamentation. Muslim rulers and the British were not blameless for damage either. The Archaeological Survey of India is doing its best to preserve the site, though most of the caves are damp, moss-covered and full of bats.

The Entrance Originally there were 3 entrances, and 28 pillars, 8 of which have been destroyed or collapsed. The 2 side entrances on the E and W have subsidiary shrines which may have been excavated and used for different ceremonies. The main entrance now is from the N. At dawn the rising sun casts its rays on the approach to the main shrine (*garbha-griha*), housed in a square structure at the W end of the main hall. On your left as you enter is a carving of Siva as Nataraj (see page 77). On the right is a much damaged carving of Siva as **Lakulisa**. Seated on a lotus, the symbol of the unconscious mind and enlightenment, the figure has a Buddha-like feel found also in the Orissan temples where Lakulisa played a prominent role in efforts to bring Buddhists back into Hinduism – see page 724. From the steps at the entrance you can see the *yoni-lingam*, the symbol of the creative power of the deity.

The Main Hall The pillars in the main hall, in a cruciform pattern, have a square base from which rises a thick column topped by a cushion-like capital. Between 5 and 6m high, they have no structural importance. At the corner of each pillar is a dwarf signifying the earth spirit (*gana*). There are also figures of Ganesh, the elephant-headed son of Siva. To the right the main **Linga Shrine** in the *garbha-griha*, 6m square and 1m above the floor of the temple, has 4 entrances, each corresponding to a cardinal point. They represent the threshold from the secular to the spiritual world and guard the idol from external influences. Each doorway is flanked by guardians (*dwarapala*). The best preserved, on the W entrance to the shrine, shows a tall elegant figure with a sacred thread over his left shoulder and a sword at his side. The foot is touched by pilgrims as an act of reverence when they enter the sanctum. In the centre of the shrine is a 1m high smooth lingam. The interior of the sanctum is bare, drawing attention more firmly to the *yoni-lingam* which the devotee must walk around, clockwise. To go the wrong way round is to invite bad luck. The male and female symbols together are in harmony or equilibrium as the creative forces of energy and spirit.

The wall panels To the N of the *garbha-griha* is **Bhairava killing the demon Andhakasura**. This extraordinarily vivid carving shows Siva at his most fearsome, with a necklace of skulls and a skull and cobra on his head, crushing the power of Andhaka, the chief of darkness. It was held that if he was wounded each drop of his blood would create a new demon. So Siva impaled him and collected his blood with a cup which he then offered to his consort Shakti to drink. In winter the best time to see this panel is in the early afternoon as the light plays on it.

Opposite, on the S side of the *garbha-griha* is the badly damaged panel of the **Marriage of Siva and Parvati**. Siva stands with Parvati on his right, a sign that it is their wedding, for normally a Hindu wife stands on her husband's left hand side. She looks demurely at the floor, perhaps out of shyness or merely respect, but her body is inclined or drawn to him. Behind Parvati stands her father Himalaya and to his left is Chandramas, the god of the moon, carrying a pot of *soma*, the food of the gods, as a gift. On Siva's left is Vishnu and below is Brahma, witness and priest respectively.

At the extreme W end of the temple are **Siva as Nataraja** (left) and **Siva as the Yogi** (right). The former shows a beautifully executed figure of Ganesh above and Parvati on his left. All the other gods watch him. Above his right shoulder is the 4 headed god of creation and intellect, Brahma. Below Brahma is the elephant-headed god Ganesh, Siva's son. Opposite by the left shoulder of Siva is Vishnu, the god of preservation. Behind him is Indra who is riding an elephant, and beneath him is Parvati.

On the S wall, opposite the entrance are 3 panels. **The Descent of the Ganga** is on the W. Originally India's holiest river flowed only in heaven but was brought to earth by her father King Bhagiratha (kneeling at Siva's right foot). Some of Bhagiratha's ancestors had disturbed a sage while he was meditating and in anger he destroyed them. The family had tried to have the curse revoked by getting Ganga to flow down from heaven over their bodies. However, Ganga was reluctant to leave heaven until Siva commanded her and the waters were let loose, flooding the plains and destroying land. When she came to Siva at Kailasa mountain, he broke her fall from heaven with his head. Ever since, Ganga is seen flowing from his matted hair. Here, Ganga is shown in the centre and her 2 tributaries, Yamuna and Saraswati on either side. These 3 rivers are believed to meet at Allahabad (see page 281).

To the left of the Descent of the Ganga is the centre piece of the whole temple, the remarkable sculpture of Siva as Lord of the Universe (*Maheshwara*), **the triple headed Siva** (Trimurti). Nearly 6m high, Siva unites all the functions of creation, preservation and destruction. Some have seen the head on the left (your right) as representing Vishnu, while others suggest that it shows a more feminine aspect of Siva and may be that of Uma. To his right is Rudra or Bhairava. He has snakes in his hair, a skull to represent ageing from which only Siva is free, and has a look of anger and vengefulness. The central face is Siva Swarupa, Siva as his true self, balancing out creation and destruction. In this mode he is passive, serene and unperturbed. He radiates peace and wisdom like the Buddha. He wears a tall crown and his right hand is held up in a calming gesture. In his left hand is a lotus bud.

The panel to the left has the 5m tall carving of **Siva as Arddhanarishvara**. This depicts Siva as the embodiment of male and female, representing wholeness and the harmony of opposites. In the rock sculpture the female half is relaxed and gentle, the mirror in the hand symbolising the woman reflecting the man. Siva has his vehicle, Nandi on the right.

To the E, opposite the *garbha-griha* was probably the original entrance. On the N is **Siva and Parvati on Mount Kailash**. Siva is the faceless figure with Parvati on his left. They are shown playing at dice. Parvati has lost and is sulking but her playful husband persuades her to return to the game. They are surrounded by the divine bull Nandi, celestial beings, an attendant carrying a child and an ascetic with his begging bowl.

On the S is **Ravana Shaking Mount Kailash**. **Ravana**, the demon king of Lanka, arrives on the scene. He worships Siva and wants to bring mount Kailash back to his own kingdom (Sri Lanka). The panel shows him trying to uproot the mountain. Siva is shown sitting on the mountain supported by 2 attendants. He is calm and unperturbed by Ravana's show of brute strength and reassures the frightened Parvati. He pins down Ravana with his toe, who fails to move the mountain, begs Siva's forgiveness and receives it.

The Subsidiary Shrines The larger shrine on the E side has a lingam. There are also damaged images of Karttikeya, Ganesh and the Matrikas.

Kanheri caves

The caves, (also known as the Mahakali Caves) 42 km N of Bombay, are on a low hill midway between Borivli and Thana. Even on recent maps the countryside around Kanheri is shown as dense jungle, and until quite recently the surroundings must have looked quite like those at Ajanta today. The hills used to form the central part of Salsette Island, but the surrounding land has long since been drained and extensively built on. Further up the ravine from the caves there are some fine views across the Bassein Fort and out to sea. Although not as impressive as the caves at Ajanta and Ellora, if time is limited, a visit to Kanheri is a compensation. **Transport** Regular suburban tours or by train to Borivli station from Bombay Central. From here you can take a taxi for the 10 km journey. On Sun and public holidays there is a bus service from the station.

The major caves The caves are set in the heart of the Borivli National Park. The entrance is from the S, the caves still shaded by a small cluster of trees. There are 109 Buddhist caves, dating from the end of the 2nd to the 9th century AD with flights of steps joining them. The most significant is the **Chaitya cave** (3) c 6th century. The last Hinayana chaitya hall to be excavated is entered through a forecourt and verandah. The pillared entrance has well carved illustrations of the donors, and the cave itself comprises a 28m long, 13m wide colonnaded hall of 34 pillars. At one end these encircle the 5m high dagoba. Some of the pillars have carvings of elephants and trees.

50m up the ravine is Darbar of the **Maharajah Cave** (10). This was a dharamshala, chapter house or resthouse. 22m long and 10m wide, it has 2 stone benches running down the sides and some cells lead off the left and back walls. Above Cave 10 is Cave 35 which was a *vihara* (monastery). This is 12m by 14m and has reliefs of a Buddha seated on a lotus and of a disciple spreading his cloak for him to walk on. Cave 14 further up on the left has some traces of painting and Cave 21 has columns similar to some of those at Elephanta, a Buddhist litany and a figure of Padmapani. All the caves have an elaborate drainage and water storage system, fresh rainwater being led into underground storage tanks. Patrons endowed the monasteries so that they could be decorated.

Bassein (Vasai)

60 km N of central Bombay, Bassein is situated at the mouth of the Ulhas river

on the mainland. Originally built by Bahadur Shah, Sultan of Gujarat, it was intended as a chain of forts against the Portuguese. However, the chain was breached, and the Portuguese re-modelled the city along Portuguese lines, re-naming it **Vasai**. From 1534 to 1739 it became so prosperous as a centre of ship-building and the export of Bassein stone that it was called the Court of the North. As a walled city it contained a cathedral, 5 convents, 13 churches and the splendid houses and palaces of the aristocracy, or *Hidalgos*, who with members of the religious orders, alone were allowed to live within the walls. Stone and timber were available locally in large quantities so buildings were grand. The Marathas took Vasai in Feb after a long and desperate siege. Almost the whole Portuguese garrison, 800 strong, was killed in the battle; the Marathas are thought to have lost 5000 men. In 1780 the British evicted the Marathas, only to return it to them 3 years later under the Treaty of Salbai. It is well worth walking round the sea face of the fort walls. The fort itself is entered from the N.

Due to silting, the fort on the Bassein Creek is now some distance from the sea. The Old Town, which you approach from the N contains the ruins of the Cathedral of St Joseph dating from 1536, the Church of St Anthony, the Jesuits' church and the convents, all belonging to Franciscans, Dominicans, Jesuits or Augustinians. **Transport Road** or **Train** From Bombay Central to Bassein (or Vasai) Road station. From there, hire a car for 11 km journey to the town.

Beaches

Kashid, virtually undiscovered, has an excellent, unspoilt, 3 km silver sand beach. It is 139 km S of Bombay near the town of Alibag, but it may not remain quiet for long as it is becoming popular with hikers and water sports enthusiasts. Less than 1 km from Kashid village Bus Stand is **C** *Kashid Beach Resort*, opened in 1992 is ½ km from the clean, uncrowded beach, 28 suites with superb views of the sea (cheaper during week), restaurant (buffets), Rs 200 full board, in large grounds, pool, health club, billiards, riding, bike hire. Across the road you can hire speed boats, windsurfers etc. A 42 ft yacht costs Rs 2000 a day to hire from *South Asian Retreats Yacht Club*. Nearby hills good for walking. Fully equipped *Campsite*. Reservations: Beacon, Munshaw House, 22 Rustom Sidhwa Marg, Fort, Bombay, T 2625406. KBR, 9th Gulmohr Cross Rd, T 6208780. **Transport** From Bombay 3½ hr by car, 4 hr on bus via Murud. Also daily 2 'Asiad' coaches from Central Bus Terminal (0545, 1200) Rs 40. Alternatively, ferry from Bombay wharf to Rewas (Rs 10) then frequent buses to Kashid, 55 km away.

Manori

Dharavi island with 3 villages, Manori, Gorai and Utan with a population of 4,000, has been recently developed for tourism. Portuguese ships docked here some centuries ago but the rural atmosphere remains. Described as "a carefree, laidback place, slow and languid" ...full of bougainvillea..."an unspoiled mini Goa". The 2 hr journey to the idyllic beach is a popular getaway from Bombay, although foreign tourists are virtually unheard of. Very 'local'. You need to book 3 months ahead for Christmas/ New Year holidays.

• **Accommodation D** *Manoribel*, 11 rm and 8 cottages, clean, but no frills, weekday discounts, restaurant, reservations: Industrial Leather Co, Ash Lane, Fort, Bombay, T 271270. **E** *Damonica Beach Resorts* with 20 rm is less sedate, catering for young 'revellers', campfire and jazz evenings by the beach, also possible to rent room in a house.

• **Transport Train** From Churchgate, on Suburban W Rly to Malad, then auto rickshaw to Marve Ferry crosses to Manori, 0515-2215. Then take a *tonga* to the hotel.

MAHARASHTRA

Contents

Maps

Maharashtra dominates the heart of the Peninsula. With over 500 km of coastline, from Daman in the N to Goa in the S, it stretches over 900 km E to the edge of the Chota Nagpur plateau. There are some beautiful and fascinating sites.

Along the sea coast there are some attractive towns such as Ratnagiri. In the Western Ghats, Maratha forts are perched precariously on the hilltops, once the home of the charismatic Sivaji. From these fastnesses, in the late 17th century the Marathas, masters in the art of guerrilla warfare, carved out a territory that stretched the width of India. He divided the country into **Swarajya** (Homeland) and **Mughlai** (territory controlled by foreigners that was the legitimate object of raids). Swaraj ('home rule') re-emerged as one of the watchwords of the Independence struggle in the 20th century.

Bombay apart, Maharashtra is predominantly agricultural, but has well developed industries. It is a distinct cultural region, Marathi, the state language, being spoken by 90% of the population.

BASICS *Population*: 79mn (Urban 39%, Scheduled Castes 7%, Scheduled Tribes 9%); *Literacy*: M 75% F 51%; *Birth rate*: *Rural* 30:1000, *Urban* 24:1000; *Death rate*: *Rural* 9:1000, *Urban* 6:1000; *Infant mortality*: *Rural* 68:1000, *Urban* 35:1000; **Religion**: Hindu 89%, Muslim 9%, Christian 1%, Buddhist 6%.

Environment

The Land

Area: 308,000 sq km, slightly less than Germany. Maharashtra borders Gujarat to the N, Madhya Pradesh to N and E, Andhra Pradesh to the SE and Karnataka to the S. The Konkan coastal lowland is widest near Bombay, but nowhere is it wider than 100 km. It is far from flat, and is crossed by a series of short streams and rivers, rarely more than 80 km in length.

Western Ghats Formed along a fault line running the length of India's W coast, they rise like a wall between the sea and the Deccan plateau, reaching over 1400m in places. Railways and roads have been built through the few gaps. Beyond the ridge line wide, often almost imperceptible valleys have been carved out by the great rivers.

Most of the State is covered by the black volcanic lavas of the **Deccan Trap**. East of Nagpur these give way to gently rolling granite hills, 250-350m above sea level, an extraordinary landscape of huge open spaces and sweeping views. Once over the ridge of the ghats, the rainfall decreases so sharply that the natural vegetation cover is always much lighter than on the Ghats or the coastal plain. Now

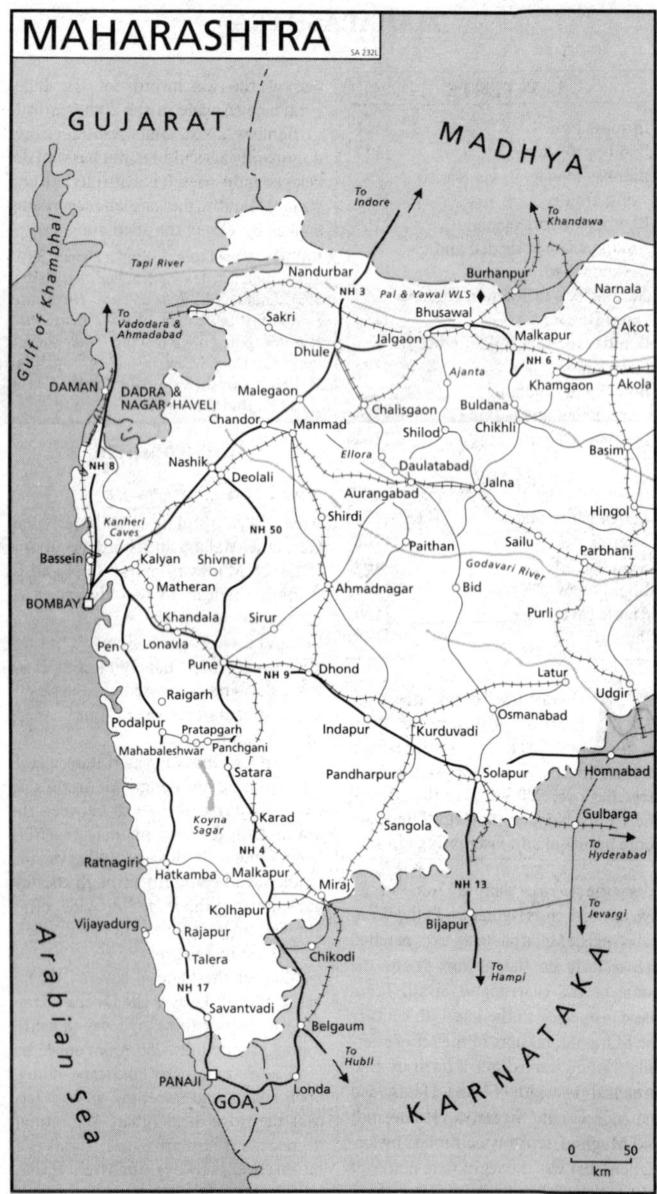
MAHARASHTRA
SA 232L
GUJARAT
MADHYA
To Indore
To Khandawa
Gulf of Khambhal
Tapi River
Nandurbar
Burhanpur
Narnala
NH 3
Pal & Yawal WLS
To Vadodara & Ahmadabad
Sakri
Bhusawal
Akot
Jalgaon
Malkapur
Dhule
NH 6
Ajanta
Khamgaon
Akola
DAMAN
DADRA & NAGAR HAVELI
Malegaon
Chalisgaon
Buldana
Chandor
Manmad
Shilod
Chikhli
NH 8
Ellora
Basim
Nashik
Deolali
Daulatabad
Jalna
Aurangabad
Shirdi
Hingol
Kanheri Caves
NH 50
Paithan
Sailu
Parbhani
Bassein
Kalyan
Shivneri
Godavari River
Matheran
Ahmadnagar
Bid
BOMBAY
Khandala
Sirur
Purli
Pen
Lonavla
Pune
NH 9
Dhond
Latur
Raigarh
Udgir
Osmanabad
Podalpur
Pratapgarh
Indapur
Kurduvadi
Mahabaleshwar
Panchgani
Satara
Pandharpur
Solapur
Homnabad
Gulbarga
Koyna Sagar
Karad
Sangola
To Hyderabad
NH 4
Ratnagiri
Hatkamba
Malkapur
Miraj
NH 13
Kolhapur
To Jevargi
Bijapur
Vijayadurg
Rajapur
Chikodi
Talera
To Hampi
NH 17
Savantvadi
Belgaum
Arabian Sea
To Hubli
PANAJI
Londa
GOA
KARNATAKA
0 50
km

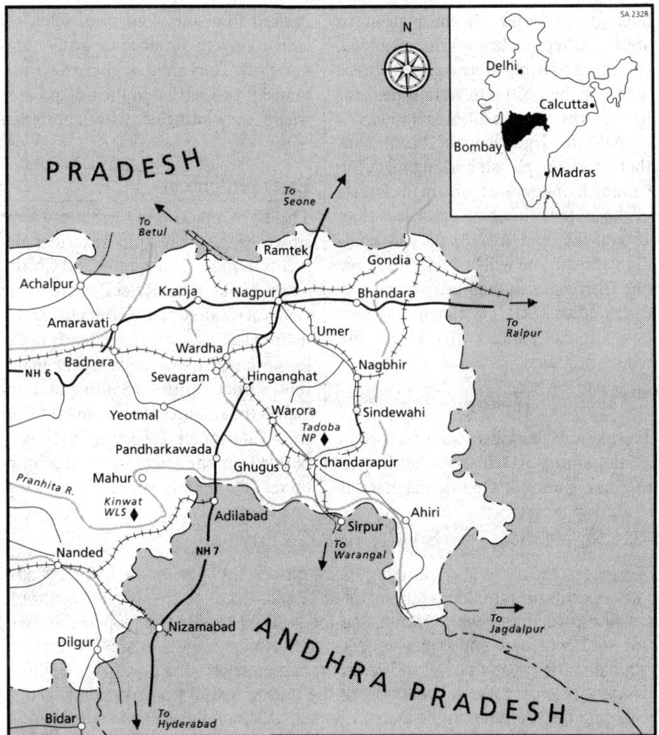

cultivated land stretches as far as the eye can see.

Rivers

A number of large and important rivers rise in the Western Ghats. The Girna flows NE to join the Tapti which drains into the Arabian Sea. All the other important rivers, such as the Godavari and the Krishna, rise within 100 km of the Arabian Sea but then flow E or SE across the Deccan plateau to the Bay of Bengal.

Climate

On the coast daily maximum temperatures are fairly uniform throughout the year at an average of 31.5°C. The daily minimum is 16°C in Jan and 26°C in Jun. In Aurangabad the average daily maximum in May is 40°C and 29°C in Jan whilst the minimum is 14°C in Jan and 25°C in May.

The SW monsoon breaks on the coast in the first week of Jun and finishes in Sep. 80% of the annual rainfall is received over this period. The coastal Konkan strip is wet while the interior upland behind is much drier. Bombay receives over 2700 mm per year, 95% of which is from Jun to Sep. Nagpur on the other hand receives 1128 mm per year, 87% of which is during the monsoon.

Flora & fauna

Vegetation On the coast mango, coconut, bamboo, teak and myrabolan (for dyeing) are found. On the plateau, in areas that receive heavy rain, magnolia, chestnut and bamboo are common. Areas with less than 650 mm of rain per year have thorny, savanna-like vegetation.

Wildlife Tiger, leopard, bison, panther, sambhar, chital, barking deer, hyena and monkeys are found in the forests of the state which now cover less than 15% of the total area. Snakes are common, though you will be lucky if you see one. Birds are numerous, particularly duck and peacock. The sanctuaries harbour drongo, paradise flycatchers and winter migrants.

History

The name **Maharashtra** was first used in a 7th century AD inscription, but its origins are unclear. One view is that it is derived from the word rathi (chariot) whose drivers formed an army (maharathis). They are thought to have migrated S and settled in the upland area where they mingled with aboriginal tribes.

Early settlement

The dry W margins of the plateau have sites from the earliest pre-historic settlements in India, and Nevasa and Chirki, on the banks of the River Pravara in the Godavari valley, have Paleolithic remains. The relatively open lands in the lee of the Ghats were one of the major routes from North to South India but lacked the resources to become the centre of a major political power. In the early period from the 8th to the 14th century there were a number of Hindu king-

Sivaji's Rise To Power

Sivaji rose rapidly to weld different Hindu groups into a powerful force. Initially attacking its neighbouring Muslim states, it rapidly expanded its power to confront the Mughal Empire which dominated the N. The Marathas developed the skills of lightning raids and highly mobile military manoeuvres, enabling them to threaten the greater power of the Mughals themselves. The last Great Mughal, Aurangzeb spent nearly the whole of the second half of his reign (1658-1707) fighting the Marathas in the Deccan Plateau. Aurangabad is named after him.

Sivaji was born in 1627 in the then Muslim Sultanate of **Ahmadnagar**. In 1646, at the age of 19, Sivaji gathered an army, took Pratapgad fort near Pune and rapidly established a powerful base. He made his reputation by a combination of brilliant campaigns, physical courage and occasional acts of astonishing cruelty towards his opponents.

Sivaji made his capital at Raigarh, and championing the Hindu cause gained the reputation of being an Indian Robin Hood and regional hero. In 1664 he sacked the Mughal port of Surat. In 1666, the Rajput Jai Singh, sent by Aurangzeb to curb Sivaji's power, succeeded in defeating him and bringing him back to the Mughal court. At this stage Sivaji obviously thought that he could not take on the Mughals and win, so he agreed to relinquish 23 of the 35 forts he had taken and to accompany Jai Singh to Agra to pay his respects to Aurangzeb.

His reception at the great Mughal's court was muddled. Aurangzeb intended to make him a gift of an elephant but was caught up in his own 50th birthday party celebrations and ignored Sivaji. The Maratha stormed out in protest but was kept under house arrest. By deceiving his guards into thinking that every day he sent a large basket of sweetmeats to Brahmins in the city, he smuggled himself out and returned to Maharashtra, dressed like a Hindu ascetic to avoid recapture. He returned to his own people and was crowned King.

doms, followed by the first Muslim dynasty in 1307. The Muslim use of Persian as a court language left its mark on the development of the Marathi language.

The Maratha confederacy

Within 4 years of his coronation Sivaji had begun to re-take the forts ceded under the treaty with Aurangzeb, and by his death in 1680 he had re-established a powerful base around Pune. He died of dysentery at the age of 53. For the next 27 years Aurangzeb battled to maintain and extend Mughal authority across the whole of his S territory. However, on his death in 1707, Sivaji's former kingdom became a confederacy under the charge of a hereditary minister called the Peshwa and 4 main Maratha chiefs – Holkar, Scindia, Gaekwad and Bhonsla. By 1750 their power reached across India to Orissa, which they occupied, and Bengal, which they attacked.

Maratha power was only decisively curbed when they were defeated at Panipat by the Afghan Ahmad Shah Abdali. In 1772, on the death of the young Peshwa, Madhao Rao I, the 5 Maratha powers became increasingly independent of one another as the 5 Deccani sultanates had done 2 centuries earlier. Weakened and divided, they were unable to resist the advance of British power.

The British period

In 1688 The East India Company leased all of the islands of Bombay from the British Government for £10 in gold per year. Initially Bombay's fortunes rested on shipbuilding. Locally available Malabar teak proved to be very durable, an ideal timber. Later Bombay took over from Surat in Gujarat as the Company's main centre on the western coast of India. Thereafter its growth was dramatic. On Independence in 1947, Bombay Presidency became Bombay state.

Culture

The People

Ethnically, Maharashtra contains a variety of peoples. The Bhil, Warli, Gond, Korku and Gowari tribal groups living in the Satpura and Sahyadri ranges in the N are Australoid aboriginals. The Kunbi Marathas are found all over the state and are believed to be the descendants of immigrants from the N at the beginning of the Christian era. Parsis arrived in the region in the 11th century from Persia.

Just over 80% of the people are Hindus with Islam and Buddhism the most numerous minority religions. The Buddhists are recent converts from among formerly outcaste Hindus. The extraordinary paintings and sculptures at the Buddhist and Hindu caves at Ajanta and Ellora cover the period from the 2nd century BC to around 650 AD.

Language

Marathi is the regional language. In addition, English (particularly in Bombay), Gujarati, Hindi, Telugu, Kannada, Urdu, Bengali and Malayalam are spoken. There are also a large number of dialects, including Konkani on the W coast, Gondi in the N.

Cuisine

Maharashtrians are predominantly vegetarians; both wheat and rice are used and vegetables are lightly spiced. Sweet and sour dishes are favoured, with a distinctive emphasis on dried and salted fish such as Bombay Duck cooked with dhal. Maharashtrians have a number of recipes that use sprouting beans.

Bombay has the heaviest concentration of Parsis in the country, so try their cuisine here – Dhansak, a special lentil curry with lamb or chicken cooked with 5 varieties of spice, or Patrani machli, fish (often pomfret) stuffed with coconut chutney and coriander, steamed in banana leaves.

Festivals

There are many festivals throughout the year, the majority of them Hindu. The *Ranga panchami* is highly colourful. *Dasara* is significant because it was the day on which the Marathas usually began their military campaigns. *Holi*, marking the beginning of spring is very popular. *Janmashtami* in Jul and Aug celebrates the birth of Lord Krishna. Men and boys form human pyramids to break pots of curds that have been hung from high places.

On *Ganesh Chaturthi* in Bombay (Aug/Sep) massive figures of the ever popular elephant god Ganesh, the bringer of good fortune, are immersed in the sea. The Muslim festival of *Mohurram* which commemorates the martyrs of Islam, is often observed by Hindus as well.

Modern Maharashtra

Government

Independence Bombay Presidency had never coincided with the area in which Marathi was the dominant language. In 1948 the former princely state of Vadodara (Baroda) and some others were merged into Bombay. The present state did not take shape until 1960, when Gujarati areas in the N and Kannada speaking areas in the S were allocated to Gujarat and Karnataka respectively.

Maharashtra, a state in the federal union, has a governor as its head. The legislature has 2 houses; the Vidhan Parishad (legislative council) and Vidhan Sabha (legislative assembly). Except for an annual meeting at Nagpur, the old Maratha capital, these meet in Bombay. The state is represented by 48 members in the Lok Sabha (Lower House) and 19 members in Rajya Sabha (Upper House) of the national parliament in New Delhi. While the Congress Party has retained a hold on power it has been challenged in some areas, especially Bombay, by the Hindu/Mahratha party the Shiv Sena. Some of the cities of the state, especially Bombay, experienced major riots in Dec-Jan 1992-93, following the destruction of the Babri mosque in Ayodhya.

Economy

Agriculture is the mainstay of the economy. Over 65% of the total area is cultivated but only 12% is irrigated. The main food crops are jowar, bajra, wheat and pulses (peas, beans, lentils). Rice is not as well suited to the dry conditions and lower rainfall as these hardy crops. The state is also a major producer of groundnuts (peanuts), sunflowers, cotton, sugarcane, tobacco, turmeric and a variety of vegetables. A substantial area is devoted to oranges, bananas, mangoes, grapes and limes. In recent years an attractive Méthode Champenoise sparkling wine called Omar Khayyam has been produced with French expertise.

Water is scarce, but the state government has given assistance to improve productivity. Higher yielding varieties of rice and wheat have been promoted. Irrigation in rain shadow areas has encouraged good sugarcane crops. Forest products include timber, bamboo, sandalwood and tendu leaves which are used for making cheap cigarettes.

Minerals Manganese, iron ore, limestone, copper, bauxite, silica salt and common salt are extracted. Bhandara, Nagpur and Chandrapur districts in the E have rich bituminous coal deposits, used by the railways and power stations. The Bombay High and the nearby Bassein North fields were first developed in 1976. Although the state has only 9% of India's population, it accounts for about 11% of the industrial units and 23% of the value of the nation's industrial output.

Industry The Bombay-Pune complex is the state's major industrial area. Bombay alone accounts for over 33% of India's total income tax revenue. Nagpur, Aurangabad, Sholapur, Thane and Kolhapur are also important industrial centres. Chemicals, pharmaceuticals, plastic ware, machine tools, electrical and non-electrical machinery and petroleum products are all important. The oldest and largest industry in the state is textiles, but it leads the country in the manufacture of sophisticated electronics equipment and produces both thermal and hydro-electricity. The atomic power station at Tarapur, 112 km N of Bombay, was India's first nuclear power plant. From the late 1970s the state government has been encouraging industry to decentralise away from Bombay and centres such as Nashik have grown very rapidly.

Tourism The Government is promoting 'Adventure tourism', water sports and 'Jungle safaris' in addition to conventional 'Holiday Resorts' where cottages and dormitories are very reasonably priced. Tents and equipment is available for hire from Maharashtra Tourism regional offices and on site.

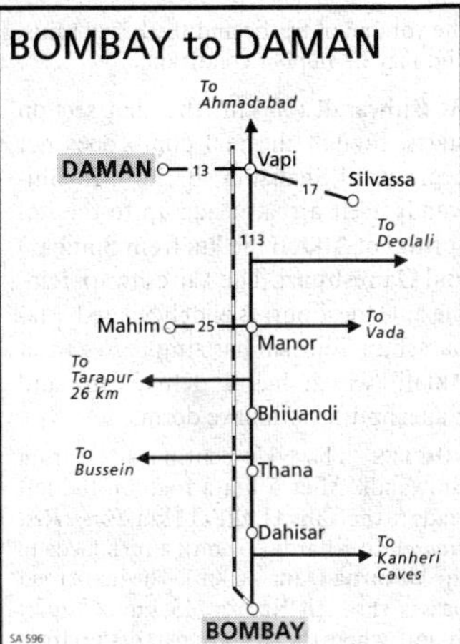

BOMBAY TO DAMAN

ROUTES This short journey leaves Bombay by the W Expressway, then travels inland over low hills and across the short streams that run from the W Ghats to the sea. The NH8, the main road to Vadodara and Ahmadabad, by-passes formerly rich Portuguese settlements such as Bassein and Thana which can make interesting short diversions. It is very busy with heavy lorry traffic.

Just before Dahisar (42 km from central Bombay) a right turn leads to the **Kanheri National Park** and the **Kanheri caves** (see above – **Excursions from Bombay**, page 1149). A little further N **Thana** (Thane) was the terminus of the first railway in India, built from Bombay in 1856. As early as 1298, however, Marco Polo had written of Thana as "a great kingdom...there is much traffic here and many ships and merchants frequent the place". It was an important Portuguese centre until the Marathas captured it in 1739. The English church in the town dates from 1825.

Bassein, further N, was also in Portuguese hands from 1534 to 1739. The walls are still standing, and it is an interesting place to stop, see page 1150. 6 km from Shirsad are the **Vrajeshwari Temple**, with hot springs, and Bhiwandi (*Population*: 391,700; *STD Code*: 02522). The route N to Daman is described below under **Routes** from Ahmadabad to Bombay see page 1252.

BOMBAY TO NAGPUR via Nashik and Dhule

ROUTES The route through the Western Ghats from Bombay to Nashik (**NH3**) is one of the busiest in India. After following the Ulhas River from Shahapur to Igatpuri it climbs through the forested slopes of the Western Ghats, where streams on the wet slopes of the ghats have been dammed to provide hydro-electricity for Bombay. The lakes offer some attractive picnic spots off the main route. The climb through the ghats is particularly beautiful before the end of the rains in Sep. Wild flowers are everywhere, and rivers and waterfalls are full. Although it is repaired periodically, sections of the road are often damaged by the volume of traffic and the heavy rains, and may be in poor condition.

At **Bhiwandi** (58 km) the ghat section starts, though the real climb does not begin until Shahapur (33 km). In Bhiwandi itself a road leads up to the hot springs of **Alkloli** (80 km from Bombay) and **Ganeshpuri**. The Vajreshwari Temple at Ganeshpuri is widely visited. Maharashtra Tourism has simple *Resorts* at Akloli (which has 2 deluxe rm) and Ganeshpuri. Both have dorm.

ROUTES The NH3 continues NE from Bhiwandi. After 5 km a road on the left leads to the **Tansa Lake** (13 km; *Forest Rest House*). In Khardi (17 km), a turn leads to the **Vaiturna Dam** (16 km). The main road passes through Kasara (13 km; *Altitude*: 300m), where the steepest part of the climb begins, gaining 320m in 15 km.

The railway through the ghats, which in this section alone passes through 10 tunnels, and over 5 viaducts and 11 bridges, was completed in 1861. It starts the Thul ghat section after 7 km, reaching the end of the ghat at **Igatpuri** (10 km; *Population*: 22,900; *Altitude*: 580m) – the 'town of difficulties'. **Kalsubai** (1540m), the highest mountain in Maharashtra, is visible to the S. One km beyond the village of Igatpuri the road passes the end of the beautiful **Beale Lake**, at the head of one of the streams that joins the Godavari downstream from Nashik.

Jawhar (*Altitude*: 518m) Formerly the capital of a tribal kingdom, Jawhar is noted for its Warli paintings. Rice paste or poster colours is used to decorate the hut walls. **Jai Vilas**, the palace, and **Bhupatgad**, the fort, still show evidence of the tribal kingdom, while there are attractive waterfalls at Dadar Kopra. **Accommodation E** *Maharashtra Tourism's Holiday Resort*, 3 rm and dorm.

From Igatpuri the NH3 goes through Ghoti (8 km) where a road on the right leads to the 150m high Wilson Dam at **Bhandardara** (32 km) which has a Maharashtra Tourism **E** *Holiday Resort*, with 20 rm, and on to Nashik (32 km).

Nashik

Nashik (*Population*: 722,100; *Altitude*: 610m; *STD Code*: 0253) is one of Hinduism's most holy sites, associated with stories from the *Ramayana* legend.

Kumbh Mela

It shares the triennial Kumbh Mela with Ujjain, Haridwar and Allahabad, see page 281, and every 12 years millions of pilgrims converge on the River Godavari, sometimes referred to as the Ganga of the Deccan, to bathe. The Godavari, which rises 30 km away at Trimbak is believed to have a common underground source with the Ganga itself. In the last 10 years it has been one of India's fastest growing cities. Benefitting from Government incentives in the 1970s to re-locate outside Bombay, private industry rapidly took up all the spaces allotted on the industrial estate.

The town itself is undoubtedly ancient, and Ghose suggests that it has an unbroken history of over 2,500 years. At Pandu Lena, within a few km of the town centre, palaeolithic settlements have been discovered. Chalcolithic pottery has been found at Gangawadi, 15 km NW of Nashik. Other finds date from the 5th century BC up to the 1st century AD, with a great deal of Northern Black Polished Ware pottery – see page 300. Roman pottery has been found in the third period levels.

Places of interest

None of Nashik's temples are very old. The Vaisnavite **Narayana Temple** (1756) on the W bank has 3 black Vishnu images. The **Ramesvara Temple** (18th century) where Rama is believed to have carried out the funeral rites for his father, and the **Rama Kund** nearby where he is thought to have bathed. It is a popular place to throw ashes of the dead into the river.

The banyan-shaded **Sita Gupha** cave on the E side of town is where Rama's wife hid from Ravana the demon. Nearby is the **Kala** (black) **Rama Temple** (1782) which stands in an enclosure with 96 pillars and has a 25m high *shikhara*.

Excursions

Pandu Lena, 8 km SW of Nashik and just off NH3 is a group of 24 rock cut Buddhist monuments, the earliest dating from the 1st C BC. They include over 20 caves. While they have nothing like the detailed decoration of the Ajanta caves, some have excellent carving, particularly on the exterior doorways. **Cave** 3 has 19 monastic cells, a carved Buddha decorates the rear of Cave 10, while the exterior of the early **Cave 18**, a chapel (*chaitya*), is finely decorated. The group are cut into the NE facing escarpment and overlook the road.

Deolali, 7 km SE on NH50 to Pune, was the transfer camp for British soldiers going home during the 2 World Wars. To go 'Doolally Tap' was to go crazy with boredom waiting there. A mental hospital accommodated these casualties.

Trimbak (*Population*: 7900) 30 km W of Nashik, is centred around the beautiful **Gangasagar Tank**, and 690 steps lead up the hill behind Trimbak to the source of the Godavari itself. The town is partly surrounded by a fantastic semi-circle of hills, topped by a near vertical scarp of about 40m. The impressive Maratha **Fort** is situated 550m above the village at 1295m. There are 2 gateways, and the **Temple of Trimbakeshwar**, an 18th century Siva sanctuary with a *Jyotirlinga*, is a pilgrimage site. Non-Hindus may not enter but may climb steps to look inside. In Feb/Mar a large fair is held, the important *Sinhastha Fair* occurring every 12 years. **E** Maharashtra Tourism *Holiday cottages*, T 43, with 11 rm with bath and dorm.

Prayag Tirth, on the road to Trimbak, has a beautiful stone-lined tank with 2 temples. Further on near **Anjaneri**, 2 300m high conical hills are on either side of the road, sweeping round in a broad arc behind the town of Trimbak.

Local information

● **Accommodation**

(Airport 5 km, rly 9 km) **D** *Green View*, 1363 Mt Trimbak Rd, T 72231, 24 rm, 14 a/c, restaurant, garden; **D** *Holiday Cottages*, Bombay Agra Rd, Vilhouli, T 2376, 40 rm, most a/c, 10 km centre, restaurant, pool; **D** *Durgesh*, New Bombay Agra Rd, T 77019, 20 rm, veg restaurant; **D** *Panchavati*, 430 Vakil Wadi (Chandak Wadi), T 75771, 41 rm, some a/c, restaurant (Indian). Slightly cheaper **D** *Panchavati Yatri*, T 71274, 54 rm, 6 comfortable a/c rm (but cold showers), restaurant (Indian veg), bar, modern, clean, good value; **D** *Samrat*, nr Central Bus Stand, opp Indian Airlines, Old Agra Rd, T 77211, 14 rm, some a/c, restaurant, permit rm, travel; **D** *Wasan's Inn*, Old Agra Rd, T 77881, 24 rm, restaurant.

E *Siddhartha*, Nashik Pune Rd, nr Airport, T 73288, 32 rm, some a/c.

● **Tourist offices**

Maharashtra Tourism, T/1 Golf Club, Old Agra Rd, T 70059. Sightseeing 0730-1500, Rs 60.

● **Transport**

Train **Bombay (VT)**: *Punjab Mail* 1038, daily, 0754, 4½ hr; *Kushinagar Exp* 1016, daily, 1104, 5¼ hr; *Bombay Mail* 3003, daily, 0630, 5 hr. **Bhopal**: *Kushinagar Exp* 1015, daily, 1547, 11½ hr; *Punjab Mail* 1037, daily, 2017, 11 hr; *Amritsar Exp* 1057, daily, 0245, 12¾ hr. **Road** Good connections with other centres in the state.

Nashik to Nagpur

The **NH3** continues NE from Nashik across the broad open agricultural land of the Deccan plateau. It passes through several small settlements to Chandvad (61 km; *Population*: 15,000), crossing the low-rising Satmala Hills (*Altitude*: 1376m) to Malegaon (36 km; *Population*: 342,400). Facilities basic.

Dhule (48 km; *Population*: 278,000) has accommodation in **E** *Hotel Dina*, Sakri Rd, reasonable modern hotel in town with little competition.

At the crossroads in Dhule turn right onto NH6 along the valley of the Tapti River to Nagpur. Although this is the main Bombay-Calcutta road it is much less heavily used than the Bombay-Delhi NH3. Passing through largely open, extensively cultivated countryside, there is a scatter of towns, some growing rapidly but still with few facilities for travellers. From Dhule continue to Jalgaon.

Jalgaon

Jalgaon (64 km; *Population*: 242,000; *Altitude*: 820m; *STD Code*: 0257) is the rail junction for the Ajanta Caves (56 km) and was once at the centre of a savannah forest region, the habitat of tigers, leopards and other game animals. Now it has become an important cotton growing area.

• **Accommodation** **D** *Morako*, 364 Navi Path between Rly and Bus Stand, T 6621, 24 rm, restaurant (Indian). **E** *Natraj*, Nehru Chowk, T 4021, also has some a/c rm; **E** *Crazy Home*, NH 6, Akashwani Chowk, T 3275, is cheaper; **E** *Shiva*, is basic; **E** *Govt Rest House*, Station Rd, 5 min from station, T 183, good rm, some with bath. **F** *Railway Retiring Rooms*.

• **Transport** **Train** Bombay (VT): *Punjab Mail* 1038, daily, 0433, 7¾ hr; *Kushinagar Exp* 1015, daily, 1120, 8¾ hr; *Bombay Mail* 3003, daily, 0305, 8¼ hr. **Bhopal**: *Punjab Mail* 1037, daily, 2325, 7¾ hr; *Amritsar Exp* 1057, daily, 0615, 9¼ hr. **Road** Good connections with other centres.

ROUTES The 437 km from Jalgaon to Nagpur runs from W to E. The road crosses from the S side of the Tapti valley into the catchment area of the S flowing tributaries of the Godavari. It lies in the heart of the rain-shadow area of the Western Ghats, with less than 750 mm of rain a year, increasing slowly to the E. On the lower land the soils are some of the best in the Peninsula – rich black soils derived from the lava, overlying basalt rocks, though on the higher land the much poorer red soils surface. Given the relative dryness of the region and the lack of irrigation, an extraordinarily high percentage is cultivated, in some districts as much as 80% of the total area, though the poorer soils are often left fallow. Another extraordinary feature is the lack of rice cultivation – less than 2% of the entire region. Sorghum (*jowar*) and cotton dominate, cotton being a short stapled variety. In the W pearl millet (*bajra*) becomes more important than sorghum. The whole route is on **NH6**.

Bhusawal (27 km; *Population*: 160,000) is an important railway junction. Robert Gill, the 19th century painter who devoted much of his life to the task of copying and preserving the Ajanta murals, is buried in the small European cemetery. The road then enters what used to be the princely state of Berar, see page 803. In 1858 the ruler was dispossessed for lending support to the 1857 mutiny. His lands, long claimed by Hyderabad state, were awarded to the Nizam as a mark of gratitude. Around here are some of the finest cotton fields in India.

Buldhana (*Altitude*: 630m; *Population*: 52,800), reached from the town of Malkapur, had a reputation as one of the coolest and pleasantest spots in the Berar district. In **Akola** (99 km; *Population*: 328,000; *Altitude*: 290m; *STD Code*: 0724) a lower Palaeolithic site has been discovered revealing a range of tools. The town is a major cotton and grain handling centre. Buses go to Aurangabad and Lonar (see below).

At **Shegaon**, 43 km from Malkapur, is a small **E** Maharashtra Tourism *Resort*, T Buldhana 100, 6 rm, fairly basic.

ROUTES The NH6 continues to Amravati.

Amravati (Amraoti)

95 km *Population*: 421,000; *STD Code*: 0721, the district HQ which has a very large cotton market.

• **Accommodation** A basic **F** *PWD Rest House*, in Maltekdi Rd.

• **Tourist office** Maharashtra Tourism office at *PWD Rest House*, Maltekdi Rd, T 74008.

• **Transport** **Train** Amaravati is the nearest railhead for Achalpur (Ellichpur) and the hill station of Chikhaldara.

Achalpur

(*Altitude*: 500m; *Population*: 96,200) Until 1853 this important market town was the capital of Berar kingdom, established in 1484 by Imad Shah. The old cantonment, which had been occupied by a regiment of the Hyderabad infantry, was abandoned in 1903.

To the N and just before reaching Chikaldara is the fort of **Gawilgarh** (Gavilgarh). An important fortress of the 15th century Shahi dynasty, the fort was taken over when the kingdom of Ahmednagar expanded in 1574. Arthur Wellesley, subsequently the Duke of Wellington, who had defeated Tipu Sultan of Mysore at Srirangapatnam just 4 years previously, captured the fort in 1803 during the 2nd Maratha War. The defences were destroyed after the Indian mutiny in 1858. Today it is a deserted ruin overgrown with scrub.

Chikhaldara (Chikhalda; *Altitude*: 1200m; *Population*: 3100) Known as the only hill station in the Vidharba region, Chikhaldara is high in the Gavilgarh Hills, a branch of the Satpura Mnts. Established as a hill station by the British in 1839, historically the hills marked the southern limits of the core region within which the epics of Hinduism were played out. It remains a tribal region, peopled largely by the Korkus, an Austric tribal group. The settlement is reputed to have taken its name from Kichaka, a prince who was killed by Bhima, one of the Pandava brothers, for having insulted Draupadi. Today the Satpura Range in which Chikaldara lies mark the southern boundary of Hindi speech. The area is also known as the northernmost coffee growing region in India and as the site of the Melghat Project Tiger reserve. The ghat road winds through increasingly grassy and wooded landscape from the intensively cultivated plains of the W-draining Chandrabaga, Purna and their tributaries to the S. The town has a municipal park with a miniature toy train.

• **Accommodation & food F** Maharashtra Tourism *Cottages* are very basic though adequate. Restaurant a short walk away. Some improved accommodation is planned.

• **Transport Train** Badnera (105 km: central rly) on the Bombay-Calcutta line is the nearest station. Amaravati is on a short spur (10 km) from Badnera. **Road** State transport buses from Amaravati, Nagpur, Wardha and Akola. Taxis are also available in Amravati (100 km).

Nagpur

Population: 1,661,400; *Altitude*: 312m; *STD Code*: 0712. Nagpur, the former capital of the Central Provinces, is one of the older towns of Central India. The Chanda dynasty of aboriginal Gonds ruled in the 10th-11th centuries – see page 333). Muhammad Bahmani (1463-82) wrested it from the Kherla rulers. The Gonds rose again in the 16th century and in 1740 Nagpur was taken by Raghuji Bhonsla. In 1861 the British annexed it on the Principle of Lapse – see page 262, Lucknow), along with the Saugor and Narbada Provinces.

Places of interest

The city stands on the Nag river and centres on the **Sitabaldi Fort** which is surrounded by cliffs and a moat. At the highest point there is a memorial to those who fell in the Battle of Sitabaldi between the Marathas and the British. The fort, HQ of the Territorial Army, is only open to the public on Aug 15 and Jan 26. British buildings are to be found mainly in the W half of the city: the red brick **Council Hall** (1912-13); the Anglican **Cathedral of All Saints** (1851); **the**

CLIMATE: NAGPUR

	Jan	Feb	Mar	Apr	May	Jun	Jul	Aug	Sep	Oct	Nov	Dec	Av/Tot
Max (°C)	29	33	36	40	43	38	31	30	31	32	30	29	34
Min (°C)	13	15	19	24	28	27	24	24	23	20	14	12	20
Rain (mm)	15	2	25	20	10	174	351	277	181	62	9	2	1128

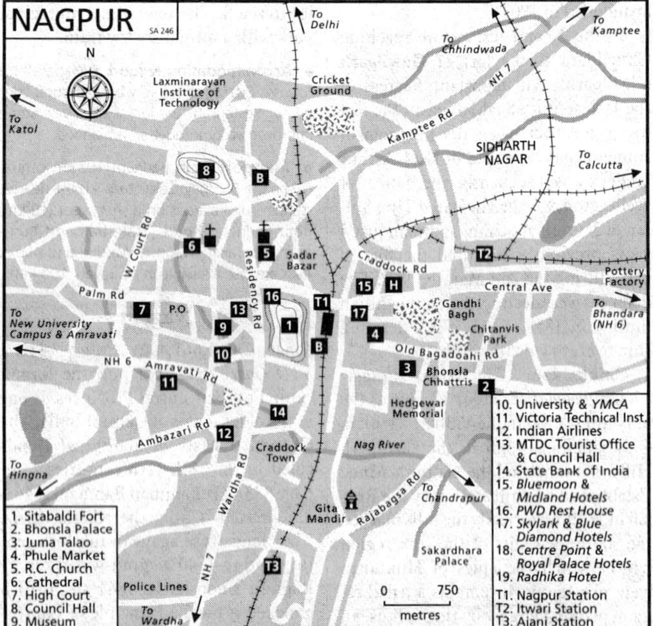

High Court (1937-42) is suggestive of Rashtrapati Bhavan in New Delhi – no coincidence, as it was designed by one of the architects who contributed designs to parts of New Delhi, Henry Medd. On the other high hill in the town is the **Raj Bhavan** (Government House). In the E half of the town, near the Nag River, were the **Bhonsla Palace** and the Gond Rajah's Palace. The former was damaged by fire in 1864. Little remains.

The **Bhonsla Chhattris** are in the Sukrawari area S of the old city. Around the town there are also a number of tanks. The **Maharaj Bagh** is an attractive park/zoo. Nagpur is famous across India for its oranges and is an important industrial centre.

Local festivals

The following are celebrated in the city and surrounding area.

Apr/May *Ram Navmi* Colourful procession in various parts of the city.

Aug/Sep *Janmashtami* Krishna's birthday is celebrated in Nagpur with the distinctive tradition of stringing clay pots full of curd high above the streets. Young men try to pull them down by forming human pyramids. *Pola* the cattle and monsoon harvest festival. *Ganesh Chaturthi* when idols of Ganesh are immersed in streams and tanks.

Local information

● Accommodation

(Airport 7-10 km, railway 2 km, most 2-3 km from centre). The **C** hotels do not have all usual facilities of the grade. **C** *Centre Point*, 24 Central Bazar Rd, Ramdaspeth, T 523093, F 7012 524279, 85 rm, restaurant, pool; **C** *Rawell Continental*, 7 Dhantoli, Wardha Rd, T 523845, 25 rm, restaurant, travel.

D *Skylark*, 119 Central Ave, T 44654, 48 rm, some a/c, restaurant, exchange, 10% travel discount; **D** *Radhika*, 3 Farmland, Wardha Rd, T 522011, 60 rm, some a/c, restaurant, bar, exchange; **D** ***Blue Diamond***, 113 Doser Chowk, Central Ave, T 47460, 71 rm, restaurant, bar; **D** ***Dua Continental***, Kamptee Rd, T 520801, 22 a/c rm, restaurant; **D** ***Saurabh International***, 3 Jaika, Civil Lines, T 250240, 34 a/c rm, restaurant; **D** ***Bluemoon***, opp Mayo Hospital, 129 Central Ave Rd, T 46061, 30 rm, 20 a/c, restaurant, bar, exchange; **D** ***Jagsons***, 30 Back Central Ave, T 48611, 32 a/c rm, restaurant, bar, travel, exchange; **D** ***Midland***, opp Mayo Hospital, Central Ave Rd, T 46131, 36 rm, some a/c, restaurant, bar, exchange; **D** ***Pal Palace***, 25 Central Ave, T 44724, 32 rm, 26 a/c; **D** ***Royal Palace***, 22 Farmland, Central Bazar Rd, T 525454, 36 rm, central a/c, restaurant.

E ***Shyam***, Pandit Malaviya Rd, Sitabaldi, T 524073, 36 rm with bath, restaurant; **E** ***Upvan***, 64 Mount Rd, Sadar, T 34704, 9 rm with bath, some a/c, central, restaurant, bar.

● Places to eat

Outside hotels in the Sadar area are: ***Ashoka*** and ***Moti Mahal***, ***Kwality***, in Rani Jhansi Sq, ***Nanking***, for Chinese. In Sitabaldi: ***Golden Gate*** and ***Anand Bhandar*** for Indian, ***Khyber*** and ***Sher Punjab*** for Tandoori. Others in Dharampeth, Ramdaspeth (inc ***Indian Coffee House***) and Central Ave.

● Banks & money changers

State Bank of India, **Punjab National Bank** and **Bank of India in Kingsway**; several others in Civil Lines, Dharampeth, Sitabaldi and Central Ave.

● Post & telecommunications

GPO and **Central Telegraph Office** nr Govt Printing Press, Itwari.

● Shopping

Main areas are Sitabaldi, Dharampeth, Sadar, Itwari, Mahatma Phule Market. ***Gangotri UP Handicrafts*** in Sadar and ***Khadi Gramudyog*** in Mahal.

● Tourist office

Maharashtra Tourism, Sanskrutik Bachat Bhavan, Sitabuldi, T 533325.

● Transport

Local Unmetered taxis from Stand opp Rly Station, T 33460 or **Blaze Car Rentals**, Sitabaldi, T 22792. Extensive coverage by city **buses**. **Coaches** from Tourist Office for sightseeing. **Auto-rickshaws**, **cycle-rickshaws** and **tongas** available. Negotiate fares.

Air Indian Airlines connects Nagpur with Bombay, Delhi and Bhubaneswar. Indian Airlines, T 33962. Airport, T 24870.

Train Bombay (VT): *Bombay Mail* 8002, daily, 1600, 15¾ hr; *Bombay Exp* 8030, daily, 1230, 17 hr; *Gitanjali Exp* 2860, daily, 0750, 14 hr. Enquiry, T 25743, Reservations, T 25633 (Class I), T 31019 (Class II).

Road MRTC, Mor Bhavan Sitabaldi, T 46221. Nr Rly Station, T 33695. Good bus services to places within the state and to neighbouring states' centres. Nagpur is connected with **Bhopal** (345 km), **Jabalpur** (240 km) on NH7.

Excursions around Nagpur

Ramtek (*Population*: 20,100) 40 km NE, just off the main road N to Jabalpur, has a fort with several Hindu temples at its western end, some dating back to the 5th century AD. The fort walls on the well-wooded 'Hill of Rama' were built in 1740 by Raghoji I, the first Bhonsla of Nagpur. The citadel is older and the principal temples are those to Rama and Sita, who are believed to have stayed here with Lakshman during their exile. It was the capital of the 4th-6th century Vakataka rulers. The fort is approached by a flight of steps from the village of Ambala. The poet Kalidasa wrote his epic *Meghdoot* here. Nearby are the Ramsagar and Lindsey lakes. There is a 15 day fair in Nov. **Accommodation F** Maharashtra Tourism *Hotel*, 4 rm with bath and dorms. Also camping. Quite basic.

Wardha

(62 km SW) Mahatma Gandhi established his **Sevagram Ashram** (Gandhian Village of Service) in 1933, 6 km from Wardha, where he spent 15 years. It is now a national institution where you can visit the residences *Nivases* and *Kutirs*, see the Mahatma's personal belongings, watch hand-spinning and attend prayers at the open-air multi-faith Prayer Ground (0430 and 1800). The **Mahatma Gandhi Research Institute of Medical Sciences** and **Kasturba Hospital**, with 325 beds, draws patients from neighbouring areas.

The **Magan Sanghralaya** (Centre of Science for Villages) is an alternative technology museum 6 km from Wardha, on the Nagpur Rd. 10 km away at **Pauna**, Vinoba Bhave, one of Gandhi's keenest disciples, set up his Ashram. He championed the 'land gift' or Bhoodan Movement, seeking with remarkable success to persuade large landowners to give away land to the poor.

• **Accommodation** E *Holiday Resort*, nr Bus Stand, rm with bath, dormitory, restaurant. Also cheaper rm in *Lodges* and *Ashrams* and *Govt Circuit House* and *PWD Rest House* in Civil Line. *Annapurna Restaurant* nr the Station, *Ambika* and *Rambharose* in Saraf Lines. The Ashram has a *Guest House* and *Yatri Niwas* where you can get meals. Check out 0800.

• **Tourist Information** Voluntary guides. Reservations: Secretary, Ashram Pratishthan, T 2172. **Post Office** nearby. Khadi cloth is sold through shops.

NB: Alcohol, smoking and non-vegetarian food are prohibited.

• **Transport Train** Wardha is on the Central Railway. **Nagpur**: *Haora Mail* 8001, 0941, 1¾ hr; *Kurla Haora Exp* 8029, 1310, 2 hr. **Haora**: *Haora Mail* 8001, 0941, 23½ hr. **Bombay**: *Bombay Mail* 8002, 1724, 12¼ hr. **Road Buses**: to Wardha from other major cities in Maharashtra incl Nagpur, 77 km. You can get to Sevagram by bus from Wardha and Nagpur.

Approx 100 km S of Nagpur and 45 km N of the nearest town is the **Taroba National Park**.

Taroba National Park

Background

The area was once in the possession of the Gond tribals. The compact 120 sq km park (*Altitude*: 200m) has rich deciduous forest – mainly teak with bamboo, gardenia, satinwood (chloroxylon swietenia), *mahua* and *jamun*. Water birds are attracted by the perennial circular lake, inc cattle egrets, purple moorhens and jacanas. It also has quite a number of marsh crocodiles with a breeding farm for the palustris species. A motorable road runs around the lake, while other roads radiate to the park perimeter. Minibuses for viewing, which is best in the evening around lake in the dry season. *Temp range*: 47°C to 9°C; *Rainfall*: 1175 mm; *Best season*: Nov-Jun.

Wildlife

The wildlife consists of several troops of langur monkeys, palm civets, gaur, jackal, wild boar, chital, bison, sambar and a few tigers (although you are more likely to see a leopard in the evening). As in Madhya Pradesh and Andhra Pradesh, there are no wild elephants in Maharashtra.

NB: No official guides but if you hire a search light, you will be accompanied by a forest guard who will act as a guide.

Park information

● **Accommodation**

E *Mayur*, Mul Rd, T 3712, 27 rm, 1 km rly, Restaurant, bar. Three *Forest Rest Houses*, around the lake, reservations: Div Forest Officer, W Chanda Div, Mul Rd, Chandrapur, canteen, needs a day's notice.

● **Transport**

Air Through Nagpur (150 km).

Train Nearest at Chandrapur (45 km).

East from Nagpur to Madhya Pradesh

ROUTES From Nagpur the NH6 continues E. Across the **Wainganga River** (2 km) it continues through open parkland scenery interspersed with cultivated fields and areas of thicker forest. Running through one of the major tribal areas of Madhya Pradesh, the town of **Durg** (77 km; *Population*: 166,800; *STD Code*: 07742) is now joined to the modern steel town of **Bhilainagar** (13 km; *Population*: 398,800), which has one of the few large hotels in the whole of the region, run essentially for visitors to the Hindustan Steel works. **Accommodation D** *Bhilai Hotel*, 124 rm, all a/c. Raipur is a further 24 km.

Raipur (*Population*: 461,900; *Altitude*: 300m; *STD Code*: 0771) is the regional centre for much of SE Madhya Pradesh. A fort, built by Raja Bhubaneshwar

Singh in 1460, has long since disappeared. A tank near the fort covered 3 sq km. The city **museum** records the major events in the town's history. The 18th century Maharajbandh Tank was built during the Maratha period, and the Dudhari Temple in 1775. The Kankali Tank in the town centre was built in the late 17th century.

• **Transport Air** Indian Airlines, Delhi, Tu,Th, 1605, 1½ hr. **Continental Aviation**, Bombay, via Bhopal and Indore, M,W,F, 1430, 4½ hr. **Train Delhi**: via Bhopal, Jhansi, Gwalior and Agra, *Link Exp* 8518, 1410, 30½ hr; **Visakhapatnam**: *Link Exp* 8517, 1425, 10 hr; **Bombay VT**: *Bombay Mail* 8002, 0928, 22 hr; **Calcutta**: *Calcutta Mail* 8001, 1715, 14 hr.

BOMBAY TO AURANGABAD

Aurangabad, the seat of the last great Mughal, Aurangzeb, is the normal access point for the caves at Ellora and Ajanta.

ROUTES The easiest road route to Aurangabad is the NH3. The road climbs up the Western Ghats to nearly 1600m. At Ghoti, a small market town on the plateau, a road runs SE to **Arthur Hill Lake** and **Bhandardara** (*Population*: 79,900). A small stream leaves the lake to cascade down the 45m Randha Falls, while Bhandardara is overlooked by the 626m high hill Mt Kalsubai. Ratangarh fort can be climbed from the town. **Accommodation** Very modest Maharashtra Tourism **F** *Resort*, 20 rm.

ROUTES The road gradually descends from Arthur Hill Lake to Sangamner following the Pravara River. From **Sangamner** (*Population*: 49,000) the route crosses the upper valley of the Godavari River to the Ahmednagar-Aurangabad crossroads. The journey to Aurangabad can be completed in a very long day. An attractive alternative is to leave the NH3 at Bhiwandi (56 km) for Kalyan.

Kalyan (72 km), once an important town and port in Thana district. The ruined fort of **Malangarh** lies 16 km to the S. Kalyan rose to prominence at the end of the 2nd century and soon became one of West India's chief markets. The Muslims renamed it Kalyan Islamabad in the 14th century. The Portuguese and British occupied the town for periods between the 16th and 18th centuries though the Marathas were only defeated finally at the end of the 18th century. There are several ruined monuments nearby which suggest its earlier magnificence.

Ambarnath, a few km SE of Ulhasnagar has the very fine 11th century **Yadava temple**. It is partly ruined but

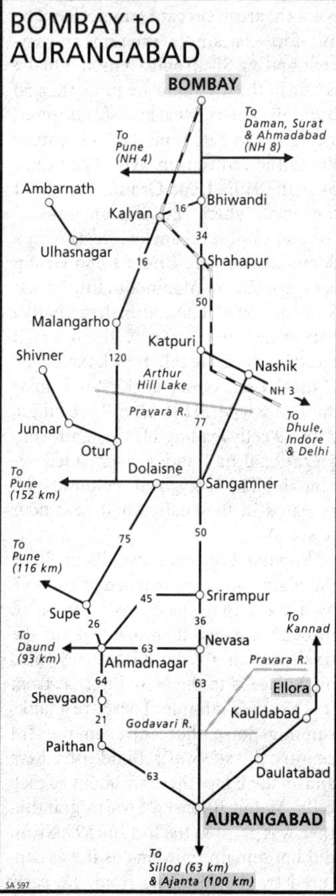

has very good sculptures of Siva dancing, Brahma, Bhairava and graceful female figures.

Titwala Just to the N of the road out of Kalyan is the pilgrim centre visited for its Mahaganesha and Vithoba Temples. **Accommodation** Maharashtra Tourism *Resort*, suites and dorm, basic.

From Kalyan drive to Junnar (approx 120 km), turning right before the village of Otur.

Junnar

The birthplace of **Sivaji** in 1627, Junnar is another rock cut cave temple site. The hill fort contains a monument commemorating Sivaji and a temple. On the E side of the hill there are more than 50 **Buddhist caves**. Most are *viharas* (monasteries) and date from the 2nd century BC to the 3rd century AD. They comprise the **Tulja Lena Group**, 2 km W of the town, which includes an unusual circular *chaitya* (chapel, Cave 3) with a dome ceiling. The **Bhuta Lena Group** is on the side of Manmodi Hill, 1.5 km S of the town. The unfinished chaitya hall (Cave 40) has a well preserved façade containing reliefs of Laxmi. The **Ganesh Lena Group** is 4 km S of Junnar on the Lenyadri Hill. Cave 7 is a vihara with 19 cells leading off the main congregational hall and a colonnaded verandah. The octagonal columns are repeated in the chaitya hall next door (Cave 6).

Shivner Fort rises over 300m above the plain and is approached from the S by a track that passes over the moat, through 4 gates, then dog-legs up the final stretch to the plateau. Sivaji's birthplace is to the N and not far from it is a ruined mosque. There are 4 tanks running down the centre. In the 3rd century the site was a Buddhist vihara and on the E face there are about 50 rock cells. Maloji Bhonsla, Sivaji's grandfather, was granted the fort in 1599. Sivaji did not remain in it long as it was captured by the Mughals from the early 1630s. Several attempts to win it back failed.

Bhimashankar Completely off the beaten track, the pilgrim site of Bhimashankar can be reached by road from Shivner or from the NH 50 at Narayangaon. However, even buses are infrequent. The site is important to Hindus for the Siva temple built by the Peshwa Nana Phadnavis to house one of Maharashtra's 5 *jyotirlingas*. At *Sivaratri* there is a famous fair. **Accommodation** Two basic Maharashtra Tourism *Bungalows*.

The shortest way by road to Ahmadnagar from Shivner is via Ghargaon. A longer way but on better roads is to go on to Dolasne, via Supe in the Harischandra Range, then NE to Ahmadnagar.

Ahmadnagar

Ahmadnagar (*Population*: 221,700; *STD Code*: 0241), an historic Muslim town, was founded in 1490 by Ahmad Nizam Shah Bahri, the son of a Brahmin from Vijayanagar who converted to Islam. The dynasty he founded ruled the region until 1636, their territory stretching from Aurangabad to Bassein, just N of Bombay. Akbar captured the fort in 1599 after a long siege. The widow of Ali Adil Shah, killed leading the defence of the fort, is buried on a hill 10 km E of the city in the Tomb of Salabat Khan. Its Islamic history reflects strong Persian influence, both architecturally in the Persian style Husaini Mosque, and theologically in the presence of Shi'a Muslims from Persia in the court.

Aurangzeb died here on 3 Mar 1707. **Alamgir's Dargah** is a small enclosure near the cantonment and marks his temporary resting place before his body was moved to Aurangabad (Ahmadnagar was where Aurangzeb had begun his long Deccan campaign 24 years earlier). The tomb faces a mosque, while to the E is a white marble **Darbar Hall**, well worth visiting for the view from the roof.

The Fort (1599) is almost 1 km to the E of the city. Circular, it has an 18m high wall reinforced with 22 bastions. Among the numerous mosques inside are the small but attractive **Qasim** Mosque (1500-8); the **Husaini**, with its Persian style dome; the **Farhad Khani** (1560) with minarets, the **Damadi** (1567) with its splendid carved stonework and the large domed **Jamal Khan's Mosque**.

The Malik-i-Maidan iron cannon now standing on the Lion Bastion at Bijapur – see page 1054, was cast at Ahmadnagar by Rumi Khan, Nizam Shah's Turkish artillery officer. He also constructed the **Mecca Mosque** (c1515). The **Farah Baksh Palace**, built between 1508 and 1583, is now in ruins. The well preserved **Tomb of Nizam Shah** is situated in a large garden on the left bank of the Sina River. **Pariabagh** (Fairy Garden), the old palace of Burhan Nizam Shah (1508-53), is 3 km S of the city.

• **Accommodation** **D** *Natraj*, Nagar Aurangabad Rd, T 6576, 24 rm, 6 a/c, restaurant, bar. **E** *Asoka Tourist*, Kings Rd, T 23607, 32 rm, some a/c, restaurant (Punjabi). **Out of town**: **D** *Bhagyalaxmi*, Shirdi, Kopargaon, T 261, 58 rm, close to Kopargaon Rly. **E** *Suvidha*, Nim Gaon Jali, Sangamner, T Ashwi 75, 6 rm, restaurant (Indian).

• **Transport Train** Pune: *Maharashtra Exp* 7384, daily, 0140, 4¼ hr. **Bhopal**: *Jhelum Exp* 4677, daily, 2046, 12½ hr. The fort is 4 km NE of the station. **Road Bus**: regular buses to Bombay, Pune and other towns in the state.

Excursion

Shirdi (65 km; *Population*: 15,100) Just S of the Godavari River, the small town of Shirdi is associated with the original **Sai Baba**. Believed to be an incarnation of the Guru Pattareya, Sai Baba died on Dasara 1918. The present Sai Baba, who lives in Karnataka, is widely believed to be a re-incarnation of the Maharashtrian Sai Baba. Large fairs are held on *Ramnavmi*, *Guru Poornima* and *Dasara*, but every Thur is also special. **Accommodation F** Maharashtra Tourism *Pilgrim's Inn*, 50 self-contained rm, basic. T Shirdi 94.

ROUTES The direct route NE from Ahmadnagar to Aurangabad is 110 km. A longer route takes in Paithan (85 km), 63 km S of Aurangabad.

Paithan

(*Population*: 27,700; *STD Code*: 02766) This is one of the oldest cities of the Deccan. On the N bank of the Godavari River as it leaves the Nath Sagar reservoir to the W, it is mentioned in Asoka's Edicts and was visited by Greek traders in the 3rd century BC. From the 2nd century BC to 2nd century AD it was the capital of the Satvahana dynasty and was known as Pratisthan. Earlier remains have been dated to the 3rd millennium BC. It is famous for its Shrine of **Sant Eknath**.

Paithan is also famous for a special kind of silk sari with brocaded gold borders and *pallu* (end-piece). Motifs of geese, parrots, peacocks and stylised leaves, flowers and creepers in dark greens, red and blue are brocaded against the golden background. **Accommodation** Maharashtra Tourism has an **E** *Lake View Resort* at Jayakwadi (Jaikwadi), 14 rm, restaurant.

The **Jayakwadi Project** at **Nath Sagar** is a large earthen dam and reservoir covering over 35,000 ha. The Left Bank scheme is already providing irrigation all the way down the Godavari to Nanded 140 km to the E, and the equivalent Right Bank scheme is in progress. Around Paithan and Jayakwadi, the **Gyaneshwar Udyan**, a large garden along the lines of the Brindavan Gardens in Mysore, is being developed. At the S and N ends of the dam are 2 viewing stations for watching indigenous and migratory birds (best season Oct-Mar).

Local festival

Every year on *Nath Shashti* (usually in Mar) the 10-day Paithan Yatra fair is held, drawing pilgrims in their thousands.

Aurangabad

Population: 592,000; *STD Code*: 02432; *Best time*: Nov-Feb. Known as the base for visiting the superb caves at Ellora and Ajanta, Aurangabad is of interest in itself. Today, it has a university, medical and engineering colleges and an airport to complement its industrial and commercial activities, and is one of India's fastest growing cities.

History

Originally known as **Khadke** it was founded in 1610 by Malik Ambar, an Abyssinian slave who became the wazir (Prime Minister) to the King of Ahmadnagar. It was later changed to Aurangabad in honour of the last great Mughal, Aurangzeb, who built a new citadel. His wife is buried in the **Bibika Maqbara** and he is buried in a simple grave at Rauza – see Excursions. It acted as the centre of operations for his Deccan campaign which occupied him for the second half of his 49 year reign.

The British **cantonment** area is in the SW quadrant of the city on the left bank of the Kham River. To the N is the **Begumpura** district in which there is the attractive Pan Chakki water mill and the Bibika Maqbara, the mausoleum of Aurangzeb's wife, both worth visiting.

Places of Interest

Aurangzeb built the 4.5m high, crenellated city walls in 1682 as defence against the Marathas. There were 4 main gates (Delhi-N, Jalna-E, Pathan-S, and Mecca-W) and 9 subsidiary gates.

The **Killa Arrak** (1692), Aurangzeb's citadel, lay between the Delhi and Mecca Gates. Little remains, though when it was Aurangzeb's capital over 50 Maharajahs and Princes attended the court. With Aurangzeb gone, the city's significance faded. At the centre in a grove of trees lies the **Jama Masjid**, a low building with minarets and a broad band carved with Koranic inscriptions running the length of the façade. Malik Ambar built half the mosque, Aurangzeb the other.

Other monuments in the old city are **Kali Masjid** (1600), a 6 pillared stone mosque built by Malik Ambar who also constructed the ruined **Naukonda Palace** (1616), with a *zenana*, Halls of Public and Private Audience, mosque and baths. In the market square is the **Shah Ganj Mosque** (c1720) which has shops on 3 sides. The **Chauk Masjid** (1665) was built by Shayista Khan, Aurangzeb's uncle, and has 5 domes. The **Lal Masjid** (1655) is in red-painted basalt. The **City Chowk**, the market in the Old City, is worth visiting.

Bibika Maqbara (1678) Beyond the Mecca Gate lies the mausoleum of Aurangzeb's wife, Rabia Daurani. Open sunrise to 2000. Re 0.75, free on Fri. Floodlit at night.

Mughal style in decline The classic lines of a garden tomb give it an impressive setting. Yet close inspection disappoints. Modelled on the Taj Mahal, which was completed 25 years earlier, it is about half its size, standing in a 137,000 sq metre walled area, see page 45. Far less money was spent – $\frac{1}{300}$th, by some estimates – and the comparative poverty of the finish is immediately obvious. It uses marble on the bottom 2m of the mausoleum and 4 of the jali

CLIMATE: AURANGABAD

	Jan	Feb	Mar	Apr	May	Jun	Jul	Aug	Sep	Oct	Nov	Dec	Av/Tot
Max (°C)	29	32	36	38	40	35	29	29	30	31	30	29	32
Min (°C)	14	16	20	24	25	23	22	21	21	20	16	14	20
Rain (mm)	3	3	4	7	17	141	189	146	179	62	32	9	792

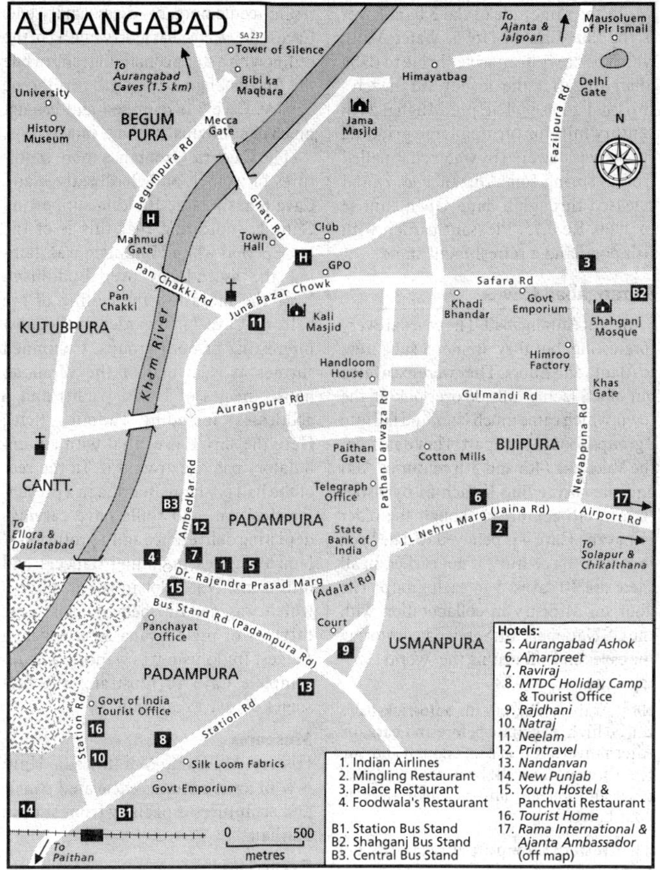

screens, but plaster elsewhere. The proportions are cramped for space and although the minarets are more than adequate in themselves, they are too heavy in relation to the main mausoleum. The decoration has become over fussy and the lines weak, and most of the carvings do not approach the quality of the Taj Mahal.

Yet despite all its failings it is one of the finest buildings of its period. The brass door carries an inscription which says Ata Ullah was the chief architect and Haibat Rai the maker of the door. An octagonal white marble *jali* screen surrounds the grave. On the tomb itself, in place of a marble slab, there is bare earth covered with a decorated cloth, a sign of humility. Light enters through a precisely angled shaft, allowing the early morning sun's rays to light the tomb for 3 min. The second tomb in the corner is said to be that of Rabi'a Daurani's nurse. To the W is a mosque.

On the same side of the Kham River is the **Pan Chakki** (1696, Water Mill), which has a white marble shrine to Baba Shah Muzaffar, the devout Aurangzeb's spiritual adviser. The pre-Mughal 17th century mill for turning large grinding stones was powered by water channelled from a spring some distance away and released through a dam. Open sunrise to 2000. Re 0.75. Pleasant garden with fish pond and a refreshment stand.

Aurangabad Caves

3 km N of Aurangabad. The caves are very interesting, but they are not a substitute to Ajanta and Ellora. They were excavated out of a S facing hillside overlooking the town, which came much later, and fall into 2 groups about 1 km apart. They date from the Vakataka (4th and 5th centuries AD) and the succeeding Kalachuri dynasties (6th to 8th centuries) though the older Hinayana Cave 4 is believed to date back to at least 1st century, if not earlier. In all there are 10 caves, 5 in each group. The Tourism Ministry in collaboration with the US National Park Service are restoring the caves and afforesting the 'World Heritage' site.

NB: Waiting charges for auto-rickshaws can be high, negotiate before and bargain. Alternatively, if it is cool enough and you feel fit, you can walk back to the edge of town and get an auto-rickshaw back to your hotel.

The **Western Group** are all *viharas* except for the earlier Cave 4 which is a *chaitya*. Cave 1 (incomplete) has finely carved pillars with figures on brackets and ornamentation around doorways and walls. Good views of the country around. Cave 2 has a shrine and columned hallways, with a large Buddha as Teacher in a seated position, with intricately carved panels. The larger Cave 3 has a plain exterior but has superb carvings on 12 pillars of the hallway which leads to the sanctuary, cut deep into the rock, with panels illustrating *jataka* stories and a fine large Buddha figure on his throne, with attendant devotees who represent contemporary dress and style. Cave 4, the *chaitya* has a rib vaulting of the ceiling with a stupa containing relics while the Buddha, figure is seated on a throne outside. Cave 5 is damaged and has not much of its original carvings intact.

The **Eastern Group** has more sculptures of women and Bodhisattvas and Cave 6 has a large Buddha supporting Ganesh, indicating that this is of the later period when Hinduism was gaining the ascendancy over Buddhism. Note the mural on the ceiling of the balcony. Cave 7 is regarded as the most interesting of both groups. Columned shrines at each end of the verandah house images of Hariti (right) and 6 goddesses, including Padmini (left). Here the shrine is central with an ambulatory passage around it. In the rear of the hall is a large Buddha in a preaching position, and walls have carvings depicting deliverance and a profusion of female figures including dancers and musicians. Not a lot to see in Cave 9 which was not finished but has some carvings of pre-Nirvana figures which suggest Buddhism was waning. The incomplete Cave 10 illustrates the first stages of cave excavation.

Museums

History Museum, Marathwada Univ, NW of town contains excavated panels and sculptures especially from sites in Paithan.

Excursions

Ellora, Daulatabad and Rauza are within easy reach for a half day excursion. Ajanta's caves are further but have magnificent paintings and rock cut cave temples. Conducted tours leave early.

NB: For visiting the caves. Take packed lunch and drinks, wear a sun hat and comfortable shoes, take a strong torch. Flash photography is allowed at Ellora but permission needed for professional cine cameras. Guides available (several foreign languages spoken) and at Ajanta 'flash lights passes' for groups wishing to see darker caves illuminated, are available (best to join a group if on your own). Painted caves open at 1000, others at 0900 – light is better in the afternoon. For the elderly and infirm, *dhoolies* (chairs carried by men) are available.

Ghrishneshwara The temple, just outside Ellora, houses one of the twelve jyotirlinga, see page 77.

Tours

Maharashtra Tourism, ITDC and ST all operate good sightseeing to Ajanta, Ellora and City sightseeing daily. **Central Bus Stand**: Ellora and City (0800-1630); Ajanta (0730-1730). **From Maharashtra Tourism** *Holiday Camp* (pick-up from major hotels): Ellora and City (0930-1730), Ajanta (0800-1730). **NB** Ellora trip visits too many places. ITDC tour tickets, from *Hotel Aurangabad Ashok*, T 24143.

Local Festivals

Feb/Mar: *Mahashivratri* large fair at the Ghrishneshwara Temple, nr Ellora and the *Ellora Yatra*.

Local information

● Accommodation

Price guide
AL Rs 3,000+ **A** Rs 2,000-3,000
B Rs 1,200-2,000 **C** Rs 600-1,200
D Rs 250-600 **E** Rs 100-250 **F** Up to Rs 100

Some offer discounts between Apr and Sep. Most will provide packed-lunch for trip to the caves. Taj Group's **A** *Residency*, 40 rm, to be opened mid-1993; **A** Welcomgroup *Rama International*, Airport Rd, R 3 Chikalthana, T 82241, 100 rm, 4 km centre, restaurant (variable), quiet, large gardens, off-season discount, some rm could be cleaner; **A** *Ajanta Ambassador*, Airport Rd, Chikalthana, T 82211, 125 rm, 4 km centre, excellent food (slow service), you can watch chef preparing meal, quiet, good service, excellent pool in pleasant gardens (open to non-residents, Rs 50).

C *Quality Inn Vedant*, Station Rd, T 25844, restaurants, pool; **C** *Aurangabad Ashok*, Dr Rajendra Prasad Marg, T 24520, 66 a/c rm, restaurant, bar, travel, shops, pool, comfortable and rec; **C** *Amarpreet*, JL Nehru Marg, T 23422, F 2792, 30 rm, central, restaurants, garden bar, travel.

D *Rajdoot*, very clean, good value, excellent Chinese restaurant, a little noisy; **D** *Raviraj*, Dr Rajendra Prasad Marg, T 27501, 40 rm, some a/c, restaurant, bar; **D** *Nandavan*, Station Rd, T 23574, 29 rm, few a/c, good restaurants, bar; **D** *Rajdhani*, a little further along Station Rd, T 27562, 30 rm with bath, some a/c.

● Budget hotels

E Maharashtra Tourism *Holiday Resort*, Station Rd, T 24259, 62 rm (6 a/c) with bath and mosquito nets, Tourist office, pleasant, good value rm, bar. **NB** Checkout 0800. Avoid restaurant. **E** *Tourist Home*, Station Rd, best in station area; **E** *New Punjab*, nr station, rec as good value; **E** *Natraj*, Station Rd, 100m from Rly, simple rm with bath, veg restaurant; **E** *Neelam*, Juna Bazar Chowk, T 24561, 28 rm with bath, some a/c, restaurant; **E** *Printravel*, Dr Ambedkar Rd, T 24707, old fashioned rm with baths and mosquito nets.

F *Youth Hostel*, Station Rd, Padampura, T 23801, clean, well run, good segregated dormitories, roof terrace, breakfast/evening meals, very good value, rec; **F** *Asoka*, Tilak Path, T 24555 and *Ambika*, nr the station are basic but cheap. Also *Railway Retiring Rms*, T 24815.

● Places to eat

Hotels rec for good food are *Ashok*, *Amarpreet*, *Ambassador* and *Printravel*. ***Mingling***, JL Nehru Marg opp *Amarpreet* has reasonably priced Chinese, rec; ***Palace***, Shahgunj, Indian (Mughlai); ***Neelam***, Jubilee Park; ***Panchavati***, nr Youth Hostel, Padampura. Best value *thalis* at the Youth Hostel and at ***Foodwalla's***, Dr Rajendra Prasad Marg, rec. Indian restaurants on Station Rd: ***Tandoor***, ½ km from Holiday Camp, popular, good value; *Nandavan* and ***Guru***, Station Rd. Punjabi. Inexpensive ***New Punjab***, nr Rly Station.

● Banks & money changers

Central Bank and State Bank of India in Kranti Chowk; **State Bank of Hyderabad** in Shahganj and Rly Station.

● Hospitals & medical services

Medical College Hospital, T 4411.

● Post & telecommunications

GPO: Juna Bazar Chowk. Cantt Post Office.

● Shopping

Usually open 1000-2000, closed Sun. The city is known for its handwoven Himru shawls (brocades occasionally with Ajanta motifs), and special textile weaves – *Mashru*, *Pathani silk* and *Kimkhab* as well as artificial silk. You can also get good decorative lacquer work, Bidri-ware and agate articles.

Main shopping areas are City Chowk, Gulmandi, Nawabpura, Station Rd, Shahganj, Sarafa, Mondha. **In Shahganj**: ***Cottage Industries*** and ***Himroo Factory Emporium***, nr Bus Stand, Station Rd: ***Silk Loom Fabrics*** and ***Govt. Emporium***, opp Holiday Camp. **At Nawabpura**: ***Khadi Gramudyog*** in Sarafa and ***Sajawat*** at Eknath Mandir.

Photography: *Mohammad Bhoy*, Chowk. *Paul Studio*, Cantt.

● **Tour comapnies & travel agents**

Aurangabad Transport Syndicate, *Rama International Hotel*, T 24872; ***Tourist Guide Service***, Shastri Nagar, Jawahar Colony, T 24262; ***Printravel***, Adalat Rd, T 24707; ***Amarmaya Travels***, T 26300.

● **Tourist offices & information**

Govt of India, Krishna Vilas, Station Rd, T 4817. Open 0830-1800 weekdays, 0830-1230 Sat. Airport Counter open at flight times. **Maharashtra Tourism**, *Holiday Resort*, Station Rd, T 23298. Open 1000-1700. Both helpful.

● **Useful addresses**

Ambulance: T 102. **Fire**: T 101. **Police**: T 100.

● **Transport**

Local Local taxis: Rates Rs 150/ 4 hr, 40 km. Rs 250/ 8 hr, 80 km. **Tongas** (no fixed rate) and **auto-rickshaws** (Rs 2.50 per km). **Bicycle hire**: ('cycle taxi') from shops nr Rly station. Rs 1.50/hr. **Bus**: services to Daulatabad fort, Ellora, Fardapur etc from Central Bus Stand.

Air The airport is 10 km from city centre. **Indian Airlines** connects Aurangabad with Bombay and New Delhi via Udaipur, Jodhpur and Jaipur daily. Indian Airlines City Office, Dr Rajendra Prasad Marg, T 24864. Airport Office, JL Nehru Rd, Chikalthana, T 82223.

Train Secunderabad (Hyderabad): *Ajanta Exp* 7552, daily, 2153, 12¾ hr. Direct service to Bombay. For Delhi change at Manmad.

Road Bus: State Transport Bus Service operates a/c coaches to Bombay (388 km) and Gatge Patil. State Transport bus services also connect Aurangabad with Pune, Hyderabad, Nashik and Nagpur. ITDC daily luxury coach to Bombay.

To Ellora

ROUTES The very pleasant drive to Ellora, 30 km NW of Aurangabad, passes through some exciting countryside with 2 interesting sites en route. Initially the road is tree lined with cultivated fields either side, becoming drier with thorny scrub.

Daulatabad

(13 km) On a volcanic lava rock towering 250m above the surrounding countryside is the fort of **Deogiri**. This dates from the Yadava period of the 11th-14th centuries although the first fort had probably been constructed in the 9th century, and before that had been a Buddhist monastery. From Ala-ud-din Khalji's capture of Deogiri in 1296 until Independence in 1947, by which time it was under the control of the Nizam of Hyderabad, the fort remained in Muslim hands. Muhammad Tughluq – see page 180 – determined to extend his

Deogiri Fortifications

The hillside around the Deogiri was made steeper to make scaling extremely difficult. The 3 concentric walls had strong gates, surrounded by a deep moat. The path climbs through the gates then up the steep slope towards the citadel. Today a new path has been cut to avoid the obstacles that were designed to prevent attackers from gaining entry; an L-shaped keep, a long tortuous tunnel which could be sealed by an iron cover at the top after firing with hot coals, and a chamber which could be filled with noxious fumes. At one point the tunnel divides and meets, to fool attackers to kill each other in the dark. The only genuine access was narrowed so that an invader would have to crawl through the last few metres, making it possible for defenders to kill them on sight. The bodies were disposed of by chutes down into the crocodile infested moat 75m below. A guide will take you through.

power S, seized Daulatabad, deciding to make it his capital and populate it with the residents from Delhi. Thousands died as a result of the shortlived experiment. The outermost of the 3 main ring walls and the bastion gates were probably built by the Muslims. It is an extraordinary site, particularly attractive in the late afternoon when the crowds have gone.

The Persian style **Chand Minar** (1435) stands at the bottom of the fort, towering as a celebration of victory like the Qutb Minar in Delhi. Its original covering of Persian blue tiles must have made it even more striking. Opposite is the **Jami Masjid** (1318), with 106 pillars taken from a Hindu temple, and a large tank. The 31m high victory tower built by Ala-ud-din Bahmani to celebrate his capture of the fort has at its base 24 chambers and a small mosque. Passing bastions, studded gates and a drawbridge, the path passes the **Chini Mahal** where Abdul Hasan Tana Shah, the last King of Golconda, was imprisoned in 1687 for 13 years. The 6.6m long **Kila Shikan** (Fort Breaker) iron cannon is on the bastion nearby. At the end of the tunnel (see box) inside the citadel is a flight of steps leading up to the **Baradari** (Pavilion), said to be the palace of the Yadavi Queen and later Shah Jahan. The **citadel** is reached by climbing 100 further steps and passing through 2 more gateways. At the top is another cannon with a ram's head on the butt. The Persian inscription around the muzzle reads 'Creator of Storms'. If you are lucky you may get the resident guide who takes visitors through the dark tunnels with a torch. Maharashtra Tourism Restaurant opp the entrance.

Beyond **Daulatabad**, the road climbs onto a plateau to **Rauza** (11 km, 630m) or Khuldabad, meaning 'Heavenly Abode', where there is the simple tomb of Aurangzeb, and over 20 tombs of other Muslim rulers in the Deccan. It was once an important town. Aurangzeb built the wall around it with 7 gates and a path and died at the age of 89 on Fri 20 Feb 1707. Since he wanted a simple grave as a sign of humility, open to the sky, his grave has no canopy. The marble screen around it was erected later by Lord Curzon and the Nizam of Hyderabad. Close to Aurangzeb's tomb are those of various saints, going back to the 14th century. Some are decorated with silver, and there are several relics – hairs of the Prophet's beard said to multiply every year, the Prophet's robe, the supposed remnants of trees miraculously converted to silver by the saint Saiyed Burhan-ud-Din (d1344). **Accommodation** **E** *Kailash* nr the caves has a good restaurant. **F** *Khuldabad Guest House* (3 km from Ellora caves) and *Local Fund Traveller's Bungalow* can be reserved through the Exec Engineer, Padampura and Zila Parishad, respectively, if free, cook available.

Ellora

The Hindu, Jain and Buddhist caves at Ellora are among the finest in India. Lying near an important ancient trade route between Ujjain in Madhya Pradesh and the W coast, the caves are thought to be the work of priests and pilgrims who used the route. Unlike the caves at Ajanta, Ellora's caves were never 'lost', but they were abandoned and forgotten. There are 34 caves, cut out of the volcanic lavas of the Deccan Trap. 12 are Buddhist (created from approximately 600-800 AD), 17 Hindu (600-900 AD) and 5 Jain (800-1100 AD). The land slopes so that most have courtyards in front. They face W and are best seen in the afternoon, and can comfortably be visited in an afternoon from Aurangabad.

NB: In order to see the caves in chronological order it is advisable if possible to stop at the E end of the caves so that you can see the Buddhist Viharas first. In this way the magnificent Hindu Kailasnatha temple is seen towards the end. However,

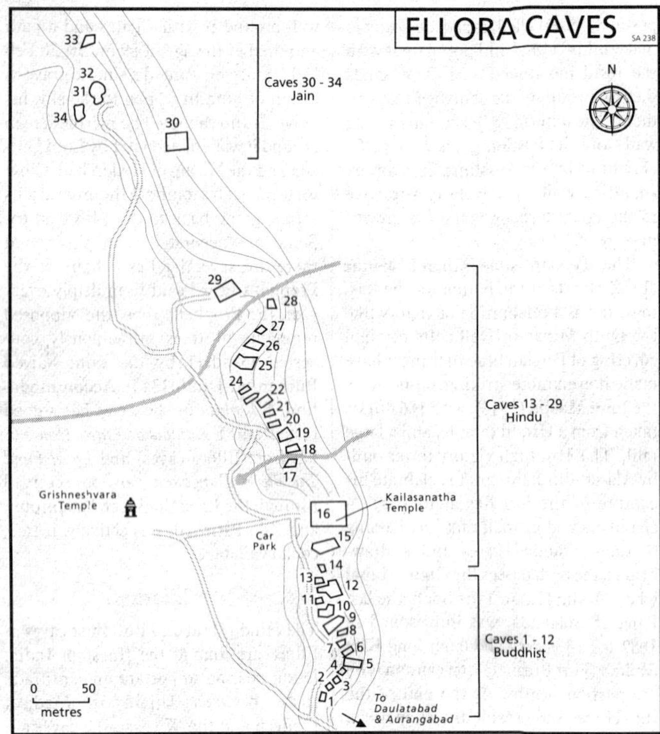

tour buses usually stop at the car park, directly in front of the Kailasnatha temple itself.

NB: Maharashtra Tourism has opened a restaurant, unexciting food, slow service; toilets and garden, souvenirs and postcards available, very attractive countryside, not suitable for disabled.

The Buddhist Caves: **Nos 1-10** (7th century) **11-12** (8th century):
These belong to the **Vajrayana** sect of the Mahayana (Greater Vehicle) School. The caves include *viharas* (monasteries) and *chaityas* (chapels) where the monks worshipped. It has been suggested that the stone cut structures were ideally suited to the climate which experienced monsoons, and rapidly became the preferred medium over more flimsy and less durable wood.

Cave 1 is a simple vihara with no pillars or carving. There are 4 cells in the S and E walls around a 13m square assembly hall. The adjoining **Cave 2** was a hall for worship and is reached by a flight of steps. At the door of the cave are *dwarapala* (guardians) flanked by windows. The interior (14.5 sq metres) comprises a hall supported by 12 pillars, some decorated with the pot and foliage motif. A gallery runs down each side. In the centre of the back wall is a 3m high seated Buddha and 2 standing Buddhas while along each of the side walls are 5 Buddhas accompanied by Boddhisattvas and *apsaras* (celestial nymphs). **Cave 3** is similar, having a square central chamber with a Buddha image, this time seated on a lotus at the far end. Around the walls are 12 meditation cells. **Cave 4** is 2-storeyed and not in very good condition. It contains a Buddha sitting under the Bo (pipal) tree.

Cave 5, the **Maharwada**, is the largest of the single storeyed caves in this group (17.6m by 36m). 2 rows of 10 columns each run the length of the cave, as do 2 raised platforms which were probably tables, suggesting that this cave was a dining hall. Note very attractive carvings on the first pillar on the left. The Buddha at the back is guarded on the left by *Padmapani* ('He who holds the lotus') a symbol of purity. On the right is *Vajrapani* ('He who wields the thunderbolt'), the symbol of esoteric knowledge and the popular deity of the sect, responsible for creating the caves. The Buddha is seated, not cross-legged on the floor as is usual, but on a chair or stool. He demonstrates some of the 32 distinctive marks: 3 folds in the neck, long ear lobes and the third eye. The hand codes (*mudras*) acted as signals to the initiated. The mudra here signifies the Buddha's first sermon at the Deer Park at Sarnath – see page 297 – and is a teaching pose.

The next 4 caves can be bypassed as they contain nothing new. **Cave 6** has a rectangular columned hall with 2 smaller subsidiary chambers, decorations of Bodhisattvas and a seated Buddha. **Cave 9** is approached through the hall of Cave 6 and consists of a small hall, open terrace with balcony and a shrine. The façade is richly decorated. **Cave 7** (under Cave 6) has 12 unfinished cells and a seated Buddha. The shrine in **Cave 8** is brought out into the hall and has a passageway around it.

Cave 10, **Viswakarma**, or Carpenter's Cave, is the only chaitya (chapel) cave in the group. It was a monastery. This is on the ground floor and above are what are presumed to have been the living quarters of the monks. In front is a large courtyard approached by a flight of steps. The galleries around it have square-based pillars at the foot of which was a lion facing outwards. At the back of these galleries are 2 elaborately carved chapels. The exterior decoration gives the impression that instead of stone, wood was the building material, hence *Viswakarma*. The façade has a trefoil window with *apsara* groups for ornamentation.

The main hall is large (26m by 13m, 10m high). The curved fluted 'beams' suggest to some the upturned hull of a ship. The chamber has 28 columns, each with a vase and foliage capital, dividing it up into a nave and aisles. The aisle runs round the decorated stupa (*dagoba*) with a colossal 4.5m 'Preaching Buddha' carved in front of it.

The upper gallery, reached by an internal flight of steps, was supposed to have subsidiary shrines at either end but the left hand one was not finished. Decorating the walls are loving couples, indicating how much Buddhism had changed from its early ascetic days. You can get a view of the friezes above the pillars which show Naga queens, symbolic precursors of the monsoon, and dwarfs as entertainers, dancing and playing musical instruments. The circular window at the entrance enables sunlight to be cast on it giving the face a truly spiritual and ethereal quality.

Caves 11 and 12 (both 8th century) are 3-storeyed and illustrate the use of the upper levels of these caves as a residence for monks and pilgrim hostels. **Cave 11** (*Do Thal* – 2-storeyed) was found to have a third storey in 1876 when the basement was discovered. The lowest level is a verandah with a shrine and 2 cells at the back of it. The middle level has 8 front pillars and 5 rear cells of which only the central 3 are completed and decorated. The upper level has a porch opening into a long colonnaded hall with a Buddha shrine at the rear. Images of Durga and Ganesh suggest that the cave was later used by Hindus. **Cave 12** (*Tin Thal* – 3 storeyed) has cells for sleeping (note stone benches) on the lower floors but it is the figures of the Buddha which are of particular interest. The rows of 7 Buddhas are symbolic of the belief that he appears on earth every 5,000 years and has already visited it 7 times.

The **Hindu Caves** (**Nos 13-29**)

These lie in the centre of the group and are the most numerous. **Cave 13** is a plain room while **Cave 14** (*Ravana ki khai*, 7th century), is single storeyed and the last of the collection from the early period. River goddesses and guardians stand at the doorway while inside is a broken image of Durga and figurative panels on the walls of the principle deities, Vishnu, Siva, Lakshmi and Parvati. **Cave 15** (*Das Avatara*, mid 8th century), reached by a flight of steps, has a large courtyard and is 2-storeyed.

Cave 16, **Kailasanatha Temple** (mid 8th century onwards). There is a car park in front of the temple. The Kailasanatha Temple is the most magnificent of all the rock cut structures at Ellora, cut out of the rock and open to the elements. It is the only building that was begun from the top.

Carved out of 85,000 cubic metres of rock, the design and execution of the full temple plan is an extraordinary triumph of imagination and craftsmanship. Excavating 3 deep trenches into the rock, carving started from the top of the cliff and worked down to the base. Enormous blocks were left intact from which the porch, the free standing pillars and other shrines were subsequently carved. The main shrine was carved on what became the upper storey, as the lower floor was cut out below. It is attributed to the Rashtrakuta King Dantidurga (725-55) and must have taken years to complete.

Mount Kailasa (6700m), the home of Siva, is a real mountain on the Tibetan plateau beyond the Himalaya. Its distinctive pyramidal shape, its isolation from other mountains, and the appearance of a swastika symbol etched by snow and ice on its rock face, imbued the mountain with great religious significance to Hindus and Buddhists alike. Kailasa was seen as the centre of the universe, and Siva is lord of Kailasa, Kailasanatha. To imitate the real snow covered peaks, the sikharas here were once covered with white plaster.

The Entrance The temple is 50m long and 33m wide and the tower rises 29m above the level of the court. At the entrance gate the threshold between the profane and sacred worlds, the goddesses **Ganga** and **Yamuna** form the door jambs. Just inside are 2 seated sages: **Vyasa**, the legendary author of the Mahabharata, and **Valmiki** to whom the Ramayana has been ascribed. In the porch 4 columns carry the North Indian vase and foliage motif, a symbol of fertility and well-being. On each side of the doorway there are images of **Kubera**, the god of wealth, with other symbols of well-being such as the conch shell and the lotus. Two more figures complete the welcoming party. They are **Ganesh** (left), the elephant headed son of Siva, the bringer of good fortune, and **Durga** (right), the vengeful form of Siva's wife Parvati.

In the antechamber opposite is **Lakshmi**, the goddess of wealth. In the courtyard, to your right and left are free standing elephants. On the left round the corner is a panel depicting **Kama**, the god of desire, carrying his bow and 5 arrows, one for each of the senses. On the far wall to your left of the entrance, behind the pillars, is the shrine of the **Three River Goddesses** – Ganga (centre), Yamuna (left) and Sarasvati (right). Symbolically they stand for purity, devotion and wisdom respectively. This is a good place to photograph the central shrine. The 2 carved monolithic pillars are probably stylised flagstaffs indicating royal patronage – a practice that Asoka popularised in the 3rd century BC.

There are 2 distinct levels taking the

worshipper from the courtyard by 2 staircases flanking the central hall, to the lower level with its processional path and then rising even higher to the upper level of the *mandapa*.

The Central Assembly Hall Around the central shrine is a colonnaded hall gouged from the rock, which in places overhangs menacingly. Inside this cloister are a series of panels portraying Siva and Vishnu myths. The whole can be viewed as a sort of instructional picture gallery, a purpose it served for worshippers from ancient times who could not read.

The S facing wall has *Ramayana* stories – Ravana offering his heads; Siva and Parvati with Nandi the bull and the lingam (creative power); Siva playing the vina; Siva and Parvati playing dice in a spirit of harmony; the marriage of Siva and Parvati; the origin of the *lingam*, the symbol of Siva and creative (male) energy; Siva dancing and Siva tricking Parvati. Note the panel on the S of the *mandapa* of Ravana shaking Mount Kailasa attempting to carry it off, disturbing Parvati and her attendants, one of whom is seen frightened and fleeing, and Siva restoring order with the movement of his toe.

Along the N facing wall are stories from the *Mahabharata* above and *Krishna* legends below. The panels include Krishna (Vishnu's 8th incarnation) stealing buttermilk; Vishnu as Narasimha, half man, half lion; Vishnu reclining on Ananda the serpent in-between incarnations; Vishnu the Preserver. Finally there is Annapurna, Goddess of Plenty.

The inner porch contains 2 panels, Siva as Lord of Knowledge and Siva as Bhairava Killing the Elephant Demon.

The Main Shrine Steps lead to the upper floor which contains a *mandapa* (central hall, 17m by 16m) of 16 stout pillars arranged in groups of 4, with aisles corresponding to the cardinal points leading to an open central area. At the far end is the *garbhagriha* (shrine) with Ganga and Yamuna as door guardians. Inside is the yoni lingam, symbol of Siva's creative power. Running around the back is a passageway with 5 small shrine rms off it, each with a replica of the main temple. Note the Nataraja painting on the *mandapa* ceiling. There are remnants of paintings on the porch ceilings (particularly to the W) where you will see *apsaras*, dwarfs and animals.

The temple rises in a pyramid, heavier and more squat looking than later towers in the N. The shape suggests enormous strength. As you leave the temple, the path to the left leads up and around the temple, giving a birds-eye view of the magnificent complex.

Cave 21 (**Ramesvara**, late 6th century) has a court with a stone Nandi bull in the middle and side shrines. A linga sanctuary leads off the verandah. This cave is celebrated for its fine sculptures of amorous couples and the gods. **Cave 29** (Dhumar Lena, late 6th century) is very similar to Elephanta – see Bombay Excursions page 1147 – in concept. Access is from 3 sides, there is a spacious hall with a separate small sanctuary with a *lingam* at the end. Wall panels depict Siva legends especially as Destroyer.

Jain Caves (Nos 30-34)

These are something of an anti-climax after the Hindu ones, but they have an aura of peace and simplicity. **Cave 30** (Chhota Kailasa, early 9th century) was intended as a smaller scale replica of the Kailasanatha temple but was not completed. The columned shrine has 22 *tirthankaras* with *Mahavira* in the sanctuary.

Cave 32 (Indra Sabha, early 9th century) is the finest of the Jain series and is dedicated to **Mahavira**. A simple gateway leads into an open court in the middle of which stands the shrine. The walls have carvings of elephants, lions and *tirthankaras*. The lower of the 2 is incomplete but the upper has carvings of Ambika and also Mahavira flanked by guardians of earlier *tirthankaras*. The ceiling is richly carved with a massive lotus at the centre and you can see signs of painted figures among clouds.

Ajanta

The drive to Ajanta (100 km) takes under 2 hr. The Jalgaon road crosses the relatively fertile plain surrounding the city, then climbs the hills behind Aurangabad. There is extensive small scale irrigation in this area. **Shilod** (Silod) (63 km) is a popular halting place and has a number of restaurants. About 10 km from Ajanta, the road descends from this plateau. There are dramatic views of the Waghora valley, where the caves are located.

There is a small settlement with a *Tourist Lodge*, restaurant, curio market and aggressive salesmen at the foot of the approach to the caves, which are carved in a horseshoe shaped cliff face. It is a short uphill walk along a well-made, stepped concrete path to the entrance. There are *dhoolis* available for hire if you wish to be carried. The admission kiosk is at the top of the steps. Open 0900-1730, Re 0.50, free on Fri. A light pass (Rs 5.00) is necessary if you want the guides to turn on the lights.

NB: You can approach the caves from the river bed in the bottom of the valley, where the bus stops. You have to buy your ticket from the kiosk first, and if there is water in the stream at the bottom you have to walk through it, but it is much shadier than the path cut out of the cliff.

The history

The caves, older than those at Ellora, date from about 200 BC to 650 AD. They are cut from the volcanic lavas of the Deccan Trap in a steep crescent shaped hillside in a forested ravine of the Sahyadri hills. After the late 7th century, the jungle took over and they lay unnoticed for centuries. Hiuen-Tsang, recorded in the 7th century (although he didn't visit it) a description of the "monastery in a deep defile...large temple with a huge stone image of the Buddha with a tier of 7 canopies."

The Caves

The terrain in which the caves were excavated was a sheer cliff facing a deeply incised river meander. At the height of Ajanta's importance the caves are thought to have housed about 200 monks (some of them artists), and numerous artists, craftsmen and labourers. The masterpieces retell the life-story of the Buddha and reveal the life and culture of the people of the times, royal court settings, family life, street scenes and superb studies of animals and birds. The Jatakas relate the Buddha's previous births – showing the progress of the soul.

Cave Painting Techniques

To prepare the rock for painting it was chiselled to leave a rough surface. 2 layers of mud-plaster containing fibrous material (grain-husk, vegetable fibres and rock grit), was applied, the first coarse, the second fine. Metal mirrors must have been used by the artists, to reflect sunlight into the dark caves. It is thought that the tempera technique was used. On a dry surface, a red cinnabar outline defined the picture, filled in, possibly initially with grey and then numerous colour pigments usually mixed with glue: the completed painting was burnished to give a lustrous finish. The pigments were mainly taken from the land around, the principle ones being red and yellow ochre, white from lime and kaoline, green from glauconite, black from lamp-black and blue from imported lapis lazuli. The shellac used in restoration after 1819 was found to be cracking. Since 1951 this has been removed by the Archaeological Survey of India, with UNESCO's help. PVA is now used.

Originally the entrance to the caves was along the river-bed and most had a flight of stairs leading up to them. The first to be excavated was Cave 10, followed by the first Hinayana (in which the Buddha is not depicted in human form) caves either side. Later Mahayana caves were discovered, completing the spectrum of Buddhist development in India.

There is a round trip walk, up the side of the valley where all the caves are located then down to the river to cross to the other side. An attractive low level walk through forest brings you back to the roadhead. **Caves 1, 2, 10, 16, 17,** have lights. **11, 19** and **26** are also particularly worth visiting.

NB: Flash photography is forbidden because of the damage that is caused by direct

AJANTA'S DISCOVERY

In 1819, a party of British army officers from Madras noticed the top of the façade of Cave 10 while tiger hunting. They investigated and discovered some of the caves, describing seeing 'figures with curled wigs'. Others made exploratory trips to the fascinating caves. In 1843, James Fergusson, horrified by the ravage of the elements, requested that the East India Company do something to preserve and protect the deteriorating caves.

In 1844 Captain **Robert Gill,** an artist, was sent to copy the paintings on the cave walls. He spent 27 years living in a small encampment outside, sending each new batch of paintings to Bombay and London. After nearly 20 years his work was almost complete. His collection was displayed in the Crystal Palace in S London. In Dec 1866 all but a few of the paintings were destroyed in a fire. Gill soldiered on for another 5 years before giving up, and died from illness soon afterwards. He is buried in the small European cemetery at **Bhusawal,** 60 km to the N.

Preservation of the murals poses enormous challenges. Repeated attempts to reproduce and to restore have faced major problems. After all but 5 of Robert Gill's paintings were destroyed by fire, the Bombay School of Arts sent out a team to copy the paintings under the guidance of the principal John Griffiths in the 1870s. He advocated that photographic plates be made of the facsimiles as soon as they reached London. However, the expense was considered too great. The paintings were stored in the Victoria and Albert Museum in London. This also had a fire in 1885, when 87 were destroyed.

In 1918 a team from Kyoto University Oriental Arts Faculty arrived at Ajanta to copy the sculptures. This they did by pressing wet rice paper against the surface to make casts which were then shipped back to Japan. In the early 1920s they were all destroyed by an earthquake.

In 1920 the paintings were cleaned by the former Hyderabad Government under whose jurisdiction the caves lay. Two Italian restorers were commissioned, whose first priority was to fix the peeling paintings to the walls of the caves. They first injected casein between the paintings and the plastered wall, then applied shellac as a fixative. The Griffiths team from Bombay had also applied a coat of varnish to bring out the colours of the paintings.

However, these varnishes darkened over the years, rendering the murals less, not more visible. They also cracked, aiding the peeling process and the accumulation of moisture between the wall and the outer membrane. The Archaeological Survey of India is now responsible for all restoration at the site.

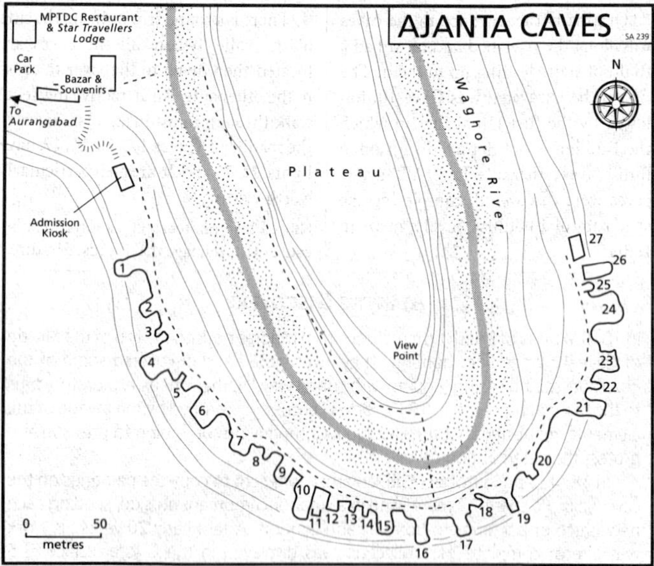

light to the paintings. It is possible to buy excellent postcards very cheaply. In the Mahayana caves with paintings there is a restriction on the number of visitors allowed in at any one time. Some caves have electricity supplied to them and lights for illuminating the paintings. These are only turned on for brief moments.

The Mahayana group

Cave 1 (Late 5th century), is one of the finest viharas (monasteries), remarkable for the number and quality of its murals. A verandah with cells and porches either side has 6 columns and 3 entrances leading into a pillared hall. Above the verandah are friezes depicting the sick man, old man, corpse and saint encountered by the Buddha, who is shown above the left porch. The hall measures 19.5 sq metres and has 20 ornamented pillars, a feature of the late period caves. Five small monks' cells lead off 3 sides, and in the centre of the back wall is a large shrine of the Buddha supported by Indra, the rain god. At the entrance are the river goddesses Yamuna and Ganga and 2 snake-hooded guardians at the base.

The **murals** are among the finest at Ajanta. In the 4 corners are panels representing groups of foreigners. The Mahajanaka jataka (where the Buddha took the form of an able and just ruler) covers much of the left hand wall including Renunciation, and the scenes where he is enticed by beautiful dancing girls.

On either side of the entrance to the antechamber of the shrine room are 2 of the best known murals at Ajanta. On the left is the Bodhisattva Padmapani (here holding a blue lotus) in a pose of spiritual of detachment, whilst on the right is the Boddhisattva Avalokitesvara. Together compassion and knowledge, the basis of Mahayana Buddhism, complement one another. Their size dwarfs the attendants to enhance the godlike stature of the boddhisattva. The Buddha inside the shrine is seated in the teaching position, flanked by the 2 carved boddhisattvas. Under the throne appears the Wheel of

Life, with deer representing Sarnath where he preached his first sermon. See page 297.

One of the sculptural tricks that a guide will display is that when the statue is lit from the left side (as you face it), the facial expression is solemn, suggesting contemplation. Yet from the other side, there is a smile of joy while from below it suggests tranquillity and peace. Note the paintings on the ceiling, particularly the elephant scattering the lotus as it rushes out of the pond, and the charging bull. Also look for the 'black princess' and the row of the dancer with musicians. On the way out look for the pillar that has 4 deer sculpted skilfully, sharing the same head.

Cave 2 (6th century) is also a *vihara* hall, 14.6 sq metres with 12 pillars, with 5 cells on each side of the left and right hand walls and 2 chapels on each side of the antechamber and shrine room. At the front is a verandah with a side chapel at each end. The doorway is richly carved. On the left hand wall is the mural depicting **The Birth of The Buddha**. Next to this is **The 'Thousand' Buddhas**, which illustrates the miracle when the Buddha multiplied himself to confuse a heretic. On the right are dancing girls before the king, shown with striking 3 dimensional effect.

The cave is remarkable for its painted ceiling, giving the effect of the draped cloth canopy of a tent. The *mandala* (circular diagram of the cosmos) is supported by demon-like figures. The Greek key designs on the border are possibly influenced by Gandharan art, 1st-3rd centuries AD. The ceiling decorations portray a number of figures of Persian appearance apparent from the style of beard and whiskers and their clothing.

The *Yaksha* (nature spirits) Shrine in the left chapel is associated with fertility and wealth. The main shrine is that of Buddha in the teaching position, again flanked by the 2 boddhisattvas, both holding the royal fly whisk. The Hariti Shrine on the right is to the ogress who liked eating children! The panel on your left as you leave the hall is a *jataka* telling the story of the Boddhisattva's life as the Pandit Vidhura.

Cave 3-7 are late 5th century. **Cave 3** has no verandah and **Cave 4** is the largest vihara at Ajanta, planned on an ambitious scale and not completed. The hall is 27 sq metres and supported on 28 pillars. Along the walls are cells whilst at the rear is a large shrine. **Cave 5** is also unfinished while **Cave 6** is on 2 levels with only 7 of the 16 octagonal pillars standing. A shrine contains a seated Buddha. **Cave 7** has no hall. The verandah has 2 porches each supported by heavy octagonal Elephanta-type columns. These lead to 4 cells. These and the antechamber are profusely carved. The shrine is that of Buddha, his hand raised in blessing.

Hinayana group

A Hinayana group comes next (**Caves 6-10** and **12**, **13** and **15**) dating from the 2nd century BC. **Cave 8** (1st century BC) is a small vihara (10m by 5m and 3m high). **Cave 9** (c100 BC), a *chaitya*, is 14m long, 7m wide and 7m high. 14 columns run the length of each side and 11 continue round the stupa. The vaulted roof was once wooden ribbed and leads back from a huge 3.4m arched *chaitya sun* window which throws light on the stupa at the rear. Two phases of wall painting have been identified. The earlier ones dating from the construction of the cave can be seen at the far left side and consist of a procession to a stupa as well as a thin band above the left colonnade. Above this are later Buddha figures from the Mahayana period when the figures of the Buddha on either side of the entrance were painted.

Cave 10 (c150 BC) is much larger and measures 30m by 12.4m and is 11m high. Like the previous cave the roof was once fitted with wooden ribs which subsequently collapsed. The long hall with an apse housing the stupa was one of the first excavated and first rediscovered by army officers. An inscription above the façade, now destroyed, dated the excavation to the 2nd century BC through a generous donation by the king. The dagoba or stupa resembles that of Cave 9 and is a double storey drum. There are also paintings dating from the Hinayana and Mahayana periods. The early ones depict figures in costumes resembling those seen at Sanchi – see page 360. Traces of later paintings survive on the pillars and aisle ceilings and later Buddha figures are often superimposed on earlier works. The main subjects of the Hinayana paintings are *jataka* stories. On the rear wall is the King (in a ceremonial head-dress) and Queen approaching the Sacred Bodhi Tree, one of the earliest Ajanta paintings.

Cave 11 (originally 2nd century BC, with 6th century alterations) has a verandah and roof painted with birds and flowers, a hall supported by 4 heavy pillars and a stone bench running along the right side. There are 5 cells and a shrine of a seated Buddha. **Caves 12** (with glauconite rock wall) and **13** (2nd century BC) are small viharas. **Cave 14** (5th century AD) was planned on a grand scale but not completed and can be missed along with **Cave 15** (5th century) which is a long hall with a Buddha carved out of the rock.

Later Mahayana period

The remaining caves all belong to the **Later Mahayana period** and date from the 5th century. **Cave 16**, with kneeling elephants at the entrance and the Cobra King, has a 20m long and 3.5m deep verandah that carries 6 plain octagonal pillars. There is a good view of the ravine from here. The magnificent 20m long columned hall inside has 6 cells on each side and a beamed ceiling. The Teaching Buddha is seated on a lion throne. On the left the 'Dying Princess' portrays Nanda's new bride being told that he has been ordained a monk and renounced the world. Her misery is shared by all and everything around her. On the right wall are the remains of a picture of Prince Siddhartha, later the Buddha, using a bow.

Cave 17 (late 5th century) is very similar to No. 16 in layout and preserves the greatest number of murals. On the left of the verandah is a painted Wheel of Life. Over the entrance door is a row of 7 Past Buddhas and the 8th, the **Maitreya** or Future Buddha, above a row of amorous Yaksha couples. Sculpted deities are carved on either side.

Murals show scenes from 17 *jatakas*: the worship of Buddha where even the god Indra descends through clouds with other celestial figures; a flying apsara to the right; the Buddha preaching; Hansa jataka, with paintings of geese; Vessantara jataka where the greedy Brahmin is portrayed, grinning; the miraculous 'Subjugation of the rogue elephant', sent to kill the Buddha; the ogress who turns into a beautiful maiden by day! There are also panels showing royal processions, warriors, an assembled congregation from which you can get an accurate and detailed picture of the times. **Cave 18** (late 5th century) has little of merit and can be missed.

Cave 19 (late 5th century) is a Mahayana chaitya hall and was painted throughout. The façade is considered to be one of the most elegant in terms of execution and elaborate ornamentation, and has the arched chaitya window set into it. The interior (14m long, 7.3m high and wide) is in the layout seen before, 2 rows of richly decorated columns leading up to and around the back of the standing Buddha which here is in front of the slender stupa. This tall shrine has a triple stone umbrella above it. Note the seated Nagaraja with attendants.

Cave 20 is comparatively small (8.5m by 7.6m) and has imitation beams carved into the ceiling.

Later caves

The final few caves belong to the 7th century and are a separate and distinct group at the farthest end of the horseshoe nr the waterfall. Only one, Cave 26 need be visited. **Cave 21** (early 7th century) has a fallen verandah with flanking chapels. Cave 24 was intended to be the largest *vihara* but was not completed.

Cave 26 is a large *chaitya hall*. A partly damaged columned façade stretches across the front with the customary side chambers at each end. The 3m high window is flanked by sculptured Buddha reliefs. Inside, 26 pillars run in an elongated semi circle around the cylindrical stupa which is decorated with Buddhas. The walls are decorated with sculpture, including the temptations by Mara's daughters, but the most striking being a 9m reclining image of the Parinirvana Buddha, about to enter Nirvana, his death mourned by his followers.

The walk back along the promenade connecting the shrines is pleasant enough but the return via the river, waterfall and forest walkway is delightful. Steps lead down from Cave 16 (with the carved elephants). The hilltop opposite the caves offers a fine view of the horseshoe shaped gorge.

NB: The *Food Wallahs* restaurant at the entrance serves good if limited food. Reasonable price, good service, clean toilets.

• **Accommodation At Ajanta**: **E** Maharashtra Tourism ***Resort***, has rm with bath, beer bar. **At Fardapur** (Phardapur): **E** Maharashtra Tourism ***Holiday Resort***, Fardapur, 10 rm with bath and dorm, 5 km from Ajanta caves, restaurant, inexpensive, simple but rec, furnished tents with electricity in the grounds are popular. Also ***Guest House*** and ***Travellers' Bungalow***, with cook but these are less comfortable, reservations: Exec Engineer, PWD, Padampura, Aurangabad, if free. ***Forest Rest House*** with cook, Reservations: Div Forest Officer, Osmanpura, Aurangabad. Land has been acquired to provide other facilities near the caves.

• **Transport Train** The caves can also be visited from Jalgaon 59 km, which has the nearest railway station. *Coromandel Exp* (convenient from Calcutta) does not stop at Jalgaon so best to get off at Bhusawal. **Road Bus**: regular bus service to Ellora and Fardapur from Aurangabad and Jalgaon. **Taxis** and **auto rickshaws** can be hired for the day for visiting the sights.

AURANGABAD TO NANDED AND NIZAMABAD

The road and railway go down the gentle slope of the great basin of the Godavari. Ancient erosion surfaces covered in some of India's richest black lava soils dominate the landscape.

NB: During the monsoon the causeways over the rivers may be flooded. Enquire in advance.

ROUTES From Aurangabad cross the River Balamarai (by causeway; 32 km) to **Jalna** (230 km; *Population*: 175,000; *STD Code*: 02482). Noted as the town to which Abul Fazl, who wrote the *Ain i Akbari*, was exiled and ultimately murdered by Bir Singh Deo of Orchha – see page 347 – at the instigation of Jahangir. The Jalna region is dotted with forts.

• **Accommodation** There is a *Dak Bungalow* and a *Rest House* in the town.

• **Transport Train** To **Aurangabad**: *Marathwada Exp* 7593, daily, 0907, 1¼ hr; *Adilabad Passenger* 577, daily, 1852, 1¾ hr. To **Nanded**: *Marathwada Exp* 7594, daily, 1856, 4 hr. To **Secunderabad via Nanded**: *Ellora Exp* 7596, daily, 1031, 4 hr and 11 hr. **Road Bus**: regular buses to Lonar (2 hr), Aurangabad (2 hr) and Nanded (5 hr).

ROUTES The road continues E to Mantha (37 km), where a road runs N to the remarkable 2 km wide meteor crater near **Lonar**(42 km; *Population*: 16,000).

• **Accommodation F** Maharashtra Tourism *Resort*, tents can be reserved, T Buldhana 443302.

• **Transport Road** To Jalna (75 km, 2 hr). To Jintur (50 km, 1½ hr). To Ajanta (137 km) via Buldana (90 km, 3 hr).

ROUTES From Jintur (*Population*: 28,300) the Nanded road continues E. After 30 km a road left turn leads to the **Sideshwar Dam** (4 km).

The road to Nanded crosses wide open cultivated land, interspersed with occasional small settlements, mainly off the road itself. It passes through the important religious settlement of **Aundah** (Aundh Nagnath) which is regarded as the first ('adya') of the twelve jyotirlinga sites. The Nagnath temple is finely carved. See page 77.

Nanded (Nander) (*Population*: 308,900; *STD Code*: 02462) is where Guru Gobind Singh, the 10th Sikh guru, was assassinated in 1708 – see page 92. There is a *gurudwara* 1.5 km from the station. Today Nanded is an important regional centre, administrative and commercial town. It is on the River Godavari. It is also on the main railway line between Hyderabad/Secunderabad and Aurangabad/ Nashik.

AURANGABAD TO SOLAPUR, GULBARGA AND BIJAPUR

ROUTES The road crosses from the great river basin of the Godavari River to the Bhima River, a tributary of the Krishna. It is the shortest route (325 km) from Aurangabad to the Muslim capitals of North Karnataka.

The slopes are often imperceptible, occasional flat-topped tablelands separated from the valley floors by short steep sided escarpments. The altitude falls gently from 525m at Aurangabad to 475m around Solapur. This is the heart of the black lava soil region. The roads are generally quiet, the only towns being small market centres with very limited facilities.

Latur (*Population*: 197,400) On 30 September 1993 the area was shaken by a devastating earthquake, focused on Latur. Registering 6.3 on the Richter scale, the quake caused an estimated 10,000 deaths, largely because it occurred in the early hours of the morning when most people were in their houses. The area, in the normally stable geological region of the central peninsula, is far removed from the main earthquake zones, and houses have not been designed to minimise damage.

ROUTES The road passes through **Bid** (Bir, Beed; 42 km; *Population*: 112,400), where the Parli Vaijnath temple enshrines one of the twelve jyotirlinga, see page 71. It continues to **Yermala** (79 km) and crosses the Barsi Light Railway (21 km), the narrow gauge railway line that links **Miraj**, 220 km to the SW (*Population*: 125,400), with Latur 70 km E.

Around **Osmanabad** (*Population*: 68,000; *STD Code*: 02472) there are groups of Jain and Vaishnavite caves dating from the 5th and 6th centuries AD. Between Osmanabad and **Tuljapur** (*Population*: 23,000) the road crosses the watershed between the Godavari and the Krishna river basins. In the town of Tuljapur the Tulja Bhavani temple, dedicated to Durga, is a focus for pilgrims from all over India. It is associated with supposedly miraculous gift of a sword by the Goddess to Sivaji which was vital to his subsequent success. Solapur is 42 km S, see page 1194.

BOMBAY TO PUNE, SOLAPUR AND HYDERABAD

ROUTES The main **NH4** crosses the narrow lowland out of Bombay to Thana. It climbs steeply onto the plateau. Pune, just in the lee of the ghats, has become a sprawling city with 2.5 million people. The **NH4** then runs across the vast open spaces of the cultivated plateau region, with spectacularly broad views of the black soil regions en route to the cotton textile centre of Solapur and on to Hyderabad.

From Bombay the NH4 passes through Thana. To the E of Mumbra, crowning the steeply scarped plateau is the Maratha fort of **Malangarh**. Continue to Panvel (*Population*: 58,800; *STD Code*: 0227). 3 km out of Panvel the climb up the ghats begins.

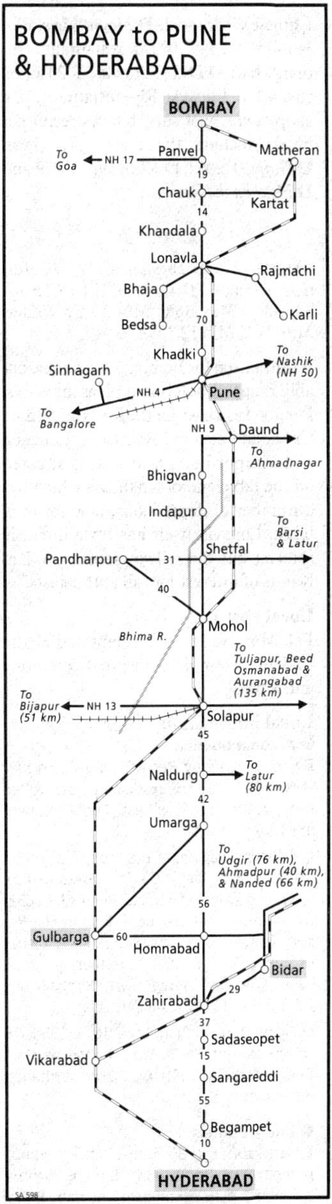

Matheran

(*Population*: 4,700; *Altitude*: 750m) Bombay's nearest hill station, Matheran maintains its quiet by banning all forms of vehicles within the town. Situated in the Sahyadari range, meaning 'Mother Forest' or 'Wooded Head', the views, the cooler air and pleasant walks are its main attractions. Particularly quiet during the week.

Light railway The most scenic route for this diversion is by the spectacular light railway through the ghats from Neral (may be closed during the monsoon). From Bombay take the Pune trains as far as **Neral** then transfer to the atmospheric narrow gauge. Each sector of the journey is about 2 hrs. On this route you appreciate the problems facing the early railway engineers – see page 1124. There are also trains from **Karjat Junction**.

Matheran sprawls out along a N-S ridge and from rocky promontories such as The Hart, Panorama Point, Chauk, Duke's Nose and Garbat there are splendid views down the almost sheer hillsides to the valleys below. From the northernmost vantage points you can see the lights of Bombay on a clear night. The layout of the town conforms with standard British Hill Station planning with central civic buildings and widely dispersed bungalows.

• **Accommodation** The hotels here are all central and nr the Rly Station. Many can be reserved in Bombay. **B** *Rugby*, Vithalrao Kotwal Rd, T 291, 52 a/c rm, restaurant.

C *The Byke*, T 316 or Bombay, T 256312, 50 rm, some a/c, restaurants, pool. **C** *Brightlands Resorts*, Maulana Azad Rd, T 244 or Bombay, T 6423856, 36 rm, 11 a/c, restaurant, travel, pool. **C** *Lord's Central*, T 228, or Bombay, T 318008, 23 rm, restaurant, bar, park, riding, not plush but clean. **C** *Regal*, opp Post Office, Kasturba Rd, T 243 or Bombay, T 325342, 75 rm, some a/c. **C** *Royal*, T 247, or Bombay, T 352784, 61 rm, 5 a/c, restaurant (Indian veg), bar, coffee shop, travel, health club, exchange, information counter.

D *Maldoonga Resort*, Malet Rd, T 204, 14 rm, restaurant. **D** *Alexander*, T 251, 24 rm, 3 a/c, restaurant. **D** *Tourist Towers*, MG Rd, T 71, 24 rm, restaurant (Indian), riding. **D** *Bombay View*, Cutting Rd, T 279, or Bombay, T 6145993, 22 rm, nr rly, restaurant, travel. **D** *Silvan*, Acharya Atre Marg, nr Charlotte Lake, T 74, 16 rm, riding. **D** *Divadkar*, opp Rly Station, rm with bath and verandah.

• **Budget hotels** **E** *Gujarat Bhavan*, Maulana Azad Rd, T 378, 22 rm, restaurant (Indian veg), garden, local folk dances. **E** *Giririhar*, Sivaji Rd, peaceful, spacious gardens, some rm with balconies. **E** *Laxmi*, M Gandhi Rd, next to PO, rm with bath. **F** *Holiday Camp*, 1 km before Matheran (Train stops at camp), T 77, cottages and dorm.

• **Places to eat** *Woodlands*, Chinoy Rd, Indian. *Kwality Fruit Juice House*, MG Rd, S of Rly Station among many. Excellent honey and *chikki* (a sweet peanut brittle). Restaurants sell beer without a permit.

• **Tourist Information Centre & Post Office** (opp Rly Station), on MG Rd.

• **Transport Local Ponies** and **rickshaws** are available for hire at negotiable rates.

ROUTES From Matheran you can proceed to Lonavla via Khandala. The ravined countryside between is stunning. On the railway line gradients of 1 in 37 were used to overcome the problems posed by 'the big step' (Ghat) the hills presented. At the **Bhor Ghat** near Karjat there was a reversing station. During the monsoon waterfalls are commonplace.

The NH4 continues from the Matheran-Neral Junc through a ghat section and tunnel to Khopoli and Khandala.

Khopoli is little more than a stopping point on the Bombay-Pune Highway. **Accommodation** **E** Maharashtra Tourism *Motel Madhughat*, with a/c suites and a restaurant. It is a convenient base for exploring local sights such as the Sri Baleshwar temple at Pali (35 km).

Khandala (27 km; *Alt*: 615m) is a quiet village overlooking a great ravine from which the Konkan region S of Bombay can be seen. **Accommodation On Bombay-Pune Rd**: **D** *Fun-n-Food*, 61 Hilltop Colony, T 2854, 35 rm, restaurant (Indian, Chinese), bar, pool; **D** *Mount View*, Plot No 415, T 2335, 16 rm, restaurants (Indian), bar; **D** *Duke's Retreat*, T 2336, 62 rm, 4 km Lonavla Rly, restaurant, bar, shop, lawns, pool, superb views, rec. Other hotels include the reasonably cheap **D** *Girija*, T 2062; **D** *Khandala*, T 239 and **D** *Hotel on the Rocks*.

Lonavla

BASICS 5 km; *Population*: 47,700; *Altitude*: 625m; *STD Code*: 021147; *Climate*: Summer: Max 36°C Min 19°C; Winter: Max 31°C Min 12.3°C.

A hill station for Bombay, it has a reasonable range of hotels and pleasant walks. It is good as a base for the Karla and Bhaja Caves and also the Rajmachi, Lohagen and Visapur Forts nearby. It is situated on the tableland of Khandala which has a number of depressions, now forming lakes. Lonavla itself has little intrinsic interest but the railway journey to Kalyan is of interest for rail enthusiasts.

Local Festivals

Feb/Mar *Sivaratri* is celebrated at the Mahadev Temple with great ceremony and a fair.

Local information

● **Accommodation**

B *Fariyas Holiday Resort*, Tungarli, Frichley Hills, T 2701, 90 rm, restaurants, bar, coffee shop, health club, solar heated pool, re-opening 1992.

C *Adarsh*, Sivaji Rd, nr Bus Stop, T 2353, 50 rm, restaurant (veg). **C** *Biji's Ingleside Inn*, New Tungarli Rd, off Bombay-Pune Rd, T 2638, 37 rm, restaurant, bar, pool. **C** *Span Hill Resort*, Tungarli Valley, Anand Giri Society, T 2153 or Bombay, T 6145166, restaurant, good value. **C** *Mount View Resort*, Bombay-Pune Rd, T 2335, 13 rm, restaurant, bar.

D *Lions Den*, Tungarli Lake Rd, T 2954, 16 rm, restaurant. **D** *Ceeking*, nr Valvan Dam Bridge, Bombay, T 398164, 30 rm, 5 cottages, restaurant.

● **Budget hotels**

E *Vishwabharat*, 80 Tungarli (nr HP Pump), Bombay-Pune Rd, T 2686, 18 rm. **E** *Purohit*, behind PO, T 2695, some rm with bath. **E** Maharashtra Tourism ***Holiday Resort***, Ryewood Park.

F ***Pitale Lodge***, Bombay-Pune Rd, T 2657, 7 rm with bath, charming old stone and wood colonial-style bungalow with verandah, restaurant, bar, good value, rec. **F** ***Sahani Holiday Home***, nr Rly Station, T 2784, 57 rm. **F** ***Woodlands***, Ryewood Rd, T 2417, 10 rm, 3 cottages. **F** ***Chandralok***, T 2294, veg restaurant.

● **Places to eat**

On Bombay-Pune Rd: *Diamond Garden*, opp Flyover Bridge (inc *Tandoori*); ***Kamat's***, veg with Tandoori in patio, rec.

In the Bazar: *Dhiraj*, for good Indian and ***Plaza*** for pizzas, snacks. Also ***Central***, opp Rly Station, ***Gulistan*** and ***Swad*** (snacks only).

● **Banks & money changers**

Bank of Maharashtra and **State Bank of India**, Lokmanya Tilak Rd.

● **Hospitals & medical services**

Shri Babasheb Dahanukar Hospital, T 2673. *Favourite Medical Stores*, Tilak Rd.

● **Post & telecommunications**

Shivaji Rd.

● **Shopping**

For the famous sweet *chikki* (peanut brittle): ***National Chikki Mart***, Marker Manzil, ***Super Chikki*** and ***Santosh Chikki***, Bombay-Pune Rd. ***Maharashtra Medical & General Stores***, nr State Bank.

● **Sports**

Swimming: swimming pools at *Biji's Ingleside Inn* and Gajanan Mahimtura.

● **Tourist office**

Nr Lonavla Rly Station.

● **Useful Services**

Municipal Office and Fire brigade: T 2286. **Police**: T 2233.

● **Transport**

Local Rickshaws: no fixed price. To the Caves by auto-rickshaw: Lonavla-Karla Rs 25, approx return Rs 60. **To Rajmachi Fort**: **Bus**: local bus service is erratic.

Train Rly Station and Enquiry, T 2215. **Bombay (VT)**: *Madras-Bombay Mail* 7010, daily, 0140, 3¼ hr; *Udyan Exp* 6530, daily, 1720, 3 hr; *Hyderabad-Bombay Exp* 7032, daily, 0955, 3 hr; *Deccan Exp* 1008, daily, 1628, 3¼ hr. **Pune**: *Indrayani Exp* 2113, daily, 0815, 1¼ hr; *Deccan Queen Exp* 2123, daily, 1925, 1¼ hr; *Sinhagad Exp* 1009, daily, 1745, 1¼ hr; *Sahyadahri Exp* 7311, daily, 2340, 1¼ hr.

Road ST Stand, T 2742. Daily MRTC buses to Lonavla from Pune (62 km) and Bombay (101 km). Taxis from Dadar station, Bombay (Rs 500-650) take ¾ hr.

Excursions Karla and Bhaja

Karli (or **Karla**) has the largest and best preserved Buddhist *chaitya** (chapel) cave in India, dating from the 2nd-1st century BC. Unlike Ajanta and Ellora it is off the beaten tourist track for foreigners, though it is much visited at weekends.

The approach is across an excavated court. At the massive entrance stands a stone column topped with 4 lions (*sinha stambha*). The Hindu temple just outside the entrance may have been built over the remains of a second pillar. The façade contains a large horse-shoe shaped window above the 3 doorways (1 for the priest and the other 2 for pilgrims). In front of the side doors were shallow water-filled troughs through which the pilgrims walked to cleanse their feet. The remarkable sun window diffused the light into the hall, falling gently onto the stupa at the end. Buddha images (c 5th century) partly decorate the exterior. There are also panels between the doorways depicting 6 pairs of donors.

The main chamber (38m by 14m), entered through a large outer porch, is supported by 37 pillars. It is 8m from floor to ceiling which is barrel vaulted and ribbed with teak beams. There are 15 octagonal columns along either side, each capital having kneeling elephants carrying an embracing couple carved on it. The stupa is similar to that in Cave No 10 at Ellora but here is topped by a wooden umbrella which is carved with delicate patterns. The other caves to the right of the entrance are of little interest.

● **Accommodation** **E** *Peshwa Holiday Resort*, nr Karla Caves, T 55, 15 rm, restaurant, children's park. **E-F** Maharashtra Tourism ***Holiday Camp***, off Bombay-Pune Road, T 30, cottages for 2-4, restaurant, contact Maharashtra Tourism at Bombay or Pune.

• **Transport** Continue on the NH4 E from Lonavla through the village of Karla (8 km). A left turn leads to the remarkable Karla caves (4 km) and the Bhaja caves (7 km).

Bhaja, has 18 caves dating from the 2nd century BC. **Cave No 12** is the best and possibly the first apsidal *chaitya* (a long hall with a semi-circular end) in India. The apse contains a *dagoba*. The vaulted roof of the chapel is supported by 27 columns. The exterior was once covered in a bas-relief, now much of this has been defaced. The last cave to the S has very fine sculptures, including the 'Dancing Couple'. On either side of the main cave are others which were probably nuns' cells and working quarters. To the S are 14 stupas, 5 of which are inside the cave.

The ruined **Lohagen Fort** is about 4 km from the caves and was twice taken and lost by Sivaji. **Visapur Fort** which stands 600m from the foot of the hill is nearby.

ROUTES The NH4 continues E from Karla to **Kamshet** (9 km). Nearby are more Buddhist rock-cut caves at **Bedsa** (6 km). The *chaitya* with 4 columns with animal carvings is like that at Karli but may have been built later. The rib vaulted roof is supported by 26 pillars.

Pune

Population: 2,485,000; *Altitude*: 560m; *STD Code*: 0212. Pune (also spelt Poona), the early home of Sivaji, became the Maratha capital in 1750. After a period under the Nizam of Hyderabad's rule it came under British control in 1817, who then developed it as a summer capital for Bombay and as a military cantonment. It is now a major industrial city. The climatic contrast between Pune and the ghats just 70 km away is astonishing. The monsoon winds of Jun-Sep drop most of their rain on the ghats themselves, and rainfall totals fall from over 3500 mm a year to Pune's 715 mm. Descriptions of the city's site range from 'absolutely flat' to 'surrounded by hills', the contrast depending on the direction from which you approach it.

For all its connections with the Marathas there are few physical reminders of their power. The city is known for its wide streets and there is much more of a British colonial feel to the town, renowned for its military cantonment, educational and scientific institutions and as a place for relaxation.

Places of interest

The city stands on the right bank of the Mutha River before its confluence with the Mula and was divided up into 19 peths (wards). Some were named after the days of their weekly market, others after well known people like the Maratha Gen Sadashiv Peth. In the E and SE are hills leading up to the plateau around Satara.

The majority of the British buildings are to the S of the rivers. Near the Rly Station is the English gothic style **Sassoon Hospital** (1867). Nearby is the Collectorate and the old Treasury. To the SW is the **Synagogue** (1867) and Sir David Sassoon's Tomb. **St Paul's Church** (1867) was consecrated by Bishop Harding and **St Mary's Church** (1825) to the S by Bishop Heber, who toured the country extensively in the 1830s. St Patrick's Cathedral is on the other side of the Racecourse. To the N are the **Empress**

CLIMATE: PUNE

	Jan	Feb	Mar	Apr	May	Jun	Jul	Aug	Sep	Oct	Nov	Dec	Av/Tot
Max (°C)	31	33	36	38	37	32	28	28	29	32	31	30	323
Min (°C)	12	13	17	21	23	23	22	21	21	19	15	12	18
Rain (mm)	2	0	3	18	35	103	187	106	127	92	37	5	715

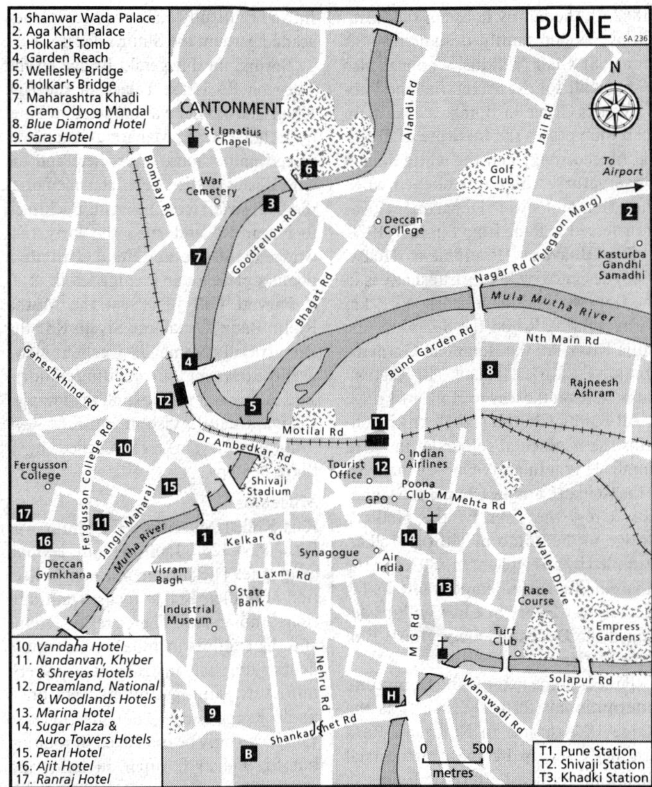

Gardens which have a fine collection of tropical trees and a small zoo.

Moving back to the W by the river are **Visram Bagh**, a very attractive Maratha Palace. Now used as a college, high school and court, the netrance and balcony have beautifully carved woodwork. The inner courts and hall are being restored by Babasaheb Purandare to their original state. The **Shanwar Wada Palace** (Saturday Palace, 1736), built by Baji Rao, the last Peshwa's grandfather, but burnt down in 1827. Only the massive outer walls remain. The main entrance is by the iron-spiked Delhi Gate. Elephants were used for crushing people to death in the nearby street (see below for Tomb of Vithoji Holkar). The gardens were irrigated and contained the Hazari Karanje (Fountain of a Thousand Jets). In fact there were only 197 jets.

Cross the river by **Lloyd Bridge** into Sivaji Rd. Along this are the Panchaleshwar Temple and Sivaji Memorial Hall and Military College (1922). A 9m high statue of Sivaji (sculpted by VP Karkomar) stands in front. To the N is **Wellesley Bridge** (1875) near the Sangam, the confluence of the rivers. Near the bridge is the Engineering College and 300m beyond this is **Garden Reach**

(1862-4), the family house of the influential Sassoon family, designed by Sir Henry St Clair Wilkins, who was also responsible for the Secretariat and Public Works Office in Bombay. The main road then passes the **Institute of Tropical Meteorology** and the white domed **Observatory**, which was opened when the Meteorological Department was transferred to Pune from Simla in 1928.

Raj Bhavan (Government House, 1866) designed by James Trubshawe is in the Ganeshkhind neighbourhood. 3 km N, in Aundha Rd on the S bank of the Mula River, are the **Botanical Gardens**. One km E is Kirkee (Khadki) Rly Station. From here on the way to Holkar's bridge is **All Saints Church** (1841) which contains the regimental colours of the 23rd Bombay Light Infantry. One km to the SE is the Roman Catholic **Chapel of St Ignatius**. Cross the river by the Holkar's Bridge to the **Tomb of Vithoji Holkar**, trampled by an elephant in 1802, and the adjacent Mahadeo Temple built in his memory. Sir Henry St Clair Wilkins designed the **Deccan College** (1864) E of Pune Station.

Pune is home to the **Osho Commune International** (formerly known as the Rajneesh Ashram) in Koregaon Park, originally set up by the controversial Bhagwan Rajneesh (Osho). Rajneesh left India (to avoid paying taxes, it is claimed by critics), to found a commune in Oregon. He returned to India where he died in 1990. The lushly landscaped 24-acre commune "spiritual Disneyland for disaffected First World Yuppies" (*Wall Street Journal*) offers numerous programmes with an emphasis on meditation. The plush 'Club Meditation' with all facilities attracts thousands daily. Tours Rs 10 (excl eating and toilet facilities). Other visitors are screened compulsorily for HIV. Day Pass, Rs 20 (incl meditation, entertainment, discussions etc). The commune has recently gone to great lengths to convert a former rubbish tip in next door Koregaon park into a beautifully maintained and landscaped garden, the Shunyo Park.

Beyond the Fitzgerald Bridge on the Talegaon Rd is the **Palace of the Aga Khan** (1860) who was attracted to Pune by the horse racing. Mahatma Gandhi was placed under house arrest here and his wife Kasturba died here. Her memorial tomb (*samadhi*) is on the estate. Backtrack to Nagar Rd and cross the Fitzgerald Bridge to the riverside **Bund Gardens**, a popular place for an evening stroll.

Parvati Hill Just S of the Mutha Right Bank Canal off Sivaji Rd, the Parvati Hill commands excellent views over the town and surrounding countryside. A popular picnic spot, the temples to Siva, Ganesh, Vishnu and Kartikeya (Subrahmanayam) are reached by a flight of steps.

Museums

Raja Kelkar Museum, 1378 Shukrawar Peth. 0830-1230, 1500-1830. Re 1. Good catalogue. The private museum collection of Dinkar Kelkar focuses on traditional Indian arts. There are 36 sections and the exhibits include carved temple doors, musical instruments, pottery, miniature paintings, nutcrackers, brass padlocks and lamps. The collection is so vast it can only be displayed in rotation but Sri Kelkar is often on hand and personally guides visitors around his wonderful display.

Mahatma Phule Museum, 1203 Sivaji Nagar. 0800-1730. Re 1 adults, Re 0.50 children. Kasturba Gandhi Samadhi, Aga Khan Palace, Nagar Rd. Daily till 1700. Rs 2. A memorial to Mahatma Gandhi, his wife Kasturba and the Independence Movement. Tribal Museum with research institute.

Parks & zoos

There is a small zoo at the Empress Gardens.

Excursions

Sinhagarh (Sinhagad) (1317m), 24 km SW. The 'Lion Fort', situated in the Bhuleshwar range, was a small hill station during the British period. On the way you pass the **Kharakwasla reservoir** on the Mutha river. The dam was constructed in 1879, the first large dam in the Deccan.

The roughly triangular ruined **fort**, stands in a beautiful setting on a hill 700m above the land below. The ascent is steep. To the N and S are cliffs topped with 12m high basalt walls. There were 2 entrances, the Pune Gate (NE) and Kalyan Gate (SW), both protected by 3 successive gates. On the W side of the hill the wall was continued across a gorge, creating a dam. Muhammad Tughluq (see page 180) captured the fort in 1328, and in 1486 Malik Ahmad, founder of Ahmadnagar took it. Nearly 200 years later the Marathas captured it in what has become a legendary feat of bravery and skill by the commanderTanaji Malasure, scaling the cliffs at night and taking the garrison by surprise. Near the dammed gorge is a monument (1937) to the leader of the campaign, Tanaji Malusara. Sinhagarh is a popular day out for people from Pune.

Tours

Maharashtra Tourism operate tours from the Rly Station Counter, opp 1st Class booking office. City tours: Daily (0800-1100, 1500-1800). Rs 35.

Panshet Maharashtra Tourism has established a base for water sports on the Panshet Lake, 45 km SW of Pune. Information from their office in Pune. **Accommodation E** *Panshet Lake Resort*, 37 rm, good restaurant.

Local information

● Accommodation

Airport 10 km, all within 2 km of centre. Some hotels offer 50% day rate (0900-1800). **B** *Blue Diamond*, 11 Koregaon Rd, T 663775, F 212 646101, 114 rm, modern, comfortable, good food, restaurant discourages informal dress, business people's spouses accommodated free. **B** *Aurora Towers*, 9 Moledina Rd, T 660130, 68 rm, all usual facilities inc good restaurants and a pool. **B** *Executive Ashok*, 5 University Rd, Sivajinagar, T 57391, 71 rm, clean, comfortable, good service, rec.

C *Sagar Plaza*, 1 Bund Garden Rd, T 661880, 80 rm, 3 km airport, modern concrete and glass tower block. **C** *Amir*, 15 Connaught Rd, T 661840, 100 rm, most a/c, 3 Restaurants, bar, coffee shop, exchange, health club, shops, Indian Airlines office, popular, flexible check-out. **C** *Regency*, 192 Dhole Patil Rd, T 669411, F 666675, 44 rm, restaurant, bar, exchange.

D *Ashirwad*, 16 Connaught Rd, T 666142, F 666121, 44 rm, modern, neat, restaurant (good *thali*), exchange, travel, shop. **D** *Deccan Park*, 299/19D Ferguson College Rd, opp Vaishali, Sivajinagar, T 345065, 21 a/c rm, restaurant, exchange, travel, management and staff very friendly, rm very clean. **D** *Span Executive*, Revenue Colony, Sivajinagar, behind Tel Exch, T 59192, 40 rm, some a/c, restaurants, bar, coffee shop, travel. **D** *Ajit*, 775/2 Deccan Gymkhana, T 339076, F 330094, 20 rm, some a/c, restaurant, permit rm, travel, shop, modern, rather characterless but quite decent. **D** *Ashiyana*, 1198 FC Rd, Sivajinagar, T 52426, 37 rm, 4 a/c, restaurant (Indian). **D** *Dreamland*, 2/14 Connaught Rd, opp Rly Station, T 662121, 35 rm, 9 a/c, restaurant (Indian veg). **D** *Marina*, 77 MG Rd, T 669141, 12 rm, some a/c, restaurant (Indian, Chinese), bar, travel, traffic noise. **D** *Nandanvan*, Deccan Gymkhana, T 55251, F 660 688, 27 rm, 10 a/c, restaurant (veg), airport transfer. **D** *Pathik*, 1263/4B, off Jungli Maharaj Rd, T 59085, 18 rm, some a/c, rm service for snacks. **D** *Raviraj*, 790 Bhandarkar Institute Rd, T 339581, 15 rm, some a/c, restaurant, bar, coffee shop, garden. **D** *Silver Inn*, 1973 Gafferbeg St, nr Contonment Market, Pune Camp, T 25041, 35 rm, some a/c, restaurant, bar. **D** *Sunderban*, 19 Koregaon Park, next to Osho Commune, T 661919, 23 rm, 5 a/c, restaurant (veg), exchange, travel, gardens. **D** *Suyash*, 1547 B, Sadashiv Peth, opp Tilak Rd, T 439377, 39 rm, 10 a/c, restaurant (Indian veg), airport transfer. **D** *Vandana,* opp Sambhaji Park, off Jangli Maharaj Rd, Deccan Gymkhana, T 59090, F 660 688, 23 rm, restaurant (veg), travel, exchange, airport transfer. **D** *Woodland*, Sadhu Vaswani Circle, nr Pune Station, T 661111, F 60688, 50 rm, 40 a/c, restaurant (Indian veg), travel, exchange, airport transfer, helpful.

● Budget hotels

E *Jinna Mansion*, 18 Wilson Garden, nr Pune rly sation. T667158. Clean and reasonable. **E** *Gauri*, nr Chinchwad Rly Station, Pune Bombay Rd, T 85588, F 660688, 22 rm, restaurant (Veg), **E** *Gulmohr*, 15A/1 Connaught Rd, nr Rly station, T 661773, 32 rm, restaurant, bar.

E *Pearl*, opp Balgandharva Rangmandir, JM Rd, T 53247, 15 rm, buffet dinner. **E** Maharashtra Tourism *Saras*, Nehru Stadium, Swargate, T 30499, nr bus station, pleasant. **E** *Shalimar*, 12A Connaught Rd, T 69191, 45 rm.

F *National*, 14 Sassoon Rd, opp Wilson Garden, T 68054, helpful staff, good value. *Railway Retiring Rooms* at Pune station.

● Places to eat

Those in hotels have extensive menus. **Outside hotels**: *Mazdana*, 22 Amludhur Rd, in pleasant garden, has character; *Apsara*, Udyog Bhavan, Tilak Rd (a/c, bar); *Dicy-Spicy*, Senapati Bapat Rd (Punjabi).

Indian: *Khyber*, 1258/2 J Maharaj Rd, (also Continental, beer bar and ice-creams); *Panchali, Ruchira* (live music) and *Poonam* on J Maharaj Rd, Deccan Gymkhana; *Supriya*, Ambedkar Rd; *Chalukya*, Garware Bridge, Deccan Gymkhana, Maharashtrian specialities; *Shreyas*, 1242 B Apte Rd, with open-air terrace; *Shabree*, nr Ferguson College, does good Maharashtrian food; *Coffee House*, N Molodina Rd, a large a/c restaurant.

North Indian: *Latif's* and *Kwality's* nearby, good for North Indian.

Chinese: *Chinese Room Oriental*, Karve Rd (bar, ice-creams); *Nanking*, opp Pune Club, Bund Garden Rd; *Kamlings* and *Chinese Room* on East St, rec.

Several good Western style restaruants near the Osho Commune, N Main Rd, Koregaon Park: *German Bakery* does great coffee and snacks; *Prems* is outdoor with fountain, set among huge shady trees, good Indian and Western food, highly rec. Further E down N Main Rd is New Arc Farm's *Sangamitra*, also in attractive garden, candlelit in evenings, incredible lemon cheese cake, paté, tofu, home-made pasta, very good but expensive. Going W along N Main Rd, across Koregaon Park Rd, is the Italian *Shriman*, tomato and mozarella salad, great pizza, pasta, fresh bread, gnucci, pleasant candlelit atmosphere.

Also several good restaurants near the Regency Hotel: *Madhuban*, excellent for Indian food. Near the university on Ferguson College Rd: South Indian *Vaishali* and *Roopali* are very popular, in lovely gardens at the back, patronised by students, highly rec.

Fast food: *Eddies Kitchen*, Synagogue St; *Dorabjee*, Dastur Meher Rd (Parsee); *Good Luck* and *Lucky*, nr Deccan Gymkhana are good cafés. For Western food try *The Sizzler*, 7 Modelina Rd. *Venky's*, 2 Wellesley Rd and *The Pub* are popular for fast foods; *Spices Health Foods*, MG Rd for brown bread, peanut butter and tofu; *Darshon*, 759 Prabhat Rd for fruit juices, milkshakes and Western meals. *Pune Coffee House*, 1256/2 Deccan Gymkhana, large, live music; *George*, 2436 Gen Thimaya Rd, part a/c, snacks and ice-creams.

● Banks & money changers

State Bank of India, Laxmi Rd. **State Bank of Hyderabad**, Laxmi Rd, for cashing TCs – be prepared to wait!

● Discos

Pune has quite an active night life. The *Kaplia Hotel* (opp Regency) has a rooftop dance party once a week (2200-0100). *The Pyramids* at the N end of N Main Rd have all night disco parties 3 times a month. Outdoors and very high tech. Membership of Ashram not necessary. Entry, approx Rs100.

● Hospitals & medical services

Pune Cantonment, Shankareth Rd, Golibar Maidan. *KEM*, Rasta Peth. *Sassoon*, Jayaprakash Narayan Rd, T 664 764.

Chemists: *Madhav & Co*, Nr DG Post Office, T 333864.

● Post & telecommunications

Head Post Office (city): Laxmi Rd.

● Shopping

The main shopping centres in Pune are in MG Rd (Camp area), Deccan Gymkhana (packed with every kind of shop), Karve Rd and Laxmi Rd (particularly noted for clothing and textiles). Pune is known for its handlooms, especially Pune saris (cotton-silk weave).

Books: *SP Pratinidhi*, 1170/27 JM Rd; *Utkarsha Book Service*, nr Garware Bridge; *Popular Book House*, 759/74/D Gymkhana; *nternational Book Service*, Deccan Gymkhana.

Boutiques & Garment Stores: on MG Rd, *Sirocco*, *Figleaf*, *Fairdeal*, *Weekenders*. Also *Sunny's Sports Boutique*, 766/3 Deccan Gymkhana.

Department Stores: on MG Rd, *Shan Hira*, *Chandan Stores*, *Dorabjee*. *Wonderland*, good for anything and everything, Moledina Rd.

Grocers: *Green Grocers*, North Main Rd, excellent baked goods and all sorts of groceries.

Textiles: on MG Rd, *Pune Saree Centre* and *Indo-Foreign Stores*. *Kundan Saree Centre*, Bhavani Peth, Ramoshi Gate.

Photography: *Pahiyar Studios*, Tilak Rd; *Colour Photo Studio*, MG Rd, Camp.

● **Sports**
The *Royal Western India Turf Club* on Race Course Rd.

● **Tour companies & travel agents**
Trade Wings, 321 MG Rd, T 668909; *Travel Corporation (India)*, *Hotel Blue Diamond*, T 665271; *Indtravels*, Atur House, Moledina Rd, T 28874; *Thomas Cook*, 13 Thakers House, T 667188.

● **Tourist offices**
Maharashtra Tourism, I Block, Central Bldg, T 668867; *Saras Hotel*, Nehru Stadium, T 30499. Information Counter, Pune Rly Station; Lohagaon Airport; *Saras Hotel*, Nehru Stadium, nr Saras Baug, T 430499.

● **Useful addresses**
Ambulance: T 101. **Fire**: T 101. **Police**: T 100.

● **Transport**
Bombay (184 km); Nashik (184 km); **Mahabaleshwar** (120 km); **Belgaum** (336 km); **Delhi** (1424 km); **Bangalore** (840 km).

Local Taxis: rates negotiable. **Auto-rickshaws**: are readily available. Extra charges for journeys outside the Municipal Corporation and Cantonment limits, and between 2400-0500. **City Buses**: on all important routes in the city and suburbs. **Bicycles** are available for hire from many places.

Air Transport to town Ex-Servicemen run coach for 8 km city transfer. **Indian Airlines**, enquiries T 664840. **Delhi**: daily except Su, 2000, 2 hr. **Bangalore and Madras**: M,W,F, 1810, 1 hr 20 min, 2½ hr.

Train Rail Booking Offices: City – Raviwar Peth, and Deccan Booking Office, Karve Rd. Mon-Sat 0900-1200, 1300-1700. Cl Sun. **Bombay (VT)**: *Madras-Bombay Mail* 7010, daily, 0033, 4¼ hr; *Udyan Exp* 6530, daily, 1618, 4 hr; *Hyderabad-Bombay Exp* 7032, daily, 0853, 4 hr; *Pune-Bombay Indrayani Exp* 2114, daily, 1845, 4½ hr. **Hyderabad**: *Bombay-Hyderabad Exp* 7031, daily, 1715, 13¼ hr. **Madras via Solapur and Guntakal**: *Madras Mail* 7009, daily, 0350, 22 hr. **Bangalore via Guntakal**: *Madras Mail* 7009, daily, 0350, 23 hr. **Delhi and Jammu Tawi** : (ND) *Jhelum Exp* 4677, daily, 1740, 27½ hr; (Hazrat Nizamuddin) *Goa Exp* 2703, daily, 1235, 26 hr. **Vasco da Gama (Goa)**: *Goa Exp* 2704, daily, 1520, 14½ hr.

Road Bus: Rly Bus Stand for the S: **Kolhapur** 0020, 0730, 0900, 1130, 1330, 1730, 1930, 2245; **Chiplun** 0500, 1430; **Panaji** 0430, 0530, 1900, 2030; **Shirdi** 0530; **Ganpatipule** 0615; **Solapur** 0640, 2300; **Mahabaleshwar** 0900, 1215, 1700; **Hubli** 0445, 2215; **Ratnagiri 2040; Belgaum** 2315.

Sivaji Nagar Bus Stand for the E/NE: **Nashik** 22 buses a day, 0530-0030; **Ahmadnagar** 0600, 0930, 1045, 1100, 1700, 2200; **Aurangabad** 0030, 0130, 0745 0915, 1300, 1500, 2245; **Nagpur** 1715; **Jalna** 1000, 1100, 1815, 2200, 2330, 2345; **Dhule 0800, 1600, 2000, 2045, 0845; Indore** 0600, 1800; **Amravati** 0500, 1530; **Akola** 0800, 1915; **Shirdi** 0700, 1615; **Vadodara** 0715; **Jalgaon** 0700, 2030; **Alibag (Kihim)** 0500, 0800, 1000, 1445, 1515,1700, 1900; **Bid** 0615, 1045, 1730, 2230, 2245; **Hyderabad** 0130; **Ahmadabad** 2100.

Swargate Bus Stand for Baneshwar, Bhargar, Daund, Khodakwasla, Morgaon, Purandhar, Saswad, Sivapur and Sinhagad. **Solapur** 0530, 0645, 0730, 0800, 1030, 1230; **Kolhapur** 0815, 0945, 1425, 1530, 1545; **Ratnagiri** 0745; **Mahabaleshwar** 0815, 1400, 1820; **Sangli** 0845, 1215, 1630, 2345; **Thane** 0630, 0730, 1045, 1215; 1600, 1700, 2015, 2130; **Mangalore** (starting from Bombay) 0115, 1000, 1130, 1500, 1545, 1930, 2300. **Belgaum** 1230, 2315.

MSRTC connects Pune by regular services with all major towns within the state. Enquiry, T 665516. **Asiad Buses** to Bombay from Pune Rly Station, every 30 min from 0530-2330. **NB**: Reserve a seat. Maharashtra Tourism, daily services to Panaji,1800; Kolhapur, 0130; Aurangabad, 0130. Southern Travels operates luxury coaches to Ahmadabad, Panaji, and Indore. Taxis from Bombay Dadar station, Rs 500-650, Maharashtra Tourism bus, Rs 115.

Pune to Solapur

ROUTES From Pune the **NH9** goes E and SE across the plateau following the Bhima River. The vast open fields and scattered settlements give the impression that this is a sparsely populated region. Only the very high proportion of land under cultivation makes clear the extent to which land throughout this rainfed agricultural belt is heavily used. It is also a region rich in archaeological sites, as it was a major centre of prehistoric settlement.

From Pune follow the NH9 to **Vadgaon** (162 km *Population*: 8,900), where a right turn leads to the pilgrimage centre of Pandharpur (31 km).

Pandharpur (*Population*: 79,800), on the S bank of the Bhima River, is regared by many as the spiritual capital of Maharashtra. It has a shrine to Vithoba, an incarnation of Vishnu, dating from 1228. Although some tourist literature puts its origins as early as 83 AD there is no evidence for this early date. There are a dozen bathing ghats on the river bank, and during the main pilgrimage season of July (the *Kartik Ekadashi Fair*) tens of thousands of pilgrims converge on the town. The Rath Yatra, or temple procession dates back to 1810.

ROUTES From **Vengaon** the **NH9** continues to Solapur (81 km).

Solapur

(*Population*: 620,500; *Altitude*: 450m) In the heart of the cotton growing area it has been a focus of the cotton trade for over a century. It is unusual among Indian towns in being almost entirely an industrial city. The town has benefitted from being on the main railway line between Madras and Bombay.

• **Accommodation** There are a few new-style hotels and plenty of small, cheap boarding houses and lodges, most very basic. The newest and best is **D** ***Pratham***, 560/61 S Sadar Bazar, T 29581, F 28724, 30 rm, half a/c with bath, comfortable, though signs of economising to provide surface glamour, good open-air restaurant, friendly service, order breakfast in rm rather than restaurant; **D** ***Surya International***, T 29501, 32 rm, 8 a/c, Indian restaurant, ice cream parlour. **E** ***Rajdhani***, 26 Rly Lines, T 23291, 74 rm, some a/c, restaurant (Indian, Chinese). **F** ***Railway Retiring Rooms*** and Dorm.

• **Transport** Solapur is very well placed on the road network, with excellent connections to Bombay, Hyderabad, Aurangabad to the N and Bijapur to the S. **Train Bombay (Dadar)**: *Chennai Exp* 6064, daily except Th,Sa, 2240, 8½ hr. **Bombay (VT)**: *Madras-Bombay Mail* 7010, daily, 1830, 10¼ hr. **Madras**: *Dadar-Madras Chennai Exp* 6063, daily except Sa,Su, 0435, 15½ hr; *Dadar-Madras Exp* 6511, daily, 2345, 17 hr; **Hyderabad**: *Minar Exp* 2101, daily, 0605, 6¼ hr; **Bangalore**: *Udyan Exp* 6529, daily, 1653, 15¼ hr. **Road Bus**: long distance Express bus services connect Solapur with Bombay, Aurangabad, Hyderabad and Bangalore.

BOMBAY TO KOLHAPUR AND BELGAUM via Pune

This route climbs the Ghats up to Pune (see above) then runs virtually due S at an altitude of about 700m along the E edge of the Ghats through often dense forests and spectacular scenery.

Purandhar Fort (1220m), a 13 km diversion from the NH9, commands a high point on the Western Ghats. Legends say that the citadel was built by Purandara or Indra, king of the gods. It is a double fort, the lower one, **Vajragad** to the E and **Purandhar** itself, which together command a narrow passage through the hills. Like other hill forts, Purandhar was defended by curtain walls, in this case 42 km in extent, relieved by 3 gateways and 6 bastions. The earliest fortifications date from 1350. On the summit of the hill farthest from Delhi Gate is the **Mahadev temple**.

Wai (57 km; *Population*: 26,300), situated on the left bank of the Krishna River. The riverside is very attractive, lined with shady temples. Behind the town the hills rise sharply. Note particularly the finely carved mandapam in front of the Mahadev temple. On top of one is the fort of **Pandavgad**, which according to local tradition was visited by the Pandava Brothers of the *Mahabharata*. The town's sanctity is enhanced by its proximity to the source of the Krishna.

Satara

To the S Satara (42 km; *Population*: 95,100; *Altitude*: 670m; *STD Code*: 02162) lies in a hollow near the confluence of the Krishna and Venna rivers. It is considered a place of great sanctity and there are several temples on the banks at **Mahuli**. The cantonment contains Sir Bartle Frere's **Residency** (1820). A 'New Palace' (1838-44) was built by the engineer responsible for the bridges over the 2 rivers.

The ruling house of Satara was descended from Sahu, Sivaji's grandson, who was brought up at the Mughal court. Their **mansion**, 200m from the New Palace, contains a number of Sivaji's weapons. These include the notorious 'tigers' claws' (*waghnakh*) with which Sivaji is reputed to have disembowelled the Bijapur General Afzal Khan. Other weapons include *Jai Bhavani*, his favourite sword (made in Genoa), and his rhinoceros hide shield. There is an **Historical Museum** (1930) which contains a fine collection of archival material on the Marathas.

Wasota Fort on the S side of the town can be reached by footpath. Reputedly built by the Raja of Panhala in the 12th century, its 14m high walls and buttresses contain the remains of the Rajah's Palace, a small temple and a bungalow. It passed to the Mughals under Aurangzeb, for a time, after he besieged the fort in 1699 but returned to the Marathas in 1705 with the help of a Brahmin agent who tricked the Mughals. **Accommodation** *Monark*, Pune-Bangalore Rd, Powai Naka, T 2789, good restaurant, clean, though traffic noise.

ROUTES The road continues S to **Karad** (53 km; *Population*: 56,700). A road on the right in Karad leads to the Koyna Dam (58 km).

Kolhapur

(*Population*: 417,300; *Altitude*: 563m; *STD Code*: 0231) Kolhapur, founded under the 10th century Yadavas, was once one of the most important Maratha states, ruled by Sivaji's younger son. The centre of rich bauxite deposits it is now one of the major industrial centres of Maharashtra. The damming of the Koyna, a tributary of the Krishna, is providing electricity for production of aluminium smelting.

Places of interest

The **Panchganga River** is considered sacred and ghats and temples, including the **Amba Bhai** or Mahalaxmi Temple to the mother goddess, stands on its banks. It has 10th century foundations (tall pyramidal tower added in the 18th) and an impressive carved ceiling to the pillared hall. Note Vishnu with the 8 *Dikpalas*, see page 728. **Brahmapuri Hill** the Brahmin cremation ground, is in the W. The **New Palace** (1881) belongs to the period when all the succession disputes had been resolved and Kolhapur was being governed as a model state. Built out of grey stone around a central courtyard dominated by a clocktower it contains elements from Jain temples and Deeg Palace.

Major Charles Mant of the Royal Engineers designed this and the **cenotaph** on the banks of the Arno River for Maharajah Rajaram and **Rajwada** (Old Palace) which was badly damaged by fire in 1810. There is a Durbar Hall and armoury which contains one of Aurangzeb's swords. Mant also designed the Town Hall (1873), General Library (1875), Albert Edward Hospital (1878) and High School (1879). The **Irwin Museum** has a bell taken from the Portuguese at Bassein in 1739. Near Brahmapuri Hill is the **Rani's Garden** where the royal family have memorial *chhattris*.

Excursions

Panhala (977m), 19 km NW of Kolhapur, is where Rajah Bhoj II, whose territory extended to the Mahadeo Hills N of Satara, had his fort. However, it is particularly associated with Sivaji, who often stayed at the fort. The Marathas and Mughals occupied it in turn until the British took it in 1844. The fort is triangular with a 7 km wall with 3 gates around it, in places rising to 9m. The Tin Darwaza (3 Doors) Gate has 2 outer doors leading to a central courtyard or 'killing chamber'; the inner gate leads to the Guard Room. The Wagh Gate (partly ruined) adopts similar principles of defence. By the ruins is a temple to Maruti, the Wind god. Inside the fort are vast granaries. The largest, the Ganga Kothi, covers 950 sq metres and has 11m high walls and enabled Sivaji to withstand a 5 month siege. To the N is the 2-storey Palace.

Local information

● Accommodation

D *Shalini Palace* (Mansingh Gr), Rankala, A Ward, T 20401, 41rm, some a/c, restaurant (Indian, slow service), garden, on the lake, comfortable (though a little neglected), very peaceful, no taxis or auto-rickshaws; **D** *Pearl*, New Sahupuri, T 20451, 28 rm, 12 a/c, restaurant, bar, exchange, garden, good service; **D** *Woodlands*, 204-E Tarabai Park, T 20941, 25 rm, 6 a/c, nr rly and centre, restaurant, bar.

● Budget hotels

E *Tourist*, 204 E Shahupuri, T 20421, 29 rm, some a/c, nr rly, restaurant, bar, lawn; **E** *Lishan*, Ward E, T 21804, 22 rm, restaurant (veg); *Samrat*, Station Rd, nr State Terminal Stand, T 27101, 20 rm, restaurant (Indian); **E** *Opal*, Pune-Bangalore Rd, T 23622, 9 rm with TV, restaurant (Maharashtrian), rec.

F *Maharaja*, 514E, opp Central Bus Station, T 20829, 26 rm, veg restaurant.

● Tourist office

Maharashtra Tourism, Kedar Complex, Station Road, Kolhapur, T 22935. Information and Booking counter at Mahalaxmi Dharmshala, Tarabai Rd.

● Transport

Train The terminus of the broad gauge line from Bombay. Trains to Kolhapur arrive via Miraj (see Goa Travel). **Bombay (VT)**: *Konya Express* 7308, daily, 0800, 13¼ hr; *Mahalaxmi Express* 7304, daily, 2150, 14¼ hr.

ROUTES The road continues S to Karnataka. The main road goes on to the important border town of Belgaum, see page 1042. A minor road leads SW to Amboli, one of the most remote hill stations in Maharashtra (see below).

BOMBAY TO GOA

ROUTES The 593 km coast road from Bombay to Goa, the NH17, runs through the **Konkan** region. It connects a string of small towns which developed at the heads of estuaries. These were transhipment points for cargos brought by sea, then hauled by pack animals over the Ghats. Although lowland it is far from flat. Many of the densely wooded slopes have been cleared, leaving the laterites bare and unproductive, alternating with patches of intensive rice cultivation and coconut groves. The coastal estuaries support mangrove swamps. It is one of the poorest and most densely populated parts of Maharashtra, and a major source of migrant workers to Bombay. The **NH17** is slow; from late May to Oct it is often flooded.

Kihim About 5 km S of Pen a road goes W from the NH17 to Alibag and Kihim (120 km S of Bombay by road).

● **Accommodation** Maharashtra Tourism has a small tented campsite on the unspoilt beach at Kihim, T 021433 8172, the tents are fully furnished. There are also some private resorts.

● **Transport Road** Direct from Bombay or by ferry except during the monsoons

At Kolad (80 km from Panvel) a road leads to the coastal fort of Murud-Janjira.

Murud-Janjira (*Population*: 12,100) The Janjira Fort, reputedly one of the strongest coastal forts in India, retains a number of remarkable buildings, including mosques and a 5-storeyed palace. The Marathas made numerous unsuccessful attempts to capture the fort, including according to one legend the digging of a tunnel under the sea. The fort can only be reached by boat from Rajpuri, where boatmen row visitors across. Five km from Murud. Cycles available for hire in Murud. One km from Murud centre is the Datta mandir. 250 steps give a commanding view.

● **Accommodation** Maharashtra Tourism has an **E** *Resort*, 6 A type cottages for 2, 8 cottages for 4, basic and poorly maintained, but still the best, popular with holidaymakers from Bombay, restaurant – food can get monotonous.

● **Transport Sea** A ferry runs periodically from the Ferry Wharf (Bhaucha Dhakka) to Rewas. Local State Transport buses from there to Murud, though there can be a long wait.

Road From Bombay State Transport buses cover the 165 km in under 6 hrs.

From Mahad (134 km from Panvel) there is a left turn off the NH17 to Sivaji's former capital of Raigad (Raigarh), high up in the Ghats (27 km).

Raigad

(869m) The fort town was Sivaji's HQ during the latter part of his reign. The views from the 3-pronged hilltop fort are magnificent, especially the stunningly beautiful panorama across the lakes to the N. Difficult to reach, the fort is little visited.

Raigarh dates from around the 12th century. Known as Rairi it was the seat of a Maratha chief. Later it came under the suzerainty of Vijayanagar and in 1479 passed to the Nizam of Ahmadnagar. The Nizam Shahi dynasty held it until 1636 when it was ceded to the Adil Shah's of Bijapur. Sivaji took it in 1648 and made it the home of his much-revered mother, Jiji Bai. In 1674 he chose it for his coronation and 6 years later, in 1680, he died at the fort. Aurangzeb acquired it in 1690 but it soon reverted back to the Marathas who surrendered it to the British in 1818.

The ascent, a climb of 1400 steps, begins at **Wadi**. The flat hilltop is approx 2500m long and 1500m at the widest central point. A bastioned wall encloses it while 2 outer curtain walls contour round the hillsides 60m and 120m below. Each of the 3 corners of this irregular triangle are heavily fortified and command fine panoramas. In Sivaji's day it was regarded as one of the strongest in India.

The main gate the **Maha Darwaza** is flanked by 2 large bastions, both 21m high, 1 concave, the other convex. Inside the fort are several buildings. The extensive **Palace** and **Queen's Chamber** are placed between the **Gangasagar** and **Kushwatra** tanks. In the courtyard is a low platform where the throne of Chattrapati stood when he was crowned and assumed the title *Chattrapati* – Lord of the Umbrella, a regal symbol. In the centre of the town was a market which had more than 40 shops in 2 parallel rows. The fort housed around 2,000 people. To the NE is **Sivaji's Samadhi** (cremation monument), as well as a chhattri for his dog. The adjacent **Temple of Jagadishwara** has a Nandi Bull outside and an inscription to Hanuman inside.

A *doolie* (basket chair carried by 4 bearers) can be hired.

• **Accommodation** There is a small *Rest House*, where you can stay overnight, this is recommended if you go up in the evening when the heat has died down, extremely atmospheric. There is also a Maharashtra Tourism **E** *Resort*, with 6 blocks of self contained rooms and 2 large dormitories (100 beds), reservations at MSTDC offices in Bombay or Pune.

• **Transport Train** Pune is the nearest railhead. **Road Bus**: buses go from both Bombay (via Mahad, 210 km) and Pune (126 km)

From **Raigad** you have to return to the **NH17**.

Pratapgarh

(38 km) The setting for this Maratha **fort** is spectacular. From the summit (1080m) on which it is sited there is a splendid view down the forested hillside. A road leads to the foot of the hill, then 500 steps run up to the top.

The fort comprises a double wall with corner bastions. The gates are studded with iron spikes. Inside are 2 *dipmal* (lantern towers), so called because their exteriors are covered with regularly placed projections like giant coat hooks. Presumably lanterns were placed on these or hung from them, the towers then acting as beacons.

Mahabaleshwar

(24 km; *Population*: 10,600; *Altitude*: 1370m; *STD Code*: 021686; *Best season*: Nov-May) One of the wettest parts of the Western Ghats during the monsoon. The town is in a pleasantly wooded set-

Sivaji and the Tiger's Claw

One of the most frequently recounted tales of Sivaji's cunning occurred near Pratapgarh when the Bijapur General Afzal Khan was invited to come unarmed to a meeting after threatening Sivaji's territory. Neither was reputed to have honoured the conditions, and Sivaji killed his opponent by embracing him with a *Waghnakh* (Tiger's Claw), a knuckleduster with sharpened spikes. Afzal Khan's head was cut off and buried beneath the Afzal Burj in the fort.

ting at the head of the Krishna River on cliffs overlooking the Bombay coast, and is the main hill station for Bombay. "Discovered" by General Lodwick in 1824, Mahabaleshwar was declared an official British sanatorium in 1828 and was once the capital of the Bombay Presidency. The altitude makes the climate very pleasant during the dry season. From **Bombay Point** and the hills around the town you can see the sea on a clear day. There are pleasant walks and waterfalls within walking distance. **Arthur's Seat** (12 km) looks out over a 600m precipice to the Konkan. The 9-hole Golf Course is built on a cliff side. **Venna Lake** has boating and fishing. The bazar sells local soft fruit and jams.

There are several typical British hill station buildings: **Christchurch** (1842, enlarged 1867); the cemetery; **Frere Hall** (1864) with its mullioned windows and the **Club**, founded in 1882; **Government House** (1829) on Mount Malcolm; The **Lodwick Monument** (1874) in honour of the town's founder and the **Beckwith Monument**.

The old town contains 3 temples including the **Krishnabai** or Panchganga, said to have 5 streams, including the Krishna flowing from it. The 13th century Yadav King Singhan built a small tank at the Krishna's source. After Bombay, Mahabaleshwar is pleasantly cool and relaxed and an ideal place to have an overnight stop. The Krishna rises from a spring at an altitude of 1360m near Mahabaleshwar, starting its 1400 km journey across the Deccan to the sea.

Tours
Maharashtra Tourism deluxe buses for sightseeing, 1430, Pratapgarh, 0700 and Panchgani, 1100. Reservations can be made at Maharashtra TDC (T 234522-482), Express Towers, Nariman Point, Bombay.

• **Accommodation** Several are family run **C** *Brightland Holiday Village*, Nakhinda Village, Kates Pt Rd, T 353 or Bombay T 2872590, 30 rm, 4 km centre, restaurants, bar, pool, gardens. Others close to town centre: **D** *Krishna*, opp Holiday Camp, T 253, 23 rm, restaurant (Indian veg); **D** *Dreamland*, T 228, 64 rm, some a/c, restaurant (Indian veg); **D** *Fountain*, opp Koyna Valley, T 227, 106 rm, some a/c, restaurant (veg); **D** *Lake View*, Satara Rd, T 412, 36 rm, some a/c, restaurant; **D** *Mayfair*, Mazda Bungalow, LC D'Souza Rd, nr State Bus Stand, T 366, 13 rm, restaurant, bar; **D** *Belmont Park Hill Resort*, Wilson Pt, T 414, 14 rm, restaurant; **D** *Executive Inn*, LC D'Souza Rd, T 432, 8 rm; **D** *Fredrick*, T 240, 32 rm, restaurant, bungalow hotel. **E** Maharashtra Tourism *Holiday Camp*, T 218, cottages, rm and garden suites, restaurant and permit rm. Also **F** Dorm. *Mahabaleshwar Club*, quiet, with character, temporary membership available to stay.

• **Banks & money changers** On Dr Sabbana Rd.

• **Tourist offices** At Kedar Complex, Station Rd, T 22935; the Bus Stand (T 271) and the *Holiday Camp* (T 7318).

• **Transport Train** Pune is the most convenient railhead. **Road** Regular services from Pune, Rs 20. Maharashtra Tourism deluxe buses (except monsoons) to Bombay 1500 (6½ hr) and from Bombay 0700 (7 hr), Rs 125.

Panchgani (*Altitude*: 1334m) Only 18 km from Mahabaleshwar, Panchgani, surrounded by the 5 hills from which it takes its name, is surrounded by spectacular scenery. The drive between Panchgani and Mahabaleshwar offers beautiful views, and Maharashtra Tourism are happy to arrange to visit some of the British and Parsi bungalows.

• **Accommodation E** Maharashtra Tourism *Five Hills* and a *Resort*, T Satara 312.

• **Transport Train** The nearest rly station is Pune (98 km). **Road Bus**: buses run from Bombay (via Mahad) and Pune.

Chiplun (*Population*: 34,300) The NH17 runs S from Podalpur through Khed (47 km) to Chiplun (26 km) on the banks of the Vashishti River, fed from the Koyna Lake, one of the largest artificial lakes in the Western Ghats. The Chiplun irrigation scheme (developed in the 1980s) between the town and the hills is one of the few canal irrigation projects on the narrow coastal fringe between the Ghats and the sea. **Accommodation** Between Khed and Chiplun, Taj Gateway **A** *Riverview Lodge*, superb view of river meandering through the Ghats 600m below, nr attractive small village and temple, comfortable rm, but restaurant and service indifferent.

ROUTES The NH 17 continues through a succession of ghat sections to Hatkamba (153 km) where there is a right turn to **Ratnagiri** (13 km 'jewel hill' *Population*: 56,500; *STD Code*: 02352). The birthplace of 2 leaders of the Independence movement, Gangadhar Tilak and GK Gokhale, Ratnagiri was also the internment home for the last king of Burma, King Thibaw, who was held here between 1886 and his death in 1916. It is the only town of any importance in S Konkan. Maharashtra Tourism has an information office at the *Zilla Parishad Office* in the town.

Ganpatipule Revered and much visited by Hindus for its *Swayambhu* ('naturally occurring' or 'self-created') image of Ganesh, Ganpatipule has a beautifully white beech to rival those of Goa further S.

• **Accommodation E** Maharashtra Tourism *Resort* has family suites and dorm.

• **Transport Road Bus**: direct State Transport buses from Bombay (375 km), Pune (331 km via Satara) and Ratnagiri (45 km).

ROUTES From Hatkamba the road S goes to Talera (93 km), where a right turn offers one of the rare chances to get to the coast, at Vijayadurg.

Vijayadurg

(Viziadurg; 52 km) The formidable structure guarding the river is on an ancient site. The Sultans of Bijapur enlarged it and Sivaji further strengthened it by adding the 3 outer walls. It has 27 bastions, an inner moat, good water supply and carried 278 guns in 1682. The Maratha pirate Kanhoji Angria made it his base in 1698, plundered European shipping and withstood assaults by the Portuguese and the British.

ROUTES You have to return on the same road to the NH17, then S to the River Petdhaval (46 km). In the small town of Kudal a road runs down to the coast at **Malvan**. Sivaji's coastal fort of **Sindhudurg** is on a low-lying island just off the coast. The fort encloses 8 ha but is now deserted. There are still several shrines – to Maruti, Bhavani, Mahadeo and unquely to Sivaji himself. There is an unconventional statue of Shivaji. Malvan itself is be ing developed as a beach resort by Maharashtra Tourism. The NH 17 goes to Vengurla on the coast, while a state road goes inland up the ghats to the minor hill station of Amboli and on the Belgaum.

Vengurla was a trading settlement on an island, now joined to the land. Only just to the N of Goa, the coast is lined with beautiful white sand beaches. Salt pans provide an important product for export from the region. The old town of Malvan has 2 well-known temples, the Sri Devi Sateri temple and the Rameshwar Mandir.

Amboli (*Altitude*: 690m) Set on the flat topped heights of the Western Ghats overlooking the coastall plain below, Amboli is a quiet and little visited resort. There are attractive walks and several waterfalls, including the Nagatta Falls. The Bauxite

Mines (10 km) can also be visited.

• **Accommodation E** Maharashtra Tourism *Resort* offers a reasonably comfortable base.

• **Transport Train** To Kolhapur or Belgaum, then by local bus. **Road** From the coastal towns of Ratnagiri (210 km) and Vengurla (50 km).

ROUTES The NH 17 continues to the Maharashtra-Goa border and Mapusa where minor roads run W to the northern Goan beaches of Anjuna and Chapora. Panaji is a further 32 km.

GOA

Contents

Maps

Brilliant lush green fields of irrigated paddy surround villages and hamlets, white painted churches standing out against occasional empty patches of startling red soil. In the background are the jungle-clad hills. Piazzas with whitewashed churches and elegant mansions splashed with the colour of bougainvillea lend the atmosphere of lethargic southern Italian villages.

With some of India's finest beaches, Goa has long been popular as a place for relaxation. It gained the reputation for being free and easy, but although cheap accommodation is still widely available there is now a wide range of hotels

BASICS *Population*: 1.168mn (Urban 41%, Scheduled Castes 2%, Scheduled Tribes 1%); *Birth rate*: *Rural* 15:1000, *Urban* 16:1000; *Death rate*: *Rural* 8:1000, *Urban* 7:1000; *Literacy*: M 74% F 59%; *Religion*: *Hindu* 66%, *Muslim* 5%, *Christian* 29%.

Environment

The Land

Area: 3800 sq km. Goa has a 97 km coastline and occupies an embayment in the forest clad Western Ghats, which rise to nearly 1300m on the E margins, and sweep down to the gently undulating coastal strip. The **Mandovi** and **Juari** rivers join at high tide in an inland creek encircling the island of Goa. Alfonso de Albuquerque grasped the advantages of this island site, large enough to give a secure food-producing base but with a defensible moat, at the same time well placed with respect to the important NW sector of the Arabian Sea. Roughly triangular in shape the island has a rocky headland and has the added advantage of having 2 harbours. It was given the name **Ilhas** (island in Portuguese).

The rich lowland soils have a high mineral content, patches of almost sterile red laterite forming upland areas between the lower lying fertile deltas. Huge reserves of manganese have been discovered and mined, along with iron ore. While the income derived from this has helped to boost Goa's foreign exchange, it scars the landscape and has had a bad effect on neighbouring agriculture.

Climate: Goa

	Jan	Feb	Mar	Apr	May	Jun	Jul	Aug	Sep	Oct	Nov	Dec	Av/Tot
Max (°C)	31	32	32	33	33	31	29	29	29	31	33	33	31
Min (°C)	19	20	23	25	27	25	24	24	24	23	22	21	23
Rain (mm)	2	0	4	17	18	580	892	341	277	122	20	37	2310

Climate

Goa experiences the full force of the SW monsoon. Mar to May are very hot, Jun to Oct very wet. The rainfall and temperature pattern for **Panaji** is shown below.

History

Early Goa

Some identify Goa in the *Mahabharata* as Gomant, where **Vishnu**, reincarnated as Parasurama, shot an arrow from the Western Ghats into the Arabian Sea and with the help of the god of the sea reclaimed the beautiful land of Gomant. Siva is also supposed to have stayed in Goa on a visit to bless 7 great sages who had performed penance for 7 million years. In the *Puranas* the small enclave of low lying land enclosed by the Ghats is referred to as Govapuri, Gove and Gomant. The ancient Hindu city of Goa was built at the southernmost point of the island. The jungle has taken over and virtually nothing survives.

Contact with the Muslim world

Arab geographers knew it as Sindabur. Ruled by the Kadamba dynasty from the

2nd century AD to 1312 and by Muslim invaders from 1312 to 1367, it was then annexed by the Hindu kingdom of **Vijayanagar** and later conquered by the **Bahamani dynasty** of Bidar in North Karnataka who founded Old Goa in 1440. It had already become an important centre for the trade in horses with the Vijayanagar Empire. When the Portuguese arrived, Yusuf Adil Shah, the Muslim King of **Bijapur**, was the ruler. At this time Goa was an important starting point for Mecca bound pilgrims, as well as continuing to be a centre importing Arab horses and a major market on the W coast of India.

The Portuguese

The Portuguese were intent on setting up a string of coastal stations to the Far East in order to control the lucrative spice trade. Goa was the first Portuguese possession in Asia and was taken by **Alfonso de Albuquerque** in Mar 1510, the city surrendering without a struggle. Three months later Yusif Adil Shah blockaded it with 60,000 men. In Nov Albuquerque returned with reinforcements, recaptured the city after a bloody struggle, massacred all the Muslims and appointed a Hindu as Governor.

The Portuguese built a series of coastal forts to protect and dominate the Arabian sea and East Indies routes. Goa's function was to supervise the Malabar coast. The forts are small compared with even the modest Indian forts, due the small number of expatriate Portuguese manning them.

The Portuguese rarely interfered with local customs except for forbidding the burning of widows (*sati*). At first they employed Hindus as officials and troops. Mutual hostility towards Muslims encouraged cordiality and trade links between Goa and the Hindu kingdom of Vijayanagar. Religion only became an issue when missionary activity in India increased. Franciscans, Dominicans and Jesuits arrived, carrying with them both religious zeal and intolerance. The Inquisition was introduced in 1540.

Goa became the capital of the Portuguese empire in the East and was granted the same civic privileges as Lisbon. It reached its greatest splendour between 1575 and 1600, to decline when the Dutch with their superior seafaring skills began to control trade in the Indian Ocean. The fall of the Vijayanagar empire in 1565 caused the lucrative trade between Goa and the Hindu state to dry up. The Dutch blockaded Goa in 1603 and 1639. They weakened but did not succeed in taking it. It was ravaged by an epidemic in 1635, and manpower was so severely depleted that the Portuguese brought criminals from Lisbon's prisons to maintain their numbers.

Distracted by the Mughals in 1683, the Marathas called off their attack on Goa which remained safe in its isolation, though it was threatened again briefly in 1739. The seat of government was shifted first to Margao (Madgaon) and then in 1759 to Panaji, mainly because of outbreaks of cholera. Over this period (1695 to 1775) the population of Old Goa dwindled from 20,000 to 1600 and by the mid 19th century only a few priests and nuns remained.

Independence

The Portuguese came under increasing pressure in 1948 and 1949 to cede Goa, Daman and Diu to India. In 1955 *satyagrahis* (non violent demonstrators) attempted to enter Goa. They were deported but later when larger numbers tried, the Portuguese used force to repel them. The problem festered until in 1961 the Indian Army, supported by a naval blockade marched in and brought to an end 450 years of Portuguese rule. Originally Goa became a Union Territory together with the old Portuguese enclaves of Daman and Diu, but on 30 May 1987 it became a full state of the Indian Union.

Culture

The People

The Goan population is a mixture of Hindu, Christian and Muslim. The Christians generally spoke Portuguese but now speak Konkani and English. The Hindus speak Konkani, Marathi and Hindi. Increasing poverty in the past caused large numbers of Goans to emigrate. Many are found in Bombay, Mozambique, Natal and elsewhere. Most are of part Portuguese descent and bear Portuguese names like de Silva and Fernandes, a direct result of Portugal's policy of encouraging inter-marriage which was seen as a way of maintaining settler populations in climates that exacted a high toll on Europeans. This intermingling has spread to the church – the complexions of the saints and madonnas are those of South Asia.

Language Portuguese was much more widely spoken in Goa than was English in most of the rest of India, but local languages remained important. The 2 most significant were *Marathi*, the language of the politically dominant majority of the neighbouring state to the N, and *Konkani*, the language commonly spoken on the coastal districts further S. The use of 3 languages is reflected in considerable confusion of the spelling of many place names, with Portuguese, Marathi and Konkani variants all in common use. Konkani was introduced as the language of instruction in Church primary schools in 1991 while Government run primary schools have switched to Marathi. There are only 8 government primary schools using Konkani medium compared with over 800 using Marathi, but the issue is still contentious.

Cuisine

Although Goan food has similarities with that in the rest of India – rice, vegetable curries and *dal* are common, for example – there are many local specialities. Not surprisingly, the food in this region is hot, making full use of the small bird's-eye chillies that are grown locally. Other common ingedients are coconut, rice and cashew (caja) nuts.Tavernas and bars are common.

Meat dishes Spicy pork or beef *vindalho* (Vindaloo), marinated in garlic and vinegar, is very popular. Goa's Christians had no qualms about using pork (not eaten by Muslims and most Hindus) in their culinary dishes. *Chourisso* is Goan sausage made of pork pieces stuffed in tripe, boiled or fried with onions and chilles. It is often eaten stuffed into bread. *Sorpotel* a highly spiced dish of pickled pig's liver and heart, seasoned with vinegar and tamarind, is perhaps the most famous of Goan meat dishes. One recipe suggests that in addition to other spices you should use 20 dry chillies for 1½ kg pork plus liver and heart, with 4 green chillies thrown in for good measure! *Yacutti* is a hot chicken or meat dish prepared with coconuts.

Seafood *Apa de camarao* is a spicy prawn-pie and *reichado* is usually prepared with a whole mackerel or pomfret, cut in half and served with a *masala* sauce. You will find lobsters, baked oysters, boiled clams and stuffed crabs as specialities. *Bangra* is Goa mackerel and fish *balchao* is a preparation of red masala and onions used as a sauce for prawns or king-fish. A less common dish, not least because it is made without coconut, is *Ambot tik*, a sour curry made with shark, squid or ray and eaten with rice.

Bread & sweets Goan bread is good and there are pleasant European style biscuits. *Unde* is a hard crust round bread, while *kankonn*, hard and crispy and shaped like a bangle is often dunked in tea. *Pole* is like chapatti, often stuffed with vegetables, and Goans prepare there own version of the South Indian *idli*, the *sanna*.The favourite dessert is *bebinca*, a layered coconut and jaggery delicacy made with egg yolks, sugar, nutmeg and ghee. Other sweets include *dodol*, a mix of jaggery and coconut with rice flour and nuts, *doce*, which looks like the North Indian *barfi*, *mangada*, a mango jam, and *bolinhas*, small round semolina cakes.

Fruit, nuts & wine Home of one of India's most famous mangoes, the *alfonso*, Goa has a wide range of fruit. The extremely rich *jackfruit* are common, as are papaya and watermelons. Cashew nuts are grown in abundance. Like pineapples (brought from South America) and papaya (brought from the Philippines) chillies and cashews were introduced to India by the Portuguese. The fermented fruit of cashew apples is distilled for the local brew *feni* (*fen*, froth) which can also be made from the sap of the coconut palm. Beer is cheaper here than in most other parts of India. Goan wines tend to be of the fortified variety and are sweet; port is particularly good.

Local festivals

With its large non-Hindu population, Christian festivals such as Christmas and Easter are popular. Check dates of special festivals with Tourist Office.

Jan *Feast of the Three Kings* (6th) celebrated in Cuelim, Chandler and Reis Magos, nr Fort Aguada, where there is also a fair.

Feb/Mar The *Carnival*, preceding Lent has been discontinued. On the Mon after the *5th Sunday in Lent* there is a procession with all 26 statues of the saints from St Andrew's in Old Goa. Dating from the 17th century, it is the only one of its kind outside Rome. A large fair is held where old fashioned hand-held fans, a local handicraft, are sold. Also actors and musicians perform in villages. *Shigmotsav* is a Hindu spring festival held at full moon, celebrated all over Goa but particularly in Panaji, Mapusa, Vasco d Gama and Margao.

Apr *Feast of Our Lady of Miracles* On the nearest Sun, 16 days after Easter, a huge fair and market is held at Mapusa; also celebrated by Hindus in honour of the Goddess Lairaya.

Jun *Feast of St Anthony* (13th) Songs in honour of the saint requesting the gift of rain. *Feast of St John the Baptist* (24th), at Calangute. A thanksgiving for the arrival of the monsoon. Young men tour the area singing for gifts. They also jump into wells! *Festival of St Peter* (29th), Fort Aguada. A floating stage is erected on fishing boats tied together and a pageant is held as they float downstream.

Aug *Feast of St Lawrence* (10th), celebrates the opening of the sandbars in the Mandovi River. *Harvest Festival of Novidade* (21st and 24th). The first sheaves of rice are offered to the priests on the 21st and to the Governor and Archbishop and placed in the Cathedral on the 24th. The festival includes a re-enactment of one of the battles between Albuquerque and the Adil Shah on the lawns of the Lieutenant Governor's Palace.

The major local Hindu festivals include:

Late Aug *Birth of Lord Krishna* Mass bathing in the Mandovi River off Diwadi Island.

Oct/Nov *Diwali* Celebrated with a big procession and fireworks.

Modern Goa

Economy

Industry & exports Goa exports coconuts, fruit, spices, manganese and iron ores, bauxite fish and salt. Its manufacturers produce fertilisers, sugar, textiles, chemicals, iron pellets and pharmaceuticals. Rice is the staple product with fruit, salt, coconuts, pulses and betel (areca nut) also produced. The Japanese are investing in a new city designed to process iron ore for export.

Tourism Tourism plays an important role in the economy and is growing fast. Householders are being encouraged to add an extra room to their home to accommodate paying guests. In the S of Goa beyond the Majorda Resort, several hotel complexes are being developed on 20 km stretch of beach; none is permitted to be built within 200m of the high-tide line. These resort hotels are situated between the sea and the river so that during the monsoon, when the sea is too rough and dangerous for swimming, water sports can proceed on the river. Although tourism brings money into the Goan economy, there is considerable opposition to the expansion of facilities for tourists. Some Goanese criticise the Government's expansion plans as bringing little benefit to the local economy, while threatening to damage traditional social and cultural values. The spread of hippy colonies in the late 1960s and 1970s was deeply resented by some, and more recently the rapid development of power, including current plans to generate nuclear power on the coast S of Panaji, have raised protests. There have also been isolated cases of violence against tourists and some cases reported of police harassment. Motorcyclists and budget travellers have been particular targets of unwarranted police attention. Demands to see your licence can lead to prolonged interrogation, the confiscation of passports and other papers and demands for money. Some tourists have been suspected of planting drugs on likely looking travellers and then arresting them, hoping for substantial bribes for their release. However difficult it may seem, if you are faced with unlawful detention by the police the best policy is to keep calm and patient. Insist on seeing the senior officer and on reporting the matter to the Chief of Police.

Communications Communications internally and with the rest of India remain underdeveloped. The bridge across the Mandovi at Panaji has been rebuilt so that there are no longer long delays for ferry crossings at this point. The NH 17 now has bridges over all the estuaries which has eased travel to the northern beaches.

PANAJI

There were 3 principal cities in Goa: **Old Goa**, **Panaji** (Panjim) or New Goa and **Margao**. Old Goa has a melancholy beauty, a city of Baroque churches, some half-hidden by jungle, dead except for the great pilgrimage to the tomb of St Francis Xavier in the magnificent cathedral of Bom Jesus. Panaji was originally a suburb of Old Goa and is built on the left bank of the Mandovi Estuary. It contains the archbishop's palace, a modern port, government buildings, hotels, bars and shops set around a number of plazas.

Panaji

(*Population*: 85,200; *STD Code*: 0832), also called **Panjim** or Ponnje, is the capital of Goa State (Daman and Diu are now Union Territories). It is a small town, laid out on a grid pattern overlooked by the *altinho* (hill) to the S. The hill offered defensive advantages which were responsible for the original decision to locate the city on this site. It is well worth walking up for the view over the estuary.

Places of Interest

The **campal** is a riverside boulevard with picturesque views across the Mandovi. At the E end is the **Idalcao Palace** of the Adil Shahs and was once their castle. The Portuguese rebuilt it in 1615 and until 1759 it was the Viceregal Palace. In 1843 it became the Secretariat, and now hoises the Passport Office. Next to it is a statue of the Abbé Faria (1755-1819). Of part negro extraction, the Abbé Faria left for theological training in Rome and after ordination went on to Paris. He made a reputation as an authority on hypnotism. Further W are the library and public rooms of the Braganza Institute, the entrance of which is decorated with blue tiles illustrating scenes from Goa's history.

Largo da Igreja, the main (Church)

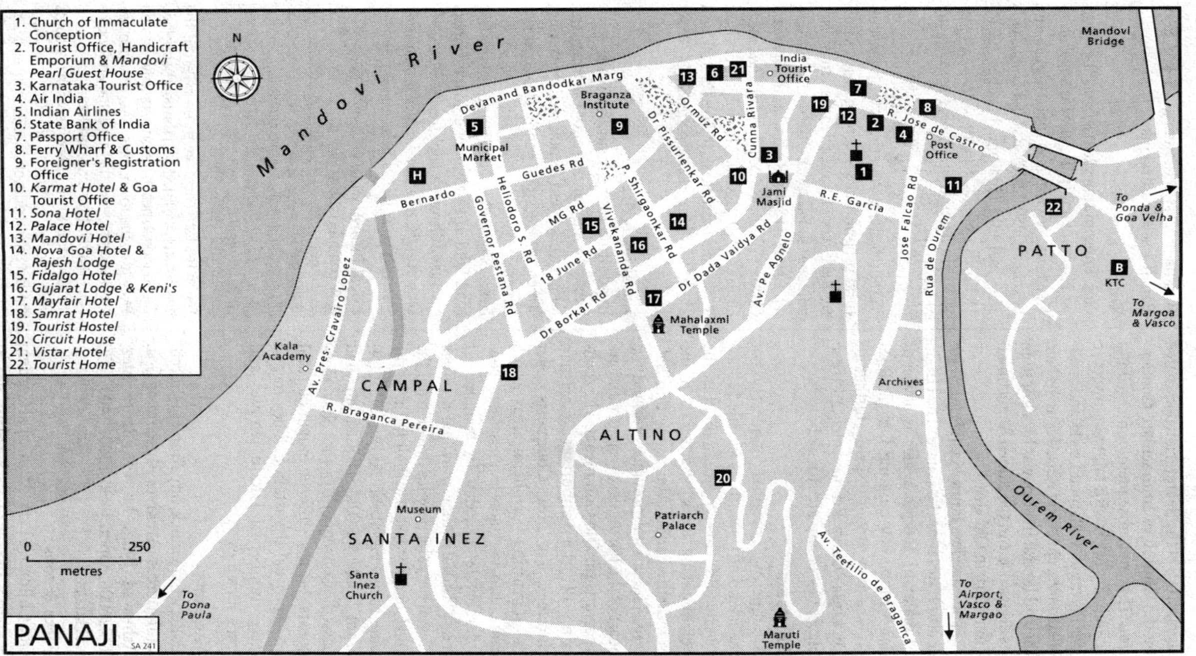
1. Church of Immaculate Conception
2. Tourist Office, Handicraft Emporium & *Mandovi Pearl Guest House*
3. Karnataka Tourist Office
4. Air India
5. Indian Airlines
6. State Bank of India
7. Passport Office
8. Ferry Wharf & Customs
9. Foreigner's Registration Office
10. *Karmat Hotel* & Goa Tourist Office
11. *Sona Hotel*
12. *Palace Hotel*
13. *Mandovi Hotel*
14. *Nova Goa Hotel & Rajesh Lodge*
15. *Fidalgo Hotel*
16. *Gujarat Lodge & Keni's*
17. *Mayfair Hotel*
18. *Samrat Hotel*
19. *Tourist Hostel*
20. *Circuit House*
21. *Vistar Hotel*
22. *Tourist Home*
N
Mandovi River
Mandovi Bridge
India Tourist Office
Devanand Bandodkar Marg
Braganza Institute
Municipal Market
Ormuz Rd
Cunna Rivara
Dr Pissurlenkar Rd
R. Jose de Castro
Post Office
Guedes Rd
Bernardo
Heliodoro S. Rd
Governor Pestana Rd
MG Rd
P. Shirgaonkar Rd
Vivekananda Rd
18 June Rd
Dr Dada Vaidya Rd
Dr Borkar Rd
Jami Masjid
R.E. Garcia
Jose Falcao Rd
Rua de Ourem
Av. Pe Agnelo
Mahalaxmi Temple
To Ponda & Goa Velha
PATTO
KTC
To Margoa & Vasco
Kala Academy
Av. Pres. Cravairo Lopez
CAMPAL
R. Braganca Pereira
Archives
ALTINO
Patriarch Palace
Museum
SANTA INEZ
Santa Inez Church
Av. Teefilio de Braganca
Ourem River
To Airport, Vasco & Margao
Maruti Temple
0 250
metres
To Dona Paula
PANAJI
SA 241

square, is S of the Secretariat, dominated by the **Church of Immaculate Conception** (1541, but subsequently enlarged and re-built in 1619) with tall twin towers in the Portuguese Baroque style and modelled on the church at Reis Magos. Its bell, the 2nd largest in Goa, was brought from its original site in the ruined Augustinian monastery in Old Goa.

The domeless **Jama Masjid** (mid-18th century) lies near the square. The Hindu **Mahalaxmi Temple**, which is now hidden behind a new building, is by the Boca de Vaca (cow's mouth) spring, further up Dr Dada Vaidya Rd on which all these places of worship are situated.

Excursions

Albuquerque's original conquest was of the island of Tiswaldi (now called Ilhas) where Old Goa is situated, plus the neighbouring areas – Bardez (N of the Mandovi), Ponda, Marmagao and Salcete. The coastal provinces formed the heart of the Portuguese territory and are known as the **Old Conquests**. They contain all the important Christian churches. The **New Conquests** cover the remaining peripheral areas which came into Portuguese possession considerably later, either by conquest or treaty. Initially they provided a refuge for not only the peoples driven from the Old Conquest but also their faith. By the time they were absorbed the full intolerant force of the Inquisition had passed. Consequently, the New Conquests did not suffer as much cultural and spiritual devastation. They have a large number of Hindu temples and some mosques.

Museums

Gallery Experanca, opp Merces Church, Vadi Merces. **Archives Museum of Goa,** Ashirwad Bldg, 1st Flr, Santa Inez, T 226006. Open 0930-1300, 1400-1730 weekdays.

Parks & zoos

Goa Children's Park; Municipal Garden; Manezes Braganza Park. Mini zoo at Bondla Forest Sanctuary, 55 km E of Panaji – see Excursions.

Tours

Goa Tourism tours leave from the Tourist Hostel, Panaji, T 226515. Several offered inc: *N Goa Tour* incl Mapusa and beaches (0930-1800), Rs 60-34206; *S Goa Tour* incl Old Goa and beaches (0915-1800), Rs 60-85; *Pilgrim Special* (0930-1230), incl Old Goa, Rs 35; *Beach Special* (1500-1900), Rs 35.

River Cruises by luxury launch on Mandovi river, sometimes with live cultural programmes. Evening cruises particularly rec. Launch leaves from jetty adjacent to Passport Office. One hr *Sunset Cruise* (1800) Rs 55, and *Sundown Cruise* (1900), Rs 55. Two hr *Full moon Cruise* (2030), Rs 90. Also longer cruises: 4 hr *Goa on waters* (0930) Rs 150 and 2½ hr *The Mangrove experience* (1430) Rs 100.

Local festivals

In addition to the major festivals:

Feb: *Mahasivaratri* and *Carnival* (no longer a big event) is marked by feasting, street processions and floats down streets.

Mar: *Shigmotsav* is a Hindu spring festival held at full moon; colourful floats are taken through the streets.

Dec 8th: *Feast of our Lady of Immaculate Conception* A fair is held.

Local information

● **Accommodation**

Price guide
AL Rs 3,000+ **A** Rs 2,000-3,000
B Rs 1,200-2,000 **C** Rs 600-1,200
D Rs 250-600 **E** Rs 100-250 **F** Up to Rs 100

The hotels listed here are those in Panaji. The beach hotels are listed with the beaches below. The principal beach resorts, mostly located away from the town, have been grouped under 3 sections – northern, central and southern, after the towns nearest them.

Many top hotels offer off-season discounts from mid-Feb or Mar to mid-Dec, the more modest offer reductions between Jul and Sep. There are other innumerable small 'hotels', often only a couple of rooms in a private house or a shack by the beach; it is worth shopping around. **NB** You can often bargain big discounts if you are staying for any length of time.

C ***Fidalgo***, 18th June Rd (Swami Vivekananda Rd), T 226291, 123 a/c rm, restaurant, bar, coffee shop, pastry shop, pool, health club, Air India Office, sometimes noisy and service slow, needs modernising, their 'New Bookshop' is rec, reasonable prices, books can be ordered, foreign newspapers, helpful; **C** ***Mandovi***, DB Bandodkar Marg, nr Mahalxmi Temple, T 226270, F 45451, 63 a/c rm in old building, good restaurant, outdoor bar, exchange, book shop, pastry shop, overlooks river, relaxing but lacks character, overpriced; **C** ***Golden Goa***, Dr Atmaram Borker Rd, off 18th June Rd, T 226231, 36 a/c rm with bath, good restaurants, exchange, travel, very clean pool; next door, sharing the pool is **C** ***Nova Goa***, T 226231, F 224090, 85 a/c rm with bath, good a/c restaurant and bar, exchange, travel, pool, clean, modern, good value.

D ***Aroma***, Cunha Rivara Rd opp Municipal Garden, T 223519, F 224811, dim public areas, 26 clean rm, central, restaurant a/c (Goan, Punjabi), bar; **D** ***Delmon***, Caetano de Albuquerque Rd, T 225616, 50 rm, clean; **D** ***Keni's***, 18th June Rd, T 224581, 38 simple rm with bath, 16 a/c, central, restaurant, bar, exchange, travel, shops, pleasant rm and garden; **D** ***Mayfair***, Dr Dada Vaidya Rd, T 225952, 27 cramped rm, some a/c rm, some with balcony, restaurant, bar; ***Rohma*** under same management has 32 larger rm. **D** ***Park Plaza,*** opp Azad Maidan, T 225635, modern hotel with 37 rm, some a/c, a/c restaurant; **D** ***Rajdhani***, Dr. Atmaram Borkar Rd, T 225362, 21 good clean rm with bath, some a/c in modern Indian business style hotel, good a/c restaurant (Gujarati, Punjabi, Chinese), travel; **D** ***Samrat***, Dr Dada Vaidya Rd, T 223318, 44 rm (some occupied 'permanantly'), central, a/c restaurant (Indian, Goan, good Chinese), bar, exchange, travel, roof-garden; **D** Goa Tourism ***Tourist Hostel***, nr Secretariat nr river, T 222303, 40 rm with balcony, some a/c, best views from top Flr, good open-air restaurant, shops, often fully booked, some complaints about service; **D** ***Vistar***, Dr Shirgaokar Rd nr Custom House, T 225411, 16 rm, some a/c, restaurant.

● Budget hotels

E ***Campal***, T 224531, 46 rm, some a/c in large house, restaurant, travel, spacious gardens, roof garden; **E** ***Republica***, Jose Falca Rd, T 222638; **E** ***Sona***, Rua de Ourem, T 224426, 21 rm with bath, restaurant, bar; **E** ***Mandovi Pearl Guest House***, T 223928, 5 large spacious rm, popular if basic; **E** ***Panjim Inn,*** nr the Cathedral, large rm with character; **E** ***Neptune***, Malacca Rd, T 224447, 37 rm, some a/c, big, modern, lacking character, good a/c restaurant, good value.

F ***Kiran Boarding and Lodging***, opp Bombay steamer jetty; **F** ***Palace***, Jose Falca Rd, cheap rm with hardboard partitions, avoid – very dirty in 1994; **F** Goa Tourism ***Tourist Home***, Patto Bridge, T 225715, 8 dorm with 9 beds, restaurant, paying guest accommodation lists from Goa Tourism, T 226515.

● Places to eat

Restaurants in *Mandovi* hotel, Dr Dada Vaidya Rd, are rec: ***Riorico*** for Indian and Continental, Chinese ***Goenchin***, ***High Tidebar*** for snacks and drinks. Also good pastry shops. ***Chit Chat*** at Tourist Hostel; good *Tandooris*, pleasant and popular.

Indian, Continental & Goan: ***Shalimar***, ***Sher-e-Punjab***, 18th June Rd. ***Venite***, rua 31st January Rd, nr Tourist Hostel, T 225537, 1st Flr of old colonial house, serves excellent local food (daily change of menu), open for breakfast, lunch and dinner, pleasant atmosphere, also 2 cheap rm often full.

Indian Veg: ***Kamat***, top of Municipal Gardens, rec for cheap *thali* meals. Also ***Taj Mahal***, MG Rd, opp Press, ***Gujarat Lodge***, 18th June Rd, and ***Shanbag Café***, next to Garden View Hotel, opp Municipal Garden Sq. Also open-air ***River Deck***, opp Hotel Mandovi, nr Jetty, but expensive. ***Shalimar***, MG Rd and ***Captain's Cabin***, Mandovi Park offer a wide choice. ***Eurasia***, Dr Dada Vaidya Rd does Italian, good pizzas (rec esp when tired of curries!). ***O Pastelaria***, Dr Dada Vaidya Rd, highly rec.

Porvorim on the Panaji-Mapusa road has some: ***O Coqueiro***, nr water tank, Alto Porvorim, with a bar, tables in or out, excellent Goan food, but avoid pork when the temp is high. Opp is ***Chinese Garden***, rec, and ***Village Nook*** in Church St, Alto-Porvorim, a garden pub with home cooking. ***Al Fresco***.

● Bars

The bars are like Mediterranean cafés; some are very pleasant.

● Airline offices

Air India, Hotel Fidalgo, T 224081. **Biman Bangladesh**, **Air France**, **Gulf Air**, **Philip-**

pine Airlines, **TWA**, at Jet Air, T 223891 and National Travel Service, T 223324 for **Kuwait Airways**, both at Jesuit House, Municipal Garden Sq. **British Airways, Kenya Airways**, Chowgule Brothers, opp Captain of Ports Office, T 225266. **PIA**, ABC, B-24 Trionora Apts, T 226190.

● Banks & money changers
Most of the larger hotels and beach resorts have foreign exchange facilities for guests. Several banks in town. Indian currency against Mastercard at **Central Bank**, Nizari Bhavan; **Andhra Bank**, Credit Card Service (Visa, Master Card) Dr Atmaram Borkar Rd, T 43513; **Bank of Baroda**, in all major towns, accepts Visa cards.

● Chambers of Commerce
Chamber of Commerce and Industry, Rua De Ormuz; **Economic Dev Corp**, Atmaram Borker Rd; **Goa Industrial Dev Corp**, Saraswati Mandir Bldg, 18th June Rd; **Small Handicrafts Dev Corp**, Gov Pestana Rd.

● Entertainment
A large variety of local drama presentations are performed in Goa, many during the festivals. The Kala Academy, Campal (on way to Miramar) with indoor and outdoor autitoria arranges puts on plays, concerts, exhibitions.

● Hospitals & medical services
Goa Medical College Hospital. CMM Poly Clinic, Altitnho, T 225918. *Laxmibai Talaulikar Memorial Hospital*, T 225626. *Mandovi Clinic*, Alto Porvorim.

● Libraries
Some hotels/hostels now run 'book exchanges'; a deposit is usually required.

● Posts & telecommunications
Courier services: *DHL*, Nagesh Apts, Rua Conde de Sarcedes, T 226487; *Skypak*, Rivera Rd, Municipal Garden Sq, T 225763. **GPO**. **Telegraph Office**: Dr Atmaram Borkar Rd, also STD, ISD and trunk services.

● Shopping
Handicrafts: (some with a Portuguese hall mark), jewellery, particularly malachite set in gold filigree and clothes, are good buys. The bazars are worth browsing through for pottery and copper goods. Some resort hotel shops have clothes, jewellery, rugs and shell carvings, while Goa Govt handicrafts shops are at Tourist Hostels and the Interstate Terminus, which also has the MP Emporium. ***Handicrafts Emporia*** in all major towns. Kashmir and Kerala handicrafts shops at *Hotel Fidalgo*, Swami Vivekananda Rd.

Photography: *Fantasy Studio*, Eldorado; *Souza Paul*, MG Rd; ***Central Studio***, Tourist Hostel; ***Lisbon Studio***, Church Sq.

● Sports
The better beach resorts have a range of activities incl windsurfing, sailing, water-skiing, parasailing etc organised by the hotels. *Yachting Assoc*, PO Box 33, T 223261. *Aqua Sport*, 2nd Flr, Ghanekar Bldg, J Falcao Rd, T 224706.

Walking: there are some beautiful walks through the forested areas of Goa. Contact the *Hiking Assoc of Goa*, 6 Anand Niwas, Swami Vivekenanda Rd or Captain of Ports Office, T 5070.

● Tour companies & travel agents
Several in Panaji: *Rauraje Deshprabhu*, Cunha Rivara Rd, Municipal Garden Sq, T 222392; *Travel Corp of India*, 1st Flr, Sukerkar Mansion, MG Rd, T 225152.

● Tourist offices
Govt of India Tourist Office, Municipal Bldg, Church Sq T 223412. **State Govt Tourist Office**, Tourist Home, Patto, T 225715; Counter at Kadamba Bus Station, T 225620, Dabolim airport, T 222644. Goa Tourism Dev Corp, Trionara Apts, Dr Alvares Costa Rd, T 226515. Also at Western Rly Station, Bombay Central, T 396288.

● Useful addresses
Fire: Panaji, T 101. **Foreigners' Regional Registration Office**: Police Headquarters, T 5360. **Police**: T 100.

● Transport
Local Bicycle/motorcyle hire: bicycles are available at popular beaches and in Panaji for around Rs 2/hr, Rs 15/day, Rs 350/month. Private motorcycles, at about Rs 150-200/day, without petrol, but much higher in some luxury resorts; usually available coastal areas (ask a beachside shop).

WARNING: Reports of police harassing motorcyclists and demanding 'fines'.

Coach and Car hire: available from *Goa Tourism*, Trionora Apts, T 223396. Worthwhile if shared (max 5). **Tourist Taxi**: A/c Deluxe cars or Ambassadors, Rs 6-10/km, min 100 km/8 hr; Non-a/c, Rs 3/km. Rs 300 for half day (100 km). Waiting charges and night halt extra. **Mini-buses** (15 and 23 seater) and larger luxury coaches also available. Car Hire with or without a driver with a choice of models: **Budget**, Camila Bldg, opp Bus Stand. Branches at airport, Leela Beach Resort etc. **Hertz**, Don Bosco High School. Offers option to begin and end hire in different major towns in India. **Private (yellow top) taxis**, unmetered. Fares negotiable. Waiting charge, Rs 10-15 per hr. **City bus service**, from Panaji Bus Stand (Main Terminal) to the city. **Auto-rickshaws** and **Motorcycle taxis** (with yellow mudguards) are easily available (uniique in Goa). A rider takes 1 passenger; useful in rough/ muddy roads or narrow lanes but can be somewhat dangerous (no helmets). Fares negotiable.

Ferries: flat-bottomed ferries charge a nominal fee to take passengers (and usually vehicles) when rivers are not bridged. ***Panaji-Betim*** ferry has now been replaced by the Nehru bridge over the Mandovi. ***Old Goa-Divar Island***. ***Dona Paula-Marmagao***. Fair weather service only, Sep-May, takes 45 min. Buses meet the ferry on each side.

Long distance transport

NH 4A, 17 and 17A pass through Goa. **Delhi** (1,904 km), **Bombay** (582 km); Taj Group's ***Chiplun Resort Hotel*** is suitable for breaking the journey from Bombay. **Calcutta** (2,114 km), **Madras** (904 km), **Bangalore** (570 km), **Hyderabad** (712 km), **Pune** (505 km).

Air Dabolim airport is 30 km from Panaji. **Transport to town**: State Transport Coach Rs 20 per person. Taxis Rs 4.30 per km. Larger hotels offer free transfer.

Indian Airlines City Office, Dempo House, DB Bandodkar Marg, T 223826. Reservations 1000-1300, 1400-1600. **Delhi**: daily except M, 1150, 2½ hr; **Bombay**: daily, 1430, 1 hr; **Kochi**: daily except M, 0830, 1 hr; **Madras**: Tu,Th,Sa, 1740, 2 hr. **Air India** Dabolim Airport, T 224081; Hotel Fidalgo, T 224081. **Bombay**: M, 1615, 1 hr. **Damania Airways**: T 226196, F 224155. **Bombay**: daily, 1600. **East West Airlines**, T 226291, F 225237. **Bombay**: daily, 1630; **Delhi**: M to Sa, 1445, 2½ hr. **Goa Way**, T 0832 44129. **Bombay**: daily. Check timing; **Kochi**: W,Th,Su, 1240, 1 hr; **Pune**: M,Sa, 1200, 1 hr. **Jet Airways Bombay**: daily, 1530. **Modiluft**, T 223508. **Bangalore**: M,W,F,Su, 1405; **Bombay**: M,W,F,Su, 1105; **Delhi**: M,W,F,Su, 1500.

Goa is a firmly established popular package tour destination. There are direct charter flights from England, Germany, Finland, Denmark and soon from Austria, Portugal, Sweden and France; worth enquiring at your local travel agent. They are often cheaper than a scheduled airfare, though you will then be expected to find your own accommodation as what is included in the 'package' is unsuitable.

Train The nearest station is in Vasco da Gama, see below. **Rail agency**, T 225620, Reservations, 0930-1300; 1430-1700. The new Konkan Railway is under construction from Bombay to Mangalore via Goa. Large sections are nearing completion although some parts of the rooute have not yet been finally approved. It should be completed by the late 1990s.

Road Share-taxis ply on certrain routes; available nr the ferry wharves, main hotels and market places (max 5). Mapusa from Panaji, approx Rs 9. State KTC (Kadamba) buses and private buses (often crowded) operate in the state; the time-table is not strictly adhered to; buses often wait until full. (Bus Terminus, T 223334.) Booking 0900-1300, 1400-1730. The minimum (for 3 km) is under a rupee. Frequent service to Old Goa, Rs 2, then to Ponda, Rs 6. **Karnataka RTC** (Bus Terminus, T 225126), Booking 0800-1100, 1400-1700. **Maharashtra RTC** (Bus Complex, T 4363), Booking 0800-1100, 1400-1630. Private operators (eg *West Coast Travels*, Old Bus Stand, T 225723), have regular services from Panaji to inter-state destinations. *Unique International Travels* run a/c buses from Goa to Bombay, Pune and Bangalore. Timings from International Travels, nr Viranis, MG Rd, T 46335.

Kadamba TC: To **Bombay**: 1500, 1515,1530, 1600 (16 hr); To **Pune**: 0615, 1800, 1900 (12 hr); To **Bangalore**: 1745 (14 hr). To **Mangalore**: 0615, 1615 (10 hr); To **Belgaum**: 0630, 0800, 1000, 1300 (5 hr); To **Miraj**: 1030. (10 hr). **Karnataka RTC**: To **Mangalore**: 0700, 0830, 0930, 2030; To **Bangalore**: 1700, 2030; To **Belgaum**: 0730, 1200, 1400, 1715; To **Hubli**: 1530, 1600; To **Mysore**: 1700. **Maharashtra RTC**: To **Bombay**: 1700, 1600, 1530; To **Ratnagiri**: 1230; To **Pune**: 0830, 1800 (12 hr); To **Miraj**: 0830, 1000; To **Mahabaleshwar**: 1900.

Sea Steamer service between Panaji and Bombay, Oct-May, Daily (exc Tues from Bombay, Wed from Panaji), 1000 (about 20 hr). Cabin and Deck Class, Rs 75-350. Enquiries: ***The Shipping Corp of India***, New Ferry Wharf, Mallet Bunder, Bombay, T 864071; ***Moghul Line***, VS Dempo, opp Capt of Ports Jetty, T 3842.

Excursion from Panaji

Old Goa

When Richard Burton, the explorer, arrived in Goa on sick leave from his Indian army unit in 1850 he described Old Goa as being a place of 'utter desolation' and the people 'as sepulchral looking as the spectacle around them'. The vegetation was dense and he had difficulty reaching the ruins. Today it is quite different.

Old Goa (or Velha Goa, page 1217) is 8 km from Panaji and may be regarded as the spiritual heart of the territory. It lies on the S bank of the Mandovi on the crest of a low lying hill. It owes its origin as Portuguese capital to Alfonso de Albuquerque, and some of its early ecclesiastical development to St Francis Xavier who was here in the mid 16th century. However, before the Portuguese arrived it was the second capital of the Bijapur kingdom. All the mosques and fortifications of that period have disappeared; only a fragment of the Sultan's palace walls remain.

Old Goa was protected by a fortified wall. In the W lay the barracks, mint, foundry and arsenal, hospital and prison. On the banks of the river were the shipyards of Ribeira des Gales and adjacent to these was the administrative and commercial centre. To the E was the market and fortress of Adil Shah whilst the true centre of the town was filled with magnificent churches.

All of the churches of Old Goa used the local red laterite as the basic building material. Basalt and fine white limestone were imported from Bassein, for decorative detail (see page 1150). The laterite exteriors were coated with a lime plaster to protect them from the weather which had to be renewed after each monsoon. When maintenance lapsed, the buildings crumbled away.

The Archaeological Survey of India is responsible for the upkeep of the churches and has published a small inexpensive booklet on the monuments: *Old Goa* by South Rajagopalan, available from the Archaeological Museum at Old Goa. An attractive and much more extensive, richly illustrated book, *Goa: A Traveller's Historical and Architectural Guide* by Anthony Hutt, is available from many hotel bookshops.

Places of interest

Holy Hill As you approach the large central monuments you go over the 'Holy Hill' with a number of churches. The **Chapel of Our Lady of the Rosary** (1526) belongs to the earliest period of church building and is described as Manueline. At the time of the conquest of Goa, Portugal was enjoying a period of prosperity under King Manuel I

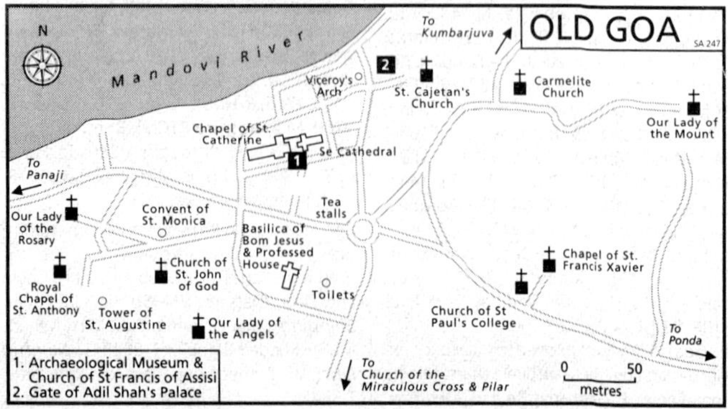

(r1495-1521), hence the term. The architectural style that evolved borrowed from Iberian decoration, but also included many local naturalistic motifs as well as Islamic elements, seen on the marble cenotaph owing to the Hindu and Muslim craftsmen employed. The church here has a 2 storey entrance, a single tower and low flanking turrets. From this site Albuquerque directed the battle against the Adil Shahi forces in 1510.

Behind is the **Royal Chapel of St Anthony** (1543), the national saint of Portugal and **Tower of St Augustine**. St Anthony's was restored by the Portuguese Govt in 1961. St Augustine's is now in ruins, except for the belfry. The church, which once boasted 8 chapels and convent were erected in 1512, but abandoned in 1835 due to religious persecution. The vault collapsed in 1842 burying the image, followed by the façade and main tower in 1931. Only 1 of the original 4, survives.

Further on is the **Convent of St Monica** (1607-27), the biggest in East Asia. The huge square building is 3-storeys high and was built around a sunken central courtyard which contained a formal garden. The church is in the S part of the building. At one time it enjoyed the status of Royal Monastery, now it is the Mater Dei Institute for Nuns, founded in 1964 for theological studies. The only other building on the Holy Hill is the **Church and Convent of St John of God** built in 1685 and abandoned in 1835. Descending from the Holy Hill you enter a broad tree lined plaza with large buildings on either side. On conducted tours this is where you leave your transport and walk.

The Basilica of Bom (the Good) Jesus (1594). Open 0900-1830. No photography. The world renowned church contains the body of St Francis Xavier, a former pupil of soldier-turned-saint, Ignatius Loyola, the founder of the Order of Jesuits. St Francis Xavier's remains form the principal spiritual treasure of the territory (see page 94). The Jesuits began work on their own church in 1594. By 1605 it was finished and consecrated. In 1613 the body of St Francis was brought there from the College of St Paul. It was moved into the church in 1624 and its present chapel in 1655 where it has remained ever since. St Francis was canonised by Pope Gregory XV in 1622 and in 1964 Pope Pius XII raised the church to a minor basilica. The order of Jesuits was suppressed in 1759 and its property confiscated by the state. The church, however, was allowed to continue services.

The church was originally lime plastered but this was recently removed to reveal the laterite base. The granite decorative elements have always been unadorned. The façade is the richest in Goa and also the least Goan in character. There are no flanking towers. It appears that the church was modelled on the earlier but now destroyed church of St Paul which in turn was based on the Gesu, the mother church in Rome. There is only 1 tower in the building and that is placed at the E end, giving it a more Italian look. On the pediment of the façade is a tablet with I.H.S (Jesus in Greek or *Iaeus Hominum Salvator*). Apart from the elaborate gilded altars, and the twisted Bernini columns, the interior of the church is very simple.

The Tomb of St Francis Xavier (1696) was the gift of one of the last of the Medicis, Cosimo III, the Grand Duke of Tuscany, and was carved by the Florentine sculptor Giovanni Batista Foggini. It took 10 years to complete. It comprises 3 tiers of marble and jasper, the upper tier having panels depicting scenes from the saint's life. The casket containing his remains is silver and has 3 locks, the keys being held by the Governor, Archbishop and Convent Administrator. Every 10 years on the anniversary of the saint's death the holy relics are displayed to the public. The next showing is in 1994. *Feast Day* 3rd Dec.

The body of St Francis has suffered

much over the years and has been gradually reduced by the removal of various parts. One devotee is reputed to have bitten off a toe in 1554 and carried it in her mouth to Lisbon where it is still supposed to be kept by her family. In 1890 another toe fell off and is displayed in the Sacristy. Part of the arm was sent to Rome in 1615 where it is idolised in the Gesu. Part of the right hand was sent to Japan in 1619.

Next to the church and connected with it, is the house for **Jesuit fathers**, a handsome 2-storey building with a typically Mediterranean open courtyard garden. It was built of plaster-coated laterite in 1589, despite much local opposition to the Jesuits. After a fire in 1633 destroyed it, it was only partially rebuilt. It now houses a few Jesuit fathers who run a small college. There is a modern **art gallery** next to the church.

The Se Cathedral, across the square, is dedicated to **St Catherine**. The largest church in Old Goa, dedicated to the saint on whose day Goa was recaptured, it is possibly the largest in Asia with a barrel vaulted ceiling. Built by the Dominicans between 1562-1623 in a Tuscan style on the exterior and Corinthian inside, the main façade faces E with the characteristic twin towers, 1 of which collapsed in 1776. The remaining 1 contains the Golden Bell (rung 0530, the 'Mid-day' Angelus at 1230 and 1830), cast at nearby Cuncolim in 1652. Good views from the top. The vast interior is divided into a nave and 2 side aisles. To your right is the granite baptismal font St Francis. On each side of the church are 4 chapels: on the right to St Anthony, St Bernard, The Cross of Miracles and the Holy Spirit; on the left to Nossa Senhora de Necessidades, the Blessed Sacrament and Nossa Senora de Boa Vida. The main altar is superbly gilded and painted with further altars in the transept.

SW of the Cathedral's front door are the ruins of the **Palace of the Inquisition**. Over 16,000 cases were heard between 1561 and 1774. The Inquisition was finally suppressed in 1814. Beneath the hall were dungeons. In the heyday of Old Goa this was the town centre. Moving back towards the main thoroughfare you can see the **Church and Convent of St Francis of Assisi**, the **Chapel of St Catherine** and the **Archaeological Museum**. All these are in the same complex as the Cathedral.

The Church and Convent of St Francis of Assisi is a broad vault of a church with 2 octagonal towers. The floor is paved with tombstones and the walls around the High Altar are decorated with paintings on wood depicting scenes from St Francis' life. The convent was begun by Franciscan friars in 1517, and later restored 1762-5. The style is Portuguese Gothic. The convent now houses the **Archaeological Museum** (1000-1700, closed Fri) which has an impressive range of stone sculptures from different ages in Goa's history and some portraits of former Viceroys. **St Catherine's Chapel** was built on the orders of Albuquerque as an act of gratitude at having beaten the forces of Bijapur in 1510. The original church was of mud and straw. Two years later a stone chapel was erected.

To the NE of the cathedral on the road towards the Mandovi River is **The Arch of the Viceroys (Ribeira dos Viceroys),** built at the end of the 16th century to commemorate the centenary of Vasco da Gama's discovery of the sea route to India. His grandson, Francisco da Gama was Viceroy (1597-1600). On the arrival of each new viceroy this would be decorated. The ornamentation includes a statue of Vasco da Gama. The arch was rebuilt in 1954. To the E of this lies the splendid domed Baroque **Convent and Church of St Cajetan** (1665) built by Italian friars of the Theatine order, sent to India by Pope Urban III. Shaped like a Greek cross, the church was modelled on St Peter's in Rome.

Beyond is **Gate of the Fortress of the Adil Shahs** comprising a lintel supported on moulded pillars mounted on a plinth, probably built by Sabaji, the ruler of Goa before the Muslim conquest of 1471. The now ruined palace was occupied by Adil Shahi sultans of Bijapur who occupied Goa before the arrival of the Portuguese in 1510. It became the Palace of the Viceroys from 1554 to 1695.

Museums

Archaeological Museum and Portrait Gallery, The Convent of St Francis of Assisi, Old Goa, T 5941. Open 1000-1200, 1300-1700, **closed Fri**. Entry free. Collection of sculptures covers the period from before the arrival of the Portuguese. Many date from the 12th-13th centuries when Goa came under the rule of the Kadamba dynasty. Also a fine collection of portraits of Portuguese Governors on the 1st Flr which provides an interesting study in the evolution of court dress.

Tours

Goa Tourism tour to Old Goa (incl in the South *Goa* and *Pilgrim Tours*) spends a short time visiting the sights. Better to go by bus or share a taxi (waiting charge Rs 10-15 per hr) to give you time to see Old Goa at leisure.

Galleries at See Cathedral, Convent of St Francis of Assisi and Basilica Bom Jesus. 0900-1230, 1500-1830; Sun from 1000.

• **Transport Road** From Panaji, frequent service, Rs 2.

Beaches near Panaji

Miramar

3 km, (Gaspar Dias) Panaji's beach on the Mandovi estuary is pleasant, with good views over the sea but very 'urban' in character. Although you can wade out a long way, there can be an undertow.

Local festivals

May: Five-day *Seafood Festival*.

• **Accommodation D** *Solmar*, Ave Gaspar Dias (BD Badodkar Marg), T 46555, 24 rm, 7 a/c, restaurant, exchange, travel, check-out 0900, clean, modern, good value. **E** *Goa International*, Tonca, T 5804, 27 rm, some with river view, central, restaurant (Indian, Goan), bar, travel. **D** *London*, T 46017, 16 rm, some a/c. **D-E** *Yatri Niwas*, T 47754, some a/c, in 2-storey blocks by shaded groves. **D** *Mayur*, T 43174, 10 rm. **E** *Royal Beach*, T 46316, 14 rm, some with balconies. **F** *Youth Hostel*, T 45433, dorms (20, 10), next to beach, on bus route to town, for members/students.

Dona Paula

(7 km from Panaji) on the headland between the Mandovi and Zuari estuaries has a small palm fringed beach, casuarina groves and is very peaceful. It is named after a viceroy's daughter who reputedly jumped from the cliffs when refused permission to marry a fisherman, Gaspar Dias. There is a fine view of the harbour. Fisherfolk turned local vendors sell straw hats, lace handkerchiefs and colourful spices to visitors who now come to enjoy its peace and the variety of water sports on offer. On the rocky promontory between the 2 river estuaries is **Raj Niwas**, once the Viceroy's house, with its enclosed circular verandah and chapel alongside. **Vainguinim** beach is close by and is part occupied by Welcomgroup's stylish *Cidade de Goa* complex.

Local festivals

Nov: Colourful *Watersports Festival*.

• **Accommodation B** *Cidade De Goa*, on the beach, T 53301, 101 rm, 26 km airport, 7 km centre, 3 restaurants, water sports, shops, pool, another imaginative modern development designed by the noted Indian architect Charles Correa, rm at various levels opening out onto balconies and small communal areas, very pleasant and secluded beach. **C** *Villa Sol*, T 45852, good restaurant, rm with balcony, small pool, built on high ground overlooking Cidade de Goa whose beach is open to residents here; **C** *Prainha Cottages*, T 44162, 13 cottages by the sea, with shower and balcony, some a/c, simple but comfortable and quiet on a secluded black sand beach, good restaurant, exchange, travel, rec. **D** *Beach Resort*,

T 47955, 17 large rm, some with balcony, small garden restaurant.

• **Places to eat** *O Pescador*, good views over jetty, rec, seafood specialities. Also a Punjabi *Dhaba*.

Bambolim

(8 km) off the NH17 S, has the site of the Goa University nearby. The dark-sand beach is secluded, free of hawkers and shaded by palms.

• **Accommodation C** *Hotel Bombolim*, on the beach, T 46499, a/c rm, though simple are airy with balcony, open-air, beach side restaurant and bar (breakfast incl), and bar, palm shaded terrace and poolside, weekly folk entertainment, taxi to Panjim usually available, peaceful, excellent service, highly rec.

• **Places to eat** *Sand & Sea Restaurant*, down the beach will cook any kind of fish dish ordered (watch out for price quoted though).

Siridao

A short drive from Panaji, Siridao is a small secluded beach often good for shells.

Local festival

Mar/Apr: *Feast of Jesus of Nazareth*, is celebrated on the 1st Sun after Easter.

Circular excursion from Panaji

A pleasant trip round central and South Goa leaves Panaji by NH4A through Old Goa and Ponda to Molem and the Bhagwan Mahaveer Sanctuary (see above). You can make a short circuit by turing S at Ponda and crossing the Zuari at Borlim bridge to visit Rachol. The NH 4A goes straight on to Molem. A right turn leads through the forested hills of Sanguem taluka to Colem and Calem railway stations and then **Sanguem**, 20 km from Molem, which is the district headquarters of the largest taluka in Goa. Although inland it has the 'backwaters' feel. The 19th century Jama Masjid (renovated 1959) has 4 minarets and 2 turrets. A district road NW towards San Vordem, turns W to Chandor.

In **Chandor** the enormous **Menezes Braganza House** (part 16th century) shows the opulent lifestyle of the old Portuguese families who established great plantation estates. From here you can reach Rachol to the NW, by district road via Curtorim, or go first to Margao (W), then take a back road along the Zuari river.

Rachol (8 km from Margao) is set in a fertile green valley. A stone archway crosses the road marking the entrance, the road coming to an abrupt end in a hamlet by the river bank. The white painted buildings of the seminary are scattered on the left. The **fort**, mostly in ruins, was one of the most ancient in Goa. Originally Muslim it was captured by the forces of Vijayanagar in 1520 and then ceded to the Portuguese. During the Maratha Wars of 1737-9 the Portuguese had about 100 cannons. During the siege that followed it was greatly damaged. Having lost the northern provinces the Portuguese paid a huge indemnity to keep the southern forts. The fort was repaired by the Marquis of Alorna in 1745 but with the threat of aggression removed most of the buildings gradually disintegrated over the ensuing years.

The **Church of Nossa Senhora das Neves** (1576, expanded in 1596) has 5 altars and contains a famous library. The seminary was transferred to Rachol from Margao in 1580 after being burnt down there in a Muslim raid in 1579 (5 years after being established. It was known originally as the College of All Saints. For successive generations it has been the most prestigious centre of education in Goa, producing some of Goa's secular as well as religious leaders. The vast stone structure of the seminary is built round a large courtyard; the exterior is lime-washed but inside the courtyard the walls are pink. There is an underground cistern.

ROUTES The road runs SE to Margao and the southern beaches. The NH17 itself runs N from Margao and crosses the Zuari estuary at **Cortalim** by a new bridge. From the N of the bridge the road runs across the island which had been at the heart of the original Portuguese settlement **Agassim** has a small white chapel by the road shaded by a large tamarind. After passing through Mercurim the road reaches Goa Velha, 6 km N of Agassim on the N bank of the Zuari.

Goa Velha, as Richards says "meaning old – being already old when the present-named Old Goa, or Velha Goa, was still young and flourishing." Goa Velha had been capital of the Bahmani Muslims, who ruled it from 1469 to 1488, when it was taken by the Sultan of Bijapur. It is difficult now to spot the site of Velha Goa. A faded notice board by a cross standing on a pedestal is the only visible remains. Nearby the **Pilar Seminary**, an ancient institution founded in 1613, is sited on a hilltop over a Siva temple. Relics of a headless *Nandi* bull and a rock carving of a Naga (serpent) were found. Good views of harbour.

ROUTES The NH 17 goes over the undulating laterite plateau to Panaji. In parts thickly wooded but also densely populated, evidence of the Portuguese Christian impact is visible in the white painted churches and the domestic architecture. Two km S of Panaji is the most striking of these churches at Santa Cruz. Set in a wide open square, this has a very large bell tower at the corner. It is fronted by a cemetery and fountain.

From Bambolim an alternative route to Panaji crosses the bare laterite plateau to the W, past the Goa Medical College and turns left to **Dona Paula**, the headland between the Mandovi River estuary and Marmagao harbour (see below).

Cabo de Raj Niwas, on the opposite side of the Mandovi Estuary from Fort Aguada, was begun in 1540. A Franciscan monastery was built alongside. During the Napoleonic Wars British troops were garrisoned at Cabo to prevent the possibility of a Napoleonic invasion. They built themselves barracks which were subsequently demolished by the Portuguese. Later the Archbishop of Goa was given the monastery as his residence which later became the governor's residence (*Raj Bhawan*). The second line of defence on this side of the estuary was Gaspar Dias near Miramar Beach. It was destroyed during the mutiny of 1835.

ROUTES The return to Panaji is along the Miramar beach, an extension of the Panaji esplanade.

OTHER TOWNS AND BEACHES

The whole coastline of Goa is one long coconut-fringed beach, indented by occasional inlets and estuaries. The road runs slightly inland, with spurs leading down to the main popular sections of beach.

Today many offer watersports – water skiing, sailing, para sailing, snorkelling, diving, water scooter and trips in glass bottom launches. There are no private beaches in Goa. Public access is guaranteed and hotels are not allowed to build within 200m of the high tide mark. On the popular stretches of sand such as Calangute there is a seemingly endless stream of local entrepreneurs selling food and simple handicrafts, or offering a massage or to tell your fortune. The more exclusive beach resorts try to protect their clients by discouraging these purveyors of goods and services. Now the public have free access to hotel and resort beaches. Even the busiest are spasely populated compared with most European beaches. The beaches further S (Palolem) are even less visited; however, the railway from Bombay, once extended to these parts may change that. The best and most expensive time to visit is mid-Nov to mid-Feb; the best discounts are available from mid-Jun to mid-Sep.

Northern Goa

Mapusa

(13 km from Panaji; *Pop* 31,600; *STD Code* 083284) This is the main town of Bardez *taluka* and periodic market centre (Fri). Municipal Gardens. It stands

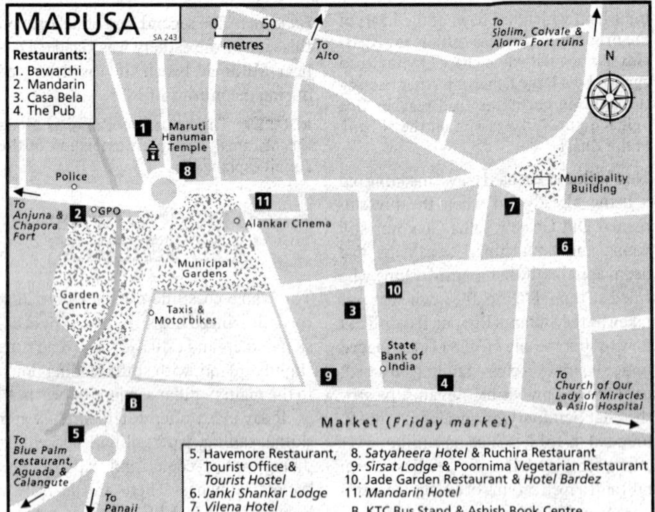

on a long ridge which runs E-W, fertile agricultural land occupying the flat valley floor right up to the edge of the town. The **Church of Our Lady of Miracles** (1594) was rebuilt in 1719 and 1838 after it was destroyed by fire. The Nosa Senhora de Milagres image is venerated by Hindus and Christians alike. Although the town has little of architectural interest it is a busy and attractive market centre.

Excursion

Alorna The Portuguese captured the important fort in the NE corner of the state at Alorna from the Bhonsla in 1746. On the N bank of the Chapora river it is now in ruins.

Local information

● Accommodation

D *Satyaheera*, nr Hanuman Temple, T 2849, 33 rm, some with a/c and TV, rooftop restaurant; **D** *Mandarin*, nr Alankar Cinema, has some decent rm.

E *Vilena*, nr Municipality, T 2824, 16 rm, some a/c; **E** *Bardez*, Coscar Corner, T 2607, has rm with bath, a/c restaurant (Chinese *Jade Garden*); **E** Goa Tourism *Tourist Hostel*, T 2794, at the roundabout, rm for 2-6, good value restaurant, beers; **E** *Shalini*, Taliwado, T 262334, simple rm, restaurant; **E** *Sirsat Lodge*, T 262419, with 40 rm and **E** *Janki Shankar*, with 20 rm are simple.

● Places to eat

Hotel Mahalaxmi, Anjuna Rd, has veg restaurant. *Bawarchi*, behind Hanuman Temple, nr Bus Stand, part a/c. A/c *Moonlight*, Shalini Bldg, 1st Flr, nr Taxi stand. *Casa Bela* and *Lobster*, 1st Flr, opp Hotel Vilena specialise in Goan food. A/c Chinese *Mandarin*, Garden Centre, opp Police Station. *Blue Palm*, Canca Parra, Mapusa-Calangute Rd. All have **bars**. *Royal-T*, Shop 96, nr Shakuntala Fountain, Municipal Market, Goan snacks, sweets and spices. Snacks also at *Xavier's*, Municipal Market and *The Pub*, 1st Flr, Dipti Chambers, opp Municipal Market. From 1630 until late, carts and stalls mainly nr Alankar Cinema, sell popular meat and seafood dishes.

● Airline office

Damania Airways, T 262694.

● Hospitals & medical services

Hospital, T 2372. *Drogaria Pharmacy*, nr Swiss Chapel, open 24 hr. *Mapusa Clinic*, T 2350.

● Post & telecommunications

Telephone & fax: several in town incl JJ Sons, 13 Garden Centre; other nr KTC Bus Stand.

● Shopping

Books: *Ashish Book Centre*, nr KTC Bus Stand.

Market: the Municipal market is well planned. The colourful Fri market from 0800-1800, is full of activity and local atmosphere; popular with backpackers too, who buy and sell belongings. Worth a visit but check goods carefully.

Photography: *Remy Studios*, Coscar Corner and Shop 8, KTC Bus Stand.

● Useful addresses

Fire: T 2231. **Police**: T 2231.

● Transport

Local Taxi: to/from Panaji when shared, Rs 8; Aldona, Rs 4; Chapora, Calangute, Baga, Rs 6; Siolim, Rs 6. **Motorcycle taxi**: to Anjuna, Rs 20.

Road To Panjim Rs 2 (about ½ hr). Anjuna, Vagator, 7 km, Rs 2. Calangute.

Northern beaches

Arambol

(Harmal) Locally called 'Hippie beach' this northernmost beach with a deserted wide stretch of white sand, is well beyond the main tourist track, across the estuary of the Chopdem (Chapora) river. Its idyllic peace may not last, as the Goan Government is in advanced negotiations with a Japanese company to set up a Japanese township of some 600 cottages in 300 ha on the Arambol coast, along with an 18-hole golf course. The plan has aroused strong local oppostion.

Mandrem

Mandrem is about 1.5 km S and is deserted, while **Morgim** is at the mouth of the Chopdem river. From the beach, a 20 min walk N by a rough track takes you to a fresh water lake; swimming possible (some found it dirty). **Getting there** To reach Arambol from Vagator (see below) walk E of Fort to Chapora village, past fish processing to cross the estuary (Rs 20 each, Rs 40 for boat). Two hr walk along coast which is well worthwhile.

Terekhol

(Tiracol) Further N, along the coast is a Goan enclave on the Maharashtra border. It stands on the N side of the Terekhol river estuary on a piece of high ground giving good views across the water. Originally a Maratha fort, it is protected from attacks from the sea, while the walls on the land side rise from a dry moat. It was captured by the Portuguese in 1776. The church inside the fort has a classic Goan façade and is large enough to have catered for the occupants of the fort and the surrounding settlements.

● Accommodation E *Terekhol Fort Tourist Rest Home*, T via Redi 48, the old fort has been converted to provide 10 rm in cottages, good views. There is basic, very spartan accommodation in Waddo, the small village, nr Arambol.

● Transport To Terekhol from Panaji, bus leaves at 1130; from Mapusa, share taxi to Siolim (Rs 8), cross river by ferry, continue to Keri by share taxi, cross river by ferry to Terekhol and walk remaining 2 km! Alternatively, avoiding ferry, a quicker, though 8 km longer route, is via Colvale (N of Mapusa) and Shiroda and Redi (both in Maharasthra), returning to Terekhol.

Vagator

(8 km W from Mapusa, *STD Code*: 083226) This is a very attractive little bay between rocky headlands with a series of small beaches to the S with shady palms. **Chapora Fort** is on a hill at the N end, only a short walk away. Now in ruins, the fort stands on the S bank of the Chapora River and dominates the estuary. It was originally built by Adil Shah. Aurangzeb's son Akbar (not Akbar the Great) used it as his headquarters. The Portuguese built it in its present form in 1717 as a secure refuge for the people of Bardez in face of Maratha attacks as well as a defence of the river mouth.

Day-tourists in buses from Panaji descend on Vagator and Anjuna at about 1100 and leave at about 1700; the beach is particularly attractive in the early morning.

• **Accommodation** **C** *Sterling Resort* (was Vagator Beach Resort, now extended), T 3276, at the foot of the Fort, 140 rm, restaurant, pool, red tiled cottages in a peaceful garden setting with shady trees, quiet, attractive, good value. **D** *Royal Resort*, T 3260, 28 rm, 10 a/c, restaurant, bar, pool. **F** *Noble Nest*, opp Chapel, Chapora, nr Post Office, restaurant.

• **Places to eat** *Laxmi* and others on beach, some serve good fresh fish.

• **Transport Road** From Panaji to Vagator takes 1¼ hr.

Anjuna

S of Vagator Beach Anjuna is now one of Goa's best known beaches, which has taken over from Calangute as the centre for hippies. Some are still here, living in cheap rooms near the beach. In Anjuna itself is the splendid **Albuquerque mansion** built in the 1920s by an expatriate Goan who had worked as a doctor in Zanzibar and then returned home. The Wed **Flea Market** is very popular – "huge and really worthwhile. You can get anything from anywhere in India, especially good for jewellery and ethnic clothes". Some disappointed – rather full of tourists (Mapusa better for 'local colour').

Windsurfing boards for hire at the S end of the beach, Rs 100 per hr, Rs 800 per week.

• **Accommodation** **C** *Bougainvillea*, has comfortable rm, excellent food, bar (wines, imported beer), very pretty garden, bit pricey but rec. **D** *Tamarind Lodge*, Kumar Vaddo, 3 km from beach, excellent restaurant (see below), bar, 27 rm, 6 a/c with modern bath in stone cottages, displaying owners art work, garden, pool. **E** *Granpa's Inn*, Gaunwadi, T Mapusa 26250, 10 rm; **E** *Poonam Guest Home*, has 16 rm; **E** *Palacete Rodrigues*, Mazalvaddo, rm and suites.

• **Places to eat** *Tamarind Lodge*, Kumar Vaddo, with bar, in traditional house with large veranda where meals are served, good meals inc Western specialities. *German Bakery*, inland from the Flea Market, outdoors, soft lighting, cane chairs, (table-tennis!), excellent espresso, capuccino, juice and snacks, 2/3 main courses (eg lasagna, tofu-burger) each night, rec. Behind this and next to a tennis court is *Gregory's*, rec for excellent Western food, esp pizzas (try with prawns). For seafood try *La franza*, and for French food *The Knock-in Wall*. *The Haystack*, Arpora Bardez, nr Anjuna (6 km from Mapusa), Goan food and wine, live contemporary music and cultural shows (leading artistes appear occasionally) on Fri (except monsoons) from 2030 – an al fresco cabaret.

Calangute

(*Pop*: 11,800; *STD Code*: 083288). **Calangute**, also called Kongutey, 10 km from Mapusa, has a post office, bank, tourist office, travel, restaurants and shops selling clothes and handicrafts, and is now a busy and developed centre. Despite fears of over-development it is still far from this. The *Youth Fête* held in 2nd week of May attracts Goa's leading musicians and dancers.

To the S of Anjuna, **Baga** is really the top end of Calangute beach. A former hippie hideaway, it has become more sedate and offers some cheap accommodation right on the beach. An attractive estuary can be waded at low tide. Calangute is popular not just because of its beach but also on account of the village houses spread out behind the beach under the palm trees, many offering accommodation. Early risers may see fishermen returning with their catch.

Local information

• **Accommodation**

Most in Calangute beach; many offer big off-season discounts. **C** *Paradise Village Beach Resort*, close to beach and town, individual cottages, comfortable, excellent service and management, rec; **C** *CSM Leisure Resorts*, Cobravaddo, T 842571, F 083227 6001, 45 suites (apartment style), restaurant, bar, shops, pool; **C** *Ronil Royale*, Baga Rd, Sauntavaddo, T 6018, F 083227 6001, 20 rm, 2 a/c, restaurant, coffee shop, shops.

D *Goan Heritage*, Gauravaddo, Candolim, T 6120, 31 airyrm with balcony, restaurant, pool; **D** *Linda Goa*, Cobravaddo, T 6066, 10 rm; **D** *Concha Beach Resort*, Umtawaddo, T 6058, 14 rm, restaurant, travel, wind surfing;

D ***Mira***, Umtawaddo, nr Chapel, T 083 276023, modern, clean rm (no TV), restaurant in roof-garden, 4 min walk from beach, nr shops and market; **D** ***Ronil Beach Resort***, Baga, T 6068, 58 rm, some a/c rm, restaurant, simple, helpful service; **D** ***Baia Del Sol***, Baga, T 6084, 23 rm, a/c cottages, restaurant (good view), water sports, excellent seafood and entertainment, simple but good, in attractive garden setting; **D** ***Varma's Beach Resort***, Umtavaddo, behind Bus Stand, T 6022, 10 clean a/c rm with verandahs facing pleasant garden, closed Jun-Oct; **D** ***Estrelo del Mar Beach Resort***, Calangute-Baga Rd, quiet, 10 rm, pleasant garden; **D** ***Bonaza***, Cobravaddo, T 6018, 10 rm; **D** ***Greenfield Cottages***, Morod, 12 rm, vary in price, good value.

● **Budget hotels**
You will be overwhelmed by the number on offer; here is a selection: **E** ***Cavala Hotels***, Baga, T 6090, 16 rm, good value; **E** ***Ancora Beach Resort***, Sauntavado, T 6096, 10 decent rm; **E** ***Riverside***, nr bridge, Baga Beach, T 6062, 12 rm, restaurant, cottages in garden setting, beautiful location; **E** ***Sea View Cottages***, on the beach, pleasant rm; Goa Tourism's **E** ***Tourist Resort***, Calangute, T 6024, rm, cottages and dorm, restaurant, bar, can be noisy; **E** ***Hacienda***, Sauntavaddo, Calangute has 10 good value rm; **E** ***Calangute Beach Guest House***, S of Beach Rd, spacious rm, restaurant; **E** ***Coco Banana***, back from beach; **E** ***Tourist Home***, Calangute-Baga Rd, T 6065, quiet and shady, restaurant, bar; **E** ***Sunshine Beach Resort***, Calangute-Baga Rd, attractive rm around a shady courtyard; **E** ***Chalston***, Cobravaddo, T 80, 12 rm, some a/c, 7 km centre, restaurant, water sports; **E** ***Calangute Beach Resort***, Umtawaddo, T 6063, 11 rm, some with bath, restaurant, bar, travel, exchange.

● **Places to eat**
Beachfront *dhaba* nr *Baia del Sol*, Baga, does good cheap Western food. There are also numerous small cafés along the beach incl ***St Anthony's***, Baga, for Goan and seafood. ***Master Joel Confectioners***, 9 Romano Chambers, opp petrol pump, making good Goan specialities.

● **Banks & money changers**
State Bank changes some travellers cheques but does not accept Visa. The **Bank of Baroda** does accept some credit cards.

● **Library**
Friends Circulating Library, Tintovaddo, keeps English French and German books.

● **Travel agent**
Space, Vila Xavier, Porvavaddo, Calangute, T 6076.

Candolim

STD Code: 083288. Calangute runs into Candolim, which has some accommodation. The beach itself is long and straight, backed by scrub-covered dunes but with little shelter.

● **Accommodation** **C** *Fisherman's Cave*, opp Taj Holiday Village, some cheaper rm, restaurant; **C** ***Aldeia Santa Rita***, T 842571, F 6001, 32 rm with balcony (some suites), restaurant, bar, pool. **D** ***Aguada Holiday Resort***, Bamonwaddo, T 6071, 40 rm; **D** ***Holiday Beach Resort***, T 2288, 22 rm, some cheaper. **E** ***Alexander Tourist Centre***, Morodvaddo, 7 rm; **E** ***Sea Shell Inn***, 8 rm.

● **Places to eat** *21 coconuts*, Restaurant and Bar, Candolim, rec for salads and health foods. *Coconut Inn* and Bar, Fort Aguada rd, by Shanti Durga temple, Candolim, typical Goan house, indoor and open-air. ***Fisherman's Nook***, Camotinvaddo, for seafood.

● **Airline office** UVI, Holiday Beach Resort, T 2088. GSA for Danair.

● **Travel agent** *Vit Yiak*, Camo Vaddo.

Sinquerim

Just N of Panaji, this is where the Taj Hotel group has set up its fabulous *Hermitage Hotel Complex* which dominates the headland around the historic Fort Aguada, partly occupying it. 45 km airport. Panaji is 13 km by road and a ferry ride away. If you want a long beach walk the firm sand is uninterrupted all the way N to Baga.

Aguada

(1612) on the N tip of the Mandovi estuary with the Neerul river to the E, Aguada was the strongest of the Portuguese coastal forts. Open 1600-1730. A channel was excavated to make the headland an island. A large well and a number of springs provided the fort and ships at harbour with drinking water (*agoa*). The main fortifications are still intact. 79 guns were placed to give the fort all round defensive fire power, the **Church of St Lawrence** (1630) standing in the centre of the fort. A 13m high lighthouse with rotating lamp, one of the first in Asia, was added in 1864, the lamp lit on the birthday of Queen Maria Pia of Portugal. Rs 2 to visit; good views from top. During WWII German prisoners of war were interned in the fortress which later served as the Central Jail. The *Taj Holiday Village*, *Fort Aguada* and *Hermitage* now occupy the area.

• **Accommodation AL** *Aguada Hermitage*, T 276201, exclusive and luxurious, 20 fully serviced 1 or 2 rm villas (US$475 peak season drops to $135 in low), each has its own spacious, tropical garden, the nightclub does not disturb the peace, good beach cafés. **AL-A** *Fort Aguada Beach Resort*, T 6701, is a standard hotel with 120 rm on a hill with good views. **A-B** *Holiday Village*, T 7515, 144 (some non a/c) villas, expensive in peak period, bus to airport and Panaji, imaginative planning, beautiful gardens of bougainvillea and palms, hotel lobby is open on the seaward side, giving a magnificent view, good restaurants, informal, helpful staff, efficient service, yhe pool at the *Village* is better than that at the *Resort*, highly rec.

Reis Magos

2.5 km E along the N bank of the Mandovi from Fort Aguada and faces Panaji across the river. It is a small town of some charm with a fort that was constructed in 1551 by Don Alfonso de Noronha. It was intended as a 2nd line of defence should an enemy, notably the Dutch, manage to sail past Aguada and Cabo on the headlands. Richards recalls that in 1604 the Dutch had succeeded in penetratingthe estuary and burning a number of ships. From this period ships had to stop at one of the forts on either side of the estuary to be cleared for passage upstream. The turreted walls are in almost perfect condition and house a local prison. The Franciscan **Church of Reis Magos** (1555) stands alongside and is one of the 1st Goan churches. Dedicated to the 3 Magi, Gaspar, Melchior and Balthazar, it was also used as a residence by dignitaries. Both stand quite high above water level and are approached by a flight of steep steps. **Accommodation D** Bamboo Motels *Noah's Ark*, Verem, Reis Magos, T 7321, 30 rm facing pool, restaurant.

Central Goa

Vasco da Gama

(30 km from Panaji, *STD Code*: 08345) Vasco da Gama (Vasco, in short) is Goa's passenger railway terminus of the Central Goa branch line. **Marmagao** (Mormugoa), the state's principal commercial port and one of India's few natural harbours is NW at a distance of 4 km (as is Dabolim airport, to the SE). A railway connects it with **Castle Rock** on the Western Ghats with *Aranyaka Jungle Camp* with its traditional huts. One km before Marmagao, is **Pilot Point**, at the base of the ruined fort, which offers excellent views over the harbour, the sea, the Zuari river and Dona Paula beach.

Virtually nothing remains of **Marmagao Fort** on the S headland of Marmagao Bay, and what does is hidden by the industrial development that has taken place. Non-combatants were moved to the fort from Old Goa when the old city was under threat in 1683 and at one time there was a scheme to shift the capital here. Along with Aguada, Marmagao was the 'throat' through which Goa breathed and is one of the finest natural harbours along the western seaboard of India.

Bogmalo beach is about 8 km away which has hotels. Hansa Beach, 4 km, in the Naval area, has a safe swimming beach (motorcycle taxis charge Rs 15). If you walk, in a cove halfway between the two is a fresh water spring, Suravali.

NB: Part of Baina Beach, 2 km, the red lght district, is notified as a high risk area for AIDS.

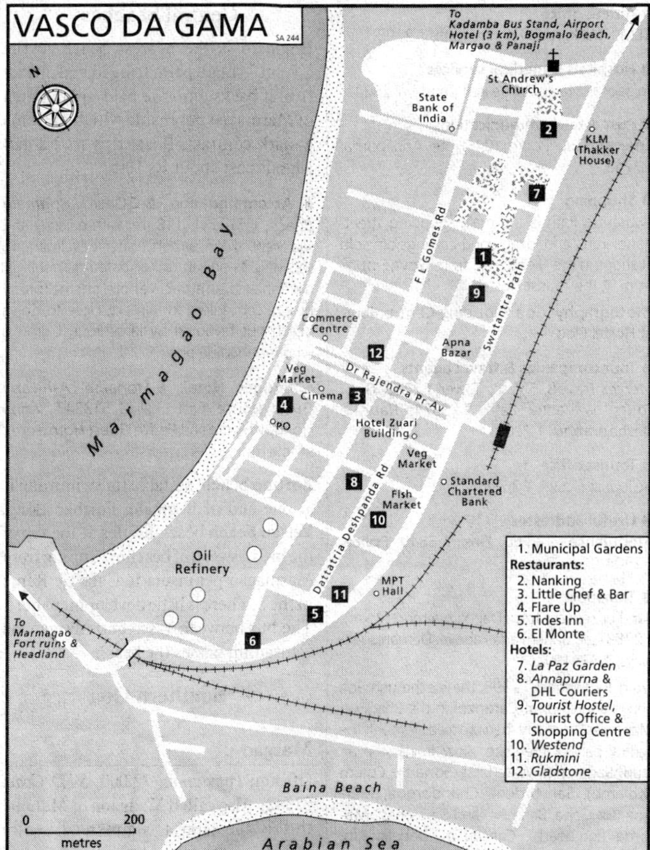

Local information

● Accommodation

C *La Paz Gardens*, Swatantra Path, T 512121, 72 rm, restaurants, exchange, free transport to airport and beach.

D *Airport*, Airport Rd (3 km from airport), T 513192, 30 a/c rm, restaurant; **D** *Maharaja*, Rua Leopoldo Flores, opp Hindustan Petroleum, T 512269, 50 rm, 18 a/c, restaurants, bar, travel.

● Budget hotels

E *Rukmini*, nr MPT Hall, T 512356, good value a/c rm, restaurant; **E** *Westend*, Mendes Mansion, Flores Gomes Rd (nr Rly), T 512288, 25 rm, some a/c, restaurant, bar, travel; **E** *Tourist Hostel*, nr Bus Stand, T 513119, 45 rm, some a/c, some 4-6-bed, limited menu restaurant, Tourist Office; **E** *Hotel Vasco*, Swatantra Path, T 513517, 21 inexpensive rm, some a/c, good value; **E** *Annapurna*, Dr Deshpande Rd, T 513645, 33 clean rm, good veg restaurant.

F *Rebelo*, Mundvel, T 512620, 30 rm.

● Places to eat

La Paz restaurants serve fast food and wide choice of meals. *Flare up* is nr the PO. *Little Chef*, FLores Gomes Rd, with Bar, is a/c, popular for snacks and simple Indian meals.

● **Airline office**
KLM, Thakkers, Swatantra Path, T 2298.

● **Hospitals & medical services**
Salgaocar Medical Research Centre, T 2524.

● **Post & telecommunications**
Courier: *DHL*, Room 104, Hotel Annapurna, T 3745.

● **Shopping**
Swatantra Path is the main shopping street. Handicrafts and local wood carvings are sold at shops in the N end; also from ***Govt Emporium*** at the Tourist Hostel.

Photography: ***Goa Shopping Centre***, Tourist Hostel Bldg.

● **Tour companies & travel agents**
Merces Travels, 6 Vasco Tower, T 2268; ***Gopi Tours***, Swatantra Path, T 3974; ***Rauraje Deshaprabhu***, T 2203.

● **Tourist office**
At Tourist Hostel, T 2673.

● **Useful addresses**
Ambulance: T 2768. **Fire**: T 3840. **Police**: T 2304.

● **Transport**
Air For services from Dabolim airport (4 km), T 2788, see under Panaji above. Damania Airways, T 513199.

Train RlyStation, T 2398. The line through Goa enters and stops at **Caranzol** in the Bhagwan Mahaveer Sanctuary then proceeds through the central part of the state. Slow trains stop at: **DudhSagar** (for Waterfalls), **Sonauli**, **Colem (Kolamb)**, **Sanvordem**, **Chandorgoa**, **Margoa** (for Colva, Benaulim and S beaches), **Majorda** (for beach), **Cansaulim**, Dabolim (for airport and Oberoi Bogmalo). **Vasco da Gama RlyStation** (35 km from Panaji) is linked by metre gauge line to Miraj which is linked with Bombay and Bangalore by broad gauge lines.

Bangalore: *Mail* 6202, daily, 1015, 20¼ hr. **Delhi via Miraj and Agra**: *Goa Exp* 7803, daily, 2030 (from Margao at 2110) 42¼ hr. **Hospet** for Hampi (Vijaynagara): *Vasco Exp* 7830, daily, 0715 via Hubli, 13 hr. **Miraj**: *Gomantak Exp* 7805, daily, 2115, (11 hr); changes to *Koyna Exp* 7308, dep Miraj 0935, 11¾ hr to **Bombay**. **Belgaum**: *Mandovi Exp* 7897, daily, 1130, 6½ hr.

Road To Panaji and Margao, Rs 5.

Sea From Marmagao, to Dona Paula, passenger launch, Rs 4.

Central beaches

Bogmalo is the nearest beach to the airport – small, palm fringed and attractive. It backs onto the bald upland area of Marmagao peninsula which presents a stark contrast. Boat trips to 2 small islands cost about Rs 100.

● **Accommodation** **B-C** Oberoi *Bogmalo Beach*, T 513311, 118 rm, with balcony and sea view, 4 km airport, older development, showing its age in rather dated furnishings, nevertheless, an attractive hotel on small pretty beach, convenient for airport, close to Colva beach but favoured by large tourist groups who monopolise pool.

● **Budget Hotel** **E** *Monalise Ashiyana Guest House*, Balli Chali, T 513347. *Vinny Holiday Home* and *Petite Guest House* offer simple rm.

Zortino beach, suitable for swimming is at one end of Bogmalo. Further along, **Velsao beach** beach nestles at the top of the broad sweep of beaches running from Marmagao peninsula to Cabo de Rama in the S. There is little development here. The bus between Vasco and Margao via Cansaulim passes the beach.

Southern Goa

Margao

(10 km; *Population*: 72,000; *STD Code*: 08342) Also called Madgaon or Margoa, this is the largest commercial centre after Panaji and the administrative capital of South Goa. A pleasant provincial town (given the status of town by Royal decree in 1778), it is HQ of the state's richest and most fertile taluka *Salcete*. The impressive Baroque **Church of the Holy Spirit** with its classic Goan façade dominates the Old Market (*Feast Day* in June) square, surrounded by a number of fine town houses. Built in 1564 over the ruins of a Hindu temple, it was sacked by Muslims in 1589 and rebuilt in 1675. In the square is a monumental cross with a mango tree beside it. The **Grace Church** is in the centre. The 17th

century **da Silva House** (also called 7 Shoulders) has sumptuous furnishings and the **de Joao Figueiredo House** has a splendid collection of Goan furniture. The covered **Market** is interesting to walk around.

Damodar Temple, 2 km from Kadamba Bus Terminal hosts the winter *Dindi Procession*. The pleasant Municipal and Children's Parks are near the City Bus Stand. **Monte Hill** a hillock, has good views over the town ('Motorcycle Taxis' charge Rs 7 for return trip, from centre).

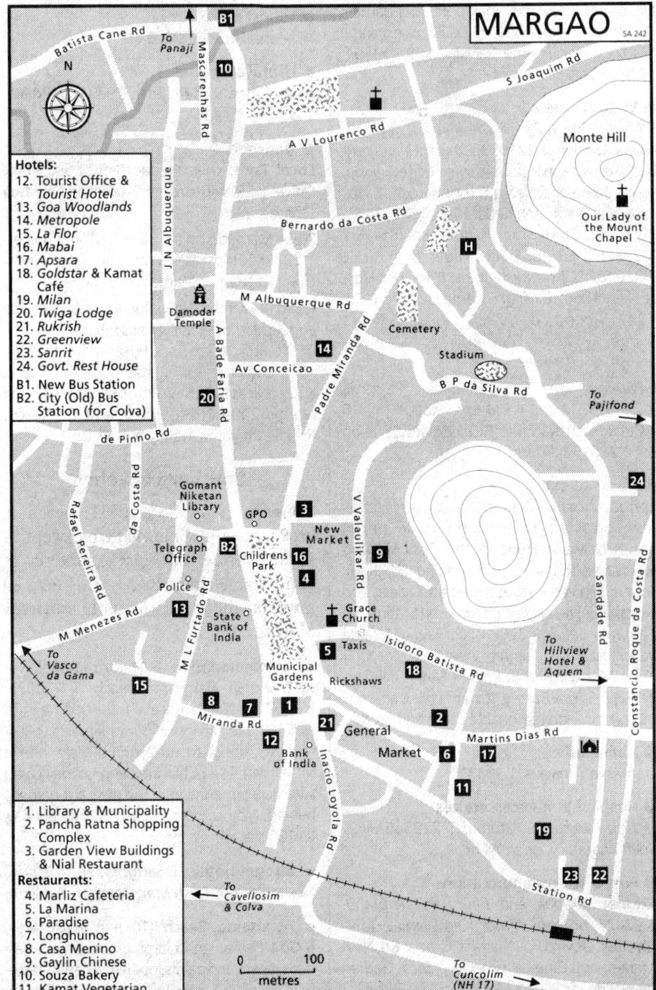

Local information

● Accommodation

Usually serves business travellers; holiday-makers head for the beaches, using Margao for an overnight stop for making travel connections. **D** *Goa Woodlands*, Furtado Rd, opp City Bus Stand, T 21121, 46 rm, 15 a/c, clean and spacious with bath, restaurant, bar, popular with business travellers; **D** *Metropole*, T 221556, 50 rm, some a/c, central, restaurant, bar, pool, roof garden; **D** *Hillview*, Aquem Alto, T 222582, 22 rm, some a/c; **D** *La Flor*, Erasmo Carvalho St, T 221591, 34 rm, 15 a/c, restaurant.

● Budget hotels

E *Mabai*, Praca Dr George Barreto, opp Municipal Garden, T 221653, 30 rm, 12 a/c, central, restaurants, permit rm, coffee shop, shops, large and pleasant roof garden; **E** *Apsara* (was Neptune), Kadar Manzil, T 221401, 20 rm; **E** *Gold Star*, Isadoro Baptista Rd, T 222153, 53 rm; **E** *Silveirado*, Monte Hill, T 220407, 22 rm, restaurant; **E** *Tourist Hostel*, T 21966; **E** *Milan Kamat*, Station Rd, T 22715, good Indian veg restaurant; **E** *Twiga Lodge*, 413 Abade Faria Rd, T 20049, 4 pleasant rm, good value.

F *Paulino*, rua de Sandade, Pajifond, T 220615, 14 rm; **F** *Rukrish*, Station Rd, 15 clean rm with balconies; **F** *Greenview*, Station Rd, T 220151, 54 rm.

● Places to eat

Longuinhos nr Municipality is open all day from breakfast time, specialises in prawn dishes. *La Marina* nr Taxi Stand. *Casa Menino* (part a/c) with Bar, Luis Miranda Rd (LIC Bldg). Four Indian veg *Kamat* restaurants, clean and good value; try a/c *Kamat Milan* on Station Rd. *Shalimar Cellar*, T 22888. A/c *Gaylin*, 1 Varde Valaulikar Rd nr Garden View Bldg, for Chinese. *Maria Luiza Bakers* nr Municipal Garden and Souza Bakery, towards the Kadamba Bus terminal do reasonable cakes and breads.

● Airline office

Damania Airways, T 20470.

● Hospital & medical services

JJ Costa Hospital, Fatorda, T 222586. *Holy Spirit Pharmacy*, open 24 hr.

● Post & telecommunications

Courier: *Skypak* and *Rau Raje Desprahu*, T 22477, nr *Hotel Mayur*, Old Market. **Telephones**: Govind Poi, Mariano Gracias Rd, New Market; opp Cine Lata (incl Fax); *Bico*, Garden View Bldg, nr PO, *La Marina*, nr Taxi Stand.

● Shopping

The Old Market has been rehoused in the New (Municipal) Market in town.

Books: *Golden Heart*, behind GPO.

Handicrafts: Tourist Hostel shop; *AJ Mavany*, Grace Estate.

Photography: *Wonder Colour Lab*, Garden View Bldg; *Lorenz*, opp Municipality.

● Tourist office

At Tourist Hostel, T 222513.

● Useful addresses

Ambulance: 21444. **Fire**: T 222175. **Police**: T 22175.

● Transport

Local Taxis: to Panaji about Rs 300. Share taxi, Colva, Rs 3. **Motorcycle Taxis** and City **bus** service.

Train Margao is on the S Central Rly. Enquiries, T 222255. Most trains originate from Vasco; *Goa Exp* stops at Margao, see above.

Road Kadamba (New) Bus Terminal is on the edge of town, then City bus into centre, Re 1 or Motorcycle Taxi Rs 8; buses arriving before 1000 and after 1900, proceed to the centre. KTC services to **Panaji**, Rs 6, **Mangalore**; from Margao 2000 (10 hr); to Margao 2100; **Vasco**, Rs 5. From Vasco, hourly bus, Rs 2.

Southern beaches

Majorda (*STD Code*: 0834) beach is broad, flat and somewhat windswept. A 12 km bus ride from Margao; motorcycle taxis charge about Rs 30; taxis take 20 min from the airport, under 15 min from Margao.

● Accommodation **B** *Majorda Beach Resort*, 2 min walk from beach, T 220025, F 220212, 108 "rustically furnished" a/c rm and 10 more expensive individual villas, 3 Restaurants, designed on a grand scale with a rather barn-like public area and holiday camp style accommodation in the pleasant gardens behind, Motorbikes on beach (Rs 600 per day, Rs 150 per hr).

● Budget hotels **E** *Sangrila*, H No 294/A, 12 simple rm; **E** *Mish Mar*, Dongrim, has 2 rm.

● At **Utorda Beach** (10 min walk away) **B** *Goa Penta*, set in large grounds with gardens, lawns and palms, opened recently, tastefully decorated rm with balcony, in 2-3 storey development, fine white-sand beach reached through the grounds.

Excursion

Quepem 15 km SE of Margao, inland, has the Chandresvar (Moon God) Temple at Paroda, on the small Chandranath Hill. Water is believed to ooze from the siva linga when touched by moonlight at each full moon (the temple is designed to make this possible). The Moon was worshipped by Bhoja kings who ruled South Goa up to the mid-8th century before the Christian arrived. The old wooden temple chariot has good carvings. Good views from the hilltop.

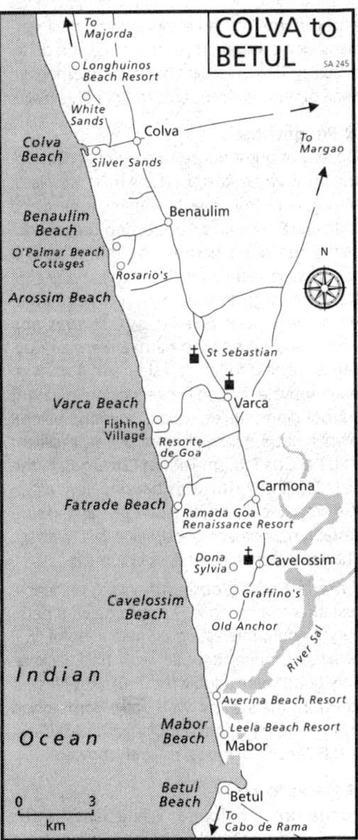

Colva beach

Colva (also called Koleam) is one of the most popular beaches in Goa, stretching 20 km along the coast. On the way you pass the large **Church of Our Lady of the Miracles** (1581) which houses an image of Jesus alleged to have been discovered on the African coast. *Annual feast* in Oct (see below). The village has a small fishing fleet and the palm-fringed beach itself is magnificent with beautiful white sand, coconut palms gently swaying in the breeze and blue waters (which can sometimes be rough). Travellers may notice the 'fishy' smell when dead fish are washed up on the beach. The narrow and attractive road S from Colva runs about 1 km inland from the sea through small villages, some with superb white painted churches. Paddy fields and palm groves alternate, and periodically roads run down to the sea, sometimes to small settlements, sometimes to deserted beaches.

Local festival

Mid-Oct *Feast of Menino Jesus* held on a Mon.

Local information

● Accommodation

Most 6-8 km from Margao Rly station. **C** *Penthouse Beach Resort*, T 221030, 68 rm in pleasant local style cottages, some a/c, exchange, good pool, garden dotted with palms, entertainment in season, good atmosphere, very helpful staff, excellent value.

D *Silver Sands*, in unimaginative building 2 min from white-sand beach, T 221645, 50 rm, some a/c with balcony, restaurant, bar, shops, travel, exchange, pool, package tour oriented, nr cafés, shops, good value, some complaints of dirty rm and pool, poor service, expensive massage, poorly maintained building; **D** *William Beach Resort*, T 221077, some a/c rm, restaurant; **D** *Colva Beach Resort*, T 221975, 19 rm, some a/c with showers; **D** *Longuinhos Beach Resort*, on water's edge, T 222918, 32 rm with balcony, 6 a/c, good restaurant, boutiques, cultural shows; **D** *Sukhsagar Beach Resort*, behind *Penthouse*, path off Margao Rd, T 221888, 22 rm with bath, 5 a/c, restaurant, bar, travel; **D** *Colmar*, White Sands, on the beach (little further from Tourist Cottages, T 221253, 26 clean rm with hot and cold, and cheap dorm, rm in cottages with small gardens, good restaurant, redecorated and partly rebuilt in 1994, pleasant hotel, more expensive than others nearby but rec for friendly service.

● **Budget hotels**

Dozens of guest houses too, offer accommodation: **E** ***Vailankanni***, H No 414/1, 4th Ward, a short walk from beach, with 6 clean rm and bath and **E** ***Glowin's Abode***, opp, are friendly, family run guest houses, the former with a good value restaurant; **E** ***Vincy's***, T 222276, has 7 rm, large and gloomy above restaurant, no longer popular; **E** ***Sea View Cottages***, opp *Silver Sands*, 4 rm with bath; **E** ***Garden Cottages***, behind *Johnny's* restaurant, 4 rm with bath, private balcony, overlooking pleasant surroundings, quiet, clean, friendly, helpful owner, but 5 min walk from beach, excellent value. **E** Goa Tourism ***Tourist Cottages***, nr the sea, T 222287, rm with balcony, few a/c in 2-storeyed building or cottages, and dorm, restaurant, garden, good value but without character, popular with Indian tourists.

F ***Maria Guest House***, 4th Ward, nr beach, restaurants and shops, 7 rm, some with bath, very friendly, interesting owners, helpful, will arrange car-hire, popular with backpackers, very good value, highly rec; **F** ***Tourist Nest***, 2 km from the sea, rm with bath, dorm, good restaurant, bike hire, popular with backpackers; **F** ***Tansy Cottages***, rm with shower.

● **Places to eat**

Longuinos and ***Colmar*** White Sands Hotels and ***Goodman's*** highly rec for excellent fresh fish and Goan dishes, value for money and friendly service. Also ***Connie M's*** and ***Lactancias Music House***; latter offers limited choice but is good value. Poor reports for food and service at *Colva Beach Resort* restaurant. Several others offer cheap Western food and beer.

● **Bar**

Splash with a dance floor is open all night. Very popular.

● **Shopping**

Small square with usual craft shops and a good bookshop. Kashmiri papier maché and Karnataka mirror-work is cheaper than in the regional centres.

● **Transport**

Road To Margao (6 km) every ½ hr, takes ½ hr, (or taxi for 8). Both Rs 3. Last bus to Margao, 1915, from Margao, 2000 (from there to Mangalore, dep 2030 takes 9½ hr, Rs 100); motorcycle taxi, Rs 15; autorickshaws Rs 25.

Benaulim (also called Banaley) this is the more tranquil end of Colva beach easily reached by private transport. Buses go as far as Maria Hall (Dangvaddo), 1 km walk from the beach. The 4 km walk or cycle-ride between Colva and Benaulim, through idyllic countryside is recommended. Cycles for hire in village.

● **Accommodation** **D** *Corina Beach Resort*, 14 rm, some a/c, with shower, others cheaper; **D** ***Palm Grove Cottages***, H No 1678, Vasvaddo, rm facilities vary, some a/c with bath, others cheaper, restaurant, bar, palm-shaded garden. **E** ***L'Amour Beach Resort***, nearest beach, T 223720, 20 rm in cottages and restaurant (incl seafood). **Note**: Take care of possessions. **F** ***Brito's Tourist Corner***, modern building nr Maria Hall, 1 km from beach, 10 clean rm with shower. **E** ***O'Palmar Beach Cottages***,, right on the beach, T 223278, rm with shower. **F** ***Come-up***, H No 807/A, Dauler, T 23268, 5 rm with shower. Many families take paying guests, charging Rs 30-60 for double rm.

● **Places to eat** Plenty of beach restaurants, often excellent, incl ***Pedro's***, ***Goodman's*** and ***Atona***; ***Johncy's*** and ***Rafael's*** rec for fresh fish and Goan dishes, value for money and friendly service. Johncy's is very pleasant (backgammon, scrabble). ***Sesha*** is nr Bus Stand at Dangvaddo. One km from Colva ***Sucorina*** is highly rec for seafood.

South of Colva

(*STD Code*: 0834) The beach runs into **Varca** and **Cavelossim** with several up-market resorts. The small village of Varca inland has notable church with a particularly striking front. To reach Cavellosim (18 km from Margao) bus journeys are uncomfortably slow; taxis charge Rs 150.

Further S, **Mabor** (or Mobor) and **Betul** beaches lie on either side of the inlet where the river Sal joins the sea. Some exclusive hotel resorts have been developed, although visually they are quite unobtrusive. Betul is an important fishing village. About 10 km to the S of Betul is **Cabo de Rama**, named after the hero of the *Ramayana* Hindu epic who is said to have lived there with his wife Sita during their period of exile. The site was chosen well as the narrow headland only needed fortification on the landward side. Its origins pre-date the arrival of the Portuguese who captured it in 1763 and was used as a prison. It is well preserved, with 21 guns. There are 2 springs, 1 of which gives out water through 2 spouts at different temperatures. Not easily accessible by road, it is best seen by boat.

• **Accommodation** **A** Ramada *Goa Renaissance Resort*, Fatrade Beach, Varca, T 245200, F 245335, new, interesting design by Mexican architects, with water sports and 9-hole golf; **A** *Leela Beach*, Mabor, T 246363, F 246352, 217 rm in villas and pavilions, all facilities, 3 restaurants, sports, for peak season (20 Dec-10 Jan) reserve 4 months ahead. **B** *Old Anchor*, 2 km S of Cavelossim, T 23005, 238 large rm in new resort replacing 2-storey self-catering apartments, between the sea and the River Sal, speciality restaurants, disco at bar, water sports, golf, tennis, fine-sand beach of the Sal, reached by paved walkway, crossing the coastal road; **B** *Resorte de Goa*, Fatrade Beach, Varca, T 245066, F 5310, 56 rm and suites in main building and smaller rm in colourful cottages, prices drop steeply in Jun-Sep; **B** *Averina Beach Resort*, Mabor, Varca, T 246303, F 246333, 144 comfortable rm (prices vary) with shady balconies in 2-storey buildings around pool and garden, all expected facilities, health club, tennis. **C** *Dona Sylvia Resort*, T 246321, F 246320, 240 comfortable a/c rm in 2-storey villas with emerging gardens, nightly entertainment in restaurant in season, bar, large pool, gym, very popular with charter groups. **D** *Graffino's Beach Resort*, Mabor, T 23439, 16 rm with shower.

Palolem

(*STD Code*: 0834) further S on the coast (40 km from Margao via Cuncolim), Palolem has an unspoilt beach, 2 km off the main road, with strange rock formations locally referred to as *Pandava's* drums and footprints. Visit rec.

• **Accommodation** **E** *Palolem Beach Resort*, T 643054, 6 basic rm with shower and toilet, 7 simple tents with shower block, clean, very quiet, shaded site.

• **Transport** From Margao, a Karwar bus will take you to Canacona junction; 2 km walk from there. Alternatively walk to Canacona Bus Depot and get an autorickshaw to Palolem beach, Rs 25.

The Goa-Karnataka border is further S, just under 1 hr bus ride. Across the border there is a marked improvement in the road surface, and the road no longer winds through forest but is relatively wide and straight along the Karnataka coast.

PANAJI TO PONDA AND MARDOL

This round trip gives an attractive view of the Western Ghats, intensively cultivated rice fields, and some interesting small villages. Allow a full day.

From Panaji cross the Mandovi to **Betim**. **Accommodation F** *Tourist Complex*, T 7362 with very basic facilities, some beds (Rs 10-30), mattresses (Rs 5) or floor space for students (Rs 3), Tourist Office.

ROUTES Take NH17, then after about 3 km a road goes right, skirting the upper waters of the Mapusa River, to **Bicholim** (*Population*: 13,700; *STD Code*: 08323).

Mayem Lake is 1 km to the S and is a popular local picnic spot, with pedal boats on the lake, on the road to Piligao. Goa Tourism's **E** *Lake Resort*, T Bicholim 2144, 16 rm, some a/c with bath, dorm. Continue to Sanguelim

Sanguelim (*Populaion*: 6,200), the 'home' area of the Rajput Ranes tribe who migrated S from Rajasthan in the late 18th century and spent the next century fighting for the Portuguese as mercenaries, then against them for arrears of pay. In 1895 one of their revolts necessitated the despatch of troops from Portugal. The **Temple of Vitthala**, an aspect of Vishnu, built in the North Indian style, has recently been renovated. Some of the original carved wooden columns have been retained. Outside is a temple cart, used to transport a Hanuman image on festive occasions. The Ranes still live in the old family house next to the temple.

ROUTES The road S goes to Tisk (25 km) which is at the intersection with NH 4A.

Bondla Sanctuary

The smallest of Goa's 3 nature reserves, is only 80 sq km in area and is situated in the foothills of the Western Ghats, which harbours sambar and wild boar. The Dept of Tourism is promoting it as an educational resource centre. The park has a botanical and rose garden to complement the jungle, a zoo and deer park (**closed Thur**). More a theme park than a national park, visitors in 1994 reported it as very unimpressive.

• **Accommodation** Goa Tourism *Tourist Cottages*, which are fairly comfortable, meals are available, advance reservations: Conservator of Forests, Junta House, Grd Flr, next to Sahakar Bhandar.

• **Transport Road** Via Ponda and Usgaon.

Molem

(18 km E along the NH4A, 1½ hr journey) is near the **Bhagwan Mahaveer Sanctuary**. This 240 sq km park is quite different, containing a herd of gaur (*Bos gaurus* – often called Indian Bison), leopard, deer, elephants and a rich bird life. The attractive **Dudhsagar waterfalls**, (600m from hilltop to valley) are in the SE corner, accessible only by train.

• **Accommodation** None in Sanctuary; carry provisions. Nearest in Molem, **E** Goa Tourism *Tourist Complex*, T 5238, with 23 simple rm, dorm, ice cold pool at the base of the waterfall is lovely for a swim. The **Devil's Canyon** is also here.

• **Transport Train** From Vasco, train dep at 0730 for Colem via Margao (dep 0800); from Colem Rly Station, the waterfalls is 10 km (1 hr). Return train dep 1500.

Molem is the start of hikes and treks in Dec/Jan. Popular routes lead to Dudhsagar (16km), the Sanctuary and Atoll Gad, 12 km, Matkonda Hill, 10 km and Tambdi Surla, 12 km. **Tambdi Surla** is in the foothills with the 13th century basalt Mahadeva Temple complex, the only example of Kadamba/Yadava architecture (there is road from Sancordem). Contact the Hiking Assoc, Captain of Ports Office, Panaji, T 45070.

ROUTES Return to Tisk and along **NH4A** to Ponda.

Ponda

(*Population*: 14,700; *STD Code*: 08343)
Not officially part of Portuguese Goa until it was ceded by the King of Sunda in 1791, it was one of the first provinces conquered by them. However, it was quickly retaken by the Adil Shah dynasty of Bijapur who built the **Safa Mosque** (1560). It has a simple rectangular chamber on a low plinth, with a pointed pitched roof, very much in the local architectural style, but the arches are distinctly Bijapuri. Built of laterite, the lower tier has been quite badly eroded. On the S side is a tank for ablutions with *maharab* designs. The large gardens and fountains here were destroyed during Portuguese rule. Today they are attractively set off by the low rising forest covered hills in the background. During the Inquisition many Hindu devotees were forced to remove images from Portuguese territory to safety. Many were taken only as far as Ponda (also called Phondya) which was just over the border. As a centre of culture, music, drama and poetry, it was known as *Antruz Mahal*.

It has some of the most important Hindu temples in Goa; there are 7 within 5 km. The **Shanti Durga Temple** (1738) the Goddess of Peace, set in a picturesque forest clearing, was erected by one of the Maratha rulers of the W Deccan. The original temple was over 400 years old. In the temple complex there is a tank and a 5-storeyed bell or lamp tower; the roof is made of long stone slabs. These pagoda like structures are peculiar to Goa and suggest the influence of Western Church ideas concerning the place of worship. The domed temple is Neo-Classical in design. Also here, (22 km from Panaji and nr Mardol), on a wooded hill is the tiny 18th century **Sri Manguesh Temple** at Priol. It is the principal shrine of Siva in Goa and is being constantly added to. Painted white, it resembles the Jain temples at Palitana – see page 1265. Inside, it has blue pillars and chandeliers.

Ponda fort was constructed by the Adil Shahi rulers and was destroyed by the Portuguese in 1549. Shivaji conquered the town in 1675 and rebuilt the fort, but it was again taken and wrecked by the Portuguese.

- **Transport Road** From Panaji, Rs 6.

Mardol

Mahalsa Narayani Temple (2 km from Sri Manguesh, 18th century). The original temple at Verna in Salcete taluka was the refuge of a group of Portuguese who were under attack from Adil Shah forces. It was re-erected at Mardol in the more European style. The goddess Mahalsa is a form of Lakshmi, Vishnu's consort. Inside is a series of carvings of the 10 avatars of Vishnu. In front of the temple, alongside the tower, is a brass Garuda pillar which rests on the back of a turtle as in Nepal. Garuda, Vishnu's vehicle sits on top. Main festival in Feb. Verna is the site of a proposed golf course.

ROUTES Return to Panaji via **Banasatri** and **Old Goa**.

GUJARAT

Contents

Maps

BASICS *Population*: 42.5mn (*Urban* 34%, *Scheduled Castes* 7%, *Scheduled Tribes* 14%); *Literacy*: M 70% F 48%; *Birth rate*: *Rural* 30:1000, *Urban* 27:1000; *Death rate*: *Rural* 10:1000, *Urban* 9:1000; *Infant mortality*: 72:1000; *Religion*: *Hindu* 89%, *Muslim* 9%, *Christian* 0.4%, *Sikh* 0.1%, *Jain* 1.4%; *Principal language*: Gujarati

Gujarat occupies an area of over 196,000 sq km, approximately the size of the United Kingdom. The *Gujara* are believed to have been a sub- tribe of the Huns who ruled the area during the 8th and 9th centuries AD. The present state was created in 1960 when Bombay state was divided between Maharashtra and Gujarat. The new city of Gandhinagar, 20 km N of Ahmadabad, is the state's capital. Gujarat has some fascinating and distinctive architecture, a wide variety of scenery and some superb beaches.

Gujarat's ports have been important centres of trade and embarkation points for Muslim pilgrims bound for Mecca. European colonial nations established factories and trading bases around the coast from the late 15th century onwards. In the 19th century many Gujaratis went to East Africa. They have subsequently scattered to England, Canada and New Zealand. At home, Gujaratis are prominent in the business community.

Historical sites

Gandhi's ashram at **Sabarmati** is just 6 km from the centre of Ahmadabad. **Baroda** (Vadodara) was the capital of the Gaekwad princely state whilst **Surat** on the coast was where Parsis settled after being driven from Persia. It was also the site of the first British factory in India in 1612. **Junagadh** is notable for its fort and numerous temples and is a suitable base for visiting the Gir forest, 1 of the state's 4 national parks and last home of the Asian lion. **Porbandar** was Mahatma Gandhi's birthplace, and **Rajkot** was where he spent his early years when his father was *diwan* (chief minister) to the Rajah of Saurashtra. The walled town of **Bhuj** is the major town of Kutch and a delightful haven off the beaten tourist track. **Palitana** in Saurashtra is an important Jain pilgrimage site.

Environment

The Land

Area 196,000 sq km. Gujarat has nearly 1,600 km of coastline, and no part of the state is more than 160 km from the sea. It is bounded by Rajasthan to the N, Madhya Pradesh to the E, Maharashtra to the S, and Pakistan to the NW.

Kachchh (Kutch) on the NW border of the peninsula, has a central ridge of Jurassic sandstones, with underlying basalts breaking through from place to place. It rises to heights of between 275m and 325m, and like the plains of the Indus into which it drops almost imperceptibly, it is almost desert. To the N of the ridge is the Great Rann of Kachchh, a 20,700 sq km salt marsh. To the S is the Little Rann. During the monsoon the Rann floods, virtually making Kachchh an island, while during the hot dry summer months it is a dusty plain. The drainage pattern has been strongly affected by earthquakes. A particularly large quake in 1819 formed a new scarp up to 6m high and 80 km long, diverting the old channels of the Indus. It has become known as Allah's Bund – *God's dyke*. To the E, the same earthquake caused widespread damage in Ahmadabad.

Saurashtra To the S of the Gulf of Kachchh, and between it and the Gulf of Khambhat (Cambay), is the **Kathiawad** or Saurashtra peninsula. A basalt platform 430 km long by 320 km wide, it is flanked by sandstones in the N. It rises from the coast to low scrub-covered hills at the centre, but is rarely more than 180m high. The 2 exceptions are to the E of Rajkot (335m) and in the Gir Range (640m). Formed of intruded igneous rocks pushed up into the surrounding Deccan lavas, the resulting plateaus have a completely radial drainage system. Over most of Kathiawad are great sheets of Deccan lavas, cut across by lava dykes. Around the ancient and holy city of Dwarka in the W and Bhavnagar in the E are limestones and clays, separated by a 50 km belt of alluvium. Some is wind blown, and at Junagadh reaches a depth of over 60m. Its creamy-coloured soft stone is widely used as Porbandar stone.

NE Gujarat is a continuation of central Kachchh and is characterised by small plains and low hills. The railway line from Bombay to Delhi runs through these hills which surround Ahmadabad. To the S of Baroda are the districts of Bharuch and Surat.

The **Western Ghats** extend into SE Gujarat, the wettest region of the state.

Rivers The Narmada which rises in Central MP has deposited large quantities of alluvium producing good agricultural land, although silting has contributed to the decline of ports such as Khambhat. The smaller but nevertheless important river Tapti rises near Pachmarhi in MP and enters the sea at Surat. The Sabarmati and Mahi also flow into the Gulf of Khambhat.

Climate

In Ahmadabad the daily winter maximum temperature is 27°C and the minimum 12°C, although sub zero cold spells have been recorded. In summer the daily max temperature can reach 48°C, though 42-43°C is more common. The summer min is 25°C. Further S the winter temperatures never fall as far, and the summer temperatures are slightly more moderate.

In the far S around Daman rainfall is still strongly affected by the SW monsoon, and totals often exceed 1500 mm, nearly all between Jun and Oct. However, because it is marginal to the main rain-bearing winds the total amounts are highly variable, falling rapidly northwards. At Ahmadabad it averages 900 mm a year, 88% of this falling during the monsoon months of Jun to Sep. West

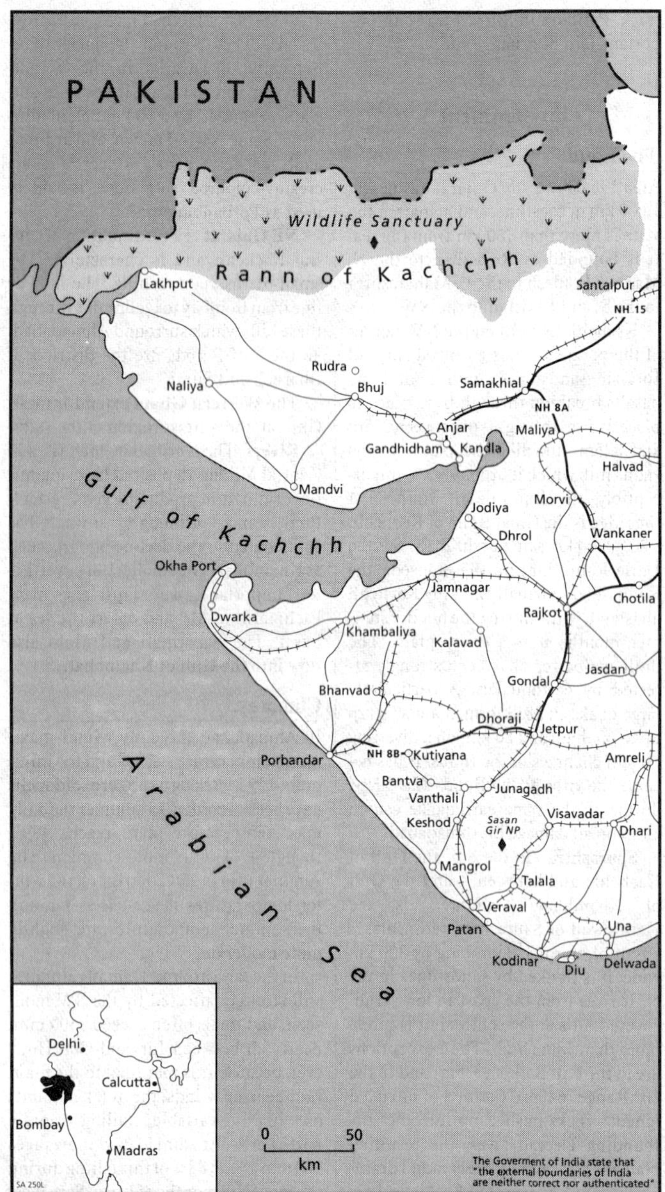
PAKISTAN
Wildlife Sanctuary
Rann of Kachchh
Lakhput
Santalpur
NH 15
Rudra
Naliya
Bhuj
Samakhial
NH 8A
Anjar
Maliya
Gandhidham
Kandla
Halvad
Mandvi
Gulf of Kachchh
Jodiya
Morvi
Dhrol
Wankaner
Okha Port
Jamnagar
Chotila
Dwarka
Rajkot
Khambaliya
Kalavad
Jasdan
Gondal
Bhanvad
Dhoraji
Jetpur
Porbandar
NH 8B
Kutiyana
Amreli
Bantva
Junagadh
Vanthali
Keshod
Sasan Gir NP
Visavadar
Dhari
Mangrol
Talala
Veraval
Patan
Una
Kodinar
Diu
Delwada
Arabian Sea
Delhi
Calcutta
Bombay
Madras
0
50
km
SA 250L
The Goverment of India state that "the external boundaries of India are neither correct nor authenticated"

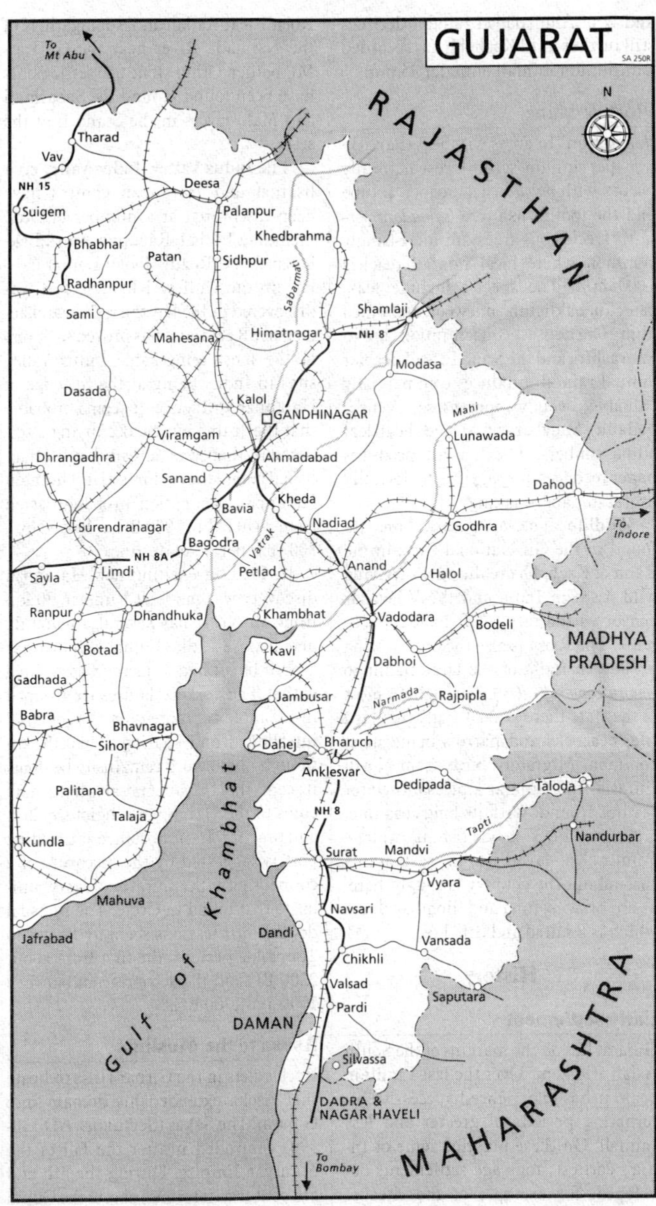
GUJARAT
SA 250R
N
RAJASTHAN
MADHYA PRADESH
MAHARASHTRA
Gulf of Khambhat
To Mt Abu
Tharad
Vav
NH 15
Deesa
Suigem
Palanpur
Khedbrahma
Bhabhar
Patan
Sidhpur
Radhanpur
Sabarmati
Shamlaji
Sami
Himatnagar
NH 8
Mahesana
Modasa
Dasada
Kalol
GANDHINAGAR
Mahi
Viramgam
Lunawada
Dhrangadhra
Ahmadabad
Sanand
Dahod
Kheda
Bavia
To Indore
Nadiad
Godhra
Surendranagar
Bagodra
Vatrak
NH 8A
Anand
Sayla
Limdi
Petlad
Halol
Ranpur
Dhandhuka
Khambhat
Vadodara
Bodeli
Botad
Kavi
Dabhoi
Gadhada
Narmada
Rajpipla
Jambusar
Babra
Bhavnagar
Sihor
Dahej
Bharuch
Anklesvar
Dedipada
Taloda
Palitana
NH 8
Talaja
Tapti
Nandurbar
Kundla
Surat
Mandvi
Vyara
Mahuva
Navsari
Jafrabad
Dandi
Vansada
Chikhli
Valsad
Saputara
Pardi
DAMAN
Silvassa
DADRA &
NAGAR HAVELI
To Bombay

and N of Ahmadabad rainfall declines still further until Kachchh has recorded a minimum rainfall of under 25 mm.

Flora & fauna

Vegetation In areas with less than 635 mm per annum scrub forest naturally occurs with *babul* acacia, caper, jujube and the toothbrush tree (*salvadora persica*). Deciduous trees are increasingly common where local rainfall reaches 1000 mm. The species include teak, catechu, bakligum, axlewood and butea gum. The densest concentrations are in Saurashtra and the S and E. Still heavier annual rainfall produces commercially valuable woolly tomentosa, vengai padauk, Malabar simal and heartleaf adina timbers. The E coast produces paper reed (*cyperus papyrus*), historically useful in paper-making.

Wildlife The last Asiatic lions are found in the Gir National Park; in the Rann of Kachchh are the only surviving wild asses in India and the Velavadar conserves the rare, swift footed blackbuck. The Rann is also the only nesting ground in India of the large flamingo (*phoenicopterus ruber*). Throughout most of the state there is a naturally rich bird life, peacocks and parrots being most common. Migratory birds from North Eurasia find Gujarat a pleasant winter resting ground. With its long coastline, Gujarat enjoys good fishing waters. Pomfret, a favourite in restaurants throughout the country is caught here, as are prawns, tuna and 'Bombay duck' which is a salted and dried fish.

History

Early settlement

Gujarat lies on the margins of the South Asian arid zone. Over the last 1 million years it has experienced successive alternating periods of greater and less rainfall. On these margins some of India's earliest stone age settlements developed, for example at the sites of Rojadi near Rajkot and Adamgarh, N of the Narmada River near the Gujarat-MP border. Other stone age settlements have been found around the Sabarmati and Mahi rivers in the S and E of the state.

The Indus Valley Indus Valley civilisation and Harappan centres have been discovered at a number of sites, including Lothal, Rangpur, Amri, Lakhabaval and Rozdi. Today Lothal is 10 km up the Gulf of Khambhat. It was discovered in 1954 by the Indian archaeologist SR Rao, and has proved to be one of the most remarkable Indus Valley sites in India, being at the SE edge of Harappan influence. It seems probable that they came by sea, occupying a settlement that was already well-established before they colonised it. The main Harappan occupation probably lasted from 2450 BC to 1900 BC, followed by a 300 year period of decline.

In 1988 an exciting new Harappan discovery was made at Kuntasi, 30 km from Morvi. It has several apparently new features. Like Lothal Kuntasi was a port, but it had a 'factory' associated with it. The workers' houses are grouped in 1 complex of more than 50 rooms, all interlinked and sharing 1 hearth. Although much work remains to be done, it seems that the site may also hold more clues to the Harappan religious beliefs and practice. Its importance as a trading port is suggested by the discovery of a copper ring with a spiral motif very similar to that found in Crete. The unusual double fortifications seem to date from 2 separate periods, the first from about 2200 BC and the second from between 1900 and 1700 BC.

Asoka to the Muslims

Rock edicts in the Girnar Hills indicate that Asoka extended his domain into Gujarat. The Sakas (Scythians; AD 130-390) controlled it after the fall of the Mauryan Empire. During the 4th and 5th centuries it formed part of the Gupta

Empire. Gujarat attained its greatest territorial extent under the Solanki dynasty, from the 9th century. The Vaghela dynasty which followed was defeated by the Muslim Ala-ud-din Khalji, the King of Delhi. There then followed a long period of Muslim rule. Ahmad I, the first independent Muslim ruler of Gujarat founded Ahmadabad in 1411.

Mughal power

The Mughal Humayun took Malwa and Gujarat in a brilliant campaign in 1534-5 but soon lost them. His son, Akbar, reclaimed both in a similarly daring and inspired military operation, securing the region for the Mughals for nearly 2 centuries, terminated by the Marathas in the mid 18th century.

Colonial power

In the scramble for trading bases the Dutch, English, French and Portuguese all established bases along the coast in the 17th century. The British East India Company's first headquarters in India was at Surat. It was later moved to Bombay. As British maritime supremacy became established all but the Portuguese at Daman and Diu withdrew. The state came under the control of the East India Company in 1818 and after the 1857 Mutiny was assumed by the Crown. It was then divided into Gujarat province, which had an area of 25,900 sq km with the rest comprising numerous princely states. Until Independence Kathiawad was one of the most highly fragmented regions of India, having 86 distinct political units in just over 55,000 sq km. The largest, Junagadh, had an area of less than 9000 sq km and a population of under 750,000 in 1947.

Art & architecture

Gujarati provincial architecture flowered between 1300 and 1550. The new Muslim rulers made full use of the already highly-developed skills of Hindu and Jain builders and craftsmen. The mosques and tombs that resulted reflect the new combination of Muslim political power and Hindu traditions. Thus, although the mosques obey strict Islamic principles they contain important features that are derived directly from Hindu and Jain precedents.

Culture

The People

Gujarat is one of the modern strongholds of Jainism. Note the '*parabdis*', special feeding places for birds, in the town. Jains devote great attention to the care of sick animals and birds and run a number of special animal hospitals. Mahatma Gandhi was strongly influenced by Jain principles, including that of *ahimsa*– see page 89. He found the deep divisions between high and low caste Hindus deeply repugnant. Re-naming the former untouchables as 'Harijans' (God's people), he fought for their rights and dignity. Caste division remains a potent political force in Gujarat today.

Language The majority of the people speak Gujarati, an Indo-Aryan language derived from Sanskrit. It was also heavily influenced by *Apabrahmsa*, which was widely spoken in North-West India from the 10th to the 14th centuries, while maritime contacts with Persia, Arabia, Portugal and England led to the introduction of many words from these languages. Persian influence was particularly strong in Ahmadabad. The great majority of the population is of Indo-Aryan origin. Nearly 20% of the population is tribal, the Bhil, Bhangi, Koli, Dhubla, Naikda and Macchi-Kharwa tribes all being represented.

Cuisine

Whilst Gujarat has a long coastline and an almost endless supply of fish and shellfish, strict Jainism in the past and orthodox Hinduism today have encouraged the widespread adoption of a vegetarian diet. Gujaratis base their diet on rice, wholemeal *chapati*, a wide variety of beans and pulses which are rich in protein, and coconut and pickles; a *thali* would include all these, the meal ending with sweetened yoghurt.

The dishes themselves are not heavily spiced, though somewhat sweeter than those of neighbouring states. Popular dishes include *kadhi*, a savoury yoghurt curry with chopped vegetables and variety of spices; *Undhyoo* a combination of potatoes, sweet potatoes, aubergines (egg plant) and beans cooked in an earthenware pot in the fire; Surat *Paunk* is made with tender kernels of millet, sugar balls, savoury twists and garlic chutney. Eating freshly prepared vegetable snacks from street vendors is popular. A large variety of *ganthia* or *farsan*: light savoury snacks prepared from chick-pea and wheat flour, is a speciality in the state. Desserts are very sweet. Surat specialises in *gharis* made with butter, dried fruits and thickened milk and rich *halwa*. *Srikhand* is saffron flavoured yoghurt with fruit and nuts.

Modern Gujarat

Government

Recent political history At Independence in 1947, Gujarat proper was incorporated into Bombay state. In 1956 Saurashtra and Kachchh were added. On 1 May 1960 Bombay state was split into present day Maharashtra and Gujarat states and in 1961 India forcibly annexed Daman and Diu. After Partition the possession of the Rann of Kachchh was disputed by India and Pakistan. In 1965 they fought over it, and following the ceasefire on 1 Jul, division of the area was referred to an international tribunal. In 1968 the tribunal recommended that 90% should remain with India and 10% pass to Pakistan.

Government With the sole exception of 1977 Gujarat remained one of the Congress Party's chief strongholds throughout the period after Independence until 1989. It produced a number of national leaders after Mahatma Gandhi, including the first Prime Minister of the Janata Govt in 1977, Morarji Desai. In Nov 1989 the Congress was reduced to holding 3 of the 26 Lok Sabha seats, the BJP taking 12 and the Janata Dal 11. The BJP fought the campaign on a strongly pro-Hindu line, gathering support from the campaign at Ayodhya to build a temple on Ram's supposed birthplace. In 1991 the Congress made up some of its lost ground, and today forms the State Government.

Economy

Agriculture Two-thirds of the working population are farmers and half the state is cultivated. The staples are wheat and *bajra* (millet), and rice in the wetter parts and where irrigation is feasible. Maize is also grown. Gujarat produces one third of India's cotton and one sixth of its tobacco. Gujarati businessmen first started investing in groundnut oil production 50 years ago. Today the districts of Rajkot, Jamnagar and Junagadh account for nearly one third of India's total production. Used for cooking and in the chemical industry, there are over 600 oil mills and solvent extraction plants in Saurashtra. Press reports suggest that the growth has been accompanied by a considerable amount of graft, as much as half the output being claimed to be sold tax free 'out of the back door'. Today the groundnut oil companies are diversifying into a wide range of other industrial goods. Other important cash crops are cumin, sugar-cane, mangoes and bananas. One of the major constraints on further increases in productivity is water. Even groundwater is in short supply. In the S of the state the water table is at a depth of about 30m, but in the N and in Kachchh it is as low as 350m, raising steeply the cost of pumping. In 1994 the state government's attempts to raise the price of electricity to farmers prompted widespread agitations for fear that water for irrigation would become prohibitively expensive.

Minerals The state is rich in limestone, manganese, gypsum, calcite, bauxite, lignite, quartz sand, agate and feldspar. Extensive exploration and production of oil and natural gas at Ankleshwar, Khambhat and Kalol has placed Gujarat at the forefront of the country's major petroleum producing states. Soda ash and salt production account for 90% and 66% respectively of national production. A thermal-power station using coal, natural gas and oil is located at Dhuvaran. Power from the Tarapur nuclear station in Maharashtra supplements the locally generated power.

Industry The most remarkable feature of Gujarat's recent industrial development has been the growth of the dairy industry, much of it conducted on a cooperative basis. There are now 15 milk processing plants with a production capacity of 3.2 million litres per day. Membership of dairying cooperatives exceeds 1 million. Of these the Kaira District Cooperative Milk Producers' Union ('Anand' products) is the best known. The state Govt plays a significant role in extending financial support and organisational expertise to the establishment of new cooperatives. To support milk production there are over 10 factories processing 1500-2000 tonnes of cattlefeed per day. There has been considerable assistance from the European Community's 'Operation Flood', using Europe's milk surpluses to guarantee adequate supply of milk while local supply was increased.

In the last 2 decades manufacturing has been energetically diversified away from its traditional base in textiles. The oil refinery at Kovali has created a rapidly expanding petrochemical industry. The pharmaceutical industry concentrated at Vadodara, Ahmadabad and Atul (Valsad) produces one-third of the country's pharmaceutical products. The cement, vegetable oil and industrial machinery and battery industries are all important, and an electronics estate has been set up at Gandhinagar to produce components for India's increasingly sophisticated consumer market. There has also been a steady growth in small scale industry with over 100,000 small scale industrial units. Handicrafts include embroidery, leather work, *bandhani* (tie-and-dye), hand-block printing. Surat's 'Tanchoi' and 'Gajee' silks and 'Kinkhab' gold brocades are famous and so is the wood inlay work. Ahmadabad produces fine jewellery and brass and copperware.

Communications

There is a good road network and Gujarat is also well connected by broad gauge railway. The main airport is Ahmadabad and is supported by a network of small regional airports. Kandla is the major international port and is supported by 39 intermediate and minor ports.

AHMADABAD

On the banks of the Sabarmati river, Ahmadabad, the former state capital (Gandhinagar is the new capital), is the largest city of Gujarat. At the end of the 16th century, 200 years after its foundation, some foreign travellers regarded it as equal to the finest European cities. The Mughal Emperor Jahangir was much less favourably impressed, calling it Gardabad – 'City of Dust'. It is now one of India's foremost industrial centres, the important trades being in cotton manufacture and commerce.

BASICS *Population*: 3.298mn; *Altitude*: 53m; *STD Code*: 0272.

The **old city** (on the left (E) bank) was founded in 1411 by Sultan Ahmad I, then King of Gujarat. He made Asaval, an old Hindu town in the S, his seat of power then expanded it to make his capital. Almost constantly at war with the neighbouring Rajputs, fortifications were essential.

The *Bhadra* towers and the square bastions of the royal citadel were among the first structures to be erected. The city walls contained 12 gates, 139 towers and nearly 6000 battlements. Although most have been demolished many monuments remain, some of them striking examples of Indian Islamic architecture. The provincial Gujarati style flourished from the mid-15th century, and in addition to the religious buildings many of the houses have façades beautifully decorated with wood carving. The *Swami Narayan Temple*, Kalipur, *Rajani Vaishnav Temple* and *Harkore Haveli*, nr Manek Chowk as well as havelis on Doshiwadani Pol illustrate traditional carving skills. Sadly, much of the old carving has been dismantled to be sold off to collectors.

The new city The newer part of the city lying on the W bank is the site of Mahatma Gandhi's famous *Sabarmati Ashram* from where he commenced his historic march in protest against the Salt Law in 1915. Modern Ahmadabad has its own share of showpieces designed by famous architects, among them Le Corbusier, Louis Kahn, Doshi and Correa. The *School of Architecture, the National Institute of Design* and the *Indian Institute of Management* (IIM) are national centres of learning.

Local crafts & industry Ahmadabad has a long tradition in craftsmanship. Under Gujarati Sultans and Mughal Viceroys it was one of the most brilliant Indian cities. Its jewellers and goldsmiths are renowned, copper and brassworkers produce very fine screens and *pandans* (betel boxes). The carpenter produce fine *shisham wood* articles. There are also skilled stonemasons, producers of lacquer boxes, ivory carvers and hand block printers using vegetable dyes and embroiderers producing exquisite pieces with beads and mirrors. These complement the modern industries such as pharmaceuticals and textiles. Large scale development of cotton mills began later than in Bombay and Ahmadabad had the benefit of Bombay's experience as well as its own natural advantages of cheap land and labour and raw material on the spot.

Places of interest

Gujarati provincial buildings

In the **Jami Masjid**, Ahmadabad contains one of the best examples of the second period of Gujarat's provincial

CLIMATE: AHMADABAD

	Jan	Feb	Mar	Apr	May	Jun	Jul	Aug	Sep	Oct	Nov	Dec	Av/Tot
Max (°C)	29	31	36	40	41	38	33	32	33	36	33	30	34
Min (°C)	12	15	19	23	26	27	26	25	24	21	16	13	21
Rain (mm)	4	0	1	2	5	100	316	213	163	13	5	1	823

Ahmadabad's 'Pols'

The old part of the city are divided into unique, self-contained *pols*, or quarters, fascinating to wander round. Huge wooden doors lead off from narrow lanes into a section of houses with decorative wooden screens and brackets where small communities of people practising a craft or skill lived. Merchants, weavers, woodworkers, printers and jewellers – each had their *pol*, their houses along winding alleys met in common courtyards and squares. Even the old city shows signs of recent rapid development, with tower blocks rising up from just inside the old city walls.

architectural development. Ahmad Shah I, the founder of a new dynasty, embarked on an extraordinary building programme. In 1411 he laid the foundations of Ahmadabad, which was to be his new capital. By 1423 the Jami Masjid, regarded by many as one of the finest mosques in India, was completed. He had taken great interest in the whole project himself, encouraging others to construct monumental buildings as well. As a result there are over 50 mosques and tombs dating from his period within the city. Mahmud I Begarha (r1459-1511) established the third phase of Gujarati provincial architecture, building some of India's most magnificent Islamic monuments.

The central city

The plan of the city The citadel of the planned city formed a rectangle facing the river. A broad street was designed to run from Ahmad Shah's fortified palace in the citadel to the centre of the city, lying due E.

The citadel The ancient citadel built by Ahmad Shah I in 1411, now known as the **Bhadra**, lies between the Nehru and Ellis bridges. It is named after an incarnation of the Hindu goddess Kali. In the E face is the **Palace**, now the Post Office, and other public buildings occupy the site, with the civil court to the S. **Sidi Sayyid's Mosque** (c1570) formed part of the wall on the NE corner but now stands isolated in a square. Ten windows of very fine stone tracery with patterns of branching tree are famous here. Note particularly those on the W wall. Women are prohibited from entering but may get a view from the gate.

In the SW corner of the Bhadra is **Ahmad Shah's Mosque** (1414), built as a private chapel and one of the oldest mosques in Ahmadabad. The façade is plain and the minarets unfinished. The internal pillars and the stone latticed ladies' gallery are thought to be part of a Hindu temple that stood here. By the entrance to the mosque is the **Ganj-i-Shahid**, the place where Muslims killed during the storming of the town, are buried.

Jami Masjid Ideally, Ahmad Shah would have wished the main entrance to the Jami Masjid to face the processional route from the citadel to the centre of the city. Such a plan was impossible because the essential orientation of the Qibla wall to Mecca meant that the main entrance to the mosque itself had to be in its E wall. Thus Ahmad Shah aligned the mosque so that the road (now the busy Mahatma Gandhi Rd) would pass its N entrance. This is still the point at which you enter, by a flight of steps which are not immediately visible until you are there. It is pleasantly quiet and peaceful inside.

The façade The beauty of the sanctuary is emphasised by the spacious courtyard paved in marble, 75m long by 65m wide with a tank in the middle. The façade has a screen of arches flanked by

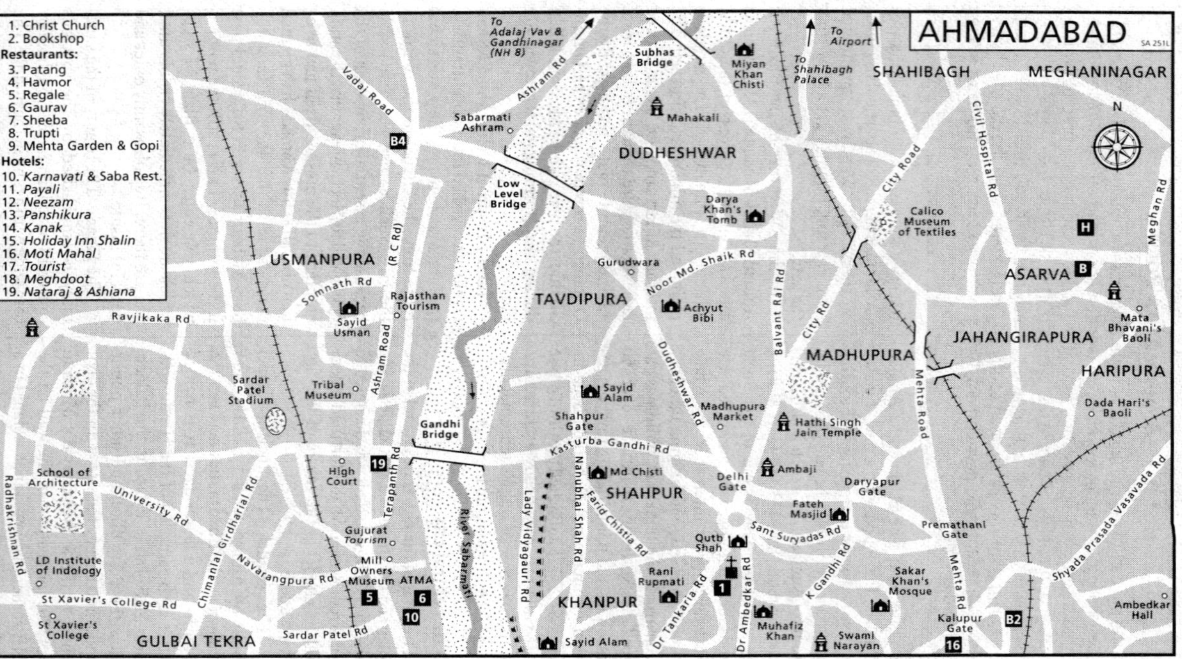
AHMADABAD
1. Christ Church
2. Bookshop
Restaurants:
3. Patang
4. Havmor
5. Regale
6. Gaurav
7. Sheeba
8. Trupti
9. Mehta Garden & Gopi
Hotels:
10. Karnavati & Saba Rest.
11. Payali
12. Neezam
13. Panshikura
14. Kanak
15. Holiday Inn Shalin
16. Moti Mahal
17. Tourist
18. Meghdoot
19. Nataraj & Ashiana
To Adalaj Vav & Gandhinagar (NH 8)
Subhas Bridge
Miyan Khan Chisti
To Shahibagh Palace
To Airport
SHAHIBAGH
MEGHANINAGAR
Vadaj Road
Ashram Rd
Sabarmati Ashram
Mahakali
DUDHESHWAR
Civil Hospital Rd
City Road
Meghan Rd
Low Level Bridge
Darya Khan's Tomb
Calico Museum of Textiles
USMANPURA
(R C Rd)
Gurudwara
Noor Md. Shaik Rd
Balvant Rai Rd
ASARVA
Somnath Rd
Rajasthan Tourism
TAVDIPURA
Achyut Bibi
City Rd
Mata Bhavani's Baoli
Ravjikaka Rd
Sayid Usman
Ashram Road
JAHANGIRAPURA
MADHUPURA
HARIPURA
Dudheshwar Rd
Sardar Patel Stadium
Tribal Museum
Sayid Alam
Madhupura Market
Hathi Singh Jain Temple
Mehta Road
Dada Hari's Baoli
Shahpur Gate
Gandhi Bridge
Kasturba Gandhi Rd
High Court
Terapanth Rd
Ambaji
School of Architecture
Md Chisti
Delhi Gate
Daryapur Gate
University Rd
Chimanlal Girdharlal Rd
SHAHPUR
Fateh Masjid
Lady Vidyagauri Rd
Nanubhai Shah Rd
Farid Chistia Rd
Premathani Gate
Gujarat Tourism
Qutb Shah
Sant Suryadas Rd
Shyada Prasada Vasavada Rd
LD Institute of Indology
Mill Owners Museum
ATMA
River Sabarmati
Radhakrishnan Rd
Navarangpura Rd
Rani Rupmati
K Gandhi Rd
Sakar Khan's Mosque
Mehta Rd
St Xavier's College Rd
KHANPUR
Dr Tankaria Rd
Dr Ambedkar Rd
Ambedkar Hall
Kalupur Gate
St Xavier's College
Muhafiz Khan
GULBAI TEKRA
Sardar Patel Rd
Sayid Alam
Swami Narayan

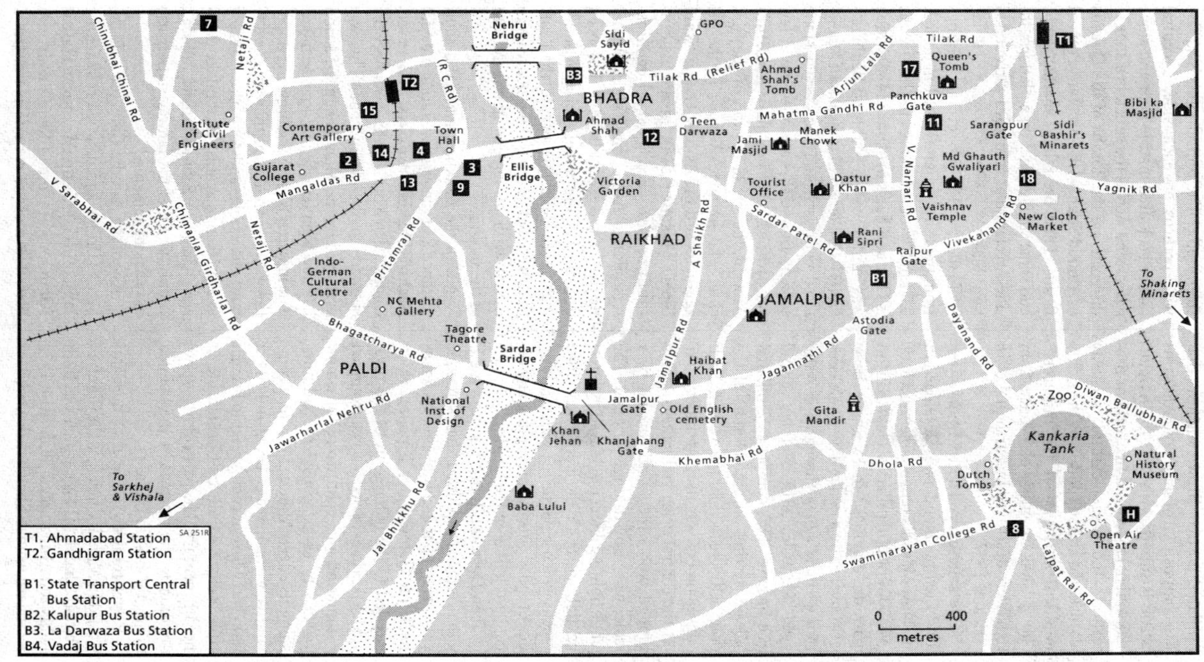
Chinubhai Chinai Rd
Netaji Rd
Nehru Bridge
Sidi Sayid
GPO
Tilak Rd
Tilak Rd (Relief Rd)
Ahmad Shah's Tomb
Arjun Lala Rd
Queen's Tomb
Panchkuva Gate
(R C Rd)
BHADRA
Institute of Civil Engineers
Contemporary Art Gallery
Town Hall
Ahmad Shah
Teen Darwaza
Mahatma Gandhi Rd
Jami Masjid
Manek Chowk
Sarangpur Gate
Sidi Bashir's Minarets
Bibi ka Masjid
Gujarat College
Mangaldas Rd
Ellis Bridge
Victoria Garden
Tourist Office
Dastur Khan
V. Narhari Rd
Md Ghauth Gwaliyari
Vaishnav Temple
Yagnik Rd
New Cloth Market
V Sarabhai Rd
Chimanlal Girdharlal Rd
Sardar Patel Rd
Rani Sipri
Raipur Gate
Vivekananda Rd
RAIKHAD
A Shaikh Rd
Pritamraj Rd
Indo-German Cultural Centre
NC Mehta Gallery
JAMALPUR
Astodia Gate
To Shaking Minarets
Bhagatcharya Rd
Tagore Theatre
Sardar Bridge
PALDI
Jamalpur Rd
Haibat Khan
Jagannathi Rd
Dayanand Rd
National Inst. of Design
Jamalpur Gate
Old English cemetery
Gita Mandir
Zoo
Diwan Ballubhai Rd
Jawarharlal Nehru Rd
Khan Jehan
Khanjahang Gate
Khemabhai Rd
Dhola Rd
Kankaria Tank
Natural History Museum
Dutch Tombs
To Sarkhej & Vishala
Baba Lului
Jai Bhikkhu Rd
Swaminarayan College Rd
Open Air Theatre
Lajpat Rai Rd
0 400 metres
T1
T2
B1
B3
2
3
4
7
8
9
11
12
13
14
15
17
18
SA 251R
T1. Ahmadabad Station
T2. Gandhigram Station
B1. State Transport Central Bus Station
B2. Kalupur Bus Station
B3. La Darwaza Bus Station
B4. Vadaj Bus Station

a pillared portico. Brown suggests that "as a composition of solids and voids this façade is superb with its 3 main openings well balanced and in excellent proportion, the large central archway accentuated and supported by the richly moulded buttresses of the minarets". The 2 'shaking minarets', once 26m high, were destroyed by earthquakes in 1819 and 1957.

The sanctuary The tradition of the Hindu temple mandapa is developed in the Jami Masjid's remarkable sanctuary. Over 300 graceful pillars, set less than 2m apart, are organised in 15 square bays, each covered by a dome. The whole rises from a single storey through the 2-storeyed side aisles to the 3-storey central aisle or nave. This comprises 2 pillared galleries resting on the columns of the lower hall, screened for the women. Such a development was itself an innovation, but the central octagonal lantern, rising through both storeys and covered by a dome, was also strikingly original. The gentle lighting effect is achieved by filtering light through the perforated stone screens which separate the galleries from the verandas outside, preventing any direct light falling in the building.

Teen Darwaza Immediately to the E of the entrance to Ahmad Shah's mosque is the triumphal archway also known as **the Triple Gateway** (or Tripolia), which once led to the outer court of the royal citadel. At a later period it was surrounded by tamarind and palm trees, but is now crowded by shops, considerably diminishing its effect. Although it is on a comparatively small scale, being only 12m high, Percy Brown compares it to Roman triple archways built by Constantine in the 4th century. He particularly draws attention to the fineness of the pointed arches, the best in India.

Royal tombs To the E of the Jami Masjid in Manek Chowk, is the **Tomb of Ahmad Shah I** (d1442), which was built by his son Muhammad Shah (d1451) in the square Ahmad Shah had designed for the purpose. The central tomb is square with porticos on each side, a central dome, a coloured marble floor and stone *jali* screens. Across the street, in a state of disrepair, are the **Tombs of the Queens of Ahmad Shah**, with a decorative carved façade. There are 8 large marble tombs and some smaller ones on a platform inside a rectangular courtyard surrounded by a cloister.

To the E and SE are several buildings from the third Gujarati Muslim period. 0.5 km SW of the Tombs of the Queens is **Dastur Khan's Mosque** (1486) which was built by one of Mahmud Beghara's Chief Ministers. This consists of a cloistered courtyard and the carved stone screens around this are very fine. A few steps to the E of the mosque is **Asa Bhil's Mound**, the site of the fort of the Bhil chief who founded Asaval. To the SE again, toward the Astodia Gate, is **Rani Sipri's Mosque** (1514). Small but beautifully proportioned, it has 2 15m minarets. Rani Asni, one of Mahmud Beghara's wives, built what has been described as "the first of a series of buildings more delicately ornate than any that preceded" (Hope). The square tomb (*rauza*) with *jali* screens stands in front of the mosque.

NE of the Astodia Gate and a short distance S of the railway station are **Sidi Bashir's Shaking Minarets**, 2 tall towers connected by a bridge which was once the entrance to the old mosque. This was destroyed by the Marathas in 1753, and has now been replaced by a modern one. The minarets 'shake' or vibrate in sympathy with one another as they are cleverly built on flexible sandstone base, possibly as a protection against earthquake damage (Rajpur **Bibi-ki-Masjid** (1454), Gomtipur, SE of the railway station also has shaking minarets).

SW of the Astodia Gate, towards the Sardar Bridge and just before reaching Jamalpur Gate, is the **Mosque of Haibat Khan**, one of Ahmad Shah's court nobles. The mosque is quite plain with a

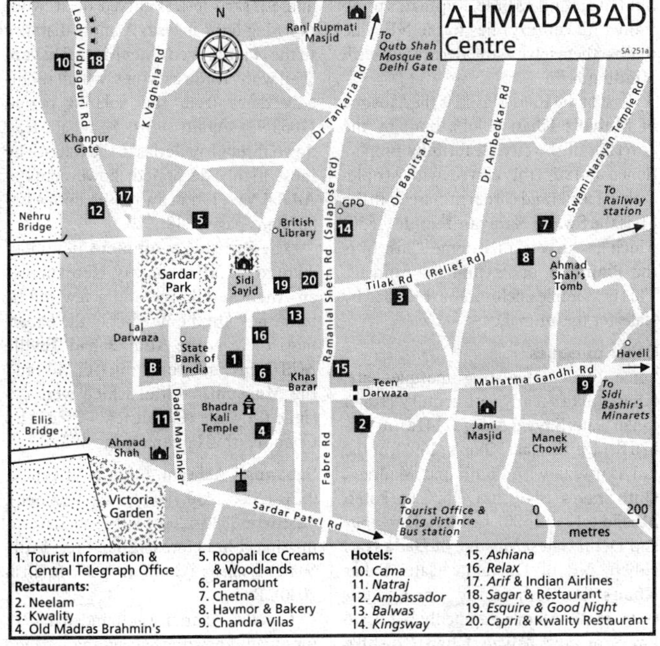

triple arched façade and small minarets. Much of the building material came from Hindu temples as the decoration of the central dome indicates. The old **English Cemetery** is close to Jamalpur Gate.

The north

Sayyid Usman's mausoleum Immediately across the Gandhi bridge, immediately W of Ashram Rd, is the *rauza* (tomb complex) of Sayyid Usman, one of the first examples of the Begarha style. Built about 1460, its pillared sanctuary is the first to have had minarets at each end. The pillars are beautifully made, though Percy Brown suggests that the building lacks a powerful central feature to give it overall unity. Notice also the shrines that are still foci of pilgrimage. Back on the E side of the Sabarmati River in the NW of the city near Shahpur Gate is the **Mosque of Shaikh Hasan Muhammad Chishti**, built in 1565. This has some of the finest tracery work in Ahmadabad.

There are several **Jain temples** in the city, the highly decorated, white marble **Hathi Singh Temple** (1848) just N of the Delhi Gate, dedicated to Dharamanath, the 5th Jain Tirthankar, is perhaps the most visited. Along the streets of Ahmadabad, it is quite common to see Jain *parabdis*.

The **Rani Rupmati Masjid** (early 16th century), in Mirzapur district, SW of Delhi Gate and just S of the *Grand Hotel*, incorporates Hindu and Islamic design. Rupmati was Princess of Dhar (MP) and the Sultan's Hindu wife. It has a high central arch and 2 minarets which were damaged in the 1819 earthquake. The roof carries 3 domes, each above an entrance. The carvings in the gallery and the *mihrabs* are particularly attractive. Note how the dome is raised to allow light in around its base. Rupmati's tomb (mid 15th century) lies to the NE. The tombs themselves are decorated with Hindu motifs.

East of the Rani Masjid is the **Mosque of Muhafiz Khan** (1465), built by the governor of the city. Beautifully proportioned and superbly carved, with a triple-arched façade and corner minarets. To the SE is the **Swami Narayan Temple** (1850) which has an octagonal dome. Close by is the **Pinjrapol**, or Asylum for Animals. This is a simple enclosure surrounded by stalls for the animals.

Other mosques

Some other interesting mosques are: **Khan Jahan's** (early 16th century), Khan Jahan Gate; **Sayyid Alam's** (1412), nr Nehru Bridge; **Shujaat Khan's** (1695), nr the Lal Darwaza with Tomb and Madrasa; **Qutb Shah's** (1449), nr Delhi Gate; **Fateh Masjid** (c1450-1500), between Daryapur and Delhi Gates; **Mosque of Dada Hari** (1499), NE of Daryapur Gate; **Sakar Khan's** (late 15th century), nr Kalupur Gate; **Malik Alam's** (reputedly 1422), 1.6 km S of city; **Miyan Khan Chishti's** (1465) nr Subhas Bridge; **Achyut Bibi's** (1469), Tavdipura; **Queen's Mosque and Tomb** (early 16th century) and **Muhammad Ghauth Gwaliyari's** (c1565) are nr Sarangpur Gate; **Rani's Masjid** (c1500-15), nr village of Kochrab; **Blessed on All Sides Mosque** (early 16th century), Isanpur, between Vatva and Rasulabad; **Baba Lului's** (1560), 2 km SW on banks of Sabarmati. There are also many other tombs.

Baolis At **Asarva**, about 1 km NE of Daryapur Gate are the Dada Hari (1499) and Mata Bhavani (c1080) baolis. The *baolis* (step wells) in Gujarat are highly distinctive and often serve a dual purpose of being a cool, secluded source of water during the summer and a place of religious sanctity. At **Dada Hari** (1499) there is a spiral staircase leading down to 3 lower platforms and a small octagonal well at the bottom, which has Arabic and Sanskrit letters carved on it. Mid-morning light is best. A short distance to the N is the even older **Mata Bhavani** Well with Hindu carvings, which reputedly dates from the Solanki period (1063-93). Again steps, 52 in all, lead down through galleries to the water. The most highly decorated, however, is at **Adalaj Vav**, 19 km away (see under Excursions page 1248).

The British **Cantonment** lies about 4 km to the NE of the city. Here there is an Anglican Church and a few public buildings. On the W bank of the Sabarmati there is the **Ahmadabad Textile Mill Owner's Association** (ATMA) and the **Museum**, both of which were designed by Le Corbusier – see also Chandigarh, Haryana (page 492).

Sabarmati Ashram, 6 km N of centre. 0830-1200, 1430-1900 (1 Apr-30 Sep), otherwise 0830-1200, 1430-1830. Last admission, 1 hr before closing. Free. Daily *Son et Lumière* (Gujarati 1930, English 2030). Rs 5.

Gandhi's Ashram was founded in 1917 (originally known an Satyagraha and then Harijan Ashram) and was the starting point for Gandhi's celebrated 24 day, 385 km march to Dandi in March 1930. He vowed not to return till India gained independence. Gandhi and 81 colleagues, followers and supporters in the Independence Movement began the march, but by the end there were 90,000 protesting against the unpopular British Salt Tax Laws (the manufacture of salt was a Govt monopoly). Salt was chosen for the protest as it was a commodity every peasant used and could understand. At Dandi beach on 6 Apr Gandhi went down to the sea and made a small amount of salt, for which he was promptly arrested. In the following months, thousands of Indians followed his example and were arrested by the British.

The **Sangrahalaya** includes a library, archives and a picture gallery depicting Gandhi's life in photographs and paintings. A 5 min film on his life is shown several times daily. The peace, quiet and simple style of the Ashram is impressively maintained. Some of the original ashram's work, such as a school for Harijan girls, continues. **Hridaya Kunj**, Gandhi's home for 15 years containing simple mats, desk, spinning wheel and some personal belongings overlooks the central prayer corner and the river, and is undisturbed, as is the unfurnished room of his wife Kasturba. **Accommodation D** Gujarat Tourism *Toran Guest House*, is across the road, opp the Ashram (see **Accommodation**).

Kankaria Lake SE of the city this remarkable artificial lake was constructed in 1451 and has 34 sides each 60m long. It is now a popular local picnic spot. There is a large zoo and children's park – see below.

Museums

Calico Museum is in an attractive old *haveli* in Shahi Bagh gardens which is of interest botanically; part of the Sarabhai Foundation. Some exhibits date from the 17th century and include rich displays of heavy brocades, fine embroideries, saris, carpets, turbans, Maharajahs' costumes and royal Mughal tents. Also weaving techniques but no weaving equipment. Regarded as one of the finest museums of its kind in the world. Part displayed in religious atmosphere; the Jain Gallery has an outstanding collection of Jain manuscripts. Secular pieces in traditional buildings around the chowk. 1015-1230, 1430-1700. Tours (incl 15th century Jain temple) 1015-1115, 1430-1530. Closed Wed. Free. Excellent library of textiles. Museum shop sells cards, reproductions and books.

Shreyas Folk Museum Comprehensive collection of folk arts, crafts and costumes from Saurashtra and Kachchh. Exhibits include embroideries, utensils, handicrafts, weapons and carts. Also children's section with costumes, puppets, folk art. 0900-1100, 1600-1900, closed Wed.

Tribal Research and Training Institute Museum Gujarat Vidyapith, Ashram Rd, T 79741. 1130-1930, closed Sun, Sat 1130-1430.

NC Mehta Gallery, S of Ellis Bridge. Rare Gujarati and Rajasthani miniature paintings. 0900-1100, 1600-1900, closed Mon.

Contemporary Art Gallery, nr Orient club, Ellis Bridge. Gujarat Kala Mandir Art Gallery nr Law College Bus Stand, Ellis Bridge. Jyoti Art Gallery, 587 Tilak Rd, T 336996. Hutheesing Visual Art, opp Gujarat University, Navrangpura. Lalit Kala Akademi, nr Ellis Bridge Gymkhana.

Sardar Valabhai Patel National Memorial, Shahibaug. 0930-1730, except Wed.

Parks & zoos

Large Deer Park next to Sarita Udyan in Indrada Village. Sundervan Snake Garden, off M Dayanand Rd with its collection of snakes. Snake handling shows daily.

Excursions

Vishala, Sarkhej Rd, Vasana, 5 km, is a purpose-built collection of traditional Gujarati village huts. It began as an excellent vegetarian restaurant in 1978 and grew to include a museum. Evening meal at 2100, accompanied by music. Traditional dancing after the meal, light is provided entirely by lanterns. You sit cross-legged at low tables, eat off green leaves and drink from clay tumblers. Fixed menu, with full dinner under Rs 120 and lunch Rs 80. Some vistors have found it slightly neglected and disappointing, but it is still popular with business people and families from Ahmadabad. The **Utensils Museum** dedicated to domestic implements has a collection of brass and copper utensils, water pots, old betel nut boxes and containers used for temple rituals. 1700-2300 weekdays, 1000-1300, 1700-2200 Sun.

Sarkhej (8 km SW of the city), once a country retreat of the Muslim rulers, is noted for its *Rauza* (1445-51), the fine architectural complex of mosque, palace, pavilions and tombs, all grouped around a stepped tank. The style shows distinct Hindu influence. The Dutch established an indigo factory nearby.

Adalaj, 17 km N of Ahmadabad on Ajmer Rd (nr Gandhinagar crossroad). The **Vav** (*baoli*) in a garden setting in the hamlet of Adalaj (1502) is one of the finest in India showing a combination of Hindu, Muslim and Buddhist styles. A long flight of steps descends over 30m, to the water. It has 4 floors, each cooler than the 1 above. Ornately carved pillars, niches and cross beams create large octagonal landings (now inaccessible) which served as resting places. Remains of the bullock ramp are still visible. Queen Rupabai is believed to have had it built to provide the traveller with a cool and pleasant refuge from the summer heat (some believe she drowned herself, rather than be forced to marry a 2nd time). Seven km E of Adalaj is the State capital of Gandhinagar.

Gandhinagar

(*Population*: 123,400; *STD Code*: 02712; 23 km N of Ahmadabad). When Bombay state was divided along linguistic lines into Maharashtra and Gujarat in 1960, a new capital city was planned for Gujarat named after Mahatma Gandhi. As with Chandigarh, Le Corbusier was instrumental in the design. The 30 residential sectors around the central government complex are similarly impersonal. Construction began in 1965 and the Secretariat was completed in 1970. In 1994 the new capital was still far from complete but was an established town with over ¼ of a million people. **Akshardham** in Sector 20, a Hindu temple cum cultural complex/ entertainment park run by volunteers. The monument is open daily 0900-1900 (Nov-Feb) and 1000-2000 (Mar-Oct). Entry (referred to as "generous support") Rs 15. It is floodlit immediately after dusk. Built in pink sandstone, the main building houses a 2m gold leaf idol of Sri Swaminarayan and associated relics. The 3 halls feature a variety of sound and light presentations relating to Sri Swaminarayan, the Vedas and the Hindu epics. Outside is a garden for meditation, the Sahajanabd Vun, where there is also a restaurant

• **Accommodation** **C** *Haveli*, Sector 11, opp Sachivalaya, T 23905, F 24057, 84 rm, restaurants (Good South indian dining hall), exchange, car-hire, free airport transfer, day rates available, smart entrance but rm and toilets below standard. The **F** *Youth Hostel* in Sector 16 is very good. **F** *Panthik Ashram*, Sector 11, is a Govt Rest House. Other *Guest Houses* around Pethapur and Sachivalaya.

• **Transport Train** Gandhinagar is linked by metre gauge railway to Ahmadabad. **Road Bus**: regular buses from Ahmadabad. ST Bus Station, Sector 11, T 22842.

Tours

Tourist Office, Ahmadabad Municipal Corp arranges city sightseeing. Enquiries and Reservations: T 353927. *Morning Tour*: 0950-1330. Sidi Sayyid, Hutheesing Jain Temple, Sardar Patel Museum, Calico Museum, Dadahari Step Well, Lake Kankaria, Geeta Mandir, Shah Alam Mosque. Rs 25. *Afternoon Tour*: 1400-1800. Gandhi Ashram, Vechaar Utensils Museum, Snake Farm and Municipal Museum. Rs 25.

Gujarat Tourism Tours by a/c coach, usually 0800-1430, about Rs 35; Full day Rs 55. *Tour 1*: Adalaj Step Well, Gandhi Ashram, Hutheesing Temple – Lunch – Badshah no Hajiro, Jama Masjid, Teen Darwaza, Calico Museum, Sarkhej, Vishala. *Tour 2*: Adalaj, Mohera – Lunch – Sharyas, Sarkhej, Vishala, Vechaar Museum. *Tour 3*: Hutheesing, Swaminarayan Temple, Ratan Pol, Manek Chowk, Rani no Hajira, Jama Masjid, Badshah No Hajira, Teen Darwaza, Shopping on Ashram Rd – Lunch – NC Mehta Collection, Airport. *Children's Special Tour*: (*Bal Yatra*) on Sun 0800 for Rs 15.

Longer tours: Gujarat Tourism also runs 2 5-day package tours: Saurashtra Darshan, every Fri, about Rs 550; North Gujarat-Rajasthan Tour, 1st and 3rd Sat in month, Rs 700.

Local festivals

Mid-Jan *Makar Sankranti* marks the end of winter. It is celebrated with kite fighting by people of all ages, accompanied by colourful street markets and festivities. The kite strings are prepared with a paste of rice flour and powdered glass and kites come in all colours, shapes and sizes, the best varieties reputedly being available in Manek Chowk and Tankshala Kalupur. The flying continues after sunset, as the kites are lit with candles. The Govt of India sponsors an international kite flying competition, setting up a special kite town 'Patand Nagar' to accommodate it. **Sep/Oct**: *Navaratri* honouring Goddess Amba (*Shakti*), has special significance in the city which prepares for it for weeks and celebrates it for 9 days with music and dancing, traditionally '*Garba Ras*' (sadly often to Westernised disco rhythm in some parts of the city). The custom of women balancing clay pots while they dance is still practised.

Local information

● Accommodation

Price guide
AL Rs 3,000+ **A** Rs 2,000-3,000
B Rs 1,200-2,000 **C** Rs 600-1,200
D Rs 250-600 **E** Rs 100-250 **F** Up to Rsl100

Airport 10 km, most nr centre, about 3 km from rly. City's new **B** ***Quality Inn Shalin***, Gujarat College Cross Rd, Ellis Bridge, T 446767, F 460022, 72 rm, restaurant, permit shop, exchange, pool, excellent food and service, rec.

C ***Rivera***, Khanpur Rd, T 24201, 69 clean, comfortable rm (some overlook river), restaurant, bar, coffee shop, exchange, free airport transfer, lawn, quiet, good value, rec; **C** ***Cama***, Khanpur Rd, T 25281, F 25285, 55 comfortable a/c rm some with river-view, good restaurant, bar, exchange, pool, lawn, modern, airport transfer, Rs 200, check-out 0900, highly rec but a little expensive; **C** ***Capri***, Tilak Rd, T 354643, some a/c rm with bath; **C** ***Natraj***, nr Ahmad Shah Mosque, Ashram Rd, T 448747, 25 rm, restaurant, comfortable; **C** ***Karnavati***, Shri Cinema Bldg, Ashram Rd, T 402161, 48 rm, restaurant, bar, coffee shop, exchange.

Several new clean very good value, cheaper **D** grade hotels have rm (some a/c) with shower and TV, in Khanpur. Those without restaurants provide good room service. **D** ***City Plaza***, Maniar House, Kadiakui, Relief Rd, T 384900, some a/c rm, restaurant, travel, noisy, not good value; **D** ***Poonam Palace***, off Ashram Rd, nr Dipali Cinema, rec; **D** ***Panshikura***, nr Town Hall, Underbridge, Ellis Bridge, T 402960, 24 a/c rm, quieter at rear, restaurant; **D** ***Ambassador***, Khanpur, T 353244, 31 rm with bath, some a/c, restaurant, check-out 24-hr, basic but clean and recently renovated; **D** ***City Palace***, opp Calico Dome, Relief Rd, T 386574, 18 rm, some a/c; **D** ***Kingsway,***, Ramanlal Sheth Rd (nr Relief Cinema), T 26221, 34 rm with bath, some a/c, restaurant; **D** ***Meghdoot***, Gupta Chambers, nr New Cloth Market, T 464324, 27 rm, some a/c, rm service; **D** ***Stay-Inn***, nr Khanpur Gate, T 354127, F 469101, 14 colourful rm (some a/c), ½ a/c, eager-to-please, 24-hr check-out and good rm service, spotless and good value; **D** ***Alif***, nr Lal Darwaza, opp BMC Bank, Khanpur, T 359440, 40 rm, 7 a/c, rm service, new, clean; **D** ***Balwas***, 6751 Relief Rd, nr Electric House, T 351135, 21 rm, ½ a/c, better at rear, good restaurant, 24-hr check-out, spotless and good value though in crowded noisy area; **D** Gujarat Tourism ***Toran Guest House***, T 483742, opp Ashram, Sabarmati, 10 rm, few a/c, 7 km, simple, rather gloomy, dining hall, out-of-town though convenient for Ashram, overpriced.

● Budget hotels

E ***Tourist***, nr Panchkuva Darwaza, T 383255, rm with bath; **E** ***Ashiana***, Murtuza Manzil, opp Soneri Masjid, Salapose Rd, T 351114, 13 rm, rm service; **E** ***Esquire***, opp Sidi Saiyid Mosque, nr the British Lib, is clean and popular; nearby **E** ***Goodnight***, T 351997, clean rm, ***Food Inn*** downstairs, excellent restaurant, very good value, rec; **E** ***Relax***, opp Central Telegraph Office, is fairly modern, rm with bath; **E** ***Railway Retiring Rooms***, Ahmadabad Junc station and the **E** ***Alankar***, opp Kalupuir Rly Station has 26 rm.

● Places to eat

Indian: dimly-lit ***Balwas*** does good Indian food. Opp Karnavati's ***Saba*** does good *thali* meals; ***Sheeba***, opp Telephone Exch, Navrangpura; ***Angithi***, Trade Centre, opp Sardar Patel Stadium; ***Side Walk***, Ship Bldg, Navrangpura; ***Regale***, National Bldg, Ashram Rd; ***Volga***, nr Dipali Cinema, Ashram Rd; ***Neelam***, Teen Darwaza; ***Paramount***, Khas Bazar; ***Old Madras Brahmin's***, opp Civil Court, South Indian; ***Chetna*** next to Krishna Cinema, Relief Rd; ***Woodlands***, CG Rd; ***Kalpi***, Advance Cinema Rd, rec. **On Ashram Rd**: ***Gaurav Dining Hall,*** Shiv Cinema and ***Mehta Garden***, for excellent *thalis*. ***Gopi***, nr VS Hospital, Ellis Bridge and ***Saurashtra Dining Hall***, opp Town Hall.

Gujarati: *Vishala Village*, Sarkhej, a re-creation of a traditional village, folk dancers, negotiate a return price with autorickshaw. See under excursions. Some recent visitors disappointed.

Ice creams: *Havmor*, with bakery upstairs on Salapose Rd, opp Krishna Cinema (and another nr Ellis Bridge) and ***Roopali*** nr Sardar Bagh are rec. ***Gandhi*** kiosk, 100m from Teen Darwaza does *lassis* and ice creams.

Multi-cuisine: Hotels *Shalin*, *Cama*, *Karnavati*, *Rivera*, *City Plaza* and are rec. ***Patang***, Chinubhai Centre, Ashram Rd, revolving restaurant with buffet or à la carte, attractive decor, live classical music at night, evening reservations essential.

Sweets: *Azad Halwai*, sells good sweets.

● Bars

Prohibition is in force. Liquor permits may be obtained by foreign nationals and for medical reasons. Some larger hotels have liquor stores which issue temporary permits.

● Airline offices

Air India, Premchand House, nr High Court, T 425644; **Air France**, T 442391; **British Airways**, T 465621; ***Delta***, T 448143; **Ethiopian Airlines**, T 406077; **Gulf Air**, T 463812; **KLM**, T 77875; **Kuwait Airways**, T 465848; **Kenya Airways**, T 406027; **Lufthansa**, T 464122; **Malaysian**, T 425840; **Singapore Airlines**, T 461335; **Swissair**, T 449149; **United**, T 401909.

● Banks & money changers

The **State Bank of India**, Tilak Rd.

● Clubs

Dariapur Gymkhana, Dariapur Dabgharwad. **Gymkhana**, opp Nursery, Netaji Rd.

● Cultural centres

The **British Library** is opp the Sidi Saiyid Mosque and is a/c with toilets, T 460693. **Alliance Francaise**, T 441551. **Indo-German Centre**, T 77429.

● Hospitals & medical services

Nagri Eye Hospital, Ellis Bridge, T 444724. *Civil Hospital*, Asarwa, T 376351. *ESIC General Hospital*, Bapunagar, T 363734. *Sardar Patel Hospital*, Maninagar, T 50573. *Sarbhai General Hospital*, Ellis Bridge, T 78123. *Victoria Jubilee Hospital*, Panchkuwa Darwaza, T 361080.

● Post & telecommunications

Central Post Office: Salapose Road, Mirzapur.

● Shopping

Books: *Kitab Kendra*, Sahitya Seva Sadan, nr Gujarat College Cross Rd.

Photography: *Ahmadabad Photo Depot*, nr Model Cinema. ***New Navrang Studio***, opp Jama Masjid, on Gandhi Rd. ***Patel Photo Studio***, Ellis Bridge.***Ahmadabad Photo Depot***, nr Model Cinema. ***New Navrang Studio***, opp Jama Masjid, on Gandhi Rd. ***Patel Photo Studio***, Ellis Bridge.

Textiles: the state produces excellent textiles, plus embroidery (bead and mirror work), tie-and-dye, zari on cloth and *Patola* silks. Also lacquered furniture and wood carvings, jewellery and pottery. Shops usually open from 0900-1900, most close on Sun. Manek Chowk is the main bazar. Other centres are Relief Rd, Ashram Rd, Lal Darwaza and Kapasia Bazar. ***Garvi*** and ***Gujari***, on Ashram Rd, nr Times of India Office, Ashram (a State Govt Undertaking). Three floors of well displayed and carefully selected handicrafts from all over the state. Textiles, rugs, lacquered and inlaid furniture, rosewood beads, wool shawls. Open 1030-1400, 1500-1900, closed Wed. Try ***Ratanpul Rd Market*** for saris and dress material. ***Sewa*** is a Muslim women's cooperative producing very fine shadow embroidery.

● Sports

Outdoor Sports at the Sardar Patel Stadium.

● Tour companies & travel agents

Travel Corp of India (TCI), nr Natraj Theatre, behind Handloom House, Ashram Rd, T 407061; ***Sita World Travels***, Suflam Buildings, Mithakhali Underbridge, Ashram Rd.

● **Tourist offices**

Gujarat (TCGL), HK House, Ashram Rd, nr *Hotel Natraj*, T 449172. Director of Tourism, Sachivalaya, Gandhinagar, T 20601. Tourist Office, Ahmadabad Municipal Corp, nr Khamasa Gate, T 365610. 1100-1800. Also at airport, T 67568. 0600-2200, and Railway station, T 347745. 0600-2200. **Rajasthan**, Karnavati Society, Usmanpura, T 490127. **MP**, T 449172. **UP**, Smrutikunj Society, opp Asia Engineering School. **Jammu** and **Kashmir**, Indian Airlines Bldg, Lal Darawaza, T 391043.

● **Useful Addresses**

Ambulance: T 102. **Fire**: T 101. **Foreigners Regional Registration Office**: Police Commissioner's Office, Shahibaug, T 333999. **Police**: T 100. **Visa extension**: Gandhinagar, T 92 20388.

● **Transport**

Bombay 492 km, **Vadodara** 113 km, **Surat** 120 km, **Udaipur** 287 km, **Rajkot** 216 km, **Porbandar** 394 km, **Palitana** 217 km and **Sasan Gir** 217 km.

Local Yellow top taxis: fares negotiable. **City Bus service**: available from main bus station, Lal Darwaza, railway station and all major points in the city. AMTS, T 352911. **Auto rickshaws**: min Rs 3.50 (ask to see rate card). Night charges are quite high. **Tourist taxis**: for hire from various agencies.

Air Airport 10 km from the city centre. **Transport to town**: Regular bus leaves from Lal Darwaza to meet flights. Approx Rs 15. **Indian Airlines**, City Office, Lal Darwaza, nr Roopalee Cinema, T 353333. 1000-1315, 1415-1715. **Delhi**: 0835, 2025 daily (1¼ hr); **Bombay**: 0735, 1950 (1 hr) direct and an additional Delhi – Jaipur – Jodhpur – Ahmadabad – Bombay flight. **Madras**: via Bangalore, W,F,Su, 1745. **East-West Airlines**, T 423311. Airport: Domestic T 869234, International T 867237.

Train Ahmadabad is on a broad gauge line from Bombay (Platforms 1-4) and a metre gauge line from Delhi (Platforms 7-12). Platforms 5 and 6 serve both according to demand and has 3 rails! The main entrance is by Platforms 1-4. **Ahmadabad Junc (Kalupur) Railway Station**, enquiries T 131. Computerised Reservations at Junc and Gandhigram stations: 1st Class 0730-1530, 2nd Class 0700-1430, 1500-2000, T 135. The following dep from Junc station: **Old Delhi**: *Aravalli Exp* 9932, daily, 0545, 23¾ hr; *Delhi Mail* 9902, daily, 0825, 23 hr; *Delhi Exp* 9904, daily, 1800, 25 hr; *Ashram Exp* 2906, daily, 1700, 17 hr. **Bombay Central**: *Bombay Gandhidham Kachchh Exp* 9032, daily, 0500, 8½ hr; *Gujarat Exp* 9012, daily, 0715, 9 hr; *Gujarat Mail* 9002, daily, 2200, 8¾ hr. **Udaipur City**: *Ahmadabad-Udaipur Exp* 9644, daily, 2315, 9 hr. **Bhopal**: *Rajkot-Bhopal Exp* 1269, daily, 1910, 13½ hr. **Jaipur**: *Delhi Mail* 9902, daily, 0825, 15½ hr; *Delhi Exp* 9904, daily, 1800, 16¼ hr; *Ashram Exp* 2906, daily, 1750, 16¼ hr. **Ajmer**: *Aravalli Exp* 9932, daily, 0545, 12¾ hr; *Delhi Mail* 9902, daily, 0825, 12 hr; *Delhi Exp* 9904, daily, 1800, 12½ hr; *Ashram Exp* 2906, daily, 1700, 8½ hr. **Ujjain**: *Rajkot-Bhopal Exp* 1269, daily, 1910, 9¼ hr; *Sabarmati Exp* 9165, daily, 2030, 9¼ hr. **Mt. Abu**: *Aravalli Exp* 9932, daily, 0545, 5 hr; *Delhi Mail* 9902, daily, 0825, 4½ hr; *Ashram Exp* 2906, daily, 1700, 3¼ hr; *Delhi Exp* 9904, daily, 1800, 4½ hr; *Surya Nagri Exp* 2908, daily, 2115, 3¼ hr. **Bhavnagar**: *Ahmadabad Bhavnagar Exp* 9810, daily, 1630, 6 hr; *Girnar Exp* 9846, daily, 2045, 8¼ hr. **Junagadh**: *Girnar Exp* 9846, daily, 2045, 10¾ hr; *Somnath Mail* 9824, daily, 2155, 12½ hr. **Veraval**: *Girnar Exp* 9846, daily, 2045, 13 hr; *Somnath Mail* 9824, daily, 2155, 15 hr. **Jamnagar**: *Saurashtra Exp* 9215, daily, 2100, 7 hr; *Saurashtra Mail* 9005, daily, 0555, 7 hr.

Road Ahmadabad is well connected with other cities and towns in Gujarat and with neighbouring states. Central Bus Station, Geeta Mandir, T 344764. Reservations 0700-1900. Advance booking for night services 1500-2300, luxury coach services 1030-1800. The State Transport Corp of Gujarat, Rajasthan, MP and Maharashtra provide services with Bombay (11 hr), Mt Abu (7 hr), Indore, Ujjain, Bhopal, Pune, Udaipur, Jaipur and Jodhpur as well as to towns within the state. **Private bus companies** also operate services, often at night. ***Punjab Travels***, Delhi Darwaza, T 449777. ***Sena Travel Agency***, outside Astodia Gate, Bhutni Ambli. **JK Travels**, Ashram Rd, Dinesh Hall. ***Pawan Travels***, Pritannagar first Dhal, Ellis Bridge.

AHMADABAD TO INDORE

The route crosses the flat plain where dozens of tiny states and principalities formed, broke up and re-formed over the centuries before the British arrived. The smallest of the states was 2 sq km and had a population of 96. Much of this area will be irrigated from the proposed Narmada High level canal if it is ever completed. The road then runs E through Dohad, climbing onto the plateau and crossing the Gujarat-MP border at an altitude of about 550m.

ROUTES The NH8 goes SE to **Chandula Lake** (5 km) and Kaira (32 km).

Kheda (Kaira)

(*Population*: 21,800; *STD Code*: 02694) An ancient settlement, Kheda possibly dates from as early as 1400 BC. The first firm evidence of its existence from Chalukya inscriptions can be dated to the 5th century AD. It was captured in 1736 by the Marathas. In 1803 the British took it and developed a military garrison.

An important trading centre on the route from Khambhat into North India, it has a **Jain temple** with superb carving and the **Church** consecrated by Bishop Heber in 1822 and an early 19th century **Town Hall**. Today **Kaira** is one of the major centres of India's dairy industry. In 1892 the British administrator Alexander Roper whote that the Kaira region that there is no richer country in the Bombay Presidency or probably in all of Hindustan.

Nadiad & surroundings

(*Population*: 170,200; *STD Code*: 0268) The largest town in Kheda District. 42 km to its N is the small walled town of **Kapadvanj**, famous for making glass and leather containers for ghee and soap. Half way between Nadiad and Kapadvanj is the small town of **Lasundra**, noted for its hot (46°C), slightly sulphurous springs.

Nearby, **Nalsarovar** lake is noted for its water-birds. Some indigenous species come here after breeding but it is the migratory ducks, flamingoes and geese that are the main attraction. Season: Nov-Feb. Dec and Jan best. Govt *Holiday Home* near the lake can be booked through the Tourist Office, Ahmadabad.

Dakor (34 km from Nadiad; *Population*: 20,400), has a large lake and a temple that is the centre of pilgrimage in Oct/Nov. The road runs right alongside the single track broad gauge spur railway line from Ghodra to Khambhat. It crosses the River Mahi by a 500m long bridge to Godhra, then climbing steadily onto the plateau to **Dohad** (48 km; *Population*: 96,800) and the great expanse of Deccan lava country to Indore.

AHMADABAD TO BOMBAY

The route from Ahmadabad crosses the fertile alluvial plains of the Sabarmati and Mahi Rivers before entering the Konkan region. The alluvial plains gradually give way S to broken hills. Inland parallel ridges reach between 500-600m. Rice dominates agriculture further S, but ragi (finger millet) and pulses are also common. The N plains are the centre of a rapidly industrialising region.

ROUTES It takes no more than 2½ hrs to reach Vadodara by bus. The **NH8** is dual carriageway for long stretches between Ahmadabad and Ankleshwar, but is very slow further S because of the heavy lorry traffic. There are clean and modern, if basic, restaurants at frequent intervals. **Kaira**, centre of a major co-operative dairying industry, is 32 km. In Kaira keep on the **NH8** for Vadodara.

Diversion to Khambhat

In Kaira, a road on the right goes to Khamhat (61 km).

Khambhat (Cambay)

(*Population*: 89,800; *STD Code*: 02698) Situated at the mouth of the Mahi river, this was Ahmadabad's seaport. Well known to Arab traders. Ala-ud-din Khalji sacked it in 1304, and until 1400 it was governed by the Kings of Anhil-

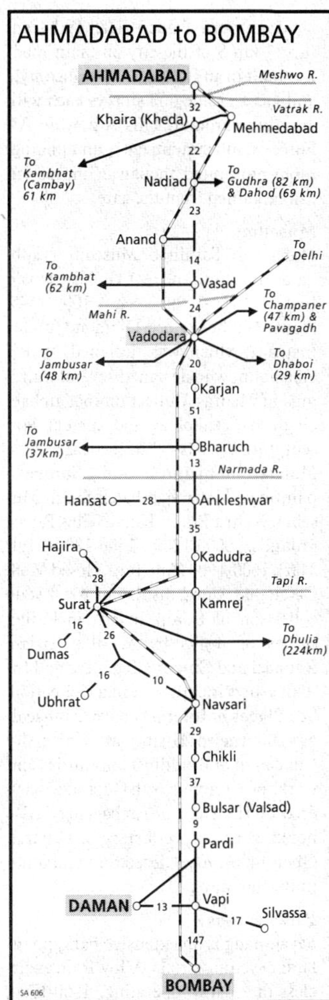

wara (Patan). Queen Elizabeth I's ambassadors to the Mughal court bore letters for Akbar that were addressed to the King of Cambay. An English factory was established in the **Nawab's Kothi** in 1600 in the wake of Dutch and Portuguese ones. Surat later developed at Cambay's expense and the port declined further when silting presented problems for shipping.

The **Jama Masjid** (1325) is built from materials taken from desecrated Hindu and Jain temples. The enclosed façade to the sanctuary is similar to that of the Quwwat-ul-Islam mosque at Delhi – see page 177). The design heavily influenced the Gujarati architectural style.

Vadodara (Baroda)

Population: 1.115mn; *Altitude*: 35m; *STD Code*: 0265. Formerly Baroda, this was the capital of one of the most powerful princely states which covered 21,144 sq km. The family name 'Gaekwad' means 'Protector of Cows'. The Gaekwad stood high in the order of precedence and was 1 of only 5 rulers who received a 21-gun salute. He was reputedly so rich that he had a carpet woven of diamonds and pearls, and cannons cast in gold. Parks, lakes, and palaces dominate the old city. It is now a rapidly expanding industrial centre, yet still a pleasant and relaxing place to visit (Kammati Bagh is beautiful). Some of the places of interest are not open to visitors.

Places of interest

The Laxmi Vilas Palace (1880-90) Unless you can obtain special permission from the military authorities, the palace can only be glimpsed from the gate. Built by RH Chisholm – see page821 – after early designs by the military engineer Mant, the façade of this extraordinary building is 150m wide, incorporating a large number of different Indian and European architectural styles. The palace is faced in red Agra sandstone with dressings of Rajasthani marble and blue trapstone from Pune. The interior is spectacular: the Durbar Hall has walls and floor in Venetian mosaic and marble is used extensively throughout, as is stained glass from London. Nearby is the **Naulakhi Well**, a well-preserved *baoli* (step well) which has galleried compartments or levels.

Also closed to the public.

Just to the S of the Palace is the **Maharajah Fateh Singh Museum**. Possibly the most original feature of this small museum is its collection of paintings by the 19th century Indian artist Raja Ravi Verma. There are also interesting exhibits of Japanese and Chinese statuary and porcelain, some European porcelain, and good copies of paintings by such European masters as Titian, Rubens and and Raphael. Further S, beyond the railway is the **Pratap Vilas Palace** (c1910), now the Railway Staff College. In the centre of town is the Kirti Mandir (early 20th century), the Gaekwad samadhi, or memorial ground. The Kothi Building (late 19th century) is to the W and now houses the Secretariat. Across the road is the **Nyaya Mandir**, (1896) not a temple as the name implies but the High Court, in Mughal and Gothic styles. The **Jami Masjid** is next door. Further along the road away from the lake is the Mandvi (1736), a square Muslim Pavilion and the spacious **Nazar Bagh Palace** (1721) which has a Shish Mahal (mirror palace), a collection of embroidered cloth and the jewel 'Star of the South'. The solid gold and silver guns, each barrel weighing 127 kg, were drawn by teams of milk-white bullocks on ceremonial occasions. Half way down Raj Mahal Rd are the remarkable buildings of the Khanderao Market. One of the old painted *havelis* the 4-storey Tambekarwada, acquired by the Archaeological Survey is well worth visiting. Directions from Tourist Office. The Vadodara College of Fine Art is an institute of national renown.

Makarpura Palace (late 19th century, 7 km S of the city on main road) was built in an Italian Renaissance style and has a façade of 3 storeys each with an arcade around. This is now an Air Force establishment, entry and photography prohibited, though an impression can be gained from the gate.

Museums

Maharajah Sayajirao Museum (Vadodara Museum) and Art Gallery, Sayaji Baug. 0100-1700, Sat 1000-1645. Housed in the Victoria Diamond Jubilee Institute which was designed by RF Chisholm, who designed several buildings in Madras. Collection incl archaeology, art, ethnology and ancient Jain sculptures. Also Industrial Arts, Mughal miniatures and European paintings. **Maharajah Fateh Singh Museum**, Nehru Rd, in Laxmi Vilas Palace grounds. 0900-1200, 1500-1800 (Jul-Mar), 1600-1900 (Apr-Jun), closed Mon. Catalogue. Good display of royal state collection of European art, including copies of works by Murillo, Titian, Raphael and Chinese, Japanese and Indian artists incl Ravi Verma Collection. See **Places of Interest** above. Archaeology and Ancient History, MS University Collection of Biuddhist antiquities and works of art from North Gujarat discovered by the Dept of Archaeology. Also noted work on pre-history of Gujarat. Open 1400-1700. Closed Sun and other public holidays.

Parks & zoos

Sayaji Baug is an extensive park, popular for evening strolls. A Toy Train encircles the park, operating 1500-1700,

CLIMATE: VADODARA

	Jan	Feb	Mar	Apr	May	Jun	Jul	Aug	Sep	Oct	Nov	Dec	Av/Tot
Max (°C)	30	33	37	40	41	37	32	31	33	35	33	31	34
Min (°C)	13	14	19	23	27	27	26	25	24	21	16	13	21
Rain (mm)	2	0	0	0	5	121	305	283	171	45	3	0	935

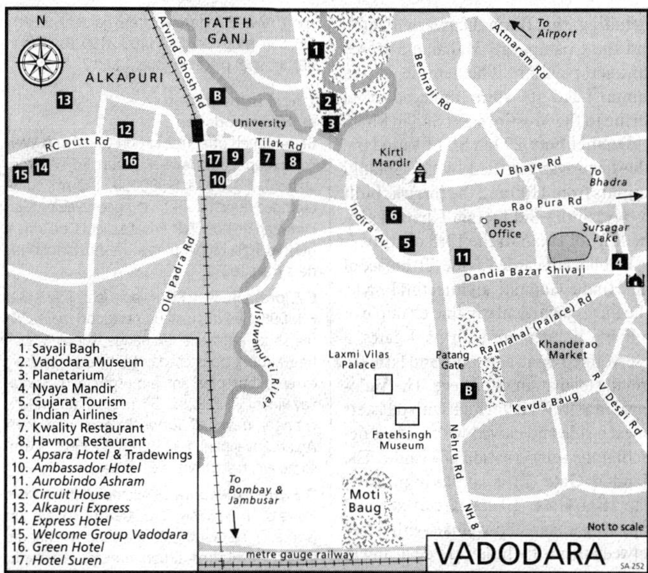

bookings from 0800-1100 at the Planetarium which has an English language performance each evening. For the children there is a Traffic Park and Elephant Rides from 1700-1800. At the entrance is a large bronze statue of HH Maharajah Sayaji Rao III; inside the park is one of Shivaji.

Excursions

A pleasant day trip by car from Vadodara could include Champaner, Pavagadh and Dabhoi Fort, 146 km via Bodeli.

Champaner, 47 km NE of Vadodara, stands on an 882m high hill in the Girnar Hills. The fortress was the old capital of the local Rajputs who lost it in 1484 to Mahmud Beghara who renamed it Muhammadabad and took 23 years to build his new city. In his campaign in Gujarat, the Mughal Emperor Humayun personally led a small team that scaled the walls of the city using iron spikes and then let the rest of the army in through the main gate. With the collapse of the Empire, Champaner passed to the Marathas.

In the **Old City**, the remains of many fine mosques and palaces show a blend of Islamic and Jain traditions, a unique style encouraged by Champaner's relative isolation. The **Jami Masjid** (1523), a large, richly ornamented mosque modelled on the Friday Mosque at Ahmadabad, is exemplary of the Gujarati style with interesting features such as oriel windows. **Accommodation E** Gujarat Tourism *Hotel Champaner*, T 41, is on a plateau (Machi Haveli), reached by cable car (closed from 1300-1400), 32 rm, and dorm.

The **Fort of Pavagadh**, 4 km SW of Champaner, dominates the skyline and is visible for miles around. Pavagadh was believed to have been part of the Himalaya carried off by the monkey god Hanuman. Occupying a large area, it rises in 3 stages; the ruined fort, then the palace and middle fort and finally the upper fort with Jain and Hindu temples. Parts of the massive walls still stand. The ascent is steep and passes several ruins including the Buria Darwaza (Gate), and the Champavati Mahal, a 3-storey summer pavilion. The temple at the summit had its spire replaced by a shrine to the Muslim saint Sadan Shah.

Dabhoi Fort 29 km SE of Vadodara. The town was fortified by the Solanki Rajputs from 1100 and the fort was built by Jayasimha Siddharaja Chapotkaha, the king of Patan in the 13th century.

Dabhoi is regarded as the birthplace of the Hindu Gujarati architectural style. The fort is a particularly fine example of military architecture with its 4 gates, a reservoir fed by an aqueduct and farms to provide food at times of siege. The **Vadodara Gate** (NW) is 9m high with pilasters on each side and carved with images depicting the reincarnation of Vishnu. The **Nandod Gate** (S) is similarly massive. The **Hira Gate** (E) has a carved relief depicting a man and woman with a tree between them. To the left is a devil and in the centre, an elephant. According to local legend, the builder is buried beneath this. **Mori Gate** (N) lies next to the old palace and on the left of this is the **Ma Kali Temple** (1225) shaped like a cross, with profuse carvings.

Tours

Gujarat Tourism (TCGL): *1. Saurashtra Darshan* (5 days), every Fri 0630. Rajkot, Jamnagar, Dwarka, Porbandar, Somnath, Sasan Gir, Veraval, Junagadh, Virpur, Palitana, Velavadar, Lothal, Ahmadabad. Price incl dorm accommodation. *2. North Gujarat and Rajasthan* (5 days), 1st and 3rd Sat, 0600. Shamlaji, Udaipur, Chittorgarh, Nathdwara, Charbhuja, Haldighati. *3. Special tour to Madhya Pradesh* (4 days). Pavagadh, Mandu, Omkareshwar, Ujjain. *4. Special Rajasthan Tour* (8 days). Shamlaji, Udaipur, Chittorgarh, Nathdwara, Pushkar, Jaipur, Jodhpur, Mount Abu etc.

Vadodara Tourist Office, T 329656: *1.* Every Tue, Wed and Fri, 1400-1800. Rs 15 (min 10). EME Temple, Sayaji Garden, Kirti Mandir, Geeta Mandir, Vadodara Dairy, Fatehsingh Museum, Aurobindo Society. *2.* Every Sat, Sun, Mon (Jul-Sep), 1700-2100. Rs 20 (min 10). Numeta (picnic spot), Ajwa (Brindavan pattern garden). *3.* Every Sat, Sun, Mon (Oct-Jun) 1400-2100. Rs 35 (min 20). Includes places in Tours 1 and 2.

Local information

● Accommodation

Better hotels offer free airport transfer. **A** Welcomgroup ***Vadodara***, RC Dutt Rd (W from station), T 330033, F 330050, 102 rm, some cramped, lunch buffet, very good value, A-la-carte can be slow. **NB** Private clients, on arrival quoted 30% higher than tariff shown for business travellers.

C ***Express***, RC Dutt Rd nr *Vadodara*, T 323131, F 330980, 64 rm, restaurants (good *thali*), coffee shop, patisserie, exchange, shops, travel, free airport transfer, day tariff, unimpressive exterior but pleasant atmosphere; **C** ***Surya***, Sayajiganj, T 328282, 51 rm, restaurant, exchange, travel; **C** ***Surya Palace***, opp Parsi Agiari, Sayajiganj, T 329999, F 325668, 80 rm, some a/c, restaurant, exchange.

D ***Express Alkapuri***, 18 Alkapuri, 0.5 km from *Express*, T 325744, F 330980, 30 a/c rm (some **C**), restaurant, coffee shop, exchange, shops, travel, free airport transfer, day tariff; **D** ***Sweet Dreams***, next to Museum, new; **D** ***Aditi***, Sardar Patel Statue, Sayajiganj, T 327722, 64 rm, some a/c, restaurant, travel. **D** Best Western ***Rama Inn***, Sayajiganj, T 32 9567, 74 rm, half a/c, nr Rly, restaurant, travel, small gym (sauna, jaccuzi on separate payment), small pool (reported dirty in 1994); **D** ***Sayaji***, opp Rajshri Cinema, T 329244, 36 a/c rm, restaurant, exchange; **D** ***Kaviraj***, RC Dutt Rd, T 323401, nr Rly, 30 rm, some a/c, nr rly, restaurant; **D** ***Utsav***, Manek Rao Rd, T 551415, 28 a/c rm, restaurants, exchange, good value.

● Budget hotels

E ***Rajdhani***, Dandia Bazar, T 541136, 22 rm, central a/c, restaurant (good *thalis* and Chinese); **E** ***Suren*** opp Rly, rm with bath. There are several cheap hotels nearby incl **E** ***Green***, opp Circuit House, T 323111, 22 rm, in old building, now a little rundown.

F ***Railway Retiring Rooms*** with the conveniently located **F** ***Municipal Corp Guesthouse*** (Pravasi Grih) opp.

● Places to eat

Many hotels have good restaurants with extensive menus, with the *Express* and *Rajdhani* serving good *thalis* (Rs 40).

Outside hotels: ***Kwality***, Sayajiganj, wide

choice, incl Italian and Peshwari dishes served indoors or in garden; ***Volga*** in Alankar Cinema grounds, Sayajiganj does good Mughlai kebabs and Chinese.

Continental: ***Copper Coin***, World Trade Centre and ***Havmor***, Yash Kamal Bldg, Sayajiganj; ***Rangoli***, Fatehgunj.

Chinese: ***Chung Fa***, RC Dutt Rd; ***Oriental Spice***, Sayajiganj.

Gujarati (thali): nr *Express Hotel*, RC Dutt Rd, ***Sahayoga*** good and cheap; ***Gokul***, Kothi Char-rasta; ***Satya Vijay***, Manjalpur; ***Iswar Bhuvan***, Dandia Bazar.

Indian/South Indian: ***Alka*** and ***Sanman***, Alkapuri.

Paan: ***Richa***, nr *Express Hotel* makes excellent *Singhoda* with 'peanut marzipan cold filling'. Try after a *thali* – you will be surprised!

● Airline offices

Air India, British Airways and **Japan Airlines** have offices on RC Dutt Rd.

● Banks & money changers

Most are in Alkapuri: **Bank of Vadodara, Bank of India**; **Indian Bank**, opp *Express Hotel*; **Indian Overseas Bank**; **State Bank of India**, opp Jamunabai Hospital, Mandvi.

● Hospitals & medical services

Sayaji Hospital, Sayajiganj. *Maharani Jamunabai Hospital*, Mandvi.

● Post & telecommunications

GPO: Raopura. **Railway Mail Service**: Railway Station.

● Shopping

Vadodara is an important centre for silver jewellery. The main shopping areas are Raopura, Mandvi, Teen Darwaza, National Plaza, Leheripura Mandir Bazar and Alkapuri Arcade. ***Khadi Bhandar***, Kothi Rd, for handlooms and local handicrafts.

Photography: ***Sharp Studio***, Sangeeta Apts, Alkapuri.

Silks & saris: ***Kala Niketan*** opp *Hotel Vadodara* and ***Chimanlal Vrajlal***, National Plaza, MG Rd. For women, Gujarati clothes from ***Rang Vesh***, National Plaza; others from ***Weekender*** nr Kala Niketan. Nearby shops sell famous local savoury *chewdo*.

● Sports

Boating: at Sursagar Lake provided by Municipal Corp.

Flying: *Gujarat Flying Club*, Airport.

Polo: *Polo Club*, Polo Ground.

Swimming: Lal Baug Pool; Sardar Baug Pool, Alkapuri; *Hotel Welcomgroup Vadodara*; *Hotel Surya Palace*.

● Tour companies & travel agents

Travel Corp of India, Vishwas Colony, nr Alkapuri Petrol Pump, T 322181; ***Travel House***, *Hotel Welcomgroup Vadodara*, RC Dutt Rd, T 320891; ***Tradewings***, Sayajiganj, T 327127.

● Tourist offices

Gujarat Tourism, Narmada Bhawan, C-Block, Indira Ave, T 540797. 1030-1810, closed Sun. Instant reservations available from Tourist Bungalows and selected private hotels in Gujarat. **Vadodara Tourist Office** (Municipal Corp), Nagar Palika Pravasi Grih, nr Rly Station, T 329656. 0900-1800. Also at Khanderao Market, Palace Rd, T 551116. 1030-1800.

● Useful addressess

Ambulance: T 101. **Fire**: T 101. **Foreigners' Regional Registration Office**: Collector's Office, Kothi Kacheri. **Police**: T 100.

● Transport

Ahmadabad (113 km), **Palitana** (325 km), **Sasan Gir** (431 km), **Ujjain** (403 km), **Indore** (348 km), **Junagadh** (372 km), **Delhi** (995 km), **Bombay** (425 km), **Jaipur** (725 km).

Local Yellow top taxis: Min Rs 10. **Auto rickshaws**: Min Rs 2. **City bus**: The ST bus service operates all round the city. **Tourist taxis**: Gujarat Tourism, Tourist Office (and other recognised travel agents). Also from *Hotel Vadodara*. Non a/c Ambassador, Rs 3.50 per km, airport drop Rs 70, airport pick-up Rs 120, 80 km/8hr Rs 350. Also **coaches** and **minibuses** for hire.

Air The airport is 6 km from the centre of town. **Transport to town**: taxi or auto rickshaw. **Indian Airlines**, City Office, Fatehgunj, T 329178; Airport, T 554433. 1000-1330, 1415-1700. **Bombay**: daily, 1645, 1 hr; **Delhi**: daily, 2005, 1½ hr. **East West Airlines**: **Bombay**: daily 0810, 1 hr 20 mins. **Continental Aviation**: **Bombay**: M,W,F, 0745, 1¼ hr.

Train Vadodara is on the main Western Railways' Delhi-Bombay broad gauge line and is well connected with other regional centres. **Bombay Central**: *Bombay Gandhidham Kutch Exp* 9032, daily, 0710, 6¼ hr; *Saurashtra Janata Exp* 9018, daily, 2237, 7½ hr; *Vadodara-Bombay Exp* 9028, daily, 2300, 6½ hr. **New Delhi**: *Rajdhani Exp* 2951, daily except Sat, 2131, 11¾ hr; *Paschim Exp* 2925, daily, 1726, 17 hr; *Frontier Mail* 2903, daily, 0256, 16 hr. **Vadodara Railway Station**, Sayajiganj. Enquiries, T 557575. Reservations T 65121. 0800-2000 (2nd class) and 0800-1800 (1st Class).

Road State Road Transport Corporations (SRTC) of Gujarat, Rajasthan, MP and Maharashtra operate between Vadodara and destinations in the region, incl Ujjain, Bombay, Pune, Udaipur and, Mount Abu. The Gujarat SRTC provides services for Gujarat. Central Bus Stand, nr Railway Station. Reservations, 0700-2200. Advance booking 0900-1300, 1330-1700.

Vadodara to Surat

ROUTES Leave Vadodara S on the NH8 to Bharuch (73 km).

Bharuch (Broach)

(*Population*: 138,200; *STD Code*: 02642) At the mouth of the Narmada River, is one of the oldest seaports in Western India and flourished in the 1st century AD. Mentioned as Barugaza by the Romans in c210 AD it was ruled by a Gurhara Prince and much later came under the rule of the Solanki Rajputs.

The **Bhrigu Rishi Temple** from which the town got its name (**Bhrigukachba**) is on the bank of the River Narmada. It subsequently developed at the lowest crossing of the river, a point of strategic importance. During the rule of Muslims from Sind (1297 to 1772) the British and the Dutch established factories in 1614 and 1617. Aurangzeb ordered the fortifications to be destroyed in 1660 which paved the way for successful attacks by the Marathas in 1675 and 1686 who rebuilt the walls.

The **Fort** overlooks the Narmada. Within it are the Collector's Office, Civil Courts, the old Dutch factory, a church, the Victoria Clocktower and other buildings. Below the fort is the **Jama Masjid** (early 14th century) which was built from a demolished Jain temple but in accordance with conventional mosque design. Just over 3 km W of the fort are some early **Dutch tombs**, overlooked by some Parsee **Towers of Silence**. Today Bharuch is well known for its textile mills and long staple cotton. **Suklatirtha**, about 10 km upstream has a *Holiday Home*.

Immediately S of Bharuch **Ankleshwar** has become a highly industrialised town. The low land along the Narmada plain is intensively cultivated under irrigation, but is relatively poor away from the river. To the S, the Tapti has cut down 3 to 4m into the floodplain as a result of geologically recent uplift of the land. There are several good new 'motels' between Bharuch and Surat. At **Kadodra**, 48 km S of Bharuch, is the **F** *Manisha Guest House and Restaurant*, and the *Alpa Restaurant*. There are also good wayside food stalls, *dabbas*.

Surat

(*Population*: 1.517mn; *STD Code*: 0261) The name is associated with 'Saurashtra' (The Good Land), the regions covering the peninsula of Gujarat. It is situated on the banks of the Tapti river and owes its development to its importance as a trading centre. It was large in 1600 and even after a decline in its fortunes the population in 1796 was estimated to be as much as 800,000.

Local crafts & industry

Surat is a centre of the jewellery business. The production of gold and silver thread and *kinkhab* brocades and wood and ivory inlay work are also important. Silk weaving is a cottage industry producing the famous *Tanchoi* and *Gajee* saris and diamond cutting is also a speciality.

History

The Parsis, driven from Persia, first arrived in India in the 8th century and many moved from their first settlement on the W coast of the peninsula to Surat in the 12th century. The Mughals, under Akbar, took the town and during their reign, the Portuguese, British, Dutch and French in turn established trading outposts here. The British were the first to establish a factory, having arrived in 1608 and Surat remained their HQ until it moved to Bombay in 1674.

During the 17th and 18th centuries, trade flourished and made Surat the mercantile capital of West India. The first dock was built in 1720 and by 1723 there were 2 shipyards. The tide turned, however, in the next century, when a fire destroyed the city centre to be followed by floods when the river Tapti burst its banks. This led many Parsis to move to Bombay. Today it is a rapidly growing industrial and commercial city, but virtually none of its history survives in its buildings.

Places of interest

The **Castle**, on the banks of the Tapti near the old bridge, provides a good vantage point for viewing the city and surrounding countryside. The **Dutch, English** and **Armenian Cemeteries** are very poorly maintained and unattractive.

The strong Muslim influence is evident in the **Nau Saiyid Mosque** (Mosque of the 9 Saiyids) which is on the W bank of the Gopi Lake, the **Khwaja Diwan Sahib's Mosque** (c1530) and the **Saiyid Idris Mosque** (1639). The **Mirza Sami Mosque** (1540) was built by Khudawand Khan who was also responsible for the castle. There are 2 **Parsi Fire Temples** (1823). The Swami Narayan Temple with its 3 white domes is a local landmark.

Excursions

At **Rander**, 5 km from the city is the site of a city dating to 200 BC. The Muslims sacked it in 1225 and built a **Jami Masjid** on the site of a Jain Temple.

There are a number of beaches near Surat: **Dumas**, 16 km is a popular health resort; **Hajira**, 28 km, with Casuarina groves and a Gujarat Tourism *Holiday Home*, 10 rm; **Ubhrat**, 42 km with palm-shaded beach and a Gujarat Tourism *Holiday Home* with well equipped cottages (various categories).

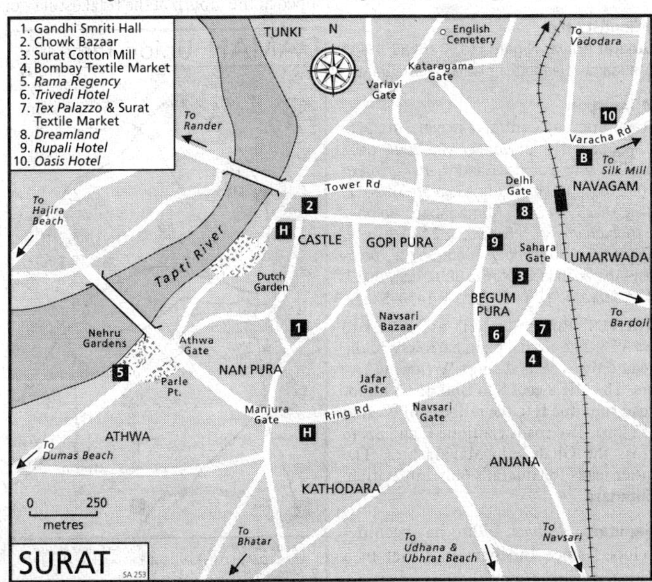

Local information

● Accommodation

A *Rama Regency*, Athwa Lines, nr Bharati Park, T 666565, F 667294, 140 rm, modern, pleasant outlook over river, good pool, very helpful service, the best hotel in Surat.

D *Oasis*, nr Vaishali Cinema, Varacha Rd, T 41124, 25 rm, some a/c, restaurants (1 garden), permit rm, coffee shop, pool; **D** *Tex Palazzo*, Ring Rd, T 623018, 43 rm, some a/c, restaurants, coffee shop, on a very busy road; **D** *Trivedi*, Ring Rd, Begumpura, is fairly new; **D** *Dhawalgiri*, Opp Collector's Bungalow, Athwa Lines, T 40040, 10 a/c rm, restaurant (incl veg health food), service rooms, run down.

E *Dreamland*, Sufi Baug, opp rly station, T 39016, 39 rm, some a/c, snacks only; **E** *Yuvraj*, T 53621, 56 rm, central a/c, restaurants (veg).

Nearby are **F** *Subras* and **F** *Rupali* with rm and dorm.

● Places to eat

Little choice outside hotels. *Tex Palazzo* (good *thalis*), revolving restaurant but the views are not spectacular. Dwahalgiri's *Health Food Restaurant* and *Sahkar*, Ajanta Apartments Corner, Ring Rd, are open all day.

● Tourist office

Gujarat Pravas Nigam Ltd, T 26586, 1/847 Athugar St, Nanpura, nr Kailash Restaurant.

● Transport

Train **Bombay Central**: *Paschim Exp* 2926, daily, 1053, 4¼ hr; *Frontier Mail* 2904, daily, 0250, 4¼ hr; *Bombay Gandhidam Kutch Exp* 1032, daily, 0916, 4¼ hr; *Gujarat Exp* 9012, daily, 1125, 4¾ hr. **Ahmadabad**: *Bombay Gandhidham Kutch Exp* 9031, 2140, 3½ hr; *Gujarat Exp* 9011, daily, 1045, 5½ hr; *Bombay-Ahmadabad Janata Exp* 9007, daily, 0033, 4 hr; *Saurashtra Exp* 9215, daily, 1410, 5¼ hr.

ROUTES Return to NH8 at Navsari to travel S. The coastal plain narrows and the road crosses several short W flowing rivers. The NH 8 goes S to Chikhli. A minor road runs due E to the railhead of Waghai (55 km). Two roads continue E and SE to cross the Ghats into Maharashtra. The latter leads to Gujarat's only hill station, **Saputara**.

Saputara (*Altitude*: 870m) has been developed since Independence. Set in a forested tribal region there is an attractive lake and the Mahal Bardipura forest wildlife sanctuary nearby. The name is derived from the snake deity of the tribal people who is worshipped here. **Accommodation** Gujarat Tourism's **E** *Toran Hill Resort*, T 26, cottages and huts, restaurant.

Tithal, 5 km from Valsad beach has a palm-fringed beach with an **E** Gujarat Tourism *Holiday Home*, T 2206, 24 rm and 2 *Hill Bungalows*.

Daman

(*Population*: 26,900; *STD Code*: 02636) 160 km N of Bombay. The 380 sq km enclave of Daman, along with Diu and Goa, were Portuguese possessions until forcibly taken over by the Indian Govt in 1961. Its association with Goa ceased when the latter became a 'State' in 1987. It is now a Union Territory with its own Pradesh Council.

Situated on the S side of the **Gulf of Khambhat** (Cambay), Daman developed at the mouth of the tidal estuary of

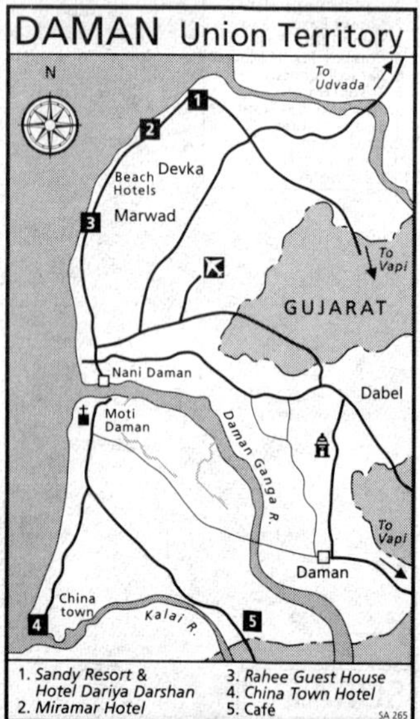

the Daman Ganga river as a Portuguese trading centre from 1531. Much of its early commerce was with the Portuguese territories in East Africa. Later (1817-1837) it was a link in the opium trade chain until this was broken by the British. The main road into Daman from the N (either from Patalia or from Vapi) enters the centre of the modern town still known as *Nani* (small) *Daman*. From the S a road leaves NH8 S of Vapi and enters the town through *Moti* (large) *Daman*.

Moti Daman

Retaining something of the Portuguese atmosphere of its colonial origins, many still speak the language and some street names still appear in Portuguese.

The landward (E) side has a moat and drawbridge. The shaded main street inside the **fort** wall runs N-S between attractive arched gateways. These carry Portuguese arms. One shows a saint carrying a sword but the sculpted giants on the doorways are modelled on the guardian *dwarpalas* at entrances to Hindu temples. The road passes the former **Governor's Palace** and other government buildings. These now serve as the administrative offices for the Union Territory. Towards the S end of the street is the former Cathedral Church of **Bom Jesus**, started in 1559 but consecrated in 1603. Large and airy when the main S door is open, the chief feature of the church is its painted and gilt wooden altar reredos and pulpit. Much of the ornamentation, notably the gold crowns of the saints, have been stolen. On the W side of the small square is the old **jail**, still in use. To the S, against the fort wall, is the **Rosario Chapel**, formerly the Church of the Madre Jesus, with a unique feature in Indian churches of carved and gilded wooden panels illustrating stories from the life of Christ. These include the adoration of the Magi, Jesus teaching in the synagogue as a child, and Mary's ascension. The ceiling features charming carved cherubs. The statue of Mary of the Rosary was placed on the altar in thanksgiving by the Portuguese commander for rescue from an attack by Sivaji, and the original statue of Mary the Mother of Jesus moved to its present position on the W wall of the nave.

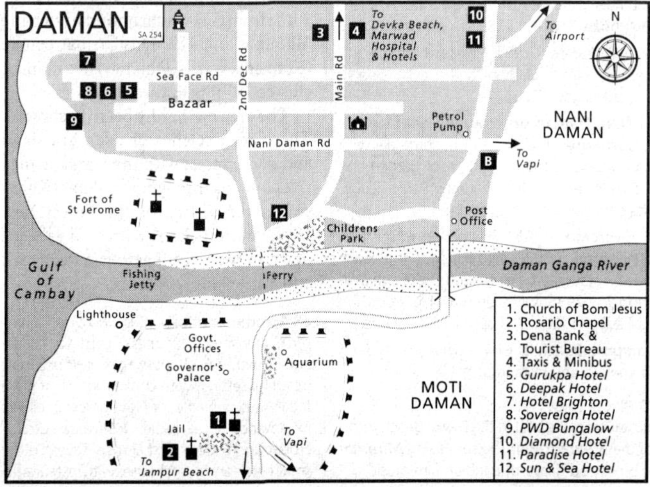

Nani Daman

This is N of the river. The bridge across Daman Ganga gives attractive views of Moti Daman's walls and the country fishing boats on either bank. On the N side of the river is a smaller **Fort**, which encloses a church and a cemetery. Some of the old houses retain beautifully carved wooden doors and lintels.

The town is thick with bars (trading on Gujarat's prohibition of alcohol) and has some basic hotels and restaurants. Two km N is an airport which ceased operating in 1991 but may reopen. A new resort complex some 2 km further N has a cluster of better hotels by the rather unattractive beach. Bathing is unsafe. There is a small resort at Jampore planted with casuarina groves, about 3 km S of Moti Daman, where the beach is sandy and swimming safe, but still not very appealing.

● Accommodation

Nr Devka Beach, 5 km from centre: **D** *Miramar*, T 2471, cottage and rm (some a/c), breezy beach restaurant, a/c indoor (1994), slightly day-tripper, holiday camp atmosphere; **D** *Dariya Darshan*, T 2286, cottages and rm (some a/c), restaurant; **D** *Sandy Resort*, T 2751, 32 rm, some a/c, restaurant, pool, the quietest – and most pleasant – of the Devka Beach hotels; **D** *Ashoka Palace*, T 2239, rm with bath.

E PWD *Rahee Guest House*, Marwad Rd, between Nani Daman and Devka Beach, T 2250, is good value.

In Nani Daman on crowded Seaface Rd: **E** *Gurukripa*, T 2846, 25 rm, some a/c with bath, good restaurant, bar, roof garden, TV; **E** *Sun 'n Sea*, opp the Childrens' Park, T 2506, has some a/c rm with balcony.

F *Sovereign*, T 2833, has better rm upstairs; **F** *Brighton*, T 2922, set back from the beach has a restaurant. **E** *Paradise*, T 2404 and *Diamond*, T 2935, with some a/c rm are nr the Taxi stand. **F** *Gokul*, is opp the PWD Office.

Jampore Beach: **D** *China Town*, T 2416, rm (some a/c) and restaurant.

● Places to eat

Restaurants are best in the Devka Beach resort and at *China Town*. The sea-facing *Miramar* is breezy but plays loud Indian film music.

● Tourist office

On Main Rd, in the Dena Bank building opp the mini-bus stand.

● Transport

Local bicycles: you can rent bicycles in Nani Daman bazar.

Train Vapi, 13 km E, is the railway station for Daman and is on a main railway line from Bombay Central to Vadodara and Ahmadabad, about 3 hr. Not all trains stop at Vapi. **Transport to town**: plenty of buses and share-taxis into towns (about Rs 6 per person).

Road Bus: regular buses to Bombay and Surat.

ROUTES From Vapi a road leads to Silvassa (14 km).

Dadra & Nagar Haveli

(*Population*: 13,900)

Silvassa

(*Population*: 11,700; 17 km), named from the Portuguese *selva*, forest. *Dadra* means a 'high (vantage) point'; the elevation still offers fine views over the Gujarat plains, and also over the unattractive industrial works in Vapi.

Silvassa is the capital of the Union Territory of Dadra and Nagar Haveli formerly administered by the Portuguese from Goa who acquired it from the Marathas in 1779. Local tribal people (Konkans, Warlis, Dhodias) live in small clusters of huts in the villages.

The area has hardly been discovered. There are stretches of open grassland and dense forest with the Damanganga river flowing through. Van Vihar (Khanvel) is the setting of the Forest Rest House with its lawns, terraced gardens down to the river. There is a deer park and a tribal museum.

● Accommodation **C-D** *Chowda Complex*, Khanvel, 2 categories of cottages, Luxury and Economy. **E** *Khanvel Forest House* in its beautiful setting, with cook who will prepare meals, it is primarily for Govt officers, reserve in advance if available. **F** *Silvassa Circuit House* and **F** *Govt Rest House*. Several other small hotels and guest houses with restaurants.

• **Transport Train** The nearest station is at Vapi which has trains from Bombay Central, about 3 hr. **Road** From Vapi, 1 hr by rickshaw or bus.

ROUTES The NH8 to Bombay continues S from Daman through Manor. In places the Western Ghats form an impressive wall. The road is very busy with slow moving lorry traffic. Approaching the outskirts of Bombay a small road leads to the coastal site of **Tarapur** (26 km) India's first nuclear power plant. The start of the W Express Highway then begins 42 km from the centre of Bombay.

AHMADABAD TO BHAVNAGAR, PALITANA AND DIU

ROUTES This route explores the E coast of the Kathiawad Peninsula. Substantial remains of Harappan culture including the dry dock can be seen at Lothal before the road skirts the marshes to reach the important town of Bhavnagar and the grasslands of the Velavadar National Park. Further on, the Jain temple city of **Shatrunjaya** rises out of the plain near **Palitana**. The road returns briefly to the coast at **Mahuva** before continuing inland along a picturesque road to the old Portuguese island enclave of **Diu**.

Dholka

This was built as the residence of the Muslim Governor of Delhi. The **Masjid of Hilal Khan Qazi** (1333) has a simple façade with 2 turrets flanking the central arch. The **Tanka Masjid** (1361) has over 100 Hindu pillars suggesting that a purely Islamic style had not yet developed – see also Qutb Minar Delhi (page 175).The other mosque, of **Alif Khan** (1453), is unlike other Gujarati mosques of the period in that it is of brick. Davies suggests that it is South Persian in design and execution, the workers migrating as a result of the coastal shipping trade.

ROUTES Continue S from Dholka to Lothal

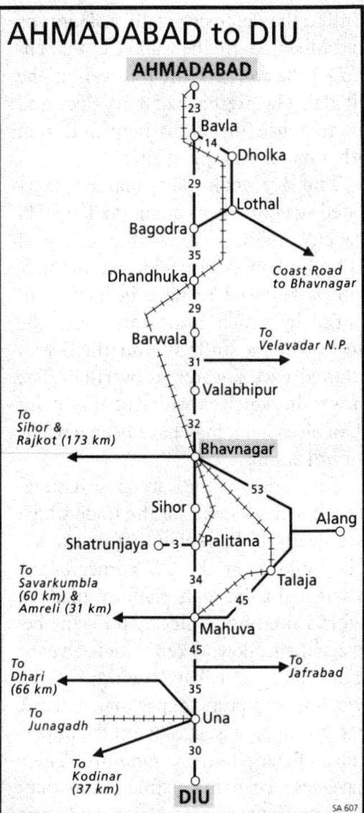

Lothal ('Mound of the dead')

Sandwiched between the Sabarmati river and the Bhogavo River, Lothal is now 10 km up from the Gulf of Khambhat. 720 km as the crow flies SE of Moenjodaro, it has some of the most substantial remains of the Harappan culture in India dating from c2500 BC-1700 BC. Its site and function as a port have led most authorities to argue that it was settled by Harappan trading communities who came by sea from the mouths of the Indus, but some believe that it may have been settled by traders moving across the overland route.

Places of interest

The site is surrounded by a mud-brick embankment 300m N-S and 400m E-W.

Unlike the defensive walls at Harappa and Moenjodaro, the wall at Lothal enclosed the workers' area as well as the citadel. The presence of a dry dock and a warehouse further distinguish it from other major Harappan sites.

The dry dock This massive excavated structure runs along the E wall of the city and has average dimensions of 214m by 36m. A 12m wide gap in the N side is believed to have been the entrance by which boats came into the dock, while a spillway over the S wall allowed excess water to overflow. The city wall, which is wider at this point than elsewhere, may have been a wharf for unloading.

Excavations of the warehouse have revealed wide evidence of the trade which was clearly the basis of Lothal's existence. The building at the SW corner of the wharf had a 4m high platform made of cubical mud-brick blocks, the gaps between them allowing ventilation. Over 65 Indus Valley seals have been discovered which show pictures of packing material, bamboo or rope, suggestive of the importance of trade to the community. There have also been many finds of pottery, semi-precious stones, beads and even necklaces made of tiny beads of gold. Rice and millet were clearly in use, and there is some evidence that horses had been domesticated.

The city Excavations show a planned city in a grid pattern, with an underground drainage system, wells, brick houses with baths and fireplaces. The raised brick platform to the SE may have been a kiln where seals and plaques were baked. Objects found include painted pottery, ivory, shell, semi-precious stone items, beads, bangles and terracotta toys. The long rectangular tank to the E may have been used as a dock. The discovery of a seal from Bahrain suggests that there was overseas trade. The cemetery to the NW had large funerary vessels indicating pit burials.

Museum

The Archaeological Museum contains various artefacts including copper and bronze implements from the site.

- **Accommodation** The *Toran Holiday Home* has 2 rm and a dormitory.

- **Transport Train** Burkhi, on the Ahmadabad-Bhavnagar line is the nearest station, but the trains are slow and inconvenient. **Road** Direct buses from Ahmadabad. Allow a full day for a round trip. It is a hard day, with not much to see at the end of it. More comfortably managed by car.

Lothal to Palitana

It is possible to take the coast road S from Lothal to Bhavnagar, but this crosses marshes, is poor quality and sometimes is not open. It is necessary to check before travelling. The alternative is via Dhingra, Barvala and Vallabhipur.

Bhavnagar

(*Population*: 405,200; *STD Code*: 0278). Founded in 1723 by the Rajput Bhavsinghji Gohil, who developed it into an important coastal town and seaport. Its principal trade is the export of cotton.

Places of interest

The palace-like **Takhtsinghji General Hospital** (1879-83) was designed by William Emerson, President of the Royal Institute of British Architects. He also designed the **Darbargadh** (Old Palace 1894-5) in the centre of town, now used as bank offices and the imposing **Town Hall**. The **Barton Museum** (1895) has a good collection of arms, armour and coins. In the same building is the more famous **Gandhi Smitri**, a library, memorial and museum dedicated to Mahatma Gandhi.

Excursions

Gaurishankar Lake is a popular picnic spot and the hilltop **Takhteshwar Temple** has good views. **Alang** beach, 50 km S of Bhavnagar, has turned into the world's largest scrapyard for dead ships, the industry yielding rich pickings from the sale of salvaged metal (steel, bronze and copper). Labourers' 'huts' line the coast road.

Velavadhar National Park The 35 sq km of flat grassland is the home for black buck, best visited from Nov-May. The road approach is from Vallabhipur.

Local information

● Accommodation

C Welcomegroup *Nilambag Palace*, T 24340, 14 a/c rm, restaurant, gardens, tennis, pool, small palace which belonged to Maharajah Krishnakumarsingh, the first Indian Prince to hand over his state to the Govt of India after Independence.

D *Apollo*, opp Central Bus Station, T 25249, 30 rm, half a/c, restaurant, fast food counter, exchange, shop; **D** *Blue Hill*, nr Pill Garden, T 26951, 38 rm, some a/c, central, restaurant, coffee shop, exchange, travel; **D** *Jubilee*, behind Pill Garden, T 26624, 30 rm, some a/c, central, restaurant, exchange, travel.

● Budget hotels

E *Mini*, Station Rd, T 23113, some a/c rm, clean, excellent value.

Basic **F** hotels include the *Evergreen Guest House*, T 4605, *Kashmir* and *Geeta*, T 3985, has rm and dorm. *Shital*, Amba Chowk, Mali Tekra, T 28360, clean and good value, rec. Also *Railway Retiring Rooms*.

● Places to eat

Limited choice outside hotels. *Nataraj*, opp Ganga Devi, and *Havmor* in the shopping area opp the covered food market are reasonable. *Mahavir Lodge*, nr the Rly Station, does good veg *thalis*.

● Transport

Air *Indian Airlines*: Bombay, M,Tu,Th,S, 1310, 50 min. *East West Airlines*: Bombay, daily, 1145, 1 hr 10 min.

Train Ahmadabad: The railway line has to take a circuitous route to skirt the marshes. It is a slow journey. *Girnar Exp* 9845, daily, 2145, 8½ hr; *Bhavnagar Ahmadabad Exp* 9809, daily, 0530, 6¼ hr.

Road Bus: there are good bus connections with Ahmadabad and other centres in the state.

Velavadar National Park

This compact game reserve with open grassland was created especially for conserving the black buck, which is associated with ancient Indian legend. The black buck is the second largest of the antelopes and the fastest long-distance runner of all animals. It can keep going at a steady 90 km per hr. It is unfortunately the most hunted animal in India, and so is an endangered species. Best time, Oct-early Jun. Jeep hire. **Accommodation** The nearest accommodation is at Bhavnagar.

Palitana

BASICS *Population*: 42,000; *Altitude*: 182m; *Area*: 13 sq km; *Climate*: Temperature Summer: Max 46°C, Min 24°C; Winter: Max 38°C, Min 17°C; *Annual rainfall*: 580 mm, mostly Jun-Sep; *Best Season*: Nov-Mar. Apr-Jun, extremely hot.

Palitana is the base for visiting the impressive Jain temple city of Shatrunjaya. It was the capital of a small princely state founded by Shahji, a Gohel Rajput who belonged to the same clan as the Maharajah of Bhavnagar. Besides being a pilgrimage centre, Palitana also has a name for horse-breeding. Local industries incl diamond cutting and manufacture of harmonium reeds and weighing scales.

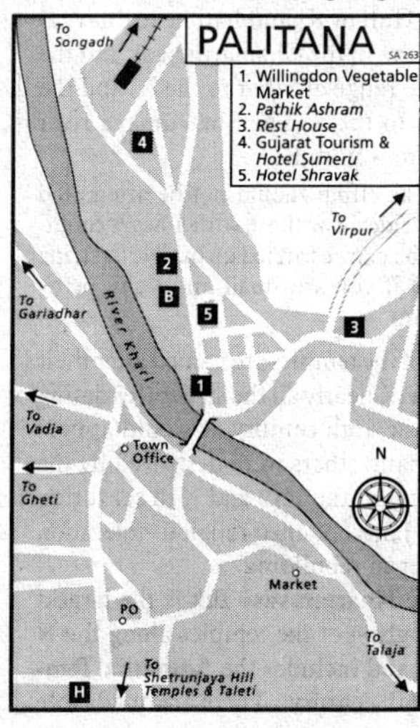

Places of interest

Shatrunjaya is the largest temple city of its kind in India and within its gates are found 863 temples. According to local tradition, Adinatha, the 1st Tirthankara, visited the hill several times and the first temple was erected by his son. Thereafter the temple builders could not stop. Jains believe that Pundarika, the chief disciple of Adinatha attained *nirvana* there. All these monuments are situated on **Shatrunjaya Hill**, a 600m climb and 3 km SW of Palitana. There are 2 series of temples strung along the 2 ridges of the hill with further temples in the hollow between linking them. All are surrounded by a tall battlement, obviously erected for defence. These fortifications are called *tuks* and have created a series of 9 enclosures.

Temples Open 0700-1900. The climb of at least 1 hr up a stepped path busy with pilgrims is extremely hard work. There are 2 long flat stretches, but even in winter it can be very hot. Arrive early, and allow 5 hr for the round trip. Take lots of water and a sun hat or parasol. No restaurant or facilities at the top. From the summit there is a superb view of the Gulf of Khambhat, near Bhavnagar to the E, the Chamardi peak and the granite range of Sihor to the N, and the plains to the S. The Shatrunjaya river runs from W to E.

NB The climb should not be attempted by the elderly or those with a heart condition. You can be carried up by *dhooli* (string chairs) if you are small and light, or by elephant.

Most of the temples are named after their founders, nearly all the structures dating from the 16th century. It would appear that many others were destroyed by the Muslims in the 14th and 15th centuries. Later, Jains obtained religious toleration and began rebuilding.

The **Khartaravasi Tuk** is the largest and highest of the temples along the N Ridge and includes the **Adinatha Temple** (16th century). There are quadruple Tirthankara images inside the sanctuary over which rises a slender tower. The **Vallabhai Temple** (19th century) with its finely clustered spires and the large **Motisah Temple** (1836) occupy the middle ground between the ridges.

The **Vimalavasi Tuk** occupies the W end of the S Ridge. In it is the **Adishvara Temple** (16th century) which dominates the site. It is similar in layout to the Adinatha temple and has a double-storey mandapa inside which is a large image of Rishabhanatha with crystal eyes and a gold crown of jewels.

Other temples in this southern group are the Temple of **Ramaji Gandharia** (16th century) and the **Bhulavani** (labyrinth, 18th century) which is a series of crypt-like chambers each surmounted with a dome. The **Hathiapol** (Elephant Gate, 19th C) faces SE.

As there is no accommodation on the hill, pilgrims and visitors must return to Palitana leaving Shatrunjaya deserted, but even during the day there is a peaceful serenity in the City of the Gods.

Museums

Stapitya Kala Sangrah, Taleti. Free. Sri Vishal Jain Kala Sansthan, Taleti Rd. Jain Art. Free.

Local information

● Accommodation

C *Nilambag Palace* at Bhavnagar is the best nearby (see above).

D Gujarat Tourism *Toran Sumeru*, Station Rd, nr Octroi Naka, T 227, 7 comfortable rm (1 a/c), 5 dorms, restaurant (serves good Eng breakfast), Tourist Office, check-out 0900, good value; **D** *Shravak*, opp ST Depot, T 328, 13 rm, some a/c with bath, dorm, 24 hr rm service.

● Budget hotels

F *Pathik Ashram*, nr ST Depot, has 9 rm; **F** *Mahavir Lodge*, is nr the State Bank of Saurashtra; PWD **F** *Ready Money Guest House*, nr Power House, T 16, reservations: Exec Engineer, Bhavnagar, T 6951.

There are over 150 *dharamshalas* with modern facilities catering primarily for Jain pilgrims. Non-Jains may be allowed to stay. Some prominent ones are: *Oswal*, T 140; *Khetlavir*,

T 384; *Nanda Bhuvan*, T 285; *Narsinatha*, T 86; *Kuchi Bhavan*, T 37; *Chandra Deepak*, T 135; *Rajendra Vihar Dadavadi*, T 148; *Sona Rupa*, T 276.

● **Places to eat**
Siddh Kshetra Jain Bhojanshala, nr Sir Mansinhji Hospital, Indian; *Siddhgiri Bhojanalaya*, Taleti Rd, Gujarati thali; *Vaishali*, Main Bazar, Gujarati *thali* and South Indian.

● **Hospitals & medical services**
Mansinhji Govt Hospital, Main Rd, T 75. *Shatrunjaya Hospital*, Taleti Rd.

● **Post & telecommunications**
Post Office: Bhairavnath Rd, T 33.

● **Shopping**
Local handicrafts incl embroidery (saris, dresses, purses, bags, wall hangings etc) and metal engraving. You can watch the craftsmen making harmonium reeds.

Photography: several in Main Rd. Nearest processing at Bhavnagar.

● **Tourist office**
The Tourist Office is at *Hotel Toran Sumeru*.

● **Useful addresses**
Ambulance: T 75. **Police**: T 50.

● **Transport**
Palitana is connected by good motorable roads with **Bhavnagar** (57 km by State Highway), **Junagadh** (215 km), **Ahmadabad** (217 km), **Porbandar** (294 km), **Dwarka** (400 km), **Gandhidham** (376 km), **Bombay** (768 km), **Delhi** (1,113 km).

Local Taxis and **tongas**, both rates negotiable. Also *dandis* for transport up the hill. Rs 150.

Air Bhavnagar (51 km NE) is the nearest airport.

Train Palitana is on the metre gauge of the Western Railway and has a connection only with Bhavnagar. The nearest major railway junction is Ahmadabad. Rly Enquiries, Palitana, T 8.

Road Gujarat State Transport services connect Palitana with Bhavnagar, Ahmadabad, Rajkot, Jamnagar, Vadodara and Surat. Res, T 68. 0800-1200, 1400-1800. Private bus companies operate regular deluxe coaches to Palitana from Bombay and Surat via Vadodara. *Paras Travels*, Owen Bridge, T 370. *Khodiar Travels*, opp State Transport depot, T 586 (to Surat only). *Shah Travels*, opp ST depot, T 396. Taxis: for up to 7 sometimes run between Bhavnagar and Palitana. Rs 10-15 per person.

75 km SW of Palitana are the hot springs at **Tulshishyam**, and a further 60 km SE the coastal town of **Mahuva** (*Population*: 64,100; *STD Code*: 02844) and 110 km to Diu. There are no places of great historical importance but it is quite picturesque.

Diu

(*Population*: 20,600; *STD Code*: 028758). The 11 km long and 3 km wide island of Diu is situated off the S tip of the Kathiawad peninsula on the N side of the Gulf of Khambhat. The island has a fascinating history, excellent cuisine and superb beaches. It is still hardly visited. Like its neighbour Daman across the gulf, it was a Portuguese colony until 1961. In 1987 its administration was separated from Goa which then became a State; Diu remains a Union Territory. With its attractively ornamented buildings with balconies and

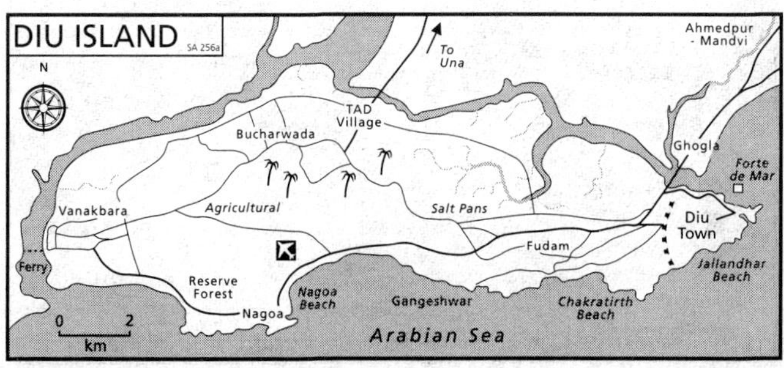

verandahs, its narrow streets and squares, the town has more of a Portuguese flavour than Daman. The fishing village of Ghogla on the mainland was also part of Diu. The N side of the island has been subject to marine deposition and comprises salt pans and marshes. The S coast has some fine limestone cliffs and sandy beaches. The Branching palms were introduced from Africa by the Portuguese. Coconut palms are also very much in evidence.

History

Fort de Mar, built in 1535, was strategically important as an easily defended base for controlling the shipping lanes on the NE part of the Arabian Sea. From the 14th to 16th centuries the Sultans of Oman held the reins of maritime power. The Portuguese failed to take it at their first attempt in 1531 but succeeded 3 years later. Like Daman it was once a port for the export of opium from Malwa (Madhya Pradesh). With the decline of Portugal as a naval power it became little more than a backwater.

Places of interest

Diu town is squeezed between the fort (E) and a large city wall (W). It has 2 churches, **St Paul's** (1691) with a baroque façade with fine wood panelling and **St Francis of Assisi**, which is a museum; there are few Christians now. The **Fort** is considered one of the most important built by the Portuguese in Asia. Constructed after the Mughal Emperor Humayun attacked the Sultan of Gujarat, with the help of the Portuguese. Skirted by the sea on 3 sides, there were 2 moats, 1 of which was tidal. Cannon and cannon balls litter the ramparts; the lighthouse stands at one end and parts of the central keep are still used as a jail.

Excursions

In **Fudam**, S side of the island, there is the **Church of Our Lady of the Remedies**, now rather dilapidated. **Vanakbara** on the W tip of the island has the **Church of Our Lady of Mercy**. There is a ferry service across to **Kotla**.

Nagoa, 7 km from Diu Town on the S of the island, facing the Arabian Sea, has a beautiful semi-circular palm-fringed beach suitable for swimming.

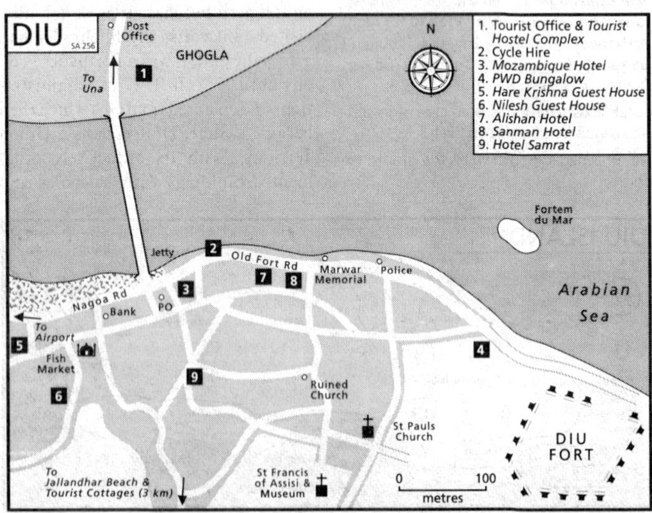

Popular with foreign visitors. **Accommodation F** *Ganga Sagar Guest House* on the beach, T 2249, 5 clean rm, restaurant does very good meals esp seafood (order in advance), bar, well located. **Bucharwada** not faraway, does not have attractive beaches but has cheap, spartan rm.

Ahmedpur-Mandvi The unspoilt beach to the N which looks out to Diu is also being developed. The Junagadh Nawabs built a fortified summer palace here. The bus from Una to Ghogla may stop if you request, otherwise take a rickshaw from Ghogla, 3 km or take a shorter path on foot along the beach. **Accommodation D** ITDC *Tourist Bungalow* and Gujarat Tourism **D** *Samudra Beach Resort*, T 116, with good rm in typical Saurashtrian huts, 14 huts, some a/c, 22 rm in '*Haveli*' and dorm. Restaurant in old palace, rec, surfing, boating, water-skiing and para-sailing.

It is 80 km along the coast to **Somnath** via Kodinar. An alternative is to go inland to **Sasan Gir** (40 km) to visit the National Park.

Local information

● Accommodation

Most are fairly basic. Only a few with a/c rm. **D** *Samrat*, T 2354, is best, 12 rm, 3 a/c, and a good restaurant; **D** *Ankur*, T 2388, 13 rm, 2 a/c; **D** *Alishan*, nr *Sanman* on seaside, T 2354, 15 rm, 2 a/c and dorm, clean, comfortable; **D** *Tourist Hostel Complex*, at Ghogla, T 2212, 14 rm, 4 a/c and dorm, simple restaurant, Tourist Office; **D** *Tourist Cottages*, on Jallandhar Beach to the S, with 6 rm, modern, good value.

● Budget hotels

E *Sanman*, formerly *Baron's Inn*, by the sea, Old Fort Rd, T 2273, 6 rm with bath, meals available, this was an impressive colonial house, now losing something of its atmosphere, Next door is **E** *Apna Guest House*, Old Fort Rd, T 2112, 17 rm some with bath (best with sea view and balcony) and dorm, rooftop terrace with restaurant and bar; **E** *Mozambique*, old colonial house off the Bunder opp Vegetable Market, T 2223, 8 rm, best with roof-terrace, restaurant, clean, quiet.

F *PWD Bungalow*, nr Fort, T 2163, 10 rm (2 a/c), best with bath and balcony to garden, good restaurant (Indian), well run, inexpensive, so very popular; **F** *Nilesh Guest House*, nr Fish Market, T 2319, 17 rm some with bath, restaurant and bar (can be noisy), spartan. Also nr Fish Market is **F** *Prince*, T 2265, 11 rm, rec; **F** *Hare Krishna Guest House*, between fish market and Tourist Office, T 2213, 5 rm and dorm, friendly staff, popular restaurant.

● Places to eat

Best at Ahmedpur Mandvi, on mainland. In addition to hotel restaurants, *Deepee* café, opp Bus Stand, serves excellent veg meals and ice-cream. *Saraswati Hotel*, opp *Goa Travels* is a tea shop, good breakfast.

● Hospitals & medical services

Manesh Medical Store is a pharmacy with a doctor in the building.

● Post & telecommunications

The main **Post Office** is on Main Sq, the other at Ghogla.

● Tourist office

At Tourist Complex, Ghogla. Mon-Fri, 0930-1315, 1400-1745.

● Transport

Local A new bridge joins Diu Town with Ghogla. **Buses**: operate from the main square which is on the N shore. There are 2 local bus services from Diu to Nagoa, 3 times daily, and Diu to Bucharwada-Vanakbara 16 times a day. **Bicycles**: at the *Shilpa Cycle Store*, Main Sq or *Kishma Cycle Store* nr the State Bank of Saurashtra, Ghogla. About Rs 15 per day.

Air No flights at present.

Train Delwada, 8 km N is the nearest railhead with trains to and from Junagadh. Shared auto rickshaws available into Diu.

Road Bus: long distance State buses from Diu and Ghogla. Daily private luxury buses to Bombay. Also services to Ahmadabad, Rajkot, Porbandar, Veraval etc from Una (12 km). *Goa Travels* runs buses to Bhavnagar, Palitana, Junagadh. A daily bus connects with Bombay via Bhavnagar (20 hr). Bombay Agent: *Hirup Travel*, Prabhakar Sadan, Khetwadi Back Rd, 12th Line, T 358816. Daman Agent: *Satish General Stores*, Nani Daman.

AHMADABAD TO RAJKOT

The road runs across northern Saurashtra, skirting the central hills of the Kathiawad Peninsula. This is one of the major groundnut growing regions of India, but other crops include millets and wheat.

Limbdi

(44 km; *Population*: 35,300), situated on the banks of the artificial Ramsagar Lake, Limbdi was the capital of a former princely state. The Rajput chief – Thakur Sahib – lived in a very attractive palace which can still be seen. The town specialised in making ivory bangles and brass ware, especially boxes. The town is 1 km from the main road. The Gujarat Tourism *Motel Ramsagar* is on the National Highway.

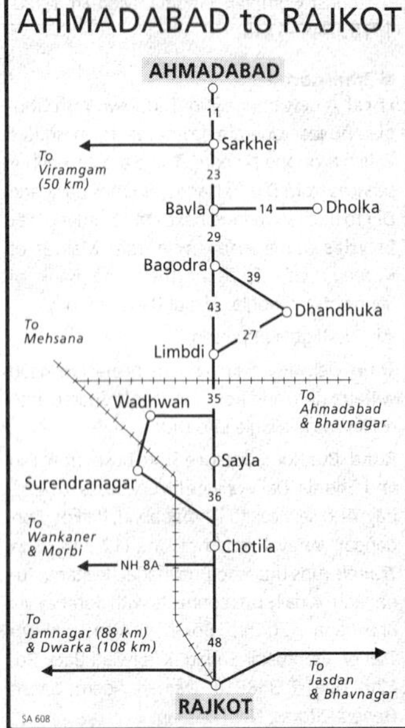

Rajkot

(*Population*: 550,000; *Altitude*: 120m; *STD Code*: 0281) Although there is an early Palaeolithic site at Rajkot, there is very little evidence of significant settlement before the modern period. The capital of a second ranking Rajput Princely State, the town is best known as the early home of Mohandas Karamchand Gandhi. His family home is now a Gandhi museum. Rajkot was the home of the British Resident for the Western Indian States.

Widely regarded as a progressive state, Rajkot still has a number of buildings and institutions dating from the late 19th century:– the Rajkumar College (1870), the Alfred High School (1875) and the Kaisar-i-Hind Bridge (1910). It has become one of India's fastest growing middle rank cities, its population nearly doubling in the last 20 years. That growth has been based on a rapid industrialisation, especially the processing of agricultural products such as groundnuts.

Places of interest

The Rajkumar College Founded in 1870, the College is now one of India's best known public schools. Gandhi was educated at the **Alfred High School**, (now Mahatma Gandhi High School) which has a statue of him outside. **The Jubilee Gardens**, in the old civil station of the town, house the **Memorial Institute** which has the Lang Library and the Connaught Hall. **Gandhi Smriti**, the Gandhi family home, has been turned into a memorial museum.

Museum

Watson Museum, Jubilee Gardens. Exhibits from Indus Valley civilisation, medieval sculpture, pottery and crafts, and colonial memorabilia.

Excursion

Tarnetar with the Trineteswar Mahadev Temple attracts large crowds to its Folk Festival in Aug/Sep. Interesting for dance, music and art and the colourful local people who attend with their striking 'umbrellas' decorated with mirror-work and embroidery. **Accommodation** Gujarat Tourism tent village.

Local information

● Accommodation

All except *Mohit International* are central, 2-3 km from rly. **D** ***Galaxy***, Jawahar Rd, T 31781, 35 very well furnished, clean rm, most a/c, restaurant, pleasant roof-garden, excellent service and good value, rec; **D** ***Samrat International***, 37 Karanpura, T 22269, 32 rm, some a/c with TV, restaurant, exchange, travel; **D** ***Tulsi***, Kante Shree Vikas Guru Rd, T 31791, some a/c rm, excellent restaurant, exchange, clean, modern hotel; **D** ***Jayson***, SVP (Canal) Rd, T 26170, 18 rm some a/c, restaurant, exchange, travel; **D** ***Ruby***, Kanak Rd, T 31722, 40 ac rm, restaurant; **D** ***Mohit International***, Sir Harilal Gosaliya Marg, T 33338, 36 rm, some a/c, 2 km centre, restaurant, exchange.

● Budget hotels

F *Babha Guest House*, Panchnath Rd, excellent veg restaurant. There are several **F** Guest Houses nr the shopping complex in Lakhajiraj Rd: ***Ashok***, Dhebar Chowk, nr Municipal Office, T 27144; ***Himalaya***, clean, good value; ***Circuit House***, Sardarbagh; ***Atithigriha*** may be available, contact Collector; ***Railway Retiring Rooms*** on 1st Flr, 3 clean rm (1 a/c), 4-bed dorm, reasonable veg restaurant, good value.

● Places to eat

Kanchan, in *Hotel Tulsi* is expensive, but excellent; ***Rainbow*** Lakhajiraj Rd, good S Indian food; Varied menu at ***Havmor***, nr *Galaxy Hotel*, good value.

● Post & telecommunications

GPO: MG Rd. **Telegraph Office**: just N of MG Rd opp Jubilee Gardens.

● Shopping

Shopping complex in Lakhajiraj Rd, a bazar to its E and a fruit market just N of Jubilee Gardens.

● Tourist office

In Jubilee Gardens, nr Watson Museum, T 31616.

● Transport

Rajkot is well connected by road to all the

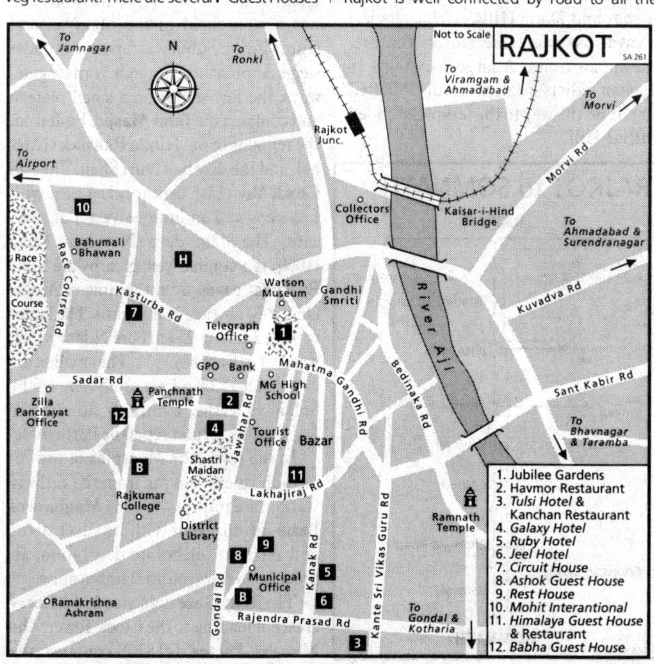

towns of the Kathiawad Peninsula, across to Kachchh and N to Rajasthan.

Air Daily *Indian Airlines*, *Angel's Hotel*, Dhebar Chowk: **Bombay** via Bhuj: W,F,Sa, 1310, 2 hr. *East West Airlines*: **Bombay**: daily, 1050, 1 hr 20 min. Airlines bus to town.

Train Bombay (Central): *Saurashtra Exp* 9216, daily 0030, 18¾ hr; *Saurashtra Janata Exp* 9018, daily 1430, 15¼ hr. **Ahmadabad**: same trains as to Bombay; 5¾ hr; 5¼ hr; **Vadodara**: same as to Bombay, 9¾ hr; 8 hr. **Porbandar**: *Saurashtra Exp* 9215, 0205, 4¾ hr.

Road Good service to main towns in Gujarat. Private Luxury buses to Ahmadabad and Bombay daily run by *Eagle Travels*. Junagadh (2 hr), Veraval (5 hr), Jamnagar and Dwarka all served regularly.

RAJKOT TO JUNAGADH, VERAVAL AND SOMNATH

Junagadh is situated on the edge of the Girnar and Datta Hills. Archaeological excavations place the site in the pre-Harappan times. A large rock with 14 Asokan edicts (dating from 250 BC) stands on the way to the temple-studded Girnar Hill.

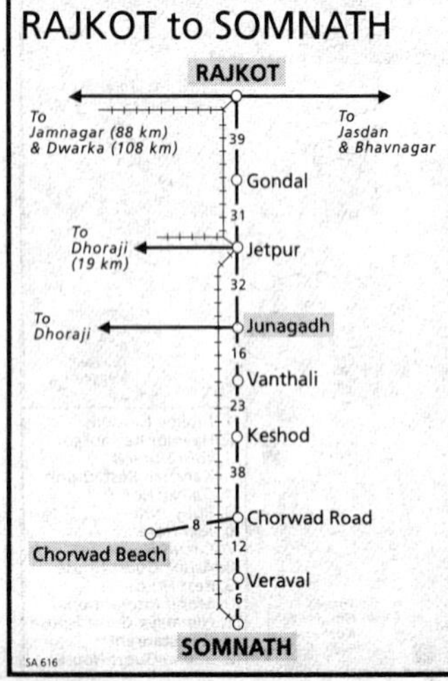

Junagadh

(*Population*: 167,100; *STD Code*: 0285) From the 2nd to 4th centuries Junagadh was the capital of Gujarat under the Kshattrapa rulers. It is also associated with the **Chadva Rajputs** who ruled from Junagadh from 875. The fort was expanded in 1472 by Mahmud Beghada, and again in 1683 and 1880. At the time of Partition, the ruler wanted his tiny princely state to join Pakistan. His subjects were predominantly Hindu and their will prevailed. He was exiled.

Places of interest

The town is surrounded by an old wall, large parts of which are now gone, but the narrow winding lanes and colourful bazars are evocative of earlier centuries. You can often find excellent embroidery work in the shops.

Uparkot citadel The old citadel of Uparkot lies in the NE of the town and was a stronghold in the Mauryan and Gupta Empires, but was repeatedly under siege. Approached through 3 ornate gateways, the fort stands on a small plateau and contains the **Jami Masjid**, built from the remains of the Hindu Ranakdevi Mahal, and the Tomb of Nuri Shah. The **Adi Chadi Vav** (15th century) is a *baoli* with 172 steps and an impressive spiral staircase. The 52m deep **Navghan Kuva** (1060) is a similar well. Nearby are some **Buddhist caves** from the time of Asoka. On the W wall are 2 large guns, The larger is the 5.2m long 25 cm bore Nilam which was cast in Egypt in 1531. The smaller, the Chudanal, is 3.8m long. Both were left by Sulaiman Pasha, a Turkish Admiral, to assist the local ruler repel the Portuguese.

In the town, the Mausolea of the Junagadh rulers, not far from the railway station, are impressive. The **Maqbara of Baha-ud-din Bhar** with its silver doors and intricate, elaborate decoration, almost has a fairground flamboyance.

The **Reay Gate** is an arcaded 2-storey crescent leading to the Clock Tower. The **Nawabs Palace** (c1870) contains the

Durbar Hall Museum which houses regal memorabilia incl portraits, palanquins and weapons.

Parks & zoos

Sakar Bagh Zoo If you are unable to go to Gir, or did not have the good fortune to see the lions there, this small zoo has some. It is well kept and in addition to the lions has tigers and leopards among others. The garden also houses a fine museum with local paintings, manuscripts, archaeological finds and natural history. Open daily except Wed, 2nd and 4th Sat in the month. **Getting there** Take bus No 1, 2 or 6. 3.5 km N of the town centre on the Rajkot Rd.

Excursions

East of the town is the 259m long, 13.5m high **Willingdon Dam** (1936). Also in this direction is the **Girnar Hill**, which rises to 900m above the surrounding plain and has been an important religious centre for the Jains from the 3rd century BC. The ascent of this worn volcanic cone by 10,000 stone steps can take about 2 hrs in the heat but fortunately there are tea stalls en route. The central peak of the ridges that form the crater is about 650m. You start just beyond **Damodar Kund** in teak forest. At the foot is the Asoka Edict, carved in the ancient Pali script on a large boulder. Later Sanskrit inscriptions were added in 150 AD and 450 AD by Sakandagupta, the last Mauryan Emperor. Open

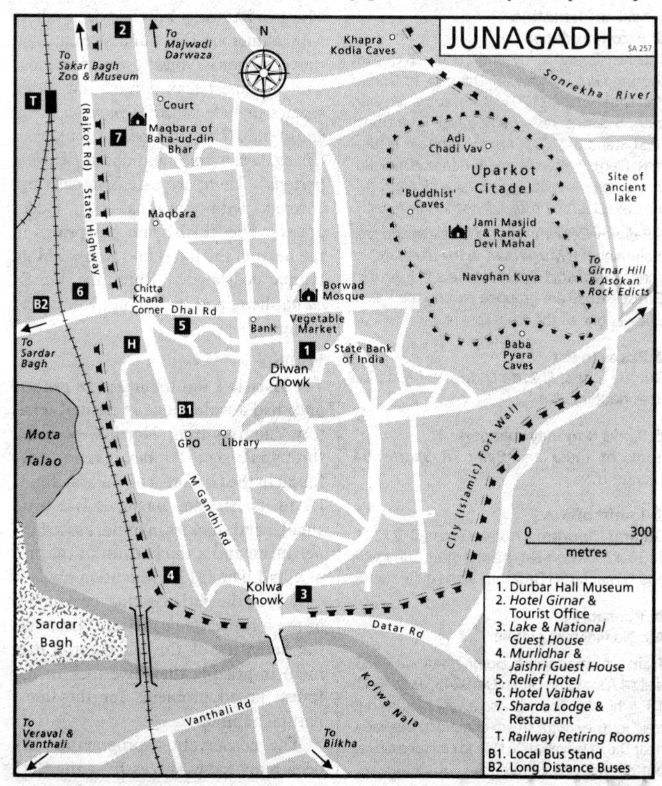

0900-1200, 1500-1800. A group of 16 Jain temples surmounts the hill. The 2 near the top are the **Neminatha** (1128), one of the oldest, and **Mallinatha** temples (1231) dedicated to the 19th Tirthankar. The corbelled domes, maidens and flying figures as decoration are typical of the Solanki period. A popular fair is held here during the Kartika Purnima Festival in Nov/Dec. There is also the **Temple of Samprati Raja** (1453), a fine example of the later period and the **Melak Vasahi Temple** (15th century). **Getting there** You can take an hourly No 3 or 4 bus from the stand opp the GPO to Girnar Taleti at the foot of the hill. It passes the Asoka edicts. About Re 1.

Local information

● Accommodation

The first 2 are nr rly and centre. **E** Gujarat Tourism *Girnar*, Majwadi Darwaja, nr Durbar Hall Museum, T 21201, 8 rm, some a/c with bath, 8 dorms, restaurant, travel; **E** *Vaibhav*, nr ST Stand, T 21070, 48 rm, some a/c, restaurant (veg), coffee shop; **E** *Relief*, Dhal Rd, dining hall, friendly, good value; **E** *National* (nr *Lake Guest House*), very good value, rec.

F *Railway Retiring Rooms* are clean and well maintained; **F** *Murlidhar*, with restaurant, its annexe **F** *Jai Shri Guest House* and **F** *Tourist Guest House* are grouped around the Kalwa Chowk, one of the main squares.

● Places to eat

Outside hotels, *Sharda Lodge* nr Rly station does good *thalis*.

● Banks & money changers

Bank of India and Bank of Saurashtra change TCs.

● Tourist offices

Gujarat Tourism, *Hotel Girnar*, T 21201, 1130-1700 Mon-Sat, helpful staff, *Junagadh and Girnar* by SH Desai on sale, is quite useful.

● Transport

Air No flights at present.

Train Ahmadabad: *Somnath Mail* 9823, daily, 1706, 12 hr; *Girnar Exp* 9845, daily, 1941, 10½ hr. **NB** There is also a very picturesque train journey (with steam engine) to Delwada, near Diu. It leaves at 0615 and can take all day, but is a very attractive ride.

Road **Bus**: regular bus services to Ahmadabad, Rajkot, Veraval, Porbandar and Sasan Gir.

Sasan Gir National Park

Approach

The Park covers a total area of 1412 sq km in the Saurashtra peninsula, of which about 10% is forest. The cattle invasion and agricultural colonisation are partly responsible for this small proportion, but much of the natural vegetation in the region was scrub jungle. Season Dec-Jun; Best Mar-May, closed during monsoons. Temp range: 42°C to 7°C. Rainfall: 1000 mm.

Background

The area has rocky hills and deep valleys with numerous rivers and streams, and the vegetation is typically semi-deciduous with dry-forest teak dominating. Other species include sadad (*Terminalia crenulata*), tendu (*Diospyros melanoxylon*), palas (*Butea monosperma*) and dudhi (*Wrightia tinctoria*). There are extensive clearings covered with savannah-like fodder grasses. The **Tulsishyam hotsprings** in the heart of the forest and **Kankai Mata temple** dedicated to Bhim, the *Mahabharata* hero, and his mother Kunti, add interest.

Wildlife

The **Asiatic Lion** (*Panthera leo persica*) once had a wide range in natural territory running from North-West India through Persia to Arabia. It is now only found in the Gir forest of Gujarat. Similar to its African cousin, it is a little smaller and stockier in build, has a thinner mane and a thicker tuft at the end of its tail. The 1913 census accounted for only 20 in the park. Gradual conversion of the forest into agricultural land and the activities of the *maldharis* (cattle men) in grazing their livestock in the forest, posed problems for the lions' natural habitat.

The conservation programme has been remarkably successful – the 1985

Census showed 239, and the 1990, 270 lions; according to a senior research fellow at the Wildlife Institute of India, far too many for the area of the sanctuary!

Apart from the lion, over 2000 nilgai and 1000 chinkara, Gir has common langur, leopard, hyena, sambar, chital, chowsingha and wild pig. The **chowsingha** is exclusively Indian and is unique in being the only wild animal where the male has 2 pairs of horns. The does are hornless. It is found on flat hilltop where there is short herbage. Like its nearest relative, the African kilpspringer, it can jump high from almost a standing start. The large population of over 8000 chital provide suitable prey for the lion in place of cattle.

Attacks There has been a spate of complaints about the rise in attacks on villagers by lions from the parks. Lions were reported as wandering up to 60 km from the park boundary. Villagers blamed the sanctuary's new policy of excluding the cattle herds of *maldharis*. They believed that stray cattle from these herds offered ideal prey for the lions, and their removal is now forcing lions to look elsewhere for food.

You can be sure of sighting the animal with the help of a tracker and guide. Jeeps with guides available.

Park information

● Accommodation

D Gujarat Tourism ***Lion Safari Lodge***, Sasan Gir, T 21, 24 rm with bath, 6 comfortable a/c, restaurant, tours of sanctuary and folk dances.

E ***Forest Dept Guesthouse***, small chalets with bath, spacious gardens, book direct 2 weeks in advance or through Gujarat Govt Office, Dhanraj Mahal, Apollo Bunder, Bombay, T 257039 or Information Centre, Baba Kharak Singh Marg, New Delhi, T 343147.

Also in the park **F** Gujarat Tourism ***Toran Holiday Home***, Tulsishyam, 4 rm, checkout 0900.

● Transport

Air Nearest airport is Keshod (86 km).

Train Daily slow train direct from Junagadh to Sasan Gir (2½ hr), continuing on to Delwada near Diu. Sasan station is 10 min walk from the Forest Lodge.

Road Service from Junagadh (54 km), 2½ hr, and one from Veraval (2 hr).

South to Somnath

ROUTES Continue SW to Vanthli (15 km). The road goes straight on, a road on the right leading to Porbandar. Continue to Keshod (20 km), the nearest point of entry to the Sasan Gir National Park (see above).

Chorwad (38 km from Keshod), is a popular beach resort. It is greener than the surrounding area with rocky outcrops on the beach.

• Accommodation D ***Palace Beach Resort***, T 96, the former summer palace of the Nawabs of Junagadh built in 1928 on the sea shore now offers 12 rm in Palace, 18 in annexe, also 40 cottages and dorm, comfortable resort hotel with a pool combining rustic charm with modern amenities, rec.

• Transport Train Chorwad Road station in 8 km from the resort.

Veraval

(*Population*: 105,000; *STD Code*: 02876) Before the rise of Surat, Veraval was the major seaport for pilgrims to Mecca. Its importance now is as a fishing port with dhows still being built by the sea. It is a noisy, extremely smelly, and not particularly attractive town, but it is a suitable base for visiting the Hindu pilgrimage centre of Somnath at Prabhas Patan – see below.

• Accommodation E Gujarat Tourism ***Toran Tourist Bungalow***, College Rd, T 20488, 6 rm, 5 dorm; **E** ***Circuit House***, nr the lighthouse have pleasant sea views. Others are noisy – The **E** ***Satkar***, nr Bus Stand, T 120, is well maintained and clean, some a/c rm plus a dormitory, restaurant. ***Railway Retiring Rooms*** and **F** ***Chandrani Guesthouse*** nearby.

• Places to eat ***Satkar*** does good *thalis*. ***La'Bela*** is quite good. ***Swati*** (a/c) and ***New Apsara*** nr rly station serve veg food.

• Transport Air Nearest airport is Keshod. Daily flight from Bombay. No Indian Airlines

Office, but *Somnath Travels*, Satta Bazar, T 162, will obtain tickets. **Train Ahmadabad**: *Somnath Mail* 9823, daily, 1445, $14\frac{1}{2}$ hr; *Girnar Express* 9845, daily, 1745, $12\frac{1}{2}$ hr. **Road** To **Keshod** (1 hr), Diu via Kodinar, Porbandar via Chorvad and Mangrol and also to **Bhavnagar** (9 hr).

Somnath

6 km E of Veraval. The **Somnath Temple**, a major Hindu pilgrimage centre, is said to have been built out of gold by Somraj, the Moon God (and subsequently in silver, wood and stone). In keeping with the legend the stone façade appears golden at sunset. Mahmud of Ghazni plundered it and removed the gates in 1024. Destroyed by successive Muslim invaders, it was rebuilt each time on the same spot.

The final reconstruction did not take place until 1950 and is still going on. Unfortunately, it lacks character but it has been built to traditional patterns with a soaring 50m high tower that rises in clusters. Dedicated to Siva, it has one of the 12 sacred *Jyotirlingas* (see page 382).

Krishna was believed to have been hit by an arrow, shot by the Bhil, Jara, when he was mistaken for a deer at Bhalka Teerth nearby, and was cremated at Triveni Ghat.

Nearby is the ruined **Rudreshvara Temple** which dates from the same time as the Somnath Temple and was laid out in a similar fashion. The sculptures on the walls and doorways give an indication of what the Somnath Temple was like.

Museum

There is a small **Archaeological Museum** with pieces from the former temples. 0900-1200, 1500-1800, closed Wed and holidays.

- **Accommodation F** *Mayuram*, Triveni Rd, restaurant, good food, clean; **F** *Shri Somnath Guest House*, nr Temple has 20 very basic rm, better accommodation at Veraval.

- **Transport** You can reach Somnath from Veraval by auto-rickshaw (Rs 15) or bus (Re 1.50).

RAJKOT TO PORBANDAR

ROUTES The road runs S past the central hills of Kathiawad Peninsula then W to Porbandar, a small port.

Porbandar

(*Population*: 160,200; *STD Code*: 0286). The former capital of the Jethwa Rajput petty princely state. It was previously named Sudamapuri, after *Krishna's* devoted friend; it has a temple dedicated to her. The tradition of *dhow* building which continues on the seashore to the present day reflects its maritime past when it traded with North Africa and Arabia. Today, Porbandar produces gold and silver trinkets, manufactures fine quality silk and cotton and has chemical and cement factories.

Places of interest

Mahatma Gandhi was born in Porbandar (1869). Next to the house with its carved balconies is **Kirti Mandir**, a small museum that traces his life and contains memorabilia and a library. The **Planetarium** here has shows in Gujarati

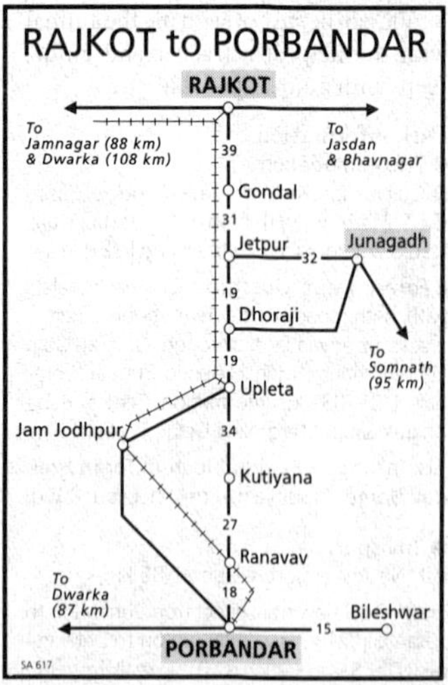

RAJKOT to PORBANDAR

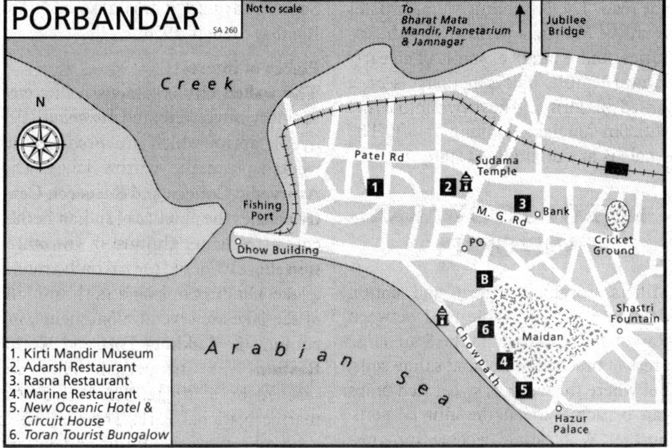

only. The architecture incorporates different religious styles illustrating Gandhi's open mind. The **Bharat Mandir Hall** is situated in Dayananda Vatika across the Jubilee (Jyubeeli) Bridge, a pleasant irrigated garden. It has a large marble relief map of India on the floor and bas reliefs of heroes from Hindu legends on the pillars. The Maharana's deserted **Hazur Palace** is near the sea front. Nearby **Arya Kanya Gurukul** is an experiment in education for girls based on ancient Indian tradition.

NB: Swimming is not recommended in the harbour.

Excursions

Bileshwar approx 15 km E of Porbandar. The **Siva Temple** dates from the early 7th century and is one of the finest examples of early Hindu architecture in Gujarat. The enclosure is later but the temple itself has a multi-storey tower (*shikhara*) which is more like a pyramid than a spire. The exterior is decorated with arch-like motifs but much of the detail has been obscured by a later plaster coating.

In the picturesque wooded valley at **Ghumli** a few km further inland there are ruins dating back to the Solanki period (10th-13th centuries). The **Vikia Vav** (early 12th century) is one of the largest step-wells in Gujarat. Pavilions were constructed over the steps with one at the entrance. All were richly carved. The well also served a religious purpose as a water sanctuary. Nearby is a ruined early 13th century **Naulakha Temple** (meaning 900,000, possibly reflecting its cost in rupees).

Local information

● Accommodation

D Gujarat Tourism *Toran Tourist Bungalow*, Chowpatty, 3 km from centre, T 22746. 20 rm, 6 large a/c, 4 dorm, checkout 0900, quiet, sea views, well kept. Nearby **D** *New Oceanic*, has 4 rm, a/c available; **D** *Sheetal*, is opp the GPO, with some a/c rm. **E** *Paradise Lodge*, SV Patel Rd. **D** *Flamingo*, with some a/c rm, and the basic **F** *Rajkamal Guest House* are on MG Rd opp State Bank of India. **E** *Rly Retiring Rooms*.

● Transport

Train Bombay Central: *Saurashtra Exp* 9216, daily, 2000, 23¼ hr. Also services with Rajkot and Ahmadabad.

Road To Veraval (3 hr).

Gop

Approximately 50 km NE of Porbandar and midway on the Porbandar-Jamnagar road. The 6th century temple dates from the Maitraka period (6th-8th centuries) and is a rare example of an early Hindu temple. The sanctuary is on a raised platform and has a pyramidal roof with an amalaka topping it off. The whole is in a dilapidated state.

RAJKOT TO DWARKA AND OKHA

Millets, sorghum, wheat and cotton dominate the cultivable land between Rajkot and the coast. To the S are large areas of brackish water and saline soils, but where the water is sweet rich crops can be achieved on the alluvial soils. Further W farming becomes progressively more marginal, and towards Dwarka clay soils are occasionally interspersed with higher limestones.

Jamnagar

(*Population*: 381,600; *STD Code*: 0288) A small 16th century pearl fishing town and capital of the Jadeja Rajputs minor princely state of Nawanagar. The famous cricketer Ranjitsinghji was its ruler from 1907-33 and his successor, Jam Sahib, became the President of Saurashtra until it was absorbed into Bombay State in 1956.

Places of interest

The walled city is famous for its embroidery, silverware and *bandhani* (tie-dyed) fabrics which are produced in workshops in the narrow lanes. The **Ayurvedic College and Research Centre** teaches the practice of Indian herbal cures (see under **Culture** in **Introduction** above). The old town is built around a lake. On Pirotan Island in the middle of the lake are several monuments, including the **Lakhota Fort** and **Kotha Bastion** with its arsenal. They are reached by a bridge. There is also a marine National Park. The fort has a good collection of sculpture and pottery found in ruined medieval villages. Open Th-Tues, 0900-1200, 1500-1800. The bastion has an old well from which water can be drawn by blowing into a small hole in the floor. The **Solarium** uses solar radiation to cure diseases.

• **Accommodation** **D** *President*, Teen Batti, T 70516, 27 rm, some a/c with TV, central, restaurant; **D** *Aashiana*, Supermarket, 3rd Flr, T 77421, has some a/c rm; **D** *Daavati*, Bagga Mansions, opp Amber Cinema. The Supermarket area has other **D** hotels on upper

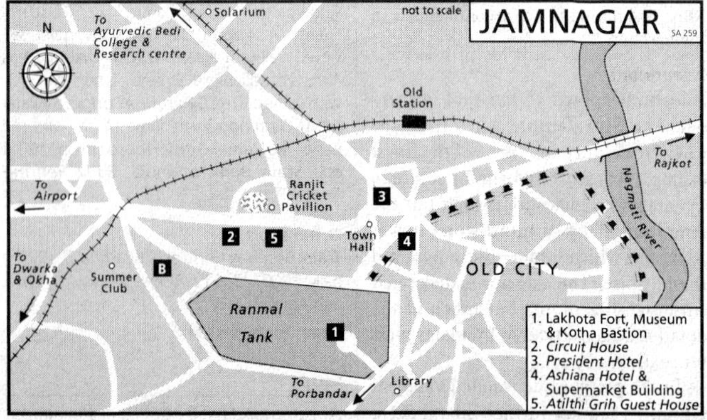

flrs. **E** Gujarat Tourism *Toran Tourist Dormitory*, has rm and dorm. Other **E** and **F** hotels on old Station Rd.

• **Transport Air** There is a daily flight from Bombay that continues on to Bhuj. **Train** Ahmadabad: *Saurashtra Exp* 9216, daily, 2251, 7½ hr; *Saurashtra Mail* 9006, daily, 1435, 7½ hr. **Bombay Central**: *Saurashtra Exp* 9216, daily, 2251, 20¼ hr; *Saurashtra Mail* 9006, daily, 1440, 17½ hr. **Road** Several buses to Rajkot and Porbandar.

Dwarka

(*Population*: 27,800; *STD Code*: 02892) Dwarka has the unique distinction of being one of Hinduism's 4 Holy Abodes as well as one of its 7 Holy Places. It is one of the most sacred sites for Vaishnavite Hindus, celebrated as Krishna's capital. A small coastal town on the tip of the Kathiawad peninsula, it is closely associated with the Krishna legend and it is believed that Krishna set up his capital here after his flight from Mathura. Archaeological excavations indicate that present day Dwarka is built on the sites of 4 former cities. Work in 1990 by the marine archaeologist SR Rao discovered triangular anchors weighing 250 kg, suggesting that ships of up to 120 tonnes had used the port. The anchors are believed to be identical to those used by ships from Cyprus and Syria during the Bronze Age, going back to the 14th century BC. Much of the town was submerged by rising sea levels. The evidence suggests that in the 15th century BC it was a large trading port, with fortifications and town planning.

The present town is largely 19th century when the Gaekwad princes developed the town as a popular pilgrimage centre and thousands of pilgrims come every year to celebrate Krishna's birthday and at Holi and Diwali. A pilgrimage to Dwarka is not complete until a visit has been made to **Beyt Dwarka**, a Hindu temple on the island off the coast. The 19th century temple contains a series of shrines and images of Krishna and his 56 consorts. Archaeological excavations have revealed Harappan artefacts dating from the 2nd millennium BC.

The 12th century **Rukmini Temple** and the mainly 16th century **Dvarakadisha Temple** attract thousands of pilgrims each year. The Rukmini Temple has beautifully carved mandapa columns and a fine sanctuary doorway, but much else is badly weathered. The Dvarakadisha Temple was supposedly built in 1 night, and some believe that the inner sanctum is 2500 years old. Non-Hindus usually cannot enter. The sanctuary walls probably date from the 12th century but Michell argues that the 50m high tower which rises in a series of balconied layers is much later. The exterior is more interesting. The soaring 5-storey tower is supported by 60 columns. The BJP started its '*Rath Yatra*' pilgrimage across India to the Babri Masjid mosque in Ayodhya here in 1989, leading to widespread communal rioting.

Local festival

Aug/Sep It is an important site for the *Janmashtami* festival – see Bombay (page 1134).

• **Accommodation** **F** *Toran Tourist Dormitories*, T 3136 rm, 12 dorms, nr Govt Guest House, checkout 0900. *Railway Retiring Room* and a number of small cheap hotels.

• **Transport Train** Ahmadabad: *Saurashtra Mail* 9006, daily, 1158, 10 hr. **Bombay Central**: *Saurashtra Mail* 9006, daily, 1203, 20 hr.

Okha

A small port at the head of the Gulf of Kachchh, Okha is about 30 km N of Dwarka. A few **F** category hotels here. The island nearby is connected with the legend of Vishnu slaying the demon.

• **Transport Train** Ahmadabad: *Saurashtra Mail* 9006, daily, 1115, 10¼ hr. **Road** Local buses connect Okha with Dwarka.

AHMADABAD TO BHUJ

ROUTES The route to Kachchh follows the NH8A out of Ahmadabad, going towards Rajkot (see above) as far as Chotila. The road continues down the gentle gradient to the waste land of the Little Rann of Kachchh, which it crosses at the narrowest point some 25 km inland of the Gulf of Kachchh. Once across the mud and salt flats the NH8A curves S to Gandhidham while the road to Bhuj goes straight across the semi desert.

Wankaner

(*Population*: 36,600) The Raja of Wankaner came to a political arrangement with the East India Company in 1807. It was then left largely to its own devices through the 19th century. Maharaja Amarsinghji (1881-1948) introduced wide-ranging reforms. He was also responsible for building the **Ranjitvilas Palace**, visible for miles across the plains. It is built in a variety of European and Indian styles. Today, the summer palace is run by Maharajah Pratapsinghji as a hotel. **Accommodation** C *Ranjitvilas Palace*, T 363621, Contact Secretary, Palace, Wankaner, price includes 3 meals per day, served in the Vijniwas Palace, 2 km from Ranjitvilas. Only really suitable if you have transport, but it is from another age – faded mosquito nets, no water in the swimming pool, lots of retainers – and a strong mosqito spray recommended in the evenings!

Morvi

(29 km; *Population*: 120,100) The capital of another tiny princely state, Morvi dominated access to the Peninsula. Making use of the trade route, it developed into a modern state under the leadership of Thakur Sahib Waghaji (r1879-1948). There are 2 palaces of interest. The older is the **Dubargadh Waghaji Palace** (1880), with a Venetian Gothic exterior and Rajput, Gothic and Indo-Saracenic features inside. It is approached by a suspension bridge. The **New Palace** (1931-44) contains some late Art Deco features, like the Umaid Bhavan Palace in Jodhpur, and similarly includes some subterranean rm.

Kachchh

Kachchh is the northwesternmost part of Gujarat, the least appealing climatically, the most sparsely populated and well and truly off the beaten tourist trail. The various communities such as Rabaris, Ahirs and Meghwals among others, each have a distinct dress and practise a particular craft.

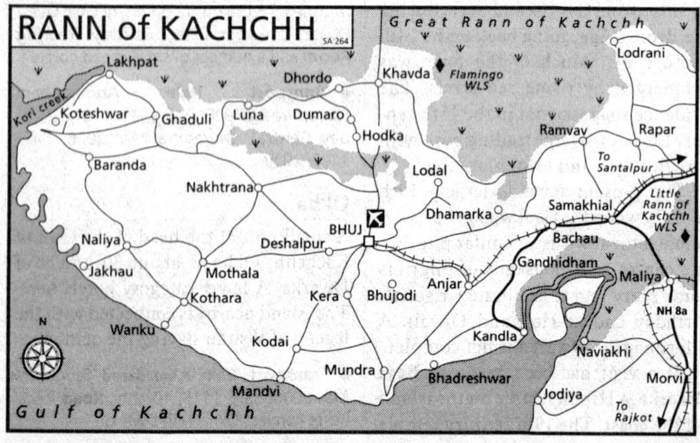

The Rann The low lying Rann of Kachchh in the N, a part of the Thar desert, is a hard smooth bed of dried mud in the dry season. Some vegetation exists, concentrated on little grassy islands called *bets*, which remain above water level when the monsoons flood the mudflats.

The **Little Rann of Kachchh Wildlife Sanctuary** is here. *Climate*: Temp: Max 42°C, Min 7°C; *Annual Rainfall*: 1000 mm; *Season*: Open to visitors Feb-May.

The Little Rann is the only place where the Asiatic wild ass (locally called *khacchar* or *ghroker*) is found. The herds of the endangered species that roam this barren area feed at night on vegetation at the edge, then retreat inland during the day and so are difficult to see. The fawn coloured ass has a dark stripe that runs down the back; it can reach a speed of 50 kmph. A sanctuary (4840 sq km) was created for them in 1973 but visiting can be difficult as it is a sensitive border area. Other mammals found here include blackbuck, blue bull, wild boar, chinkara, wolf and desert cat. **Accommodation** Dhrangadhra Govt *Rest Houses* and *Desert Coursers Camp*. Gujarat Tourism plans to open a Tourist complex.

The monsoon With the arrival of the SW monsoon in May the saltwater of the Gulf of Kachchh invades the Rann and the Rajasthan rivers pour fresh water into it. It then becomes an inland sea and very dangerous for those who get trapped in it. In ancient times armies have perished there. At this time Kachchh virtually becomes an island. From Dec to Feb, The **Great Rann** is the winter home of migratory flamingoes when they arrive near Khevda. You will also see sand-grouse, Imperial grouse, pelicans and avocets.

An important activity is **salt** production and railway lines back into the Rann to facilitate the transport of it.

Handicrafts Local traditional embroidery and weaving is particularly prized. When the monsoons flooded vast areas of Kachchh, farming had to be abandoned, handicrafts flourished which not only gave expression to artistic skills, but also provided a means of earning a living. Mirrorwork, Kachchh appliqué and embroidery with beads, *bandhni* (tie-and-dye), embroidery on leather, gold and silver jewellery, gilding and enamelling and colourful wool-felt *namda* rugs are available (see also **Craft villages** below). The *Desert Festival*, where craftsmen demonstrate their skills, is held in Feb/Mar.

Gandhidhem

(*Population*: 104,600; *STD Code*: 02836). Gandhidham was founded by the Maharaos of Kachchh to accommodate refugees from Sindh in Pakistan after Partition in 1947. **Accommodation** **D** *Shiv*, 360 Ward 12-B (1 km from rly station, T 21297, 39 rm, some a/c, restaurant, travel.

Bhadreshwar, 36 km W along the coast from Gandhidam was important as an ancient seaport and has a temple and 2 mosques. The **Jain Temple** (1248) is attractive where the main building is surrounded by small shrines which together reproduce the shape and form of the temple itself. The archway leading into the enclosure, added in the mid 12th century, shows Islamic influence. The more important of the 2 mosques is the **Solah Khambi Masjid** which is the only known Islamic structure that existed before the Muslim conquests. All its original features are intact. A further 27 km to the S of Gandhidham is the new port of **Kandla**, built to take some of the trade from the Punjab which had been handled by Karachi before Independence.

Bhuvad 19 km SW of Anjar on the Mundra Rd, Bhuvad has the ruined 13th century temple of **Bhuvaneshwar Mahadev**. The 10m by 12m mandapa is supported by 34 pillars of rather unusual design, having a square base up to a third of their height surmounted by a round upper section. The inscription on the right of the shrine gives the dates 1289-90. A local legend describes how the headless body of the chieftain Bhuvad, who was killed in battle about 1320, fought its way to the village. The District Gazetteer records that a shrine with a red painted headless figure is dedicated to him, while the nearby tall shrines are said to have been raised over warriors killed in the same battle.

Bhuj

(*Population*: 120,000; *STD Code*: 02832). Despite its rapid growth since Independence, a result of the location of several state and central government offices in the town, Bhuj retains much of its picturesque character. The **Bhujia Fort** (1718-41) stands on a hill to the SE, while it is bounded on the W by the Hamirsagar Lake and the often dry Desalsar to the E. The Fort, 75m above the cantonment has a temple to the guardian deity *Bhujang Naag* (serpent). The town's 10.5m high stone defensive wall forming an irregular polygon studded with towers and 5 gates, is a reminder of Bhuj's medieval defences; the local raja Rao Khengarji I chose this to be his capital in 1548. The existing walls were built in 1723, though subsequently the town fell twice to attacking forces, on the latter occasion to the British in 1819. Far greater damage was caused in the same year, by the great earthqauke of Gujarat, which is reported to have destroyed 7000 houses and killed over 1000 people. Some of the older buildings survived and can still be seen. The E wall of the city was knocked down after Independence to allow for the growth of the town, but the old part of the town is still a tightly packed maze of winding streets, full of character.

Places of interest

Aina Mahal Among the palace buildings is **Rao Lakha's Palace** (c 1750) a large white mansion with carvings and fretwork which contained a Darbar Hall, the State Apartments and the noted **Aina Mahal** (Mirror Palace) which displays the Maharao's collection. Surrounded by a verandah, the 14m long Mahal cost a fortune (£200,000). It has exquisite ivory inlaid doors (c1708), china tiles on the floor and marble walls covered with mirrors and gilt decorations, the roof and pillars decorated with rich gold mouldings. In 1823, Col Tod described the English and Dutch chiming clocks on the floor, all playing at once! There are portraits, 18th century lithographs, crystals and paintings. In the centre of the State Apartments nearby is Rao Lakha's small square bedroom with the central platform ('bed') surrounded by water, where the Maharao sat in cool comfort. Ingenious pumps, designed by Ramsingh Malam, raise water to the tank with sprinkling fountains. Near the entrance is the **Tourist office**.

Rao Pragmalji's Palace is across the courtyard. Designed by the British engineer Col Wilkins, the palace was begun in 1865 to replace some stables and outhouses. It contained a vast Darbar Hall (25m x 12m) and 12m high with verandahs, corner towers and *zenanas* all opulantly decorated with carving, gilding, Minton tiles and marble. It is now used as Govt offices so only the Darbar Hall is open to visitors (0900-1130, 1500-1730; closed Wed, 2nd and 4th Sat in month). The **Tourist Office** is near the entrance. There are good views of the Rann of Kachchh from the tall clock-tower connected to the palace by covered galleries. The colourful new **Swaminarayan Temple** is behind the Palace and near the bazar. The busy bazar sells local crafts and textiles among more mundane necessities.

The **Maharaos' chhattris** (locally called *chatedis*), or memorial tombs, built of red sandstone just outside the town walls to the W, were severely damaged in the 1819 earthquake. Rao Lakha's polygonal chhattri (1770) has a

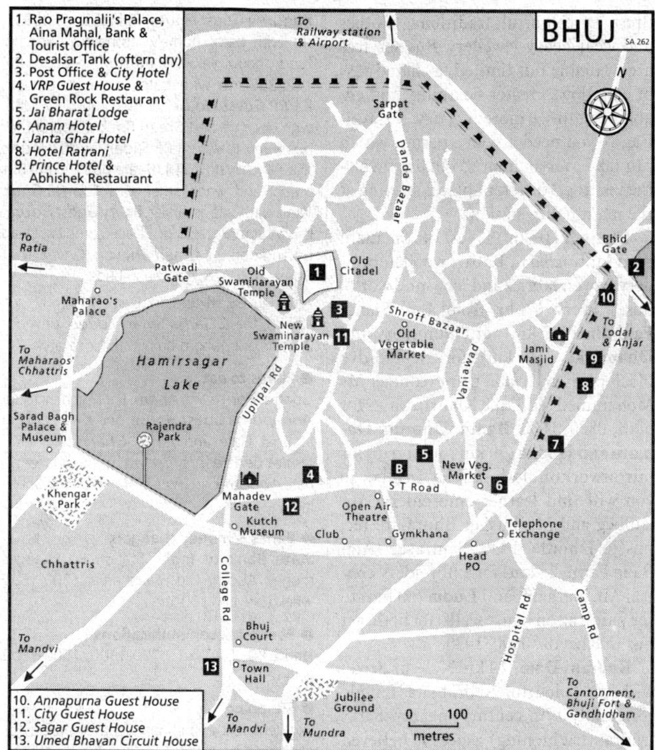

carved roof supported by pillars and contains beautiful statues of deities, Rao Lakha on horseback and tablets of 15 court musicians who committed *jauhar* after his death. That of Rao Pragmalji's father, Rao Desalji, has impressively carved wall panels, while Rao Pragmalji's own cenotaph has some excellent modern carving.

Museums

The Kachchh Museum, (formerly Fergusson Museum, 1877) nr the Mahadev Gate, built facing the lake in an Italianate style, is the oldest in Gujarat. Exhibits include the largest collection of Kshatrap inscriptions, the earliest going back to 89 AD, textiles, weaponry, paintings and an anthropological section. Well maintained. **Aina Mahal Museum** see above. Both open daily 0900-1130, 1500-1730; closed Wed, 2nd and 4th Sat in month.

Excursions

Craft villages A visit to nearby villages can be a memorable experience. The rural population live in small communities; round mud houses (*bhungas*) which have a central pole supporting the thatched or tiled roof are built around a courtyard; colourful embroidered hangings, and typical local pottery with limepaste and mirrorwork decoration brighten the interiors; weaving communities have pit looms at home. They still dress in colourful traditional clothes and wear heavy jewellery. Bus services are available but limited; a shared taxi or car allows greater flexibility and enables you to see more in a day. If travelling N you need a police permit which can take over an hour to obtain, involving visiting 3 different places starting at the main police station.

Bhujodi (10 km) is just off the main road for *bandhani*, Rabari wool embroidery, woven fabrics and "cowmud work"; buses every ½ hr from Bus Stand. **Padhdhar** (22 km) for embroidery and **Dhamarka** (50 km) for tie-and-dye block print and *chuni* print (contact Mr Mohammed Siddique Khatri); buses for both, 0820, 1000. **Banni**, **Dhordo**, **Dumaro** and **Hodka** (70 km round trip) for mirrorwork on cloth and clay. In Dhordo you will find leather embroidery; Mr. Gulbeg and Mr. Basher Bhura are rec; bus to Dhordo, 1330. **Samrasar** (Ami Baug Farm, 24 km) for embroidery contact Mr. Nathani, and **Ludia** (60 km) to see painting on house walls; for both, get bus to Khevda, 0900, 1430.

Rudrani Dam (14 km N, ½ hr drive) with the colourful Rudramata Temple (originally 17th century) nearby. Sati's 'rudra' (frightening) aspect is believed to have fallen on this spot and is hence a place of pilgrimage; see page 71 and **Accommodation** below.

Local festivals

Feb/Mar: Four day *Rann Festival* organised by Gujarat Tourism attracts tribal craftsmen, dancers and traders and provides an excellent insight into the cultural life in Bhun and surrounding villages.

Local information

● Accommodation

D *Prince*, Station Rd, T 20370, some a/c rm with bath, good restaurant, the reception also arranges excellent guided tours of local villages for Rs 325 per day plus a km charge for the car; **D** *Anam*, end of Station Rd, T 21390, some a/c rm with bath, good a/c veg restaurant, good value, rec.

F *Nilkanth Guest House* is nearby; **F** *Annapurna Guest House*, Bhid Gate, T 20831, rm with bath, homely, authentic Kachchhi food, good value; **F** *Ratrani*, Station Rd, T 22388, rm with bath, Indian restaurant; **F** *VRP Guest House*, nr Bus Stand, T 21388, with clean rm and *Green Rock* restaurant for good veg *thalis*, and **F** *Sagar Guest House*, Jilla Panchayat, T 21479, are both nr the Bus Station and hence rather noisy; **F** *Janta Ghar*, Vaniawad Gate, is similar; **F** *City Guest House*, Langa St in Bazar, S of Palace complex, clean rm and dorm; **F** *Umed Bhavan*, Govt Circuit House, T 20828, has cheap beds.

Alternatively, at Rudrani Dam (14 km N, see above), the **C** *Garha Safari Lodge*, provides 20 huts or *bhungas* built in the local style.

● Places to eat

Good at *Prince* and *Anam*. For Kutchchi food: *Annapurna Guest House*, and *Kisan Lodge* at Bhid Gate and *Janta Ghar* Station Rd. *Omlet Centre* for breakfast, nr the bus terminal. *Abhishek* nr *Prince Hotel* serves South Indian snacks.

● Banks & money changers

State Bank of India, Station Rd changes money. Also nr Old Palace area, 1100-1500 weekdays, till 1300 Sat.

● Post & telecommunications

Head PO: Lal Takri. 0700-1300, 1500-1800 (Mon-Sat).

● Shopping

Excellent folk embroidery, leather shoes, appliqué, mirrorwork, block-printed fabrics, painted pottery and local weaving are sold in the bazar. In Dandi Bazar: *Kutch Handicraft Society* and *Bandhani Ghar*. Also *Anand Store* in Langa St. *Mr. Shah's Handicrafts shop*. Mr. Shah's Handicrafts shop is particularly good for embroidery. Silver work is sold in Shroff Bazar. Villages nearby can offer real bargains.

● Tourist office

The Tourist Office is in the Aina Mahal. 0900-1200, 1500-1800, closed Sat. Town map, helpful staff.

● Useful addresses

Fire: T 21490. **Police**: T 20892.

● Transport

Local Taxis: (about Rs 350/day plus km charge); auto and cycle rickshaws.

Air The airport is 4 km from town; airlines bus or taxi. *Indian Airlines*, Station Rd, T 130, have daily flights from Bombay to Bhuj via Jamnagar. Dep M,Tu,Th,Sa,Su, 0830, 1hr. Because it is so near the Pakistan border, the security at the airport is tight. Pack cameras away in your checked luggage, along with knives, scissors and batteries.

Train The new station is just N of the city. Daily rail connection with Ahmadabad, but very slow. Also trains between Bhuj and Kandla Port. The most convenient train is the *Bombay-Gandhidham Kutch Exp* 9031, daily, 1715, 14½ hr, then 2 hr by bus or train to Bhuj. The same train departs Ahmadabad 0143, 6 hr.

Road Bus: there are buses to Ahmadabad (411 km) and other centres in Gujarat. Bus (or shared taxi) to Wankaner 3 hr, Rajkot 5 hr; 2 days to Jaisalmer via Barmer.

Mandvi

(*Population*: 37,000) Mandvi, 54 km SW of Bhuj, used to be the main port for Kachchh, though it has now been replaced by Kandla. It is a desert town, but today is home to important agricultural research for the Kachchh region. The Gujarat Agricultural University and the Vivekenand Research and Training Institute, a charitable trust, are carrying out a range of experiments to improve farming in the often hostile regional environment. Dry farming techniques including new water harvesting measures to improve ground water recharge are matched by the introduction of a new range of crops, notably those which tolerate saline soils. Sunflower, mustard, pomegranates, dates and figs are among the new commercial varieties being tested on the Gujarat Agricultural University's 10 ha plot outside the town. A recent report claims that rural de-population resulting from the lack of water is a continuing problem, over 770 of the 960 villages in the area having no safe water source. It is hoped that planting of drought tolerant trees like the *neem* or the saline tolerant fruit tree, the *pilu*, will raise the water table, allowing wells to be revived.

The Vijay Vilas Palace (1930s) near the beach was once the Maharaos' summer palace, and is being returned to its former glory. It had been stripped of its furniture and decorations when, for a time, the followers of Bhagwan Rajneesh (see page 1188) negotiated to purchase it. The caretaker will often take visitors around. Good views.

Lakhpat Situated at the NE end of the Kori Creek and the S edge of the Gt Rann of Kachchh, at Independence in 1947 Lakhpat was a town of 40,000 people. After Partition it became India's westernmost town, but the hostility between India and Pakistan ended the trade between Sindh and Gujarat on which it had depended. Today it is a ghost town with no more than 250 people, although the district still has a population of nearly 40,000.

AHMADABAD TO MOUNT ABU

ROUTES The **NH8** crosses the plains of the Sabarmati, following the railway line all the way to Abu Road. The fertile irrigated land immediately N of Ahmadabad gives way to increasingly arid northwards towards Rajasthan. Towards Mehsana there are signs of the growing economy; an oil and natural gas Commission project, a fertiliser plant, the very large milk processing plant, Dudhsagar, and a rape seed oil processing plant. There is a growing number of basic but modern and clean motels, such as the *Fun and Food Restaurant*, the *Hotel Asu Palace*, and the *Kausal*, 15, 20 and 25 km S of Mehsana respectively. In Mar the road between Mehsana and Modhera is lined with the stalls of wholesalers of chillies, now an important cash crop.

Modhera

Today Modhera is a virtually deserted hamlet. However, the partially ruined **Surya (Sun) Temple** (1026), built during the reign of Bhimdev I, and consecrated in 1026-27, 2 centuries before the Sun Temple at Konark, is one of the finest Hindu temples in Gujarat, a product of the great Solanki period (8th-13th centuries). Despite its partial destruction by subsequent earthquakes which may have accounted for the destruction of its tower, it remains an outstanding monument, set against the backdrop of a barren landscape. Superb carvings of goddesses, birds, beasts and blossoms on the pillars decorate the remaining pillars. Over the last 20 years it has undergone major restoration by the Archaeological Survey of India which is continuing as funds permit. Unlike the Sun Temple at Konark, the main temple stands well above the surrounding land, raised by a high brick terrace faced with stone.

The entrance A rectangular pool (kund, now dry), over 50m long and 20m wide, with flights of steps and subsidiary shrines, face the E front of the temple. It is a remarkable structure, and although many of the images in the subsidiary shrines are much weathered it is still possible to gain an impression of the excellence of the carving as well as of the grandiose scale on which the whole plan was conceived. On the W side of the tank a steep flight of steps lead up to the main entrance of the E mandapa through a beautifully carved torana, of which only the pillars now remain. **The sabha mandapa** The pillared hall is 15m square. Note the cusped arches which became such a striking feature of Mughal buildings 600 years later. The corbelled roof of this entry hall, which has been reconstructed, is a low stepped pyramid. Beautiful columns and magnificent carvings decorate the hall. **The raised sanctuary** The W part of the temple contains the inner sanctuary within its oblong plan. The upper storeys have been completely destroyed, though it clearly consisted of a low pyramidal roof in front of the tall sikhara (tower) over the sanctuary itself. Surya's image in the sanctuary (now missing) was once illuminated by the first rays of the rising sun at each solar equinox, though images of Surya and Agni are among the better preserved carvings on the external walls. Unlike the exterior, the interior walls were plain other than for niches to house images of Surya.

• **Accommodation** Gujarat Tourism ***Toran*** restaurant serves drinks and light meals. The **F *PWD Rest House*** has basic accommodation.

• **Transport** Far more off the beaten track and much less well known than the Sun Temple at Konark, Modhera retains a great deal of its atmosphere and charm. There are direct buses to Modhera from Ahmadabad. Alternatively, you can take the train to Mehsana (same as for Patan) and take a bus for the 35 km road trip to the site.

Patan

In the 8th century, Patan was the capital of the Hindu kings of Gujarat. Mahmud of Ghazni sacked it in 1024, and it was taken by Ala-ud-din Khalji's brother Alaf Khan in 1306. Off the beaten track, Patan has over 100 beautifully carved **Jain temples** and many attractive traditional carved wooden houses. It is a centre for fine textiles, particularly silk *patola* saris produced by the characteristic *ikat* technique. Little remains of the old city except some of the walls, **Rani Vav** (Queen's Well, late 11th century), a step well recently renovated, and the **Sahasra Linga** (1000 Linga) 12th century **Tank**.

• **Transport Train** Patan is 25 km N of Mehsana, the most suitable place for getting off the train.

BHUTAN

Contents

MAPS

OFFICIAL NAME *Druk-Yul*

CAPITAL Thimphu

NATIONAL FLAG Saffron and orange red, divided diagonally, with a white dragon in the centre.

OFFICIAL LANGUAGE Dzongkha

MEDIUM OF INSTRUCTION IN SCHOOLS English

BASICS *Population*: 1993 650,000. Urban 4%, Drukpas 70%, Nepali origin about 30%; *Birth rate*: 38:1000; *Death rate*: 17:1000; *Life expectancy*: 48; *Literacy*: 32%, M 45%, F 19%; *Land use*: forested, 70% permanent pasture and agriculture 9%, other 21%; *GNP per capita*: US$468; *Religion*: Buddhist 70%, Hindu 25%, Muslim 5%.

Land and life

Bhutan, dwarfed by its great neighbours India and China, and only one third the size of Nepal, is none the less slightly larger than Switzerland. Its official name, Druk-Yul, means 'Land of the Thunder Dragon', portrayed on the flag. It is perhaps the most mysterious and the least modernised country in South Asia. Never colonised, the country is today fully independent and maintains excellent relations with India. Consistently cautious with respect to contact with the outside world, the flow of tourists is tightly controlled. The government is making great efforts to uphold the country's religious and cultural traditions.

Geology and landscape

Location

Bhutan lies between 89° and 92°E and 27° and 28°N. India lies along the entire length of its S border with Tibet to its N, from which it is separated by the relatively narrow part of the High Himalaya.

The Land

To the N lies a chain of glacier mountains with several peaks over 7000m. The highest is **Kangkar Punsum** (7540m) and the most famous and picturesque is **Chomolhari** (7313m). In the W the watershed of the Tibetan Chumbi valley forms the border whose alignment has been repeatedly disputed by China.

The border with India was established by the British in the 18th and 19th centuries. In the S it generally runs along the base of the abruptly rising Himalayan foothills and in some areas it includes the N rim of the Brahmaputra river lowlands called the *Duars* (Hindi – gates), 18 of which have been cut by the Himalayan rivers. All the motor roads from the S pass through the Duars. In the W the boundary with Sikkim was also established by the British and accepted by India.

The largest part of the country is part of the middle Himalayan range with altitudes ranging from 1600 to 5000m. The rivers tend to run N-S and the Black Mountain Range forms a divide between the W and E parts of the country and is crossed by the **Pele La** (3369m).

Vegetation

The wet Duars are covered in lush forest with bamboos, ferns, hanging plants and giant orchids on banyan, giant sal and teak trees. As you move higher the forest thins out but there is still a wide range of trees: poplar, ash, aspen, magnolia, oak, conifers and beautiful rhododendron. Above 3000m bamboo and conifer forests take over, with fir, larch, cypress and pine. At 4000m birch, pine and rhododendron dominate and then give way to juniper and other bushes. Mosses and lichens can occasionally be found at high altitude and it is only in East Bhutan that the forest reaches the otherwise bleak N side of the main Himalaya range.

Wildlife

Monkeys, deer, buffalo, wild boars, bears, leopards, tigers and rhino are common. The rare and protected *bharal* blue sheep and takins live above 4000m. The **blue sheep** (*Pseudois nayaur*) rare elsewhere in the Himalaya, have thick sheep-like horns but goat-like legs with dark stripes on the flanks. They prefer plateaus for grazing and have a split lip which enables them to pull grass straight out of the ground rather than crop it. Takins (*Budorcas taxicolor*) are larger (over 1m at the shoulders), and short-legged. They have a shaggy dark brown coat with a lighter back; the snout is swollen and their thick horns splay out and then up and back. They live in small herds, often above the tree-line, and in spite of their stocky appearance are remarkably agile on steep slopes. The winter draws them down to bamboo and rhododendron forests, from which they emerge to graze in meadows, morning and evening.

There are also many kinds of birds and butterflies, and various reptiles. Manas Wildlife Park which stretches across the border into Assam, may be entered from the Indian side (closed at present, see page 690).

Climate

The monsoon begins in Jun and lasts until end of Sep when 85% of the annual rainfall is received. The windward S facing mountain slopes are the wettest areas.

Rainfall

In the Duars Plain and up to 1500m, the climate is sub-tropical with high humidity and heavy rainfall (2000-5000 mm). From 3000–4500m it is temperate with cold winters and cool summers. Here the rainfall averages 1000 mm-1500 mm per year. In the winter snowfall can close many passes. Above 4500m an alpine/arctic climate prevails with most areas permanently covered with snow and ice.

The climate within the mountains varies greatly according to sunshine, precipitation and wind conditions, yet is basically similar to the middle European climate. The daily air mass exchange between highland and lowlands often causes stormy winds frequently preventing rain in the middle portions of cross valleys so that between 900 to 1800m it is quite dry, requiring irrigation for farming while higher up it is often wet.

Temperature

Min temperatures range from -10°C (Paro, Thimphu) to 15°C (Southern Foothills); Max from 30°C (Southern Foothills) to 35°C (Paro, Thimphu).

History

Bhutan's recorded history dates the Buddhist monasteries of **Kyichu** in the W (Paro district) and the **Jampey Lhakhang** in the centre (Bumthang district) to the 7th century but liitle is known of the early history of the country and its inhabitants. In the 8th century Bhutan is believed to have been converted to Buddhism by the Tantric saint Padmasambhava. Following the disintegration of the Tibetan empire in the 9th century, waves of people came from Tibet to settle in Bhutan. Between the 11th and 15th century, the major Tibetan schools of Buddhism established monasteries in the country and cultural and economic ties with Tibet became important. Shabdrung Ngawang Namgyel is

considered the founder of unified Bhutan and was a lama of the Drukpa sect. He ruled the country as spiritual and secular leader in the 17th century and successfully repelled Tibetan and Mongolian attacks. His successors were believed to be reincarnations of his person. Spiritual and secular power were divided, however, between the *Shebdrung* (spiritual) and *Desi* (secular). The various valley districts were ruled over by governors (*Penlops*) who resided in the fortified monasteries called *dzongs*.

The dual system existed for 300 years and was only discontinued in the 20th century when no successor could be found for the *Shebdrung*. The *Desi* temporarily took on both responsibilities until, with British support, Ugyen Wangchuk, the *penlop* of Tongsa province, was elected hereditary Maharajah of the country in 1907. Secular and religious rule was vested in his family.

In the 18th century Bhutan became a tributary of **Tibet** and confronted the East India Company along its S borders into the 19th century. Warren Hastings sent a mission into the "Land of the Thunder Dragon" in the 1770s, headed by George Bogle (who was also ordered to plant potatoes there!). In 1841 the **British** annexed the Duars plain and created the present boundary, agreeing to pay a small annual subsidy as long as the Bhutanese remained peaceful. However, Bhutanese raiders continued to make forays across the border, carrying off Indians as slaves. In 1863, the visit of a British representative who forced his way into Bhutan, did not please the Bhutanese and so he was not treated well. A war followed but the British failed to invade Bhutan. The Duars were regained by the British in exchange for monetary compensation to the Bhutanese. In 1907, Ugyen Wangchuck, the Tongsa Penlop became the first hereditary King of Bhutan.

In 1910, in return for an increase in its annual subsidy, Bhutan agreed to accept British guidance in its external affairs. Bhutan, however, did not receive help in building roads, expanding communications and developing the economy as did Sikkim which was a British protectorate. The pace of development was therefore much slower.

The Bhutanese rulers had always been wary of the outside world. However, the invasion of Tibet by China in 1959 changed their outlook and Bhutan started opening up slowly. In 1971, it joined the UN and is now member of many international organisations. Up to the 20th century the S remained uninhabitated until small numbers of Nepali moved into the southern foothills. The numbers remained relatively small as Nepali forest labourers were brought in, who later settled as tenant farmers and then acquired Bhutanese nationality in 1958. However, with the opening up of the country and the endeavour to develop the infrastructure, large numbers of economic migrants entered and settled in the S, the majority of them ethnic Nepali. These latecomers were declared illegal immigrants in 1991. The Nepalis outnumber the indigenous Bhutanese in the 5 southern districts.

CULTURE

People and language

About 70% of the population are Drukpas of Tibetan origin. The Nepali speaking *Lhotshampas* (about 30%), belong mainly to the high castes and to the Rai, Gurung and Limbu tribes and because of their different language and religion they have not intermingled with the Drukpas. There are also tiny indigenous groups such as the Doyas in SW Bhutan and the Monpas in South Central Bhutan. There are also other tribal groups such as the Lepcha, an indigenous people – see Sikkim, page 1313, and the Santal who migrated from North Bihar.

Since 1959 immigration from Nepal has been banned and the Govt wishes to avoid a repetition of what happened in Sikkim (where, in 1975 the King was overthrown by the majority Nepali speaking population). The problem of the people of Nepali origin who left Bhutan since 1990 for refugee camps in SE Nepal is the subject of talks between Nepal and Bhutan.

Bhutan has the lowest population density in South Asia. Most people live along the S border and in the high valleys to the N, particularly along the E-W trade route that passes through Thimphu and Punakha. In the mountain region the Drukpas are predominant, whilst the S is predominantly settled by Nepalis.

National language The Drukpas share a common Tibetan heritage of culture, language and religion. The teaching of the national language, Dzongkha (affiiliated to Tibetan) is compulsory at all levels of education, although English is the medium of instruction. Primary education has been encouraged since the 1960s with the opening of state funded schools throughout the country.

Daily life

National dress The people take pride in their clothing which is influenced by the harsh climate. The men wear a long *kho* or *baku* (robe), hitched up to the knees with a sash, and long boots, while women wear an *onju* or *gyenja* (blouse), a *kira* (ankle-length robe, wrapped around from under the arm, held by silver brooches), a belt, and a *togo* (short jacket). Traditionally, special ceremonial scarves are worn – the king wears yellow, the ministers orange, senior officials red and the ordinary subjects white, while the women wear red flowery printed scarves.

Village houses with mud walls have a lower floor for animals; the upper floor for living is made of wood and bamboo lattices covered with mud plaster. Shuttered windows with a trefoil arch shape are colourfully painted. Roofs are covered with wooden shingles weighted down with stones. In North and Central Bhutan, house walls are made of stones and in the E, bamboo houses are built on stilts. Lighting is provided by butter lamps.

Religion

Religion plays a crucial role in social affairs. The **Drukpa Kagyupa** school of Tantric Buddhism is the state religion but the **Nyingmapa** school is well represented in the centre and E of the country.

Tantric Buddhism, which came from Tibet, is practised, but in contrast to the

DZONGS

These were originally built as monasteries/fortresses, strategically sited to defend the country from hostile Tibetans who enviously looked on to the cultivated terraced hillsides of Bhutan. They became centres of religious as well as secular power. Traditionally they have been the centres of artistic and intellectual life and their construction, ornamentation and maintenance have absorbed much of the nation's wealth. The high whitewashed walls are made of earth and stone (mud is trampled into wooden brick moulds, the labour being provided by the community). The wooden windows and balconies (built without nails) are richly ornamented. The interior walls are usually covered with murals depicting episodes in Buddhist mythology.

The villagers congregate at the *dzong* for the major festivals and for seasonal agricultural feasts which provide them an opportunity to wear their finest clothes and for merrymaking after the religious ceremony. *Tsechus*, held on the 10th day of the month, are celebrated in different parts of the kingdom, through the year, to commemorate the deeds of Guru Rimpoche. In the non-religious festivals, the participating monks do so as cultivators or archers (archery being a highly popular sport, associated with all celebrations; archers aim at targets at a distance of about 150m and every village has its own range). The circular cloth umbrella-like flags are to carry the spiritual teachings in every direction. Religious *Cham* dances can be very colourful and spectacular, performed in special costumes and masks to the accompaniment of drums and cymbals. Mask makers can sometimes be seen at work during festivals. They often enact the victory of Good over Evil, and may conclude with the display of a prized *thankha*.

predominating Gelugpa sects in Tibet, Bhutan is the stronghold of the Drukpa Kagyupa school, hence the name of the country, Druk. The Drukpa school is a branch of the Kagyupa School and came into existence in the 12th century in Tibet. It was introduced in Bhutan in the 13th century and became the predominant school in the 17th when the country was unified by the Drukpa hierarch who had fled persecution in Tibet.

There are around 5000 monks in Bhutan, the larger dzongs housing several hundred. Monks are highly respected by the community (and the government) for whom they provide spiritual comfort and guidance through prayers and rituals. Although monks are now supported by the State, people contribute towards their support, as giving to monks acquires merit. The performance of rituals by monks is essential for Bhutanese people especially at the time of death. At the time of religious festivals, monks and trained laymen perform sacred dances which have a symbolic meaning.

There are also a large number of private temples belonging to Nyingmapa priests who marry and pass their teachings and properties to their heirs.

Religious festivals are a wonderful occasion for people from the same region to gather and enjoy themselves. It is also an occasion for them to renew their faith and receive teachings by watching sacred dances. The dances are performed by monks and laymen in gorgeous costumes, and in some cases, in impressive masks. Most of the festivals started in the 17th century and called **Tscechu** are dedicated to Padmasambhava who introduced Buddhism in Bhutan. In Paro, Wangdi, Mongar and Tashigang, a big *thngdrel* is exhibited for a few hours on one day. A **thongdrel** is a thangka (a banner which 'brings liberation by sight') and people throng to get blessed on that auspicious day.

Religious dances (*cham*) can be didactic (with a moral), 'purificatory' and protect against evil spirits, or those celebrating proclaiming victory of Buddhism and glorifying Padmasambhava. Famous dances include the Black Hat dance when dancers wear large hats, high boots, silk brocade costumes and are accompanied by drummers. In the Dance of the Fearsome Gods, dancers wear terrifying masks of angry deities. In the colourful Dance of the Heroes, there is much leaping and whirling by dancers in bright yellow skirts and skull masks on their heads. The accompanying musicians play long trumpets, drums, pipes, gongs, cymbals and conch shells.

Crafts

Traditional handicrafts include handloom textiles, metal and wood work, paper manufacture, baskets and embroidery. Handloom cloth in traditional patterns and weaves, using raw silk, cotton, wool or yak hair, is very striking. The jewellery, mainly in silver sometimes set with turquoise, coral and pearl, is very distinctive.

MODERN BHUTAN

Government

After independence in 1947, India continued to take responsibility for Bhutan's foreign affairs, maintaining its roads and remaining the major source of foreign aid. King Jigme Dorje Wangchuk (1952-1972) brought in changes to allow for a National Assembly, the *Tshogdu*, to assume some representative power with 110 out of 150 members being elected by a limited electorate (village elders and heads of households). In 1971, Bhutan joined the UN and since then has exercised considerable independence in its foreign policy. Although the present King Jigme Singye Wangchuk wields considerable power, the 15 districts into which the country is divided have been given increasingly more administrative power and a greater say in economic policy. However, there is no written constitution and no independent legal system. His reign has been marked by a great improvement in the country's infrastructure; in the development of roads, buildings, telecommunication. The emphasis is also on developing agriculture, private enterprise and environmental conservation. Priority is given to education and healthcare (both are free). From the mid-70s political and administrative decentralisation has been taking place with the setting up of DDCs (District Development Committees) and more recently Committees at *gewog* (village group) level.

Recent developments The early 1990s have been marked by major unrest in the neighbouring Indian state of Assam and parts of North India. The response of the Bhutan government was to strengthen its programme of self-reliance and to underline its commitment to maintaining traditional Bhutanese values. The King has toured extensively and renewed support for the wearing of national dress has come from many parts of the country, especially in the S, bordering India. Language posed a particular problem, as English was increasingly becoming the lingua franca of the educated. While promoting the use of Dzongka, the King also took steps to encourage the Hindu population of the S to feel integrated with the Buddhist population, himself taking part in one of the major Hindu festivals.

In 1990, a new census declared many Nepalis illegal immigrants, which sparked off anti-government propaganda by dissidents and terrorism which led many Nepalis to leave the country. By the end of 1992, 70,000

Nepalis were in refugee camps in E. Nepal. Dissidents formed the political organisation BNDP. In September 1990 violent mass demonstrations were mounted and government offices ransacked in South Bhutan protesting against 'racism', the denial of democratic and human rights, and ethnic cleansing. The King threatened to abdicate but was persuaded to remain by the National Assembly. He then granted amnesty to hundreds of detainees and announced exemption of rural and labour tax in 1992 for all Lhotshampas and encouraged them not to leave the country. Schools, development projects and health services which had been suspended since 1990 because of the unrest, were ordered to reopen in 1993.

The plea put forward is that without military and economic might, the very survival of the tiny country, the last bastion of Mahayana Buddhism, depends on Bhutan retaining its cultural identity.

Bhutan has played an active part in the SAARC meetings, and has welcomed contacts with the outside world, increasing the tourist quota to 4000. Satellite dishes are not permitted and there is no national TV but video rental shops flourish and they are uncensored.

Economy

In 1991, the per capita income was US$425. 80% was in the rural sector but it contributed less than 2% in tax revenue. Airline services and modern satellite communication systems now link Bhutan with the outside world. Out of necessity it is rapidly emerging from the medieval, feudal religious-state which existed up to the 1950s.

Agriculture

Over 91% of the population depends on agriculture and livestock rearing. The most important area is in the Duars and the middle sections of the large river valleys. Maize is the most important crop (output 40,000 tonnes), with rice second (33,000 tonnes), cultivated on the valley floors and on more level slopes up to 2400m, terraced and irrigated, wherever possible. Between 2400m and 2900m, millet, wheat, buckwheat and barley are also grown. Hot pepper is the favoured vegetable in kitchen gardens all over the country. Apples and potatoes are particularly important cash crops for the central valleys while at altitudes between 300m and 1300m, oranges are a particularly important cash crop. Farming is at the subsistence level and in recent years rice has had to be imported. Cattle, pigs, horses and sheep contribute greatly to the economy; yaks are the main livestock over 3500m.

The extensive forests are scientifically managed, but are nonetheless damaged by shifting cultivation in the E and also by ageing and pests throughout. The Bhutanese government is very conservation oriented and is assisted in this task by various international organizations. A small dairy farm was started in central Bhutan with Swiss help and produces excellent cheese.

The ending of trade with Tibet in 1959 encouraged economic dependence on India and smuggling. Trade with India is contributing to Bhutan's economic development, with road building, small industries (fruit processing) and hydro-electric power plant construction. Smuggling over the Tibetan border has increased. Grain and sugar are carried on yak trains into Tibet and watches, thermos flasks and 'trainers' (shoes) from China are brought into the country.

Industry and resources

Bhutan has no oil or natural gas. It is mining dolomite and limestone for export to India, along with gypsum and slate. It also mines 30,000 tonnes of coal a year. The main industries are cement and distillery products, but Bhutan is also producing veneer woods and plywood, and high density polythene pipe.

Its main exports, all to India, are cement, timber, block boards, cardamom, fruit and alcoholic drinks.

Tourism

This is deliberately kept on a small scale with 4000 tourists planned for in 1993-4. Tourists are only allowed in minimum groups of 6. As late as the early 1960's the only way to Thimphu was either on foot or by pack animal. The building of roads had been forbidden until 1959 and began in 1960 on the issue of a royal decree. By 1964 the first all-weather road was completed from Paro to the new capital Thimphu.

Tourists are required to spend a minimum of US$220 daily, a lot by South Asian standards. Consequently only affluent tourists from Western countries, virtually all in tour groups, see this marvellous, peaceful country with its charming and friendly people. There are however, small signs that this exclusive destination will continue to open its doors to an increasing number of visitors; the Tourist Agency has been privatised and more hotels are being built.

Philately

Bhutan joined the Universal Postal Union only in 1969 but since then has made a specialty of exporting stamps, producing novelty stamps (3-dimensional, circular, on silk and metal) and they are now a significant source of foreign exchange.

THIMPHU

Population: 26,000 approx; *Altitude*: 2350m. Thimphu is a relatively new town, having been built by the late King Jigme Dorje Wangchuk to become the new permanent capital from 1955 (the old capital was Punakha). By Bhutanese standards Thimphu is busy and lively, though to an outsider it may appear an uncrowded haven.

Places of interest

The 400 year old **Tashichho Dzong** originally occupied the site although the present sprawling building with a tiered roof was built in the 1960s using traditional techniques and modelled on the original. The mud walls are 2m thick in places. The **Dzong** stands on the outskirts of the town, next to a 9-hole golf course, the only one in the country. With fine rose bushes at its entrance, it houses the **Central Secretariat**, the summer headquarters of the Central Monk Authority where the 150 member National Assembly meets. The present King's father, who died in 1972, initiated popular rule by voluntarily giving up his absolute powers. The gilded throne room and the King's Headquarters are also here. Half of the Dzong is an active monastery to which non-Buddhists are not allowed when monks are in residence (summer). **Note** This is true of all monasteries.

A **New Central Secretariat** which is also a conference centre has been completed in 1993. In traditional style, it stands on the other side of the river opposite the dzong.

A short distance away is a **chorten** (1974) to the late king which has paintings inside. Across the Thimphu river and up the valley is the **Dechenchholing Palace**. Nearby you can watch gold and silversmiths at work. 5 km downstream is **Simtoka** (1627), Bhutan's oldest dzong. This now houses the school for dzongkha and traditional studies (foreign tourists not permitted).

Excursions

Punakha Valley

Punakha is close enough to Thimphu to make a long day-trip feasible. A 2-hr drive on the new road goes over the spectacular Dochu-La Pass (2743m) with excellent views of the northern peaks early morning from Oct to Mar.

The pass is 45 min drive from Thimphu. *Dochu-La Cafe* serves refreshments. The valley is in a rainshadow area, at 1300m, lower than most midland valleys with a mild climate allowing rice, oranges and a variety of vegetables to be grown. Beautifully located *Zandopelri Hotel* opened in 1994, 10 km before Punakha.

Punakha **Dechen Phodrang Dzong** stands at the confluence of the Pho Chu (Father) and Mo Chu (Mother) rivers. Built in 1637, it was subsequently damaged by fires in the 17th and 18th centureis and when the moraine lake flooded in 1897; the present King has had it restored. It was the winter capital of Bhutan and is still the winter headquarters of the Head Abbot. Open to foreigners in summer when the monks are in Thimphu; courtyard only, when dzong is in use in winter.

Wangdiphodrang

South of Punakha is the gateway to central and eastern Bhutan. The large 1638 dzong standing on a rocky outcrop is impressive (closed to visitors except at Tshechu). Two hr drive from Wangdi, branching off the main road to Pelela pass, a 7 km road leads to **Phobjika valley** (3000m). It is the site of the beautiful **Gantey** monastery (17th century) and the winter ground for the amazing black-neck cranes which circle over the fields (Nov-Mar). The higher pastures above the valley are ideal for yaks; there is a Yak Dairy Research Station at Gogona. Local handicrafts include bamboo work and stone and slate carving.

• **Accommodation** In town, a small, spartan ***Guest House***, with 6 clean rm, some with bath, simple meals, camping on lawn, suitable overnight stop for trekkers. The lovely ***Dechen Cottages*** in Mendeygang, are 15 km before Wangdi, on the Thimphu road.

Local information

● Accommodation

On the upper outskirts of Thimphu, to the W: BTCL ***Mothigang***, in a park, at 2560m, is built in traditional style but with modern comforts, this large hotel is also used for official guests. Lower down, ***Zandopelri***, off Thori Lam, Mutithang, is small and cozy. ***Bhutan***, has rm with terraces, good views.

In town: *Jomolhari*, T 22747, and ***Druk*** are conveniently located with all modern facilities. The small ***Druk Sherig Guest House*** is the favourite of returning visitors. All have rm with bath, restaurant, bar, exchange.

● Places to eat

All hotels offer Indian, Chinese, Continental and a few local dishes incl the fiery *emadatsi* (cheese with hot peppers). Non-residents should book in advance at *Zandopelri*. For *momos, chowmien* and *thukpas* the tiny and spartan ***Beneez*** is excellent while ***Sambaral*** serves hot Chinese food. ***Golf Canteen*** in the dzong with great views, offers sandwiches and good Chinese. ***Gahsel*** coffee-shop, 32 Norzim Lam (0900-2100), serves good *shay phalay* and *emadatsi*. For Bhutanese delicacies, ***Rabten*** is the place (on order only). The popular ***Swiss Bakery***, a white octagonal cottage off Norzim Lam, nr crossroad, uphill from *Hotel Druk* does Western snacks (closed Th). ***Plum Café*** is equally good for snacks as is ***Jichudrake Bakery*** up the same road for good cakes and bread.

● Airline offices

Druk Air, Lower Market, nr *Druk Hotel*.

● Banks & money changers

American Express and Bank of Bhutan, Norzim Lam, 0900-1600. BTCL also changes money.

● Entertainment

Thimphu is very quiet by Western standards. Royal Academy of Performing Arts, puts on shows.

● Hospitals & medical services

General Hospital, T 22496.

● Post & telecommunications

Post Office: off Norzim Lam nr bank, 0830-1230, 1330-1630, Sat 0900-1230. **Couriers & fax**: *DHL*, at Sonam Peldon Stationery shop nr Druk Air.

● Shopping

The sprawling capital has rows of neat, traditionally painted shops in the Bazar. Most accept only Bhutanese currency. Usually open 0800-2000, Mon-Sat. There is a Sunday Market.

Books and cards: *Yangchenma Bookshop*, Gatoen Lam, and ***National Library Bookstore***.

Handicrafts: *Handicrafts Emporium*, Norzim Lam, extensive range including old sculptures, textiles, masks, jewellery and paintings. An excellent handicrafts shop has opened in *Druk Hotel*, American Express accepted. *Kelzang Handicrafts and Jewellery*, by Druk Shopping Complex and *Norling Handicrafts*, shop 37, Norzim Lam, are worth a visit. For masks go to *Choeki Handicrafts*.

Maps: newspaper stand nr the cinema hall, which also sells maps of Thimphu and Paro.

Photography: films and processing at *Photofield* and *Sunrise*.

Stamps for collectors from *Philatelic Bureaue*, inside GPO.

Textiles: *Pel Jorkhang*, Crossroads, specialises in local textiles. *Sengay Buddha* and *Dorji Gyeltshen*, shops 33 and 35, Line 2, Norzim Lam, are rec for traditional clothes. Also *Tshering Dolkar* and *Ethometho*, Tourism Bldg by Cinema, for handicrafts and cloth. The latter stocks books, postcards and stamps.

WARNING Do not bargain. Foreigners are not allowed to buy antiques (see **Information for Visitors** below).

● **Sports**

Golf: there is a golf course, towards Tashichho Dzong.

Health clubs: at *Druk Hotel* and *Sakteng* on Gatoen Lam.

● **Tourist office**

Tourist Authority of Bhutan (TAB), PO Box 126, T 23251, F 23695.

● **Tour companies**

See **Information for Visitors** below.

● **Transport**

Road Most places of interest are now linked by bus. Private vehicle hire with a driver is possible. Paro (59 km, 1½ hr); Punakha and Wangdi 2 hr; Phuntsholing, 6 hr.

AROUND BHUTAN

Paro

Most foreign visitors arrive by air at Paro which has the only airstrip. It is a 90 min drive to Thimphu. The Paro Valley with its forests of blue pine is considered the most beautiful of Bhutan's main valleys. The vast white **Paro Dzong** dominates the skyline and life of Paro, with its small bazar and a farming population living in groups of traditional shingle-roofed houses surrounded by paddy fields. The dzong stands on the site of an old temple built in the 14th century by a famous Drukpa lama.

The imposing 5-storeyed dzong was built by Ngawang Namgyal in 1646 with a covered drawbridge on one side and dungeons; you can see their narrow window slits on the other 3 steep sides. For 250 years it served as a bastion against invasions from the N. It burnt down in 1907 and all the treasures except the enormous **Thongdel thangka** (30m x 45m) were destroyed. The thangka depicts Padmasambhava (Guru Rinpoche) flanked by his 2 consorts and surrounded by his 8 manifestations. On the last day of the Paro Tshechu, it is unfurled for a few hours and dances are performed in front of it.

The present monastery was built immediately after the fire and has fine woodwork, large sections of logs slotted into each other, held together without any nails. The informal interior (closed at present) contrasts with the forbidding exterior. Above the dzong is the largest of the original watchtowers (c1775) which houses the **National Museum of Bhutan** with a varied collection of paintings, sculptures and traditional articles in daily use, and a collection of ancient and modern costumes and jewellery. 0900-1600. Closed Mon. Free. Carry a flashlight (erratic electric supply) and allow 1 hr to see all floors.

Close to the main village, you can catch a glimpse of the lovely **Ugyen Pelri Palace** modelled on the heavenly palace of Padmasambhava and build at the beginning of this century. The unique chorten-shaped **Dungtse Lhakhang** stands on the other side of the river. This temple first built in the 15th century by **Thangtong Gyelpo**, a famous saint and builder (who also built the famous iron chain bridges, see under **Trekking**). The building was restored in the early 19th century and is an extraordinary repository of Buddhist iconography. The walls of the 3 storeys, connected by a steep ladder, are covered with paintings representing the whole pantheon. Permission needed for a visit; flashlight essential.

A few km N the **Kyichu Lhakhang**, (closed to foreigners) surrounded by prayer flags, is one of Bhutan's oldest temples, built in the 7th century "on the left foot of a demoness" by the Tibetan king Songtsen Gampo. It had the gold roof added in 1830; the courtyard and decoration are particularly attractive. A 2nd temple built in the 1960s in the same style is attached to the old one.

A few km further, at the end of the valley stands the 17th century **Drukgyel Dzong** (the dzong of the victorious Drukpas) built to commemorate victory over the Tibetans but ruined by fire in 1954. Situated on a hill, it stands against the Chomolhari, protected by 3 towers and approached only from one direction, and gives the impression of shutting off the Paro valley. Its position ensured that no one could travel on the Paro-Tibet road without being seen.

The **Taktsang Monastery** (Tiger's Lair) seems to hang on the face of the almost sheer 1000m cliff above the Paro valley. It is an impressive sight but far from inaccessible. The buildings date from the late 17th century but the site itself was rendered sacred by Padmasambhava who is said to have meditated here in the 8th century after arriving on the back of a flying tiger. It is a popular pilgrimage place. **NOTE** Foreigners are only allowed to within 100m of the monastery.

You can also stop at the *Taktsang Tea House* on the way, which has breathtaking views of the monastery; it serves refreshments, warm lunches, and sells handicrafts. Although horses can be arranged on request, it is better to walk up as Bhutanese saddles are memorably uncomfortable. The beautiful walk up from the Satsam chorten (10 min drive from Paro village; 2 hr from Thimphu) through oaks and pine trees to the *Tea House*, is quite strenuous and usually takes 2 hr (3 hr to reach the highest point). Higher still, though not in such a spectacular setting, is the 300 yr old **Sangtog Monastery**.

• **Accommodation** BTCL *Olathang*, in a beautiful hillside setting overlooking valley, 3 km from the village, pleasant rm with bath in main building and in 14 cottages spread around the large grounds, restaurant, bar, shop. *Gantey Resort*, refurbished and located in an old traditional manor opp the dzong, is charming. *New Druk Hotel*, shaped like a dzong above the airport is very grand. *Eye of the Tiger* cottages opp Taktsang monastery are simpler but very pleasant.

• **Shopping** *Lam Dorji's*, has local handicrafts and clothing. There is also a shop at the airport.

Phuntsholing

The border town is 3-4 hr by road from Bagdogra in West Bengal. A traditionally painted gateway welcomes you to Bhutan. Commercially it is an important town with small-scale industries (dairy, soft drinks, matches). All imported goods to the capital Thimphu transit through Phuntsholing so each morning trucks (and buses) roar through the streets. The town is not particularly attractive, but has an interesting mix of population and a definite tropical air about it.

The town is at the foot of the Himalaya and the spectacular 175 km road from here to Thimphu and Paro reaches altitudes of 3000m. The first stop is at **Kharbandi Monastery** above the town with fine views over the foothills and the Bengal plains. The 8 *chortens* nearby commemorate the important events the Buddha's life. **Accommodation** Phuntsholing is the usual night halt for travellers by road. Welcomgroup *Druk*, T 2426, and *Namgay*, PO Box 99, T 2293, are the best with good restaurants. For a simple Indian meal *Kunga* opp *Druk* is fine. *Kharbandi*, 5 km, nr the monastery, has a good restaurant. All are comfortable.

Tongsa

2200m (130 km E of Wangdiphodrang) has the largest and most impressive dzong in Bhutan standing on a spur above a deep gorge and dominated by a 2-wing watchtower, the **Ta dzong**. Established in the 16th century and enlarged several times, the huge, many-levelled **Tongsa dzong** with its 20 temples and a maze of courtyards and covered passages, was the ancestral home of Bhutan's royal family (tourists need a permit to visit). The dzong contains frescoes, and figures of the Buddha, Tara and past kings and among the treasures is a collection of rhino horn sculptures.

In the 19th century, Tongsa was the seat of the most powerful governor of the country; the Tongsa Penlop commanded the whole of the central and eastern region. One of them, Ugyen Wangchuck, became the first hereditary King of Bhutan in 1907. The village above the dzong was built in the 1980s. **Accommodation** BTCL *Sherubling Lodge*, nr the school, has 6 simple heated rm and 6 cottages with bath, limited catering. *Yangkhil* in town is simpler but great for excellent meals in the warm kitchen.

Central Bhutan

A trip to central Bhutan allows you to discover different aspects of Bhutan but be prepared for long drives and rustic comfort at the lodges. Allow about 10 days for a worthwhile trip. From Jun-Sep the roads are sometimes blocked by landslides.

Bumthang

A rural area which was developed with Swiss assistance, it is also the religious heart of Bhutan with beautiful monasteries and small temples scattered in the valleys. It is also a fantastic area for day-walks. The area's 4 high valleys (Chume, Choekhor, Tang and Ura) have Jakar as the principal town but Bumthang is the most popular and important. With beautifully painted wooden facades of houses, it looks best in the autumn when the buckwheat paints the fields deep orange. Though accessible by road, most of the interesting sights are only accessible to trekkers. See below.

Eastern Bhutan

The best time for a trip E is Apr/May and Oct/Nov. The E is wonderful in winter as it is warmer than western Bhutan but there can be snow on the road from Bumthang to Mongar.

After passing the big village of **Ura**, the last in Bumthang, the road ascends the **Thumsing la** pass at 3650m. From there in 3 hr you make a dramatic descent to 700m and a semi-tropical area; it is a spectacular drive. **Mongar** (1600m) is a small, sleepy town with a lovely restored dzong. From there you can drive straight to Tashigang or take a 3-day side trip to **Lhuntse dzong** in the N. The road goes through a gorge for almost 70 km before reaching the massive 17th century Lhuntse dzong. This area is with its mountain villages is known for its fine weaving and the village women spend most of their days at the loom. The steep terrain is really suitable for exploring on foot.

From Mongar it is a quick 3 hr journey to **Tashigang** (1100m), the biggest and busiest town in the E. The town looks attractive with its painted houses among bougainvilleas, its tiny shops, and the 'square' and cafés which hum with activity at the end of the day. Tropical fruits and crops thrive; apple is pressed into juice to produce cider and brandy. The local *endi* silk is spun from silkworms bred on castor oil plants. The **Dzong** which stands on a spur overlooking the Manas river 400m below, was built in 1656.

A day-trip to **Chorten Kora** and **Tashiyangtse** (2 hrs drive from Tashigang) is really worthwhile. A lush narrow valley at 1700m, Tashiyangtse is famous for its huge white chorten in Nepalese style and an old drawbridge covered with bamboo mats below the small dzong.

Tashigang is a 7 hr drive from **Samdrupjongkhar**, a market town on the border from where one can go to Guwahati airport in Assam (special permission needed)..

• **Accommodation** Mongar has ***Shongar Lodge*** nr the dzong and Tashigang has ***Kellling Lodge***. These simple BTCL guest houses are basic, with electricity and water supply still erratic.

TREKKING IN BHUTAN

Trekking in Bhutan offers not only spectacular scenery but also a chance to see the people in their villages carrying out ancient skills and crafts. Bhutan is really off-the-beaten-track, has wonderful landscapes, amazing flora and kind, affectionate people who are very proud of their life-style. The attractions of trekking here include the relatively clear paths and the accessibility of good fishing. See this **Trekking** section for detailed advice, page 114.

Planning a trek

Trekking conditions are very different from Nepal since it is much wetter; the season is much shorter and for some high-altitude treks choosing a period between snow and rain can be difficult. The best months are Mar-Apr and Oct-Nov. Treks start at 2400m generally rising to 4000m quite rapidly. With Bhutan's small, scattered population you might trek for hours, and sometimes days, without seeing a single house, and only passing the odd person with pack animals along the track. The trails are not mapped or well-defined so it is easy to lose one's way; high-altitude rescue is non-existent.

The fast mountain streams are crossed by ingenious log or liana and split bamboo bridges, while wider rivers may have more substantial wooden ones – often protected by prayer flags. The famous 15th century iron chain bridges were built by Thangtong Gyelpo. The chains were often made in Bhutan (using a small quantity of arsenic to reduce the melting point of iron) and transported great distances. Over 50 bridges were erected across the Himalaya; some had 9 lengths of chain suspended to form the frame of a bridge which would then be tied with wire and have matting put underfoot.

For **accommodation** there are no 'tea houses' or cosy lodges with hot-water to welcome you after a hard day's trek. In the countryside. The Bhutanese are fully occupied tending animals and with work in the fields and do not have time, or the need, to take in guests be they Bhutanese or foreigners – the traces of fire camps in rock shelters provide ample proof of this. Because of the inaccessablity of most of the countryside, people are reluctant to sell any food since a shop could be 3 days' walk away. In remote areas, barter is a standard mode of exchange; salt or edible oil are more likely to see eggs materialise than a bank-note!

The economy is not dependent on tourism and so the Bhutanese do not hire themselves as porters; yaks and mules carry all belongings on treks. Since the trekking months coincide with the busy period in the fields, the owners of pack animals have to be contacted well in advance, and be flattered and cajoled before they agree.

Trekking in Bhutan is logistically complicated because it is still a wild country. However, tour operators here know the problems well; they will help you with the choice of trek and the season, taking into account your own preferences and physical fitness. Small groups are provided with a guide, helpers, a wonderful cook, tents, mattresses, pack-animals and all the food needed, as there is nothing available on the way; you are advised to bring your own sleeping bags. In the monsoons some paths can be very muddy and below 2000m, leeches can be a problem.

Ecology and the environment have recently become the main concern of tour operators who do not want trekkers (and local staff) to litter the still pristine countryside. Please follow the Himalayan Code of Practice given in the Trekking section.

North Western Bhutan

Paro to Haa via the Chelila

From Paro, most of the early part is through dense forest. As you reach Chelila, broad panoramas of the mountains around Chomolhari open out. Above the forest, the trekking is across yak pastures. There are 2 important passes, the Kalai La and Sage La, both important burial areas. Towards the finish, you will descend into deciduous forest and the Paro Valley. Although comparatively short (under 7 days), the variation in altitude and vegetation plus the rich flora and fauna and stunnng views make it an exceptionally good trek in Oct-Nov and Apr.

Paro-Thimphu Trek (Druk Path)

Although most people drive from Paro to Thimphu, you can do a 3-day easy trek along a path, instead of the road, going through a 3900m pass. It gives the not-so-energetic a wonderful, relaxed insight into Bhutanese life. There are some fine ridge views of the mountains and pleasant stretches through lush forest. In Apr-May the rhododendrons are in bloom and are a spectacular sight. On the way, there are beautiful lakes and the famous monastery of **Phajoding** (3058m) with its 18th century temples housing art works and paintings, which can also be visited from Thimphu on a day excursion but involves a 3-hr climb.

Chomolhari Base Camp

This is more demanding, and takes around 7 days. Best season Late Apr, May, Oct. You get excellent views of the mountains and glaciers and pass gorges and waterfalls, cross rivers and see yaks in their pasture and alpine flowers, rhododendrons and orchids according to the season.

From **Drukyel dzong** in Paro the path rises steadily up to the ruined **Soi dzong** at the foot of the **Chomolhari** (7313m), a truly dramatic sight. Then the trail crosses a pass at 4400m before descending to the valley where the hilltop **Lingshi Dzong** once guarded the frontier with Tibet. From there you have splendid views of the Jichudrake (6793m) and Tseringkhang mountains. The path then continues through yak pastures to the Yelela pass (4900m) before descending through the spectacular Wang river gorge, up to **Dodina** in the upper part of the Thimphu valley.

Gaza-Laya Trek

This can be combined with the Chomolhari trek which makes it a strenuous 15-day trek going over several 4000m passes. Alternatively, starting and finishing in Punakha in a semi-tropical region would take 11 days, with 4 days into the Laya region at 4200m. The change in vegetation is spectacular – from thick forest to open meadow.

Gaza is in the Mo Chu valley, once the market where the yak caravans congregated. Gaza is also known for its Dzong and its healing hotsprings. **Laya** (3850m) is the 2nd highest village in Bhutan at the foot of the Masagang (7200m) where the Layas still worship Bon gods and guard their villages of painted wooden houses with wood images. Here, yak herders dressed in a very distinctive costume, live and tend their yaks; the women too look different with their long hair and plaited cane pointed hats. You will see herdsmen in blackened yak-hair tents or stone houses, and prayer flags around 'ghost catchers' made of wood and stone. In the higher reaches there are large flocks of blue sheep, and the takin which is rare elsewhere in the Himalaya. Bears are relatively common, and the guides often make a lot of noise so as not to take them by surprise.

You can drive to **Dodina** from Thimphu (1 hr), reach the Base camp in 4-5 days and return to Paro via the **Drugkel Dzong**.

Lunana Trek

One of the most difficult of all, this takes 18 days, and is for the very fit, experienced trekker as it crosses 5 passes over 5000m. Best season: Aug-Sep.

The trail goes first from Punakha to **Laya** (see above) in 4 days. Then it is 3 days' demanding trekking, traversing the **Ganlakarchung Pass** (5100m) the first of the 3 steep passes over 5000m which gives superb views over the East Himalaya and on to **Woche** (3850m) in the beautiful northern region of Lunana. Then trek for 2 days through **Thega, Chozo** Valley with its dzong, and to the regional capital **Thaanza** (4050m) before the 5-day trail to **Nikacchu Bridge** where you can get transport back to Tongsa or Thimphu. The mountain views are spectacular and you pass lakes, glacial rivers and moraines, and beautiful forests with Himalayan birds and flowers in the meadows. Uncertain weather conditions add to the difficulty of this trek.

Central Bhutan

The 4 valleys that make up the area gives the visitor an opportunity to see the remote countryside where life has remained virtually unchanged for centuries. **Jakar** (also spelt Byakar) (2800m, 70 km from Tongsa) is the main town with **Jakar Dzong** (the dzong of the White Bird) keeping vigil over the Choekhor valley.

Gantey Gompa trek

This easy 3-4 day trek takes you from Phobjika valley where you see the beautiful Gantey gompa, up to **Wangdiphodrang** through small villages and splendid forests of giant junipers, daphne bushes, rhododendrons and magnolia. The rhododendron season (Apr) is highly recommended, when you can see hundreds in bloom.

Bumthang Trek

The easy 5-6 day trek remains below 3500m and gives you a chance to see typical villages of Central Bhutan. You can watch people producing baskets, weaving on traditional looms or making hand-made paper from daphne bark. Best season: Apr-May, late Sep to mid-Nov. The trail which starts near **Kuje Lhakhang** takes you to **Ngang Lhakhang**, an old temple, before crossing a pass and reaching the very rural valley where you will see **Ugyenchöling dzong**.

There are important religious places which can be included ona 5-6 day trek: **Jampey Lhakhang** was founded in the 7th century 'on the left knee of the demoness', by the Tibetan King Songsten Gampo. **Kuje Lhakhang** where Padmasambhava is believed to have meditated and left his body print in the rock; it is the site of 3 imposing temples with the funeral chorten of the 3 kings in front of them. **Tamshing Lhakhang**, a charming monastery, established by the great nyingmapa saint **Pemalingpa** in the early 16th century has superb paintings of the period. **Note** Most of the temples require a permit to be visited.

- **Accommodation** The small BTCL *Wangdichöling Lodge* nr an old 19th century palace is full of charm with its painted bungalows and its large elaborately decorated dining room. Heated rm with bath, simple meals (Continental and Bhutanese), handicrafts shop. ***Swiss Guest House***, above the Swiss Farm is simple but has excellent food and cosy atmosphere, favourite with returning visitors. A new guest house is scheduled to open nr Tamshing monastery.

INFORMATION FOR VISITORS

Contents

Before you go

Entry requirements

● Visas

Valid passports and entry visa are essential. There is a fixed government quota on the number of tourists most of which is taken up by tour companies, hence the only way to see Bhutan is as a member of a commercially organised tour group. Tour prices, all inclusive, range from US$ 130 to 250 per day according to the season.

Visas cannot be obtained at Bhutanese embassies. Foreigners can only go through a travel agent abroad or one in Bhutan who will obtain a visa for you and make all your bookings. This can take about 3 weeks (Fax is very reliable within Bhutan). You pay for the visa (US$ 20) on arrival in Bhutan. The regulations are simpler for Indian national who do not need to go through a travel agent. **NB** Special permission is needed to visit monasteries and dzongs. **Buddhists** are given special permits to restricted dzongs and gompas.

● Tourist authority

The Tourism Authority of Bhutan, (TAB) is the only government body; all other outlets are private travel agents. There is no tourism office abroad. You can write for information to TAB, PO Box 126, Thimphu, T 975 223251, F 223695. Information can also be obtained from Bhutan Embassies/Missions in Dhaka, Kuwait, Delhi, Geneva and New York.

● Embassies abroad

Royal Bhutan Embassy: **India**: Chandra Gupta Marg, Chanakyapuri, T 604076, New Delhi 11021; 48 Tivoli Court, 1A Ballygunge Circular Rd, Calcutta. **Bangladesh**: 58, Rd No 3A, Dhanmondi RA, Dhaka, T 545018. **USA**: 120 E 56th St, New York, NY 10022.

● Tour Companies and travel agents

Bhutan: In Thimphu: *Bhutan Himalaya Trekking*, PO Box 236, (code 975) T 223293, F 222897; *BTCL* (Bhutan Tourism Corp Ltd), PO Box 159, T 222647, F 222479; *Chhundu Travels*, PO Box 149, T 222592, F 222645; *Ethometho Tours*, PO Box 360, T 223693, F 222884; *Lhomen Tours and Trekking*, T/F 23243; *Mandala Tours*, PO Box 397, T 223676, F 223675; *Reekor Tours*, PO Box 304, T 222733, F 223541; *Takin Tours*, PO Box 454, T 223129, F 223130; *Yangphel Tours*, PO Box 326, T 223293, F 222897; *YuDruk*, PO Box 140, T 223461, F 222116.

Nepal: *President Travels & Tours*, Durbar Marg, Kathmandu, T 226744.

UK: *Himalayan Kingdoms*, 20 The Mall, Clifton, Bristol, BS8 4DR, T 0272 237163; *Worldwide Safaris*, Chelsea Reach, 2nd Fl, 79-89 Lots Rd, London SW10 0RN, T 071 3510298.

USA: *Bhutan Travel*, 120E, 56th St, Suite 1430, New York, NY 10022, T 212 838 6382; *Inner Asia*, 2627 Lombard St, San Francisco, Ca 94123, T 4159220448, F 3465535; *Mountain Travel*, 6420 Fairmount Ave, El Cerrito, CA 94530, T 415 527 8100.

When to go

● Best time for a visit

Mar-May and Sep-Nov, either side of the rainy season.

Health

Protection is *recommended* against cholera, typhoid, tetanus, polio, hepatitis, malaria and rabies, and *optional* for meningitis. See Health in South Asia Introduction, page 13.

WARNING Thimphu Valley has been experiencing increased incidence of rabies because of the growing number of stray dogs.

Money

● Currency

The national currency is the Ngultrum (Nu). 100 Chetrum = 1 Nu. Exchange rate is approx. US $1 = Nu 30. Indian Rupees circulate at par. American Express credit card accepted in a few shops. No other credit card is accepted so far.

● Money changing

Bank of Bhutan in Thimphu and Phuntsholing will change travellers cheques and hard currency. The **Bank of Bhutan** has 26 branches across the country. Head Office is at Phuntsholing. Money-changers prefer travellers cheques to currency notes. Carry enough Nu when trekking or touring.

Getting there

● Air

The airport is at Paro. **Transport to Thimphu**: 1½ hr drive by Druk Air coach. Druk Air, the national carrier (2 BAe 146), has connections with Delhi (3 hr), US$580, via Kathmandu (¾ hr) US$330 on Mon and Th. From Bangkok (4 hr), US$670, via Calcutta (1½ hr), US$330 Wed, return Sun, and via Dhaka (1 hr), US$330, Sun, return Wed. **NB** Bad weather can delay flights during monsoons. Dep from Paro 0730; To Paro from Delhi 1125; Kathmandu 1410; Dhaka 1610, Bangkok 1355. *Druk Air*, 48 Tivoli Court, Ballygunge Circular Rd, Calcutta. There are also offices in Delhi, Dhaka, Bangkok and Kathmandu but **note** bookings must be done through your travel agent. Always recheck your flight time. A visa fee of US$ 20 is payable at Paro airport; the airport tax Nu 300.

● Road

The road from Bagdogra (the nearest Indian airport) enters Bhutan at Phuntsholing, the border town. It is a 3-4 hr drive from Bagdogra airport (see page 652) which can be reached by plane from Calcutta and Delhi. From Darjiling or Gangtok, it can take 7 hr to Phuntsholing. It takes about 6 hr to negotiate the winding 179 km road from Phuntsholing through to Thimphu (or Paro).

● Customs

8 mm cameras are allowed. No 16 mm cameras. Permits are needed for video cameras and for filming (for a fee). Contact BTCL, Box 159, Thimphu. You may not take antiquities, plants or animal products out of the country – all old items must have a certificate clearing them from the Dept of Antiquities.

When you arrive

● Clothing

Cottons and light woollens in summer (Jun-Sep). Heavy woollens and jackets the rest of the year. Take an umbrella for the monsoons and comfortable shoes. Shorts, revealing T-shirts or clothes are not suitable. For trekking gear, see **India, Infomation for visitors**, see page 114.

● Hints on social behaviour

Useful words include – *Kadrinche* (thank you), *Kousousangpo* (good morning) and *Lass* (when leavetaking). The interiors of some monasteries were closed because the tourists were disturbing the lamas and stealing mementos. When visiting a dzong, **do not** smoke, wear a hat, interrupt prayers or enter the dance area during the *tshechu*. Ask before photographing. See also page 120.

● Official time

Bhutanese time is 30 min ahead of Indian National Time or GMT +6 hrs.

● Photography

There is some spectacular scenery, but if you go during the wet season make sure to protect film against humidity. Carry plenty of films and batteries.

● Safety

The crime rate in this unspoilt country is very low.

● Shopping

Traditional handicrafts, jewellery, baskets, masks, textiles. Paintings and woodcarving make good buys. See **Thimphu Shopping** above. Get a receipt and please do not attempt to bargain.

● Tipping

Tipping is forbidden by law.

● Voltage

230-240 volts, 50 cycles A.C. The current is variable.

● Weights and measures

Metric – the same as in India.

Where to stay

Bhutan has only been accepting foreign visitors for the last 15 years and limited the numbers to 2000-3000 so there is neither a well developed hotel industry nor category **A-C** hotels. In Phuntsholing, Thimphu and Paro there are some comfortable hotels with Bhutanese decor and modern facilities. BTCL accommodation in Bumthang, Tongsa, Mongar and Tashigang is simpler but has modern plumbing and helpful staff (water and electricity supply can be erratic). Elsewhere Guest Houses are very basic.

Food and drink

● Food

Rice is the staple, eaten with spicy and hot vegetables and meat curries; buckwheat pancakes or noodles, and barley or wheat flour is eaten in some high valleys. Hot chillies and melted cheese (*emadatsi*) is the national dish. Dumpling (momos), and noodles are great favourites. Pork and beef are the most common meat; chicken is also becoming popular. Yak meat is the favourite but available only in the winter. Desserts are not served but delicious fruits are available in season.

● Drink

Sweet milk tea, beer and fruit juices are available but no real coffee, only Nescafé. Butter tea is drunk at home for special occasions and local alcoholic drinks (*chang*, *ara* and *tomba*) are brewed or distilled at home. Bottled mineral water can be bought in the towns. Spirits (whisky, gin, fruit brandies and rum) are produced in Bhutan.

Getting around

● Road

The road network is not extensive and the principal means of road transport is by public bus. 4-wheel drive and Japanese cars are available for hire. Cars are always hired with driver.

Communications

● Postal services

A postal service was introduced in 1962 which covers most of the country. Allow at least 14 days for delivery to Australia and Europe and longer for the Americas. Attractive country stamps are sold at the GPO, Thimphu and Philatelic Bureau, Phuntsholing.

● Telephone services

Most of the country is now internally connected and international phone calls can be made from Paro, Thimphu, Bumthang, Mongar and Tashigang. The connections are excellent and the fax services are also very reliable.

Bhutan international dialing code is 975. Area codes: Thimphu and Paro 2; Tongsa, Bumthang and Galeyphu 3; Mongar, Tashigang and Samdrupjongkhar 4.

Entertainment

● Media

Kuensel the only national weekly (English) but international magazines are on sale. BBS is the national radio. BBC and VOA reception is good. No TV.

Holidays and festivals

● National holidays

Dates sometimes vary according to the lunar calendar.

1994

Sep 22 Blessed Rainy Day.
Oct 14 Dasain; **26** Descending of Lord Buddha.
Nov 11-13 Birthday of the present King.
Dec 17 National Day (everything closes).

1995

Jan 2 Winter Solstice; **8** Meeting of Nine Evils; **31** Traditional day of offerings.
Mar 1 New Year.
May 2 Birth anniversary of the 3rd King.
June 2 Coronation Day.
July 21 Death anniversary of the 3rd King.

● Festivals

Most religious festivals take place in the spring and autumn, see page 1291. Check with your travel agent who is sent a list by TAB, well ahead of time. Only authorised festivals are listed.

Thimphu Tshechu 14-16 Sep 94.
Wangdiphodrang Tshechu 12-14 Sep 94.
Tongsa Tshechu 10-12 Dec 94.
Bumthang Tamshing Phala Choepa 14-16 Sept 94; Thangbi Manicham 19-21; Jampey Lhakhang 19-23 Oct 94; Prakhar 21-22 Oct 94.
Mongar Tshechu 9-12 Nov 94.
Tashigang Tshechu 11-13 Nov 94.
Lhuntsi Tshechu 10-13 Dec 94.
Punakha Dromchoe 5-7 Mar 95; Serda 9 Mar 95.
Chorten Kora 31 Mar-2 Apr 95.
Paro Tshechu 11-15 Apr 95.

SRI LANKA

Contents

Maps

OFFICIAL NAME *Sri Lanka Prajatantrika Samajawadi Janarajaya* (Democratic Socialist Republic of Sri Lanka)

CAPITAL Colombo

NATIONAL FLAG a dark red field, within a golden border, a golden lion passant holding a sword in its right paw, and a representation of a bo-leaf coming from each corner; to its right, 2 vertical saffron and green stripes (representing Hindu and Muslim minorities), also within a golden border.

NATIONAL ANTHEM *Namo Namo Matha* (We all stand together).

BASICS *Population*: 1994 17.8mn; *Annual growth rate*: 1.6%; *Crude birth rate*: 2.4%; *Crude death rate*: 0.6%; *Urban population*: 21%; *Infant mortality*: 2.9% of live births; *Adult literary*: M 93% F 84%; *Area*: 66,000 sq km; *Population density*: 256 per sq km; *GDP per capita*: US$550; *Average Annual growth rate*: 1965-93 2.9%.

Land and life

Geology and landscape

Location

Situated between 5°55'-9°51'N, Sri Lanka is at the heart of the Indian Ocean trading routes. After the opening of the route round the Cape of Good Hope by Vasco da Gama in 1498 the island was brought into direct contact with Western Europe. The opening of the Suez Canal in 1869 further strengthened the trading links with the West.

The land

Geologically Sri Lanka is a continuation of the Indian Peninsula, from which it was separated less than 10,000 years ago by the 10m deep and 35 km wide **Palk Straits**. Its area of 65,610 sq km makes Sri Lanka a little smaller than Belgium and the Netherlands combined. It is 435 km long and at its broadest 225 km wide. Its 1600 km of coastline is lined with fine sandy beaches, coral reefs and lagoons.

Virtually the whole of Sri Lanka is underlain by crystalline rocks dating from between 570 mn and 3500 mn years ago. See page 22. Today these rocks form a highland massif with its centre of gravity somewhat to the SW of the geographical centre of the pear-shaped island. From *Piduratalaga* (Sri Lanka's highest mountain at 2524m) and sacred *Adam's Peak*, the hills descend in 3 great steps to the coastal lowlands. Recent evidence suggests that the very early folding of the ancient rocks, followed by erosion at different speeds, formed the scarps and plateaus, often deeply cut by the rivers which radiate from the centre of the island. In the central highlands the Khondalite series of metamorphosed sandstones are widespread. Most of the Jaffna Peninsula in the N is covered by limestone laid down in shallow seas between 7 mill and 26 mill years ago.

Rivers and lakes

The only river of any length is the Mahaweli Ganga which rises about 50 km S of Kandy and flows N then NE to the sea at Trincomalee, covering a distance of 320 km. A number of the rivers have now been developed both for irrigation and power, the Victoria project of development on the Mahaweli Ganga being one of the biggest in Asia – and one of the most controversial. It has created Sri Lanka's largest lake.

Wildlife

Sri Lanka's 24 wildlife sanctuaries are home to a wide range of native species, eg elephants, leopard, sloth bear, the unique loris, a variety of deer, the purple-faced langur monkey, the endangered wild boar, porcupines and ant-eaters. Reptiles include the marsh crocodile. The 3 largest sanctuaries are the National Parks at **Ruhuna** (Yala), **Wilpattu** and **Gal Oya**. Among the 16 amphibians unique to the island are the **Nanophrys frogs** in the hills. Most of the fish are river or marsh dwelling – the trout, introduced by the British, being found in the cool streams of the Horton Plains.

The indigenous 240 (of the total of 440) species of butterflies are seen below 1000m and Mar/Apr is the period of seasonal migration. Sri Lanka is also an ornithologist's paradise with over 250 resident species, mostly found in the Wet Zone, including the Grackle, whistling thrush, yellow-eared Bulbul, Malkoha and brown-capped Babbler. The **Sinharaja Reserve** and the highland **Peak Wilderness Sanctuary** nr Adam's Peak, are famous. The winter migrants come from distant Siberia and W Europe, the reservoirs attracting vast numbers of waterbirds (stilts, sandpipers, terns and plover, as well as herons, egrets and storks). The forests attract species of warblers, thrushes, cuckoo and many others. The **Kumana** in the E, and **Bundala** (famed for flamingoes), **Kalametiya** and **Wirawila** between Tissemaharam and Hambantota in the S, all with lagoons, are the principal Bird Sanctuaries. The Wildlife Conservation programme is undertaken by the government with an office in Colombo.

Climate

Rainfall

Sri Lanka is divided into 2 unequal climatic regions. About three quarters of the island – the entire N and E region – comprises the 'dry zone'. In the rainshadow of the central highlands during the SW monsoon, this area receives most of its rain during the Oct-Dec period of the retreating monsoon, yet despite the term 'dry zone', it can be very wet indeed. The SW quarter of the island receives rain both from the NE and from the SW monsoon, and in the wetter highlands the total rises to over 5500 mm. The timing of the monsoons is very irregular, and the wetter times of year are also extremely humid.

Temperatures

The major temperature differences reflect contrasts in altitude. On the plains temperature reflects the degree of cloud cover, but maximum temperatures are rarely as high as in India. Because it lies so close to the Equator there is little variation in temperature from month to month. Colombo, virtually at sea level, has minimum of 25°C in Dec and a maximum of 28°C in May. At Nuwara Eliya, the average daytime temperatures hover around 16°C, but you need to be prepared for the chill in the evenings. Only the NE occasionally experiences temperatures of up to 38°C.

History

Prehistory

Stone tools from the Middle Palaeolithic Age have been found in several places, evidence of settlement in Sri Lanka perhaps as much as 500,000 years ago. However, no Neolithic tools have been found, and the Copper Age which is so well represented in peninsular India from the 2nd millennium BC is unrepresented. The picture changes with the arrival of the Iron Age, for the megalithic graves, associated with black and red pottery, suggest that Sri Lanka had direct contact with South India well before the Aryans immigrated from North

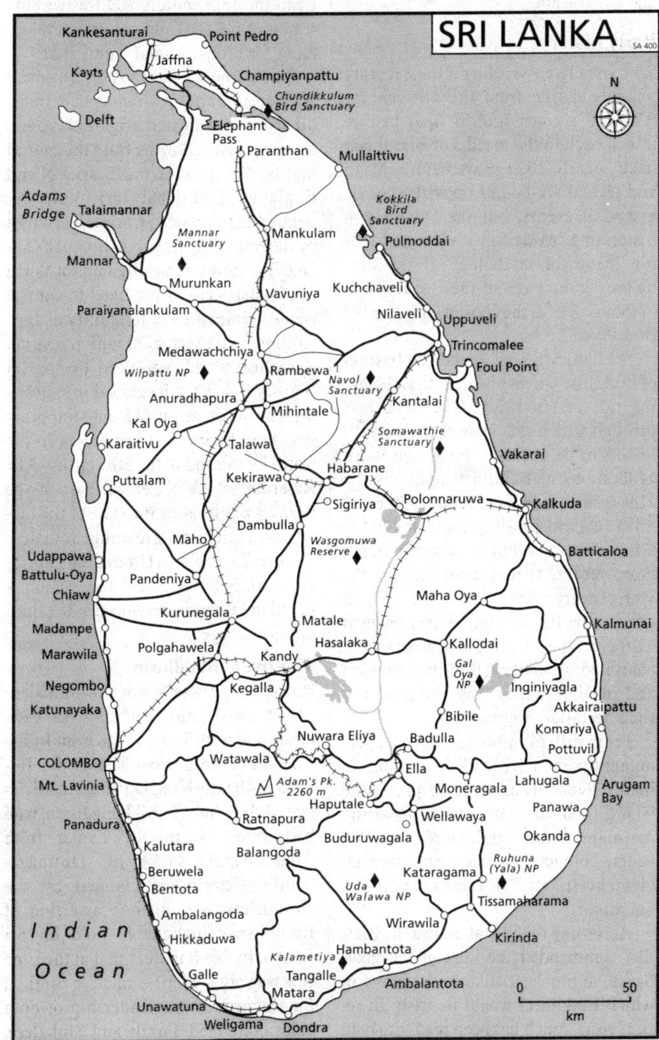

India from around 500 BC. However Sri Lanka's archaeological record is comparatively sparse, with barely any evidence with which to date the development of Stone Age cultures or the later spread of domesticated animals and cultivation.

Early history

Sri Lanka has a written political history possibly dating from the 6th century AD, and a conception of that history traced back to the origins of Buddhism itself, nearly 1000 years before. Myth and legend are bound up with specific historical events, but the Sri Lankan historian K M de Silva has noted that the historical mythology of the Sinhalese "is the basis of their conception of themselves as the chosen guardians of Buddhism."

Sri Lanka is seen as the last bastion of Buddhist sanctity against the advancing tide of Hinduism. The basic text through which this view of the island's history has been passed on by successive generations of Buddhist monks is the *Mahavansa* (the *Great Lineage*), which de Silva suggests possibly goes back to the 6th century AD, but is probably much more recent. It was continued in the 13th century text the *Culavamsa*, which gives a very full account of the medieval history of the island. These works were compiled by *bhikkus* (Buddhist monks) and inevitably they have the marks of their sectarian origins.

Proximity to India has played a permanent part in Sri Lanka's developing history. Not only have the peoples of the island themselves originated from the mainland, but through more than 2000 years, contact has been an essential element in all Sri Lanka's political equations.

According to the Mahavansa the Buddha commanded the king of the gods, Sakra, to protect Lanka as the home in which Buddhism would flourish. In recent years, much has been read into both the text and to more recent history to suggest that Sinhalese have always been at war with the Tamils. The truth is far more complicated. The earliest settlement of the island took place in the NE, the region now known as the dry zone. Until the 13th century AD this was the region of political and cultural development for Sinhalese and Tamil alike.

The economy and the culture developed around the creation of an extraordinarily sophisticated irrigation system, using the rivers flowing from the central highlands across the much drier N and E plains. Traditional agriculture depended entirely on the rainfall brought by the retreating monsoon between Oct-Dec. The developing kingdoms of North Sri Lanka realised the need to control water to improve the reliability of agriculture, and a system of tank irrigation was already well advanced by the 1st century BC. This developed into possibly the most advanced contemporary system of hydraulic engineering in the world by the end of the 5th century AD. **Rajarata** in the N central part of the island's plains grew into one of the major core regions of developing Sinhalese culture. To its N was **Uttaradesa** ('northern country'), while in the SE region of the island **Rohana** developed as the third political centre.

The rise of Buddhism

Periodically these centres of Sinhalese power came into conflict with each other, and with Tamil kings from India. The Mahavansa records how the Rohana Sinhalese King Dutthagamani defeated the Chola Tamil King Elara, who had ruled North Sri Lanka from Anuradhapura, in 140 BC. Dutthagamani's victory was claimed by the chroniclers as a historic assertion of Buddhism's inalienable hold on Sri Lanka. In fact it is clear that at the time this was not a Tamil-Sinhalese conflict, for the armies and leadership of both sides contained Tamils and Sinhalese.

By that time Buddhism had already been a power in the island for 2 centuries, when the king *Devanampiya Tissa* (307-267 BC) converted to Buddhism, probably under the influence of missionaries sent by the Mauryan Emperor Asoka led by Mahinda, who was either Asoka's son or brother.

Buddhism became the state religion, identified with the growth of Sinhalese culture and political power. The power of the central kingdom based at *Anuradhapura* was rarely unchallenged or complete. Power was decentralised, with a large measure of local autonomy. Furthermore, provincial centres periodically established their independence. Anuradhapura became one of Asia's pre-eminent cities, but from the 11th century AD *Polonnaruwa* took over as capital.

The Tamil involvement Buddhist power was predominant in Sri Lanka from the 1st century BC, but Sri Lankan kings often deliberately sought Tamil support in their own disputes. As a result Sri Lanka was affected by political developments in South India, and the rise of the expansionist Tamil kingdoms of the Pandiyas, Pallavas and Cholas from the 5th century AD increased the scope for interaction with the mainland. In de Silva's words, "South Indian auxiliaries became in time a vitally important, if not the most powerful element in the armies of the Sinhalese rulers, and an unpredictable, turbulent group who were often a threat to political stability. They were also the nucleus of a powerful Tamil influence in the court."

It was not a one way flow. Occasionally the Sinhalese were themselves drawn in to attack Tamil kings in India, as in the 9th century when they attacked the Cholas. The Chola Emperor Rajaraja I responded by invading North Sri Lanka and adding Jaffna and the N plains, including Anuradhapura, to his empire. See pages 802 and 871. The Cholas ruled from Polonnaruva for 75 years, finally being driven out by the Rohana king Vijayabahu I in 1070 AD. He established peace and a return to some prosperity in the N before civil war broke out and disrupted the civil administration again. Only the 33 year rule of Parakramabahu I (1153-1186) interrupted the decline. Some of Sri Lanka's most remarkable monuments date from his reign, including the massive irrigation embankment 12m high and 15 km long which enclosed the *Parakrama Samudra (Sea of Parakrama)* at Polonnaruwa. However, it was the collapse of this kingdom and its ultimate annihilation by the Tamils in the 13th century that left not only its physical imprint on the North Sri Lankan landscape but also an indelible psychological mark on the Sri Lankan perception of neighbouring Tamil Hindus.

The Sinhalese move South

Other factors, such as the spread of malaria which occurred with the deterioration in maintenance of the irrigation system, may have led to the progressive desertion of the N and E plains and the movement S of the centre of gravity of the Island's population. Between the 12th and 17th centuries Sinhalese moved from the dry to the wet zone. This required a change in agriculture from irrigated to rainfed crops. Trade also increased, especially in cinnamon, an activity controlled by the rising population of Muslim seafarers. A Tamil kingdom was set up in Jaffna for the first time, briefly coming back under Sinhalese power (under the Sinhalese king Parakramabahu VI, 1412-67, based in his capital at *Kotte*), but generally remaining independent, and a frequent threat to the power of the Sinhalese kingdoms to the S. Other threats came from overseas. As early as the 13th century, a Buddhist king from Malaya invaded Sri Lanka twice to try and capture the tooth relic and the Buddha's alms bowl. In the early 15th century the Island was even invaded by a fleet of Chinese junks sent by the Ming Emperors.

The Kandyan kingdom

Between the S and N kingdoms, Kandy became the capital of a new kingdom around 1480. Establishing its base in the central highlands, it became a powerful independent kingdom by the end of the 15th century. By the early 16th century the Sinhalese kingdom of Kotte in the S was hopelessly fragmented, giving impetus to Kandy's rise to independent power. Its remote and inaccessible position gave it added protection from the early colonial invasions. Using both force and diplomacy to capitalise on its geographical advantages, it survived as the last independent Sinhalese kingdom until 1815. It had played the game of seeking alliances with one colonial power against another with considerable success, first seeking the help of the Dutch against the Portuguese, then of the British against the Dutch. However, this policy ran out of potential allies when the British established their supremacy over the Island in 1796, and by 1815 the last Kandyan King, a Tamil Hindu converted to Buddhism, was deposed by his Sinhalese chiefs, who sought an accord with the new British rulers in exchange for retaining a large measure of their own power.

Colonial power

The succession of 3 colonial powers, the Portuguese, Dutch and the British, finally ended the independent Sinhalese and Tamil rule. There also lay the threat of expanding Islam, evidenced in the conversion of the inhabitants of islands on the Arab trading routes such as the Maldives and the Laccadives as well as significant numbers on the SW coast of India. The Portuguese arrived in Sri Lanka 1605 and established control over some of the island's narrow coastal plains around Colombo. They were responsible for large-scale conversions to Roman Catholicism which today accounts for 90% of the island's Christians, leaving both a linguistic legacy and an imprint on the population, evidenced today in many names of Portuguese origin.

During this period the rest of the island was dominated by the rulers of Sitavaka, who overpowered the Kotte kingdom in 1565 and dominated the whole of the SW apart from Colombo. For 10 years they occupied Kandy itself, nearly evicted the Portuguese and came close to reasserting Sinhalese power in the far N.

By 1619 the **Portuguese** had annexed Jaffna, which thereafter was treated by the **Dutch**, and more importantly the British, as simply part of the Island state. They were less successful in subjugating Kandy, and in 1650 they were ousted by the Dutch, who extended colonial control from Negombo (40 km N of Colombo), S right round the coast to Trincomalee, as well as the entire N peninsula, leaving the Kandyan kingdom in charge of the remainder. Because the Portuguese and Dutch were interested in little other than the spice

Handling The Police

Dealings with the police can be very difficult and in the worst regions even dangerous. The paper work involved in reporting losses can be time consuming and irritating, and your own documentation (e.g. passport and visas) may be demanded. In some states the police themselves sometimes demand bribes, though tourists should not assume, however, that if procedures move slowly they are automatically being expected to offer a bribe. If you have to go to a police station if possible take someone with you. If you face really serious problems, for example in connection with driving accidents, you should contact your consular offices as quickly as possible.

trade, they bent most of their efforts to producing the goods necessary for their trade. The British replaced the Dutch in 1795-6 when British power was being consolidated in South India at the expense of the French and the Mysore Muslim Raja, Tipu Sultan, see page 994. Their original purpose was to secure the important Indian Ocean port of Trincomalee. B.H. Farmer points out that by 1802 "it was apparent that Madras-trained officials were, apart from other disabilities, quite unable to understand the language and customs of the Sinhalese, and Ceylon became a Crown Colony."

When the **British** came to control the whole island after 1815 they established a quite distinctive imprint on the island's society and economy. This was most obvious in the introduction of plantation agriculture. During the British period coffee took over from cinnamon, but by the beginning of the 20th century, even though coffee had largely been wiped out by disease, plantation agriculture was the dominant pillar of the cash economy. Rice production stagnated and then declined, and Sri Lanka became dependent on the export of cash crops and the import of food. In 1948 it was only producing about 35% of its rice needs. Society too underwent radical changes, with the widespread adoption of English education among the urban middle class.

The moves to Independence

Buddhist and Sinhalese dominated in its early stages, no one in the Independence movement at the turn of the century would have believed that British rule would end within 50 years – nor would many have wanted it to. The **Ceylon National Congress**, formed in 1919, was conservative and pragmatic, but the pressures of imminent democratic self-rule made themselves felt throughout the 1930s, as minority groups pressed to protect their position. Universal suffrage came in 1931, along with the promise of self rule from the British Government. It had the positive benefit of encouraging the development of welfare policies such as health care, nutrition and public education. However, it also had the immediate impact of encouraging a resurgence of nationalism linked with Buddhist revivalism.

Sinhalese Stupas

The Sinhalese classify the domes into six different types, such as bell-shaped, or bubble-shaped. On top of the dome is a small square enclosure (*hataraes kotuwa*), which contained valuable offerings, surrounded by a railed pavilion. Above it is the ceremonial umbrella (*chatta*). The Sri Lankan parasols are furled into a staff-like shape (see page 1312). Percy Brown suggests that they are more reminiscent of the totem poles of the Veddas, and may be derived from aboriginal symbols. Originally the cubical box housed the sacred relics themselves. However, the post left little room for the relics and offerings. A compartment was then hollowed out of the brickwork immediately below the staff. Into it was lowered the 'mystic stone', a granite block carved with 9 recesses to contain the relics and offerings. The finial staff then sealed and surmounted the relic stone and the whole dagoba.

Many of these buildings are immense, and enormous effort went into ensuring that they would last. The Mahavansa records how King Dutthagamani prepared their foundations. The base was laid of round stones, crushed by pounding and then trampled by huge elephants with leather shoes to protect their feet. Clay was then spread over the hard core, followed by a layer of iron, another layer of stones and then a layer of ordinary stone.

Serendipity – The Island Of The Lion

Sri Lanka has had many different names in its long history. To the Greeks and Romans it was Taprobane, a word derived from Pali and Sanskrit names, Tambavanna, Tambrapani and Tambapanni. In the form of Tamraparni it remains the name today of the major river of Tirunelveli District in Tamil Nadu, across the Palk Straits. Other names were derived from the Pali word for lion, ***Sihalam***. Thus Salai, Siele, Sielidiba, Sielendiba and Serendip have all been used at one time or another. Serendip could have evolved from 'Swarandwip' (golden isle) and hence 'Sarandip'. Serendib gave English the word serendipity, coined by the writer Horace Walpole, to describe the gift of making happy and unexpected discoveries purely by accident. From 1802, when the Island became a British Crown Colony, until 1972, when the island took its present name of Sri Lanka (the 'hallowed island') it was known as Ceylon. This too had a number of forms – among them Ceilan, Ceyllan, Sailan and Zeilan. Lanka itself had the early form of Lankadipa, and the more recent Lankava. It was a name that crossed the straits to India, for the Tamils knew the island not only as Eelam or Ilanare but as Elankai, in which form it figured in a wide range of Hindu myths.

Independence came with scarcely a murmur on 4 February 1948, 6 months after that of India and Pakistan. Ceylon's first Prime Minister was Don Stephen Senanayake. His son **Dudley Senanayake**, who followed, was identified with a pragmatic nationalism. The heart of his programme was the recolonisation of the deserted Sinhalese heartlands of the dry zone.

Art and architecture

Sri Lankan architecture has many features in common with Buddhist and Hindu Indian traditions, but the long period of relative isolation, and the determined preservation of Buddhism long after its demise in India, have contributed to some very distinctive features.

Buddhist architecture

Stupas were the most striking feature of Buddhist architecture in India, see page 774. Originally they were funeral mounds, built to house the remains of the Buddha and his disciples. The tradition was developed by Sri Lanka's Sinhalese kings, notably in golden age of the 4th and 5th centuries AD, and the revival during the 11th-12th centuries AD. Some of the stupas (*Dagobas*) are huge structures, and even those such as the 4th century *Jetavana* at Anuradhapura, now simply a grassed-over brick mound, is impressively large.

Few of the older Buddhist monuments are in their original form, either having become ruins or been renovated. Hemispherical mounds built of brick and filled with brick and rubble, they stand on a square terrace, surmounted by 3 concentric platforms. In its original or its restored form, the brick mound is covered with plaster and painted white. Surrounding it on a low platform (*vahalakadas*) is the ambulatory, or circular path, reached from the cardinal directions by stone stairways. Around some of the dagobas there are fine sculptures on these circular paths at the head of each stairway.

The design is filled with symbolic meaning. The hemisphere is the dome of heaven, the axis of the cosmos being represented by the central finial on top, while the umbrella-like tiers are the rising heavens of the gods. Worshippers walk round the stupa on the raised platform in a clockwise direction (*pradakshina*), following the rotational movement of the celestial bodies.

Many smaller stupas were built within circular buildings. These were covered with a metal and timber roof resting on concentric rows of stone pillars. Today the roofs have disappeared, but examples such as the *Vatadage* at Polonnaruwa can still be seen. King Parakramabahu I also built another feature of Sri Lankan architecture at Polonnaruwa, a large rectangular hall in which was placed an image of the Buddha. Most of Sri Lanka's early secular architecture has disappeared. Made of wood, there are remnants of magnificent royal palaces at both Anuradhapura and Sigiriya.

Moonstones

Sri Lanka's moonstones (not the gem) are among the world's finest artistic achievements. Polished semi-circular granite, they are carved in concentric semi-circular rings ('half-moons', about 1m in radius) portraying various animals, flowers and birds, and normally placed at the foot of flights of steps or entrances to important buildings. There are particularly fine examples in Anuradhapura and Polonnaruwa.

Hindu architecture

Sri Lankan Hindu architecture bears close resemblances with the Dravida styles of neighbouring Tamil Nadu, see page 807.

Sculpture

Early Sri Lankan sculpture shows close links with Indian Buddhist sculpture. The first images of the Buddha, some of which are still in Anuradhapura, are similar to 2nd-3rd century AD images from Andhra Pradesh. The middle period of the 5th to 11th centuries AD contains some magnificent sculptures on rocks, but there is a range of other sculpture, notably moonstones. There are decorated bands of flower motifs, geese and a variety of animals, both Anuradhapura and Polonnaruwa having outstanding examples. While the moonstones are brilliant works in miniature, Sri Lankan sculptors also produced outstanding colossal works, such as the 13m high Buddha at Avukana or the reclining Buddha at Polonnaruwa.

Painting

Sri Lanka's most famous art is its rock paintings from Sigiriya, dating from the 6th century AD. The heavenly nymphs (*apsaras*), scattering flowers from the clouds, are shown with extraordinary grace and beauty. Polonnaruwa saw a later flowering of the painting tradition in the 12th and 13th centuries, but thereafter Sri Lankan art declined.

Culture

People and language

The earliest occupants were aboriginal tribes of Australoid, Negrito and Mediterranean stock, now almost entirely absorbed in the settled populations. Evidence of their origins is limited, but megalithic burial sites suggest that there may well have been migrations from South India from before the major migrations that brought Buddhism and Hinduism into the island up until about 100 BC. The earliest named culture is that of **Balangoda**, distributed across the whole island between 5000 and 500 BC. The **Veddas** are the only inhabitants today whose ancestors were in Sri Lanka before the Aryan migrations. Related to the Dravidian jungle peoples in South India, they dwelt in caves and rock shelters, and lived by hunting and gathering. They practised a cult of the dead, communicating with ancestors through reincarnated spirits. Today the Veddas have been largely absorbed into the Sinhalese community and have virtually ceased to have a separate existence. In the mid 1960s their numbers had shrunk to under 800, from over 5000 at the beginning of the century.

Migration from India The overwhelming majority of the present population of Sri Lanka owes its origins to successive waves of migration from 2 different regions of India. Most people are of Indo-Aryan origin and came from North India. **Sinhala**, the language of the Sinhalese, is an Indo-European language with East Indian affinities (Bihar) unlike the Dravidian language Tamil. The earliest migrations from North India may have taken place as early as the 5th century BC. Although these migrants brought with them their North Indian language, they were not yet Buddhists, for Buddhism did not arrive in Sri Lanka until the 3rd century BC. The origins of Tamil settlement are unclear, but are thought to go back at least to the 3rd century BC, when there is clear evidence of trade between Sri Lanka and South India.

Today the *Sinhalese* make up 74% of the total population. Sri Lanka's *Tamil* population comprises the long settled Tamils of the N and E (12.6%) and the migrant workers on the tea plantations in the central highlands (5.5%) who settled in Sri Lanka from the late 19th century onwards. By 1992 over 340,000 adults from this Tamil community had been repatriated to India. The so-called '**Moors**', Tamil speaking Muslims of Indian-Arab descent, were traders on the E coast and now number over 1.1 million (7.7%). A much smaller but highly distinct community is that of the **Burghers**, numbering about 50,000. The Dutch (mainly members of the Dutch Reformed Church), and the Portuguese intermarried with local people, and their descendants were urban and ultimately English speaking. There are similar numbers of Malays and smaller groups of Kaffirs. The Malays are Muslims who were brought by the Dutch from Java. The Kaffirs were brought by the Portuguese from Mozambique and other parts of East Africa as mercenaries.

Religion

Sri Lankan Buddhism

Sri Lankan Buddhism survived in the Hinayana form which became extinct in mainland India, See introduction, page 85. King **Devanampiya Tissa** (d207 BC), converted by Asoka's son Mahinda, established the Mahavihara monastery. Successors repeatedly struggled to preserve its distinct identity from that of neighbouring Hinduism and Tantrism. It was also constantly struggling with Mahayana Buddhism, which gained the periodic support of successive royal patrons. King Mahasena (AD 276-303) and his son Sri Meghavarna, who brought the famous 'tooth of the Buddha' to the island, both advocated Mahayana forms of the faith.

Sri Lanka's Buddhism is not strictly orthodox. The personal character of the Buddha is emphasised, as was the virtue of being a disciple of the Buddha. *Maitreya*, the 'future' Buddha, is recognised as the only Bodhisattva, and it has been a feature of Buddhism in the island for kings to identify themselves with this incarnation of the Buddha.

The Sinhalese see themselves as guardians of the original Buddhist faith. They believe that Pali scripture was first written down by King **Vattagamani Abhaya** in the 1st century BC. The *Pali canon* of scripture is referred to as 3 'baskets', because the palm leaf texts on which they were written were stored in baskets. They are '**conduct**' (*vinaya*), or rules; '**sermon**' (*sutta*), the largest and most important of the 3; and '**metaphysics**' (*Abhidhamma*). There are also several works that lack the full authority of the canon but are none the less important. Basham suggests that the main propositions of the literature are psychological rather than metaphysical. Suffering, sorrow and dissatisfaction are the nature of ordinary life, and can only be eliminated by giving up desire. In turn, desire is a result of the misplaced belief in the reality of individual existence. In its

Theravada form, Hinanaya Buddhism taught that there is no soul and ultimately no god. Nirvana was a state of rest beyond the universe, once found never lost.

The cosmology Although the Buddha discouraged the development of cosmologies, the Hinayana Buddhists produced a cyclical view of the universe, evolving through 4 time periods. Period 1 Man slowly declines until everything is destroyed except the highest heaven. The good go to this heaven, the remainder to various hells. Period 2 A quiescent phase. Period 3 Evolution begins again. However, 'the good *karma* of beings in the highest heaven' (see page 69) now begins to fail, and a lower heaven evolves, a *world of form*. During this period a great being in the higher heaven dies, and is re-born in the world of form as Brahma. Feeling lonely, he wishes that others were with him. Soon other beings from the higher heaven die and are reborn in this world. Brahma interprets these people as his own creation, and himself as The Creator. Period 4 The first men, who initially had supernatural qualities, deteriorate and become earthbound, and the period fluctuates between advance and deterioration.

The 4-period cycles continue for eternity, alternating between 'Buddha cycles' – one of which we live in today – and 'empty cycles'. It is believed that in the present cycle 4 Buddhas – *Krakucchanda*, *Kanakamuni*, *Kasyapa*, and *Sakyamuni* – have already taught, and one, *Maitreya*, is still to come.

In Sri Lanka the scriptures came to be attributed with almost magical powers. Close ties developed between Buddhist belief and Sinhalese nationalism. The Sinhalese scholar *Buddhaghosa* translated Sinhalese texts into Pali in the 5th century AD. At the beginning of the 11th century Sri Lankan missionaries were responsible for the conversion of Thailand, Burma, Cambodia and Laos to Theravadin Buddhism. In the face of continued threats to their continued survival, Sri Lanka's Buddhist monks had to be re-ordained into the valid line of Theravadin lineage by monks from SE Asia. Buddhist links with Thailand remain close.

Buddhist practice

By the time Buddhism was brought to Sri Lanka there was a well developed religious organisation which had strong links with secular authorities. Developments in Buddhist thought and belief had made it possible for peasants and lay people to share in the religious beliefs of the faith. As it developed in Sri Lanka the main outlines of practice became clearly defined. The king and the orders of monks became interdependent; a monastic hierarchy was established; most monks were learning and teaching, rather than practising withdrawal from the world. Most important, Buddhism accepted a much wider range of goals for living than simply the release from permanent rebirth.

The most important of these was 'good rebirth', the prevention of misfortune and the increase in good fortune during the present life. These additions to original Buddhist thought led to a number of contradictions and tensions, summarised by Tambiah as: the Buddha as a unique individual, rather than a type of person (*Bodhisattva*) coming into the world periodically to help achieve release from *samsara* (rebirth), or rebirth into a better life; Buddhism as a path to salvation for all, or as a particular, nationalist religion; Buddhism as renunciation of the world and all its obligations, in contrast with playing a positive social role; and finally, whether monasteries should be run by the monks themselves, or with the support and involvement of secular authorities. These tensions are reflected in many aspects of Buddhism in Sri Lanka today, as in debates between monks who argue for political action as against withdrawal from the world.

Until the 16th century Buddhism in Sri Lanka enjoyed the active support of the state. It remained longest in Kandy, but was withdrawn steadily after the British took control in 1815. The 18th century revival of Buddhism in the wet zone was sponsored by the landowning village headmen, not by royalty, and castes such as the Goyigama and Salagama played a prominent role. Through the 19th century they became the dominant influence on Buddhist thought, while the remaining traditional Buddhist authority in Kandy, the Siyam Nikaya, suffered permanent loss of influence. This new, independent, Buddhism, became active and militant. It entered into direct competition with Christians in proselytising, and in setting up schools, special associations and social work.

After Independence, political forces converged to encourage State support for Buddhism. The lay leadership pressed the government to protect Buddhists from competition with other religious groups. The Sinhalese political parties saw benefits in emphasising the role of Buddhism in society.

Hinduism

Hindu beliefs are outlined in the introduction, see page 67. Hinduism in North Sri Lanka was brought over by successive Tamil kings and their followers. Most Hindus in Sri Lanka are Saivite.

Jaffna was subject to Christian missionary work, especially through education, from the early 19th century. It produced a Hindu response, and a Hindu renaissance took place in the late 19th century under the leadership of *Arumuga Navalar*. Setting up an extensive network of schools, he was anxious to strengthen orthodox Saivism, on the one hand through restoring temples and on the other by publishing religious texts.

Virtually all Hindu temples in Sri Lanka were destroyed by the Portuguese and the Dutch. Those that have been rebuilt never had the resources available to compare with those in India, not having had their lands restored in the post colonial period, so they are generally small. However, they play a prominent part in Hindu life. De Silva suggests that Navalar's failure to argue for social reform meant that caste – and untouchability – were virtually untouched. The high caste **Vellalas**, a small minority of the total Hindu population, maintained their power unchallenged until after Independence. Removal of caste disabilities started in the 1950s. The struggle by Tamils for Independence may well have transformed the whole basis of caste discrimination far more thoroughly than any programme of social reform.

Islam

Islam was brought to Sri Lanka by Arab traders. However, numbers were swelled by conversion from both Buddhists and Hindus, and by immigrant Muslims from South India who fled the Portuguese along the W coast of India. There are also Muslims of Malay origin. Both in Kandy and the coastal districts Muslims have generally lived side by side with Buddhists, often sharing common interests against the colonial powers. However, one of the means by which Muslims maintained their identity was to refuse to be drawn into colonial education. As a result, by the end of the 19th century the Muslims were among the least educated groups. A Muslim lawyer, *Siddi Lebbe*, helped to change attitudes and encourage participation by Muslims.

In 1915 there were major Sinhalese-Muslim riots, and Muslims began a period of active collaboration with the British, joining other minorities led by the Tamils in the search for security and protection of their rights against the Sinhalese. The Muslims have been particularly anxious to maintain Muslim family law, and to gain concessions on education. One of the chief of these is the teaching of Arabic in government schools to Muslim children. Until 1974 Muslims were unique among minorities in having the right to choose which of 3 languages – Sinhala, Tamil or English – would be their medium of instruction. Since then a new category of Muslim schools has been set up, allowing them to distance themselves from the Tamil Hindu community, whose language most of them speak.

Christianity

Christianity was introduced by the Portuguese. Unlike India, where Christian missionary work from the late 18th century was often carried out in spite of colonial government rather than with its active support, in Sri Lanka missionary activity enjoyed various forms of state backing. One Sinhalese king, Dharmapala, was converted, endowing the church, and even some high caste families became Christian. When the Dutch evicted the Portuguese they tried to suppress Roman Catholicism, and the Dutch Reformed Church found some converts. Other Protestant denominations followed the arrival of the British, though not always with official support or encouragement. Many of the churches remained dependent on outside support. Between the 2 World Wars Christian influence in government was radically reduced. Denominational schools lost their protection and special status, and since the 1960s have had to come to terms with a completely different role in Sri Lanka.

Caste

The elements of the caste system were probably present in pre-Buddhist Sri Lanka, with both the priestly caste of Brahmins and a range of low caste groups such as scavengers. Although Buddhism encouraged its followers to eradicate distinction based on caste, the system clearly survived. There are 25 castes among the contemporary Sinhalese. The highest is the *goyigama* caste of cultivators. Unlike India, where fishing is a low caste occupation, the *Karava* caste of fishermen among the Sinhalese is high caste. Service castes are at the bottom of the hierarchy. The Tamil Hindus have evolved a distinct caste hierarchy from their Indian neighbours, having no significant Brahmin community. The *Vellalas*, who control land rights, carried out priestly functions, and are top of the hierarchy in North Sri Lanka. At the bottom of the scale were the landless labourers such as the Pallas and Nallavas. The tea plantation workers are all regarded as low caste.

Crafts

Local craft skills are still practised widely in households across the country. Pottery, coir fibre, carpentry, handloom weaving and metalwork all receive government assistance. Some of the crafts are concentrated in just a few villages. **Brasswork**, for example, is restricted to a small area around Kandy, where the 'city of arts', Kalapura, has over 70 families of craftsmen making superb brass, wood, silver and gold items. Fine **gold and silver chain work** is done both in the Pettah area of Colombo and in Jaffna. **Batiks**, from wall hangings to sarongs, and a wide range of handloom household linen are widely available. **Silver jewellery** (also from Kandy), trays, ornaments and inlay work is a further specialisation. **Masks** are a popular product in the SW of the island, based on traditional masks used in dance dramas while Galle and the S is famous for lace-making.

MODERN SRI LANKA

Government

In its first 30 years of Independence Sri Lanka held 8 general elections, sometimes accompanied by radical changes in political direction. Between 1956 and

1977 the governing party always lost. Power alternated between the socialist **Sri Lanka Freedom Party** (SLFP), and the free-market **United National Party** (UNP), which had formed the first government after Independence. Neither has succeeded in achieving the economic success which could keep pace with the growing demands of an increasingly young and literate population, struggling for jobs. Education has been one of the triumphs, with the country, high adult literacy figures. It has the 6th highest pupil-teacher ratio in the world, with 14 primary pupils per teacher (Asiaweek).

There has been a series of moves to turn away from British institutions and styles of government. Both parties have competed in the search for more and more potent symbols of national identity, largely Buddhist and Sinhalese. The last decade has seen the divisions worked out in ethnic conflict of these 2 fundamental aspects of political development.

Since July 1983, when an anti-Tamil pogrom devastated many Tamil areas of Colombo and led to the loss of hundreds of Tamil lives, Sri Lanka has been locked in a bitter conflict between the government forces and Tamil guerrillas. Over 150,000 Tamils fled as refugees to India. In the N and E, Tamil militancy rapidly gained ground, and between 1983 and 1987 the **Liberation Tigers of Tamil Eelam** (LTTE or just 'the Tigers') waged an increasingly successful battle for control of what they regarded as the Tamil homeland, both against rival Tamil groups and against the Sri Lankan armed forces. In response the Government mounted increasingly strong attacks into the N, and in summer 1987 launched what was hailed as a final offensive.

The conflict had been watched with growing concern by the Indian government, which opposed the creation of a separate Tamil State in Sri Lanka but feared the domestic political consequences of failing to support Sri Lankan Tamils in the face of increasingly genocidal attacks. In July 1987 the Indian Prime Minister Rajiv Gandhi forced President Jayawardene and the Sri Lankan Government to accept a peace accord, under which the Indian army would enter Sri Lanka to restore law and order and elections would be held to elect Provincial Councils.

In the event the Indian army became bogged down in a conflict with the Tigers themselves. At the same time the presence of the Indian forces roused fierce opposition from the Sinhalese, and the angry upsurge of support among young people for the fiercely anti-Tamil **JVP party** in the S of the island was accompanied by escalating violence and disruption. Many people 'disappeared' (presumed dead) at this time.

In November 1989 the 2 key leaders of the JVP were killed, and the new Sri Lankan Government of President Premadasa claimed its first major success. Soon it was able to claim another, for it appeared to have succeeded in reaching an agreement with the Tigers on a withdrawal of the Indian Peace Keeping Force, finally completed in March 1990. That accord soon broke down. Although the S was now quiet, in mid 1994 civil war continued in the far the N of the Island. The assassination of President Premadasa on 1 May 1993 at a Labour Day parade in Colombo marked a further destructive twist in the island's violent fabric. Following less than 2 weeks after the assasination of another high ranking former cabinet minister, Lalith Athulathmudali, President Premadasa's assassination by a suicide bomber was believed by the government to be at the hands of the Tamil Tigers (the LTTE). They disclaimed responsibility, though the method used was very similar to that of the woman LTTE member who was responsible for the death of Rajiv Gandhi in India in May 1991, and for which at the time the leadership had also disclaimed responsibilty. The Sri Lankan Prime Minister, Dingiri Banda Wijetunga, was elected President in Mr Premadasa's place on 7 May 1993.

District elections in 1994 suggested that there was a strong tide flowing against the UNP government. Mrs Bandaranaike's Sri Lanka Freedom Party, weakened for many years by internal factionalism and defeat at the hands of the UNP, was making a strong comeback. The SLFP itself underwent important changes in its leadership, Mrs Bandaranaike's son Anura deserting the party for the UNP, while her daughter Chandrika took up the mantle as her mother's chosen successor. In July 1994 President Wijetunga dissolved the Assembly and called elections for August 1994, ahead of the Presidential election scheduled for December.

Economy

Agriculture and fishing

About 25% of Sri Lanka's area is cultivated by sedentary farmers or under cultivated forests, a further 15% being under shifting cultivation. About half is under forest, grassland, swamp and waste land. In the wet zone virtually all the cultivable land is now taken up.

Sri Lanka has not produced enough food to meet the needs of its population since the 18th century, yet in many respects it has been the most obviously prosperous state in South Asia. In the 1970s more than half the money earned from the export of tea, rubber and coconuts was spent on importing foodgrains, leaving little for investment. Attempts to increase rice production have ranged from land reform to the introduction of high yielding varieties (hyv).

Sri Lanka has 2 main rice growing seasons. The *Maha* crop is harvested between Jan and Mar, the *Yala* crop between Aug-Sep. By the early 1980s there was virtually a 100% takeup of new varieties. Yields have increased to over 4 tonnes per ha, and production has risen towards 80% of domestic needs despite the speed of population growth. In addition to the intensification programme the Government has also carried out major colonisation schemes, bringing new land under rice cultivation. This has been expensive and certainly not always cost effective, but in part has been a response to political pressures to reclaim land for Sinhalese cultivators.

The cash crops of tea, rubber and coconuts continue to contribute the lion's share of Sri Lanka's foreign exchange earnings. In 1950 this stood at 96%. In 1992 over 50% of foreign exchange earnings still came from these 3 products alone. **Tea** has suffered from inadequate investment and fierce competition from expanding production in other countries of cheaper, lower quality tea. The area cropped under tea fell steadily, but production nearly doubled between 1948 and 1965. It declined to around 180 million kg in 1983. Since then it has risen again to over 210 million kg in 1991 though severe drought threatened to reduce the crop in 1992. Tea alone still accounts for Rs 10.6 bn of exports, 33% of the total value of exports, followed by rubber (Rs 3 bn) and coconuts (Rs 1.4 bn).

Potentially rich fishery resources have yet to be fully developed. Fresh water stocking programmes have increased the yield of rivers and lakes, and brackish water fishing is becoming increasingly commercialised. However, nearly 40% of households which depend on fishing have no boats or equipment, and despite the potential of the export market production does not meet domestic demand.

Resources and industry

Sri Lanka has few fossil fuels or metallic minerals. Gemstones, graphite (crystalline carbon) and heavy mineral sands are the most valuable resources, though clays, sands and limestones are abundant. Gemstones include sapphires, rubies, topaz, zircon, tourmaline and many others. Gem bearing gravels are common, especially in the SW around the appropriately named Ratnapura (*city of gems*). Other minerals are also concentrated in the SW. The greatest concentration of heavy mineral sands – ilmenite, rutile and monazite – is N of Trincomalee, where deposits are 95% pure. Monazite is found on the W coast. There are scattered deposits of iron ore in the SW, and some veins of magnetite in the NW interior. High evaporation rates make shallow lagoons, as in the NE, suitable for salt manufacture. The most important salterns are at Puttalam, Elephant Pass and Hambantota in the S.

Due to the lack of fossil fuel resources, 95% of the island's electricity is now generated by hydro power. The first HEP project was opened in the 1930s, but firewood still accounts for 60% of all energy used. Supplies are under increasing pressure, and the Mahaveli Project undertaking has meant that most of the HEP is now developed.

Sri Lanka had very little industry at Independence, manufacturing accounting for less than 5% of the GDP. By 1990 a number of new industries had been developed – cement, mineral sands, ceramics, cloth. These were all planned originally in the state controlled sector. The socialist government under Mrs Bandaranaike envisaged public ownership of all major industries, but the United National Party government elected under President Jayawardene's leadership in 1977 reversed this policy, moving towards a free trade economy.

Among the leading sectors of the new policy was tourism, with particular efforts to exploit the superb beaches and equable climate. This programme has been severely hit by the political troubles which have dogged the island since 1983. In the 1990s, however, barring trouble spots in the N, tourists have been returning with confidence. Sub-marine fauna and the opportunities for water-sports have made some beaches particularly attractive along the SW, S and the SE of the island.

In 1992 the total value of industrial production was just under Rs 50 bn, the food and beverages industry, textiles and leather, and chemicals each contributing about Rs 14 bn. The present government is pushing still harder towards ending all public subsidies and state involvement in economic activity.

COLOMBO

Population: 1.9mn; *Altitude*: sea level. Sheltered from the SW Monsoon by a barely perceptible promontory jutting out into the sea, Colombo's bay was an important site for Muslim traders before the colonial period. However, it is essentially a colonial city, whose rise to preeminence did not start until the 19th century and the establishment of British power. Before that it was a much less important town than Galle, but when the British took control of Kandy and encouraged the development of commercial estates, the Island's economic centre of gravity moved N. The capital, Colombo offered 2 easy routes into the Kandyan highlands.

Introduction

Colombo's small promontory offered little protection for larger ships, and in the late 19th century the British started work on a series of breakwaters which were to provide an effective harbour round the year. The SW breakwater, over 1000m long, was completed in 1885. It has the pilot station at its head. The NE breakwater, a rubble embankment 350m long, was completed in 1902, followed in 1907 by the NW breakwater. This 'island' work has a S entrance 250m wide and a N entrance 220m wide. Overall the breakwaters enclose an area of 3 sq km more than 8m deep.

The growth in shipping during the early 20th century reflected the advantages of Colombo's position on the Indian Ocean Sea route between Europe, the Far East and Australasia. However, the city also benefitted from its central position on the rapidly expanding transport system within the Island, and the road and rail networks both focused on Colombo. Since Independence it has retained its dominant position.

The Centre and North

The Fort area

The **Fort**, no more than 500m square, lies immediately S of the harbour, the commercial centre of the city. Little remains of either the Portuguese or Dutch periods. Marine Drive runs down the coast to the *Intercontinental Hotel* and across the wide open space of the Galle Face. Immediately inland of its N section is the narrow road now called Galle Buck, an English corruption of the old name Gal Bokka – rocky belly. From the N end of Marine Drive, Church St runs E, past **St Peter's Church** on the right. Part of the former residence of Dutch Governors, the Church cemetery contains the tombs of several British residents, including William Tolfrey (1778-1817), an army officer and the first translator of the Bible into Pali and Sinhalese. The nave of the church was originally a reception and banqueting hall, first converted into a church in 1804 and consecrated in 1821.

To the E is the *Hotel Taprobane*, renamed *Grand Oriental*, from which **York St**, one of the main shopping areas, runs due S. Half way down it is **Sir Baron Jayatilleke Mawatha**, the main bank-

CLIMATE: COLOMBO

	Jan	Feb	Mar	Apr	May	Jun	Jul	Aug	Sep	Oct	Nov	Dec	Av/Tot
Max (°C)	32	32	32	33	32	31	30	30	30	31	31	30	31
Min (°C)	22	23	24	26	26	26	25	26	24	24	23	23	24
Rain (mm)	70	88	121	286	388	186	154	99	216	396	329	193	2526

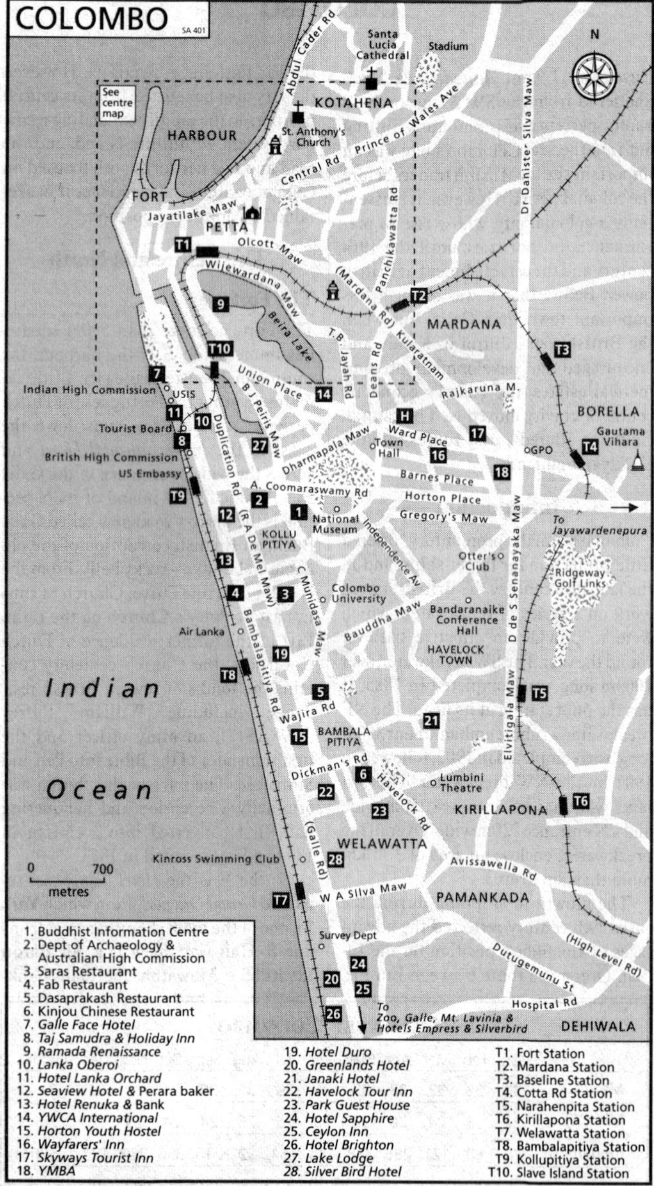
COLOMBO
SA 401
See centre map
HARBOUR
FORT
PETTA
KOTAHENA
MARDANA
BORELLA
KOLLU PITIYA
HAVELOCK TOWN
BAMBALA PITIYA
KIRILLAPONA
WELAWATTA
PAMANKADA
DEHIWALA
Indian Ocean
Santa Lucia Cathedral
Stadium
St. Anthony's Church
Abdul Cader Rd
Prince of Wales Ave
Central Rd
Dr Danister Silva Maw
Jayatilake Maw
Olcott Maw
Wijewardana Maw
Beira Lake
(Mardana Rd)
Panchikawatta Rd
Kularatnam
T.B. Jayah Rd
Deans Rd
Union Place
B J Peiris Maw
Rajkaruna M.
Ward Place
Town Hall
Dharmapala Maw
Barnes Place
Horton Place
Gregory's Maw
A. Coomaraswamy Rd
National Museum
Independence Av
Duplication Rd
(R A De Mel Maw)
C Munidasa Maw
Colombo University
Otter's Club
Bauddha Maw
Bandaranaike Conference Hall
D de S Senanayaka Maw
Elvitigala Maw
Ridgeway Golf Links
Gautama Vihara
GPO
To Jayawardenepura
Indian High Commission
USIS
Tourist Board
British High Commission
US Embassy
Air Lanka
Bambalapitiya Rd
Wajira Rd
Dickman's Rd
Havelock Rd
Lumbini Theatre
(Galle Rd)
Kinross Swimming Club
Avissawella Rd
W A Silva Maw
Survey Dept
(High Level Rd)
Dutugemunu St
Hospital Rd
To Zoo, Galle, Mt. Lavinia & Hotels Empress & Silverbird
0 700 metres
N
1. Buddhist Information Centre
2. Dept of Archaeology & Australian High Commission
3. Saras Restaurant
4. Fab Restaurant
5. Dasaprakash Restaurant
6. Kinjou Chinese Restaurant
7. Galle Face Hotel
8. Taj Samudra & Holiday Inn
9. Ramada Renaissance
10. Lanka Oberoi
11. Hotel Lanka Orchard
12. Seaview Hotel & Perara baker
13. Hotel Renuka & Bank
14. YWCA International
15. Horton Youth Hostel
16. Wayfarers' Inn
17. Skyways Tourist Inn
18. YMBA
19. Hotel Duro
20. Greenlands Hotel
21. Janaki Hotel
22. Havelock Tour Inn
23. Park Guest House
24. Hotel Sapphire
25. Ceylon Inn
26. Hotel Brighton
27. Lake Lodge
28. Silver Bird Hotel
T1. Fort Station
T2. Mardana Station
T3. Baseline Station
T4. Cotta Rd Station
T5. Narahenpita Station
T6. Kirillapona Station
T7. Welawatta Station
T8. Bambalapitiya Station
T9. Kollupitiya Station
T10. Slave Island Station

ing street. Nearly all the buildings are in red brick. Hospital St, running W at the S end of York St, is a lively centre of low cost restaurants, fruit sellers, and pavement merchants.

Running S from Church St to the W of St Peter's Church is **Janadhipathi Mawatha** (formerly Queen St). At the N end are Gordon Gardens, with a statue of Queen Victoria and a stone bearing the Portuguese Coat of Arms. Threats of terrorist violence have led to entrance to the Gordon Gardens being restricted, as it lies in Republic Square, alongside the offices of the Prime Minister and Cabinet. The N end of Janadhipathi Mawatha is normally closed to the public. Colombo is not graced with many fine buildings, but the GPO, on the E side of Janadhipathi Mawatha is a good example of Victorian colonial building. Opposite it is the President's House, *Janadhipathi Medura*. The Chartered Bank building is another imposing commercial structure, decorated with reliefs of domesticated elephants.

The statue in front of the **President's House** is of the 19th century British Governor Edward Barnes. An adjutant of the Duke of Wellington during the Battle of Waterloo, in Sri Lanka he is better known for building the Colombo-Kandy road. His statue is the point from which the distances of all towns in Sri Lanka from Colombo are measured. Just to the S again is the **Lighthouse Clock Tower** (1837), now replaced as a lighthouse by the new tower on Marine Drive. Sir Baron Jayatilleka Mawatha runs E, immediately N of the GPO, with a number of impressive commercial buildings, including a good example of inter-war architecture in the Bank of India.

East of the *Grand Oriental Hotel* is the Central YMCA, next to the Moors Islamic Cultural Home in Bristol St. Across Duke St is the Young Mens Buddhist Association. The shrine houses a noted modern image of the Buddha. The Fort Mosque, in a building of the Dutch period, is to the S on Chatham St.

The Pettah

While the Fort is the centre of Colombo's modern commercial activity, the Pettah (Tamil: *'pettai'* – 'suburb'; Sinhalese: *'pitakotuwa'* – outer fort) is the hub of its traditional markets. The small shops and narrow streets are covered in advertising hoardings. Specialist streets house such craftsmen and traders as goldsmiths (Sea St), fruit and vegetable dealers (the end of Main St) and ayurvedic herbs and medicines (Gabo's Lane).

At the SE edge of the Pettah is the Fort Railway Station. In the market area to the N, Arabs, Portuguese, Dutch and British traded. Half way along Main St on the left hand side after 2nd Cross St is the **Jami ul Alfar** mosque. Entry permitted on removing shoes. At the end of Main St, Central Road goes E from a large roundabout, just N of the Market. A left turn off Central Rd immediately after the roundabout, Brass Founder St, leads to a right fork, Ratnajothi Saravana Mawatha, formerly Wolfendahl St. At the end is the **Wolfendahl Church**. Built in 1749 on the site of an earlier Portuguese church, it is prominently placed on a hill, where its massive cruciform shape stands out, commanding a view over the harbour. Its Doric façade is solid and heavy, and inside it has many tombstones and memorial tablets to Dutch officials. It is the most interesting surviving Dutch monument in Sri Lanka.

To its NE is the most remarkable Roman Catholic cathedral in the island, **Santa Lucia**. With a classical façade, inside are the tombs of 3 French bishops. Begun in 1876 it was completed in 1910, but there is little of interest inside. To the S in New Moor St is the Grand Mosque, a modern building in the style, as one critic puts it, of a modern international airport covered in metallic paint.

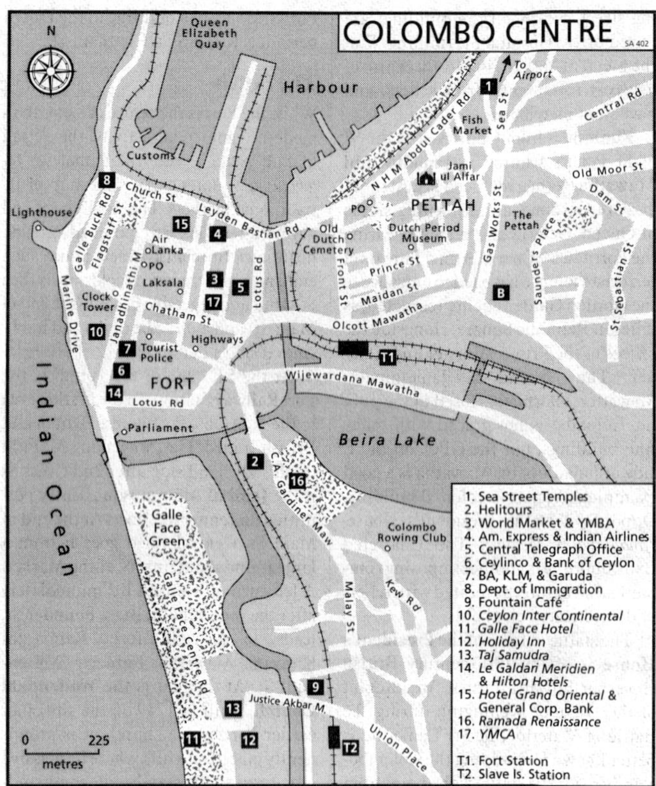

Also in the Pettah are 3 modest Hindu temples, of little architectural interest, but giving an insight into Hindu building style and worship. Perhaps the most striking is that of **Sri Ponnambula Vanesvara** at 38 Sri Ramanathan Rd. The gopuram (entrance gateway) has typical sculptures of gods from the Hindu pantheon. A Siva lingam is in the innermost shrine, with a Nandi in front and a dancing Siva (*Nataraja*) to one side, see page 75.

Borella, 6 km E of the Fort, the modest building of the Gotami Vihara at Borella contains impressive modern murals depicting the life of the Buddha by the Sri Lankan artist George Keyt.

Further NE across the Kelaniya River is the **Raja Maha Vihara**, 13 km from the centre of the city and, after the temple of the tooth in Kandy, the most visited Buddhist temple in Sri Lanka. In the 13th century *Kelaniya* was an impressive city, but its chief attraction today is the legendary visit of the Buddha to the site. The Mahavansa recorded that the original stupa enshrined a gem-studded throne on which the Buddha sat when he supposedly visited Sri Lanka. Ultimately destroyed by the Portuguese, the present dagoba is in the shape of a heap of paddy. There is a famous image of the reclining Buddha, but there are also many images of Hindu deities. The temple is the meeting place for the **Duruthu Perahera** in January every year, which draws thousands of pilgrims from all over the Island.

The first city on the site was believed to have been built by King Yatala Tissa. According to legend this was destroyed by a flood from the sea, which was a punishment given to the king for mistreating the Buddhist *sangha*. He tried to placate the sea by setting his daughter afloat on a golden boat. Having drifted ashore in the S of the island she married King Kavan Tissa, and became the mother of one of Sri Lanka's great heroes, King Dutugemunu. The city is subsequently believed to have been destroyed by Tamil invasions, and was only re-built in the 13th century by King Vijayabahu. The present temple dates from about 1300.

The South

There are some attractive walks and drives to the S of the Fort area and Beira Lake. Galle Rd runs almost due S across the windswept open space of the Galle Face in the N, gradually moving away from the sea southwards, and separated from it by the railway. Inland and parallel with it runs R.A. de Mel Mawatha, built up all the way S. Inland again lies the most prestigious residential area of Colombo, Cinnamon Gardens – widely referred to by its postal code, Colombo 7. Wide roads and shaded avenues make it a very attractive area. The Town Hall was completed in 1927, and there is a range of parks, the national museum and conference facilities. The **Viharamahadevi Park**, now named after an early Sri Lankan Queen, but originally named after Queen Victoria, faces the Town Hall. It has a range of tropical trees, including ebony, mahogany, sal and lemon eucalyptus, and a wide variety of birds. Early morning is an excellent time to visit (open 0700). A series of rectangular lakes to the E of the park lead to a golden statue of the seated Buddha.

Museums

National Museum, 8 Marcus Fernando Mawatha, (Albert Crescent). 0900-1700, Sun-Th, closed on public holidays. Rs 45. (Bus 114, 138). Opened in 1877 – collection of paintings, sculptures, furniture and porcelain. Also masks and Kandyan ragalia; and the library houses a unique collection of over 4000 *Ola* (palm manuscripts). An extremely rich archaeological and artistic collection. Very well labelled and organised, a visit is an excellent introduction to a tour of Sri Lanka. Exhibits include an outstanding collection of 10th-12th century bronzes from Polonnaruwa, and the lion throne of King Nissankamalla, which has become the symbol of Sri Lanka.

The ground floor displays Buddhist and Hindu sculptures, incl a striking 1500 year old stone statue of the Buddha from Toluvila. Demon dance masks line the stairs to the 1st floor, where there are superbly executed scale reproductions of the wall paintings at Sigiriya and Polonnaruwa. Other exhibits incl ancient jewellery and carvings in ivory and wood.

Natural History Museum, behind the National Museum has good natural history and geological galleries.

Dutch Period Museum, Prince St, Pettah. 0900-1700, Mon-Fri. The fine old Dutch town hall, which has been used as a hospital, police station and a post office before being renovated to house the museum.

Bandaranaike Museum, Bauddhaloka Maw. 0900-1600 except Mon and *Poya* holidays. Devoted to the life and times of the late prime minister.

National Art Gallery, 106 Ananda Coomaraswamy Maw. Open 0900-1800, closed Poya Days. Permanant collection, mainly portraits.

Parks & Zoos

Dehiwala Zoo, Dharmapala Maw (Allan Ave), 10 km SW from centre. 0830-1700. Entry Rs 30, plus charge for photography. One of the most attractive in Asia. 15 ha undulating ground, beautifully laid out with shrubs, flowering trees and plants, orchids, lakes and fountains. Over 2000 animals include sloth bear, leopard, civets and other small cats, many kinds of lizard, crocodiles and snakes. Lions, tigers, jaguars, black panthers, and many exotic species such as hippopotami, rhinos, giraffes and kangaroos. The zoo also has an aquarium with over 500 species of fish, and is particularly noted for its collection of birds. There is a troupe of trained elephants which are shown every afternoon. **Getting there** Bus no 132 or 176, also train to Dehiwala Station.

Vihara Mahadevi Park (formerly Victoria Park), on the site of the old Cinnamon Gardens. Now re-named after the mother of the Sinhalese King Dutthagamani. A botanical garden, including named species ranging from a bo tree to an enormous profusion of climbing plants, parasites and rare orchids.

Tours

City tours: by car with a chauffeur/Guide for 3 – Half day: 40 km, Buddhist Temple, Hindu Temple, Zoo and residential area. Full Day: also includes Kelaniya Temple. For nature safaris, hiking and birdwatching contact Wildlife and Nature Protection Soc, Chaitiya Rd, Marine Drive, Fort, T 25248.

Local information

● Accommodation

Colombo now has several world class hotels, but is poorly provided with good cheap accommodation; it can be difficult to find a suitable room. Mount Lavinia (listed separately), has the widest range of choice.

AL *Ceylon Intercontinental*, 48 Jandhipathi Maw, Fort, T 421221, F 547326, 250 rm, all with superb sea-view, 9-storey seafront hotel, roof-top *Cats Eye* restaurant (good buffet lunches), *Pearl* for seafood and bar with panoramic views, Snackbar serves Sinhalese specialities, open-air dining with live music, in season, well located, good bookshop; **AL** *Le Galdari Meridien*, 64 Lotus Rd, corner of Janadhipathi Maw, T 544544, F 549875, 500 rm, in business centre, overlooking Indian Ocean with golf nearby, french restaurant, *Café Fleuri* and *Colombo 2000* nightclub, good rooftop pool; **AL** *Ramada Renaissance*, 115C Gardiner Maw, T 544200, F 449184, 356 rm, one of city's newest, 4 speciality restaurants, casino and turkish bath; **AL** *Taj Samudra*, 25 Galle Face Rd, overlooking sea and Green, T 546622, F 546348, 400 rm, well designed, ideally situated in large well kept gardens; **AL** *Lanka Oberoi*, 56/2 Galle Rd, Steuart Pl, opp *Galle Face Hotel*, T 437437, F 449280, 500 rm, with sea or lake-view, many recently refurbished, unimpressive exterior but atrium and long Batik hangings very attractive in public area, roof-top night club, 9 restaurants include excellent oriental cuisine in *Ran Malu* and Western in *London Grill*; **AL** *Holiday Inn*, 30 Sir M Markar Maw, T 422001, F 547977, 100 rm in attractive Moghul style building, open-air pool and specialist *Alhambra* Restaurant for Muslim cuisine, *Golden Seer* for fish, rec; **AL** *Hilton*, 67 Lotus Rd, Echelon Sq, T 544644, F 544657, 387 rm, some non-smoking, Japanese floor, special facilities for ladies; **AL** *Colombo Marriott*, 64 Lotus Rd, T 445860, F 575662, Europcar rentals.

A *Palm Village*, Uswetakeiyawa, T 530766, F 446838, 50 rm, attractive location by seaside nr airport, an Aitken Spence hotel; **A** *Galle Face*, Fort, 2 Kollupitiya Rd, S of the Green, T 541010, 54 rm, many refurbished, some very large, quiet and best with sea-view, Raj-style, with character in 1894 building with grand, spacious public rooms, good restaurant, terrace overlooking the green, indoor garden for breakfast and drinks, nice pool in excellent location by the sea, rec; **A** *Pegasus Reef*, Santa Maria Maw, Hendala, Wattala, by old Dutch canal, 11 km from city centre, 18 km airport, T 530205, F 549790, 150 rm, 500m of coconut-fringed beach, good restaurants, pool.

Most in the **B** category are comfortable with a/c, restaurant, exchange, shop and pool. **B** *Havelock Tour Inn*, 20 Dickman's Rd, Bambalapitya, T 85251, charming, in quiet residential area, tropical garden and excellent restaurant, rec; **B** *Grand Oriental*, 2 York St,

Fort, overlooking harbour, T 20391, 60 comfortable rm, reception next to large bar, the old hotel for travellers arriving by sea, still full of sailors from port!, ***Harbour Room*** restaurant on top floor with excellent views, good bookshop; **B** ***Ceylinco***, 69 Janadhipathi Maw, Fort, T 20431, small with 15 rm in modern building, restaurant below has superb views; **B** ***Renuka***, 328 Galle Rd, Colombo 3, towards Mt Lavinia, T 573598, 44 a/c rm with TV, central a/c, basement ***Palmyrah*** restaurant serves good Sri Lankan curries.

C ***Lanka Orchard***, 6 Galle Rd, Colombo 6, T 580809, modern, central, further S, along Galle Rd, which is busy and noisy, are several moderately priced hotels which vary: price is not always the best guide so you would do well to visit before booking; **C** ***Ranmuthu***, 112 Galle Rd, Colombo 3, T 433968, 54 rm, central a/c, restaurant, bar, exchange, pool; **C** ***Brighton***, 57 Ramakrishna Rd, Wellawatte, T 585211, 62 rm in a modern hotel on seafront close to rly line but away from busy rd; **C** ***Empress***, 383 de Mel Maw, Colombo 3, T 27205, 33 rm; **C** ***Galaxy***, Union Place, Col 2, T 696372, 52 a/c rm, restaurant, 24 hr coffee shop, bar, business centre, travel, pool; **C** ***Sapphire***, 371 Galle Rd, Wellawatte, T 583306, 40 rm, 20 a/c, good beach nearby, restaurant, exchange, car hire; **C** ***Ceylon Inns***, 501 Galle Rd, Wellawatte, T 580474, 74 rm some a/c, popular with tour groups, restaurant, bar, exchange, pool; nearby **C** ***Silver Bird***, 382 Galle Rd, Wellawatte, T 83143, 50 rm; **C** ***Duro***, 429 Kollupitiya Rd, T 85338, 27 rm; **C** ***Skyways Tourist Inn***, 28 Cross Rd, off Ward Pl, Col 8, T 698313, some a/c rm, restaurant, exchange, tours, pool; **C** ***Lake Lodge*** 20, Alvis Terrace (off Dharmapala Maw), Col 3, T 26443, 16 rm, 1 a/c, central, good value; **C** ***Sea View***, 15 Sea View Av, Colombo 3, T 573570, fairly large rm but generally shabby and dirty – horrifc wiring, quiet, around large central courtyard, overpriced.

D ***Wayfarer's Inn***, 77 Rosmead Pl, Col 7, nr Town Hall, T 93936, some a/c rm, restaurant, car hire, tours, pool, garden; **D** ***Orchid Inn***, 571/6 Galle Rd, Colombo 6, T 83916; **D** ***YWCA International***, 393 Union Place, Colombo 2, 20 rm with bath (for women and couples), well located, in residential area, good restaurant and spice shop.

E ***YWCA*** *Rotunda Guest House*, 7 Rotunda Gardens, Col 3 nr Lanka Oberoi, rm with bath and dorms; **E** ***Lanka Inns***, 239 Galle Rd, Colombo 4, T 84220. F ***YMCA***, 39 Bristol St, Fort, T 25252, 58 dorm beds, inexpensive, self-service cafeteria.

● Youth Hostel

At 35/1 Horton Pl, Colombo 7, E of Viharamanadevi Park, affiliated to international YHA, some rm and dorm, restaurant and cooking facilities.

● Places to eat

Some of the best restaurants are in hotels, but there is a wide range of restaurants outside. Chinese, Indian and continental specialties are all available. The list below contains some suggestions, but enquire locally for completely up-to-date advice.

Buffets: coffee shops in the city's top hotels offer a wide choice of dishes at lunch-time charging about Rs 300-350 plus tax (*Hilton* charges Rs 450); the *Inter-Continental* (rec) and the *Marriott* offer theirs' at a reduced rate if you choose not to have dessert. The venue gives you the added benefit of sitting in cool comfort during the hottest part of the day!

Chinese: ***Peking Palace***, 3 Sellamuttu Ave, Col 3; ***Nanking***, 33 Chatham St, Col 1; ***Park View Lodge***, 70, Park St, Col 2; ***Lotus Motel***, 265 Galle Rd, Col 3; ***Jade Garden***, 126 Havelock Rd, Col 5; ***Flower Drum*** Thurstan Rd, quiet atmosphere, excellent food, reasonable prices, rec; ***Kinjou***, 33 Amarsekera Maw, Col 5 opp BBC Grounds.

Fast foods: ***Nectar***, Mudalige Maw, corner of York St, Fort for snacks, ice creams. ***Fountain Café***, 199 Union Pl, garden, all day for cold drinks, ice creams, good value. ***Peera***, 217 Galle Rd, Col 3, for cakes, snacks, breads, mainly take-away.

Indian: ***Kohinoor***, 49 Dharmapala Maw, Col 3; ***Saras Indian Restaurant***, 25 Charles Drive, Col 3. For good vegetarian try ***Dasaprakash***, 237 Galle Rd, Col 4; ***Crowns***, next to *Laksala*, York St, South Indian style, simple, friendly, cheap, rec.

Japanese: ***Kyoto***, 19 De Vos Ave, Col 4; ***Nippon***, 123 Kumaran Ratnam Rd, Col 2; ***Sakura***, 14 Rhineland Place, Kollupitya, Col 3.

Korean: ***Ari Rang***, 16 Abdul Gafoor Maw, Col 3, with barbecues at tables, special eel dishes, also Chinese. ***Sam Gyup Sal*** and ***Sobul Gogi*** rec.

Sri Lankan: ***Fountain Café***, Bridge St, Col 2, Local and European food, excellent.

Western & seafood: ***Seafish***, 5 Sir Chittampalam Gardiner Maw, Col 2, excellent fish, very reasonable prices, though lacks atmosphere, rec; ***Alt Heidelberg***, 11 Galle Court 2, Col 3.

German: ***The Fab***, Kolpiti, 474 Galle Rd, Western food and excellent patisserie.

Italian: ***Da Guido***, 47/4 Dharmapala Maw, Col 7, excellent; ***Ginza Araliya***, 286 Galle Rd, Col 3.

● Bars

All the main hotels have bars.

Entertainment & shopping

● Cultural centres

Buddhist Cultural Centre, 125 Anderson Rd Nedimala, Deliwala, T 714256, F 723767, 8 km S of town centre, information, instruction and meditation by prior arrangement. Most have a library and reading room and have regular music and film programmes. ***Buddhist Information Centre***, 50 Ananda Coomaraswamy Maw. ***Alliance Française***, 54 Ward Place, Col 7. ***British Council***, 49 Alfred House Gdns, Col 3, T 580301. ***German (Geothe) Cultural Institute***, 39 Gregory's Rd, Col 7, T 694562, open 0900-1300, 1500-1700 weekdays. ***Soviet Cultural Centre***, 10 Independence Ave, Col 7, T 685429, open weekdays 0900-1700. ***USIS***, 44 Galle Rd, Col 3, T 332725, open Tue-Sat, 1000-1800.

● Entertainment

Cinemas: the larger a/c cinemas along Galle Rd sometimes have English language films.

Cultural shows: performances of Sinhala dance and music can be seen at the YMBA Hall, Borella, Navarangahala, Cumaratunga Munidasa Maw, and at Lionel Wendt Hall, 19 Guildford Crescent both at Col 7. Lumbini Hall, Havelock Town specialises in Sinhalese theatre. Some top hotels put on regular folk dance shows and also have Western floor shows and live music for dancing, open to non-residents.

● Libraries

See **Cultural Centres** above. ***Colombo Public Library***, Ananda Coomaraswamy Maw, Col 7, T 695156, open daily except Wed and public holidays, 0800-1845, Rs 2 entry fee.

● Shopping

Gemstones, Batik, handlooms, silver jewellery, crafts (lac, reed, wood, brass, Demon dance masks, betel-nut boxes etc), spices and tea are best buys. You can shop with confidence at govt run shops although it may be interesting to wander in the bazaars and look for good bargains – ***Sunday Bazaar*** on Main St, Pettah and Duke St, Fort. The top hotels have good shopping arcades but prices are often higher than elsewhere. The shops in the Fort tend to be good but more expensive than equally good quality items in Kollupitiya. There are several new shopping complexes such as Liberty Plaza on Dharmapala Maw, Kollupitiya, World Market, nr Fort Railway Station, Majestic City and Unity Plaza on Galle Rd; the boutiques in Pettah are worth a visit too. Most shops are open 1000-1900 on weekdays and 0845-1500 on Sat.

Duty Free Complex at Katunayake International Airport stocks the usual articles, to be paid for in foreign currency and noted in your passport. City shop on Galle Rd, Kollupitiya. ***Travel Information Centre***, 78 Steuart Pl, Col 3, has cassettes of words and music on pilgrim sites, booklets on the ancient cities, posters and picture post cards. ***The Philatelic Bureau***, 4th Flr, Ceylinco House, Janadhipathi Maw, Fort has a good stock of stamps.

Books: good shops in the *Inter-Continental* and *Grand Oriental* Hotels. ***Lakehouse***, 100 Sir C Gardiner Maw; ***KVG de Silva***, 415 Galle Rd, Col 4; ***MD Gunasena***, Olcott Maw, Col 11; others on Sir Baron Jayatilleka Maw, Fort. Second-hand books from ***Ashok Trading***, 183 Galle Rd, Col 4 and antiquarian from ***Serendib***, 100 Galle Rd. ***Children's Bookshop***, 20 Bogala Bldg, Janadhipathi Maw, nr Fort clocktower for Sri Lankan music cassettes. Books on Buddhism from ***Buddhist Information Centre***, 50 Ananda Coomaraswamy Maw, Col 7.

Gemstones, silver & gold: articles should only be bought at reputable shops – eg arcades in the top hotels; ***State Gem Corp*** Showroom, 24 York St, Col 1, T 23377, guarantees all it sells and will test purchases from other jewellers, free at their laboratory. Branches at *Hotel Intercontinental* and at Airport. ***Premadasa***, 17 Sir Baron Jayatilleke Maw and 20 Duke St, Col 1; ***Zam Gems***, 81 Galle Rd, Col 4 with a few branches; ***Janab***, 9 Temple Lane, Col 3. Sea St in Pettah has a number of private Jewellers; ***Hemchandra***, 229 Galle Rd, Col 3.

Handloom & handicrafts: Govt outlets incl ***Laksala***, Australia House, York St, Col 1 which carries a wide range. Other branches in Galle Face and Bambalapitiya. Open 0900-1700, except Sat and Sun, Apr-Oct. ***Viskam Niwasa*** (Dept of Industries), Bauddhaloka Maw, Col 7 also has high quality craft goods. ***Handloom Shop***, 71 Galle Rd, Col 4. ***Ceylon Ceramics Corpn*** showroom in Bambalapitiya also has terracotta ware. ***Lakmedura***, 113 Dharmapala Maw, Col 7. For good batiks try ***Serendib***, 100 Galle Rd, Col 4, ***Fantasy Lanka***, 302 (1st Flr), Unity Plaza, 2 Galle Rd, Col 4, ***Barbara Sansoni***, Galle Rd, Bambalipitiya and ***Ena de Silva***, Duplication Rd, Kollupitiya.

Maps: *Survey Dept, Map Sales Branch*, Kirula Rd, Narahenpita and ***Map Sales Centre***, York St, Col 1. Govt restrictions prohibit the sale of most large scale maps and town plans. Some can be consulted.

Photography: numerous in town. ***Hayleys***, 303 Galle Rd, Col 3 offers special 1 hr service.

Supermarkets: in the centre include ***Cornell's*** nr the Duty Free Centre; also ***YWCA Spice Shop***, Union Pl; ***Sri Lanka Tea Board***, 574 Galle Rd, Col 3; ***Mlesna Tea Centre***, Liberty Plaza.

● Sports

Visitors may take out temporary membership at various local clubs.

Golf: *Royal Colombo Golf Club*, Model Farm Rd, Col 8, temporary membership.

Rowing: *Colombo Rowing Club*, C Gardiner Maw, Col 2 (entrance opp Lake House Bookshop), T 433758, temp membership.

Squash: at the *Oberoi*, *Intercontinental*, *Taj Samudra* and *Ramada* Hotels. Also at ***Gymkhana Club***, 31 Maitland Crescent, Col 7 and Sri Lanka Ladies Squash Assoc, T 696256.

Swimming: *Colombo Swimming Club*, Storm Lodge, Galle Rd, Col 3; ***Kinross Swimming & Lifesaving Club***, 10 Station Ave, Wellawatte, and leading hotels allow temporary membership.

Tennis: at major hotels.

Yachting: *Royal Colombo Yacht Club*, welcomes experienced sailors.

Services

● Airline offices

Airlanka, 14 Sir Baron Jayatilleke Maw, T 21291. **Aeroflot**, 79/81 Hemas Bldg, York St, T 25580. **Air France**, 4 Leyden Bastion Rd, T 35333. **British Airways**, *Ramada Renaissance Hotel*, 115 C Gardiner Maw, T 20231. **Cathay Pacific**, 94 York St, T 23048. **Gulf Air**, 11 York St, T 547627. **Indian Airlines and Maldives International**, 95 Sir Baron Jayatilleke Maw, T 26844. **Japan Airlines**, T 545480, and **Emirates**, T 540709, *Meridien Hotel*, 64 Lotus Rd. **KLM**, 61 Janadhipathi Maw, T 545531. **Lufthansa**, 8 Galle Face Rd, Col 3, T 35536. **Phillippine Airlines**, 41 Janadhipadhi Maw, T 44831. **PIA**, 432 Galle Rd, Col 3, T 573475. **Qantas**, 5 Upper Chatham St, T 20551. **Royal Nepal Airlines**, 434 Galle Rd, Col 3, T 24045. **Singapore Airlines**, 15A Jayatilleke Maw, T 22711. **SAS** 16 Janadhipathi Maw, T 36201. **Thai International**, *Intercontinental Hotel*. **Ethiopian Airlines**, T 436724, and **TWA**, T 26611, 51 Janadhipathi Maw.

● Banks & money changers

Bank of Ceylon, Bureau de Change, Ground Flr, York St, T 22730, 0900-1800; weekends and holidays 0900-1600. Also at New HQ Bldg, 1st Flr, Janadhipathi Maw, 0900-1300 Mon, 0900-1330 Tue-Fri. Airport counter, T 030 2424, open 24 hr. Airlanka Office, GCEC Bldg, Sir Baron Jayatilleke Maw, issues Traveller's cheques, daily 0900-1530. **People's Bank**, Foreign Branch, 27 MICH Bldg, Bristol St, T 20651, 0900-1330 Mon-Fri. Night Service at HQ Branch, Sir Chittampalam A Gardiner Maw, T 36948. **Card Centre**, 1st Flr, 20 CA Gardiner Maw, Col 2, T 434147.

● Chambers of Commerce

Dept of Small Industries, 71 Galle Rd, Col 4, T 501209; **Investment Promotion Dept**, Greater Colombo Economic Commission, PO Box 1768, 14 Sir Baron Jayatileke Maw, Col 1, T 22447.

● High commissions & consulates

Australia, 3 Cambridge Pl, T 59876. **Austria**, Col 2, T 91613. **Bangladesh**, Col 7, T 502397. **Canada**, 6 Gregory's Rd, T 595841. **France**, Col 5, T 583621. **Germany**, 40 Alfred House Av, T 580531. **India**, 18-3/1 Sir Baron Jayatilleka Maw, T 21604. **Indonesia**, 1 Police Park Terrace, T 580113. **Italy**, Col 5, T 588622. **Japan**, Col 7, T 93831. **Malaysia**, 63A Ward Pl, T 94837. **Maldives**, 25 Melbourne Av, T 586762. **Nepal**, Col 4, T 586762. **Netherlands**, 25 Torrington Av, T 589626. **Pakistan**, 211 De Saram Pl, T 596301. **Sweden**, 315 Vauxhall St, T 20201. **Thailand**, 26 Gregory's Rd, T 597406. **UK**, 190 Galle Rd, Col 3, T 27611. **USA**, Col 3, T 548007. **USSR**, Col 3, T 573555.

● Hospitals & medical services

Chemists: a number on Galle Rd, Union Place, Pettah and Fort. State Pharmaceutical outlets at Hospital Junc, Col 7; Main St, Fort.

Hospitals: *General Hospital*, Regent St, T 691111 (24-'hr Accident and Emergency), Cardiology Unit, T 93059. Private hospitals incl *Nawaloka*, T 944444 (24-hr). Ministry of Indigenous Medicine, 385 Deans Rd, T 597345, has list of practitioners. Homeopathy and herbal medicine from *Govt Ayurvedic Hospital*, Cotta Rd, Borella, T 595855. *Siddhalepa Ayurveda Hospital,* Mt Lavinia (see below).

● Post & telecommunications

GPO: Janadhipathi Maw, Col 1. **Telegraph office**: Lower Chatham St, Col 1, T 31967. **Telephones**: there are a few International Direct Dialling centres outside hotels offering 24 hr service and far cheaper rates. One of the most accessible is in the Liberty Plaza, R.De Mel mawatha (Duplication Rd).

● Tour companies & travel agents

Aitken Spence, 13 Sir Baron Jayatilleke Maw, Col 1; ***Aset***, 315 Vauxhall St, Col 2, T 440480, excellent car hire and tour service; ***Ceylon Tours***, Col 2, T 21722; ***Thomas Cook***, 15 Sir Baron Jayatilleka Maw, T 54597; ***Cox & Kings***, Col 2, T 34295; ***Paradise Holidays***, 5 Palmyra Ave, Col 3, T 380106; ***Gemini Tours***, 40 Wijerama Maw, Col 7, T 598 446.

● Tourist offices

TIC, Ceylon Tourist Board, 78 Steuart Pl, Galle Rd, T 437059, F 437953. Open 0830-1615, Mon-Fri, 0800-1230, weekends and public holidays. Free literature in English, German, French, Italian, Swedish and Japanese to personal callers. Guide service arranged. Tickets and permits for ancient archaeological sites.

● Useful addresses

Automobile Association of Ceylon: 40 Sir Mohammad Macan Marker Maw, Galle Face, Col 3, T 21528. **Dept of Immigration and Emigration**: Chaitya Rd, T 29851. **For visiting ancient sites**: Ministry of Cultural Affairs, Malay St, Col 2, T 587912. Open 0830-1615, Dept of Archaeology, Marcus Fernando Maw, Col 7 and Cultural Triangle Office, 212 Bauddalaka Maw, Col 7. **Police**: T 33333. Police Station, S of Maradana Rly Station, Kollupitya, Bambalapitya and Wellawatte. **Tourist Police**: 12, Hospital St, New Secretariat Bldg, Fort, T 26941.

Transport

● Local transport

Bus: good network of buses and mini-buses. Ceylon Transport Board (CTB), private and mini-buses compete on popular routes. Local CTB buses have white signs, yellow for long-distance. Central Bus Stand, Olcott Maw, SE corner of Pettah. Enquiries, T 28081.

Car hire: Avis, Hertz and **Europcar** are represented in town and also at the airport. Europcar, International airport, T 452388, F 575662. Self-drive cars for 25-65 year olds are available, though it is easier (and safer!) to have a chauffeur-driven car charged at a similar rate (about US$28-35 depending on type covering 100 km per day). Excellent car hire (usually Japanese cars) and tour service; ***Ceylon Tours***, Col 2, T 21722; ***Mackinnons*** (Avis), 4 Leyden Bastian Rd, Col 1, T 29881; ***Aban Tours***, (Europcar) 498 Galle Rd, Col 3, T 574160. ***Quickshaw's*** (Hertz), 3 Kalinga Place, Col 5, T 583133; ***Inter Rent and Dollar***, Mercantile Tours, 51 Janadhipathi Maw, T 28708; ***Mercantile Tours***, 586 Galle Rd, Col 3, T 501946; ***Sudans***, 18-1/2 Mudalige Maw, T 431 865 or at Airport; they will also arrange holidays in the Maldives.

Motor bike hire: ***Gold Wing Motors***, 346 Deans Rd Colombo 10, T 685750, F 698787, rental on daily, weekly or monthly terms.

Scooter-rickshaws: ('trishaws') for 2 passengers, price has to be negotiated.

Taxis: metered taxis have yellow tops and red-on-white number plates. Make certain that the driver has understood where you wish to go and fix a rate for long-distance travel. 'Radio Cabs' are rec (available at airport and in town) which have a higher min charge (Rs 28) but the meters are more dependable. ***Quick Radio Cabs***, 911/1 Galle Rd, Col 4, T 502888, 24 hr, no extra for 15 km of city, sp rates for return trips of 60+ km. ***Ace Radio Cabs***, T 5015024.

Trains: suburban services to Bambalapitya, Kollupitiya, Dehiwala and Mt Lavinia all along the Galle Rd. The Fort Station, SW corner of Pettah.

WARNING Beware of pickpockets on public transport.

● Long distance connections

Air: International Airport, Katunayake, T 030 2911. TIC, 030 2411 (Flight times, day and night). Ratmalana Airport, T 716261. **Transport to town**: Airport Express, T 687037, 24-hr, one-way a/c, Rs 500. Upali Travels charter helicopter services to places of interest and resort hotels and charter aircraft for domestic airports. Air Taxi Ltd flies 5 passengers on Cessna aircraft and helicopters with landing facilities at Batticaloa, Hingurakgoda, Vavuniya, Anuradhapura, Kankesanthurai, Koggala, Sigiriya, Amparai, Puttalam, Katunayake and Trincomalee. Contact Thomas Cook, 15 Sir Baron Jayatilleke Maw, Col 1, T 545971.

Train: trains to all important places of interest. **Anuradhapura**: *Yal Devi*, 77, daily, 0545, 4 hr; *Rajarata Rajini*, 85, daily, 1405, 4¾ hr. **Polonnaruwa**: *Udaya Devi*, 79, daily, 0605, 6 hr 20; *Mail*, 93, daily, 2000, 7½ hr. **Kandy**: *Podi Menike*, 5, daily, 0555, 2¾ hr; *Intercity Express*, 9, daily, 0655, 2½ hr; *Intercity Express*, 29, daily, 1535, 2½ hr. **Galle**: (no 1st class on this service) 50, daily, 0730, 2¾ hr; 52, daily, 0845, 2¾ hr; *Galu Kumari*, 56, daily, 1335, 2¾ hr; 775, daily, 1915, 3¼ hr. **Matara**: (no 1st class on this service), 50, daily, 0730, 4½ hr; 52, daily, 0845, 4½ hr; *Galu Kumari*, 56, daily, 1335, 4½ hr. **Nanu-Oye (Nuwara Eliya)**: *Podi Menike*, 5, daily, 0555, 7½ hr; *123 Express*, daily, 0945, 6 hr; *Colombo-Kandy Mail*, 45, daily, 2015, 8 hr. **Bandarawela**: *Podi Menike*, 5, daily, 0555, 7½ hr; *123 Express*, daily, 0945, 8 hr; *Colombo-Kandy Mail*, 45, daily, 2015, 8¼ hr.

Special a/c Hitachi trains for day tours to Kandy and Hikkaduwa. Inter-city Expresses to Kandy and Bandarawela. Occasional tours on vintage steam trains – details from the Railway Tourist Office, Fort Station, T 35838.

Road: The Sri Lanka Transport Board has a good island-wide network and travel is cheap. Principal towns have an Express Service every ½ hr; Regular buses leave every 15 from Pettah and a fast Inter-city service operates to Kandy. Central Bus Stand, Olcott Maw, Pettah. Enquiries, T 28081. Frequent services to Kandy, Galle, Ratnapura, Anuradhapura, Kurunegala, Matara. Eight buses daily to Kataragama, 2 to Medawachchiya. Minibuses also leave from the bus stop and from the Rly station.

Short excursions from Colombo

Mt Lavinia

Galle Rd continues S to Mt Lavinia, one of the most popular excursions just 13 km from Colombo, and 3 km beyond the Dehiwala zoo. It takes its name from a corruption of the Sinhalese 'Lihinia Kanda' – *gull rock*. An attractive picnic spot, the original *Mt Lavinia Hotel* was Governor Edward Barnes' weekend retreat. He was forced to sell the house by the Government in England who approved neither the expenditure nor the luxurious style.

• **Accommodation AL** *Mount Lavinia*, T 715221, F 715228, 275 a/c rm, once British Governor's residence, now radically renovated and extended, massive white building – enormous public rooms, labryinthine corridors, excellent terrace with pool overlooking the ocean which gets blisteringly hot, guests avoid the indifferent, seedy beach, good evening buffet meals, good bar and shops, some non a/c rooms, cheaper; **AL** *Mount Royal Beach*, 36 College Av, T 714001, F 713030, 90 rm, private beach huts.

B *Riviras*, 50/2 De Saram Rd, T 717786, 16 rm, some a/c, villa style; **B** *Saltaire*, 50/5 De Saram Rd, T 717731, wooden cabanas, in a large garden nr the sea, typical package hotel appearance; **B** *Ranwali Holiday Village*, T 031 2136, 84 rm; **B** *Lak-Mahal's Inn*, 8 Vihara Rd, T/F 734848, German restaurant with rooms.

C *Sea Breeze Tour Inn*, De Saram Rd, T 714017, 23 rm; **C** *Mt Lavinia Inn*, De Saram Av, mainly package tour groups; **C** *Tropic Inn*, 6 College Inn Av, dark, small rm, overpriced; **C** *Ratna Inn*, Barnes Av, large, quiet family house, friendly.

D *Cottage Gardens*, College Av, bungalows in small garden; **D** *Oceanview*, along railway line from Royal Beach; **D** *Shore Lanka Beach Inn*, De Alwis Av, slightly cheaper than others in the category; **D** *Sunray Beach VIllas*, 3 De Saram Rd, T 716272, a guest house with 3 rm in a comfortable house with garden; **D** *Palm Beach*, 52 De Saram Rd, T 712713, F 94 1 4376953, 30 rm, 10 a/c, restaurant, bar, exchange; **D** *Estoril Beach Resort*, 30 Sri Dharmapala Rd, 25 rm.

On the seaward side of Galle Rd, S of St Mary's Church, there is some **E** category accommodation.

Siddhalepa Ayurveda Hospital, 106 Templer's Rd, Mt Lavinia, T 722524, F 725465, herbal and ayurvedic health programmes incl herbal/ steam baths and massage, large a/c rm with TV, about Rs 2,200 for 3 days (2 nights) incl treatment.

Jayawardenepura-Kotte

The Gramodaya Folk Arts Centre (11 ha) has craftsmen working with brass, silver, leather, coir and producing jewellery, pottery, natural silk, lace and reed baskets. There is a shop, a herbal health drink counter, an aquarium and a restaurant serving Sri Lankan specialities.

NEGOMBO, PUTTALAM AND ANURADHAPURA

The coastal route to Puttalam (A3) runs due N through apparently endless groves of coconut palms. It passes the International Airport about 4 km S of Negombo, then runs close to the coast and coastal lagoons all the way to Puttalam. The road from Puttalam to Anuradhapura crosses much more open terrain, the dryness leading to much less dense forest and sparser cultivation.

ROUTES The A1 runs N, 3 or 4 km inland of the coast. At **Dalugama** The A3 leaves the A1 to go N to *Wattala* (11 km from the city centre). It passes the *Pegasus Reef Hotel* (see above), through some built up areas and an industrial estate. Half way to Negombo it passes through **Ja-ela**, at the heart of what used to be one of Sri Lanka's main cinnamon producing areas. Now the road runs through coconut groves, following the line of a Dutch canal up to the Negombo lagoon and beyond to Chilaw.

Negombo

Population: 55,000; *Altitude*: sea level. 6 km N of the international airport. The Dutch had captured it from the Portuguese in 1644, and made it an important centre. It has a high reputation for its brasswork, and today the Negombo Lagoon has become the country's main fishing port, and a centre for prawn and shrimp fishing and research.

It is Sri Lanka's biggest tourist resort complex, with some pollution problems to match. There is a major AIDS problem here and the town sometimes has an unpleasant atmosphere with the obvious presence of police. However, tourists come here for the exciting diving it offers and for other water sports. Scuba diving allows you to get excellent views of corals within 10-20m and the marine life includes barracuda, blue-ringed angels and unusual star fish. The reef is 3 km W of the beach hotel area.

Places of interest

The town still has a few remains from its period as a Dutch settlement, notably the residence of the District Judge, the Dutch church, and the impressive gateway to the Fort (1672). **St Mary's Church** is one of many that bears witness to the extent of Portuguese conversions to Roman Catholicism, especially among the fishermen in Negombo District. The fishermen use catamarans and outrigger canoes, and bring up their catch onto the beach every day – seer, skipjack, herring, mullet, pomfret, amber-jack, and sometimes sharks, are usually landed in the afternoon. Prawns and lobster are caught in the lagoon.

WARNING It is often dangerous to swim, particularly during the SW monsoon, May-Oct. Warning notices are now posted on the beach.

Local festivals

Jul *Fishermen's festival*, St Mary's Church. A major regional festival.

Local information

● Accommodation

Many hotels and guest houses have been built, most along Lewis Place, which is the beach road, due N of the lagoon. Some are a few km out of Negombo. Meals normally included in price, especially in season. Resort hotels offer watersports. **NB** Some hotels do not allow Sri Lankans accompanying tourists to stay.

Best in the region, **AL** *Dolphin*, Kammala S, Waikkal, T 031 3129, 76 a/c rm, traditional decor, good seafood restaurant, surrounded by a garden of palm trees, superb swimming pool; **AL** *Browns Beach Hotel* 175 Lewis Place, T 031 20 31, F 031 2639, 145 a/c rm, 10 bungalows, large slightly characterless hotel on Negombo sea front; **AL** *Royal Oceanic*, Ethukala, T 031 2377, 85 large a/c rm with sea view, tropical garden.

Cheaper **A** *Blue Oceanic*, next door, 30m from beach, some a/c rm. The 'garden hotel'; **A** *Golden Sands*, Ethukala, T 031 3564, F 94-31 4227, 75 rm with balcony and sea view; **A** *Blue Lagoon*, Talahena, T 01 433268, 28 rm with garden or lagoon view.

B *Golden Star Beach*, 163 Lewis Place, T 031 3564, F 031 4266, 61 rm, Sri Lankan/ Dutch management.

C *Catamaran Beach*, 89 Lewis Place, T 031 2342, 48 rm; **C** *Don's Beach*, 75 Lewis Place, T 031 2342, 60 rm.

● Cheap accommodation

E *Rainbow Guest House*, 3 Carron Place, T 031 2082, excellent food, rec; **E** *Beach View Guest House*, Lewis Place (next to *Blue Oceanic Hotel*), clean, well rec; **E** *Interline Beach*, 5 Carron Pl (off Lewis Place), T 031 2350, 25 rm, all with sea view.

F There are lots of cheap guest houses along Lewis Place. Among the best value for money is *Seaforth*, 31 Customs House Rd.

● Places to eat

Sea food is the speciality of many hotels and restaurants. Lobsters, crabs and prawns are all excellent.

● Transport

Local Car and cycle hire: the flat roads make a short trip out of Negombo attractive. *Nishal Travel*, 274 Lewis Pl, opp *Golden Sands Hotel*, T 031 2725. **Warning** Check car well before hiring as often the one shown when enquiring is in far better condition. Cars also available from jeweller's shop opposite. **Motor bike hire**: *Gold Wing Motors*, 546 Colombo Rd, Negombo, T 031 2895, rental on daily, weekly or monthly terms.

Train/Road Regular bus and train services to Colombo.

Negombo to Puttalam

The A3 goes on to **Marawila** (20 km), one of many villages with large Roman Catholic churches. Strongly influenced by the Portuguese, the coastal strip has a high proportion of Catholics. In 1992 23% of the population immediately inland from Negombo was Christian, increasing N to 38%. Crossing the estuary the road passes between the coastal lagoon and the railway through **Madampe** (13 km; known for its Coconut Research Institute) to **Chilaw** (12 km). A small village, but an important Roman Catholic centre, with another very large church. There is also an interesting Saivite Temple at **Munneswaram** (Munnessarama, 5 km E of Chilaw) with Tamil inscriptions. It is an important pilgrimage centre.

The road runs due N. A left turn at Battulu Oya leads to **Udappawa**, 12 km N of Chilaw. A tiny Tamil Hindu village, it is noted for its firewalking ceremonies which take place in Jul-Aug every year. Experiments conducted in 1935-36 showed that the coals were heated to about 500° C during the ceremony.

Marshes and lagoons lie between the road and the sea for much of the route N to Puttalam, which crosses a series of minor rivers and a few major ones such as the **Battulu Oya**. At Palavi, 3 km S of **Puttalam**, a left turn goes up the W side of the Puttalam lagoon to Kalpitya.

Kalpitya (25 km), with an excellent road. The town has an old Dutch Fort and an attractive 18th century church. Continuing up the main road to Puttalam is the Lake View Restaurant, 139 Colombo Road. Clean and good food. You can cross the Puttalam Lagoon by ferry to Karaitivu, travelling S to complete a round trip to Puttalam.

ROUTES From Puttalam the **A12** goes NE to Anuradhapura, fringing the Wilpattu National Park. 30 km before Anuradhapura, turn off the A 12 to reach the entrance to the park (7 km).

Wilpattu National Park

Approach

The Park covers 1900 sq km and is particularly famous for its leopards and sloth bears. The park entrance is 7 km from Timbriwewa, 29 km from Anuradhapura. Due to the unstable political situation the park remained closed from the mid-80s; enquire about access from the Dept of Wildlife Conservation, State Timber Corp Bldg, 82 Rajamalwatte Rd, Battaramulla nr Sri Jayawardenepuram-Kotte.

About 300 km of jeep track cover the area. In addition to paying an entrance fee, if you have not come on a tour from Kala Oya, you will have to choose between hiring a jeep with driver/guide (min charge is high) or taking a seat in a mini-bus. Although a jeep is more expensive, unless you can share with others, it is by far the best way to get a glimpse of a leopard and see the sloth bear. Other wildlife includes a variety of deer, mongoose, wild buffaloes and wild boar; Kumbukwila and Nelunwila have watch-huts.

Wildlife

The largest reserve in Sri Lanka, this is best seen by staying at **Kala Oya** (30 km) and taking advantage of the government organised tours. Private cars are not allowed into the reserve, which, unlike some of the island's other parks, has some dense jungle, interspersed with savannah and sand dunes. A number of *villus* – the small lakes which attract animals to drink, have crocodiles; Wil-pattu means 'the land of lakes'. Some of these were used by earlier kingdoms as reservoirs.

Viewing

Early morning or late afternoon are the best times for a visit, to avoid the heat of the day and also to see the animals. First light is best for viewing birds and deer. From 0800-1100, if you drive around the park you may spot leopard by the lakes and a variety of deer. At mid-day, sloth bear sometimes bask in the sun on sandy patches; true to its name, the bear is slow to move and survives on honey, soft fruit and white ants (termites). After 1600, you will again see activity in the park; leopards possibly and certainly bear near the *villus*. In the dry season (Aug-Sep), elephants can be spotted as they come out to the water-holes.

The park is good for birdwatching with a large variety of water birds, especially winter migrants from Nov-Jan, as well as those of the dry-zone jungle. Some Sinhalese ruins have been discovered in the forested areas to the E.

Park information

● Accommodation

Several very basic ***Park Bungalows*** are located within the perimeter, which can be reserved through Wildlife Dept, Transwork House, Col 1, T 33787. You need to bring your bedding and food (cook provided).

At **Maradanmaduwa**, 15 km from main gate, by the *villu*, ***Bungalow***, sleeps 10, ***Log Cabin***, 4, very good for bird-watching and spotting elephants in the dry months. 18 km away at **Manikapolauttu**, nr the centre of the park with several *villus* around, the ***Bungalow*** is nr a small lake with crocodiles, good viewing from verandah! 8 km away, 3 km E of the old Great North Rd, is **Kalivillu** which has the ***Bungalow*** on the water's edge, good for spotting leopards, and in the dry season, elephants which frequent the large *villu*. On the N boundary, by Moeragam Aru, a river attracting anglers, is the **Kokomattai** *Bungalow*. **Talawila** was once hunting territory; the ***Bungalow*** overlooks a lake. ***Nature and Wildlife Conservation Soc*** can sleep up to 10, reservations: Soc Offices, Chaitiya Rd, Marine Drive, Fort, Col, T 25248. At **Kala Oya C** ***Wilpattu Hotel***, T 29 752, 41 rm with fan, shower and mosquito nets, dining room overlooks Kala Oya river, excellent bungalows, rec. ***Pershamel Safari Hotel***, Pahamaragahawewa has 12 rm.

● Transport

Road Bus: from Anuradhapura, twice daily; also jeep or taxis.

Nochchiyagama From Kala Oya the road passes NE through this small Tamil village of potters, famous for producing black clay cooking pots known as *Chutties*.

It is about 20 km to Anuradhapura along the rather poor quality A12. See below for description.

ANURADHAPURA AND JAFFNA

The route runs NE from Colombo across the coastal plain. Lush and beautiful scenery continues 65 km, through paddy fields interspersed with coconut and areca nut palms and endless bananas and above all pineapples. It then climbs gently over attractive rolling low hills, the site of *chena* (shifting) cultivation for generations. Leaving the wet zone just N of Colombo, rainfall declines steadily NW.

Sapugaskanda Leaving Colombo on A1 a right turn at 12 km leads to the minor temple of Sapugaskanda, on a low hill 3 km away. There are beautiful views from the terrace of the small stupa, but the temple is famous for its murals which show the arrival of the Burmese saint Jagara Hamuduruvo in Sri Lanka.

ROUTES The A1 goes through **Mahara** (15 km; excellent *Rest House*). The small town was once a Dutch cantoonment. Five km off the main road to the left, just before Yekwala, is Heneratgoda.

Heneratgoda Botanical Gardens

Near Gampaha (well signed). It is a beautiful garden town and particularly famous as the nursery of Asia's first rubber trees introduced from the Amazon basin over a century ago. Several of the early imports are now magnificent specimens; the first tree planted carrying the No 6 is over 100 years old, but the most famous is No 2 because of its remarkable yield. The trees include *Hevea brasiliensis*, *Uncaria gambier*, rubber producing lianas (*Landolphia*), and the drug *ipecacuanha*. A female of the Coco de Mer was imported from the Seychelles and bore fruit in 1915.

The road passes by the former estate of Sir Solomon Dias Bandaranaike, aide de camp to the British Governor at the time of World War I. His son, **Solomon Western Ridgway Dias Bandaranaike**, became Prime Minister of independent Ceylon in 1956, but was assassinated in 1959. His memorial is by the side of the road 38 km out of Colombo. His widow succeeded him as Prime Minister. The family home, where visitors such as King George V and Jawaharlal Nehru stayed, can be seen nearby. After a further 7 km **Pasyala** is on the W edge of the central highland massif. The area is noted for its graphite (*plumbago*) mines and betel nuts. Passing through **Cadjugama** ('village of cashew nuts') note the many cashew nut stalls along the roadside.

ROUTES The road passes through a series of small villages and towns including Warakapola and Ambepussa, where the A1 turns E to Kandy, via Kegalla (see below). For Anuradhapura the A6 goes straight on, through **Polgahawela** ('the field of the coconut') to Kurunegala.

Kurunegala

(37 km) The town is surrounded by a chain of bare rocks which look like animals – elephant rock, tortoise rock etc. It is at the foot of the 325m rock **Etagala**. Excellent views from top. 18 km NE of Kurunegala is an ancient Buddhist temple, some of the doors being carved and inlaid with ivory. There is an attractive artificial lake at the foot of the hills. **Accommodation D** *Rest House*, overlooks the lake, clean and pleasant.

ROUTES From Kurunegala 2 routes go N to Anuradhapura. The W route (106 km) goes N from Pandeniya to **Maho** (19 km), the base from which to see the 13th century capital of Yapahuwa.

Yapahuwa

(4 km) From Maho take the road to the left, which leads to the foot of the rock on which the **fortress** stands. The tooth relic, now enshrined at Kandy, was carried from the temple here to India, then recovered in 1288 by Parakramabahu III. It was built as the fortress capital of the Sinhalese kings in 1301, and when abandoned, was inhabited by Buddhist monks and religious ascetics.

A vast granite rock rising 100m abruptly from the surrounding plain, is encircled by a 1 km long path rising to the top. The fort is surrounded by a moat and ramparts, and there are signs of other ancient means of defence. The impressive ornamental staircase is still well preserved, and the ruins at the head of the remarkable flight of granite steps are unique. One of the 2 window frames is now exhibited in the Colombo Museum.

Return to the main road and turn N to **Mahagalkadawala** (24 km; turn left in town to see Rajagane 1 km), and Anuradhapura (37 km). The road into Anuradhapura enters past the lake, *Tissa Wewa*, on the right, and passes some of the main dagobas before reaching the new town.

The E route to Anuradhapura (116 km) goes to Dambulla (an area known for its mangoes), where there are famous rock caves and temples, only 15 km from the magnificent and dramatic site of Sigiriya.

Anuradhapura

Anuradhapura is Sri Lanka's most sacred town. From its origins as a settlement in the 6th century BC, it was made capital in 377 BC by King Pandukhabhaya who started the great irrigation works on which it depended, and named it after the constellation Anuradha. Although the city has remained a symbol of Sinhalese regal power and of Buddhist orthodoxy its period as a centre of real political power had ended by the 12th century AD, though for 500 years before that it had suffered widely fluctuating fortunes. By the 19th century it was completely deserted. 'Re-discovered' in the early 19th century by Ralph Backhaus, archaeological research, excavation and restoration have been going on ever since. The new town was started in the 1950s.

At its height it may have stretched 25 km. Its ruins and monuments today are widely scattered, which makes a thorough tour time consuming, but it more than repays the effort.

The first era of religious building followed the conversion of King Devanampiyatissa. In his 40 year reign these included the Thuparama Dagoba, Vihara, and the Maha Vihara. A branch of the **Bodhi tree** (see below) under which the Buddha was believed to have gained his enlightenment was brought from India and successfully transplanted. It is one of the holiest Buddhist sites in the world.

Anuradhapura remained a capital city until the 9th century AD, when it reached its peak of power and vigour. After the 13th century it almost entirely disappeared, the irrigation works on which it had depended falling into total disuse, and its political functions taken over first by Polonnaruwa, and then by capitals to the S. The earliest restoration work began in 1872, and has continued ever since. The town is now the headquarters of the Sri Lanka Archaeological Survey.

Places of interest

ENTRY Individual entry to the Anuradhapura sites is US$7. Combined tickets for the triangle of ancient sites can be obtained from Colombo. See page 1330.

PHOTOGRAPHY Permits are essential, obtainable from the Office of Antiquities, next to the Archaeological Museum.

NB: The sites of interest are scattered, and the most enjoyable way of seeing them is by bicycle. Some guest houses can provide cycles or arrange hire. Cars may also be hired.

The **Archaeological Museum** is central to the site and makes a good starting point for a tour. Immediately to its W is the Basawakkulama Tank, the oldest artificial lake in the city, built by King Pandukabhaya in the 4th century BC. **Ruvanwelisiya Dagoba** is opposite the museum. The renovation has flattened the shape of the dome, and some of the painting is of questionable style, but it remains a remarkably striking monument. The dome is 80m in diameter at its base and 55m high. It was begun by King

CLIMATE: ANURADHAPURA

	Jan	Feb	Mar	Apr	May	Jun	Jul	Aug	Sep	Oct	Nov	Dec	Av/Tot
Max (°C)	31	35	37	38	35	34	35	35	33	34	31	30	34
Min (°C)	21	22	24	25	25	26	25	26	25	24	23	23	24
Rain (mm)	94	47	71	178	89	10	34	40	67	263	244	223	1360

Dutthagamani (*Dutugemunu*) to house relics, and priests from all over India were recorded as being present at the enshrinement of the relics in 140 BC. A small passage leads to the relic chamber. At the cardinal points are 4 'chapels' which were reconstructed in 1873, when renovation started.

Mirisawetiya Dagoba (originally from the 2nd century BC) is near the *Tissawewa Rest House*, 1 km to the SW. It was completely rebuilt during the reign

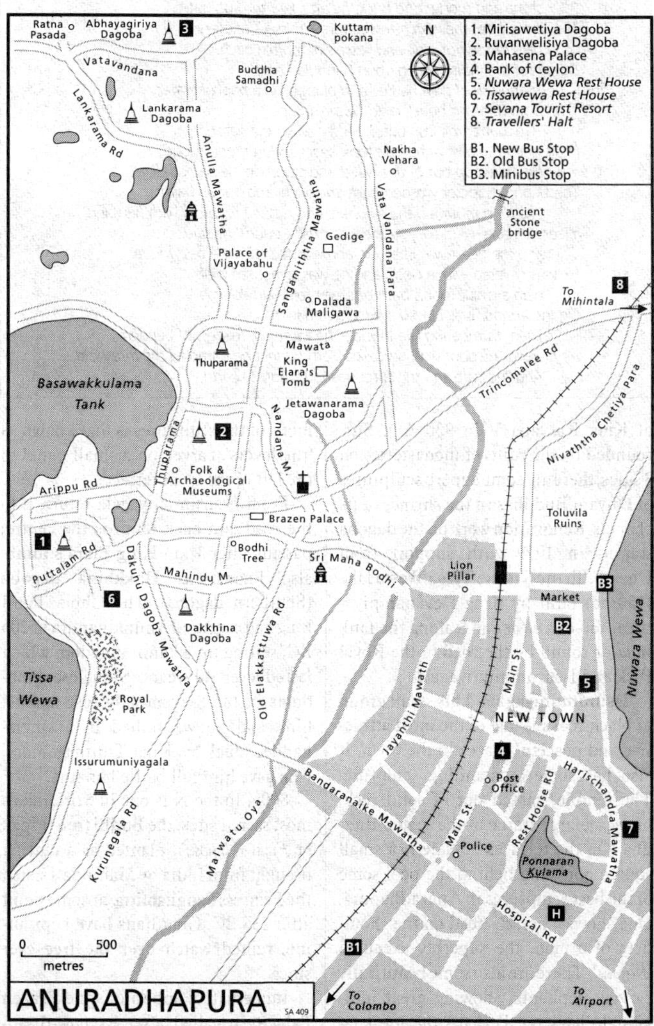

DUTTHAGAMANI: BATTLE WITH ELARA

A.L. Basham gives a flavour of the Mahavansa's account of the battle between Dutthagamani's and Elara's forces:

The city had three moats, And was guarded by a high wall.
Its gate was covered with iron, Hard for foes to shatter.
The elephant knelt on his knees, and battering with his tusks
stone and mortar and brick, he attacked the iron gate.
The Tamils from the watch-tower, threw missiles of every kind,
balls of red hot iron and vessels of molten pitch.
Down fell the molten pitch upon Kandula's back.
In anguish of pain he fled and plunged in a pool of water.
"This is no drinking bout!" cried Gothaimbara.
"Go, batter the iron gate! Batter down the gate!!"
In his pride the best of tuskers took heart and trumpeted loud.
He reared up out of the water and stood on the bank defiant.
The elephant-doctor washed away the pitch, and put on balm.
The King mounted the elephant and rubbed his brow with his hand.
'Dear Kandula, I'll make you the lord of all Ceylon!' he said,
and the beast was cheered, and was fed with the best fodder.
He was covered with a cloth, and he was armoured well
with armour for his back of seven-fold buffalo hide.
On the armour was placed a skin soaked in oil.
Then, trumpeting like thunder, he came on, fearless of danger.
He pierced the door with his tusks. With his feet he trampled the threshold.
And the gate and the lintel crashed loudly to earth.

of King Kasyapa V in 930 AD. Surrounded by the ruins of monasteries on 3 sides, there are some superb sculptures of Dhyani Buddhas in the shrines of its chapels. Renovation work on the dagoba started in 1979 with support from Unesco. To the S is the **Tissa Wewa** lake (150 ha) built by King Devanampiyatissa. You can either go S along the tank *bund* or round by the road to the Royal Park and Issurummuniyagala.

Issurumuniyagala This small group of black rocks is one of the most attractive and peaceful places in the town. It also has some outstanding sculpture. The temple, carved out of solid rock, houses a large statue of the seated Buddha. On the terraces outside is a small square pool, and behind the pool some of the best sculptures in Anuradhapura. One shows a horse's head on the shoulders of a man, the superbly executed '*Kapila*'. There are also some beautifully carved elephants, showing great individual character. Perhaps the most famous of the sculptures is that known as 'the lovers', carved on a small panel to the left of the front terrace.

From Issurumuniyagala return E to the road and back towards the centre, passing after 1 km **King Elara's tomb**, also known as **Dakkhina dagoba** (Southern dagoba). The Chola Tamil king had captured Anuradhapura in 205 BC, setting up a Tamil kingdom which lasted over 40 years. Sinhalese kingdoms in the S eventually rose against him, and he was killed in a single-handed duel by King Dutthagamani, who gave him full battle honours.

800m to the N is one of Sri Lanka's most sacred sites, the **Bodhi tree** (Pipal, or *Ficus religiosa*), planted as a cutting brought from India by Mahinda's sister, the **Princess Sanghamitta**, at some point after 236 BC. Guardians have kept uninterrupted watch over the tree ever since.

Immediately opposite is the **Brazen Palace**, so called after its now-disappeared roof, reputedly made of bronze, the most remarkable of many monastic buildings scattered across the site. Described in the *Mahavansa* as having 9 storeys, there are 600 pillars laid out over an area 70m square. The pillars, just under 4m high, supported the first floor. You need imagination to visualise the scale of the building as it may have been, for there is no hint of its structural style or decoration. The walls between the pillars were made of brick, while the upper floors were wooden. Built in 161 BC by Dutthagamani, it was the heart of the monastic life of the city, the *Mahavihara*. Much of what is visible today is the reconstruction of King Parakramabahu I in the last quarter of the 11th century, making use of the remnants of former buildings.

The road E between the Brazen Palace and the Bo tree goes to the new town, the railway station and the **Nuwarawewa**, the largest of Anuradhapura's artificial lakes (1000 ha) completed about 20 BC.

Going E from the Brazen Palace (along the Trincomalee and Mihintale Rd), a left fork after 800m goes N to the ruined Jetawarama Dagoba. Along the Malwatu Oya, N of the road are ruins of ancient stone bridges with pillars and slabs – these may have been used as elephant crossings.

Jetavanarama Dagoba was named after the first Buddhist monastery (names of the Jetawarama and Abhayagiriya dagobas are sometimes reversed). The largest dagoba in Anuradhapura, it is also being renovated with help from Unesco. Started by King Mahasena (AD 275-292), the paved platform on which it stands covers more than 3 ha and it has a diameter of over 100m. In 1860 Emerson Tennet, in his book *Ceylon*, calculated that it had enough bricks to build a 3m high brick wall 25 cm thick from London to Edinburgh, equal to the distance from the southern tip of Sri Lanka to Jaffna and back down the coast to Trincomalee. Its massive scale was designed in a competitive spirit to rival the orthodox Maha Vihara.

Continuing N from the Jetavanarama Dagoba, turn left at the crossroads to the oldest dagoba, the **Thuparama**. Built by Devanampitiya in 307 BC, the 19m high dagoba has retained its beautiful bell shape, despite restoration work. It is surrounded by concentric circles of graceful granite monolithic pillars, possibly originally designed to support an over-arching thatched cover. It is a centre of active pilgrimage, highly decorated with flags and lights. Immediately to its NE was the original **Dalada Maligawa**, where the Tooth Relic was first enshrined when it was brought to Ceylon in AD 313. Fa Hien gave a vivid description of its display.

The road N (Sanghamitta Maw) goes 1.5 km through the site of the 11th century palace of Vijayabahu I to the superb statue of the serene **Samadhi Buddha**; some think the expression changes as the sun's light moves across it. Roofed to protect it from the weather, it probably dates from the 4th century AD.

Across the Vatavandana Para, a little to the N, you turn right for the **Kuttan-Pokuna** – recently restored 8th and 9th century ritual baths. Though called 'twin' ponds, one is over 10m longer than the other. You can see the underground water supply channel at one end of the 2nd bath. They were probably for the use of the monastery or for the university nearby.

Abhayagiriya Dagoba is left from the crossroads. It is 400m round and supposedly 135m high in its original form, part of the pinnacle has disappeared. It is now about 110m high. Built in 88 BC by Valagam Bahu, the temple and its associated monastery were built in an attempt to weaken the political hold of the Hinayana Buddhists, and to give shelter to monks of the Mahayana school. There are 2 splendid sculpted guardians at the threshold.

To the W of the Abhayagiriya Dagoba are the ruins of the **Ratnaprasada**. The area had once been the 'undesirable' outskirts of Anuradhapura where the cremation grounds were sited. In protest against the King's rule, an ascetic community of monks set up a *tapovana* community of which this is an architectural example. Though they lived an austere life, the buildings here were superbly crafted and curiously, contained elaborately carved lavatories (examples in the Archaelogical Museum)! This type of monastery typically had 2 pavilions connected by a stone bridge within a high-walled enclosure which contained a pond. The main entrance was from the E, with a porch above the entrance. Here the Ratnaprasada did not remain a peaceful haven but was the scene of bloody massacres when a rebellious group took refuge with the monks and were subsequently beheaded by the King's men; their turn to have their heads roll in the dust followed another bloody revolt. The nearby **Mahasena Palace** has a particularly fine carved stone tablet and one of the most beautifully carved moonstones, see page 1313.

ROUTES You can return to Museums by taking the road Lankarama Rd to the S.

Museums

Archaeological Museum, 0800-1600 (closed Tue), an excellent small museum, with some beautiful pieces of sculpture, incl finds from Mihintale. **Folk Museum** reflects rural life in the North Central Province.

Excursion

Mihintale 16 km E of Anuradhapura, Mihintale is revered as the place where Mahinda converted King Devanampiya Tissa to Buddhism in 243 BC, thereby enabling Buddhism to spread to the whole island. It is a beautiful site. The legend tells how King Tissa was chasing a stag during a hunting expedition. The stag reached Mahintale and fled up the hill side, followed by the King, until he reached a place surrounded by hills, where he was astonished to find a man. It was Mahinda, Asoka's son, who had come to preach the Buddha's teachings.

The top of the hill became a monastery, reached by a flight of 1840 broad granite steps, lined with frangipani. The climb starts gently, rising in a broad stairway of 350 steps. This is followed by a flat platform, then a steep flight of steps up to the dagoba of **Kantaka Cetiya**, built before 60 BC. Unearthed in 1932-35, it had been severely damaged. Over 130m round, today it is only about 12m high, compared with its original height of perhaps 30m. At the 4 cardinal points it has some beautiful sculptures – geese, dwarves, and a variety of animals – and several rock cells around it. Return to the main path.

The climb continues up a 2nd and then a 3rd flight of steps. Half way up on the left is a path to a stone aqueduct and bathing trough beyond. Further up is a ruined shrine, at the entrance of which are slabs covered in 10th century inscriptions giving detailed rules about access to the sacred site. Return to the third flight of steps and continue to the top, where there is a refectory for the priests, the **Bhojana Salava**. It is also possible to travel this far by road.

The final steps lead up to the **Ambasthala** ('mango tree') **Dagoba**, with a diversion to the right about half way up to the Naga Pokuna, a 40m bathing pool carved out of solid rock. Shoes must be removed before climbing to the Ambasthala dagoba, the holiest part of the site. Walking on to the NE of the dagoba, built on the traditional site of the meeting between King Tissa and Mahinda, is the stone couch of Mahinda, carved out of bare rock. A short path to the SW leads to the summit (310m) and the **Mahasewa Dagoba**. This was supposedly built on the orders of King Tissa as a reliquary for a lock of the Buddha's hair, or relics of Mahinda. The views across Anuradhapura are magnificent.

Local festivals

Jun At the full moon in *Poson*, the introduction of Buddhism to Sri Lanka is celebrated with huge processions when many pilgrims visit the town.

Local information

● Accommodation

The **C** *Rest Houses* are excellent value. There are many small guesthouses and hotels in the new town. Most will arrange car/cycle hire. **C** ***Nuwarawewa Rest House***, T 025 2565, nr New Town, 60 rm, 35 a/c, restaurant, bar, exchange, shop, entertainment, pool, restaurant serves excellent mild curries (ask for a selection), evening meals European but curries to order, on the edge of the lake in attractive garden, friendly and helpful staff, good value and rec; slightly cheaper **C** ***Tissawewa Rest House***, T 025 2299, 25 rm, 2 a/c, near Tissawewa tank, formerly the *Grand Hotel*, the charming colonial house is beautifully situated in a secluded parkland with lots of monkeys, within the religious area hence no alcohol served, excellent and very good value, but often heavily booked, good restaurant, exchange. **C/D** ***Miridya***, Rowing Club Rd, T 025 2519, 40 rm, some a/c rm with view over Lake Nuwarawewa, restaurant, bar, exchange, entertainment, shop, lake fishing.

D ***Rajarata***, Rowing Club Rd, T 025 2578, 100 rm, 70 a/c, restaurant, exchange, pool; **D** ***Ashok***, Rowing Club Rd, T 025 2753, 26 rm; **D** ***Monara House***, 63 Freeman Maw, T 025 2110, 8 rm, basic.

E ***Sevana Tourist Rest***, 394/8 Harishchandra Maw, next door to the *Miridya Hotel*, simple, but clean and good value. F ***Youth Hostel***, Travellers' Hotel, 15 Jafna Junc, T 290, has 15 beds; 13 F ***Railway Retiring Rooms***.

● Transport

Train Colombo: *Rajarata Rajini*, 86, daily, 0505, 4 hr 35; *78 Express*, daily, 1428, $4^1/4$ hr; 868, daily, 1540, 5 hr. **Jaffna**: *Yal Devi*, 77, daily, 0945, 5 hr; *91 Mail*, daily, 0045, 6 hr. **Talaimannar**: 463, daily, 1335, $5^1/4$ hr; *97 Mail*, daily, 0112, 4 hr. **NB**: Services to Jaffna and Talaimannar may be disrupted.

Road Bus: frequent bus service to Mihintale, Colombo ($6^1/2$ hr) and Kandy (5 hr). In normal times the journey to Jaffna is 6 hr, but the service is currently completely unreliable.

Sea In mid-1991 the ferry service to India was not operating; enquire locally.

Anuradhapura to Jaffna

WARNING The civil war continues to claim many lives in northern Sri Lanka in mid-1994. It is impossible to travel to the Jaffna peninsula and some neighbouring areas at the time of writing without Government approval. Below is a brief summary of the route to Jaffna.

ROUTES From Anuradhapura take the A12 Trincomalee road for 1 km then fork left on the A20 to **Rambewa** (15 km) where you join the A9 from the S and turn N to **Medawachchiya** (10 km). The main road to Jaffna goes due N to **Vavuniya** (26 km) and Kilinochchi (77 km), across the Jaffna lagoon (15 km) through the **Elephant Pass** onto the Jaffna Peninsula. The road then runs W into **Jaffna** (49 km; *Population*: 120,000). The change in scenery is dramatic, palmyra palms suddenly replacing coconuts at the Elephant Pass, reflecting the much greater aridity of the N peninsula.

SIGIRIYA AND TRINCOMALEE

The A1 and A6 go NE to Kurunegala, skirting the N fringe of the Central Highlands to Dambulla, then passing through the heart of the Dry Zone and shifting '*chena*' cultivation across the gently sloping plain to **Trincomalee** (85 km). Irrigated rice is interspersed with

CLIMATE: JAFFNA

	Jan	Feb	Mar	Apr	May	Jun	Jul	Aug	Sep	Oct	Nov	Dec	Av/Tot
Max (°C)	29	32	33	34	33	31	31	31	30	31	30	28	31
Min (°C)	23	25	26	27	29	28	29	27	27	26	25	24	26
Rain (mm)	59	28	25	57	50	20	20	32	41	258	337	257	1184

extensive tracts of mixed jungle, including teak, bamboo and eucalyptus, and the road passes through the Minneriya-Giritale Sanctuary.

Dambulla a gigantic granite outcrop, towers more than 160m above the surrounding land. The rock is more than 1.5 km around its base and the summit is at an altitude of 550m. **The caves** Open 0600-1100; 1400-1900. Entry US$5. The caves were the refuge of King Valagam Bahu when he was in exile for 14 years. When he returned to the throne at Anuradhapura in the 1st century BC, he had a magnificent rock temple built at Dambulla. From the carpark it is a hot and tiring climb, first across bare rock, then up a series of steps. The caves are about half way to the top of the hill, and now form part of a temple complex. Shoes and hats must be removed, and shorts must be covered with a sarong (provided at the entrance). They have a mixture of Buddhist and Hindu painting and sculpture. There are several reclining Buddhas, including the 15m long sculpture of the dead Buddha in Cave 1, with other Buddhist figures. The frescoes on the walls and ceilings date from the 15th-18th centuries. Cave 2 is the largest and most impressive, containing over 150 statues, illustrating the Mahayana influences on Buddhism at the time through introducing Hindu deities such as Vishnu and Ganesh. The ceiling frescoes show scenes from the Buddha's life and Sinhalese history. The rock is best visited in the early morning. Panoramic views from the top of surrounding jungle and lakes, and of Sigiriya, 19 km away. **Accommodation D** *Dambulla Rest House*, T 066 8299, close to caves, pleasant, rec.

Excursion

Aukana Direct buses run from Dambulla to the remarkable 13m high statue of the standing Buddha, carved out of the rock. Dating from the 5th century, it is near the Kalawewa Tank.

From Dambulla, take the main road NE to Trincomalee. After about 9 km, turn right at Inamaluwa to see the rock fort at Sigiriya, 11 km. Frequent buses from Dambulla, fewer in the afternoon. From Kandy, direct bus daily to Sigiriya.

Sigiriya

STD Code: 066. The rewards of the site justify the steep climb. There are stunning views. Very early morning is beautiful, the site still very quiet until 0730, but the late afternoon light is better for the frescoes. In addition to the rock fortress, there are extensive grounds at the foot of the hill.

Entry US$7. See page 1313. Allow 2-3 hr for a visit. Refreshments at the *Rest House* nr the entrance. Carry your drink if you want to avoid paying an excessive price at the kiosk half way up.

NB: There can be long queues on public holidays.

WARNING Visitors suffering from vertigo are advised not to attempt it. Not suitable for the frail or unfit.

The vast flat-topped 200m high **Lion Rock** (*Sinha-Giri*) stands starkly above the surrounding countryside of the central forest. It was an exceptional natural site for a fortress, taking its name because lions were believed to occupy the caves. Hieroglyphs suggest that it was occupied by humans from very early times, long before the fortress was built. The royal citadel (477-495 AD) was surrounded by an impressive wall and moat; the city had the Palace and quarters for the ordinary people who built the royal pavilions, pools and fortifications. The top of the rock has a surface area of 1.5 ha, to the NW of which was the palace, built on the precipitous edge.

When the citadel ceased to be a palace, it was inhabited by monks until 1155, and then abandoned. It was rediscovered by archaeologists in 1828. The Mahavansa records that King Kasyapa, having killed his father to gain the throne, lived in terror that his half-brother, who had taken refuge in India, would return to kill him. He did come back, after 18 years, to find that Kasyapa had built a combination of pleasure palace and massive fortress. Kasyapa came down from the hill to face his half brother's army on elephant back. Mistakenly thinking he had been abandoned, he killed himself with his dagger.

At Sigiriya, Kasyapa intended to reproduce on earth the legendary palace of *Kubera*, the God of Wealth, and so had it decorated lavishly with impressive gardens, cisterns and ponds. For the famous frescoes he gathered together the best artists of his day. Excavations have revealed surface and underground drainage systems.

At the western approach to the rock are the 5th century water gardens, restored by the Central Cultural Fund sponsored by UNESCO, with walks, pavilions, ponds and fountains which are gravity fed from the moats as they were 1500 years ago. At the foot of the climb, the **Cobra hood Cave** has 2nd century inscriptions. Nearby is a water tank or cistern. Steps then lead up to the **Fresco gallery**, painted under an overhanging rock and reached by a spiral staircase. Of the 500 or so frescoes, which vie with those in Ajanta (see page 1178), only 21 remain. They are remarkably well preserved, as they are sheltered from the elements in a niche. In the style of Ajanta, the first drawing was done on wet plaster and then painted with red, yellow, green and black. The figures are 'portraits' of celestial nymphs and attendants above clouds – offering flowers, scattering petals or bathing-beauties.

Immediately beyond the foot of the spiral staircase the path is protected on the outer side by the 3m high **Mirror Wall**, a highly polished plaster wall believed to have been coated with egg white and wild honey. After 15 centuries it still has a reflective sheen. Visitors and pilgrims have written tiny Sinhalese 'graffiti', prompted by the frescoes.

The main path takes you to the top of the rock up the steep W and N sides. The original staircase that led up to the top is in ruins, but there are well-made steps. The path reaches the **Lion Terrace** on the N ledge where it leads through the giant plaster-covered brick paws of the lion – steep steps and railings go to the top. To reach the palace there were 25 flights of steps. On the top the **Summer Palace** had bathing pools for the royal family. You can see the granite throne, audience hall, niches to hold oil lamps, and precariously positioned platforms for guards at the top.

The small **Museum** is at the beginning of the path up, and there is a dagoba and other ruins on the roadside just over a km away.

• **Accommodation** The best 2 are 1 km away. They are comfortable with restaurants, games, shops and pools. **A** *Sigiriya*, T 8311, 50 comfortable rm in bungalows with terrace in a picturesque location set against the rock, in a large garden; **A** *Sigiriya Village*, by the rock, T 8216, 120 a/c rm in bungalows with terraces, both pools are open to non-residents for a fee. **D** *Rest House*, T 8324, moderately priced, conveniently close to the entrance, 15 rm, 2 a/c, good restaurant, comfortable, rec. Some smaller *Guest Houses* nr the rock including the F *Ajantha* which provides good food.

• **Transport Road Bus**: there is a bus hourly to Dambulla (½ hr). Daily bus to Kandy (2½-3 hr) and Colombo.

ROUTES From Sigiriya rejoin the main A6 at Habarana.

Habarana

(24 km), an important crossroads. **NB** The quality of the accommodation and the central location make this an excellent place to stay if you are travelling by car. There is an attractive Buddhist temple, with excellent paintings. Behind the tank next to the temple is a rock, with superb views from the top over the forest to Sigiriya. **Accommodation AL** *The Lodge*, T 066 8321, 150 rm, in bunga-

lows, excellent; **AL** *Village Habarana*, T 066 8316, 106 cottages, enormous gardens, excellent food, warm welcome, highly rec. **D** *Habarana Rest House*, 4 rm, good value alternative.

Take the **A11** E from Habarana through the **Minneriya-Giritale sanctuary**. 26 km from Polonnaruwa is King Mahasena's magnificent Minneriya Tank (4th century AD), covering 3000 ha. A further 12 km away is the Giritale Tank (7th century AD). **Accommodation** Two hotels overlook the lake in beautiful settings, and can make a convenient base for Polonnaruwa. **A** *The Royal Lotus*, 54 rm, some a/c, T 6316 or Colombo 548850, close to lakeside, good food, excellent views. **A** *Giritale Hotel*, 40 rm, some a/c, T 631, up the hill, superb views from restaurant and terrace, good facilities. Polonnaruwa is another 13 km.

Polonnaruwa

STD Code: 027. The Sinhalese kings of Anuradhapura in 369 AD used Polonnaruwa as their residence but it did not rank as a capital until the 8th century. The Cholas destroyed the Sinhalese kingdom at the beginning of the 11th century, and taking control of most of the island, they established their capital at Polonnaruwa. In 1056 King Vijayabahu I defeated the Cholas, setting up his own capital in the city. It remained a vibrant centre of Sinhalese culture under his successors, notably Parakramabahu I (1153-1186) who maintained very close ties with India, importing architects and engineers, and Nissankamalla (1187-1196). The rectangular shaped city was enclosed by 3 concentric walls, and was made attractive with parks and gardens. After them the kingdom went into terminal decline and the city was finally abandoned in 1288, after the tank embankment was breached.

Many of the remains are in an excellent state of repair though several of the residential buildings remain to be excavated. The restoration at the site is by the UNESCO sponsored Central Cultural Fund. Allow a day to get some impression of this ancient site. You can cover part of the tour by taxi and part on foot. Guides are available although at the monuments officials are happy to answer questions or explain details (with expectations of a tip). Entry US$7. See page 1376.

Polonnaruwa owes much of its glory to the artistic conception of King Parakramabahu I who planned the whole as an expression and statement of imperial power. In its imperial intentions, and the brevity of its existence, it may be compared to the great Mughal emperor Akbar's city of Fatehpur Sikri, see page 321. Its great artificial lake, covering over 2500 ha, provided defence along its entire W flank, cooling breezes through the city, and water for irrigation. The bund is over 14 km long and 12m high, and the tank irrigates over 90 sq km of paddy fields. Fed by a 40 km long canal and a link from the Giritale tank, it was named after its imperial designer, the **Sea of Parakrama** (Topa Wewa). Today it attracts numerous water birds, including cormorants and pelicans.

Places of interest

If you are staying at the lakeside *Rest House*, or one of the hotels nearby you can start the tour by going 1.5 km S towards the village.

The **Southern Group** You will first see the giant 3.5m high **statue** of a bearded figure, now believed to be King Parakramabahu himself, looking away from the city he restored, holding in his hand the palm leaf manuscript of the 'Book of Law' (some suggest it represents 'the burden of royalty' in the shape of a rope. To its S is the now restored **Potha Gul Vihara**, a circular *gedige* type building which is circular (instead of being corbelled from 2 sides), with 4 small solid *dagobas*. It has been reno-

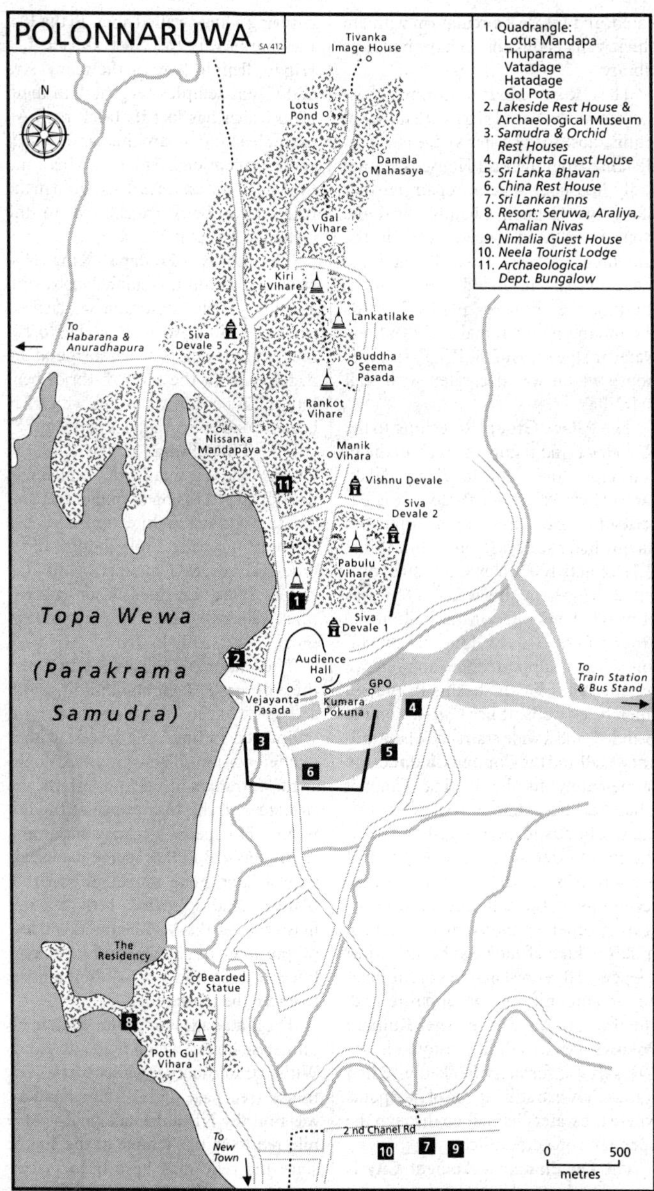
POLONNARUWA
SA 412
N
1. Quadrangle:
Lotus Mandapa
Thuparama
Vatadage
Hatadage
Gol Pota
2. Lakeside Rest House &
Archaeological Museum
3. Samudra & Orchid
Rest Houses
4. Rankheta Guest House
5. Sri Lanka Bhavan
6. China Rest House
7. Sri Lankan Inns
8. Resort: Seruwa, Araliya,
Amalian Nivas
9. Nimalia Guest House
10. Neela Tourist Lodge
11. Archaeological
Dept. Bungalow
Tivanka
Image House
Lotus
Pond
Damala
Mahasaya
Gal
Vihare
Kiri
Vihare
Lankatilake
To
Habarana &
Anuradhapura
Siva
Devale 5
Buddha
Seema
Pasada
Rankot
Vihare
Nissanka
Mandapaya
Manik
Vihara
Vishnu Devale
Siva
Devale 2
Pabulu
Vihare
Topa Wewa
(Parakrama
Samudra)
Siva
Devale 1
Audience
Hall
To
Train Station
& Bus Stand
GPO
Vejayanta
Pasada
Kumara
Pokuna
The
Residency
Bearded
Statue
Poth Gul
Vihara
2 nd Chanel Rd
To
New
Town
0
500
metres

vated, and inside a circular rm with 5m thick walls is thought to have housed a library.

The **Rest House Group** Nissankamalla's 'New' Palace with its Royal Baths, close to the water's edge is a short distance from the Rest House. They are sadly in a poor state of repair. Further along the Council Chamber had the stone Lion throne (now housed in the Colombo National Museum) and the stone pillars inscribed with names, marking the Ministers' places. Towards the mound which remains above flood water are the ruins of the King's summer house which was decorated with wall paintings.

The **Palace Group** Returning to the *Rest House* and taking the path to the E, you cross the road to King Parakramabahu's Vejayanta Pasada. It is described in the Chronicles as originally having had 7 storeys (hence, Sath Mahal Palace) and 1000 rooms, but most of it was destroyed by fire as much of it was of wood. The large central hall on the ground floor, 31m by 13m, has 30 columns which supported the roof; you can see the holes for the beams in the 3m thick brick walls. It has porticos on the E and W and a wide stairway. The **Audience Hall** and the **Council Chamber** are immediately to the E. The Council Chamber has superb friezes of elephants, lions and dwarves, which follow the entire exterior of the base. The hall has 4 rows of 10 sculpted columns. Inscriptions on the columns indicate the seating order in the council chamber, from the king at the head to the record keepers and representatives of the business community at the opposite end. Nearby, to the SE, is the **Kumara Pokuna** (Prince's Bath), restored in the 1930s. It was formerly flanked by 2 lion statues. You can still see one of the spouts where the water channelled through the open jaws of a crocodile.

The **Quadrangle – Ancient City** is immediately to the N of the Citadel covering a huge walled area. To the E of the entrance is the **Siva Devale I**, a Hindu Temple (one of the many Siva and Vishnu temples here) built in about 1200 which has lost its brick roof. An example of Indian architectural style, it shows exceptional stone carving, and the fine bronze statues discovered in the ruins have been transferred to the Colombo Museum.

The **Lotus Mandapa** King Nissankamalla built this small dagoba with a stone fence imitating a latticed wooden railing with posts. The ornamental stone pillars which surround the dagoba are in the form of thrice-bent lotus buds on stalks, a design which has become one of Sri Lanka's emblem.

The **Thuparama**, in the S of the Quadrangle is a small *gedige* which was developed as a fusion of Indian and Sinhalese Buddhist architecture. This has the only surviving vaulted dome of its type and houses a number of Buddha statues. It has very thick plaster-covered brick walls with a staircase embedded in them, now usually locked.

The **Vatadage** ('hall of the relic') near the entrance is a circular building with a dagoba on concentric terraces with sculptured railings, the largest with a diameter of 18m. There are guardstones at the entrances of the 2nd terrace; the *moonstone* to the N entrance of the top terrace is superb. The dagoba at the centre has 4 Buddhas (some damaged) with a later stone screen. A superbly planned and executed 12th century masterpiece, the Vatadage has modest proportions but remarkably graceful lines. It was almost certainly intended to house the tooth relic.

The **Hatadage** is opposite "built in 60 Sinhalese hours" which made up a day. With extraordinary *moonstones* at its entrance (see page 1313), the sanctuary was built by **Nissankamalla** and is also referred to as the **Temple of the Tooth**, since the relic may have been placed here for a time. To the E of the Hatadage (also known as the Atadaga – 'house of 8 relics') is the **Gal Pota** ('Book of Stone'). According to the inscription it weighs 25 tons, and was brought over 90 km from Mihintale. It is in the form of a palm leaf measuring over 9m by 1.2m, over 60 cm thick in places, with Sinhalese inscriptions praising the works of the King Nissankamalla.

The **Hindu temples** belong to different periods. If you walk past the **Pabulu Vihare**, a squat stupa up to the N wall of the ancient city, you come to one of the earliest temples with Tamil inscriptions, **Siva Devala 2**. Built of stone by the Indian Cholas in a style they were developing in Tamil Nadu (as at Thanjavur, see page 871) but using brick rather than stone. Another group of scattered monuments is further N. To the left of the path is the **Rankot Vihara**, the 4th largest dagoba on the island with a height of 55m, built by **Nissankamalla** in the 12th century. Note the perfection of the spire and the clarity of the statues round the drum.

Alahana Parivena (Royal Cremation Ground) was set aside by Parakramabahu. There are exellent views from the Chapter House, reached just before the large *gedige* **Jetavanarama** (see **Anuradhapura** above) or **Lankatilaka** ('ornament of Lanka'). The latter has walls which are 4m thick and still stand 17m high, although the roof has crumbled. The design illustrates the development in thinking which underlay the massive building, for it marks a turning away from the abstract form of the dagoba to a much more personalised faith in the Buddha in human form. The building is essentially a shrine, built to focus the attention of worshippers on the 18m high statue of the Buddha at the end of the nave. They are built of brick and covered in stucco, but the overall design of the building shows strong Tamil influence. The exterior bas relief sculpture sheds light on contemporary architectural styles.

Queen Subhadra is believed to have built the 'milk white' **Kiri Vihara** next to it, so named because of the unspoilt white plasterwork when it was first discovered. It remains the best preserved of the island's unrestored dagobas. In addition this separate group also has the *mandapa* with carved columns and a Hall, just S of the Jetawanarama.

The **Gal Vihara** (Cave of the Spirits of Knowledge) is N again from the Kiri Vihara. It is the principle attraction of Polonnaruwa, forming a part of Parakramabahu's monastery where a gigantic Buddha seated on a pedestal under a canopy, was carved out of an 8m high rock. On either side of the rock shrine are further vast carvings of a seated and a 14m recumbent Buddha. The grain of the rock is beautiful as is the expression. Near the head of the reclining figure of the Parinirvana Buddha, the 7m standing image with folded arms, was believed to be his grieving disciple Ananda but is now thought to be of the Buddha himself. Drink stalls nearby.

The Northern monuments A path continues N to rejoin the road. Opposite, a path leads to the **Lotus Pond** a little further along, a small bathing pool with 5 concentric circles of 8 petals which form the steps down which bathers stepped down into the water. The road ends at the **Tivanka Image House** where the Buddha image is in the unusual 'thrice bent' posture associated with a female figure, possibly emphasising his gentle aspect. This is the largest brick-built shrine, now substantially renovated, and there are excellent frescoes inside depicting scenes from the *Jatakas* and delightful carvings of dwarves on the plinth.

Museums

Archaeological Museum nr the *Rest House* is small but interesting.

Local information

● Accommodation

C *Rest House*, T 2411, 15 rm, 5 a/c, built on

the occasion of Queen Elizabeth II's visit in the 1950s, pleasant though now a little old-fashioned, well located for visiting the site with superb views over lake and popular, so advance reservations advisable, restaurant, bar, exchange, boating, fishing.

D *Araliya*, which was temporarily closed, the National Holiday Complex nr the Poth Gul Vihara, has the best accommodation in a group of 3 hotels by the lakeside further S, but 3 km from old town, hence transport essential, bikes for hire; **D** *Seruwa*, T 2411, 40 a/c rm, some with bath, restaurant, comfortable; **D** *Amalian Nivas*, T 2405, 36 rm, some a/c, rm service, both have a bar, exchange, boating, use of pool.

The best of the less expensive hotels in the **E** category are also nr the New Town some distance from the site, so you need transport. Alternatively, you can get a bus from the rly station or the Old Town bus stop to the New Town and take the path signposted beyond the Statue, for a km to the E. **D** *Nimalia Guest House*, 2nd Channel Rd, good restaurant; **D** *Sri n Inns*, 2nd Channel Rd, T 2403, nearby has 17 rm with baths around a court, scrupulously clean, good restaurant, rec. **E** *Gajaba Guest House*, nr Lake, Kuruppu Gardens, T 2392, 15 rm with bath, restaurant, garden. The small **E** *Neela Tourist Lodge* has 5 rm.

The Old Town nr the site offers a choice of inexpensive hotels. Towards the Rly Station and Bus Stop, on the Batticaloa Rd, are a couple of simple hotels which have rm with baths. The **E** *Rankheta Guest House*, Batiicaloa Rd, T 2080, with a good restaurant and **E** *Sri Lanka Bhavan*, off the road, nearer the centre of the Old Town are cheaper hotels with rm with or without bath. F *Samudra*, nr Lake is basic; F *Free Tourist Resort*, is simple with a reasonable restaurant. **E** *Archaelogical Bungalow*, by Lakeside, has 2 rm.

● **Places to eat**

Mainly in the hotels. If you are in the Old Town, the *Rest House* and *Ranketha* offer the best food.

● **Transport**

Train The Rly Station is a few km W of the Old Town on the Batticaloa Rd. **Colombo**: *Udaya Devi*, 80, daily, 1225, 6 hr; *Mail*, 94, daily, 2147, 8 hr.

Road Bus: the out-of-town Bus Stop is nr the Rly station. Several buses daily to Colombo (6 hr), via Dambulla (2 hr); minibuses to/from Anuradhapura (3 hr), Kandy (4 hr), Sigiriya and Batticaloa.

ROUTES Habarane take the **A6** NE direct to Trincomalee.

Trincomalee

STD Code: 026. Known above all for its excellent natural harbour. In the 1770s the future Lord Nelson described it as 'the best in the world', and it remains an outstandingly well-sheltered deep port with an area of more than 80 sq km. The harbour has often been fiercely contested, and it was a crucial naval base for the British during World War II. The town itself has never been very important, but that reflects its location in Sri Lanka's dry NE region, where the interior has been difficult to cultivate and malaria-infested for centuries. Only today, with the completion of the Victoria Dam and the re-settlement scheme of colonisers using irrigation from the Mahaweli Ganga Project, is the region inland developing into an important agricultural region. However, it is also torn by political strife, and in 1994 there was little sign that the civil war which continues to take a sporadic toll of life is coming to a close.

Local information

● **Accommodation**

AL *Club Oceanic*, T 2307, 83 rm, superb facilities in delightful palm tree garden setting right

CLIMATE: TRINCOMALEE

	Jan	Feb	Mar	Apr	May	Jun	Jul	Aug	Sep	Oct	Nov	Dec	Av/Tot
Max (°C)	28	31	33	34	36	36	35	35	35	33	29	28	33
Min (°C)	25	24	25	27	28	27	26	26	26	25	22	24	25
Rain (mm)	169	89	48	59	52	25	63	92	97	235	344	345	1618

on the beach; **AL** ***Seven Islands***, Orrs Hill Rd, T 2373, 25 rm, each with individual terrace, an old hotel, fully renovated, it dominates the promontory and has magnificent views, The old Naval Officers' Club now has most of the surrounding land taken over by the Naval Base.

There are several small guesthouses, both in Trincomalee and in beach resorts along the coast.

D ***Rest House***, corner of Dockyard Rd and Kachcheri Rd, T 25, 9 rm, good restaurant; **D** ***Rainbow Beach***, 322 Dyke St, T 2365, nr waterfront, some rm with bath, good open-air restaurant.

E ***Newland***, 87 Raja Varothayam Rd, nr the Clock Tower, T 2668, some rm with bath, clean, friendly, good sea-food. Also a modest F ***Chinese Guest House***, Duke St, backing onto beach, T 2455, basic; F ***Votre Maison***, 45 Green Rd, backing onto Nelson Cinema, simple, but good food; F 6 ***Railway Retiring Rooms***.

● **Places to eat**

Some of the hotels serve good sea food specialities. Chinese along Ehamparam Rd, best being ***Chinese Eastern***, nr the Clock Tower. Fast food, ice creams and cold drinks along Dockyard Rd – ***Flora Fountain***, rec. Cheap local food nr the Bus Station.

● **Banks & money changers**

Bank of Ceylon on Inner Harbour Rd, nr Customs Rd.

● **Post & telecommunications**

Post Office: corner of Power House Rd and Kachcheri Rd.

● **Transport**

Train Colombo (change at Gal Oya): *883*, daily, 0745, 10¾ hr.

Road Bus: frequent buses to Anuradhapura. Three to Colombo (7-8 hr), Kandy (5 hr) and 1 to Polonnaruwa daily.

KANDY AND BATTICALOA

Taking 11 years to complete, the trunk road from Colombo to Kandy was the first modern road to be opened in Sri Lanka (in 1832), when the first mail service ran between the 2 cities. Although the road route is quicker the train often gives better views. Some beautiful hill scenery lies between Kegalle and Mawanella.

Kegalla is a long straggling town in a picturesque setting. The first part of the route follows the A1 to Warakapola. Then after a right turn the road begins to climb into the hills at **Rambukkana** and on to Kegalla (19 km). On either side the vegetation is stunningly rich. At the top of the **Balana Pass** is a precipice called Sensation Point. The railway goes through 2 tunnels to Peradeniya (10 km), where the road crosses the Mahaweli Ganga, Sri Lanka's longest river.

Pinnawela, 3 km S of Rambukkana and just 45 min SW of Kandy, has the government's **Elephant Orphanage** where several dozen young animals, some only a few weeks' old and a metre high, are kept in parkland. Set up by the Government in 1975 to rescue orphaned baby elephants, the babies are introduced to the herd once they have been thoroughly checked. Babies are fed 'baby milk' 5 times daily. Tourists are sometimes allowed to help feed.You can watch them browsing, bathing, being hand-fed or trained to work. Down the road is the **Concept Elephant Bath**. You can ride elephants, either on land or through water.

Peradeniya

(*Altitude*: 500m) Famous for its magnificent Royal Botanic Gardens, Peradeniya is also the home of the Sri Lanka University and almost a suburb of Kandy (5 km).

Places of interest

The Botanic Gardens Entry Rs 20. Conceived originally in 1371 as the Queen's pleasure garden, Peradeniya became the residence of a Kandyan Prince between 1741-1782 where royal visitors were entertained. The park was converted into a 60 ha Botanical Garden in 1821, 6 years after the fall of the last Kandyan King. It is still beautifully maintained. Best to visit in early morning or late afternoon.

There are extensive well-kept lawns,

pavilions, an Orchid House with an outstanding collection, an Octagon Conservatory, Fernery, banks of bamboo and numerous flower borders with cannas, hibiscus, chrysanthemums, croton and colourful bougainvilleas. The central tank has water plants including the giant water lily and papyrus reeds. You will see unusual exotic species, especially palms (palmyra, talipot, royal, cabbage), and *Ficus elastica* (latex-bearing fig or 'Indian rubber tree' with buttress roots) and some magnificent old specimen trees. There is also a line of double coconut (*Coco de Mer*), unique in their native habitat to the island of *Praslin* in the Seychelles.

A bridge across the river, takes you to the **School of Tropical Agriculture** at Gannoruwa, where research is undertaken into various important spices and medicinal herbs as well as into tea, coffee, cocoa, rubber, coconuts and varieties of rice and other cash crops. The **Economic Museum** has botanical and agricultural exhibits. There is a reasonable at the *Rest House* nr the entrance and the *Royal Park Cafeteria* which is worth trying at lunchtime if you are visiting. The **University** (1942) is nearby, built in the old Kandyan style in an impressive setting of a large park with the river Mahaveli Ganga and the surrounding hillocks.

Kandy

Population: 50,000; *Altitude*: 488m. Kandy is one of the most important symbols of Sinhalese national identity. The last bastion of Buddhist political power against colonial forces, the home of the Temple of the Buddha's tooth relic, and the site of one of the world's most impressive annual festivals, the city is the gateway to the higher hills and the tea plantations. Its architectural monuments date mainly from a final surge of grandiose building by King Vikrama Raja Sinha in the early 19th century, so extravagant, and achieved only with such enormous costs for the people of Kandy, that his nobles betrayed him to the British rather than continue enduring his excesses. The result is some extraordinary buildings, none of great architectural merit, but sustaining a genuinely Kandyan style going back to the 16th century, and rich in symbolic significance of the nature of the king's view of his world.

History

Although the city of Kandy (originally *Senkadagala*) is commonly held to have been founded by a general named Vikramabahu in 1472, there was a settlement on the site for at least 150 years before that. On asserting his independence from the reigning monarch, Vikramabahu made Kandy his capital. He built a palace for his mother and a shrine on pillars. In 1542 the **Tooth Relic** was brought to the city, stimulating a flurry of new religious building – a 2 storey house for the relic itself, and 86 houses for the monks. As in Anuradhapura and Polonnaruwa, the Tooth temple was built next to the Palace.

Defensive fortifications probably only came with the attacks of the Portuguese. Forced to withdraw from the town in 1594, King Vimala Dharma

CLIMATE: KANDY

	Jan	Feb	Mar	Apr	May	Jun	Jul	Aug	Sep	Oct	Nov	Dec	Av/Tot
Max (°C)	29	33	34	35	31	29	29	28	28	30	29	28	30
Min (°C)	18	18	20	22	22	21	21	22	20	20	19	19	20
Rain (mm)	90	82	83	207	154	150	129	113	140	298	296	203	1945

Suriya set half the city on fire, a tactic that was repeated by several successors in the face of expulsion by foreign armies. However, he won it back, and promptly set about building a massive wall, interspersed with huge towers. In-

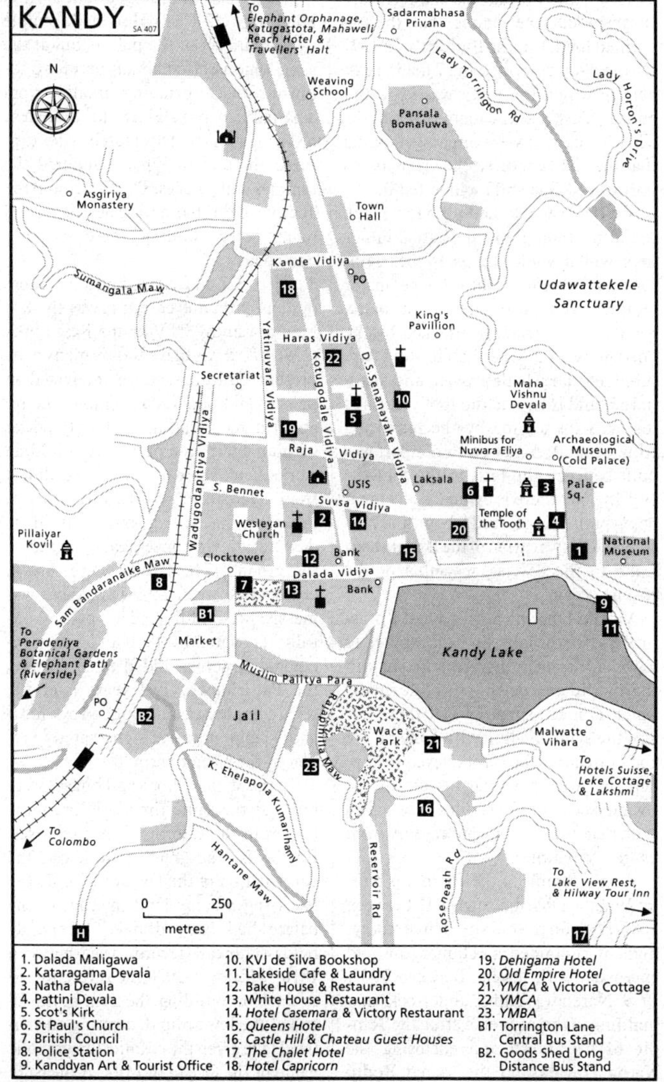

side, a new palace replaced the one destroyed by fire, and the city rapidly gained a reputation as a cosmopolitan centre of splendour and wealth. As early as 1597 some Portuguese showed scepticism about the claims that the enshrined tooth was the Buddha's. In 1597 De Quezroy described the 7 golden caskets in which the tooth was kept, but added that it was the tooth of a buffalo. The Portuguese were already claiming that they had captured the original, exported it to Goa and incinerated it.

By 1602 the city had probably taken the form (though not the actual buildings) which would survive to the beginning of the 19th century. The major temples were also already in place. Kandy was repeatedly attacked by the Portuguese. In 1611 the city was captured and largely destroyed, and again in 1629 and 1638, and the Tooth relic was removed for a time by the retreating King Senarat. A new earth rampart was built between the hills in the S of the city. In 1681 there is evidence of a moat being built using forced labour, and possibly the first creation of the **Bogambara Lake** to the SW, as a symbol of the cosmic ocean.

Vimala Dharma Suriya I had a practical use for the lake, for he is reputed to have kept some of his treasure sunk in the middle, guarded by crocodiles in the water. Duncan suggests that there was also the symbolic link with Kubera, the god of wealth, who was believed to have kept his wealth at the bottom of the cosmic ocean. Crocodiles are often shown on the dragon gateways (*makara torana*) of temples.

A new Temple of the Tooth was built by Vimala Dharma Suriya II between 1687-1707, on the old site. Three storeys high, it contained a reliquary of gold encrusted with jewels. Between 1707-1739 Narendra Sinha undertook new building in the city, renovating the **Temple of the Tooth** and enclosing the **Natha Devala** and the sacred **Bodhi tree**. He established the validity of his royal line by importing princesses from Madurai, and set aside a separate street for them in the town.

Major new building awaited King Kirti Sri (1747-1782). He added a temple to Vishnu NW of the palace, but at the same time asserted his support for Buddhism, twice bringing monks from Thailand to re-validate the Sinhalese order of monks. The Dutch, who captured the city in 1765, plundered the temples and palaces. The Palace and the Temple of the Tooth were destroyed and many other buildings were seriously damaged.

Kirti Sri started re-building, more opulently than ever, but it was the last king of Kandy, Sri Vikrama Raja Sinha (1798-1815) who gave Kandy many of its present buildings. More interested in palaces and parks than temples, he set about demonstrating his kingly power with an exhibition of massive building works. Once again he had started almost from scratch, for in 1803 the city was taken by the British, but to avoid its desecration was once again burned to the ground. The British were thrown out, and between 1809-1812 there was massive re-building. The palace was fully renovated by 1810 and a new octagonal structure added to the palace, the **Pattiripuwa**. Two years later the royal complex was surrounded by a moat and a single massive stone gateway replaced the earlier entrances.

In the W new shops and houses were built, at the same time building more houses in the E for his Tamil relatives. But by far the greatest work was the construction of the lake. Previously the low lying marshy land in front of the palace had been drained for paddy fields. Duncan records that between 1810-1812 up to 3000 men were forced to work on building the dam at the W end of the low ground, creating an artificial lake given the cosmically symbolic name of the Ocean of Milk. A pleasure

Worship Of The 'Tooth Relic'

The eyewitness account of **Bella Sidney Woolf** in 1914 captures something of the atmosphere: "the relic is only shown to royal visitors, or on certain occasions to Burmese and other pilgrims. If the passenger happens to be in Kandy at such a time he should try to see the Tooth, even though it may mean many hours of waiting. It is an amazing sight. The courtyard is crammed with worshippers of all ages, bearing offerings in their hands, leaves of young coconut, scent, flowers, fruit. As the door opens, they surge up the dark and narrow stairway to the silver and ivory doors behind which lies the Tooth.

The doors are opened and a flood of hot heavy scented air pours out. The golden 'Karandua' or outer casket of the tooth stands revealed dimly behind gilded bars. In the weird uncertain light of candles in golden candelabra the yellow-robed priests move to and fro. The Tooth is enclosed in five Karanduas and slowly and solemnly each is removed in turn; some of them are encrusted with rubies, emeralds and diamonds.

At last the great moment approaches. The last Karandua is removed – in folds of red silk lies the wondrous relic – the centre point of the faith of millions. It is a shock to see a tooth of discoloured ivory at least 3 inches long – unlike any human tooth ever known. The priest sets it in a golden lotus – the Temple Korala gives a sharp cry – the tom-toms and conches and pipes blare out – the kneeling worshippers, some with tears streaming down their faces, stretch out their hands in adoration."

house was built in the middle of the lake, connected by drawbridge to the palace. At last the city had taken virtually its present form.

Places of interest

The chief focus of interest is the Palace area, with the Temple of the Tooth and associated buildings. The entrance is in Palace Square opposite the Natha Devala. Entry US$7. See page 1376.

The original **Temple of the Tooth** (*Dalada Maligawa*) dated from the 16th century, though most of the present building and the *Pathiruppuwa*, or Octagon, were built in the early 19th century. The gilded roof over the relic chamber is a recent addition. The oldest part is the inner shrine, built by Kirti Sri after 1765. The drawbridge, moat and gateway were the work of Sri Wickrama Raja Sinha. There is a moonstone step at the entrance to the archway, and a stone depicting Lakshmi against the wall facing the entrance. The main door to the temple is in the wall of the upper veranda, covered in restored frescoes depicting Buddhist conceptions of hell. The doorway is a typical *makrana torana* showing mythical beasts. A second Kandyan style door leads into the courtyard, across which is the building housing the Tooth Relic. The door has ivory, inlay work, with copper and gold handles. The **Udmale** – upper storey – houses the Relic.

Caged behind gilded iron bars is the large outer casket (*karanduwa*), made of silver. Inside it are 7 smaller caskets, each made of gold studded with jewels. Today the temple is controlled by a layman (the *Diyawadne*) elected by the high priests of the monasteries in Kandy and Asgiriya. The administrator holds the key to the iron cage, but there are 3 different keys to the caskets themselves, one held by the administrator, one each by the high priests of Malwatte and Asgiriya, so that the caskets can only be opened when all 3 are present.

The sanctuary is opened at dawn. Ceremonies start at 0530, 0930 and 1830.

Kandy's Esala Perahera

The entire organisation of the Perahera was designed to symbolise the flow of cosmic power through the god-chosen king to the people – and to enable it to be renewed for the following year. It was rich with potent symbolism. Seneviratne shows how the ritual pole used in the processions represents the cosmic axis. Cut specially each year from a male tree with milk-like sap, symbolising fertility, milk and semen, the chosen tree was encircled with a magic symbol to transform it into the axis of the world. An E facing branch (the auspicious direction) would be cut and divided into 4 sections, one for each of the four temples: each piece (*kapa*) would then be taken to its respective temple, linking the temple with the cosmic axis and thereby renewing its access to the source of all power. Further rituals at each of the temples, in which the kapa were taken round the temple 3 times, linked the temple directly with the 3 worlds. The planting of the kapa then inaugurated the Perahera.

In the 2nd stage – ***Kumbal Perahera,*** the symbols of the 4 gods were joined with the Tooth Relic and processed for the first time with elephants. Duncan suggests that at this stage there were 5 processions joined in one; that of the *Tooth Relic*, which was started by King Kirti Sri in 1747; of *Natha*, the next Buddha; of *Vishnu*, due to be Buddha after Natha; of *Katagarama*, the general; and of the goddess *Pattini.* This procession marched round the sacred Bo tree in the centre of the square for several nights in succession, drawing on the strength which flowed through the Bo tree as another representation of the central axis of the city and of the world.

The 3rd and last stage – ***Randoli Perahera***, saw the procession move out to encompass the whole city, at which point the king made his first entry. He would be seen first at the windows of the *Pattirippuwa*, and then went to the Temple of the Tooth, raised the relic and placed it on the elephant. Duncan points out that the 8-sided building symbolically controlled the 8 directions, and that it was built specifically for this ritual purpose. The procession then moved off clockwise round the city, the king and the representatives of the 21 Kandyan provinces, in a parade that was itself intended to secure fertility. The 21 days of the festival may themselves have been symbolic of the 21 provinces. Seneviratne has suggested that the Perahera was believed to be capable of producing light rains, symbolised by the flowers strewed in front of the elephant carrying the Tooth Relic. Elephants themselves were seen as able to bring rain, for grey and massive, like rain clouds themselves, they could attract the clouds of heaven.

These are moments when the temple comes to life with pilgrims, making offerings of flowers amidst clouds of incense and the beating of drums. You are very unlikely to be allowed to see the relic itself, which for many years has only been displayed to the most important of visitors.

The **Audience Hall** was rebuilt in the Kandyan style with a wooden pillared hall (1784). The historic document ending the Kandyan kingdom was signed, and the territory was handed over to the British. There is excellent carving on the pillars.

On the lakeside is the 18th century **Malwatte Vihara** (Flower Garden) decorated with ornate wood and metal work where important ordinations take place. This and the **Asigiriya** are particularly important monasteries because of the senior position of their incumbents. There is a large recumbent Buddha statue at the latter, and the mound of the old Royal Burial Ground nearby.

The lake walk An attractive 4 km walk round the lake, named by its creator King Vikrama the 'ocean of milk' after its cosmic parallel. Some beautiful views, especially of the island pavilion in the lake. The Royal Palace Park (*Wace Park*), overlooks the lake and also has superb views.

Museums

Archaeological Museum, Palace Sq. Open 0900-1700, closed Tues. Superb sculptures, wood and stone housed in what remains of the old Palace. Some architectural pieces, notably columns and capitals from the Kandyan kingdom. **Kandy National Museum** in the Queen's Palace, behind Temple of the Tooth. Open 0900-1700, closed Fri. A vivid history of the development and culture of the Kandyan kingdom. Jewels, armaments, ritual objects, sculptures, clothes, games, medical instruments – an enormous range of everyday and exceptional objects.

Local festivals

Jul-Aug *Esala Perahera* Sri Lanka's greatest festival is of special significance. It is held in the lunar month in which the Buddha was conceived and in which he left his father's home. It has also long been associated with rituals to ensure renewed fertility for the year ahead. The last Kandy kings turned the Perahera into a mechanism for reinforcing their own power, trying to identify themselves with the gods who needed to be appeased. By focusing on the Tooth relic, the Tamil kings hoped to establish their own authority and their divine legitimacy within the Buddhist community. The Sri Lankan historian Seneviratne has suggested that fear both of the king and of divine retribution encouraged nobles and peasants alike to come to the Perahera, and witnessing the scale of the spectacle reinforced their loyalty.

Today the festival is a magnificent 15-day spectacle of elephants, musicians, dancers and tens of thousands of pilgrims in procession, Buddhists drawn to the temple by the power of the Tooth Relic rather than by that of the King's authority. The power of the Relic certainly long preceded that of the Kandyan dynasty. **Fa Hien** described the annual festival in Anuradhapura in 399 AD, which even then was a lavish procession in which roads were vividly decorated, elephants covered in jewels and flowers, and models of figures such as Bodhisattvas were paraded. When the tooth was moved to Kandy, the Perahera moved with it. However, today the tooth relic itself is no longer taken out.

The first 5 days of the festival are celebrated only within the grounds of the 4 Hindu *devalas* (temples). On the 6th night the torchlight processions set off from the temples for the Temple of the Tooth. Every night the procession grows, moving from the *Dalada Maligawa* along *Dalada Vidiya* and *Trincomalee St* to the *Adahanamaluwa*, where the relic casket is left in the keeping of the temple trustees. The separate temple processions go back to their temples, coming out in the early morning for the water cutting ceremony. Originally, the temple guardians went to the lake with golden water pots to empty water collected the previous year. They would then be refilled and taken back to the temple for the following year, symbolising the fertility protected by the gods. On the last day of the festival a daylight procession accompanies the return of the Relic to the Temple of the Tooth.

NOTE Change in street names: Gregory Rd to *Rajapihilla Mawatha*; Lady Horton's Drive to *Vihara Mahadevi Mawatha*; Lady McCallum Drive to *Srimath Kuda Ratwatte Mawatha*; Lady Blacke's Drive to *Devani Rajasinghe Mawatha*, etc.

Local information

● Accommodation

Owing to its elevation, a/c is not normally necessary.

NB: Prices during Perahera are highly inflated and accommodation difficult to find; out-of-town accommodation can be expensive to reach by taxi (or auto) and are sometimes off the main road reached by bus and can involve a climb up-hill.

WARNING Hotel touts are extremely persistent (sometimes boarding trains before they arrive at Kandy) and should be avoided at all costs. Insist on choosing your own hotel as otherwise prices for you will be raised by small hotels and guest houses to pay off the tout. You can telephone a hotel and reserve a rm and may then be sent transport or have the taxi fare paid.

AL *Citadel*, 124 Srimanth Kuda, Ratwatte Maw, T 25314, F 447087, 93 rm on 3 flower-filled terraces, good restaurant, modern but in local architectural style by River Mahaveli, 5 km out of town, hence inconvenient, tour groups make it noisy (ineffective soundproofing);. **AL** ***Mahaweli Reach***, 35 Siyambalagastenna Rd, by Katugastota Bridge, T 32062, 50 non a/c rm, striking, modern hotel, 5 km from town in commanding position overlooking river, family run, relaxed atmosphere; **AL** ***Suisse***, 130 Sangaraja Maw, T 22637, F 32083, 100 rm, 15 a/c, rm vary, best with balcony on lakeside, good pool, sports, night club, colonial style hotel in quiet lakeside location in parkland, 15 min walk from Temple.

A *Queens* (Oberoi), Dalada Vidiya, T 22121, 100 rm, garden side best, others noisy, good restaurant, bar, beer garden, pool, nr lake and palace, one of the oldest in the country (est. in 1860s), the advantage of its position opp the Temple of the Tooth, allows most guests excellent vantage point for seeing the procession from their balcony.

B *Tourmaline*, Anniewatte, 1.6 km from town, T 32326, F 32073, 30 a/c rm with balconies with mountain views; **B** *Hill Top*, 200 Bahirawakanda, on rd to Peradeniya, T 24162, 57 rm, 15 a/c, attractive and comfortable; **B** *Thilanka*, 3 Sangamitta Maw, behind the Temple of the Tooth, T 22060, 65 well furnished rm, 1st Flr better, good restaurant and pool, very clean, beautiful views, rec.

C ***Castle Hill Guest House***, 22 Rajapihilla Maw, T 24376, 4 large tastefully decorated rm, 2 on garden-side, meals in dining room; **C** ***Olde Empire Hotel***, 21 Temple St, T 24284, 10 clean rm with bath, good restaurant, well placed for temple and lake, rec; **C** ***Casamara***, 12 Kotugodale Vidiya, T 224051, 35 rm, ***Victory*** restaurant; **C** ***Dehigama***, 84 Raja Vidiya, T 22709, 20 rm; **C** ***Topaz***, Anniwatte, T 32073, 80 rm, 7 a/c, restaurant, bar, exchange, shops, travel, pool, tennis, well kept, quiet, good mountain views; **C** ***The Chalet***, 32 Rajapihilla Maw, T 24353, 31 rm, good restaurant, bar, tennis, small pool, boating, 1.5 km centre, beautifully located among wooded hills, by the lake, rec; **C** ***Hill Valley Inn***, Ampitya, 3 km from town centre (buses available), comfortable large rm with bath in Sri Lankan home, good food, peaceful, rec.

● Guest houses

There are several small, family guest houses by the lake with meals available and within easy reach of the *Hotel Suisse* swimming pool. Most will offer transport from station on request – **C** ***Chateau***, 20 Rajapihilla Maw, T 23608, 3 rm with bath, good views, peaceful, rec; **C** ***Lake Inn***, 43 Saranankara Rd, T 22208, has 10 rm; **C** ***Lake Cottage***, 28 Sangaraja Maw, T 23234, adjoins *Hotel Suisse*; **C** ***Lake View Rest***, 71 Rajapihilla Maw, T 32034, 30 rm with good views and **C** ***Hilway Tour Inn***, 90A/1 Rajapihilla Maw (15 min walk from centre), T 25430, with 2 rm. All have a bar, exchange, boating, pool.

D *Blue Star*, 30 Hewatha Rd, T 24392, cabanas, good restaurant, rec; **D** *Gem Inn*, 39 Anagarika Dharmapala Maw, out of town (E), T 24239, pleasantly located on a ridge with good views, good rm with bath.

Many good-value rooms in **private homes** are available; ask locally. The Tourist Office has a list of small guest houses. Inexpensive **D** category incl ***Lakshmi***, 57 Sanankara Rd, uphill nr the *Suisse*, T 22154, has clean rm; ***Victoria Cottage***, 6 Victoria Drive, next to YMCA on the lake which has rm with bath; ***Kandy City Mission***, 125 Trincomalee St, 150m from Dalada Maligawa, 12 good rm, restaurant rec as good value for snacks, clean, comfortable, home made bread and cheese.

● Budget accommodation & youth hostels

YMCA, 90 Kotugodale Vidiya, T 3529, 32 beds in dorm. The cheaper **E** *YMCA* is at 4 Sangaraja Maw, on lakeside, 10 rm, basic. *YMBA* (Young Men's Buddhist Assoc), 5 Rajapihilla Maw, nr Wace Park, overlooking lake. *Rly Retiring Rm* at Kandy station. *Youth Hostel*, Trinity College. *Travellers Halt*, 53/4 Siyambalagastenna, Katugastota, 25 beds, 4 km from centre. Bus from opp Police Station (Rly Crossing Bus Stop) to Katugastota, where you cross the bridge to reach the youth hostel.

27 km out of town in **Elkaduwa**, higher in the

hills, is the modern Jetwing hotel, **B *Hunas Falls***, T 08 76402, 31 rm, the most up-to-date in the area, it has 40 a/c rm, restaurant, bar, exchange, pool, boating, fishing, tennis, beautifully located in a tea garden, by a waterfall with excellent walks, visits to tea estate, factory and spice gardens.

● Places to eat

The hotels in the town are good but can be expensive and slow to serve. In the same class, ***Flower Song***, 137 Kotugodale Vidiya, serves excellent Chinese; good portions. In town, try ***Royal Garden***, 72 Sangaraja Maw, nr Tourist Office, ***Bake House***, 36 Dalada Vidiya, the ***White House***, open (slow service), ***Devon***, 4E Sangaraja Maw, (1st Flr) opp on Lakeside, and ***Lyon's*** on Peradeniya Rd, nr main roundabout, which are inexpensive and good value.

● Banks & money changers

Bank of Ceylon on Dalada Vidya.

● Entertainment

Daily performances of highland Kandyan dancing in different parts of the town. At Amungama, 10 km away is the Kandyan Dance Academy where the art and skill is handed down from father to son. Keppetipola Hall and the Lake Club performances are rec. The show usually lasts about 90 mins, ending with the fire dance.

● Libraries

Alliance Française, 412 Peradeniya Rd. **British Council** is opp the Clock Tower, the **USIS** on Kotugodale Vidiya and **United Services Library** by the Lake, opp the Temple of the Tooth.

● Posts & telecommunications

Post Offices: are opp the Rly Station and on Senanayake Vidiya (crossing with Kande Vidiya).

● Shopping

Numerous shops sell handicrafts, batik and jewellery. ***Laksala*** and ***Kandyan Art Association*** (Tourist Office) are govt sales outlets where you can watch weavers and craftsmen working on wood, silver, copper and brass, and buy lacquer ware and batik. ***Dalada Vidya*** nr the Temple of the Tooth. Several antique shops, many along the lake. Good batiks from ***Fresco***, 901 Peradeniya Rd, ***Presar*** and ***Kjreil***. Books from ***KVJ de Silva***, 86 DS Senanayake Vidiya. The **crafts village** set up with govt help is at ***Kalapuraya Nattaropotha***, 7 km away in the beautiful Dumbara Valley where craft skills have been handed down from father to son. A visit to the ***Municipal Market***, W of the lake is worthwhile even if you are not planning to bargain for superb Sri Lankan fruit. The ***Wheel*** by the Lake sells Buddhist literature.

● Tourist office

Kandy Art Assoc Bldg, Sangaraja Maw.

● Transport

Local Taxis and autos: available for transport to hotel (see **Warning** under **Accommodation**).

Train Colombo: *Intercity Express*, 30, daily, 0630, 2½ hr; *24 Express*, daily, 1000, 3 hr; *Intercity Express*, 10, daily, 1500, 2½ hr. **Nanu Oya** (for Nuwara Eliya): *Podi Menike*, 5, daily, 0906, 4¼ hr. **Badulla**: *Podi Menike*, 5, daily, 0906, 7¾ hr; *Mail*, 45, daily, 2355, 7¾ hr.

Road Bus: local buses use the Central/Torrington Bus Stand near the market. Long distance buses leave from the Goods shed Bus Stand nr the station. CTB buses leave from the Central Bus Stand, in front of the market. Frequent buses to Colombo, Nuwara Eliya (mini bus from behind the Temple, (2½ hr) and all major cities on the island.

Excursions around Kandy

The Elephant bath

In Mahaveli Ganga nr *Mahaveli Reach Hotel* at **Katugastota**. Elephants are brought to the river for their bath twice a day and their mahouts brush, sponge and splash them with water (essential for the animals' health). The trip out to the Katugastota Elephant Orphanage makes a pleasant diversion. Best to visit at feeding times when the orphans receive their bottled milk. Rides available; you may have to pay to take photographs. Getting there: Bus 625 from Kandy. Also at riverside on **Rajasinghe Mawatha** opp Military Cemetery, 4 km. 0900-1800. Entry fee.

Western Shrines

On the Kadugannawa-Peradeniya Rd, 16 km away, is a group of 14th century temples. The **Gadaladeniya Temple** is in a beautiful setting, built on a rock, about a km from the main road. The stone temple, influenced by Indian temple architecture has lacquered doors, carvings and frescoes and a moonstone at the entrance of the shrine. Three km away along the road is the 2nd of the group. You climb up a rock cut stairway to the **Lankatilleke Temple**, with a large Buddha, with 6 other divinities, carved wooden doors and well preserved frescoes. It is one of oldest and best examples of the Kandyan temple style. A path, leads to the **Embekke Temple** (dedicated to God *Kataragama* or *Skanda*) 1.5 km away. It is famous for its carved wooden pillars (which may have once adorned the Audience Hall in Kandy) with vibrant figures of soldiers, wrestlers, dancers, musicians, mythical animals and birds. You can see similar carved pillars at the remains of the old **Pilgrim's Rest** nearby. The village has craftsmen working on silver, brass and copper. **Getting there** Buses from Kandy to the temples and to the Botanical Gardens.

Galmaduwa Temple

The unusual incomplete 14th Galmaduwa Temple, 6 km SE on the Kundasala road, was an attempt to combine the features of Sinhalese, Indian, Islamic and Christian architectural styles. **Getting there** Bus 655 from the Market Bus Stop drops you at the bridge, across the river from the temple.

Medawela Temple

10 km NE, though built in the 18th century is on an ancient site. The interesting features include the shrine room built in wood and wattle and daub similar to the old Kandyan grain stores and the wall paintings. **Getting there** Bus 603 from Market Bus Stop.

Road to Nalanda

A very attractive road runs from Kandy N to **Nalanda**, **Dambulla** and **Sigirya**. It passes through spice gardens and plantations – coffee, cocoa and rubber – around the small town of **Matale**.

- **Accommodation** *Home Seas*, restaurant, modern and very clean, rec.
- **Banks & money changers** Bank of Ceylon.

Nalanda, 49 km from Kandy and right in the centre of Sri Lanka, has a small *gedige* temple, probably built in the 7th-8th centuries. It has similarities with the Pallava shore temples at Mamallapuram, see page 849. If time is very limited it is possible to take a car for the day from Kandy to visit Dambulla, Sigiriya and Polonnaruwa in 1 day. While this is a full day it can be very rewarding. Total cost for 4 people approx US$130 plus entrance fee to sites. Contact Tourist Office or hotel travel desk.

Kandy to Batticaloa

The direct route (A26) goes through the eastern highlands to Madugoda and drops steeply to Mahinyangana and across the Mahaweli Ganga. The A5 then goes NE across the Dry Zone through Waywatta and Maha Oya to Chenkaladi at the northern edge of the lagoon. The A15 runs SE to Batticaloa and N along the coast to Trincomalee. An alternative route from Kandy to Batticaloa by road goes via the tea country surrounding Nuwara Eliya and Badulla. These are described in the next route. It is then possible to go due E to the coast at Arugam Bay, driving up all along the coast to Batticaloa. The coastal road was devastated by a cyclone in 1978, and the damage to housing is still visible. It is a desolate journey. Alternatively you can follow the **A5** due N from Passala to Kehelulla, leaving the hills, and turning NE to Eravur. Here a road turns SE to Batticaloa. The old direct route from Kandy due E has now been flooded by the Victoria Dam project.

Batticaloa

This old Dutch town is called the town of Tamarinds by its predominantly Tamil population. The Dutch fortified the town in 1602, the remains of which can be seen near the present day *Rest*

House, but today it is famous for its singing fish, heard in the middle of the lagoon on still nights. The centre of the lagoon bridge is reputed to be the best place for listening to the extraordinary resonating sounds.

WARNING has been the centre of repeated violent fighting between the Tamil Tigers and the Army. Check locally whether it is possible and safe to go.

• **Accommodation** In 1994 the only suitable one for travellers was **C** *Lake View Inn*, 22 Mudaliyar St, T 065 2593, 3 rm, restaurant with good seafood, rec. The following may be available: near the Dutch Fort on Arugam Bay side, the rebuilt **D** *Rest House*. **E** *Sunshine Inn*, 118 Bar Rd, on the other side of the rly track from the station, clean, in a pleasant garden. F *Rly Retiring Rm*, T 065 2271, 8 rm, 5 km from town. At the end of the bus route are: **E** *Beach House Guest House*, Bar Rd, nr Lighthouse, quiet, good food; and **E** *East Winds*, next door.

NUWARA ELIYA, BADULLA AND ARUGAM BAY

The most attractive route runs S from Colombo, along the S bank of the Kelaniya River. It is a scenically beautiful route up into the hills, past Adam's Peak, the second highest mountain in Sri Lanka, and through the great tea estates of the Hatton-Dikoya region to the most popular holiday resort for Sri Lankans at Nuwara Eliya.

The **A4** runs SE through Nugegoda. The slower but more attractive route follows the left (S) bank of the Kelaniya River. *Kelani River Villa*, on the river bank, 20 min drive from Colombo on Biyagama Main Rd, for rent, T 536820. **Kaduwela** (16 km) has a *Rest House* in beautiful position overlooking the river with a constant succession of varied river traffic. There is a fairly large Buddhist temple and irrigation tank of Mulleriyawa. Continuing along the Kelaniya River the road passes through **Hanwella** (33 km), where there is another excellent *Rest House*, again with a beautiful view up and down the river. On the site of a Portuguese fort, Hanwella is noted as the place where the last king of Kandy, Sri Vikrama Raja Sinha, was defeated.

At Hanwella the road joins the **A4** and turns left towards **Avisawella** (18 km), the centre of rubber industry, in beautiful wooded surroundings. The ruins of a royal palace and temple destroyed by Portuguese on opposite bank of the river. The *Rest House* is recommended. Continue on the **A7** to the **Ginigathena Pass** (38 km). Magnificent views at the top.

From here on the road runs through tea country. Ginighathena is a small bazaar for the tea estates and their workers. The road winds up through a beautiful valley, surrounded by green, evenly picked tea bushes to **Watawala** (10 km). The air becomes noticeably cooler, and occasionally there are views right across the plains to Colombo and the Kelaniya Valley. At Watawala the Carolina Falls are spectacular in the wet season. Follow the lower road to Hatton (12 km).

Hatton is one of the major centres of Sri Lanka's tea industry, and the base from which most pilgrims and tourists trek to the top of Adam's Peak. Hotels will arrange tours. Buses run the tortuously winding route from Hatton to **Maskeliya** (20 km; *Altitude*: 1280m) and on to Dalhousie. By car it takes about an hour, going through some of the most productive tea growing areas towards **Norwood**. Keep to the Maskeliya road up the Pass before Norwood. The air is already strikingly fresh, and the higher road is lined with tropical ferns. The bus journey takes about 2 hr to **Dalhousie**, where the climb itself starts. There are *Tea shops* in Dalhousie, but nowhere good to stay.

Adam's Peak (2260m)

A steep footpath leads to the peak sacred to Buddhists, Hindus and Muslims, one of Sri Lanka's main centres of pilgrimage. The object of pilgrimage on the summit is the giant footprint – of the Buddha, of Adam, of Siva? – covered by a huge stone slab, in which has been carved another print. Local Buddhist tradition promises any woman who succeeds in climbing by this route that she will be re-born in the next life as a man.

The climb to the top from Maskeliya takes about 3 hr. The path is clearly marked throughout, beginning fairly easily but rapidly become steeper. Most people do the walk by moonlight, arriving in time to see the dawn when the conical peak, only 50m square, forms an extraordinary shadow across the plains to the W. It is completely safe, even the steepest parts being protected, and steps and chains provided where necessary. The route is ancient – **Marco Polo** commented on the chains provided for pilgrims in the 13th century. An alternative route, much steeper and more difficult, comes up from the Ratnapura side.

NB: It is very cold on top of the peak until well after sunrise. It is essential to take warm clothing, as well as some food and drink.

From Hatton the road crosses the railway line and winds up through the tea estates of **Dimbula** to **Talawakele** (10 km). Sri Lanka's Tea Research Institute (sometimes open to visitors) has played a major role in improving Sri Lanka's tea production. A right turn after Talawakele leads up a beautiful mountain road to **Agrapatana**, but the main road continues through Nanu Oya, and finally down into Nuwara Eliya.

Nuwara Eliya

Nuwara Eliya is the highest town in Sri Lanka and a major hill resort. Semi-enclosed by hills on the W, 'The City of Light' was a favourite hill station of the British. Some feel its charm has faded, but it retains some distinctive features.

Nuwara Eliya (*Noo-rail-eeya*; *Altitude*: 1990m) has retained all the paraphernalia of a British hill station, with its colonial houses, parks, an 18 hole golf course, and trout streams; there are brown trout in the lake for anglers. It offers a cool escape (it can be very cold at night) from the plains and is particularly popular during the New Year holidays in April when hotels tend to raise their prices and are still full. The Golf Course is thought to be exceptionally good and for added entertainment there are horse races during the 3 week holiday.

Places of interest

Some of the buildings are of Georgian and Queen Anne periods, and there are attractive walks round the small town, which has lawns, parks, an Anglican church and the *Hill Club*. The **Horton Plains** nearby, the island's highest and most isolated plateau, harbours many wild animals and is rich in bird life. A bridle path leads to the **World's End** which has a spectacular precipice with a 1050m drop.

The **Hakgala Gardens** (10 km) was once a Cinchona Plantation and then a Botanical Garden, but now is famous for its roses. The name Hakgala or 'Jaw Rock' comes from the story in the epic *Ramayana* where the Monkey god, takes back a part of the mountainside in his

CLIMATE: NUWARA ELIYA

	Jan	Feb	Mar	Apr	May	Jun	Jul	Aug	Sep	Oct	Nov	Dec	Av/Tot
Max (°C)	20	24	25	25	23	20	20	19	19	21	20	20	21
Min (°C)	9	9	9	11	13	14	13	14	14	12	11	12	12
Rain (mm)	116	87	69	170	185	215	185	161	177	245	222	213	2045

jaw, when asked by Rama to seek out a special herb! The *Humbugs Restaurant* and bar is beautifully located and does good meals and snacks. You will pass the **Sita Eliya Temple** to Rama's wife a short distance before you reach the gardens which is thought to mark the spot where she was kept a prisoner by King Ravana. There are buses from Nuwara Eliya. There are magnificent views.

Excursions

Pidurutalagala (Mt Pedro) is the island's highest peak (2524m) and is a 2 hr climb up the track from nr the RC Church, N of the town, in places still through dense forest. It is a steep but quite manageable climb.

Local information

● Accommodation

NB Beware of hotel touts – see note under **Kandy**. The 2 best are by the Golf Course and are in the Raj style. Well kept, good restaurants, with plenty of atmosphere. **A** *The Grand*, Grand Hotel Rd, T 052 2881, 114 rm, considerable Colonial character, ball-room sized restaurant (buffets catering for package tourists), golf, tennis, cultural shows; **A** *St Andrews*, 10 St Andrews Drive, overlooking Golf Course, T 2445, 52 rm, good restaurant, rec; **A** *Glendower*, 5 Grand Hotel Rd, T 2749, 7 rm, just below *The Grand*, very attractive modern bungalow-style guest house, large rooms, pleasant lounge; **A** *Hill Club*, up path from Grand Hotel Rd, 22 rm in century old Coffee Planters' club (building 1930s), formal restaurant (tie essential for dinner), 5 min walk from Golf course, billiards, rather run-down and over priced.

B *The Windsor*, Kandy Rd, T 2554, modern style hotel, good restaurant. **C** *Princess Guest House*, 12 Wedderburn Rd, T 2462, 7 rm in 19th century home.

D *The Rest*, off the Hakgala Rd, T 2436, is less expensive and has a restaurant, govt run; **D** *Tourinn*, Park Rd, T 052 2410, 7 rm; **D** *The Grosvenor*, 4 Haddon Hill Rd, T 052 2307, 19 rm, in charming old Colonial house, rec; **D** *Alpen Guest House*, Hadden Hill Rd nr the Grosvenor, T 3009, 13 rm, various prices, good food, comfortable and friendly; **D** *Oatlands*, St Andrews Drive, T 2572, 5 rm, small, family run guest house serving good food. Several others along Upper Lake Drive. **D** *Collingwood*, Badulla Rd, in old Planter's house, retaining its old-world British character, only 1 guest rm.

● Places to eat

DeSilva Food Centre, Central market.

● Bars

Ceylon Brewery's English style Pub serves draught stout as well as in bottles. Closes 2030!

● Banks & money changers

Bank of Ceylon, nr Post Office, Cargills.

● Hospitals & medical services

Chemists: Kandy Rd.

● Sports

Golf: beautiful and superbly maintained golf course. Temp membership Rs 100, Rs 600 per day.

● Transport

Train The nearest station is *Nanu Oya*, a short bus ride away. It is too far to walk. **Colombo**: *Uda Rakamenike*, 16, daily, 0936, 6 hr; *Podi Menike Exp*, 6, daily, 1244, 7¼ hr; *Mail*, 46, daily, 2206, 7½ hr. **Kandy**: *Podi Menike Exp*, 6, daily, 1244, 4¼ hr.

Road Bus: frequent buses to Badulla and Kandy. Two CTB buses a day to Colombo (6½ hr).

Nuwara Eliya to Arugam Bay

From Nuwara Eliya the A 5 continues E to Badulla. Just past the **Hakgala Gardens** (10 km) is a superb view SE across the hills of Bandarawela and over the baked plains of the E coastlands. The road drops rapidly through to **Welimada**, where a right turn leads to Bandarawela (see below), past terraced fields of paddy and across occasional streams. This area is already in the rainshadow of the hills to the W, sheltered from the SW monsoon and much drier than Nuwara Eliya. Rubber plantations cover some of the slopes before

Badulla

(45 km; *Altitude*: 675m; *STD Code*: 055) The capital of Uva Province, it is one of the oldest towns in Sri Lanka though there are no traces of the earlier settlement. The Portuguese once occupied it

but set the town on fire before leaving.

Surrounded by paddy fields along the banks of the river Gallanda Oya which has an ancient wooden bridge with an unusual tiled roof in the Kandyan style. It has an old fort against a backcloth of mountains and a small lake. There are 2 large **temples**, the Buddhist Mutiyangane Vihare (the ancient core is believed to be 2000 years old) and the Hindu Kataragama Devale (note the plaster-on-wood statues and wooden pillars). Both are on sites of earlier temples, and there is also a revered Bo tree. At one time it was an extremely active social centre for planters, with a race course, golf, tennis and cricket clubs, long since fallen into disuse. The park was once a small botanic garden. The Duhinda Falls are about 6 km away (buses take you to a point below the falls).

• **Accommodation D** *Duhinda Falls Inn*, 35/11 -1/1 Bandaranayake Maw, T 2406, 12 rm, restaurant, bar, exchange, car/cycle hire, visits to tea gardens; **D** *Rest House* in town centre, is good value; **D** *Riverside Holiday Inn*, 27 Lower King St (no river here!), T 2501; **D** *Tourist Resort*, 97 Duhinda Rd, towards the waterfall, good value; **D** *Eagle's Nest*, 159 Lower St, T 2501.

Local families take in paying guests and offer good home cooking. Some rec: 5/2 Malla Gastenne, not far from Rly and Bus Stand and 28 Passara Rd, well kept with a garden.

• **Transport Train** Colombo: *Uda Rakamenike*, 16, daily, 0555, 9¾ hr; *Podi Menike Express*, 6, daily, 0850, 11¾ hr; *Mail*, 46, daily, 1745, 12 hr. **Kandy**: *Podi Menike Express*, 6, daily, 0850, 8 hr. **Road Bus**: frequent buses to Nuwara Eliya (2 hr), Bandarawela. Occasional buses to E coast.

The Uva Province is associated with the Buddha who made 2 visits to the area. It has some high water falls, spectacular 'gaps' in its precipitous ridges, some interesting wildlife and is also famous for spices and Ayurvedic herbs which grow in the SW of the province.

From Badulla, take A22 E to Hulandawa (53 km) and continue along the A4 towards Arugam Bay. As a detour, or to travel to Batticaloa from here, at Siyambalamduwa (36 km) turn left taking the A25 N. At Wadingala (25 km), there is a road to the left to **Inginiyagala** where you can stay to visit the Gal Oya National Park early in the morning.

Gal Oya National Park

The Park, inland from the E Coast, covers 540 sq km, and is famous for its elephants and the large number of water birds which are attracted by the huge lake, Senanayaka Samudra. Best visited in the early morning for watching elephants and white buffaloes which come down to the lake, the crocodiles in the water and the birds. You can take motor boat tours on the lake, lasting 2-3 hr. **Accommodation AL** *Inginiyagala Safari Inn*, superbly situated, booked through Mercantile Tours, T 063 2499 or in Colombo, T 91805, 22 comfortable rm, restaurant, a 10 min walk brings you to the lake, picturesque at sunset, the hotel will organise tours into the Park and also a Vedda village.

If you do not wish to visit the National Park continue on **A22** towards Arugam Bay. At **Lahugala Sanctuary** (20 km) by a large tank, you can stop to see the numerous species of birds and the large elephant herds that come down to the water in the dry season (Aug-Oct). A few km on, to the S of the main rd is **Magul Maha Vihara** – ruins in a jungle setting of a Vatadage and a dagoba with impressive *moonstones* and guardstones.

Arugam Bay

(15 km passing through Pottuvil) The Bay with its beautiful beach is particularly interesting for not only those keen on water sports (it has excellent surf), and underwater photography but also offers exciting possibilities for divers keen to explore wrecked ships. The lagoon here attracts water birds; take a sailing boat at dawn and dusk. You can visit old temple ruins by walking over the dunes. **Accommodation** Large

number of moderately priced simple hotels, cabanas and beach cottages to choose from; the cheaper places S of the bridge. **C** *Stardust Beach Hotel*, just on S edge of mouth of lagoon, 3 km S of Pottuvil in a superb location between the sea, 20 well-appointed, thatched bungalows, good restaurant, bar, laundry, Danish owned, attentive service, highly rec, arranges trips to Yala National Park (20 km), cycle hire available. **D** *Rest House*, on the beach, 3 rm, restaurant, pleasant and comfortable.

The coastal road S of Arugam Bay takes you to **Kumana Bird Sanctuary** (40 km). Kumana, to the E of the larger Yala National Park, is visited for its resident and migratory aquatic birds including flamingoes, ibis, herons, pheasants, particularly impressive in May and June. **Accommodation** There are 2 simple *Bungalows* with warden/cook, bring your bedding and food, reservations: Wildlife Dept, Transwork House, Col 1, T 33787.

RATNAPURA AND BANDARAWELA

The most attractive route to Ratnapura goes via Avissawella through the wet zone, before reaching the centre of Sri Lanka's gem producing region. It is a gentle drive to the foot of the hills, with superb views of Adam's Peak and the hills. From Ratnapura the A4 circles to the S of Adam's Peak, climbing into the hills through Balangoda to Bandarawela. The A8, which also runs through attractive countryside, offers an alternative route to Ratnapura.

NB: The option of high level road from Colombo through the suburb of Nugegoda and the new capital of Jayawardenepuram-Kotte to Homagama, Ingiriya and Ratnapura. This avoids the danger of floods in the wet season.

The S route to Ratnapura, the A8, goes S to **Panadura** (27 km) then turns left to **Horana** (16 km). The **D** *Rest House* (good value) is built in the remains of an ancient Buddhist monastery. On the opposite side of road is a large Buddhist temple with a particularly noteworthy bronze candlestick, over 2m tall. From Nambapane (29 km) the road keeps quite close to the Kalu Ganga River, staying in its valley to

Ratnapura

(21 km; *STD Code*: 045) The climate of Ratnapura has been likened to a Turkish bath. The vegetation is correspondingly luxuriant, but the city is best known for its gem stones, washed down the river bed so it is aptly named the 'City of Gems'.

The quality of Ratnapura's gems is legendary. In the 7th century Hiuen Tsang claimed that there was a ruby on the spire of the temple at Anuradhapura whose magnificence illuminated the sky. Today sapphires are much more important. A number of precious stones are found nearby including sapphire, ruby, topaz, amethyst, cat's eye, alexandrite, aquamarine, tourmaline, garnet and zircon. Several are mined from pits dug into a special form of gravel. Genuine stones are common; valuable stones by definition are rarer. Advice given to travellers at the beginning of the century

CLIMATE: RATNAPURA

	Jan	Feb	Mar	Apr	May	Jun	Jul	Aug	Sep	Oct	Nov	Dec	Av/Tot
Max (°C)	34	36	36	36	34	31	31	31	30	33	32	31	33
Min (°C)	22	23	24	24	25	25	24	24	23	23	23	23	24
Rain (mm)	120	52	215	359	479	420	305	270	388	453	355	221	3637

still holds: "As regards buying stones, it is a risky business unless the passenger has expert knowledge or advice. It is absolute folly to buy stones from itinerant vendors. It is far better to go to one of the large Colombo jewellers and take the chance of paying more and obtaining a genuine stone."

Ratnapura is surrounded by rubber and tea estates in a lush and beautiful setting, and gives better views of Adam's Peak than almost anywhere else on the island. It is well worth going to the top of the fort for the views. Driving up to Gilimale from the bridge gives you a chance to see the massive curtain wall of the central highlands to the N. Three km W of Ratnapura is Maha Saman Dewale, the richest Buddhist temple in Sri Lanka.

Museums

Ratnapura National Museum Small exhibition of pre-historic fossil skeletons from the region of elephants, hippos and rhinoceros found in gem pits. Also jewellery, gems, textiles and flags. **Gem Museum** Getangama Gems from different parts of Sri Lanka and an exhibition of gem polishing. **NB** Travel agents can organise visits to gem mines.

Excursions

Adam's Peak This is the base for the much steeper and more strenuous route leads to Adam's Peak. Route: Malwala (8 km) on the Kalu Ganga to Palabadalla (11 km 375m), then a very steep path to Heramitipana (13 km 1100m) and the summit (5 km 2260m). The imprint of the Buddha's foot gives it the name Sripada. **Accommodation A** *Ratnaloka Tour Inns*, Kosgala, Kahangama (6 km from town), T 2455, 53 rm, central a/c, good restaurant, open to non-residents, gem museum. **D** *Rest House*, T 2299, 11 rm, above the town, outstanding views and delightful site, food also excellent value. F *Traveller's Rest*, 66 Inner Circular Rd, basic. Other basic hotels nr bus stand.

The road between Ratnapura and Pelmadulla (18 km) continues across the fertile and undulating low country. A diversion is possible from Pelmadulla, to **Madampe** (13 km). The **A17** then goes S through **Rakwana**, the chief village of a tea-growing district. Good **D** *Rest House*, with views that are some of the most beautiful in Sri Lanka. Beautiful flowering trees in season, notably *Dendrodium maccarthii*. It continues S to Galle or Matara. The **A18** goes SE from Madampe to **Maduwanwela** (35 km), one of best known *walauwas* of the Kandyan chiefs where small inward-looking courtyards were built on the "Pompeiian plan".

It continues SE into the Dry Zone and through areas with over 90% of the land under shifting cultivation. At the small village of **Embilipitiya**, on the edge of a great rice growing area, is a paper mill set up to use rice straw. Intended to be an environmentally friendly development, it is causing some water pollution problems with its waste. The road joins the **A2** on the coast at Nonagama.

The **A4** continues to **Balangoda** (24 km) through superb scenery all the way, rubber estates being important. Adam's Peak and the Maskeliya Range rise magnificently to the N, although during the SW monsoon they are almost permanently covered in cloud. The densely forested land to the E has now largely been cleared, and the road goes on through **Belihuloya** (19 km) with tea estates, then rising to **Haldummulla** (15 km; *Altitude*: 1020m). There are excellent views across to the sea. The A16 goes NE shortly after Haldummulla, a short but steep climb to Haputale.

Haputale

(*Altitude*: 1400m) Magnificent views of the dawn over the Low Country to the E. On a clear day you can see the salt pans at Hambantota to the S, and the horizon is the sea. To the N in magnificent contrast are the hills.

• **Accommodation** The new **C** *Rest House*, 100 Bandarawela Rd (1 km centre), T 8099, 6 rm with bath, simple but comfortable with very good food and bar, very pleasant garden, rec. The old **D** ***Rest House*** nr Rly Station in town centre has the best views, 5 rm, noisy, not very clean with smelly toilets.

● **Transport Train** Trains to Colombo and Kandy. **Road** To Wellawaya and Matara.

DIVERSION The A4 turns right after Haldummulla to Koslande, past the Diyaluma waterfall (170m) to Wellawaya.

Wellawaya *STD Code*: 055. **Accommodation C** *Saranga Holiday Inn*, 37 Old Ella Rd, T 4891, with some a/c rm, good 2 rm. **D** *Rest House*, a short distance N of Haldumulla-Moneragala-Pottuvil Rd. It then continues E across the plains to Arugam Bay (105 km).

Bandarawela

(*Altitude*: 1230m; *STD Code*: 057) The rain shadow of the Central Highlands gives it a drier SW monsoon than the hills immediately to the W, and Bandarawela has possibly the best climate in Sri Lanka, and the most renowned tea. A small and straggling town, it is a good base for pleasant walks.

● **Accommodation B** *Bandarawela Hotel*, 14 Welimada Rd, T 2501, F 2834, 36 rm, central, built 1893, renovated retaining period furniture, but still not very exciting; **B** ***Orient***, 10 Dharmapala Maw, T 2501, 50 rm, restaurant, huge concrete barracks like building. **C** ***Ideal Resort***, Welimada Rd, T 2476, 6 rm; **C** ***Alpine Inn***, Haputale Rd, Ellatota, T 2569, 5 rm; **C** ***Rest House***, nr *Orient Hotel*, 9 large rm, restaurant, good location and value; **C** ***Madhu***, T 2504, 30 rm, wide range of services, 3 km out of town; **C** ***Rose Villa***, off Poonagala Rd, T 2329. **D** ***Queens***, Badulla Rd, T 2806.

● **Transport Train** Colombo: *Uda Rakamenike*, 16, daily, 0726, 8¼ hr; *Podi Menike Exp*, 6, daily, 1244, 7¼ hr; *Mail*, 46, daily, 2206, 7½ hr. **Kandy**: *Podi Menike Exp*, 6, daily, 1022, 6¼ hr. **Road Bus**: frequent buses to Haputale, Badulla and Ella. Nuwara Eliya direct bus takes just over 1 hr.

Ella

(13 km; *STD Code*: 057) To reach Ella from Bandarawela keep on the A 16. After 7 km turn right. At this junction the road to **Badulla** goes straight on (20 km). Alternatively, it is a pleasant walk along the railway line; there are only a few trains and the route is well used by local people.

6 km S from Ella is the Ravana Ella Falls, while close to the Rest House is the vast cave which is associated with the *Ramayana* story: Ravana imprisoned Rama's wife Sita in the cave. The cave is filled by a lake which has hindered exploration. **Accommodation C** CHC *Rest House*, T 2636, 6 rm, very popular, so book in advance, superb views from its position high above the plains.

GALLE, HAMBANTOTA AND TISSAMAHARAMA

This route follows close to the coast, with its magnificent bays and sandy beaches. It is a wholly distinctive drive, contrasting sharply with the routes into and through the hills or across the dry zone of the N and E. Some of the beaches are now developed, but even so they retain their largely rural settings. The railway line hugs the ocean as it goes S and is an exhilarating journey. Recommended.

ROUTES Take the **A2** S of Colombo, through Mount Lavinia to **Moratuwa** (28

CLIMATE: BANDARAWELA

	Jan	Feb	Mar	Apr	May	Jun	Jul	Aug	Sep	Oct	Nov	Dec	Av/Tot
Max (°C)	23	28	28	29	27	28	27	27	26	26	24	23	26
Min (°C)	14	13	14	15	17	17	18	18	17	16	15	16	16
Rain (mm)	125	98	108	193	121	45	58	77	115	262	256	203	1661

km), noted for its furniture making and its college. Cross the 300m wide River Kalu Ganga ('Black River') to

Kalutara

(24 km) The Portuguese built a fort on the site of a Buddhist temple, the Dutch took it over and the British Agent converted it to his residence. It now has a Buddhist shrine again. Wild hog deer, introduced by Dutch from the Ganga Delta, are reputedly still found. The centre of the arrack industry, Kalutara is known for its basket making. Leaves of the wild date are dyed red, orange, green and black, and woven into hats and baskets. The area is also famous for its mangosteen fruit, and graphite is mined.

Kalutara has a huge stretch of fine sand. South is one of the most densely populated parts of the Island. Many people depend on fishing, and every day fishermen bring in their catch at numerous points along the coast. The coconut palms that also line the shore all the way down to Galle and beyond provide fibre for local use as well as for export. **Accommodation** **AL** *Tangerine Beach*, T 034 22640, 175 rm, beautifully laid out, enormous lawn stretches beneath the coconut palms to the sea. **A** *Hibiscus Beach*, T 034 22704, 50 rm, more modest than some, but pleasantly laid out.

Beruwela (16 km S; derived from the Sinhalese word Baeruala – the place where the sail is lowered), the spot where the first Muslim settlers are believed to have landed. The Kitchimalai mosque, on a headland, is worth seeing. It is a major pilgrimage centre at the end of Ramadan. You can also go out to the lighthouse raised on a small island offshore. There is an excellent view of the coastline from the top. Most of the hotels cater for package tours. **Accommodation** **AL** *Neptune*, T 034 75218, F 034 75301, 104 a/c rm, full board, beach and shady trees in front, highly praised, good food, an Aitken Spence hotel, contact Colombo T 326767; **AL** *Wornels Reef*, Moragella, T 034 7430, 119 rm, 23 a/c, shaded garden fronting beach. **A** *Tropical Villas*, Moragalle, T/F 034 76156, opened Nov 1993, 54 suites set in gardens around pool, not directly on beach; **A** *Berberyn Reef*, T 034 79582, 84 rm, some a/c, cottage style, self catering arrangements if req. **E** *Rest House*, view of the harbour and mosque on quiet village road away from tourist hotels, pleasant.

Road and rail continue S to **Aluthgama** (5 km), the main bus and railway station for the beaches to both N and S. The town is famous for its oysters, and as a weekend resort from Colombo.

Bentota

(3 km S) The resort is built entirely for foreign tourists as a specially designed beach complex mainly catering for groups. The sand spit which separates the river from the sea, where most of the hotels are built, gives excellent waters for wind surfing and sailing. A full range of watersports is available plus tennis, mini golf, pool etc. The sea is best, Oct-Apr. The accommodation is listed from N to S.

- **Accommodation** **AL** *Robinson Club*, Paradise Island, T 347 5167, F 347 5172, 150 a/c rm, in pagoda style buildings in tropical gardens, formerly private club, water sports and activities, 99% German package tour clientele; **AL** *Bentota Beach*, T 09 57023, 133 rm, extensive gardens, luxurious layout, full range activities; **AL** *Serendib*, T 034 75248, 90 rm. **A** *Italian Club*, smaller and more modest guest house between the big hotels; **A** *Ceysands*, between sea and river, T Col 20862, 80 rm, 32 a/c, beautifully built, wide choice of activities, floating Disco and food, approached by ferry; **A** *Lihiniya Surf*, T 034 75126, 86 rm, the feel of a beach-side motel. **B** *Warahena Walauwa*, 2 min from beach, 20 rm in old building furnished with antiques, good, reasonable restaurant.

- **Places to eat** Outside hotels *Sea View* in National Tourist Resort Complex. No sea-view but good food all day esp sea-food and rice dishes, within walking distance of many hotels, garden.

From here to Galle the road is nearly always in sight of the sea.

Kosgoda, just S of Bentota, with the **AL** *Kosgoda Beach Resort*, T 09 54017, between sea and lagoon, rm with open-air showers, lovely pool, excellent restaurant.

Ahungalla, a further 6 km S, has one of the region's most luxurious hotels at the **AL** *Triton*, in coconut groves, T 09 54041, 125 rm, superb in every detail on excellent beach. Also, for aimed at Austrian/German tourists; **AL** *Lotus Villa*, T 54082, F 54083, an exclusive, beachside villa with 14 rm, Austrian speciality restaurant, ayurvedic and herbal therapy, boating etc.

Ambalangoda is the home of Devil Dancing and mask making. Traditional masks are available on the N edge of the town. You can watch craftsmen at the **Mask Museum**. The colourful fishmarket is worth visiting early morning. **Accommodation D** *Princess Guest House*, 418 Main St, Patabendimulla, nr Museum, 5 rm, good home cooking, pleasant atmosphere, rec, good value. **E** *Rest House*, Beach Rd, 7 rm with bath, T 09 27299, next to the sea and good swimming, good food (excellent club-sandwich) but plaqued by flies, originally it was a Dutch warehouse for cinnamon and coconuts, the new, characterless wing has 8 rm, old building houses restaurants and some rm. About 2 km inland **D** *Sena's Lake View House*, Maha Ambalangoda, very quiet, by attractive lake, rec.

Meetiyagoda, 6 km, has a moonstone quarry. **Seenigama** 6 km has a Devil's Temple by roadside; Sri Lankan travellers pay their respects here bringing most traffic comes to a temporary halt.

Hikkaduwa

(13 km) This has become the most popular and developed beach on the W Coast. Excellent swimming and a wide range of facilities for snorkelling and scuba diving with 3 stations, incl Poseiden on Main Road, T 3294. Famous for its 'Coral Gardens' – you can hire a glass-bottomed boat which can be hired from near the *Coral Gardens Hotel*, to view the splendid underwater collection. The town is thriving again, and the guest houses and hotels are returning to normal, along with the shops and restaurants which line the road. Hikkaduwa is unique on this stretch of coast in having a full range of accommodation with over 50 hotels. Cheaper guest houses are along the S end of the beach, also the better end for surfing. Bikes and motor bikes can be hired in many places (shack opp *Hikkaduwa Beach Resort*, ask for Neel) and there is a wide range of shops. However, the main road is a death trap – the traffic moves very fast.

Excursion

Baddegama (11 km) is within easy reach of Hikkaduwa by bicycle or motor bike. It is a very attractive road through coconut and banana groves, followed by several small plantations – rubber, tea and spices. About half way the road passes the Nigro Dharama Mahavira (stupa) in Gopinuwala. On a hill above the river in the grounds of Christ Church Girls College is the first Anglican church in Sri Lanka, built in 1818 and consecrated by Bishop Heber in 1825. It has noteworthy ironwood pillars. **Accommodation C** *Plantation Hotel*, Halpatota, Baddegama, 4 rm, breakfast incl, reservations: T Col 587454, set in small tea estate, this guest house is quite exceptional, surrounded by a beautiful quiet wooded garden, it has the feel of an old planter's house, though the house is quite new, food excellent, hosts very welcoming, well worth a visit.

Local information

● Accommodation

Negotiate discounts for longer stays. Off-season upto 50% cheaper. **Warning** Many touts offer cheap rooms, drugs, etc; Best avoided.

AL *Reefcomber*, T 092 3374, 54 a/c rm, all facing beach; **AL** *Coral Gardens*, T 57023, top of its class, excellent restaurants (buffets reasonably priced, rec); **AL** *Coral Sands*, T 57436, 50 rm, 30 facing sea, 5 a/c, newest and best scuba diving equipment, German instructor.

B *Ocean Beach Club*, Main Rd, 3 km from town centre, 25 clean, comfortable rm, excellent restaurant, rec; **B** *Sunil's Beach*, just S of the marine gardens, 56 seaview rm, Sinhala architecture, new; **B** *Hikkaduwa Beach Resort*, Galle Rd, modern block, slightly above average; **B** *Lanka Supercorals*, T 22897, 93 rm, large package tour hotel, beginning to fade; **B** *Ozone Tourist Rest*, 374 Galle Rd, 5 rm, basic.

C *Golden Sand Beach*, clean, quite smart, rec; **C** *Blue Note Cabanas*, 424 Galle Rd, restaurant, very clean, *cabana* rooms.

D *Sea View*, 295 Galle Rd, nr Coral Gardens, T 22014, 6 large rm with bath, restaurant good for Italian and fish dishes, noisy main road; **D** *Tandem*, Main Rd, 100 km post, 6 rm with bath, modern, clean, comfortable.

E *Casalanka*, Galle Rd, hippie haven, together, one long block of barracks-style rm. F *Hansa Surf*, adequate but very basic.

● Places to eat

Plenty of choice, especially for sea food. *Refresh*, 384 Galle Rd, for sea food, pleasant ambiance. Nearby *Francis*, 389 Galle Rd, for Chinese and Western. *Blue Fox*, large, popular restaurant, good food but service sometimes slow. *Cool Spot*, 327 Galle Rd, good breakfasts. *Greenline*, opp Sunil's Beach, good food, grumpy staff. *Farmhouse*, 341 Galle Rd, offers wide range of other services.

● Travel agents

Sri Lanka Travels and Tours (opp *Reefcomber Hotel*), minibus and taxis to Katunayake Airport.

Dodanduwa (6 km), further to the S, has a beautiful lake and a fine Buddhist temple approached by a long steep and narrow flight of stone stairs. After 15 km the road crosses the Dutch Canal to enter Galle.

Galle

Galle is the most important town in the S and has retained much of its colonial atmosphere. The Portuguese, Dutch and British used the natural harbour as their main port until 1875, when reconstruction of breakwaters and the enlarged harbour made Colombo the island's major port. Its origins as a port go back well before the Portuguese. Ibn Battuta, the great Moroccan traveller, visited it in 1344. The historian of Ceylon Sir Emerson Tennant claimed that Galle was the ancient city of Tarshish, which had traded not only with Persians and Egyptians, but with King Solomon.

The Portuguese Lorenzo de Almeida drifted into Galle by accident in 1505. It was a further 82 years before the Portuguese captured it from the Sinhala Kings, and they controlled the port until the Dutch laid siege in 1640. The old Portuguese Fort on a promontory was strengthened by the Dutch.

Places of interest

The Dutch left their mark on the town building brick-lined sewers which the tides automatically flushed twice a day. The **Dutch Reformed Church** (1754), built as a result of a vow taken by the Dutch Governor of Galle, Casparaous de Jong, contains a number of interesting memorials, and in the quiet backstreets of the fort there are still some fine houses. Over the gateway of the citadel which leads to the port are the monogrammed arms of the Dutch East India Company, VOC – *Vereenigde Oost Indische Campagnie* – dated 1699, the year when the fortifications were completed. The Government offices on Hospital St were once the Dutch warehouse ('factory'). All Saints Church, whose bright red pinnacle roof is a landmark for miles from the town, was consecrated in 1871. The Old Dutch Goernment House is now Walker & Sons.

The ramparts of the **Fort** are over 2.5 km long. Surrounded on 3 sides by the sea, they make a very pleasant walk. They are marked by a series of bastions covering the promontory. Nearest to the harbour were 2 bastions – The *Sun* and *Zwart* which controlled the traffic into the harbour. They were followed by the *Aurora* and *Point Utrecht* bastions before the lighthouse, then *Triton*, *Neptune*, *Clippenburg*, *Aeolus*, *Star* and *Moon*.

The crescent-shaped shoreline was dotted with islands, though some have now been joined up or altered by the harbour developments. The lighthouse is nearly 20m high.

Local information

● Accommodation

A *New Oriental (NOH)*, 10 Church St, Fort, T/F 94 932191, also contact in UK, T/F 44 51 625 9157, 36 large rm (best 1st Flr), well maintained old hotel (building dating from 1684) in a lovely garden, good atmosphere, good value, managed by Mrs Nesta Brohier's family since 1899; **A** *Closenberg*, 11 Closenberg Rd, Magalle, overlooking Harbour, T 23073, 20 comfortable rm, on the promontory overlooking the bay 3 km E of Galle with boating, sea fishing, colonial house built in 1858, with character and attractive atmosphere, restaurant pleasant and quiet in the evenings (not lunch), out of town but rec. **NB**: Beach nearby polluted; Bus to Matara (bathing) stops close to hotel.

C *Old Dutch House*, 46 Lighthouse St inside Fort, T 22370, 8 rm, good restaurant, laundry, spotless, excellent service, rec, old Dutch fur-

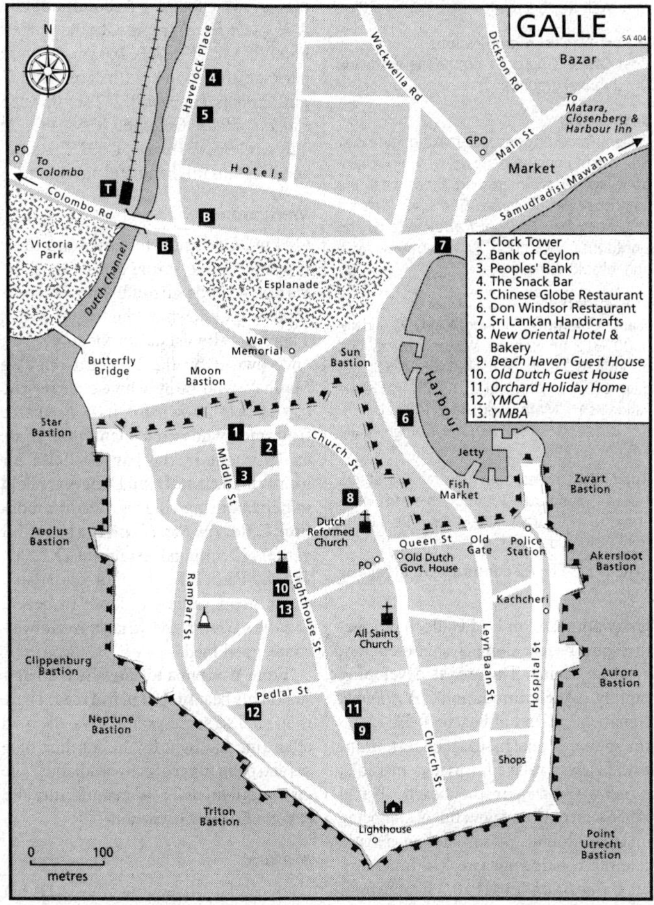

niture and architectural features, rec; **C** ***Beach Haven GH***, 65 Lighthouse St in Fort, T 22663, 4 rm, 1 a/c, excellent restaurant, immaculate and highly rec. F ***Rly Retiring Rm***.

● Places to eat

Best at the *New Oriental*, which has a bakery next door. ***Chinese Globe Restaurant***, 38 Havelock Pl, opp Rly station and ***Snack Bar***, nearby. ***Don Windsor*** on Harbour for seafood. ***New Shan Lanka***, Rampart St for Chinese, more expensive than it looks. On the 1st floor of the ***Seleka Shopping Precinct***, by the Bus Stand, is a good, clean and reasonable restaurant, well worth a try.

● Post & telecommunications

Post Office: Church St (on the site of the old Dutch burial ground).

● Shopping

Galle is famous for its lace-making, gem polishing and ebony carving, all of which make good souvenirs. Interesting shops near the lighthouse incl ***Universal Gems***, 42 A Jiffriya St (Cripps Rd). ***Lihinya Trades***, just by the Lighthouse, very good, with knowledgeable and reliable owner.

● Transport

Train Colombo: *Samudra Devi*, 327, daily, 0500, 3¼ hr; *Ruhunu Kumari Express*, 57, daily, 0825, 2½ hr; 51, daily, 1456, 2¾ hr; 53, daily, 1700, 2½ hr. 2nd Cl, Rs 55, seat reservation Rs 15. **Matara**: 50, daily, 1022, 1¼ hr; 52, daily, 1123, 52; *Ruhunu Kumari*, daily, 1815, 1 hr.

Road Bus: buses from Central Bus Stand, Pettah, Colombo. Less comfortable and picturesque than by train. Rs 25. **Taxi**: Rs 3,000+ from Colombo.

ROUTES The **A2** continues SE along the coast.

Unawatuna, 5 km E of Galle, has a picturesque beach along a sheltered bay, good for diving. The area is developing rapidly. **Accommodation A** *Milton's*, Ganahena, E end of beach, T 53312, 25 rm, sheltered pool in sea, good restaurant with views, relaxed, diving possible; **A** *Secret Garden*, nr the beach, T Col 685564, an old bungalow, full of character, in large grounds, 4 rm sharing a bath, catering, bookings for a week (min), peaceful. **B** *Bay Beach*, T 0415 201 en route from Galle, 56 rm, restaurant, pool; **B** *Beach Resort*, T 22147, 45 good rm, good seafacing restaurant, boating, diving. **C** *Sun-n-Sea*, E end of beach, nr Milton's, 8 rm by the sea, excellent restaurant, rec. Many cheaper **D/E** rooms in private houses by the beach and along the main road; ask locally and inspect. Even cheaper a little inland. Guest House opp *Sun-n-Sea* rec, rm with bath better.

Koggala, 3 km, has a free trade zone and there is some light industry, with plans to expand. **Accommodation A** *Koggala Beach*, reputedly the longest hotel in Asia, T 53260, 200 rm, 30 a/c, a package tour hotel, with large restaurant, 2 pools. *Horizon*, T 2528 or through *Ruhunu Hotel*, Colombo T 580493. At **Talpe**, **C** *Beach Haven*, T 53362, 25 rm, good restaurant, beautiful situation.

Weligama

(23 km). One km before the town there is a huge stone statue of Kushta Raja. Various legends surround him, and he is sometimes known as the 'Leper King'. There is a tiny island in the lovely bay, once owned by the French Count de Maunay, who built a house on it. The bay is best known for its remarkable fishermen who perch silently for hours on stilts out in the bay, and also for locally made lace. Devil Dances are held in neighbouring villages. **Accommodation C** *Bay Inn Rest House*, in a beautiful garden, 12 rm, good restaurant. **D** *Sam's*, 484 By-Pass Rd, nr main crossroad., clean, good value rm, close to beach; **D** *Raja's GH*, in the village, warm welcome, good food.

From Weligama to **Tangalle** is an outstandingly beautiful stretch of road. There is an endless succession of bays, the road often running right by the startling blue sea and palm fringed rocky headlands. The district is famous for the manufacture and export of citronella perfume.

Matara

(15 km) This lively town has 2 Dutch

forts – the gateway (1770) to the Coral Star Fort (which houses the library) is particularly picturesque. The fort itself is private property. The Buddhist hermitage, *Chula Lanka*, on a tiny island joined by causeway to the mainland, was founded by a Thai Prince priest. As with several of the coastal towns, a local delicacy is the fine curd.

• **Accommodation C** *Rest House*, in main Fort, by the sea, nr Clock Tower and Bus Stop, T 2291, 20 rm, better in new part with bath, very attractive, good food, good value. At **Polhena**, 3 km away, the more comfortable **C** *Polhena Reef Garden*, T 2478, off the main rd, is good for water sports and underwater exploring. **E** *Sepalika*, opp School, simple rm, good food, 100m from sea.

• **Transport Train** Trains to Colombo, (4 hr).

The road crosses the Nilwala Ganga. After 5 km a road to the left goes to what has been described as a new Buddhist sanctuary at Werahena, in 'stupefyingly bad taste'. There is a statue of the Buddha 40m high. Perahera at Nov/Dec full moon. The road goes on to **Dondra** (7 km), a fishing village which marks the southernmost point of Sri Lanka. The temple was destroyed by Portuguese. There is a modern vihara, and the lighthouse at the S promontory was built in 1899. Perehara processions (Jul/Aug) for 12 days. The road passes through **Dikwella** (12 km) where there are superb statues and tableaux, and a Buddhist temple. **Accommodation A** *Dikwella Village Resort* (Relais Club), T 2961, 44 bungalows, good restaurant, very attractive location on the promontory, Italian owned and managed, beautifully laid out, cultural shows and activities.

Tangalle (16 km; *STD Code*: 047), is famous for its turtles and its beach of pink sand. An attractive fishing port with a palm fringed bay. There is extensive irrigation to N.

• **Accommodation B** *Tangalle Bay*, Pallikudawa, T 40346, 34 rm, designed like a ship, standing on rocky promontory, attractive setting, pool, rec. **C** *Rest House*, on promontory overlooking harbour in town centre, T 40229, 26 rm, better in new building, Dutch reception building 1774, overpriced; **C** *Palm Paradise Cabanas*, Goyam Bokka, 2 km W, T Col 717517, 15 Cabanas on beach, tour groups. **D** *Manaraha Beach*, Moraketiyara, 2 km W, by the sea in large grounds, good food, clean, good value, rec; **D** *Touristen Gast Haus*, T 40370, 4 rm with bath, spotless, good service, rec. **E** *Tourist Guest House*, nr *Tangalle Bay Hotel*, T 40389, 4 clean rm with bath, breakfast incl, quiet, good value. **D** *Gayana Guest House*, Medketiya Beach (E, beyond the lagoon bridge), 8 rm, better on beachside, restaurant, basic but friendly; **D** *Anail's*, Medketiya Beach, restaurant. **NB** Avoid *Samon's Tourist House*, 75 Wijaya Rd, unpleasant management.

• **Places to eat** Many serve seafood, especially nr the *Tangalle Bay Hotel* incl *Chalet*.

Going W, you pass from the wet zone to the dry zone, through **Ranna** (12 km) where there is a Buddhist temple on summit of hill, and Ambalantota (16 km) to Hambantota (14 km). **Hambantota** a small fishing port with a large Muslim population. It is the centre for producing salt from evaporated sea water. The *lewayas*, or shallow salt pans, are by the road. The small bay offers excellent swimming, but the beaches are not so good. There are sand dunes immediately around the town. **Accommodation A** *Peacock Beach Hotel*, on the seaside at Galwala, is the best, T 20377, 80 a/c rm, some non-a/c cheaper, secluded, but indifferent gardens, pool amidst frangipanis, often full with tour groups, self contained resort with security guards. **C** *Rest House*, T 20299, situated in a superb position on a promontory, with a restaurant, described as 'the bright spot of Hambantota'. On the beach at Galwala: **D** *Seaspray*, 1 km from Bus stop, T 20212, some a/c rm. Other accommodation is fairly basic.

Tissamaharama

32 km NE of Hambantota, is one of oldest

of the abandoned royal cities. The ruins had been hidden in jungle for centuries. King Dutthagamani had his capital here before recapturing Anuradhapura.

The tank at Tissawewa, thought to have been created at the end of the 3rd century BC, was restored with 2 others and attracts a lot of water birds. Numerous dagobas, including one 50m high, which too had been lost under the sand having been destroyed by the invading Dravidians, have been restored entirely by local Buddhists. Other buildings resemble a palace and a multi-storeyed monastery.

Excursions

Kataragama, 16 km from Tissamaharama, is a tiny village which comes vividly to life at the Esala (Jul-Aug) festival. Pilgrims flock to the temple, and which ends with fire walking and 'water cutting' ceremonies. The pilgrims come to perform penance for sins they have committed, and some of the scenes of self-mutilation, performed in a trance, are horrific. **Accommodation** **C** *New Rest House*, T 35299, 18 rm. **D** *Kataragama Rest House*, nr the river, has 23 simple rm. Enquire in Colombo about rm at the attractive *Bank of Ceylon* guest house. **Getting there** Services in all directions, incl direct bus to Nuwara Eliya.

Kirinda, on the coast, is 10 km SE of Tissamaharama, and has a good beach and some Buddhist ruins on the rocks. It is historically linked to the King Dutthagamani. His mother, having been banished by her father, landed at the village and married the local king. Although popular with scuba divers who are attracted by the reefs at Great and Little Basses off the coast, the currents can be treacherous.

Yala in the dry zone, also known as **Ruhuna National Park**, is 20 km from Tissamaharama. **Kumana** (see above) to the E is a Bird Sanctuary, reached from Pottuvil and Arugam Bay. You need to spend a day at the 1260 sq km park which varies from open parkland, scrub, to dense jungle on the plains, rocky outcrops and streams, small lakes and lagoons and has a picturesque ocean frontage. With the Lahugala Sanctuary bordering it, the elephants are the main attraction, with deer, wild boar, buffaloes and numerous species of birds. Best time to visit is Oct-Dec, early morning or late afternoon. Buses or jeep tours within the Park, 0530, 1500. Safari tours, about Rs 200 per person in a jeep carrying 6 passengers, last 3 hr. Some are disappointed by difficulty of seeing wildlife. **Accommodation** Six *Park Bungalows*, have a cook, bring your own bedding and food, reservations: Wildlife Dept, Transwork House, Col 1, T 33787. *Yala Safari Beach Hotel*, Amaduwa. *Brown's Safari Beach*, Amaduwa, has 8 rm.

• **Accommodation** The **B** *Tissamaharama Rest House*, T 047 37299, in gardens on the lakeside is very comfortable, 63 rm, 5 a/c, restaurant, open-air bar, pool, lacks personal touch, but still rec, very popular, book ahead. Others nearby are simpler guest house. **C** *Priyanka Inn*, Kataragama Rd, T 3246, 12 rm, pleasant restaurant, good atmosphere, very clean. **D** *Singha Tourist Inn*, nr Rest House, residential block is in family home's garden, rm rather dark, friendly, rec, often full; **D** *Chandrika*, Kataragama Rd, 8 rm, good restaurant. **E** *Hatari*, Kataragama Rd, 7 rm, modest, Chinese restaurant.

Climate: Tissamaharama

	Jan	Feb	Mar	Apr	May	Jun	Jul	Aug	Sep	Oct	Nov	Dec	Av/Tot
Max (°C)	31	31	31	32	31	31	31	31	30	30	30	30	31
Min (°C)	23	23	24	26	26	26	26	25	24	24	24	24	25
Rain (mm)	81	56	57	98	91	58	55	49	67	141	193	127	1073

INFORMATION FOR VISITORS

Contents

Before you go

Entry requirements

● Visas

Nationals of the following countries as tourists require a valid passport but do not need a visa for a period of 30 days: Australia, Austria, Bahrain, Bangladesh, Belgium, Britain, Bangladesh, Bahrain, Canada, Denmark, Eire, Finland, France, Germany, Indonesia, Italy, Japan, Kuwait, Luxembourg, Malaysia, the Maldives, Nepal, Netherlands, New Zealand, Norway, Oman, Pakistan, Philippines, Qatar, Saudi Arabia, Singapore, South Korea, Spain, Sweden, Switzerland, Thailand, UAE, USA and Yugoslavia. **NB** All tourists should have a valid visa for the country that is their next destination if that country requires a visa. Nationals of all other countries require a visa. Check with your nearest Sri Lankan representative.

● Extensions

Extensions beyond 1 month provided you have US$30 to spend per day, a valid passport and an onward or return ticket. Proof of daily spending US$30 during the first month may be required. Apply to Dept Immigration and Emigration, Galle Buck Rd, Colombo 1, T 29851.

Visitors require sufficient funds to maintain themselves and a return (or onward) ticket or foreign exchange to purchase a ticket.

● Innoculations

A valid certificate of vaccination against yellow fever if you are travelling from a yellow fever infected areas. Protection against tetanus, typhoid, hepaitits and malaria is advised.

● Registration

Tourists from non-Commonwealth countries granted an extension of their tourist visa must register at the Aliens Bureau, Grd Flr, New Secretariat Bldg, Colombo 1.

● Work permits

All foreigners intending to work require work permits. Apply to the Sri Lankan Representative in your country of origin.

● Representation overseas

Australia, 35 Empire Circuit, Forrest, Canberra ACT 2603; **Belgium**, 21-22 Ave des Arts (4e étage), 1040 Brussels, T 513 98 92; **Canada**, 102-104, 85 Range Rd, Ottawa, Ontario K1M 8J6; **France**, 15 Rue d'Astorg, 75008 Paris, T 266-35-01. 0900-1200, 1400-1700, Mon-Fri; **Germany**, Rolandstrasse 52, 5300 Bonn 2; **India**, 27 Kautilya Marg, Chanakyapuri, New Delhi 110021; **Indonesia**, 70 Jalan Diponegoro, Jakarta; **Singapore**, 1207-1212 Goldhill Plaza, Singapore 11; **Thailand**, Lailart Bldg, 87 Sukhumvit Rd, Bangkok; **Switzerland**, 56 Rue de Moillebeau, 1211, Geneva 19; **UK**, 13 Hyde Park Gardens, London W2 2LU; **USA**, 2148 Wyoming Av, NW, Washington DC 20008, T 483 4025, F 282 7181.

● Ceylon Tourist Board offices overseas

Australia, 241 Abercrombie St, Chippendale NSW 2008, T 02 698 5226; **Canada**, Ontario M5B 1K2; **Thailand**, PO Box 316, 1/8 Soi 10, Sukhumvit Rd, Bangkok, T 251 8062, F 662 2544820; **France**, 19 rue de Quatre Septembre, 75002 Paris, T 42 60 49 99; **Japan**, Dowa

Bldg 7-2-22, Ginza Chuo-Ku, T 3289 0771, F 3289 0772; **Germany**, Allerheiligentor 2-4, D 6000 Frankfurt/Main 1, T 287734, F 288371; **UK**, 13 Hyde Park Gardens, London W2 2LU, T 071 262 5009, F 071 262 7970.

● **Tour companies**

The following tour companies (among others) operate from the UK – ***Coromandel***, 081 995 3642; ***Kuoni***, T 0306 740500; ***Hayes & Jarvis***, T 081 748 5050; ***Explore Worldwide***, T 0252 319448; ***Thomsons***, T 071 431 2005; ***Allegro Holidays***, T 0737 221323; ***BA Worldwide***, T 0293 611611; ***Sri Lanka Tours***, T 071 434 3921; ***Young World***, T 0273 203764; ***Paradise***, T 071 2297686. Also ***Cosmos***, ***Sri Lanka Tours***, ***JBS Study Tours***, ***Annis Travels*** and *Eleanor Travels*.

Money

● **Currency**

The Sri Lanka rupee is made up of 100 cents. Notes in denominations of Rs 1000, 500, 100, 50, 20, 10, 5, 2; coins of Rs 5, 2, and 1, and of 50, 25, 10, 5, 2, and 1c. Keep plenty of small change and low denomination notes as they can be difficult to find, and changing a large note can also be difficult.

● **Credit cards**

Shops accept most major credit cards although some may try to add a surcharge which is not authorised. The Hong Kong Bank, 24 Sir Baron Jayatilleke Maw, Colombo allows Visa and Master Card holders to obtain cash and travellers cheques. See note above on exchange transactions. However, American Express is not widely accepted.

● **Money changing**

Banking Hours: 0900-1300 Mon and 0900-1330 Tue-Fri. The **Bank of Ceylon** in York St, Fort, is open 0800-2000 every day, incl holidays. It is easier to get cash using a Visa card in Sri Lanka than elsewhere in South Asia. The **Bank of Ceylon** may accept UK cheques backed by Visa cards, and the **Bank of America** head branch will give cash on a Visa card. **NB** All foreign exchange transactions must be made through authorised banks and exchanges and entered on the Customs and Immigration form. Unspent rupees may be reconverted at time of departure at a commercial bank. Govt approved hotels and shops are allowed to deal in foreign currency. Keep the receipts when you change money. For visa extension you may need to show proof of spending US$30 a day during the first month.

● **Travellers cheques**

Travellers cheques are widely acceptable by commercial banks and authorised dealers, and get a better rate of exchange than other forms of currency.

Getting there

● **Air**

Air Lanka, the National airline and several international carriers (with phone nos in London) linking airports around the world with Colombo incl: **Air France**, 081 742 6600, **Gulf Air**, 071 408 1717, **Emirates**, 071 930 5356, **KLM**, 081 750 9000, **Kuwait Airways**, T 071 412 0007, **PIA**, T 071 734 5544, **Royal Jordanian**, T 071 734 2557). **Indian Airlines** also flies to Colombo daily from Madras and twice weekly from Trivandrum.

Air Lanka, T Colombo 21161. In South Asia it flies to Bombay (M,Th), Delhi (W,Sa, excellent Airbus service), Madras (daily), Trivandrum (M,Tu,Th,F,Sa), Tiruchirappalli (Th,Su), Male and Karachi. Trivandrum is marginally cheaper than Tiruchirappalli. Overseas offices: Amsterdam 717733; Bangkok 2360159; Bombay 223299; Frankfurt 069 740941; Hong Kong 5 252171; Karachi 514421; London 071 930 2099; Madras 867932; Male 3459; New York 838 5120; Paris 429 74344; Tokyo 5734261; Thiruvananthapuram 68767. Sri Lanka's modern International Airport at **Katunayake**, 35 km N of the capital, has several facilities, including a duty-free shop, bank and an expensive restaurant. The Bank of Ceylon exchange counter, airport restaurant, day rooms and the tobacco counter are open 24 hr. The Tourist Information Centre and the Tea Centre (behind Customs area) are open for flight arrivals and departures. Porter, left luggage and bond baggage service are available, as well as assistance with meeting passengers.

● **Customs**

You are permitted to bring in items for 'personal use' provided they are not intended for sale. You must declare all currency including travellers cheques, drafts etc, precious metals and gem stones, firearms, weapons, drugs, narcotics and any goods in commercial quantities (see **Prohibited and restricted** items below). In addition to completing Part II of the Immigration Landing Card, a tourist may be asked by the Customs Officer to complete a Baggage Declaration Form. Foreign currency in excess of US$5000 must be declared on

Exchange Control, Form D. Up to Rs 250 may be imported or exported. On departure Sri Lankan money must be changed back before Customs.

● **Duty Free Allowances**
200 cigarettes or 50 cigars or 375g of tobacco (or in combination). Two bottles of wine and 1.5 litres of spirits. A small quantity of perfume and 250 ml of toilet water. Travel souvenirs up to a max value of Rs 1000. Customs should be satisfied that other articles will be re-exported on departure.

● **Prohibited and restricted items**
Export of the following without a permit is forbidden: precious metals (gold, platinum and silver), antiques (rare books, palm leaf manuscripts, rare anthropological material etc), ivory, precious and semi-precious stones (even when set in jewellery), narcotics, firearms, explosives, dangerous weapons, and fauna and flora. A max of Rs 250 in local currency, 3 kg of tea and goods purchased for personal use, using foreign currency can be exported. See '**Money changing**' below for regulations on reconverting unspent rupees.

Import of all the items listed above and in addition, Indian and Pakistani currency, obscene and seditious literature or pictures is prohibited.

Warning It is illegal to purchase items made from wild animals and reptiles.

When you arrive

● **Arrival and departure**
Arrival Tourists must hand in completed, Part I of the Immigration Landing Card and present Part II for certification by the Customs officer. This should be retained and produced at the time of departure.

Connections to the city It is worth buying the monthly guide *This month in Sri Lanka* at the airport bookshop before leaving. Airport Taxis (up to 3 passengers), a/c coaches, minibuses and local buses are available for transfer to Colombo and Negombo. Tickets are for sale in the airport arrivals hall. Local bus Nos. 187, 300 and 875 – often crowded, but the cheapest way. Tickets on the bus. In addition there are train services to the city at 0746, 0820, 1632 and 1720. There is now a helicopter service to the city centre.

Departure Tax Embarkation Tax of Rs 500 payable after check-in. Tourists may take out 3 kg of tea.

● **Clothing**
Light and loose cottons throughout the year. Some warmer clothes for the hills, especially in the evenings. Topless bathing is prohibited; heavy fines can be imposed. See list in India, Information for visitors.

● **Cost of living**
Both the standard and the cost of living are higher than in India, but much less than in Europe or the United States.

● **Hours of business**
0830-1630 Mon-Fri. Some open on Sat 0830-1300. Shops often close for lunch from 1300-1400 on weekdays, most close on Sun. Sunday street bazaars in some areas. **NB** *Poya* (Full moon) days are holidays.

● **Maps**
Ceylon Tourist Board, 78 Steuart Place, Colombo 3, T 437059, F 437953, gives out a Sri Lanka itinerary map. Nelles Verlag 1:450,000 Sri Lanka is conventional with 4 city insets. The new Sarvodaya Vishva Lekha (41 Lumbini Ave, Ratmalana, T 722932, F 722932) is 1:500,000. It has 4 fold-outs in a handy format with added advantage of an index.

Many large scale maps are available for consultation at the Survey Dept, Map Sales Branch, Kirula Rd, Narahenpita, T 585111 and Map Sales Centre, York St, Colombo 1 T 35328. Most large scale maps and town plans are not for sale for security reasons.

● **Official time**
5½ hr ahead of GMT.

● **Photography**
For photography of museum exhibits at the ancient sites you need a permit from the Dept of Archaeology, Marcus Fernando Maw, Col 7. Filming permits are obtainable from Cultural Triangle Office, 212 Bauddalaka Maw, Col 7. Individual site offices also issue permits with tickets from 0600-1800. Please ask before taking photographs of local people.

● **Shopping**
Batik, tea, spices, silverware, coir articles, leather goods, jewellery and gem stones are good buys. See **Handicrafts** in **Introduction**, page 1317. Govt *Laksala* shops in Colombo, Kandy, Galle, Nuwara Eliya, Matara, Kegalle, Kalutara, Kurunegala, Udagama, Batticaloa, Anuradhapura, Bentota, Hikkaduwa, Negombo, Ratnapura and Medawachchiya.

Social behaviour

Greeting "Ayubowan" (may you have long life) is the traditional welcome greeting.

Visiting religious sites Visitors to Buddhist temples are welcome everywhere. Parts of Hindu temples are sometimes closed to non-Hindus. Visitors to both Buddhist and Hindu temples should be properly dressed – shorts and swim wear are not suitable. Shoes should be left at the entrance and any head covering taken off. (Best to visit early in the day and to take socks for protection against the hot stone.)

Do not attempt to shake hands or be photographed with Buddhist *bhikkus* (monks) or to pose for photos with statues of the Buddha or other deities and paintings. Remember that monks are not permitted to touch money so donations should be put in temple offering boxes. Monks renounce all material possessions and so live on offerings. (However, you are advised not to give to ordinary beggars.)

Tourist Information Centres will help with providing trained English speaking guides (and occasionally speaking a European language, Malay or Japanese). Fees are specified. Alternatively ask at hotel.

Note Entry fees to ancient archaeological sites, museums etc are much higher for foreign visitors than for Sri Lankans. Inclusive tickets US$20. Most individual sites US$5 each. Children under 12 – half price.

Tipping

The same principles apply as in India – see page 136. Remember, the average weekly wage is about Rs 500. **Note** A 10% Service Charge is now common in even the most basic hotels and restaurants in the tourist area. This is levied even though the quality of service may be poor.

Voltage

230-240 volts, 50 cycles A.C. The current is variable.

Weights and measures

Sri Lanka now uses metric weights and measures.

Where to stay

Accommodation

The Tourist Board issues lists at the International Airport and at their office at 78 Steuart Pl, Galle Rd, Colombo. From international class hotels in the capital with a full range of facilities (min US$75), the choice ranges from moderately priced comfortable accommodation in the city (Rs 300-450 for a double rm) to *Rest Houses* in converted colonial houses, often in superb locations and very simple Wildlife Conservation Dept bungalows in the parks. It is also possible to book rooms in plantation estate bungalows or private homes in towns and cities; this is a good alternative for those on a low budget.

HOTEL CLASSIFICATION

Many higher range hotels quote their prices in US dollars. The **price categories** for Sri Lanka used in the Handbook are: **AL** US$90+; **A** US$60-90; **B** US$35-60; **C** Rs 500-1000; **D** Rs 300-500; **E** Rs 150-300; F Rs 150 or less.

Food and drink

Food

Rice and curry are the staple main course food of Sri Lanka, but that term conceals an enormous variety of subtle flavours. Coriander, chillies, mustard, cumin, pepper, cinnamon and garlic are just some of the common ingredients which add flavour to both sea food and meat curries. Fresh sea food – crab, lobster and prawn, as well as fish – is excellent, and meat is cheap. Rice forms the basis of many Sri Lankan sweet dishes, palm treacle being used as the main traditional sweetener. This is also served on curd as a delicious dessert. Sadly, it is not easy to get good Sri Lankan food in most hotels which concentrate on Western dishes. A meal in a first class restaurant could cost as little as Rs 250.

Sri Lanka has a wide variety of tropical fruit throughout the year, pineapple, papaya and banana being particularly good. The extraordinarily rich jack fruit are also available all year. Seasonal fruit include mangosteen (no relation of mangos), passion fruit, custard apples, avocado pears, durian and rambutan from July-Oct. In addition to ordinary green coconuts, Sri Lanka is also home to the distinctive King Coconut (*thambili*). The milk is particularly sweet and nutritious.

Many spices are grown in the island and are widely available in the markets and shops. Cinnamon, nutmeg, cloves, cardomom and pepper are all grown, the Kandy region being a major centre of spice production. Many private spice gardens are open to the public.

● **Drink**

All big hotels will serve filtered water and mineral water, and there is a wide range of bottled soft drinks. Always take great care with water. Alcoholic drinks are widely available, though imported drinks (wines) are very expensive. Local beer (*Lion* and *Three Coins*) is acceptable. The local spirit *arrack*, is distilled from coconut toddy. **Note** Alcohol is not sold on *Poya* (monthly full-moon) days.

Getting around

Warning The civil war continued in the NE and the extreme N which remained dangerous and closed to visitors in 1994. Conditions for tourists returned to normal in the rest of the island and large numbers are visiting the island now. ***Government Rest Houses*** still often offer the best accommodation in the lower price range, though in Sri Lanka these are not as cheap as in India. However, some are outstanding value, in beautiful settings.

● **Air**

All internal air services are unscheduled. Upali Travels and Air Taxi Ltd operate charter helicopter and fixed winged aircraft to destinations of tourist interest and to domestic airports from the Ratmalana Airport, Colombo. Details under Colombo. Also from Government Tourist Offices and Thomas Cook, 15 Sir Baron Jayatilleka Maw, Col 1, T 545971-4.

● **Train**

Although the network is restricted there are train services to a number of major destinations, and journeys are comparatively short. Special a/c trains operate to Kandy and Hikkaduwa, and there is an inter-city express service (one class) Colombo-Kandy and Colombo-Bandarawela. The Colombo Matara line is now being extended and eventually will reach Kataragama. The first leg to Dikwella is expected to be open in 1994. There are now direct trains from Matara to Kandy and Anuradhapura, which saves the change which used to be necessary. 3rd Cl has hard seats, 1st is relatively comfortable. Fares are low, about US$1 for 80 km on 2nd Cl.

● **Road**

Bus The nationalised bus service (CTB) has competition from a range of private operators, especially minibuses. CTB buses carry white signs for local routes and yellow signs for long distance routes. Though cheap, long distances can be exhausting.

Car There are several self drive car hire firms based in Colombo including some of the main international operators. International driving permit needed to obtain temporary local licence. Contact Automobile Association of Sri Lanka. However, it may actually be cheaper (and more relaxing) to hire a car with driver, available through travel agents and tour operators for about US$ 50 a day. One excellent agency is ASET (Aitken Spence Travel).

Taxis Taxis have yellow tops with red numbers on white plates. Available in most towns. Negotiate price for long journeys, unless metered. About Rs 30 min, Rs 15 for extra km. Colombo has **auto rickshaws**.

Travel tips No distances are great, and roads are generally good, though they are slow. If travelling by train hang on to your baggage at the station. Beware: porters will take charge of you unless you negotiate firmly first.

Communications

● **Postal services**

Details of postal rates to other countries can be obtained from major hotels, or from the Inquiries Counter of the GPO in Janadhipathi Maw, Colombo 1. A Poste Restante service is available. Information in Colombo T 26203. The GPO is open 24 hr for the sale of stamps and for local telephone calls. DHL Worldwide Express Parcel Service, 130 Glennie St, Colombo 2, T 541285.

● **Telephone services**

International phone calls can be made from the GPO between 0700 and 2100. Foreign cables also accepted at GPO. Directory Enquiries, T 161, International Calls, T 100, Trunk Calls, T 101. There is now a growing number of International Direct Dialling centres. In Colombo these operate at reasonably competitive international rates. Elsewhere and in hotels rates may be as much as 3 times as high.

Entertainment

● **Newspapers**

The Daily News and *The Island* are national daily newspapers published in English. In Colombo and some other hotels a wide range of international daily and periodical newspapers and magazines is available. The *Lanka Guardian* is a respected monthly.

● **Radio and television**

Sri Lanka Broadcasting Corporation operates

in 9 languages, between 0530 and 2300. Two TV channels. *ITN* from 1830. News in English at 2200. *Rupavahini* – English newscast at 2130. Liberalisation has opened the door to several private channels and an ever growing number of private radio stations.

Holidays and festivals

Sat and Sun are always holidays. Poya (full moon) days, are also holidays. No liquor is sold (you can order drinks at your hotel, the day before) and all places of entertainment are closed. Some other festivals and public holidays in Sri Lanka are determined by the lunar calendar and therefore change from year to year.

● **1994**

Sep *Binara* Poya Day.

Oct *Wap* Poya Day; *Milad-un-Nabi* Prophet Mohammad's birthday; *Deepavali* Festival.

Nov *Il* Poya Day.

Dec *Unduwap* Poya Day; **25** Christmas Day; **31** Special Bank Holiday.

● **1995**

Jan *Duruthu* Poya day. Sri Lankan Buddhists believe that the Buddha visited the island and celebrate with Colombo's biggest annual festival. *Tamil Thai Pongal* day.

Feb 4 National Day. Processions, dances, parades. *Navam* Poya Day. A large celebration with elephant processions in Colombo. *Maha Sivarathri* Day.

Mar *Medin* Poya Day.

Apr *Bak* Poya Day. Good Friday; **13-14** Sinhala and Tamil New Year Day. The celebrations are accompanied by closure of many shops and restaurants. *Eid ul Fitr* (Ramazan).

May 1 May Day; *Wesak* Poya Day and day following. The major Poya holiday, celebrating the key events in the Buddha's life: his birth, enlightenment and death. Lamps are light across the island. **22** National Heroes Day.

Jun *Poson* Poya Day, celebrating Mahinda's arrival in Sri Lanka as the first Buddhist missionary. **30** Bank Holiday.

Jul *Esala* Poya Day. This is the most important Sri Lankan festival with a great procession honouring the Sacred Tooth of the Buddha in Kandy. It lasts 10 days.

Aug *Nikini* Poya Day.

Further reading

Handbook for the Ceylon Traveller, 2nd ed. Studio Times, Colombo, 1983. **American Women's Assoc** *Colombo Handbook*, Colombo. **de Silva, K. M.** *A History of Sri Lanka*. London, OUP, 1981. **Malangoda, K.** *Buddhism in Sinhalese Society, 1750-1900*. Berkeley, 1976. **Moore, M.P.** *The State and Peasant Politics in Sri Lanka*. London, 1985. **McGowan, W.** *Only man is vile: The Tragedy if Sri Lanka*. Picador, 1983. **Obeyesekere, R. & Fernando, C.** Eds. *An anthology of modern writing from Sri Lanka*. Tucson, Arizona, 1981. **Reynolds, C.H.B.** Ed. *An anthology of Sinhalese Literature of the 20th century*. London, 1987. **Goonetilleke, D.C.R.A.** Ed. *The Penguin New Writing in Sri Lanka*. India, 1992.

MALDIVES

CONTENTS

MAPS

OFFICIAL NAME Divehi Jumhuriya (Republic of Maldives)

CAPITAL Male

NATIONAL FLAG Green rectangle with a red border; a white crescent in the centre.

EMBLEM Coconut palm, crescent and star, 2 crossed national flags and the title of the state.

OFFICIAL LANGUAGE Dhivehi

OFFICIAL RELIGION Islam

NATIONAL ANTHEM "Qawmee mi ekuveri kan mathee thibegen kureeme salaam" (In National Unity we salute our nation).

BASICS *Population*: 213,215 (1990 census), 48.5% Women, Male 60,000, *Urban* 30%, *Rural* 70%; *Religion*: Islam (Sunni) 100%; *Population growth rate (1991)*: 3.2%; *Birth rate*: 39/1000; *Death rate*: 9/1000; *Infant mortality rate*: 56/1000; *Life expectancy*: 63 years; *GNP per capita*: US$470; *Annual per capita income*: US$600; *Literacy*: 98.2%.

ENVIRONMENT

Land

Dhivehi Jumhuriyya, the Republic of the Maldives (pronounced 'a' as in all, 'i' as in give) is the smallest member state of the UN. It comprises a group of islands stretching over 823 km N to S and nearly 130 km from E to W approximately 650 km SW of the S tip of India. Of the 1190 coral islands many of which are no more than sandbanks, only 202 are inhabited. 67 have been turned into tourist resorts, scattered around 5 central atolls of North and South Male, Ari, Lhaviyani and Vaavu plus Gan which has a tourist resort. The tiny islands are grouped around the fringes of shallow lagoons, collectively known by the Maldivian word which has entered the English language, **atoll**. Huvadhu atoll, to the S is the world's largest true atoll, enclosing a lagoon area of 2240 sq km. In regions with the greatest depth, the sea is 200 fathoms deep; the islands themselves are rarely more than 2.5m above sea level. There are 19 administrative groups of atolls each named after a letter of the **Dhivehi** alphabet.

The approach by air is dramatic. A line of white waves indicates the reefs nearing but often not breaking the surface. Inside, are the aquamarine and turquoise shallows, with the coral clearly visible beneath, and then tiny patches of islands.

Soil

The thin (15 cm) surface covering of dark sandy humus contains some parent coral rock making it very alkaline. The sandstone layer underneath gives way to a layer of sand which retains a lens of fresh-water on many islands which can be tapped by wells.

Flora & Fauna

Flora

Most islands, including the uninhabited ones, have a substantial cover of tall coconut palms, screw pines, salt-resistant bushy plants and breadfruit. On some of the inhabited islands. Fruit and vegetables including mangoes, papayas, sweet potatoes, pumpkins and bananas as well as cereals are grown.

Fauna

Though the island lacks land-based fauna, the coral reefs harbour a rich variety of tropical reef fish. Big fish include tunas, sharks, barracudas, manta rays and bonitos. Groupers and red snappers are fairly easily caught.

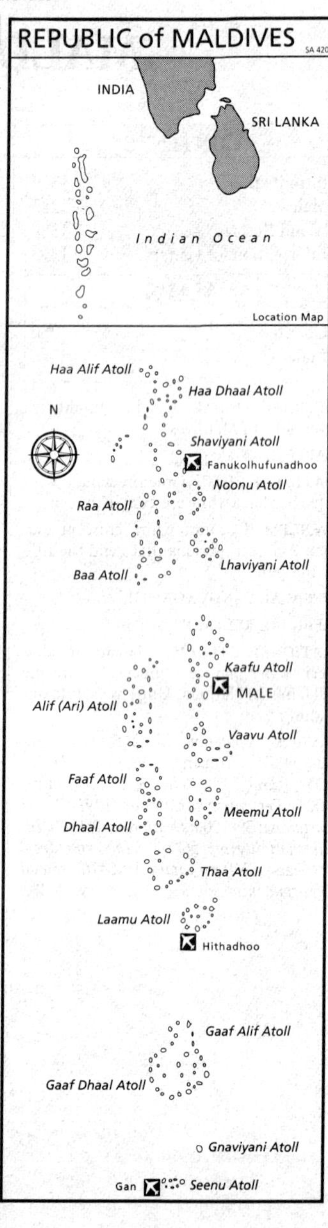

Climate

Best season

There is no really unsuitable time to visit. Jan-Feb are the driest and the best period, but it can rain heavily at any time. End of May-Jun and Nov are likely to be most showery although these are not persistent. The High Season (Nov-Apr) is mostly dry with occasional showers and calm seas. On a few islands higher rates apply in Aug. The Low Season (May-Oct) has higher humidity, more rain (though not prolonged) and rough seas.

Temperatures

The Maldives' climate reflects its equatorial oceanic position; the islands have no winter season. Temperatures remain almost the same throughout the year, remaining between 25.7°C and 30.4°C. Minor variations reflecting differences in cloud cover more than the apparent movement of the sun. Water temperatures are similarly equable and high.

Rainfall

Rainfall is spread throughout the year with an annual average of 1950 mm. The monsoons are not as pronounced as in the rest of South Asia. The 2 periods are: SW monsoon (May-Oct) which brings rain and the NE Monsoon (Nov-Apr) which is marked by stronger winds. Since the islands are situated in the doldrums, they do not get cyclones. The tidal range usually remains below a metre.

HISTORY

Early history

Recording of history only began with the arrival of Islam in the 12th century but prior to that, the islands have been referred to classical writer and by the Alexandrian Pappus as early as the 4th century. The Maldives archipelago was originally probably referred to as the Lakshadweeps (100,000 islands) and included at least the southern Minicoy Island of the present group (now a part of India) which was ruled from Male up to the 18th century and with which it has strong cultural and linguistic links (see page 1112).

The Sultanate

The Maldives remained an independent country with a sultanate until the Portuguese arrived in Male in 1513 and with the consent of the Sultan built a fort there. They ruled briefly for 15½ years from 1558 to 1573 when they were driven out by Muhammad Takarufanu. In the 17th century the Dutch considered the islands a protectorate while they ruled over Ceylon (Sri Lanka). Then the Malabari Moplas from South India attacked Male in 1752 and remained in power for the brief period of 3 months and 20 days. The country was once again liberated by the founder of the Huraagé dynasty which ruled the islands until it became a Republic.

The Maldives became a British Protectorate in 1887 though the country in effect remained a sultanate. In 1953 an attempt to found a Republic failed after 7 months and the sultanate returned (though in name only in the latter years). The country enjoyed British defence protection until independence on 26 July 1965 with the British keeping the island of Gan under lease as an RAF base until 1978 when they prematurely terminated the lease.

The Republic

As an independent state it joined the United Nations in Sep 1965. Three years later, after a referendum, the Sultanate was abolished and country was declared a Republic on 1 Apr 1968. Ibrahim Nasir (who had held the post of Prime Minister since1958 and had negotiated independent status) was elected President of the new republic on 11 November 1968.

CULTURE

People

The Maldivian people are descended from Aryan, Dravidian, Arab and Negro ancestors. The original population may have been Dravidians from South India followed by Indo-Aryan settlers from India and Sri Lanka and by 500 AD the Buddhists dominated the islands; archaeologists have found remains of temples and stupas in some atolls.

Language

Dhivehi, the Maldivian language, is related to Sinhalese from Sri Lanka which belongs to the Indo-Aryan group. It also shows strong Arabic influence, the script being written right to left. The language is another common link between Minicoy (Maliku) in the Lakshadweeps where Mahl is spoken (see page 1112).

Religion

From the mid-7th century Arab traders landed on Maldivian islands when sailing back from Malacca and China and although the Berber Abul Barakaath (see **Medhu Ziayarath** below) is remembered as the bringer of Islam to the country, the long association with Muslim Arab sailors paved the way for its adoption. In 1153 the ruler Sultan Mohammed ibn Abdullah (King Dovemi Kalaminja) was converted to Islam and declared it the religion of his kingdom. He was subsequently followed by the whole population.

MODERN MALDIVES

Government

The President is the Head of State & Chief Executive, nominated by the Citizens' Majlis and elected by a public referendum, for a 5 year term. The Majlis (Parliament) comprises 48 members (2 elected from each atoll and 8 nominated by the President); there is no party system. Ibrahim Nasir, the first President resigned in 1978, succeeded by Maumoon Abdul Gayoom.

Recent developments The Maldives joined the Commonwealth in 1982 and is also a member of the principal international financial institutions. 20th century modernisation has been making an impact on the Maldivians since the 1960; changes have also been brought about by developing the tourist atolls. The young population (47% under 15 years) however, is no longer guaranteed a job on finishing high school giving rise to frustration and discontent. There have been occasional attempts at overthrowing the present government; in Nov 1988 a coup attempt had to be crushed with Indian help.

There is a strong lobby suggesting that 'global warming' through environmental change can pose a serious threat to these low-lying islands. The high tidal swell in 1987 which caused severe damage to the airport island and Male brought the issue to the forefront. Figures quoted in 1990 by the Inter governmental Panel on Climate Change claim that if conditions remain unchanged, the sea level may rise by 1m by the year 2100.

Economy

The Maldivians depended heavily on trade in the past, exchanging fish, coconut products, ambergrise and cowries (which was used as currency on the subcontinent and beyond), for grain (particularly rice) and cloth. Even today the fishing and coconut growing remain major activities.

Agriculture Natural constraints such as poor, alkaline soil which retains some coral rock with low water-retentive quality, the scarcity of fresh-water, the unfavourable climate, leaves only 10% of the land area of 300 sq km on these small islands suitable for agriculture. Maldivians depend on the wet SW monsoon as the principal source of rain-water supplemented by a small amount of fresh-water available. In spite of this, a growing amount of cash crops are grown.

Coconut palm is the chief crop, its products, especially the wood being used for boat-building and construction. This is followed by breadfruit, mango, papaya, lime and banana among tropical fruit, as well as some vegetables and chilli, which is in great demand. The government is trying to improve conditions by limiting pest damage, improving seed varieties and distribution of seeds, encouraging new ventures eg bee-keeping (which could also increase crop yields), poultry farming (for meat and eggs which have to be imported in large quantities) and growing cereals other than rice, and also through education.

Tourism Since the the building of the first resort in 1972 tourism has transformed the economy, and now contributes nearly 20% to the GDP, employing 5% of the workforce and is the largest earner of foreign exchange (60%). Europeans form the largest group of tourists (led by the Germans and Italians) while tourist numbers from Japan and Australia are growing very fast. In 1993 over 220,000 tourists visited the islands. This sector has enabled some enterprising Maldivians to become rich overnight; they lease uninhabited islands from the government for a nominal rent and re-lease these to foreign developers who pay large sums to turn them into resorts.

Fishing has remained the traditional occupation of the islands for centuries; today's exports are canned (particularly Tuna), frozen and salted, and trade is mainly with the Far East and Europe. The vessel mechanisation programme since 1974 has greatly increased yields. Fishing employs 25% of the workforce and is the 2nd largest contributor of foreign exchange.

Another 25% (mostly women) are occupied in the traditional boatbuilding, mat-weaving, rope-making and craft industries. In the modern sector fish canning and garment lead the export oriented group. Major trading partners include UK, USA, Sri Lanka, Thailand, Germany, Singapore, Japan, the Netherlands and Hong Kong.

Shipping From the mid-1960s upto the early 80s the National Ship Management Ltd handled enough trade to become a significant source of foreign exchange. However, the decline in world trade has resulted in the industry shrinking considerably to remain economic.

Communication The Satellite Earth Station on Villingili island provides the country with international direct dialling telephones, telex and fax services. Between the atolls communication is through HF transceivers although UHF and VHF telephones are in use between many islands.

MALE

BASICS *Population*: 56,000.

The capital, Male is in one of the central atolls of the archipelago. It covers about 3 sq km and houses ¼ of the nation's population. You can walk from one end of the island to the other in 20 mins, or cover it by motor bike in under 5 min, and to find all the major streets and restaurants. Overcrowding in the tiny capital has resulted in a temporary solution; the shallow waters within the western and southern reefs have been reclaimed to increase the area by a third.

Though the resident population is small, Male also has a floating population of many thousands from the atolls who come to carry out business, buy and sell products and to receive medical treatment not available on the other islands. Government and private schools also attract large numbers of pupils although each inhabited island has a government school.

Male is divided into 4 wards: Heneveiru (NE) with the finer houses, the residential area of Maafannu (NW and W) with some guest houses, and the smaller 2 Galolhu (centre and SW) and Machchangolhi (C and SE). The Inner Harbour with the jetties to the N is enclosed by a coral stone breakwater which was first built between 1620 and 1648. The Outer Harbour beyond the breakwater demarkated by 3 neighbouring islands, is used for shipping; ocean going vessels anchor there, the cargo being transported by small towed boats to and from the new wharf near Male Customs.

CLIMATE: MALE

	Jan	Feb	Mar	Apr	May	Jun	Jul	Aug	Sep	Oct	Nov	Dec
Air (°C)	30	31	31	31	30	30	29	29	29	29	30	30
Water (°C)	27	27	28	28	29	29	28	28	27	27	27	27

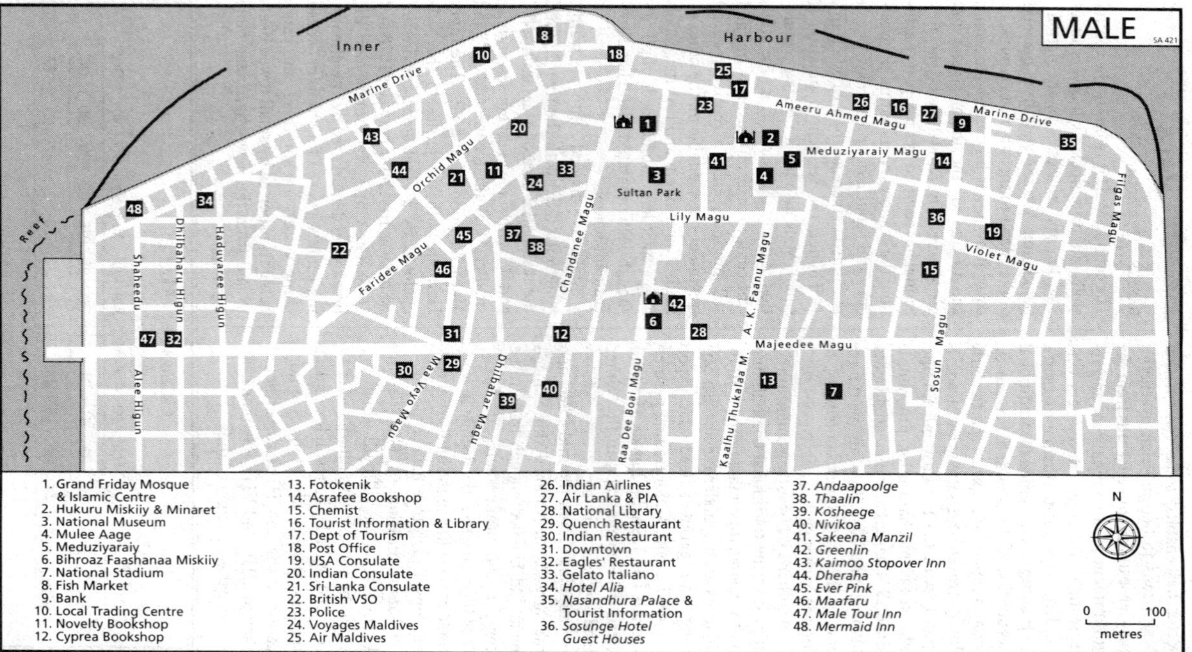
MALE
SA 421
Inner
Harbour
Reef
Marine Drive
Ameeru Ahmed Magu
Marine Drive
Meduziyaraiy Magu
Filgas Magu
Orchid Magu
Sultan Park
Lily Magu
Violet Magu
Faridee Magu
Chandanee Magu
A. K. Faanu Magu
Shaheedu
Dhilbaharu Higun
Haduvaree Higun
Majeedee Magu
Sosun Magu
Maa Veyo Magu
Dhilbahar Magu
Raa Dee Boai Magu
Kaalhu Thukalaa M.
Alee Higun
1. Grand Friday Mosque & Islamic Centre
2. Hukuru Miskiiy & Minaret
3. National Museum
4. Mulee Aage
5. Meduziyaraiy
6. Bihroaz Faashanaa Miskiiy
7. National Stadium
8. Fish Market
9. Bank
10. Local Trading Centre
11. Novelty Bookshop
12. Cyprea Bookshop
13. Fotokenik
14. Asrafee Bookshop
15. Chemist
16. Tourist Information & Library
17. Dept of Tourism
18. Post Office
19. USA Consulate
20. Indian Consulate
21. Sri Lanka Consulate
22. British VSO
23. Police
24. Voyages Maldives
25. Air Maldives
26. Indian Airlines
27. Air Lanka & PIA
28. National Library
29. Quench Restaurant
30. Indian Restaurant
31. Downtown
32. Eagles' Restaurant
33. Gelato Italiano
34. *Hotel Alia*
35. *Nasandhura Palace* & Tourist Information
36. *Sosunge Hotel Guest Houses*
37. *Andaapoolge*
38. *Thaalin*
39. *Kosheege*
40. *Nivikoa*
41. *Sakeena Manzil*
42. *Greenlin*
43. *Kaimoo Stopover Inn*
44. *Dheraha*
45. *Ever Pink*
46. *Maafaru*
47. *Male Tour Inn*
48. *Mermaid Inn*
N
0 100
metres

Places of interest

Most of Male's sights can be seen in a day; they are clustered to the N of the island. **Grand Friday Mosque**, (Masjid-al- Sultan Mohamed Thakurufaan Al-A'z'am) 3 storeys high, is the country's largest and is the **Islamic Centre** with a library and conference hall. Named after the national hero who defeated the Portuguese in 1573, it was completed in 1984. The prayer hall with its large gold coloured dome, decorated with beautiful woodcarving and arabic calligraphy, can accommodate about 5000 worshippers. The minaret is over 40m high. Non-Muslim visitors are welcome from 0900-1700 except at prayer times. Late morning and mid-afternoon are suitable times. Visitors must dress modestly, remove their shoes and wash their feet before entering.

Hukuru Miskiiy, the old Friday Mosque on Meduziyaraiy Magu, had the foundation stone laid in 1656 during the reign of Sultan Ibrahim Iskandhar. Built of stone, it has the tombs of Sultan Ibrahim Iskandhar and the royal family who reigned after him as well as other famous Maldivians. Verses of the Koran and an account of the conversion of the Maldivian people to Islam are carved on the walls. To prevent further deterioration of the coral stone structure, the western end has been protected from the sun by rather ugly corrugated iron sheets. **Munnaaru**, the white minaret at its gate was built 1675, inspired by Mecca after the King's visit and was originally used for calling the people to prayer.

Medhu Ziayarath opposite the old mosque, a shrine commemorating the Moroccon Abul Barakaath-al Barbarie who is believed to have brought Islam to the Maldives in 1153; some believe it was Yusuf Shamsuddin of Tabriz. **Mulee-Aage** (c1913) The official residence of the President is nearby. Built by Sultan Shamsuddeen III for his son and heir, it shows colonial rather than Islamic architectural influence. The Sultan however, was deposed and his family never used it. Used as government offices for many years, it was subsequently altered and enlarged; since the Maldives was declared a Republic in 1953 it has become the Presidential Palace.

Markets The colourful vegetable, fruit and firewood markets on Marine Drive are worth visiting. The Fish Market is particularly busy in the late afternoon/ early evening when the fishermen return.

Local industries

On the outlying islands boat building and fishing continue to be the most important means of gaining a livelihood while coir production provides some employment. Attempts are being made to diversify with small scale textile printing and lace making for the tourist market.

Museums

The **National Museum** is behind the Islamic Centre. Allow an hr. Open 0900-1140, 1500-1740. Entry Rf 5, children under twelve Rf 2. Attractively housed in one of Male's older wooden 2 storey houses, it includes collections of early sculptures, mainly in coral, some in wood, probably of the pre-Islamic Buddhist period in the Maldives. Some wooden boards show examples of early Divehi script. Dates of most of the early artefacts are uncertain, and are broadly listed as 11th century. More recent exhibits include royal memorabilia (furniture, clothes, transport such as palanquins, and arms); coins from the time of the first Sultan (Mohamad Imaadudin) in 1620, up to recent and contemporary items such as 2 motorbikes hit by bullets during the Nov 1988 coup attempt.

Parks

Sultan Park The space occupied by the Sultan's Palace complex which was demolished when the Maldives became a Republic for the 2nd time in 1968 was declared a public park; the huge iron gate at the main entrance has been retained. The only surviving building houses the National Museum.

Local information

Accommodation

All the accommodation on Male is simple, the most expensive charging about US$100 per rm in high season. It is the only island on which it is possible to stay quite cheaply, but it is not a place for a long visit. There are no beaches (it is now almost completely built up), and it is easily possible to see the sights of interest in a day. Some hotels have a/c rooms but there are also guest house rooms with fan and attached shower, and inexpensive rooms in private homes which usually do not provide meals. Several are 'Govt Registered', charging between US$15-30 per night. Most are small (less than 10 rooms), with a very limited range of services, but those listed here are clean and good value.

Sosunge, Sosun Magu, few blocks from Marine Drive, T 323025, 4 rm, former government guest house, now the most expensive small hotel in town, fresh water. ***Nasandhura Palace***, Marine Drive, E end, T 323380, F 320822, 31 rm, some a/c with bath, phone and TV, restaurant, bar, fresh water. ***Alia***, 32 Marine Drive, Haveeree Higun W end, T 322080, F 322197, 18 rm, some a/c with bath, restaurant, bar, fresh water.

Guest houses

With attached baths. ***Nivikoa***, Chandanee Magu, T 322942, 7 rm, rec. ***Mermaid Inn***, Marine Drive, W end, T 323329. ***Sony***, Janavaree Magu, T 323249, 6 rm. ***Araarootuge***, Madhoshi Goalhi, T 322661, bed and breakfast. ***Gadhoo***, Marine Drive, E end, T 323222, 3 rm, bed and breakfast. ***Maagri, Big Coral*** Guest House, Marine Drive, T 322576, small and friendly.

The following are conveniently situated fairly close to the shops, sights and restaurants. Ask around for private rooms (some under US$10) in the Tel office area. One opp crossing with small red plate (US$25), others around Kosheege (US$15). ***Male Tour Inn***, T 326220. ***Sakeena Manzil***, Meduziyaraiy Magu, T 323281, dining hall, but crowded rm, you may be woken early by the call to prayer from nearby mosque. ***Greenlin***, T 322279. ***Andaapoolge***, T 322173. ***Thaalin***, T 324036. ***Kosheege***, T 323585. ***Ever Pink***, T 324751. ***Maafaru***, T 322220. ***Kaimoo Stop Over Inn***, T 323241. ***Dheraha***, T 323018.

Places to eat

Most are on Majeedee Magu, and menus are limited. ***Downtown*** is very popular. ***Quench***, across the road has tables outside or under a thatch, Indian, continental and American fast food style menu. ***Eagle Restaurant*** is close to the *Male Tour Inn* with a specialist ***Indian Restaurant***. ***Gelato Italiano*** for coffee, ice creams and soft drinks is more upmarket than other cafes. The ***Canteen*** is opp the Indoor Sports Centre. ***New Pot*** on Marine Drive is rec.

Cafés: the cafés open early and close late. A plate of savoury and sweet snacks are put on the table to have with a drink of tea or sweetened milk. ***Seagull Café House***, Majeedee Uafa and ***Junction Hotel*** are at the crossing of Chandanee Magu and Faridee Magu nr the Museum.

Soft drinks: there are shops clustered just behind Marine Drive where the boats from the airport and other islands berth. Soft drinks are twice as expensive immediately around the jettys as they are in the small local stores just a little further inland.

Bars

Tourist hotels serve a full range of alcoholic drinks.

Airline offices

Scheduled: **Air Lanka**, Ameer Ahmed Magu, T 323459. **Air Maldives**, Maldives Air Services Ltd, Marine Drive, T 322436. **Alitalia**, c/o Air Maldives, T 322436. **Emirates Air**, Marine Drive, T 325675. **Indian Airlines**, Sifaa, Marine Drive, T 323003. **Pakistan International**, 4 Luxwood, 1 Marine Drive, T 323532. **Royal Nepal Airlines**, c/o Air Maldives, Marine Drive, T 322436. **Singapore Airlines**, 2nd Flat, MHA Bldg, T 320777.

Charter: **Balkan**, **Tarom**, **ZAS**, Maldives Air Services Ltd, Marine Drive, T 322436. **Lauda Air**, c/o Fantasy Travels, Faridee Magu, T 324668. **LTU/LTS**, c/o Faihu Agency, H Maaleythila, T 323202.

From Dusseldorf, Frankfurt, Munich: **Condor**, c/o Universal Travel Dept., 18 Marine Drive, T 323116. **Air 2000**, **Air Europe**, **Belair**, **Sterling Airways**, c/o Voyages Maldives, 2 Faridee Magu, T 323617.

Banks & money changers

Open 0900-1300, Sun-Th. They are the only authorised money changers. **Bank of Ceylon**, Alia Building, Gr Fl, Orchid Magu. **Bank of Credit and Commerce** and **Habib Bank** on

Chandanee Magu. **Bank of Maldives, Maldives Monetary Authority** and **State Bank of India** on Marine Drive.

● Chambers of Commerce

Ministry of Trade and Industries, F/1 Ghazee Building, Ameeru Ahmed Magu, T 323668.

● Entertainment

See under '**Island Resorts**' below.

● Foreign representations

Most European countries have their embassy and consular staff based in Sri Lanka. Their telephone numbers are given in the Sri Lanka section (see page 1329). In an emergency they should be contacted by telephone, which can be done readily from Male and from some other islands.

High Commissions: **India**, Maafannu Aage, T 323716, F 324778. **Pakistan**, 2 Moonimaage, T 323005, F 321823. **Sri Lanka**, Sakeena Manzil, T 323338, F 321652.

Honorary Consuls & others: **Bangladesh**, c/o Universal Enterprises, T 323080. **France**, 27 Chandanee Magu, T 324132, F 322516. **Denmark, Norway, Sweden**, 25 Marine Drive, T 3222451, F 323523. **UK**, c/o Dhiraagu Pvt Ltd, PO Box 2082, T 322802, F 325704. **USA**, Mandhu-edhuruge, Violet-Magu, T 321981.

● Hospitals & medical services

Central Hospital, Sosun Magu, Henveira, T 322400. New *Indira Gandhi Hospital*. *Flying Swiss Ambulance Clinic*, Huvadhoo, Marine Drive, T 324508. Emergency T 324500 (24 hr). A small private health clinic service having own speedboat to reach outlying islands with European medical staff. To insure in advance, contact Head Office, Postfach 259, FL-9495, Triesen, Switzerland. The Inter-Atoll Flying Boat Service helps to transport emergency cases.

● Libraries

The Library is on Majeedee Magu, open daily, 0900-1200, 1400-1700, closed Fri. The private library on Amir Ahmed Magu, belonging to the Didi family which has some good reference books and books about the islands, open daily 1400-2200, 1730-2000 during Ramazan, monthly subscription and deposit.

● Post & telecommunications

The **Post Office** (with poste restante) is at the corner of Marine Drive and Chandanee Magu, open 0730-1330, 1600-1750 (though often closed 1245-1330), closed Fri.

● Shopping

Open daily except Fri, 0800-2300. The shopping streets are 5 mins' walk from the wharf. It is best to browse before buying and ignore the advice of local 'guides'. The duty free shopping complex is in ***Umar Shopping Arcade***, Chandanee Magu which stock electrical goods, watches and cosmetics etc. The Airport ***Duty free*** shop is small but well stocked and competitively priced. **NB** Take your passport with you. ***Lemon Souvenir Shop***, Chandanee Magu, sells jewellery made from tortoise shell, mother of pearl, and red and black coral, colourful T-shirts and books and postcards. The ***Crafts Market*** is worth visiting. ***Asrafee***, Orchid Magu, ***Cyprea*** and ***Novelty Bookshop***, Faridee Magu, sell books and postcards.

Photography: *Fototeknik*, *Fotogenic* and *Centofoto* are on Majeedee Magu.

● Sports

See under '**Island Resorts**' below.

● Tour operators & travel agents

A selection of internal travel, cruises and accommodation on the islands: ***Cyprea***, 25 Marine Drive, T 322451, F 323523. ***Galena Maldives***, Orchid Magu, T 324743, F 324465. ***Sun Travel and Tours***, Manaage, Machchangolhi, Maaveyo Magu, T 325975, F 320419, they offer resort holidays and 'Diving and Cruising safaris' which usually stop at an island for the night. ***Treasure Island Enterprise***, agents for American Express, 8 Marine Drive, PO Box 2009, T 322165, F 322798, they organise diving holidays on 3 resorts with special diving bases (Full Moon Island, Maayafushi and Bathala) and other island holidays. ***Voyages Maldives***, PO Box 2019, 2 Faridee Magu, T 323019, F 325336, they offer special 'Divers' Dream' min 8 days, 'Sailing Safaris' min 8 days, 'Adventure Sailing' or simply a beach holiday. ***ZSS Hotels and Travel Service***, 5, Fiyaathoshi Goalhi, Henveiru, also offer similar special packages.

● Tourist office & information

Ministry of Tourism, F/2 Ghazee Building, Ameeru Ahmed Magu, T 323224. **Information Unit** at the airport. **Dept of Information & Broadcasting**, F/3 Huravee Bldg, Ameeru Ahmed Magu, T 323836, F 326211.

● Transport

Local The usual mode of transport on Male is **bicycles**. However, all sightseeing and shopping areas are within walking distance and although taxis are available, you are not likely to need one except perhaps when you arrive and leave Male. **Taxis**: can be contacted by phone; it is best to agree the fare in advance – Rf 15-20. *Dialcab*, T 323132, and others.

ISLAND RESORTS

The resort islands are scattered around 5 atolls – North and South Male (**Kaafu atoll**) where only 9 out of the 81 islands are inhabited, **Ari** or Alif atoll where 18 of the 76 islands are inhabited. There is one resort on Lhaviyani, 2 on Vaavu Atoll and one on Gan. Travel agents and tour operators offer packages to the Maldives either flying direct to the islands for 2-4 weeks or as an extension to a holiday in India or Sri Lanka. You can choose to visit 2 or more islands.

Resort categories & transfer from airport

Resorts offer comfortable to fairly simple rooms, mostly a/c with attached bathrooms with hot and cold freshwater or desalinated water to showers (occasionally bath tubs). The resorts listed below offer a good selection of water sports and prices often include full board; some charge luxury hotel prices but naturally do not offer city hotel facilities; are still good value. The price category is based on high-season rates which apply from Nov-Apr and are nearly double that in May-Oct. A few charge more in Aug; there is an extra 15% surcharge over Christmas and New Year.

The hotel categories are based on the price in US$ per person per day sharing a double room on an island (this often includes half or full board). **AL** US$150 and over. **A** US$100-150; **B** US$70-100; **C** US$40-70; **D** up to US$40.

The transfer cost (payable in US$) is for return travel between the airport and the resort either by local boat, occasionally speed boat or seaplane or helicopter for the distant resorts. Travel between islands can be fairly expensive. Most travellers with pre-booked holidays are met by a resort representative at the airport. Others may phone resort to enquire about transfer arrangements.

Resorts on Ari Atoll and others a long way away are not possible to reach in the dark (after about 1830). Late arrivals have to spend a night in Male since the boat ride takes 3-4 hrs. Those catching early morning flights out of the Maldives similarly must arrive in Male the night before. There are no inter-island flight at night.

Entertainment & Sports

Entertainment

Some resorts have live bands and/or discos, beach barbecues and 'local' dances. It is government policy to keep tourists apart from the local population as far as reasonably possible. This means that all the holiday islands are separate from the settled islands, and there are no authentic indigenous cultural activities or entertainments accessible to outsiders.

Sports

Scuba diving, snorkelling, fishing, windsurfing, waterskiing, parasailing are all available on various islands.

Diving can be enjoyed by the beginner and the experienced in the ideal underwater reefs off the islands; wrecks are found near some islands. Expert instruction is available in many resorts; diving school prices vary. All equipment is available including cameras in some resorts; bring your own torch and batteries if you are planning to go out at night and your log book if you have dived before. Scuba diving is safe provided you make sure you have taken professional advice and have all the necessary equipment. **NB** Scuba diving is not covered by most holiday insurance policies so extra cover should be taken out.

The big fish, eg tunas, sharks, barracudas, bonitos and a rich variety of coral fish can be seen from all islands. Manta rays are around in the low season when there is more plankton in the river. Catches of groupers and red snappers when you go fishing are fairly common. Other sports incl tennis, football and volleyball.

Dhoni Safaris A few wooden sailing boats have been refurbished and fitted with diesel engines. Others are purpose built 12 to 15m long 'Dhoni Yachts' with lateen rig, diesel engines and radio. They can take groups of 8 with a crew of 3 or 4 on trips around the islands. The sleeping accommodation for the tourists is separate but very basic, usually on bunk in saloons. Meals are provided and windsurfing, snorkelling and diving equipment is usually taken. Contact Male Travel Agents.

Maldive Travel, 3 Esher House, 11 Edith Terrace, London SW10 0TH, T 352 2246, F 351 3382, the only specialist company in the UK, offers 'Magic' tours on a new traditionally built '80ft' Dhoni boat. Twin cabins with shower and WC Comfortable, freedom to choose your pace and destination, all safety precautions. Support boat for diving gear, compressor and to take you ashore. The whole boat for 12 must be chartered for weekly periods.

Resorts

AL *Nika Hotel* (Kuda Folliudhoo), T 450516, F 450577. North end of Ari atoll, is 70 km and 2½ hr by speed boat (US$250) or 35 min by helicopter, from the airport; helicopter pad is 10 min boat ride away (late arrivals have to spend a night in a private apartment in Male). It is one of the most exclusive resorts in the Maldives.

26 very spacious fan-cooled thatched bungalows of unusual design, built partly out of coral and wood. Each has a solarium and showers with hot/cold fresh water in private garden, practically private beach. Italian, other continental and eastern dishes, with barbecue and a Maldivian supper twice a week. Very well equipped diving school and all other water sports, and volleyball, badminton and tennis. Strong Italian character. Male, 10 Faridi Magu, T 325087, F 325097. In Italy, contact Nika Hotel, 5 Via Albricci, 20122, Milan, Italy, T 02/8077983.

AL *Cocoa Island* or Makunufushi on the E side of the South Male atoll is 30 km from the airport (US$200 by sea), T 343713, F 441919. Expensive, with eye-catching design, the 8 cottages are built of striking white coral with high thatched roofs lined with palm leaves. Raised sleeping area is up some stairs. Restaurant and bar have a good reputation. **NB** No hot or fresh water. Windsurfing, diving, catamaran, fishing and waterskiing. Male T/F 322326.

A *Rhiveli Beach Resort* (Mahaana Elhi Huraa) is on the S side of the South Male atoll about 40 km from Male (US$135), T/F 443731. 46 rm. A silver sand resort with Island of Birds and Rising Sun Island within easy reach. French owned with particularly good restaurant and bar. Watersports includes windsurfing, sailing, waterskiing and tennis. Package incl 2-day cruise around nearby islands. Male T 323767, F 322964.

A *Kuda Rah Island Resort* SouthEast of Ari atoll, 84 km from the airport, 30 min helicopter transfer (helipads on nearby islands), 10 by dhoni boat (US$50) or speedboat; dep by seaplane (20 min) optional, T 450549, F 450550. A small uncrowded island with plenty of vegetation, a virgin reef and ample white sand. '30 spacious a/c bungalows and 5 water-bungalows with steps down to the sea, bath tubs, hot/cold freshwater, private garden. Imaginative cuisine, boutique, disco, doctor and infirmary. Snorkelling, windsurfing, day/night fishing, canoeing, sailing, PADI diving (all equipment incl in price). Male T 325847, 322335.

A *Kurumba Village* (Vihamana Fushi) Maldive's first resort island on North Male atoll, recently modernised. Small island only 3 km from airport, 20 min transfer by boat (US$12), T 443, F 443885. 169 comfortable rooms in single/double storey bungalows or deluxe cottages, set apart from the main reception area. All have a/c and hot/cold fresh water to bathrooms. Four restaurants, regular entertainment, pools and tennis. Full range of water sports. About US$25 for single dives. Not as idyllic as far-off islands since you can see Male. Conference centre and modern business facilities. Male, Universal Enterprises, T 322971, F 322678.

A *Vabinfaru Paradise Island* 17 km NW of the airport in the North Male atoll is about 1½ hr by boat (US$50), T 443147, F 443843. Small French run resort with 31 thatched rondavels. Good food and a variety of water sports (some free). Popular with Australians and Italians.

A ***Bandos Island Resort*** South of the North Male atoll, 9 km from the airport; transfer 45 min by local boat or 15 min by speed launch (US$40), T 443310, F 443877. One of the larger tourist islands from which you can cross to uninhabited and attractive Kuda Bandos nearby but do not swim across as currents are strong. 203 comfortable rooms recently upgraded, half a/c, with terraces and unheated spring water showers. A/c restaurant, bar, 24-hr open-air coffee shop and aquarium. Swimming pool and sports complex (squash, gym, sauna). Excellent watersports and diving school, large decompression chamber, new medical centre. Good for families (babysitting). Male, Dhirham Travels, T 323369, F 324752.

A ***Laguna Beach Resort*** previously Velassaru is on the N tip of the South Male atoll, only 10 km from the airport (US$40), 30 min transfer, T/F 343041. 100 comfortable a/c rm, some in individual bungalows, phones, fresh water for bath. Italian and Chinese restaurants, disco, pool, gym, tennis, beach barbecue. All facilities incl diving school, windsurfing, parasailing and night fishing. Elegant resort with good diving. Male, Universal Enterprise, T 322971, F 322678.

B ***Vadoo Diving Paradise*** Eight km from the airport in the South Male atoll is about 15 min by speed boat (US$30), T 443976, F 443397. Small island straddling Vaadhoo channel with 24 a/c rm in a 'colonial' style villa and 7 'Sunset Wing' floating cottages with illuminated glass-top table for viewing and feeding the tropical fish! Attractive Hut Bar over the water; snorkelling, glass-bottomed boat, night fishing and good diving. Male T 325844.

B ***Veligandhu Huraa*** 50 km from the airport in the South Male atoll is about 1¼ hr by speed boat (US$80), T/F 450519. 63 rm, incl 16 deluxe bungalows, bath tubs, hot freshwater. Restaurants incl Thai, bar, outdoor buffets. Most watersports available. A sophisticated island with a bar (classical music) on the walkway to Digufinolhu island nearby, which has a livelier clientele and occasional disco! A small deserted island between the two. Male T 322432, F 324009.

B ***Digufinolhu Tourist Resort*** (US$50), T 443599, F 443886. 50 a/c semi-detached bungalows and 10 new a/c 2-storey sea-facing units with patio. Hot/cold reshwater showers/bath tubs, coffee shop, beach BBQ, small shop. Dive School (PADI), good windsurfing, sailing, day/night fishing. Friendly, family island. Male T/F 327058.

B ***Biyadoo Island Resort*** 29 km from the airport in the South Male atoll, close to Cocoa Island, transfer by boat (US$35), T 447171, F 447272. 96 comfortable a/c rooms on 2 storeys with hot freshwater showers and patio/balcony. A/c restaurant and bar, weekly barbecue, disco, local and Indian folk evenings. Virtually every kind of water sport including parasailing; night fishing catches can be barbecue. 'Nautico' watersports centre, PADI diving and decompression chamber. Two housereefs for shore diving with 5 passages each on this and Villivaru. Speedboats and dhonis available for trip to Male or helipad for helicopter 'flips'. Male T 324699, F 327014.

B ***Villivaru Island Resort***, nr Biyadoo, 29 km from Male (US$35), T 447070, F 343742. Smaller than Biyadoo with landscaped gardens. 60 a/c rooms with hot/cold freshwater showers (all water is desalinated), private patios open on to beach. A/c restaurant and bar. Snorkelling and diving. The coral reef harbouring a large variety of fish is approximately 30m offshore and excellent for experienced divers (PADI). Daily ferry service to Biyadoo. Male T 324699, F 327014.

B ***Nakatchafushi*** is on the W side of the North Male atoll, 24 km from the airport and about 1½ hr boat ride (US$50), T 443847, F 442665. This pretty island has Maldivian character. 52 secluded, simply furnished a/c 'rondavels', some with thatch, with fresh water for baths. Small open-air Chinese restaurant, good coffee shop, pleasant terrace bar over water, dance floor for parties. All kinds of water sports. German diving school. Ideal for honeymooners. Male T 322971, F 322678.

B ***Farukolufushi*** in the North Male atoll, just N of the airport so a quick transfer but on the flight path, T 343021. French run, typical Club Med resort which is one of the largest – guests must stay minimum of a week. No a/c rm. No day-trippers allowed. The large thatched restaurant serves good food. Usual water sports but no water skiing.

B ***Bathala Island Resort*** is a small island on the NE edge of the Ari atoll about 85 km and under 3 hr by boat from the airport (US$150), T 450587, F 450558. The island is completely encircled by the reef, the inner reef being only

30m from the waters' edge. 37 round bungalows have pointed palm thatch roofs, some deluxe with a/c. Simply furnished with hard water outdoor showers in private walled gardens. Restaurant (fish caught daily) and bar are open-sided. Watersports include catamaran, waterskiing and windsurfing (currents can be strong), expert diving instruction. A 'Treasure Island Enterprise' informal resort popular with the young. Male T 323323, F 324628.

B ***Baros Holiday Resort*** Oval shaped, small island 16 km from the airport on the North Male atoll, 1 hr by boat (US$40), T 442672, F 443497. 56 upgraded a/c rm wiith verandah and 12 new luxury water-bungalows with steps down to lagoon, all with freshwater showers. One of the oldest, popular with British tourists. Restaurant, bar, new beach coffee shop and barbecue area, small gift shop and dive shop. Good housereef – the coral and fish make diving and snorkelling particularly interesting for beginners, while windsurfing on the lagoon and waterskiing are also excellent. Ideal for families, friendly. Male, Universal Enterprises, T 322971, F 322678.

B ***Full Moon Island*** (Furana) Just N of Male, nr the airport and reached in 20 min (US$40), T 443878, F 443879. Larger island – 1½ hr to walk around, with banyan trees and plenty of birds. White sandy beaches with a large lagoon. You can visit nearby fishing village or deserted islands. 65 rm on stilts plus 92 rm in blocks of 4, all sea facing. Desalinated water. Restaurants, barbecue terrace deck extending onto sea open at night, disco, piano bar and coffee shop. Freshwater pool, business centre, shop, gym, tennis, diving school (located on the E outer reef, diving waters are 15 min away). The large lagoon offers plenty of scope for windsurfing, sailing and waterskiing. It is one of the few with a big game Fishing Club; night fishing excursions possible. Male, Universal Enterprise, opened in June 1993, T 322971, F 322678.

B ***Kanifinolhu Resort*** On the E edge of the North Male atoll, 16 km from the airport, transfer 30 min by speedboat (US$30), T 443152, F 444859. A ¾ km semicircular island with a sheltered lagoon. 106 rooms in semi-detached bungalows, from non-a/c to comfortable luxury a/c suites with verandahs. New deluxe rm, double storied, furnished to high standard. All on the beach side, with fresh water to showers. Restaurant (with à la carte), bar, coffee shop, gift shop. Weekly disco and occasional live band. Most kinds of watersports incl good diving, good snorkelling to the S, also tennis. Lively – popular with under 35s. Also suitable for families with children. Male, Cyprea, T 322451, F 323523.

B ***Rangali Tourist Village*** On the South Ari atoll is 104 km away from the airport, 2½ hr transfer by boat (US$100) or 35 min by helicopter, T 450629, F 450619. Fairly new, 41 a/c bungalows with verandas to beach. Most watersports, pool, diving, tennis, bathrom with freshwater. Male, T 324701, F 324009.

B-C ***Kuramathi Tourist Island*** Rashdu Atoll, on the N fringe of the Ari atoll 60 km W of Male, transfer time about 2 hr by speed boat (US$100), ½ hr by helicopter, T 450527, F 450556. One of the larger islands, attractive for diving and snorkelling. The N tip is occupied by the **B** ***Blue Lagoon Club*** with its own private pier. 50 comfortable units with hot/cold desalinated water. The 20 thatched cottages on the E side, built on stilts, are reached by walkways; private terrace with steps down to water. The Lagoon restaurant (with à la carte) and terrace bar. At low tide it is possible to walk a long distance out beyond the N tip – take care not to get stranded! The **C** ***Kuramathi Village*** in the SE corner of the island is less expensive. 122 a/c units, some thatched round houses. Restaurant, bar and coffee shop are all open-sided. Live entertainment weekly and discos on other evenings. The **C** ***Cottage Club*** is the 3rd centre. Water sports include snorkelling, diving (with a dive shop) and windsurfing school and day/night fishing. You may see hammerhead sharks nearby. Also tennis and archery. Male, Universal Enterprise, T 322971, F 322678.

C ***Fun Island Resort***, (Bodu Finolhu) is on the E reef of the South Male atoll, 40 km from the airport, about 3 hr by boat (US$70), T 444558, F 443958. A very small island which may feel a little overcrowded but has a shallow lagoon making it possible to walk across to 2 tiny neighbouring uninhabited islands at low tide. 100 comfortable rooms in blocks of 2/3/4, all a/c, with verandah, and baths with hot/cold desalinated water. Comfortable open-sided restaurant, bar and coffee shop with an attractive terrace overhanging the lagoon. Disco and weekly cultural shows ('boduberu') in season, recreation complex, new photo lab and clinic. Diving, windsurfing, snorkelling, fishing and waterskiing. Male T 324478, F 327845.

C ***Maayafushi Tourist Resort*** On NE fringe

of the Ari atoll 65 km W of Male, 4 hr transfer (US$100), T 450588, F 450568. 60 small thatched units in rows with terraces with showers. Restaurant serving hot/cold buffets and bar. Expert diving instruction (the house reef is only 70m away); boats to farther reefs twice daily. For non-divers there is a large lagoon for snorkelling, windsurfing, water skiing, parasailing and sailing. Visits to other islands possible. A 'Treasure Island Enterprise' resort popular with under 35s. Male T 320097, F 326658.

C ***Lhohifushi Tourist Resort*** is a smaller quieter island with pretty, lush vegetation, to the N of Kanifinolhu, 18 km from Hulule. Transfer time, 1½ hr (US$30), T 441909, F 441908. The resort is unsophisticated and has attempted to retain Maldivian character in its buildings. 105, some a/c simply furnished rooms with small verandahs have island water to showers. Open-sided restaurant and bar/lounge, open-air coffee shop with balcony overhanging the sea. Water sports are limited to diving, windsurfing and sailing. Male T 323378, F 324783.

C ***Hudhuveli Beach Resort*** is a very small island on the North Male atoll 10 km from the airport, about 45 min by Dhoni (US$30), T 443396, F 443849. 44 units, some rondavels and some terraced bungalows, all thatched and painted white. Restaurant (fresh fish daily), bar and open-air coffee shop. The island claims to be the cleanest in the Maldives, with the best water in the whole atoll and no mosquitos! Diving (either in the inner coral reef or in the outer reef close to larger fish), snorkelling, windsurfing, fishing and waterskiing. Also volleyball, badminton and table tennis. Male T 322844, F 321026.

C ***Ocean Reef Club*** has opened on Gan; the transfer by air costs US$160. Offers snorkelling, diving, tennis. Phoenix Hotels and Resorts in Male will book rooms, T 323181, F 325499

D ***Meerufenfushi Island Resort*** or 'sweet water island' is to the E of the North Male atoll, T 443157, F 445946. It is 40 km from the airport, about 2½ hr by boat (US$50). Rec for sight-seeing – a roundtrip from Male costs about US$45. One of the larger island resorts (28 ha) with a large lagoon – pleasant and green with coral sand on beach and only islands on the horizon. Takes ½ hr to walk round. You can swim to Fishman Island 100m away (take towel and shirt). Rec as best in the lower-price group, popular with British tour groups.

164 non-a/c simply furnished rooms in single storey bungalows close to the beach with unheated island water showers. Restaurant, open-sided bar, gift shop. Price incl half-board. Midday coffee shop meal US$6, good value. Diving, expensive compared to some others (eg US$50 for single, certification US$500), windsurfing, snorkelling, night fishing, volleyball and table tennis. Sailboarding popular on the lagoon. Friendly service. Popular with German and Swedish groups. Male T 324910, F 324711.

D ***Eriyadu Island Resort*** is 29 km NW of Male and 3 hr by local boat (US$50), T 444487, F 445925. One of the cheaper resort islands, quite informal, with 46 sea-facing rooms (some family rm for 4), in simple, whitewashed bungalows with fans and fresh water. Restaurant and bar. Wide stretch of beach, shaded, pretty lagoon and good housereef. Diving (Swiss sub-aqua), snorkelling, windsurfing, day/night fishing and volleyball. Male T 326483, F 326482.

D ***Helengeli Tourist Village*** in the far N of the North Male atoll, is about 50 km from the airport (US$68), T/F 444615. Small resort, 30 rm with salt water showers. Limited water sports; good coral reef so convenient for snorkelling and unlimited diving (reasonable charges). Male T 325587, F 325625.

INFORMATION FOR VISITORS

Contents

Before you go

Entry requirements

● Visas

All tourists holding a full passport are given 30 days permit to enter the Maldives free of charge (no photo required) byt Israeli Passport holders are NOT allowed to visit the Maldives. Indians, Pakistanis, Bangladeshis and Italians are given staying permits for 30 days on arrival. The stay can be extended for a nominal fee. An international certificate of innoculation against yellow fever is required if coming from or through an infected country. Tourists must carry US$25 minimum per day of stay except those travelling with a tour company or coming on recruitment to an Agency.

● Representations overseas

Honorary Consuls & trade representatives

Austria: G Wiedler, 1190 Wien, Weimarerstrasse 104, T 345273, F 043222. **Belgium**: FE Drion, rue de Vignes 16, 1020 Brussels, T 4781426, F 4785682. **Egypt**: Md AAA Daem, 16 Ahmed Omar Rd, 4th Flr, Flat 7, El-Helmeya-El Adida, Cairo, T 391052, F 94062. **France**: Dr JP Laboureau, Zone Artisanale, 5 rue de Lafontaine, 21560 Arc sur Tille, T 80372660, F 80372661. **Germany**: G Muecke, Immanuel Kant Str Be 16, D-6380 Bad Homburg, T 69066789, F 69692102. **Hong Kong**: BN Harelela, 201-5 Kowloon Centre, 29-39 Ashley Rd, Kowloon, T 3762114, F 37662366. **India**: AS Nathani, 202 Sethi Bhavan, 7 Rajendra Place, North Delhi 110000, T 5718590, F 5725991 and Nathan Rd, Vidyavihar, Bombay 400086, T 22515111, F 225146311. **Italy**: M. Giacoma, via Calderini 68/D, INT 800196, Rome, T 519115., F 534115. **Japan**: H Shimuzu, Chiyoda Bldg 1-2, 2 Chome, Marunochi, Chiyodaku, Tokyo, T 32115463, F 32116921. **Pakistan**: AS Tapal, PO Box 51, Karachi T 737945, F 737817. **Saudi Arabia**: HE Sh Md Saleh Bahareth, PO Box 404, Jeddah 21411, T 6423666. **Singapore**: Trade Representative, 10 Anson Rd, 18-12 International Plaza, Singapore 0207, T 225 8955, F 224 6050. **Switzerland**: MA Odermatt, Gerechtigkeitsgasse 23 8002 Zurich, T 2028448, F 2027505. **UK**: Trade Representative, Unit 9, Printing House Yard, 15A Hackney Rd, London E2 7PR, T 081 729571, 081 7291374.

● Tour operators & travel agents

UK: *Maldive Travel*, 3 Esher House, 11 Edith Terrace, London SW10 0TH, T 071 352 2246, F 071 351 3382. This is the only specialist company for the Maldives.

● Tourism representatives

Japan: Mr T. Asakura, 3-32-13 Horikiri, Katsushika-ku, Tokyo 124, T 6924455, F 6913785. **Norway**: H Hussain Afeef, Stubbratan 20, 1352 Kolsas, T 02137221. **Sweden**: S Ericsson, Heimdalsvagen 5 A, S-756 52 Uppsala. **UK**: Toni de Laroque – The Maldive Lady, 3 Esher House, 11 Edith Terrace, London SW10 0TH, T 071 352 2246, F 071 351 3382.

Health

Health care is far from comprehensive in the Maldives and facilities are basic. Maldivians themselves have to go abroad for any specialist treatment. Come prepared with reasonable precautions. Know your blood group and be properly insured, as good health care is not cheap. Take a high protection factor suntan lotion, wear a straw hat and a T-shirt for the first few days to avoid over-exposure. Avoid sunburn when snorkelling.

Money

● Currency
The unit of currency is the Ruffiyaa divided into 100 Laari. Notes are in denominations of 100, 50, 20, 10, 5 and 2 Rufiyaa. Coins are in denominations of 1 Rufiya, 50, 20, 10 and 5 Laari.

● Money changing
The law requires all transactions to be conducted in Maldivian currency. Most banks, shops and tourist resorts will convert foreign currency, American dollars being the commonest.

● Travellers' cheques & credit cards
Hotels are authorised to accept foreign currency and travellers' cheques; US$ TCs are preferred. Among credit cards, most common are American Express, Visa, Master Card, Diners and Euro Card. Some shops accept travellers' cheques or foreign currency, and give change in dollars.

● Unauthorised dealing
Do not convert your currency with an unauthorised dealer. Keep your exchange receipts as you may need them when you re-convert any Maldivian currency when you depart. There is no restriction on the amount of foreign currency that visitors may bring in or take out.

Getting there

● Air
Most tourists arrive by air at Male International Airport on Hulule Island. The airport departure tax is US$10.

From India **Indian Airlines** operate 5 flights a week from **Trivandrum** (M,Tu,Th,F,Sa), but they are extremely heavily booked. Dep Triv, 1430; Dep Male, 1610 (40 min), Fare US$62. It is often necessary to make a reservation 4 weeks in advance to obtain an OK ticket. Waiting lists are long, but it is sometimes possible to fly even if well down the waiting list. The only travel agent who has direct links with the Maldives in Trivandrum is ***Aries Travels***, Ayswarya Building, Press Rd, Trivandrum 695001, T 65417.

From Sri Lanka **Air Lanka** at least 1 flight daily *from Colombo* to Male.

From UK *From London*: **Air Lanka** via Colombo. **Br Caledonian** (charter) operated by Kuoni. Gatwick/Heathrow via Dubai. **Singapore Airlines** from Heathrow.

From Asia & Africa *From Colombo*: **Air Lanka**. *From Dubai*: **Emirates Airlines**. *From Karachi*: **Pakistan International**. *From Kathmandu*: **Royal Nepal Airlines**.

From Europe Scheduled Airlines: *From Rome*: **Alitalia**. *From Amsterdam, Brussels, Paris, Singapore, Vienna, Zurich*: **Singapore Airlines**.

Charter Airlines: *From Dusseldorf, Munich*: **LTU/LTS**. *From Dusseldorf, Frankfurt, Munich*: **Condor**. *From Vienna*: **Lauda Air** and **Austrian Airlines**. *From Copenhagen, Stockholm, Helsinki, Greece*: **Sterling Airways**. *From Milan, Zurich:* **Balair**.

● Sea
It is very unusual for foreign tourists to arrive by sea but if you are in Colombo in Sri Lanka or in Tuticorin in Tamil Nadu, India, you may wish to enquire from Shipping agents whether they will allow passengers on their cargo boats.

● Customs regulations
NB **Prohibited items**: Any alcohol carried by passengers will be kept at the airport (resorts are well-stocked). It can be reclaimed on departure. You are also not allowed to bring in drugs, pork products, pornographic magazines (incl Playboy) or videos. Landing cards have to be completed on board the plane before arrival, and it is necessary to state where you will be staying. **Other restrictions**: Nudity is banned. You may not pick up shells or coral and spear fishing is prohibited.

When you arrive

The **airport** on Hulule island is 15 min boat ride to the N of Male. There is a **bank** at the airport; it is worth changing money immediately, as banks on Male are only open in the mornings. A **travel agent** is available at the airport on arrival. A boat jetty lies directly outside the airport exit and help is available to carry bags if required. The boat fare to Male from the airport is US$5, and taxi fares on Male are up to US$3. Fares to other islands depend on distance. See map for details.

● Clothing
Light cottons are best. Nudity is forbidden and tourists visiting inhabited islands should be clothed modestly. The Dept of Tourism advises "Minimum dress – Men: T-shirts and shorts,

but jeans or long trousers are preferable. Women: T-shirts, blouses or shirts and skirts or adequate shorts which cover the thighs, made of non-seethrough or diaphanous material; a piece of cloth simply wrapped around the torso is not acceptable or indeed permitted". Sun hat and beach shoes are essential. Bring all toiletry requirements; plenty of shampoo to counteract hard water!

● Hours of business

Most offices are open from Sat to Th, although banks are also open on Sun. Banks: 0900-1300; Government offices: 0730-1330; Shops are open daily 0600-2300, some remaining closed on Fri morning. During the day shops and restaurants close their doors for 15 min a few times a day when there are calls to prayer. If you are in a café or restaurant, you are not expected to leave but can carry on eating.

● Official time

The Maldives are 5 hrs ahead of GMT.

● Safety

Crime is virtually unknown on the islands.

● Shopping

Opportunities for shopping are extremely limited. Local sea shells and some coral are available, but most other goods for sale have been imported, largely from India, Sri Lanka and Southeast Asia. The range is generally narrow, the quality rather mediocre and the price comparatively high, but it is possible to find attractive items reasonably priced.

● Voltage

Islands generate their own electricity at 240 volts.

● Weights & measures

Metric.

Where to stay

If you do not have accommodation fixed, ask for assistance at the Airport Tourist Information Unit before completing customs formalities.

Hotel and guest house accommodation on Male is limited. During the season book well in advance. Private rooms in Male can cost less than US$5 but are not well advertised, so ask around. The 60 outlying resort islands can cater for about 7500 visitors. They are all small with self-contained communities and it will take you 15-30 mins to walk around each. The accommodation is mainly in bungalow style rooms or in 'rondavels' (round thatched houses) with modern conveniences; attractive 'water-bungalows' with immediate access to the sea are being built. Many offer a/c rooms, and have open-air restaurants and bars and a few have discos and other entertainment. Do not expect a television (though a few offer videos) and telephone in every room and newspapers daily! The islands have beautiful, pollution free beaches and a wealth of water sports; several have diving schools.

The hotel categories are based on the price in US$ per person per day sharing a double room on an island (this often includes half or full board). **AL** US$150 and over. **A** US$100-150; **B** US$70-100; **C** US$40-70; **D** up to US$40. In comfort, facilities and sophistication, however, they don't compare with what is expected in similarly priced hotels in western seaside resorts and you may be surprised by the sand floors in some of the hotels' public areas.

Food & drink

● Food

Local and continental cuisine is available, often heavily dependent on freshly caught fish (*mas*) and a variety of sea food, with occasional buffets and barbecues organised for guests. Unlike some other tropical resorts, the islands produce very little by way of fruit and vegetables, although the coconut (*kurumba*) palm thrives and there are some bananas (*donkeo*), mangoes (*don ambu*), breadfruit (*bambukeyo*) and pawpaws (*falor*). The Maldivians usually eat rice (*bai*), sometimes unleavened bread similar to a *roti* or *chapati* (*roshi*) with a fish dish, curried (*mas riha*), fried (*teluli mas*), smoked (*valo mas*) or as a soup (*garudia*) accompanied by pickles. Meat and chicken are only eaten on special occasions. Drink – Tea, which is invariably with milk and sugar already added (*sa*) and milk (*kiru*) which too is often served sweetened. If you prefer your tea unsweetened ask for *hakuru naala sa* and for black tea *kiri naala sa*.

● Drink

Alcohol is readily available for visitors on tourist islands. You may not import it or offer it to Maldivian nationals. The local toddy *raa*, can be an acquired taste, which is drunk after the juice from the palm has been left to ferment, but freshly tapped is considered delicious by those who don't wish to take alcohol.

NB Water supply can be erratic and different

from what you are accustomed to. 'Island water' is sea water pumped and filtered and remains slightly salty. It is adequate for showers and washing but you will find it quite hard. Some resorts have desalination plants or rain water reservoirs while a few provide fresh water. Most resorts only supply unheated water although this does not create a problem as it is usually luke-warm. During the peak season and dry periods the supply of fresh water and rain water may be restricted.

Getting around

There is no centralised transport between the islands. Local boats (**dhonis**) are the commonest form of transport which average about 13 kmph. *Dhonis* and speedboats are available for hire. Tourist resorts have their own boats and the transfer charges appear above (in US$).

Hummingbird Helicopters, Luxwood 2, Marine Drive, Male, T 325708, offers 'flips' which are 15 min flights from the airport which capture the magic of the local reefs. Away-day excursions take you to distant atolls and include lunch or beach barbecue, diving and snorkelling. Pick-ups offered when a resort has a landing site. Airport-resort transfers are available; contact at airport Main Arrivals behind the Tourist Information desk.

Maldivian Airtaxis (float planes) operate inter-island services by Twin Otter (for 18) and Cesna 208 Caravan (for 9) including island-hopping, excursions and Male shopping. Their airport transfer takes about 20-30 min; boat-transfer time is 3-5 hr for distant resorts. Contact at airport, T 315201, F 315203.

Seagull Helicopters and *Superspeed* (a large hovercraft) also operate between islands.

Air Maldives operates domestic flights to 2 southern and 1 northern atoll.

Communications

● Postal services

Post Offices are open 0745-1245, 1600-1750, Sat-Thurs.

● Telephone services

International telephone, Telefax, Telex and Telegraph services are available 24 hrs. International calls are handled by operator at 190. Phonecards may be bought from post offices. Some shops permit you to use their telephones for a small charge.

Entertainment

● Media

The one Male daily, the 'Haveeru', carries a section in English. Entertainments are also advertised in English. Fortnightly English 'News Bulletin' published locally. Some weekly international news magazines are also available at the Male bookshops. Don't expect daily newspapers in every hotel bedroom.

Holidays & festivals

1 Jan: New Year's Day
5 Feb: Martyr's Day commemorating the death of Sultan Ali VI in 1558
26-27 Jul: Independence Day
29-30 Aug: National Day
3 Nov: Victory Day
11-12: Republic Day commemorating the 2nd Republic, 1968. Huravee Day marks the defeat of the Malabar Indians in 1752.

In addition, Muslim festivals are observed: Beginning of Ramadan, Eid-ul-Fitr, Haj Day, Eid-ul-Adah, Islamic New Year, Prophet Mohammed's Birthday.

Further reading

Anderson, Charles & Hafiz, Ahmad *Common Reef Fishes of the Maldive Islands*, 1987, and **Anderson, RC** *Living reefs of the Maldives*, 1991. Both from Male, Novelty Printers. **Ellis, Kirsten** *Introduction to the Maldives*, Hongkong, The Guidebook Co, 1991. **Dept of Information and Broadcasting** *Maldives, a historical overview*, Male, 1986. **Mohamed Amin** *Introduction to Maldives*. **Webb, Paul A** *Maldives – people and environment*, Bangkok, Media Transasia, 1988. Reynolds, C.H.B, Maldives, a bibliography, Clio Press 1993.

Glossary of architectural terms

A

abacus square or rectangular table resting on top of a pillar (phalaka/ palagai)
Acanthus thick-leaved plant, common decoration on pillars, esp Greek
alinda verandah
amla/amalaka circular ribbed pattern (based on a gourd) at the top of a temple tower
ambulatory processional path
anda lit 'egg,' spherical part of the stupa
antarala vestibule, chamber in front of shrine or cella
antechamber chamber in front of the sanctuary
apsara heavenly nymph figure
apse semi-circular plan, as in apse of a church
arabesque ornamental decoration with intertwining lines
architrave horizontal beam across posts or gateways
ardha mandapam chamber in front of main hall of temple
asana a seat or throne
astanah threshold
atrium court open to the sky in the centre In modern architecture, enclosed in glass

B

bada cubical portion of a temple up to the roof or spire
badgir rooftop structure to channel cool breeze into the house (mainly Pakistan and N and W India)
bagh garden
baluster (balustrade) a small pillar or column supporting a handrail
Bangla (Bangaldar) curved roof, based on thatched roofs in Bengal; imitated in brick temples
baoli or wav rectangular well surrounded by steps; esp in Gujarat and W India
baradari lit 'twelve pillared,' a portico or pavilion with columns
barrel-vault semi-cylindrical shaped roof or ceiling
basement lower part of walls, usually adorned with decorated mouldings
basti Jain temple
bas-relief carving of low projection
batter slope of a wall, esp in a fort
bedi platform for reading the holy books or vedas
beki circular stone below the amla in the finial of a building
belvedere summer house; small room on a house roof
bhadra flat face of the sikhara (tower)
bhavan building or house
bhoga-mandapa the refectory hall of a temple, particularly in Orissa
bhumi 'earth'; refers to a horizontal moulding of a shikhara
bo-tree *Ficus religiosa*, large spreading tree
brahma-kanda column with a rectangular section
burj tower or bastion

C

capital upper part of a column or pilaster
caryatid sculptured human female figure used as a support for columns
cave temple rock-cut shrine or monastery
cella small chamber, compartment for the image of a deity
cenotaph commemorative monument, usually an open domed pavilion
chajja overhanging cornice or eaves
chakra sacred Buddhist wheel of the law; also Vishnu's discus
chala Bengali curved roof
chamfer bevelled surface, obtained by cutting away a corner
chandra moon
chankrama place of the promenade of the Buddha at Bodh Gaya

char bangla (char-chala) four temples in Bengal, built like huts

char bagh formal Mughal garden, divided into quarters

chatta ceremonial umbrella on stupa (Buddhist)

chauki recessed space between pillars: also entrance to a porch

chaultri travellers' rest house; pillared hall adjoining Dravidian temple

chaumukha Jain sanctuary with a quadruple image, approached through four doorways

chauri fly-whisk, symbol for royalty

chhatra honorific umbrella; a pavilion (Buddhist)

chhatri umbrella shaped dome or pavilion. See also cenotaph

chillah khanah room to which Muslim hermits retreat for 40 days

chlorite soft greenish stone that hardens on exposure, permitting intricate carving

chokhang Tibetan Buddhist prayer hall

chowk open space or court yard

chunam lime plaster or stucco made from burnt seashells which can be polished to shine like marble

circum-ambulation clockwise movement around a stupa or shrine while worshipping

clerestory upper section of the walls of a building which allowed light in

cloister passage usually around an open square

corbel horizontal block supporting a vertical structure or covering an opening

cornice horizontal band at the top of a wall

crenellated having battlements

cupola small dome

curvilinear gently curving shape, generally of a tower

cusp, cusped projecting point between small sections of an arch

cutcherry (kutchery) a court; an office where any public business is conducted

D

dado part of a pedestal between its base and cornice; also the lower section of walls

dagoba stupa (Sinhalese)

dais raised platform

dargah a Muslim tomb complex

darwaza gateway, door

daulat khana treasury

dentil small block used as part of a cornice

deul in Bengal and Orissa, generic name for temple; also used to signify the sanctuary only

deval memorial pavilion built to mark royal funeral pyre

devala temple or shrine, (Buddhist or Hindu)

dharmachakra wheel of 'moral' law (Buddhist)

dhvajastam-bham tall pillar in front of temple

dikka raised platform around ablution tank

dikpala guardian of one of the cardinal directions (N,S,E or W)

dipdan lamp pillar

divan (diwan) smoking-room; also a chief minister

diwan-i-am hall of public audience

diwan-i-khas hall of private audience

do-chala rectangular Bengali style roof

double dome composed of an inner and outer shell of masonry

drum circular wall on which the dome rests

dry masonry stones laid without mortar

dvarpala doorkeeper

dvipa lamp-column, generally of stone or brass-covered wood

dzong Tibetan lamasery or monastery

E

eave overhang that shelters a porch or verandah

epigraph carved inscription

F

faience coloured tilework, earthenware or porcelain

fan-light fan-shaped window over door

fenestration	with windows or openings
filigree	ornamental work or delicate tracery
finial	emblem at the summit of a stupa, tower, dome, or at the end of a parapet; generally in the form of a tier of umbrella-like motifs, or a pot
foliation	ornamental design derived from foliage
frieze	horizontal band of figures or decorative designs

G

gable	end of an angled roof
gaddi	throne
gana	child figures in art
gandharvas	celestial musicians of Indra
garbhagriha	Lit 'womb-chamber'; a temple sanctuary
Garuda	vehicle (riding bird) of Vishnu
gedige	ancient Sinhalese architectural style, extremely thick walls and a corbelled roof
ghanta	bell
godown	warehouse
gola	conical-shaped storehouse
gompa	Tibetan Buddhist monastery
gopura	towered gateway in S Indian temples
gudi	temple (Karnataka)
gumbaz	(gumbad) dome
gumpha	monastery, cave temple
gurudwara	(Lit 'entrance to the house of God'); Sikh religious complex, usually with a temple and rest-house

H

hammam	Turkish bath
harem	women's quarters (Muslim), from 'haram', Arabic for 'forbidden by law'
harmika	the finial of a stupa in the form of a pedestal where the shaft of the honorific umbrella was set
hathi pol	elephant gate
haveli	usually a merchant's house in Rajasthan, particularly finely decorated
hawa mahal	palace of the winds
hippogryph	fabulous griffin-like creature with body of a horse
hiti	a water channel; a bath or tank with water spouts
huzra	a Muslim tomb chamber
hypostyle	hall with pillars

I

icon	statue or image of worship in a temple
imambara	tomb of a Shiite Muslim holy man; focus of Muharram procession
iwan	main arch in mosque

J

jaga mohan	audience hall or ante-chamber of an Orissan temple in front of the sanctuary
jagati	railed parapet
jala durga	water fort
jali	lit 'net'; any lattice or perforated pattern
jamb	vertical side slab of doorway
Jami masjid	(Jama, Jumma) Friday mosque, used for congregational worship
jangha	broad band of sculpture on the outside of the temple wall
jarokha	balcony
jawab	lit 'answer,' a building which duplicates another to provide symmetry
jaya stambha	victory tower
jhilmil	projecting canopy over a window or door opening
jorbangla	double hut-like temple in Bengal
Jyotirlinga	Luminous energy of Siva manifested at 12 holy places (including Kedarnath, Prabhas Patan, Srisailam, Ujjain, Varanasi), miraculously formed lingams having special significance

K

kailasa	Siva's heaven
kalasha	pot-like finial of a tower
kalyan mandapa	hall with columns, used for the symbolic marriage ceremony of the temple deity
kashi-work	special kind of glazed tiling, probably derived from Kashan in Persia
keep	tower of a fort, stronghold

keystone central wedge-shaped block in a masonry arch

khondalite crudely grained basalt

kirti-stambha 'pillar of fame,' free standing pillar in front of temple

kos minars Mughal mile stones, common along Grand Trunk Road

kothi house

kotla citadel

kovil temple in Tamil Nadu

kumbha a vase-like motif

kund well or pool

kutcha mud built with sun-dried bricks

kwabgah bedroom; lit 'palace of dreams'

L

lat pillar, column (also stambha)

lattice screen of cross laths: perforated

lena cave, usually a rock-cut sanctuary

lingam (linga) Siva as the phallic emblem

lintel horizontal beam over doorway

liwan cloisters of a mosque

lunette semicircular window opening

M

madrassa Islamic theological school or college

mahal palace, grand building

maha-mandapam large enclosed hall in front of main shrine

makara crocodile-shaped mythical creature symbolizing the river Ganga

manastambha free-standing pillar in front of temple

mandala geometric diagram symbolizing the structure of the Universe, the basis of a temple plan; orders deities into pantheons

mandapa columned hall preceding the sanctuary in a Jain or Hindu temple

mandir temple

mani (mani wall) stones with sacred inscriptions at Buddhist sites

maqbara chamber of a Muslim tomb

maqsura screen or arched façade of a mosque

masjid lit 'place of prostration'; mosque

math Hindu or Jain monastery

mausoleum large tomb building

medallion circle or part-circle framing a figure or decorative motif

mihrab niche or arched recess in the western wall of a mosque towards which worshippers turn for prayer

mimbar pulpit in mosque

minar (minaret) slender tower of a mosque from which the muezzin calls the faithful to prayer

mithuna couple in sexual embrace

monolith single block of stone shaped into a pillar or monument

moonstone the semi-circular stone step before a shrine (also chandrasila)

mukha mandapa hall for shrine

muqarna Muslim stalactite design

mural wall decoration

N

nakkar khana drum house; arched structure or gateway for musicians (also naubat khana)

nal staircase

nal mandapa porch over a staircase

nandi mandapa portico or pavilion erected over the sacred bull (nandi)

nata mandapa (nat-mandir; nritya sala) dancing hall in a temple (usually the middle structure in Orissa)

navagraha nine planets, represented usually on the lintel or architrave of the front door of a temple

navaranga central hall of temple

niche wall recess containing a sculpted image or emblem, mostly framed by a pair of pilasters

nirvana enlightenment; (lit 'extinguished')

niwas small palace

O

obelisk	tapering and usually monolithic shaft of stone with pyramidal apex
ogee	form of moulding or arch comprising a double curved line made up of a concave and convex part
oriel	projecting window

P

pada	foot or base
padma	lotus, moulding having the curves of the lotus petal (padmasana, lotus throne)
paga	projecting pilaster-like surface of an Orissan temple (exterior)
pagoda	tall structure in several stories
parapet	wall extending above the roof
parterre	level space in a garden occupied by flower-beds
patina	green film that covers materials exposed to the air
pediment	mouldings, often in a triangular formation above an opening or niche
pendant	hanging, generally refers to a motif depicted upside down
peristyle	range of columns surrounding a court or temple
pida	(pitha) basement
pida deul	hall with a pyramidal roof in an Orissan temple
pietra dura	inlaid mosaic of hard and expensive stones
pilaster	ornamental small column, with capital and bracket, usually forming part of the wall construction
pinjra	lattice work
pitha	base, pedestal
podium	stone bench; low pedestal wall
pokana	bathing tank (Sri Lanka)
pol	fortified gateway
porch	covered entrance to a shrine or hall, generally open and with columns
portico	space enclosed between columns
potgul	library
pradakshina patha	processional passage or ambulatory, also vedika
prakaram	open courtyard
pukka	solidly built, reliable; lit 'ripe' or 'finished'
pushkarani	sacred pool or tank

Q

qabr	Muslim grave
qibla	direction for Muslim prayer
qila	fort
qutb	axis or pivot

R

ranga mandapa	painted hall or theatre
ratha	temple chariot; sometimes also refers to a temple model
rekha	curvilinear portion of a spire or sikhara (rekha deul, sanctuary, curved tower of an Orissan temple)
reredos	screen behind an altar

S

sabha	columned hall (sabha mandapa, assembly hall)
sahn	open courtyard of a mosque
sal	hall
samadhi	funerary memorial, like a temple but enshrining an image of the deceased
samudra	large tank or inland sea
sangarama	monastery
sankha	a shell, emblem of the god Vishnu
sangrahalaya	rest-house for Jain pilgrims
sarai	caravansarai, halting place
sati stone/pillar	stone commemorating self-immolation of a widow
schist	grey or green finely grained stone in North-Western Pakistan
shala	barrel-vaulted roof
sheesh mahal	palace apartment enriched with mirror work
shikhara	curved temple tower or spire
sileh khana	armoury
sinha stambha	lion pillar
soma sutra	spout to carry away oblations in the shrine of a temple
spandrel	triangular space between the curve of an arch and the square enclosing it

squinch	arch across an interior angle
sridhara	pillar with octagonal shaft and square base
stalactite	system of vaulting remotely resembling stalactite formations in a cave
stambha	free-standing column or pillar, often with lamps or banners
steatite	finely grained grey mineral
stele	upright inscribed slab or pillar used as a gravestone
stellate	arranged like a star, radiating
stucco	plasterwork
stupa	hemispheric funerary mound; principal votive monument in a Buddhist religious complex
stylobate	base or sub-structure on which a colonnade is placed
sun window	chaitya window, large arched opening in the facade of a chaitya hall or Buddhist temple
superstructure	tower rising over a sanctuary or gateway, roof above a hall
suraj-mukh	'sun-face,' a symbolic decorative element
surya	the sun god
sutradhara	chief architect

T

taikhana	underground apartments, cool retreats from the fierce summer heat
talar	tank
tandava	dance of Siva
tank	reservoir; in temple architecture a masonry-lined body of water, often with stepped sides
tatties	cane or grass screens used for shade
tempera	distemper; method of mural painting by means of a 'body,' such as white pigment
terracotta	burnt clay used as building material
thakur bari	sanctuary (Bengal)
thangka	(thanka) Traditional religious painting on cloth (often silk)
torana	gateway with two posts linked by architraves
trisula	trident, emblem of Siva
tuk	fortified enclosure containing Jain shrines
tykhana	an underground room in a house in Upper India for use in hot weather
tympanum	triangular space within the cornices of a pediment

V

vahana mandapa	(Chalukyan) hall in which the vahanas or temple vehicles are stored
vatadage	ancient Sinhalese architectural style; 'circular relic house'
vedi	altar, also a wall or screen
verandah	enlarged porch in front of a hall
vihara	Buddhist or Jain monastery with cells opening off a central court
vilas	house or pleasure palace
vimana	towered sanctuary containing the cell in which the deity is enshrined
vyala	leogryph, lion-like sculpture

W

Wav	step-well, particularly in Gujarat and W India (baoli)

Y

yagasala	hall where the sacred fire is maintained and worshipped; place of sacrifice
yaksha	semi-divine being
yali	hippopotamus-like creature in the ornamentation of Chalukyan temples
yashti	stick, pole or shaft, (Buddhist)
yoni	a hole in a stone, symbolising the vagina or female sexuality

Z

zarih	cenotaph in a Muslim tomb
zenana	segregated women's apartments
ziarat	holy Muslim tomb

Glossary of Names

A

Adinatha First of the 24 Tirthankaras, distinguished by his bull mount

Agastya Legendary sage who brought the Vedas to S India

Agni Vedic fire divinity, intermediary between gods and men; guardian of the SE

Ananda The Buddha's chief disciple

Ananta A huge snake on whose coils Vishnu rests

Andhaka Demon killed by Siva

Annapurna Goddess of abundance; one aspect of Devi

Ardhanarisvara Siva represented as half-male and half-female

Arjuna Hero of the Mahabharata, to whom Krishna delivered the Bhagavad Gita

Aruna Charioteer of Surya, the Sun God; Red

Ashta Matrikas The 8 mother goddesses who attended on Siva or Skanda

Avalokitesh-wara Lord who looks down; Bodhisattva, the Compassionate

B

Balabhadra Balarama, elder brother of Krishna, also an incarnation of Vishnu

Bhadrakali Tantric goddess and consort of Bhairav

Bhagiratha The king who prayed to Ganga to descend to earth

Bhairava Siva, the Fearful

Bharata Half-brother of Rama

Bhima Pandava hero of the Mahabharata, famous for his strength

Bhimsen Deity worshipped for his strength and courage

Bodhisattva Enlightened One, destined to become Buddha

Bon Pre-Buddhist religion of Tibet, incorporating animism and sorcery

Brahma Universal self-existing power; Creator in the Hindu Triad. Often represented in art, with four heads

Buddha The enlightened One; founder of Buddhism who is worshipped as god by certain sects

C

Chamunda Terrifying form of the goddess Durga

Chandra Moon; a planetary deity

D

Dakshineshvara Lord of the South; name of Siva

Dasaratha King of Ayodhya and father of Rama in the Ramayana

Dattatraya Syncretistic deity; an incarnation of Vishnu, a teacher of Siva, or a cousin of the Buddha

Devi Goddess; later, the Supreme Goddess; Siva's consort, Parvati

Dikpala Guardian of the directions; mostly appear in a group of eight

Draupadi Wife-in-common of the five Pandava brothers in the Mahabharata

Durga Principal goddess of the Shakti cult; riding on a tiger and armed with the weapons of all the gods, she slays the demon (Mahisha)

G

Ganesh (Ganapati) Lord of the Ganas; popular elephant-headed son of Siva and Parvati, the god of good fortune and remover of obstacles

Gandharva Semi-divine flying figure; celestial musician

Ganga Goddess personifying the Ganga river

Garuda Mythical eagle, half-human Vishnu's vehicle

Gauri 'Fair One'; Parvati; Gaurishankara, Siva with Parvati

Gopala	(Govinda) Cowherd; a name of Krishna
Gopis	Cowherd girls; milk maids who played with Krishna
Gorakhnath	Historically, an 11th-century yogi who founded a Saivite cult; an incarnation of Siva

H

Hanuman	Monkey hero of the Ramayana; devotee of Rama; bringer of success to armies
Hara	(Hara Siddhi) Siva
Hari	Vishnu Harihara, Vishnu-Siva as a single divinity
Hariti	Goddess of prosperity and patroness of children, consort of Kubera
Hasan	The murdered eldest son of Ali, commemorated at Muharram
Hidimba Devi	Durga worshipped at Manali, India, as an angry goddess
Hiranyakashipu	Demon king killed by Narasimha
Hussain	The second murdered son of Ali, commemorated at Muharram

I

Indra	King of the gods; God of rain; guardian of the East
Ishana	Guardian of the North East
Ishvara	Lord; Siva

J

Jagadambi	lit Mother of the World; Parvati
Jagannath	lit Lord of the World; particularly, Krishna worshipped at Puri (Orissa, India)
Jamuna	Hindu goddess who rides a tortoise
Janaka	Father of Sita in the Ramayana
Jina	lit 'victor'; spiritual conqueror or Tirthankara, after whom Jainism is named
Jogini	Mystical goddess

K

Kailasa	Mountain home of Siva
Kali	lit 'black'; terrifying form of the goddess Durga, wearing a necklace of skulls/heads
Kalki	Future incarnation of Vishnu on horseback
Kartikkeya/ Kartik	Son of Siva, God of war Also known as Skanda or Subrahmanyam
Krishna	8th incarnation of Vishnu; the mischievious child, the cowherd (Gopala, Govinda) playing with gopis; the charioteer of Arjuna in the Mahabharata epic (see above)
Kubera	Chief of the yakshas; keeper of the treasures of the earth, Guardian of the North
Kumari	Virgin; Durga

L

Lakshmana	Younger brother of Rama in the Ramayana
Lakshmi	Goddess of wealth and good fortune, associated with the lotus; consort of Vishnu
Lakulisha	Founder of the Pashupata sect, believed to be an incarnation of Siva, seen holding a club
Lingaraja	Siva worshipped at Bhubaneswar
Lokeshwar	'Lord of the World', Avalokiteshwara to Buddhists and of Siva to Hindus

M

Machhendra	The guardian deity of the Kathmandu Valley, guarantor of rain and plenty; worshipped as the *Rato* (Red) Machhendra in Patan and the *Seto* (White) Machhendra in Kathmandu
Mahabharata	Story of the Great Bharatas; ancient Sanskrit epic about the battle between the Pandavas and Kauravas
Mahadeva	lit 'Great Lord'; Siva
Mahavira	lit 'Great Hero'; last of the 24 Tirthankaras, teacher contemporary with Buddha, founder of Jainism
Mahesha	(Maheshvara) Great Lord; Siva
Mahisha	Buffalo demon killed by Durga
Maitreya	The future Buddha

Manjushri	Legendary Buddhist patron of the Kathmandu Valley; God of learning, destroyer of falsehood/ ignorance
Makara	Mythical aquatic creature
Manasa	Snake goddess; form of Sakti
Mara	Tempter, who sent his daughters (and soldiers) to disturb the Buddha's meditation
Meru	Axial mountain supporting the heavens
Minakshi	lit 'fish-eyed'; Parvati worshipped at Madurai, India
Mohammad	'the praised'; The Prophet; founder of Islam

N

Naga	(nagi/nagini) Snake deity; associated with fertility and protection
Nandi	A bull, Siva's vehicle and a symbol of fertility
Narayana	Vishnu as the creator of life
Nataraja	Siva, Lord of the cosmic dance
Nihang	Lit 'crocodile': followers of Guru Gobind Singh (Sikh)

P

Parvati	Daughter of the Mountain; Siva's consort, sometimes serene, sometimes fearful
Pashupati	lit Lord of the Beasts; Siva

R

Radha	Krishna's favourite consort
Rama	Seventh incarnation of Vishnu; hero of the Ramayana epic
Ravana	Demon king of Lanka; kidnapper of Sita, killed by Rama in the battle of the Ramayana

S

Saiva	(Shaiva) the cult of Siva
Saraswati	Wife of Brahma and goddess of knowledge; usually seated on a swan, holding a veena
Sati	Wife of Siva who destroyed herself by fire
Shakti	Energy; female divinity often associated with Siva; also a name of the cult
Shankara	Siva
Shesha	(Sesha) serpent who supports Vishnu
Shitala Mai	A former ogress who became a protector of children, worshipped at Swayambhunath
Siva	The Destroyer among Hindu gods; often worshipped as a lingam or phallic symbol
Sivaratri	Lit 'Siva's night'; festival (Feb-Mar) dedicated to Siva
Sita	Rama's wife, heroine of the Ramayana epic. Worshipped by Hindus, esp in Janakpur, India, her legendary birthplace
Skanda	The Hindu god of war
Subrahmanya	Skanda, one of Siva's sons; Kartikkeya in S India
Surya	Sun; the Sun God who rides in a seven-horse chariot

T

Tara	Historically a Nepalese princess, now worshipped by Buddhists and Hindus, particularly in Nepal
Tirthankara	lit 'ford-maker'; title given to twenty-four saviours or teachers, worshipped by Jains
Trimurti	Triad of Hindu divinities, Brahma, Vishnu and Siva

U

Uma	Siva's consort in one of her many forms

V

Valmiki	Sage, author of the Ramayana epic
Vamana	Dwarf incarnation of Vishnu
Varaha	Boar incarnation of Vishnu
Varuna	Guardian of the West, accompanied by Makara (see above)
Vayu	Guardian of the North-West; wind
Vishnu	A principal Hindu deity; creator and preserver of universal order; appears in 10 incarnations (Dashavatara)

Y

Yaksha	(Yakshi) a demi-god, associated with nature in folk religion
Yama	God of death, judge of the living; guardian of the south

Glossary of terms

Words in *italics* are common elements of words, often making up part of a place name

A

aarti	(arati) Hindu worship with lamps
abad	peopled
achalam	hill (Tamil)
acharya	religious teacher
Adi Granth	Guru Granth Sahib, holy book of the Sikhs
agarbathi	incense
aghani	wet season (Bengal)
ahimsa	non-harming, non-violence
ajrak	Hyderabadi handloom fabric (Pakistan)
akhand path	unbroken reading of the Guru Granth Sahib
aman	wet season rice crop (Jul-Dec) Bengal
amrita	ambrosia; drink of immortality
ananda	joy
anicut	irrigation channel (Tamil)
anna	(ana) one sixteenth of a rupee (still occasionally referred to)
apsara	celestial nymph
aram	pleasure garden
aru	river (Tamil)
arrack	whisky fermented from potatoes or grain
Aryans	lit 'noble' (Sanskrit); prehistoric peoples who settled in Persia and N India
ashram	hermitage or retreat
atman	philosophical concept of universal soul or spirit
aus	summer rice crop (Apr-Aug) Bengal
avatara	'descent'; incarnation of a divinity, usually Vishnu's incarnations
ayacut	irrigation command area (Tamil)
ayah	nursemaid, especially for children

B

baba	old man
babu	clerk
badlands	eroded landscape with deforestation and gullying
bahadur	title, meaning 'the brave'
baksheesh	tip
bandh	strike
bandhani	tie dyeing (W India, Rajasthan)
bania	merchant caste
banian	vest
baranni	rainfed agricultural land (Pakistan)
barkandaz	guard watchman; doorkeeper
basti	temple (Kanarese)
bazaar	market
begum	Muslim princess; Muslim woman's courtesy title
bhaati	An inn or tea shop in Nepal especially those of the Thakali people
bhaat	cooked rice also refers to a meal (of rice)
bhabar	coarse alluvium at foot of Himalayas
bhadoi	season of early rain (Bengal)
Bhagavad-Gita	Song of the Lord; section of the Mahabharata in which Krishna preaches a sermon to Arjuna explaining the Hindu ways of knowledge, duty and devotion
bhai	brother
bhakti	adoration of a particular god or goddess
bhang	Indian hemp
bharal	Bhutanese blue sheep
bhavan	house, home
bhikku	Buddhist monk
bhisti	A water-carrier
bhit	sand dune (Pakistan)
bidi	(beedi) tobacco leaf rolled into small cigarette

bigha	measure of land - normally about one-third of an acre
bodi	tuft of hair on back of the shaven head (also Tikki)
Bon	an animist religion
Brahmachari	religious student, accepting rigorous discipline imposed for a set period, including absolute chastity
Brahman	(Brahmin) highest Hindu (and Jain) caste of priests
Brahmanism	Ancient Indian religion, precursor of modern Hinduism and Buddhism
bund	An embankment; a causeway
burqa	An over-dress worn by Muslim women observing purdah (see below)
bustee	slum, squatter settlement

C

cantonment	large planned military or civil area in town
catamaran	log raft, logs (*maram*) tied (*kattu*) together (Tamil)
chaam	Himalayan Buddhist masked dance
chadar	sheet worn as clothing by men and women
chai	tea
chakra	wheel, the Buddhist wheel of the law
chapatti	unleavened Indian bread cooked on a griddle
chaprassi	messenger or often orderly usually wearing a badge
char	sand-bank or island in the bed of a river
charka	spinning wheel
charpai	'four legs' – wooden frame string bed
chaukidar	(chowkidar) night-watchman; guard
charan	foot print
chauth	25% tax raised for revenue by Marathas
chena	shifting cultivation (Sri Lanka)
cheri	outcaste settlement; urban huts, slum (Tamil Nadu)
cheruva	tank (Telugu)
chhetri	Hindu warrior caste second in status only to brahmins
chhang	strong mountain beer of fermented barley maize rye or millet
chikan	shadow embroidery on fine cotton (especially in Lucknow)
chikki	nut crunch, a speciality of Lonavla
chiya	Nepalese tea, brewed together with milk, sugar and spices
chitrakar	picture maker
chit sabha	hall of wisdom (Tamil)
chogyal	heavenly king (Sikkim)
choli	blouse
chorten	Himalayan Buddhist relic shrine or memorial stupa
choultry	travellers' rest house (from Telugu)
chowk	(chauk) a block; open place in a city where the market is held; a square
chowkidar	watchman
crewel work	chain stitching
crore	10 million

D

dabba	meals: stainless steel meal containers (Pakistan and West India)
dacoit	bandit
dada	(dadu) grandfather; elder brother
dahi	yoghurt
dak	post
dak bungalow	rest house for official travellers
dakini	sorceress
dan	gift
dandi	wooden palanquin carried by bearers
darbar	(durbar) a royal gathering
dargah	Muslim tomb complex
darshan	(darshana) viewing of a deity
Dasain	principal Nepalese festival, Sep/Oct
Dasara	(dassara/dussehra/dassehra) 10 day festival (Sep-Oct)
deodar	Himalayan cedar; from *deva-daru*, the 'wood of the gods'
dervish	member of Muslim brotherhood, committed to poverty
devasthanam	temple trust
dhaba	roadside restaurant, especially in N India and Pakistan, truck drivers' rest stop

dhal (daal) lentil 'soup'
dhansak special Parsi dish made with lentils
dharma moral and religious duty
dharamshala (dharamsala) pilgrims' rest-house
dharo river (Sindi)
dhobi washerman
dhol drums
dholi swinging chair on a pole, carried by bearers
dhoti loose loincloth worn by Indian men
dhyana meditation
digambara lit 'sky-clad'; one of the two main Jain sects in which the monks go naked
dighi village pond (Bengal)
dikshitar person who makes oblations or offerings
distributary river that flows away from main channel, usually in deltas
Diwali festival of lights (Sep-Oct) usually marks the end of the rainy season
diwan chief financial minister
dokra tribal name for lost wax metal casting (cire perdu)
doab interfluve, land between two rivers
dosai (dosa) thin pancake
drug (*durg*) fort (Tamil, Telugu)
duar (dwar) door, gateway
dun valley
dupatta long scarf (usually very thin) worn by Punjabi women
durrie (dhurrie) thick handloom rug
durwan watchman
dzong Tibetan lamasery, monastery

E

ek the number 1, a symbol of unity
ekka one horse carriage
eri tank (Tamil)

F

fakir religious mendicant, normally Muslim
firman edict or grant issued by a sovereign

G

gadba woollen blanket (Kashmir)
gadi/gari car, cart, train
gali (galli) lane; an alley
ganj market
ganja Indian hemp
gaon village
garh fort
Gelugpa Tibetan sect
ghagra (ghongra) long flared skirt with many gathers
ghat hill range, hill road; landing place; steps on the river bank
ghazal Urdu lyric poetry/love songs, often erotic
ghee clarified butter for cooking
gherao industrial action, surrounding home or office of politician or industrial manager
giri hill
Gita Govinda Jayadeva's poem of the Krishnalila
godown warehouse
goncha loose woollen robe, tied at waist with wide coloured band (Leh)
gosain monk or devotee (Hindi)
gram chick pea, pulse
gram village; gramadan, gift of village
gur palm sugar
gur gur salted butter tea (Leh)
guru teacher; spiritual leader, Sikh religious leader

H

Haj (Hajj) annual Muslim pilgrimage to Mecca (Haji, One who has performed the Haj)
hakim judge; a physician (usually Muslim)
halwa a special sweet meat
handi Punjabi dish cooked in a pot
haor tectonic depression, flooded during rainy season (Bengal)
hartal general strike
hat market
hathi (hati) elephant
hauz tank or reservoir
havildar army sergeant
hindola swing
Holi spring festival (Feb-Mar) associated with Krishna
hookah 'hubble bubble' or smoking vase. Smoke is drawn through water by sucking on long flexible pipe

horst block mountain
howdah seat on elephant's back, sometimes canopied
hundi temple offering
hypothecated mortgaged

I

Id principal Muslim festivals
Idgah open space for the Id prayers, on the W of town
idli steamed rice cake (Tamil)
ikat 'resist-dyed' woven fabric
imam Muslim religious leader in a mosque
Impeyan Nepal's national bird; a species of the pheasant
Isvara Lord (Sanskrit)

J

jadu magic
jaggery brown sugar, made from the sap of a variety of palm
jahaz ship: building constructed in form of ship
Jambudvipa Continent of the Rose-Apple Tree; the earth
jataka stories Buddhist accounts of the previous lives of the Buddha
jatra Bengali folk theatre
jawan army recruit, soldier
jelebi snack prepared by frying circles of batter and soaking in syrup
jhankri shaman or sorcerer (Nepal)
jheel (jhil) lake; a marsh; a swamp
-ji (jee) honorific suffix added to names out of reverence and/or politeness; also abbreviated 'yes' (Hindi/Urdu)
jihad striving in the way of god; holy war by Muslims against non-believers
johar (jauhar) mass suicide by fire of women, particularly in Rajasthan, to avoid capture

K

kabalai (kavalai) well irrigation using bullock power (Tamil Nadu)
kabigan folk debate in verse
kachcha man's underpants (one of 5 'ks': Sikh symbols worn or carried on the person)
kadal wooden bridge (Kashmir)
kadhi savoury yoghurt curry (Gujarat/ N India)
kadu forest (Tamil)
kalamkari special painted cotton hanging from Andhra
kameez women's shirt
kanga comb
kankar limestone pieces, used for road making
kantha Bengali quilting
kapok the silk cotton tree
kara steel bracelet (one of 5 'ks': Sikh symbols worn or carried on the person)
karma present consequences of past lives; impurity resulting from past misdeeds
kata ceremonial scarf presented to high Tibetan Buddhist figures
katcheri (cutchery) public office or court
kati-roll Muslim snack of meat rolled in a 'paratha' bread
kattakat mixed brain, liver and kidney (Gujarat)
kebab variety of meat dishes
kere tank (Kanarese)
khadi woven cotton cloth made from home-spun cotton (or silk) yarn. A pre-Independence symbol of national self-sufficiency
khal creek; a canal
khave khana tea shop
khana suffix for room/office/place; also food or meal
kharif monsoon season crop
kheda enclosure in which wild elephants are caught; elephant depot
khet field
khola river or stream in Nepal
khukri traditional curved knife best known as the weapon of Gurkha soldiers
khutba Muslim Friday sermon
khyaung Buddhist temple (Chittagong Hill tracts)
kikar gum arabic
kirpan sabre, dagger
kofta meat balls
kohl antimony, used as eye shadow
konda hill (Telugu)

korma	rich curry using cubes of meat
kot	(kota/kottai//kotte) fort
kothi	house
kovil	temple (Tamil)
kritis	S Indian devotional music
kulam	tank or pond (Tamil)
kumar	a young man
kumari	young unmarried girl; young virgin regarded as a living goddess in Kathmandu Valley towns
kumhar	potter
kumbha	pot
Kumbhayog	auspicious time for bathing to wash away sins
kund	lake
kundan	jewellery setting of uncut gems (Pakistan and Rajasthan)
kuppam	hamlet
kurta	Punjabi shirt
kurti-kanchali	small blouse
kutcha	(cutcha/kacha) raw; crude; unpaved

L

la	Himalayan mountain pass
laddu	round sweet snack
lakh	100,000
lama	Buddhist priest in Tibet
lassi	iced yoghurt drink
lath	monolithic pillar
lathi	bamboo stick with metal bindings, used by police
lingam	phallus, Siva's symbol
lungi	wrapped-around loin cloth, normally checked

M

madrassa	school, usually attached to a mosque
maha	great
maha	the winter rice crop (Sri Lanka)
Mahabodhi	Great Enlightenment of Buddha
mahalla	(mohulla)division of a town; a quarter; a ward
mahant	head of a monastery
maharaja	great king; maharajkumar, crown prince
maharani	great queen
maharishi	(Maharshi) lit 'great teacher'
mahout	elephant driver/keeper
Mahayana	The Greater Vehicle; form of Buddhism practised in East Asia, Tibet and Nepal
mahseer	large freshwater fish found especially in Himalayan rivers
maidan	large open grassy area in a city or town
makhan	butter
malai	hill (Tamil)
mali	gardener
mandalam	region, tract of country (Tamil)
mandi	market
mantra	sacred chant for meditation by Hindus and Buddhists
marg	wide roadway
mata	mother
maulana	scholar (Muslim)
maulvi	religious teacher (Muslim)
maund	measure of weight about 20 kilos
maya	illusion
meena	enamel work
mela	festival or fair, usually Hindu
memsahib	married European woman, term used mainly before Independence
mithai	Indian sweets
mofussil	the country or hinterland, as distinct from the town
mohalla	quarter of a town inhabited by members of one caste or religion
momos	Tibetan stuffed pastas, somewhat like ravioli
moksha	salvation, enlightenment; lit 'release'
mouza	(mowza) village; a parcel of lands having a separate name in the revenue records
mridangam	barrel-shaped drum
muballigh	second prayer leader
mudra	symbolic hand gesture
muezzin	mosque official who calls the faithful to prayer
Muharram	Period of mourning in remembrance of Hasan and Hussain, two murdered sons of Ali
mullah	religious teacher (Muslim)
mund	Toda village
muri	a dry measure equal to about 75 litres It contains 30 'paathis' or 160 'manas' (Nepal)
musalla	prayer mat

muta	limited duration marriage (Leh)
muthi	measure equal to 'a handful'
muzzaffar-khana	traditional dormitory accommodation for travellers (Pakistan)

N

naan	unleavened bread cooked in a special clay oven, tandoor
nadi	river
nadu	region, country (Tamil)
nagara	city, sometimes capital
nallah	(nullah) ditch, channel
namaste	common Hindu greeting (with joined palms) translated as: 'I salute all divine qualities in you'
namaaz	Muslim prayers, worship
namda	rug
namkeen	(nimkee) savory snacks
nara durg	type of large fort built on a flat plain
nath	lit'place' eg Amarnath
natya	the art of dance
nautch	display by dancing girls
navaratri	lit '9 nights'; name of the Dasara festival
nawab	prince, wealthy Muslim, sometimes used as a title
nihari	sheep's thigh cooked in spices (Pakistan)
nirvana	enlightenment; lit 'extinguished'
nritya	pure dance

O

ola	palm manuscripts (Sri Lanka)

P

padam	dance which tells a story
padma	lotus flower Padmasana, lotus seat; posture of meditating figures
pahar	hill
paisa	(poisa) one hundredth of a rupee or taka (currency in India, Nepal, Pakistan and Bengal)
palanquin	covered litter (bed-shaped vehicle) for one, carried on poles by men
palayam	minor kingdom (Tamil)
pali	language of Buddhist scriptures
palli	village
pan	leaf of the betel vine; sliced areca nut, lime and other ingredients wrapped in leaf for chewing
panchayat	A 'council of five'; a government system of elected councils at local and regional levels
pandal	marquee made of bamboo and cloth
pandas	temple priests
pandit	teacher or wise man sometimes used as a title; a Sanskrit scholar
pankah	(punkha) fan, formerly pulled by a cord
parabdis	special feeding place for birds (Jain)
paratha	unleavened bread prepared with flour and fat
pargana	sub-division of a district usually comprising many villages; a fiscal unit
Parinirvana	the Buddha's state prior to nirvana, shown usually as a reclining figure
parishads	political division of group of villages
Parsi	(Parsee) Zoroastrians who fled from Iran to W India in the 9th century to avoid persecution
pashmina	a fine mountain goat's wool found mainly in Kashmir and Ladakh (pashm, goat's wool)
pata	painted hanging scroll
patan	town or city (Sanskrit)
patel	village headman
pattachitra	specially painted cloth (especially Orissan)
pau	measure for vegetables and fruit equal to 250 grams
paya	soup
payasam	sweet rice or vermicelli pudding
peon	servant, messenger (from Portuguese *peao*)
perak	black hat, studded with turquoise and lapis lazuli (Ladakh)
Persian wheel	well irrigation system using bucket lift and bullock power
pettah	suburbs, outskirts of town (Tamil:*pettai*); the market outside the Fort in Colombo

pice (old form) 1/100th of a rupee
picottah water lift using horizontal pole pivoted on vertical pole (Tamil Nadu)
pinjrapol animal hospital (Jain)
pipal Ficus religiosa, the Bodhi tree
pir Muslim holy man
pithasthana place of pilgrimage
pralaya the end of the world
prasadam consecrated temple food
prayag confluence considered sacred by Hindus
puja ritual offerings to the gods; worship (Hindu)
pujari worshipper; one who performs puja (Hindu)
punya merit earned through actions and religious devotion (Buddhist)
Puranas Sanskrit sacred poems; lit 'the old'
purdah seclusion of Muslim women from public view (lit curtains)
puri fried Indian 'bread'

Q

qila fort
Quran holy Muslim scriptures

R

rabi winter/spring season crop in northern areas of S Asia
raj rule or government
raja king, ruler (variations include rao rawal); prefix 'maha' means great
rajbari palaces of a small kingdom
Rajput dynasties of western and central India
Rakshakas Earth spirits
Ramayana Ancient Sanskrit epic - the story of Rama
Ramazan (Ramadan) Muslim month of fasting
rana warrior (Nepal)
rani queen
rath chariot or temple car
rawal head priest
rasam clear pepper soup (Tamil)
rickshaw 3-wheeled bicycle-powered (or 2-wheeled hand-powered) vehicle to transport passengers
Rig Veda (Rg) Oldest and most sacred of the Vedas
Rimpoche blessed incarnation; abbot of a Tibetan Buddhist monastery (gompa)
rishi 'seer'; inspired poet, philosopher or wise man
rumal handkerchief, specially painted in Chamba (Himachal Pradesh)
rupee Unit of currency in India, Pakistan, Nepal, and Sri Lanka
ryot (rayat/raiyat) a subject; a cultivator; a farmer

S

sabzi vegetables, vegetable curry
sadhu ascetic; religious mendicant, holy man
sadar (sadr/saddar) chief, main
safa turban (Rajasthan)
sagar lake; reservoir
sahib title of address, like 'sir'
sal hardwood tree of the lower slopes of Himalayan foothills
salaam greeting (Muslim); lit 'peace'
salwar (shalwar) loose trousers (Punjab)
samadh (samadhi) Hindu memorial
sambar lentil and vegetable soup dish, accompanying main meal (Tamil)
samsara eternal transmigration of the soul
sangam junction of rivers
sangha ascetic order founded by Buddha
sankha (shankha) the conch shell (symbolically held by Vishnu); the shell bangle worn by Bengali women
sanyasi wandering ascetic; final stage in the ideal life of a man
saranghi small four-stringed viola shaped from a single piece of wood and played with a horsehair bow
sarkar the government; the state; a writer; an accountant
sarod Indian stringed musical instrument
sarvodaya uplift, improvement of all
sati (suttee) a virtuous woman; later applied to the act of self-immolation on a husband's funeral pyre

satyagraha	'truth force'; passive resistance
sayid	title (Muslim)
seer	(ser) unit of weight equal to about 1 kg
sepoy	(sepai) Indian soldier, private
serow	a wild Himalayan antelope
seth	merchant, businessman
seva	voluntary service
shahtush	very fine wool from the Tibetan antelope
shalagrama	stone containing fossils worshipped as a form of Vishnu
shaman	doctor/priest, using magic
shamiana	cloth canopy
sharia	corpus of Muslim theological law
shastras	Ancient texts setting norms of conduct for temple architecture, use of images and worship
shastri	religious title (Hindu)
shehnai	(shahnai) Indian wind instrument similar to an oboe
sherwani	knee-length coat for men
shikar	hunting
shikhara	boat (Kashmir)
shisham	a valuable building timber
shloka	Sanskrit sacred verse
shola	patch of forest or wood (Tamil)
sindur	vermilion powder often combined with mustard oil used in temple ritual; applied in the parting of the hair by women as a sign of marriage in parts of E India
singh	(sinha) lion; also Rajput caste name adopted by Sikhs
sirdar	a guide, usually a Sherpa, who leads trekking groups
sitar	classical Indian stringed musical instrument with a gourd for soundbox
soma	sacred drink mentioned in the Vedas
sri	(shri) honorific title, often used for 'Mr'; repeated as sign of great respect
sthan	place
subahdar	(subedar) the governor of a province; viceroy under the Mughal government
sudra	lowest of the Hindu castes
sufis	Muslim mystics; sufism, Muslim mystic worship
sultan	Muslim prince (sultana, wife of sultan)
svami	(swami) holy man; also used as a suffix for temple deities
svastika	(swastika) auspicious Hindu/ Buddhist emblem
swadeshi	home made goods
swaraj	home rule
swatantra	freedom
syce	groom, attendant who follows a horseman or carriage

T

tabla	a pair of drums
tahr	wild Himalayan goat
tahsildar	tax-collector; a collector of revenue
taka	unit of currency in Bangladesh
takht	throne
tale	tank (Sinhalese)
taluk	administrative subdivision of a district; talukdar petty proprietor
tamasha	spectacle, festive celebration
tank	lake created for irrigation
tapas	(tapasya) ascetic meditative self-denial
tareeqat	'spirituality' (Islamic)
tari	fermented palm wine drunk by hill tribes from the Chittagong Hill Tracts
tarkashi	Orissan silver filigree
Teej	Hindu festival
tehsil	administrative subdivision of a district (N India)
tempo	3 wheeler vehicle, used for goods or passengers
terai	narrow strip of land along Himalayan foothills
teri	soil formed from wind blown sand (Tamil nadu)
thali	S and W Indian vegetarian meal
thana	a police jurisdiction; police station
thangka	(thankha) cloth (often silk) painted with a Tibetan Mahayana deity
thakur	high Hindu caste
thug	member of a group of professional robbers or murderers in north central India
thukba	thick Tibetan soup
tiffin	snack, light meal

tika	(tilak) vermilion powder applied by Hindus to the forehead as a symbol of the divine; auspicious mark on the forehead; now usually simply decorative
tikka	tender pieces of meat, marinated and barbecued
tillana	abstract dance
tirtha	ford, bathing place, holy spot (Sanskrit)
tole	street (Nepal)
tonga	2 wheeled horse or pony carriage
topi	(topee) pith helmet, formerly believed to prevent sunstroke
tottam	garden (Tamil)
tribhanga	favourite triple-bended posture for standing figures of deities
tripolia	triple gateway
trisul	the trident chief symbol of the god Siva
triveni	triple-braided
tsampa	ground and roasted barley, sometimes eaten dry. Often mixed with milk, tea or water (Himalayan)
tulsi	sacred basil plant

U

untouchable	'outcastes', with whom contact of any kind was believed by high caste Hindus to be defiling
Upanishads	Ancient Sanskrit philosophical texts, part of the Vedas
ur	village (Tamil)
usta	painted camel leather goods
ustad	master
uttarayana	northwards

V

vaisya	the 'middle-class' caste of merchants and farmers
vana	grove, forest
varam	village (Tamil)
varna	'colour'; social division of Hindus into Brahmin, Kshatriya, Vaishya and Sudra
varnam	S Indian musical etude, conforming to a raga
Veda	(Vedic) Oldest known religious texts; include hymns to Agni, Indra and Varuna, adopted as Hindu deities
vina	plucked stringed instrument, relative of sitar
villu	small lake (Sri Lanka)

W

-wallah	suffix often used with a occupational name, eg rickshaw-wallah
wazir	chief minister of a raja (from Turkish 'vizier')
wazwan	ceremonial meal (Kashmir)
wewa	tank or lake (Sinhalese)

Y

yagya	(yajna) major ceremonial sacrifice
yala	summer rice crop (Sri Lanka)
yantra	magical diagram used in meditation; machine
yatra	pilgrimage
yeti	mythical Himalayan animal often referred to as 'the abominable snowman'
yoga	school of philosophy concentrating on different mental and physical disciplines (yogi, a practitioner)
yura	water channel (Ladakh)

Z

zamindar	landlord granted a right to land (zamin) and income by Moghul rulers
zeenat	decoration
zilla	(zillah) district

INDEX TO MAPS

A-D

E-K

L-R

S-Z

ROUTE MAPS

NORTH INDIA

EAST INDIA

SOUTH INDIA

WEST INDIA

TREKKING IN THE HIMALAYA

The Himalaya has some of the best trekking routes available anywhere in the world. The Handbook has extensive sections on trekking in the regional sections, which are summarised here in the following quick reference listing.

A wide selection of walks and full scale treks is given, as well as trips and side excursions from mountain.

You will find useful notes on **Organising a Trek** (page 114), **Practical Information** (page 119) and **Equipment and Clothing** (page 121), which apply to all trekking areas.

In addition you should read the **Health Information** (page 119) especially the notes on Altitude, which covers mountain sickness and other problems encountered in the high Himalaya.

It is also essential to check with the appropriate authorities before travelling, to ensure you can gain access to the places you want to visit. Many trekking routes pass through sensitive 'Inner Line' border areas like Kashmir. Permits are often required and some areas may be closed to visitors altogether.

TEMPERATURE CONVERSION TABLE

°C	°F	°C	°F	°C	°F	°C	°F	°C	°F
1	34	11	52	21	70	31	88	41	106
2	36	12	54	22	72	32	90	42	108
3	38	13	56	23	74	33	92	43	109
4	39	14	57	24	75	34	93	44	111
5	41	15	59	25	77	35	95	45	113
6	43	16	61	26	79	36	97	46	115
7	45	17	63	27	81	37	99	47	117
8	46	18	64	28	82	38	100	48	118
9	48	19	66	29	84	39	102	49	120
10	50	20	68	30	86	40	104	50	122

The formula for converting °C to °F is: °C x 9 ÷ 5 + 32 = °F

WEIGHTS AND MEASURES

Metric	**British and US**
Weight:	
1 kilogram (kg) = 2,205 pounds	1 pound (lb) = 454 grams
1 metric ton = 1.102 short tons	1 short ton (2,000lb) = 0.907 metric ton
= 0.984 long ton	1 long ton (2,240lb) = 1.016 metric tons
Length:	
1 millimetre (mm) = 0.03937 inch	1 inch = 25.417 millimetres
1 metre = 3.281 feet	1 foot (ft) = 0.305 metre
1 kilometre (km) = 0.621 mile	1 mile = 1.609 kilometres
Area:	
1 hectare = 2.471 acres	1 acre = 0.405 hectare
1 square km (km^2) = 0.386 sq mile	1 square mile (sq mile) = 2,590 km^2
Capacity:	
1 litre = 0.220 Imperial gallon	1 Imperial gallon = 4.546 litres
= 0.264 US gallon	1 US gallon = 3.785 litres

(5 Imperial gallons are approximately equal to 6 US gallons)

Volume:	
1 cubic metre (m^3) = 35.31 cubic feet	1 cubic foot (cu ft) = 0.028 m^3
= 1.31 cubic yards	1 cubic yard (cu yd) = 0.765 m^3

NB The *manzana,* used in Central America, is about 0.7 hectare (1.73 acres).

INDEX

A

B

C

E

F

G

L

W

Y

Z

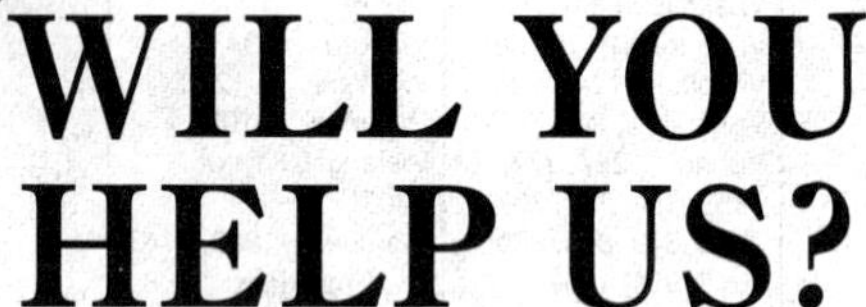

We do all we can to get our facts right in the **INDIA HANDBOOK**. Each section is thoroughly revised each year, but the territory is vast and our eyes cannot be everywhere. If you have enjoyed a tour, trek, train trip, beach, museum, temple, fort or any other activity and would like to share it, please write with all the details. We are always pleased to hear about any restaurants, bars or hotels you have enjoyed. When writing, please give the year on the cover of your *Handbook* and the page number referred to. In return we will send you details of our special guidebook offer.

Thank you very much indeed for your help.

Write to The Editor, *India Handbook*, Trade & Travel,
6 Riverside Court, Lower Bristol Road, Bath BA2 3DZ. England